A Classical Dictionary Of Biography, Mythology, And Geography Based On The Larger Dictionaries

𝔇r. 𝔚m. Smith's Ancient Atlas.

Complete in One Volume, Folio, £6. 6s., half-bound.

ATLAS OF ANCIENT GEOGRAPHY,
BIBLICAL AND CLASSICAL.

COMPILED UNDER THE SUPERINTENDENCE OF

WILLIAM SMITH, D.C.L., AND SIR GEORGE GROVE, D.C.L.

THIS important Work has been undertaken to supply an acknowledged want, as well as in Illustration of Dr. WM. SMITH's BIBLICAL and CLASSICAL DICTIONARIES, The SPEAKER'S COMMENTARY, &c.

The Maps are on a large scale, and have been executed by the most eminent engravers in Paris and London. They contain the modern names along with the ancient ones. There is also a series of smaller Maps, exhibiting each country at different historical periods. To the larger Maps a full Index is appended. The CLASSICAL Maps have been prepared by Dr. KARL MÜLLER, under the superintendence of Dr. SMITH. Those of the HOLY LAND and MOUNT SINAI include the recent observations and positions obtained by the Officers of Royal Engineers, and have been prepared under the superintendence of Sir GEORGE GROVE.

The Maps are of the same size as those of KEITH JOHNSTON'S ROYAL ATLAS OF MODERN GEOGRAPHY, with which the present Atlas will range. The descriptive Letterpress gives an account of the authorities employed in constructing each Map.

LIST OF MAPS.

'The students of Dr. Smith's admirable Dictionaries must have felt themselves in want of an Atlas constructed on the same scale of precise and minute information with the article they were reading. This want has at length been supplied by the superb work before us. The indices are full, the engraving is exquisite, and the delineation of the natural features very minute and beautiful. It may safely be pronounced—and higher praise can scarcely be bestowed—to be a worthy companion of the volumes which it is intended to illustrate.'

GUARDIAN.

'Whether large or small, we have certainly no such thoroughly satisfactory set of maps elsewhere; and this Atlas may almost claim an international value, for it has profited by both English and foreign help, and the maps have been executed by the most eminent engravers both in London and Paris.'

ACADEMY.

JOHN MURRAY, Albemarle Street.

Dr. Wm. Smith's Classical Dictionaries.

With Illustrations, 6 vols. Medium 8vo. 28s. each.

AN ENCYCLOPÆDIA OF CLASSICAL ANTI-

QUITY. Containing Greek and Roman Antiquities, Biography, Mythology, and Geography. By VARIOUS WRITERS. Edited by WM. SMITH, D.C.L. and LL.D.

NOTICE.—These important Dictionaries—written by eminent scholars, and edited by Dr. WM. SMITH—have been long acknowledged to be indispensable to every Library and every Student. But as their cost has hitherto prevented many from possessing them, it has been decided to place them within the reach of a much larger number of readers by *issuing the works at the following reduced prices :—*

I. A DICTIONARY OF GREEK AND ROMAN ANTI-

QUITIES. Including the Laws, Institutions, Domestic Usages, Painting, Sculpture, Music, the Drama, &c. (1,300 pp.) With 500 Illustrations. Medium 8vo. 28s.

II. A DICTIONARY OF BIOGRAPHY AND MYTHO-

LOGY. Containing a History of the Ancient World, Civil, Literary, and Ecclesiastical. (3,700 pp.) With 560 Illustrations. 3 vols. Medium 8vo. 84s.

III. A DICTIONARY OF GREEK AND ROMAN GEO-

GRAPHY. Including the Political History of both Countries and Cities, as well as their Geography (2,500 pp.) With 534 Illustrations. 2 vols. Medium 8vo. 56s.

'A work of so much utility to the student of ancient history, and of such general importance to classical education and the progress of knowledge that its extensive circulation, wherever the English language is spoken or read, may confidently be anticipated.'—*William Martin Leake, F.R.S.*

'I have for some time been in the habit of using the Dictionaries of Antiquity and Ancient Biography, as well as the Dictionary of Ancient Geography, and I have no hesitation in saying from my knowledge of them that they are far superior to any other publications of the same sort in our language. They are works which every student of ancient literature ought to consult habitually, and which are indispensable to every person engaged in original researches into any department of antiquity.'—*Sir G. Cornewall Lewis.*

'It is an honour to this College to have presented to the world so distinguished a scholar as Dr. Wm. Smith, who has, by his valuable manuals of classical antiquity, and classical history and biography, done as much as any man living to promote the accurate knowledge of the Greek and Roman world among the students of this age.'—*Mr. Grote, at the London University.*

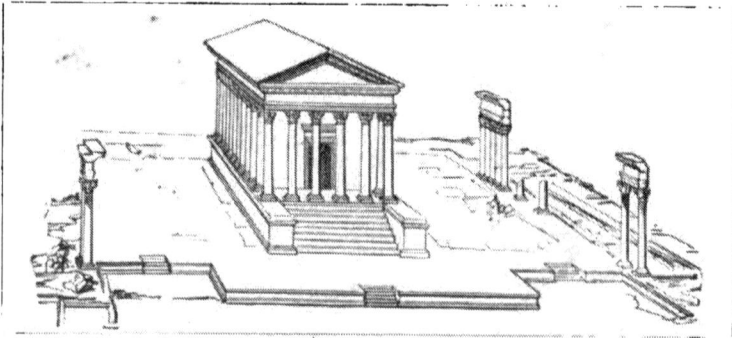

Temple at Nemausus, now called the Maison Carrée.

Temple of Venus at Pompeii. (The Forum and Temple of Jupiter in the background)

Street of the Tombs at Pompeii.

A

CLASSICAL DICTIONARY

OF

BIOGRAPHY, MYTHOLOGY, AND GEOGRAPHY

BASED ON THE LARGER DICTIONARIES

BY WILLIAM SMITH, D.C.L., LL.D.

EDITOR OF THE

"LATIN-ENGLISH AND ENGLISH-LATIN DICTIONARIES"

EIGHTEENTH EDITION

WITH 750 ILLUSTRATIONS

LONDON

JOHN MURRAY, ALBEMARLE STREET

1883

DR. WM. SMITH'S DICTIONARIES.

A DICTIONARY of GREEK and ROMAN ANTIQUITIES. With 500 Illustrations. Medium 8vo. 28s.

A SMALLER DICTIONARY of GREEK and ROMAN ANTIQUITIES. Abridged from the above Work. With 200 Woodcuts. Crown 8vo. 7s. 6d.

A DICTIONARY of GREEK and ROMAN BIOGRAPHY and MYTHOLOGY. With 564 Illustrations. 3 vols. medium 8vo. £4. 4s.

A DICTIONARY of GREEK and ROMAN GEOGRAPHY. With 534 Illustrations. 2 vols. medium 8vo. 56s.

A CLASSICAL DICTIONARY of MYTHOLOGY, BIOGRAPHY, and GEOGRAPHY (abridged from the above works), for the HIGHER FORMS in Schools. With 750 Woodcuts. 8vo. 18s.

A SMALLER CLASSICAL DICTIONARY of MYTHOLOGY, BIOGRAPHY, and GEOGRAPHY. Abridged from the above Work. With 200 Woodcuts. Crown 8vo. 7s. 6d.

A COMPLETE LATIN-ENGLISH DICTIONARY. With Tables of the Roman Calendar, Measures, Weights, and Money. Medium 8vo. 21s.

A SMALLER LATIN-ENGLISH DICTIONARY. Abridged from the above Work. Square 12mo. 7s. 6d.

A COPIOUS and CRITICAL ENGLISH-LATIN DICTIONARY. Compiled from original sources. Medium 8vo. 21s.

A SMALLER ENGLISH-LATIN DICTIONARY. Abridged from the above Work. Square 12mo. 7s. 6d.

A DICTIONARY of the BIBLE. Its Antiquities, Biography, Geography, and Natural History. By Various Writers. With Illustrations. 3 vols. medium 8vo. £5. 5s.

A CONCISE BIBLE DICTIONARY: comprising its Antiquities, Biography, Geography, and Natural History. Condensed from the above Work. With Maps and 300 Illustrations. Medium 8vo. 21s.

A SMALLER BIBLE DICTIONARY: comprising its Antiquities, Biography, Geography, and Natural History. Abridged from the above Work. With Maps and Illustrations. Crown 8vo. 7s. 6d.

A DICTIONARY of CHRISTIAN ANTIQUITIES. The History, Institutions, and Antiquities of the Christian Church, in continuation of the above Work. By Various Writers. With Illustrations. 2 vols. medium 8vo. £3. 13s. 6d.

A DICTIONARY of CHRISTIAN BIOGRAPHY, LITERATURE, SECTS, and DOCTRINES. From the time of the Apostles to the Age of Charlemagne. By Various Writers. Vols. I. to III. Medium 8vo. 31s. 6d. each. (To be completed in 4 vols.)

PREFACE.

Tns great progress which classical studies have made in Europe, and more especially
in Germany during the present century, has superseded most of the Works usually
employed in the elucidation of the Greek and Roman writers. It had long been felt
by our best scholars and teachers that something better was required than we yet
possessed in the English language for illustrating the Antiquities, Literature, Mythology, and Geography of the Ancient Writers, and for enabling a diligent student
to read them in the most profitable manner. It was with a view of supplying this
acknowledged want that the series of Classical Dictionaries was undertaken; and the
very favourable manner in which these Works have been received by the Scholars and
Teachers of this country demands from the Editor his most grateful acknowledgments.
The approbation with which he has been favoured has encouraged him to proceed in
the design which he had formed from the beginning, of preparing a series of works
which might be useful not only to the scholar and the more advanced student, but
also to those who were entering on their classical studies. The Dictionaries of
" Greek and Roman Antiquities," of " Greek and Roman Biography and Mythology,"
and of " Greek and Roman Geography," are intended to meet the wants of the more
advanced scholar; but these Works are on too extended a scale, and enter too much
into details, to be suitable for the use of junior students. For the latter class of persons
a work is required of the same kind as Lempriere's well-known Dictionary, containing
in a single volume the most important names, Biographical, Mythological, and Geographical, occurring in the Greek and Roman writers usually read in our public
schools. It is invidious for an author to speak of the defects of his predecessors; but
it may safely be said that Lempriere's work, which originally contained the most
serious mistakes, has long since become obsolete; and that since the time it was com-

a

piled we have attained to more correct knowledge on a vast number of subjects comprised in that work

The present Dictionary is designed, as already remarked, chiefly to elucidate the Greek and Roman writers usually read in schools; but at the same time it has not been considered expedient to omit any proper names connected with classical antiquity, of which it is expected that some knowledge ought to be possessed by every person who aspires to a liberal education. Accordingly, while more space has been given to the prominent Greek and Roman writers, and to the more distinguished characters of Greek and Roman history, other names have not been omitted altogether, but only treated with greater brevity. The chief difficulty which every Author has to contend with in a Work like the present is the vastness of his subject and the copiousness of his materials. It has therefore been necessary in all cases to study the greatest possible brevity; to avoid all discussions; and to be satisfied with giving simply the results at which the best modern scholars have arrived. The Writer is fully aware that in adopting this plan he has frequently stated dogmatically conclusions which may be open to much dispute; but he has thought it better to run this risk, rather than to encumber and bewilder the junior student with conflicting opinions. With the view likewise of economising space few references have been given to ancient and modern writers. In fact such references are rarely of service to the persons for whom such a Work as the present is intended, and serve more for parade than for any useful purpose; and it has been the less necessary to give them in this Work, as it is supposed that the persons who really require them will be in possession of the larger Dictionaries

The present Work may be divided into three distinct parts, Biography, Mythology, and Geography, on each of which a few words may be necessary.

The Biographical portion may again be divided into the three departments of History, Literature, and Art. The Historical articles include all the names of any importance which occur in the Greek and Roman writers, from the earliest times down to the extinction of the Western Empire in the year 476 of our era. Very few names are inserted which are not included in this period; but still there are some persons who lived after the fall of the Western Empire who could not with propriety be omitted in a Classical Dictionary. Such is the case with Justinian, whose legislation has exerted such an important influence upon the nations of Western Europe; with Theodoric, king of the Ostrogoths, at whose court lived Cassiodorus and Boëthius; and with a few others. The lives of the later Western Emperors and their contemporaries are given with greater brevity than the lives of such persons as lived in the more important epochs of Greek and Roman history, since the students for whom the present Work is intended will rarely require information respecting the later period of the empire. The Romans, as a general rule, have been given under the cognomens, and not under the gentile names; but in cases where a person is more usually mentioned under the name of his gens than under that of his cognomen, he will be found under the former. Thus, for example, the two celebrated conspirators against Caesar, Brutus and Cassius, are given under these names respectively; though uniformity would require, either that Cassius should be inserted under his cognomen of Longinus, or Brutus under his gentile name of Junius. But in this, as in all other cases, it has been considered more advisable to consult utility, than to adhere to any prescribed rule, which would be attended with practical inconveniences.

To the Literary articles considerable space has been devoted. Not only are all Greek and Roman writers inserted whose works are extant, but also all such as exercised any important influence upon Greek and Roman literature, although their writings have not come down to us. It has been thought quite unnecessary, however, to give the vast number of writers mentioned only by Athenaeus, Stobaeus, the Lexicographers, and the Scholiasts; for though such names ought to be found in a complete history of Greek and Roman Literature, they would be clearly out of place in a Work like the present. In the case of all writers whose works are extant, a brief account of their works, as well as of their lives, is given; and at the end of each article one or two of the best modern editions are specified. As the present work is designed for the elucidation of the Classical writers, the Christian writers are omitted, with the exception of the more distinguished Fathers, who form a constituent part of the history of Greek and Roman literature. The Byzantine historians are, for the same reason, inserted; though in their case, as well as in the case of the Christian Fathers, it has been impossible to give a complete account either of their lives or of their writings.

The lives of all the more important Artists have been inserted, and an account has also been given of their extant works. The history of ancient Art has received so little attention from the scholars of this country, that it has been deemed advisable to devote as much space to this important subject as the limits of the Work would allow. Accordingly, some artists are noticed on account of their celebrity in the history of Art, although their names are not even mentioned in the ancient writers. This remark applies to Agasias, the sculptor of the Borghese gladiator, which is still preserved in the Louvre at Paris: to Agesander, one of the sculptors of the group of Laocoön; to Glycon, the sculptor of the Farnese Hercules; and to others. On the contrary, many of the names of the artists in Pliny's long list are omitted, because they possess no importance in the history of Art.

In writing the Mythological articles care has been taken to avoid, as far as possible, all indelicate allusions, as the Work will probably be much in the hands of young persons. It is of so much importance to discriminate between the Greek and Roman mythology, that an account of the Greek divinities is given under their Greek names, and of the Roman divinities under their Latin names, a practice which is universally adopted by the continental writers, which has received the sanction of some of our own scholars, and which is moreover of such great utility in guarding against endless confusions and mistakes as to require no apology for its introduction into this Work.

In the Geographical articles, besides the original sources, use has been made of the best modern treatises on the subject, and of the valuable works of travels in Greece, Italy, and the East, which have appeared within the last few years, both in England and in Germany. It would have been impossible to give references to these treatises, without interfering with the general plan of the present Work; but this omission is supplied in the " Dictionary of Greek and Roman Geography." It is hoped that in the Geographical portion of the Work very few omissions will be discovered of names occurring in the chief classical writers; but the great number of names found only in Strabo, Pliny, Ptolemy, and the Itineraries, have been purposely omitted, except in cases where such names have become of historical celebrity, or have given rise to important towns in modern times. At the commencement of every geographical article the Ethnic name and the modern name have been given, whenever they could be ascertained.

The present Edition has been revised, and Illustrations have been inserted for the first time. These illustrations, which exceed 750 in number, have reference to the Mythological, Biographical, and Geographical articles, and will, it is believed, add considerably to the value and usefulness of the Work. The Mythological illustrations, taken from ancient works of art, give numerous representations of the Greek and Roman divinities, with their various attributes, of the most celebrated heroes, and of other mythical beings. The Biographical illustrations consist of coins drawn from originals in the British Museum, and exhibit a complete series of the rulers of the chief nations of antiquity, such as the Roman emperors from Augustus to the last emperor of the West, the monarchs of the Greek kingdoms founded by the successors of Alexander, and various others. The Geographical illustrations contain, in addition to coins of the more important places, representations of public buildings and of other ancient monuments.

WILLIAM SMITH

London : January 1, 1858.

Gate of Signia

A

CLASSICAL DICTIONARY,

BIOGRAPHICAL, MYTHOLOGICAL, AND GEOGRAPHICAL.

Abacaenum ('Αβακαῖνον or τὰ 'Αβάκαινα: Αβακαινῖνος: nr. *Tripi*, Ru.), an ancient town of the Siculi in Sicily, W. of Messana, and S. of Tyndaris.

Abae ("Αβαι: 'Αβαῖος: nr. *Exarcho*, Ru.), an ancient town of Phocis, on the boundaries of Boeotia, said to have been founded by the Argive Abas, but see ABANTES. It possessed an ancient temple and oracle of Apollo, who hence derived the surname of *Abaeus*. The temple was destroyed by the Persians in the invasion of Xerxes, and a second time by the Boeotians in the sacred war: it was rebuilt by Hadrian.

Abantes ("Αβαντες), the ancient inhabitants of Euboea. (Hom. *Il.* ii. 536.) They are said to have been of Thracian origin, to have first settled in Phocis, where they built Abae, and afterwards to have crossed over to Euboea. The Abantes of Euboea assisted in colonising several of the Ionic cities of Asia Minor.

Abantiades ('Αβαντιάδης), any descendant of Abas, but especially Perseus, great-grandson of Abas, and Acrisius, son of Abas. A female descendant of Abas, as Danaë and Atalante, was called Abantias.

Abantias. [ABANTIADES.]

Abantidas ('Αβαντίδας), son of Paseas, became tyrant of Sicyon, after murdering Clinias, the father of Aratus, B. C. 264, but was soon after assassinated.

Abaris ("Αβαρις), son of Seuthes, was a Hyperborean priest of Apollo, and came from the country about the Caucasus to Greece, while his own country was visited by a plague. In his travels through Greece he carried with him an arrow as the symbol of Apollo, and gave oracles. His history is entirely mythical, and is related in various ways: he is said to have taken no earthly food, and to have ridden on his arrow, the gift of Apollo, through the air. He cured diseases by incantations, and delivered the world from a plague. Later writers ascribe to him several works; but if such works were really current in ancient times, they were not genuine. The time of his appearance in Greece is stated differently: he may perhaps be placed about B. C. 570.

Abarnis ('Αβαρνις or "Αβαρνος: Αβαρνεύς), a

town and promontory close to Lampsacus on the Asiatic side of the Hellespont.

Abas ("Αβας). 1. Son of Metanira, was changed by Demeter into a lizard, because he mocked the goddess when she had come on her wanderings into the house of his mother, and drank eagerly to quench her thirst. —2. Twelfth king of Argos, son of Lynceus and Hypermnestra, grandson of Danaus, and father of Acrisius and Proetus. When he informed his father of the death of Danaus, he was rewarded with the shield of his grandfather, which was sacred to Hera. This shield performed various marvels, and the mere sight of it could reduce a revolted people to submission. He is described as a successful conqueror. and as the founder of the town of Abae in Phocis, and of the Pelasgic Argos in Thessaly.

Abdēra (τὰ "Αβδηρα, Abdera, ae, and Abdera, orum: 'Αβδηρίτης, Abdērītes and Abdērīta). 1. (*Polystilo*), a town of Thrace, near the mouth of the Nestus, which flowed through the town. According to mythology, it was founded by Hercules in honour of his favourite ABDERUS; but according to history, it was colonised by Timesius of Clazomenae about B. C. 656. Timesius was expelled by the Thracians, and the town was colonised a second time by the inhabitants of Teos in Ionia, who settled there after their own town had been taken by the Persians B. C. 544. Abdera was a flourishing town when Xerxes invaded Greece, and continued a place of importance under the Romans, who made it a free city. It was the birthplace of Democritus, Protagoras, Anaxarchus, and other distinguished men; but its inhabitants notwithstanding were accounted stupid, and an "Abderite" was a term of reproach. — 2. (*Adra*), a town of Hispania Baetica on the coast, founded by the Phoenicians.

Abdērus ("Αβδηρος), a favourite of Hercules, was torn to pieces by the mares of Diomedes, which Hercules had given him to pursue the Bistones. Hercules is said to have built the town of Abdera in honour of him.

Abdōlōnȳmus or **Abdălōnīmus**, also called Ballonymus, a gardener, but of royal descent, was made king of Sidon by Alexander the Great.

Abella or **Avella** (Abellānus: *Avella vecchia*), a town of Campania, not far from Nola, founded by the Chalcidians in Euboea. It was celebrated for its apples, whence Virgil (*Aen.* vii. 740) calls it *mālĭfĕra*, and for its great hazel-nuts, *nuces Avellānae*.

Abellīnum (Abellīnas: *Avellino*), a town of the Hirpini in Samnium, near the sources of the Sabatus.

Abgărus, Acbărus, or **Augārus** ("Aβγαρος, 'Aκβαρος, Aυγαρος), a name common to many rulers of Edessa, the capital of the district of Oarhoëne in Mesopotamia. Of these rulers one is supposed by Eusebius to have been the author of a letter written to Christ, which he found in a church at Edessa and translated from the Syriac. The letter is believed to be spurious.

Abĭa (ἡ Aβία: nr. *Zarnata*), a town of Messenia, on the Messenian gulf. It is said to have been the same town as the Ire of the Iliad (ix. 292), and to have acquired the name of Abia in honour of Abia, the nurse of Hyllus, a son of Hercules. At a later time Abia belonged to the Achaean League.

Abĭi ("Aβιοι), a tribe mentioned by Homer (*Il.* xiii. 6), and apparently a Thracian people. This matter is discussed by Strabo (p. 296).

Abĭla (τὰ "Aβιλα: 'Aβιληνός), a town of Coele-Syria, afterwards called Claudiopolis, and the capital of the tetrarchy of Abilēne (Luke, iii. 1). The position seems doubtful. A town of the same name is mentioned by Josephus as being 60 stadia E. of the Jordan.

Abisăres ('Aβισάρης), also called Embisarus, an Indian king beyond the river Hydaspes, sent embassies to Alexander the Great, who not only allowed him to retain his kingdom, but increased it, and on his death appointed his son his successor.

Abnŏba Mons, the range of hills covered by the Black Forest in Germany, not a single mountain.

Abōnitĭchos ('Aβώνου τεῖχος), a town of Paphlagonia on the Black Sea, with a harbour, afterwards called Ionopolis ('Iωνόπολις), whence its modern name *Ineboli,* the birth-place of the pretended prophet ALEXANDER, of whom Lucian has left us an account.

Abŏrĭgĭnes, the original inhabitants of a country, equivalent to the Greek αὐτόχθονες. But the Aborigines in Italy are not in the Latin writers the original inhabitants of all Italy, but the name of an ancient people who drove the Siculi out of Latium, and there became the progenitors of the Latini.

Aborrhas ('Aβόρῥας: *Khabur*), a branch of the Euphrates, which joins that river on the east side near Arcesium. It is called the Araxes by Xenophon (*Anab.* i. 4. § 19), and was crossed by the army of Cyrus the Younger in the march from Sardis to the neighbourhood of Babylon, B. c. 401. A branch of this river, which rises near Nisibis, and is now called Jakhjakhah, is probably the ancient Mygdonius. The Khabur rises near Orfah, and is joined near the lake of Khatuniyah by the Jakhjakhah, after which the united stream flows into the Euphrates. The course of the Khabur is very incorrectly represented in the maps.

Abradātas ('Aβραδάτας), a king of Susa and an ally of the Assyrians against Cyrus, according to Xenophon's Cyropaedia. His wife Panthĕa was taken on the conquest of the Assyrian camp. In consequence of the honourable treatment which she received from Cyrus, Abradatas joined the latter with his forces. He fell in battle, while fighting against the Egyptians. Inconsolable at her loss, Panthea put an end to her own life. Cyrus had a high mound raised in honour of them.

Abrincatŭi, a people of Gallia Lugdunensis in the neighbourhood of the modern *Avranches.*

Abrŏcōmas ('Aβροκόμας), one of the satraps of Axtaxerxes Mnemon, was sent with an army, to oppose Cyrus on his march into Upper Asia, B. c. 401. He retreated on the approach of Cyrus, but did not join the king in time for the battle of Cunaxa.

Abrŏnўchus ('Aβρώνυχος), an Athenian, served in the Persian war, B. c. 480, and was subsequently sent as ambassador to Sparta with Themistocles and Aristides respecting the fortifications of Athens.

Abrŏtŏnum, mother of THEMISTOCLES.

Abrŏtŏnum ('Aβρότονον: *Sabart* or *Old Tripoli*), a city on the coast of Africa, between the Syrtes, founded by the Phoenicians; a colony under the Romans. It was also called Sabrăta and Neapolis, and it formed, with Oea and Leptis Magna, the African Tripolis.

Absyrtĭdes or **Apsyrtĭdes,** sc. insulae ('Aψυρτίδες: *Cherso* and *Osero*), the name of two islands off the coast of Illyricum. According to one tradition Absyrtus was slain in these islands by his sister Medĕa and by Jason.

Absyrtus or **Apsyrtus** ("Aψυρτος), son of Aeëtes, king of Colchis, and brother of Medĕa. When Medea fled with Jason, she took her brother Absyrtus with her; and when she was nearly overtaken by her father, she murdered Absyrtus, cut his body in pieces and strewed them on the road, that her father might thus be detained by gathering the limbs of his child. Tomi, the place where this horror was committed, was believed to have derived its name from τέμνω, "cut." According to another tradition Absyrtus did not accompany Medea, but was sent out by his father in pursuit of her. He overtook her in Corcyra, where she had been kindly received by king Alcinous, who refused to surrender her to Absyrtus. When he overtook her a second time in certain islands off the Illyrian coast, he was slain by Jason. The son of Aeëtes, who was murdered by Medea, is called by some writers Aegialeus.

Abŭlītes ('Aβουλίτης), the satrap of Susiana, surrendered Susa to Alexander. The satrapy was restored to him by Alexander, but he and his son Oxyathres were afterwards executed by Alexander for the crimes they had committed.

Aburnus Valens. [VALENS.]

Abus (*Humber*), a river in Britain.

Abydēnus ('Aβυδηνός), a Greek historian, wrote a history of Assyria. His date is uncertain: he made use of the works of Megasthenes and Berosus, and he wrote in the Ionic dialect. His work was particularly valuable for chronology. The fragments of his history have been published by Scaliger, *De Emendatione Temporum,* and Richter, *Berosi Chaldaeorum Historiae,* &c., Lips. 1825.

Abўdos ("Aβυδος: 'Aβυδηνός). 1. A town of the Troad on the Hellespont, and a Milesian colony. It was nearly opposite to Sestos, but a little lower down the stream. The bridge of boats which Xerxes constructed over the Hellespont, B. c. 480, commenced a little higher up than Abydos, and touched the European shore between Sestos and Madўtus. The site of Abydos is a little N. of Sultania or the old castle of Asia, which is opposite to the old castle of Europe.—**2.** (Nr. *Arabat el Matfoon* and *El Birbeh,* Ru.), a city of Upper Egypt, near the W. bank of the Nile ; once second only to Thebes, but in Strabo's time (A. D. 14) a small village. It had a temple of Osiris and a *Memnonium,* both still standing, and an oracle. Here was found the inscription known as the *Table of Abydos,* which contains a list of the Egyptian kings.

Abỹla or **Abīla Mons** or **Columna** ('Aϐúλη or 'Aϐíλη στήλη or ὅρος: *Jebel Zatout,* i. e. *Apes' Hill,* above *Ceuta*), a mountain in Mauretania Tingitana, forming the E. extremity of the S. or African coast of the Fretum Gaditanum. This and M. Calpe (*Gibraltar*), opposite to it on the Spanish coast, were called the *Columns of Hercules,* from the fable that they were originally one mountain, which was torn asunder by Hercules.

Acacallis ('Aκακαλλίς), daughter of Minos, by whom Apollo begot a son Miletus, as well as other children. Acacallis was in Crete a common name for a narcissus.

Acacesium ('Aκακήσιον: 'Aκακήσιος), a town of Arcadia, at the foot of a hill of the same name.

Acacesius ('Aκακήσιος), a surname of Hermes, for which Homer uses the form *Acacetes.* Some writers derive it from the Arcadian town of Acacesium, in which he was believed to have been brought up ; others from κακός, and suppose it to mean " the god who does not hurt." The same surname is given to Prometheus, whence it may be inferred that its meaning is that of benefactor or deliverer from evil.

Acacetes. [ACACESIUS.]

Acādēmīa ('Aκαδήμεια or 'Aκακδήμια : also Academia in the older Latin writers), a piece of land on the Cephissus, 6 stadia from Athens, originally belonging to the hero ACADEMUS, and subsequently a gymnasium, which was adorned by Cimon with plane and olive plantations, statues, and other works of art. Here taught Plato, who possessed a piece of land in the neighbourhood, and after him his followers, who were hence called the *Academici,* or Academic philosophers. When Sulla besieged Athens in B. C. 87, he cut down the plane trees in order to construct his military machines ; but the place was restored soon afterwards. Cicero gave the name of Academia to his villa near Puteoli, where he wrote his " Quaestiones Academicae."

Acādēmīci. [ACADEMIA.]

Acādēmus ('Aκάδημος), an Attic hero, who betrayed to Castor and Pollux, when they invaded Attica to liberate their sister Helen, that she was kept concealed at Aphidnae. For this the Tyndarids always showed him gratitude, and whenever the Lacedaemonians invaded Attica, they spared the land belonging to Academus. [ACADEMIA.]

Acalandrus (*Salandrella*), a river in Lucania, flowing into the gulf of Tarentum.

Acāmas ('Aκάμας). **1.** Son of Theseus and Phaedra, accompanied Diomedes to Troy to demand the surrender of Helen. During his stay at Troy he won the affection of Laodice, daughter of Priam, and begot by her a son, Munitus. He was one of the Greeks concealed in the wooden horse at the taking of Troy. The Attic tribe Acamantis derived its name from him. —**2.** Son of Antenor and Theano, one of the bravest Trojans, slain by Meriones. —**3.** Son of Eussorus, one of the leaders of the Thracians in the Trojan war, slain by the Telamonian Ajax.

Acanthus ('Aκανθος: 'Aκάνθιος). **1.** (Nr. *Erso,* Ru.), a town on the Isthmus, which connects the peninsula of Athos with Chalcidice. It was founded by the inhabitants of Andros, and continued to be a place of considerable importance from the time of Xerxes to that of the Romans.—**2.** (*Dashur*), a town on the W. bank of the Nile, 120 stadia S. of Memphis, with a temple of Osiris.

Acarnan ('Aκαρνάν, -âνος), one of the Epigoni, son of Alcmaeon and Callirrhoë, and brother of Amphoterus. Their father was murdered by Phegeus, when they were very young, and Callirrhoë prayed to Zeus to make her sons grow quickly, that they might be able to avenge the death of their father. The prayer was granted, and Acarnan with his brother slew Phegeus, his wife, and his two sons. The inhabitants of Psophis, where the sons had been slain, pursued the murderers as far as Tegea, where, however, they were received and rescued. They afterwards went to Epirus, where Acarnan founded the state called after him Acarnania.

Acarnānĭa ('Aκαρνανία: 'Aκαρνάν, -âνος), the most westerly province of Greece, was bounded on the N. by the Ambracian gulf, on the W. and S. W. by the Ionian Sea, on the N. E. by Amphilochia, which is sometimes included in Acarnania, and on the E. by Aetolia, from which at a later time it was separated by the Achelous. The name of Acarnania does not occur in Homer. In the most ancient times the land was inhabited by the Taphii, Teleboae, and Leleges, and subsequently by the Curetes, who emigrated from Aetolia and settled there. At a later time a colony from Argos, said to have been led by ACARNAN, the son of Alcmaeon, settled in the country. In the seventh century B. C. the Corinthians founded several towns on the coast. The Acarnanians first emerge from obscurity at the beginning of the Peloponnesian war, B. C. 431. They were then a rude people, living by piracy and robbery, and they always remained behind the rest of the Greeks in civilization and refinement. They were good slingers, and are praised for their fidelity and courage. The different towns formed a League with a Strategus at their head in the time of war : the members of the League met at Stratos, and subsequently at Thyrium or Leucas. Under the Romans Acarnania formed part of the province of Macedonia.

Acastus ('Aκαστος), son of Pelias, king of Iolcus, and of Anaxibia or Philomache. He was one of the Argonauts, and also took part in the Calydonian hunt. His sisters were seduced by Medea to cut up their father and boil him, in order to make him young again. Acastus, in consequence, drove Jason and Medea from Iolcus, and instituted funeral games in honour of his father. During these games Astydamia, the wife of Acastus, also called Hippolyte, fell in love with Peleus, whom Acastus had purified from the murder of Eurytion. When Peleus refused to listen to her addresses, she accused him to her husband of having attempted her dishonour. Shortly afterwards, when Acastus and Peleus were hunting on mount Pelion, and the latter had fallen asleep, Acastus took his sword from him, and left him alone. He was in consequence nearly destroyed by the Centaurs ; but he was saved by Chiron or Hermes, returned to Acastus, and killed him together with his wife.

Acbarus. [ABGARUS.]

Acca Laurentia or **Larentia,** a mythical

woman in early Roman story. According to one account, in the reign of Ancus Martius a servant (*aedituus*) of the temple of Hercules invited the god to a game of dice, promising that if he should lose the game, he would treat the god with a repast and a beautiful woman. When the god had conquered the servant, the latter shut up Acca Laurentia together with a well-stored table in the temple of Hercules. On the following morning the god advised her to gain the affection of the first wealthy man she should meet. She succeeded in making Carutius or Tarrutius, an Etruscan, love and marry her. After his death she inherited his large property, which she left to the Roman people. Ancus, in gratitude for this, allowed her to be buried in the Velabrum, and instituted an annual festival, the Larentalia, at which sacrifices were offered to the Lares. According to another account, Acca Laurentia was the wife of the shepherd Faustulus and the nurse of Romulus and Remus after they had been taken from the she-wolf. According to other accounts again she was not the wife of Faustulus, but a prostitute who from her mode of life was called lupa by the shepherds, and who left the property she gained in that way to the Roman people. Thus much seems certain, whatever we may think of the stories, that she was of Etruscan origin, and connected with the worship of the Lares, from which her name Larentia seems to be derived.

L. **Accius** or **Attius**, an early Roman tragic poet and the son of a freedman, was born B. C. 170, and lived to a great age. Cicero, when a young man, frequently conversed with him. His tragedies were chiefly imitated from the Greek, but he also wrote some on Roman subjects (*Praetextata*); one of which, entitled Brutus, was probably in honour of his patron D. Brutus. We possess only fragments of his tragedies, but they are spoken of in terms of admiration by the ancient writers. Accius also wrote *Annales* in verse, containing the history of Rome, like those of Ennius; and a prose work, *Libri Didascalion*, which seems to have been a history of poetry. The fragments of his tragedies are given by Bothe, *Poet. Scenici Latin.* vol. v. Lips. 1834: and those of the Didascalia by Madvig, *De L. Attii Didascaliis Comment.* Hafniae, 1831.

Acco, a chief of the Senones in Gaul, who induced his countrymen to revolt against Caesar, B. C. 53, by whom he was put to death.

Acê. [PTOLEMAIS.]

Acerbas, a Tyrian priest of Hercules, who married Elissa, the sister of king Pygmalion. He had concealed his treasures in the earth, knowing the avarice of Pygmalion, but he was murdered by Pygmalion, who hoped to obtain his treasures through his sister. The prudence of Elissa saved the treasures, and she emigrated from Phoenicia. In this account, taken from Justin, Acerbas is the same person as Sichaeus, and Elissa the same as Dido in Virgil (*Aen.* i. 343, seq.). The names in Justin are undoubtedly more correct than in Virgil; for Virgil here, as in other cases, has changed a foreign name into one more convenient to him.

Acerrae (Acerrānus). 1. (*Acerra*), a town in Campania on the Clanius, received the Roman franchise in B. C. 332. It was destroyed by Hannibal, but was rebuilt.—2. (*Gerra*), a town of the Insubres in Gallia Transpadana.

Acersecomes (Ἀκερσεκόμης), a surname of Apollo expressive of his beautiful hair which was never cut or shorn.

Acesas (Ἀκεσᾶς), a native of Salamis in Cyprus, famed for his skill in weaving cloth with variegated patterns (*polymitarius*). He and his son Helicon were the first who made a peplus for Athena Polias. They must have lived before the time of Euripides and Plato, who mention this peplus.

Acesines (Ἀκεσίνης). 1. (*Chenaub*), a river in India, into which the Hydaspes flows, and which itself flows into the Indus.—2. (*Alcantara*), a river in Sicily, near Tauromenium.

Acestes (Ἀκέστης), son of a Trojan woman of the name of Egesta or Segesta, who was sent by her father to Sicily, that she might not be devoured by the monsters which infested the territory of Troy. When Egesta arrived in Sicily, the river-god Crimisus begot by her a son Acestes, who was afterwards regarded as the hero who had founded the town of Segesta. Aeneas, on his arrival in Sicily, was hospitably received by Acestes.

Acestor (Ἀκέστωρ). 1. Surnamed *Sacas*, on account of his foreign origin, was a tragic poet at Athens, and a contemporary of Aristophanes.—2. A sculptor of Cnossus, who flourished about B. C. 452.

Achaea (Ἀχαία, from ἄχος, "grief"), "the distressed one," a surname of Demeter at Athens, so called on account of her sorrow for the loss of her daughter.

Achaei (Ἀχαιοί), one of the chief Hellenic races, were according to tradition descended from Achaeus, who was the son of Xuthus and Creusa, and grandson of Hellen. The Achaei originally dwelt in Thessaly, and from thence migrated to Peloponnesus, the whole of which became subject to them with the exception of Arcadia, and the country afterwards called Achaia. As they were the ruling nation in Peloponnesus in the heroic times, Homer frequently gives the name of Achaei to the collective Greeks. On the conquest of the greater part of Peloponnesus by the Heraclidae and the Dorians 80 years after the Trojan war, many of the Achaei under Tisamenus, the son of Orestes, left their country and took possession of the northern coast of Peloponnesus then called Aegialea, and inhabited by the Ionians, whom they expelled from the country, which was henceforth called Achaia. The expelled Ionians migrated to Attica and Asia Minor. The Achaei settled in 12 cities: Pellene, Aegira, Aegae, Bura, Helice, Aegium, Rhypae, Patrae, Pharae, Olenus, Dyme, and Tritaea. These cities are said to have been governed by Tisamenus and his descendants till Ogyges, upon whose death a democratical form of government was established in each state; but the twelve states formed a league for mutual defence and protection. In the Persian war the Achaei took no part; and they had little influence in the affairs of Greece till the time of the successors of Alexander. In B.C. 281 the Achaei, who were then subject to the Macedonians, resolved to renew their ancient league for the purpose of shaking off the Macedonian yoke. This was the origin of the celebrated Achaean League. It at first consisted of only four towns, Dyme, Patrae, Tritaea, and Pharae, but was subsequently joined by the other towns of Achaia with the exception of Olenus and Helice. It did not, however, obtain much importance till B. C. 251, when Aratus united to it his native town, Sicyon. The example of Sicyon was followed by Corinth and many other towns in Greece, and the League soon became the chief political power in Greece. At length the Achaei declared war against the Romans, who destroyed the League, and thus put an end to the independence of Greece. Corinth, then the chief town of the League, was taken by the Roman general Mummius, in B. c. 146, and the whole of southern Greece made a Roman province under the name of ACHAIA. The different states composing the Achaean League had equal rights. The assemblies of the League were held twice a year, in the spring and autumn, in a grove of Zeus Homagyrius near Aegium. At these assemblies all the business of the League was conducted, and at the spring meeting the public functionaries were chosen. These were:—1. a Strategus (στρατηγός) or General, and an Hipparchus (Ίππαρχος) or commander of the cavalry; 2. a Secretary (γραμματεύς); and 3. ten Demiurgi (δημιουργοί, also called ἄρχοντες), who appear to have had the right of convening the assembly. For further particulars see Dict. of Ant., art Achaicum Foedus.

Achaemenes ('Αχαιμένης). 1. The ancestor of the Persian kings, who founded the family of the Achaemenidae ('Αχαιμενίδαι), which was the noblest family of the Pasargadae, the noblest of the Persian tribes. The Roman poets use the adjective Achaemenius in the sense of Persian. — 2. Son of Darius I., governor of Egypt, commanded the Egyptian fleet in the expedition of Xerxes against Greece, B. C. 480. He was defeated and killed in battle by Inarus the Libyan, B. c. 460.

Achaemenides, or Achemenides, son of Adamastus of Ithaca, and a companion of Ulysses, who left him behind in Sicily, when he fled from the Cyclops. Here he was found by Aeneas, who took him with him.

Achaeus ('Αχαιός). 1. Son of Xuthus, the mythical ancestor of the ACHAEI. — 2. Governor under Antiochus III. of all Asia W. of mount Taurus. He revolted against Antiochus, but was defeated by the latter, taken prisoner at Sardis, and put to death, B. c. 214. — 3. Of Eretria in Euboea, a tragic poet, born B. c. 484. In 447, he contended with Sophocles and Euripides, and though he subsequently brought out many dramas, according to some as many as 34 or 40, he nevertheless only gained the prize once. In the satyrical drama he possessed considerable merit. The fragments of his pieces have been published by Urlichs, Bonn, 1834.

Achaïa ('Αχαΐα: 'Αχαιός). 1. The northern coast of the Peloponnesus, originally called Aegialea (Αἰγιάλεια) or Aegialus (Αἰγιαλός), i. e. the coast-land, was bounded on the N. by the Corinthian gulf and the Ionian sea, on the S. by Elis and Arcadia, on the W. by the Ionian sea, and on the E. by Sicyonia. It was a narrow slip of country sloping down from the mountains to the sea. The coast is generally low, and has few good ports. Respecting its inhabitants see ACHAEI. — 2. A district in Thessaly, which appears to have been the original seat of the Achaei. It retained the name of Achaia in the time of Herodotus. — 3. The Roman province, included Peloponnesus and northern Greece S. of Thessaly. It was formed on the dissolution of the Achaean League in B. c. 146, and hence derived its name.

Acharnae ('Αχαρναί: 'Αχαρνεύς, Pl. 'Αχαρνῆς), the principal demus of Attica, belonging to the tribe

Oeneis, 60 stadia N. of Athens, possessed a rough and warlike population, who were able to furnish 3000 hoplitae at the commencement of the Peloponnesian war. Their land was fertile and they carried on a considerable traffic in charcoal. One of the plays of Aristophanes bears the name of the inhabitants of this demus.

Acharrae, a town in Thessaliotis in Thessaly, on the river Pamisus.

Achates (Dirillo), a river in southern Sicily, between Camarina and Gela, in which the first agate is said to have been found.

Acheloides, a surname of the Sirens, the daughters of Achelous and a Muse: also a surname of water-nymphs.

Achelous ('Αχελῷος, 'Αχελώιος in Hom.: Aspro Potamo), more anciently called Thoas, Axenus, and Thestius, the largest river in Greece. It rises in Mount Pindus, and flows southward, forming the boundary between Acarnania and Aetolia, and falls into the Ionian sea opposite the islands called Echinades. It is about 130 miles in length. The god of this river is described as the son of Oceanus and Tethys, and as the eldest of his 3000 brothers. He fought with Hercules for Deïanira, but was conquered in the contest. He then took the form of a bull, but was again overcome by Hercules, who deprived him of one of his horns, which however he recovered by giving up the horn of Amalthea. According to Ovid (Met. ix. 87), the Naiads changed the horn which Hercules took from Achelous into the horn of plenty. Achelous was from the earliest times considered to be a great divinity throughout Greece, and was invoked in prayers, sacrifices, &c. On several coins of Acarnania the god is represented as a bull with the head of an old man. — Achelous was also the name of a river in Arcadia, and of another in Thessaly.

Achemenides [ACHAEMENIDES.]

Acheron ('Αχέρων), the name of several rivers, all of which were, at least at one time, believed to be connected with the lower world.—1. A river in Thesprotia in Epirus, which flows through the lake Acherusia into the Ionian sea. — 2. A river in Elis which flows into the Alphēus. — 3. A river in southern Italy in Bruttii, on which Alexander of Epirus perished. — 4. The river of the lower world, round which the shades hover, and into which the Pyriphlegethon and Cocytus flow. In late writers the name of Acheron is used in a general sense to designate the whole of the lower world. The Etruscans were acquainted with the worship of Acheron (Acheruns) from very early times, as we must infer from their Acheruntici libri, which treated of the deification of souls, and of the sacrifices (Acheruntia sacra) by which this was to be effected.

Acherontia. 1. (Acerenza), a town in Apulia on a summit of Mount Vultur, whence Horace (Carm. iii. 4. 14) speaks of celsae nidum Acherontiae. — 2. A town on the river Acheron, in Bruttii. [ACHERON, No. 3.]

Acherusia ('Αχερουσία λίμνη or 'Αχερουσίς), the name of several lakes and swamps, which, like the various rivers of the name of Acheron, were at some time believed to be connected with the lower world, until at last the Acherusia came to be considered to be in the lower world itself. The lake to which this belief seems to have been first attached was the Acherusia in Thesprotia, through which the Acheron flowed. Other lakes or swamps of the same name were near Hermione in Argolis, between Cumae and cape Misenum in Campania, and lastly in Egypt, near Memphis. — Acherusia was also the name of a peninsula, near Heraclēa in Bithynia, with a deep chasm, into which Hercules is said to have descended to bring up the dog Cerberus.

Achetum, a small town in Sicily, the site of which is uncertain.

Achilla or **Acholla** (Ἄχολλα: Ἀχολλαῖος, Achillitanus: *El Aliah*, Ru.), a town on the seacoast of Africa, in the Carthaginian territory (Byzacena), a little above the northern point of the Syrtis Minor.

Achillas (Ἀχιλλᾶς), one of the guardians of the Egyptian king Ptolemy Dionysus, and commander of the troops, when Pompey fled to Egypt, B. C. 48. It was he and L. Septimius who killed Pompey. He subsequently joined the eunuch Pothinus in resisting Caesar, and obtained possession of the greatest part of Alexandria. He was shortly afterwards put to death by Arsinoë, the youngest sister of Ptolemy, B. C. 47.

Achilles (Ἀχιλλεύς), the great hero of the Iliad. — *Homeric story.* Achilles was the son of Peleus, king of the Myrmidones in Phthiotis, in Thessaly, and of the Nereid Thetis. From his father's name he is often called *Pelīdes, Peleïades*, or *Pelīon*, and from his grandfather's, *Aeacides*. He was educated by Phoenix, who taught him eloquence and the arts of war, and accompanied him to the Trojan war. In the healing art he was instructed by Chiron, the centaur. His mother Thetis foretold him that his fate was either to gain glory and die early, or to live a long but inglorious life. The hero chose the former, and took part in the Trojan war, from which he knew that he was not to return. In 50 ships he led his hosts of Myrmidones, Hellenes, and Achaeans against Troy. Here the swift-footed Achilles was the great bulwark of the Greeks, and the worthy favourite of Athena and Hera. Previous to the dispute with Agamemnon, he ravaged the country around Troy, and destroyed 12 towns on the coast and 11 in the interior of the country. When Agamemnon was obliged to give up Chryseïs to her father, he threatened to take away Briseïs from Achilles, who surrendered her on the persuasion of Athena, but at the same time refused to take any further part in the war, and shut himself up in his tent. Zeus, on the entreaty of Thetis, promised that victory should be on the side of the Trojans, until the Achaeans should have honoured her son. The affairs of the Greeks declined in consequence, and they were at last pressed so hard, that an embassy was sent to Achilles, offering him rich presents and the restoration of Briseïs; but in vain. Finally, however, he was persuaded by Patroclus, his dearest friend, to allow him to make use of his men, his horses, and his armour. Patroclus was slain, and when this news reached Achilles, he was seized with unspeakable grief. Thetis consoled him, and promised new arms, to be made by Hephaestus, and Iris appeared to rouse him from his lamentations, and exhorted him to rescue the body of Patroclus. Achilles now rose, and his thundering voice alone put the Trojans to flight. When his new armour was brought to him, he hurried to the field of battle, disdaining to take any drink or food until the death of his friend

should be avenged. He wounded and slew numbers of Trojans, and at length met Hector, whom he chased thrice around the walls of the city. He then slew him, tied his body to his chariot, and dragged him to the ships of the Greeks. After this, he burnt the body of Patroclus, together with twelve young captive Trojans, who were sacrificed to appease the spirit of his friend; and subsequently gave up the body of Hector to Priam, who came in person to beg for it. Achilles himself fell in the battle at the Scaean gate, before Troy was taken. His death itself does not occur in the Iliad, but it is alluded to in a few passages (xxii. 358, xxi. 278). It is expressly mentioned in the Odyssey (xxiv. 36), where it is said that his fall — his conqueror is not mentioned — was lamented by gods and men, that his remains together with those of Patroclus were buried in a golden urn which Dionysus had given as a present to Thetis, and were deposited in a place on the coast of the Hellespont, where a mound was raised over them. Achilles is the principal hero of the Iliad: he is the handsomest and bravest of all the Greeks; he is affectionate towards his mother and his friends; formidable in battles, which are his delight; openhearted and without fear, and at the same time susceptible of the gentle and quiet joys of home. His greatest passion is ambition, and when his sense of honour is hurt, he is unrelenting in his revenge and anger, but withal submits obediently to the will of the gods. — *Later traditions.* These chiefly consist in accounts which fill up the history of his youth and death. His mother wishing to make her son immortal, is said to have concealed him by night in the fire, in order to destroy the mortal parts he had inherited from his father, and by day to have anointed him with ambrosia. But Peleus one night discovered his child in the fire, and cried out in terror. Thetis left her son and fled, and Peleus entrusted him to Chiron, who educated and instructed him in the arts of riding, hunting, and playing the phorminx, and also changed his original name, Ligyron, i. e. the "whining," into Achilles. Chiron fed his pupil with the hearts of lions and the marrow of bears. According to other accounts, Thetis endeavoured to make Achilles immortal by dipping him in the river Styx, and succeeded with the exception of the ankles, by which she held him. When he was nine years old, Calchas declared that Troy could not be taken without his aid, and Thetis knowing that this war would be fatal to him, disguised him as a maiden, and introduced him among the daughters of Lycomedes of Scyros, where he was called by the name of Pyrrha on account of his golden locks. But his real character did not remain concealed long, for one of his companions, Deïdamia, became mother of a son, Pyrrhus or Neoptolemus, by him. Ulysses at last discovered his place of concealment, and Achilles immediately promised his assistance. During the war against Troy, Achilles slew Penthesilēa, an Amazon. He also fought with Memnon and Troïlus. The accounts of his death differ very much, though all agree in stating that he did not fall by human hands, or at least not without the interference of the god Apollo. According to some traditions, he was killed by Apollo himself; according to others, Apollo assumed the appearance of Paris in killing him, while others say that Apollo merely directed the weapon of Paris against Achilles, and thus caused his death, as had been suggested by the dying Hector. Others again relate that Achilles loved Polyxena, a daughter of Priam, and tempted by the promise that he should receive her as his wife, if he would join the Trojans, he went without arms into the temple of Apollo at Thymbra, and was assassinated there by Paris. His body was rescued by Ulysses and Ajax the Telamonian; his armour was promised by Thetis to the bravest among the Greeks, which gave rise to a contest between the two heroes who had rescued his body. [AJAX.] After his death, Achilles became one of the judges in the lower world, and dwelled in the islands of the blessed, where he was united with Medēa or Iphigenīa.

Achilles Tatīus, or as others call him Achilles Statius, an Alexandrine rhetorician, lived in the latter half of the fifth or the beginning of the sixth century of our era. He is the author of a Greek romance in eight books, containing the adventures of two lovers, Clitophon and Leucippe, which has come down to us. The best edition is by Fr. Jacobs, Lips. 1821. Suidas ascribes to this Achilles a work on the sphere (περὶ σφαίρας), a fragment of which professing to be an introduction to the Phaenomena of Aratus is still extant. But this work was written at an earlier period. It is printed in Petavius, *Uranologia*, Paris, 1630, and Amsterdam, 1703.

Achillēum ('Αχίλλειον), a town near the promontory Sigēum in the Troad, where Achilles was supposed to have been buried. There was a place of the same name on the Cimmerian Bosporus, or Straits of Kaffa, on the Asiatic side.

Achilleus, assumed the title of emperor under Diocletian, and reigned over Egypt for some time. He was taken by Diocletian after a siege of 8 months in Alexandria, and put to death, A. D. 296.

Achillēus Drōmos ('Αχίλλειος δρόμος : *Tendera* or *Tendra*), a narrow tongue of land in the Euxine Sea, not far from the mouth of the Borysthenes, where Achilles is said to have made a race-course. Before it lay the celebrated Island of Achilles (*Insula Achillis*) or Leuce (Λευκή), where there was a temple of Achilles.

Achillēus Portus ('Αχίλλειος λιμήν), a harbour in Laconia, near the promontory Taenarum.

Achillīdes, a patronymic of Pyrrhus, son of Achilles.

Achillis Insūla. [ACHILLEUS DROMOS.]

Achirŏe ('Αχιρόη), daughter of Nilus, and wife of Belus, by whom she became the mother of Aegyptus and Danaus.

Achīvi, the name of the Achaei in the Latin writers, and frequently used, like Achaei, to signify the whole Greek nation. [ACHAEI.]

Acholla. [ACHILLA.]

Acholŏē. [HARPYIAE.]

Achrādīna or **Acrādīna.** [SYRACUSAE.]

Acichŏrīus ('Ακιχώριος), one of the leaders of the Gauls, who invaded Thrace and Macedonia in B. C. 280. In the following year he accompanied Brennus in his invasion of Greece. Some writers suppose that Brennus and Acichorius are the same persons, the former being only a title and the latter the real name.

Acidālia, a surname of Venus, from the well Acidalius near Orchomenos, where she used to bathe with the Graces.

Acidīnus, L. Manlīus. 1. One of the Roman generals in the second Punic war, praetor urbanus

B. C. 210, served against Hasdrubal in 207, and was sent into Spain in 206, where he remained till 199.—2. Surnamed FULVIANUS, because he originally belonged to the Fulvia gens, praetor B. C. 188 in Nearer Spain, and consul in 179 with his own brother Q. Fulvius Flaccus, which is the only instance of two brothers holding the consulship at the same time.

Acilia Gens, plebeian. Its members are mentioned under the family-names of AVIOLA, BALBUS, and GLABRIO.

Acis ('Ακις), son of Faunus and Symaethis, was beloved by the nymph Galatea: Polyphemus the Cyclop, jealous of him, crushed him under a huge rock. His blood gushing forth from under the rock was changed by the nymph into the river Acis or Acinius at the foot of Mount Aetna (now *Fiume di Jaci*). This story, which is related only by Ovid (*Met.* xiii. 750, seq.), is perhaps no more than a happy fiction suggested by the manner in which the little river springs forth from under a rock.

Acmōnīa ('Ακμονία : 'Ακμονίτης, *Acmonensis*), a city of the Greater Phrygia.

Acmōnīdes, one of the three Cyclopes in Ovid, is the same as Pyracmon in Virgil, and as Arges in most other accounts of the Cyclopes.

Acoetes ('Ακοίτης), son of a poor fisherman of Maeonia, who served as a pilot in a ship. After landing at the island of Naxos, the sailors brought with them on board a beautiful boy asleep, whom they wished to take with them: but Acoetes, who recognised in the boy the god Bacchus, dissuaded them from it, but in vain. When the ship had reached the open sea, the boy awoke, and desired to be carried back to Naxos. The sailors promised to do so, but did not keep their word. Hereupon the god disclosed himself to them in his majesty; vines began to twine round the vessel, tigers appeared, and the sailors, seized with madness, jumped into the sea and perished. Acoetes alone was saved and conveyed back to Naxos, where he was initiated in the Bacchic mysteries This is the account of Ovid (*Met.* iii. 582, &c.). Other writers call the crew of the ship Tyrrhenian pirates, and derive the name of the Tyrrhenian sea from them.

Acontīus ('Ακόντιος), a beautiful youth of the island of Ceos. On one occasion he came to Delos to celebrate the annual festival of Diana, and fell in love with Cydippe, the daughter of a noble Athenian. In order to gain her, he had recourse to a stratagem. While she was sitting in the temple of Diana, he threw before her an apple upon which he had written the words "I swear by the sanctuary of Diana to marry Acontius." The nurse took up the apple and handed it to Cydippe, who read aloud what was written upon it, and then threw the apple away. But the goddess had heard her vow, and the repeated illness of the maiden, when she was about to marry another man, at length compelled her father to give her in marriage to Acontius. This story is related by Ovid (*Heroid.* 20, 21), who borrowed it from a lost poem of Callimachus, entitled "Cydippe."

Acŏris ('Ακορις), king of Egypt, assisted Evagoras king of Cyprus, against Artaxerxes king of Persia, about B. C. 385. He died about 374, before the Persians entered Egypt, which was in the following year.

Acrae ('Ακραι) 1. (Nr. *Palazzolo*, Ru.), a town

in Sicily, W. of Syracuse, and 10 stadia from the river Anapus, was founded by the Syracusans 70 years after the foundation of their own city.—2. A town in Aetolia.

Acraea ('Ακραία), and Acraeus, are surnames given to various goddesses and gods whose temples were situated upon hills, such as Zeus, Hera, Aphrodite, Pallas, Artemis, and others.

Acraepheus. [ACRAEPHIA.]

Acraephia, Acraephiae, or Acraephion ('Ακραιφία, 'Ακραιφίαι, 'Ακραίφιον : 'Ακραίφιος, 'Ακραιφιαῖος: Kardhitza), a town in Boeotia, on the lake Copais, said to have been founded by Acraepheus, the son of Apollo.

Acragas. [AGRIGENTUM.]

Acratus, a freedman of Nero, sent into Asia and Achaia (A. D. 64) to plunder the temples and take away the statues of the gods.

Acriae ('Ακριαί, or 'Ακραῖαι), a town in Laconia, not far from the mouth of the Eurotas.

Acrillae, a town in Sicily between Agrigentum and Acrae.

Acrisione ('Ακρισιώνη), a patronymic of Danaë, daughter of Acrisius. Perseus, grandson of Acrisius, was called in the same way Acrisioniades.

Acrisius ('Ακρίσιοs), son of Abas, king of Argos, and of Ocalia, grandson of Lynceus, and great-grandson of Danaus. His twin-brother was Proetus, with whom he is said to have quarrelled even in the womb of his mother. Acrisius expelled Proetus from his inheritance ; but, supported by his father-in-law Iobates, the Lycian, Proetus returned, and Acrisius was compelled to share his kingdom with his brother by giving up to him Tiryns, while he retained Argos for himself. An oracle had declared that Danaë, the daughter of Acrisius, would give birth to a son who would kill his grandfather. For this reason he kept Danaë shut up in a subterraneous apartment, or in a brazen tower. But here she became mother of Perseus, notwithstanding the precautions of her father, according to some accounts by her uncle Proetus, and according to others by Zeus, who visited her in the form of a shower of gold. Acrisius ordered mother and child to be exposed on the wide sea in a chest ; but the chest floated towards the island of Seriphus, where both were rescued by Dictys. As to the manner in which the oracle was subsequently fulfilled, see PERSEUS.

Acritas ('Ακρείτας: C. Gallo), the most southerly promontory in Messenia.

Acroceraunia (τὰ 'Ακροκεραύνια, sc. ὄρη: C. Linguetta), a promontory in Epirus, jutting out into the Ionian sea, was the most westerly part of the CERAUNII MONTES. The coast of the Acroceraunia was dangerous to ships, whence Horace (Carm. i. 3. 20) speaks of infames scopulos Acroceraunia.

Acrocorinthus. [CORINTHUS.]

Acrolissus. [LISSUS.]

Acron. 1. King of the Caeninenses, whom Romulus slew in battle, and whose arms he dedicated to Jupiter Feretrius as Spolia Opima.—2. An eminent physician of Agrigentum in Sicily, is said to have been in Athens during the great plague (B. C. 430) in the Peloponnesian war, and to have ordered large fires to be kindled in the streets for the purpose of purifying the air, which proved of great service to several of the sick. This fact, however, is not mentioned by Thucydides. The medical sect of the Empirici, in order to boast

of a greater antiquity than the Dogmatici (founded about B. C. 400), claimed Acron as their founder, though they did not really exist before the third century B. C.

Acron, Helenius, a Roman grammarian, probably of the fifth century A. D., wrote notes on Horace, part of which are extant, and also, according to some critics, the scholia which we have on Persius.

Acropolis. [ATHENAE.]

Acropolita, Georgius (Γεώργιος 'Ακροπολίτης), a Byzantine writer, was born at Constantinople in A. D. 1220, and died in 1282. He wrote several works which have come down to us. The most important of them is a history of the Byzantine empire, from the taking of Constantinople by the Latins in 1204, down to the year 1261, when Michael Palaeologus delivered the city from the foreign yoke. Edited by Leo Allatius, Paris, 165?, reprinted at Venice, 1729.

Acrorea (ἡ 'Ακρώρεια), a mountainous tract of country in the north of Elis.

Acrotatus ('Ακρότατος). 1. Son of Cleomenes II. king of Sparta, sailed to Sicily in B. C. 314 to assist the Agrigentines against Agathocles of Syracuse. On his arrival at Agrigentum he acted with such tyranny that the inhabitants compelled him to leave the city. He returned to Sparta, and died before his father, leaving a son, Areus.—2. Grandson of the preceding, and the son of Areus I. king of Sparta ; bravely defended Sparta against Pyrrhus in B. C. 272 ; succeeded his father as king in 265, but was killed in the same year in battle against Aristodemus, the tyrant of Megalopolis.

Acrothoum or Acrothoi ('Ακρόθωον, 'Ακρόθωοι : 'Ακροθωΐτης : Lavra), afterwards called Uranopolis, a town near the extremity of the peninsula of Athos.

Actaea ('Ακταία), daughter of Nereus and Doris.

Actaeon ('Ακταίων). 1. A celebrated huntsman, son of Aristaeus and Autonoë, a daughter of Cadmus, was trained in the art of hunting by the centaur Chiron. One day as he was hunting, he saw Artemis with her nymphs bathing in the vale of Gargaphia, whereupon the goddess changed him into a stag, in which form he was torn to pieces by his 50 dogs on Mount Cithaeron. Others relate that he provoked the anger of the goddess by boasting that he excelled her in hunting.—2. Son of Melissus, and grandson of Abron, who had fled from Argos to Corinth for fear of the tyrant Phidon. Archias, a Corinthian, enamoured with the beauty of Actaeon, endeavoured to carry him off; but in the struggle which ensued between Melissus and Archias, Actaeon was killed. [ARCHIAS.]

Actaeus ('Ακταῖος), son of Erisichthon, and the earliest king of Attica. He had three daughters, Agraulos, Herse, and Pandrosus, and was succeeded by Cecrops, who married Agraulos.

Acte, the concubine of Nero, was originally a slave from Asia Minor. Nero at one time thought of marrying her ; whence he pretended that she was descended from king Attalus. She survived Nero.

Acte ('Ακτή), properly a piece of land running into the sea, and attached to another larger piece of land, but not necessarily by a narrow neck. 1. An ancient name of Attica, used especially by the poets.—2. The eastern coast of Peloponnesus near Troezen and Epidaurus.—3. The peninsula between the Strymonic and Singitic gulfs, on which Mount Athos is.

Actiăcus. [ACTIUM.]

Actisănes ('Ακτισάνης), a king of Ethiopia, who conquered Egypt and governed it with justice, in the reign of Amasis. This Amasis is a more ancient king than the contemporary of Cyrus.

Actium ("Ακτιον : "Ακτιος : La Punta not Azio), a promontory, and likewise a place, in Acarnania, at the entrance of the Ambracian gulf, off which Augustus gained the celebrated victory over Antony and Cleopatra, on September 2, B. C. 31. At Actium there was originally no town, but only a temple of Apollo, who was hence called *Actiacus* and *Actius*. This temple was beautified by Augustus, who established, or rather revived, a festival to Apollo, called *Actia* (see *Dict. of Ant. s. v.*), and erected NICOPOLIS on the opposite coast, in commemoration of his victory. A few buildings sprung up around the temple at Actium, but the place was only a kind of suburb of Nicopolis.

Actius. [ATTIUS.]

Actor ('Ακτωρ). 1. Son of Deion and Diomede, father of Menoetius, and grandfather of Patroclus. — 2. Son of Phorbas and Hyrmine, and husband of Molione. — 3. A companion of Aeneas, of whose conquered lance Turnus made a boast. This story seems to have given rise to the proverb *Actoris spolium* (Juv. ii. 100), for any poor spoil.

Actŏrĭdes or **Actŏrĭon** ('Ακτορίδης or 'Ακτορίων), patronymics of descendants of an Actor, such as Patroclus, Erithus, Eurytus, and Cteatus.

Actuarĭus, Joannes, a Greek physician of Constantinople, probably lived in the reign of Andronicus II. Palaeologus, A. D. 1281—1328. He was the author of several medical works, which are extant.

C. Aculĕo, an eminent Roman lawyer, who married the sister of Helvia, the mother of Cicero: his son was C. Visellius Varro ; whence it would appear that Aculeo was only a surname given to the father from his acuteness, and that his full name was C. Visellius Varro Aculeo.

Acūsilāus ('Ακουσίλαος), of Argos, one of the earlier Greek logographers, flourished about B. C. 525. Three books of his Genealogies are quoted, which were for the most part only a translation of Hesiod into prose. He wrote in the Ionic dialect. His fragments are published by Sturtz, Lips. 1824, and in Didot's *Fragm. Histor. Graec.* p. 100, seq.

Ada ("Αδα), daughter of Hecatomnus, king of Caria, and sister of Mausolus, Artemisia, Idrieus, and Pixodarus. She was married to her brother Idrieus, on whose death (B. C. 344) she succeeded to the throne of Caria, but was expelled by her brother Pixodarus in 340. When Alexander entered Caria in 334, Ada, who was in possession of the fortress of Alinda, surrendered this place to him. After taking Halicarnassus, Alexander committed the government of Caria to her.

Adamantĕa. [AMALTHEA.]

Adamantĭus. ('Αδαμάντιος), a Greek physician, flourished about A. D. 415, the author of a Greek treatise on Physiognomy, which is borrowed in a great measure from Polemo's work on the same subject. Edited by Franzius, in *Scriptores Physiognomiae Veteres,* 1780, 8vo.

Addŭa (*Adda*), a river of Gallia Cisalpina, which rises in the Rhaetian Alps, and flows through

the Lacus Larius (*L. di Como*) into the Po, about 8 miles above Cremona.

Adherbal ('Ατάρβας), son of Micipsa, and grandson of Masinissa, had the kingdom of Numidia left to him by his father in conjunction with his brother Hiempsal and Jugurtha, B. C. 118. After the murder of his brother by Jugurtha, Adherbal fled to Rome and was restored to his share of the kingdom by the Romans in 117. But he was again stripped of his dominions by Jugurtha and besieged in Cirta, where he was treacherously killed by Jugurtha in 112.

Adiabēnē ('Αδιαβηνή), a district of Assyria, E. of the Tigris, and between the river Lycus, called Zabatus in the Anabasis of Xenophon, and the Caprus, both of which are branches of the Tigris.

Adīmantus ('Αδείμαντος). 1. The commander of the Corinthian fleet, when Xerxes invaded Greece (B. C. 480), vehemently opposed the advice of Themistocles to give battle to the Persians. — 2. An Athenian, one of the commanders at the battle of Aegospotami, B. C. 405, where he was taken prisoner. He was accused of treachery in this battle, and is ridiculed by Aristophanes in the " Frogs." — 3. The brother of Plato, frequently mentioned by the latter.

Adis ('Αδίς : *Rhades ?*), a considerable town on the coast of Africa, in the territory of Carthage (Zeugitana), a short distance E. of Tunis. Under the Romans it appears to have been supplanted by a new city, named Maxula.

Admētē ('Αδμήτη). 1. Daughter of Oceanus and Thetys. — 2. Daughter of Eurystheus and Antimache or Admete. Hercules was obliged by her father to fetch for her the girdle of Ares, which was worn by Hippolyte, queen of the Amazons.

Admētus ('Αδμητος). 1. Son of Pheres and Periclymene or Clymene, was king of Pherae in Thessaly. He took part in the Calydonian hunt and in the expedition of the Argonauts. He sued for the hand of Alcestis, the daughter of Pelias, who promised her to him on condition that he should come to her in a chariot drawn by lions and boars. This task Admetus performed by the assistance of Apollo, who served him, according to some accounts, out of attachment to him, or, according to others, because he was obliged to serve a mortal for one year for having slain the Cyclops. On the day of his marriage with Alcestis, Admetus neglected to offer a sacrifice to Artemis, but Apollo reconciled the goddess to him, and at the same time induced the Moirae to grant to Admetus deliverance from death, if at the hour of his death his father, mother, or wife would die for him. Alcestis died in his stead, but was brought back by Hercules from the lower world. — 2. King of the Molossians, to whom THEMISTOCLES fled for protection, when pursued as a party to the treason of Pausanias.

Adōnis ("Αδωνις), a beautiful youth, beloved by Aphrodite. He was, according to Apollodorus, a son of Cinyras and Medarme, or, according to the cyclic poet Panyasis, a son of Theias, king of Assyria, and Smyrna (Myrrha). The ancient story ran thus : Smyrna had neglected the worship of Aphrodite, and was punished by the goddess with an unnatural love for her father. With the assistance of her nurse she contrived to share her father's bed. When he discovered the crime he wished to kill her ; but she fled, and on being nearly overtaken, prayed to the gods to make her invisible. They were moved to pity and changed her into a tree called σμύρνα. After the lapse of 9 months the tree burst, and Adonis was born. Aphrodite was so much charmed with the beauty of the infant, that she concealed it in a chest which she entrusted to Persephone ; but the latter refused to give it up. Zeus decided the dispute by declaring that during 4 months of every year Adonis should be left to himself, during 4 months he should belong to Persephone, and during the remaining 4 to Aphrodite. Adonis, however, preferring to live with Aphrodite, also spent with her the four months over which he had control. Adonis afterwards died of a wound which he received from a boar during the chase. The grief of the goddess at the loss of her favourite was so great, that the gods of the lower world allowed him to spend 6 months of every year with Aphrodite upon the earth. The worship of Adonis, which in later times was spread over nearly all the countries round the Mediterranean, was, as the story itself sufficiently indicates, of Asiatic, or more especially of Phoenician origin. Thence it was transferred to Assyria, Egypt, Greece, and even to Italy, though of course with various modifications. In the Homeric poems no trace of it occurs, and the later Greek poets changed the original symbolic account of Adonis into a poetical story. In the Asiatic religions Aphrodite was the fructifying principle of nature, and Adonis appears to have reference to the death of nature in winter and its revival in spring — hence he spends 6 months in the lower and 6 in the upper world. His death and his return to life were celebrated in annual festivals (*Adonia*) at Byblos, Alexandria in Egypt, Athens, and other places

Adōnis ("Αδωνις), a small river of Phoenicia, which rises in the range of Libanus.

Adramyttium ('Αδραμύττειον or 'Αδραμύττιον: 'Αδραμυττηνός : *Adramyti*), a town of Mysia near the head of the gulf of Adramyttium, and opposite to the island of Lesbos.

Adrāna (*Eder*), a river in Germany, which flows into the Fulda near Cassel.

Adrānum or **Hadrānum** ("Αδρανον, "Αδρανον: 'Αδρανίτης : *Aderno*), a town in Sicily, on the river Adranus, at the foot of M. Aetna, was built by Dionysius, and was the seat of the worship of the god Adranus.

Adrānus ('Αδρανός). [ADRANUM.]

Adrastīa ('Αδράστεια). 1. A Cretan nymph, daughter of Melisseus, to whom Rhea entrusted the infant Zeus to be reared in the Dictaean grotto. —2. A surname of Nemesis, derived by some writers from Adrastus, who is said to have built the first sanctuary of Nemesis on the river Asopus, and by others from the verb διδράσκειν, i. e. the goddess whom none can escape.

Adrastus ("Αδραστος). 1. Son of Talaus, king of Argos, and Lysimache, or Lysianassa or Eurynome. Adrastus was expelled from Argos by Amphiaräus, and fled to Polybus, king of Sicyon, whom he succeeded on the throne of Sicyon, and instituted the Nemean games. Afterwards he became reconciled to Amphiaraus, and returned to his kingdom of Argos. He married his two daughters Deipyle and Argīa, the former to Tydeus of Calydon, and the latter to Polynices of Thebes, both fugitives from their native countries. He now prepared to restore Polynices to Thebes, who had been expelled by his brother Eteocles, although Amphiaraus foretold that all who should engage in the war should perish,

with the exception of Adrastus. Thus arose the celebrated war of the " Seven against Thebes," in which Adrastus was joined by six other heroes, viz. Polynices, Tydeus, Amphiaraus, Capaneus, Hippomedon, and Parthenopaeus. Instead of Tydeus and Polynices other legends mention Eteocles and Mecisteus. This war ended as unfortunately as Amphiaraus had predicted, and Adrastus alone was saved by the swiftness of his horse Arion, the gift of Hercules. Creon of Thebes refusing to allow the bodies of the six heroes to be buried, Adrastus went to Athens and implored the assistance of the Athenians. Theseus was persuaded to undertake an expedition against Thebes ; he took the city and delivered up the bodies of the fallen heroes to their friends for burial. Ten years after this Adrastus persuaded the seven sons of the heroes who had fallen in the war, to make a new attack upon Thebes, and Amphiaraus now promised success. This war is known as the war of the "Epigoni" ('Επίγονοι) or descendants. Thebes was taken and razed to the ground. The only Argive hero that fell in this war, was Aegialeus, the son of Adrastus : the latter died of grief at Megara on his return to Argos, and was buried in the former city. He was worshipped in several parts of Greece, as at Megara, at Sicyon, where his memory was celebrated in tragic choruses, and in Attica. The legends about Adrastus and the two wars against Thebes furnished ample materials for the epic as well as tragic poets of Greece.—2. Son of the Phrygian king Gordius, having unintentionally killed his brother, fled to Croesus, who received him kindly. While hunting he accidentally killed Atys, the son of Croesus, and in despair put an end to his own life.

Adria or **Hadria**. 1. (*Adria*), also called Atria, a town in Gallia Cisalpina, between the mouths of the Po and the Athesis (*Adige*), from which the Adriatic sea takes its name. It was originally a powerful town of the Etruscans. —2 (*Atri*), a town of Picenum in Italy, probably an Etruscan town originally, afterwards a Roman colony, at which place the family of the emperor Hadrian lived.

Adria ('Αδρίας, Ion. 'Αδρίης), or **Mare Adriaticum**, also **Mare Superum**, so called from the town Adria [No. 1], was in its widest signification the sea between Italy on the W., and Illyricum, Epirus, and Greece, on the E. By the Greeks the name Adrias was only applied to the northern part of this sea, the southern part being called the Ionian Sea.

Adriānus. [HADRIANUS.]

Adriānus ('Αδριανός), a Greek rhetorician, born at Tyre in Phoenicia, was the pupil of Herodes Atticus, and obtained the chair of philosophy at Athens during the lifetime of his master. He was invited by M. Antonius to Rome, where he died about A. D. 192. Three of his declamations are extant, edited by Walz in *Rhetores Graeci*, vol. i. 1832.

Adrumētum. [HADRUMETUM.]

Aduatūca, a castle of the Eburones in Gaul, probably the same as the later Aduaca Tongrorum (*Tongern*).

Aduatūci or **Aduatīci**, a powerful people of Gallia Belgica in the time of Caesar, were the descendants of the Cimbri and Teutoni, and lived between the Scaldis (*Schelde*) and Mosa (*Maas*).

Adūla Mons. [ALPES.]

Adūle or **Adūlis** ('Αδούλη, 'Αδουλις, and also other forms: 'Αδουλίτης, Adulitānus: *Arkiko* or *Zula*, Ru.), a maritime city of Aethiopia, on a bay of the Red Sea, called Adulitanus Sinus ('Αδουλιτικὸς κόλπος, *Annesley Bay*). It was believed to have been founded by slaves who fled from Egypt, and afterwards to have fallen into the power of the Auxumitae, for whose trade it became the great emporium. Cosmas Indicopleustes (A. D. 535) found here the *Monumentum Adulitanum*, a Greek inscription recounting the conquests of Ptolemy II. Euergetes in Asia and Thrace.

Adyrmāchīdae ('Αδυρμαχίδαι), a Libyan people, who appear to have once possessed the whole coast of Africa from the Canopic mouth of the Nile to the Catabathmus Major, but were afterwards pressed further inland. In their manners and customs they resembled the Egyptians, to whom they were the nearest neighbours.

Aea (Αἶα), sometimes with the addition of the word Colchis, may be considered either a part of Colchis or another name for the country. (Herod. i. 2.

Aeāces (Αἰάκης), son of Syloson, and grandson of Aeaces, was tyrant of Samos, but was deprived of his tyranny by Aristagoras, when the Ionians revolted from the Persians, B. C. 500. He then fled to the Persians, who restored him to the tyranny of Samos, B. C. 494.

Aeācēum (Αἰάκειον). [AEGINA.]

Aeācīdes (Αἰακίδης), a patronymic of the descendants of Aeacus, as Peleus, Telamon, and Phocus, sons of Aeacus; Achilles, son of Peleus and grandson of Aeacus; Pyrrhus, son of Achilles and great-grandson of Aeacus; and Pyrrhus, king of Epirus, who claimed to be a descendant of Achilles.

Aeācīdes, son of Arymbas, king of Epirus, succeeded to the throne on the death of his cousin Alexander, who was slain in Italy, B. C. 326. Aeacides married Phthia, by whom he had the celebrated PYRRHUS. He took an active part in favour of Olympias against Cassander; but his subjects disliked the war, rose against their king, and drove him from the kingdom. He was recalled to his kingdom by his subjects in B. C. 313: Cassander sent an army against him under Philip, who conquered him the same year in two battles, in the last of which he was killed.

Aeācus (Αἶακος), son of Zeus and Aegina, a daughter of the river-god Asopus. He was born in the island of Oenone or Oenopia, whither Aegina had been carried by Zeus, and from whom this island was afterwards called Aegina. Some traditions related that at the birth of Aeacus, Aegina was not yet inhabited, and that Zeus changed the ants (μύρμηκες) of the island into men (Myrmidones) over whom Aeacus ruled. Ovid (*Met.* vii. 520) relates the story a little differently. Aeacus was renowned in all Greece for his justice and piety, and was frequently called upon to settle disputes not only among men, but even among the gods themselves. He was such a favourite with the gods, that, when Greece was visited by a drought, rain was at length sent upon the earth in consequence of his prayers. Respecting the temple which Aeacus erected to Zeus Panhellenius, and the Aeacēum, where he was worshipped by the Aeginetans, see AEGINA. After his death Aeacus became one of the three judges in Hades. The Aeginetans regarded him as the tutelary deity of their island.

Aeaea (Αἰαία). 1. A surname of Circe, the sister of Aeëtes. Her son Telegonus is likewise mentioned with this surname.—2. A surname of Calypso, who was believed to have inhabited a small island of the name of Aeaea in the straits between Italy and Sicily.

Aebūra (*Cuerva*), a town of the Carpetani in Hispania Tarraconensis.

Aebūtīa Gens, patrician, was distinguished in the early ages of the Roman republic, when many of its members were consuls, viz. in B. C. 499, 463, and 442.

Aeca or **Aecae** (Aecānus), a town of Apulia on the road from Aquilonia in Samnium to Venusia.

Aeculānum or **Aeclānum**, a town of the Hirpini in Samnium, a few miles S. of Beneventum.

Aedepsus (Αἴδηψος: Αἰδήψιος: *Dipso*), a town on the W. coast of Euboea, N. of Chalcis, with warm baths sacred to Hercules, which the dictator Sulla used.

Aēdon ('Αηδών), daughter of Pandareus of Ephesus, wife of Zethus king of Thebes, and mother of Itylus. Envious of Niobe, the wife of her brother Amphion, who had six sons and six daughters, she resolved to kill the eldest of Niobe's sons, but by mistake slew her own son Itylus. Zeus relieved her grief by changing her into a nightingale, whose melancholy tunes are represented by the poets as Aëdon's lamentations about her child. Aëdon's story is related differently in a later tradition.

Aedūi or **Haedūi**, one of the most powerful people in Gaul, lived between the Liger (*Loire*) and the Arar (*Saone*). They were the first Gallic people who made an alliance with the Romans, by whom they were called " brothers and relations." On Caesar's arrival in Gaul, B. C. 58, they were subject to Ariovistus, but were restored by Caesar to their former power. In B. C. 52 they joined in the insurrection of Vercingetorix against the Romans, but were at the close of it treated leniently by Caesar. Their principal town was BIBRACTE. Their chief magistrate, elected annually by the priests, was called Vergobretus.

Aeētes or **Aeēta** (Αἰήτης), son of Helios (the Sun) and Perseïs, and brother of Circe, Pasiphaë, and Perses. His wife was Idyia, a daughter of Oceanus, by whom he had two daughters, Medea and Chalciope, and one son, Absyrtus. He was king of Colchis at the time when Phrixus brought thither the golden fleece. For the remainder of his history, see ABSYRTUS, ARGONAUTAE, JASON, MEDEA.

Aeētis, **Aeētias**, and **Aeētīne**, patronymics of Medea, daughter of Aeëtes.

Aega (Αἴγη), daughter of Olenus, who with her sister Helice, nursed the infant Zeus in Crete, and was changed by the god into the constellation Capella.

Aegae (Αἰγαί: Αἰγαῖος). 1. A town in Achaia on the Crathis, with a celebrated temple of Poseidon, was originally one of the twelve Achaean towns, but its inhabitants subsequently removed to Aegira. — 2. A town in Emathia in Macedonia, the burial-place of the Macedonian kings, was probably a different place from EDESSA.—3. A town in Euboea with a celebrated temple of Poseidon, who was hence called Aegaeus. — 4. Also **Aegaeae** (Αἰγαῖαι: Αἰγεάτης), one of the twelve cities of Aeolis in Asia Minor, N. of Smyrna, on the river Hyllus: it suffered greatly from an earthquake in the time of Tiberius. — 5. (*Ayas*), a seaport town of Cilicia.

Aegaeon (Αἰγαίων), son of Uranus by Gaea. Aegaeon and his brothers Gyges and Cottus are known under the name of the Uranids, and are described as huge monsters with a hundred arms (ἑκατόγχειρες) and fifty heads. Most writers mention the third Uranid under the name of Briareus instead of Aegaeon, which is explained by Homer (*Il.* i. 403), who says that men called him Aegaeon, but the gods Briareus. According to the most ancient tradition Aegaeon and his brothers conquered the Titans when they made war upon the gods, and secured the victory to Zeus, who thrust the Titans into Tartarus, and placed Aegaeon and his brothers to guard them. Other legends represent Aegaeon as one of the giants who attacked Olympus ; and many writers represent him as a marine god living in the Aegaean sea. Aegaeon and his brothers must be regarded as personifications of the extraordinary powers of nature, such as earthquakes, volcanic eruptions, and the like.

Aegaeum Mare (τὸ Αἰγαῖον πέλαγος, ὁ Αἰγαῖος πόντος), the part of the Mediterranean now called the *Archipelago*. It was bounded on the N. by Thrace and Macedonia, on the W. by Greece, and on the E. by Asia Minor. It contains in its southern part two groups of islands, the Cyclades, which were separated from the coasts of Attica and Peloponnesus by the Myrtoan sea, and the Sporades, lying off the coasts of Caria and Ionia. The part of the Aegaean which washed the Sporades was called the Icarian sea, from the island Icaria, one of the Sporades. The origin of the name of Aegaean is uncertain ; some derive it from Aegeus, the king of Athens, who threw himself into it ; others from Aegaea, the queen of the Amazons, who perished there ; others from Aegae in Euboea ; and others from αἰγίς, a squall, on account of its storms.

Aegaeus (Αἰγαῖος). [AEGAE, No. 3.]

Aegaleos (Αἰγάλεως, τὸ Αἰγάλεων ὄρος : *Skaramanga*), a mountain in Attica opposite Salamis, from which Xerxes saw the defeat of his fleet. B. C. 480.

Aegates, the goat-islands, were three islands off the W. coast of Sicily, between Drepanum and Lilybaeum, near which the Romans gained a naval victory over the Carthaginians, and thus brought the first Punic war to an end, B. C. 241. The islands were Aegusa (Αἰγοῦσσα) or Capraria (*Favignana*), Phorbantia (*Levanzo*) and Hiera (*Maretimo*).

Aegeria or **Egeria**, one of the Camenae in Roman mythology, from whom Numa received his instructions respecting the forms of worship which he introduced. The grove in which the king had his interviews with the goddess, and in which a well gushed forth from a dark recess, was dedicated by him to the Camenae. The Roman legends point out two distinct places sacred to Aegeria, one near Aricia, and the other near Rome at the Porta Capena, in the valley now called *Caparella*. Aegeria was regarded as a prophetic divinity, and also as the giver of life, whence she was invoked by pregnant women.

Aegesta. [SEGESTA.]

Aegestus. [ACESTES.]

Aegeus (Αἰγεύς). 1. Son of Pandion and king of Athens. He had no children by his first two wives, but he afterwards begot THESEUS by Aethra at Troezen. When Theseus had grown up to manhood, he went to Athens and defeated the 50 sons of his uncle Pallas, who had made war upon Aegeus and had deposed him. Aegeus was now restored. When Theseus went to Crete to deliver Athens from the tribute it had to pay to Minos, he promised his father that on his return he would hoist white sails as a signal of his safety. On approaching the coast of Attica he forgot his promise, and his father, perceiving the black sail, thought that his son had perished and threw himself into the sea, which according to some traditions received from this event the name of the Aegean. Aegeus was one of the eponymous heroes of Attica ; and one of the Attic tribes (Aegeis) derived its name from him. — 2. The eponymous hero of the phyle called the Aegidae at Sparta, son of Oeolycus, and grandson of Theras, the founder of the colony in Thera. All the Aegeïds were believed to be Cadmeans, who formed a settlement at Sparta previous to the Dorian conquest.

Aegiae (Αἰγειαί, Αἰγαῖαι), a small town in Laconia, not far from Cythium, the Augiae of Homer (*Il.* ii. 583).

Aegiale or **Aegialea** (Αἰγιάλη, Αἰγιάλεια), daughter of Adrastus and Amphithea, or of Aegialeus the son of Adrastus, whence she is called Adrastine. She was married to Diomedes, who, on his return from Troy, found her living in adultery with Cometes. The hero attributed this misfortune to the anger of Aphrodite, whom he had wounded in the war against Troy : when Aegiale threatened his life, he fled to Italy.

Aegialea, Aegialos. [ACHAIA ; SICYON.]

Aegialeus (Αἰγιαλεύς). 1. Son of Adrastus, the only one among the Epigoni that fell in the war against Thebes. [ADRASTUS.] — 2. Son of Inachus and the Oceanid Melia, from whom the part of Peloponnesus afterwards called Achaia derived its name Aegialea ; he is said to have been the first king of Sicyon. — 3. Son of Aeëtes, and brother of Medea, commonly called Absyrtus.

Aegides (Αἰγείδης), a patronymic from Aegeus, especially his son Theseus.

Aegila (τὰ Αἴγιλα), a town of Laconia with a temple of Demeter.

Aegilia (Αἰγιλία : Αἰγιλιεύς). 1. A demus of Attica belonging to the tribe Antiochis, celebrated for its figs. — 2. (*Cerigotto*), an island between Crete and Cythera. — 3. An island W. of Euboea and opposite Attica.

Aegimius (Αἰγίμιος), the mythical ancestor of the Dorians, whose king he was when they were yet inhabiting the northern parts of Thessaly. Involved in a war with the Lapithae, he called Hercules to his assistance, and promised him the third part of his territory, if he delivered him from his enemies. The Lapithae were conquered. Hercules did not take the territory for himself, but left it to the king who was to preserve it for the sons of Hercules. Aegimius had two sons, Dymas and Pamphylus, who migrated to Peloponnesus, and were regarded as the ancestors of two branches of the Doric race (Dymanes and Pamphylians), while the third branch derived its name from Hyllus (Hylleans), the son of Hercules, who had been adopted by Aegimius. There existed in antiquity an epic poem called *Aegimius*, which described the war of Aegimius and Hercules against the Lapithae.

Aegimūrus (Αἰγίμουρος, Aegīmŏri Arae, Plin., and probably the Arae of Virg. *Aen.* i. 108 ; *Zowamour* or *Zembra*), a lofty island, surrounded by cliffs, off the African coast, at the mouth of the Gulf of Carthage.

Aegina (Αἴγινα : Αἰγινήτης : *Eghina*), a rocky island in the middle of the Saronic gulf, about 200 stadia in circumference. It was originally called Oenone or Oenopia, and is said to have obtained the name of Aegina from Aegina, the daughter of the river god Asopus, who was carried to the island by Zeus, and there bore him a son Aeacus. As the island had then no inhabitants, Zeus changed the ants into men (Myrmidones), over whom Aeacus ruled. [AEACUS.] It was first colonized by Achaeans, and afterwards by Dorians from Epidaurus, whence the Doric dialect and customs prevailed in the island. It was at first closely connected with Epidaurus, and was subject to the Argive Phidon, who is said to have established a silver-mint in the island. It early became a place of great commercial importance, and its silver coinage was the standard in most of the Dorian states. In the sixth century B. C. Aegina became independent, and for a century before the Persian war was a prosperous and powerful state. The Aeginetans fought with 30 ships against the fleet of Xerxes at the battle of Salamis, B. C. 480, and are allowed to have distinguished themselves above all the other Greeks by their bravery. After this time its power declined. In B. C. 429 the Athenians took possession of the island and expelled its inhabitants, and though a portion of them was restored by Lysander in B. C. 404, the island never recovered its former prosperity. In the NW. of the island there was a city of the same name, which contained the Aeacēum or temple of Aeacus, and on a hill in the NE. of the island was the celebrated temple of Zeus Panhellenius, said to have been built by Aeacus, the ruins of which are still extant. The sculptures which occupied the tympana of the pediment of this temple were discovered in 1811, and are now preserved at Munich. In the half century preceding the Persian war, and for a few years afterwards, Aegina was the chief seat of Greek art : the most eminent artists of the Aeginetan school were CALLON, ANAXAGORAS, GLAUCIAS, SIMON, and ONATAS.

Aeginēta Paulus. [PAULUS AEGINETA.]

Aeginĭum (Αἰγίνιον : Αἰγινιεύς : *Stagus*), a town of the Tymphaei in Thessaly on the confines of Athamania.

Aegĭŏchus (Αἰγίοχος), a surname of Zeus, because he bore the Aegis.

Aegĭpan (Αἰγίπαν), that is, Goat-Pan, was, according to some, a being distinct from Pan, while others regard him as identical with Pan. His story appears to be of late origin. [PAN.]

Aegiplanctus Mons (τὸ Αἰγίπλαγκτον ὄρος), a mountain in Megaris.

Aegĭra (Αἴγειρα : Αἰγειράτης), formerly Hyperesia (Ὑπερησία), a town in Achaia on a steep hill, with a sea-port about 12 stadia from the town. [AEGAE, No. 1.]

Aegirūssa (Αἰγιρόεσσα, Αἰγιροῦσσα), one of the 12 cities of AEOLIS in Asia Minor.

Aegisthus (Αἴγισθος), son of Thyestes, who unwittingly begot him by his own daughter Pelopia. Immediately after his birth he was exposed, but was saved by shepherds and suckled by a goat (αἴξ), whence his name. His uncle Atreus

brought him up as his son. When Pelopia lay with her father, she took from him his sword, which she afterwards gave to Aegisthus. This sword was the means of revealing the crime of Thyestes, and Pelopia thereupon put an end to her own life. Aegisthus murdered Atreus, because he had ordered him to slay his father Thyestes, and he placed Thyestes upon the throne, of which he had been deprived by Atreus. Homer appears to know nothing of these tragic events ; and we learn from him only that Aegisthus succeeded his father Thyestes in a part of his dominions. According to Homer Aegisthus took no part in the Trojan war, and during the absence of Agamemnon, the son of Atreus, Aegisthus seduced his wife Clytemnestra. Aegisthus murdered Agamemnon on his return home, and reigned 7 years over Mycenae. In the 8th Orestes, the son of Agamemnon, avenged the death of his father by putting the adulterer to death. [AGAMEMNON, CLYTEMNESTRA, ORESTES.]

Aegithallus (Αἰγίθαλλος ; *C. di S. Teodoro*), a promontory in Sicily, between Lilybaeum and Drepanum, near which was the town Aegithallum.

Aegitĭum (Αἰγίτιον), a town in Aetolia, on the borders of Locris.

Aegĭum (Αἴγιον : Αἰγιεύς : *Vostitza*), a town of Achaia, and the capital after the destruction of Helice. The meetings of the Achaean league were held at Aegium in a grove of Zeus called Homarium.

Aeglē (Αἴγλη), that is "Brightness" or "Splendour," is the name of several mythological females, such as, 1. The daughter of Zeus and Neaera, the most beautiful of the Naiads ;—2. A sister of Phaëton ;—3. One of the Hesperides ;—4. A nymph beloved by Theseus, for whom he forsook Ariadne ;—5. One of the daughters of Aesculapius.

Aeglētes (Αἰγλήτης), that is, the radiant god, a surname of Apollo.

Aegŏcĕrus (Αἰγόκερως), a surname of Pan, descriptive of his figure with the horns of a goat, but more commonly the name of one of the signs of the Zodiac, *Capricornus.*

Aegos-Pŏtămos (Αἰγὸς ποταμός), the " goat's-river," a small river, with a town of the same name on it, in the Thracian Chersonesus, flows into the Hellespont. Here the Athenians were defeated by Lysander, B. C. 405.

Aegosthēna (Αἰγόσθενα : Αἰγοσθενεύς, Αἰγοσθενίτης), a town in Megaris on the borders of Boeotia, with a sanctuary of Melampus.

Aegus and **Roscillus,** two chiefs of the Allobroges, who had served Caesar with fidelity in the Gallic war, deserted to Pompey in Greece (B. C. 48).

Aegūsa. [AEGATES.]

Aegypsus or **Aegysus,** a town of Moesia on the Danube.

Aegyptus (Αἴγυπτος), son of Belus and Anchinoe or Achiroe, and twin-brother of Danaus. Belus assigned Libya to Danaus, and Arabia to Aegyptus, but the latter subdued the country of the Melampodes, which he called Aegypt after his own name. Aegyptus by his several wives had 50 sons, and his brother Danaus 50 daughters. Danaus had reason to fear the sons of his brother, and fled with his daughters to Argos in Peloponnesus. Thither he was followed by the sons of Aegyptus, who demanded his daughters for their wives, and promised faithful alliance. Danaus complied with their request, and distributed his daughters among them, but to each of them he gave a dagger, with which they were to kill their husbands in the bridal night. All the sons of Aegyptus were thus murdered, with the exception of Lynceus, who was saved by Hypermnestra. The Danaids buried the heads of their murdered husbands in Lerna, and their bodies outside the town, and were afterwards purified of their crime by Athena and Hermes at the command of Zeus.

Aegyptus (ἡ Αἴγυπτος: Αἰγύπτιος, Aegyptius: *Egypt*), a country in the N. E. corner of Africa, bounded on the N. by the Mediterranean, on the E. by Palestine, Arabia Petraea, and the Red Sea, on the S. by Ethiopia, the division between the two countries being at the First or Little Cataract of the Nile, close to Syene (*Assouan*; Lat. 24° 8′), and on the W. by the Great Libyan Desert. This is the extent usually assigned to the country ; but it would be more strictly correct to define it as that part of the basin of the Nile which lies below the First Cataract.— 1. *Physical Description of Egypt.* The river Nile, flowing from S. to N. through a narrow valley, encounters, in Lat. 24° 8′, a natural barrier, composed of two islands (Philae and Elephantine) and between them a bed of sunken rocks, by which it is made to fall in a series of cataracts, or rather rapids (τὰ Κατάδουπα, ὁ μικρὸς Καταῤῥάκτης, Catarrhactes Minor, comp. CATARRHACTES), which have always been regarded as the southern limit assigned by nature to Egypt. The river flows due N. between two ranges of hills, so near each other as to leave scarcely any cultivable land, as far as Silsilis (*Jebel Selseleh*), about 40 miles below Syene, where the valley is enlarged by the W. range of hills retiring from the river. Thus the Nile flows for about 500 miles, through a valley whose average breadth is about 7 miles, between hills which in one place (W. of Thebes) attain the height of 1000 or 1200 feet above the sea, to a point some few miles below Memphis, where the W. range of hills runs to the N. W., and the E. range strikes off to the E., and the river divides into branches (seven in ancient time, but now only two), which flow through a low alluvial land, called, from its shape, the *Delta*, into the Mediterranean. To this valley and Delta must be added the country round the great natural lake Moeris (*Birket-el-Keroun*), called Nomos Arsinoïtes (*Faioum*), lying N. W. of Heracleopolis, and connected with the valley of the Nile by a break in the W. range of hills. The whole district thus described is periodically laid under water by the overflowing of the Nile from April to October. The river, in subsiding, leaves behind a rich deposit of fine mud, which forms the soil of Egypt. All beyond the reach of the inundation is rock or sand. Hence Egypt was called the "Gift of the Nile." The extent of the cultivable land of Egypt is in the Delta about 4500 square miles, in the valley about 2255, in *Faioum* about 340, and in all about 7095 square miles. The outlying portions of ancient Egypt consisted of 3 cultivable valleys (called Oases), in the midst of the Western or Libyan Desert, a valley in the W. range of hills on the W. of the Delta, called Nomos Nitriotes from the Natron Lakes which it contains, some settlements on the coast of the Red Sea and in the mountain passes between it and the Nile, and a strip of coast on the Mediterranean, extending E. as far as Rhinocolura (*El-Arish*), and W. as far (according to some of the ancients) as the Catabathmus Magnus (Long. about 25° 10′ E.). The only river of

Egypt is the Nile [NILUS]. A great artificial canal (*Bahr-Yussouf*, i. e. *Joseph's Canal*) runs parallel to the river, at the distance of about 6 miles, from Diospolis Parva in the Thebais to a point on the W. mouth of the river about half-way between Memphis and the sea. Many smaller canals were cut to regulate the irrigation of the country. A canal from the E. mouth of the Nile to the head of the Red Sea was commenced under the native kings, and finished by Darius, son of Hystaspes. There were several lakes in the country, respecting which see MOERIS, MAREOTIS, BUTOS, TANIS, SIRBONIS, and LACUS AMARI. — 2. *Ancient History.* At the earliest period, to which civil history reaches back, Egypt was inhabited by a highly civilized agricultural people, under a settled monarchical government, divided into castes, the highest of which was composed of the priests, who were the ministers of a religion based on a pantheistic worship of nature, and having for its sacred symbols not only images but also living animals and even plants. The priests were also in possession of all the literature and science of the country and all the employments based upon such knowledge. The other castes were, 2nd, the soldiers, 3rd, the husbandmen, 4th, the artificers and tradesmen, and last, held in great contempt, the shepherds or herdsmen, poulterers, fishermen, and servants. The Egyptians possessed a written language, which appears to have had affinities with both the great families of Language, the Semitic and the Indo-European ; and the priestly caste had, moreover, the exclusive knowledge of a sacred system of writing, the characters of which are known by the name of *Hieroglyphics*, in contradistinction to which the common characters are called *Enchorial* (i. e. *of the country*). They were acquainted with all the processes of manufacture which are essential to a highly civilized community : they had made great advances in the fine arts, especially architecture and sculpture (for in painting their progress was impeded by a want of knowledge of perspective) : they were deterred from commercial enterprize by the policy of the priests, but they obtained foreign productions to a great extent, chiefly through the Phoenicians, and at a later period they engaged in maritime expeditions : in science they do not seem to have advanced so far as some have thought, but their religion led them to cultivate astronomy and its application to chronology, and the nature of their country made a knowledge of geometry (in its literal sense) indispensable, and their application of its principles to architecture is attested by their extant edifices. There can be little doubt that the origin of this remarkable people and of their early civilization is to be traced to the same Asiatic source as the early civilization of Assyria and India. The ancient history of Egypt may be divided into 4 great periods :—(1) From the earliest times to its conquest by Cambyses ; during which it was ruled by a succession of native princes, into the difficulties of whose history this is not the place to inquire. The last of them, Psammenitus, was conquered and dethroned by Cambyses in B. C. 525, when Egypt became a province of the Persian empire. During this period Egypt was but little known to the Greeks. The Homeric poems show some slight acquaintance with the country and its river (which is also called Αἴγυπτος, *Od.* xiv. 25), and refer to the wealth and splendour of " Thebes with the Hundred Gates." In the latter part of the period learned men among the Greeks began to travel to Egypt for the sake of studying its institutions : among others it was visited by Pythagoras, Thales, and Solon. (2) From the Persian conquest in B. C. 525, to the transference of their dominion to the Macedonians in B. C. 332. This period was one of almost constant struggles between the Egyptians and their conquerors, until B. C. 340, when Nectanebo II., the last native ruler of Egypt, was defeated by Darius Ochus. It was during this period that the Greeks acquired a considerable knowledge of Egypt. In the wars between Egypt and Persia, the two leading states of Athens and Sparta at different times assisted the Egyptians, according to the state of their relations to each other and to Persia ; and, during the intervals of those wars, Egypt was visited by Greek historians and philosophers, such as Hellanicus, Herodotus, Anaxagoras, Plato, and others, who brought back to Greece the knowledge of the country which they acquired from the priests and personal observation. (3) The dynasty of Macedonian kings, from the accession of Ptolemy, the son of Lagus, in B. C. 323, down to B. C. 30, when Egypt became a province of the Roman empire. When Alexander invaded Egypt in B. C. 332, the country submitted to him without a struggle ; and, while he left it behind him to return to the conquest of Persia, he conferred upon it the greatest benefit that was in his power, by giving orders for the building of Alexandria. In the partition of the empire of Alexander after his death in B. C. 323, Egypt fell to the share of Ptolemy, the son of Lagus, who assumed the title of king in B. C. 306, and founded the dynasty of the Ptolemies, under whom the country greatly flourished, and became the chief seat of Greek learning. But soon came the period of decline. Wars with the adjacent kingdom of Syria, and the vices, weaknesses, and dissensions of the royal family, wore out the state, till in B. C. 81 the Romans were called upon to interfere in the disputes for the crown, and in B. C. 55 the dynasty of the Ptolemies came to be entirely dependent on Roman protection, and, at last, after the battle of Actium and the death of Cleopatra, who was the last of the Ptolemies, Egypt was made a Roman province, B. C. 30. (4) Egypt under the Romans, down to its conquest by the Arabs in A. D. 638. As a Roman province, Egypt was one of the most flourishing portions of the empire. The fertility of its soil, and its position between Europe and Arabia and India, together with the possession of such a port as Alexandria, gave it the full benefit of the two great sources of wealth, agriculture and commerce. Learning continued to flourish at Alexandria, and the patriarchs of the Christian Church in that city became so powerful as to contend for supremacy with those of Antioch, Constantinople, and Rome, while a succession of teachers, such as Origen and Clement of Alexandria, conferred real lustre on the ecclesiastical annals of the country. When the Arabs made their great inroad upon the Eastern empire, the geographical position of Egypt naturally caused it to fall an immediate victim to that attack, which its wealth and the peaceful character of its inhabitants invited. It was conquered by Amrou, the lieutenant of the Caliph Omar, in A. D. 638. — 3. *Political Geography.* — From the earliest times the country was divided into (1) The Delta or Lower Egypt

(τὸ Δέλτα, ἡ κάτω χώρα, *El-Bahari*, *El-Kebli*) (2) The Heptanomis, or Middle Egypt, Ἑπτανομίς, ἡ μεταξὺ χώρα, *Mesr Mostani*) ; (3) The Thebaïs, or Upper Egypt (Θηβαΐς, ἡ ἄνω χώρα, *Said*) : and it was further subdivided into 36 nomes or governments. Respecting the Oases, see OASIS.

Aegys (Αἴγυς, Αἰγύτης : nr. *Ghiorgitza*), a town of Laconia on the borders of Arcadia.

Aelāna (Αἴλανα : Αἰλανίτης), a town on the northern arm of the Red Sea, near the Bahr-el-Akaba, which was called by the Greeks Aelanites from the name of the town. It is the Elath of the Hebrews, and one of the sea-ports of which Solomon possessed himself.

Aelia Gens, plebeian, the members of which are given under their surnames, GALLUS, LAMIA, PAETUS, SEJANUS, STILO, TUBERO.

Aelia, a name given to Jerusalem after its restoration by the Roman emperor Aelius Hadrianus.

Aeliānus, Claudius, was born at Praeneste in Italy, and lived at Rome about the middle of the 3rd century of the Christian era. Though an Italian, he spoke and wrote Greek as well as a native Athenian. He never married, and lived to the age of 60. Two of his works have come down to us: one a collection of miscellaneous history (Ποικίλη Ἱστορία) in 14 books, commonly called *Varia Historia ;* and the other a work on the peculiarities of animals (Περὶ Ζώων ἰδιότητος) in 17 books, commonly called *De Animalium Natura.* The former work contains short narrations and anecdotes, historical, biographical, antiquarian, &c., selected from various authors, generally without their names being given, and on a great variety of subjects. The latter work is of the same kind, scrappy and gossipping. It is partly collected from older writers, and partly the result of his own observations both in Italy and abroad. There are also attributed to him 20 letters on husbandry (Ἀγροικικαὶ Ἐπιστολαί), written in a rhetorical style and of no value. — *Editions.* Of the *Varia Historia*, by Perizonius, Leyden, 1701 ; by Gronovius, Leyden, 1731 ; and by Kühn, Leipzig, 1780. Of the *De Animalium Natura*, by Gronovius, Lond. 1744 ; by J. Schneider, Leipzig, 1784 ; and by Fr. Jacobs, Jena, 1832. Of the *Letters*, by Aldus Manutius, in his *Collectio Epistolarum Graecarum*, Venice, 1499, 4to.

Aeliānus Meccius, an ancient physician, who must have lived in the 2nd century after Christ, as he is mentioned by Galen as the oldest of his tutors.

Aeliānus Tacticus, a Greek writer, who lived in Rome and wrote a work on the Military Tactics of the Greeks (Περὶ Στρατηγικῶν Τάξεων Ἑλληνικῶν), dedicated to the emperor Hadrian. He also gives a brief account of the constitution of a Roman army at that time. — *Editions.* By Franciscus Robortellus, Venice, 1552 ; and by Elzevir, Leyden, 1613.

Aello, one of the Harpies. [HARPYIAE.]

Aellŏpus (Ἀελλόπους), a surname of Iris, the messenger of the gods, by which she is described as swift-footed as a storm-wind.

Aemilia. 1. The 3rd daughter of L. Aemilius Paulus, who fell in the battle of Cannae, was the wife of Scipio Africanus 1. and the mother of the celebrated Cornelia, the mother of the Gracchi. — 2. Aemilia Lepida. [LEPIDA.] — 3. A Vestal virgin, put to death B. C. 114 for having committed incest upon several occasions.

Aemilia Gens, one of the most ancient patrician gentes at Rome, said to have been descended from Mamercus, who received the name of Aemilius on account of the persuasiveness of his language (διʼ αἱμυλίαν λόγου). This Mamercus is represented by some as the son of Pythagoras, and by others as the son of Numa. The most distinguished members of the gens are given under their surnames Barbula, Lepidus, Mamercus or Mamercinus, Papus, Paulus, Regillus, Scaurus.

Aemilia Via, made by M. Aemilius Lepidus, cos. B. C. 187, continued the Via Flaminia from Ariminum, and traversed the heart of Cisalpine Gaul through Bononia, Mutina, Parma, Placentia (where it crossed the Po) to Mediolanum. It was subsequently continued as far as Aquileia.

Aemilianus. 1. The son of L. Aemilius Paulus Macedonicus, was adopted by P. Cornelius Scipio, the son of P. Cornelius Scipio Africanus, and was thus called P. Cornelius Scipio Aemilianus Africanus. [Scipio.]—2. The governor of Pannonia and Moesia in the reign of Gallus, was proclaimed emperor by his soldiers in A. D. 253, but was slain by them after reigning a few months.—3. One of the 30 tyrants (A. D. 259—268), assumed the purple in Egypt, but was taken prisoner and strangled by order of Gallienus.

Aemilius Probus. [Nepos, Cornelius.]

Aemōna or **Emōna** (*Laibach*), a fortified town in Pannonia, and an important Roman colony, said to have been built by the Argonauts.

Aenāria, also called **Pithēcūsa** and **Inārīme** (*Ischia*), a volcanic island off the coast of Campania, at the entrance of the bay of Naples, under which the Roman poets represented Typhoeus as lying.

Aenēa (Αἴνεια: Αἰνειεύς, Αἰνεάτης), a town in Chalcidice, on the Thermaic gulf.

Aeneădes (Αἰνειάδης), a patronymic from Aeneas, given to his son Ascanius or Iulus, and to those who were believed to be descended from him, such as Augustus, and the Romans in general.

Aeneas (Αἰνείας). 1. *Homeric Story.* Aeneas was the son of Anchises and Aphrodite, and born on mount Ida. On his father's side he was a great-grandson of Tros, and thus nearly related to the royal house of Troy, as Priam himself was a grandson of Tros. He was educated from his infancy at Dardanus, in the house of Alcathous, the husband of his sister. At first he took no part in the Trojan war; and it was not till Achilles attacked him on mount Ida, and drove away his flocks, that he led his Dardanians against the Greeks. Henceforth he and Hector are the great bulwarks of the Trojans against the Greeks, and Aeneas appears beloved by gods and men. On more than one occasion he is saved in battle by the gods: Aphrodite carried him off when he was wounded by Diomedes, and Poseidon, when he was on the point of perishing by the hands of Achilles. Homer makes no allusion to the emigration of Aeneas after the capture of Troy, but on the contrary he evidently conceives Aeneas and his descendants as reigning at Troy after the extinction of the house of Priam.—*Later Stories.* The later stories present the greatest variations respecting the conduct of Aeneas at the capture of Troy and in the events immediately following. Most accounts, however, agree that after the city had fallen, he withdrew to mount Ida with his friends and the images of the gods, especially that of Pallas (*Palladium*); and that from thence he crossed over to Europe, and finally settled at Latium in Italy, where he became the ancestral hero of the Romans. A description of the wanderings of Aeneas before he reached Latium, and of the various towns and temples he was believed to have founded during his wanderings, is given by Dionysius of Halicarnassus (i. 50, &c.), whose account is on the whole the same as the one followed by Virgil in his Aeneid, although the latter makes various embellishments and additions, some of which, such as his landing at Carthage and meeting with Dido, are irreconcilable with mythical chronology. From Pallene, where Aeneas stayed the winter after the taking of Troy, he sailed with his companions to Delos, Cythera, Boiae in Laconia, Zacynthus, Leucas, Actium, Ambracia, and to Dodona, where he met the Trojan Helenus. From Epirus he sailed across the Ionian sea to Italy, where he landed at the Iapygian promontory. Thence he crossed over to Sicily, where he met the Trojans, Elymus and Aegestus (Acestes), and built the towns of Elyme and Aegesta. From Sicily he sailed back to Italy, landed in the port of Palinurus, came to the island of Leucasia, and at last to the coast of Latium. Various signs pointed out this place as the end of his wanderings, and he and his Trojans accordingly settled in Latium. The place where they had landed was called Troy. Latinus, king of the Aborigines, prepared for war, but afterwards concluded an alliance with the strangers, gave up to them part of his dominions, and with their assistance conquered the Rutulians. Aeneas founded the town of Lavinium, called after Lavinia, the daughter of Latinus, whom he married. A new war then followed between Latinus and Turnus, in which both chiefs fell, whereupon Aeneas became sole ruler of the Aborigines and Trojans, and both nations were united into one. Soon after this Aeneas fell in a battle with the Rutulians, who were assisted by Mezentius, king of the Etruscans. As his body was not found after the battle, it was believed that it had been carried up to heaven, or that he had perished in the river Numicius. The Latins erected a monument to him, with the inscription *To the father and native god.* Virgil represents Aeneas landing in Italy 7 years after the fall of Troy, and comprises all the events in Italy from the landing to the death of Turnus, within the space of 20 days. The story of the descent of the Romans from the Trojans through Aeneas was believed at an early period, but probably rests on no historical foundation.—2. **Aeneas Silvius**, son of Silvius, and grandson of Ascanius, is the 3rd in the list of the mythical kings of Alba in Latium: the Silvii regarded him as the founder of their house.

Aeneas Gazaeus, so called from Gaza, his birthplace, flourished A. D. 487. He was at first a Platonist and a Sophist, but afterwards became a Christian, when he composed a dialogue, On the Immortality of the Soul, called *Theophrastus.* — *Editions.* By Barthius, Lips. 1655; by Boissonade, Par. 1836.

Aeneas Tacticus, a Greek writer, *may* be the same as the Aeneas of Stymphalus, the general of the Arcadians, B. C. 362 (Xen. *Hell.* vii. 3. § 1); and he probably lived about that period. He wrote a work on the art of war, of which a portion only is preserved, commonly called *Commentarius Poliorceticus*, showing how a siege should be resisted. An epitome of the whole book was made by Cineas.

Aesculapius and a Sick Man.
(Millin, Gal. Myth., tav. 32, No. 105.) Page 19.

Amphitrite.
(From a Bas-relief published by Winckelmann.) Page 46.

Death of Achilles. (Raoul-Rochette, Mon. Ined., pl. 53.) Page 6.

Achilles seizing Arms at Scyros.
(A Painting found at Pompeii.) Page 6.

Actaeon.
(British Museum.) Page 8.

[To face p. 16.

Aemilianus, Roman Emperor, A.D. 253.   Page 16.

M. Agrippa, General of Augustus.   Page 18.

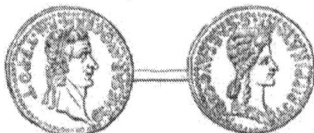

Agrippina I.   Head of Caligula on the obverse.   Page 28.

Agrippina II.   Head of Claudius on the reverse.   Page 62.

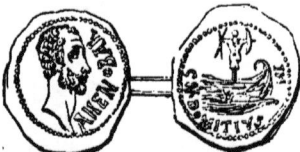

Cn. Domitius Ahenobarbus.   Page 29.   AHENOBARBUS, No. 8.

Albinus Clodius, Roman Emperor, A.D. 197.   Page 31.
To face p. 17.]

Alexander I., King of Epirus, B.C. 336–326.   Page 35.

Alexander II., King of Epirus, B.C. 272.   Page 35.

Alexander I., King of Macedonia, B.C. 507–455.   Page 35.

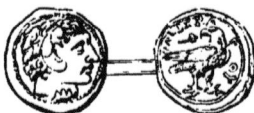

Alexander II., King of Macedonia, B.C. 369–367.   Page 35.

Alexander III., King of Macedonia, B.C. 336–323.
Pages 35—37.

Alexander Balas, King of Syria, B.C. 150—146.   Page 37.

(Cic. *ad Fam.* ix. 25.)—*Editions.* By Ernesti, Lips. 1763 ; by Orelli, Lips. 1818.

Aenesidemus (Αἰνησίδημος), a celebrated sceptic, born at Cnossus in Crete, probably lived a little later than Cicero. He differed on many points from the ordinary sceptics. The grand peculiarity of his system was the attempt to unite scepticism with the earlier philosophy, to raise a positive foundation for it by accounting from the nature of things for the never-ceasing changes both in the material and spiritual world. None of the works of Aenesidemus have come down to us. To them Sextus Empiricus was indebted for a considerable part of his work.

Aenianes (Αἰνιᾶνες, Ion. Ἐνιῆνες), an ancient Greek race, originally near Ossa, afterwards in southern Thessaly, between Oeta and Othrys, on the banks of the Sperchēus.

Aenus (Αἶνος: Αἴνιος, Αἰνιάτης: Eno), an ancient town in Thrace, near the mouth of the Hebrus, mentioned in the Iliad. It was colonized by the Aeolians of Asia Minor. Virgil (*Aen.* iii. 18) supposes Aenos to have been built by Aeneas, but he confounds it with ARNRA in Chalcidice. Under the Romans Aenos was a free town, and a place of importance.

Aenus (*Inn*) a river in Rhaetia, the boundary between Rhaetia and Noricum.

Aeoles or **Aeolii** (Αἰολεῖς), one of the chief branches of the Hellenic race, supposed to be descended from Aeolus, the son of Hellen. [AEOLUS, No. 1.] They originally dwelt in Thessaly, from whence they spread over various parts of Greece, and also settled in AEOLIS in Asia Minor, and in the island of LESBOS.

Aeoliae Insulae (*al* Αἰόλου νῆσοι: *Lipari Islands*), a group of islands N. E. of Sicily, where Aeolus, the god of the winds, reigned. Homer (*Od.* x. 1) mentions only one Aeolian island, and Virgil (*Aen.* i. 52) accordingly speaks of only one Aeolia (sc. *insula*), where Aeolus reigned, supposed to be Strongyle or Lipara. These islands were also called *Hephaestiades* or *Vulcaniae*, because Hephaestus or Vulcan was supposed to have had his workshop in one of them called Hiera. (Virg. *Aen.* viii. 415, seq.) They were also named *Liparenses*, from Lipära, the largest of them. The names of these islands were, Lipära (*Lipari*); Hiěra (*Volcano*); Strongỹle (*Stromboli*); Phoenicūsa (*Felicudi*); Ericūsa (*Alicudi*); Euonymus (*Panaria*); Didyme (*Salina*); Hicesia (*Lisca Bianca*); Basilidia (*Basilixxo*); Osteodes (*Ustica*).

Aeolides (Αἰολίδης), a patronymic given to the sons of Aeolus, as Athamas, Cretheus, Sisyphus, Salmoneus, &c., and to his grandsons, as Cephalus, Ulysses and Phrixus. Aeolis is the patronymic of the female descendants of Aeolus, given to his daughters Canace and Alcyone.

Aeolis (Αἰολίς) or **Aeolia**, a district of Mysia in Asia Minor, was peopled by Aeolian Greeks, whose cities extended from the Troad along the shores of the Aegaean to the river Hermus. In early times their 12 most important cities were independent and formed a League, the members of which celebrated an annual festival (*Panaeolium*) at Smyrna. The 12 cities comprising this League were Cyme, Larissae, Neontichos, Temnus, Cilla, Notium, Aegirūsa, Pitane, Aegacae, Myrina, Grynēa, and Smyrna ; but SMYRNA subsequently became a member of the Ionian confederacy. (Herod. i. 149, seq.) These cities were subdued by

Croesus, and were incorporated in the Persian empire on the conquest of Croesus by Cyrus.

Aeolus (Αἴολος). 1. Son of Hellen and the nymph Orseïs, and brother of Dorus and Xuthus. He was the ruler of Thessaly, and the founder of the Aeolic branch of the Greek nation. His children are said to have been very numerous ; but the most ancient story mentioned only four sons, viz. Sisyphus, Athamas, Cretheus, and Salmoneus. The great extent of country which this race occupied probably gave rise to the varying accounts about the number of his children.—2. Son of Hippotes, or, according to others, of Poseidon and Arne, a descendant of the previous Aeolus. His story probably refers to the emigration of a branch of the Aeolians to the west. His mother was carried to Metapontum in Italy, where she gave birth to Aeolus and his brother Boeotus. The two brothers afterwards fled from Metapontum, and Aeolus went to some islands in the Tyrrhenian sea, which received from him the name of the Aeolian islands. Here he reigned as a just and pious king, taught the natives the use of sails for ships, and foretold them the nature of the winds that were to rise. In these accounts Aeolus, the father of the Aeolian race, is placed in relationship with Aeolus the ruler and god of the winds. In Homer, however, Aeolus, the son of Hippotes, is neither the god nor the father of the winds, but merely the happy ruler of the Aeolian island, to whom Zeus had given dominion over the winds, which he might soothe or excite according to his pleasure. (*Od.* x. 1, seq.) This statement of Homer and the etymology of the name of Aeolus from ἀέλλω led to Aeolus being regarded in later times as the god and king of the winds, which he kept enclosed in a mountain. It is therefore to him that Juno applies when she wishes to destroy the fleet of the Trojans. (Virg. *Aen.* i. 78.) The Aeolian island of Homer was in later times believed to be Lipara or Strongyle, and was accordingly regarded as the place in which the god of the winds dwelt. [AEOLIAE INSULAE.]

Aepea (Αἴπεια: Αἰπεάτης). 1. A town in Messenia on the sea-coast, afterwards THURIA.—2. A town in Cyprus, afterwards SOLI.

Aepy (Αἶπυ), a town in Elis, situated on a height, as its name indicates.

Aepytus (Αἴπυτος). 1. A mythical king of Arcadia, from whom a part of the country was called Aepytis. — 2. Youngest son of the Heraclid Cresphontes, king of Messenia, and of Merope, daughter of the Arcadian king Cypselus. When his father and brothers were murdered during an insurrection, Aepytus alone, who was with his grandfather Cypselus, escaped the danger. The throne of Cresphontes was in the meantime occupied by the Heraclid Polyphontes, who also forced Merope to become his wife. When Aepytus had grown to manhood, he returned to his kingdom, and put Polyphontes to death. From him the kings of Messenia were called Aepytids instead of the more general name Heraclids. — 3. Son of Hippothous, king of Arcadia, and great-grandson of the Aepytus mentioned first.

Aequi, Aequicoli, Aequiculae, Aequiculani, an ancient warlike people of Italy, dwelling in the upper valley of the Anio in the mountains forming the eastern boundary of Latium, and between the Latini, Sabini, Hernici, and Marsi. In conjunction with the Volsci, who were of the same race, they carried on constant hostilities with Rome, but were finally subdued in B.C. 302. One of their chief seats was Mount Algidus, from which they were accustomed to make their marauding expeditions.

Aequi Falisci. [FALERII.]

Aequimaelium. [MAELIUS.]

Aëropē ('Αερόπη), daughter of Catreus, king of Crete, and granddaughter of Minos. Her father, who had received an oracle that he should lose his life by one of his children, gave her and her sister Clymene to Nauplius, who was to sell them in a foreign land. Aerope married Plisthenes, the son of Atreus, and became by him the mother of Agamemnon and Menelaus. After the death of Plisthenes Aerope married Atreus; and her two sons, who were educated by Atreus, were generally believed to be his sons. Aerope was faithless to Atreus, being seduced by Thyestes.

Aesăcus (Αἴσακος), son of Priam and Alexirrhoë. He lived far from his father's court in the solitude of mountain-forests. Hesperia, however, the daughter of Cebren, kindled love in his heart, and on one occasion while he was pursuing her, she was stung by a viper and died. Aesacus in his grief threw himself into the sea and was changed by Thetis into an aquatic bird. This is the story related by Ovid (*Met.* xi. 750), but it is told differently by Apollodorus.

Aesar, the name of the deity among the Etruscans.

Aesar or **Aesărus** (*Esaro*), a river near Croton in Bruttii, in southern Italy.

Aeschĭnes (Αἰσχίνης). 1. The Athenian orator born B.C. 389, was the son of Atrometus and Glaucothea. According to Demosthenes, his political antagonist, his parents were of disreputable character and not even citizens of Athens; but Aeschines himself says that his father was descended from an honourable family, and lost his property during the Peloponnesian war. In his youth Aeschines appears to have assisted his father in his school; he next acted as secretary to Aristophon, and afterwards to Eubulus; he subsequently tried his fortune as an actor, but was unsuccessful; and at length, after serving with distinction in the army, came forward as a public speaker and soon acquired great reputation. In 347 he was sent along with Demosthenes as one of the 10 ambassadors to negotiate a peace with Philip: from this time he appears as the friend of the Macedonian party and as the opponent of Demosthenes. Shortly afterwards Aeschines formed one of the second embassy sent to Philip to receive the oath of Philip to the treaty which had been concluded with the Athenians; but as the delay of the ambassadors in obtaining the ratification had been favourable to the interests of Philip, Aeschines on his return to Athens was accused by Timarchus. He evaded the danger by bringing forward a counter-accusation against Timarchus (345), and by showing that the moral conduct of his accuser was such that he had no right to speak before the people. The speech in which Aeschines attacked Timarchus is still extant: Timarchus was condemned and Aeschines gained a brilliant triumph. In 343 Demosthenes renewed the charge against Aeschines of treachery during his second embassy to Philip. This charge of Demosthenes (περὶ παραπρεσβείας) was not spoken, but published as a memorial, and Aeschines answered it in a similar memorial on the embassy (περὶ παραπρεσβείας), which was likewise published. Shortly after the battle of Chaeronēa in 338, which gave Philip the supremacy in Greece, Ctesiphon proposed that Demosthenes should be rewarded for his services with a golden crown in the theatre at the great Dionysia. Aeschines in consequence accused Ctesiphon; but he did not prosecute the charge till 8 years later, 330. The speech which he delivered on the occasion is extant, and was answered by Demosthenes in his celebrated oration on the crown (περὶ στεφάνου). Aeschines was defeated, and withdrew from Athens. He went to Asia Minor, and at length established a school of eloquence at Rhodes. On one occasion he read to his audience in Rhodes his speech against Ctesiphon, and when some of his hearers expressed their astonishment at his defeat, he replied, "You would cease to be astonished if you had heard Demosthenes." From Rhodes he went to Samos, where he died in 314. Besides the 3 orations extant, we also possess 12 letters which are ascribed to Aeschines, but which are the work of late sophists.—*Editions.* In the editions of the Attic orators [DEMOSTHENES], and by Bremi, Zurich, 1823. — 2. An Athenian philosopher and rhetorician, and a disciple of Socrates. After the death of his master, he went to Syracuse; but returned to Athens after the expulsion of Dionysius, and supported himself, receiving money for his instructions. He wrote several dialogues, but the 3 which have come down to us under his name are not genuine. — *Editions.* By Fischer, Lips. 1786; by Böckh, Heidel. 1810; and in many editions of Plato. — 3. Of Neapolis, a Peripatetic philosopher, who was at the head of the Academy at Athens, together with Charmades and Clitomachus about B.C. 109. — 4. Of Miletus, a contemporary of Cicero, and a distinguished orator in the Asiatic style of eloquence.

Aeschrĭon (Αἰσχρίων). 1. Of Syracuse, whose wife Pippa was one of the mistresses of Verres, and who was himself one of the scandalous instruments of Verres.—2. An iambic poet, a native of Samos. There was an epic poet of the same name, who was a native of Mytilene and a pupil of Aristotle, and who accompanied Alexander on some of his expeditions. He may perhaps be the same person as the Samian.—3. A native of Pergamus, and a physician in the second century after Christ, was one of Galen's tutors.

Aeschȳlus (Αἰσχύλος). 1. The celebrated tragic poet, was born at Eleusis in Attica, B.C. 525, so that he was 35 years of age at the time of the battle of Marathon, and contemporary with Simonides and Pindar. His father Euphorion was probably connected with the worship of Demeter, and Aeschylus himself was, according to some authorities, initiated in the mysteries of this goddess. At the age of 25 (B.C. 499), he made his first appearance as a competitor for the prize of tragedy, without being successful. He fought with his brothers Cynaegirus and Aminius, at the battle of Marathon (490), and also at those of Salamis (480) and Plataea (479). In 484 he gained the prize of tragedy; and in 472 he gained the prize with the trilogy, of which the Persae, the earliest of his extant dramas, was one piece. In 468 he was defeated in a tragic contest by his younger rival Sophocles; and he is said in consequence to have quitted Athens in disgust, and to have gone to the court of Hiero, king of Syracuse, where he found Simonides the lyric poet. In 467, his friend and patron king

Hiero died ; and in 458, it appears that Aeschylus was again at Athens, from the fact that the trilogy of the Oresteia was produced in that year. In the same or the following year, he again visited Sicily, and he died at Gela in 456, in the 69th year of his age. It is said that an eagle, mistaking the poet's bald head for a stone, let a tortoise fall upon it to break the shell, and so fulfilled an oracle, according to which Aeschylus was fated to die by a blow from heaven. The alterations made by Aeschylus in the composition and dramatic representation of Tragedy were so great, that he was considered by the Athenians as the father of it, just as Homer was of Epic poetry and Herodotus of History. Even the improvements and alterations introduced by his successors were the natural results and suggestions of those of Aeschylus. The first and principal alteration which he made was the introduction of a second actor (δευτεραγωνιστής), and the consequent formation of the dialogue properly so called, and the limitation of the choral parts. This innovation was of course adopted by his contemporaries, just as Aeschylus himself followed the example of Sophocles, in subsequently introducing a third actor. But the improvements of Aeschylus were not limited to the composition of tragedy : he added the resources of art in its exhibition. Thus, he is said to have availed himself of the skill of Agatharchus, who painted for him the first scenes which had ever been drawn according to the principles of linear perspective. He also furnished his actors with more suitable and magnificent dresses, with significant and various masks, and with the thick-soled cothurnus, to raise their stature to the height of heroes. He moreover bestowed so much attention on the choral dances, that he is said to have invented various figures himself, and to have instructed the choristers in them without the aid of the regular ballet-masters. With him also arose the usage of representing at the same time a *trilogy* of plays connected in subject, so that each formed one act, as it were, of a great whole, which might be compared with some of Shakspeare's historical plays. Even before the time of Aeschylus, it had been customary to contend for the prize of tragedy with 3 plays exhibited at the same time, but it was reserved for him to show how each of 3 tragedies might be complete in itself, and independent of the rest, and nevertheless form a part of an harmonious and connected whole. The only example still extant of such a trilogy is the Oresteia, as it was called. A satyrical play commonly followed each tragic trilogy. Aeschylus is said to have written 70 tragedies. Of these only 7 are extant, namely, the *Persians*, the *Seven against Thebes*, the *Suppliants*, the *Prometheus*, the *Agamemnon*, the *Choephori*, and *Eumenides* ; the last three forming, as already remarked, the trilogy of the *Oresteia*. The *Persians* was acted in 472, and the *Seven against Thebes* a year afterwards. The *Oresteia* was represented in 458 ; the *Suppliants* and the *Prometheus* were brought out some time between the *Seven against Thebes* and the *Oresteia*. It has been supposed from some allusions in the *Suppliants*, that this play was acted in 461, when Athens was allied with Argos.—*Editions.* By Wellauer, Lips. 1823, W Dindorf, Lips. 1827, and Scholefield, Camb. 1830.

Aesculapius ('Ασκληπιός), the god of the medical art. In the Homeric poems Aesculapius is not a divinity, but simply the "blameless physi-

cian" (ἰητὴρ ἀμύμων), whose sons, Machaon and Podalīrius, were the physicians in the Greek army, and ruled over Tricca, Ithome, and Oechalia. Homer says nothing of the descent of Aesculapius. The common story relates that he was a son of Apollo and Coronis, and that when Coronis was with child by Apollo, she became enamoured with Ischys, an Arcadian. Apollo, informed of this by a raven, which he had set to watch her, or, according to others, by his own prophetic powers, sent his sister Artemis to kill Coronis. Artemis accordingly destroyed Coronis in her own house at Lacerīa in Thessaly, on the shore of lake Baebia. According to Ovid (*Met.* ii. 605), it was Apollo himself who killed Coronis and Ischys. When the body of Coronis was to be burnt, either Apollo or Hermes saved the child Aesculapius from the flames, and carried it to Chiron, who instructed the boy in the art of healing and in hunting. There are various other narratives respecting his birth, according to some of which he was a native of Epidaurus, and this was a common opinion in later times. After he had grown up, reports spread over all countries, that he not only cured all the sick, but called the dead to life again. But while he was restoring Glaucus to life, Zeus killed him with a flash of lightning, as he feared lest men might contrive to escape death altogether, or, because Pluto had complained of Aesculapius diminishing the number of the dead. But, on the request of Apollo, Zeus placed Aesculapius among the stars. Aesculapius is also said to have taken part in the expedition of the Argonauts and in the Calydonian hunt. He was married to Epione, and besides the two sons spoken of by Homer, we also find mention of the following children of his : Ianiscus, Alexenor, Aratus, Hygieia, Aegle, Iaso, and Panaceia, most of whom are only personifications of the powers ascribed to their father. Aesculapius was worshipped all over Greece. His temples were usually built in healthy places, on hills outside the town, and near wells which were believed to have healing powers. These temples were not only places of worship, but were frequented by great numbers of sick persons, and may therefore be compared to modern hospitals. The principal seat of his worship in Greece was Epidaurus, where he had a temple surrounded with an extensive grove. Serpents were everywhere connected with his worship, probably because they were a symbol of prudence and renovation, and were believed to have the power of discovering herbs of wondrous powers. For these reasons, a peculiar kind of tame serpents, in which Epidaurus abounded, was not only kept in his temple, but the god himself frequently appeared in the form of a serpent. At Rome the worship of Aesculapius was introduced from Epidaurus at the command of the Delphic oracle or of the Sibylline books, in B. C. 293, for the purpose of averting a pestilence. The supposed descendants of Aesculapius were called by the patronymic name *Asclepiadae* ('Ασκληπιάδαι), and their principal seats were Cos and Cnidus. They were an order or caste of priests, and for a long period the practice of medicine was intimately connected with religion. The knowledge of medicine was regarded as a sacred secret, which was transmitted from father to son in the families of the Asclepiadae. Respecting the festivals of Aesculapius, see *Dict. of Antiq.*

Aesepus (Αἴσηπος), a river which rises in the mountains of Ida, and flows by a N. E. course into the Propontis, which it enters W. of Cyzicus and E. of the Granicus.

Aesernia (*Aeserninus*: *Isernia*), a town in Samnium, made a Roman colony in the first Punic war.

Aesis (*Esino* or *Fiumesino*), a river which formed the boundary between Picenum and Umbria, was anciently the S. boundary of the Senones, and the N.E. boundary of Italy proper.

Aesis or **Aesium** (Aesinas: *Jesi*), a town and a Roman colony in Umbria on the river Aesis, celebrated for its cheese, *Aesinas caseus*.

Aeson (Αἴσων), son of Cretheus, the founder of Iolcus, and of Tyro, the daughter of Salmoneus, and father of Jason and Promachus. He was excluded from the throne by his half-brother Pelias, who endeavoured to keep the kingdom to himself by sending Jason away with the Argonauts. Pelias subsequently attempted to get rid of Aeson by force, but the latter put an end to his own life. According to Ovid (*Met.* vii. 162, seq.), Aeson survived the return of the Argonauts, and was made young again by Medea.

Aesopus (Αἴσωπος). 1. A writer of Fables, lived about B. C. 570, and was a contemporary of Solon. He was originally a slave, and received his freedom from his master Iadmon the Samian. Upon this he visited Croesus, who sent him to Delphi, to distribute among the citizens 4 minae apiece; but in consequence of some dispute on the subject, he refused to give any money at all, upon which the enraged Delphians threw him from a precipice. Plagues were sent upon them from the gods for the offence, and they proclaimed their willingness to give a compensation for his death to any one who could claim it. At length Iadmon, the grandson of his old master, received the compensation, since no nearer connection could be found. A life of Aesop prefixed to a book of fables purporting to be his, and collected by Maximus Planudes, a monk of the 14th century, represents Aesop as a perfect monster of ugliness and deformity; a notion for which there is no authority whatever in the classical authors. Whether Aesop left any written works at all, is a question which affords considerable room for doubt; though it is certain that fables, bearing Aesop's name, were popular at Athens in its most intellectual age. We find them frequently noticed by Aristophanes. They were in prose, and were turned into poetry by several writers. Socrates turned some of them into verse during his imprisonment; and Demetrius Phalereus (B. c. 320) imitated his example. The only Greek versifier of Aesop, of whose writings any whole fables are preserved, is Babrius. [BABRIUS.] Of the Latin writers of Aesopean fables, Phaedrus is the most celebrated. [PHAEDRUS.] The fables now extant in prose, bearing the name of Aesop, are unquestionably spurious, as is proved by Bentley in his dissertation on the Fables of Aesop appended to his celebrated letters on Phalaris.— *Editions.* By Ernesti, Lips. 1781, and by Schaefer, Lips. 1820.—2. A Greek historian, who wrote a life of Alexander the Great. The original is lost, but there is a Latin translation of it by Julius VALERIUS.

Aesopus, Claudius, or **Clodius,** was the greatest tragic actor at Rome, and a contemporary of Roscius, the greatest comic actor; and both of them lived on intimate terms with Cicero. Aesopus appeared for the last time on the stage at an advanced age at

the dedication of the theatre of Pompey (B. c. 55), when his voice failed him, and he could not go through with the speech. Aesopus realized an immense fortune by his profession, which was squandered by his son, a foolish spendthrift. It is said, for instance, that he dissolved in vinegar and drank a pearl worth about 8000*l.*, which he took from the ear-ring of Caecilia Metella.

Aestii, Aestyi, or **Aestui,** a people dwelling on the sea-coast, in the N. E. of Germany, probably in the modern *Kurland,* who collected amber, which they called *glessum.* Their customs, says Tacitus, resembled the Suevic, and their language the British. They were probably a Sarmatian or Slavonic race, and not a Germanic.

Aesula (Aesulānus), a town of the Aequi on a mountain between Praeneste and Tibur. (Aesulae *declive* arvum," Hor. *Carm.* iii. 29.)

Aethalia (Αἰθαλία, Αἰθάλη), called Ilva (*Elba*) by the Romans, a small island in the Tuscan sea, opposite the town of Populonia, celebrated for its iron mines. It had on the N. E. a good harbour, "Argous Portus" (*Porto Ferraio*), in which the Argonaut Jason is said to have landed.

Aethalides (Αἰθαλίδης), son of Hermes and Eupolemia, the herald of the Argonauts. He had received from his father the faculty of remembering every thing, even in Hades, and was allowed to reside alternately in the upper and in the lower world. His soul, after many migrations, at length took possession of the body of Pythagoras, in which it still recollected its former migrations.

Aether (Αἰθήρ), a personified idea of the mythical cosmogonies, in which Aether was considered as one of the elementary substances out of which the Universe was formed. Aether was regarded by the poets as the pure upper air, the residence of the gods, and Zeus as the Lord of the Aether, or Aether itself personified.

Aethices (Αἴθικες), a Thessalian or Epirot people, near M. Pindus.

Aethicus, Hister or **Ister,** a Roman writer of the 4th century after Christ, a native of Istria, the author of a geographical work, called *Aethici Cosmographia,* which appears to have been chiefly drawn up from the measurement of the whole Roman world ordered by Julius Caesar, B. c. 44, and from other official documents. Edited by Gronovius, in his edition of Pomponius Mela, Leyden, 1722.

Aethilla (Αἴθιλλα or Αἴθυλλα), daughter of Laomedon and sister of Priam, became after the fall of Troy the prisoner of Protesilaus.

Aethiopes (Αἰθίοπες, said to be from αἴθω and ἄψ, but perhaps really a foreign name corrupted), was a name applied (1) most generally to all black or dark races of men; (2) to the inhabitants of all the regions S. of those with which the early Greeks were well acquainted, extending even as far N. as Cyprus and Phoenicia; (3) to all the inhabitants of Inner Africa, S. of Mauretania, the Great Desert, and Egypt, from the Atlantic to the Red Sea and Indian Ocean, and to some of the dark races of Asia; and (4) most specifically to the inhabitants of the land S. of Egypt, which was called AETHIOPIA.

Aethiopia (Αἰθιοπία, Αἰθ. ὑπὲρ Αἰγύπτου: Αἰθίοψ, Αἰθιοπεύς, Hom., fem. Αἰθιοπίς, Aethiops: *Nubia, Kordofan, Sennaar, Abyssinia*), a country of Africa, S. of Egypt, the boundary of the countries being at Syene (*Assouan*) and the Smaller Cataract of the Nile, and extending on the E. to the Red Sea, and to the S. and S.W. indefinitely, as far apparently as the knowledge of the ancients extended. In its most exact political sense the word Aethiopia seems to have denoted the kingdom of MEROE; but in its wider sense it included also the kingdom of the AXOMITAE, besides several other peoples, such as the Troglodytes and the Ichthyophagi on the Red Sea, the Blemmyes and Megabari and Nubae in the interior. The country was watered by the Nile and its tributaries, the Astapus (*Bahr-el-Azrek* or *Blue Nile*) and the Astaboras (*Atbara* or *Tacazze*). The people of Ethiopia seem to have been of the Caucasian race, and to have spoken a language allied to the Arabic. Monuments are found in the country closely resembling those of Egypt, but of an inferior style. The religion of the Ethiopians appears to have been similar to that of the Egyptians, but free from the grosser superstitions of the latter, such as the worship of animals. Some traditions made Meroë the parent of Egyptian civilization, while others ascribed the civilization of Ethiopia to Egyptian colonization. So great was the power of the Ethiopians, that more than once in its history Egypt was governed by Ethiopian kings; and even the most powerful kings of Egypt, though they made successful incursions into Ethiopia, do not appear to have had any extensive or permanent hold upon the country. Under the Ptolemies Graeco-Egyptian colonies established themselves in Ethiopia, and Greek manners and philosophy had a considerable influence on the upper classes; but the country was never subdued. The Romans failed to extend their empire over Ethiopia, though they made expeditions into the country, in one of which C. Petronius, prefect of Egypt under Augustus, advanced as far as Napata, and defeated the warrior queen Candace (B. C. 22). Christianity very early extended to Ethiopia, probably in consequence of the conversion of the treasurer of queen Candace (Acts, viii. 27). The history of the downfall of the great Ethiopian kingdom of Meroë is very obscure.

Aethlius ('Αέθλιος), first king of Elis, father of Endymion, was son of Zeus and Protogenia, daughter of Deucalion, or son of Aeolus.

Aethra (Αἴθρα). 1. Daughter of Pittheus of Troezen, was mother of Theseus by Aegeus. She afterwards lived in Attica, from whence she was carried off to Lacedaemon by Castor and Pollux, and became a slave of Helen, with whom she was taken to Troy. At the capture of Troy she was restored to liberty by her grandson Acamas or Demophon. — **2**. Daughter of Oceanus, by whom Atlas begot the 12 Hyades and a son Hyas.

Aëtion ('Αετίων). 1. A sculptor of Amphipolis, flourished about the middle of the 3rd century B.C.—**2**. A celebrated painter, whose best picture represented the marriage of Alexander and Roxana. It is commonly supposed that he lived in the time of Alexander the Great; but the words of Lucian (*Herod.* 4) show that he must have lived about the time of Hadrian and the Antonines.

Aëtius. 1. A celebrated Roman general, defended the Western empire against the barbarians during the reign of Valentinian III. In A. D. 451 he gained a great victory over Attila, near Chalons in Gaul; but he was treacherously murdered by Valentinian in 454.—**2**. A Greek medical writer, born at Amida in Mesopotamia, lived at the end of the 5th or the beginning of the 6th century after

Christ. His work Βιβλία 'Ιατρικὰ 'Εκκαίδεκα, "Sixteen Books on Medicine," is one of the most valuable medical remains of antiquity, as being a judicious compilation from many authors whose works are lost. The whole of it has never appeared in the original Greek, but a corrupt translation of it into Latin was published by Cornarius, Basil. 1542, often reprinted, and in H. Stephens's *Medicae Artis Principes*, Paris, 1567.

Aetna (Αἴτνη). 1. (*Monte Gibello*), a volcanic mountain in the N. E. of Sicily between Tauromenium and Catana. It is said to have derived its name from Aetna, a Sicilian nymph, a daughter of Uranus and Gaea, or of Briareus. Zeus buried under it Typhon or Enceladus; and in its interior Hephaestus and the Cyclops forged the thunderbolts for Zeus. There were several eruptions of M. Aetna in antiquity. One occurred in B. C. 475, to which Aeschylus and Pindar probably allude, and another in B. C. 425, which Thucydides says (iii. 116) was the third on record since the Greeks had settled in Sicily. The form of the mountain seems to have been much the same in antiquity as it is at present. Its base covers an area of nearly 90 miles in circumference, and its highest point is 10,874 feet above the level of the sea. The circumference of the crater is variously estimated from 2½ to 4 miles, and the depth from 600 to 800 feet.—**2**. (Aetnenses: *S. Maria di Licodia*), a town at the foot of M. Aetna, on the road to Catana, formerly called Inessa or Innesa. It was founded in B. C. 461, by the inhabitants of Catana, who had been expelled from their own town by the Siculi. They gave the name of Aetna to Inessa, because their own town Catana had been called Aetna by Hiero I.

Aetnaeus (Αἰτναῖος), an epithet of several gods and mythical beings connected with Mount Aetna; — of Zeus, of whom there was a statue on Mount Aetna, and to whom a festival was celebrated there, called Aetnea; of Hephaestus; and of the Cyclops.

Aetolia (Αἰτωλία: Αἰτωλός), a division of Greece, was bounded on the W. by Acarnania, from which it was separated by the river Achelous, on the N. by Epirus and Thessaly, on the E. by the Ozolian Locrians, and on the S. by the entrance to the Corinthian gulf. It was divided into two parts, Old Aetolia, from the Achelous to the Evenus and Calydon, and New Aetolia, or the Acquired (ἐπίκτητος), from the Evenus and Calydon to the Ozolian Locrians. On the coast the country is level and fruitful, but in the interior mountainous and unproductive. The mountains contained many wild beasts, and were celebrated in mythology for the hunt of the Calydonian boar. The country was originally inhabited by Curetes and Leleges, but was at an early period colonized by Greeks from Elis, led by the mythical AETOLUS. The Aetolians took part in the Trojan war, under their king Thoas. They continued for a long time a rude and uncivilized people, living to a great extent by robbery; and even in the time of Thucydides (B. C. 410) many of their tribes spoke a language which was not Greek, and were in the habit of eating raw flesh. Like the other Greeks, they abolished at an early time the monarchical form of government, and lived under a democracy. They appear to have been early united by a kind of League, but this League first acquired political importance about the middle of the 3rd century B. C., and became a formidable rival to the Macedonian monarchs and the Achaean League. The Aetolian League at one time included not only Aetolia 'roper, but Acarnania, part of Thessaly, Locris, and the island of Cephallenia ; and it also had close alliances with Elis and several towns in the Peloponnesus, and likewise with Cius on the Propontis. Its annual meetings, called *Panaetolica*, were held in the autumn at Thermus, and at them were chosen a General (στρατηγός), who was at the head of the League, an Hipparchus, or Master of the Horse, a Secretary, and a select committee called Apocleti (ἀπόκλητοι). For further particulars respecting the constitution of the League, see *Dict. of Ant.* art. *Aetolicum Foedus.* The Aetolians took the side of Antiochus III. against the Romans, and on the defeat of that monarch B. c. 189, they became virtually the subjects of Rome. On the conquest of the Achaeans, B. c. 146, Aetolia was included in the Roman province of Achaia. After the battle of Actium, B. c. 31, a considerable part of the population of Aetolia was transplanted to the city of Nicopolis, which Augustus built in commemoration of his victory.

Aetōlus (Αἰτωλός), son of Endymion and Neïs, or Iphianassa, married Pronoë, by whom he had two sons, Pleuron and Calydon. He was king of Elis, but was obliged to leave Peloponnesus, because he had slain Apis, the son of Jason or Salmoneus. He went to the country near the Achelous, which was called Aetolia after him.

Aexōnē (Αἰξωνή and Αἰξωνῆς: Αἰξωνεύς : *Asani* ?), an Attic demus of the tribe Cecropis or Pandionis. Its inhabitants had the reputation of being mockers and slanderers.

Afer, Domitĭus, of Nemausus (Nismes) in Gaul, was the teacher of Quintilian, and one of the most distinguished orators in the reigns of Tiberius, Caligula, Claudius, and Nero, but he sacrificed his character by conducting accusations for the government. He was consul suffectus in A. D. 39, and died in 60. Quintilian mentions several works of his on oratory, which are all lost.

Afrānĭus. 1. L. A Roman comic poet, flourished about B. c. 100. His comedies described Roman scenes and manners (*Comoediae togatae*), and the subjects were mostly taken from the life of the lower classes. (*Comoediae tabernariae.*) They were frequently polluted with disgraceful amours ; but he depicted Roman life with such accuracy, that he is classed with Menander (Hor. *Ep.* ii. 1. 57). His comedies continued to be acted under the empire. The names and fragments of between 20 and 30 are still preserved.—2. L., a person of obscure origin, and a faithful adherent of Pompey. He served under Pompey against Sertorius and Mithridates, and was, through Pompey's influence, made consul, B. c. 60. When Pompey obtained the provinces of the two Spains in his second consulship (B. c. 55), he sent Afranius and Petreius to govern them, while he himself remained in Rome. In B. c. 49, Afranius and Petreius were defeated by Caesar in Spain. Afranius thereupon passed over to Pompey in Greece ; was present at the battle of Pharsalia, B. c. 48 ; and subsequently at the battle of Thapsus in Africa, B. c. 46. He then attempted to fly into Mauretania, but was taken prisoner by P. Sittius, and killed.

Afrĭca ('Αφρίκη: Africānus), was used by the ancients in two senses, (1) for the whole continent of *Africa*, and (2) for the portion of N. Africa which constituted the territory of Carthage, and which the Romans erected into a province, under the name of Africa Propria.—1. In the more general sense the name was not used by the Greek writers ; and its use by the Romans arose from the extension to the whole continent of the name of a part of it. The proper Greek name for the continent is Libya (Λιβύη). Considerably before the historical period of Greece begins, the Phoenicians extended their commerce over the Mediterranean, and founded several colonies on the N. coast of Africa, of which Carthage was the chief. [CARTHAGO.] The Greeks knew very little of the country until the foundation of the Dorian colony of Cyrene (B. c. 620), and the intercourse of Greek travellers with Egypt in the 6th and 5th centuries ; and even then their knowledge of all but the part near Cyrene was derived from the Egyptians and Phoenicians, who sent out some remarkable expeditions to explore the country. A Phoenician fleet sent by the Egyptian king Pharaoh Necho (about B. c. 600), was said to have sailed from the Red Sea, round Africa, and so into the Mediterranean : the authenticity of this story is still a matter of dispute. We still possess an authentic account of another expedition, which the Carthaginians despatched under Hanno (about B. c. 510), and which reached a point on the W. coast nearly, if not quite, as far as lat. 10° N. On the opposite side of the continent, the coast appears to have been very little known beyond the S. boundary of Egypt, till the time of the Ptolemies. In the interior, the Great Desert (*Sahara*) interposed a formidable obstacle to discovery ; but even before the time of Herodotus the people on the northern coast told of individuals who had crossed the Desert and had reached a great river flowing towards the E., with crocodiles in it, and black men living on its banks ; which, if the story be true, was probably the *Niger* in its upper course, near *Timbuctoo.* That the Carthaginians had considerable intercourse with the regions S. of the *Sahara*, has been inferred from the abundance of elephants they kept. Later expeditions and inquiries extended the knowledge which the ancients possessed of the E. coast to about 10° S. lat., and gave them, as it seems, some further acquaintance with the interior, about *Lake Tchad*, but the southern part of the continent was so totally unknown, that Ptolemy, who finally fixed the limits of ancient geographical science, recurred to the old notion, which seems to have prevailed before the time of Herodotus, that the S. parts of Africa met the S. E. part of Asia, and that the Indian Ocean was a vast lake. The greatest geographers who lived before Ptolemy, namely, Eratosthenes and Strabo, had accepted the tradition that Africa was circumnavigable. The shape of the continent they conceived to be that of a rightangled triangle, having for its hypotenuse a line drawn from the Pillars of Hercules to the S. of the Red Sea ; and, as to its extent, they did not suppose it to reach nearly so far as the Equator. Ptolemy supposed the W. coast to stretch N. and S. from the Pillars of Hercules, and he gave the continent an indefinite extent towards the S. There were also great differences of opinion as to the boundaries of the continent. Some divided the whole world into only two parts, Europe and Asia, and they were not agreed to which of these two Libya (i. e. Africa) belonged ; and those who recognised three divisions differed again in placing the boundary between Libya and Asia either on the W. of Egypt, or along the Nile, or at the isthmus of Suez and the Red Sea: the last opinion gradually prevailed. As to the subdivision of the country itself, Herodotus distributes it into Aegyptus, Aethiopia (i. e. all the regions S. of Egypt and the *Sahara*), and Libya, properly so called; and he subdivides Libya into three parts, according to their physical distinctions, namely, (1) the Inhabited Country along the Mediterranean, in which dwelt the Nomad Libyans (οἱ παραθαλάσσιοι τῶν νομάδων Λιβύων: the *Barbary States*); (2) the Country of Wild Beasts (ἡ θηριώδης), S. of the former, that is, the region between the Little and Great Atlas, which still abounds in wild beasts, but takes its name from its prevailing vegetation (*Bcled-el-Jerid*, i. e. the *Country of Palms*), and (3) the Sandy Desert (ἡ ψάμμος; the *Sahara*), that is, the table land bounded by the Atlas on the N. and the margin of the Nile-valley on the E., which is a vast tract of sand broken only by a few habitable islands, called Oases. As to the people, Herodotus distinguishes four races, two native, namely, the Libyans and Ethiopians, and two foreign, namely, the Phoenicians and the Greeks. The Libyans, however, were a Caucasian race: the Ethiopians of Herodotus correspond to our Negro races. The Phoenician colonies were planted chiefly along, and to the W. of, the great recess in the middle of the N. coast, which formed the two SYRTES, by far the most important of them being Carthage; and the Greek colonies were fixed on the coast along and beyond the E. side of the Syrtes; the chief of them was CYRENE, and the region was called Cyrenaïca. Between this and Egypt were Libyan tribes, and the whole region between the Carthaginian dominions and Egypt, including Cyrenaïca, was called by the same name as the whole continent, Libya. The chief native tribes of this region were the ADYRMACHIDAE, MARMARIDAE, PSYLLI, and NASAMONES. The last extended into the Carthaginian territory. To the W. of the Carthaginian possessions, the country was called by the general names of NUMIDIA and MAURETANIA, and was possessed partly by Carthaginian colonies on the coast, and partly by Libyan tribes under various names, the chief of which were the NUMIDAE, MASSYLII, MASSAESYLII, and MAURI, and to the S. of them the GAETULI. The whole of this northern region fell successively under the power of Rome, and was finally divided into provinces as follows: — (1) Aegypt; (2) Libya, including (a) Libyae Nomos or Libya Exterior, (b) Marmarica, (c) Cyrenaïca; (3) Africa Propria, the former empire of Carthage (see below, No. 2); (4) Numidia; (5) Mauretania, divided into (a) Sitifensis, (b) Caesariensis, (c) Tingitana: these, with (6) Aethiopia, make up the whole of Africa, according to the divisions recognised by the latest of the ancient geographers. The northern district was better known to the Romans than it is to us, and was extremely populous and flourishing; and, if we may judge by the list of tribes in Ptolemy, the interior of the country, especially between the Little and Great Altars, must have supported many more inhabitants than it does at present. Further information respecting the several portions of the country will be found in the separate articles. — 2. **Africa Propria** or Provincia, or simply Africa,

was the name under which the Romans, after the Third Punic War (B. C. 146), erected into a province the whole of the former territory of Carthage. It extended from the river Tusca, on the W., which divided it from Numidia, to the bottom of the Syrtis Minor, on the S. E. It was divided into two districts (regiones), namely, (1) Zeugis or Zeugitana, the district round Carthage, (2) Byzacium or Byzacena, S. of Zeugitana, as far as the bottom of the Syrtis Minor. It corresponds to the modern regency of *Tunis*. The province was full of flourishing towns, and was extremely fertile, especially Byzacena: it furnished Rome with its chief supplies of corn. The above limits are assigned to the province by Pliny: Ptolemy makes it extend from the river Ampsaga on the W., to the borders of Cyrenaica, at the bottom of the Great Syrtis, on the E., so as to include Numidia and Tripolitana.

Africānus, a surname given to the Scipios on account of their victories in Africa. [SCIPIO.]

Africānus. 1. **Sex. Caecilius**, a Roman juris-consult, lived under Antoninus Pius (A. D. 138—161), and wrote *Libri IX. Quaestionum*, from which many extracts are made in the Digest.—2. **Julius**, a celebrated orator in the reign of Nero, is much praised by Quintilian, who speaks of him and Domitius Afer as the best orators of their time.—3. **Sex. Julius**, a learned Christian writer at the beginning of the 3rd century, passed the greater part of his life at Emmaus in Palestine, and afterwards lived at Alexandria. His principal work was a *Chronicon* in five books, from the creation of the world, which he placed in 5499 B.C., to A. D. 221. This work is lost, but part of it is extracted by Eusebius in his *Chronicon*, and many fragments of it are preserved by Georgius Syncellus, Cedrenus, and in the Paschale Chronicon. There was another work written by Africanus, entitled *Cesti* (Κεστοί), that is, embroidered girdles, so called from the celebrated *Cestus* of Aphrodite (Venus). It treated of a vast variety of subjects—medicine, agriculture, natural history, the military art, &c. The work itself is lost, but some extracts from it are published by Thevenot in the *Mathematici Veteres*, Paris, 1693, and also in the *Geoponica*.

Africus (Λίψ by the Greeks), the S. W. wind, so called because it blew from Africa, frequently brought storms with it (*creberque procellis Africus*, Virg. *Aen.* i. 85).

Agamēdē ('Αγαμήδη), daughter of Augias and wife of Mulius, who, according to Homer (*Il.* xi. 739), was acquainted with the healing powers of all the plants that grow upon the earth.

Agamēdes ('Αγαμήδης), commonly called son of Erginus, king of Orchomenus, and brother of Trophonius; though his family connexions are related differently by different writers. Agamedes and Trophonius distinguished themselves as architects: they built a temple of Apollo at Delphi, and a treasury of Hyrieus, king of Hyria in Boeotia. The story about this treasury resembles the one which Herodotus (ii. 121) relates of the treasury of the Egyptian king Rhampsinitus. In the construction of the treasury of Hyrieus, Agamedes and Trophonius contrived to place one stone in such a manner, that it could be taken away outside, and thus formed an entrance to the treasury, without any body perceiving it. Agamedes and Trophonius now constantly robbed the treasury; and the king, seeing that locks and seals were un-injured while his treasures were constantly decreasing, set traps to catch the thief. Agamedes was thus ensnared, and Trophonius cut off his head to avert the discovery. After this Trophonius was immediately swallowed up by the earth. On this spot there was afterwards, in the grove of Lebadēa, the cave of Agamedes with a column by the side of it. Here also was the oracle of Trophonius, and those who consulted it first offered a ram to Agamedes and invoked him. A tradition mentioned by Cicero (*Tusc. Quaest.* i. 47) states that Agamedes and Trophonius, after building the temple of Apollo at Delphi, prayed to the god to grant them in reward for their labour what was best for men. The god promised to do so on a certain day, and when the day came, the two brothers died.

Agamemnon ('Αγαμέμνων), son of Plisthenes and Aërope or Eriphyle, and grandson of Atreus, king of Mycenae ; but Homer and others call him a son of Atreus and grandson of Pelops. Agamemnon and his brother Menelaus were brought up together with Aegisthus, the son of Thyestes, in the house of Atreus. After the murder of Atreus by Aegisthus and Thyestes, who succeeded Atreus in the kingdom of Mycenae [AEGISTHUS], Agamemnon and Menelaus went to Sparta, where Agamemnon married Clytemnestra, the daughter of Tyndareus, by whom he became the father of Iphianassa (Iphigenīa), Chrysothemis, Laodice (Electra), and Orestes. The manner in which Agamemnon obtained the kingdom of Mycenae, is differently related. From Homer, it appears as if he had peaceably succeeded Thyestes, while, according to others, he expelled Thyestes, and usurped his throne. He now became the most powerful prince in Greece. A catalogue of his dominions is given in the Iliad (ii. 569, &c.). When Homer attributes to Agamemnon the sovereignty over all Argos, the name Argos signifies Peloponnesus, or the greater part of it, for the city of Argos was governed by Diomedes. When Helen, the wife of Menelaus, was carried off by Paris, and the Greek chiefs resolved to recover her by force of arms, Agamemnon was chosen their commander in chief. After two years of preparation, the Greek army and fleet assembled in the port of Aulis in Boeotia. At this place Agamemnon killed a stag which was sacred to Artemis, who in return visited the Greek army with a pestilence, and produced a calm which prevented the Greeks from leaving the port. In order to appease her wrath, Agamemnon consented to sacrifice his daughter Iphigenia ; but at the moment she was to be sacrificed, she was carried off by Artemis herself to Tauris and another victim was substituted in her place. The calm now ceased, and the army sailed to the coast of Troy. Agamemnon alone had 100 ships, independent of 60 which he had lent to the Arcadians. In the tenth year of the siege of Troy we find Agamemnon involved in a quarrel with Achilles respecting the possession of Briseïs, whom Achilles was obliged to give up to Agamemnon. Achilles withdrew from the field of battle, and the Greeks were visited by successive disasters. The danger of the Greeks at last induced Patroclus, the friend of Achilles, to take part in the battle, and his fall led to the reconciliation of Achilles and Agamemnon. [ACHILLES.] Agamemnon, although the chief commander of the Greeks, is not the hero of the Iliad, and in chivalrous spirit, bravery, and character, altogether inferior to Achilles. But he nevertheless rises above

all the Greeks by his dignity, power, and majesty. his eyes and head are likened to those of Zeus, his girdle to that of Ares, and his breast to that of Poseidon. The emblem of his power is a sceptre, the work of Hephaestus, which Zeus had once given to Hermes, and Hermes to Pelops, from whom it descended to Agamemnon. At the capture of Troy he received Cassandra, the daughter of Priam, as his prize. On his return home he was murdered by Aegisthus, who had seduced Clytemnestra during the absence of her husband. The tragic poets make Clytemnestra alone murder Agamemnon : her motive is in Aeschylus her jealousy of Cassandra, in Sophocles and Euripides her wrath at the death of Iphigenīa.

Agamemnōnĭdes ('Αγαμεμνονίδης), the son of Agamemnon, i. e. Orestes.

Agănippe ('Αγανίππη), a nymph of the well of the same name at the foot of Mount Helicon, in Boeotia, which was considered sacred to the Muses (who were hence called *Aganippides*), and which was believed to have the power of inspiring those who drank of it. The fountain of Hippocrēne has the epithet *Aganippis* (Ov. *Fast.* v. 7), from its being sacred to the Muses, like that of Aganippe.

Agapēnor ('Αγαπήνωρ), son of Ancaeus king of the Arcadians, received 60 ships from Agamemnon, in which he led his Arcadians to Troy. On his return from Troy he was cast by a storm on the coast of Cyprus, where he founded the town of Paphus, and in it the famous temple of Aphrodite

Agarista ('Αγαρίστη). 1. Daughter of Clisthenes, tyrant of Sicyon, wife of Megacles, and mother of Clisthenes who divided the Athenians into ten tribes, and of Hippocrates.—2. Daughter of the above-mentioned Hippocrates, and granddaughter of No. 1, wife of Xanthippus, and mother of Pericles.

Agasĭas ('Αγασίας), son of Dositheus, a sculptor of Ephesus, probably a contemporary of Alexander the Great (B. C. 330), sculptured the statue known by the name of the Borghese gladiator, which is still preserved in the gallery of the Louvre. This statue, as well as the Apollo Belvidere, was discovered among the ruins of a palace of the Roman emperors on the site of the ancient Antium (*Capo d'Anzo*). From the attitude of the figure it is clear, that the statue represents not a gladiator, but a warrior contending with a mounted combatant. Perhaps it was intended to represent Achilles fighting with Penthesilēa.

Agasicles, Agesicles, or **Hegesicles** ('Αγασικλῆς, 'Αγησικλῆς, 'Ηγησικλῆς), king of Sparta, succeeded his father Archidamus I., about B. C. 600 or 590.

Agatharchĭdes ('Αγαθαρχίδης) or **Agatharchus** ('Αγάθαρχος), a Greek grammarian, born at Cnidos, lived at Alexandria, probably about B. C. 130. He wrote a considerable number of geographical and historical works ; but we have only an epitome of a portion of his work on the Erythraean sea, which was made by Photius : it is printed in Hudson's *Geogr. Script. Gr. Minores.*

Agatharchus ('Αγάθαρχος), an Athenian artist, said to have invented scene-painting, and to have painted a scene for a tragedy which Aeschylus exhibited. It was probably not till towards the end of Aeschylus's career that scene-painting was introduced, and not till the time of Sophocles that it was generally made use of ; which may account for Aristotle's assertion (*Poët.* iv. 16) that scene-painting was introduced by Sophocles. — **2.** A Greek painter, a native of Samos, and son of Eudemus. He was a contemporary of Alcibiades and Zeuxis, and must not be confounded with the contemporary of Aeschylus.

Agathēmērus ('Αγαθήμερος), the author of "A sketch of Geography in epitome" (τῆς γεωγραφίας ὑποτυπώσεις ἐν ἐπιτομῇ), probably lived about the beginning of the 3rd century after Christ. The work consists chiefly of extracts from Ptolemy and other earlier writers. It is printed in Hudson's *Geogr. Script. Gr. Minores.*

Agathīas ('Αγαθίας), a Byzantine writer, born about A. D. 536 at Myrina in Aeolia, practised as an advocate at Constantinople, whence he obtained his surname *Scholasticus* (which word signified an advocate in his time), and died about A. D. 582. He wrote many poems, of which several have come down to us; but his principal work was his History in five books, which is also extant, and is of considerable value. It contains the history from A. D. 553—558, a period remarkable for important events, such as the conquest of Italy by Narses and the exploits of Belisarius over the Huns and other barbarians. The best edition is by Niebuhr, Bonn, 1828.

Agathŏclēa ('Αγαθόκλεια), mistress of Ptolemy IV. Philopator, king of Egypt, and sister of his minister Agathocles. She and her brother were put to death on the death of Ptolemy (B. c. 205).

Agathŏcles ('Αγαθοκλῆς). **1.** A Sicilian, raised himself from the station of a potter to that of tyrant of Syracuse and king of Sicily. Born at Thermae, a town of Sicily subject to Carthage, he is said to have been exposed when an infant, by his father, Carcinus of Rhegium, in consequence of a succession of troublesome dreams, portending that he would be a source of much evil to Sicily. His mother, however, secretly preserved his life, and at 7 years old he was restored to his father, who had long repented of his conduct to the child. By him he was taken to Syracuse and brought up as a potter. His strength and personal beauty recommended him to Damas, a noble Syracusan, who drew him from obscurity, and on whose death he married his rich widow, and so became one of the wealthiest citizens in Syracuse. His ambitious schemes then developed themselves, and he was driven into exile. After several changes of fortune, he collected an army which overawed both the Syracusans and Carthaginians, and was restored under an oath that he would not interfere with the democracy, which oath he kept by murdering 4000 and banishing 6000 citizens. He was immediately declared sovereign of Syracuse, under the title of Autocrator, B. c. 317. In the course of a few years the whole of Sicily, which was not under the dominion of Carthage, submitted to him. In B. c. 310 he was defeated at Himera by the Carthaginians, under Hamilcar, who straightway laid siege to Syracuse; whereupon he formed the bold design of averting the ruin which threatened him, by carrying the war into Africa. His successes were most brilliant and rapid. He constantly defeated the troops of Carthage, but was at length summoned from Africa by the affairs of Sicily, where many cities had revolted from him, B. c. 307. These he reduced, after making a treaty with the Carthaginians. He had previously assumed the title of king of Sicily. He afterwards plun-

dered the Lipari isles, and also carried his arms into Italy in order to attack the Bruttii. But his last days were embittered by family misfortunes. His grandson Archagathus murdered his son Agathocles, for the sake of succeeding to the crown, and the old king feared that the rest of his family would share his fate. He accordingly sent his wife Texena and her two children to Egypt, her native country; and his own death followed almost immediately, B. c. 289, after a reign of 28 years, and in the 72nd year of his age. Other authors relate an incredible story of his being poisoned by Maeno, an associate of Archagathus. The poison, we are told, was concealed in the quill with which he cleaned his teeth, and reduced him to so frightful a condition, that he was placed on the funeral pile and burnt while yet living, being unable to give any signs that he was not dead. — **2.** Of Pella, father of Lysimachus. — **3.** Son of Lysimachus, was defeated and taken prisoner by Dromichaetis, king of the Getae, about B. c. 292, but was sent back to his father with presents. In 287, he defeated Demetrius Poliorcetes. At the instigation of his stepmother, Arsinoë, Lysimachus cast him into prison, where he was murdered (284) by Ptolemaeus Ceraunus. — **4.** Brother of AGATHOCLES. — **5.** A Greek historian, of uncertain date, wrote the history of Cyzicus, which was extensively read in antiquity, and is referred to by Cicero (*de Div.* i. 24).

Agăthŏdaemon ('Αγαθοδαίμων or 'Αγαθὸς ϑεὸς). **1.** The "Good Deity," in honour of whom the Greeks drank a cup of unmixed wine at the end of every repast. — **2.** Of Alexandria, the designer of some maps to accompany Ptolemy's Geography. Copies of these maps are found appended to several MSS. of Ptolemy.

Agăthon ('Αγάθων), an Athenian tragic poet, born about B. c. 447, of a rich and respectable family, was a friend of Euripides and Plato. He gained his first victory in 416: in honour of which Plato represents the Symposium to have been given, which he has made the occasion of his dialogue so called. In 407, he visited the court of Archelaus, king of Macedonia, where his friend Euripides was also a guest at the same time. He died about 400, at the age of 47. The poetic merits of Agathon were considerable, but his compositions were more remarkable for elegance and flowery ornaments than force, vigour, or sublimity. In the *Thesmophoriazusae* of Aristophanes he is ridiculed for his effeminacy, being brought on the stage in female dress.

Agathyrna, Agathyrnum ('Αγάθυρνα, -ον: 'Αγαθυρναῖος: *Agatha*), a town on the N. coast of Sicily.

Agăthyrsi ('Αγάθυρσοι), a people in European Sarmatia, on the river Maris (*Maroseh*) in Transylvania. From their practice of painting or tatooing their skin, they are called by Virgil (*Aen.* iv. 146) *picti Agathyrsi.*

Agăvē ('Αγαυή), daughter of Cadmus, wife of Echion, and mother of Pentheus. When Pentheus attempted to prevent the women from celebrating the Dionysiac festivals on mount Cithaeron, he was torn to pieces there by his own mother Agave, who in her frenzy believed him to be a wild beast. [PENTHEUS.] — One of the Nereids, one of the Danaids, and one of the Amazons were also called Agavae.

Agbatăna. [ECBATANA.]

Agdistis ('Αγδίστις), an androgynous deity, the

offspring of Zeus and Earth, connected with the Phrygian worship of Attes or Atys.

Ageladas ('Αγελάδας), an eminent statuary of Argos, the instructor of the three great masters, Phidias, Myron, and Polycletus. Many modern writers suppose that there were two artists of this name; one an Argive, the instructor of Phidias, born about B. C. 540, the other a native of Sicyon, who flourished about B. C. 432.

Agelaus ('Αγέλαος). 1. Son of Hercules and Omphale, and founder of the house of Croesus. —2. Son of Damastor and one of the suitors of Penelope, slain by Ulysses.—3. A slave of Priam, who exposed the infant Paris on mount Ida, in consequence of a dream of his mother.

Agendicum or Agedicum (Sens), the chief town of the Senones in Gallia Lugdunensis.

Agenor ('Αγήνωρ). 1. Son of Poseidon and Libya, king of Phoenicia, twin-brother of Belus, and father of Cadmus, Phoenix, Cylix, Thasus, Phineus, and according to some of Europa also. Virgil (Aen. i. 338) calls Carthage the city of Agenor, since Dido was descended from Agenor. —2. Son of Jasus, and father of Argus Panoptes, king of Argos.—3. Son and successor of Triopas, in the kingdom of Argos.—4. Son of Pleuron and Xanthippe, and grandson of Aetolus.—5. Son of Phegeus, king of Psophis, in Arcadia. He and his brother Pronous slew Alcmaeon, when he wanted to give the celebrated necklace and peplus of Harmonia to his second wife Calirrhoë. [Phegeus.] The two brothers were afterwards killed by Amphoterus and Acarnan, the sons of Alcmaeon and Callirrhoë.—6. Son of the Trojan Antenor and Theano, one of the bravest among the Trojans, was wounded by Achilles, but rescued by Apollo.

Agenorides ('Αγηνορίδης), a descendant of an Agenor, such as Cadmus, Phineus, and Perseus.

Agesander, a sculptor of Rhodes, who, in conjunction with Polydorus and Athenodorus, sculptured the group of Laocoon, one of the most perfect specimens of art. This celebrated group was discovered in the year 1506, near the baths of Titus on the Esquiline hill: it is now preserved in the museum of the Vatican. The artists probably lived in the reign of Titus, and sculptured the group expressly for that emperor.

Agesilaus ('Αγησίλαος), kings of Sparta. 1. Son of Doryssus, reigned 44 years, and died about B. C. 886. He was contemporary with the legislation of Lycurgus. — 2. Son of Archidamus II., succeeded his half-brother Agis II., B. C. 398, excluding, on the ground of spurious birth, and by the interest of Lysander, his nephew Leotychides. From 396 to 394 he carried on the war in Asia Minor with great success, and was preparing to advance into the heart of the Persian empire, when he was summoned home to defend his country against Thebes, Corinth, and Argos, which had been induced by Artaxerxes to take up arms against Sparta. Though full of disappointment, he promptly obeyed; and in the course of the same year (394), he met and defeated at Coronea in Boeotia the allied forces. During the next 4 years he regained for his country much of its former supremacy, till at length the fatal battle of Leuctra, 371, overthrew for ever the power of Sparta, and gave the supremacy for a time to Thebes. For the next few years Sparta had almost to struggle for its existence amid dangers without and within, and it was chiefly owing to the skill, courage, and pre-

sence of mind of Agesilaus that she weathered the storm. In 361 he crossed with a body of Lacedaemonian mercenaries into Egypt. Here, after displaying much of his ancient skill, he died, while preparing for his voyage home, in the winter of 361—360, after a life of above 80 years and a reign of 38. His body was embalmed in wax, and splendidly buried at Sparta. In person Agesilaus was small, mean-looking, and lame, on which last ground objection had been made to his accession, an oracle, curiously fulfilled, having warned Sparta of evils awaiting her under a "lame sovereignty." In his reign, indeed, her fall took place, but not through him, for he was one of the best citizens and generals that Sparta ever had.

Agesipolis ('Αγησίπολις), kings of Sparta. 1. Succeeded his father Pausanias, while yet a minor, in B. C. 394, and reigned 14 years. As soon as his minority ceased, he took an active part in the wars in which Sparta was then engaged with the other states of Greece In 390 he invaded Argolis with success; in 385 he took the city of Mantinea; in 381 he went to the assistance of Acanthus and Apollonia against the Olynthians, and died in 380 during this war in the peninsula of Pallene. — 2. Son of Cleombrotus, reigned one year B. C. 371.—3. Succeeded Cleomenes in B. C. 220, but was soon deposed by his colleague Lycurgus: he afterwards took refuge with the Romans.

Agetor ('Αγήτωρ), "the leader," a surname of Zeus at Lacedaemon, of Apollo, and of Hermes, who conducts the souls of men to the lower world.

Aggenus Urbicus, a writer on the science of the Agrimensores, may perhaps have lived at the latter part of the 4th century of our era. His works are printed in Goesius, Rei Agrariae Auctores.

Aggrammes or Xandrames (Ξανδράμης), the ruler of the Gangaridae and Prasii in India, when Alexander invaded India, B. C. 327.

Agias ('Αγίας), a Greek epic poet, erroneously called Augias, a native of Troezen, flourished about B. C. 740, and was the author of a poem called Nosti (Νόστοι), i. e. the history of the return of the Achaean heroes from Troy.

Aginnum (Agen), the chief town of the Nitiobriges in Gallia Aquitanica.

Agis ('Αγις), kings of Sparta. 1. Son of Eurysthenes, the founder of the family of the Agidae.—2. Son of Archidamus II., reigned B. C. 427—398. He took an active part in the Peloponnesian war, and invaded Attica several times. While Alcibiades was at Sparta he was the guest of Agis, and is said to have seduced his wife Timaea; in consequence of which Leotychides, the son of Agis, was excluded from the throne as illegitimate.—3. Son of Archidamus III., reigned B. C. 338—330, attempted to overthrow the Macedonian power in Europe, while Alexander the Great was in Asia, but was defeated and killed in battle by Antipater in 330.—4. Son of Eudamidas II., reigned B. C. 244—240. He attempted to re-establish the institutions of Lycurgus, and to effect a thorough reform in the Spartan state; but he was resisted by his colleague Leonidas II. and the wealthy, was thrown into prison, and was there put to death by command of the ephors, along with his mother Agesistrata, and his grandmother Archidamia.

Agis, a Greek poet of Argos, a notorious flatterer of Alexander the Great.

Aglāïa ('Αγλαΐα), "the bright one." 1. One of the CHARITES or Graces.—2. Wife of Charopus and mother of Nireus, who came from the island of Sime against Troy.

Aglaophāmē. [SIRENES.]

Aglaophon ('Αγλαοφῶν). 1. Painter of Thasos, father and instructor of Polygnotus and Aristophon, lived about B. C. 500.—2. Painter, lived about B. C. 420, probably grandson of No. 1.

Aglāus ('Αγλαός), a poor citizen of Psophis in Arcadia, whom the Delphic oracle declared happier than Gyges king of Lydia, on account of his contented disposition. Pausanias places him in the time of Croesus.

Agnōdīcē ('Αγνοδίκη), an Athenian maiden, was the first of her sex to learn midwifery, which a law at Athens forbade any woman to learn. Dressed as a man, she obtained instruction from a physician named Hierophilus, and afterwards practised her art with success. Summoned before the Areopagus by the envy of the other practitioners, she was obliged to disclose her sex, and was not only acquitted, but obtained the repeal of the obnoxious law. This tale, though often repeated, does not deserve much credit, as it rests on the authority of Hyginus alone.

Agnōnīdes ('Αγνωνίδης), an Athenian demagogue, induced the Athenians to sentence Phocion to death (B. C. 318), but was shortly afterwards put to death himself by the Athenians.

Agoracrītus ('Αγοράκριτος), a statuary of Paros, flourished B. C. 440—428, and was the favourite pupil of Phidias. His greatest work was a statue of Aphrodite, which he changed into a statue of Nemesis, and sold it to the people of Rhamnus, because he was indignant that the Athenians had given the preference to a statue by Alcamenes, who was another distinguished pupil of Phidias.

Agŏraea and **Agŏraeus** ('Αγοραία and 'Αγοραίος), epithets of several divinities who were considered as the protectors of the assemblies of the people in the *agora*, such as Zeus, Athena, Artemis, and Hermes.

Agraei ('Αγραίοι), a people of Aetolia on the Achelous.

Agraulē ('Αγραυλή and 'Αγρύλη : 'Αγρυλεύς), an Attic demus of the tribe Erechtheis, named after AGRAULOS, No. 2.

Agraulos ('Αγραυλος, also "Αγλαυρος). 1. Daughter of Actaeus, first king of Athens, and wife of Cecrops.—2. Daughter of Cecrops and Agraulos, is an important personage in the legends of Attica, and there were three different stories about her. 1. According to some writers Athena gave Erichthonius in a chest to Agraulos and her sister Herse, with the command not to open it ; but unable to control their curiosity, they opened it, and thereupon were seized with madness at the sight of Erichthonius, and threw themselves down from the Acropolis. 2. According to Ovid (*Met.* ii. 710) Agraulos and her sister survived opening the chest, but Agraulos was subsequently punished by being changed into a stone by Hermes, because she attempted to prevent the god from entering the house of Herse, when he had fallen in love with the latter. 3. The third legend relates that Athens was once involved in a long-protracted war, and that Agraulos threw herself down from the Acropolis because an oracle had declared that the Athenians would conquer if some one would sacrifice himself for his country. The Athenians in gratitude built her a temple on the Acropolis, in which it became customary for the young Athenians, on receiving their first suit of armour, to take an oath that they would always defend their country to the last. One of the Attic *demi* (Agraule) derived its name from this heroine, and a festival and mysteries (*Agraulia*) were celebrated at Athens in honour of her.

Agreus ('Αγρεύς), a hunter, a surname of Pan and Aristaeus.

Agri Decumātes, tithe lands, the name given by the Romans to a part of Germany, E. of the Rhine and N. of the Danube, which they took possession of when the Germans retired eastward, and which they gave to Gauls and subsequently to their own veterans on the payment of a tenth of the produce (*decuma*). Towards the end of the first or the beginning of the second century after Christ, these lands were incorporated in the Roman empire.

Agrīcōla, Cn. Jūlĭus, born June 13th, A. D. 37, at Forum Julii (*Fréjus* in Provence), was the son of Julius Graecinus, who was executed by Caligula, and of Julia Procilla. He received a careful education ; he first served in Britain, A. D. 60, under Suetonius Paulinus ; was quaestor in Asia in 63 ; was governor of Aquitania from 74 to 76 ; and was consul in 77, when he betrothed his daughter to the historian Tacitus, and in the following year gave her to him in marriage. In 78 he received the government of Britain, which he held for 7 years, during which time he subdued the whole of the country with the exception of the highlands of Caledonia, and by his wise administration introduced among the inhabitants the language and civilization of Rome. He was recalled in 85 through the jealousy of Domitian, and on his return lived in retirement till his death in 93, which according to some was occasioned by poison, administered by order of Domitian. His character is drawn in the brightest colours by his son-in-law Tacitus, whose Life of Agricola has come down to us.

Agrĭgentum ('Ακράγας : 'Ακραγαντῖνος, Agrigentinus : *Girgenti*), a town on the S. coast of Sicily, about 2½ miles from the sea, between the rivers Acragas (*Fiume di S. Biagio*), and Hypsas (*Fiume Drago*). It was celebrated for its wealth and populousness, and till its destruction by the Carthaginians (B. C. 405) was one of the most splendid cities of the ancient world. It was the birthplace of Empedocles. It was founded by a Doric colony from Gela, about B. C. 579, was under the government of the cruel tyrant Phalaris (about 560), and subsequently under that of Theron (488—472), whose praises are celebrated by Pindar. After its destruction by the Carthaginians, it was rebuilt by Timoleon, but it never regained its former greatness. After undergoing many vicissitudes it at length came into the power of the Romans (210), in whose hands it remained. There are still gigantic remains of the ancient city, especially of the Olympiëum, or temple of the Olympian Zeus.

Agrĭnĭum ('Αγρίνιον), a town in Aetolia, perhaps near the sources of the Thermissus.

Agrippa, first a praenomen, and afterwards a cognomen among the Romans, signifies a child presented at its birth with its feet foremost.

Agrippa, Herōdes. 1. Called " Agrippa the Great," son of Aristobulus and Berenice, and grandson of Herod the Great. He was educated at Rome with the future emperor Claudius, and Drusus the son of Tiberius. Having given offence to Tiberius he was thrown into prison ; but Caligula, on his accession (A. D. 37), set him at liberty, and gave him the tetrarchies of Abilene, Batanaea, Trachonitis, and Auranitis. On the death of Caligula (41), Agrippa, who was at the time in Rome, assisted Claudius in gaining possession of the empire. As a reward for his services, Judaea and Samaria were annexed to his dominions. His government was mild and gentle, and he was exceedingly popular amongst the Jews. It was probably to increase his popularity with the Jews that he caused the apostle James to be beheaded, and Peter to be cast into prison (44). The manner of his death, which took place at Caesarea in the same year, is related in *Acts* xii. By his wife Cypros he had a son Agrippa, and three daughters, Berenice, Mariamne, and Drusilla.—2. Son of Agrippa I., was educated at the court of Claudius, and at the time of his father's death was 17 years old. Claudius kept him at Rome, and sent Cuspius Fadus as procurator of the kingdom, which thus again became a Roman province. On the death of Herodes, king of Chalcis (48), his little principality was given to Agrippa, who subsequently received an accession of territory. Before the outbreak of the war with the Romans, Agrippa attempted in vain to dissuade the Jews from rebelling. He sided with the Romans in the war ; and after the capture of Jerusalem, he went with his sister Berenice to Rome, and died in the 70th year of his age, A. D. 100. It was before this Agrippa that the apostle Paul made his defence, A. D. 60 (*Acts* xxv. xxvi.).

Agrippa, M. Vipsānĭus, born in B. C. 63, of an obscure family, studied with young Octavius (afterwards the emperor Augustus) at Apollonia in Illyria ; and upon the murder of Caesar in 44, was one of the friends of Octavius, who advised him to proceed immediately to Rome. In the civil wars which followed, and which terminated in giving Augustus the sovereignty of the Roman world, Agrippa took an active part ; and his military abilities, combined with his promptitude and energy, contributed greatly to that result. In 41 Agrippa, who was then praetor, commanded part of the forces of Augustus in the Perusinian war. In 38 he obtained great successes in Gaul and Germany ; in 37 he was consul ; and in 36 he defeated Sex. Pompey by sea. In 33 he was aedile, and in this office expended immense sums of money upon great public works. He restored old aqueducts, constructed a new one, to which he gave the name of the Julian, in honour of Augustus, and also erected several public buildings. In 31 he commanded the fleet of Augustus at the battle of Actium ; was consul a second time in 28, and a third time in 27, when he built the Pantheon. In 21 he married Julia, daughter of Augustus. He had been marred twice before, first to Pomponia, daughter of T. Pomponius Atticus, and next to Marcella, niece of Augustus. He continued to be employed in various military commands in Gaul, Spain, Syria, and Pannonia, till his death in B. C. 12. By his first wife Pomponia, Agrippa had Vipsania, married to Tiberius, the successor of Augustus ; and by his third wife, Julia, he had 2 daughters, Julia, married to L. Aemilius Paulus, and Agrippina, married

to Germanicus, and 3 sons, Caius Caesar, Lucius Caesar [CAESAR], and Agrippa Postumus, who was banished by Augustus to the island of Planasia, and was put to death by Tiberius at his accession, A. D. 14.

Agrippīna. 1. Daughter of M. Vipsanius Agrippa and of Julia, the daughter of Augustus, married Germanicus, by whom she had nine children, among whom was the emperor Caligula, and Agrippina, the mother of Nero. She was distinguished for her virtues and heroism, and shared all the dangers of her husband's campaigns. On his death in A. D. 17 she returned to Italy ; but the favour with which she was received by the people increased the hatred and jealousy which Tiberius and his mother Livia had long entertained towards her. For some years Tiberius disguised his hatred, but at length under the pretext that she was forming ambitious plans, he banished her to the island of Pandataria (A. D. 30), where she died 3 years afterwards, A. D. 33, probably by voluntary starvation.—2. Daughter of Germanicus and Agrippina [No. 1.], and mother of the emperor Nero, was born at Oppidum Ubiorum, afterwards called in honour of her Colonia Agrippina, now *Cologne*. She was beautiful and intelligent, but licentious, cruel, and ambitious. She was first married to Cn. Domitius Ahenobarbus (A. D. 28), by whom she had a son, afterwards the emperor Nero ; next to Crispus Passienus ; and thirdly to the emperor Claudius (49), although she was his niece. In 50, she prevailed upon Claudius to adopt her son, to the prejudice of his own son Britannicus ; and in order to secure the succession for her son, she poisoned the emperor in 54. Upon the accession of her son Nero, who was then only 17 years of age, she governed the Roman empire for a few years in his name. The young emperor soon became tired of the ascendency of his mother, and after making several attempts to shake off her authority, he caused her to be assassinated in 59.

Agrippīnenses. [COLONIA AGRIPPINA.]

Agrīus (Ἄγριος), son of Porthaon and Euryte, and brother of Oeneus, king of Calydon in Aetolia: his six sons deprived Oeneus of his kingdom, and gave it to their father ; but Agrius and his sons were afterwards slain by Diomedes, the grandson of Oeneus.

Agroecĭus or **Agroetĭus**, a Roman grammarian, probably lived in the 5th century after Christ, and wrote an extant work *De Orthographia et Differentia Sermonis*, which is printed in Putschius, *Grammaticae Latinae Auctores Antiqui*, pp. 2266 —2275.

Agron (Ἄγρων). 1. Son of Ninus, the first of the Lydian dynasty of the Heraclīdae.—2. Son of Pleuratus, king of Illyria, died B. C. 231, and was succeeded by his wife Teuta, though he left a son Pinnes or Pinneus by his first wife, Triteuta, whom he had divorced.

Agrŏtĕra (Ἀγροτέρα), the huntress, a surname of Artemis. There was a festival celebrated to her honour at Athens under this name. (See *Dict. of Antiq.*)

Agryle. [AGRAULE.]

Agyieus (Ἀγυιεύς), a surname of Apollo, as the protector of the streets and public places.

Agylla (Ἄγυλλα), the ancient Greek name of the Etruscan town of CAERE.

Agyrĭum (Ἀγύριον : Ἀγυριναῖος, Agyrinensis

S. Filipo d'Argiro), a town in Sicily on the Cyamosorus, N. W. of Centuripae and N. E. of Enna, the birth-place of the historian Diodorus.

Agyrrhius ('Αγύρριος), an Athenian, after being in prison many years for embezzlement of public money, obtained about B. C. 395 the restoration of the Theoricon, and also tripled the pay for attending the assembly: hence he became so popular, that he was appointed general in 389.

Ahala, Servilius, the name of several distinguished Romans, who held various high offices in the state from B. C. 478 to 342. Of these the best known is C. Servilius Ahala, magister equitum in 439 to the dictator L. Cincinnatus, when he slew Sp. Maelius in the forum, because he refused to appear before the dictator. Ahala was afterwards brought to trial, and only escaped condemnation by a voluntary exile.

Aharna, a town in Etruria, N. E. of Volsinii.

Ahenobarbus, Domitius, the name of a distinguished Roman family. They are said to have obtained the surname of Ahenobarbus, i. e. "Brazen-Beard" or "Red-Beard," because the Dioscuri announced to one of their ancestors the victory of the Romans over the Latins at lake Regillus (B. C. 496), and, to confirm the truth of what they said, stroked his black hair and beard, which immediately became red.—**1. Cn.,** plebeian aedile B. C. 196, praetor 194, and consul 192, when he fought against the Boii.—**2. Cn.,** son of No. 1, consul suffectus in 162.—**3. Cn.,** son of No. 2, consul 122, conquered the Allobroges in Gaul, in 121, at the confluence of the Sulga and Rhodanus. He was censor in 115 with Caecilius Metellus. The Via Domitia in Gaul was made by him.—**4. Cn.,** son of No. 3, tribune of the plebs 104, brought forward the law (*Lex Domitia*), by which the election of the priests was transferred from the collegia to the people. The people afterwards elected him Pontifex Maximus out of gratitude. He was consul in 96, and censor in 92, with Licinius Crassus, the orator. In his censorship he and his colleague shut up the schools of the Latin rhetoricians: but otherwise their censorship was marked by their violent disputes.—**5. L.,** brother of No. 4, praetor in Sicily, probably in 96, and consul in 94, belonged to the party of Sulla, and was murdered at Rome in 82, by order of the younger Marius.—**6. Cn.,** son of No. 4, married Cornelia, daughter of L. Cinna, consul in 87, and joined the Marian party. He was proscribed by Sulla in 82, and fled to Africa, where he was defeated and killed by Cn. Pompey in 81.—**7. L.,** son of No. 4, married Porcia, the sister of M. Cato, and was a stanch and courageous supporter of the aristocratical party. He was aedile in 61, praetor in 58, and consul in 54. On the breaking out of the civil war in 49 he threw himself into Corfinium, but was compelled by his own troops to surrender to Caesar. He next went to Massilia, and, after the surrender of that town, repaired to Pompey in Greece: he fell in the battle of Pharsalia (48), where he commanded the left wing, and, according to Cicero's assertion in the second Philippic, by the hand of Antony.—**8. Cn.,** son of No. 7, was taken with his father at Corfinium (49), was present at the battle of Pharsalia (48), and returned to Italy in 46, when he was pardoned by Caesar. After Caesar's death in 44, he commanded the republican fleet in the Ionian sea. He afterwards became reconciled to Antony whom he accompanied in his

campaign against the Parthians in 36. He was consul in 32, and deserted to Augustus shortly before the battle of Actium.—**9. L.,** son of No. 8 married Antonia, the daughter of Antony by Octavia; was aedile in 22, and consul in 16; and after his consulship, commanded the Roman army in Germany and crossed the Elbe. He died A. D. 25.—**10. Cn.,** son of No. 9, consul A. D. 32, married Agrippina, daughter of Germanicus, and was father of the emperor Nero. [AGRIPPINA.]

Ajax (Αἴας). **1.** Son of Telamon, king of Salamis, by Periboea or Eriboea, and grandson of Aeacus. Homer calls him Ajax the Telamonian, Ajax the Great, or simply Ajax, whereas the other Ajax, son of Oïleus, is always distinguished from the former by some epithet. He sailed against Troy in 12 ships, and is represented in the Iliad as second only to Achilles in bravery, and as the hero most worthy, in the absence of Achilles, to contend with Hector. In the contest for the armour of Achilles, he was conquered by Ulysses, and this, says Homer, was the cause of his death. (*Od.* xi. 541, seq.) Homer gives no further particulars respecting his death; but later poets relate that his defeat by Ulysses threw him into an awful state of madness; that he rushed from his tent and slaughtered the sheep of the Greek army, fancying they were his enemies; and that at length he put an end to his own life. From his blood there sprang up a purple flower bearing the letters ai on its leaves, which were at once the initials of his name and expressive of a sigh. Homer does not mention his mistress TECMESSA. Ajax was worshipped in Salamis, and was honoured with a festival (Αἰάντεια). He was also worshipped at Athens, and one of the Attic tribes (*Aeantis*) was called after him.—**2.** Son of Oïleus, king of the Locrians, also called the lesser Ajax, sailed against Troy in 40 ships. He is described as small of stature, and wears a linen cuirass (λινοθώρηξ), but is brave and intrepid, skilled in throwing the spear, and, next to Achilles, the most swift-footed among the Greeks. On his return from Troy his vessel was wrecked on the Whirling Rocks (Γυραὶ πέτραι); he himself got safe upon a rock through the assistance of Poseidon; but as he boasted that he would escape in defiance of the immortals, Poseidon split the rock with his trident, and Ajax was swallowed up by the sea. This is the account of Homer, but his death is related somewhat differently by Virgil and other writers, who also tell us that the anger of Athena was excited against him, because, on the night of the capture of Troy, he violated Cassandra in the temple of the goddess, where she had taken refuge. The Opuntian Locrians worshipped Ajax as their national hero.

Aides ('Αΐδης). [HADES.]

Aidoneus ('Αϊδωνεύς). **1.** A lengthened form of *Aides*. [HADES.]—**2.** A mythical king of the Molossians in Epirus, husband of Persephone, and father of Core. When Theseus and Pirithous attempted to carry off Core, Aïdoneus had Pirithous killed by Cerberus, and kept Theseus in captivity till he was released by Hercules.

Aius Locutius or **Loquens,** a Roman divinity. A short time before the Gauls took Rome (B. C. 390) a voice was heard at Rome in the Via nova, during the silence of night, announcing that the Gauls were approaching. No attention was at the time paid to the warning, but the Romans afterwards erected on the spot where the voice had been heard, an altar with a sacred enclosure around it, to Aius Locutius, or the " Announcing Speaker."

Alābanda (ἡ Ἀλάβανδα or τὰ Ἀλάβανδα: Ἀλαβανδεύς or Ἀλάβανδος: *Arabissar*), an inland town of Caria, near the Marsyas, to the S. of the Maeander, was situated between two hills : it was a prosperous place, but one of the most corrupt and luxurious towns in Asia Minor. Under the Romans it was the seat of a conventus juridicus.

Alābon (Ἀλαβών), a river and town in Sicily, N. of Syracuse.

Alagōnīa (Ἀλαγωνία), a town of the Eleuthero-Laconians on the frontiers of Messenia.

Alaloōmēnae (Ἀλαλκομεναί: Ἀλαλκομεναῖος, Ἀλαλκομενεύς). 1. (*Sulinari*), an ancient town of Boeotia, E. of Coronēa, with a temple of Athene, who is said to have been born in the town, and who was hence called *Alalcomenēis* (Ἀλαλκομενηίς, ίδος). The name of the town was derived either from Alalcomenia, a daughter of Ogyges, or from the Boeotian hero Alalcomenes. —2. A town in Ithaca, or in the island Asteria, between Ithaca and Cephallenia.

Alalīa. [ALERIA.]

Alāni (Ἀλανοί, Ἀλαυνοί, i. e. *mountaineers*, from the Sarmatian word *ala*), a great Asiatic people, included under the general name of Scythians, but probably a branch of the Massagetae. They were a nation of warlike horsemen. They are first found about the E. part of the Caucasus, in the country called Albania, which appears to be only another form of the same name. In the reign of Vespasian they made incursions into Media and Armenia ; and at a later time they pressed into Europe, as far as the banks of the Lower Danube, where, towards the end of the 5th century, they were routed by the Huns, who then compelled them to become their allies. In A. D. 406, some of the Alani took part with the Vandals in their irruption into Gaul and Spain, where they gradually disappear from history.

Alāricus, in German *Al-ric*, i. e. "All-rich," elected king of the Visigoths in A. D. 398, had previously commanded the Gothic auxiliaries of Theodosius. He twice invaded Italy, first in A. D. 402—403, when he was defeated by Stilicho at the battle of Pollentia, and a second time in 408—410 ; in his second invasion he took and plundered Rome, 24th of August, 410. He died shortly afterwards at Consentia in Bruttium, while preparing to invade Sicily.

Alastor (Ἀλάστωρ). 1. A surname of Zeus as the avenger of evil, and also in general any deity who avenges wicked deeds.—2. A Lycian, and companion of Sarpedon, slain by Ulysses.

Alba Silvīus, one of the mythical kings of Alba, son of Latinus, reigned 39 years.

Alba. 1. (*Abla*), a town of the Bastitani in Spain.—2. (*Alvanna*), a town of the Barduli in Spain.—3. Augusta (*Aulps*, nr. Durance), a town of the Elicoci in Gallia Narbonensis.—4. Fūcentia or Fucentis (Albenses: *Alba* or *Albi*), a town of the Marsi, and subsequently a Roman colony, was situated on a lofty rock near the lake Fucinus. It was a strong fortress, and was used by the Romans as a state prison.—5. Longa (Albāni), the most ancient town in Latium, is said to have been built by Ascanius, and to have founded Rome. It was called Longa, from its stretching in a long line down the Alban Mount towards the Alban Lake, perhaps near the

modern convent of *Palazzolo*. It was destroyed by Tullus Hostilius, and was never rebuilt: its inhabitants were removed to Rome. At a later time the surrounding country, which was highly cultivated and covered with vineyards, was studded with the splendid villas of the Roman aristocracy and emperors (Pompey's, Domitian's, &c.), each of which was called *Albanum*, and out of which a new town at length grew, also called Albanum (*Albano*), on the Appian road, ruins of which are extant.—6. Pompeia (Albenses Pompeiani: *Alba*), a town in Liguria, founded by Scipio Africanus I., and colonized by Pompeius Magnus, the birth-place of the emperor Pertinax.

Albānīa (Ἀλβανία : Ἀλβανοί, Albāni ; *Schirwan* and part of *Daghestan*, in the S.E. part of *Georgia*), a country of Asia on the W. side of the Caspian, extending from the rivers Cyrus and Araxes on the S. to M. Ceraunius (the E. part of the Caucasus) on the N., and bounded on the W. by Iberia. It was a fertile plain, abounding in pasture and vineyards ; but the inhabitants were fierce and warlike. They were a Scythian tribe, probably a branch of the Massagetae, and identical with the ALANI. The Romans first became acquainted with them at the time of the Mithridatic war, when they encountered Pompey with a large army.

Albānum. [ALBA, No. 5.]

Albānus Lacus (*Lago di Albano*), a small lake about 5 miles in circumference, W. of the Mons Albanus between Bovillae and Alba Longa, is the crater of an extinct volcano, and is many hundred feet deep. The emissarium which the Romans bored through the solid rock during the siege of Veii, in order to carry off the superfluous water of the lake, is extant at the present day.

Albānus Mons (*Monte Cavo* or *Albano*), was, in its narrower signification, the mountain in Latium on whose declivity the town of Alba Longa was situated. It was the sacred mountain of the Latins, on which their religious festivals of the Latin League were celebrated (*Feriae Latinae*), and on its highest summit was the temple of Jupiter Latiaris, to which the Roman generals ascended in triumph, when this honour was denied them in Rome. The Mons Albanus in its wider signification included the Mons ALGIDUS and the mountains about Tusculum.

Albi Montes, a lofty range of mountains in the W. of Crete, 300 stadia in length, covered with snow the greater part of the year.

Albīci (Ἀλβίοικοι, Ἀλβιεῖς), a warlike Gallic people, inhabiting the mountains north of Massilia.

Albingaunum. [ALBIUM INGAUNUM.]

Albinovānus, C. Pedo, a friend of Ovid, who addresses to him one of his Epistles from Pontus (iv. 10). Three Latin elegies are attributed to Albinovanus, printed by Wernsdorf, in his *Poëtae Latini Minores*, vol. iii. iv., and by Meinecke, Quedlinburg, 1819.

Albinovānus, P. Tullīus, belonged to the Marian party, was proscribed in B. C. 87, but was pardoned by Sulla in 81, in consequence of his putting to death many of the officers of Norbanus, whom he had invited to a banquet at Ariminum.

Albīnus or **Albus, Postumīus**, the name of a patrician family at Rome, many of the members of which held the highest offices of the state from the commencement of the republic to its downfal.—1. A., surnamed *Regillensis*, dictator B. C. 498, when he conquered the Latins in the great battle near lake Regillus, and consul 496, in which year some of the annals placed the battle.—2. Sp., consul 466, and a member of the first decemvira'e 451.—3. Sp., consul 344, and again 321. In the latter year he marched against the Samnites, but was defeated near Caudium, and obliged to surrender with his whole army, who were sent under the yoke. The senate, on the advice of Albinus, refused to ratify the peace which he had made with the Samnites, and resolved that all persons who had sworn to the peace should be given up to the Samnites, but they refused to accept them.—4. L., consul 234, and again 229. In 216 he was praetor, and was killed in battle by the Boii.—5. Sp., consul in 186, when the senatusconsultum was passed, which is extant, for suppressing the worship of Bacchus in Rome. He died in 179.—6. A., consul 180, when he fought against the Ligurians, and censor 174. He was subsequently engaged in many public missions. Livy calls him Luscus, from which it would seem that he was blind of one eye. —7. L., praetor 180, in Further Spain, where he remained two years, and conquered the Vaccaei and Lusitani. He was consul in 173, and afterwards served under Aemilius Paulus in Macedonia in 168.—8. A., consul 151, accompanied L. Mummius into Greece in 146. He was well acquainted with Greek literature, and wrote in that language a poem and a Roman history, which is censured by Polybius.— 9. Sp., consul 110, carried on war against Jugurtha in Numidia, but effected nothing. When Albinus departed from Africa, he left his brother Aulus in command, who was defeated by Jugurtha. Spurius was condemned by the Mamilia Lex, as guilty of treasonable practices with Jugurtha.—10. A., consul B.C. 99, with M. Antonius, is said by Cicero to have been a good speaker.

Albīnus ('Αλβῖνος), a Platonic philosopher, lived at Smyrna in the 2nd century after Christ, and wrote an *Introduction to the Dialogues of Plato*, which contains hardly any thing of importance.— *Editions.* In the first edition of Fabricius's *Bibl. Graec.* vol. ii., and prefixed to Etwall's edition of three dialogues of Plato, Oxon. 1771 ; and to Fischer's four dialogues of Plato, Lips. 1783.

Albīnus, Clōdīus, whose full name was *Decimus Clodius Ceionius Septimius Albinus*, was born at Adrumetum in Africa. The emperor Commodus made him governor of Gaul and afterwards of Britain, where he was on the death of Commodus in A.D. 192. In order to secure the neutrality of Albinus, Septimius Severus made him Caesar ; but after Severus had defeated his rivals, he turned his arms against Albinus. A great battle was fought between them at Lugdunum (Lyons), in Gaul, the 19th of February, 197, in which Albinus was defeated and killed.

Albīon or Albīon ('Αλβίων, 'Αλεβίων), son of Poseidon and brother of Dercynus or Bergion, with whom he attacked Hercules, when he passed through their country (Liguria) with the oxen of Geryon. They were slain by Hercules.

Albīon, another name of BRITANNIA, the *white* land, from its white cliffs opposite the coast of Gaul.

Albis (*Elbe*), one of the great rivers in Germany, the most easterly which the Romans became acquainted with, rises according to Tacitus in the country of the Hermunduri. The Romans reached the Elbe for the first time in B.C. 9 under Drusus, and crossed it for the first time in B.C. 3 under Domitius Ahenobarbus. The last Roman general who saw the Elbe was Tiberius in A.D. 5.

Albīum Ingaunum or Albingaunum (*Albengo*), a town of the Ingauni on the coast of Liguria, and a municipium.

Albīum Intemelīum or Albintemelīum (*Vintimiglia*), a town of the Intemelii on the coast of Liguria, and a municipium.

T. Albūcīus or Albūtīus, studied at Athens, and belonged to the Epicurean sect ; he was well acquainted with Greek literature, but was satirized by Lucilius on account of his affecting on every occasion the Greek language and philosophy. He was praetor in Sardinia in B.C. 105 ; and in 103 was accused of repetundae by C. Julius Caesar, and condemned. He retired to Athens and pursued the study of philosophy.

Albūla, an ancient name of the river TIBER.

Albūlae Aquae [ALBUNEA.]

Albūnēa or Albūna, a prophetic nymph or Sybil, to whom a grove was consecrated in the neighbourhood of Tibur (Tivoli), with a fountain and a temple. This fountain was the largest of the Albulae aquae, still called *Acque Albule*, sulphureous springs at Tibur, which flow into the Anio. Near it was the oracle of Faunus Fatidicus. The temple is still extant at Tivoli.

Alburnus Mons, a mountain in Lucania, covered with wood, behind Paestum.

Alcaeus ('Αλκαῖος), son of Perseus and Andromeda, and father of Amphitryon and Anaxo.

Alcaeus. 1. Of Mytilene in Lesbos, the earliest of the Aeolian lyric poets, began to flourish about B.C. 611. In the war between the Athenians and Mytilenaeans for the possession of Sigeum (B.C. 606) he incurred the disgrace of leaving his arms on the field of battle : these arms were hung up as a trophy by the Athenians in the temple of Pallas at Sigeum. Alcaeus took an active part in the struggles between the nobles and people of Mytilene : he belonged by birth to the nobles and was driven into exile with his brother Antimenidas, when the popular party got the upper hand. He attempted by force of arms to regain his country ; but all his attempts were frustrated by PITTACUS, who had been chosen by the people Aesymnetes or dictator for the purpose of resisting him and the other exiles. Alcaeus and his brother afterwards travelled into various countries : the time of his death is uncertain. Some fragments of his poems which remain, and the excellent imitations of Horace, enable us to understand something of their character. Those which have received the highest praise are his warlike odes, in which he tried to rouse the spirits of the nobles, the *Alcaei minaces Camenae* of Horace (*Carm.* iv. 9. 7). In others he described the hardships of exile, and his perils by sea (*dura navis, dura fugae mala, dura belli,* Hor. *Carm.* ii. 13. 27). Alcaeus is said to have invented the well-known Alcaic metre.— *Editions.* By Matthiae, *Alcaei Mytilenaei reliquiae,* Lips. 1827 ; and by Bergk, in *Poetae Lyrici Graeci,* Lips. 1843.—2. A comic poet at Athens, flourished about B.C. 388, and exhibited plays of that mixed comedy, which formed the transition between the old and the middle—3. Of Messene, the author of 22 epigrams in the Greek anthology, written between B.C. 219 and 196.

Alcāmēnes ('Αλκαμένης). 1. Son of Teleclus, king of Sparta, from B.C. 779 to 742.—2. A statuary of Athens flourished from B.C. 444 to 400 and was the most famous of the pupils of Phidias. His greatest work was a statue of Aphrodite.

Alcander ('Αλκανδρος), a young Spartan, who thrust out one of the eyes of Lycurgus, when his fellow-citizens were discontented with the laws he proposed. Lycurgus pardoned the outrage, and thus converted Alcander into one of his warmest friends.

Alcăthŏē or Alcĭthŏē ('Αλκαθόη or 'Αλκιθόη), daughter of Minyas, refused with her sisters Leucippe and Arsippe to join in the worship of Dionysus when it was introduced into Boeotia, and were accordingly changed by the god into bats, and their work into vines. See *Dict. of Ant.* art. *Agrionia.*

Alcăthŏus ('Αλκάθοος). 1. Son of Pelops and Hippodamia, brother of Atreus and Thyestes, obtained as his wife Euaechme, the daughter of Megareus, by slaying the Cithaeronian lion, and succeeded his father-in-law as king of Megara. He restored the walls of Megara, in which work he was assisted by Apollo. The stone upon which the god used to place his lyre while he was at work, was believed, even in late times, to give forth a sound, when struck, similar to that of a lyre (Ov. *Met.* viii. 15).—2. Son of Aesyetes and husband of Hippodamia, the daughter of Anchises and sister of Aeneas, was one of the bravest of the Trojan leaders in the war of Troy, and was slain by Idomeneus.

Alcestis or Alcestē ('Αλκηστις or 'Αλκέστη), daughter of Pelias and Anaxibia, wife of Admetus, died in place of her husband. [ADMETUS.]

Alcĕtas ('Αλκέτας), two kings of Epirus. 1. Son of Tharypus, was expelled from his kingdom, and was restored by the elder Dionysius of Syracuse. He was the ally of the Athenians in B. c. 373.—2. Son of Arymbas, and grandson of Alcetas I., reigned B. c. 313—303, and was put to death by his subjects.

Alcĕtas. 1. King of Macedonia, reigned 29 years, and was father of Amyntas I.—2. Brother of Perdiccas and son of Orontes, was one of Alexander's generals. On the death of Alexander, he espoused his brother's party, and upon the murder of the latter in Egypt in 321, he joined Eumenes. He killed himself at Termessus in Pisidia in 320, to avoid falling into the hands of Antigonus.

Alcĭbĭădes ('Αλκιβιάδης), son of Clinias and Dinomache, was born at Athens about B. c. 450, and on the death of his father in 447, was brought up by his relation Pericles. He possessed a beautiful person, transcendent abilities, and great wealth, which received a large accession through his marriage with Hipparēte, the daughter of Hipponicus. His youth was disgraced by his amours and debaucheries, and Socrates, who saw his vast capabilities, attempted to win him to the paths of virtue, but in vain. Their intimacy was strengthened by mutual services. At the battle of Potidaea (B. c. 432) his life was saved by Socrates, and at that of Delium (424) he saved the life of Socrates. He did not take much part in public affairs till after the death of Cleon (422), but he then became one of the leading politicians, and the head of the war party in opposition to Nicias. Enraged at the affront put upon him by the Lacedaemonians, who had not chosen to employ his intervention in the negotiations which ended in the peace of 421, and had preferred Nicias to him, he induced the Athenians to form an alliance with Argos, Mantineia, and Elis, and to attack the allies of

Sparta. In 415 he was foremost among the advocates of the Sicilian expedition, which he believed would be a step towards the conquest of Italy, Carthage, and Peloponnesus. While the preparations for the expedition were going on, there occurred the mysterious mutilation of the Hermes-busts, which the popular fears connected in some unaccountable manner with an attempt to overthrow the Athenian constitution. Alcibiades was charged with being the ringleader in this attempt. He had been already appointed along with Nicias and Lamachus as commander of the expedition to Sicily, and he now demanded an investigation before he set sail. This, however, his enemies would not grant; as they hoped to increase the popular odium against him in his absence. He was therefore obliged to depart for Sicily ; but he had not been there long, before he was recalled to stand his trial. On his return homewards, he managed to escape at Thurii, and thence proceeded to Sparta, where he acted as the avowed enemy of his country. At Athens sentence of death was passed upon him, and his property was confiscated. At Sparta he rendered himself popular by the facility with which he adopted the Spartan manners ; but the machinations of his enemy AGIS II. induced him to abandon the Spartans and take refuge with Tissaphernes (412), whose favour he soon gained. Through his influence Tissaphernes deserted the Spartans and professed his willingness to assist the Athenians, who accordingly recalled Alcibiades from banishment in 411. He did not immediately return to Athens, but remained abroad for the next 4 years, during which the Athenians under his command gained the victories of Cynossema, Abydos, and Cyzicus, and got possession of Chalcedon and Byzantium. In 407 he returned to Athens, where he was received with great enthusiasm, and was appointed commander-in-chief of all the land and sea forces. But the defeat at Notium, occasioned during his absence by the imprudence of his lieutenant, Antiochus, furnished his enemies with a handle against him, and he was superseded in his command (B. c. 406). He now went into voluntary exile to his fortified domain at Bisanthe in the Thracian Chersonesus, where he made war on the neighbouring Thracians. Before the fatal battle of Aegos-Potami (405), he gave an ineffectual warning to the Athenian generals. After the fall of Athens (404), he was condemned to banishment, and took refuge with Pharnabazus ; he was about to proceed to the court of Artaxerxes, when one night his house was surrounded by a band of armed men, and set on fire.' He rushed out sword in hand, but fell, pierced with arrows (404). The assassins were probably either employed by the Spartans, or by the brothers of a lady whom Alcibiades had seduced. He left a son by his wife Hipparete, named Alcibiades, who never distinguished himself. It was for him that Isocrates wrote the speech Περὶ τοῦ Ζεύγους.

Alcĭdămas ('Αλκιδάμας), a Greek rhetorician, of Elaea in Aeolis, in Asia Minor, was a pupil of Gorgias, and resided at Athens between B. c. 432 and 411. His works were characterised by pompous diction and the extravagant use of poetical epithets and phrases. There are two declamations extant which bear his name, entitled *Ulysses*, and *On the Sophists*, but they were probably not written by him. *Editions.*—In Reiske's *Oratores Graeci*, vol. viii., and in Bekker's *Oratores Attici*, vol. vii.

Patroclus. (Aegina Marbles.)

Temple of Athena (Minerva) at Aegina, restored. Page 13.

Ajax. (Aegina Marbles.)

Hector. (Aegina Marbles.)

[To face p. 32.

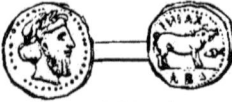

Abacaenum in Sicily. Page 1.

Abdera in Thrace. Page 1.

Abydos on the Hellespont. Page 2.

Acanthus in Chalcidice. Page 3.

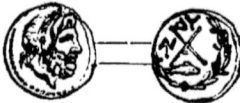

Achaia. Page 5.

Acmonia in Greater Phrygia. Page 7.

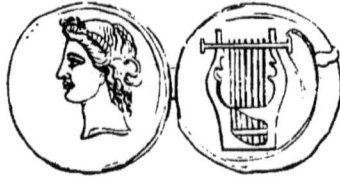

Adranum in Sicily. Page 10.

Adria in Picenum. Page 10.

Aegina. Page 13.

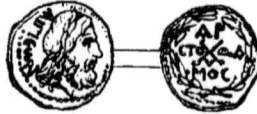

Aegium in Achaia. Page 13.

Aegospotamos. Page 13.

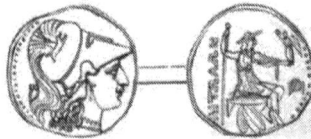

Aetolia. Page 21.

To face p. 33.]

Alcĭdas ('Αλκίδας Dor. = 'Αλκείδης), a Spartan commander of the fleet in the Peloponnesian war, B. C. 428—427. In the former year he was sent to Mytilene, and in the latter to Corcyra.

Alcīdes ('Αλκείδης), a name of Amphitryon, the son of Alcaeus, and more especially of Hercules, the grandson of Alcaeus.

Alcĭmĕdē ('Αλκιμέδη), daughter of Phylacus and Clymene, wife of Aeson, and mother of Jason.

Alcīmus (Avitus) Alethĭus, the writer of 7 short poems, a rhetorician in Aquitania, in Gaul, is spoken of in terms of praise by Sidonius Apollinaris, and Ausonius.—*Editions.* In Meier's *Anthologia Latina*, ed. 254—260, and in Wernsdorf's *Poëtae Latini Minores*, vol. vi.

Alcĭnŏus ('Αλκίνοος). 1. Son of Nausithous, and grandson of Poseidon, is celebrated in the story of the Argonauts, and still more in the Odyssey. Homer represents him as the happy ruler of the Phaeacians in the island of Scheria, who has by Arete five sons and one daughter, Nausicaa. The way in which he received Ulysses, and the stories which the latter related to the king about his wanderings, occupy a considerable portion of the Odyssey (books vi. to xiii.).—2. A Platonic philosopher, who probably lived under the Caesars, wrote a work entitled *Epitome of the Doctrines of Plato.—Editions.* By Fell, Oxon. 1667, and by J. F. Fischer, Lips. 1783, 8vo.

Alcĭphron ('Αλκίφρων), the most distinguished of the Greek epistolary writers, was perhaps a contemporary of Lucian, about A. D. 180. The letters (113 in number, in 3 books) are written by fictitious personages, and the language is distinguished by its purity and elegance. The new Attic comedy was the principal source from which the author derived his information respecting the characters and manners which he describes, and for this reason they contain much valuable information about the private life of the Athenians of that time. — *Editions.* By Bergler, Lips. 1715, and by Wagner, ips. 1798.

Alcĭthŏe. [ALCATHOE.]

Alcmaeon ('Αλκμαίων). 1. Son of Amphiaraüs and Eriphyle, and brother of Amphilochus. His mother was induced by the necklace of Harmonia, which she received from Polynices, to persuade her husband Amphiaraus to take part in the expedition against Thebes ; and as he knew he should perish there, he enjoined his sons to kill their mother as soon as they should be grown up. Alcmaeon took part in the expedition of the Epigoni against Thebes, and on his return home after the capture of the city, he slew his mother according to the injunction of his father. For this deed he became mad, and was haunted by the Erinnyes. He went to Phegeus in Psophis, and being purified by the latter, he married his daughter Arsinoë or Alphesiboea, to whom he gave the necklace and peplus of Harmonia. But as the land of this country ceased to bear on account of its harbouring a matricide, he left Psophis and repaired to the country at the mouth of the river Achelous. The god Achelous gave him his daughter Callirrhoë in marriage ; and as the latter wished to possess the necklace and peplus of Harmonia, Alcmaeon went to Psophis and obtained them from Phegeus, under the pretext of dedicating them at Delphi ; but when Phegeus heard that the treasures were fetched for Callirrhoë, he caused his sons to murder Alcmaeon. Alcmaeon was worshipped as a hero at Thebes,

and at Psophis his tomb was shown, surrounded with cypresses. — 2. Son of Megacles, was greatly enriched by Croesus.—3. Of Crotona in Italy, said to have been a pupil of Pythagoras, though this is very doubtful. He is said to have been the first person who dissected animals, and he made some important discoveries in anatomy and natural philosophy. He wrote several medical and philosophical works, which are lost.

Alcmaeŏnĭdae ('Αλκμαιωνίδαι), a noble family at Athens, members of which fill a space in Grecian history from B. C. 750 to 400. They were a branch of the family of the Nelidae, who were driven out of Pylus in Messenia by the Dorians, and settled at Athens. In consequence of the way in which Megacles, one of the family, treated the insurgents under CYLON (B. C. 612), they brought upon themselves the guilt of sacrilege, and were in consequence banished from Athens, about 595. About 560 they returned from exile, but were again expelled by Pisistratus. In 548 they contracted with the Amphictyonic council to rebuild the temple of Delphi, and obtained great popularity throughout Greece by executing the work in a style of magnificence which much exceeded their engagement. On the expulsion of Hippias in 510, they were again restored to Athens. They now joined the popular party, and Clisthenes, who was at that time the head of the family, gave a new constitution to Athens. [CLISTHENES.]

Alcman ('Αλκμάν, also called 'Αλκμαίων), the chief lyric poet of Sparta, by birth a Lydian of Sardis, was brought to Laconia as a slave, when very young, and was emancipated by his master, who discovered his genius. He probably flourished about B. C. 631, and most of his poems were composed after the conclusion of the second Messenian war. He is said to have died, like Sulla, of the *morbus pedicularis.* Alcman's poems were comprised in 6 books : many of them were erotic, and he is said by some ancient writers to have been the inventor of erotic poetry. His metres were very various. The Cretic hexameter was named Alcmanic, from his being its inventor. His dialect was the Spartan Doric, with an intermixture of the Aeolic. The Alexandrian grammarians placed Alcman at the head of their canon of the 9 lyric poets. The fragments of his poems are edited by Welcker, Giessen, 1815 ; and by Bergk, in *Poetae Lyrici Graeci,* 1843.

Alcmēnē ('Αλκμήνη), daughter of Electryon, king of Mycenae, by Anaxo or Lysidice. The brothers of Alcmene were slain by the sons of Pterelaus ; and their father set out to avenge their death, leaving to Amphitryon his kingdom and his daughter Alcmene, whom Amphitryon was to marry. But Amphitryon having unintentionally killed Electryon before the marriage, Sthenelus expelled both Amphitryon and Alcmene, who went to Thebes. But here, instead of marrying Amphitryon, Alcmene declared that she would only marry the man who should avenge the death of her brothers. Amphitryon undertook the task, and invited Creon of Thebes to assist him. During his absence, Zeus, in the disguise of Amphitryon, visited Alcmene, and, pretending to be her husband, related in what way he had avenged the death of her brothers. Amphitryon himself returned the next day ; Alcmene became the mother of Hercules by Zeus, and of Iphicles by Amphitryon. [HERCULES.] After the death of Amphitryon, Alcmene

D

married Rhadamanthys, at Ocalia in Boeotia. When Hercules was raised to the rank of a god, Alcmene, fearing Eurystheus, fled with the sons of Hercules to Athens.

Alcўŏnē or **Halcўŏnē** ('Αλκυόνη). 1. A Pleiad, daughter of Atlas and Pleione, and beloved by Poseidon. — 2. Daughter of Aeolus and Enarete or Aegiale, and wife of Ceÿx. They lived so happily that they were presumptuous enough to call each other Zeus and Hera, for which Zeus metamorphosed them into birds, alcyon and ceÿx. Others relate that Ceÿx perished in a shipwreck, that Alcyone for grief threw herself into the sea, and that the gods, out of compassion, changed the two into birds. It was fabled, that during the seven days before, and as many after, the shortest day of the year, while the bird alcyon was breeding, there always prevailed calms at sea.

Alcўŏneus ('Αλκυονεύς), a giant, killed by Hercules at the Isthmus of Corinth.

Alcўŏnĭum Măre (ἡ 'Αλκυονὶς θάλασσα), the E. part of the Corinthian gulf.

Alēa ('Αλέα), a surname of Athena, under which she was worshipped at Alea, Mantinea, and Tegea. Her temple at the latter place was one of the most celebrated in Greece. It is said to have been built by Aleus, son of Aphĭdas, king of Tegea, from whom the goddess is supposed to have derived this surname.

Alēa ('Αλέα: 'Αλεύς), a town in Arcadia, E. of the Stymphalian lake, with a celebrated temple of Athena, the ruins of which are near Piali.

Alebĭon. [ALBION.]

Alecto. [EUMENIDES.]

Alemanni or **Alamanni** or **Alamani** (from the German alle Männer, all men), a confederacy of German tribes, chiefly of Suevic extraction, between the Danube, the Rhine, and the Main, though we subsequently find them extending their territories as far as the Alps and the Jura. The different tribes of the confederacy were governed by their own kings, but in time of war they obeyed a common leader. They were brave and warlike, and proved formidable enemies to the Romans. They first came into contact with the Romans in the reign of Caracalla, who assumed the surname of Alemannicus on account of a pretended victory over them (A. D. 214). They were attacked by Alexander Severus (234), and by Maximin (237). They invaded Italy in 270, but were driven back by Aurelian, and were again defeated by Probus in 282. After this time they continually invaded the Roman dominions in Germany, and, though defeated by Constantius I., Julian (357), Valentinian, and Gratian, they gradually became more and more powerful, and in the fifth century were in possession of Alsace and of German Switzerland.

Alěrĭa ('Αλερία: 'Αλαλία in Herod.), one of the chief cities of Corsica, on the E. of the island, on the S. bank of the river Rhotanus (Tavignano) near its mouth. It was founded by the Phocaeans B. C. 564, was plundered by L. Scipio in the first Punic war, and was made a Roman colony by Sulla.

Alēsa. [HALESA.]

Alēsĭa ('Αλεσία), an ancient town of the Mandubii in Gallia Lugdunensis, said to have been founded by Hercules, and situated on a high hill (now Auxois), which was washed by the two rivers Lutosa (Oze) and Osera (Ozerain). It was taken and destroyed by Caesar, in B. C. 52. after a memorable siege, but was afterwards rebuilt.

Alěsĭae ('Αλεσίαι), a town in Laconia, W. of Sparta, on the road to Pherae.

Alēsĭum ('Αλείσιον), a town in Elis, not far from Olympia, afterwards called Alesiaeum.

Alēsĭus Mons (τὸ 'Αλήσιον ὄρος), a mountain in Arcadia, with a temple of Poseidon Hippius and a grove of Demeter.

Alētes ('Αλήτης), son of Hippotes and a descendant of Hercules, is said to have taken possession of Corinth, and to have expelled the Sisyphids, 30 years after the first invasion of Peloponnesus by the Heraclĭda. His family, called the Aletidae, maintained themselves at Corinth down to the time of Bacchis.

Alētĭum (Aletinus), a town of Calabria.

Aletrĭum or **Alatrĭum** (Aletrinas, -ātis: Alatri), an ancient town of the Hernici, subsequently a municipium and a Roman colony, W. of Sora and E. of Anagnia.

Aleuădae. [ALEUAS.]

Aleuas ('Αλεύας), a descendant of Hercules, was the ruler of Larissa in Thessaly, and the reputed founder of the celebrated family of the Aleuadae. Before the time of Pisistratus (B. C. 560), the family of the Aleuadae appears to have become divided into two branches, the Aleuadae and the Scopadae. The Scopadae inhabited Crannon and perhaps Pharsalus also, while the main branch, the Aleuadae, remained at Larissa. The influence of the families, however, was not confined to these towns, but extended more or less over the greater part of Thessaly. They formed in reality a powerful aristocratic party in opposition to the great body of the Thessalians. In the invasion of Greece by Xerxes (480), the Aleuadae espoused the cause of the Persians, and the family continued to be the predominant one in Thessaly for a long time afterwards. But after the end of the Peloponnesian war (404), another Thessalian family, the dynasts of Pherae, gradually rose to power and influence, and gave a great shock to the power of the Aleuadae. The most formidable of these princes was Jason of Pherae, who succeeded, after various struggles, in raising himself to the dignity of Tagus, or supreme ruler of Thessaly. [JASON.]

Aleus. [ALEA.]

Alex or **Hălex** (Alece), a small river in S. Italy, was the boundary between the territory of Rhegium and of the Locri Epizephyrii.

Alexander ('Αλέξανδρος), the usual name of PARIS in the Iliad.

Alexander Sevĕrus. [SEVERUS.]

Alexander. I. Minor Historical Persons.

1. Son of Aeropus, a native of the Macedonian district called Lyncestis, whence he is usually called Alexander Lyncestes. He was an accomplice in the murder of Philip, B. C. 336, but was pardoned by Alexander the Great. He accompanied Alexander to Asia; but in 334 he was detected in carrying on a treasonable correspondence with Darius, was kept in confinement and put to death in 330. — 2. Son of Antonius the triumvir, and Cleopatra, born with his twin-sister Cleopatra, B. C. 40. After the battle of Actium they were taken to Rome by Augustus, and were generously educated by Octavia, the wife of Antonius, with her own children. — 3. Eldest son of Aristobulus II., king of Judaea, rose in arms in B. C. 57, against Hyrcanus, who was supported by the Romans. Alexander was defeated by the Romans in 56 and 55, and was put to death by Pompey at Antioch

in 49.—4. Third son of Cassander, king of Macedonia, by Thessalonica, sister of Alexander the Great. In his quarrel with his elder brother Antipater for the government [ANTIPATER], he called in the aid of Pyrrhus of Epirus and Demetrius Poliorcetes, by the latter of whom he was murdered B. c. 294.—5. Jannaeus, the son of Joannes Hyrcanus, and brother of Aristobulus I., king of the Jews B. c. 104—77. At the commencement of his reign he was engaged in war with Ptolemy Lathyrus, king of Cyprus ; and subsequently he had to carry on for six years a dangerous struggle with his own subjects, to whom he had rendered himself obnoxious by his cruelties and by opposing the Pharisees. He signalized his victory by the most frightful butchery of his subjects.—6. Surnamed Isius, the chief commander of the Aetolians, took an active part in opposing Philip of Macedonia (B. c. 198, 197), and in the various negotiations with the Romans.—7. Tyrant of Pherae, was a relation of Jason, and succeeded either Polydorus or Polyphron, as Tagus of Thessaly, about B. c. 369. In consequence of his tyrannical government the Thessalians applied for aid first to Alexander II., king of Macedonia, and next to Thebes. The Thebans sent Pelopidas into Thessaly to succour the malcontents ; but having ventured incautiously within the power of the tyrant, he was seized by Alexander, and thrown into prison B. c. 368. The Thebans sent a large army into Thessaly to rescue Pelopidas, but they were defeated in the first campaign, and did not obtain their object till the next year, 367. In 364 Pelopidas again entered Thessaly with a small force, but was slain in battle by Alexander. The Thebans now sent a large army against the tyrant, and compelled him to become a dependent ally of Thebes. We afterwards hear of Alexander making piratical descents on many of the Athenian dependencies and even on Attica itself. He was murdered in 367, by his wife Thebe, with the assistance of her three brothers.—8. Son of Polysperchon, the Macedonian, was chiefly employed by his father in the command of the armies which he sent against Cassander. Thus he was sent against Athens in B. c. 318, and was engaged in military operations during the next year in various parts of Greece. But in 315 he became reconciled to Cassander, and we find him in 314 commanding on behalf of the latter. He was murdered at Sicyon in 314.—9. Ptolemaeus. [PTOLEMAEUS.] —10. Tiberius, born at Alexandria, of Jewish parents, and nephew of the writer Philo. He deserted the faith of his ancestors, and was rewarded for his apostacy by various public appointments. In the reign of Claudius he succeeded Fadius as procurator of Judaea (A. D. 46), and was appointed by Nero procurator of Egypt. He was the first Roman governor who declared in favour of Vespasian ; and he accompanied Titus in the war against Judaea, and was present at the taking of Jerusalem.

II. Kings of Epirus.

1. Son of Neoptolemus and brother of Olympias, the mother of Alexander the Great. Philip made him king of Epirus in place of his cousin Aeacides, and gave him his daughter Cleopatra in marriage (B. c. 336). In 332, Alexander, at the request of the Tarentines, crossed over into Italy, to aid them against the Lucanians and Bruttii. After meeting

with considerable success, he was defeated and slain in battle in 326, near Pandosia, on the banks of the Acheron in Southern Italy.—2. Son of Pyrrhus and Lanassa, daughter of the Sicilian tyrant Agathocles, succeeded his father in B. c. 272, and drove Antigonus Gonatas out of Macedonia. He was shortly afterwards deprived of both Macedonia and Epirus by Demetrius, the son of Antigonus ; but he recovered Epirus by the aid of the Acarnanians.

III. Kings of Macedonia.

1. Son of Amyntas I., distinguished himself in the life-time of his father by killing the Persian ambassadors who had come to demand the submission of Amyntas, because they attempted to offer indignities to the ladies of the court, about B. c. 507. He succeeded his father shortly afterwards, was obliged to submit to the Persians, and accompanied Xerxes in his invasion of Greece (B. c. 480). He gained the confidence of Mardonius, who sent him to Athens to propose peace to the Athenians, which was rejected. He was secretly inclined to the cause of the Greeks, and informed them the night before the battle of Plataeae of the intention of Mardonius to fight on the following day. He died about B. c. 455, and was succeeded by Perdiccas II.—2. Son of Amyntas II., whom he succeeded, reigned B. c. 369—367. A usurper of the name of Ptolemy Alorites, having risen against him, Pelopidas, who was called in to mediate between them, left Alexander in possession of the kingdom, but took with him to Thebes several hostages ; among whom was Philip, the youngest brother of Alexander, afterwards king of Macedonia. Alexander was shortly afterwards murdered by Ptolemy Alorites.—3. Surnamed Great, son of Philip II. and Olympias, was born at Pella, B. c. 356. His early education was committed to Leonidas and Lysimachus ; and he was also placed under the care of Aristotle, who acquired an influence over his mind and character, which was manifest to the latest period of his life. At the age of 16 Alexander was entrusted with the government of Macedonia by his father, while he was obliged to leave his kingdom to march against Byzantium. He first distinguished himself, however, at the battle of Chaeronea (338), where the victory was mainly owing to his impetuosity and courage. On the murder of Philip (336), Alexander ascended the throne, at the age of 20, and found himself surrounded by enemies on every side. He first put down rebellion in his own kingdom, and then rapidly marched into Greece. His unexpected activity overawed all opposition ; Thebes, which had been most active against him, submitted when he appeared at its gates ; and the assembled Greeks at the Isthmus of Corinth, with the sole exception of the Lacedaemonians, elected him to the command against Persia, which had previously been bestowed upon his father. He now directed his arms against the barbarians of the north, marched (early in 335) across mount Haemus, defeated the Triballi, and advanced as far as the Danube, which he crossed ; and on his return subdued the Illyrians and Taulantii. A report of his death having reached Greece, the Thebans once more took up arms. But a terrible punishment awaited them. He advanced into Boeotia by rapid marches took Thebes by assault, destroyed all the buildings, with the exception of

D 2

the house of Pindar, killed most of the inhabitants, and sold the rest as slaves. Alexander now prepared for his great expedition against Persia. In the spring of 334, he crossed the Hellespont, with about 35,000 men. Of these 30,000 were foot and 5000 horse ; and of the former only 12,000 were Macedonians. Alexander's first engagement with the Persians was on the river Granicus in Mysia (May 334), where they were entirely defeated by him. This battle was followed by the capture or submission of the chief towns on the W. coast of Asia Minor. Halicarnassus was not taken till late in the autumn, after a vigorous defence by Memnon, the ablest general of Darius, and whose death in the following year (333) relieved Alexander from a formidable opponent. He now marched along the coast of Lycia and Pamphylia, and then N. into Phrygia and to Gordium, where he cut or untied the celebrated Gordian knot, which, it was said, was to be loosened only by the conqueror of Asia. In 333, he marched from Gordium through the centre of Asia Minor into Cilicia, where he nearly lost his life at Tarsus by a fever, brought on by his great exertions, or through throwing himself, when heated, into the cold waters of the Cydnus. Darius meantime had collected an army of 500,000 or 600,000 men, with 30,000 Greek mercenaries, whom Alexander defeated in the narrow plain of Issus. Darius escaped across the Euphrates by the ford of Thapsacus ; but his mother, wife, and children fell into the hands of Alexander, who treated them with the utmost delicacy and respect. Alexander now directed his arms against the cities of Phoenicia, most of which submitted ; but Tyre was not taken till the middle of 332, after an obstinate defence of seven months. Next followed the siege of Gaza, which again delayed Alexander two months. Afterwards, according to Josephus, he marched to Jerusalem, intending to punish the people for refusing to assist him, but he was diverted from his purpose by the appearance of the high priest, and pardoned the people. This story is not mentioned by Arrian, and rests on questionable evidence.—Alexander next marched into Egypt, which willingly submitted to him, for the Egyptians had ever hated the Persians. At the beginning of 331, Alexander founded at the mouth of the W. branch of the Nile, the city of ALEXANDRIA, and about the same time visited the temple of Jupiter Ammon, in the desert of Libya, and was saluted by the priests as the son of Jupiter Ammon. —In the spring of the same year (331), Alexander set out to meet Darius, who had collected another army. He marched through Phoenicia and Syria to the Euphrates, which he crossed at the ford of Thapsacus ; thence he proceeded through Mesopotamia, crossed the Tigris, and at length met with the immense hosts of Darius, said to have amounted to more than a million of men, in the plains of Gaugamela. The battle was fought in the month of October, 331, and ended in the complete defeat of the Persians. Alexander gave the fugitives to Arbela (*Erbil*), which place has given its name to the battle, though distant about 50 miles from the spot where it was fought. Darius, who had left the field of battle early in the day, fled to Ecbatana (*Hamadan*), in Media. Alexander was now the conqueror of Asia, and began to adopt Persian habits and customs, by which he conciliated the affections of his new subjects. From Arbela he marched to Babylon, Susa,

and Persepolis, all of which surrendered to him. He is said to have set fire to the palace of Persepolis, and, according to some accounts, in the revelry of a banquet, at the instigation of Thais, an Athenian courtezan.—At the beginning of 330 Alexander marched from Persepolis into Media, in pursuit of Darius, whom he followed through Rhagae and the passes of the Elburz mountains, called by the ancients the Caspian Gates, into the deserts of Parthia, where the unfortunate king was murdered by Bessus, satrap of Bactria, and his associates. Alexander sent his body to Persepolis, to be buried in the tombs of the Persian kings. Bessus escaped to Bactria, and assumed the title of king of Persia. Alexander was engaged during the remainder of the year in subduing the N. provinces of Asia between the Caspian and the Indus, namely, Hyrcania, Parthia, Aria, the Drangae and Sarangae. It was during this campaign that PHILOTAS, his father PARMENION, and other Macedonians, were executed on the charge of treason. In 329 Alexander crossed the mountains of the Paropamisus (the *Hindoo Koosh*), and marched into Bactria against Bessus, whom he pursued across the Oxus into Sogdiana. In this country Bessus was betrayed to him, and was put to death. From the Oxus he advanced as far as the Jaxartes (the *Sir*), which he crossed, and defeated several Scythian tribes N. of that river. After founding a city Alexandria on the Jaxartes, he retraced his steps, and returned to Zariaspa or Bactra, where he spent the winter of 329. It was here that he killed his friend Clitus in a drunken revel. — In 328, Alexander again crossed the Oxus to complete the subjugation of Sogdiana, but was not able to effect it in the year, and accordingly went into winter quarters at Nautaca, a place in the middle of the province. At the beginning of 327, he took a mountain fortress, in which Oxyartes, a Bactrian prince, had deposited his wife and daughters. The beauty of Roxana, one of the latter, captivated the conqueror, and he accordingly made her his wife. This marriage with one of his Eastern subjects was in accordance with the whole of his policy. Having completed the conquest of Sogdiana, he marched S. into Bactria, and made preparations for the invasion of India. While in Bactria another conspiracy was discovered for the murder of the king. The plot was formed by Hermolaus with a number of the royal pages, and Callisthenes, a pupil of Aristotle, was involved in it. All the conspirators were put to death. Alexander did not leave Bactria till late in the spring of 327, and crossed the Indus, probably near the modern Attock. He met with no resistance till he reached the Hydaspes, where he was opposed by Porus, an Indian king, whom he defeated after a gallant resistance, and took prisoner. Alexander restored to him his kingdom, and treated him with distinguished honour. He founded two towns, one on each bank of the Hydaspes : one called Bucephala, in honour of his horse Bucephalus, who died here, after carrying him through so many victories ; and the other Nicaea, to commemorate his victory. From thence he marched across the Acesines (the *Chinab*) and the Hydraotes (the *Ravee*), and penetrated as far as the Hyphasis (*Gurra*). This was the furthest point which he reached, for the Macedonians, worn out by long service, and tired of the war, refused to advance further ; and Alexander, notwithstanding his entreaties and prayers, was obliged to lead them back. He returned to the Hydaspes, where he had previously given orders for the building of a fleet, and then sailed down the river with about 8000 men, while the remainder marched along the banks in two divisions. This was late in the autumn of 327. The people on each side of the river submitted without resistance, except the Malli, in the conquest of one of whose places Alexander was severely wounded. At the confluence of the Acesines and the Indus, Alexander founded a city, and left Philip as satrap, with a considerable body of Greeks. Here he built some fresh ships, and continued his voyage down the Indus, founded a city at Pattala, the apex of the delta of the Indus, and sailed into the Indian ocean, which he reached about the middle of 326. Nearchus was sent with the fleet to sail along the coast to the Persian gulf [NEARCHUS]; and Alexander marched with the rest of his forces through Gedrosia, in which country his army suffered greatly from want of water and provisions. He reached Susa at the beginning of 325. Here he allowed himself and his troops some rest from their labours; and anxious to form his European and Asiatic subjects into one people, he assigned to about 80 of his generals Asiatic wives, and gave with them rich dowries. He himself took a second wife, Barsine, the eldest daughter of Darius, and according to some accounts, a third, Parysatis, the daughter of Ochus. About 10,000 Macedonians followed the example of their king and generals, and married Asiatic women. Alexander also enrolled large numbers of Asiatics among his troops, and taught them the Macedonian tactics. He moreover directed his attention to the increase of commerce, and for this purpose had the Euphrates and Tigris made navigable, by removing the artificial obstructions which had been made in the river for the purpose of irrigation. The Macedonians, who were discontented with several of the new arrangements of the king, rose in mutiny against him, which he quelled with some difficulty. Towards the close of the same year (325) he went to Ecbatana, where he lost his great favourite HEPHAESTION. From Ecbatana he marched to Babylon, subduing in his way the Cossaei, a mountain tribe; and before he reached Babylon he was met by ambassadors from almost every part of the known world. Alexander entered Babylon in the spring of 324, about a year before his death, notwithstanding the warnings of the Chaldaeans, who predicted evil to him if he entered the city at that time. He intended to make Babylon the capital of his empire, as the best point of communication between his eastern and western dominions. His schemes were numerous and gigantic. His first object was the conquest of Arabia, which was to be followed, it was said, by the subjugation of Italy, Carthage, and the West. But his views were not confined merely to conquest. He ordered a fleet to be built on the Caspian, in order to explore that sea. He also intended to improve the distribution of waters in the Babylonian plain, and for that purpose sailed down the Euphrates to inspect the canal called Pallacopas. On his return to Babylon he was attacked by a fever, probably brought on by his recent exertions in the marshy districts around Babylon, and aggravated by the quantity of wine he had drunk at a banquet given to his principal officers. He died after an illness of 11 days, in the month of May or June B. C. 323, at the age of 32, after a reign of 12 years and 8 months.

He appointed no one as his successor, but just before his death he gave his ring to Perdiccas. Roxana was with child at the time of his death, and afterwards bore a son who is known by the name of Alexander Aegus.—The history of Alexander forms an important epoch in the history of mankind. Unlike other Asiatic conquerors, his progress was marked by something more than devastation and ruin; at every step of his course the Greek language and civilization took root and flourished; and after his death Greek kingdoms were formed in all parts of Asia, which continued to exist for centuries. By his conquests the knowledge of mankind was increased; the sciences of geography, natural history and others, received vast additions; and it was through him that a road was opened to India, and that Europeans became acquainted with the products of the remote East.—4. Aegus, son of Alexander the Great and Roxana, was born shortly after the death of his father, in B. C. 323, and was acknowledged as the partner of Philip Arrhidaeus in the empire, under the guardianship of Perdiccas, Antipater, and Polysperchon in succession. Alexander and his mother Roxana were imprisoned by Cassander, when he obtained possession of Macedonia in 316, and remained in prison till 311, when they were put to death by Cassander.

IV. *Kings of Syria.*

1. Surnamed Balas, a person of low origin, pretended to be the son of Antiochus IV. Epiphanes, and reigned in Syria B. C. 150—146. He defeated and slew in battle Demetrius I. Soter, but was afterwards defeated and dethroned by Demetrius II. Nicator.—2. Surnamed Zebina or Zabinas, son of a merchant, was set up by Ptolemy Physcon as a pretender to the throne of Syria, shortly after the return of Demetrius II. Nicator from his captivity among the Parthians, B c. 128. He defeated Demetrius in 125, but was afterwards defeated by Antiochus Grypus, by whom he was put to death, 122.

V. *Literary.*

1. Of Aegae, a peripatetic philosopher at Rome in the first century after Christ, was tutor to the emperor Nero.—2. The Aetolian, of Pleuron in Aetolia, a Greek poet, lived in the reign of Ptolemaeus Philadelphus (B. C. 285—247), at Alexandria, where he was reckoned one of the seven tragic poets who constituted the tragic pleiad. He also wrote other poems besides tragedies. His fragments are collected by Capellmann, *Alexandri Aetoli Fragmenta*, Bonn, 1829.—3. Of Aphrodisias, in Caria, the most celebrated of the commentators on Aristotle, lived about A. D. 200. About half his voluminous works were edited and translated into Latin at the revival of literature; there are a few more extant in the original Greek, which have never been printed, and an Arabic version is preserved of several others. His most important treatise is entitled *De Fato*, an inquiry into the opinions of Aristotle on the subject of Fate and Freewill: edited by Orelli, Zurich, 1824. —4. Cornelius, surnamed Polyhistor, a Greek writer, was made prisoner during the war of Sulla in Greece (B. C. 87—84), and sold as a slave to Cornelius Lentulus, who took him to Rome, made him the teacher of his children, and subsequently restored him to freedom. The surname of Polyhistor was given to him on account of his prodigious

learning. He is said to have written a vast number of works, all of which have perished: the most important of them was one in 42 books, containing historical and geographical accounts of nearly all countries of the ancient world. — 5. Surnamed **Lychnus**, of Ephesus, a Greek rhetorician and poet, lived about B.C. 30. A few fragments of his geographical and astronomical poems are extant. — 6. Of **Myndus**, in Caria, a Greek writer on zoology of uncertain date. — 7. **Numenius**, a Greek rhetorician, who lived in the second century of the Christian aera. Two works are ascribed to him, one *De Figuris Sententiarum et Elocutionis*, from which Aquila Romanus took his materials for his work on the same subject; and the other *On Show-speeches ;* which was written by a later grammarian of the name of Alexander. Edited in Walz's *Rhetores Graeci*, vol. viii. — 8. The **Paphlagonian**, a celebrated impostor, who flourished about the beginning of the second century after Christ, of whom Lucian has given an amusing account, chiefly of the various contrivances by which he established and maintained the credit of an oracle. The influence he attained over the populace seems incredible ; indeed, the narrative of Lucian would appear to be a mere romance, were it not confirmed by some medals of Antoninus and M. Aurelius. — 9. Surnamed **Peloplaton**, a Greek rhetorician of Seleucia in Cilicia, was appointed Greek secretary to M. Antoninus, about A.D. 174. At Athens he conquered the celebrated rhetorician Herodes Atticus, in a rhetorical contest. All persons, however, did not admit his abilities ; for a Corinthian of the name of Sceptes said that he had found in Alexander " the clay (Πῆλος), but not Plato." This saying gave rise to the surname of Peloplaton. — 10. **Philalethes**, an ancient Greek physician, lived probably towards the end of the first century B.C., and succeeded Zeuxis as head of a celebrated Herophilean school of medicine, established in Phrygia between Laodicea and Carura. — 11. Of **Tralles** in Lydia, an eminent physician, lived in the 6th century after Christ, and is the author of two extant Greek works: — 1. *Libri Duodecim de Re Medica ;* 2. *De Lumbricis.*

Alexandrīa, oftener -**Ia**, rarely -**ēa** ('Αλεξάνδρεια: 'Αλεξανδρεύς, Alexandrinus), the name of several cities founded by, or in memory of Alexander the Great. — 1. (*Alexandria*, Arab. *Iskanderia*), the capital of Egypt under the Ptolemies, ordered by Alexander to be founded in B.C. 332. It was built on the narrow neck of land between the Lake Mareotis and the Mediterranean, opposite to the I. of Pharos, which was joined to the city by an artificial dyke, called Heptastadium, which formed, with the island, the two harbours of the city, that on the N.E. of the dyke being named the Great Harbour (now the *New Port*), that on the S.W. Eunostos (εὔνοστος, the *Old Port*). These harbours communicated with each other by two channels cut through the Heptastadium, one at each end of it ; and there was a canal from the Eunostos to the Lake Mareotis. The city was built on a regular plan; and was intersected by two principal streets, above 100 feet wide, the one extending 30 stadia from E. to W., the other across this, from the sea towards the lake, to the length of 10 stadia. At the E. extremity of the city was the royal quarter, called Bruchium, and at the other end of the chief street, outside of the city, the Ne-

cropolis or cemetery. A great lighthouse was built on the I. of Pharos in the reign of Ptolemy Philadelphus (B.C. 283). Under the care of the Ptolemies, as the capital of a great kingdom and of the most fertile country on the earth, and commanding by its position all the commerce of Europe with the East, Alexandria soon became the most wealthy and splendid city of the known world. Greeks, Jews, and other foreigners flocked to it ; and its population probably amounted to three quarters of a million. But a still greater distinction was conferred upon it through the foundation, by the first two Ptolemies, of the Museum, an establishment in which men devoted to literature were maintained at the public cost, and of the Library, which contained 90,000 distinct works, and 400,000 volumes, and the increase of which made it necessary to establish another library in the Serapeum (Temple of Serapis), which reached to 42,800 volumes, but which was destroyed by the bishop Theophilus, at the time of the general overthrow of the heathen temples under Theodosius (A.D. 389). The Great Library suffered severely by fire when Julius Caesar was besieged in Alexdria, and was finally destroyed by Amrou, the lieutenant of the Caliph Omar, in A.D. 651. These institutions made Alexandria the chief centre of literary activity. When Egypt became a Roman province [AEGYPTUS], Alexandria was made the residence of the Praefectus Aegypti. It retained its commercial and literary importance, and became also a chief seat of Christianity and theological learning. Its site is now covered by a mass of ruins, among which are the remains of the cisterns by which the whole city was supplied with water, house by house ; the two obelisks (vulg. *Cleopatra's Needles*), which adorned the gateway of the royal palace, and, outside the walls, to the S., the column of Diocletian (vulg. *Pompey's Pillar*). The modern city stands on the dyke uniting the island of Pharos to the mainland. — 2. A. **Troas**, also Troas simply ('A. ἡ Τρωάς: *Eskistamboul*, i.e. the *Old City*), on the sea-coast S.W. of Troy, was enlarged by Antigonus, hence called Antigonia, but afterwards it resumed its first name. It flourished greatly, both under the Greeks and the Romans ; it was made a colonia ; and both Julius Caesar and Constantine thought of establishing the seat of empire in it. — 3. A. **ad Issum** ('A. κατὰ 'Ισσόν : *Iskenderoon, Scanderoun, Alexandrette*), a sea-port at the entrance of Syria, a little S. of Issus. — 4. In Susiana, aft. *Antiochia*, aft. *Charax Spasini* (Χάραξ Πασίνου or Σπασ.), at the mouth of the Tigris, built by Alexander ; destroyed by a flood ; restored by Antiochus Epiphanes : birthplace of Dionysius Periegetes and Isidorus Characenus. — 5. A. **Ariae** ('A. ἡ ἐν 'Αρίοις : *Herat*), founded by Alexander on the river Arius, in the Persian province of Aria, a very flourishing city, on the great caravan road to India. — 6. A. **Arachosiae** or **Alexandropolis** (*Kandahar ?*), on the river Arachotus, was probably not founded till after the time of Alexander. — 7. A. **Bactriana** ('A. κατὰ Βάκτρα : prob. *Khooloom*, Ru.), E. of Bactra (*Balkh*). — 8. A. **ad Caucasum**, or *apud* Paropamisidas ('A. ἐν Παροπαμισάδαις), at the foot of M. Paropamisus (*Hindoo Koosh*), probably near *Cabool.* — 9. A. **Ultima** or **Alexandrescata** ('A. ἡ ἐσχάτη: *Kokand ?*), in Sogdiana, on the Jaxartes, a little E. of Cyropolis or Cyreschata, marked the furthest point reached by Alexander in his

Scythian expedition.—These are not all the cities of the name.

Alexicācus ('Αλεξίκακος), the averter of evil, a surname of several deities, but particularly of Zeus, Apollo, and Hercules.

Alexīnus ('Αλεξῖνος), of Elis, a philosopher of the Dialectic or Megarian school, and a disciple of Eubulides, lived about the beginning of the 3rd century B. C.

Alexis ('Αλεξις). 1. A comic poet, born at Thurii in Italy, and an Athenian citizen. He was the uncle and instructor of Menander, was born about B. C. 394, and lived to the age of 106. Some of his plays, of which he is said to have written 245, belonged to the Middle, and others to the New Comedy.—2. A sculptor and statuary, one of the pupils of Polycletus.

Alfēnus Varus. [VARUS.]

Algidum or Algĭdus (nr. Cava ?), a small but strongly fortified town of the Aequi on one of the hills of M. Algidus, of which all trace has now disappeared.

Algidus Mons, a range of mountains in Latium, extending S. from Praeneste to M. Albanus, cold, but covered with wood, and containing good pasturage (gelido Algido, Hor. Carm. i. 21. 6 ; nigrae feraci frondis in Algido, Id. iv. 4. 58). It was an ancient seat of the worship of Diana. From it the Aequi usually made their incursions into the Roman territory.

Aliēnus Caecina. [CAECINA.]

Alimentus, L. Cincius, a celebrated Roman annalist, antiquary, and jurist, was praetor in Sicily, B. C. 209, and wrote several works, of which the best known was his Annales, which contained an account of the second Punic war.

Alinda (τὰ Ἄλινδα : 'Αλινδεύς), a fortress and small town, S.E. of Stratonīce, where Ada, queen of Caria, fixed her residence, when she was driven out of Halicarnassus (B. C. 340).

Aliphēra ('Αλίφειρα, 'Αλίφηρα: 'Αλιφειραῖος, 'Αλιφηρεύς: nr. Nerovitza, Ru.), a fortified town in Arcadia, situated on a mountain on the borders of Elis, S. of the Alphēus, said to have been founded by the hero Alipherus, son of Lycaon.

Aliphērus. [ALIPHERA.]

Aliso (Elsen), a strong fortress built by Drusus B. C. 11, at the confluence of the Luppia (Lippe) and the Eliso (Alme).

Alīsontia (Alsitz), a river flowing into the Mosella (Mosel).

Allectus, the chief officer of Carausius in Britain, whom he murdered in A. D. 293. He then assumed the imperial title himself, but was defeated and slain in 296 by the general of Constantius.

Allīa or more correctly Alīa, a small river, which rises about 11 miles from Rome, in the neighbourhood of Crustumerium, and flows into the Tiber about 6 miles from Rome. It is memorable by the defeat of the Romans by the Gauls on its banks, July 16th, B. C. 390 ; which day, dies Alliensis, was hence marked as an unlucky day in the Roman calendar.

A. Alliēnus. 1. A friend of Cicero, was the legate of Q. Cicero in Asia, B. C. 60, praetor in 49, and governor of Sicily on behalf of Caesar in 46 and 47.—2. A legate of Dolabella, by whom he was sent into Egypt in 43.

Allīfae or Alīfae (Allifanus: Allife), a town of Samnium, on the Vulturnus, in a fertile country.

It was celebrated for the manufacture of its large drinking-cups (Allifana sc. pocula, Hor. Sat. ii. 8. 39).

Allobrŏges (Nom. Sing. Allŏbrox : 'Αλλόβρογες, 'Αλλόβρυγες, 'Αλλόβριγες : perhaps from the Celtic aill, " rock " or " mountain," and brog, " dwelling," consequently " dwellers in the mountains "), a powerful people of Gaul dwelling between the Rhodanus (Rhone) and the Isara (Isère), as far as the L. Lemannus (Lake of Geneva), consequently in the modern Dauphiné and Savoy. Their chief town was VIENNA on the Rhone. They are first mentioned in Hannibal's invasion, B. C. 218. They were conquered, in B. C. 121, by Q. Fabius Maximus Allobrogicus, and made subjects of Rome, but they bore the yoke unwillingly, and were always disposed to rebellion. In the time of Ammianus the eastern part of their country was called Sapaudia, i. e. Savoy.

Almo (Almone), a small river, rises near Bovillae, and flows into the Tiber S. of Rome, in which the statues of Cybele were washed annually.

Almōpes ('Αλμῶπες), a people in Macedonia, inhabiting the district Almopia between Eordaea and Pelagonia.

Alŏeus ('Αλωεύς), son of Poseidon and Canace, married Iphimedia, the daughter of Triops. His wife was beloved by Poseidon, by whom she had two sons, Otus and Ephialtes, who are usually called the Aloïdae, from their reputed father Aloeus. They were renowned for their extraordinary strength and daring spirit. When they were 9 years old, each of their bodies measured 9 cubits in breadth and 27 in height. At this early age, they threatened the Olympian gods with war, and attempted to pile Ossa upon Olympus, and Pelion upon Ossa. They would have accomplished their object, says Homer, had they been allowed to grow up to the age of manhood ; but Apollo destroyed them before their beards began to appear (Od. xi. 305, seq.). They also put the god Ares in chains, and kept him imprisoned for 13 months. Other stories are related of them by later writers.

Aloïdae. [ALOEUS.]

Alonta ('Αλόντα : Terek), a river of Albania, in Sarmatia Asiatica, flowing into the Caspian.

Alŏpe ('Αλόπη), daughter of Cercyon, became by Poseidon the mother of HIPPOTHOUS. She was put to death by her father, but her body was changed by Poseidon into a well, which bore the same name.

Alŏpe ('Αλόπη : 'Αλοπεύς, 'Αλοπίτης). 1. A town in the Opuntian Locris, opposite Euboea. —2. A town in Phthiotis in Thessaly (Il. ii. 682).

Alŏpĕce ('Αλωπεκή and 'Αλωπεκαί : 'Αλωπεκεύς), a demus of Attica, of the tribe Antiochis, 11 stadia E. of Athens, on the hill Anchesmus.

Alopeconnēsus ('Αλωπεκόννησος : 'Αλωπεκοννήσιοι : Alexi ?), a town in the Thracian Chersonesus, founded by the Aeolians.

Alpēnus ('Αλπηνός, 'Αλπηνοί), a town of the Epicnemidii Locri at the entrance of the pass of Thermopylae.

Alpes (al Ἄλπεις, ἡ Ἄλπις, τὰ Ἄλπεινά ὄρη, τὰ Ἄλπεια ὄρη ; probably from the Celtic Alb or Alp, " a height "), the mountains forming the boundary of northern Italy, are a part of the great mountain-chain, which extends from the

Gulf of Genoa across Europe to the Black Sea, of which the Apennines and the mountains of the Grecian peninsula may be regarded as off-shoots. Of the Alps proper, the Greeks had very little knowledge, and included them under the general name of the Rhipaean mountains. The Romans first obtained some knowledge of them by Hannibal's passage across them: this knowledge was gradually extended by their various wars with the inhabitants of the mountains, who were not finally subdued till the reign of Augustus. In the time of the emperors the different parts of the Alps were distinguished by the following names, most of which are still retained. We enumerate them in order from W. to E. 1. ALPES MARITIMAE, the *Maritime* or *Ligurian Alps*, from Genua (*Genoa*), where the Apennines begin, run W. as far as the river Varus (*Var*) and M. Cema (*la Caillole*), and then N. to M. Vesulus (*Monte Viso*), one of the highest points of the Alps. — 2. ALPES COTTIAE or COTTIANAE, the *Cottian Alps* (so called from a king Cottius in the time of Augustus), from Monte Viso to Mont Cenis, contained M. Matrona, afterwards called M. Janus or Janna (*Mont Genèvre*), across which Cottius constructed a road, which became the chief means of communication between Italy and Gaul: this road leads from the valley of the Durance in France to Segusio (*Susa*) and the valley of the Dora in Piedmont. The pass over Mont Cenis, now one of the most frequented of the Alpine passes, appears to have been unknown ·in antiquity.— 3. ALPES GRAIAE, also *Saltus Graius* (the name is probably Celtic, and has nothing to do with Greece), the *Graian Alps*, from Mont Cenis to the Little St. Bernard inclusive; contained the Jugum Cremonis (*le Cramont*) and the Centronicae Alpes, apparently the Little St. Bernard and the surrounding mountains. The Little St. Bernard, which is sometimes called Alpis Graia, is probably the pass by which Hannibal crossed the Alps; the road over it, which was improved by Augustus, led to Augusta (*Aosta*) in the territory of the Salassi.— 4. ALPES PENNINAE, the *Pennine Alps*, from the Great St. Bernard to the Simplon inclusive, the highest portion of the chain, including Mont Blanc, Monte Rosa, and Mont Cervin. The Great St. Bernard was called M. Penninus, and on its summit the inhabitants worshipped a deity, whom the Romans called Jupiter Penninus. The name is probably derived from the Celtic *pen*, " a height." —5. ALPES LEPONTIORUM or LEPONTIAE, the *Lepontian* or *Helvetian Alps*, from the Simplon to the St. Gothard. — 6. ALPES RHAETICAE, the *Rhaetian Alps*, from the St. Gothard to the Orteler by the pass of the Stelvio. M. Adula is usually supposed to be the St. Gothard, but it must be another name for the whole range, if Strabo is right in stating that both the Rhine and the Adda rise in M. Adula. The Romans were acquainted with two passes across the Rhaetian Alps, connecting Curia (*Coire*) and Milan, one across the Splügen and the other across Mont Septimer, and both meeting at Clavenna (*Chiavenna*). — 7. ALPES TRIDENTINAE, the mountains of southern Tyrol, in which the Athesis (*Adige*) rises, with the pass of the Brenner. — 8. ALPES NORICAE, the *Noric Alps*, N. E. of the Tridentine Alps, comprising the mountains in the neighbourhood of Salzburg. — 9. ALPES CARNICAE, the *Carnic Alps*, E. of the Tridentine, and S. of the Noric, to Mount

Terglu. — 10. ALPES JULIAE, the *Julian Alps*, from Mount Terglu to the commencement of the Illyrian or Dalmatian mountains, which are known by the name of the Alpes Dalmaticae, further north by the name of the Alpes Pannonicae. The Alpes Juliae were so called because Julius Caesar or Augustus constructed roads across them: they are also called Alpes Venetae.

Alphēnus Varus. [VARUS.]

Alphěsibœa ('Αλφεσίβοια). 1. Mother of Adonis. [ADONIS.] — 2. Daughter of Phegeus, who married Alcmaeon. [ALCMAEON.]

Alphěus Mytilēnaeus ('Αλφεῖος Μυτιληναῖος), the author of about 12 epigrams in the Greek Anthology, was probably a contemporary of the emperor Augustus.

Alphěus ('Αλφειός: Dor. 'Αλφεός; *Alfeo, Rofeo, Rufo, Rufea*), the chief river of Peloponnesus, rises at Phylace in Arcadia, shortly afterwards sinks under ground, appears again near Asea, and then mingles its waters with those of the Eurōtas. After flowing 20 stadia, the two rivers disappear under ground: the Alpheus again rises at Pegae in Arcadia, and increased by many affluents, flows N. W. through Arcadia and Elis, not far from Olympia, and falls into the Ionian sea. The subterranean descent of the river, which is confirmed by modern travellers, gave rise to the story about the river-god Alphēus and the nymph Arethusa. The latter, pursued by Alpheus, was changed by Artemis into the fountain of Arethusa in the island of Ortygia at Syracuse, but the god continued to pursue her under the sea, and attempted to mingle his stream with the fountain in Ortygia. Hence it was said that a cup thrown into the Alpheus would appear again in the fountain of Arethusa in Ortygia. Other accounts related that Artemis herself was beloved by Alpheus: the goddess was worshipped, under the name of *Alpheaea*, both in Elis and Ortygia.

Alphīus Avītus. [AVITUS.]

Alpīnus, a name which Horace gives in ridicule to a bombastic poet. He probably means BIBACULUS.

Alsīum (Alsiensis: *Palo*), one of the most ancient Etruscan towns on the coast near Caere, and a Roman colony after the 1st Punic war. In its neighbourhood Pompey had a country-seat (*villa Alsiensis*).

Althaea ('Αλθαία), daughter of the Aetolian king Thestius and Eurythemis, married Oeneus, king of Calydon, by whom she became the mother of several children, and among others of MELEAGER, upon whose death she killed herself.

Althaea, the chief town of the Olcades in the country of the Oretani in Hispania Tarraconensis.

Althēmēnes ('Αλθημένης or 'Αλθαιμένης), son of Catreus, king of Crete. In consequence of an oracle, that Catreus would lose his life by one of his children, Althemenes quitted Crete and went to Rhodes. There he unwittingly killed his father, who had come in search of his son.

Altīnum (Altīnas: *Altino*), a wealthy municipium in the land of the Veneti in the N. of Italy, at the mouth of the river Silis and on the road from Patavium to Aquileia, was a wealthy manufacturing town, and the chief emporium for all the goods which were sent from southern Italy to the countries of the north. Goods could be brought from Ravenna to Altinum through the Lagoons and the numerous canals of the Po, safe from storms and pirates. There were many beautiful villas around the town. (Mart. iv. 25.)

Altis ("Αλτις), the sacred grove of Zeus at OLYMPIA.

Aluntium or **Haluntium** ('Αλούντιον), a town on the N. coast of Sicily on a steep hill, celebrated for its wine.

Alus or **Halus** ('Αλος, "Αλος: 'Αλεύς: nr. *Kefalosi*, Ru.), a town in Phthiotis in Thessaly, at the extremity of M. Othrys, built by the hero **Athamas.**

Alyattes ('Αλυάττης), king of Lydia, B.C. 617—560, succeeded his father Sadyattes, and was himself succeeded by his son Croesus. He carried on war with Miletus from 617 to 612, and with Cyaxares, king of Media, from 590 to 585; an eclipse of the sun, which happened in 585 during a battle between Alyattes and Cyaxares, led to a peace between them. Alyattes drove the Cimmerians out of Asia and took Smyrna. The tomb of Alyattes, N. of Sardis, near the lake Gygaea, which consisted of a large mound of earth, raised upon a foundation of great stones, still exists. Mr. Hamilton says that it took him about ten minutes to ride round its base, which would give it a circumference of nearly a mile.

Alyba ('Αλύβη), a town on the S. coast of the Euxine. (Hom. *Il.* ii. 857.)

Alypius ('Αλύπιος), of Alexandria, probably lived in the 4th century of the Christian aera, and is the author of a Greek musical treatise entitled "Introduction to Music" (εἰσαγωγὴ μουσική), printed by Meibomius in *Antiquae Musicae Auctores Septem*, Amstel. 1652.

Alyzia or **Alyzea** ('Αλυζία, 'Αλύζεια: 'Αλυζαίος; Ru. in the valley of *Kandili*), a town in Acarnania near the sea opposite Leucas, with a harbour and a temple both sacred to Hercules. The temple contained one of the works of Lysippus representing the labours of Hercules, which the Romans carried off.

Amadocus ('Αμάδοκος) or **Medocus** (Μήδοκος). 1. King of the Odrysae in Thrace, when Xenophon visited the country in B.C. 400. He and Seuthes, who were the most powerful Thracian kings, were frequently at variance, but were reconciled to one another by Thrasybulus, the Athenian commander, in 390, and induced by him to become the allies of Athens. — 2. A ruler in Thrace, who, in conjunction with Berisades and Cersobleptes, succeeded Cotys in 358.

Amagetobria. [MAGETOBRIA.]

Amalthea ('Αμάλθεια). 1. The nurse of the infant Zeus in Crete. According to some traditions Amalthea is the goat who suckled Zeus, and who was rewarded by being placed among the stars. [AEGA.] According to others, Amalthea was a nymph, daughter of Oceanus, Helios, Haemonius, or of the Cretan king Melisseus, who fed Zeus with the milk of a goat. When this goat broke off one of her horns, Amalthea filled it with fresh herbs and gave it to Zeus, who placed it among the stars. According to other accounts Zeus himself broke off one of the horns of the goat Amalthea, and gave it to the daughters of Melisseus, and endowed it with the wonderful power of becoming filled with whatever the possessor might wish. This is the story about the origin of the celebrated horn of Amalthea, commonly called the horn of plenty or cornucopia, which was used in later times as the symbol of plenty in general. — 2. One of the Sibyls, iden-

tified with the Cumaean Sibyl, who sold to king Tarquinius the celebrated Sibylline books.

Amaltheum or **Amalthea**, a villa of Atticus on the river Thyamis in Epirus, was perhaps originally a shrine of the nymph Amalthea, which Atticus adorned with statues and bas-reliefs, and converted into a beautiful summer retreat. Cicero, in imitation, constructed a similar retreat on his estate at Arpinum.

Amantia ('Αμαντία: Amantinus, Amantianus, or Amantes, pl.: *Nivitza*), a Greek town and district in Illyricum: the town, said to have been founded by the Abantes of Euboea, lay at some distance from the coast, E. of Oricum.

Amanus (ὁ Ἀμανός, τὸ Ἀμανόν: 'Αμανίτης, Amaniensis: *Almadagh*), a branch of Mt. Taurus, which runs from the head of the Gulf of Issus N.E. to the principal chain, dividing Syria from Cilicia and Cappadocia. There were two passes in it; the one, called the Syrian Gates (αἱ Συρίαι πύλαι, Syriae Portae: *Bylan*) near the sea; the other, called the Amanian Gates ('Αμανίδες or 'Αμανικαὶ πύλαι: Amanicae Pylae, Portae Amani Montis: *Demir Kapu*, i. e. the *Iron Gate*), further to the N. The former pass was on the road from Cilicia to Antioch, the latter on that to the district Commagene; but, on account of its great difficulty, the latter pass was rarely used, until the Romans made a road through it. The inhabitants of Amanus were wild banditti.

Amardi or **Mardi** ("Αμαρδοι, Μάρδοι), a powerful, warlike, and predatory tribe who dwelt on the S. shore of the Caspian Sea.

Amardus or **Mardus** ("Αμαρδος, Μάρδος: *Kizil Ozien*), a river flowing through the country of the Mardi into the Caspian Sea.

Amarynceus ('Αμαρυγκεύς), a chief of the Eleans, is said by some writers to have fought against Troy; but Homer only mentions his son Diores (*Amaryncides*) as taking part in the Trojan war.

Amarynthus ('Αμάρυνθος: 'Αμαρύνθιος), a town in Euboea 7 stadia from Eretria, to which it belonged, with a celebrated temple of Artemis, who was hence called *Amarynthia* or *Amarysia*, and in whose honour there was a festival of this name both in Euboea and Attica. (See *Dict. of Antiq.* art. *Amarynthia*.)

Amasenus (*Amaseno*), a river in Latium, rises in the Volscian mountains, flows by Privernum, and after being joined by the Ufens (*Ufente*), which flows from Setia, falls into the sea between Circeii and Terracina, though the greater part of its waters are lost in the Pontine marshes.

Amasia or **-ea** ('Αμάσεια: 'Αμασεύς: *Amasiah*), the capital of the kings of Pontus, was a strongly fortified city on both banks of the river Iris. It was the birthplace of Mithridates the Great and of the geographer Strabo.

Amasis ('Αμασις). 1. King of Egypt, B.C. 570—526, succeeded Apries, whom he dethroned. During his long reign Egypt was in a very prosperous condition; and the Greeks were brought into much closer intercourse with the Egyptians than had existed previously. Amasis married Ladice, a Cyrenaic lady, contracted an alliance with Cyrene and Polycrates of Samos, and also sent presents to several of the Greek cities. — 2. A Persian, sent in the reign of Cambyses (B.C. 525) against Cyrene, took Barca, but did not succeed in taking Cyrene.

Amastris ('Αμαστρις, Ion. "Αμηστρις). 1. Wife

of Xerxes, and mother of Artaxerxes I., was of a cruel and vindictive character. — 2. Also called *Amastrine*, niece of Darius, the last king of Persia. She married, 1. Craterus ; 2. Dionysius, tyrant of Heraclea in Bithynia, B. C. 322 ; and 3. Lysimachus, B. C. 302. Having been abandoned by Lysimachus upon his marriage with Arsinoë, she retired to Heraclea, where she reigned, and was drowned by her two sons about 288.

Amastris ('Αμιστρις; 'Αμαστριανός: *Amasera*), a large and beautiful city, with two harbours, on the coast of Paphlagonia, built by Amastris after her separation from Lysimachus (about B. C. 300), on the site of the old town of Sesamus, which name the citadel retained. The new city was built and peopled by the inhabitants of Cytorus and Cromna.

Amāta, wife of king Latinus and mother of Lavinia, opposed Lavinia being given in marriage to Aeneas, because she had already promised her to Turnus. When she heard that Turnus had fallen in battle, she hung herself.

Amāthūs, -untis ('Αμαθοῦς, -οῦντος: 'Αμαθούσιος: *Limasol*), an ancient town on the S. coast of Cyprus, with a celebrated temple of Aphrodite, who was hence called *Amathūsia*. There were coppermines in the neighbourhood of the town (*fecundam Amathunta metalli*, Ov. *Met.* x. 220).

Amātīus, surnamed *Pseudomarius*, pretended to be either the son or grandson of the great Marius, and was put to death by Antony in B. C. 44. Some call him Herophilus.

Amāzōnes ('Αμαζόνες), a mythical race of warlike females, are said to have come from the Caucasus, and to have settled in the country about the river Thermodon, where they founded the city Themiscýra, in the neighbourhood of the modern Trebizond. Their country was inhabited only by the Amazons, who were governed by a queen: but in order to propagate their race, they met once a year the Gargareans in Mount Caucasus. The children of the female sex were brought up by the Amazons, and each had her right breast cut off ; the male children were sent to the Gargareans or put to death. The foundation of several towns in Asia Minor and in the islands of the Aegean is ascribed to them, *e. g.* of Ephesus, Smyrna, Cyme, Myrina, and Paphos. The Greeks believed in their existence as a real historical race down to a late period ; and hence it is said that Thalestris, the queen of the Amazons, hastened to Alexander, in order to become a mother by the conqueror of Asia. This belief of the Greeks may have arisen from the peculiar way in which the women of some of the Caucasian districts lived, and performed the duties which in other countries devolve upon men, as well as from their bravery and courage, which are noticed as remarkable even by modern travellers. Vague and obscure reports about them probably reached the inhabitants of western Asia and the Greeks, and these reports were subsequently worked out and embellished by popular tradition and poetry. The following are the chief mythical adventures with which the Amazons are connected : — they are said to have invaded Lycia in the reign of Iobates, but were destroyed by Bellerophontes, who happened to be staying at the king's court. [BELLEROPHONTES ; LAOMEDON.] They also invaded Phrygia, and fought with the Phrygians and Trojans when Priam was a young man. The ninth among the labours imposed upon Hercules by

Eurystheus, was to take from Hippolyte, the queen of the Amazons, her girdle, the ensign of her kingly power, which she had received as a present from Ares. [HERCULES.] In the reign of Theseus they invaded Attica. [THESEUS.] Towards the end of the Trojan war, the Amazons, under their queen Penthesilëa, came to the assistance of Priam ; but she was killed by Achilles. The Amazons and their battles are frequently represented in the remains of ancient Greek art.

Amāzōnīci or -ius Mons, a mountain range parallel and near to the coast of Pontus, containing the sources of the Thermodon and other streams which water the supposed country of the Amazons.

Ambarri, a people of Gaul, on the Arar (*Saone*) E. of the Aedui, and of the same stock as the latter.

Ambiāni, a Belgic people, between the Bellovaci and Atrebates, conquered by Caesar in B. C. 57. Their chief town was Samarobrīva afterwards called Ambiani, now *Amiens*.

Ambiatīnus Vicus, a place in the country of the Treviri near Coblentz, where the emperor Caligula was born.

Ambibāri, an Armoric people in Gaul, near the modern *Ambières* in Normandy.

Ambiliāti, a Gallic people, perhaps in Brittany.

Ambīōrix, a chief of the Eburones in Gaul, cut to pieces, in conjunction with Cativolcus, the Roman troops under Sabinus and Cotta, who were stationed for the winter in the territories of the Eburones, B. C. 54. He failed in taking the camp of Q. Cicero, and was defeated on the arrival of Caesar, who was unable to obtain possession of the person of Ambiorix, notwithstanding his active pursuit of the latter.

Ambivareti, the clientes or vassals of the Aedui, probably dwelt N. of the latter.

Ambivariti, a Gallic people, W. of the Maas, in the neighbourhood of Namur.

Ambivīus Turpio. [TURPIO.]

Amblada (τὰ 'Αμβλαδα : 'Αμβλαδεύς), a town in Pisidia, on the borders of Caria ; famous for its wine.

Ambrācia ('Αμπρακία, afterwards 'Αμβρακία : 'Αμβρακιώτης, 'Αμβρακιεύς, Ambraciensis: *Arta*), a town on the left bank of the Arachthus, 80 stadia from the coast, N. of the Ambracian gulf, was originally included in Acarnania, but afterwards in Epirus. It was colonised by the Corinthians about B. C. 660, and at an early period acquired wealth and importance. It became subject to the kings of Epirus about the time of Alexander the Great. Pyrrhus made it the capital of his kingdom, and adorned it with public buildings and statues. At a later time it joined the Aetolian League, was taken by the Romans in B. C. 189, and stripped of its works of art. Its inhabitants were transplanted to the new city of NICOPOLIS, founded by Augustus after the battle of Actium, B. C. 31. South of Ambracia on the E. of the Arachthus, and close to the sea was the fort *Ambracus*.

Ambracius Sinus ('Αμπρακινὸς or 'Αμβρακικὸς κόλπος: *G. of Arta*), a gulf of the Ionian sea between Epirus and Acarnania, said by Polybius to be 300 stadia long and 100 wide, and with an entrance only 5 stadia in width. Its real length is 25 miles and its width 10 : the narrowest part of the entrance is only 700 yards, but its general width is about half a mile.

Ambrōnes ('Αμβρωνες), a Celtic people, who

joined the Cimbri and Teutoni in their invasion of the Roman dominions, and were defeated by Marius near Aquae Sextiae (*Aix*) in B. C. 102.

Ambrōsĭus, usually called **St. Ambrose**, one of the most celebrated Christian fathers, was born in A. D. 340, probably at Augusta Trevirorum (*Treves*). After a careful education at Rome, he practised with great success as an advocate at Milan ; and about A. D. 370 was appointed prefect of the provinces of Liguria and Aemilia, whose seat of government was Milan. On the death of Auxentius, bishop of Milan, in 374, the appointment of his successor led to an op··n conflict between the Arians and Catholics. Ambrose exerted his influence to restore peace, and addressed the people in a conciliatory speech, at the conclusion of which a child in the further part of the crowd cried out "*Ambrosius episcopus.*" The words were received as an oracle from heaven, and Ambrose was elected bishop by the acclamation of the whole multitude, the bishops of both parties uniting in his election. It was in vain that he adopted the strangest devices to alter the determination of the people ; nothing could make them change their mind ; and at length he yielded to the express command of the emperor (Valentinian I.), and was consecrated on the eighth day after his baptism, for at the time of his election he was only a catechumen. Ambrose was a man of eloquence, firmness, and ability, and distinguished himself by maintaining and enlarging the authority of the church. He was a zealous opponent of the Arians, and thus came into open conflict with Justina, the mother of Valentinian II., who demanded the use of one of the churches of Milan for the Arians. Ambrose refused to give it ; he was supported by the people ; and the contest was at length decided by the miracles which are reported to have attended the discovery of the reliques of two martyrs, Gervasius and Protasius. Although these miracles were denied by the Arians, the impression made by them upon the people in general was so strong, that Justina thought it prudent to give way. The state of the parties was quite altered by the death of Justina in 387, when Valentinian became a Catholic, and still more completely by the victory of Theodosius over Maximus (388). This event put the whole power of the empire into the hands of a prince who was a firm Catholic, and over whom Ambrose acquired such influence, that, after the massacre at Thessalonica in 390, he refused Theodosius admission into the church of Milan for a period of 8 months, and only restored him after he had performed a public penance. The best edition of the works of Ambrose is that of the Benedictines, Paris, 1686 and 1690.

Ambrȳsus or **Amphrȳsus** ('Αμβρυσος : 'Αμφρυσεύς: nr. *Dhistomo*), a town in Phocis strongly fortified, S. of M. Parnassus : in the neighbourhood were numerous vineyards.

Ambustus, Făbĭus. 1. M., pontifex maximus in the year that Rome was taken by the Gauls, B. C. 390. His three sons, Kaeso, Numerius, and Quintus, were sent as ambassadors to the Gauls, when the latter were besieging Clusium, and took part in a sally of the besieged against the Gauls (B. C. 391). The Gauls demanded that the Fabii should be surrendered to them for violating the law of nations ; and upon the senate refusing to give up the guilty parties, they marched against Rome. The three sons were in the same year elected consular tribunes. — **2. M.**, consular tribune in B. C.

381 and 369, and censor in 363, had two daughters, of whom the elder was married to Ser. Sulpicius, and the younger to C. Licinius Stolo, the author of the Licinian Rogations. According to the story recorded by Livy, the younger Fabia induced her father to assist her husband in obtaining the consulship for the plebeian order, into which she had married. — **3. M.**, thrice consul, in B. C. 360, when he conquered the Hernici, a second time in 356, when he conquered the Falisci and Tarquinienses, and a third time in 354, when he conquered the Tiburtes. He was dictator in 351. He was the father of the celebrated Q. Fabius Maximus Rullianus. [MAXIMUS.]

Amēnănus ('Αμενανός, Dor. 'Αμένας), a river in Sicily near Catana, only flowed occasionally (*nunc fluit, interdum suppressis fontibus aret,* Ov. *Met.* xv. 280).

Amĕrĭa (Amĕrīnus: *Amelia*), an ancient town in Umbria, and a municipium, the birth-place of Sex. Roscius defended by Cicero, was situate in a district rich in vines (Virg. *Georg.* i. 265).

Amerĭŏla, a town in the land of the Sabines, destroyed by the Romans at a very early period.

Amestrātus (Amestratīnus : *Mistretta*), a town in the N. of Sicily not far from the coast, the same as the *Myttistratum* of Polybius, and the *Amastra* of Silius Italicus, taken by the Romans from the Carthaginians in the first Punic war.

Amestris. [AMASTRIS.]

Amīda (ἡ Ἄμιδα: *Diarbekr*), a town in Sophene (Armenia Major) on the upper Tigris.

Amilcar. [HAMILCAR.]

Aminĭas ('Αμεινίας), brother of Aeschylus, distinguished himself at the battle of Salamis (B. C. 480) : he and Eumenes were judged to have been the bravest on this occasion among all the Athenians.

Amipsĭas ('Αμειψίας), a comic poet of Athens, contemporary with Aristophanes, whom he twice conquered in the dramatic contests, gaining the second prize with his *Connus* when Aristophanes was third with the *Clouds* (B. C. 423), and the first with his *Comastae* when Aristophanes gained the second with the *Birds* (B. C. 414).

Amisĭa or **Amisĭus** (*Ems*), a river in northern Germany well known to the Romans, on which Drusus had a naval engagement with the Bructeri, B. C. 12.

Amisĭa (*Emden ?*), a fortress on the left bank of the river of the same name.

Amisŏdărus ('Αμισώδαρος), a king of Lycia, said to have brought up the monster Chimaera: his sons Atymnius and Maris were slain at Troy by the sons of Nestor.

Amīsus ('Αμισός: 'Αμισηνός, Amisēnus: *Samsun*), a large city on the coast of Pontus, on a bay of the Euxine Sea, called after it (Amisenus Sinus). Mithridates enlarged it, and made it one of his residences.

Amiternum (Amiternīnus: *Amatrica* or *Torre d'Amiterno*), one of the most ancient towns of the Sabines, on the Aternus, the birth-place of the historian Sallust.

Ammĭānus ('Αμμιανός), a Greek epigrammatist, but probably a Roman by birth, the author of nearly 30 epigrams in the Greek Anthology, lived under Trajan and Hadrian.

Ammĭānus Marcellīnus, by birth a Greek, and a native of Syrian Antioch, was admitted at an early age among the imperial body guards. He served many years under Ursicinus, one of the generals of Constantius, both in the West and East, and he subsequently attended the emperor Julian in his campaign against the Persians (A. D. 363). Eventually he established himself at Rome, where he composed his history, and was alive at least as late as 390. His history, written in Latin, extended from the accession of Nerva, A. D. 96, the point at which the histories of Tacitus terminated, to the death of Valens, A. D. 378, comprising a period of 282 years. It was divided into 31 books, of which the first 13 are lost. The remaining 18 embrace the acts of Constantius from A. D. 353, the 17th year of his reign, together with the whole career of Gallus, Julianus, Jovianus, Valentinianus, and Valens. The portion preserved was the more important part of the work, as he was a contemporary of the events described in these books. The style of Ammianus is harsh and inflated, but his accuracy, fidelity, and impartiality, deserve praise. — *Editions.* By Gronovius, Lugd. Bat. 1693; by Ernesti, Lips. 1773 ; by Wagner and Erfurdt, Lips. 1808.

Ammon ('Αμμων), originally an Aethiopian or Libyan, afterwards an Egyptian divinity. The real Egyptian name was Amun or Ammun ; the Greeks called him Zeus Ammon, the Romans Jupiter Ammon, and the Hebrews Amon. The most ancient seat of his worship was Meroe, where he had an oracle : thence it was introduced into Egypt, where the worship took the firmest root at Thebes in Upper Egypt, which was therefore frequently called by the Greeks Diospolis, or the city of Zeus. Another famous seat of the god, with a celebrated oracle, was in the oasis of Ammonium (*Siwah*) in the Libyan desert ; the worship was also established in Cyrenaica. The god was represented either in the form of a ram, or as a human being with the head of a ram ; but there are some representations in which he appears altogether as a human being with only the horns of a ram. It seems clear that the original idea of Ammon was that of a protector and leader of the flocks. The Aethiopians were a nomad people, flocks of sheep constituted their principal wealth, and it is perfectly in accordance with the notions of the Aethiopians as well as Egyptians to worship the animal which is the leader and protector of the flock. This view is supported by the various stories related about Ammon.

Ammonium. [OASIS.]

Ammonius ('Αμμώνιος). 1. Grammaticus, of Alexandria, left this city on the overthrow of the heathen temples in A. D. 389, and settled at Constantinople. He wrote, in Greek, a valuable work, *On the Differences of Words of like Signification* (περὶ ὁμοίων καὶ διαφόρων λέξεων). — *Editions.* By Valckenaer, Lugd. Bat. 1739; by Schäfer, Lips. 1822. — 2. Son of Hermeas, studied at Athens under Proclus (who died A. D. 484), and was the master of Simplicius, Damascius, and others. He wrote numerous commentaries in Greek on the works of the earlier philosophers. His extant works are *Commentaries on the Isagoge of Porphyry, or the Five Predicables,* first published at Venice in 1500 ; and *On the Categories of Aristotle* and *De Interpretatione,* published by Brandis in his edition of the Scholia on Aristotle. — 3. Of Lamprae in Attica, a Peripatetic philosopher, lived in the first century of the Christian aera, and was the instructor of Plutarch. — 4. Surnamed Saccas, or sack-carrier, because his employment

was carrying the corn, landed at Alexandria, as a public porter, was born of Christian parents. Some writers assert, and others deny, that he apostatised from the faith. At any rate he combined the study of philosophy with Christianity, and is regarded by those who maintain his apostasy as the founder of the later Platonic School. Among his disciples were Longinus, Herennius, Plotinus, and Origen. He died A. D. 243, at the age of more than 80 years.

Amnisus ('Αμνισός), a town in the N. of Crete and the harbour of Cnossus, situated on a river of the same name, the nymphs of which, called *Amnisiades,* were in the service of Artemis.

Amor, the god of love, had no place in the religion of the Romans, who only translate the Greek name Eros into Amor. [EROS.]

Amorgus ("Αμοργος : 'Αμοργῖνος : *Amorgo*), an island in the Grecian Archipelago, one of the Sporades, the birth-place of Simonides, and under the Roman emperors a place of banishment.

Amorium ('Αμόριον), a city of Phrygia Major or Galatia, on the river Sangarius ; the reputed birth-place of Aesop.

Ampe ("Αμπη, Herod.) or Ampelone (Plin.), a town at the mouth of the Tigris, where Darius I. planted the Milesians whom he removed from their own city after the Ionian revolt (B. C. 494).

L. Ampelius, the author of a small work, entitled *Liber Memorialis,* probably lived in the 2nd or 3rd century of the Christian aera. His work is a sort of common-place-book, containing a meagre summary of the most striking natural objects and of the most remarkable events, divided into 50 chapters. It is generally printed with Florus, and has been published separately by Beck, Lips. 1826.

Ampelus ("Αμπελος), a promontory at the extremity of the peninsula Sithonia in Chalcidice in Macedonia near Torone.

Ampelusia ('Αμπελουσία : *C. Espartel*), the promontory at the W. end of the S. or African coast of the Fretum Gaditanum (*Straits of Gibraltar*). The natives of the country called it Cotes (*al Kóteis*).

Amphaxitis ('Αμφαξῖτις), a district of Mygdonia in Macedonia, at the mouths of the Axius and Echedorus.

Amphea ('Αμφεια : 'Αμφεύς), a small town of Messenia on the borders of Laconia and Messenia, conquered by the Spartans in the first Messenian war.

Amphiaraus ('Αμφιάραος), son of Oicles and Hypermnestra, daughter of Thestius, was descended on his father's side from the famous seer Melampus, and was himself a great prophet and a great hero at Argos. By his wife Eriphyle, the sister of Adrastus, he was the father of Alcmaeon, Amphilochus, Eurydice, and Demonassa. He took part in the hunt of the Calydonian boar, and in the Argonautic voyage. He also joined Adrastus in the expedition against Thebes, although he foresaw its fatal termination, through the persuasions of his wife Eriphyle, who had been induced to persuade her husband by the necklace of Harmonia which Polynices had given her. On leaving Argos, however, he enjoined his sons to punish their mother for his death. During the war against Thebes, Amphiaraus fought bravely, but could not escape his fate. Pursued by Periclymenus, he fled towards the river Ismenius, and the earth swallowed him up together with his chariot, before he was overtaken by his enemy. Zeus made him immortal, and henceforth he was worshipped as a hero, first at Oropus and afterwards in all Greece. His oracle between Potniae and Thebes, where he was said to have been swallowed up, enjoyed great celebrity. (See *Dict. of Ant.* art. *Oraculum.*) His son, Alcmaeon, is called *Amphiaraides.*

Amphicaea or **Amphiclea** ('Αμφίκαια, 'Αμφίκλεια: 'Αμφικαιεύς: *Dhadhi* or *Oglunitza?*), a town in the N. of Phocis, with an adytum of Dionysus, was called for a long time *Ophitëa* ('Οφιτεία) by command of the Amphictyons.

Amphictyon ('Αμφικτυών), a son of Deucalion and Pyrrha. Others represent him as a king of Attica, who expelled from the kingdom his father-in-law Cranaus, ruled for 12 years, and was then in turn expelled by Erichthonius. Many writers represent him as the founder of the amphictyony of Thermopylae; in consequence of this belief a sanctuary of Amphictyon was built in the village of Anthela on the Asopus, which was the most ancient place of meeting of this amphictyony.

Amphidamas ('Αμφιδάμας), son, or, according to others, brother of Lycurgus, one of the Argonauts.

Amphilochia ('Αμφιλοχία), the country of the Amphilochi ('Αμφίλοχοι), an Epirot race, at the E. end of the Ambracian gulf, usually included in Acarnania. Their chief town was ARGOS AMPHILOCHICUM.

Amphilochus ('Αμφίλοχος), son of Amphiaraus and Eriphyle, and brother of Alcmaeon. He took an active part in the expedition of the Epigoni against Thebes, assisted his brother in the murder of their mother [ALCMAEON], and afterwards fought against Troy. On his return from Troy, together with Mopsus, who was himself a seer, he founded the town of Mallos in Cilicia. Hence he proceeded to his native place, Argos, but returned to Mallos, where he was killed in single combat by Mopsus. Others relate (Thuc. ii. 68), that after leaving Argos, Amphilochus founded Argos Amphilochium on the Ambracian gulf. He was worshipped at Mallos in Cilicia, at Oropus, and at Athens.

Amphilytus ('Αμφίλυτος), a celebrated seer in the time of Pisistratus (B. c. 559), is called both an Acarnanian and an Athenian: he may have been an Acarnanian who received the franchise at Athens.

Amphimachus ('Αμφίμαχος). 1. Son of Cteatus, grandson of Poseidon, one of the four leaders of the Epeans against Troy, was slain by Hector. — 2. Son of Nomion, with his brother Nastes, led the Carians to the assistance of the Trojans, and was slain by Achilles.

Amphimalla (τὰ 'Αμφίμαλλα), a town on the N. coast of Crete, on a bay called after it (*G. of Armiro*).

Amphimedon ('Αμφιμέδων), of Ithaca, a guest-friend of Agamemnon, and a suitor of Penelope. was slain by Telemachus.

Amphion ('Αμφίων). 1. Son of Zeus and Antiope, the daughter of Nycteus of Thebes, and twin-brother of Zethus. (Ov. *Met.* vi. 110, seq.) Amphion and Zethus were born either at Eleutherae in Boeotia or on Mount Cithaeron, whither their mother had fled, and grew up among the shepherds, not knowing their descent. Hermes (according to others, Apollo, or the Muses) gave Amphion a lyre, who henceforth practised song

and music, while his brother spent his time in hunting and tending the flocks. (Hor. *Ep.* i. 18. 41.) Having become acquainted with their origin they marched against Thebes, where Lycus reigned, the husband of their mother Antiope, whom he had repudiated, and had then married Dirce in her stead. They took the city, and as Lycus and Dirce had treated their mother with great cruelty, the two brothers killed them both. They put Dirce to death by tying her to a bull, who dragged her about till she perished; and they then threw her body into a well, which was from this time called the well of Dirce. After they had obtained possession of Thebes, they fortified it by a wall. It is said, that when Amphion played his lyre, the stones moved of their own accord and formed the wall (*movit Amphion lapides canendo,* Hor. *Carm.* iii. 11). Amphion afterwards married Niobe, who bore him many sons and daughters, all of whom were killed by Apollo. His death is differently related: some say, that he killed himself from grief at the loss of his children (Ov. *Met.* vi. 270), and others tell us that he was killed by Apollo because he made an assault on the Pythian temple of the god. Amphion and his brother were buried at Thebes. The punishment inflicted upon Dirce is represented in the celebrated Farnese bull, the work of Apollonius and Tauriscus, which was discovered in 1546, and placed in the palace Farnese at Rome. — 2. Son of Jasus and father of Chloris. In Homer, this Amphion, king of Orchomenos, is distinct from Amphion, the husband of Niobe; but in earlier traditions they seem to have been regarded as the same person.

Amphipolis ('Αμφίπολις; 'Αμφιπολίτης: *Neokhorio,* in Turkish *Jeni-Kessi*), a town in Macedonia on the left or eastern bank of the Strymon, just below its egress from the lake Cercinitis, and about 3 miles from the sea. The Strymon flowed almost round the town, nearly forming a circle, whence its name Amphi-polis. It was originally called 'Εννεα ὁδοί, "the Nine Ways," and belonged to the Edonians, a Thracian people. Aristagoras of Miletus first attempted to colonize it, but was cut off with his followers by the Edonians in B. c. 497. The Athenians made a next attempt with 10,000 colonists, but they were all destroyed by the Edonians in 465. In 437 the Athenians were more successful, and drove the Edonians out of the "Nine Ways," which was henceforth called Amphipolis. It was one of the most important of the Athenian possessions, being advantageously situated for trade on a navigable river in the midst of a fertile country, and near the gold mines of M. Pangaeus. Hence the indignation of the Athenians when it fell into the hands of Brasidas (B. c. 424) and of Philip (358). Under the Romans it was a free city, and the capital of *Macedonia prima*: the Via Egnatia ran through it. The port of Amphipolis was EION.

Amphis ('Αμφις), an Athenian comic poet, of the middle comedy, contemporary with the philosopher Plato. We have the titles of 26 of his plays, and a few fragments of them.

Amphissa ('Αμφισσα: 'Αμφισσεύς, 'Αμφισσαῖος: *Salona*), one of the chief towns of the Locri Ozolae on the borders of Phocis, 7 miles from Delphi, said to have been named after Amphissa, daughter of Macareus, and beloved by Apollo. In consequence of the Sacred War declared against Amphissa by the Amphictyons, the town was destroyed by Philip, B. c. 338, but it was soon afterwards rebuilt, and under the Romans was a free state.

Amphistrătus ('Αμφίστρατος) and his brother Rhecas, the charioteers of the Dioscuri, were said to have taken part in the expedition of Jason to Colchis, and to have occupied a part of that country which was called after them *Heniochia*, as *heniochus* (ἡνίοχος) signifies a charioteer.

Amphitrītě ('Αμφιτρίτη), a Nereid or an Oceanid, wife of Poseidon and goddess of the sea, especially of the Mediterranean. In Homer Amphitrite is merely the name of the sea, and she first occurs as a goddess in Hesiod. Later poets again use the word as equivalent to the sea in general. She became by Poseidon the mother of Triton, Rhode or Rhodos, and Benthesicyme.

Amphitrŏpě ('Αμφιτρόπη: 'Αμφιτροπαιεύς), an Attic demus belonging to the tribe Antiochis, in the neighbourhood of the silver-mines of Laurium.

Amphitryon or **Amphitrŭo** ('Αμφιτρύων), son of Alcaeus, king of Tiryns, and Hipponome. Alcaeus had a brother Electryon, who reigned at Mycenae. Between Electryon and Pterelaus, king of the Taphians, a furious war raged, in which Electryon lost all his children except Licymnius, and was robbed of his oxen. Amphitryon recovered the oxen, but on his return to Mycenae accidentally killed his uncle Electryon. He was now expelled from Mycenae, together with Alcmene the daughter of Electryon, by Sthenelus the brother of Electryon, and went to Thebes, where he was purified by Creon. In order to win the hand of Alcmene, Amphitryon prepared to avenge the death of Alcmene's brothers on the Taphians, and conquered them, after Comaetho, the daughter of Pterelaus, through her love for Amphitryon, cut off the one golden hair on her father's head, which rendered him immortal. During the absence of Amphitryon from Thebes, Jupiter visited ALCMENE, who became by the god the mother of Hercules ; the latter is called *Amphitryoniades* in allusion to his reputed father. Amphitryon fell in a war against Erginus, king of the Minyans. The comedy of Plautus, called *Amphitruo*, is a ludicrous representation of the visit of Zeus to Alcmene in the disguise of her lover Amphitryon.

Amphŏtěrus ('Αμφότερος). [ACARNAN.]

Amphrÿsus ('Αμφρυσός). 1. A small river in Thessaly which flowed into the Pagasaean gulf, on the banks of which Apollo fed the herds of Admetus (*pastor ab Amphryso*, Virg. *Georg.* iii. 2).—2. See AMBRYSUS.

Ampsăga (*Wad-el-Kabir*, or *Sufjimar*), a river of N. Africa, which divided Numidia from Mauretania Sitifensis. It flows past the town of Cirta (*Constantina*).

Ampsanctus or **Amsanctus Lacus** (*Lago d'Ansanti* or *Mufiti*), a small lake in Samnium near Aeculanum, from which mephitic vapours arose. Near it was a chapel of the god Mephitis with a cavern from which mephitic vapours also came, and which was therefore regarded as an entrance to the lower world. (Virg. *Aen.* vii. 563, seq.)

Ampsivarii. [ANSIBARII.]

Ampÿcus ('Αμπυκος). 1. Son of Pelias, husband of Chloris, and father of the famous seer Mopsus, who is hence called *Ampicides*. Pausanias calls him Ampyx.—2. Son of Japetus, a bard and priest of Ceres, killed by Pettalus at the marriage of Perseus.

Ampyx. [AMPYCUS.]

Amūlius. [ROMULUS.]

Amỹclae. 1. ('Αμύκλαι: 'Αμυκλαιεύς, 'Αμυκλαῖος: *Sklavokhori* or *Aïa Kyriaki*?), an ancient town of Laconia on the Eurotas, in a beautiful country, 20 stadia S. E. of Sparta. It is mentioned in the Iliad (ii. 584), and is said to have been founded by the ancient Lacedaemonian king Amyclas, father of Hyacinthus, and to have been the abode of Tyndarus, and of Castor and Pollux, who are hence called *Amyclaei Fratres*. After the conquest of Peloponnesus by the Dorians, the Achaeans maintained themselves in Amyclae for a long time ; and it was only shortly before the first Messenian war that the town was taken and destroyed by the Lacedaemonians under Teleclus. The tale ran that the inhabitants had been so often alarmed by false reports of the approach of the enemy, that they passed a law that no one should speak of the enemy ; and accordingly when the Lacedaemonians at last came, and no one dared to announce their approach, " Amyclae perished through silence : " hence arose the proverb *Amyclis ipsis taciturnior*. After its destruction by the Lacedaemonians Amyclae became a village, and was only memorable by the festival of the Hyacinthia (see *Dict. of Ant. s. v.*) celebrated at the place annually, and by the temple and colossal statue of Apollo, who was hence called *Amyclaeus*.—2. (Amyclanus), an ancient town of Latium, E. of Terracina, on the Sinus Amyclanus, was, according to tradition, an Achaean colony from Laconia. In the time of Augustus the town had disappeared ; the inhabitants were said to have deserted it on account of its being infested by serpents ; whence Virgil (*Aen.* x. 564) speaks of *tacitae Amyclae*, though some commentators suppose that he transfers to this town the epithet belonging to the Amyclae in Laconia [No. 1]. Near Amyclae was the Spelunca (*Sperlonga*), or natural grotto, a favourite retreat of the emperor Tiberius.

Amỹclas. [AMYCLAE.]

Amỹclides, a name of Hyacinthus, as the son of Amyclas.

Amỹcus ('Αμυκος), son of Poseidon and Bithynia, king of the Bebryces, was celebrated for his skill in boxing, and used to challenge strangers to box with him. When the Argonauts came to his dominions, Pollux accepted the challenge and killed him.

Amymōně ('Αμυμώνη), one of the daughters of Danaus and Elephantis. When Danaus arrived in Argos, the country was suffering from a drought and Danaus sent out Amymone to fetch water. She was attacked by a satyr, but was rescued from his violence by Poseidon, who appropriated her to himself, and then showed her the wells at Lerna. According to another account he bade her draw his trident from the rock, from which a threefold spring gushed forth, which was called after her the well and river of Amymone. Her son by Poseidon was called Nauplius.

Amynander ('Αμύνανδρος), king of the Athamanes in Epirus, an ally of the Romans in their war with Philip of Macedonia, about B. C. 198, but an ally of Antiochus, B. C. 189.

Amyntas ('Αμύντας). 1. I. King of Macedonia, reigned from about B. C. 540 to 500, and was succeeded by his son Alexander I.—2. II. King of Macedonia, son of Philip, the brother of Perdiccas II., reigned B. C. 393—369, and obtained the crown by the murder of the usurper Pausanias. Soon after his accession he was driven from Macedonia by the Illyrians, but was restored to his kingdom by the Thessalians. On his return he was engaged in war with the Olynthians, in which he was assisted by the Spartans, and by their aid Olynthus was reduced in 379. Amyntas united himself also with Jason of Pherae, and carefully cultivated the friendship of Athens. Amyntas left by his wife Eurydice three sons, Alexander, Perdiccas, and the famous Philip. — 3. Grandson of Amyntas II., was excluded by Philip from the succession on the death of his father Perdiccas III. in B. c. 360. He was put to death in the first year of the reign of Alexander the Great, 336, for a plot against the king's life. — 4. A Macedonian officer in Alexander's army, son of Andromenes. He and his brothers were accused of being privy to the conspiracy of Philotas in 330, but were acquitted. Some little time after he was killed at the siege of a village. — 5. A Macedonian traitor, son of Antiochus, took refuge at the court of Darius, and became one of the commanders of the Greek mercenaries. He was present at the battle of Issus (B. c. 333), and afterwards fled to Egypt, where he was put to death by Mazaces, the Persian governor. — 6. A king of Galatia, supported Antony, and fought on his side against Augustus at the battle of Actium (B. c. 31). He fell in an expedition against the town of Homonada or Homona. — 7. A Greek writer of a work entitled *Stathmi* (Σταθμοί), probably an account of the different halting-places of Alexander the Great in his Asiatic expedition.

Amyntor ('Αμύντωρ), son of Ormenus of Eleon in Thessaly, where Autolycus broke into his house, and father of PHOENIX, whom he cursed on account of unlawful intercourse with his mistress. According to Apollodorus he was a king of Ormenium, and was slain by Hercules, to whom he refused a passage through his dominions, and the hand of his daughter ASTYDAMIA. According to Ovid (*Met.* xii. 364) he was king of the Dolopes.

Amyrtaeus ('Αμυρταῖος), an Egyptian, assumed the title of king, and joined Inarus the Libyan in the revolt against the Persians in B. c. 460. They at first defeated the Persians [ACHAEMENES], but were subsequently totally defeated, 455. Amyrtaeus escaped, and maintained himself as king in the marshy districts of Lower Egypt till about 414, when the Egyptians expelled the Persians, and Amyrtaeus reigned 6 years.

Amyrus ('Άμυρος), a river in Thessaly, with a town of the same name upon it, flowing into the lake Boebeis: the country around was called the 'Αμύρικὸν πεδίον.

Amythāon ('Αμυθάων), son of Cretheus and Tyro, father of Bias and of the seer Melampus, who is hence called *Amythāōnius* (Virg. *Georg.* iii. 550). He dwelt at Pylus in Messenia, and is mentioned among those to whom the restoration of the Olympian games was ascribed.

Anābon ('Άνάβων), a district of the Persian province of Aria, S. of Aria Proper, containing 4 towns, which still exist, Phra (*Ferrah*), Bis (*Beest* or *Bost*), Gari (*Ghore*), Nii (*Neh*).

Anāces ("Άνακες). [ANAX, No. 2.]

Anacharsis ('Ανάχαρσις), a Scythian of princely rank, left his native country to travel in pursuit of knowledge, and came to Athens, about B. c. 594. He became acquainted with Solon, and by his ta-

lents and acute observations, he excited general admiration. The fame of his wisdom was such, that he was even reckoned by some among the seven sages. He was killed by his brother Saulius on his return to his native country. Cicero (*Tusc. Disp.* v. 32) quotes from one of his letters, of which several, but spurious, are still extant.

Anacreōn ('Ανακρέων), a celebrated lyric poet, born at Teos, an Ionian city in Asia Minor. He removed from his native city, with the great body of its inhabitants, to Abdera, in Thrace, when Teos was taken by the Persians (about B. c. 540), but lived chiefly at Samos, under the patronage of Polycrates, in whose praise he wrote many songs. After the death of Polycrates (522), he went to Athens at the invitation of the tyrant Hipparchus, where he became acquainted with Simonides and other poets. He died at the age of 85, probably about 478, but the place of his death is uncertain. The universal tradition of antiquity represents Anacreon as a consummate voluptuary ; and his poems prove the truth of the tradition. He sings of love and wine with hearty good will ; and we see in him the luxury of the Ionian inflamed by the fervour of the poet. The tale that he loved Sappho is very improbable. Of his poems only a few genuine fragments have come down to us ; for the "Odes" attributed to him are now admitted to be spurious. — *Editions*: by Fischer, Lips. 1793 ; Bergk, Lips. 1834.

Anactōrium ('Ανακτόριον ; 'Ανακτόριος), a town in Acarnania, built by the Corinthians, upon a promontory of the same name (near *La Madonna*) at the entrance of the Ambracian gulf. Its inhabitants were removed by Augustus after the battle of Actium (B. c. 31) to Nicopolis.

Anădyŏmēnē ('Αναδυομένη), the goddess rising out of the sea, a surname given to Aphrodite, in allusion to the story of her being born from the foam of the sea. This surname had not much celebrity before the time of Apelles, but his famous painting of Aphrodite Anadyomene excited the emulation of other artists, painters as well as sculptors. [APELLES.]

Anagnia (Anagninus: *Anagni*), an ancient town of Latium, the chief town of the Hernici, and subsequently both a municipium and a Roman colony. It lay in a very beautiful and fertile country on a hill, at the foot of which the *Via Lavicana* and *Via Praenestina* united (*Compitum Anagninum*). In the neighbourhood Cicero had a beautiful estate, *Anagninum* (sc. *praedium*).

Anagyrūs ('Αναγυροῦς, -οῦντος : 'Αναγυράσιος, 'Αναγυρουντόθεν : nr. *Vari*, Ru.), a demus of Attica, belonging to the tribe Erectheis, not, as some say, Aeantis, S. of Athens, near the promontory Zoster.

Anaïtica ('Αναϊτική), a district of Armenia, in which the goddess Anaïtis was worshipped ; also called Acilisene.

Anaïtis ('Αναῖτις), an Asiatic divinity, whose name is also written *Anaea*, *Aneitis*, *Tanaïs*, or *Nanaea*. Her worship prevailed in Armenia, Cappadocia, Assyria, Persia. &c., and seems to have been a part of the worship so common among the Asiatics, of the creative powers of nature, both male and female. The Greek writers sometimes identify Anaitis with Artemis, and sometimes with Aphrodite.

Anamari or -res, a Gallic people in the plain of the Po, in whose land the Romans founded Placentia.

Anānes, a Gallic people, W. of the Trebia, between the Po and the Apennines.

Ananĭus ('Aνάνιος), a Greek iambic poet, contemporary with Hipponax, about B. C. 540.

Anăphē ('Aνάφη: 'Aναφαῖος : *Anaphi, Nanfio*), a small island in the S. of the Aegean sea, E. of Thera, with a temple of Apollo Aegletes, who was hence called *Anaphaeus.*

Anaphlystus ('Aνάφλυστος: 'Aναφλύστιος : *Anavyso*), an Attic demus of the tribe Antiochis on the S. W. coast of Attica, opposite the island Eleussa, called after Anaphlystus, son of Poseidon.

Anāpus ("Aναπος). 1. A river in Acarnania, flowing into the Achelous.—2. (*Anapo*), a river in Sicily, flowing into the sea S. of Syracuse through the marshes of Lysimelīa.

Anartes or -ti, a people of Dacia, N. of the Theiss.

Anas ("Aνας : *Guadiana*), one of the chief rivers of Spain, rises in Celtiberia in the mountains near Laminium, forms the boundary between Lusitania and Baetica, and flows into the ocean by two mouths (now only one).

Anatŏlĭus. 1. Bishop of Laodicea, A. D. 270, an Alexandrian by birth, was the author of several mathematical and arithmetical works, of which some fragments have been preserved.—2. An eminent jurist, was a native of Berytus, and afterwards P. P. (*praefectus praetorio*) of Illyricum. He died A. D. 361. A work on agriculture, often cited in the Geoponica, and a treatise *concerning Sympathies and Antipathies*, are assigned by many to this Anatolius. The latter work, however, was probably written by Anatolius the philosopher, who was the master of Iamblichus, and to whom Porphyry addressed *Homeric Questions.*—3. Professor of law at Berytus, is mentioned by Justinian among those who were employed in compiling the Digest. He wrote notes on the Digest, and a very concise commentary on Justinian's Code. Both of these works are cited in the Basilica. He perished A. D. 557, in an earthquake at Byzantium, whither he had removed from Berytus.

Anaurus ('Aναυρός), a river of Thessaly flowing into the Pagasaean gulf.

Anāva ('Aνανα), an ancient, but early decayed, city of Great Phrygia, on the salt lake of the same name, between Celaenae and Colossae (*Hages Ghiosel*).

Anax ("Aναξ). 1. A giant, son of Uranus and Gaea, and father of Asterius.—2. An epithet of the gods in general, characterising them as the rulers of the world ; but the plural forms, "Aνακες, or "Aνακτες, or "Aνακες παῖδες, were used to designate the Dioscuri.

Anaxăgŏras ('Aναξαγόρας), a celebrated Greek philosopher of the Ionian school, was born at Clazomenae in Ionia, B. C. 500. He gave up his property to his relations, as he intended to devote his life to higher ends, and went to Athens at the age of 20; here he remained 30 years, and became the intimate friend and teacher of the most eminent men of the time, such as Euripides and Pericles. His doctrines gave offence to the religious feelings of the Athenians; and the enemies of Pericles availed themselves of this circumstance to accuse him of impiety, B. C. 450. It was only through the eloquence of Pericles that he was not put to death ; but he was sentenced to pay a fine of 5 talents and to quit Athens. He retired to Lampsacus, where he died in 428, at the age of 72. Anaxa-

goras was dissatisfied with the systems of his predecessors, the Ionic philosophers, and struck into a new path. The Ionic philosophers had endeavoured to explain nature and its various phenomena by regarding matter in its different forms and modifications as the cause of all things. Anaxagoras, on the other hand, conceived the necessity of seeking a higher cause, independent of matter, and this cause he considered to be *nous* (νοῦς), that is, mind, thought, or intelligence.

Anaxander ('Aνάξανδρος), king of Sparta, son of Eurycrates, fought in the 2nd Messenian war, about B. C. 668.

Anaxandrĭdes ('Aναξανδρίδης). 1. Son of Theopompus, king of Sparta. — 2. King of Sparta, son of Leon, reigned from about B. C. 560 to 520. Having a barren wife whom he would not divorce, the ephors made him take with her a second. By her he had Cleomenes ; and after this by his first wife Dorieus, Leonidas, and Cleombrotus.— 3. An Athenian comic poet of the middle comedy, a native of Camirus in Rhodes, began to exhibit comedies in B. C. 376. Aristotle held him in high esteem.

Anaxarchus ('Aνάξαρχος), a philosopher of Abdera, of the school of Democritus, accompanied Alexander into Asia (B. C. 334), and gained his favour by flattery and wit. After the death of Alexander (323), Anaxarchus was thrown by shipwreck into the power of Nicocreon, king of Cyprus, to whom he had given mortal offence, and who had him pounded to death in a stone mortar.

Anaxarĕte ('Aναξαρέτη), a maiden of Cyprus, remained unmoved by the love of Iphis, who at last, in despair, hung himself at her door. She looked with indifference at the funeral of the youth, but Venus changed her into a stone statue.

Anaxĭbĭa ('Aναξιβία), daughter of Plisthenes, sister of Agamemnon, wife of Strophius, and mother of Pylades.

Anaxĭbĭus ('Aναξίβιος), the Spartan admiral stationed at Byzantium on the return of the Cyrean Greeks from Asia, B. C. 400. In 389 he succeeded Dercyllidas in the command in the Aegaean, but fell in a battle against Iphicrates, near Antandrus, in 388.

Anaxĭdāmus ('Aναξίδαμος), king of Sparta, son of Zeuxidamus, lived to the conclusion of the 2nd Messenian war, B. C. 668.

Anaxĭlāus ('Aναξίλαος) or **Anaxĭlas** ('Aναξίλας). 1. Tyrant of Rhegium, of Messenian origin, took possession of Zancle in Sicily about B. C. 494, peopled it with fresh inhabitants, and changed its name into Messene. He died in 476.—2. Of Byzantium, surrendered Byzantium to the Athenians in B. C. 408.—3. An Athenian comic poet of the middle comedy, contemporary with Plato and Demosthenes. We have a few fragments, and the titles of 19 of his comedies. — 4. A physician and Pythagorean philosopher, born at Larissa, was banished by Augustus from Italy, B. C. 28, on the charge of magic.

Anaximander ('Aναξίμανδρος), of Miletus, was born B. C. 610 and died 547, in his 64th year. He was one of the earliest philosophers of the Ionian school, and the immediate successor of Thales, its first founder. He first used the word ἀρχή to denote the origin of things, or rather the material out of which they were formed : he held that this ἀρχή was the infinite (τὸ ἄπειρον), everlasting, and divine, though not attributing to it a spiritual or intelligent nature; and that it was the sub-

Alexander Zebina, King of Syria, B.C. 128—122. Page 37.

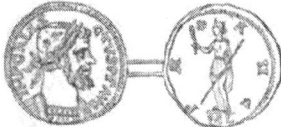

Antigonus Gonatas, King of Macedonia, B.C. 243—239. Page 54.

Allectus, Roman Emperor, A.D. 293—296. Page 39.

Antinous, favourite of Hadrian, ob. A.D. 122. Page 54.

Amastris, Queen of Heracleia, ob. B.C. 288. Page 42.

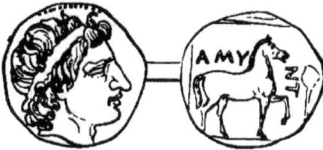

Antiochus I. Soter, King of Syria, B.C. 280—261. Page 55.

Amyntas II., King of Macedonia, B.C. 393—369. Page 46.

Antiochus II. Theos, King of Syria, B.C. 261—246. Page 55.

Amyntas, King of Galatia. Page 47. No. 6.

Antiochus III. the Great, King of Syria, B.C. 223—187. Page 55.

Antigonus, King of Asia, ob. B.C. 301. Page 54.

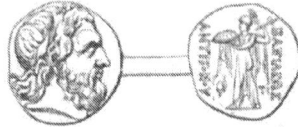

Antiochus IV. Epiphanes, King of Syria, B.C. 175—164. Page 55.

[To face p. 48.

Antiochus V. Eupator, King of Syria, B.C. 164—162.
Page 56.

Antiochus VI. Theos, King of Syria, B.C. 144—142.
Page 56.

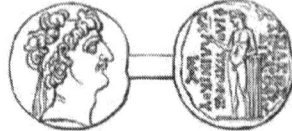

Antiochus VII. Sidetes, King of Syria, B.C. 137—128.
Page 56.

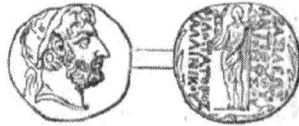

Antiochus VIII. Grypus, King of Syria, B.C. 125—96.
Page 56.

Antiochus IX. Cyzicenus, King of Syria, B.C. 112—96.
Page 56.

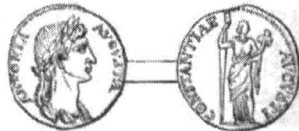

Antiochus X. Eusebes, King of Syria, B.C. 95. Page 56.

To face p. 49.]

Antiochus XI. Epiphanes, King of Syria. Page 56.

Antiochus XII. Dionysus, King of Syria. Page 56.

Antiochus XIII. Asiaticus, King of Syria, B.C. 69—65.
Page 56.

Antiochus IV., King of Commagene, A.D. 38—72. Page 56.

Antonia Minor, mother of Germanicus. Page 56.

Antoninus Pius, Roman Emperor, A.D. 138—161. Page 56.

stance into which all things were resolved on their dissolution. He was a careful observer of nature, and was distinguished by his astronomical, mathematical, and geographical knowledge: he is said to have introduced the use of the Gnomon into Greece.

Anaximēnes ('Αναξιμένης). 1. Of Miletus, the third in the series of Ionian philosophers, flourished about B. C. 544; but as he was the teacher of Anaxagoras. B. C. 480, he must have lived to a great age. He considered air to be the first cause of all things, the primary form, as it were, of matter, into which the other elements of the universe were resolvable.—2. Of Lampsacus, accompanied Alexander the Great to Asia (B.C. 334), and wrote a history of Philip of Macedonia; a history of Alexander the Great; and a history of Greece in 12 books, from the earliest mythical ages down to the death of Epaminondas. He also enjoyed great reputation as a rhetorician, and is the author of a scientific treatise on rhetoric, the Ῥητορική πρὸς 'Αλέξανδρον, usually printed among the works of Aristotle. He was an enemy of Theophrastus, and published under the name of the latter a work calumniating Sparta, Athens, and Thebes, which produced great exasperation against Theophrastus.

Anazarbus or -a ('Αναζαρβός or -d: 'Αναζαρβεύς, Anazarbēnus: *Anasarba* or *Naversa*, Ru.), a considerable city of Cilicia Campestris, on the left bank of the river Pyramus, at the foot of a mountain of the same name. Augustus conferred upon it the name of Caesarea (ad Anazarbum); and, on the division of Cilicia into the two provinces of Prima and Secunda, it was made the capital of the latter. It was almost destroyed by earthquakes in the reigns of Justinian and Justin.

Ancaeus ('Αγκαῖος). 1. Son of the Arcadian Lycurgus and Creophile or Eurynome, and father of Agapenor. He was one of the Argonauts, and took part in the Calydonian hunt, in which he was killed by the boar.—2. Son of Poseidon and Astypalaea or Alta, king of the Leleges in Samos, husband of Samia, and father of Perilaus, Enodos, Samos, Alitherses, and Parthenope. He seems to have been confounded by some mythographers with Ancaeus, the son of Lycurgus. The son of Poseidon is also represented as one of the Argonauts, and is said to have become the helmsman of the ship Argo after the death of Tiphys. A well-known proverb is said to have originated with this Ancaeus. He had been told by a seer that he would not live to taste the wine of his vineyard; and when he was afterwards on the point of drinking a cup of wine, the growth of his own vineyard, he laughed at the seer, who, however, answered, πολλὰ μεταξὺ κύλικός τε καὶ χειλέων ἄκρων, "There is many a slip between the cup and the lip." At the same instant Ancaeus was informed that a wild boar was near. He put down his cup, went out against the animal, and was killed by it.

Ancalites, a people of Britain, probably a part of the **Atrebates**.

Q. Ancharius, tribune of the plebs, B. C. 59, took an active part in opposing the agrarian law of Caesar. He was praetor in 56; and succeeded L. Piso in the province of Macedonia.

Anchesmus ('Αγχεσμός), a hill not far from Athens, with a temple of Zeus, who was hence called *Anchesmius*.

Anchĭălē and -lus ('Αγχιάλη). 1. (*Akiali*), a town in Thrace on the Black Sea, on the borders

of Moesia.—2. Also **Anchialos**, an ancient city of Cilicia, W. of the Cydnus near the coast, said to have been built by Sardanapalus.

Anchises ('Αγχίσης), son of Capys and Themis, the daughter of Ilus, king of Dardanus on Mount Ida. In beauty he equalled the immortal gods, and was beloved by Aphrodite, by whom he became the father of Aeneas, who is hence called *Anchisiades*. The goddess warned him never to betray the real mother of the child; but as on one occasion he boasted of his intercourse with the goddess, he was struck by a flash of lightning, which according to some traditions killed, but according to others only blinded or lamed him. Virgil in his Aeneid makes Anchises survive the capture of Troy, and Aeneas carries his father on his shoulders from the burning city. He further relates that Anchises died soon after the first arrival of Aeneas in Sicily, and was buried on mount Eryx. This tradition seems to have been believed in Sicily, for Anchises had a sanctuary at Egesta, and the funeral games celebrated in Sicily in his honour continued down to a late period.

Anchisia ('Αγχισία), a mountain in Arcadia, N. W. of Mantinea, where Anchises is said to have been buried, according to one tradition.

Ancon (Λευκοσύρων 'Αγκών), a harbour and town at the mouth of the river Iris (*Yeshil-ermark*) in Pontus.

Ancōna or **Ancon** ('Αγκών: Anconitānus: *Ancona*), a town in Picenum on the Adriatic sea, lying in a bend of the coast between two promontories, and hence called *Ancon* or an "elbow." It was built by the Syracusans, who settled there about B. C. 392, discontented with the rule of the elder Dionysius; and under the Romans, who made it a colony, it became one of the most important seaports of the Adriatic. It possessed an excellent harbour, completed by Trajan, and it carried on an active trade with the opposite coast of Illyricum. The town was celebrated for its temple of Venus and its purple dye: the surrounding country produced good wine and wheat.

Ancorārius Mons, a mountain in Mauretania Caesariensis, S. of Caesarea, abounding in citron trees, the wood of which was used by the Romans for furniture.

Andöre. [**Nicaea**.]

Ancus Marcius, fourth king of Rome, reigned 24 years, B. C. 640—616, and is said to have been the son of Numa's daughter. He conquered the Latins, took many Latin towns, transported the inhabitants to Rome, and gave them the Aventine to dwell on: these conquered Latins formed the original Plebs. He also founded a colony at Ostia, at the mouth of the Tiber; built a fortress on the Janiculum as a protection against Etruria, and united it with the city by a bridge across the Tiber; dug the ditch of the Quirites, which was a defence for the open ground between the Caelian and the Palatine; and built a prison. He was succeeded by Tarquinius Priscus.

Ancyra ('Αγκύρα: 'Αγκυρανός, Ancyrānus). 1. (*Angora*), a city of Galatia in Asia Minor, in 39° 56′ N. lat. In the time of Augustus, when Galatia became a Roman province, Ancyra was the capital: it was originally the chief city of a Gallic tribe named the Tectosages, who came from the S. of France. Under the Roman empire it had the name of Sebaste, which in Greek is equivalent to Augusta in Latin. When Augustus recorded the

E

chief events of his life on bronze tablets at Rome, the citizens of Ancyra had a copy made, which was cut on marble blocks and placed at Ancyra in a temple dedicated to Augustus and Rome. This inscription is called the *Monumentum Ancyranum*. The Latin inscription was first copied by Tournefort in 1701, and it has been copied several times since. One of the latest copies has been made by Mr. Hamilton, who also copied as much of the Greek inscription as is legible. — 2. A town in Phrygia Epictetus on the borders of Mysia.

Andānĭa ('Ανδανία: 'Ανδανιεύς, 'Ανδάνιος), a town in Messenia, between Megalopolis and Messene, the capital of the kings of the race of the Leleges, abandoned by its inhabitants in the second Messenian war, and from that time only a village.

Andĕcăvi, Andĕgăvi, or Andes, a Gallic people N. of the Loire, with a town of the same name, also called Juliomagus, now *Angers*.

Andematunnum. [LINGONES.]

Andēra (τὰ 'Άνδειρα: 'Ανδειρηνός), a city of Mysia, celebrated for its temple of Cybele surnamed 'Ανδειρηνή.

Anderĭtum (*Anterieux*), a town of the Gabali in Aquitania.

Andes. 1. See ANDECAVI.—2. (*Pietola*), a village near Mantua, the birth-place of Virgil.

Andŏcĭdes ('Ανδοκίδης), one of the ten Attic orators, son of Leogoras, was born at Athens in B. C. 467. He belonged to a noble family, and was a supporter of the oligarchical party at Athens. In 436 he was one of the commanders of the fleet sent by the Athenians to the assistance of the Corcyreans against the Corinthians. In 415 he became involved in the charge brought against Alcibiades for having profaned the mysteries and mutilated the Hermae, and was thrown into prison; but he recovered his liberty by promising to reveal the names of the real perpetrators of the crime. He is said to have denounced his own father among others, but to have rescued him again in the hour of danger. But as Andocides was unable to clear himself entirely, he was deprived of his rights as a citizen, and left Athens. He returned to Athens on the establishment of the government of the Four Hundred in 411, but was soon obliged to fly again. In the following year he ventured once more to return to Athens, and it was at this time that he delivered the speech still extant, *On his Return*, in which he petitioned for permission to reside at Athens, but in vain. He was thus driven into exile a third time, and went to reside at Elis. In 403 he again returned to Athens upon the overthrow of the tyranny of the Thirty by Thrasybulus, and the proclamation of the general amnesty. He was now allowed to remain quietly at Athens for the next 3 years, but in 400 his enemies accused him of having profaned the mysteries: he defended himself in the oration still extant, *On the Mysteries*, and was acquitted. In 394 he was sent as ambassador to Sparta to conclude a peace, and on his return in 393 he was accused of illegal conduct during his embassy (παραπρεσβείας); he defended himself in the extant speech *On the Peace with Lacedaemon*, but was found guilty, and sent into exile for the fourth time. He seems to have died soon afterwards in exile. Besides the three orations already mentioned there is a fourth against Alcibiades, said to have been delivered in 415, but which is in all probability spurious. —

Editions. In the collections of the Greek orators: also separately by Baiter and Sauppe, Zürich, 1838.

Andraemon ('Ανδραίμων). 1. Husband of Gorge, daughter of Oeneus king of Calydon, in Aetolia, whom he succeeded, and father of Thoas, who is hence called *Andraemonides*.—2. Son of Oxylus, and husband of Dryope, who was mother of Amphissus by Apollo.

Andriscus ('Ανδρίσκος), a man of low origin, who pretended to be a natural son of Perseus, king of Macedonia, was seized by Demetrius, king of Syria, and sent to Rome. He escaped from Rome, assumed the name of Philip, and obtained possession of Macedonia, B. C. 149. He defeated the praetor Juventius, but was conquered by Caecilius Metellus, and taken to Rome to adorn the triumph of the latter, 148.

Andrŏcles ('Ανδροκλῆς), an Athenian demagogue and orator. He was an enemy of Alcibiades; and it was chiefly owing to his exertions that Alcibiades was banished. After this event, Androcles was for a time at the head of the democratical party; but in B. C. 411 he was put to death by the oligarchical government of the Four Hundred.

Andrŏclus, the slave of a Roman consular, was sentenced to be exposed to the wild beasts in the circus; but a lion which was let loose upon him, instead of springing upon his victim, exhibited signs of recognition, and began licking him. Upon inquiry it appeared that Androclus had been compelled by the severity of his master, while in Africa, to run away from him. Having one day taken refuge in a cave from the heat of the sun, a lion entered, apparently in great pain, and seeing him, went up to him and held out his paw. Androclus found that a large thorn had pierced it, which he drew out, and the lion was soon able to use his paw again. They lived together for some time in the cave, the lion catering for his benefactor. But at last, tired of this savage life, Androclus left the cave, was apprehended by some soldiers, brought to Rome, and condemned to the wild beasts. He was pardoned, and presented with the lion, which he used to lead about the city.

Andrŏgĕŏs ('Ανδρόγεως), son of Minos and Pasiphaë, or Crete, conquered all his opponents in the games of the Panathenaea at Athens. This extraordinary good luck, however, became the cause of his destruction, though the mode of his death is related differently. According to some accounts Aegeus sent the man he dreaded to fight against the Marathonian bull, who killed him; according to others, he was assassinated by his defeated rivals on his road to Thebes, whither he was going to take part in a solemn contest. A third account related that he was assassinated by Aegeus himself. Minos made war on the Athenians in consequence of the death of his son, and imposed upon them the shameful tribute, from which they were delivered by THESEUS. He was worshipped in Attica as a hero, and games were celebrated in his honour every year in the Ceramicus. (*Dict. of Ant.* art. *Androgeonia.*)

Andrŏmăchē ('Ανδρομάχη), daughter of Eëtion, king of the Cilician Thebes, and one of the noblest and most amiable female characters in the Iliad. Her father and her 7 brothers were slain by Achilles at the taking of Thebes, and her mother, who had purchased her freedom by a large ransom, was killed by Artemis. She was married to Hector, by whom she had a son Scamandrius (Astyanax), and for whom she entertained the most tender love. On the taking of Troy her son was hurled from the wall of the city, and she herself fell to the share of Neoptolemus (Pyrrhus), the son of Achilles, who took her to Epirus, and to whom she bore 3 sons, Molossus, Pielus, and Pergamus. She afterwards married Helenus, a brother of Hector, who ruled over Chaonia, a part of Epirus, and to whom she bore Cestrinus. After the death of Helenus, she followed her son Pergamus to Asia, where an heroum was erected to her.

Andrŏmăchus ('Ανδρόμαχος). 1. Ruler of Tauromenium in Sicily about B. C. 344, and father of the historian Timaeus.—2. Of Crete, physician to the emperor Nero, A. D. 54—68; was the first person on whom the title of *Archiater* was conferred, and was celebrated as the inventor of a famous compound medicine and antidote called *Theriaca Andromachi*, which retains its place in some foreign Pharmacopoeias to the present day. Andromachus has left the directions for making this mixture in a Greek elegiac poem, consisting of 174 lines, edited by Tidicaeus, Tiguri, 1607, and Leinker, Norimb. 1754.

Andrŏmĕda ('Ανδρομέδη), daughter of the Aethiopian king, Cepheus and Cassiopēa. Her mother boasted that the beauty of her daughter surpassed that of the Nereids, who prevailed on Poseidon to visit the country by an inundation, and a sea-monster. The oracle of Ammon promised deliverance if Andromeda was given up to the monster; and Cepheus, obliged to yield to the wishes of his people, chained Andromeda to a rock. Here she was found and saved by Perseus, who slew the monster and obtained her as his wife. Andromeda had previously been promised to Phineus, and this gave rise to the famous fight of Phineus and Perseus at the wedding, in which the former and all his associates were slain. (Ov. *Met.* v. 1, seq.) After her death, she was placed among the stars.

Andronicus ('Ανδρονίκος). 1. *Cyrrhestes,* so called from his native place, Cyrrha, probably lived about B. C. 100, and built the octagonal tower at Athens, vulgarly called " the tower of the winds " (see *Dict. of Ant.* p. 616, 2d ed., where a drawing of the building is given).—2. **Livius Andronicus**, the earliest Roman poet, was a Greek, probably a native of Tarentum, and the slave of M. Livius Salinator, by whom he was manumitted, and from whom he received the Roman name Livius. He obtained at Rome a perfect knowledge of the Latin language. He wrote both tragedies and comedies in Latin, and we still possess the titles and fragments of at least 14 of his dramas, all of which were borrowed from the Greek: his first drama was acted in B. C. 240. He also wrote an *Odyssey* in the Saturnian verse and *Hymns.* (See Düntzer, *Livii Andronici Fragmenta collecta, &c.* Berlin, 1835.)—3. Of **Rhodes**, a Peripatetic philosopher at Rome, about B. C. 58. He published a new edition of the works of Aristotle and Theophrastus, which formerly belonged to the library of Apellicon, and which were brought to Rome by Sulla with the rest of Apellicon's library in B. C. 84. Tyrannio commenced this task, but apparently did not do much towards it. The arrangement which Andronicus made of Aristotle's writings seems to be the one which forms the basis of our present editions. He wrote many commentaries upon the works of Aristotle;

but none of these is extant, for the paraphrase of the Nicomachean Ethics, which is ascribed to Andronicus of Rhodes, was written by some one else, and may have been the work of Andronicus Callistus of Thessalonica, who was professor in Italy, in the latter half of the 15th century.

Andrŏpŏlis ('Ανδρῶν πόλις: *Chabur*), a city of Lower Egypt, on the W. bank of the Canopic branch of the Nile, was the capital of the Nomos Andropolites, and, under the Romans, the station of a legion.

Andros ("Ανδρος: "Ανδριος: *Andro*), the most northerly and one of the largest islands of the Cyclades, S. E. of Euboea, 21 miles long and 8 broad, early attained importance, and colonised Acanthus and Stagira about B. C. 654. It was taken by the Persians in their invasion of Greece, was afterwards subject to the Athenians, at a later time to the Macedonians, and at length to Attalus III., king of Pergamus, on whose death (B. C. 133) it passed with the rest of his dominions to the Romans. It was celebrated for its wine, whence the whole island was regarded as sacred to Dionysus. Its chief town, also called Andros, contained a celebrated temple of Dionysus, and a harbour of the name of Gaureleon, and a fort Gaurion.

Andrŏtĭon ('Ανδροτίων). 1. An Athenian orator, and a contemporary of Demosthenes, against whom the latter delivered an oration, which is still extant.—2. The author of an Atthis, or a work on the history of Attica.

Anemōrēa, afterwards **Anemōlēa** ('Ανεμωρεια, 'Ανεμώλεια: 'Ανεμωριεύς), a town on a hill on the borders of Phocis and Delphi.

Anemūrium ('Ανεμούριον: *Anamur,* Ru.), a town and promontory at the S. point of Cilicia, opposite to Cyprus.

Angerŏna or **Angerŏnĭa**, a Roman goddess, respecting whom we have different statements, some representing her as the goddess of silence, others as the goddess of anguish and fear, that is, the goddess who not only produces this state of mind, but also relieves men from it. Her statue stood in the temple of Volupia, with her mouth bound and sealed up. Her festival, *Angeronalia,* was celebrated yearly on the 12th of December.

Angites ('Αγγίτης: *Anghista*), a river in Macedonia, flowing into the Strymon.

Angitia or **Anguitia**, a goddess worshipped by the Marsians and Marrubians, who lived about the shores of the lake Fucinus.

Angli or **Anglii**, a German people of the race of the Suevi, on the left bank of the Elbe, afterwards passed over with the Saxons into Britain, which was called after them England. [SAXONES.] A portion of them appear to have settled in *Angeln* in Schleswig.

Angrivarii, a German people dwelling on both sides of the Visurgis (*Weser*), separated from the Cherusci by an agger or mound of earth. The name is usually derived from *Angern,* that is, meadows. They were generally on friendly terms with the Romans, but rebelled in A. D. 16, and were subdued. Towards the end of the first century they extended their territories southwards, and in conjunction with the Chamavi, took possession of part of the territory of the Bructeri, S. and E. of the Lippe, the Angaria or Engern of the middle ages.

Anicetus, a freedman of Nero, and formerly his tutor, was employed by the emperor in the execu-

E 2

tion of many of his crimes: he was afterwards banished to Sardinia where he died.

Anīcīus Gallus. [GALLUS.]

Anīgrus ('Ανιγρος: *Mauro-Potamo*), a small river in the Triphylian Elis, the *Minyeius* (Μινυήϊος) of Homer (*Il.* xi. 721), rises in M. Lapithas, and flows into the Ionian sea near Samicum: its waters have a disagreeable smell, and its fish are not eatable. Near Samicum was a cave sacred to the Nymphs *Anigrides* ('Ανιγρίδες or 'Ανιγρίδες), where persons with cutaneous diseases were cured by the waters of the river.

Anīo, anciently **Anīen** (hence Gen. Aniĕnis: *Teverone* or *l'Aniene*), a river, the most celebrated of the tributaries of the Tiber, rises in the mountains of the Hernici near Treba (*Trevi*), flows first N.W. and then S.W. through narrow mountain-valleys, receives the brook Digentia (*Licenza*) above Tibur, forms at Tibur beautiful water-falls (hence *praeceps Anio*, Hor. *Carm.* i. 7. 13), and flows, forming the boundary between Latium and the land of the Sabines, into the Tiber, 3 miles above Rome, where the town of Antemnae stood. The water of the Anio was conveyed to Rome by two Aqueducts, the *Anio vetus* and *Anio novus*. (See *Dict. of Ant.* pp. 110, 111, 2d ed.)

Anīus ('Ανιος), son of Apollo by Creüsa, or Rhoeo, and priest of Apollo at Delos. By Dryope he had three daughters, Oeno, Spermo, and Elais, to whom Dionysus gave the power of producing at will any quantity of wine, corn, and oil, — whence they were called *Oenotrōpae*. With these necessaries they are said to have supplied the Greeks during the first 9 years of the Trojan war. After the fall of Troy, Aeneas was kindly received by Anius.

Anna, daughter of Belus and sister of Dido. After the death of the latter, she fled from Carthage to Italy, where she was kindly received by Aeneas. Here she excited the jealousy of Lavinia, and being warned in a dream by Dido, she fled and threw herself into the river Numicius. Henceforth she was worshipped as the nymph of that river under the name of ANNA PERENNA. There are various other stories respecting the origin of her worship. Ovid relates that she was considered by some as Luna, by others as Themis, by others as Io, daughter of Inachus, by others as the Anna of Bovillae, who supplied the plebs with food, when they seceded to the Mons Sacer. (Ov. *Fast.* iii. 523.) Her festival was celebrated on the 15th of March. She was in reality an old Italian divinity, who was regarded as the giver of life, health, and plenty, as the goddess whose powers were most manifest at the return of spring when her festival was celebrated. The identification of this goddess with Anna, the sister of Dido, is undoubtedly of late origin.

Anna Comnēna, daughter of Alexis I. Comnenus (reigned A. D. 1081—1118), wrote the life of her father Alexis in 15 books, which is one of the most interesting and valuable histories of the Byzantine literature. — *Editions.* By Possinus, Paris, 1651 ; by Schopen, Bonn, 1839.

Annālis, a cognomen of the Villia Gens, first acquired by L. Villius, tribune of the plebs, in B. C. 179, because he introduced a law fixing the year (*annus*) at which it was lawful for a person to be a candidate for each of the public offices.

M. Anneius, legate of M. Cicero during his government of Cilicia, B. C. 51.

T. Anniānus, a Roman poet, lived in the time of Trajan and Hadrian, and wrote Fescennine verses.

Annicĕris ('Αννίκερις), a Cyrenaic philosopher, of whom the ancients have left us contradictory accounts. Many modern writers have supposed that there were two philosophers of this name, the one contemporary with Plato, whom he is said to have ransomed for 20 minae from Dionysius of Syracuse, and the other with Alexander the Great.

Annīus Cimber. [CIMBER.]

Annīus Milo. [MILO.]

Anser, a poet of the Augustan age, a friend of the triumvir M. Antonius, and one of the detractors of Virgil. Hence Virgil plays upon his name (*Ecl.* ix. 36). Ovid (*Trist.* ii. 435) calls him *procax*.

Ansibariī or **Ampsivariī,** a German people, originally dwelt S. of the Bructeri, between the sources of the Ems and the Weser: driven out of their country by the Chauci in the reign of Nero (A. D. 59), they asked the Romans for permission to settle in the Roman territory between the Rhine and the Yssel, but when their request was refused they wandered into the interior of the country to the Cherusci, and were at length extirpated, according to Tacitus. We find their name, however, among the Franks in the time of Julian.

Antaeŏpŏlis ('Ανταιόπολις: nr. *Gau-el-Kebir*), an ancient city of Upper Egypt (the Thebaïs), on the E. side of the Nile, but at some distance from the river, was the capital of the Nomos Antaeopolites, and one of the chief seats of the worship of Osiris.

Antaeus ('Ανταῖος), son of Poseidon and Ge, a mighty giant and wrestler in Libya, whose strength was invincible so long as he remained in contact with his mother earth. The strangers who came to his country were compelled to wrestle with him ; the conquered were slain, and out of their skulls he built a house to Poseidon. Hercules discovered the source of his strength, lifted him from the earth, and crushed him in the air. The tomb of Antaeus (*Antaei collis*), which formed a moderate hill in the shape of a man stretched out at full length, was shown near the town of Tingis in Mauretania down to a late period.

Antagŏras ('Ανταγόρας), of Rhodes, flourished about B. C. 270, a friend of Antigonus Gonatas and a contemporary of Aratus. He wrote an epic poem entitled *Thebais,* and also epigrams of which specimens are still extant.

Antalcĭdas ('Ανταλκίδας), a Spartan, son of Leon, is chiefly known by the celebrated treaty concluded with Persia in B. C. 387, usually called the peace of Antalcidas, since it was the fruit of his diplomacy. According to this treaty all the Greek cities in Asia Minor, together with Clazomenae and Cyprus, were to belong to the Persian king: the Athenians were allowed to retain only Lemnos, Imbros, and Scyros ; and all the other Greek cities were to be independent.

Antander ('Αντανδρος), brother of Agathocles, king of Syracuse, wrote the life of his brother.

Antandrus ('Αντανδρος: 'Αντανδριος; *Antandro*), a city of Great Mysia, on the Adramyttian Gulf, at the foot of Mount Ida ; an Aeolian colony. Virgil represents Aeneas as touching here after leaving Troy (*Aen.* iii. 106).

Antărādus ('Αντάραδος: *Tortosa*), a town on the N. border of Phoenicia, opposite the island of Aradus.

Antēa or **Antīa** (Ἄντεια), daughter of the Lycian king Iobates, wife of Proetus of Argos. She is also called Stheneboea. Respecting her love for Bellerophontes, see BELLEROPHONTES.

Antemnae (Antemnas, -atis), an ancient Sabine town at the junction of the Anio and the Tiber, destroyed by the Romans in the earliest times.

Antēnor (Ἀντήνωρ). 1. A Trojan, son of Aesyetes and Cleomestra, and husband of Theano. According to Homer, he was one of the wisest among the elders at Troy: he received Menelaus and Ulysses into his house when they came to Troy as ambassadors, and advised his fellow-citizens to restore Helen to Menelaus. Thus he is represented as a traitor to his country, and when sent to Agamemnon, just before the taking of Troy, to negotiate peace, he concerted a plan of delivering the city, and even the palladium, into the hands the Greeks. On the capture of Troy Antenor was spared by the Greeks. His history after this event is related differently. Some writers relate that he founded a new kingdom at Troy; according to others, he embarked with Menelaus and Helen, was carried to Libya, and settled at Cyrene; while a third account states that he went with the Heneti to Thrace, and thence to the western coast of the Adriatic, where the foundation of Patavium and several towns is ascribed to him. The sons and descendants of Antenor were called *Antēnŏrĭdae*. —2. Son of Euphranor, an Athenian sculptor, made the first bronze statues of Harmodius and Aristogīton, which the Athenians set up in the Ceramīcus, B. C. 509. These statues were carried off to Susa by Xerxes, and their place was supplied by others made either by Callias or by Praxiteles. After the conquest of Persia, Alexander the Great sent the statues back to Athens, where they were again set up in the Ceramīcus.

Antěros. [EROS.]

Antevorta, also called **Porrima** or **Prorsa**, together with **Postvorta**, are described either as the two sisters or companions of the Roman goddess Carmenta; but originally they were only two attributes of the one goddess Carmenta, the former describing her knowledge of the future, and the latter that of the past, analogous to the two-headed Janus.

Anthēdōn (Ἀνθηδών: Ἀνθηδόνιος: Lukisi?), a town of Boeotia with a harbour, on the coast of the Euboean sea, at the foot of M. Messapius, said to have derived its name from a nymph Anthedon, or from Anthedon, son of Glaucus, who was here changed into a god. (Ov. Met. vii. 232, xiii. 905.) The inhabitants chiefly lived by fishing.

Anthēmius, emperor of the West, A. D. 467—472, was killed on the capture of Rome by Ricimer, who made Olybrius emperor.

Anthēmūs (Ἀνθεμοῦς -οῦντος: Ἀνθεμούσιος), a Macedonian town in Chalcidice.

Anthēmūsĭa or **Anthēmus** (Ἀνθεμουσία), a city of Mesopotamia, S.W. of Edessa, and a little E. of the Euphrates. The surrounding district was called by the same name, but was generally included under the name of OSRHOENE.

Anthēnē (Ἀνθήνη), a place in Cynuria, in the Peloponnesus.

Anthylla (Ἄνθυλλα), a considerable city of Lower Egypt, near the mouth of the Canopic branch of the Nile, below Naucratis, the revenues of which, under the Persians, were assigned to the wife of the satrap of Egypt, to provide her with shoes.

Antĭas, Q. Valerĭus, a Roman historian, flourished about B. C. 80, and wrote the history of Rome from the earliest times down to those of Sulla. He is frequently referred to by Livy, who speaks of him as the most lying of all the annalists, and seldom mentions his name without terms of reproach: there can be little doubt that Livy's judgment is correct.

Anticlēa (Ἀντίκλεια), daughter of Autolycus, wife of Laërtes, and mother of Ulysses, died of grief at the long absence of her son. It is said that before marrying Laërtes, she lived on intimate terms with Sisyphus; whence Euripides calls Ulysses a son of Sisyphus.

Anticlīdes (Ἀντικλείδης), of Athens, lived after the time of Alexander the Great, and was the author of several works, the most important of which was entitled *Nosti* (Νόστοι), containing an account of the return of the Greeks from their mythical expeditions.

Antĭcȳra, more anciently **Anticirrha** (Ἀντίκιρρα, or Ἀντίκυρα: Ἀντικυρεύς, Ἀντικυραῖος). 1. (*Aspra Spitia*), a town in Phocis, with a harbour on a peninsula on the W. side of the Sinus Anticyranus, a bay of the Crissaean gulf, called in ancient times Cyparissus. It continued to be a place of importance under the Romans.—2. A town in Thessaly, on the Spercheus, not far from its mouth. Both towns were celebrated for their hellebore, the chief remedy in antiquity for madness: hence the proverb, Ἀντικίρρας σε δεῖ, when a person acted senselessly, and *Naviget Anticyram.* (Hor. Sat. ii. 3. 166.)

Antigēnes (Ἀντιγένης), a general of Alexander the Great, on whose death he obtained the satrapy of Susiana, and espoused the side of Eumenes. On the defeat of the latter in B. C. 316, Antigenes fell into the hands of his enemy Antigonus, and was burnt alive by him.

Antigĕnĭdas (Ἀντιγενίδας), a Theban, a celebrated flute-player, and a poet, lived in the time of Alexander the Great.

Antĭgŏnē (Ἀντιγόνη), daughter of Oedipus by his mother Jocaste, and sister of Ismene, and of Eteocles and Polynīces. In the tragic story of Oedipus Antigone appears as a noble maiden, with a truly heroic attachment to her father and brothers. When Oedipus had blinded himself, and was obliged to quit Thebes, he was accompanied by Antigone, who remained with him till he died in Colonus, and then returned to Thebes. After her two brothers had killed each other in battle, and Creon, the king of Thebes, would not allow Polynices to be buried, Antigone alone defied the tyrant, and buried the body of her brother. Creon thereupon ordered her to be shut up in a subterraneous cave, where she killed herself. Haemon, the son of Creon, who was in love with her, killed himself by her side.

Antĭgŏnēa and **-īa** (Ἀντιγόνεια, Ἀντιγονία). 1. (*Tepeleni*), a town in Epirus (Illyricum), at the junction of a tributary with the Aous, and near a narrow pass of the Acroceraunian mountains.—2. A Macedonian town in Chalcidice.—3. See MANTINEA.—4. A town on the Orontes in Syria, founded by Antigonus as the capital of his empire (B. C. 306), but most of its inhabitants were transferred by Seleucus to ANTIOCHIA, which was built in its neighbourhood.—5. A town in Bithynia, afterwards Nicaea.—6. A town in the Troas. [ALEXANDRIA, No. 2.]

Antĭgŏnus ('Αντίγονος). 1. King of ASIA, surnamed the One-eyed, son of Philip of Elymiotis, and father of Demetrius Poliorcetes by Stratonĭce. He was one of the generals of Alexander the Great, and in the division of the empire after the death of the latter (B. C. 323), he received the provinces of the Greater Phrygia, Lycia, and Pamphylia. On the death of the regent Antipater in 319, he aspired to the sovereignty of Asia. In 316 he defeated and put Eumenes to death, after a struggle of nearly 3 years. From 315 to 311 he carried on war, with varying success, against Seleucus, Ptolemy, Cassander, and Lysimachus. By the peace made in 311, Antigonus was allowed to have the government of all Asia; but peace did not last more than a year. After the defeat of Ptolemy's fleet in 306, Antigonus assumed the title of king, and his example was followed by Ptolemy, Lysimachus, and Seleucus. In the same year Antigonus invaded Egypt, but was compelled to retreat. His son Demetrius carried on the war with success against Cassander in Greece; but he was compelled to return to Asia to the assistance of his father, against whom Cassander, Seleucus, Ptolemy, and Lysimachus, had formed a fresh confederacy. Antigonus and Demetrius were defeated by Lysimachus at the decisive battle of Ipsus in Phrygia, in 301. Antigonus fell in the battle in the 81st year of his age. — 2. **Gonătas**, son of Demetrius Poliorcetes, and grandson of the preceding. He assumed the title of king of Macedonia after his father's death in Asia in B. C. 283, but he did not obtain possession of the throne till 277. He was driven out of his kingdom by Pyrrhus of Epirus in 273, but recovered it in the following year: he was again expelled by Alexander, the son of Pyrrhus, and again recovered his dominions. He attempted to prevent the formation of the Achaean league, and died in 239. He was succeeded by Demetrius II. His surname Gonatas is usually derived from Gonnos or Gonni in Thessaly; but some think that Gonatas is a Macedonian word, signifying an iron plate protecting the knee. — 3. **Doson** (so called because he was always about to give but never did), son of Demetrius of Cyrene, and grandson of Demetrius Poliorcetes. On the death of Demetrius II. in B. C. 229, he was left guardian of his son Philip, but he married the widow of Demetrius, and became king of Macedonia himself. He supported Aratus and the Achaean league against Cleomenes, king of Sparta, whom he defeated at Sellasia in 221, and took Sparta. On his return to Macedonia, he defeated the Illyrians, and died a few days afterwards, 220. — 4. **King of Judaea**, son of Aristobulus II., was placed on the throne by the Parthians in B. C. 40, but was taken prisoner by Sosius, the lieutenant of Antony, and was put to death by the latter in 37. — 5. Of **Carystus**, lived at Alexandria about B. C. 250, and wrote a work still extant, entitled *Historiae Mirabiles*, which is only of value from its preserving extracts from other and better works. — *Editions*. By J. Beckmann, Lips. 1791, and by Westermann in his *Paradoxographi*, Bruns. 1839.

Antĭlĭbănus ('Αντιλίβανος: *Jebel-es-Sheikh* or *Anti-Lebanon*), a mountain on the confines of Palestine, Phoenicia, and Syria, parallel to Libanus (*Lebanon*), which it exceeds in height. Its highest summit is M. Hermon (also *Jebel-es-Sheikh*).

Antĭlŏchus ('Αντίλοχος), son of Nestor and Anaxibia or Eurydice, accompanied his father to Troy, and distinguished himself by his bravery. He was slain before Troy by Memnon the Ethiopian, and was buried by the side of his friends Achilles and Patroclus.

Antĭmăchus ('Αντίμαχος). 1. A Trojan, persuaded his countrymen not to surrender Helen to the Greeks. He had three sons, two of whom were put to death by Menelaus. — 2. Of Claros or Colophon, a Greek epic and elegiac poet, was probably a native of Claros, but was called a Colophonian, because Claros belonged to Colophon. (*Clarius poeta*, Ov. *Trist.* i. 6. 1.) He flourished towards the end of the Peloponnesian war; his chief work was an epic poem of great length called *Thebais* (Θηβαίς). Antimachus was one of the forerunners of the poets of the Alexandrine school, who wrote more for the learned than for the public at large. The Alexandrine grammarians assigned to him the second place among the epic poets, and the emperor Hadrian preferred his works even to those of Homer. He also wrote a celebrated elegiac poem called *Lyde*, which was the name of his wife or mistress, as well as other works. There was likewise a tradition that he made a recension of the text of the Homeric poems.

Antĭnŏŏpŏlis ('Αντινόου πόλις or 'Αντινόεια: *Ensench*, Ru.), a splendid city, built by Hadrian, in memory of his favourite ANTINOUS, on the E. bank of the Nile, upon the site of the ancient Besa, in Middle Egypt (Heptanomis). It was the capital of the Nomos Antinoïtes, and had an oracle of the goddess Besa.

Antĭnŏus ('Αντίνοος). 1. Son of Eupithes of Ithaca, and one of the suitors of Penelope, was slain by Ulysses. — 2. A youth of extraordinary beauty, born at Claudiopolis in Bithynia, was the favourite of the emperor Hadrian, and his companion in all his journeys. He was drowned in the Nile, A. D. 122, whether accidentally or on purpose, is uncertain. The grief of the emperor knew no bounds. He enrolled Antinous amongst the gods, caused a temple to be erected to him at Mantinea, and founded the city of ANTINOOPOLIS in honour of him. A large number of works of art of all kinds were executed in his honour, and many of them are still extant.

Antĭŏchĭa and **-a** ('Αντιόχεια: 'Αντιοχεύς and -όχειος, fem. 'Αντιοχίς and -όχισσα, Antiochēnus), the name of several cities of Asia, 16 of which are said to have been built by Seleucus I. Nicator, and named in honour of his father Antiochus. 1. A. **Epĭdaphnes**, or **ad Daphnem**, or **ad Orontem** ('A. ἐπὶ Δάφνῃ: so called from a neighbouring grove: 'A. ἐπὶ 'Ορόντῃ: *Antakia*, Ru.), the capital of the Greek kingdom of Syria, and long the chief city of Asia and perhaps of the world, stood on the left bank of the Orontes, about 20 miles (geog.) from the sea, in a beautiful valley, about 10 miles long and 5 or 6 broad, enclosed by the ranges of Amanus on the N.W. and Casius on the S.E. It was built by Seleucus Nicator, about B. C. 300, and peopled chiefly from the neighbouring city of ANTIGONIA. It flourished so rapidly as soon to need enlargement; and other additions were again made to it by Seleucus II. Callinicus (about B. C. 240), and Antiochus IV. Epiphanes (about B. C. 170). Hence it obtained the name of Tetrapolis (τετραπόλις, i. e. 4 cities). Besides being the capital of the greatest kingdom of the world, it had a considerable commerce, the Orontes being navigable up to the city, and the high road between Asia and Europe passing through it. Under the Romans it was the residence of the proconsuls of Syria ; it was favoured and visited by emperors ; and was made a colonia with the Jus Italicum by Antoninus Pius. It was one of the earliest strongholds of the Christian faith ; the first place where the Christian name was used (Acts, xi. 26) ; the centre of missionary efforts in the Apostolic age ; and the see of one of the four chief bishops, who were called Patriarchs. Though far inferior to Alexandria as a seat of learning, yet it derived some distinction in this respect from the teaching of Libanius and other sophists ; and its eminence in art is attested by the beautiful gems and medals still found among its ruins. It was destroyed by the Persian king Chosroës (A. D. 540), but rebuilt by Justinian, who gave it the new name of Thëüpŏlis (Θεούπόλις). The ancient walls which still surround the insignificant modern town are probably those built by Justinian. The name of Antiochia was also given to the surrounding district, i. e. the N.W. part of Syria, which bordered upon Cilicia. — 2. A. ad Maeandrum ('A. πρὸς Μαίανδρῳ: nr. Yenishehr, Ru.), a city of Caria, on the Maeander, built by Antiochus I. Soter on the site of the old city of Pythopolis. — 3. A. Pisidiae or ad Pisidiam ('A. Πισιδίας or πρὸς Πισιδίᾳ), a considerable city on the borders of Phrygia Paroreios and Pisidia ; built by colonists from Magnesia ; declared a free city by the Romans after their victory over Antiochus the Great (B. C. 189) ; made a colony under Augustus, and called Caesarea. It was celebrated for the worship and the great temple of Men Arcaeus (Μὴν 'Αρκαῖος, the Phrygian Moon-god), which the Romans suppressed. — 4. A. Margiāna ('A. Μαργιανή: Meru Shah-Jehan ?), a city in the Persian province of Margiana, on the river Margus, founded by Alexander, and at first called Alexandria ; destroyed by the barbarians, rebuilt by Antiochus I. Soter, and called Antiochia. It was beautifully situated, and was surrounded by a wall 70 stadia (about 8 miles) in circuit. Among the less important cities of the name were : (5.) A. ad Taurum in Commagene ; (6.) A. ad Cragum, and (7.) A. ad Pyramum, in Cilicia. The following Antiochs are better known by other names : A. ad Sarum [ADANA] ; A. Characenes [CHARAX] ; A. Callirrhoë [EDESSA] ; A. ad Hippum [GADARA] ; A. Mygdoniae [NISIBIS] ; in Cilicia [TARSUS] ; in Caria or Lydia [TRALLES].

Antiŏchus ('Αντίοχος). I. *Kings of Syria.*

1. Soter (reigned B. C. 280—261), was the son of Seleucus I., the founder of the Syrian kingdom of the Seleucidae. He married his stepmother Stratonice, with whom he fell violently in love, and whom his father surrendered to him. He fell in battle against the Gauls in 261. — 2. Theos (B. C. 261—246), son and successor of No. 1. The Milesians gave him his surname of *Theos,* because he delivered them from their tyrant, Timarchus. He carried on war with Ptolemy Philadelphus, king of Egypt, which was brought to a close by his putting away his wife Laodice, and marrying Berenice, the daughter of Ptolemy. After the death of Ptolemy, he recalled Laodice, but in revenge for the insult she had received, she caused Antiochus and Berenice to be murdered. During the reign of Antiochus, Arsaces founded the Parthian empire (250), and Theodotus established an independent kingdom at Bactria. He was succeeded by his

son Seleucus Callinicus. His younger son Antiochus Hierax also assumed the crown, and carried on war some years with his brother. [SELEUCUS II.] — 3. The Great (B. C. 223—187), second son of Seleucus Callinicus, succeeded to the throne on the death of his brother Seleucus Ceraunus, when he was only in his 15th year. After defeating (220) Molon, satrap of Media, and his brother Alexander, satrap of Persia, who had attempted to make themselves independent, he carried on war against Ptolemy Philopator, king of Egypt, in order to obtain Coele-Syria, Phoenicia, and Palestine, but was obliged to cede these provinces to Ptolemy, in consequence of his defeat at the battle of Raphia near Gaza, in 217. He next marched against Achaeus, who had revolted in Asia Minor, and whom he put to death, when he fell into his hands in 214. [ACHAEUS.] Shortly after this he was engaged for 7 years (212—205) in an attempt to regain the E. provinces of Asia, which had revolted during the reign of Antiochus II. ; but though he met with great success, he found it hopeless to effect the subjugation of the Parthian and Bactrian kingdoms, and accordingly concluded a peace with them. In 205 he renewed his war against Egypt with more success, and in 198 conquered Palestine and Coele-Syria, which he afterwards gave as a dowry with his daughter Cleopatra upon her marriage with Ptolemy Epiphanes. In 196 he crossed over into Europe, and took possession of the Thracian Chersonese. This brought him into contact with the Romans, who commanded him to restore the Chersonese to the Macedonian king ; but he refused to comply with their demand ; in which resolution he was strengthened by Hannibal, who arrived at his court in 195. Hannibal urged him to invade Italy without loss of time ; but Antiochus did not follow his advice, and it was not till 192, that he crossed over into Greece. In 191 he was defeated by the Romans at Thermopylae, and compelled to return to Asia : his fleet was also vanquished in two engagements. In 190 he was again defeated by the Romans under L. Scipio, at Mount Sipylus, near Magnesia, and compelled to sue for peace, which was granted in 188, on condition of his ceding all his dominions E. of Mount Taurus, paying 15,000 Euboic talents within 12 years, giving up his elephants and ships of war, and surrendering the Roman enemies ; but he allowed Hannibal to escape. In order to raise the money to pay the Romans, he attacked a wealthy temple in Elymais, but was killed by the people of the place (187). He was succeeded by his son Seleucus Philopator. — 4. Epiphanes (B. C. 175—164), son of Antiochus III., was given as a hostage to the Romans in 188, and was released from captivity in 175 through his brother Seleucus Philopator, whom he succeeded in the same year. He carried on war against Egypt from 171—168 with great success, in order to obtain Coele-Syria and Palestine, which had been given as a dowry with his sister, and he was preparing to lay siege to Alexandria in 168, when the Romans compelled him to retire. He endeavoured to root out the Jewish religion and to introduce the worship of the Greek divinities ; but this attempt led to a rising of the Jewish people, under Mattathias and his heroic sons the Maccabees, which Antiochus was unable to put down. He attempted to plunder a temple in Elymais in 164, but he was repulsed, and died shortly afterwards

E 4

in a state of raving madness, which the Jews and Greeks equally attributed to his sacrilegious crimes. His subjects gave him the name of *Epimanes* (" the madman") in parody of *Epiphanes*. — **5. Eupator** (B.C. 164—162), son and successor of Epiphanes, was 9 years old at his father's death, and reigned under the guardianship of Lysias. He was dethroned and put to death by Demetrius Soter, the son of Seleucus Philopator, who had hitherto lived at Rome as a hostage. — **6. Theos**, son of Alexander Balas. He was brought forward as a claimant to the crown in 144, against Demetrius Nicator by Tryphon, but he was murdered by the latter, who ascended the throne himself in 142. — **7. Sidetes** (B.C. 137—128), so called from Side in Pamphylia, where he was brought up, younger son of Demetrius Soter, succeeded Tryphon. He married Cleopatra, wife of his elder brother Demetrius Nicator, who was a prisoner with the Parthians. He carried on war against the Parthians, at first with success, but was afterwards defeated and slain in battle in 128. — **8. Grypus**, or Hook-nosed (B.C. 125 — 96), second son of Demetrius Nicator and Cleopatra. He was placed upon the throne in 125 by his mother Cleopatra, who put to death his eldest brother Seleucus, because she wished to have the power in her own hands. He poisoned his mother in 120, and subsequently carried on war for some years with his half-brother A. IX. Cyzicenus. At length, in 112, the two brothers agreed to share the kingdom between them, A. Cyzicenus having Coele-Syria and Phoenicia, and A. Grypus the remainder of the provinces. Grypus was assassinated in 96. — **9. Cyzicenus**, from Cyzicus, where he was brought up, son of A. VII. Sidetes and Cleopatra, reigned over Coele-Syria and Phoenicia from 112 to 96, but fell in battle in 95 against Seleucus Epiphanes, son of A. VIII. Grypus. — **10. Eusebes**, son of A. IX. Cyzicenus, defeated Seleucus Epiphanes, who had slain his father in battle, and maintained the throne against the brothers of Seleucus. He succeeded his father Antiochus IX. in 95. — **11. Epiphanes**, son of A. VIII. Grypus and brother of Seleucus Epiphanes, carried on war against A. X. Eusebes, but was defeated by the latter, and drowned in the river Orontes. — **12. Dionysus**, brother of No. 11, held the crown for a short time, but fell in battle against Aretas, king of the Arabians. The Syrians, worn out with the civil broils of the Seleucidae, offered the kingdom to Tigranes, king of Armenia, who united Syria to his own dominions in 83, and held it till his defeat by the Romans in 69. — **13. Asiaticus**, son of A. X. Eusebes, became king of Syria on the defeat of Tigranes by Lucullus in 69; but he was deprived of it in 65 by Pompey, who reduced Syria to a Roman province. In this year the Seleucidae ceased to reign.

II. *Kings of Commagene.*

1. Made an alliance with the Romans, about B.C. 64. He assisted Pompey with troops in 49, and was attacked by Antony in 38. He was succeeded by Mithridates I. about 31. — **2** Succeeded Mithridates I., and was put to death at Rome by Augustus in 29. — **3.** Succeeded Mithridates II., and died in A.D. 17. Upon his death, Commagene became a Roman province, and remained so till A.D. 38. — **4.** Surnamed Epiphanes, apparently a son of Antiochus III.,

received his paternal dominion from Caligula in A.D. 38. He was subsequently deposed by Caligula, but regained his kingdom on the accession of Claudius in 41. He was a faithful ally of the Romans, and assisted them in their wars against the Parthians under Nero, and against the Jews under Vespasian. At length in 72, he was accused of conspiring with the Parthians against the Romans, was deprived of his kingdom, and retired to Rome, where he passed the remainder of his life.

III. *Literary.*

1. Of **Aegae** in Cilicia, a sophist, or, as he himself pretended to be, a Cynic philosopher. He flourished about A.D. 200, during the reign of Severus and Caracalla. During the war of Caracalla against the Parthians, he deserted to the Parthians together with Tiridates. He was one of the most distinguished rhetoricians of his time, and also acquired some reputation as a writer. — **2.** Of **Ascalon**, the founder of the fifth Academy, was a friend of Lucullus and the teacher of Cicero during his studies at Athens (B.C. 79); but he had a school at Alexandria also, as well as in Syria, where he seems to have ended his life. His principal teacher was Philo, who succeeded Plato, Arcesilas, and Carneades, as the founder of the fourth Academy. He is, however, better known as the adversary than the disciple of Philo; and Cicero mentions a treatise called *Sosus*, written by him against his master, in which he refutes the scepticism of the Academica. — **3.** Of **Syracuse**, a Greek historian, lived about B.C. 423, and wrote histories of Sicily and Italy.

Antiope ('Αντιόπη). **1.** Daughter of Nycteus and Polyxo, or of the river god Asopus in Boeotia, became by Zeus the mother of Amphion and Zethus. [AMPHION.] Dionysus threw her into a state of madness on account of the vengeance which her sons had taken on Dirce. In this condition she wandered through Greece, until Phocus, the grandson of Sisyphus, cured and married her. — **2.** An Amazon, sister of Hippolyte, wife of Theseus, and mother of Hippolytus.

Antipater ('Αντίπατρος). **1.** The Macedonian, an officer greatly trusted by Philip and Alexander the Great, was left by the latter regent in Macedonia, when he crossed over into Asia in B.C. 334. In consequence of dissensions between Olympias and Antipater, the latter was summoned to Asia in 324, and Craterus appointed to the regency of Macedonia, but the death of Alexander in the following year prevented these arrangements from taking effect. Antipater now obtained Macedonia again, and in conjunction with Craterus, who was associated with him in the government, carried on war against the Greeks, who endeavoured to establish their independence. This war, usually called the Lamian war, from Lamia, where Antipater was besieged in 323, was terminated by Antipater's victory over the confederates at Crannon in 322. This was followed by the submission of Athens and the death of Demosthenes. In 321 Antipater crossed over into Asia in order to oppose Perdiccas; but the murder of Perdiccas in Egypt put an end to this war, and left Antipater supreme regent. Antipater died in 319, after appointing Polysperchon regent, and his own son Cassander to a subordinate position. — **2.** Grandson of the preceding, and second son of Cassander and Thessalonica. After the death of his elder brother Philip

IV. (B. C. 295), great dissensions ensued between Antipater and his younger brother Alexander, for the kingdom of Macedonia. Antipater, believing that Alexander was favoured by his mother, put her to death. The younger brother upon this applied for aid at once to Pyrrhus of Epirus and Demetrius Poliorcetes. The remaining history is related differently : but so much is certain, that both Antipater and Alexander were subsequently put to death, either by Demetrius or at his instigation, and that Demetrius became king of Macedonia.—3. Father of Herod the Great, son of a noble Idumaean of the same name, espoused the cause of Hyrcanus against his brother Aristobulus. He ingratiated himself with the Romans, and in B. C. 47 was appointed by Caesar procurator of Judaea, which appointment he held till his death in 43, when he was carried off by poison which Malichus, whose life he had twice saved, bribed the cup-bearer of Hyrcanus to administer to him. —4. Eldest son of Herod the Great by his first wife, Doris, brought about the death of his two half-brothers, Alexander and Aristobulus, in B. C. 6, but was himself condemned as guilty of a conspiracy against his father's life, and was executed five days before Herod's death.—5. Of Tarsus, a Stoic philosopher, the successor of Diogenes and the teacher of Panaetius, about B. C. 144. —6. Of Tyre, a Stoic philosopher, died shortly before B. C. 45, and wrote a work on Duties (de Officiis).—7. Of Sidon, the author of several epigrams in the Greek Anthology, flourished about B. C. 108—100, and lived to a great age.—8. Of Thessalonica, the author of several epigrams in the Greek Anthology, lived in the latter part of the reign of Augustus.

Antipāter, L. Caellus, a Roman jurist and historian, and a contemporary of C. Gracchus (B. C. 123) and L. Crassus, the orator, wrote Annales, which were epitomized by Brutus, and which contained a valuable account of the 2nd Punic war.

Antipatria ('Αντιπάτρια : Berat ?), a town in Illyricum on the borders of Macedonia, on the left bank of the Apsus.

Antiphānes ('Αντιφάνηι). 1. A comic poet of the middle Attic comedy, born about B. C. 404, and died 330. He wrote 365, or at the least 260 plays, which were distinguished by elegance of language.—2. Of Berga in Thrace, a Greek writer on marvellous and incredible things.—3. An epigrammatic poet, several of whose epigrams are still extant in the Greek Anthology, lived about the reign of Augustus.

Antiphātes ('Αντιφάτης), king of the mythical Laestrygones in Sicily, who are represented as giants and cannibals. They destroyed 11 of the ships of Ulysses, who escaped with only one vessel.

Antiphellus ('Αντίφελλος : Antiphilo), a town on the coast of Lycia, between Patara and Aperlae, originally the port of PHELLUS.

Antiphēmus ('Αντίφημος), the Rhodian, founder of Gela in Sicily, B. C. 690.

Antiphilus ('Αντίφιλος). 1. Of Byzantium, an epigrammatic poet, author of several excellent epigrams in the Greek Anthology, was a contemporary of the emperor Nero.—2. Of Egypt, a distinguished painter, the rival of Apelles, painted for Philip and Alexander the Great.

Antiphon ('Αντιφῶν). 1. The most ancient of the 10 orators in the Alexandrine canon, was a son of Sophilus the Sophist, and born at Rhamnus in Attica, in B. c. 480. He belonged to the oligarchical party at Athens, and took an active part in the establishment of the government of the Four Hundred (B. c. 411), after the overthrow of which he was brought to trial, condemned, and put to death. The oratorical powers of Antiphon are highly praised by the ancients. He introduced great improvements in public speaking, and was the first who laid down theoretical laws for practical eloquence ; he opened a school in which he taught rhetoric, and the historian Thucydides is said to have been one of his pupils. The orations which he composed were written for others ; and the only time that he spoke in public himself was when he was accused and condemned to death. This speech, which was considered in antiquity a master-piece of eloquence, is now lost. (Thuc. viii. 68 ; Cic. Brut. 12.) We still possess 15 orations of Antiphon, 3 of which were written by him for others, and the remaining 12 as specimens for his school, or exercises on fictitious cases. They are printed in the collections of the Attic orators, and separately, edited by Baiter and Sauppe, Zürich, 1838, and Mätzner, Berlin, 1838.—2. A tragic poet, whom many writers confound with the Attic orator, lived at Syracuse, at the court of the elder Dionysius, by whom he was put to death.—3. Of Athens, a sophist and an epic poet, wrote a work on the interpretation of dreams, which is referred to by Cicero and others. He is the same person as the Antiphon who was an opponent of Socrates. (Xen. Mem. i. 6.)

Antiphus ('Αντιφος). 1. Son of Priam and Hecuba, slain by Agamemnon.—2. Son of Thessalus, and one of the Greek heroes at Troy.

Antipōlis ('Αντίπολις : Antibes, pronounced by the inhabitants Antiboul), a town in Gallia Narbonensis on the coast, in the territory of the Deciates, a few miles W. of Nicaea, was founded by Massilia ; the muria, or salt pickle made of fish, prepared at this town, was very celebrated.

Antirrhium ('Αντίρριον : Castello di Romelia), a promontory on the borders of Aetolia and Locris, opposite Rhium (Castello di Morea) in Achaia, with which it formed the narrow entrance of the Corinthian gulf: the straits are sometimes called the Little Dardanelles.

Antissa ('Αντισσα: 'Αντισσαῖος : Kalas Limneonas), a town in Lesbos with a harbour, on the W. coast between Methymna and the promontory Sigrium, was originally on a small island opposite Lesbos, which was afterwards united with Lesbos. It was destroyed by the Romans, B. c. 168, and its inhabitants removed to Methymna, because they had assisted Antiochus.

Antisthēnes ('Αντισθένης), an Athenian, founder of the sect of the Cynic philosophers. His mother was a Thracian. In his youth he fought at Tanagra (B. c. 426), and was a disciple first of Gorgias, and then of Socrates, whom he never quitted, and at whose death he was present. He died at Athens, at the age of 70. He taught in the Cynosarges, a gymnasium for the use of Athenians born of foreign mothers ; whence probably his followers were called Cynics (κυνικοί), though others derive their name from their dog-like neglect of all forms and usages of society. His writings were very numerous, and chiefly dialogues ; his style was pure and elegant ; and he possessed considerable powers of wit and sarcasm. Two declamations of his are preserved, named Ajax and Ulysses, which are purely rhetorical. He was an enemy to all speculation, and thus was opposed to Plato, whom he attacked furiously in one of his dialogues. His philosophical system was confined almost entirely to ethics, and he taught that virtue is the sole thing necessary. He showed his contempt of all the luxuries and outward comforts of life by his mean clothing and hard fare. From his school the Stoics subsequently sprung. In one of his works entitled *Physicus*, he contended for the Unity of the Deity. (Cic. *de Nat. Deor.* i. 13.)

Antistius, P., tribune of the plebs, B.C. 88, a distinguished orator, supported the party of Sulla, and was put to death by order of young Marius in 82. His daughter Antistia was married to Pompeius Magnus.

Antistius Labeo. [LABEO.]

Antistius Vetus. [VETUS.]

Antitaurus ('Αντίταυρος : *Ali-Dagh*), a chain of mountains, which strikes off N.E. from the main chain of the Taurus on the S. border of Cappadocia, in the centre of which district it turns to the E. and runs parallel to the Taurus as far as the Euphrates. Its average height exceeds that of the Taurus ; and one of its summits, Mount Argaeus, near Mazaca, is the loftiest mountain of Asia Minor.

Antium (Antias : *Torre* or *Porto d' Anzo*), a very ancient town of Latium on a rocky promontory running out some distance into the Tyrrhenian sea. It was founded by Tyrrhenians and Pelasgians, and in earlier and even later times was noted for its piracy. Although united by Tarquinius Superbus to the Latin League, it generally sided with the Volscians against Rome. It was taken by the Romans in B. c. 468, and a colony was sent thither, but it revolted, was taken a second time by the Romans in B. c. 338, was deprived of all its ships, the beaks of which (*Rostra*) served to ornament the platform of the speakers in the Roman forum, was forbidden to have any ships in future, and received another Roman colony. But it gradually recovered its former importance, was allowed in course of time again to be used as a seaport, and in the latter times of the republic and under the empire, became a favourite residence of many of the Roman nobles and emperors. The emperor Nero was born here, and in the remains of his palace the celebrated Apollo Belvedere was found. Antium possessed a celebrated temple of Fortune (*O Diva, gratum quas regis Antium,* Hor. *Carm.* i. 35), of Aesculapius, and at the port of Ceno, a little to the E. of Antium, a temple of Neptune, on which account the place is now called *Nettuno.*

Antius Restio. [RESTIO.]

Antonia. 1. *Major*, elder daughter of M. Antonius and Octavia, husband of L. Domitius Ahenobarbus, and mother of Cn. Domitius, the father of the emperor Nero. Tacitus calls this Antonia the younger daughter. — 2. *Minor*, younger sister of the preceding, husband of Drusus, the brother of the emperor Tiberius, and mother of Germanicus, the father of the emperor Caligula, of Livia or Livilla, and of the emperor Claudius. She died A. D. 38, soon after the accession of her grandson Caligula. She was celebrated for her beauty, virtue, and chastity. — 3. Daughter of the emperor Claudius, married first to Pompeius Magnus, and afterwards to Faustus Sulla. Nero wished to marry her after the death of his wife Poppaea, A. D. 66 ; and on her refusal he caused her to be put to death on a charge of treason.

Antonia Turris, a castle on a rock at the N.W. corner of the Temple at Jerusalem, which commanded both the temple and the city. It was at first called Baris. Herod the Great changed the name in honour of M. Antonius. It contained the residence of the Procurator Judaeae.

Antonini Itinerarium, the title of an extant work, which is a very valuable itinerary of the whole Roman empire, in which both the princ pal and the cross-roads are described by a list of all the places and stations upon them, the distances from place to place being given in Roman miles. It is usually attributed to the emperor M. Aurelius Antoninus, but it appears to have been commenced by order of Julius Caesar and to have been completed in the reign of Augustus ; though it is probable that it received important additions and revision under one or both of the Antonines.—*Editions :* by Wesseling, Amst. 1735 ; by Parthey and Pinder, Berlin, 1848.

Antoninopolis ('Αντωνινόπολις: *-ίτης*, anus), a city of Mesopotamia, between Edessa and Dara, *aft.* Maximianopolis, and *aft.* Constantia.

Antoninus, M. Aurelius. [M. AURELIUS.]

Antoninus Pius, Roman emperor, A. D. 138— 161. His name in the early part of his life, at full length, was *Titus Aurelius Fulvus Boionius Arrius Antoninus.* His paternal ancestors came from Nemausus (*Nismes*) in Gaul ; but Antoninus himself was born near Lanuvium, September 19th, A. D. 86. From an early age he gave promise of his future worth. In 120 he was consul, and subsequently proconsul of the province of Asia : on his return to Rome he lived on terms of the greatest intimacy with Hadrian, who adopted him on February 25th, 138. Henceforward he bore the name of *T. Aelius Hadrianus Antoninus Caesar,* and on the death of Hadrian, July 2nd, 138, he ascended the throne. The senate conferred upon him the title of *Pius,* or the *dutifully affectionate,* because he persuaded them to grant to his father Hadrian the apotheosis and the other honours usually paid to deceased emperors, which they had at first refused to bestow upon Hadrian. The reign of Antoninus is almost a blank in history — a blank caused by the suspension for a time of war, violence, and crime. He was one of the best princes that ever mounted a throne, and all his thoughts and energies were dedicated to the happiness of his people. No attempt was made to achieve new conquests, and various insurrections among the Germans, Dacians, Jews, Moors, Egyptians, and Britons, were easily quelled by his legates. In all the relations of private life the character of Antoninus was without reproach. He was faithful to his wife Faustina, notwithstanding her profligate life, and after her death loaded her memory with honours. He died at Lorium, March 7th, 161, in his 75th year. He was succeeded by M. Aurelius, whom he had adopted, when he himself was adopted by Hadrian, and to whom he gave his daughter FAUSTINA in marriage.

Antoninus Liberalis, a Greek grammarian, probably lived in the reign of the Antonines, about A. D. 147, and wrote a work on Metamorphoses (Μεταμορφώσεων συναγωγή) in 41 chapters, which is extant.—*Editions :* by Verheyk, Lugd. Bat. 1774 ; by Koch, Lips. 1832 ; by Westermann, in his *Paradoxographi,* Brunsv. 1839.

Antonius. L M., the orator, born B. c. 143 quaestor in 113 ; praetor in 104, when he fought against the pirates in Cilicia; consul in 99; and censor in 97. He belonged to Sulla's party, and was put to death by Marius and Cinna when they entered Rome in 87: his head was cut off and placed on the Rostra. Cicero mentions him and L. Crassus as the most distinguished orators of their age; and he is introduced as one of the speakers in Cicero's *De Oratore.* — **2. M.**, surnamed CRETICUS, elder son of the orator, and father of the triumvir, was praetor in 75, and received the command of the fleet and all the coasts of the Mediterranean, in order to clear the sea of pirates; but he did not succeed in his object, and used his power to plunder the provinces. He died shortly afterwards in Crete, and was called *Creticus* in derision. — **3. C.**, younger son of the orator, and uncle of the triumvir, was expelled the senate in 70, and was the colleague of Cicero in the praetorship (65) and consulship (63). He was one of Catiline's conspirators, but deserted the latter by Cicero's promising him the province of Macedonia. He had to lead an army against Catiline, but unwilling to fight against his former friend, he gave the command on the day of battle to his legate, M. Petreius. At the conclusion of the war Antony went into his province, which he plundered shamefully; and on his return to Rome in 59 was accused both of taking part in Catiline's conspiracy and of extortion in his province. He was defended by Cicero, but was condemned, and retired to the island of Cephallenia. He was subsequently recalled, probably by Caesar, and was in Rome at the beginning of 44. — **4. M.**, the Triumvir, was son of No. 2. and Julia, the sister of L. Julius Caesar, consul in 64, and was born about 83. His father died while he was still young, and he was brought up by Cornelius Lentulus, who married his mother Julia, and who was put to death by Cicero in 63 as one of Catiline's conspirators: whence he became a personal enemy of Cicero. Antony indulged in his earliest youth in every kind of dissipation, and his affairs soon became deeply involved. In 58 he went to Syria, where he served with distinction under A. Gabinius. He took part in the campaigns against Aristobulus in Palestine (57, 56), and in the restoration of Ptolemy Auletes to Egypt in 55. In 54 he went to Caesar in Gaul, and by the influence of the latter was elected quaestor. As quaestor (52) he returned to Gaul, and served under Caesar for the next two years (52, 51). He returned to Rome in 50, and became one of the most active partizans of Caesar. He was tribune of the plebs in 49, and in January fled to Caesar's camp in Cisalpine Gaul, after putting his veto upon the decree of the senate which deprived Caesar of his command. He accompanied Caesar in his victorious march into Italy, and was left by Caesar in the command of Italy, while the latter carried on the war in Spain. In 48 Antony was present at the battle of Pharsalia, where he commanded the left wing; and in 47 he was again left in the command of Italy during Caesar's absence in Africa. In 44 he was consul with Caesar, when he offered him the kingly diadem at the festival of the Lupercalia. After Caesar's murder on the 15th of March, Antony endeavoured to succeed to his power. He therefore used every means to appear as his representative; he pronounced the speech over Caesar's body and read his will to the people; and he also obtained the papers and private property of Caesar. But he found a new and unex-

pected rival in young Octavianus, the adopted son and great-nephew of the dictator, who came from Apollonia to Rome, assumed the name of Caesar, and at first joined the senate in order to crush Antony. Towards the end of the year Antony proceeded to Cisalpine Gaul, which had been previously granted him by the senate; but Dec. Brutus refused to surrender the province to Antony and threw himself into Mutina, where he was besieged by Antony. The senate approved of the conduct of Brutus, declared Antony a public enemy, and entrusted the conduct of the war against him to Octavianus. Antony was defeated at the battle of Mutina, in April 43, and was obliged to cross the Alps. Both the consuls, however, had fallen, and the senate now began to show their jealousy of Octavianus. Meantime Antony was joined by Lepidus with a powerful army: Octavianus became reconciled to Antony; and it was agreed that the government of the state should be vested in Antony, Octavianus, and Lepidus, under the title of *Triumviri Reipublicae Constituendae*, for the next 5 years. The mutual enemies of each were proscribed, and in the numerous executions that followed, Cicero, who had attacked Antony in the most unmeasured manner in his *Philippic Orations*, fell a victim to Antony. In 42 Antony and Octavianus crushed the republican party by the battle of Philippi, in which Brutus and Cassius fell. Antony then went to Asia, which he had received as his share of the Roman world. In Cilicia he met with Cleopatra, and followed her to Egypt, a captive to her charms. In 41 Fulvia, the wife of Antony, and his brother L. Antonius, made war upon Octavianus in Italy. Antony prepared to support his relatives, but the war was brought to a close at the beginning of 40, before Antony could reach Italy. The opportune death of Fulvia facilitated the reconciliation of Antony and Octavianus, which was cemented by Antony marrying Octavia, the sister of Octavianus. Antony remained in Italy till 39, when the triumvirs concluded a peace with Sext. Pompey, and he afterwards went to his provinces in the East. In this year and the following Ventidius, the lieutenant of Antony, defeated the Parthians. In 37 Antony crossed over to Italy, when the triumvirate was renewed for 5 years. Then he returned to the East, and shortly afterwards sent Octavia back to her brother, and surrendered himself entirely to the charms of Cleopatra. In 36 he invaded Parthia, but he lost a great number of his troops, and was obliged to retreat. He was more successful in his invasion of Armenia in 34, for he obtained possession of the person of Artavasdes, the Armenian king, and carried him to Alexandria. Antony now laid aside entirely the character of a Roman citizen, and assumed the pomp and ceremony of an Eastern despot. His conduct, and the unbounded influence which Cleopatra had acquired over him, alienated many of his friends and supporters; and Octavianus thought that the time had now come for crushing his rival. The contest was decided by the memorable sea-fight off Actium, September 2nd, 31, in which Antony's fleet was completely defeated. Antony, accompanied by Cleopatra, fled to Alexandria, where he put an end to his own life in the following year (30), when Octavianus appeared before the city. — **5. C.**, brother of the triumvir, was praetor in Macedonia in 44, fell into the hands of M. Brutus in

43, and was put to death by Brutus in 42, to revenge the murder of Cicero. — **6. L.**, youngest brother of the triumvir, was consul in 41, when he engaged in war against Octavianus at the instigation of Fulvia, his brother's wife. He was unable to resist Octavianus, and threw himself into the town of Perusia, which he was obliged to surrender in the following year: hence the war is usually called that of Perusia. His life was spared, and he was afterwards appointed by Octavianus to the command of Iberia. Cicero draws a frightful picture of Lucius' character. He calls him a gladiator and a robber, and heaps upon him every term of reproach and contempt. Much of this is of course exaggeration. — **7. M.**, called by the Greek writers *Antyllus*, which is probably only a corrupt form of Antonillus (young Antonius), elder son of the triumvir by Fulvia, was executed by order of Octavianus, after the death of his father in 30. — **8. Julus**, younger son of the triumvir by Fulvia, was brought up by his step-mother Octavia at Rome, and received great marks of favour from Augustus. He was consul in B. C. 10, but was put to death in 2, in consequence of his adulterous intercourse with Julia, the daughter of Augustus.

Antōnĭus Felix. [FELIX.]
Antōnĭus Musa. [MUSA.]
Antōnĭus Primus. [PRIMUS.]

Antron ('Αντρών and οἱ 'Αντρῶνες: 'Αντρώνιος: *Fano*), a town in Phthiotis in Thessaly, at the entrance of the Sinus Maliacus.

Antunnacum (*Andernach*), a town of the Ubii on the Rhine.

Anūbis ("Ανουβις), an Egyptian divinity, worshipped in the form of a human being with a dog's head. He was originally worshipped simply as the representative of the dog, which animal, like the cat, was sacred in Egypt; but his worship was subsequently mixed up with other religious systems, and Anubis thus assumed a symbolical or astronomical character, at least with the learned. His worship prevailed throughout Egypt, but he was most honoured at Cynopolis in middle Egypt. Later myths relate that Anubis was the son of Osiris and Nephthys, born after the death of his father; and that Isis brought him up, and made him her guard and companion, who thus performed to her the same service that dogs perform to men. In the temples of Egypt Anubis seems to have been represented as the guard of other gods, and the place in the front of a temple was particularly sacred to him. The Greeks identified him with their own Hermes, and thus speak of Hermanuphis in the same manner as of Zeus Ammon. His worship was introduced at Rome towards the end of the republic, and under the empire spread very widely both in Greece and at Rome.

Anxur. [TARRACINA.]

Anxūrus, an Italian divinity, who was worshipped in a grove near Anxur (Tarracina) together with Feronia. He was regarded as a youthful Jupiter, and Feronia as Juno. On coins his name appears as Axur or Anxur.

Anysis ("Ανυσις), an ancient king of Egypt, in whose reign Egypt was invaded by the Ethiopians under their king Sabaco.

Anÿtē ('Ανύτη), of Tegea, the authoress of several epigrams in the Greek Anthology, flourished about B. C. 700, and not 300, as is usually supposed. The epigrams are for the most part in the style of the ancient Doric choral songs.

Anÿtus ("Ανυτος), a wealthy Athenian, son of Anthemion, the most influential and formidable of the accusers of Socrates, B. C. 399 (hence Socrates is called *Anyti reus*, Hor. *Sat.* ii. 4. 3). He was a leading man of the democratical party, and took an active part, along with Thrasybulus, in the overthrow of the 30 Tyrants. The Athenians, having repented of their condemnation of Socrates, sent Anytus into banishment.

Aōn ("Αων), son of Poseidon, and an ancient Boeotian hero, from whom the Aones, an ancient race in Boeotia, were believed to have derived their name. *Aonia* was the name of the part of Boeotia, near Phocis, in which were Mount Helicon and the fountain Aganippe (*Aonias aquae*, Ov. *Fast.* iii. 456). The Muses are also called *Aonides*, since they frequented Helicon and the fountain of Aganippe. (Ov. *Met.* v. 333.)

Aōnĭdes. [AON.]

Aorsi ("Αορσοι) or **Adorsi**, a powerful people of Asiatic Sarmatia, who appear to have had their original settlements on the N.E. of the Caspian, but are chiefly found between the Palus Maeotis (*Sea of Azof*) and the Caspian, to the S.E. of the river Tanaïs (*Don*), whence they spread far into European Sarmatia. They carried on a considerable traffic in Babylonian merchandise, which they fetched on camels out of Media and Armenia.

Aōus or **Aeas** ('Αῷος or Αἴας: *Viosa, Viussa*, or *Vovussa*), the principal river of the Greek part of Illyricum, rises in M. Lacmon, the N. part of Pindus, and flows into the Ionian sea near Apollonia.

Apāmēa or **-īa** ('Απάμεια: 'Απαμιεύς, Apamēus, -ēnus, -ensis), the name of several Asiatic cities, three of which were founded by Seleucus I. Nicator, and named in honour of his wife Apama. **1. A. ad Orontem** (*Famiah*), the capital of the Syrian province Apamene, and, under the Romans, of Syria Secunda, was built by Seleucus Nicator on the site of the older city of PELLA, in a very strong position on the river Orontes or Axius, the citadel being on the left (W.) bank of the river, and the city on the right. It was surrounded by rich pastures, in which Seleucus kept a splendid stud of horses and 500 elephants. — **2. In Osroëne** in Mesopotamia (*Balasir*), a town built by Seleucus Nicator on the E. bank of the Euphrates, opposite to ZEUGMA, with which it was connected by a bridge, commanded by a castle, called Seleucia. In Pliny's time (A. D. 77) it was only a ruin. — **3. A. Cibōtus** or **ad Maeandrum** ('A. ἡ Κιβωτός, or πρὸς Μαίανδρον), a great city of Phrygia, on the Maeander, close above its confluence with the Marsyas. It was built by Antiochus I. Soter, who named it in honour of his mother Apama, and peopled it with the inhabitants of the neighbouring Celaenae. It became one of the greatest cities of Asia within the Euphrates; and under the Romans it was the seat of a Conventus Juridicus. The surrounding country, watered by the Maeander and its tributaries, was called Apamēna Regio. — **4. A. Myrlēon**, in Bithynia. [MYRLEA.] — **5. A** town built by Antiochus Soter, in the district of Assyria called Sittacene, at the junction of the Tigris with the Royal Canal which connected the Tigris with the Euphrates, and at the N. extremity of the island called Mesene, which was formed by this canal and the 2 rivers. — **6. A. Mesene** (*Korna*), in Babylonia, at the S. point of the same island of Mesene, and at the junction of the Tigris and Euphrates. — **7. A. Rhagiana** ('A. ἡ πρὸς Ῥαγαῖς), a Greek city in the district of Choarene in Parthia (formerly in Media), S. of the Caspian Gates.

Apelles ('Απελλῆς), the most celebrated of Grecian painters, was born, most probably, at Colophon in Ionia, though some ancient writers call him a Coan and others an Ephesian. He was the contemporary and friend of Alexander the Great (B. C. 336—323), whom he probably accompanied to Asia, and who entertained so high an opinion of him, that he was the only person whom Alexander would permit to take his portrait. After Alexander's death he appears to have travelled through the western parts of Asia. Being driven by a storm to Alexandria, after the assumption of the regal title by Ptolemy (B. C. 306), whose favour he had not gained while he was with Alexander, his rivals laid a plot to ruin him, which he defeated by an ingenious use of his skill in drawing. We are not told when or where he died. Throughout his life Apelles laboured to improve himself, especially in drawing, which he never spent a day without practising. Hence the proverb *Nulla dies sine linea*. A list of his works is given by Pliny (xxxv. 36). They are for the most part single figures, or groups of a very few figures. Of his portraits the most celebrated was that of Alexander wielding a thunderbolt; but the most admired of all his pictures was the " Venus Anadyomene " (ἡ ἀναδυομένη 'Αφροδίτη), or Venus rising out of the sea. The goddess was wringing her hair, and the falling drops of water formed a transparent silver veil around her form. He commenced another picture of Venus, which he intended should surpass the Venus Anadyomene, but which he left unfinished at his death.

Apellicon ('Απελλικῶν), of Teos, a Peripatetic philosopher and great collector of books. His valuable library at Athens, containing the autographs of Aristotle's works, was carried to Rome by Sulla (B. C. 83): Apellicon had died just before.

Apenninus Mons (ὁ 'Απέννινος and τὸ 'Απέννινον ὄρος, probably from the Celtic *Pen* "a height "), the *Apennines*, a chain of mountains which runs throughout Italy from N. to S., and forms the backbone of the peninsula. It is a continuation of the Maritime Alps [ALPES], begins near Genua, and ends at the Sicilian sea, and throughout its whole course sends off numerous branches in all directions. It rises to its greatest height in the country of the Sabines, where one of its points (now *Monte Corno*) is 9521 feet above the sea; and further S., at the boundaries of Samnium, Apulia, and Lucania, it divides into two main branches, one of which runs E. through Apulia and Calabria, and terminates at the Salentine promontory, and the other W., through Bruttium, terminating apparently at Rhegium and the straits of Messina, but in reality continued throughout Sicily. The greater part of the Apennines is composed of limestone, abounding in numerous caverns and recesses, which in ancient as well as modern times were the resort of numerous robbers: the highest points of the mountains are covered with snow, even during most of the summer (*nivali vertice se attollens Apenninus*, Virg. *Aen.* xii. 703).

M. Aper, a Roman orator and a native of Gaul, rose by his eloquence to the rank of quaestor, tribune, and praetor, successively. He is one of the speakers in the Dialogue *de Oratoribus*, attributed to Tacitus.

Aper, Arrius, praetorian prefect, and son-in-law of the emperor Numerian, whom he was said to have murdered: he was himself put to death by Diocletian on his accession in A. D. 284.

Aperantia, a town and district of Aetolia near the Achelous, inhabited by the Aperantii.

Apēsas ('Απέσας: *Fuka* ?), a mountain on the borders of Phliasia and Argolis, with a temple of Zeus, who was hence called *Apesantius*, and to whom Perseus here first sacrificed.

Aphāca (τὰ 'Αφακα: *Afka* ?), a town of Coele-Syria, between Heliopolis and Byblus, celebrated for the worship and oracle of Aphrodite Aphacitis ('Αφακῖτις).

Aphāreus ('Αφαρεύς), son of the Messenian king Perieres and Gorgophone, and founder of the town of Arene in Messenia, which he called after his wife. His two sons Idas and Lynceus, the *Apharetidae* (*Apharēïa proles*, Ov. *Met.* viii. 304), are celebrated for their fight with the Dioscuri, which is described by Pindar. (*Nem.* x. 111.) —2. An Athenian orator and tragic poet, flourished B. C. 369—342. After the death of his father, his mother married the orator Isocrates, who adopted Aphareus as his son. He wrote 35 or 37 tragedies, and gained 4 prizes.

Aphētae ('Αφέται and *Aperai*: 'Αφεταῖος), a sea-port and promontory of Thessaly, at the entrance of the Sinus Maliacus, from which the ship Argo is said to have sailed.

Aphidas ('Αφείδας), son of Arcas, obtained from his father Tegea and the surrounding territory. He had a son, Aleus.

Aphidna ('Αφίδνα and 'Αφίδναι: 'Αφιδναῖος), an Attic demus not far from Decelea, originally belonged to the tribe Aeantis, afterwards to Leontis, and last to Hadrianis. It was in ancient times one of the 12 towns and districts into which Cecrops is said to have divided Attica: in it Theseus concealed Helen, but her brothers Castor and Pollux took the place and rescued their sister.

Aphrodisias ('Αφροδισίας·'Αφροδισιεύς: Aphrodisiensis), the name of several places famous for the worship of Aphrodite. 1. A. Carise (*Gheira*, Ru.), on the site of an old town of the Leleges, named Ninoë: under the Romans a free city and asylum, and a flourishing school of art.—2. Veneris Oppidum (*Porto Cavaliere*), a town, harbour, and island, on the coast of Cilicia, opposite to Cyprus.—3. A town, harbour, and island, on the coast of Cyrenaica in N. Africa.—4. See GADES.

Aphrodite ('Αφροδίτη), one of the great divinities of the Greeks, the goddess of love and beauty. In the Iliad she is represented as the daughter of Zeus and Dione, and in later traditions as a daughter of Cronos and Euonyme, or of Uranus and Hemera; but the poets most frequently relate that she was sprung from the foam (ἀφρός) of the sea, whence they derive her name. She is commonly represented as the wife of Hephaestus; but she proved faithless to her husband, and was in love with Ares, the god of war, to whom she bore Phobos, Deimos, Harmonia, and, according to later traditions, Eros and Anteros also. She also loved the gods Dionysus, Hermes, and Poseidon, and the mortals ANCHISES, ADONIS, and BUTES. She surpassed all the other goddesses in beauty, and hence received the prize of beauty from Paris. She likewise had the power of granting beauty and invincible charms to others, and whoever wore her magic girdle, immediately became an object of love and desire. In the vegetable kingdom the myrtle, rose, apple, poppy, &c., were sacred to her. The animals sacred to her, which are often mentioned as drawing her chariot or serving as her messengers, are the sparrow, the dove, the swan, the swallow, and a bird called iynx. The planet Venus and the spring-month of April were likewise sacred to her. The principal places of her worship in Greece were the islands of Cyprus and Cythera. The sacrifices offered to her consisted mostly of incense and garlands of flowers, but in some places animals were sacrificed to her. Respecting her festivals, see *Dict. of Antiq.* art. *Adonia, Anagogia, Aphrodisia, Catagogia.* Her worship was of Eastern origin, and probably introduced by the Phoenicians to the islands of Cyprus, Cythera, and others, from whence it spread all over Greece. She appears to have been originally identical with Astarte, called by the Hebrews Ashtoreth, and her connection with Adonis clearly points to Syria. Respecting the Roman goddess Venus, see VENUS.

Aphroditŏpŏlis ('Αφροδίτης πόλις), the name of several cities in Egypt. 1. In Lower Egypt: (1) In the Nomos Leontopolites, in the Delta, between Arthribis and Leontopolis: (2) (*Chybĕn-el-Koum*) in the Nomos Prosopites, in the Delta, on a navigable branch of the Nile, between Naucratis and Sais; probably the same as Atarbechis, which is an Egyptian name of the same meaning as the Greek Aphroditopolis. — 2. In Middle Egypt or Heptanomis, (*Atfyh*) a considerable city on the E. bank of the Nile; the chief city of the Nomos Aphroditopolites. — 3. In Upper Egypt, or the Thebaïs: (1) Veneris Oppidum (*Tachta*), a little way from the W. bank of the Nile; the chief city of the Nomos Aphroditopolis: (2) In the Nomos Hermonthites (*Deir*, N.W. of Esneh), on the W bank of the Nile.

Aphthŏnĭus ('Αφθόνιος), of Antioch, a Greek rhetorician, lived about A. D. 315, and wrote the introduction to the study of rhetoric, entitled *Progymnasmata* (προγυμνάσματα). It was constructed on the basis of the *Progymnasmata* of Hermogenes, and became so popular that it was used as the common school-book in this branch of education for several centuries. On the revival of letters it recovered its ancient popularity, and during the 16th and 17th centuries was used everywhere, but more especially in Germany, as the text-book for rhetoric. The number of editions and translations which were published during that period is greater than that of any other ancient writer. The best edition is in Walz's *Rhetores Graeci*, vol. i. Aphthonius also wrote some Aesopic fables, which are extant.

Aphj̆tis ('Αφύτις: *Alhyto*), a town in the peninsula Pallene in Macedonia, with a celebrated temple and oracle of Jupiter Ammon.

Apĭa ('Απία, sc. γῆ), the *Apian land*, an ancient name of Peloponnesus, especially Argolis, said to have been so called from Apis, a mythical king of Argos.

Apĭcāta, wife of Sejanus, was divorced by him, A. D. 23, after she had borne him three children, and put an end to her own life on the execution of Sejanus in 31.

Apĭcĭus, the name of three notorious gluttons. — 1. The first lived in the time of Sulla, and is said to have procured the condemnation of Rutilius Rufus, B. C. 92. — 2. The second and most re-

nowned, *M. Gabius Apicius*, flourished under Tiberius. After squandering upwards of 800,000 pounds upon his stomach, he found that little more than 80,000 remained; upon which, despairing of being able to satisfy the cravings of hunger from such a pittance, he forthwith hanged himself. But he was not forgotten. Sundry cakes (*Apicia*) and sauces long kept alive his memory; Apion, the grammarian, composed a work upon his luxurious labours, and his name passed into a proverb in all matters connected with the pleasures of the table — 3. A contemporary of Trajan, sent to this emperor, when he was in Parthia, fresh oysters, preserved by a skilful process of his own. — The treatise we now possess, bearing the title CAELII APICII *de Opsoniis et Condimentis*, sive *de Re Culinaria, Libri decem*, is a sort of Cook and Confectioner's Manual, containing a multitude of receipts for cookery. It was probably compiled at a late period by some one who prefixed the name of Apicius, in order to insure the circulation of his book. — *Editions.* By Almeloveen, Amstelod. 1709. and by Bernhold, Ansbach. 1806.

Apĭdănus ('Απιδανός, Ion. 'Ηπιδανός), a river in Thessaly, which flows into the Enipeus near Pharsalus.

Apĭōlae, a town of Latium, destroyed by Tarquinius Priscus.

Apĭon ('Απίων), a Greek grammarian, and a native of Oasis in Egypt, studied at Alexandria, and taught rhetoric at Rome in the reigns of Tiberius and Claudius. In the reign of Caligula he left Rome, and in A. D. 38 he was sent by the inhabitants of Alexandria at the head of an embassy to Caligula to bring forward complaints against the Jews residing in their city. Apion was the author of many works, all of which are now lost. Of these the most celebrated were upon the Homeric poems. He is said not only to have made the best recension of the text of the poems, but to have written explanations of phrases and words in the form of a Dictionary (Λέξεις 'Ομηρικαί). He also wrote a work on Egypt in 5 books, and a work against the Jews, to which Josephus replied in his treatise *Against Apion.*

Apĭon, Ptolemaeus. [PTOLEMAEUS, APION.]

Apĭs ('Απις). 1. Son of Phoroneus and Laodice, king of Argos, from whom Peloponnesus was called APIA: he ruled tyrannically, and was killed by Thelxion and Telchis. — 2. The Bull of Memphis, worshipped with the greatest reverence as a god among the Egyptians. The Egyptians believed that he was the offspring of a young cow, fructified by a ray from heaven. There were certain signs by which he was recognised to be the god. It was requisite that he should be quite black, have a white square mark on the forehead, on his back a figure similar to that of an eagle, have two kinds of hair in his tail, and on his tongue a knot resembling an insect called *cantharus*. When all these signs were discovered, the animal was consecrated with great pomp, and was conveyed to Memphis, where he had a splendid residence, containing extensive walks and courts for his amusement. His birthday, which was celebrated every year, was his most solemn festival; it was a day of rejoicing for all Egypt. The god was allowed to live only a certain number of years, probably 25. If he had not died before the expiration of that period, he was killed and buried in a sacred well, the place of which was unknown except to the initiated.

But if he died a natural death, he was buried publicly and solemnly; and as his birth filled all Egypt with joy and festivities, so his death threw the whole country into grief and mourning. The worship of Apis was originally nothing but the simple worship of the bull; but in the course of time the bull, like other animals, was regarded as a symbol, and Apis is hence identified with Osiris or the Sun.

Apis (Ἆπις), a city of Egypt, on the coast of the Mediterranean, on the border of the country towards Libya, about 10 stadia W. of Paraetonium; celebrated for the worship of the god Apis.

Apobathmi (Ἀπόβαθμοι), a place in Argolis on the sea not far from Thyrea, where Danaus is said to have landed.

Apodoti and Apodeotae (Ἀπόδωτοι and Ἀποδοτοί), a people in the S. E. of Aetolia, between the Evenus and Hylaethus.

Apollināris, Sidōnīus. [SIDONIUS.]

Apollinis Pr. (Ἀπόλλωνος ἄκρον: C. Zibeeb or C. Farina), a promontory of Zeugitana in N. Africa, forming the W. point of the Gulf of Carthage.

Apollo (Ἀπόλλων), one of the great divinities of the Greeks, son of Zeus and Leto and twin brother of Artemis, was born in the island of Delos, whither Leto had fled from the jealous Hera. [LETO.] After 9 days' labour, the god was born under a palm or olive tree at the foot of mount Cynthus, and was fed by Themis with ambrosia and nectar. The powers ascribed to Apollo are apparently of different kinds, but all are connected with one another, and may be said to be only ramifications of one and the same, as will be seen from the following classification. He is — 1. *The god who punishes*, whence some of the ancients derived his name from ἀπόλλυμι, destroy. (Aesch. Agam. 1081.) As the god who punishes he is represented with bow and arrows, the gift of Hephaestus; whence his epithets, ἕκατος, ἑκάεργος, ἑκατηβόλος, κλυτότοξος, and ἀργυρότοξος, arcitenens, &c. All sudden deaths were believed to be the effect of the arrows of Apollo; and with them he sent the plague into the camp of the Greeks. — 2. *The god who affords help and wards off evil.* As he had the power of punishing men, so he was also able to deliver men, if duly propitiated: hence his epithets, ἀκέσιος, ἀκέστωρ, ἀλεξίκακος, σώτηρ, ἀποτρόπαιος, ἐπικούριος, ἰατρομάντις, opifer, salutifer, &c. From his being the god who afforded help, he is the father of Aesculapius, the god of the healing art, and was also identified in later times with Paeëon, the god of the healing art in Homer. [PAEEON.] — 3. *The god of prophecy.* Apollo exercised this power in his numerous oracles, and especially in that of Delphi. (Dict. of Ant. art. Oraculum.) He had also the power of communicating the gift of prophecy both to gods and men, and all the ancient seers and prophets are placed in some relationship to him. — 4. *The god of song and music.* We find him in the Iliad (i. 603) delighting the immortal gods with his phorminx; and the Homeric bards derived their art of song either from Apollo or the Muses. Later traditions ascribed to Apollo even the invention of the flute and lyre, while it is more commonly related that he received the lyre from Hermes. Respecting his musical contests, see MARSYAS, MIDAS. — 5. *The god who protects the flocks and cattle* (νόμιος θεός, from νομός or νομή, a meadow or pasture land). There are in Homer only a few allusions to this feature in the character of Apollo, but in later writers it assumes a very prominent form, and in the story of Apollo tending the flocks of Admetus at Pherae in Thessaly, the idea reaches its height. — 6. *The god who delights in the foundation of towns and the establishment of civil constitutions.* Hence a town or a colony was never founded by the Greeks without consulting an oracle of Apollo, so that in every case he became, as it were, their spiritual leader.—7. *The god of the Sun.* In Homer, Apollo and Helios, or the Sun, are perfectly distinct, and his identification with the Sun, though almost universal among later writers, was the result of later speculations and of foreign, chiefly Egyptian, influence. — Apollo had more influence upon the Greeks than any other god. It may safely be asserted, that the Greeks would never have become what they were, without the worship of Apollo; in him the brightest side of the Grecian mind is reflected. Respecting his festivals, see Dict. of Ant. art. Apollonia, Thargelia, and others. — In the religion of the early Romans there is no trace of the worship of Apollo. The Romans became acquainted with this divinity through the Greeks, and adopted all their notions and ideas about him from the latter people. There is no doubt that the Romans knew of his worship among the Greeks at a very early time, and tradition says that they consulted his oracle at Delphi even before the expulsion of the kings. But the first time that we hear of his worship at Rome is in B. C. 430, when, for the purpose of averting a plague, a temple was raised to him, and soon after dedicated by the consul, C. Julius. A second temple was built to him in 350. During the second Punic war, in 212, the ludi Apollinares were instituted in his honour. (Dict. of Ant. art. Ludi Apollinares.) His worship, however, did not form a very prominent part in the religion of the Romans till the time of Augustus, who, after the battle of Actium, dedicated to him a portion of the spoils, built or embellished his temple at Actium, and founded a new one at Rome on the Palatine, and instituted quinquennial games at Actium.—The most beautiful and celebrated among the extant representations of Apollo are the Apollo Belvedere at Rome, which was discovered in 1503 at Rettuno and the Apollino at Florence. In the Apollo Belvedere, the god is represented with commanding but serene majesty; sublime intellect and physical beauty are combined in the most wonderful manner.

Apollocrates (Ἀπολλοκράτης), elder son of Dionysius, the Younger, was left by his father in command of the island and citadel of Syracuse, but was compelled by famine to surrender them to Dion, about B. C. 354.

Apollodorus (Ἀπολλόδωρος).—1. Of Amphipolis, one of the generals of Alexander the Great, was intrusted in B. C. 331, together with Menes, with the administration of Babylon and of all the satrapies as far as Cilicia.—2. Tyrant of Cassandrea (formerly Potidaea) in the peninsula of Pallene, obtained the supreme power in B. C. 379, and exercised it with the utmost cruelty. He was conquered and put to death by Antigonus Gonatas. —3. Of Carystus, a comic poet, probably lived B. C. 300—260, and was one of the most distinguished of the poets of the new Attic comedy. It was from him that Terence took his Hecyra and Phormio. — 4. Of Gela in Sicily, a comic poet and a contemporary of Menander, lived B. C. 340—290. He is frequently confounded with Apollodorus of Carystus. — **5.** A **Grammarian** of Athens, son of Asclepiades, and pupil of Aristarchus and Panaetius, flourished about B. c. 140. He wrote a great number of works, all of which have perished with the exception of his *Bibliotheca*. This work consists of 3 books, and is by far the best among the extant works of the kind. It contains a well-arranged account of the mythology and the heroic age of Greece: it begins with the origin of the gods, and goes down to the time of Theseus, when the work suddenly breaks off. — *Editions.* By Heyne, Göttingen, 1803, 2d ed. ; by Clavier, Paris, 1805, with a French translation ; and by Westermann in the *Mythographi*, Brunswick, 1843. Of the many other works of Apollodorus, one of the most important was a chronicle in iambic verses, comprising the history of 1040 years, from the destruction of Troy (1184) down to his own time, B. c. 143.—**6.** Of **Pergamus**, a Greek rhetorician, taught rhetoric at Apollonia in his advanced age, and had as a pupil the young Octavius, afterwards the emperor Augustus —**7.** A painter of Athens, flourished about B. c 408, with whom commenced a new period in the history of the art. He made a great advance in colouring, and invented chiaroscuro. — **8.** An architect of Damascus, lived under Trajan and Hadrian, by the latter of whom he was put to death.

Apollōnīa (Ἀπολλωνία: Ἀπολλωνιάτης). **1.** (*Pollina* or *Pollona*), an important town in Illyria or New Epirus, not far from the mouth of the Aous, and 60 stadia from the sea. It was founded by the Corinthians and Corcyraeans, and was equally celebrated as a place of commerce and of learning ; many distinguished Romans, among others the young Octavius, afterwards the emperor Augustus, pursued their studies here. Persons travelling from Italy to Greece and the E., usually landed either at Apollonia or Dyrrhachium ; and the Via Egnatia, the great high road to the East, commenced at Apollonia or, according to others, at Dyrrhachium. [EGNATIA VIA.] — **2.** (*Polina*), a town in Macedonia, on the Via Egnatia, between Thessalonica and Amphipolis, and S. of the lake of Bolbe. — **3.** (*Sizeboli*), a town in Thrace on the Black Sea, with two harbours, a colony of Miletus, afterwards called Sozopolis, whence its modern name : it had a celebrated temple of Apollo, from which Lucullus carried away a colossus of this god, and erected it on the Capitol at Rome.—**4.** A castle or fortified town of the Locri Ozolae, near Naupactus.—**5.** A town in Sicily, on the N. coast, of uncertain site. —**6.** (*Abullionte*), a town in Bithynia on the lake Apolloniatis, through which the river Rhyndacus flows. — **7.** A town on the borders of Mysia and Lydia, between Pergamus and Sardis. — **8.** A town in Palestina, between Caesarea and Joppa. — **9.** A town in Assyria, in the district of Apolloniatis, through which the Delas or Durus (*Diala*) flows. —**10.** (*Marza Susa*), a town in Cyrenaica and the harbour of Cyrene, one of the 5 towns of the Pentapolis in Libya: it was the birthplace of Eratosthenes.

Apollōnis (Ἀπολλωνίς), a city in Lydia, between Pergamus and Sardis, named after Apollonis, the mother of king Eumenes. It was one of the 12 cities of Asia, which were destroyed by an earthquake in the reign of Tiberius (A. D. 17).

Apollōnīus (Ἀπολλώνιος). **1.** Of **Alabanda** in Caria, a rhetorician, taught rhetoric at Rhodes about B. c. 100. He was a very distinguished teacher of rhetoric, and used to ridicule and despise

philosophy. He was surnamed ὁ Μαλακός, and must be distinguished from the following. — **2.** Of **Alabanda**, surnamed **Molo**, likewise a rhetorician, taught rhetoric at Rhodes, and also distinguished himself as a pleader in the courts of justice. In B. c. 81, when Sulla was dictator, Apollonius came to Rome as ambassador of the Rhodians, on which occasion Cicero heard him ; Cicero also received instruction from Apollonius at Rhodes a few years later. — **3.** Son of **Archebulus**, a grammarian of Alexandria, in the first century of the Christian aera, and a pupil of Didymus. He wrote an Homeric Lexicon, which is still extant, and though much interpolated, is a work of great value. — *Editions.* By Villoison, Paris, 1773 ; by H. Tollius, Lugd. Bat. 1788 ; and by Bekker, Berlin, 1833. — **4.** Surnamed **Dyscolus**, " the ill-tempered," a grammarian at Alexandria, in the reigns of Hadrian and Antoninus Pius (A. D. 117—161), taught at Rome as well as Alexandria. He and his son HERODIANUS are called by Priscian the greatest of all grammarians. Apollonius was the first who reduced grammar to any thing like a system. Of his numerous works only 4 are extant. 1. Περὶ συντάξεως τοῦ λόγου μερῶν, " de Constructione Orationis," or " de Ordinatione sive Constructione Dictionum," in 4 books ; edited by Fr. Sylburg, Frankf. 1590, and by I. Bekker, Berlin, 1817. 2. Περὶ ἀντωνυμίας, " de Pronomine ;" edited by I. Bekker, Berlin, 1814. 3. Περὶ συνδέσμων, " de Conjunctionibus," and 4. Περὶ ἐπιῤῥημάτων, " de Adverbiis," printed in Bekker's *Anecdot.* ii. p. 477, &c. Among the works ascribed to Apollonius by Suidas there is one περὶ κατεψευσμένης ἱστορίας, on fictitious or forged histories: this has been erroneously supposed to be the same as the extant work Ἱστορίαι θαυμασίαι, which purports to be written by an Apollonius (published by Westermann, *Paradoxographi*, Brunswick, 1839) ; but it is now admitted that the latter work was written by an Apollonius who is otherwise unknown. — **5. Pergaeus**, from Perga in Pamphylia, one of the greatest mathematicians of antiquity, commonly called the " Great Geometer," was educated at Alexandria under the successors of Euclid, and flourished about B. c. 250—220. His most important work was a treatise on Conic Sections in 8 books, of which the first 4, with the commentary of Eutocius, are extant in Greek ; and all but the eighth in Arabic. We have also introductory lemmata to all the 8, by Pappus. Edited by Halley, " Apoll. Perg. Conic. lib. viii., &c.," Oxon. 1710, fol. The eighth book is a conjectural restoration founded on the introductory lemmata of Pappus. — **6. Rhodius**, a poet and grammarian, son of Silleus or Illeus and Rhode, was born at Alexandria, or, according to one statement, at Naucratis, and flourished in the reigns of Ptolemy Philopator and Ptolemy Epiphanes (B. c. 222—181). In his youth he was instructed by Callimachus ; but they afterwards became bitter enemies. Their tastes were entirely different ; for Apollonius admired and imitated the simplicity of the ancient epic poets, and disliked and despised the artificial and learned poetry of Callimachus. When Apollonius read at Alexandria his poem on the Argonautic expedition (*Argonautica*), it did not meet with the approbation of the audience : he attributed its failure to the intrigues of Callimachus, and revenged himself by writing a bitter epi-

Hercules and Alcestis. (From a Bas-relief at Florence.)
See ADMETUS, p. 2.

Death of Adonis.
(A Painting found at Pompeii.) Page 9.

Andromeda and Perseus.
(From a Terra-cotta.) Page 51.

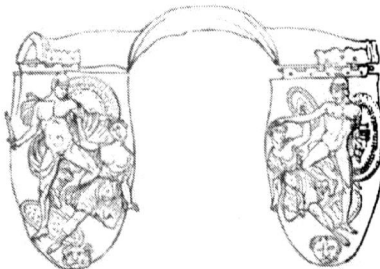

Zethus and Amphion.
(From a Bas-relief at Rome.) Page 45.

Amazons.
(From Bronzes of Siris in the British Museum.) Page 42.

Amazons. (From a Sarcophagus in the Capitol at Rome.) Page 42.

[To face p. 64.

Agrigentum. Page 27.

Amisus in Pontus. Page 43.

Agyrium in Sicily. Page 28.

Amphipolis. Page 45.

Aluntium in Sicily. Page 41.

Anactorium in Acarnania. Page 47.

Alyzia in Acarnania. Page 41.

Ancona in Italy. Page 49.

Amastris in Paphlagonia. Page 47.

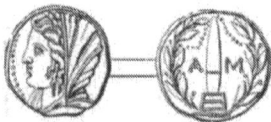

Ancyra in Phrygia. Page 49.

Ambracia. Page 47.

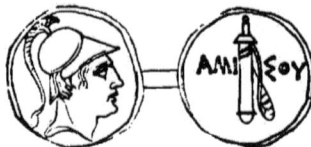

Andros. Page 51.

To face p. 65.]

gram on Callimachus which is still extant. (*Anth. Graec.* xi. 275.) Callimachus in return attacked Apollonius in his *Ibis*, which was imitated by Ovid in a poem of the same name. Apollonius now left Alexandria and went to Rhodes, where he taught rhetoric with so much success, that the Rhodians honoured him with their franchise: hence he was called the " Rhodian." He afterwards returned to Alexandria, where he read a revised edition of his *Argonautica* with great applause. He succeeded Eratosthenes as chief librarian at Alexandria, in the reign of Ptolemy Epiphanes, about B. C. 194, and appears to have held this office till his death. The *Argonautica*, which consists of 4 books, and is still extant, gives a straightforward and simple description of the adventures of the Argonauts: it is a close imitation of the Homeric language and style, but exhibits marks of art and labour, and thus forms, notwithstanding its many resemblances, a contrast with the natural and easy flow of the Homeric poems. Among the Romans the work was much read, and P. Terentius Varro Atacinus acquired great reputation by his translation of it. The *Argonautica* of Valerius Flaccus is only a free imitation of it. — *Editions.* By Brunck, Argentorat. 1780 ; by G. Schaefer, Lips. 1810—13 ; by Wellauer, Lips. 1828. Apollonius wrote several other works which are now lost. — **7. Tyanensis** or **Tyanaeus,** *i. e.* of Tyāna in Cappadocia, a Pythagorean philosopher, was born about 4 years before the Christian aera. At a period when there was a general belief in magical powers, it would appear that Apollonius obtained great influence by pretending to them ; and we may believe that his Life by Philostratus gives a just idea of his character and reputation, however inconsistent in its facts, and absurd in its marvels. Apollonius, according to Philostratus, was of noble ancestry, and studied first under Euthydemus, of Tarsus ; but, being disgusted at the luxury of the inhabitants, he retired to the neighbouring town of Aegae, where he studied the whole circle of the Platonic, Sceptic, Epicurean, and Peripatetic philosophy, and ended by giving his preference to the Pythagorean. He devoted himself to the strictest asceticism, and subsequently travelled throughout the East, visiting Nineveh, Babylon, and India. On his return to Asia Minor, we first hear of his pretensions to miraculous power, founded, as it would seem, on the possession of some divine knowledge derived from the East. From Ionia he crossed over into Greece, and from thence to Rome, where he arrived just after an edict against magicians had been issued by Nero. He accordingly remained only a short time at Rome, and next went to Spain and Africa ; at Alexandria was of assistance to Vespasian, who was preparing to seize the empire. The last journey of Apollonius was to Ethiopia, whence he returned to settle in the Ionian cities. On the accession of Domitian, Apollonius was accused of exciting an insurrection against the tyrant : he voluntarily surrendered himself and appeared at Rome before the emperor : but as his destruction seemed impending, he escaped by the exertion of his supernatural powers. The last years of his life were spent at Ephesus, where he is said to have proclaimed the death of the tyrant Domitian at the instant it took place. Many of the wonders, which Philostratus relates in connection with Apollonius, curiously coincide with the Christian miracles. The proclamation of the birth of Apollonius to his mother by Proteus, and

the incarnation of Proteus himself, the chorus of swans which sang for joy on the occasion, the casting out of devils, raising the dead, and healing the sick, the sudden disappearances and reappearances of Apollonius, his adventures in the cave of Trophonius, and the sacred voice which called him at his death, to which may be added his claim as a teacher having authority to reform the world — cannot fail to suggest the parallel passages in the Gospel history. We know, too, that Apollonius was one among many rivals set up by the Eclectics to our Saviour, an attempt renewed by the English freethinkers Blount and Lord Herbert. Still it must be allowed that the resemblances are very general, and on the whole it seems probable that the life of Apollonius was not written with a controversial aim, as the resemblances, although real, only indicate that a few things were borrowed, and exhibit no trace of a systematic parallel. [PHILOSTRATUS.] — **8.** Of **Tyre**, a Stoic philosopher, who lived in the reign of Ptolemy Auletes, wrote a history of the Stoic philosophy from the time of Zeno. — **9. Apollonius** and **Tauriscus** of Tralles, were two brothers, and the sculptors of the group which is commonly known as the Farnese bull, representing the punishment of Dirce by Zethus and Amphion. [DIRCE.] It was taken from Rhodes to Rome by Asinius Pollio, and afterwards placed in the baths of Caracalla, where it was dug up in the sixteenth century, and deposited in the Farnese palace. It is now at Naples. Apollonius and Tauriscus probably flourished in the first century of the Christian aera.

Apollophānes ('Ἀπολλοφάνης), a poet of the old Attic comedy, of whose comedies a few fragments are extant, lived about B. C. 400.

Apŏnus or **Apŏni Fons** (*Abano*), warm medicinal springs, near Patavium, hence called Aquae Patavinae, were much frequented by the sick.

Appia or **Apia** ('Ἀππία, 'Ἀπία), a city of Phrygia Pacatiana.

Appia Via, the most celebrated of the Roman roads (*regina viarum*, Stat. *Silv.* ii. 2. 12), was commenced by Ap. Claudius Caecus, when censor, B. C. 312, and was the great line of communication between Rome and southern Italy. It issued from the *Porta Capena*, and passing through *Aricia, Tres Tabernae, Appii Forum, Turracina, Fundi, Formiae, Minturnae, Sinuessa,* and *Casilinum,* terminated at *Capua,* but was eventually extended through *Calatia* and *Caudium* to *Beneventum,* and finally thence through *Venusia, Tarentum,* and *Uria,* to *Brundusium.*

Appiānus ('Ἀππιανός), the Roman historian, was born at Alexandria, and lived at Rome during the reigns of Trajan, Hadrian, and Antoninus Pius. He wrote a Roman history ('Ῥωμαϊκὰ, or 'Ῥωμαϊκὴ ἱστορία), in 24 books, arranged not synchronistically, but ethnographically, that is, he did not relate the history of the Roman empire as a whole in chronological order ; but he gave a separate account of the affairs of each country, till it was finally incorporated in the Roman empire. The subjects of the different books were : 1. The kingly period. 2. Italy. 3. The Samnites. 4. The Gauls or Celts. 5. Sicily and the other islands. 6. Spain. 7. Hannibal's wars. 8. Libya, Carthage, and Numidia. 9. Macedonia. 10. Greece and the Greek states in Asia Minor. 11. Syria and Parthia. 12. The war with Mithridates. 13—21. The civil wars, in 9 books, from those of Marius and Sulla to the battle of Actium. 22. Ἐκατονταετία, comprised the history of a hundred years, from the battle of Actium to the beginning of Vespasian's reign. 23. The wars with Illyria. 24. Those with Arabia. We possess only 11 of these complete ; namely, the 6th, 7th, 8th, 11th, 12th, 13th, 14th, 15th, 16th, 17th, and 23rd : there are fragments of several of the others. The Parthian history, which has come down to us as part of the 11th book, is not a work of Appian, but merely a compilation from Plutarch's Lives of Antony and Crassus. Appian's work is a compilation. His style is clear and simple ; but he possesses few merits as an historian, and he frequently makes the most absurd blunders. Thus, for instance, he places Saguntum on the N. of the Iberus, and states that it takes only half a day to sail from Spain to Britain. The best edition is that of Schweighäuser, Lips. 1785.

Appias, a nymph of the Appian well, which was situated near the temple of Venus Genetrix in the forum of Julius Caesar. It was surrounded by statues of nymphs, called *Appiades*.

Appii Forum. [FORUM APPII.]

Appuleius or **Apuleius**, of Madura in Africa, was born about A. D. 130, of respectable parents. He received the first rudiments of education at Carthage, and afterwards studied the Platonic philosophy at Athens. He next travelled extensively, visiting Italy, Greece, and Asia, and becoming initiated in most mysteries. At length he returned home, but soon afterwards undertook a new journey to Alexandria. On his way thither he was taken ill at the town of Oea, and was hospitably received into the house of a young man, Sicinius Pontianus, whose mother, a very rich widow of the name of Pudentilla, he married. Her relatives, being indignant that so much wealth should pass out of the family, impeached Appuleius of gaining the affections of Pudentilla by charms and magic spells. The cause was heard at Sabrata before Claudius Maximus, proconsul of Africa, A. D. 173, and the defence spoken by Appuleius is still extant. Of his subsequent career we know little : he occasionally declaimed in public with great applause. The most important of the extant works of Appuleius are : I. *Metamorphoseon seu de Asino Aureo Libri XI.* This celebrated romance, together with the *Asinus* of Lucian, is said to have been founded upon a work bearing the same title by a certain Lucius of Patrae. It seems to have been intended simply as a satire upon the hypocrisy and debauchery of certain orders of priests, the frauds of juggling pretenders to supernatural powers, and the general profligacy of public morals. There are some, however, who discover a more recondite meaning, and especially bishop Warburton, in his Divine Legation of Moses, who has at great length endeavoured to prove, that the Golden Ass was written with the view of recommending the Pagan religion in opposition to Christianity, and especially of inculcating the importance of initiation into the purer mysteries. The well-known and beautiful episode of Cupid and Psyche is introduced in the 4th, 5th, and 6th books. This, whatever opinion we may form of the principal narrative, is evidently an allegory, and is generally understood to shadow forth the progress of the soul to perfection. II. *Floridorum Libri IV.* An Anthology, containing select extracts from various orations and dissertations, collected probably by some admirer. III. *De*

Deo Socratis Liber. IV. *De Dogmate Platonis Libri tres.* The first book contains some account of the *speculative doctrines* of Plato, the second of his *morals*, the third of his *logic.* V. *De Mundo Liber.* A translation of the work περὶ κόσμου, at one time ascribed to Aristotle. VI. *Apologia* sive *De Magia Liber.* The oration described above, delivered before Claudius Maximus. The best edition of the whole works of Appuleius is by Hildebrand, Lips. 1842.

Appuleius Saturninus. [SATURNINUS.]

Apriës (Ἀπρίης, Ἀπρίας), a king of Egypt, the Pharaoh-Hophra of Scripture, succeeded his father Psammis, and reigned B. C. 595—570. After an unsuccessful attack against Cyrene he was dethroned and put to death by AMASIS.

Apronius. 1. Q., one of the worst instruments of Verres in oppressing the Sicilians.—2. L., served under Drusus (A. D. 14) and Germanicus (15) in Germany. In 20 he was proconsul of Africa, and praetor of Lower Germany, where he lost his life in a war against the Frisii. Apronius had two daughters : one of whom was married to Plautius Silvanus ; the other to Lentulus Gaetulicus, consul in 26.

Apsilae (Ἀψίλαι), a Scythian people in Colchis, N. of the river Phasis.

Apsines (Ἀψίνης), of Gadara in Phoenicia, a Greek sophist and rhetorician, taught rhetoric at Athens about A. D. 235. Two of his works are extant : Περὶ τῶν μέρων τοῦ πολιτικοῦ λόγου τέχνη, which is much interpolated ; and Περὶ τῶν ἐσχηματισμένων προβλημάτων, both of which are printed in Walz. *Rhetor. Graec.*

Apsus (Crevasta), a river in Illyria (Nova Epirus), which flows into the Ionian sea.

Apsyrtus. [ABSYRTUS.]

Apta Julia (Apt), chief town of the Vulgientes in Gallia Narbonensis, and a Roman colony.

Aptěra (Ἄπτερα : Ἀπτεραῖος : Palaeokastron on the G. of Suda), a town on the W. coast of Crete, 80 stadia from Cydonia.

Apuāni, a Ligurian people on the Macra, were subdued by the Romans after a long resistance and transplanted to Samnium, B. C. 180.

Apuleius. [APPULEIUS.]

Apulia (Apulus), included, in its widest signification, the whole of the S.E. of Italy from the river Frento to the promontory Iapygium, and was bounded on the N. by the Frentani, on the E. by the Adriatic, on the S. by the Tarentine gulf, and on the W. by Samnium and Lucania, thus including the modern provinces of Bari, Otranto, and Capitanata, in the kingdom of Naples. Apulia in its narrower sense was the country E. of Samnium on both sides of the Aufidus, the Daunia and Peucetia of the Greeks : the whole of the S.E. part was called Calabria by the Romans. The Greeks gave the name of Daunia to the N. part of the country from the Frento to the Aufidus, of Peucetia to the country from the Aufidus to Tarentum and Brundusium, and of Iapygia or Messapia to the whole of the remaining S. part : though they sometimes included under Iapygia all Apulia in its widest meaning. The N.W. of Apulia is a plain, but the S. part is traversed by the E. branch of the Apennines, and has only a small tract of land on the coast on each side of the mountains. The country was very fertile, especially in the neighbourhood of Tarentum, and the mountains afforded excellent pasturage. The population was of a mixed nature : they were for the most part of Illyrian origin, and are said to have settled in the country under the guidance of Iapyx, Daunius, and Peucetius, three sons of an Illyrian king, Lycaon. Subsequently many towns were founded by Greek colonists. The Apulians joined the Samnites against the Romans, and became subject to the latter on the conquest of the Samnites.

Aquae, the name given by the Romans to many medicinal springs and bathing-places : — 1. Aurelia or Colonia Aurelia Aquensis (*Baden-Baden*). 2. Calidae or Solis (*Bath*) in Britain. 3. Cutiliae, mineral springs in Samnium near the ancient town of Cutilia, which perished in early times, and E. of Reate. There was a celebrated lake in its neighbourhood with a floating island, which was regarded as the umbilicus or centre of Italy. Vespasian died at this place. 4. Mattiacae or Fontes Mattiaci (*Wiesbaden*), in the land of the Mattiaci in Germany. 5. Patavinae [Aponi Fons]. 6. Sextiae (*Aix*), a Roman colony in Gallia Narbonensis, founded by Sextius Calvinus, B. C. 122 ; its mineral waters were long celebrated, but were thought to have lost much of their efficacy in the time of Augustus. Near this place Marius defeated the Teutoni, B. C. 102. 7. Statiellae (*Acqui*), a town of the Statielli in Liguria, celebrated for its warm baths.

Aquae, in Africa. 1. (*Meriga*, Ru.), in the interior of Mauretania Caesariensis.—2. Calidae (*Gurbos* or *Hammam l'Enf*), on the gulf of Carthage.—3. Regiae (*Hamnam Truzza*), in the N. part of Byzacena.—4. Tacapitanae (*Hammat el-Khabs*), at the S. extremity of Byzacena, close to the large city of Tacape (*Khabs*).

Aquila. 1. Of Pontus, translated the Old Testament into Greek, in the reign of Hadrian, probably about A. D. 130. Only a few fragments remain, which have been published in the editions of the Hexapla of Origen.—2. **Julius Aquila**, a Roman jurist quoted in the Digest, probably lived under or before the reign of Septimius Severus, A. D. 193—198.—3. L. **Pontius Aquila**, a friend of Cicero, and one of Caesar's murderers, was killed at the battle of Mutina, B. C. 43.—4. **Aquila Romanus**, a rhetorician, who probably lived in the third century after Christ, wrote a small work entitled *De Figuris Sententiarum et Elocutionis*, which is usually printed with Rutilius Lupus.—*Editions.* By Ruhnken, Lugd. Bat. 1768, reprinted with additional notes by Frotscher, Lips. 1831.

Aquillaria (*Alhowareah*), a town on the coast of Zeugitana in Africa, on the W. side of Hermaeum Pr. (*C. Bon*), the E. extremity of the Gulf of Carthage. It was a good landing-place in summer.

Aquileia (Aquileiensis: *Aquileia* or *Aglar*), a town in Gallia Transpadana at the very top of the Adriatic, between the rivers Sontius and Natiso, about 60 stadia from the sea. It was founded by the Romans in B. C. 182 as a bulwark against the N. barbarians, and is said to have derived its name from the favourable omen of an eagle (*aquila*) appearing to the colonists. As it was the key of Italy on the N.E., it was made one of the strongest fortresses of the Romans. From its position it became also a most flourishing place of commerce : the Via Aemilia was continued to this town, and from it all the roads to Rhaetia, Noricum, Pannonia, Istria, and Dalmatia branched off. It was taken and completely destroyed by Attila in A. D.

452 : its inhabitants escaped to the Lagoons, where Venice was afterwards built.

Aquillia Via, began at *Capua*, and ran S. through *Nola* and *Nuceria* to *Salernum* ; from thence it ran through the very heart of Lucania and Bruttii, passing *Nerulum, Interamnia, Cosentia, Vibo*, and *Medma*, and terminated at *Rhegium*.

Aquillius or **Aquilius**. 1. **M'.**, consul B. C. 129, finished the war against Aristonicus, son of Eumenes of Pergamus. On his return to Rome he was accused of maladministration in his province, but was acquitted by bribing the judges. — 2. **M'.**, consul in B. C. 101, conquered the slaves in Sicily, who had revolted under Athenion. In 98 he was accused of maladministration in Sicily, but was acquitted. In 88 he went into Asia as one of the consular legates in the Mithridatic war : he was defeated and handed over by the inhabitants of Mytilene to Mithridates, who put him to death by pouring molten gold down his throat.

Aquillius Gallus. [Gallus.]

Aquilonia (Aquilōnus), a town of Samnium, E of Bovianum, destroyed by the Romans in the Samnite wars.

Aquinum (Aquinas: *Aquino*), a town of the Volscians, E. of the river Melpis, in a fertile country ; a Roman municipium and afterwards a colony ; the birth-place of Juvenal ; celebrated for its purple dye. (Hor. *Ep.* i. 10. 27.)

Aquitania. 1. The country of the Aquitani, extended from the Garumna (*Garonne*) to the Pyrenees, and from the ocean to Gallia Narbonensis : it was first conquered by Caesar's legates, and again upon a revolt of the inhabitants in the time of Augustus. — 2. The Roman province of Aquitania, formed in the reign of Augustus, was of much wider extent, and was bounded on the N. by the Ligeris (*Loire*), on the W. by the ocean, on the S. by the Pyrenees, and on the E. by the Mons Cevenna, which separated it from Gallia Narbonensis.—The *Aquitani* were one of the three races which inhabited Gaul ; they were of Iberian or Spanish origin, and differed from the Gauls and Belgians in language, customs, and physical peculiarity.

Ara Ubiorum, a place in the neighbourhood of Bonn in Germany, perhaps *Godesberg* : others suppose it to be another name of Colonia Agrippina (*Cologne*).

Arabia (ἡ 'Ἀραβία : 'Ἀραψ, pl. 'Ἀραβες, 'Ἀραβοι, Arabs, Ἀράβης, pl. Ἀράβες, Ἀράβι : *Arabia*), a country at the S.W. extremity of Asia, forming a large peninsula, of a sort of hatchet shape, bounded on the W. by the Arabicus Sinus (*Red Sea*), on the S. and the E. by the Erythraeum Mare (*Gulf of Bab-el-Mandeb* and *Indian Ocean*), and on the N.E. by the Persicus Sinus (*Persian Gulf*). On the N. or land side its boundaries were somewhat indefinite, but it seems to have included the whole of the desert country between Egypt and Syria, on the one side, and the banks of the Euphrates on the other ; and it was often considered to extend even further on both sides, so as to include, on the E., the S. part of Mesopotamia along the left bank of the Euphrates, and, on the W., the part of Palestine E. of the Jordan, and the part of Egypt between the Red Sea and the E. margin of the Nile valley, which, even as a part of Egypt, was called Arabiae Nomos. In the stricter sense of the name, which confines it to the peninsula itself, Arabia may be considered as bounded on the N. by a line from the head of the Red Sea

F 2

(at *Suez*) to the mouth of the Tigris (*Shat-el-Arab*) which just about coincides with the parallel of 30° N. lat. It was divided into 3 parts: (1) **Arabia Petraea** (ή πετραία 'Αραβία: N.W. part of *El-Hejaz*), including the triangular piece of land between the two heads of the Red Sea (the peninsula of M. Sinai) and the country immediately to the N. and N. E.; and called from its capital Petra, while the literal signification of the name " Rocky Arabia" agrees also with the nature of the country: (2) **Arabia Deserta** (*El-Jebel*), including the great Syrian Desert and a portion of the interior of the Arabian peninsula: (3) **Arabia Felix** (*El-Nejed*, *El-Hejaz*, *El-Yemen*, *El-Hadramaut*, *Oman*, and *El-Hejer*) consisted of the whole country not included in the other two divisions; the ignorance of the ancients respecting the interior of the peninsula leading them to class it with Arabia Felix, although it properly belongs to Arabia Deserta, for it consists, so far as it is known, of a sandy desert of steppes and table land, interspersed with Oases (*Wadis*), and fringed with mountains, between which and the sea, especially on the W. coast, lies a belt of low land (called *Tehāmah*), intersected by numerous mountain torrents, which irrigate the strips of land on their banks, and produce that fertility which caused the ancients to apply the epithet of Felix to the whole peninsula. The width of the *Tehamah* is, in some places on the W. coast, as much as from one to two days' journey, but on the other sides it is very narrow, except at the E. end of the peninsula (about *Muskat* in Oman) where for a small space its width is again a day's journey.—The inhabitants of Arabia were of the race called Semitic or Aramaean, and closely related to the Israelites. The N.W. district (Arabia Petraea) was inhabited by the various tribes which constantly appear in Jewish history: the Amalekites, Midianites, Edomites, Moabites, Ammonites, &c. The Greeks and Romans called the inhabitants by the name of NABATHAEI, whose capital was Petra. The people of Arabia Deserta were called Arabes Scenitae (Σκηνῖται), from their dwelling in tents, and Arabes Nomadae (Νομάδες), from their mode of life, which was that of wandering herdsmen, who supported themselves partly by their cattle, and to a great extent also by the plunder of caravans, as their unchanged descendants, the *Bedouins* or *Bedawees*, still do. The people of the *Tehamah* were (and are) of the same race; but their position led them at an early period to cultivate both agriculture and commerce, and to build considerable cities. Their chief tribes were known by the following names, beginning S. of the Nabathaei, on the W. coast: the Thamydēni and Minaei (in the S. part of *Hejaz*) in the neighbourhood of Macoraba (*Mecca*); the Sabaei and Homeritae in the S. W. part of the peninsula (*Yemen*); on the S. E. coast, the Chatramolitae and Adramītae (in *El-Hadramaut*, a country very little known, even to the present day); on the E. and N. E. coast the Omanītae and Darachēni (in *Oman*, and *El-Ahsa* or *El-Hejer*). — From the earliest known period a considerable traffic was carried on by the people in the N. (especially the Nabathaei) by means of caravans, and by those on the S. and E. coast by sea, in the productions of their own country (chiefly gums, spices, and precious stones), and in those of India and Arabia. Besides this peaceful intercourse with the neighbouring countries, they seem to have made military

expeditions at an early period, for there can be no doubt that the Hyksos or " Shepherd-kings," who for some time ruled over Lower Egypt, were Arabians. On the other hand, they have successfully resisted all attempts to subjugate them. The alledged conquests of some of the Assyrian kings could only have affected small portions of the country on the N. Of the Persian empire we are expressly told that they were independent. Alexander the Great died too soon even to attempt his contemplated scheme of circumnavigating the peninsula and subduing the inhabitants. The Greek kings of Syria made unsuccessful attacks upon the Nabathaei. Under Augustus, Aelius Gallus, assisted by the Nabathaei, made an expedition into Arabia Felix, but was compelled to retreat into Egypt to save his army from famine and the climate. Under Trajan, Arabia Petraea was conquered by A. Cornelius Palma (A. D. 107), and the country of the Nabathaei became a Roman province. Some partial and temporary footing was gained at a much later period, on the S.W. coast by the Ethiopians; and both in this direction and from the N. Christianity was early introduced into the country, where it spread to a great extent, and continued to exist side by side with the old religion (which was Sabaeism, or the worship of heavenly bodies), and with some admixture of Judaism, until the total revolution produced by the rise of Mohammedanism in 622. While maintaining their independence, the Arabs of the Desert have also preserved to this day their ancient form of government, which is strictly patriarchal, under the heads of tribes and families (*Emirs* and *Sheiks*). In the more settled districts, the patriarchal authority passed into the hands of kings; and the people were divided into the several castes of scholars, warriors, agriculturists, merchants, and mechanics. The Mohammedan revolution lies beyond our limits.

Arābīcus Sinus (ὁ 'Αραβικὸς κόλπος: *Red Sea*), a long narrow gulf between Africa and Arabia, connected on the S. with the *Indian Ocean* by the Angustiae Divae (*Straits of Bab-el-Mandeb*), and on the N. divided into two heads by the peninsula of Arabia Petraea (*Penins. of Sinai*), the E. of which was called Sinus Aelanites or Aelaniticus (*Gulf of Akaba*), and the W. Sinus Heroopolites or Heroopoliticus (*Gulf of Suez*). The upper part of the sea was known at a very early period; but it was not explored in its whole extent till the maritime expeditions of the Ptolemies. Respecting its other name see ERYTHRAEUM MARE.

Arābis ('Αραβις, also 'Αράβιος, 'Αρβις, 'Αραβις, and 'Αράβιος: *Poorally* or *Agbor*), a river of Gedrosia, falling into the Indian Ocean 1000 stadia (100 geog. miles) W. of the mouth of the Indus, and dividing the Oritae on its W. from the Arabitae or Arbies on its E., who had a city named Arbis on its E. bank.

Arabītae. [ARABIS.]

Arachnaeum ('Αραχναῖον), a mountain forming the boundary between Argolis and Corinthia.

Arachnē, a Lydian maiden, daughter of Idmon of Colophon, a famous dyer in purple. Arachne excelled in the art of weaving, and, proud of her talent, ventured to challenge Athena to compete with her. Arachne produced a piece of cloth in which the amours of the gods were woven, and as Athena could find no fault with it, she tore the work to pieces. Arachne in despair hung herself: the goddess loosened the rope and saved her life but the rope was changed into a cobweb and Arachne herself into a spider (ἀράχνη), the animal most odious to Athena. (Ov. *Met.* vi. 1, seq.) This fable seems to suggest the idea that man learnt the art of weaving from the spider, and that it was invented in Lydia.

Arāchōsĭā ('Αραχωσία: 'Αραχωτοί or -ῶται: *S. E. part of Afghanistan* and *N. E. part of Beloochistan*), one of the extreme E. provinces of the Persian (and afterwards of the Parthian) Empire, bounded on the E. by the Indus, on the N. by the Paropamisadae, on the W. by Drangiana, and on the S. by Gedrosia. It was a fertile country, watered by the river Arachotus ('Αράχωτος), some distance from which stood a city of the same name, Arachotus, which was said to have been built by Semiramis, and which was the capital of the province until the foundation of ALEXANDRIA. The shortest road from Persia to India passed through Arachosia.

Arāchōtus. [ARACHOSIA.]

Arachthus or **Arētho** ("Αραχθος or 'Αρέθων: *Arta*), a river of Epirus, rises in M. Lacmon or the Tymphean mountains, and flows into the Ambracian gulf, S. of Ambracia: it is deep and difficult to cross, and navigable up to Ambracia.

Aracynthus ('Αράκυνθος: *Zigos*), a mountain on the S.W. coast of Aetolia near Pleuron, sometimes placed in Acarnania. Later writers erroneously make it a mountain between Boeotia and Attica, and hence mention it in connection with Amphion, the Boeotian hero. (Propert. iii. 13. 41 ; *Actaeo* (i. e. Attico) *Aracyntho*, Virg. *Ecl.* ii. 24.)

Arādus ("Αραδος: 'Αράδιος, Arādius : in O. T. Arvad : *Ruad*), an island off the coast of Phoenicia, at the distance of 20 stadia (2 geog. miles), with a city which occupied the whole surface of the island, 7 stadia in circumference, which was said to have been founded by exiles from Sidon, and which was a very flourishing place under its own kings, under the Seleucidae, and under the Romans. It possessed a harbour on the mainland, called ANTARADUS.

Arae Philaenorum. [PHILAENORUM ARAE.]

Araethyrēa ('Αραιθυρέα), daughter of Aras, an autochthon who was believed to have built Arantea, the most ancient town in Phliasia. After her death, her brother Aoris called the country of Phliasia Araethyrea, in honour of his sister.

Arāphēn ('Αραφήν : 'Αραφήνιος, 'Αραφήνοθεν: *Rafina*), an Attic demus belonging to the tribe Aegaeis, on the E. of Attica, N. of the river Erasinus, not far from its mouth.

Arar or **Arăris** (*Saône*), a river of Gaul, rises in the Vosges, receives the Dubis (*Doubs*) from the E., after which it becomes navigable, and flows with a quiet stream into the Rhone at Lugdunum (*Lyon*). In the time of Ammianus (A. D. 370) it was also called *Sauconna*, and in the middle ages *Sangona*, whence its modern name *Saône*.

Ararōs ('Αραρώς), an Athenian poet of the Middle Comedy, son of Aristophanes, flourished B. C. 375.

Aras. [ARAETHYREA.]

Araspes ('Αράσπης), a Mede, and a friend of the elder Cyrus, is one of the characters in Xenophon's Cyropaedia. He contends with Cyrus that love has no power over him, but shortly afterwards refutes himself by falling in love with Panthea, whom Cyrus had committed to his charge. [ABRADATAS.]

Arātus ("Αρατος). 1. The celebrated general of the Achaeans, son of Clinias, was born at Sicyon, B. C. 271. On the murder of his father by ABANTIDAS, Aratus, who was then a child, was conveyed to Argos, where he was brought up. When he had reached the age of 20 he gained possession of his native city, B. C. 251, deprived the usurper Nicocles of his power, and united Sicyon to the Achaean league, which gained in consequence a great accession of power. [ACHAEI.] In 245 he was elected general of the league, which office he frequently held in subsequent years. Through his influence a great number of the Greek cities joined the league ; but he excelled more in negotiation than in war, and in his war with the Aetolians and Spartans he was often defeated. In order to resist these enemies he cultivated the friendship of Antigonus Doson, king of Macedonia, and of his successor Philip ; but as Philip was evidently anxious to make himself master of all Greece, dissensions arose between him and Aratus, and the latter was eventually poisoned in 213 by the king's order. Divine honours were paid to him by his countrymen, and an annual festival ('Αράτεια, see *Dict of Antiq.*) established. Aratus wrote *Commentaries*, being a history of his own times down to B. C. 220 : at which point POLYBIUS commenced his history.—2. Of Soli, afterwards Pompeiopolis, in Cilicia, or (according to one authority) of Tarsus, flourished B. C. 270, and spent all the latter part of his life at the court of Antigonus Gonatas, king of Macedonia. He wrote two astronomical poems, entitled *Phaenomena* (Φαινόμενα), consisting of 732 verses, and *Diosemeia* (Διοσημεῖα), of 422. The design of the *Phaenomena* is to give an introduction to the knowledge of the constellations, with the rules for their risings and settings. The *Diosemeia* consists of prognostics of the weather from astronomical phaenomena, with an account of its effects upon animals. It appears to be an imitation of Hesiod, and to have been imitated by Virgil in some parts of the Georgics. The style of these two poems is distinguished by elegance and accuracy ; but it wants originality and poetic elevation. That they became very popular both in the Grecian and Roman world (*cum sole et luna semper Aratus erit*, Ov. *Am.* i. 15. 16), is proved by the number of commentaries and Latin translations. Parts of three poetical Latin translations are preserved. One written by Cicero when very young, one by Caesar Germanicus, the grandson of Augustus, and one by Festus Avienus.— *Editions.* By Voss, Heidelb. 1824, with a German poetical version ; by Buttmann, Berol. 1826 ; and by Bekker, Berol. 1828.

Arauris (*Herault*), erroneously Rauraris in Strabo, a river in Gallia Narbonensis, rises in M. Cevenna, and flows into the Mediterranean.

Arausĭo (*Orange*), a town of the Cavari or Cavares, and a Roman colony, in Gallia Narbonensis, on the road from Arelate to Vienna : it still contains remains of an amphitheatre, circus, aqueduct, triumphal arch, &c.

Araxes ('Αράξης), the name of several rivers. —1. In Armenia Major (*Eraskh* or *Aras*), rises in M. Aba or Abus (nr. *Erzeroum*), from the opposite side of which the Euphrates flows ; and, after a great bend S.E. and then N.E., joins the Cyrus (*Kour*), which flows down from the Caucasus, and falls with it into the Caspian by two mouths, in about 39° 20' N. Lat. The lower part,

F 3

past ARTAXATA, flows through a plain, which was called τὸ 'Αραξηνὸν πεδίον. The Araxes was proverbial for the force of its current ; and hence Virgil (*Aen.* viii. 728), says *pontem indignatus Araxes*, with special reference to the failure of both Xerxes and Alexander in throwing a bridge over it. It seems to be the Phasis of Xenophon. —2. In Mesopotamia. [ABORRHAS.]—3. In Persis (*Bend-Emir*), the river on which Persepolis stood, rises in the mountains E. of the head of the Persian Gulf, and flows S.E. into a salt lake (*Bakhtegan*) not far below Persepolis. — 4. It is doubtful whether the Araxes of Herodotus is the same as the OXUS, JAXARTES, or *Volga.*—5. The PENEUS, in Thessaly, was called Araxes from the violence of its torrent (fr. ἀράσσω)

Araxus ('Άραξος: *C. Papa*), a promontory of Achaia near the confines of Elis.

Arbaces ('Αρβάκης), the founder of the Median empire, according to Ctesias, is said to have taken Nineveh in conjunction with Belesis, the Babylonian, and to have destroyed the old Assyrian empire under the reign of Sardanapalus, B. C. 876. Ctesias assigns 28 years to the reign of Arbaces, B. C. 876—848, and makes his dynasty consist of 8 kings. This account differs from that of Herodotus, who makes DEIOCES the first king of Media, and assigns only 4 kings to his dynasty.

Arbēla (τὰ Άρβηλα: *Erbille*), a city of Adiabene in Assyria, between the rivers Lycus and Caprus ; celebrated as the head-quarters of Darius Codomannus, before the last battle in which he was overthrown by Alexander (B. C. 331), which is hence frequently called the battle of Arbela, though it was really fought near GAUGAMELA, about 50 miles W. of Arbela. The district about Arbela was called Arbelitis ('Αρβηλῖτις).

Arbis. [ARABIS.]

Arbucăla or **Arbocăla** (*Villa Fasila ?*), the chief town of the Vaccaei in Hispania Tarraconensis, taken by Hannibal after a long resistance.

Arbuscŭla, a celebrated female actor in pantomimes in the time of Cicero.

Arca or **-ae** ('Άρκη, or -αι: *Tell-Arka*), a very ancient city in the N. of Phoenicia, not far from the sea-coast, at the foot of M. Lebanon : a colony under the Romans, named Arca Caesarea or Caesarea Libani : the birthplace of the emperor Alexander Severus.

Arcădĭa ('Αρκαδία: Άρκας, pl. 'Αρκάδες), a country in the middle of Peloponnesus, was bounded on the E. by Argolis, on the N. by Achaia, on the W. by Elis, and on the S. by Messenia and Laconica. Next to Laconica it was the largest country in the Peloponnesus : its greatest length was about 50 miles, its breadth from 35 to 41 miles. It was surrounded on all sides by mountains, which likewise traversed it in every direction, and it may be regarded as the Switzerland of Greece. Its principal mountains were Cyllene and Erymanthus in the N., Artemisius in the E., and Parthenius, Maenalus, and Lycaeus in the S. and S.W. The Achelous, the greatest river of Peloponnesus, rises in Arcadia, and flows through a considerable part of the country, receiving numerous affluents. The N. and E. parts of the country were barren and unproductive ; the W. and S. were more fertile, with numerous valleys where corn was grown. The Arcadians, said to be descended from the eponymous hero ARCAS, regarded themselves as the most ancient people in Greece : the

Greek writers call them indigenous (αὐτόχθονες) and Pelasgians. In consequence of the physical peculiarity of the country, they were chiefly employed in hunting and the tending of cattle, whence their worship of Pan, who was especially the god of Arcadia, and of Artemis. They were a people simple in their habits and moderate in their desires : they were passionately fond of music, and cultivated it with great success (*soli cantare periti Arcades*, Virg. *Ecl.* x. 32), which circumstance was supposed to soften the natural roughness of their character. The Arcadians experienced fewer changes than any other people in Greece, and retained possession of their country upon the conquest of the rest of Peloponnesus by the Dorians. Like the other Greek peoples, they were originally governed by kings, but are said to have abolished monarchy towards the close of the second Messenian war, and to have stoned to death their last king Aristocrates, because he betrayed his allies the Messenians. The different towns then became independent republics, of which the most important were MANTINEA, TEGEA, ORCHOMENUS, PSOPHIS, and PHENEOS. Like the Swiss, the Arcadians frequently served as mercenaries, and in the Peloponnesian war, they were found in the armies of both the Lacedaemonians and Athenians. The Lacedaemonians made many attempts to obtain possession of parts of Arcadia, but these attempts were finally frustrated by the battle of Leuctra (B. C. 371) ; and in order to resist all future aggressions on the part of Sparta, the Arcadians, upon the advice of Epaminondas, built the city of MEGALOPOLIS, and instituted a general assembly of the whole nation, called the *Myrii* (Μύριοι, *Dict. of Antiq. s. v.*). They subsequently joined the Achaean League, and finally became subject to the Romans.

Arcădĭus, emperor of the East (A. D. 395—408), elder son of Theodosius I., was born in Spain, A. D. 383. On the death of Theodosius, he became emperor of the East, while the West was given to his younger brother Honorius. Arcadius possessed neither physical nor intellectual vigour, and was entirely governed by unworthy favourites. At first he was ruled by Rufinus, the praefect of the East ; and on the murder of the latter soon after the accession of Arcadius, the government fell into the hands of the eunuch Eutropius. Eutropius was put to death in 399, and his power now devolved upon Gainas, the Goth ; but upon his revolt and death in 401 Arcadius became entirely dependent upon his wife Eudoxia, and it was through her influence that St. Chrysostom was exiled in 404. Arcadius died on the 1st of May, 408, leaving the empire to his son Theodosius II., who was a minor.

Arcănum. [ARPINUM.]

Arcas ('Άρκας), king and eponymous hero of the Arcadians, son of Zeus and Callisto, grandson of Lycaon and father of Aphidas and Elatus. Arcas was the boy whose flesh his grandfather Lycaon placed before Zeus, to try his divine character. Zeus upset the table (τράπεζα) which bore the dish, and destroyed the house of Lycaon by lightning, but restored Arcas to life. When Arcas had grown up, he built on the site of his father's house the town of Trapezus. Arcas and his mother were placed by Zeus among the stars.

Arcĕsĭlāus or **Arcĕsĭlas** ('Αρκεσίλαος, 'Αρκεσίλας), a Greek philosopher, son of Seuthes or Scythes, was born at Pitane in Aeolis, and floueisned about B. C. 250. He studied at first in his native town under Autolycus, a mathematician, and afterwards went to Athens, where he became the disciple first of Theophrastus and next of Polemo and of Crantor. He succeeded Crates about B. C. 241 in the chair of the Academy, and became the founder of the second or middle (μέση) Academy. He is said to have died in his 76th year from a fit of drunkenness. His philosophy was of a sceptical character, though it did not go so far as that of the followers of Pyrrhon. He did not doubt the existence of truth in itself, only our capacities for obtaining it, and he combated most strongly the dogmatism of the Stoics.

Arcesilaus ('Αρκεσίλαος). 1. Son of Lycus and Theobule, leader of the Boeotians in the Trojan war, slain by Hector. — 2. The name of four kings of Cyrene. [BATTUS and BATTIADAE.]

Arcesius ('Αρκείσιος), son of Zeus and Euryodia, father of Laërtes, and grandfather of Ulysses. Hence both Laërtes and Ulysses are called *Arcesiades* ('Αρκεισιάδης).

Archaeopolis ('Αρχαιόπολις), the later capital of Colchis; near the river Phasis.

Archandropolis ('Αρχάνδρου πόλις), a city of Lower Egypt, on the Nile, between Canopus and Cercasorus.

Archedemus ('Αρχέδημος; Dor. 'Αρχέδαμος). 1. A popular leader at Athens, took the first step against the generals who had gained the battle of Arginusae, B. C. 406. The comic poets called him " blear-eyed " (γλάμων), and said that he was a foreigner, and had obtained the franchise by fraud. — 2. An Aetolian (called Archidamus by Livy), commanded the Aetolian troops which assisted the Romans in their war with Philip (B. C. 199—197). He afterwards took an active part against the Romans, and eventually joined Perseus, whom he accompanied in his flight after his defeat in 168. — 3. Of Tarsus, a Stoic philosopher, mentioned by Cicero, Seneca, and other ancient writers.

Archedicus ('Αρχέδικος), an Athenian comic poet of the new comedy, supported Antipater and the Macedonian party.

Archegetes ('Αρχηγέτης), a surname of Apollo, probably in reference to his being a leader of colonies. It was also a surname of other gods.

Archelais ('Αρχελαΐς). 1. In Cappadocia (Akserai), on the Cappadox, a tributary of the Halys, a city founded by Archelaus, the last king of Cappadocia, and made a Roman colony by the emperor Claudius. — 2. A town of Palestine, near Jericho, founded by Archelaus, the son of Herod the Great.

Archelaus ('Αρχέλαος). 1. Son of HEROD the Great, was appointed by his father as his successor, and received from Augustus Judaea, Samaria, and Idumaea, with the title of ethnarch. In consequence of his tyrannical government, the Jews accused him before Augustus in the 10th year of his reign (A. D. 7): Augustus banished him to Vienna in Gaul, where he died.—2. King of MACEDONIA (B. C. 413—399), an illegitimate son of Perdiccas II., obtained the throne by the murder of his half-brother. He improved the internal condition of his kingdom, and was a warm patron of art and literature. His palace was adorned with magnificent paintings by Zeuxis ; and Euripides, Agathon, and other men of eminence, were among his guests. According to some accounts Archelaus was accidentally slain in a hunting party by his favourite, Craterus or Crateuas ; but according to

other accounts he was murdered by Craterus. — 3. A distinguished general of MITHRIDATES. In B. C. 87 he was sent into Greece by Mithridates with a large fleet and army ; at first he met with considerable success, but was twice defeated by Sulla in 86, near Chaeronea and Orchomenos in Boeotia, with immense loss. Thereupon he was commissioned by Mithridates to sue for peace, which he obtained : but subsequently being suspected of treachery by the king, he deserted to the Romans just before the commencement of the second Mithridatic war, B. C. 81. — 4. Son of the preceding, was raised by Pompey, in B. C. 63, to the dignity of priest of the goddess (Enyo or Bellona) at Comana in Pontus or Cappadocia. In 56 or 55 Archelaus became king of Egypt by marrying Berenice, the daughter of Ptolemy Auletes, who after the expulsion of her father had obtained the sovereignty of Egypt. Archelaus, however, was king of Egypt only for 6 months, for Gabinius marched with an army into Egypt in order to restore Ptolemy Auletes, and in the battle which ensued, Archelaus perished. — 5. Son of No. 4, and his successor in the office of high-priest of Comana, was deprived of his dignity by Julius Caesar in 47. — 6. Son of No. 5., received from Antony, in B. C. 36, the kingdom of Cappadocia — a favour which he owed to the charms of his mother Glaphyra. After the battle of Actium Octavianus not only left Archelaus in the possession of his kingdom, but subsequently added to it a part of Cilicia and Lesser Armenia. But having incurred the enmity of Tiberius by the attention which he had paid to C. Caesar, he was summoned to Rome soon after the accession of Tiberius and accused of treason. His life was spared, but he was obliged to remain at Rome, where he died soon after, A. D. 17. Cappadocia was then made a Roman province. — 7. A philosopher, probably born at Athens, though others make him a native of Miletus, flourished about B. C. 450. The philosophical system of Archelaus is remarkable, as forming a point of transition from the older to the newer form of philosophy in Greece. As a pupil of Anaxagoras he belonged to the Ionian school, but he added to the physical system of his teacher some attempts at moral speculation. — 8. A Greek poet, in Egypt, lived under the Ptolemies, and wrote epigrams, some of which are still extant in the Greek Anthology.—9. A sculptor of Priene, son of Apollonius, made the marble bas-relief representing the Apotheosis of Homer, which formerly belonged to the Colonna family at Rome, and is now in the Townley Gallery of the British Museum. He probably lived in the reign of Claudius.

Archemorus ('Αρχέμορος), or OPHELTES, son of the Nemean king Lycurgus and Eurydice. When the Seven heroes on their expedition against Thebes stopped at Nemea to obtain water, Hypsipyle, the nurse of the child Opheltes, while showing the way to the Seven, left the child alone. In the meantime, the child was killed by a dragon, and buried by the Seven. But as Amphiaraus saw in this accident an omen boding destruction to him and his companions, they called the child Archemorus, that is, " Forerunner of Death," and instituted the Nemean games in honour of him.

Archestratus ('Αρχέστρατος), of Gela or Syracuse, about B. C. 350, wrote a poem on the Art of Cookery, which was imitated or translated by Ennius in his *Carmina Hedypathetica* or *Hedypathica* (from ἡδυπάθεια).

F 4

Archias ('Αρχίας). **1.** An Heraclid of Corinth, left his country in consequence of the death of ACTAEON, and founded Syracuse, B. C. 734, by command of the Delphic oracle.—**2. A. Licinius Archias**, a Greek poet, born at Antioch in Syria, about B. C. 120, very early obtained celebrity by his verses. In 102 he came to Rome, and was received in the most friendly way by many of the Roman nobles, especially by the Luculli, from whom he afterwards obtained the gentile name of Licinius. After a short stay at Rome he accompanied L. Lucullus, the elder, to Sicily, and followed him, in the banishment to which he was sentenced for his management of the slave war in that island, to Heraclea in Lucania, in which town Archias was enrolled as a citizen ; and as this town was a state united with Rome by a *foedus*, he subsequently obtained the Roman franchise in accordance with the lex Plautia Papiria passed in B. C. 89. At a later time he accompanied L. Lucullus the younger to the Mithridatic war. Soon after his return, a charge was brought against him in 61 of assuming the citizenship illegally, and the trial came on before Q. Cicero, who was praetor this year. He was defended by his friend M. Cicero in the extant speech *Pro Archia*, in which the orator, after briefly discussing the legal points of the case, rests the defence of his client upon his surpassing merits as a poet, which entitled him to the Roman citizenship. We may presume that Archias was acquitted, though we have no formal statement of the fact. Archias wrote a poem on the Cimbric war in honour of Marius ; another on the Mithridatic war in honour of Lucullus ; and at the time of his trial was engaged on a poem in honour of Cicero's consulship. No fragments of these works are extant ; and it is doubtful whether the epigrams preserved under the name of Archias in the Greek Anthology were really written by him.

Archidāmus ('Αρχίδαμος), the name of 5 kings of Sparta. **1.** Son of Anaxidamus, contemporary with the Tegeatan war, which followed soon after the second Messenian, B. C. 668.—**2.** Son of Zeuxidamus, succeeded his grandfather Leotychides, and reigned B. C. 469—427. During his reign, B. C. 464, Sparta was made a heap of ruins by a tremendous earthquake ; and for the next 10 years he was engaged in war against the revolted Helots and Messenians. Towards the end of his reign the Peloponnesian war broke out : he recommended his countrymen not rashly to embark in the war, and he appears to have taken a more correct view of the real strength of Athens than any other Spartan. After the war had been declared (B. C. 431) he invaded Attica, and held the supreme command of the Peloponnesian forces till his death in 429.—**3.** Grandson of No. 2, and son of Agesilaus II., reigned B. C. 361—338. During the lifetime of his father he took an active part in resisting the Thebans and the various other enemies of Sparta, and in 367 he defeated the Arcadians and Argives in the " Tearless Battle," so called because he had won it without losing a man. In 362 he defended Sparta against Epaminondas. In the third Sacred war (B. C. 356—346) he assisted the Phocians. In 338 he went to Italy to aid the Tarentines against the Lucanians, and there fell in battle.—**4.** Grandson of No. 3, and son of Eudamidas I., was king in B. C. 296, when he was defeated by Demetrius Poliorcetes.—**5.** Son of Eudamidas II., and the brother of Agis IV. On the

murder of Agis, in B. C. 240, Archidamus fled from Sparta, but afterwards obtained the throne by means of Aratus. He was, however, slain almost immediately after his return to Sparta. He was the last king of the Eurypontid race.

Archigĕnes ('Αρχιγένης), an eminent Greek physician, born at Apamea in Syria, practised at Rome in the time of Trajan, A. D. 98—117. He published a treatise on the pulse, on which Galen wrote a Commentary. He was the most eminent physician of the sect of the Eclectici, and is mentioned by Juvenal as well as by other writers. Only a few fragments of his works remain.

Archilŏchus ('Αρχίλοχος), of Paros, was one of the earliest Ionian lyric poets, and the first Greek poet who composed Iambic verses according to fixed rules. He flourished about B. C. 714—676. He was descended from a noble family, who held the priesthood in Paros. His grandfather was Tellis, his father Telesicles, and his mother a slave, named Enipo. In the flower of his age (between B. C. 710 and 700), Archilochus went from Paros to Thasos with a colony, of which one account makes him the leader. The motive for this emigration can only be conjectured. It was most probably the result of a political change, to which cause was added, in the case of Archilochus, a sense of personal wrongs. He had been a suitor to Neobule, one of the daughters of Lycambes, who first promised and afterwards refused to give his daughter to the poet. Enraged at this treatment, Archilochus attacked the whole family in an Iambic poem, accusing Lycambes of perjury, and his daughters of the most abandoned lives. The verses were recited at the festival of Demeter, and produced such an effect, that the daughters of Lycambes are said to have hung themselves through shame. The bitterness which he expresses in his poems towards his native island seems to have arisen in part also from the low estimation in which he was held, as being the son of a slave. Neither was he more happy at Thasos. He draws the most melancholy picture of his adopted country, which he at length quitted in disgust. While at Thasos, he incurred the disgrace of losing his shield in an engagement with the Thracians of the opposite continent ; but, instead of being ashamed of the disaster, he recorded it in his verse. At length he returned to Paros, and in a war between the Parians and the people of Naxos, he fell by the hand of a Naxian named Calondas or Corax. Archilochus shared with his contemporaries, Thaletas and Terpander, in the honour of establishing lyric poetry throughout Greece. The invention of the elegy is ascribed to him, as well as to Callinus ; but it was on his satiric Iambic poetry that his fame was founded. His Iambics expressed the strongest feelings in the most unmeasured language. The licence of Ionian democracy and the bitterness of a disappointed man were united with the highest degree of poetical power to give them force and point. The emotion accounted most conspicuous in his verses was " rage," " Archilochum proprio *rabies* armavit iambo." (Hor. *Ar. Poët.* 79.) The fragments of Archilochus are collected in Bergk's *Poet. Lyrici Graec.*, and by Liebel, *Archilochi Reliquiae*, Lips. 1812, 8vo.

Archimēdes ('Αρχιμήδης), of Syracuse, the most famous of ancient mathematicians, was born B. C. 287. He was a friend, if not a kinsman, of

Hiero, though his actual condition in life does not seem to have been elevated. In the early part of his life he travelled into Egypt, where he studied under Conon the Samian, a mathematician and astronomer. After visiting other countries, he returned to Syracuse. Here he constructed for Hiero various engines of war, which, many years afterwards, were so far effectual in the defence of Syracuse against Marcellus, as to convert the siege into a blockade, and delay the taking of the city for a considerable time. The accounts of the performances of these engines are evidently exaggerated ; and the story of the burning of the Roman ships by the reflected rays of the sun, though very current in later times, is probably a fiction. He superintended the building of a ship of extraordinary size for Hiero, of which a description is given in Athenaeus (v. p. 206, d.), where he is also said to have moved it to the sea by the help of a screw. He invented a machine called, from its form, Cochlea, and now known as the water-screw of Archimedes, for pumping the water out of the hold of this vessel. His most celebrated performance was the construction of a *sphere ;* a kind of orrery, representing the movements of the heavenly bodies. When Syracuse was taken (B. C. 212), Archimedes was killed by the Roman soldiers, being at the time intent upon a mathematical problem. Upon his tomb was placed the figure of a sphere inscribed in a cylinder. When Cicero was quaestor in Sicily (75) he found this tomb near one of the gates of the city, almost hid amongst briars, and forgotten by the Syracusans. The intellect of Archimedes was of the very highest order. He possessed, in a degree never exceeded, unless by Newton, the inventive genius which discovers new provinces of inquiry, and finds new points of view for old and familiar objects ; the clearness of conception which is essential to the resolution of complex phaenomena into their constituent elements ; and the power and habit of intense and persevering thought, without which other intellectual gifts are comparatively fruitless. The following works of Archimedes have come down to us : 1. *On Equiponderants and Centres of Gravity.* 2. *The Quadrature of the Parabola.* 3. *On the Sphere and Cylinder.* 4. *On Dimension of the Circle.* 5. *On Spirals.* 6. *On Conoids and Spheroids.* 7. The *Arenarius.* 8. *On Floating Bodies.* 9. *Lemmata.* The best edition of his works is by Torelli, Oxon. 1792. There is a French translation of his works, with notes, by F. Peyrard, Paris, 1808, and an English translation of the Arenarius by G. Anderson, London, 1784.

Archinus ('Ἀρχῖνος), one of the leading Athenians, who, with Thrasybulus and Anytus, overthrew the government of the Thirty, B. C. 403.

Archippus ("Ἀρχιππος), an Athenian poet of the old comedy, about B. C. 415.

Archytas ('Ἀρχύτας). 1. Of Amphissa, a Greek epic poet, flourished about B. C. 300. — **2.** Of Tarentum, a distinguished philosopher, mathematician, general, and statesman, probably lived about B. C. 400, and onwards, so that he was contemporary with Plato, whose life he is said to have saved by his influence with the tyrant Dionysius. He was 7 times the general of his city, and he commanded in several campaigns, in all of which he was victorious. After a life which secured to him a place among the very greatest men of antiquity, he was drowned while upon a voyage on the

Adriatic. (Hor. *Carm.* i. 28.) As a philosopher, he belonged to the Pythagorean school, and he appears to have been himself the founder of a new sect. Like the Pythagoreans in general, he paid much attention to mathematics. Horace calls him *maris et terrae numeroque carentis arenae Mensorem.* To his theoretical science he added the skill of a practical mechanician, and constructed various machines and automatons, among which his wooden flying dove in particular was the wonder of antiquity. He also applied mathematics with success to musical science, and even to metaphysical philosophy. His influence as a philosopher was so great, that Plato was undoubtedly indebted to him for some of his views ; and Aristotle is thought by some writers to have borrowed the idea of his categories, as well as some of his ethical principles, from Archytas.

Arconnēsus ('Ἀρκόννησος : 'Ἀρκοννήσιος). **1.** An island off the coast of Ionia, near Lebedus, also called *Aspis* and *Macris.* — **2.** (*Orak Ada*), an island off the coast of Caria, opposite Halicarnassus, of which it formed the harbour.

Arctinus ('Ἀρκτῖνος), of Miletus, the most distinguished among the cyclic poets, probably lived about B. C. 776. Two epic poems were attributed to him. 1. The *Aethiopis,* which was a kind of continuation of Homer's Iliad : its chief heroes were Memnon, king of the Ethiopians, and Achilles, who slew him. 2. The *Destruction of Ilion,* which contained a description of the destruction of Troy, and the subsequent events until the departure of the Greeks.

Arctophylax. [ARCTOS.]

Arctos ("Ἀρκτος), "the Bear," two constellations near the N. Pole. **1.** THE GREAT BEAR ("Ἀρκτος μεγάλη : *Ursa Major*), also called the *Waggon* (ἅμαξα : *plaustrum*). The ancient Italian name of this constellation was *Septem Triones,* that is, the *Seven Ploughing Oxen,* also *Septentrio,* and with the epithet *Major* to distinguish it from the *Septentrio Minor,* or *Lesser Bear :* hence Virgil (*Aen.* iii. 356) speaks of *geminosque Triones.* The Great Bear was also called *Helice* (ἑλίκη) from its sweeping round in a curve. — **2.** THE LESSER or LITTLE BEAR ("Ἀρκτος μικρά : *Ursa Minor*), likewise called the *Waggon,* was first added to the Greek catalogues by Thales, by whom it was probably imported from the East. It was also called *Phoenice* (Φοινίκη), from the circumstance that it was selected by the Phoenicians as the guide by which they shaped their course at sea, the Greek mariners with less judgment employing the Great Bear for the purpose ; and *Cynosura* (Κυνόσουρα), *dog's tail,* from the resemblance of the constellation to the upturned curl of a dog's tail. The constellation before the Great Bear was called *Boötes* (Βοώτης), *Arctophylax* ('Ἀρκτοφύλαξ), or *Arcturus* ('Ἀρκτοῦρος from οὖρος, *guard*) ; the two latter names suppose the constellation to represent a man upon the watch, and denote simply the position of the figure in reference to the Great Bear, while *Boötes,* which is found in Homer, refers to the *Waggon,* the imaginary figure of Boötes being fancied to occupy the place of the driver of the team. At a later time *Arctophylax* became the general name of the constellation, and the word *Arcturus* was confined to the chief star in it. All these constellations are connected in mythology with the Arcadian nymph CALLISTO, the daughter of Lycaon. Metamorphosed by Zeus upon the earth into a she-bear, Callisto was pursued by her son Arcas in the chase, and when he was on the point of killing her, Zeus placed them both among the stars, Callisto becoming the Great Bear and Arcas the Little Bear or Boötes. In the poets the epithets of these stars have constant reference to the family and country of Callisto: thus we find them called *Lycaonis Arctos: Maenalia Arctos* and *Maenalis Ursa* (from M. Maenalus in Arcadia): *Erymanthis Ursa* (from M. Erymanthus in Arcadia): *Parrhasides stellae* (from the Arcadian town Parrhasia). — Though most traditions identified Boötes with Arcas, others pronounced him to be Icarus or his daughter Erigone. Hence the Septentriones are called *Boves Icarii.* (See *Dict. of Antiq* pp. 147, 148, 159, 2nd ed.)

Arctûrus. [ARCTOS.]

Arděa (Ardeas, -ätis: *Ardea*). 1. The chief town of the Rutuli in Latium, a little to the left of the river Numicus, 3 miles from the sea, was situated on a rock surrounded by marshes, in an unhealthy district. It was one of the most ancient places in Italy, and was said to have been the capital of Turnus. It was conquered and colonized by the Romans, B. C. 442, from which time its importance declined. In its neighbourhood was the Latin Aphrodisium or temple of Venus, which was under the superintendence of the Ardeates. — 2. (*Ardekán ?*), an important town in Persia, S.W. of Persepolis.

Arduenna Silva, *the Ardennes*, a vast forest, in the N.W. of Gaul, extended from the Rhine and the Treviri to the Nervii and Remi, and N. as far as the Scheldt : there are still considerable remains of this forest, though the greater part of it has disappeared.

Ardys ('Αρδυς), son of Gyges, king of Lydia, reigned B. C. 678—629 : he took Priene and made war against Miletus.

Areê or **Arětīās** ('Αρεια or 'Αρητίας νῆσος, i. e. the island of Ares: *Kerasunt Ada*), also called Chalceritis, an island off the coast of Pontus, close to Pharnacěa, celebrated in the legend of the Argonauts.

Arěíthŏūs ('Αρηΐθοος), king of Arne in Boeotia, and husband of Philomedusa, is called in the Iliad (vii. 8) κορυνήτης, because he fought with a club : he fell by the hand of the Arcadian Lycurgus.

Arelāte, Arělas, or **Arelātum** (Arelatensis : *Arles*), a town in Gallia Narbonensis at the head of the delta of the Rhone on the left bank, and a Roman colony founded by the soldiers of the sixth legion, *Colonia Arelate Sextanorum.* It is first mentioned by Caesar, and under the emperors it became one of the most flourishing towns on this side of the Alps. Constantine the Great built an extensive suburb on the right bank, which he connected with the original city by a bridge. The Roman remains at Arles attest the greatness of the ancient city : there are still to be seen an obelisk of granite, and the ruins of an aqueduct, theatre, amphitheatre, palace of Constantine, and a large Roman cemetery.

Aremŏrĭca. [ARMORICA.]

Arenacum (*Arnheim* or *Aert ?*), a town of the Batavi in Gallia Belgica.

Arěŏpăgus. [ATHENAE.]

Ares ('Αρης), the Greek god of war and one of the great Olympian gods, is represented as the son of Zeus and Hera. The character of Ares in Greek mythology will be best understood by comparing it with that of other divinities who are likewise in some way connected with war. Athena represents thoughtfulness and wisdom in the affairs of war, and protects men and their habitations during its ravages. Ares, on the other hand, is nothing but the personification of bold force and strength, and not so much the god of war as of its tumult, confusion, and horrors. His sister Eris calls forth war, Zeus directs its course, but Ares loves war for its own sake, and delights in the din and roar of battles, in the slaughter of men, and the destruction of towns. He is not even influenced by party-spirit, but sometimes assists the one and sometimes the other side, just as his inclination may dictate ; whence Zeus calls him ἀλλοπρόσαλλος. (*Il.* v. 889.) This savage and sanguinary character of Ares makes him hated by the other gods and by his own parents. It was contrary to the spirit of the Greeks to represent a being like Ares, with all his overwhelming physical strength, as always victorious ; and when he comes in contact with higher powers, he is usually conquered. He was wounded by Diomedes, who was assisted by Athena, and in his fall he roared like ten thousand warriors. The gigantic Aloïdae had likewise conquered him, and kept him a prisoner for 13 months, until he was delivered by Hermes. He was also conquered by Hercules, with whom he fought on account of his son Cycnus, and was obliged to return to Olympus. This fierce and gigantic, but withal handsome god loved and was beloved by Aphrodite. [APHRODITE.] When Aphrodite loved Adonis, Ares in his jealousy metamorphosed himself into a bear, and killed his rival. [ADONIS.] According to a late tradition, Ares slew Halirrhothius, the son of Poseidon, when he was on the point of violating Alcippe, the daughter of Ares. Hereupon Poseidon accused Ares in the Areopagus, where the Olympian gods were assembled in court. Ares was acquitted, and this event was believed to have given rise to the name Areopagus. The warlike character of the tribes of Thrace led to the belief that the god's residence was in that country, and here and in Scythia were the principal seats of his worship. In Scythia he was worshipped under the form of a sword, to which not only horses and other cattle, but men also were sacrificed. In Greece itself the worship of Ares was not very general. All the stories about Ares and his worship in the countries N. of Greece seem to indicate that his worship was introduced into the latter country from Thrace. The Romans identified their god Mars with the Greek Ares. [MARS.]

Arestor ('Αρέστωρ), father of Argus, the guardian of Io, who is therefore called *Arestorides.*

Arětaeus ('Αρεταῖος), the Cappadocian, one of the most celebrated of the ancient Greek physicians, probably lived in the reign of Vespasian. He wrote in Ionic Greek a general treatise on diseases in 8 books, which is still extant. The best edition is by C. G. Kühn, Lips. 1828.

Arětas ('Αρέτας), the name of several kings of Arabia Petraea. 1. A contemporary of Pompey, invaded Judaea in B. C. 65, in order to place Hyrcanus on the throne, but was driven back by the Romans, who espoused the cause of Aristobulus. His dominions were subsequently invaded by Scaurus, the lieutenant of Pompey. — 2. The father-in-law of Herod Antipas, invaded Judaea, because Herod had dismissed the daughter of Aretas in consequence of his connection with Herodias. This Aretas seems to have been the same who had possession of Damascus at the time of the conversion of the Apostle Paul, A. D. 31.

Arētē ('Αρήτη). 1. Wife of Alcinous, king of the Phaeacians, received Ulysses with hospitality. — 2. Daughter of the elder Dionysius and Aristomache, wife of Thearides, and after his death of her uncle Dion. After Dion had fled from Syracuse, Arete was compelled by her brother to marry Timocrates, one of his friends ; but she was again received by Dion as his wife, when he had obtained possession of Syracuse and expelled the younger Dionysius. After the assassination of Dion in 353, she was drowned by his enemies. — 3. Daughter of Aristippus, the founder of the Cyrenaic school of philosophy, was instructed by him in the principles of his system, which she transmitted to her son the younger Aristippus.

Arethūsa ('Αρέθουσα), one of the Nereids, and the nymph of the famous fountain of Arethusa in the island of Ortygia near Syracuse. For details, see ALPHEUS. Virgil (Eclog. iv. 1, x. 1) reckons her among the Sicilian nymphs, and as the divinity who inspired pastoral poetry.—There were several other fountains in Greece, which bore the name of Arethusa, of which the most important was one in Ithaca, now Lebado, and another in Euboea near Chalcis.

Arēthūsa ('Αρέθουσα : Er-Restun), a town and fortress on the Orontes, in Syria : in Strabo's time the seat of a petty Arabian principality.

Arētīas. [AREA.]

Arētīum. [ARRETIUM.]

Areus ('Αρεύς), two kings of Sparta. 1. Succeeded his grandfather, Cleomenes II., since his father Acrotatus had died before him, and reigned a. c. 309—265. He made several unsuccessful attempts to deliver Greece from the dominion of Antigonus Gonatas, and at length fell in battle against the Macedonians in 265, and was succeeded by his son Acrotatus. — 2. Grandson of No. 2, reigned as a child for 8 years under the guardianship of his uncle Leonidas II., who succeeded him about B. C. 256.

Arēvācae or **Arēvāci**, the most powerful tribe of the Celtiberians in Spain, near the sources of the Tagus, derived their name from the river Areva (Arianzo), a tributary of the Durius (Duero).

Argaeus ('Αργαῖος). 1. King of Macedonia, son and successor of Perdiccas I., the founder of the dynasty. — 2. A pretender to the Macedonian crown, dethroned Perdiccas II. and reigned 2 years

Argaeus Mons ('Αργαῖος : Erdjish), a lofty snow-capped mountain nearly in the centre of Cappadocia ; an offset of the Anti-Taurus. At its foot stood the celebrated city of Mazaca or Caesarea.

Arganthōnīus ('Αργανθώνιος), king of Tartessus in Spain, in the 6th century B.C., is said to have reigned 80 years, and to have lived 120.

Arganthōnīus or **Arganthus Mons** (τὸ 'Αργανθώνιον ὄρος : Katirli), a mountain in Bithynia, running out into the Propontis, forming the Prom. Posidium (C. Bozz), and separating the bays of Cios and Astacus.

Argennum or **Arginum** ('Αργεννον, 'Αργινον : C. Bianco), a promontory on the Ionian coast, opposite to Chios.

Argentēus, a small river in Gallia Narbonensis, which flows into the Mediterranean near Forum Julii.

Argentorātum or -tus (Strassburg), an important town on the Rhine in Gallia Belgica, the head-quarters of the 8th legion, and a Roman municipium. In its neighbourhood Julian gained a brilliant victory over the Alemanni, A. D. 357. It was subsequently called Strateburgum and Stratisburgum, whence its modern name.

Arges. [CYCLOPES.]

Argīa ('Αργεία), daughter of Adrastus and Amphithea, and wife of Polynices.

Argīa ('Αργεία). [ARGOS.]

Argilētum, a district in Rome, which extended from the S. of the Quirinal to the Capitoline and the Forum. It was chiefly inhabited by mechanics and booksellers. The origin of the name is uncertain : the most obvious derivation is from argilla " potter's clay ; " but the more common explanation in antiquity was Argi letum, " death of Argus," from a hero Argus who was buried there.

Argīlus ("Αργιλος : 'Αργίλιος), a town in Bisaltia, the E. part of Mygdonia in Macedonia, between Amphipolis and Bromiscus, a colony of Andros.

Arginūsae ('Αργινοῦσαι or 'Αργινοῦσσαι), 3 small islands off the coast of Aeolia, opposite Mytilene in Lesbos, celebrated for the naval victory of the Athenians over the Lacedaemonians under Callicratidas, B. C. 406.

Argīphontes ('Αργειφόντης), " the slayer of Argus," a surname of HERMES.

Argippaei ('Αργιππαῖοι), a Scythian tribe in Sarmatia Asiatica, who appear, from the description of them by Herodotus (iv. 23), to have been of the Calmuck race.

Argissa. [ARGURA.]

Argithēa, the chief town of Athamania in Epirus.

Argīva, a surname of Hera or Juno from Argos, where, as well as in the whole of Peloponnesus, she was especially honoured. [ARGOS.]

Argīvi. [ARGOS.]

Argo. [ARGONAUTAE.]

Argōlis. [ARGOS.]

Argōnautae ('Αργοναῦται), the Argonauts, "the sailors of the Argo," were the heroes who sailed to Aea (afterwards called Colchis) for the purpose of fetching the golden fleece. The story of the Argonauts is variously related by the ancient writers, but the common tale ran as follows. In Iolcus in Thessaly reigned Pelias, who had deprived his half-brother AESON of the sovereignty. In order to get rid of JASON the son of Aeson, PELIAS persuaded Jason to fetch the golden fleece, which was suspended on an oak-tree in the grove of Ares in Colchis, and was guarded day and night by a dragon. Jason willingly undertook the enterprize, and commanded Argus, the son of Phrixus, to build a ship with 50 oars ; which was called Argo ('Αργώ) after the name of the builder. Jason was accompanied by all the great heroes of the age, and their number is usually said to have been 50. Among these were Hercules, Castor and Pollux, Zetes and Calais, the sons of Boreas, the singer Orpheus, the seer Mopsus, Philammon, Tydeus, Theseus, Amphiaraus, Peleus, Nestor, Admetus, &c. After leaving Iolcus they first landed at Lemnos, where they united themselves with the women of the island, who had just before murdered their fathers and husbands. From Lemnos they sailed to the Doliones at Cyzicus, where king Cyzicus received them hospitably. They left the country during the night, and being thrown back on the coast by a contrary wind, they were taken for Pelasgians, the enemies of the Doliones, and a struggle ensued, in which Cyzicus was slain ; but being recognised by the Argonauts, they buried him and mourned over his fate. They next landed in Mysia, where they left behind Hercules and Polyphemus, who had gone into the country in search of Hylas, whom a nymph had carried off while he was fetching water for his companions. In the country of the Bebryces, king Amycus challenged the Argonauts to fight with him ; and when Pollux was killed by him, the Argonauts in revenge slew many of the Bebryces, and sailed to Salmydessus in Thrace, where the seer Phineus was tormented by the Harpies. When the Argonauts consulted him about their voyage, he promised his advice on condition of their delivering him from the Harpies. This was done by Zetes and Calais, two sons of Boreas ; and Phineus now advised them, before sailing through the Symplegades, to mark the flight of a dove, and to judge from its fate what they themselves would have to do. When they approached the Symplegades, they sent out a dove, which in its rapid flight between the rocks lost only the end of its tail. The Argonauts now, with the assistance of Hera, followed the example of the dove, sailed quickly between the rocks, and succeeded in passing without injury to their ship, with the exception of some ornaments at the stern. Henceforth the Symplegades stood immoveable in the sea. On their arrival at the Mariandyni, the Argonauts were kindly received by their king, Lycus. The seer Idmon and the helmsman Tiphys died here, and the place of the latter was supplied by Ancaeus. They now sailed along the coast until they arrived at the mouth of the river Phasis. The Colchian king Aeëtes promised to give up the golden fleece, if Jason alone would yoke to a plough two fire-breathing oxen with brazen feet, and sow the teeth of the dragon which had not been used by Cadmus at Thebes, and which he had received from Athena. The love of Medea furnished Jason with means to resist fire and steel, on condition of his taking her as his wife ; and she taught him how he was to kill the warriors that were to spring up from the teeth of the dragon. While Jason was engaged upon his task, Aeëtes formed plans for burning the ship Argo and for killing all the Greek heroes. But Medea's magic powers sent to sleep the dragon who guarded the golden fleece ; and after Jason had taken possession of the treasure, he and his Argonauts, together with Medea and her young brother Absyrtus, embarked by night and sailed away. Aeëtes pursued them, but before he overtook them, Medea murdered her brother, cut him into pieces, and threw his limbs overboard, that her father might be detained in his pursuit by collecting the limbs of his child. Aeëtes at last returned home, but sent out a great number of Colchians, threatening them with the punishment intended for Medea, if they returned without her. While the Colchians were dispersed in all directions, the Argonauts had already reached the mouth of the river Eridanus. But Zeus, angry at the murder of Absyrtus, raised a storm which cast the ship from its course. When driven on the Absyrtian islands, the ship began to speak, and declared that the anger of Zeus would not cease, unless they sailed towards Ausonia, and got purified by Circe. They now sailed along the coasts of the Ligyans and Celts, and through the sea of

Sardinia, and continuing their course along the coast of Tyrrhenia, they arrived in the island of Aeaea, where Circe purified them. When they were passing by the Sirens, Orpheus sang to prevent the Argonauts being allured by them. Butes, however, swam to them, but Aphrodite carried him to Lilybaeum. Thetis and the Nereids conducted them through Scylla and Charybdis and between the whirling rocks (πέτραι πλαγκταί) ; and sailing by the Trinacian island with its oxen of Helios, they came to the Phaeacian island of Corcyra, where they were received by Alcinous. In the meantime, some of the Colchians, not being able to discover the Argonauts, had settled at the foot of the Ceraunian mountains ; others occupied the Absyrtian islands near the coast of Illyricum ; and a third band overtook the Argonauts in the island of the Phaeacians. But as their hopes of recovering Medea were deceived by Arete, the queen of Alcinous, they settled in the island, and the Argonauts continued their voyage. During the night they were overtaken by a storm ; but Apollo sent brilliant flashes of lightning which enabled them to discover a neighbouring island, which they called Anaphe. Here they erected an altar to Apollo, and solemn rites were instituted, which continued to be observed down to very late times. Their attempt to land in Crete was prevented by Talus, who guarded the island, but was killed by the artifices of Medea. From Crete they sailed to Aegina, and from thence between Euboea and Locris to Iolcus. Respecting the events subsequent to their arrival in Iolcus, see AESON, MEDEA, JASON, PELIAS. The story of the Argonauts probably arose out of accounts of commercial enterprises which the wealthy Minyans, who lived in the neighbourhood of Iolcus, made to the coasts of the Euxine. The expedition of the Argonauts is related by Pindar in the 4th Pythian ode, by Apollonius Rhodius in his *Argonautica*, and by his Roman imitator Valerius Flaccus.

Argos (τὸ Ἄργος, -εος), is said by Strabo (p. 372) to have signified a plain in the language of the Macedonians and Thessalians, and it may therefore contain the same root as the Latin word *ager*. In Homer we find mention of the Pelasgic Argos, that is, a town or district of Thessaly, and of the Achaean Argos, by which he means sometimes the whole Peloponnesus, sometimes Agamemnon's kingdom of Argos of which Mycenae was the capital, and sometimes the town of Argos. As Argos frequently signifies the whole Peloponnesus, the most important part of Greece, so the Ἀργεῖοι often occur in Homer as a name of the whole body of the Greeks, in which sense the Roman poets also use *Argivi*.—1. **Argos**, a district of Peloponnesus, called *Argolis* (ἡ Ἀργολίς) by Herodotus, but more frequently by other Greek writers either *Argos*, *Argīa* (ἡ Ἀργεία), or *Argolice* (ἡ Ἀργολική). Under the Romans Argolis became the usual name of the country, while the word Argos or Argi was confined to the town. Argolis under the Romans signified the country bounded on the N. by the Corinthian territory, on the W. by Arcadia, on the S. by Laconia, and included towards the E. the whole Acte or peninsula between the Saronic and Argolic gulfs : but during the time of Grecian independence Argolis or Argos was only the country lying round the Argolic gulf, bounded on the W. by the Arcadian mountains, and separated on the N. by a range of mountains from Corinth,

Cleonae, and Phlius. Argolis, as understood by the Romans, was for the most part a mountainous and unproductive country : the only extensive plain adapted for agriculture was in the neighbourhood of the city of Argos. Its rivers were insignificant and mostly dry in summer : the most important was the Inachus. The country was divided into the districts of Argia or Argos proper, EPIDAURIA, TROEZENIA, and HERMIONIS. The original inhabitants of the country were, according to mythology, the Cynurii ; but the main part of the population consisted of Pelasgi and Achaei, to whom Dorians were added after the conquest of Peloponnesus by the Dorians. See below, No. 2.—2. Argos, or Argi, -orum, in the Latin writers, now *Argo*, the capital of Argolis, and, next to Sparta, the most important town in Peloponnesus, situated in a level plain a little to the W. of the Inachus. It had an ancient Pelasgic citadel, called Larissa, and another built subsequently on another height (*duas arces habent Argi*, Liv. xxxiv. 25). It possessed numerous temples, and was particularly celebrated for the worship of Hera, whose great temple, *Heraeum*, lay between Argos and Mycenae. The remains of the Cyclopian walls of Argos are still to be seen. The city is said to have been built by INACHUS or his son PHORONEUS, or grandson ARGUS. The descendants of Inachus, who may be regarded as the Pelasgian kings, reigned over the country for 9 generations, but were at length deprived of the sovereignty by DANAUS, who is said to have come from Egypt. The descendants of Danaus were in their time obliged to submit to the Achaean race of the Pelopidae. Under the rule of the Pelopidae Mycenae became the capital of the kingdom, and Argos was a dependent state. Thus Mycenae was the royal residence of Atreus and of his son Agamemnon ; but under Orestes Argos again recovered its supremacy. Upon the conquest of Peloponnesus by the Dorians Argos fell to the share of Temenus, whose descendants ruled over the country ; but the great bulk of the population continued to be Achaean. All these events belong to mythology ; and Argos first appears in history about B.C. 750, as the chief state of Peloponnesus, under its ruler PHIDON. After the time of Phidon its power declined, and it was not even able to maintain its supremacy over the other towns of Argolis. Its power was greatly weakened by its wars with Sparta. The two states long contended for the district of Cynuria, which lay between Argolis and Laconia, and which the Spartans at length obtained by the victory of their 300 champions, about B.C. 550. In B.C. 524 Cleomenes, the Spartan king, defeated the Argives with such loss near Tiryns, that Sparta was left without a rival in Peloponnesus. In consequence of its weakness and of its jealousy of Sparta, Argos took no part in the Persian war. In order to strengthen itself, Argos attacked the neighbouring towns of Tiryns, Mycenae, &c., destroyed them, and transplanted their inhabitants to Argos. The introduction of so many new citizens was followed by the abolition of royalty and of Doric institutions, and by the establishment of a democracy, which continued to be the form of government till later times, when the city fell under the power of tyrants. In the Peloponnesian war Argos sided with Athens against Sparta. In B.C. 243 it joined the Achaean League, and on the conquest of the latter by the Romans, 146, it became a part of the Roman pro-

vince of Achaia. At an early time Argos was distinguished by its cultivation of music and poetry [SACADAS ; TELESILLA] ; but at the time of the intellectual greatness of Athens, literature and science seem to have been entirely neglected at Argos. It produced some great sculptors, of whom AGELADAS and POLYCLETUS are the most celebrated.

Argos Amphilochĭcum ('Άργος τὸ 'Αμφιλοχικόν), the chief town of Amphilochia in Acarnania, situated on the Ambracian gulf, and founded by the Argive AMPHILOCHUS.

Argos Hippĭum. [ARPL]

Argŏus Portus (*Porto Ferraio*), a town and harbour in the island of Ilva (*Elba*).

Argūra ('Άργουρα), a town in Pelasgiotis in Thessaly, called Argissa by Homer (*Il.* ii. 738).

Argus ('Άργος). 1. Son of Zeus and Niobe, 3rd king of Argos, from whom Argos derived its name. — 2. Surnamed *Panoptes*, " the all-seeing," because he had a hundred eyes, son of Agenor, Arestor, Inachus, or Argus. Hera appointed him guardian of the cow into which Io had been metamorphosed ; but Hermes, at the command of Zeus, put Argus to death, either by stoning him, or by cutting off his head after sending him to sleep by the sweet notes of his flute. Hera transplanted his eyes to the tail of the peacock, her favourite bird. — 3. The builder of the Argo, son of Phrixus, Arestor, or Polybus, was sent by Aeëtes, his grandfather, after the death of Phrixus, to take possession of his inheritance in Greece. On his voyage thither he suffered shipwreck, was found by Jason in the island of Aretias, and carried back to Colchis.

Argÿra ('Αργυρᾶ), a town in Achaia near Patrae, with a fountain of the same name.

Argÿrĭpa. [ARPL]

Aria ('Αρεία, 'Αρία : "Αρειος, "Αριος : *the E. part of Khorassan, and the W. and N.W. part of Afghanistan*), the most important of the E. provinces of the ancient Persian Empire, was bounded on the E. by the Paropamisadae, on the N. by Margiana and Hyrcania, on the W. by Parthia, and on the S. by the great desert of Carmania. It was a vast plain, bordered on the N. and E. by mountains, and on the W. and S. by sandy deserts ; and, though forming a part of the great sandy tableland, now called the Desert of Iran, it contained several very fertile oases, especially in its N. part, along the base of the Sariphi (*Kohistan* and *Hazarah*) mountains, which was watered by the river **Arius** or -as (*Herirood*), on which stood the later capital Alexandria (*Herat*). The river is lost in the sand. The lower course of the great river ETYMANDRUS (*Helmund*) also belonged to Aria, and the lake into which it falls was called **Aria Lacus** (*Zurrah*). From Aria was derived the name under which all the E. provinces were included. [ARIANA.]

Aria Lacus. [ARIA.]

Ariabignes ('Αριαβίγνης), son of Darius Hystaspis, one of the commanders of the fleet of Xerxes, fell in the battle of Salamis, B.C. 480.

Ariadnē ('Αριάδνη), daughter of Minos and Pasiphaë or Creta, fell in love with Theseus, when he was sent by his father to convey the tribute of the Athenians to Minotaurus, and gave him the clue of thread by means of which he found his way out of the Labyrinth, and which she herself had received from Hephaestus. Theseus in return promised to marry her, and she accordingly left Crete with him ; but on their arrival in the island of Dia (Naxos), she was killed by Artemis. This is the Homeric account (Od. xi. 322) ; but the more common tradition related that Theseus left Ariadne in Naxos alive, either because he was forced by Dionysus to leave her, or because he was ashamed to bring a foreign wife to Athens. Dionysus found her at Naxos, made her his wife, and placed among the stars the crown which he gave her at their marriage. There are several circumstances in the story of Ariadne which offered the happiest subjects for works of art, and some of the finest ancient works, on gems as well as paintings, are still extant, of which Ariadne is the subject.

Ariaeus ('Αριαῖος) or **Aridaeus** ('Αριδαῖος), the friend of Cyrus, commanded the left wing of the army at the battle of Cunaxa, B. C. 401. After the death of Cyrus he purchased his pardon from Artaxerxes by deserting the Greeks.

Ariamnes ('Αριάμνης), the name of two kings of Cappadocia, one the father of Ariarathes I., and the other the son and successor of Ariarathes II.

Ariāna ('Αριανή : *Iran*), derived from ARIA, from the specific sense of which it must be carefully distinguished, was the general name of the E. provinces of the ancient Persian Empire, and included the portion of Asia bounded on the W. by an imaginary line drawn from the Caspian to the mouth of the Persian Gulf, on the S. by the Indian Ocean, on the E. by the Indus. and on the N. by the great chain of mountains called by the general name of the Indian Caucasus, embracing the provinces of Parthia, Aria, the Paropamisadae, Arachosia, Drangiana, Gedrosia, and Carmania (*Khorassan*, *Afghanistan*, *Beloochistan*, and *Kirman*). But the name was often extended to the country as far W. as the margin of the Tigris-valley, so as to include Media and Persia, and also to the provinces N. of the Indian Caucasus, namely Bactria and Sogdiana (*Bokhara*). The knowledge of the ancients respecting the greater part of this region was confined to what was picked up in the expeditions of Alexander and the wars of the Greek kings of Syria, and what was learned from merchant caravans.

Ariarāthes ('Αριαράθης), the name of several kings of Cappadocia.—**1.** Son of Ariamnes I., assisted Ochus in the recovery of Egypt, B. C. 350. Ariarathes was defeated by Perdiccas, and crucified, 322. Eumenes then obtained possession of Cappadocia.—**2.** Son of Holophernes, and nephew of Ariarathes I.,recovered Cappadocia after the death of Eumenes, B.C. 315. He was succeeded by Ariamnes II.—**3.** Son of Ariamnes II., and grandson of No. 2, married Stratonice, daughter of Antiochus II., king of Syria.—**4.** Son of No. 3, reigned B.C. 220—162. He married Antiochis, the daughter of Antiochus III., king of Syria, and assisted Antiochus in his war against the Romans. After the defeat of Antiochus, Ariarathes sued for peace in 188, which he obtained on favourable terms. In 183—179, he assisted Eumenes in his war against Pharnaces.—**5.** Son of No. 4, previously called Mithridates, reigned B. c. 163—130. He was surnamed Philopator, and war distinguished by the excellence of his character and his cultivation of philosophy and the liberal arts. He assisted the Romans in their war against Aristonicus of Pergamus, and fell in this war, 130.—**6.** Son of No. 5, reigned B. c. 130—96. He married Laodice, sister of Mithridates

VI., king of Pontus, and was put to death by Mithridates by means of Gordius. On his death the kingdom was seized by Nicomedes, king of Bithynia, who married Laodice, the widow of the late king. But Nicomedes was soon expelled by Mithridates, who placed upon the throne,—**7.** Son of No. 6. He was, however, also murdered by Mithridates in a short time, who now took possession of his kingdom. The Cappadocians rebelled against Mithridates, and placed upon the throne, —**8.** Second son of No. 6 ; but he was speedily driven out of the kingdom by Mithridates, and shortly afterwards died. Both Mithridates and Nicomedes attempted to give a king to the Cappadocians ; but the Romans allowed the people to choose whom they pleased. and their choice fell upon Ariobarzanes.—**9.** Son of Ariobarzanes II., reigned B. c. 42—36. He was deposed and put to death by Antony, who appointed Archelaus as his successor.

Ariaspae or **Agriaspae** ('Αριάσπαι, 'Αγριάσπαι), a people in the S. part of the Persian province of Drangiana, on the very borders of Gedrosia, with a capital city, Ariaspe ('Αριάσπη). In return for the services which they rendered to the army of Cyrus the Great, when he marched through the desert of Carmania, they were honoured with the name of Εὐεργέται, and were allowed by the Persians to retain their independence, which was confirmed to them by Alexander as the reward of similar services to himself.

Aricīa (Aricīnus : *Aricūa* or *Riccia*), an ancient town of Latium at the foot of the Alban Mount, on the Appian Way, 16 miles from Rome. It was a member of the Latin confederacy, was subdued by the Romans, with the other Latin towns, in B. C. 338. and received the Roman franchise. In its neighbourhood was the celebrated grove and temple of Diana Aricīna, on the borders of the Lacus Nemorensis (*Nemi*). Diana was worshipped here with barbarous customs : her priest, called *rex nemorensis*, was always a run-away slave, who obtained his office by killing his predecessor in single combat. The priest was obliged to fight with any slave who succeeded in breaking off a branch of a certain tree in the sacred grove.

Aridaeus. [ARIAEUS ; ARRHIDAEUS.]

Arii, is the name applied to the inhabitants of the province of ARIA, but it is probably also a form of the generic name of the whole Persian race, derived from the root *ar*, which means *noble*, and which forms the first syllable of a great number of Persian names. [Comp. ARTAEI.]

Arimaspi ('Αριμασποί), a people in the N. of Scythia, of whom a fabulous account is given by Herodotus (iv. 27). The germ of the fable is perhaps to be recognised in the fact that the Ural Mountains abound in gold.

Arimāxes ('Αριμάζης) or **Ariomāxes** ('Αριομάζης), a chief in Sogdiana, whose fortress was taken by Alexander in B. c. 328. In it Alexander found Roxana, the daughter of the Bactrian chief, Oxyartes, whom he made his wife.

Arimi ("Αριμοι) and **Arimă** (τὰ "Αριμα sc. ὄρη), the names of a mythical people, district, and range of mountains in Asia Minor, which the old Greek poets made the scene of the punishment of the monster Typhoeus. Virgil (*Aen.* ix. 716) has misunderstood the εἰν 'Αρίμοις of Homer (*Il.* ii. 783), and made Typhoeus lie beneath Inarime, an island off the coast of Italy, namely, Pithecusa or Aenaria (*Ischia*).

Ariminum (Ariminensis: *Rimini*), a town in Umbria on the coast at the mouth of the little river Ariminus (*Marocchia*). It was originally inhabited by Umbrians and Pelasgians, was afterwards in the possession of the Senones, and was colonised by the Romans in B. C. 268, from which time it appears as a flourishing place. After leaving Cisalpine Gaul, it was the first town which a person arrived at in the N. E. of Italia proper.

Ariobarzānes ('Αριοβαρζάνης). I. *Kings or Satraps of Pontus.*—1. Betrayed by his son Mithridates to the Persian king, about B. C. 400.—2. Son of Mithridates I., reigned B. C. 363—337. He revolted from Artaxerxes in 362, and may be regarded as the founder of the kingdom of Pontus. —3. Son of Mithridates III., reigned 266—240, and was succeeded by Mithridates IV.—II. *Kings of Cappadocia.*—1. Surnamed *Philoromaeus*, reigned B. C. 93—63, and was elected king by the Cappadocians, under the direction of the Romans. He was several times expelled from his kingdom by Mithridates, but was finally restored by Pompey in 63, shortly before his death.—2. Surnamed *Philopator*, succeeded his father in 63. The time of his death is not known; but it must have been before 51, in which year his son was reigning.—3. Surnamed *Eusebes* and *Philoromaeus*, son of No. 2, whom he succeeded about 51. He assisted Pompey against Caesar in 48, but was nevertheless pardoned by Caesar, who even enlarged his territories. He was slain in 42 by Cassius, because he was plotting against him in Asia.

Arion ('Αρίων). 1. Of Methymna in Lesbos, an ancient Greek bard and a celebrated player on the cithara, is called the inventor of the dithyrambic poetry, and of the name dithyramb. He lived about B. C. 625, and spent a great part of his life at the court of Periander, tyrant of Corinth. Of his life scarcely any thing is known beyond the beautiful story of his escape from the sailors with whom he sailed from Sicily to Corinth. On one occasion, thus runs the story, Arion went to Sicily to take part in some musical contest. He won the prize, and, laden with presents, he embarked in a Corinthian ship to return to his friend Periander. The rude sailors coveted his treasures, and meditated his murder. After trying in vain to save his life, he at length obtained permission once more to play on the cithara. In festal attire he placed himself in the prow of the ship and invoked the gods in inspired strains, and then threw himself into the sea. But many song-loving dolphins had assembled round the vessel, and one of them now took the bard on its back and carried him to Taenărus, from whence he returned to Corinth in safety, and related his adventure to Periander. Upon the arrival of the Corinthian vessel Periander inquired of the sailors after Arion, who replied that he had remained behind at Tarentum; but when Arion, at the bidding of Periander, came forward, the sailors owned their guilt, and were punished according to their desert. In the time of Herodotus and Pausanias there existed at Taenarus a brass monument, representing Arion riding on a dolphin. Arion and his cithara (lyre) were placed among the stars. A fragment of a hymn to Poseidon, ascribed to Arion, is contained in Bergk's *Poetae Lyrici Graeci*, p. 566, &c.—2. A fabulous horse, which Poseidon begot by Demeter; for, in order to escape from the pursuit of Poseidon, the goddess had metamorphosed herself into a mare, and Poseidon de-

ceived her by assuming the figure of a horse. There were many other traditions respecting the origin of this horse, but all make Poseidon its father, though its mother is different in the various legends.

Ariovistus, a German chief, who crossed the Rhine at the request of the Sequani, when they were hard pressed by the Aedui. He subdued the Aedui, but appropriated to himself part of the territory of the Sequani, and threatened to take still more. The Sequani now united with the Aedui in imploring the help of Caesar, who defeated Ariovistus about 50 miles from the Rhine, B. C. 58. Ariovistus escaped across the river in a small boat.

Aristaenětus ('Αρισταίνετος), the reputed author of 2 books of Love-Letters, taken almost entirely from Plato, Lucian, Philostratus, and Plutarch. Of the author nothing is known. The best edition is by Boissonade, Paris, 1822.

Aristaenus ('Αρίσταινος), of Megalopolis, sometimes called *Aristaenetus*, was frequently strategus or general of the Achaean league from B. C. 198 to 185. He was the political opponent of Philopoemen, and a friend of the Romans.

Aristaeus ('Αρισταῖος), a divinity worshipped in various parts of Greece, was once a mortal, who became a god through the benefits he had conferred upon mankind. The different accounts about him seem to have arisen in different places and independently of one another, so that they referred to several distinct beings, who were subsequently identified and united into one. He is described either as a son of Uranus and Ge, or, according to a more general tradition, as the son of Apollo and Cyrene. His mother Cyrene had been carried off by Apollo from mount Pelion to Libya, where she gave birth to Aristaeus. Aristaeus subsequently went to Thebes in Boeotia; but after the unfortunate death of his son ACTAEON, he left Thebes and visited almost all the Greek colonies on the coasts of the Mediterranean. Finally he went to Thrace, and after dwelling for some time near mount Haemus, where he founded the town of Aristaeon, he disappeared. Aristaeus is one of the most beneficent divinities in ancient mythology: he was worshipped as the protector of flocks and shepherds, of vine and olive plantations; he taught men to keep bees, and averted from the fields the burning heat of the sun and other causes of destruction.

Aristagŏras ('Αρισταγόρας), of Miletus, brother-in-law of Histiaeus, was left by the latter during his stay at the Persian court, in charge of the government of Miletus. Having failed in an attempt upon Naxos (B. C. 501), which he had promised to subdue for the Persians, and fearing the consequences of his failure, he induced the Ionian cities to revolt from Persia. He applied for assistance to the Spartans and Athenians; the former refused, but the latter sent him 20 ships and some troops. In 499 his army captured and burnt Sardis, but was finally chased back to the coast. The Athenians now departed; the Persians conquered most of the Ionian cities; and Aristagoras in despair fled to Thrace where he was slain by the Edonians in 497.

Aristander ('Αρίστανδρος), the most celebrated soothsayer of Alexander the Great, wrote a work on prodigies.

Aristarchus ('Αρίσταρχος). 1. An Athenian, one of the leaders in the revolution of the " Four Hundred," B. C. 411. He was afterwards put to death by the Athenians, not later than 406.—2

A Lacedaemonian, succeeded Cleander as harmost of Byzantium in 400, and in various ways ill treated the Cyrean Greeks, who had recently returned from Asia. — 3. Of TEGEA, a tragic poet at Athens, contemporary with Euripides, flourished about B. c. 454, and wrote 70 tragedies. — 4. Of SAMOS, an eminent mathematician and astronomer at Alexandria, flourished between B. c. 280 and 264. He employed himself in the determination of some of the most important elements of astronomy; but none of his works remain, except a treatise on the magnitudes and distances of the sun and moon (περὶ μεγεθῶν καὶ ἀποστημάτων ἡλίου καὶ σελήνης). Edited by Wallis, Oxon, 1688, and reprinted in vol. iii. of his works. There is a French translation, and an edition of the text, Paris, 1810. — 5. Of SAMOTHRACE, the celebrated grammarian, flourished B. c. 156. He was educated in the school of Aristophanes of Byzantium, at Alexandria, where he himself founded a grammatical and critical school. At an advanced age he left Alexandria, and went to Cyprus, where he is said to have died at the age of 72, of voluntary starvation, because he was suffering from incurable dropsy. Aristarchus was the greatest critic of antiquity. His labours were chiefly devoted to the Greek poets, but more especially to the Homeric poems, of which he published a recension, which has been the basis of the text from his time to the present day. The great object of his critical labours was to restore the genuine text of the Homeric poems, and to clear it of all later interpolations and corruptions. He marked those verses which he thought spurious with an obelos, and those which he considered as particularly beautiful with an asterisk. He divided the Iliad and Odyssey into 24 books each. He did not confine himself to a recension of the text, but also explained and interpreted the poems: he opposed the allegorical interpretation which was then beginning to find favour, and which at a later time became very general. His grammatical principles were attacked by many of his contemporaries: the most eminent of his opponents was CRATES of Mallus.

Aristĕas ('Αριστέας), of Proconnesus, an epic poet of whose life we have only fabulous accounts. His date is quite uncertain: some place him in the time of Croesus and Cyrus; but other traditions make him earlier than Homer, or a contemporary and teacher of Homer. The ancient writers represent him as a magician, who rose after his death, and whose soul could leave and re-enter his body according to its pleasure. He was connected with the worship of Apollo, which he was said to have introduced at Metapontum. He is said to have travelled through the countries N. and E. of the Euxine, and to have visited the Issedones, Arimaspae, Cimmerii, Hyperborei, and other mythical nations, and after his return to have written an epic poem in 3 books, called *The Arimaspēa* (τὰ Ἀριμάσπεια). This work is frequently mentioned by the ancients, but it is impossible to say who was the real author of it.

Aristĕas or **Aristaeus**, an officer of Ptolemy Philadelphus (B. c. 285—247), the reputed author of a Greek work, giving an account of the manner in which the translation of the Septuagint was executed, but which is generally admitted by the best critics to be spurious. Printed at Oxford, 1692, 8vo.

Aristīdes ('Αριστείδης). 1. An Athenian, son of Lysimachus, surnamed the "Just," was of an ancient and noble family. He was the political disciple of Clisthenes, and partly on that account, partly from personal character, opposed from the first to Themistocles. Aristides fought as the commander of his tribe at the battle of Marathon, B. c. 490; and next year, 489, he was archon. In 483 or 482 he suffered ostracism, probably in consequence of the triumph of the maritime and democratic policy of his rival. He was still in exile in 480 at the battle of Salamis, where he did good service by dislodging the enemy, with a band raised and armed by himself, from the islet of Payttaleia. He was recalled from banishment after the battle, was appointed general in the following year (479), and commanded the Athenians at the battle of Plataea. In 477, when the allies had become disgusted with the conduct of Pausanias and the Spartans, he and his colleague Cimon had the glory of obtaining for Athens the command of the maritime confederacy: and to Aristides was by general consent entrusted the task of drawing up its laws and fixing its assessments. This first tribute (φόρος) of 460 talents, paid into a common treasury at Delos, bore his name, and was regarded by the allies in after times, as marking their Saturnian age. This is his last recorded act. He died after 471, the year of the ostracism of Themistocles, and very likely in 468. He died so poor that he did not leave enough to pay for his funeral: his daughters were portioned by the state, and his son Lysimachus received a grant of land and of money. — 2. The author of a work entitled *Milesiaca*, which was probably a romance, having Miletus for its scene. It was written in prose, and was of a licentious character. It was translated into Latin by L. Cornelius Sisenna, a contemporary of Sulla, and it seems to have become popular with the Romans. Aristides is reckoned as the inventor of the Greek romance, and the title of his work gave rise to the term *Milesian*, as applied to works of fiction. His age and country are unknown, but the title of his work is thought to favour the conjecture that he was a native of Miletus. — 3. Of THEBES, a celebrated Greek painter, flourished about B. c. 360—330. The point in which he most excelled was in depicting the feelings, expressions, and passions which may be observed in common life. His pictures were so much valued that long after his death Attalus, king of Pergamus, offered 600,000 sesterces for one of them. — 4. P. Aelius Aristides, surnamed THEODORUS, a celebrated Greek rhetorician, was born at Adriani in Mysia, in A. D. 117. He studied under Herodes Atticus at Athens, and subsequently travelled through Egypt, Greece, and Italy. The fame of his talents and acquirements was so great that monuments were erected to his honour in several towns which he had honoured with his presence. Shortly before his return he was attacked by an illness which lasted for 13 years, but this did not prevent him from prosecuting his studies. He subsequently settled at Smyrna, and when this city was nearly destroyed by an earthquake in 178, he used his influence with the emperor M. Aurelius to induce him to assist in rebuilding the town. The Smyrnaeans showed their gratitude to Aristides by offering him various honours and distinctions, most of which he refused: he accepted only the office of priest of Asclepius, which he held until his death, about A. D. 180. The works of Aristides which have come down to us, are 55 orations and

Apollo Musagetes.
(Osterley, Denk. der alten Kunst, tav. 32.) Page 63.

Ares (Mars).
(Ludovisi Statue in Rome.) Page 74.

The Pythian Apollo.
(Audian, Proportion du Corps Humain, pl. 18.) Page 63.

Apollo, with Lyre and Bow.
(Zoëga, Bassirilievi, tav. 98.) Page 63.

Bacchus and Ariadne drawn by Tigers.
(From a Bas-relief in the Vatican.) Pages 77, 78.

Ariadne.
(From a Painting found at Pompeii.) Pages 77, 78.

[To face p. 80.

Antioch. Page 54, No. 1.

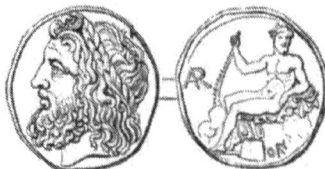

Apamea in Phrygia. Page 66, No. 3.

Aphrodisias in Caria. Page 61.

Aptera in Crete. Page 66.

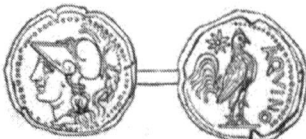

Aquinum, a town of the Volscians. Page 67.

Aradus in Phoenicia. Page 69.

Arcadia. Page 76.

Argos in Peloponnesus. Page 77.

Argos Amphilochicum. Page 77.

Arpi. Page 84.

Aspendus in Pamphylia. Page 96.

Assorus. Page 98.

declamations, and 2 treatises on rhetorical subjects of little value. His orations are much superior to those of the rhetoricians of his time. His admirers compared him to Demosthenes, and even Aristides did not think himself much inferior. This vanity and self-sufficiency made him enemies and opponents ; but the number of his admirers was far greater, and several learned grammarians wrote commentaries on his orations, some of which are extant. The best edition of Aristides is by W. Dindorf, Lips. 1829.—5. **Quintilianus Aristides**, the author of a treatise in 3 books on music, probably lived in the 1st century after Christ. His work is perhaps the most valuable of all the ancient musical treatises ; it is printed in the collection of Meibomius entitled *Antiquae Musicae Auctores Septem*, Amst. 1652.

Aristion ('Aριστίων), a philosopher either of the Epicurean or Peripatetic school, made himself tyrant of Athens through the influence of Mithridates. He held out against Sulla in B. C. 87 ; and when the city was taken by storm, he was put to death by Sulla's orders.

Aristippus ('Aρίστιππος). 1. Son of Aritades, born at Cyrene, and founder of the Cyrenaic school of Philosophy, flourished about B. C. 370. The fame of Socrates brought him to Athens, and he remained with the latter almost up to the time of his execution, B. C. 399. Though a disciple of Socrates, he wandered both in principle and practice very far from the teaching and example of his great master. He was luxurious in his mode of living : he indulged in sensual gratifications and the society of the notorious Lais ; and he took money for his teaching (being the first of the disciples of Socrates who did so). He passed part of his life at the court of Dionysius, tyrant of Syracuse ; but he appears at last to have returned to Cyrene, and there to have spent his old age. The anecdotes which are told of him, however, do not give us the notion of a person who was the mere slave of his passions, but rather of one who took a pride in extracting enjoyment from all circumstances of every kind, and in controlling adversity and prosperity alike. They illustrate and confirm the two statements of Horace (*Ep.* i. l. 18), that to observe the precepts of Aristippus is *mihi res, non me rebus subjungere*, and (l. 17, 23) that, *omnis Aristippum decuit color et status et res*. Thus when reproached for his love of bodily indulgences, he answered, that there was no shame in enjoying them, but that it would be disgrace! ; if he could not at any time give them up. To Xenophon and Plato he was very obnoxious, as we see from the *Memorabilia* (ii. l.) where he maintains an odious discussion against Socrates in defence of voluptuous enjoyment, and from the *Phaedo*, where his absence at the death of Socrates, though he was only at Aegina, 200 stadia from Athens, is doubtless mentioned as a reproach. He imparted his doctrine to his daughter Arete, by whom it was communicated to her son, the younger Aristippus.—2. Two tyrants of Argos, in the time of Antigonus Gonatas. See ARISTOMACHUS, Nos. 3 and 4.

Aristo, T., a distinguished Roman jurist, lived under the emperor Trajan, and was a friend of the Younger Pliny. His works are occasionally mentioned in the Digest, but there is no direct extract from any of them in that compilation. He wrote notes on the *Libri Posteriorum* of Labeo, on Cassius, whose pupil he had been, and on Sabinus.

Aristo. [ARISTON.]

Aristobūlus ('Aριστόβουλος), princes of Judaea. 1. Eldest son of Joannes Hyrcanus, assumed the title of king of Judaea, on the death of his father in B. C. 107. He put to death his brother Antigonus, in order to secure his power, but died in the following year, 106.—2. Younger son of Alexander Jannaeus and Alexandra. After the death of his mother in B. C. 70, there was a civil war for some years between Aristobulus and his brother Hyrcanus, for the possession of the crown At length in B. C. 63, Aristobuius was deprived of the sovereignty by Pompey and carried away as a prisoner to Rome. In 57, he escaped from his confinement at Rome, with his son Antigonus, and, returning to Judaea, renewed the war ; but he was taken prisoner, and sent back to Rome by Gabinius. In 49, he was released by Julius Caesar, who sent him into Judaea, but he was poisoned on the way by some of Pompey's party.—3. Grandson of No 2, son of Alexander and brother of Herod's wife Mariamne. He was made high-priest by Herod, when he was only 17 years old, but was afterwards drowned at Jericho, by order of Herod, B. C. 35. —4. Son of Herod the Great by Mariamne, was put to death in B. C. 6, with his brother Alexander, by order of their father, whose suspicions had been excited against them by their brother ANTIPATER. —5. Surnamed "the Younger," son of Aristobulus and Berenice, and grandson of Herod the Great. He was educated at Rome with his two brothers, Agrippa I. and Herod the future king of Chalcis. He died, as he had lived, in a private station.— 6. Son of Herod king of Chalcis, grandson of No. 4, and great-grandson of Herod the Great. In A. D. 55, Nero made him king of Armenia Minor, and in 61 added to his dominions some portion of the Greater Armenia which had been given to Tigranes. He joined the Romans in the war against Antiochus, king of Commagene, in 73.

Aristobūlus. 1. Of Cassandrea, served under Alexander the Great in Asia, and wrote a history of Alexander, which was one of the chief sources used by Arrian in the composition of his work.— 2. An Alexandrine Jew, and a Peripatetic philosopher, lived B. C. 170, under Ptolemy VI. Philometor. He is said to have been the author of commentaries upon the books of Moses, the object of which was to prove that the Greek philosophy was taken from the books of Moses ; but it is now admitted that this work was written by a later writer, whose object was to induce the Greeks to pay respect to the Jewish literature.

Aristōcles ('Aριστοκλῆς). 1. Of Rhodes, a Greek grammarian and rhetorician, a contemporary of Strabo.—2. Of Pergamus, a sophist and rhetorician, and a pupil of Herodes Atticus, lived under Trajan and Hadrian.—3. Of Messene, a Peripatetic philosopher, probably lived about the beginning of the third century after Christ. He wrote a work on philosophy, some fragments of which are preserved by Eusebius.—4. Sculptors. There were two sculptors of this name : Aristocles the elder, who is called both a Cydonian and a Sicyonian, probably because he was born at Cydonia and practised his art in Sicyon ; and Aristocles the younger, of Sicyon, grandson of the former, son of Cleoetas, and brother of Canachus. These artists founded a school of sculpture at Sicyon, which secured an hereditary reputation, and of which we have the heads for 7 genera-

G

tions, namely, Aristocles, Cleoetas, Aristocles and Canachus, Synnoön, Ptolichus, Sostratus, and Pantias. The elder Aristocles probably lived about B. C. 600—568 ; the younger about 540—508.

Aristocrates ('Αριστοκράτης). 1. Last king of Arcadia, was the leader of the Arcadians in the 2nd Messenian war, when they assisted the Messenians against the Spartans. Having been bribed by the Spartans, he betrayed the Messenians, and was in consequence stoned to death by the Arcadians, about B. C. 668, who now abolished the kingly office.—2. An Athenian of wealth and influence, son of Scellias, was one of the Athenian generals at the battle of Arginusae, B. C. 406, and on his return to Athens was brought to trial and executed.

Aristodemus ('Αριστόδημος). 1. A descendant of Hercules, son of Aristomachus, and father of Eurysthenes and Procles. According to some traditions Aristodemus was killed at Naupactus by a flash of lightning, just as he was setting out on his expedition into Peloponnesus ; but a Lacedaemonian tradition related, that Aristodemus himself came to Sparta, was the first king of his race, and died a natural death.—2. A Messenian, one of the chief heroes in the first Messenian war. As the Delphic oracle had declared that the preservation of the Messenian state demanded that a maiden of the house of the Aepytids should be sacrificed, Aristodemus offered his own daughter. In order to save her life, her lover declared that she was with child by him, but Aristodemus, enraged at this assertion, murdered his daughter and opened her body to refute the calumny. Aristodemus was afterwards elected king in place of Euphnes, who had fallen in battle against the Spartans. He continued the war against the Spartans, till at length, finding further resistance hopeless, he put an end to his life on the tomb of his daughter, about B. C. 723.—3. Tyrant of Cumae in Campania, at whose court Tarquinius Superbus died, B. C. 496.—4. One of the 300 Spartans at Thermopylae (B. C. 480), was not present at the battle in which his comrades fell, either in consequence of sickness, or because he had been sent on an errand from the camp. The Spartans punished him with *Atimia*, or civil degradation. Stung with this treatment he met his death at Plataea in the following year (479), after performing the wildest feats of valour.—5. A tragic actor of Athens in the time of Demosthenes, took a prominent part in the political affairs of his time, and advocated peace with Macedonia. He was employed by the Athenians in their negotiations with Philip, with whom he was a great favourite.—6. Of Miletus, a friend and flatterer of Antigonus, king of Asia, who sent him into Greece in B. C. 315, in order to promote his interests there.—7. There were many literary persons of this name referred to by the ancient grammarians, whom it is difficult to distinguish from one another. Two were natives of Nysa in Caria, both grammarians, one a teacher of Pompey, and the other of Strabo. There was also an Aristodemus of Elis, and another of Thebes, who are quoted as writers.

Aristogiton ('Αριστογείτων). 1. The conspirator against the sons of Pisistratus. See HARMODIUS.—2. An Athenian orator and adversary of Demosthenes, Hyperides, and Dinarchus. He was often accused by Demosthenes and others, and defended himself in a number of orations which

are lost. Among the extant speeches of Demosthenes there are 2 against Aristogiton, and among those of Dinarchus there is one.

Aristomache ('Αριστομάχη), daughter of Hipparinus of Syracuse, sister of Dion, and wife of the elder Dionysius, who married her and Doris of Locri on the same day. She afterwards perished with her daughter ARETE.

Aristomachus ('Αριστόμαχος). 1. Son of Talaus and brother of Adrastus.—2. Son of Cleodemus or Cleodaeus, grandson of Hyllus, great-grandson of Hercules, and father of Temenus, Cresphontes, and Aristodemus. He fell in battle when he invaded Peloponnesus ; but his three sons were more successful and conquered Peloponnesus.—3. Tyrant of Argos, under the patronage of Antigonus Gonatas, was assassinated, and succeeded by Aristippus II.—4. Tyrant of Argos, succeeded Aristippus II.: he resigned his power upon the death of Demetrius in B. C. 229, and induced Argos to join the Achaean league. He afterwards deserted the Achaeans, and again assumed the tyranny of Argos ; but the city having been taken by Antigonus Doson, Aristomachus fell into the hands of the Achaeans, and was by them put to death.

Aristomenes ('Αριστομένης). 1. The Messenian, the hero of the 2nd war with Sparta, belongs more to legend than to history. He was a native of Andania, and was sprung from the royal line of Aepytus. Tired of the yoke of Sparta, he began the war in B. C. 685, 39 years after the end of the 1st war. Soon after its commencement he so distinguished himself by his valour, that he was offered the throne, but refused it, and received the office of supreme commander. After the defeat of the Messenians in the 3rd year of the war, through the treachery of Aristocrates, the Arcadian leader, Aristomenes retreated to the mountain fortress of Ira, and there maintained the war for 11 years, constantly ravaging the land of Laconia. In one of his incursions, however, the Spartans overpowered him with superior numbers, and carrying him with 50 of his comrades to Sparta, cast them into the pit (κεάδας) where condemned criminals were thrown. The rest perished ; not so Aristomenes, the favourite of the gods ; for legends told how an eagle bore him up on its wings as he fell, and a fox guided him on the 3rd day from the cavern. But having incurred the anger of the Twin Brothers, his country was destined to ruin. The city of Ira, which he had so long successfully defended, fell into the hands of the Spartans ; Aristomenes, after performing prodigies of valour, was obliged to leave his country, which was again compelled to submit to the Spartans, B. C. 668. He afterwards settled at Ialysus in Rhodes, where he died. Damagetus, king of Ialysus, had been enjoined by the Delphic oracle " to marry the daughter of the best of the Greeks," and he therefore took to wife the daughter of Aristomenes, who accompanied him to Rhodes. The Rhodians honoured Aristomenes as a hero, and from him were descended the illustrious family of the Diagoridae. —2. An Acarnanian, who governed Egypt with justice and wisdom during the minority of Ptolemy V. Epiphanes, but was put to death by Ptolemy in 192.—3. A comic poet of Athens, flourished during the Peloponnesian war.

Ariston ('Αρίστων). 1. Of Chios, a Stoic philosopher, and a disciple of Zeno, flourished about B. C. 260. Though he professed himself a Stoic yet he differed from Zeno in several points, and became the founder of a small school. He is said to have died of a *coup de soleil*. — **2.** A Peripatetic philosopher of Julis in the island of Ceos, succeeded Lycon as head of the Peripatetic school, about B. C. 230. He wrote several philosophical works which are lost. — **3.** Of Alexandria, a Peripatetic philosopher and a contemporary of Strabo, wrote a work on the Nile.

Aristonautae ('Αριστοναῦται), a town in Achaia, the harbour of Pallene.

Aristonicus ('Αριστόνικος). **1.** A natural son of Eumenes II. of Pergamus. Upon the death of his brother Attalus III., B. C. 133, who left his kingdom to the Romans, Aristonicus laid claim to the crown. At first he met with considerable success. He defeated in 131 the consul P. Licinius Crassus ; but in 130 he was defeated and taken prisoner by M. Perperna, was carried to Rome by M'. Aquillius in 129, and was there put to death. — **2.** An Alexandrine grammarian, a contemporary of Strabo, and the author of several works, most of which related to the Homeric poems.

Aristonymus ('Αριστώνυμος), a comic poet and contemporary of Aristophanes and Amipsias.

Aristophanes ('Αριστοφάνης). **1.** The celebrated comic poet, was born about B. C. 444 and probably at Athens. His father Philippus had possessions in Aegina, and may originally have come from that island, whence a question arose whether Aristophanes was a genuine Athenian citizen : his enemy Cleon brought against him more than one accusation to deprive him of his civic rights (ξενίας γραφαί), but without success. He had three sons, Philippus, Araros, and Nicostratus, but of his private history we know nothing. He probably died about B. C. 380. The comedies of Aristophanes are of the highest historical interest, containing as they do an admirable series of caricatures on the leading men of the day, and a contemporary commentary on the evils existing at Athens. Indeed, the caricature is the only feature in modern social life which at all resembles them. Aristophanes was a bold and often a wise patriot. He had the strongest affection for Athens, and longed to see her restored to the state in which she was flourishing in the previous generation, and almost in his own childhood, before Pericles became the head of the government, and when the age of Miltiades and Aristides had but just passed away. The first great evil of his own time against which he inveighs, is the Peloponnesian war, which he regards as the work of Pericles. To this fatal war, among a host of evils, he ascribes the influence of demagogues like Cleon at Athens. Another great object of his indignation was the recently adopted system of education which had been introduced by the Sophists, acting on the speculative and inquiring turn given to the Athenian mind by the Ionian and Eleatic philosophers, and the extraordinary intellectual development of the age following the Persian war. The new theories introduced by the Sophists threatened to overthrow the foundations of morality, by making persuasion and not truth the object of man in his intercourse with his fellows, and to substitute a universal scepticism for the religious creed of the people. The worst effects of such a system were seen in Alcibiades, who combined all the elements which Aristophanes most disliked, heading the war party in politics, and protecting the sophistical school in philosophy and also in literature. Of this latter

school — the literary and poetical Sophists — Euripides was the chief, whose works are full of that μετεωροσοφία which contrasts so offensively with the moral dignity of Aeschylus and Sophocles, and for which Aristophanes introduces him as soaring in the air to write his tragedies. Another feature of the times was the excessive love for litigation at Athens, the consequent importance of the dicasts, and disgraceful abuse of their power ; all of which enormities are made by Aristophanes objects of continual attack. But though he saw what were the evils of his time, he had not wisdom to find a remedy for them, except the hopeless and undesirable one of a movement backwards ; and therefore, though we allow him to have been honest and bold, we must deny him the epithet of great. The following is a list of his extant comedies, with the year in which they were performed:—425. *Acharnians*. Produced in the name of Callistratus. First prize.—424. 'Ιππεῖς, *Knights* or *Horsemen*. The first play produced in the name of Aristophanes himself. First prize ; second Cratinus. — 423. *Clouds*. First prize, Cratinus ; second, Amipsias. —422. *Wasps*. Second prize. — *Clouds* (second edition). failed in obtaining a prize. Some writers place this B. C. 411, and the whole subject is very uncertain. — 419. *Peace*. Second prize ; Eupolis first. — *Birds*. Second prize ; Amipsias, first ; Phrynichus, third. — 411. *Lysistrata*. — *Thesmophoriazusae*. During the Oligarchy.—408. First *Plutus*. — 405. *Frogs*. First prize ; Phrynichus, second ; Plato, third. Death of Sophocles.—392. *Ecclesiazusae*. — 388. Second edition of the *Plutus*. — The last two comedies of Aristophanes were the *Aeolosicon* and *Cocalus*, produced about B. C. 387 (date of the peace of Antalcidas) by Araros, one of his sons. — Suidas tells us, that Aristophanes was the author, in all, of 54 plays. As a poet Aristophanes possessed merits of the highest order. His works contain snatches of lyric poetry which are quite noble, and some of his chorusses, particularly one in the *Knights*, in which the horses are represented as rowing triremes in an expedition against Corinth, are written with a spirit and humour unrivalled in Greek, and are not very dissimilar to English ballads. He was a complete master of the Attic dialect, and in his hands the perfection of that glorious language is wonderfully shown. No flights are too bold for the range of his fancy: animals of every kind are pressed into his service ; frogs chaunt chorusses, a dog is tried for stealing a cheese, and an iambic verse is composed of the grunts of a pig. — *Editions.* The best of the collective plays are by Invernizzi, completed by Beck and Dindorf. 13 vols. Lips. 1794—1826, and by Bekker, 5 vols. 8vo., London, 1829. — **2.** Of Byzantium, son of Apelles, and one of the most eminent Greek grammarians at Alexandria. He was a pupil of Zenodotus and Eratosthenes, and teacher of the celebrated Aristarchus. He lived about B. C. 264, in the reign of Ptolemy II. and Ptolemy III., and had the supreme management of the library at Alexandria. Aristophanes was the first who introduced the use of accents in the Greek language. He devoted himself chiefly to the criticism and interpretation of the Greek poets, and more especially of Homer, of whose works he made a new and critical edition (διόρθωσις). The philosophers Plato and Aristotle likewise engaged his attention, and of the former, as of several of the poets, he made new and critical editions.

All we possess of his numerous works consists of fragments scattered through the Scholia on the poets, some argumenta to the plays of the tragic poets and of Aristophanes, and a part of his Λέξεις, which is printed in Boissonade's edition of Herodian's *Partitiones*, London, 1819, pp. 283—289.

Aristŏphon ('Αριστόφων). 1. Of the demus of Azenia in Attica, one of the most distinguished Athenian orators about the close of the Peloponnesian war. The number of laws which he proposed may be inferred from his own statement, as preserved by Aeschines, that he was accused 75 times of having made illegal proposals, but that he had always come off victorious. In B. C. 354 he accused Iphicrates and Timotheus, and in the same year he came forward in the assembly to defend the law of Leptines against Demosthenes. The latter treats him with great respect, and reckons him among the most eloquent orators. — 2. Of the demus of Colyttus, a contemporary of Demosthenes, and an orator of great distinction and influence. It was this Aristophon whom Aeschines served as a clerk, and in whose service he was trained for his public career. [AESCHINES.] — 3. A comic poet of the middle comedy. — 4. A painter of some distinction, son and pupil of Aglaophon, and brother of Polygnotus.

Aristŏtĕles ('Αριστοτέλης), the philosopher, was born at Stagīra, a town in Chalcidice in Macedonia, B. C. 384. His father, Nicomachus, was physician in ordinary to Amyntas II., king of Macedonia, and the author of several treatises on subjects connected with natural science: his mother Phaestis (or Phaestias), was descended from a Chalcidian family. The studies and occupation of his father account for the early inclination manifested by Aristotle for the investigation of nature, an inclination which is perceived throughout his whole life. He lost his father before he had attained his 17th year, and he was entrusted to the guardianship of one Proxenus of Atarneus in Mysia, who was settled in Stagira. In 367, he went to Athens to pursue his studies, and there became a pupil of Plato upon the return of the latter from Sicily about 365. Plato soon distinguished him above all his other disciples. He named him the " intellect of his school," and his house, the house of the "reader." Aristotle lived at Athens for 20 years, till 347. During the whole of this period the good understanding which subsisted between teacher and scholar continued, with some trifling exceptions, undisturbed ; for the stories of the disrespect and ingratitude of the latter towards the former are nothing but calumnies invented by his enemies. During the last 10 years of his first residence at Athens, Aristotle gave instruction in rhetoric, and distinguished himself by his opposition to Isocrates. It was at this time that he published his first rhetorical writings. Upon the death of Plato (347) Aristotle left Athens, perhaps he was offended by Plato having appointed Speusippus as his successor in the Academy. He first repaired to his friend Hermias at Atarneus, where he married Pythias, the adoptive daughter of the prince. On the death of Hermias, who was killed by the Persians (344), Aristotle fled from Atarneus to Mytilene. Two years afterwards (342) he accepted an invitation from Philip of Macedonia, to undertake the instruction of his son Alexander, then 13 years of age. Here Aristotle was treated with the most marked respect. His native city,

Stagira, which had been destroyed by Philip, was rebuilt at his request, and Philip caused a gymnasium (called Nymphaeum) to be built there in a pleasant grove expressly for Aristotle and his pupils. Several of the youths of the Macedonian nobles were educated by Aristotle along with Alexander. Aristotle spent 7 years in Macedonia ; but Alexander enjoyed his instruction without interruption for only 4. Still with such a pupil even this short period was sufficient for a teacher like Aristotle to fulfil the highest purposes of education, and to create in his pupil that sense of the noble and great, which distinguishes Alexander from all those conquerors who have only swept like a hurricane through the world. On Alexander's accession to the throne in 335, Aristotle returned to Athens. Here he found his friend Xenocrates president of the Academy. He himself had the Lycēum, a gymnasium sacred to Apollo Lyceus, assigned to him by the state. He soon assembled round him a large number of distinguished scholars, to whom he delivered lectures on philosophy in the shady walks (περίπατοι) which surrounded the Lyceum, while walking up and down (περιπατῶν), and not sitting, which was the general practice of the philosophers. From one or other of these circumstances the name *Peripatetic* is derived, which was afterwards given to his school. He gave two different courses of lectures every day. Those which he delivered in the morning (ἑωθινὸς περίπατος) to a narrower circle of chosen (esoteric) hearers, and which were called *acroamatic* or *acroatic*, embraced subjects connected with the more abstruse philosophy (theology), physics, and dialectica. Those which he delivered in the afternoon (δειλινὸς περίπατος) and intended for a more promiscuous circle (which accordingly he called *exoteric*), extended to rhetoric, sophistica, and politics. He appears to have taught not so much in the way of conversation, as in regular lectures. His school soon became the most celebrated at Athens, and he continued to preside over it for 13 years (335—323). During this time he also composed the greater part of his works. In these labours he was assisted by the truly kingly liberality of his former pupil, who not only presented him with 800 talents, but also caused large collections of natural curiosities to be made for him, to which posterity is indebted for one of his most excellent works, the *History of Animals*. Meanwhile various causes contributed to throw a cloud over the latter years of the philosopher's life. In the first place, he felt deeply the death of his wife Pythias, who left behind her a daughter of the same name: he lived subsequently with a friend of his wife's, the slave Herpyllis, who bore him a son, Nicomachus. But a source of still greater grief was an interruption of the friendly relation in which he had hitherto stood to his royal pupil. This was occasioned by the conduct of Callisthenes, the nephew and pupil of Aristotle, who had vehemently and injudiciously opposed the changes in the conduct and policy of Alexander. Still Alexander refrained from any expression of hostility towards his former instructor, although their former cordial connection no longer subsisted undisturbed. The story that Aristotle had a share in poisoning the king, is a fabrication of a later age ; and moreover it is certain that Alexander died a natural death. After the death of Alexander (323) Aristotle was looked upon with suspision at Athens as a friend of Macedonia ; but as it was not easy to bring any political accusation against him, he was accused of impiety (ἀσεβείας) by the hierophant Eurymedon. He withdrew from Athens before his trial, and escaped in the beginning of 322 to Chalcis in Euboea, where he died in the course of the same year, in the 63rd year of his age, of a chronic disease of the stomach. His body was transported to his native city Stagira, and his memory was honoured there, like that of a hero, by yearly festivals. He bequeathed to Theophrastus his well-stored library and the originals of his writings. In person Aristotle was short and of slender make, with small eyes, and a lisp in his pronunciation, using L for R, and with a sort of sarcastic expression in his countenance. He exhibited remarkable attention to external appearance, and bestowed much care on his dress and person. He is described as having been of weak health, which, considering the astonishing extent of his studies, shows all the more the energy of his mind. — The numerous works of Aristotle may be divided into the following classes according to the subjects of which they treat : we only mention the most important in each class. I. Dialectics and Logic.—The extant logical writings are comprehended as a whole under the title Organon ('Ὄργανον, i. e. instrument of science). They are occupied with the investigation of the method by which man arrives at knowledge. An insight into the nature and formation of conclusions and of proof by means of conclusions, is the common aim and centre of all the separate 6 works composing the Organon : these separate works are, 1. Κατηγορίαι, Praedicamenta, in which Aristotle treats of the (10) comprehensive generic ideas, under which all the attributes of things may be subordinated as species. 2. Περὶ ἑρμηνείας, De Interpretatione, concerning the expression of thought by means of speech. 3, 4. Ἀναλυτικὰ πρότερα and ὕστερα, Analytica, each in 2 books, on the theory of conclusions, so called from the resolution of the conclusion into its fundamental component parts. 5. Τοπικὰ, De Locis, in 8 books, of the general points of view (τόποι), from which conclusions may be drawn. 6. Περὶ σοφιστικῶν ἐλέγχων, concerning the fallacies which only apparently prove something. The best edition of the Organon is by Waitz, Lips. 1844. — II. Theoretical Philosophy, consisting of Metaphysics, Mathematics, and Physics, on all of which Aristotle wrote works. 1. The Metaphysics, in 14 books (τῶν μετὰ τὰ φυσικὰ), originally consisted of distinct treatises, independent of one another, and were put together as one work after Aristotle's death. The title also is of late origin, and was given to the work from its being placed after (μετὰ) the Physics (τὰ φυσικὰ). The best edition is by Brandis, Berol. 1823. — 2. In Mathematics we have 2 treatises by Aristotle : (1.) Περὶ ἀτόμων γραμμῶν, i. e. concerning indivisible lines ; 2. Μηχανικὰ προβλήματα, Mechanical Problems. — 3. In Physics, we have, — (1). Physics (φυσικὴ ἀκρόασις, called also by others περὶ ἀρχῶν), in 8 books. In these Aristotle develops the general principles of natural science. (Cosmology.) (2.) Concerning the Heaven (περὶ οὐρανοῦ), in 4 books. (3.) On Production and Destruction (περὶ γενέσεως καὶ φθορᾶς, de Generatione et Corruptione), in 2 books, develop the general laws of production and destruction. (4.) On Meteorology (μετεωρολογικά, de Meteoris), in 4 books. (5.) On the Universe (περὶ

κόσμου, de Mundo), a letter to Alexander, treats the subject of the last 2 works in a popular tone and a rhetorical style altogether foreign to Aristotle. The whole is probably a translation of a work with the same title by Appuleius. (6.) The History of Animals (περὶ ζώων ἱστορία), in 9 books, treats of all the peculiarities of this division of the natural kingdom, according to genera, classes, and species ; especially giving all the characteristics of each animal according to its external and internal vital functions ; according to the manner of its copulation, its mode of life, and its character. The best edition is by Schneider, Lips. 1811. The observations in this work are the triumph of ancient sagacity, and have been confirmed by the results of the most recent investigations. (Cuvier.) (7.) On the parts of Animals (περὶ ζώων μορίων), in 4 books, in which Aristotle, after describing the phaenomena in each species, develops the causes of these phaenomena by means of the idea to be formed of the purpose which is manifested in the formation of the animal. (8.) On the Generation of Animals (περὶ ζώων γενέσεως), in 5 books, treats of the generation of animals and the organs of generation. (9.) De Incessu Animalium (περὶ ζώων πορείας). (10.) Three books on the Soul (περὶ ψυχῆς). Aristotle defines the soul to be " the internal formative principle of a body which may be perceived by the senses, and is capable of life." Best edition by Trendelenburg, Jenae, 1833. Several anatomical works of Aristotle have been lost. He was the first person who in any especial manner advocated anatomical investigations, and showed the necessity of them for the study of the natural sciences. He frequently refers to investigations of his own on the subject. — III. Practical Philosophy or Politics. —All that falls within the sphere of practical philosophy is comprehended in three principal works : the Ethics, the Politics, and the Oeconomics. 1. The Nicomachean Ethics (Ἠθικὰ Νικομάχεια), in 10 books. Aristotle here begins with the highest and most universal end of life, for the individual as well as for the community in the state. This is happiness (εὐδαιμονία) ; and its conditions are, on the one hand, perfect virtue exhibiting itself in the actor, and on the other hand, corresponding bodily advantages and favourable external circumstances. Virtue is the readiness to act constantly and consciously according to the laws of the rational nature of man (ὀρθὸς λόγος). The nature of virtue shows itself in its appearing as the medium between two extremes. In accordance with this, the several virtues are enumerated and characterized. Best editions by Zell, Heidelb. 1820 ; Corais, Paris, 1822 ; Cardwell, Oxon. 1828 ; Michelet, Berol. 1828. — 2. The Eudemean Ethics (Ἠθικὰ Εὐδήμεια), in 7 books, of which only books i. ii. iii. and vii. are independent, while the remaining books iv. v. and vi. agree word for word with books v. vi. and vii. of the Nicomachean Ethics. This ethical work is perhaps a recension of Aristotle's lectures, edited by Eudemus. — 3. Ἠθικὰ Μεγάλα, in 2 books. — 4. Politics (Πολιτικά), in 8 books. The Ethics conduct us to the Politics. The connection between the two works is so close, that in the Ethics by the word ὕστερον reference is made by Aristotle to the Politics, and in the latter by πρότερον to the Ethics. The Politics show how happiness is to be attained for the human community in the state ; for the object of the state is not merely the external preservation of life, but " happy life, as it is attained by means of virtue " (ἀρετή, perfect development of the whole man). Hence also *ethics* form the first and most general foundation of political life, because the state cannot attain its highest object, if morality does not prevail among its citizens. The house, the family, is the element of the state. Accordingly Aristotle begins with the doctrine of domestic economy, then proceeds to a description of the different forms of government, after which he gives a delineation of the most important Hellenic constitutions, and then investigates which of the constitutions is the best (the ideal of a state). The doctrine concerning education, as the most important condition of this best state, forms the conclusion. Best editions, by Schneider, Francof. ad Viadr. 1809 ; Corais, Paris, 1821 ; Göttling, Jenae, 1824 ; Stahr, with a German translation, Lips. 1837 ; Barthélémy St. Hilaire, with a French translation, Paris. 1837.— 5. *Oeconomics* (οἰκονομικά), in 2 books, of which only the first is genuine. — IV. WORKS ON ART, which have for their subject the exercise of the creative faculty, or Art. To these belong the *Poetics* and *Rhetoric*. 1. *The Poetics* (Περὶ ποιητικῆς). Aristotle penetrated deeper than any of the ancients into the essence of Hellenic art. He is the father of the *aesthetics of poetry*, as he is the completer of Greek rhetoric as a science. The greatest part of the treatise contains a theory of Tragedy.; nothing else is treated of, with the exception of the epos ; comedy is merely alluded to. . Best editions by Tyrwhitt, Oxon. 1794 ; Hermann, Lips. 1802 ; Gräfenhan, Lips. 1821 ; Bekker, Berol. 1832 ; Ritter, Colon. 1839. — 2. *The Rhetoric* (τέχνη ῥητορική), in 3 books. Rhetoric, as a science, according to Aristotle, stands side by side with Dialectics. The only thing which makes a scientific treatment of rhetoric possible is the argumentation which awakens conviction : he therefore directs his chief attention to the theory of oratorical argumentation. The second main division of the work treats of the production of that favourable disposition in the hearer, in consequence of which the orator appears to him to be worthy of credit. The third part treats of oratorical expression and arrangement. — According to a story current in antiquity Aristotle bequeathed his library and MSS. to Theophrastus, his successor in the Academy. On the death of Theophrastus, the libraries and MSS. both of Aristotle and Theophrastus are said to have come into the hands of his relation and disciple, Neleus of Scepsis. This Neleus sold both libraries to Ptolemy II. king of Egypt, for the Alexandrine library ; but he retained for himself, as an heirloom, the original MSS. of the works of these two philosophers. The descendants of Neleus, who were subjects of the king of Pergamus, knew of no other way of securing them from the search of the Attali, who wished to rival the Ptolemies in forming a large library, than concealing them in a cellar, where for a couple of centuries they were exposed to the ravages of damp and worms. It was not till the beginning of the century before the birth of Christ that a wealthy book-collector, the Athenian Apellicon of Teos, traced out these valuable relics, bought them from the ignorant heirs, and prepared from them a new edition of Aristotle's works. After the capture of Athens, Sulla conveyed Apellicon's library to Rome, B. C. 84. [APELLICON.] From this story an error arose, which has been handed down from the time

of Strabo to the present day. It was concluded from this account, that neither Aristotle nor Theophrastus had published their writings, with the exception of some exoteric works, which had no im portant bearing on their system ; and that it was not till 200 years later that they were brought to light by the above-mentioned Apellicon, and published to the philosophical world. That, however, was by no means the case. Aristotle indeed did not prepare a complete edition, as we call it, of his writings. Nay, it is certain that death overtook him before he could finish some of his works and put the finishing hand to others. Nevertheless it cannot be denied that Aristotle destined all his works for publication, and published several in his life-time. This is indisputably certain with regard to the exoteric writings. Those which had not been published by Aristotle himself, were given to the world by Theophrastus and his disciples in a complete form. — *Editions.* The best edition of the complete works of Aristotle is by Bekker, Berlin, 1831—1840, 4to. text, 2 vols., and a Latin translation in one volume. This edition has been reprinted at Oxford in 11 vols. 8vo. There is a stereotyped edition published by Tauchnitz, Leipzig, 1832, 16mo. in 16 vols., and another edition of the text by Weise, in one volume, Leipzig, 1843.

Aristoxĕnus ('Αριστόξενος), of Tarentum, a Peripatetic philosopher and a musician, flourished about B. C. 318. He was a disciple of Aristotle, whom he appears to have rivalled in the variety of his studies. According to Suidas, he produced works to the number of 453 upon music, philosophy, history, in short every department of literature. We know nothing of his philosophical opinions, except that he held the soul to be a *harmony* of the body (Cic. *Tusc.* i. 10), a doctrine which had been already discussed by Plato in the *Phaedo.* Of his numerous works the only one extant is his *Elements of Harmony* (ἁρμονικὰ στοιχεῖα), in 3 books : edited by Meibomius, in the *Antiquae Musicae Auctores Septem,* Amst. 1652.

Aristus ("Αριστος). 1. Of Salamis in Cyprus, wrote a history of Alexander the Great.—2. An Academic philosopher, a contemporary and friend of Cicero, and teacher of M. Brutus.

Arius, river. [ARIA.]

Arilūsĭa (ἡ Ἀριουσία χώρα), a district on the N. coast of Chios, where the best wine in the island was grown (*Ariusium Vinum,* Virg. *Ecl.* v. 71).

Armĕnē ('Αρμένη, or -ήνη : *Akliman*), a town on the coast of Paphlagonia, where the 10,000 Greeks, during their retreat, rested 5 days, entertained by the people of Sinope, a little to the W. of which Armene stood.

Armĕnĭa ('Αρμενία: 'Αρμένιος, Armenius: *Armenia*), a country of Asia, lying between Asia Minor and the Caspian, is a lofty table-land, backed by the chain of the Caucasus watered by the rivers Cyrus and Araxes, containing the sources also of the Tigris and of the Euphrates, the latter of which divides the country into 2 unequal parts, which were called Major and Minor. 1. **Armenia Major** or **Propria** ('A. ἡ μεγάλη or ἡ ἰδίως καλουμένη : *Erzerum, Kars, Van,* and *Erivan*), was bounded on the N.E. and N. by the Cyrus (*Kur*), which divided it from Albania and Iberia ; on the N.W. and W. by the Moschici mountains (the prolongation of the chain of the Anti-Taurus), and the Euphrates (*Frat*), which divided it from Colchis and Armenia Minor ; and on the S. and S.E.

by the mountains called Masius, Niphates, and Gordiaei (the prolongation of the Taurus), and the lower course of the ARAXES, which divided it from Mesopotamia, Assyria. and Media: on the E. the country comes to a point at the confluence of the Cyrus and Araxes. It is intersected by chains of mountains, between which run the two great rivers ARAXES, flowing E. into the Caspian, and the Arsanias or S. branch of the Euphrates (*Murad*), flowing W. into the main stream (*Frat*) just above M. Masius. The E. extremity of the chain of mountains which separates the basins of these two rivers, and which is an offshoot of the Anti-Taurus, forms the Ararat of Scripture. In the S. of the country is the great lake of *Van*, Arsissa Palus, enclosed by mountain chains which connect Ararat with the S. range of mountains. — **2. Armenia Minor** ('A. μικρά or βραχυτέρα), was bounded on the E. by the Euphrates, which divided it from Armenia Major, on the N. and N.W. by the mountains Scodiaes, Paryadres, and Anti-Taurus, dividing it from Pontus and Cappadocia, and on the S. by the Taurus, dividing it from Commagene in N. Syria, so that it contained the country E. and S. of the city of *Sivas* (the ancient Cabira or Sebaste) as far as the Euphrates and the Taurus. The boundaries between Armenia Minor and Cappadocia varied at different times ; and indeed the whole country up to the Euphrates is sometimes called Cappadocia, and, on the other hand, the whole of Asia Minor E. of the Halys seems at one time to have been included under the name of Armenia.—The people of Armenia claimed to be aboriginal ; and there can be little doubt that they were one of the most ancient families of that branch of the human race which is called Caucasian. Their language, though possessing some remarkable peculiarities of its own, was nearly allied to the Indo-Germanic family ; and their manners and religious ideas were similar to those of the Medes and Persians, but with a greater tendency to the personification of the powers of nature, as in the goddess Analtis, whose worship was peculiar to Armenia. They had commercial dealings with Assyria and Phoenicia. In the time of Xenophon they had preserved a great degree of primitive simplicity, but 400 years later Tacitus gives an unfavourable view of their character. — The earliest Armenian traditions represent the country as governed by native kings, who had perpetually to maintain their independence against attacks from Assyria. They were said to have been conquered by Semiramis, but again threw off the yoke at the time of the Median and Babylonian revolt. Their relations to the Medes and Persians seem to have varied between successful resistance, unwilling subjection, and friendly alliance. A body of Armenians formed a part of the army which Xerxes led against Greece ; and they assisted Darius Codomannus against Alexander, and in this war they lost their king, and became subject to the Macedonian empire (B. C. 328). After another interval of successful revolt (B. C. 317— 274), they submitted to the Greek kings of Syria ; but when Antiochus the Great was defeated by the Romans (B. C. 190), the country again regained its independence, and it was at this period that it was divided into the two kingdoms of Armenia Major and Minor, under two different dynasties, founded respectively by the nobles who headed the revolt, Artaxias and Zariadras. Ultimately,

Armenia Minor was made a Roman province by Trajan ; and Armenia Major, after being a perpetual object of contention between the Romans and the Parthians, was subjected to the revived Persian empire by its first king Artaxerxes (Ardeshir) in A. D. 226

Armenius Mons (τὸ 'Αρμένιον ὄρος), a branch of the Anti-Taurus chain in Armenia Minor.

Arminius (the Latinized form of *Hermann*, " the chieftain"), son of Sigimer, " the conqueror," and chief of the tribe of the Cherusci, who inhabited the country to the north of the Hartz mountains, now forming the S. of Hanover and Brunswick. He was born in B. C. 18 ; and in his youth, he led the warriors of his tribe as auxiliaries of the Roman legions in Germany, where he learnt the language and military discipline of Rome, and was admitted to the freedom of the city, and enrolled amongst the equites. In A. D. 9, Arminius, who was now 27 years old, and had succeeded his father as chief of his tribe, persuaded his countrymen to rise against the Romans, who were now masters of this part of Germany, and which seemed destined to become, like Gaul, a Roman province. His attempt was crowned with success. Quintilius Varus, who was stationed in the country with 3 legions, was destroyed with almost all his troops [VARUS] ; and the Romans had to relinquish all their possessions beyond the Rhine. In 14, Arminius had to defend his country against Germanicus. At first he was successful ; the Romans were defeated, and Germanicus withdrew towards the Rhine, followed by Arminius. But having been compelled by his uncle, Inguiomer, against his own wishes, to attack the Romans in their entrenched camp, his army was routed, and the Romans made good their retreat to the Rhine. It was in the course of this campaign that Thusnelda, the wife of Arminius, fell into the hands of the Romans, and was reserved with the infant boy to whom she soon after gave birth in her captivity, to adorn the triumph of Germanicus at Rome. In 16, Arminius was again called upon to resist Germanicus, but he was defeated, and his country was probably only saved from subjection by the jealousy of Tiberius, who recalled Germanicus in the following year. At length Arminius aimed at absolute power, and was in consequence cut off by his own relations in the 37th year of his age, A. D. 19.

Armorica or **Aremorica**, the name of the N.W. coast of Gaul from the Ligeris (*Loire*) to the Sequana (*Seine*), derived from the Celtic *ar*, *air*, " upon," and *muir*, *môr*, " the sea." The *Armoricae civitates* are enumerated by Caesar (*B. G.* vii. 75):

Arna (Arnas, -tis : *Civitella d'Arno*), a town in Umbria near Perusia.

Arnae ("Αρναι), a town in Chalcidice in Macedonia, S. of Aulon and Bromiscus.

Arne ("Αρνη), a town in Boeotia mentioned by Homer (*Il.* ii. 507), supposed by Pausanias to be the same as Chaeronēa, but placed by others near Acraephium on the E. of the lake Copais.

Arnissa ("Αρνισσα : *Ostrova* ?), a town in Eordaea in Macedonia.

Arnobius. 1. The elder, a native of Africa, lived about A. D. 300, in the reign of Diocletian. He was at first a teacher of rhetoric at Sicca in Africa, but afterwards embraced Christianity ; and to remove all doubts as to the reality of his con-

G 4

version, he wrote, while yet a catechumen, his celebrated work against the Pagans, in 7 books (*Libri septem adversus Gentes*), which we still possess. The best edition is by Orelli, Lips. 1816. —2. The Younger, lived about A. D. 460, and was probably a bishop or presbyter in Gaul. He wrote a commentary on the Psalms, still extant, which shows that he was a Semi-Pelagian.

Arnŏn ('Αρνων: *Wad-el Mojib*), a considerable river of E. Palestine, rising in the Arabian Desert, and flowing W. through a rocky valley into the Lacus Asphaltites (*Dead Sea*). The surrounding district was called Arnonas ; and in it the Romans had a military station, called Castra Arnonensia.

Arnus (*Arno*), the chief river of Etruria, rises in the Apennines, flows by Pisae, and falls into the Tyrrhenian sea. It gave the name to the *Tribus Arniensis*, formed B. C. 387.

Arŏa ('Αρόα or 'Αρόη), the ancient name of PATRAE.

Arŏmătă (τὰ 'Αρώματα, 'Αρωμάτων ἄκρον: *Cape Guardafui*), the E.-most promontory of Africa, at the S. extremity of the Arabian Gulf: also the surrounding district was called Aromata or Aromatophora Regio, with a town 'Αρωμάτων ἐμπόριον : so named from the abundance of spices which the district produced.

Arpi (Arpānus : *Arpi*), an inland town in the Daunian Apulia, founded, according to tradition, by Diomedes, who called it "Αργος 'Ιππιον, from which its later names of Argyrippa or Argyripa and Arpi are said to have arisen (*Illa* (Diomedes) *urbem Argyripam, patriae cognomine gentis*, Virg. *Aen.* xi. 246). During the time of its independence it was a flourishing commercial town, using Salapia as its harbour. It was friendly to the Romans in the Samnite wars, but revolted to Hannibal after the battle of Cannae, B. C. 216 : it was taken by the Romans in 213, deprived of its independence, and never recovered its former prosperity.

Arpīnum (Arpīnas, -ātis : *Arpino*), a town of Latium on the small river Fibrenus (*Fibreno*), originally belonging to the Volscians and afterwards to the Samnites, from whom the Romans wrested it, was a Roman municipium, and received the *jus suffragii*, or right of voting in the Roman comitia, B. C. 188. It was the birthplace of Marius and Cicero, the latter of whom was born in his father's villa, situated on a small island formed by the river Fibrenus. Cicero's brother Quintus had an estate S. of Arpinum, called *Arcanum*.

Arrētium or **Arētium** (Arretīnus : *Arezzo*), one of the most important of the 12 cities of Etruria, was situated in the N. E. of the country at the foot of the Apennines, and possessed a fertile territory near the sources of the Arnus and the Tiber, producing good wine and corn. It was thrice colonised by the Romans, whence we read of *Arretini Veteres, Fidenates, Julienses*. It was particularly celebrated for its pottery, which was of red ware. The Cilnii, from whom Maecenas was descended, were a noble family of Arretium. The ruins of a city 2 or 3 miles to the S. E. of Arezzo, on a height called *Poggio di San Cornelio*, or *Castel Secco*, are probably the remains of the ancient Arretium.

Arrhapachītis ('Αρραπαχίτις), a district of Assyria, between the rivers Lycus and Choatras.

Arrhibaeus ('Αρρίβαιος), chieftain of the Macedonians of Lyncus, revolted against king Perdiccas in the Peloponnesian war. It was to reduce him

that Perdiccas sent for Brasidas (B. C. 424), and against him took place the unsuccessful joint expedition, in which Perdiccas deserted Brasidas, and Brasidas effected his bold and skilful retreat.

Arrhidaeus ('Αρριδαῖος) or **Aridaeus** ('Αριδαῖος). 1. A half-brother of Alexander the Great, son of. Philip and a female dancer, Philinna of Larissa, was of imbecile understanding. He was at Babylon at the time of Alexander's death, B. C. 323, and was elected king under the name of Philip. The young Alexander, the infant son of Roxana, was associated with him in the government. In 322, Arrhidaeus married Eurydice. On their return to Macedonia, Eurydice attempted to obtain the supreme power in opposition to Polysperchon ; but Arrhidaeus and Eurydice were made prisoners, and put to death by order of Olympias, 317. —2. One of Alexander's generals, obtained the province of the Hellespontine Phrygia, at the division of the provinces in 321 at Triparadisus, but was deprived of it by Antigonus in 319.

Arria. 1. Wife of Caecina Paetus. When her husband was ordered by the emperor Claudius to put an end to his life, A. D. 42, and hesitated to do so, Arria stabbed herself, handed the dagger to her husband, and said, " Paetus, it does not pain me."—2. Daughter of the preceding, and wife of Thrasea.

Arriānus ('Αρριανός). 1. Of Nicomedia in Bithynia, born about A. D. 90, was a pupil and friend of Epictetus, and first attracted attention as a philosopher by publishng at Athens the lectures of his master. In 124, he gained the friendship of Hadrian during his stay in Greece, and received from the emperor the Roman citizenship ; from this time he assumed the name of Flavius. In 136, he was appointed praefect of Cappadocia, which was invaded the year after by the Alani or Massagetae, whom he defeated. Under Antoninus Pius, in 146, Arrian was consul ; and about 150 he withdrew from public life, and from this time lived in his native town of Nicomedia, as priest of Demeter and Persephone. He died at an advanced age in the reign of M. Aurelius. Arrian was one of the most active and best writers of his time. He was a close imitator of Xenophon both in the subjects of his works and in the style in which they were written. He regarded his relation to Epictetus as similar to that of Xenophon to Socrates ; and it was his endeavour to carry out that resemblance. With this view he published, 1. the philosophical lectures of his master (Διατριβαὶ 'Επικτήτου) in 8 books, the first half of which is still extant. Edited in Schweighäuser's *Epicteteae Philosophiae Monumenta*, vol. iii., and in Coraes' Πάρεργα 'Ελλην. Βιβλιοθ. vol. viii.— 2. An abstract of the practical philosophy of Epictetus ('Εγχειρίδιον 'Επικτήτου), which is still extant. This celebrated work maintained its authority for many centuries, both with Christians and Pagans. The best editions are those of Schweighäuser and Coraes, in the collections above referred to. He also published other works relating to Epictetus, which are now lost. His original works are : — 3. A treatise on the chase (Κυνηγητικός), which forms a kind of supplement to Xenophon's work on the same subject, and is printed in most editions of Xenophon's works. — 4. The History of the Asiatic expedition of Alexander the Great ('Ανάβασις 'Αλεξάνδρου), in 7 books, the most important of Arrian's works. This great work reminds the

•

reader of Xenophon's Anabasis, not only by its title, but also by the ease and clearness of its style. It is also of great value for its historical accuracy, being based upon the most trustworthy histories written by the contemporaries of Alexander, especially those of Ptolemy, the son of Lagus, and of Aristobulus, the son of Aristobulus. — 5. On India ('Ινδική or τὰ 'Ινδικά), which may be regarded as a continuation of the Anabasis, at the end of which it is usually printed. This work is written in the Ionic dialect, probably in imitation of Ctesias of Cnidus, whose work on the same subject Arrian wished to supplant by a more trustworthy and correct account. The best editions of the *Anabasis* are by Ellendt, Regimontii, 1832, and by C. W. Krüger, Berlin, 1835 ; of the *Indica* by Schmieder, Halle, 1798. — 6. A description of a voyage round the coasts of the Euxine (περίπλους πόντου Εὐξείνου), which had undoubtedly been made by Arrian himself during his government of Cappadocia. This Periplus has come down to us together with a Periplus of the Erythraean, and a Periplus of the Euxine and the Palus Maeotis, both of which also bear the name of Arrian, but they belong undoubtedly to a later period. The best editions are in Hudson's *Geographi Minores*, vol. i., and in Gail's and Hoffmann's collections of the minor Geographers. — 7. A work on Tactics (λόγος τακτικὸς or τέχνη τακτική), of which we possess at present only a fragment: printed in Blancard's collection of the minor works of Arrian. Arrian also wrote numerous other works, all of which are now lost. — 2. A Roman jurisconsult, probably lived under Trajan, and is perhaps the same person with the orator Arrianus, who corresponded with the younger Pliny. He wrote a treatise *de Interdictis*, of which the 2d book is quoted in the Digest.

Arrĭbas, Arrўbas, Arymbas, or Tharrytas ('Αρρίβας, 'Αρρύβας, 'Αρύμβας, or Θαρρύτας), a descendant of Achilles, and one of the early kings of the Molossians in Epirus. He is said to have been educated at Athens, and on his return to his native country to have framed for the Molossians a code of laws, and established a regular constitution.

Q. Arrĭus. 1. Praetor, B. C. 72, defeated Crixus, the leader of the runaway slaves, but was afterwards conquered by Spartacus. In 71, Arrius was to have succeeded Verres as propraetor in Sicily, but died on his way to Sicily. — 2. A son of the preceding, was an unsuccessful candidate for the consulship, B. c. 59. He was an intimate friend of Cicero.

Arrĭus Aper. [APER.]

L. Arruntĭus. 1. Proscribed by the triumvirs in B. c. 43, but escaped to Sext. Pompey in Sicily, and was restored to the state with Pompey. He subsequently commanded the left wing of the fleet of Octavianus at the battle of Actium, 31, and was consul in 22. — 2. Son of the preceding, consul A. D. 6. Augustus declared in his last illness, that Arruntius was not unworthy of the empire, and would have boldness enough to seize it, if an opportunity presented. This rendered him an object of suspicion to Tiberius. He was charged in A. D. 37, as an accomplice in the crimes of Albucilla, and put an end to his own life.

Arsa (*Azunga*), a town in Hispania Baetica.

Arsăces ('Αρσάκης), the name of the founder of the Parthian empire, which was also borne by all his successors, who were hence called the *Arsacidae*.
1. He was of obscure origin, and seems to have

come from the neighbourhood of the Ochus. He induced the Parthians to revolt from the Syrian empire of the Seleucidae, and he became the first monarch of the Parthians. This event probably took place about B. c. 250, in the reign of Antiochus II. ; but the history of the revolt, as well as of the events which immediately followed, is stated very differently by different historians. Arsaces reigned only 2 years, and was succeeded by his brother Tiridates. — 2. Tiridâtes, reigned 37 years, B. c. 248—211, and defeated Seleucus Callinicus, the successor of Antiochus II. — 3. Artabânus I., son of the preceding, was attacked by Antiochus III. (the Great), who, however, was unable to subdue his country, and at length recognised him as king, about 210. — 4. Priapatius, son of the preceding, reigned 15 years, and left 3 sons, Phraates, Mithridates, and Artabanus. — 5. Phraâtes I., subdued the Mardi, and, though he had many sons, left the kingdom to his brother Mithridates. — 6. Mithridâtes I., son of Arsaces IV., greatly enlarged the Parthian empire by his conquests. He defeated Demetrius Nicator, king of Syria, and took him prisoner in 138. Mithridates treated Demetrius with respect, and gave him his daughter Rhodogune in marriage. Mithridates died during the captivity of Demetrius, between 138 and 130. — 7. Phraâtes II., son of the preceding, carried on war against Antiochus VII. Sidetes, whom Phraates defeated and slew in battle, B. c. 128. Phraates himself was shortly after killed in battle by the Scythians, who had been invited by Antiochus to assist him against Phraates, but who did not arrive till after the fall of the former. — 8. Artabânus II., youngest brother of Arsaces VI., and youngest son of Arsaces IV., fell in battle against the Thogarii or Tochari, apparently after a short reign. — 9. Mithridâtes II., son of the preceding, prosecuted many wars with success, and added many nations to the Parthian empire, whence he obtained the surname of Great. It was in his reign that the Romans first had any official communication with Parthia. Mithridates sent an ambassador to Sulla, who had come into Asia B. c. 92, and requested alliance with the Romans. — 10. (Mnascires ?) Nothing is known of the successor of Arsaces IX. Even his name is uncertain. — 11. Sanatroces, reigned 7 years, and died about B.C. 70.— 12. Phraâtes III., son of the preceding. He lived at the time of the war between the Romans and Mithridates of Pontus, by both of whom he was courted. He contracted an alliance with the Romans, but he took no part in the war. At a later period misunderstandings arose between Pompey and Phraates, but Pompey thought it more prudent to avoid a war with the Parthians, although Phraates had invaded Armenia, and Tigranes, the Armenian king, implored Pompey's assistance. Phraates was murdered soon afterwards by his 2 sons, Mithridates and Orodes. — 13. Mithridâtes III., son of the preceding, succeeded his father during the Armenian war. On his return from Armenia, Mithridates was expelled from the throne, on account of his cruelty, and was succeeded by his brother Orodes. Mithridates afterwards made war upon his brother, but was taken prisoner and put to death. — 14. Orôdes I., brother of the preceding, was the Parthian king, whose general Surenas defeated Crassus and the Romans, B. c. 53. [CRASSUS.] After the death of Crassus,

Orodes gave the command of the army to his son Pacorus, who entered Syria in 51 with a small force, but was driven back by Cassius. In 50 Pacorus again crossed the Euphrates with a much larger army, and advanced as far as Antioch, but was defeated near Antigonēa by Cassius. The Parthians now remained quiet for some years. In 40 they crossed the Euphrates again, under the command of Pacorus and Labienus, the son of T. Labienus. They overran Syria and part of Asia Minor, but were defeated in 39 by Ventidius Bassus, one of Antony's legates: Labienus was slain in the flight, and the Parthians retired to their own dominions. In 38, Pacorus again invaded Syria, but was completely defeated and fell in the battle. This defeat was a severe blow to the aged king Orodes, who shortly afterwards surrendered the crown to his son, Phraates, during his life-time. —15. **Phraātes IV.**, commenced his reign by murdering his father, his 30 brothers, and his own son, who was grown up, that there might be none of the royal family whom the Parthians could place upon the throne in his stead. In consequence of his cruelty many of the Parthian nobles fled to Antony (37), who invaded Parthia in 36, but was obliged to retreat after losing a great part of his army. A few years afterwards the cruelties of Phraates produced a rebellion against him ; he was driven out of the country, and Tiridates proclaimed king in his stead. Phraates, however, was soon restored by the Scythians, and Tiridates fled to Augustus, carrying with him the youngest son of Phraates. Augustus restored his son to Phraates, on condition of his surrendering the Roman standards and prisoners taken in the war with Crassus and Antony. They were given up in 20: their restoration caused universal joy at Rome, and was celebrated not only by the poets, but by festivals and commemorative monuments. Phraates also sent to Augustus as hostages his 4 sons, with their wives and children, who were carried to Rome. In A. D. 2, Phraates was poisoned by his wife Thermusa, and her son Phraataces. —16. **Phraataces**, reigned only a short time, as he was expelled by his subjects on account of his crimes. The Parthian nobles then elected as king Orodes, who was of the family of the Arsacidae. —17. **Orōdes II.**, also reigned only a short time, as he was killed by the Parthians on account of his cruelty. Upon his death the Parthians applied to the Romans for Vonones, one of the sons of Phraates IV., who was accordingly granted to them. —18. **Vonōnes I.**, son of Phraates IV., was also disliked by his subjects, who therefore invited Artabanus, king of Media, to take possession of the kingdom. Artabanus drove Vonones out of Parthia, who resided first in Armenia, next in Syria, and subsequently in Cilicia. He was put to death in A. D. 19, according to some accounts by order of Tiberius on account of his great wealth. —19. **Artabānus III.**, obtained the Parthian kingdom soon after the expulsion of Vonones, about A. D. 16. Artabanus placed Arsaces, one of his sons, over Armenia, and assumed a hostile attitude towards the Romans. His subjects, whom he oppressed, despatched an embassy to Tiberius to beg him to send to Parthia Phraates, one of the sons of Phraates IV. Tiberius willingly complied with the request ; but Phraates upon arriving in Syria was carried off by a disease, A. D. 35. As soon as Tiberius heard of his death, he set up Ti-

ridates, another of the Arsacidae, as a claimant to the Parthian throne: Artabanus was obliged to leave his kingdom, and to fly for refuge to the Hyrcanians and Carmanians. Hereupon Vitellius, the governor of Syria, crossed the Euphrates, and placed Tiridates on the throne. Artabanus was, however, recalled next year (36) by his fickle subjects. He was once more expelled by his subjects, and once more restored. He died soon after his last restoration, leaving two sons, Bardanes and Gotarzes, whose civil wars are related differently by Josephus and Tacitus. — 20. **Gotarzes**, succeeded his father, Artabanus III., but was defeated by his brother Bardanes and retired into Hyrcania. — 21. **Bardanes**, brother of the preceding, was put to death by his subjects in 47, whereupon Gotarzes again obtained the crown. But as he ruled with cruelty, the Parthians secretly begged the emperor Claudius to send them from Rome Meherdates, grandson of Phraates IV. Claudius complied with their request, and commanded the governor of Syria to assist Meherdates, but the latter was defeated in battle, and taken prisoner by Gotarzes. — 22. **Vonōnes II.**, succeeded Gotarzes about 50. His reign was short. — 23. **Vologēses I.**, son of Vonones II. or Artabanus III. Soon after his accession, he conquered Armenia, which he gave to his brother Tiridates. In 55 he gave up Armenia to the Romans, but in 58 he again placed his brother over Armenia and declared war against the Romans. This war terminated in favour of the Romans: the Parthians were repeatedly defeated by Domitius Corbulo, and Tiridates was driven out of Armenia. At length, in 62, peace was concluded between Vologeses and the Romans on condition that Nero would surrender Armenia to Tiridates, provided the latter would come to Rome and receive it as a gift from the Roman emperor. Tiridates came to Rome in 63, where he was received with extraordinary splendour, and obtained from Nero the Armenian crown. Vologeses afterwards maintained friendly relations with Vespasian, and seems to have lived till the reign of Domitian. — 24. **Pacōrus**, succeeded his father, Vologeses I., and was a contemporary of Domitian and Trajan. — 25. **Chosrŏes** or **Osrŏes**, succeeded his brother Pacorus during the reign of Trajan. His conquest of Armenia occasioned the invasion of Parthia by Trajan, who stripped it of many of its provinces, and made the Parthians for a time subject to Rome. [TRAJANUS.] Upon the death of Trajan in A. D. 117, the Parthians expelled Parthamaspates whom Trajan had placed upon the throne, and recalled their former king, Chosroes. Hadrian relinquished the conquests of Trajan, and made the Euphrates, as before, the eastern boundary of the Roman empire. Chosroes died during the reign of Hadrian. — 26. **Vologēses II.**, succeeded his father Chosroes, and reigned from about 122 to 149. — 27. **Vologēses III.**, began to reign in 149. He invaded Syria in 162, but the generals of the emperor Verus drove him back into his own dominions, invaded Mesopotamia and Assyria, and took Seleucia and Ctesiphon ; and Vologeses was obliged to purchase peace by ceding Mesopotamia to the Romans. From this time to the downfall of the Parthian empire, there is great confusion in the list of kings. — 28. **Vologēses IV.**, probably ascended the throne in the reign of Commodus. His dominions were invaded by Septimius Severus, who took Ctesiphon in 199. On the death of Volo-

geses IV., at the beginning of the reign of Caracalla, Parthia was torn asunder by contests for the
crown between the sons of Vologeses. — 29. Volo-
géses V., son of Vologeses IV., was attacked by
Caracalla in 215, and about the same time was
dethroned by his brother Artabanus. — 30. Artabānus IV., the last king of Parthia. The war
commenced by Caracalla against Vologeses, was
continued against Artabanus ; but Macrinus, the
successor of Caracalla, concluded peace with the
Parthians. In this war Artabanus had lost the
best of his troops, and the Persians seized the opportunity of recovering their long-lost independence. They were led by Artaxerxes (Ardshir),
the son of Sassan, and defeated the Parthians in
three great battles, in the last of which Artabanus
was taken prisoner and killed, A. D. 226. Thus
ended the Parthian empire of the Arsacidae, after
it had existed 476 years. The Parthians were
now obliged to submit to Artaxerxes, the founder
of the dynasty of the Sassanidae, which continued
to reign till A. D. 651.

Arsacia ('Αρσακία : Ru. S.E. of *Teheran*), a
great city of Media, S. of the Caspiae Portae, originally named Rhagae ('Ραγαι) ; rebuilt by Seleucus Nicator, and called Europus (Εὐρωπός) ;
again destroyed in the Parthian Wars and rebuilt
by Arsaces, who named it after himself.

Arsacidae, the name of a dynasty of Parthian
kings. [ARSACES.] It was also the name of a
dynasty of Armenian kings, who reigned in Armenia from B. C. 149 to A. D. 428. This dynasty
was founded by ARTAXIAS I., who was related
to the Parthian Arsacidae.

Arsamōsătă ('Αρσαμόσατα, also wrongly abbrev.
'Αρμόσατα : *Shemshat*), a town and strong fortress
in Armenia Major, between the Euphrates and the
sources of the Tigris, near the most frequented pass
of the Taurus.

Arsanias, -ius, or -us ('Αρσανίας, &c.), the
name of two rivers of Great Armenia. — 1. (*Murad*),
the S. arm of the Euphrates. [ARMENIA.] — 2.
(*Arsias ?*), a small stream rising near the sources of
the Tigris, and flowing W. into the Euphrates near
Melitene.

Arsenaria, or -enn- ('Αρσηναρία : *Arzew*, Ru.),
a town in Mauretania Caesariensis, 3 miles (Rom.)
from the sea : a Roman colony.

Arsene. [ARSANENE.]

Arses, Narses, or **Oarses** ("Αρσης, Νάρσης, or
Oάρσης), youngest son of king Artaxerxes III.
Ochus, was raised to the Persian throne by the
eunuch Bagoas after he had poisoned Artaxerxes,
B. c. 339. but he was murdered by Bagoas in the 3rd
year of his reign, when he attempted to free himself
from the bondage in which he was kept. After the
death of Arses, Bagoas made Darius III. king.

Arsia (*Arsa*), a river in Istria, forming the
boundary between Upper Italy and Illyricum, with
a town of the same name upon it.

Arsia Silva, a wood in Etruria celebrated for
the battle between the Tarquins and the Romans.

Arsinŏe ('Αρσινόη). I. *Mythological*. 1. Daughter
of Phegeus, and wife of Alcmaeon. As she disapproved of the murder of Alcmaeon, the sons of
Phegeus put her into a chest and carried her to
Agapenor at Tegea, where they accused her of
having killed Alcmaeon. [ALCMAEON, AGENOR.]
— 2. Nurse of Orestes, saved the latter from the
hands of Clytemnestra, and carried him to Strophius,
father of Pylades. Some accounts call her Lao-

damia. — 3. Daughter of Leucippus and Philodice,
became by Apollo mother of Eriopis and Aesculapius. — II. *Historical*. 1. Mother of Ptolemy I.,
was a concubine of Philip, father of Alexander the
Great, and married Lagus, while she was pregnant
with Ptolemy. — 2. Daughter of Ptolemy I. and
Berenice, married Lysimachus, king of Thrace, in
B. c. 300 ; after the death of Lysimachus in 281,
she married her half-brother, Ptolemy Ceraunus,
who murdered her children by Lysimachus ; and,
lastly, in 279, she married her own brother Ptolemy II. Philadelphus. Though Arsinoë bore
Ptolemy no children, she was exceedingly beloved
by him ; he gave her name to several cities, called
a district (νομός) of Egypt Arsinoïtes after her,
and honoured her memory in various ways. — 3.
Daughter of Lysimachus, married Ptolemy II.
Philadelphus soon after his accession, B. c. 285.
In consequence of her plotting against her namesake [No. 2], when Ptolemy fell in love with her,
she was banished to Coptos in Upper Egypt. She
had by Ptolemy three children, Ptolemy III. Evergetes, Lysimachus, and Berenice.—4. Also called
Eurydice and *Cleopatra*, daughter of Ptolemy III.
Evergetes, wife of her brother Ptolemy IV. Philopator, and mother of Ptolemy V. Epiphanes. She
was killed by Philammon by order of her husband.
—5. Daughter of Ptolemy XI. Auletes, escaped
from Caesar, when he was besieging Alexandria
in B. c. 47, and was recognised as queen by the
Alexandrians. After the capture of Alexandria
she was carried to Rome by Caesar, and led in
triumph by him in 46. She was afterwards dismissed by Caesar, and returned to Alexandria ;
but her sister Cleopatra persuaded Antony to have
her put to death in 41.

Arsinŏe ('Αρσινόη : 'Αρσινοεύς, or -οήτης), the
name of several cities of the times of the successors
of Alexander, each called after one or other of the
persons of the same name (see above). — 1. In
Aetolia, formerly Κωνώπα. — 2. On the N. coast
of Cyprus, on the site of the older city of Marium
(Μάριον), which Ptolemy I. had destroyed. —3
A port on the W. coast of Cyprus. — 4. (*Fama-
gosta*), on the S.E. coast of Cyprus, between Salamis and Leucolla. — 5. In Cilicia, E. of Anemurium. — 6. (*Ajeroud* or *Suez*), in the Nomos
Heroöpolites in Lower Egypt, near or upon the
head of the Sinus Heroöpolites or W. branch of
the Red Sea (*Gulf of Suez*). It was afterwards
called Cleopatris. — 7. (*Medinet-el-Faioum*, Ru.),
the chief city of the Nomos Arsinoïtes in the Heptanomis or Middle Egypt [AEGYPTUS, p. 15, b.] ;
formerly called Crŏcŏdīlopŏlis (Κροκοδείλων πόλις), and the district Nomos Crocodilopolites, from
its being the chief seat of the Egyptian worship of
the crocodile. This nomos also contained the Lake
Moeris and the labyrinth. — 8. In Cyrenaica, also
called Taucheira. — 9. On the coast of the Troglodytae on the Red Sea, E. of Egypt. Its probable position is a little below the parallel of
Thebes. — Some other cities called Arsinoë are
better known by other names, such as EPHESUS in
Ionia and PATARA in Lycia.

Arsissa or **Mantiāna** ('Αρσίσσα, ἡ Μαντιανή :
Van), a great lake, abounding in fish, in the S. of
Armenia Major. [ARMENIA.]

Artabānus ('Αρτάβανος). 1. Son of Hystaspes
and brother of Darius, is frequently mentioned in
the reign of his nephew Xerxes, as a wise and
frank counsellor. — 2. An Hyrcanian, commander

of the body-guard of Xerxes, assassinated this king
in B. C. 465, with the view of setting himself upon
the throne of Persia, but was shortly afterwards
killed by Artaxerxes.—3. I. II. III. IV., kings
of Parthia. [ARSACES, III. VIII. XIX. XXXI.]

Artabāzus ('Αρτάβαζος). 1. A Mede, acts a
prominent part in Xenophon's account of Cyrus the
Elder.—2. A distinguished Persian, a son of Pharnaces, commanded the Parthians and Choasmians,
in the expedition of Xerxes into Greece, B. C. 480.
He served under Mardonius in 479, and after the
defeat of the Persians at Plataea, he fled with
40,000 men, and reached Asia in safety.—3. A
general of Artaxerxes I., fought against Inarus in
Egypt, B. C. 462.—4. A Persian general, fought
under Artaxerxes II., against Datames, satrap of
Cappadocia, B. C. 362. Under Artaxerxes III.,
Artabasus, who was then satrap of W. Asia, revolted in B. C. 356, but was defeated and obliged
to take refuge with Philip of Macedonia. He was
afterwards pardoned by Artaxerxes, and returned
to Persia ; and he was one of the most faithful
adherents of Darius III. Codomannus, who raised
him to high honours. On the death of Darius
(330) Artabazus received from Alexander the satrapy of Bactria. One of his daughters, Barsine,
became by Alexander the mother of Hercules ; a
second, Artocama, married Ptolemy son of Lagus ;
and a third, Artonis, married Eumenes.

Artabri, afterwards Arotrēbae, a Celtic people
in the N. W. of Spain, near the Promontory Nerium or Celticum, also called Artabram after them
(C. Finisterre).

Artacē ('Αρτάκη : Artaki), a sea-port town of
the peninsula of Cyzicus, in the Propontis : also a
mountain in the same peninsula.

Artachaees ('Αρταχαίης), a distinguished Persian in the army of Xerxes, died while Xerxes
was at Athos. The mound which the king raised
over him is still in existence.

Artācoānā ('Αρταχόανα, or -κάννα: Sekhvan ?),
the ancient capital of ARIA, not far from the site
of the later capital, ALEXANDRIA.

Artaei ('Αρταῖοι), was, according to Herodotus
(vi. 61), the old native name of the Persians. It
signifies noble, and appears, in the form Αρτα, as
the first part of a large number of Persian proper
names. [Comp. ARII.]

Artānes ('Αρτάνης). 1. A river in Thrace,
falling into the Ister.—2. A river in Bithynia.

Artaphernes ('Αρταφέρνης). 1. Son of Hystaspes and brother of Darius. He was satrap of
Sardis at the time of the Ionian revolt, B. C. 500.
See ARISTAGORAS.—2. Son of the former, commanded, along with Datis, the Persian army of
Darius, which was defeated at the battle of Marathon, B. C. 490. Artaphernes commanded the Lydians and Mysians in the invasion of Greece by
Xerxes in 480.

Artaunum (Salburg near Homburg ?), a Roman
fortress in Germany on M. Taunus, built by Drusus
and restored by Germanicus.

Artavasdes ('Αρταουάσδης or 'Αρταβάσδης) or
Artabāzes ('Αρταβάζης). 1. King of the Greater
Armenia, succeeded his father Tigranes. In the expedition of Crassus against the Parthians, B. C. 54,
Artavasdes was an ally of the Romans ; but after the
defeat of the latter, he concluded a peace with the
Parthian king. In 36 he joined Antony in his
campaign against the Parthians, and persuaded him
to invade Media, because he was at enmity with

his namesake Artavasdes, king of Media : but he
treacherously deserted Antony in the middle of the
campaign. Antony accordingly invaded Armenia in-
34, contrived to entice Artavasdes into his camp,
where he was immediately seized, carried him to-
Alexandria, and led him in triumph. He remained
in captivity till 30, when Cleopatra had him killed
after the battle of Actium, and sent his head to
his old enemy, Artavasdes of Media, in hopes of
obtaining assistance from the latter. This Artavasdes was well acquainted with Greek literature,
and wrote tragedies, speeches, and historical works.
—2. King of Armenia, probably a grandson of
No. 1, was placed upon the throne by Augustus,
but was deposed by the Armenians.—3. King of
Media Atropatene, and an enemy of Artavasdes I.,
king of Armenia. Antony invaded his country
in 36, at the instigation of the Armenian king, but
he was obliged to retire with great loss. Artavasdes afterwards concluded a peace with Antony,
and gave his daughter Iotape in marriage to Alexander, the son of Antony. Artavasdes was subsequently engaged in wars with the Parthians and
Armenians. He died shortly before 20.

Artaxāta or -ae (τὰ 'Αρτάξατα, or -ξίατα : Ru.
above Nakshivan), the later capital of Great Armenia, built by ARTAXIAS, under the advice of
Hannibal, on a peninsula, surrounded by the river
Araxes. After being burnt by the Romans under
Corbulo (A. D. 58), it was restored by Tiridates,
and called Neroniana. It was still standing in
the 4th century.

Artaxerxes or Artoxerxes ('Αρταξέρξης or 'Αρ-
τοξέρξης), the name of 4 Persian kings, is compounded of Arta, which means "honoured," and
Xerxes, which is the same as the Zend, ksathra,
"a king:" consequently Artaxerxes means "the
honoured king."—1. Surnamed Longimānus,
from the circumstance of his right hand being longer
than his left, reigned B. C. 465—425. He ascended
the throne after his father, Xerxes I., had been murdered by Artabanus, and after he himself had put
to death his brother Darius on the instigation of Artabanus. His reign was disturbed by several dangerous insurrections of the satraps. The Egyptians
also revolted in 460, under Inarus, who was supported by the Athenians. The first army which
Artaxerxes sent under his brother Achaemenes was
defeated and Achaemenes slain. The second army
which he sent, under Artabazus and Megabyzus,
was more successful. Inarus was defeated in 456
or 455, but Amyrtaeus, another chief of the insurgents, maintained himself in the marshes of Lower
Egypt. At a later period (449) the Athenians
under Cimon sent assistance to Amyrtaeus ; and
even after the death of Cimon, the Athenians gained
two victories over the Persians, one by land and
the other by sea, in the neighbourhood of Salamis
in Cyprus. After this defeat Artaxerxes is said to-
have concluded peace with the Greeks on terms
very advantageous to the latter. Artaxerxes was
succeeded by his son Xerxes II.—2. Surnamed
Mnēmon, from his good memory, succeeded his
father, Darius II., and reigned B. C. 405—359.
Cyrus, the younger brother of Artaxerxes, who
was satrap of W. Asia, revolted against his brother,
and, supported by Greek mercenaries, invaded
Upper Asia. In the neighbourhood of Cunaxa, near
Babylon, a battle was fought between the armies
of the two brothers, in which Cyrus fell, B. C. 401.
[CYRUS.] Tissaphernes was appointed satrap of

W. Asia in the place of Cyrus, and was actively engaged in wars with the Greeks. [THIMBRON ; DERCYLLIDAS ; AGESILAUS.] Notwithstanding these perpetual conflicts with the Greeks, the Persian empire maintained itself by the ˈdisunion among the Greeks themselves, which was fomented and kept up by Persian money. The peace of Antalcidas, in B. C. 388, gave the Persians even greater power and influence than they had possessed before. [ANTALCIDAS.] But the empire was suffering from internal disturbances, and Artaxerxes had to carry on frequent wars with tributary princes and satraps, who endeavoured to make themselves independent. Thus he maintained a long struggle against Evagoras of Cyprus, from 385 to 376 ; he also had to carry on war against the Cardusians, on the shores of the Caspian sea ; and his attempts to recover Egypt were unsuccessful. Towards the end of his reign he put to death his eldest son Darius, who had formed a plot to assassinate him. His last days were still further embittered by the unnatural conduct of his son Ochus, who caused the destruction of two of his brothers, in order to secure the succession for himself. Artaxerxes was succeeded by Ochus, who ascended the throne under the name of Artaxerxes III.—3. Also called Ochus, reigned B. C. 359—338. In order to secure his throne, he began his reign with a merciless extirpation of the members of his family. He himself was a cowardly and reckless despot ; and the great advantages which the Persian arms gained during his reign, were owing only to his Greek generals and mercenaries. These advantages consisted in the conquest of the revolted satrap Artabazus [ARTABAZUS, No. 4], and in the reduction of Phoenicia, of several revolted towns in Cyprus, and of Egypt, 350. The reins of government were entirely in the hands of the eunuch Bagoas, and of Mentor the Rhodian. At last he was poisoned by Bagoas, and was succeeded by his youngest son, ARSES.—4. The founder of the dynasty of the SASSANIDAE.

Artaxias (ˈΑρταξίας) or **Artaxes** (Ἀρτάξης), the name of 3 kings of Armenia.—1. The founder of the Armenian kingdom, was one of the generals of Antiochus the Great, but revolted from him about B. C. 188, and became an independent sovereign. Hannibal took refuge at the court of Artaxias, and he superintended the building of ARTAXATA, the capital of Armenia. Artaxias was conquered and taken prisoner by Antiochus IV. Epiphanes, about 165.—2. Son of Artavasdes, was made king by the Armenians when his father was taken prisoner by Antony in 34. In 20 Augustus, at the request of the Armenians, sent Tiberius into Armenia, in order to depose Artaxias and place Tigranes on the throne, but Artaxias was put to death before Tiberius reached the country. Tiberius, however, took the credit to himself of a successful expedition : whence Horace (*Epist.* i. 12. 26) says, *Claudi virtute Neronis Armenius cecidit.* — 3. Son of Polemon, king of Pontus, was proclaimed king of Armenia by Germanicus, in A. D. 18. He died about 35.

Artayctes (ˈΑρταΰκτης), Persian governor of Sestus on the Hellespont, when the town was taken by the Greeks in B. C. 478, met with an ignominious death on account of the sacrilegious acts which he had committed against the tomb of the hero Protesilaus.

Artemidorus (ˈΑρτεμίδωρος). 1. Surnamed Aristophanius, from his being a disciple of the celebrated grammarian Aristophanes, was himself a grammarian, and the author of several works now lost.—2. Of **Cnidus**, a friend of Julius Caesar, was a rhetorician, and taught the Greek language at Rome.—3. **Daldianus**, a native of Ephesus, but called Daldianus, from Daldis in Lydia, his mother's birth-place, to distinguish him from the geographer Artemidorus. He lived at Rome in the reigns of Antoninus Pius and M. Aurelius (A. D. 138 —180), and wrote a work on the interpretation of dreams (ˈΟνειροκριτικά), in 5 books, which is still extant. The object of the work is to prove, that the future is revealed to man in dreams, and to clear the science of interpreting them from the abuses with which the fashion of the time had surrounded it. The style is simple, correct, and elegant. The best edition is by Reiff, Lips. 1805. — 4. Of **Ephesus**, a Greek geographer, lived about B. C. 100. He made voyages round the coasts of the Mediterranean, in the Red Sea, and apparently even in the S. ocean. He also visited Iberia and Gaul. The work, in which he gave the results of his investigations, consisted of 11 books, of which Marcianus afterwards made an abridgement. The original work is lost ; but we possess fragments of Marcianus' abridgement, which contain the periplus of the Pontus Euxinus, and accounts of Bithynia and Paphlagonia. These fragments are printed in Hudson's *Geographi Minores*, vol. i.

Artemis (ˈΑρτεμις), one of the great divinities of the Greeks. According to the most ancient account, she was the daughter of Zeus and Leto, and the twin-sister of Apollo, born with him in the island of Delos. She was regarded in various points of view by the Greeks, which must be carefully distinguished.—1. *Artemis as the sister of Apollo,* is a kind of female Apollo, that is, she as a female divinity represented the same idea that Apollo did as a male divinity. As sister of Apollo, Artemis is like her brother armed with a bow, quiver, and arrows, and sends plagues and death among men and animals. Sudden ˈdeaths, but more especially those of women, are described as the effect of her arrows. As Apollo was not only a destructive god, but also averted evils, so Artemis likewise cured and alleviated the sufferings of mortals. In the Trojan war she sided, like Apollo, with the Trojans. She was more especially the protectress of the young ; and from her watching over the young of females, she came to be regarded as the goddess of the flocks and the chase. In this manner she also became the huntress among the immortals. Artemis, like Apollo, is unmarried ; she is a maiden-divinity never conquered by love. She slew ORION with her arrows, according to one account, because he made an attempt upon her chastity ; and she changed ACTAEON into a stag, simply because he had seen her bathing. With her brother Apollo, she slew the children of NIOBE, who had deemed herself superior to Leto. When Apollo was regarded as identical with the sun or Helios, nothing was more natural than that his sister should be regarded as Selene or the moon, and accordingly the Greek Artemis is, at least in later times, the goddess of the moon. Hence Artemis is represented in love with the fair youth ENDYMION, whom she kissed in his sleep, but this legend properly relates to Selene or the Moon, and is foreign to the character of Artemis, who, as we have observed, was a goddess unmoved by love. — 2. *The Arcadian Artemis* is a goddess of the nymphs, and was worshipped as such in Arcadia in very early times. She hunted with her nymphs on the Arcadian mountains, and her chariot was drawn by 4 stags with golden antlers. There was no connection between the Arcadian Artemis and Apollo. — 3. *The Taurian Artemis.* The worship of this goddess was connected, at least in early times, with human sacrifices. According to the Greek legend there was in Tauris a goddess, whom the Greeks for some reason identified with their own Artemis, and to whom all strangers thrown on the coast of Tauris were sacrificed. Iphigenia and Orestes brought her image from thence, and landed at Brauron in Attica, whence the goddess derived the name of Brauronia. The Brauronian Artemis was worshipped at Athens and Sparta, and in the latter place the boys were scourged at her altar till it was besprinkled with their blood. This cruel ceremony was believed to have been introduced by Lycurgus, instead of the human sacrifices which had until then been offered to her. Iphigenia, who was at first to have been sacrificed to Artemis, and who then became her priestess, was afterwards identified with the goddess, who was worshipped in some parts of Greece, as at Hermione, under the name of Iphigenia. Some traditions stated that Artemis made Iphigenia immortal, in the character of Hecate, the goddess of the moon. — 4. *The Ephesian Artemis,* was a divinity totally distinct from the Greek goddess of the same name. She seems to have been the personification of the fructifying and all-nourishing powers of nature. She was an ancient Asiatic divinity whose worship the Greeks found established in Ionia, when they settled there, and to whom they gave the name of Artemis. Her original character is sufficiently clear from the fact, that her priests were eunuchs, and that her image in the magnificent temple of Ephesus represented her with *many* breasts (πολυμαστός). The representations of the Greek Artemis in works of art are different according as she is represented either as a huntress, or as the goddess of the moon. As the huntress, she is tall, nimble, and has small hips; her forehead is high, her eyes glancing freely about, and her hair tied up, with a few locks floating down her neck; her breast is covered, and the legs up to the knees are naked, the rest being covered by the chlamys. Her attributes are the bow, quiver, and arrows, or a spear, stags, and dogs. As the goddess of the moon, she wears a long robe which reaches down to her feet, a veil covers her head, and above her forehead rises the crescent of the moon. In her hand she often appears holding a torch. The Romans identified their goddess Diana with the Greek Artemis.

Artemisia (Ἀρτεμισία). 1. Daughter of Lygdamis, and queen of Halicarnassus in Caria, accompanied Xerxes in his invasion of Greece, with 5 ships, and in the battle of Salamis (B.C. 480) greatly distinguished herself by her prudence and courage, for which she was afterwards highly honoured by the Persian king. — 2. Daughter of Hecatomnus, and sister, wife, and successor of the Carian prince Mausolus, reigned B.C. 352–350. She is renowned in history for her extraordinary grief at the death of her husband Mausolus. She is said to have mixed his ashes in her daily drink; and to perpetuate his memory she built at Halicarnassus the celebrated monument, *Mausoleum,*

which was regarded as one of the 7 wonders of the world, and whose name subsequently became the generic term for any splendid sepulchral monument.

Artemisium (Ἀρτεμίσιον), properly a temple of Artemis. 1. A tract of country on the N. coast of Euboea, opposite Magnesia, so called from the temple of Artemis belonging to the town of Hestiaea : off this coast the Greeks defeated the fleet of Xerxes, B.C. 480. — 2. A promontory of Caria near the gulf Glaucus, so called from the temple of Artemis in its neighbourhood.

Artemita (Ἀρτεμίτα). — 1. (*Sherebas ?*) a city on the Sillas, in the district of Apolloniatis in Assyria. — 2. A city of Great Armenia, S. of the lake Arsissa.

Artemon (Ἀρτέμων), a Lacedaemonian, built the military engines for Pericles in his war against Samos in B.C. 441. — There were also several writers of this name, whose works are lost.

M. Artorius, a physician at Rome, was the friend and physician of Augustus, whom he attended in his campaign against Brutus and Cassius, B.C. 42. He was drowned at sea shortly after the battle of Actium, 31.

Arverni, a Gallic people in Aquitania in the country of the M. Cebenna, in the modern *Auvergne.* In early times they were the most powerful people in the S. of Gaul : they were defeated by Domitius Ahenobarbus and Fabius Maximus in B.C. 121, but still possessed considerable power in the time of Caesar (58). Their capital was Nemossus, also named Augustonemetum or Arverni on the Eléver (*Allier*), with a citadel, called at least in the middle ages Clarus Mons, whence the name of the modern town, *Clermont.*

Arvina, a cognomen of the Cornelia gens, borne by several of the Cornelii, of whom the most important was A. Cornelius Cossus Arvina, consul B.C. 343 and 322, and dictator 320. He commanded the Roman armies against the Samnites, whom he defeated in several battles.

Aruns, an Etruscan word, was regarded by the Romans as a proper name, but perhaps signified a younger son in general. — 1. Younger brother of Lucumo, i. e. L. Tarquinius Priscus. — 2. Younger brother of L. Tarquinius Superbus, was murdered by his wife. — 3. Younger son of Tarquinius Superbus, fell in combat with Brutus. — 4. Son of Porsena, fell in battle before Aricia. — 5. Of Clusium, invited the Gauls across the Alps.

Aruntius. [ARRUNTIUS.]

Arusianus, Messus or **Messius,** a Roman grammarian, lived about A.D. 450, and wrote a Latin phrase-book, entitled *Quadriga, vel Exempla Elocutionum ex Virgilio, Sallustio, Terentio, et Cicerone per literas digesta.* It is called Quadriga from its being composed from 4 authors. The best edition is by Lindemann, in his *Corpus Grammaticorum Latin.* vol. i. p. 199.

Arxata (Ἀρξάτα: *Nakshivan*), the capital of Great Armenia, before the building of Artaxata, lay lower down upon the Araxes, on the confines of Media.

Aryandes (Ἀρυάνδης), a Persian, who was appointed by Cambyses governor of Egypt, but was put to death by Darius, because he coined silver money of the purest metal, in imitation of the gold money of that monarch.

Arycanda (Ἀρύκανδα), a small town of Lycia, E. of Xanthus, on the river Arycandus, a tributary of the Limyrus.

Arzănēne ('Αρζανηνή), a district of Armenia Major, bounded on the S. by the Tigris, on the W. by the Nymphius, and containing in it the lake Arsēne ('Αρσηνή : Erzen). It formed part of GORDYENE.

Arzĕn or **-ĕs**, or **Atranutzin** ('Αρζήν, 'Αρζες, 'Ατράνουτζιν : Erzeroum), a strong fortress in Great Armenia, near the sources of the Euphrates and the Araxes, founded in the 5th century.

Assai ('Ασαῖοι), a people of Sarmatia Asiatica, near the mouth of the Tanaïs (Don).

Asander ('Ασανδρος). 1. Son of Philotas, brother of Parmenion, and one of the generals of Alexander the Great. After the death of Alexander in 323 he obtained Caria for his satrapy, and took an active part in the wars which followed. He joined Ptolemy and Cassander in their league against Antigonus, but was defeated by Antigonus in 313. — 2. A general of Pharnaces II., king of Bosporus. He put Pharnaces to death in 47, after the defeat of the latter by Julius Caesar, in hopes of obtaining the kingdom. But Caesar conferred the kingdom upon Mithridates of Pergamus, with whom Asander carried on war. Augustus afterwards confirmed Asander in the sovereignty.

Asbystae ('Ασβύσται), a Libyan people, in the N. of Cyrenaica. Their country was called 'Ασβυστίς.

Asca ("Ασκα), a city of Arabia Felix.

Ascalăbus, son of Misme, respecting whom the same story is told, which we also find related of ABAS, son of Metanira. [ABAS. No. 1.]

Ascalăphus ('Ασκάλαφος). 1. Son of Ares and Astyoche, led, with his brother Ialmenus, the Minyans of Orchomenos against Troy, and was slain by Deïphobus. — 2. Son of Acheron and Gorgyra or Orphne. When Persephone was in the lower world, and Pluto gave her permission to return to the upper, provided she had not eaten anything, Ascalaphus declared that she had eaten part of a pomegranate. Demeter punished him by burying him under a huge stone, and when this stone was subsequently removed by Hercules, Persephone changed him into an owl (ἀσκάλαφος), by sprinkling him with water from the river Phlegethon.

Ascălon ('Ασκάλων : 'Ασκαλωνείτης : Askalán), one of the chief cities of the Philistines, on the coast of Palestine, between Azotus and Gaza.

Ascănĭa (ἡ 'Ασκανία λίμνη). 1. (Lake of Iznik), in Bithynia, a great fresh-water lake, at the E. end of which stood the city of Nicaea (Iznik). The surrounding district was also called Ascania. — 2. (Lake of Burdur), a salt-water lake on the borders of Phrygia and Pisidia, which supplied the neighbouring country with salt.

Ascănĭus ('Ασκάνιος), son of Aeneas by Creusa. According to some traditions, Ascanius remained in Asia after the fall of Troy, and reigned either at Troy itself or at some other town in the neighbourhood. According to other accounts he accompanied his father to Italy. Other traditions again gave the name of Ascanius to the son of Aeneas and Lavinia. Livy states that on the death of his father Ascanius was too young to undertake the government, and that after he had attained the age of manhood, he left Lavinium in the hands of his mother, and migrated to Alba Longa. Here he was succeeded by his son Silvius. Some writers relate that Ascanius was also called Ilus or Julus. The gens Julia at Rome traced its origin from Julus or Ascanius.

Asciburgĭum (Asburg near Mörs), an ancient place on the left bank of the Rhine, founded, according to fable, by Ulysses.

Ascii (ἄσκιοι, i. e. shadowless), a term applied to the people living about the Equator, between the tropics, who have, at certain times of the year, the sun in their zenith at noon, when consequently erect objects can cast no shadow.

Asclēplădae, the reputed descendants of Aesculapius. [AESCULAPIUS.]

Asclēplădes ('Ασκληπιάδης). 1. A lyric poet, who is said to have invented the metre called after him (Metrum Asclepiadĕum), but of whose life no particulars are recorded. — 2. Of Tragilus in Thrace, a contemporary and disciple of Isocrates, about B. C. 360, wrote a work called Τραγῳδούμενα in 6 books, being an explanation of the subjects of the Greek tragedies. — 3. Of Myrlēa in Bithynia, in the middle of the first century B. C., wrote several grammatical works. — 4. There were a great many physicians of this name, the most celebrated of whom was a native of Bithynia, who came to Rome in the middle of the first century B. C., where he acquired a great reputation by his successful cures. Nothing remains of his writings but a few fragments published by Gumpert, Asclepiadis Bithyni Fragmenta, Vinar. 1794.

Asclēplŏdōrus ('Ασκληπιόδωρος). 1. A general of Alexander the Great, afterwards made satrap of Persia by Antigonus, B. C. 317. — 2. A celebrated Athenian painter, a contemporary of Apelles.

Asclēplus. [AESCULAPIUS.]

Q. Ascōnius Pedĭănus, a Roman grammarian, born at Patavium (Padua), about B. C. 2, lost his sight in his 73rd year in the reign of Vespasian, and died in his 85th year in the reign of Domitian. His most important work was a Commentary on the speeches of Cicero, and we still possess fragments of his Commentaries on the Divinatio, the first 2 speeches against Verres, and a portion of the third, the speeches for Cornelius (i. ii.), the speech In toga candida, for Scaurus, against Piso, and for Milo. They are written in very pure language, and refer chiefly to points of history and antiquities, great pains being bestowed on the illustration of those constitutional forms of the senate, the popular assemblies, and the courts of justice, which were fast falling into oblivion under the empire. This character, however, does not apply to the notes on the Verrine orations, which were probably written by a later grammarian. Edited in the 5th volume of Cicero's works by Orelli and Baiter. There is a valuable essay on Asconius by Madvig, Hafniae, 1828.

Ascordus, a river in Macedonia, which rises in M. Olympus and flows between Agassa and Dium into the Thermaic gulf.

Ascra ('Ασκρα : 'Ασκραῖος), a town in Boeotia on M. Helicon, where Hesiod resided, who had removed thither with his father from Cyme in Aeolis, and who is therefore called Ascraeus.

Ascŭlum. 1. Picēnum (Asculānus. Ascoli), the chief town of Picenum and a Roman municipium, was destroyed by the Romans in the Social War (B. C. 89), but was afterwards rebuilt. — 2. Apŭlum (Asculinus : Ascoli di Satriano), a town of Apulia in Daunia on the confines of Samnium, near which the Romans were defeated by Pyrrhus, B. C. 279.

Ascŭris (Exero), a lake in M. Olympus in Perrhaebia in Thessaly, near Lapathus

Asdrŭbal. [HASDRUBAL.]

Asĕa (ἡ Ἀσία), a town in Arcadia, not far from Megalopolis.

Asellĭo, P. Semprōnĭus, tribune of the soldiers under P. Scipio Africanus at Numantia, B. C. 133, wrote a Roman history from the Punic wars inclusive to the times of the Gracchi.

Asellus, Tib. Claudĭus, a Roman eques, was deprived of his horse by Scipio Africanus Minor, when censor, B. C. 142, and in his tribuneship of the plebs in 139 accused Scipio Africanus before the people.

Asĭa (Ἀσία), daughter of Oceanus and Tethys, wife of Iapetus, and mother of Atlas, Prometheus, and Epimetheus. According to some traditions, the continent of Asia derived its name from her.

Asĭa (Ἀσία: Ἀσιεύς, -ιανός, -ιάτης, -ατικός: Asia), also in the poets **Asĭs** (ἄσις), one of the 3 great divisions which the ancients made of the known world. It is doubtful whether the name is of Greek or Eastern origin; but, in either case, it seems to have been first used by the Greeks for the W. part of Asia Minor, especially the plains watered by the river Cayster, where the Ionian colonists first settled; and thence, as their geographical knowledge advanced, they extended it to the whole country E., N.E., and S.E. The first knowledge which the Greeks possessed of the opposite shores of the Aegean Sea dates before the earliest historical records. The legends respecting the Argonautic and the Trojan expeditions, and other mythical stories, on the one hand, and the allusions to commercial and other intercourse with the people of Asia Minor, Syria, and Egypt, on the other hand, indicate a certain degree of knowledge of the coast from the mouth of the Phasis, at the E. extremity of the Black Sea, to the mouth of the Nile. This knowledge was improved and increased by the colonization of the W., N., and S. coasts of Asia Minor, and by the relations into which these Greek colonies were brought, first with the Lydian, and then with the Persian empires, so that, in the middle of the 5th century B. C., Herodotus was able to give a pretty complete description of the Persian empire, and some imperfect accounts of the parts beyond it; while some knowledge of S. Asia was obtained by way of Egypt; and its N. regions, with their wandering tribes, formed the subject of marvellous stories which the traveller heard from the Greek colonists on the N. shores of the Black Sea. The conquests of Alexander, besides the personal acquaintance which they enabled the Greeks to form with those provinces of the Persian empire hitherto only known to them by report, extended their knowledge over the regions watered by the Indus and its 4 great tributaries (*the Punjab and Scinde*); the lower course of the Indus and the shores between its mouth and the head of the Persian Gulf were explored by Nearchus; and some further knowledge was gained of the nomad tribes which roamed (as they still do) over the vast steppes of Central Asia by the attempt of Alexander to penetrate on the N.E. beyond the Jaxartes (*Sihoun*); while, on all points, the Greeks were placed in advanced positions from which to acquire further information, especially at Alexandria, whither voyagers constantly brought accounts of the shores of Arabia and India, as far as the island of Taprobane, and even beyond this, to the Malay peninsula and the coasts of Cochin China. On the E. and N. the wars and commerce of the

Greek kingdom of Syria carried Greek knowledge of Asia no further, except in the direction of India to a small extent, but of course more acquaintance was gained with the countries already subdued, until the conquests of the Parthians shut out the Greeks from the country E. of the Tigris-valley; a limit which the Romans, in their turn, were never able to pass. They pushed their arms, however, further N. than the Greeks had done, into the mountains of Armenia, and they gained information of a great caravan route between India and the shores of the Caspian, through Bactria, and of another commercial track leading over Central Asia to the distant regions of the Seres. This brief sketch will show that all the accurate knowledge of the Greeks and Romans respecting Asia was confined to the countries which slope down S.-wards from the great mountain-chain formed by the Caucasus and its prolongation beyond the Caspian to the Himalayas: of the vast elevated steppes between these mountains and the central range of the Altai (from which the N. regions of Siberia again slope down to the Arctic Ocean) they only knew that they were inhabited by nomad tribes, except the country directly N. of Ariana, where the Persian empire had extended beyond the mountain-chain, and where the Greek kingdom of Bactria had been subsequently established. — The notions of the ancients respecting the size and form of Asia were such as might be inferred from what has been stated. Distances computed from the accounts of travellers are always exaggerated; and hence the S. part of the continent was supposed to extend much further to the E. than it really does (about 60° of long. too much, according to Ptolemy), while to the N. and N.E. parts, which were quite unknown, much too small an extent was assigned. However, all the ancient geographers, except Pliny, agreed in considering it the largest of the 3 divisions of the world, and all believed it to be surrounded by the ocean, with the curious exception of Ptolemy, who recurred to the early notion, which we find in the poets, that the E. parts of Asia and the S.E. parts of Africa were united by land which enclosed the Indian Ocean on the E. and S. The different opinions about the boundaries of Asia on the side of Africa are mentioned under AFRICA: on the side of Europe the boundary was formed by the river Tanais (*Don*), the Palus Maeotis (*Sea of Azof*), Pontus Euxinus (*Black Sea*), Propontis (*Sea of Marmora*), and the Aegean (*Archipelago*). — The most general division of Asia was into 2 parts, which were different at different times, and known by different names. To the earliest Greek colonists the river Halys, the E. boundary of the Lydian kingdom, formed a natural division between *Upper* and *Lower Asia* (ἡ ἄνω Ἀ., or τὰ ἄνω Ἀσίης, ἡ κάτω Ἀ., or τὰ κάτω τῆς Ἀσίης, or Ἀ. ἡ ἐντὸς Ἅλυος ποταμοῦ); and afterwards the Euphrates was adopted as a more natural boundary. Another division was made by the Taurus into *A. intra Taurum*, i. e. the part of Asia N. and N.W. of the Taurus, and *A. extra Taurum*, all the rest of the continent (Ἀ. ἐντὸς τοῦ Ταύρου, and Ἀ. ἐκτὸς τοῦ Ταύρου). The division ultimately adopted, but apparently not till the 4th century of our era, was that of *A. Major* and *A. Minor.* — 1. **Asia Major** (Ἀ. ἡ μεγάλη) was the part of the continent E. of the Tanais, the Euxine, an imaginary line drawn from the Euxine at Trapezus (*Trebizond*) to the

Athena (Minerva). (Bartoli, Admiranda, pl. 41.) Pages 101, 102.

Aphrodite (Venus) and Eros (Cupid).
(Causei, Museum Romanum, vol. 1, tav. 40.) Page 61.

Athena (Minerva) superintending the Building of the Argo.
(Zoëga, Bassirilievi, tav. 45.) Page 75.

[To face p. 96.

M. Antonius, the Triumvir, ob. B.C. 30. Page 59.

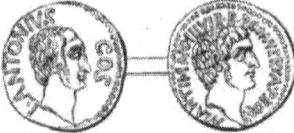

Ariarathes VI., King of Cappadocia, B.C. 130—96. Page 78.

L. Antonius, brother of the Triumvir. The head on the obverse is that of the Triumvir. Page 60.

Ariarathes VII., King of Cappadocia.

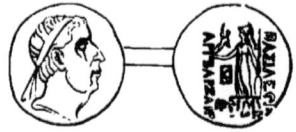

Arcadius, Roman Emperor, A.D. 395—408. Page 70.

Ariobarzanes I., King of Cappadocia, B.C. 93—63. Page 79.

Archelaus, King of Cappadocia, ob. A.D. 17. Page 71, No. 9.

Ariobarzanes III., King of Cappadocia, ob. B.C. 42. Page 79.

Aretas, King of Arabia Petraea. Page 74.

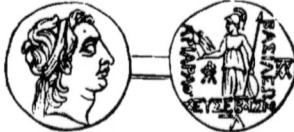

Arsaces I. (Artabanus I.), King of Parthia. Page 89.

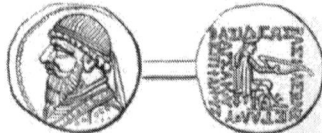

Ariarathes IV., King of Cappadocia, B.C. 220—162. Page 78.

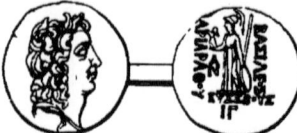

Arsaces V. (Phraates I.), King of Parthia. Page 89.

Ariarathes V., King of Cappadocia, B.C. 163—130. Page 78.
To face p. 97.]

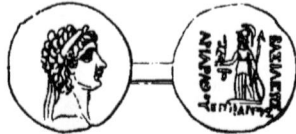

Arsaces VI. (Mithridates I.), King of Parthia. Page 89.

Gulf of Issus, and the Mediterranean : thus it included the countries of Sarmatica Asiatica with all the Scythian tribes to the E., Colchis, Iberia, Albania, Armenia, Syria, Arabia, Babylonia, Mesopotamia, Assyria, Media, Susiana, Persis, Ariana, Hyrcania, Margiana, Bactriana, Sogdiana, India, the land of the Sinae and Serica ; respecting which, see the several articles. — 2. **Asia Minor** ('Aσία ἡ μικρά : *Anatolia*), was the peninsula on the extreme W. of Asia, bounded by the Euxine, Aegean, and Mediterranean on the N., W., and S. ; and on the E. by the mountains on the W. of the upper course of the Euphrates. It was for the most part a fertile country, intersected with mountains and rivers, abounding in minerals, possessing excellent harbours, and peopled, from the earliest known period, by a variety of tribes from Asia and from Europe. For particulars respecting the country, the reader is referred to the separate articles upon the parts into which it was divided by the later Greeks, namely, Mysia, Lydia, and Caria, on the W., Lycia, Pamphylia, and Cilicia, on the S. ; Bithynia, Paphlagonia, and Pontus, on the E. ; and Phrygia, Pisidia, Galatia, and Cappadocia, in the centre: see also the articles TROAS, AEOLIA, IONIA, DORIA, LYCAONIA, PERGAMUS, HALYS, SANGARIUS, TAURUS, &c. — 3. **Asia Propria** ('A. ἡ ἰδίως καλουμένη), or simply **Asia**, the Roman province, formed out of the kingdom of Pergamus, which was bequeathed to the Romans by ATTALUS III. (B. C. 130), and the Greek cities on the W. coast, and the adjacent islands, with Rhodes. It included the districts of Mysia, Lydia, Caria, and Phrygia; and was governed at first by propraetors, afterwards by proconsuls. Under Constantine the Great, a new division was made, and Asia only extended along the coast from the Prom. Lectum to the mouth of the Maeander.

Asinārus ('Aσίναρος: *Fiume di Noto* or *Freddo* ?), a river on the E. side of Sicily, on which the Athenians were defeated by the Syracusans, B. C. 413: the Syracusans celebrated here an annual festival called *Asinaria*.

Asīnē ('Aσίνη : 'Aσιναῖος). 1. A town in Laconica on the coast between Taenarum and Gythium. — 2. A town in Argolis, W. of Hermione, was built by the Dryopes, who were driven out of the town by the Argives after the first Messenian war, and built No. 3. — 3. (*Saratza*?), an important town in Messenia, near the Promontory Acritas, on the Messenian gulf, which was hence also called the Asinaean gulf.

Asinia Gens, plebeian, came from Teate, the chief town of the Marrucini ; and the first person of the name mentioned is Herius Asinius, the leader of the Marrucini in the Marsic war, B. C. 90. The Asinii are given under their surnames, GALLUS and POLLIO.

Asius ("Aσιος). 1. Son of Hyrtacus of Arisbe, and father of Acamas and Phaenops, an ally of the Trojans, slain by Idomeneus. — 2. Son of Dymas and brother of Hecuba, whose form Apollo assumed when he roused Hector to fight against Patroclus. — 3. Of Samos, one of the earliest Greek poets, lived probably about B. C. 700. He wrote epic and elegiac poems, which have perished with the exception of a few fragments.

Asmiraea, a district and city of Serica in the N. of Asia, near mountains called **Asmiraei Montes**, which are supposed to be the *Altai* range, and the city to be *Khamil*, in the centre of Chinese Tartary.

Asōpus ('Aσωπός). 1. (*Basilikos*), a river in Peloponnesus rises near Phlius, and flows through the Sicyonian territory into the Corinthian gulf. Asopus, the god of this river, was son of Oceanus and Tethys, husband of Metope, and father o Evadne, Euboea, and Aegina, each of whom was therefore called *Asopis* ('Aσωπίς). When Zeus carried off Aegina, Aesopus attempted to fight with him, but he was smitten by the thunderbolt of Zeus, and from that time the bed of the river contained pieces of charcoal. By Aegina Asopus became the grandfather of Aeacus, who is therefore called *Asopiades*. — 2. (*Asopo*), a river in Boeotia, forms the N. boundary of the territory of Plataeae, flows through the S. of Boeotia, and falls into the Euboean sea near Delphinium in Attica. — 3. A river in Phthiotis in Thessaly, rises in M. Oeta, and flows into the Maliac gulf near Thermopylae. — 4. A river in Phrygia, flows past Laodicēa into the Lycus. — 5. A town in Laconica on the E. side of the Laconian gulf.

Aspadāna ('Aσπαδάνα : *Ispahan*?), a town of the district Paraetacene in Persis.

Asparagium (*Isoarpar*), a town in the territory of Dyrrhachium in Illyria.

Aspasia ('Aσπασία). 1. The elder, of Miletus daughter of Axiochus, the most celebrated of the Greek Hetaerae (see *Dict. of Antiq. s. v.*), came to reside at Athens, and there gained and fixed the affections of Pericles, not more by her beauty than by her high mental accomplishments. Having parted with his wife, Pericles attached himself to Aspasia during the rest of his life as closely as was allowed by the law, which forbade marriage with a foreign woman under severe penalties. The enemies of Pericles accused Aspasia of impiety (ἀσέβεια), and it required all the personal influence of Pericles, who defended her, and his most earnest entreaties and tears, to procure her acquittal. The house of Aspasia was the centre of the best literary and philosophical society of Athens, and was frequented even by Socrates. On the death of Pericles (B. C. 429), Aspasia is said to have attached herself to one Lysicles, a dealer in cattle, and to have made him by her instructions a first-rate orator. The son of Pericles by Aspasia was legitimated by a special decree of the people, and took his father's name. — 2. The Younger, a Phocaean, daughter of Hermotimus, was the favourite concubine of Cyrus the Younger, who called her Aspasia after the mistress of Pericles, her previous name having been Milto. After the death of Cyrus at the battle of Cunaxa (B. C. 401), she fell into the hands of Artaxerxes, who likewise became deeply enamoured of her. When Darius, son of Artaxerxes, was appointed successor to the throne, he asked his father to surrender Aspasia to him. The request could not be refused as coming from the king elect ; Artaxerxes, therefore, gave her up ; but he soon after took her away again, and made her a priestess of a temple at Ecbatana, where strict celibacy was requisite.

Aspasii. [ASPII.]

Aspasius ('Aσπάσιος). 1. A peripatetic philosopher, lived about A. D. 80, and wrote commentaries on most of the works of Aristotle. A portion of his commentaries on the Nicomachean Ethics is still preserved. — 2. Of Byblus, a Greek sophist, lived about A. D. 180, and wrote commentaries on Demosthenes and Aeschines, of which a few extracts are preserved.

K

Aspendus (Ἄσπενδος: Ἀσπένδιος, Aspendius: *Dashashkehr* or *Manaugat*), a strong and flourishing city of Pamphylia, on the small navigable river Eurymedon, 60 stadia (6 geog. miles) from its mouth: said to have been a colony of the Argives.

Asper, Aemilius, a Roman grammarian, who wrote commentaries on Terence and Virgil, must be distinguished from another grammarian, usually called *Asper Junior*, the author of a small work entitled *Ars Grammatica*, printed in the *Grammat. Lat. Auctores*, by Putschius, Hanov. 1605.

Asphaltites Lacus or **Mare Mortuum** (Ἀσφαλ-τῖτις or Σοδομῖτις λίμνη, or ἡ Ξάλασσα ἡ νέκρα), the great salt and bituminous lake in the S.E. of Palestine, which receives the water of the Jordan. It has no visible outlet, and its surface is considerably below the level of the Mediterranean. The tales about fish not living in it and birds dropping down dead as they fly over it, are now proved to be fabulous.

Aspii or **Aspasii** (Ἄσπιοι, Ἀσπάσιοι), an Indian tribe, in the district of the Paropamisadae, between the rivers Choes (*Kama*) and Indus, in the N.E. of *Afghanistan* and the N.W. of the *Punjab*.

Aspis (Ἀσπίς). 1. **Clypea** (*Klibiah*), a city on a promontory of the same name, near the N.E. point of the Carthaginian territory, founded by Agathocles, and taken in the first Punic War by the Romans, who called it Clypea, the translation of Ἀσπίς.— 2. (*Marsa-Zaffran ?* Ru.), in the African Tripolitana, the best harbour on the coast of the Great Syrtis.— 3. [ARCONNESUS.]

Aspledon (Ἀσπληδών: Ἀσπληδόνιος), or **Spledon**, a town of the Minyae in Boeotia on the river Melas, near Orchomenus; built by the mythical Aspledon, son of Poseidon and Midëa.

Assa (Ἄσσα: Ἀσσαῖος), a town in Chalcidice in Macedonia, on the Singitic gulf.

Assaceni (Ἀσσακηνοί), an Indian tribe, in the district of the Paropamisadae, between the rivers Cophen (*Cabool*) and Indus, in the N.W. of the *Punjab*.

Assaracus (Ἀσσάρακος), king of Troy, son of Tros, father of Capys, grandfather of Anchises, and great-grandfather of Aeneas. Hence the Romans, as descendants of Aeneas, are called *domus Assaraci* (Virg. *Aen.* i. 284).

Assesus (Ἀσσησός), a town of Ionia near Miletus, with a temple of Athena surnamed Ἀσσησία.

Assorus (Ἀσσωρός or Ἀσσώριον: Ἀσσωρῖνος: *Asaro*), a small town in Sicily between Enna and Agyrium.

Assus (Ἄσσος: Ἄσσιος, Ἀσσεύς: *Asso*, Ru., near *Berani*), a flourishing city in the Troad, on the Adramyttian Gulf, opposite to Lesbos: afterwards called Apollonia: the birthplace of Cleanthes the Stoic.

Assyria (Ἀσσυρία: Ἀσσύριος, Assyrius: *Kur-distan*). 1. The country properly so called, in the narrowest sense, was a district of W. Asia, extending along the E. side of the Tigris, which divided it on the W. and N.W. from Mesopotamia and Babylonia, and bounded on the N. and E. by M. Niphates and M. Zagrus, which separated it from Armenia and Media, and on the S.E. by Susiana. It was watered by several streams, flowing into the Tigris from the E.; two of which, the Lycus or Zabatus (*Great Zab*), and the Caprus or Zabas or Anzabas (*Little Zab*), divided the country into three parts: that between the Upper Tigris and the Lycus was called Aturia (a mere dialectic variety of Assyria), was probably the most ancient seat of the monarchy, and contained the capital, Nineveh or NINUS: that between the Lycus and the Caprus was called Adiabene: and the part S.E. of the Caprus contained the districts of Apolloniatis and Sittacene. Another division into districts, given by Ptolemy, is the following: Arrhapachitis, Calacine, Adiabene, Arbelitis, Apolloniatis and Sittacene.— 2. In a wider sense the name was applied to the whole country watered by the Euphrates and the Tigris, between the mountains of Armenia on the N., those of *Kurdistan* on the E., and the Arabian Desert on the W., so as to include, besides Assyria Proper, Mesopotamia and Babylonia; nay, there is sometimes an apparent confusion between Assyria and Syria, which gives ground for the supposition that the terms were originally identical.— 3. By a further extension the word is used to designate the Assyrian Empire in its widest sense. The early history of this great monarchy is too obscure to be given here in any detail; and indeed it is only just now that new means of investigating it are being acquired. The germ of this empire was one of the first great states of which we have any record, and was probably a powerful and civilized kingdom as early as Egypt. Its reputed founder was Ninus, the builder of the capital city; and in its widest extent it included the countries just mentioned, with Media, Persia, and portions of the countries to the E. and N.E., Armenia, Syria, Phoenicia, and Palestine, except the kingdom of Judah; and, beyond these limits, some of the Assyrian kings made incursions into Arabia and Egypt. The fruitless expedition of Sennacherib against the latter country and the miraculous destruction of his army before Jerusalem (B.C. 714), so weakened the empire, that the Medes revolted and formed a separate kingdom, and at last, in B.C. 606, the governor of Babylonia united with Cyaxares, the king of Media, to conquer Assyria, which was divided between them, Assyria Proper falling to the share of Media, and the rest of the empire to Babylon. The Assyrian king and all his family perished, and the city of Ninus was rased to the ground. [Comp. BABYLON and MEDIA.] It must be noticed as a caution, that some writers confound the Assyrian and Babylonian empires under the former name.

Asta (Astensis). 1. (*Asti* in Piedmont), an inland town of Liguria on the Tanarus, a Roman colony.— 2. (*Mesa de Asta*), a town in Hispania Baetica, near Gades, a Roman colony with the surname *Regia*.

Astaboras (Ἀσταβόρας: *Atbarah* or *Tacazza*) and **Astapus** (Ἀστάπους, *Bahr-el-Azak* or *Blue Nile*), two rivers of Aethiopia, having their sources in the highlands of *Abyssinia*, and uniting in about 17° N. Lat. to form the Nile. The land enclosed by them was the island of MEROE.

Astacus (Ἄσταχος), father of Ismarus, Leades, Asphodicus, and Melanippus.

Astacus (Ἄστακος: Ἀστακηνός). 1. (*Dragomestre*), a city of Acarnania, on the Acheloüs.— 2. A celebrated city of Bithynia, at the S.E. corner of the *Sinus Astacenus* (Ἀστακηνὸς κόλπος), a bay of the Propontis, was a colony from Megara, but afterwards received fresh colonists from Athens, who called the place *Olbia* (Ὀλβία). It was destroyed by Lysimachus, but rebuilt on a neighbouring site, at the N.E. corner of the gulf, by Nicomedes I., who named his new city NICOMEDIA.

Astăpa (*Estepa*), a town in Hispania Baetica.

Astăpus. [ASTABORAS.]

Astartē. [APHRODITE and SYRIA DEA.]

Astĕlĕphus ('Αστέλεφος), a river of Colchis, 120 stadia (12 geog. miles) S. of Sebastopolis.

Astĕrĭa ('Αστερία), daughter of the Titan Coeus and Phoebe, sister of Leto (Latona), wife of Perses, and mother of Hecate. In order to escape the embraces of Zeus, she is said to have taken the form of a quail (*ortyx*, ὄρτυξ), and to have thrown herself down from heaven into the sea, where she was metamorphosed into the island *Asteria* (the island which had fallen from heaven like a star), or *Ortygia*, afterwards called Delos.

Astĕrĭon or **Astĕrĭus** ('Αστερίων or 'Αστέριος). 1. Son of Teutamus, and king of the Cretans, married Europa after she had been carried to Crete by Zeus, and brought up the three sons, Minos, Sarpedon, and Rhadamanthys, whom she had by the father of the gods. — 2. Son of Cometes, Pyremus, or Priscus, by Antigone, daughter of Pheres, was one of the Argonauts.

Astĕris or **Astĕria** ('Αστερίς, 'Αστερία), a small island between Ithaca and Cephallenia.

Astĕrĭum ('Αστέριον), a town in Magnesia in Thessaly.

Astĕrŏpaeus ('Αστεροπαῖος), son of Pelegon, leader of the Paeonians, and an ally of the Trojans, was slain by Achilles.

Astigi, a town in Hispania Baetica on the river Singulis, a Roman colony with the surname *Augusta Firma.*

Astraea ('Αστραία), daughter of Zeus and Themis, or, according to others, of Astraeus and Eos. During the golden age, this star-bright maiden lived on earth and among men, whom she blessed ; but when that age had passed away, Astraea, who tarried longest amongst men, withdrew, and was placed among the stars, where she was called Παρθένος or *Virgo.* Her sister Αἰδώς or *Pudicitia*, left the earth along with her (*ad superos Astraea recessit, hac (Pudicitia) comite,* Juv. vi. 19).

Astraeus ('Αστραῖος), a Titan, son of Crius and Eurybia, husband of Eos (Aurora), and father of the winds Zephyrus, Boreas, and Notus, Eosphorus (the morning star) and all the stars of heaven. Ovid (*Met.* xiv. 545) calls the winds *Astraei* (adj.) *fratres,* the "Astraean brothers."

Astūra. 1. (*La Stura*), a river in Latium, rises in the Alban mountains, and flows between Antium and Circeii into the Tyrrhenian sea. At its mouth it formed a small island with a town upon it, also called Astura (*Torre d' Astura*): here Cicero had an estate. — 2. (*Ezla*), a river in Hispania Tarraconensis, flowing into the Durius.

Astūres, a people in the N. W. of Spain, bounded on the E. by the Cantabri and Vaccaei, on the W. by the Gallaeci, on the N. by the Ocean, and on the S. by the Vettones, thus inhabiting the modern *Asturias* and the northern part of *Leon* and *Valladolid.* They contained 22 tribes and 240,000 freemen, and were divided into the Augustani and Transmontani, the former of whom dwelt S. of the mountains as far as the Durius, and the latter N. of the mountains down to the sea-coast. The country of the Astures was mountainous, rich in minerals and celebrated for its horses : the people themselves were rude and warlike. Their chief town was Asturica Augusta (*Astorga*).

Astyăges ('Αστυάγης), son of Cyaxares, last king of Media, reigned B. C. 594—559. Alarmed by a dream, he gave his daughter Mandane in marriage to Cambyses, a Persian of good family. Another dream induced him to send Harpagus to destroy the offspring of this marriage. The child, the future conqueror of the Medes, was given to a herdsman to expose, but he brought it up as his own. Years afterwards, circumstances occurred which brought the young Cyrus under the notice of Astyages, who, on inquiry, discovered his parentage. He inflicted a cruel punishment on Harpagus, who waited his time for revenge. When Cyrus had grown up to man's estate, Harpagus induced him to instigate the Persians to revolt, and, having been appointed general of the Median forces, he deserted with the greater part of them to Cyrus. Astyages was taken prisoner, and Cyrus mounted the throne. He treated the captive monarch with mildness, but kept him in confinement till his death. This is the account of Herodotus, and is to be preferred to that of Xenophon, who makes Cyrus the grandson of Astyages, but says, that Astyages was succeeded by his son Cyaxares II., on whose death Cyrus succeeded peaceably to the vacant throne.

Astyănax ('Αστυάναξ), son of Hector and Andromache : his proper name was Scamandrius, but he was called Astyanax or "lord of the city" by the Trojans, on account of the services of his father. After the taking of Troy the Greeks hurled him down from the walls, that he might not restore the kingdom of Troy.

Astȳdămas ('Αστυδάμας), a tragic poet, son of Morsimus and of a sister of the poet Aeschylus, and a pupil of Isocrates, wrote 240 tragedies, and gained the prize 15 times. His first tragedy was acted B. C. 399.

Astȳdămīa ('Αστυδάμεια). 1. Daughter of Amyntor and mother of Tlepolemus by Hercules. — 2. Wife of ACASTUS.

Astȳnŏmē ('Αστυνόμη), daughter of Chryses, better known under her patronymic CHRYSEIS.

Astȳŏchē or **Astȳŏchīa** ('Αστυόχη or 'Αστυόχεια). 1. Daughter of Actor, by whom Ares begot Ascalaphus and Ialmenus. — 2. Daughter of Phylas, king of Ephyra in Thesprotia, became by Hercules the mother of Tlepolemus.

Astȳŏchus ('Αστύοχος), the Lacedaemonian admiral in B. C. 412, commanded on the coast of Asia Minor, where he was bribed by the Persians to remain inactive.

Astȳpălaea ('Αστυπάλαια : 'Αστυπαλαιεύς,'Αστυπαλαιάτης : *Stampalia*), one of the Sporades in the S. part of the Grecian archipelago, with a town of the same name, founded by the Megarians, which was under the Romans a libera civitas. (*Astypalēia regna*, i. e. *Astypalaea,* Ov. *Met.* vii. 461.) The inhabitants worshipped Achilles.

Astȳra (τὰ 'Αστυρα), a town of Mysia, N.W. of Adramyttium, on a marsh connected with the sea, with a grove sacred to Artemis surnamed 'Αστυρίνη or -ηνή.

Asychis ('Ασυχίς), an ancient king of Egypt, succeeded Mycerinus.

Atăbŭlus, the name in Apulia of the parching S. E. wind, the Sirocco, which is at present called *Altino* in Apulia.

Atabȳris or **Atabȳrium** ('Αταβύριον), the highest mountain in Rhodes on the S.W. of that island, on which was a celebrated temple of Zeus Atabyrius, said to have been founded by Althaemenes, the grandson of Minos.

Atāgis. [ATHESIS.]

Atălanta ('Αταλάντη). 1. The *Arcadian Atalanta*, was a daughter of Iasus (Iasion or Iasius) and Clymene. Her father, who had wished for a son, was disappointed at her birth, and exposed her on the Parthenian (virgin) hill, where she was suckled by a she-bear, the symbol of Artemis. After she had grown up she lived in pure maidenhood, slew the centaurs who pursued her, and took part in the Calydonian hunt. Her father subsequently recognised her as his daughter; and when he desired her to marry, she required every suitor who wanted to win her, to contend with her first in the foot-race. If he conquered her, he was to be rewarded with her hand; if not, he was to be put to death. This she did because she was the most swift-footed of mortals, and because the Delphic oracle had cautioned her against marriage. She conquered many suitors, but was at length overcome by Milanion with the assistance of Aphrodite. The goddess had given him 3 golden apples, and during the race he dropped them one after the other: their beauty charmed Atalanta so much, that she could not abstain from gathering them, and Milanion thus gained the goal before her. She accordingly became his wife. They were subsequently both metamorphosed into lions, because they had profaned by their embraces the sacred grove of Zeus. — 2. The *Boeotian Atalanta*. The same stories are related of her as of the Arcadian Atalanta, except that her parentage and the localities are described differently. Thus she is said to have been a daughter of Schoenus, and to have been married to Hippomenes. Her foot-race is transferred to the Boeotian Onchestus, and the sanctuary which the newly married couple profaned by their love, was a temple of Cybele, who metamorphosed them into lions, and yoked them to her chariot.

Atalantē ('Αταλάντη: 'Αταλανταῖος). 1. A small island in the Euripus, on the coast of the Opuntian Locri, with a small town of the same name. — 2. A town of Macedonia on the Axius, in the neighbourhood of Gortynia and Idomene.

Atărantes ('Ατάραντες), a people in the E. of Libya, described by Herodotus (iv. 184).

Atarbēchis. [APHRODITOPOLIS.]

Atarneus ('Αταρνεύς: *Dikeli*), a city on M. Cane, on the coast of Mysia, opposite to Lesbos: a colony of the Chians: the residence of the tyrant Hermias, with whom Aristotle resided some time: destroyed before the time of Pliny.

Ataulphus, Athaulphus, Adaulphus (*i.e.* Athaulf, "sworn helper," the same name as that which appears in later history under the form of Adolf or Adolphus), brother of Alaric's wife. He assisted Alaric in his invasion of Italy, and on the death of that monarch in A. D. 410, he was elected king of the Visigoths. He then made a peace with the Romans, married Placidia, sister of Honorius, retired with his nation into the S. of Gaul, and finally withdrew into Spain, where he was murdered at Barcelona.

Atax (*Aude*), originally called Narbo, a river in Gallia Narbonensis, rises in the Pyrenees, and flows by Narbo Martius into the Lacus Rubresus or Rubrensis, which is connected with the sea. From this river the poet P. Terentius Varro obtained the surname *Atacinus.* [VARRO.]

Atē ("Ατη), daughter of Eris or Zeus, was an ancient Greek divinity, who led both gods and men into rash and inconsiderate actions. She once even induced Zeus, at the birth of Hercules, to take an oath by which Hera was afterwards enabled to give to Eurystheus the power which had been destined for Hercules. When Zeus discovered his rashness, he hurled Ate from Olympus and banished her for ever from the abodes of the gods. In the tragic writers Ate appears in a different light: she avenges evil deeds and inflicts just punishments upon the offenders and their posterity, so that her character is almost the same as that of Nemesis and Erinnys. She appears most prominent in the dramas of Aeschylus, and least in those of Euripides, with whom the idea of Dike (justice) is more fully developed.

Atēius, surnamed *Praetextatus,* and *Philologus,* a celebrated grammarian at Rome, about B. C. 40, and a friend of Sallust, for whom he drew up an Epitome (*Breviarium*) of Roman History. After the death of Sallust Ateius lived on intimate terms with Asinius Pollio, whom he assisted in his literary pursuits.

Atēius Căpĭto. [CAPITO.]

Atella (Atellānus; *Aversa*), a town in Campania between Capua and Neapolis, originally inhabited by the Oscans, afterwards a Roman municipium and a colony. It revolted to Hannibal (B. C. 216) after the battle of Cannae, and the Romans in consequence transplanted its inhabitants to Calatia, and peopled the town by new citizens from Nuceria. Atella owes its celebrity to the *Atellanae Fabulae* or Oscan farces, which took their name from this town. (*Dict. of Antiq.* p. 347, 2d ed.)

Aternum (*Pescara*), a town in central Italy on the Adriatic, at the mouth of the river Aternus (*Pescara*), was the common harbour of the Vestini, Marrucini, and Peligni.

Aternus. [ATERNUM.]

Atestē (Atestīnus: *Este*), a Roman colony in the country of the Veneti in Upper Italy.

Athācus, a town in Lyncestis in Macedonia.

Athamānia ('Αθαμανία: 'Αθαμάν, -ᾶνος), a mountainous country in the S. of Epirus, on the W. side of Pindus, of which Argithea was the chief town. The Athamanes were a Thessalian people, who had been driven out of Thessaly by the Lapithae. They were governed by independent princes, the last of whom was AMYNANDER.

Athāmas ('Αθάμας), son of Aeolus and Enarete, and king of Orchomenus in Boeotia. At the command of Hera, Athamas married Nephele, by whom he became the father of PHRIXUS and Helle. But he was secretly in love with the mortal Ino, the daughter of Cadmus, by whom he begot Learchus and Melicertes ; and Nephele, on discovering that Ino had a greater hold on his affections than herself, disappeared in anger. Having thus incurred the anger both of Hera and of Nephele, Athamas was seized with madness, and in this state killed his own son, Learchus: Ino threw herself with Melicertes into the sea, and both were changed into marine deities, Ino becoming Leucothea, and Melicertes Palaemon. Athamas, as the murderer of his son, was obliged to flee from Boeotia, and settled in Thessaly. — Hence we have *Athamantiădes,* son of Athamas, i. e. Palaemon ; and *Athamantis,* daughter of Athamas, i. e. Helle.

Athanagia (*Agramunt ?*), the chief town of the Ilergetes in Hispania Tarraconensis.

Athanaricus, king of the Visi-Goths during their stay in Dacia. In A. D. 367—369 he carried on war with the emperor Valens, with whom he finally concluded a peace. In 374 Athanaric was defeated by the Huns, and, after defending himself for some time in a stronghold in the mountains of Dacia, was compelled to fly in 380, and take refuge in the Roman territory. He died in 381.

Athanasius ('Αθανάσιος), St., one of the most celebrated of the Christian fathers, was born at Alexandria about A. D. 296, and was elected archbishop of the city on the death of Alexander in 326. The history of his episcopate is full of stirring incidents and strange transitions of fortune. He was the great champion of the orthodox faith, as it had been expounded at the council of Nice in 325, and was therefore exposed to persecution whenever the Arians got the upper hand in the state. He was thrice driven from his see into exile, and thrice recalled. He died in 373. The Athanasian creed was not composed by Athanasius: its real author is unknown. The best edition of his works is by Montfaucon, Paris, 1698, reprinted at Padua. 1777.

Athēnā ('Αθήνη or 'Αθηνᾶ), one of the great divinities of the Greeks. Homer calls her a daughter of Zeus, without any allusion to the manner of her birth ; but later traditions related that she was born from the head of Zeus, and some added that she sprang forth with a mighty war-shout and in complete armour. The most ancient tradition, as preserved by Hesiod, stated that Metis, the first wife of Zeus, was the mother of Athena, but that Metis, when pregnant with her, was, on the advice of Gaea and Urania, swallowed up by Zeus, and that Zeus afterwards gave birth himself to Athena, who sprang from his head. Another set of traditions regarded her as the daughter of Pallas, the winged giant, whom she afterwards killed on account of his attempting to violate her chastity ; and a third set carried her to Libya, and called her a daughter of Poseidon and Tritonis. These various traditions about Athena arose, as in most other cases, from local legends and from identifications of the Greek Athena with other divinities. But according to the general belief of the Greeks, she was the daughter of Zeus ; and if we take Metis to have been her mother, we have at once the clue to the character which she bears in the religion of Greece ; for, as her father was the most powerful and her mother the wisest among the gods, so Athena was a combination of the two, a goddess in whom power and wisdom were harmoniously blended. From this fundamental idea may be derived the various aspects under which she appears in the ancient writers. She seems to have been a divinity of a purely ethical character ; her power and wisdom appear in her being the preserver of the state and of everything which gives to the state strength and prosperity.—As the protectress of agriculture, Athena is represented as inventing the plough and rake : she created the olive tree (see below), taught the people to yoke oxen to the plough, took care of the breeding of horses, and instructed men how to tame them by the bridle, her own invention. Allusions to this feature of her character are contained in the epithets βούδεια, βοαρμία, ἀγρίφα, ἱππία, or χαλινῖτις. She is also represented as the patron of various kinds of science, industry, and art, and as inventing numbers, the trumpet, the chariot and navigation. She was further believed to have invented nearly

every kind of work in which women were employed, and she herself was skilled in such work. Hence we have the tale of the Lydian maiden Aracline, who ventured to compete with Athena in the art of weaving. [ARACHNE.] Athena is in fact the patroness of both the useful and elegant arts. Hence she is called ἐργάνη, and later writers make her the goddess of all wisdom, knowledge, and art, and represent her as sitting on the right hand of her father Zeus, and supporting him with her counsel. She is therefore characterized by various epithets and surnames, expressing the keenness of her sight or the vigour of her intellect, such as ὀπτιλέτις, ὀφθαλμῖτις, ὀξυδερκής, γλαυκῶπις, πολύβουλος, πολύμητις, and μηχανῖτις.—As the patron divinity of the state she was at Athens the protectress of the phratries and houses which formed the basis of the state The festival of the Apaturia had a direct reference to this particular point in the character of the goddess. (Dict. of Ant. art. Apaturia.) She also maintained the authority of the law, justice, and order in the courts and the assembly of the people. This notion was as ancient as the Homeric poems, in which she is described as assisting Ulysses against the lawless conduct of the suitors. (Od. xiii. 394.) She was believed to have instituted the ancient court of the Areopagus, and in cases where the votes of the judges were equally divided, she gave the casting one in favour of the accused. The epithets which have reference to this part of the goddess's character are ἀξιόποινος, the avenger, βουλαῖα, and ἀγυραῖα.—As Athena promoted the internal prosperity of the state, so she also protected the state from outward enemies, and thus assumes the character of a warlike divinity, though in a very different sense from Ares, Eris, or Enyo According to Homer she does not even keep arms, but borrows them from Zeus ; she preserves men from slaughter when prudence demands it, and repels Ares's savage love of war, and conquers him. The epithets which she derives from her warlike character are ἀγελεία, λάφρια, ἀλκιμάχη, λαόσσοος, and others. In times of war, towns, fortresses, and harbours, are under her especial care, whence she is designated as ἐρυσίπτολις, ἀλαλκομενηΐς, πολιάς, πολιοῦχος, ἀκραία, ἀκρία, κληδοῦχος, πυλαῖτις, προμαχόρμα, and the like. In the war of Zeus against the giants, she assisted her father and Hercules with her counsel, and also took an active part in it, for she buried Enceladus under the island of Sicily, and slew Pallas. In the Trojan war she sided with the Greeks, though on their return home she visited them with storms, on account of the manner in which the Locrian Ajax had treated Cassandra in her temple. As a goddess of war and the protectress of heroes, Athena usually appears in armour, with the aegis and a golden staff. — The character of Athena, as we have here traced it, holds a middle place between the male and female, whence she is a virgin divinity, whose heart is inaccessible to the passion of love. Tiresias was deprived of sight for having seen her in the bath ; and Hephaestus, who had made an attempt upon her chastity, was obliged to take to flight. For this reason, the ancient traditions always describe the goddess as dressed ; and when Ovid makes her appear naked before Paris, he abandons the genuine story.—Athena was worshipped in all parts of Greece. Her worship was introduced from the ancient towns on the lake Copais at a very early period into Attica, where she became the great national divinity of the city and the country. Here she was regarded as the Δεὰ σώτειρα, ὑγίεια, and παιωνία. The tale ran that in the reign of Cecrops both Poseidon and Athena contended for the possession of Athens. The gods resolved that whichever of them produced a gift most useful to mortals should have possession of the land. Poseidon struck the ground with his trident and straightway a horse appeared. Athena then planted the olive. The gods thereupon decreed that the olive was more useful to man than the horse, and gave the city to the goddess, from whom it was call Athenae. At Athens the magnificent festival of the *Panathenaea* was celebrated in honour of the goddess. At this festival took place the grand procession, which was represented on the frieze of the Parthenon. (*Dict. of Ant.* art. *Panathenaea.*) At Lindus in Rhodes her worship was likewise very ancient. Respecting its introduction into Italy, and the modifications which her character underwent there, see MINERVA. Among the things sacred to her we may mention the owl, serpent, cock, and olive-tree, which she was said to have created in her contest with Poseidon about the possession of Attica. The sacrifices offered to her consisted of bulls, rams, and cows. Athena was frequently represented in works of art, in which we generally find some of the following characteristics:— 1. The helmet, which she usually wears on her head, but in a few instances carries in her hand. It is generally ornamented in the most beautiful manner with griffins, heads of rams, horses, and sphinxes. 2. The aegis, which is represented on works of art, not as a shield, but as a goat-skin, covered with scales, set with the appalling Gorgon's head, and surrounded with tassels. (*Dict. of Ant.* art. *Aegis.*) 3. The round Argolic shield, in the centre of which the head of Medusa likewise appears. 4. Objects sacred to her, such as an olive branch, a serpent, an owl, a cock, and a lance. Her garment is usually the Spartan tunic without sleeves, and over it she wears a cloak, the peplus, or, though rarely, the chlamys.

Athēnae ('Αθῆναι, also 'Αθήνη in Homer: 'Αθηναιος, ή 'Αθηναία, Athēniensis: *Athens*), the capital of Attica, about 30 stadia from the sea, on the S. W. slope of Mount Lycabettus, between the small rivers Cephissus on the W. and Ilissus on the E., the latter of which flowed through the town. The most ancient part of it, the *Acropolis*, is said to have been built by the mythical Cecrops, but the city itself is said to have owed its origin to Theseus, who united the 12 independent states or townships of Attica into one state, and made Athens their capital. The city was burnt by Xerxes in B. c. 480, but was soon rebuilt under the administration of Themistocles, and was adorned with public buildings by Cimon and especially by Pericles, in whose time (B. c. 460—429) it reached its greatest splendour. Its beauty was chiefly owing to its public buildings, for the private houses were mostly insignificant, and its streets badly laid out. Towards the end of the Peloponnesian war, it contained 10,000 houses (Xen. *Mem.* iii. 6. § 14), which at the rate of 12 inhabitants to a house would give a population of 120,000, though some writers make the inhabitants as many as 180,000. Under the Romans Athens continued to be a great and flourishing city, and retained many privileges and immunities when S. Greece was formed into the Roman province of Achaia. It suffered greatly on its capture by Srlla,

B. c. 86, and was deprived of many of its privileges. It was at that time, and also during the early centuries of the Christian aera, one of the chief seats of learning, and the Romans were accustomed to send their sons to Athens, as to an University, for the completion of their education. Hadrian, who was very partial to Athens and frequently resided in the city (A. D. 122, 128), adorned it with many new buildings, and his example was followed by Herodes Atticus, who spent large sums of money upon beautifying the city in the reign of M. Aurelius. — Athens consisted of 2 distinct parts: I. *The City* (τὸ ἄστυ), properly so called, divided into, 1. The Upper City or Acropolis (ή ἄνω πόλις, ἀκρόπολις), and, 2. The Lower City (ή κάτω πόλις), surrounded with walls by Themistocles. II. The 3 harbour-towns of Piraeus, Munychia, and Phalērum, also surrounded with walls by Themistocles, and connected with the city by means of the *long walls* (τὰ μακρὰ τείχη), built under the administration of Pericles. The long walls consisted of the wall to Phalērum on the E., 35 stadia long (about 4 miles), and of the wall to Piraeus on the W., 40 stadia long (about 4½ miles); between these two, at a short distance from the latter and parallel to it, another wall was erected, thus making 2 walls leading to the Piraeus (sometimes called τὰ σκέλη), with a narrow passage between them. There were therefore 3 long walls in all; but the name of *Long Walls* seems to have been confined to the two leading to the Piraeus, while the one leading to Phalerum was distinguished by the name of the *Phalerian Wall* (τὸ Φαληρικὸν τείχος). The entire circuit of the walls was 174½ stadia (nearly 22 miles), of which 43 stadia (nearly 5½ miles) belonged to the city, 75 stadia (9½ miles) to the long walls, and 56½ (7 miles) to Piraeus, Munychia, and Phalerum. — 1. **Topography of the Acropolis or Upper City.** The Acropolis, also called *Cecropia* from its reputed founder, was a steep rock in the middle of the city, about 150 feet high, 1150 feet long, and 500 broad; its sides were naturally scarped on all sides except the W. end. It was originally surrounded by an ancient Cyclopian wall said to have been built by the Pelasgians; at the time of the Peloponnesian war only the N. part of this wall remained, and this portion was still called the *Pelasgic Wall;* while the S. part, which had been rebuilt by Cimon, was called the *Cimonian Wall.* On the W. end of the Acropolis, where access is alone practicable, were the magnificent PROPYLAEA, "the Entrances," built by Pericles, before the right wing of which was the small temple of Νίκη 'Άπτερος. The summit of the Acropolis was covered with temples, statues of bronze and marble, and various other works of art. Of the temples, the grandest was the PARTHENON, sacred to the "Virgin" goddess Athena; and N. of the Parthenon was the magnificent ERECHTHEUM, containing 3 separate temples, one of Athena Polias (Πολίας), or the "Protectress of the State," the *Erechthēum* proper, or sanctuary of Erechtheus, and the *Pandrosium*, or sanctuary of Pandrosos, the daughter of Cecrops. Between the Parthēnon and Erechthēum was the colossal statue of Athena Promachos (Πρόμαχος), or the "Fighter in the Front," whose helmet and spear was the first object on the Acropolis visible from the sea. — **2. Topography of the Lower City.** — The lower city was built in the plain round the Acropolis, but this plain

The Bema of the Pnyx at Athens.

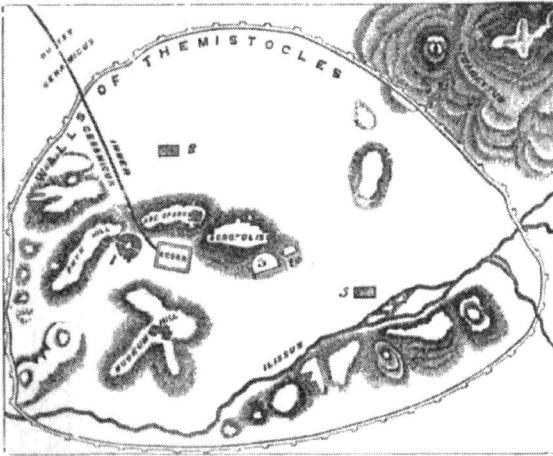

Plan of Athens.

1. Pnyx Ecclesia.
2. Theseum.
3. Theatre of Dionysus.

4. Odĕum of Pericles.
5. Temple of the Olympian Jove.

The Acropolis restored.

[To face p. 102.

The Parthenon, Athena Promachus, and the Cave of Pan. (From a Coin.)

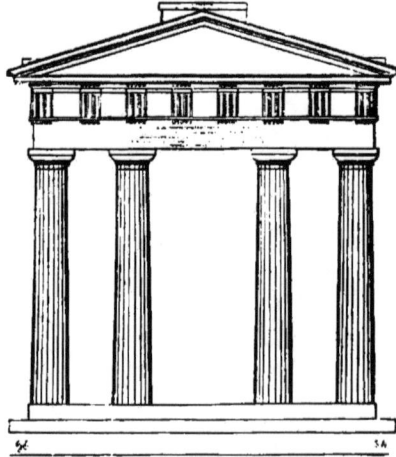

Choragic Monument of Lysicrates.

Portico of Athena Archegetis.

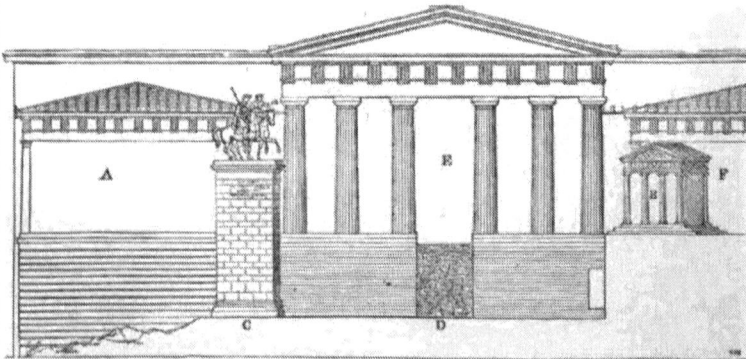

The Propylaea restored.

A. Pinacotheca.
B. Temple of Nike Apteros.
C. Pedestal of Agrippa.

D. Road leading to the central entrance.
E. Central entrance.

F. Hall corresponding to the Pinacotheca.

To face p. 103.]

also contained several hills, especially in the S.W. part. — **Walls.** The ancient walls embraced a much greater circuit than the modern ones. On the W. they included the hill of the Nymphs and the Pnyx, on the S. they extended a little beyond the Ilissus, and on the E. they crossed the Ilissus, near the Lyceum, which was outside the walls. — **Gates.** Their number is unknown, and the position of many of them is uncertain ; but the following list contains the most important. On the W. side were : — 1. *Dipylum* (Δίπυλον, more anciently Θριασίαι or Κεραμικαί), the most frequented gate of the city, leading from the inner Ceramīcus to the outer Ceramicus, and to the Academy. — 2. *The Sacred Gate* (αἱ Ἱεραὶ Πύλαι), where the sacred road to Eleusis began. — 3. *The Knight's Gate* (αἱ Ἱππάδες π.), probably between the hill of the Nymphs and the Pnyx. — 4. *The Piraean Gate* (ἡ Πειραϊκὴ π.), between the Pnyx and the Museum, leading to the carriage road (ἁμάξιτος) between the Long Walls to the Piraeus. — 5. *The Melitian Gate* (αἱ Μελιτίδες π.), so called because it led to the demus Melite, within the city. On the S. side, going from W. to E. : — 6. *The Gate of the Dead* (αἱ Ἠρίαι π.) in the neighbourhood of the Museum, placed by many authorities on the N. side. — 7. *The Itonian Gate* (αἱ Ἰτώνιαι π.), near the Ilissus, where the road to Phalērum began. On the E. side, going from S. to N. : — 8. *The Gate of Diochares* (αἱ Διοχάρους π.), leading to the Lyceum. — 9. *The Diomēan Gate* (ἡ Διόμεια π.), leading to Cynosarges and the demus Diomea. On the N. side. — 10. *The Acharnian Gate* (αἱ Ἀχαρνικαί π.), leading to the demus Acharnae. — **Chief Districts.** The inner *Ceramicus* (Κεραμεικός), or " Potter's Quarter," in the W. of the city, extending N. as far as the gate Dipylum, by which it was separated from the outer Ceramīcus ; the S. part of the inner Ceramicus contained the *Agora* (ἀγορά), or " market-place," the only one in the city (for there were not 2 market-places, as some suppose), lying S.W. of the Acropolis, and between the Acropolis, the Areopagus, the Pnyx, and the Museum. The demus *Melite*, S. of the inner Ceramicus, and perhaps embracing the hill of the Museum. The demus *Scambonidae*, W. of the inner Ceramicus, between the Pnyx and the hill of the Nymphs. The *Collytus*, S. of Melite. *Coele*, a district S. of Collytus and the Museum, along the Ilissus, in which were the graves of Cimon and Thucydides. *Limnae*, a district E. of Melite and Collytus, between the Acropolis and the Ilissus. *Diomea*, a district in the E. of the city, near the gate of the same name and the Cynosarges. *Agrae*, a district S. of Diomea. — **Hills.** The *Arēopăgus* (Ἀρείου πάγος or Ἄρειος πάγος), the " Hill of Ares," W. of the Acropolis, which gave its name to the celebrated council that held its sittings there (*Dict. of Ant. s. v.*), was accessible on the S. side by a flight of steps cut out of the rock. The *Hill of the Nymphs*, N.W. of the Areopagus. The *Pnyx* (Πνύξ), a semicircular hill, S.W. of the Areopagus, where the assemblies of the people were held in earlier times, for afterwards the people usually met in the Theatre of Dionysus. (See *Dict. of Ant.* p. 440, b, 2d ed.) The *Musēum*, S. of the Pnyx and the Areopagus, on which was the monument of Philopappus, and where the Macedonians built a fortress. — **Streets.** Of these we have little information. We read of the *Piraean Street*, which led from the Piraean gate to the

Agora ; of the *Street of the Hermae*, which ran along the Agora between the Stoa Basilēos and Stoa Poecile ; of the *Street of the Tripods*, on the E. of the Acropolis, &c. — **Public Buildings.** 1. *Temples.* Of these the most important was the *Olympiēum* (Ὀλυμπίειον), or Temple of the Olympian Zeus, S. E. of the Acropolis, near the Ilissus and the fountain Callirrhoë, which was long unfinished, and was first completed by Hadrian. *Thesēum* (Θησεῖον) or Temple of Theseus, on a hill N. of the Areopagus, now converted into the Museum of Athens. The *Temple of Ares*, S. of the Areopagus and W. of the Acropolis. *Metrōum* (Μητρῷον), or temple of the mother of the gods, E. of the Agora, and S. of the Acropolis, near the Senate House, and the Odeum of Herodes Atticus. Besides these, there was a vast number of other temples in all parts of the city. — 2. The *Senate House* (βουλευτήριον), at the S. end of the Agora. — 3. The *Tholus* (θόλος), a round building close to the Senate House, which served as the new Prytanēum, in which the Prytanes took their meals and offered their sacrifices. (*Dict. of Ant. s. v.*) — 4. The *Prytanēum* (Πρυτανεῖον), at the N.E. foot of the Acropolis, where the Prytanes used more anciently to take their meals, and where the laws of Solon were preserved. — 5. *Stoae* (στοαί), or *Halls*, supported by pillars, and used as places of resort in the heat of the day, of which there were several in Athens. (*Dict. of Ant.* p. 944, 2d ed.) In the Agora there were 3 ; the *Stoa Basilēus* (στοὰ βασίλειος), the court of the King-Archon, on the W. side of the Agora ; the *Stoa Poecilē* (στοὰ ποικίλη), so called because it was adorned with fresco painting of the battle of Marathon by Polygnotus ; and the *Stoa Eleutherius* (στοὰ ἐλευθέριος), or Hall of Zeus Eleutherius, both on the S. side of the Agora. — 6. *Theatres* The *Theatre of Dionysus*, on the S.E. slope of the Acropolis, was the great theatre of the state (*Dict. of Ant.* p. 1120, 2d ed.) ; besides this there were three *Odēa* (ᾠδεῖα), for contests in vocal and instrumental music (*Dict. of Ant. s. v.*), an ancient one near the fountain Callirrhoë, a second built by Pericles, close to the theatre of Dionysus, on the S.E. slope of the Acropolis, and a third built by Herodes Atticus, in honour of his wife Regilla, on the S.W. slope of the Acropolis, of which there are still considerable remains. — 7. *Stadium* (τὸ Στάδιον), S. of the Ilissus, in the district Agrae. — 8. *Monuments.* The *Monument of Andronicus Cyrrhestes*, formerly called the *Tower of the Winds*, an octagonal building N. of the Acropolis, still extant, was an horologium. (*Dict. of Ant.* p. 616, 2d ed.) The *Choragic Monument of Lysicrates*, frequently but erroneously called the *Lantern of Demosthenes*, still extant, in the Street of the Tripods. The *Monument of Harmodius and Aristogiton* in the Agora, just before the ascent to the Acropolis. — **Suburbs.** The *Outer Ceramīcus* (ὁ ἔξω καλούμενος), N.W. of the city, was the finest suburb of Athens : here were buried the Athenians who had fallen in war, and at the further end of it was the ACADEMIA, 6 stadia from the city. *Cynosarges* (τὸ Κυνόσαργες), E. of the city, before the gate Diomea, a gymnasium sacred to Hercules, where Antisthenes, the founder of the Cynic school, taught. *Lycēum* (τὸ Λύκειον), S. E. of the Cynosarges, a gymnasium sacred to Apollo Lycēus, where Aristotle and the Peripatetics taught

Athēnae ('Αθῆναι: *Atenah*), a seaport town of Pontus, named from its temple of Athena.

Athēnaeum ('Αθήναιον), in general a temple of Athena, or any place consecrated to this goddess. The name was specially given to a school founded by the emperor Hadrian at Rome about A. D. 133, for the promotion of literary and scientific studies. It was in the neighbourhood of the forum, and at the foot of the Aventine Hill: it had a staff of professors paid by the government, and continued in repute till the 5th century of our era. (*Dict. of Ant. s. v.*) — **Athenaeum** was also the name of a town in Arcadia, not far from Megalopolis, and of a place in Athamania in Epirus.

Athēnaeus ('Αθήναιος). **1.** A contemporary of Archimedes, the author of an extant work Περὶ Μηχανημάτων (on warlike engines), addressed to Marcellus (probably the conqueror of Syracuse); printed in Thevenot's *Mathematici Veteres*, Paris, 1693. — **2.** A learned Greek grammarian, of Naucratis in Egypt, lived about A. D. 230, first at Alexandria and afterwards at Rome. His extant work is entitled the *Deipnosophistae* (Δειπνοσοφισταί), *i. e.* the *Banquet of the Learned*, in 15 books, of which the first 2 books, and parts of the 3rd, 11th, and 15th, exist only in an Epitome. The work may be considered one of the earliest collections of what are called *Ana*, being an immense mass of anecdotes, extracts from the writings of poets, historians, dramatists, philosophers, orators, and physicians, of facts in natural history, criticisms, and discussions on almost every conceivable subject, especially on Gastronomy. Athenaeus represents himself as describing to his friend Timocrates, a full account of the conversation at a banquet at Rome, at which Galen, the physician, and Ulpian, the jurist, were among the guests. — *Editions.* By Casaubon, Genev. 1597; by Schweighäuser, Argentorati, 1801–1807; and by W. Dindorf, Lips. 1827. — **3.** A celebrated physician, founder of the medical sect of the Pneumatici, was born at Attalia in Cilicia, and practised at Rome about A. D. 50.

Athēnagōras ('Αθηναγόρας), an Athenian philosopher, converted to the Christian religion in the 2d century of our aera, is the author of two extant works, *An Apology for Christians*, addressed to the emperors M. Aurelius and his son Commodus, and a treatise in defence of the tenet of the resurrection. — *Editions.* By Fell, Oxon. 1682; Rechenberg, Lips. 1684–85; Dechair, Oxon. 1706.

Athēnaĭs ('Αθηναΐς). **1.** Surnamed *Philostorgus*, wife of Ariobarzanes II., king of Cappadocia, and mother of Ariobarzanes III. — **2.** Daughter of Leontius, afterwards named EUDOCIA.

Athēnĭon ('Αθηνίων), a Cilician, one of the commanders of the slaves in the 2nd servile war in Sicily, maintained his ground for some time successfully, and defeated L. Licinius Lucullus, but was at length conquered and killed in B. C. 101 by the consul M'. Aquillius.

Athēnŏdōrus ('Αθηνόδωρος). **1.** Of Tarsus, a Stoic philosopher surnamed *Cordylio*, was the keeper of the library at Pergamus, and afterwards removed to Rome, where he lived with M. Cato, at whose house he died. — **2.** Of Tarsus, a Stoic philosopher, surnamed *Cananites*, from Cana in Cilicia, the birthplace of his father, whose name was Sandon. He was a pupil of Posidonius at Rhodes, and afterwards taught at Apollonia in Epirus, where the young Octavius (subsequently the emperor Au-

gustus) was one of his disciples. He accompanied the latter to Rome, and became one of his intimate friends and advisers. In his old age he returned to Tarsus, where he died at the age of 82. He was the author of several works which are not extant. — **3.** A sculptor, the son and pupil of Agesander of Rhodes, whom he assisted in executing the group of Laocoon. [AGESANDER.]

Athēsis (*Adige* or *Etsch*), rises in the Rhaetian Alps, receives the **Atāgis** (*Eisach*), flows through Upper Italy past Verona, and falls into the Adriatic by many mouths.

Athmōne ('Αθμονή, also 'Αθμονία and "Αθμονον: 'Αθμονεύς, fem. 'Αθμονίς), an Attic demus belonging to the tribe Cecropis, afterwards to the tribe Attalis.

Athōs ("Αθως, also "Αθων: 'Αθωΐτης: *Haghion Oros*, *Monte Santo*, i. e. *Holy Mountain*), the mountainous peninsula, also called Acte, which projects from Chalcidice in Macedonia. At the extremity of the peninsula the mountain rises abruptly from the sea to a height of 6349 feet; there is no anchorage for ships at its base, and the voyage round it was so dreaded by mariners, that Xerxes had a canal cut through the isthmus, which connects the peninsula with the mainland, to afford a passage to his fleet. The isthmus is about 1½ mile across; and there are most distinct traces of the canal to be seen in the present day; so that we must not imitate the scepticism of Juvenal (x. 174), and of many modern writers, who refused to believe that the canal was ever cut. The peninsula contained several flourishing cities in antiquity, and is now studded with numerous monasteries, cloisters, and chapels, whence it derives its modern name. In these monasteries some valuable MSS. of ancient authors have been discovered.

Athrĭbis ('Αθρίβις), a city in the Delta of Egypt; capital of the Nomos Athribites.

Atia, mother of AUGUSTUS.

Atilia or **Atilia Gens**, the principal members of which are given under their surnames CALATINUS, REGULUS, and SERRANUS.

Atilicīnus, a Roman jurist, who probably lived about A. D. 50, is referred to in the Digest.

Atilius. **1.** L., one of the earliest of the Roman jurists who gave public instruction in law, probably lived about B. C. 100. He wrote commentaries on the laws of the Twelve Tables. — **2. M.**, one of the early Roman poets, wrote both tragedies and comedies, but apparently a greater number of the latter than of the former.

Atina (Atinas, -ātis: *Atina*), a town of the Volsci in Latium, afterwards a Roman colony.

Atintānes ('Ατιντᾶνες), an Epirot people in Illyria, on the borders of Macedonia; their country, *Atintania*, was reckoned part of Macedonia.

Atius Varus. [VARUS.]

Atlantĭcum Māre. [OCEANUS.]

Atlantis ('Ατλαντίς, sc. νῆσος), according to an ancient tradition, a great island W. of the Pillars of Hercules in the Ocean, opposite Mount Atlas: it possessed a numerous population, and was adorned with every beauty; its powerful princes invaded Africa and Europe, but were defeated by the Athenians and their allies: its inhabitants afterwards became wicked and impious, and the island was in consequence swallowed up in the ocean in a day and a night. This legend is given by Plato in the *Timaeus*, and is said to have been

Ruins of the Olympieum.

Theatre of Dionysus. (From Coin.)

Theatre of Dionysus. (From a Vase.)

Ionic Temple on the Ilissus.

Street of the Tripods at Athens. (From a Bas-relief.)

[To face p. 104.

Arsaces VII. (Mithridates II)., King of Parthia. Page 89.

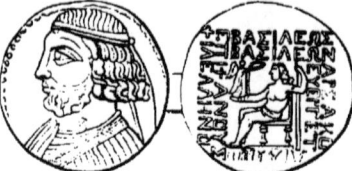

Augustus, when Triumvir, on a Coin of Balbus. Page 109.

Arsaces XIV. (Orodes I.), King of Parthia. Page 89.

Augustus, Roman Emperor, ob. A.D. 14. Pages 108—110.

Arsaces XXVII. (Vologeses III.), King of Parthia. Page 90.

Aurelianus, Roman Emperor, A.D. 270—275. Page 110.

Arsinoe, daughter of Ptolemy I., and wife of Ptolemy II. Page 91.

M. Aurelius Antoninus, Roman Emperor, A.D. 161—180. Page 111.

Arsinoe, daughter of Ptolemy III., and wife of Ptolemy IV. Page 91.

Avitus, Roman Emperor, A.D. 445. Page 113.

Attalus, Roman Emperor, A.D. 409—410. Page 106.
To face p. 106.

Balbinus, Roman Emperor, A.D. 238. Page 115.

related to Solon by the Egyptian priests. The Canary Islands, or the Azores, which perhaps were visited by the Phoenicians, may have given rise to the legend ; but some modern writers regard it as indicative of a vague belief in antiquity in the existence of the W. hemisphere.

Atlas ("Ατλας), son of Iapetus and Clymene, and brother of Prometheus and Epimetheus. He made war with the other Titans upon Zeus, and being conquered, was condemned to bear heaven on his head and hands : according to Homer Atlas bears the long columns which keep asunder heaven and earth. The myth seems to have arisen from the idea that lofty mountains supported the heaven. Later traditions distort the original idea still more, by making Atlas a man who was metamorphosed into a mountain. Thus Ovid (*Met.* iv. 626, seq.) relates that Perseus came to Atlas and asked for shelter, which was refused, whereupon Perseus, by means of the head of Medusa, changed him into M. Atlas, on which rested heaven with all its stars. Others go still further, and represent Atlas as a powerful king, who possessed great knowledge of the courses of the stars, and who was the first who taught men that heaven had the form of a globe. Hence the expression that heaven rested on his shoulders was regarded as a merely figurative mode of speaking. At first, the story of Atlas referred to one mountain only, which was believed to exist on the extreme boundary of the earth ; but, as geographical knowledge extended, the name of Atlas was transferred to other places, and thus we read of a Mauretanian, Italian, Arcadian, and even of a Caucasian, Atlas. The common opinion, however, was, that the heaven-bearing Atlas was in the N.W. of Africa. See below. Atlas was the father of the Pleiades by Pleione or by Hesperis ; of the Hyades and Hesperides by Aethra ; and of Oenomaus and Maia by Sterope. Dione and Calypso, Hyas and Hesperus, are likewise called his children. — *Atlantiades*, a descendant of Atlas, especially Mercury, his grandson by Maia (comp. *Mercuri facunde nepos Atlantis*, Hor. *Carm.* i. 10), and Hermaphroditus, son of Mercury. — *Atlantias* and *Atlantis*, a female descendant of Atlas, especially the Pleiads and Hyads.

Atlas Mons ("Ατλας: *Atlas*), was the general name of the great mountain range which covers the surface of N. Africa between the Mediterranean and Great Desert (*Sahara*), on the N. and S., and the Atlantic and the Lesser Syrtis on the W. and E. ; the mountain chains S.E. of the Lesser Syrtis, though connected with the Atlas, do not properly belong to it, and were called by other names. The N. and S. ranges of this system were distinguished by the names of **Atlas Minor** and **Atlas Major**, and a distinction was made between the 3 regions into which they divided the country. [AFRICA, p. 23, a.]

Atossa ("Ατοσσα), daughter of Cyrus, and wife successively of her brother Cambyses, of Smerdis the Magian, and of Darius Hystaspis, over whom she possessed great influence. She bore Darius 4 sons, Xerxes, Masistes, Achaemenes, and Hystaspes.

Atrae or **Hatra** ("Ατραι, τὰ "Ατρα : 'Ατρηνός, Ατρēnus ; *Hadr*, S.W. of *Mosul*), a strongly fortified city on a high mountain in Mesopotamia, inhabited by people of the Arab race.

Sempronius, Atratinus. 1. A., consul B. C. 497 and 491. — **2. L.,** consul 444 and censor 443. — **3. C.,** consul 423, fought unsuccessfully against the Volscians, and was in consequence condemned to pay a heavy fine. — **4. L.,** accused M. Caelius Rufus, whom Cicero defended, 57.

Atrax ("Ατραξ : 'Ατράκιος), a town in Pelasgiotis in Thessaly, inhabited by the Perrhaebi, so called from the mythical Atrax, son of Peneus and Bura, and father of Hippodamia and Caenis.

Atrebates, a people in Gallia Belgica, in the modern *Artois*, which is a corruption of their name. In Caesar's time (B. C. 57) they numbered 15,000 warriors : their capital was NEMETOCENNA. Part of them crossed over to Britain, where they dwelt in the upper valley of the Thames, *Oxfordshire* and *Berkshire*.

Atreus ('Ατρεύς), son of Pelops and Hippodamia, grandson of Tantalus, and brother of Thyestes and Nicippe. [PELOPS.] He was first married to Cleola, by whom he became the father of Plisthenes ; then to Aërope, the widow of his son Plisthenes, who was the mother of Agamemnon, Menelaus, and Anaxibia, either by Plisthenes or by Atreus [AGAMEMNON]; and lastly to Pelopia, the daughter of his brother Thyestes. The tragic fate of the house of Tantalus afforded ample materials to the tragic poets of Greece, who relate the details in various ways. In consequence of the murder of their half-brother Chrysippus, Atreus and Thyestes were obliged to take to flight ; they were hospitably received at Mycenae ; and, after the death of Eurystheus, Atreus became king of Mycenae. Thyestes seduced Aërope, the wife of Atreus, and was in consequence banished by his brother : from his place of exile he sent Plisthenes, the son of Atreus, whom he had brought up as his own child, in order to slay Atreus ; but Plisthenes fell by the hands of Atreus, who did not know that he was his own son. In order to take revenge, Atreus, pretending to be reconciled to Thyestes, recalled him to Mycenae, killed his 2 sons, and placed their flesh before their father at a banquet, who unwittingly partook of the horrid meal. Thyestes fled with horror, and the gods cursed Atreus and his house. The kingdom of Atreus was now visited by famine, and the oracle advised Atreus to call back Thyestes. Atreus, who went out in search of him, came to king Thesprotus, and as he did not find him there, he married his third wife, Pelopia, the daughter of Thyestes, whom Atreus believed to be a daughter of Thesprotus. Pelopia was at the time with child by her own father. This child, Aegisthus, afterwards slew Atreus because the latter had commanded him to slay his own father Thyestes. [AEGISTHUS.] The treasury of Atreus and his sons at Mycenae, which is mentioned by Pausanias, is believed by some to exist still ; but the ruins which remain are above ground, whereas Pausanias speaks of the building as underground.

Atria. [ADRIA.]

Atrides ('Ατρείδης), a descendant of Atreus, especially Agamemnon and Menelaus.

Atropatene ('Ατροπατηνή), or Media Atropatia ('Ατροπατία or -οs Μηδία), the N.W. part of Media, adjacent to Armenia, named after Atropātes, a native of the country, who, having been made its governor by Alexander, founded there a kingdom, which long remained independent alike of the Seleucidae, the Parthians, and the Romans, but was at last subdued by the Parthians.

Atropătes ('Ατροπάτης), a Persian satrap, fought at the battle of Gaugamela, B. c. 331, and after the death of Darius, was made satrap of Media by Alexander. His daughter was married to Perdiccas in 324 ; and he received from his father-in-law, after Alexander's death, the province of the Greater Media. In the N.W. of the country, called after him Media Atropatēne, he established an independent kingdom, which continued to exist down to the time of the emperor Augustus.

Atrŏpos. [MOIRAE.]

Atta, T. Quintius, a Roman comic poet, died B. C. 78. His surname Atta was given him from a defect in his feet, to which circumstance Horace probably alludes (*Ep.* ii. l. 79). His plays were very popular, and were acted even in the time of Augustus.

Attaginus ('Ατταγῖνος), son of Phrynon, a Theban, betrayed Thebes to Xerxes, B.C. 480. After the battle of Plataeae (479) the other Greeks required Attaginus to be delivered up to them, but he made his escape.

Attālia ('Ατταλεια, 'Ατταλεώτης or -ατης).— 1. A city of Lydia, formerly called Agroïra ('Αγρόειρα).— 2. (*Laara*), a city on the coast of Pamphylia, near the mouth of the river Catarrhactes, founded by Attalus II. Philadelphus, and subdued by the Romans under P. Servilius Isauricus.

Attālus ("Ατταλος). 1. A Macedonian, uncle of Cleopatra, whom Philip married in B. C. 337. At the nuptials of his niece, Attalus offered an insult to Alexander, and, on the accession of the latter, was put to death by his order in Asia Minor, whither Philip had previously sent him to secure the Greek cities to his cause.— 2. Son of Andromenes the Stymphaean, and one of Alexander's officers ; after the death of Alexander (B. C. 323), he served under Perdiccas, whose sister, Atalante, he had married ; and after the death of Perdiccas (321), he joined Alcetas, the brother of Perdiccas ; but their united forces were defeated in Pisidia by Antigonus in 320. — 3. *Kings of Pergamus.* — (I.) Son of Attalus, a brother of Philetaerus, succeeded his cousin, Eumenes I., and reigned B. C. 241—197. He took part with the Romans against Philip and the Achaeans. He was a wise and just prince, and was distinguished by his patronage of literature. — (II.) Surnamed *Philadelphus*, 2nd son of Attalus I., succeeded his brother Eumenes II., and reigned 159—138. Like his father he was an ally of the Romans, and he also encouraged the arts and sciences. — (III.) Surnamed *Philometor*, son of Eumenes II. and Stratonice, succeeded his uncle Attalus II., and reigned 138—133. He is known to us chiefly for the extravagance of his conduct and the murder of his relations and friends. In his will, he made the Romans his heirs ; but his kingdom was claimed by Aristonicus. [ARISTONICUS.] — 4. Roman emperor of the West, was raised to the throne by Alaric, but was deposed by the latter, after a reign of one year (A. D. 409, 410), on account of his acting without Alaric's advice. — 5. A Stoic philosopher in the reign of Tiberius, was one of the teachers of the philosopher Seneca, who speaks of him in the highest terms.

Attegŭa, a town in Hispania Baetica, of uncertain site.

Atthis or Attis ("Ατθις or "Αττις), daughter of Cranaus, from whom Attica was believed to have derived its name. The two birds into which Philomele and her sister Procne were metamorphosed, were likewise called Attis.

Attica (ἡ 'Αττική, sc. γῆ), a division of Greece,

has the form of a triangle, two sides of which are washed by the Aegaean sea, while the third is separated from Boeotia on the N. by the mountains Cithaeron and Parnes. Megaris, which bounds it on the N.W, was formerly a part of Attica. In ancient times it was called *Acte* and *Actice* ('Ακτή and 'Ακτική), or the "coastland" [ACTE], from which the later form *Attica* is said to have been derived : but according to traditions it derived its name from *Atthis*, the daughter of the mythical king Cranaus ; and it is not impossible that *Att-ica* may contain the root *Att* or *Ath*, which we find in *Atthis* and *Athenae.* Attica is divided by many ancient writers into 3 districts. 1. *The Highlands* (ἡ διακρία, also ὀρεινὴ 'Αττική), the N.E. of the country, containing the range of Parnes and extending S. to the promontory Cynosura : the only level part of this district was the small plain of Marathon opening to the sea. 2. *The Plain* (ἡ πεδίας, τὸ πέδιον), the N.W. of the country, included both the plain round Athens and the plain round Eleusis, and extended S. to the promontory Zoster. 3. *The Sea-coast District* (ἡ παραλία), the S. part of the country, terminating in the promontory Sunium. Besides these 3 divisions we also read of a 4th, *The Midland District* (μεσόγαια), still called *Mesogia*, an undulating plain in the middle of the country, bounded by M. Pentelicus on the N., M. Hymettus on the W., and the sea on the E. The soil of Attica is not very fertile : the greater part of it is not adapted for growing corn ; but it produces olives, figs, and grapes, especially the 2 former, in great perfection. The country is dry : the chief river is the Cephissus, which rises in Parnes and flows through the Athenian plain. The abundance of wild flowers in the country made the honey of M. Hymettus very celebrated in antiquity. Excellent marble was obtained from the quarries of Pentelicus, N.E. of Athens, and a considerable supply of silver from the mines of Laurium near Sunium. The area of Attica, including the island of Salamis, which belonged to it, contained between 700 and 800 square miles ; and its population in its flourishing period was probably about 500,000, of which nearly 4-5ths were slaves. Attica is said to have been originally inhabited by Pelasgians. Its most ancient political division was into 12 independent states, attributed to CECROPS, who according to some legends came from Egypt. Subsequently Ion, the grandson of Hellen, divided the people into 4 tribes, *Geleontes, Hopletes, Argades,* and *Aegicores;* and Theseus, who united the 12 independent states of Attica into one political body, and made Athens the capital, again divided the nation into 3 classes, the *Eupatridae, Geomori,* and *Demiurgi.* Clisthenes (B. C. 510) abolished the old tribes and created 10 new ones, according to a geographical division : these tribes were subdivided into 174 demi or townships. (For details, see *Dict. of Ant.* art. *Tribus.*)

Atticus Herōdes, Tĭbĕrius Claudius, a celebrated Greek rhetorician, born about A. D. 104, at Marathon in Attica. He taught rhetoric both at Athens and at Rome, and his school was frequented by the most distinguished men of the age. The future emperors M. Aurelius and L. Verus were among his pupils, and Antoninus Pius raised him to the consulship in 143. He possessed immense wealth, a great part of which he spent in embellishing Athens. He died at the age of 76, in 180

He wrote numerous works, none of which have come down to us, with the exception of an oration, entitled Περὶ πολιτείας, the genuineness of which, however, is very doubtful. It is printed in the collections of the Greek orators, and by Fiorillo, in *Herodis Attici quae supersunt*, Lips. 1801.

Atticus, T. Pomponius, a Roman eques, born at Rome, B. C. 109. His proper name after his adoption by Q. Caecilius, the brother of his mother, was Q. Caecilius Pomponianus Atticus. His surname, Atticus, was given him on account of his long residence in Athens and his intimate acquaintance with the Greek language and literature. He was educated along with L. Torquatus, the younger C. Marius, and M. Cicero. Soon after the breaking out of the civil war between Marius and Sulla, he resolved to take no part in the contest, and accordingly removed to Athens. During the remainder of his life, he kept aloof from all political affairs, and thus lived on the most intimate terms with the most distinguished men of all parties. He was equally the friend of Caesar and Pompey, of Brutus and Cassius, of Antony and Augustus; but his most intimate friend was Cicero, whose correspondence with him, beginning in 68 and continued down to Cicero's death, is one of the most valuable remains of antiquity. He purchased an estate at Buthrotum in Epirus, in which place, as well as at Athens and Rome, he spent the greater part of his time, engaged in literary pursuits and commercial undertakings. He died in 32, at the age of 77, of voluntary starvation, when he found that he was attacked by an incurable illness. His wife Pilia, to whom he was married in 56, when he was 53 years of age, bore him only one child, a daughter, Pomponia or Caecilia, whom Cicero sometimes calls Attica and Atticula. She was married in the life-time of her father to M. Vipsanius Agrippa. The sister of Atticus, Pomponia, was married to Q. Cicero, the brother of the orator. The life of Atticus by Cornelius Nepos is to be regarded rather as a panegyric upon an intimate friend, than strictly speaking a biography. In philosophy Atticus belonged to the Epicurean sect. He was thoroughly acquainted with the whole circle of Greek and Roman literature. So high an opinion was entertained of his taste and critical acumen, that many of his friends, especially Cicero, were accustomed to send him their works for revision and correction. None of his own writings have come down to us.

Attila ('Αττήλας or 'Αττίλας, German, *Etzel*, Hungarian, *Ethele*), king of the Huns, attained in A. D. 434, with his brother Bleda (in German *Blödel*), to the sovereignty of all the northern tribes between the frontier of Gaul and the frontier of China, and to the command of an army of at least 500,000 barbarians. He gradually concentrated upon himself the awe and fear of the whole ancient world, which ultimately expressed itself by affixing to his name the well-known epithet of " the Scourge of God." His career divides itself into two parts. The first (A. D. 445—450) consists of the ravage of the Eastern empire between the Euxine and the Adriatic and the negotiations with Theodosius II., which followed upon it. They were ended by a treaty which ceded to Attila a large territory S. of the Danube and an annual tribute. The second part of his career was the invasion of the Western empire (450—452). He crossed the Rhine at Strasburg, but was defeated at Chalons by Aëtius,

and Theodoric, king of the Visigoths, in 451. He then crossed the Alps, and took Aquileia in 452. after a siege of 3 months, but he did not attack Rome, in consequence, it is said, of his interview with Pope Leo the Great. He recrossed the Alps towards the end of the year, and died in 453, on the night of his marriage with a beautiful girl, variously named Hilda, Ildico, Mycolth, by the bursting of a blood-vessel. In person Attila was, like the Mongolian race in general, a short thickset man, of stately gait, with a large head, dark complexion, flat nose, thin beard, and bald with the exception of a few white hairs, his eyes small, but of great brilliancy and quickness.

Attilius. [ATILIUS.]

Attius. [ACCIUS.]

Attius or Attus Navius. [NAVIUS.]

Attius Tullius. [TULLIUS.]

Atūria ('Ατουρία). [ASSYRIA.]

Atūrus (*Adour*), a river in Aquitania, rises in the Pyrenees and flows through the territory of the Tarbelli into the ocean.

Atymnius ('Ατύμνιος or Ἄτυμνος), son of Zeus and Cassiopēa, a beautiful boy, beloved by Sarpedon. Others call him son of Phoenix.

Atys, Attys, Attes, Attis, or **Attin** (Ἄτυς, Ἄττυς, Ἄττης, Ἄττις, or Ἄττιν). 1. Son of Nana, and a beautiful shepherd of the Phrygian town, Celaenae. He was beloved by Cybele, but as he proved unfaithful to her, he was thrown by her into a state of madness, in which he unmanned himself. Cybele thereupon changed him into a fir-tree, which henceforth became sacred to her, and she commanded that, in future, her priests should be eunuchs. Such is the account in Ovid (*Fast.* iv. 221), but his story is related differently by other writers. Atys was worshipped in the temples of Cybele in common with this goddess. His worship appears to have been introduced into Greece at a comparatively late period. It is probable that the mythus of Atys represents the twofold character of nature, the male and female concentrated in one. — 2. Son of Manes, king of the Maeonians, from whose son Lydus, his son and successor, the Maeonians were afterwards called Lydians. — 3. A Latin chief, son of Alba, and father of Capys, from whom the Atia Gens derived its origin, and from whom Augustus was believed to be descended on his mother's side. — 4. Son of Croesus, slain by ADRASTUS.

Aufidēna (Aufidēnas, -ātis: *Alfidena*), a town in Samnium on the river Sagrus.

Aufidius. 1. Cn., a learned historian, celebrated by Cicero for the equanimity with which he bore blindness, was quaestor B. C. 119, tribunus plebis, 114, and finally praetor 108.— 2. T., a jurist, quaestor B. C. 86, and afterwards propraetor in Asia. — 3. Bassus. [BASSUS.] — 4. Lurco. [LURCO.] — 5. Orestes. [ORESTES.]

Aufidus (*Ofanto*), the principal river of Apulia, rises in the Apennines in the territory of the Hirpini in Samnium, flows at first with a rapid current (hence *violens* and *acer*, Hor. *Carm.* iii. 30. 10, *Sat.* i. 1. 58), and then more slowly (*stagna Aufida*, Sil. Ital. x. 171) into the Adriatic. Venusia, the birth-place of Horace, was on the Aufidus.

Augărus. [ACBARUS.]

Augē or Augia (Αὔγη or Αὐγεία), daughter of Aleus and Neaera, was a priestess of Athena, and mother by Hercules of TELEPHUS. She afterwards married Teuthras, king of the Mysians.

Augĕas or **Augĭas** (Αὐγέας or Αὐγείας), son of Phorbas or Helios (the Sun), and king of the Epeans in Elis. He had a herd of 3000 oxen, whose stalls had not been cleansed for 30 years. It was one of the labours imposed upon Hercules by Eurystheus to cleanse these stalls in one day. As a reward the hero was to receive the tenth part of the oxen ; but when he had accomplished his task by leading the rivers Alpheus and Peneus through the stables, Augeas refused to keep his promise. Hercules thereupon killed him and his sons, with the exception of Phyleus, who was placed on the throne of his father. Another tradition represents Augeas as dying a natural death at an advanced age, and as receiving heroic honours from Oxylus.

Augĭla (τὰ Αὔγιλα: *Aujilah*), an oasis in the Great Desert of Africa, about 3½° S. of Cyrene, and 10 days' journey W. of the Oasis of Ammon, abounding in date palms, to gather the fruit of which a tribe of the Nasamones, called Augïlae (Αὐγίλαι), resorted to the Oasis, which at other times was uninhabited.

Augurīnus, Genucĭus. 1. T., consul B. c. 451, and a member of the first decemvirate in the same year. — **2.** M., brother of the preceding, consul 445.

Augurīnus, Minucĭus. 1. M., consul B. c. 497 and 491. He took an active part in the defence of Coriolanus, who was brought to trial in 491, but was unable to obtain his acquittal. — **2.** L., consul 458, carried on war against the Aequians, and was surrounded by the enemy on Mt. Algidus, but was delivered by the dictator Cincinnatus. — **3.** L., was appointed praefect of the corn-market (*praefectus annonae*) 439, as the people were suffering from grievous famine. The ferment occasioned by the assassination of Sp. Maelius in this year was appeased by Augurinus, who is said to have gone over to the plebs from the patricians, and to have been chosen by the tribunes one of their body. Augurinus lowered the price of corn in 3 market days, fixing as the maximum an *as* for a modius. The people in their gratitude presented him with an ox having its horns gilt, and erected a statue to his honour outside the Porta Trigemina, for which every body subscribed an ounce of brass.

Augusta, the name of several towns founded or colonised by Augustus. **1.** A. **Asturĭca**. [ASTURES.] — **2.** A. **Emerīta** (*Merida*), in Lusitania on the Anas (*Guadiana*), colonised by Augustus with the veterans (emeriti) of the 5th and 10th legions, was a place of considerable importance. — **3.** A. **Firma**. [ASTIGI.] — **4.** A. **Praetorĭa** (*Aosta*), a town of the Salassi in Upper Italy, at the foot of the Graian and Pennine Alps, colonised by Augustus with soldiers of the praetorian cohorts. The modern town still contains many Roman remains : the most important of which are the town gates and a triumphal arch. — **5.** A. **Rauracorum** (*Augst*), the capital of the Rauraci, colonised by Munatius Plancus under Augustus, was on the left of the Rhine near the modern *Basle* : the ruins of a Roman amphitheatre are still to be seen. — **6.** A. **Suessonum** (*Soissons*), the capital of the Suessones in Gallia Belgica, probably the *Noviodūnum* of Caesar. — **7.** A. **Taurinorum** (*Turin*), more anciently called *Taurasia*, the capital of the Taurini on the Po, was an important town in the time of Hannibal, and was colonised by Augustus. — **8.** **Trevirorum**. [TREVIRI.] — **9.** **Tricastinorum**

(*Aouste*), the capital of the Tricastini in Gallia Narbonensis. — **10.** A. **Vindělicorum** (*Augsburg*), capital of Vindelicia or Rhaetia Secunda on the Licus (*Lech*), colonised by Drusus under Augustus, after the conquest of Rhaetia, about B. c. 14.

Augustīnus, Aurelĭus, usually called **St. Augustine**, the most illustrious of the Latin fathers, was born A. D. 354, at Tagaste, an inland town in Numidia. His mother was a sincere Christian, who exerted herself in training up her son in the practice of piety, but for a long time without effect. He studied rhetoric at Carthage, where he embraced the Manichaean heresy, to which he adhered for 9 years. He afterwards became a teacher of rhetoric at Carthage, but in 383 he went to Italy, and in Milan was led by the preaching and conversation of Ambrose to abandon his Manichaean errors and embrace Christianity. He was baptized by Ambrose in 387, and then returned to Africa, where he passed the next 3 years in seclusion, devoting himself to religious exercises. In 391 he was ordained a priest by Valerius, then bishop of Hippo, and in 395 he was ordained bishop of Hippo. His history, from the time of his elevation to the see of Hippo, is so closely implicated with the Donatistic and Pelagian controversies, that it would be impracticable to pursue its details within our limits. He died at Hippo in 430, when the city was besieged by the Vandals. Of his numerous works the 2 most interesting are : 1. His *Confessions*, in 13 books, written in 397, containing an account of his early life. 2. *De Civitate Dei*, in 22 books, commenced about 413, and not finished before 426. The first 10 books contain a refutation of the various systems of false religion, the last 12 present a systematic view of the true religion. — The best edition of the collected works of Augustine is the Benedictine, 11 vols. fol. Paris, 1679—1700.

Augustobŏna (*Troyes*), afterwards called *Tricassae*, the capital of the Tricasii or Tricasses in Gallia Lugdunensis.

Augustodūnum. [BIBRACTE.]
Augustonemětum. [ARVERNI.]
Augustorītum. [LEMOVICES.]

Augustus, the first Roman emperor, was born on the 23rd of September, B. c. 63, and was the son of C. Octavius by Atia, a daughter of Julia, the sister of C. Julius Caesar. His original name was C. Octavius, and, after his adoption by his great-uncle, C. Julius Caesar Octavianus, but for the sake of brevity we shall call him Augustus, though this was only a title given him by the senate and the people in 27, to express their veneration for him. Augustus lost his father at 4 years of age, but his education was conducted with great care by his grandmother Julia, and by his mother and step-father, L. Marcius Philippus, whom his mother married soon after his father's death. C. Julius Caesar, who had no male issue, also watched over his education with solicitude. He joined his uncle in Spain in 45, in the campaign against the sons of Pompey, and in the course of the same year was sent by Caesar to Apollonia in Illyricum, where some legions were stationed, that he might acquire a more thorough practical training in military affairs, and at the same time prosecute his studies. He was at Apollonia, when the news reached him of his uncle's murder at Rome in March 44, and he forthwith set out for Italy, accompanied by Agrippa and a few other friends.

On landing near Brundusium at the beginning of April, he heard that Caesar had adopted him in his testament and made him his heir. He now assumed the name of Caesar, and was so saluted by the troops. On reaching Rome about the beginning of May he demanded nothing but the private property which Caesar had left him, but declared that he was resolved to avenge the murder of his benefactor. The state of parties at Rome was most perplexing ; and one cannot but admire the extraordinary tact and prudence which Augustus displayed, and the skill with which a youth of barely 20 contrived to blind the most experienced statesmen in Rome, and eventually to carry all his designs into effect. Augustus had to contend against the republican party as well as against Antony ; for the latter foresaw that Augustus would stand in the way of his views, and had therefore attempted, though without success, to prevent Augustus from accepting the inheritance which his uncle had left him. Augustus, therefore, resolved to crush Antony first as the more dangerous of his two enemies, and accordingly made overtures to the republican party. These were so well received, especially when 2 legions went over to him, that the senate conferred upon him the title of praetor, and sent him with the 2 consuls of the year, C. Vibius Pansa and A. Hirtius, to attack Antony, who was besieging D. Brutus in Mutina. Antony was defeated and obliged to fly across the Alps ; and the death of the 2 consuls gave Augustus the command of all their troops. The senate now became alarmed, and determined to prevent Augustus from acquiring further power. But he soon showed that he did not intend to become the senate's servant. Supported by his troops he marched upon Rome and demanded the consulship, which the terrified senate was obliged to give him. He was elected to the office along with Q. Pedius, and the murderers of the dictator were outlawed. He now marched into the N. of Italy, professedly against Antony, who had been joined by Lepidus, and who was descending from the Alps along with the latter at the head of 17 legions. Augustus and Antony now became reconciled ; and it was agreed that the empire should be divided between Augustus, Antony, and Lepidus, under the title of *triumviri rei publicae constituendae*, and that this arrangement should last for the next 5 years. They published a *proscriptio* or list of all their enemies, whose lives were to be sacrificed and their property confiscated : upwards of 2000 equites and 300 senators were put to death, among whom was Cicero. Soon afterwards Augustus and Antony crossed over to Greece, and defeated Brutus and Cassius at the decisive battle of Philippi in 42, by which the hopes of the republican party were ruined. The triumvirs thereupon made a new division of the provinces. Lepidus obtained Africa, and Augustus returned to Italy to reward his veterans with the lands he had promised them. Here a new war awaited him (41), excited by Fulvia, the wife of Antony. She was supported by L. Antonius, the consul and brother of the triumvir, who threw himself into the fortified town of Perusia, which Augustus succeeded in taking in 40. Antony now made preparations for war, but the opportune death of Fulvia led to a reconciliation between the triumvirs, who concluded a peace at Brundusium. A new division of the provinces was again made : Augustus obtained all

the parts of the empire W. of the town of Scodra in Illyricum, and Antony the E. provinces, while Italy was to belong to them in common. Antony married Octavia, the sister of Augustus, in order to cement their alliance. In 39 Augustus concluded a peace with Sex. Pompey, whose fleet gave him the command of the sea, and enabled him to prevent corn from reaching Rome. But this peace was only transitory. As long as Pompey was independent, Augustus could not hope to obtain the dominion of the West, and he therefore eagerly availed himself of the pretext that Pompey allowed piracy to go on in the Mediterranean, for the purpose of declaring war against him. In 36 the contest came to a final issue. The fleet of Augustus, under the command of M. Agrippa, gained a decisive victory over that of Pompey, who abandoned Sicily and fled to Asia. Lepidus, who had landed in Sicily to support Augustus, was impatient of the subordinate part which he had hitherto played, and claimed the island for himself ; but he was easily subdued by Augustus, stripped of his power, and sent to Rome, where he resided for the remainder of his life, being allowed to retain the dignity of pontifex maximus. In 35 and 34 Augustus was engaged in war with the Illyrians and Dalmatians. Meantime, Antony had repudiated Octavia, and had alienated the minds of the Roman people by his arbitrary and arrogant proceedings in the East. Augustus found that the Romans were quite prepared to desert his rival, and accordingly in 32 the senate declared war against Cleopatra, for Antony was looked upon only as her infatuated slave. The remainder of the year was occupied by preparations for war on both sides. In the spring of 31 Augustus passed over to Epirus, and in September in the same year his fleet gained a brilliant victory over Antony's near the promontory of Actium in Acarnania. In the following year (30) Augustus sailed to Egypt. Antony and Cleopatra, who had escaped in safety from Actium, put an end to their lives to avoid falling into the hands of the conqueror ; and Augustus now became the undisputed master of the Roman world. He returned to Rome in 29, and after restoring order in all parts of the government he proposed in the senate to lay down his powers, but pretended to be prevailed upon to remain at the head of affairs for 10 years longer. This plan was afterwards repeated several times, and he apparently allowed himself to be always persuaded to retain his power either for 10 or 5 years more. He declined all honours and distinctions which were calculated to remind the Romans of kingly power ; but he accepted in 33 the *imperium proconsulare* and the *tribunitia potestas* for life, by which his inviolability was legally established, while by the imperium proconsulare he became the highest authority in all the Roman provinces. On the death of Lepidus in 12 he became pontifex maximus ; but though he had thus united in his own person all the great offices of state, yet he was too prudent to show to the Romans by any display of authority that he was the sole master. He had no ministers, in our sense of the word ; but on state matters, which he did not choose to be discussed in public, he consulted his personal friends, C. Cilnius Maecenas, M. Vipsanius Agrippa, M. Valerius Messalla Corvinus, and Asinius Pollio. The people retained their republican privileges, though they were mere forms : they still met in their assemblies, and elected consuls and other magistrates ; but only such persons were elected as had been proposed or recommended by the emperor. The almost uninterrupted festivities, games, distributions of corn, and the like, made the people forget the substance of their republican freedom, and obey contentedly their new ruler. The wars of Augustus were not aggressive, but were chiefly undertaken to protect the frontiers of the Roman dominions. Most of them were carried on by his relations and friends, but he conducted some of them in person. Thus, in 27, he attacked the warlike Cantabri and Astures in Spain, whose subjugation, however, was not completed till 19 by Agrippa. In 21 Augustus travelled through Sicily and Greece, and spent the winter following at Samos. Next year (20) he went to Syria, where he received from Phraätes, the Parthian monarch, the standards and prisoners which had been taken from Crassus and Antony. In 16 the Romans suffered a defeat on the Lower Rhine by some German tribes ; whereupon Augustus went himself to Gaul, and spent 4 years there, to regulate the government of that province, and to make the necessary preparations for defending it against the Germans. In 9 he again went to Gaul, where he received German ambassadors, who sued for peace ; and from this time forward, he does not appear to have again taken any active part in the wars that were carried on. Those in Germany were the most formidable, and lasted longer than the reign of Augustus. He died at Nola, on the 29th of August, A. D. 14, at the age of 76. Augustus was first married, though only nominally, to Clodia, a daughter of Clodius and Fulvia. His 2nd wife, Scribonia, bore him his only daughter, Julia. His 3rd wife was Livia Drusilla, the wife of Tiberius Nero. Augustus had at first fixed on M. Marcellus as his successor, the son of his sister Octavia, who was married to his daughter Julia. After his death Julia was married to Agrippa, and her 2 sons, Caius and Lucius Caesar, were now destined by Augustus as his successors. On the death of these 2 youths, Augustus was persuaded to adopt Tiberius, the son of Livia, and to make him his colleague and successor. [TIBERIUS.]

Augustŭlus, Romŭlus, last Roman emperor of the West, was placed upon the throne by his father Orestes (A. D. 475), after the latter had deposed the emperor Julius Nepos. In 476 Orestes was defeated by Odoacer and put to death: Romulus Augustulus was allowed to live, but was deprived of the sovereignty.

Aulerci, a powerful Gallic people dwelling between the Sequana (*Seine*) and the Liger (*Loire*), were divided into 3 great tribes. 1. **A. Eburovices**, near the coast on the left bank of the Seine in the modern Normandy : their capital was Mediolanum, afterwards called Eburovices (*Evreux*). —2. **A. Cenomăni**, S.W. of the preceding near the Liger : their capital was Subdinnum (*le Mans*). At an early period some of the Cenomani crossed the Alps and settled in Upper Italy.—3. **A. Brannovices**, E. of the Cenomani near the Aedui, whose clients they were. The *Diablintes* mentioned by Caesar are said by Ptolemy to have been likewise a branch of the Aulerci.

Aulis (Αὐλίς), a harbour in Boeotia on the Euripus, where the Greek fleet assembled before sailing against Troy : it had a temple of Artemis.

Aulon (Αὐλών: Αὐλωνίτης). 1. A district and town on the borders of Elis and Messenia, with a temple of Aesculapius, who hence had the surname *Aulonius.* —2. A town in Chalcidice in Macedonia, on the Strymonic gulf.— 3. (*Melone*), a fertile valley near Tarentum celebrated for its wine (*amicus Aulon fertili Baccho*, Hor. *Carm.* ii. 6. 18).

Auranitis (Αὐρανῖτις : *Hauran*), a district S. of Damascus and E. of Ituraea and Batanaea, on the E. side of the Jordan, belonging either to Palestine or to Arabia.

Aurĕa Chersonĕsus (ἡ Χρυσῆ Χερσόνησος), the name given by the late geographers to the *Malay Peninsula*. They also mention an Aurea Regio beyond the Ganges, which is supposed to be the country round *Ava.*

Aurĕlĭa, the wife of C. Julius Caesar, by whom she became the mother of C. Julius Caesar, the dictator, and of 2 daughters. She carefully watched over the education of her children, and always took a lively interest in the success of her son. She died in B. C. 54, while Caesar was in Gaul.

Aurĕlĭa Gens, plebeian, of which the most important members are given under their family names, COTTA, ORESTES, and SCAURUS.

Aurĕlĭa Orestilla, a beautiful but profligate woman, whom Catiline married. As Aurelia at first objected to marry him, because he had a grown-up son by a former marriage, Catiline is said to have killed his own offspring in order to remove this impediment to their union.

Aurĕlĭa Via, the great coast road from Rome to Transalpine Gaul, at first extended no further than *Pisae*, but was afterwards continued along the coast to *Genua* and *Forum Julii* in Gaul.

Aureliāni. [GENABUM.]

Aurĕlĭānus, Roman emperor, A. D. 270—275, was born about A. D. 212, at Sirmium in Pannonia. He entered the army as a common soldier, and by his extraordinary bravery was raised to offices of trust and honour by Valerian and Claudius II. On the death of the latter, he was elected emperor by the legions at Sirmium. His reign presents a succession of brilliant exploits, which restored for a while their ancient lustre to the arms of Rome. He first defeated the Goths and Vandals, who had crossed the Danube, and were ravaging Pannonia. He next gained a great victory over the Alemanni and other German tribes ; but they succeeded notwithstanding in crossing the Alps. Near Placentia they defeated the Romans, but were eventually overcome by Aurelian in two decisive engagements in Umbria. After crushing a formidable conspiracy at Rome, Aurelian next turned his arms against Zenobia, queen of Palmyra, whom he defeated, took prisoner, and carried with him to Rome. [ZENOBIA.] On his return to Italy he marched to Alexandria and put Firmus to death, who had assumed the title of emperor. He then proceeded to the West, where Gaul, Britain, and Spain were still in the hands of Tetricus, who had been declared emperor a short time before the death of Gallienus. Tetricus surrendered to Aurelian in a battle fought near Chalons. [TETRICUS.] The emperor now devoted his attention to domestic improvements and reforms. Many works of public utility were commenced : the most important of all was the erection of a new line of strongly fortified walls, embracing a much more ample circuit than the old ones, which had long since fallen into ruin ; but this vast plan was not completed until the reign of Probus. After a short residence in the city, Aurelian visited the provinces on the Danube. He now entirely abandoned Dacia, which had been first conquered by Trajan, and made the S. bank of the Danube, as in the time of Augustus, the boundary of the empire. A large force was now collected in Thrace in preparation for an expedition against the Persians ; but while the emperor was on the march between Heraclea and Byzantium, he was killed by some of his officers. They had been induced to conspire against him by a certain Mnestheus, the freedman of the emperor and his private secretary, who had betrayed his trust, and fearful of punishment, had, by means of forged documents, organised the conspiracy.

Aurēliānus, Caelius or Coelius, a very celebrated Latin physician, was a native of Numidia, and probably lived in the 4th century after Christ. Of his writings we possess 3 books *On Acute Diseases* " Celerum Passionum," (or " De Morbis Acutis,") and 5 books *On Chronic Diseases,* " Tardarum Passionum " (or " De Morbis Chronicis"). Edited by Amman, Amstel. 1709.

M. Aurēlius Antōnīnus, Roman emperor, A. D. 161—180, commonly called " the philosopher," was born at Rome on the 20th of April, A. D. 121. He was adopted by Antoninus Pius immediately after the latter had been himself adopted by Hadrian, received the title of Caesar, and married Faustina, the daughter of Pius (138). On the death of the latter in 161, he succeeded to the throne, but he admitted to an equal share of the sovereign power L. Ceionius Commodus, who had been adopted by Pius at the same time as Marcus himself. The two emperors henceforward bore respectively the names of M. Aurelius Antoninus and L. Aurelius Verus. Soon after their accession Verus was despatched to the East, and for 4 years (A. D. 162—165) carried on war with great success against Vologeses III., king of Parthia, over whom his lieutenants, especially Avidius Cassius, gained many victories. At the conclusion of the war both emperors triumphed, and assumed the titles of *Armeniacus, Parthicus Maximus,* and *Medicus.* Meantime Italy was threatened by the numerous tribes dwelling along the northern limits of the empire, from the sources of the Danube to the Illyrian border. Both emperors set out to encounter the foe ; and the contest with the northern nations was continued with varying success during the whole life of M. Aurelius, whose head-quarters were generally fixed in Pannonia. After the death of Verus in 169, Aurelius prosecuted the war against the Marcomanni with great success, and in consequence of his victories over them he assumed in 172 the title of Germanicus, which he also conferred upon his son Commodus. In 174 he gained a decisive victory over the Quadi, mainly through a violent storm, which threw the barbarians into confusion. This storm is said to have been owing to the prayers of a legion chiefly composed of Christians. It has given rise to a famous controversy among the historians of Christianity upon what is commonly termed the Miracle of the Thundering Legion. The Marcomanni and the other northern barbarians concluded a peace with Aurelius in 175, who forthwith set out for the East, where Avidius Cassius, urged on by Faustina, the unworthy wife of Aurelius, had risen in rebellion and proclaimed himself emperor. But before Aurelius reached the East, Cassius had been slain by his own officers. On his arrival in the East, Aurelius

acted with the greatest clemency ; none of the accomplices of Cassius were put to death, and to establish perfect confidence in all, he ordered the papers of Cassius to be destroyed without suffering them to be read. During this expedition, Faustina, who had accompanied her husband, died, according to some by her own hands. Aurelius returned to Rome towards the end of 176 ; but in 178 he set out again for Germany, where the Marcomanni and their confederates had again renewed the war. He gained several victories over them, but died in the middle of the war on March 17th, 180, in Pannonia, either at Vindobona (*Vienna*) or at Sirmium, in the 59th year of his age and 20th of his reign. — The leading feature in the character of M. Aurelius was his devotion to philosophy and literature. When only 12 years old, he adopted the dress and practised the austerities of the Stoics, and he continued throughout his life a warm adherent and a bright ornament of the Stoic philosophy. We still possess a work by M. Aurelius, written in the Greek language, and entitled Τὰ εἰς ἑαυτὸν, or *Meditations,* in 12 books. It is a sort of common-place book, in which were registered from time to time the thoughts and feelings of the author upon moral and religious topics, without an attempt at order or arrangement. No remains of antiquity present a nobler view of philosophical heathenism. The best edition of the Meditations is by Gataker, Cantab. 1652. and Lond. 1697. — The chief and perhaps the only stain upon the memory of Aurelius is his 2 persecutions of the Christians ; in the former of which, 166, the martyrdom of Polycarp occurred, and in the latter, 177, that of Irenaeus. — Aurelius was succeeded by his son Commodus.

Aurēlius Victor. [VICTOR.]

Aurĕŏlus, one of the *Thirty Tyrants* (A. D. 260 —267), who assumed the title of Augustus during the feeble rule of Gallienus. Aureolus was proclaimed emperor by the legions of Illyria in 267, and made himself master of N. Italy, but he was defeated and slain in battle in 268, by Claudius II., the successor of Gallienus.

Aurōra. [EOS.]

Aurunci. [ITALIA.]

Auruncŭleius Cotta. [COTTA.]

Ausa. [AUSETANI.]

Ausci or Auscii, a powerful people in Aquitania, who possessed the Latin franchise : their capital was called Climberrum or Elimberrum, also Augusta and Ausci (now *Auch*).

Ausētāni, a Spanish people in the modern Catalonia : their capital was Ausa (*Vique*).

Auson (Αὔσων), son of Ulysses and Calypso or Circe, from whom the country of the Auruncans was believed to have been called Ausonia.

Ausŏnes, Ausōnĭa. [ITALIA.]

Ausōnĭus, Decĭmus Magnus, a Roman poet, born at Burdigāla (*Bourdeaux*), about A. D. 310, taught grammar and rhetoric with such reputation at his native town, that he was appointed tutor of Gratian, son of the emperor Valentinian, and was afterwards raised to the highest honours of the state. He was appointed by Gratian praefectus of Latium, of Libya, and of Gaul, and in 379 was elevated to the consulship. After the death of Gratian, in 383, he retired from public life, and ended his days in a country retreat near Bourdeaux, perhaps about 390. It is most probable that he was a Christian and not a heathen. His extant works are — 1. *Epigrammatum Liber*, a collection of 150 epigrams. 2. *Ephemeris*, containing an account of the business and proceedings of a day. 3. *Parentalia*, a series of short poems addressed to friends and relations on their decease. 4. *Professores*, notices of the Professors of Bourdeaux. 5. *Epitaphia Heroum*, epitaphs on the heroes who fell in the Trojan war and a few others. 6. A metrical catalogue of the first 12 Caesars. 7. *Tetrasticha*, on the Caesars from Julius to Elagabalus. 8. *Clarae Urbes*, the praises of 14 illustrious cities. 9. *Ludus Septem Sapientum*, the doctrines of the 7 sages expounded by each in his own person. 10. *Idyllia*, a collection of 20 poems. 11. *Eclogarium*, short poems connected with the Calendar, &c. 12. *Epistolae*, 25 letters, some in verse and some in prose. 13. *Gratiarum Actio pro Consulatu*, in prose, addressed to Gratian. 14. *Periochae*, short arguments to each book of the Iliad and Odyssey. 15. *Tres Praefatiunculae.* — Of these works the Idyls have attracted most notice, and of them the most pleasing is the *Mosella*, or a description of the river Moselle. Ausonius possesses skill in versification, but is destitute of all the higher attributes of a poet. The best edition of his complete works is by Tollius, Amstel. 1671.

Auster, called *Notus* (Νότος) by the Greeks, the S. wind or strictly the S.W. wind, is personified as the god of the S. wind, son of Astraeus and Eos. It frequently brought with it fogs and rain; but at certain seasons of the year it was a dry sultry wind (hence called *plumbeus Auster*, Hor. *Sat.* ii. 6. 18), injurious both to man and to vegetation, the *Sirocco* of the modern Italians.

Autariātae (Αὐταριᾶται), an Illyrian people in the Dalmatian mountains, extinct in Strabo's time.

Autesiodŏrum, -ūrum (*Auxerre*), a town of the Senones in Gallia Lugdunensis.

Autĕsĭon (Αὐτεσίων), son of Tisamenus, father of Theras and Argia, left Thebes at the command of an oracle, and joined the Dorians in Peloponnesus.

Autochthŏnes (αὐτόχθονες). [ABORIGINES.]

Autŏlŏles, or -ae (Αὐτολόλαι), a Gaetulian tribe on the W. coast of Africa, S. of the Atlas mountains.

Autŏlўcus (Αὐτόλυκος). 1. Son of Hermes and Chione, father of Anticlĕa, and thus maternal grandfather of Ulysses. He lived on mount Parnassus, and was renowned for his cunning and robberies. Ulysses, when staying with him on one occasion, was wounded by a boar on Parnassus, and it was by the scar of this wound that he was recognized by his aged nurse, when he returned from Troy. — 2. A Thessalian, son of Deïmachus, one of the Argonauts, and the founder of Sinope.— 3. A mathematician of Pitane in Aeolis, lived about B. c. 340, and wrote 2 astronomical treatises, which are the most ancient existing specimens of the Greek mathematics 1. *On the Motion of the Sphere* (περὶ κινουμένης σφαίρας). 2. *On the risings and settings of the fixed stars* (περὶ ἐπιτολῶν καὶ δύσεων). Edited by Dasypodius in his *Sphaericae Doctrinae Propositiones*, Argent. 1572.

Autŏmăla (τὰ Αὐτόμαλα), a fortified place on the Great Syrtis in N. Africa.

Autŏmĕdon (Αὐτομέδων). 1. Son of Diores, the charioteer and companion of Achilles, and, after the death of the latter, the companion of his son Pyrrhus. Hence Automedon is the name of any skilful charioteer. (Cic. *pro Rosc. Am.* 35;

Juv. i. 61.) — 2. Of Cyzicus, a Greek poet, 12 of whose epigrams are in the Greek Anthology, lived in the reign of Nerva, A. D. 96—98.

Automŏli (Αὐτόμολοι), as a proper name, was applied to the Egyptian soldiers, who were said to have deserted from Psammetichus into Aethiopia, where they founded the kingdom of MEROË.

Autŏnŏë (Αὐτονόη), daughter of Cadmus and Harmonia, wife of Aristaeus, and mother of Actaeon. With her sister Agave, she tore Pentheus to pieces in their Bacchic fury: her tomb was shown in the territory of Megara.

Autrigŏnes, a people in Hispania Tarraconensis between the ocean (Bay of Biscay) and the upper course of the Iberus: their chief town was FLAVIOBRIGA.

Autronius Paetus. [PAETUS.]

Auxĕsĭa (Αὐξησία), the goddess who grants growth and prosperity to the fields, honoured at Troezen and Epidaurus, was another name for Persephone. Damia, who was honoured along with Auxesia at Epidaurus and Troezen, was only another name for Demeter.

Auxĭmum (Auximas, -ătis: *Osimo*), an important town of Picenum in Italy, and a Roman colony.

Auxūme or **Ax-** (Αὐξούμη, or Ἀξώμη, and other forms: Αὐξουμῖται, or Ἀξωμῖται, &c.: *Axum*, Ru. S.W. of *Adowa*), the capital of a powerful kingdom in Ethiopia, to the S. E. of Meroë, in *Habesh* or *Abyssinia*, which either first arose or first became known to the Greeks and Romans in the early part of the 2nd century of our aera. It grew upon the decline of the kingdom of Meroë, and extended beyond the *Straits of Bab-el-Mandeb* into Arabia. Being a mountainous region, watered by the numerous upper streams of the Astaboras and Astapus, and intersected by the caravan routes from the interior of Africa to the Red Sea and the Gulf of Bab-el-Mandeb, the country possessed great internal resources and a flourishing commerce.

Auzĕa, or -ia, or **Audia** (*Sur-Guzlan* or *Hamza*, Ru.), a city in the interior of Mauretania Caesariensis; a Roman colony under M. Aurelius Antoninus.

Avālĭtes (Αὐαλίτης: *Zeilah*), an emporium in S. Aethiopia, on a bay of the Erythraean Sea, called Avālĭtes Sĭnus (Ἀ. κόλπος), probably the *Gulf of Bab-el-Mandeb*, or its innermost part, S. of the Straits. A people, Avalitae, are also mentioned in these parts.

Avarĭcum. [BITURIGES.]

Avella. [ABELLA.]

Avenĭo (*Avignon*), a town of the Cavares in Gallia Narbonensis on the left bank of the Rhone.

Aventĭcum (*Avenches*), the chief town of the Helvetii, and subsequently a Roman colony with the name *Pia Flavia Constans Emerita*, of which ruins are still to be seen in the modern town.

Aventinensis, Genucĭus. 1. L., consul B. c. 365, and again 362, was killed in battle against the Hernicans in the latter of these years, and his army routed. — **2.** Cn., consul 363.

Aventīnus, son of Hercules and the priestess Rhea.

Aventīnus Mons. [ROMA.]

Avernus Lacus (ἡ Ἄορνος λίμνη: *Lago Averno*), a lake close to the promontory which runs out into the sea between Cumae and Puteoli. This lake fills the crater of an extinct volcano; it is circular, about 1½ mile in circumference, is very deep,

Athena (Minerva). (From the Museum
at Florence.) Pages 101, 102.

Artemis (Diana), the Huntress.
(Museum Capitolinum, vol. 4, tav. 37.) Pages 93, 94.

Artemis (Diana), goddess of the Moon.
(Gorii, Mus. Flor., vol. 2, tav. 88.) Pages 93, 94.

Athena (Minerva). (From the Museum
at Dresden.) Pages 101, 102.

[To face p. 112.

Athena (Minerva).
(From a Statue in the possession of Mr. Hope.) Pages 101, 102.

Athena (Minerva).
(Aegina Marbles). Pages 101, 102.

Athena (Minerva).
(From the Museum at Naples.) Pages 101, 102.

Atlas.
(From the Farnese Collection now at Naples.) Page 105.

To face p. 113.]

and is surrounded by high banks, which in antiquity were covered by a gloomy forest sacred to Hecate. From its waters mephitic vapours arose, which are said to have killed the birds that attempted to fly over it, from which circumstance its Greek name was supposed to be derived (from *a* priv. and ὄρνις). The lake was celebrated in mythology on account of its connection with the lower world. On its banks dwelt the Cimmerians in constant darkness, and near it was the cave of the Cumaean Sibyl, through which Aeneas descended to the lower world. Agrippa, in the time of Augustus, cut down the forest which surrounded the lake, and connected the latter with the Lucrine lake ; he also caused a tunnel to be made from the lake to Cumae, of which a considerable part remains and is known under the name of *Grotta di Sibylla.* The Lucrine lake was filled up by an eruption in 1530, so that Avernus is again a separate lake.

Aviānus, Flavius, the author of 42 Aesopic fables in Latin elegiac verse, which are of very little merit both as respects the matter and the style. The date of Avianus is uncertain ; he probably lived in the 3rd or 4th century of the Christian aera.—*Editions.* By Cannegieter, Amstel. 1731 ; by Nodell, Amstel. 1787 ; and by Lachmann, Berol. 1845.

Aviānus, Rufus Festus, a Latin poet towards the end of the 4th century of the Christian aera. His poems are chiefly descriptive, and are some of the best specimens of the poetry of that age. His works are :—1. *Descriptio Orbis Terrae,* also called *Metaphrasis Periegeseos Dionysii,* in 1394 hexameter lines, derived directly from the περιήγησις of Dionysius, and containing a succinct account of the most remarkable objects in the physical and political geography of the known world.— 2. *Ora Maritima,* a fragment in 703 Iambic trimeters, describing the shores of the Mediterranean from Marseilles to Cadiz. — 3. *Aratea Phaenomena,* and *Aratea Prognostica,* both in Hexameter verse, the first containing 1325, the second 552 lines, being a paraphrase of the two works of Aratus. The poems are edited by Wernsdorf, in his *Poetae Latini Minores,* vol. v. pt. ii., which, however, does not include the Aratea.

Aviōnes, a people in the N. of Germany, whose position is uncertain.

Avitus, Alphius, a Latin poet under Augustus and Tiberius, the fragments of some of whose poems are preserved in the *Anthologia Latina.*

Avitus, Cluentius. [CLUENTIUS.]

Avitus, M. Maecilius, emperor of the West, was raised to the throne by the assistance of Theodoric II. king of the Visigoths in A. D. 455 ; but, after a year's reign, was deposed by Ricimer.

Axēnus. [EUXINUS PONTUS.]

Axia (*Castell d' Asso*), a fortress in the territory of Tarquinii in Etruria.

Axion ('Αξίων), son of Phegeus, brother of Temenus, along with whom he killed Alcmaeon.

Axiothēa ('Αξιοθέα), a maiden of Phlius, who came to Athens, and putting on male attire, was for some time a hearer of Plato, and afterwards of Speusippus.

Axius, Q., an intimate friend of Cicero and Varro, one of the speakers in the 3d book of Varro's *De Re Rustica.*

Axius ("Αξιος: *Wardar* or *Vardhari*), the chief river in Macedonia, rises in Mt Scordus, re-

ceives many affluents, of which the most important is the Erigon, and flows S.E. through Macedonia into the Thermaic gulf. As a river-god, Axius begot by Periboea a son Pelegon, the father of ASTEROPAEUS.

Axōna (*Aisne*), a river in Gallia Belgica, which falls into the Isara (*Oise*).

Axūme. [AUXUME.]

Azan ('Αζάν), son of Arcas and the nymph Erato, brother of Aphidas and Elatus. The part of Arcadia which he received from his father was called *Azania :* it was on the borders of Elis.

Azāni ('Αζανοί: 'Αζανίτης), a town of Phrygia, on the river Rhyndacus, and 20 miles S.W. of Cotyaeium (*Kiutayah*). The ruins of columns, capitals, and other architectural fragments are scattered over the ground. There are also the remains of a splendid temple, and of a theatre. This ancient site was discovered by Mr. Keppel.

Azanīa or **Barbarīa** ('Αζανία, Βαρβαρία: *Ajan*), the region on the E. coast of Africa, S. of Aromata Pr. (C. Guardafui), as far as Rhaptum Pr. (C. Formosa ?)

Azēnīa ('Αζηνία: 'Αζηνιεύς), a demus in the S.W. of Attica, near Sunium, belonging to the tribe Hippothoontis.

Azeus ('Αζεύς), son of Clymenus of Orchomenos, brother of Erginus, Stratius, Arrhon, and Pyleus, father of Actor and grandfather of Astyoche.

Azōrus or **Azōrium** ("Αζωρος, 'Αζώριον : 'Αζωρίτης, 'Αζωριδάτης, 'Αζωρεύς), a town in the N. of Thessaly, on the W. slope of Olympus, formed, with Doliche and Pythium, the Perrhaebian Tripolis.

Azōtus ("Αζωτος: 'Αζώτιος: *Ashdod* or *Ashdoud*), a city of Palestine, near the sea-coast, 9 miles N.E. of Ascalon. It was one of the free cities of the Philistines, which were included within the portion of the tribe of Judah.

B.

Babrius (Βάβριος), a Greek poet, probably in the time of Augustus, turned the fables of Aesop into verse, of which only a few fragments were known, till within the last few years, when a manuscript containing 123 fables was discovered on Mount Athos. Edited by Lachmann, Berol. 1845 ; by Orelli and Baiter, Turic. 1845 ; by Lewis, Lond. 1847.

Babylon (Βαβυλών: Βαβυλώνιος, fem. Βαβυλωνίς : Babel in O. T. : Ru. at and around *Hillah*), one of the oldest and greatest cities of the ancient world, the capital of a great empire, was built on both banks of the river Euphrates, in about 32° 28' N. lat. Its foundation, and the establishment of a kingdom by Nimrod, with the city for a capital, are among the first recorded facts subsequent to the Deluge (*Gen.* x. 9, 10, xi.)—9). Secular history ascribes its origin to Belus (i. e. the god Baal), and its enlargement and decoration to Ninus or his wife Semiramis ; or, according to another tradition, the country was subdued by Ninus, and the city was subsequently built by Semiramis, who made it the capital of the Assyrian empire. At all events it is pretty clear that Babylon was subject to the Assyrian kings of Nineveh from a very early period ; and the time at which the governors of Babylon first succeeded in making themselves virtually independent, cannot be determined with any certainty until we know more of the history of the early Assyrian dynasties. [Comp. NABO-NASSAR.] The Babylonian empire begins with the reign of Nabopolassar, the father of Nebuchadnezzar, who, with the aid of the Median king Cyaxares, overthrew the Assyrian monarchy, and destroyed Nineveh (B. C. 606), and soon afterwards defended his kingdom against the aggressions (at first successful) of Necho, king of Egypt, in the battle of Circesium, B. C. 604. Under his son and successor, Nebuchadnezzar (B. C. 604—562), the Babylonian empire reached its height, and extended from the Euphrates to Egypt, and from the mountains of Armenia to the deserts of Arabia. After his death it again declined, until it was overthrown by the capture of Babylon by the Medes and Persians under Cyrus (B. C. 538), who made the city one of the capitals of the Persian empire, the others being Susa and Ecbatana. Under his successors the city rapidly sank. Darius I. dismantled its fortifications, in consequence of a revolt of its inhabitants ; Xerxes carried off the golden statue of Belus, and the temple in which it stood became a ruin. After the death of Alexander, Babylon became a part of the Syrian kingdom of Seleucus Nicator, who contributed to its decline by the foundation of SELEUCIA on the Tigris, which soon eclipsed it. At the commencement of our era, the greater part of the city was in ruins ; and at the present day all its *visible* remains consist of mounds of earth, ruined masses of brick walls, and a few scattered fragments. Its very site has been turned into a dreary marsh by repeated inundations from the river. — The city of Babylon had reached the summit of its magnificence in the reign of Nebuchadnezzar. It formed a square, each side of which was 120 stadia (12 geog. miles) in length. The walls, of burnt brick, were 200 cubits high and 50 thick ; in them were 250 towers and 60 bronze gates ; and they were surrounded by a deep ditch. The Euphrates, which divided the city into 2 equal parts, was embanked with walls of brick, the openings of which at the ends of the transverse streets were closed by gates of bronze. A bridge, built on piers of hewn stone, united the 2 quarters of the city ; and at each end of it stood a royal palace: these erections were ascribed to Semiramis. Of two other public buildings of the greatest celebrity, the one was the temple of Belus, rising to a great height, and consisting of 8 stories, gradually diminishing in width, and ascended by a flight of steps, which wound round the whole building on the outside ; in the uppermost story was the golden statue of Belus, with a golden altar and other treasures: this building also was ascribed to Semiramis. The other edifice referred to was the "hanging gardens" of Nebuchadnezzar, laid out upon terraces which were raised above one another on arches. The houses of the city were 3 or 4 stories in height, and the streets were straight, intersecting one another at right angles. The buildings were almost universally constructed of bricks, some burnt and some only sun-dried, cemented together with hot bitumen and in some cases with mortar. — The Babylonians were certainly a Semitic race ; but the ruling class, to which the kings and priests and the men of learning belonged, were the Chaldaeans, whose origin and affinities are somewhat doubtful ; the most probable opinion, however, is that they were a tribe of invaders, who descended from the mountains on the borders of Armenia,

and conquered the Babylonians. — The religion of the Chaldaeans was Sabaeism, or the worship of the heavenly bodies, not purely so, but symbolized in the forms of idols, besides whom they had other divinities, representing the powers of nature. The priests formed a caste, and cultivated science, especially astronomy ; in which they knew the apparent motions of the sun, moon, and 5 of the planets, the calculation of eclipses of the moon, the division of the zodiac into 12 constellations, and of the year into 12 months, and the measurement of time by the sun-dial. They must also have had other instruments for measuring time, such as the water-clock, for instance ; and it is highly probable that the definite methods of determining such quantities, which the Chaldaean astronomers invented, were the origin of the systems of weights and measures used by the Greeks and Romans. Their buildings prove their knowledge of mechanics ; and their remains, slight as they are, show considerable progress in the fine arts. — The Babylonian government was an unlimited monarchy : the king appears to have lived in almost total seclusion from his people, surrounded by his court ; and the provinces were administered by governors, like the Persian satraps, responsible only to the monarch, whose commands they obeyed or defied according to his strength or weakness. — The position of the city on the lower course of the Euphrates, by which it was connected with the Persian Gulf, and at the meeting of natural routes between E. Asia and India on the one side, and Europe, Asia Minor, Syria, Egypt, and Arabia, on the other, made it the seat of a flourishing commerce and of immense wealth and luxury. — The district around the city, bounded by the Tigris on the E., Mesopotamia on the N., the Arabian Desert on the W., and extending to the head of the Persian Gulf on the S., was known in later times by the name of **Babylonia** (*Irak Arabi*), sometimes also called Chaldaea. [But comp. CHALDAEA.] This district was a plain, subject to continual inundations from the Tigris and Euphrates, which were regulated by canals, the chief of which was the Naarmalcha, i. e. *Royal River* or *Canal* (ποταμὸς βασίλειος, διῶρυξ βασιλική, flumen regium), which extended from the Tigris at Seleucia due W. to the Euphrates, and was navigable. The country was fertile, but deficient in trees.

Babylon (Βαβυλών: nr. *Fostat* or *Old Cairo*), a fortress in Lower Egypt, on the right bank of the Nile, exactly opposite to the pyramids, and at the beginning of the canal which connected the Nile with the Red Sea. Its origin was ascribed by tradition to a body of Babylonian deserters. It first became an important place under the Romans. Augustus made it the station of one of the 3 Egyptian legions.

Babylonia. [BABYLON.]

Bacchae (Βάκχαι), also called *Maenades* and *Thyiades*. 1. The female companions of Dionysus or Bacchus in his wanderings through the East, are represented as crowned with vine-leaves, clothed with fawn-skins, and carrying in their hands the *thyrsus* (see *Dict. of Ant. s. v.*). — **2.** Priestesses of Dionysus, who by wine and other exciting causes worked themselves up to frenzy at the Dionysiac festivals.

Bacchiadae (Βακχιάδαι), an Heraclid clan, derived their name from Bacchis, king of Corinth, and retained the supreme rule in that state, first under a monarchical form of government, and next as a close oligarchy, till their deposition by Cypselus, about B. C. 657. They were for the most part driven into banishment, and are said to have taken refuge in different parts of Greece and even Italy.

Bacchius (Βακχεῖος). 1. The author of a short musical treatise called εἰσαγωγὴ τέχνης μουσικῆς, printed by Meibomius, in the *Antiquae Musicae Auctores Septem*, Amst. 1652. — 2. Of Tanagra in Boeotia, one of the earliest commentators on the writings of Hippocrates: his writings have perished. — 3. Of Miletus, the author of a work on agriculture.

Bacchus. [DIONYSUS.]

Bacchylides (Βακχυλίδης), one of the great lyric poets of Greece, born at Iulis in Ceos, and nephew as well as fellow-townsman of Simonides. He flourished about B. C. 470, and lived a long time at the court of Hiero in Syracuse, together with Simonides and Pindar. He wrote in the Doric dialect Hymns, Paeans, Dithyrambs, &c.; but all his poems have perished, with the exception of a few fragments, and 2 epigrams in the Greek Anthology. The fragments have been published by Neue, *Bacchylidis Cei Fragmenta*, Berol. 1823, and by Bergk, *Poëtae Lyrici Graeci*, p. 820.

Bacenis Silva, a forest which separated the Suevi from the Cherusci, probably the W. part of the Thuringian Forest.

Bacis (Βάκις), the name of several prophets, of whom the most celebrated was the Boeotian seer, who delivered his oracles in hexameter verse at Heleon in Boeotia. In later times there existed a collection of his oracles, similar to the Sibylline books at Rome.

Bactra or **Zariaspa** (τὰ Βάκτρα, τὰ Ζαρίασπα and ἡ Ζαρί 'σπη : *Balkh*), the capital of BACTRIA, appears to have been founded by the early Persian kings, but not to have been a considerable city till the time of Alexander, who settled in it his Greek mercenaries and his disabled Macedonian soldiers. It stood at the N. foot of the M. Paropamisus (the *Hindoo Koosh*) on the river Bactrus (*Adirsiah* or *Dehas*), about 25 miles S. of its junction with the Oxus. It was the centre of a considerable traffic. The existing ruins, 20 miles in circuit, are all of the Mohammedan period.

Bactria or **-iana** (Βακτριανή: Βάκτροι, -ιοι, -ιανοί : *Bokhara*), a province of the Persian empire, bounded on the S. by M. Paropamisus, which separated it from Ariana, on the E. by the N. branch of the same range, which divided it from the Sacae, on the N.E. by the Oxus, which separated it from Sogdiana, and on the W. by Margiana. It was inhabited by a rude and warlike people, who were subdued by Cyrus or his next successors. It was included in the conquests of Alexander, and formed a part of the kingdom of the Seleucidae, until B. C. 255, when Theodotus, its governor, revolted from Antiochus II., and founded the Greek kingdom of Bactria, which lasted till B. C. 134 or 125, when it was overthrown by the Parthians, with whom, during its whole duration, its kings were sometimes at war, and sometimes in alliance against Syria. This Greek kingdom extended beyond the limits of the province of Bactria, and included at least a part of Sogdiana. Bactria was watered by the Oxus and its tributaries, and contained much fertile land; and much of the commerce between W. Asia and India passed through it.

Baduhennae Lucus, a wood in W. Friesland.

Baebia Gens, plebeian, the most important members of which are given under their surnames, DIVES, SULCA, TAMPHILUS.

Baecula, a town in Hispania Tarraconensis, W. of Castulo, in the neighbourhood of silver mines.

Baeterrae (*Beziers*), also called **Biterrensis urbs**, a town in Gallia Narbonensis on the Obris, not far from Narbo, and a Roman colony: its neighbourhood produced good wine.

Baetica [HISPANIA.]

Baetis (*Guadalquiver*), a river in S. Spain, formerly called **Tartessus**, and by the inhabitants **Certis**, rises in Hispania Tarraconensis in the territory of the Oretani, flows S.W. through Baetica, to which it gives its name, past the cities of Corbuda and Hispalis, and falls into the Atlantic Ocean by 2 mouths, N. of Gades.

Bagacum (*Bavai*), the chief town of the Nervii in Gallia Belgica: there are many Roman remains in the modern town.

Bagaudae, a Gallic people, who revolted under Diocletian, and were with difficulty subdued by Maximian, A. D. 286.

Bagoas (Βαγώας), an eunuch, highly trusted and favoured by Artaxerxes III. (Ochus), whom he poisoned, B. C. 338. He was put to death by Darius III. Codomannus, whom he had attempted likewise to poison, 336. The name Bagoas frequently occurs in Persian history, and is sometimes used by Latin writers as synonymous with an eunuch.

Bagradas (Βαγράδας : *Mejerdah*), a river of N. Africa, falling into the Gulf of Carthage near Utica.

Baiae (Baïanus), a town in Campania, on a small bay W. of Naples, and opposite Puteoli, was situated in a beautiful country, which abounded in warm mineral springs. The baths of Baiae were the most celebrated in Italy, and the town itself was the favourite watering-place of the Romans, who flocked thither in crowds for health and pleasure; it was distinguished by licentiousness and immorality. The whole country was studded with the palaces of the Roman nobles and emperors, which covered the coast from Baiae to Puteoli: many of these palaces were built out into the sea. (Hor. *Carm.* ii. 18. 20.) The site of ancient Baiae is now for the most part covered by the sea.

Balbinus, D. Caelius, was elected emperor by the senate along with M. Clodius Pupienus Maximus, after the murder of the two Gordians in Africa at the beginning of A. D. 238; but the new emperors were slain by the soldiers at Rome in June in the same year.

Balbus, M'. Acilius, the name of 2 consuls, one in B. C. 150, and the other in 114.

Balbus, T. Ampius, tribune of the plebs B. C. 63, was a supporter of Pompey, whom he joined in the civil war B. C. 49. He was pardoned by Caesar through the intercession of Cicero, who wrote to him on the occasion (*ad Fam.* vi. 12).

Balbus, M. Atius, of Aricia, married Julia, the sister of Julius Caesar, who bore him a daughter, Atia, the mother of Augustus Caesar.

Balbus, L. Cornelius. 1. Of Gades, served under Q. Metellus and Pompey against Sertorius in Spain, and received from Pompey the Roman citizenship. He accompanied Pompey on his return to Rome, B. C. 71, and was for a long time one of his most intimate friends. At the same time he gained the friendship of Caesar, who placed great confidence in him. As the friend of Caesar and Pompey, he had numerous enemies, who accused him in 56 of having illegally assumed the Roman citizenship; he was defended by Cicero, whose speech has come down to us, and was acquitted. In the civil war, 49, Balbus did not take any open part against Pompey; but he attached himself to Caesar, and, in conjunction with Oppius, had the entire management of Caesar's affairs at Rome. After the death of Caesar (44) he was equally successful in gaining the favour of Octavian, who raised him to the consulship in 40. Balbus wrote a diary (*Ephemeris*), which has not come down to us, of the most remarkable occurrences in Caesar's life. He took care that Caesar's Commentaries on the Gallic war should be continued; and we accordingly find the 8th book dedicated to him.—2. Nephew of the preceding, received the Roman franchise along with his uncle. He served under Caesar in the civil war; he was quaestor of Asinius Pollio in Further Spain in B. C. 43, and while there added to his native town Gades a suburb; many years afterwards he was proconsul of Africa, and triumphed over the Garamantes in 19. He built a magnificent theatre at Rome, which was dedicated in 13.

Balbus, Lucillus. 1. L., a jurist, and brother of the following.—**2. Q.**, a Stoic philosopher, and a pupil of Panaetius, is introduced by Cicero as one of the speakers in his *De Natura Deorum*.

Balbus, Octavius, a contemporary of Cicero, bore a high character as a judex; he was put to death by the triumvirs, B. C. 43.

Balbus, Sp. Thorius, tribune of the plebs, about B. C. 111, proposed an agrarian law. See *Dict. of Ant.*, art. *Lex Thoria*.

Baleares (Βαλεαρίδες, Βαλιαρίδες), also called **Gymnesiae** (Γυμνησίαι) by the Greeks, 2 islands in the Mediterranean, off the coast of Spain, distinguished by the epithets *Major* and *Minor*, whence their modern names *Majorca* and *Minorca*. They were early known to the Carthaginians, who established settlements there for the purposes of trade; they afterwards received colonies from Rhodes; and their population was at a later time of a very mixed kind. Their inhabitants, also called *Baleares*, were celebrated as slingers, and were employed as such in the armies of the Carthaginians and Romans. In consequence of their piracies they provoked the hostility of the Romans, and were finally subdued B. c. 123, by Q. Metellus, who assumed accordingly the surname Balearicus.

Balista, prefect of the praetorians under Valerian, whom he accompanied to the East. After the defeat and capture of that emperor (A. D. 260), he rallied a body of Roman troops, and defeated the Persians in Cilicia. His subsequent career is obscure; he is mentioned as one of the Thirty Tyrants, and was probably put to death, about 264, by Odenathus.

Bambalio, M. Fulvius, father of Fulvia, the wife of M. Antonius, the triumvir, received the nickname of Bambalio on account of a hesitancy in his speech.

Bambyce. [HIERAPOLIS].

Banasa (*Mamora?* Ru.), a city of Mauretania Tingitana, on the river Subur (*Sebou*), near the W. coast: a colony under Augustus.

Bandusiae Fons (*Sambuco*), a fountain in Apulia, 6 miles from Venusia. (Hor. *Carm.* iii. 13.)

Bantia (Bantinus; *Banzi* or *Vanzi*), a town in Apulia, near Venusia, in a woody district (*saltus Bantini,* Hor. *Carm.* iii. 4. 15).

Barbana (*Bojana*), a river in Illyria, flows through the Palus Labeatis.

Barbari (Βάρβαροι), the name given by the Greeks to all foreigners, whose language was not Greek, and who were therefore regarded by the Greeks as an inferior race. The Romans applied the name to all people, who spoke neither Greek nor Latin.

Barbaria. [AZANIA.]

Barbatio, commander of the household troops under Gallus, whom he arrested by command of Constantius, A. D. 354. In 355 he was made general of the infantry, and sent into Gaul to assist Julian against the Alemanni. He was put to death by Constantius in 359.

Barbatus, M. Horatius, consul B. c. 449 with Valerius Publicola after the overthrow of the decemvirs. [PUBLICOLA.]

Barbosthenes, a mountain E. of Sparta.

Barbula, Aemilius. 1. Q., consul B. C. 317, when he subdued Apulia, and consul again in 311, when he fought against the Etruscans.—**2. L.,** consul in 281, carried on war against the Tarentines, Samnites, and Sallentines.—**3. M.,** consul in 230, carried on war against the Ligurians.

Barca, the surname of HAMILCAR, the father of Hannibal, is probably the same as the Hebrew *Barak,* which signifies lightning. His family was distinguished subsequently as the "Barcine family," and the democratical party, which supported this family, as the "Barcine party."

Barca or **-e** (Βάρκη: Βαρκίτης, Βαρκαῖος, Barcaeus). 1. (*Merjeh,* Ru.), the second city of Cyrenaica, in N. Africa, 100 stadia (10 geog. miles) from the sea, appears to have been at first a settlement of a Libyan tribe, the Barcaei, but about B. c. 560 was colonized by the Greek seceders from Cyrene, and became so powerful as to make the W. part of Cyrenaica virtually independent of the mother city. In B. C. 510 it was taken by the Persians, who removed most of its inhabitants to Bactria, and under the Ptolemies its ruin was completed by the erection of its port into a new city, which was named PTOLEMAIS, and which took the place of Barca as one of the cities of the Cyrenaic Pentapolis.—**2.** A town in Bactria peopled by the removed inhabitants of the Cyrenaic Barca.

Barcino (*Barcelona*), a town of the Laeetani, in Hispania Tarraconensis, afterwards a Roman colony: the town was not large, but it possessed an excellent harbour.

Bardanes. [ARSACES XXI.]

Bardylis or **Bardyllis** (Βάρδυλις, Βάρδυλλις), an Illyrian chieftain, carried on frequent wars with the Macedonians, but was at length defeated and slain in battle by Philip, the father of Alexander the Great, B. c. 359.

Barea Soranus, consul suffectus in A. D. 52 under Claudius, and afterwards proconsul of Asia, was a man of justice and integrity. He was accused of treason in the reign of Nero, and was condemned to death together with his daughter Servilia. The chief witness against him was P. Egnatius Celer, a Stoic philosopher, and the teacher of Soranus. (See Juv. iii. 116.)

Bargūsii, a people in the N.E. of Spain, between the Pyrenees and the Iberus.

Bărĭum (Barinus: *Bari*), a town in Apulia, on the Adriatic, a municipium, and celebrated for its fisheries (*Barium piscosum*, Hor. *Sat.* i. 5. 97).

Barsaentes (Βαρσαέντης) or **Barzaentus** (Βαρ-ζάεντος), satrap of the Arachoti and Drangae, took part in the murder of Darius III., and afterwards fled to India, where he was seized by the inhabitants and delivered up to Alexander, who put him to death.

Barsĭnē (Βαρσίνη). 1. Daughter of Artabazus, and wife of Memnon the Rhodian, subsequently married Alexander the Great, to whom she bore a son, Hercules. She and her son were put to death by Polysperchon in 309. — 2. Also called **Statira**, elder daughter of Darius III., whom Alexander married at Susa, B.C. 324. Shortly after Alexander's death she was murdered by Roxana.

Basănitis. [BATANAEA.]

Basilia (*Basel* or *Bâle*), a town on the Rhine, in the neighbourhood of which Valentinian built a fortress.

Basilīna, the mother of Julian the apostate, being the second wife of Julius Constantius, brother of Constantine the Great.

Basilĭus, commonly called Basil the Great, was born A.D. 329, at Caesarēa. He studied at Antioch or Constantinople under Libanius, and subsequently continued his studies for 4 years (351—355) at Athens, chiefly under the sophists Himerius and Proaeresius. Among his fellow-students were the emperor Julian and Gregory Nazianzen, the latter of whom became his most intimate friend. After acquiring the greatest reputation as a student for his knowledge of rhetoric, philosophy, and science, he returned to Caesarea, where he began to plead causes, but soon abandoned his profession and devoted himself to a religious life. He now led an ascetic life for many years; he was elected bishop of Caesarea in 370 in place of Eusebius; he died in 379. — The best edition of his works is by Garnier, Paris, 1721—1730.

Basilĭus, **L. Minucĭus**, served under Caesar in Gaul, and commanded part of Caesar's fleet in the civil war. He was one of Caesar's assassins (B.C. 44), and in the following year was murdered by his own slaves.

Bassāreus (Βασσαρεύς), a surname of Dionysus, probably derived from βασσάρις, a fox-skin, worn by the god himself and the Maenads in Thrace.

Bassus, **Aufidĭus**, an orator and historian under Augustus and Tiberius, wrote an account of the Roman wars in Germany, and a work upon Roman history of a more general character, which was continued in 31 books by the elder Pliny.

Bassus, **Q. Caecilĭus**, a Roman eques, and an adherent of Pompey, fled to Tyre after the battle of Pharsalia B.C. 48. Shortly afterwards he obtained possession of Tyre, and was joined by most of the troops of Sex. Caesar, the governor of Syria, who had been killed by his own soldiers at the instigation of Bassus. He subsequently settled down in Apamea, where he maintained himself for 3 years (46—43) against C. Antistius Vetus, and afterwards against Statius Murcus and Marcius Crispus. On the arrival of Cassius in Syria in 43, the troops of Bassus went over to Cassius.

Bassus, **Caesĭus**, a Roman lyric poet, and a friend of Persius, who addresses his 6th satire to him, was destroyed along with his villa in A.D. 79

by the eruption of Vesuvius which overwhelmed Herculaneum and Pompeii.

Bassus, **Saleius**, a Roman epic poet of considerable merit, contemporary with Vespasian.

Bastarnae or **Basternae**, a warlike German people, who migrated to the country near the mouth of the Danube. They are first mentioned in the wars of Philip and Perseus against the Romans, and at a later period they frequently devastated Thrace, and were engaged in wars with the Roman governors of the province of Macedonia. In B.C. 30, they were defeated by M. Crassus, and driven across the Danube; and we find them, at a later time, partly settled between the Tyras (*Dneister*) and Borysthenes (*Dnieper*), and partly at the mouth of the Danube, under the name of *Peucini*, from their inhabiting the island of Peuce, at the mouth of this river.

Bastitāni (also **Bastetani**, **Bastuli**), a people in Hispania Baetica on the coast.

Bătănaea or **Basanitis** (Βαταναία, Βασανῖτις: O. T. Bashan, Basan), a district of Palestine, E. of the Jordan, extending from the river Jabbok on the S. to Mt. Hermon, in the Antilibanus chain, on the N. The **s** and **t** are mere dialectic varieties.

Bătăvi or **Bătăvi**, a Celtic people who abandoned their homes in consequence of civil dissensions, before the time of Julius Caesar, and settled in the island formed by the Rhine, the Waal, and the Maas, which island was called after them *Insula Batavorum*. They were for a long time allies of the Romans in their wars against the Germans, and were of great service to the former by their excellent cavalry; but at length, exasperated by the oppressions of the Roman officers, they rose in revolt under Claudius Civilis, in A.D. 69, and were with great difficulty subdued. On their subjugation, they were treated by the Romans with mildness, and were exempt from taxation. Their country, which also extended beyond the island S. of the Maas and the Waal, was called, at a later time, **Batavia**. Their chief towns were *Lugdunum* (*Leyden*) and *Batavodurum*, between the Maas and the Waal. The *Canninefates* or *Canninefates* were a branch of the Batavi, and dwelt in the W. of the island.

Batavodūrum. [BATAVI.]

Bathycles (Βαθυκλῆς), a celebrated artist of Magnesia on the Maeander, constructed for the Lacedaemonians the colossal throne of the Amyclaean Apollo. He probably flourished about the time of Solon, or a little later.

Băthyllus. 1. Of Samos, a beautiful youth beloved by Anacreon. — 2. Of Alexandria, the freedman and favourite of Maecenas, brought to perfection, together with Pylades of Cilicia, the imitative dance or ballet called *Pantomimus*. Bathyllus excelled in comic, and Pylades in tragic personifications.

Batnae (Βάτναι: Βατναῖος). 1. (*Saruj*), a city of Osroëne in Mesopotamia, E. of the Euphrates, and S.W. of Edessa, at about equal distances; founded by the Macedonians, and taken by Trajan; celebrated for its annual fair of Indian and Syrian merchandize. — 2. (*Dahab*), a city of Cyrrhestice, in Syria, between Beroea and Hierapolis.

Bato (Βάτων). 1. The charioteer of Amphiaraus, was swallowed up by the earth along with AMPHIARAUS. — 2. The name of 2 leaders of the

Pannonians and Dalmatians in their insurrection in the reign of Augustus, A. D. 6. Tiberius and Germanicus were both sent against them, and obtained some advantages over them, in consequence of which the Pannonians and Dalmatians concluded a peace with the Romans in 8. But the peace was of short duration. The Dalmatian Bato put his namesake to death, and renewed the war. Tiberius now finally subdued Dalmatia ; Bato surrendered to him in 9 upon promise of pardon ; he accompanied Tiberius to Italy, and his life was spared.

Battǐădae (Βαττιάδαι), kings of Cyrene during 8 generations. 1. **Battus I.,** of Thera, led a colony to Africa at the command of the Delphic oracle, and founded Cyrene about B. c. 631. He was the first king of Cyrene, his government was gentle and just, and after his death in 599 he was worshipped as a hero. — 2. **Arcesilaus I.,** son of No. 1, reigned B. c. 599—583. — 3. **Battus II.,** surnamed " the Happy," son of No. 2, reigned B. c. 583—560 ? In his reign, Cyrene received a great number of colonists from various parts of Greece ; and in consequence of the increased strength of his kingdom Battus was able to subdue the neighbouring Libyan tribes, and to defeat Apries, king of Egypt (570), who had espoused the cause of the Libyans. — 4. **Arcesilaus II.,** son of No. 3, surnamed " the Oppressive," reigned about B. c. 560 —550. In consequence of dissensions between himself and his brothers, the latter withdrew from Cyrene, and founded Barca. He was strangled by his brother or friend, Learchus. — 5. **Battus III.,** or " the Lame," son of No. 4, reigned about B. c. 550—530. In his time, Demonax, a Mantinean, gave a new constitution to the city, whereby the royal power was reduced within very narrow limits. — 6. **Arcesilaus III.,** son of No. 5, reigned about B. c. 530—514, was driven from Cyrene in an attempt to recover the ancient royal privileges, but recovered his kingdom with the aid of Samian auxiliaries. He endeavoured to strengthen himself by making submission to Cambyses in 525. He was, however, again obliged to leave Cyrene ; he fled to Alazir, king of Barca, whose daughter he had married, and was there slain by the Barcaeans and some Cyrenaean exiles. — 7. **Battus IV.,** probably son of No. 6, of whose life we have no accounts. — 8. **Arcesilaus IV.,** probably son of No. 7, whose victory in the chariot-race at the Pythian games, B. c. 466, is celebrated by Pindar in his 4th and 5th Pythian odes. At his death, about 450, a popular government was established.

Battus (Βάττος), a shepherd whom Hermes turned into a stone, because he broke a promise which he made to the god.

Batǐlum, a town in Campania of uncertain site.

Baucis. [PHILEMON.]

Bauli (*Bacolo*), a collection of villas rather than a town, between Misenum and Baiae in Campania.

Bǎvǐus and **Maevǐus,** 2 malevolent poetasters, who attacked the poetry of Virgil and Horace.

Bazǐra or **Bezǐra** (Βάζιρα: Βάζιροι: *Bajour*, N.W. of *Peshawur*), a city in the Paropamisus, taken by Alexander on his march into India.

Bebrўces (Βέβρυκες). 1. A mythical people in Bithynia, said to be of Thracian origin, whose king, Amycus, slew Pollux [p. 76, a.]. — 2. An ancient Iberian people on the coast of the Mediterranean, N. and S. of the Pyrenees : they possessed numerous herds of cattle.

Bedriǎcum, a small place in Cisalpine Gaul between Cremona and Verona, celebrated for the defeat both of Otho and of the Vitellian troops, A. D. 69.

Belbǐna (Βέλβινα: Βελβινίτης). 1. (*St. George d'Arbori*), an island in the Aegaean sea, off the S. coast of Attica. — 2. See BELEMINA.

Belemǐna (Βελεμίνα), also called *Belmina* and *Belbina*, a town in the N.W. of Laconia, on the borders of Arcadia. The surrounding district was called *Belminatis* and *Belbinatis*.

Belěsis or **Belěsys** (Βέλεσις, Βέλεσυς), a Chaldaean priest at Babylon, who is said, in conjunction with Arbaces, the Mede, to have overthrown the old Assyrian empire. [ARBACES.] Belesis afterwards received the satrapy of Babylon from Arbaces.

Belgae, one of the 3 great people, into which Caesar divides the population of Gaul. They were bounded on the N. by the Rhine, on the W. by the ocean, on the S. by the Sequana (*Seine*) and Matrona (*Marne*), and on the E. by the territory of the Treviri. They were of German origin, and had settled in the country, expelling or reducing to subjection the former inhabitants. They were the bravest of the inhabitants of Gaul, were subdued by Caesar after a courageous resistance, and were the first Gallic people who threw off the Roman dominion. The Belgae were subdivided into the tribes of the NERVII, BELLOVACI, REMI, SUESSIONES, MORINI, MENAPII, ADUATICI, and others ; and the collective forces of the whole nation were more than a million.

Belgǐca [GALLIA.]

Belgǐum, the name generally applied to the territory of the BELLOVACI, and of the tribes dependent upon the latter, namely, the Atrebates, Ambiani, Velliocasses, Aulerci, and Caleti. Belgium did not include the whole country inhabited by the Belgae, for we find the Nervii, Remi, &c., expressly excluded from it. (Caes. *B. G.* v. 24.)

Belisǎrius, the greatest general of Justinian, was a native of Illyria and of mean extraction. In A. D. 534, he overthrew the Vandal kingdom in Africa, which had been established by Genseric about 100 years previously, and took prisoner the Vandal king, Gelimer, whom he led in triumph to Constantinople. In 535—540, Belisarius carried on war against the Goths in Italy, and conquered Sicily, but he was recalled by the jealousy of Justinian. In 541—544 he again carried on war against the Goths in Italy, but was again recalled by Justinian, leaving his victories to be completed by his rival Narses in the complete overthrow of the Gothic kingdom, and the establishment of the exarchate of Ravenna. The last victory of Belisarius was gained in repelling an inroad of the Bulgarians, 559. In 563 he was accused of a conspiracy against the life of Justinian ; according to a popular tradition, he was deprived of his property, his eyes were put out, and he wandered as a beggar through Constantinople; but according to the more authentic account, he was merely imprisoned for a year in his own palace, and then restored to his honours. He died in 565.

Bellěrǒphon or **Bellěrǒphontes** (Βελλεροφῶν or Βελλεροφόντης), son of the Corinthian king Glaucus and Eurymede, and grandson of Sisyphus, was originally called *Hipponous*, and received the name Bellerophon from slaying the Corinthian Bellerus. To be purified from the murder he fled to

Proetus, whose wife Antēa fell in love with the young hero; but as her offers were rejected by him, she accused him to her husband of having made improper proposals to her. Proetus, unwilling to kill him with his own hands, sent him to his father-in-law, Iobates, king of Lycia, with a letter in which the latter was requested to put the young man to death. Iobates accordingly sent him to kill the monster Chimaera, thinking that he was sure to perish in the contest. After obtaining possession of the winged horse, Pegasus, Bellerophon rose with him in the air, and killed the Chimaera with his arrows. Iobates, thus disappointed, sent Bellerophon against the Solymi and next against the Amazons. In these contests he was also victorious; and on his return to Lycia, being attacked by the bravest Lycians, whom Iobates had placed in ambush for the purpose, Bellerophon slew them all. Iobates, now seeing that it was hopeless to kill the hero, gave him his daughter (Philonoë, Anticlēa, or Cassandra) in marriage, and made him his successor on the throne. Bellerophon became the father of Isander, Hippolochus, and Laodamia. At last Bellerophon drew upon himself the hatred of the gods, and, consumed by grief, wandered lonely through the Aleïan field, avoiding the paths of men. This is all that Homer says respecting Bellerophon's later fate: some traditions related that he attempted to fly to heaven upon Pegasus, but that Zeus sent a gad-fly to sting the horse, which threw off the rider upon the earth, who became lame or blind in consequence. (Hor. Carm. iv. 11, 26.)

Belli, a Celtiberian people in Hispania Tarraconensis.

Bellōna, the Roman goddess of war, was probably a Sabine divinity. She is frequently mentioned by the Roman poets as the companion of Mars, or even as his sister or his wife, and is described as armed with a bloody scourge. (Virg. Aen. viii. 703). During the Samnite wars, in B.C. 296, App. Claudius Caecus vowed a temple to her, which was erected in the Campus Martius. Her priests, called *Bellonarii*, wounded their own arms or legs when they offered sacrifices to her.

Bellovăci, the most powerful of the Belgae, dwelt in the modern *Beauvais*, between the Seine, Oise, Somme, and Bresle. In Caesar's time they could bring 100,000 men into the field, but they were subdued by Caesar with the other Belgae.

Bělon or **Baelon** (Βελών, Βαιλών, nr. *Bolonia*, Ru.), a sea-port town in Hispania Baetica on a river of the same name (now *Barbate*), the usual place for crossing over to Tingis in Mauretania.

Bēlus (Βῆλος), son of Poseidon and Libya or Eurynome, twin-brother of Agenor, and father of Aegyptus and Danaus. He was believed to be the ancestral hero and national divinity of several eastern nations, from whom the legions about him were transplanted to Greece and there became mixed up with Greek myths.

Bēlus (Βῆλος: *Nahr Naman*), a river of Phoenicia, rising at the foot of M. Carmel, and falling into the sea close to the S. of Ptolemais (*Acre*), celebrated for the tradition that its fine sand first led the Phoenicians to the invention of glass.

Benācus Lacus (*Lago di Garda*), a lake in the N. of Italy (Gallia Transpadana), out of which the Mincius flows.

Běněventum (*Benevento*), a town in Samnium on the Appia Via, at the junction of the two val-

leys, through which the Sabatus and Calor flow, formerly called *Maleventum* on account, it is said, of its bad air. It was one of the most ancient towns in Italy, having been founded, according to tradition, by Diomede. In the Samnite wars it was subdued by the Romans, who sent a colony thither in B.C. 268, and changed its name Maleventum into Beneventum. It was colonised a second time by Augustus, and was hence called *Colonia Julia Concordia Augusta Felix*. The modern town has several Roman remains, among others a triumphal arch of Trajan.

Běrěcyntia (Βερεκυντία), a surname of Cybele, which she derived from Mt. Berecyntus where she was worshipped.

Běrěnīcē (Βερενίκη), a Macedonic form of *Pherenīcē* (Φερενίκη), i. e. "Bringing Victory." — 1. First the wife of an obscure Macedonian, and afterwards of Ptolemy I. Soter, who fell in love with her when she came to Egypt in attendance on his bride Eurydice, Antipater's daughter. She was celebrated for her beauty and virtue, and was the mother of Ptolemy II. Philadelphus. — 2. Daughter of Ptolemy II. Philadelphus, and wife of Antiochus Theos, king of Syria, who divorced Laodice in order to marry her, B.C. 249. On the death of Ptolemy, B.C. 247, Antiochus recalled Laodice, who notwithstanding caused him to be poisoned, and murdered Berenice and her son. — 3. Daughter of Magas, king of Cyrene, and wife of Ptolemy III. Euergetes. She was put to death by her son Ptolemy IV. Philopator on his accession to the throne, 221. The famous hair of Berenice, which she dedicated for her husband's safe return from his Syrian expedition in the temple of Arsinoë at Zephyrium, was said to have become a constellation. It was celebrated by Callimachus in a poem, of which we have a translation by Catullus. — 4. Otherwise called *Cleopatra*, daughter of Ptolemy VIII. Lathyrus, succeeded her father on the throne, B.C. 81, and married Ptolemy X. (Alexander II.), but was murdered by her husband 19 days after her marriage. — 5. Daughter of Ptolemy XI. Auletes, and eldest sister of the famous Cleopatra, was placed on the throne by the Alexandrines when they drove out her father, B.C. 58. She next married Archelaus, but was put to death with her husband, when Gabinius restored Auletes, 55. — 6. Sister of Herod the Great, married Aristobulus, who was put to death, B.C. 6. She afterwards went to Rome, where she spent the remainder of her life. She was the mother of Agrippa I. — 7. Daughter of Agrippa I., married her uncle Herod, king of Chalcis, by whom she had 2 sons. After the death of Herod, A.D. 48, Berenice, then 20 years old, lived with her brother Agrippa II., not without suspicion of an incestuous commerce with him. She gained the love of Titus, who was only withheld from making her his wife by fear of offending the Romans by such a step.

Běrěnīcē (Βερενίκη: Βερενικεύς), the name of several cities of the period of the Ptolemies. 1. Formerly Eziongeber (Ru. nr. *Akabah*), in Arabia, at the head of the Sinus Aelanites, or E. branch of the Red Sea. — 2. In Upper Egypt (for so it was considered, though it lay a little S. of the parallel of Syene), on the coast of the Red Sea, on a gulf called Sinus Immundus (ἀκάθαρτος κόλπος, now *Foul Bay*), where its ruins are still visible. It was named after the mother of Ptolemy II. Philadelphus, who built it, and made a road hence to

Coptos, so that it became a chief emporium for the commerce of Egypt with Arabia and India. Under the Romans it was the residence of a praefectus.— 3. B. Panchrȳsos (B. πάγχρυσος or ἡ κατὰ Σάβας), on the Red Sea coast in Aethiopia, considerably S. of the above.—4. B. Epidīres (B. ἐπὶ Δειρῆς), on the Prom. Dira, on the W. side of the entrance to the Red Sea (*Straits of Bub-el-Mandeb*).—5. (*Ben Ghazi*, Ru.), in Cyrenaica, formerly Hesperis ('Εσπερίς), the fabled site of the Gardens of the Hesperides. It took its later name from the wife of Ptolemy III. Euergetes, and was the W.-most of the 5 cities of the Lybian Pentapolis. — There were other cities of the name.

Bergistāni, a people in the N. E. of Spain between the Iberus and the Pyrenees, whose capital was Bergium.

Bergŏmum (Bergomas, -atis : *Bergamo*), a town of the Orobii in Gallia Cisalpina, between Comum and Brixia, afterwards a municipium.

Berŏë (Βερόη), a Trojan woman, wife of Doryclus, one of the companions of Aeneas, whose form Iris assumed when she persuaded the women to set fire to the ships of Aeneas in Sicily.

Beroea (Βέροια, also Βέῤῥοια, Βερόη: Βεροιεύς, Βεροιαῖος). 1. (*Verria*), one of the most ancient towns of Macedonia, on one of the lower ranges of Mt. Bermius, and on the Astraeus, a tributary of the Haliacmon, S.W. of Pella, and about 20 miles from the sea. — 2. (*Beria*), a town in the interior of Thrace, was under the later Roman empire, together with Philippopolis, one of the most important military posts. — 3. (*Aleppo* or *Haleb*), a town in Syria near Antioch, enlarged by Seleucus Nicator, who gave it the Macedonian name of Beroea. It is called *Helbon* or *Chelbon* in Ezekiel (xxvii. 18), and *Chalep* in the Byzantine writers, a name still retained in the modern *Haleb*, for which Europeans have substituted Aleppo.

Bērōsus (Βηρωσός or Βηρωσσός), a priest of Belus at Babylon, lived in the reign of Antiochus II. (B. c. 261—246), and wrote in Greek a history of Babylonia, in 3 books (called Βαβυλωνικά, and sometimes Χαλδαϊκά or Ἰστορίαι Χαλδαϊκαί). It embraced the earliest traditions about the human race, a description of Babylonia and its population, and a chronological list of its kings down to the time of the great Cyrus. Berosus says that he derived the materials for his work from the archives in the temple of Belus. The work itself is lost, but considerable fragments of it are preserved in Josephus, Eusebius, Syncellus, and the Christian fathers: the best editions of the fragments are by Richter, Lips. 1825, and in Didot's *Fragmenta Historicorum Graecorum*, vol. ii Paris, 1848.

Bērȳtus (Βηρυτός: Βηρύτιος: *Beirut*, Ru.), one of the oldest sea-ports of Phoenicia, stood on a promontory near the mouth of the river Magoras (*Nahr Beirut*), half way between Byblus and Sidon. It was destroyed by the Syrian king Tryphon (B. c. 140), and restored by Agrippa under Augustus, who made it a colony. It afterwards became a celebrated seat of learning.

Bēsa. [ANTINOÖPOLIS.]

Bessi, a fierce and powerful Thracian people, who dwelt along the whole of Mt. Haemus as far as the Euxine. After the conquest of Macedonia by the Romans (B. c. 168), the Bessi were attacked by the latter, and subdued after a severe struggle.

Bessus (Βῆσσος), satrap of Bactria under Darius III., seized Darius soon after the battle of

Arbela, B. c. 331. Pursued by Alexander in the following year, Bessus put Darius to death, and fled to Bactria, where he assumed the title of king. He was betrayed by two of his followers to Alexander, who put him to death.

Bestia, Calpurnīus. 1. L., tribune of the plebs, B. c. 121, and consul 111, when he carried on war against Jugurtha, but having received large bribes he concluded a peace with the Numidian. On his return to Rome he was in consequence accused and condemned. — 2. L., one of the Catilinarian conspirators, B. c. 63, was at the time tribune of the plebs designatus, and not actually tribune as Sallust says. In 59 he was aedile, and in 57 was an unsuccessful candidate for the praetorship, notwithstanding his bribery, for which offence he was brought to trial in the following year and condemned, although he was defended by Cicero.

Betasii, a people in Gallia Belgica, between the Tungri and Nervii in the neighbourhood of *Beets* in Brabant.

Bezira. [BAZIRA.]

Biānor. 1. Also called Ocnus or Aucnus, son of Tiberis and Manto, is said to have built the town of Mantua, and to have called it after his mother. — 2. A Bithynian, the author of 21 epigrams in the Greek Anthology, lived under Augustus and Tiberius.

Bias (Βίας). 1. Son of Amythaon, and brother of the seer Melampus. He married Pero, daughter of Neleus, whom her father had refused to give to any one unless he brought him the oxen of Iphiclus. These Melampus obtained by his courage and skill, and so won the princess for his brother. Melampus also gained for Bias a third of the kingdom of Argos, in consequence of his curing the daughters of Proetus and the other Argive women of their madness. — 2. Of Priene in Ionia, one of the Seven Sages of Greece, flourished about B. c. 550.

Bibacŭlus, M. Furius, a Roman poet, born at Cremona, B. c. 103, wrote iambics, epigrams, and a poem on Caesar's Gaulish wars ; the opening line in the latter poem is parodied by Horace. (*Furius hibernas cana nive conspuet Alpes, Sat.* ii. 5. 41.) It is probable that Bibaculus also wrote a poem entitled *Aethiopis*, containing an account of the death of Memnon by Achilles, and that the *turgidus Alpinus* of Horace (*Sat.* i. 10. 36) is no other than Bibaculus. The attacks of Horace against Bibaculus may probably be owing to the fact that the poems of Bibaculus contained insults against the Caesars. (Tac. *Ann.* iv. 34.)

Bibracte (*Autun*), the chief town of the Aedui in Gallia Lugdunensis, afterwards *Augustodunum*.

Bibrax (*Bièvre*), a town of the Remi in Gallia Belgica, not far from the Aisne.

Bibŭlus Calpurnīus. 1.M., curule aedile B. c. 65, praetor 62, and consul 59, in each of which years he had C. Julius Caesar as his colleague. He was a staunch adherent of the aristocratical party, but was unable in his consulship to resist the powerful combination of Caesar, Pompey, and Crassus. After an ineffectual attempt to oppose Caesar's agrarian law, he withdrew from the popular assemblies altogether ; whence it was said in joke, that it was the consulship of Julius and Caesar. In 51 Bibulus was proconsul of Syria ; and in the civil war he commanded Pompey's fleet in the Adriatic, and died (48) while holding this command off Corcyra. He married Porcia, the daughter of Cato Uticensis, by whom he had 5 sons, 2 of whom were murdered by the soldiers of Gabinius, in Egypt, 50. — 2. L., son of No. 1, was a youth at his father's death, and was brought up by M. Brutus, who married his mother Porcia. He fought with Brutus at the battle of Philippi in 42, but he was afterwards pardoned by Antony, and was intrusted by the latter with important commands. He died shortly before the battle of Actium.

Bidis (Bidinus, Bidensis), a small town in Sicily, W. of Syracuse.

Bigerra (Becerra?), a town of the Oretani in Hispania Tarraconensis.

Bigerriōnes or **Bigerri**, a people in Aquitania near the Pyrenees.

Bilbĭlis (Baubola), a town of the Celtiberi in Hispania Tarraconensis, a municipium with the surname Augusta, on the river Salo, also called Bilbilis (Xalon), was the birth-place of the poet Martial, and was celebrated for its manufactories in iron and gold.

Billaeus (Βιλλαῖος: Filbas), a river of Bithynia, rising in the Hypii M., and falling into the Pontus Euxinus 20 stadia (2 geog. miles) E. of Tium. Some made it the boundary between Bithynia and Paphlagonia.

Bingĭum (Bingen), a town on the Rhine in Gallia Belgica.

Bĭon (Βίων). 1. Of Smyrna, a bucolic poet, flourished about B. C. 280, and spent the last years of his life in Sicily, where he was poisoned. He was older than Moschus, who laments his untimely death, and calls himself the pupil of Bion. (Mosch. Id. iii.) The style of Bion is refined, and his versification fluent and elegant, but he is inferior to Theocritus in strength and depth of feeling. — Editions, including Moschus, by Jacobs, Gotha, 1795 ; Wakefield, London, 1795 ; and Manso, Leipzig, 1807. — 2. Of Borysthenes, near the mouth of the Dnieper, flourished about B. C. 250. He was sold as a slave, when young, and received his liberty from his master, a rhetorician. He studied at Athens, and embraced the later Cyrenaic philosophy, as expounded by Theodorus, the Atheist. He lived a considerable time at the court of Antigonus Gonatas, king of Macedonia. Bion was noted for his sharp sayings, whence Horace speaks of persons delighting Bionnis sermonibus et sale nigro. (Epist. ii. 2. 60.)

Bisaltia (Βισαλτία: Βισάλτης), a district of Macedonia on the W. bank of the Strymon. The Bisaltae were Thracians, and at the invasion of Greece by Xerxes (B. C. 480) they were ruled by a Thracian prince, who was independent of Macedonia ; but at the time of the Peloponnesian war we find them subject to Macedonia.

Bisanthē (Βισάνθη: Βισανθηνός: Rodosto), subsequently Rhaedestum or Rhaedestus, a town in Thrace on the Propontis, with a good harbour, was founded by the Samians, and was in later times one of the great bulwarks of the neighbouring Byzantium.

Bistŏnes (Βίστονες), a Thracian people between Mt. Rhodope and the Aegean sea, on the lake **Bistonis** in the neighbourhood of Abdera, through whose land Xerxes marched on his invasion of Greece (B. C. 480). — From the worship of Dionysus in Thrace the Bacchic women are called Bistonides. (Hor. Carm. ii. 19. 20).

Bithynia (Βιθυνία: Βιθυνός), a district of Asia Minor, bounded on the W. by Mysia, on the N. by the Pontus Euxinus, on the E. by Paphlagonia, and on the S. by Phrygia Epictetus. was possessed at an early period by Thracian tribes from the neighbourhood of the Strymon, called Thyni (Θυνοί) and Bithyni (Βιθυνοί), of whom the former dwelt on the coast, the latter in the interior. The earlier inhabitants were the Bebryces, Caucones, and Mygdones, and the N.E. part of the district was possessed by the Mariandyni. The country was subdued by the Lydians, and afterwards became a part of the Persian empire under Cyrus, and was governed by the satraps of Phrygia. During the decline of the Persian empire, the N. part of the country became independent, under native princes, called ὕπαρχοι, who resisted Alexander and his successors, and established a kingdom, which is usually considered to begin with Zipoetes (about B. C. 287) or his son Nicomedes I. (B. C. 278), and which lasted till the death of Nicomedes III. (B. C. 74), who bequeathed his kingdom to the Romans. By them it was at first attached to the province of Asia, afterwards to that of Pontus, and, under Augustus, it was made a proconsular province. Several changes were made in its boundaries under the later emperors. — It was a fertile country, intersected with wooded mountains, the highest of which was the Mysian Olympus, on its S. border. Its chief rivers were the Sangarius and the Billaeus.

Bithynĭum (Βιθύνιον), aft. Claudiopolis, an inland city of Bithynia, the birth-place of Hadrian's favourite Antinous.

Biton (Βίτων), a mathematician, the author of an extant work on Military Machines (κατασκευαὶ πολεμικῶν ὀργάνων καὶ καταπελτικῶν), whose history is unknown. The work is printed in Vet. Mathem. Op. Paris, 1693, p. 105, seq.

Biton and Cleŏbis (Κλέοβις), sons of Cydippe, a priestess of Hera at Argos. They were celebrated for their affection to their mother, whose chariot they once dragged during a festival to the temple of Hera, a distance of 45 stadia. The priestess prayed to the goddess to grant them what was best for mortals ; and during the night they both died while asleep in the temple.

Bitŭitus, in inscriptions Betultus king of the Arverni in Gaul, joined the Allobroges in their war against the Romans. Both the Arverni and Allobroges were defeated B.C. 121, at the confluence of the Rhone and the Isara, by Q. Fabius Maximus. Bituitus was subsequently taken prisoner and sent to Rome.

Bitŭriges, a numerous and powerful Celtic people in Gallia Aquitanica, had in early times the supremacy over the other Celts in Gaul. (Liv. v. 34.) They were divided into, 1. Bit. Cubi, separated from the Carnutes and Aedui by the Liger, and bounded on the S. by the Lemovices, in the country of the modern Bourges; their capital was Avaricum. 2. Bit. Vivisci or Ubisci on the Garumna: their capital was Burdigala.

Blādus, Blandus, or **Blaudus** (Βλά-, Βλαν-, Βλαῦδος: Βλαυδηνός: Blaudesius), a city of Phrygia, near the borders of Mysia and Lydia.

Blaesus, C. Sempronĭus, consul with Cn. Servilius Caepio, B. C. 253, in the 1st Punic war. The 2 consuls sailed to the coast of Africa, and on their return were overtaken off cape Palinurus by a tremendous storm, in which 150 ships perished.

Blaesus, Junius, governor of Pannonia at the

death of Augustus, A. D. 14, when the formidable insurrection of the legions broke out in that province. He obtained the government of Africa in 21, where he gained a victory over Tacfarinas. On the fall of his uncle Sejanus in 31, he was deprived of the priestly offices which he held, and in 36 put an end to his own life, to avoid falling by the hand of the executioner.

Blanda. 1. (*Blaños*), a town of the Lacetani in Hispania Tarraconensis. — 2. (*St. Biasio*), a town in Lucania.

Blascon (*Brescou*), a small island in the Gallicus Sinus, off the town of Agatha.

Blasio, M. Helvius, praetor B. C. 197, defeated the Celtiberi in Spain, and took Illiturgi.

Blavia (*Blaye*), a town of the Santones, in Gallia Aquitanica, on the Garumna.

Blemyes (Βλέμυες, Βλέμμυες), an Aethiopian people, on the borders of Upper Egypt, to which their predatory incursions were very troublesome in the times of the Roman emperors.

Blera (Bleranus : *Bieda*), a town in Etruria, on the Via Clodia, between Forum Clodii and Tuscania: there are many remains of the ancient town at *Bieda*.

Blosius or **Blossius,** the name of a noble family in Campania. — One of this family, C. Blosius of Cumae, was a philosopher, a disciple of Antipater of Tarsus, and a friend of Tib. Gracchus. After the death of Gracchus (B. C. 133) he fled to Aristonicus, king of Pergamus, and on the conquest of Aristonicus by the Romans, Blosius put an end to his own life for fear of falling into the hands of the Romans.

Boadicea, queen of the Iceni in Britain, having been shamefully treated by the Romans, who even ravished her 2 daughters, excited an insurrection of the Britons against their oppressors during the absence of Suetonius Paulinus, the Roman governor, on an expedition to the island of Mona. She took the Roman colonies of Camalodunum, Londinium, and other places, and slew nearly 70,000 Romans and their allies. She was at length defeated with great loss by Suetonius Paulinus, and put an end to her own life, A. D. 61.

Boagrius (Βοάγριος), a river in Locris, also called **Manes,** flows past Thronium into the Sinus Maliacus.

Bocchus (Βόκχος). 1. King of Mauretania, and father-in-law of Jugurtha, with whom at first he made war against the Romans, but whom he afterwards delivered up to Sulla, the quaestor of Marius, B. C. 106. — 2. Son of the preceding, reigned along with his brother Bogud, over Mauretania. Bocchus and Bogud assisted Caesar in his war against the Pompeians in Africa, B. C. 46 ; and in 45 Bogud joined Caesar in his war in Spain. After the murder of Caesar, Bocchus aided with Octavianus, and Bogud with Antony. When Bogud was in Spain in 38, Bocchus usurped the sole government of Mauretania, in which he was confirmed by Octavianus. He died about 33, whereupon his kingdom became a Roman province. Bogud had previously betaken himself to Antony, and was killed on the capture of Methone by Agrippa in 31.

Bodencus or **Bodincus.** [PADUS.]

Bodiocasses, a people in Gallia Lugdunensis ; their capital was **Augustodurum** (*Bayeux*).

Bodotria or **Boderia Aestuarium** (*Firth of Forth*), an aestuary on the E. coast of Scotland.

Boeae (Βοίαί : Βοιάτης: *Vatka*), a town in the S. of Laconica, near C. Malea.

Boebe (Βοίβη : Βοιβεύς), a town in Pelasgiotis in Thessaly, on the W. shore of the lake **Boebeis** (Βοιβηΐς), into which several rivers of Thessaly flow.

Boedromius (Βοηδρόμιος), "the helper in distress," a surname of Apollo at Athens, because he had assisted the Athenians. (See *Dict. of Ant.* art. *Boedromia.*)

Boeotia (Βοιωτία: Βοιωτός: part of *Livadia*), a district of Greece, bounded N. by Opuntian Locris, E. by the Euboean sea, S. by Attica, Megaris, and the Corinthian Gulf, and W. by Phocis. It is nearly surrounded by mountains, namely Helicon and Parnassus on the W., Cithaeron and Parnes on the S., the Opuntian mountains on the N., and a range of mountains along the whole sea-coast on the E. The country contains several fertile plains, of which the two most important were the valley of the Asopus in the S., the inhabitants of which were called Parosopii, and the valley of the Cephissus in the N. (the upper part of which, however, belonged to Phocis), the inhabitants of which were called Epicephisii. In the former valley the chief towns were THEBAE, TANAGRA, THESPIAE, and PLATAEAE ; in the latter the chief towns were ORCHOMENUS, CHAERONEA, CORONEA, LEBADEA, and HALIARTUS ; the latter valley included the lake COPAIS. The surface of Boeotia is said to be 1080 square miles. The atmosphere was damp and thick, to which circumstance some of the ancients attributed the dullness of the Boeotian intellect, with which the Athenians frequently made merry ; but the deficiency of the Boeotians in this respect was more probably owing, as has been well remarked, to the extraordinary fertility of their country, which probably depressed their intellectual and moral energies.—In the earliest times Boeotia was inhabited by various tribes, the Aones (whence the country was called Aonia), Temmices, Hyantes, Thracians, Leleges, &c. Orchomenus was inhabited by the powerful tribe of the Minyans, and Thebes by the Cadmeans, the reputed descendants of CADMUS. The Boeotians were an Aeolian people, who originally occupied Arne in Thessaly, from which they were expelled by the Thessalians 60 years after the Trojan war, and migrated into the country called after them Boeotia, partly expelling and partly incorporating with themselves the ancient inhabitants of the land. Boeotia was then divided into 14 independent states, which formed a league, with Thebes at its head. The chief magistrates of the confederacy were the Boeotarchs, elected annually, 2 by Thebes and 1 by each of the other states ; but as the number of the states was different at different times, that of the Boeotarchs also varied. The government in most states was an aristocracy. (See *Dict. of Ant.* art. *Boeotarches.*)

Boethius, whose full name was ANICIUS MANLIUS SEVERINUS BOETHIUS, a Roman statesman and author, was born between A. D. 470 and 475. He was famous for his general learning, and especially for his knowledge of Greek philosophy, which according to a common account (though of doubtful authority), he studied under Proclus at Athens. He was consul in 510, and was treated with great distinction by Theodoric the Great ; but having incurred the suspicions of the latter, by advocating the cause of the Italians against the oppressions of the Goths, he was put to death by Theodoric about 524. During his imprisonment he wrote his celebrated work *De Consolatione Philosophiae*, in 5 books, which is composed alternately in prose and verse. The diction is pure and elegant, and the sentiments are noble and exalted, showing that the author had a real belief in prayer and in Providence, though he makes no reference to Christianity. Boëthius was the last Roman of any note who understood the language and studied the literature of Greece. He translated many of the works of the Greek philosophers, especially of Aristotle, and wrote commentaries upon them, several of which have come down to us. He also wrote a commentary, in 6 books, upon the *Topica* of Cicero, which is also extant. In the ignorance of Greek writers which prevailed from the 6th to the 14th century, Boëthius was looked upon as the head and type of all philosophers, as Augustin was of all theology and Virgil of all literature ; but after the introduction of the works of Aristotle into Europe in the 13th century, Boëthius's fame gradually died away. — The best edition of his collective works was printed at Basel, 1570 ; the last edition of his *De Consolatione* is by Obbarius, Jenae, 1843.

Boëthus (Βοηθός). 1. A Stoic philosopher of uncertain date, wrote several works, from one of which Cicero quotes. — 2. A Peripatetic philosopher, was a native of Sidon in Phoenicia, a disciple of Andronicus of Rhodes, and an instructor of the philosopher Strabo. He therefore flourished about B. C. 30. He wrote several works, all of which are now lost.

Boeum (Βοιόν, Βόϊον, Βοῖον: Βοιώτης), an ancient town of the Dorian Tetrapolis.

Bogud. [BOCCHUS, No. 2.]

Boii, one of the most powerful of the Celtic people, said to have dwelt originally in Gaul (Transalpina), but in what part of the country is uncertain. At an early time they migrated in two great swarms, one of which crossed the Alps and settled in the country between the Po and the Apennines ; the other crossed the Rhine and settled in the part of Germany called Boihemum (*Bohemia*) after them, and between the Danube and the Tyrol. The Boii in Italy long carried on a fierce struggle with the Romans, but they were at length subdued by the consul P. Scipio in B. C. 191, and were subsequently incorporated in the province of Gallia Cisalpina. The Boii in Germany maintained their power longer, but were at length subdued by the Marcomanni, and expelled from the country. We find 32,000 Boii taking part in the Helvetian migration ; and after the defeat of the Helvetians (B. C. 58), Caesar allowed these Boii to dwell among the Aedui.

Boiorix, a chieftain of the Boii, fought against the Romans in Cisalpine Gaul, B. C. 194.

Bola, Bolae or **Volae** (Bolānus), an ancient town of the Aequi, belonging to the Latin league not mentioned in later times.

Bolanus, Vettius, governor of Britain in A. D. 69, is praised by Statius in the poem (*Silv.* v. 2), addressed to Crispinus, the son of Bolanus.

Bolbe (Βόλβη: *Beshek*), a lake in Macedonia, empties itself by a short river into the Strymonic gulf near Bromiscus and Aulon : the lake is now about 12 miles in length, and 6 or 8 in breadth. — There was a town of the same name upon the lake.

Bolbitine (Βολβιτίνη: Βολβιτινήτης: *Rosetta*), a city of Lower Egypt, near the mouth of a branch

of the Nile (the W.-most but one), which was called the Bolbitine mouth (τὸ Βολβίτινον στόμα).

Boline (Βολίνη: Βολιναῖος), a town in Achaia, the inhabitants of which Augustus transplanted to Patrae.

Bolissus (Βολισσός: Βολίσσιος), a town on the W. coast of Chios.

Bomilcar (Βομίλκας, Βομίλκας). 1. Commander, with Hanno, of the Carthaginians against Agathocles, when the latter invaded Africa, B. C. 310. In 308 he attempted to seize the government of Carthage, but failed, and was crucified. — 2. Commander of the Carthaginian supplies sent to Hannibal after the battle of Cannae, 216. He afterwards attempted to relieve Syracuse, when besieged by Marcellus, but was unable to accomplish any thing. — 3. A Numidian, deep in the confidence of Jugurtha. When Jugurtha was at Rome, 109, Bomilcar effected for him the assassination of Massiva. In 107 he plotted against Jugurtha.

Bomius Mons (Βόμιος and οἱ Βωμοί), the W. part of Mt. Oeta in Aetolia, inhabited by the Bomienses (Βωμιεῖς).

Bona Dea, a Roman divinity, is described as the sister, wife, or daughter of Faunus, and was herself called *Fauna, Fatua,* or *Oma.* She was worshipped at Rome as a chaste and prophetic divinity ; she revealed her oracles only to females, as Faunus did only to males. Her festival was celebrated every year on the 1st of May, in the house of the consul or praetor, as the sacrifices on that occasion were offered on behalf of the whole Roman people. The solemnities were conducted by the Vestals, and no male person was allowed to be in the house at one of the festivals. P. Clodius profaned the sacred ceremonies, by entering the house of Caesar in the disguise of a woman, B. C. 62.

Bonifacius, a Roman general, governor of Africa under Valentinian III. Believing that the empress Placidia meditated his destruction, he revolted against the emperor, and invited Genseric, king of the Vandals, to settle in Africa. In 430 he was reconciled to Placidia, and attempted to drive the Vandals out of Africa, but without success. He quitted Africa in 431, and in 432 he died of a wound received in combat with his rival Aëtius.

Bonna (*Bonn*), a town on the left bank of the Rhine in Lower Germany, and in the territory of the Ubii, was a strong fortress of the Romans and the regular quarters of a Roman legion. Here Drusus constructed a bridge across the Rhine.

Bononia (Bononiensis). 1. (*Bologna*), a town in Gallia Cispadana, originally called **Felsina**, was in ancient times an Etruscan city, and the capital of N. Etruria. It afterwards fell into the hands of the Boii, but it was colonised by the Romans on the conquest of the Boii, B. C. 191, and its name of Felsina was then changed into Bononia. It fell into decay in the civil wars, but it was enlarged and adorned by Augustus, 32. — 2. (*Boulogne*) a town in the N. of Gaul. See GESORIACUM. — 3 (*Banostor ?*), a town of Pannonia on the Danube.

Bonosus, a Spaniard by birth, served with distinction under Aurelian, and usurped the imperial title in Gaul in the reign of Probus. He was defeated and slain by Probus, A. D. 280 or 281.

Boötes. [ARCTURUS.]

Borbetomagus (*Worms*), also called **Vangiones**, at a later time **Wormatia**, a town of the Vangiones on the left bank of the Rhine in Upper Germany.

Albion, the son of Neptune. — The Britons were Celts, belonging to that branch of the race called Cymry, and were apparently the aboriginal inhabitants of the country. Their manners and customs were in general the same as the Gauls; but separated more than the Gauls from intercourse with civilised nations, they preserved the Celtic religion in a purer state than in Gaul, and hence Druidism, according to Caesar, was transplanted from Gaul to Britain. The Britons also retained many of the barbarous Celtic customs, which the more civilised Gauls had laid aside. They painted their bodies with a blue colour extracted from woad, in order to appear more terrible in battle, and they had wives in common. At a later time the Belgae crossed over from Gaul, and settled on the S. and E. coasts, driving the Britons into the interior of the island. — It was not till a late period that the Greeks and Romans obtained any knowledge of Britain. In early times the Phoenicians visited the Scilly islands and the coast of Cornwall for the purpose of obtaining tin; but whatever knowledge they acquired of the country they jealously kept secret, and it only transpired that there were Cassiterides or *Tin Islands* in the N. parts of the ocean. The first certain knowledge which the Greeks obtained of Britain was from the merchants of Massilia about the time of Alexander the Great, and especially from the voyages of PYTHEAS, who sailed round a great part of Britain. From this time it was generally believed that the island was in the form of a triangle, an error which continued to prevail even at a later period. Another important mistake, which likewise prevailed for a long time, was the position of Britain in relation to Gaul and Spain. As the N.W. coast of Spain was supposed to extend too far to the N., and the W. coast of Gaul to run N. E., the lower part of Britain was believed to lie between Spain and Gaul. — The Romans first became personally acquainted with the island by Caesar's invasion. He twice landed in Britain (B. C. 55, 54), and though on the second occasion he conquered the greater part of the S. E. of the island, yet he did not take permanent possession of any portion of the country, and after his departure the Britons continued as independent as before. The Romans made no further attempts to conquer the island for nearly 100 years. In the reign of Claudius (A. D. 43) they again landed in Britain, and permanently subdued the country S. of the Thames. They now began to extend their conquests over the other parts of the island; and the great victory (61) of Suetonius Paulinus over the Britons who had revolted under BOADICEA, still further consolidated the Roman dominions. In the reign of Vespasian, Petilius Cerealis and Julius Frontinus made several successful expeditions against the SILURES and the BRIGANTES; and the conquest of S. Britain was at length finally completed by Agricola, who in 7 campaigns (78—84), subdued the whole of the island as far N. as the Frith of Forth and the Clyde, between which he erected a series of forts to protect the Roman dominions from the incursions of the barbarians in the N. of Scotland. The Roman part of Britain was now called *Britannia Romana*, and the N. part inhabited by the Caledonians *Britannia Barbara* or *Caledonia*. The Romans however gave up the N. conquests of Agricola in the reign of Hadrian, and made a ram-

part of turf from the Aestuarium Ituna (*Solway Frith*) to the German Ocean, which formed the N. boundary of their dominions. In the reign of Antoninus Pius the Romans again extended their boundary as far as the conquests of Agricola, and erected a rampart connecting the Forth and the Clyde, the remains of which are now called *Grimes Dyke*, Grime in the Celtic language signifying great or powerful. The Caledonians afterwards broke through this wall; and in consequence of their repeated devastations of the Roman dominions, the emperor Severus went to Britain in 208, in order to conduct the war against them in person. He died in the island at Eboracum (*York*) in 211, after erecting a solid stone wall from the Solway to the mouth of the Tyne, a little N. of the rampart of Hadrian. After the death of Severus, the Romans relinquished for ever all their conquests N. of this wall. In 287 Carausius assumed the purple in Britain, and reigned as emperor, independent of Diocletian and Maximian, till his assassination by Allectus in 293. Allectus reigned 3 years, and Britain was recovered for the emperors in 296. Upon the resignation of the empire by Diocletian and Maximian (305), Britain fell to the share of Constantius, who died at Eboracum in 306, and his son Constantine assumed in the island the title of Caesar. Shortly afterwards the Caledonians, who now appear under the names of Picts and Scots, broke through the wall of Severus, and the Saxons ravaged the coasts of Britain; and the declining power of the Roman empire was unable to afford the province any effectual assistance. In the reign of Valentinian I., Theodosius, the father of the emperor of that name, defeated the Picts and Scots (367); but in the reign of Honorius, Constantine, who had been proclaimed emperor in Britain (407), withdrew all the Roman troops from the island, in order to make himself master of Gaul. The Britons were thus left exposed to the ravages of the Picts and Scots, and at length, in 447, they called in the assistance of the Saxons, who became the masters of Britain. — The Roman dominions of Britain formed a single province till the time of Severus, and were governed by a legatus of the emperor. Severus divided the country into 2 provinces, *Britannia Superior* and *Inferior*, of which the latter contained the earlier conquests of the Romans in the S. of the island, and the former the later conquests in the N., the territories of the Silures, Brigantes, &c. Upon the new division of the provinces in the reign of Diocletian, Britain was governed by a *Vicarius*, subject to the *Praefectus Praetorio* of Gaul, and was divided into 4 provinces, (1) *Britannia prima*, the country S. of the Thames: (2) *Britannia Secunda*, Wales: (3) *Maxima Caesariensis*, the country between the Thames and the Humber: (4) *Flavia Caesariensis*, the country between the Humber and the Roman wall. Besides these, there was also a fifth province, *Valentia*, which existed for a short time, including the conquests of Theodosius beyond the Roman wall.

Britannicus, son of the emperor Claudius and Messalina, was born A. D. 42. Agrippina, the second wife of Claudius, induced the emperor to adopt her own son, and give him precedence over Britannicus. This son, the emperor Nero, ascended the throne in 54, and caused Britannicus to be poisoned in the following year.

Britomartis (Βριτόμαρτις, usually derived from

βριτύ, sweet or blessing, and μάρτις, a maiden) was a Cretan nymph, daughter of Zeus and Carme, and beloved by Minos, who pursued her 9 months, till at length she leaped into the sea and was changed by Artemis into a goddess. She seems to have been originally a Cretan divinity who presided over the sports of the chase ; on the introduction of the worship of Artemis into Crete she was naturally placed in some relation with the latter goddess ; and at length the 2 divinities became identified, and Britomartis is called in one legend the daughter of Leto. At Aegina Britomartis was worshipped under the name of Aphaea.

Brixellum (Brixellanus : *Bregella* or *Brescellus*), a town on the right bank of the Po in Gallia Cisalpina, where the emperor Otho put himself to death, A. D. 69.

Brixia (Brixianus : *Brescia*), a town in Gallia Cisalpina on the road from Comum to Aquileia, through which the river Mella flowed (*flavus quam molli percurrit flumine Mella*, Catull. lxvii. 33). It was probably founded by the Etruscans, was afterwards a town of the Libui and then of the Cenomani, and finally became a Roman municipium with the rights of a colony.

Bromius (Βρόμιος), a surname of Dionysus, i. e. the noisy god, from the noise of the Bacchic revelries (from βρέμω).

Brontes. [CYCLOPES.]

Bruchium. [ALEXANDRIA.]

Bructeri, a people of Germany, dwelt on each side of the Amisia (*Ems*) and extended S. as far as the Luppia (*Lippe*). The Bructeri joined the Batavi in their revolt against the Romans in A. D. 69, and the prophetic virgin, VELEDA, who had so much influence among the German tribes, was a native of their country. A few years afterwards the Bructeri were almost annihilated by the Chamavi and Angrivarii. (Tac. *Germ.* 33.)

Brundusium or **Brundisium** (Βρεντήσιον, Βρεντέσιον : Brundusinus : *Brindisi*), a town in Calabria, on a small bay of the Adriatic, forming an excellent harbour, to which the place owed its importance. The Appia Via terminated at Brundusium, and it was the usual place of embarkation for Greece and the East. It was an ancient town, and probably not of Greek origin, although its foundation is ascribed by some writers to the Cretans, and by others to Diomede. It was at first governed by kings of its own, but was conquered and colonized by the Romans, B. C. 245. The poet Pacuvius was born at this town, and Virgil died here on his return from Greece, B. C. 19.

Bruttium, Bruttius and **Bruttiorum Ager** (Βρέττια : Bruttius), more usually called **Bruttii** after the inhabitants, the S. extremity of Italy, separated from Lucania by a line drawn from the mouth of the Laus to Thurii, and surrounded on the other 3 sides by the sea. It was the country called in ancient times Oenotria and Italia. The country is mountainous, as the Apennines run through it down to the Sicilian Straits ; it contained excellent pasturage for cattle, and the valleys produced good corn, olives, and fruit. — The earliest inhabitants of the country were Oenotrians. Subsequently some Lucanians, who had revolted from their countrymen in Lucania, took possession of the country, and were hence called *Bruttii* or *Brettii*, which word is said to mean "rebels" in the language of the Lucanians. This people, however, inhabited only the interior of the land ; the coast was almost entirely in the possession of the Greek colonies. At the close of the 2nd Punic war, in which the Bruttii had been the allies of Hannibal, they lost their independence and were treated by the Romans with great severity. They were declared to be public slaves, and were employed as lictors and servants of the magistrates.

Brutus, Junius. 1. L., son of M. Junius and of Tarquinia, the sister of Tarquinius Superbus. His elder brother was murdered by Tarquinius, and Lucius escaped his brother's fate only by feigning idiotcy, whence he received the surname of Brutus. After Lucretia had stabbed herself, Brutus roused the Romans to expel the Tarquins ; and upon the banishment of the latter he was elected first consul with Tarquinius Collatinus. He loved his country better than his children, and put to death his 2 sons, who had attempted to restore the Tarquins. He fell in battle the same year, fighting against Aruns, the son of Tarquinius. Brutus was the great hero in the legends about the expulsion of the Tarquins, but we have no means of determining what part of the account is historical. — **2. D.**, surnamed SCAEVA, magister equitum to the dictator Q. Publilius Philo, B. C. 339, and consul in 325, when he fought against the Vestini. — **3. D.**, surnamed SCAEVA, consul 292, conquered the Faliscans. — **4. M.**, tribune of the plebs 195, praetor 191, when he dedicated the temple of the Great Idaean Mother, one of the ambassadors sent into Asia 189, and consul 178, when he subdued the Istri. He was one of the ambassadors sent into Asia in 171. — **5. P.**, tribune of the plebs 195, curule aedile 192, praetor 190, propraetor in Further Spain, 189. — **6. D.**, surnamed GALLAECUS (CALLAECUS) or CALLAICUS, consul 138, commanded in Further Spain, and conquered a great part of Lusitania. From his victory over the Gallaeci he obtained his surname. He was a patron of the poet L. Accius, and well versed in Greek and Roman literature. — **7. D.**, son of No. 6, consul 77, and husband of Sempronia, who carried on an intrigue with Catiline. — **8. D.**, adopted by A. Postumius Albinus, consul 99, and hence called *Brutus Albinus.* He served under Caesar in Gaul and in the civil war. He commanded Caesar's fleet at the siege of Massilia, 49, and was afterwards placed over Further Gaul. On his return to Rome Brutus was promised the praetorship and the government of Cisalpine Gaul for 44. Nevertheless, he joined the conspiracy against Caesar. After the death of the latter (44) he went into Cisalpine Gaul, which he refused to surrender to Antony, who had obtained this province from the people. Antony made war against him, and kept him besieged in Mutina, till the siege was raised in April 43 by the consuls Hirtius and Pansa, and Octavianus. But Brutus only obtained a short respite. Antony was preparing to march against him from the N. with a large army, and Octavianus, who had deserted the senate, was marching against him from the S. His only resource was flight, but he was betrayed by Camillus, a Gaulish chief, and was put to death by Antony, 43. — **9. M.**, praetor 88, belonged to the party of Marius, and put an end to his own life in 82, that he might not fall into the hands of Pompey, who commanded Sulla's fleet. — **10. L.**, also called DAMASIPPUS, praetor 82, when the younger Marius was blockaded at Praeneste, put to death at Rome by order of Marius several of the most eminent senators of the opposite party. — 11. M., married Servilia, the half-sister of Cato of Utica. He was tribune of the plebs, 83 ; and in 77 he espoused the cause of Lepidus, and was placed in command of the forces in Cisalpine Gaul, where he was slain by command of Pompey. — 12. M., the so-called tyrannicide, son of No. 11 and Servilia. He lost his father when he was only 8 years old, and was trained by his uncle Cato in the principles of the aristocratical party. Accordingly, on the breaking out of the civil war, 49, he joined Pompey, although he was the murderer of his father. After the battle of Pharsalia, 48, he was not only pardoned by Caesar, but received from him the greatest marks of confidence and favour. Caesar made him governor of Cisalpine Gaul in 46, and praetor in 44, and also promised him the government of Macedonia. But notwithstanding all the obligations he was under to Caesar, he was persuaded by Cassius to murder his benefactor under the delusive idea of again establishing the republic. [CAESAR.] After the murder of Caesar Brutus spent a short time in Italy, and then took possession of the province of Macedonia. He was joined by Cassius who commanded in Syria, and their united forces were opposed to those of Octavian and Antony. Two battles were fought in the neighbourhood of Philippi (42), in the former of which Brutus was victorious though Cassius was defeated, but in the latter Brutus also was defeated and put an end to his own life. — Brutus's wife was PORCIA, the daughter of Cato. — Brutus was an ardent student of literature and philosophy, but he appears to have been deficient in judgment and original power. He wrote several works, all of which have perished. He was a literary friend of Cicero, who dedicated to him his *Tusculanae Disputationes*, *De Finibus*, and *Orator*, and who has given the name of *Brutus* to his dialogue on illustrious orators.

Bryaxis (Βρύαξις), an Athenian statuary in stone and metal, lived B. C. 372—312.

Brygi or **Bryges** (Βρύγοι, Βρίγες), a barbarous people in the N. of Macedonia, probably of Illyrian or Thracian origin, who were still in Macedonia at the time of the Persian war. The Phrygians were believed by the ancients to have been a portion of this people, who emigrated to Asia in early times. [PHRYGIA.]

Bubassus (Βύβασσος), an ancient city of Caria, E. of Cnidus, which gave name to the bay (Bubassius Sinus) and the peninsula (ἡ Χερσόνησος ἡ Βυβασσίη), on which it stood. Ovid speaks of *Bubasides nurus* (*Met.* ix. 643).

Bubastis (Βούβαστις), daughter of Osiris and Isis, an Egyptian divinity, whom the Greeks identified with Artemis, since she was the goddess of the moon. The cat was sacred to her, and she was represented in the form of a cat, or of a female with the head of a cat.

Bubastis or **-us** (Βούβαστις or -ος: Βούβαστίτης: *Tel Basta*, Ru.), the capital of the Nomos Bubastites in Lower Egypt, stood on the E. bank of the Pelusiac branch of the Nile, and was the chief seat of the worship of Bubastis, whose annual festival was kept here. Under the Persians the city was dismantled, and lost much of its importance.

Bubulcus, C. Junius, consul B. C. 317, a second time in 313, and a third time in 311 ; in the last of these years he carried on the war against the Samnites with great success. He was censor in 309, and dictator in 302, when he defeated the

Aequians ; in his dictatorship he dedicated the temple of Safety which he had vowed in his third consulship. The walls of this temple were adorned with paintings by C. Fabius Pictor.

Bucephala or **-ia** (Βουκέφαλα or -άλεια: *Jhelum*), a city on the Hydaspes (*Jhelum*) in N. India (the *Punjab*), built by Alexander, after his battle with Porus, in memory of his favourite charger Bucephalus, whom he buried here. It stood at the place where Alexander crossed the river, and where General Gilbert crossed it (Feb. 1849) after the battle of Goojerat.

Bucephalus (Βουκέφαλος), the celebrated horse of Alexander the Great, which Philip purchased for 13 talents, and which no one was able to break in except the youthful Alexander. This horse carried Alexander through his Asiatic campaigns, and died in India B. C. 327. See BUCEPHALA.

Budalia, a town in Lower Pannonia near Sirmium, the birth-place of the emperor Decius.

Budini (Βουδῖνοι), a Scythian people, who dwelt N. of the Sauromatae in the steppes of S. Russia. Herodotus (iv. 108) calls the nation γλαυκόν τε καὶ πυῤῥόν, which some interpret " with blue eyes and red hair," and others " painted blue and red."

Budoron (Βούδορον), a fortress in Salamis on a promontory of the same name opposite Megara.

Bulis (Βοῦλις) and **Sperthias** (Σπερθίης), two Spartans, voluntarily went to Xerxes and offered themselves for punishment to atone for the murder of the heralds whom Darius had sent to Sparta but they were dismissed uninjured by the king.

Bulis (Βοῦλις: Βούλιος), a town in Phocis on the Corinthian gulf, and on the borders of Boeotia.

Bullis (Bullinus, Bullio -ōnis, Bulliensis), a town of Illyria on the coast, S. of Apollonia.

Bupalus and his brother **Athēnis**, sculptors of Chios, lived about B. C. 500, and are said to have made caricatures of the poet Hipponax, which the poet requited by the bitterest satires.

Buphras (Βουφράς), a mountain in Messenia near Pylos.

Buprasium (Βουπράσιον: -σιεύς, -σίων, -σίδης), an ancient town in Elis, mentioned in the Iliad, which had disappeared in the time of Strabo.

Bura (Βοῦρα: Βουραῖος, Βούριος), one of the 12 cities of Achaia, destroyed by an earthquake, together with Helice, but subsequently rebuilt.

Burdigala (Βουρδίγαλα: *Bordeaux*), the capital of the Bituriges Vivisci in Aquitania, on the left bank of the Garumna (*Garonne*), was a place of great commercial importance, and at a later time one of the chief seats of literature and learning. It was the birth-place of the poet Ausonius.

Burgundiōnes or **Burgundii**, a powerful nation of Germany, dwelt originally between the Viadus (*Oder*) and the Vistula, and were of the same race as the Vandals or Goths. They pretended, however, to be descendants of the Romans, whom Drusus and Tiberius had left in Germany as garrisons, but this descent was evidently invented by them to obtain more easily from the Romans a settlement W. of the Rhine. They were driven out of their original abodes between the Oder and the Vistula by the Gepidae, and the greater part of them migrated W. and settled in the country on the Main, where they carried on frequent wars with their neighbours the Alemanni. In the 5th century they settled W. of the Alps in Gaul, where they founded the powerful kingdom of *Burgundy*. Their chief towns were Geneva and Lyons.

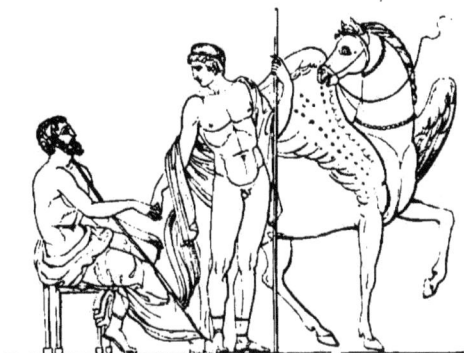

Bellerophon taking leave of Proetus.
(Tischbein, Hamilton Vases, vol. 3, pl. 38.)   Pages 118, 119.

Boreas.
(Relief from Temple of the Winds at Athens.)   Page 124.

Bellerophon, Pegasus, and Chimaera.
(Tischbein, Hamilton Vases, vol. 1, pl. 1.)   Pages 118, 119.

[To face p. 128.

Assus in the Troad.   Page 98.

Beneventum in Samnium.   Page 119.

Athens.   Page 102.

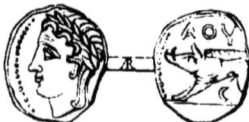

Beroea in Syria.   Page 120.

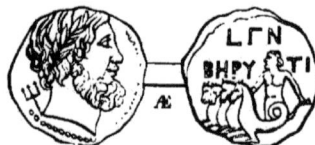

Avenio in Gaul.   Page 112.

Berytus in Phoenicia.   Page 120.

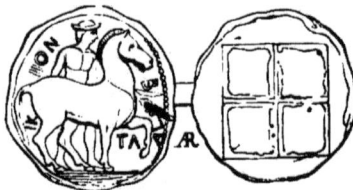

Azani in Phrygia.   Page 113.

Bisaltis.   Page 121.

Barca in Africa.   Page 116.

Boeotia.   Page 122.

Barium in Apulia.   Page 117.

Brundusium.   Page 127.

To face p. 130.]

Burii, a people of Germany, dwelt near the sources of the Oder and Vistula, and joined the Marcomanni in their war against the Romans in the reign of M. Aurelius.

Burrus, Afranius, was appointed by Claudius praefectus praetorio, A. D. 52, and in conjunction with Seneca conducted the education of Nero. He opposed Nero's tyrannical acts, and was at length poisoned by command of the emperor, 63.

Bursa. [PLANCUS.]

Bursao (Bursaoensis, Bursavolensis), a town of the Autrigonae in Hispania Tarraconensis.

Busiris (Βούσιρις), king of Egypt, son of Poseidon and Lysianassa, is said to have sacrificed all foreigners that visited Egypt. Hercules, on his arrival in Egypt, was likewise seized and led to the altar, but he broke his chains, and slew Busiris. This myth seems to point out a time when the Egyptians were accustomed to offer human sacrifices to their deities.

Busiris (Βούσιρις : Βουσιρίτης). 1. (*Abousir,* Ru.), the capital of the Nomos Busirites in Lower Egypt, stood just in the middle of the Delta, on the W. bank of the Nile, and had a great temple of Isis, the remains of which are still standing. — 2. (*Abousir* near *Jizeh*), a small town, a little N.W. of Memphis.

Buteo, Fabius. 1. N., consul B. C. 247, in the first Punic war, was employed in the siege of Drepanum. — 2. M., consul 245, also in the first Punic war. In 216 he was appointed dictator to fill up the vacancies in the senate occasioned by the battle of Cannae. — 3. Q., praetor 181, with the province of Cisalpine Gaul. In 179 he was one of the triumvirs for founding a Latin colony in the territory of the Pisani.

Butes (Βούτης), son of either Teleon or Pandion or Amycus, and Zeuxippe. He was one of the Argonauts, and priest of Athena and of the Erechthean Poseidon. The Attic family of the Butadae or Eteobutadae derived their origin from him; and in the Erechtheum on the Acropolis there was an altar dedicated to Butes.

Buthrotum (Βουθρωτόν : Βουθρώτιος : *Butrinto*), a town of Epirus on a small peninsula, opposite Corcyra, was a flourishing sea-port and was colonized by the Romans.

Buto (Βουτώ), an Egyptian divinity, worshipped principally in the town of BUTO. She was the nurse of Horus and Bubastis, the children of Osiris and Isis, and she saved them from the persecutions of Typhon by concealing them in the floating island of Chemnis. The Greeks identified her with Leto, and represented her as the goddess of night. The shrew-mouse (μυγαλή) and the hawk were sacred to her.

Buto (Βουτώ, Βούτη, or Βοῦτος : Βουτοίτης : *Baltim* ? Ru.), the chief city of the Nomos Chemmites in Lower Egypt, stood near the Sebennytic branch of the Nile, on the Lake of Buto (Βουτικὴ λίμνη, also Σεβεννυτική), and was celebrated for its oracle of the goddess Buto, in honour of whom a festival was held at the city every year.

Buxentum (Buxentinus, Buxentius : *Policastro*), originally **Pyxus** (Πυξοῦς), a town on the W. coast of Lucania and on the river Buxentius, was founded by Micythus, tyrant of Messana, B. C. 471, and was afterwards a Roman colony.

Byblini Montes (τὰ Βύβλινα ὄρη), the mountains whence the Nile is said to flow in the mythical geography of Aeschylus (*Prom.* 811).

Byblis (Βυβλίς), daughter of Miletus and Idothea, was in love with her brother Caunus, whom she pursued through various lands, till at length worn out with sorrow, she was changed into a fountain.

Byblus (Βύβλος : Βύβλιος : *Jebeil*), a very ancient city on the coast of Phoenicia, between Berytus and Tripolis, a little N. of the river Adonis. It was the chief seat of the worship of Adonis. It was governed by a succession of petty princes, the last of whom was deposed by Pompey.

Bylazora (Βυλάζωρα), a town in Paeonia, in Macedonia, on the river Astycus.

Byrsa (Βύρσα), the citadel of CARTHAGO.

Byzacium or **Byzacena Regio** (Βυζάκιον, Βυζακὶς χώρα : S. part of *Tunis*), the S. portion of the Roman province of Africa. [AFRICA, p. 23, b.]

Byzantini Scriptores, the general name of the historians, who have given an account of the Eastern or Byzantine empire from the time of Constantine the Great, A. D. 325, to the destruction of the empire, 1453. They all wrote in Greek, and may be divided into different classes. 1. The historians, whose collected works form an uninterrupted history of the Byzantine empire, and whose writings are therefore called *Corpus Historiae Byzantinae.* They are: (1) ZONARAS, who begins with the creation of the world, and brings his history down to 1188. (2) NICEPHORUS ACOMINATUS, whose history extends from 1188 to 1206. (3) NICEPHORUS GREGORAS, whose history extends from 1204 to 1331. (4) LAONICUS CHALCONDYLES, whose history extends from 1297 to 1462: his work is continued by an anonymous writer to 1565. — 2. The chronographers, who give a brief chronological summary of universal history from the creation of the world to their own times. These writers are very numerous : the most important of them are GEORGIUS SYNCELLUS, THEOPHANES, NICEPHORUS, CEDRENUS, SIMEON METAPHRANTES, MICHAEL GLYCAS, the authors of the *Chronicon Paschale,* &c. — 3. The writers who have treated of separate portions of Byzantine history, such as ZOSIMUS, PROCOPIUS, AGATHIAS, ANNA COMNENA, &c. — 4. The writers who have treated of the constitution, antiquities, &c., of the empire, such as LAURENTIUS LYDUS, CONSTANTINUS VI. PORPHYROGENNETUS. — A collection of the Byzantine writers was published at Paris by command of Louis XIV. in 36 vols. fol. 1645—1711. A reprint of this edition, with additions, was published at Venice in 23 vols. fol. 1727—1733. A new edition of the Byzantine writers was commenced by Niebuhr, Bonn, 1828, 8vo., and is still in course of publication.

Byzantium (Βυζάντιον ; Βυζάντιος, Byzantius : *Constantinople*), a town on the Thracian Bosporus, founded by the Megarians, B. C. 658, is said to have derived its name from Byzas, the leader of the colony and the son of Poseidon. It was situated on 2 hills, was 40 stadia in circumference, and its acropolis stood on the site of the present seraglio. Its favourable position, commanding as it did the entrance to the Euxine, soon rendered it a place of great commercial importance. It was taken by Pausanias after the battle of Plataea, B. C. 479 ; and it was alternately in the possession of the Athenians and Lacedaemonians during the Peloponnesian war. The Lacedaemonians were expelled from Byzantium by Thrasybulus in 390, and the city remained independent for some years. After-

K

wards it became subject in succession to the Macedonians and the Romans. In the civil war between Pescennius Niger and Severus, it espoused the cause of the former: it was taken by Severus A. D. 196 after a siege of 3 years, and a considerable part of it was destroyed. A new city was built by its side (330) by Constantine, who made it the capital of the empire, and changed its name into CONSTANTINOPOLIS.

C.

Căbālia or **-is** (Καβαλία, Καβαλίς: Καβαλεύς, Καβάλιος), a small district of Asia Minor, between Lycia and Pamphylia, with a town of the same name.

Căbăsa or **-us** (Κάβασος: Καβασίτης), the chief city of the Nomos Cabasites, in Lower Egypt.

Cabillōnum (*Châlons-sur-Saône*), a town of the Aedui on the Arar (*Saône*) in Gallia Lugdunensis, was a place of some commercial activity when Caesar was in Gaul (B. C. 53). At a later time the Romans kept a small fleet here.

Cabīra (τὰ Κάβειρα: *Sivas*), a place in Pontus, on the borders of Armenia, near M. Paryadres: a frequent residence of Mithridates, who was defeated here by Lucullus, B. C. 71. Pompey made it a city, and named it Diospolis. Under Augustus it was called Sebaste.

Cabīri (Κάβειροι), mystic divinities who occur in various parts of the ancient world. The meaning of their name, their character and nature, are quite uncertain. They were chiefly worshipped at Samothrace, Lemnos, and Imbros, and their mysteries at Samothrace were solemnized with great splendour. (See *Dict. of Ant.* art. *Cabeiria.*) They were also worshipped at Thebes, Anthedon, Pergamus, and elsewhere. Most of the early writers appear to have regarded them as the children of Hephaestus and as inferior divinities dwelling in Samothrace, Lemnos, and Imbros. Later writers identify them with Demeter, Persephone, and Rhea, and regard their mysteries as solemnized in honour of one of these goddesses. Other writers identify the Cabiri with the Dioscuri (Castor and Pollux), and others again with the Roman Penates ; but the latter notion seems to have arisen with those writers who traced every ancient Roman institution to Troy, and thence to Samothrace.

Cabȳlē (Καβύλη: Καβυληνός: *Golowitza*), a town in the interior of Thrace, conquered by M. Lucullus, probably the Goloë of the Byzantine writers.

Cācus, son of Vulcan, was a huge giant, who inhabited a cave on Mt. Aventine, and plundered the surrounding country. When Hercules came to Italy with the oxen which he had taken from Geryon in Spain, Cacus stole part of the cattle while the hero slept ; and, as he dragged the animals into his cave by their tails, it was impossible to discover their traces. But when the remaining oxen passed by the cave, those within began to bellow, and were thus discovered, whereupon Cacus was slain by Hercules. In honour of his victory, Hercules dedicated the *ara maxima*, which continued to exist ages afterwards in Rome.

Cacȳpăris (Κακύπαρις or Κακόπαρις: *Cassibili*), a river in Sicily, S. of Syracuse.

Cadēna (τὰ Κάδηνα), a strong city of Cappadocia, the residence of the last king, Archelaüs.

Cădi (Κάδοι: Καδηνός: *Kodus*), a city of Phrygia Epictetus, on the borders of Lydia.

Cadmēa. [THEBAE.]

Cadmus (Κάδμος). 1. Son of Agenor, king of Phoenicia, and of Telephassa, and brother of Europa. Another legend makes him a native of Thebes in Egypt. When Europa was carried off by Zeus to Crete, Agenor sent Cadmus in search of his sister, enjoining him not to return without her. Unable to find her, Cadmus settled in Thrace, but having consulted the oracle at Delphi, he was commanded by the god to follow a cow of a certain kind, and to build a town on the spot where the cow should sink down with fatigue. Cadmus found the cow in Phocis and followed her into Boeotia, where she sank down on the spot on which Cadmus built Cadmea, afterwards the citadel of Thebes. Intending to sacrifice the cow to Athena, he sent some persons to the neighbouring well of Ares to fetch water. This well was guarded by a dragon, a son of Ares, who killed the men sent by Cadmus. Thereupon Cadmus slew the dragon, and, on the advice of Athena, sowed the teeth of the monster, out of which armed men grew up called *Sparti* or the *Sown*, who killed each other, with the exception of 5, who were the ancestors of the Thebans. Athena assigned to Cadmus the government of Thebes, and Zeus gave him Harmonia for his wife. The marriage solemnity was honoured by the presence of all the Olympian gods in the Cadmea. Cadmus gave to Harmonia the famous peplus and necklace which he had received from Hephaestus or from Europa, and he became by her the father of Autonoë, Ino, Semele, Agave, and Polydorus. Subsequently Cadmus and Harmonia quitted Thebes, and went to the Enchelians ; this people chose Cadmus as their king, and with his assistance they conquered the Illyrians. After this, Cadmus had another son, whom he called Illyrius. In the end, Cadmus and Harmonia were changed into serpents, and were removed by Zeus to Elysium. — Cadmus is said to have introduced into Greece from Phoenicia or Egypt an alphabet of 16 letters, and to have been the first who worked the mines of mount Pangaeon in Thrace. The story of Cadmus seems to suggest the immigration of a Phoenician or Egyptian colony into Greece, by means of which the alphabet, the art of mining, and civilization, came into the country. But many modern writers deny the existence of any such Phoenician or Egyptian colony, and regard Cadmus as a Pelasgian divinity. — 2. Of Miletus, son of Pandion, the earliest Greek historian or logographer, lived about B. C. 540. He wrote a work on the foundation of Miletus and the earliest history of Ionia generally, in 4 books, but the work extant in antiquity under the latter name was considered a forgery.

Cadmus (Κάδμος). 1. (*M. Baba*) a mountain in Caria, on the borders of Phrygia, containing the sources of the rivers Cadmus and Lycus. — 2. A small river of Phrygia, flowing N. into the Lycus.

Cadurci, a people in Gallia Aquitanica, in the country now called *Querci* (a corruption of Cadurci), were celebrated for their manufactories of linen, coverlets, &c. Their capital was **Divona**, afterwards **Civitas Cadurcorum**, now *Cahors*, where are the remains of a Roman amphitheatre and of an aqueduct. A part of the town still bears the name *les Cadurcas*.

Cadūsii (Καδούσιοι), or **Gēlae** (Γῆλαι), a power-tul Scythian tribe in the mountains S.W. of the Caspian, on the borders of Media Atropatene. Under the Medo-Persian empire they were troublesome neighbours, but the Syrian kings appear to have reduced them to tributary auxiliaries.

Cadytis (Κάδυτις), according to Herodotus, a great city of the Syrians of Palestine, not much smaller than Sardis, was taken by Necho, king of Egypt, after his defeat of the "Syrians" at Magdolus. It is now pretty well established that by Cadytis is meant Jerusalem, and that the battle mentioned by Herodotus is that in which Necho defeated and slew king Josiah at Megiddo, B. C. 608. (Comp. Herod. ii. 159, iii. 5, with 2 *Kings* xxiii. and 2 *Chron.* xxxv. xxxvi.)

Caecilia. 1. Caia, the Roman name of TANAQUIL, wife of Tarquinius Priscus. — **2. Metella**, daughter of L. Metellus Dalmaticus, consul B. C. 119, was first married to M. Aemilius Scaurus, consul in 115, and afterwards to the dictator Sulla. She fell ill in 81, during the celebration of Sulla's triumphal feast ; and as her recovery was hopeless, Sulla for religious reasons sent her a bill of divorce, and had her removed from his house, but honoured her memory with a splendid funeral.—**3.** Daughter of T. Pomponius Atticus, called Caecilia, because her father took the name of his uncle, Q. Caecilius, by whom he was adopted. She was married to M. Vipsanius Agrippa. [ATTICUS.]

Caecilia Gens, plebeian, claimed descent from CAECULUS, the founder of Praeneste, or Caecas, the companion of Aeneas. Most of the Caecilii are mentioned under their cognomens, BASSUS, METELLUS, RUFUS: for others see below.

Caecilius. 1. Q., a wealthy Roman eques, who adopted his nephew Atticus in his will, and left the latter a fortune of 10 millions of sesterces. — **2. Caecilius Calactinus**, a Greek rhetorician at Rome in the time of Augustus, was a native of Cale Acte in Sicily (whence his name Calactinus). He wrote a great number of works on rhetoric, grammar, and historical subjects. All these works are now lost ; but they were in great repute with the rhetoricians and critics of the imperial period. — **3. Caecilius Statius**, a Roman comic poet, the immediate predecessor of Terence, was by birth an Insubrian Gaul, and a native of Milan. Being a slave he bore the servile appellation of *Statius*, which was afterwards, probably when he received his freedom, converted into a sort of cognomen, and he became known as Caecilius Statius. He died B. C. 168. We have the titles of 40 of his dramas, but only a few fragments of them are preserved. They appear to have belonged to the class of *Palliatae*, that is, were free translations or adaptations of the works of Greek writers of the new comedy. The Romans placed Caecilius in the first rank of comic poets, classing him with Plautus and Terence.

Caecina, the name of a family of the Etruscan city of Volaterrae, probably derived from the river Caecina, which flows by the town. — **1. A. Caecina**, whom Cicero defended in a law-suit, B. C. 69. — **2. A. Caecina**, son of the preceding, published a libellous work against Caesar, and was in consequence sent into exile after the battle of Pharsalia, B. C. 48. He afterwards joined the Pompeians in Africa, and upon the defeat of the latter in 46, he surrendered to Caesar, who spared his life. Cicero wrote several letters to Caecina, and speaks of him as a man of ability. Caecina was the author of a work on the *Etrusca Disciplina*. —

3. A. Caecina Severus, a distinguished general in the reigns of Augustus and Tiberius. He was governor of Moesia in A. D. 6, when he fought against the two Batos in the neighbouring provinces of Dalmatia and Pannonia. [BATO.] In 15 he fought as the legate of Germanicus, against Arminius, and in consequence of his success received the insignia of a triumph. — **4. Caecina Tuscus**, son of Nero's nurse, appointed governor of Egypt by Nero, but banished for making use of the baths which had been erected in anticipation of the emperor's arrival in Egypt. He returned from banishment on the death of Nero, A. D. 68.— **5. A. Caecina Alienus**, was quaestor in Baetica in Spain at Nero's death, and was one of the foremost in joining the party of Galba. He was rewarded by Galba with the command of a legion in Upper Germany ; but, being detected in embezzling some of the public money, the emperor ordered him to be prosecuted. Caecina, in revenge, joined Vitellius, and was sent by the latter into Italy with an army of 30,000 men towards the end of 68. After ravaging the country of the Helvetii, he crossed the Alps by the pass of the Great St. Bernard, and laid siege to Placentia, from which he was repulsed by the troops of Otho, who had succeeded Galba. Subsequently he was joined by Fabius Valens, another general of Vitellius, and their united forces gained a victory over Otho's army at Bedriacum. Vitellius having thus gained the throne, Caecina was made consul on the 1st of September, 69, and was shortly afterwards sent against Antonius Primus, the general of Vespasian. But he again proved a traitor, and espoused the cause of Vespasian. Some years afterwards (79), he conspired against Vespasian, and was slain by order of Titus. — **6. Decius Albinus Caecina**, a Roman satirist in the time of Arcadius and Honorius.

Caecinus (Καικινός or Καικῖνος), a river in Bruttium flowing into the Sinus Scylacius by the town Caecinum.

Caecubus Ager, a marshy district in Latium, bordering on the gulf of Amyclae close to Fundi, celebrated for its wine (*Caecubum*) in the age of Horace. In the time of Pliny the reputation of this wine was entirely gone. (See *Dict. of Ant.* p. 1207, a, 2nd ed.)

Caeculus, an ancient Italian hero, son of Vulcan, is said to have founded Praeneste.

Caeles or **Caelius Vibenna**, the leader of an Etruscan army, is said to have come to Rome in the reign either of Romulus or of Tarquinius Priscus, and to have settled with his troops on the hill called after him the Caelian.

Caelius or **Coelius**. 1. **Antipater**. [ANTIPATER.] — **2**. Aurelianus. [AURELIANUS.] — **3. Caldus**. [CALDUS.] — **4. Rufus**. [RUFUS.]

Caelius or **Coelius Mons**. [ROMA.]

Caenae (Καιναί: *Senn*), a city of Mesopotamia, on the W. bank of the Tigris, opposite the mouth of the Lycus.

Caene, Caenepolis, or **Neapolis** (Καινὴ πόλις, Νέη πόλις : *Keneh*), a city of Upper Egypt, on the right bank of the Nile, a little below Coptos and opposite to Tentyra.

Caeneus (Καινεύς), one of the Lapithae, son of Elatus or Coronus, was originally a maiden named Caenis, who was beloved by Poseidon, and was by this god changed into a man, and rendered invulnerable. As a man he took part in the Argonautic

K 2

expedition and the Calydonian hunt. In the battle between the Lapithae and the Centaurs at the marriage of Pirithous, he was buried by the Centaurs under a mass of trees, as they were unable to kill him, but he was changed into a bird. In the lower world Caeneus recovered his female form. (Virg. *Aen.* vi. 448.)

Caeni or **Caenĭci**, a Thracian people between the Black Sea and the Panyeus.

Caenĭna (Caeninensis), a town of the Sabines in Latium, whose king Acron is said to have carried on the first war against Rome. After their defeat, most of the inhabitants removed to Rome.

Caenis. [CAENEUS.]

Caenys (Καῖνυς: *Capo di Cavallo* or *Coda di Volpe*), a promontory of Bruttium opposite Sicily.

Caepārĭus, M., of Tarracina, one of Catiline's conspirators, was to induce the shepherds in Apulia to rise: he escaped from the city, but was overtaken in his flight, and was executed with the other conspirators B. C. 63.

Caepĭo, Servĭlĭus. 1. Cn., consul B. C. 253, in the first Punic war, sailed with his colleague, C. Sempronius Blaesus, to the coast of Africa.— **2.** Cn., curule aedile 207, praetor 205, and consul 203, when he fought against Hannibal near Croton in the S. of Italy. He died in the pestilence in 174.— **3.** Cn., son of No. 2, curule aedile 179, praetor 174, with Spain as his province, and consul in 169.— **4.** Q., son of No. 3, consul 142, was adopted by Q. Fabius Maximus. [MAXIMUS.]— **5.** Cn., son of No. 3, consul 141, and censor 125.— **6.** Cn., son of No. 3, consul 140, carried on war against Viriathus in Lusitania, and induced two of the friends of Viriathus to murder the latter.— **7.** Q., son of No. 6, was consul 106, when he proposed a law for restoring the judicia to the senators, of which they had been deprived by the Sempronia lex of C. Gracchus. He was afterwards sent into Gallia Narbonensis to oppose the Cimbri, and was in 105 defeated by the Cimbri, along with the consul Cn. Mallius or Manlius. 80,000 soldiers and 40,000 camp-followers are said to have perished. Caepio survived the battle, but 10 years afterwards (95) he was brought to trial by the tribune C. Norbanus on account of his misconduct in this war. He was condemned and cast into prison, where according to one account he died, but it was more generally stated that he escaped from prison, and lived in exile at Smyrna. — **8.** Q., quaestor urbanus 100, opposed the lex frumentaria of Saturninus. In 91 he opposed the measures of Drusus, and accused two of the most distinguished senators, M. Scaurus and L. Philippus. He fell in battle in the Social War, 90.

Caepĭo, Fannĭus, conspired with Murena against Augustus B. C. 22, and was put to death.

Caerē (Caerites, Caeretes, Caeretani : *Cervetri*), called by the Greeks **Agylla** (Ἀγυλλα : *Agyllina urbs*, Virg. *Aen.* vii. 652), a city in Etruria situated on a small river (Caeritis amnis), W. of Veii and 50 stadia from the coast. It was an ancient Pelasgic city, the capital of the cruel Mezentius, and was afterwards one of the 12 Etruscan cities, with a territory extending apparently as far as the Tiber. In early times Caere was closely allied with Rome ; and when the latter city was taken by the Gauls, B. C. 390, Caere gave refuge to the Vestal virgins. It was from this event that the Romans traced the origin of their word *caerimonia*. The Romans out of gratitude are said to have

conferred upon the Caerites the Roman franchise without the suffragium * though it is not improbable that the Caerites enjoyed this honour previously. In 353, however, Caere joined Tarquinii in making war against Rome, but was obliged to purchase a truce with Rome for 100 years by the forfeiture of half of its territory. From this time Caere gradually sunk in importance, and was probably destroyed in the wars of Marius and Sulla. It was restored by Drusus, who made it a municipium ; and it continued to exist till the 13th century, when part of the inhabitants removed to a site about 3 miles off, on which they bestowed the same name (now *Ceri*), while the old town was distinguished by the title of *Vetus* or *Caere Vetere*, corrupted into *Cervetri*, which is a small village with 100 or 200 inhabitants. Here have been discovered, within the last few years, the tombs of the ancient Caere, many of them in a state of complete preservation. — The country round Caere produced wine and a great quantity of corn, and in its neighbourhood were warm baths which were much frequented. Caere used as its sea-port the town of PYRGI.

Caerellĭa, a Roman lady frequently mentioned in the correspondence of Cicero as distinguished for her acquirements and her love of philosophy.

Caesar, the name of a patrician family of the Julia gens, which traced its origin to Iulus, the son of Aeneas. [JULIA GENS.] Various etymologies of the name are given by the ancient writers ; but it is probably connected with the Latin word *caes-ar-ies*, and the Sanskrit *kêsa*, " hair," for it is in accordance with the Roman custom for a surname to be given to an individual from some peculiarity in his personal appearance. The name was assumed by Augustus as the adopted son of the dictator C. Julius Caesar, and was by Augustus handed down to his adopted son Tiberius. It continued to be used by Caligula, Claudius, and Nero, as members either by adoption or female descent of Caesar's family ; but though the family became extinct with Nero, succeeding emperors still retained the name as part of their titles, and it was the practice to prefix it to their own name, as for instance, *Imperator Caesar Domitianus Augustus*. When Hadrian adopted Aelius Verus, he allowed the latter to take the title of Caesar ; and from this time, though the title of *Augustus* continued to be confined to the reigning prince, that of *Caesar* was also granted to the second person in the state and the heir presumptive to the throne.

Caesar, Jūlĭus. 1. Sex., praetor B. C. 208, with Sicily as his province.— **2.** Sex., curule aedile, 165, when the Hecyra of Terence was exhibited at the Megalesian games, and consul 157. — **3.** L., consul 90, fought against the Socii, and in the course of the same year proposed the *Lex Julia de Civitate*, which granted the citizenship to the Latins and the Socii who had remained faithful to Rome. Caesar was censor in 89 ; he belonged to the aristocratical party, and was put to death by Marius in 87.— **4.** C., surnamed STRABO VOPISCUS, brother of No. 3, was curule aedile 90, was a candidate for the consulship in 88, and was slain along with his

---

* The Caerites appear to have been the first body of Roman citizens who did not enjoy the suffrage. Thus, when a Roman citizen was struck out of his tribe by the Censors and made an aerarian, he was said to become one of the Caerites, since he had lost the suffrage : hence we find the expressions *in tabulas Caeritum referre* and *aerarium facere* used as synonymous.

brother by Marius in 87. He was one of the chief orators and poets of his age, and is one of the speakers in Cicero's dialogue *De Oratore*. Wit was the chief characteristic of his oratory; but he was deficient in power and energy. The names of 2 of his tragedies are preserved, the *Adrastus* and *Tecmessa*.—5. L., son of No. 3, and uncle by his sister Julia of M. Antony the triumvir. He was consul 64, and belonged, like his father, to the aristocratical party. He appears to have deserted this party afterwards; we find him in Gaul in 52 as one of the legates of C. Caesar, and he continued in Italy during the civil war. After Caesar's death (44) he sided with the senate in opposition to his uncle Antony, and was in consequence proscribed by the latter in 43, but obtained his pardon through the influence of his sister Julia. — 6. L., son of No. 5, usually distinguished from his father by the addition to his name of *filius* or *adolescens*. He joined Pompey on the breaking out of the civil war in 49, and was sent by Pompey to Caesar with proposals of peace. In the course of the same year, he crossed over to Africa, where the command of Clupea was entrusted to him. In 46 he served as proquaestor to Cato in Utica, and after the death of Cato he surrendered to the dictator Caesar, and was shortly afterwards put to death, but probably not by the dictator's orders.—7. C., the father of the dictator, was praetor, but in what year is uncertain, and died suddenly at Pisae in 84.—8. Sex., brother of No. 7, consul 91.—9. C., the Dictator, son of No. 7 and of Aurelia, was born on the 12th of July, 100, in the consulship of C. Marius (VI.) and L. Valerius Flaccus, and was consequently 6 years younger than Pompey and Cicero. He had nearly completed his 56th year at the time of his murder, 15th of March, 44. Caesar was closely connected with the popular party by the marriage of his aunt Julia with the great Marius; and in 83, though only 17 years of age, he married Cornelia, the daughter of L. Cinna, the chief leader of the Marian party. Sulla commanded him to put away his wife, but he refused to obey him, and was consequently proscribed. He concealed himself for some time in the country of the Sabines, till his friends obtained his pardon from Sulla, who is said to have observed, when they pleaded his youth, " that that boy would some day or another be the ruin of the aristocracy, for that there were many Mariuses in him." Seeing that he was not safe at Rome, he went to Asia, where he served his first campaign under M. Minucius Thermus, and, at the capture of Mytilene (80), was rewarded with a civic crown for saving the life of a fellow-soldier. On the death of Sulla in 78, he returned to Rome, and in the following year gained great renown as an orator, though he was only 22 years of age, by his prosecution of Cn. Dolabella on account of extortion in his province of Macedonia. To perfect himself in oratory, he resolved to study in Rhodes under Apollonius Molo, but on his voyage thither he was captured by pirates, and only obtained his liberty by a ransom of 50 talents. At Miletus he manned some vessels, overpowered the pirates, and conducted them as prisoners to Pergamus, where he crucified them, a punishment with which he had frequently threatened them in sport when he was their prisoner. He then repaired to Rhodes, where he studied under Apollonius, and shortly afterwards returned to Rome. He now devoted all his ener-

gies to acquire the favour of the people. His liberality was unbounded, and as his private fortune was not large, he soon contracted enormous debts. But he gained his object, and became the favourite of the people, and was raised by them in succession to the high offices of the state. He was quaestor in 68, and aedile in 65, when he spent enormous sums upon the public games and buildings. He was said by many to have been privy to Catiline's conspiracy in 63, but there is no satisfactory evidence of his guilt, and it is improbable that he would have embarked in such a rash scheme. In the debate in the senate on the punishment of the conspirators, he opposed their execution in a very able speech, which made such an impression, that their lives would have been spared but for the speech of Cato in reply. In the course of this year (63), Caesar was elected Pontifex Maximus, defeating the other candidates, Q. Catulus and Servilius Isauricus, who had both been consuls, and were two of the most illustrious men in the state.—In 62 Caesar was praetor, and took an active part in supporting the tribune Metellus in opposition to his colleague Cato; in consequence of the tumults that ensued, the senate suspended both Caesar and Metellus from their offices, but were obliged to reinstate him in his dignity after a few days. In the following year (61) Caesar went as propraetor into Farther Spain, where he gained great victories over the Lusitanians. On his return to Rome. he became a candidate for the consulship, and was elected notwithstanding the strenuous opposition of the aristocracy, who succeeded however in carrying the election of Bibulus as his colleague, who was one of the warmest supporters of the aristocracy. After his election, but before he entered upon the consulship, he formed that coalition with Pompey and M. Crassus, usually known by the name of the first triumvirate. Pompey had become estranged from the aristocracy, since the senate had opposed the ratification of his acts in Asia and an assignment of lands which he had promised to his veterans. Crassus in consequence of his immense wealth was one of the most powerful men at Rome, but was a personal enemy of Pompey. They were reconciled by means of Caesar, and the 3 entered into an agreement to support one another, and to divide the power in the state between them.—In 59 Caesar was consul, and being supported by Pompey and Crassus he was able to carry all his measures. Bibulus, from whom the senate had expected so much, could offer no effectual opposition, and, after making a vain attempt to resist Caesar, shut himself up in his own house, and did not appear again in public till the expiration of his consulship. Caesar's first measure was an agrarian law, by which the rich Campanian plain was divided among the poorer citizens. He next gained the favour of the equites by relieving them from 1-3rd of the sum which they had agreed to pay for the farming of the taxes in Asia. He then obtained the confirmation of Pompey's acts. Having thus gratified the people, the equites, and Pompey, he was easily able to obtain for himself the provinces which he wished. By a vote of the people, proposed by the tribune Vatinius, the provinces of Cisalpine Gaul and Illyricum were granted to Caesar with 3 legions for 5 years; and the senate added to his government the province of Transalpine Gaul, with another legion, for 5 years also, as they saw that a bill would be proposed to the people for that purpose, if they did not grant the province themselves. Caesar foresaw that the struggle between the different parties at Rome must eventually be terminated by the sword, and he had therefore resolved to obtain an army, which he might attach to himself by victories and rewards. In the course of the same year Caesar united himself more closely to Pompey by giving him his daughter Julia in marriage. During the next 9 years Caesar was occupied with the subjugation of Gaul. He conquered the whole of Transalpine Gaul, which had hitherto been independent of the Romans, with the exception of the S. E. part called Provincia ; he twice crossed the Rhine, and twice landed in Britain, which had been previously unknown to the Romans. — In his 1st campaign (58) Caesar conquered the Helvetii, who had emigrated from Switzerland with the intention of settling in Gaul. He next defeated Ariovistus, a German king, who had taken possession of part of the territories of the Aedui and Sequani, and pursued him as far as the Rhine. At the conclusion of the campaign Caesar went into Cisalpine Gaul to attend to the civil duties of his province and to keep up his communication with the various parties at Rome. During the whole of his campaigns in Gaul, he spent the greater part of the winter in Cisalpine Gaul. — In his 2nd campaign (57) Caesar carried on war with the Belgae, who dwelt in the N.E. of Gaul between the Sequana (*Seine*) and the Rhine, and after a severe struggle completely subdued them. — Caesar's 3rd campaign in Gaul (56) did not commence till late in the year. He was detained some months in the N. of Italy by the state of affairs at Rome. At Luca (*Lucca*) he had interviews with most of the leading men at Rome, among others with Pompey and Crassus, who visited him in April. He made arrangements with them for the continuance of their power ; it was agreed between them that Crassus and Pompey should be the consuls for the following year, that Crassus should have the province of Syria, Pompey the 2 Spains, and that Caesar's government, which would expire at the end of 54, should be prolonged for 5 years after that date. After making these arrangements he crossed the Alps, and carried on war with the Veneti and the other states in the N.W. of Gaul, who had submitted to Crassus, Caesar's legate, in the preceding year, but who had now risen in arms against the Romans. They were defeated and obliged to submit to Caesar, and during the same time Crassus conquered Aquitania. Thus, in 3 campaigns, Caesar subdued the whole of Gaul ; but the people made several attempts to recover their independence ; and it was not till their revolts had been again and again put down by Caesar, and the flower of the nation had perished in battle, that they learnt to submit to the Roman yoke.—In his 4th campaign (55) Caesar crossed the Rhine in order to strike terror into the Germans, but he only remained 18 days on the further side of the river. Late in the summer he invaded Britain, but more with the view of obtaining some knowledge of the island from personal observation, than with the intention of permanent conquest at present. He sailed from the port Itius (probably *Witsand*, between Calais and Boulogne), and effected a landing somewhere near the South Foreland, after a severe struggle with the natives. The late period of the year compelled him to return to Gaul after remaining only a short time in the island. In this year, according to his arrangement with Pompey and Crassus, who were now consuls, his government of the Gauls and Illyricum was prolonged for 5 years, namely, from the 1st of January, 53, to the end of December, 49. — Caesar's 5th campaign (54) was chiefly occupied with his 2nd invasion of Britain. He landed in Britain at the same place as in the former year, defeated the Britons in a series of engagements, and crossed the Tamesis (*Thames*). The Britons submitted, and promised to pay an annual tribute ; but their subjection was only nominal, for Caesar left no garrisons or military establishments behind him, and Britain remained nearly 100 years longer independent of the Romans. During the winter one of the Roman legions, which had been stationed under the command of T. Titurius Sabinus and L. Aurunculeius Cotta, in the country of the Eburones, was cut to pieces by Ambiorix and the Eburones. Ambiorix then proceeded to attack the camp of Q. Cicero, the brother of the orator, who was stationed with a legion among the Nervii ; but Cicero defended himself with bravery, and was at length relieved by Caesar in person. In September of this year, Julia, Caesar's only daughter and Pompey's wife, died in childbirth. — In Caesar's 6th campaign (53) several of the Gallic nations revolted, but Caesar soon compelled them to return to obedience. The Treviri, who had revolted, had been supported by the Germans, and Caesar accordingly again crossed the Rhine, but made no permanent conquests on the further side of the river. — Caesar's 7th campaign (52) was the most arduous of all. Almost all the nations of Gaul rose simultaneously in revolt, and the supreme command was given to Vercingetorix, by far the ablest general that Caesar had yet encountered. After a most severe struggle in which Caesar's military genius triumphed over every obstacle, the war was brought to a conclusion by the defeat of the Gauls before Alesia and the surrender of this city.— The 8th and 9th campaigns (51. 50) were employed in the final subjugation of Gaul, which had entirely submitted to Caesar by the middle of 50. Meanwhile, an estrangement had taken place between Caesar and Pompey. Caesar's brilliant victories had gained him fresh popularity and influence ; and Pompey saw with ill-disguised mortification that he was becoming the second person in the state. He was thus led to join again the aristocratical party, by the assistance of which he could alone hope to retain his position as the chief man in the Roman state. The great object of this party was to deprive Caesar of his command, and to compel him to come to Rome as a private man to sue for the consulship. They would then have formally accused him, and as Pompey was in the neighbourhood of the city at the head of an army, the trial would have been a mockery, and his condemnation would have been certain. Caesar offered to resign his command if Pompey would do the same ; but the senate would not listen to any compromise. Accordingly, on the 1st of January, 49, the senate passed a resolution that Caesar should disband his army by a certain day, and that if he did not do so, he should be regarded as an enemy of the state. Two of the tribunes, M. Antonius and Q. Cassius, put their veto upon this resolution, but their opposition was set at nought, and they fled for refuge to Caesar's camp. Under the plea of protecting the tribunes,

Caesar crossed the Rubicon, which separated his province from Italy, and marched towards Rome. Pompey, who had been entrusted by the senate with the conduct of the war, soon discovered how greatly he had overrated his own popularity and influence. His own troops deserted to his rival in crowds ; town after town in Italy opened its gates to Caesar, whose march was like a triumphal progress. The only town which offered Caesar any resistance was Corfinium, into which L. Domitius Ahenobarbus had thrown himself with a strong force ; but even this place was obliged to surrender at the end of a few days. Meantime, Pompey, with the magistrates and senators, had fled from Rome to Capua, and now, despairing of opposing Caesar in Italy, he marched from Capua to Brundusium, and on the 17th of March embarked for Greece. Caesar pursued Pompey to Brundusium, but he was unable to follow him to Greece for want of ships. He therefore marched back from Brundusium, and repaired to Rome, having thus in 3 months become master of the whole of Italy. After remaining a short time in Rome, he set out for Spain, where Pompey's legates, Afranius, Petreius, and Varro, commanded powerful armies. After defeating Afranius and Petreius, and receiving the submission of Varro, Caesar returned to Rome, where he had meantime been appointed dictator by the praetor M. Lepidus. He resigned the dictatorship at the end of 11 days, after holding the consular comitia, in which he himself and P. Servilius Vatia Isauricus were elected consuls for the next year. — At the beginning of January, 48, Caesar crossed over to Greece, where Pompey had collected a formidable army. At first the campaign was in Pompey's favour ; Caesar was repulsed before Dyrrhachium with considerable loss, and was obliged to retreat towards Thessaly. In this country on the plains of Pharsalus or Pharsalia, a decisive battle was fought between the 2 armies on the 9th of August, 48, in which Pompey was completely defeated. Pompey fled to Egypt, pursued by Caesar, but he was murdered before Caesar arrived in the country. [POMPEIUS.] His head was brought to Caesar, who turned away from the sight, shed tears at the untimely death of his rival, and put his murderers to death. When the news of the battle of Pharsalia reached Rome, various honours were conferred upon Caesar. He was appointed dictator for a whole year and consul for 5 years, and the tribunician power was conferred upon him for life. He declined the consulship, but entered upon the dictatorship in September in this year (48), and appointed M. Antony his master of the horse. On his arrival in Egypt, Caesar became involved in a war, which gave the remains of the Pompeian party time to rally. This war, usually called the Alexandrine war, arose from the determination of Caesar that Cleopatra, whose fascinations had won his heart, should reign in common with her brother Ptolemy ; but this decision was opposed by the guardians of the young king, and the war which thus broke out, was not brought to a close till the latter end of March, 47. It was soon after this, that Cleopatra had a son by Caesar. [CAESARION.] Caesar returned to Rome through Syria and Asia Minor, and on his march through Pontus attacked Pharnaces, the son of Mithridates the Great, who had assisted Pompey. He defeated Pharnaces near Zela with such ease, that he informed the senate of his victory by the words, *Veni, vidi, vici.* He reached Rome in September (47), was appointed consul for the following year, and before the end of September set sail for Africa, where Scipio and Cato had collected a large army. The war was terminated by the defeat of the Pompeian army at the battle of Thapsus, on the 6th of April, 46. Cato, unable to defend Utica, put an end to his own life. — Caesar returned to Rome in the latter end of July. He was now the undisputed master of the Roman world, but he used his victory with the greatest moderation. Unlike other conquerors in civil wars, he freely forgave all who had borne arms against him, and declared that he would make no difference between Pompeians and Caesarians. His clemency was one of the brightest features of his character. At Rome all parties seemed to vie in paying him honour: the dictatorship was bestowed on him for 10 years, and the censorship, under the new title of *Praefectus Morum*, for 3 years. He celebrated his victories in Gaul, Egypt, Pontus, and Africa by 4 magnificent triumphs. Caesar now proceeded to correct the various evils which had crept into the state, and to obtain the enactment of several laws suitable to the altered condition of the commonwealth. The most important of his measures this year (46) was the reformation of the calendar. As the Roman year was now 3 months in advance of the real time, Caesar added 90 days to this year, and thus made the whole year consist of 445 days ; and he guarded against a repetition of similar errors for the future by adapting the year to the sun's course. (*Dict. of Ant.* art. *Calendarium.*) — Meantime the 2 sons of Pompey, Sextus and Cneius, had collected a new army in Spain. Caesar set out for Spain towards the end of the year, and brought the war to a close by the battle of Munda, on the 17th of March, 45, in which the enemy were only defeated after a most obstinate resistance. Cn. Pompey was killed shortly afterwards, but Sextus made good his escape. Caesar reached Rome in September, and entered the city in triumph. Fresh honours awaited him. His portrait was to be struck on coins ; the month of Quintilis was to receive the name of Julius in his honour ; he received the title of imperator for life ; and the whole senate took an oath to watch over his safety. To reward his followers, Caesar increased the number of senators and of the public magistrates, so that there were to be 16 praetors, 40 quaestors, and 6 aediles. He began to revolve vast schemes for the benefit of the Roman world. Among his plans of internal improvement, he proposed to frame a digest of all the Roman laws, to establish public librarics, to drain the Pomptine marshes, to enlarge the harbour of Ostia, and to dig a canal through the isthmus of Corinth. To protect the boundaries of the Roman empire, he meditated expeditions against the Parthians and the barbarous tribes on the Danube, and had already begun to make preparations for his departure to the East. Possessing royal power, he now wished to obtain the title of king, and Antony accordingly offered him the diadem in public on the festival of the Lupercalia (the 15th of February) ; but, seeing that the proposition was not favourably received by the people, he declined it for the present. — But Caesar's power was not witnessed without envy. The Roman aristocracy, who had been so long accustomed to rule the Roman world and to pillage it at their pleasure, could ill brook a master, and resolved to remove him by assassination. The conspiracy against Caesar's life had been set afoot by Cassius, a personal enemy of Caesar's, and there were more than 60 persons privy to it. Many of these persons had been raised by Caesar to wealth and honour; and some of them, such as M. Brutus, lived with him on terms of the most intimate friendship. It has been the practice of rhetoricians to speak of the murder of Caesar as a glorious deed, and to represent Brutus and Cassius as patriots; but the mask ought to be stripped off these false patriots; they cared not for the republic, but only for themselves; and their object in murdering Caesar was to gain power for themselves and their party. Caesar had many warnings of his approaching fate, but he disregarded them all, and fell by the daggers of his assassins on the Ides or 15th of March, 44. At an appointed signal the conspirators surrounded him; Casca dealt the first blow, and the others quickly drew their swords and attacked him; Caesar at first defended himself, but when he saw that Brutus, his friend and favourite, had also drawn his sword, he exclaimed *Tu quoque Brute!* pulled his toga over his face, and sunk pierced with wounds at the foot of Pompey's statue. — Julius Caesar was the greatest man of antiquity. He was gifted by nature with the most various talents, and was distinguished by the most extraordinary attainments in the most diversified pursuits. He was at one and the same time a general, a statesman, a lawgiver, a jurist, an orator, a poet, an historian, a philologer, a mathematician, and an architect. He was equally fitted to excel in all, and has given proofs that he would have surpassed almost all other men in any subject to which he devoted the energies of his extraordinary mind. During the whole of his busy life he found time for literary pursuits, and was the author of many works, the majority of which has been lost. The purity of his Latin and the clearness of his style were celebrated by the ancients themselves, and are conspicuous in his *Commentarii*, which are his only works that have come down to us. They relate the history of the first 7 years of the Gallic war in 7 books, and the history of the Civil war down to the commencement of the Alexandrine in 3 books. Neither of these works completed the history of the Gallic and Civil wars. The history of the former was completed in an 8th book, which is usually ascribed to Hirtius, and the history of the Alexandrine, African, and Spanish wars were written in 3 separate books, which are also ascribed to Hirtius, but their authorship is uncertain. The lost works of Caesar are: — 1. *Anticato*, in reply to Cicero's *Cato*, which Cicero wrote in praise of Cato after the death of the latter in 46. 2. *De Analogia*, or, as Cicero explains it, *De Ratione Latine loquendi*, dedicated to Cicero, contained investigations on the Latin language, and were written by Caesar while he was crossing the Alps. 3. *Libri Auspiciorum*, or *Auguralia*. 4. *De Astris.* 5. *Apophthegmata*, or *Dicta collectanea*, a collection of good sayings. 6. *Poemata.* Two of these written in his youth, *Laudes Herculis* and a tragedy *Oedipus*, were suppressed by Augustus. Of the numerous editions of Caesar's Commentaries the best are by Oudendorp, Lugd. Bat. 1737, Stuttgard, 1822; by Morus, Lips. 1780; and by Oberlin, Lips. 1805, 1819.

C. Caesar and L. Caesar, the sons of M. Vip-

sanius Agrippa and Julia, and the grandsons of Augustus. L. Caesar died at Massilia, on his way to Spain, A. D. 2, and C. Caesar in Lycia, A. D. 4, of a wound which he had received in Armenia.

Caesaraugusta (*Zaragoza or Saragossa*), more anciently Salduba, a town of the Edetani on the Iberus in Hispania Tarraconensis, was colonized by Augustus B. C. 27, and was the seat of a Conventus Juridicus. It was the birth-place of the poet Prudentius.

Caesarēa (Καισάρεια: Καισαρεύς: Caesariensis), a name given to several cities of the Roman empire in honour of one or other of the Caesars. — 1. C. ad Argaeum, formerly Mazaca, also Eusebia (K. ἡ πρὸς τῷ Ἀργαίῳ, τὰ Μάζακα, Εὐσέβεια: Kesarieh, Ru.), one of the oldest cities of Asia Minor, stood upon Mount Argaeus, about the centre of Cappadocia, in the district (praefectura) called Cilicia. It was the capital of Cappadocia, and when that country was made a Roman province by Tiberius (A. D. 18), it received the name of Caesarea. It was ultimately destroyed by an earthquake. — 2. C. Philippi or Panēas (K. ἡ Φιλίππου, N. T.; K. Πανειάς: Banias), a city of Palestine, at the S. foot of M. Hermon, on the Jordan, just below its source [PANIUM], built by Philip the tetrarch, B. C. 3; King Agrippa called it Neronias, but it soon lost this name. — 3. C. Palaestinae, formerly Stratōnis Turris (Στράτωνος πύργος: Kaisariyeh, Ru.), an important city of Palestine, on the seacoast, just above the boundary line between Samaria and Galilee. It was surrounded with a wall and decorated with splendid buildings by Herod the Great (B. C. 13), who called it Caesarea, in honour of Augustus. He also made a splendid harbour for the city. Under the Romans it was the capital of Palestine and the residence of the procurator. Vespasian made it a colony, and Titus conferred additional favours upon it; hence it was called Colonia Flavia. — 4. C. Mauretaniae, formerly Iol (Ἰὸλ Καισάρεια: Zershell, Ru.), a Phoenician city on the N. coast of Africa, with a harbour, the residence of King Juba, who named it Caesarea, in honour of Augustus. When Claudius erected Mauretania into a Roman province, he made Caesarea a colony, and the capital of the middle division of the province, which was thence called Mauretania Caesariensis. — 5. C. ad Anazarbum. [ANAZARBUS.] There are several others, which are better known by other names, and several which are not important enough to be mentioned here.

Caesarion, son of C. Julius Caesar and of Cleopatra, originally called Ptolemaeus as an Egyptian prince, was born B. C. 47. In 42 the triumvirs allowed him to receive the title of king of Egypt, and in 34 Antony conferred upon him the title of king of kings. After the death of his mother in 30 he was executed by order of Augustus.

Caesarodūnum (*Tours*), chief town of the Turōnes or Turōni, subsequently called Turoni, on the Liger (*Loire*) in Gallia Lugdunensis.

Caesaromāgus. 1. (*Beauvais*), chief town of the Bellovaci in Gallia Belgica. — 2. (*Chelmsford*), a town of the Trinobantes in Britain.

Caesēna (Caesenas -ātis: *Cesena*), a town in Gallia Cispadana on the Via Aemilia not far from the Rubico.

Caesennius Lento. [LENTO.]
Caesennius Paetus. [PAETUS.]
Caesetius Flavus. [FLAVUS.]

Caesia, a surname of Minerva, a translation of the Greek γλαυκῶπις.

Caesia Silva (*Hässerwald*), a forest in Germany between the Lippe and the Yssel.

Caesonia, first the mistress and afterwards the wife of the emperor Caligula, was a woman of the greatest licentiousness, and was put to death with Caligula together with her daughter, A. D. 41.

M. Caesonius, a judex at the trial of Oppianicus for the murder of Cluentius, B. C. 74, and aedile with Cicero in 69.

Caicus (Καϊκός: *Akson* or *Bakir*), a river of Mysia, rising in M. Temnus and flowing past Pergamus into the Cumaean Gulf.

Caieta (Caietānus: *Gaeta*), a town in Latium on the borders of Campania, 40 stadia S. of Formiae, situated on a promontory of the same name and on a bay of the sea called after it **Sinus Caietanus**. It possessed an excellent harbour (Cic. *pro Leg. Man.* 12), and was said to have derived its name from *Caieta*, the nurse of Aeneas, who, according to some traditions, was buried at this place.

Caius, the jurist. [GAIUS.]

Caius Caesar. [CALIGULA.]

Calaber. [QUINTUS SMYRNAEUS.]

Calabria (Calabri), the peninsula in the S. E. of Italy, extending from Tarentum to the Prom. Iapygium, formed part of APULIA.

Calacta (Καλὴ 'Ακτή: Καλακτῖνος: nr. *Caronia*, Ru.), a town on the N. coast of Sicily, founded by Ducetius, a chief of the Sicels, about B. C. 447. Calacta was, as its name imports, originally the name of the coast. (Herod. vi. 22.)

Calactinus. [CAECILIUS CALACTINUS.]

Calagurris (Calagurritānus: *Calahorra*), a town of the Vascones and a Roman municipium in Hispania Tarraconensis near the Iberus, memorable for its adherence to Sertorius and for its siege by Pompey and his generals, in the course of which mothers killed and salted their children, B. C. 71. (Juv. xv. 93.) It was the birth-place of Quintilian.

Calais, brother of Zetes. [ZETES.]

Calama. 1. (*Kalma*, Ru.) an important town in Numidia, between Cirta and Hippo Regius, on the E. bank of the Rubricatus (*Seibous*). — 2. (*Kalat-al-Wad*), a town in the W. of Mauretania Caesariensis, on the E. bank of the Malva, near its mouth.

Calamine, in Lydia, a lake with floating islands, sacred to the nymphs.

Calamis (Κάλαμις), a statuary and embosser at Athens, of great celebrity, was a contemporary of Phidias, and flourished B. C. 467—429.

Calamus (Κάλαμος: *El-Kulmon*), a town on the coast of Phoenicia, a little S. of Tripolis.

Calanus (Κάλανος), an Indian gymnosophist, followed Alexander the Great from India, and having been taken ill, burnt himself alive in the presence of the Macedonians, 3 months before the death of Alexander (B. C. 325), to whom he had predicted his approaching end.

Calasiries (Καλασίριες), one of the two divisions (the other being the Hermotybii) of the warrior-caste of Egypt. Their greatest strength was 250,000 men, and their chief abode in the W. part of the Delta. They formed the king's body guard.

Calatia (Calatīnus: *Cajazzo*), a town in Samnium on the Appia Via between Capua and Bene-

ventum, was conquered by the Romans B. C. 313, and was colonized by Julius Caesar with his veterans.

Calatinus, A. Atilius, consul B. C. 258, in the first Punic war, carried on the war with success in Sicily. He was consul a 2nd time, 254, when he took Panormus ; and was dictator, 249, when he again carried on the war in Sicily, which was the first instance of a dictator commanding an army out of Italy.

Calaurea -ia (Καλαύρεια, Καλαυρία: Καλαυρείτης : *Poro*), a small island in the Saronic gulf off the coast of Argolis and opposite Troezen, possessed a celebrated temple of Poseidon, which was regarded as an inviolable asylum. Hither Demosthenes fled to escape Antipater, and here he took poison, B. C. 322. This temple was the place of meeting of an ancient Amphictyonia. (See *Dict. of Ant.* p. 79, b, 2d ed.)

Calavius, the name of a distinguished family at Capua, the most celebrated member of which was Pacuvius Calavius, who induced his fellow-citizens to espouse the cause of Hannibal after the battle of Cannae, B. C. 216.

Calbis (ὁ Κάλβις), also Indus (*Quingi* or *Tunas*) a considerable river of Caria, which rises in M. Cadmus, above Cibyra, and after receiving (according to Pliny) 60 small rivers and 100 mountain torrents, falls into the sea W. of Caunus and opposite to Rhodes.

Calchas (Κάλχας), son of Thestor of Mycenae or Megara, the wisest soothsayer among the Greeks at Troy, foretold the length of the Trojan war, explained the cause of the pestilence which raged in the Greek army, and advised the Greeks to build the wooden horse. An oracle had declared that Calchas should die if he met with a soothsayer superior to himself ; and this came to pass at Claros, near Colophon, for here Calchas met the soothsayer Mopsus, who predicted things which Calchas could not. Thereupon Calchas died of grief. After his death he had an oracle in Daunia.

Caldus, C. Caelius. 1. Rose from obscurity by his oratory, was tribune of the plebs B. C. 107, when he proposed a lex tabellaria, and consul 94. In the civil war between Sulla and the party of Marius, he fought on the side of the latter, 83. — 2. Grandson of the preceding, was Cicero's quaestor in Cilicia, 50.

Cale (*Oporto*), a port-town of the Callaeci in Hispania Tarraconensis at the mouth of the Durius. From *Porto Cale* the name of the country *Portugal* is supposed to have come.

Caledonia. [BRITANNIA.]

Calentum, a town probably of the Calenses Emanici in Hispania Baetica, celebrated for its manufacture of bricks so light as to swim upon water.

Calenus, Q. Fufius, tribune of the plebs, B. C. 61, when he succeeded in saving P. Clodius from condemnation for his violation of the mysteries of the Bona Dea. In 59 he was praetor, and from this time appears as an active partisan of Caesar. In 51 he was legate of Caesar in Gaul, and served under Caesar in the civil war. In 49 he joined Caesar at Brundusium and accompanied him to Spain, and in 48 he was sent by Caesar from Epirus to bring over the remainder of the troops from Italy, but most of his ships were taken by Bibulus. After the battle of Pharsalia (48) Calenus took many cities in Greece. In 47 he was made consul by Caesar. After Caesar's death (44) Calenus joined M. Antony, and subsequently had the command of Antony's legions in the N. of Italy. At the termination of the Perusinian war (41) Calenus died, and Octavianus was thus enabled to obtain possession of his army.

Cales or **-ex** (Κάλης or -ηξ: *Halabli*), a river of Bithynia, S.W. of Heraclēa Pontica. (Thuc. iv. 75.)

Cāles (-is, usually Pl. Cales -ium: Calenus: *Calvi*), chief town of the Caleni, an Ausonian people in Campania, on the Via Latina, said to have been founded by Calais, son of Boreas, and therefore called *Threïcia* by the poets. Cales was taken and colonized by the Romans, B. C. 335. It was celebrated for its excellent wine.

Calētes or **-i**, a people in Belgic Gaul near the mouth of the Seine: their capital was JULIOBONA.

Calētor (Καλήτωρ), son of Clytius, slain at Troy by the Telamonian Ajax.

Calidīus. 1. Q., tribune of the plebs B. C. 99, carried a law for the recall of Q. Metellus Numidicus from banishment. He was praetor 79, and had the government of one of the Spains, and on his return was accused by Q. Lollius, and condemned. — **2. M.**, son of the preceding, distinguished as an orator. In 57 he was praetor, and supported the recal of Cicero from banishment. In 51 he was an unsuccessful candidate for the consulship, and on the breaking out of the civil war, 49, he joined Caesar, who placed him over Gallia Togata, where he died in 48.

Caligula, Roman emperor, A. D. 37—41, son of Germanicus and Agrippina, was born A. D. 12, and was brought up among the legions in Germany. His real name was *Caius Caesar*, and he was always called *Caius* by his contemporaries: *Caligula* was a surname given him by the soldiers from his wearing in his boyhood small *caligae*, or soldiers' boots. Having escaped the fate of his mother and brother, he gained the favour of Tiberius, who raised him to offices of honour, and held out to him hopes of the succession. On the death of Tiberius (37), which was either caused or accelerated by Caligula, the latter succeeded to the throne. He was saluted by the people with the greatest enthusiasm as the son of Germanicus. His first acts gave promise of a just and beneficent reign. He pardoned all the persons who had appeared as witnesses or accusers against his family; he released all the state-prisoners of Tiberius; he restored to the magistrates full power of jurisdiction without appeal to his person, and promised the senate to govern according to the laws. Towards foreign princes he behaved with great generosity. He restored Agrippa, the grandson of Herod, to his kingdom of Judaea, and Antiochus IV. to his kingdom of Commagene. But at the end of 8 months the conduct of Caligula became suddenly changed. After a serious illness, which probably weakened his mental powers, he appears as a sanguinary and licentious madman. He put to death Tiberius, the grandson of his predecessor, compelled his grandmother Antonia and other members of his family to make away with themselves, often caused persons of both sexes and of all ages to be tortured to death for his amusement while taking his meals, and on one occasion, during the exhibition of the games in the Circus, he ordered a great number of the spectators to be seized, and to be thrown before the wild beasts. Such was his love of blood that he wished the Roman

people had only one head, that he might cut it off with a blow. His obscenity was as great as his cruelty. He carried on an incestuous intercourse with his own sisters, and no Roman woman was safe from his attacks. His marriages were disgracefully contracted and speedily dissolved; and the only woman who exercised a permanent influence over him was his last wife Caesonia. In his madness he considered himself a god; he even built a temple to himself as Jupiter Latiaris, and appointed priests to attend to his worship. He sometimes officiated as his own priest, making his horse Incitatus, which he afterwards raised to the consulship, his colleague. His monstrous extravagancies soon exhausted the coffers of the state. One instance may show the senseless way in which he spent his money. He constructed a bridge of boats between Baiae and Puteoli, a distance of about 3 miles, and after covering it with earth he built houses upon it. When it was finished, he gave a splendid banquet in the middle of the bridge, and concluded the entertainment by throwing numbers of the guests into the sea. To replenish the treasury he exhausted Italy and Rome by his extortions, and then marched into Gaul in 40, which he plundered in all directions. With his troops he advanced to the ocean, as if intending to cross over into Britain; he drew them up in battle array, and then gave them the signal — to collect shells, which he called the spoils of conquered Ocean. The Roman world at length grew tired of such a mad tyrant. Four months after his return to the city, on the 24th of January 41, he was murdered by Cassius Chaerea, tribune of a praetorian cohort, Cornelius Sabinus and others. His wife Caesonia and his daughter were likewise put to death.

Calingae, a numerous people of India intra Gangem, on the E. coast, below the mouths of the Ganges.

Calinipaxa (*Canonge?* a little above 27° N. lat.), a city on the Ganges, N. of its confluence with the Jomanes (*Jumna*), said to have been the furthest point in India reached by Seleucus Nicator.

Callaïci, Callaeci. [GALLAECI.]

Callatis (Κάλλατις, Κάλατις: Καλατιανοs: *Kollat, Kollati*), a town of Moesia, on the Black Sea, originally a colony of Miletus, and afterwards of Heraclea.

Calliärus (Καλλίαρος), a town in Locris, mentioned by Homer.

Callias and **Hipponicus** (Καλλίας, Ἱππόνικος), a noble Athenian family, celebrated for their wealth. They enjoyed the hereditary dignity of torch-bearer at the Eleusinian mysteries, and claimed descent from Triptolemus. **1. Hipponicus I.**, acquired a large fortune by fraudulently making use of the information he had received from Solon respecting the introduction of his σεισάχθεια, B. C. 594. (Plut. *Sol.* 15.) — **2. Callias I.**, son of Phaenippus, an opponent of Pisistratus, and a conqueror at the Olympic and Pythian games. — **3. Hipponicus II.**, surnamed Ammon, son of No. 2. — **4. Callias II.**, son of No. 3, fought at the battle of Marathon, 490. He was afterwards ambassador from Athens to Artaxerxes, and according to some accounts negotiated a peace with Persia, 449, on terms most humiliating to the latter. On his return to Athens, he was accused of having taken bribes, and was condemned to a fine of 50 talents. — **5. Hipponicus III.**, son of No. 4, one of the Athenian generals in their incursion into the territory of Tanagra, 426, also commanded at the battle of Delium, 424, where he was killed. It was his divorced wife, and not his widow, whom Pericles married. His daughter Hipparete was married to Alcibiades, with a dowry of 10 talents: another daughter was married to Theodorus, and became the mother of Isocrates the orator.—**6. Callias III.**, son of No. 5, by the lady who married Pericles, dissipated all his ancestral wealth on sophists, flatterers, and women. The scene of Xenophon's *Banquet*, and also that of Plato's *Protagoras* is laid at his house. He is said to have ultimately reduced himself to absolute beggary. In 400 he was engaged in the attempt to crush Andocides. In 392 he commanded the Athenian heavy-armed troops, when Iphicrates defeated the Spartans; and in 371 he was one of the envoys empowered to negotiate peace with Sparta.

Callias. 1. A wealthy Athenian, who, on condition of marrying Cimon's sister, Elpinice, paid for him the fine of 50 talents which had been imposed on Miltiades. He appears to have been unconnected with the nobler family of Callias and Hipponicus.—**2.** Tyrant of Chalcis in Euboea, and the rival of Plutarchus, tyrant of Eretria. He was defeated by the Athenians under Phocion, B. C. 350, and thereupon betook himself to the Macedonian court; but as he could not obtain aid from Philip, he formed an alliance with the Athenians, and by their means obtained the supremacy in the island.—**3.** A poet of the old comedy, flourished B. C. 412; the names of 6 of his comedies are preserved.—**4.** Of Syracuse, a Greek historian, was a contemporary of Agathocles, and wrote a history of Sicily in 22 books, embracing the reign of Agathocles, B. C. 317—289.

Callicrătes (Καλλικράτης). **1.** An Achaean, exerted all his influence in favour of the Romans. On the conquest of Macedonia by the Romans, B. C. 168, Callicrates pointed out 1000 Achaeans, as having favoured the cause of Perseus, who were taken to Rome; and among them was the historian Polybius. Callicrates died at Rhodes, 149.—**3.** One of the architects of the Parthenon on the Acropolis of Athens.—**4.** A Lacedaemonian sculptor, made ants and other animals out of ivory, so small that one could not distinguish the different limbs.

Callicrătĭdas (Καλλικρατίδας), a Spartan, succeeded Lysander as admiral of the Lacedaemonian fleet, B. C. 406, took Methymna, and shut up Conon in Mytilene; but the Athenians sent out a fleet of 150 sail, and defeated Callicratidas off the Arginusae. Callicratidas fell in the battle. Callicratidas was a plain, blunt Spartan of the old school. Witness his answer, when asked what sort of man the Ionians were: " Bad freemen, but excellent slaves."

Callidrŏmus or -**um** (Καλλίδρομος), part of the range of Mt. Oeta, near Thermopylae.

Callifae (Callifānus: *Calvisi*), a town in Samnium, perhaps in the territory of Allifae.

Callimăchus (Καλλίμαχος). **1.** The Athenian polemarch, commanded the right wing at Marathon, where he was slain, after behaving with much gallantry, B. C. 490. This is the last recorded instance of the polemarch performing the military duties which his name implies.—**2.** A celebrated Alexandrine grammarian and poet, was a native of Cyrene in Africa, and a descendant of the Battiadae, whence he is sometimes called *Bat-*

tiades. He lived at Alexandria in the reign of Ptolemy Philadelphus and Euergetes, and was chief librarian of the famous library of Alexandria, from about B. C. 260 until his death about 240 He founded a celebrated grammatical school at Alexandria, and among his pupils were Eratosthenes, Aristophanes of Byzantium, and Apollonius Rhodius. We have no other particulars of the life of Callimachus except his enmity with his former pupil Apollonius Rhodius, which is related elsewhere. [APOLLONIUS, No. 6.] He is said to have written 800 works, in prose and in verse, on an infinite variety of subjects, but of these we possess only some of his poems, which are characterized rather by labour and learning than by real poetical genius. Hence Ovid (*Am.* i. 15. 14) says of Callimachus, *Quamvis ingenio non valet, arte valet.* The extant works of Callimachus are 6 *Hymns* in hexameter verse, 5 in the Ionic dialect, and 1, on the bath of Pallas, in the Doric dialect, and 72 *Epigrams*, which belong to the best specimens of this kind of poetry, and were incorporated in the Greek Anthology at an early time. We have only a few fragments of his elegies, which enjoyed great celebrity, and were imitated by the Roman poets, the most celebrated of whose imitations is the *De Coma Berenices* of Catullus. Of the lost poems of Callimachus the most important were, Αἴτια, *Causes*, an epic poem in 4 books, on the causes of the various mythical stories, &c., and an epic poem entitled *Hecale*, the name of an aged woman who received Theseus hospitably when he went out to fight against the Marathonian bull. — *Editions.* By Spanheim, Ultraj. 1697. re-edited by Ernesti, Lugd. Batav. 1761; by Blomfield, Lond. 1815; by Volzer, Lips. 1817.—**3.** An architect and statuary, of uncertain country, who is said to have invented the Corinthian column, and who must have lived before B. C. 396. He was so anxious to give his works the last touch of perfection that he lost the grand and sublime; whence Dionysius compares him to the orator Lysias. Callimachus was never satisfied with himself, and therefore received the epithet κακιζότεχνος, which Pliny interprets as *calumniator sui*.

Callimĕdon (Καλλιμέδων), one of the orators at Athens in the Macedonian interest, and a friend of Phocion, was condemned to death by the Athenians in his absence, B. C. 317.

Callinĭcus Seleucus. [SELEUCUS.]

Callinus (Καλλῖνος), of Ephesus, the earliest Greek elegiac poet, probably flourished about B. C. 700. Only one of his elegies is extant, consisting of 21 lines, in which he exhorts his countrymen to courage and perseverance against their enemies. Printed in Bergk's *Poetae Lyrici Graeci*, p. 303.

Calliŏpa. [MUSAE.]

Calliŏpe (Καλλιόπη), a considerable city in the W. of Parthia, founded, or else enlarged, by Seleucus Nicator.

Calliphon (Καλλιφῶν), a Greek philosopher, and probably a disciple of Epicurus, is condemned by Cicero as making the chief good of man to consist in an union of virtue (*honestas*) and bodily pleasure (ἡδονή, *voluptas*).

Callipŏlis (Καλλίπολις; Καλλιπολίτης). **1.** (*Gallipoli*), a Greek town on the Tarentine gulf in Calabria. — **2.** A town on the E. coast of Sicily not far from Aetna. — **3.** (*Gallipoli*), a town in the Thracian Chersonese opposite Lampsacus. — **4.** A town in Aetolia. See CALLIUM.

Callippĭdes (Καλλιππίδης), of Athens, a celebrated tragic actor, a contemporary of Alcibiades and Agesilaus.

Callippus (Κάλλιππος). 1. An Athenian, accompanied Dion to Syracuse, where he murdered the latter B. C. 353. Callippus now usurped the government of Syracuse, but was expelled the city at the end of 13 months, and after wandering about Sicily with his mercenaries was at length put to death by his own friends. — 2. An astronomer of Cyzicus, came to Athens, where he assisted Aristotle in rectifying and completing the discoveries of Eudoxus. Callippus invented the period or cycle of 76 years, called after him the *Callippic*, which commenced B. C. 330.

Callirrhŏë (Καλλιρρόη). 1. Daughter of Oceanus, wife of Chrysaor, and mother of Geryones and Echidna. — 2. Daughter of Achelous and wife of Alcmaeon, induced her husband to procure her the peplus and necklace of Harmonia, by which she caused his death. [ALCMAEON.] — 3. Daughter of Scamander, wife of Tros, and mother of Ilus and Ganymedes.

Callirrhŏë (Καλλιρρόη), afterwards called Ennĕacrūnus (Ἐννεάκρουνος) or the "Nine Springs," because its water was distributed by 9 pipes, was the most celebrated well in Athens, and still retains its ancient name *Callirrhoe*. It was situated in the S. E. extremity of the city between the Olympiëum and the Ilissus.

Callisthĕnes (Καλλισθένης), of Olynthus, a relation and a pupil of Aristotle, accompanied Alexander the Great to Asia. In his intercourse with Alexander he was arrogant and bold, and took every opportunity of exhibiting his independence. He expressed his indignation at Alexander's adoption of Oriental customs, and especially at the requirement of the ceremony of adoration. He thus rendered himself so obnoxious to the king, that he was accused of being privy to the plot of Hermolaus to assassinate Alexander; and after being kept in chains for 7 months, was either put to death or died of disease. Callisthenes wrote an account of Alexander's expedition; a history of Greece, in 10 books, from the peace of Antalcidas to the seizure of the Delphic temple by Philomelus (B. C. 387—357); and other works, all of which have perished.

Callisto (Καλλιστώ), an Arcadian nymph, hence called *Nonacrina virgo* (Ov. *Met.* ii. 409) from Nonacris, a mountain in Arcadia, was daughter either of Lycaon or of Nycteus or of Ceteus, and a companion of Artemis in the chase. She was beloved by Zeus, who metamorphosed her into a she-bear that Hera might not become acquainted with the amour. But Hera learnt the truth, and caused Artemis to slay Callisto during the chase. Zeus placed Callisto among the stars under the name of *Arctos*, or the Bear. ARCAS was her son by Zeus. According to Ovid Jupiter (Zeus) overcame the virtue of Callisto by assuming the form of Artemis; Juno (Hera) then metamorphosed Callisto into a bear; and when Arcas during the chase was on the point of killing his mother Jupiter placed both among the stars. [ARCTOS.] — According to a modern scholar Callisto is merely another form of Calliste, a surname of Artemis, and she is therefore the same as this goddess. The she-bear was the symbol of the Arcadian Artemis.

Callistrātĭa (Καλλιστρατία), a town in Paphlagonia, on the coast of the Euxine.

Callistrātus (Καλλίστρατος). 1. An Athenian orator, son of Callicrates of Aphidna. His oratory was greatly admired by Demosthenes, and his speech on the affair of Oropus, B. C. 366, is said to have excited the emulation of Demosthenes, and to have caused the latter to devote himself to oratory. After taking an active part in public affairs, generally in favour of Sparta, Callistratus was condemned to death by the Athenians in 361, and went into banishment to Methone in Macedonia. He ultimately returned to Athens, and was put to death. During his exile he is said to have founded the city of Datum, afterwards Philippi. — 2. A Greek grammarian, and a disciple of Aristophanes of Byzantium. — 3. A Roman jurist, frequently cited in the Digest, wrote at least as late as the reign (A. D. 198—211) of Severus and Antoninus (*i. e.* Septimius Severus and Caracalla).

Callistus, C. Jūlĭus, a freedman of Caligula, possessed great influence in the reigns of Caligula and Claudius, and is the person to whom the physician Scribonius Largus dedicates his work.

Callĭum (Κάλλιον : Καλλιεύς), called **Callipolis** by Livy (xxxvi. 30), a town in Aetolia in the valley of the Spercheus, S.W. of Hypata.

Callixĕnus (Καλλίξενος), the leader in the prosecution of the Athenian generals who had conquered at Arginusae, B. C. 406. Not long after the execution of the generals, the Athenians repented of their unjust sentence, and decreed the institution of criminal accusations against Callixenus, but he escaped from Athens. On the restoration of democracy, 403, Callixenus took advantage of the general amnesty, and returned to Athens, but no man would give him either water or light for his fire, and he perished miserably of hunger.

Callon (Κάλλων). 1. An artist of Aegina, flourished B.C. 516. — 2. An artist of Elis, lived before B. C. 436.

Calor. 1. A river in Samnium, flows past Beneventum and falls into the Vulturnus. — 2. (*Calore*), a river in Lucania, falls into the Silarus.

Calpē (Κάλπη : *Gibralter*), a mountain in the S. of Spain on the Straits between the Atlantic and Mediterranean. This and M. Abyla opposite to it on the African coast, were called the *Columns of Hercules*. [ABYLA.]

Calpe (Κάλπη : *Kirpeh*), a river, promontory, and town on the coast of Bithynia, between the rivers Psilis and Sangarius.

Calpurnĭa, daughter of L. Calpurnius Piso, consul B. C. 58, and last wife of the dictator Caesar, to whom she was married in 59. The reports respecting the conspiracy against Caesar's life filled Calpurnia with the liveliest apprehensions; she in vain entreated her husband not to leave home on the Ides of March, 44.

Calpurnĭa Gens, plebeian, pretended to be descended from Calpus, a son of Numa. It was divided into the families of BESTIA, BIBULUS, FLAMMA, and PISO.

T. Calpurnĭus Sicŭlus, the author of 11 Eclogues in Latin verse, which are close imitations of Virgil, perhaps lived about A. D. 290. — *Editions.* In the *Poetae Latini Minores* of Wernsdorff; and by Glaeser, Gotting. 1842.

Calva, a surname of Venus at Rome, probably in honour of the Roman women, who are said, during the war with the Gauls, to have cut off their hair for the purpose of making bow-strings.

Calventĭus, an Insubrian Gaul, of the town of

Placentia, whose daughter married L. Piso, the father of L. Piso Caesoninus, consul B. C. 58. In his speech against the latter, Cicero upbraids him with the low origin of his mother, and calls him *Caesoninus Semiplacentinus Calventius.*

Calvinus, Domitius. 1. Cn., curule aedile, B. C. 299, consul 283, and dictator and censor 280. In his consulship he, together with his colleague Dolabella, defeated the Gauls and Etruscans, and hence received the surname *Maximus.*—2. Cn., tribune of the plebs, 59, when he supported Bibulus against Caesar, praetor 56, and consul 53, through the influence of Pompey. In the civil war he joined Caesar. In 49 he fought under Curio in Africa ; and in 48 he fought under Caesar in Greece, and commanded the centre of Caesar's army at the battle of Pharsalia. In 47 he had the command of Asia, and in 46 he fought in Africa against the Pompeian party. After Caesar's death (44) he fought under Octavian and Antony against the republicans. In 40 he was consul a 2nd time, and in 39 went as proconsul to Spain, where he defeated the revolted Cerretani.

Calvinus, L. Sextius, consul B. C. 124, defeated the Salluvii and other people in Transalpine Gaul, and in 123 founded the colony of Aquae Sextiae (*Aix*).

Calvinus, T. Veturius, twice consul, B. C. 334 and 321. In his second consulship he and his colleague Sp. Postumius Albinus were defeated by the Sabines at Caudium. For details see ALBINUS, No. 3.

Calvisius Sabinus. [SABINUS.]
Calvus, Licinius. [LICINIUS.]
Calycadnus (Καλύκαδνος). 1. (*Ghiuk Sooyoo*), a considerable river of Cilicia Tracheia, navigable as far up as Seleucia.—2. The promontory of this name, mentioned by Polybius (xxii. 26) and Livy (xxxviii. 38), appears to be the same as ANEMURIUM.

Calydnae (Καλύδναι νῆσοι). 1. Two small islands off the coast of Troas, between Tenedos and the Prom. Lectum.—2. A group of islands off the coast of Caria, N.W. of Cos, belonging to the Sporades. The largest of them was called Calydna, and afterwards Calymna (now *Kalimno*).

Calydon (Καλυδών: Καλυδώνιος), an ancient town of Aetolia on the Evenus in the land of the Curetes, said to have been founded by Aetolus or his son Calydon. The surrounding country produced wine, oil, and corn ; and in the mountains in the neighbourhood took place the celebrated hunt of the Calydonian boar. The inhabitants were removed by Augustus to NICOPOLIS.

Calymna. [CALYDNAE.]
Calynda (Κάλυνδα: Καλυνδεύς), a city of Caria, E. of Caunus, and 60 stadia (6 geog. miles) from the sea. The Calyndians formed a part of the fleet of Xerxes, under their king Damasithymus : afterwards they were subject to the Caunians ; and both cities were added by the Romans to the territory of Rhodes.

Calypso (Καλυψώ), daughter of Oceanus and Tethys, or of Nereus, or, according to Homer, of Atlas, was a nymph inhabiting the island of Ogygia, on which Ulysses was shipwrecked. Calypso loved the unfortunate hero, and promised him immortality if he would remain with her. Ulysses refused, and after she had detained him 7 years, the gods compelled her to allow him to continue his journey homewards.

Camalodunum (*Colchester*), the capital of the Trinobantes in Britain, and the first Roman colony in the island, founded by the emperor Claudius, A. D. 43.

Camarina (Καμάρινα: Καμαριναῖος: *Camerina*), a town on the S. coast of Sicily, at the mouth of the Hipparis, founded by Syracuse, B. C. 599. It was several times destroyed by Syracuse ; and in the 1st Punic war it was taken by the Romans, and most of the inhabitants sold as slaves. Scarcely any vestiges of the ancient town remain. In the neighbourhood was a marsh, which the inhabitants drained contrary to the command of an oracle, and thus opened a way to their enemies to take the town : hence arose the proverb μὴ κίνει Καμαρίναν, *ne moveas Camarinam.*

Cambuni Montes, the mountains which separate Macedonia and Thessaly.

Cambysene (Καμβυσηνή), a district of Armenia Major, on the borders of Iberia and Colchis.

Cambyses (Καμβύσης). 1. Father of CYRUS the Great.—2. Second king of Persia, succeeded his father Cyrus, and reigned B. C. 529—522. In 525 he conquered Egypt ; but an army which he sent against the Ammonians perished in the sands, and the forces, which he led in person against the Aethiopians S. of Egypt, were compelled by failure of provisions to return. On his return to Memphis he treated the Egyptians with great cruelty ; he insulted their religion, and slew their god Apis with his own hands. He also acted tyrannically towards his own family and the Persians in general. He caused his own brother Smerdis to be murdered ; but a Magian personated the deceased prince, and set up a claim to the throne. [SMERDIS.] Cambyses forthwith set out from Egypt against this pretender, but died in Syria, at a place named Ecbatana, of an accidental wound in the thigh, 522.

Cambyses (Καμβύσης). 1. (*Iora*), a river of Iberia and Albania, which, after uniting with the Alazon (*Alasan*), falls into the Cyrus.—2. A small river of Media, falling into the Caspian between the Araxes and the Amardus.

Camenae (not *Camoenae*), also called *Casmenae, Carmenae.* The name is connected with *carmen,* a "prophecy." The Camenae accordingly were prophetic nymphs, and they belonged to the religion of ancient Italy, although later traditions represent their worship as introduced into Italy from Arcadia, and some accounts identify them with the Muses. The most important of these goddesses was Carmenta or Carmentis, who had a temple at the foot of the Capitoline hill, and altars near the porta Carmentalis. Respecting her festival see *Dict. of Ant.* art. *Carmentalia.* The traditions which assigned a Greek origin to her worship, state that her original name was Nicostrate, and that she was the mother of EVANDER by Hermes, with whom she fled to Italy.

Cameria (*Camerinum*), an ancient town of Latium conquered by Tarquinius Priscus.

Camerinum or Camarinum, more anciently Camers (Camertes : *Camerino*), a town in Umbria on the borders of Picenum, an ally of the Romans against the Etruscans, B. C. 308, and also an ally of the Romans in the 2nd Punic war, subsequently a Roman colony.

Camerinus, the name of a patrician family of the Sulpicia gens, the members of which frequently held the consulship in the early times of the republic

(B.C. 500, 490, 461, 393, 345). After B.C. 345 the Camerini disappear from history for 400 years, but they are mentioned again as one of the noblest Roman families in the early times of the empire.

Camerīnus, a Roman poet, contemporary with Ovid, wrote a poem on the capture of Troy by Hercules.

Camīcus (Καμικός: Καμίκιος), an ancient town of the Sicani on the S. coast of Sicily on a river of the same name, occupied the site of the citadel of AGRIGENTUM.

Camilla, daughter of king Metabus of the Volscian town of Privernum, was one of the swift-footed servants of Diana, accustomed to the chase and to war. She assisted Turnus against Aeneas, and after slaying numbers of the Trojans was at length killed by Aruns.

Camillus, Furius. 1. M., one of the great heroes of the Roman republic. He was censor B.C. 403, in which year Livy erroneously places his first consular tribunate. He was consular tribune for the first time in 401, and for the second time in 398. In 396 he was dictator, when he gained a glorious victory over the Faliscans and Fidenates, took Veii, and entered Rome in triumph, riding in a chariot drawn by white horses. In 394 he was consular tribune for the third time, and reduced the Faliscans. The story of the schoolmaster who attempted to betray the town of Falerii to Camillus, belongs to this campaign. In 391, Camillus was accused of having made an unfair distribution of the booty of Veii, and went voluntarily into exile at Ardea. Next year (390) the Gauls took Rome, and laid siege to Ardea. The Romans in the Capitol recalled Camillus, and appointed him dictator in his absence. Camillus hastily collected an army, attacked the Gauls, and defeated them completely. [BRENNUS.] His fellow-citizens saluted him as the Second Romulus. In 389 Camillus was dictator a third time, and defeated the Volscians, Aequians, and other nations. In 386 he was consular tribune for the fourth, in 384 for the fifth, and in 381 for the sixth time. In 368 he was appointed dictator a fourth time to resist the rogations of C. Licinius Stolo. Next year, 367, he was dictator a fifth time, and though 80 years of age, he completely defeated the Gauls. He died of the pestilence, 365. Camillus was the great general of his age, and the resolute champion of the patrician order. His history has received much legendary and traditional fable, and requires a careful critical sifting.—**2. Sp.**, son of No. 1., first praetor 367.—**3. L.**, also son of No. 1, was dictator 350 in order to hold the comitia, and consul 349, when he defeated the Gauls.—**4. L.**, son of No. 2, consul 338, when he took Tibur, and in conjunction with his colleague Maenius completed the subjugation of Latium. In 325 he was consul a second time.—**5. M.**, proconsul of Africa in the reign of Tiberius, defeated the Numidian Tacfarinas, A.D. 17.—**6. M.**, surnamed SCRIBONIANUS, consul A.D. 32, under Tiberius. At the beginning of the reign of Claudius he was legate of Dalmatia, where he revolted, but was conquered, 42, sent into exile, and died 53.

Camīrus (Κάμειρος: Καμειρεύς), a Dorian town on the W. coast of the island of Rhodes, said to have been founded by Camirus, son of Cercaphus and Cydippe, and the principal town in the island before the foundation of Rhodes. It was the birth-place of the poet Pisander.

Camīsa (Κάμισα), a fortress in Cappadocia, 23 Roman miles E. of Sebaste.

Camoenae. [CAMENAE.]

Campānia (Campanus: *Terra di Lavoro*), a district of Italy, the name of which is probably derived from *campus* "a plain," was bounded on the N.W. by Latium, N. and E. by Samnium, S.E. by Lucania, and S. and S.W. by the Tyrrhenian sea. It was separated from Latium by the river Liris, and from Lucania at a later time by the river Silarus, though in the time of Augustus it did not extend further S. than the promontory of Minerva. In still earlier times the *Ager Campanus* included only the country round Capua. The country along the coast from the Liris to the Promontory of Minerva is a plain inclosed by the Apennines which sweeps round it in the form of a semicircle. Campania is a volcanic country, to which circumstance it was mainly indebted for its extraordinary fertility, for which it was celebrated in antiquity above all other lands. It produced corn, wine, oil, and every kind of fruit in the greatest abundance, and in many parts crops could be gathered 3 times in the year. The fertility of the soil, the beauty of the scenery, and the softness of the climate, the heat of which was tempered by the delicious breezes of the sea, procured for Campania the epithet *Felix*, a name which it justly deserved. It was the favourite retreat in summer of the Roman nobles, whose villas studded a considerable part of its coast, especially in the neighbourhood of BAIAE. The principal river was the VULTURNUS: the minor rivers were the LIRIS, SAVO, CLANIUS, SEBETHUS, SARNUS, and SILARUS. The chief lakes were LUCRINUS, ACHERUSIA, AVERNUS, and LITERNA, most of them craters of extinct volcanos.—The earliest inhabitants of the country were the AUSONES and OSCI or OPICI. They were subsequently conquered by the Etruscans, who became the masters of almost all the country. In the time of the Romans we find 3 distinct people, besides the Greek population of CUMAE: 1. The *Campani*, properly so called, a mixed race, consisting of Etruscans and the original inhabitants of the country, dwelling along the coast from Sinuessa to Paestum. They were the ruling race: their history is given under CAPUA, their chief city. 2. SIDICINI, an Ausonian people, in the N.W. of the country on the borders of Samnium. 3. PICENTINI in the S. E. of the country.

Campē (Κάμπη), a monster which guarded the Cyclops in Tartarus, was killed by Zeus when he wanted the assistance of the Cyclops against the Titans.

Campi Lapidēi (πεδίον λιθῶδες; *la Crau*), "Plain of Stones" in the S. of Gaul, E. of the Rhone, near the Mediterranean, and on the road from Arles to Marseilles. These stones were probably deposited by the Rhone and the Druentia (*Durance*), when their course was different from what it is at present. This singular plain was known even to Aeschylus, who says that Zeus rained down these stones from heaven to assist Hercules in his fight with the Ligurians, after the hero had shot away all his arrows. A sweet herbage grows underneath and between the stones, and consequently in ancient as well as in modern times, flocks of sheep were pastured on this plain.

Campi Macri (Μακροὶ Κάμποι), the "Long Plains," a tract of country between Parma and

Modena, celebrated for the wool of its sheep. There appears to have been a place of the same name, where annual meetings of the neighbouring people were held even in the time of Strabo.

Campi Raudii, a plain in the N. of Italy near Vercella, where Marius and Catulus defeated the Cimbri, B. C. 101.

Campus Martius, the "Plain of Mars," frequently called the **Campus** simply, was, in its widest signification, the open plain at Rome outside the city-walls, lying between the Tiber and the hills Capitolinus, Quirinal, and Pincius ; but it was more usually used to signify the N. W. portion of the plain lying in the bend of the Tiber, which nearly surrounded it on 3 sides. The S. portion of the plain in the neighbourhood of the Circus Flaminius was called **Circus Flaminius** or **Campus Flaminius** or **Prata Flaminia**. The Campus Martius is said to have belonged originally to the Tarquins, and to have become the property of the state, and to have been consecrated to Mars upon the expulsion of the kings. Here the Roman youths were accustomed to perform their gymnastic and warlike exercises, and here the comitia of the centuries were held. At a later time it was surrounded by porticoes, temples, and other public buildings. It was included within the city walls by Aurelian. — Some modern writers make 3 divisions of the Campus Martius, and suppose that there was a portion of the plain lying between the Campus Martius proper and the Circus Flaminius, called **Campus Tiberinus** or **Campus Minor**, but this supposition does not rest on sufficient evidence. The Campus Minor mentioned by Catullus (lv. 3) probably refers to another Campus altogether. Respecting the other Campi see ROMA.

Canae (Κάναι), a sea-port of Aeolis, in Asia Minor, opposite to Lesbos.

Cānācē (Κανάκη), daughter of Aeolus and Enarete, had several children by Poseidon. She entertained an unnatural love for her brother Macareus, and on this account was killed by her own father ; but according to others, she put an end to her life.

Cānāchus (Κάναχος). 1. A Sicyonian artist, flourished B. C. 540—508, and executed, among other works, a colossal statue of Apollo Philesius at Miletus, which was carried to Ecbatana by Xerxes, 479. — 2. A Sicyonian artist, probably grandson of the former, from whom he is not distinguished by the ancients. He and Patrocles cast the statues of 2 Spartans, who had fought in the battle of Aegospotamos, B. C. 405.

Canastrum or **Canastraeum** (Κάναστρον, Καναστραῖον, sc. ἀκρωτήριον, ἡ Καναστραίη ἄκρη : C. Paillari), the S. E. extremity of the peninsula Pallene in Macedonia.

Candace (Κανδάκη), a queen of the Aethiopians of Meroë, invaded Egypt B. C. 22, but was driven back and defeated by Petronius, the Roman governor of Egypt. Her name seems to have been common to all the queens of Aethiopia.

Candaules (Κανδαύλης), also called Myrsilus, last Heraclid king of Lydia. His wife compelled Gyges to put her husband to death, because he had exhibited to Gyges her unveiled charms. Gyges then married the queen and mounted the throne, B. C. 716.

Candavia, Candāvii Montes, the mountains separating Illyricum from Macedonia, across which the Via Egnatia ran.

Candidum Pr. (Ras-el-Abiad, Cap Bianco), N.W. of Hippo Zaritus on the N. coast of Zeugitana, in Africa, forms the W. headland of the Sinus Hipponensis.

Canicula. [CANIS.]

Canidia, whose real name was Gratidin, was a Neapolitan courtezan beloved by Horace ; but when she deserted him, he revenged himself by holding her up to contempt as an old sorceress. (Epod. 5, 17, Sat. i. 8.)

Caninius Gallus. [GALLUS.]

Caninius Rebilus. [REBILUS.]

Cānis (Κύων), the constellation of the Great Dog. The most important star in this constellation was specially named Canis or Canicula, and also Sirius. About B. C. 400 the heliacal rising of Sirius at Athens, corresponding with the entrance of the sun into the sign Leo, marked the hottest season of the sea, and this observation being taken on trust by the Romans, without considering whether it suited their age and country, the Dies Caniculares became proverbial among them, as the Dog Days are among ourselves. — The constellation of the Little Dog was called Procyon (Προκύων), literally translated Ante canem, Antecanis, because in Greece this constellation rises heliacally before the Great Dog. When Boötes was regarded as Icarius [ARCTOS], Procyon became Maera, the dog of Icarius.

Cannae (Cannensis : Canne), a village in Apulia, N. E. of Canusium, situated in an extensive plain E. of the Aufidus and N. of the small river Vergellus, memorable for the defeat of the Romans by Hannibal, B. C. 216.

Canninefates. [BATAVI.]

Canōbus or **Canōpus** (Κάνωβος or Κάνωπος), according to Grecian story, the helmsman of Menelaus, who on his return from Troy died in Egypt, and was buried on the site of the town of Canobus, which derived its name from him.

Cānōbus or **Canōpus** (Κάνωβος, Κάνωπος: Κανωβίτης: Ru. W. of Aboukir), an important city on the coast of Lower Egypt, near the W.-most mouth of the Nile, which was hence called the Canopic Mouth (τὸ Κανωβικὸν στόμα). It was 120 stadia (12 geog. miles) E. of Alexandria, and was (at least at one time) the capital of the Nomos Menelaïtes. It had a great temple of Serapis, and a considerable commerce ; and its inhabitants were proverbial for their luxury (Κανωβισμός). After the establishment of Christianity, the city rapidly declined.

Cantābri, a people in the N. of Spain. The Romans originally gave this name to all the people on the N. coast of Spain ; but when they became better acquainted with the country, the name was restricted to the people bounded on the E. by the Astures and on the W. by the Autrigones. The Cantabri were a fierce and warlike people, and were only subdued by Augustus after a struggle of several years (B. C. 25—19).

Canthārus (Κάνθαρος), a statuary and embosser of Sicyon, flourished about B. C. 268.

Canthus (Κάνθος), an Argonaut, son of Canethus or of Abas of Euboea, was slain in Libya by Cephalion or Caphaurus.

Cantium (Cantii : Kent), a district of Britain, nearly the same as the modern Kent, but included LONDINIUM.

Canulēius, C., tribune of the plebs, B. C. 445, proposed the law, establishing connubium, or the

right of intermarriage, between the patricians and
plebs. He also proposed that the people should
have the right of choosing the consuls from either
the patricians or the plebs; but this proposal was
not carried, and it was resolved instead, that military tribunes, with consular power, should be
elected from either order in place of the consuls.

Canŭsĭum (Canusinus: *Canosa*), a town in
Apulia, on the Aufidus, and on the high road from
Rome to Brundusium, founded, according to tradition, by Diomede, whence the surrounding country was called *Campus Diomedis.* It was at all
events a Greek colony, and both Greek and Oscan
were spoken there in the time of Horace. (*Canu-
sini more bilinguis,* Hor. *Sat.* i. 10. 30.) Canusium
was a town of considerable importance, but suffered
greatly, like most of the other towns in the S. of
Italy, during the 2nd Punic war. Here the remains of the Roman army took refuge after their
defeat at Cannae, B. C. 216. It was celebrated for
its mules and its woollen manufactures, but it had
a deficient supply of water. (Hor. *Sat.* i. 5. 91.)
There are still ruins of the ancient town near
Canosa.

Canŭtĭus, or **Cannŭtĭus. 1.** P., a distinguished
orator, frequently mentioned in Cicero's oration for
Cluentius. — **2. Ti.,** tribune of the plebs, B. C. 44,
a violent opponent of Antony, and, after the establishment of the triumvirate, of Octavian also. He
was taken prisoner at the capture of Perusia, and
was put to death by Octavian, 40.

Capăneus (Καπανεύς), son of Hipponous and
Astynome or Laodice, and father of Sthenelus,
was one of the 7 heroes who marched from Argos
against Thebes. He was struck by Zeus with
lightning, as he was scaling the walls of Thebes,
because he had dared to defy the god. While his
body was burning, his wife Evadne leaped into the
flames and destroyed herself.

Capella, the star. [CAPRA.]

Capella, Martiānus Mineus Felix, a native of
Carthage, probably flourished towards the close of
the fifth century of our aera. He is the author of a
work in 9 books, composed in a medley of prose
and various kinds of verse, after the fashion of the
Satyra Menippea of Varro. It is a sort of encyclopaedia, and was much esteemed in the middle
ages. The first two books, which are an introduction to the rest, consist of an allegory, entitled the
Nuptials of Philology and Mercury, while in the
remaining 7 are expounded the principles of the 7
liberal arts, Grammar, Dialectics, Rhetoric, Geometry, Arithmetic, Astronomy, and Music, including Poetry. — *Editions.* By Hugo Grotius,
Lugd. Bat. 1599; and by Kopp, Francf. 1836.

Capēna (Capenas, -ātis: *Civitucola,* an uninhabited hill), an ancient Etruscan town founded by
and dependent on Veii, submitted to the Romans
s. c. 395, the year after the conquest of Veii, and
subsequently became a Roman municipium. In its
territory was the celebrated grove and temple of
*F*eronia on the small river Capenas. [FERONIA.]

Capēna Porta. [ROMA.]

Caper, Flavĭus, a Roman grammarian of uncertain date, whose works are quoted repeatedly by
Priscian, and of whom we have 2 short treatises
extant: printed by Putschius, *Grammat. Latin. Auct.
Antiqu.,* pp. 2239—2248, Hanov. 1605.

Capētus Silvĭus. [SILVIUS.]

Caphāreus (Καφηρεύς: *Capo d' Oro*), a rocky
and dangerous promontory on the S. E. of Euboea,

where the Greek fleet is said to have been wrecked
on its return from Troy.

Caphyae (Καφύαι: Καφυεύς, Καφυάτης), a
town in Arcadia, N. W. of Orchomenus.

Capĭto, C. Atēĭus. 1. Tribune of the plebs
B. C. 55, when he opposed the triumvirs. — **2.** Son
of No. 1, an eminent Roman jurist, was appointed *Curator aquarum publicarum* in A. D.
13, and held this office till his death, 22. He
gained the favour of both Augustus and Tiberius by flattery and obsequiousness. He wrote
numerous legal works, which are cited in the
Digest and elsewhere. Capito and his contemporary Labeo were reckoned the highest legal
authorities of their day, and were the founders of
2 legal schools, to which most of the great jurists
belonged. The schools took their respective names
from distinguished disciples of those jurists. The
followers of Capito were called from Masurius
Sabinus, *Sabiniani;* and afterwards from Cassius
Longinus, *Cassiani.* The followers of Labeo took
from Proculus the name *Proculeiani.*

Capĭto, C. Fontēĭus, a friend of M. Antony,
accompanied Maecenas to Brundisium, B. C. 37,
when the latter was sent to effect a reconciliation
between Octavianus and Antony. (Hor. *Sat.* i. 5.
32.) Capito remained with Antony, and went
with him to the East.

Căpĭtōlīnus, Jŭlĭus, one of the *Scriptores Historiae Augustae,* lived in the reign of Diocletian
(A. D. 284—305), and wrote the lives of 9 emperors: — 1. Antoninus Pius, 2. M. Aurelius, 3. L.
Verus, 4. Pertinax, 5. Clodius Albinus, 6. Opilius
Macrinus, 7. the 2 Maximini, 8. the 3 Gordiani,
9. Maximus and Balbinus. The best editions of
the *Scriptores Historiae Augustae* are by Salmasius,
Par. 1620; Schrevelius, Lugd. Bat. 1671.

Căpĭtōlīnus, Manlĭus. [MANLIUS.]

Căpĭtōlīnus Mons. [CAPITOLIUM: ROMA.]

Căpĭtōlīnus, Petillĭus, was, according to the
Scholiast on Horace (*Sat.* i. 4. 94), entrusted with
the care of the temple of Jupiter on the Capitol
(whence he was called Capitolinus), and was accused of having stolen the crown of Jupiter, but
was acquitted by the judges in consequence of his
being a friend of Augustus. The surname Capitolinus appears, however, to have been a regular
family-name of the gens.

Căpĭtōlīnus, Quintĭus. [QUINTIUS.]

Căpĭtōlĭum, the temple of Jupiter Optimus
Maximus at Rome, was situated on the Mons Capitolinus, which derived its name from the temple.
This hill is in figure an irregular oblong, with two
more elevated summits at the N. and S. ends.
The N. summit, which is somewhat higher and
steeper, was the Arx or citadel of Rome, and is
now occupied by the church of *Ara Celi:* while the
S. summit, which is now covered in part by the
Palazzo Caffarelli, was the site of the Capitolium.
The temple is said to have been called the Capitolium, because a human head (*caput*) was discovered in digging the foundations. The building of
it was commenced by Tarquinius Priscus, and it
was finished by Tarquinius Superbus, but was not
dedicated till the 3rd year of the republic, B. C.
507, by the consul M. Horatius. It was burnt
down in the civil wars, 83, but was rebuilt by
Sulla, and was dedicated by Q. Catulus, 69. It
was burnt down a 2nd time by the soldiers of
Vitellius, A. D. 69, and was rebuilt by Vespasian;
but it was burnt down a 3rd time in the reign of

Temple of Jupiter Capitolinus restored. Pages 144, 145.

Temple of Jupiter Capitolinus. (From a Coin of Vespasian.) Pages 144, 145.

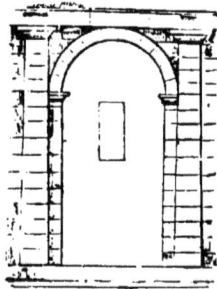

Arch of Tabularium on the Capitoline Hill. (See Dict. of Geography, Vol. II., p. 770.

Supposed Tarpeian Rock. Pages 144, 145.

[To face p. 144.

Bruttium.   Page 127.

Capua.   Page 146.

Byzantium.   Page 129.

Cardia in the Thracian Chersonese.   Page 147.

Caesarea Mazaca.   Page 146.

Carmo in Spain.   Page 148.

Calacta in Sicily.   Page 137.

Cartela in Spain.   Page 148.

Cales in Campania.   Page 138.

Camarina in Sicily.   Page 141.

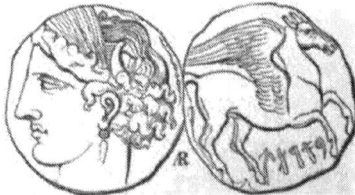

Carthage.   Page 149.

To face p. 145.]

Titus, 80, and was again rebuilt by Domitian with greater splendour than before. The Capitol contained 3 cells under the same roof: the middle cell was the temple of Jupiter, hence described as " *media* qui sedet aede Deus" (Ov. *ex Pont.* iv. 9. 32), and on either side were the cells of his attendant deities, Juno and Minerva. The Capitol was one of the most imposing buildings at Rome, and was adorned as befitted the majesty of the king of the gods. It was in the form of a square, namely, 200 feet on each side, and was approached by a flight of 100 steps. The gates were of bronze, and the ceilings and tiles gilt. The gilding alone of the building cost Domitian 12,000 talents. In the Capitol were kept the Sibylline books. Here the consuls upon entering on their office offered sacrifices and took their vows ; and hither the victorious general, who entered the city in triumph, was carried in his triumphal car to return thanks to the Father of the gods.—Although the words *Arx Capitoliumque* are properly used to signify the whole hill, yet we sometimes find the term *Arx* applied alone to the whole hill, since the hill itself constituted a natural citadel to the city, and sometimes the term *Capitolium* to the whole hill, on account of the importance and reverence attaching to the temple. Moreover, as the Capitol was nearly as defensible as the Arx, it is sometimes called *Arx Tarpeia* or *Capitolina*, but the epithet Tarpeia or Capitolina is applied to distinguish it from the Arx properly so called.

Cappădŏcĭa (Καππαδοκία: Καππάδοξ, Cappădox), a district of Asia Minor, to which different boundaries were assigned at different times. Under the Persian empire it included the whole country inhabited by a people of Syrian origin, who were called (from their complexion) White Syrians (Λευκόσυροι), and also Cappadoces, which appears to have been a word of Persian origin. Their country seems to have embraced the whole N. E. part of Asia Minor E. of the Halys and N. of the Taurus. Afterwards (but whether under the Persians or after the Macedonian conquest, is a disputed point) the country was divided into two parts, which were named respectively from their proximity to the Euxine and to the Taurus, the N. part being called Cappadocia ad Pontum and then simply **Pontus**, the S. part Cappadocia ad Taurum, and then simply Cappadocia : the former was also called Cappadocia Minor and the latter Cappadocia Major. Under the Persian Empire, the whole country was governed by a line of hereditary satraps, who traced their descent from Anaphas, an Achaemenid, one of the 7 chieftains that slew the pseudo-Smerdis, and who soon raised themselves to the position of tributary kings. After a temporary suspension of their power during the wars between the successors of Alexander, when Ariarathes I. was defeated and slain by Perdiccas (B. C. 322), the kings of S. Cappadocia (respecting the other part see **Pontus**) recovered their independence under Ariarathes II., whose history and that of his successors will be found under **Ariarathes** and **Ariobarzanes**. In A. D. 17, Archelaus, the last king, died at Rome, and Tiberius made Cappadocia a Roman province. [**Archelaus**, No. 6.] Soon afterwards the districts of Cataonia and Melitene, which had before belonged to Cilicia, were added to Cappadocia, and the province then comprised the 10 praefecturae of Melitene, Cataonia, Cilicia, Tyanitis, Garsauritis, La-

viniasene, Sargarausene, Sarauravene, Chamanene, and Morimene. There were other divisions under the later emperors. Cappadocia was a rough and generally sterile mountain region; bordered by the chains of the **Paryadres** on the N., the **Scydisses** on the E., and the **Taurus** on the S., and intersected by that of the **Anti-Taurus**, on the side of whose central mountain, **Argaeus**, stood the capital Mazaca, aft. **Caesarea ad Argaeum**. Its chief rivers were the **Halys** and the **Melas**. Its fine pastures supported abundance of good horses and mules.

Cappădox (Καππάδοξ : *Konae*), a tributary of the Halys, rising in M. Lithrus, in the chain of Paryadres, and forming the N.W. boundary of Cappadocia, on the side of Galatia.

Capra, or **Capella** (Αἴξ), the brightest star in the constellation of the *Auriga*, or *Charioteer*, is sometimes called *Olenia Capella*, because it rested on the shoulder (ἐπὶ τῆς ὠλένης) of the Auriga. This star was said to have been originally the nymph or goat who nursed the infant Zeus in Crete. [**Aega** ; **Amalthea**.] Its heliacal rising took place soon before the winter solstice, and thus it was termed *signum pluviale*.

Caprārĭa or **Caprāsĭa**. 1. (*Capraja*), a small island off the coast of Etruria between Populonia and the N. extremity of Corsica, inhabited only by wild goats, whence its name: called by the Greeks Αἰγίλων.—2. (*Cabrera*), a small island off the S. of the Balearis Major (*Majorca*), dangerous to ships.—3. See **Aegates**.—4. See **Fortunatae Insulae.**

Caprĕae (*Capri*), a small island, 9 miles in circumference, off Campania, at the S. entrance of the gulf of Puteoli, and 2¼ miles from the promontory of Minerva, from which the island had been separated by an earthquake. It is composed of calcareous rocks, which rise to 2 summits, the highest of which is between 1600 and 1700 feet above the sea. The scenery is beautiful, and the climate soft and genial. According to tradition, it was originally inhabited by the Teleboae, but afterwards belonged to the inhabitants of Neapolis, from whom Augustus either purchased it or obtained it in exchange for the island Pithecusa. Here Tiberius lived the last 10 years of his reign, indulging in secret debauchery, and accessible only to his creatures. He erected many magnificent buildings on the island, the chief of which was the Villa Jovis, and the ruins of which are still to be seen.

Capria (Καπρία), a large salt lake in Pamphylia, near the coast, between Perge and Aspendus.

Capricornus (Αἰγόκερως), *the Goat*, a sign of the Zodiac, between the Archer and the Waterman, is said to have fought with Jupiter against the Titans.

Caprus (Κάπρος). 1. (*Little Zab*), a river of Assyria, rising in Mt. Zagros (*Mts. of Kurdistan*), and flowing S.W. into the Tigris, opposite to Caenae.—2. A little river of Phrygia, rising at the foot of M. Cadmus, and flowing N. into the Lycus.

Capsa (Capsetānus: *Ghafsah*), a strong and ancient city in the S.W. of Byzacena in N. Africa, in a fertile oasis, surrounded by a sandy desert abounding in serpents. Its foundation was ascribed by tradition to the Libyan Hercules. In the war with Jugurtha, who used it as a treasure-city, it was destroyed by Marius ; but it was afterwards rebuilt and erected into a colony.

Capŭa (Capuanus, Capuensis, but more commonly Campānus: *Capua*), originally called **Vulturnum**, the chief city of Campania after the fall of CUMAE, is said to have derived its name from Capys. Capua was either founded or colonised by the Etruscans, according to some 50 years before the foundation of Rome, and it became at an early period the most prosperous, wealthy, and luxurious city in the S. of Italy. In B. C. 420 it was conquered by the warlike Samnites; and the population, which had always been of a mixed nature, now consisted of Ausonians, Oscans, Etruscans, and Samnites. At a later time Capua, again attacked by the Samnites, placed itself under the protection of Rome, 343. It revolted to Hannibal after the battle of Cannae, 216, but was taken by the Romans in 211, was fearfully punished, and never recovered its former prosperity. It was now governed by a Praefectus, who was sent annually to the city from Rome. It received a Roman colony by the lex agraria of Julius Caesar, 59, and under Nero a colony of veterans was settled there. It was subsequently destroyed by the barbarians who invaded Italy. The modern town of Capua is built about 3 miles from the ancient one, the site of which is indicated by the ruins of an amphitheatre.

Caput Vada Prom. [BRACHODES.]

Căpys (Κάπυς). 1. Son of Assaracus and Hieromnemone, and father of Anchises.—2. A companion of Aeneas, from whom Capua was said to have derived its name.

Căpys Silvius. [SILVIUS.]

Capytium or **Capitium** (*Capizzi*), called by Cicero *Capitina Civitas*, a town in Sicily near Mt. Aetna.

Car (Κάρ), son of Phoroneus, and king of Megara, from whom the acropolis of this town was called Caria.

Cărăcalla, emperor of Rome, A. D. 211—217, was son of Septimius Severus and his 2nd wife Julia Domna, and was born at Lyons, A. D. 188. He was originally called *Bassianus* after his maternal grandfather, but afterwards *M. Aurelius Antoninus*, which became his legal name, and appears on medals and inscriptions. *Caracalla* was a nickname derived from a long tunic worn by the Gauls, which he adopted as his favourite dress after he became emperor. In 198 Caracalla, when 10 years old, was declared Augustus, and in the same year accompanied his father Severus in the expedition against the Parthians. He returned with Severus to Rome in 202, and married Plautilla, daughter of Plautianus, the praetorian praefect. In 208 he went with Severus to Britain; and on the death of the latter at York, 211, Caracalla and his brother Geta succeeded to the throne, according to their father's arrangements. Caracalla's first object was to obtain the sole government by the murder of his brother; and after making several unsuccessful attempts upon the life of Geta, he at length pretended to be reconciled with him, and having thus thrown him off his guard, he caused him to be murdered in the arms of his mother, 212. The assassination of Geta was followed by the execution of many of the most distinguished men of the state, whom Caracalla suspected of favouring his brother's cause: the celebrated jurist Papinian was one of his victims. His cruelties and extravagancies knew no bounds; and after exhausting Italy by his extortions. he resolved to visit the different provinces of the empire, which became the scenes of fresh atrocities. In 214 he visited Gaul, Germany, Dacia, and Thrace; and, in consequence of a campaign against the Alemanni, he assumed the surname *Alemannicus*. In 215 he went to Syria and Egypt; his sojourn at Alexandria was marked by a general slaughter of the inhabitants, in order to avenge certain sarcastic pleasantries in which they had indulged against himself and his mother. In 216 he crossed the Euphrates, laid waste Mesopotamia, and returned to Edessa, where he wintered. Next year he again took the field, intending to cross the Tigris, but was murdered near Edessa by Macrinus, the praetorian praefect. Caracalla gave to all free inhabitants of the empire the name and privileges of Roman citizens.

Caractācus, king of. the Silures in Britain, bravely defended his country against the Romans, in the reign of Claudius. He was at length defeated by the Romans, and fled for protection to Cartimandua, queen of the Brigantes; but she betrayed him to the Romans, who carried him to Rome, A. D. 51. When brought before Claudius, he addressed the emperor in so noble a manner that the latter pardoned him and his friends.

Carālis or **Carāles** (Caralitānus: *Cagliari*), the chief town of Sardinia, with an excellent harbour, situated on the Sinus Caralitanus and on a promontory of the same name (*Capo S. Elia*). It was founded by the Carthaginians; under the Romans it was the residence of the praetor, and at a later period enjoyed the Roman franchise.

Cărambis (Κάραμβις ἄκρα: *Kerempe*), a promontory, with a city of the same name, on the coast of Paphlagonia, almost exactly opposite the Kriu Metopon or S. promontory of the Chersonesus Taurica (*Crimea*). An imaginary line joining these two headlands would make an almost equal division of the Euxine, which was hence called διθύμη θάλασσα (Soph. *Antig.* 978.)

Cărānus (Κάρανος). 1. Of Argos, a descendant of Hercules, and a brother of Phidon, is said to have settled at Edessa in Macedonia with an Argive colony about B. C. 750, and to have become the founder of the dynasty of Macedonian kings. —2. Son of Philip and half-brother of Alexander the Great. — 3. A general of Alexander the Great.

Carausius, born among the Menapii in Gaul, was entrusted by Maximian with the command of the fleet which was to protect the coasts of Gaul against the ravages of the Franks. But Maximian, having become dissatisfied with the conduct of Carausius in this command, gave orders for the execution of the latter. Carausius forthwith crossed over to Britain, where he assumed the title of Augustus, A. D. 287. After several ineffectual attempts to subdue him, Diocletian and Maximian acknowledged him as their colleague in the empire, and he continued to reign in Britain till 293, when he was murdered by his chief officer, Allectus.

Carbo, Papirius. 1. C., a distinguished orator, and a man of great talents, but of no principle. He commenced public life as one of the 3 commissioners or triumvirs for carrying into effect the agrarian law of Tib. Gracchus. His tribuneship of the plebs, B. C. 131, was characterised by the most vehement opposition to the aristocracy; and he was thought even to have murdered Scipio Africanus, the champion of the aristocratical party, 129. But after the death of C. Gracchus (121), he suddenly deserted the popular party, and in his consulship (120) actually undertook the defence of Opimius, who had murdered C. Gracchus. In 119 Carbo was accused by L. Licinius Crassus, who brought a charge against him, and as he foresaw his condemnation, he put an end to his life.—2. Cn., consul 113, was defeated by the Cimbri near Noreia, and being afterwards accused by M. Antonius, he put an end to his own life.—3. C., with the surname Arvina, son of No. 1, was a supporter of the aristocracy. In his tribuneship (90), Carbo and his colleague, M. Plautius Silvanus, carried a law (Lex Papiria Plautia), giving the Roman franchise to the citizens of the federate towns. Carbo was murdered in 82, by the praetor Brutus Damasippus, at the command of the younger Marius. [BRUTUS, No. 10.] —4. Cn., son of No. 2, was one of the leaders of the Marian party. He was thrice consul, namely, in 85, 84, and 82. In 82 he carried on war against Sulla and his generals, but was at length obliged to abandon Italy: he fled to Sicily, where he was taken prisoner, and put to death by Pompey at Lilybaeum, in the course of the same year.

Carcāso (Carcassone), a town of the Tectosages in Gallia Narbonensis.

Carcāthiŏcerta (Καρκαθιόκερτα: Kartpurt or Diarbekr), the capital of the district of Sophene in Armenia Major.

Carcīnus (Καρκίνος). 1. A comic poet and a contemporary of Aristophanes (Nub. 1263, Pax, 794). — 2. A tragic poet, lived about B.C. 380.

Cardămȳle (Καρδαμύλη: Καρδαμυλίτης). 1. A town in Messenia, one of the 7 towns promised by Agamemnon to Achilles. — 2. An island near or perhaps a town in Chios.

Cardēa, a Roman divinity protecting the hinges of doors (cardo), was a nymph beloved by Janus, who rewarded her for her favours by giving her the protection of the hinges of doors, and the power of preventing evil daemons from entering houses. Ovid (Fast. vi. 101, seq.) confounds this goddess with CARNA.

Cardĭa (Καρδία: Καρδιανός), a town on the W. side of the Thracian Chersonese on the gulf of Melas, founded by Miletus and Clazomenae, and subsequently colonized by the Athenians under Miltiades. It was destroyed by Lysimachus, who built the town of LYSIMACHIA in its immediate neighbourhood. Cardia was the birth-place of Eumenes and of the historian Hieronymus.

Cardūchi (Καρδοῦχοι), a powerful and warlike people in the S.E. of Great Armenia, on the N.E. margin of the Tigris valley, probably the same as the Γορδυαῖοι and Γορδυηνοί of the late geographers and the Kurds of modern times. They dwelt in the mountains which divided Assyria on the N.E. from Armenia (Mts. of Kurdistan), and were never thoroughly subdued by the Persians, Greeks, or Romans.

Carēsus (Κάρησος), a town of the Troad, on a river of the same name flowing into the Aesepus: destroyed before the time of Strabo.

Cārīa (Καρία: Κάρ), a district of Asia Minor, in its S.W. corner, bounded on the N. and N.E. by the mountains Messogis and Cadmus, which divided it from Lydia and Phrygia, and adjacent to Phrygia and Lycia on the E. and S.E. It is intersected by low mountain chains running out far into the sea in long promontories, the N.-most of which was called Mycale or Trogilium (opposite to Samos), the next Posidium (on which stood

Milet.s and Branchidae), the next is the long tongue of land terminated by the 2 headlands of Zephyrium and Termerium (with Halicarnassus on its S. side), next the Cnidian Chersonesus, terminated by the cape Triopium and the city of Cnidus, then the Rhodian Chersonesus, the S. point of which was called Cynossema, opposite to Rhodes, and, lastly, Pedalium or Artemisium, forming the W. headland of the bay of Glaucus. The chief gulfs formed by these promontories were the Maeandrian, between Trogilium and Posidium; the Iassian, between Posidium and Zephyrium; and the Ceraunian or Dorian, between Termerium and Triopium. The valleys between these mountain chains were well watered and fertile. The chief river was the Maeander, between the chains of Messogis and Latmus, to the S. of which the country was watered by its tributaries, the Marsyas, Harpasus, and Mosynus, besides some streams flowing W. and S. into the sea, the most considerable of which was the Calbis. (See the articles.) The chief products of the country were corn, wine, oil, and figs; for the last of which Caunus, on the S. coast, was very famous. An extensive commerce was carried on by the Greek colonies on the coast. — Even before the great colonization of the coasts of Asia Minor, Dorian settlements existed on the Triopian and Cnidian promontories, and this part of Caria, with the adjacent islands, received at that time other Dorian colonies, and obtained the name of DORIS; while to the N. of the Iassian Gulf, the coast was occupied by Ionian colonies, and thus formed the S. part of IONIA. The inhabitants of the rest of the country were Carians (Κᾶρες), a wide-spread race of the Indo-Germanic stock, nearly allied to the Lydians and Mysians, which appears, in the earliest times of which we know any thing, to have occupied the greater part of the W. coast of Asia Minor and several islands of the Aegean, in conjunction with the LELEGES, from whom the Carians are not easily distinguishable. The connection between the Carians, Lydians, and Mysians is attested by their common worship of Zeus Carios at Mylasa: the Carians had also a common sanctuary of Zeus Chrysaoreus. — Their language was reckoned by the Greeks as a barbarian tongue (i. e. unintelligible), though it early received an intermixture of Greek. The people were considered mean and stupid, even for slaves. — The country was governed by a race of native princes, who fixed their abode at Halicarnassus after its exclusion from the Dorian confederacy. [HALICARNASSUS.] These princes were subject allies of Lydia and Persia, and some of them rose to great distinction in war and peace. [See ARTEMISIA, MAUSOLUS, and ADA.] After the Macedonian conquest, the S. portion of the country became subject to Rhodes [RHODUS], and the N. part to the kings of PERGAMUS. Under the Romans, Caria formed a part of the province of ASIA.

Carīnae. [ROMA.]

Carīnus, M. Aurelius, the elder of the 2 sons of Carus, was associated with his father in the government, A.D. 283, and remained in the W., while his father and brother Numerianus proceeded to the E. to carry on war against the Persians. On the death of his father, in the course of the same year, Carinus and Numerianus succeeded to the empire. In 284 Numerianus was slain, and Carinus marched into Moesia to oppose Diocletian, who had been proclaimed emperor. A decisive battle was fought near Margum, in which Carinus gained the victory, but, in the moment of triumph, he was slain by some of his own officers, whose wives he had seduced, 285. Carinus was one of the most profligate and cruel of the Roman emperors.

Carmāna (Κάρμανα: *Kerman*, Ru.), the capital of Carmania Propria, 3° long. E. of Persepolis.

Carmānīa (Καρμανία: *Kirman*), a province of the ancient Persian empire, bounded on the W. by Persis, on the N. by Parthia, on the E. by Gedrosia, and on the S. by the Indian Ocean. It was divided into 2 parts, C. Propria and C De-serta, the former of which was well watered by several small streams, and abounded in corn, wine, and cattle. The country also yielded gold, silver, copper, salt, and cinnabar. The people were akin to the Persians.

Carmānor (Καρμάνωρ), a Cretan, said to have purified Apollo and Artemis, after slaying the monster Python.

Carmēlus, and -um (Κάρμηλος: *Jebel-Elyas*), a range of mountains in Palestine, branching off, on the N. border of Samaria, from the central chain (which extends S. and N. between the Jordan and the Mediterranean), and running N. and N. W. through the S. W. part of Galilee, till it termi-nates in the promontory of the same name (*Cape Carmel*), the height of which is 1200 feet above the Mediterranean.

Carmenta, Carmentis. [CAMENAE.]

Carmo (*Carmona*), a fortified town in Hispania Baetica, N. E. of Hispalis.

Carna, a Roman divinity, whose name is pro-bably connected with *caro*, flesh, for she was re-garded as the protector of the physical well-being of man. Her festival was celebrated June 1st, and was believed to have been instituted by Brutus in the first year of the republic. Ovid confounds this goddess with CARDEA.

Carnĕādes (Καρνεάδης), a celebrated philoso-pher, born at Cyrene about B. C. 213, was the founder of the Third or New Academy at Athens. In 155 he was sent to Rome, with Diogenes and Critolaus, by the Athenians, to deprecate the fine of 500 talents which had been imposed on the Athenians for the destruction of Oropus. At Rome he attracted great notice from his eloquent decla-mations on philosophical subjects, and it was here that he first delivered his famous orations on Jus-tice. The 1st oration was in commendation of the virtue, and the next day the 2nd answered all the arguments of the 1st, and showed that justice was not a virtue, but a matter of compact for the main-tenance of civil society. Thereupon Cato moved the senate to send the philosopher home to his school, and save the Roman youth from his de-moralising doctrines. Carneades died in 129, at the age of 85. He was a strenuous opponent of the Stoics, and maintained that neither our senses nor our understanding supply us with a sure criterion of truth.

Carnēus (Καρνεῖος), a surname of Apollo, under which he was worshipped by the Dorians, is derived by some from Carnus, a son of Zeus and Leto, and by others from Carnus, an Acarnanian soothsayer. The latter was murdered by HIPPOTES, and it was to propitiate Apollo that the Dorians introduced his worship under the surname of Carneus. The festival of the *Carnĕa*, in honour of Apollo, was one of the great national festivals of the Spartans. (*Dict. of Ant. s. v.*)

Carni, a Celtic people, dwelling N. of the Ve-neti in the Alpes Carnicae. [See p. 40.]

Carnuntum (Καρνοῦς, -οῦντος: Ru. between *Deutsch-Altenburg* and *Petronell*), an ancient Celtic town in Upper Pannonia on the Danube, E. of Vindobona (*Vienna*), and subsequently a Roman municipium or a colony. It was one of the chief fortresses of the Romans on the Danube, and was the residence of the emperor M. Aurelius during his wars with the Marcomanni and Quadi. It was the station of the Roman fleet on the Danube and the regular quarters of the 14th legion. It was destroyed by the Germans in the 4th century, but was rebuilt and was finally destroyed by the Hun-garians in the middle ages.

Carnus. [CARNEUS.]

Carnūtes or -i, a powerful people in Gallia Lug-dunensis between the Liger and Sequana: their capital was GENABUM.

Carpasia (Καρπασία: *Karpass*), a town in the S. E. of Cyprus.

Carpātes, also called **Alpes Bastarnicae** (*Car-pathian Mountains*), the mountains separating Dacia from Sarmatia.

Carpăthus (Κάρπαθος: *Scarpanto*), an island between Crete and Rhodes, in the sea named after it : its chief towns were Posidium and Nisyrus.

Carpētāni, a powerful people in Hispania Tarra-conensis, with a fertile territory on the rivers Anas and Tagus, in the modern *Castille* and *Estrema-dura* : their capital was TOLETUM.

Carpi or **Carpiāni**, a German people between the Carpathian mountains and the Danube.

Carrae or **Carrhae** (Κάρραι: Haran or Charran, S.S. : *Harran*), a city of Osroëne in Mesopotamia, not far from Edessa. It was here that Crassus met his death after his defeat by the Parthians, B. C. 53.

Carrīnas or **Carīnas.** 1. C., one of the com-manders of the Marian party, fought B. C. 83 against Pompey, and in 82 against Sulla and his generals. After the battle at the Colline gate at Rome, in which the Marian army was defeated, Carrinas took to flight, but was seized, and put to death. — 2. C., son of No. 1, was sent by Caesar, in 45, into Spain against Sext. Pompeius, but he did not accomplish anything. In 43 he was consul, and afterwards served as one of the generals of Octa-vian against Sext. Pompeius in Sicily, in 36, and as proconsul in Gaul in 31. — 3. Secundus, a rhetorician, expelled by Caligula from Rome, be-cause he had, by way of exercise, declaimed against tyrants in his school.

Carsĕŏli (Carseolānus: *Carsoli*), a town of the Aequi in Latium, colonized by the Romans at an early period.

Carsŭlae (Carsulānus: *Monte Castrilli*), a town in Umbria, originally of considerable importance, but afterwards declined.

Carteia (also called Carthaea, Carpia, Carpes-sus : *Orantia*), more anciently Tartessus, a cele-brated town and harbour in the S. of Spain, at the head of the gulf of which M. Calpe forms one side, founded by the Phoenicians, and colonized B. C. 170 by 4000 Roman soldiers, whose mothers were Spanish women.

Cartenna or **Cartinna** (*Tennez*), a colony on the coast of Mauretania Caesariensis in N. Africa, founded by Augustus.

Carthaea (Καρθαία: *Poles*, Ru.), a town on the S. side of the island of Ceos.

Carthago, Magna Carthago (Καρχηδών: Καρχηδόνιος, Carthaginiensis, Poenus: Ru. near *El-Marsa*, N.E. of Tunis), one of the most celebrated cities of the ancient world, stood in the recess of a large bay (Sinus Carthaginiensis) enclosed by the headlands Apollinis and Mercurii (*C. Farina* and *C. Bon*), in the middle and N.-most part of the N. coast of Africa, in lat. about 36° 55′ N., and long. about 10° 20′ E. The coast of this part of Africa has been much altered by the deposits of the river Bagradas and the sand which is driven seawards by the N. W. winds. In ancient times Carthage stood upon a peninsula surrounded by the sea on all sides except the W.: but now the whole space between the N. side of this peninsula and the S side of the Apollinis Pr. (*C. Farina*), is filled up and converted into a marsh ; Utica, which was on the sea-shore, being left some miles inland ; and the course of the Bagradas itself being turned considerably N. of its original channel, so that, instead of flowing about half-way between Utica and Carthage, it now runs close to the ruins of Utica, and falls into the sea just under *C. Farina*. The N. E. and S. E. sides of the peninsula are still open to the sea, which has indeed rather encroached here, for ruins are found under water. The S. side of the peninsula was formed by an enclosed bay, connected with the sea only by a narrow opening (now called the *Goletta*, or, in Arabic, *Halvet-el-Wad*, i. e. *Throat of the River*), which still forms the port of *Tunis* (anc. Tunes), which stands at its furthest end ; but it is nearly choked up with the deposit of the sewers of the city. The circuit of the old peninsula may be estimated at about 30 miles : the width of the isthmus is 3 miles. The greatest circumference of the city itself was probably about 15 miles. The original city appears to have stood on the N. E. part of the peninsula, between *Ras Ghammart* and *Ras Bousaid* (*C. Carthage*), where the remains of cisterns are seen under water: these, and the aqueduct, whose ruins may be traced for 52 miles to *Zaghwan*, are the only remains of the old city. Its port, called Cothon, was on the N. W. side of the peninsula, where a little village (now inland) still retains the name of *El-Marsa*, i. e. *the Port*. The Roman city, which was built after the destruction of the original Carthage, lay to the S. of it. — The Tyrian colony of Carthage was founded, according to tradition, about 100 years before the building of Rome, that is, about B. C. 853. There were several more ancient Phoenician colonies along the same coast, between 2 of which, Utica and Tunes, the new settlement was fixed, about 27 miles (Roman) from the former, and 10 from the latter. The mythical account of its foundation is given under Dido. The part of the city first built was called, in the Phoenician language, Betzura or Bosra, i. e. *a castle*, which was corrupted by the Greeks into Byrsa (Βύρσα), i. e. *a hide*, and hence probably arose the story of the way in which the natives were cheated out of the ground. As the city grew, the Byrsa formed the citadel: it stood on a low hill ; but its site can no longer be identified, as there are several such hills within the circuit of the ancient city. The Cothon, or *Port*, is said to have been excavated, and the quarter of the city adjoining to it built, 40 years later, B. C. 813 This Cothon was the inner harbour, and was used for ships of war: the outer harbour, divided from it by a tongue of land 300 feet wide, was the sta-

tion for the merchant ships. The fortifications of the city consisted of a single wall on the side towards the sea, where the steep shore formed a natural defence, and a triple wall of great height, with battlements and towers, on the land side ; — on this side were barracks for 40,000 soldiers, and stables for 300 elephants and 4000 horses. Beyond the fortifications was a large suburb, called Magara or Magalia, containing many beautiful gardens and villas. The aqueduct already mentioned is supposed, on good grounds, to have been built at an early period of the existence of the city. The most remarkable buildings mentioned within the city were the temple of the god whom the Greeks and Romans identified with Aesculapius, and that of Apollo (Baal or the Sun) in the market-place. The population of Carthage, at the time of the 3rd Punic war, is stated at 700,000. — The constitution of Carthage was a municipal oligarchy, somewhat resembling that of Venice. The two chief magistrates, called Suffetes (probably the same word as the Hebrew Shophetim, i. e. *Judges*) appear to have been elected for life ; the Greek and Roman writers call them kings. The generals and foreign governors were usually quite distinct from the suffetes ; but the 2 offices were sometimes united in the same person. The governing body was a Senate, partly hereditary and partly elective, within which there was a select body of 100 or 104, called Gerusia, whose chief office was to controul the magistrates, and especially the generals returning from foreign service, who might be suspected of attempts to establish a tyranny. The Gerusia was first formed about B. C. 400, when the power of the house of Mago excited suspicion ; and its efficacy was shown in the defeat of the attempts made by Hanno (B. C. 340) and Hamilcar (B. C. 306) to seize the supreme power. Its members are said by Aristotle to have been elected by the pentarchies, bodies of which we have very little information, but which appear to have been committees of five, chosen from the most eminent members of the senate, and entrusted with the controul of the various departments of the government. Important questions, especially those on which the senate and the suffetes disagreed, were referred to a general assembly of the citizens ; but concerning the mode of proceeding in this assembly, and the extent of its powers, we know very little. It seems to have elected the magistrates ; the senate having either the power of previous nomination or of a veto, it is not clear which. The generals were chosen by the gerusia, and approved by the assembly of the citizens. — The general tone of social morality at Carthage appears to have been high, at least during its earlier history : there was a censorship of public morals, under the care of the gerusia ; and all the magistrates were required, during their term of office, to abstain from wine: the magistrates were also unpaid. Their punishments were very severe, and the usual mode of inflicting death was by crucifixion. — The religion of Carthage was that of the mother country : especial mention is made of the cruel rites of their tutelar deity Melcarth (i. e. *king of the city*, no doubt the same as Moloch), which were abolished by the treaty with Gelon of Syracuse, B. C. 480 ; and also of the worship of Ashtaroth and Astarte, and Aesculapius. — The chief occupations of the people were commerce and agriculture : in the former they rivalled the mother city, Tyre ; and the latter they pursued with such success that the country around the city was one of the best cultivated districts in the ancient world, and a great work on agriculture, in 28 books, was composed by Mago, a suffete. — The revenues of the state were derived from the subject provinces; and its army was composed of mercenaries from the neighbouring country, among whom the Numidian cavalry were especially distinguished. — Of the *History of Carthage* a brief sketch will suffice; as the most important portions of it are related in the ordinary histories of Rome. The first colonists preserved the character of peaceful traders, and maintained friendly relations with the natives of the country, to whom they long continued to pay a rent or tribute for the ground on which the city was built. Gradually, however, as their commerce brought them power and wealth, they were enabled to reduce the natives of the district round the city, first to the condition of allies, and then to that of tributaries. Meanwhile, they undertook military expeditions at sea, and possessed themselves, first of the small islands near their own coast, and afterwards of Malta, and the Lipari and Balearic islands: they also sent aid to Tyre, when it was besieged by Nebuchadnezzar (B. c. 600), and took part in wars between the Etruscans and the Phocaean colonies. On the coast of Africa they founded numerous colonies, from the Pillars of Hercules to the bottom of the Great Syrtis, where they met the Greek colonists of Cyrenaica: the people of these colonies became intermixed with the Libyans around them, forming a population who are called Libyo-Phoenicians. In connection with their commercial enterprizes, they no doubt sent forth various expeditions of maritime discovery; among which we have mention of 2, which were undertaken during the long peace which followed the war with Gelon in B. c. 480, to explore the W. coasts of Europe and Africa respectively. The record of the latter expedition, under Hanno, is still preserved to us in a Greek translation [HANNO], from which we learn that it reached probably as far S. as 10° N. lat., if not further. The relations of the Carthaginians with the interior of N. Africa appear to have been very extensive, but the country actually subject to them, and which formed the true Carthaginian territory, was limited to the district contained between the river Tusca (*Zain*) on the W. and the lake and river Triton, at the bottom of the Lesser Syrtis, on the S., corresponding very nearly to the modern regency of *Tunis*; and even within this territory there were some ancient Phoenician colonies, which, though in alliance with Carthage, preserved their independent municipal government, such as Hippo Zaritus, Utica, Hadrumetum, and Leptis. — The first great development of the power of Carthage for foreign conquest was made by Mago (about B. c. 550—500), who is said to have first established a sound discipline in the armies of the republic, and to have freed the city from the tribute which it still paid to the Libyans. His sons, Hasdrubal and Hamilcar, reduced a part of the island of Sardinia, where the Carthaginians founded the colonies of Caralis and Sulci; and by this time the fame of Carthage had spread so far, that Darius is said to have sent to ask her aid against the Greeks, which, however, was refused. The Carthaginians, however, took advantage of the Persian war to attempt the conquest of Sicily, whither Hamilcar was sent with a great force, in B. c. 480, but his army was de-

stroyed and himself killed in a great battle under the walls of Himera, in which the Sicilian Greeks were commanded by Gelon the tyrant of Syracuse, and which was said to have been fought on the same day as the battle of Salamis. Their next attempt upon Sicily, in B. c. 410, led to a protracted war, which resulted in a treaty between the Syracusans, under Timoleon, and the Carthaginians, by which the latter were confirmed in the possession of the W. part of the island, as far as the river Halicus. From B. c. 310—307 there was another war between Syracuse and the Carthaginians, which was chiefly remarkable for the bold step taken by Agathocles, who invaded the Carthaginian territory in Africa, and thus, though unable to maintain himself there, set an example which was followed a century later by Scipio, with fatal results to Carthage. Passing over the wars with PYRRHUS and HIERO, we come to the long struggle between Rome and Carthage, known as the Punic Wars, which are fully related in the Histories of Rome. [See also HAMILCAR.] The first lasted from B. c. 265—242, and resulted in the loss to Carthage of Sicily and the Lipari islands. It was followed by a fierce contest of some years between Carthage and her disbanded mercenaries, which is called the Libyan War, and which was terminated by Hamilcar Barcas. After a hollow peace, during which the Romans openly violated the last treaty, and the Carthaginians conquered Spain as far as the Iberus (*Ebro*), the Second Punic War, the decisive contest between the two rival states, which were too powerful to co-exist, began with the siege of Saguntum (B. c. 218) and terminated (B. c. 201) with a peace by which Carthage was stripped of all her power. [HANNIBAL; SCIPIO.] Her destruction was now only a question of time, and, though she scrupulously observed the terms of the last peace for 50 years, in spite of every provocation from the Romans and their ally Masinissa, the king of Numidia, a pretext was at length found for a new war (B. c. 149), which lasted only 3 years, during which the Carthaginians, driven to despair by the terms proposed to them, sustained a siege so destructive that, out of 700,000 persons, who were living in the city at its commencement, only 50,000 surrendered to the Romans. The city was razed to the ground, and remained in ruins for 30 years. At the end of that time a colony was established on the old site by the Gracchi, which remained in a feeble condition till the times of Julius and Augustus, under whom a new city was built S. of the former, on the S. E. side of the peninsula, with the name of **Colonia Carthago.** It soon grew so much as to cover a great part (if not the whole) of the site of the ancient Tyrian city: it became the first city of Africa, and occupied an important place in ecclesiastical as well as in civil history. It was taken by the Vandals in A. D. 439, retaken by Belisarius in A. D. 533, and destroyed by the Arab conquerors in A. D. 698. — Respecting the territory of Carthage under the Romans, see AFRICA, No. 2.

Carthāgo Nŏva (Καρχηδὼν ἡ νέα: *Carthagena*), a town on the E. coast of Hispania Tarraconensis, founded by the Carthaginians under Hasdrubal, B. c. 243, and subsequently conquered and colonized by the Romans, from which time its full name was *Colonia Victrix Julia Nova Carthago.* It is situated on a promontory running out into the sea, and possesses one of the finest harbours in the world; at the entrance of the harbour was a small island called **Scombraria**, from the great number of scombri or mackerel caught here, from which such famous pickle was made. In ancient times Carthago Nova was one of the most important cities in all Spain ; its population was numerous, its trade flourishing, and its temples and other public buildings handsome and imposing. It was, together with Tarraco, the residence of the Roman governor of the province. In the neighbourhood were valuable silver mines ; and the country produced an immense quantity of *Spartum* or broom, whence the town bore the surname *Spartaria*, and the country was called *Campus Spartarius*.

Carūra (τὰ Καρουρά : *Sarikivi*), a Phrygian city, in the territory of Caria, on the left bank of the Maeander, celebrated for its hot springs and its temple of Men Carus.

Cārus, M. Aurēlius, Roman empéror A. D. 282 —283, probably born at Narbo in Gaul, was praefectus praetorio under Probus, and on the murder of the latter was elected emperor. After defeating the Sarmatians, Carus invaded the Persian dominions, took Seleucia and Ctesiphon, and was preparing to push his conquests beyond the Tigris, when he was struck dead by lightning, towards the close of 283. He was succeeded by his sons CARINUS and NUMERIANUS. Carus was a victorious general and able ruler.

Carūsa (ἡ Καρούσα : *Kerzek*), a city on the coast of Paphlagonia, S. of Sinope.

Carventum, a town of the Volsci, to which the **Carventana Arx** mentioned by Livy belonged, a town of the Volsci between Signia and the sources of the Trerus.

Carvilius Maxĭmus. 1. Sp., twice consul, B. C. 293 and 273, both times with L. Papirius Cursor. In their first consulship they gained brilliant victories over the Samnites, and in their second they brought the Samnite war to a close. — **2. Sp.**, son of the preceding, twice consul, 234 and 228, was alive at the battle of Cannae, 216, after which he proposed to fill up the vacancies in the senate from the Latins. This Carvilius is said to have been the first person at Rome who divorced his wife.

Carȳae (Καρύαι : Καρυάτης, fem. Καρυᾶτις), a town in Laconia near the borders of Arcadia, originally belonged to the territory of Tegea in Arcadia. It possessed a temple of Artemis Caryatis, and an annual festival in honour of this goddess was celebrated here by the Lacedaemonian maidens with national dances. Respecting the female figures in architecture called *Caryatides*, see *Dict. of Ant. s. v.*

Caryanda (τὰ Καρύανδα : Καρυανδεύς : *Karakoyun*), a city of Caria, on a little island, once probably united with the mainland, at the N.W. extremity of the peninsula on which Halicarnassus stood. It once belonged to the Ionian league ; and it was the birthplace of the geographer Scylax.

Carȳātis. [CARYAE.]

Carystīus (Καρύστιος), a Greek grammarian of Pergamus, lived about B. C. 120, and wrote numerous works, all of which are lost.

Carystus (Κάρυστος : Καρύστιος : *Karysto* or *Castel Rosso*), a town on the S. coast of Euboea, at the foot of Mount Oche, founded by Dryopes ; called, according to tradition, after Carystus, son of Chiron. In the neighbourhood was excellent marble, which was exported in large quantities ; and the mineral, called Asbestos, was also found here.

Casca, P. Servīlius, tribune of the plebs, B. C. 44, was one of the conspirators against Caesar, and aimed the first stroke at his assassination. He fought in the battle of Philippi (42), and died shortly afterwards. — C. Casca, the brother of the preceding, was also one of the conspirators against Caesar.

Cascellīus, A., an eminent Roman jurist (Hor. *Ar. Poët.*, 371), contemporary with Caesar and Augustus, was a man of stern republican principles, and spoke freely against the proscriptions of the triumvirs.

Casĭlīnum (Casilinas, -ātis), a town in Campania on the Vulturnus, and on the same site as the modern Capua, celebrated for its heroic defence against Hannibal B. C. 216. It received Roman colonists by the Lex Julia, but had greatly declined in the time of Pliny.

Casīnum (Casīnas, -ātis : *S. Germano*), a town in Latium on the river Casinus, and on the Via Latina near the borders of Campania ; colonised by the Romans in the Samnite wars ; subsequently a municipium ; its citadel containing a temple of Apollo occupied the same site as the celebrated convent *Monte Cassino :* the ruins of an amphitheatre are found at S. Germano.

Casĭōtis. [CASIUS.]

Casĭus. 1. (*Ras Kasaroun*), a mountain on the coast of Egypt, E. of Pelusium, with a temple of Jupiter on its summit. Here also was the grave of Pompey. At the foot of the mountain, on the land side, on the high road from Egypt to Syria, stood the town of Casium (*Katieh*). The surrounding district was called Casiōtis.— **2.** (*Jebel Okrah*), a mountain on the coast of Syria, S. of Antioch and the Orontes, 5318 feet above the level of the sea. The name of Casiōtis was applied to the district on the coast S. of Casius, as far as the N. border of Phoenicia.

Casměna, -ae (Κασμένη, Herod. : Κασμέναι, Thuc. : Κασμεναῖος), a town in Sicily, founded by Syracuse about B. C. 643.

Caspěrĭa or **Caspěrŭla**, a town of the Sabines, N. W. of Cures, on the river Himella (*Aspra*).

Caspĭae Portae or **Pylae** (Κάσπιαι πύλαι, i. e. *the Caspian Gates*), the principal pass from Media into Parthia and Hyrcania, through the CASPII MONTES, was a deep ravine, made practicable by art, but still so narrow that there was only room for a single waggon to pass between the lofty overhanging walls of rock, from the sides of which a constant drip of salt water fell upon the road. The Persians erected iron gates across the narrowest part of the pass, and maintained a guard for its defence. This pass was near the ancient Rhagae or Arsacia ; but there were other passes through the mountains round the Caspian, which are called by the same name, especially that on the W. shore of the Caspian, through the Caucasus near *Derbent*, which was usually called Albaniae or Caucasiae Portae. The Caspian gates, being the most important pass from Western to Central Asia, were regarded by many of the ancients as a sort of central point, common to the boundaries between W. and E. Asia and N. and S. Asia ; and distances were reckoned from them.

Caspĭi (Κάσπιοι), the name of certain Scythian tribes near the Caspian Sea, is used rather loosely by the ancient geographers. The Caspii of Strabo are on the W. side of the sea, and their country, Caspiâne, forms a part of Albania. Those of Herodotus and Ptolemy are in the E. of Media, on the borders of Parthia, in the neighbourhood of the CASPIAE PYLAE. Probably it would not be far wrong to apply the name generally to the people round the S. W. and S. shores of the Caspian in and about the CASPII MONTES.

Caspii Montes (τὰ Κάσπια ὄρη: *Elburz Mts.*) or **Caspius Mons**, is a name applied generally to the whole range of mountains which surround the Caspian Sea, on the S. and S. W., at the distance of from 15 to 30 miles from its shore, on the borders of Armenia, Media, Hyrcania, and Parthia; and more specifically to that part of this range S. of the Caspian, in which was the pass called CASPIAE PYLAE. The term was also loosely applied to other mountains near the Caspian, especially, by Strabo, to the E. part of the Caucasus, between Colchis and the Caspian.

Caspiri or **Caspiraei** (Κάσπειροι, Κασπιραῖοι), a people of India, whose exact position is doubtful: they are generally placed in *Cashmeer* and *Nepaul.*

Caspium Mare (ἡ Κασπία θάλασσα, *the Caspian Sea*), also called **Hyrcanium, Albanum,** and **Scythicum,** all names derived from the people who lived on its shores, is a great salt-water lake in Asia, according to the ancient division of the continents, but now on the boundary between Europe and Asia. Its average width from E. to W. is about 210 miles, and its length from N. to S., in a straight line, is about 740 miles; but, as its N. part makes a great bend to the E., its true length, measured along a curve drawn through its middle, is about 900 miles; its area is about 180,000 square miles. The notions of the ancients about the Caspian varied very much; and it is curious that two of the erroneous opinions of the later Greek and Roman geographers, namely, that it was united both with the Sea of Aral and with the Arctic Ocean, expressed what, at some remote period, were probably real facts. Their other error, that its greatest length lay W. and E., very likely arose from its supposed union with the Sea of Aral. Another consequence of this error was the supposition that the rivers Oxus and Jaxartes flowed into the Caspian. That the former really did so at some time subsequent to the separation of the two lakes (supposing that they were once united) is pretty well established; but whether this has been the case within the historical period cannot be determined [OXUS]. The country between the two lakes has evidently been greatly changed, and the sand-hills which cover it have doubtless been accumulated by the force of the E. winds bringing down sand from the steppes of Tartary. Both lakes have their surface considerably below that of the Black Sea, the Caspian between nearly 350 feet, and the Aral about 200 feet, lower than the level of the Black Sea, and both are still sinking by evaporation. Moreover, the whole country between and around them for a considerable distance is a depression, surrounded by lofty mountains on every side, except where the valley of the *Irtish* and *Obi* stretches away to the Arctic Ocean. Besides a number of smaller streams, two great rivers flow into the Caspian; the Rha (*Volga*) on the N., and the united Cyrus and Araxes (*Kour*) on the W.; but it loses more by evaporation than it receives from these rivers.

Cassandane (Κασσανδάνη), wife of Cyrus the Great, and mother of Cambyses.

Cassander (Κάσσανδρος), son of Antipater. His father, on his death-bed (B. c. 319), appointed Polysperchon regent, and conferred upon Cassander only the secondary dignity of Chiliarch. Being dissatisfied with this arrangement, Cassander strengthened himself by an alliance with Ptolemy and Antigonus, and entered into war with Polysperchon. In 318 Cassander obtained possession of Athens and most of the cities in the S. of Greece. In 317 he was recalled to Macedonia to oppose Olympias. He kept her besieged in Pydna throughout the winter of 317, and on her surrender in the spring of the ensuing year, he put her to death. The way now seemed open to him to the throne of Macedon. He placed Roxana and her young son, Alexander Aegus, in custody at Amphipolis, not thinking it safe as yet to murder them; and he connected himself with the regal family by a marriage with Thessalonica, half-sister to Alexander the Great. In 315 Cassander joined Seleucus, Ptolemy, and Lysimachus in their war against Antigonus, of whose power they had all become jealous. This war was upon the whole unfavourable to Cassander, who lost most of the cities in Greece. By the general peace of 311, it was provided that Cassander was to retain his authority in Europe till Alexander Aegus should be grown to manhood. Cassander thereupon put to death the young king and his mother Roxana. In 310 the war was renewed, and Hercules, the son of Alexander by Barsine, was brought forward by Polysperchon as a claimant to the Macedonian throne; but Cassander bribed Polysperchon to murder the young prince and his mother, 309. In 306 Cassander took the title of king, when it was assumed by Antigonus, Lysimachus, and Ptolemy. In the following years, Demetrius Poliorcetes, the son of Antigonus, carried on the war in Greece with great success against Cassander; but in 302 Demetrius was obliged to pass into Asia, to support his father; and next year, 301, the decisive battle of Ipsus was fought, in which Antigonus and Demetrius were defeated, and the former slain, and which gave to Cassander Macedonia and Greece. Cassander died of dropsy in 297, and was succeeded by his son Philip.

Cassandra (Κασσάνδρα), daughter of Priam and Hecuba, and twin-sister of Helenus. She and her brother, when young, were left asleep in the sanctuary of Apollo, when their ears were purified by serpents, so that they could understand the divine sounds of nature and the voices of birds. Cassandra sometimes used to sleep afterwards in the same temple; and when she grew up her beauty won the love of Apollo. The god conferred upon her the gift of prophecy, upon her promising to comply with his desires; but when she had become possessed of the prophetic art, she refused to fulfil her promise. Thereupon the god in anger ordained that no one should believe her prophecies. She predicted to the Trojans the ruin that threatened them, but no one believed her; she was looked upon as a madwoman, and, according to a late account, was shut up and guarded. On the capture of Troy she fled into the sanctuary of Athena, but was torn away from the statue of the goddess by Ajax, son of Oïleus, and, according to some accounts, was even ravished by him in the sanctuary. On the division of the booty, Cassandra fell to the lot of Agamemnon, who took her with him to Mycenae. Here she was killed by Clytaemnestra.

Cassandrēa. [POTIDAEA.]

Cassia Gens. [CASSIUS.]

Cassiŏpēa, Cassiŏpēa, or **Cassiŏpē** (Κασσιέπεια, Κασσιόπεια, or Κασσιόπη), wife of Cepheus in Aethiopia, and mother of Andromeda, whose beauty she extolled above that of the Nereids. [ANDROMEDA.] She was afterwards placed among the stars.

Cassiodŏrus, Magnus Aurēlĭus, a distinguished statesman, and one of the few men of learning at the downfal of the Western Empire, was born about A. D. 468, at Scylacium in Bruttium, of an ancient and wealthy Roman family. He enjoyed the full confidence of Theodoric the Great and his successors, and under a variety of different titles he conducted for a long series of years the government of the Ostrogothic kingdom. At the age of 70 he retired to the monastery of Viviers, which he had founded in his native province, and there passed the last 30 years of his life. His time was devoted to study and to the composition of elementary treatises on history, metaphysics, the 7 liberal arts, and divinity; while his leisure hours were employed in the construction of philosophical toys, such as sun-dials, water-clocks, &c. Of his numerous writings the most important is his *Variarum (Epistolarum) Libri XII.*, an assemblage of state papers drawn up by Cassiodorus in accordance with the instructions of Theodoric and his successors. The other works of Cassiodorus are of less value to us. The principal are: 1. *Chronicon*, a summary of Universal History; 2. *De Orthographia Liber*; 3. *De Arte Grammatica ad Donati Mentem*; 4. *De Artibus ac Disciplinis Liberalium Literarum*, much read in the middle ages; 5. *De Anima*; 6. *Libri XII. De Rebus Gestis Gothorum*, known to us only through the abridgement of Jornandes; 7. *De Institutione Divinarum Literarum*, an introduction to the profitable study of the Scriptures. There are also several other ecclesiastical works of Cassiodorus extant. — The best edition of his collected works is by D. Garet, Rouen, 1679, 2 vols. fol., reprinted at Venice, 1729.

Cassiŏpē (Κασσιόπη), a town in Corcyra on a promontory of the same name, with a good harbour and a temple of Zeus.

Cassiopēa. [CASSIEPEA.]

Cassitērĭdes. [BRITANNIA, p. 126, a.]

Cassĭus, the name of one of the most distinguished of the Roman gentes, originally patrician, afterwards plebeian. 1. **Sp. Cassĭus Viscellinus,** thrice consul: first B. C. 502, when he conquered the Sabines; again 493, when he made a league with the Latins; and, lastly, 486, when he made a league with the Hernicans, and carried his celebrated agrarian law, the first which was proposed at Rome. It probably enacted that the portion of the patricians in the public land should be strictly defined, and that the remainder should be divided among the plebeians. In the following year he was accused of aiming at regal power, and was put to death. The manner of his death is related differently, but it is most probable that he was accused before the comitia curiata by the quaestores parricidii, and was sentenced to death by his fellow patricians. His house was razed to the ground, and his property confiscated. His guilt is doubtful; he had made himself hateful to the patricians by his agrarian law, and it is most likely that the accusation was invented for the purpose of getting rid of a dangerous opponent. He left 3 sons; but

as all the subsequent Cassii are plebeians, his sons were perhaps expelled from the patrician order, or may have voluntarily passed over to the plebeians, on account of the murder of their father. — 2. **C. Cass. Longinus,** consul 171, obtained as his province Italy and Cisalpine Gaul, and without the authority of the senate attempted to march into Macedonia through Illyricum, but was obliged to return to Italy. In 154 he was censor with M. Messala; and a theatre, which these censors had built, was pulled down by order of the senate, at the suggestion of P. Scipio Nasica, as injurious to public morals. — 3. **Q. Cass. Longinus,** praetor urbanus B. C. 167, and consul 164, died in his consulship. — 4. **L. Cass. Longinus Ravilla,** tribune of the plebs, 137, when he proposed a law for voting by ballot (*tabellaria lex*); consul 127, and censor 125. He was very severe and just as a judex. — 5. **L. Cass. Longinus,** praetor 111, when he brought Jugurtha to Rome; consul 107, with C. Marius, and received as his province Narbonese Gaul, in order to oppose the Cimbri, but was defeated and killed by the Tigurini. — 6. **L. Cass. Longinus,** tribune of the plebs 104, brought forward many laws to diminish the power of the aristocracy. — 7. **C. Cass. Longinus Varus,** consul 73, brought forward, with his colleague M. Terentius, a law (*lex Terentia Cassia*), by which corn was to be purchased and then sold in Rome at a small price. In 72 he was defeated by Spartacus near Mutina; in 66 he supported the Manilian law for giving the command of the Mithridatic war to Pompey; and in his old age was proscribed by the triumvirs and killed, 43. — 8. **C. Cass. Longinus,** the murderer of Julius Caesar. In 53 he was quaestor of Crassus in his campaign against the Parthians, in which he greatly distinguished himself by his prudence and military skill. After the death of Crassus, he collected the remains of the Roman army, and made preparations to defend Syria against the Parthians. In 52 he defeated the Parthians, who had crossed the Euphrates, and in 51 he again gained a still more important victory over them. Soon afterwards he returned to Rome. In 49 he was tribune of the plebs, joined the aristocratical party in the civil war, and fled with Pompey from Rome. In 48 he commanded the Pompeian fleet; after the battle of Pharsalia he went to the Hellespont, where he accidentally fell in with Caesar, and surrendered to him. He was not only pardoned by Caesar, but in 44 was made praetor, and the province of Syria was promised him for the next year. But Cassius had never ceased to be Caesar's enemy; it was he who formed the conspiracy against the dictator's life, and gained over M. Brutus to the plot. After the death of Caesar, on the 15th of March, 44 [CAESAR], Cassius remained in Italy for a few months, but in July he went to Syria, which he claimed as his province, although the senate had given it to Dolabella, and had conferred upon Cassius Cyrene in its stead. He defeated Dolabella, who put an end to his own life; and after plundering Syria and Asia most unmercifully, he crossed over to Greece with Brutus in 42, in order to oppose Octavian and Antony. At the battle of Philippi, Cassius was defeated by Antony, while Brutus, who commanded the other wing of the army, drove Octavian off the field; but Cassius, ignorant of the success of Brutus, commanded his freedman to put an end to his life. Brutus mourned over his companion, calling him the last of the Romans. Cassius was married to Junia Tertia or Tertulla, half-sister of M. Brutus. Cassius was well acquainted with Greek and Roman literature; he was a follower of the Epicurean philosophy; his abilities were considerable, but he was vain, proud, and revengeful. — 9. L. Cass. Longinus, brother of No. 8, assisted M. Laterensis in accusing Cn. Plancius, who was defended by Cicero in 54. He joined Caesar at the commencement of the civil war, and was one of Caesar's legates in Greece in 48. In 44 he was tribune of the plebs, but was not one of the conspirators against Caesar's life. He subsequently espoused the side of Octavian, in opposition to Antony; and on their reconciliation in 43, he fled to Asia: he was pardoned by Antony in 41. — 10. Q. Cass. Longinus, the *frater* or first-cousin of No. 8. In 54 he went as the quaestor of Pompey into Spain, where he was universally hated on account of his rapacity and cruelty. In 49 he was tribune of the plebs, and a warm supporter of Caesar, but was obliged to leave the city and take refuge in Caesar's camp. In the same year he accompanied Caesar to Spain, and after the defeat of Afranius and Petreius, the legates of Pompey, Caesar left him governor of Further Spain. His cruelty and oppressions excited an insurrection against him at Corduba, but this was quelled by Cassius. Subsequently 2 legions declared against him, and M. Marcellus, the quaestor, put himself at their head. He was saved from this danger by Lepidus, and left the province in 47, but his ship sank, and he was lost, at the mouth of the Iberus. — 11. L. Cass. Longinus, a competitor with Cicero for the consulship for 63; was one of Catiline's conspirators, and undertook to set the city on fire; he escaped the fate of his comrades by quitting Rome before their apprehension. — 12. L. Cass. Longinus, consul A. D. 30, married to Drusilla, the daughter of Germanicus, with whom her brother Caligula afterwards lived. Cassius was proconsul in Asia A. D. 40, and was commanded by Caligula to be brought to Rome, because an oracle had warned the emperor to beware of a Cassius: the oracle was fulfilled in the murder of the emperor by Cassius Chaerea. — 13. C. Cass. Longinus, the celebrated jurist, governor of Syria, A. D. 50, in the reign of Claudius. He was banished by Nero in A. D. 66, because he had, among his ancestral images, a statue of Cassius, the murderer of Caesar. He was recalled from banishment by Vespasian. Cassius wrote 10 books on the civil law (*Libri Juris Civilis*), and Commentaries on Vitellius and Urseius Ferox, which are quoted in the Digest. He was a follower of the school of Ateius Capito; and as he reduced the principles of Capito to a more scientific form, the adherents of this school received the name of *Cassiani*. — 14. L. Cass. Hemina, a Roman annalist, lived about B. C. 140, and wrote a history of Rome from the earliest times to the end of the 3rd Punic war. — 15. Cass. Parmensis, so called from Parma, his birth-place, was one of the murderers of Caesar, B. C. 43; took an active part in the war against the triumvirs; and, after the death of Brutus and Cassius, carried over the fleet which he commanded to Sicily, and joined Sex. Pompey; upon the defeat of Pompey, he surrendered himself to Antony, whose fortunes he followed until after the battle of Actium, when he went to Athens, and was there put to death by the command of Octavian, B. C. 30. Cassius was a

poet, and his productions were prized by Horace (*Ep.* i. 4. 3.). He wrote 2 tragedies, entitled *Thyestes* and *Brutus*, epigrams, and other works. — 16. Cass. Etruscus, a poet censured by Horace (*Sat.* i. 10. 61), must not be confounded with No. 15. — 17. Cass. Avidius, an able general of M. Aurelius, was a native of Syria. In the Parthian war (A. D. 162—165), he commanded the Roman army as the general of Verus, and after defeating the Parthians, he took Seleucia and Ctesiphon. He was afterwards appointed governor of all the Eastern provinces, and discharged his trust for several years with fidelity; but in A. D. 175 he proclaimed himself emperor. He reigned only a few months, and was slain by his own officers, before M. Aurelius arrived in the East. [See p. 111.] — 18. Dionysius Cassius, of Utica, a Greek writer, lived about B. C. 40, and translated into Greek the work of the Carthaginian Mago on agriculture. — 19. Cass. Felix, a Greek physician, probably lived under Augustus and Tiberius; wrote a small work entitled Ἰατρικαὶ Ἀπορίαι καὶ Προβλήματα Φυσικά, *Quaestiones Medicae et Problemata Naturalia:* printed in Ideler's *Physici et Medici Graeci Minores*, Berol. 1841. — 20. Cass. Chaerea. [CHAEREA.] — 21. Cass. Dion. [DION CASSIUS.] — 22. Cass. Severus. [SEVERUS.]

Cassivelaunus, a British chief, ruled over the country N. of the Tamesis (*Thames*), and was entrusted by the Britons with the supreme command on Caesar's 2nd invasion of Britain, B. C. 54. He was defeated by Caesar, and was obliged to sue for peace.

Cassōpē (Κασσώπη: Κασσωπαῖος), a town in Thesprotia near the coast.

Castăbăla (τὰ Καστάβαλα). 1. A city of Cappadocia, near Tyana, celebrated for its temple of Artemis Perasia. — 2. A town in Cilicia Campestris, near Issus.

Castălĭa (Κασταλία), a celebrated fountain on Mt. Parnassus, in which the Pythia used to bathe; sacred to Apollo and the Muses, who were hence called Castălĭdes; said to have derived its name from Castalia, daughter of Achelous, who threw herself into the fountain when pursued by Apollo.

Castor, brother of Pollux. [DIOSCURI].

Castor (Κάστωρ). 1. A Greek grammarian, surnamed *Philoromaeus*, probably lived about B. C. 150, and wrote several books; a portion of his Τέχνη ῥητορική is still extant and printed in Walz's *Rhetores Graeci*, vol. iii. p. 712, seq. — 2. Grandson of Deiotarus. [DEIOTARUS.]

Castra, a "camp," the name of several towns, which were originally the stationary quarters of the Roman legions. 1. Constantia, in Gaul, near the mouth of the Sequana (*Seine*). — 2. Hannibalis, in Bruttium, on the S. E. coast, N. of Scylacium, arose out of the fortified camp which Hannibal maintained there during the latter years of the 2nd Punic war. — 3. Herculis, in Batavia, perhaps near *Heussen*. — 4. Minervae (*Castro*), in Calabria, with a temple of Minerva, S. of Hydruntum; the most ancient town of the Salentini, subsequently colonized by the Romans; its harbour was called Portus Veneris (*Porto Badisco*). — 5. Vetera (*Xanten*), in Gallica Belgica, on the Rhine: many Roman remains have been found at *Xanten*. — 6. Cornělĭa (*Ghellah*), a place in the Carthaginian territory (Zeugitana) in N. Africa, where Scipio Africanus the elder established his camp when he invaded Africa in the Second Punic War.

It was between Utica and Carthage, on the N. side of the river Bagradas, but its site is now S. of the river in consequence of the alterations described under CARTHAGO.

Castrum. 1. Inui, a town of the Rutuli, on the coast of Latium, confounded by some writers with No. 2. — 2. Novum (*Torre di Chiaruccia*), a town in Etruria, and a Roman colony on the coast. — 3. Novum (*Giulia Nova*), a town in Picenum, probably at the mouth of the small river Batinum (*Salinello*), colonized by the Romans, B. C. 264, at the commencement of the 1st Punic war.

Castŭlo (Κασταλόν: *Caslona*), a town of the Oretani on the Baetis, and near the frontiers of Baetica, at the foot of a mountain which bore a great resemblance to Parnassus, was under the Romans an important place, a municipium with the Jus Latii, and included in the jurisdiction of Carthago Nova : its inhabitants were called *Caesari venales*. In the mountains (*Saltus Castuloensis*) in the neighbourhood were silver and lead mines. The wife of Hannibal was a native of Castulo.

Casuentus (*Basiento*), a river in Lucania, flows into the sea near Metapontum.

Casystes (Κασύστης: *Chismek*), a fine sea-port on the coast of Ionia ; the harbour of ERYTHRAE.

Catabathmus Magnus (Καταβαθμός, i. e. *descent ; Marsa Sollem*, i. e. *Port of the Ladder*), a mountain and sea-port, at the bottom of a deep bay on the N. coast of Africa (about 25° 5′ E. long.), was generally considered the boundary between Egypt and Cyrenaica. Ptolemy distinguishes from this a place called Catabathmus Parvus, in the interior of Africa, near the borders of Egypt, above Paraetonium.

Catadŭpa or -i (τὰ Κατάδουπα, οἱ Κατάδουποι), a name given to the cataracts of the Nile, and also to the parts of Aethiopia in their neighbourhood. [NILUS.]

Catalauni or Catelauni, a people in Gaul in the modern *Champagne*, mentioned only by later writers : their capital was Durocatalauni or Catelauni (*Châlons sur Marne*), in the neighbourhood of which Attila was defeated by Aëtius and Theodoric, A. D. 451.

Catamitus, the Roman name for Ganymedes, of which it is only a corrupt form.

Catăna or Catĭna (Κατάνη: Καταναῖος: *Catania*), an important town in Sicily on the E. coast at the foot of Mt. Aetna, founded B. C. 730 by Naxos, which was itself founded by the Chalcidians of Euboea. In B. C. 476 it was taken by Hiero I., who removed its inhabitants to Leontini, and settled 5000 Syracusans and 5000 Peloponnesians in the town, the name of which he changed into Aetna. Soon after the death of Hiero (467), the former inhabitants of Catana again obtained possession of the town, and called it by its original name, Catana. Subsequently Catana was conquered by Dionysius, was then governed by native tyrants, next became subject to Agathocles, and finally in the 1st Punic war fell under the dominion of Rome. It was colonized by Augustus with some veterans. Catana frequently suffered from earthquakes and eruptions of Mt. Aetna. It is now one of the most flourishing cities in Sicily.

Cataŏnia (Καταονία), a district in the S. E. part of Cappadocia, to which it was first added under the Romans, with Melitene, which lies E. of it.

These two districts form a large and fertile plain, lying between the Anti-Taurus and the Taurus and Amanus, and watered by the river Pyramus. Cataonia had no large towns, but several strong mountain fortresses.

Catarrhactes (Καταρρáκτης). 1. (*Duden-Soo*), a river of Pamphylia, which descends from the mountains of Taurus, in a great broken waterfall (whence its name, fr. καταρρήγνυμι), and which, after flowing beneath the earth in two parts of its course, falls into the sea E. of Attalia. — 2. The term is also applied, first by Strabo, to the cataracts of the Nile, which are distinguished as C. Major and C. Minor [NILUS], in which use it must of course be regarded as a common noun, equivalent to the Latin *cataracta*, but whether derived from the name of the Pamphylian river, or at once from the Greek verb, cannot be determined.

Catelauni. [CATALAUNI.]

Cathaei (Καθαῖοι), a great and warlike people of India intra Gangem, upon whom Alexander made war. Some of the best Orientalists suppose the name to be that, not of a tribe but, of the warrior caste of the Hindoos, the *Kshatriyas*.

Catilina, L. Sergius, the descendant of an ancient patrician family which had sunk into poverty. His youth and early manhood were stained by every vice and crime. He first appears in history as a zealous partizan of Sulla ; and during the horrors of the proscription, he killed, with his own hand, his brother-in-law, Q. Caecilius, a quiet inoffensive man, and put to death by torture M. Marius Gratidianus, the kinsman and fellow-townsman of Cicero. He was suspected of an intrigue with the vestal Fabia, sister of Terentia, and was said and believed to have made away with his first wife and afterwards with his son, in order that he might marry Aurelia Orestilla, who objected to the presence of a grown-up step-child ; but notwithstanding this infamy he attained to the dignity of praetor in B. C. 68, was governor of Africa during the following year, and returned to Rome in 66, in order to sue for the consulship. The election for 65 was carried by P. Autronius Paetus and P. Cornelius Sulla, both of whom were soon after convicted of bribery, and their places supplied by their competitors and accusers, L. Aurelius Cotta and L. Manlius Torquatus. Catiline had been disqualified for becoming a candidate, in consequence of an impeachment for oppression in his province, preferred by P. Clodius Pulcher, afterwards so celebrated as the enemy of Cicero. Exasperated by their disappointment, Autronius and Catiline formed a project, along with Cn. Piso, to murder the new consuls when they entered upon their office upon the 1st of January. This design is said to have been frustrated solely by the impatience of Catiline, who, upon the appointed day, gave the signal prematurely, before the whole of the armed agents had assembled. Encouraged rather than disheartened by a failure which had so nearly proved a triumph, Catiline now determined to organize a more extensive conspiracy, in order to overthrow the existing government, and to obtain for himself and his followers all places of power and profit. Having been acquitted in 65 upon his trial for extortion, he was left unfettered to mature his plans. The time was propitious to his schemes. The younger nobility were thoroughly demoralised, with ruined for-

tunes, and eager for any change which might relieve them from their embarrassments ; the Roman
populace were restless and discontented, ready to
follow at the bidding of any demagogue ; while
many of the veterans of Sulla, who had squandered
their ill-gotten wealth, were now anxious for a renewal of those scenes of blood which they had
found so profitable. Among such men Catiline
soon obtained numerous supporters ; and his great
mental and physical powers, which even his enemies admitted, maintained his ascendency over his
adherents. The most distinguished men who
joined him, and were present at a meeting of the
conspirators which he called in June, 64, were P.
Cornelius Lentulus Sura, who had been consul in
B. C. 71, but having been passed over by the censors, had lost his seat in the senate, which he
was now seeking to recover by standing a second
time for the praetorship ; C. Cornelius Cethegus,
distinguished throughout by his headstrong impetuosity and sanguinary violence ; P. Autronius,
spoken of above ; L. Cassius Longinus, at this
time a competitor for the consulship ; L. Vargunteius, who had been one of the colleagues of Cicero
in the quaestorship, and had subsequently been
condemned for bribery ; L. Calpurnius Bestia,
tribune elect ; Publius and Servius Sulla, nephews of the dictator ; M. Porcius Laeca, &c.
The first object of Catiline was to obtain the
consulship for himself and C. Antonius, whose co-
operation he confidently anticipated. But in this
object he was disappointed : Cicero and Antonius
were elected consuls. This disappointment rendered him only more vigorous in the prosecution of
his designs ; more adherents were gained, and troops
were levied in various parts of Italy, especially in
the neighbourhood of Faesulae, under the superintendence of C. Manlius, one of the veteran centurions of Sulla. Meantime, Cicero, the consul, was
unrelaxing in his efforts to preserve the state from the
threatened danger. Through the agency of Fulvia,
the mistress of Curius, one of the conspirators, he
became acquainted with every circumstance as soon
as it occurred, and was enabled to counteract all
the machinations of Catiline. Cicero at the same
time gained over his colleague Antonius, by promising him the province of Macedonia. At length
Cicero openly accused Catiline, and the senate, now
aware of the danger which threatened the state,
passed the decree, " that the consuls should take
care that the republic received no harm," in virtue
of which the consuls were invested for the time
being with absolute power, both civil and military.
In the consular elections which followed soon afterwards, Catiline was again rejected. On the night
of the 6th of November, B. C. 63 he met the ringleaders of the conspiracy at the dwelling of M.
Porcius Laeca, and informed them that he had resolved to wait no longer, but at once to proceed to
open action. Cicero, informed as usual of these
proceedings, summoned the senate on the 8th of
November, and there delivered the first of his
celebrated orations against Catiline, in which he
displayed a most intimate acquaintance with all
the proceedings of the conspirators. Catiline, who
was present, attempted to justify himself, but
scarcely had he commenced when his words were
drowned by the shouts of " enemy " and " parricide " which burst from the whole assembly.
Finding that he could at present effect nothing
at Rome, he quitted the city in the night (8th—

9th November), and proceeded to the camp of
Manlius, after leaving the chief controul of affairs
at Rome in the hands of Lentulus and Cethegus.
On the 9th, when the flight of Catiline was
known, Cicero delivered his second speech, addressed to the people in the forum, in which he
justified his recent conduct. The senate declared
Catiline and Manlius public enemies, and soon
afterwards Cicero obtained legal evidence of the
guilt of the conspirators within the city, through
the ambassadors of the Allobroges. These men
had been solicited by Lentulus to join the plot, and
to induce their own countrymen to take part in the
insurrection. They revealed what they had heard
to Q. Fabius Sanga, the patron of their state, who
in his turn acquainted Cicero. By the instructions
of the latter, the ambassadors affected great zeal in
the undertaking, and having obtained a written
agreement, signed by Lentulus, Cethegus, and
Statilius, they quitted Rome soon after midnight
on the 3d of December, but were arrested on
the Milvian bridge, by Cicero's order. Cicero
instantly summoned the leaders of the conspiracy to his presence, and conducted them to
the senate, which was assembled in the temple of
Concord (4th of December). He proved the guilt of
the conspirators by the testimony of witnesses and
their own signatures. They were thereupon consigned to the charge of certain senators. Cicero
then summoned the people, and delivered what
is called his 3d oration against Catiline, in
which he informed them of all that had taken
place. On the following day, the nones (5th) of
December, the day so frequently referred to by
Cicero in after times with pride, the senate was
called together to deliberate respecting the punishment of the conspirators. After an animated debate, of which the leading arguments are expressed
in the 2 celebrated orations assigned by Sallust to
Caesar and to Cato, a decree was passed, that Lentulus and the conspirators should be put to death.
The sentence was executed the same night in
the prison. Cicero's speech in the debate in the
senate is preserved in his 4th oration against Catiline. The consul Antonius was then sent against
Catiline, and the decisive battle was fought early
in 62. Antonius, however, unwilling to fight
against his former associate, gave the command on
the day of battle to his legate, M. Petreius. Catiline fell in the engagement, after fighting with the
most daring valour. — The history of Catiline's
conspiracy has been written by Sallust.

CĂTĬUS, an Epicurean philosopher, a native of
Gallia Transpadana (Insuber), composed a treatise in 4 books on the nature of things and on the
chief good (de Rerum Natura et de summo Bono);
died B. C. 45.

CĂTŎ, Dionўsĭus, the author of a small work,
entitled Disticha de Moribus ad Filium, consisting
of a series of sententious moral precepts. Nothing
is known of the author or the time when he lived,
but many writers place him under the Antonines.
The best edition is by Arntzenius, Amsterdam,
1754.

CĂTŎ, Porcĭus. 1. M., frequently surnamed
Censorius or Censor, also Cato Major, to distinguish him from his great-grandson Cato Uticensis
[No. 8]. Cato was born at Tusculum, B. C. 234,
and was brought up at his father's farm, situated
in the Sabine territory. In 217 he served his
first campaign in his 17th year, and during the

remaining years of the 2d Punic war, he greatly distinguished himself by his courage and military abilities. In the intervals of war, he returned to his Sabine farm, which he had inherited from his father, and there led the same frugal and simple life, which characterised him to his last days. Encouraged by L. Valerius Flaccus, a young nobleman in the neighbourhood, he went to Rome, and became a candidate for office. He obtained the quaestorship in 204, and served under the proconsul Scipio Africanus in Sicily and Africa. From this time we may date the enmity which Cato always displayed towards Scipio; their habits and views of life were entirely different; and Cato on his return to Rome denounced in the strongest terms the luxury and extravagance of his commander. On his voyage home he is said to have touched at Sardinia, and to have brought the poet Ennius from the island to Italy. In 199 he was aedile, and in 198 praetor; he obtained Sardinia as his province, which he governed with justice and economy. He had now established a reputation for pure morality and strict virtue. In 195 he was consul with his old friend and patron L. Valerius Flaccus. He carried on war in Spain with the greatest success, and received the honour of a triumph on his return to Rome in 194. In 191 he served, under the consul M'. Acilius Glabrio, in the campaign against Antiochus in Greece, and the decisive victory at Thermopylae was mainly owing to Cato. From this time Cato's military career, which had been a brilliant one, appears to have ceased. He now took an active part in civil affairs, and distinguished himself by his vehement opposition to the Roman nobles, who introduced into Rome Greek luxury and refinement. It was especially against the Scipios that his most violent attacks were directed and whom he pursued with the bitterest animosity. He obtained the condemnation of L. Scipio, the conqueror of Antiochus, and compelled his brother P. Scipio to quit Rome in order to avoid the same fate. [SCIPIO.] In 184 he was elected censor with L. Valerius Flaccus, having been rejected in his application for the office in 189. His censorship was a great epoch in his life. He applied himself strenuously to the duties of his office, regardless of the enemies he was making; but all his efforts to stem the tide of luxury which was now setting in proved unavailing. His strong national prejudices appear to have diminished in force as he grew older and wiser. He applied himself in old age to the study of Greek literature, with which in youth he had no acquaintance, although he was not ignorant of the Greek language. But his conduct continued to be guided by prejudices against classes and nations, whose influence he deemed to be hostile to the simplicity of the old Roman character. He had an antipathy to physicians, because they were mostly Greeks, and therefore unfit to be trusted with Roman lives. When Athens sent Carneades, Diogenes, and Critolaus as ambassadors to Rome, he recommended the senate to send them from the city an account of the dangerous doctrines taught by Carneades. [CARNEADES.] Cato retained his bodily and mental vigour in his old age. In the year before his death he was one of the chief instigators of the third Punic war. He had been one of the Roman deputies sent to Africa to arbitrate between Masinissa and the Carthaginians, and he was so struck with the flourishing condition of Carthage that

on his return home he maintained that Rome would never be safe as long as Carthage was in existence. From this time forth, whenever he was called upon for his vote in the senate, though the subject of debate bore no relation to Carthage, his words were *Delenda est Carthago*. Very shortly before his death, he made a powerful speech in accusing Galba on account of his cruelty and perfidy in Spain. He died in 149, at the age of 85. — Cato wrote several works, of which only the *De Re Rustica* has come down to us, though even this work is not exactly in the form in which it proceeded from his pen: it is printed in the *Scriptores Rei Rusticae*, edited by Gesner (Lips. 1773—4), and Schneider (Lips. 1794—7). His most important work was entitled *Origines*, but only fragments of it have been preserved. The 1st book contained the history of the Roman kings; the 2d and 3d treated of the origin of the Italian towns, and from these two books the whole work derived its title. The 4th book treated of the first Punic war, the 5th book of the second Punic war, and the 6th and 7th continued the narrative to the year of Cato's death. — **2. M.**, son of No. 1., by his first wife Licinia, and thence called *Licinianus*, was distinguished as a jurist. In the war against Perseus, 168, he fought with great bravery under the consul Aemilius Paulus, whose daughter, Aemilia Tertia, he afterwards married. He died when praetor designatus, about 152. — **3. M.**, son of No. 1, by his second wife Salonia, and thence called *Salonianus*, was born 154, when his father had completed his 80th year. — **4. M.**, son of No. 2, consul 118, died in Africa in the same year. — **5. C.**, also son of No. 2, consul 114, obtained Macedonia as his province, and fought unsuccessfully against the Scordisci. He was accused of extortion in Macedonia, and was sentenced to pay a fine. He afterwards went to Tarraco in Spain, and became a citizen of that town. — **6. M.**, son of No. 3, tribunus plebis, died when a candidate for the praetorship. — **7. L.**, also son of No. 3, consul 89, was killed in battle against the Socii. — **8. M.**, son of No. 6 by Livia, great-grandson of Cato the Censor, and surnamed *Uticensis* from Utica, the place of his death, was born 95. In early childhood he lost both his parents, and was brought up in the house of his mother's brother M. Livius Drusus, along with his sister Porcia and the children of his mother by her second husband, Q. Servilius Caepio. In early years he discovered a stern and unyielding character; he applied himself with great zeal to the study of oratory and philosophy, and became a devoted adherent of the Stoic school; and among the profligate nobles of the age he soon became conspicuous for his rigid morality. He served his first campaign as a volunteer, 72, in the servile war of Spartacus, and afterwards, about 67, as tribunus militum in Macedonia. In 65 he was quaestor, when he corrected numerous abuses which had crept into the administration of the treasury. In 63 he was tribune of the plebs, and supported Cicero in proposing that the Catilinarian conspirators should suffer death. [CATILINA.] He now became one of the chief leaders of the aristocratical party, and opposed with the utmost vehemence the measures of Caesar, Pompey, and Crassus. In order to get rid of him, he was sent to Cyprus in 58 with the task of uniting the island to the Roman dominions. He returned in 56 and continued to oppose the triumvirs; but all his efforts were vain, and he was rejected when he became a candidate for the praetorship. On the breaking out of the civil war (49), he was entrusted, as propraetor, with the defence of Sicily ; but, on the landing of Curio with an overwhelming force, he abandoned the island and joined Pompey in Greece. After Pompey's victory at Dyrrhachium, Cato was left in charge of the camp, and thus was not present at the battle of Pharsalia (48). After this battle, he set sail for Corcyra, and thence crossed over to Africa, where he joined Metellus Scipio, after a terrible march across the desert. The army wished to be led by Cato ; but he yielded the command to the consular Scipio. In opposition to the advice of Cato, Scipio fought with Caesar, and was utterly routed at Thapsus (April 6th, 46). All Africa now, with the exception of Utica, submitted to Caesar. Cato wanted the Romans in Utica to stand a siege ; but when he saw that they were inclined to submit, he resolved to die rather than fall alive into the hands of the conqueror. Accordingly, after spending the greater part of the night in perusing Plato's Phaedo several times, he stabbed himself below the breast. In falling he overturned an abacus : his friends, hearing the noise, ran up, found him bathed in blood, and, while he was fainting, dressed his wound. When, however, he recovered feeling, he tore open the bandages, let out his entrails, and expired at the age of 49. — Cato soon became the subject of biography and panegyric. Shortly after his death appeared Cicero's *Cato*, which provoked Caesar's *Anticato*. In Lucan the character of Cato is a personification of godlike virtue. In modern times, the closing events of his life have been often dramatised ; and few dramas have gained more celebrity than the *Cato* of Addison. — **9. M.**, a son of No. 8, fell at the battle of Philippi, 42.

Cătŏ, Valērĭus, a distinguished grammarian and poet, lost his property in his youth during the usurpation of Sulla. He is usually considered the author of an extant poem in 183 hexameter verses, entitled *Dirae*. Edited by Putsch, Jena, 1828.

Catti or Chatti, whose name is connected with the old German word *cat* or *cad* " war," one of the most important nations of Germany, bounded by the Visurgis (*Weser*) on the E., the Agri Decumates on the S., and the Rhine on the W., in the modern *Hesse* and the adjacent countries. They were a branch of the Hermiones, and are first mentioned by Caesar under the erroneous name of Suevi. Although defeated by Drusus, Germanicus, and other Roman generals, they were never completely subjugated by the Romans; and their power was greatly augmented on the decline of the Cherusci. Their capital was MATTIUM.

Cătullus, Valērĭus, a Roman poet, born at Verona or in its immediate vicinity, B. C. 87. Catullus inherited considerable property from his father, who was the friend of Julius Caesar; but he squandered a great part of it by indulging freely in the pleasures of the metropolis. In order to better his fortunes, he went to Bithynia in the train of the praetor Memmius, but it appears that the speculation was attended with little success. It was probably during this expedition that his brother died in the Troad — a loss which he deplores in the affecting elegy to Hortalus. On his return he continued to reside at Rome or at his country-seats on the promontory of Sirmio and at Tibur. He probably died about B. C. 47. The extant works of Catullus consist of

116 poems, on a variety of topics, and composed in different styles and metres. Some are lyrical, others elegies, others epigrams ; while the Nuptials of Peleus and Thetis, in 409 Hexameter lines, is an heroic poem. Some of his poems are translations or imitations from the Greek, as, for instance, his *De Coma Berenices*, which was taken from Callimachus. In consequence of the intimate acquaintance which Catullus displays with Greek literature and mythology, he was called *doctus* by Tibullus, Ovid, and others. Catullus adorned all he touched, and his shorter poems are characterised by original invention and felicity of expression. — *Editions.* By Volpi, Patav. 1710 ; by Doering, Altona, 1834, 2nd ed. ; and by Lachmann, Berol. 1829.

Cătŭlus, Lutātĭus. 1. C., consul B. C. 242, defeated as proconsul in the following year the Carthaginian fleet off the Aegates islands, and thus brought the first Punic war to a close, 241. — **2. Q.**, consul 102 with C. Marius IV., and as proconsul next year gained along with Marius a decisive victory over the Cimbri near Vercellae (*Vercelli*), in the N. of Italy. Catulus claimed the entire honour of this victory, and asserted that Marius did not meet with the enemy till the day was decided ; but at Rome the whole merit was given to Marius. Catulus belonged to the aristocratical party ; he espoused the cause of Sulla ; was included by Marius in the proscription of 87 ; and as escape was impossible, put an end to his life by the vapours of a charcoal fire. Catulus was well acquainted with Greek literature, and famed for the grace and purity with which he spoke and wrote his own language. He was the author of several orations, of an historical work on his own Consulship and the Cimbric war, and of poems; but all these have perished with the exception of 2 epigrams. — **3. Q.**, son of No. 2, a distinguished leader of the aristocracy, also won the respect and confidence of the people by his upright character and conduct. Being consul with M. Lepidus in 78, he resisted the efforts of his colleague to abrogate the acts of Sulla, and the following spring he defeated Lepidus in the battle of the Milvian bridge, and forced him to take refuge in Sardinia. He opposed the Gabinian and Manilian laws which conferred extraordinary powers upon Pompey (67 and 66). He was censor with Crassus in 65, and died in 60.

Cătŭrĭges, a Ligurian people in Gallia Narbonensis, near the Cottian Alps : their chief towns were EBURODUNUM, and **Caturigae or Caturimagus** (*Chorges*).

Cătus Deciānus, procurator of Britain in the reign of Nero, was by his extortion one of the chief causes of the revolt of the people under Boadicea, A. D. 62. He fled to Gaul.

Cauca (*Coca*), a town of the Vaccaei in Hispania Tarraconensis ; birth-place of the emperor Theodosius 1.

Caucăsĭae Pylae. [CAUCASUS.]

Caucăsus, Caucasii Montes (ὁ Καύκασος, τὸ Καυκάσιον ὄρος, τὰ Καυκάσια ὄρη: *Caucasus*). **1.** A great chain of mountains in Asia, extending W. N. W. and E. S. E. from the E. shore of the Pontus Euxinus (*Black Sea*) to the W. shore of the Caspian. Its length is about 700 miles ; its greatest breadth 120, its least 60 or 70. Its greatest height exceeds that of the Alps, its loftiest summit (*Mt. Elbrooz*, nearly in 43° N. lat. and 43° E. long.), being 16,800 feet above the sea, and to the E. of this there are several other summits above the line of perpetual snow, which, in the Caucasus, is from 10,000 to 11,000 feet above the sea. The W. part of the chain is much lower, no summit W. of *Mt. Elbrooz* rising above the snow line. At both extremities the chain sinks down to low hills. There are two chief passes over the chain, both of which were known to the ancients: the one, between its E. extremity and the Caspian, near *Derbent*, was called Albaniae and sometimes CASPIAE PYLAE: the other, nearly in the centre of the range, was called Caucasiae Pylae (*Pass of Dariel*). In ancient times, as is still the case, the Caucasus was inhabited by a great variety of tribes, speaking different languages (Strabo says, at least 70), but all belonging to that family of the human race, which has peopled Europe and W. Asia, and which has obtained the name of Caucasian from the fact that in no other part of the world are such perfect examples of it found, as among the mountaineers of the Caucasus. — That the Greeks had some vague knowledge of the Caucasus in very early times, is proved by the myths respecting Prometheus and the Argonauts, from which it seems that the Caucasus was regarded as at the extremity of the earth, on the border of the river Oceanus. The account which Herodotus gives is good as far as it goes (i. 203); but it was not till the march of Pompey, in the Mithridatic War, extended to the banks of the Cyrus and Araxes and to the foot of the great chain, that means were obtained for that accurate description of the Caucasus which Strabo gives in his 11th book. The country about the E. part of the Caucasus was called ALBANIA: the rest of the chain divided IBERIA and COLCHIS, on the S., from SARMATIA ASIATICA on the N. — **2.** When the soldiers of Alexander advanced to that great range of mountains which formed the N. boundary of Ariana, the Paropamisus, they supposed that they had reached the great Caucasian chain at the extremity of the world mentioned by the early poets, and they applied to it the name of Caucasus: afterwards, for the sake of distinction, it was called Caucasus Indicus. [PAROPAMISUS.]

Cauci. [CHAUCI.]

Cauc̄nes (Καύκωνες), the name of peoples both in Greece and Asia, but whether of the same or different tribes cannot be determined with certainty. The Caucones in the N.W. of Greece, in Elis and Achaia, were supposed by the ancient geographers to be an Arcadian people. The Caucones in the N.W. of Asia Minor are mentioned by Homer as allies of the Trojans, and are placed in Bithynia and Paphlagonia by the geographers, who regarded them as Pelasgians, though some thought them Scythians.

Caudium (Caudīnus), a town in Samnium on the road from Capua to Beneventum. In the neighbourhood were the celebrated **Furculae Caudinae**, or *Caudine Forks*, narrow passes in the mountains, where the Roman army surrendered to the Samnites, and was sent under the yoke, B. C. 321: it is now called the valley of *Arpaia*.

Caulōn or **Caulōnia** (Cauloniata: *Castel Vetere*), a town in Bruttium, N. E. of Locri, originally called Aulon or Aulonia; founded by the inhabitants of Croton or by the Achaeans; destroyed by Dionysius the elder, who removed its inhabitants to Syracuse and gave its territory to Locri; afterwards rebuilt, but again destroyed in the war with

Pyrrhus; rebuilt a third time and destroyed a third time in the 2nd Punic war. It was celebrated for its worship of the Delphian Apollo. Its name is preserved in the hill *Caulone* in the neighbourhood of *Castel Vetere*.

Caunus. [BYBLIS.]

Caunus (ἡ Καῦνος: Καύνιος: *Kaigues*), one of the chief cities of Caria, on its S. coast, a little E. of the mouth of the Calbis, in a very fertile but unhealthy situation. It had a citadel called Imbros, an enclosed harbour for ships of war, and safe roads for merchant vessels. It was founded by the Cretans. Its dried figs (Cauneae ficus) were highly celebrated. The painter Protogenes was born here.

Caurus, the Argestes (Ἀργέστης) of the Greeks, the N.W. wind, is in Italy a stormy wind.

Cavăres, or -i, a people in Gallia Narbonensis, E. of the Rhone, between the Druentia and the Isara.

Cavarīnus, a Senonian, whom Caesar made king of his people, was expelled by his subjects and compelled to fly to Caesar, B. C. 54.

Caÿstrus (Κάϋστρος, Ion. Καΰστρως: *Kara Su*, i. e. the *Black River*, or *Kuchuk-Meinder*, i. e. *Little Maeander*), a celebrated river of Lydia and Ionia, rising in the Cilbiani M. (the E. part of Tmolus), and flowing between the ranges of Tmolus and Messogis into the Aegean, a little N. W. of Ephesus. To this day it abounds in swans, as it did in Homer's time. The valley of the Caÿstrus is called by Homer " the Asian meadow," and is probably the district to which the name of Asia was first applied. There was an inland town of the same name on its S. bank.

Cebenna Mons or **Gebenna** (τὸ Κέμμενον ὅρος: *Cevennes*), mountains in the S. of Gaul, 2000 stadia in length, extending N. as far as Lugdunum and separating the Arverni from the Helvii: Caesar found them in the winter covered with snow 6 feet deep.

Cēbēs (Κέβης), of Thebes, a disciple and friend of Socrates, was present at the death of his teacher. He wrote 3 philosophical works, one of which, entitled Πίναξ or *Table*, is extant. This work is an allegorical picture of human life, which is explained by an old man to a circle of youths. The drift of the book is to show, that only the development of our mind and the possession of real virtue can make us happy. Few works have enjoyed a greater popularity. Of the numerous editions the best are by Schweighäuser, Argent. 1806, and by Cornes in his edition of Epictetus, Paris, 1826.

Cebrēnē (Κεβρήνη), a city in the Troad, on M. Ida, which fell into decay when Antigonus transplanted its inhabitants to Alexandria Troas. A little river, which flowed past it, was called Cebren (Κεβρήν), and the surrounding district Cebrenia (Κεβρηνία).

Cecrŏpia. [ATHENAE, p. 102, b.]

Cecrops (Κέκροψ), a hero of the Pelasgic race, said to have been the first king of Attica. He was married to Agraulos, daughter of Actaeus, by whom he had a son, Erysichthon, who succeeded him as king of Athens, and 3 daughters, Agraulos, Herse, and Pandrosos. In his reign Poseidon and Athena contended for the possession of Attica, but Cecrops decided in favour of the goddess. [ATHENA.] Cecrops is said to have founded Athena, the citadel of which was called Cecropia after him, to have divided Attica into 12 communities, and to have introduced the first elements of civilized life; he instituted marriage, abolished bloody sacrifices, and taught his subjects how to worship the gods. He is sometimes called διφυής or *geminus*, an epithet which some explain by his having instituted marriage, while others suppose it to have reference to the legends, in which the upper part of his body was represented as that of a man and the lower part as that of a serpent. The later Greek writers describe Cecrops as a native of Sais in Egypt, who led a colony of Egyptians into Attica, and thus introduced from Egypt the arts of civilized life; but this account is rejected by some of the ancients themselves, and by the ablest modern critics.

Cecryphalia (Κεκρυφάλεια), a small island in the Saronic gulf, between Aegina and Epidaurus.

Cedreae (Κεδρέαι or -εῖαι, Κεδρεάτης or -αῖος), a town of Caria, on the Ceramic Gulf.

Cedrēnus, Georgĭus, a Byzantine writer, of whose life nothing is known, the author of an historical work, which begins with the creation of the world, and goes down to A. D. 1057. The last edition is by Bekker, Bonn, 1838–39.

Cēlaenae (Κελαιναί, Κελαινίτης), the greatest city of S. Phrygia, before the rise of its neighbour, Apamea Cibotus, reduced it to insignificance. It lay at the sources of the rivers Maeander and Marsyas. In the midst of it was a citadel built by Xerxes, on a precipitous rock, at the foot of which, in the Agora of the city, the Marsyas took its rise, and near the river's source was a grotto celebrated by tradition as the scene of the punishment of Marsyas by Apollo. Outside of the city was a royal palace, with pleasure-gardens and a great park (παράδεισος) full of game, which was generally the residence of a satrap. The Maeander took its rise in the very palace, and flowed through the park and the city, below which it received the Marsyas.

Cēlaeno (Κελαινώ). 1. A Pleiad, daughter of Atlas and Pleione, beloved by Poseidon.—2. One of the Harpies. [HARPYIAE.]

Celēĭa (*Cilly*), an important town in the S. E. of Noricum, and a Roman colony with the surname *Claudia*, was in the middle ages the capital of a Slavonic state called Zellia; hence the modern name of the town, which possesses Roman remains.

Cēlendĕris (Κελένδερις: *Khelindreh*), a sea-port town of Cilicia, said to have been founded by Sandarus the Syrian, and afterwards colonized by the Samians.

Cēler, together with Severus, the architect of Nero's immense palace, the golden house. He and Severus began digging a canal from the lake Avernus to the mouth of the Tiber.

Cēler, P. Egnātĭus. [BAREA.]

Celetrum (*Kastoria*), a town in Macedonia on a peninsula of the Lacus Castoria, probably the same town afterwards called **Diocletianopolis.**

Cĕleus (Κηλεός), king of Eleusis, husband of Metanira, and father of Demophon and Triptolemus. He received Demeter with hospitality at Eleusis, when she was wandering in search of her daughter. The goddess, in return, wished to make his son Demophon immortal, and placed him in the fire in order to destroy his mortal parts; but Metanira screamed aloud at the sight, and Demophon was destroyed by the flames. Demeter then bestowed great favours upon Triptolemus. [TRIPTOLEMUS.] Celeus is described as the first priest and his daughters as the first priestesses of Demeter at Eleusis.

Celsa (*Velilla* Ru., nr. *Xelsa*), a town in Hispania Tarraconensis on the Iberus, with a stone bridge over this river, and a Roman colony with the name *Victrix Julia Celsa.*

Celsus. 1. One of the 30 tyrants, usurped the purple in Africa, and was slain on the 7th day of his reign, A. D. 265.—2. An Epicurean philosopher, lived in the time of the Antonines, and was a friend of Lucian. He is supposed to be the same as the Celsus who wrote the work against Christianity called Λόγος ἀληθής, which acquired so much notoriety from the answer written to it by Origen. [ORIGENES.]—3. A. Cornelius Celsus, probably lived under the reigns of Augustus and Tiberius. He wrote several works, of which only one remains entire, his treatise *De Medicina*, "On Medicine," in 8 books. The first two books are principally occupied by the consideration of diet, and the general principles of therapeutics and pathology; the remaining books are devoted to the consideration of particular diseases and their treatment; the third and fourth to internal diseases; the fifth and sixth to external diseases, and to pharmaceutical preparations; and the last two to those diseases which more particularly belong to surgery. The work has been much valued from the earliest times to the present day. — *Editions.* By Milligan, Edinb. 1826; by Ritter and Albers, Colon. ad Rhen. 1835.—4. **Julius Celsus**, a scholar at Constantinople in the 7th century after Christ, made a recension of the text of Caesar's Commentaries. Many modern writers have attributed to him the life of Caesar, which was in reality written by Petrarch. — 5. **P. Juventius Celsus**, two Roman jurists, father and son, both of whom are cited in the Digest. Very little is known of the elder Celsus. The younger Celsus, who was the more celebrated, lived under Nerva and Trajan, by whom he was highly favoured. He wrote *Digesta* in 39 books, *Epistolae*, *Quaestiones*, and *Institutiones* in 7 books. — 6. **P. Marius Celsus**, an able general first of Galba and afterwards of Otho. After the defeat of Otho's army at the battle of Bedriacum, Celsus was pardoned by Vitellius, and was allowed by him to enter on the consulship in July (A. D. 69).

Celtae, a powerful race, which occupied a great part of W. Europe. The Greek and Roman writers call them by 3 names, which are probably only variations of one name, namely **Celtae** (Κελταί, Κελτοί), **Galatae** (Γαλάται), and **Galli** (Γάλλοι). Their name was originally given to all the people of N. and W. Europe, who were not Iberians, and it was not till the time of Caesar that the Romans made any distinction between the Celts and the Germans: the name of Celts then began to be confined to the people between the Pyrenees and the Rhine. The Celts belonged to the great Indo-Germanic race, as their language proves. Like the other Indo-Germanic races, they came from the East, and, at a period long antecedent to all historical records, settled in the W. of Europe. The most powerful part of the nation appears to have taken up their abode in the centre of the country called after them GALLIA, between the Garumna in the S. and the Sequana and Matrona in the N. From this country they spread over various parts of Europe, and they appear in early times as a migratory race, ready to abandon their homes, and settle in any district which their swords could win. Besides the Celts in Gallia, there were 8 other different settlements of the nation, which may be dis-

Charites (the Graces).
(From a Coin of Germa.) Page 166,

Charites (the Graces).
(Pitture d'Ercolano, vol. 3, tav. 11). Page 166.

Cassandra and Apollo. (Pitture d'Ercolano, vol. 2, tav. 17.) Page 152.

Calypso.
(From a Painted Vase.) Page 141.

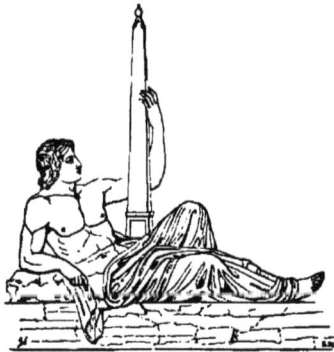

Personification of the Campus Martius.
(Visconti, Mus. Pio Clem., vol. 6, tav. 1.) Page 143.

[To face p. 160.

Berenice, wife of Ptolemy I. Soter, King of Egypt.
Page 119, No. 1.

Caligula, Roman Emperor, A.D. 37—41.   On the reverse
is the head of Augustus.   Page 138.

Berenice, wife of Ptolemy III. Euergetes, King of Egypt.
Page 119, No. 3.

Caracalla, Roman Emperor, A.D. 211—217.   Page 146.

Britannicus, son of Claudius, ob. A.D. 55.   Page 126.

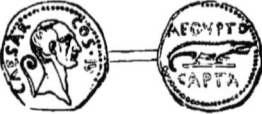

Carausius, Roman Emperor, A.D. 287—293.   Page 146.

C. Julius Caesar, the Dictator, ob. B.C. 44.   In the latter
coin, the natural baldness of his head is concealed by a
crown of laurel.   Page 133.

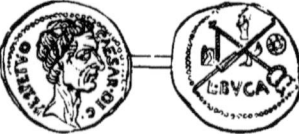

Carinus, Roman Emperor, A.D. 283—285.   Page 147.

Carus, Roman Emperor, A.D. 282—283.   Page 151.

C. Caesar and L. Caesar, grandsons of Augustus.   Page 136.

Claudius I., Roman Emperor, A.D. 41—54.   On the reverse
is the head of his wife Agrippina.   Page 179.

To face p. 161.]

tinguished by the following names:—1. Iberian Celts, who crossed the Pyrenees and settled in Spain. [CELTIBERI.] 2. British Celts, the most ancient inhabitants of Britain. [BRITANNIA.] 3. Belgic Celts, the earliest inhabitants of Gallia Belgica, at a later time much mingled with Germans. 4. Italian Celts, who crossed the Alps at different periods, and eventually occupied the greater part of the N. of Italy, which was called after them GALLIA CISALPINA. 5. Celts in the Alps and on the Danube, namely the Helvetii, Gothini, Osi, Vindelici, Raeti, Norici, and Carni. 6. Illyrian Celts, who, under the name of Scordisci, settled on Mt. Scordus. 7. Macedonian and Thracian Celts, who had remained behind in Macedonia, when the Celts invaded Greece, and who are rarely mentioned. 8. Asiatic Celts, the Tolistobogi, Trocmi and Tectosages, who founded the kingdom of GALATIA. — Some ancient writers divided the Celts into two great races, one consisting of the Celts in the S. and centre of Gaul, in Spain, and in the N. of Italy, who were the proper Celts, and the other consisting of the Celtic tribes on the shores of the Ocean and in the E. as far as Scythia, who were called Gauls: to the latter race the Cimbri belonged, and they are considered by some to be identical with the Cimmerii of the Greeks. This twofold division of the Celts appears to correspond to the two races into which the Celts are at present divided in Great Britain, namely the Gael and the Kymry, who differ in language and customs, the Gael being the inhabitants of Ireland and the N. of Scotland, and the Kymry of Wales. — The Celts are described by the ancient writers as men of large stature, of fair complexion, and with flaxen or red hair. They were brave and warlike, impatient of control and prone to change. They fought with long swords; their first charge in battle was the most formidable, but if firmly resisted, they usually gave way. They were long the terror of the Romans: once they took Rome, and laid it in ashes (B.C. 390).—For details respecting their later history and political organization, see GALLIA.

Celtibēri (Κελτιβῆρες), a powerful people in Spain, consisting of Celts, who crossed the Pyrenees at an early period, and became mingled with the Iberians, the original inhabitants of the country. They dwelt chiefly in the central part of Spain, in the highlands which separate the Iberus from the rivers which flow towards the W., and in which the Tagus and the Durius rise. They were divided into various tribes, the AREVACAE, BERONES, and PELENDONES, which were the 3 most important, the LUSONES, BELLI, DITTANI, &c. Their chief towns were SEGOBRIGA, NUMANTIA, BILBILIS, &c. Their country called Celtiberia was mountainous and unproductive. They were a brave and warlike people, and proved formidable enemies to the Romans. They submitted to Scipio Africanus in the 2nd Punic war, but the oppressions of the Roman governors led them to rebel, and for many years they successfully defied the power of Rome. They were reduced to submission on the capture of Numantia by Scipio Africanus the younger (B.C. 134), but they again took up arms under Sertorius, and it was not till his death (72) that they began to adopt the Roman customs and language.

Celtici. 1. A Celtic people in Lusitania between the Tagus and Anas. — 2. A Celtic people

in Gallaecia near the promontory Nerium, which was called Celticum after them (C. Finisterre).

Cenaeum (Κηναῖον ἄκρον: Kanaia or Litar), the N.W. promontory of Euboea, opposite Thermopylae, with a temple of Zeus Cenaeus.

Cenchrēae (Κεγχρέαι). 1. The E. harbour of Corinth on the Saronic gulf, important for the trade and commerce with the E. — 2. A town in Argolis, S. of Argos, on the road to Tegea.

Cenomāni, a powerful Gallic people, originally a branch of the AULERCI, crossed the Alps at an early period, and settled in the N. of Italy in the country of Brixia, Verona, and Mantua, and extended N. as far as the confines of Rhaetia. They were at constant feud with the neighbouring tribes of the Insubres, Boii, &c., and hence usually assisted the Romans in their wars with these people.

Censorinus. 1. One of the 30 tyrants, assumed the purple at Bologna, A. D. 270, but was shortly afterwards put to death by his own soldiers. — 2. Author of a treatise entitled de Die Natali, which treats of the generation of man, of his natal hour, of the influence of the stars and genii upon his career, and discusses the various methods employed for the division and calculation of time. The book is dedicated to Q. Cerellius, and was composed A. D. 238. A fragment de Metris and lost tracts de Accentibus and de Geometria are ascribed to this Censorinus. — Editions. By Havercamp, Lug. Bat. 1743; by Gruber, Noremb. 1805.

Censorinus, Marcius. 1. C., son of C. Marcius Rutilus, first plebeian dictator (B. C. 356), was originally called Rutilus, and was the first member of the family who had the surname Censorinus. He was consul in B.C. 310, and conducted the war in Samnium. He was censor 294, and a second time 265, the only instance in which a person held the office of censor twice. — 2. L., consul 149, the first year of the third Punic war, conducted the war against Carthage with his colleague M'. Manilius. — 3. C., one of the leaders of the Marian party, fought against Sulla in the battle near the Colline gate, was taken prisoner, and put to death by Sulla's order. Censorinus was one of the orators of his time, and versed in Greek literature. — 4. L., a partizan of M. Antony, praetor 43, and consul 39. — 5. C., consul B. C. 8, died in Asia A. D. 2, while in attendance upon C. Caesar, the grandson of Augustus.

Centauri (Κένταυροι), that is, the Bull-killers, were an ancient race, inhabiting Mount Pelion in Thessaly. They led a wild and savage life, and are hence called φῆρες or θῆρες in Homer. In later accounts they were represented as half-horses and half-men. Their origin is variously related. According to the most ancient account Centaurus, the offspring of Ixion and a cloud, begot the Hippocentaurs by mixing with Magnesian mares. From most accounts it would appear that the Centaurs and Hippocentaurs were originally regarded as two distinct classes of beings, although the name of Centaurs is applied to both by ancient as well as modern writers. The Centaurs are particularly celebrated in ancient story for their fight with the Lapithae, which arose at the marriage-feast of Pirithous. This fight is sometimes placed in connexion with a combat of Hercules with the Centaurs. It ended by the Centaurs being expelled from their country, and taking refuge on mount Pindus, on the frontiers of Epirus. Chiron is the most celebrated among the Centaurs. [CHIRON.]

M

We know that hunting the bull on horseback was a national custom in Thessaly, and that the Thessalians were celebrated riders. Hence may have arisen the fable that the Centaurs were half-men and half-horses, just as the Americans, when they first saw a Spaniard on horseback, believed horse and man to be one being. The Centaurs were frequently represented in ancient works of art, and generally, as men from the head to the loins, while the remainder of the body is that of a horse with its 4 feet and tail.

Centrites (Κεντρίτης: *Bodlis*), a small river of Armenia, which it divided from the land of the Carduchi, N. of Assyria. It rises in the mountains S. of the Arsissa Palus (*L. Van*), and flows into the Tigris.

Centumălus, Fulvĭus. 1. Cn., legate of the dictator M. Valerius Corvus B. C. 301; consul 298, when he gained a victory over the Samnites; and propraetor 295, when he defeated the Etruscans. — **2.** Cn., consul 229, defeated the Illyrians subject to the queen Teuta. — **3.** Cn., curule aedile 214; praetor 213, with Suessula as his province; and consul 211; in the next year he was defeated by Hannibal near Herdonia in Apulia, and was killed in the battle. — **4.** M., praetor urbanus 192, superintended the preparations for the war against Antiochus the Great.

Centum Cellae (*Civita Vecchia*), a sea-port town in Etruria, first became a place of importance under Trajan, who built a villa here and constructed an excellent harbour. It was destroyed by the Saracens in the 9th century, but was rebuilt on its ancient site, and was hence called *Civita Vecchia.*

Centŭrīpae (τὰ Κεντόριπα, αἱ Κεντούριπαι: Κεντοριπῖνοι, in Thuc. οἱ Κεντόριπες, Centuripīnus: *Centorbi*), an ancient town of the Siculi in Sicily, at the foot of Mt. Aetna, on the road from Catana to Panormus, and not far from the river Symaethus; in its neighbourhood a great quantity of corn was grown, and it became under the Romans one of the most flourishing cities in the island.

Cĕōs (Κέως, Ion. Κέος: Κεῖος, Ion. Κήϊος, Cĕus: *Zea*), an island in the Aegean Sea, one of the Cycladea, between the Attic promontory Sunium and the island Cythnus, celebrated for its fertile soil and its genial climate. It was inhabited by Ionians, and originally contained 4 towns, Iūlia, Carthaea, Coressus, and Poeëessa; but the two latter perished by an earthquake. Simonides was a native of Iulis in Ceos, whence we read of the *Ceae munera neniae.* (Hor. *Carm.* ii. 1. 38.)

Cĕphălē (Κεφαλή), an Attic demus, on the right bank of the Erasinus, belonging to the tribe Acamantis.

Cĕphallēnĭa (Κεφαλληνία, Κεφαληνία: Κεφαλλήν, pl. Κεφαλλῆνες: *Cephalonia*), called by Homer Same (Σάμη) or Samos (Σάμος), the largest island in the Ionian sea, separated from Ithaca on the E. by a narrow channel, contains 348 square miles. It is said to have been originally inhabited by Taphians, and to have derived its name from the mythical Cephalus. Even in Homer its inhabitants are called Cephallenes, and are the subjects of Ulysses: but the name Cephallenia first occurs in Herodotus. The island is very mountainous (παιπαλόεσση); and the highest mountain, called Aenos, on which stood a temple of Zeus, rises more than 4000 feet above the sea. Cephallenia was a tetrapolis, containing the 4

towns, Same, Pale, Cranii, and Proni. It never attained political importance. In the Persian wars the inhabitants of Pale are alone mentioned. In the Peloponnesian war Cephallenia surrendered to the Athenians. Same ventured to oppose the Romans, but was taken by M. Fulvius, B. C. 189. In modern times the island was for a long while in possession of the Venetians, but is now one of the 7 Ionian islands under the protection of Great Britain.

Cĕphăloedĭum (Κεφαλοίδιον: Cephaloeditānus; *Cefalù* or *Cephalu*), a town on the N. coast of Sicily in the territory of Himera.

Cĕphălus (Κέφαλος). **1.** Son of Hermes and Herse, was carried off by Eos (Aurora), who became by him the mother of Tithonus in Syria. — **2.** Son of Deion and Diomede, and husband of Procris or Procne, daughter of Erechtheus, whom he tenderly loved. He was beloved by Eos, but as he rejected her advances from love to his wife, she advised him to try the fidelity of Procris. The goddess then metamorphosed him into a stranger, and sent him with rich presents to his house. Procris was tempted by the brilliant presents to yield to the stranger, who then discovered himself to be her husband, whereupon she fled in shame to Crete. Artemis made her a present of a dog and a spear, which were never to miss their object, and then sent her back to Cephalus in the disguise of a youth. In order to obtain this dog and spear, Cephalus promised to love the youth, who then made herself known to him as his wife Procris. This led to a reconciliation between them. Procris however still feared the love of Eos, and therefore jealously watched Cephalus when he went out hunting, but on one occasion he killed her by accident with the never-erring spear. A somewhat different version of the same story is given by Ovid. (*Met.* vii. 685, seq.) Subsequently Cephalus fought with Amphitryon against the Teleboans, upon the conquest of whom he was rewarded with the island which he called after his own name Cephallenia. — **3.** A Syracusan, and father of the orator Lysias, came to Athens at the invitation of Pericles. He is one of the speakers in Plato's Republic. — **4.** An eminent Athenian orator of the Collytean demus, flourished B. C. 402.

Cĕpheus (Κηφεύς). **1.** King of Ethiopia, son of Belus, husband of Cassiepeia, and father of Andromeda, was placed among the stars after his death. — **2.** Son of Aleus and Nearea or Cleobule, one of the Argonauts. He was king of Tegea in Arcadia, and perished, with most of his sons, in an expedition against Hercules.

Cĕphisĭa or **Cephissia** (Κηφισία more correct than Κηφισσία: Κηφισιεύς: *Kivisia*), one of the 12 Cecropian towns of Attica, and afterwards a demus belonging to the tribe Erechtheis, N. E. of Athens, on the W. slope of Mt. Pentelicus.

Cĕphisŏdōrus (Κηφισόδωρος). **1.** An Athenian comic poet of the old comedy, flourished B. C. 402. — **2.** An Athenian orator, a disciple of Isocrates, wrote an apology for Isocrates against Aristotle, entitled αἱ πρὸς Ἀριστοτέλη ἀντιγραφαί.

Cĕphisŏdŏtus (Κηφισόδοτος). **1.** An Athenian general and orator, is mentioned on various occasions from B. C. 371 to 355. — **2.** An Athenian sculptor, whose sister was the first wife of Phocion, flourished 372. He belonged to that younger school of Attic artists, who had abandoned the stern and majestic beauty of Phidias, and adopted a more animated and graceful style.—3. An Athenian sculptor, usually called the Younger, a son of the great Praxiteles, flourished 300.

Cephisŏphon (Κηφισοφῶν), a friend of Euripides, is said not only to have been the chief actor in his dramas, but also to have aided him with his advice in the composition of them.

Cephisus or **Cephissus** (Κηφισός, Κηφισσός). 1. The chief river in Phocis and Boeotia, rises near Lilaea in Phocis, flows through a fertile valley in Phocis and Boeotia, and falls into the lake Copais, which is hence called *Cephisis* in the Iliad (v. 709). [COPAIS.]—2. The largest river in Attica, rises in the W. slope of Mt. Pentelicus, and flows past Athens on the W. into the Saronic gulf near Phalerum.—3. There was also a river of this name in Argolis, Salamis, Sicyonia, and Scyros.

Cer (Κήρ), the personified necessity of death (Κήρ or Κῆρες θανάτοιο). The Κῆρες are described by Homer as formidable, dark, and hateful, because they carry off men to the joyless house of Hades. According to Hesiod, they are the daughters of Nyx (Night) and sisters of the Moerae, and punish men for their crimes.

Cerāmus (ἡ Κέραμος: *Keramo*), a Dorian seaport town on the N. side of the Cnidian Chersonesus on the coast of Caria, from which the Ceramic gulf (ὁ Κεραμεικὸς κόλπος: *Gulf of Kos*, or, *Golfo di Stanco*) took its name. [CARIA.]

Cerăsus (Κερασοῦς: Κερασούντιος: nr. *Kheresoun*), a flourishing colony of Sinope, on the coast of Pontus, at the mouth of a river of the same name; chiefly celebrated as the place from which Europe obtained both the cherry and its name. Lucullus is said to have brought back plants of the cherry with him to Rome, but this refers probably only to some particular sorts, as the Romans seem to have had the tree much earlier.—Cerasus fell into decay after the foundation of Pharnacia (*Kheresoun*).

Cerăta (τὰ Κέρατα), the Horns, a mountain on the frontiers of Attica and Megaris.

Ceraunii Montes (Κεραύνια ὄρη: *Khimara*), a range of mountains extending from the frontier of Illyricum along the coast of Epirus, derived their name from the frequent thunder-storms which occurred among them (κεραυνός). These mountains made the coast of Epirus dangerous to ships. They were also called Acroceraunia, though this name was properly applied to the promontory separating the Adriatic and Ionian seas. The inhabitants of these mountains were called *Ceraunii*.

Cerbĕrus (Κέρβερος), the dog that guarded the entrance of Hades, is mentioned as early as the Homeric poems, but simply as "the dog," and without the name of Cerberus. (*Il.* viii. 368, *Od.* xi. 623.) Hesiod calls him a son of Typhaon and Echidna, and represents him with 50 heads. Later writers describe him as a monster with only 3 heads, with the tail of a serpent and with serpents round his neck. Some poets again call him many-headed or hundred-headed. The den of Cerberus is usually placed on the further side of the Styx, at the spot where Charon landed the shades of the departed.

Cercasōrum, or -na, or -sūra (Κερκάσωρος πόλις, Herod., Κερκέσουρα, Strab.: *El-Arkas*), a city of Lower Egypt, on the W. bank of the Nile, at the point where the river divided into its 3 principal branches, the E. or Pelusiac, the W. or Canopic, and the N. between them.

Cercĕtae or -ii (Κερκέται, probably the *Circassians*), a people of Sarmatia Asiatica, beyond the Cimmerian Bosporus, on the E. coast of the Palus Maeotis (*Sea of Azov*).

Cercetĭus, a mountain in Thessaly, part of the range of Pindus.

Cercĭna and **Cercĭnitis** (Κερκίνα, Κερκινῖτις: *Karkenah Is., Ramlah* and *Gherba*), 2 low islands off the N. coast of Africa, in the mouth of the Lesser Syrtis, united by a bridge, and possessing a fine harbour. Cercina was the larger, and had on it a town of the same name.

Cercĭnē (Κερκίνη: *Kara-dagh*), a mountain in Macedonia, between the Axius and Strymon, forming the boundary between Sintice and Paeonia.

Cercĭnitis (Κερκινῖτις), a lake in Macedonia, near the mouth of the Strymon, through which this river flows.

Cercinium, a town in Thessaly on the lake Bobeis.

Cerco, Q. Lutātĭus, consul with A. Manlius Torquatus, B. C. 241, in which year the first Punic war was brought to a close by the victory of C. Lutatius Catulus at the Aegates. Cerco, in conjunction with his colleague, subdued the Falisci or people of Falerii, who revolted from the Romans.

Cercōpes (Κέρκωπες), droll and thievish gnomes, robbed Hercules in his sleep, but were taken prisoners by him, and either given to Omphale, or killed, or set free again. Some placed them at Thermopylae (Herod. vii. 216); but the comic poem *Cercopes*, which bore the name of Homer, probably placed them at Oechalia in Euboea. Others transferred them to Lydia, or the islands called Pithecusae, which derived their name from the Cercopes who were changed into monkeys by Zeus for having deceived him.

Cercops (Κέρκωψ). 1. One of the oldest Orphic poets, also called a Pythagorean, was the author of an epic poem, "on the descent of Orpheus to Hades."—2. Of Miletus, the contemporary and rival of Hesiod, is said to have been the author of an epic poem called *Aegimius*, which is also ascribed to Hesiod.

Cercўon (Κερκύων), son of Poseidon or Hephaestus, a cruel tyrant at Eleusis, put to death his daughter ALOPE, and killed all strangers whom he overcame in wrestling; he was in the end conquered and slain by Theseus.

Cerdylĭum (Κερδύλιον), a small town in Macedonia on the right bank of the Strymon, opposite Amphipolis.

Cereālis, Petīlĭus, served under Vettius Bolanus in Britain, A. D. 61; was one of the generals who supported the claim of Vespasian to the empire, 69; suppressed the revolt of Civilis on the Rhine, 70; and was governor of Britain, 71, when he conquered a great part of the Brigantes.

Cereātae, a town of the Hernici in Latium, between Sora and Anagnia.

Cĕrēs. [DEMETER.]

Cerilli (*Cirella Vecchia*), a town in Bruttium on the coast, a little S. of the mouth of the Laus.

Cerinthus (Κήρινθος), a town on the E. coast of Euboea, on the river Budorus.

Cernē (Κέρνη), an island off the W. coast of Africa, to which the Phoenicians appear to have traded. Its position is uncertain, and Strabo even denied its existence.

Ceron, a fountain in Histiaeotis in Thessaly

said to have made all the sheep black which drank of it.

Cerretāni, an Iberian people in Hispania Tarraconensis, inhabited the modern *Cerdagne* in the Pyrenees, and were subsequently divided into the 2 tribes of the Juliani and Augustani : they were celebrated for their hams.

Cersobleptes (Κερσοβλέπτης), son of Cotys, king of Thrace, on whose death in B. C. 358 he inherited the kingdom in conjunction with Berisades and Amadocus, who were probably his brothers. As an ally of the Athenians Cersobleptes became involved in war with Philip, by whom he was frequently defeated, and was at length reduced to the condition of a tributary, 343.

Cersus (Κέρσος : *Merkes*), a river of Cilicia, flowing through the Pylae Syro-Ciliciae, into the E. side of the Gulf of Issus.

Certōnĭum (Κερτόνιον), a town in Mysia, mentioned only by Xenophon (*Anab.* vii 8. § 8).

Cervidĭus Scaevōla. [SCAEVOLA.]

Cēryx (Κήρυξ), an Attic hero, son of Hermes and Aglauros, from whom the priestly family of the Ceryces at Athens derived their origin.

Cestrus (Κέστρος : *Ak-su*), a considerable river of Pamphylia, flowing from the Taurus S.-wards into the Mediterranean. It was navigable in its lower course, at least as far as the city of Perge, which stood on its W. bank, 60 stadia (10 geog. miles) above its mouth.

Cētēi (Κήτειοι), a people of Mysia, the old inhabitants of the country which Homer (*Od.* xi. 521). Their name is evidently connected with that of the river CETIUS.

Cethēgus, Cornēlĭus, an ancient patrician family. They seem to have kept up an old fashion of wearing their arms bare, to which Horace alludes in the words *cinctuti Cethegi* (*Ars Poët.* 50); and Lucan (ii. 543) describes the associate of Catiline thus, *exsertique manus vesana Cethegi*. 1. M., curule aedile and pontifex maximus B. C. 213 ; praetor 211, when he had the charge of Apulia ; censor 209, and consul 204. In the next year he commanded as proconsul in Cisalpine Gaul, where he defeated Mago, brother of Hannibal. He died 196. His eloquence was rated very high, so that Ennius gave him the name of *Suada medulla*, and Horace twice refers to him as an ancient authority for the usage of Latin words. (*Epist.* ii. 2. 116, *Ars. Poët.* 50.) — 2. C., commanded in Spain as proconsul 200; was aedile 199; consul 197, when he defeated the Insubrians and Cenomanians in Cisalpine Gaul ; and censor 194. — 3. P., curule aedile 187, praetor 185, and consul 181. The grave of Numa was discovered in his consulship. — 4. M., consul 160, when he drained a part of the Pontine Marshes. — 5. P., a friend of Marius, proscribed by Sulla, 88, but in 83 went over to Sulla, and was pardoned. — 6. C., one of Catiline's crew, was a profligate from his early youth. When Catiline left Rome, 63, after Cicero's first speech, Cethegus stayed behind under the orders of Lentulus. His charge was to murder the leading senators ; but the tardiness of Lentulus prevented anything being done. Cethegus was arrested and condemned to death with the other conspirators.

Cētĭus (Κήτειος), a small river of Mysia, flowing from the N. through the district of Elaïtis, and falling into the Caïcus close to Pergamus.

Ceutrōnes or Centrōnes, a people in Gallia Belgica, dependents of the Nervii.

Cēyx (Κήϋξ), king of Trachys, husband of Alcyone. His death is differently related. [ALCYONE.] He was the father of Hippasus, who fell fighting as the ally of Hercules.

Chabōras. [ABORRHAS.]

Chabrĭas (Χαβρίας), a celebrated Athenian general. In B. C. 392 he succeeded Iphicrates in the command of the Athenian forces at Corinth. In 388 he assisted Evagoras in Cyprus against the Persians. In 378 he was one of the commanders of the forces sent to the aid of Thebes against Agesilaus, when he adopted for the first time that manoeuvre for which he became so celebrated,—ordering his men to await the attack with their spears pointed against the enemy and their shields resting on one knee. A statue was afterwards erected at Athens to Chabrias in this posture. In 376 he gained an important victory off Naxos over the Lacedaemonian fleet under the command of Pollis. In 361 he took the command of the naval force of Tachos, king of Egypt, who was in rebellion against Persia. In 358 he was sent as the Athenian commander in Thrace, but was compelled by Charidemus to make a peace unfavourable to Athens. On the breaking out of the Social war in 357, Chabrias commanded the Athenian fleet. At the siege of Chios he sailed into the harbour before the rest of the fleet, and, when his ship was disabled, he refused to save his life by abandoning it, and fell fighting.

Chaerea, C. Cassĭus, tribune of the praetorian cohorts, formed the conspiracy by which the emperor Caligula was slain, A. D. 41. Chaerea was put to death by Claudius upon his accession.

Chaerēmon (Χαιρήμων). 1. One of the most celebrated of the later tragic poets at Athens, flourished B. C. 380. He is erroneously called a comic poet by some writers. There are 3 epigrams ascribed to Chaeremon in the Greek Anthology. — 2. Of Alexandria, a Stoic philosopher, chief librarian of the Alexandrian library, was afterwards called to Rome, and became the preceptor of Nero, in conjunction with Alexander of Aegae. He wrote a history of Egypt, on Hieroglyphics, on Comets, and a grammatical work. Martial (xi. 56) wrote an epigram upon him.

Chaerēphon (Χαιρεφῶν), a well-known disciple of Socrates, was banished by the Thirty tyrants, and returned to Athens on the restoration of democracy, B. C. 403. He was dead when the trial of Socrates took place, 399.

Chaerōnēa (Χαιρώνεια: Χαιρωνεύς: *Capurna*), the Homeric Arne according to Pausanias, a town in Boeotia on the Cephisus near the frontier of Phocis, memorable for the defeat of the Athenians and the Boeotians in B.C. 338 by Philip, king of Macedon, and for Sulla's victory over the army of Mithridates, 86. Chaeronea was the birthplace of Plutarch. Several remains of the ancient city are to be seen at Capurna, more particularly a theatre excavated in the rock, an aqueduct, and the marble lion (broken in pieces) which adorned the sepulchre of the Boeotians who fell at the battle of Chaeronea.

Chalaeum (Χάλαιον : Χαλαῖος), a port-town of the Locri Ozolae on the Crissaean gulf, on the frontiers of Phocis.

Chalastra (Χαλάστρα, in Herod. Χαλέστρη : Χαλαστραῖος : *Culacia*), a town in Mygdonia in Macedonia, at the mouth of the river Axius.

Chalcē or -ae or -ĭa (Χάλκη, Χάλκεαι, Χαλκία :

Χαλκαῖος or -ίτης: *Charki*), an island of the Carpathian sea, near Rhodes, with a town of the same name, and a temple of Apollo.

Chalcēdon (Χαλκηδών, more correctly, Καλχηδών: Χαλκηδόνιος: *Chalkedon*, Grk., *Kadi-Kioi*, Turk., Ru.), a Greek city of Bithynia, on the coast of the Propontis at the entrance of the Bosporus, nearly opposite to Byzantium, was founded by a colony from Megara in B. c. 685. After a long period of independence (only interrupted by its captur by the Persians and its recovery by the Athenians), it became subject to the kings of Bithynia, and suffered the transference of most of its inhabitants to the new city of Nicomedia (B. c. 140). The Romans restored its fortifications, and made it the chief city of the province of Bithynia, or Pontica Prima. After various fortunes under the empire, it was entirely destroyed by the Turks. — The fourth oecumenical council of the Church met here, A. D. 451.

Chalcidice (Χαλκιδίκη), a peninsula in Macedonia between the Thermaic and Strymonic gulfs, runs out into the sea like a 3-pronged fork, terminating in 3 smaller peninsulas, PALLENE, SITHONIA, and ACTE or ATHOS. It derived its name from Chalcidian colonists. [CHALCIS, No. 1.]

Chalcidius, a Platonic philosopher who lived probably in the 6th century of the Christian aera. translated into Latin the Timaeus of Plato, on which he likewise wrote a voluminous commentary. Edited by Meursius, Leyden, 1617, and by Fabricius, Hamburg, 1718, at the end of the 2nd volume of the works of Hippolytus.

Chalcioecus (Χαλκίοικος), "the goddess of the brazen house," a surname of Athena at Sparta, from the brazen temple which she had in that city.

Chalcis (Χαλκίς: Χαλκιδεύς, Chalcidensis). 1. (*Egripo* or *Negroponte*), the principal town of Euboea, situated on the narrowest part of the Euripus, and united with the mainland by a bridge. It was a very ancient town, originally inhabited by Abantes or Curetes, and colonized by Attic Ionians under Cothus. Its flourishing condition at an early period is attested by the numerous colonies which it planted in various parts of the Mediterranean. It founded so many cities in the peninsula in Macedonia between the Strymonic and Thermaic gulfs, that the whole peninsula was called Chalcidice. In Italy it founded Cuma and in Sicily Naxos. Chalcis was usually subject to Athens during the greatness of the latter city, and afterwards passed into the hands of the Macedonians, Antiochus, Mithridates, and the Romans. It was a place of great military importance, as it commanded the navigation between the N. and S. of Greece, and hence it was often taken and retaken by the different parties contending for the supremacy in Greece. — The orator Isaeus and the poet Lycophron were born at Chalcis, and Aristotle died here. — 2. A town in Aetolia at the mouth of the Evenus, situated at the foot of the mountain Chalcis, and hence also called *Hypochalcis*. — 3. (*Kinnesrin*, Ru.), a city of Syria, in a fruitful plain, near the termination of the river Chalus; the chief city of the district of Chalcidice, which lay to the E. of the Orontes. — 4. A city of Syria on the Belus, in the plain of Marsyas.

Chalcocondyles, or, by contraction, **Chalcondyles, Laonicus** or **Nicolaus**, a Byzantine historian, flourished A. D. 1446, and wrote a history of

the Turks and of the later period of the Byzantine empire, from the year 1298 down to the conquest of Corinth and the invasion of the Peloponnesus by the Turks in 1463, thus including the capture of Constantinople in 1453. Edited by Fabrot, Paris, 1650.

Chaldaea (Χαλδαία: Χαλδαῖος), in the narrower sense, was a province of Babylonia, about the lower course of the Euphrates, the border of the Arabian Desert, and the head of the Persian Gulf. It was intersected by numerous canals, and was extremely fertile. In a wider sense, the term is applied to the whole of Babylonia, and even to the Babylonian empire, on account of the supremacy which the Chaldaeans acquired at Babylon. [BABYLON.] Xenophon mentions Chaldaeans in the mountains N. of Mesopotamia; and we have other statements respecting this people, from which it is very difficult to deduce a clear view of their early history. The most probable opinion is, that their original seat was in the mountains of Armenia and Kurdistan, whence they descended into the plains of Mesopotamia and Babylonia. Respecting the Chaldaeans as the ruling class in the Babylonian monarchy, see BABYLON.

Chalus (Χάλος: *Koweik*), a river of N. Syria, flowing S. past Beroea and Chalcis, and terminating in a marshy lake.

Chalybes (Χάλυβες), a remarkable Asiatic people, about whom we find various statements in the ancient writers. They are generally represented, both in the early poetic legends, and in the historical period, as dwelling on the S. shore of the Black Sea, about Themiscyra and the Thermodon (and probably to a wider extent, for Herodotus clearly mentions them among the nations W. of the Halys), and occupying themselves in the working of iron. Xenophon mentions Chalybes in the mountains on the borders of Armenia and Mesopotamia, who seem to be the same people that he elsewhere calls Chaldaeans; and several of the ancient geographers regarded the Chalybes and Chaldaei as originally the same people.

Chalybon (Χαλυβών: O. T. Helbon), a considerable city of N. Syria, probably the same as BEROEA. The district about it was called Chalybonitis.

Chamaeleon (Χαμαιλέων), a Peripatetic philosopher of Heraclea on the Pontus, one of the immediate disciples of Aristotle, wrote works on several of the ancient Greek poets, and likewise on philosophical subjects.

Chamāvi, a people in Germany, who were compelled by the Roman conquests to change their abodes several times. They first appear in the neighbourhood of the Rhine, but afterwards migrated E., defeated the Bructeri, and settled between the Weser and the Harz. At a later time they dwelt on the Lower Rhine, and are mentioned as auxiliaries of the Franks.

Chāones (Χάονες), a Pelasgian people, one of the 3 peoples which inhabited EPIRUS, were at an earlier period in possession of the whole of the country, but subsequently dwelt along the coast from the river Thyamis to the Acroceraunian promontory, which district was therefore called Chaonia. By the poets *Chaonius* is used as equivalent to Epirot.

Chāos (Χάος), the vacant and infinite space which existed according to the ancient cosmogonies previous to the creation of the world and out of which the gods, men, and all things arose. Chaos was called the mother of Erebos and Nyx.

Charadra (Χαράδρα: Χαραδραῖος). 1. A town in Phocis on the river Charadrus, situated on an eminence not far from Lilaea. — 2. A town in Epirus, N.W. of Ambracia. — 3. A town in Messenia, built by Pelops.

Charadrus (Χάραδρος). 1. A small river in Phocis, a tributary of the Cephisus. — 2. A small river in Argolis, a tributary of the Inachus. — 3. A small river in Messenia, rises near Oechalia.

Charax (Χάραξ), of Pergamus, an historian, wrote a work in 40 books, called Ἑλληνικά, and another named Χρονικά.

Chărax (Χάραξ, i. e. *a palisaded camp :* Χαρακηνός), the name of several cities, which took their origin from military stations. The most remarkable of them stood at the mouth of the Tigris. [ALEXANDRIA, No. 4.] There were others, which only need a bare mention, in the Chersonesus Taurica, in N. Media, near Celaenae in Phrygia, in Corsica, and on the Great Syrtis in Africa, and a few more.

Charaxus (Χάραξος) of Mytilene, son of Scamandronymus and brother of Sappho, fell in love with RHODOPIS.

Chărēs (Χάρης). 1. An Athenian general, who for a long series of years contrived by profuse corruption to maintain his influence with the people, in spite of his very disreputable character. In B. C. 367 he was sent to the aid of the Phliasians, who were hard pressed by the Arcadians and Argives, and he succeeded in relieving them. In the Social war, after the death of Chabrias, 356, he had the command of the Athenian fleet along with Iphicrates and Timotheus. His colleagues having refused, in consequence of a storm, to risk an engagement, Chares accused them to the people, and they were recalled. Being now left in the sole command, and being in want of money, he entered into the service of Artabazus, the revolted satrap of Western Asia, but was recalled by the Athenians on the complaint of Artaxerxes III In the Olynthian war, 349, he commanded the mercenaries sent from Athens to the aid of Olynthus. In 340 he commanded the force sent to aid Byzantium against Philip ; but he effected nothing, and was accordingly superseded by Phocion. In 338 he was one of the Athenian commanders at the battle of Chaeronea. When Alexander invaded Asia in 334, Chares was living at Sigeum ; and in 333 he commanded for Darius at Mytilene.—2. Of Mytilene, an officer at the court of Alexander the Great, wrote a history of Alexander in 10 books. — 3. Of Lindus in Rhodes, a statuary in bronze, the favourite pupil of Lysippus, flourished B. C. 290. His chief work was the statue of the Sun, which, under the name of "The Colossus of Rhodes," was celebrated as one of the 7 wonders of the world. Its height was upwards of 105 English feet, it was 12 years in erecting, and cost 300 talents. It stood at the entrance of the harbour of Rhodes, but there is no authority for the statement that its legs extended over the mouth of the harbour. It was overthrown and broken to pieces by an earthquake 56 years after its erection, B. C. 224. The fragments remained on the ground 923 years, till they were sold by the general of the caliph Othman IV., to a Jew of Emesa, who carried them away on 900 camels, A. D. 672.

Chăriclēs (Χαρικλῆς). 1. An Athenian demagogue, son of Apollodorus, was one of the commissioners appointed to investigate the affair of the mutilation of the Hermae, B. C. 415 ; was one of the commanders of the Athenian fleet, 413 ; and one of the 30 tyrants on the capture of Athens by Lysander, 404. — 2. An eminent physician at Rome, attended the emperor Tiberius.

Chăriclō (Χαρικλώ). 1. A nymph, daughter of Apollo, wife of the centaur Chiron, and mother of Carystus and Ocyroë. — 2. A nymph, wife of Eueres and mother of Tiresias.

Chărĭdēmus (Χαρίδημος). 1. Of Oreus in Euboea, of mean origin, became the captain of a band of mercenaries, and served in this capacity under the Athenian generals Iphicrates and Timotheus. He next entered the service of the satrap Artabazus, who had revolted against Artaxerxes III., and subsequently of Cotys, king of Thrace, whose daughter he married. On the murder of Cotys, 358, Charidemus adhered to the cause of his son Cersobleptes, and on behalf of the latter carried on the struggle with the Athenians for the possession of the Chersonesus. In 349 he was appointed by the Athenians commander in the Olynthian war, but next year was superseded and replaced by Chares.—2. An Athenian, one of the orators whose surrender was required by Alexander in B. C. 335, after the destruction of Thebes, fled to Asia, and took refuge with Darius, by whose orders he was put to death, 333, shortly before the battle of Issus.

Chărĭlāus, or **Charillus** (Χαρίλαος, Χάριλλος), king of Sparta, son of Polydectes, is said to have received his name from the general joy excited by the justice of his uncle Lycurgus when he placed him, yet a new-born infant, on the royal seat, and bade the Spartans acknowledge him for their king. He carried on war against Argos and Tegea ; he was taken prisoner by the Tegeans, but was dismissed without ransom on giving a promise (which he did not keep), that the Spartans should abstain in future from attacking Tegea.

Chăris (Χάρις), the personification of Grace and Beauty. In the Iliad (xviii. 382) Charis is described as the wife of Hephaestus, but in the Odyssey Aphrodite appears as the wife of Hephaestus, from which we may infer, if not the identity of Aphrodite and Charis, at least a close connection in the notions entertained about the 2 divinities. The idea of personified grace and beauty was at an early period divided into a plurality of beings, and even in the Homeric poems the plural Charites occurs several times. — The *Charites*, called *Gratiae* by the Romans, are usually described as the daughters of Zeus, and as 3 in number, namely, Euphrosyne, Aglaia, and Thalia. The names of the Charites sufficiently express their character. They were the goddesses who enhanced the enjoyments of life by refinement and gentleness. They are mostly described as in the service of other divinities, and they lend their grace and beauty to every thing that delights and elevates gods and men. The gentleness and gracefulness which they impart to man's ordinary pleasures are expressed by their moderating the exciting influence of wine (Hor. *Carm.* iii. 19. 15), and by their accompanying Aphrodite and Eros. Poetry, however, is the art which is especially favoured by them, and hence they are the friends of the Muses, with whom they live together in Olympus. In early times the Charites were represented dressed, but afterwards their figures were always naked: specimens of both representations of the Charites are still extant. They appear unsuspicious maidens in the full bloom of life, and they usually embrace each other.

Charisius. 1. Aurelius Arcadius, a Roman jurist, lived in the reign of Constantine the Great, and wrote 3 works, *De Testibus, De Muneribus civilibus,* and *De Officio Praefecti praetorio,* all of which are cited in the Digest.—2. **Flavius Sosipater,** a Latin grammarian, who flourished A. D. 400, author of a treatise in 5 books, drawn up for the use of his son, entitled *Institutiones Grammaticae,* which has come down to us in a very imperfect state. Edited by Putschius in *Grammaticae Latinae Auctores Antiqui,* Hanov. 1605, and by Lindemann, in *Corpus Grammat. Latin. Veterum,* Lips. 1840.

Charites. [CHARIS.]

Chariton (Χαρίτων), of Aphrodisias, a town of Caria, the author of a Greek romance, in 8 books, on the Loves of Chaereas and Callirrhoë. The name is probably feigned (from χάρις and 'Αφροδίτη), as the time and position of the author certainly are. He represents himself as the secretary of the orator Athenagoras, evidently referring to the Syracusan orator mentioned by Thucydides (vi. 35, 36) as the political opponent of Hermocrates. Nothing is known respecting the real life or the time of the author; but he probably did not live earlier than the 5th century after Christ. Edited by D'Orville, 3 vols. Amst. 1750, with a valuable commentary; reprinted with additional notes by Beck, Lips. 1783.

Charmandê (Χαρμάνδη: nr. *Haditha* or *Hit*), a great city of Mesopotamia, on the Euphrates.

Charmides (Χαρμίδης). 1. An Athenian, son of Glaucon, cousin to Critias, and uncle by the mother's side to Plato, who introduces him in the dialogue which bears his name as a very young man at the commencement of the Peloponnesian war. In B. C. 404 he was one of the Ten, and was slain fighting against Thrasybulus at the Piraeus.—2. Called also **Charmadas** by Cicero, a friend of Philo of Larissa, in conjunction with whom he is said by some to have been the founder of a 4th Academy. He flourished B. C. 100.

Charon (Χάρων). 1. Son of Erebos, conveyed in his boat the shades of the dead across the rivers of the lower world. For this service he was paid with an obolus or danace, which co¹ was placed in the mouth of every corpse previous its burial. He is represented as an aged man with a dirty beard and a mean dress.—2. A distinguished Theban, concealed Pelopidas and his fellow-conspirators in his house, when they returned to Thebes with the view of delivering it from the Spartans, B. C. 379.—3. An historian of Lampsacus, flourished B. C. 464, and wrote works on Aethiopia, Persia, Greece, &c., the fragments of which are collected by Müller, *Fragm. Histor. Graec.* Paris, 1841.

Charondas (Χαρώνδας), a lawgiver of Catana, who legislated for his own and the other cities of Chalcidian origin in Sicily and Italy. His date is uncertain. He is said by some to have been a disciple of Pythagoras; and he must have lived before the time of Anaxilaus, tyrant of Rhegium, B. C. 494—476, for the Rhegians used the laws of Charondas till they were abolished by Anaxilaus. The latter fact sufficiently refutes the common account that Charondas drew up a code of laws for Thurii, since this city was not founded till 443. A tradition relates that Charondas one day forgot to lay aside his sword before he appeared in the assembly, thereby violating one of his own laws, and that on being reminded of this by a citizen, he exclaimed, " By Zeus, I will establish it," and immediately stabbed himself. The laws of Charondas were probably in verse.

Charops (Χάροψ). 1. A chief among the Epirots, sided with the Romans in their war with Philip V., B. C. 198.—2. A grandson of the above. He received his education at Rome, and after his return to his own country adhered to the Roman cause; but he is represented by Polybius as a monster of cruelty. He died at Brundisium, 157.

Charybdis. [SCYLLA.]

Chasuari, or **Chasuarii,** or **Chattuarii,** a people of Germany, allies or dependents of the Cherusci. Their position is uncertain. They dwelt N. of the Chatti; and in later times they appear between the Rhine and the Maas as a part of the Franks.

Chatti. [CATTI.]

Chauci or **Cauci,** a powerful people in the N. E. of Germany between the Amisia (*Ems*) and the Albis (*Elbe*), divided by the Visurgis (*Weser*), which flowed through their territory into Majores and Minores, the former W. and the latter E. of the river. They are described by Tacitus as the noblest and the justest of the German tribes. They formed an alliance with the Romans A. D. 5, and assisted the latter in their wars against the Cherusci; but this alliance did not last long. They were at war with the Romans in the reigns of Claudius and Nero, but were never subdued. They are mentioned for the last time in the 3rd century, when they devastated Gaul, but their name subsequently became merged in the general name of Saxons.

Chelidon, the mistress of C. Verres, often mentioned by Cicero.

Chelidonis (Χελιδονίς), wife of Cleonymus, to whom she proved unfaithful in consequence of a passion for Acrotatus, son of Areus I.

Chelidoniae Insulae (Χελιδόνιαι νῆσοι: *Khelidoni*), a group of 5 (Strabo only mentions 3) small islands, surrounded by dangerous shallows, off the promontory called Hiera or Chelidonia (*Khelidoni*) on the S. coast of Lycia.

Chelonatas (Χελωνάτας: *C. Tornese*), a promontory in Elis, opposite Zacynthus, the most westerly point of the Peloponnesus.

Chemmis aft. **Panopolis** (Χέμμις, Πανόπολις: Χεμμίτης: *Ekhmim,* Ru.), a great city of the Thebais, or Upper Egypt, on the E. bank of the Nile, celebrated for its manufactures of linen, its stone-quarries, and its temples of Pan and Perseus. It was the birthplace of the poet Nonnus.

Chenoboscia (Χηνοβοσκία: *Kasees-Said,* Ru.), a city of Upper Egypt, on the right bank of the Nile, opposite Diospolis Parva.

Cheops (Χέοψ), an early king of Egypt, godless and tyrannical, reigned 50 years, and built the first and largest pyramid by the compulsory labour of his subjects.

Chephren (Χεφρήν), king of Egypt, brother and successor of Cheops, whose example of tyranny he followed, reigned 56 years, and built the second pyramid. The Egyptians so hated the memory of these brothers, that they called the pyramids, not by their names, but by that of Philition, a shepherd who at that time fed his flocks near the place.

Chersiphron (Χερσίφρων) or Ctesiphon, an architect of Cnossus in Crete, in conjunction with his son Metagenes, built, or commenced building, the great temple of Artemis at Ephesus. He flourished B. C. 560.

Chersŏnēsus (Χερσόνησος, Att. Χερρόνησος), "a land-island," that is, "a peninsula" (from χέρσος "land" and νῆσος "island"). 1. Ch. Thracica (Peninsula of the Dardanelles or of Gallipoli), usually called at Athens "The Chersonesus" without any distinguishing epithet, the narrow slip of land, 420 stadia in length, running between the Hellespont and the Gulf of Melas, and connected with the Thracian mainland by an isthmus, which was fortified by a wall, 36 stadia across, near Cardia. The Chersonese was colonized by the Athenians under Miltiades, the contemporary of Pisistratus. — 2. Taurica or Scythica (Crimea), the peninsula between the Pontus Euxinus, the Cimmerian Bosporus, and the Palus Maeotis, united to the mainland by an isthmus 40 stadia in width. The ancients compared this peninsula with the Peloponnesus both in form and size. It produced a great quantity of corn, which was exported to Athens and other parts of Greece. The E. part of the peninsula was called Τρηχέη or the Rugged (Herod. iv. 99). Respecting the Greek kingdom established in this country see Bosporus. — There was a town on the S. coast of this peninsula called Chersonesus, founded by the inhabitants of the Pontic Heraclēa, and situated on a small peninsula, called ἡ μικρὰ Χερ. to distinguish it from the larger, of which it formed a part. — 3. Cimbrica (Jutland.) See Cimbri. — 4. (C. Chersonisi) a promontory in Argolis between Epidaurus and Troezen. — 5. (Chersoneso). a town in Crete on the Prom. Zephyrium, the harbour of Lyctus in the interior.

Cherusci, the most celebrated of all the tribes of ancient Germany. The limits of their territory cannot be fixed with accuracy, since the ancients did not distinguish between the Cherusci proper and the nations belonging to the league of which the Cherusci were at the head. The Cherusci proper dwelt on both sides of the Visurgis (Weser), and their territories extended to the Harz and the Elbe. They were originally in alliance with the Romans, but they subsequently formed a powerful league of the German tribes for the purpose of expelling the Romans from the country, and under the chief Arminius they destroyed the army of Varus and drove the Romans beyond the Rhine, A. D. 9. In consequence of internal dissensions among the German tribes the Cherusci soon lost their influence. Their neighbours the Catti succeeded to their power.

Chēsĭum (Χήσιον), a promontory of Samos, with a temple of Artemis, who was worshipped here under the surname of Χησίας. Near it was a little river Chesius, flowing past a town of the same name.

Chĭlon (Χείλων, Χίλων), of Lacedaemon, son of Damagetus, and one of the Seven Sages, flourished B. C. 590. It is said that he died of joy when his son gained the prize for boxing at the Olympic games. The institution of the Ephoralty is erroneously ascribed by some to Chilon.

Chimaera (Χίμαιρα), a fire-breathing monster, the fore part of whose body was that of a lion, the hind part that of a dragon, and the middle that of a goat. According to Hesiod, she was a daughter of Typhaon and Echidna, and had 3 heads, one of each of the 3 animals before mentioned. She made great havoc in Lycia and the surrounding countries, and was at length killed by Bellerophon. Virgil places her together with other monsters at the entrance of Orcus. The origin of the notion of this fire-breathing monster must probably be sought for in the volcano of the name of Chimaera near Phaselis, in Lycia. In the works of art recently discovered in Lycia, we find several representations of the Chimaera in the simple form of a species of lion still occurring in that country.

Chimĕrĭon, a promontory and harbour of Thesprotia in Epirus.

Chion (Χίων), of Heraclēa on the Pontus, a disciple of Plato, put to death Clearchus, the tyrant of his native town, and was in consequence killed, B. C. 353. There are extant 13 letters which are ascribed to Chion, but which are undoubtedly of later origin. Edited by Coberus, Lips. and Dresd. 1765, and by Orelli, in his edition of Memnon, Lips. 1816.

Chĭŏnē (Χιόνη). 1. Daughter of Boreas and Orithyia, became by Poseidon the mother of Eumolpus. — 2. Daughter of Daedalion, beloved by Apollo and Hermes, gave birth to twins, Autolycus and Philammon, the former a son of Hermes and the latter of Apollo. She was killed by Artemis for having compared her beauty to that of the goddess.

Chionĭdes (Χιωνίδης and Χιονίδης), an Athenian poet of the old comedy, flourished B. C. 460, and was the first poet who gave the Athenian comedy that form which it retained down to the time of Aristophanes.

Chĭos (Χίος : Χῖος, Χῖus : Grk. Khio, Ital. Scio, Turk. Saki-Andassi, i. e. Mastio-island), one of the largest and most famous islands of the Aegean, lay opposite to the peninsula of Clazomenae, on the coast of Ionia, and was reckoned at 900 stadia (90 geog. miles) in circuit. Its length from N. to S. is about 30 miles, its greatest breadth about 10, and the width of the strait, which divides it from the mainland, about 8. It is said to have borne, in the earliest times, the various names of Aethalia, Macris, and Pityusa, and to have been inhabited by Tyrrhenian Pelasgians and Leleges. It was colonized by the Ionians at the time of their great migration, and became an important member of the Ionian league ; but its population was mixt. It remained an independent and powerful maritime state, under a democratic form of government, till the great naval defeat of the Ionian Greeks by the Persians, B. C. 494, after which the Chians, who had taken part in the fight with 100 ships, were subjected to the Persians, and their island was laid waste and their young women carried off into slavery. The battle of Mycale, 479, freed Chios from the Persian yoke, and it became a member of the Athenian league, in which it was for a long time the closest and most favoured ally of Athens ; but an unsuccessful attempt to revolt, in 412, led to its conquest and devastation. It recovered its independence, with Cos and Rhodes, in 358, and afterwards shared the fortunes of the other states of Ionia. — Chios is covered with rocky mountains, clothed with the richest vegetation. It was celebrated for its wine, which was among the best known to the ancients, its figs, gum-mastic, and other natural products, also for its marble and pottery, and for the beauty of its women, and the

:uxurious life of its inhabitants. — Of all the states which aspired to the honour of being the birthplace of Homer, Chios was generally considered by the ancients to have the best claim; and it numbered among its natives the tragedian Ion, the historian Theopompus, the poet Theocritus, and other eminent men. Its chief city, Chios (*Khio*), stood on the E. side of the island, at the foot of its highest mountain, Pelinaeus: the other principal places in it were Posidium, Phanae, Notium, Elaeus, and Leuconium.

Chirisophus (Χειρίσοφος), a Lacedaemonian, was sent by the Spartans to aid Cyrus in his expedition against his brother Artaxerxes, B. C. 401. After the battle of Cunaxa and the subsequent arrest of the Greek generals, Chirisophus was appointed one of the new generals, and in conjunction with Xenophon had the chief conduct of the retreat.

Chiron (Χείρων), the wisest and justest of all the Centaurs, son of Cronos and Philyra, and husband of Naïs or Chariclo, lived on mount Pelion. He was instructed by Apollo and Artemis, and was renowned for his skill in hunting, medicine, music, gymnastics, and the art of prophecy. All the most distinguished heroes of Grecian story, as Peleus, Achilles, Diomedes, &c., are described as the pupils of Chiron in these arts. His friendship with Peleus, who was his grandson, is particularly celebrated. Chiron saved him from the other Centaurs, who were on the point of killing him, and he also restored to him the sword which Acastus had concealed. Chiron further informed him in what manner he might gain possession of Thetis, who was destined to marry a mortal. Hercules, too, was his friend; but one of the poisoned arrows of this hero was nevertheless the cause of his death. While fighting with the other Centaurs, one of the poisoned arrows of Hercules struck Chiron, who, although immortal, would not live any longer, and gave his immortality to Prometheus. According to others, Chiron, in looking at one of the arrows, dropped it on his foot, and wounded himself. Zeus placed Chiron among the stars.

Chitone (Χιτώνη), a surname of Artemis, derived either from the Attic demus of Chitone, or because the goddess is represented with a short chiton.

Chloe (Χλόη), the Blooming, a surname of Demeter as the protectress of the green fields: hence Sophocles (*Oed. Col.* 1600) calls her Δημήτηρ εὔχλοος.

Chloris (Χλωρίς). 1. Daughter of the Theban Amphion and Niobe: she and her brother Amyclas were the only children of Niobe not killed by Apollo and Artemis. She is often confounded with No. 2. — 2. Daughter of Amphion of Orchomenos, wife of Neleus, king of Pylos, and mother of Nestor. — 3. Wife of Zephyrus, and goddess of flowers, identical with the Roman Flora.

Choarene (Χοαρηνή), a fertile valley in the W. of Parthia, on the borders of Media, between 2 ranges of the Caspii M.

Choaspes (Χοάσπης). 1. (*Kerah*, or *Kura-Su*), a river of Susiana, falling into the Tigris. Its water was so pure that the Persian kings used to carry it with them in silver vessels, when on foreign expeditions. It is wrongly identified by some geographers with the EULAEUS.—2. (*Attock*), a river in the Paropamisus, falling into the Cophes (*Cabul*), apparently identical with the Suastus of

Ptolemy and the Guraeus of Arrian; and if so the Choes of Arrian is probably the *Kama*: but the proper naming of these rivers is very difficult.

Choerades (Χοιράδες), two small rocky islands off the coast of Italy, near Tarentum.

Choerilus (Χοιρίλος or Χοίριλλος). 1. Of Athens, a tragic poet, contemporary with Thespis, Phrynichus, and Aeschylus, exhibited tragedies for 40 years, B. C. 523—483, and gained the prize 13 times. — 2. Of Samos, the author of an epic poem on the Persian wars; the chief action of the poem appears to have been the battle of Salamis. He was born about 470, and died at the court of Archelaus, king of Macedonia, consequently not later than 399, which was the last year of Archelaus. — 3. Of Iasos, a worthless epic poet in the train of Alexander the Great, is said to have received from Alexander a gold stater for every verse of his poem. (Hor. *Ep.* ii. 1. 232, *Art. Poët.* 357.)

Choes. [CHOASPES, No. 2.]

Chollidae (Χολλεῖδαι or Χολλίδαι: Χολλεῖδης -ίδης), a demus in Attica belonging either to the tribe Leontis or Acamantis.

Chonia (Χωνία), the name in early times of a district in the S. of Italy, inhabited by the **Chones** (Χῶνες), an Oenotrian people, who derived their name from the town of **Chone** (Χώνη). Chonia appears to have included the S. E. of Lucania and the whole of the E. of Bruttium as far as the promontory Zephyrium.

Chorasmii (Χωράσμιοι), a people of Sogdiana, who inhabited the banks and islands of the lower course of the Oxus. They were a branch of the Sacae or Massagetae.

Chosroes. 1. King of Parthia. [ARSACES XXV.] — 2. King of Persia. [SASSANIDAE.]

Chrysa or **-e** (Χρύσα, -η), a city on the coast of the Troad, near Thebes, with a temple of Apollo Smintheus; celebrated by Homer, but destroyed at an early period, and succeeded by another city of the same name, on a height further from the sea, near Hamaxitos. This second city fell into decay in consequence of the removal of its inhabitants to ALEXANDRIA TROAS.

Chrysantas (Χρυσάντας), described by Xenophon in the Cyropaedia as a brave and wise Persian, high in the favour of Cyrus, who rewarded him with the satrapy of Lydia and Ionia.

Chrysaor (Χρυσάωρ). 1. Son of Poseidon and Medusa, husband of Callirrhoë, and father of Geryones and Echidna.—2. The god with the golden sword, a surname of several divinities, as Apollo, Artemis, and Demeter.

Chrysas (Χρύσας), a small river in Sicily, an affluent of the Symaethus, was worshipped as a god in Assorus, in the neighbourhood of which there was a *Fanum Chrysae*.

Chryseis (Χρυσηΐς), daughter of Chryses, priest of Apollo at Chryse, was taken prisoner by Achilles at the capture of Lyrnessus or the Hypoplacian Thebe. In the distribution of the booty she was given to Agamemnon. Her father Chryses came to the camp of the Greeks to solicit her ransom, but was repulsed by Agamemnon with harsh words. Thereupon Apollo sent a plague into the camp of the Greeks, and Agamemnon was obliged to restore her to her father to appease the anger of the god. Her proper name was Astynome.

Chryses. [CHRYSEIS.]

Chrysippus (Χρύσιππος). 1. Son of Pelops and

Axioche, was hated by his step-mother Hippodamīa, who induced her sons Atreus and Thyestes to kill him. — 2. A Stoic philosopher, son of Apollonius of Tarsus, born at Soli in Cilicia, B. C. 280. When young, he lost his paternal property, and went to Athens, where he became the disciple of the Stoic Cleanthes. Disliking the Academic scepticism, he became one of the most strenuous supporters of the principle, that knowledge is attainable and may be established on certain foundations. Hence, though not the founder of the Stoic school, he was the first person who based its doctrines on a plausible system of reasoning, so that it was said, " if Chrysippus had not existed, the Porch could not have been." He died 207, aged 73. He possessed great acuteness and sagacity, and his industry was so great, that he is said to have seldom written less than 500 lines a-day, and to have left behind him 705 works. — 3. Of Cnidos, a physician, sometimes confounded with the Stoic philosopher, but he lived about a century earlier. He was son of Erineus, and pupil of Eudoxus of Cnidos: his works, which are not now extant, are quoted by Galen.

Chrysŏcĕras, the " Golden Horn," the promontory on which part of Constantinople was built.

Chrysŏgŏnus, L. Cornelĭus, a favourite freedman of Sulla, and a man of profligate character, was the false accuser of Sex. Roscius, whom Cicero defended, B. C. 80.

Chrysŏpŏlis (Χρυσόπολις : Scutari), a fortified place on the Bosporus, opposite to Byzantium, at the spot where the Bosporus was generally crossed. It was originally the port of Chalcedon.

Chrysorrhŏas (Χρυσορρόας : Barrada), also called Bardines, a river of Coele-Syria, flowing from the E. side of Anti-Libanus, past Damascus, into a lake now called Bahr-el-Merj.

Chrysostŏmus, Joannes (Χρυσόστομος, golden-mouthed, so surnamed from the power of his eloquence), usually called St. Chrysostom, was born at Antioch, of a noble family, A. D. 347. He received instruction in eloquence from Libanius; and after being ordained deacon (381) and presbyter (386) at Antioch, he became so celebrated as a preacher that he was chosen archbishop of Constantinople, on the death of Nectarius, 397. Chrysostom soon gave great offence at Constantinople by the simplicity of his mode of living, by the sternness with which he rebuked the immorality of the higher classes, and by the severity which he showed to the worldly-minded monks and clergy. Among his enemies was the empress Eudoxia; and they availed themselves of a dispute which had arisen between Chrysostom and Theophilus, patriarch of Alexandria, to accuse Chrysostom of Origenism, and to obtain his deposition by a synod held at Chalcedon in 403. But the same causes which had brought on Chrysostom the hatred of the higher orders had made him the idol of the people. A few days after he had left the city an earthquake happened, which the enraged people considered as a proof of the divine anger at his banishment. Eudoxia, fearing a popular insurrection, recalled him, but 2 months after his return he again excited the anger of the empress, and was banished a second time to the desolate town of Cucusus, on the borders of Isauria and Cilicia. He met with much sympathy from other churches, and his cause was advocated by Innocent, bishop of Rome; but all this excited

jealousy at Constantinople, and he was ordered to be removed to Pityus in Pontus. He died on the journey at Comana in Pontus, 407, in the 60th year of his age. His bones were brought back to Constantinople in 438, and he received the honour of canonization. His works are most voluminous. They consist of: 1. Homilies, Sermons on different parts of Scripture and points of doctrine and practice. 2. Commentaries on the Scriptures. 3. Epistles. 4. Treatises on various subjects, e. g. the Priesthood, Providence, &c. 5. Liturgies. The best edition of his works is by Montfaucon, Paris, 1718–38, 13 vols. fo.

Chthŏnĭus (Χθόνιος) and Chthŏnĭa (Χθόνια), epithets of the gods and goddesses of the lower world (from χθών, " the earth,") as Hades, Hecate, Demeter, Persephone, &c.

Chytri (Χύτροι). 1. (Chytri), a town in Cyprus on the road from Cerynia to Salamis. — 2. Warm springs at Salamis.

Cĭlĭca, a border fortress of the Romans, in Lesser Armenia.

Cibălae or Cibălis, a town in Pannonia on the lake Hiulcas between the Dravus and Savus, near which Constantine gained a decisive victory over Licinius, A. D. 314: the birth-place of Valentinian and Gratian.

Cibōtus. [ALEXANDRIA, No. 1; APAMEA, No. 3.]

Cĭbyra (Κίβυρα : Κιβυράτης : Cibyrata). 1. Magna (ἡ μεγάλη : Buruz or Arondon ? Ru.), a great city of Phrygia Magna, in the fertile district of Milyas, on the borders of Caria, said to have been founded by the Lydians, but afterwards peopled by the Pisidians. In Strabo's time, 4 native dialects were spoken in it, besides Greek, namely, those of the Lydians, the Pisidians, the Milyae, and the Solymi. Under its native princes, the city ruled over a large district called Cibyratis (Κιβυρᾶτις), and could send into the field an army of 30,000 men. In B. C. 83, it was added to the Roman empire, and was made the seat of a conventus juridicus. After being nearly destroyed by an earthquake, it was restored by Tiberius, under the names of Caesarea and Civitas Cibyratica. The city was very celebrated for its manufactures, especially in iron. — 2. Parva (Κ. μικρά : Ibura), a city of Pamphylia, on the borders of Cilicia.

C. Cicerĕĭus, secretary of the elder Scipio Africanus, was a candidate for the praetorship, B. C. 174, along with Scipio's son, but resigned in favour of the latter. He was praetor in the following year, and conquered the Corsicans, but was refused a triumph. In 172 and 167 he was one of the ambassadors sent to the Illyrian king, Gentius; and in 168 he dedicated on the Alban mount a temple to Juno Moneta.

Cĭcĕro, Tullĭus. 1. M., grandfather of the orator, lived at his native town Arpinum, which received the full Roman franchise in B. C. 188. — 2. M., son of No. 1, also lived at Arpinum, and died 64. — 3. L., brother of No. 2, was a friend of M. Antonius the orator. — 4. L., son of No. 3, schoolfellow of the orator, died 68, much regretted by his cousin. — 5. M., the orator, eldest son of No. 2 and Helvia, was born on the 3rd of January, B. C. 106, at the family residence in the vicinity of Arpinum. He was educated along with his brother Quintus, and the two brothers displayed such aptitude for learning that his father removed with them to Rome, where they received instruction from the best teachers in the capital. One of their most celebrated teachers was the poet Archias of Antioch. After receiving the manly gown (91) the young Marcus was placed under the care of Q. Mucius Scaevola, the augur, from whom he learnt the principles of jurisprudence. In 89 he served his 1st and only campaign under Cn. Pompeius Strabo in the Social war. During the civil wars between Marius and Sulla, Cicero identified himself with neither party, but devoted his time to the study of law, philosophy, and rhetoric. He received instruction in philosophy from Phaedrus the Epicurean, Philo, the chief of the New Academy, and Diodotus the Stoic, and in rhetoric from Molo the Rhodian. Having carefully cultivated his powers, Cicero came forward as a pleader in the forum, as soon as tranquillity was restored by the final overthrow of the Marian party. His first extant speech was delivered in 81, when he was 26 years of age, on behalf of P. Quintius. Next year (80) he defended Sex. Roscius of Ameria, charged with parricide by Chrysogonus, a favourite freedman of Sulla. Shortly afterwards (79) Cicero went to Greece, ostensibly for the improvement of his health, which was very delicate, but perhaps because he dreaded the resentment of Sulla. He first went to Athens, where he remained 6 months, studying philosophy under Antiochus of Ascalon, and rhetoric under Demetrius Syrus; and here he made the acquaintance of Pomponius Atticus, who remained his firm friend to the close of his life. From Athens he passed over to Asia Minor, receiving instruction from the most celebrated rhetoricians in the Greek cities of Asia; and finally passed some time at Rhodes (78), where he once more placed himself under the care of Molo. After an absence of 2 years, Cicero returned to Rome (77), with his health firmly established and his oratorical powers greatly improved. He again came forward as an orator in the forum, and soon obtained the greatest distinction. His success in the forum paved for him the way to the high offices of state. In 75 he was quaestor in Sicily under Sex. Peducaeus, praetor of Lilybaeum, and discharged the duties of his office with an integrity and impartiality which secured for him the affections of the provincials. He returned to Rome in 74, and for the next 4 years was engaged in pleading causes In 70 he distinguished himself by the impeachment of VERRES, and in 69 he was curule aedile. In 66 he was praetor, and while holding this office he defended Cluentius in the speech still extant, and delivered his celebrated oration in favour of the Manilian law, which appointed Pompey to the command of the Mithridatic war. Two years afterwards he gained the great object of his ambition, and although a *novus homo* was elected consul with C. Antonius as a colleague. He entered upon the office on the 1st of January, 63. Hitherto Cicero had taken little part in the political struggles of his time. As far as he had interfered in public affairs, he had sided with the popular party, which had raised him to power; but he appears never to have had any real sympathy with that party; and as soon as he had gained the highest office in the state he deserted his former friends, and connected himself closely with the aristocracy. The consulship of Cicero was distinguished by the outbreak of the conspiracy of Catiline, which was suppressed and finally crushed by Cicero's prudence and energy. [CATILINA.] For this service

Cicero received the highest honours; he was addressed as "father of his country," and thanksgivings in his name were voted to the gods. But as soon as he had laid down the consulship, the friends of the conspirators, who had been condemned to death by the senate, and whose sentence had been carried into execution by Cicero, accused him loudly of having put Roman citizens to death illegally. Cicero had clearly been guilty of a violation of the fundamental principles of the Roman constitution, which declared, that no citizen could be put to death until sentenced by the whole body of the people assembled in the comitia. Cicero's enemies were not slow in availing themselves of this vulnerable point. The people, whose cause he had deserted, soon began to show unequivocal signs of resentment against him. Shortly afterwards (62) he mortally offended Clodius by bearing witness against him, when the latter was accused of a violation of the mysteries of the Bona Dea. Clodius vowed deadly vengeance against Cicero. To accomplish his purpose more securely, Clodius was adopted into a plebeian family, was then elected tribune of the plebs, and as tribune (58) brought forward a bill, interdicting from fire and water (i. e. banishing) any one who should be found to have put a Roman citizen to death untried. The triumvirs, Caesar, Pompey, and Crassus, left Cicero to his fate; and despairing of offering any successful opposition to the measure of Clodius, Cicero voluntarily retired from Rome before it was put to the vote, and crossed over to Greece. He took up his residence at Thessalonica in Macedonia. Here he gave way to unmanly despair; and his letters during this period are filled with groans, sobs, and tears. Meanwhile his friends at Rome had not deserted him; and, notwithstanding the vehement opposition of Clodius, they obtained his recall from banishment in the course of next year. In August, 57, Cicero landed at Brundisium, and in September he was again at Rome, where he was received with distinguished honour. Taught by experience Cicero would no longer join the senate in opposition to the triumvirs, and retired to a great extent from public life. In 52 he was compelled much against his will to go to the East as governor of Cilicia. Here he distinguished himself by his integrity and impartial administration of justice, but at the same time made himself ridiculous by the absurd vanity which led him to assume the title of imperator and to aspire to the honours of a triumph on account of his subduing some robber tribes in his province. He returned to Italy towards the end of 50, and arrived in the neighbourhood of Rome on the 4th of January 49, just as the civil war between Caesar and Pompey broke out. After long hesitating which side to join, he finally determined to throw in his lot with Pompey, and crossed over to Greece in June. After the battle of Pharsalia (48), Cicero abandoned the Pompeian party and returned to Brundisium, where he lived in the greatest anxiety for many months, dreading the vengeance of Caesar. But his fears were groundless: he was not only pardoned by Caesar, but, when the latter landed at Brundisium in September, 47, he greeted Cicero with the greatest kindness and respect, and allowed him to return to Rome. Cicero now retired into privacy, and during the next 3 or 4 years composed the greater part of his philosophical and rhetorical works. The murder of Caesar on the

15th of March, 44, again brought Cicero into public life. He put himself at the head of the republican party, and in his Philippic orations attacked M. Antony with unmeasured vehemence. But this proved his ruin. On the formation of the triumvirate between Octavian, Antony, and Lepidus (27th of November, 43), Cicero's name was in the list of the proscribed. Cicero was warned of his danger while at his Tusculan villa, and embarked at Antium, intending to escape by sea, but was driven by stress of weather to Circeii, from whence he coasted along to Formiae, where he landed at his villa. From Formiae his attendants carried him in a litter towards the shore, but were overtaken by the soldiers before they could reach the coast. They were ready to defend their master with their lives, but Cicero commanded them to desist, and stretching forward called upon his executioners to strike. They instantly cut off his head and hands, which were conveyed to Rome, and, by the orders of Antony, nailed to the Rostra. Cicero perished on the 7th of December, 43, and at the time of his death had nearly completed his 64th year. — By his first wife Terentia Cicero had 2 children, a daughter TULLIA, whose death in 45 caused him the greatest sorrow, and a son Marcus. [No. 7.] His wife Terentia, to whom he had been united for 30 years, he divorced in 46, in consequence, it would appear, of some disputes connected with pecuniary transactions ; and soon afterwards he married a young and wealthy maiden, PUBLILIA, his ward, but, as might have been anticipated, found little comfort in this new alliance, which was speedily dissolved. — As a statesman and a citizen Cicero cannot command our respect. He did good service to his country by the suppression of the conspiracy of Catiline ; but this was almost the only occasion on which he showed vigour and decision of character. His own letters condemn him. In them his inordinate vanity, pusillanimity, and political tergiversation, appear in the clearest colours. — It is as an author that Cicero deserves the highest praise. In his works the Latin language appears in the greatest perfection. They may be divided into the following subjects.—I. Rhetorical Works. 1. *Rhetoricorum s. De Inventione Rhetorica Libri II.* This appears to have been the earliest of Cicero's prose works. It was intended to exhibit in a systematic form all that was most valuable in the works of the Greek rhetoricians, but it was never completed. — 2. *De Partitione Oratoria Dialogus.* A catechism of Rhetoric, according to the method of the middle Academy, by way of question and answer, drawn up by Cicero for the instruction of his son Marcus, written in 46. — 3. *De Oratore ad Quintum Fratrem Libri III.* A systematic work on the art of Oratory, written in 55 at the request of his brother Quintus. This is the most perfect of Cicero's rhetorical works. Best edition by Ellendt, Regiomont 1840.—4. *Brutus s. De Claris Oratoribus.* It contains a critical history of Roman eloquence, from the earliest times down to Hortensius inclusive. Editions by Meyer, Halae, 1838, and by Ellendt, Regiomont. 1844. — 5. *Ad M. Brutum Orator,* in which Cicero gives his views of a faultless orator : written 45. Edited by Meyer, Lips. 1827. — 6. *De Optimo Genere Oratorum.* An introduction to Cicero's translation of the orations of Aeschines and Demosthenes in the case of Ctesiphon : the translation itself has been lost. — 7. *Topica ad C.*

Trebatium. An abstract of the Topics of Aristotle, illustrated by examples derived chiefly from Roman law instead of from Greek philosophy : it was written in July 44. — 8. *Rhetoricorum ad C. Herennium Libri IV.* The author of this work is uncertain, but it was certainly not written by Cicero. — II. Philosophical Works. I. POLITICAL PHILOSOPHY. — 1. *De Republica Libri VI.* A work on the best form of government and the duty of the citizen, in the form of a dialogue, founded on the Republic of Plato ; written in 54. This work disappeared in the 10th or 11th century of our aera with the exception of the episode of the Somnium Scipionis, which had been preserved by Macrobius ; but in 1822, Angelo Mai found among the Palimpsests in the Vatican a portion of the lost treasure. Thus the greater part of the 1st and 2nd books and a few fragments of the others were discovered. Editions by Mai, Rome, 1822, and by Creuzer and Moser, Frankf. 1826.— 2. *De Legibus Libri III.* A dialogue, founded on the Laws of Plato ; probably written 52. A portion of the 3 books is lost, and it originally consisted of a greater number. Edited by Moser and Creuzer, Frankf. 1824, and by Bake, Lugd. Bat. 1842. — II. PHILOSOPHY OF MORALS. 1. *De Officiis Libri III.* Written in 44 for the use of his son Marcus, at that time residing at Athens. The first 2 books were chiefly taken from Panaetius, and the 3rd book was founded upon the work of the Stoic Hecato ; but the illustrations are taken almost exclusively from Roman history and Roman literature. Edited by Beier, Lips. 1820—1821, 2 vols. — 2. *Cato Major s. De Senectute,* addressed to Atticus, and written at the beginning of 44 : it points out how the burden of old age may be most easily supported. — 3. *Laelius s. De Amicitia,* written after the preceding, to which it may be considered as forming a companion : also addressed to Atticus. — 4. *De Gloria Libri II.,* written 44, is now lost, though Petrarch possessed a MS. of the work. — 5. *De Consolatione s. De Luctu mi nuendo,* written 45, soon after the death of his daughter Tullia, is also lost. — III. SPECULATIVE PHILOSOPHY. 1. *Academicorum Libri II.,* a treatise upon the Academic philosophy, written 45 Edited by Goerenz, Lips. 1810, and Orelli, Turic. 1827. — 2. *De Finibus Bonorum et Malorum Libri V.* Dedicated to M. Brutus, in which are discussed the opinions of the Epicureans, Stoics, and Peripatetics, on the Supreme Good, that is, the *finis,* or end, towards which all our thoughts and actions are or ought to be directed. Written in 45. Edited by Otto, Lips. 1831, and by Madvig, Copenhagen, 1839. — 3. *Tusculanarum Disputationum Libri V.* This work, addressed to M. Brutus, is a series of discussions on various important points of practical philosophy supposed to have been held in the Tusculanum of Cicero. Written in 45. Edited by Kühner, Jenae, 1835, and by Moser, Hannov. 3 vols. 1836—1837. — 4. *Paradoxa,* 6 favourite Paradoxes of the Stoics explained in familiar language, written early in 46. — 5. *Hortensius s. De Philosophia,* a dialogue in praise of philosophy, of which fragments only are extant, written in 45. — 6. *Timaeus s. De Universo,* a translation of Plato's Timaeus, of which we possess a fragment. — IV. THEOLOGY. 1. *De Natura Deorum Libri III.* An account of the speculations of the Epicureans, the Stoics, and the Academicians, on the existence, attributes, and providence of a Divine Being; dedicated to M. Brutus, and written early in 44. Edited by Moser and Creuzer, Lips. 1818. — 2. *De Divinatione Libri II.*, a continuation of the preceding work. It presents the opinions of the different schools of philosophy upon the reality of the science of divination. Written in 44, after the death of Caesar. Edited by Creuzer, Kayser, and Moser, Frankf. 1828. — 3. *De Fato Liber Singularis*, only a fragment. — III. **Orations.** The following is a list of Cicero's extant speeches, with the date at which each was delivered. Some account of each oration is given separately with the biography of the person principally concerned. 1. Pro P. Quintio, B.C. 81.—2. Pro Sex. Roscio Amerino, 80. — 3. Pro Q. Roscio Comoedo, 76. — 4. Pro M. Tullio, 71. — 5. In Q. Caecilium, 70. — 6. In Verrem Actio I., 5th August, 70. — 7. In Verrem Actio II. Not delivered. — 8. Pro M. Fonteio, 69. — 9. Pro A. Caecina, 69, probably. — 10. Pro Lege Manilia, 66. — 11. Pro A. Cluentio Avito, 66. — 12. Pro C. Cornelio, 55. — 13. Oratio in Toga Candida, 64. — 14. De Lege Agraria, 3 orations, 63. — 15. Pro C. Rabirio, 63. — 16. In Catilinam, 4 orations, 63. — 17. Pro Murena, 63. — 18. Pro P. Cornelio Sulla, 62. — 19. Pro A. Licinio Archia, 61. — 20. Pro L. Valerio Flacco, 59. — 21. Post Reditum in Senatu, 5th Sept. 57. — 22. Post Reditum ad Quirites, 6th or 7th Sept. 57. — 23. Pro Domo sua ad Pontifices, 29th Sept. 57. — 24. De Haruspicum Responsis, 56. — 25. Pro P. Sextio, 56. — 26. In Vatinium, 56. — 27. Pro M. Caelio Rufo, 56. — 28. Pro L. Cornelio Balbo, 56. —29. De Provinciis Consularibus, 56.— 30. In L. Pisonem, 55. — 31. Pro Cn. Plancio, 55. — 32. Pro C. Rabirio Postumo, 54. — 33. Pro M. Aemilio Scauro, 54. — 34. Pro T. Annio Milone, 52. — 35. Pro M. Marcello, 47. — 36. Pro Q. Ligario, 46. — 37. Pro Rege Deiotaro, 45. — 38. Orationes Philippicae, 14 orations against M. Antonius, 44 and 43. — IV. **Epistles.** Cicero during the most important period of his life maintained a close correspondence with Atticus and with a wide circle of literary and political friends and connexions. We now have upwards of 800 letters, undoubtedly genuine, extending over a space of 26 years, and commonly arranged in the following manner: — 1. *Epistolarum ad Familiares s. Epistolarum ad Diversos Libri XVI*, a series of 426 epistles, commencing with a letter to Pompey, written in 62, and terminating with a letter to Cassius, July 43. They are not placed in chronological order, but those addressed to the same individuals, with their replies, where these exist, are grouped together without reference to the date of the rest. — 2. *Epistolarum ad T. Pomponium Atticum Libri XVI*, a series of 396 epistles addressed to Atticus, of which 11 were written in 68, 67, 65, and 62, the remainder after the end of 62, and the last in Nov. 44. They are for the most part in chronological order, although dislocations occur here and there. — 3. *Epistolarum ad Q. Fratrem Libri III*, a series of 29 epistles addressed to his brother, the first written in 59, the last in 54. — 4. We find in most editions *Epistolarum ad Brutum Liber*, a series of 18 epistles all written after the death of Caesar. To these are added 8 more, first published by Cratander. The genuineness of these 2 books is doubtful. — The most useful edition of Cicero's letters is by Schütz, 6 vols. 8vo., 1809—1812, in which they are ar-

ranged in chronological order. — Cicero also wrote a great number of other works on historical and miscellaneous works, all of which are lost. He composed several poems, most of them in his earlier years, but 2 at a later period, containing a history of his consulship, and an account of his exile and recall. A line in one of these poems contained the unlucky jingle so well known to us from Juvenal (x. 122), *O fortunatam natam me consule Romam.* —The best edition of the collected works of Cicero is by Orelli, Turic. 1826—1837, 9 vols. 8vo., in 13 parts. — 6. Q., brother of the orator, was born about 102, and was educated along with his brother. In 67 he was aedile, in 62 praetor, and for the next 3 years governed Asia as propraetor. He returned to Rome in 58, and warmly exerted himself to procure the recall of his brother from banishment. In 55 he went to Gaul as legatus to Caesar, whose approbation he gained by his military abilities and gallantry: he distinguished himself particularly by the resistance he offered to a vast host of Gauls, who had attacked his camp, when he was stationed for the winter with one legion in the country of the Nervii. In 51 he accompanied his brother as legate to Cilicia; and on the breaking out of the civil war in 49 he joined Pompey. After the battle of Pharsalia, he was pardoned by Caesar. He was proscribed by the triumvirs, and was put to death in 43. Quintus wrote several works, which are all lost, with the exception of an address to his brother, entitled *De Petitione Consulatus.* Quintus was married to Pomponia, sister of Atticus; but, from incompatibility of temper, their union was an unhappy one. — 7. **M.**, only son of the orator and his wife Terentia, was born 65. He accompanied his father to Cilicia, and served in Pompey's army in Greece, although he was then only 16 years of age. In 45 he was sent to Athens to pursue his studies, but there fell into irregular and extravagant habits. On the death of Caesar (44) he joined the republican party, served as military tribune under Brutus in Macedonia, and after the battle of Philippi (42) fled to Sex. Pompey in Sicily. When peace was concluded between the triumvirs and Pompey in 39, Cicero returned to Rome, was favourably received by Octavian, who at length assumed him as his colleague in the consulship. (B. C. 30, from 13th Sept.) By a singular coincidence, the despatch announcing the capture of the fleet of Antony, which was immediately followed by his death, was addressed to the new consul in his official capacity, and thus, says Plutarch, "the divine justice reserved the completion of Antony's punishment for the house of Cicero." — 8. Q., son of No. 6, and of Pomponia, sister of Atticus, was born 66 or 67, and perished with his father in the proscription, 43.

Cichyrus (Κίχυρος), called **Ephyra** ('Εφύρη) in Homer, a town of Thesprotia in Epirus, between the Acherusian lake and the sea.

Cicones (Κίκονες), a Thracian people on the Hebrus, and near the coast.

Cicynna (Κίκυννα: Κικυννεύς), a demus of Attica, belonging to the tribe Cecropis, and afterwards to the tribe Acamantis.

Cilicia (Κιλικία: Κίλιξ, fem. Κίλισσα), a district in the S. E. of Asia Minor, bordering to the E. on Syria, to the N. on Cappadocia and Lycaonia, to the N. W. and W. on Pisidia and Pamphylia. On all sides, except the W., it is enclosed by natural boundaries, namely, the Mediterranean on the S., M. Amanus on the E., and M. Taurus on the N. The W. part of Cilicia is intersected by the offshoots of the Taurus, while in its E. part the mountain chains enclose much larger tracts of level country: and hence arose the division of the country into C. Aspera (K. ἡ τραχεῖα, or τραχειῶτις), and C. Campestris (K. ἡ πεδιάς) ; the latter was also called Cilicia Propria (ἡ ἰδίως K.). Numerous rivers, among which are the PYRAMUS, SARUS, CYDNUS, CALYCADNUS, and smaller mountain streams, descend from the Taurus. The E. division, through which most of the larger rivers flow, was extremely fertile, and the narrower valleys of Cilicia Aspera contained some rich tracts of land ; the latter district was famed for its fine breed of horses. The first inhabitants of the country are supposed to have been of the Syrian race. The mythical story derived their name from Cilix, the son of Agenor, who started, with his brothers Cadmus and Phoenix, for Europe, but stopped short on the coast of Asia Minor, and peopled with his followers the plain of Cilicia. The country remained independent till the time of the Persian Empire, under which it formed a satrapy, but appears to have been still governed by its native princes. Alexander subdued it on his march into Upper Asia ; and, after the division of his empire, it formed a part of the kingdom of the Seleucidae : its plains were settled by Greeks, and the old inhabitants were for the most part driven back into the mountains of C. Aspera, where they remained virtually independent, practising robbery by land and piracy by sea, till Pompey drove them from the sea in his war against the pirates, and, having rescued the level country from the power of Tigranes, who had overrun it, he erected it into a Roman province, B. C. 67—66. The mountain country was not made a province till the reign of Vespasian. The people bore a low character among the Greeks and Romans. The Carians, Cappadocians, and Cilicians, were called the 3 bad K's.

Cilicīae Pylae or **Portae** (αἱ Πύλαι τῆς Κιλικίας : *Kolinboghas*), the chief pass between Cappadocia and Cilicia, through the Taurus, on the road from Tyana to Tarsus. This was the way by which Alexander entered Cilicia.

Cilicīum Mare (ἡ Κιλικία Θάλασσα), the N. E. portion of the Mediterranean, between Cilicia and Cyprus, as far as the Gulf of Issus.

Cīlix (Κίλιξ), son of Agenor and Telephassa, was, with his brothers, Cadmus and Phoenix, sent out by their father in search of Europa, who had been carried off by Zeus. Cilix settled in the country called after him Cilicia.

Cilla (Κίλλα), a small town in the Troad, on the river Cilleus, at the foot of M. Cillaeus, in the range of Gargarus, celebrated for its temple of Apollo surnamed Cillaeus. Its foundation was ascribed to Pelops.

Cilnii, a powerful family in the Etruscan town of Arretium, were driven out of their native town in B. C. 301, but were restored by the Romans. The Cilnii were nobles or Lucumones in their state, and some of them in ancient times may have held even the kingly dignity. (Comp. Hor. *Carm.* i. 1.) The name has been rendered chiefly memorable by C. Cilnius Maecenas. [MAECENAS.]

Cimber, C. Annius, had obtained the praetorship from Caesar, and was one of Antony's sup-

porters, B. C. 43, on which account he is attacked by Cicero. He was charged with having killed his brother, whence Cicero calls him ironically *Philadelphus.*

Cimber, L. Tillius (not Tullius), a friend of Caesar, who gave him the province of Bithynia, but subsequently one of Caesar's murderers, B. C. 44. On the fatal day, Cimber was foremost in the ranks, under pretence of presenting a petition to Caesar praying for his brother's recall from exile. After the assassination, Cimber went to his province and raised a fleet, with which he rendered service to Cassius and Brutus.

Cimbri, a Celtic people, probably of the same race as the Cymry. [CELTAE.] They appear to have inhabited the peninsula, which was called after them **Chersonesus Cimbrica** (*Jutland*), though the greatest uncertainty prevailed among the ancients respecting their original abode. In conjunction with the Teutoni and Ambrones, they migrated S., with their wives and children, towards the close of the 2nd century B. C. ; and the whole host is said to have contained 300,000 fighting men. They defeated several Roman armies, and caused the greatest alarm at Rome. In B. C. 113 they defeated the consul Papirius Carbo, near Noreia, and then crossed over into Gaul, which they ravaged in all directions. In 109 they defeated the consul Junius Silanus, in 107 the consul Cassius Longinus, who fell in the battle, and in 105 they gained their most brilliant victory near the Rhone over the united armies of the consul Cn. Mallius and the proconsul Servilius Caepio. Instead of crossing the Alps, the Cimbri, fortunately for Rome, marched into Spain, where they remained 2 or 3 years. The Romans meantime had been making preparations to resist their formidable foes, and had placed their troops under the command of Marius. The barbarians returned to Gaul in 102. In that year the Teutoni were defeated and cut to pieces by Marius, near Aquae Sextiae (*Aix*) in Gaul ; and next year (101) the Cimbri and their allies were likewise destroyed by Marius and Catulus, in the decisive battle of the Campi Raudii, near Verona, in the N. of Italy. In the time of Augustus, the Cimbri, who were then a people of no importance, sent an embassy to the emperor.

Ciminus or **Ciminius Mons** (*Monte Cimino*, also *M. Fogliano*), a range of mountains in Etruria, thickly covered with wood (Saltus Ciminius, Silva Ciminia), near a lake of the same name, N. W. of Tarquinii between the Lacus Vulsiniensis and Soracte.

Cimmĕrii (Κιμμέριοι), the name of a mythical and of a historical people. The mythical Cimmerii, mentioned by Homer, dwelt in the furthest W. on the ocean, enveloped in constant mists and darkness. Later writers sought to localise them, and accordingly placed them either in Italy near the lake Avernus, or in Spain, or in the Tauric Chersonesus. — The historical Cimmerii dwelt on the Palus Maeotis (*Sea of Azov*), in the Tauric Chersonesus, and in Asiatic Sarmatia. Driven from their abodes by the Scythians, they passed into Asia Minor on the N. E., and penetrated W. as far as Aeolis and Ionia. They took Sardis B. C. 635 in the reign of Ardys, king of Lydia, but they were expelled from Asia by Alyattes, the grandson of Ardys.

Cimmĕrius Bospŏrus. [BOSPORUS.]

Cimōlis (Κίμωλις : *Cimoli* or *Argentiera*), an

island in the Aegaean sea, one of the Cyclades, between Siphnos and Melos, celebrated for its fine white earth, used by fullers for cleaning cloths.

Cīmon (Κίμων). 1. Son of Stesagoras, and father of Miltiades, victor at Marathon, gained 3 Olympic victories with his four-horse chariot, and after his 3rd victory was secretly murdered by order of the sons of Pisistratus. — 2. Grandson of the preceding, and son of the great Miltiades. On the death of his father (B. C. 489), he was imprisoned because he was unable to pay his fine of 50 talents, which was eventually paid by Callias on his marriage with Elpinice, Cimon's sister. Cimon first distinguished himself on the invasion of Greece by Xerxes (480), and after the battle of Plataea was brought forward by Aristides. He frequently commanded the Athenian fleet in their aggressive war against the Persians. His most brilliant success was in 466, when he defeated a large Persian fleet, and on the same day landed and routed their land forces also on the river Eurymedon in Pamphylia. The death of Aristides and the banishment of Themistocles left Cimon without a rival at Athens for some years. But his influence gradually declined as that of Pericles increased. In 461 Cimon marched at the head of some Athenian troops to the assistance of the Spartans, who were hard pressed by their revolted subjects. The Athenians were deeply mortified by the insulting manner in which their offers of assistance were declined, and were enraged with Cimon who had exposed them to this insult. His enemies in consequence succeeded in obtaining his ostracism this year. He was subsequently recalled, in what year is uncertain, and through his intervention a 5 year's truce was made between Athens and Sparta, 450. In 449 the war was renewed with Persia, Cimon received the command, and with 200 ships sailed to Cyprus; here, while besieging Citium, illness or the effects of a wound carried him off. — Cimon was of a cheerful convivial temper; frank and affable in his manners. Having obtained a great fortune by his share of the Persian spoils, he displayed unbounded liberality. His orchards and gardens were thrown open; his fellow demesmen were free daily to his table, and his public bounty verged on ostentation. With the treasure he brought from Asia the S. wall of the citadel was built, and at his own private charge the foundation of the long walls to the Piraeus was laid down. — 3. Of Cleonae, a painter of great renown, flourished about B. C. 460, and appears to have been the first painter of perspective.

Cinādon (Κινάδον), the chief of a conspiracy against the Spartan peers (ὅμοιοι) in the first year of Agesilaus II. (B. C. 398—397.) The plot was discovered, and Cinadon and the other conspirators were put to death.

Cinaethon (Κιναίθων), of Lacedaemon, one o the most fertile of the Cyclic poets, flourished B. C. 765.

Cinăra or Cinărus (Zinara), a small island in the Aegaean sea, E. of Naxos, celebrated for its artichokes (κινάρα).

Cincinnătus, L. Quintius, a favourite hero of the old Roman republic, and a model of old Roman frugality and integrity. He lived on his farm, cultivating the land with his own hand. In B. C. 460 he was appointed consul suffectus in the room of P. Valerius. In 458 he was called from the plough to the dictatorship, in order to deliver the Roman consul and army from the perilous position in which they had been placed by the Aequians. He saved the Roman army, defeated the enemy, and, after holding the dictatorship only 16 days, returned to his farm. In 439, at the age of 80, he was a 2nd time appointed dictator to oppose the alleged machinations of Sp. Maelius. — Several of the descendants of Cincinnatus held the consulship and consular tribunate, but none of them is of sufficient importance to require a separate notice.

Cincius Alimentus. [ALIMENTUS.]

Cineas (Κινέας), a Thessalian, the friend and minister of Pyrrhus, king of Epirus. He was the most eloquent man of his day, and reminded his hearers of Demosthenes, whom he heard speak in his youth. Pyrrhus prized his persuasive powers so highly, that "the words of Cineas (he was wont to say) had won him more cities than his own arms." The most famous passage in his life is his embassy to Rome, with proposals for peace from Pyrrhus, after the battle of Heraclea (B. C. 280). Cineas spared no arts to gain favour. Thanks to his wonderful memory, on the day after his arrival he was able (we are told) to address all the senators and knights by name. The senate, however, rejected his proposals mainly through the dying eloquence of old App. Claudius Caecus. The ambassador returned and told the king that there was no people like that people, — their city was a temple, their senate an assembly of kings. Two years after (278), when Pyrrhus was about to cross over into Sicily, Cineas was again sent to negotiate peace. He appears to have died in Sicily shortly afterwards.

Cinesias (Κινησίας), a dithyrambic poet of Athens, of no merit, ridiculed by Aristophanes and other comic poets. But he had his revenge; for he succeeded in procuring the abolition of the Choragia, as far as regarded comedy, about B. C. 390.

Cinga (Cinca), a river in Hispania Tarraconensis, falls with the Sicoris into the Iberus.

Cingetorix, a Gaul, one of the first men in the city of the Treviri (Trèves, Trier), attached himself to the Romans, though son-in-law to Indutiomarus, the head of the independent party. When this leader had been put to death by Caesar, he became chief of his native city.

Cingŭlum (Cingulanus: Cingpio), a town in Picenum on a rock, built by Labienus, shortly before the breaking out of the civil war, B. C. 49.

Cinna, Cornēlĭus. 1. L., the famous leader of the popular party during the absence of Sulla in the East. (B. C. 87—84.) In 87 Sulla allowed Cinna to be elected consul with Cn. Octavius, on condition of his taking an oath not to alter the constitution as then existing. But as soon as Sulla had left Italy, he began his endeavour to overpower the senate, and to recall Marius and his party. He was, however, defeated by his colleague Octavius in the forum, was obliged to fly the city, and was deposed by the senate from the consulate. But he soon returned; with the assistance of Marius, who came back to Italy, he collected a powerful army, and laid siege to Rome. The capture of the city, and the massacre of Sulla's friends which followed, more properly belong to the life of MARIUS. For the next 3 years (86, 85, 84) Cinna was consul. In 84 Sulla prepared to return from Greece; and Cinna was slain by his own troops, when he ordered them to cross over from

Italy to Greece, where he intended to encounter Sulla.—2. L., son of No. 1., joined M. Lepidus in his attempt to overthrow the constitution of Sulla 78 ; and on the defeat and death of Lepidus in Sardinia, he went with M. Perperna to join Sertorius in Spain. Caesar procured his recall from exile. He was made praetor by Caesar in 44 ; but was notwithstanding one of the enemies of the dictator. Though he would not join the conspirators, he approved of their act ; and so great was the rage of the mob against him, that they nearly murdered him. See below CINNA, HELVIUS.

Cinna, C. Helvius, a poet of considerable renown, the friend of Catullus. In B. C. 44 he was tribune of the plebs, when he was murdered by the mob, who mistook him for his namesake Cornelius Cinna, though he was at the time walking in Caesar's funeral procession. His principal work was an epic poem entitled *Smyrna.*

Cinnamus, Joannes ('Ιωάννης Κίνναμος), one of the most distinguished Byzantine historians, lived under the emperor Manuel Comnenus (who reigned A. D. 1143—1180), and wrote the history of this emperor and of his father Calo-Joannes, in 6 books, which have come down to us. Edited by Du Cange, Paris, 1670, fol., and by Meineke, Bonn, 186, 8vo.

Cinyps or Cinyphus (Κίνυψ, Κίνυφος: *Wad-Khakan* or *Kinifo*), a small river on the N. coast of Africa, between the Syrtes, forming the E. boundary of the proper territory of the African Tripolis. The district about it was called by the same name, and was famous for its fine-haired goats.

Cinyras (Κινύρας), son of Apollo, king of Cyprus, and priest of the Paphian Aphrodite, which latter office remained hereditary in his family, the Cinyradae. He was married to Metharne, the daughter of the Cyprian king Pygmalion, by whom he had several children, and among them was Adonis. According to some traditions, he unwittingly begot Adonis by his own daughter Smyrna, and killed himself on discovering the crime he had committed. According to other traditions, he had promised to assist Agamemnon ; but as he did not keep his word, he was cursed by Agamemnon, and perished in a contest with Apollo.

Cipus or Cippus, Genucius, a Roman praetor, on whose head it is said that horns suddenly grew, as he was going out of the gates of the city, and, as the haruspices declared that if he returned to the city he would be king, he imposed voluntary exile upon himself.

Circe (Κίρκη), a mythical sorceress, daughter of Helios (the Sun) by the Oceanid Perse, and sister of Aeëtes, lived in the island of Aeaea. Ulysses tarried a whole year with her, after she had changed several of his companions into pigs. By Ulysses she became the mother of Agrius and Telegonus. The Latin poets relate that she metamorphosed Scylla, and Picus king of the Ausonians.

Circeii (Circeiensis : *Circello,* and the Ru. *Citta Vecchia*), an ancient town of Latium on the promontory Circeium, founded by Tarquinius Superbus, never became a place of importance, in consequence of its proximity to the unhealthy Pontine marshes. The oysters caught off Circeii were celebrated. (Hor. *Sat.* ii. 4. 33 ; Juv. iv. 140.) Some writers suppose Circe to have resided on this promontory, and that hence it derived its name.

Circesium (Κιρκήσιον: *Kerkesiah*), a city of Mesopotamia, on the E. bank of the Euphrates, at the mouth of the Aborrhas: the extreme border fortress of the Roman Empire.

Circus. [ROMA.]

Cirphis (Κίρφις), a town in Phocis, on a mountain of the same name, which is separated by a valley from Parnassus.

Cirrha. [CRISSA.]

Cirta, aft. Constantina (*Constantineh,* Ru.), a city of the Massylii in Numidia, 50 Roman miles from the sea ; the capital of Syphax, and of Masinissa and his successors. Its position on a height, surrounded by the river Ampsagas, made it almost impregnable, as the Romans found in the Jugurthine, and the French in the Algerine, wars. It was restored by Constantine the Great, in honour of whom it received its later name.

Cisseus (Κισσεύς), a king in Thrace, and father of Theano, or, according to others, of Hecuba, who is hence called Cisseïs (Κισσηΐς).

Cissia (Κισσία), a very fertile district of Susiana, on the Choaspes. The inhabitants (Κίσσιοι) were a wild free people, resembling the Persians in their manners.

Cissus (Κισσός), a town in Macedonia on a mountain of the same name, S. of Thessalonica, to which latter place its inhabitants were transplanted by Cassander.

Cisthene (Κισθήνη). 1. A town on the coast of Mysia, on the promontory of Pyrrha, on the Gulf of Adramyttium.—2. (*Castel-Roffo*), an island and town on the coast of Lycia.—3. In the mythical geography of Aeschylus (*Prom.* 799) the "plains of Cisthene" are made the abode of the Gorgons.

Cithaeron (Κιθαιρών ; *Cithaeron,* and its highest summit *Elatia*), a lofty range of mountains, separated Boeotia from Megaris and Attica. It was covered with wood, abounded in game, and was the scene of several celebrated legends in mythology. It was said to have derived its name from Cithaeron, a mythical king of Boeotia. Its highest summit was sacred to the Cithaeronian Zeus, and here was celebrated the festival called *Daedala.* (*Dict. of Ant. s. v.*)

Citharista, a sea-port town (*Ceireste*), and a promontory (*C. d'Aigle*) in Gallia Narbonensis, near Massilia.

Citium (Κίτιον: Κιτιεύς). 1. (Nr. *Larneca,* Ru.), one of the 9 chief towns of Cyprus, with a harbour and salt-works, 200 stadia from Salamis, near the mouth of the Tetius: here Cimon, the celebrated Athenian, died, and Zeno, the founder of the Stoic school, was born.—2. A town in Macedonia, on a mountain Citius, N. W. of Beroea.

Cius (Κίος : Κίος or Κείος, Cianus : *Ghio,* also *Ghemlic* and *Kemlik*), an ancient city in Bithynia, on a bay of the Propontis called Cianus Sinus, was colonized by the Milesians, and became a place of much commercial importance. It joined the Aetolian league, and was destroyed by Philip III., king of Macedonia ; but was rebuilt by Prusias, king of Bithynia, from whom it was called Prusias.

Civilis, Claudius, sometimes called Julius, the leader of the Batavi in their revolt from Rome, A. D. 69—70. He was of the Batavian royal race, and, like Hannibal and Sertorius, had lost an eye. His brother Julius Paulus was put to death on a false charge of treason by Fonteius Capito (A. D. 67 or 68), who sent Civilis in chains to Nero at Rome, where he was heard and acquitted by Galba.

View of Corinth and the Acrocorinthus. Page 190.

View of Delphi and Mount Parnassus. Page 211.

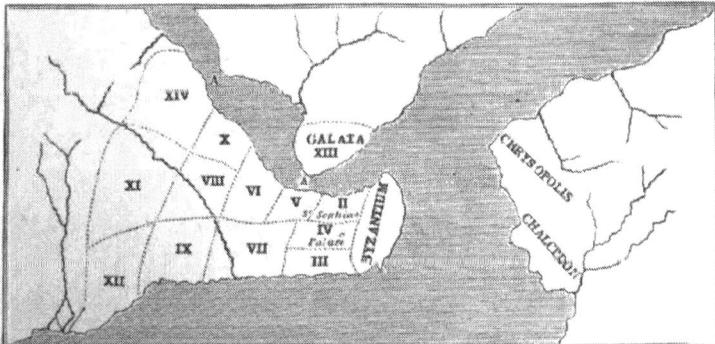

Plan of Constantinople. (A, Chrysoceras, Golden Horn.) The Roman numerals indicate the 14 regions into which the city was divided. Page 187.

[To face p. 176.

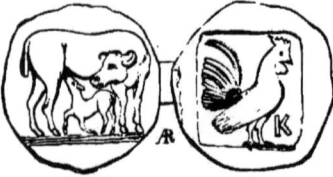

Carystus in Euboea. Page 151.

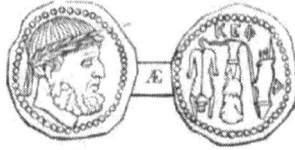

Cephaloedium in Sicily. Page 163.

Cassope in Thesprotia. Page 154.

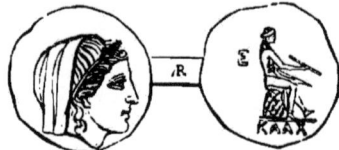

Chalcedon. Page 165.

Catana in Sicily. Page 155.

Chalcidice in Macedonia. Page 165.

Caulon or Caulonia in Bruttium. Page 159.

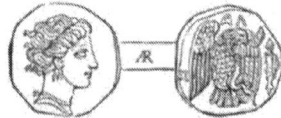

Chalcis in Euboea. Page 165.

Celenderis in Cilicia. Page 160.

Chersonesus in Crete. Page 168.

Centuripae in Sicily. Page 162.

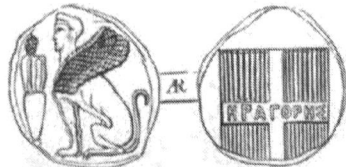

Chios. Page 165.

To face p. 177.]

He was afterwards prefect of a cohort, but under Vitellius he became an object of suspicion to the army, and with difficulty escaped with his life. He vowed vengeance. His countrymen, who were shamefully treated by the officers of Vitellius, were easily induced to revolt, and they were joined by the Canninefates and Frisii. He took up arms under pretence of supporting the cause of Vespasian, and defeated in succession the generals of Vitellius in Gaul and Germany, but he continued in open revolt even after the death of Vitellius. In 70 Civilis gained fresh victories over the Romans, but was at length defeated in the course of the year by Petilius Cerealis, who had been sent into Germany with an immense army. Peace was concluded with the Batavi on terms favourable to the latter, but we do not know what became of Civilis.

Cizara (Κίζαρα), a mountain fortress in the district of Phazemonitis in Pontus ; once a royal residence, but destroyed before Strabo's time.

Cladaus (Κλάδαος or Κλάδεος), a river in Elis, flows into the Alpheus at Olympia.

Clampetia, called by the Greeks Lampetia (Λαμπετία, Λαμπέτεια), a town of Bruttium, on the W. coast : in ruins in Pliny's time.

Clanis. 1. (Chiano), a river of Etruria, rises S. of Arretium, forms 2 small lakes near Clusium, W. of lake Trasimenus, and flows into the Tiber E. of Vulsinii. — 2. The more ancient name of the Liris. — 3. (Glan in Steiermark), a river in the Noric Alps.

Clanius. [LITERNUS.]

Clarus (ἡ Κλάρος), a small town on the Ionian coast, near Colophon, with a celebrated temple and oracle of Apollo, surnamed Clarius.

Clarus, Sex. Erucius, a friend of the younger Pliny, fought under Trajan in the E., and took Seleucia, A. D. 115. — His son Sextus was a patron of literature, and was consul under Antoninus Pius, A. D. 146.

Classicus, Julius, a Trevir, was prefect of an ala of the Treviri in the Roman army under Vitellius, A. D. 69, but afterwards joined Civilis in his rebellion against the Romans. [CIVILIS.]

Clastidium (Casteggio or Schiateggio), a fortified town of the Ananes in Gallia Cispadana, not far from the Po, on the road from Dertona to Placentia.

Claterna, a fortified town in Gallia Cispadana, not far from Bononia ; its name is retained in the small river Quaderna.

Claudia. 1. Quinta, a Roman matron, not a Vestal Virgin, as is frequently stated. When the vessel conveying the image of Cybele from Pessinus to Rome, had stuck fast in a shallow at the mouth of the Tiber, the soothsayers announced that only a chaste woman could move it. Claudia, who had been accused of incontinency, took hold of the rope, and the vessel forthwith followed her, B. C. 204. — 2. Or Clodia, eldest of the 3 sisters of P. Clodius Pulcher, the enemy of Cicero, married Q. Marcius Rex. — 3. Or Clodia, second sister of P. Clodius, married Q. Metellus Celer, but became infamous for her debaucheries, and was suspected of having poisoned her husband. Cicero in his letters frequently calls her Βοῶπις. — 4. Or Clodia, youngest sister of P. Clodius, married L. Lucullus, to whom she proved unfaithful. All 3 sisters are said to have had incestuous intercourse with their brother Publius.

Claudia Gens, patrician and plebeian. The patrician Claudii were of Sabine origin and came to Rome in B. C. 504, when they were received among the patricians. [CLAUDIUS, No. 1.] They were noted for their pride and haughtiness, their disdain for the laws, and their hatred of the plebeians. They bore various surnames, which are given under CLAUDIUS, with the exception of those with the cognomen NERO, who are better known under the latter name. — The plebeian Claudii were divided into several families, of which the most celebrated was that of MARCELLUS.

Claudianus, Claudius, the last of the Latin classic poets, flourished under Theodosius and his sons Arcadius and Honorius. He was a native of Alexandria and removed to Rome, where we find him in A. D. 395. He enjoyed the patronage of the all-powerful Stilicho, by whom he was raised to offices of honour and emolument. A statue was erected to his honour in the Forum of Trajan by Arcadius and Honorius, the inscription on which was discovered at Rome in the 15th century. He also enjoyed the patronage of the empress Serena, through whose interposition he gained a wealthy wife. The last historical allusion in his writings belongs to 404 ; whence it is supposed that he may have been involved in the misfortunes of Stilicho, who was put to death 408. He was a heathen. His extant works are : — 1. The 3 panegyrics on the 3rd, 4th, and 6th consulships of Honorius. 2. A poem on the nuptials of Honorius and Maria. 3. Four short Fescennine lays on the same subject. 4. A panegyric on the consulship of Probinus and Olybrius. 5. The praises of Stilicho, in 2 books, and a panegyric on his consulship, in 1 book. 6. The praises of Serena, the wife of Stilicho. 7. A panegyric on the consulship of Flavius Mallius Theodorus. 8. The Epithalamium of Palladius and Celerina. 9. An invective against Rufinus, in 2 books. 10. An invective against Eutropius, in 2 books. 11. De Bello Gildonico, the first book of an historical poem on the war in Africa against Gildo. 12. De Bello Getico, an historical poem on the successful campaign of Stilicho against Alaric and the Goths, concluding with the battle of Pollentia. 13. Raptus Proserpinae, 3 books of an unfinished epic on the rape of Proserpine. 14. Gigantomachia, a fragment extending to 128 lines only. 15. 5 short epistles. 16. Eidyllia, a collection of 7 poems chiefly on subjects connected with natural history. 17. Epigrammata, a collection of short occasional pieces. — The Christian hymns found among his poems in most editions are certainly spurious. — The poems of Claudian are distinguished by purity of language, and real poetical genius. The best edition is by Burmann, Amst. 1760.

Claudiopolis (Κλαυδιόπολις), the name of some cities called after the emperor Claudius, the chief of which were : 1. In Bithynia [BITHYNIUM]. 2. A colony in the district of Cataonia, in Cappadocia.

Claudius, patrician. See CLAUDIA GENS. — 1. App. Claudius Sabinus Regillensis, a Sabine of the town of Regillum or Regilli, who in his own country bore the name of Attus Clausus, being the advocate of peace with the Romans, when hostilities broke out between the two nations, withdrew with a large train of followers to Rome, B. C. 504. He was received into the ranks of the patricians, and lands beyond the Anio were assigned to his followers, who were formed into a new tribe called the Claudian. He exhibited the characteristics which marked his descendants, and showed the most bitter

N

hatred towards the plebeians. He was consul 495, and his conduct towards the plebeians led to their secession to the Mons Sacer 494.— **2. App. Cl. Sab. Regill.**, son of No. 1, consul 471, treated the soldiers whom he commanded with such severity, that his troops deserted him. Next year he was impeached by 2 of the tribunes, but, according to the common story, he died or killed himself before the trial.—**3. C. Cl. Sab. Regill.**, brother of No. 2, consul 460, when App. Herdonius seized the Capitol. Though a staunch supporter of the patricians, he warned the decemvir Appius against an immoderate use of his power. His remonstrances being of no avail, he withdrew to Regillum, but returned to defend Appius when impeached.—**4. App. Cl. Crassus Regill. Sab.**, the decemvir, commonly considered son of No. 2, but more probably the same person. He was consul 451, and on the appointment of the decemvirs in that year, he became one of them, and was reappointed the following year. His real character now betrayed itself in the most tyrannous conduct towards the plebeians, till his attempt against Virginia led to the overthrow of the decemvirate. App. was impeached by Virginius, but did not live to abide his trial. He either killed himself, or was put to death in prison by order of the tribunes.—**5. App. Claudius Caecus**, became blind before his old age. In his censorship (312), to which he was elected without having been consul previously, he built the Appian aqueduct, and commenced the Appian road, which was continued to Capua. He retained the censorship 4 years in opposition to the law which limited the length of the office to 18 months. He was twice consul in 307 and 296 ; and in the latter year he fought against the Samnites and Etruscans. In his old age, Appius by his eloquent speech induced the senate to reject the terms of peace which Cineas had proposed on behalf of Pyrrhus. Appius was the earliest Roman writer in prose and verse whose name has come down to us. He was the author of a poem known to Cicero through the Greek, and he also wrote a legal treatise, *De Usurpationibus.* He left 4 sons and 5 daughters.— **6. App. Cl. Caudex**, brother of No. 5, derived his surname from his attention to naval affairs. He was consul 264, and conducted the war against the Carthaginians in Sicily.— **7. P. Cl. Pulcher**, son of No. 5, consul 249, attacked the Carthaginian fleet in the harbour of Drepana, in defiance of the auguries, and was defeated, with the loss of almost all his forces. He was recalled and commanded to appoint a dictator, and thereupon named M. Claudius Glycias or Glicia, the son of a freedman, but the nomination was immediately superseded. He was impeached and condemned. —**8. C. Cl. Centho** or **Cento**, son of No. 5, consul 240, and dictator 213.— **9. Tib. Cl. Nero**, son of No. 5. An account of his descendants is given under NERO.— **10. App. Cl. Pulcher**, son of No. 7, aedile 217, fought at Cannae 216, and was praetor 215, when he was sent into Sicily. He was consul 212, and died 211 of a wound which he received in a battle with Hannibal before Capua. — **11. App. Cl. Pulcher**, son of No. 10, served in Greece for some years under Flamininus, Baebius, and Glabrio (197—191). He was praetor 187 and consul 185, when he gained some advantages over the Ingaunian Ligurians. He was sent as ambassador to Greece 184 and 176.— **12. P. Cl. Pulcher**, brother of No. 11, curule aedile 189, praetor

188, and consul 184. — **13. C. Cl. Pulcher**, brother of Nos. 11 and 12, praetor 180 and consul 177, when he defeated the Istrians and Ligurians. He was censor 160 with Ti. Sempronius Gracchus. He died 167.—**14. App. Cl. Cento**, aedile 178 and praetor 175, when he fought with success against the Celtiberi in Spain. He afterwards served in Thessaly (173), Macedonia (172), and Illyricum (170).—**15. App. Cl. Pulcher**, son of No. 11, consul 143, defeated the Salassi, an Alpine tribe. On his return a triumph was refused him; and when one of the tribunes attempted to drag him from his car, his daughter Claudia, one of the Vestal Virgins, walked by his side up to the capitol. He was censor 136. He gave one of his daughters in marriage to Tib. Gracchus, and in 133 with Tib. and C. Gracchus was appointed triumvir for the division of the lands. He died shortly after Tib. Gracchus. — **16. C. Claudius Pulcher**, curule aedile 99, praetor in Sicily 95, consul in 92. —**17. App. Cl. Pulcher**, consul 79, and afterwards governor of Macedonia. — **18. App. Cl. Pulcher**, praetor 89, belonged to Sulla's party, and perished in the great battle before Rome 82. — **19. App. Cl. Pulcher**, eldest son of No. 18. In 70 he served in Asia under his brother-in-law, Lucullus ; in 57 he was praetor, and though he did not openly oppose Cicero's recall from banishment, he tacitly abetted the proceedings of his brother Publius. In 56 he was propraetor in Sardinia ; and in 54 was consul with L. Domitius Ahenobarbus, when a reconciliation was brought about between him and Cicero, through the intervention of Pompey. In 53 he went as proconsul to Cilicia, which he governed with tyranny and rapacity. In 51 he was succeeded in the government by Cicero, whose appointment Appius received with displeasure. On his return to Rome he was impeached by Dolabella, but was acquitted. In 50 he was censor with L. Piso, and expelled several of Caesar's friends from the senate. On the breaking out of the civil war, 49, he fled with Pompey from Italy, and died in Greece before the battle of Pharsalia. He was an augur, and wrote a work on the augural discipline, which he dedicated to Cicero. He was also distinguished for his legal and antiquarian knowledge. — **20. C. Cl. Pulcher**, second son of No. 18, was a legatus of Caesar, 58, praetor 56, and propraetor in Asia 55. On his return he was accused of extortion by M. Servilius, who was bribed to drop the prosecution. He died shortly afterwards.— **21. P. Cl. Pulcher**, usually called **Clodius** and not Claudius, the youngest son of No. 18, the notorious enemy of Cicero, and one of the most profligate characters of a profligate age. In 70 he served under his brother-in-law, L. Lucullus in Asia ; but displeased at not being treated by Lucullus with the distinction he had expected, he encouraged the soldiers to mutiny. He then betook himself to his other brother-in-law, Q. Marcius Rex, proconsul in Cilicia, and was entrusted by him with the command of the fleet. He fell into the hands of the pirates, who however dismissed him without ransom, through fear of Pompey. He next went to Antioch, and joined the Syrians in making war on the Arabians. On his return to Rome in 65 he impeached Catiline for extortion in his government of Africa, but was bribed by Catiline to let him escape. In 64 he accompanied the propraetor L. Murena to Gallia Transalpina, where he resorted to the most nefarious methods of procuring money.

In 62 he profaned the mysteries of the Bona Dea, which were celebrated by the Roman matrons in the house of Caesar, who was then praetor, by entering the house disguised as a female musician, in order to meet Pompeia, Caesar's wife, with whom he had an intrigue. He was discovered, and next year, 61, when quaestor, was brought to trial, but obtained an acquittal by bribing the judges. He had attempted to prove an alibi, but Cicero's evidence shewed that Clodius was with him in Rome only 3 hours before he pretended to have been at Interamna. Cicero attacked Clodius in the senate with great vehemence. In order to revenge himself upon Cicero, Clodius was adopted into a plebeian family that he might obtain the formidable power of a tribune of the plebs. He was tribune 58, and, supported by the triumvirs Caesar, Pompey, and Crassus, drove Cicero into exile ; but notwithstanding all his efforts he was unable to prevent the recall of Cicero in the following year. [Cicero.] In 56 Clodius was aedile and attempted to bring his enemy Milo to trial. Each had a large gang of gladiators in his pay, and frequent fights took place in the streets of Rome between the 2 parties. In 53, when Clodius was a candidate for the praetorship, and Milo for the consulship, the contests between them became more violent and desperate than ever. At length, on the 20th of January, 52, Clodius and Milo met, apparently by accident, on the Appian road near Bovillae. An affray ensued between their followers, in which Clodius was murdered. The mob was infuriated at the death of their favourite ; and such tumults followed at the burial of Clodius, that Pompey was appointed sole consul in order to restore order to the state. For the proceedings which followed see Milo. The second wife of Clodius was the notorious Fulvia. — 22. App. Cl. Pulcher, the elder son of No. 20, was one of the accusers of Milo on the death of P. Clodius, 52. — 23. App. Cl. Pulcher, brother of No. 21, joined his brother in prosecuting Milo. As the two brothers both bore the praenomen Appius, it is probable that one of them was adopted by their uncle Appius. [No. 19].— 24. Sex. Clodius, probably a descendant of a freedman of the Claudia gens, was a man of low condition, and the chief instrument of P. Clodius in all his acts of violence. On the death of the latter in 52, he urged on the people to revenge the death of his leader. For his acts of violence on this occasion, he was brought to trial, was condemned, and after remaining in exile 8 years, was restored in 44 by M. Antonius.

Claudius I., Roman emperor A. D. 41—54. His full name was Tib. Claudius Drusus Nero Germanicus. He was the younger son of Drusus, the brother of the emperor Tiberius, and of Antonia, and was born on August 1st, B. c. 10, at Lyons in Gaul. In youth he was weak and sickly, and was neglected and despised by his relatives. When he grew up he devoted the greater part of his time to literary pursuits, but was not allowed to take any part in public affairs. He had reached the age of 50, when he was suddenly raised by the soldiers to the imperial throne after the murder of Caligula. Claudius was not cruel, but the weakness of his character made him the slave of his wives and freedmen, and thus led him to consent to acts of tyranny which he would never have committed of his own accord. He was married 4 times. At the time of his accession he was married

to his 3rd wife, the notorious Valeria Messalina, who governed him for some years, together with the freedmen Narcissus, Pallas, and others. After the execution of Messalina, 48, a fate which she richly merited, Claudius was still more unfortunate in choosing for his wife his niece Agrippina. She prevailed upon him to set aside his own son, Britannicus, and to adopt her son, Nero, that she might secure the succession for the latter. Claudius soon after regretted this step, and was in consequence poisoned by Agrippina, 54. — Several public works of great utility were executed by Claudius. He built, for example, the famous Claudian aqueduct (Aqua Claudia), the port of Ostia, and the emissary by which the water of lake Fucinus was carried into the river Liris. In his reign the southern part of Britain was made a Roman province, and Claudius himself went to Britain in 43, where he remained, however, only a short time, leaving the conduct of the war to his generals. — Claudius wrote several historical works, all of which have perished. Of these one of the most important was a history of Etruria, in the composition of which he made use of genuine Etruscan sources.

Claudius II. (M. Aurelius Claudius, surnamed Gothicus), Roman emperor A. D. 268— 270, was descended from an obscure family in Dardania or Illyria, and by his military talents rose to distinction under Decius, Valerian, and Gallienus. He succeeded to the empire on the death of Gallienus (268), and soon after his accession defeated the Alemanni in the N. of Italy. Next year he gained a great victory over an immense host of Goths near Naissus in Dardania, and received in consequence the surname Gothicus. He died at Sirmium in 270, and was succeeded by Aurelian.

Clazomenae (αἱ Κλαζομεναί : Κλαζομένιος : Kelisman), an important city of Asia Minor, and a member of the Ionian Dodecapolis, lay on the N. coast of the Ionian peninsula, upon the gulf of Smyrna. The city was said to have been founded by the Colophonians under Paralus, on the site of the later town of Chytrium, but to have been removed further E., as a defence against the Persians, to a small island, which Alexander afterwards united to the mainland by a causeway. It was one of the weaker members of the Ionian league, and was chiefly peopled, not by Ionians, but by Cleonaeans and Phliasians. Under the Romans it was a free city. It had a considerable commerce, and was celebrated for its temple of Apollo, Artemis, and Cybele, and still more as the birthplace of Anaxagoras.

Cleander (Κλέανδρος). 1. Tyrant of Gela, reigned 7 years, and was murdered B. c. 498. He was succeeded by his brother Hippocrates, one of whose sons was also called Cleander. The latter was deposed by Gelon when he seized the government, 491. — 2. A Lacedaemonian, harmost at Byzantium 400, when the Cyrean Greeks returned from Asia. — 3. One of Alexander's officers, was put to death by Alexander in Carmania, 325, in consequence of his oppressive government in Media. — 4. A Phrygian slave, and subsequently the profligate favourite and minister of Commodus. In a popular tumult, occasioned by a scarcity of corn, he was torn to death by the mob.

Cleanthes (Κλεάνθης). 1. A Stoic, born at Assos in Troas about B. c. 300. He entered life as a boxer, and had only 4 drachmas of his own when he began to study philosophy. He first placed himself under Crates, and then under Zeno, whose disciple he continued for 19 years. In order to support himself, he worked all night at drawing water from gardens ; but as he spent the whole day in philosophical pursuits, and had no visible means of support, he was summoned before the Areopagus to account for his way of living. The judges were so delighted by the evidence of industry which he produced, that they voted him 10 minae, though Zeno would not permit him to accept them. He was naturally slow, but his iron industry overcame all difficulties ; and on the death of Zeno in 263, Cleanthes succeeded him in his school. He died about 220, at the age of 80, of voluntary starvation. A hymn of his to Zeus is still extant, and contains some striking sentiments. Edited by Sturz, 1785, and Mersdorf, Lips. 1835. — 2. An ancient painter of Corinth.

Cleärchus (Κλέαρχος). 1. A Spartan, distinguished himself in several important commands during the latter part of the Peloponnesian war, and at the close of it persuaded the Spartans to send him as general to Thrace, to protect the Greeks in that quarter against the Thracians. But having been recalled by the Ephors, and refusing to obey their orders, he was condemned to death. He thereupon crossed over to Cyrus, collected for him a large force of Greek mercenaries, and marched with him into Upper Asia, 401, in order to dethrone his brother Artaxerxes, being the only Greek who was aware of the prince's real object. After the battle of Cunaxa and the death of Cyrus, Clearchus and the other Greek generals were made prisoners by the treachery of Tissaphernes, and were put to death. — 2. A citizen of Heraclëa on the Euxine, obtained the tyranny of his native town, B. C. 365, by putting himself at the head of the popular party. He governed with cruelty, and was assassinated 353, after a reign of 12 years. He is said to have been a pupil both of Plato and of Isocrates. — 3. Of Soli, one of Aristotle's pupils, author of a number of works, none of which are extant, on a great variety of subjects. — 4. An Athenian poet of the new comedy, whose time is unknown.

Clëmens. 1. T. Flavïus, cousin of the emperor Domitian, by whom he was put to death. He appears to have been a Christian. — 2. **Romänus,** bishop of Rome at the end of the first century, probably the same as the Clement whom St. Paul mentions (Phil. iv. 3). He wrote 2 epistles in Greek to the Corinthian Church, of which the 1st and part of the 2nd are extant. The 2nd, however, is probably not genuine. The Recognitiones, which bear the name of Clement, were not written by him. The epistles are printed in the Patres Apostolici, of which the most convenient editions are by Jacobson, Oxford, 1838 ; and by Hefele, Tübingen, 1839. — 3. **Alexandrïnus,** so called from his long residence at Alexandria, was ardently devoted in early life to the study of philosophy, which had a great influence upon his views of Christianity. He embraced Christianity through the teaching of Pantaenus at Alexandria, was ordained presbyter about A. D. 190, and died about 220. Hence he flourished under the reigns of Severus and Caracalla, 193—217. His 3 principal works constitute parts of a whole. In the Hortatory Address to the Greeks (Λόγος Προτρεπτικός, &c.) his design was to convince the Heathens and

to convert them to Christianity. The Paedagogus (Παιδαγωγός) takes up the new convert at the point to which he is supposed to have been brought by the hortatory address, and furnishes him with rules for the regulation of his conduct. The Stromata (Στρωματεῖς) are in 8 books : the title (Stromata, i. e. patch-work) indicates its miscellaneous character. It is rambling and discursive, but contains much valuable information on many points of antiquity, particularly the history of philosophy. The principal information respecting Egyptian hieroglyphics is contained in the 5th book. The object of the work was to delineate the perfect Christian or Gnostic, after he had been instructed by the Teacher and thus prepared by sublime speculations in philosophy and theology. — Editions. By Potter, Oxon. 1715, fol. 2 vols. ; by Klotz, Lips. 1830—34, 8vo. 4 vols.

Cleöbis. [BITON.]

Clëöbülïnä (Κλεοβυλίνη), or **Clëöbülä** (Κλεοβούλη), daughter of Cleobulus of Lindus, celebrated for her skill in riddles, of which she composed a number in hexameter verse ; to her is ascribed a well-known one on the subject of the year : — " A father has 12 children, and each of these 30 daughters, on one side white, and on the other side black, and though immortal they all die."

Cleobülus (Κλεόβουλος), one of the Seven Sages, of Lindus in Rhodes, son of Evagoras, lived about B. C. 580. He wrote lyric poems, as well as riddles, in verse ; he was said by some to have been the author of the riddle on the year, generally attributed to his daughter Cleobuline. He was greatly distinguished for strength and beauty of person.

Cleöchäres (Κλεοχάρης), a Greek orator of Myrlea in Bithynia, contemporary with the orator Demochares and the philosopher Arcesilas, towards the close of the 3rd century B. C.

Cleombrötus (Κλεόμβροτος). 1. Son of Anaxandrides, king of Sparta, became regent after the battle of Thermopylae, B. C. 480, for Plistarchus, infant son of Leonidas, but died in the same year, and was succeeded in the regency by his son Pausanias. — 2. I. King of Sparta, son of Pausanias, succeeded his brother Agesipolis I., and reigned B. C. 380—371. He commanded the Spartan troops several times against the Thebans, and fell at the battle of Leuctra (371), after fighting most bravely. — 3. II. King of Sparta, son-in-law of Leonidas II., in whose place he was made king by the party of AGIS IV. about 243. On the return of Leonidas, Cleombrotus was deposed and banished to Tegea, about 240. — 4. An Academic philosopher of Ambracia, said to have killed himself, after reading the Phaedon of Plato ; not that he had any sufferings to escape from, but that he might exchange this life for a better.

Cleomēdes (Κλεομήδης). 1. Of the island Astypalaea, an athlete of gigantic strength. — 2. A Greek mathematician, probably lived in the 2nd and 3rd centuries of the Christian aera ; the author of a Greek treatise in 2 books on the Circular Theory of the Heavenly Bodies (Κυκλικῆς Θεωρίας Μετεώρων Βιβλία δύο), which is still extant. It is rather an exposition of the system of the universe than of the geometrical principles of astronomy. Edited by Balfour, Burdigal. 1605 ; by Bake, Lugd. Bat. 1820 ; and by Schmidt, Lips. 1832.

Cleomēnes (Κλεομένης). 1. King of Sparta, son of Anaxandrides, reigned B. C. 520—491. He was a man of an enterprising but wild character.

His greatest exploit was his defeat of the Argives, in which 6000 Argive citizens fell ; but the date of this event is doubtful. In 510 he commanded the forces by whose assistance Hippias was driven from Athens, and not long after he assisted Isagoras and the aristocratical party, against Clisthenes. By bribing the priestess at Delphi, he effected the deposition of his colleague DEMARATUS, 491. Soon afterwards he was seized with madness and killed himself. — 2. King of Sparta, son of Cleombrotus I., reigned 370—309 ; but during this long period we have no information about him of any importance. — 3. King of Sparta, son of Leonidas II., reigned 236—222. While still young, he married Agiatis, the widow of Agis IV. ; and following the example of the latter, he endeavoured to restore the ancient Spartan constitution, and to regenerate the Spartan character. He was endowed with a noble mind, strengthened and purified by philosophy, and possessed great energy of purpose. His first object was to gain for Sparta her old renown in war ; and for that purpose he attacked the Achaeans, and carried on war with the League with great success. Having thus gained military renown he felt himself sufficiently strong in the winter of 226—225 to put the Ephors to death and restore the ancient constitution. The Achaeans now called in the aid of Antigonus Doson, king of Macedonia, and for the next 3 years Cleomenes carried on war against their united forces. He was at length completely defeated at the battle of Sellasia (222), and fled to Egypt, where he was kindly received by Ptolemy Euergetes, but on the death of that king he was imprisoned by his successor Philopator. He escaped from prison, and attempted to raise an insurrection, but finding no one join him, he put himself to death, 220.

Cleomênes. 1. A Greek of Naucratis in Egypt, appointed by Alexander the Great nomarch of the Arabian district (νόμος) of Egypt, and receiver of the tribute from the districts of Egypt, B. C. 331. His rapacity knew no bounds, and he collected immense wealth by his extortions. After Alexander's death he was put to death by Ptolemy, who took possession of his treasures. — 2. A sculptor, son of Apollodorus of Athens, executed the celebrated statue of the Venus de Medici, as appears from an inscription on the pedestal. He lived between B. C. 363 and 146.

Clêôn (Κλέων), son of Cleaenetus, was originally a tanner, and first came forward ·in public as an opponent of Pericles. On the death of this great man, B. C. 429, Cleon became the favourite of the 'people, and for about 6 years of the Peloponnesian war (428—422) was the head of the party opposed to peace. He is represented by Aristophanes as a demagogue of the lowest kind, mean, ignorant, cowardly, and venal ; and this view of his character is confirmed by Thucydides. But much weight cannot be attached to the satire of the poet ; and the usual impartiality of the historian may have been warped by the sentence of his banishment, if it be true, as has been conjectured with great probability, that it was through Cleon that Thucydides was sent into exile. Cleon may be considered as the representative of the middle classes of Athens, and by his ready, though somewhat coarse, eloquence, gained great influence over them. In 427 he strongly advocated in the assembly that the Mytilenaeans should be put to death. In 424 he obtained his greatest glory by

taking prisoners the Spartans in the island of Sphacteria, and bringing them in safety to Athens. Puffed up by this success, he obtained the command of an Athenian army, to oppose Brasidas in Thrace ; but he was defeated by Brasidas, under the walls of Amphipolis, and fell in the battle, 422. — The chief attack of Aristophanes upon Cleon was in the *Knights* (424), in which Cleon figures as an actual dramatis persona, and, in default of an artificer bold enough to make the mask, was represented by the poet himself with his face smeared with wine lees.

Cleônae (Κλεωναί : Κλεωναῖος). 1. An ancient town in Argolis, on the road from Corinth to Argos, on a river of the same name which flows into the Corinthian gulf, and at the foot of Mt. Apesas ; said to have been built by Cleones, son of Pelops. — 2. A town in the peninsula Athos in Chalcidice. — 3. **Hyampolis.**

Cleônymus (Κλεώνυμος). 1 An Athenian, frequently attacked by Aristophanes as a pestilent demagogue. — 2. A Spartan, son of Sphodrias, much beloved by Archidamus, the son of Agesilaus : he fell at Leuctra, B. C. 371. — 3. Younger son of Cleomenes II., king of Sparta, was excluded from the throne on his father's death, 309, in consequence of his violent and tyrannical temper. In 303 he crossed over to Italy to assist the Tarentines against the Lucanians. He afterwards withdrew from Italy, and seized Corcyra ; and in 272 he invited Pyrrhus to attempt the conquest of Sparta. [ACROTATUS.]

Cleopatra (Κλεοπάτρα). 1. (Myth.) Daughter of Idas and Marpessa, and wife of Meleager, is said to have hanged herself after her husband's death, or to have died of grief. Her real name was Alcyone. — 2. (Hist.) Niece of Attalus, married Philip, B. C. 337, on whose murder she was put to death by Olympias. — 3. Daughter of Philip and Olympias, and sister of Alexander the Great, married Alexander, king of Epirus, 336. It was at the celebration of her nuptials that Philip was murdered. Her husband died 326. After the death of her brother she was sought in marriage by several of his generals, and at length promised to marry Ptolemy ; but having attempted to escape from Sardis, where she had been kept for years in a sort of honourable captivity, she was assassinated by Antigonus. — 4. Daughter of Antiochus III. the Great, married Ptolemy V. Epiphanes, 193. — 5. Daughter of Ptolemy V. Epiphanes and No. 4, married her brother Ptolemy VI. Philometor, and on his death, 146, her other brother Ptolemy VI. Physcon. She was soon afterwards divorced by Physcon, and fled into Syria. — 6. Daughter of Ptolemy VI. Philometor and of No. 5, married first Alexander Balas (150), the Syrian usurper, and on his death Demetrius Nicator. During the captivity of the latter in Parthia, jealous of the connexion which he there formed with Rhodogune, the Parthian princess, she married Antiochus VII. Sidetes, his brother, and also murdered Demetrius on his return. She likewise murdered Seleucus, her son by Nicator, who on his father's death assumed the government without her consent. Her other son by Nicator, Antiochus VIII. Grypus, succeeded to the throne (125) through her influence ; and he compelled her to drink the poison which she had prepared for him also. [ANTIOCHUS VIII.] She had a son by Sidetes, Antiochus IX., surnamed Cyzicenus. — 7. Another daughter of Pto-

N 3

lemy VI. Philometor and No. 5, married her uncle Physcon, when the latter divorced her mother. On the death of Physcon she reigned in conjunction with her elder son, Ptolemy VIII. Lathyrus, and then in conjunction with her younger son Alexander. She was put to death by the latter in 89.—8. Daughter of Ptolemy Physcon and No. 7, married first her brother Ptolemy VIII. Lathyrus, and next Antiochus IX. Cyzicenus. She was put to death by Tryphaena, her own sister, wife of Antiochus Grypus.—9. Usually called Selene, another daughter of Ptolemy Physcon, married 1st her brother Lathyrus (on her sister No. 8 being divorced), 2dly Antiochus XI. Epiphanes, and 3rdly Antiochus X. Eusebes.—10. Daughter of Ptolemy VIII. Lathyrus, usually called Berenice. [BERENICE, No. 4.] —11. Eldest daughter of Ptolemy Auletes, celebrated for her beauty and fascination, was 17 at the death of her father (51), who appointed her heir of his kingdom in conjunction with her younger brother, Ptolemy, whom she was to marry. She was expelled from the throne by Pothinus and Achillas, his guardians. She retreated into Syria, and there collected an army with which she was preparing to enter Egypt, when Caesar arrived in Egypt in pursuit of Pompey, 47. Her charms gained for her the support of Caesar, who replaced her on the throne in conjunction with her brother. This led to the Alexandrine war, in the course of which young Ptolemy perished. Cleopatra thus obtained the undivided rule. She was, however, associated by Caesar with another brother of the same name, and still quite a child, to whom she was also nominally married. She had a son by Caesar, called CAESARION, and she afterwards followed him to Rome, where she appears to have been at the time of his death, 44. She then returned to Egypt, and in 41 she met Antony in Cilicia. She was now in her 28th year, and in the perfection of matured beauty, which, in conjunction with her talents and eloquence, completely won the heart of Antony, who henceforth appears as her devoted lover and slave. He returned with her to Egypt, but was obliged to leave her for a short time, in order to marry Octavia, the sister of Augustus. But Octavia was never able to gain his affections ; he soon deserted his wife and returned to Cleopatra, upon whom he conferred the most extravagant titles and honours. In the war between Octavian and Antony, Cleopatra accompanied her lover, and was present at the battle of Actium (31), in the midst of which she retreated with her fleet, and thus hastened the loss of the day. She fled to Alexandria, where she was joined by Antony. Seeing Antony's fortunes desperate, she entered into negotiations with Augustus, and promised to make away with Antony. She fled to a mausoleum she had built, and then caused a report of her death to be spread. Antony, resolving not to survive her, stabbed himself, and was drawn up into the mausoleum, where he died in her arms. She then tried to gain the love of Augustus, but her charms failed in softening his colder heart. Seeing that he determined to carry her captive to Rome, she put an end to her own life, either by the poison of an asp, or by a poisoned comb, the former supposition being adopted by most writers. She died in the 39th year of her age (B. C. 30), and with her ended the dynasty of the Ptolemies in Egypt, which was now made a Roman province.—12. Daughter of Antony and No. 11, born with her twin brother

Alexander in 40, along with whom she was carried to Rome after the death of her parents. Augustus married her to Juba, king of Numidia.—13. A daughter of Mithridates, married Tigranes, king of Armenia.

Cleopatris. [ARSINOE, No. 6.]

Cleophon (Κλεοφῶν), an Athenian demagogue, of obscure, and, according to Aristophanes, of Thracian origin, vehemently opposed peace with Sparta in the latter end of the Peloponnesian war. During the siege of Athens by Lysander, B. c. 404, he was brought to trial by the aristocratical party, and was condemned and put to death.

Cleostratus (Κλεόστρατος), an astronomer of Tenedos, said to have introduced the division of the Zodiac into signs, probably lived between B. c. 548 and 432.

Clevum, also **Glevum** and **Glebon** (*Gloucester*), a Roman colony in Britain.

Clides (*ai* Κλεῖδες: *C. S. Andre*), "the Keys," a promontory on the N. E. of Cyprus, with 2 islands of the same name lying off it.

Climax (Κλῖμαξ: *Ekder*), the name applied to the W. termination of the Taurus range, which extends along the W. coast of the Pamphylian Gulf, N. of Phaselis in Lycia. Alexander made a road between it and the sea. There were other mountains of the same name in Asia and Africa.

Climberrum. [AUSCI.]

Clinias (Κλεινίας). 1. Father of the famous Alcibiades, fought at Artemisium B. c. 480, in a ship built and manned at his own expense : he fell 447, at the battle of Coronea.—2. A younger brother of the famous Alcibiades.—3. Father of Aratus of Sicyon, was murdered by Abantidas, who seized the tyranny, 264.—4. A Pythagorean philosopher, of Tarentum, a contemporary and friend of Plato.

Clio. [MUSAE.]

Clisthenes (Κλεισθένης). 1. Tyrant of Sicyon. In B. c. 595, he aided the Amphictyons in the sacred war against Cirrha, which ended, after 10 years, in the destruction of the guilty city. He also engaged in war with Argos. His death cannot be placed earlier than 582, in which year he won the victory in the chariot-race at the Pythian games. His daughter Agarista was given in marriage to Megacles the Alcmaeonid.—2. An Athenian, son of Megacles and Agarista, and grandson of No. 1, appears as the head of the Alcmaeonid clan on the banishment of the Pisistratidae. Finding, however, that he could not cope with his political rival Isagoras except through the aid of the commons, he set himself to increase the power of the latter. The principal change which he introduced was the abolition of the 4 ancient tribes and the establishment of 10 new ones in their stead, B. c. 510. He is also said to have instituted ostracism. Isagoras and his party called in the aid of the Spartans, but Clisthenes and his friends eventually triumphed.—3. An Athenian, whose foppery and effeminate profligacy brought him under the lash of Aristophanes.

Clitarchus (Κλείταρχος). 1. Tyrant of Eretria in Euboea, was supported by Philip against the Athenians, but was expelled from Eretria by Phocion, B. c. 341.—2. Son of the historian Dinon, accompanied Alexander the Great in his Asiatic expedition, and wrote a history of it. This work was deficient in veracity and inflated in style, but appears nevertheless to have been much read.

Cliternum or Cliternia (Cliterninus), a town of the Frentani, in the territory of Larinum.

Clitomachus (Κλειτόμαχος), a Carthaginian by birth, and called Hasdrubal in his own language, came to Athens in the 40th year of his age, and there studied under Carneades, on whose death he became the head of the New Academy, B. C. 129. Of his works, which amounted to 400 books, only a few titles are preserved. His main object in writing them was to make known the philosophy of his master Carneades. When Carthage was taken in 146, he wrote a work to console his unfortunate countrymen.

Clitor or Clitorium (Κλείτωρ: Κλειτόριος: nr. Mazi, Ru.), a town in the N. of Arcadia on a river of the same name, a tributary of the Aroanius: there was a fountain in the neighbourhood, the waters of which are said to have given to persons who drank of them a dislike for wine. (Ov. Met. xv. 322.)

Clitumnus (Clitumno), a small river in Umbria, springs from a beautiful rock in a grove of cypress-trees, where was a sanctuary of the god Clitumnus, and falls into the Tinia, a tributary of the Tiber.

Clitus (Κλεῖτος or Κλειτός). 1. Son of Bardylis, king of Illyria, defeated by Alexander the Great, B. C. 335.——2. A Macedonian, one of Alexander's generals and friends, surnamed the Black (Μέλας). He saved Alexander's life at the battle of Granicus, 334. In 328 he was slain by Alexander at a banquet, when both parties were heated with wine, and Clitus had provoked the king's resentment by insolent language. Alexander was inconsolable at his friend's death.——3. Another of Alexander's officers, surnamed the White (Λευκός) to distinguish him from the above.——4. An officer who commanded the Macedonian fleet for Antipater in the Lamian war, 323, and defeated the Athenian fleet. In 321, he obtained from Antipater the satrapy of Lydia, from which he was expelled by Antigonus, 319. He afterwards commanded the fleet of Polysperchon, and was at first successful, but his ships were subsequently destroyed by Antigonus, and he was killed on shore, 318.

Cloacina or Cluacina, the "Purifier" (from cloare or cluere, "to wash" or "purify"), a surname of Venus at Rome.

Clodius, another form of the name Claudius, just as we find both caudex and codex, claustrum and clostrum, cauda and coda. [CLAUDIUS.]

Clodius Albinus. [ALBINUS.]

Clodius Macer. [MACER.]

Cloelia, a Roman virgin, one of the hostages given to Porsena, is said to have escaped from the Etruscan camp, and to have swum across the Tiber to Rome. She was sent back by the Romans to Porsena, who was so struck with her gallant deed, that he not only set her at liberty, but allowed her to take with her a part of the hostages. Porsena also rewarded her with a horse adorned with splendid trappings, and the Romans with the statue of a female on horseback, which was erected in the Sacred Way.

Cloelia or Cluilia Gens, of Alban origin, said to have been received among the patricians on the destruction of Alba. A few of its members with the surname Siculus obtained the consulship in the early years of the republic.

Clonas (Κλονᾶς), a poet, and one of the earliest musicians of Greece, either an Arcadian, or a Boeotian, probably lived about B. C. 620.

Clonius (Κλόνιος), leader of the Boeotians in the war against Troy, slain by Agenor.

Clota Aestuarium (Frith of Clyde), on the W. coast of Scotland.

Clotho. [MOIRAE.]

Cluentius Habitus, A., of Larinum, accused in B. C. 74 his own step-father, Statius Albius Oppianicus, of having attempted to procure his death by poison. Oppianicus was condemned, and it was generally believed that the judges had been bribed by Cluentius. In 66, Cluentius was himself accused by young Oppianicus, son of Statius Albius who had died in the interval, of 3 distinct acts of poisoning. He was defended by Cicero in the oration still extant.

Clunia (Ru. on a hill between Coruña del Conde and Peñalba de Castro), a town of the Arevacae in Hispania Tarraconensis, and a Roman colony.

Clupea or Clypea. [ASPIS.]

Clusium (Clusinus: Chiusi), one of the most powerful of the 12 Etruscan cities, situated on an eminence above the river Clanis, and S. W. of the Lacus Clusinus (L. di Chiusi). It was more anciently called Camers or Camars, whence we may conclude that it was founded by the Umbrian race of the Camertes. It was the royal residence of Porsena, and in its neighbourhood was the celebrated sepulchre of this king in the form of a labyrinth, of which such marvellous accounts have come down to us. (Dict. of Ant. art. Labyrinthus.) Subsequently Clusium was in alliance with the Romans, by whom it was regarded as a bulwark against the Gauls. Its siege by the Gauls, B. C. 391, led, as is well known, to the capture of Rome itself by the Gauls. Clusium probably became a Roman colony, since Pliny speaks of Clusini Veteres et Novi. In its neighbourhood were cold baths. (Hor. Ep. i. 15. 9.)

Clusius (Chiese), a river in Cisalpine Gaul, a tributary of the Ollius, forming the boundary between the Cenomani and Insubres.

Cluvius, a family of Campanian origin, of which the most important person was M. Cluvius Rufus, consul suffectus A.D. 45, and governor of Spain under Galba, A. D. 69, on whose death he espoused the cause of Vitellius. He was an historian, and wrote an account of the times of Nero, Galba, Otho, and Vitellius.

Clymene (Κλυμένη). 1. Daughter of Oceanus and Tethys, and wife of Iapetus, to whom she bore Atlas, Prometheus, and others.——2. Daughter of Iphis or Minyas, wife of Phylacus or Cephalus, to whom she bore Iphiclus and Alcimede. According to Hesiod and others she was the mother of Phaëton by Helios.——3. A relative of Menelaus and a companion of Helena, with whom she was carried off by Paris.

Clytaemnestra (Κλυταιμνήστρα), daughter of Tyndareus and Leda, sister of Castor, and half-sister of Pollux and Helena. She was married to Agamemnon. During her husband's absence at Troy she lived in adultery with Aegisthus, and on his return to Mycenae she murdered him with the help of Aegisthus. [AGAMEMNON.] She was subsequently put to death by her son Orestes, who thus avenged the murder of his father. For details see ORESTES.

Cnemis (Κνῆμις), a range of mountains on the frontiers of Phocis and Locris, from which the N. Locrians were called Epicnemidii. A branch of these mountains runs out into the sea, forming the promontory **Cnemides** (Κνημῖδες), with a town of the same name upon it, opposite the promontory Cenaeum in Euboea.

Cneph (Κνήφ), or **Cnuphus** (Κνοῦφις), an Egyptian divinity, worshipped in the form of a serpent, and regarded as the creator of the world.

Cnidus or **Gnidus** (Κνίδος: Κνίδιος: Ru. at Cape *Krio*), a celebrated city of Asia Minor, on the promontory of Triopium on the coast of Caria, was a Lacedaemonian colony, and the chief city of the Dorian Hexapolis. It was built partly on the mainland and partly on an island joined to the coast by a causeway, and had two harbours. It had a considerable commerce; and it was resorted to by travellers from all parts of the civilized world, that they might see the statue of Aphrodite by Praxiteles, which stood in her temple here. The city possessed also temples of Apollo and Poseidon. The great naval defeat of Pisander by Conon (B. C. 394) took place off Cnidus. Among the celebrated natives of the city were Ctesias, Eudoxus, Sostratus, and Agatharcides. It is said to have been also called, at an early period, Triopia, from its founder Triopas, and, in later times, Stadia.

Cnosus or **Gnosus**, subsequently **Cnossus** or **Gnossus** (Κνωσός, Γνωσός, Κνωσσός, Γνωσσός: Κνώσιος, Κνώσσιος: *Makro Teikho*), an ancient town of Crete, and the capital of king Minos, was situated in a fertile country on the river **Caeratus** (which was originally the name of the town), at a short distance from the N. coast. It was at an early time colonized by Dorians, and from it Dorian institutions spread over the island. Its power was weakened by the growing importance of Gortyn and Cydonia; and these towns, when united, were more than a match for Cnosus. — Cnossus is frequently mentioned by the poets in consequence of its connection with Minos, Ariadne, the Minotaur, and the Labyrinth; and the adjective Cnossius is frequently used as equivalent to Cretan.

Cobus or **Cohibus** (Κῶβος), a river of Asia, flowing from the Caucasus into the E. side of the Euxine.

Cocalus (Κώκαλος), a mythical king of Sicily, who kindly received Daedalus on his flight from Crete, and with the assistance of his daughters put Minos to death, when the latter came in pursuit of Daedalus.

Cocceius Nerva. [NERVA.]

Coche (Κωχή), a city on the Tigris, near Ctesiphon.

Cocinthum or **Cocintum** (*Punta di Stilo*), a promontory on the S. E. of Bruttium in Italy, with a town of the same name upon it.

Cocles, Horatius, that is, Horatius the "one-eyed," a hero of the old Roman lays, is said to have defended the Sublician bridge along with Sp. Lartius and T. Herminius against the whole Etruscan army under Porsena, while the Romans broke down the bridge behind them. When the work was nearly finished, Horatius sent back his 2 companions. As soon as the bridge was quite destroyed, he plunged into the stream and swam across to the city in safety amid the arrows of the enemy. The state raised a statue to his honour, which was placed in the comitium, and allowed him as much land as he could plough round in one day. Polybius relates that Horatius defended the bridge alone, and perished in the river.

Cocossates, a people in Aquitania in Gaul, mentioned along with the Tarbelli.

Cocylium (Κοκύλιον), an Aeolian city in Mysia, whose inhabitants (Κοκυλῖται) are mentioned by Xenophon; but which was abandoned before Pliny's time.

Cocytus (Κωκυτός), a river in Epirus, a tributary of the Acheron. Like the Acheron, the Cocytus was supposed to be connected with the lower world, and hence came to be described as a river in the lower world. Homer (*Od.* x. 513) makes the Cocytus a tributary of the Styx; but Virgil (*Aen.* vi. 295) represents the Acheron as flowing into the Cocytus.

Codanus Sinus, the S. W. part of the Baltic, whence the Danish islands are called **Codanonia**.

Codomannus. [DARIUS.]

Codrus (Κόδρος). 1. Son of Melanthus, and last king of Athens. When the Dorians invaded Attica from Peloponnesus (about B. C. 1068 according to mythical chronology), an oracle declared, that they should be victorious if the life of the Attic king was spared. Codrus thereupon resolved to sacrifice himself for his country. He entered the camp of the enemy in disguise, commenced quarrelling with the soldiers, and was slain in the dispute. When the Dorians discovered the death of the Attic king, they returned home. Tradition adds, that as no one was thought worthy to succeed such a patriotic king, the kingly dignity was abolished, and Medon, son of Codrus, was appointed archon for life instead. — 2. A Roman poet, ridiculed by Virgil. Juvenal also speaks of a wretched poet of the same name. The name is probably fictitious, and appears to have been applied by the Roman poets to those poetasters who annoyed other people by reading their productions to them.

Coela (τὰ κοῖλα τῆς Εὐβοίας), "the Hollows of Euboea," the W. coast of Euboea, between the promontories Caphareus and Chersonesus, very dangerous to ships: here a part of the Persian fleet was wrecked, B. C. 480.

Coele (Κοίλη), an Attic demus belonging to the tribe Hippothoontis, a little way beyond the Melitian gate at Athens: here Cimon and Thucydides were buried.

Coelesyria (ἡ Κοίλη Συρία, i. e. *Hollow Syria*), was the name given, after the Macedonian conquest, to the great valley (*El-Bukaa*), between the two ranges of M. Lebanon (Libanus and Anti-Libanus), in the S. of Syria, bordering upon Phoenicia on the W. and Palestine on the S. In the wars between the Ptolemies and the Seleucidae, the name was applied to the whole of the S. portion of Syria, which became subject for some time to the kings of Egypt; but, under the Romans, when Phoenicia and Judaea were made distinct provinces, the name of Coelesyria was confined to Coelesyria proper together with the district E. of Anti-Libanus, about Damascus, and a portion of Palestine E. of the Jordan; and this is the most usual meaning of the term. Under the later emperors, it was considered as a part of Phoenicia, and was called Phoenice Libanesia. The country was for the most part fertile, especially the E. district about the river Chrysarrhoas: the valley of Coelesyria proper was watered by the Leontes. The inhabitants were a mixt people of Syrians, Phoenicians, and Greeks, called Syrophoenicians (Συροφοίνικες).

Coeletae or **Coelaletae**, a people of Thrace, divided into Majores and Minores. in the district

Coeletica, between the Hebrus and the gulf of Melas.

Coelius. [CAELIUS.]

Coelossa (Κοίλωσσα), a mountain in the Sicyonian territory, near Phlius, an offshoot of the Arcadian mountain Cyllene.

Coelus (Κοιλὸς λίμην) or Coela (Κοῖλα), a seaport town in the Thracian Chersonese, near which was the Κυνὸς σῆμα, or the grave of Hecuba. [CYNOSSEMA.]

Coenus (Κοῖνος), son-in-law of Parmenion, one of the ablest generals of Alexander the Great, died on the Hyphasis, B. C. 327.

Coenyra (Κοίνυρα), a place in the island Thasos, opposite Samothrace.

Cöes (Κώης), of Mytilene, dissuaded Darius Hystaspis, in his Scythian expedition, from breaking up his bridge of boats over the Danube. For this good counsel he was rewarded by Darius with the tyranny of Mytilene. On the breaking out of the Ionian revolt, B. C. 501, he was stoned to death by the Mytilenaeans.

Colapis (Κόλαψ in Dion Cass.: Kulpa), a river in Pannonia, flows into the Savus: on it dwelt the Colapiani.

Colchis (Κολχίς: Κόλχος), a country of Asia, bounded on the W. by the Euxine, on the N. by the Caucasus, on the E. by Iberia; on the S. and S.W. the boundaries were somewhat indefinite, and were often considered to extend as far as Trapezus (Trebizond). The land of Colchis (or Aea), and its river Phasis are famous in the Greek mythology. [ARGONAUTAE.] The name of Colchis is first mentioned by Aeschylus and Pindar. The historical acquaintance of the Greeks with the country may be ascribed to the commerce of the Milesians. It was a very fertile country, and yielded timber, pitch, hemp, flax, and wax, as articles of commerce; but it was most famous for its manufactures of linen, on account of which, and of certain physical resemblances, Herodotus supposed the Colchians to have been a colony from Egypt. The land was governed by its native princes, until Mithridates Eupator made it subject to the kingdom of Pontus. After the Mithridatic war, it was overrun by the Romans, but they did not subdue it till the time of Trajan. Under the later emperors the country was called Lazica, from the name of one of its principal tribes, the Lazi.

Cölias (Κωλιάs), a promontory on the W. coast of Attica, 20 stadia S. of Phalerum, with a temple of Aphrodite, where some of the Persian ships were cast after the battle of Salamis. Colias is usually identified with the cape called the Three Towers (Τρεῖς Πύργοι), but it ought to be placed S.E. near Ἅγιος Κοσμᾶς.

Collātia (Collatinus). 1. (Castellaccio), a Sabine town in Latium, near the right bank of the Anio, taken by Tarquinius Priscus.—2. A town in Apulia, only mentioned under the empire.

Collatinus, L. Tarquinius, son of Egerius, and nephew of Tarquinius Priscus, derived the surname Collatinus from the town Collatia, of which his father had been appointed governor. He was married to Lucretia, and it was the rape of the latter by Sex. Tarquinius that led to the dethronement of Tarquinius Superbus. Collatinus and L. Junius Brutus were the first consuls; but as the people could not endure the rule of any of the hated race of the Tarquins, Collatinus resigned his office and retired from Rome to Lavinium.

Collina Porta. [ROMA.]

Collytus (Κολλυτός, also Κολυττός: Κολλυτεύς), a demus in Attica, belonging to the tribe Aegeis, was included within the walls of Athens, and formed one of the districts into which the city was divided: it was the demus of Plato and the residence of Timon the misanthrope.

Colonae (Κολωναί), a small town in the Troad, mentioned in Greek history, but destroyed before the time of Pliny.

Colonia Agrippina or Agrippinensis (Cologne on the Rhine), originally the chief town of the Ubii, and called Oppidum or Civitas Ubiorum, was a place of small importance till A. D. 51, when a Roman colony was planted in the town by the emperor Claudius, at the instigation of his wife Agrippina, who was born here, and from whom it derived its new name. Its inhabitants received the jus Italicum. It soon became a large and flourishing city, and was the capital of Lower Germany. At Cologne there are still several Roman remains, an ancient gate, with the inscription C. C. A. A. i. e. Colonia Claudia Augusta Agrippinensis, the foundations of the Roman walls, &c.

Colonia Equestris. [NOVIODUNUM]

Colonus (Κολωνός: Κολωνεύς -νίτης, -νιάτης), a demus of Attica, belonging to the tribe Aegeis, afterwards to the tribe Antiochis, 10 stadia, or a little more than a mile N.W. of Athens; near the Academy, lying on and round a hill; celebrated for a temple of Poseidon (hence called Κολωνὸς Ἵππειος), a grove of the Eumenides, and the tomb of Oedipus. Sophocles, who was a native of this demus, has described the scenery and religious associations of the spot, in his Oedipus Coloneus. — There was a hill at Athens called Colonus Agoraeus (Κολωνὸς ὁ ἀγοραῖος).

Colophon (Κολοφών: Zille, Ru.), one of the 12 Ionian cities of Asia Minor, was said to have been founded by Mopsus, a grandson of Tiresias. It stood about 2 miles from the coast, on the river Halesus, which was famous for the coldness of its water, between Lebedus and Ephesus, 120 stadia (12 geog. miles) from the former and 70 stadia (7 g. m.) from the latter: its harbour was called Notium. It was one of the most powerful members of the Ionian confederacy, possessing a considerable fleet and excellent cavalry; but it suffered greatly in war, being taken at different times by the Lydians, the Persians, Lysimachus, and the Cilician pirates. It was made a free city by the Romans after their war with Antiochus the Great. Besides claiming to be the birth-place of Homer, Colophon was the native city of Mimnermus, Hermesianax, and Nicander. It was also celebrated for the oracle of Apollo Clarius in its neighbourhood. [CLARUS.]

Colossae (Κολοσσαί, aft. Κολάσσαι: Κολοσσηνός, Strab., Κολοσσαεύς, N. T.; Khonas, Ru.), a city of Great Phrygia on the river Lycus, once of great importance, but so reduced by the rise of the neighbouring cities of Laodicea and Hierapolis, that the later geographers do not even mention it, and it might have been forgotten but for its place in the early history of the Christian Church. In the middle ages it was called Χῶναι, and hence the modern name of the village on its site.

Colotes (Κολώτης). 1. Of Lampsacus, a hearer of Epicurus, against whom Plutarch wrote 2 of his works. — 2. A sculptor of Paros, flourished B. C. 444, and assisted Phidias in executing the colossus of Zeus at Olympia.

Cŏlŭmella, L. Jūnīus Mŏdĕrātus, a native of Gades in Spain, and a contemporary of Seneca. We have no particulars of his life ; it appears, from his own account, that at some period of his life, he visited Syria and Cilicia ; but Rome appears to have been his ordinary residence. He wrote a work upon agriculture (*De Re Rustica*), in 12 books, which is still extant. It treats not only of agriculture proper, but of the cultivation of the vine and the olive, of gardening, of rearing cattle, of bees, &c. The 10th book, which treats of gardening, is composed in dactylic hexameters, and forms a sort of supplement to the Georgics. There is also extant a work *De Arboribus*, in one book. The style of Columella is easy and ornate. The best edition of his works is by Schneider, in the *Scriptores Rei Rusticae*, 4 vols. 8vo., Lips. 1794.

Columnae Herculis. [ABYLA ; CALPE.]

Colūthus (Κόλουθος), a Greek epic poet of Lycopolis in Egypt, lived at the beginning of the 6th century of our era. He is the author of an extinct poem on " The Rape of Helen " ('Ελένης ἁρπαγή), consisting of 392 hexameter lines. Edited by Bekker, Berl. 1816, and Schaefer, Lips. 1825.

Colyttus. [COLLYTUS.]

Comāna (Κόμανα). 1. C. Pontica (*Guminik*, Ru.), a flourishing city of Pontus, upon the river Iris, celebrated for its temple of Artemis Taurica, the foundation of which tradition ascribed to Orestes. The high-priests of this temple took rank next after the king, and their domain was increased by Pompey after the Mithridatic war.— 2. Cappadociae, or C. Chryse (*Bostan*), lay in a narrow valley of the Anti-Taurus, in Cataonia, and was also celebrated for a temple of Artemis Taurica, the foundation of which was likewise ascribed by tradition to Orestes.

Combrēa (Κόμβρεια), a town in the Macedonian district of Crossaea.

Comīnīum, a town in Samnium, destroyed by the Romans in the Samnite wars.

Commăgēne (Κομμαγηνή), the N. E.-most district of Syria, was bounded on the E. and S. E. by the Euphrates, on the N. and N.W. by the Taurus, and on the S. by Cyrrhestice. It formed a part of the Greek kingdom of Syria, after the fall of which it maintained its independence under a race of kings who appear to have been a branch of the family of the Seleucidae, and was not united to the Roman empire till the reign of Vespasian. Under Constantine, if not earlier, it was made a part of Cyrrhestice. The district was remarkable for its fertility.

Commīus, king of the Atrebates, was advanced to that dignity by Caesar, who had great confidence in him. He was sent by Caesar to Britain to accompany the ambassadors of the British states on their return to their native country, but he was cast into chains by the Britons, and was not released till the Britons had been defeated by Caesar, and found it expedient to sue for peace. In B. C. 52 he joined the other Gauls in their great revolt against the Romans, and continued in arms even after the capture of Alesia.

Commŏdus, L. Ceiōnīus, was adopted by Hadrian, A. D. 136, when he took the name of L. AELIUS VERUS CAESAR. His health was weak ; he died on the 1st of January, 138, and was interred in the mausoleum of Hadrian. His son L. Aurelius Verus was the colleague of Antoninus Pius in the empire. [VERUS.]

Commŏdus, L. Aurēlīus, Roman emperor, A. D. 180—192, son of M. Aurelius and the younger Faustina, was born at Lanuvium, 161, and was thus scarcely 20, when he succeeded to the empire. He was an unworthy son of a noble father. Notwithstanding the great care which his father had bestowed upon his education, he turned out one of the most sanguinary and licentious tyrants that ever disgraced a throne. It was after the suppression of the plot against his life, which had been organised by his sister Lucilla, 183, that he first gave uncontrolled sway to his ferocious temper. He resigned the government to various favourites who followed each other in rapid succession (Perennis, Cleander, Laetus, and Eclectus), and abandoned himself without interruption to the most shameless debauchery. But he was at the same time the slave of the most childish vanity, and sought to gain popular applause by fighting as a gladiator, and slew many thousands of wild beasts in the amphitheatre with bow and spear. In consequence of these exploits he assumed the name of Hercules, and demanded that he should be worshipped as that god, 191. In the following year his concubine Marcia found on his tablets, while he was asleep, that she was doomed to perish along with Laetus and Eclectus and other leading men in the state. She forthwith administered poison to him, but as its operation was slow, Narcissus, a celebrated athlete, was introduced, and by him Commodus was strangled, Dec. 31st, 192.

Comnēna. [ANNA COMNENA.]

Complūtum, a town of the Carpetani in Hispania Tarraconensis, between Segovia and Bilbilis.

Compsa (Compsānus : Conza), a town of the Hirpini in Samnium, near the sources of the Aufidus.

Cōmum (Comensis : Como), a town in Gallia Cisalpina, at the S. extremity of the W. branch of the Lacus Larius (*L. di Como*). It was originally a town of the Insubrian Gauls, and was colonized by Pompeius Strabo, by Cornelius Scipio, and by Julius Caesar. Caesar settled there 6000 colonists, among whom were 500 distinguished Greek families; and this new population so greatly exceeded the number of the old inhabitants, that the town was called *Novum Comum*, a name, however, which it did not retain. Comum was celebrated for its iron-manufactories: it was the birthplace of the younger Pliny.

Cōmus, the god of festive mirth and joy, is represented as a winged youth.

Concordĭa, a Roman goddess, the personification of concord, had several temples at Rome. The earliest was built by Camillus in commemoration of the reconciliation between the patricians and plebeians, after the enactment of the Licinian rogations, B. C. 367. In this temple the senate frequently met. Concordia is represented on coins as a matron, holding in her left hand a cornucopia, and in her right either an olive branch or a patera.

Condāte, the name of many Celtic towns, said to be equivalent in meaning to Confluentes, *i. e.* the union of two rivers.

Condrūsi, a German people in Gallia Belgica, the dependents of the Treviri, dwelt between the Eburones and the Treviri in the district of *Condros* on the Maas and Ourthe.

Confluentes (*Coblenz*), a town in Germany at the confluence of the Moselle and the Rhine.

Conisalus (Κονίσαλος), a deity worshipped at Athens along with Priapus.

Conōn (Κόνων). 1. A distinguished Athenian general, held several important commands in the latter part of the Peloponnesian war. After the defeat of the Athenians by Lysander at Aegos Potami (B. C. 405), Conon, who was one of the generals, escaped with 8 ships, and took refuge with Evagoras in Cyprus, where he remained for some years. He was subsequently appointed to the command of the Persian fleet along with Pharnabazus, and in this capacity was able to render the most effectual service to his native country. In 394 he gained a decisive victory over Pisander, the Spartan admiral, off Cnidus. After clearing the Aegean of the Spartans, he returned to Athens in 393, and commenced restoring the long walls and the fortifications of Piraeus. When the Spartans opened their negotiations with Tiribazus, the Persian satrap, Conon, was sent by the Athenians to counteract the intrigues of Antalcidas, but was thrown into prison by Tiribazus. According to some accounts, he was sent into the interior of Asia, and there put to death. But according to the most probable account, he escaped to Cyprus, where he died. — 2. Son of Timotheus, grandson of the preceding, lived about 318. — 3. Of Samos, a distinguished mathematician and astronomer, lived in the time of the Ptolemies Philadelphus and Euergetes (B. C. 283—222), and was the friend of Archimedes, who praises him in the highest terms. None of his works are preserved — 4. A grammarian of the age of Augustus, author of a work entitled Διηγήσεις, a collection of 50 narratives relating to the mythical and heroic period. An epitome of the work is preserved by Photius.

Cōnōpa (Κωνώπα; Κωνωπεύς—πίτης—παῖος), a village in Aetolia on the Achelous, enlarged by Arsinoë, wife of Ptolemy II., and called after her name.

Consentes Dii, the 12 Etruscan gods who formed the council of Jupiter. They consisted of 6 male and 6 female divinities: we do not know the names of all of them, but it is certain that Juno, Minerva, Summanus, Vulcan, Saturn, and Mars were among them.

Consentia (Consentinus : *Cosenza*), chief town of the Bruttii on the river Crathis: here Alaric died.

P. Consentīus, a Roman grammarian, probably flourished in the 5th century of the Christian era, and is the author of 2 extant grammatical works, one published in the Collection of grammarians by Putschius, Hanov. 1605 (*De Duabus Partibus Orationis, Nomine et Verbo*), and the other by Buttman, Berol. 1817.

C. Consīdīus Longus, propraetor in Africa, left his province shortly before the breaking out of the civil war B. C. 49, entrusting the government to Q. Ligarius. He returned to Africa soon afterwards, and held Adrumetum for the Pompeian party. After the defeat of the Pompeians at Thapsus, he attempted to fly into Mauretania, but was murdered by the Gaetulians.

Constans, youngest of the 3 sons of Constantine the Great and Fausta, received after his father's death (A. D. 337) Illyricum, Italy, and Africa as his share of the empire. After successfully resisting his brother Constantine, who was slain in invading his territory (340), Constans became master of the whole West. His weak and profligate character rendered him an object of contempt, and he was slain in 350 by the soldiers of the usurper MAGNENTIUS.

Constantīa. 1. Daughter of Constantius Chlorus and half-sister of Constantine the Great, married to Licinius, the colleague of Constantine in the empire. — 2. Daughter of Constantius II. and grand-daughter of Constantine the Great, married the emperor Gratian.

Constantīa, the name of several cities, all of which are either of little consequence, or better known by other names. 1. In Cyprus, named after Constantius [SALAMIS]. 2. In Phoenicia, after the same [ANTARADUS]. 3. In Palestine, the port of GAZA, named after the sister of Constantine the Great, and also called Magiuna. 4. In Mesopotamia. [ANTONINOPOLIS.]

Constantīna, daughter of Constantine the Great and Fausta, married to Hannibalianus, and after the death of the latter to Gallus Caesar.

Constantīna, the city. [CIRTA.]

Constantīnŏpŏlis (Κωνσταντίνου πόλις : *Constantinople*), built on the site of the ancient BYZANTIUM by Constantine the Great, who called it after his own name and made it the capital of the Roman empire. It was solemnly consecrated A. D. 330. It was built in imitation of Rome. Thus it covered 7 hills, was divided into 14 regiones, and was adorned with various buildings in imitation of the capital of the Western world. Its extreme length was about 3 Roman miles ; and its walls included eventually a circumference of 13 or 14 Roman miles. It continued the capital of the Roman empire in the E. till its capture by the Turks in 1453. An account of its topography and history does not fall within the scope of the present work.

Constantīnus. 1. I. Surnamed "the Great," Roman emperor, A. D. 306—337, eldest son of the emperor Constantius Chlorus and Helena, was born A. D. 272, at Naissus (*Nissa*), a town in upper Moesia. He was early trained to arms, and served with great distinction under Galerius in the Persian war. Galerius became jealous of him and detained him for some time in the E.; but Constantine at last contrived to join his father in Gaul just in time to accompany him to Britain on his expedition against the Picts, 306. His father died at York in the same year, and Constantine laid claim to a share of the empire. Galerius, who dreaded a struggle with the brave legions of the West, acknowledged Constantine as master of the countries beyond the Alps, but with the title of Caesar only The commencement of Constantine's reign, however, is placed in this year, though he did not receive the title of Augustus till 308. Constantine took up his residence at Treviri (*Trèves*), where the remains of his palace are still extant. He governed with justice and firmness, beloved by his subjects, and feared by the neighbouring barbarians. It was not long however before he became involved in war with his rivals in the empire. In the same year that he had been acknowledged Caesar (306), Maxentius, the son of Maximian, had seized the imperial power at Rome. Constantine entered into a close alliance with Maxentius by marrying his sister Fausta. But in 310 Maximian formed a plot against Constantine, and was put to death by his son-in-law at Massilia. Maxentius resented the death of his father, and began to make preparations to attack Constantine in Gaul. Constantine anticipated his movements, and invaded Italy at the head of a large army. The struggle was brought to a close by the defeat of Maxentius at the village of Saxa Rubra near Rome, October 27th, 312. Maxentius tried to escape over the Milvian bridge into Rome, but perished in the river. It was in this campaign that Constantine is said to have been converted to Christianity. On his march from he N. to Rome, either at Autun in Gaul, or near Andernach on the Rhine, or at Verona, he is said to have seen in the sky a luminous cross with the inscription ἐν τούτῳ νίκα, BY THIS, CONQUER; and on the night before the last and decisive battle with Maxentius, a vision is said to have appeared to Constantine in his sleep, bidding him inscribe the shields of his soldiers with the sacred monogram of the name of Christ. The tale of the cross seems to have grown out of that of the vision, and even the latter is not entitled to credit. It was Constantine's interest to gain the affections of his numerous Christian subjects in his struggle with his rivals; and it was probably only self-interest which led him at first to adopt Christianity. But whether sincere or not in his conversion, his conduct did little credit to the religion which he professed. The miracle of his conversion was commemorated by the imperial standard of the *Labarum*, at the summit of which was the monogram of the name of Christ. Constantine, by his victory over Maxentius, became the sole master of the W. Meantime important events took place in the E. On the death of Galerius in 311, Licinius and Maximinus had divided the East between them; but in 313 a war broke out between them, Maximin was defeated, and died at Tarsus. Thus there were only two emperors left, Licinius in the E. and Constantine in the W.; and between them also war broke out in 314, although Licinius had married in the preceding year Constantia, the sister of Constantine. Licinius was defeated at Cibalis in Pannonia and afterwards at Adrianople. Peace was then concluded on condition that Licinius should resign to Constantine Illyricum, Macedonia, and Achaia, 314. This peace continued undisturbed for 9 years, during which time Constantine was frequently engaged in war with the barbarians on the Danube and the Rhine. In these wars his son Crispus greatly distinguished himself. In 323 the war between Constantine and Licinius was renewed. Licinius was again defeated in 2 great battles, first near Adrianople, and again at Chalcedon. He surrendered himself to Constantine on condition of having his life spared, but he was shortly afterwards put to death at Thessalonica by order of Constantine. Constantine was now sole master of the empire. He resolved to remove the seat of empire to Byzantium, which he called after his own name Constantinople, or the city of Constantine. The new city was solemnly dedicated in 330. Constantine reigned in peace for the remainder of his life. In 325 he supported the orthodox bishops at the great Christian council of Nicaea (Nice), which condemned the Arian doctrine by adopting the word ὁμοούσιον. In 324 he put to death his eldest son Crispus on a charge of treason, the truth of which however seems very doubtful. He died in May, 337, and was baptized shortly before his death by Eusebius. His three sons Constantine, Constantius and Constans succeeded him in the empire.—3. II. Roman emperor, 337—340, eldest of the 3 sons of Constantine the Great, by Fausta, received Gaul, Britain, Spain, and part of Africa at his father's death. Dissatisfied with his share of the empire,

he made war upon his younger brother Constans, who governed Italy, but was defeated and slain near Aquileia. — 3. An usurper, who assumed the purple in Britain in the reign of Arcadius and Honorius, 407. He also obtained possession of Gaul and Spain, and took up his residence in the former country. He reigned 4 years, but was defeated in 411 by Constantius, the general of Honorius, was taken prisoner and carried to Ravenna, where he was put to death. — 4. Constantine is likewise the name of many of the later emperors of Constantinople. Of these Constantine VII. Porphyrogenitus, who reigned 911—959, was celebrated for his literary works, many of which have come down to us.

Constantius. 1. I. Surnamed **Chlorus**, "the pale," Roman emperor, A. D. 305-306, was the son of Eutropius, a noble Dardanian, and of Claudia, daughter of Crispus, brother of Claudius II. He was one of the two Caesars appointed by Maximian and Diocletian in 292, and received the government of Britain, Gaul, and Spain with Treviri (*Trèves*) as his residence. At the same time he married Theodora, the daughter of the wife of Maximian, divorcing for that purpose his wife Helena. As Caesar he rendered the empire important services. His first effort was to reunite Britain to the empire, which after the murder of Carausius was governed by Allectus. After a struggle of 3 years (293—296) with Allectus, Constantius established his authority in Britain. He was equally successful against the Alemanni, whom he defeated with great loss. Upon the abdication of Diocletian and Maximian, in 305, Constantius and Galerius became the Augusti. Constantius died 15 months afterwards (July, 306) at Eboracum (York) in Britain, on an expedition against the Picts, in which he was accompanied by his son Constantine, afterwards the Great, who succeeded him in his share of the government. — 2. II. Roman emperor, 337—361, third son of Constantine the Great by his second wife Fausta. On the death of his father in 337, he received the E. as his share of the empire. Upon his accession he became involved in a serious war with the Persians, which was carried on with a few interruptions during the greater part of his reign. This war prevented him from taking any part in the struggle between his brothers Constantine and Constans, which ended in the defeat and death of the former, and the accession of the latter to the sole empire of the W., 340. After the death of Constans in 350, Constantius marched into the W. in order to oppose Magnentius and Vetranio, both of whom had assumed the purple. Vetranio submitted to Constantius, and Magnentius was finally crushed in 353. Thus the whole empire again became subject to one ruler. In 354 Constantius put to death his cousin Gallus, whom he had left in command of the E., while he marched against the usurpers in the W. In 355 Constantius made Julian, the brother of Gallus, Caesar, and sent him into Gaul to oppose the barbarians. In 360 Julian was proclaimed Augustus by the soldiers at Paris. Constantius prepared for war and set out for Europe, but died on his march in Cilicia, 361. He was succeeded by Julian. — 3. III. Emperor of the West (A. D. 421), a distinguished general of Honorius. He defeated the usurper Constantine in 411, and also fought successfully against the barbarians. He was rewarded for these services with the hand of

Placidia, the sister of Honorius. In 421 he was declared Augustus by Honorius, but died in the 7th month of his reign.

Consus, an ancient Roman divinity, who was identified by some in later times with Neptune. Hence Livy (i. 9) calls him Neptunus Equestris. He was regarded by some as the god of secret deliberations, but he was most probably a god of the lower world. Respecting his festival of the Consualia, see Dict. of Ant. s. v.

Contrebia, one of the chief towns of the Celtiberi in Hispania Tarraconensis, S. E. of Saragossa.

Convenae, a people in Aquitania near the Pyrenees and on both sides of the Garumna, a mixed race which had served under Sertorius, and were settled in Aquitania by Pompey. They possessed the Jus Latii. Their chief town was Lugdunum (St. Bertrand de Comminges), situated on a solitary rock: in its neighbourhood were celebrated warm baths, Aquae Convenarum (Bagnères).

Copae (Κῶπαι : Κωπαιεύς : nr. Topoglia), an ancient town in Boeotia on the N. side of the lake Copais, which derived its name from this place. It was originally situated on an island in the lake, which island was subsequently connected with the mainland by a mole.

Copais (Κωπαῒς λίμνη), a lake in Boeotia, and the largest lake in Greece, formed chiefly by the river Cephisus, the waters of which are emptied into the Euboean sea by several subterraneous canals, called Katabothra by the modern Greeks. The lake was originally called Cephisis, under which name it occurs in Homer, and subsequently different parts of it were called after the towns situated on it, Haliartus, Orchomenus, Onchestus, Copae, &c.; but the name Copais eventually became the most common, because near Copae the waters of the lake are the deepest and are never dried up. In the summer the greater part of the lake is dry, and becomes a green meadow, in which cattle are pastured. The eels of this lake were much prized in antiquity, and they retain their celebrity in modern times.

Cophenor, Cophes (Κωφήν, Arrian., Κόφης Strab. Cabul), the only grand tributary river which flows into the Indus from the W. It was the boundary between India and Ariana.

C. Coponius, praetor B. C. 49, fought on the side of Pompey; he was proscribed by the triumvirs in 43, but his wife obtained his pardon from Antony by the sacrifice of her honour.

Coprates (Κοπράτης : Abzal), a river of Susiana, flowing from the N. into the Pasitigris on its W. side.

Copreus (Κοπρεύς), son of Pelops, who after murdering Iphitus, fled from Elis to Mycenae, where he was purified by Eurystheus.

Coptos (Κοπτός : Koft, Ru.), a city of the Thebaïs or Upper Egypt, lay a little to the E. of the Nile, some distance below Thebes. Under the Ptolemies, it was the central point of the commerce with Arabia and India, by way of Berenice and Myos-Hormos. It was destroyed by Diocletian, but again became a considerable place. The neighbourhood was celebrated for its emeralds and other precious stones, and produced also a light wine.

Cora (Coranus: Cori), an ancient town in Latium in the Volscian mountains, S.E. of Velitrae, said to have been founded by the Argive Corax. At Cori there are remains of Cyclopian walls and of an ancient temple.

Coracesium (Κοοακήσιον : Alaya), a very strong city of Cilicia Aspera, on the borders of Pamphylia, standing upon a steep rock, and possessing a good harbour. It was the only place in Cilicia which opposed a successful resistance to Alexander, and, after its strength had been tried more than once in the wars of the Seleucidae, it became at last the head-quarters of the Cilician pirates, and was taken by Pompey.

Corassiae (Κορασσίαι), a group of small islands in the Icarian sea, S.W. of Icaria. They must not be confounded, as they often are, with the islands Corsiae or Corsiae (Κόρσεαι or Κόρσιαι), off the Ionian coast and opposite the promontory Ampelos in Samos.

Corax (Κόραξ), a Sicilian rhetorician, who acquired so much influence over the citizens by his oratorical powers, that he became the leading man in Syracuse, after the expulsion of Thrasybulus, B. C. 467. He wrote the earliest work on the art of rhetoric, and his treatise (entitled Τέχνη) was celebrated in antiquity.

Corbulo, Cn. Domitius, a distinguished general under Claudius and Nero. In A. D. 47 he carried on war in Germany with success, but his fame rests chiefly upon his glorious campaigns against the Parthians in the reign of Nero. Though beloved by the army he continued faithful to Nero, but his only reward was death. Nero, who had become jealous of his fame and influence, invited him to Corinth. As soon as he landed at Cenchreae, he was informed that orders had been issued for his death, whereupon he plunged his sword into his breast, exclaiming, " Well deserved ! "

Corcyra (Κέρκυρα, later Κόρκυρα : Κερκυραῖος : Corfu from the Byzantine Κορυφώ), an island in the Ionian sea, off the coast of Epirus, about 58 miles in length, but of very unequal breadth. It is generally mountainous, but possesses many fertile vallies. Its two chief towns were Corcyra, the modern town of Corfu, in the middle of the E. coast, and Cassiope, N. of the former. The ancients universally regarded this island as the Homeric Scheria (Σχερίη), where the enterprising and sea-loving Phaeacians dwelt, governed by their king Alcinous. The island is said to have also borne the name of Drepane (Δρεπάνη) or the " Sickle " in ancient times. About B. C. 700 it was colonised by the Corinthians under Chersicrates, one of the Bacchiadae, who drove out the Liburnians, who were then inhabiting the island. It soon became rich and powerful by its extensive commerce; it founded many colonies on the opposite coast, Epidamnus, Apollonia, Leucas, Anactorium; and it exercised such influence in the Ionian and Adriatic seas as to become a formidable rival to Corinth. Thus the two states early became involved in war, and about B. C. 664 a battle was fought between their fleets, which is memorable as the most ancient sea-fight on record. At a later period Corcyra by invoking the aid of Athens against the Corinthians became one of the proximate causes of the Peloponnesian war, 431. Shortly afterwards her power declined in consequence of civil dissensions, in which both the aristocratical and popular parties were guilty of the most horrible atrocities against each other. At last it became subject to the Romans with the rest of Greece. — Corfu is at present one of the 7 Ionian islands under the protection of Great Britain and the seat of government.

Corcyra Nigra (Cursola, in Slavonic Karkar)

an island off the coast of Illyricum, surnamed the "Black," on account of its numerous forests, to distinguish it from the more celebrated Corcyra. It contained a Greek town of the same name founded by Cnidos.

Corduba (*Cordova*), one of the largest cities in Spain, and the capital of Baetica, on the right bank of the Baetis ; made a Roman colony B. C. 152, and received the surname Patricia, because some Roman patricians settled there; taken by Caesar in 45 because it sided with the Pompeians; birthplace of the two Senecas and of Lucan. In the middle ages it was the capital of the kingdom of the Moors, but is now a decaying place with 55,000 inhabitants.

Corduēnē. [GORDYENE.]

Cordus, Cremūtius, a Roman historian under Augustus and Tiberius, was accused in A. D. 25 of having praised Brutus and denominated Cassius "the last of the Romans." As the emperor had determined upon his death, he put an end to his own life by starvation. His works were condemned to be burnt, but some copies were preserved by his daughter Marcia and by his friends.

Cŏrē (*Κόρη*), the Maiden, a name by which Persephone is often called. [PERSEPHONE.]

Coressus (*Κόρησσος*). 1. A lofty mountain in Ionia, 40 stadia (4 geog. miles) from Ephesus, with a place of the same name at its foot. — 2. A town in the island of Ceos.

Coressus. [CEOS.]

Corfīnium (*Corfiniensis*), chief town of the Peligni in Samnium, not far from the Aternus, strongly fortified, and memorable as the place which the Italians in the Social war destined to be the new capital of Italy in place of Rome, on which account it was called *Italica.*

Cŏrinna (*Κόριννα*), a Greek poetess, of Tanagra in Boeotia, sometimes called the Theban on account of her long residence in Thebes. She flourished about B. C. 490, and was a contemporary of Pindar, whom she is said to have instructed, and over whom she gained a victory at the public games at Thebes. Her poems were written in the Aeolic dialect. They were collected in 5 books, and were chiefly lyrical. Only a few fragments have been preserved.

Corinthīǎcus Isthmus (*'Ισθμὸς Κορίνθου*), often called simply the **Isthmus,** lay between the Corinthian and Saronic gulfs, and connected the Peloponnesus with the mainland or Hellas proper. In its narrowest part it was 40 stadia or 5 Roman miles across : here was the temple of Poseidon and the Isthmian games were celebrated : and here also was the *Diolcos* (*Δίολκος*), or road by which ships were dragged across from the bay of Schoenus to the harbour of Lechaeum. Four unsuccessful attempts were made to dig a canal across the Isthmus, namely, by Demetrius Poliorcetes, Julius Caesar, Caligula, and Nero.

Corinthīǎcus Sinus (*Κορινθιακὸς* or *Κορίνθιος κόλπος*: *G. of Lepanto*), the gulf between the N. of Greece and Peloponnesus, begins, according to some, at the mouth of the Achelous in Aetolia and the promontory Araxus in Achaia, according to others, at the straits between Rhium and Antirrhium. In early times it was called the Crissaean Gulf (*Κρισσαῖος κόλπος*), and its eastern part the Alcyonian Sea (*ἡ 'Αλκυονὶς θάλασσα*).

Cŏrinthus (*Κόρινθος*: *Κορίνθιος*), called in Homer **Ephyra** (*'Εφύρη*), a city on the above-men-

tioned Isthmus. Its territory, called **Corinthia** (*Κορινθία*), embraced the greater part of the Isthmus with the adjacent part of the Peloponnesus : it was bounded N. by Megaris and the Corinthian gulf, S. by Argolis, W. by Sicyonia and Phliasia, and E. by the Saronic gulf. In the N. and S. the country is mountainous, but in the centre it is a plain with a solitary and steep mountain rising from it, the **Acrocorinthus** (*'Ακροκόρινθος*), 1900 feet in height, which served as the citadel of Corinth. The city itself was built on the N. side of this mountain ; and the walls, which included the Acrocorinthus, were 86 stadia in circumference. It had 2 harbours, **CENCHREAE** on the E. or Saronic gulf, and **LECHAEUM** on the W. or Crissaean gulf. Its favourable position between two seas, the difficulty of carrying goods round Peloponnesus, and the facility with which they could be transported across the Isthmus, raised Corinth in very early times to great commercial prosperity, and made it the emporium of the trade between Europe and Asia. Its navy was numerous and powerful. At Corinth the first triremes were built, and the first sea-fight on record was between the Corinthians and their colonists the Corcyraeans. Its greatness at an early period is attested by numerous colonies, Ambracia, Corcyra, Apollonia, Potidaea, &c. It was adorned with magnificent buildings, and in no other city of Greece, except Athens, were the fine arts prosecuted with so much vigour and success. Its commerce brought great wealth to its inhabitants ; but with their wealth, they became luxurious and licentious. Thus the worship of Aphrodite (Venus) prevailed in this city, and in her temples a vast number of courtezans was maintained. — Corinth was originally inhabited by the Aeolic race. Here ruled the Aeolic Sisyphus and his descendants. On the conquest of Peloponnesus by the Dorians, the royal power passed into the hands of the Heraclid Alētes. The conquering Dorians became the ruling class, and the Aeolian inhabitants subject to them. After Aletes and his descendants had reigned for 5 generations, royalty was abolished ; and in its stead was established an oligarchical form of government, confined to the powerful family of the Bacchiadae. This family was expelled B. C. 655 by CYPSELUS, who became tyrant and reigned 30 years. He was succeeded, 625, by his son PERIANDER, who reigned 40 years. On the death of the latter, 585, his nephew Psammetichus reigned for 3 years, and on his fall in 581, the government again became an aristocracy. In the Peloponnesian war Corinth was one of the bitterest enemies of Athens. In 346 Timophanes attempted to make himself master of the city, but he was slain by his brother Timoleon. It maintained its independence till the time of the Macedonian supremacy, when its citadel was garrisoned by Macedonian troops. This garrison was expelled by Aratus in 243, whereupon Corinth joined the Achaean league, to which it continued to belong, till it was taken and destroyed in 146 by L. Mummius, the Roman consul, who treated it in the most barbarous manner. Its inhabitants were sold as slaves; its works of art, which were not destroyed by the Roman soldiery, were conveyed to Rome; its buildings were razed to the ground; and thus was destroyed the *lumen totius Graeciae,* as Cicero calls the city. For a century it lay in ruins; only the buildings on the Acropolis and a few temples remained standing. In 46 it was rebuilt by Caesar, who peopled it with a colony of veterans and descendants of freedmen. It was now called *Colonia Julia Corinthus*; it became the capital of the Roman province of Achaia, and soon recovered much of its ancient prosperity, but at the same time it became noted for its former licentiousness, as we see from St. Paul's epistles to the inhabitants. — The site of Corinth is indicated by 7 Doric columns, which are the only remains of the ancient city.

Coriōlānus, the hero of one of the most beautiful of the early Roman legends. His original name was *C.* or *Cn. Marcius*, and he received the surname Coriolanus from the heroism he displayed at the capture of the Volscian town of Corioli. His haughty bearing towards the commons excited their fear and dislike, and when he was a candidate for the consulship, they refused to elect him. After this, when there was a famine in the city, and a Greek prince sent corn from Sicily, Coriolanus advised that it should not be distributed to the commons, unless they gave up their tribunes. For this he was impeached and condemned to exile, B. C. 491. He now took refuge among the Volscians, and promised to assist them in war against the Romans. Attius Tullius, the king of the Volscians, appointed Coriolanus general of the Volscian army. Coriolanus took many towns, and advanced unresisted till he came to the *fossa Cluilia*, or Cluilian dyke close to Rome, 489. Here he encamped, and the Romans in alarm sent to him embassy after embassy, consisting of the most distinguished men of the state. But he would listen to none of them. At length the noblest matrons of Rome, headed by Veturia, the mother of Coriolanus, and Volumnia his wife, with his 2 little children, came to his tent. His mother's reproaches, and the tears of his wife and the other matrons, bent his purpose. He led back his army, and lived in exile among the Volscians till his death; though other traditions relate that he was killed by the Volscians on his return to their country.

Coriōli (Coriolānus), a town in Latium, capital of the Volsci, from the capture of which in B. C. 493, C. Marcius obtained the surname of Coriolanus.

Cormāsa (Κόρμασα), an inland town of Pamphylia, or of Pisidia, taken by the consul Manlius.

Cornēlia. 1. One of the noble women at Rome, guilty of poisoning the leading men of the state, B. C. 331. — 2. Elder daughter of P. Scipio Africanus the elder, married to P. Scipio Nasica. — 3. Younger sister of No. 2, married to Ti. Sempronius Gracchus, censor 169, was by him the mother of the two tribunes Tiberius and Caius. She was virtuous and accomplished, and united in her person the severe virtues of the old Roman matron, with the superior knowledge and refinement which then began to prevail in the higher classes at Rome. She superintended with the greatest care the education of her sons, whom she survived. She was almost idolized by the people, who erected a statue to her, with the inscription CORNELIA, MOTHER OF THE GRACCHI. — 4. Daughter of L. Cinna, married to C. Caesar, afterwards dictator. She bore him his daughter Julia, and died in his quaestorship, 68. — 5. Daughter of Metellus Scipio, married first to P. Crassus, the son of the triumvir, who perished in the expedition against the Parthians, 53. Next year she married Pompey the Great, by whom she was

tenderly loved. She accompanied Pompey to Egypt after the battle of Pharsalia, and saw him murdered. She afterwards returned to Rome, and received from Caesar the ashes of her husband, which she preserved on his Alban estate.

Cornēlia Orestilla. [ORESTILLA.]

Cornēlia Gens, the most distinguished of all the Roman gentes. All its great families belonged to the patrician order. The names of the patrician families are:—ARVINA, CETHEGUS, CINNA, COSSUS, DOLABELLA, LENTULUS, MALUGINENSIS, MAMMULA, MERULA, RUFINUS, SCIPIO, SISENNA, and SULLA. The names of the plebeian families are BALBUS and GALLUS, and we also find various cognomens, as CHRYSOGONUS, &c. given to freedmen of this gens.

Cornēlius Nepos. [NEPOS.]

Cornĭcŭlum (Corniculānus), a town in Latium in the mountains N. of Tibur, taken and destroyed by Tarquinius Priscus, and celebrated as the residence of the parents of Servius Tullius.

Cornĭfĭcĭus. 1. Q., a friend of Cicero, was tribune of the plebs, B. C. 69, and one of Cicero's competitors for the consulship in 64. When the Catilinarian conspirators were arrested, Cethegus was committed to his care. — 2. Q., son of No. 1. In the civil war (48) he was quaestor of Caesar, who sent him into Illyricum with the title of propraetor: he reduced this province to obedience. In 45 he was appointed by Caesar governor of Syria, and in 44 governor of the province of Old Africa, where he was at the time of Caesar's death. He maintained this province for the senate, but on the establishment of the triumvirate was defeated and slain in battle by T. Sextius. Cornificius was well versed in literature. Many have attributed to him the authorship of the " Rhetorica ad Herennium," usually printed with Cicero's works; but this is only a conjecture. The Cornificius who is mentioned by Quintilian as the author of a work on rhetoric, was probably a different person from the one we are speaking of. — 3. L., one of the generals of Octavianus in the war against Sex. Pompey, and consul 35.

Cornus, a town on the W. of Sardinia.

Cornūtus, L. Annaeus, a distinguished Stoic philosopher, was born at Leptis in Libya. He came to Rome, probably as a slave, and was emancipated by the Annaei. He was the teacher and friend of the poet Persius, who has dedicated his 5th satire to him, and who left him his library and money. He was banished by Nero, A. D. 68, for having too freely criticised the literary attempts of the emperor. He wrote a large number of works, all of which are lost: the most important of them was on Aristotle's Categories.

Coroebus (Κόροιβος). 1. A Phrygian, son of Mygdon, loved Cassandra, and for that reason fought on the side of the Trojans: he was slain by Neoptolemus or Diomedes.—2. An Elean, who gained the victory in the stadium at the Olympic games, B. C. 776: from this time the Olympiads begin to be reckoned.

Corōnē (Κορώνη : Κορωνεύς -ναιεύς), a town in Messenia on the W. side of the Messenian gulf, founded B. C. 371 by the Messenians after their return to their native country, with the assistance of the Thebans: it possessed several public buildings, and in its neighbourhood was a celebrated temple of Apollo.

Corōnēa (Κορώνεια: Κορωναῖος, Κορώνειος, -ρεος).

1. A town in Boeotia, S.W. of the lake Copais, situate on a height between the rivers Phalarus and Curalius; a member of the Boeotian League; in its neighbourhood was the temple of Athena Itorica, where the festival of the Pamboeotia was celebrated. Near Coronea the Boeotians gained a memorable victory over the Athenians under Tolmides, B. C. 447; and here Agesilaus defeated the allied Greeks, 394. — 2. A town in Phthiotis in Thessaly.

Corōnis (Κορωνίς). 1. The mother of AESCU-LAPIUS. — 2. Daughter of Phoroneus, king of Phocis, metamorphosed by Athena into a crow, when pursued by Poseidon.

Corsĕae. [CORASSIAE.]

Corsĭa (Κορσεία, also Κηρσιαί), a town in Boeotia on the borders of Phocis.

Corsĭca, called Cyrnus by the Greeks (Κύρνος: Κύρνιος, Κυρναῖος, Corsus: Corsica), an island N. of Sardinia, spoken of by the ancients as one of the 7 large islands in the Mediterranean. The ancients, however, exaggerate for the most part the size of the island; its greatest length is 116 miles, and its greatest breadth about 51. It is mountainous and was not much cultivated in antiquity. A range of mountains running from S. to N. separates it into 2 parts, of which the E. half was more cultivated, while the W. half was covered almost entirely with wood. Honey and wax were the principal productions of the island; but the honey had a bitter taste from the yew-trees with which the island abounded. (Cyrneas taxos, Virg. Eol. ix. 30.) The inhabitants were a rude mountain race, addicted to robbery, and paying little attention to agriculture. Even in the time of the Roman empire their character had not much improved, as we see from the description of Seneca, who was banished to this island. The most ancient inhabitants appear to have been Iberians; but in early times Ligurians, Tyrrhenians, Carthaginians, and even Greeks [ALERIA], settled in the island. It was subject to the Carthaginians at the commencement of the 1st Punic war, but soon afterwards passed into the hands of the Romans, and subsequently formed a part of the Roman province of Sardinia. The Romans founded several colonies in the island, of which the most important were MARIANA and ALERIA.

Corsōtē (Κορσωτή: Erzey, Ru.), a city of Mesopotamia, on the Euphrates, near the mouth of the Mascas or Saocoras (Wady-el-Seba), which Xenophon found already deserted.

Cortōna. (Cortonensis: Cortona), one of the 12 cities of Etruria, lay N.W. of the Trasimene lake, and was one of the most ancient cities in Italy. It is said to have been orginally called Corythus from its reputed founder Corythus, who is represented as the father of Dardanus. It is also called Croton, Cothornia, Cyrtonium, &c. The Creston mentioned by Herodotus (i. 57) was probably Creston in Thrace and not Cortona, as many modern writers have supposed. Crotona is said to have been originally founded by the Umbrians, then to have been conquered by the Pelasgians, and subsequently to have passed into the hands of the Etruscans. It was afterwards colonized by the Romans, but under their dominion sunk into insignificance. The remains of the Pelasgic walls of this city are some of the most remarkable in all Italy: there is one fragment 120 feet in length, composed of blocks of enormous magnitude.

Coruncānĭus, Tĭ., consul B. c. 280, with P. Valerius Laevinus, fought with success against the Etruscans and Pyrrhus. He was the first plebeian who was created pontifex maximus. He was one of the most remarkable men of his age, possessed a profound knowledge of pontifical and civil law, and was the first person at Rome who gave regular instruction in law.

Corvīnus Messala. [MESSALA.]

Corvus, M. Vălĕrĭus, one of the most illustrious men in the early history of Rome. He obtained the surname of Corvus, or "Raven," because, when serving as military tribune under Camillus, B. c. 349, he accepted the challenge of a gigantic Gaul to single combat, and was assisted in the conflict by a raven which settled upon his helmet, and flew in the face of the barbarian. He was 6 times consul, B. c. 348, 346, 343, 335, 300, 299, and twice dictator, 342, 301, and by his military abilities rendered the most memorable services to his country. His most brilliant victories were gained in his third consulship, 343, when he defeated the Samnites at Mt. Gaurus and at Suessula; and in his other consulships he repeatedly defeated the Etruscans and other enemies of Rome. He reached the age of 100 years, and is frequently referred to by the later Roman writers as a memorable example of the favours of fortune.

Cōrўbantes, priests of Cybele or Rhea in Phrygia, who celebrated her worship with enthusiastic dances, to the sound of the drum and the cymbal. They are often identified with the Curetes and the Idaean Dactyli, and thus are said to have been the nurses of Zeus in Crete. They were called Galli at Rome.

Cōrўcĭa (Κωρυκία or Κωρυκίς), a nymph, who became by Apollo the mother of Lycorus or Lycoreus, and from whom the Corycian cave in mount Parnassus was believed to have derived its name The Muses are sometimes called by the poets Corycides Nymphae.

Cōrўcus (Κώρυκος: Κωρύκιος, Corycius). 1. (Korakis), a high rocky hill on the coast of Ionia, forming the S.W. promontory of the Erythraean peninsula. — 2. A city of Pamphylia, near Phaselis and Mt. Olympus; colonized afresh by Attalus II. Philadelphus; taken, and probably destroyed, by P. Servilius Isauricus. — 3. (Ru. opp. the island ot Khorgos), a city in Cilicia Aspera, with a good harbour, between the mouths of the Lamus and the Calycadnus. 20 stadia (2 geog. miles) from the city, was a grotto or glen in the mountains, called the Corycian Cave (Κωρύκιον ἄντρον) celebrated by the poets, and also famous for its saffron. At the distance of 100 stadia (10 geog. miles) from Corycus, was a promontory of the same name.

Corydallus (Κορυδαλλός: Κορυδαλλεύς), a demus in Attica belonging to the tribe Hippothoontis, situate on the mountain of the same name, which divides the plain of Athens from that of Eleusis.

Coryphasĭum (Κορυφάσιον), a promontory in Messenia, enclosing the harbour of Pylos on the N., with a town of the same name upon it.

Corўthus (Κόρυθος), an Italian hero, son ot Jupiter, husband of Electra, and father of Iasius and Dardanus, is said to have founded Corythus (Cortona).

Cōs, Cōōs, Cōüs (Κῶς, Κόως; Κῶος, Cōüs; Κος, Stanco), one of the islands called Sporades, lay off the coast of Caria, at the mouth of the Ceramic Gulf, opposite to Halicarnassus. In early times it was called

Centaur.   (Metope from the Parthenon.)   Page 161.

Cerberus.   (From a Bronze Statue.)   Page 163.

Danaids.   (Visconti, Mus. Pio Clem., vol. 4, tav. 36.)   Page 207.

Cybele and Corybantes with Infant Zeus (Jupiter).
(Museo Capitolino).   Page 192.

Charon, Hermes or Mercury, and Soul.
(From a Roman Lamp.)   Page 167.

[To face p. 192.

Cibyra Magna in Caria.   Page 170.

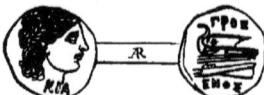

Cius in Bithynia.   Page 176.

Clazomenae in Asia Minor.   Page 179.

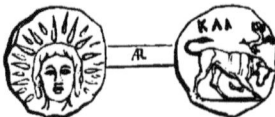

Cleonae in Argolis.   Page 181.

Cnidus.   Page 184.

Cnosus in Crete.   Page 184.

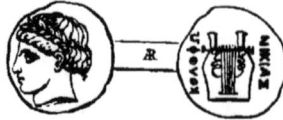

Colophon in Asia Minor.   Page 184.

Comana in Pontus.   Page 186.

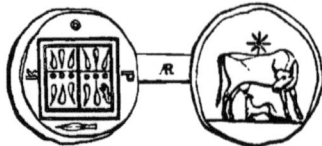

Corcyra.   Page 189.

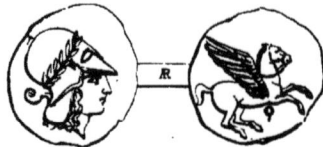

Corinth.   Page 190.

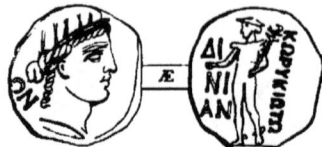

Corycus in Cilicia.   Page 192.

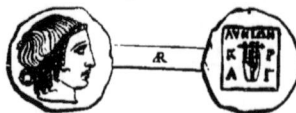

Cragus in Cilicia.   194.

To face p. 193.]

Meröpis and Nymphaea. It was colonized by Aeolians, but became a member of the Dorian confederacy. Its chief city, Cos, stood on the N.E. side of the island, in a beautiful situation, and had a good harbour. Near it stood the Asclepiěum, or temple of Asclepius, to whom the island was sacred, and from whom its chief family, the Asclepiadae, claimed their descent. The island was very fertile ; its chief productions were wine, ointments, and the light transparent dresses called " Coae vestes." It was the birthplace of the physician Hippocrates, who was an Asclepiad, of the poet Philetas, and of the painter Apelles, whose pictures of Antigonus and of Venus Anadyomene adorned the Asclepiěum. Under the Romans, Cos was favoured by Claudius, who made it a free state, and by Antoninus Pius, who rebuilt the city of Cos after its destruction by an earthquake.

Côsa or **Cossa** (Cossânus). 1. (Ansedonia, about 5 miles S. E. of Orbetello), a city of Etruria near the sea, with a good harbour, called Herculis Portus, was a very ancient place ; and after the fall of Falerii one of the 12 Etruscan cities. It was colonized by the Romans B. c. 273, and received in 197 an addition of 1000 colonists. There are still extensive ruins of its walls and towers, built of polygonal masonry. — **2.** A town in Lucania near Thurii.

Coseönius. 1. C., praetor in the Social war, B. c. 89, defeated the Samnites. — **2.** C., praetor in the consulship of Cicero 63 ; governed in the following year the province of Further Spain ; was one of the 20 commissioners, in 59, to carry into execution the agrarian law of Julius Caesar, but died in this year. — **3.** C., tribune of the plebs 59, aedile 57, and one of the judices at the trial of P. Sextius, 56.

Cosmas (Κοσμᾶς), commonly called INDICO-PLEUSTES (Indian navigator), an Egyptian monk, flourished in the reign of Justinian, about A. D. 535. In early life he followed the employment of a merchant, and visited many foreign countries, of which he gave an account in his Τοπογραφία Χριστιανική, Topographia Christiana, in 12 books, of which the greater part is extant.

Cosroës. 1. King of Parthia. [ARSACES XXV.] — **2.** King of Persia. [SASSANIDAE.]

Cossaea (Κοσσαία), a district in and about M. Zagros, on the N.E. side of Susiana, and on the confines of Media and Persia, inhabited by a rude, warlike, predatory people, the Cossaei (Κοσσαῖοι), whom the Persian kings never subdued, but on the contrary, purchased their quiet by paying them tribute. Alexander conquered them (B. c. 325–24), and with difficulty kept them in subjection ; after his death, they soon regained their independence. Their name is supposed to have been the origin of the modern name of Susiana, Khuzistan, and is possibly connected with the Cush of the O. T.

Cossus, Cornělius, the name of several illustrious Romans in the early history of the republic. Of these the most celebrated was Ser. Cornelius Cossus, consul B. c. 428, who killed Lar Tolumnius, the king of the Veii, in single combat, and dedicated his spoils in the temple of Jupiter Feretrius — the 2nd of the 3 instances in which the spolia opima were won.

Cossutius, a Roman architect, who rebuilt at the expense of Antiochus Epiphanes the temple of the Olympian Zeus at Athens, about B. c. 168, in the most magnificent Corinthian style.

Cosyra (Pantelaria), also written Coasyra, Cosyra, Cosura, Cossura, a small island in the Mediterranean near Malta.

Cöthon. [CARTHAGO.]

Côtiso, a king of the Dacians, conquered in the reign of Augustus by Lentulus.

Cotta, Aurělius. 1. C., consul B. c. 252 and 248, in both of which years he fought in Sicily against the Carthaginians with success. — **2.** C., consul 200, fought against the Boii and the other Gauls in the N. of Italy. — **3.** L., tribune of the plebs 154, and consul 144. — **4.** L., consul 119, opposed C. Marius, who was then tribune of the plebs. — **5.** C., was accused under the lex Varia, 91, of supporting the claims of the Italian allies, and went into voluntary exile. He returned to Rome when Sulla was dictator, 82; and in 75 he was consul with L. Octavius. He obtained the government of Gaul, and died immediately after his return to Rome. He was one of the most distinguished orators of his time, and is introduced by Cicero as one of the speakers in the De Oratore, and the De Natura Deorum, in the latter of which works he maintains the cause of the Academics. — **6. M.,** brother of No. 5, consul 74, with L. Licinius Lucullus, obtained Bithynia for his province, and was defeated by Mithridates near Chalcedon. — **7. L.,** brother of Nos. 5 and 6, praetor 70, when he carried the celebrated law (lex Aurelia judiciaria) which entrusted the judicia to the senators, equites, and tribuni aerarii. He was consul 65 with L. Manlius Torquatus, after the consuls elect, P Sulla and P. Autronius Paetus, had been condemned of ambitus. He supported Cicero during his consulship, and proposed his recall from exile. In the civil war he joined Caesar, whom he survived.

Cotta, Aurunculěius, one of Caesar's legates in Gaul, perished along with Sabinus in the attack made upon them by Ambiorix, B. c. 54. [AMBIORIX.]

Cottius, son of Donnus, king of several Ligurian tribes in the Cottian Alps, which derived their name from him. [ALPES.] He submitted to Augustus, who granted him the sovereignty over 12 of these tribes, with the title of Praefectus. Cottius thereupon made roads over the Alps, and erected (B. c. 8) at Seguaio (Susa), a triumphal arch in honour of Augustus, extant at the present day. His authority was transmitted to his son, upon whom Claudius conferred the title of king. On his death, his kingdom was made a Roman province by Nero.

Cottus, a giant with 100 hands, son of Uranus and Gaea.

Cotyla, L. Varius, one of Antony's most intimate friends, fought on his side at Mutina, B. c. 43.

Cötylus (Κότυλος), the highest peak of M. Ida in the Troad, containing the sources of the rivers Scamander, Granicus, and Aesepus.

Cötyöra (Κοτύωρα), a colony of Sinope, in the territory of the Tibareni, on the coast of Pontus Polemoniacus, at the W. end of a bay of the same name, celebrated as the place where the 10,000 Greeks embarked for Sinope. The foundation of Pharnacia reduced it to insignificance.

Cötys or **Cötytto** (Κότυς or Κοτυττώ), a Thracian divinity, whose festival, the Cotyttia (Dict. of Ant. s. v.), resembled that of the Phrygian Cybele, and was celebrated with licentious revelry. In later times her worship was introduced at Athens and Corinth. Those who celebrated her festival were

o

called *Baptae*, from the purifications which were originally connected with the solemnity.

Cŏtys (Κότυς). 1. King of Thrace, B. C. 382—358, was for a short time a friend of the Athenians, but carried on war with them towards the close of his reign. He was cruel and sanguinary, and was much addicted to gross luxury and drunkenness. He was murdered by two brothers whose father he had injured.—2. King of the Odrysae in Thrace, assisted Perseus against Rome, B. C. 168. His son was taken prisoner and carried to Rome, whereupon he sued for peace and was pardoned by the Romans.—3. A king of Thrace, who took part against Caesar with Pompey, 48.—4. King of Thrace, son of Rhoemetalces, in the reigns of Augustus and Tiberius. He carried on war with his uncle Rhescuporis, by whom he was murdered, A. D. 19. Ovid, during his exile at Tomi, addressed an epistle to him (*Ex Pont.* ii. 9).

Crăgus (Κράγος), a mountain consisting of 8 summits, being a continuation of Taurus to the W., and forming, at its extremity, the S.W. promontory of Lycia (*Yedy-Booroom*, i. e. *Seven Capes*). Some of its summits show traces of volcanic action, and the ancients had a tradition to the same effect. At its foot was a town of the same name, on the sea-shore, between Pydna and Patara. Parallel to it, N. of the river Glaucus, was the chain of Anticrăgus. The greatest height of Cragus exceeds 3000 feet.

Cranae (Κρανάη), the island to which Paris first carried Helen from Peloponnesus (Hom. *Il.* iii. 445), is said by some to be an island off Gythium in Laconia, by others to be the island Helena off Attica, and by others again to be Cythera.

Cranăus (Κραναός), king of Attica, the son-in-law and successor of Cecrops. He was deprived of his kingdom by his son-in-law Amphictyon.

Cranii-ium (Κράνιοι, Κράνιον: Κράνιος: *Krania* nr. *Argostoli*), a town of Cephallenia on the S. coast.

Crănōn or **Crannōn** (Κρανών, Κραννών: Κραννώνιος), in ancient times **Ephyra**, a town in Pelasgiotis in Thessaly, not far from Larissa.

Crantor (Κράντωρ), of Soli in Cilicia, an Academic philosopher, studied at Athens under Xenocrates and Polemo, and flourished B. C. 300. He was the author of several works, all of which are lost, and was the first who wrote commentaries on Plato's works. Most of his writings related to moral subjects (Hor. *Ep.* i. 2. 4). One of his most celebrated works was *On Grief*, of which Cicero made great use in the 3rd book of his Tusculan Disputations, and in the *Consolatio*, which he composed on the death of his daughter, Tullia.

Crassipes, Furius, Cicero's son-in-law, the second husband of Tullia, whom he married B. C. 56, but from whom he was shortly afterwards divorced.

Crassus, Licinius. 1. P., praetor B.C. 176, and consul 171, when he carried on the war against Perseus.—2. Q., brother of No. 1, praetor 172, and consul 168.—3. C., probably son of No. 2, tribune of the plebs 145, was distinguished as a popular leader.—4. P., surnamed *Dives* or *Rich*, elected pontifex maximus 212, curule aedile 211, praetor 208, and consul 205 with Scipio Africanus, when he carried on war against Hannibal in the S. of Italy. He died 183.—5. P., surnamed *Dives Mucianus*, son of P. Mucius Scaevola, was adopted by the son of No. 4. In 131 he was consul and pontifex maximus, and was the first

priest of that rank who went beyond Italy. He carried on war against Aristonicus in Asia, but was defeated and slain. He was a good orator and jurist.—6. M., surnamed *Agelastus*, because he is said never to have laughed, was grandfather of Crassus the triumvir.—7. P., surnamed *Dives*, son of No. 6, and father of the triumvir. He was the proposer of the lex Licinia, to prevent excessive expense in banquets, but in what year is uncertain. He was consul 97, and carried on war in Spain for some years. He was censor 89 with L. Julius Caesar. In the civil war he took part with Sulla, and put an end to his own life, when Marius and Cinna returned to Rome at the end of 87.—8. M., surnamed *Dives*, the triumvir, younger son of No. 7. His life was spared by Cinna, after the death of his father; but fearing Cinna, he afterwards escaped to Spain, where he concealed himself for 8 months. On the death of Cinna in 84, he collected some forces and crossed over into Africa, whence he passed into Italy in 83 and joined Sulla, on whose side he fought against the Marian party. On the defeat of the latter, he was rewarded by donations of confiscated property, and thus greatly increased his patrimony. His ruling passion was money, and he devoted all his energies to its accumulation. He was a keen and sagacious speculator. He bought multitudes of slaves, and, in order to increase their value, had them instructed in lucrative arts. He worked silver mines, cultivated farms, and built houses, which he let at high rents. In 71 he was appointed praetor in order to carry on the war against Spartacus and the gladiators; he defeated Spartacus, who was slain in the battle, and he was honoured with an ovation. In 70 Crassus was consul with Pompey; he entertained the populace at a banquet of 10,000 tables, and distributed corn enough to supply the family of every citizen for 3 months. He did not, however, co-operate cordially with Pompey, of whose superior influence he was jealous. He was afterwards reconciled to Pompey by Caesar's mediation, and thus was formed between them, in 60, the so-called triumvirate. [See p. 133, b.] In 55 Crassus was again consul with Pompey, and received the province of Syria, where he hoped both to increase his wealth and to acquire military glory by attacking the Parthians. He set out for his province before the expiration of his consulship, and continued his march notwithstanding the unfavourable omens which occurred to him at almost every step. After crossing the Euphrates in 54, he did not follow up the attack upon Parthia, but returned to Syria, where he passed the winter. In 53 he again crossed the Euphrates; he was misled by a crafty Arabian chieftain to march into the plains of Mesopotamia, where he was attacked by Surenas, the general of the Parthian king, Orodes. In the battle which followed Crassus was defeated with immense slaughter, and retreated with the remainder of his troops to Carrhae (the Haran of Scripture). The mutinous threats of his troops compelled him to accept a perfidious invitation from Surenas, who offered a pacific interview, at which he was slain either by the enemy, or by some friend who desired to save him from the disgrace of becoming a prisoner. His head was cut off and sent to Orodes, who caused melted gold to be poured into the mouth of his fallen enemy, saying, "Sate thyself now with that metal of which in life thou wert so greedy."—9. M., surnamed *Dives*, son of No. 8, served under Caesar in Gaul.

and at the breaking out of the civil war in 49, was praefect in Cisalpine Gaul. — **10.** P., younger son of No. 8., was Caesar's legate in Gaul from 58 to 55. In 54 he followed his father to Syria, and fell in the battle against the Parthians. — **11.** L., the celebrated orator. At the age of 21 (B. C. 119), he attracted great notice by his prosecution of C. Carbo. He was consul in 95 with Q. Scaevola, when he proposed a law to compel all who were not citizens to depart from Rome: the rigour of this law was one of the causes of the Social war. He was afterwards proconsul of Gaul. In 92 he was censor, when he caused the schools of the Latin rhetoricians to be closed. He died in 91, a few days after opposing in the senate the consul L. Philippus, an enemy of the aristocracy. Crassus was fond of elegance and luxury. His house upon the Palatium was one of the most beautiful at Rome, and was adorned with costly works of art. As an orator he surpassed all his contemporaries. In the treatise *De Oratore* Cicero introduces him as one of the speakers, and he is understood to express Cicero's own sentiments.

Crastīnus, one of Caesar's veterans, commenced the battle of Pharsalia, B. C. 48, and died fighting bravely in the foremost line.

Cratērus (Κρατερός). 1. A distinguished general of Alexander the Great, on whose death (B. C. 323) he received in common with Antipater the government of Macedonia and Greece. He arrived in Greece in time to render effectual assistance to Antipater in the Lamian war. At the close of this war he married Phila, the daughter of Antipater. Soon after he accompanied Antipater in the war against the Aetolians, and in that against Perdiccas in Asia. He fell in a battle against Eumenes, in 321. — **2.** Brother of Antigonus Gonatas, compiled historical documents relative to the history of Attica. — **3.** A Greek physician, who attended the family of Atticus, mentioned also by Horace (*Sat.* ii. 3. 161).

Crātēs (Κράτης). 1. An Athenian poet of the old comedy, began to flourish B. C. 449, and was one of the most celebrated of the comic poets. He excelled chiefly in mirth and fun, and was the first Attic poet who brought drunken persons on the stage. — **2.** Of Tralles, an orator or rhetorician of the school of Isocrates. — **3.** Of Thebes, a pupil of the Cynic Diogenes, and one of the most distinguished of the Cynic philosophers, flourished about 320. Though heir to a large fortune, he renounced it all, and lived and died as a true Cynic, disregarding all external pleasures, and restricting himself to the most absolute necessaries. He received the surname of the "Door-opener," because it was his practice to visit every house at Athens, and rebuke its inmates. He married Hipparchia, the daughter of a family of distinction, who threatened to commit suicide when her parents opposed her union with the philosopher. He wrote several works which are lost, for the epistles extant under his name are not genuine. — **4.** Of Athens, the pupil and friend of Polemo, and his successor in the chair of the Academy, about 270. He was the teacher of Arcesilaüs, Theodorus, and Bion Borysthenites. — **5.** Of Mallus in Cilicia, a celebrated grammarian. He was brought up at Tarsus, whence he removed to Pergamos, where he founded the Pergamene school of grammar, in opposition to the Alexandrian. He wrote a commentary on the Homeric poems, in opposition to Aristarchus, and

supported the system of *anomaly* (ἀνωμαλία) against that of *analogy* (ἀναλογία). He also wrote commentaries on the other Greek poets, and works on other subjects, of which only fragments have come down to us. In 157 he was sent by Attalus as an ambassador to Rome, where he introduced for the first time the study of grammar.

Crāthis (Κρᾶθις). 1. (*Crata*), a river in Achaia, rises in a mountain of the same name in Arcadia, receives the Styx flowing down from Nonacris, and falls into the sea near Aegae. — **2.** (*Crati*), a river in lower Italy, forming the boundary on the E. between Lucania and Bruttii, and falling into the sea near Sybaris. At its mouth was a celebrated temple of Minerva: its waters were fabled to dye the hair blond.

Crātīnus (Κρατῖνος). 1. One of the most celebrated of the Athenian poets of the old comedy, was born B. C. 519, but did not begin to exhibit till 454, when he was 65 years of age. He exhibited 21 plays and gained 9 victories. He was *the poet* of the old comedy. He gave it its peculiar character, and he did not, like Aristophanes, live to see its decline. Before his time the comic poets had aimed at little beyond exciting the laughter of their audience: he was the first who made comedy a terrible weapon of personal attack, and the comic poet a severe censor of public and private vice. He is frequently attacked by Aristophanes, who charges him with habitual intemperance, an accusation which was admitted by Cratinus himself, who treated the subject in a very amusing way in his Πυτίνη. This play was acted in 423, when the poet was 96 years of age; it gained the prize over the *Connus* of Amipsias and the *Clouds* of Aristophanes. Cratinus died in the following year, at the age of 97. — **2.** The younger, an Athenian poet of the middle comedy, a contemporary of Plato the philosopher, flourished as late as 324.

Crātippus (Κράτιππος). 1. A Greek historian and contemporary of Thucydides, whose work he completed. — **2.** A Peripatetic philosopher of Mytilene, a contemporary of Pompey and Cicero, the latter of whom praises him highly. He accompanied Pompey in his flight after the battle of Pharsalia, B. C. 48. He afterwards settled at Athens, where young M. Cicero was his pupil in 44. Through the influence of Cicero, Cratippus obtained from Caesar the Roman citizenship.

Crātos (Κράτος), the personification of strength, a son of Uranus and Ge.

Cratŷlus (Κρατυλος), a Greek philosopher, a pupil of Heraclitus, and one of Plato's teachers. Plato introduces him as one of the speakers in the dialogue which bears his name.

Cremēra, a small river in Etruria, which falls into the Tiber a little above Rome: memorable for the death of the 300 Fabii.

Cremna (Κρῆμνα: *Ghermè,* Ru.), a strongly fortified city of Pisidia, built on a precipitous rock in the Taurus range, and noted for repeated obstinate defences: a colony under Augustus.

Cremni (Κρημνοί), an emporium of the free Scythians on the W. side of the Palus Maeotis.

Crēmōna (Cremonensis: *Cremona*), a Roman colony in the N. of Italy, N. of the Po, and at no great distance from the confluence of the Addua and the Po, was founded together with Placentia B. C. 219 as a protection against the Gauls and Hannibal's invading army. It soon became a place of great importance and one of the most flourishing cities in the N. of Italy; but having espoused the cause of Vitellius, it was totally destroyed by the troops of Vespasian, A. D. 69. It was rebuilt by Vespasian, but never recovered its former greatness.

Cremōnis Jugum. [ALPES.]

Cremūtius Cordus. [CORDUS.]

Crĕŏn (Κρέων). 1. King of Corinth, son of Lycaethus, whose daughter, Glauce or Creusa, married Jason. Medĕa, thus forsaken, sent Glauce a garment which burnt her to death when she put it on; the palace took fire, and Creon perished in the flames. — 2. Son of Menoeceus, and brother of Jocaste, the wife of Laius. After the death of Laius, Creon governed Thebes for a short time, and then surrendered the kingdom to Oedipus, who had delivered the country from the Sphinx. [OEDIPUS.] When Eteocles and Polynīces, the sons of Oedipus, fell in battle by each other's hands, Creon became king of Thebes. His cruelty in forbidding burial to the corpse of Polynīces, and his sentencing Antigone to death for disobeying his orders, occasioned the death of his own son Haemon. For details see ANTIGONE.

Crĕŏphȳlus (Κρεώφυλος), of Chios, one of the earliest epic poets, said to have been the friend or son-in-law of Homer. The epic poem Οἰχαλία or Οἰχαλίας ἅλωσις, ascribed to him, related the contest which Hercules, for the sake of Iole, undertook with Eurytus, and the capture of Oechalia.

Cresphontes (Κρησφόντης), an Heraclid, son of Aristomachus, and one of the conquerors of Peloponnesus, obtained Messenia for his share. During an insurrection of the Messenians, he and two of his sons were slain. A third son, Aepytus, avenged his death. [AEPYTUS.]

Crestōnia (Κρηστωνία: ἡ Κρηστωνική), a district in Macedonia between the Axius and Strymon, near Mt. Cercine, inhabited by the **Crestonaei** (Κρηστωναῖοι), a Thracian people: their chief town was Creston or Crestōne (Κρήστων, Κρηστώνη), founded by the Pelasgians. This town is erroneously supposed by some writers to be the same as CORTONA in Italy.

Crēta (Κρήτη: Κρηταῖος: *Candia*), one of the largest islands in the Mediterranean sea, nearly equidistant from Europe, Asia, and Africa, but always reckoned as part of Europe. Its length from E. to W. is about 160 miles: its breadth is very unequal, being in the widest part about 35 miles, and in the narrowest only 6. A range of mountains runs through the whole length of the island from E. to W., sending forth spurs N. and S.: in the centre of the island rises Mt. Ida far above all the others. [IDA.] The rivers of Crete are numerous, but are little more than mountain-torrents, and are for the most part dry in summer. The country was celebrated in antiquity for its fertility and salubrity. — Crete was inhabited at an early period by a numerous and civilized population. Homer speaks of its hundred cities (Κρήτη ἑκατόμπολις, *Il.* ii. 649); and before the Trojan war mythology told of a king MINOS, who resided at Cnossus, and ruled over the greater part of the island. He is said to have given laws to Crete, and to have been the first prince who had a navy, with which he suppressed piracy in the Aegaean. After his descendants had governed the island for some generations, royalty was abolished, and the cities became independent republics, of which

Cnossus and Gortyna were the most important, and exercised a kind of supremacy over the rest. The ruling class were the Dorians who settled in Crete about 60 years after the Dorian conquest of Peloponnesus, and reduced the former inhabitants, the Pelasgians and Achaeans, to subjection. The social and political institutions of the island thus became Dorian, and many of the ancients supposed that the Spartan constitution was borrowed from Crete. The chief magistrates in the cities were the *Cosmi*, 10 in number, chosen from certain families: there was also a *Gerusia*, or senate; and an *Ecclesia* or popular assembly, which, however, had very little power. (For details, see *Dict. of Ant.* art. *Cosmi.*) At a later time the power of the aristocracy was overthrown and a democratical form of government established. The ancient Doric customs likewise disappeared, and the people became degenerate in their morals and character. The historian Polybius accuses them of numerous vices, and the Apostle Paul, quoting the Cretan poet Epimenides, describes them as "alway liars, evil beasts, slow bellies" (*Titus*, i. 12). — The Cretans were celebrated as archers, and frequently served as mercenaries in the armies of other nations. The island was conquered by Q. Metellus, who received in consequence the surname Creticus (B.C. 68—66), and it became a Roman province. Crete and Cyrenaica subsequently formed one province.

Crēteus or **Catreus** (Κρητεύς), son of Minos by Pasiphaë or Crete, and father of Althemenes.

Crētheus (Κρηθεύς), son of Aeolus and Enarete, wife of Tyro, and father of Aeson, Pheres, Amythaon, and Hippolyte: he was the founder of Iolcus.

Crētŏpŏlis (Κρητόπολις), a town in the district of Milyas in Asia Minor, assigned sometimes to Pisidia, sometimes to Pamphylia.

Crēūsa (Κρέουσα). 1. A Naiad, daughter of Oceanus, became by Peneus the mother of Hypseus and Stilbe. — 2. Daughter of Erechtheus and Praxithea, wife of Xuthus, and mother of Achaeus and Ion. She is said to have been beloved by Apollo, whence Ion is sometimes called her son by this god. — 3. Daughter of Priam and Hecuba, wife of Aeneas, and mother of Ascanius. She perished on the night of the capture of Troy, having been separated from her husband in the confusion. — 4. Daughter of Creon, who fell a victim to the vengeance of Medea. [CREON, No. 1.]

Creusis or **Creûsa** (Κρεῦσις, Κρέουσα: Κρευσιεύς), a town on the E. coast of Boeotia, the harbour of Thespiae.

Crimīsa or **Crimissa** (Κρίμισα, Κρίμισσα: *C. dell' Alice*), a promontory on the E. coast of Bruttium, with a town of the same name upon it, said to have been founded by Philoctetes, a little S. of the river Crimisus.

Crimīsus or **Crimissus** (Κριμισός, Κριμισσός), a river in the W. of Sicily, falls into the Hypsa: on its banks Timoleon defeated the Carthaginians, B. C. 339.

Crinăgŏras (Κριναγόρας), of Mytilene, the author of 50 epigrams in the Greek Anthology, lived in the reign of Augustus.

Crispīnus, a person ridiculed by Horace (*Sat.* i. l. 120), is said to have written bad verses on the Stoic philosophy, and to have been surnamed Aretalogus.

Crispus, Flavius Julius, eldest son of Constantine the Great, was appointed Caesar A. D. 317, and gained great distinction in a campaign against the Franks and in the war with Licinius. But having excited the jealousy of his step-mother Fausta, he was put to death by his father, 326.

Crispus Passiēnus, husband of Agrippina, and step-father of the emperor Nero, was distinguished as an orator.

Crispus, Vibius, of Vercelli, a contemporary of Quintilian, and a distinguished orator.

Crissa or Crisa (Κρίσσα, Κρίσα : Κρισσαῖος), and Cirrha (Κίῤῥα : Κιῤῥαῖος), towns in Phocis, regarded by some ancient, as well as by some modern writers as the same; but it seems most probable that Crissa was a town inland S. W. of Delphi, and that Cirrha was its port in the Crissaean gulf. The inhabitants of these towns levied contributions upon the pilgrims frequenting the Delphic oracle, in consequence of which the Amphictyons declared war against them, B. C. 595, and eventually destroyed them. Their territory, the rich Crissaean plain, was declared sacred to the Delphic god, and was forbidden to be cultivated. The cultivation of this plain by the inhabitants of Amphissa led to the Sacred War, in which Philip was chosen general of the Amphictyons, 338. Crissa remained in ruins, but Cirrha was afterwards rebuilt, and became the harbour of Delphi.

Critias (Κριτίας). 1. Son of Dropides, a contemporary and relation of Solon's.— 2. Son of Callaeschrus, and grandson of the above, was one of the pupils of Socrates, by whose instructions he profited but little in a moral point of view. He was banished from Athens, and on his return he became leader of the oligarchical party. He was one of the 30 tyrants established by the Spartans B. C. 404, and was conspicuous above all his colleagues for rapacity and cruelty. He was slain at the battle of Munychia in the same year, fighting against Thrasybulus and the exiles. He was a distinguished orator, and some of his speeches were extant in the time of Cicero. He also wrote poems, dramas, and other works. Some fragments of his elegies are still extant.

Critōlāus (Κριτόλαος). 1. Of Phaselis in Lycia, studied philosophy at Athens under Ariston of Ceos, whom he succeeded as the head of the Peripatetic school. In B. C. 155 he was sent by the Athenians as ambassador to Rome with Carneades and Diogenes. [CARNEADES.] He lived upwards of 82 years, but we have no further particulars of his life.— 2. General of the Achaean League, 147, distinguished by his bitter enmity to the Romans. He was defeated by Metellus, and was never heard of after the battle.

Criton (Κρίτων). 1. Of Athens, a friend and disciple of Socrates, whom he supported with his fortune. He had made every arrangement for the escape of Socrates from prison, and tried, in vain, to persuade him to fly, as we see from Plato's dialogue named after him. Criton wrote 17 dialogues on philosophical subjects, which are lost.— 2. A physician at Rome in the 1st or 2nd century after Christ, perhaps the person mentioned by Martial (Epigr. xi. 60.6): he wrote several medical works.

Criū-mětŏpon (Κριοῦ μέτωπον), i. e. "Ram's Front."—1. A promontory at the S. of the Tauric Chersonesus.— 2. A promontory at the S. W. of Crete.

Crius (Κρῖος), one of the Titans, son of Uranus and Ge.

Crŏcŏdīlŏpŏlis (Κροκοδείλων πόλις). 1. (Embeshunda?), a city of Upper Egypt, in the Nomos Aphroditopolites.— 2. [ARSINOE, No. 7.]

Crŏcus, the beloved friend of Smilax, was changed by the gods into a saffron plant.

Crocylēa (τὰ Κροκύλεια), according to Homer (Il. ii. 633), a place in Ithaca, but according to Strabo, in Leucas in Acarnania.

Croesus (Κροῖσος), last king of Lydia, son of Alyattes, reigned B. C. 560—546, but was probably associated in the kingdom during his father's life. The early part of his reign was most glorious. He subdued all the nations between the Aegaean and the river Halys, and made the Greeks in Asia Minor tributary to him. The fame of his power and wealth drew to his court at Sardis all the wise men of Greece, and among them Solon, whose interview with the king was celebrated in antiquity. In reply to the question who was the happiest man he had ever seen, the sage taught the king that no man should be deemed happy till he had finished his life in a happy way. Alarmed at the growing power of the Persians, Croesus sent to consult the oracle of Apollo at Delphi, whether he should march against the Persians. Upon the reply of the oracle, that, if he marched against the Persians, he would overthrow a great empire, he collected a vast army and marched against Cyrus. Near Sinope an indecisive battle was fought between the two armies; whereupon he returned to Sardis, and disbanded his forces, commanding them to reassemble in the following spring. But Cyrus appeared unexpectedly before Sardis; Croesus led out the forces still remaining with him, but was defeated, and the city was taken after a siege of 14 days. Croesus, who was taken alive, was condemned to be burnt to death. As he stood before the pyre, the warning of Solon came to his mind, and he thrice uttered the name of Solon. Cyrus inquired who it was that he called on; and, upon hearing the story, repented of his purpose, and not only spared the life of Croesus, but made him his friend. Croesus survived Cyrus, and accompanied Cambyses in his expedition against Egypt.

Crommyōn or Cromyōn (Κρομμυών, Κρομμυών), a town in Megaris on the Saronic gulf, afterwards belonged to Corinth; celebrated in mythology on account of its wild sow, which was slain by Theseus.

Cronius Mons (Κρόνιον ὄρος), a mountain in Elis near Olympia, with a temple of Cronus.

Cronus (Κρόνος), the youngest of the Titans, son of Uranus and Ge, father by Rhea of Hestia, Demeter, Hera, Hades, Poseidon, and Zeus. At the instigation of his mother, Cronus unmanned his father for having thrown the Cyclopes, who were likewise his children by Ge, into Tartarus. Out of the blood thus shed sprang up the Erinnyes. When the Cyclopes were delivered from Tartarus, the government of the world was taken from Uranus and given to Cronus, who in his turn lost it through Zeus, as was predicted to him by Ge and Uranus. [ZEUS.] The Romans identified their Saturnus with Cronus. [SATURNUS.]

Cropia (Κρωπεία), an Attic demus belonging to the tribe Leontis.

Crŏtōn or Crotōna (Crotoniensis, Crotonensis, Crotoniata : Crotona), a Greek city on the E. coast of Bruttium, on the river Aesarus, and in a very healthy locality, was founded by the Achaeans

o 3

under Myscellus of Aegae, assisted by the Spartans, B. C. 710. Its extensive commerce, the virtue of its inhabitants, and the excellence of its institutions, made it the most powerful and flourishing town in the S. of Italy. It owed much of its greatness to Pythagoras, who established his school here. Gymnastics were cultivated here in greater perfection than in any other Greek city; and one of its citizens, Milo, was the most celebrated athlete in Greece. It attained its greatest power by the destruction of Sybaris in 510; but it subsequently declined in consequence of the severe defeat it sustained from the Locrians on the river Sagras. It suffered greatly in the wars with Dionysius, Agathocles, and Pyrrhus; and in the 2nd Punic war a considerable part of it had ceased to be inhabited. It received a colony from the Romans in 195.

Crustumēria, -rĭum, also **Crustumĭum** (Crustumĭnus), a town of the Sabines, situated in the mountains near the sources of the Allia, was conquered both by Romulus and Tarquinius Priscus, and is not mentioned in later times.

Cteatus. [MOLIONES.]

Ctēsĭas (Κτησίας), of Cnidus in Caria, a contemporary of Xenophon, was private physician of Artaxerxes Mnemon, whom he accompanied in his war against his brother Cyrus, B. C. 401. He lived 17 years at the Persian court, and wrote in the Ionic dialect a great work on the history of Persia (Περσικὰ), in 23 books. The first 6 contained the history of the Assyrian monarchy down to the foundation of the kingdom of Persia. The next 7 contained the history of Persia down to the end of the reign of Xerxes, and the remaining 10 carried the history down to the time when Ctesias left Persia, i. e. to the year 398. All that is now extant is a meagre abridgment in Photius and a number of fragments preserved in Diodorus and other writers. The work of Ctesias was compiled from Oriental sources, and its statements are frequently at variance with those of Herodotus. Ctesias also wrote a work on India (Ἰνδικὰ) in one book, of which we possess an abridgment in Photius. This work contains numerous fables, but it probably gives a faithful picture of India, as it was conceived by the Persians. The abridgment which Photius made of the Persica and Indica of Ctesias has been printed separately by Lion, Göttingen, 1823, and by Bähr, Frankfort, 1824.

Ctēsĭbĭus (Κτησίβιος), celebrated for his mechanical inventions, lived at Alexandria in the reigns of Ptolemy Philadelphus and Euergetes, about B. C. 250. His father was a barber, but his own taste led him to devote himself to mechanics. He is said to have invented a clepsydra or water-clock, a hydraulic organ (ὕδραυλις), and other machines, and to have been the first to discover the elastic force of air and apply it as a moving power. He was the teacher, and has been supposed to have been the father of Hero Alexandrinus.

Ctēsĭphōn (Κτησιφῶν), son of Leosthenes of Anaphlystus, was accused by Aeschines for having proposed the decree, that Demosthenes should be honoured with the crown. [AESCHINES.]

Ctesĭphon (Κτησιφῶν: Κτησιφώντιος: *Takti Kesra,* Ru.), a city of Assyria, on the E. bank of the Tigris, 3 Roman miles from Seleucia on the W. bank, first became an important place under the Parthians, whose kings used it for some time as a winter residence, and afterwards enlarged and fortified it, and made it the capital of their empire. It is said to have contained at least 100,000 inhabitants. In the wars of the Romans with the Parthians and Persians, it was taken, first by Trajan (A. D. 115), and by several of the later emperors, but Julian did not venture to attack it, even after his victory over the Persians before the city.

Ctesĭppus (Κτήσιππος). 1. Two sons of Hercules, one by Deianira, and the other by Astydamia. — 2. Son of Polytherses of Same, one of the suitors of Penelope, killed by Philoetius, the cow-herd.

Cŭlăro, afterwards called **Gratianŏpŏlis** (*Grenoble*) in honour of the emperor Gratian, a town in Gallia Narbonensis on the Isara (*Isère*).

Cŭllĕo or **Cŭlĕo, Q. Terentĭus.** 1. A senator of distinction, was taken prisoner in the second Punic war, and obtained his liberty at the conclusion of the war, B. C. 201. To show his gratitude to P. Scipio, he followed his triumphal car, wearing the pileus or cap of liberty, like an emancipated slave. In 187 he was praetor peregrinus, and in this year condemned L. Scipio Asiaticus, on the charge of having misappropriated the money gained in the war with Antiochus. — 2. Tribune of the plebs, 58, exerted himself to obtain Cicero's recall from banishment. In the war which followed the death of Caesar (43), Culleo was one of the legates of Lepidus.

Cūmae (Κύμη: Κυμαῖος, Cumānus), a town in Campania, and the most ancient of the Greek colonies in Italy and Sicily, was founded by Cumae in Aeolis, in conjunction with Chalcis and Eretria in Euboea. Its foundation is placed in B. C. 1050, but this date is evidently too early. It was situated on a steep hill of Mt. Gaurus, a little N. of the promontory Misenum. It became in early times a great and flourishing city; its commerce was extensive; its territory included a great part of the rich Campanian plain; its population was at least 60,000; and its power is attested by its colonies in Italy and Sicily, — Puteoli, Palaeopolis, afterwards Neapolis, Zancle, afterwards Messana. But it had powerful enemies to encounter in the Etruscans and the Italian nations. It was also weakened by internal dissensions, and one of its citizens Aristodemus made himself tyrant of the place. Its power became so much reduced that it was only saved from the attacks of the Etruscans by the assistance of Hiero, who annihilated the Etruscan fleet, 474. It maintained its independence till 417, when it was taken by the Campanians and most of its inhabitants sold as slaves. From this time CAPUA became the chief city of Campania; and although Cumae was subsequently a Roman municipium and a colony, it continued to decline in importance. At last the Acropolis was the only part of the town that remained, and this was eventually destroyed by Narses in his wars with the Goths. — Cumae was celebrated as the residence of the earliest Sibyl, and as the place where Tarquinius Superbus died.—Its ruins are still to be seen between the Lago di Patria and Fusaro.

Cūnaxa (Κούναξα), a small town in Babylonia, on the Euphrates, famous for the battle fought here between the younger Cyrus and his brother Artaxerxes Mnemon, in which the former was killed (B. C. 401). Its position is uncertain. Plutarch (*Artax.* 8) places it 500 stadia (50 geog. miles) above Babylon; Xenophon, who does not mention it by name, makes the battle field 360 stadia (36 geog. miles) from Babylon.

Cupiennĭus, attacked by Horace (*Sat.* i. 2. 36), is said by the Scholiast to have been a friend of Augustus, but is probably a fictitious name.

Cupra (Cuprensis). **1. Maritima** (*Marano* at the mouth of the *Monecchia*), a town in Picenum, with an ancient temple of Juno, founded by the Pelasgians and restored by Hadrian. — **2. Montana**, a town near No. 1 in the mountains.

Cūres (Gen. Curium), an ancient town of the Sabines, celebrated as the birth-place of T. Tatius and Numa Pompilius: from this town the Romans are said to have derived the name of Quirites.

Cūrētes (Κουρῆτες), a mythical people, said to be the most ancient inhabitants of Acarnania and Aetolia; the latter country was called Curetis from them. They also occur in Crete as the priests of Zeus, and are spoken of in connexion with the Corybantes and Idaean Dactyli. The infant Zeus was entrusted to their care by Rhea; and by clashing their weapons in a warlike dance, they drowned the cries of the child, and prevented his father Cronus from ascertaining the place where he was concealed.

Curĭas. [Curium.]

Cūrĭätii, a celebrated Alban family. 3 brothers of this family fought with 3 Roman brothers, the Horatii, and were conquered by the latter. In consequence of their defeat, Alba became subject to Rome.

Curiātĭus Maternus. [Maternus.]

Cūrĭo, C. Scribonĭus. 1. Praetor B. c. 121, was one of the most distinguished orators of his time. — **2.** Son of No. 1, tribune of the plebs, B. c. 90; afterwards served under Sulla in Greece; was praetor 82; consul 76; and after his consulship obtained the province of Macedonia, where he carried on war against the barbarians as far N. as the Danube. He was a personal enemy of Caesar, and supported P. Clodius, when the latter was accused of violating the sacra of the Bona Dea. In 57 he was appointed pontifex maximus, and died 53. He had some reputation as an orator, and was a friend of Cicero. — **3.** Son of No. 2, also a friend of Cicero, was a most profligate character. He was married to Fulvia, afterwards the wife of Antony. He at first belonged to the Pompeian party, by whose influence he was made tribune of the plebs, 50; but he was bought over by Caesar, and employed his power as tribune against his former friends. On the breaking out of the civil war (49), he was sent by Caesar to Sicily with the title of propraetor. He succeeded in driving Cato out of the island, and then crossed over to Africa, where he was defeated and slain by Juba and P. Attius Varus.

Curiosolĭtae, a Gallic people on the Ocean in Armorica near the Veneti, in the country of the modern *Corseult* near St. Malo.

Curĭum (Κούριον: Κουριεύς: nr. *Piscopia* Ru.), a town on the S. coast of Cyprus, near the promontory *Curĭas*, W. of the mouth of the Lycus.

Cūrĭus Dentātus. [Dentatus.]

Cūrĭus, M.', an intimate friend of Cicero and Atticus, lived for several years as a negotiator at Patrae in Peloponnesus. In his will he left his property to Atticus and Cicero. Several of Cicero's letters are addressed to him.

Cursor, L. Păpīrĭus. 1. A distinguished Roman general in the 2nd Samnite war, was 5 times

consul (B. c. 333, 320, 319, 315, 313), and twice dictator (325, 309). He frequently defeated the Samnites, but his greatest victory over them was gained in his 2nd dictatorship. Although a great general, he was not popular with the soldiers on account of his severity. — **2.** Son of No. 1, was, like his father, a distinguished general. In both his consulships (293, 272) he gained great victories over the Samnites, and in the 2nd he brought the 3rd Samnite war to a close.

Curtĭus, Mettus or **Mettĭus**, a distinguished Sabine, fought with the rest of his nation against Romulus. According to one tradition, the *Lacus Curtius*, which was part of the Roman forum, was called after him; because in the battle with the Romans he escaped with difficulty from a swamp, into which his horse had plunged. But the more usual tradition respecting the name of the Lacus Curtius related that in B. c. 362 the earth in the forum gave way, and a great chasm appeared, which the soothsayers declared could only be filled up by throwing into it Rome's greatest treasure; that thereupon M. Curtius, a noble youth, mounted his steed in full armour; and declaring that Rome possessed no greater treasure than a brave and gallant citizen, leaped into the abyss, upon which the earth closed over him.

Curtĭus Montānus. [Montanus.]

Curtĭus Rūfus, Q., the Roman historian of Alexander the Great. Respecting his life, and the time at which he lived, nothing is known with certainty. Some critics place him as early as the time of Vespasian, and others as late as Constantine; but the earlier date is more probable than the later. The work itself, entitled *De Rebus Gestis Alexandri Magni*, consisted of 10 books, but the first 2 are lost, and the remaining 8 are not without considerable gaps. It is written in a pleasing though somewhat declamatory style. It is taken from good sources, but the author frequently shows his ignorance of geography, chronology, and tactics. The best editions are by Zumpt, Berlin, 1826, and Mützell, Berlin, 1843.

Cutillae Aquae. [Aquae, No. 3.]

Cȳănē (Κυάνη), a Sicilian nymph and playmate of Proserpine, changed into a fountain through grief at the loss of the goddess.

Cyanĕae Insŭlae (Κυανέαι νῆσοι or πέτραι, *Urek-Jaki*), 2 small rocky islands at the entrance of the Thracian Bosporus into the Euxine, the **Planctae** (Πλάγκται) and **Symplēgădes** (Συμπληγάδες) of mythology, so called because they are said to have been once moveable and to have rushed together, and thus destroyed every ship that attempted to pass through them. After the ship Argo had passed through them in safety, they became stationary. [See p. 76, a.]

Cyaxares (Κυαξάρης), king of Media B. c. 634 —594, son of Phraortes, and grandson of Deioces. He was the most warlike of the Median kings, and introduced great military reforms. He defeated the Assyrians, who had slain his father in battle, and he laid siege to Ninus (Nineveh). But while he was before the city, he was defeated by the Scythians, who held the dominion of Upper Asia for 28 years (634—607), but were at length driven out of Asia by Cyaxares. After the expulsion of the Scythians, Cyaxares again turned his arms against Assyria, and with the aid of the king of Babylon (probably the father of Nebuchadnezzar), he took and destroyed Ninus, in 606. He subsequently carried on war for 5 years against Alyattes, king of Lydia. [ALYATTES.] Cyaxares died in 594, and was succeeded by his son Astyages. — Xenophon speaks of a Cyaxares II., king of Media, son of Astyages, respecting whom see CYRUS.

Cўbĕlĕ. [RHEA.]

Cybistra (τὰ Κυβίστρα), an ancient city of Asia Minor, several times mentioned by Cicero (*Ep. ad Fam.* xv. 2, 4, *ad Att.* v. 18, 20), who describes it as lying at the foot of Mt. Taurus, in the part of Cappadocia bordering on Cilicia. Strabo places it 300 stadia (30 geog. miles) from Tyana. Mention is made of a place of the same name (now *Kara Hissar*), between Tyana and Caesarea ad Argaeum; but this latter can hardly be believed to be identical with the former.

Cyclădes (Κυκλάδες), a group of islands in the Aegaean sea, so called because they lay in a circle (ἐν κύκλῳ) around Delos, the most important of them. According to Strabo they were 12 in number; but their number is increased by other writers. The most important of them were DELOS, CEOS, CYTHNOS, SERIPHOS, RHENIA, SIPHNOS, CIMOLOS, NAXOS, PAROS, SYROS, MYCONOS, TENOS, ANDROS.

Cyclōpes (Κύκλωπες), that is, creatures with round or circular eyes, are described differently by different writers. Homer speaks of them as a gigantic and lawless race of shepherds in Sicily, who devoured human beings and cared nought for Zeus: each of them had only one eye in the centre of his forehead: the chief among them was POLYPHEMUS. According to Hesiod the Cyclops were Titans, sons of Uranus and Ge, were 3 in number, Arges, Steropes, and Brontes, and each of them had only one eye on his forehead. They were thrown into Tartarus by Cronus, but were released by Zeus, and in consequence they provided Zeus with thunderbolts and lightning, Pluto with a helmet, and Poseidon with a trident. They were afterwards killed by Apollo for having furnished Zeus with the thunderbolts to kill Aesculapius. A still later tradition regarded the Cyclopes as the assistants of Hephaestus. Volcanoes were the workshops of that god, and Mt. Aetna in Sicily and the neighbouring isles were accordingly considered as their abodes. As the assistants of Hephaestus they make the metal armour and ornaments for gods and heroes. Their number is no longer confined to 3; and besides the names mentioned by Hesiod, we also find those of Pyracmon and Acamas. The name of Cyclopian walls was given to the walls built of great masses of unhewn stone, of which specimens are still to be seen at Mycenae and other parts of Greece, and also in Italy. They were probably constructed by the Pelasgians; and later generations, being struck by their grandeur, ascribed their building to a fabulous race of Cyclops.

Cycnus (Κύκνος). 1. Son of Apollo by Hyrie, lived in the district between Pleuron and Calydon, and was beloved by Phyllius; but as Phyllius refused him a bull, Cycnus leaped into a lake and was metamorphosed into a swan. — 2. Son of Poseidon, was king of Colonae in Troas, and father of Tenes and Hemithea. His second wife Philonome fell in love with Tenes, her step-son, and as he refused her offers, she accused him to his father, who threw Tenes with Hemithea in a chest into the sea. Tenes escaped and became king of Tenedos. [TENES.] In the Trojan War both Cycnus and Tenes assisted the Trojans, but both

were slain by Achilles. As Cycnus could not be wounded by iron, Achilles strangled him with the thong of his helmet, or killed him with a stone. When Achilles was going to strip Cycnus of his armour, the body disappeared, and was changed into a swan. — 3. Son of Ares and Pelopia, slain by Hercules at Itone. — 4. Son of Ares and Pyrene, likewise killed by Hercules. — 5. Son of Sthenelus, king of the Ligurians, and a friend and relation of Phaethon. While he was lamenting the fate of Phaethon on the banks of the Eridanus, he was metamorphosed by Apollo into a swan, and placed among the stars.

Cydias, a celebrated painter from the island of Cythnus, B. C. 364, whose picture of the Argonauts was exhibited in a porticus by Agrippa at Rome.

Cўdippĕ. [ACONTIUS.]

Cydnus (Κύδνος: *Tersoos-Chai*), a river of Cilicia Campestris, rising in the Taurus, and flowing through the midst of the city of Tarsus, where it is 120 feet wide (Kinneir: Xenophon says 2 plethra=202 feet). It was celebrated for the clearness and coldness of its water, which was esteemed useful in gout and nervous diseases, but by bathing in which Alexander nearly lost his life. At its mouth the river spread into a lagune, which formed the harbour of Tarsus, but which is now choked with sand. In the middle ages the river was called Hierax.

Cydōnĭa, more rarely Cydōnis (Κυδωνία, Κυδωνίς: Κυδωνιάτης: *Khania*), one of the chief cities of Crete, the rival and opponent of CNOSSUS and GORTYNA, was situated on the N. W. coast, and derived its name from the Cydōnes (Κύδωνες), a Cretan race, placed by Homer in the W. part of the island. At a later time a colony of Zacynthians settled in Cydonia; they were driven out by the Samians about B. C. 524; and the Samians were in their turn expelled by the Aeginetans. Cydonia was the place from which quinces (*Cydonia mala*) were first brought to Italy, and its inhabitants were some of the best Cretan archers (*Cydonio arcu*, Hor. *Carm.* iv. 19. 17).

Cyllārus (Κύλλαρος), a beautiful centaur, killed at the wedding feast of Pirithous. The horse of Castor was likewise called Cyllarus.

Cyllēnē (Κυλλήνη). 1. (*Zyria*), the highest mountain in Peloponnesus on the frontiers of Arcadia and Achaia, sacred to Hermes (Mercury), who had a temple on the summit, was said to have been born there, and was hence called Cyllenius. — 2. A sea-port town of Elis.

Cylon (Κύλων), an Athenian of noble family, married the daughter of Theagenes, tyrant of Megara, and gained an Olympic victory B. C. 640. Encouraged by the Delphic oracle, he seized the Acropolis, intending to make himself tyrant of Athens. Pressed by famine, Cylon and his adherents were driven to take refuge at the altar of Athena, whence they were induced to withdraw by the archon Megacles, the Alcmaeonid, on a promise that their lives should be spared. But their enemies put them to death as soon as they had them in their power.

Cymē (Κύμη; Κυμαῖος: *Sandakli*), the largest of the Aeolian cities of Asia Minor, stood upon the coast of Aeolis, on a bay named after it, Cumaeus (also Elaïticus) Sinus (ὁ Κυμαῖος κόλπος: *Gulf of Sandakli*), and had a good harbour. It was founded by a colony of Locrians from Mt. Phricius, and hence it had the epithet Φρικωνίς. It was the native place of Hesiod and Ephorus, and the mother city of Side in Pamphylia and Cumae in Campania.

Cyna. [CYNANE.]

Cynaegīrus (Κυναίγειρος), brother of the poet Aeschylus, distinguished himself by his valour at the battle of Marathon, B.C. 490. According to Herodotus, when the Persians were endeavouring to escape by sea, Cynaegirus seized one of their ships to keep it back, but fell with his right hand cut off. In the later versions of the story Cynaegirus is made to perform still more heroic deeds.

Cynaetha (Κύναιθα: Κυναιθεύς, -θαιεύς), a town in the N. of Arcadia, whose inhabitants, unlike the other Arcadians, had a dislike to music, to which circumstance Polybius attributes their rough and demoralized character.

Cynane, Cyna, or **Cynna** (Κυνάνη, Κύνα, Κύννα), half-sister to Alexander the Great, daughter of Philip by Audata, an Illyrian woman. She was married to her cousin Amyntas ; and after the death of Alexander she crossed over to Asia, intending to marry her daughter Eurydice to Arrhidaeus, who had been chosen king. Her project alarmed Perdiccas, by whose order she was put to death.

Cyněsii or **Cynětes** (Κυνήσιοι, Κύνητες), a people, according to Herodotus, dwelling in the extreme W. of Europe, beyond the Celts, apparently in Spain.

Cynisca (Κυνίσκα), daughter of Archidamus II. king of Sparta, was the first woman who kept horses for the games, and the first who gained an Olympic victory.

Cynŏpŏlis (Κυνὸς πόλις : Samallout), a city of the Heptanomis, or Middle Egypt, on an island in the Nile ; the chief seat of the worship of Anubis. There was a city of the same name in the Delta.

Cynos (Κῦνος : Κύνιος, Κυναῖος), the chief seaport in the territory of the Locri Opuntii.

Cynosarges (τὸ Κυνόσαργες), a gymnasium, sacred to Hercules, outside Athens, E. of the city and before the gate Diomēa, for the use of those who were not of pure Athenian blood : here taught Antisthenes, the founder of the Cynic school.

Cynoscěphălae(Κυνὸς κεφαλαί), "Dog's Heads." 1. Two hills near Scotussa in Thessaly, where Flaminius gained his celebrated victory over Philip of Macedonia, B.C. 197.—2. A hill between Thebes and Thespiae in Boeotia.

Cynossēma (Κυνὸς σῆμα), "Dog's Tomb," a promontory in the Thracian Chersonesus near Madytus, so called because it was supposed to be the tomb of Hecuba, who had been previously changed into a dog.

Cynosūra (Κυνόσουρά), an Idaean nymph, and one of the nurses of Zeus, who placed her among the stars. [ARCTOS.]

Cynosūra (Κυνόσουρα), "Dog's Tail," a promontory in Attica, S. of Marathon.

Cynthia and **Cynthius** (Κυνθία and Κύνθιος), surnames respectively of Artemis and Apollo, which they derived from Mt. Cynthus in the island of Delos, their birthplace.

Cynūria (Κυνουρία : Κυνούριος), a district on the frontiers of Argolis and Laconia, for the possession of which the Argives and Spartans carried on frequent wars, and which the Spartans at length obtained about B.C. 550. [See p. 77, a.] The inhabitants were Ionians.

Cyparissīa (Κυπαρισσία). 1. A town in Messenia on the W. coast, S. of the river Cyparissus, and on a promontory and bay of the same name. Homer (Il. ii. 593) speaks of a town **Cyparissēeis** (Κυπαρισσήεις) subject to Nestor, which is probably the same as the preceding, though Strabo places it in Triphylia. — 2. A town in Laconia on a peninsula near the Asopus.

Cyparissus (Κυπάρισσος), son of Telephus, beloved by Apollo or Silvanus. Having inadvertently killed his favourite stag, he was seized with immoderate grief, and metamorphosed into a cypress.

Cyparissus (Κυπάρισσος), a small town in Phocis on Parnassus near Delphi.

Cyphanta (τὰ Κύφαντα), a town on the E. coast of Laconia near Brasiae.

Cypria, Cypris, surnames of Aphrodite, from the island of CYPRUS.

Cypriānus, a celebrated father of the Church, was a native of Africa. He was a Gentile by birth, and before his conversion to Christianity he taught rhetoric with distinguished success. He was converted about A.D. 246, was ordained a presbyter 247, and was raised to the bishopric of Carthage 248. When the persecution of Decius burst forth (250), Cyprian fled from the storm, and remained 2 years in retirement. A few years afterwards the emperor Valerian renewed the persecution against the Christians. Cyprian was banished by Paternus the proconsul to the maritime city of Curubia, where he resided 11 months. He was then recalled by the new governor, Galerius Maximus, and was beheaded in a spacious plain without the walls A.D. 258. He wrote several works which have come down to us. They are characterised by lucid arrangement, and eloquent, though declamatory style. The best editions are by Fell, Oxford, 1682, fol., to which are subjoined the Annales Cypriānici of Pearson ; and that commenced by Baluze, and completed by a monk of the fraternity of St. Maur, Paris, 1726, fol.

Cyprus (Κύπρος : Κύπριος : Cyprus, called by the Turks Kebris), a large island in the Mediterranean, S. of Cilicia and W. of Syria. It is called by various names in the poets, Cerastia or Cerastis, Macaria, Sphecia, Acamantis, Amathusia, and also Paphos. The island is of a triangular form : its length from E. to W. is about 140 miles ; its greatest breadth, which is in the W. part, is about 50 miles from N. to S., but it gradually narrows towards the E. A range of mountains, called Olympus by the ancients, runs through the whole length of the island from E. to W., and rises in one part more than 7000 feet in height. The plains are chiefly in the S. of the island, and were celebrated in ancient as well as in modern times for their fertility. The largest plain, called the Salaminian plain, is in the E. part of the island near Salamis. The rivers are little more than mountain torrents, mostly dry in summer. — Cyprus was colonized by the Phoenicians at a very early period ; and Greek colonies were subsequently planted in the island, according to tradition soon after the Trojan war. We read at first of 9 independent states, each governed by its own king, SALAMIS, CITIUM, AMATHUS, CURIUM, PAPHOS, MARIUM, SOLI, LAPETHUS, CERYNIA. The island was subdued by Amasis, king of Egypt, about B.C. 540. Upon the downfal of the Egyptian monarchy, it became subject to the Persians ; but EVAGORAS of Salamis, after a severe struggle with the Persians, established its independence about 385, and handed down the sovereignty to his son NICOCLES. It eventually fell to the share of the Ptolemies in Egypt, and was governed by them, sometimes united to Egypt, and sometimes by separate princes of the royal family. In 58 the Romans made Cyprus one of their provinces, and sent M. Cato to take possession of it. — Cyprus was one of the chief seats of the worship of Aphrodite (Venus), who is hence called *Cypris* or *Cypria*, and whose worship was introduced into the island by the Phoenicians.

Cypséla (τὰ Κύψελα: Κυψελῖνος, -ληνός). 1. A town in Arcadia on the frontiers of Laconia. — 2. A town in Thrace on the Hebrus and the Egnatia Via.

Cypsélus (Κύψελος). 1. Father of Merope and grandfather of Aepytus. [AEPYTUS.] — 2. Of Corinth, son of Aëtion. The mother of Cypselus belonged to the house of the Bacchiadae, that is, to the Doric nobility of Corinth. According to tradition, she married Aëtion, because, being ugly, she met with no one among the Bacchiadae who would have her as his wife. As the oracle of Delphi had declared that her son would prove formidable to the ruling party at Corinth, the Bacchiadae attempted to murder the child. But his mother concealed him in a chest (κυψέλη), from which he derived his name, Cypselus. When he had grown up to manhood, he expelled the Bacchiadae, with the help of the people, and then established himself as tyrant. He reigned 30 years, B. C. 655—625, and was succeeded by his son Periander. The celebrated chest of Cypselus, consisting of cedar wood, ivory, and gold, and richly adorned with figures in relief, is described at length by Pausanias (v. 17, &c.).

Cyraunis (Κύραυνις), an island off the N. coast of Africa mentioned by Herodotus (iv. 95); probably the same as CERCINE.

Cyrēnāĭca (ἡ Κυρηναία, ἡ Κυρηναίη χώρη, Herod: *Dernah* or *Jebel-Akhdar*, i. e. the *Green Mountain*, the N. E. part of *Tripoli*), a district of N. Africa, between Marmarica on the E. and the Regio Syrtica on 'the W., was considered to extend in its widest limits from the Philaenorum Arae at the bottom of the Great Syrtis to the Chersonesus Magna or N. headland of the Gulf of Platea (*G. of Bomba*), or even to the Catabathmus Magnus (*Marsa Sollum*); but the part actually possessed and cultivated by the Greek colonists can only be considered as beginning at the N. limit of the sandy shores of the Great Syrtis, at Boreum Pr. (*Ras Teyonas*, S. of *Ben-Ghazi*), between which and the Chersonesus Magna the country projects into the Mediterranean in the form of a segment of a circle, whose chord is above 150 miles long and its are above 200. From its position, formation, climate, and soil, this region is perhaps one of the most delightful on the surface of the globe. Its centre is occupied by a moderately elevated table-land, whose edge runs parallel to the coast, to which it sinks down in a succession of terraces, clothed with verdure, intersected by mountain streams running through ravines filled with the richest vegetation, exposed to the cool sea-breezes from the N., and sheltered by the mass of the mountain from the sands and hot winds of the Sahara. These slopes produced the choicest fruits, vegetables, and flowers, and some very rare plants, such as the silphium and the

ὁπὸς Κυρηναῖος. The various harvests, at the different elevations, lasted for 8 months of the year. With these physical advantages, the people naturally became prone to luxury. The country was, however, exposed to annual ravages by locusts. The belt of mountainous land extends inwards from the coast about 70 or 80 miles. — The first occupation of this country by the Greeks, of which we have any clear account, was effected by BATTUS, who led a colony from the island of Thera, and first established himself on the island of Platea at the E. extremity of the district, and afterwards built CYRENE (B. C. 631), where he founded a dynasty, which ruled over the country during 8 reigns, though with comparatively little power over some of the other Greek cities. Of these the earliest founded were TEUCHIRA and HESPERIS, then BARCA, a colony from Cyrene; and these, with Cyrene itself and its port APOLLONIA, formed the original Libyan Pentapolis, though this name seems not to have come into general use till under the Ptolemies. The comparative independence of Barca, and the temporary conquest of the country by the Persians under Cambyses, diminished the power of the later kings of Cyrene, and at last the dynasty was overthrown and a republic established in the latter part of the 5th century B. C. When Alexander invaded Egypt, the Cyrenaeans formed an alliance with him; but their country was made subject to Egypt by Ptolemy the son of Lagus. It appears to have flourished under the Ptolemies, who pursued their usual policy of raising new cities at the expense of the ancient ones, or restoring the latter under new names. Thus Hesperis became Berenice, Teuchira was called Arsinoë, Barca was entirely eclipsed by its port, which was raised into a city under the name of Ptolemaïs, and Cyrene suffered from the favours bestowed upon its port Apollonia. The country was now usually called Pentapolis, from the 5 cities of Cyrene, Apollonia, Ptolemaïs, Arsinoë, and Berenice. In B. C. 95, the last Egyptian governor, Apion, an illegitimate son of Ptolemy Physcon, made the country over to the Romans, who at first gave the cities their freedom, and afterwards formed the district, under the name of Cyrenaica, with the island of Crete, into a province. Under Constantine Cyrenaica was separated from Crete, and made a distinct province, under the name of Libya Superior. The first great blow to the prosperity of the country was given by the murderous conflict which ensued on an insurrection of the Jews (who had long settled here in great numbers) in the reign of Trajan. As the Roman empire declined, the attacks of the native Libyan tribes became more frequent and formidable, and the sufferings caused by their inroads and by locusts, plague, and earthquakes, are most pathetically described by Synesius, bishop of Ptolemaïs, in the 5th century. In the 7th century the country was overrun by the Persians, and soon afterwards it fell a final prey to the great Arabian invasion.

Cyrēnē (Κυρήνη), daughter of Hypseus, mother of Aristaeus by Apollo, was carried by the god from Mt. Pelion to Libya, where the city of Cyrene derived its name from her.

Cyrēnē (Κυρήνη, Κυρηναῖος: *Ghrennah*, very large Ru.), the chief city of CYRENAICA in N. Africa, was founded by Battus (B. C. 631) over a fountain consecrated to Apollo, and called Cyre (Κύρη: Ἀπόλλωνος κρήνη), which supplied the city with water, and then ran down to the sea through a beautiful ravine. The city stood 80 stadia (8 geog. miles) from the coast, on the edge of the upper of two terraces of table land, at the height of 1800 feet above the sea, in one of the finest situations in the world. The road which connected it with its harbour, Apollonia, still exists, and the ruins of Cyrene, though terribly defaced, are very extensive, comprising streets, aqueducts, temples, theatres, tombs, paintings, sculpture, and inscriptions. In the face of the terrace on which the city stands is a vast subterraneous necropolis. For the history of the city and surrounding country, see CYRENAICA. Among its celebrated natives were the philosopher Aristippus, the poet Callimachus, and the Christian bishop and orator Synesius.

Cyreschăta or Cyrŏpŏlis (Κυρέσχατα, Κύρα, Κύρου πόλις), a city of Sogdiana, on the Jaxartes, the furthest of the colonies founded by Cyrus, and the extreme city of the Persian empire: destroyed, after many revolts, by Alexander. Its position is doubtful, but it was probably not far from Alexandreschata (Kokand).

Cyrillus (Κύριλλος). — 1. Bishop of Jerusalem, A. D. 351—386, was a firm opponent of the Arians, by whose influence he was banished 3 times from Jerusalem. His works are not numerous. The most important are lectures to catechumens, &c., and a letter to the emperor Constantius, giving an account of the luminous cross which appeared at Jerusalem, 351. The best editions are by Milles, Oxford, 1703, fol., and by Touttee, Paris, 1720, fol. — 2. Bishop of Alexandria, A. D. 412—444, of which city he was a native. He was fond of power, and of a restless and turbulent spirit. He persecuted the Jews, whom he expelled from Alexandria; and after a long protracted struggle he procured the deposition of Nestorius, bishop of Constantinople. He was the author of a large number of works, many of which are extant; but in a literary view they are almost worthless. The best edition is by Aubert, Paris, 1638, 6 vols. fol.

Cyrrhestĭcē (Κυῤῥεστική), the name given under the Seleucidae to a province of Syria, lying between Commagene on the N. and the plain of Antioch on the S., between Mt. Amanus on the W. and the Euphrates on the E. After the time of Constantine, it was united with Commagene into one province, under the name of Euphratesia.

Cyrrhus or Cyrus (Κύῤῥος, Κύρος: Korus?), a city of Syria, founded under the Seleucidae, and called after the city of the same name in Macedonia; chiefly remarkable as the residence and see of Theodoret, who describes its poverty, which he did much to relieve. Justinian rebuilt the walls, and erected an aqueduct.

Cyrrhus, a town in Macedonia, near Pella.

Cyrus (Κύρος). 1. The Elder, the founder of the Persian empire. The history of his life was overlaid in ancient times with fables and romances, and is related differently by Herodotus, Ctesias, and Xenophon. The account of Herodotus best preserves the genuine Persian legend, and is to be preferred to those of Ctesias and Xenophon. It is as follows: — Cyrus was the son of Cambyses, a noble Persian, and of Mandane, daughter of the Median king Astyages. In consequence of a dream, which seemed to portend that his grandson should be master of Asia, Astyages sent for his daughter, when she was pregnant; and upon her giving birth to a son, he committed it to Harpagus, his confidential attendant, with orders to kill it. Harpagus gave it to a herdsman of Astyages, who was to expose it. But the wife of the herdsman having brought forth a still-born child, they substituted the latter for the child of Mandane, who was reared as the son of the herdsman. When he was 10 years old, his true parentage was discovered by the following incident. In the sports of his village, the boys chose him for their king. One of the boys, the son of a noble Median named Artembares, disobeyed his commands, and Cyrus caused him to be severely scourged. Artembares complained to Astyages, who sent for Cyrus, in whose person and courage he discovered his daughter's son. The herdsman and Harpagus, being summoned before the king, told him the truth. Astyages forgave the herdsman, but revenged himself on Harpagus by serving up to him at a banquet the flesh of his own son. As to his grandson, by the advice of the Magians, who assured him that his dreams were fulfilled by the boy's having been a king in sport, he sent him back to his parents in Persia. When Cyrus grew up, he conspired with Harpagus to dethrone his grandfather. He induced the Persians to revolt from the Median supremacy, and at their head marched against Astyages. The latter had given the command of his forces to Harpagus, who deserted to Cyrus. Astyages thereupon placed himself at the head of his troops, but was defeated by Cyrus and taken prisoner, B. C. 559. The Medes accepted Cyrus for their king, and thus the supremacy which they had held passed to the Persians. It was probably at this time that Cyrus received that name, which is a Persian word (Kohr), signifying the Sun. — Cyrus now proceeded to conquer the other parts of Asia. In 546 he overthrew the Lydian monarchy, and took Croesus prisoner. [CROESUS.] The Greek cities in Asia Minor were subdued by his general Harpagus. He next turned his arms against the Assyrian empire, of which Babylon was then the capital. After defeating the Babylonians in battle, he laid siege to the city, and after a long time he took it by diverting the course of the Euphrates, which flowed through the midst of it, so that his soldiers entered Babylon by the bed of the river. This was in 538. Subsequently he crossed the Araxes, with the intention of subduing the Massagetae, a Scythian people, but he was defeated and slain in battle. Tomyris, the queen of the Massagetae, cut off his head, and threw it into a bag filled with human blood, that he might satiate himself (she said) with blood. He was killed in 529. He was succeeded by his son CAMBYSES. — Xenophon represents Cyrus as brought up at his grandfather's court, as serving in the Median army under his uncle Cyaxares II., the son and successor of Astyages, of whom Herodotus and Ctesias know nothing; as making war upon Babylon simply as the general of Cyaxares; as marrying the daughter of Cyaxares; and at length dying quietly in his bed, after a sage and Socratic discourse to his children and friends. Xenophon's account is preserved in the Cyropaedia, in which he draws a picture of what a wise and just prince ought to be. The work must not be regarded as a genuine history. -- In the East Cyrus was long regarded as the greatest hero of antiquity, and hence the fables by which his history is obscured. His sepulchre at Pasargadae was visited by Alexander the Great. The tomb has perished, but his name is found on monuments at Murghab, N. of Persepolis. — **2. The Younger,** the 2nd of the 4 sons of Darius Nothus, king of Persia, and of Parysatis, was appointed by his father commander of the maritime parts of Asia Minor, and satrap of Lydia, Phrygia, and Cappadocia, B. C. 407. He assisted Lysander and the Lacedaemonians with large sums of money in their war against the Athenians. Cyrus was of a daring and ambitious temper. On the death of his father and the accession of his elder brother Artaxerxes Mnemon, 404, Cyrus formed a plot against the life of Artaxerxes. His design was betrayed by Tissaphernes to the king, who condemned him to death ; but, on the intercession of Parysatis, he spared his life and sent him back to his satrapy. Cyrus now gave himself up to the design of dethroning his brother. He collected a powerful native army, but he placed his chief reliance on a force of Greek mercenaries. He set out from Sardis in the spring of 401, and, having crossed the Euphrates at Thapsacus, marched down the river to the plain of Cunaxa, 500 stadia from Babylon. Here he found Artaxerxes prepared to meet him. Artaxerxes had from 400,000 to a million of men ; Cyrus had about 100,000 Asiatics and 13,000 Greeks. The battle was at first altogether in favour of Cyrus. His Greek troops on the right routed the Asiatics who were opposed to them ; and he himself pressed forward in the centre against his brother, and had even wounded him, when he was killed by one of the king's body-guard. Artaxerxes caused his head and right hand to be struck off, and sought to have it believed that Cyrus had fallen by his hand. The character of Cyrus is drawn by Xenophon in the brightest colours. It is enough to say that his ambition was gilded by all those brilliant qualities which win men's hearts. — **3.** An architect at Rome, who died on the same day as Clodius. 52.

Cyrus (Κῦρος: Kour), one of the two great rivers of Armenia, rises in the Caucasus, flows through Iberia, and after forming the boundary between Albania and Armenia, unites with the Araxes, and falls into the W. side of the Caspian. — There were small rivers of the same name in Media and Persia.

Cyta or **Cytaea** (Κύτα, Κύταια: Κυταῖος, Κυταιεύς), a town in Colchis on the river Phasis, where Medea was said to have been born.

Cythera (Κύθηρα: Κυθήριος: Cerigo), a mountainous island off the S. E. point of Laconia, with a town of the same name in the interior, the harbour of which was called **Scandea** (Σκανδεία). It was colonized at an early time by the Phoenicians, who introduced the worship of Aphrodite into the island, for which it was celebrated. This goddess was hence called **Cytheraea, Cytheréis** ; and, according to some traditions, it was in the neighbourhood of this island that she first rose from the foam of the sea. The Argives subsequently took possession of Cythera, but were driven out of it by the Lacedaemonians, who added it to their dominions.

Cytheris, a celebrated courtezan, the mistress of Antony, and subsequently of the poet Gallus, who mentioned her in his poems under the name of Lycoris.

Cytherus (Κύθηρος: Κυθήριος), one of the 12 ancient towns of Attica and subsequently a demus, belonging to the tribe Pandionis.

Cythnus (Κύθνος: Κύθνιος: Thermia), an island in the Aegaean sea, one of the Cyclades, with a town of the same name, celebrated for its cheese, and also for its warm springs, whence its modern name.

Cytinium (Κυτίνιον: Κυτινιάτης), one of the 4 cities in Doris, on Parnassus.

Cytorus or **-um** (Κύτωρος or -ον: Kidros), a town on the coast of Paphlagonia, between Amastris and the promontory Carambis, was a commercial settlement of the people of Sinope. It stood upon or near the mountain of the same name, which is mentioned by the Romans as abounding in box-trees.

Cyzicus (Κύζικος), son of Aeneus and Aenete, the daughter of Eusorus, or son of Eusorus, or son of Apollo by Stilbe. He was king of the Doliones at Cyzicus on the Propontis. For his connection with the Argonauts see p. 75, b.

Cyzicus (Κύζικος: Κυζικηνός: Bal Kiz or Chisico, Ru.), one of the most ancient and powerful of the Greek cities in Asia Minor, stood upon an island of the same name in the Propontis (Sea of Marmara). This island, the earlier name of which was Arctonnēsus ("Ἀρκτων νῆσος), lay close to the shore of Mysia, to which it was united by two bridges, and afterwards (under Alexander the Great) by a mole, which has accumulated to a considerable isthmus. The city of Cyzicus stood on the S. side of the island, at the N. end of the isthmus, on each side of which it had a port. Tradition ascribed the foundation of the city to the Doliones, a tribe of Thessalian Pelasgians, who had been driven from their homes by the Aeolians. It was said to have been afterwards colonized by the Milesians. It was one of the finest cities of the ancient world, for the beauty of its situation and the magnificence of its buildings: it possessed an extensive commerce, and was celebrated for the excellence of its laws and government. Its staters were among the most esteemed gold coins current in Greece. It took no conspicuous place in history till about 22 years after the peace of Antalcidas, when it made itself independent of Persia. It preserved its freedom under Alexander and his successors, and was in alliance with the kings of Pergamus, and afterwards with the Romans. Its celebrated resistance against Mithridates, when he besieged it by sea and land (B. C. 75), was of great service to the Romans, and obtained for it the rank of a "libera civitas," which it lost again under Tiberius. Under Constantine it became the chief city of the new province of Hellespontus. It was greatly injured by an earthquake in A. D. 443, and finally ruined by its conquest by the Arabians in 675.

D.

Diae. [DAHAE.]

Dachinabades (Δαχιναβάδης), a general name for the S. part of the Indian peninsula, derived from the Sanscrit dakshina, the S. wind, and connected with the modern name Deccan.

Dacia (Dacus), as a Roman province, was bounded on the S. by the Danube, which separated it from Moesia, on the N. by the Carpathian mountains, on the W. by the river Tysia (Theiss), and on the E. by the river Hierasus (Pruth), thus comprehending the modern Transylvania, Wallachia, Moldavia, and part of Hungary. The Daci were of the same race and spoke the same language as the Getae, and are therefore usually said to be of Thracian origin. They were a brave and warlike people. In the reign of Augustus they crossed the Danube and plundered the allies of Rome, but were defeated and driven back into their own country by the generals of Augustus. In the reign of Domitian they became so formidable under their king DECEBALUS, that the Romans were obliged to purchase a peace of them by the payment of tribute. Trajan delivered the empire from this disgrace; he crossed the Danube, and after a war of 5 years (A. D. 101—106), conquered the country, made it a Roman province, and colonized it with inhabitants from all parts of the empire. At a later period Dacia was invaded by the Goths; and as Aurelian considered it more prudent to make the Danube the boundary of the empire, he resigned Dacia to the barbarians, removed the Roman inhabitants to Moesia, and gave the name of Dacia (Aureliani) to that part of the province along the Danube where they were settled.

Dactýli (Δάκτυλοι), fabulous beings to whom the discovery of iron and the art of working it by means of fire was ascribed. Their name Dactyls, that is, Fingers, is accounted for in various ways; by their number being 5 or 10, or by the fact of their serving Rhea just as the fingers serve the hand, or by the story of their having lived at the foot (ἐν δακτύλοις) of mount Ida. Most authorities describe mount Ida in Phrygia as the original seat of the Dactyls, whence they are usually called Idaean Dactyls. In Phrygia they were connected with the worship of Rhea. They are sometimes confounded or identified with the Curetes, Corybantes, Cabiri, and Telchines. This confusion with the Cabiri also accounts for Samothrace being in some accounts described as their residence. Other accounts transfer them to mount Ida in Crete, of which island they are said to have been the original inhabitants. Their number appears to have been originally 3: Celmis (the smelter), Damnameneus (the hammer), and Acmon (the anvil). Their number was afterwards increased to 5, 10 (5 male and 5 female), 52 and 100.

Dadastána (ἡ Δαδαστάνα: Torbaleh or Kestabeg?), a fortress on the borders of Bithynia and Galatia, where the emperor Jovian died suddenly, A. D. 364.

Daedála (τὰ Δαίδαλα), a city in Asia Minor, upon the Gulf of Glaucus, on the borders of Caria and Lycia. The same name was given to a mountain overhanging the town.

Daedálus (Δαίδαλος). 1. A mythical personage, under whose name the Greek writers personified the earliest development of the arts of sculpture and architecture, especially among the Athenians and Cretans. The ancient writers generally represent Daedalus as an Athenian, of the royal race of the Erechthidae. Others called him a Cretan, on account of the long time he lived in Crete. He is said to have been the son of Metion, the son of Eupalamus, the son of Erechtheus. Others make nim the son of Eupalamus, or of Palamaon. His mother is called Alcippe, or Iphinoë, or Phrasimede. He devoted himself to sculpture, and made great improvements in the art. He instructed his sister's son, Calos, Talus, or Perdix, who soon came to surpass him in skill and ingenuity, and Daedalus killed him through envy. [PERDIX.] Being condemned to death by the Areopagus for this

murder, he went to Crete, where the fame of his skill obtained for him the friendship of Minos. He made the well-known wooden cow for Pasiphaë; and when Pasiphaë gave birth to the Minotaur, Daedalus constructed the labyrinth, at Cnossus, in which the monster was kept. For his part in this affair, Daedalus was imprisoned by Minos; but Pasiphaë released him, and, as Minos had seized all the ships on the coast of Crete, Daedalus procured wings for himself and his son Icarus, and fastened them on with wax. Daedalus himself flew safe over the Aegean, but, as Icarus flew too near the sun, the wax by which his wings were fastened on was melted, and he dropped down and was drowned in that part of the Aegean which was called after him the Icarian sea. Daedalus fled to Sicily, where he was protected by Cocalus, the king of the Sicani. When Minos heard where Daedalus had taken refuge, he sailed with a great fleet to Sicily, where he was treacherously murdered by Cocalus or his daughters. According to some accounts Daedalus first alighted in his flight from Crete at Cumae in Italy, where he erected a temple to Apollo, in which he dedicated the wings with which he had fled from Crete. Several other works of art were attributed to Daedalus, in Greece, Italy, Libya, and the islands of the Mediterranean. They belong to the period when art began to be developed. The name of Daedala was given by the Greeks to the ancient wooden statues, ornamented with gilding and bright colours and real drapery, which were the earliest known forms of the images of the gods, after the mere blocks of wood or stone, which were at first used for symbols of them. — 2. Of Sicyon, a statuary in bronze, son and disciple of Patrocles, flourished B. C. 400.

Dähae (Δάαι), a great Scythian people, who led a nomad life over a great extent of country on the E. of the Caspian, in Hyrcania (which still bears the name of Daghestan), on the banks of the Margus, the Oxus, and even the Jaxartes. Some of them served as cavalry and horse-archers in the armies of Darius Codomannus, Alexander, and Antiochus the Great, and they also made good foot-soldiers.

Daimáchus (Δαΐμαχος), of Plataeae, was sent by Seleucus as ambassador to Sandrocottus, king of India, about B. C. 312, and wrote a work on India, which is lost.

Dalmátia or Delmátia (Δαλματία: Δαλμάτης, more anciently Δαλματεύς, Dalmata), a part of the country along the E. coast of the Adriatic sea included under the general name of Illyricum, was separated from Liburnia on the N. by the Titius (Kerka), and from Greek Illyria on the S. by the Drilo (Drino), and extended inland to the Bebian mountains and the Drinus, thus nearly corresponding to the modern Dalmatia. The capital was Dalminium or Delminium, from which the country derived its name. The next most important town was SALONA, the residence of Diocletian. The Dalmatians were a brave and warlike people, and gave much trouble to the Romans. In B. C. 119 their country was overrun by L. Metellus, who assumed in consequence the surname Dalmaticus, but they continued independent of the Romans. In 39 they were defeated by Asinius Pollio, of whose Dalmaticus triumphus Horace speaks (Carm. ii. 1. 16); but it was not till the year 23 that they were finally subdued by Statilius Taurus. They took part in the great Pannonian revolt under their leader Bato, but after a 3 years' war were again reduced to subjection by Tiberius, A. D. 9.

Dalmatius. [DELMATIUS.]

Dalminium. [DALMATIA.]

Damagētus (Δαμάγητος), king of Ialysus in Rhodes, married, in obedience to the Delphic oracle, the daughter of Aristomenes of Messene, and from this marriage sprang the family of the Diagoridae, who were celebrated for their victories at Olympia. [ARISTOMENES.]

Dāmālis or **Bous** (Δάμαλις, ἡ Βοῦς), a small place in Bithynia, on the shore of the Thracian Bosporus, N. of Chalcedon ; celebrated by tradition as the landing-place of Io, the memory of whose passage was preserved by a bronze cow set up here by the Chalcedonians.

Damarătus. [DEMARATUS.]

Damascius (Δαμάσκιος), the Syrian, of Damascus, whence he derived his name, the last of the renowned teachers of the Neo-Platonic philosophy at Athens, was born about A. D. 480. He first studied at Alexandria and afterwards at Athens, under Marinus and Zenodotus, whom he succeeded. When Justinian closed the heathen schools of philosophy at Athens in 529, Damascius emigrated to King Chosroës of Persia. He afterwards returned to the W., since Chosroës had stipulated in a treaty that the heathen adherents of the Platonic Philosophy should be tolerated by the Byzantine emperor. The only work of Damascius which has been printed, is entitled " Doubts and Solutions of the first Principles," edited by Kopp, Francof. 1828, 8vo.

Damascus (ἡ Δαμασκός: Δαμασκηνός: Damshk, Damascus, Esh-Sham), one of the most ancient cities of the world, mentioned as existing in the time of Abraham (Gen. xiv. 15), stood in the district afterwards called Coele-Syria, upon both banks of the river Chrysorrhoas or Bardines (Burada), the waters of which, drawn off by canals and aqueducts, fertilised the plain around the city. This plain is open on the S. and E., and sheltered on the W. and N. by an offshoot of the Antilibanus ; its fruits were celebrated in ancient, as in modern times ; and altogether the situation of the city is one of the finest on the globe. In the earliest times, except during the short period for which David subjected it to the Hebrew monarchy, Damascus was the seat of an independent kingdom, called the kingdom of Syria, which was subdued by the Assyrians, and passed successively under the dominion of the Babylonians, the Persians, the Greek kings of Syria, and the Romans, the last of whom obtained possession of it after the conquest of Tigranes, and assigned it to the province of Syria. It flourished greatly under the emperors, and is called by Julian (Epist. 24) " the Eye of all the East." Diocletian established in it a great factory for arms ; and hence the origin of the fame of Damascus blades. Its position on one of the high roads from Lower to Upper Asia gave it a considerable trade. The surrounding district was called Δαμασκηνή.

Damasippus, L. Junius Brutus. [BRUTUS, No. 10.]

Damasippus, Licinius. 1. A Roman senator, fought on the side of the Pompeians in Africa, and perished B. C. 47. — 2. A contemporary of Cicero, who mentions him as a lover of statues, and speaks of purchasing a garden from Damasippus. He is probably the same person as the Damasippus ridi-

culed by Horace. (Sat. ii. 3. 16, 64.) It appears from Horace that Damasippus had become bankrupt, in consequence of which he intended to put an end to himself ; but he was prevented by the Stoic Stertinius, and then turned Stoic himself, or at least affected to be one by his long beard. — The Damasippus mentioned by Juvenal (Sat. viii. 147, 151, 167) is a fictitious name, under which the satirist ridiculed some noble lover of horses.

Damastes (Δαμάστης), of Sigeum, a Greek historian, and a contemporary of Herodotus and Hellanicus of Lesbos: his works are lost.

Damia. [AUXESIA.]

Damnonii. 1. Or **Dumnonii** or **Dumnunii,** a powerful people in the S.W. of Britain, inhabiting Cornwall, Devonshire, and the W. part of Somersetshire, from whom was called the promontory **Damnonium,** also **Ocrinum** (C. Lizard) in Cornwall. — 2. Or **Damnii,** a people in N. Britain, inhabiting parts of Perth, Argyle, Stirling, and Dubmarton-shires.

Damo (Δαμώ), a daughter of Pythagoras and Theano, to whom Pythagoras entrusted his writings, and forbad her to give them to any one. This command she strictly observed, although she was in extreme poverty, and received many requests to sell them.

Damocles (Δαμοκλῆς), a Syracusan, one of the companions and flatterers of the elder Dionysius. Damocles having extolled the great felicity of Dionysius on account of his wealth and power, the tyrant invited him to try what his happiness really was, and placed him at a magnificent banquet, in the midst of which Damocles saw a naked sword suspended over his head by a single horse-hair — a sight which quickly dispelled all his visions of happiness. The story is alluded to by Horace. (Carm. iii. 1. 17.)

Damon (Δάμων). 1. Of Athens, a celebrated musician and sophist. He was a pupil of Lamprus and Agathocles, and the teacher of Pericles, with whom he lived on the most intimate terms. He is also said to have taught Socrates, but this statement is more doubtful. In his old age he was banished from Athens, probably on account of the part he had taken in politics. — 2. A Pythagorean, and friend of Phintias (not Pythias). When the latter was condemned to die for a plot against Dionysius I. of Syracuse, he asked leave of the tyrant to depart for the purpose of arranging his domestic affairs, promising to find a friend who would be pledge for his appearance at the time appointed for his punishment. To the surprise of Dionysius, Damon unhesitatingly offered himself to be put to death instead of his friend, should he fail to return. Phintias arrived just in time to redeem Damon, and Dionysius was so struck with this instance of firm friendship on both sides, that he pardoned the criminal, and entreated to be admitted as a third into their bond of brotherhood.

Damoxēnus (Δαμόξενος), an Athenian comic poet of the new comedy, and perhaps partly of the middle.

Dana (Δάνα), a great city of Cappadocia (Xen. Anab. i. 2. § 20), probably the same as the later TYANA.

Dānāë (Δανάη), daughter of Acrisius and mother of Perseus. [ACRISIUS.] An Italian legend related that Danae came to Italy, built the town of Ardea, and married Pilumnus, by whom she became the mother of Daunus, the ancestor of Turnus.

Danāi. [DANAUS.]

Dănăïdes (Δαναΐδες), the 50 daughters of Danaus. [DANAUS.]

Danāla (τὰ Δάναλα), a city in the territory of the Trocini, in the N. E. of Galatia, notable in the history of the Mithridatic War as the place where Lucullus resigned the command to Pompey.

Danapris. [BORYSTHENES.]

Danastris. [TYRAS.]

Dănāus (Δαναός), son of Belus and twin-brother of Aegyptus. Belus had assigned Libya to Danaüs, but the latter, fearing his brother and his brother's sons, fled with his 50 daughters to Argos. Here he was elected king by the Argives in place of Gelanor, the reigning monarch. The story of the murder of the 50 sons of Aegyptus by the 50 daughters of Danaüs (the Danaïdes) is given under AEGYPTUS. There was one exception to the murderous deed. The life of Lynceus was spared by his wife Hypermnestra ; and according to the common tradition he afterwards avenged the death of his brothers by killing his father-in-law, Danaüs. According to the poets the Danaïdes were punished in Hades by being compelled everlastingly to pour water into a sieve (*inane lymphae dolium fundo pereuntis imo*, Hor. *Carm.* iii. 11. 26). — From Danaüs the Argives were called *Danai*, which name, like that of the Argives, was often applied by the poets to the collective Greeks.

Danūbīus (*Danube*, in Germ. *Donau*), also **Danuvius** on coins and inscriptions, called ISTER (Ἴστρος) by the Greeks, one of the chief rivers of Europe, rises in the Black Forest, and after flowing 1770 miles falls into the Black sea. It is mentioned by Hesiod, but the Greeks knew very little about it. According to Herodotus it rises at the city Pyrene among the Celts and flows through the whole of Europe. The Romans first obtained some accurate information concerning the river at the commencement of the empire. Tiberius in his campaign against the Vindelicians, visited the sources of the Danube, which, according to Tacitus, rises in M. ABNOBA. The Danube formed the N. boundary of the empire, with the exception of the time that DACIA was a Roman province. In the Roman period the upper part of the river from its source as far as Vienna was called Danubius, while the lower part to its entrance on the Black Sea was named Ister.

Daorsi or **Daorizi**, a tribe in Dalmatia.

Daphnae Pēlūsiae (Δάφναι αἱ Πελούσιαι : *Safnas*), a border fortress of Lower Egypt against Arabia and Syria, stood on the right hand of the Nile, 16 Roman miles S. W. of Pelusium. Many Jews settled here after the destruction of Jerusalem by the Babylonians.

Daphnē (Δάφνη). 1. Daughter of the river-god Ladon in Arcadia, by Ge (the earth), or of the river-god Peneus in Thessaly. She was extremely beautiful, and was loved by Apollo and Leucippus, son of Oenomaus, but she rejected both their suits. In order to win her, Leucippus disguised himself as a maiden, but Apollo's jealousy caused his discovery and he was killed by the companions of Daphne. Apollo now pursued Daphne, and as she was on the point of being overtaken by him, she prayed for aid, and was metamorphosed into a laurel-tree (δάφνη), which became in consequence the favourite tree of Apollo. — 2. Daughter of Tiresias, better known under the name of MANTO.

Daphnē (Δάφνη). 1. (*Beit-el-Mois*, or *Babyla ?*), a beautiful spot, 5 miles S. of Antioch in Syria, to which it formed a sort of park or pleasure garden. Here was a grove of laurels and cypresses, 80 stadia in circuit, watered by fresh springs and consecrated by Seleucus Nicator to Apollo, to whom also a magnificent temple was built by Antiochus Epiphanes, and adorned with a splendid statue of the god by Bryaxis. To this temple were attached periodical games and the privilege of asylum. Daphne was a royal residence of the Seleucidae and of the later Roman emperors, and a favourite resort of the people of Antioch, who, however, carried the pleasures they enjoyed here so far beyond the bounds of moderation, that the phrase *Daphnici mores* passed into a proverb. It was from this place that Antioch received its distinguishing name, 'A. ἐπὶ Δάφνης. — 2. A place in Upper Galilee on the lake Semechonitis.

Daphnis (Δάφνις), a Sicilian hero, to whom the invention of bucolic poetry is ascribed. He was the son of Hermes by a nymph. His mother placed him when an infant in a charming valley in a laurel grove, from which he received his name of Daphnis. He was brought up by nymphs ; was taught by Pan to play on the flute ; he became a shepherd, and tended his flocks on Mt. Aetna winter and summer. A Naiad fell in love with him, and made him swear that he would never love any other maiden, threatening him with blindness if he broke his oath. For a time the handsome shepherd resisted the numerous temptations to which he was exposed, but at last he forgot himself, having been made intoxicated by a princess. The Naiad accordingly punished him with blindness, or, as others relate, changed him into a stone. Previous to this time he had composed bucolic poetry, and with it delighted Artemis during the chase. After having become blind, he invoked his father to help him. The god accordingly raised him up to heaven, and caused a well to gush forth on the spot where this happened. The well bore the name of Daphnis, and at it the Sicilians offered an annual sacrifice.

Daphnūs (Δάφνους -οῦντος : Δαφνούσιοι), a town of the Locri Opuntii on the coast, in earlier times belonging to Phocis.

Darādax (Δαράδαξ : *Abu-Ghalgal ?*), a river of Upper Syria, flowing into the Euphrates, 30 parasangs from the R. Chalos, and 15 from Thapsacus.

Dardāni (Δάρδανοι), a people in Upper Moesia, who also occupied part of Illyricum, and extended as far as the frontiers of Macedonia.

Dardānīa (Δαρδανία), a district of the Troad, lying along the Hellespont, S. W. of Abydos, and adjacent on the land side to the territories of Ilium and Scepsis. Its people (Δάρδανοι) appear in the Trojan War, under Aeneas, in close alliance with the Trojans, with whose name theirs is often interchanged, especially by the Roman poets. [DARDANUS.]

Dardānus (Δάρδανος), son of Zeus and Electra. His native place in the various traditions is Arcadia, Crete, Troas, or Italy. Dardanus is the mythical ancestor of the Trojans, and through them of the Romans. The Greek traditions usually made him a king in Arcadia. He first emigrated to Samothrace, and afterwards passed over to Asia, where he received a tract of land from king Teucer, on which he built the town of Dardania. He married Batea, daughter of Teucer, or Arisbe of Crete, by whom he became the father of Erichthonius. His grandson was Tros, who removed to Troy the Palladium, which had belonged to his grandfather. According to the Italian traditions, Dardanus was the son of Corythus, an Etruscan prince of Corythus (Cortona), or of Zeus by the wife of Corythus ; and, as in the Greek tradition, he afterwards emigrated to Phrygia.

Dardānus (ἡ Δάρδανος: Δαρδανεύς), also, -um and -ium, a Greek city in the Troad on the Hellespont, near the Prom. Dardanis or Dardanium and the mouth of the river Rhodius, 12 Roman miles from Ilium, and 9 (or 70 stadia) from Abydus. It was built by Aeolian colonists, at some distance from the site of the ancient city Dardania (Δαρδανίη), which is mentioned by Homer (Il. ii. 216) as founded by Dardanus before the building of Ilium. The Romans, after the war with Antiochus the Great, made Dardanus and Ilium free cities, as an act of filial piety. The peace between Sulla and Mithridates was made here, B.C. 84. From Dardanus arose the name of the Castles of the Dardanelles, after which the Hellespont is now called.

Dārēs (Δάρης), a priest of Hephaestus at Troy, mentioned in the Iliad (v. 9), to whom was ascribed in antiquity an Iliad, which was believed to be more ancient than the Homeric poems. This work, which was undoubtedly the composition of a sophist, is lost ; but there is extant a Latin work in prose in 44 chapters, on the destruction of Troy, bearing the title Daretis Phrygii de Excidio Trojae Historia, and purporting to be a translation of the work of Dares by Cornelius Nepos. But the Latin work is evidently of much later origin ; it is the production of a person of little education and of bad taste ; and it is supposed by some to have been written even as late as the 12th century. It is usually printed with Dictys Cretensis: the best edition is by Dederich, Bonn, 1837, 8vo.

Darīus (Δαρεῖος). I. King of Persia, B.C. 521 —485, was the son of Hystaspes, satrap of the province of Persia, and of the royal family of the Achaemenidae. He was one of the 7 Persian chiefs who destroyed the usurper SMERDIS. The 7 chiefs agreed that the one of them whose horse neighed first at an appointed time and place, should become king ; and as the horse of Darius neighed first, he was declared king. He married Atossa and Artystone, the 2 daughters of Cyrus, and Parmys, the daughter of Cyrus's son Smerdis, and Phaedime, the daughter of Otanes, one of the 7 chiefs. He then began to set in order the affairs of his vast empire, which he divided into 20 satrapies, assigning to each its amount of tribute. Persis proper was exempted from all taxes, except those which it had formerly been used to pay. It was in the reign of Darius that the consolidation of the empire was effected, for Cyrus and Cambyses had been engaged in continual wars. — A few years after his accession the Babylonians revolted, but after a siege of 20 months, Babylon was taken by a stratagem of ZOPYRUS, about 516. The reduction of Babylon was followed by the invasion of Scythia (about 508). Darius crossed the Danube, and marched far into the interior of modern Russia ; but after losing a large number of men by famine, and being unable to meet with the enemy, he was obliged to retreat. On his return to Asia, he sent part of his forces, under Megabazus, to subdue Thrace and Macedonia, which thus became subject to the Persian empire. The most important event

in the reign of Darius was the commencement of the great war between the Persians and the Greeks. The history of this war belongs to the biographies of other men. In 501 the Ionian Greeks revolted ; they were assisted by the Athenians, who burnt Sardis, and thus provoked the hostility of Darius. [ARISTAGORAS ; HISTIAEUS.] In 492 Mardonius was sent with a large army to invade Greece, but he lost a great part of his fleet off Mt. Athos. and the Thracians destroyed a vast number of his land forces. [MARDONIUS.] He was, in consequence, recalled, and Datis and Artaphernes appointed to the command of the invading army. They took Eretria in Euboea, and landed in Attica, but were defeated at Marathon by the Athenians under the command of Miltiades. [MILTIADES.] Darius now resolved to call out the whole force of his empire for the purpose of subduing Greece ; but, after 3 years of preparation, his attention was called off by the rebellion of Egypt. He died in 485, leaving the execution of his plans to his son XERXES.—II. King of Persia, 424—405, named Ochus (Ὦχος) before his accession, and then surnamed Nothus (Νόθος), or the Bastard, from his being one of the bastard sons of Artaxerxes I. Darius obtained the crown by putting to death his brother SOGDIANUS, who had murdered Xerxes II. He married Parysatis, daughter of Xerxes I., by whom he had 2 sons, Artaxerxes II., who succeeded him, and Cyrus the younger. Darius was governed by eunuchs, and the weakness of his government was shown by repeated insurrections of his satraps. In 414 the Persians were expelled from Egypt by Amyrtaeus, who reigned there 6 years, and at whose death (408) Darius was obliged to recognise his son Pausiris as his successor.—III. Last king of Persia, 336—331, named Codomannus before his accession, was the son of Arsames and Sisygambis, and a descendant of Darius II. He was raised to the throne by Bagoas, after the murder of ARSES. The history of his conquest by Alexander the Great, and of his death, is given in the life of ALEXANDER.

Dascon (Δάσκων: Δασκώνιος), a fortress near Syracuse, situated on a bay of the same name.

Dascÿlium (Δασκύλιον or -εῖον: Δασκυλίτης : Diaskili), a town of Bithynia, on the Propontis, near a lake called Dascylitis.

Dasēa (Δασέα, also Δασέαι: Δασεάτης), a small town in Arcadia near Megalopolis.

Dassarētii or Dassarītae, Dassarētae (Δασσαρήτιοι, Δασσαρῖται), a people in Greek Illyria on the borders of Macedonia : their chief town was Lychnidus (Λύχνιδος) on a hill, on the N. side of the lake Lychnītis, which was so called after the town.

Datāmes (Δατάμης), a distinguished Persian general, a Carian by birth, son of Camissares by a Scythian mother. He succeeded his father as satrap of Cilicia, under Artaxerxes II. (Mnemon), but, in consequence of the machinations of his enemies at the Persian court, he threw off his allegiance to the king, and made common cause with the other satraps who had revolted from Persia. He defeated the generals who were sent against him, but was assassinated by Mithridates, son of Ariobarzanes, about B.C. 362. Cornelius Nepos, who has written his life, calls him the bravest and most able of all barbarian generals, except Hamilcar and Hannibal.

Datis (Δᾶτις), a Mede, commanded, along with

Daedalus and Icarus.
(Zoëga, Bassirilievi di Roma, tav. 44.) Page 205.

Dido. (MS. Vatican Virgil, p. 93.) Page 219.

Demeter (Ceres).
(Mus. Bor., vol. 9, tav. 35.) Page 212.

Dionysus (Bacchus).
(Millingen, Peintures Antiques, pl. 53). Pages 226, 227.

Dionysus (Bacchus) drawn by Tigers. (Museum Capitolinum, vol. 4, tav. 63.) Pages 226, 227.

[To face p. 208.

Claudius II., Roman Emperor, A.D. 268—270.   Page 179.

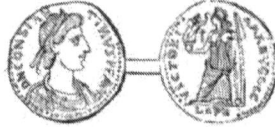

Constantinus II., Roman Emperor, A.D. 337—340.

Cleopatra and her son Antiochus VIII. Grypus.
Page 181, No. 6.

Constantinus, Roman Usurper. A.D. 407—411.
Page 188, No. 3.

Cleopatra, Queen of Egypt, ob. B.C. 30.   The head of Antony
is on the obverse, and that of Cleopatra on the reverse.
Page 132, No. 11.

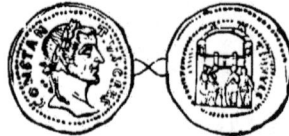

Constantius I., Roman Emperor, A.D. 305—306.   Page 118.

Commodus, Roman Emperor, A.D. 180—182.   Page 186.

Constantius II., Roman Emperor, A.D. 337—361.   Page 188.

Constans, Roman Emperor, A.D. 337—350.   Page 187.

Constantius III., Roman Emperor, A.D. 421.   Page 188.

Constantinus I. the Great, Roman Emperor, A.D. 306—337.
Page 187.

Decentius, Roman Caesar, A.D. 351—353.   Page 209.

To face p. 209.]

Artaphernes, the Persian army of Darius, which was defeated at Marathon, B. C. 490.

Datum or **Datus** (Δάτον, Δάτος: Δατηνός), a Thracian town on the Strymonic gulf, subject to Macedonia, with gold mines in Mt. Pangaeus in the neighbourhood, whence came the proverb a "Datum of good things."

Daulis or **Daulia** (Δαυλίς -ίδος, Δαυλία: Δαυλιεύς, Δαύλιος), an ancient town in Phocis on the road from Chaeronēa and Orchomenus to Delphi, situated on a lofty hill: celebrated in mythology as the residence of the Thracian king TEREUS, and as the scene of the tragic story of PHILOMELA and PROCNE. Hence **Daulias** (Δαυλιάς) is the surname both of Procne and Philomela.

Daunia. [APULIA.]

Daunus (Δαῦνος). 1. Son of Lycaon, and brother of Iapyx and Peucetius. The 3 brothers crossed over from Illyria, and settled in Apulia, which was divided into 3 parts, and named after them. The poets sometimes gave the name of Daunia to the whole of Apulia: Horace (*Carm.* i. 22. 14) uses the adjective *Daunias* (sc. *terra*). — 2. Son of Pilumnus and Danaë, wife of Venilia, and ancestor of Turnus.

Decebalus (Δεκέβαλος), a celebrated king of the Dacians during the reigns of Domitian and Trajan. For 4 years (A. D. 86—90) he carried on war against the Romans with such success, that Domitian was at length glad to conclude peace with him by the payment of an annual tribute. Trajan refused to continue this disgraceful payment, and renewed the war. He defeated the Dacians, and compelled Decebalus to sue for peace, which was granted (101—103). But in 104 the war broke out again ; Decebalus was again defeated, and put an end to his own life ; and Dacia became a Roman province, 106.

Decelea or **-ia** (Δεκέλεια: Δεκελεύς: *Biala-Castro*), a demus of Attica, belonging to the tribe Hippothoöntis, lay N.W. of Athens, on the borders of Boeotia, near the sources of the Cephissus. In the 19th year of the Peloponnesian War (B. C. 413), the Peloponnesians under Agis seized and fortified Decelea, and thereby annoyed the Athenians in many ways during the remainder of the war.

Decentius Magnus, brother or cousin of Magnentius, by whom he was created Caesar, A. D. 351. After the death of MAGNENTIUS, he put an end to his own life, 353.

Decetia (*Decize*), a city of the Aedui, in Gallia Lugdunensis, on an island in the Liger (*Loire*).

Deciates, a Ligurian people on the coast and about the sources of the Druentia (*Durance*). Their chief city, Deciatum (Δεκίητον), lay between Nicaea and Antipolis.

Decidius Saxa. [SAXA.]

P. **Decius Mus,** plebeians. 1. Consul B. C. 340 with T. Manlius Torquatus in the great Latin war. Each of the consuls had a vision in the night before fighting with the Latins, announcing that the general of one side and the army of the other were devoted to death. The consuls thereupon agreed that the one whose wing first began to waver should devote himself and the army of the enemy to destruction. Decius commanded the left wing, which began to give way, whereupon he devoted himself and the army of the enemy to destruction, according to the formula prescribed by the pontifex maximus, then rushed into the thickest of the enemy, and was slain, leaving the victory to the

Romans. — 2. Son of the preceding, 4 times consul, 312, 308, 297, and 295. In his 4th consulship he commanded the left wing at the battle of Sentinum, where he was opposed to the Gauls, and when his troops began to give way, he imitated the example of his father, devoted himself and the enemy to destruction, and fell as a sacrifice for his nation. — 3. Son of No. 2, consul 279, in the war against Pyrrhus. According to some he sacrificed himself in battle like his father and grandfather, but this is not true, for he survived the war with Pyrrhus.

Decius, Roman emperor, A. D. 249—251, whose full name was C. MESSIUS QUINTUS TRAJANUS DECIUS, was born at Bubalia in Pannonia. He was sent by the emperor Philippus in 249 to restore subordination in the army of Moesia, but the troops compelled him to accept the purple under threats of death. Decius still assured Philippus of his fidelity; but the latter not trusting these professions, hastened to meet his rival in the field, was defeated near Verona, and slain. The short reign of Decius was chiefly occupied in warring against the Goths. He fell in battle against the Goths together with his son in 251. In his reign the Christians were persecuted with great severity.

Decumates Agri. [AGRI DECUMATES.]

Deïanira (Δηϊάνειρα), daughter of Althaea by either Oeneus, or Dionysus, or Dexamenus, and sister of Meleager. Achelous and Hercules both loved Deïanira, and fought for the possession of her. Hercules was victorious, and she became his wife. She was the unwilling cause of her husband's death by presenting him with the poisoned robe, which the centaur Nessus gave her. In despair she put an end to her own life. For details see HERCULES.

Deïdamia (Δηϊδάμεια). 1. Daughter of Lycomedes in the island of Scyros. When Achilles was concealed there in maiden's attire, she became by him the mother of Pyrrhus or Neoptolemus. — 2. Wife of Pirithous, commonly called HIPPODAMIA. — 3. Sister of Pyrrhus, married Demetrius Poliorcetes.

Deïoces (Δηϊόκης), first king of Media, after the Medes had thrown off the supremacy of the Assyrians, was the son of Phraortes, and reigned B. C. 709—656. He built the city of Ecbatana, which he made the royal residence. His administration of justice was severe, and he kept a body of spies and informers throughout the whole country. He was succeeded by his son, PHRAORTES.

Deïon (Δηΐων), son of Aeolus and Enarete, king in Phocis, husband of Diomede, and father of Asteropia, Aenetus, Actor, Phylacus, and Cephalus.

Deïone (Δηϊόνη), mother of Miletus, who is hence called **Deïonides.** (Ov. *Met.* ix. 442.)

Deïotarus (Δηϊόταρος). 1. Tetrarch of Galatia, adhered firmly to the Romans in their wars in Asia against Mithridates, and was rewarded by the senate with the title of king, and the addition of Armenia Minor to his dominions. In the civil war he sided with Pompey, and was present at the battle of Pharsalia, B. C. 48. In 47 he applied to Domitius Calvinus, Caesar's legate in Asia, for aid against Pharnaces, who had taken possession of Armenia Minor. When Caesar, in the same year, came into Asia from Egypt, Deïotarus received him with submission, and endeavoured to excuse the aid he had given to Pompey. Caesar deprived

P

him of part of his dominions, but allowed him to retain his regal title. Two years afterwards (45) his grandson Castor accused him of having formed a design against Caesar's life, when he received Caesar in Galatia. He was defended by Cicero before Caesar, in the house of the latter at Rome, in the speech (*pro Rege Deiotaro*) still extant. The result of the trial is not known. After Caesar's death he obtained from Antony the restitution of his dominions by paying Fulvia a large sum of money. In 42, he joined the party of Brutus and Cassius, and died shortly afterwards at a great age. — **2.** Son and successor of the above. In the war between Antony and Octavian he took part with the former, but went over from him to the enemy in the battle of Actium, 31.

Deïphŏbē (Δηΐφόϐη), the Sibyl at Cumae, daughter of Glaucus. [SIBYLLA.]

Deïphŏbus (Δηΐφοϐος), a son of Priam and Hecuba, and next to Hector, the bravest among the Trojans. He always supported Paris in his refusal to deliver up Helen to the Trojans; and he married her after the death of Paris. Accordingly, on the fall of Troy, the vengeance of the Greeks was chiefly directed against him. His house was one of the first committed to the flames, and he was slain and fearfully mangled by Menelaus. In this dreadful condition he was found in the lower world by Aeneas, who erected a monument to him on cape Rhoeteum.

Deïphontes (Δηΐφόντης), son of Antimachus, and husband of Hyrnetho, the daughter of Temenus the Heraclid, became king of Argos, after Temenus had been murdered by his own sons. Pausanias (ii. 19) gives a different account.

Dēlĭum (Δήλιον: *Dhilessi*), a town on the coast of Boeotia, in the territory of Tanagra, near the Attic frontier, named after a temple of Apollo similar to that at Delos. The Athenians used it as a fortress in the early part of the Peloponnesian War, and in B. C. 424 they were defeated here by the Boeotians.

Dēlĭus and **Dēlĭa** (Δήλιος, Δηλία), surnames of Apollo and Artemis respectively, from the island of DELOS.

Dellĭus, Q., a Roman eques, who frequently changed sides in the civil wars. In B. C. 44 he joined Dolabella in Asia, afterwards went over to Cassius, and then united himself to M. Antony. He deserted to Octavian shortly before the battle of Actium, 31. He appears to have become a personal friend of Octavian and Maecenas, and is therefore addressed by Horace in one of his Odes (ii. 3). He wrote a history of Antony's war against the Parthians, in which he had himself fought.

Delmātĭus or **Dalmātĭus.** 1. Son of Constantius Chlorus and his second wife Theodora. From his half-brother, Constantine the Great, he received the title of censor: he died before A. D. 335. — **2.** Son of the preceding, was created Caesar by Constantine the Great, 335; and, upon the division of the empire, received Thrace, Macedonia, and Achaia, as his portion. He was put to death in 337 on the death of Constantine.

Dēlos or **Dēlus** (ἡ Δῆλος: Δήλιος: *Delo, Deli, Dili,* or *Sdilli,* Ru.), the smallest of the islands called Cyclades, in the Aegean Sea, lay in the strait between Rhenea and Myconus. It was also called, in earlier times, Asteria, Ortygia, and Chlamydia. According to a legend, founded perhaps on some tradition of its late volcanic origin, it was

called out of the deep by the trident of Poseidon, but was a floating island until Zeus fastened it by adamantine chains to the bottom of the sea, that it might be a secure resting-place to Leto, for the birth of Apollo and Artemis. Apollo afterwards obtained possession of Delos, by giving Calauria to Poseidon in exchange for it; and it became the most holy seat of the worship of Apollo. Such is the mythical story: we learn from history that Delos was peopled by the Ionians, for whom it was the chief centre of political and religious union in the time of Homer: it was also the seat of an Amphictyony, comprising the surrounding islands. In the time of Pisistratus, Delos became subject to the Athenians; it was made the common treasury of the Greek confederacy for carrying on the war with Persia; but the transference of the treasury to Athens, and the altered character of the league, reduced the island to a condition of absolute political dependence upon Athens. It still possessed, however, a very extensive commerce, which was increased by the downfal of Corinth, when Delos became the chief emporium for the trade in slaves; and it was one of the principal seats of art in Greece, especially for works in bronze, of which metal one of the most esteemed mixtures was called the Delian. An especial sanctity was attached to Delos from its connection with the worship of Apollo; and the peculiar character assigned to the island by the traditions of its origin was confirmed by the remarkable fact that, though of volcanic origin, and in the midst of islands very subject to earthquakes, Delos enjoyed an almost entire exemption from such visitations, so that its being shaken by an earthquake was esteemed a marked prodigy. The city of Delos stood on the W. side of the island, at the foot of Mt. Cynthus (whence the god's surname of Cynthius), near a little river called Inopus. It contained a temple of Leto, and the great temple of Apollo. The latter was built near the harbour, and possessed an oracle. Though enriched with offerings from all Greece, and defended by no fortifications, it was so protected from plunder by the sanctity of the place, that even the Persians, when sailing against Greece, not only passed it by uninjured, but sent rich presents to the god. With this temple were connected games, called Delia, which were celebrated every 4 years, and were said to have been founded by Theseus. A like origin is ascribed to the sacred embassy (θεωρία) which the Athenians sent to Delos every year. (*Dict. of Ant.* art. *Theori.*) The temple and oracle were visited by pilgrims from every quarter, even from the regions of Scythia. The greatest importance was attached to the preservation of the sanctity of the island. It was twice purified by the Athenians; once under Pisistratus, when all tombs within sight of the temple were taken away; and again in B. C. 426, when all human and animal remains were removed entirely from the island, which was henceforth forbidden to be polluted by births or deaths, or by the presence of dogs: all persons about to die or bring forth children were to be removed to the adjacent island of Rhenea. Delos continued in a flourishing condition, and under the rule of the Athenians, who were confirmed in the possession of it by the Romans, until the Mithridatic War, when Menophanes, one of the generals of Mithridates, inflicted upon it a devastation, from which it never again recovered.

Delphi (οἱ Δελφοί: Δελφός: *Kastri*), a small town in Phocis, but one of the most celebrated in Greece, on account of its oracle of Apollo. It was 16 stadia in circumference, was situated on a steep declivity on the S. slope of Mt. Parnassus, and its site resembled the cavea of a great theatre. It was shut in on the N. by a barrier of rocky mountains, which were cleft in the centre into 2 great cliffs with peaked summits, between which issued the waters of the Castalian spring. It was originally called **Pytho** (Πυθώ), by which name it is alone mentioned in Homer. The origin of the name of Delphi is uncertain. The ancients derived it from an eponymous hero, Delphus, a descendant of Deucalion ; but it has been conjectured, with great probability, that *Delphi* is connected with *adeiphos*, "brother," and that it was indebted for its name to the twin peaks mentioned above. Delphi was colonised at an early period by Doric settlers from the neighbouring town of Lycorea, on the heights of Parnassus. The government was an oligarchy, and was in the hands of a few distinguished families of Doric origin. From them were taken the chief magistrates, the priests, and a senate consisting of a very few members. Delphi was regarded as the central point of the whole earth, and was hence called the "navel of the earth." It was said that 2 eagles sent forth by Jupiter, one from the E. and the other from the W., met at Delphi at the same time. — Delphi was the principal seat of the worship of Apollo. Besides the great temple of Apollo, it contained numerous sanctuaries, statues, and other works of art. The Pythian games were also celebrated here, and it was one of the 2 places of meeting of the Amphictyonic council. — The temple of Apollo was situated at the N. W. extremity of the town. The first stone temple was built by Trophonius and Agamedes ; and when this was burnt down B. C. 548, it was rebuilt by the Amphictyons with still greater splendour. The expense was defrayed by voluntary subscriptions, to which even Amasis, king of Egypt, contributed. The architect was Spintharus of Corinth ; the Alcmaeonidae contracted to build it, and liberally substituted Parian marble for the front of the building, instead of the common stone which they had agreed to employ. The temple contained immense treasures ; for not only were rich offerings presented to it by kings and private persons, who had received favourable replies from the oracle, but many of the Greek states had in the temple separate *thesauri*, in which they deposited, for the sake of security, many of their valuable treasures. The wealth of the temple attracted Xerxes, who sent part of his army into Phocis to obtain possession of its treasures, but the Persians were driven back by the god himself, according to the account of the Delphians. The Phocians plundered the temple to support them in the war against Thebes and the other Greek states (357—346) ; and it was robbed at a later time by Brennus and by Sulla. — In the centre of the temple there was a small opening (χάσμα) in the ground, from which, from time to time, an intoxicating vapour arose, which was believed to come from the well of Cassotis. No traces of this chasm or of the mephitic exhalations are now any where observable. Over this chasm there stood a tripod, on which the priestess, called Pythia, took her seat whenever the oracle was to be consulted. The words which she uttered after exhaling the

vapour, were believed to contain the revelations of Apollo. They were carefully written down by the priests, and afterwards communicated in hexameter verse to the persons who had come to consult the oracle. If the Pythia spoke in prose, her words were immediately turned into verse by a poet employed for the purpose. The oracle is said to have been discovered by its having thrown into convulsions some goats which had strayed to the mouth of the cave. — For details respecting the oracle and its influence in Greece, see *Dict. of Ant.* art. *Oraculum.*

Delphines. [DELPHINIUS.]

Delphinium (Δελφίνιον). 1. A temple of Apollo Delphinius at Athens, said to have been built by Aegeus, in which the Ephetae sat for trying cases of intentional, but justifiable homicide. — 2. The harbour of Oropus in Attica, on the borders of Boeotia, called ὁ ἱερὸς λιμήν. — 3. A town on the E. coast of the island Chios.

Delphinius (Δελφίνιος), a surname of Apollo, derived either from his slaying the dragon Delphines (usually called Python), or because in the form of a dolphin (δελφίς) or riding on a dolphin, he showed the Cretan colonists the way to Delphi.

Delphus (Δελφός). 1. Son of Poseidon and Melantho, to whom the foundation of Delphi was ascribed. — 2. Son of Apollo and Celaeno, who is also said to have founded Delphi.

Delta. [AEGYPTUS.]

Demades (Δημάδης, a contraction of Δημεάδης), an Athenian orator, was of very low origin, but rose by his talents to a prominent position at Athens. He belonged to the Macedonian party, and was a bitter enemy of Demosthenes. He was taken prisoner at the battle of Chaeronea, B. C. 338, but was dismissed by Philip with distinguished marks of honour. After Philip's death he was the subservient supporter of Alexander, but notwithstanding frequently received bribes from the opposite party. He was put to death by Antipater in 318, because the latter had discovered a letter of Demades, urging the enemies of Antipater to attack him. Demades was a man without principle, and lived in a most profligate and dissolute manner. But he was a brilliant orator. He always spoke extempore, and with such irresistible force that he was a perfect match for Demosthenes himself. There is extant a large fragment of an oration bearing the name of Demades (περὶ δωδεκαετίας), in which he defends his conduct during the period of Alexander's reign. It is printed in the collections of the Attic orators, but its genuineness is doubtful. Cicero and Quintilian both state that Demades left no orations behind him.

Demaratus (Δημάρατος, Dor. Δαμάρατος). 1. King of Sparta, reigned from about B. C. 510 to 491. He was at variance with his unscrupulous colleague Cleomenes, who at length accused him before the Ephors of being an illegitimate son of Ariston, and obtained his deposition by bribing the Delphic oracle, B. C. 491. Demaratus thereupon repaired to the Persian coast, where he was kindly received by Darius. He accompanied Xerxes in his invasion of Greece, and recommended the king not to rely too confidently upon his countless hosts. His family continued long in Asia. — 2. A merchant-noble of Corinth, and one of the Bacchiadae. When the power of his clan had been overthrown by Cypselus, about B. C. 657, he fled from Corinth, and settled at Tarquinii in Etruria, where he married an Etruscan wife, by whom he had 2 sons, Aruns and Lucumo, afterwards L. Tarquinius Priscus.

Demetae, a people of Britain, in the S.W. of Wales : their chief towns were Maridunum (*Carmarthen*) and Luentinum.

Dēmētēr (Δημήτηρ), one of the great divinities of the Greeks, was the goddess of the earth, and her name probably signified *Mother-Earth* (γῆ μήτηρ). She was the protectress of agriculture and of all the fruits of the earth. She was the daughter of Cronus and Rhea, and sister of Zeus, by whom she became the mother of Persephone (Proserpina). Zeus, without the knowledge of Demeter, had promised Persephone to Aïdoneus (Pluto) ; and while the unsuspecting maiden was gathering flowers in the Nysian plain in Asia, the earth suddenly opened and she was carried off by Aïdoneus. Her mother, who heard only the echo of her voice, immediately set out in search of her daughter. For 9 days she wandered about without obtaining any tidings of her, but on the tenth she met Hecate, who told her that she had heard the cries of Persephone, but did not know who had carried her off. Both then hastened to Helios (the Sun), who revealed to them that it was Aïdoneus who had carried off Persephone with the consent of Zeus. Thereupon Demeter in her anger avoided Olympus, and dwelt upon earth among men, conferring blessings wherever she was kindly received, and severely punishing those who repulsed her. In this manner she came to Celeus at Eleusis. [CELEUS.] As the goddess still continued angry, and did not allow the earth to produce any fruits, Zeus first sent Iris and then all the gods to persuade Demeter to return to Olympus. But she was deaf to all their entreaties, and refused to return to Olympus, and to restore fertility to the earth, till she had seen her daughter again. Zeus accordingly sent Hermes into Erebus to fetch back Persephone. Aïdoneus consented, but gave Persephone part of a pomegranate to eat. Hermes then took her to Eleusis to her mother, who received her with unbounded joy. At Eleusis both were joined by Hecate, who henceforth became the attendant of Persephone. Demeter now returned to Olympus with her daughter, but as the latter had eaten in the lower world, she was obliged to spend one third of the year with Aïdoneus, but was allowed to continue with her mother the remainder of the year. The earth now brought forth fruit again. Before Demeter left Eleusis, she instructed Triptolemus, Diocles, Eumolpus, and Celeus in the mode of her worship and in the mysteries. This is the ancient legend as preserved in the Homeric hymn, but it is variously modified in later traditions. In the Latin poets the scene of the rape is near Enna in Sicily ; and Ascalaphus, who had alone seen Persephone eat any thing in the lower world, revealed the fact and was in consequence turned into an owl by Demeter. [ASCALAPHUS.] In the Iliad and Odyssey there is no mention of this legend, and there appears no connexion between Demeter and Persephone. The meaning of the legend is obvious. Persephone, who is carried off to the lower world, is the seed-corn, which remains concealed in the ground part of the year ; Persephone, who returns to her mother, is the corn which rises from the ground and nourishes men and animals. Later philosophical writers, and perhaps the mysteries also, referred the disappearance and return of Persephone to the burial of the body of man

and the immortality of his soul.—The other legends about Demeter are of less importance. To escape the pursuit of Poseidon she changed herself into a mare, but the god effected his purpose, and she became the mother of the celebrated horse Arion [ARION, No. 2.] According to some traditions she also bore to Poseidon a daughter Despoena (*i. e* Persephone). — She fell in love with Iasion and lay with him in a thrice-ploughed field in Crete : their offspring was Plutus (*Wealth*). [IASION.] — She punished with fearful hunger Erysichthon, who had cut down her sacred grove. [ERYSICHTHON.]—The chief seats of the worship of Demeter and Persephone were Attica, Arcadia and Sicily. In Attica she was worshipped with great splendour. The Athenians pretended that agriculture was first practised in their country, and that Triptolemus of Eleusis, the favourite of Demeter, was the first who invented the plough and sowed corn. [TRIPTOLEMUS.] Every year at Athens the festival of the *Eleusinia* was celebrated in honour of these goddesses. The festival of the Thesmophoria was also celebrated in her honour as well at Athens as in other parts of Greece : it was intended to commemorate the introduction of the laws and the regulations of civilised life, which were ascribed to Demeter, since agriculture is the basis of civilisation. (*Dict. of Ant.* arts. *Eleusinia, Thesmophoria.*)—In works of art Demeter was represented sometimes in a sitting attitude, sometimes walking, and sometimes riding in a chariot drawn by horses or dragons, but always in full attire. Around her head she wore a garland of corn-ears or a simple riband, and in her hand she held a sceptre, corn-ears or a poppy, sometimes also a torch and the mystic basket. — The Romans received from Sicily the worship of Demeter, to whom they gave the name of Ceres. The first temple of Ceres at Rome was vowed by the dictator A. Postumius Albinus, in B. C. 496, for the purpose of averting a famine with which Rome was threatened during a war with the Latins. The Romans instituted a festival with games in honour of her (*Dict. of Ant. s. v. Cerealia*). She was looked upon by the Romans much in the same light as Tellus. Pigs were sacrificed to both divinities, in the seasons of sowing and in harvest time, and also at the burial of the dead. Her worship acquired considerable political importance at Rome. The property of traitors against the republic was often made over to her temple. The decrees of the senate were deposited in her temple for the inspection of the tribunes of the people. If we further consider that the aediles had the special superintendence of this temple, it is very probable that Ceres, whose worship was, like the plebeians themselves, introduced at Rome from without, had some peculiar relation to the plebeian order.

Dēmētrias (Δημητριάς : Δημητριεύς). 1. A town in Magnesia in Thessaly, on the innermost recess of the Pagasaean bay, founded by Demetrius Poliorcetes, and peopled by the inhabitants of Iolcus and the surrounding towns : it soon became one of the most important towns in the N. of Greece, and is frequently mentioned in the wars between the Macedonians and Romans.—2. A town in Assyria, not far from Arbela.—3. An Athenian tribe, added to the 10 old tribes, B. C. 307, and named in honour of Demetrius Poliorcetes.

Dēmētrius (Δημήτριος). 1. A Greek of the island of Pharos in the Adriatic. He was a general of Teuta, the Illyrian queen, and treacherously surrendered Corcyra to the Romans, who rewarded him with a great part of the dominions of Teuta, 228. Subsequently he ventured on many acts of piratical hostility against the Romans, thinking that they were too much occupied with the Gallic war and the impending danger of Hannibal's invasion to take notice of him. The Romans, however, immediately sent the consul L. Aemilius Paulus over to Illyria (219), who took Pharos itself, and obliged Demetrius to fly for refuge to Philip, king of Macedonia. At the court of this prince he spent the remainder of his life.— 2. Younger son of Philip V., king of Macedonia, was sent as a hostage to Rome after the battle of Cynoscephalae (198). Five years afterwards he was restored to his father, who subsequently sent him as his ambassador to Rome. But having incurred the jealousy of his father and his brother, Perseus, by the favourable reception he had met with from the Romans, he was secretly put to death by his father's order.

I. *Kings of Macedonia.* 1. Surnamed **Poliorcetes** (Πολιορκητής), or the Besieger, son of Antigonus, king of Asia, and Stratonice. At an early age he gave proofs of distinguished bravery. He accompanied his father in his campaigns against Eumenes (B. C. 317, 316), and a few years afterwards was left by his father in the command of Syria, which he had to defend against Ptolemy. In 312 he was defeated by Ptolemy near Gaza, but soon after retrieved his disaster in part by defeating one of the generals of Ptolemy. In 311 a general peace was concluded among the successors of Alexander, but it was only of short duration. In 307 Demetrius was despatched by his father with a powerful fleet and army to wrest Greece from Cassander and Ptolemy. He met with great success. At Athens he was received with enthusiasm by the people as their liberator. Demetrius the Phalerean, who had governed the city for Cassander, was expelled, and the fort at Munychia taken. Demetrius took up his abode for the winter at Athens, where divine honours were paid him under the title of "the Preserver" (ὁ Σωτήρ). He was recalled from Athens by his father to take the command of the war in Cyprus against Ptolemy. Here also he was successful, and in a great naval battle he annihilated the fleet of Ptolemy (306). Next year (305) he laid siege to Rhodes, because the Rhodians had refused to support him against Ptolemy. It was in consequence of the gigantic machines which Demetrius constructed to assail the walls of Rhodes, that he received the surname of Poliorcetes. But all his exertions were unavailing, and after the siege had lasted above a year, he at length concluded a treaty with the Rhodians (304). — Demetrius then crossed over to Greece, which had meanwhile been almost conquered by Cassander. He soon compelled Cassander to evacuate all Greece S. of Thermopylae, and for the next 2 years continued to prosecute the war with success. But in 302 he was obliged to return to Asia in order to support his father Antigonus. In 301 their combined forces were totally defeated by those of Lysimachus and Seleucus in the battle of Ipsus, and Antigonus himself slain. Demetrius, to whose impetuosity the loss of the battle would seem to be in great measure owing, fled to Ephesus, and from thence set sail for Athens; but the Athenians declined to receive him into their city. The jealousies of his enemies soon changed the face of his affairs;

and Ptolemy having entered into a closer union with Lysimachus, Seleucus married Stratonice, daughter of Demetrius. By this alliance Demetrius obtained possession of Cilicia, and he had never lost Cyprus, Tyre, and Sidon. In 297 he determined to make an effort to recover his dominions in Greece. He appeared with a fleet on the coast of Attica, but was at first unsuccessful. The death of Cassander, however, in the course of the same year gave a new turn to affairs. Demetrius made himself master of Aegina, Salamis, and finally of Athens, after a long blockade (295). In 294 he marched into Peloponnesus against the Spartans, and was on the point of taking their city when he was suddenly called away by the state of affairs in Macedonia. Here the dissensions between Antipater and Alexander, the 2 sons of Cassander, had led Alexander to call in foreign aid to his support; and he sent embassies at once to Demetrius and to Pyrrhus. Pyrrhus was the nearest at hand, and had already defeated Antipater and established Alexander on the throne, when Demetrius arrived with his army. He was received with apparent friendliness, but mutual jealousies quickly arose. Demetrius caused the young king to be assassinated at a banquet, and was thereupon acknowledged as king by the Macedonian army. Demetrius kept possession of Macedonia for 7 years (294—287). His reign was a series of wars. In 292 he marched against the Thebans, who had risen against him, and took their city. In 291 he took advantage of the captivity of Lysimachus among the Getae to invade Thrace; but he was recalled by the news of a fresh insurrection in Boeotia. He repulsed Pyrrhus, who had attempted by invading Thessaly to effect a diversion in favour of the Boeotians, and again took Thebes after a long siege (290). In 289 he carried on war against Pyrrhus and the Aetolians, but he concluded peace with Pyrrhus that he might march into Asia with the view of recovering his father's dominions. His adversaries however forestalled him. In 287 Ptolemy sent a powerful fleet against Greece, while Pyrrhus (notwithstanding his recent treaty) on the one side and Lysimachus on the other simultaneously invaded Macedonia. Demetrius was deserted by his own troops, who proclaimed Pyrrhus king of Macedonia. He then crossed over to Asia, and after meeting with alternate success and misfortune, was at length obliged to surrender himself prisoner to Seleucus (286). That king kept him in confinement, but did not treat him with harshness. Demetrius died in the 3rd year of his imprisonment and the 56th of his age (283). He was one of the most remarkable characters of his age: in restless activity of mind, fertility of resource, and daring promptitude in the execution of his schemes, he has perhaps never been surpassed. His besetting sin was his unbounded licentiousness. Besides Lamia and his other mistresses, he was regularly married to 4 wives, Phila, Eurydice, Deïdamia, and Ptolemaïs, by whom he left 4 sons. The eldest of these, Antigonus Gonatas, eventually succeeded him on the throne of Macedonia. — 2. Son of Antigonus Gonatas, succeeded his father, and reigned B. C. 239—229. He carried on war against the Aetolians, and was opposed to the Achaean League. He was succeeded by Antigonus Doson.

II. *Kings of Syria.* 1. **Soter** (reigned B. C. 162

—150), was the son of Seleucus IV. Philopator and grandson of Antiochus the Great. While yet a child, he had been sent to Rome by his father as a hostage, and remained there during the whole of the reign of Antiochus IV. Epiphanes. After the death of Antiochus, being now 23 years old, he demanded of the senate to be set at liberty; but as his request was refused by the senate, he fled secretly from Rome, by the advice of the historian Polybius, and went to Syria. The Syrians declared in his favour; and the young king Antiochus V. Eupator, with his tutor Lysias, was seized by his own guards and put to death. By valuable presents Demetrius obtained from the Romans his recognition as king. But having alienated his own subjects by his luxury and intemperance, they sided with an impostor of the name of Balas, who took the title of Alexander. By him Demetrius was defeated in battle and slain. He left 2 sons, Demetrius Nicator and Antiochus Sidetes, both of whom subsequently ascended the throne.—2. Nicator (B. C. 146—142, and again 128—125), son of Demetrius Soter. He had been sent by his father for safety to Cnidus, when Alexander Balas invaded Syria; and after the death of his father he continued in exile for some years. With the assistance of Ptolemy Philometor he defeated Balas, and recovered his kingdom; but, having like his father rendered himself odious to his subjects by his vices and cruelties, he was driven out of Syria by Tryphon, who set up Antiochus, the infant son of Alexander Balas, as a pretender against him. Demetrius retired to Babylon, and from thence marched against the Parthians, by whom he was defeated and taken prisoner, 138. He remained as a captive in Parthia 10 years, but was kindly treated by the Parthian king Mithridates (Arsaces VI.), who gave him his daughter Rhodogune in marriage. Meanwhile, his brother, Antiochus VII. Sidetes, having overthrown the usurper Tryphon, engaged in war with Parthia, in consequence of which Phraates, the successor of Mithridates, brought forward Demetrius, and sent him into Syria to operate a diversion against his brother. In the same year Antiochus fell in battle, and Demetrius again obtained possession of the Syrian throne, 128. Having engaged in an expedition against Egypt, Ptolemy Physcon set up against him the pretender Alexander Zebina, by whom he was defeated and compelled to fly. His wife Cleopatra, who could not forgive him his marriage with Rhodogune in Parthia, refused to afford him refuge at Ptolemais, and he fled to Tyre, where he was assassinated, 125.—3. Eucaerus, son of Antiochus VIII. Grypus, and grandson of Demetrius II. During the civil wars that followed the death of Antiochus Grypus (96), Demetrius and his brother Philip for a time held the whole of Syria. But war broke out between them; Demetrius was taken prisoner and sent to Parthia, where he remained in captivity till his death.

III. *Literary.* 1. Of **Adramyttium**, surnamed Ixion, a Greek grammarian of the time of Augustus, lived partly at Pergamus and partly at Alexandria, and wrote commentaries on Homer and Hesiod and other works.— 2. **Magnes**, that is, of Magnesia, a Greek grammarian, and a contemporary of Cicero and Atticus. He wrote a work On concord (περὶ ὁμονοίας), and another on poets and other authors who bore the same name (Περὶ ὁμωνύμων ποιητῶν καὶ συγγραφέων).—3. **Phalereus**, so called from

his birthplace, the Attic demos of Phalerus, where he was born about B. C. 345. His parents were poor, but by his talents and perseverance he rose to the highest honours at Athens, and became distinguished both as an orator, a statesman, a philosopher, and a poet. He was educated, together with the poet Menander, in the school of Theophrastus. He began his public career about 325, and acquired great reputation by his eloquence. In 317 the government of Athens was entrusted to him by Cassander, and he discharged the duties of his office for 10 years with such general satisfaction, that the Athenians conferred upon him the most extraordinary distinctions, and erected no less than 360 statues to his honour. But during the latter period of his administration he seems to have become intoxicated with his good fortune, and he abandoned himself to dissipation. When Demetrius Poliorcetes approached Athens, in 307, Demetrius Phalereus was obliged to take to flight, and his enemies induced the Athenians to pass sentence of death upon him. He went to Ptolemy Lagi at Alexandria, with whom he lived for many years on the best terms; and it was probably owing to the influence of Demetrius that the great Alexandrine library was formed. His successor, Ptolemy Philadelphus, was hostile towards Demetrius, because he had advised his father to appoint another of his sons as his successor. He banished Demetrius to Upper Egypt, where he is said to have died from the bite of a snake.—Demetrius Phalereus was the last among the Attic orators worthy of the name; but even his orations bore evident marks of the decline of oratory, and were characterised rather by grace and elegance than by force and sublimity. His numerous writings, the greater part of which were probably composed in Egypt, embraced subjects of the most varied kinds; but none of them has come down to us, for the work on elocution (περὶ ἑρμηνείας), extant under his name, is probably the work of an Alexandrine sophist of the name of Demetrius.— 4. Of **Scepsis**, a Greek grammarian of the time of Aristarchus, wrote a learned commentary on the Catalogue in the 2nd book of the Iliad.—5. Of **Sunium**, a Cynic philosopher, lived from the reign of Caligula to that of Domitian, and was banished from Rome in consequence of the freedom with which he rebuked the powerful.

Democedes (Δημοκήδης), a celebrated physician of Crotona. He practised medicine successively at Aegina, Athens, and Samos. He was taken prisoner along with Polycrates, in B. C. 522, and was sent to Susa to the court of Darius. Here he acquired great reputation by curing the king's foot, and the breast of the queen Atossa. Notwithstanding his honours at the Persian court, he was always desirous of returning to his native country. In order to effect this, he pretended to enter into the views and interests of the Persians, and procured by means of Atossa that he should be sent with some nobles to explore the coast of Greece, and ascertain in what parts it might be most successfully attacked. When they arrived at Tarentum, the king, Aristophilides, out of kindness to Democedes, seized the Persians as spies, which afforded the physician an opportunity of escaping to Crotona. Here he settled, and married the daughter of the famous wrestler, Milo; the Persians having followed him to Crotona, and in vain demanded that he should be restored.

Dēmŏchărēs (Δημοχάρης), an Athenian, son of the sister of Demosthenes. He was probably trained by his uncle in oratory, and inherited his patriotic sentiments. After the restoration of the Athenian democracy in B.C. 307 by Demetrius Poliorcetes, Demochares was at the head of the patriotic party and took an active part in public affairs for the next 20 or 30 years. He left behind him several orations, and an extensive history of his own times.

Dēmŏclēs (Δημοκλῆς), an Attic orator, and an opponent of Demochares.

Dēmŏcrătēs (Δημοκράτης), a Pythagorean philosopher, of whose life nothing is known, the author of an extant collection of moral maxims, called the golden sentences (γνῶμαι χρυσαῖ). They are printed with DEMOPHILUS.

Dēmŏcritus (Δημόκριτος), a celebrated Greek philosopher, was born at Abdera in Thrace, about B.C. 460. His father, Hegesistratus, — or, as others called him, Damasippus or Athenocritus, — was possessed of so large a property, that he was able to entertain Xerxes on his march through Abdera. Democritus spent the inheritance, which his father left him, on travels into distant countries, which he undertook to satisfy his extraordinary thirst for knowledge. He travelled over a great part of Asia, and spent some time in Egypt. The many anecdotes preserved about Democritus show that he was a man of a most sterling and honourable character. His diligence was incredible: he lived exclusively for his studies, and his disinterestedness, modesty, and simplicity, are attested by many features which are related of him. Notwithstanding the great property he had inherited from his father, he died in poverty, but highly esteemed by his fellow-citizens. He died in 361 at a very advanced age. There is a tradition that he deprived himself of his sight, that he might be less disturbed in his pursuits; but this tradition is one of the inventions of a later age, which was fond of piquant anecdotes. It is more probable that he may have lost his sight by too severe application to study. This loss, however, did not disturb the cheerful disposition of his mind, which prompted him to look, in all circumstances, at the cheerful side of things, which later writers took to mean, that he always laughed at the follies of men. His knowledge was most extensive. It embraced not only the natural sciences, mathematics, mechanics, grammar, music, and philosophy, but various other useful arts. His works were composed in the Ionic dialect, though not without some admixture of the local peculiarities of Abdera. They are nevertheless much praised by Cicero on account of the liveliness of their style, and are in this respect compared even with the works of Plato. The fragments of them are collected by Mullach, *Democriti Abderitae Operum Fragmenta*, Berlin, 1843. Leucippus appears to have had most influence upon the philosophical opinions of Democritus, and these 2 philosophers were the founders of the theory of atoms. In order to explain the creation of all existing things, Democritus maintained that there were in infinite space an infinite number of atoms or elementary particles, homogeneous in quality, but heterogeneous in form. He further taught that these atoms combine with one another, and that all things arise from the infinite variety of the form, order, and position of the atoms in forming combinations. The cause of these combinations he

called chance (τύχη), in opposition to the νοῦς of Anaxagoras; but he did not use the word chance in its vulgar acceptation, but to signify the necessary succession of cause and effect. In his ethical philosophy Democritus considered the acquisition of peace of mind (εὐθυμία) as the end and ultimate object of our actions.

Dēmŏdŏcus (Δημόδοκος), the celebrated bard at the court of Alcinoüs who sang of the loves of Ares and Aphrodite, while Ulysses sat at the banquet of Alcinoüs. He is also mentioned as the bard who advised Agamemnon to guard Clytaemnestra, and to expose Aegisthus in a desert island. Later writers, who looked upon this mythical minstrel as an historical person, related that he composed a poem on the destruction of Troy, and on the marriage of Hephaestus and Aphrodite.

Dēmōnax (Δημώναξ), of Cyprus, a Cynic philosopher in the time of Hadrian. We owe our knowledge of his character to Lucian, who has painted it in the most glowing colours, representing him as almost perfectly wise and good. Demonax appears to have been free from the austerity and moroseness of the sect, though he valued their indifference to external things. He was nearly 100 years old at the time of his death.

Dēmōnēsi Insŭlae (Δημόνησοι), a group of islands in the Propontis (*Sea of Marmora*), belonging to Bithynia: of these the most important were Pityōdes and Chalcitis, also called Demonesus.

Dēmŏphĭlus (Δημόφιλος). 1. Son of Ephorus, continued his father's history by adding to it the history of the Sacred War.—2. An Athenian comic poet of the new comedy, from whose 'Ονάγός Plautus took his *Asinaria*.—3. A Pythagorean philosopher, of whose life nothing is known, wrote a work entitled βίου θεράπεια, part of which is extant, in the form of a selection, entitled γνωμικὰ ὁμοιώματα. Best edition by Orelli, in his *Opusc. Graec. Vet. Sentent*. Lips. 1819.

Dēmŏphōn or **Dēmŏphŏōn** (Δημοφῶν or Δημοφόων). 1. Son of Celeus and Metanira, whom Demeter wished to make immortal. For details see CELEUS.—2. Son of Theseus and Phaedra, accompanied the Greeks against Troy, and there procured the liberation of his grandmother Aethra, who lived with Helen as a slave. On his return from Troy, he gained the love of Phyllis, daughter of the Thracian king Sithon, and promised to marry her. Before the nuptials were celebrated, he went to Attica to settle his affairs, and as he tarried longer than Phyllis had expected, she thought that she was forgotten, and put an end to her life; but she was metamorphosed into a tree. Demophon became king of Athens. He marched out against Diomedes, who on his return from Troy had landed on the coast of Attica, and was ravaging it. He took the Palladium from Diomedes, but had the misfortune to kill an Athenian in the struggle. For this murder he was summoned before the court ἐπὶ Παλλαδίῳ—the first time that a man was tried by that court.

Dēmosthĕnēs (Δημοσθένης). 1. Son of Alcisthenes, a celebrated Athenian general in the Peloponnesian War. In B.C. 426 he was sent with a fleet to ravage the coast of Peloponnesus: he afterwards landed at Naupactus, and made a descent into Aetolia; he was at first unsuccessful, and was obliged to retreat; but he subsequently gained a brilliant victory over the Ambraciots. In 425, though not in office, he sailed with the Athenian fleet, and was allowed by the Athenian commanders to remain with 5 ships at Pylos, which he fortified in order to assail the Lacedaemonians in their own territories. He defended Pylos against all the attempts of the Lacedaemonians, till he was relieved by an Athenian fleet of 40 ships. The Spartans, who in their siege of the place had occupied the neighbouring island of Sphacteria, were now cut off and blockaded. Later in the same year he rendered important assistance to Cleon, in making prisoners of the Spartans in the island of Sphacteria, though the whole glory of the success was given to Cleon. In 413 he was sent with a large fleet to Sicily, to assist Nicias. Fortune was unfavourable to the Athenians. Demosthenes now counselled an immediate departure, but Nicias delayed returning till it was too late. The Athenian fleet was destroyed, and when Demosthenes and Nicias attempted to retreat by land, they were obliged to surrender to the enemy with all their forces. Both commanders were put to death by the Syracusans. — **2.** The greatest of Athenian orators, was the son of Demosthenes, and was born in the Attic demos of Paeania, about B. C. 385. At 7 years of age he lost his father, who left him and his younger sister to the care of 3 guardians, Aphobus and Demophon, 2 relations, and Therippides, an old friend. These guardians squandered the greater part of the property of Demosthenes, and neglected his education to a great extent. He nevertheless received instruction from the orator Isaeus ; but it is exceedingly doubtful whether he was taught by Plato and Isocrates, as some of the ancients stated. At the age of 18 Demosthenes called upon his guardians to render him an account of their administration of his property ; but by intrigues they contrived to defer the business for 2 years. At length, in 364, Demosthenes accused Aphobus before the archon, and obtained a verdict in his favour. Aphobus was condemned to pay a fine of 10 talents. Emboldened by this success, Demosthenes ventured to come forward as a speaker in the public assembly. His first effort was unsuccessful, and he is said to have been received with ridicule ; but he was encouraged to persevere by the actor Satyrus, who gave him instruction in action and declamation. In becoming an orator, Demosthenes had to struggle against the greatest physical disadvantages. His voice was weak and his utterance defective ; he could not pronounce the ρ, and constantly stammered, whence he derived the nickname of βάταλος. It was only owing to the most unwearied exertions that he succeeded in overcoming the obstacles which nature had placed in his way. Thus it is said that he spoke with pebbles in his mouth, to cure himself of stammering ; that he repeated verses of the poets as he ran up hill, to strengthen his voice ; that he declaimed on the sea-shore to accustom himself to the noise and confusion of the popular assembly ; that he lived for months in a cave under ground, engaged in constantly writing out the history of Thucydides, to form a standard for his own style. These tales are not worthy of much credit ; but they nevertheless attest the common tradition of antiquity respecting the great efforts made by Demosthenes to attain to excellence as an orator. — It was about 355 that Demosthenes began to obtain reputation as a speaker in the public assembly. It was in this year that he delivered the oration against Leptines, and from this time we have a

series of his speeches on public affairs. His eloquence soon gained him the favour of the people. The influence which he acquired he employed for the good of his country, and not for his own aggrandisement. He clearly saw that Philip had resolved to subjugate Greece, and he therefore devoted all his powers to resist the aggressions of the Macedonian monarch. For 14 years he continued the struggle against Philip, and neither threats nor bribes could turn him from his purpose. It is true he failed ; but the failure must not be considered his fault. The history of his struggle is best given in the life of Philip. [PHILIPPUS.] It is sufficient to relate here that it was brought to a close by the battle of Chaeronëa (338), by which the independence of Greece was crushed. Demosthenes was present at the battle, and fled like thousands of others. His enemies reproached him with his flight, and upbraided him as the cause of the misfortunes of his country ; but the Athenians judged better of his conduct, requested him to deliver the funeral oration upon those who had fallen at Chaeronea, and celebrated the funeral feast in his house. At this time many accusations were brought against him. Of these one of the most formidable was the accusation of Ctesiphon by Aeschines, but which was in reality directed against Demosthenes himself. Aeschines accused Ctesiphon for proposing that Demosthenes should be rewarded for his services with a golden crown in the theatre. Aeschines maintained that the proposal was not only made in an illegal form, but that the conduct of Demosthenes did not give him any claim to such a distinction. The trial was delayed for reasons unknown to us till 330, when Demosthenes delivered his oration on the crown (περὶ στεφάνου). Aeschines was defeated and withdrew from Athens. [AESCHINES.] — Meantime important events had taken place in Greece. The death of Philip in 336 roused the hopes of the patriots, and Demosthenes, although he had lost his daughter only 7 days before, was the first to proclaim the joyful tidings of the king's death, and to call upon the Greeks to unite their strength against Macedonia. But Alexander's energy, and the frightful vengeance which he took upon Thebes, compelled Athens to submit and sue for peace. Alexander demanded the surrender of Demosthenes and the other leaders of the popular party, and with difficulty allowed them to remain at Athens. During the life of Alexander, Athens made no open attempt to throw off the Macedonian supremacy. In 325 Harpalus fled from Babylon with the treasure entrusted to his care by Alexander, and came to Athens, the protection of which he purchased by distributing his gold among the most influential demagogues. The reception of such an open rebel was viewed as an act of hostility towards Macedonia itself ; and accordingly Antipater called upon the Athenians to deliver up the rebel and to try those who had accepted his bribes. Demosthenes was one of those who were suspected of having received money from Harpalus. His guilt is doubtful ; but he was condemned, and thrown into prison, from which however he escaped, apparently with the connivance of the Athenian magistrates. He now resided partly at Troezene and partly in Aegina, looking daily across the sea towards his beloved native land. But his exile did not last long. On the death of Alexander (323) the Greek states rose in arms against Macedonia. Demosthenes was recalled from exile ; a trireme was sent to Aegina to fetch him, and his progress to the city was a glorious triumph. But in the following year (322) the confederate Greeks were defeated by Antipater at the battle of Cranon, and were obliged to sue for peace. Antipater demanded the surrender of Demosthenes, who thereupon fled to the island of Calauria, and took refuge in the temple of Poseidon. Here he was pursued by the emissaries of Antipater ; he thereupon took poison, which he had for some time carried about his person, and died in the temple, 322.—There existed 65 orations of Demosthenes in antiquity ; but of these only 61 have come down to us, including the letter of Philip, which is strangely enough counted as an oration. Several of the orations, however, are spurious, or at least of very doubtful authenticity. Besides these orations, there are 56 *Exordia* to public orations, and 6 letters which bear the name of Demosthenes, but are probably spurious. — The orations may be divided into the following classes : (I.) 17 *Political orations* (λόγοι συμβουλευτικοί), of which the 12 Philippic orations are the most important. They bear the following titles : — 1. The 1st.Philippic, delivered 352. 2—4. The 3 Olynthiac orations, delivered 349. 5. On the Peace, 346. 6. The 2nd Philippic, 344. 7. On Halonesus, 343, not genuine, probably written by Hegesippus. 8. On the affairs of the Chersonesus, 342. 9. The 3rd Philippic, 342. 10. The 4th Philippic, not genuine, 341. 11. On the letter of Philip, 340, also spurious. 12. The letter of Philip.—(II.) 42 *Judicial Orations* (λόγοι δικανικοί), of which the most important are : Against Midias, written 355, but never delivered ; Against Leptines, 355 ; On the dishonest conduct of Aeschines during his embassy to Philip (Περὶ τῆς Παραπρεσβείας), 342 ; On the Crown, 330. — (III.) 2 *Show Speeches* (λόγοι ἐπιδεικτικοί), namely the Ἐπιτάφιος and Ἐρωτικός, both of which are spurious. The orations of Demosthenes are contained in the collections of the Attic orators by Reiske, Lips. 1770—1775 ; Bekker, Oxon. 1823 ; Dobson, Lond. 1828 ; Baiter and Sauppe, Turic. 1845.

Denseletae or **Denthelētae**, a Thracian people on the Haemus, between the Strymon and Nessus.

Dentātus, M'. Curius, a favourite hero of the Roman republic, was celebrated in later times as a noble specimen of old Roman frugality and virtue. He was of Sabine origin, and the first of his family who held any of the high offices of state (consequently a *homo novus*). He was consul B.C. 290 with P. Cornelius Rufinus. The 2 consuls defeated the Samnites, and brought the Samnite wars to a close. In the same year Dentatus also defeated the Sabines, who appear to have supported the Samnites. In 283 he fought as praetor against the Senones. In 275 he was consul a second time, and defeated Pyrrhus near Beneventum and in the Arusinian plain so completely, that the king was obliged to quit Italy. The booty which he gained was immense, but he would keep nothing for himself. In 274 he was consul a third time, and conquered the Lucanians, Samnites, and Bruttians, who still continued in arms after the defeat of Pyrrhus. Dentatus now retired to his small farm in the country of the Sabines, and cultivated the land with his own hands. Once the Samnites sent an embassy to him with costly presents ; they found him sitting at the hearth and roasting turnips. He rejected their presents, telling them that

he preferred ruling over those who possessed gold, to possessing it himself. He was censor in 272, and in that year executed public works of great importance. He commenced the aqueduct which carried the water from the river Anio into the city (Aniensis Vetus) ; and by a canal he carried off the water of the lake Velinus into the river Nar, in consequence of which the inhabitants of Reate gained a large quantity of excellent land.

Dēō (Δηώ), another name for Demeter: hence her daughter Persephone is called by the patronymic **Dēōis** and **Dēōine**.

Derbē (Δέρβη: Δερβήτης, Δερβαῖος), a town in Lycaonia, on the frontiers of Isauria. It is first mentioned as the residence of the tyrant Antipater of Derbe, a friend of Cicero, whom Amyntas put to death.

Derbiccae or **Derbices**, a Scythian people in Margiana, dwelling on the Oxus, near its entrance into the Caspian sea. They worshipped the earth as a goddess, neither sacrificed nor ate any female animals, and killed and ate all their old men above 70 years of age.

Dercětis, Dercěto (Δερκέτις, Δερκετώ), also called *Atargatis*, a Syrian goddess. She offended Aphrodite (Venus), who in consequence inspired her with love for a youth, to whom she bore a daughter Semiramis ; but ashamed of her frailty, she killed the youth, exposed her child in a desert, and threw herself into a lake near Ascalon. Her child was fed by doves, and she herself was changed into a fish. The Syrians thereupon worshipped her as a goddess. The upper part of her statue represented a beautiful woman, while the lower part terminated in the tail of a fish. She appears to be the same as Dagon mentioned in the Old Testament as a deity of the Philistines.

Dercyllīdas (Δερκυλλίδας), a Spartan, succeeded Thimbron, B.C. 399, in the command of the army which was employed in the protection of the Asiatic Greeks against Persia. He carried on the war with success. Tissaphernes and Pharnabazus were at length glad to sue for peace. In 396 he was superseded by Agesilaus.

Dertōna (*Tortona*), an important town in Liguria, and a Roman colony with the surname Julia, on the road from Genua to Placentia.

Dertōsa (*Tortosa*), a town of the Ilercaones on the Iberus in Hispania Tarraconensis, and a Roman colony.

Despoena (Δέσποινα), the mistress, a surname of several divinities, as Aphrodite, Demeter, and more especially Persephone, who was worshipped under this name in Arcadia.

Deucălion (Δευκαλίων). 1. Son of Prometheus and Clymene, king of Phthia, in Thessaly. When Zeus, after the treatment he had received from Lycaon, had resolved to destroy the degenerate race of men, Deucalion and his wife Pyrrha were, on account of their piety, the only mortals saved. On the advice of his father, Deucalion built a ship, in which he and his wife floated in safety during the 9 days' flood, which destroyed all the other inhabitants of Hellas. At last the ship rested on mount Parnassus in Phocis, or, according to other traditions, on mount Othrys in Thessaly, on mount Athos, or even on Aetna in Sicily. When the waters had subsided, Deucalion offered up a sacrifice to Zeus Phyxius (Φύξιος), and he and his wife then consulted the sanctuary of Themis how the race of man might be restored. The goddess bade them cover their heads and throw the bones of their mother behind them. After some doubts and scruples respecting the meaning of this command, they agreed in interpreting the bones of their mother to mean the stones of the earth. They accordingly threw stones behind them, and from those thrown by Deucalion there sprang up men, from those thrown by Pyrrha women. Deucalion then descended from Parnassus, and built his first abode at Opus or at Cynus. Deucalion became by Pyrrha the father of Hellen, Amphictyon, Protogenia, and others. — **2.** Son of Minos and Pasiphaë, and father of Idomeneus, was an Argonaut and one of the Calydonian hunters.

Deva. 1. (*Chester*), the principal town of the Cornavii in Britain, on the Seteia (*Dee*), and the head-quarters of the Legio XX. Victrix. — **2.** (*Dee*), an estuary in Scotland. on which stood the town Devana, near the modern Aberdeen.

Dexamenus (Δεξάμενος), a Centaur who lived in Bura in Achaia. According to others, he was king of Olenus, and father of Deïanira, who is usually represented as daughter of Oeneus.

Dexippus (Δέξιππος). **1.** Called also *Dioxippus*, a physician of Cos, one of the pupils of Hippocrates, lived about B. C. 380, and attended the children of Hecatomnus, prince of Caria. — **2. P. Herennius**, a Greek rhetorician and historian, was a native of Attica, and held the highest offices at Athens. He distinguished himself in fighting against the Goths, when they invaded Greece in A. D. 262. He was the author of 3 historical works: — 1. A history of Macedonia from the time of Alexander. 2. A chronological history from the mythical ages down to the accession of Claudius Gothicus, A. D. 268. 3. An account of the war of the Goths or Scythians, in which Dexippus himself had fought. The fragments of Dexippus, which are considerable, are published by Bekker and Niebuhr in the first volume of the *Scriptores Historiae Byzantinae*, Bonn, 1829, 8vo. — **3.** A disciple of the philosopher Iamblichus, lived about A. D. 350, and wrote a commentary on the Categories of Aristotle, of which a Latin translation appeared at Paris, 1549, 8vo., and at Venice, 1546, fo. after the work of Porphyry *In Praedicam.*

Dia (Δία), daughter of Deioneus and wife of Ixion. By Ixion, or according to others, by Zeus, she became the mother of Pirithous.

Dia (Δία). **1.** The ancient name of Naxos. — **2.** An island near Amorgos. — **3.** A small island off Crete, opposite the harbour of Cnossus. — **4.** An island in the Arabian gulf, on the W. coast of Arabia.

Diablintes. [AULERCI.]

Diacria (ἡ Διακρία), a mountainous district in the N. E. of Attica, including the plain of Marathon. [ATTICA.] The inhabitants of this district (Διακριεῖς, Διάκριοι), formed one of the 3 parties into which the inhabitants of Attica were divided in the time of Solon: they were the most democratical of the 3 parties.

Diadumenianus or **Diadumenus**, son of the emperor Macrinus, received the title of Caesar, when his father was elevated to the purple, A. D. 217, and was put to death in the following year about the same time with Macrinus.

Diaeus (Δίαιος), of Megalopolis, general of the Achaean league B. C. 149 and 147, took an active part in the war against the Romans. On the death

of Critolaüs in 146, he succeeded to the command of the Achaeans, but was defeated by Mummius near Corinth, whereupon he put an end to his own life, after slaying his wife to prevent her falling into the enemy's power.

Diagoras (Διαγόρας). **1.** Son of Damagetus, of Ialysus in Rhodes, was very celebrated for his own victories and those of his sons and grandsons, in the Grecian games. His fame was celebrated by Pindar in the 7th Olympic ode. He was victor in boxing twice in the Olympian games, four times in the Isthmian, twice in the Nemean, and once at least in the Pythian. He had therefore the high honour of being a περιοδονίκης, that is, one who had gained crowns at all the 4 great festivals. When an old man, he accompanied his sons, Acusilaüs and Damagetus, to Olympia. The young men, having both been victorious, carried their father through the assembly, while the spectators showered garlands upon him, and congratulated him as having reached the summit of human happiness. He gained his Olympic victory, B. C. 464. — **2.** Surnamed the **Atheist** ("Αθεος), a Greek philosopher and poet, was the son of Teleclides, and was born in the island of Melos, one of the Cyclades. He was a disciple of Democritus of Abdera, and in his youth he acquired considerable reputation as a lyric poet. He was at Athens as early as B. C. 424, for Aristophanes in the *Clouds* (830), which were performed in that year, alludes to him as a well-known character. In consequence of his attacks upon the popular religion, and especially upon the Eleusinian mysteries, he was formally accused of impiety B. C. 411, and fearing the results of a trial, fled from Athens. He was condemned to death in his absence, and a reward set upon his head. He first went to Pallene, and afterwards to Corinth, where he died. One of the works of Diagoras was entitled Φρύγιοι λόγοι, in which he probably attacked the Phrygian divinities.

Diana, an ancient Italian divinity, whom the Romans identified with the Greek Artemis. Her worship is said to have been introduced at Rome by Servius Tullius, who dedicated a temple to her on the Aventine; and she appears to have been originally worshipped only by the plebeians. At Rome Diana was the goddess of light, and her name contains the same root as the word *dies*. As Dianus (Janus), or the god of light, represented the sun, so Diana, the goddess of light, represented the moon. The attributes of the Greek Artemis were afterwards ascribed to the Roman Diana. See **ARTEMIS.**

Dianium. 1. (*Giannuti*), a small island in the Tyrrhenian sea, opposite the gulf of Cosa. — **2.** (*Denia*), called **Hemeroscopion** ('Ημεροσκοπεῖον) by Strabo, a town in Hispania Tarraconensis on a promontory of the same name (*C. Martin*) founded by the Massilians. Here stood a celebrated temple of Diana, from which the town derived its name; and here Sertorius kept most of his military stores.

Dicaea (Δίκαια), a town in Thrace, on the lake Bistonis.

Dicaearchia. [PUTEOLI.]

Dicaearchus (Δικαίαρχος), a celebrated Peripatetic philosopher, geographer, and historian, was born at Messana in Sicily, but passed the greater part of his life in Greece Proper, and especially in Peloponnesus. He was a disciple of Aristotle and a friend of Theophrastus. He wrote a vast number of works, of which only fragments are extant. His most important work was entitled Βίος τῆς Ἑλλάδος: it contained an account of the geography, history, and moral and religious condition of Greece. See Fuhr, *Dicaearchi Messenii quae supersunt composita et illustrata*, Darmstadt, 1841.

DĬCĔ (Δίκη), the personification of justice, a daughter of Zeus and Themis, and the sister of Eunomia and Eirene. She was considered as one of the Horae, and is frequently called the attendant or councillor (πάρεδρος or ξύνεδρος) of Zeus. In the tragedians, she appears as a divinity who severely punishes all wrong, watches over the maintenance of justice, and pierces the hearts of the unjust with the sword made for her by Aesa. In this capacity she is closely connected with the Erinnyes, though her business is not only to punish injustice, but also to reward virtue.

Dictaeus. [Dicte.]

Dictamnum (Δίκταμνον), a town on the N. coast of Crete with a sanctuary of Dictynna, from whom the town itself was also called Dictynna.

Dictē (Δίκτη), a mountain in the E. of Crete, where Zeus is said to have been brought up. Hence he bore the surname *Dictaeus*. The Roman poets frequently employ the adjective Dictaeus as synonymous with Cretan.

Dictynna (Δίκτυννα), a surname both of Britomartis and Diana, which two divinities were subsequently identified. The name is connected with δίκτυον, a hunting-net, and was borne by Britomartis and Diana as goddesses of the chase. One tradition related that Britomartis was so called, because when she had thrown herself into the sea to escape the pursuit of Minos, she was saved in the nets of fishermen.

Dictys Cretensis, the reputed author of an extant work in Latin on the Trojan war, divided into 6 books, and entitled *Ephemeris Belli Trojani*, professing to be a journal of the leading events of the war. In the preface to the work we are told that it was composed by Dictys of Cnossus, who accompanied Idomeneus to the Trojan war, and was inscribed in Phoenician characters on tablets of lime wood or paper made from the bark. The work was buried in the same grave with the author, and remained undisturbed till the sepulchre was burst open by an earthquake in the reign of Nero, and the work was discovered in a tin case. It was carried to Rome by Eupraxia, whose slaves had discovered it, and it was translated into Greek by order of Nero. It is from this Greek version that the extant Latin work professes to have been translated by a Q. Septimius Romanus. Although its alleged origin and discovery are quite unworthy of credit, it appears nevertheless to be a translation from a Greek work, which we know to have been extant under the name of Dictys, since it is frequently quoted by the Byzantine writers. The work was probably written in Greek by Eupraxis in the reign of Nero, but at what time the Latin translation was executed is quite uncertain. The work contains a history of the Trojan war, from the birth of Paris down to the death of Ulysses. The compiler not unfrequently differs widely from Homer, adding many particulars, and recording many events of which we find no trace elsewhere. All miraculous events and supernatural agency are entirely excluded. The compilations ascribed to Dictys and Dares [Dares], are of considerable importance in the history of modern literature, since they are the chief fountains from which the legends of Greece first flowed into the romances of the middle ages, and then mingled with the popular tales and ballads of England, France, and Germany.—The best edition of Dictys is by Dederich, Bonn, 1835.

Dīdĭus. 1. T., praetor in Macedonia, B. c. 100, where he defeated the Scordiscans, consul 98, and subsequently proconsul in Spain, where he defeated the Celtiberians. He fell in the Marsic war, 89.—2. C., a legate of Caesar, fell in battle in Spain fighting against the sons of Pompey, 46.—3. M. Dīdĭus Salvĭus Jūlĭānus, bought the Roman empire of the praetorian guards, when they put up the empire for sale after the death of Pertinax, A. D. 193. Flavius Sulpicianus, praefect of the city, and Didius bid against each other, but it was finally knocked down to Didius, upon his promising a donative to each soldier of 25,000 sesterces. Didius, however, held the empire for only 2 months, from March 28th to June 1st, and was murdered by the soldiers when Severus was marching against the city.

Dīdō (Διδώ), also called Elissa, the reputed founder of Carthage. She was daughter of the Tyrian king Belus or Agenor or Mutgo, and sister of Pygmalion, who succeeded to the crown after the death of his father. Dido was married to her uncle, Acerbas or Sichaeus, a priest of Hercules, and a man of immense wealth. He was murdered by Pygmalion, who coveted his treasures; but Dido secretly sailed from Tyre with the treasures, accompanied by some noble Tyrians, who were dissatisfied with Pygmalion's rule. She first went to Cyprus, where she carried off 80 maidens to provide the emigrants with wives, and then crossed over to Africa. Here she purchased as much land as might be covered with the hide of a bull; but she ordered the hide to be cut up into the thinnest possible stripes, and with them she surrounded a spot, on which she built a citadel called Byrsa (from βύρσα, i. e. the hide of a bull). Around this fort the city of Carthage arose, and soon became a powerful and flourishing place. The neighbouring king Hiarbas, jealous of the prosperity of the new city, demanded the hand of Dido in marriage, threatening Carthage with war in case of refusal. Dido had vowed eternal fidelity to her late husband; but seeing that the Carthaginians expected her to comply with the demands of Hiarbas, she pretended to yield to their wishes, and under pretence of soothing the manes of Acerbas by expiatory sacrifices, she erected a funeral pile, on which she stabbed herself in presence of her people. After her death she was worshipped by the Carthaginians as a divinity.—Virgil has inserted in his Aeneid the legend of Dido with various modifications. According to the common chronology, there was an interval of more than 300 years between the capture of Troy (B. c. 1184) and the foundation of Carthage (B. c. 853); but Virgil nevertheless makes Dido a contemporary of Aeneas, with whom she falls in love on his arrival in Africa. When Aeneas hastened to seek the new home which the gods had promised him, Dido in despair destroyed herself on a funeral pile.

Dīdȳma. [Branchidae.]

Dīdȳmē. [Aeoliae Insulae.]

Dīdȳmus (Δίδυμος), a celebrated Alexandrine grammarian, a contemporary of Julius Caesar and Augustus, was a follower of the school of Aristarchus, and received the surname χαλκέντερος, on

account of his indefatigable and unwearied application to study. He is said to have written 4000
works, the most important of which were commentaries on Homer. The greater part of the
extant *Scholia minora* on Homer was at one time
considered the work of Didymus, but is really taken
from the commentaries of Didymus and of other
grammarians.

Diespīter. [JUPITER.]

Dīgentia (*Licenza*), a small stream in Latium,
beautifully cool and clear, which flows into the
Anio near the modern *Vicovaro*. It flowed through
the Sabine farm of Horace. Near its source, which
was also called Digentia (*fons etiam rivo dare
nomen idoneus*, Hor. *Ep.* i. 16. 12), stood the house
of Horace (*vicinus tecto jugis aquae fons*, Hor. *Sat.*
ii. 6. 2).

Dimallum, a town in Greek Illyria.

Dīnarchus (Δείναρχος), the last and least important of the 10 Attic orators, was born at Corinth about B. C. 361. He was brought up at
Athens, and studied under Theophrastus. As he
was a foreigner, he could not come forward himself
as an orator, and was therefore obliged to content
himself with writing orations for others. He belonged to the friends of Phocion and the Macedonian party. When Demetrius Poliorcetes advanced against Athens in 307, Dinarchus fled to
Chalcis in Euboea, and was not allowed to return
to Athens till 292, where he died at an advanced
age. Only 3 of his speeches have come down to
us: they all refer to the question about HARPA-
LUS. They are printed in the collections of the
Attic orators.

Dindỹmēne. [DINDYMUS.]

Dindỹmus or Dindỹma, -ōrum (Δίνδυμος: τὰ
Δίνδυμα). 1. A mountain in Phrygia on the
frontiers of Galatia, near the town Pessinus, sacred
to Cybele, the mother of the gods, who is hence
called Dindymēne. — 2. A mountain in Mysia
near Cyzicus, also sacred to Cybele.

Dīnocrătes (Δεινοκράτης), a distinguished Macedonian architect in the time of Alexander the
Great. He was the architect of the new temple
of Artemis at Ephesus, which was built after the
destruction of the former temple by Herostratus.
He was employed by Alexander, whom he accompanied into Egypt, in the building of Alexandria.
He formed a design for cutting mount Athos into
a statue of Alexander; but the king forbad the
execution of the project. The right hand of the
figure was to have held a city, and in the left there
would have been a basin, in which the water of
all the mountain streams was to pour, and thence
into the sea. He commenced the erection of a
temple to Arsinoë, the wife of Ptolemy II., of
which the roof was to be arched with loadstones,
so that her statue made of iron might appear to
float in the air, but he died before completing the
work.

Dīnŏmăchus (Δεινόμαχος), a philosopher, who
agreed with CALLIPHON in considering the chief
good to consist in the union of virtue with bodily
pleasure.

Dīnŏmēnes (Δεινομένης), a statuary, whose
statues of Io and Callisto stood in the Acropolis at
Athens in the time of Pausanias: he flourished
B. C. 400.

Dinon (Δείνων, Δίνων), father of the historian
Clitarchus, wrote himself a history of Persia.

Dio. [DION.]

Diocaesarĕa (Διοσκαισάρεια: *Sefurieh*), more
anciently Sepphōris (Σεπφώρις), in Galilee, was
a small place until Herodes Antipas made it the
capital of Galilee, under the name of Diocaesarea.
It was destroyed in the 4th century by Gallus, on
account of an insurrection which had broken out
there.

Dioclea or Doclea (Δόκλεα), a place in Dalmatia, near Salona, the birth-place of Diocletian.

Diŏcles (Διοκλῆς). 1. A brave Athenian, who
lived in exile at Megara. Once in a battle he protected with his shield a youth whom he loved, but
he lost his own life in consequence. The Megarians rewarded him with the honours of a hero,
and instituted the festival of the Dioclea, which
they celebrated in the spring of every year. —
2. A Syracusan, the leader of the popular party in
opposition to Hermocrates. In B. C. 412 he was
appointed with several others to draw up a new
code of laws. This code, which was almost exclusively the work of Diocles, became very celebrated, and was adopted by many other Sicilian
cities. — 3. Of Carystus in Euboea, a celebrated
Greek physician, lived in the 4th century B. C.
He wrote several medical works, of which only
some fragments remain.

Dioclet. ănŏpŏlis. [CELETRUM.]

Dioclētiānus, Valĕrius, Roman emperor, A. D.
284—305, was born near Salona in Dalmatia, in
245, of most obscure parentage. From his mother,
Doclea, or Dioclea, who received her name from
the village where she dwelt, he inherited the appellation of *Docles* or *Diocles*, which, after his
assumption of the purple, was expanded into Diocletianus, and attached as a cognomen to the high
patrician name of Valerius. Having entered the
army, he served with high reputation under Probus and Aurelian, followed Carus to the Persian
war, and, after the fate of Numerianus became
known at Chalcedon, was proclaimed emperor by
the troops, 284. He slew with his own hands
Arrius Aper, who was arraigned of the murder of
Numerianus, in order, according to some authorities, that he might fulfil a prophecy delivered to
him in early youth by a Gaulish Druidess, that he
should mount a throne as soon as he had slain the
wild-boar (*Aper*). Next year (285) Diocletian
carried on war against Carinus, on whose death he
became undisputed master of the empire. But as
the attacks of the barbarians became daily more
formidable, he resolved to associate with himself a
colleague in the empire, and accordingly selected
for that purpose Maximianus, who was invested
with the title of Augustus in 286. Maximian had
the care of the Western empire, and Diocletian
that of the Eastern. But as the dangers which
threatened the Roman dominions from the attacks
of the Persians in the E., and the Germans and
other barbarians in the W., became still more imminent, Diocletian made a still further division of
the empire. In 292, Constantius Chlorus and
Galerius were proclaimed Caesars, and the government of the Roman world was divided between
the 2 Augusti and the 2 Caesars. Diocletian had
the government of the E. with Nicomedia as his
residence; Maximian, Italy, and Africa, with
Milan, as his residence; Constantius, Britain, Gaul,
and Spain, with Treves, as his residence; Galerius, Illyricum, and the whole line of the Danube,
with Sirmium, as his residence. The wars in the
re'gn of Diocletian are related in the lives of his

colleagues, since Diocletian rarely commanded the armies in person. It is sufficient to state here that Britain, which had maintained its independence for some years under CARAUSIUS and AL-LECTUS, was restored to the empire (296) ; that the Persians were defeated and obliged to sue for peace (298) ; and that the Marcomanni and other barbarians in the N. were also driven back from the Roman dominions. But after an anxious reign of 21 years Diocletian longed for repose. Accordingly on 1st of May, 305, he abdicated at Nicomedia, and compelled his reluctant colleague Maximian to do the same at Milan. Diocletian retired to his native Dalmatia, and passed the remaining 8 years of his life near Salona in philosophic retirement, devoted to rural pleasures and the cultivation of his garden. He died 313. One of the most memorable events in the reign of Diocletian was his fierce persecution of the Christians (303), to which he was instigated by his colleague Galerius.

Diŏdŏrus (Διόδωρος). 1. Surnamed **Cronus**, of Iasus in Caria, lived at Alexandria in the reign of Ptolemy Soter, who is said to have given him the surname of Cronus on account of his inability to solve at once some dialectic problem proposed by Stilpo, when the 2 philosophers were dining with the king. Diodorus is said to have taken that disgrace so much to heart, that after his return from the repast, and writing a treatise on the problem, he died in despair. According to another account he derived his surname from his teacher Apollonius Cronus. He belonged to the Megaric school of philosophy, of which he was the head. He was celebrated for his great dialectic skill, for which he is called ὁ διαλεκτικός, or διαλεκτικώτατος. — 2. **Siculus**, of Agyrium in Sicily, was a contemporary of Julius Caesar and Augustus. In order to collect materials for his history, he travelled over a great part of Europe and Asia, and lived a long time at Rome. He spent altogether 30 years upon his work. It was entitled Βιβλιοθήκη ἱστορική, The Historical Library, and was an universal history, embracing the period from the earliest mythical ages down to the beginning of Caesar's Gallic wars. It was divided into 3 great sections and into 40 books. The 1st section, which consisted of the first 6 books, contained the history of the mythical times previous to the Trojan war. The 2nd section, which consisted of 11 books, contained the history from the Trojan war down to the death of Alexander the Great. The 3rd section, which contained the remaining 23 books, treated of the history from the death of Alexander down to the beginning of Caesar's Gallic wars. Of this work only the following portions are extant entire: the first 5 books, which contain the early history of the Eastern nations, the Egyptians, Aethiopians, and Greeks ; and from book 11 to book 20, containing the history from the 2nd Persian war, B. C. 480, down to 302. Of the remaining portion there are extant a number of fragments and the Excerpta, which are preserved partly in Photius, and partly in the Eclogae made at the command of Constantine Porphyrogenitus. The work of Diodorus is constructed upon the plan of annals, and the events of each year are placed one after the other without any internal connection. In compiling his work Diodorus exercised no judgment or criticism. He simply collected what he found in his different authorities, and thus jumbled together history, mythus, and fiction: he frequently mis-

understood authorities, and not seldom contradicts in one passage what he has stated in another. But nevertheless the compilation is of great importance to us, on account of the great mass of materials which are there collected from a number of writers whose works have perished. The best editions are by Wesseling, Amsterd. 1746, 2 vols. fol., reprinted at Bipont, 1793, &c., 11 vols. 8vo. ; and by Dindorf, Lips. 1828, 6 vols. 8vo.— 3. Of Sinope, an Athenian comic poet of the middle comedy, flourished 353.—4. Of Tyre, a peripatetic philosopher, a disciple and follower of Critolaüs, whom he succeeded as the head of the Peripatetic school at Athens. He flourished B. C. 110.

Diŏdŏtus (Διόδοτος), a Stoic philosopher and a teacher of Cicero, in whose house he lived for many years at Rome. In his later years, Diodotus became blind : he died in Cicero's house, B. C. 59, and left to his friend a property of about 100,000 sesterces.

Diŏgĕnes (Διογένης). 1. Of **Apollonia** in Crete, an eminent natural philosopher, lived in the 5th century B. C., and was a pupil of Anaximenes. He wrote a work in the Ionic dialect, entitled Περὶ Φύσεως, On Nature, in which he appears to have treated of physical science in the largest sense of the words.—2. The **Babylonian**, a Stoic philosopher, was a native of Seleucia in Babylonia, was educated at Athens under Chrysippus, and succeeded Zeno of Tarsus as the head of the Stoic school at Athens. He was one of the 3 ambassadors sent by the Athenians to Rome in B. C. 155. [CARNEADES : CRITOLAUS.] He died at the age of 88. — 3. The **Cynic** philosopher, was born at Sinope in Pontus, about B. C. 412. His father was a banker named Icesias or Icetas, who was convicted of some swindling transaction, in consequence of which Diogenes quitted Sinope and went to Athens. His youth is said to have been spent in dissolute extravagance ; but at Athens his attention was arrested by the character of Antisthenes, who at first drove him away. Diogenes, however, could not be prevented from attending him even by blows, but told him that he would find no stick hard enough to keep him away. Antisthenes at last relented, and his pupil soon plunged into the most frantic excesses of austerity and moroseness. In summer he used to roll in hot sand, and in winter to embrace statues covered with snow ; he wore coarse clothing, lived on the plainest food, slept in porticoes or in the street, and finally, according to the common story, took up his residence in a tub belonging to the Metroum, or temple of the Mother of the Gods. The truth of this latter tale has, however, been reasonably disputed. In spite of his strange eccentricities, Diogenes appears to have been much respected at Athens, and to have been privileged to rebuke anything of which he disapproved. He seems to have ridiculed and despised all intellectual pursuits which did not directly and obviously tend to some immediate practical good. He abused literary men for reading about the evils of Ulysses, and neglecting their own ; musicians for stringing the lyre harmoniously while they left their minds discordant ; men of science for troubling themselves about the moon and stars, while they neglected what lay immediately before them ; orators for learning to say what was right, but not to practise it. — On a voyage to Aegina he was taken prisoner by pirates,

and carried to Crete to be sold as a slave. Here
when he was asked what business he understood,
he answered, " How to command men." He was
purchased by Xeniades of Corinth, over whom he
acquired such influence, that he soon received from
him his freedom, was entrusted with the care of
his children, and passed his old age in his house.
During his residence at Corinth his celebrated interview with Alexander the Great is said to have
taken place. The conversation between them begun
by the king's saying, " I am Alexander the Great;"
to which the philosopher replied, " And I am Diogenes the Cynic." Alexander then asked whether
he could oblige him in any way, and received no
answer except, " Yes, you can stand out of the
sunshine." We are further told that Alexander
admired Diogenes so much that he said, " If I were
not Alexander, I should wish to be Diogenes."
Diogenes died at Corinth at the age of nearly 90,
B. C. 323. — 4. **Laertius**, of Laërte in Cilicia, of
whose life we have no particulars, probably lived
in the 2nd century after Christ. He wrote the
Lives of the Philosophers in 10 books: the work
is entitled περὶ βίων, δογμάτων, καὶ ἀποφθεγμάτων
τῶν ἐν φιλοσοφίᾳ εὐδοκιμησάντων. According to
some allusions which occur in it, he wrote it for a
lady of rank, who occupied herself with philosophy,
and who, according to some, was Arria, the friend
of Galen. In this work Diogenes divides the philosophy of the Greeks into the Ionic — which commences with Anaximander and ends with Clitomachus, Chrysippus, and Theophrastus — and the
Italian, which was founded by Pythagoras, and
ends with Epicurus. He reckons the Socratic
school, with its various ramifications, as a part of
the Ionic philosophy, of which he treats in the first
7 books. The Eleatics, with Heraclitus and the
Sceptics, are included in the Italian philosophy,
which occupies the 8th and 9th books. Epicurus
and his philosophy are treated of in the 10th book
with particular minuteness, which has led some
writers to the belief that Diogenes himself was an
Epicurean. The work is of great value to us, as
Diogenes made use of a great number of writers on
the history of philosophy, whose works are now
lost ; but it is put together without plan, criticism,
or connection, and the author had evidently no
conception of the real value and dignity of philosophy. The best editions are by Meibom, Amsterd.
1692, 2 vols. 4to., and Hübner, Lips. 2 vols. 8vo.
1828—1831.—**5. Oenomäus**, a tragic poet, who
began to exhibit at Athens B. C. 404.

Diogeniänus (Διογενειανός), of Heraclea on the
Pontus, a distinguished grammarian in the reign
of Hadrian, wrote a Greek Lexicon, from which
the Lexicon of Hesychius seems to have been
almost entirely taken. A portion of it is still
extant, containing a collection of proverbs first
printed by Schottus, with the proverbs of Zenobius
and Suidas, Antv. 1612, 4to., and subsequently in
other editions of the *Paroemiographi Graeci.*

Dioméa (τὰ Διόμεια : Διομειεύς, Διομεύς), a
demus in Attica belonging to the tribe Aegeis,
with a temple of Hercules ; the Diomean gate in
Athens led to this demus. [See p. 103, a.]

Diomedëae Insülae, 5 small islands in the
Adriatic sea, N. of the promontory Garganum in
Apulia, named after Diomedes. [DIOMEDES.] The
largest of these, called Diomedea Insula or Trimerus
(*Tremiti*), was the place where Julia, the grand-
daughter of Augustus, died

Diomëdes (Διομήδης). 1. Son of Tydeus and
Deïpyle, whence he is constantly called Tydïdes
(Τυδείδης), succeeded Adrastus as king of Argos.—
Homeric Story. Tydeus fell in the expedition
against Thebes, while his son Diomedes was yet a
boy ; but Diomedes was afterwards one of the
Epigoni who took Thebes. He went to Troy with
80 ships, and was, next to Achilles, the bravest
hero in the Greek army. He enjoyed the especial
protection of Athena ; he fought against the
most distinguished of the Trojans, such as Hector
and Aeneas, and even with the gods who espoused
the cause of the Trojans. He thus wounded both
Aphrodite and Ares. — *Later Stories.* Diomedes
and Ulysses carried off the palladium from the
city of Troy, since it was believed that Troy
could not be taken so long as the palladium was
within its walls. Diomedes carried the palladium
with him to Argos ; but according to others it
was taken from him by Demophon in Attica,
where he landed one night on his return from
Troy, without knowing where he was. [DEMO-
PHON.] Another tradition stated, that Diomedes
restored the palladium to Aeneas. On his arrival
in Argos Diomedes found his wife Aegialea living in
adultery with Hippolytus, or, according to others,
with Cometes or Cyllabarus. This misfortune
befell him through the anger of Aphrodite, whom
he had wounded before Troy. He therefore quitted
Argos, either of his own accord, or he was expelled
by the adulterers, and went to Aetolia. He subsequently attempted to return to Argos, but on his
way home a storm threw him on the coast of
Daunia in Italy, where he was kindly received by
Daunus, the king of the country. Diomedes assisted Daunus in his war against the Messapians,
married Euippe, the daughter of Daunus, and settled in Daunia, where he died at an advanced age.
He was buried in one of the islands off cape Garganum, which were called after him the Diomedean
islands. His companions were inconsolable at his
loss, and were metamorphosed into birds (*Aves
Diomedëae*), which, mindful of their origin, used
to fly joyfully towards the Greek ships, but to
avoid those of the Romans. According to others
Diomedes returned to Argos, or disappeared in one
of the Diomedean islands, or in the country of the
Heneti. A number of towns in the E. part of Italy,
such as Beneventum, Argos Hippion (afterwards
Argyripa or Arpi), Venusia, Canusium, Venafrum,
Brundusium, &c. were believed to have been
founded by Diomedes. A plain of Apulia, near
Salapia and Canusium, was called *Diomedii Campi*
after him. He was worshipped as a divine being,
especially in Italy, where statues of him existed
at Argyripa, Metapontum, Thurii, and other places.
— **2.** Son of Ares and Cyrene, king of the Bistones in Thrace, killed by Hercules on account of
his mares, which he fed with human flesh.

Diomëdes, a Latin grammarian, probably lived
in the 4th or 5th century after Christ, and is the
author of an extant work, *De Oratione et Partibus
Orationis et Vario Genere Metrorum libri III.,*
printed in the *Grammaticae Latinae Auctores Antiqui* of Putschius, 4to. Hanov. 1605.

Diomëdon (Διομέδων), an Athenian commander
during the Peloponnesian war. He was one of the
commanders at the battle of Arginusae (B. C. 406),
and was put to death with 5 of his colleagues on
his return to Athens.

Dion (Δίων), a Syracusan, son of Hipparinus,

and a relation of Dionysius. His sister Aristomache was the second wife of the elder Dionysius ; and Dion himself was married to Arete, the daughter of Dionysius by Aristomache. Dion was treated by Dionysius with the greatest distinction, and was employed by him in many services of trust and confidence. Of this close connection and favour with the tyrant he seems to have availed himself to amass great wealth. He made no opposition to the succession of the younger Dionysius to his father's power, but he became an object of suspicion to the youthful tyrant, to whom he also made himself personally disagreeable by the austerity of his manners. Dion appears to have been naturally a man of a proud and stern character, and having become an ardent disciple of Plato when that philosopher visited Syracuse in the reign of the elder Dionysius, he carried to excess the austerity of a philosopher, and viewed with undisguised contempt the debaucheries and dissolute pleasures of his nephew. From these he endeavoured to withdraw him by persuading him to invite Plato a second time to Syracuse ; but the philosopher, though received at first with the utmost distinction, failed in obtaining a permanent hold on the mind of Dionysius; and the intrigues of the opposite party, headed by Philistus, were successful in procuring the banishment of Dion. Dion retired to Athens, where he lived in habitual intercourse with Plato and his disciples ; but Plato having failed in procuring his recall (for which purpose he had a third time visited Syracuse), and Dionysius having confiscated his property, and compelled his wife to marry another person, he determined on attempting the expulsion of the tyrant by force. He sailed from Zacynthus with only a small force and obtained possession of Syracuse without opposition during the absence of Dionysius in Italy. Dionysius returned shortly afterwards, but found himself obliged to quit Syracuse and sail away to Italy, leaving Dion undisputed master of the city, B. C. 356. His despotic conduct however soon caused great discontent, and the people complained with justice that they had only exchanged one tyrant for another. He caused his chief opponent, Heraclídes, to be put to death, and confiscated the property of his adversaries. Callippus, an Athenian, who had accompanied him from Greece, formed a conspiracy against him, and caused him to be assassinated in his own house, 353.

Dion Cassius, the historian, was the son of a Roman senator, Cassius Apronianus, and was born A. D. 155, at Nicaea in Bithynia. He also bore the surname Cocceianus, which he derived from the orator Dion Chrysostomus Cocceianus, his maternal grandfather. He was educated with great care ; he accompanied his father to Cilicia, of which he had the administration ; and after his father's death, he went to Rome, about 180. He was straightway made a senator, and frequently pleaded in the courts of justice. He was aedile and quaestor under Commodus, and praetor under Septimius Severus, 194. He accompanied Caracalla on his journey to the East; he was appointed by Macrinus to the government of Pergamus and Smyrna, 218 ; was consul about 220; proconsul of Africa 224, under Alexander Severus, by whom he was sent as legate to Dalmatia in 226, and to Pannonia in 227. In the latter province he restored strict discipline among the troops ; which excited the discontent of the praetorians at Rome, who de-

manded his life of Alexander Severus But the emperor protected him and raised him to his second consulship 229. Dion, however, retired to Campania, and shortly afterwards obtained permission of the emperor to return to his native town Nicaea, where he passed the remainder of his life and died.—Dion wrote several historical works, but the most important was a History of Rome ('Ρωμαικὴ Ἱστορία), in 80 books, from the landing of Aeneas in Italy to A. D. 229, the year in which Dion returned to Nicaea. Unfortunately, only a comparatively small portion of this work has come down to us entire. Of the first 34 books we possess only fragments ; but since Zonaras in his Annals chiefly followed Dion Cassius, we may regard the Annals of Zonaras as to some extent an epitome of Dion Cassius. Of the 35th book we possess a considerable fragment, and from the 36th book to the 54th the work is extant complete, and embraces the history from the wars of Lucullus and Cn. Pompey against Mithridates, down to the death of Agrippa, B. c. 10. Of the remaining books we have only the epitomes made by Xiphilinus and others. Dion Cassius treated the history of the republic with brevity, but gave a more minute account of these events, of which he had been himself an eyewitness. He consulted original authorities, and displayed great judgment and discrimination in the use of them. He had acquired a thorough knowledge of his subject, and his notions of the ancient Roman institutions were far more correct than those of some of his predecessors, such as Dionysius of Halicarnassus. The best editions are by Reimarus, Hamb. 1750—52, 2 vols. fol., and by Sturz, Lips. 1824, 9 vols. 8vo.

Dion Chrysostŏmus, that is, the golden-mouthed, a surname given to him on account of his eloquence. He also bore the surname Cocceianus, which he derived from the emperor Cocceius Nerva, with whom he was very intimate. He was born at Prusa in Bithynia, about the middle of the first century of our era. He received a careful education, increased his knowledge by travelling in different countries, and came to Rome in the reign of Vespasian, but having incurred the suspicions of Domitian, was obliged to leave the city. On the advice of the Delphic oracle, he put on a beggar's dress, and in this condition visited Thrace, Mysia, Scythia, and the country of the Getae. After the murder of Domitian, A. D. 96, Dion used his influence with the army stationed on the frontier in favour of his friend Nerva, and seems to have returned to Rome immediately after his accession. Trajan also entertained the highest esteem for Dion, and showed him the most marked favour. Dion died at Rome about A. D. 117.—Dion Chrysostom is the most eminent of the Greek rhetoricians and sophists in the time of the Roman empire. There are extant 80 of his orations ; but they are more like essays on political, moral, and philosophical subjects than real orations, of which they have only the form. We find among them λόγοι περὶ βασιλείας or λόγοι βασιλικοί, 4 orations addressed to Trajan on the virtues of a sovereign; Διογένης ἢ περὶ τυραννίδος, on the troubles to which men expose themselves by deserting the path of nature, and on the difficulties which a sovereign has to encounter ; essays on slavery and freedom ; on the means of attaining eminence as an orator ; political discourses addressed to various towns ; on subjects of ethics and practical philosophy; and lastly, orations on mythical subjects and show-speeches. All these orations are written in pure Attic Greek, and, although tainted with the rhetorical embellishments of the age, are distinguished by their refined and elegant style. The best editions are by Reiske, Lips. 1784, 2 vols. and by Emperius, Bruns. 1844.

Dionaea.   [DIONE.]

Dione (Διώνη), daughter of Oceanus and Tethys, or of Uranus and Ge, or of Aether and Ge. She was beloved by Zeus, by whom she became the mother of Aphrodite (Venus). She received her daughter in Olympus, when she was wounded by Diomedes. — Aphrodite is hence called **Dionaea**, and this epithet is frequently applied to any thing sacred to Aphrodite. Hence we find *Dionaeum antrum* (Hor. *Carm.* ii. 1. 39), and *Dionaeus Caesar* (Virg. *Ecl.* ix. 47), because Caesar claimed descent from Venus. Aphrodite is sometimes also called Dione.

Dionysius (Διονύσιος) I. *Historical.* — 1. The Elder, tyrant of Syracuse, son of Hermocrates, born B. C. 430. He was born in a private but not low station, and began life as a clerk in a public office. He was one of the partizans of Hermocrates, the leader of the aristocratical party, and was severely wounded in the attempt which Hermocrates made to effect by force his restoration from exile. He subsequently served in the great war against the Carthaginians, who had invaded Sicily under Hannibal, the son of Gisco, and successively reduced and destroyed Selinus, Himera, and Agrigentum. These disasters, and especially the failure of the Syracusan general, Daphnaeus, to relieve Agrigentum, had created a general spirit of discontent and alarm, of which Dionysius skilfully availed himself. He succeeded in procuring a decree for deposing the existing generals, and appointing others in their stead, among whom was Dionysius himself, B.C. 406. His efforts were from this time directed towards supplanting his new colleagues and obtaining the sole direction of affairs. These efforts were crowned with success. In the following year (405), the other generals were deposed, and Dionysius, though only 25 years of age, was appointed sole general, with full powers. From this period we may date the commencement of his reign, or tyranny, which continued without interruption for 38 years. His first step was to procure the appointment of a body-guard, which he speedily increased to the number of 1000 men: at the same time he induced the Syracusans to double the pay of all the troops, and took every means to ingratiate himself with the mercenaries. By his marriage with the daughter of Hermocrates he secured to himself the support of all the remaining partizans of that leader. He converted the island of Ortygia into a strong fortress, in which he took up his own residence. After concluding a peace with Carthage, and putting down a formidable insurrection in Syracuse, he began to direct his arms against the other cities of Sicily. Naxos, Catana, and Leontini, successively fell into his power, either by force or treachery. For several years after this he made preparations for renewing the war with Carthage. At first he met with great success, but in 395 his fleet was totally defeated, and he was obliged to shut himself up within the walls of Syracuse, where he was besieged by the Carthaginians both by sea and land. A pestilence shortly after broke out in the Carthaginian camp,

and greatly reduced the enemy; whereupon Dionysius suddenly attacked the enemy both by sea and land, defeated the army, and burnt great part of their fleet. The Carthaginians were now obliged to withdraw. In 393 they renewed the war with no better success, and in 392 they concluded a peace with Dionysius. This treaty left Dionysius at leisure to continue the ambitious projects in which he had previously engaged against the Greek cities in Italy. He formed an alliance with the Lucanians, and crossed over into Italy. He subdued Caulonia, Hipponium, and Rhegium, 387. He was in close alliance with the Locrians; and his powerful fleets gave him the command both of the Tyrrhenian and Adriatic seas. He was now at the summit of his greatness, and during the 20 years that elapsed from this period to his death, he possessed an amount of power and influence far exceeding those enjoyed by any other Greek before the time of Alexander. During this time he was twice engaged again in war with Carthage, namely in 383, when a treaty was concluded, by which the river Halycus was fixed as the boundary of the two powers; and again in 368, in the middle of which war Dionysius died at Syracuse, 367. His last illness is said to have been brought on by excessive feasting; but according to some accounts, his death was hastened by his medical attendants, in order to secure the succession for his son. After the death of his first wife, Dionysius had married almost exactly at the same time — some said even on the same day — Doris, a Locrian of distinguished birth, and Aristomache, a Syracusan, the daughter of his supporter Hipparinus, and the sister of Dion. By Doris he had 3 children, of which the eldest was his successor, Dionysius. The character of Dionysius has been drawn in the blackest colours by many ancient writers; he appears indeed to have become a sort of type of a tyrant, in its worst sense. In his latter years he became extremely suspicious, and apprehensive of treachery even from his nearest friends, and is said to have adopted the most excessive precautions to guard against it. Many of these stories have however an air of great exaggeration. (Cic. *Tusc.* v. 20.) He built the terrible prison, called Lautumiae, which was cut out of the solid rock in the part of Syracuse, named Epipolae. (See *Dict. of Ant.* art. *Lautumiae.*) Dionysius was fond of literature and the arts. He adorned Syracuse with splendid temples and other public edifices, so as to render it unquestionably the greatest of all Greek cities. He was himself a poet, and repeatedly contended for the prize of tragedy at Athens. Here he several times obtained the second and third prizes; and, finally, just before his death, bore away the first prize at the Lenaea, with a play called "The Ransom of Hector." He sought the society of men distinguished in literature and philosophy, entertaining the poet Philoxenus at his table, and inviting Plato to Syracuse. He however soon after sent the latter away from Sicily in disgrace; and though the story of his having caused him to be sold as a slave, as well as that of his having sent Philoxenus to the stone quarries for ridiculing his bad verses, are probably gross exaggerations, they may well have been so far founded in fact, that his intercourse with these persons was interrupted by some sudden burst of capricious violence. — 2. The Younger, son of the preceding, succeeded his father as tyrant of Syracuse, B. C. 367. He was at this time under 30 years

Dionysus (Bacchus) enthroned. (Ponce, Bains de Titus, No. 12.) Pages 226, 227.

Adventures of Dionysus (Bacchus). (From the Choragic Monument of Lysicrates.)
Pages 226, 227. See illustrations opposite pp. 240, 272.

Bacchante, with Snake-bound Hair. (Thiersch, über die
hellenischen bemalten Vasen.) Pages 226, 227.

Dionysus (Bacchus). (From a Painting at Pompeii.)
Pages 226, 227.

[To face p. 224.

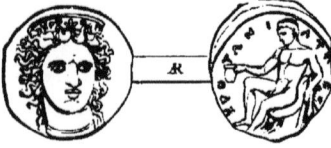

Croton in Bruttium. Page 197.

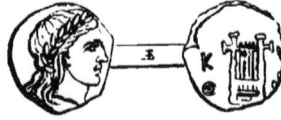

Cumae in Campania. Page 198.

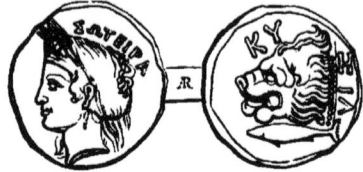

Cyconia in Crete. Page 200.

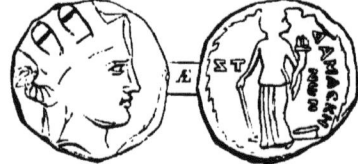

Cyme in Aeolis. Page 200.

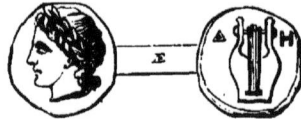

Cyparissia in Messenia. Page 201.

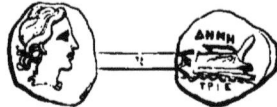

Cyrene in Africa. Page 202.

Cythnus. Page 204.

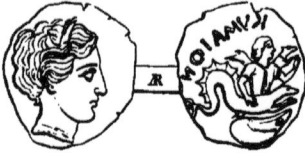

Cyzicus. Page 204.

Damascus. Page 206.

Delos. Page 210.

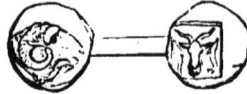

Delphi. Page 211.

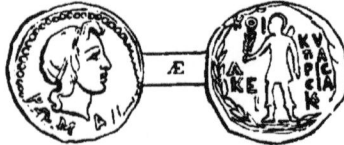

Demetrias. Page 212.

Dionysopolis in Phrygia. Page 226.

of age : he had been brought up at his father's court in idleness and luxury, and studiously precluded from taking any part in public affairs. The ascendancy which Dion, and through his means Plato, obtained for a time over his mind was undermined by flatterers and the companions of his pleasures. Yet his court was at this time a great place of resort for philosophers and men of letters : besides Plato, whom he induced by the most urgent entreaties to pay him a second visit, Aristippus of Cyrene, Eudoxus of Cnidus, Speusippus, and others, are stated to have spent some time with him at Syracuse ; and he cultivated a friendly intercourse with Archytas and the Pythagoreans of Magna Graecia. Dion, who had been banished by Dionysius, returned to Sicily in 357, at the head of a small force, with the avowed object of dethroning Dionysius. The latter was absent from Syracuse at the time that Dion landed in Sicily; but he instantly returned to Syracuse, where the citadel still held out for him. But finding it impossible to retain his power, he sailed away to Italy with his most valuable property, and thus lost the sovereignty after a reign of 12 years, 356. He now repaired to Locri, the native city of his mother, Doris, where he was received in the most friendly manner; but he made himself tyrant of the city, and is said to have treated the inhabitants with the utmost cruelty. After remaining at Locri 10 years, he availed himself of the internal dissensions at Syracuse to recover possession of his power in that city, 346. The Locrians took advantage of his absence to revolt against him, and wreaked their vengeance in the most cruel manner on his wife and daughters. He continued to reign in Syracuse for the next 3 years, till Timoleon came to Sicily, to deliver the Greek cities of the island from the tyrants. As he was unable to resist Timoleon, he surrendered the citadel into the hands of the latter, on condition of being allowed to depart in safety to Corinth, 343. Here he spent the remainder of his life in a private condition, and is said to have frequented low company, and sunk gradually into a very degraded and abject state. According to some writers, he was reduced to support himself by keeping a school ; others say, that he became one of the attendants on the rites of Cybele, a set of mendicant priests of the lowest class.— 3. Tyrant of Heraclea on the Euxine, son of Clearchus, succeeded his brother Timotheus in the tyranny about B. c. 338. He is said to have been the mildest and justest of all the tyrants that had ever lived. He married Amastris, niece of Darius. In 306 he assumed the title of king, and died shortly afterwards at the age of 55. He is said to have been choked by his own fat.

II. *Literary.* 1. Surnamed **Areopagita**, because he was one of the council of the Areopagus, was converted by St. Paul's preaching at Athens. There are extant several works under his name, which however could scarcely have been written before the 5th century of our era.— **2. Cato.** [CATO.]— 3. Surnamed **Chalcus** (ὁ Χαλκοῦς), an Attic poet and orator, who derived his surname from his having advised the Athenians to coin brass money for the purpose of facilitating traffic. Of his oratory we know nothing ; but his poems, chiefly elegies, are often referred to and quoted. He was one of the leaders of the colony to Thurii in Italy, B. c. 444. — **4.** Of **Halicarnassus**, a celebrated rhetorician, came to Rome about B. c. 29, for the purpose of

making himself acquainted with the Latin language and literature. He lived at Rome on terms of friendship with many distinguished men, such as Q. Aelius Tubero, and the rhetorician Caecilius, and he remained in the city for 22 years, till his death, B. c. 7. His principal work, which he composed at Rome at the later period of his life, was a history of Rome in 22 books, entitled 'Ρωμαϊκὴ 'Αρχαιολογία. It contained the history of Rome from the mythical times down to B. c. 264, in which year the history of Polybius begins with the Punic wars. The first 9 books alone are complete ; of the 10th and 11th we have the greater part ; and of the remaining 9 we possess nothing but fragments and extracts. Dionysius treated the early history of Rome with great minuteness. The 11 books extant do not carry the history beyond B. c. 441, so that the 11th book breaks off very soon after the decemviral legislation. This peculiar minuteness in the early history, however, was in a great measure the consequence of the object he had proposed to himself, and which, as he himself states, was to remove the erroneous notions which the Greeks entertained with regard to Rome's greatness. Dionysius had no clear notions about the early constitution of Rome, and was led astray by the nature of the institutions which he saw in his own day ; and thus makes innumerable mistakes in treating of the history of the constitution. He introduces numerous speeches in his work, which, though written with artistic skill, nevertheless show that Dionysius was a rhetorician, not an historian, and still less a statesman. — Dionysius also wrote various rhetorical and critical works, which abound with the most exquisite remarks and criticisms on the works of the classical writers of Greece. They show that he was a greater critic than historian. The following are the extant works of this class : 1. Τέχνη ῥητορική, addressed to one Echecrates, part of which is certainly spurious. 2. Περὶ συνθέσεως ὀνομάτων, treats of oratorical power, and on the combination of words according to the different styles of oratory. 3. Τῶν ἀρχαίων κρίσις, contains characteristics of poets, from Homer down to Euripides, of some historians, such as Herodotus, Thucydides, Philistus, Xenophon, and Theopompus, and lastly, of some philosophers and orators. 4. Περὶ τῶν ἀρχαίων ῥητόρων ὑπομνηματισμοί, contains criticisms on the most eminent Greek orators, of which we now possess only the first 3 sections, on Lysias, Isocrates, and Isaeus. The other 3 sections treated of Demosthenes, Hyperides, and Aeschines ; but they are lost, with the exception of the 1st part of the 4th section, which treated of the oratorical power of Demosthenes. 5. 'Επιστολὴ πρὸς 'Αμμαῖον, a letter to his friend Ammaeus, in which he shows that most of the orations of Demosthenes had been delivered before Aristotle wrote his Rhetoric, and consequently that Demosthenes had derived no instruction from Aristotle. 6. 'Επιστολὴ πρὸς Γναῖον Πομπήϊον, was written by Dionysius with a view of justifying the unfavourable opinion which he had expressed upon Plato, and which Pompey had censured. 7. Περὶ τοῦ Θουκυδίδου χαρακτῆρος καὶ τῶν λοιπῶν τοῦ συγγραφέως ἰδιωμάτων, was written by Dionysius at the request of his friend Tubero for the purpose of explaining more minutely what he had written on Thucydides. As Dionysius in this work looks at the great historian from his rhetorical point of view, his judgment is often unjust and incorrect. 8. Περὶ τῶν τοῦ Θουκυδίδου ἰδιω-μάτων, addressed to Ammaeus. 9. Δείναρχος, a very valuable treatise on the life and orations of Dinarchus. The best editions of the complete works of Dionysius are by Sylburg, Frankf. 1586, 2 vols. fol. reprinted at Leipzig, 1691 ; by Hudson, Oxon. 1704, 2 vols. fol. ; and by Reiske, Lips. 1774. — 5. Of Heraclea, son of Theophantus, was a pupil of Zeno, and adopted the tenets of the Stoics. But in consequence of a most painful complaint, he abandoned the Stoic philosophy, and joined the Eleatics, whose doctrine, that ἡδονή and the absence of pain was the highest good, had more charms for him than the austere ethics of the Stoa. This renunciation of his former creed drew upon him the nickname of μεταθέμενος, i. e. the renegade. He died in his 80th year of voluntary starvation. He wrote several works, all of which are lost. Cicero censures him for having mixed up verses with his prose, and for his want of elegance and refinement. — 6. Of Magnesia, a distinguished rhetorician, taught in Asia between B. C. 79 and 77, when Cicero visited the E. — 7. Of Miletus, one of the earliest Greek historians, and a contemporary of Hecataeus, wrote a history of Persia. — 8. Of Mytilene, surnamed Scytobrachion, taught at Alexandria in the 1st century B. C. He wrote a prose work on the Argonauts, which was consulted by Diodorus Siculus. — 9. Surnamed Periēgētēs, from his being the author of a περιήγησις τῆς γῆς, which is still extant; probably lived about A. D. 300. The work contains a description of the whole earth, in hexameter verse, and is written in a terse and elegant style. It enjoyed great popularity in ancient times. Two translations or paraphrases of it were made by Romans, one by Rufus Festus Avienus [AVIENUS], and the other by the grammarian Priscian. [PRISCIANUS.] The best edition of the original is by Bernhardy, Lips. 1828. — 10. Of Sinope, an Athenian comic poet of the middle comedy. — 11. Surnamed Thrax, from his father being a Thracian, was himself a native either of Alexandria or Byzantium. He is also called a Rhodian, because at one time he resided at Rhodes, and gave instructions there. He also taught at Rome, about B. C. 80. He was a very celebrated grammarian ; but the only one of his works come down to us is a small treatise, entitled τέχνη γραμματική, which became the basis of all subsequent grammars, and was a standard book in grammar schools for many centuries.

III. Artists. — 1. Of Argos, a statuary, flourished B. C. 476. — 2. Of Colophon, a painter, contemporary with Polygnotus of Thasos, whose works he imitated in every other respect except in grandeur. Aristotle (Poët. 2) says that Polygnotus painted the likenesses of men better than the originals, Pauson made them worse, and Dionysius just like them (ὁμοίους). It seems from this that the pictures of Dionysius were deficient in the ideal.

Dionysopolis (Διονύσου πόλις), a town in Phrygia, belonging to the conventus juridicus of Apameia, founded by Attalus and Eumenes.

Dionysus (Διόνυσος or Διώνυσος), the youthful, beautiful, but effeminate god of wine. He is also called both by Greeks and Romans Bacchus (Βάκχος), that is, the noisy or riotous god, which was originally a mere epithet or surname of Dionysus, and does not occur till after the time of Herodotus. According to the common tradition, Dionysus was the son of Zeus and Semele, the daughter of Cadmus of Thebes ; though other traditions give him a different parentage and a different birth-place. It was generally believed that when Semele was pregnant, she was persuaded by Hera, who appeared to her in disguise, to request the father of the gods to appear to her in the same glory and majesty in which he was accustomed to approach his own wife Hera. Zeus unwillingly complied, and appeared to her in thunder and lightning. Semele was terrified and overpowered by the sight, and being seized by the flames, she gave premature birth to a child. Zeus saved the child from the flames, sewed him up in his thigh, and thus preserved him till he came to maturity. Various epithets which are given to the god refer to that occurrence, such as πυριγενής, μηρορραφής, μηρο-τραφής, and ignigena. After the birth of Dionysus, Zeus entrusted him to Hermes, or, according to others, to Persephone or Rhea, who took the child to Ino and Athamas at Orchomenos, and persuaded them to bring him up as a girl. Hera was now urged on by her jealousy to throw Ino and Athamas into a state of madness. Zeus, in order to save his child, changed him into a ram, and carried him to the nymphs of Mt. Nysa, who brought him up in a cave, and were afterwards rewarded by Zeus, by being placed as Hyades among the stars. Mt. Nysa, from which the god was believed to have derived his name, was placed in Thrace ; but mountains of the same name are found in different parts of the ancient world where he was worshipped, and where he was believed to have introduced the cultivation of the vine. Various other nymphs are also said to have reared him When he had grown up, Hera drove him mad, in which state he wandered about through various parts of the earth. He first went to Egypt, where he was hospitably received by king Proteus. He thence proceeded through Syria, where he flayed Damascus alive, for opposing the introduction of the vine. He then traversed all Asia, teaching the inhabitants of the different countries of Asia the cultivation of the vine, and introducing among them the elements of civilization. The most famous part of his wanderings in Asia is his expedition to India, which is said to have lasted several years. On his return to Europe, he passed through Thrace, but was ill received by Lycurgus, king of the Edones, and leaped into the sea to seek refuge with Thetis, whom he afterwards rewarded for her kind reception with a golden urn, a present of Hephaestus. All the host of Bacchantic women and Satyrs, who had accompanied him, were taken prisoners by Lycurgus, but the women were soon set free again. The country of the Edones thereupon ceased to bear fruit, and Lycurgus became mad and killed his own son, whom he mistook for a vine. After this his madness ceased, but the country still remained barren, and Dionysus declared that it would remain so till Lycurgus died. The Edones, in despair, took their king and put him in chains, and Dionysus had him torn to pieces by horses. He then returned to Thebes, where he compelled the women to quit their houses, and to celebrate Bacchic festivals on Mt. Cithaeron, or Parnassus. Pentheus, who then ruled at Thebes, endeavoured to check the riotous proceedings, and went out to the mountains to seek the Bacchic women ; but his own mother, Agave, in her Bacchic fury, mistook him for an animal, and tore him to pieces. Dionysus next went to Argos, where the people first refused to acknowledge him, but after punishing the women with frenzy, he was recognised as a god and temples were erected to him. His last feat was performed on a voyage from Icaria to Naxos. He hired a ship which belonged to Tyrrhenian pirates ; but the men, instead of landing at Naxos, steered towards Asia to sell him there as a slave. Thereupon the god changed the mast and oars into serpents, and himself into a lion ; ivy grew around the vessel, and the sound of flutes was heard on every side ; the sailors 'were seized with madness, leaped into the sea, and were metamorphosed into dolphins. After he had thus gradually established his divine nature throughout the world, he took his mother out of Hades, called her Thyone, and rose with her into Olympus. — Various mythological beings are described as the offspring of Dionysus ; but among the women, both mortal and immortal, who won his love, none is more famous in ancient story than Ariadne. [ARIADNE.] The extraordinary mixture of traditions respecting the history of Dionysus seems evidently to have arisen from the traditions of different times and countries, referring to analogous divinities, and transferred to the Greek Dionysus. The worship of Dionysus was no part of the original religion of Greece, and his mystic worship is comparatively of late origin. In Homer he does not appear as one of the great divinities, and the story of his birth by Zeus and the Bacchic orgies are not alluded to in any way : Dionysus is there simply described as the god who teaches man the preparation of wine, whence he is called the "drunken god" ($\mu\alpha\iota\nu\acute{o}\mu\epsilon\nu\sigma$), and the sober king Lycurgus will not, for this reason, tolerate him in his kingdom. (Hom. *Il.* vi. 132, *Od.* xviii. 406, comp. xi. 325.) As the cultivation of the vine spread in Greece, the worship of Dionysus likewise spread further ; the mystic worship was developed by the Orphici, though it probably originated in the transfer of Phrygian and Lydian modes of worship to that of Dionysus. After the time of Alexander's expedition to India, the celebration of the Bacchic festivals assumed more and more their wild and dissolute character.—As far as the nature and origin of the god Dionysus is concerned, he appears in all traditions as the representative of the productive, overflowing, and intoxicating power of nature, which carries man away from his usual quiet and sober mode of living. Wine is the most natural and appropriate symbol of that power, and it is therefore called "the fruit of Dionysus." Dionysus is, therefore, the god of wine, the inventor and teacher of its cultivation, the giver of joy, and the disperser of grief and sorrow. As the god of wine, he is also both an inspired and an inspiring god, that is, a god who has the power of revealing the future to man by oracles. Thus, it is said, that he had as great a share in the Delphic oracle as Apollo, and he himself had an oracle in Thrace. Now, as prophetic power is always combined with the healing art, Dionysus is, like Apollo, called $\iota\alpha\tau\rho\acute{o}s$, or $\acute{v}\gamma\iota\alpha\tau\acute{\eta}s$, and is hence invoked as a $\vartheta\epsilon\grave{o}s$ $\sigma\omega\tau\acute{\eta}\rho$ against raging diseases. The notion of his being the cultivator and protector of the vine was easily extended to that of his being the protector of trees in general, which is alluded to in various epithets and surnames given him by the poets of antiquity, and he thus comes into close connection with Demeter. This character is still further developed in the notion of

his being the promoter of civilization, a law-giver, and a lover of peace. As the Greek drama had grown out of the dithyrambic choruses at the festivals of Dionysus, he was also regarded as the god of tragic art, and as the protector of theatres. The orgiastic worship of Dionysus seems to have been first established in Thrace, and to have thence spread southward to Mts. Helicon and Parnassus, to Thebes, Naxos, and throughout Greece, Sicily, and Italy, though some writers derived it from Egypt. Respecting his festivals and the mode of their celebration, and especially the introduction and suppression of his worship at Rome, see *Dict. of Ant.* art. *Dionysia.* — In the earliest times the Graces or Charites were the companions of Dionysus. This circumstance points out the great change which took place in the course of time in the mode of his worship, for afterwards we find him accompanied in his expeditions and travels by Bacchantic women, called Lenae, Maenades, Thyiades, Mimallones, Clodones, Bassarae or Bassarides, all of whom are represented in works of art as raging with madness or enthusiasm, in vehement motions, their heads thrown backwards, with dishevelled hair, and carrying in their hands thyrsus-staffs (entwined with ivy, and headed with pine-cones), cymbals, swords, or serpents. Sileni, Pans, satyrs, centaurs, and other beings of a like kind, are also the constant companions of the god.—The temples and statues of Dionysus were very numerous in the ancient world. The animal most commonly sacrificed to him was the ram. Among the things sacred to him, we may notice the vine, ivy, laurel, and asphodel ; the dolphin, serpent, tiger, lynx, panther, and ass ; but he hated the sight of an owl. In later works of art he appears in 4 different forms : 1. As an infant handed over by Hermes to his nurses, or fondled and played with by satyrs and Bacchae. 2. As a manly god with a beard, commonly called the Indian Bacchus. He there appears in the character of a wise and dignified Oriental monarch ; his beard is long and soft, and his Lydian robes ($\beta\alpha\sigma\sigma\acute{\alpha}\rho\alpha$) are long and richly folded. 3. The youthful or so-called Theban Bacchus was carried to ideal beauty by Praxiteles. The form of his body is manly and with strong outlines, but still approaches to the female form by its softness and roundness. The expression of the countenance is languid, and shows a kind of dreamy longing ; the head, with a diadem, or a wreath of vine or ivy, leans somewhat on one side ; his attitude is easy, like that of a man who is absorbed in sweet thoughts, or slightly intoxicated. He is often seen leaning on his companions, or riding on a panther, ass, tiger, or lion. The finest statue of this kind is in the villa Ludovisi. 4. Bacchus with horns, either those of a ram or of a bull. This representation occurs chiefly on coins, but never in statues.

Diophánes ($\Delta\iota\sigma\phi\acute{\alpha}\nu\eta s$). 1. Of Mytilene, a distinguished Greek rhetorician, came to Rome, where he instructed Tib. Gracchus, and became his intimate friend. After the murder of Gracchus, Diophanes was also put to death.—2. Of Nicaea, in Bithynia, in the 1st century B. C., abridged the agricultural work of Cassius Dionysius for the use of king Deiotarus.

Diophantus ($\Delta\iota\acute{o}\phi\alpha\nu\tau\sigma s$). 1. An Attic orator and contemporary of Demosthenes, with whom he opposed the Macedonian party. — 2. Of Alexandria, the only Greek writer on Algebra. His period

Q 2

is unknown; but he probably ought not to be placed before the end of the 5th century of our era. He wrote *Arithmetica*, in 13 books, of which only 6 are extant, and 1 book, *De Multangulis Numeris*, on polygonal numbers. These books contain a system of reasoning on numbers by the aid of general symbols, and with some use of symbols of operation; so that, though the demonstrations are very much conducted in words at length, and arranged so as to remind us of Euclid, there is no question that the work is algebraical: not a treatise *on algebra*, but an algebraical treatise on the relations of integer numbers, and on the solution of equations of more than one variable in integers. Editions by Bachet de Meziriac, Paris, 1621, fol., and by Fermat, Toulouse, 1670, fol.

Diopithes (Διωπείθης). 1 A half-fanatic, half-impostor, who made at Athens an apparently thriving trade of oracles: he was much satirised by the comic poets. — 2. An Athenian general, father of the poet Menander, was sent out to the Thracian Chersonesus about B. C. 344, at the head of a body of Athenian settlers or κληροῦχοι. In the Chersonese he became involved in disputes with the Cardians, who were supported by Philip. The latter sent a letter of remonstrance to Athens, and Diopithes was arraigned by the Macedonian party, but was defended by Demosthenes in the oration, still extant, on the Chersonese, B. C. 341, in consequence of which he was permitted to retain his command.

Dioscoridis Insula (Διοσκορίδου νῆσος : Socotra), an island off the S. coast of Arabia, near the promontory Syagrus. The island itself was marshy and unproductive, but it was a great commercial emporium; and the N. part of the island was inhabited by Arabian, Egyptian, and Greek merchants.

Dioscorides (Διοσκορίδης). 1. A disciple of Isocrates, and a Greek grammarian, wrote upon Homer. — 2. The author of 39 epigrams in the Greek Anthology, seems to have lived in Egypt about the time of Ptolemy Euergetes. — 3. **Pedacius** or **Pedanius**, of Anazarba in Cilicia, a Greek physician, probably lived in the 2nd century of the Christian era. He has left behind him a Treatise on Materia Medica (Περὶ Ὕλης Ἰατρικῆς), in 5 books, a work of great labour and research, and which for many ages was received as a standard production. It consists of a description of all the articles then used in medicine, with an account of their supposed virtues. The other works extant under the name of Dioscorides are probably spurious. The best edition is by Sprengel, Lips. 1829, 1830, 2 vols. 8vo. — 4. Surnamed **Phacas** on account of the moles or freckles on his face, probably lived in the 1st century B. C.

Dioscuri (Διόσκουροι), that is, sons of Zeus, the well-known heroes, **Castor** (Κάστωρ) and **Pollux** or Polydeuces (Πολυδεύκης). The two brothers were sometimes called **Castores** by the Romans.—According to Homer they were the sons of Leda and Tyndareus, king of Lacedaemon, and consequently brothers of Helen. Hence they are often called by the patronymic *Tyndaridae*. Castor was famous for his skill in taming and managing horses, and Pollux for his skill in boxing. Both had disappeared from the earth before the Greeks went against Troy. Although they were buried, says Homer, yet they came to life every other day, and they enjoyed honours like those of the gods. —

According to other traditions both were the sons of Zeus and Leda, and were born at the same time with their sister Helen out of an egg. [LEDA.] According to others again, Pollux and Helen only were children of Zeus, and Castor was the son of Tyndareus. Hence, Pollux was immortal, while Castor was subject to old age and death like every other mortal. They were born, according to different traditions, at different places, such as Amyclae, mount Taygetus, the island of Pephnos or Thalamae. — The fabulous life of the Dioscuri is marked by 3 great events. 1. *Their expedition against Athens.* Theseus had carried off their sister Helen from Sparta, and kept her in confinement at Aphidnae, under the superintendence of his mother Aethra. While Theseus was absent from Attica, the Dioscuri marched into Attica, and ravaged the country round the city. Academus revealed to them that Helen was kept at Aphidnae; the Dioscuri took the place by assault, carried away their sister Helen, and made Aethra their prisoner. 2. *Their part in the expedition of the Argonauts,* as they had before taken part in the Calydonian hunt. During the voyage of the Argonauts, it once happened that when the heroes were detained by a vehement storm, and Orpheus prayed to the Samothracian gods, the storm suddenly subsided, and stars appeared on the heads of the Dioscuri. On their arrival in the country of the Bebryces, Pollux fought against Amycus, the gigantic son of Poseidon, and conquered him. During the Argonautic expedition they founded the town of Dioscurias. 3. *Their battle with the sons of Aphareus.* Once the Dioscuri, in conjunction with Idas and Lynceus, the sons of Aphareus, had carried away a herd of oxen from Arcadia. Idas appropriated the herd to himself, and drove it to his home in Messene. The Dioscuri then invaded Messene, drove away the cattle of which they had been deprived, and much more in addition. Hence arose a war between the Dioscuri and the sons of Aphareus, which was carried on in Messene or Laconia. Castor, the mortal, fell by the hands of Idas, but Pollux slew Lynceus, and Zeus killed Idas by a flash of lightning. Pollux then returned to his brother, whom he found breathing his last, and he prayed to Zeus to be permitted to die with him. Zeus gave him the option, either to live as his immortal son in Olympus, or to share his brother's fate, and to live alternately one-day under the earth, and the other in the heavenly abodes of the gods. According to a different form of the story, Zeus rewarded the attachment of the two brothers by placing them among the stars as *Gemini.* — These heroic youths received divine honours at Sparta. Their worship spread from Peloponnesus over Greece, Sicily, and Italy. Their principal characteristic was that of θεοὶ σωτῆρες, that is, mighty helpers of man, whence they were sometimes called ἄνακες or ἄνακτες. They were worshipped more especially as the protectors of travellers by sea, for Poseidon had rewarded their brotherly love by giving them power over winds and waves, that they might assist the shipwrecked. (*Fratres Helenae, lucida sidera,* Hor. *Carm.* i. 3.) Whenever they appeared they were seen riding on magnificent white steeds. They were regarded as presidents of the public games. They were further believed to have invented the war-dance and warlike music, and poets and bards were favoured by them. Owing to their warlike character, it was customary at Sparta for the 2 kings, whenever they went to war, to be accompanied by symbolic representations of the Dioscuri (δόκανα). Respecting their festivals, see *Dict. of Ant.*, arts. *Anacoia, Dioscuria*. Their usual representation in works of art is that of 2 youthful horsemen with egg-shaped helmets, crowned with stars, and with spears in their hands.—At Rome, the worship of the Dioscuri was introduced at an early time. They were believed to have assisted the Romans against the Latins in the battle of Lake Regillus; and the dictator, A. Postumius Albinus, during the battle vowed a temple to them. It was erected in the Forum, on the spot where they had been seen after the battle, opposite the temple of Vesta. It was consecrated on the 15th of July, the anniversary of the battle of Regillus. The equites regarded the Dioscuri as their patrons. From the year B.C. 305, the equites went every year, on the 15th of July, in a magnificent procession on horseback, from the temple of Mars through the main streets of the city, across the Forum, and by the ancient temple of the Dioscuri.

Dioscūrīas (Διοσκουριάς: Διοσκουριεύς: *Iskuria* or *Isgaur*), an important town in Colchis on the river Anthemus, N. W. of the Phasis, founded by the Milesians, was a great emporium for all the surrounding people: under the Romans it was called Sebastopolis.

Dios-Hiĕron (Διὸς Ἱερὸν: Διοσιερίτης), a small town on the coast of Ionia, between Lebedus and Colophon.

Diospŏlis (Διόσπολις: Διοσπολίτης). 1. D. **Magna**, the later name of Thebes in Egypt. [THEBAE.]—2. D. **Parva**, called by Pliny Jovis Oppidum, the capital of the Nomos Diospolites in Upper Egypt.—3. A town in Lower Egypt in the Delta near Mendes, in the midst of marshes.—4. (*Ludd, Lydd*), the name given by the Greek and Roman writers to the LYDDA of the Scriptures.—5. A town in Pontus, originally called CABIRA.

Diovis, an ancient Italian (Umbrian) name of Jupiter.

Diphĭlus (Δίφιλος), one of the principal Athenian comic poets of the new comedy and a contemporary of Menander and Philemon, was a native of Sinope. He is said to have exhibited 100 plays. Though, in point of time, Diphilus belonged to the new comedy, his poetry seems to have had more of the character of the middle. This is shown, among other indications, by the frequency with which he chose mythological subjects for his plays, and by his bringing on the stage the poets Archilochus, Hipponax, and Sappho. The Roman comic poets borrowed largely from Diphilus. The *Casina* of Plautus is a translation of his Κληρούμενοι. His Συναποθνήσκοντες was translated by Plautus in the lost play of the *Commorientes*, and was partly followed by Terence in his *Adelphi*. The *Rudens* of Plautus is also a translation of a play of Diphilus, but the title of the Greek play is not known.

Dipoenus and **Scyllis** (Δίποινος καὶ Σκύλλις), very ancient Greek statuaries, who are always mentioned together, flourished about B.C. 560. They were natives of Crete, whence they went to Sicyon, which was for a long time the chief seat of Grecian art. Their disciples were Tectaeus and Angelion, Learchus of Rhegium, Doryclidas and his brother Medon, Dontas, and Theocles, who were all 4 Lacedaemonians. Dipoenus and

Scyllis are sometimes called sons of Daedalus, by which we are only to understand that they belonged to the Daedalian style of art. [DAEDALUS.]

Dirae, a name of the Furiae. [EUMENIDES.]

Dircē (Δίρκη), daughter of Helios and wife of Lycus. Her story is related under AMPHION.

Dirphys (Δί, φυς), a mountain in Euboea.

Dis, contracted from Dives, a name sometimes given to Pluto, and hence also to the lower world.

Dīum (Δῖον: Διεύς, Διαστής). 1. An important town in Macedonia on the Thermaic gulf, so called after a temple of Zeus. Here were placed the equestrian statues by Lysippus of the Macedonians who had fallen at the battle of the Granicus. —2. A town in Chalcidice in Macedonia, on the Strymonic gulf.—3. A town in Euboea, not far from the promontory Cenaeum.

Dīvĭco, the leader of the Helvetians in the war against L. Cassius in B.C. 107, was at the head of the embassy sent to Julius Caesar, nearly 50 years later, B.C. 58, when he was preparing to attack the Helvetians.

Dīvĭtĭācus, an Aeduan noble and brother of Dumnorix, was a warm adherent of the Romans and of Caesar, who, in consideration of his entreaties, pardoned the treason of Dumnorix in B.C. 58. In the same year he took the most prominent part among the Gallic chiefs in requesting Caesar's aid against Ariovistus; he had some time before gone even to Rome to ask the senate for their interference, but without success. During this visit he was the guest of Cicero.

Divodūrum (*Metz*), subsequently Mediomatrici, and still later Metis or Mettis, the capital of the Mediomatrici in Gallia Belgica.

Divŏna. [CADURCI.]

Diyllus (Δίυλλος), an Athenian, who wrote a history of Greece and Sicily in 26 or 27 books, from the seizure of the Delphic temple by Philomelus. The exact period at which he flourished cannot be ascertained, but he belongs to the age of the Ptolemies.

Dobērus (Δόβηρος), a town in Paeonia in Macedonia, E. of the river Echedorus.

Docĭmĭa or **Docimēum** (Δοκιμία, Δοκίμειον: Δοκιμεύς, Δοκιμηνός), a town in Phrygia, not far from Synnada: in its neighbourhood were celebrated marble quarries.

Dōdōna (Δωδώνη), the most ancient oracle in Greece, was situated in Epirus, and probably at the S. E. extremity of the lake of Joannina near Kastritza. It was founded by the Pelasgians, and was dedicated to Zeus. The responses of the oracle were given from lofty oaks or beech trees, probably from a grove consisting of these trees. The will of the god was declared by the wind rustling through the trees; and in order to render the sounds more distinct, brazen vessels were suspended on the branches of the trees, which being set in motion by the wind came in contact with one another. These sounds were in early times interpreted by men, but afterwards, when the worship of Dione became connected with that of Zeus, by 2 or 3 aged women, who were called πελειάδες or πέλαιαι, because pigeons were said to have brought the command to found the oracle. There were, however, also priests, called Selli or Helli, who had the management of the temple. The oracle of Dodona had less influence in historical times than in the heroic age. It was chiefly consulted by the neighbouring tribes, the Aetolians, Acarnanians, and

Q 3

Epirots, and by those who would not go to Delphi on account of its partiality for the Dorians. In B. C. 219, the temple was destroyed by the Aetolians, and the sacred oaks cut down. But the town continued to exist, and we hear of a bishop of Dodona in the council of Ephesus.

Dŏlăbella, Cornēlĭus. 1. P., consul B. C. 283, conquered the Senones.—2. Cn., curule aedile 105, in which year he and his colleague, Sex. Julius Caesar, had the Hecyra of Terence performed at the festival of the Megalesia. In 159 he was consul.—3. Cn., a partisan of Sulla, by whom he was made consul, 81. He afterwards received Macedonia for his province. In 77 he was accused by the young Julius Caesar of having been guilty of extortion in his province, but he was acquitted.—4. Cn., praetor urbanus 81, when the cause of P. Quintius was tried: Cicero charges him with having acted on that occasion unjustly. The year after he had Cilicia for his province; C. Malleolus was his quaestor, and the notorious Verres his legate. Dolabella not only tolerated the extortions and robberies committed by them, but shared in their booty. On his return to Rome, Dolabella was accused by M. Aemilius Scaurus of extortion in his province, and on that occasion Verres deserted his accomplice and furnished the accuser with all the necessary information. Dolabella was condemned, and went into exile.—5. P., the son-in-law of Cicero, whose daughter Tullia he married after divorcing his wife Fabia, 51. He was one of the most profligate men of his age, and his conduct caused Cicero great uneasiness. On the breaking out of the civil war he joined Caesar and fought on his side at the battle of Pharsalia (48), in Africa (46), and in Spain (45). Caesar raised him to the consulship in 44, notwithstanding the opposition of Antony. After the murder of Caesar, he forthwith joined the assassins of his benefactor ; but when Antony gave him the province of Syria, with the command against the Parthians, all his republican enthusiasm disappeared at once. On his way to his province he plundered the cities of Greece and Asia Minor, and at Smyrna he murdered Trebonius, who had been appointed by the senate proconsul of Asia. When his proceedings became known at Rome, he was declared a public enemy ; and Cassius, who had received Syria from the senate, marched against him. Dolabella threw himself into Laodicēa, which was besieged by Cassius, who at length succeeded in taking it. Dolabella, in order not to fall into the hands of his enemies, ordered one of his soldiers to kill him, 43.

Dŏlĭchē (Δολίχη). 1. The ancient name of the island Icarus.—2. A town in Thessaly on the W. slope of Olympus. — 3. A town in Commagene, between Zeugma and Germanicia, also called Dolichene, celebrated for the worship of Jupiter. — 4. Or Dulichium. [ECHINADES.]

Dŏlĭchistē (Δολιχίστη : Kakava), an island off the coast of Lycia, opposite the promontory Chimaera.

Dŏlĭōnes (Δολίονες), a Pelasgic people in Mysia, who dwelt between the rivers Aesepus and Rhyndacus, and in the neighbourhood of Cyzicus, which was called after them Doliōnis.

Dŏlōn (Δόλων), a Trojan, sent by night to spy the Grecian camp, was taken prisoner by Ulysses and Diomedes, compelled to give intelligence respecting the Trojans, and then slain by Diomedes.

The 10th book of the Iliad was therefore called Δολώνεια or Δολωνοφονία.

Dolonci (Δόλογκοι), a Thracian people in the Thracian Chersonesus.

Dolŏpes (Δόλοπες), a powerful people in Thessaly, dwelt on the Enipeus, and fought before Troy. (Hom. Il. ix. 484.) At a later time they dwelt at the foot of Mt. Pindus ; and their country, called Dolopia (Δολοπία), was reckoned part of Epirus.

Dŏmĭtĭa. 1. Sister of Cn. Domitius Ahenobarbus [AHENOBARBUS, No. 10], and consequently an aunt of the emperor Nero. She was the wife of Crispus Passienus, and was murdered in her old age by Nero, who wished to get possession of her property.—2. Lepĭda, sister of the preceding, wife of M. Valerius Messala Barbatus, and mother of Messalina, was put to death by Claudius at the instigation of Agrippina.—3. Longīna, daughter of Domitius Corbulo, was first married to L. Lamia Aemilianus, and afterwards to the emperor Domitian. In consequence of her adulterous intercourse with Paris, an actor, Domitian repudiated her, but was afterwards reconciled to her. She was privy to Domitian's murder.

Dŏmĭtĭa Gens, plebeian, was divided into the 2 illustrious families of AHENOBARBUS and CALVINUS.

Dŏmĭtĭānus, or with his full name T. Flavius Domitianus Augustus, Roman emperor A. D. 81 —96, was the younger son of Vespasian, and was born at Rome, A. D. 51. When Vespasian was proclaimed emperor by the legions in the E. (69), Domitian, who was then at Rome, narrowly escaped being murdered by Vitellius, and concealed himself until the victory of his father's party was decided. After the fall of Vitellius, Domitian was proclaimed Caesar, and obtained the government of the city till the return of his father. In this short time he gave full proofs of his sanguinary and licentious temper. Vespasian entrusted Domitian with no public affairs, and during the 10 years of his reign (69—79), Domitian lived as a private person on an estate near the Alban Mount, surrounded by a number of courtezans, and devoting a great part of his time to the composition of poetry and the recitation of his productions. During the reign of his brother Titus (79-81), he was also not allowed to take any part in public affairs. On the death of Titus (81), which was in all probability the work of Domitian, he was proclaimed emperor by the soldiers. During the first few years of his reign he kept a strict superintendence over the governors of provinces, enacted several useful laws, endeavoured to correct the licentious conduct of the higher classes ; and though he indulged himself in strange passions, his government was much better than had been expected. But his conduct was soon changed for the worse. His wars were mostly unfortunate ; and his want of success both wounded his vanity and excited his fears, and thus led him to delight in the misfortunes and sufferings of others. In 83 he undertook an expedition against the Chatti, which was attended with no result, though on his return to Rome in the following year, he celebrated a triumph, and assumed the name of Germanicus. In 85 Agricola, whose success and merits excited his jealousy, was recalled to Rome. [AGRICOLA.] From 86 to 90 he had to carry on war with Decebalus and the Dacians, who defeated the Roman armies, and at length compelled Domitian to purchase peace on very humiliating terms. [DECEBALUS.] It was after the Dacian war especially, that he gave full sway to his cruelty and tyranny. No man of distinction was safe, unless he would degrade himself to flatter the tyrant. The silent fear which prevailed in Rome and Italy during the latter years of Domitian's reign are briefly but energetically described by Tacitus in the introduction to his Life of Agricola, and his vices and tyranny are exposed in the strongest colours by the withering satire of Juvenal. All the philosophers who lived at Rome were expelled. Christian writers attribute to him a persecution of the Christians likewise, but there is some doubt upon the matter; and the belief seems to have arisen from the strictness with which he exacted the tribute from the Jews, and which may have caused much suffering to the Christians also. Many conspiracies had been formed against his life, and at length 3 officers of his court, assisted by Domitia, the emperor's wife, had him murdered by Stephanus, a freedman, on the 18th of September, 96.

Domitilla, Flavia, the first wife of Vespasian, and mother of Titus, Domitian, and Domitilla.

Domitius Afer. [AFER.]

Domitius Corbŭlo. [CORBULO.]

Domitius Marsus. [MARSUS.]

Domitius Ulpiānus. [ULPIANUS.]

Domna, Julia, of Emesa, was born of humble parents, and married the emperor Septimius Severus, when he was in a private station. She was beautiful and profligate, but at the same time gifted with strong powers of mind, and fond of literature and of the society of literary men. She had great influence over her husband, and after his death was entrusted by her son Caracalla with the administration of the most important affairs of state. After the murder of Caracalla, she was at first kindly treated by Macrinus; but having incurred the suspicions of Macrinus, and being commanded to quit Antioch, she put an end to her own life by voluntary starvation, A. D. 217.

Donātus. 1. A celebrated grammarian, who taught at Rome in the middle of the 4th century, and was the preceptor of Saint Jerome. His most famous work is a system of Latin Grammar, which has formed the groundwork of most elementary treatises upon the same subject, from his own time to the present day. It has been usually published in the form of 2 separate tracts: 1. *Ars s. Editio Prima, de literis, syllabis, pedibus, et tonis*; 2. *Editio Secunda, de octo partibus orationis;* to which are commonly annexed *De barbarismo, De soloecismo, De ceteris vitiis; De metaplasmo; De schematibus; De tropis;* but in the recent edition of Lindemann (in *Corpus Gramm. Latin.* Lips. 1831) these are all combined under one general title, *Donati Ars Grammatica tribus libris comprehensa.* We also possess introductions (*enarrationes*) and scholia, by Donatus, to 5 out of the 6 plays of Terence, those to the Heautontimorumenos having been lost. They are attached to all complete editions of Terence. — **2. Tiberius Claudius,** the author of a life of Virgil in 25 chapters, prefixed to many editions of Virgil. Nothing is known with regard to this Donatus; but it has been conjectured that some grammarian, who flourished about the commencement of the 5th century, may have drawn up a biography which formed the groundwork of the piece we now possess.

Donūsa or **Donūsia** (Δονουσία. Δονουσιος: Stenosa), one of the smaller Sporades in the Aegean

sea, S. of Naxos, subject to the Rhodians in early times. It produced green marble, whence Virgil (*Aen.* iii. 125) calls the island *viridis.* Under the Roman emperors it was used as a place of banishment.

Dōra, Dōrus, Dōrum (τὰ Δῶρα, Δῶρος : Δωρίτης), called DOR in the O. T., the most southerly town of Phoenicia on the coast, on a kind of peninsula at the foot of Mt. Carmel. It was an ancient town, formerly the residence of a Canaanitish king, and afterwards belonged to the tribe of Manasseh. Under the Seleucidae it was a strong fortress, and was included in Coele-Syria. It subsequently fell into decay, but was restored and again made a fortified place by the Roman general Gabinius.

Dōrieus (Δωριεύς). 1. Eldest son of Anaxandrides, king of Sparta, by his first wife, was however born after the son of the second marriage, Cleomenes, and therefore excluded from the immediate succession. [ANAXANDRIDES.] On the accession of Cleomenes to the throne, Dorieus left Sparta to establish for himself a kingdom elsewhere. He led his colony first to Libya; but driven away thence, he passed over to Eryx in Sicily, where he fell in a battle with the Egestaeans and Carthaginians, about B. C. 508. — **2.** Son of Diagoras of Rhodes [DIAGORAS], was celebrated for his victories in all the great Grecian games. He settled in Thurii, and from this place, after the defeat of the Athenians at Syracuse, he led 30 galleys to the aid of the Spartan cause in Greece, B. C. 412. He continued to take an active part in the war till 407, when he was captured by the Athenians; but the people, in admiration of his athletic size and noble beauty, dismissed him without so much as exacting a ransom. He is said at a later time to have been put to death by the Spartans.

Dōris (Δωρίς). 1. Daughter of Oceanus and Thetis, wife of her brother Nereus, and mother of the Nereides. The Latin poets sometimes use the name of this divinity for the sea itself. (Virg. *Eclog.* x. 5.) — **2.** One of the Nereides, daughter of the preceding.

Dōris (Δωρίς). 1. A small and mountainous country in Greece, formerly called **Dryŏpis** (Δρυοπίς), was bounded by Thessaly on the N., by Aetolia on the W., by Locris on the S., and by Phocis on the E. It contained 4 towns, Boum, Citinium, Erineus, and Pindus, which formed the Dorian tetrapolis. These towns never attained any consequence, and in the time of the Romans were in ruins; but the country is of importance as the home of the Dorians (Δωριεῖς: Dores), one of the great Hellenic races, who claimed descent from the mythical Dorus. [DORUS.] The Dorians, however, had not always dwelt in this land. Herodotus relates (i. 56), that they first inhabited Phthiotis in the time of Deucalion; that next, under Dorus, they inhabited Histiaeotis at the foot of Ossa and Olympus; that, expelled from thence by the Cadmeans, they settled on Mt. Pindus; and that they subsequently took up their abode in Dryopis, afterwards called Doris. Their 5th and last migration was to Peloponnesus, which they conquered, according to tradition, 80 years after the Trojan war. It was related that Aegimius, the king of the Dorians, had been driven from his dominions by the Lapithae, but was reinstated by Hercules; that the children of Hercules hence took refuge in this land when they had been expelled from Peloponnesus; and that it was to restore them to their rights that the Dorians invaded Peloponnesus. Accordingly, the conquest of Peloponnesus by the Dorians is usually called the Return of the Heraclidae. See HERACLIDAE. — The Dorians were divided into 3 tribes: the *Hylleis* ('Υλλεῖς), *Pamphyli* (Πάμφυλοι), and *Dymanes* (Δυμᾶνες). The first derived their name from Hyllus, son of Hercules, the two last from Pamphylus and Dymas, sons of Aegimius. The Dorians were the ruling class throughout Peloponnesus; the old inhabitants were reduced to slavery, or became subjects of the Dorians under the name of *Perioeci* (Περίοικοι). (*Dict. of Antiq.* art. *Perioeci.*) — 2. A district in Asia Minor consisting of the Dorian settlements on the coast of Caria and the neighbouring islands. 6 of these towns formed a league, called the Dorian hexapolis, consisting of Lindus, Ialysus, and Camīrus in the island of Rhodes, the island Cos, and Cnidus and Halicarnassus on the mainland. There were also other Dorian settlements in the neighbourhood, but they were never admitted to the league. The members of the hexapolis were accustomed to celebrate a festival with games on the Triopian promontory near Cnidus, in honour of the Triopian Apollo; the prizes in those games were brazen tripods, which the victors had to dedicate in the temple of Apollo; and Halicarnassus was struck out of the league, because one of her citizens carried the tripod to his own house instead of leaving it in the temple. The hexapolis thus became a pentapolis.

Doriscus (Δορίσκος), a town in Thrace at the mouth of the Hebrus, in the midst of an extensive plain of the same name, where Xerxes reviewed his vast forces.

Dorso, C. Fabius, greatly distinguished himself when the Capitol was besieged by the Gauls, B. C. 390. The Fabian gens was accustomed to celebrate a sacrifice at a fixed time on the Quirinal hill, and accordingly, at the appointed time, C. Dorso, who was then a young man, descended from the Capitol, carrying the sacred things in his hands, passed in safety through the enemy's posts, and, after performing the sacrifice, returned in safety to the Capitol.

Dōrus (Δῶρος), the mythical ancestor of the Dorians, is described either as a son of Hellen, the nymph Orseïs, and a brother of Xuthus and Aeolus, or as a son of Apollo and Phthia, and a brother of Laodocus and Polypoetes.

Dorylaeum (Δορύλαιον: Δορυλαεύς: *Eski-Shehr*), a town in Phrygia Epictetus, on the river Thymbris, with warm baths which are used at the present day; important under the Romans as the place from which the roads diverged to Pessinus, Iconium, and Apamea.

Dosiādas (Δωσιάδας), of Rhodes, the author of 2 poems in the Greek Anthology, the verses of which are so arranged that each poem presents the profile of an altar.

Dosītheus (Δωσίθεος), surnamed Magister, a Greek grammarian, taught at Rome about A. D. 207. He has left behind him a work entitled 'Ερμηνεύματα, of which the 1st and 2nd books contain a Greek grammar written in Latin, and Greek-Latin and Latin-Greek glossaries. The third book, which is the most important, contains translations from Latin authors into Greek, and *vice versâ*, and has been published separately by Böcking, Bonn, 1832.

Dossennus Fabius, or **Dorsennus,** an ancient Latin comic dramatist, censured by Horace (*Ep.* ii. 1. 173) on account of the exaggerated buffoonery of his characters. It appears that the name Dossennus (like that of *Maccius*) was appropriated to one of the standard characters in the Atellane farces. Hence some have supposed that Dossennus in Horace is not the name of a real person.

Dōtium (Δώτιον: Δωτιεύς), a town and plain in Thessaly S. of Mt. Ossa, on the lake Bobeïs.

Drabescus (Δράβησκος, also Δράβισκος), a town in the district Edōnis in Macedonia, on the Strymon.

Dracănon (Δράκανον), a town and promontory in the island Icaria.

Dracon (Δράκων), the author of the first written code of laws at Athens, which were called θεσμοί, as distinguished from the νόμοι of Solon. In this code he affixed the penalty of death to almost all crimes — to petty thefts, for instance, as well as to sacrilege and murder — which gave occasion to the remark that his laws were written not in ink, but in blood. We are told that he himself defended this extreme harshness by saying that small offences deserved death, and that he knew no severer punishment for great ones. His legislation is placed in B. C. 621. After the legislation of Solon (594), most of the laws of Dracon fell into disuse; but some of them were still in force at the end of the Peloponnesian war, as for instance the law which permitted the injured husband to slay the adulterer, if taken in the act. We are told that Dracon died at Aegina, being smothered by the number of hats and cloaks showered upon him as a popular mark of honour in the theatre.

Drangiāna (Δραγγιανή: *Sedjestân*), a part of Ariana, was bounded by Gedrosia, Carmania, Arachosia, and Aria. It sometimes formed a separate satrapy, but was more usually united to the satrapies either of Arachosia or of Gedrosia, or of Aria. The chief product of the country was tin: the chief river was the Erymanthus or Erymandrus (*Hilmend* or *Hindmend*). In the N. of the country dwelt the Drangae (Δράγγαι), a warlike people, from whom the province derived its name: their capital was Prophthasia. The Zarangae, Sarangae, or Darandae, who are also mentioned as inhabitants of the country, are probably only other forms of the name Drangae. The Ariaspae inhabited the S. part of the province. [ARIASPAE.]

Draudācum (*Dardasso*), a fortress of the Penestae in Greek Illyria.

Drāvus (*Drave*), a tributary of the Danube, rises in the Noric Alps near Aguntum, flows through Noricum and Pannonia; and, after receiving the Murius (*Muhr*), falls into the Danube E. of Mursa (*Essek*).

Drēcānum (Δρέκανον), a promontory on the W. side of the island Cos.

Drepānius, Latinus Pacātus, a friend of Ausonius, and a correspondent of Symmachus, delivered a panegyric on the emperor Theodosius, A. D. 391, after the victory of the latter over Maximus. This panegyric, which is extant, is the 11th in the collection of the *Panegyrici Veteres.*

Drĕpănum (Δρέπανον: Δρεπανεύς), that is, a sickle. 1. Also Drepăna (τὰ Δρέπανα), more rarely Drĕpăne (*Trapani*), a seaport town in the N. W. corner of Sicily, so called because the land on which it was built was in the form of a sickle. It was founded by the Carthaginian Hamilcar, at the commencement of the 1st Punic War, and was one of the chief naval stations of the Carthaginians. Under the Romans it was an important commercial town. It was here that Anchises died, according to Virgil. — **2.** A promontory in Achaia. [RHIUM.] — **3.** The ancient name of CORCYRA. — **4.** Also **Drěpǎne**, a town in Bithynia, on the Sinus Astacenus, the birth-place of Helena, mother of Constantine the Great, in whose honour it was called **Helenopolis**, and made an important place. In its neighbourhood were warm medicinal baths, which Constantine the Great frequently used in the latter part of his life.

Drepsa (Δρέψα, also Ἄδραψα, Δδραψα, Δράψα-κα: *Anderab* or *Inderab*), a town in the N.E. of Bactriana, on the frontiers of Sogdiana.

Drilae (Δρίλαι), a brave people in Pontus, on the frontiers of Colchis, near Trapezus.

Drilo, a river in Illyricum, flows into the Adriatic near Lissus.

Dromichaetes (Δρομιχαίτης), a king of the Getae, who took Lysimachus prisoner. [LYSIMACHUS.]

Dromos Achillěus. [ACHILLEUS DROMOS.]

Druentia (*Durance*), a large and rapid river in Gallia Narbonensis, rises in the Alps, and flows into the Rhone near Avenio (*Avignon*).

Drūna (*Drôme*), a small river in Gallia Narbonensis, rises in the Alps, and flows into the Rhone S. of Valencia (*Valence*).

Drusilla. 1. Livia, mother of the emperor Tiberius and wife of Augustus. [LIVIA.] — **2.** Daughter of Germanicus and Agrippina, married 1st to L. Cassius Longinus, and afterwards to M. Aemilius Lepidus ; but she lived in incestuous intercourse with her brother Caligula, whose passion for her exceeded all bounds. On her death, in A. D. 38, he commanded that she should be worshipped, by the name Panthea, with the same honours as Venus. — **3.** Daughter of Herodes Agrippa I., king of the Jews, married 1st Azizus, king of Emesa, whom she divorced, and 2ndly Felix, the procurator of Judaea. She was present with her husband when St. Paul preached before Felix in A. D. 60.

Drūsus, the name of a distinguished family of the Livia gens. It is said that one of the Livii acquired the cognomen Drusus for himself and his descendants by having slain in close combat one Drausus, a Gallic chieftain ; but this statement deserves little credit. — **1. M. Livius Drusus,** tribune of the plebs with C. Gracchus, B.C. 122. He was a staunch adherent of the aristocracy, and after putting his veto upon the laws proposed by Gracchus, he brought forward almost the very same measures, in order to gain popularity for the senate, and to impress the people with the belief that the optimates were their best friends. The success of this system earned for him the designation *patronus senatus*. Drusus was consul 112, obtained Macedonia as his province, and conquered the Scordisci. — **2. M. Livius Drusus,** son of No. 1, an eloquent orator, and a man of great energy and ability. He was tribune of the plebs, 91, in the consulship of L. Marcius Philippus and Sex. Julius Caesar. Although, like his father, he belonged to the aristocratical party, he meditated the most extensive and organic changes in the Roman state. To conciliate the people he renewed several of the measures of the Gracchi. He proposed and carried laws for the distribution of corn or for its sale at a low price, and ⸺

the assignation of public land. He also gained the support of the Latini and the Socii by promising to secure for them the Roman citizenship. Thus strengthened, he proposed to transfer the judicia from the equites to the senate ; but as a compensation to the former order, he further proposed that the senate, now reduced below the regular number of 300, should be reinforced by the introduction of an equal number of new members selected from the equites. This measure proved unsatisfactory to both parties. The Roman populace also were opposed to the Roman franchise being given to the Latins and the Socii. The senate, perceiving the dissatisfaction of all parties, voted that all the laws of Drusus, being carried against the auspices, were null and void from the beginning. Drusus now began to organise a formidable conspiracy against the government ; but one evening as he was entering the hall of his own house, he was stabbed and died a few hours afterwards. The assassin was never discovered, and no attempts were made to discover him. Caepio and Philippus were both suspected of having suborned the crime ; but Cicero attributes it to Q. Varius. The death of Drusus destroyed the hopes of the Socii, and was thus immediately followed by the Social War. — **3. Livius Drusus Claudianus,** father of Livia, who was the mother of the emperor Tiberius. He was one of the gens Claudia, and was adopted by a Livius Drusus. It was through this adoption that the Drusi became connected with the imperial family. The father of Livia, after the death of Caesar, espoused the cause of Brutus and Cassius, and, after the battle of Philippi (42), being proscribed by the conquerors, he killed himself in his tent. — **4. Nero Claudius Drusus,** commonly called by the moderns **Drusus Senior,** to distinguish him from No. 5, was the son of Tib. Claudius Nero and Livia, and younger brother of the emperor Tiberius. He was born in the house of Augustus 3 months after the marriage of Livia and Augustus, 38. Drusus, as he grew up, was more liked by the people than was his brother. His manners were affable, and his conduct without reproach. He married Antonia, the daughter of the triumvir, and his fidelity to his wife was a theme of admiration in a profligate age. He was greatly trusted by Augustus, who employed him in important offices. He carried on the war against the Germans, and penetrated far into the interior of the country. In 12 he drove the Sicambri and their allies out of Gaul, crossed the Rhine, then followed the course of the river down to the ocean, and subdued the Frisians. It was apparently during this campaign that Drusus dug a canal (*Fossa Drusiana*) from the Rhine near Arnheim to the Yssel, near Doesberg ; and he made use of this canal to sail from the Rhine into the ocean. In his 2nd campaign (11), Drusus subdued the Usipetes, invaded the country of the Sicambri, and passed on through the territory of the Cherusci as far as the Visurgis (*Weser*). On his return he was attacked by the united forces of the Germans, and defeated them with great slaughter. — In his 3rd campaign (10), he conquered the Chatti and other German tribes, and then returned to Rome, where he was made consul for the following year. — In his 4th campaign (9), which he carried on as consul, he advanced as far as the Albia (*Elbe*), sweeping every thing before him. It is said that he had resolved to cross the Elbe, but was deterred by the apparition of a woman of dimensions greater than human, who said to him in the Latin tongue, "Whither goest thou, insatiable Drusus? The Fates forbid thee to advance. Away! The end of thy deeds and thy life is nigh." On the return of the army to the Rhine, Drusus died in consequence of a fracture of his leg, which happened through a fall from his horse. Upon receiving tidings of the dangerous illness of Drusus, Tiberius immediately crossed the Alps, and after travelling with extraordinary speed arrived in time to close the eyes of his brother. Tiberius brought the body to Italy: it was burnt in the field of Mars, and the ashes deposited in the tomb of Augustus. — 5. **Drusus Caesar**, commonly called by modern writers Drusus Junior, was the son of the emperor Tiberius by his 1st wife, Vipsania. He married Livia, the sister of Germanicus. After the death of Augustus, A. D. 14, he was sent into Pannonia to quell the mutiny of the legions. In 15 he was consul, and in 16 he was sent into Illyricum: he succeeded in fomenting dissension among the Germanic tribes, and destroyed the power of Maroboduus. In 21 he was consul a 2nd time; and in 22 he received the *tribunicia potestas*, by which he was pointed out as the intended successor to the empire. But Sejanus, the favourite of Tiberius, aspired to the empire. He seduced Livia, the wife of Drusus, and persuaded her to become the murderer of her husband. A poison was administered to Drusus, which terminated his life by a lingering disease, that was supposed at the time to be the consequence of intemperance, A. D. 23. — 6. **Drusus**, 2nd son of Germanicus and Agrippina. After the death of Drusus, the son of Tiberius [No. 5], Drusus and his elder brother Nero became the heirs to the imperial throne. Sejanus therefore resolved to get rid of them both. He first engaged Drusus in the plots against his elder brother, which ended in the banishment and death of that prince. [NERO.] The turn of Drusus came next. He was accused in 30, and condemned to death as an enemy of the state. Tiberius kept him imprisoned for 3 years, and then starved him to death, 33.

Dryades. [NYMPHAE.]

Dryas (Δρύας), father of the Thracian king Lycurgus, who is hence called **Dryantides.**

Drymaea or **Drymus** (Δρυμαία, Δρυμός: Δρυμιεύς: Baba ?), a town in Phocis, a little S. of the Cephissus, was destroyed by Xerxes.

Drymus (Δρυμός). 1. See DRYMAEA. — 2. A strong place in Attica, on the frontiers of Boeotia.

Drymussa (Δρυμοῦσσα: Δρυμουσσαῖος), an island in the Hermaean gulf, off the coast of Ionia, opposite Clazomenae; given by the Romans to Clazomenae.

Dryope (Δρυόπη), daughter of king Dryops, and the playmate of the Hamadryades on Mt. Oeta. She was beloved by Apollo, who, to gain possession of her, metamorphosed himself into a tortoise. Dryope took the creature into her lap, whereupon the god changed himself into a serpent. The nymphs fled away in affright, and thus Apollo remained alone with Dryope. Soon after she married Andraemon, but became, by Apollo, the mother of AMPHISSUS, who built the town of Oeta, and a temple to Apollo. Dryope was afterwards carried off by the Hamadryades, and became a nymph.

Dryopes (Δρύοπες), a Pelasgic people, descended from a mythical ancestor Dryops, dwelt first in Thessaly, from the Spercheus to Parnassus, and afterwards in Doris, which was called from them **Dryopis** (Δρυοπίς). Driven out of Doris by the Dorians, they migrated to other countries, and settled in Peloponnesus, Euboea, and Asia Minor.

Dryops (Δρύοψ), son of the river-god Spercheus and the Danaid Polydora, or of Lycaon and Dia, the daughter of Lycaon, the mythical ancestor of the Dryopes.

Dryos Cephalae (Δρυὸς Κεφαλαί), a narrow pass of Mt. Cithaeron, between Athens and Plataeae.

Dubis (Doubs), a river in Gaul, rises in M. Jurassus (Jura), flows past Vesontio (Besançon), and falls into the Arar (Saône) near Cabillonum (Châlons).

Dubris Portus (Dover), a seaport town of the Cantii, in Britain: here was a fortress erected by the Romans against the Saxon pirates.

Ducas, Michael, a Byzantine historian, held a high office under Constantine XIII., the last emperor of Constantinople. After the capture of Constantinople, A. D. 1453, he fled to Lesbos. His history extends from the death of John VI. Palaeologus, 1355, to the capture of Lesbos by the Turks, 1462. The work is written in barbarous Greek, but gives a clear and impartial account of events. The best edition is by Bekker, Bonn, 1834.

Ducetius (Δουκέτιος), a chief of the Sicelians, or Sicels, the native tribes in the interior of Sicily, carried on a formidable war in the middle of the 5th century B. C. against the Greeks in the island. Having been at last defeated in a great battle by the Syracusans, he repaired to Syracuse as a suppliant, and placed himself at their mercy. The Syracusans spared his life, but sent him into an honourable exile at Corinth. He returned soon afterwards to Sicily, and founded the city of Calacte. He died about B. C. 440.

Duilius. 1. **M.,** tribune of the plebs B. C. 471. He was one of the chief leaders of the plebeians, and it was on his advice that the plebeians migrated from the Aventine to the Mons Sacer, just before the overthrow of the decemvirs. He was then elected tribune of the plebs a 2nd time, 449. — 2. **K.,** one of the decemvirs, 450, on whose overthrow he went into voluntary exile. —3. **C.,** consul 260, with Cn. Cornelius Scipio Asina, in the 1st Punic War. In this year the Romans built their first fleet, using for their model a Carthaginian vessel which had been thrown on the coast of Italy. The command of this fleet was given to Scipio, who was defeated by the Carthaginians off Lipara. Thereupon Duilius was entrusted with the command, and as he perceived the disadvantages under which the clumsy ships of the Romans were labouring, he devised the well-known grappling irons, by means of which the enemy's ships might be drawn towards his, and the sea-fight thus changed into a land-fight. By this means he gained a brilliant victory over the Carthaginian fleet near Mylae, and then prosecuted the war in Sicily with success, relieving Egesta, and taking Macella by assault. On his return to Rome, Duilius celebrated a splendid triumph, for it was the first naval victory that the Romans had ever gained, and the memory of it was perpetuated by a column which was erected in the forum, and adorned with the beaks of the conquered ships (Columna Rostrata). It is generally believed that the original inscription which adorned the basis of the column is still extant. It was dug out of the ground in the 16th century, in a mutilated condition, and it has since often been printed with attempts at restoration. There are, however, in that inscription some orthographical peculiarities, which suggest, that the present inscription is a later restoration of the original one. Duilius was further rewarded for this victory, by being permitted, whenever he returned home from a banquet at night, to be accompanied by a torch and a flute-player.

Dulgibini, a people in Germany, dwelt S.E. of the Angrivarii, on the W. bank of the Weser.

Dulichium. [ECHINADES.]

Dumnŏrix, a chieftain of the Aedui, conspired against the Romans, B.C. 58, but was then pardoned by Caesar in consequence of the entreaties of his brother, Divitiacus. When Caesar was going to Britain in 54, he suspected Dumnorix too much to leave him behind in Gaul, and he insisted therefore on his accompanying him. Dumnorix, upon this, fled from the Roman camp with the Aeduan cavalry, but was overtaken and slain.

Dunium. [DUROTRIGES.]

Dūra (τὰ Δοῦρα: Δουρηνός). 1. A town in Mesopotamia, on the Euphrates, not far from Circesium, founded by the Macedonians, and hence surnamed Nicanoris; also called Eurōpus (Εὐρωπός) by the Greeks. In the time of Julian it was deserted.—2. (*Dor*), a town in Assyria, on the Tigris.

Dūranius (*Dordogne*), a river in Aquitania, which falls into the Garumna.

Dūria (*Dora Baltea*), a river which rises in the S. of the Alps, flows through the country of the Salassi, bringing gold dust with it, and falls into the Po.

Dūris (Δοῦρις), of Samos, the historian, was a descendant of Alcibiades, and lived in the reign of Ptolemy Philadelphus. He obtained the tyranny of his native island, though it is unknown by what means. He wrote a considerable number of works, of which the most important was a history of Greece, from B.C. 370 to 281. He does not appear to have enjoyed any very great reputation as an historian among the ancients. His fragments have been collected by Hulleman, *Duridis Samii quae supersunt*, Traject. ad Rhen. 1841.

Dūrius (Δούριος, Δέριος: *Duero, Douro*), one of the chief rivers of Spain, rises among the Pelendones, at the foot of M. Idubeda near Numantia, and flows into the Atlantic; it was auriferous, and is navigable a long way from its mouth.

Durobrivae (*Rochester*), a town of the Cantii in Britain.

Durocasis (*Dreux*) a town of the Carnutes in Gallia Lugdunensis.

Durocatelauni. [CATALAUNI.]

Durocortorum (*Rheims*), the capital of the Remi in Gallia Belgica, and subsequently called Remi, was a populous and powerful town.

Duronia, a town in Samnium in Italy, W. of the Caudine passes.

Durotrīges, a people in Britain, in Dorsetshire and the W. of Somersetshire: their chief town was Dunium (*Dorchester*).

Durovernum or **Darvernum** (*Canterbury*), a town of the Cantii in Britain, afterwards called Cantuaria.

Dyardanes or **Oedanes** (*Brahmaputra*), a river in India, falls into the Ganges on the E. side.

Dȳmas (Δύμας), son of Aegimius, from whom the Dymanes, one of the 3 tribes of the Dorians, were believed to have derived their name.

Dȳmē or **Dymae** (Δύμη, Δῦμαι: Δυμαῖος, Dymaeus; nr. *Karavostasi*, Ru.), a town in the W of Achaia, near the coast; one of the 12 Achaean towns; it founded, along with Patrae, the 2nd Achaean league; and was at a later time colonised by the Romans.

Dyras (Δύρας), a small river in Phthiotis in Thessaly, falls into the Sinus Maliacus.

Dyrrhāchium (Δυρράχιον: Δυρράχιος, Δυρραχηνός, Dyrrachīnus: *Durazzo*), formerly called **Epidamnus** ('Επίδαμνος: 'Επιδάμνιος), a town in Greek Illyria, on a peninsula in the Adriatic sea. It was founded by the Corcyraeans, and received the name Epidamnus; but since the Romans regarded this name a bad omen, as reminding them of *damnum*, they changed it into Dyrrhachium, when they became masters of the country. Under the Romans it became an important place; it was the usual place of landing for persons who crossed over from Brundisium. Commerce and trade were carried on here with great activity, whence it is called *Taberna Adriae* by Catullus (xxxvi.15); and here commenced the great Egnatia Via, leading to the E. In the civil war it was the head-quarters of Pompey, who kept all his military stores here. In A.D. 345 it was destroyed by an earthquake.

Dysōrum (τὸ Δύσωρον), a mountain in Macedonia with gold mines, between Chalcidice and Odomantice.

Dyspontium (Δυσπόντιον: Δυσπόντιος), an ancient town of Pisatis in Elis, N. of the Alpheus, was destroyed by the Eleans; whereupon its inhabitants removed to Epidamnus and Apollonia.

E.

Ebŏra. 1. Or **Ebūra Cerealis,** a small town in Hispania Baetica, perhaps in the neighbourhood of the modern *Sta. Cruz.*—2. Surnamed **Liberalitas Julia** (*Evora*), a Roman municipium in Lusitania. —3. Or **Ebūra** (*S. Lucar de Barrameda*), a town in Hispania Baetica, near the mouth of the Baetis. —4. A fortress of the Edetani in Hispania Tarraconensis.

Eborācum or **Eburācum** (*York*), a town of the Brigantes in Britain, was made a Roman station by Agricola, and soon became the chief Roman settlement in the whole island. It was both a municipium and a colony. It was the head-quarters of the sixth legion, and the residence of the Roman emperors when they visited Britain. Here the emperors Septimius Severus and Constantius Chlorus died. Part of the ancient Roman walls still exist at York; and many Roman remains have been found in the modern city.

Eborolācum (*Evreule* on the river *Sioule*), a town in Aquitania.

Ebrodūnum (*Embrun*), a town in Gallia Narbonensis, in the Cottian Alps.

Ebūdae or **Hebūdae** (*Hebrides*), islands in the Western Ocean off Britain. They were 5 in number, according to Ptolemy, 2 called Ebudae, Maleus, Epidium, and Ricina.

Eburomāgus or **Hebromagus** (nr. *Bram* or *Villerazons*), a town in Gallia Narbonensis.

Eburōnes, a German people, who crossed the Rhine and settled in Gallia Belgica, between the Rhine and the Mosa (*Maas*) in a marshy and woody district. They were dependants (*clientes*) of the Treviri, and were in Caesar's time under the rule of Ambiorix and Cativolcus. Their insurrection against the Romans, B. C. 54, was severely punished by Caesar, and from this time they disappear from history.

Eburovices. [AULERCI.]

Ebusus or **Ebūsus** (*Iviza*), the largest of the Pityusae insulae, off the E. coast of Spain, reckoned by some writers among the Baleares. It was celebrated for its excellent figs. Its capital, also called Ebusus, was a civitas foederata, possessed an excellent harbour, was well built, and carried on a considerable trade.

Ecbătănă (τὰ Ἐκβάτανα, Ion. and Poët. Ἀγβάτανα: *Hamadan*), a great city, most pleasantly situated, near the foot of Mt. Orontes, in the N. of Great Media, was the capital of the Median kingdom, and afterwards the summer residence of the Persian and Parthian kings. Its foundation was more ancient than any historical record: Herodotus ascribes it to Deioces, and Diodorus to Semiramis. It had a circuit of 240 stadia, and was surrounded by 7 walls, each overtopping the one before it, and crowned with battlements of different colours: these walls no longer existed in the time of Polybius. The citadel, of great strength, was used as the royal treasury. Below it stood a magnificent palace, the tiles of which were silver, and the capitals, entablatures, and wainscotings, of silver and gold; treasures which the Seleucidae coined into money, to the amount of 4000 talents. The circuit of this palace was 7 stadia.

Ecetra (Ecetranus), an ancient town of the Volsci, and, according to Dionysius, the capital of this people, was destroyed by the Romans at an early period.

Echedŏrus (Ἐχέδωρος, in Herod. Ἐχείδωρος), a small river in Macedonia, rises in Crestonia, flows through Mygdonia, and falls into the Thermaic gulf.

Echělīdae (Ἐχελίδαι: Ἐχελίδης), an Attic demus E. of Munychia, called after a hero Echelus.

Echěmus (Ἔχεμος), son of Aëropus and grandson of Cepheus, succeeded Lycurgus as king of Arcadia. In his reign the Dorians invaded Peloponnesus, and Echemus slew, in single combat, Hyllus, the son of Hercules. In consequence of this battle, which was fought at the Isthmus, the Heraclidae were obliged to promise not to repeat their attempt upon Peloponnesus for 50 years.

Echestrătus (Ἐχέστρατος), king of Sparta, son of Agis I., and father of Labotas or Leobotes.

Echetla (Ἐχέτλα), a town in Sicily, W. of Syracuse in the mountains.

Echĕtus (Ἔχετος), a cruel king of Epirus. His daughter, Metope or Amphissa, who had yielded to her lover Aechmodicus, was blinded by her father, and Aechmodicus was cruelly mutilated.

Echidna (Ἔχιδνα), daughter of Tartarus and Ge, or of Chrysaor and Callirrhoë, or of Peiras and Styx. The upper part of her body was that of a beautiful maiden with black eyes, while the lower part was that of a serpent, of a vast size. She was a horrible, and blood-thirsty monster. She became by Typhon the mother of the Chimaera, of the many-headed dog Orthus, of the hundred-headed dragon who guarded the apples of the Hesperides, of the Colchian dragon, of the Sphinx, of Cerberus (hence called *Echidnaeus canis*), of Scylla, of Gorgon, of the Lernaean Hydra (*Echidna Lernaea*), of the eagle which consumed the liver of Prometheus, and of the Ne-

mean lion. She was killed in her sleep by Argus Panoptes. According to Hesiod she lived with Typhon in a cave in the country of the Arimi, but another tradition transported her to Scythia, where she became by Hercules the mother of Agathyrsus, Gelonus, and Scythes. (Herod. iv. 8—10.)

Echinădes (Ἐχινάδες or Ἐχῖναι: *Curzolari*), a group of small islands at the mouth of the Achelous, belonging to Acarnania, said to have been formed by the alluvial deposits of the Achelous. The legend related that they were originally Nymphs, who dwelt on the mainland at the mouth of the Achelous, and that on one occasion having forgotten to present any offerings to the god Achelous, when they sacrificed to the other gods, the river-god, in wrath, tore them away from the mainland with the ground on which they were sacrificing, carried them out to sea, and formed them into islands. — The Echinades appear to have derived their name from their resemblance to the Echinus or sea-urchin. — The largest of these islands was named **Dulichium** (Δουλίχιον). It is mentioned by Homer, and from it Meges, son of Phyleus, went to the Trojan War. At the present day it is united to the mainland.

Echion (Ἐχίων). 1. One of the 5 surviving Sparti who had grown up from the dragon's teeth, which Cadmus had sown. He married Agave, by whom he became the father of Pentheus: he assisted Cadmus in the building of Thebes.—2. Son of Hermes and Antianira, twin-brother of Erytus or Eurytus, with whom he took part in the Calydonian hunt, and in the expedition of the Argonauts. — 3. A celebrated Grecian painter, flourished B. C. 352. One of his most noted pictures was Semiramis passing from the state of a handmaid to that of a queen; in this picture the modesty of the new bride was admirably depicted. The picture in the Vatican, known as "the Aldobrandini Marriage," is supposed by some to be a copy from the "Bride" of Echion.

Echo (Ἠχώ), an Oread who, according to the legend related by Ovid, used to keep Juno engaged by incessantly talking to her, while Jupiter was sporting with the nymphs. Juno, however, found out the trick that was played upon her, and punished Echo by changing her into an echo, that is, a being with no control over its tongue, which is neither able to speak before anybody else has spoken, nor to be silent when somebody else has spoken. Echo in this state fell desperately in love with Narcissus; but as her love was not returned, she pined away in grief, so that in the end there remained of her nothing but her voice. (Ov. *Met.* iii. 356—401.)

Ecphantīdes (Ἐκφαντίδης), one of the earliest poets of the old Attic comedy, flourished about B. C. 460, a little before Cratinus. The meaning of the surname of Καπνίας, which was given to him by his rivals, seems to imply a mixture of subtilty and obscurity. He ridiculed the rudeness of the old Megaric comedy, and was himself ridiculed on the same ground by Cratinus and Aristophanes.

Edessa or **Antiochia Callirrhoë** (Ἔδεσσα, Ἀντιόχεια ἡ ἐπὶ Καλλιρρόῃ, or Ἀ. μιξοβάρβαρος: O. T. UR: *Urfah*), a very ancient city in the N. of Mesopotamia, the capital of Osroëne, and the seat of an independent kingdom from B. C. 137 to A. D. 216. [ABGARUS.] It stood on the river Scirtus or Bardesanes, which often inundated and damaged the city. It was here that Caracalla was murdered.

Having suffered by an earthquake in the reign of Justin I., the city was rebuilt and named Justinopolis. — The Edessa of Strabo is evidently a different place, namely the city usually called Bambyce or Hierapolis.

Edĕtāni or Sedĕtāni, a people in Hispania Tarraconensis, E. of the Celtiberi. Their chief towns were VALENCIA, SAGUNTUM, CAESAR-AUGUSTA, and Edeta, also called Liria (Lyria).

Edōni or Edōnes ('Ηδωνοί, 'Ηδῶνες), a Thracian people, between the Nestus and the Strymon. They were celebrated for their orgiastic worship of Bacchus ; whence Edōnis in the Latin poets signifies a female Bacchante, and Horace says (Carm. ii. 7. 26), Non ego sanius bacchabor Edonis.— The poets frequently use Edoni as synonymous with Thracians.

Eĕtĭon ('Ηετίων), king of-the Placian Thebé in -Cilicia, and father of Andromache, the wife of Hector. He and 7 of his sons were slain by Achilles, when the latter took Thebae.

Egelasta, a town of the Celtiberi in Hispania Tarraconensis.

    Egĕrĭa. [AEGERIA.]

    Egesta. [SEGESTA.]

Egnātĭa (Torre d' Anazzo), a town in Apulia, on the coast, called Gnatia by Horace (Sat. i. 5. 97), who speaks of it as Lymphis (i. e. Nymphis) iratis exstructa, probably on account of its bad or deficient supply of water. It was celebrated for its miraculous stone or altar, which of itself set on fire frankincense and wood ; a prodigy which afforded amusement to Horace and his friends, who looked upon it as a mere trick. — Egnatia owed its chief importance to being situated on the great high road from Rome to Brundisium. This road reached the sea at Egnatia, and from this town to Brundisium it bore the name of the Via Egnatia. The continuation of this road on the other side of the Adriatic from Dyrrhachium to Byzantium also bore the name of the Via Egnatia. It was the great military road between Italy and the E. Commencing at Dyrrhachium, it passed by Lychnidus, Heraclēa, Lyncestis, Edessa, Thessalonica, Amphipolis, Philippi, and traversing the whole of Thrace, finally reached Byzantium.

Egnātĭi, a family of Samnite origin, some of whom settled at Teanum. 1. GELLIUS EGNATIUS, leader of the Samnites in the 3rd Samnite war, fell in battle against the Romans, B.C. 295.— 2. MARIUS EGNATIUS, one of the leaders of the Italian allies in the Social War, was killed in battle, 89.— 3. M. EGNATIUS RUFUS, aedile 20 and praetor 19, was executed in the following year, in consequence of his having formed a conspiracy against the life of Augustus.— 4. P. EGNATIUS CELER. [BAREA.]

Eĭon ('Ηΐων: 'Ηΐονεύς: Contessa or Rendina), a town in Thrace, at the mouth of the Strymon, 25 stadia from Amphipolis, of which it was the harbour. Brasidas, after obtaining possession of Amphipolis, attempted to seize Eion also, but was prevented by the arrival of Thucydides with an Athenian fleet, B. C. 424.

Eĭōnes ('Ηϊόνες), a town in Argolis with a harbour, subject to Mycenae in the time of Homer, but not mentioned in later times.

Elaea ('Ελαία: Kazlu), an ancient city on the coast of Aeolis in Asia Minor, said to have been founded by Mnestheus, stood 12 stadia S. of the mouth of the Caïcus, and 120 stadia (or 16 Roman miles) from Pergamus, to which city, in the time of

the Pergamene kingdom, it served for a harbour (ἐπίνειον). It was destroyed by an earthquake in B. C. 90. The gulf on which it stood, which forms a part of the great Gulf of Adramyttium, was named after it Sinus Elaïticus ('Ελαϊτικὸς κόλπος, G. of Chandeli).

Elaeūs ('Ελαιοῦς, -οῦντος : 'Ελαιοῦσιος). 1. Or Elĕūs ('Ελεοῦς: Critia), a town on the S.E. point of the Thracian Chersonese, with a harbour and an heroum of Protesilaus.— 2. (Mesolonghi), a town in Aetolia, S. of Pleuron.— 3. A town in Argolis.— 4. A demus in Attica, belonging to the tribe Hippothoontis.

Elagăbălus, Roman emperor, A. D. 218—222, son of Julia Soemias and Varius Marcellus, was born at Emesa about 205, and was originally called VARIUS AVITUS BASSIANUS. While almost a child he became, along with his first cousin Alexander Severus, priest of Elagabalus, the Syro-Phoenician Sun-god, to whose worship a temple was dedicated in his native city. It was from this circumstance that he obtained the name Elagabalus, by which he is usually known. He owed his elevation to the purple to the intrigues of his grandmother Julia Maesa, who circulated the report that Elagabalus was the offspring of a secret commerce between Soemias and Caracalla, and induced the troops in Syria to salute him as their sovereign by the title of M. AURELIUS ANTONINUS, the 16th of May, 218. Macrinus forthwith marched against Elagabalus, but was defeated near Antioch, June 8th, and was shortly afterwards put to death. Elagabalus was now acknowledged as emperor by the senate, and in the following year came to Rome. The reign of this prince, who perished at the age of 18, after having occupied the throne nearly 4 years, was characterised throughout by an accumulation of the most fantastic folly and superstition, together with impurity so bestial that the particulars almost transcend the limits of credibility. In 221 he adopted his first cousin Alexander Severus, and proclaimed him Caesar. Having become jealous of Alexander, he attempted to put him to death, but was himself slain along with his mother Soemias by the soldiers, with whom Alexander was a great favourite.

Elāna. [AELANA.]

Elāra ('Ελάρα), daughter of Orchomenus or Minyas, bore to Zeus the giant Tityus. Zeus, from fear of Hera, concealed her under the earth.

Elatēa ('Ελάτεια: 'Ελατεύς). 1. (Nr. Elephtha Ru.), a town in Phocis, and the most important place in the country next to Delphi, was situated near the Cephissus in a fertile valley, which was an important pass from Thessaly to Boeotia. Elatea was thus frequently exposed to hostile attacks. It is said to have been founded by Elatus, son of Arcas.— 2. A town in Pelasgiotis in Thessaly, near Gonni.— 3. Or Elatrēa, a town in Epirus, near the sources of the Cocytus.

Elătus ("Ελατος). 1. Son of Arcas and Leanira, king of Arcadia, husband of Laodice, and father of Stymphalus, Aepytus, Cyllen, and Pereus. He resided on mount Cyllene, and went from thence to Phocis, where he founded the town of Elatea.— 2. A prince of the Lapithae at Larissa in Thessaly, husband of Hippea, and father of Caeneus and Polyphemus. He is sometimes confounded with the Arcadian Elatus.

Elăver (Allier), subsequently Elaris or Elauris, a river in Aquitania, a tributary of the Liger.

Elbo ('Eλεώ), an island on the coast of the Delta of Egypt, in the midst of the marshes between the Phatnitic and the Tanitic mouths of the Nile, was the retreat of the blind Pharoah Anysis from the Aethiopian Sabacon, and afterwards of Amyrtaeus from the Persians.

Elea. [VELIA.]

Electra ('Hλέκτρα), i. e. the bright or brilliant one. 1. Daughter of Oceanus and Tethys, wife of Thaumas, and mother of Iris and the Harpies, Aëllo and Ocypete. — 2. Daughter of Atlas and Pleïone, one of the 7 Pleiades, and by Zeus mother of Iasion and Dardanus. According to an Italian tradition, she was the wife of the Italian king Corythus, by whom she had a son Iasion; whereas by Zeus she was the mother of Dardanus. It was through her means, according to another tradition, that the Palladium came to Troy; and when she saw the city of her son Dardanus perishing in flames, she tore out her hair for grief, and was placed among the stars as a comet. According to others, Electra and her 6 sisters were placed among the stars as the 7 Pleiades, and lost their brilliancy on seeing the destruction of Ilium. — 3. Sister of Cadmus, from whom the Electrian gate at Thebes was said to have received its name.—4. Daughter of Agamemnon and Clytaemnestra, also called Laodice, sister of Iphigenia and Orestes. After the murder of her father by her mother, she saved the life of her young brother Orestes, by sending him under the protection of a slave to king Strophius at Phanote in Phocis, who had the boy educated together with his own son Pylades. When Orestes had grown up to manhood, Electra excited him to avenge the death of Agamemnon, and assisted him in slaying their mother, Clytaemnestra. [ORESTES.] After the death of the latter, Orestes gave her in marriage to his friend Pylades. The history and character of Electra form the subject of the " Choëphori " of Aeschylus, the " Electra " of Euripides, and the " Electra " of Sophocles.

Electrides Insulae. [ERIDANUS.]

Electryon ('Hλεκτρύων), son of Perseus and Andromeda, king of Mycenae, husband of Anaxo, and father of Alcmene, the wife of Amphitryon. For details see AMPHITRYON.

Electryone ('Hλεκτρυώνη). 1. Daughter of Helios and Rhodos. — 2. A patronymic from Electryon, given to his daughter, Alcmene.

Eleon ('Eλέων), a town in Boeotia, near Tanagra.

Eleos ('Eλεος), the personification of pity or mercy, worshipped by the Athenians alone.

Elephantine or **Elephantis** ('Eλεφαντίνη, 'Eλεφαντίς: Jezirah-el-Zahir, or Jezirah-el-Assouan), an island in the Nile, with a city of the same name, opposite to Syene, and 7 stadia below the Little Cataract, was the frontier station of Egypt towards Ethiopia, and was strongly garrisoned under the Persians and the Romans. The island was extremely fertile, the vine and the fig-tree never shedding their leaves: it had also great quarries. Among the most remarkable objects in it were the temple of Cnuphis and a Nilometer; and it is still celebrated for the ruins of its rock-hewn temples.

Elephantis, a Greek poetess under the early Roman emperors, wrote certain amatory works (molles Elephantidos libelli), which are referred to by Martial and Suetonius.

Elephenor ('Eλεφήνωρ), son of Chalcodon and of Imenarete or Melanippe, and prince of the Abantes in Euboea, whom he led against Troy. He was one of the suitors of Helen; he was killed before Troy by Agenor.

Eleusis ('Eλευσίς, later 'Eλευσίν: 'Eλευσίνιος: Leosina or Lessina), a town and demus of Attica, belonging to the tribe Hippothoontis, was situated N.W. of Athena, on the coast near the frontiers of Megara. It possessed a magnificent temple of Demeter, and it gave its name to the great festival and mysteries of the Eleusinia, which were celebrated in honour of Demeter and Persephone. The Eleusinia were originally a festival peculiar to Eleusis, which was an independent state; but after the Eleusinians had been conquered by the Athenians in the reign of Erechtheus, according to tradition, the Eleusinia became a festival common to both cities, though the superintendence of the festival remained with the descendants of Eumolpus, the king of Eleusis. For an account of the festival see Dict. of Antiq. art. Eleusinia.

Eleutherae ('Eλευθεραί: 'Eλευθερεύς), a town in Attica on the frontiers of Boeotia, originally belonged to the Boeotian confederacy, and afterwards voluntarily united itself to Attica.

Eleutherius ('Eλευθέριος), a surname of Zeus, as the Deliverer. (Dict. of Ant. art. Eleutheria.)

Eleutherna ('Eλευθέρνα: 'Eλευθερναῖος), a town in the interior of Crete.

Eleutherus ('Eλεύθερος: Nahr-el-Kebir, i. e. Great River), a river forming the boundary between Syria and Phoenice, rose in Mt. Bargylus, the N. prolongation of Lebanon, and fell into the sea between Antaradus and Tripolis.

Elicius, a surname of Jupiter at Rome, where king Numa dedicated to Jupiter Elicius an altar on the Aventine. The origin of the name is referred to the Etruscans, who by certain prayers and sacrifices called forth (eliciebant or evocabant) lightning, or invited Jupiter to send lightning. The object of calling down lightning was according to Livy's explanation to elicit prodigies (ad prodigia elicienda, Liv. i. 20.).

Elimberrum. [AUSCI.]

Elimea, **-ia**, or **Elimiotis** ('Eλίμεια, 'Eλιμία, 'Eλιμιῶτις), a district of Macedonia, on the frontiers of Epirus and Thessaly, originally belonged to Illyria, and was bounded by the Cambunian mountains on the S. and the Tymphaean mountains on the W. Its inhabitants, the Elimaei ('Eλειμιῶται), were Epirots.

Elis ('Hλις, Dor. ᾽Αλις, 'Hλεία: 'Hλεῖος, Dor. ᾽Αλιος, whence Alii in Plautus), a country on the W. coast of Peloponnesus, bounded by Achaia on the N., Arcadia on the E., Messenia on the S., and the Ionian sea on the W. The country was fertile, watered by the ALPHEUS and its tributaries, and is said to have been the only country in Greece which produced flax. The PENEUS is the only other river in Elis of any importance. Elis was divided into 3 parts:—1. **Elis Proper** or **Hollow Elis** (ἡ Κοίλη 'Hλις), the N. part, watered by the Peneus, of which the capital was also called Elis.— 2. **Pisatis** (ἡ Πισᾶτις), the middle portion, of which the capital was PISA.— 3. **Triphylia** (ἡ Τριφυλία), the S. portion, of which PYLOS was the capital, lay between the Alpheus and the Neda. — In the heroic times we find the kingdom of Nestor and the Pelīdae in the S. of Elis; while the N. of the country was inhabited by the Epeans ('Eπειοί), with whom some Aetolian tribes were mingled. On the conquest of Peloponnesus by the Heraclidae, the Aetolian chief Oxylus received Elis as his share of the conquest ; and it was the union of his Aetolian and Dorian followers with the Epeans, which formed the subsequent population of the country, under the general name of Eleans. Elis owed its importance in Greece to the worship of Zeus at Olympia near Pisa, in honour of whom a splendid festival was held every 4 years. [OLYMPIA.] In consequence of this festival being common to the whole of Greece, the country of Elis was declared sacred, and its inhabitants possessed priestly privileges. Being exempt from war and the dangers of invasion, the Eleans became prosperous and wealthy ; their towns were unwalled and their country was richly cultivated. The prosperity of their country was ruined by the Peloponnesian War ; the Athenians were the first to disregard the sanctity of the country ; and from that time it frequently had to take part in the other contests of the Greeks. — The town of Elis was situated on the Peneus, and was built at the time of the Persian War by the inhabitants of 8 villages, who united together, and thus formed one town. It originally had no walls, being sacred like the rest of the country, but subsequently it was fortified. The inhabitants of Elis formed a close alliance with the Spartans, and by their means destroyed the rival city of Pisa, and became the ruling city in the country, B. C. 572. In the Peloponnesian War they quarrelled with the Spartans, because the latter had espoused the cause of Lepraeum, which had revolted from Elis. The Eleans retaliated upon the Spartans by excluding them from the Olympic games.

Eliso. [ALISO.]

Elissa. [DIDO.]

Ellŏpia ('Ελλοπία). 1. A district in the N. of Euboea, near the promontory Cenaeum, with a town of the same name which disappeared at an early period : the whole island of Euboea is sometimes called Ellopia. — **2.** An ancient name of the district about Dodona in Epirus.

Elŏnē ('Ηλώνη), a town of the Perrhaebi in Thessaly, afterwards called Limone (Λειμώνη).

Elpēnor ('Ελπήνωρ), one of the companions of Ulysses, who were metamorphosed by Circe into swine, and afterwards back into men. Intoxicated with wine, Elpenor one day fell asleep on the roof of Circe's residence, and in his attempt to rise he fell down and broke his neck. When Ulysses was in the lower world, he met the shade of Elpenor, who implored him to burn his body. After his return to the upper world, Ulysses complied with this request of his friend.

Elpĭnĭcē ('Ελπινίκη), daughter of Miltiades, and sister of Cimon, married Callias. [CALLIAS.]

Elusātes, a people in Aquitania in the interior of the country. Their chief town was **Elūsa.** (Nr. Euse or Eause.) It was the birthplace of Rufinus, the minister of Arcadius.

Elymaei, Elymi. [ELYMAIS.]

Elymāis, a district of Susiana, extending from the river Eulaeus on the W. to the Oroatis on the E., derived its name from the Elymaei or Elymi ('Ελυμαῖοι, 'Ελυμοι), a warlike and predatory people, who are also found in the mountains of Great Media : in the Persian armies they served as archers. These Elymaei were probably among the most ancient inhabitants of the country N. of the head of the Persian Gulf: in the O. T. Susiana is called Elam.

Elymi. [ELYMUS.]

Elymiōtis. [ELIMEA.]

Elymus ('Ελυμος), a Trojan, natural son of Anchises and brother of Eryx. Previous to the emigration of Aeneas, Elymus and Aegestus had fled from Troy to Sicily, and had settled on the banks of the river Crimisus. When afterwards Aeneas also arrived there, he built for them the towns of Aegesta and Elyme. The Trojans who settled in that part of Sicily called themselves Elymi, after Elymus.

Elyrus ('Ελυρος), a town in the W. of Crete, S. of Cydonia.

Elysium ('Ηλύσιον πέδιον, later simply 'Ηλύσιον), the Elysian fields. In Homer (Od. iv. 563) Elysium forms no part of the realms of the dead ; he places it on the W. of the earth, near Ocean, and describes it as a happy land, where there is neither snow, nor cold, nor rain, and always fanned by the delightful breezes of Zephyrus. Hither favoured heroes, like Menelaus, pass without dying, and live happy under the rule of Rhadamanthys. — The Elysium of Hesiod and Pindar are in the Isles of the Blessed (μακάρων νῆσοι), which they place in the Ocean. From these legends arose the fabulous island of ATLANTIS. — The Elysium of Virgil is part of the lower world, and the residence of the shades of the Blessed.

Emathia ('Ημαθία: 'Ημαθιεύς), a district of Macedonia, between the Haliacmon and the Axius, formerly part of Paeonia, and the original seat of the Macedonian monarchy. The poets frequently give the name of Emathia to the whole of Macedonia, and sometimes even to the neighbouring Thessaly.

Emathides, the 9 daughters of Pierus, king of Emathia.

Emathion ('Ημαθίων), son of Tithonus and Eos, brother of Memnon, was slain by Hercules.

Embŏlima ('Εμβόλιμα), a city of the Paropamisadae in N. India, near the fortress of Aornos, 16 days' march from the Indus. (Q. Curt.)

Emĕsa or **Emissa** ('Εμεσα, 'Εμισσα: 'Εμεσηνός : Hums or Homs), a city of Syria, on the E. bank of the Orontes, in the province of Apamene, but afterwards the capital of Phoenice Libanesia, was in Strabo's time the residence of independent Arabian princes ; but under Caracalla it was made a colony with the Jus Italicum. It is a remarkable place in the history of the Roman empire, being the native city of Julia Domna, the wife of Septimius Severus, of Elagabalus, who exchanged the high priesthood of the celebrated temple of the Sun in this city for the imperial purple, and of the emperor Alexander Severus ; and also the scene of the decisive battle between Aurelian and Zenobia, A. D. 273.

Emmĕnĭdae ('Εμμενίδαι), a princely family at Agrigentum, which traced their origin to the mythical hero Polynices. Among its members we know Emmenides (from whom the family derived its name) the father of Aenesidamus, whose sons Theron and Xenocrates are celebrated by Pindar as victors at the great games of Greece.

Emōdi Montes, or -us, or -es, or -on (τὰ 'Ημωδὰ ὄρη, τὸ 'Ημωδὸν ὄρος, or ὁ 'Ημωδός : Himalaya M.), a range of mountains N. of India, forming the prolongation E.wards of the Paropamisus.

Empĕdŏcles ('Εμπεδοκλῆς), of Agrigentum in Sicily, flourished about B. C. 444. Although he was descended from an ancient and wealthy family, he joined the revolution in which Thrasydaeus, the son and successor of Theron, was expelled. His zeal in the establishment of political equality is said to have been manifested by his magnanimous support of the poor, by his severity in persecuting the overbearing conduct of the aristocrats, and in his declining the sovereignty which was offered to him. His brilliant oratory, his penetrating knowledge of nature, and the reputation of his marvellous powers, which he had acquired by curing diseases, by his successful exertions in removing marshy districts and in averting epidemics and obnoxious winds, spread a lustre around his name. He was called a magician (γόης), and he appears to have attributed to himself miraculous powers. He travelled in Greece and Italy, and made some stay at Athens. His death is said to have been marvellous, like his life. One tradition represented him as having been removed from the earth, like a divine being ; and another related that he threw himself into the flames of mount Aetna, that by his sudden disappearance he might be believed to be a god ; but it was added that the volcano threw up one of his sandals, and thus revealed the manner of his death. The rhetorician Gorgias was a disciple of Empedocles. — The works of Empedocles were all in verse. The two most important were a didactic poem on nature (Περὶ Φύσεως), of which considerable fragments are extant, and a poem, entitled Καθαρμοί, which seems to have recommended good moral conduct as the means of averting epidemics and other evils. Lucretius, the greatest of all didactic poets, speaks of Empedocles with enthusiasm, and evidently makes him his model. Empedocles was acquainted with the theories of the Eleatics and the Pythagoreans ; but he did not adopt the fundamental principles of either school, although he agreed with the latter in his belief in the migration of souls, and in a few other points. With the Eleatics he agreed in thinking that it was impossible to conceive any thing arising out of nothing. Aristotle with justice mentions him among the Ionic physiologists, and places him in very close relation to the atomistic philosophers and to Anaxagoras. Empedocles first established the number of 4 elements, which he called the roots of things.

Empŏriae or **Emporium** ('Ἐμπορίαι, 'Ἐμπορεῖον, 'Ἐμπόριον : 'Ἐμπορίτης : *Ampurias*), a town of the Indigetes in Hispania Tarraconensis near the Pyrenees, was situated on the river Clodianus, which formed the harbour of the town. It was founded by the Phocaeans from Massilia, and was divided into 2 parts, at one time separated from each other by a wall : the part near the coast being inhabited by the Greeks, and the part towards the interior by the Indigetes. It was subsequently colonised by Julius Caesar. Its harbour was much frequented : here Scipio Africanus first landed when he came to Spain in the 2nd Punic War.

Empŭlum (*Ampiglione ?*), a small town in Latium, near Tibur.

Empūsa ('Ἔμπουσα), a monstrous spectre, which was believed to devour human beings. It could assume different forms, and was sent by Hecate to frighten travellers. It was believed usually to appear with one leg of brass and the other of an ass, whence it was called ὀνοσκελίς or ὀνοκώλη. The Lamiae and Mormolyceia, who assumed the form of handsome women for the purpose of attracting young men, and then sucked their blood like vampyrs and ate their flesh, were reckoned among the Empusae.

Enarĕphŏrus ('Ἐναρήφορος), son of Hippocoön, a passionate suitor of Helen, when she was yet quite young. Tyndareus, therefore, entrusted the maiden to the care of Theseus. Enarephorus had a heroum at Sparta.

Encĕlădus ('Ἐγκέλαδος), son of Tartarus and Ge, and one of the hundred-armed giants who made war upon the gods. He was killed, according to some, by a flash of lightning, by Zeus, who buried him under mount Aetna ; according to others, Athena killed him with her chariot, or threw upon him the island of Sicily.

Enchĕles ('Ἐγχελεῖς, also 'Ἐγχελέαι, 'Ἐγχέλιοι), an Illyrian tribe.

Endoeus ('Ἔνδοιος), an Athenian statuary, is called a disciple of Daedalus, whom he is said to have accompanied on his flight from Crete. This statement must be taken to express, not the time at which he lived, but the style of art which he practised. It is probable that he lived in the time of Pisistratus and his sons, about B. c. 560.

Endȳmĭon ('Ἐνδυμίων), a youth distinguished by his beauty, and renowned in ancient story for his perpetual sleep. Some traditions about Endymion refer us to Elis, and others to Caria, and others again are a combination of the two. According to one set of legends, he was a son of Aëthlius and Calyce, or of Zeus and Calyce, and succeeded Aëthlius in the kingdom of Elis. Others related that he had come from Elis to mount Latmus in Caria, whence he is called the Latmian (*Latmius*). As he slept on Latmus, his surprising beauty warmed the cold heart of Selene (the moon), who came down to him, kissed him, and lay by his side. His eternal sleep on Latmus is assigned to different causes ; but it was generally believed that Selene had sent him to sleep, that she might be able to kiss him without his knowledge. By Selene he had 50 daughters. There is a beautiful statue of a sleeping Endymion in the British Museum.

Engȳum ('Ἔγγυον or 'Ἔγγυον: 'Ἐγγύινος, Enguinus: *Gangi*), a town in the interior of Sicily near the sources of the Monalus, was originally a town of the Siculi, but is said to have been colonised by the Cretans under Minos: it possessed a celebrated temple of the great mother of the gods.

Enīpeus ('Ἐνιπεύς). 1. A river in Thessaly, rises in Mt. Othrys, receives the Apidanus near Pharsalus, and flows into the Peneus. Poseidon assumed the form of the god of this river in order to obtain possession of Tyro, who was in love with Enipeus. She became by Poseidon the mother of Pelias and Neleus. Ovid relates (*Met.* vi. 116) that Neptune (Poseidon) having assumed the form of Enipeus, became by Iphimedia the father of Otus and Ephialtes. — 2. A small river in Pisatis (Elis) flows into the Alpheus near its mouth. — 3. A small river in Macedonia, which rises in Olympus.

Enna or **Henna** ('Ἔννα: 'Ἐνναῖος: *Castro Giovanni*), an ancient and fortified town of the Siculi in Sicily, on the road from Catana to Agrigentum, said to be the centre of the island (ὀμφαλὸς Σικελίας). It was surrounded by fertile plains, which bore large crops of wheat ; it was one of the chief seats of the worship of Demeter (Ceres), and possessed a celebrated temple of this goddess. According to later tradition it was in a flowery mea-

Dioscuri (Castor and Pollux).
(From a Coin in the British Museum.) Page 228.

Dioscuri (Castor and Pollux).
(Millin. Gal. Myth., pl. 108.) Page 228.

Dirce. (Group at Naples.)
(Maffei, pl. 48.) Pages 229, 45.

Eros (Cupid) whetting his Darts.
(De la Chausse, Gemme Antiche.)

Eros (Cupid).
(Museum Capitolinum, vol. 4, tav. 57.)

Eros (Cupid). (From a Gem.)

Adventures of Dionysus (Bacchus).
(From the Choragic Monument of Lysicrates.) See illustrations opposite pp. 224, 227.

[To face p. 240.

Decius, Roman Emperor, A.D. 249—251. Page 209.

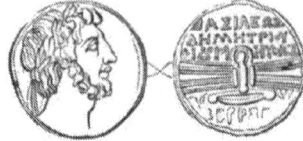

Demetrius III. Eucaerus, King of Syria, ob. B.C. 84.
Page 214.

Deiotarus, Tetrarch of Galatia. Page 209.

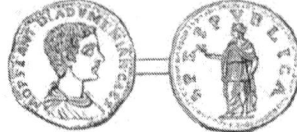

Diadumenianus, Roman Caesar, A.D. 217.

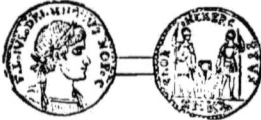

Delmatius, Roman Caesar, ob. A.D. 337. Page 210.

Diocletianus, Roman Emperor, A.D. 284—305. Page 220.

Demetrius Poliorcetes, King of Macedonia, ob. B.C. 283.
Page 213.

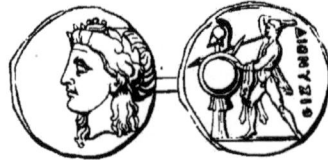

Dionysius of Heraclea, B.C. 306. Page 225.

Demetrius I. Soter, King of Syria, ob. B.C. 150.
Pages 213, 214.

Domitia, wife of Domitian. Page 230.

Demetrius II. Nicator, King of Syria, ob. B.C. 125. Page 214.
To face p. 241.

Domitian, Roman Emperor, A.D. 81—96. Pages 230, 231.

dow in the neighbourhood of Enna that Pluto carried off Proserpine, and the cave was shown through which the god passed as he carried off his prize. Its importance gradually declined from the time of the 2nd Punic war, when it was severely punished by the Romans, because it had attempted to revolt from the Carthaginians.

Ennius, Q., the Roman poet, was born at Rudiae, in Calabria, B. C. 239. He was a Greek by birth, but a subject of Rome, and served in the Roman armies. In 204 Cato, who was then quaestor, found Ennius in Sardinia, and brought him in his train to Rome. In 189 Ennius accompanied M. Fulvius Nobilior during the Aetolian campaign, and shared his triumph. Through the son of Nobilior, Ennius, when far advanced in life, obtained the rights of a Roman citizen. He dwelt in a humble house on the Aventine, and maintained himself by acting as a preceptor to the youths of the Roman nobles. He lived on terms of the closest intimacy with the elder Scipio Africanus. He died 169, at the age of 70. He was buried in the sepulchre of the Scipios, and his bust was allowed a place among the effigies of that noble house. Ennius was regarded by the Romans as the father of their poetry (*alter Homerus*, Hor. *Ep.* ii. 1. 50). Cicero calls him *Summus poëta noster*; and Virgil was not ashamed to borrow many of his thoughts, and not a few of his expressions. All the works of Ennius are lost with the exception of a few fragments. His most important work was an epic poem, in dactylic hexameters, entitled *Annalium Libri* XVIII., being a history of Rome, commencing with the loves of Mars and Rhea, and reaching down to his own times. The beautiful history of the kings in Livy may have been taken from Ennius. No great space, however, was allotted to the earlier records, for the contest with Hannibal, which was described with great minuteness, commenced with the 7th book, the first Punic war being passed over altogether. He wrote numerous tragedies, which appear to have been all translations or adaptations from the Greek, the metres of the originals being in most cases closely imitated. He wrote also a few comedies, and several other works, such as *Satirae*, composed in a great variety of metres, from which circumstance they probably received their name; a didactic poem, entitled *Epicharmus*; a panegyric on Scipio; Epigrams, &c. The best collection of the fragments of Ennius is by Hieronymus Columna, Neapol. 4to. 1590, reprinted with considerable additions, by Hesselius, Amstel. 4to. 1707.

Enōpe ('Ενόπη), a town in Messenia, mentioned by Homer, supposed to be the same as GERENIA.

Entella ('Εντελλα: Entellinus, Entellensis: *Entella*), an ancient town of the Sicani in the interior of the island on the W. side, said to have been founded by Entellus, one of the companions of the Trojan Aegestus. It was subsequently seized and peopled by the Campanian mercenaries of Dionysius.

Enyalius ('Ενυάλιος), the Warlike, frequently occurs in the Iliad (never in the Odyssey) as an epithet of Ares. At a later time Enyalius and Ares were distinguished as 2 different gods of war; Enyalius was looked upon as a son of Ares and Enyo, or of Cronos and Rhea. The name is evidently derived from ENYO.

Enyo ('Ενυώ), the goddess of war, who delights in bloodshed and the destruction of towns, and accompanies Ares in battles. Respecting the Roman goddess of war, see BELLONA.

Eordaea ('Εορδαία, also 'Εορδία), a district and town in the N. W. of Macedonia, inhabited by the **Eordi** ('Εορδοί, also 'Εορδαίοι).

Eös ('Ηώς, Att. "Εως), in Latin **Aurōra**, the goddess of the morning red, daughter of Hyperion and Thia or Euryphassa; or of Pallas, according to Ovid. At the close of every night she rose from the couch of her spouse Tithonus, and on a chariot drawn by the swift horses Lampus and Phaëton she ascended up to heaven from the river Oceanus, to announce the coming light of the sun to the gods as well as to mortals. In the Homeric poems Eos not only announces the coming Sun, but accompanies him throughout the day, and her career is not complete till the evening; hence she came to be regarded as the goddess of the daylight, and was completely identified by the tragic writers with Hemera. She carried off several youths distinguished for their beauty, such as ORION, CEPHALUS, and TITHONUS, whence she is called by Ovid *Tithonia conjux*. She bore Memnon to Tithonus. [MEMNON.] By Astraeus she became the mother of Zephyrus, Boreas, Notus, Heosphorus, and other stars.

Epaminondas ('Επαμεινώνδας, 'Επαμινώνδας), the Theban general and statesman, son of Polymnis, was born and reared in poverty, though his blood was noble. His close and enduring friendship with Pelopidas is said to have originated in the campaign in which they served together on the Spartan side against Mantinea, where Pelopidas having fallen in a battle, apparently dead, Epaminondas protected his body at the imminent risk of his own life, B. C. 385. After the Spartans had been expelled from Thebes, 379, Epaminondas took an active part in public affairs. In 371 he was one of the Theban commanders at the battle of Leuctra, so fatal to the Lacedaemonians, in which the success of Thebes is said to have been owing mainly to the tactics of Epaminondas. He it was who most strongly urged the giving battle, while he employed all the means in his power to raise the courage of his countrymen, not excluding even omens and oracles, for which, when unfavourable, he had but recently expressed his contempt. In 369 he was one of the generals in the 1st invasion of Peloponnesus by the Thebans; and before leaving Peloponnesus he restored the Messenians to their country and established a new city, named Messene. On their return home Epaminondas and Pelopidas were impeached by their enemies, on a capital charge of having retained their command beyond the legal term. The fact itself was true enough; but they were both honourably acquitted, Epaminondas having expressed his willingness to die if the Thebans would record that he had been put to death because he had humbled Sparta and taught his countrymen to face and to conquer her armies. In 368 he again led a Theban army into the Peloponnesus, but did not advance far, and, on his return, was repulsed by Chabrias in an attack which he made on Corinth. In the same year we find him serving, but not as general, in the Theban army which was sent into Thessaly to rescue Pelopidas from Alexander of Pherae, and which was saved from utter destruction only by the ability of Epaminondas. In 367 he was sent at the head of another force to release Pelopidas, and accomplished his object without even striking a blow, and by

R

the mere prestige of his name. In 366 he invaded the Peloponnesus for the 3rd time, and in 362 for the 4th time. In the latter year he gained a brilliant victory over the Lacedaemonians at Mantinēa ; but in the full career of victory he received a mortal wound. He was told that his death would follow directly on the javelin being extracted from the wound ; and he would not allow this to be done till he had been assured that his shield was safe, and that the victory was with his countrymen. It was a disputed point by whose hand he fell : among others, the honour was assigned to Gryllus, the son of Xenophon. Epaminondas was one of the greatest men of Greece. He raised Thebes to the supremacy of Greece, which she lost almost as soon as he died. Both in public and in private life he was distinguished by integrity and uprightness, and he carried into daily practice the lessons of philosophy, of which he was an ardent student.

Epaphrŏdītus ('Επαφρόδιτος). 1. A freedman and favourite of the emperor Nero. He assisted Nero in killing himself, and he was afterwards put to death by Domitian. The philosopher Epictetus was his freedman.—**2. M. Mettīus Epaphrodītus,** of Chaeronea, a Greek grammarian, the slave and afterwards the freedman of Modestus, the praefect of Egypt. He subsequently went to Rome, where he resided in the reign of Nero and down to the time of Nerva. He was the author of several grammatical works and commentaries.

Epăphus ("Επαφος), son of Zeus and Io, born on the river Nile, after the long wanderings of his mother. He was concealed by the Curetes, at the request of Hera, but was discovered by Io in Syria. He subsequently became king of Egypt, married Memphis, a daughter of Nilus, or, according to others, Cassiopea, and built the city of Memphis.. He had a daughter Libya, from whom Libya (Africa) received its name.

Epēi. [ELIS.]

Epētĭum ('Επέτιον : nr. *Strobrecz*, Ru.), a town of the Lisaii in Dalmatia with a good harbour.

Epēus ('Επειός). 1. Son of Endymion, king in Elis, from whom the Epei are said to have derived their name.—**2.** Son of Panopeus, went with 30 ships from the Cyclades to Troy. He built the wooden horse with the assistance of Athena.

Ephēsus ("Εφεσος : 'Εφέσιος : Ru. near *Ayasaluk*, i. e. "Αγιος Θεόλογος, the title of St. John), the chief of the 12 Ionian cities on the coast of Asia Minor, was said to have been founded by Carians and Leleges, and to have been taken possession of by Androclus, the son of Codrus, at the time of the great Ionian migration. It stood a little S. of the river Caÿster, near its mouth, where a marshy plain, extending S. from the river, is bounded by two hills, Prion or Lepre on the E., and Coressus on the S. The city was built originally on Mt. Coressus, but, in the time of Croesus, the people transferred their habitations to the valley, whence Lysimachus, the general of Alexander, compelled them again to remove to M. Prion. On the N. side of the city was a lake, communicating with the Caÿster, and forming the inner harbour, now a marsh ; the outer harbour (πάνορμος) was formed by the mouth of the river. In the plain, E. of the lake, and N.E. of the city, beyond its walls, stood the celebrated temple of Artemis, which was built in the 6th century B. C., by an architect named Chersiphron, and, after being burnt down by Herostratus in the night on which

Alexander the Great was born (Oct. 13—14, B.C. 356), was restored by the joint efforts of all the Ionian states, and was regarded as one of the wonders of the world : nothing now remains of the temple, except some traces of its foundations. The temple was also celebrated as an asylum, till Augustus deprived it of that privilege. The other buildings at Ephesus, of which there are any ruins, are the agora, theatre, odeum; stadium, gymnasium, and baths, temples of Zeus Olympius and of Julius Caesar, and a large building near the inner harbour: the foundations of the walls may also be traced.—With the rest of Ionia, Ephesus fell under the power successively of Croesus, the Persians, the Macedonians, and the Romans. It was always very flourishing, and became even more so as the other Ionian cities decayed. It was greatly favoured by its Greek rulers, especially by Lysimachus, who, in honour of his second wife, gave it her name, Arsinoë, which, however, it did not long retain. Attalus II. Philadelphus constructed docks for it, and improved its harbours. Under the Romans it was the capital of the province of Asia, and by far the greatest city of Asia Minor. It is conspicuous in the early history of the Christian Church, both St. Paul and St. John having laboured in it, and addressed epistles to the church of Ephesus ; and at one time its bishop possessed the rank and power of a patriarch over the churches in the province of Asia. Its position, and the excellence of its harbours, made it the chief emporium for the trade of all Asia within the Taurus ; and its downfall was chiefly owing to the destruction of its harbours by the deposits of the Caÿster.— In the earliest times Ephesus was called by various names, Alope, Ortygia, Morges, Smyrna Tracheia, Samornia, and Ptelea.

Ephialtes ('Εφιάλτης). 1. One of the Aloïdae. [ALOEUS.]—**2.** A Malian, who in B.C. 480, when Leonidas was defending the pass of Thermopylae, guided a body of Persians over the mountain path, and thus enabled them to fall on the rear of the Greeks.—**3.** An Athenian statesman, was a friend and partisan of Pericles, whom he assisted in carrying his political measures. He is mentioned in particular as chiefly instrumental in that abridgment of the power of the Areopagus, which inflicted such a blow on the oligarchical party, and against which the *Eumenides* of Aeschylus was directed. His services to the democratic cause excited the rancorous enmity of some of the oligarchs, and led to his assassination during the night, probably in 456.

Ephippus ("Εφιππος). 1. An Athenian poet of the middle comedy.—**2.** Of Olynthus, a Greek historian of Alexander the Great.

Ephŏrus ("Εφορος), of Cymae in Aeolis, a celebrated Greek historian, was a contemporary of Philip and Alexander, and flourished about B. C. 340. He studied rhetoric under Isocrates, of whose pupils he and Theopompus were considered the most distinguished. On the advice of Theopompus he wrote *A History* ('Ιστορίαι) in 30 books, which began with the return of the Heraclidae, and came down to the siege of Perinthus in 341. It treated of the history of the barbarians as well as of the Greeks, and was thus the first attempt at writing a universal history that was ever made in Greece. It embraced a period of 750 years, and each of the 30 books contained a compact portion of the history, which formed a complete whole by itself.

Ephorus did not live to complete the work, and it was finished by his son Demophilus. Diyllus began his history at the point at which the work of Ephorus left off. Ephorus also wrote a few other works of less importance, of which the titles only are preserved by the grammarians. Of the history likewise we have nothing but fragments. It was written in a clear and polished style, but was at the same time deficient in power and energy. Ephorus appears to have been faithful and impartial in the narration of events; but he did not always follow the best authorities, and in the later part of his work he frequently differed from Herodotus, Thucydides, and Xenophon, on points on which they are entitled to credit. Diodorus Siculus made great use of the work of Ephorus. The fragments of his work have been published by Marx, Carlsruhe, 1815, and in Müller's *Fragm. Historicor. Graec.* Paris, 1841.

Ephyra ('Εφύρα). 1. The ancient name of Corinth [CORINTHUS.] — 2. An ancient town of the Pelasgi near the river Selleis in Elis. — 3. A town in Thessaly, afterwards called CRANON. — 4. A town in Epirus, afterwards called CICHYRUS. — 5. A small town in the district of Agraea in Aetolia.

Epicastē ('Επικάστη), commonly called JOCASTE.

Epicēphēsia ('Επικηφισία : 'Επικηφήσιος), a demus in Attica, belonging to the tribe Oeneis.

Epicharmus ('Επίχαρμος), the chief comic poet among the Dorians, was born in the island of Cos, about B. C. 540. His father, Elothales, was a physician, of the race of the Asclepiads. At the age of 3 months, Epicharmus was carried to Megara, in Sicily; thence he removed to Syracuse, when Megara was destroyed by Gelon (484 or 483). Here he spent the remainder of his life, which was prolonged throughout the reign of Hieron, at whose court Epicharmus associated with the other great writers of the time, and among them with Aeschylus. He died at the age of 90 (450), or, according to Lucian, 97 (443). Epicharmus was a Pythagorean philosopher, and spent the earlier part of his life in the study of philosophy, both physical and metaphysical. He is said to have followed for some time his father's profession of medicine; and it appears that he did not commence writing comedies till his removal to Syracuse. Comedy had for some time existed at Megara in Sicily, which was a colony from Megara on the Isthmus, the latter of which towns disputed with the Athenians the invention of comedy. But the comedy at the Sicilian Megara before Epicharmus seems to have been little more than a low buffoonery. It was he, together with Phormis, who gave it a new form, and introduced a regular plot. The number of his comedies is differently stated at 52, or at 35. There are still extant 35 titles. The majority of them are on mythological subjects, that is, travesties of the heroic myths, and these plays no doubt very much resembled the satyric dramas of the Athenians. But besides mythology, Epicharmus wrote on other subjects, political, moral, relating to manners and customs, &c. The style of his plays appears to have been a curious mixture of the broad buffoonery which distinguished the old Megarian comedy, and of the sententious wisdom of the Pythagorean philosopher. His language was remarkably elegant: he was celebrated for his choice of epithets: his plays abounded, as the extant fragments prove, with philosophical and moral maxims. He was

imitated by Crates, and also by Plautus, as we learn from the line of Horace (*Epist.* ii. 1. 58),—

" Plautus ad exemplar Siculi properare Epicharmi."

The parasite, who forms so conspicuous a character in the plays of the new comedy, is first found in Epicharmus.

Epicnemidii Locri. [LOCRIS.]

Epicrātes ('Επικράτης). 1. An Athenian, took part in the overthrow of the 30 Tyrants; but afterwards, when sent on an embassy to the Persian king Artaxerxes, he was accused of corruption in receiving money from Artaxerxes. He appears to have been acquitted this time; but he was tried on a later occasion, on another charge of corruption, and only escaped death by a voluntary exile. He was ridiculed by the comic poets for his large beard, and for this reason was called σακεσφορός. — 2. Of Ambracia, an Athenian poet of the middle comedy.

Epictētus ('Επίκτητος), of Hierapolis in Phrygia, a celebrated Stoic philosopher, was a freedman of Epaphroditus, who was himself a freedman of Nero. [EPAPHRODITUS.] He lived and taught first at Rome, and, after the expulsion of the philosophers by Domitian, at Nicopolis in Epirus. Although he was favoured by Hadrian, he does not appear to have returned to Rome; for the discourses which Arrian took down in writing were delivered by Epictetus when an old man at Nicopolis. Only a few circumstances of his life are recorded, such as his lameness, which is spoken of in different ways, his poverty, and his few wants. Epictetus did not leave any works behind him, and the short manual (*Enchiridion*), which bears his name, was compiled from his discourses by his faithful pupil Arrian. Arrian also wrote the philosophical lectures of his master in 8 books, from which, though 4 are lost, we are enabled to gain a complete idea of the way in which Epictetus conceived and taught the Stoic philosophy. [ARRIANUS.] Being deeply impressed with his vocation as a teacher, he aimed in his discourses at nothing else but winning the minds of his hearers to that which was good, and no one was able to resist the impression which they produced.

Epictētus Phrygia. [PHRYGIA.]

Epicūrus ('Επίκουρος), a celebrated Greek philosopher, and the founder of a philosophical school called, after him, the Epicurean. He was a son of Neocles and Charestrata, and was born B. C. 342, in the island of Samos, where his father had settled as one of the Athenian cleruchi; but he belonged to the Attic demos of Gargettus, and hence is sometimes called the Gargettian. (Cic. *ad Fam.* xv. 16.) At the age of 18 Epicurus came to Athens, and there probably studied under Xenocrates, who was then at the head of the academy. After a short stay at Athens he went to Colophon, and subsequently resided at Mytilene and Lampsacus, in teaching philosophy. In 306, when he had attained the age of 35, he again came to Athens, where he purchased for 80 minae a garden — the famous Κῆποι 'Επικούρου — in which he established his philosophical school. Here he spent the remainder of his life, surrounded by numerous friends and pupils. His mode of living was simple, temperate, and cheerful; and the aspersions of comic poets and of later philosophers, who were opposed to his philosophy and describe him as a person devoted to sensual pleasures, do not seem entitled to the least credit. He took no part in public affairs. He died in 270, at the age of 72, after a long and painful illness, which he endured with truly philosophical patience and courage. — Epicurus is said to have written 300 volumes. Of these the most important was one On Nature (Περὶ Φύσεως), in 37 books. All his works are lost ; but some fragments of the work on Nature were found among the rolls at Herculaneum, and were published by Orelli, Lips. 1818. In his philosophical system, Epicurus prided himself in being independent of all his predecessors ; but he was in reality indebted both to Democritus and the Cyrenaics. Epicurus made ethics the most essential part of his philosophical system, since he regarded human happiness as the ultimate end of all philosophy. His ethical theory was based upon the dogma of the Cyrenaics, that pleasure constitutes the highest happiness, and must consequently be the end of all human exertions. Epicurus, however, developed and ennobled this theory in a manner which constitutes the real merit of his philosophy, and which gained for him so many friends and admirers both in antiquity and in modern times. Pleasure with him was not a mere momentary and transitory sensation, but he conceived it as something lasting and imperishable, consisting in pure and noble mental enjoyments, that is, in ἀταραξία and ἀπονία, or the freedom from pain and from all influences which disturb the peace of our mind, and thereby our happiness, which is the result of it. The summum bonum, according to him, consisted in this peace of mind ; and this was based upon φρόνησις, which he described as the beginning of everything good, as the origin of all virtues, and which he hence therefore occasionally treated as the highest good itself. — In the physical part of his philosophy, he followed the atomistic doctrines of Democritus and Diagoras. His views are well known from Lucretius's poem De Rerum Natura. We obtain our knowledge and form our conceptions of things, according to him, through εἴδωλα, i. e. images of things which are reflected from them, and pass through our senses into our minds. Such a theory is destructive of all absolute truth, and a mere momentary impression upon our senses or feelings is substituted for it. The deficiencies of his system are most striking in his views concerning the gods, which drew upon him the charge of atheism. His gods, like every thing else, consisted of atoms, and our notions of them are based upon the εἴδωλα which are reflected from them and pass into our minds. They were and always had been in the enjoyment of perfect happiness, which had not been disturbed by the laborious business of creating the world ; and as the government of the world would interfere with their happiness, he conceived them as exercising no influence whatever upon the world or man. The pupils of Epicurus were very numerous, and were attached to their master in a manner which has rarely been equalled either in ancient or modern times. But notwithstanding the extraordinary devotion of his pupils, there is no philosopher in antiquity who has been so violently attacked as Epicurus. This has been owing partly to a superficial knowledge of his philosophy, and partly to the conduct of men who called themselves Epicureans, and who, taking advantage of the facility with which his ethical theory was made the handmaid of a sensual life, gave themselves up to the enjoyment of sensual pleasures.

Epicȳdes (Ἐπικύδης), a Syracusan by origin, but born and educated at Carthage. He served, together with his elder brother Hippocrates, with much distinction in the army of Hannibal, both in Spain and Italy ; and when, after the battle of Cannae (B. C. 216), Hieronymus of Syracuse sent to make overtures to Hannibal, that general selected the 2 brothers as his envoys to Syracuse. They soon induced the young king to desert the Roman alliance. Upon the murder of Hieronymus shortly after, they were the leaders of the Carthaginian party at Syracuse, and eventually became masters of the city, which they defended against Marcellus. Epicydes fled to Agrigentum, when he saw that the fall of Syracuse was inevitable.

Epidamnus. [DYRRHACHIUM.]

Epidaurus (Ἐπίδαυρος; Ἐπιδαύριος). 1. (Epidauro), a town in Argolis on the Saronic gulf, formed with its territory Epidauria (Ἐπιδαυρία), a district independent of Argos, and was not included in Argolis till the time of the Romans. It was originally inhabited by Ionians and Carians, whence it was called Epicarus, but it was subdued by the Dorians under Deiphontes, who thus became the ruling race. Epidaurus was the chief seat of the worship of Aesculapius, and was to this circumstance indebted for its importance. The temple of this god, which was one of the most magnificent in Greece, was situated about 5 miles S. W. of Epidaurus. A few ruins of it are still extant. The worship of Aesculapius was introduced into Rome from Epidaurus. See AESCULAPIUS.—2. Surnamed Limēra (ἡ Λιμηρά: Monembasia or Old Malvasia), a town in Laconia, on the E. coast, said to have been founded by Epidaurus in Argolis, possessed a good harbour.—3. (Old Ragusa), a town in Dalmatia.

Epidēlium (Ἐπιδήλιον), a town in Laconia on the E. coast, S. of Epidaurus Limera, with a temple of Apollo and an image of the god, which once thrown into the sea at Delos is said to have come to land at this place.

Epigĕnes (Ἐπιγένης). 1. An Athenian poet of the middle comedy, flourished about B. C. 380.—2. Of Sicyon, who has been confounded by some with his namesake the comic poet, preceded Thespis, and is said to have been the most ancient writer of tragedy. It is probable that Epigenes was the first to introduce into the old dithyrambic and satyrical τραγῳδία other subjects than the original one of the fortunes of Dionysus.—3. Of Byzantium, a Greek astronomer, mentioned by Seneca, Pliny, and Censorinus. He professed to have studied in Chaldea, but his date is uncertain.

Epigŏni (Ἐπίγονοι), that is, " the Descendants," the name in ancient mythology of the sons of the 7 heroes who perished before Thebes. [ADRASTUS.] Ten years after their death, the descendants of the 7 heroes marched against Thebes to avenge their fathers. The names of the Epigoni are not the same in all accounts ; but the common lists contain Alcmaeon, Aegialeus, Diomedes, Promachus, Sthenelus, Thersander, and Euryalus. Alcmaeon undertook the command, in accordance with an oracle, and collected a considerable body of Argives. The Thebans marched out against the enemy, under the command of Laodamas, after whose death they fled into the city. On the part of the Epigoni, Aegialeus had fallen. The seer Tiresias, knowing that the city was doomed to fall, persuaded the inhabitants to quit it, and take their wives and children with them. The Epigoni thereupon took possession of Thebes, and razed it to the ground. They sent a portion of the booty and Manto, the daughter of Tiresias, to Delphi, and then returned to Peloponnesus. The war of the Epigoni was made the subject of epic and tragic poems.

Epimenides (Ἐπιμενίδης). 1. A celebrated poet and prophet of Crete, whose history is to a great extent mythical. He was reckoned among the Curetes, and is said to have been the son of a nymph. He was a native of Phaestus in Crete, and appears to have spent the greatest part of his life at Cnossus, whence he is sometimes called a Cnossian. There is a legend that when a boy, he was sent out by his father in search of a sheep, and that seeking shelter from the heat of the midday sun, he went into a cave, and there fell into a deep sleep, which lasted 57 years. On waking and returning home, he found to his great amazement that his younger brother had in the mean time grown an old man. He is further said to have attained the age of 154, 157, or even of 229 years. — His visit to Athens, however, is an historical fact, and determines his date. The Athenians, who were visited by a plague in consequence of the crime of Cylon [CYLON], consulted the Delphic oracle about the means of their delivery. The god commanded them to get their city purified, and the Athenians invited Epimenides to come and undertake the purification. Epimenides accordingly came to Athens, about B. C. 596, and performed the desired task by certain mysterious rites and sacrifices, in consequence of which the plague ceased. Epimenides was reckoned by some among the 7 wise men of Greece ; but all that tradition has handed down about him suggests a very different character from that of the seven ; he must rather be ranked in the class of priestly bards and sages who are generally comprised under the name of the Orphici. Many works, both in prose and verse, were attributed to him by the ancients, and the Apostle Paul has preserved (*Titus,* i. 12) a celebrated verse of his against the Cretans.

Epimetheus. [PROMETHEUS and PANDORA.]

Epiphanes, a surname of Antiochus IV. and Antiochus XI., kings of Syria.

Epiphania or **êa** (Ἐπιφάνεια). 1. In Syria (O. T. Hamath : *Hamah*), in the district of Casiotis, on the left bank of the Orontes, an early colony of the Phoenicians ; may be presumed, from its later name, to have been restored or improved by Antiochus Epiphanes. — 2. In Asia Minor (*Urzin*), on the S. E. border of Cilicia, close to the Pylae Amanides, was formerly called Oeniandus, and probably owed its new name to Antiochus Epiphanes. Pompey repeopled this city with some of the pirates whom he had conquered. — There were some other Asiatic cities of the name.

Epiphanius (Ἐπιφάνιος), one of the Greek fathers, was born near Eleutheropolis in Palestine, about A. D. 320, of Jewish parents. He went to Egypt when young, and there appears to have been tainted with Gnostic errors, but afterwards fell into the hands of some monks, and by them was made a strong advocate for the monastic life. He returned to Palestine, and lived there for some time as a monk, having founded a monastery near his native place. In A. D. 367 he was chosen bishop of Constantia, the metropolis of Cyprus, formerly called Salamis. His writings shew him to have been a man of great reading ; for he was acquainted with Hebrew, Syriac, Greek, Egyptian, and Latin. But he was entirely without critical or logical power ; of real piety, but also of a very bigoted and dogmatical turn of mind. He distinguished himself by his opposition to heresy, and especially to Origen's errors. He died 402. His most important work is entitled *Panarium,* being a discourse against heresies. The best edition of his works is by Petavius, Paris, 1622, and Lips. 1682, with a commentary by Valesius.

Epipolae. [SYRACUSAE.]

Epirus (Ἤπειρος : Ἠπειρώτης, fem. Ἠπειρῶτις : *Albania*), that is, " the mainland," a country in the N. W. of Greece, so called to distinguish it from Corcyra and the other islands off the coast. Homer gives the name of Epirus to the whole of the W. coast of Greece, thus including Acarnania in it. Epirus was bounded by Illyria and Macedonia on the N., by Thessaly on the E., by Acarnania and the Ambracian gulf on the S., and by the Ionian sea on the W. The principal mountains were the Acroceraunii, forming the N. W. boundary, and Pindus, forming the E. boundary ; besides which there were the mountains Tomarus in the E., and Crania in the S. The chief rivers were the Celydnus, Thyamis, Acheron, and Arachthus. — The inhabitants of Epirus were numerous, but were not of pure Hellenic blood. The original population appears to have been Pelasgic ; and the ancient oracle of Dodona in the country was always regarded as of Pelasgic origin. These Pelasgians were subsequently mingled with Illyrians, who at various times invaded Epirus and settled in the country. Epirus contained 14 different tribes. Of these the most important were the CHAONES, THESPROTI and MOLOSSI, who gave their names to the 3 principal divisions of the country CHAONIA, THESPROTIA, and MOLOSSIS. The different tribes were originally governed by their own princes. The Molossian princes, who traced their descent from Pyrrhus (Neoptolemus), son of Achilles, subsequently acquired the sovereignty over the whole country, and took the title of kings of Epirus. The first who bore this title was Alexander, who invaded Italy to assist the Tarentines against the Lucanians and Bruttii, and perished at the battle of Pandosia, B. C. 326. The most celebrated of the later kings was PYRRHUS, who carried on war with the Romans. About B. C. 200 the Epirots established a republic ; and the Romans, after the conquest of Philip, 197, guaranteed its independence. But in consequence of the support which the Epirots afforded to Antiochus and Perseus, Aemilius Paulus received orders from the senate to punish them with the utmost severity. He destroyed 70 of their towns, and sold 150,000 of the inhabitants for slaves. In the time of Augustus the country had not yet recovered from the effects of this devastation.

Epirus Nova. [ILLYRICUM.]

Epona (from *epus,* that is, *equus*), a Roman goddess, the protectress of horses. Images of her, either statues or paintings, were frequently seen in niches of stables.

Epopeus (Ἐπωπεύς). 1. Son of Poseidon and Canace, came from Thessaly to Sicyon, of which place he became king. He carried away from Thebes the beautiful Antiope, daughter of Nycteus, who therefore made war upon Epopeus. The two kings died of the wounds which they received in the war. — 2. One of the Tyrrhenian pirates, who attempted to carry off Bacchus, but were changed by the god into dolphins.

Eporēdia (*Ivrea*), a town in Gallia Cisalpina on the Duria in the territory of the Salassi, colonised by the Romans, B. c. 100, on the command of the Sibylline books, to serve as a bulwark against the neighbouring Alpine tribes.

Eporedŏrix, a chieftain of the Aedui, was one of the commanders of the Aeduan cavalry, which was sent to Caesar's aid against Vercingetorix, in B. c. 52; but he himself revolted soon afterwards and joined the enemy.

Epȳtus, a Trojan, father of Periphas, who was a companion of Iulus, and is called by the patronymic Epytides.

Equester (Ἵππιος), a surname of several divinities, but especially of Poseidon (Neptune), who had created the horse, and in whose honour horse-races were held.

Equus Tūtīcus or **Aequum Tūtīcum**, a small town of the Hirpini in Samnium, 21 miles from Beneventum. The Scholiast on Horace (*Sat.* i. 5. 87), supposes, but without sufficient reasons, that it is the town, *quod versu dicere non est.*

Erae (Ἔραι: *Sighajik ?*), a small but strong seaport town on the coast of Ionia, N. of Teos.

Erāna, a town in M. Amanus, the chief seat of the Eleutherocilices in the time of Cicero.

Erannobŏas (Ἐραννοβόας: *Gunduk*), a river of India, one of the chief tributaries of the Ganges, into which it fell at Palimbothra.

Erasinīdes (Ἐρασινίδης), one of the Athenian commanders at the battle of Arginusae. He was among the 6 commanders who returned to Athens after the victory, and were put to death, B. c. 406.

Erasĭnus (Ἐρασῖνος). 1. (*Kephalari*), the chief river in Argolis, rises in the lake Stymphalus, then disappears under the earth, rises again out of the mountain Chaon, and after receiving the river Phrixus, flows through the Lernaean marsh into the Argolic gulf. — 2. A small river near Brauron in Attica.

Erasistrătus (Ἐρασίστρατος), a celebrated physician and anatomist, was born at Iulis in the island of Ceos. He was a pupil of Chrysippus of Cnidos, Metrodorus, and apparently Theophrastus. He flourished from B. c. 300 to 260. He lived for some time at the court of Seleucus Nicator, king of Syria, where he acquired great reputation by discovering that the illness of Antiochus, the king's eldest son, was owing to his love for his mother-in-law, Stratonice, the young and beautiful daughter of Demetrius Poliorcetes, whom Seleucus had lately married. Erasistratus afterwards lived at Alexandria, which was at that time beginning to be a celebrated medical school. He gave up practice in his old age, that he might pursue his anatomical studies without interruption. He prosecuted his experiments in this branch of medical science with great success, and with such ardour that he is said to have dissected criminals alive. He had numerous pupils and followers, and a medical school bearing his name continued to exist at Smyrna in Ionia about the beginning of the Christian era.

Erātĭdae (Ἐρατίδαι), an illustrious family of Ialysus in Rhodes, to which Damagetus and his son Diagoras belonged.

Erāto (Ἐρατώ). 1. Wife of Arcas, and mother of Elatus and Aphidas. [ARCAS.]—2. One of the Muses. [MUSAE.]

Eratosthĕnes (Ἐρατοσθένης), of Cyrene, was born B. c. 276. He first studied in his native city and then at Athens. He was taught by Ariston of Chius, the philosopher; Lysanias of Cyrene, the grammarian; and Callimachus, the poet. He left Athens at the invitation of Ptolemy Evergetes, who placed him over the library at Alexandria. Here he continued till the reign of Ptolemy Epiphanes. He died at the age of 80, about B. c. 196, of voluntary starvation, having lost his sight, and being tired of life. He was a man of very extensive learning, and wrote on almost all the branches of knowledge then cultivated — astronomy, geometry, geography, philosophy, history, and grammar. He is supposed to have constructed the large *armillas* or fixed circular instruments which were long in use at Alexandria. His works have perished, with the exception of some fragments. His most celebrated work was a systematic treatise on geography, entitled Γεωγραφικά, in 3 books. The first book, which formed a sort of introduction, contained a critical review of the labours of his predecessors from the earliest to his own times, and investigations concerning the form and nature of the earth, which, according to him, was an immovable globe. The second book contained what is now called mathematical geography. He was the first person who attempted to measure the magnitude of the earth, in which attempt he brought forward and used the method which is employed to the present day. The third book contained political geography, and gave descriptions of the various countries, derived from the works of earlier travellers and geographers. In order to be able to determine the accurate site of each place, he drew a line parallel with the equator, running from the pillars of Hercules to the extreme east of Asia, and dividing the whole of the inhabited earth into two halves. Connected with this work was a new map of the earth, in which towns, mountains, rivers, lakes, and climates were marked according to his own improved measurements. This important work of Eratosthenes forms an epoch in the history of ancient geography. Strabo, as well as other writers, made great use of it. Eratosthenes also wrote 2 poems on astronomical subjects: one entitled Ἑρμῆς or Καταστερισμοί, which treated of the constellations; and another entitled Ἠριγόνη: but the poem Καταστερισμοί, which is still extant under his name, is not the work of Eratosthenes. He wrote several historical works, the most important of which was a chronological work entitled Χρονογραφία, in which he endeavoured to fix the dates of all the important events in literary, as well as political history. The most celebrated of his grammatical works was *On the Old Attic Comedy* (Περὶ τῆς Ἀρχαίας Κωμῳδίας). The best collection of his fragments is by Bernhardy, *Eratosthenica*, Berol. 1822.

Erbessus (Ἐρβησσός), a town in Sicily, N.E. of Agrigentum near the sources of the Acragas, which must not be confounded with the town Herbessus near Syracuse.

Erota (Ἐἱρκτή or Εἱρκταί), a fortress in Sicily on a hill with a harbour near Panormus.

Erĕbus (Ἔρεβος), son of Chaos, begot Aether and Hemera (Day) by Nyx (Night), his sister. The name signifies darkness, and is therefore applied also to the dark and gloomy space under the earth, through which the shades pass into Hades.

Erechthēum. [ERICHTHONIUS.]

Erechtheus. [ERICHTHONIUS.]

Erĕsus or **Eressus** (Ἔρεσος, Ἔρεσσος: Ἐρέσιος), a town on the W. coast of the island of Lesbos, the birthplace of Theophrastus and Phanias, and, according to some, of Sappho.

Eretria (Ἐρέτρια: Ἐρετριεύς: *Palaeo-Castro*), an ancient and important town in Euboea on the Euripus, with a celebrated harbour Porthmos (*Porto Bufalo*), was founded by the Athenians, but had a mixed population, among which was a considerable number of Dorians. Its commerce and navy raised it in early times to importance; it contended with Chalcis for the supremacy of Euboea; it ruled over several of the neighbouring islands, and planted colonies in Macedonia and Italy. It was destroyed by the Persians, B. C. 490, and most of its inhabitants were carried away into slavery. Those who were left behind built, at a little distance from the old city, the town of New Eretria, which, however, never became a place of importance.—**2.** A town in Phthiotis in Thessaly near Pharsalus.

Erginus (Ἐργῖνος), son of Clymenus, king of Orchomenos. After Clymenus had been killed at Thebes, Erginus, who succeeded him, marched against Thebes, and compelled them to pay him an annual tribute of 100 oxen. The Thebans were released from the payment of this tribute by Hercules, who killed Erginus.

Erichthonius (Ἐριχθόνιος), or **Erechtheus** (Ἐρεχθεύς). In the ancient myths these two names indicate the same person; but later writers mention 2 heroes, one of whom is usually called Erichthonius or Erechtheus I. and the other Erechtheus II. Homer knows only one Erechtheus, as an autochthon and king of Athens; and the first writer who distinguishes 2 personages is Plato. —**1. Erichthonius** or **Erechtheus I.**, son of Hephaestus and Atthis, the daughter of Cranaus. Athena reared the child without the knowledge of the other gods, and entrusted him to Agraulos, Pandrosos, and Herse, concealed in a chest. They were forbidden to open the chest, but they disobeyed the command. Upon opening the chest they saw the child in the form of a serpent, or entwined by a serpent, whereupon they were seized with madness, and threw themselves down the rock of the acropolis, or, according to others, into the sea. When Erichthonius had grown up, he expelled Amphictyon, and became king of Athens. His wife Pasithea bore him a son Pandion. He is said to have introduced the worship of Athena, to have instituted the festival of the Panathenaea, and to have built a temple of Athena on the acropolis. When Athena and Poseidon disputed about the possession of Attica, Erichthonius declared in favour of Athena. He was further the first who used a chariot with 4 horses, for which reason he was placed among the stars as auriga. He was buried in the temple of Athena, and was worshipped as a god after his death. His famous temple, the Erechthēum, stood on the acropolis, and contained 3 separate temples; one of Athena Polias or the protectress of the state, the *Erechthēum* proper or sanctuary of Erechtheus, and the *Pandrosium* or sanctuary of Pandrosos.—**2. Erechtheus II.**, grandson of the former, son of Pandion by Zeuxippe, and brother of Butes, Procne, and Philomela. After his father's death, he succeeded him as king of Athens, and was regarded in later times as one of the Attic eponymi. He was married to Praxithea, by whom he became the father of Cecrops, Pandoros, Metion, Orneus, Procris, Creusa, Chthonia, and Orithyia. In the war between the

Eleusinians and Athenians, Eumolpus, the son of Poseidon, was slain; whereupon Poseidon demanded the sacrifice of one of the daughters of Erechtheus. When one was drawn by lot, her 3 sisters resolved to die with her; and Erechtheus himself was killed by Zeus with a flash of lightning at the request of Poseidon.

Erichthonius, son of Dardanus and Batëa, husband of Astyoche or Callirrhoë, and father of Tros or Assaracus. He was the wealthiest of all mortals; 3000 mares grazed in his fields, which were so beautiful, that Boreas fell in love with them. He is mentioned also among the kings of Crete.

Ericinium, a town in Thessaly near Gomphi.

Eridanus (Ἠριδανός), a river god, a son of Oceanus and Tethys, and father of Zeuxippe. He is called the king of rivers, and on his banks amber was found. In Homer the name does not occur, and the first writer who mentions it is Hesiod. The position which the ancient poets assign to the river Eridanus differed at different times. In later times the Eridanus was supposed to be the same as the Padus, because amber was found at its mouth. Hence the *Electrides Insulae* or " Amber Islands " are placed at the mouth of the Po, and here Phaethon was supposed to have fallen when struck by the lightning of Zeus. The Latin poets frequently give the name of Eridanus to the Po. [PADUS.]

Erigon (Ἐρίγων), a tributary of the Axius in Macedonia the Agrianus of Herodotus. [AXIUS.]

Erigone (Ἠριγόνη). 1. Daughter of Icarius, beloved by Bacchus. For the legend respecting her, see ICARIUS.—**2.** Daughter of Aegisthus and Clytaemnestra, and mother of Penthilus by Orestes. Another legend relates that Orestes wanted to kill her with her mother, but that Artemis removed her to Attica, and there made her her priestess. Others state that Erigone put an end to herself when she heard that Orestes was acquitted by the Areopagus.

Erineus (Ἐρινεός or Ἐρινεόν: Ἐρινεύς, Ἐρινεώτης). 1. A small but ancient town in Doris, belonging to the Tetrapolis. [DORIS.]—**2.** A town in Phthiotis in Thessaly.

Erinna (Ἤριννα), a Greek poetess, a contemporary and friend of Sappho (about B. C. 612), who died at the age of 19, but left behind her poems which were thought worthy to rank with those of Homer. Her poems were of the epic class: the chief of them was entitled Ἠλακάτη, *the Distaff*: it consisted of 300 lines, of which only 4 are extant. It was written in a dialect which was a mixture of the Doric and Aeolic, and which was spoken at Rhodes, where, or in the adjacent island of Telos, Erinna was born. She is also called a Lesbian and a Mytilenaean, on account of her residence in Lesbos with Sappho. There are several epigrams upon Erinna, in which her praise is celebrated, and her untimely death is lamented. 3 epigrams in the Greek Anthology are ascribed to her, of which the first has the genuine air of antiquity; but the other two, addressed to Baucis, seem to be a later fabrication.—Eusebius mentions another Erinna, a Greek poetess, contemporary with Demosthenes and Philip of Macedon, B. C. 352 ; but this statement ought probably to be rejected.

Erinyes. [EUMENIDES.]

Eriphus (Ἔριφος), an Athenian poet of the middle comedy.

Eriphyle (Ἐριφύλη), daughter of Talaus and

Lysimache, and wife of Amphiaraus, whom she betrayed for the sake of the necklace of Harmonia. For details see AMPHIARAUS, ALCMAEON, HARMONIA.

Eris (Ἔρις), the goddess of Discord. Homer describes her as the friend and sister of Ares, and as delighting with him in the tumult of war and the havoc and anguish of the battle-field. According to Hesiod she was a daughter of Night, and the poet describes her as the mother of a variety of allegorical beings, which are the causes or representatives of man's misfortunes. It was Eris who threw the apple into the assembly of the gods, the cause of so much suffering and war. [PARIS.] —Virgil introduces Discordia as a being similar to the Homeric Eris; for Discordia appears in company with Mars, Bellona, and the Furies, and Virgil is evidently imitating Homer.

Erisa (τὰ Ἔριζα: Ἐριζηνός), a city of Caria, on the borders of Lycia and Phrygia, on the river Chalis (or rather Calis). The surrounding district was called Asia Erizēna.

Eros (Ἔρος), in Latin, **Amor** or **Cupīdo**, the god of Love. In order to understand the ancients properly we must distinguish 3 gods of this name: 1. The Eros of the ancient cosmogonies; 2. The Eros of the philosophers and mysteries, who bears great resemblance to the first; and 3. The Eros whom we meet with in the epigrammatic and erotic poets. Homer does not mention Eros, and Hesiod, the earliest author who speaks of him, describes him as the cosmogonic Eros. First, says Hesiod, there was Chaos, then came Ge, Tartarus, and Eros, the fairest among the gods, who rules over the minds and the council of gods and men. By the philosophers and in the mysteries Eros was regarded as one of the fundamental causes in the formation of the world, inasmuch as he was the uniting power of love, which brought order and harmony among the conflicting elements of which Chaos consisted. The Orphic poets described him as a son of Cronus, or as the first of the gods who sprang from the world's egg; and in Plato's Symposium he is likewise called the oldest of the gods. The Eros of later poets, who gave rise to that notion of the god which is most familiar to us, is one of the youngest of all the gods. The parentage of this Eros is very differently described. He is usually represented as a son of Aphrodite (Venus), but his father is either Ares (Mars), Zeus (Jupiter), or Hermes (Mercury). He was at first represented as a handsome youth; but shortly after the time of Alexander the Great the epigrammatists and erotic poets represented him as a wanton boy, of whom a thousand tricks and cruel sports were related, and from whom neither gods nor men were safe. In this stage Eros has nothing to do with uniting the discordant elements of the universe, or with the higher sympathy or love which binds human kind together; but he is purely the god of sensual love, who bears sway over the inhabitants of Olympus as well as over men and all living creatures. His arms consist of arrows, which he carries in a golden quiver, and of torches which no one can touch with impunity. His arrows are of different power: some are golden, and kindle love in the heart they wound; others are blunt and heavy with lead, and produce aversion to a lover. Eros is further represented with golden wings, and as fluttering about like a bird. His eyes are sometimes covered, so that he acts blindly. He is the

usual companion of his mother Aphrodite, and poets and artists represent him moreover as accompanied by such allegorical beings as Pothos, Himeros, Tyche, Peitho, the Charites or Muses. — **Antĕros**, which literally means return-love, is usually represented as the god who punishes those who did not return the love of others: thus he is the avenging Eros, or a *deus ultor* (Ov. *Met.* xiii. 750). But in some accounts he is described as a god opposed to Eros and struggling against him. — The number of Erotes (Amores and Cupidines) is playfully extended ad libitum by later poets, and these Erotes are described either as sons of Aphrodite or of nymphs. — Among the places distinguished for the worship of Eros, Thespiae in Boeotia stands foremost: there a quinquennial festival, the Erotidia or Erotia, was celebrated in his honour. In ancient works of art, Eros is represented either as a full-grown youth of the most perfect beauty, or as a wanton and sportive boy. — Respecting the connection between Eros and Psyche, see PSYCHE.

Erotiānus (Ἐρωτιανός), a Greek grammarian or physician in the reign of Nero, wrote a work still extant, entitled Τῶν παρ' Ἱπποκράτει Λέξεων Συναγωγή, *Vocum, quae apud Hippocratem sunt, Collectio*, which is dedicated to Andromachus, the archiater of the emperor. The best edition is by Franz, Lips. 1780.

Erubrus (*Ruber*), a small tributary of the Moselle, near Trèves.

Erȳmanthus (Ἐρύμανθος). 1. A lofty mountain in Arcadia on the frontiers of Achaia and Elis, celebrated in mythology as the haunt of the savage Erymanthian boar destroyed by Hercules. [HERCULES.]—The Arcadian nymph Callisto, who was changed into a she-bear, is called *Erymanthis ursa*, and her son Arcas *Erymanthidis ursae custos.* [ARCTOS.]—2. A river in Arcadia, which rises in the above-mentioned mountain, and falls into the Alpheus.

Erȳmanthus or **Etȳmandrus** (Ἐρύμανθος, Ἐτύμανδρος Arrian.: *Helmund*), a considerable river in the Persian province of Arachosia, rising in M. Paropamisus, and flowing S.W. and W. into the lake called Aria (*Zarah*). According to other accounts, it lost itself in the sand, or flowed on through Gedrosia into the Indian Ocean.

Erysichthon (Ἐρυσίχθων), that is, "the Tearer up of the Earth." 1. Son of Triopas, cut down trees in a grove sacred to Demeter, for which he was punished by the goddess with fearful hunger.— 2. Son of Cecrops and Agraulos, died without issue in his father's lifetime on his return from Delos, from whence he brought to Athens the ancient image of Ilithyia.

Erythīni (Ἐρυθῖνοι), a city on the coast of Paphlagonia, between Cromna and Amastris. A range of cliffs near it was called by the same name.

Erythrae (Ἐρυθραί: Ἐρυθραῖος). 1. (Nr. *Pigadia* Ru.), an ancient town in Boeotia, not far from Plataeae and Hysia, and celebrated as the mother city of Erythrae in Asia Minor. — 2. A town of the Locri Ozŏlae, but belonging to the Aetolians, E. of Naupactus. — 3. (*Ritri*, Ru.), one of the 12 Ionian cities of Asia Minor, stood at the bottom of a large bay, on the W. side of the peninsula which lies opposite to Chios. Tradition ascribed its foundation to a mixed colony of Cretans, Lycians, Carians, and Pamphylians, under Erythros the son of Rhadamanthus; and the leader of the Ionians, who afterwards took possession of it, was said to have been Cnopus, the son of Codrus, after whom the city was also called Cnōpŏpŏlis (Κνωπούπολιs). The little river Aleos (or rather Axus, as it appears on coins) flowed past the city, and the neighbouring sea-port towns of Cyssus or Casystes, and Phoenicus, formed its harbours. Erythrae contained a temple of Hercules and Athena Polias, remarkable for its antiquity ; and on the coast near the city was a rock called Nigrum Promontorium (ἄκρα μέλαινα), from which excellent mill-stones were hewn.

Erythraeum Mare (ἡ Ἐρυθρὰ Θάλασσα, also rarely Ἐρυθραῖος πόντος), was the name applied originally to the whole expanse of sea between Arabia and Africa on the W., and India on the E., including its two great gulfs (the Red Sea and Persian Gulf). In this sense it is used by Herodotus, who also distinguishes the Red Sea by the name of Ἀράβιος κόλπος. [ARABICUS SINUS.] Supposing the shores of Africa and Arabia to trend more and more away from each other the further S. you go, he appears to have called the head of the sea between them ὁ Ἀράβιος κόλπος, and the rest of that sea, as far S. as it extended, and also E.wards to the shores of India, ἡ Ἐρυθρὴ Θάλασσα, and also ἡ Νοτίη Θάλασσα ; though there are, again, some indications of a distinction between these 2 terms, the latter being applied to the whole expanse of ocean S. of the former ; in one passage, however, they are most expressly identified (ii. 158). Afterwards, when the true form of these seas became to be better known, through the progress of maritime discovery under the Ptolemies, their parts were distinguished by different names, the main body of the sea being called Indicus Oceanus, the Red Sea Arabicus Sinus, the Persian Gulf Persicus Sinus, and the name Erythraeum Mare being confined by some geographers to the gulf between the Straits of Bab-el-Mandeb and the Indian Ocean, but far more generally used as identical with Arabicus Sinus, or the corresponding genuine Latin term, Mare Rubrum (Red Sea). Still, however, even long after the commencement of our era, the name Erythraeum Mare was sometimes used in its ancient sense, as in the Περίπλους τῆς Ἐρυθρᾶς θαλάσσης, ascribed to Arrian, but really the work of a later period, which is a description of the coast from Myos Hormos on the Red Sea to the shores of India. The origin of the name is doubtful, and was disputed by the ancients : it is generally supposed that the Greek Ἐρυθρὰ Θάλασσα is a significant name, identical in meaning with the Latin and English names of the Red Sea ; but why red no very satisfactory reason has been given ; the Hebrew name signifies the sedgy sea.

Eryx (Ἔρυξ). 1. Also Erycus Mons (S. Giuliano), a steep and isolated mountain in the N.W. of Sicily near Drepanum. On the summit of this mountain stood an ancient and celebrated temple of Aphrodite (Venus), said to have been built by Eryx, king of the Elymi, or, according to Virgil, by Aeneas, but more probably by the Phoenicians, who introduced the worship of Aphrodite into Sicily. [APHRODITE.] From this temple the goddess bore the surname Erycina, under which name her worship was introduced at Rome about the beginning of the 2nd Punic war. At present there is standing on the summit of the mountain the remains of a castle, originally built by the Saracens. — 2. The town of this name was on the W. slope of the mountain. It was destroyed by the Cartha-

ginians in the time of Pyrrhus ; was subsequently rebuilt; but was again destroyed by the Carthaginians in the 1st Punic war, and its inhabitants removed to Drepanum.

Esdraëla (Ἐσδρανλά) and Esdraëlon or Esdrēlon, or -om (Ἐσδρηλών or -ώμ), the Greek names for the city and valley of Jezreel in Palestine.

Esquiliae. [ROMA.]

Essui, a people in Gaul, W. of the Sequana, probably the same as the people elsewhere called Esubii and Sesuvii.

Estiōnes, a people in Rhaetia Secunda or Vindelicia, whose capital was Campodūnum (Kempten) on the Iller.

Eteocles (Ἐτεοκλῆς.) 1. Son of Andreus and Evippe, or of Cephisus ; said to have been the first who offered sacrifices to the Charites at Orchomenos in Boeotia. — 2. A son of Oedipus and Jocaste. After his father's flight from Thebes, he and his brother Polynices undertook the government of Thebes by turns. But, disputes having arisen between them, Polynices fled to Adrastus, who then brought about the expedition of the Seven against Thebes. [ADRASTUS.] When many of the heroes had fallen, Eteocles and Polynices resolved upon deciding the contest by single combat, and both the brothers fell.

Eteoclus (Ἐτέοκλος), a son of Iphis, was, according to some traditions, one of the 7 heroes who went with Adrastus against Thebes. He had to make the attack upon the Neïtian gate, where he was opposed by Megareus.

Eteōnus (Ἐτεωνός), a town in Boeotia, belonging to the district Parasopia, mentioned by Homer, subsequently called Scarphe.

Etēsiae (Ἐτησίαι, sc. ἄνεμοι), the Etesian Winds, derived from ἔτος " year," signified any periodical winds, but the word was used more particularly by the Greeks to indicate the northerly winds, which blew in the Aegean for 40 days from the rising of the dog star.

Etis or Etia (Ἦτις, Ἦτεια : Ἤτιος, Ἠτεῖος), a town in the S. of Laconia near Boeae, said to have been founded by Aeneas, and named after his daughter Etias. Its inhabitants were transplanted at an early time to Boeae, and the place disappeared.

Etovissa, a town of the Edetani in Hispania Tarraconensis.

Etruria or Tuscia, called by the Greeks Tyrrhēnia or Tyrsēnia (Τυῤῥηνία, Τυρσηνία), a country in central Italy. The inhabitants were called by the Romans Etrusci or Tusci, by the Greeks Tyrrhēni or Tyrsēni (Τυῤῥηνοί, Τυρσηνοί), and by themselves Rasēna. Etruria was bounded on the N. and N.W. by the Apennines and the river Macra, which divided it from Liguria, on the W. by the Tyrrhene sea or Mare Inferum, on the E. and S. by the river Tiber, which separated it from Umbria and Latium, thus comprehending almost the whole of modern Tuscany, the Duchy of Lucca, and the Transtiberine portion of the Roman states. It was intersected by numerous mountains, offshoots of the Apennines, consisting of long ranges of hills in the N., but in the S. lying in detached masses, and of smaller size. The land was celebrated in antiquity for its fertility, and yielded rich harvests of corn, wine, oil, and flax. The upper part of the country was the most healthy, namely, the part at the foot of the Apennines, near the sources of the Tiber and the Arnus, in the neighhourhood of Arretium, Cortona, and Perusia. The lower part of the country on the coast was marshy and unhealthy, like the Maremma at the present day. — The early history of the population of Etruria has given rise to much discussion in modern times. It is admitted on all hands that the people known to the Romans under the name of Etruscans were not the original inhabitants of the country, but a mixed race. The most ancient inhabitants appear to have been Ligurians in the N. and Siculians in the S., both of whom were subsequently expelled from the country by the Umbrians. So far most accounts agree ; but from this point there is great difference of opinion. The ancients generally believed that a colony of Lydians, led by Tyrsenus, son of the king of Lydia, settled in the country, to which they gave the name of their leader ; and it has been maintained by some modern writers that the Oriental character of many of the Etruscan institutions is in favour of this account of their origin. But most modern critics adopt an entirely different opinion. They believe that a Pelasgic race, called Tyrrheni, subdued the Umbrians, and settled in the country, and that these Tyrrhene-Pelasgians were in their turn conquered by a powerful Rhaetian race, called Rasena, who descended from the Alps and the valley of the Po. Hence it was from the union of the Tyrrhene-Pelasgians and the Rasena that the Etruscan nation was formed. It is impossible, however, to come to any definite conclusion respecting the real origin of the Etruscans ; since we are entirely ignorant of the language which they spoke; and the language of a people is the only means by which we can pronounce with certainty respecting their origin. But whatever may have been the origin of the Etruscans, we know that they were a very powerful nation when Rome was still in its infancy, and that they had at an early period extended their dominion over the greater part of Italy, from the Alps and the plains of Lombardy on the one hand, to Vesuvius and the gulf of Sarento on the other. These dominions may be divided into 3 great districts : Circumpadane Etruria in the N., Etruria Proper in the centre, and Campanian Etruria in the S. In each of these districts there were 12 principal cities or states, who formed a confederacy for mutual protection. Through the attacks of the Gauls in the N., and of the Sabines, Samnites, and Greeks in the S., the Etruscans became confined within the limits of Etruria Proper, and continued long to flourish in this country, after they had disappeared from the rest of Italy. Of the 12 cities, which formed the confederacy in Etruria Proper, no list is given by the ancients. They were most probably CORTONA, ARRETIUM, CLUSIUM, PERUSIA, VOLATERRAE, VETULONIA, RUSELLAE, VOLSINII, TARQUINII, VALERII, VEII, CAERE more anciently called Agylla. Each state was independent of all the others. The government was a close aristocracy, and was strictly confined to the family of the Lucumones, who united in their own persons the ecclesiastical as well as the civil functions. The people were not only rigidly excluded from all share in the government, but appear to have been in a state of vassalage or serfdom. From the noble and priestly families of the Lucumones a supreme magistrate was chosen, who appears to have been sometimes elected for life, and to have borne the title of king ; but his power was much fettered by the noble families. At a later time the

kingly dignity was abolished, and the government entrusted to a senate. A meeting of the confederacy of the 12 states was held annually in the spring, at the temple of Voltumna near Volsinii.— The Etruscans were a highly civilised people, and from them the Romans borrowed many of their religious and political institutions. The 3 last kings of Rome were undoubtedly Etruscans, and they left in the city enduring traces of Etruscan power and greatness. The Etruscans paid the greatest attention to religion ; and their religious system was closely interwoven with all public and private affairs. The principal deities were divided into 2 classes. The highest class were the " Shrouded Gods," who did not reveal themselves to man, and to whom all the other gods were subject. The 2nd class consisted of the 12 great gods, 6 male and 6 female, called by the Romans Dii Consentes. They formed the council of Tina or Tinia, the Roman Jupiter, and the 2 other most powerful gods of the 12 were Cupra, corresponding to Juno and Menrva or Menerva, corresponding to the Roman Minerva. Besides these 2 classes of gods, there was a great number of other gods, penates and lares, to whom worship was paid. The mode in which the gods were worshipped was prescribed in certain sacred books, said to have been written by TAGES. These books contained the " Etrusca Disciplina," and gave minute directions respecting the whole of the ceremonial worship. They were studied in the schools of the Lucumones, to which the Romans also were accustomed to send some of their noblest youths for instruction ; since it was from the Etruscans that the Romans borrowed most of their arts of divination. — In architecture, statuary, and painting, the Etruscans attained to great eminence. They were acquainted with the use of the arch at an early period, and they employed it in constructing the great cloacae at Rome. Their bronze candelabra were celebrated at Athens even in the time of Pericles ; and the beauty of their bronze statues is still attested by the She Wolf of the Capitol and the Orator of the Florence Gallery. The beautiful vases, which have been discovered in such numbers in Etruscan tombs, cannot be cited as proofs of the excellence of Etruscan workmanship, since it is now admitted by the most competent judges, that these vases were either made in Greece, or by Greek artists settled in Italy. — Of the private life of the Etruscans we have a lively picture from the paintings discovered in their tombs ; but into this subject our limits forbid us to enter. — The later history of Etruria is a struggle against the rising power of Rome, to which it was finally compelled to yield. After the capture of Veii by the dictator Camillus, B. C. 396, the Romans obtained possession of the E. part of Etruria ; and the Ciminian forest, instead of the Tiber, now became the boundary of the 2 people. The defeat of the Etruscans by Q. Fabius Maximus in 310, was a great blow to their power. They still endeavoured to maintain their independence with the assistance of the Samnites and the Gauls ; but after their decisive defeat by Cornelius Dolabella in 283, they became the subjects of Rome. In 91 they received the Roman franchise. The numerous military colonies established in Etruria by Sulla and Augustus destroyed to a great extent the national character of the people, and the country thus became in course of time completely Romanised.

Euboea (Εὔβοια: Εὐβοιεύς, Εὐβοεύς, fem. Εὔβοϊς). 1. (*Negropont*), the largest island of the Aegaean sea, lying along the coasts of Attica, Boeotia, and the S. part of Thessaly, from which countries it is separated by the Euboean sea, called the Euripus in its narrowest part. Euboea is about 90 miles in length : its extreme breadth is 30 miles, but in the narrowest part it is only 4 miles across. Throughout the length of the island runs a lofty range of mountains, which rise in one part as high as 7266 feet above the sea. It contains nevertheless many fertile plains, and was celebrated in antiquity for the excellence of its pasturage and cornfields. According to the ancients it was once united to Boeotia, from which it was separated by an earthquake. In Homer the inhabitants are called Abantes, and are represented as taking part in the expedition against Troy. In the N. of Euboea dwelt the Histiaei, from whom that part of the island was called Histiaea ; below these were the Ellopii, who gave the name of Ellopia to the district, extending as far as Aegae and Cerinthus ; and in the S. were the Dryopes. The centre of the island was inhabited chiefly by Ionians. It was in this part of Euboea that the Athenians planted the colonies of CHALCIS and ERETRIA, which were the 2 most important cities in the island. After the Persian wars Euboea became subject to the Athenians, who attached much importance to its possession ; and consequently Pericles made great exertions to subdue it, when it revolted in B.C. 445. Under the Romans Euboea formed part of the province of Achaia.—Since Cumae in Italy was a colony from Chalcis in Euboea, the adjective *Euboicus* is used by the poets in reference to the former city. Thus Virgil (*Aen.* vi. 2) speaks of *Euboicis Cumarum oris.*—2. A town in the interior of Sicily, founded by Chalcis in Euboea, but destroyed at an early period.

Eubulides (Εὐβουλίδης), of Miletus, a philosopher of the Megaric school. He was a contemporary of Aristotle, against whom he wrote with great bitterness; and he is stated to have given Demosthenes instruction in dialectics. He is said to have invented the forms of several of the most celebrated false and captious syllogisms.

Eubulus (Εὔβουλος). 1. An Athenian, of the demus Anaphlystus, a distinguished orator and statesman, was one of the most formidable opponents of Demosthenes. It was with him that Aeschines served as secretary in the earlier part of his life.—2. An Athenian, son of Euphranor, of the Cettian demus, a distinguished poet of the middle comedy, flourished B.C. 376. He wrote 104 plays, of which there are extant more than 50 titles. His plays were chiefly on mythological subjects. Several of them contained parodies of passages from the tragic poets, and especially from Euripides.

Euclides (Εὐκλείδης). 1. The celebrated mathematician, who has almost given his own name to the science of geometry, in every country in which his writings are studied ; but we know next to nothing of his private history. The place of his birth is uncertain. He lived at Alexandria in the time of the first Ptolemy, B.C. 323—283, and was the founder of the Alexandrian mathematical school. He was of the Platonic sect, and well read in its doctrines. It was his answer to Ptolemy, who asked if geometry could not be made easier, that there was no royal road. Of the nu-

merous works attributed to Euclid the following are still extant :—1. Στοιχεῖα, the *Elements*, in 13 books, with a 14th and 15th added by HYPSICLES. 2. Δεδομένα, the *Data*, containing 100 propositions, with a preface by Marinus of Naples. 3. Εἰσαγωγὴ Ἁρμονική, a *Treatise on Music* ; and 4. Κατατομὴ Κανόνος, *the Division of the Scale* : one of these works, most likely the former, must be rejected. 5. Φαινόμενα, the *Appearances* (of the heavens). 6. Ὀπτικά, on *Optics* ; and 7. Κατοπτρικά, on *Catoptrics*. The only complete edition of all the reputed works of Euclid is that published at Oxford, 1703, folio, by David Gregory, with the title Εὐκλείδου τὰ σωζόμενα. The Elements and the Data were published in Greek, Latin, and French, in 3 vols. 4to. Paris, 1814—16—18, by Peyrard. The most convenient edition for scholars of the Greek text of the Elements is the one by August, Berol. 1826, 8vo.—2. Of Megara, was one of the chief of the disciples of Socrates, but before becoming such, he had studied the doctrines, and especially the dialectics, of the Eleatica. Socrates on one occasion reproved him for his fondness for subtle and captious disputes. On the death of Socrates (B.C. 399), Euclides took refuge in Megara, and there established a school which distinguished itself chiefly by the cultivation of dialectics. The doctrines of the Eleatics formed the basis of his philosophical system. With these he blended the ethical and dialectical principles of Socrates. He was the author of 6 dialogues, none of which however have come down to us. He has frequently been erroneously confounded with the mathematician of the same name. The school which he founded was called sometimes the Megaric, sometimes the Dialectic or Eristic.

Eucratides (Εὐκρατίδης), king of Bactria, from about B.C. 181 to 161, was one of the most powerful of the Bactrian kings, and made great conquests in the N. of India.

Euctemon, the astronomer. [METON.]

Eudamidas (Εὐδαμίδας). I. King of Sparta, reigned from B.C. 330 to about 300. He was the younger son of Archidamus III. and succeeded his brother Agis III.—II. King of Sparta, was son of Archidamus IV., whom he succeeded, and father of Agis IV.

Eudemus (Εὔδημος). 1. Of Cyprus, a Peripatetic philosopher, to whom Aristotle dedicated the dialogue Εὔδημος ἢ περὶ ψυχῆς, which is lost.—2. Of Rhodes, also a peripatetic philosopher, and one of the most important of Aristotle's disciples. He edited many of Aristotle's writings ; and one of them even bears the name of Eudemus, namely, the Ἠθικὰ Εὐδήμεια, which work was in all probability a recension of Aristotle's lectures edited by Eudemus. [See p. 85, b.]—3. The physician of Livilla, the wife of Drusus Caesar, who assisted her and Sejanus in poisoning her husband, A.D. 23.

Eudocia (Εὐδοκία). 1. Originally called Athenais, daughter of the sophist Leontius, was distinguished for her beauty and attainments. She married the emperor Theodosius II., A.D. 421 ; and on her marriage she embraced Christianity, and received at her baptism the name of Eudocia. She died at Jerusalem, A.D. 460. She wrote several works ; and to her is ascribed by some the extant poem *Homero-Centones*, which is composed of verses from Homer, and relates the history of the fall and of the redemption of man by Jesus Christ ; but its genuineness is very doubtful.—2.

Of Macrembolis, wife of the emperors Constantine XI. Ducas and Romanus IV. Diogenes (A. D. 1059 —1071), wrote a dictionary of history and mythology, which she called Ἰωνιά, *Violarium*, or *Bed of Violets*. It was printed for the first time by Villoison, in his *Anecdota Graeca*, Venice, 1781. The sources from which the work was compiled are nearly the same as those used by Suidas.

Eudoses, a people in Germany near the Varini, probably in the modern *Mecklenburg*.

Eudoxus (Εὔδοξος). 1. Of Cnidus, son of Aeschines, a celebrated astronomer, geometer, physician, and legislator, lived about B. C. 366. He was a pupil of Archytas and Plato, and also went to Egypt, where he studied some time with the priests. He afterwards returned to Athens, but it would appear that he must have spent some time in his native place, for Strabo says that the observatory of Eudoxus at Cnidus was existing in his time. He died at the age of 53. He is said to have been the first who taught in Greece the motions of the planets ; and he is also stated to have made separate spheres for the stars, sun, moon, and planets. He wrote various works on astronomy and geometry, which are lost ; but the substance of his Φαινόμενα is preserved by Aratus, who turned into verse the prose work by Eudoxus with that title. — 2. An Athenian comic poet of the new comedy, was by birth a Sicilian and the son of Agathocles — 3. Of Cyzicus, a geographer, who went from his native place to Egypt, and was employed by Ptolemy Evergetes and his wife Cleopatra, in voyages to India ; but afterwards being robbed of all his property by Ptolemy Lathyrus, he sailed away down the Red Sea, and at last arrived at Gades. He afterwards made attempts to circumnavigate Africa in the opposite direction, but without success. He lived about B. C. 130.

Eugamon (Εὐγάμων), one of the Cyclic poets, was a native of Cyrene, and lived about B. C. 568. His poem (Τηλεγονία) was a continuation of the Odyssey, and formed the conclusion of the epic cycle. It concluded with the death of Ulysses.

Euganeï, a people who formerly inhabited Venetia on the Adriatic sea, and were driven towards the Alps and the Lacus Benacus by the Henetí or Veneti. According to some traditions they founded Patavium and Verona, in the neighbourhood of which were the Euganei Colles. They possessed numerous flocks of sheep, the wool of which was celebrated. (Juv. viii. 15.)

Euhēmērus (Εὐήμερος), probably a native of Messene in Sicily, lived at the court of Cassander in Macedonia, about B. C. 316. Cassander furnished him with the means to undertake a voyage of discovery. He is said to have sailed down the Red Sea and round the southern coasts of Asia, until he came to an island called Panchaea. After his return he wrote a work entitled Ἱερὰ Ἀναγραφή, or a *Sacred History*, in 9 books. He gave this title to his work, because he pretended to have derived his information from Ἀναγραφαί, or inscriptions in temples, which he had discovered in his travels, especially in the island of Panchaea. Euhemerus had been trained in the school of the Cyrenaics, who were notorious for their scepticism in matters connected with the popular religion; and the object of his work was to exclude every thing supernatural from the popular religion, and to dress up the myths as so many plain histories. In his work the several gods were represented as

having originally been men who had distinguished themselves either as warriors, or benefactors of mankind, and who after their death were worshipped as gods by the grateful people. Zeus, for example, was a king of Crete, who had been a great conqueror ; and he asserted that he had seen in the temple of Zeus Triphylius a column with an inscription detailing all the exploits of the kings Uranus, Cronus, and Zeus. The book was written in an attractive style, and became very popular, and many of the subsequent historians, such as Diodorus, adopted his mode of dealing with myths. The great popularity of the work is attested by the circumstance that Ennius made a Latin translation of it. But the pious believers, on the other hand, called Euhemerus an atheist. The Christian writers often refer to him to prove that the pagan mythology was nothing but a heap of fables invented by men.

Eulaeus (Εὐλαῖος : O. T. Ulai : *Karoon*), a river in Susiana, on the borders of Elymaïs, rising in Great Media, flowing S. through Mesobatene, passing E. of Susa, and, after uniting with the Pasitigris, falling into the head of the Persian Gulf. Some of the ancient geographers make the Eulaeus fall into the Choaspes, and others identify the two rivers.

Eumaeus (Εὔμαιος), the faithful swineherd of Ulysses, was a son of Ctesius, king of the island of Syrie ; he had been carried away from his father's house by a Phoenician slave, and Phoenician sailors sold him to Laërtes, the father of Ulysses.

Eumēlus (Εὔμηλος). 1. Son of Admetus and Alcestis, went with 11 ships from Pherae to Troy. He was distinguished for his excellent horses, which had once been under the care of Apollo, and with which Eumelus would have gained the prize at the funeral games of Patroclus, if his chariot had not been broken. His wife was Iphthima, daughter of Icarius. — 2. Of Corinth, one of the Bacchiadae, an ancient Epic poet, belonged, according to some, to the Epic cycle. His name is significant, referring to his skill in poetry. He flourished about B. C. 760. His principal poem seems to have been his *Corinthian History*.

Eumēnes (Εὐμένης). 1. Of CARDIA, served as private secretary to Philip and Alexander, whom he accompanied throughout his expedition in Asia, and who treated him with marked confidence and distinction. After the death of Alexander (B. C. 323) Eumenes obtained the government of Cappadocia, Paphlagonia, and Pontus, which provinces had never yet been conquered by the Macedonians. Eumenes entered into a close alliance with Perdiccas, who subdued these provinces for him. When Perdiccas marched into Egypt against Ptolemy, he committed to Eumenes the conduct of the war against Antipater and Craterus in Asia Minor. Eumenes met with great success; he defeated Neoptolemus, who had revolted from Perdiccas; and subsequently he again defeated the combined armies of Craterus and Neoptolemus: Craterus himself fell, and Neoptolemus was slain by Eumenes with his own hand, after a deadly struggle in the presence of the 2 armies. Meantime the death of Perdiccas in Egypt changed the aspect of affairs. Antigonus now employed the whole force of the Macedonian army to crush Eumenes. The struggle was carried on for some years (320—316). It was conducted by Eumenes with consummate skill; and notwithstanding the numerical inferiority of his forces, he maintained his ground against his enemies, till he was surrendered by the Argyraspids to Antigonus, by whom he was put to death, 316. He was 45 years old at the time of his death. Of his ability, both as a general and a statesman, no doubt can be entertained ; and it is probable that he would have attained a far more important position among the successors of Alexander, had it not been for the accidental disadvantage of his birth. But as a Greek of Cardia, and not a native Macedonian, he was constantly looked upon with dislike both by his opponents and companions in arms. — **2. I.** King of PERGAMUS, reigned B. C. 263—241; and was the successor of his uncle Philetaerus. He obtained a victory near Sardis over Antiochus Soter, and thus established his dominion over the provinces in the neighbourhood of his capital.—**3. II.** King of PERGAMUS, reigned B. C. 197—159; and was the son and successor of Attalus I. He inherited from his predecessor the friendship and alliance of the Romans, which he took the utmost pains to cultivate. He supported the Romans in their war against Antiochus ; and after the conquest of the latter (190) he received from the senate Mysia, Lydia, both Phrygias, and Lycaonia, as well as Lysimachia, and the Thracian Chersonese. By this means he was at once raised from a state of comparative insignificance to be the sovereign of a powerful monarchy. Subsequently he was involved in war with Pharnaces, king of Pontus, and Prusias, king of Bithynia, but both wars were brought to a close by the interposition of the Romans. At a later period Eumenes was regarded with suspicion by the Roman senate, because he was suspected of having corresponded secretly with Perseus, king of Macedonia, during the war of the latter with the Romans. Eumenes assiduously cultivated all the arts of peace: Pergamus became under his rule a great and flourishing city, which he adorned with splendid buildings, and in which he founded that celebrated library which rose to be a rival even to that of Alexandria.

Eumenia (Εὐμένεια or Εὐμενία : Ishekli), a city of Great Phrygia, on the rivers Glaucus and Cludrus, N. of the Maeander, named by Attalus II. after his brother and predecessor Eumenes II. There are indications which seem to connect the time of its foundation with that of the destruction of Corinth.

Eumenides (Εὐμενίδες), also called **Erinyes**, not Erinnyes ('Ερινύες, 'Εριννῦς), and by the Romans **Furiae** or **Dirae**, the Avenging Deities, were originally only a personification of curses pronounced upon a criminal. The name Erinys is the more ancient one ; its etymology is uncertain, but the Greeks derived it from ἐρίνω or ἐρευνάω, I hunt up or persecute, or from the Arcadian ἐρινύω, I am angry ; so that the Erinyes were either the angry goddesses, or the goddesses who hunt up or search after the criminal. The name Eumenides, which signifies " the well-meaning," or " soothed goddesses," is a mere euphemism, because people dreaded to call these fearful goddesses by their real name. It was said to have been first given them after the acquittal of Orestes by the Areopagus, when the anger of the Erinyes had become soothed. It was by a similar euphemism that at Athens the Erinyes were called σεμναὶ θεαί, or the venerable goddesses. — Homer sometimes mentions an *Erinys*, but more frequently *Erinyes*

in the plural. He represents them as inhabitants of Erebos, where they remain quiet until some curse pronounced upon a criminal calls them into activity. The crimes which they punish are disobedience towards parents, violation of the respect due to old age, perjury, murder, violation of the law of hospitality, and improper conduct towards suppliants. They took away from men all peace of mind, and led them into misery and misfortune. Hesiod says that they were the daughters of Ge, and sprang from the drops of blood that fell upon her from the body of Uranus. Aeschylus calls them the daughters of Night ; and Sophocles of Darkness and Ge. In the Greek tragedians neither the names nor the number of the Erinyes are mentioned. Aeschylus describes them as divinities more ancient than the Olympian gods, dwelling in the deep darkness of Tartarus, dreaded by gods and men ; with bodies all black, serpents twined in their hair, and blood dripping from their eyes. Euripides and other later poets describe them as winged. With later writers their number is usually limited to 3, and their names are Tisiphŏnĕ, Alecto, and **Megaera**. They gradually assumed the character of goddesses who punished men after death, and they seldom appeared upon earth. The sacrifices offered to them consisted of black sheep and nephalia, *i. e.* a drink of honey mixed with water. They were worshipped at Athens, where they had a sanctuary and a grotto near the Areopagus : their statues, however, had nothing formidable, and a festival Eumenidea was there celebrated in their honour. Another sanctuary, with a grove which no one was allowed to enter, existed at Colonus.

Eumenius, a Roman rhetorician of Augustodunum (*Autun*) in Gaul, held a high office under Constantius Chlorus. He is the author of four panegyrics in the " Panegyrici Veteres," namely : 1. *Oratio pro instaurandis scholis*, a lecture delivered on the re-establishment by Constantius Chlorus of the school at Autun, A. D. 296 or 297. 2. *Panegyricus Constantio Caesari dictus*, delivered 296 or 297. 3. *Panegyricus Constantino Augusto dictus*, delivered 310. 4. *Gratiarum actio Constantino Augusto Flaviensium nomine*, delivered 311.

Eumolpus (Εὔμολπος), that is " the good singer," a Thracian bard, usually represented as a son of Poseidon and Chione, the daughter of Boreas. As soon as he was born, he was thrown into the sea by his mother, who was anxious to conceal her shame, but was preserved by his father Poseidon, who had him educated in Ethiopia by his daughter Benthesicyma. When he had grown up, he married a daughter of Benthesicyma; but as he made an attempt upon the chastity of his wife's sister, he was expelled together with his son Ismarus. They went to the Thracian king Tegyrius, who gave his daughter in marriage to Ismarus; but as Eumolpus drew upon himself the suspicion of Tegyrius, he was again obliged to take to flight, and came to Eleusis in Attica, where he formed a friendship with the Eleusinians. After the death of his son Ismarus, he returned to Thrace at the request of Tegyrius. The Eleusinians, who were involved in a war with Athens, called Eumolpus to their assistance. Eumolpus came with a numerous band of Thracians, but he was slain by Erechtheus. Eumolpus was regarded as the founder of the Eleusinian mysteries, and as the first priest of Demeter and Dionysus. He was succeeded in the priestly office by his son Ceryx (who was, according to some accounts, the son of Hermes), and his family, the *Eumolpidae*, continued till the latest times the priests of Demeter at Eleusis. — The legends connected Eumolpus with Hercules, whom he is said to have instructed in music, or initiated into the mysteries. There were so many different traditions about Eumolpus that some of the ancients supposed that there were 2 or 3 persons of that name.

Eunapius (Εὐνάπιος), a Greek sophist, was born at Sardis A. D. 347, and lived and taught at Athens as late as the reign of Theodosius II. He wrote, 1. Lives of Sophists (Βίοι φιλοσόφων καὶ σοφιστῶν), still extant, containing 23 biographies of sophists, most of whom were contemporaries of Eunapius, or had lived shortly before him. Though these biographies are extremely brief, and the style is intolerably inflated, yet they supply us with important information respecting a period, on which we have no other information. Eunapius was an enthusiastic admirer of the philosophy of the New Platonists, and a bitter enemy of Christianity. Edited by Boissonade, Amsterdam, 1822. 2. A continuation of the history of Dexippus (Μετὰ Δέξιππον χρονικὴ ἱστορία), in 14 books, began with A. D. 270, and went down to 404. Of this work we have only extracts, which are published along with Dexippus. [Dexippus.]

Euneus (Εὔνηος or Εὔνευς), a son of Jason and Hypsipyle in Lemnos, supplied the Greeks with wine during their war against Troy. He purchased Lycaon of Patroclus for a silver urn.

Eunomia. [Horae.]

Eunomus (Εὔνομος), king of Sparta, is described by some as the father of Lycurgus and Polydectes. Herodotus, on the contrary, places him in his list after Polydectes. In all probability, the name was invented with reference to the Lycurgean Εὐνομία, and Eunomus, if not wholly rejected, must be identified with Polydectes.

Eunus (Εὔνους), a Sicilian slave, and a native of Apamea in Syria, was the leader of the Sicilian slaves in the servile war. He first attracted attention by pretending to the gift of prophecy, and by interpreting dreams ; to the effect of which he added by appearing to breathe flames from his mouth and other similar juggleries. He was proclaimed king, and soon collected formidable forces, with which he defeated several Roman armies. The insurrection now became so formidable that for 3 successive years (B. C. 134—132) 3 consuls were sent against the insurgents, and it was not till the 3rd year (132) that the revolt was finally put down by the consul Rupilius. Eunus was taken prisoner, and died in prison at Morgantia, of the disease called *morbus pedicularis*.

Eupalium or **Eupolium** (Εὐπάλιον, Εὐπόλιον : Εὐπαλιεύς), a town of the Locri Ozolae, N. of Naupactus, subsequently included in Aetolia Epictetus.

Eupator (Εὐπάτωρ), a surname assumed by many of the kings in Asia after the time of Alexander the Great. See Antiochus, Mithridates.

Eupatoria or **Eupatoria** (Εὐπατόριον, Εὐπατορία) a town in the Chersonesus Taurica, founded by Mithridates Eupator, and named after him.

Euphaes (Εὐφάης), king of the Messenians, fell in battle against the Spartans in the first Messenian war. He was succeeded by Aristodemus.

Euphemus (Εὔφημος), son of Poseidon by Europe, the daughter of Tityus, or by Mecionice or Oris, a daughter of Orion or Eurotas. According to one account he was an inhabitant of Panopeus

on the Cephissus in Phocis, and according to another of Hyria in Boeotia, and afterwards lived at Taenarus. He was married to Laonome, the sister of Hercules ; he was one of the Calydonian hunters, and the helmsman of the vessel of the Argonauts, and, by a power which his father had granted to him, he could walk on the sea just as on firm ground. He is mentioned also as the ancestor of Battus, the founder of Cyrene.

Euphorbus (Εὔφορβος). 1. Son of Panthous, one of the bravest of the Trojans, was slain by Menelaus, who subsequently dedicated the shield of Euphorbus in the temple of Hera, near Mycenae. Pythagoras asserted that he had once been the Trojan Euphorbus, and in proof of his assertion took down at first sight the shield of Euphorbus from the temple of Hera (*clipeo Trojana refixo tempora testatus*, Hor. *Carm.* i. 28. 11).—2. Physician of Juba II., king of Mauretania, about the end of the first century B. C., and brother to Antonius Musa, the physician to Augustus.

Euphorion (Εὐφορίων). 1. Father of the poet Aeschylus.—2. Son of Aeschylus, and himself a tragic poet.—3. Of Chalcis in Euboea, an eminent grammarian and poet, son of Polymnetus, was born about B. C. 274. He became the librarian of Antiochus the Great, 221, and died in Syria, either at Apamea, or at Antioch. The following were the most important of the poems of Euphorion in heroic verse : — 1. Ἡσίοδος, probably an agricultural poem. 2. Μοψοπία, so called from an old name of Attica, the legends of which country seem to have been the chief subject of the poem. 3. Χιλιάδες, a poem written against certain persons, who had defrauded Euphorion of money which he had entrusted to their care. It probably derived its title from each of its books consisting of 1000 verses. He also wrote epigrams, which were imitated by many of the Latin poets, and also by the emperor Tiberius, with whom he was a great favourite. Euphorion likewise wrote many historical and grammatical works. All his works are lost, but the fragments are collected by Meineke, in his *Analecta Alexandrina*, Berol. 1843.

Euphranor (Εὐφράνωρ), a distinguished statuary and painter, was a native of the Corinthian isthmus, but practised his art at Athens. He flourished about B. C. 336. His most celebrated statue was a Paris, which expressed alike the judge of the goddesses, the lover of Helen, and the slayer of Achilles ; the very beautiful sitting figure of Paris, in marble, in the Museo Pio-Clementino is, no doubt, a copy of this work. His best paintings were preserved in a porch in the Ceramicus at Athens. On the one side were the 12 gods; and on the opposite wall, Theseus, with Democracy and Demos. —Euphranor also wrote works on proportion and on colours (*de Symmetria et Coloribus*), the two points in which his own excellence seems chiefly to have consisted. Pliny says that he was the first who properly expressed the dignity of heroes, by the proportions he gave to their statues. He made the bodies somewhat more slender, and the heads and limbs larger.

Euphrates (Εὐφράτης), an eminent Stoic philosopher, was a native of Tyre, or, according to others, of Byzantium. He was an intimate friend of the younger Pliny. In his old age he became tired of life, and asked and obtained from Hadrian permission to put an end to himself by poison.

Euphrates (Εὐφράτης : O. T. Phrat : *El-Frat*),

a great river of W. Asia, forming the boundary of Upper and Lower Asia, consists, in its upper course, of 2 branches, both of which rise in the mountains of Armenia. The N. branch (*Kara-Sou*), which is the true Euphrates, rises in the mountain above *Erzeroum* (the M. Abus or Capotes of the ancients) and flows W. and S.W. to a little above lat. 39° and E. of long. 39°, where it breaks through the chain of the Anti-Taurus, and, after receiving the S. branch (*Mourad-Chai*), or, as the ancients called it, the ARSANIAS, it breaks through the main chain of the Taurus between Melitene and Samosata, and then flows in a general S. direction, till it reaches lat. 36°, whence it flows in a general S. E. direction, till it approaches the Tigris opposite to Seleucia, where the distance between the 2 rivers was reckoned at only 200 stadia. Then it flows through the plain of Babylonia, at first receding further from the Tigris, and afterwards approaching it again, till it joins it about 60 miles above the mouth of the Persian Gulf, having already had its waters much diminished by numerous canals, which irrigated the country in ancient times, but the neglect of which at present has converted much of the once fertile district watered by the Euphrates into a marshy desert. The whole length of the Euphrates is between 500 and 600 miles. In its upper course, before reaching the Taurus, its N. branch and a part of the united stream divided Armenia Major from Colchis and Armenia Minor, and its lower course divided Mesopotamia from Syria. Its chief tributary, besides the Arsanias, was the *Aborrhas*.

Euphron (Εὔφρων), an Athenian poet of the new comedy, whose plays, however, partook largely of the character of the middle comedy.

Euphrŏsȳnă, one of the Charites or Graces. [CHARIS.]

Eupŏlis (Εὔπολις), son of Sosipolis, an Athenian poet of the old comedy, and one of the 3 who are distinguished by Horace, in his well-known line, " Eupolis, atque Cratinus, Aristophanesque poetae," above all the . . . " alii quorum prisca comoedia virorum est." He was born about B. C. 446, and is said to have exhibited his first drama in his 17th year, 429, two years before Aristophanes. The date of his death is uncertain. The common story was, that Alcibiades, when sailing to Sicily (415), threw Eupolis into the sea, in revenge for an attack which he had made upon him in his *Βάπται*; but this cannot be true, as we know that Eupolis produced plays after the Sicilian expedition. He probably died in 411. The chief characteristic of the poetry of Eupolis seems to have been the liveliness of his fancy, and the power which he possessed of imparting its images to the audience. In elegance he is said to have even surpassed Aristophanes, while in bitter jesting and personal abuse he emulated Cratinus. Among the objects of his satire was Socrates, on whom he made a bitter, though less elaborate attack than that in the *Clouds* of Aristophanes. The dead were not exempt from his abuse, for there are still extant some lines of his, in which Cimon is most unmercifully treated.—A close relation subsisted between Eupolis and Aristophanes, not only as rivals, but as imitators of each other. Cratinus attacked Aristophanes for borrowing from Eupolis, and Eupolis in his *Βάπται* made the same charge, especially with reference to the *Knights*. The Scholiasts specify the last Parabasis of the *Knights* as borrowed from Eupolis. On the other hand, Aristophanes, in the second (or third) edition

of the *Clouds*, retorts upon Eupolis the charge of imitating the *Knights* in his *Maricas*, and taunts him with the further indignity of jesting on his rival's baldness.

Eupompus (Εὔπομπος), of Sicyon, a distinguished Greek painter, was the contemporary of Zeuxis, Parrhasius, and Timanthes, and the instructor of Pamphilus, the master of Apelles. The fame of Eupompus led to the creation of a 3rd school of Greek art, the Sicyonian, at the head of which he was placed.

Euripides (Εὐριπίδης). 1. The distinguished tragic poet, was the son of Mnesarchus and Clito, and is said to have been born at Salamis, B. C. 480, on the very day that the Greeks defeated the Persians off that island, whither his parents had fled from Athens on the invasion of Xerxes. Some writers relate that his parents were in mean circumstances, and his mother is represented by Aristophanes as a herb-seller, and not a very honest one either ; but much weight cannot be accorded to these statements. It is more probable that his family was respectable. We are told that the poet, when a boy, was cup-bearer to a chorus of noble Athenians at the Thargelian festival,—an office for which nobility of blood was requisite. We know also that he was taught rhetoric by Prodicus, who was certainly not moderate in his terms for instruction, and who was in the habit of seeking his pupils among youths of high rank. It is said that the future distinction of Euripides was predicted by an oracle, promising that he should be crowned with " sacred garlands," in consequence of which his father had him trained to gymnastic exercises ; and we learn that, while yet a boy, he won the prize at the Eleusinian and Thesean contests, and offered himself, when 17 years old, as a candidate at the Olympic games, but was not admitted because of some doubt about his age. But he soon abandoned gymnastic pursuits, and studied the art of painting, not, as we learn, without success. To philosophy and literature he devoted himself with much interest and energy, studying physics under Anaxagoras, and rhetoric, as we have already seen, under Prodicus. He lived on intimate terms with Socrates, and traces of the teaching of Anaxagoras have been remarked in many passages of his plays. He is said to have written a tragedy at the age of 18 ; but the first play, which was exhibited in his own name, was the *Peliades*, when he was 25 years of age (B. C. 455). In 441 he gained for the first time the first prize, and he continued to exhibit plays until 408, the date of the *Orestes*. Soon after this he left Athens for the court of Archelaüs, king of Macedonia, his reasons for which step can only be matter of conjecture. Traditionary scandal has ascribed it to his disgust at the intrigue of his wife with Cephisophon, and the ridicule which was showered upon him in consequence by the comic poets. But the whole story has been refuted by modern writers. Other causes more probably led him to accept an invitation from Archelaüs, at whose court the highest honours awaited him. The attacks of Aristophanes and others had probably not been without their effect ; and he must have been aware that his philosophical tenets were regarded with considerable suspicion. He died in Macedonia in 406, at the age of 75. Most testimonies agree in stating that he was torn in pieces by the king's dogs, which, according to some, were set upon him through envy by Arrhidaeus and Crateuas, two rival poets. The regret of Sophocles for his death is said to have been so great, that at the representation of his next play he made his actors appear uncrowned. The accounts which we find in some writers of the profligacy of Euripides are mere idle scandal, and scarcely worthy of serious refutation. Nor does there appear to be any better foundation for that other charge which has been brought against him, of hatred to the female sex. This is said to have been occasioned by the infidelity of his wife; but, as has been already remarked, this tale does not deserve credit. He was a man of a serious and austere temper: and it was in consequence of this that the charge probably originated. It is certain that the poet who drew such characters as Antigone, Iphigenia, and, above all, Alcestis, was not blind to the gentleness, the strong affection, the self-abandoning devotedness of women. With respect to the world and the Deity, he seems to have adopted the doctrines of Anaxagoras, not unmixed apparently with pantheistic views. [ANAXAGORAS.] To class him with atheists, as some have done, is undoubtedly unjust. At the same time, it must be confessed that we look in vain in his plays for the high faith of Aeschylus; nor can we fail to admit that the pupil of Anaxagoras could not sympathise with the popular religious system around him, nor throw himself cordially into it. He frequently altered in the most arbitrary manner the ancient legends. Thus, in the *Orestes*, Menelaüs comes before us as a selfish coward, and Helen as a worthless wanton; in the *Helena*, the notion of Stesichorus is adopted, that the heroine was never carried to Troy at all, and that it was a mere εἴδωλον of her for which the Greeks and Trojans fought; Andromache, the widow of Hector and slave of Neoptolemus, seems almost to forget the past in her quarrel with Hermione and the perils of her present situation; and Electra, married by the policy of Aegisthus to a peasant, scolds her husband for inviting guests to dine without regard to the ill-prepared state of the larder. In short, with Euripides tragedy is brought down into the sphere of every-day life; men are represented, according to the remark of Aristotle, not as they ought to be, but as they are; under the names of the ancient heroes, the characters of his own time are set before us; it is not Medea, or Iphigenia, or Alcestis that is speaking, but abstractedly a mother, a daughter, or a wife. All this, indeed, gave fuller scope, perhaps, for the exhibition of passion and for those scenes of tenderness and pathos in which Euripides especially excelled; and it will serve also to account in great measure for the preference given to his plays by the practical Socrates, who is said to have never entered the theatre unless when they were acted, as well as for the admiration felt for him by Menander and Philemon, and other poets of the new comedy. The most serious defects in his tragedies, artistically speaking, are: his constant employment of the "Deus ex machina;" the disconnexion of his choral odes from the subject of the play; the extremely awkward and formal character of his prologues; and the frequent introduction of frigid γνῶμαι and of philosophical disquisitions, making Medea talk like a sophist, and Hecuba like a free thinker, and aiming rather at subtilty than simplicity. On the same principles on which he brought his subjects and characters to the level of common life, he adopted

also in his style the every-day mode of speaking. According to some accounts, he wrote, in all, 75 plays; according to others, 92. Of these, 18 are extant, if we omit the *Rhesus*, which is probably spurious. A list is subjoined of the extant plays of Euripides, with their dates, ascertained or probable:—*Alcestis*, B. C. 438. This play was brought out as the last of a tetralogy, and stood therefore in the place of a satyric drama, to which indeed it bears, in some parts, great similarity, particularly in the representation of Hercules in his cups. *Medea*, 431. *Hippolytus Coronifer*, 428, gained the first prize. *Hecuba*, exhibited before 423. *Heraclidae*, about 421. *Supplices*, about 421. *Ion*, of uncertain date. *Hercules Furens*, of uncertain date. *Andromache*, about 420—417. *Troades*, 415. *Electra*, about 415—413. *Helena*, 412. *Iphigenia at Tauri* of uncertain date. *Orestes*, 408. *Phoenissae*, of uncertain date. *Bacchae*: this play was apparently written for representation at Macedonia, and therefore at a very late period of the life of Euripides. *Iphigenia at Aulis*: this play, together with the *Bacchae* and the *Alcmaeon*, was brought out at Athens, after the poet's death, by the younger Euripides. *Cyclops*, of uncertain date: it is interesting as the only extant specimen of the Greek satyric drama. Besides the plays, there are extant 5 letters, purporting to have been written by Euripides, but they are spurious.—*Editions*. By Musgrave, Oxford, 1778; by Beck, Leipsig, 1778—88; by Matthiae, Leipsig, 1813—29; and a variorum edition, Glasgow, 1821. Of separate plays there have been many editions, e. g. by Porson, Elmsley, Valckenaer, Monk, Pflugk, and Hermann.—2. The youngest of the 3 sons of the above. After the death of his father he brought out 3 of his plays at the great Dionysia, viz. the *Alcmaeon* (no longer extant), the *Iphigenia at Aulis*, and the *Bacchae*.

Euripus (Εὔριπος), any part of the sea where the ebb and flow of the tide were remarkably violent, is the name especially of the narrow strait which separates Euboea from Boeotia, in which the ancients asserted that the sea ebbed and flowed 7 times in the day. The extraordinary tides of the Euripus have been noticed by modern observers: the water sometimes runs as much as 8 miles an hour. At Chalcis there was a bridge over the Euripus, uniting Euboea with the mainland.

Eurōmus (Εὔρωμος: *Jaklys*), a small town of Caria, at the foot of Mt. Grion (a ridge parallel to Mt. Latmus), in the conventus juridicus of Alabanda. It lay 8 English miles N.W. of Mylasa.

Eurōpa (Εὐρώπη), according to the Iliad (xiv. 321), a daughter of Phoenix, but according to the common tradition a daughter of the Phoenician king Agenor. Her surpassing beauty charmed Zeus, who assumed the form of a bull and mingled with the herd as Europa and her maidens were sporting on the sea-shore. Encouraged by the tameness of the animal, Europa ventured to mount his back; whereupon Zeus rushed into the sea, and swam with her in safety to Crete. Here she became by Zeus the mother of Minos, Rhadamanthus, and Sarpedon. She afterwards married Asterion, king of Crete, who brought up the children whom she had had by the king of the gods.

Eurōpa (Εὐρώπη), one of the 3 divisions of the ancient world. The name is not found in the Iliad and Odyssey, and first occurs in the Homeric Hymn to Apollo (251), but even there it does not

The Erechtheum restored. Page 247.

One of the Caryatides supporting the southern portico of the Erechtheum.

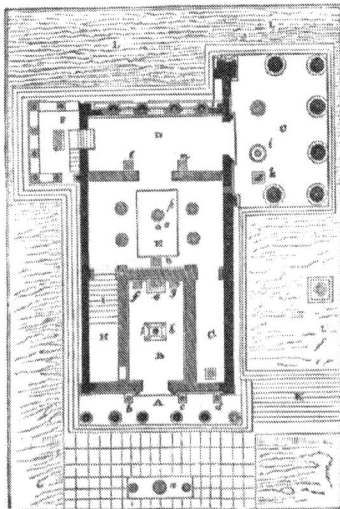

Ground Plan of the Erechtheum. (For a description of the building, see Dict. of Geog. Vol. I. pp. 275—280.)

Divisions.

Temple of Athena Polias, Pandroseum, divided into { Pandroseum proper. { Cecropium.

A. Eastern portico : entrance to the temple of Athena Polias.

B. Temple of Athena Polias.
   a. Altar of Zeus Hypatos.
   b. c. d. Altars of Poseidon-Erechtheus, of Butes, and of Hephaestus.
   e. Palladium.
   f. g. Statue of Hermes. Chair of Daedalus.
   h. Golden Lamp of Callimachus.

C. Northern portico : entrance to the Pandroseum.
   i. The salt well.
   k. Opening in the pavement, by which the traces of Poseidon's trident might be seen.

D. Pronaos of the Pandroseum, serving also as an entrance to the Cecropium.
   l. m. Altars, of which one was dedicated to Thallo.

E. Cella of Pandrosus.
   n. Statue of Pandrosus.
   o. The olive tree.
   p. Altar of Zeus Hyrceus.

F. Southern portico : the Cecropium.

G. Passage on the level of the Pandroseum, leading to the souterrains of the building.

H. Passage of communication by means of the steps I. between the temples of Polias and Pandrosus.

K. Steps leading down to the Temenos.

L. Temenos or sacred enclosure of the building.

[To face p. 296.

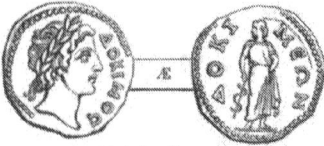

Docimia. Page 279.

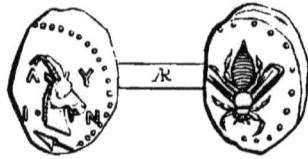

Elyrus in Crete. Page 239.

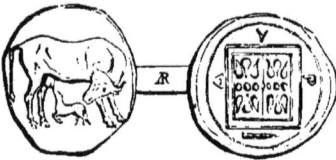

Dyrrhachium. Page 755.

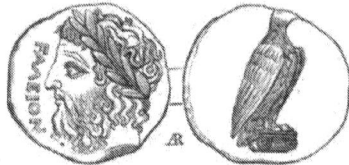

Elis. Page 238.

Edessa in Mesopotamia. Page 238.

Emesa. Page 239.

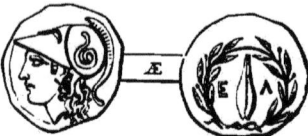

Elaea. Page 237.

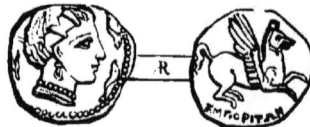

Emporiae. Page 240.

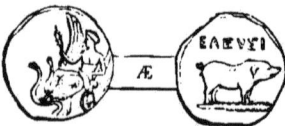

Eleusis. Page 236.

Enna in Sicily. Page 240.

Eleutherna in Crete. Page 234.

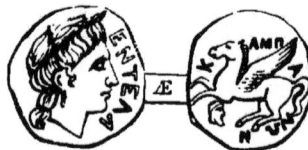

Entella in Sicily. Page 241.

To face p. 237.]

indicate the continent, but simply the mainland of Hellas proper, in opposition to Peloponnesus and the neighbouring islands. Herodotus is the first writer who uses it in the sense of one of the divisions of the world. The origin of the name is doubtful; but the most probable of the numerous conjectures is that which supposes that the Asiatic Greeks called it Europa (from εὐρύς, "broad," and the root ὄπ, "to see"), from the wide extent of its coast. Most of the ancients supposed the name to be derived from Europa, the daughter of Agenor. The boundaries of Europe on the E. differed at various periods. In earlier times the river Phasis was usually supposed to be its boundary, and sometimes even the Araxes and the Caspian sea; but at a later period the river Tanais and the Palus Maeotis were usually regarded as the boundaries between Asia and Europe. The N. of Europe was little known to the ancients, but it was generally believed, at least in later times, that it was bounded on the N. by the Ocean.

Europus. [TITARESIUS.]

Europus (Εὔρωπος). 1. A city of Caria, afterwards named Idrias.—2. (*Yeraboius*, or *Kulat-el-Nejin?*), a city in the district of Cyrrhestice in Syria, on the W. bank of the Euphrates, a few miles S. of Zeugma; called after the town of the same name in Macedonia.—3. Europus was the earlier name of Dura Nicanoris in Mesopotamia; and (4) it was also given by Seleucus Nicator to Rhagae in Media. [ARSACIA.]

Eurotas (Εὐρώτας). 1. (*Basilipotamo*), the chief river in Laconia, but not navigable, rises in Mt. Boreum in Arcadia, then disappears under the earth, rises again near Sciritis, and flows S.wards, passing Sparta on the E., through a narrow and fruitful valley, into the Laconian gulf. — 2. See TITARESIUS.

Euryalus (Εὐρύαλος). 1. Son of Mecisteus, one of the Argonauts, and of the Epigoni, accompanied Diomedes to Troy, where he slew several Trojans. — 2. One of the suitors of Hippodamia.

Euryanassa. [PELOPS.]

Eurybates (Εὐρυβάτης). 1. Called *Eribotes* by Latin writers, son of Teleon, and one of the Argonauts.—2. The herald of Ulysses, whom he followed to Troy.

Eurybatus (Εὐρύβατος), an Ephesian, whom Croesus sent with a large sum of money to the Peloponnesus to hire mercenaries for him in his war with Cyrus. He, however, went over to Cyrus, and betrayed the whole matter to him. In consequence of this treachery, his name passed into a proverb amongst the Greeks.

Eurybia (Εὐρυβία), daughter of Pontus and Ge, mother by Crius of Astraeus, Pallas, and Perses.

Eurybiades. [THEMISTOCLES.]

Euryclea (Εὐρύκλεια), daughter of Ops, was purchased by Laërtes and brought up Telemachus. When Ulysses returned home, she recognised him by a scar, and afterwards faithfully assisted him against the suitors.

Eurydice (Εὐρυδίκη). 1. Wife of Orpheus [ORPHEUS.]. — 2. An Illyrian princess, wife of Amyntas II., king of Macedonia, and mother of the famous Philip.—3. An Illyrian, wife of Philip of Macedon, and mother of Cynane or Cynna.—4. Daughter of Amyntas, son of Perdiccas III., king of Macedonia, and Cynane, daughter of Philip. After the death of her mother in Asia [CYNANE], Perdiccas gave her in marriage to the king Arrhi-

daeus. She was a woman of a masculine spirit, and entirely ruled her weak husband. On her return to Europe with her husband, she became involved in war with Polysperchon and Olympias, but she was defeated in battle, taken prisoner, and compelled by Olympias to put an end to her life, B.C. 317. — 5. Daughter of Antipater, and wife of Ptolemy the son of Lagus. She was the mother of 3 sons, viz. Ptolemy Ceraunus, Meleager, and a third (whose name is not mentioned); and of 2 daughters, Ptolemaïs, afterwards married to Demetrius Poliorcetes, and Lysandra, the wife of Agathocles, son of Lysimachus. —6. An Athenian, of a family descended from the great Miltiades. She was first married to Ophellas, the conqueror of Cyrene, and after his death returned to Athens, where she married Demetrius Poliorcetes, on occasion of his first visit to that city.

Eurylochus (Εὐρύλοχος). 1. Companion of Ulysses in his wanderings, was the only one that escaped from the house of Circe, when his friends were metamorphosed into swine. Another personage of the same name is mentioned among the sons of Aegyptus. —2. A Spartan commander, in the Peloponnesian war, B.C. 426, defeated and slain by Demosthenes at Olpae.

Eurymedon (Εὐρυμέδων). 1. One of the Cabiri, son of Hephaestus and Cabiro, and brother of Alcon. — 2. An attendant of Nestor. —3. Son of Ptolemaeus, and charioteer of Agamemnon. —4. Son of Thucles, an Athenian general in the Peloponnesian war. He was one of the commanders in the expedition to Corcyra, B.C. 428, and also in the expedition to Sicily, 425. In 414, he was appointed, in conjunction with Demosthenes, to the command of the second Syracusan armament, and fell in the first of the two sea-fights in the harbour of Syracuse.

Eurymedon (Εὐρυμέδων: *Kapri-Su*), a small river in Pamphylia, navigable as far up as the city of ASPENDUS, through which it flowed; celebrated for the victory which Cimon gained over the Persians on its banks (B.C. 469).

Eurymenae (Εὐρυμεναί), a town in Magnesia in Thessaly, E. of Ossa.

Eurynome (Εὐρυνόμη). 1. Daughter of Oceanus. When Hephaestus was expelled by Hera from Olympus, Eurynome and Thetis received him in the bosom of the sea. Before the time of Cronos and Rhea, Eurynome and Ophion had ruled in Olympus over the Titans. — 2. A surname of Artemis at Phigalea in Arcadia, where she was represented half woman and half fish.

Euryphon (Εὐρυφῶν), a celebrated physician of Cnidos in Caria, was a contemporary of Hippocrates, but older. He is quoted by Galen, who says that he was considered to be the author of the ancient medical work entitled Κνίδιαι Γνῶμαι, and also that some persons attributed to him several works included in the Hippocratic Collection.

Eurypon, otherwise called **Eurytion** (Εὐρυπῶν, Εὐρυτίων), grandson of Procles, was the third king of that house at Sparta, and thenceforward gave it the name of Eurypontidae.

Eurypylus (Εὐρύπυλος). 1. Son of Euaemon and Ops, appears in different traditions as king either of Ormenion, or Hyria, or Oyrene. In the Iliad he is represented as having come from Ormenion to Troy with 40 ships. He slew many Trojans, and when wounded by Paris, he was nursed and cured by Patroclus. Among the heroes of Hyria, he is mentioned as a son of Poseidon and Celaeno, who went to Libya where he ruled in the country afterwards called Cyrene, and there became connected with the Argonauts. He married Sterope, the daughter of Helios, by whom he became the father of Lycaon and Leucippus. — 2. Son of Poseidon and Astypalaea, king of Cos, was killed by Hercules who on his return from Troy landed in Cos, and being taken for a pirate, was attacked by its inhabitants. According to another tradition Hercules attacked the island of Cos, in order to obtain possession of Chalciope, the daughter of Eurypylus, whom he loved. — 3. Son of Telephus and Astyoche, king of Mysia or Cilicia, was induced by the presents which Priam sent to his mother or wife, to assist the Trojans against the Greeks. Eurypylus killed Machaon, but was himself slain by Neoptolemus.

Eurȳsăces (Εὐρυσάκης), son of the Telamonian Ajax and Tecmessa, named after the " broad shield" of his father. An Athenian tradition related, that Eurysaces and his brother Philaeus had given up to the Athenians the island of Salamis, which they had inherited from their grandfather, and that the 2 brothers received in return the Attic franchise. Eurysaces was honoured like his father, at Athens, with an altar.

· Eurysthĕnes (Εὐρυσθένης), and Procles (Προκλῆς), the twin sons of Aristodemus, were born, according to the common account before, but, according to the genuine Spartan story, after their father's return to Peloponnesus and occupation of his allotment of Laconia. He died immediately after the birth of his children, and had not even time to decide which of the 2 should succeed him. The mother professed to be unable to name the elder, and the Lacedaemonians applied to Delphi, and were instructed to make them both kings, but give the greater honour to the elder. The difficulty thus remaining was at last removed at the suggestion of Panites, a Messenian, by watching which of the children was first washed and fed by the mother; and the first rank was accordingly given to Eurysthenes and retained by his descendants. From these 2 brothers, the 2 royal families in Sparta were descended, and were called respectively the Eurysthenidae and Proclidae. The former were also called the Agidae from Agis, son of Eurysthenes; and the latter Eurypontidae from Eurypon, grandson of Procles.

Eurystheus. [HERCULES.]

Eurȳtus (Εὔρυτος). 1. Son of Melaneus and Stratonice, was king of Oechalia, probably the Thessalian town of this name. He was a skilful archer and married to Antioche, by whom he became the father of Iole, Iphitus, Molion or Deïon, Clytius, and Toxeus. He was proud of his skill in using the bow, and is said to have instructed even Hercules in his art. He offered his daughter Iole as a prize to him who should conquer him and his sons in shooting with the bow. Hercules won the prize, but Eurytus and his sons, with the exception of Iphitus, refused to give up Iole, because they feared lest Hercules should kill the children he might have by her. Hercules accordingly marched against Oechalia with an army, took the place and killed Eurytus and his sons. According to Homer, on the other hand, Eurytus was killed by Apollo whom he presumed to rival in using the bow. (Od. viii. 226.) — 2. Son of Actor and Molione of Elis. [MOLIONES.] — 3. Son of Hermes and Antianira,

and brother of Echion, was one of the Argonauts. — 4. An eminent Pythagorean philosopher, a disciple of Philolaus.

Eusēbius (Εὐσέβιος), surnamed Pamphili to commemorate his devoted friendship for Pamphilus, bishop of Caesarea. Eusebius was born in Palestine about A. D. 264, was made bishop of Caesarea 315, and died about 340. He had a strong leaning towards the Arians, though he signed the creed of the council of Nicaea. He was a man of great learning. His most important works are :—1. The Chronicon (χρονικὰ παντοδαπῆς ἱστορίας), a work of great value to us in the study of ancient history. It is in 2 books. The first, entitled χρονογραφία, contains a sketch of the history of several ancient nations, as the Chaldaeans, Assyrians, Medes, Persians, Lydians, Hebrews, and Egyptians. It is chiefly taken from the work of Africanus [AFRICANUS], and gives lists of kings and other magistrates, with short accounts of remarkable events from the creation to the time of Eusebius. The second book consists of synchronological tables, with similar catalogues of rulers and striking occurrences, from the time of Abraham to the celebration of Constantine's Vicennalia at Nicomedia, A. D. 327, and at Rome, A. D. 328. The Greek text of the Chronicon is lost, but there is extant part of a Latin translation of it by Jerome, published by Scaliger, Leyden, 1606, of which another enlarged edition appeared at Amsterdam, 1658. There is also extant an Armenian translation, which was discovered at Constantinople, and published by Mai and Zohrab at Milan, 1818, and by Aucher, Venice, 1818.—2. The Praeparatio Evangelica (εὐαγγελικῆς ἀποδείξεως προπαρασκευή) in 15 books, is a collection of various facts and quotations from old writers, by which it was supposed that the mind would be prepared to receive the evidences of Christianity. This book is almost as important to us in the study of ancient philosophy, as the Chronicon is with reference to history, since in it are preserved specimens from the writings of almost every philosopher of any note whose works are not now extant. Edited by R. Stephens, Paris, 1544, and again in 1628, and by F. Viger, Cologne, 1688. — 3. The Demonstratio Evangelica (εὐαγγελικὴ ἀπόδειξις) in 20 books, of which 10 are extant, is a collection of evidences, chiefly from the Old Testament, addressed principally to the Jews. This is the completion of the preceding work, giving the arguments which the Praeparatio was intended to make the mind ready to receive. Edited with the Praeparatio in the editions both of R. Stephens and Viger. — 4. The Ecclesiastical History (ἐκκλησιαστικὴ ἱστορία), in 10 books, containing the history of Christianity from the birth of Christ to the death of Licinius, A. D. 324. Edited with the other Ecclesiastical historians by Reading, Cambridge, 1720, and separately by Burton, Oxford, 1838. — 5. De Martyribus Palaestinae, being an account of the persecutions of Diocletian and Maximin from A. D. 303 to 310. It is in one book, and generally found as an appendix to the eighth of the Ecclesiastical History.—6. Against Hierocles. Hierocles had advised Diocletian to begin his persecution, and had written 2 books, called λόγοι φιλαληθεῖς, comparing our Lord's miracles to those of Apollonius of Tyana. In answering this work, Eusebius reviews the life of Apollonius by Philostratus. It is published with the works of PHILOSTRATUS. — 7. Against Marcellus, bishop of Ancyra, in 2 books

8. *De Ecclesiastica Theologia*, a continuation of the former work. — 9. *De Vita Constantini*, 4 books, a panegyric rather than a biography. It has generally been published with the Ecclesiastical History, but edited separately by Heinichen, 1830. — 10. *Onomasticon de Locis Hebraicis*, a description of the towns and places mentioned in Holy Scripture, arranged in alphabetical order. It was translated into Latin by Jerome.

Eustathius (Εὐστάθιος). 1. Of Cappadocia, a Neo-Platonic philosopher, was a pupil of Iamblichus and Aedesius. In A. D. 358, he was sent by Constantius as ambassador to king Sapor, and remained in Persia, where he was treated with the greatest honour. — 2. Or **Eumathius**, probably lived as late as the twelfth century of our era. He wrote a Greek romance in 11 books, still extant, containing an account of the loves of Hysminias and Hysmine. The tale is wearisome and improbable, and shows no power of invention on the part of its author. Edited by Gaulmin, Paris, 1617, and by Teucher, Lips. 1792. — 3. Archbishop of Thessalonica, was a native of Constantinople, and lived during the latter half of the twelfth century. He was a man of great learning and wrote numerous works, the most important of which is his commentary on the Iliad and Odyssey (Παρεκβολαὶ εἰς τὴν Ὁμήρου Ἰλιάδα καὶ Ὀδυσσείαν), or rather his collection of extracts from earlier commentators on those two poems. This vast compilation was made from the numerous and extensive works of the Alexandrian grammarians and critics; and as nearly all the works from which Eustathius made his extracts are lost, his commentary is of incalculable value to us. Editions: At Rome, 1542—1550, 4 vols. fol.; at Basle, 1559-60; at Leipzig, 1825-26, containing the commentary on the Odyssey, and at Leipzig, 1827-29, the commentary on the Iliad. There is also extant by Eustathius a commentary on Dionysius Periegetes, which is published with most editions of Dionysius. Eustathius likewise wrote a commentary on Pindar, which seems to be lost. — 4. Usually called **Eustathius Romanus**, a celebrated Graeco-Roman jurist, filled various high offices at Constantinople, from A. D. 960 to 1000.

Eustratius (Εὐστράτιος), one of the latest commentators on Aristotle, lived about the beginning of the twelfth century after Christ, under the emperor Alexius Comnenus, as metropolitan of Nicaea. Of his writings only two are extant, and these in a very fragmentary state: viz. 1. A Commentary on the 2nd book of the Analytica. 2. A Commentary on the *Ethica Nicomachea*.

Euterpe. [MUSAE.]

Euthydemus (Εὐθύδημος). 1. A sophist, was born at Chios, and migrated with his brother Dionysodorus to Thurii in Italy. Being exiled thence, they came to Athens, where they resided many years. The pretensions of Euthydemus and his brother are exposed by Plato in the dialogue which bears the name of the former. — 2. King of Bactria, was a native of Magnesia. We know nothing of the circumstances attending his elevation to the sovereignty of Bactria. He extended his power over the neighbouring provinces, so as to become the founder of the greatness of the Bactrian monarchy. His dominions were invaded about B. C. 212, by Antiochus the Great, with whom he eventually concluded a treaty of peace.

Euthymus (Εὔθυμος), a hero of Locri in Italy,

son of Astycles or of the river-god Caecinus. He was famous for his strength and skill in boxing, and delivered the town of Temesa from the evil spirit Polites, to whom a fair maiden was sacrificed every year. Euthymus himself disappeared at an advanced age in the river Caecinus.

Eutocius (Εὐτόκιος) of Ascalon, the commentator on Apollonius of Perga and on Archimedes, lived about A. D. 560. His commentaries are printed in the editions of APOLLONIUS and ARCHIMEDES.

Eutrapelus, P. Volumnius, a Roman knight, obtained the surname of Eutrapelus (Εὐτράπελος), on account of his liveliness and wit. He was an intimate friend of Antony, and a companion of his pleasures and debauches. Cytheris, the mistress of Antony, was originally the freedwoman and mistress of Volumnius Eutrapelus, whence we find her called Volumnia, and was surrendered to Antony by his friend. Eutrapelus is mentioned by Horace. (*Epist.* i. 18. 31.)

Eutresii (Εὐτρήσιοι), the inhabitants of a district in Arcadia, N. of Megalopolis.

Eutresis (Εὔτρησις), a small town in Boeotia between Thespiae and Plataeae, with a temple and oracle of Apollo, who hence had the surname Eutresites.

Eutropius. 1. An eunuch, the favourite of Arcadius, became the virtual governor of the E. on the death of Rufinus, A. D. 395. He was consul in 399, but in that year was deprived of his power by the intrigues of the empress Eudoxia and Gainas, the Goth; he was first banished to Cyprus, was shortly afterwards recalled and put to death at Chalcedon. The poet Claudian wrote an invective against Eutropius. — 2. A Roman historian, held the office of a secretary under Constantine the Great, was patronised by Julian the Apostate, whom he accompanied in the Persian expedition, and was alive in the reign of Valentinian and Valens. He is the author of a brief compendium of Roman history in 10 books, from the foundation of the city to the accession of Valens, A. D. 364, to whom it is inscribed. In drawing up this abridgment Eutropius appears to have consulted the best authorities, and to have executed his task in general with care. The style is in perfect good taste and keeping with the nature of the undertaking, being plain, precise, and simple. The best editions are by Tzschucke, Lips. 1796, and by Grosse, Hal., 1813.

Eutychides (Εὐτυχίδης), of Sicyon, a statuary, and a disciple of Lysippus, flourished B. C. 300.

Euxinus Pontus. [PONTUS EUXINUS.]

Evadne (Εὐάδνη). 1. Daughter of Poseidon and Pitane, who was brought up by the Arcadian king Aepytus, and became by Apollo the mother of Iamus. — 2. Daughter of Iphis (hence called Iphias), or Philax, and wife of Capaneus. For details see CAPANEUS.

Evagoras (Εὐαγόρας), king of Salamis in Cyprus. He was sprung from a family which claimed descent from Teucer, the reputed founder of Salamis; and his ancestors appear to have been during a long period the hereditary rulers of that city under the supremacy of Persia. They had, however, been expelled by a Phoenician exile, who obtained the sovereignty for himself, and transmitted it to his descendants. Evagoras succeeded in recovering his hereditary kingdom, and putting the reigning tyrant to death, about B. C. 410. His rule was distinguished for its mildness and equity, and he greatly increased the power of Salamis, specially by the formation of a powerful fleet. He gave a friendly reception to Conon, when the latter took refuge at Salamis after the defeat of the Athenians at Aegospotami, 405 ; and it was at his intercession that the king of Persia allowed Conon the support of the Phoenician fleet. But his growing power excited the jealousy of the Persian court, and at length war was declared against him by Artaxerxes. Evagoras received the assistance of an Athenian fleet under Chabrias, and at first met with great success ; but the fortune of war afterwards turned against him, and he was glad to conclude a peace with Persia, by which he resigned his conquests in Cyprus, but was allowed to retain possession of Salamis, with the title of king. This war was brought to a close in 385. Evagoras was assassinated in 374, together with his eldest son Pnytagoras. He was succeeded by his son Nicocles. There is still extant an oration of Isocrates in praise of Evagoras, addressed to his son Nicocles.

Evagrius (Εὐάγριος), of Epiphania in Syria, born about A. D. 536, was by profession a " scholasticus" (advocate or pleader), and probably practised at Antioch. He wrote *An Ecclesiastical History*, still extant, which extends from A. D. 431 to 594. It is published with the other Ecclesiastical Historians, by Reading, Camb. 1720.

Evander (Εὔανδρος). 1. Son of Hermes by an Arcadian nymph, called Themis or Nicostrata, and in Roman traditions Carmenta or Tiburtis. About 60 years before the Trojan war, Evander is said to have led a Pelasgian colony from Pallantium in Arcadia into Italy, and there to have built a town, Pallantium, on the Tiber, at the foot of the Palatine Hill, which town was subsequently incorporated with Rome. Evander taught his neighbours milder laws and the arts of peace and of social life, and especially the art of writing, with which he himself had been made acquainted by Hercules, and music ; he also introduced among them the worship of the Lycaean Pan, of Demeter, Poseidon, and Hercules. Virgil (*Aen.* viii. 51) represents Evander as still alive at the time when Aeneas arrived in Italy, and as forming an alliance with him against the Latins. Evander was worshipped at Pallantium in Arcadia, as a hero. At Rome he had an altar at the foot of the Aventine. — 2. A Phocian, was the pupil and successor of Lacydes as the head of the Academic School at Athens, about B. C. 215.

Evenus (Εὔηνος). 1. Son of Ares and Demonice, and father of Marpessa. For details see MARPESSA. — 2. Two elegiac poets of Paros. One of these poets, though it is uncertain whether the elder or the younger, was a contemporary of Socrates, whom he is said to have instructed in poetry ; and Plato in several passages refers to Evenus, somewhat ironically, as at once a sophist or philosopher and a poet. There are 16 epigrams in the Greek Anthology bearing the name of Evenus, but it is difficult to determine which of them should be assigned to the elder and which to the younger Evenus.

Evenus (Εὐηνός: *Fidhari*). formerly called Lycormas, rises in Mt. Oeta, and flows with a rapid stream through Aetolia into the sea, 120 stadia W. of Antirrhium.

Evenus (Εὔηνος: *Sandarli*), a river of Mysia,

rising in Mt. Temnus, flowing S. through Aeolis, and falling into the Sinus Elaiticus near Pitane. The city of Adramyttium, which stood nearly due W. of its sources, was supplied with water from it by an aqueduct.

Evergetes (Εὐεργέτης), the " Benefactor," a title of honour, frequently conferred by the Greek states upon those from whom they had received benefits. It was assumed by many of the Greek kings in Egypt and elsewhere [PTOLEMAEUS.]

Evius (Εὔιος), an epithet of Bacchus, given him from the cheering and animating cry, εὔα, εὐοῖ (Lat. *evoe*), in the festivals of the god.

Exadius ('Εξάδιος), one of the Lapithae, fought at the nuptials of Pirithoüs.

Exsuperantius, Julius, a Roman historian, who lived perhaps about the 5th or 6th century of our era. He is the author of a short tract entitled *De Marii, Lepidi, ac Sertorii bellis civilibus*, which many suppose to have been abridged from the Histories of Sallust. It is appended to several editions of Sallust.

Exiongeber. [BERENICE, No. 1.]

F.

Fibaris or Farfarus (*Farfa*), a small river in Italy in the Sabine territory between Reate and Cures.

Fabatus, L. Roscius, one of Caesar's lieutenants in the Gallic war, and praetor in B. C. 49. He espoused Pompey's party, and was twice sent with proposals of accommodation to Caesar. He was killed in the battle at Mutina, B. C. 43.

Fabatus, Calpurnius, a Roman knight, accused in A. D. 64, but escaped punishment. He was grandfather to Calpurnia, wife of the younger Pliny, many of whose letters are addressed to him.

Faberius. 1. A debtor of M. Cicero. — 2. One of the private secretaries of C. Julius Caesar.

Fabia, 2 daughters of M. Fabius Ambustus. The elder was married to Ser. Sulpicius, a patrician, and one of the military tribunes B. C. 376, and the younger to the plebeian C. Licinius Stolo.

Fabia Gens, one of the most ancient patrician gentes at Rome, which traced its origin to Hercules and the Arcadian Evander. The Fabii occupy a prominent part in history soon after the commencement of the republic ; and 3 brothers belonging to the gens are said to have been invested with 7 successive consulships, from B. C. 485 to 479. The house derived its greatest lustre from the patriotic courage and tragic fate of the 306 Fabii in the battle on the Cremera, B. C. 477. [VIBULANUS.] The principal families of this gens bore the names of AMBUSTUS, BUTEO, DORSO, LABEO, MAXIMUS, PICTOR, and VIBULANUS.

Fabianus, Papirius, a Roman rhetorician and philosopher in the time of Tiberius and Caligula. He wrote works on philosophy and physics, which are referred to by Seneca and Pliny.

Fabrateria (Fabraternus: *Falvaterra*), a town in Latium on the right bank of the Trerus, originally belonged to the Volscians, but was subsequently colonised by the Romans.

Fabricii belonged originally to the Hernican town of Aletrium, where some of this name lived as late as the time of Cicero. 1. C. Fabricius Luscinus, was probably the first of his family who quitted Aletrium and settled at Rome. He was one of the most popular heroes in the Roman annals, and, like Cincinnatus and Curius, is the representative of the purity and honesty of the good old times. In his first consulship, B. C. 282, he defeated the Lucanians, Bruttians, and Samnites, gained a rich booty ánd brought into the treasury more than 400 talents. Fabricius probably served as legate in the unfortunate campaign against Pyrrhus in 280 ; and at its close he was one of the Roman ambassadors sent to Pyrrhus at Tarentum to negotiate a ransom or exchange of prisoners. The conduct of Fabricius on this occasion formed one of the most celebrated stories in Roman history, and was embellished in every possible way by subsequent writers. So much, however, seems certain,—that Pyrrhus used every effort to gain the favour of Fabricius ; that he offered him the most splendid presents, and endeavoured to persuade him to enter into his service, and accompany him to Greece ; but that the sturdy Roman was proof against all his seductions, and rejected all his offers. On the renewal of the war in the following year (279), Fabricius again served as legate, and shared in the defeat at the battle of Asculum. In 278 Fabricius was consul a second time, and had the conduct of the war against Pyrrhus. The king was anxious for peace ; and the generosity with which Fabricius sent back to Pyrrhus the traitor who had offered to poison him, afforded an opportunity for opening negotiations, which resulted in the evacuation of Italy by Pyrrhus. Fabricius then subdued the allies of the king in the S. of Italy. He was censor in 275, and distinguished himself by the severity with which he attempted to repress the growing taste for luxury. His censorship is particularly celebrated, from his expelling from the senate P. Cornelius Rufinus, on account of his possessing ten pounds' weight of silver plate. The love of luxury and the degeneracy of morals which had already commenced, brought out still more prominently the simplicity of life and the integrity of character which distinguished Fabricius as well as his contemporary Curius Dentatus ; and ancient writers love to tell of the frugal way in which they lived on their hereditary farms, and how they refused the rich presents which the Samnite ambassadors offered them. Fabricius died as poor as he had lived ; he left no dowry for his daughters, which the senate, however, furnished ; and in order to pay the greatest possible respect to his memory, the state interred him within the pomaerium, although this was forbidden by the 12 Tables.—2. L. Fabricius, curator viarum in B. C. 62, built a new bridge of stone. which connected the city with the island in the Tiber, and which was, after him, called *pons Fabricius.* The name of its author is still seen on the remnants of the bridge, which now bears the name of *ponte quattro capi.* — 3. Q. Fabricius, tribune of the plebs, 57, proposed as early as the month of January of that year, that Cicero should be recalled from exile ; but this attempt was frustrated by P. Clodius by armed force.

Fadus, Cuspius, appointed by the emperor Claudius procurator of Judaea in A. D. 44. He was succeeded by Tiberius Alexander.

Faesūlae (Faesulānus: *Fiesole*), a city of Etruria, situated on a hill 3 miles N.E. of Florence, was probably not one of the 12 cities of the League. Sulla sent to it a military colony ; and it was the head-quarters of Catiline's army. There are still to be seen the remains of its ancient walls, of a theatre, &c.

Falacrine or Falacrinum, a Sabine town at the foot of the Apennines on the Via Salaria between Asculum and Reate, the birthplace of the emperor Vespasian.

Falĕrii or Falĕrium, a town in Etruria, situated on a steep and lofty height near Mt. Soracte, was an ancient Pelasgic town, and is said to have been founded by Halesus, who settled there with a body of colonists from Argos. Its inhabitants were called Falisci, and were regarded by many as of the same race as the Aequi, whence we find them often called Aequi Falisci. Falerii afterwards became one of the 12 Etruscan cities ; but its inhabitants continued to differ from the rest of the Etruscans both in their language and customs even in the time of Augustus. After a long struggle with Rome, the Faliscans yielded to Camillus B. C. 394. They subsequently joined their neighbours several times in warring against Rome, but were finally subdued. At the close of the 1st Punic war, 241, they again revolted. The Romans now destroyed Falerii and compelled the Faliscans to build a new town in the plain. The ruins of the new city are to be seen at *Falleri* ; while the remains of the more ancient one are at *Civita Castellana.* The ancient town of Falerii was afterwards colonised by the Romans under the name of " Colonia Etruscorum Falisca," or " Colonia Junonia Faliscorum," but it never became again a place of importance. The ancient town was celebrated for its worship of Juno Curitis or Quiritis, and it was in honour of her that the Romans founded the colony. Minerva and Janus were also worshipped in the town.—Falerii had extensive linen manufactories, and its white cows were prized at Rome as victims for sacrifice.

Falernus Ager, a district in the N. of Campania, extending from the Massic hills to the river Vulturnus. It produced some of the finest wine in Italy, which was reckoned only second to the wine of Setia. Its choicest variety was called Faustianum. It became fit for drinking in 10 years, and might be used when 20 years old.

Falesia Portus, a harbour in Etruria, S. of Populonium, opposite the island Ilva.

Falisci. [FALERII.]

Faliscus, Gratius, a contemporary of Ovid, and the author of a poem upon the chase, entitled *Cynegeticon Liber,* in 540 hexameter lines. Printed in Burmann's and Wernsdorf's *Poet. Lat. Min.*

Fannia. 1. A woman of Minturnae, who hospitably entertained Marius, when he came to Minturnae in his flight, B. C. 88, though he had formerly pronounced her guilty of adultery.—2. The second wife of Helvidius Priscus.

Fannius. 1. C., tribune of the plebs, B. C. 187. —2. L., deserted from the Roman army in 84, with L. Magius, and went over to Mithridates, whom they persuaded to enter into negotiations with Sertorius in Spain. Fannius afterwards commanded a detachment of the army of Mithridates against Lucullus. — 3. C., one of the persons who signed the accusation brought against P. Clodius in 61. In 59 he was mentioned by L. Vettius as an accomplice in the alleged conspiracy against Pompey. — 4. C., tribune of the plebs, 59, opposed the *lex agraria* of Caesar. He belonged to Pompey's party, and in 49 went as praetor to Sicily.—5. C., a contemporary of the younger Pliny, the author of a work, very popular at the time, on the deaths of persons executed or exiled by Nero.

Fannius Caepio. [CAEPIO.]

Fannius Strabo. [STRABO.]

Fannius Quadratus. [QUADRATUS.]

Fanum Fortunae (*Fano*), an important town in Umbria at the mouth of the Metaurus, with a celebrated temple of Fortuna, whence the town derived its name. Augustus sent to it a colony of veterans, and it was then called " Colonia Julia Fanestris." Here was a triumphal arch in honour of Augustus.

Farfarus. [FABARIS.]

Fascinus, an early Latin divinity, and identical with Mutinus or Tutinus. He was worshipped as the protector from sorcery, witchcraft, and evil daemons; and represented in the form of a phallus, the genuine Latin for which is *fascinum*, as this symbol was believed to be most efficacious in averting all evil influences.

Faula or **Fauna,** according to some, a concubine of Hercules in Italy; according to others, the wife or sister of Faunus. [FAUNUS.]

Faunus, son of Picus, grandson of Saturnus, and father of Latinus, was the third in the series of the kings of the Laurentes. Faunus acts a very prominent part in the mythical history of Latium, and was in later times worshipped in 2 distinct capacities: first, as the god of fields and shepherds, because he had promoted agriculture and the breeding of cattle; and secondly, as an oracular divinity, because he was one of the great founders of the religion of the country. The festival of the Faunalia, celebrated on the 5th of December by the country people, had reference to him as the god of agriculture and cattle. As a prophetic god, he was believed to reveal the future to man, partly in dreams, and partly by voices of unknown origin, in certain sacred groves, one near Tibur, around the well Albunea, and another on the Aventine, near Rome. What Faunus was to the male sex, his wife Faula or Fauna was to the female. — At Rome there was a round temple of Faunus, surrounded with columns, on Mount Caelius; and another was built to him, in B.C. 196, on the island in the Tiber, where sacrifices were offered to him on the ides of February. — As the god manifested himself in various ways, the idea arose of a plurality of Fauns (Fauni), who are described as half men, half goats, and with horns. Faunus gradually came to be identified with the Arcadian Pan, and the Fauni with the Greek Satyrs.

Fausta. 1. Cornelia, daughter of the dictator Sulla, and twin sister of Faustus Sulla, was born about B.C. 88. She was first married to C. Memmius, and afterwards to Milo. She was infamous for her adulteries, and the historian Sallust is said to have been one of her paramours, and to have received a severe flogging from Milo when he was detected on one occasion in the house of the latter. Villius was another of her paramours, whence Horace calls him "Sullae gener." (*Sat.* i. 2. 64.) — — 2. **Flavia Maximiana,** daughter of Maximianus, and wife of Constantine the Great, to whom she bore Constantinus, Constantius, and Constans.

Faustina. 1. Annia Galeria, commonly distinguished as *Faustina Senior*, the wife of Antoninus Pius, died in the 3d year of his reign, A.D. 141. Notwithstanding the profligacy of her life, her husband loaded her with honours both before and after her decease. It was in honour of her that Antoninus established a hospital for the education and support of young females, who were called after her *puellae alimentariae Faustinianae* — 2. **Annia,** or *Faustina Junior*, daughter of the elder Faustina, was married to M. Aurelius in A.D. 145 or 146, and she died in a village on the skirts of Mount Taurus, in 175, having accompanied the emperor to Syria. Her profligacy was so open and infamous, that the good nature or blindness of her husband, who cherished her fondly while alive, and loaded her with honours after her death, appears truly marvellous.—3. **Annia,** grand-daughter or great-grand-daughter of M. Aurelius, the third of the numerous wives of Elagabalus.

Faustulus. [ROMULUS.]

Faventia (Faventinus: *Faenza*), a town in Gallia Cisalpina on the river Anemo and on the Via Aemilia, celebrated for its linen manufactories.

Favonii Portus (*Porto Favone*), a harbour on the coast of Corsica.

M. Favonius, an imitator of Cato Uticensis, whose character and conduct he copied so servilely as to receive the nickname of Cato's ape. He was always a warm supporter of the party of the optimates, and actively opposed all the measures of the first triumvirate. On the breaking out of the civil war in B.C. 49, he joined Pompey, notwithstanding his personal aversion to the latter, and opposed all proposals of reconciliation between Caesar and Pompey. He served in the campaign against Caesar in Greece in 48, and after the defeat of his party at Pharsalus, he accompanied Pompey in his flight, and showed him the greatest kindness and attention. Upon Pompey's death he returned to Italy, and was pardoned by Caesar. He took no part in the conspiracy against Caesar's life, but after the murder of the latter, he espoused the side of Brutus and Cassius. He was taken prisoner in the battle of Philippi in 42, and was put to death by Octavianus.

Favorinus, a philosopher and sophist in the reign of Hadrian, was a native of Arles in Gaul. He resided at different periods of his life in Rome, Greece, and Asia Minor, and obtained high distinctions. He was intimate with some of his most distinguished contemporaries, among others, with Plutarch, who dedicated to him his treatise on the principle of cold, and with Herodes Atticus, to whom he bequeathed his library and house at Rome. He wrote several works on various subjects, but none of them are extant.

Febris, the goddess, or rather the averter, of fever. She had 3 sanctuaries at Rome, in which amulets were dedicated which people had worn during a fever.

Februus, an ancient Italian divinity, to whom the month of February was sacred, for in the latter half of that month general purifications and lustrations were celebrated. The name is connected with *februare* (to purify), and *februae* (purifications). Februus was also regarded as a god of the lower world, and the festival of the dead (*Feralia*) was celebrated in February.

Felicitas, the personification of happiness, to whom a temple was erected by Lucullus in B.C. 75, which was burnt down in the reign of Claudius. Felicitas is frequently seen on Roman medals, in the form of a matron, with the staff of Mercury (*caduceus*) and a cornucopia.

Felix, Antonius, procurator of Judaea, in the

reigns of Claudius and Nero, was a brother of the freedman Pallas, and was himself a freedman of the emperor Claudius. Hence he is also called *Claudius* Felix. In his private and his public character alike Felix was unscrupulous and profligate. Having fallen in love with Drusilla, daughter of Agrippa I., and wife of Azizus, king of Emesa, he induced her to leave her husband ; and she was still living with him in 60, when St. Paul preached before him " of righteousness, temperance, and judgment to come." His government, though cruel and oppressive, was strong ; he suppressed all disturbances, and cleared the country of robbers. He was recalled in 62, and succeeded by Porcius Festus ; and the Jews having lodged accusations against him at Rome, he was saved from condign punishment only by the influence of his brother Pallas with Nero.

Fèlix, M. Minŭcius, a Roman lawyer, who flourished about A. D. 230, wrote a dialogue entitled *Octavius*, which occupies a conspicuous place among the early Apologies for Christianity. Edited by Gronovius, Lug. Bat. 1707 ; by Ernesti, ibid. 1773 ; and by Muralto, Turic. 1836.

Felsina. [BONONIA.]

Feltria (Feltrinus : *Feltre*), a town in Rhaetia, a little N. of the river Plavis.

Fenestella, a Roman historian, who lived in the time of Augustus, and died A. D. 21, in the 70th year of his age. His work, entitled *Annales*, extended to at least 22 books. The few fragments preserved relate to events subsequent to the Carthaginian wars ; and we know that it embraced the greater part of Cicero's career. A treatise, *De Sacerdotiis et Magistratibus Romanorum Libri II.*, ascribed to Fenestella, is a modern forgery.

Fenni, a savage people living by the chase, whom Tacitus (*Germ.* 46) reckons among the Germans. They appear to have dwelt in the further part of E. Prussia, and to have been the same as the modern Finns.

Ferentinum (Ferentinas, Ferentinus). 1. (*Ferento*), a town of Etruria, S. of Volsinii, the birthplace of the emperor Otho. It is called both a colonia and a municipium. There are still remains of its walls, of a theatre and of sepulchres at Ferento. — 2. (*Ferento*), an ancient town of the Hernici in Latium, S.W. of Anagnia, colonised by the Romans in the 2nd Punic war. There are still remains of its ancient walls. In its neighbourhood was the source of the sacred brook Ferentina, at which the Latins used to hold their meetings.

Ferentum. [FORENTUM.]

Feretrius, a surname of Jupiter, derived from *ferire*, to strike ; for persons who took an oath called upon Jupiter to strike them if they swore falsely, as they struck the victim which they sacrificed to him. Others derived it from *ferre*, because he was the giver of peace, or because people dedicated (*ferebant*) to him spolia opima.

Feronia, an ancient Italian divinity, who originally belonged to the Sabines and Faliscans, and was introduced by them among the Romans. It is difficult to form a definite notion of the nature of this goddess. Some consider her to have been the goddess of liberty ; others look upon her as the goddess of commerce and traffic, and others again regard her as a goddess of the earth or the lower world. Her chief sanctuary was at Terracina, near mount Soracte.

Ferox, Urseius, a Roman jurist, who probably

flourished between the time of Tiberius and Vespasian.

Ferrātus Mons (*Jebel-Jurjurah*), one of the principal mountain-chains in the Lesser Atlas system, in N. Africa, on the borders of Mauretania Caesariensis and Mauretania Sitifensis.

Fescennium or Fescennia (Fescenninus), a town of the Falisci in Etruria, and consequently like Falerii of Pelasgic origin. [FALERII.] From this town the Romans are said to have derived the Fescennine songs. The site of the town is uncertain ; it may perhaps be placed at *S. Silvesto*. Many writers place it at *Civita Castellana*, but this was the site of Falerii.

Festus, Sext. Pompeius, a Roman grammarian, probably lived in the 4th century of our era. His name is attached to a dictionary or glossary of Latin words and phrases, divided into 20 books, and commonly called *Sexti Pompeii Festi de Verborum Significatione*. It was abridged by Festus from a work with the same title by M. Verrius Flaccus, a celebrated grammarian in the reign of Augustus. Festus made a few alterations and criticisms of his own, and inserted numerous extracts from other writings of Verrius ; but altogether omitted those words which had fallen into disuse, intending to make these the subject of a separate volume. Towards the end of the 8th century, Paul, son of Warnefrid, better known as Paulus Diaconus, from having officiated as a deacon of the church at Aquileia, abridged the abridgment of Festus. The original work of Verrius Flaccus has perished with the exception of one or two inconsiderable fragments. Of the abstract by Festus one imperfect MS. only has come down to us. The numerous blanks in this MS. have been ingeniously filled up by Scaliger and Ursinus, partly from conjecture and partly from the corresponding paragraphs of Paulus, whose performance appears in a complete form in many MSS. The best edition of Festus is by K. O. Müller, Lips. 1839, in which the text of Festus is placed face to face with the corresponding text of Paulus, so as to admit of easy comparison. The work is one of great value, containing a rich treasure of learning upon many points connected with antiquities, mythology, and grammar.

Festus, Porcius, succeeded Antonius Felix as procurator of Judaea in A. D. 62, and died not long after his appointment. It was he who bore testimony to the innocence of St. Paul, when he defended himself before him in the same year.

Fibrēnus. [ARPINUM.]

Ficāna (Ficanensis), one of the ancient Latin towns destroyed by Ancus Martius.

Ficulēa (Ficuleas, -ātis, Ficolensis), an ancient town of the Sabines, E. of Fidenae, said to have been founded by the Aborigines, but early sunk into decay.

Fidēnae, sometimes Fidena (Fidenas, -ātis : *Castel Giubileo*), an ancient town in the land of the Sabines, 40 stadia (5 miles) N.E. of Rome, situated on a steep hill, between the Tiber and the Anio. It is said to have been founded by Alba Longa, and also to have been conquered and colonised by Romulus ; but the population appears to have been partly Etruscan, and it was probably colonised by the Etruscan Veii, with which city we find it in close alliance. It frequently revolted and was frequently taken by the Romans. Its last revolt was in B. C. 438, and in the following year it was de-

s 4

stroyed by the Romans. Subsequently the town was rebuilt; but it is not mentioned again till the reign of Tiberius; when in consequence of the fall of a temporary wooden theatre in the town 20,000, or, according to some accounts, 50,000 persons lost their lives.

Fidentia (Fidentīnus: *Borgo S. Donino*), a town in Cisalpine Gaul on the Via Aemilia between Parma and Placentia, memorable for the victory which Sulla's generals gained over Carbo, B. c. 82.

Fides, the personification of fidelity or faithfulness. Numa is said to have built a temple to Fides publica, on the Capitol, and another was built there in the consulship of M. Aemilius Scaurus, B. c. 115. She was represented as a matron wearing a wreath of olive or laurel leaves, and carrying in her hand corn ears, or a basket with fruit.

Fidius, an ancient form of *filius*, occurs in the connection of *Dius Fidius*, or *Medius Fidius*, that is, *me Dius* (Διός) *filius*, or the son of Jupiter, that is, Hercules. Hence the expression *medius fidius* is equivalent to *me Hercules*, scil. *juvet*. Sometimes Fidius is used alone. Some of the ancients connected *fidius* with *fides*.

Figulus, C. Marcius. 1. Consul B. c. 162, and again consul 156, when he carried on war with the Dalmatae in Illyricum. — 2. Consul 64, supported Cicero in his consulship.

Figulus, P. Nigidius, a Pythagorean philosopher of high reputation, who flourished about B. c. 60. Mathematical and physical investigations appear to have occupied a large share of his attention; and such was his fame as an astrologer, that it was generally believed, in later times at least, that he had predicted the future greatness of Octavianus on hearing the announcement of his birth. He, moreover, possessed considerable influence in political affairs; was one of the senators selected by Cicero to take down the depositions of the witnesses who gave evidence with regard to Catiline's conspiracy, B. c. 63; was praetor, 59; took an active part in the civil war on the side of Pompey; was compelled in consequence by Caesar to live abroad, and died in exile, 44.

Fimbria, C. Flavius. 1. A *homo novus*, who rose to the highest honours through his own merits and talents. Cicero praises him both as a jurist and an orator. He was consul B. c. 104, and was subsequently accused of extortion in his province, but was acquitted. — 2. Probably son of the preceding, was one of the most violent partizans of Marius and Cinna during the civil war with Sulla. In B. c. 86 he was sent into Asia as legate of Valerius Flaccus, and took advantage of the unpopularity of his commander with the soldiers to excite a mutiny against him. Flaccus was killed at Chalcedon, and was succeeded in the command by Fimbria, who carried on the war with success against the generals of Mithridates. In 84 Sulla crossed over from Greece into Asia, and, after concluding peace with Mithridates, marched against Fimbria. The latter was deserted by his troops, and put an end to his life.

Fines, the name of a great number of places, either on the borders of Roman provinces or of different tribes. These places are usually found only in the Itineraries, and are not of sufficient importance to be enumerated here.

Firmānus, Tarutius, a mathematician and astrologer, contemporary with M. Varro and Cicero. At Varro's request Firmanus took the horoscope of Romulus, and from the circumstances of the life and death of the founder determined the era of Rome.

Firmānus Symposius, Caelius, of uncertain age and country, the author of 100 insipid riddles, each comprised in 3 hexameter lines, collected, as we are told in the prologue, for the purpose of promoting the festivities of the Saturnalia. Printed in the *Poet. Lat. Min.* of Wernsdorf, vol. vi.

Firmicus Maternus, Julius, or perhaps Vilius, the author of a work entitled *Matheseos Libri VIII.*, which is a formal introduction to judicial astrology, according to the discipline of the Egyptians and Babylonians. The writer lived in the time of Constantine the Great, and had during a portion of his life practised as a forensic pleader. There is also ascribed to this Firmicus Maternus a work in favour of Christianity, entitled *De Errore Profanarum Religionum ad Constantium et Constantem*. This work was, however, probably written by a different person of the same name, since the author of the work on astrology was a pagan.

Firmum (Firmānus: *Fermo*), a town in Picenum, 3 miles from the coast, and S. of the river Tinna, colonised by the Romans at the beginning of the 1st Punic war. On the coast was its strongly fortified harbour, **Castellum Firmānum** or **Firmanorum** (*Porto di Fermo*).

M. Firmus, a native of Seleucia, the friend and ally of Zenobia, seized upon Alexandria, and proclaimed himself emperor, but was defeated and slain by Aurelian, A. D. 273.

Flaccus, Calpurnius, a rhetorician in the reign of Hadrian, whose 51 declamations are frequently printed with those of Quintilian.

Flaccus, Fulvius. 1. M., consul with App. Claudius Caudex, B. c. 264, in which year the first Punic war broke out. — 2. Q., son of No. 1, consul 237, fought against the Ligurians in Italy. In 224 he was consul a 2nd time, and conquered the Gauls and Insubrians in the N. of Italy. In 215 he was praetor, after having been twice consul; and in the following year (214) he was re-elected praetor. In 213 he was consul for the 3rd time, and carried on the war in Campania against the Carthaginians. He and his colleague, Ap. Claudius Pulcher, took Hanno's camp by storm, and then laid siege to Capua, which they took in the following year (212). In 209 he was consul for the 4th time, and continued the war against the Carthaginians in the S. of Italy. — 3. Cn., brother of No. 2, was praetor 212, and had Apulia for his province: he was defeated by Hannibal near Herdonea. In consequence of his cowardice in this battle he was accused before the people, and went into voluntary exile before the trial. — 4. Q., son of No. 2, was praetor 182, and carried on war in Spain against the Celtiberians, whom he defeated in several battles. He was consul 179 with his brother, L. Manlius Acidinus Fulvianus, who had been adopted by Manlius Acidinus. In his consulship he defeated the Ligurians. In 174 he was censor with A. Postumius Albinus. Shortly afterwards he became deranged, and hung himself in his bedchamber. — 5. M., nephew of No. 4, and a friend of the Gracchi, was consul 125, when he subdued the Transalpine Ligurians. He was one of the triumvirs for carrying into execution the agrarian law of Tib. Gracchus, and was slain together with C. Gracchus in 121. He was a man of a bold and determined character, and was more ready to have recourse to violence and open force than C. Gracehus.— 6. Q., praetor in Sardinia, 187, and consul 180.—7. Ser., consul 135, subdued the Vardaeans in Illyricum.

Flaccus, Granius, a contemporary of Julius Caesar, wrote a book, *De Jure Papiriano*, which was a collection of the laws of the ancient kings of Rome, made by Papirius. [PAPIRIUS].

Flaccus, Horatius. [HORATIUS.]

Flaccus, Hordeonius, consular legate of Upper Germany at Nero's death, A. D. 68. He was secretly attached to the cause of Vespasian, for which reason he made no effectual attempt to put down the insurrection of Civilis [CIVILIS]. His troops, who were in favour of Vitellius, compelled him to give up the command to VOCULA, and shortly afterwards put him to death.

Flaccus, C. Norbanus, a general of Octavian and Antony in the campaign against Brutus and Cassius, B. C. 42. He was consul in 38.

Flaccus, Perslus. [PERSIUS.]

Flaccus Siculus, an agrimensor by profession, probably lived about the reign of Nerva. He wrote a treatise entitled *De Conditionibus Agrorum*, of which the commencement is preserved in the collection of Agrimensores. [FRONTINUS.]

Flaccus, Valerius. 1. L., curule aedile B. C. 201, praetor 200, and consul 195. with M. Porcius Cato. In his consulship, and in the following year, he carried on war, with great success, against the Gauls in the N. of Italy. In 184 he was the colleague of M. Cato in the censorship, and in the same year was made princeps senatus. He died 180.—2. L., consul 131, with P. Licinius Crassus.—3. L., consul 100 with C. Marius, when he took an active part in putting down the insurrection of Saturninus. In 97 he was censor with M. Antonius, the orator. In 86 he was chosen consul in place of Marius, who had died in his 7th consulship, and was sent by Cinna into Asia to oppose Sulla, and to bring the war against Mithridates to a close. The avarice and severity of Flaccus made him unpopular with the soldiers, who at length rose in mutiny at the instigation of Fimbria. Flaccus was then put to death by order of Fimbria. [FIMBRIA.]—4. L., the interrex, who proposed that Sulla should be made dictator, 82, and who was afterwards made by Sulla his magister equitum.—5. C., praetor 98, consul 93, and afterwards proconsul in Spain.—6. L., praetor 63, and afterwards propraetor in Asia, where he was succeeded by Q. Cicero. In 59 he was accused by D. Laelius of extortion in Asia; but, although undoubtedly guilty, he was defended by Cicero (in the oration *pro Flacco*, which is still extant) and Q. Hortensius, and was acquitted.—7. C., a poet, was a native of Padua, and lived in the time of Vespasian. He is the author of the *Argonautica*, an unfinished heroic poem in 8 books, on the Argonautic expedition, in which he follows the general plan and arrangement of Apollonius Rhodius. The 8th book terminates abruptly, at the point where Medea is urging Jason to make her the companion of his homeward journey. Flaccus is only a second-rate poet. His diction is pure; his general style is free from affectation; his versification is polished and harmonious; his descriptions are lively and vigorous; but he displays no originality, nor any of the higher attributes of genius. Editions by Burmannus, Leid. 1724; by Harles, Altenb. 1781; and by Wagner, Gotting. 1805.

Flaccus, Verrius, a freedman by birth, and a distinguished grammarian, in the reign of Augustus, who entrusted him with the education of his grandsons, Caius and Lucius Caesar. He died at an advanced age, in the reign of Tiberius. At the lower end of the market-place at Praeneste was a statue of Verrius Flaccus, fronting the Hemicyclium, on the inner curve of which were set up marble tablets, inscribed with the Fasti Verriani. These Fasti were a calendar of the days and vacations of public business— *dies fasti, nefasti,* and *intercisi*—of religious festivals, triumphs, &c., especially including such as were peculiar to the family of the Caesars. In 1770 the foundations of the Hemicyclium of Praeneste were discovered, and among the ruins were found fragments of the Fasti Verriani. They are given at the end of Wolf's edition of Suetonius, Lips. 1802.— Flaccus wrote numerous works on philology, history, and archaeology. Of these the most celebrated was his work *De Verborum Significatione,* which was abridged by Festus. [FESTUS.]

Flamininus, Quintius. 1. T., a distinguished general, was consul B. C. 198, and had the conduct of the war against Philip of Macedonia, which he carried on with ability and success. He pretended to have come to Greece to liberate the country from the Macedonian yoke, and thus induced the Achaean league, and many of the other Greek states, to give him their support. The war was brought to a close in 197, by the defeat of Philip by Flamininus, at the battle of Cynoscephalae in Thessaly; and peace was shortly afterwards concluded with Philip. Flamininus continued in Greece for the next 3 years, in order to settle the affairs of the country. At the celebration of the Isthmian games at Corinth in 196, he caused a herald to proclaim, in the name of the Roman senate, the freedom and independence of Greece. In 195 he made war against Nabis, tyrant of Sparta, whom he soon compelled to submit to the Romans; and in 194 he returned to Rome, having won the affections of the Greeks by his prudent and conciliating conduct. In 192 he was again sent to Greece as ambassador, and remained there till 190, exercising a sort of protectorate over the country. In 183 he was sent as ambassador to Prusias of Bithynia, in order to demand the surrender of Hannibal. He died about 174.—2. L., brother of the preceding, was curule aedile 200, praetor 199, and afterwards served under his brother as legate in the war against Macedonia. He was consul in 192, and received Gaul as his province, where he behaved with the greatest barbarity. On one occasion he killed a chief of the Boii who had taken refuge in his camp, in order to afford amusement to a profligate favourite. For this and similar acts of cruelty he was expelled from the senate in 184, by M. Cato, who was then censor. He died in 170.—3. T., consul 150, with M'. Acilius Balbus.—4. T., consul 123, with Q. Metellus Balearicus. Cicero says that he spoke Latin with elegance, but that he was an illiterate man.

Flaminius. 1. C., was tribune of the plebs, B. C. 232, in which year, notwithstanding the violent opposition of the senate, he carried an agrarian law, ordaining that the *Ager Gallicus Picenus*, which had recently been conquered, should be distributed among the plebeians. In 227, in which year 4 praetors were appointed for the first time, he was one of them, and received Sicily for his province, where he earned the goodwill of the provincials by his integrity and justice. In 223 he was consul, and marched against the Insubrian Gauls. As the senate were anxious to deprive Flaminius of his office, they declared that the consular election was not valid on account of some fault in the auspices, and sent a letter to the consuls, with orders to return to Rome. But as all preparations had been made for a battle against the Insubrians, the letter was left unopened until the battle was gained. In 220 he was censor, and executed 2 great works, which bore his name, viz. the *Circus Flaminius* and the *Via Flaminia.* In 217 he was consul a second time, and marched against Hannibal, but was defeated by the latter at the fatal battle of the Trasimene lake, on the 23d of June, in which he perished with the greater part of his army. — **2.** C., son of No. 1, was quaestor of Scipio Africanus in Spain, 210; curule aedile 196, when he distributed among the people a large quantity of grain at a low price, which was furnished him by the Sicilians as a mark of gratitude towards his father and himself; was praetor 193, and obtained Hispania Citerior as his province, where he carried on the war with success; and was consul 185, when he defeated the Ligurians.

Flanaticus or **Flanonicus Sinus** (*Gulf of Quarnaro*), a bay of the Adriatic sea on the coast of Liburnia, named after the people **Flanates** and their town **Flanona** (*Fianona*).

Flavia, a surname given to several towns in the Roman empire in honour of the Flavian family.

Flavia gens, celebrated as the house to which the emperor Vespasian belonged. During the later period of the Roman empire, the name Flavius descended from one emperor to another, Constantius, the father of Constantine the Great, being the first in the series.

Flavia Domitilla. [DOMITILLA.]

Flavius, Cn., the son of a freedman, became secretary to App. Claudius Caecus, and, in consequence of this connection, attained distinguished honours in the commonwealth. He is celebrated in the annals of Roman law for having been the first to divulge certain technicalities of procedure, which previously had been kept secret as the exclusive patrimony of the pontiffs and the patricians. He was elected curule aedile B. C. 303, in spite of his ignominious birth.

Flavius Fimbria. [FIMBRIA.]
Flavius Josephus. [JOSEPHUS.]
Flavius Vopiscus. [VOPISCUS.]

Flavus, L. Caesetius, tribune of the plebs, B. C. 44, was deposed from his office by C. Julius Caesar, because, in concert with C. Epidius Marullus, one of his colleagues in the tribunate, he had removed the crowns from the statues of the dictator, and imprisoned a person who had saluted Caesar as "king."

Flavus or **Flavius, Subrius**, tribune in the Praetorian guards, was the most active agent in the conspiracy against Nero, A. D. 66, which, from its most distinguished member, was called Piso's conspiracy.

Flevum, a fortress in Germany at the mouth of the Amisia (*Ems*).

Flevum, Flevo. [RHENUS.]

Flora, the Roman goddess of flowers and spring. The writers, whose object was to bring the Roman religion into contempt, relate that Flora was a courtezan, who had accumulated a large property, and bequeathed it to the Roman people, in return for which she was honoured with the annual festival of the Floralia. But her worship was established at Rome in the very earliest times, for a temple is said to have been vowed to her by king Tatius, and Numa appointed a flamen to her. The resemblance between the names Flora and Chloris led the later Romans to identify the two divinities. Her temple at Rome was situated near the Circus Maximus, and her festival was celebrated from the 28th of April till the 1st of May, with extravagant merriment and lasciviousness. (*Dict. of Ant.* art. *Floralia.*)

Florentia (Florentinus). **1.** (*Firenze, Florence*), a town in Etruria on the Arnus, was a Roman colony, and was probably founded by the Romans during their wars with the Ligurians. In the time of Sulla it was a flourishing municipium, but its greatness as a city dates from the middle ages. — **2.** (*Fiorenzuola*), a town in Cisalpine Gaul on the Aemilia Via between Placentia and Parma.

Florentinus, a jurist, one of the council of the emperor Severus Alexander, wrote *Institutiones* in 12 books, which are quoted in the Corpus Juris.

Florianus, M. Annius, the brother, by a different father, of the emperor Tacitus, upon whose decease he was proclaimed emperor at Rome, A. D. 276. He was murdered by his own troops at Tarsus, after a reign of about 2 months, while on his march against Probus, who had been proclaimed emperor by the legions in Syria.

Florus, Annaeus. 1 L., a Roman historian, lived under Trajan and Hadrian, and wrote a summary of Roman history, divided into 4 books, extending from the foundation of the city to the establishment of the empire under Augustus, entitled *Rerum Romanarum Libri IV.*, or *Epitome de Gestis Romanorum.* This compendium presents within a very moderate compass a striking view of the leading events comprehended by the above limits. It is written in a declamatory style, and the sentiments frequently assume the form of tumid conceits expressed in violent metaphors. The best editions are, by Duker, Lug. Bat. 1722, 1744, reprinted Lips. 1832; by Titze, Prag. 1819; and by Seebode, Lips. 1821. — **2.** A Roman poet in the time of Hadrian.

Florus, Gessius, a native of Clazomenae, succeeded Albinus as procurator of Judaea, A. D. 64—65. His cruel and oppressive government was the main cause of the rebellion of the Jews. He is sometimes called Festus and Cestius Florus.

Florus, Julius, addressed by Horace in 2 epistles (i. 3, ii. 2). was attached to the suite of Claudius Tiberius Nero, when the latter was despatched by Augustus to place Tigranes upon the throne of Armenia. He was both a poet and an orator.

Foca or **Phocas**, a Latin grammarian, author of a dull, foolish life of Virgil in hexameter verse, of which 119 lines are preserved. Printed in the *Anthol. Lat.* of Burmann and Wernsdorf.

Foeniculārius Campus, i. e., the Fennel Fields, a plain covered with fennel, near Tarraco in Spain.

Fontēius, M., governed as propraetor Narbonese Gaul, between B. C. 76—73, and was accused of extortion in his province by M. Plaetorius in 69. He was defended by Cicero in an oration (*pro M. Fonteio*), part of which is extant.

Fontēius Căpĭto. [CAPITO.]

Fontus, a Roman divinity, son of Janus, had an altar on the Janiculus, which derived its name from his father, and on which Numa was believed to be buried. The name of this divinity is connected with *fons*, a fountain ; and he was the personification of the flowing waters. On the 13th of October the Romans celebrated the festival of the fountains called Fontinalia, at which the fountains were adorned with garlands.

Fŏrentum or **Fĕrentum** (Forentanus : *Forenza*), a town in Apulia, surrounded by fertile fields and in a low situation, according to Horace (*arvum pingue humile Forenti, Carm.* iii. 4. 16). Livy (ix. 20) describes it as a fortified place, which was taken by C. Junius Bubulcus, B. c. 317. The modern town lies on a hill.

Formĭae (Formianus : nr. *Mola di Gaëta*, Ru.), a town in Latium, on the Appia Via, in the innermost corner of the beautiful Sinus Caietanus (*Gulf of Gaëta*). It was a very ancient town, founded by the Pelasgic Tyrrhenians ; and it appears to have been one of the head-quarters of the Tyrrhenian pirates, whence later poets supposed the city of Lamus, inhabited by the Laestrygones, of which Homer speaks (*Od.* x. 81), to be the same as Formiae. Formiae became a municipium and received the Roman franchise at an early period. The beauty of the surrounding country induced many of the Roman nobles to build villas at this spot : of these the best known is the Formianum of Cicero, in the neighbourhood of which he was killed. The remains of Cicero's villa are still to be seen at the *Villa Marzana* near *Castiglione*. The hills of Formiae produced good wine. (Hor. *Carm.* i. 20.)

Formĭo (*Formione, Rusano*), a small river, forming the N. boundary of Istria.

Fornax, a Roman goddess, said to have been worshipped that she might ripen the corn, and prevent its being burnt in baking in the oven (*fornax*). Her festival, the Fornacalia, was announced by the curio maximus.

Fortūna (Τύχη), the goddess of fortune, was worshipped both in Greece and Italy. Hesiod describes her as a daughter of Oceanus ; Pindar in one place calls her a daughter of Zeus the Liberator, and in another place one of the Moerae or Fates. She was represented with different attributes. With a rudder, she was conceived as the divinity guiding and conducting the affairs of the world ; with a ball, she represents the varying unsteadiness of fortune ; with Plutos or the horn of Amalthea, she was the symbol of the plentiful gifts of fortune. She was worshipped in most cities in Greece. Her statue at Smyrna held with one hand a globe on her head, and in the other carried the horn of Amalthea. Fortuna was still more worshipped by the Romans than by the Greeks. Her worship is traced to the reigns of Ancus Martius and Servius Tullius, and the latter is said to have built 2 temples to her, the one in the forum boarium, and the other on the banks of the Tiber. The Romans mention her with a variety of surnames and epithets, as *publica, privata, muliebris* (said to have originated at the time when Coriolanus was prevented by the entreaties of the women from destroying Rome), *regina, conservatrix, primigenia, virilis*, &c. Fortuna Virginensis was worshipped by newly-married women, who dedicated their maiden garments and girdle in her temple. Fortuna Virilis was worshipped by women, who prayed

to her that she might preserve their charms, and thus enable them to please their husbands. Her surnames, in general, express either particular kinds of good fortune, or the persons or classes of persons to whom she granted it. Her worship was of great importance also at Antium and Praeneste, where her *sortes* or oracles were very celebrated.

Fortunātae or **-orum Insŭlae** (*αἱ τῶν μακάρων νῆσοι*, i. e. the Islands of the Blessed). The early Greeks, as we learn from Homer, placed the Elysian fields, into which favoured heroes passed without dying, at the extremity of the earth, near the river Oceanus. [ELYSIUM.] In poems later than Homer, an island is clearly spoken of as their abode ; and though its position was of course indefinite, both the poets, and the geographers who followed them, placed it beyond the pillars of Hercules. Hence when, just after the time of the Marian civil wars, certain islands were discovered in the Ocean, off the W. coast of Africa, the name of Fortunatae Insulae was applied to them. As to the names of the individual islands, and the exact identification of them by their modern names, there are difficulties : but it may be safely said, generally, that the Fortunatae Insulae of Pliny, Ptolemy, and others, are the *Canary Islands*, and probably the *Madeira* group ; the latter being perhaps those called by Pliny (after Juba) Purpurariae.

Fortunatiānus, Atilĭus, a Latin grammarian, author of a treatise (*Ars*) upon prosody, and the metres of Horace, printed in the collection of Putschius.

Fortunatiānus, Curĭus or **Chirĭus**, a Roman lawyer, flourished about A. D. 450. He is the author of a compendium of technical rhetoric, in 3 books, under the title *Curii Fortunatiani Consulti Artis Rhetoricae Scholicae Libri tres*, which at one period was held in high esteem as a manual. Printed in the *Rhetores Latini Antiqui*, of Pithou, Paris, 1599.

Fŏrum, an open space of ground, in which the people met for the transaction of any kind of business. At Rome the number of fora increased with the growth of the city. They were level pieces of ground of an oblong form, and were surrounded by buildings, both private and public. They were divided into 2 classes ; *fora civilia*, in which justice was administered and public business transacted, and *fora venalia*, in which provisions and other things were sold, and which were distinguished as the *forum boarium, olitorium, suarium, piscarium, &c.* The principal fora at Rome were : 1. **Forum Romanum**, also called simply the *Forum*, and at a later time distinguished by the epithets *vetus* or *magnum*. It is usually described as lying between the Capitoline and Palatine hills ; but to speak more correctly, it lay between the Capitoline and the Velian ridge, which was a hill opposite the Palatine. It ran lengthwise from the foot of the Capitol or the arch of Septimius Severus in the direction of the arch of Titus ; but it did not extend so far as the latter, and came to an end at the commencement of the ascent to the Velian ridge, where was the temple of Antoninus and Faustina. Its shape was that of an irregular quadrangle, of which the 2 longer sides were not parallel, but were much wider near the Capitol than at the other end. Its length was 630 French feet, and its breadth varied from 190 to 100 feet, an extent undoubtedly small for the greatness of Rome ; but it must be recollected that the limits of the forum were fixed in the early days of Rome and never underwent any alteration. The origin of the forum is ascribed to Romulus and Tatius, who are said to have filled up the swamp or marsh which occupied its site, and to have set it apart as a place for the administration of justice and for holding the assemblies of the people. The forum in its widest sense included the forum properly so called, and the Comitium. The Comitium occupied the narrow or upper end of the forum, and was the place where the patricians met in their comitia curiata: the forum, in its narrower sense, was originally only a market-place, and was not used for any political purpose. At a later time the forum in its narrower sense was the place of meeting for the plebeians in their comitia tributa, and was separated from the comitium by the Rostra or platform, from which the orators addressed the people. The most important of the public buildings which surrounded the forum in early times was the Curia Hostilia, the place of meeting of the senate, which was said to have been erected by Tullus Hostilius. It stood on the N. side of the Comitia. In the time of Tarquin the forum was surrounded by a range of shops, probably of a mean character, but they gradually underwent a change, and were eventually occupied by bankers and money-changers. The shops on the N. side underwent this change first, whence they were called *Novas* or *Argentariae Tabernae*; while the shops on the S. side, though they subsequently experienced the same change, were distinguished by the name of *Veteres Tabernae*. As Rome grew in greatness, the forum was adorned with statues of celebrated men, with temples and basilicae, and with other public buildings. The site of the ancient forum is occupied by the *Campo Vaccino.*—2. **Forum Julium** or **Forum Caesaris**, was built by Julius Caesar, because the old forum was found too small for the transaction of public business. It was close by the old forum, behind the church of St. Martina. Caesar built here a magnificent temple of Venus Genitrix.—3. **Forum Augusti**, built by Augustus, because the 2 existing fora were not found sufficient for the great increase of business which had taken place. It stood behind the Forum Julium, and its entrance at the other end was by an arch, now called *Arco de' Pantani*. Augustus adorned it with a temple of Mars Ultor, and with the statues of the most distinguished men of the republic. This forum was used for *causae publicae* and *sortitiones judicum.* — 4. **Forum Nervae** or **Forum Transitorium**, was a small forum lying between the Temple of Peace and the fora of Julius Caesar and Augustus. The Temple of Peace was built by Vespasian; and as there were private buildings between it and the fora of Caesar and Augustus, Domitian resolved to pull down those buildings, and thus form a 4th forum, which was not, however, intended like the other 3 for the transaction of public business, but simply to serve as a passage from the Temple of Peace to the fora of Caesar and Augustus: hence its name *Transitorium*. The plan was carried into execution by Nerva, whence the forum is also called by the name of this emperor.— 5. **Forum Trajani**, built by the emperor Trajan, who employed the architect Apollodorus for the purpose. It lay between the forum of Augustus and the Campus Martius. It was the most splendid of all the fora, and considerable remains of it are still extant. Here were the *Basilica Ulpia* and *Biblio-*

theca Ulpia, the celebrated *Columna Trajani*, an equestrian statue and a triumphal arch of Trajan, and a temple of Trajan built by Hadrian.

Fŏrum, the name of several towns in various parts of the Roman empire, which were originally simply markets or places for the administration of justice. 1. **Aliēni** (*Ferrara ?*), in Cisalpine Gaul.— 2. **Appii** (nr. *S. Donato*, Ru.), in Latium, on the Appia Via, in the midst of the Pomptine marshes, 43 miles S. E. of Rome, founded by the censor Appius Claudius when he made the Appia Via. Here the Christians from Rome met the Apostle Paul (*Acts,* xxviii.15).—3. **Amēlii** or **Amelium** (*Montalto*), in Etruria on the Aurelia Via. — 4. **Cassii**, in Etruria on the Cassia Via, near Viterbo. —5. **Clōdii** (*Oriulo*), in Etruria. — 6. **Cornēlii** (*Imola*), in Gallia Cispadana, on the Aemilia Via, between Bononia and Faventia, a colony founded by Cornelius Sulla. —7. **Flaminii**, in Umbria on the Flaminia Via.—8. **Fulvii**, surnamed **Valentinum** (*Valenza*), in Liguria on the Po, on the road from Dertona to Asta.—9. **Gallorum** (*Castel Franco*), in Gallia Cisalpina on the Aemilia Via between Mutina and Bononia, memorable for the 2 battles fought between Antonius and the consuls Pansa and Hirtius.—10. **Hadriāni** (*Voorburg*), in the island of the Batavi in Gallia Belgica, where several Roman remains have been found. — 11. **Julii** or **Julium** (Forojuliensis: *Frejus*), a Roman colony founded by Julius Caesar, B. C. 44, in Gallia Narbonensis, on the river Argenteus and on the coast, 600 stadia N. E. of Massilia. It possessed a good harbour, and was the usual station of a part of the Roman fleet. It was the birthplace of Agricola. At Frejus are the remains of a Roman aqueduct, circus, arch, &c. — 12. **Julii** or **Julium** (*Friaul*), a fortified town and a Roman colony in the country of the Carni, N. E. of Aquileia: in the middle ages it became a place of importance.—13. **Julium**. See ILLITURGIS.—14. **Livii** (*Forli*), in Cisalpine Gaul, in the territory of the Boii, on the Aemilia Via, S. W. of Ravenna: here the Gothic king Athaulf married Galla Placidia.—15. **Popilii** (*Forlimpopoli*), in Gallia Cisalpina, E. of No. 14, and on the same road.—16. **Popilii** (*Polla*), in Lucania, E. of Paestum on the Tanger and on the Popilia Via. On the wall of an inn at Polla was discovered an inscription respecting the praetor Popilius. —17. **Segusiānōrum** (*Feurs*), in Gallia Lugdunensis, on the Liger, and W. of Lugdunum, a town of the Segusiani and a Roman colony with the surname Julia Felix.—18. **Semprōnii** (Forosemproniensis: *Fossombrone*), a municipium in Umbria, on the Flaminia Via.—19. **Vocontii** (*Vidaubon* E. of Canet), a town of the Salyes in Gallia Narbonensis.

Fosi, a people of Germany, the neighbours and allies of the Cherusci, in whose fate they shared. [CHERUSCI.] It is supposed that their name is retained in the river *Fuse* in Brunswick.

Fossa or **Fossae**, a canal. 1. **Clōdia**, a canal between the mouth of the Po and Altinum in the N. of Italy: there was a town of the same name upon it.—2. **Cluilia** or **Cluiliae**, a trench about 5 miles from Rome, said to have been the ditch with which the Alban king Cluilius protected his camp, when he marched against Rome in the reign of Tullus Hostilius. —3. **Corbulōnis**, a canal in the island of the Batavi, connecting the Maas and the Rhine, dug by command of Corbulo in the reign of Claudius. — 4. **Drusiānae** or **Drusinae**, a canal which Drusus caused his soldiers to dig in B. C. 11

uniting the Rhine with the Yssel. It probably commenced near Arnheim on the Rhine and fell into the Yssel near Doesberg. — 5. **Mariāna** or **Mariānae**, a canal dug by command of Marius during his war with the Cimbri, in order to connect the Rhone with the Mediterranean, and thus make an easier passage for vessels into the Rhone, because the mouths of the river were frequently choked up with sand. The canal commenced near Arelate, but in consequence of the frequent changes in the course of the Rhone, it is impossible now to trace the course of the canal. — 6. **Xerxis.** See ATHOS.

Franci, i. e., " the Free men," a confederacy of German tribes, formed on the Lower Rhine in the place of the ancient league of the Cherusci, and consisting of the Sigambri, the chief tribe, the Chamavi, Ampsivarii, Bructeri, Chatti, &c. They are first mentioned about A. D. 240. After carrying on frequent wars with the Romans, they at length settled permanently in Gaul, of which they became the rulers under their great king Clovis, A. D. 496.

Fregellae (Fregellānus: *Ceprano*), an ancient and important town of the Volsci on the Liris in Latium, conquered by the Romans, and colonised B. C. 328. It took part with the allies in the Social war, and was destroyed by Opimius.

Fregēnae, sometimes called **Fregellae** (*Torre Maccarese*), a town of Etruria on the coast between Alsium and the Tiber, on a low swampy shore, colonised by the Romans, B. C. 245.

Frentāni, a Samnite people, inhabiting a fertile and well watered territory on the coast of the Adriatic, from the river Sagrus on the N. (and subsequently almost as far N. as from the Aternus) to the river Frento on the S., from the latter of which rivers they derived their name. They were bounded by the Marrucini on the N., by the Peligni and by Samnium on the W., and by Apulia on the S. They submitted to the Romans in B. C. 304, and concluded a peace with the republic.

Frento (*Fortore*), a river in Italy forming the boundary between the Frentani and Apulia, rises in the Apennines and falls into the Adriatic sea.

Friniātes, a people in Liguria, probably the same as the Briniates, who, after being subdued by the Romans, were transplanted to Samnium.

Frisiabōnes, probably a tribe of the Frisii, inhabiting the islands at the mouth of the Rhine.

Frisii, a people in the N. W. of Germany, inhabited the coast from the E. mouth of the Rhine to the Amisia (*Ems*), and were bounded on the S. by the Bructeri, consequently in the modern *Friesland*, *Gröningen*, &c. Tacitus divided them into *Majores* and *Minores*, the former probably in the E., and the latter in the W. of the country. The Frisii were on friendly terms with the Romans from the time of the first campaign of Drusus till A. D. 28, when the oppressions of the Roman officers drove them to revolt. In the 5th century we find them joining the Saxons and Angli in their invasion of Britain.

Frontinus, Sex. Julius, was praetor A. D. 70, and in 75 succeeded Cerealis as governor of Britain, where he distinguished himself by the conquest of the Silures, and maintained the Roman power unbroken until superseded by Agricola in 78. In 97 Frontinus was nominated *curator aquarum*. He died about 106. Two works undoubtedly by this author are still extant :— 1. *Strategematicon Libri IV.*, a sort of treatise on the art of war, developed in a collection of the sayings and doings of the most renowned leaders of antiquity. 2. *De Aquaeductibus Urbis Romae Libri II.*, which forms a valuable contribution to the history of architecture. The best editions of the *Strategematica* are, by Oudendorp, Lug. Bat. 1779, and by Schwebel, Lips. 1772 ; of the *De Aquaeductibus* by Polenus, Patav. 1722. — In the collection of the *Agrimensores* or *Rei Agrariae Auctores* (ed. Goesius, Amst. 1674 ; ed. Lachmann, Berlin, 1848), are preserved some treatises usually ascribed to Sex. Julius Frontinus. The collection consists of fragments connected with the art of measuring land and ascertaining boundaries. It was put together without skill, pages of different works being mixed up together, and the writings of one author being sometimes attributed to another.

Fronto, M. Cornēlius, was born at Cirta in Numidia, in the reign of Domitian, and came to Rome in the reign of Hadrian, where he attained great celebrity as a pleader and a teacher of rhetoric. He was entrusted with the education of the future emperors, M. Aurelius and L. Verus, and was rewarded with wealth and honours. He was raised to the consulship in 143. So great was his fame as a speaker, that a sect of rhetoricians arose who were denominated *Frontoniani*. Following the example of their founder, they avoided the exaggeration of the Greek sophistical school, and bestowed especial care on the purity of their language and the simplicity of their style. Fronto lived till the reign of M. Aurelius. The latest of his epistles belongs to the year 166. — Up to a recent period no work of Fronto was known to be in existence, with the exception of a corrupt and worthless tract entitled *De Differentiis Vocabulorum*, and a few fragments preserved by the grammarians. But about the year 1814 Angelo Mai discovered on a palimpsest in the Ambrosian library at Milan a considerable number of letters which had passed between Fronto, Antoninus Pius, M. Aurelius, L. Verus, and various friends, together with some short essays. These were published by Mai at Milan in 1815, and in an improved form by Niebuhr, Buttmann and Heindorf, Berlin, 1816. Subsequently Mai discovered on a palimpsest in the Vatican library at Rome, upwards of 100 new letters ; and he published these at Rome in 1823, together with those which had been previously discovered.

Fronto, Papirius, a jurist, who probably lived about the time of Antoninus Pius, or rather earlier.

Frusino (Frusinas, -ātis : *Frosinone*), a town of the Hernici in Latium, in the valley of the river Cosas, and subsequently a Roman colony. It was celebrated for its prodigies, which occurred here almost more frequently than at any other place.

Fucentis, Fucentia. [ALBA, No. 4.]

Fucinus Lacus (*Lago di Celano* or *Capistrano*), a large lake in the centre of Italy and in the country of the Marsi, about 30 miles in circumference, into which all the mountain streams of the Apennines flow. As the water of this lake had no visible outlet, and frequently inundated the surrounding country, the emperor Claudius constructed an emissarium or artificial channel for carrying off the waters of the lake into the river Liris. This emissarium is still nearly perfect : it is almost 3 miles in length. It appears that the actual drainage was relinquished soon after the death of Claudius, for it was reopened by Hadrian.

Fufius Calēnus. [CALENUS.]

Fufīdīus, a jurist, who probably lived between the time of Vespasian and Hadrian.

Fulgentīus, Fabīus Planciādes, a Latin grammarian of uncertain date, probably not earlier than the 6th century after Christ, appears to have been of African origin. He is the author of: 1. *Mythologiarum Libri III. ad Catum Presbyterum*, a collection of the most remarkable tales connected with the history and exploits of gods and heroes. 2. *Expositio Sermonum Antiquorum cum Testimoniis ad Chalcidicum Grammaticum*, a glossary of obsolete words and phrases ; of very little value. 3. *Liber de Expositione Virgilianae Continentiae ad Chalcidicum Grammaticum*, a title which means, an *explanation of what is contained in Virgil*, that is to say, of the esoteric truths allegorically conveyed in the Virgilian poems. — The best edition of these works is in the *Mythographi Latini* of Muncker, Auct. 1681, and of Van Staveren, Lug. Bat. 1742.

Fulgīnīa, Fulgīnīum (Fulginas, -ātis: *Foligno*), a town in the interior of Umbria on the Via Flaminia, was a municipium.

Fulvīa. 1. The mistress of Q. Curius, one of Catiline's conspirators, divulged the plot to Cicero. — 2 A daughter of M. Fulvius Bambalio of Tusculum, thrice married, 1st to the celebrated P. Clodius, by whom she had a daughter Clodia, afterwards the wife of Octavianus ; 2ndly to C. Scribonius Curio, and 3rdly to M. Antony, by whom she had 2 sons. She was a bold and ambitious woman. In the proscription of B. C. 43 she acted with the greatest arrogance and brutality: she gazed with delight upon the head of Cicero, the victim of her husband. Her turbulent and ambitious spirit excited a new war in Italy in 41. Jealous of the power of Octavianus, and anxious to withdraw Antony from the E., she induced L. Antonius, the brother of her husband, to take up arms against Octavianus. But Lucius was unable to resist Octavianus, and threw himself into Perusia, which he was obliged to surrender in the following year (40). Fulvia fled to Greece and died at Sicyon in the course of the same year.

Fulvīa Gens, plebeian, but one of the most illustrious Roman gentes. It originally came from Tusculum. The principal families in the gens are those of CENTUMALUS, FLACCUS, NOBILIOR, and PAETINUS.

Fundānīus. 1. C., father of Fundania, the wife of M. Terentius Varro, is one of the speakers in Varro's dialogue, *De Re Rustica*. — 2. M., defended by Cicero, B. C. 65; but the scanty fragments of Cicero's speech do not enable us to understand the nature of the charge. — 3. A writer of comedies praised by Horace (*Sat.* i. 10. 41, 42).

Fundi (Fundanus: *Fondi*), an ancient town in Latium on the Appia Via, at the head of a narrow bay of the sea running a considerable way into the land, called the Lacus Fundānus. Fundi was a municipium, and was subsequently colonised by the veterans of Augustus. The surrounding country produced good wine. There are still remains at Fondi of the walls of the ancient town.

Furcīlae Caudīnae. [CAUDIUM.]

Furia Gens, an ancient patrician gens, probably came from Tusculum. The most celebrated families of the gens bore the names of CAMILLUS, MEDULLINUS, PACILUS, and PHILUS. For others of less note see BIBACULUS, CRASSIPES, PURPUREO.

Furīae. [EUMENIDES.]

Furīna, an ancient Roman divinity, who had a sacred grove at Rome. Her worship seems to have become extinct at an early time. An annual festival (*Furinalia* or *Furinales feriae*) had been celebrated in honour of her, and a flamen (*flamen Furinalis*) conducted her worship. She had also a temple in the neighbourhood of Satricum.

C. Furnīus, a friend and correspondent of Cicero, was tribune of the plebs B. C. 50; sided with Caesar in the civil war ; and after Caesar's death was a staunch adherent of Antony. After the battle of Actium, 31, he was reconciled to Augustus, through the mediation of his son, was appointed consul in 29, and was prefect of Hither Spain in 21.

Fuscus. 1. **Arellīus**, a rhetorician at Rome in the latter years of Augustus, instructed in rhetoric the poet Ovid. He declaimed more frequently in Greek than in Latin, and his style of declamation is described by Seneca, as more brilliant than solid, antithetical rather than eloquent. His rival in teaching and declaiming was Porcius Latro. [LATRO.] — 2. **Aristīus**, a friend of the poet Horace, who addressed to him an ode (*Carm.* i. 22) and an epistle (*Ep.* i. 10), and who also introduces him elsewhere (*Sat.* i. 9. 61; 10. 83). — 3. **Cornēlīus**, one of the most active adherents of Vespasian in his contest for the empire, A. D. 69. In the reign of Domitian he was sent against the Dacians, by whom he was defeated. Martial wrote an epitaph on Fuscus (*Ep.* vi. 76), in which he refers to the Dacian campaign.

G.

Gābae (Γάβαι). 1. (*Darabgherd ?*), a fortress and royal residence in the interior of Persis, S. E. of Pasargadae, near the borders of Carmania. — 2. Or Gabaza, or Cazaba, a fortress in Sogdiana, on the confines of the Massagetae.

Gābāla (Γάβαλα), a sea-port town of Syria Seleucis, S. of Laodicea ; whence good storax was obtained.

Gabāli, a people in Gallia Aquitanica, whose country possessed silver mines and good pasturage. Their chief town was Anderitum (*Anterieux*).

Gābīāna or **-ēnē** (Γαβιανή, Γαβινή), a fertile district in the Persian province of Susiana, W. of M. Zagros.

Gābīī (Gabīnus: nr. *Castiglione* Ru.), a town in Latium, on the Lacus Gabinus (*Lago di Gavi*), between Rome and Praeneste, was in early times one of the most powerful Latin cities ; a colony from Alba Longa ; and the place, according to tradition, where Romulus was brought up. It was taken by Tarquinius Superbus by stratagem, and it was in ruins in the time of Augustus (*Gabiis desertior vicus*, Hor. *Ep.* i. 11. 7). The *cinctus Gabinus*, a peculiar mode of wearing the toga at Rome, appears to have been derived from this town. In the neighbourhood of Gabii are the immense stone quarries, from which a part of Rome was built.

A. Gabīnīus, dissipated his fortune in youth by his profligate mode of life. He was tribune of the plebs B. C. 66, when he proposed and carried a law conferring upon Pompey the command of the war against the pirates. He was praetor in 61, and consul in 58 with L. Piso. Both consuls supported Clodius in his measures against Cicero, which resulted in the banishment of the orator. In 57 Gabinius went to Syria as proconsul. His first attention was directed to the affairs of Judea.

He restored Hyrcanus to the high priesthood, of which he had been dispossessed by Alexander, the son of Aristobulus. He next marched into Egypt, and restored Ptolemy Auletes to the throne. The restoration of Ptolemy had been forbidden by a decree of the senate, and by the Sibylline books ; but Gabinius had been promised by the king a sum of 10,000 talents for this service, and accordingly set at nought both the senate and the Sibyl. His government of the province was marked in other respects by the most shameful venality and oppression. He returned to Rome in 54. He was accused of *majestas* or high treason, on account of his restoration of Ptolemy Auletes, in defiance of the Sibyl, and the authority of the senate. He was acquitted on this charge ; but he was forthwith accused of *repetundae*, for the illegal receipt of 10,000 talents from Ptolemy. He was defended by Cicero, who had been persuaded by Pompey, much against his will, to undertake the defence. Gabinius, however, was condemned on this charge, and went into exile. He was recalled from exile by Caesar in 49, and in the following year (48) was sent into Illyricum by Caesar with some newly levied troops, in order to reinforce Q. Cornificius. He died in Illyricum about the end of 48, or the beginning of the following year.

Gădăra (Γάδαρα : Γαδαρηνός : Um-Keis), a large fortified city of Palestine, one of the 10 which formed the Decapolis in Peraea, stood a little S. of the Hieromax (*Yarmuk*), an eastern tributary of the Jordan. The surrounding district, S. E. of the Lake of Tiberias, was called Gadăris, and was very fertile. Gadara was probably favoured by the Greek kings of Syria, as it is sometimes called Antiochia and Seleucia ; it was restored by Pompey : Augustus presented it to king Herod, after whose death it was assigned to the province of Syria. It was made the seat of a Christian bishopric. There were celebrated baths in its neighbourhood, at Amatha.

Gădes (τὰ Γάδειρα : Γαδειρεύς : *Cadiz*), a very ancient town in Hispania Baetica, W. of the Pillars of Hercules, founded by the Phoenicians, and one of the chief seats of their commerce in the W. of Europe, was situated on a small island of the same name (*I. de Leon*), separated from the mainland by a narrow channel, which in its narrowest part was only the breadth of a stadium, and over which a bridge was built. Herodotus says (iv. 8) that the island of Erythīa was close to Gadeira ; whence most later writers supposed the island of Gades to be the same as the mythical island of Erythia, from which Hercules carried off the oxen of Geryon. A new town was built by Cornelius Balbus, a native of Gades, and the circumference of the old and new towns together was only 20 stadia. There were, however, several inhabitants on the mainland opposite the island, as well as on a smaller island (*S. Sebastian* or *Trocadero*) in the immediate neighbourhood of the larger one. After the 1st Punic War Gades came into the hands of the Carthaginians ; and in the 2nd Punic war it surrendered of its own accord to the Romans. Its inhabitants received the Roman franchise from Julius Caesar. It became a municiplum, and was called *Augusta urbs Julia Gaditana*.—Gades was from the earliest to the latest times an important commercial town. Its inhabitants were wealthy, luxurious, and licentious ; and their lascivious dances were celebrated at

Rome. (Juv. xi. 162.) Gades possessed cele brated temples of Cronus and Hercules. Its drink- ing water was as bad in antiquity as it is in the present day.—Gades gave its name to the **Fretum Gaditānum**, the straits at the entrance of the Me- diterranean between Europe and Africa (*Straits of Gibraltar*).

Gaea or **Ge** (Γαῖα or Γῆ), the personification of the earth. Homer describes her as a divine being, to whom black sheep were sacrificed, and who was invoked by persons taking oaths ; and he calls her the mother of Erechtheus and Tithyus. In Hesiod she is the first being that sprang from Chaos, and gave birth to Uranus and Pontus. By Uranus she became the mother of Oceanus, Coeus, Crius, Hyperion, Iapetus, Thia, Rheia, Themis, Mnemosyne, Phoebe, Thetys, Cronos, the Cyclopes, Brontes, Steropes, Arges, Cottus, Briareus, and Gyges. These children were hated by their father, and Ge therefore concealed them in the bosom of the earth ; but she made a large iron sickle, gave it to her sons, and requested them to take vengeance upon their father. Cronos undertook the task, and mutilated Uranus. The drops of blood, which fell from him upon the earth (Ge), became the seeds of the Erinnyes, the Gigantes, and the Melian nymphs. Subsequently Ge became, by Pontus, the mother of Nereus, Thaumas, Phorcys, Ceto, and Eurybia. Ge belonged to the gods of the nether world (θεοὶ χθόνιοι), and hence she is frequently mentioned where they are invoked. The surnames and epithets given to her have more or less refer- ence to her character as the all-producing and all-nou- rishing mother (*mater omniparens et alma*). Her worship appears to have been universal among the Greeks, and she had temples or altars in almost all the cities of Greece. At Rome the earth was worshipped under the name of **Tellus** (which is only a variation of *Terra*). She was regarded by the Romans also as one of the gods of the nether world (*Inferi*), and is mentioned in connection with Dis and the Manes. A temple was built to her by the consul P. Sempronius Sophus, in B. C. 304. Her festival was celebrated on the 15th of April, and was called Fordicidia or Hordicidia. The sacrifice, consisting of cows, was offered up in the Capitol in the presence of the Vestals.

Gaeson, Gaesus, or **Gessus** (Γαίσων), a river of Ionia in Asia Minor, falling into the Gulf of Maeander near the promontory of Mycale.

Gaetūlĭa (Γαιτουλία), the interior of N. Africa, S. of Mauretania, Numidia, and the region border- ing on the Syrtes, reaching to the Atlantic Ocean on the W., and of very indefinite extent towards the E. and S. The people included under the name Gaetūli (Γαιτοῦλοι), in its widest sense, were the inhabitants of the region between the countries just mentioned and the Great Desert, and also in the Oases of the latter, and nearly as far S. as the river Niger. They were a great nomad race, including several tribes, the chief of whom were the Autololes and Pharusii on the W. coast, the Darae, or Gaetuli-Darae, in the steppes of the Great Atlas, and the Melanogaetuli, a black race resulting from the intermixture of the Gaetuli with their S. neighbours, the Nigritae. The pure Gaetulians were not an Aethiopic (*i. e.* negro), but a Libyan race, and were most probably of Asiatic origin. They are supposed to have been the ancestors of the *Berbers.*

Gainas. [ARCADIUS.]

Gāius or Cāius, a celebrated Roman jurist, wrote under Antoninus Pius and M. Aurelius. His works were very numerous, and great use was made of them in the compilation of the Digest. One of his most celebrated works was an elementary treatise on Roman law, entitled *Institutiones*, in 4 books. This work was for a long time the ordinary text book used by those who were commencing the study of the Roman law; but it went out of use after the compilation of the Institutiones of Justinian, and was finally lost. This long lost work was discovered by Niebuhr in 1816 in the library of the Chapter at Verona. The MS. containing Gaius was a palimpsest one. The original writing of Gaius had on some pages been washed out, and on others scratched out, and the whole was re-written with the Letters of St. Jerome. The task of deciphering the original MS. was a very difficult one, and some parts were completely destroyed. It was first published by Göschen in 1821 : a second edition appeared in 1824, and a third in 1842.

Gagae (Γάγαι), a town on the coast of Lycia, E. of Myra, whence was obtained the mineral called Gagātes lapis, that is, *jet*, or, as it is still called in German, *gagat*.

Galanthis. [GALINTHIAS.]

Gălătēa (Γαλάτεια), daughter of Nereus and Doris. For details, see ACIS.

Gălātĭa (Γαλατία: Γαλάτης: in the E. part of *Anadoli* and the W. part of *Rumili*), a country of Asia Minor, composed of parts of Phrygia and Cappadocia, and bounded on the W., S., and S. E. by those countries, and on the N. E., N., and N. W. by Pontus, Paphlagonia, and Bithynia. It derived its name from its inhabitants, who were Gauls that had invaded and settled in Asia Minor at various periods during the 3d century B. C. First, a portion of the army which Brennus led against Greece, separated from the main body, and marched into Thrace, and, having pressed forward as far as the shores of the Propontis, some of them crossed the Hellespont on their own account, while others, who had reached Byzantium, were invited to pass the Bosporus by Nicomedes I., king of Bithynia, who required their aid against his brother Zipoetus (B. C. 279). They speedily overran all Asia Minor within the Taurus, and exacted tribute from its various princes, and served as mercenaries not only in the armies of these princes, but also of the kings of Syria and Egypt ; and, according to one account, a body of them found their way to Babylon. During their ascendancy, other bodies of Gauls followed them into Asia. Their progress was at length checked by the arms of the kings of Pergamus : Eumenes fought against them with various fortune ; but Attalus I. gained a complete victory over them (B. C. 230), and compelled them to settle down within the limits of the country thenceforth called Galatia, and also, on account of the mixture of Greeks with the Celtic inhabitants, which speedily took place, Graeco-Galatia and Gallograecia. The people of Galatia adopted to a great extent Greek habits and manners and religious observances, but preserved their own language, which is spoken of as resembling that of the Treviri. They retained also their political divisions and forms of government. They consisted of 3 great tribes, the Tolistobogi, the Trocmi, and the Tectosages, each subdivided into 4 parts, called by the Greeks τετραρχίαι. At the head of each of these 12 Tetrarchies was a chief,

or Tetrarch, who appointed the chief magistrate (δικαστής), and the commander of the army (στρατοφύλαξ), and 2 lieutenant-generals (ὑποστρατοφύλακες). The 12 tetrarchs together had the general government of the country, but their power was checked by an assistant senate of 300, who met in a place called Drynaemetum (or, probably, Dryanetum, *i. e.* the *oak-grove*), and had jurisdiction in all capital cases. This form of government had a natural tendency to monarchy, according as either of the 12 tetrarchs became more powerful than the rest, especially under the protection of the Romans, to whom Galatia became virtually subject as the result of the campaign which the consul Cn. Mánlius undertook against the Gauls, to punish them for the assistance they had given to Antiochus the Great (B. C. 189). At length one of the tetrarchs, DEIOTARUS, was rewarded for his services to the Romans in the Mithridatic War, by the title of king, together with a grant of Pontus and Armenia Minor ; and after the death of his successor Amyntas, Galatia was made by Augustus a Roman province (B. C. 25). It was soon after enlarged by the addition of Paphlagonia. Under Constantine it was restricted to its old limits, and under Valens it was divided into 2 provinces, Galatia Prima and Galatia Secunda. The country was beautiful and fertile, being watered by the rivers Halys and Sangarius. Its only important cities were, in the S.W. PESSINUS, the capital of the Tolistobogi ; in the centre ANCYRA, the capital of the Tectosages ; and in the N. E., TAVIUM, the capital of the Trocmi. — From the Epistle of St. Paul to the Galatians, we learn not only that many Christian churches had been formed in Galatia during the apostolic age, but also that those churches consisted, in great part, of Jewish converts.

Galaxĭus (Γαλάξιος), a small river in Boeotia, on which stood a temple of Apollo Galaxios : it derived its name from its milky colour, which was owing to the chalky nature of the soil through which it flowed.

Galba, Sulpĭcĭus, patrician. 1. P., consul B. C. 211, received Macedonia as his province, where he remained as proconsul till 204, and carried on the war against Philip. In 200, he was consul a second time, and again obtained Macedonia as his province ; but he was unable to accomplish any thing of importance against Philip, and was succeeded in the command in the following year by Villius Tappulus. He was one of the 10 commissioners sent to Greece in 196, after the defeat of Philip by Flamininus, and was one of the ambassadors sent to Antiochus in 193. — 2. Ser., was praetor 151, and received Spain as his province. His name is infamous on account of his treacherous and atrocious murder of the Lusitanians, with their wives and children, who had surrendered to him on the promise of receiving grants of land. Viriathus was one of the few Lusitanians, who escaped from the bloody scene. [VIRIATHUS.] On his return to Rome in 149, he was brought to trial on account of his horrible massacre of the Lusitanians. His conduct was denounced in the strongest terms by Cato, who was then 85 years old, but he was nevertheless acquitted. He was consul 144. Cicero praises his oratory in the highest terms. — 3. Ser., great-grandfather of the emperor Galba, served under Caesar in the Gallic war, and was praetor in 54. After Caesar's death he served

Faunus.
(Gori, Gem. Ant. Flor., vol. 1, pl. 94.) Page 262

Fortuna. (Bronze, in the British
Museum.) Page 267.

Furies. (From a Painted Vase.)

Fury. (From a Painted Vase.) See EUMENIDES, p. 253.

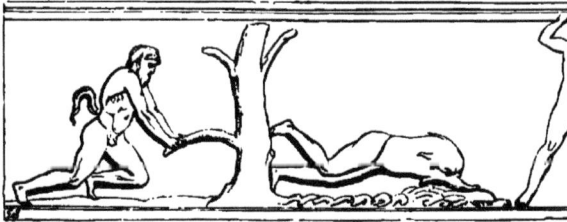

Adventures of Dionysus (Bacchus). (From the Choragic Monument of Lysicrates.)
See illustrations opposite pp. 234, 340.

[To face p. 272.

Domitilla Flavia, wife of Vespasian. Page 231.

Euthydemus. King of Bactria, about B.C. 212. Page 259.

Domna Julia, wife of Septimius Severus. Page 231.

Flavia Maximiana Fausta, wife of Constantine the Great.
Page 262.

Claudius Drusus, brother of the Emperor Tiberius,
ob. B.C. 9. Page 233, No. 4.

Faustina senior, wife of Antoninus Pius, ob. A.D. 141. The
reverse of the coin commemorates the institution of the
Puellae Alimentariae Faustinae. Page 262.

Drusus Caesar, son of the Emperor Tiberius, ob. A.D. 23.
Page 234, No. 5.

Faustina junior, wife of M. Aurelius, ob. A.D. 175. Page 262.

Elagabalus, Roman Emperor, A.D. 218—227. Page 23 .

Faustina, wife of Elagabalus. Page 263.

Eucratides, King of Bactria, about B.C. 181—161. Page 251.
To face p. 273.]

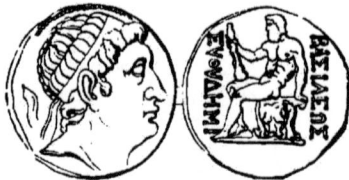

Florianus, Roman Emperor, A.D. 276. Page 266.

against Antony in the war of Mutina.—4. C., father of the emperor Galba, was consul in A. D. 22.

Galba, Ser. Sulpicius, Roman emperor, from June A. D. 68 to January, A. D. 69. He was born near Terracina, on the 24th of December, B. C. 3. Both Augustus and Tiberius are said to have told him, that one day he would be at the head of the Roman world, from which we must infer that he was a young man of more than ordinary talents. From his parents he inherited great wealth. He was invested with the curule offices before attaining the legitimate age. He was praetor A. D. 20, and consul 33. After his consulship he had the government of Gaul, 39, where he carried on a successful war against the Germans, and restored discipline among the troops. On the death of Caligula many of his friends urged him to seize the empire, but he preferred living in a private station. Claudius entrusted him, in 45, with the administration of Africa, which he governed with wisdom and integrity. In the reign of Nero he lived for several years in retirement, through fear of becoming the victim of the tyrant's suspicion; but in 61, Nero gave him the government of Hispania Tarraconensis, where he remained for 8 years. In 68 Vindex rebelled in Gaul. About the same time Galba was informed that Nero had sent secret orders for his assassination. He therefore resolved at once to follow the example of Vindex; but he did not assume the imperial title, and professed to act only as the legate of the Roman senate and people. Shortly afterwards Nero was murdered; and Galba thereupon proceeded to Rome, where he was acknowledged as emperor. But his severity and avarice soon made him unpopular with his new subjects, and especially with the soldiers. His powers had also become enfeebled by age, and he was completely under the sway of favourites, who perpetrated many enormities in his name. Perceiving the weakness of his government, he adopted Piso Licinianus, a noble young Roman, as his successor. But this only hastened his ruin. Otho, who had hoped to be adopted by Galba, formed a conspiracy among the soldiers, who rose in rebellion 6 days after the adoption of Piso. Galba was murdered, and Otho was proclaimed emperor.

Galēnus, Claudius, commonly called Galen, a very celebrated physician, whose works have had a longer and more extensive influence on the different branches of medical science than those of any other individual either in ancient or modern times. He was born at Pergamum in A. D. 130. His father Nicon, who was an architect and geometrician, carefully superintended his education. In his 17th year (146), his father, who had hitherto destined him to be a philosopher, altered his intentions, and, in consequence of a dream, chose for him the profession of Medicine. He at first studied medicine in his native city. In his 20th year (149), he lost his father, and about the same time he went to Smyrna for the purpose of studying under Pelops the physician, and Albinus the Platonic philosopher. He afterwards studied at Corinth and Alexandria. He returned to Pergamum in his 29th year (158), and was immediately appointed physician to the school of gladiators, an office which he filled with great reputation and success. In 164 he quitted his native country on account of some popular commotions, and went to Rome for the first time. Here he stayed about 4 years, and gained great reputation from his skill in anatomy and medicine. He

returned to Pergamum in 168, but had scarcely settled there, when he received a summons from the emperors M. Aurelius and L. Verus to attend them at Aquileia in Venetia. From Aquileia Galen followed M. Aurelius to Rome in 170. When the emperor again set out, to conduct the war on the Danube, Galen with difficulty obtained permission to be left behind at Rome, alleging that such was the will of Aesculapius. Before leaving the city the emperor committed to the medical care of Galen his son Commodus, who was then 9 years of age. Galen stayed at Rome some years, during which time he employed himself in lecturing, writing, and practising, with great success. He subsequently returned to Pergamum, but whether he again visited Rome is uncertain. He is said to have died in the year 200, at the age of 70, in the reign of Septimius Severus; but it is not improbable that he lived some years longer. Galen wrote a great number of works on medical and philosophical subjects. The works still extant under the name of Galen consist of 83 treatises acknowledged to be genuine; 19 whose genuineness has been doubted; 45 undoubtedly spurious; 19 fragments; and 15 commentaries on different works of Hippocrates. Galen attached himself exclusively to none of the medical sects into which the profession was divided, but chose from the tenets of each what he believed to be good and true, and called those persons slaves who designated themselves as followers of Hippocrates, Praxagoras, or any other man. The best edition of his works is by Kühn, Lips. 1821—1833, 20 vols. 8vo.

Galepsus (Γαληψός; Γαλήψιος), a town in Macedonia, on the Toronaic gulf.

Galĕrius Maximiānus. [MAXIMIANUS.]

Galĕrius Trachălus. [TRACHALUS.]

Galēsus (Galeso), a river in the S. of Italy, flows into the gulf of Tarentum, through the meadows where the sheep fed whose wool was so celebrated in antiquity (dulos pellitis ovibus Galaesi flumen, Hor. Carm. ii. 6. 10.)

Galĕus (Γάλεος), that is, "the lizard," son of Apollo and Themisto, the daughter of the Hyperborean king Zabius. In pursuance of an oracle of the Dodonean Zeus, Galeus emigrated to Sicily, where he built a sanctuary to his father Apollo. The Galeotae, a family of Sicilian soothsayers, derived their origin from him. The principal seat of the Galeotae was the town of Hybla, which was hence called Galeotis or Galeatis.

Galilaea (Γαλιλαία), at the birth of Christ, was the N.-most of the 3 divisions of Palestine W. of the Jordan. It lay between the Jordan and the Mediterranean on the E. and W., and the mountains of Hermon and Carmel on the N. and S. It was divided into Upper or N. Galilee, and Lower or S. Galilee. It was very fertile and densely peopled; but its inhabitants were a mixed race of Jews, Syrians, Phoenicians, Greeks, and others, and were therefore despised by the Jews of Judaea. [PALAESTINA.]

Galinthĭas or Galanthis (Ov. Met. ix. 306), daughter of Proetus of Thebes and a friend of Alcmene. When Alcmene was on the point of giving birth to Hercules, and the Moerae and Ilithyiae, at the request of Hera, were endeavouring to delay the birth, Galinthias suddenly rushed in with the false report that Alcmene had given birth to a son. The hostile goddesses were so surprised at this information that they dropped their arms,

Thus the charm was broken, and Alcmene was enabled to give birth to Hercules. The deluded goddesses avenged the deception practised upon them by metamorphosing Galinthias into a weasel or cat (γαλῆ). Hecate, however, took pity upon her, and made her her attendant, and Hercules afterwards erected a sanctuary to her. At Thebes it was customary at the festival of Hercules first to offer sacrifices to Galinthias.

Galla. 1. Wife of Constantius, son of the emperor Constantius Chlorus. She was the mother of Gallus Caesar. [GALLUS.]—2. Daughter of the emperor Valentinian I., and 2nd wife of Theodosius the Great.—3. GALLA PLACIDIA or simply PLACIDIA, daughter of Theodosius the Great by No. 2. She fell into the hands of Alaric, when he took Rome, A. D. 410; and Ataulphus, the Gothic king, married her in 414. After the death of Ataulphus, she was restored to Honorius; and in 417 she was married to Constantius, to whom she bore the emperor Valentinian III. During the minority of the latter she governed the Western empire. She died about 450.

Gallaecia, the country of the Gallaeci (Καλλαϊκοί), in the N. of Spain, between the Astures and the Durius, was in earlier times included in Lusitania. Gallaecia was sometimes used in a wider sense to include the country of the Astures and the Cantabri. It produced tin, gold, and a precious stone called *gemma Gallaica*. Its inhabitants were some of the most uncivilised in Spain. They were defeated with great slaughter by D. Brutus, consul B. C. 138, who obtained in consequence the surname of Gallaecus.

Gallia (ἡ Κελτική, Γαλατία), was used before the time of Julius Caesar, to indicate all the land inhabited by the Galli or Celtae, and consequently included not only the later Gaul and the N. of Italy, but a part of Spain, the greater part of Germany, the British isles, and other countries. The early history of the Celtic race, and their various settlements in different parts of Europe, are related under CELTAE.—1. Gallia, also called Gallia Transalpina or Gallia Ulterior, to distinguish it from Gallia Cisalpina, or the N. of Italy. Gallia Braccata and Gallia Comata are also used in contradistinction to Gallia Togata or the N. of Italy, but these names are not identical with the whole of Gallia Transalpina. *Gallia Braccata* was the part of the country first subdued by the Romans, the later Provincia, and was so called, because the inhabitants wore *braccae* or trowsers. *Gallia Comata* was the remainder of the country, excluding Gallia Braccata, and derived its name from the inhabitants wearing their hair long. The Romans were acquainted with only a small portion of Transalpine Gaul till the time of Caesar. In the time of Augustus it was bounded on the S. by the Pyrenees and the Mediterranean; on the E. by the river Varus and the Alps, which separated it from Italy, and by the river Rhine, which separated it from Germany; on the N. by the German Ocean and the English Channel; and on the W. by the Atlantic; thus including not only the whole of France and Belgium, but a part of Holland, a great part of Switzerland, and all the provinces of Germany W. of the Rhine. The greater part of this country is a plain, well watered by numerous rivers. The principal mountains were Mons CEBENNA or Gebenna in the S.; the lofty range of Mons JURA in the E., separating the Sequani and the Helvetii; and Mons VOSEGUS or VOGESUS, a continuation

of the Jura. The chief forest was the Silva Arduenna, extending from the Rhine and the Treviri as far as the Scheldt. The principal rivers were, in the E. and N., the RHENUS (*Rhine*), with its tributaries the MOSA (*Maas*) and MOSELLA (*Moselle*); the SEQUANA (*Seine*), with its tributary the MATRONA: in the centre the LIGERIS (*Loire*); in the W. the GARUMNA (*Garonne*); and in the S. the RHODANUS (*Rhone*). The country was celebrated for its fertility in ancient times, and possessed a numerous and warlike population.—The Greeks, at a very early period, became acquainted with the S. coast of Gaul, where they founded, in B. C. 600, the important town of MASSILIA, which in its turn founded several colonies, and exercised a kind of supremacy over the neighbouring districts. The Romans did not attempt to make any conquests in Transalpine Gaul till they had finally conquered not only Africa, but Greece and a great part of Western Asia. In B. C. 125 the consul M. Fulvius Flaccus commenced the subjugation of the Salluvii in the S. of Gaul. In the next 3 years (124—122) the Salluvii were completely subdued by Sextius Calvinus, and the colony of Aquae Sextiae (*Aix*) was founded in their country. In 121 the Allobroges were defeated by the proconsul Domitius Ahenobarbus; and in the same year Q. Fabius Maximus gained a great victory over the united forces of the Allobroges and Arverni, at the confluence of the Isara and the Rhone. The S. of Gaul was now made a Roman province; and in 118 was founded the colony of Narbo Martius (*Narbonne*), which was the chief town of the province. In Caesar's Commentaries the Roman province is called simply *Provincia*, in contradistinction to the rest of the country: hence comes the modern name of *Provence*. The rest of the country was subdued by Caesar after a struggle of several years (58—50). At this time Gaul was divided into 3 parts, *Aquitania*, *Celtica*, and *Belgica*, according to the 3 different races by which it was inhabited. The Aquitani dwelt in the S.W. between the Pyrenees and the Garumna; the Celtae, or Galli proper, in the centre and W., between the Garumna and the Sequana and the Matrona; and the Belgae in the N.E. between the two last mentioned rivers and the Rhine. The different tribes inhabiting Aquitania and Belgica are given elsewhere. [AQUITANIA: BELGAE.] The most important tribes of the Celtae or Galli were: 1. *Between the Sequana and the Liger*: the ARMORICI, the name of all the tribes dwelling on the coast between the mouths of these 2 rivers; the AULERCI, dwelling inland close to the Armorici; the NAMNETES, ANDECAVI or ANDES on the banks of the Liger; E. of them the CARNUTES; and on the Sequana, the PARISII, SENONES, and TRICASSES.—2. *Between the Liger and the Garumna*: on the coast the PICTONES and SANTONES; inland the TURONES, probably on both sides of the Liger, the BITURIGES CUBI, LEMOVICES, PETROCORII, and CADURCI; E. of these, in the mountains of Cebenna, the powerful ARVERNI (in the modern *Auvergne*); and S. of them the RUTENI.—3. *On the Rhone and in the surrounding country*, between the Rhone and the Pyrenees, the VOLCAE; between the Rhone and the Alps, the SALYES or SALLUVII; N. of them the CAVARES; between the Rhone, the Isara, and the Alps, the ALLOBROGES; and further N. the AEDUI, SEQUANI, and HELVETII, 3 of the most powerful people in all Gaul.—Augustus divided Gaul into 4 provinces. 1. *Gallia Narbonensis*, the same as the old Provincia. 2. *G. Aquitanica*, which extended from the Pyrenees to the Liger. 3. *G. Lugdunensis*, the country between the Liger, the Sequana, and the Arar, so called from the colony of Lugdunum (*Lyon*), founded by Munatius Plancus. 4. *G. Belgica*, the country between the Sequana, the Arar, and the Rhine. Shortly afterwards the portion of Belgica bordering on the Rhine, and inhabited by German tribes, was subdivided into 2 new provinces, called *Germania Prima* and *Secunda*, or *Germania Superior* and *Inferior*. At a later time the provinces of Gaul were still further subdivided, till at length, under the emperor Gratian, they reached the number of 17.—Gallia Narbonensis belonged to the senate, and was governed by a proconsul; the other provinces belonged to the emperor, and were governed by imperial legati. After the time of Claudius, when a formidable insurrection of the Gauls was suppressed, the country became more and more Romanized. The Latin language gradually became the language of the inhabitants, and Roman civilisation took deep root in all parts of the country. The rhetoricians and poets of Gaul occupy a distinguished place in the later history of Roman literature; and Burdigala, Narbo, Lugdunum, and other towns, possessed schools, in which literature and philosophy were cultivated with success. On the dissolution of the Roman empire, Gaul, like the other Roman provinces, was overrun by barbarians, and the greater part of it finally became subject to the Franci or Franks, under their king Clovis, about A. D. 496. —2. Gallia Cisalpīna, also called G. Citerior and G. Togāta, a Roman province in the N. of Italy, was bounded on the W. by Liguria and Gallia Narbonensis (from which it was separated by the Alps), on the N. by Rhaetia and Noricum, on the E. by the Adriatic and Venetia (from which it was separated by the Athesis), and on the S. by Etruria and Umbria (from which it was separated by the river Rubico). It was divided by the Po into Gallia Transpadāna, also called Italia Transpadāna, in the N., and Gallia Cispadāna in the S. The greater part of the country is a vast plain, drained by the Padus (*Po*) and its affluents, and has always been one of the most fertile countries of Europe. It was originally inhabited by Ligurians, Umbrians, Etruscans, and other races; but its fertility attracted the Gauls, who at different periods crossed the Alps, and settled in the country, after expelling the original inhabitants. We have mention of 5 distinct immigrations of Gauls into the N. of Italy. The 1st was in the reign of Tarquinius Priscus, and is said to have been led by Bellovesus, who settled with his followers in the country of the Insubres, and built Milan. The 2nd consisted of the Cenomani, who settled in the neighbourhood of Brixia and Verona. The 3rd of the Salluvii, who pressed forward as far as the Ticinus. The 4th of the Boii and Lingones, who crossed the Po, and took possession of the country as far as the Apennines, driving out the Etruscans and Umbrians. The 5th immigration was the most important, consisting of the warlike race of the Senones, who invaded Italy in immense numbers, under the command of Brennus, and took Rome in B. C. 390. Part of them subsequently recrossed the Alps and returned home; but a great number of them remained in the N. of Italy, and were for

more than a century a source of terror to the Romans. After the 1st Punic war the Romans resolved to make a vigorous effort to subdue their dangerous neighbours. In the course of 4 years (225—222) the whole country was conquered, and upon the conclusion of the war (222) was reduced to the form of a Roman province. The inhabitants, however, did not bear the yoke patiently, and it was not till after the final defeat of the Boii in 191 that the country became submissive to the Romans. — The most important tribes were: In Gallia Transpadana, in the direction of W. to E., the Taurini, Salassi, Libici, Insubres, Cenomani: in G. Cispadana, in the same direction, the Boii, Lingones, Senones.

Galliēnus, with his full name, P. Licinius Valerianus Egnatius Galliēnus, Roman emperor A. D. 260—268. He succeeded his father Valerian, when the latter was taken prisoner by the Persians in 260; but he had previously reigned in conjunction with his father from his accession in 253. Gallienus was indolent, profligate, and indifferent to the public welfare; and his reign was one of the most ignoble and disastrous in the history of Rome. The barbarians ravaged the fairest portion of the empire, and the inhabitants were swept away by one of the most frightful plagues recorded in history. This pestilence followed a long protracted famine. When it was at its greatest height, 5000 sick are said to have perished daily at Rome; and, after the scourge had passed away, it was found that the inhabitants of Alexandria were diminished by nearly two thirds. The complete dissolution of the empire was averted mainly by a series of internal rebellions. In every district able officers sprang up, who asserted and strove to maintain the dignity of independent princes. The armies levied by these usurpers, who are commonly distinguished as *The Thirty Tyrants*, in many cases arrested the progress of the invaders, and restored order in the provinces which they governed. Gallienus was at length slain by his own soldiers in 268, while besieging Milan, in which the usurper Aureolus had taken refuge.

Gallinārīa. 1. (*Galinara*), an island off the coast of Liguria, celebrated for its number of hens; whence its name. — 2. Silva, a forest of pine-trees near Cumae in Campania.

Gallīo, Jūnīus. 1. A Roman rhetorician, and a friend of M. Annaeus Seneca, the rhetorician, whose son he adopted. He was put to death by Nero. In early life he had been a friend of Ovid (*Ex Pont.* iv. 11). — 2. Son of the rhetorician M. Annaeus Seneca, and an elder brother of the philosopher Seneca, was adopted by No. 1.

Q. Gallĭus, was a candidate for the praetorship in B. C. 64, and was accused of ambitus or bribery by M. Calidius. He was defended on that occasion by Cicero in an oration of which a few fragments have come down to us. He was praetor urbanus B. C. 63, and presided at the trial of C. Cornelius. — He left two sons, Q. Gallĭus, who was praetor in 43, and was put to death by the triumvirs; and M. Gallĭus, who is mentioned as one of Antony's partizans in 43.

Gallograecĭa. [Galatia.]

Gallōnĭus, a public crier at Rome, probably contemporary with the younger Scipio, whose wealth and gluttony passed into the proverb " to live like Gallonius." He was satirised by Horace (*Sat.* ii. 2. 46).

Gallus, Aelīus. 1. A jurist, contemporary with Cicero and Varro, though probably rather older than either. He was the author of a treatise, *De Verborum, quae ad Jus Civile pertinent, Significatione*, which is frequently cited by the grammarians. — 2. An intimate friend of the geographer Strabo, was praefect of Egypt in the reign of Augustus. In B. C. 24 he invaded Arabia, and after his army had suffered dreadfully from the heat and want of water, he was obliged to retreat with great loss.

Gallus, L. Anicĭus, praetor B. C. 168, conducted the war against Gentius, king of the Illyrians, whom he compelled to submit to the Romans.

Gallus, C. Aquillĭus, a distinguished Roman jurist, was a pupil of Q. Mucius Scaevola, and the instructor of Serv. Sulpicius. He was praetor along with Cicero, B. C. 66. He is often cited by the jurists in the Digest, but there is no direct extract from his own works in the Digest.

Gallus Salonīnus, L. Asinĭus, son of C. Asinius Pollio, was consul B. C. 8. He was hated by Tiberius, because he had married Vipsania, the former wife of Tiberius. In A. D. 30, Tiberius got the senate to sentence him to death, and kept him imprisoned for 3 years, on the most scanty supply of food. He died in prison of starvation, but whether his death was compulsory or voluntary is unknown. Gallus wrote a work, entitled *De Comparatione patris ac Ciceronis*, which was unfavourable to the latter, and against which the emperor Claudius wrote his defence of Cicero.

Gallus, L. Caninĭus, was tribune of the plebs, B. C. 56, when he supported the views of Pompey. During the civil war he appears to have remained neutral. He died in 44.

Gallus, Cestĭus, governor of Syria (*legatus*, A. D. 64, 65), under whom the Jews broke out into the rebellion which ended in the destruction of their city and temple by Titus.

Gallus, Constantĭus, son of Julius Constantius and Galla, grandson of Constantius Chlorus, nephew of Constantine the Great, and elder brother by a different mother, of Julian the Apostate. In A. D. 351 he was named Caesar by Constantius II., and was left in the command of the E., where he conducted himself with the greatest haughtiness and cruelty. In 354 he went to the W. to meet Constantius at Milan, but was arrested at Petovio in Pannonia, and sent to Pola in Istria, where he was beheaded in a prison.

Gallus, C. Cornēlĭus, was born at Forum Julii (*Frejus*) in Gaul, of poor parents, about B. C. 66. He went to Italy at an early age, and began his career as a poet when he was about 20. He had already attained considerable distinction at the time of Caesar's death, 44 ; and upon the arrival of Octavian in Italy after that event, Gallus embraced his party, and soon acquired great influence with him. In 41 he was one of the triumviri appointed by Octavian to distribute lands in the N. of Italy among his veterans, and on that occasion he afforded protection to the inhabitants of Mantua and to Virgil. He afterwards accompanied Octavian to the battle of Actium, 31, and commanded a detachment of the army. After the battle, Gallus was sent with the army to Egypt, in pursuit of Antony ; and when Egypt was made a Roman province, Octavian appointed Gallus the first prefect of the province. He remained in Egypt for nearly 4 years ; but he incurred at length the enmity of Octavian, though the exact nature of his

offence is uncertain. According to some accounts he spoke of the emperor in an offensive and insulting manner ; he erected numerous statues of himself in Egypt, and had his own exploits inscribed on the pyramids. The senate deprived him of his estates, and sent him into exile ; whereupon he put an end to his life by throwing himself upon his own sword, B. C. 26. The intimate friendship existing between Gallus and the most eminent men of the time, as Asinius Pollio, Virgil, Varus, and Ovid, and the high praise they bestow upon him, prove that he was a man of great intellectual powers and acquirements. Ovid (*Trist.* iv. 10. 5) assigns to him the first place among the Roman elegiac poets ; and we know that he wrote a collection of elegies in 4 books, the principal subject of which was his love of Lycoris. But all his productions have perished ; for the 4 epigrams in the Latin Anthology attributed to Gallus could not have been written by a contemporary of Augustus. Gallus translated into Latin the poems of Euphorion of Chalcis, but this translation is also lost. Some critics attribute to him the poem Ciris, usually printed among the works of Virgil, but the arguments do not appear satisfactory.

Gallus, Sulpicĭus, a distinguished orator, was praetor B. C. 169, and consul 166, when he fought against the Ligurians. In 168 he served as tribune of the soldiers under Aemilius Paulus in Macedonia, and during this campaign predicted an eclipse of the moon.

Gallus, Treboniānus, Roman emperor, A. D. 251 -254. His full name was C. VIBIUS TREBONIANUS GALLUS. He served under Decius in the campaign against the Goths, 251, and he is said to have contributed by his treachery to the disastrous issue of the battle, which proved fatal to Decius and his son Herennius. Gallus was thereupon elected emperor, and Hostilianus, the surviving son of Decius, was nominated his colleague. He purchased a peace of the Goths by allowing them to retain their plunder, and promising them a fixed annual tribute. In 253 the Goths again invaded the Roman dominions, but they were driven back by Aemilianus, whose troops proclaimed him emperor in Moesia. Aemilianus thereupon marched into Italy ; and Gallus was put to death by his own soldiers, together with his son Volusianus, before any collision had taken place between the opposing armies. The name of Gallus is associated with nothing but cowardice and dishonour. In addition to the misery produced by the inroads of the barbarians during this reign, a deadly pestilence broke out in 252, and continued its ravages over every part of the empire for 15 years.

Gallus. 1. A river in Bithynia, rising near Modra, on the borders of Phrygia, and falling into the Sangarius near Leucae (*Lefkeh*). — 2. A river in Galatia, which also fell into the Sangarius, near Pessinus. From it the priests of Cybele are said to have obtained their name of Galli.

Gamelĭi (γαμήλιοι θεοί), the divinities protecting and presiding over marriage. These divinities are usually regarded as the protectors of marriage. Respecting the festival of the Gamelia see *Dict. of Antiq. s. v.*

Gandārae (Γανδάραι), an Indian people in the Paropamisus, on the N.W. of the *Punjab*, between the rivers Indus and Suastus. Under Xerxes they were subjects of the Persian empire. Their country was called Gandaritis (Γανδαρῖτις).

Gandaridae or **Gandaritae** (Γανδαρίδαι, Γανδαρῖται), an Indian people, in the middle of the Punjab, between the rivers Acesines (*Chenab*) and Hydraotes (*Ravee*), whose king, at the time of Alexander's invasion, was a cousin and namesake of the celebrated Porus. Whether they were different from the GANDARAE is uncertain. Sanskrit writers mention the *Ghandlára* in the centre of the Punjab.

Gangaridae (Γαγγαρίδαι), an Indian people about the mouths of the Ganges.

Ganges (Γάγγης: *Ganges* or *Ganga*), the greatest river of India, which it divided into the 2 parts named by the ancients India intra Gangem (*Hindustan*) and India Extra Gangem (*Burmah, Cochin China, Siam*, and the *Malay Peninsula*). It rises in the highest part of the Emodi Montes (*Himalaya*), and flows in a general S. E. direction till it falls by several mouths into the head of the Gangeticus Sinus (*Bay of Bengal*). Like the Nile, it overflows its banks periodically, and these inundations render its valley the most fertile part of India. The knowledge of the ancients respecting it was very imperfect, and they give very various accounts of its source, its size, and the number of its mouths. The breadth, which Diodorus Siculus assigns to it in the lower part of its course, 32 stadia, or about 3 miles, is perfectly correct. The following rivers are mentioned as its tributaries: Cainas, Jomanes or Diamunas, Sarabus, Condochates, Oedanes, Cosoagus or Cossoanus, Erannobnas, Sonus or Soas, Sittocestis, Solomatis, Sambus, Magon, Agoranis, Omalia, Commenases, Cacuthis, Andomatis, Amystis, Oxymagis, and Errhenysis.—The name is also applied to a city in the interior of India, on the Ganges, where it makes its great bend to the E., perhaps *Allahabad*.

Gangra (Γάγγρα: *Kankari*), a city of Paphlagonia, near the confines of Galatia, was originally a fortress ; in the time of king Deiotarus, a royal residence; and under the later emperors, the capital of Paphlagonia.

Ganos (Γάνος), a fortress in Thrace, on the Propontis.

Ganymedes (Γανυμήδης), son of Tros and Callirrhoë, and brother of Ilus and Assaracus, was the most beautiful of all mortals, and was carried off by the gods that he might fill the cup of Zeus, and live among the eternal gods. This is the Homeric account; but other traditions give different details. Some call him son of Laomedon, others son of Ilus, and others again of Erichthonius or Assaracus. The manner in which he was carried away from the earth is likewise differently described ; for while Homer mentions the gods in general, later writers state that Zeus himself carried him off, either in his natural shape, or in the form of an eagle, or by means of his eagle. There is, further, no agreement as to the place where the event occurred ; though later writers usually represent him as carried off from Mount Ida (*captus ab Ida*, Hor. *Carm.* iv. 4). The early legend simply states that Ganymedes was carried off that he might be the cup-bearer of Zeus, in which office he was conceived to have succeeded Hebe; but later writers describe him as the beloved and favourite of Zeus, without allusion to his office. Zeus compensated the father for his loss by a pair of divine horses. Astronomers have placed Ganymedes among the stars under the name of Aquarius. The Romans called him by a corrupt form of his name, **Catamitus**.

Garama. [GARAMANTES.]

Garamantes (Γαράμαντες), the S.most people known to the ancients in N. Africa, dwelt far S. of the Great Syrtis in the region called Phazania (*Fezzan*), where they had a capital city, Gărămā (Γάραμα: *Mourzouk*, lat. 25° 53′ N., long. 14° 10′ E.). They are mentioned by Herodotus as a weak unwarlike people; he places them 19 days' journey from Aethiopia and the shores of the Indian Ocean, 15 days' journey from Ammonium, and 30 days' journey from Egypt. The Romans obtained fresh knowledge of them by the expedition of Cornelius Balbus into their country, in B. C. 43.

Garganus Mons (*Monte Gargano*), a mountain and promontory in Apulia, on which were oak forests (*quercæta Gargani*, Hor. *Carm.* ii. 9. 7.)

Gargara, -on, or -us (Γάργαρα, ον, os : Γαργαρεύς). 1. (*Kaz-Dagh*) the S. summit of M. Ida, in the Troad.—2. A city at the foot of M. Ida, on the shore of· the Gulf of Adramyttium, between Assus and Antandrus ; said to have been founded originally on the summit of the mountain by the Leleges ; afterwards colonised from Miletus ; and removed to the lower site on account of the inclemency of its situation on the mountain. Its neighbourhood was rich in corn.

Gargettus (Γαργηττός: Γαργήττιος), a demus in Attica, belonging to the tribe Aegeis, on the N.W. slope of Mt. Hymettus ; the birthplace of the philosopher Epicurus.

Garites, a people in Aquitania, neighbours of the Ausci, in the modern *Comté de Gaure*.

Garocēli, a people in Gallia Narbonensis, near Mt. Cenis, in the neighbourhood of *St. Jean de Maurienne*.

Garsaŭris, or -itis (Γαρσαουρία, or -ῖτις), a praefectura in Cappadocia, on the borders of Lycaonia and Tyanitis. Its chief town was called Γαρσάουρα.

Garuli, a people of Liguria in the Apennines.

Garumna (*Garonne*), one of the chief rivers of Gaul, rises in the Pyrenees, flows N.W. through Aquitania, and becomes a bay of the sea below Burdigala (*Bordeaux*).

Garumni, a people in Aquitania on the Garumna.

Gathēae (Γαθέαι), a town in Arcadia on the **Gatheātas**, a river which flows into the Alphēus, W.S.W. of Megalopolis.

Gaugamēla (τὰ Γαυγάμηλα: *Karmelis*), a village in the district of Aturia in Assyria, the scene of the last and decisive battle between Alexander and Darius Codomannus, B. C. 331, commonly called the battle of ARBELA.

Gaulanitis (Γαυλα- or -ονῖτις: *Jaulan*), a district in the N. of Palestine, on the E. side of the Lake of Tiberias, as far S. as the river Hieromax, named from the town of Golan (Γαύλανα).

Gaulos (Γαῦλος: Γαυλίτης: *Gozzo*), an island in the Sicilian sea near Melite (*Malta*).

Gaurelĕon, Gaurion. [ANDROS.]

Gaurus Mons, Gauranus or -ni M. (*Monte Gauro*), a volcanic range of mountains in Campania, between Cumae and Neapolis, in the neighbourhood of Puteoli, which produced good wine, and was memorable for the defeat of the Samnites by M. Valerius Corvus, B. C. 343.

Gaza (Γάζα). 1. (*Ghuzzeh*), the last city on the S. W. frontier of Palestine, and the key of the country on the side of Egypt, stood on an eminence about 2 miles from the sea, and was, from the very earliest times of which we have any record, very

strongly fortified. It was one of the 5 cities of
the Philistines; and, though taken from them more
than once by the Jews, was each time recovered.
It was taken by Cyrus the Great, and remained
in the hands of the Persians till the time of Alexander, who only gained possession of it after an
obstinate defence of several months. In B. C. 315,
it fell into the power of Ptolemy the son of Lagus,
as the result of his victory over Demetrius before
the city, and was destroyed by him. But it again
recovered, and was possessed alternately by the
kings of Syria and Egypt, during their prolonged
wars, and afterwards by the Asmonaean princes of
Judaea, one of whom, Alexander Jannaeus, again
destroyed it, B. C. 96. It was rebuilt by Gabinius;
given by Augustus to Herod the Great; and, after
Herod's death, united to the Roman province of Syria.
In A. D. 65, it was again destroyed in an insurrection of its Jewish inhabitants; but it recovered once
more, and remained a flourishing city till it fell
into the hands of the Arabs in A. D. 634. In addition to its importance as a military post, it possessed an extensive commerce, carried on through
its port, Majuma, or CONSTANTIA. — 2. (Ghas), a
city in the Persian province of Sogdiana, between
Alexandria and Cyropolis; one of the 7 cities which
rebelled against Alexander in B. C. 328.

Gazaca (Γάζακα: *Tubreex*), a city in the N. of
Media Atropatene, equidistant from Artaxata and
Ecbatana, was a summer residence of the kings of
Media.

Gaziura (Γαζίουρα), a city in Pontus Galaticus,
on the river Iris, below Amasia, was the ancient
residence of the kings of Pontus; but in Strabo's
time it had fallen to decay.

Gobalene (Γεβαληνή), the district of Arabia
Petraea around the city of Petra.

Gebenna Mons. [CEBENNA.]

Gedrosia (Γεδρωσία, and Γαδρωσία: S.E. part of
Beloochistan), the furthest province of the Persian
empire on the S. E., and one of the subdivisions of
ARIANA, was bounded on the W. by Carmania, on
the N. by Drangiana and Arachosia, on the E. by
India (or, as the country about the lower course of
the Indus was called, Indo-Scythia), and on the S.
by the Mare Erythraeum, or Indian Ocean. It is
formed by a succession of sandy steppes, rising from
the sea-coast towards the table land of Ariana, and
produced little besides aromatic shrubs. The slip
of land between the coast and the lowest mountain
range is watered by several rivers, the chief of
which was called Arabis (*Dooaee?*); but even this
district is for the most part only a series of salt
marshes. Gedrosia is known in history chiefly
through the distress suffered for want of water, in
passing through it, by the armies of Cyrus and of
Alexander. The inhabitants were divided by the
Greek writers into 2 races, the Ichthyophagi on the
sea coast, and the Gedrosi in the interior. The
latter were a wild nomade people, whom even
Alexander was only able to reduce to a temporary
subjection. The whole country was divided into 8
districts. Its chief cities were Rhambacia and
Pura, or Parsis.

Gegania Gens, traced its origin to the mythical
Gyas, one of the companions of Aeneas. It was
one of the most distinguished Alban houses, transplanted to Rome on the destruction of Alba by
Tullus Hostilius, and enrolled among the Roman
patricians. There appears to have been only one
family in this gens, that of *Macerinus*, many mem-

bers of which filled the highest offices in the state
in the early times of the republic.

Gela (ἡ Γέλα, Ion. Γέλη: Γελῷος, Gelensis.
nr. *Terra Nuova* Ru.), a city on the S. coast of
Sicily, on a river of the same name (*Fiume di Terra
Nuova*), founded by Rhodians from Lindos, and
by Cretans, B. C. 690. It soon obtained great
power and wealth; and, in 582, it founded Agrigentum, which, however, became more powerful
than the mother city. Like the other cities of
Sicily, it was subject to tyrants, of whom the most
important were HIPPOCRATES, GELON, and HIE-
RON. Gelon transported half of its inhabitants to
Syracuse; the place gradually fell into decay, and
in the time of Augustus was no longer inhabited.
The poet Aeschylus died here. — N. of Gela were
the celebrated *Campi Geloi*, which produced rich
crops of wheat.

Gelae. [CADUSII.]

Gelanor (Γελάνωρ), king of Argos, was expelled
by Danaus.

Gelduba (*Gelb*, below *Cologne*), a fortified place
of the Ubii on the Rhine in Lower Germany.

Gellia Gens, plebeian, was of Samnite origin,
and afterwards settled at Rome. There were 2
generals of this name in the Samnite wars, Gellius
Statius in the 2nd Samnite war, who was defeated
and taken prisoner, B. C. 305, and Gellius Egnatius
in the 3rd Samnite war. [EGNATIUS.] The chief
family of the Gellii at Rome bore the name of
PUBLICOLA.

Gellius. 1. Cn., a contemporary of the Gracchi,
the author of a history of Rome from the earliest
epoch down to B. C. 145 at least. The work is
lost, but it is frequently quoted by later writers.
— 2. Aulus, a Latin grammarian of good family,
was probably a native of Rome. He studied rhetoric under T. Castricius and Sulpicius Apollinaris,
philosophy under Calvisius Taurus and Peregrinus
Proteus, and enjoyed also the friendship and instructions of Favorinus, Herodes Atticus, and Cornelius Fronto. While yet a youth he was appointed by the praetor to act as an umpire in civil
causes. The precise date of his birth and death is
unknown; but he must have lived under Hadrian,
Antoninus Pius, and M. Aurelius, A. D. 117—180.
He wrote a work entitled *Noctes Atticae*, because
it was composed in a country house near Athens,
during the long nights of winter. It is a sort of
miscellany, containing numerous extracts from
Greek and Roman writers, on a variety of topics
connected with history, antiquities, philosophy, and
philology, interspersed with original remarks, the
whole thrown together into 20 books, without any
attempt at order or arrangement. The 8th book
is entirely lost with the exception of the index. —
The best editions are by Jac. Gronovius, Lug. Bat.
1706 (reprinted by Conradi, Lips. 1762), and by
Lion, Gotting. 1824. — 3. Publicius, a jurist, one
of the disciples of Ser. Sulpicius.

Gelon (Γέλων). 1. Son of Dinomenes, tyrant
of Gela, and afterwards of Syracuse, was descended
from one of the most illustrious families in Gela.
He held the chief command of the cavalry in the
service of Hippocrates, tyrant of Gela; shortly after
whose death he obtained the supreme power, B. C.
491. In 485 he availed himself of the internal
dissensions of Syracuse to make himself master of
this city also. From this time he neglected Gela,
and bent all his efforts to the aggrandisement of
Syracuse, to which place he removed many of the

inhabitants of the other cities of Sicily. In 480 he gained a brilliant victory at Himera over the Carthaginians, who had invaded Sicily with an army, amounting, it is said, to the incredible number of 300,000 men. Scarcely any of this vast host survived to carry the news to Carthage. The victory is said to have been gained on the very same day as that of Salamis. He died in 478 of a dropsy, after reigning 7 years at Syracuse. He was succeeded by his brother HIERON. He is represented as a man of singular leniency and moderation, and as seeking in every way to promote the welfare of his subjects ; and his name even appears to have become almost proverbial as an instance of a good monarch. A splendid tomb was erected to him by the Syracusans at the public expense, and heroic honours were decreed to his memory — 2. Son of Hieron II., king of Syracuse, who died before his father, at the age of more than 50 years. He received the title of king in the lifetime of his father.

Gělŏni (Γελωνοί), a Scythian people, who dwelt in Sarmatia Asiatica, to the E. of the river Tanaïs (Don). They were said to have been of Greek origin, and to have migrated from the shores of the Euxine; but they intermixed with the Scythians so as to lose all traces of their Hellenic race. Their chief city was called Gelonus (Γελωνός).

Gemīnus (Γεμῖνος), an astronomer, was a native of Rhodes, and flourished about B. C. 77. He is the author of an extant work, entitled Εἰσαγωγὴ εἰς τὰ Φαινόμενα, which is a descriptive treatise on elementary astronomy, with a great deal of historical allusion. It is printed in the Uranologion of Petavius, Paris, 1630, and in Halma's edition of Ptolemy, Paris, 1819.

Gěmĭnus, Servīlius. 1. P., twice consul with C. Aurelius Cotta in the 1st Punic war, namely, in B. C. 252 and 248. In both years he carried on war against the Carthaginians. — 2. Cn., son of No. 1, was consul 217 with C. Flaminius, in the 2nd Punic war, and ravaged the coast of Africa. He fell in the battle of Cannae, 216. — 3. M., also surnamed Pulex, consul 202 with Tib. Claudius Nero, obtained Etruria for his province. He is mentioned on several occasions subsequently.

Gemonīae (scalae) or Gemonii (gradus), a flight of steps cut out of the Aventine, down which the bodies of criminals strangled in the prison were dragged, and afterwards thrown into the Tiber.

Genăbum or Cenăbum (Orleans), a town in Gallia Lugdunensis, on the N. bank of the Ligeris, was the chief town of the Carnutes : it was plundered and burnt by Caesar, but subsequently rebuilt. In later times it was called Civitas Aurelianorum or Aurelianensis Urbs, whence its modern name.

Genauni, a people in Vindelicia, the inhabitants of the Alpine valley, now called Valle di Non, were subdued by Drusus. (Hor. Carm. iv. 14. 10.)

Genēsius, Josěphus, lived about A. D. 940, and wrote in 4 books a history of the Byzantine emperors from A. D. 813 to 886, consequently of the reigns of Leo V., Michael II., Theophilus, Michael III., and Basil I. Edited by Lachmann, Bonn, 1834.

Genetaeus (Γενηταῖος), a surname of Zeus, from Cape Genetus on the Euxine, where he was worshipped as εὔξεινος, i.e. " the hospitable."

Genetyllis (Γενετυλλίς), the protectress of births, occurs both as a surname of Aphrodite,

and as a distinct divinity and a companion of Aphrodite. We also find the plural, Γενετυλλίδες, or Γενναΐδες, as a class of divinities presiding over generation and birth, and as companions of Aphrodite Colias.

Gěněva or Genāva (Genevensis : Geneva), the last town of the Allobroges, on the frontiers of the Helvetii, was situated on the S. bank of the Rhone, at the spot where the river flowed out of the Lacus Lemannus. There was a bridge here over the Rhone.

Gěnĭtrix, that is, " the mother," is used by Ovid (Met. xiv. 536) as a surname of Cybele, in the place of mater, or magna mater ; but it is better known as a surname of Venus, to whom Caesar dedicated a temple at Rome, as the mother of the Julia Gens.

Gěnĭus, a protecting spirit, analogous to the guardian angels invoked by the Church of Rome. The belief in such spirits existed both in Greece and at Rome. The Greeks called them δαίμονες, Daemons, and appear to have believed in them from the earliest times, though Homer does not mention them. Hesiod says that the Daemons were 30,000 in number, and that they dwelled on earth unseen by mortals, as the ministers of Zeus, and as the guardians of men and of justice. He further conceives them to be the souls of the righteous men who lived in the golden age of the world. The Greek philosophers took up this idea, and developed a complete theory of daemons. Thus we read in Plato, that daemons are assigned to men at the moment of their birth, that they accompany men through life, and after death conduct their souls to Hades. Pindar, in several passages, speaks of γενέθλιος δαίμων, that is, the spirit watching over the fate of man from the hour of his birth. The daemons are further described as the ministers and companions of the gods, who carry the prayers of men to the gods, and the gifts of the gods to men, and accordingly float in immense numbers in the space between heaven and earth. There was also a distinct class of daemons, who were exclusively the ministers of the gods. — The Romans seem to have received their notions respecting the genii from the Etruscans, though the name Genius itself is Latin (it is connected with gi-gn-o, gen-ui, and equivalent in meaning to generator or father). The genii of the Romans are the powers which produce life (dii genitales), and accompany man through it as his second or spiritual self. They were further not confined to man, but every living being, animal as well as man, and every place had its genius. Every human being at his birth obtained (sortitur) a genius, whom he worshipped as sanctus et sanctissimus deus, especially on his birthday, with libations of wine, incense, and garlands of flowers. The bridal bed was sacred to the genius, on account of his connection with generation, and the bed itself was called lectus genialis. On other merry occasions, also, sacrifices were offered to the genius, and to indulge in merriment was not unfrequently expressed by genio indulgere, genium curare, or placare. The whole body of the Roman people had its own genius, who is often seen represented on coins of Hadrian and Trajan. He was worshipped on sad as well as joyous occasions ; thus, sacrifices were offered to him at the beginning of the 2nd year of the war with Hannibal. The genii are usually represented in works of art as winged beings. The genius of a place appears in the form of a serpent eating fruit placed before him.

Gensĕric, king of the Vandals, and the most terrible of all the barbarian invaders of the empire. In A. D. 429 he crossed over from Spain to Africa, and ravaged the country with frightful severity. Hippo was taken by him in 431, but Carthage did not fall into his hands till 439. Having thus become master of the whole of the N.W. of Africa, he attacked Italy itself. In 455 he took Rome and plundered it for 14 days, and in the same year he destroyed Capua, Nola, and Neapolis. Twice the empire endeavoured to revenge itself, and twice it failed: the first was the attempt of the Western emperor Majorian (457), whose fleet was destroyed in the bay of Carthagena. The 2nd was the expedition sent by the Eastern emperor Leo (468), which was also baffled by the burning of the fleet off Bona. Genseric died in 477, at a great age. He was an Arian; and in the cruelties exercised under his orders against his Catholic subjects he exhibited the first instance of persecution carried on upon a large scale by one body of Christians against another.

Gentĭus, son of Pleuratus, a king of the Illyrians. As early as B. c. 180, he had given offence to the Romans on account of the piracies of his subjects; and in 168 he entered into an alliance with Perseus, king of Macedonia. In the following year the praetor L. Anicius Gallus was sent against him. The war was finished within 30 days. Gentius was defeated in battle, and then surrendered himself to Anicius, who carried him to Rome to adorn his triumph. He was afterwards kept as a prisoner at Spoletium.

Genŭa (Genuas, -ātis, Genuensis: Genoa), an important commercial town in Liguria, situated at the extremity of the Ligurian gulf (Gulf of Genoa), was in the possession of the Romans at the beginning of the 2nd Punic war, but towards the end of the war was held for some time by the Carthaginian Mago. It was a Roman municipium, but it did not become of political importance till the middle ages, when it was commonly called Janua.

Gentĭcĭa Gens, patrician, of which the principal families bore the names of AVENTINENSIS and AUGURINUS.

Gentĭsus (Iskumi), a river in Greek Illyria, N. of the Apsus.

Gephyraei (Γεφυραῖοι), an Athenian family, to which Harmodius and Aristogiton belonged. They said that they came originally from Eretria in Euboea. Herodotus believed them to be of Phoenician descent, to have followed Cadmus into Boeotia, and from thence to have emigrated to Athens. They dwelt on the banks of the Cephissus, which separated the territory of Athens from that of Eleusis, and their name was said to have been derived from the bridge (γέφυρα), which was built over the river at this point. Such a notion, however, is quite untenable, since " bridge " appears to have been a comparative recent meaning of γέφυρα. We find that there were temples at Athens, belonging peculiarly to the Gephyraei, to the exclusion of the rest of the Athenians, especially one to Demeter Achaea, whose worship they seem to have brought with them from Boeotia.

Gepĭdae, a Gothic people, who came from Scandinavia, and first settled in the country between the Oder and the Vistula, from which they expelled the Burgundiones. Subsequently they joined the numerous hosts of Attila; and after his death they settled in Dacia, on the banks of the Danube. As they were dangerous neighbours to the Eastern empire, Justinian invoked the aid of the Langobardi or Lombards, who conquered the Gepidae and destroyed their kingdom.

Ger or Gir (Γείρ: Ghir or Mansolig), a river of Gaetulia in Africa, S. of Mauretania Caesariensis; flowing S. E. from the S. slope of M. Atlas, till it is lost in the desert. It first became known to the Romans through the expedition of Suetonius Paulinus in the reign of Nero.

Geraestus (Γεραιστός: Γεραίστιος), a promontory and harbour at the S. extremity of Euboea, with a celebrated temple of Poseidon, in whose honour the festival of the Geraestia (Γεραίστια) was here celebrated.

Geranĕa (ἡ Γεράνεια), a range of mountains, beginning at the S.W. slope of Cithaeron, and running along the W. coast of Megaris, till it terminated in the promontory Olmiae in the Corinthian territory; but the name is sometimes confined to the mountain in the Corinthian territory.

Gerēnĭa (Γερηνία), an ancient town in Messenia, the birthplace of Nestor, who is hence called Gerenian (Γερήνιος). It was regarded by some as the same place as the Homeric Enope.

Gergis, or Gergĭtha, or -es, or -us, (Γέργις, Γέργιθα, or -ες, or -ος: Γεργίθιος), a town in the Troad, N. of the Scamander, inhabited by Teucrians. Attalus removed the inhabitants to the sources of the Caïcus, where mention is made of a place called Gergētha or Gergithion, in the territory of Cyme.

Gergŏvĭa. 1. A fortified town of the Arverni in Gaul, situated on a high and inaccessible hill, W. or S.W. of the Elaver (Allier). Its site is uncertain; but it was probably in the neighbourhood of the modern Clermont. — 2. A town of the Boii in Gaul, of uncertain site.

Germa (Γέρμη), the name of 3 cities in Asia Minor. 1. (Germaslu, Ru.) in Mysia Minor, near Cyzicus.—2. (Yermatepe) in Mysia, between Pergamus and Thyatira.—3. (Yerma), in Galatia, between Pessinus and Ancyra; a colonia.

Germānĭa, was bounded by the Rhine on the W., by the Vistula and the Carpathian mountains on the E., by the Danube on the S., and by the German Ocean and the Baltic on the N. It thus included much more than modern Germany on the N. and E., but much less in the W. and S. The N. and N.E. of Gallia Belgica were likewise called Germania Prima and Secunda under the Roman emperors [see p. 275, a.]; and it was in contradistinction to these provinces that Germania proper was also called Germania Magna or G. Transrhenāna or G. Barbăra. It was not till Caesar's campaigns in Gaul (B. c. 58—50) that the Romans obtained any accurate knowledge of the country. The Roman writers represent Germany as a dismal land, covered for the most part with forests and swamps, producing little corn, and subject to intense frosts and almost eternal winter. Although these accounts are probably exaggerated, yet there can be no doubt that, before the immense woods were cleared and the morasses drained, the climate of Germany was much colder than it is at present. — The N. of Germany is a vast plain, but in the S. there are many mountains, which were covered in antiquity with vast forests, and thus were frequently called Silvae. Of these the most important was the HERCYNIA SILVA.—The chief rivers were the RHENUS (*Rhine*), DANUBIUS (*Danube*), VISTULA, AMISIA (*Ems*), VISURGIS (*Weser*), ALBIS (*Elbe*), VIADUS (*Oder*). — The inhabitants were called GERMANI by the Romans. Tacitus says (*Germ.* 2) that Germani was the name of the Tungri, who were the first German people that crossed the Rhine. It would seem that this name properly belonged only to those tribes who were settled in Gaul ; and as these were the first German tribes with which the Romans came into contact, they extended the name to the whole nation. The etymology of the name is uncertain. Some modern writers derive it from the German *ger*, *gwer*, *Heer*, *Wehr*, so that the word would be equivalent to *Wehrman*, *Wehrmänner*, that is, warriors. The Germans themselves do not appear to have used any one name to indicate the whole nation ; for there is no reason to believe, as some have done, that the name *Teutones* (i. e. *Teuten*, *Deutsche*), was the general name of the nation in the time of the Romans. The Germans regarded themselves as indigenous in the country ; but there can be no doubt that they were a branch of the great Indo-Germanic race, who, along with the Celts, migrated into Europe from the Caucasus and the countries around the Black and Caspian seas, at a period long anterior to historical records. They are described as a people of high stature and of great bodily strength, with fair complexions, blue eyes, and yellow or red hair. Notwithstanding the severity of their climate, they wore little clothing, and their children went entirely naked. They had scarcely any defensive armour : their chief offensive weapon was the *framea*, a long spear with a narrow iron point, which they either darted from a distance or pushed in close combat. Their houses were only low huts, made of rough timber, and thatched with straw. A number of these were of course often built near each other ; but they could not be said to have any towns properly so called. Many of their tribes were nomad, and every year changed their place of abode. —The men found their chief delight in the perils and excitement of war. In peace they passed their lives in listless indolence, only varied by deep gaming and excessive drinking. Their chief drink was beer ; and their carouses frequently ended in bloody brawls. The women were held in high honour. Their chastity was without reproach. They accompanied their husbands to battle, and cheered them on by their presence, and frequently by their example as well. Both sexes were equally distinguished for their unconquerable love of liberty ; and the women frequently destroyed both themselves and their children, rather than fall into the power of their husbands' conquerors. — In each tribe we find the people divided into 4 classes : the nobles ; the freemen ; the freedmen or vassals ; and the slaves. All questions relating to peace and war, and the general interests of the tribe, were decided in the popular assembly, in which each freeman had a right to take part. In these assemblies a king was elected from among the nobles ; but his power was very limited, and he only acted as the supreme magistrate in time of peace ; for when a war broke out, the people elected a distinguished warrior as their leader, upon whom the prerogatives of the king devolved. — The religion of the Germans is known to us only from the Greek and Roman writers, who have confused the

subject by seeking to identify the gods of the Germans with their own divinities. We know that they worshipped the Sun, the Moon, and the Stars. They are also said to have paid especial honour to Mercury, who was probably the German *Wodan* or *Odin*. Their other chief divinities were Isis (probably *Freia*, the wife of Odin) ; Mars (*Tyr* or *Zio*, the German god of war) ; the mother of the gods, called *Nerthus* (less correctly *Herthus* or *Hertha*) ; and Jupiter (*Thor*, or the god of thunder). The worship of the gods was simple. They had both priests and priestesses to attend to their service ; and some of the priestesses, such as Veleda among the Bructeri, were celebrated throughout Germany for their prophetic powers. — The Germani first appear in history in the campaigns of the Cimbri and Teutones (B. C. 113), the latter of whom were undoubtedly a Germanic people. [TEUTONES.] About 50 years afterwards Ariovistus, a German chief, crossed the Rhine, with a vast host of Germans, and subdued a great part of Gaul ; but he was defeated by Caesar with great slaughter (58), and driven beyond the Rhine. Caesar twice crossed this river (55, 53), but made no permanent conquest on the E. bank. In the reign of Augustus, his step-son Drusus carried on war in Germany with great success for 4 years (12—9), and penetrated as far as the Elbe. On his death (9), his brother Tiberius succeeded to the command ; and under him the country between the Rhine and the Visurgis (*Weser*) was entirely subjugated, and bid fair to become a Roman province. But in A. D. 9, the impolitic and tyrannical conduct of the Roman governor Quintilius Varus, provoked a general insurrection of the various German tribes, headed by Arminius, the Cheruscan. Varus and his legions were defeated and destroyed, and the Romans lost all their conquests E. of the Rhine. [VARUS.] The defeat of Varus was avenged by the successful campaigns of Germanicus, who would probably have recovered the Roman dominions E. of the river, had not the jealousy of Tiberius recalled him to Rome, A. D. 16. From this time the Romans abandoned all further attempts to conquer Germany ; but in consequence of the civil dissensions which broke out in Germany soon after the departure of Tiberius, they were enabled to obtain peaceable possession of a large portion of the S. W. of Germany between the Rhine and the Danube, to which they gave the name of the AGRI DECUMATES. [See p. 27, b.] On the death of Nero, several of the tribes in W. Germany joined the Batavi in their insurrection against the Romans (A. D. 69—71). Domitian and Trajan had to repel the attacks of some German tribes ; but in the reign of Antoninus Pius, the Marcomanni, joined by various other tribes, made a more formidable attack upon the Roman dominions, and threatened the empire with destruction. From this time the Romans were often called upon to defend the left bank of the Rhine against their dangerous neighbours, especially against the 2 powerful confederacies of the Alemanni and Franks [ALEMANNI ; FRANCI] ; and in the 4th and 5th centuries the Germans obtained possession of some of the fairest provinces of the empire. — The Germans are divided by Tacitus into 3 great tribes : 1. *Ingaevones*, on the Ocean. 2. *Hermiones*, inhabiting the central parts. 3. *Istaevones*, in the remainder of Germany, consequently in the E. and

&. parts. These 3 names were said to be derived from the 3 sons of Mannus, the son of Tuisco. Pliny makes 5 divisions: 1. *Vindili*, including Burgundiones, Varini, Carini, and Guttones. 2. *Ingaevones*, including Cimbri, Teutones, and Chauci. 3. *Istaevones*, including the midland Cimbri. 4. *Hermiones*, including the Suevi, Hermunduri, Chatti, and Cherusci. 5. *Peucini* and *Bastarnae*, bordering on the Dacians. But whether we adopt the division of Tacitus or Pliny, we ought to add the inhabitants of the Scandinavian peninsula, the Hilleviones, divided into the Sinones and Sitones. It is difficult to fix with accuracy the position of the various tribes, as they frequently migrated from one spot to another. An account of each is given under the name of the tribe. See CHAUCI, CHERUSCI, CIMBRI, SUEVI, &c.

Germanicus Caesar, son of Nero Claudius Drusus and Antonia, the daughter of the triumvir Antony, was born B. C. 15. He was adopted by his uncle Tiberius in the lifetime of Augustus, and was raised at an early age to the honours of the state. He assisted Tiberius in the war against the Pannonians and Dalmatians (A. D. 7—10), and also fought along with Tiberius against the Germans in the 2 following years (11, 12). He had the command of the legions in Germany, when the alarming mutiny broke out among the troops in Germany and Illyricum, upon the death of Augustus (14). Germanicus was a favourite with the soldiers, and they offered to place him at the head of the empire; but he rejected their proposal, and exerted all his influence to quell the mutiny, and reconcile them to their new sovereign. After restoring order among the troops, he crossed the Rhine, and laid waste the country of the Marsi with fire and sword. In the following year (15), he again crossed the Rhine, and marched into the interior of the country. He penetrated as far as the Saltus Teutoburgiensis, N. of the Lippe, in which forest the army of Quintilius Varus had been destroyed by the Germans. Here his troops gathered up the bones of their ill-fated comrades, and paid the last honours to their memory. But meantime Arminius had collected a formidable army, with which he attacked the Romans; and it was not without considerable loss that Germanicus made good his retreat to the Rhine. It was in this campaign that Thusnelda, the wife of Arminius, fell into the hands of Germanicus. [ARMINIUS.] Next year (16) Germanicus placed his troops on board a fleet of 1000 vessels, and sailed through the canal of his father, Drusus [see p. 233, b.], and the Zuydersee to the ocean, and from thence to the mouth of the Amisia (*Ems*), where he landed his forces. After crossing the Ems and the Weser, he fought 2 battles with Arminius, in both of which the Germans were completely defeated. The Germans could no longer offer him any effectual resistance, and Germanicus needed only another year to reduce completely the whole country between the Rhine and the Elbe. But the jealousy of Tiberius saved Germany. Upon pretence of the dangerous state of affairs in the E., the emperor recalled Germanicus to Rome, which he entered in triumph on the 26th of May, 17. In the same year all the Eastern provinces were assigned to Germanicus; but Tiberius placed Cn. Piso in command of Syria, with secret instructions to check and thwart Germanicus. Piso soon showed his hostility to Germanicus; and

his wife Plancina, in like manner, did every thing in her power to annoy Agrippina, the wife of Germanicus. In 18, Germanicus proceeded to Armenia, where he placed Zeno on the throne, and in the following year (19) he visited Egypt, and on his return he was seized with a dangerous illness, of which he died. He believed that he had been poisoned by Piso, and shortly before he died, he summoned his friends, and called upon them to avenge his murder. He was deeply and sincerely lamented by the Roman people; and Tiberius was obliged to sacrifice Piso to the public indignation. [PISO.] By Agrippina he had 9 children, of whom 6 survived him. Of these the most notorious were the emperor Caligula, and Agrippina, the mother of Nero. Germanicus was an author of some repute. He wrote several poetical works. We still possess the remains of his Latin translation of the *Phaenomena* of Aratus. The latest edition of this work is by Orelli at the end of his Phaedrus, Zurich, 1831.

Germanicia or Caesarea Germanica (Γερμανίκεια, Καισάρεια Γερμανική), a town in the Syrian province of Commagene, near the borders of Cappadocia; the birthplace of the heretic Nestorius.

Gerra (Γέῤῥα: near *El-Katif*), one of the chief cities of Arabia, and a great emporium for the trade of Arabia and India, stood on the N. E. coast of Arabia Felix, 200 stadia (20 geog. miles) from the shore of the Sinus Gerraeus or Gerraicus (*Elwah Bay?*), a bay on the W. side of the Persian Gulf, 2400 stadia (240 geog. miles=4° of lat.) from the mouth of the Tigris. The city was 5 Roman miles in circuit. The inhabitants, called Gerraei (Γεῤῥαῖοι) were said to have been originally Chaldaeans, who were driven out of Babylon. There was a small place of the same name on the N. E. frontier of Egypt, between Pelusium and M. Casius, 50 stadia or 8 Roman miles from the former.

Gerrhus (Γέῤῥος), a river of Scythia, flowing through a country of the same name, was a branch of the Borysthenes, and flowed into the Hypacyris, dividing the country of the Nomad Scythians from that of the Royal Scythians.

Gerunda (*Gerona*), a town of the Ausetani in Hispania Tarraconensis, on the road from Tarraco to Narbo in Gaul.

Geryon or Geryones (Γηρυόνης), son of Chrysaor and Callirrhoë, a monster with 3 heads, or, according to others, with 3 bodies united together, was a king in Spain, and possessed magnificent oxen, which Hercules carried away. For details see HERCULES.

Gesoriacum (*Boulogne*), a port of the Morini in Gallia Belgica, at which persons usually embarked to cross over to Britain: it was subsequently called Bononia, whence its modern name.

Gessius Florus. [FLORUS.]

Geta, Septimius, brother of Caracalla, by whom he was assassinated, A. D. 212. For details see CARACALLA.

Getae, a Thracian people, called Daci by the Romans. Herodotus and Thucydides place them S. of the Ister (*Danube*) near its mouths; but in the time of Alexander the Great they dwelt beyond this river and N. of the Triballi. They were driven by the Sarmatians further W. towards Germany. For their later history see DACIA.

Gigantes (Γίγαντες), the giants. According to Homer, they were a gigantic and savage race of men, dwelling in the distant W. in the island of

Trinacia, and were destroyed on account of their insolence towards the gods. — Hesiod considers them as divine beings, who sprang from the blood that fell from Uranus upon the earth, so that Ge (the earth) was their mother. Neither Homer nor Hesiod know any thing about their contest with the gods. — Later poets and mythographers frequently confound them with the Titans, and represent them as enemies of Zeus and the gods, whose abode on Olympus they attempt to take by storm. Their battle with the gods seems to be only an imitation of the revolt of the Titans against Uranus. Ge, it is said, indignant at the fate of her former children, the Titans, gave birth to the Gigantes, who were beings of a monstrous size, with fearful countenances and the tails of dragons. They were born, according to some, in the Phlegraean plains in Sicily, Campania, or Arcadia, and, according to others, in the Thracian Pallene. In their native land they made an attack upon heaven, being armed with huge rocks and trunks of trees. The gods were told that they could not conquer the giants without the assistance of a mortal; whereupon they summoned Hercules to their aid. The giants Alcyoneus and Porphyrion distinguished themselves above their brethren. Alcyoneus was immortal so long as he fought in his native land; but Hercules dragged him away to a foreign land, and thus killed him. Porphyrion was killed by the lightning of Zeus and the arrows of Hercules. The other giants, whose number is said to have been 24, were then killed one after another by the gods and Hercules, and some of them were buried by their conquerors under (volcanic) islands. — It is worthy of remark, that most writers place the giants in volcanic districts; and it is probable that the story of their contest with the gods took its origin from volcanic convulsions.

Gigōnus (Γίγωνος: Γιγώνιος), a town and promontory of Macedonia on the Thermaic gulf.

Gildo, or **Gildon**, a Moorish chieftain, governed Africa for some years as a subject of the Western empire; but in A. D. 397, he transferred his allegiance to the Eastern empire, and the emperor Arcadius accepted him as a subject. Stilicho, guardian of Honorius, sent an army against him. Gildo was defeated; and being taken prisoner, he put an end to his own life by hanging himself (398). The history of this war forms the subject of one of Claudian's poems (*De Bello Gildonico*).

Gindārus (Γίνδαρος: *Gindaries*), a very strong fortress in the district of Cyrrhestice in Syria, N. E. of Antioch.

Girba, a city on the island of Meninx (*Jerbah*), at the S. extremity of the Lesser Syrtis, in N. Africa: celebrated for its manufactures of purple.

Gisco or **Gisgo** (Γίσκων or Γέσκων). 1. Son of Hamilcar who was defeated and killed in the battle of Himera, B. C. 480. In consequence of this calamity, Gisgo was banished from Carthage. He died at Selinus in Sicily. — 2. Son of Hanno, was in exile when the Carthaginians were defeated at the river Crimissus by Timoleon, 339. He was then recalled from exile, and sent to oppose Timoleon, but was unable to accomplish any thing of importance. — 3. Commander of the Carthaginian garrison at Lilybaeum, at the end of the first Punic war. After the conclusion of peace, 241, he was deputed by the government to treat with the mercenaries who had risen in revolt, but he was seized by them and put to death.

Gitiādas (Γιτιάδας), a Lacedaemonian architect statuary, and poet. He completed the temple of Athena Poliouchos at Sparta, and ornamented it with works in bronze, from which it was called the Brazen House, and hence the goddess received the surname of Χαλκοοῖκος. He composed a hymn to the goddess, besides other poems. He flourished about B. C. 516, and is the last Spartan artist of any distinction.

Glabrio, **Acilius**, plebeians. 1. C., quaestor B. C. 203, and tribune of the plebs 197. He acted as interpreter to the Athenian embassy in 155, when the 3 philosophers, Carneades, Diogenes, and Critolaus came as envoys to Rome. He wrote in Greek a history of Rome from the earliest period to his own times. It was translated into Latin by one Claudius, and his version is cited by Livy, under the titles of *Annabes Aciliani* (xxv. 39) and *Libri Aciliani* (xxxv. 14). — 2. M'., tribune of the plebs 201, praetor 196, and consul 191. In his consulship he defeated Antiochus at Thermopylae, and subsequently the Aetolians likewise. — 3. M'., married a daughter of M. Aemilius Scaurus, consul 115, whom Sulla, in 82, compelled him to divorce. Glabrio was praetor urbanus in 70, when he presided at the impeachment of Verres. He was consul in 67, and in the following year proconsul of Cilicia. He succeeded L. Lucullus in the command of the war against Mithridates, but remained inactive in Bithynia. He was superseded by Cn. Pompey. — 4. M'., son of No. 3, was born in the house of Cn. Pompey, B. C. 81, who married his mother after her compulsory divorce from the elder Glabrio. Aemilia died in giving birth to him. In the civil war, Glabrio was one of Caesar's lieutenants; commanded the garrison of Oricum in Epirus in 48, and was stationed in Sicily in 46. He was twice defended on capital charges by Cicero, and acquitted.

Glanis, more usually written CLANIS.

Glānum Livii (nr. *St. Remy* Ru.), a town of the Salyes in Gallia Narbonensis.

Glaphyra. [ARCHELAUS, No. 6.]

Glaucē (Γλαύκη). 1. One of the Nereides, the name Glauce being only a personification of the colour of the sea. — 2. Daughter of Creon of Corinth, also called Creusa. For details see CREON.

Glaucia, C. **Servilius**, praetor B. C. 100, the chief supporter of Saturninus, with whom he was put to death in this year. [SATURNINUS.]

Glaucias (Γλαυκίας). 1. King of the Taulantians, one of the Illyrian tribes, fought against Alexander the Great, B. C. 335. In 316 he afforded an asylum to the infant Pyrrhus, and refused to surrender him to Cassander. In 307 he invaded Epirus, and placed Pyrrhus, then 12 years old, upon the throne. — 2. A Greek physician, who probably lived in the 3rd or 2nd century B. C. — 3. A statuary of Aegina, who made the bronze chariot and statue of Gelon, flourished B. C. 488.

Glaucon (Γλαύκων). 1. Son of Critias, brother of Callaeschrus, and father of Charmides and of Plato's mother, Perictione. — 2. Brother of Plato, who makes him one of the speakers in the Republic.

Glaucus (Γλαύκος). 1. Grandson of Aeolus, son of Sisyphus and Merope, and father of Bellerophontes. He lived at Potniae, despised the power of Aphrodite, and did not allow his mares to breed, that they might be the stronger for the horse race. According to others he fed them with human flesh. This excited the anger of Aphrodite, who destroyed him. According to some accounts his horses became frightened and threw him out of his chariot, as he was contending in the funeral games celebrated by Acastus in honour of his father Pelias. According to others, his horses tore him to pieces, having drunk from the water of a sacred well in Boeotia, in consequence of which they were seized with madness. Glaucus of Potniae (Γλαῦκος Ποτνιεύς) was the title of one of the lost tragedies of Aeschylus. — 2. Son of Hippolochus, and grandson of Bellerophontes, was a Lycian prince, and assisted Priam in the Trojan war. He was connected with Diomedes by ties of hospitality ; and when they recognised one another in the battle, they abstained from fighting, and exchanged arms with one another. Glaucus was slain by Ajax. — 3. Son of the Messenian king Aepytus, whom he succeeded on the throne. — 4. One of the sons of the Cretan king Minos by Pasiphaë or Crete. When a boy, he fell into a cask full of honey, and was smothered. Minos searched for his son in vain, and was at length informed by Apollo or the Curetes that the person who should devise the most appropriate comparison between a cow, which could assume 3 different colours, and any other object, would find the boy. The soothsayer Polyidus of Argos solved the problem by likening the cow to a mulberry, which is at first white, then red, and in the end black. By his prophetic powers he then discovered the boy. Minos now required Polyidus to restore his son to life ; but as he could not accomplish this, Minos ordered him to be entombed alive with the body of Glaucus. When Polyidus was thus shut up in the vault, he saw a serpent approaching the dead body, and killed the reptile. Presently another serpent came, and placed a herb upon the dead serpent, which was thereby restored to life. Thereupon Polyidus covered the body of Glaucus with the same herb, and the boy at once rose into life again. The story of Glaucus and Polyidus was a favourite subject with the ancient poets and artists. — 5. Of Anthedon in Boeotia, a fisherman, who became immortal by eating of the divine herb which Cronos had sown. His parentage is differently stated : some called his father Copeus, others Polybus, the husband of Euboea, and others again Anthedon or Poseidon. He was further said to have been a clever diver, to have built the ship Argo, and to have accompanied the Argonauts as their steersman. In the sea-fight of Jason against the Tyrrhenians, Glaucus alone remained unhurt ; he sank to the bottom of the sea, where he was visible to none save Jason. From this moment he became a marine deity, and was of service to the Argonauts. The story of his sinking or leaping into the sea was variously modified in the different traditions. There was a belief in Greece that once in every year Glaucus visited all the coasts and islands, accompanied by marine monsters, and gave his prophecies. Fishermen and sailors paid particular reverence to him, and watched his oracles, which were believed to be very trustworthy. He is said to have even instructed Apollo in the prophetic art. Some writers stated that he dwelt in Delos, where he prophesied in conjunction with the nymphs ; but the place of his abode varied in different traditions. The stories about his various loves were favourite subjects with the ancient poets. — 6. Of Chios, a statuary in metal, distinguished as the inventor of the art of soldering metals (κόλ-

λησις), flourished B. C. 490. His most noted work was an iron base (ὑποκρητηρίδιον), which, with the silver bowl it supported, was presented to the temple at Delphi by Alyattes, king of Lydia.

Glaucus (Γλαῦκος). 1. A small river of Phrygia, falling into the Maeander near Eumenia. — 2. A small river of Lycia, on the borders of Caria, flowing into the Sinus Glaucus (Gulf of Makri).

Glaucus Sinus. [GLAUCUS.]

Glessaria (Ameland), an island off the coast of the Frisii, so called from "glessum" or amber which was found there : its proper name was Austeravia.

Glisas (Γλῖσας: Γλισάντιος), an ancient town in Boeotia, on Mt. Hypaton. It was in ruins in the time of Pausanias.

Glycas, Michael, a Byzantine historian, the author of a work entitled Annals (βίβλος χρονική), containing the history of the world from the creation to the death of Alexis I. Comnenus, A. D. 1118. Edited by Bekker, Bonn, 1836.

Glycēra (Γλυκέρα), "the sweet one," a favourite name of hetairae. The most celebrated hetairae of this name are, 1. The daughter of Thalassis, and the mistress of Harpalus. — 2. Of Sicyon, and the mistress of Pausias. — 3. A favourite of Horace.

Glycerius, became emperor of the W. A. D. 473, after the death of Olybrius, by the assistance of Gundobald the Burgundian. But the Byzantine court did not acknowledge Glycerius, and proclaimed Julius Nepos emperor, by whom Glycerius was dethroned (474), and compelled to become a priest. He was appointed bishop of Salona in Dalmatia.

Glycon (Γλύκων), an Athenian sculptor, known to us by his magnificent colossal marble statue of Hercules, commonly called the "Farnese Hercules." It was found in the baths of Caracalla, and, after adorning the Farnese palace for some time, was removed to the royal museum at Naples. It represents the hero resting on his club, after one of his labours. The swollen muscles admirably express repose after severe exertion. Glycon probably lived under the early Roman emperors.

Gnipho, M. Antōnius, a Roman rhetorician, was born B. C. 114, in Gaul, but studied at Alexandria. He afterwards established a school at Rome, which was attended by many distinguished men, and among others by Cicero, when he was praetor.

Gnōsus, Gnossus. [CNOSUS.]

Gōbryas (Γωβρύας), a noble Persian, one of the 7 conspirators against Smerdis the Magian. He accompanied Darius into Scythia. He was doubly related to Darius by marriage : Darius married the daughter of Gobryas, and Gobryas married the sister of Darius.

Golgi (Γολγοί: Γόλγιος), a town in Cyprus, of uncertain site, was a Sicyonian colony, and one of the chief seats of the worship of Aphrodite (Venus).

Gomphi (Γόμφοι: Γομφεύς), a town in Hestiaeotis in Thessaly, was a strong fortress on the confines of Epirus, and commanded the chief pass between Thessaly and Epirus : it was taken and destroyed by Caesar (B. C. 48), but was afterwards rebuilt.

Gonni, Gonnus (Γόννοι, Γόννος: Γόννιος), a strongly fortified town of the Perrhaebi in Thessaly, on the river Peneus and at the entrance of the vale of Tempe, was, from its position, of great military importance ; but it is not mentioned after the time of the wars between the Macedonians and Romans.

Gordiānus, M. Antōnius, the name of 3 Roman emperors, father, son, and grandson. 1. Surnamed Africanus, son of Metius Marullus and Ulpia Gordiana, possessed a princely fortune, and was distinguished alike by moral and intellectual excellence. In his 1st consulship, A. D. 213, he was the colleague of Caracalla ; in his 2nd of Alexander Severus ; and soon afterwards was nominated proconsul of Africa. After governing Africa for several years with justice and integrity, a rebellion broke out in the province in consequence of the tyranny of the procurator of Maximinus. The ringleaders of the conspiracy compelled Gordian, who was now in his 80th year, to assume the imperial title. He entered on his new duties at Carthage in the month of February, associated his son with him in the empire, and despatched letters to Rome, announcing his elevation. Gordianus and his son were at once proclaimed Augusti by the senate, and preparations were made in Italy to resist Maximinus. But meantime a certain Capellianus, procurator of Numidia, refused to acknowledge the authority of the Gordiani and marched against them. The younger Gordianus was defeated by him, and slain in the battle ; and his aged father thereupon put an end to his own life, after reigning less than 2 months. — 2. Son of the preceding and of Fabia Orestilia, was born A. D. 192, was associated with his father in the purple, and fell in battle, as recorded above. — 3. Grandson of the elder Gordianus, either by a daughter or by the younger Gordianus. The soldiers proclaimed him emperor in July, A. D. 238, after the murder of Balbinus and Pupienus, although he was a mere boy, probably not more than 12 years old. He reigned 6 years, from 238 to 244. In 241 he married the daughter of Misitheus, and in the same year set out for the E. to carry on the war against the Persians. With the assistance of Misitheus, he defeated the Persians in 242. Misitheus died in the following year ; and Philippus, whom Gordian had taken into his confidence, excited discontent among the soldiers, who at length rose in open mutiny, and assassinated Gordian in Mesopotamia, 244. He was succeeded by PHILIPPUS.

Gordium (Γόρδιον, Γορδίου Κώμη), the ancient capital of Phrygia, the royal residence of the kings of the dynasty of Gordius, and the scene of Alexander's celebrated exploit of " cutting the Gordian knot." [GORDIUS]. It was situated in the W. of that part of Phrygia which was afterwards called Galatia, N. of Pessinus, on the N. bank of the Sangarius. In the reign of Augustus it received the name of Juliopolis (Ἰουλιούπολις).

Gordius (Γόρδιος), an ancient king of Phrygia, and father of Midas, was originally a poor peasant. Internal disturbances having broken out in Phrygia, an oracle informed the inhabitants that a waggon would bring them a king, who should at the same time put an end to the disturbances. When the people were deliberating on these points, Gordius, with his wife and son, suddenly appeared riding in his waggon in the assembly of the people, who at once acknowledged him as king. Gordius, out of gratitude, dedicated his chariot to Zeus, in the acropolis of Gordium. The pole was fastened to the yoke by a knot of bark ; and an oracle declared that whosoever should untie the knot should reign over all Asia. Alexander, on his arrival at Gordium, cut the knot with his sword, and applied the oracle to himself.

Gordiuteichos (Γορδίου τεῖχος), a town in Caria, near the borders of Phrygia, between Antiochia ad Maeandrum and Tabae.

Gordyaei. [GORDYENE.]

Gordyaei Montes (τὰ Γορδυαῖα ὄρη: Mountains of Kurdistan), the name given by Strabo to the N. part of the broad belt of mountains, which separates the Tigris valley from the great table land of Iran, and which divided Mesopotamia and Assyria from Armenia and Media. They are connected with the mountains of Armenia at Ararat, whence they run S. E. between the Arsissa Palus (Lake Van) and the sources of the Tigris and its upper confluents as far as the confines of Media, where the chain turns more to the S. and was called ZAGROS.

Gordyene or Corduene (Γορδυηνή, Κορδουηνή), a mountainous district in the S. of Armenia Major, between the Arsissa Palus (Lake Van) and the GORDYAEI MONTES. After the Mithridatic War, it was assigned by Pompey to Tigranes, with whom its possession had been disputed by the Parthian king Phraates. Trajan added it to the Roman empire; and it formed afterwards a constant object of contention between the Romans and the Parthian and Persian kings, but was for the most part virtually independent. Its warlike inhabitants, called Γορδυαῖοι or Corduēni, were no doubt the same people as the CARDUCHI of the earlier Greek geographers, and the Kurds of modern times.

Gorge (Γόργη), daughter of Oeneus and Althea. She and her sister Deianira alone retained their original forms, when their other sisters were metamorphosed by Artemis into birds.

Gorgias (Γοργίας). 1. Of Leontini, in Sicily, a celebrated rhetorician and orator, sophist and philosopher, was born about B. C. 480, and is said to have lived 105, or even 109 years. Of his early life we have no particulars ; but when he was of advanced age (B. C. 427) he was sent by his fellow-citizens as ambassador to Athens, for the purpose of soliciting its protection against Syracuse. He seems to have returned to Leontini only for a short time, and to have spent the remaining years of his vigorous old age in the towns of Greece Proper, especially at Athens and the Thessalian Larissa, enjoying honour everywhere as an orator and teacher of rhetoric. The common statement that Pericles and the historian Thucydides were among his disciples, cannot be true, as he did not go to Athens till after the death of Pericles ; but Alcibiades, Alcidamas, Aeschines, and Antisthenes, are called either pupils or imitators of Gorgias, and his oratory must have had great influence upon the rhetorician Isocrates. The high estimation in which he was held at Athens appears from the way in which he is introduced in the dialogue of Plato, which bears his name. The eloquence of Gorgias was chiefly calculated to tickle the ear by antitheses, alliterations, the symmetry of its parts, and similar artifices. Two declamations have come down to us under the name of Gorgias, viz. the Apology of Palamedes, and the Encomium on Helena, the genuineness of which is doubtful. Besides his orations, which were mostly what the Greeks called Epideitic or speeches for display, such as his oration addressed to the assembled Greeks at Olympia, Gorgias also wrote loci communes, probably as rhetorical exercises ; a work on dissimilar and homogeneous words, and another on rhetoric. The works of Gorgias did not even contain the elements of a scientific theory of oratory, any more than his oral instructions. He confined himself to teaching his pupils a variety of rhetorical artifices, and made them learn by heart certain formulas relative to them. — **2.** Of Athens, gave instruction in rhetoric to young M. Cicero, when he was at Athens. He wrote a rhetorical work, a Latin abridgment of which by Rutilius Lupus is still extant, under the title *De Figuris Sententiarum et Elocutionis.*

Gorgo and **Gorgones** (Γοργώ and Γόργονες). Homer mentions only one Gorgo, who appears in the Odyssey (xi. 633) as one of the frightful phantoms in Hades: in the Iliad the Aegis of Athena contains the head of Gorgo, the terror of her enemies. Hesiod mentions 3 Gorgones, **Stheno, Euryale,** and **Medusa,** daughters of Phorcys and Ceto, whence they are sometimes called **Phorcÿdes.** Hesiod placed them in the far W. in the Ocean, in the neighbourhood of Night and the Hesperides; but later traditions transferred them to Libya. They were frightful beings; instead of hair, their heads were covered with hissing serpents; and they had wings, brazen claws, and enormous teeth. Medusa, who alone of her sisters was mortal, was, according to some legends, at first a beautiful maiden, but her hair was changed into serpents by Athena, in consequence of her having become by Poseidon the mother of Chrysaor and Pegasus, in one of Athena's temples. Her head now became so fearful that every one who looked at it was changed into stone. Hence the great difficulty which Perseus had in killing her. [PERSEUS.] Athena afterwards placed the head in the centre of her shield or breastplate.

Gortyn, Gortÿna (Γόρτυν, Γόρτυνα: Γορτύνιος). 1. (Nr. *Hagios Dheka* Ru., 6 miles from the foot of Mt. Ida), one of the most ancient cities in Crete, on the river Lethaeus, 90 stadia from its harbour Lebën, and 130 stadia from its other harbour Matalia. It was one of the chief seats of the worship of Europa, whence it was called *Hellotis*; and it was subsequently peopled by Minyans and Tyrrhene-Pelasgians, whence it also bore the name of Larissa. It was the 2nd city in Crete, being only inferior to Cnossus; and on the decline of the latter place under the Romans, it became the metropolis of the island. — **2.** Also **Gortys** (Nr. *Atsikolo* Ru.), a town in Arcadia on the river Gortynius, a tributary of the Alpheus.

Gortynïa (Γορτυνία), a town in Emathia in Macedonia, of uncertain site.

Gotarzes. [ARSACES XX. XXI.]

Gothi, Gothönes, Guttönes, a powerful German people, who played an important part in the overthrow of the Roman empire. They originally dwelt on the Prussian coast of the Baltic at the mouth of the Vistula, where they are placed by Tacitus; but they afterwards migrated S., and at the beginning of the 3rd century, they appear on the coasts of the Black Sea, where Caracalla encountered them on his march to the E. In the reign of the emperor Philippus (A. D. 244—249), they obtained possession of a great part of the Roman province of Dacia; and in consequence of their settling in the countries formerly inhabited by the Getae and Scythians, they are frequently called both Getae and Scythians by later writers. From the time of Philippus the attacks of the Goths against the Roman empire became more frequent and more destructive. In A. D. 272 the emperor Aurelian surrendered to them the whole of Dacia. It is about

this time that we find them separated into 2 great divisions, the Ostrogoths or E. Goths, and the Visigoths or W. Goths. The Ostrogoths settled in Moesia and Pannonia, while the Visigoths remained N. of the Danube. — The Visigoths under their king Alaric invaded Italy, and took and plundered Rome (410). A few years afterwards they settled permanently in the S. W. of Gaul, and established a kingdom of which Tolosa was the capital. From thence they invaded Spain, where they also founded a kingdom, which lasted for more than 2 centuries, till it was overthrown by the Arabs. — The Ostrogoths meantime had extended their dominions almost up to the gates of Constantinople; and the emperor Zeno was glad to get rid of them by giving them permission to invade and conquer Italy. Under their king Theodoric the Great they obtained possession of the whole of Italy (493). Theodoric took the title of king of Italy, and an Ostrogothic dynasty reigned in the country, till it was destroyed by Narses, the general of Justinian, A. D. 553. — The Ostrogoths embraced Christianity at an early period; and it was for their use that Ulphilas translated the sacred Scriptures into Gothic, about the middle of the 4th century.

Gothini, a Celtic people in the S. E. of Germany, subject to the Quadi.

Gracchānus, M. Jūnius, assumed his cognomen on account of his friendship with C. Gracchus. He wrote a work, *De Potestatibus,* which gave an account of the Roman constitution and magistracies from the time of the kings. It was addressed to T. Pomponius Atticus, the father of Cicero's friend. This work, which appears to have been one of great value, is lost, but some parts of it are cited by Joannes Lydus. [LYDUS.]

Gracchus, Semprōnius, plebeians. — **1.** Tib., a distinguished general in the 2nd Punic war. In B.C. 216 he was magister equitum to the dictator, M. Junius Pera; in 215 consul for the first time; and in 213 consul for the 2nd time. In 212 he fell in battle against Mago, at Campi Veteres, in Lucania. His body was sent to Hannibal, who honoured it with a magnificent burial. — **2.** Tib., was tribune of the plebs in 187; and although personally hostile to P. Scipio Africanus, he defended him against the attacks of the other tribunes, for which he received the thanks of the aristocratical party. Soon after this occurrence Gracchus was rewarded with the hand of Cornelia, the youngest daughter of P. Scipio Africanus. In 181 he was praetor, and received Hispania Citerior as his province, where he carried on the war with great success against the Celtiberians. After defeating them in battle, he gained their confidence by his justice and kindness. He returned to Rome in 178; and was consul in 177, when he was sent against the Sardinians, who revolted. He reduced them to complete submission in 176, and returned to Rome in 175. He brought with him so large a number of captives, that they were sold for a mere ·trifle, which gave rise to the proverb *Sardi venales*. In 169 he was censor with C. Claudius Pulcher, and was consul a 2nd time in 163. — He had 12 children by Cornelia, all of whom died at an early age, except the 2 tribunes, Tiberius and Caius, and a daughter, Cornelia, who was married to P. Scipio Africanus the younger. — **3.** Tib., elder son of No. 2, lost his father at an early age. He was educated together with his brother Caius by his illustrious mother, Cornelia, who made it the object of her life to render her sons worthy at their father and of her own ancestors. She was assisted in the education of her children by eminent Greeks, who exercised great influence upon the minds of the two brothers, and among whom we have especial mention of Diophanes of Mytilene, Menelaus of Marathon, and Blossius of Cumae. Tiberius was 9 years older than his brother Caius; and although they grew up under the same influence, and their characters resembled each other in the main outlines, yet they differed from each other in several important particulars. Tiberius was inferior to his brother in talent, but surpassed him in the amiable traits of his gentle nature : the simplicity of his demeanour, and his calm dignity, won for him the hearts of the people. His eloquence, too, formed a strong contrast with the passionate and impetuous harangues of Caius ; for it was temperate, graceful, persuasive, and, proceeding as it did from the fulness of his own heart, it found a ready entrance into the hearts of his hearers. Tiberius served in Africa under P. Scipio Africanus the younger, who had married his sister, and was present at the destruction of Carthage (146). In 137 he was quaestor, and in that capacity he accompanied the consul, Hostilius Mancinus, to Hispania Citerior, where he gained both the affection of the Roman soldiers, and the esteem and confidence of the victorious enemy. The distressed condition of the Roman people had deeply excited the sympathies of Tiberius. As he travelled through Etruria on his journey to Spain, he observed with grief and indignation the deserted state of that fertile country; thousands of foreign slaves in chains were employed in cultivating the land and tending the flocks upon the immense estates of the wealthy, while the poorer classes of Roman citizens, who were thus thrown out of employment, had scarcely their daily bread or a clod of earth to call their own. He resolved to use every effort to remedy this state of things by endeavouring to create an industrious middle class of agriculturists, and to put a check upon the unbounded avarice of the ruling party, whose covetousness, combined with the disasters of the 2nd Punic war, had completely destroyed the middle class of small landowners. With this view, he offered himself as a candidate for the tribuneship, and obtained it for the year 133. The agrarian law of Licinius, which enacted that no one should possess more than 500 jugera of public land, had never been repealed, but had for a long series of years been totally disregarded. The first measure, therefore, of Tiberius was to propose a bill to the people, renewing and enforcing the Licinian law, but with the modification, that besides the 500 jugera allowed by that law, any one might possess 250 jugera of the public land for each of his sons. This clause, however, seems to have been limited to 2 ; so that a father of 2 sons might occupy 1000 jugera of public land. The surplus was to be taken from them and distributed in small farms among the poor citizens. The business of measuring and distributing the land was to be entrusted to triumvirs, who were to be elected as a permanent magistracy. This measure encountered the most vehement opposition from the senate and the aristocracy, and they got one of the tribunes M. Octavius, to put his *intercessio* or veto upon the bill. When neither persuasions nor threats would induce Octavius to withdraw his opposition, the people, upon the proposition of Tiberius, deposed Octavius from his office. The law was then passed;

and the triumvirs appointed to carry it into execution were Tib. Gracchus, App. Claudius, his father-in-law, and his brother C. Gracchus, who was then little more than 20 years old, and was serving in the camp of P. Scipio at Numantia. About this time Attalus died, bequeathing his kingdom and his property to the Roman people. Gracchus thereupon proposed that this property should be distributed among the people, to enable the poor, who were to receive lands, to purchase the necessary implements, cattle and the like. When the time came for the election of the tribunes for the following year, Tiberius again offered himself as a candidate. The senate declared that it was illegal for any one to hold this office for 2 consecutive years ; but Tiberius paid no attention to the objection. While the tribes were voting, a band of senators, headed by P. Scipio Nasica, rushed from the senate house into the forum and attacked the people. Tiberius was killed as he was attempting to escape. He was probably about 35 years of age at the time of his death. Whatever were the errors of Tiberius in legislation, his motives were pure ; and he died the death of a martyr in the protection of the poor and oppressed. All the odium that has for many centuries been thrown upon Tiberius and his brother Caius arose from party prejudice, and more especially from a misunderstanding of the nature of a Roman agrarian law, which did not deal with private property, but only with the public land of the state. (See *Dict. of Antiq.* art. *Agrariae Leges.*) —4. C., brother of No. 3, was in Spain at the time of his brother's murder, as has been already stated. He returned to Rome in the following year (132), but kept aloof from public affairs for some years. In 126 he was quaestor, and went to Sardinia, under the consul L. Aurelius Orestes ; and there gained the approbation of his superiors and the attachment of the soldiers. The senate attempted to keep him in Sardinia, dreading his popularity in Rome; but after he had remained there 2 years, he left the province without leave, and returned to the city in 124. Urged on by the popular wish, and by the desire of avenging the cause of his murdered brother, he became a candidate for the tribuneship of the plebs, and was elected for the year 123. His reforms were far more extensive than his brother's, and such was his influence with the people that he carried all he proposed; and the senate were deprived of some of their most important privileges. His first measure was the renewal of the agrarian law of his brother. He next carried several laws for the amelioration of the condition of the poor, enacting, that the soldiers should be equipped at the expense of the republic ; that no person under the age of 17 should be drafted for the army ; and that every month corn should be sold at a low fixed price to the poor. In order to weaken the power of the senate, he enacted, that the judices in the judicia publica, who had hitherto been elected from the senate, should in future be chosen from the equites ; and that in every year, before the consuls were elected, the senate should determine the 2 provinces which the consuls should have. No branch of the public administration appears to have escaped his notice. He gave a regular organisation to the province of Asia, which had for many years been left unsettled. In order to facilitate intercourse between the several parts of Italy, and at the same time to give employment to the poor, he made new roads in all directions, repaired the old ones, and set up milestones along them. — Caius was elected tribune again for the following year, 122. The senate, finding it impossible to resist the measures of Caius, resolved if possible to destroy his influence with the people, that they might retain the government in their own hands. For this purpose they persuaded M. Livius Drusus, one of the colleagues of Caius, to propose measures still more popular than those of Caius. The people allowed themselves to be duped by the treacherous agent of the senate, and the popularity of Caius gradually waned. During his absence in Africa, whither he had gone as one of the triumvirs to establish a colony at Carthage, in accordance with one of his own laws, his party had been considerably weakened by the influence of Drusus and the aristocracy, and many of his friends had deserted his cause. He failed in obtaining the tribuneship for the following year (121); and when his year of office expired, his enemies began to repeal several of his enactments. Caius appeared in the forum to oppose these proceedings. One of the attendants of the consul Opimius was slain by the friends of Caius. Opimius gladly availed himself of this pretext to persuade the senate to confer upon him unlimited power to act as he thought best for the good of the republic. Fulvius Flaccus, and the other friends of Caius, called upon him to repel force by force; but he refused to arm, and while his friends fought in his defence, he fled to the grove of the Furies, where he fell by the hands of his slave, whom he had commanded to put him to death. The bodies of the slain, whose number is said to have amounted to 3000, were thrown into the Tiber, their property was confiscated, and their houses demolished. All the other friends of Gracchus who fell into the hands of their enemies were thrown into prison, and there strangled.

Gradivus, i. e. the marching (probably from *gradior*), a surname of Mars, who is hence called *gradivus pater* and *res gradivus*. Mars Gradivus had a temple outside the porta Capena on the Appian road, and it is said that king Numa appointed 12 Salii as priests of this god.

Graeae (Γραῖαι), that is, "the old women," daughters of Phorcys and Ceto, were 3 in number, *Pephredo*, *Enyo*, and *Dino*, and were also called *Phorcÿdes*. They had grey hair from their birth; and had only one tooth and one eye in common, which they borrowed from each other when they wanted them. They were perhaps marine deities, like the other children of Phorcys.

Graecia or **Hellas** (ἡ Ἑλλάς), a country in Europe, the inhabitants of which were called **Graeci** or **Hellēnes** (Ἕλληνες). Among the Greeks *Hellas* did not signify any particular country, bounded by certain geographical limits, but was used in general to signify the abode of the *Hellenes*, wherever they might happen to be settled. Thus the Greek colonies of Cyrene in Africa, of Syracuse in Sicily, of Tarentum in Italy, and of Smyrna in Asia, are said to be in Hellas. In the most ancient times Hellas was a small district of Phthiotis in Thessaly, in which was situated a town of the same name. As the inhabitants of this district, the Hellenes, gradually spread over the surrounding country, their name was adopted by other tribes, who became assimilated in language, manners and customs to the original Hellenes; till at length the whole of the N. of Greece from the Ceraunian and Cambunian mountains to the Corinthian isthmus was

designated by the name of Hellas.[*] Peloponnesus was generally spoken of during the flourishing times of Greek independence, as distinct from Hellas proper; but subsequently Peloponnesus and the Greek islands were also included under the general name of Hellas, in opposition to the land of the barbarians. Still later even Macedonia, and the S. part of Illyria were sometimes reckoned part of Hellas. The Romans called the land of the Hellenes *Graecia*, whence we have derived the name of Greece. They probably gave this name to the country from their first becoming acquainted with the tribe of the *Graeci*, who were said to be descended from Graecus, a son of Thessalus, and who appear at an early period to have dwelt on the W. coast of Epirus.—Hellas or Greece proper, including Peloponnesus, lies between the 36th and 46th degrees of N. latitude, and between the 21st and 26th degrees of E. longitude. Its greatest length from Mt. Olympus to Cape Taenarus is about 250 English miles: its greatest breadth from the W. coast of Acarnania to Marathon in Attica is about 180 miles. Its area is somewhat less than that of Portugal. On the N. it was separated by the Cambunian and Ceraunian mountains from Macedonia and Illyria; and on the other 3 sides it is bounded by the sea, namely, by the Ionian sea on the W., and by the Aegaean on the E. and S. It is one of the most mountainous countries of Europe, and possesses few extensive plains and few continuous valleys. The inhabitants were thus separated from one another by barriers which it was not easy to surmount, and were naturally led to form separate political communities. At a later time the N. of Greece was generally divided into 10 districts: EPIRUS, THESSALIA, ACARNANIA, AETOLIA, DORIS, LOCRIS, PHOCIS, BOEOTIA, ATTICA and MEGARIS. The S. of Greece or Peloponnesus was usually divided into 10 districts likewise: CORINTHIA, SICYONIA, PHLIASIA, ACHAIA, ELIS, MESSENIA, LACONICA, CYNURIA, ARGOLIS and ARCADIA. An account of the geography, early inhabitants, and history of each of these districts is given in separate articles. It is only necessary to remark here that before the Hellenes had spread over the country, it was inhabited by various tribes, whom the Greeks call by the general name of barbarians. Of these the most celebrated were the Pelasgians, who had settled in most parts of Greece, and from whom a considerable part of the Greek population was undoubtedly descended. These Pelasgians were a branch of the great Indo-Germanic race, and spoke a language akin to that of the Hellenes, whence the amalgamation of the 2 races was rendered much easier. [PELASGI.] The Hellenes traced their origin to a mythical ancestor Hellen, from whose sons and grandsons they were divided into the 4 great tribes of Dorians, Aeolians, Achaeans and Ionians. [HELLEN.]

Graecia Magna or **G. Major** (ἡ μεγάλη Ἑλλάς), a name given to the districts in the S. of Italy, inhabited by the Greeks. This name was never used simply to indicate the S. of Italy; it was always confined to the Greek cities and their territories, and did not include the surrounding districts, inhabited by the Italian tribes. It appears to have been applied chiefly to the cities on the Tarentine

---

[*] *Epirus* is, for the sake of convenience, usually included in Hellas by modern geographers, but was excluded by the Greeks themselves, as the Epirots were not regarded as genuine Hellenes.

The Gorgon Medusa.
(Florentine Gem.) Page 286.

The Gorgon Medusa.
(Marble Head, at Munich.) Page 286.

Hermes (Mercury) presenting a Soul to Hades (Pluto) and Persephone (Proserpine).
(Pict. Aut. Sepolcri Nasonum, pl. 8.) Pages 290, 291.

Ganymedes. (Visconti, Mus. Pio. Clem. vol. 3, tav.
49.) Page 277. See illustrations opposite p. 304.

Hades (Pluto). (From a Statue in the
Vatican.) Pages 290, 291.

[To face p. 286.

Ephesus. Page 242.

Epirus. Page 245.

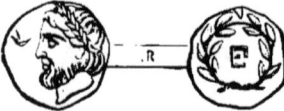

Epidaurus. Page 244.

Epiphania in Syria. Page 245.

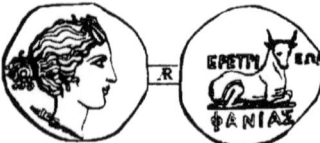

Eretria in Euboea. Page 247.

Erythrae in Asia Minor. Page 248.

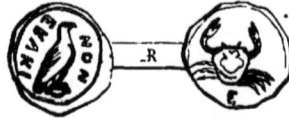

Eryx in Sicily. Page 249.

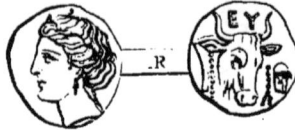

Euboea. Page 251.

Gades. Page 271.

Galatia. Page 272.

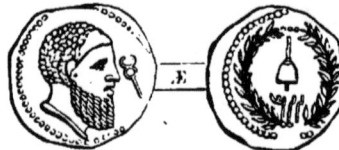

Gaulos. Page 277.

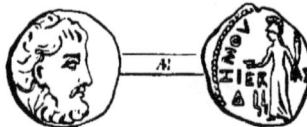

Gaza in Palestine. Page 277.

gulf, Tarentum, Sybaris, Croton, Caulonia, Siris (Heraclea), Metapontum, Locri and Rhegium; but it also included the Greek cities on the W. coast, such as Cumae and Neapolis. Strabo extends the appellation even to the Greek cities of Sicily. The origin of the name is doubtful; whether it was given to the Greek cities by the Italian tribes from their admiring the magnificence of these cities, or whether it was assumed by the inhabitants themselves out of vanity and ostentation, to show their superiority to the mother country.

Grampius Mons (*Grampian Hills*), a range of mountains in Britannia Barbara or Caledonia, separating the Highlands and Lowlands of Scotland. Agricola penetrated as far as these mountains and defeated Galgacus at their foot.

Granicus (Γράνικος : *Koja-Chai*), a river of Mysia Minor, rising in M. Cotylus, the N. summit of Ida, flowing N.E. through the plain of Adrastea, and falling into the Propontis (*Sea of Marmara*) E. of Priapus: memorable as the scene of the first of the 3 great victories by which Alexander the Great overthrew the Persian empire (B. C. 334), and, in a less degree, for a victory gained upon its banks by Lucullus over Mithridates, B. C. 73.

Granis (Γράνις : *Khisht*), a river of Persis, with a royal palace on its banks. It fell into the Persian Gulf near Taoce.

Q. Granius, a clerk employed by the auctioneers at Rome to collect the money at sales, lived about B. C. 110. Although his occupation was humble, his wit and caustic humour rendered him famous among his contemporaries, and have transmitted his name to posterity.

Granua (Γρανούα : *Graan*), a river in the land of the Quadi and the S. E. of Germany, and a tributary of the Danube, on the banks of which M. Aurelius wrote the 1st book of his Meditations.

Grātiae. [CHARITES.]

Grātiānus. 1. Emperor of the Western Empire, A. D. 367—383, son of Valentinian I., was raised by his father to the rank of Augustus in 367, when he was only 8 years old. On the death of Valentinian in 375, Gratian did not succeed to the sole sovereignty ; as Valentinian II., the half brother of Augustus, was proclaimed Augustus by the troops. By the death of his uncle, Valens (378), the Eastern empire devolved upon him ; but the danger to which the E. was exposed from the Goths led Gratian to send for Theodosius, and appoint him emperor of the E. (379). Gratian was fond of quiet and repose, and was greatly under the influence of ecclesiastics, especially of Ambrose of Milan. He became unpopular with the army. Maximus was declared emperor in Britain, and crossed over to Gaul, where he defeated Gratian, who was overtaken and slain in his flight after the battle.—2. A usurper, who assumed the purple in Britain, and was murdered by his troops about 4 months after his elevation (407). He was succeeded by Constantine. [CONSTANTINUS, No. 3.]

Gratianopolis. [CULARO.]

Gratiārum Collis (Χαρίτων λόφος, Herod. iv. 175 : *Hills of Tarhownah*), a range of wooded hills running parallel to the coast of N. Africa between the Syrtes, and containing the source of the CINYPS and the other small rivers of that coast.

Grātius Faliscus. [FALISCUS.]

Grātus, Valērius, procurator of Judaea from A. D. 15. to 27, and the immediate predecessor of Pontius Pilate.

Graviscae, an ancient city of Etruria, subject to Tarquinii, was colonised by the Romans B. C. 183, and received new colonists under Augustus. It was situated in the Maremma, and its air was unhealthy (*intempestae Graviscae*, Virg. *Aen.* x. 184); whence the ancients ridiculously derived its name from *aër gravis*. Its ruins are on the right bank of the river *Marta*, about 2 miles from the sea, where are the remains of a magnificent arch.

Gregōras, Nicēphŏrus, one of the most important Byzantine historians, was born about A. D. 1295, and died about 1359. His principal work is entitled *Historia Byzantina*. It is in 38 books, of which only 24 have been printed. It begins with the capture of Constantinople by the Latins in 1204, and goes down to 1359 ; the 24 printed books contain the period from 1204 to 1351. Edited by Schopen, Bonn, 1829.

Gregōrius (Γρηγόριος). 1. Surnamed **Naziansēnus**, and usually called **Gregory Nazianzen**, was born in a village near Nazianzus in Cappadocia about A. D. 329. His father took the greatest pains with his education, and he afterwards prosecuted his studies at Athens, where he earned the greatest reputation for his knowledge of rhetoric, philosophy, and mathematics. Among his fellow students was Julian, the future emperor, and Basil, with the latter of whom he formed a most intimate friendship. Gregory appears to have remained at Athens about 6 years (350—356), and then returned home. Having received ordination, he continued to reside at Nazianzus, where he discharged his duties as a presbyter, and assisted his aged father, who was bishop of the town. In 372 he was associated with his father in the bishopric ; but after the death of the latter in 374, he refused to continue bishop of Nazianzus, as he was averse from public life, and fond of solitary meditation. After living some years in retirement, he was summoned to Constantinople in 379, in order to defend the orthodox faith against the Arians and other heretics. In 380 he was made bishop of Constantinople by the emperor Theodosius ; but he resigned the office in the following year (381), and withdrew altogether from public life. He lived in solitude at his paternal estate at Nazianzus, and there he died in 389 or 390. His extant works are, 1 Orations or Sermons ; 2. Letters ; 3. Poems. His discourses, though sometimes really eloquent, are generally nothing more than favourable specimens of the rhetoric of the schools. He is more earnest than Chrysostom, but not so ornamental. He is more artificial, but also more attractive, than Basil. Edited by Morell, Paris, 2 vols. fol., 1609—1611, reprinted 1630. Of the Benedictine edition, only the first volume containing the discourses, was published, Paris, 1778. — 2. **Nyssēnus**, bishop of Nyssa in Cappadocia, was the younger brother of Basil, and was born at Caesarea in Cappadocia, about 331. He was made bishop of Nyssa about 372, and, like his brother Basil and their friend Gregory Nazianzen, was one of the pillars of orthodoxy. He died soon after 394. Like his brother, he was an eminent rhetorician, but his oratory often offends by its extravagance. His works are edited by Morell and Gretser, 2 vols. fol. Paris, 1615—1618. — 3. Surnamed **Thaumaturgus**, from his miracles, was born at Neocaesarea in Cappadocia, of heathen parents. He was converted to Christianity by Origen, about 234, and subsequently became the bishop of his native

U

town. He died soon after 265. His works are not numerous. The best edition is the one published at Paris, 1622.

Grudii, a people in Gallia Belgica, subject to the Nervii, N. of the Scheldt.

Grumentum (Grumentīnus : *Il Palazzo*), a town in the interior of Lucania on the road from Beneventum to Heraclea, frequently mentioned in the 2nd Punic war.

Gryllus (Γρύλλος), elder son of Xenophon, fell at the battle of Mantinea, B. C. 362, after he had, according to some accounts, given Epaminondas his mortal wound.

Grynīa or -ium (Γρύνεια, Γρύνιον), a very ancient fortified city on the coast of the Sinus Elaïticus, in the S. of Mysia, between Elaea and Myrina, 70 stadia from the former and 40 from the latter; celebrated for its temple and oracle of Apollo, who is hence called Grynaeus Apollo (Virg. *Aen.* iv. 345). It possessed also a good harbour. Parmenion, the general of Alexander, destroyed the city and sold the inhabitants as slaves. It was never again restored.

Gryps or Gryphus (Γρύψ), a griffin, a fabulous animal, dwelling in the Rhipaean mountains, between the Hyperboreans and the one-eyed Arimaspians, and guarding the gold of the north. The Arimaspians mounted on horseback, and attempted to steal the gold, and hence arose the hostility between the horse and the griffin. The body of the griffin was that of a lion, while the head and wings were those of an eagle. It is probable that the origin of the belief in griffins must be looked for in the East, where it seems to have been very ancient. They are also mentioned among the fabulous animals which guarded the gold of India.

Gugerni or Guberni, a people of Germany, probably of the same race as the Sigambri, crossed the Rhine, and settled on its left bank, between the Ubii and Batavi.

Gulussa, a Numidian, 2nd son of Masinissa, and brother to Micipsa and Mastanabal. On the death of Masinissa, in B. C. 149, he succeeded along with his brothers to the dominions of their father. He left a son, named MASSIVA.

Gūraeus (Γουραῖος, Γαββοίας), a river of India, flowing through the country of the Guraei (in the N.W. of the *Punjab*), into the Cophen.

Guttōnes. [GOTHI]

Gyārus or Gyāra (ἡ Γύαρος, τὰ Γύαρα : Γυαρεύς : *Chiara* or *Jura*), one of the Cyclades, a small island S. W. of Andros, poor and unproductive, and inhabited only by fishermen. Under the Roman emperors it was a place of banishment. (*Aude aliquid brevibus Gyaris et carcere dignum*, Juv. i. 73.)

Gȳēs or Gyges (Γύης, Γύγης), son of Uranus (Heaven) and Ge (Earth), one of the giants with 100 hands, who made war upon the gods.

Gygaeus Lacus (ἡ Γυγαίη λίμνη : *Lake of Marmora*), a small lake in Lydia, between the rivers Hermus and Hyllus, N. of Sardis, the necropolis of which city was on its banks. It was afterwards called Coloë.

Gygēs (Γύγης), the first king of Lydia of the dynasty of the Mermnadae, dethroned Candaules, and succeeded to the kingdom, as related under CANDAULES. He reigned B. C. 716—678. He sent magnificent presents to Delphi, and carried on various wars with the cities of Asia Minor, such as Miletus, Smyrna, Colophon, and Magnesia. " The riches of Gyges" became a proverb.

Gylippus (Γύλιππος), a Spartan, son of Cleandridas, was sent as the Spartan commander to Syracuse, to oppose the Athenians, B. C. 414. Under his command the Syracusans annihilated the great Athenian armament, and took Demosthenes and Nicias prisoners, 413. In 404 he was commissioned by Lysander, after the capture of Athens, to carry home the treasure ; but by opening the seams of the sacks underneath, he abstracted a considerable portion. The theft was discovered, and Gylippus went at once into exile. — The syllable Γυλ- in the name of Gylippus is probably identical with the Latin *Gilvus*.

Gynaecōpŏlis (Γυναικόπολις, or Γυναικῶν πόλις), a city in the Delta of Egypt, on the W. bank of the Canopic branch of the Nile, between Hermopolis and Momemphis. It was the capital of the Nomos Gynaecopolites.

Gyndes (Γύνδης), a river of Assyria, rising in the country of the Matieni (in the mountains of *Kurdistan*), and flowing into the Tigris, celebrated through the story that Cyrus the Great drew off its waters by 360 channels. (Herod. i. 189.) It is very difficult to identify this river : perhaps it is the same as the Delas or Silla (*Diala*), which falls into the Tigris just above Ctesiphon and Seleucia. It is also doubtful whether the Sindes of Tacitus (*Ann.* xi. 10.) is the same river.

Gyrtōn, Gyrtōna (Γυρτών, Γυρτώνη : Γυρτώνιος : nr. *Tatari* Ru.), an ancient town in Pelasgiotis in Thessaly, on the Peneus.

Gythēum, Gythĭum (τὸ Γύθειον, Γύθιον : Γυθεάτης : *Palaeopolis* nr. *Marathonisi*), an ancient town on the coast of Laconia, founded by the Achaeans, lay near the head of the Laconian bay, S. W. of the mouth of the river Eurotas. It served as the harbour of Sparta, and was important in a military point of view. In the Persian war the Lacedaemonian fleet was stationed at Gytheum, and here the Athenians under Tolmides burnt the Lacedaemonian arsenal, B. C. 455. After the battle of Leuctra (370) it was taken by Epaminondas. In 195 it was taken by Flamininus, and made independent of Nabis, tyrant of Sparta ; whereupon it joined the Achaean league.

Gyzantes (Γύζαντες), a people in the W. part of Libya (N. Africa), whose country was rich in honey and wax. They seem to have dwelt in Byzacium.

H.

Hādēs or Plūto ("Αιδης, Πλούτων, or poetically 'Αΐδης, 'Αϊδωνεύς, Πλουτεύς), the God of the Nether World. Plato observes that people preferred calling him Pluto (the giver of wealth) to pronouncing the dreaded name of Hades or Aïdes. Hence we find that in ordinary life and in the mysteries the name Pluto became generally established, while the poets preferred the ancient name Aïdes or the form Pluteus. The Roman poets use the names Dis, Orcus, and Tartarus, as synonymous with Pluto, for the god of the Nether World. Hades was son of Cronus and Rhea, and brother of Zeus and Poseidon. His wife was Persephŏne or Proserpĭna, the daughter of Demeter, whom he carried off from the upper world, as is related elsewhere. [See p. 212.] In the division of the world among the 3 brothers, Hades obtained the

Nether World, the abode of the shades, over which he ruled. Hence he is called the infernal Zeus (Ζεὺς καταχθόνιος), or the king of the shades (ἄναξ ἐνέρων). He possessed a helmet which rendered the wearer invisible, and later traditions stated that this helmet was given him as a present by the Cyclopes after their delivery from Tartarus. Ancient story mentions both gods and men who were honoured by Hades with the temporary use of this helmet. His character is described as fierce and inexorable, whence of all the gods he was most hated by mortals. He kept the gates of the lower world closed (and is therefore called Πυλάρτης), that no shades might be able to escape or return to the region of light. When mortals invoked him, they struck the earth with their hands ; the sacrifices which were offered to him and Persephone consisted of black sheep ; and the person who offered the sacrifice had to turn away his face. The ensign of his power was a staff, with which, like Hermes, he drove the shades into the lower world. There he sat upon a throne with his consort Persephone. Like the other gods, he was not a faithful husband ; the Furies are called his daughters ; the nymph Mintho, whom he loved, was metamorphosed by Persephone into the plant called mint ; and the nymph Leuce, with whom he was likewise in love, was changed by him after her death into a white poplar, and transferred to Elysium. Being the king of the lower world, Pluto is the giver of all the blessings that come from the earth : he is the possessor and giver of all the metals contained in the earth, and hence his name Pluto. He bears several surnames referring to his ultimately assembling all mortals in his kingdom, and bringing them to rest and peace ; such as *Polydegmon, Polydectes, Clymenus*, &c. He was worshipped throughout Greece and Italy. We possess few representations of this divinity, but in those which still exist, he resembles his brother Zeus and Poseidon, except that his hair falls down his forehead, and that his appearance is dark and gloomy. His ordinary attributes are the key of Hades and Cerberus. In Homer Aïdes is invariably the name of the god ; but in later times it was transferred to his house, his abode or kingdom, so that it became a name for the nether world.

Hadranum. [ADRANUM.]

Hadria. [ADRIA.]

Hadrianopolis ('Αδριανόπολις : 'Αδριανοπολίτης : *Adrianople*), a town in Thrace on the right bank of the Hebrus, in an extensive plain, founded by the emperor Hadrian. It was strongly fortified ; possessed an extensive commerce ; and in the middle ages was the most important town in the country after Constantinople.

Hadrianothera or -ae ('Αδριανοθήρα), a city in Mysia, between Pergamus and Miletopolis, founded by the emperor Hadrian.

Hadrianus, P. Aelius, usually called **Hadrian**, Roman emperor, A. D. 117—138, was born at Rome, A. D. 76. He lost his father at the age of 10, and was brought up by his kinsman Ulpius Trajanus (afterwards emperor) and by Caelius Attianus. From an early age he studied with zeal the Greek language and literature. At the age of 15 he went to Spain, where he entered upon his military career ; and he subsequently served as military tribune in Lower Moesia. After the elevation of Trajan to the throne (98), he married Julia Sabina, a grand-daughter of Trajan's sister Marciana. This mar-

riage was brought about through the influence of Plotina, the wife of Trajan ; and from this time Hadrian rose rapidly in the emperor's favour. He was raised successively to the quaestorship (101), praetorship (107), and consulship (109). He accompanied Trajan in most of his expeditions, and distinguished himself in the second war against the Dacians, 104—106 ; was made governor of Pannonia in 108 ; and subsequently fought under Trajan against the Parthians. When Trajan's serious illness obliged him to leave the E., he placed Hadrian at the head of the army. Trajan died at Cilicia on his journey to Rome (117). Hadrian, who pretended that he had been adopted by Trajan, was proclaimed emperor by the legions in Syria, and the senate ratified the election. Hadrian's first care was to make peace with the Parthians, which he obtained by relinquishing the conquests of Trajan, E. of the Euphrates. He returned to Rome in 118 ; but almost immediately afterwards set out for Moesia, in consequence of the invasion of this province by the Sarmatians. After making peace with the Sarmatians, and suppressing a formidable conspiracy which had been formed against his life by some of the most distinguished Roman nobles, all of whom he put to death, he returned to Rome in the course of the same year. He sought to gain the goodwill of the senate by gladiatorial exhibitions and liberal largesses, and he also cancelled all arrears of taxes due to the state for the last 15 years. The remainder of Hadrian's reign was disturbed by few wars. He spent the greater part of his reign in travelling through the various provinces of the empire, in order that he might inspect personally the state of affairs in the provinces, and apply the necessary remedies wherever mismanagement was discovered. He commenced these travels in 119, visiting first Gaul, Germany, and Britain, in the latter of which countries he caused a wall to be built from the Solway to the mouth of the river Tyne. He afterwards visited Spain, Africa, and the E., and took up his residence at Athens for 3 years (123—126). Athens was his favourite city, and he conferred upon its inhabitants many privileges. The most important war during his reign was that against the Jews, which broke out in 131. The Jews had revolted in consequence of the establishment of a colony under the name of Aelia Capitolina on the site of Jerusalem, and of their having been forbidden to practise the rite of circumcision. The war was carried on by the Jews as a national struggle with the most desperate fury, and was not brought to an end till 136, after the country had been nearly reduced to a wilderness. During the last few years of Hadrian's life, his health failed. He became suspicious and cruel, and put to death several persons of distinction. As he had no children, he adopted L. Aelius Verus, and gave him the title of Caesar in 136. Verus died on the 1st of January, 138, whereupon Hadrian adopted Antoninus, afterwards surnamed Pius, and conferred upon him likewise the title of Caesar. In July in the same year, Hadrian himself died in his 62nd year, and was succeeded by ANTONINUS. — The reign of Hadrian may be regarded as one of the happiest periods in Roman history. His policy was to preserve peace with foreign nations, and not to extend the boundaries of the empire, but to secure the old provinces, and promote their welfare. He paid particular attention to the administration of justice in the provinces as well as in Italy. His reign forms an epoch in the history of Roman jurisprudence. It was at Hadrian's command that the jurist Salvius Julianus drew up the *edictum perpetuum*, which formed a fixed code of laws. Some of the laws promulgated by Hadrian are of a truly humane character, and aimed at improving the public morality of the time. The various cities which he visited received marks of his favour or liberality; in many places he built aquaeducts, and in others harbours or other public buildings, either for use or ornament. But what has rendered his name more illustrious than any thing else are the numerous and magnificent architectural works which he planned and commenced during his travels, especially at Athens, in the S. part of which he built an entirely new city, Adrianopolis. We cannot here enter into an account of the numerous buildings he erected; it is sufficient to direct attention to his villa at Tibur, which has been a real mine of treasures of art, and his mausoleum at Rome, which forms the groundwork of the present castle of St. Angelo. Hadrian was a patron of learning and literature, as well as of the arts, and he cultivated the society of poets, scholars, rhetoricians, and philosophers. He founded at Rome a scientific institution under the name of the Athenaeum, which continued to flourish for a long time after him. He was himself an author, and wrote numerous works both in prose and in verse, all of which are lost, with the exception of a few epigrams in the Greek and Latin Anthologies.

Hadriānus, the rhetorician. [ADRIANUS.]

Hadrūmētum or Adrūmētum (Ἀδρύμη: *Hammeím*), a flourishing city founded by the Phoenicians in N. Africa, on the E. coast of Byzacena, of which district it was the capital under the Romans. Trajan made it a colony; and it was afterwards called Justinianopolis.

Haemon (Αἵμων). 1. Son of Pelasgus and father of Thessalus, from whom the ancient name of Thessaly, **Haemonia** or **Aemonia**, was believed to be derived. The Roman poets frequently use the adjective *Haemonius* as equivalent to Thessalian. — 2. Son of Lycaon, and the reputed founder of Haemonia in Arcadia. — 3. Son of Creon of Thebes, was destroyed, according to some accounts, by the sphinx. But, according to other traditions, he was in love with Antigone, and killed himself on hearing that she was condemned by his father to be entombed alive.

Haemŏnīa (Αἱμονία). [HAEMON, No. 1.]

Haemus (Αἷμος), son of Boreas and Orithyia, wife of Rhodope, and father of Hebrus. As he and his wife presumed to assume the names of Zeus and Hera, both were metamorphosed into mountains.

Haemus (ὁ Αἷμος, τὸ Αἷμον: *Balkan*), a lofty range of mountains, separating Thrace and Moesia, extended from M. Scomius, or, according to Herodotus, from M. Rhodope on the W. to the Black Sea on the E. The name is probably connected with the Sanscrit *hîma* (whence comes the word *Himalaya*), the Greek χειμών, and the Latin *hiems;* and the mountains were so called on account of their cold and snowy climate. The height of these mountains was greatly exaggerated by the ancients: the mean height does not exceed 3000 or 4000 feet above the sea. There are several passes over them; but the one most used in antiquity was in the W. part of the range, called "Succi" or "Succorum angustiae," also "Porta Trajani"

(*Soulu Derbend*), between Philippopolis and Serdica. The later province of "Haemimontus" in Thrace derived its name from this mountain.

Hagnūs (Ἁγνοῦς, -οῦντος: Ἁγνούσιος: nr. *Markopulo*), a demus in Attica, W. of Paeania, belonging to the tribe Acamantis.

Halae (Ἁλαί, Ἅλαι, Ἁλαί: Ἁλαιεύς). 1. **H. Araphēnĭdes** (Ἀραφηνίδες), a demus in Attica, belonging to the tribe Aegeis, was situated on the E. coast of Attica, and served as the harbour of Brauron: it possessed a temple of Artemis.—2. **H. Aexōnĭdes** (Αἰξωνίδες), a demus in Attica, belonging to the tribe Cecropis, situated on the W. coast. —3. A town, formerly of the Opuntii Locri, afterwards of Boeotia, situated on the Opuntian gulf.

Hales (Ἅλης). 1. A river of Ionia in Asia Minor, near Colophon, celebrated for the coldness of its water.— 2. A river in the island of Cos.

Halēsa (Ἅλαισα: Halesinus: *Torre di Pittineo*), a town on the N. coast of Sicily, on the river **Halēsus** (*Pittineo*), was founded by the Greek mercenaries of Archonides, a chief of the Siculi, and was originally called **Archonidion**. It became a place of considerable importance, and was in later times a municipium, exempt from taxes.

Halēsus, a chief of the Auruncans and Oscans, the son of a soothsayer, and an ally of Turnus, was slain by Evander. He came to Italy from Argos in Greece, whence he is called *Agamemnonius, Atrides,* or *Argolicus.* He is said to have founded the town of Falerii.

Halex. [ALEX.]

Haliacmon (Ἁλιάκμων: *Vistriza*), an important river in Macedonia, rises in the Tymphaean mountains, flows first S.E. through Elimaea, then N.E. forming the boundary between Eordaea and Pieria, and falls into the Thermaic gulf in Bottiaeis. Caesar (*B. C.* iii. 36) incorrectly makes it the boundary between Macedonia and Thessaly.

Haliartus (Ἁλίαρτος: Ἁλιάρτιος: *Mazi*), an ancient town in Boeotia on the S. of the lake Copais. It was destroyed by Xerxes in his invasion of Greece (B. C. 480), but was rebuilt, and appears as an important place in the Peloponnesian war. Under its walls Lysander lost his life (395). It was destroyed by the Romans (171), because it supported Perseus, king of Macedonia, and its territory was given to the Athenians.

Halĭas (Ἁλιας: Ἁλιεύς), a district on the coast of Argolis between Asine and Hermione, so called because fishing was the chief occupation of its inhabitants. Their town was called **Haliae** (Ἁλιαί) or **Haliēs** (Ἁλιεῖς).

Hălĭcarnassus (Ἁλικαρνασσός, Ion. Ἁλικαρνησσός: Ἁλικαρνασσεύς, Halicarnassensis, Halicarnassius: *Budrum*, Ru.), a celebrated city of Asia Minor, stood in the S.W. part of Caria, on the N. coast of the Sinus Ceramicus, opposite to the island of Cos. It was said to have been founded by Dorians from Troezene, and was at first called Zephyra. It was one of the 6 cities that originally formed the Dorian Hexapolis, but it was early excluded from the confederacy, as a punishment for the violation, by one of its citizens, of a law connected with the common worship of the Triopian Apollo. (Herod. i. 144.) With the rest of the coast of Asia Minor, it fell under the dominion of the Persians, at an early period of whose rule Lygdamis made himself tyrant of the city, and founded a dynasty which lasted for some generations. His daughter Artemisia assisted Xerxes in his expedition against Greece [ARTEMISIA, No.

]. Her grandson Lygdamis was overthrown by a revolution, in which Herodotus is said to have taken part [HERODOTUS]. In the Peloponnesian War, we find Halicarnassus, with the other Dorian cities of Caria, on the side of the Athenians; but we do not know what was its form of government, until the reestablishment, by HECATOMNUS, of a dynasty ruling over all Caria, with its capital first at Mylasa, and afterwards at Halicarnassus, and virtually independent of Persia; before B. C. 380. It seems not unlikely that both this and the older dynasty of tyrants of Halicarnassus, were a race of native Carian princes, whose ascendancy at Halicarnassus may be accounted for by the prevalence of the Carian element in its population at an early period. Hecatomnus left 3 sons and 2 daughters, who all succeeded to his throne in the following order, Mausolus, Artemisia, Idrieus, Ada, Pixodarus, and Ada again. In B. C. 334, Alexander took the city, after an obstinate defence by the Persian general Memnon, and destroyed it. From this blow it never recovered, although it continued to be celebrated for the Mausoleum, a magnificent edifice which Artemisia II. built as a tomb for Mausolus, and which was adorned with the works of the most eminent Greek sculptors of the age. Fragments of these sculptures, which were discovered built into the walls of the citadel of *Budrum*, are now in the British Museum. With the rest of Caria, Halicarnassus was assigned by the Romans, after their victory over Antiochus the Great, to the government of Rhodes, and was afterwards united to the province of Asia. The city was very strongly fortified, and had a fine harbour, which was protected by the island of ARCONNESUS: its citadel was called Salmacis (Σαλμακίς) from the name of a spring which rose from the hill on which it stood. Halicarnassus was the birthplace of the historians HERODOTUS and DIONYSIUS.

Halicyae ('Αλικύαι: Halicyensis), a town in the N.W. of Sicily, between Entella and Lilybaeum, was long in the possession of the Carthaginians, and in Cicero's time was a municipium, exempt from taxes.

Halimūs ('Αλιμοῦς ·οῦντος: 'Αλιμούσιος), a demus of Attica, belonging to the tribe Leontis, on the W. coast, a little S. of Athens.

Halipēdon ('Αλίπεδον), a plain near the Piraeus, probably between the Piraeus and the Academy.

Halirrhöthius ('Αλιρρόθιος), son of Poseidon and Euryte, attempted to violate Alcippe, daughter of Ares and Agraulos, but was slain by Ares. Ares was brought to trial by Poseidon for this murder, on the hill at Athens, which was hence called Areopagus, or the Hill of Ares.

Halitisa ('Αλιούσα? *Karavi*), an island in the Argolic gulf.

Halizōnes ('Αλίζωνες, and -οι), a people of Bithynia, with a capital city Alybe ('Αλύβη), mentioned by Homer as allies of the Trojans.

Halmydessus. [SALMYDESSUS.]

Halmȳris ('Αλμυρίς, sc. λίμην), a bay of the sea in Moesia formed by the S. mouth of the Danube, with a town of the same name upon it.

Halonēsus ('Αλόνησος, 'Αλόννησος: 'Αλονήσιος, 'Αλοννήσιος: *Khiliodromia*), an island of the Aegean sea, off the coast of Thessaly, and E. of Sciathos and Peparethos, with a town of the same name upon it. The possession of this island occasioned great disputes between Philip and the Athenians: there is a speech on this subject among the extant orations of Demosthenes, but it was probably written by Hegesippus.

Halōsydnē ('Αλοσύδνη), "the Sea-born," a surname of Amphitrite and Thetys.

Haluntium. [ALUNTIUM.]

Halus. [ALUS.]

Halȳcus ("Αλυκος: *Platani*), a river in the S. of Sicily, which flows into the sea near Heraclea Minoa.

Halys ("Αλυς: *Kizil-Irmak*, i. e. *the Red River*), the greatest river of Asia Minor, rises in that part of the Anti-Taurus range called Paryadres, on the borders of Armenia Minor and Pontus, and after flowing W. by S. through Cappadocia, turns to the N. and flows through Galatia to the borders of Paphlagonia, where it takes a N. E. direction, dividing Paphlagonia from Pontus, and at last falls into the Euxine (*Black Sea*) between Sinope and Amisus. In early times it was a most important boundary, ethnographical as well as political. It divided the Indo-European races which peopled the W. part of Asia Minor from the Semitic (Syro-Arabian) races of the rest of S. W. Asia; and it separated the Lydian empire from the Medo-Persian, until, by marching over it to meet Cyrus, Croesus began the contest which at once ended in the overthrow of the former and the extension of the latter to the Aegean Sea.

Hamadryādes. [NYMPHAE.]

Hamaxitus ('Αμαξιτός), a small town on the coast of the Troad, near the promontory Lectum; said to have been the first settlement of the Teucrian immigrants from Crete. The surrounding district was called 'Αμαξιτία. Lysimachus removed the inhabitants to Alexandria Troas.

Hamaxōbii ('Αμαξόβιοι), a people in European Sarmatia, in the neighbourhood of the Palus Maeotis, were a nomad race, as their name signifies.

Hamilcar ('Αμίλκας). The 2 last syllables of this name are the same as *Melcarth*, the tutelary deity of the Tyrians, called by the Greeks Hercules, and the name probably signifies "the gift of Melcarth." 1. Son of Hanno, or Mago, commander of the great Carthaginian expedition to Sicily, B. C. 480, which was defeated and almost destroyed by Gelon at Himera. [GELON.] Hamilcar fell in the battle.—2. Surnamed Rhodanus, was sent by the Carthaginians to Alexander after the fall of Tyre, B. C. 332. On his return home he was put to death by the Carthaginians for having betrayed their interests.—3. Carthaginian governor in Sicily at the time that Agathocles was rising into power. At first he supported the party at Syracuse, which had driven Agathocles into exile, but he afterwards espoused the cause of Agathocles, who was thus enabled to make himself master of Syracuse, 317.—4. Son of Gisco, succeeded the preceding as Carthaginian commander in Sicily, 311. He carried on war against Agathocles, whom he defeated with great slaughter, and then obtained possession of the greater part of Sicily; but he was taken prisoner while besieging Syracuse, and was put to death by Agathocles.—5. A Carthaginian general in the 1st Punic war, must be carefully distinguished from the great Hamilcar Barca [No. 6.]. In the 3d year of the war (262) he succeeded Hanno in the command in Sicily, and carried on the operations by land with success. He made himself master of Enna and Camarina, and fortified Drepanum. In 257

he commanded the Carthaginian fleet on the N.
coast of Sicily, and fought a naval action with the
Roman consul C. Atilius Regulus. In the following year (256), he and Hanno commanded the
great Carthaginian fleet, which was defeated by
the 2 consuls M. Atilius Regulus and L. Manlius
Vulso, off Ecnomus, on the S. coast of Sicily. He
was afterwards one of the commanders of the land
forces in Africa opposed to Regulus. — 6. Surnamed Barca, an epithet supposed to be related
to the Hebrew *Barak*, and to signify " lightning."
It was merely a personal appellation, and is not to
be regarded as a family name, though from the
great distinction that he obtained, we often find
the name of Barcine applied either to his family or
his party in the state. He was appointed to the
command of the Carthaginian forces in Sicily, in
the 18th year of the 1st Punic War, 247. At
this time the Romans were masters of the whole
of Sicily, with the exception of Drepanum and
Lilybaeum, both of which were blockaded by them
on the land side. Hamilcar established himself
with his whole army on a mountain named Herctè
(*Monte Pollegrino*), in the midst of the enemy's
country, and in the immediate neighbourhood of
Panormus, one of their most important cities.
Here he succeeded in maintaining his ground,
to the astonishment alike of friends and foes,
for nearly 3 years. In 244 he abruptly quitted
Herctè, and took up a still stronger position on Mt.
Eryx, after seizing the town of that name. Here
he also maintained himself in spite of all the efforts
of the Romans to dislodge him. After the great
naval defeat of the Carthaginians by Lutatius Catulus (241), Hamilcar, who was still at Eryx, was
entrusted by the Carthaginian government with
the conclusion of the peace with the Romans. —
On his return home, he had to carry on war in
Africa with the Carthaginian mercenaries, whom
he succeeded in subduing after an arduous struggle
of 3 years (240—238). Hamilcar now formed
the project of establishing in Spain a new empire,
which should not only be a source of strength
and wealth to Carthage, but should be the
point from whence he might at a subsequent period renew hostilities against Rome. He crossed
over into Spain soon after the termination of the
war with the mercenaries ; but we know nothing
of his operations in the country, save that he obtained possession of a considerable portion of Spain,
partly by force of arms, and partly by negotiation.
After remaining in Spain nearly 9 years, he fell in
battle (229) against the Vettones. He was succeeded in the command by his son-in-law Hasdrubal. He left 3 sons, the celebrated Hannibal,
Hasdrubal, and Mago. — 7. Son of Gisco, Carthaginian governor of Melite (*Malta*), which surrendered to the Romans, 218. — 8. Son of Bomilcar,
one of the generals in Spain, 215, with Hasdrubal and Mago, the 2 sons of Barca. The
3 generals were defeated by the 2 Scipios, while
besieging Illiturgi. — 9. A Carthaginian, who excited a general revolt of the Gauls in Upper Italy,
about 200, and took the Roman colony of Placentia. On the defeat of the Gauls by the consul
Cethegus in 197, he was taken prisoner.

Hannibal (Ἀννίβας). The name signifies " the
grace or favour of Baal ; " the final syllable *bal*, of
such common occurrence in Punic names, always
having reference to this tutelary deity of the
Phoenicians. — 1. Son of Gisco, and grandson of

HAMILCAR [No. 1]. In 409 he was sent to Sicily,
at the head of a Carthaginian army to assist the
Segestans against the Selinuntines. He took Selinus, and subsequently Himera also. In 406 he
again commanded a Carthaginian army in Sicily
along with Himilco, but died of a pestilence while
besieging Agrigentum. — 2. Son of Gisco, was
the Carthaginian commander at Agrigentum, when
it was besieged by the Romans, 262. After standing a siege of 7 months, he broke through the
enemy's lines, leaving the town to its fate. After
this he carried on the contest by sea, and for the
next year or two ravaged the coast of Italy; but in
260 he was defeated by the consul Duilius. In
259 he was sent to the defence of Sardinia. Here
he was again unfortunate, and was seized by his
own mutinous troops, and put to death. — 3. Son
of Hamilcar (perhaps HAMILCAR, No. 5), succeeded
in carrying succours of men and provisions to Lilybaeum, when it was besieged by the Romans, 250.
— 4. A general in the war of the Carthaginians
against the mercenaries (240—238), was taken
prisoner by the insurgents, and crucified. — 5. Son
of Hamilcar Barca, and one of the most illustrious
generals of antiquity, was born B. C. 247. He was
only 9 years old when his father took him with
him into Spain, and it was on this occasion that
Hamilcar made him swear upon the altar eternal
hostility to Rome. Child as he then was, Hannibal
never forgot his vow, and his whole life was one
continual struggle against the power and domination
of Rome. He was early trained in arms under the
eye of his father, and was present with him in the
battle in which Hamilcar perished (229). Though
only 18 years old at this time, he had already displayed so much courage and capacity for war, that
he was entrusted by Hasdrubal (the son-in-law and
successor of Hamilcar) with the chief command of
most of the military enterprises planned by that
general. He secured to himself the devoted attachment of the army under his command ; and,
accordingly, on the assassination of Hasdrubal (221),
the soldiers unanimously proclaimed their youthful
leader commander-in-chief, which the government
at Carthage forthwith ratified. Hannibal was at
this time in the 26th year of his age. There can
be no doubt that he already looked forward to the
invasion and conquest of Italy as the goal of his
ambition ; but it was necessary for him first to
complete the work which had been so ably begun
by his 2 predecessors, and to establish the Carthaginian power as firmly as possible in Spain. In
2 campaigns he subdued all the country S. of the
Iberus, with the exception of the wealthy town of
Saguntum. In the spring of 219 he proceeded to
lay siege to Saguntum, which he took after a desperate resistance, which lasted nearly 8 months.
Saguntum lay S. of the Iberus, and was therefore
not included under the protection of the treaty
which had been made between Hasdrubal and the
Romans ; but as it had concluded an alliance with
the Romans, the latter regarded its attack as a
violation of the treaty between the 2 nations. On
the fall of Saguntum, the Romans demanded the
surrender of Hannibal; and when this demand was
refused, war was declared, and thus began the long
and arduous struggle called the 2nd Punic War.
In the spring of 218 Hannibal quitted his winter-
quarters at New Carthage and commenced his
march for Italy. He crossed the Pyrenees, and
marched along the S. coast of Gaul. The Romans

sent the consul P. Scipio to oppose him in Gaul ; but when Scipio arrived in Gaul, he found that Hannibal had already reached the Rhone, and that it was impossible to overtake him. After Hannibal had crossed the Rhone, he continued his march up the left bank of the river as far as its confluence with the Isère. Here he struck away to the right and commenced his passage across the Alps. He probably crossed the Alps by the pass of the Little St. Bernard, called in antiquity the Graian Alps. His army suffered much from the attacks of the Gaulish mountaineers, and from the natural difficulties of the road, which were enhanced by the lateness of the season (the beginning of October, at which time the snows have already commenced in the high Alps). So heavy were his losses, that when he at length emerged from the valley of Aosta into the plains of the Po, he had with him no more than 20,000 foot and 6000 horse. During Hannibal's march over the Alps, P. Scipio had sent on his own army into Spain, under the command of his brother Cneius, and had himself returned to Italy. He forthwith hastened into Cisalpine Gaul, took the command of the praetor's army, which he found there, and led it against Hannibal. In the first action, which took place near the Ticinus, the cavalry and light-armed troops of the two armies were alone engaged ; the Romans were completely routed, and Scipio himself severely wounded. Scipio then crossed the Po and withdrew to the hills on the left bank of the Trebia, where he was soon after joined by the other consul, Ti. Sempronius Longus. Here a second and more decisive battle was fought. The Romans were completely defeated, with heavy loss, and the remains of their army took refuge within the walls of Placentia. This battle was fought towards the end of 218. Hannibal was now joined by all the Gaulish tribes, and he was able to take up his winter-quarters in security. Early in 217 he descended by the valley of the Macra into the marshes on the banks of the Arno. In struggling through these marshes great numbers of his horses and beasts of burthen perished, and he himself lost the sight of one eye by a violent attack of ophthalmia. The consul Flaminius hastened to meet him, and a battle was fought on the lake Trasimenus, in which the Roman army was destroyed; thousands fell by the sword, among whom was the consul himself; thousands more perished in the lake, and no less than 15,000 prisoners fell into the hands of Hannibal. Hannibal now marched through the Apennines into Picenum, and thence into Apulia, where he spent a great part of the summer. The Romans had collected a fresh army, and placed it under the command of the dictator Fabius Maximus, who had prudently avoided a general action, and only attempted to harass and annoy the Carthaginian army. Meanwhile the Romans had made great preparations for the campaign of the following year (216). The 2 new consuls, L. Aemilius Paulus and C. Terentius Varro, marched into Apulia, at the head of an army of little less than 90,000 men. To this mighty host Hannibal gave battle in the plains on the right bank of the Aufidus, just below the town of Cannae. The Roman army was again annihilated : between 40 and 50 thousand men are said to have fallen in the field, among whom was the consul Aemilius Paulus, both the consuls of the preceding year, above 80 senators, and a multitude of the wealthy knights who composed the Roman cavalry. The

other consul, Varro, escaped with a few horsemen to Venusia, and a small band of resolute men forced their way from the Roman camp to Canusium ; all the rest were killed, dispersed, or taken prisoners. This victory was followed by the revolt from Rome of most of the nations in the S. of Italy. Hannibal established his army in winter-quarters in Capua, which had espoused his side. Capua was celebrated for its wealth and luxury, and the enervating effect which these produced upon the army of Hannibal became a favourite theme of rhetorical exaggeration in later ages. The futility of such declamations is sufficiently shown by the simple fact that the superiority of that army in the field remained as decided as ever. Still it may be truly said that the winter spent at Capua, 216—215, was in great measure the turning point of Hannibal's fortune, and from this time the war assumed an altered character. The experiment of what he could effect with his single army had now been fully tried, and, notwithstanding all his victories, it had decidedly failed ; for Rome was still unsubdued, and still provided with the means of maintaining a protracted contest. From this time the Romans in great measure changed their plan of operations, and, instead of opposing to Hannibal one great army in the field, they hemmed in his movements on all sides, and kept up an army in every province of Italy, to thwart the operations of his lieutenants, and check the rising disposition to revolt. It is impossible here to follow the complicated movements of the subsequent campaigns, during which Hannibal himself frequently traversed Italy in all directions. In 215 Hannibal entered into negotiations with Philip, king of Macedonia, and Hieronymus of Syracuse, and thus sowed the seeds of 2 fresh wars. From 214 to 212 the Romans were busily engaged with the siege of Syracuse, which was at length taken by Marcellus in the latter of these years. In 212 Hannibal obtained possession of Tarentum; but in the following year he lost the important city of Capua, which was recovered by the Romans after a long siege. In 209 the Romans also recovered Tarentum. Hannibal's forces gradually became more and more weakened; and his only object now was to maintain his ground in the S. until his brother Hasdrubal should appear in the N. of Italy, an event to which he had long looked forward with anxious expectation. In 207 Hasdrubal at length crossed the Alps, and descended into Italy ; but he was defeated and slain on the Metaurus. [HASDRUBAL, No. 3.] The defeat and death of Hasdrubal was decisive of the fate of the war in Italy. From this time Hannibal abandoned all thoughts of offensive operations, and collected together his forces within the peninsula of Bruttium. In the fastnesses of that wild and mountainous region he maintained his ground for nearly 4 years (207—203). He crossed over to Africa towards the end of 203 in order to oppose P. Scipio. In the following year (202) the decisive battle was fought near Zama. Hannibal was completely defeated with great loss. All hopes of resistance were now at an end, and he was one of the first to urge the necessity of an immediate peace. The treaty between Rome and Carthage was not finally concluded until the next year (201). By this treaty Hannibal saw the object of his whole life frustrated, and Carthage effectually humbled before her imperious rival. But his enmity to Rome was unabated ; and though now more than 45 years old, he set himself to work to prepare the means for renewing the contest at no distant period. He introduced the most beneficial reforms into the state, and restored the ruined finances; but having provoked the enmity of a powerful party at Carthage, they denounced him to the Romans as urging on Antiochus III. king of Syria, to take up arms against Rome. Hannibal was obliged to flee from Carthage, and took refuge at the court of Antiochus, who was at this time (193) on the eve of war with Rome. Hannibal in vain urged the necessity of carrying the war at once into Italy, instead of awaiting the Romans in Greece. On the defeat of Antiochus (190), the surrender of Hannibal was one of the conditions of the peace granted to the king. Hannibal, however, foresaw his danger, and took refuge at the court of Prusias, king of Bithynia. Here he found for some years a secure asylum ; but the Romans could not be at ease so long as he lived ; and T. Quintius Flamininus was at length despatched to the court of Prusias to demand the surrender of the fugitive. The Bithynian king was unable to resist; and Hannibal, perceiving that flight was impossible, took poison, to avoid falling into the hands of his enemies, about the year 183. Of Hannibal's abilities as a general it is unnecessary to speak : all the great masters of the art of war, from Scipio to the emperor Napoleon, have concurred in their homage to his genius. But in comparing Hannibal with any other of the great leaders of antiquity, we must ever bear in mind the peculiar circumstances in which he was placed. Feebly and grudgingly supported by the government at home, he stood alone, at the head of an army composed of mercenaries of many nations. Yet not only did he retain the attachment of these men, unshaken by any change of fortune, for a period of more than 15 years, but he trained up army after army ; and long after the veterans that had followed him over the Alps had dwindled to an inconsiderable remnant, his new levies were still as invincible as their predecessors.

Hanniballiānus. 1. Son of Constantius Chlorus and his second wife Theodora, and half-brother of Constantine the Great. He was put to death in 337 on the death of Constantine. — **2.** Son of the elder, brother of the younger Delmatius, was also put to death on the death of Constantine.

Hannibālis Castra. [CASTRA, No. 2.]

Hanno ('Αννων), one of the most common names at Carthage. Only the most important persons of the name can be mentioned. — **1.** One of the Carthaginian generals who fought against Agathocles in Africa, B. C. 310. — **2.** Commander of the Carthaginian garrison at Messana, at the beginning of the 1st Punic war, 264. In consequence of his surrendering the citadel of this city to the Romans, he was crucified on his return home. — **3.** Son of Hannibal, was sent to Sicily by the Carthaginians with a large force immediately after the capture of Messana, 364, where he carried on the war against the Roman consul Ap. Claudius. In 262 he again commanded in Sicily, but failed in relieving Agrigentum, where Hannibal was kept besieged by the Romans. [HANNIBAL, No. 2.] In 256 he commanded the Carthaginian fleet, along with Hamilcar, at the great battle of Ecnomus. — **4.** Commander of the Carthaginian fleet, which was defeated by Lutatius Catulus off the Aegates, 241. On his return home, he was crucified. — **5.** Surnamed the Great, apparently for his successes in Africa. We do not, however, know against what nations of

Africa his arms were directed, nor what was the occasion of the war. He was one of the commanders in the war against the mercenaries in Africa after the end of the 1st Punic war (240—238). From this time forward he appears to have taken no active part in any of the foreign wars or enterprises of Carthage. But his influence in her councils at home was great; he was the leader of the aristocratic party, and, as such, the chief adversary of Hamilcar Barca and his family. On all occasions, from the landing of Barca in Spain till the return of Hannibal from Italy, a period of above 35 years, Hanno is represented as thwarting the measures of that able and powerful family, and taking the lead in opposition to the war with Rome, the great object to which all their efforts were directed. He survived the battle of Zama, 202.—**6.** A Carthaginian officer left in Spain by Hannibal when that general crossed the Pyrenees, 218. He was shortly afterwards defeated by Cn. Scipio, and taken prisoner. —**7.** Son of Bomilcar, one of the most distinguished of Hannibal's officers. He commanded the right wing at the battle of Cannae (216), and is frequently mentioned during the succeeding years of the war. In 203 he took the command of the Carthaginian forces in Africa, which he held till the arrival of Hannibal.—**8.** A Carthaginian general, who carried on the war in Sicily after the fall of Syracuse, 211. He left Sicily in the following year, when Agrigentum was betrayed to the Romans. —**9.** The last commander of the Carthaginian garrison at Capua, when it was besieged by the Romans (212—211).—**10.** A Carthaginian navigator, under whose name we possess a *Periplus* (περίπλους), which was originally written in the Punic language, and afterwards translated into Greek. The author had held the office of suffetes, or supreme magistrate at Carthage, and he is said by Pliny to have undertaken the voyage when Carthage was in a most flourishing condition. Hence it has been conjectured that he was the same as the Hanno, the father or son of Hamilcar, who was killed at Himera, B. C. 480; but this is quite uncertain. In the Periplus itself Hanno says that he was sent out by his countrymen to undertake a voyage beyond the Pillars of Hercules, and to found Libyphoenician towns, and that he sailed with a body of colonists to the number of 30,000. On his return from his voyage, he dedicated an account of it, inscribed on a tablet, in the temple of Cronos. It is therefore presumed that our periplus is a Greek version of the contents of that Punic tablet. Edited by Falconer, Lond. 1797, with an English translation.

Harma (τὸ Άρμα : 'Αρματεύς). **1.** A small place in Boeotia near Tanagra, said to have been so called from the *harma* or chariot of Adrastus, which broke down here, or from the chariot of Amphiaraus, who was here swallowed up by the earth along with his chariot. — **2.** A small place in Attica, near Phyle.

Harmātūs ('Αρματοῦς), a city and promontory on the coast of Aeolis in Asia Minor, on the N. side of the Sinus Elaïticus.

Harmŏdĭus and **Aristogīton** ('Αρμόδιος, 'Αριστογείτων), Athenians, of the blood of the Gephyraei, were the murderers of Hipparchus, brother of the tyrant Hippias, in B. C. 514. Aristogiton was strongly attached to the young and beautiful Harmodius, who returned his affection with equal warmth. Hipparchus endeavoured to withdraw the youth's love to himself, and, failing in this, resolved to avenge the slight by putting upon him a public insult. Accordingly, he took care that the sister of Harmodius should be summoned to bear one of the sacred baskets in some religious procession, and when she presented herself for the purpose, he caused her to be dismissed and declared unworthy of the honour. This fresh insult determined the 2 friends to slay both Hipparchus and his brother Hippias as well. They communicated their plot to a few friends ; and selected for their enterprise the day of the festival of the great Panathenaea, the only day on which they could appear in arms without exciting suspicion. When the appointed time arrived, the 2 chief conspirators observed one of their accomplices in conversation with Hippias. Believing, therefore, that they were betrayed, they slew Hipparchus. Harmodius was immediately cut down by the guards. Aristogiton at first escaped, but was afterwards taken, and was put to the torture ; but he died without revealing any of the names of the conspirators. Four years after this Hippias was expelled, and thenceforth Harmodius and Aristogiton obtained among the Athenians of all succeeding generations the character of patriots, deliverers, and martyrs, — names often abused indeed, but seldom more grossly than in the present case. Their deed of murderous vengeance formed a favourite subject of drinking songs. To be born of their blood was esteemed among the highest of honours, and their descendants enjoyed an immunity from public burdens. Their statues, made of bronze by Antenor, were set up in the Agora. When Xerxes took the city, he carried these statues away, and new ones, the work of CRITIAS, were erected in 477. The original statues were afterwards sent back to Athens by Alexander the Great.

Harmŏnĭa ('Αρμονία), daughter of Ares and Aphrodite, or, according to others, of Zeus and Electra, the daughter of Atlas, in Samothrace. When Athena assigned to Cadmus the government of Thebes, Zeus gave him Harmonia for his wife, and all the gods of Olympus were present at the marriage. On the wedding-day Cadmus received a present of a necklace, which afterwards became fatal to all who possessed it. Harmonia accompanied Cadmus when he was obliged to quit Thebes, and shared his fate. [CADMUS.] Polynices, who inherited the fatal necklace, gave it to Eriphyle, that she might persuade her husband, Amphiaraus, to undertake the expedition against Thebes. Through Alcmaeon, the son of Eriphyle, the necklace came into the hands of Arsinoë, next into those of the sons of Phegeus, Pronous and Agenor, and lastly into those of the sons of Alcmaeon, Amphoterus and Acarnan, who dedicated it in the temple of Athena Pronoea at Delphi.

Harpăgĭa, or -ĭum ('Αρπαγεῖα, or -άγιον), a small town in Mysia, between Cyzicus and Priapus, the scene of the rape of Ganymedes, according to some legends.

Harpăgus ("Αρπαγος). 1. A noble Median, whose preservation of the infant Cyrus, with the events consequent upon it, are related under CYRUS. He became one of the generals of Cyrus, and conquered the Greek cities of Asia Minor. — 2. A Persian general, under Darius I., took Histiaeus prisoner.

Harpălus ("Αρπαλος). 1. A Macedonian of noble birth, accompanied Alexander the Great to Asia, as superintendent of the treasury. After the conquest of Darius, he was left by Alexander in charge of the royal treasury, and with the administration of the wealthy satrapy of Babylon. Here, during Alexander's absence in India, he gave himself up to the most extravagant luxury and profusion, and squandered the treasures entrusted to him. When he heard that Alexander, contrary to his expectations, was returning from India, he fled from Babylon with about 5000 talents and a body of 6000 mercenaries, and crossed over to Greece, B. C. 324. He took refuge at Athens, where he employed his treasures to gain over the orators, and induce the people to support him against Alexander and his vicegerent, Antipater. Among those whom he thus corrupted are said to have been Demades, Charicles, the son-in-law of Phocion, and even Demosthenes himself. [DEMOSTHENES.] But he failed in his general object, for Antipater, having demanded his surrender from the Athenians, it was resolved to place him in confinement until the Macedonians should send for him. He succeeded in making his escape from prison, and fled to Crete, where he was assassinated soon after his arrival, by Thimbron, one of his own officers. — 2. A Greek astronomer, introduced some improvements into the cycle of CLEOSTRATUS. Harpalus lived before METON.

Harpălyce ('Αρπαλύκη). 1. Daughter of Harpalycus, king in Thrace. As she lost her mother in infancy, she was brought up by her father with the milk of cows and mares, and was trained in all manly exercises. After the death of her father, she lived in the forests as a robber, being so swift in running that horses were unable to overtake her. At length she was caught in a snare by shepherds, who killed her. — 2. Daughter of Clymenus and Epicaste, was seduced by her own father. To revenge herself she slew her younger brother, and served him up as food before her father. The gods changed her into a bird.

Harpăsa ("Αρπασα : Arepas), a city of Caria, on the river HARPASUS.

Harpăsus ("Αρπασος). 1. (Arpa-Su), a river of Caria, flowing N. into the Maeander, into which it falls opposite to Nysa. — 2. (Harpa-Su), a river of Armenia Major, flowing S. into the Araxes. Xenophon, who crossed it with the 10,000 Greeks, states its width as 4 plethra (about 400 feet).

Harpĭna or **Harpinna** ("Αρπινα, "Αρπιννα), a town in Elis Pisatis, near Olympia, said to have been called after a daughter of Asopus.

Harpocrătion, Valerĭus, a Greek grammarian of Alexandria, of uncertain date, the author of an extant dictionary to the works of the 10 Attic orators, entitled Περὶ τῶν λέξεων τῶν δέκα ῥητόρων, or Λεξικὸν τῶν δέκα ῥητόρων. It contains not only explanations of legal and political terms, but also accounts of persons and things mentioned in the Attic orators, and is a work of great value. The best editions are the one published at Leipzig, 1824, and the one by Bekker, Berlin, 1833.

Harpyiae ("Αρπυιαι), the Harpies, that is, the Robbers or Spoilers, are in Homer nothing but personified storm winds, who are said to carry off any one who had suddenly disappeared from the earth. Thus they carried off the daughters of king Pandareus, and gave them as servants to the Erinnyes. — Hesiod describes them as daughters of Thaumas by the Oceanid Electra, fair-locked and winged maidens, who surpassed winds and birds in the rapidity of their flight. But even in Aeschylus they appear as ugly creatures with wings; and later writers represent them as most disgusting monsters, being birds with the heads of maidens, with long claws and with faces pale with hunger. They were sent by the Gods to torment the blind Phineus, and whenever a meal was placed before him, they darted down from the air and carried it off; later writers add, that they either devoured the food themselves, or rendered it unfit to be eaten. Phineus was delivered from them by Zetes and Calais, sons of Boreas, and 2 of the Argonauts. [See p. 76, a.] Hesiod mentions 2 Harpies, Ocypete and Aëllo: later writers 3; but their names are not the same in all accounts. Besides the 2 already mentioned, we find Aëllopos, Nicothoë, Ocythoë, Ocypode, Celaeno, Acholoë. Virgil places them in the islands called Strophades, in the Ionian sea (*Aen.* iii. 210), where they took up their abode after they had been driven away from Phineus.— In the famous Harpy monument recently brought from Lycia to this country, the Harpies are represented in the act of carrying off the daughters of Pandareus.

Harudes, a people in the army of Ariovistus (B. C. 58), supposed to be the same as the Charūdes mentioned by Ptolemy, and placed by him in the Chersonesus Cimbrica.

Hasdrūbal (Ἀσδρούβας), a Carthaginian name, probably signifies one whose help is Baal. 1. Son of Hanno, a Carthaginian general in the 1st Punic war. He was one of the 2 generals defeated by Regulus B. C. 256. In 254 he was sent into Sicily, with a large army, and remained in the island 4 years. In 250, he was totally defeated by Metellus, and was put to death on his return to Carthage. — 2. A Carthaginian, son-in-law of Hamilcar Barca, on whose death in 229, he succeeded to the command in Spain. He ably carried out the plans of his father-in-law for extending the Carthaginian dominions in Spain, and entrusted the conduct of most of his military enterprises to the young Hannibal. He founded New Carthage, and concluded with the Romans the celebrated treaty which fixed the Iberus as the boundary between the Carthaginian and Roman dominions. He was assassinated by a slave, whose master he had put to death (221), and was succeeded in the command by HANNIBAL. — 3. Son of Hamilcar Barca, and brother of Hannibal. When Hannibal set out for Italy (218), Hasdrubal was left in the command in Spain, and there fought for some years against the 2 Scipios. In 207 he crossed the Alps and marched into Italy, in order to assist Hannibal; but he was defeated on the Metaurus, by the consuls C. Claudius Nero and M. Livius Salinator, his army was destroyed, and he himself fell in the battle. His head was cut off and thrown into Hannibal's camp. — 4. One of Hannibal's chief officers, commanded the left wing of the Carthaginian army at the battle of Cannae (216). — 5. Surnamed the Bald (Calvus), commander of the Carthaginian expedition to Sardinia in the 2nd Punic war, 215. He was defeated by the Roman praetor, T. Manlius, taken prisoner, and carried to Rome. — 6. Son of Gisco, one of the Carthaginian generals in Spain during the 2nd Punic war. He fought in Spain from 214 to 206. After he and Mago had been defeated by Scipio in the latter of these years, he crossed over to Africa, where he succeeded in obtaining the alliance of Syphax by giving him his daughter So-

phonisba in marriage. In conjunction with Syphax, Hasdrubal carried on war against Masinissa, but he was defeated by Scipio, who landed in Africa in 204. He was condemned to death for his ill success by the Carthaginian government, but he still continued in arms against the Romans. On the arrival of Hannibal from Italy his sentence was reversed; but the popular feeling against him had not subsided, and in order to escape death from his enemies, he put an end to his life by poison.— 7. Commander of the Carthaginian fleet in Africa in 203, must be distinguished from the preceding. —8. Surnamed the Kid (*Haedus*), one of the leaders of the party at Carthage favourable to peace towards the end of the 2nd Punic war. — 9. General of the Carthaginians in the 3rd Punic war. When the city was taken, he surrendered to Scipio, who spared his life. After adorning Scipio's triumph, he spent the rest of his life in Italy.

Haterius, Q., a senator and rhetorician in the age of Augustus and Tiberius, died A. D. 26, in the 89th year of his age.

Hēbē (Ἥβη), called **Juventas** by the Romans, the goddess of youth, was a daughter of Zeus and Hera. She waited upon the gods, and filled their cups with nectar, before Ganymedes obtained this office; and she is further represented as assisting her mother Hera in putting the horses to her chariot, and in bathing and dressing her brother Ares. She married Hercules after he was received among the gods, and bore to him 2 sons, Alexiares and Anicetus. Later traditions represent her as a divinity who had it in her power to make aged persons young again. At Rome there were several temples of Juventas. She is even said to have had a chapel on the Capitol before the temple of Jupiter was built there.

Hebromāgus. [EBUROMAGUS.]

Hebron (Ἑβρών, Χεβρών· Ἑβρώνιος: El-Khalil), a city in the S. of Judaea, as old as the times of the patriarchs, and the first capital of the kingdom of David, who reigned there 7½ years, as king of Judah only.

Hebrus (Ἕβρος: Maritza), the principal river in Thrace, rises in the mountains of Scomius and Rhodope, flows first S.E. and then S.W., becomes navigable for smaller vessels at Philippopolis, and for larger ones at Hadrianopolis, and falls into the Aegean sea near Aenos, after forming by another branch an estuary called Stentoris Lacus. — The Hebrus was celebrated in Greek legends. On its banks Orpheus was torn to pieces by the Thracian women; and it is frequently mentioned in connexion with the worship of Dionysus.

Hēcaergē (Ἑκαέργη). 1. Daughter of Boreas, and one of the Hyperborean maidens, who were believed to have introduced the worship of Artemis in Delos. — 2. A surname of Artemis, signifying the goddess who hits at a distance.

Hēcălē (Ἑκάλη), a poor old woman, who hospitably received Theseus, when he had gone out for the purpose of killing the Marathonian bull. She vowed to offer to Zeus a sacrifice for the safe return of the hero; but as she died before his return, Theseus ordained that the inhabitants of the Attic tetrapolis should offer a sacrifice to her and Zeus Hecalus, or Hecaleius.

Hecataeus (Ἑκαταῖος). 1. Of Miletus, one of the earliest and most distinguished Greek historians and geographers. He was the son of Hegesander, and belonged to a very ancient and illustrious family. We have only a few particulars of his life. In B. C. 500 he endeavoured to dissuade his countrymen from revolting from the Persians; and when this advice was disregarded, he gave them some sensible counsel respecting the conduct of the war, which was also neglected. Previous to this, Hecataeus had visited Egypt and many other countries. He survived the Persian wars, and appears to have died about 476. He wrote 2 works: — 1. Περίοδος γῆς, or Περιήγησις, divided into 2 parts, one of which contained a description of Europe, and the other of Asia, Egypt, and Libya. Both parts were subdivided into smaller sections, which are sometimes quoted under their respective names, such as Hellespontus, &c.—2. Γενεαλογίαι or Ἱστορίαι, in 4 books, contained an account of the poetical fables and traditions of the Greeks. His work on geography was the more important, as it embodied the results of his numerous travels. He also corrected and improved the map of the earth drawn up by ANAXIMANDER. Herodotus knew the works of Hecataeus well, and frequently controverts his opinions. Hecataeus wrote in the Ionic dialect in a pure and simple style. The fragments of his works are collected by Klausen, *Hecataei Milesii Fragmenta*, Berlin, 1831, and by C. and Th. Müller, *Frag. Hist. Graec.* Paris, 1841. — 2. Of Abdera, a contemporary of Alexander the Great and Ptolemy, the son of Lagus, appears to have accompanied the former on his Asiatic expedition. He was a pupil of the Sceptic Pyrrho, and is himself called a philosopher, critic, and grammarian. In the reign of the first Ptolemy he travelled up the Nile as far as Thebes. He was the author of several works, of which the most important were: — 1. A History of Egypt. — 2. A work on the Hyperboreans. — 3. A History of the Jews, frequently referred to by Josephus and other ancient writers. This work was declared spurious by Origen: modern critics are divided in their opinions.

Hĕcătē (Ἑκάτη) a mysterious divinity, commonly represented as a daughter of Persaeus or Perses and Asteria, and hence called Perseis. She is also described as a daughter of Zeus and Demeter, or of Zeus and Pheraea or Hera, or of Leto or Tartarus. Homer does not mention her. According to the most genuine traditions, she appears to have been an ancient Thracian divinity, and a Titan, who ruled in heaven, on the earth, and in the sea, bestowing on mortals wealth, victory, wisdom, good luck to sailors and hunters, and prosperity to youth and to the flocks of cattle. She was the only one among the Titans who retained this power under the rule of Zeus, and she was honoured by all the immortal gods. The extensive power possessed by Hecate was probably the reason that she was subsequently identified with several other divinities, and at length became a mystic goddess, to whom mysteries were celebrated in Samothrace and in Aegina. In the Homeric hymn to Demeter, she is represented as taking an active part in the search after Proserpina, and when the latter was found as remaining with her as her attendant and companion. [See p. 212, a.] She thus became a deity of the lower world, and is described in this capacity as a mighty and formidable divinity. In consequence of her being identified with other divinities, she is said to have been Selene or Luna in heaven, Artemis or Diana in earth, and Persephone or Proserpina in the lower world. Being

thus as it were a 3-fold goddess, she is described with 3 bodies or 3 heads, the one of a horse, the 2nd of a dog, and the 3rd of a lion. Hence her epithets *Tergeminus, Triformis, Triceps,* &c. From her being an infernal divinity, she came to be regarded as a spectral being, who sent at night all kinds of demons and terrible phantoms from the lower world, who taught sorcery and witchcraft, and dwelt at places where 2 roads crossed, on tombs, and near the blood of murdered persons. She herself wandered about with the souls of the dead, and her approach was announced by the whining and howling of dogs. — At Athens there were very many small statues or symbolical representations of Hecate (ἑκάταια), placed before or in houses, and on spots where 2 roads crossed: it would seem that people consulted such Hecataea as oracles. At the close of every month dishes with food were set out for her and other averters of evil at the points where 2 roads crossed; and this food was consumed by poor people. The sacrifices offered to her consisted of dogs, honey, and black female lambs.

Hecatomnus (Ἑκατόμνως), king or dynast of Caria, in the reign of Artaxerxes III. He left 3 sons, Mausolus, Idrieus, and Pixodarus, all of whom, in their turn, succeeded him in the sovereignty; and 2 daughters, Artemisia and Ada.

Hecatompÿlos (Ἑκατόμπυλος, i. e. *having* 100 *gates*). 1. An epithet of Thebes in Egypt [THEBAE]. — 2. A city in the middle of Parthia, 1260 stadia or 133 Roman miles from the Caspiae Pylae; enlarged by Seleucus; and afterwards used by the Parthian kings as a royal residence.

Hěcăton (Ἑκάτων), a Stoic philosopher, a native of Rhodes, studied under Panaetius, and wrote numerous works, all of which are lost.

Hecatonnēsi (Ἑκατόννησοι: *Mosko-nisi*), a group of small islands, between Lesbos and the coast of Aeolis, on the S. side of the mouth of the Gulf of Adramyttium. The name, 100 *islands*, was indefinite; the real number was reckoned by some at 20, by others at 40. Strabo derives the name, not from ἕκατον, 100, but from Ἕκατος, a surname of Apollo.

Hector (Ἕκτωρ), the chief hero of the Trojans in their war with the Greeks, was the eldest son of Priam and Hecuba, the husband of Andromache, and father of Scamandrius. He fought with the bravest of the Greeks, and at length slew Patroclus, the friend of Achilles. The death of his friend roused Achilles to the fight. The other Trojans fled before him into the city. Hector alone remained without the walls, though his parents implored him to return; but when he saw Achilles, his heart failed him, and he took to flight. Thrice did he race round the city, pursued by the swift-footed Achilles, and then fell pierced by Achilles' spear. Achilles tied Hector's body to his chariot, and thus dragged him into the camp of the Greeks · but later traditions relate that he first dragged the body thrice around the walls of Ilium. At the command of Zeus, Achilles surrendered the body to the prayers of Priam, who buried it at Troy with great pomp. Hector is one of the noblest conceptions of the poet of the Iliad. He is the great bulwark of Troy, and even Achilles trembles when he approaches him. He has a presentiment of the fall of his country, but he perseveres in his heroic resistance, preferring death to slavery and disgrace. Besides these virtues of a warrior, he is distinguished also by those of a man: his heart is open to the gentle feelings of a son, a husband, and a father.

Hecŭba ('Εκάβη), daughter of Dymas in Phrygia, or of Cisseus, king of Thrace. She was the wife of Priam, king of Troy, to whom she bore Hector, Paris, Deiphobus, Helenus, Cassandra, and many other children. On the capture of Troy, she was carried away as a slave by the Greeks. According to the tragedy of Euripides, which bears her name, she was carried by the Greeks to Chersonesus, and there saw her daughter Polyxena sacrificed. On the same day the waves of the sea washed on the coast the body of her last son Polydorus, who had been murdered by Polymestor, king of the Thracian Chersonesus, to whose care he had been entrusted by Priam. Hecuba thereupon killed the children of Polymestor, and tore out the eyes of their father. Agamemnon pardoned her the crime, and Polymestor prophesied that she should be metamorphosed into a she-dog, and should leap into the sea at a place called Cynossema. It was added that the inhabitants of Thrace endeavoured to stone her, but that she was metamorphosed into a dog, and in this form howled through the country for a long time. — According to other accounts she was given as a slave to Ulysses, and in despair leaped into the Hellespont; or being anxious to die, she uttered such invectives against the Greeks, that the warriors put her to death, and called the place where she was buried Cynossema, with reference to her impudent invectives.

Hēdўlus ("Ἡδυλος), son of Melicertus, was a native of Samos or of Athens, and an epigrammatic poet. 11 of his epigrams are in the Greek Anthology. He was a contemporary and rival of Callimachus, and lived therefore about the middle of the 3rd century B. C.

Hēdўlius Mons ('Ἡδύλειον), a range of mountains in Boeotia, W. of the Cephissus.

Hēgēmon ('Ἡγήμων), of Thasos, a poet of the old comedy at Athens, but more celebrated for his parodies, of which kind of poetry he was the inventor. He was nicknamed Φακῆ, on account of his fondness for that kind of pulse. He lived in the time of the Peloponnesian war; and his parody of the Gigantomachia was the piece to which the Athenians were listening, when the news was brought to them in the theatre of the destruction of the expedition to Sicily.

Hēgēmŏnē ('Ἡγεμόνη), the leader or ruler, is the name of one of the Athenian Charites or Graces. Hegemone was also a surname of Artemis at Sparta, and in Arcadia.

Hēgēsĭānax ('Ἡγησιάναξ), an historian of Alexandria, is said to have been the real author of the work called Troica, which went under the name of Cephalon, or Cephalion. He appears to be the same as the Hegesianax, who was sent by Antiochus the Great as one of his envoys to the Romans in B. C. 196 and 193.

Hēgēsĭas ('Ἡγησίας). 1. Of Magnesia, a rhetorician and historian, lived about B. C. 290, and wrote the history of Alexander the Great. He was regarded by some as the founder of that degenerate style of composition which bore the name of the Asiatic. His own style was destitute of all vigour and dignity, and was marked chiefly by childish conceits and minute prettinesses. — 2. Of Salamis, supposed by some to have been the author of the Cyprian poem, which, on better authority, is ascribed to Stasinus. — 3. A Cyrenaic philosopher, who lived

at Alexandria in the time of the Ptolemies, perhaps about B. C. 260. He wrote a work containing such gloomy descriptions of human misery, that it drove many persons to commit suicide ; hence he was surnamed Peisithanatos (Πεισιθάνατος). He was, in consequence, forbidden to teach by Ptolemy.

Hēgēsĭas ('Ἡγησίας) and Hēgĭas ('Ἡγίας), 2 Greek statuaries, whom many scholars identify with one another. They lived at the period immediately preceding that of Phidias. The chief work of Hegesias was the statues of Castor and Pollux, which are supposed to be the same as those which now stand on the stairs leading to the Capitol.

Hēgēsīnus ('Ἡγησίνους), of Pergamum, the successor of Evander and the immediate predecessor of Carneades in the chair of the Academy, flourished about B. C. 185.

Hēgēsippus ('Ἡγήσιππος). 1. An Athenian orator, and a contemporary of Demosthenes, to whose political party he belonged. The grammarians ascribe to him the oration on Halonesus, which has come down to us under the name of Demosthenes. — 2. A poet of the New Comedy, flourished about B. C. 300. — 3. A Greek historian of Mecyberna, wrote an account of the peninsula of Pallene.

Hēgēsĭpġla ('Ἡγησιπύλη), daughter of Olorus, king of Thrace, and wife of Miltiades.

Hēgĭas. [HEGESIAS.]

Hēlēna ('Ἑλένη), daughter of Zeus and Leda, and sister of Castor and Pollux (the Dioscuri). She was of surpassing beauty. In her youth she was carried off by Theseus and Pirithous to Attica. When Theseus was absent in Hades, Castor and Pollux undertook an expedition to Attica, to liberate their sister. Athens was taken, Helen delivered, and Aethra, the mother of Theseus, made prisoner, and carried as a slave of Helen, to Sparta. According to some accounts she bore to Theseus a daughter Iphigenia. On her return home, she was sought in marriage by the noblest chiefs from all parts of Greece. She chose Menelaus for her husband, and became by him the mother of Hermione. She was subsequently seduced and carried off by Paris to Troy. [For details, see PARIS and MENELAUS.] The Greek chiefs who had been her suitors, resolved to revenge her abduction, and accordingly sailed against Troy. Hence arose the celebrated Trojan war, which lasted 10 years. During the course of the war she is represented as showing great sympathy with the Greeks. After the death of Paris towards the end of the war, she married his brother Deiphobus. On the capture of Troy, which she is said to have favoured, she betrayed Deiphobus to the Greeks, and became reconciled to Menelaus, whom she accompanied to Sparta. Here she lived with him for some years in peace and happiness ; and here, according to Homer, Telemachus found her solemnising the marriage of her daughter Hermione with Neoptolemus. The accounts of Helen's death differ. According to the prophecy of Proteus in the Odyssey, Menelaus and Helen were not to die, but the gods were to conduct them to Elysium. Others relate that she and Menelaus were buried at Therapne in Laconia, where their tomb was seen by Pausanias. Others again relate, that after the death of Menelaus she was driven out of Peloponnesus by the sons of the latter and fled to Rhodes, where she was tied to a tree and strangled by Polyxo: the Rhodians expiated the crime by dedicating a temple to her under the name of Helena Dendritis. According to another tradition she married Achilles in the island of Leuce, and bore him a son Euphorion. — The Egyptian priests told Herodotus that Helen never went to Troy, but that when Paris reached Egypt with Helen on his way to Troy, she was detained by Proteus, king of Egypt ; and that she was restored to Menelaus when he visited Egypt in search of her after the Trojan war, finding that she had never been at Troy.

Hĕlĕna, Flāvĭa Jŭlĭa. 1. The mother of Constantine the Great. When her husband Constantius was raised to the dignity of Caesar by Diocletian, A. D. 292, he was compelled to repudiate his wife, to make way for Theodora, the step-child of Maximianus Herculius. Subsequently, when her son succeeded to the purple, Helena was treated with marked distinction and received the title of Augusta. She died about 328. She was a Christian, and is said to have discovered at Jerusalem the sepulchre of our Lord, together with the wood of the true cross. — 2. Daughter of Constantine the Great and Fausta, married her cousin Julian the Apostate, 355, and died 360.

Hĕlĕna ('Ελένη). 1. (*Makronisi*), a small and rocky island, between the S. of Attica and Ceos, formerly called Cranaë. — 2. The later name of ILLIBERRIS in Gaul.

Hĕlĕnus ("Ελενος). 1. Son of Priam and Hecuba, was celebrated for his prophetic powers, and also fought against the Greeks in the Trojan war. In Homer we have no further particulars about Helenus ; but in later traditions he is said to have deserted his countrymen and joined the Greeks. There are likewise various accounts respecting his desertion of the Trojans. According to some he did it of his own accord ; according to others, he was ensnared by Ulysses, who was anxious to obtain his prophecy respecting the fall of Troy. Others, again, relate that, on the death of Paris, Helenus and Deiphobus contended for the possession of Helena, and that Helenus being conquered, fled to Mt. Ida, where he was taken prisoner by the Greeks. After the fall of Troy, he fell to the share of Pyrrhus. He foretold Pyrrhus the sufferings which awaited the Greeks who returned home by sea, and prevailed upon him to return by land to Epirus. After the death of Pyrrhus he received a portion of the country, and married Andromache, by whom he became the father of Cestrinus. When Aeneas in his wanderings arrived in Epirus, he was hospitably received by Helenus, who also foretold him the future events of his life. — 2. Son of Pyrrhus, king of Epirus, by Lanassa, daughter of Agathocles. He accompanied his father to Italy B. C. 280, and was with him when Pyrrhus perished at Argos, 272. He then fell into the hands of Antigonus Gonatas, who however sent him back in safety to Epirus.

Hĕlĭădae and **Hĕlĭădes** ('Ηλιάδαι and 'Ηλιάδες), the sons and daughters of Helios (the Sun). The name *Heliades* is given especially to *Phaëthusa*, *Lampetie* and *Phoebe*, the daughters of Helios and the nymph Clymene, and the sisters of Phaëton. They bewailed the death of their brother Phaëton so bitterly on the banks of the Eridanus, that the gods in compassion changed them into poplar-trees and their tears into amber. [See ERIDANUS.]

Hĕlĭce ('Ελίκη), daughter of Lycaon, was beloved by Zeus, but Hera, out of jealousy, metamorphosed her into a she-bear, whereupon Zeus placed her among the stars, under the name of the Great Bear.

Hĕlĭcē ('Ελίκη : 'Ελικώνιος, 'Ελικεύς). 1. The ancient capital of Achaia, said to have been founded by Ion, possessed a celebrated temple of Poseidon, which was regarded as the great sanctuary of the Achaean race. Helice was swallowed up by an earthquake together with Bura, B. C. 373. The earth sunk deep into the ground, and the place on which the cities stood was ever afterwards covered by the sea. — 2. An ancient town in Thessaly, which disappeared in early times.

Hĕlĭcon ('Ελικών), son of Acesas, a celebrated artist. [ACESAS.]

Hĕlĭcon ('Ελικών : *Helicon, Palaeo-Buni*, Turk. *Zagora*), a celebrated range of mountains in Boeotia, between the lake Copais and the Corinthian gulf, was covered with snow the greater part of the year, and possessed many romantic ravines and lovely vallies. Helicon was sacred to Apollo and the Muses, the latter of whom are hence called 'Ελικώνιαι παρθένοι and 'Ελικωνιάδες νύμφαι by the Greek poets, and *Heliconiades* and *Heliconides* by the Roman poets. Here sprung the celebrated fountains of the Muses, AGANIPPE and HIPPOCRENE. At the fountain of Hippocrene was a grove sacred to the Muses, which was adorned with some of the finest works of art. On the slopes and in the valleys of the mountains grew many medicinal plants, which may have given occasion to the worship of Apollo, as the healing god.

Hĕlĭŏdōrus ('Ηλιόδωρος). 1. An Athenian, surnamed *Periegetes* (Περιηγητής), probably lived about B. C. 164, and wrote a description of the works of art in the Acropolis at Athens. This work was one of the authorities for Pliny's account of the Greek artists. — 2. A rhetorician at Rome in the time of Augustus, whom Horace mentions as the companion of his journey to Brundisium (*Sat.* i. 5. 2, 3.) — 3. A Stoic philosopher at Rome, who became a *delator* in the reign of Nero. (Juv. *Sat.* i. 33.) — 4. A rhetorician, and private secretary to the emperor Hadrian. — 5. Of Emesa in Syria, lived about the end of the 4th century of our era, and was bishop of Tricca in Thessaly. Before he was made bishop, he wrote a romance in 10 books, entitled *Aethiopica*, because the scene of the beginning and the end of the story is laid in Aethiopia. This work has come down to us, and is far superior to the other Greek romances. It relates the loves of Theagenes and Chariclea. Though deficient in those characteristics of modern fiction which appeal to the universal sympathies of our nature, the romance of Heliodorus is interesting on account of the rapid succession of strange and not altogether improbable adventures, the many and various characters introduced, and the beautiful scenes described. The language is simple and elegant. The best editions are by Mitscherlich in his *Scriptores Graeci Erotici*, Argentorat. 1798, and by Coraës, Paris, 1804. — 6. Of Larissa, the author of a short work on optics, still extant, chiefly taken from Euclid's *Optics*: edited by Matani, Pistor. 1758.

Heliogabălus. [ELAGABALUS.]

Heliopŏlis ('Ηλίου πόλις or 'Ηλιούπολις, i. e. the *City of the Sun*). 1. (Heb. Baalath : *Baalbek*, Ru.), a celebrated city of Syria, a chief seat of the worship of Baal, one of whose symbols was the Sun, and whom the Greeks identified with Apollo, as well as with Zeus : hence the Greek name of the city. With the worship of Baal, here as elsewhere, was associated that of Astarte, whom the Greeks identified with Aphrodite. It was situated in the middle of Coele-Syria, at the W. foot of Anti-Libanus, on a rising ground at the N. E. extremity of a large plain which reaches almost to the sea, and which is well watered by the river Leontes (*Nahr-el-Kasimiyeh*), near whose sources Heliopolis was built: the sources of the Orontes also are not far N. of the city. The situation of Heliopolis necessarily made it a place of great commercial importance, as it was on the direct road from Egypt and the Red Sea and also from Tyre to Syria, Asia Minor, and Europe; and hence, probably, the wealth of the city, to which its ruins still bear witness. We know, however, very little of its history. It was made a Roman colony by the name of Colonia Julia Augusta Felix Heliopolitana, and colonised by veterans of the 5th and 8th legions, under Augustus. Antoninus Pius built the great temple of Jupiter (i. e. Baal), of which the ruins still exist; and there are medals which shew, in addition to other testimony, that it was favoured by several of the later emperors. All the existing ruins are of the Roman period, and most of them probably of later date than the great temple just mentioned; but it is impossible to determine their exact times. They consist of a large quadrangular court in front of the great temple, another hexagonal court outside of this, and, in front of all, a portico, or propylaea, approached by a flight of steps. Attached to one corner of the quadrangular court is a smaller, but more perfect, temple; and, at some distance from all these buildings, there is a circular edifice, of a unique and very interesting architectural form. There is also a single Doric column on a rising ground, and traces of the city walls. — 2. (O. T. On, or Bethshemesh: *Matarieh*, Ru. N.E. of *Cairo*), a celebrated city of Lower Egypt, capital of the Nomos Heliopolites, stood on the E. side of the Pelusiac branch of the Nile, a little below the apex of the Delta, and near the canal of Trajan, and was, in the earliest period of which we have any record, a chief seat of the Egyptian worship of the Sun. Here also was established the worship of Mnevis, a sacred bull similar to Apis. The priests of Heliopolis were renowned for their learning. It suffered much during the invasion of Cambyses; and by the time of Strabo it was entirely ruined.

Hēlios ("Ηλιος or 'Hέλιος), called **Sol** by the Romans, the god of the sun. He was the son of Hyperion and Thea, and a brother of Selene and Eos. From his father, he is frequently called **Hyperiōnides**, or **Hyperion**, the latter of which is an abridged form of the patronymic, **Hyperionion**. In the Homeric hymn on Helios, he is called a son of Hyperion and Euryphaëssa. Homer describes Helios as giving light both to gods and men: he rises in the E. from Oceanus, traverses the heaven, and descends in the evening into the darkness of the W. and Oceanus. Later poets have marvellously embellished this simple notion. They tell of a most magnificent palace of Helios in the E., containing a throne occupied by the god, and surrounded by personifications of the different divisions of time. They also assign him a second palace in the W., and describe his horses as feeding upon herbs growing in the islands of the Blessed. The manner in which Helios during the night passes from the western into the eastern ocean is not mentioned either by Homer or Hesiod, but later poets make him sail in a golden boat, the work of Hephaestus, round one-half of the earth, and thus arrive in the E. at the point from which he has to rise again.

Others represent him as making his nightly voyage while slumbering in a golden bed. The horses and chariot with which Helios traverses the heavens are not mentioned in the Iliad and Odyssey, but first occur in the Homeric hymn on Helios, and both are described minutely by later poets.—Helios is described as the god who sees and hears every thing, and was thus able to reveal to Hephaestus the faithlessness of Aphrodite, and to Demeter the abduction of her daughter. At a later time Helios became identified with Apollo, though the 2 gods were originally quite distinct; but the identification was never carried out completely, for no Greek poet ever made Apollo ride in the chariot of Helios through the heavens, and among the Romans we find this idea only after the time of Virgil. The representations of Apollo with rays around his head, to characterise him as identical with the sun, belong to the time of the Roman empire. — The island of Thrinacia (Sicily) was sacred to Helios, and there he had flocks of sheep and oxen, which were tended by his daughters Phaetusa and Lampetia. Later traditions ascribe to him flocks also in the island of Erythia; and it may be remarked in general, that sacred flocks, especially of oxen, occur in most places where the worship of Helios was established.—His descendants are very numerous; and the surnames and epithets given him by the poets are mostly descriptive of his character as the sun. Temples of Helios (ἡλιεῖα) existed in Greece at a very early time; and in later times we find his worship established in various places, and especially in the island of Rhodes, where the famous colossus was a representation of the god. The sacrifices offered to him consisted of white rams, boars, bulls, goats, lambs, especially white horses, and honey. Among the animals sacred to him, the cock is especially mentioned. The Roman poets, when speaking of the god of the sun (Sol), usually adopt the notions of the Greeks. The worship of Sol was introduced at Rome, especially after the Romans had become acquainted with the East, though traces of the worship of the sun and moon occur at an early period.

Helissōn ('Ελισσών or 'Ελισσοῦς), a small town in Arcadia, on a river of the same name, which falls into the Alphēus.

Hellānīcus ('Ελλάνικος). 1. Of Mytilene in Lesbos, the most eminent of the Greek logographers, or early Greek historians, was in all probability born about B. c. 496, and died 411. We have no particulars of his life, but we may presume that he visited many of the countries, of whose history he gave an account. He wrote a great number of genealogical, chronological and historical works, which are cited under the titles of *Troica*, *Aeolica*, *Persica*, &c. One of his most popular works was entitled *Ἱέρειαι τῆς Ἥρας*: it contained a chronological list of the priestesses of Hera at Argos, compiled from the records preserved in the temple of the goddess of this place. This work was one of the earliest attempts to regulate chronology, and was made use of by Thucydides, Timaeus and others. The fragments of Hellanicus are collected by Sturz, *Hellanici Lesbii Fragmenta*, Lips. 1826; and by C. and Th. Müller, *Fragm. Histor. Graec.* Paris, 1841.—2. A Greek grammarian, a disciple of Agathocles, and apparently a contemporary of Aristarchus, wrote on the Homeric poems.

Hellas, Hellēnes. [GRAECIA.]

Hellē ("Ελλη), daughter of Athamas and Nephèle, and sister of Phrixus. When Phrixus was to be sacrificed [PHRIXUS], Nephele rescued her 2 children, who rode away through the air upon the ram with the golden fleece, the gift of Hermes; but, between Sigeum and the Chersonesus, Helle fell into the sea, which was thence called the sea of Helle (*Hellespontus*). Her tomb was shown near Pactya, on the Hellespont.

Hellēn ("Ελλην), son of Deucalion and Pyrrha, or of Zeus and Dorippe, husband of Orseis, and father of Aeolus, Dorus, and Xuthus. He was king of Phthia in Thessaly, and was succeeded by his son Aeolus. He is the mythical ancestor of all the Hellenes; from his 2 sons Aeolus and Dorus were descended the Aeolians and Dorians; and from his 2 grandsons Achaeus and Ion, the sons of Xuthus, the Achaeans and Ionians.

Hellespontus ('Ελλήσποντος: *Straits of the Dardanelles,* or *of Gallipoli,* Turk. *Stambul Denghis*), the long narrow strait connecting the Propontis (*Sea of Marmara*) with the Aegean Sea, and through which the waters of the Black Sea discharge themselves into the Mediterranean in a constant current. The length of the strait is about 50 miles, and the width varies from 6 miles at the upper end to 2 at the lower, and in some places it is only 1 mile wide, or even less. The narrowest part is between the ancient cities of SESTUS and ABYDUS, where Xerxes made his bridge of boats, [XERXES] and where the legend related that Leander swam across to visit Hero. [LEANDER.] The name of the Hellespont (i. e. the *Sea of Helle*) was derived from the story of Helle's being drowned in it [HELLE]. The Hellespont was the boundary of Europe and Asia, dividing the Thracian Chersonese in the former from the Troad and the territories of Abydus and Lampsacus in the latter. The district just mentioned, on the S. side of the Hellespont, was also called 'Ελλήσποντος, its inhabitants 'Ελλησπόντιοι, and the cities on its coast 'Ελλησπόντιαι πόλεις. — 2. Under the Roman empire, Hellespontus was the name of a proconsular province, composed of the Troad and the N. part of Mysia, and having Cyzicus for its capital.

Hellŏmĕnum ('Ελλόμενον), a seaport town of the Acarnanians on the island Leucas.

Hellŏpĭa. [ELLOPIA.]

Helōrus or **Helōrum** (ἡ "Ελωρος: 'Ελωρίτης), a town on the E. coast of Sicily, S. of Syracuse, at the mouth of the river Helorus. There was a road from Helorus to Syracuse (ὁδὸς 'Ελωρίνη, Thuc. vi. 70, vii. 80).

Hālos (τὸ "Ελος: 'Ελεῖος, 'Ελεάτης). 1. A town in Laconia, on the coast, in a marshy situation, whence its name (ἕλος=*marsh*). The town was in ruins in the time of Pausanias. It was commonly said that the Spartan slaves, called Helotes (Εἵλωτες), were originally the Achaean inhabitants of this town, who were reduced by the Dorian conquerors to slavery; but this account of the origin of the Helotes seems to have been merely an invention, in consequence of the similarity of their name to that of the town of Helos. (See *Dict. of Antiq.* art. *Helotae.*) — 2. A town or district of Elis on the Alphēus.

Helvecōnae, a people in Germany, between the Viadus and the Vistula, S. of the Rugii, and N. of the Burgundiones, reckoned by Tacitus among the Ligii.

Helvĕtĭi, a brave and powerful Celtic people, who dwelt between M. Jurassus (*Jura*), the Lacus

Lemannus (*Lake of Geneva*), the Rhone, and the Rhine as far as the Lacus Brigantinus (*Lake of Constance*). They were thus bounded by the Sequani on the W., by the Nantuates and Lepontii in Cisalpine Gaul on the S., by the Rhaeti on the E., and by the German nations on the N. beyond the Rhine. Their country, called *Ager Helvetiorum* (but never *Helvetia*), thus corresponded to the W. part of Switzerland. Their chief town was AVENTICUM. They were divided into 4 *pagi* or cantons, of which the *Pagus Tigurinus* was the most celebrated. We only know the name of one of the 3 others, namely the *Vicus Verbigenus,* or, more correctly, *Urbigenus.* — The Helvetii are first mentioned in the war with the Cimbri. In B. C. 107 the Tigurini defeated and killed the Roman consul L. Cassius Longinus, on the lake of Geneva, while another division of the Helvetii accompanied the Cimbri and Teutones in their invasion of Gaul. Subsequently the Helvetii invaded Italy along with the Cimbri; and they returned home in safety, after the defeat of the Cimbri by Marius and Catulus in 101. About 40 years afterwards, they resolved, upon the advice of Orgetorix, one of their chiefs, to migrate from their country with their wives and children, and seek a new home in the more fertile plains of Gaul. In 58 they endeavoured to carry their plan into execution, but they were defeated by Caesar, and driven back into their own territories. The Romans now planted colonies and built fortresses in their country (Noviodunum, Vindonissa, Aventicum), and the Helvetii gradually adopted the customs and language of their conquerors. They were severely punished by the generals of Vitellius (A. D. 70), whom they refused to recognise as emperor; and after that time they are rarely mentioned as a separate people. — The Helvetii were included in Gallia Lugdunensis, according to Strabo, but in Gallia Belgica, according to Pliny: most modern writers adopt Pliny's statement. When Gaul was subdivided into a greater number of provinces under the later emperors, the country of the Helvetii formed, with that of the Sequani and the Rauraci, the province of *Maxima Sequanorum.*

Helvia, mother of the philosopher SENECA.

Helvidius Priscus. [PRISCUS.]

Helvii, a people in Gaul, between the Rhone and Mt. Cebenna, which separated them from the Arverni, were for a long time subject to Massilia, but afterwards belonged to the province of Gallia Narbonensis. Their country produced good wine.

Helvius. 1. **Blasio.** [BLASIO.] — 2. **Cinna.** [CINNA.] — 3. **Mancia.** [MANCIA.] — 4. **Pertĭnax.** [PERTINAX.]

Hēmĕrēsĭa ('Ημερησία), the soothing goddess, a surname of Artemis, under which she was worshipped at the fountain Lusi (Λουσοί), in Arcadia.

Hēmĕrŏscŏpĭon. [DIANIUM, No. 2.]

Hemina, Cassĭus. [CASSIUS, No. 14.]

Hĕnĕtĭ ('Ενετοί), an ancient people in Paphlagonia, dwelling on the river Parthenius, fought on the side of Priam against the Greeks, but had disappeared before the historical times. They were regarded by many ancient writers as the ancestors of the Veneti in Italy. [VENETI.]

Hĕnĭŏchi ('Ηνίοχοι), a people in Colchis, N. of the Phasis, notorious as pirates.

Henna. [ENNA.]

Hephaestĭa ('Ηφαιστία). 1. ('Ηφαιστιεύς), a town in the N.W. of the island of Lemnos. — 2.

('Ηφαιστίδης -τείδης), a demus in Attica, belonging to the tribe Acamantis.

Hephaestíades Insúlae. [AEOLIAE.]

Hephaestíon ('Ηφαιστίων). 1. Son of Amyntor, a Macedonian of Pella, celebrated as the friend of Alexander the Great, with whom he had been brought up. Alexander called Hephaestion his own private friend, but Craterus the friend of the king. Hephaestion accompanied Alexander to Asia, and was employed by the king in many important commands. He died at Ecbatana, after an illness of only 7 days, B. C. 325. Alexander's grief for his loss was passionate and violent. A general mourning was ordered throughout the empire, and a funeral pile and monument erected to him at Babylon, at a cost of 10,000 talents. — 2. A Greek grammarian, who instructed the emperor Verus in Greek, and accordingly lived about A. D. 150. He was perhaps the author of a *Manual on Metres* ('Εγχειρίδιον περὶ μέτρων), which has come down to us under the name of Hephaestion. This work is a tolerably complete manual of Greek metres, and forms the basis of all our knowledge on that subject. Edited by Gaisford, Oxon. 1810.

Hephaestus ("Ηφαιστος), called Vulcánus by the Romans, the god of fire. He was, according to Homer, the son of Zeus and Hera. Later traditions state that he had no father, and that Hera gave birth to him independent of Zeus, as she was jealous of Zeus having given birth to Athena independent of her. He was born lame and weak, and was in consequence so much disliked by his mother, that she threw him down from Olympus. The marine divinities, Thetis and Eurynome, received him, and he dwelt with them for 9 years in a grotto, beneath Oceanus, making for them a variety of ornaments. He afterwards returned to Olympus, though we are not told through what means, and he appears in Homer as the great artist of the gods of Olympus. Although he had been cruelly treated by his mother, he always showed her respect and kindness ; and on one occasion took her part, when she was quarrelling with Zeus, which so much enraged the father of the gods, that he seized Hephaestus by the leg, and hurled him down from heaven. Hephaestus was a whole day falling, but in the evening he alighted in the island of Lemnos, where he was kindly received by the Sintians. Later writers describe his lameness as the consequence of this fall, while Homer makes him lame from his birth. He again returned to Olympus, and subsequently acted the part of mediator between his parents. On that occasion he offered a cup of nectar to his mother and the other gods, who burst out into immoderate laughter on seeing him busily hobbling from one god to another. — Hephaestus appears to have been originally the god of fire simply ; but as fire is indispensable in working metals, he was afterwards regarded as an artist. His palace in Olympus was imperishable and shining like stars. It contained his workshop, with the anvil and 20 bellows, which worked spontaneously at his bidding. It was there that he made all his beautiful and marvellous works, both for gods and men. The ancient poets abound in descriptions of exquisite workmanship which had been manufactured by the god. All the palaces in Olympus were his workmanship. He made the armour of Achilles ; the fatal necklace of Harmonia ; the

fire-breathing bulls of Aeëtes, king of Colchis, &c. In later accounts, the Cyclops are his workmen and servants, and his workshop is no longer in Olympus, but in some volcanic island. In the Iliad the wife of Hephaestus is Charis: in Hesiod Aglaia, the youngest of the Charites ; but in the Odyssey, as well as in later accounts, Aphrodite appears as his wife. Aphrodite proved faithless to her husband, and was in love with Ares ; but Helios disclosed their amours to Hephaestus, who caught the guilty pair in an invisible net, and exposed them to the laughter of the assembled gods. — The favourite abode of Hephaestus on earth was the island of Lemnos ; but other volcanic islands also, such as Lipara, Hiera, Imbros, and Sicily, are called his abodes or workshops. — Hephaestus, like Athena, gave skill to mortal artists, and, conjointly with her, he was believed to have taught men the arts which embellish and adorn life. Hence at Athens they had temples and festivals in common. The epithets and surnames, by which Hephaestus is designated by the poets, generally allude to his skill in the plastic arts or to his lameness. The Greeks frequently placed small dwarf-like statues of the god near the hearth. During the best period of Grecian art, he was represented as a vigorous man with a beard, and is characterised by his hammer or some other instrument, his oval cap, and the chiton, which leaves the right shoulder and arm uncovered. — The Roman Vulcanus was an old Italian divinity. [VULCANUS.]

Heptánomis. [AEGYPTUS.]

Hera ("Ηρα or "Ηρη), called Juno by the Romans. The Greek Hera, that is, *Mistress*, was a daughter of Cronos and Rhea, and sister and wife of Zeus. Some call her the eldest daughter of Cronos, but others give this title to Hestia. According to Homer she was brought up by Oceanus and Tethys, and afterwards became the wife of Zeus, without the knowledge of her parents. This simple account is variously modified in other traditions. Being a daughter of Cronos, she, like his other children, was swallowed by her father, but afterwards released ; and, according to an Arcadian tradition, she was brought up by Temenus, the son of Pelasgus. The Argives, on the other hand, related that she had been brought up by Euboea, Prosymna, and Acraea, the 3 daughters of the river Asterion. Several parts of Greece claimed the honour of being her birthplace, and more especially Argos and Samos, which were the principal seats of her worship. Her marriage with Zeus offered ample scope for poetical invention, and several places in Greece also claimed the honour of having been the scene of the marriage, such as Euboea, Samos, Cnossus in Crete, and Mount Thornax, in the S. of Argolis. Her marriage, called the *Sacred Marriage* (ἱερὸς γάμος), was represented in many places where she was worshipped. At her nuptials all the gods honoured her with presents, and Ge presented to her a tree with golden apples, which was watched by the Hesperides, at the foot of the Hyperborean Atlas. — In the Iliad Hera is treated by the Olympian gods with the same reverence as her husband. Zeus himself listens to her counsels, and communicates his secrets to her. She is, notwithstanding, far inferior to him in power, and must obey him unconditionally. She is not, like Zeus, the queen of gods and men, but simply the wife of the supreme god. The idea of her being the queen

Ganymedes. (Zannoni, Gal. di Firenze, serie 4, vol. 2, pl. 101.) Page 277. See illustrations opposite p. 298.

Helios (the Sun). (Coin of Rhodes, in the British Museum). Page 302.

Wine Genius. (A Mosaic, from Pompeii.) Page 279.

Flora.
(From an Ancient Statue.) Page 226.

Hebe.
(From a Bas-relief at Rome.) Page 298.

[To face p. 304.

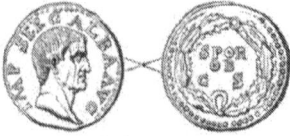

Ser. Sulpicius Galba, Roman Emperor, A.D. 68—69.
Page 273.

Galla Placidia, daughter of Theodosius the Great, ob. A.D. 450.
Page 274.

Gallienus, Roman Emperor, A.D. 260—268. Page 275.

Gelon II., King of Syracuse. Page 279. No. 2.

Germanicus Caesar, ob. A.D. 19. Page 282.

Geta, Roman Emperor, A.D. 212. Page 282.

Gordianus I., Roman Emperor, A.D. 238. Page 285.

Gordianus II., Roman Emperor, A.D. 238. Page 285.

Gordianus III., Roman Emperor, A.D. 238—244. Page 285.

·Gratianus, Roman Emperor, A.D. 367—383. Page 289.

Hadrianus, Roman Emperor, A.D. 117—138. Page 291.

Helena, wife of Constantius Chlorus, and mother of
Constantine the Great. Page 301.

To face p. 360.)

of heaven, with regal wealth and power, is of much later date. Her character, as described by Homer, is not of a very amiable kind ; and her jealousy, obstinacy, and quarrelsome disposition, sometimes make her husband tremble. Hence arise frequent disputes between Hera and Zeus ; and on one occasion Hera, in conjunction with Poseidon and Athena, contemplated putting Zeus into chains. Zeus, in such cases, not only threatens, but beats her. Once he even hung her up in the clouds, with her hands chained, and with two anvils suspended from her feet ; and on another occasion, when Hephaestus attempted to help her, Zeus hurled him down from Olympus. — By Zeus she was the mother of Ares, Hebe, and Hephaestus.— Hera was, properly speaking, the only really married goddess among the Olmpians, for the marriage of Aphrodite with Hephaestus can scarcely be taken into consideration. Hence, she is the goddess of marriage and of the birth of children. Several epithets and surnames, such as Εἰλείθυια, Γαμηλία, Ζυγία, Τελεία, &c., contain allusions to this character of the goddess, and the Ilithyiae are described as her daughters. — She is represented in the Iliad riding in a chariot drawn by 2 horses, in the harnessing and unharnessing of which she is assisted by Hebe and the Horae. Owing to the judgment of Paris [PARIS], she was hostile to the Trojans, and in the Trojan war she accordingly sided with the Greeks. She persecuted all the children of Zeus by mortal mothers, and hence appears as the enemy of Dionysus, Hercules, and others. In the Argonautic expedition she assisted Jason. It is impossible here to enumerate all the events of mythical story in which Hera acts a part ; and the reader must refer to the particular deities or heroes with whose story she is connected. — Hera was worshipped in many parts of Greece, but more especially at Argos, in the neighbourhood of which she had a splendid temple, on the road to Mycenae. Her great festival at Argos is described in the *Dict. of Ant.* art. *Heraea.* She also had a splendid temple in Samos. — The ancients gave several interpretations respecting the real significance of Hera ; but we must in all probability regard her as the great goddess of nature, who was worshipped every where from the earliest times. The worship of the Roman *Juno* is spoken of in a separate article. [JUNO.] Hera was usually represented as a majestic woman of mature age, with a beautiful forehead, large and widely opened eyes, and with a grave expression commanding reverence. Her hair was adorned with a crown or a diadem. A veil frequently hangs down the back of her head, to characterise her as the bride of Zeus, and the diadem, veil, sceptre, and peacock, are her ordinary attributes.

Hēraclēa (Ἡράκλεια: Ἡρακλεώτης : Heracleōtes). I. *In Europe.* 1. H., in Lucania, on the river Siris, founded by the Tarentines. During the independency of the Greek states in the S. of Italy, congresses were held in this town under the presidency of the Tarentines. It sunk into insignificance under the Romans. — 2. In Acarnania on the Ambracian gulf. — 3. In Pisatis Elis, in ruins in the time of Strabo. —4. The later name of Perinthus in Thrace. [PERINTHUS.] — 5. H. Caccabaria Porbaria, in Gallia Narbonensis on the coast, a sea-port of the Massilians. — 6. H. Lyncestis (Λύγκηστις), also called Pelagonia (*Bitoglia* or *Bitolia*), in Macedonia, on the Via Egnatia, W.

of the Erigon, the capital of one of the 4 districts into which Macedonia was divided by the Romans. —7. H. Minōa (Μινώα : nr. *Torre di Capo Bianco* Ru.), on the S. coast of Sicily, at the mouth of the river Halycus, between Agrigentum and Selinus. According to tradition it was founded by Minos, when he pursued Daedalus to Sicily, and it may have been an ancient colony of the Cretans. We know, however, that it was afterwards colonised by the inhabitants of Selinus, and that its original name was *Minoa*, which it continued to bear till about B. c. 500, when the town was taken by the Lacedaemonians under Euryleon, who changed its name into that of *Heraclea ;* but it continued to bear its ancient appellation as a surname to distinguish it from other places of the same name. It fell at an early period into the hands of the Carthaginians, and remained in their power till the conquest of Sicily by the Romans, who planted a colony there. — 8. H. Sintĭca (Σιντική), in Macedonia, a town of the Sinti, on the left bank of the Strymon, founded by Amyntas, brother of Philip. — 9. H. Trachīnĭae, in Thessaly. See TRACHIS. — II. *In Asia* 1. H. Pontĭca (Ἡ. ἡ Ποντική, or Πόντου, or ἐν Πόντῳ : *Harakli* or *Ereyli*), a city on the S. shore of the Pontus Euxinus, on the coast of Bithynia, in the territory of the Mariandyni, was situated 20 stadia N. of the river Lycus, upon a little river called Acheron or Soonautes, and near the base of a peninsula called Acherusia, and had a fine harbour. It was founded about B. c. 550, by colonists from Megara and from Tanagra in Boeotia (not, as Strabo says, from Miletus). After various political struggles, it settled down under a monarchical form of government. It reached the height of its prosperity in the reign of Darius Codomannus, when it had an extensive commerce, and a territory reaching from the Parthenius to the Sangarius. It began to decline in consequence of the rise of the kingdom of Bithynia and the foundation of Nicomedia, and the invasion of Asia Minor by the Gauls ; and its ruin was completed in the Mithridatic war, when the city was taken and plundered, and partly destroyed, by the Romans under Cotta. It was the native city of HERACLIDES PONTICUS, and perhaps of the painter ZEUXIS. — 2. H. ad Latmum (Ἡ. Λάτμου, or ἡ ὑπὸ Λάτμῳ : Ru. near the *Lake of Baffi*), a town of Ionia, S.E. of Miletus, at the foot of Mt. Latmus and upon the Sinus Latmicus ; formerly called Latmus. Near it was a cave, with the tomb of Endymion. — There was another city of the same name in Caria, one in Lydia, 2 in Syria, one in Media, and one in India, none of which require special notice here.

Hēracleŏpŏlis (Ἡρακλεούπολις). 1. Parva (ἡ μικρά), also called Sethron, a city of Lower Egypt, in the Nomos Sethroites, 22 Roman miles W. of Pelusium. — 2. Magna (ἡ μεγάλη, also ἡ ἄνω), the capital of the fertile Nomos Heracleopolites or Heracleotes, in the Heptanomis, or Middle Egypt ; a chief seat of the worship of the ichneumon.

Hēraclēum (Ἡράκλειον), the name of several promontories and towns, of which none require special notice except : 1. A town in Macedonia at the mouth of the Apilas, near the frontiers of Thessaly. — 2. The harbour of Cnossus in Crete. — 3. A town on the coast of the Delta of Egypt, a little W. of Canopus ; from which the Canopic mouth of the Nile was often called also the Heracleotic mouth. — 4. A place near Gindarus in the Syrian province of Cyrrhestice, where Ventidius, the legate of M. Antony, gained his great victory over the Parthians under Pacorus, in B. C. 38.

Hēracliānus ('Ηρακλειανός), one of the officers of Honorius, put Stilicho to death (A. D. 408), and received, as the reward of that service, the government of Africa. He rendered good service to Honorius during the invasion of Italy by Alaric, and the usurpation of Attalus. In 413 he revolted against Honorius, and invaded Italy ; but his enterprize failed, and on his return to Africa he was put to death at Carthage.

Hēraclidae ('Ηρακλειδαι), the descendants of Hercules, who, in conjunction with the Dorians, conquered Peloponnesus. It had been the will of Zeus, so ran the legend, that Hercules should rule over the country of the Perseids, at Mycenae and Tiryns. But through Hera's cunning, Eurystheus had been put into the place of Hercules, who had become the servant of the former. After the death of Hercules, his claims devolved upon his sons and descendants. At the time of his death, Hyllus, the eldest of his 4 sons by Deïaníra, was residing with his brothers at the court of Ceyx at Trachis. As Eurystheus demanded their surrender, and Ceyx was unable to protect them, they fled to various parts of Greece, until they were received as suppliants at Athena, at the altar of Eleos (Mercy). According to the Heraclidae of Euripides, the sons of Hercules were first staying at Argos, thence went to Trachis in Thessaly, and at length came to Athens. Demophon, the son of Theseus, received them, and they settled in the Attic tetrapolis. Eurystheus, to whom the Athenians refused to surrender the fugitives, now marched against the Athenians with a large army, but was defeated by the Athenians under Iolaus, Theseus, and Hyllus, and was slain with his sons. The battle itself was celebrated in Attic story as the battle of the Scironian rock, on the coast of the Saronic gulf, though Pindar places it in the neighbourhood of Thebes. After the battle, the Heraclidae entered Peloponnesus, and themselves there for one year. This was their 1st invasion of Peloponnesus. But a plague, which spread over the whole peninsula, compelled them to return to Attica, where, for a time, they again settled in the Attic tetrapolis. From thence they proceeded to Aegimius, king of the Dorians, whom Hercules had assisted in his war against the Lapithae, and who had promised to preserve a 3rd of his territory for the children of Hercules. [ÆGIMIUS.] The Heraclidae were hospitably received by Aegimius, and Hyllus was adopted by the latter. After remaining in Doris 3 years, Hyllus, with a band of Dorians, undertook an expedition against Atreus, who had married a daughter of Eurystheus, and had become king of Mycenae and Tiryns. Hyllus marched across the Corinthian isthmus, and first met Echemus of Tegea, who fought for the Pelopidae, the principal opponents of the Heraclidae. Hyllus fell in single combat with Echemus, and, according to an agreement which had been made before the battle, the Heraclidae were not to make any further attempt upon Peloponnesus for the next 50 years. Thus ended their 2nd invasion. They now retired to Tricorythus, where they were allowed by the Athenians to take up their abode. During the period which followed (10 years after the death of Hyllus), the Trojan war took place ; and 30 years after the Trojan war Cleodaeus, son

of Hyllus, again invaded Peloponnesus, which was the 3rd invasion. About 20 years later Aristomachus, the son of Cleodaeus, undertook the 4th expedition ; but both heroes fell. Not quite 30 years after Aristomachus (that is, about 80 years after the destruction of Troy), the Heraclidae prepared for their 5th and final attack. Temenus, Cresphontes, and Aristodemus, the sons of Aristomachus, upon the advice of an oracle, built a fleet on the Corinthian gulf ; but this fleet was destroyed, because Hippotes, one of the Heraclidae, had killed Carnus, an Acarnanian soothsayer ; and Aristodemus was killed by a flash of lightning. An oracle now ordered them to take a 3-eyed man for their commander. He was found in the person of Oxylus, the son of Andraemon, an Aetolian, but descended from a family in Elis. The expedition now successfully sailed from Naupactus towards Rhium in Peloponnesus. Oxylus, keeping the invaders away from Elis, led them through Arcadia. The Heraclidae and Dorians conquered Tisamenus, the son of Orestes, who ruled over Argos, Mycenae, and Sparta. After this they became masters of the greater part of Peloponnesus, and then distributed by lot the newly acquired possessions. Temenus obtained Argos ; Procles and Eurystheus, the twin sons of Aristodemus, Lacedaemon ; and Cresphontes, Messenia. — Such are the traditions about the Heraclidae and their conquest of Peloponnesus. They are not purely mythical, but contain a genuine historical substance, notwithstanding the various contradictions in the accounts. They represent the conquest of the Achaean population by Dorian invaders, who henceforward appear as the ruling race in the Peloponnesus. The conquered Achaeans became partly the slaves and partly the subjects of the Dorians. (See Dict. of Ant. art. Perioeci.)

Hēraclidēs ('Ηρακλείδης). 1. A Syracusan, son of Lysimachus, one of the generals when Syracuse was attacked by the Athenians, B. C. 415. — 2. A Syracusan, who held the chief command of the mercenary forces under the younger Dionysius. Being suspected by Dionysius, he fled from Syracuse, and afterwards took part with Dion in expelling Dionysius from Syracuse. After the expulsion of the tyrant, a powerful party at Syracuse looked up to Heraclides as their leader, in consequence of which Dion caused him to be assassinated, 354. — 3. Son of Agathocles, accompanied his father to Africa, where he was put to death by the soldiers, when they were deserted by Agathocles, 307. — 4. Of Tarentum, one of the chief counsellors of Philip V. king of Macedonia. — 5. Of Byzantium, sent as ambassador by Antiochus the Great to the 2 Scipios, 190. — 6. One of the 3 ambassadors sent by Antiochus Epiphanes to the Romans, 169. Heraclides was banished by Demetrius Soter, the successor of Antiochus (162), and in revenge gave his support to the impostor of Alexander Balas. — 7. Surnamed Ponticus, because he was born at Heraclēa in Pontus. He was a person of considerable wealth, and migrated to Athens, where he became a pupil of Plato. He paid attention also to the Pythagorean system, and afterwards attended the instructions of Speusippus, and finally of Aristotle. He wrote a great number of works upon philosophy, mathematics, music, history, politics, grammar, and poetry ; but almost all these works are lost. There has come down to us a small work, under the name of Heraclides, entitled περὶ Πολιτειῶν, of which the best editions are by Köler, Halle, 1804, and by Coraes, in his edition of Aelian, Paris, 1805. Another extant work, 'Αλληγορίαι 'Ομηρικαί, which also bears the name of Heraclides, was certainly not written by him. Diogenes Laërtius, in his life of Heraclides, says that " Heraclides made tragedies, and put the name of Thespis to them." This sentence has given occasion to a learned disquisition by Bentley (*Phalaris*, p. 239), to prove that the fragments attributed to Thespis are really cited from these counterfeit tragedies of Heraclides. Some childish stories are told about Heraclides keeping a pet serpent, and ordering one of his friends to conceal his body after his death, and place the serpent on the bed, that it might be supposed that he had been taken to the company of the gods. It is also said that he killed a man who had usurped the tyranny in Heraclea, and there are other traditions about him scarcely worth relating. — 8. An historian, who lived in the reign of Ptolemy Philopator (222—205), and wrote several works, quoted by the grammarians. — 9. A physician of Tarentum, lived in the 3rd or 2nd century B. C., and wrote some works on Materia Medica, and a commentary on all the works in the Hippocratic Collection. — 10. A physician of Erythrae in Ionia, was a pupil of Chrysermus, and a contemporary of Strabo in the 1st century B. C.

Heraclitus ('Ηράκλειτος.) 1. Of Ephesus, a philosopher generally considered as belonging to the Ionian school, though he differed from their principles in many respects. In his youth he travelled extensively, and after his return to Ephesus the chief magistracy was offered him, which, however, he transferred to his brother. He appears afterwards to have become a complete recluse, rejecting even the kindnesses offered by Darius, and at last retreating to the mountains, where he lived on pot-herbs; but, after some time, he was compelled by the sickness consequent on such meagre diet to return to Ephesus, where he died. He died at the age of 60, and flourished about B. C. 513. — Heraclitus wrote a work *On Nature* (περὶ φύσεως), which contained his philosophical views. From the obscurity of his style, he gained the title of the *Obscure* (σκοτεινός). He considered fire to be the primary form of all matter; but by fire he meant only to describe a clear light fluid, " self-kindled and self-extinguished," and therefore not differing materially from the air of Anaximenes. — 2. An Academic philosopher of Tyre, a friend of Antiochus, and a pupil of Clitomachus and Philo. — 3. The reputed author of a work, Περὶ 'Απίστων, published by Westermann, in his *Mythographi*, Brunsvig. 1843.

Heraea ('Ηραία: 'Ηραιεύς: nr. *St. Joannes*, Ru.), a town in Arcadia, on the right bank of the Alpheus, near the borders of Elis. Its territory was called **Heraeatis** ('Ηραιᾶτις).

Heraei Montes (τὰ "Ηραια ὄρη: *Monti Sori*), a range of mountains in Sicily, running from the centre of the island S.E., and ending in the promontory Pachynum.

Heraeum. [ARGOS, p. 77, a.]

Herbessus. [ERBESSUS.]

Herbīta ('Ερβῖτα: 'Ερβιταῖος, Herbitensis), a town in Sicily, N. of Agyrium, in the mountains, was a powerful place in early times under the tyrant Archonides, but afterwards declined in importance.

Herculānĕum, a town in Samnium, conquered

by the consul Carvilius, B. C. 293 (Liv. x. 45), must not be confounded with the more celebrated town of this name mentioned below.

Herculanĕum, Herculanīum, Herculānum, Herculense Oppidum, Herculĕa Urbs ('Ηράκλειον), an ancient city in Campania, near the coast, between Neapolis and Pompeii, was originally founded by the Oscans, was next in the possession of the Tyrrhenians, and subsequently was chiefly inhabited by Greeks, who appear to have settled in the place from other cities of Magna Graecia, and to have given it its name. It was taken by the Romans in the Social war (B. C. 89, 88), and was colonised by them. In A. D. 63 a great part of it was destroyed by an earthquake; and in 79 it was overwhelmed, along with Pompeii and Stabiae, by the great eruption of Mt. Vesuvius. It was buried under showers of ashes and streams of lava, from 70 to 100 feet under the present surface of the ground. On its site stand the modern *Portici* and part of the village of *Resina*: the Italian name of *Ercolano* does not indicate any modern place, but only the part of Herculaneum that has been disinterred. The ancient city was accidentally discovered by the sinking of a well in 1720, since which time the excavations have been carried on at different periods; and many works of art have been discovered, which are deposited in the Royal Museum at Portici. It has been found necessary to fill up again the excavations which were made, in order to render Portici and Resina secure, and therefore very little of the ancient city is to be seen. The buildings that have been discovered are a theatre capable of accommodating about 10,000 spectators, the remains of 2 temples, a large building, commonly designated as a *forum civile*, 228 feet long and 132 broad, and some private houses, the walls of which were adorned with paintings, many of which, when discovered, were in a state of admirable preservation. There have been also found at Herculaneum many MSS., written on rolls of papyrus; but the difficulty of unrolling and deciphering them was very great; and the few which have been deciphered are of little value, consisting of a treatise of Philodemus on music, and fragments of unimportant works on philosophy.

Herculĕs ('Ηρακλῆς), the most celebrated of all the heroes of antiquity. His exploits were celebrated not only in all the countries round the Mediterranean, but even in the more distant lands of the ancient world. I. **Greek Legends.** The Greek traditions about Hercules appear in their national purity down to the time of Herodotus. But the poets of the time of Herodotus and of the subsequent periods introduced considerable alterations, which were probably derived from the East or Egypt, for every nation possesses some traditions respecting heroes of superhuman strength and power. Now while in the earliest Greek legends Hercules is a purely human hero, a conqueror of men and cities, he afterwards appears as the subduer of monstrous animals, and is connected in a variety of ways with astronomical phaenomena. According to Homer, Hercules was the son of Zeus by Alcmene of Thebes in Boeotia. His stepfather was Amphitryon. Amphitryon was the son of Alcaeus, the son of Perseus; and Alcmene was a grand-daughter of Perseus. Hence Hercules belonged to the family of Perseus. Zeus visited Alcmene in the form of Amphitryon, while the latter was absent warring against the Taphians; and he, pretending to be her husband, became by her the father of Hercules. [For details, see ALC-MENE, AMPHITRYON.] On the day on which Hercules was to be born, Zeus boasted of his becoming the father of a hero who was to rule over the race of Perseus. Hera prevailed upon him to swear that the descendant of Perseus born that day should be the ruler. Thereupon she hastened to Argos, and there caused the wife of Sthenelus to give birth to Eurystheus; whereas, by keeping away the Ilithyiae, she delayed the birth of Hercules, and thus robbed him of the empire which Zeus had destined for him. Zeus was enraged at the imposition practised upon him, but could not violate his oath. Alcmene brought into the world 2 boys, Hercules, the son of Zeus, and Iphicles, the son of Amphitryon, who was one night younger than Hercules. Nearly all the stories about the childhood and youth of Hercules, down to the time when he entered the service of Eurystheus, seem to be inventions of a later age. At least in Homer and Hesiod we are only told that he grew strong in body and mind, that confiding in his own powers he defied even the immortal gods, and wounded Hera and Ares, and that under the protection of Zeus and Athena he escaped the dangers which Hera prepared for him. To these simple accounts, various particulars are added in later writers. As he lay in his cradle, Hera sent 2 serpents to destroy him, but the infant hero strangled them with his own hands. As he grew up, he was instructed by Amphitryon in driving a chariot, by Autolycus in wrestling, by Eurytus in archery, by Castor in fighting with heavy armour, and by Linus in singing and playing the lyre. Linus was killed by his pupil with the lyre, because he had censured him; and Amphitryon, to prevent similar occurrences, sent him to feed his cattle. In this manner he spent his life till his 18th year. His first great adventure happened while he was still watching the oxen of his father. A huge lion, which haunted Mt. Cithaeron, made great havoc among the flocks of Amphitryon and Thespius (or Thestius), king of Thespiae. Hercules promised to deliver the country of the monster; and Thespius, who had 50 daughters, rewarded Hercules by making him his guest so long as the chase lasted, and by giving up his daughters to him, each for one night. Hercules slew the lion, and henceforth wore its skin as his ordinary garment, and its mouth and head as his helmet. Others related that the lion's skin of Hercules was taken from the Nemean lion. On his return to Thebes, he met the envoys of king Erginus of Orchomenos, who were going to fetch the annual tribute of 100 oxen, which they had compelled the Thebans to pay. Hercules cut off the noses and ears of the envoys, and thus sent them back to Erginus. The latter thereupon marched against Thebes; but Hercules defeated and killed Erginus, and compelled the Orchomenians to pay double the tribute which they had formerly received from the Thebans. In this battle against Erginus Hercules lost his father Amphitryon, though the tragedians make him survive the campaign. Creon rewarded Hercules with the hand of his daughter, Megara, by whom he became the father of several children. The gods, on the other hand, made him presents of arms: Hermes gave him a sword, Apollo a bow and arrows, Hephaestus a golden coat of mail, and

Athena a peplus. He cut for himself a club in the neighbourhood of Nemea, while, according to others, the club was of brass, and the gift of Hephaestus. Soon afterwards Hercules was driven mad by Hera, and in this state he killed his own children by Megara and 2 of Iphicles. In his grief he sentenced himself to exile, and went to Thespius, who purified him. Other traditions place this madness at a later time, and relate the circumstances differently. He then consulted the oracle of Delphi as to where he should settle. The Pythia first called him by the name of Hercules — for hitherto his name had been Alcides or Alcaeus, — and ordered him to live at Tiryns, and to serve Eurystheus for the space of 12 years, after which he should become immortal. Hercules accordingly went to Tiryns, and did as he was bid by Eurystheus. — The accounts of the 12 labours which Hercules performed at the bidding of Eurystheus, are found only in the later writers. The only one of the 12 labours mentioned by Homer is his descent into the lower world to carry off Cerberus. We also find in Homer the fight of Hercules with a sea-monster; his expedition to Troy, to fetch the horses which Laomedon had refused him; and his war against the Pylians, when he destroyed the whole family of their king Neleus, with the exception of Nestor. Hesiod mentions several of the feats of Hercules distinctly, but knows nothing of their number 12. The selection of these 12 from the great number of feats ascribed to Hercules is probably the work of the Alexandrines. They are usually arranged in the following order. 1. *The fight with the Nemean lion.* The valley of Nemea, between Cleonae and Phlius, was inhabited by a monstrous lion, the offspring of Typhon and Echidna. Eurystheus ordered Hercules to bring him the skin of this monster. After using in vain his club and arrows against the lion, he strangled the animal with his own hands. He returned carrying the dead lion on his shoulders; but Eurystheus was so frightened at the gigantic strength of the hero, that he ordered him in future to deliver the account of his exploits outside the town. — 2. *Fight against the Lernaean hydra.* This monster, like the lion, was the offspring of Typhon and Echidna, and was brought up by Hera. It ravaged the country of Lernae near Argos, and dwelt in a swamp near the well of Amymone. It had 9 heads, of which the middle one was immortal. Hercules struck off its heads with his club; but in the place of the head he cut off, 2 new ones grew forth each time. A gigantic crab also came to the assistance of the hydra, and wounded Hercules. However, with the assistance of his faithful servant Iolaus, he burned away the heads of the hydra, and buried the ninth or immortal one under a huge rock. Having thus conquered the monster, he poisoned his arrows with its bile, whence the wounds inflicted by them became incurable. Eurystheus declared the victory unlawful, as Hercules had won it with the aid of Iolaus. — 3. *Capture of the Arcadian stag.* This animal had golden antlers and brazen feet. It had been dedicated to Artemis by the nymph Taygete, because the goddess had saved her from the pursuit of Zeus. Hercules was ordered to bring the animal alive to Mycenae. He pursued it in vain for a whole year: at length he wounded it with an arrow caught it, and carried it away on his shoulders. While in Arcadia, he was met by Artemis, who was angry with him for having outraged the animal

THE TWELVE LABOURS OF HERCULES.

See pp. 308—310.

I. Hercules and Nemean Lion.
(From a Roman Lamp.)

II. Hercules and Hydra.
(From a Marble at Naples.)

III. Hercules and Arcadian Stag.
(From a Statue at Naples.)

IV. Hercules and Boar, with Eurystheus.
(From a Marble at Naples.)

V. Hercules cleaning the Stables of Augeas.
(From a Relief at Rome.)

VI. Hercules and the Stymphalian Birds.
(From a Gem at Florence.)

[To face p. 308.

THE TWELVE LABOURS OF HERCULES.

See pp. 308—310.

VII. Hercules and Bull.
(From a Bas-relief in the Vatican.)

VIII. Hercules and Horses of Diomedes.
(From the Museo Borbonico.)

IX. Hercules and Geryon. (Museo Borbonico.)

XI. Hercules and the Hesperides.
(From a Bas-relief at Rome.)

XII. Hercules and Cerberus.
(Millin, Tombeaux de Canosa.)

To face p. 309.]

sacred to her; but he succeeded in soothing her anger, and carried his prey to Mycenae. According to some statements, he killed the stag. — 4. *Destruction of the Erymanthian boar.* This animal, which Hercules was ordered to bring alive to Eurystheus, had descended from mount Erymanthus into Psophis. Hercules chased him through the deep snow, and having thus worn him out, he caught him in a net, and carried him to Mycenae. Other traditions place the hunt of the Erymanthian boar in Thessaly, and some even in Phrygia. It must be observed that this and the subsequent labours of Hercules are connected with certain subordinate labours, called *Parerga* (Πάρεργα). The first of these parerga is the fight of Hercules with the Centaurs. In his pursuit of the boar he came to the centaur Pholus, who had received from Dionysus a cask of excellent wine. Hercules opened it, contrary to the wish of his host, and the delicious fragrance attracted the other centaurs, who besieged the grotto of Pholus. Hercules drove them away; they fled to the house of Chiron; and Hercules, eager in his pursuit, wounded Chiron, his old friend, with one of his poisoned arrows; in consequence of which Chiron died. [CHIRON.] Pholus likewise was wounded by one of the arrows, which by accident fell on his foot and killed him. This fight with the centaurs gave rise to the establishment of mysteries, by which Demeter intended to purify the hero from the blood he had shed against his own will. — 5. *Cleansing of the stables of Augeas.* Eurystheus imposed upon Hercules the task of cleansing in one day the stalls of Augeas, king of Elis. Augeas had a herd of 3000 oxen, whose stalls had not been cleansed for 30 years. Hercules, without mentioning the command of Eurystheus, went to Augeas, and offered to cleanse his stalls in one day, if he would give him the 10th part of his cattle. Augeas agreed to the terms; and Hercules after taking Phyleus, the son of Augeas, as his witness, led the rivers Alpheus and Peneus through the stalls, which were thus cleansed in a single day. But Augeas, who learned that Hercules had undertaken the work by the command of Eurystheus, refused to give him the reward. His son Phyleus then bore witness against his father, who exiled him from Elis. Eurystheus however declared the exploit null and void, because Hercules had stipulated with Augeas for a reward for performing it. At a later time Hercules invaded Elis, and killed Augeas and his sons. After this he is said to have founded the Olympic games. — 6. *Destruction of the Stymphalian birds.* These voracious birds had been brought up by Ares. They had brazen claws, wings, and beaks, used their feathers as arrows, and ate human flesh. They dwelt on a lake near Stymphalus in Arcadia, from which Hercules was ordered by Eurystheus to expel them. When Hercules undertook the task, Athena provided him with a brazen rattle, by the noise of which he startled the birds; and, as they attempted to fly away, he killed them with his arrows. According to some accounts, he only drove the birds away; and they appeared again in the island of Aretias, where they were found by the Argonauts. — 7. *Capture of the Cretan bull.* According to some this bull was the one which had carried Europa across the sea. According to others, the bull had been sent out of the sea by Poseidon, that Minos might offer it in sacrifice. But Minos was so charmed with the beauty of the animal, that he

kept it, and sacrificed another in its stead. Poseidon punished Minos, by driving the bull mad, and causing it to commit great havoc in the island. Hercules was ordered by Eurystheus to catch the bull, and Minos willingly allowed him to do so. Hercules accomplished the task, and brought the bull home on his shoulders; but he then set the animal free again. The bull now roamed through Greece, and at last came to Marathon, where we meet it again in the stories of Theseus. — 8. *Capture of the mares of the Thracian Diomedes.* This Diomedes, king of the Bistones in Thrace, fed his horses with human flesh. Eurystheus ordered Hercules to bring these animals to Mycenae. With a few companions, he seized the animals, and conducted them to the sea coast. But here he was overtaken by the Bistones. During the fight he entrusted the mares to his friend Abderus, who was devoured by them. Hercules defeated the Bistones, killed Diomedes whose body he threw before the mares, built the town of Abdera in honour of his unfortunate friend, and then returned to Mycenae, with the mares which had become tame after eating the flesh of their master. The mares were afterwards set free, and destroyed on Mt. Olympus by wild beasts. — 9. *Seizure of the girdle of the queen of the Amazons.* Hippolyte, the queen of the Amazons possessed a girdle, which she had received from Ares. Admete, the daughter of Eurystheus, wished to obtain this girdle; and Hercules was therefore sent to fetch it. He was accompanied by a number of volunteers, and after various adventures in Europe and Asia, he at length reached the country of the Amazons. Hippolyte at first received him kindly, and promised him her girdle; but Hera having excited the Amazons against him, a contest ensued, in which Hercules killed their queen. He then took her girdle, and carried it with him. In this expedition Hercules killed the 2 sons of Boreas, Calais and Zetes; and he also begot 3 sons by Echidna, in the country of the Hyperboreans. On his way home he landed in Troas, where he rescued Hesione from the monster sent against her by Poseidon; in return for which service her father Laomedon promised him the horses he had received from Zeus as a compensation for Ganymedes. But, as Laomedon did not keep his word, Hercules on leaving threatened to make war against Troy. He landed in Thrace, where he slew Sarpedon, and at length returned through Macedonia to Peloponnesus. — 10. *Capture of the oxen of Geryones in Erythia.* Geryones, the monster with 3 bodies, lived in the fabulous island of Erythia (the reddish), so called because it lay under the rays of the setting sun in the W. This island was originally placed off the coast of Epirus, but was afterwards identified either with Gades or the Balearic islands, and was at all times believed to be in the distant W. The oxen of Geryones were guarded by the giant Eurytion and the two-headed dog Orthrus; and Hercules was commanded by Eurystheus to fetch them. After traversing various countries, he reached at length the frontiers of Libya and Europe, where he erected 2 pillars (Calpe and Abyla) on the 2 sides of the straits of Gibraltar, which were hence called the pillars of Hercules. Being annoyed by the heat of the sun, Hercules shot at Helios, who so much admired his boldness, that he presented him with a golden cup or boat, in which he sailed to Erythia. He there slew Eurytion and his dog, as well as Geryones, and sailed with his booty to Tartessus, where he returned the golden cup (boat) to Helios. On his way home he passed through Gaul, Italy, Illyricum and Thrace, and met with numerous adventures, which are variously embellished by the poets. Many attempts were made to deprive him of the oxen, but he at length brought them in safety to Eurystheus, who sacrificed them to Hera. These 10 labours were performed by Hercules in the space of 8 years and 1 month; but as Eurystheus declared 2 of them to have been performed unlawfully, he commanded him to accomplish 2 more. — 11. *Fetching the golden apples of the Hesperides.* This was particularly difficult, since Hercules did not know where to find them. They were the apples which Hera had received at her wedding from Ge, and which she had entrusted to the keeping of the Hesperides and the dragon Ladon, on Mt. Atlas, in the country of the Hyperboreans. [For details see HESPER-IDES.] After various adventures in Europe, Asia and Africa, Hercules at length arrived at Mt. Atlas. On the advice of Prometheus, he sent Atlas to fetch the apples, and in the meantime bore the weight of heaven for him. Atlas returned with the apples, but refused to take the burden of heaven on his shoulders again. Hercules, however, contrived by a stratagem to get the apples, and hastened away. On his return Eurystheus made him a present of the apples; but Hercules dedicated them to Athena, who restored them to their former place. Some traditions add that Hercules killed the dragon Ladon. — 12. *Bringing Cerberus from the lower world.* This was the most difficult of the 12 labours of Hercules. He descended into Hades, near Tae-narum in Laconia, accompanied by Hermes and Athena. He delivered Theseus and Ascalaphus from their torments. He obtained permission from Pluto to carry Cerberus to the upper world, provided he could accomplish it without force of arms. Hercules succeeded in seizing the monster and carrying it to the upper world; and after he had shown it to Eurystheus, he carried it back again to the lower world. Some traditions connect the descent of Hercules into the lower world with a contest with Hades, as we see even in the Iliad (v. 397), and more particularly in the Alcestis of Euripides (24, 846). — Besides these 12 labours, Hercules performed several other feats without being commanded by Eurystheus. These feats were called *Parerga* by the ancients. Several of them were interwoven with the 12 labours and have been already described: those which had no connection with the 12 labours are spoken of below. After Hercules had performed the 12 labours, he was released from the servitude of Eurystheus, and returned to Thebes. He there gave Megara in marriage to Iolaus; and he wished to gain in marriage for himself Iole, the daughter of Eurytus, king of Oechalia. Eurytus promised his daughter to the man who should conquer him and his sons in shooting with the bow. Hercules defeated them; but Eurytus and his sons, with the exception of Iphitus, refused to give Iole to him, because he had murdered his own children. Soon afterwards the oxen of Eurytus were carried off, and it was suspected that Hercules was the offender. Iphitus again defended Hercules, and requested his assistance in searching after the oxen. Hercules agreed; but when the 2 had arrived at Tiryns, Hercules, in a fit of madness, threw his friend down from the wall, and killed him. Dei-phobus of Amyclae purified Hercules from this

murder, but he was, nevertheless, attacked by a severe illness. Hercules then repaired to Delphi to obtain a remedy, but the Pythia refused to answer his questions. A struggle ensued between Hercules and Apollo, and the combatants were not separated till Zeus sent a flash of lightning between them. The oracle now declared that he would be restored to health, if he would serve 3 years for wages, and surrender his earnings to Eurytus, as an atonement for the murder of Iphitus. Thereupon he became a servant to Omphale, queen of Lydia, and widow of Tmolus. Later writers describe Hercules as living effeminately during his residence with Omphale: he span wool, it is said, and sometimes put on the garments of a woman, while Omphale wore his lion's skin. Accord-ing to other accounts he nevertheless performed several great feats during this time. He undertook an expedition to Colchis, which brought him into connection with the Argonauts; he took part in the Calydonian hunt, and met Theseus on his landing from Troezene on the Corinthian isthmus. An expedition to India, which was mentioned in some traditions, may likewise be inserted in this place. —When the time of his servitude had expired, he sailed against Troy, took the city, and killed Lao-medon, its king. On his return from Troy, a storm drove him on the island of Cos, where he was attacked by the Meropes; but he defeated them and killed their king, Eurypylus. It was about this time that the gods sent for him in order to fight against the Gigantes. [GIGANTES]. — Soon after his return to Argos, he marched against Augeas, as has been related above. He then proceeded against Pylos, which he took, and killed Periclymenus, a son of Neleus. He next advanced against Lacedaemon, to punish the sons of Hippo-coon, for having assisted Neleus and slain Oeonus, the son of Licymnius. He took Lacedaemon, and assigned the government of it to Tyndareus. On his return to Tegea, he became, by Auge, the father of Telephus [AUGE]; and he then proceeded to Calydon, where he obtained Deianira, the daughter of Oeneus, for his wife, after fighting with Achelous for her. [DEIANIRA; ACHELOUS.] After Hercules had been married to Deianira nearly 3 years, he accidentally killed at a banquet in the house of Oeneus, the boy Eunomus. In accordance with the law Hercules went into exile, taking with him his wife Deianira. On their road they came to the river Evenus, across which the centaur Nessus carried travellers for a small sum of money. Her-cules himself forded the river, but gave Deianira to Nessus to carry across. Nessus attempted to outrage her: Hercules heard her screaming, and shot an arrow into the heart of Nessus. The dying centaur called out to Deianira to take his blood with her, as it was a sure means of preserving the love of her husband. He then conquered the Dryopes, and assisted Aegimius, king of the Dorians, against the Lapithae. [AEGIMIUS.] After this he took up his abode at Trachis, whence he marched against Eurytus of Oechalia. He took Oechalia killed Eurytus and his sons, and carried off his daughter Iole as a prisoner. On his return home he landed at Cenaeum, a promontory of Euboea, erected an altar to Zeus, and sent his companion, Lichas, to Trachis, in order to fetch him a white garment, which he intended to use during the sacrifice. Deianira, afraid lest Iole should supplant her in the affections of her husband, steeped the white garment he had demanded in the blood of Nessus. This blood had been poisoned by the arrow with which Hercules had shot Nessus; and accordingly as soon as the garment become warm on the body of Hercules, the poison penetrated into all his limbs, and caused him the most excruciating agony. He seized Lichas by his feet, and threw him into the sea. He wrenched off the garment, but it stuck to his flesh, and with it he tore away whole pieces from his body. In this state he was conveyed to Trachis. Deianira, on seeing what she had unwittingly done, hung herself. Hercules commanded Hyllus, his eldest son, by Deianira, to marry Iole as soon as he should arrive at the age of manhood. He then ascended Mt. Oeta, raised a pile of wood, on which he placed himself, and ordered it to be set on fire. No one ventured to obey him, until at length Poeas the shepherd, who passed by, was prevailed upon to comply with the desire of the suffering hero. When the pile was burning, a cloud came down from heaven, and amid peals of thunder carried him to Olympus, where he was honoured with immortality, became reconciled to Hera, and married her daughter Hebe, by whom he became the father of Alexiares and Anicetus. Immediately after his apotheosis, his friends offered sacrifices to him as a hero; and he was in course of time worshipped throughout all Greece both as a god and as a hero. His worship however prevailed more extensively among the Dorians than among any other of the Greek races. The sacrifices offered to him consisted principally of bulls, boars, rams and lambs.—The works of art in which Hercules was represented were extremely numerous, and of the greatest variety, for he was represented at all the various stages of his life, from the cradle to his death. But whether he appears as a child, a youth, a struggling hero, or as the immortal inhabitant of Olympus, his character is always one of heroic strength and energy. Specimens of every kind are still extant. The finest representation of the hero that has come down to us is the so-called Farnese Hercules, which was executed by Glycon. The hero is resting, leaning on his right arm, and his head reclining on his left hand: the whole figure is a most exquisite combination of peculiar softness with the greatest strength.—**II. Roman Traditions.** The worship of Hercules at Rome and in Italy is connected by Roman writers, with the hero's expedition to fetch the oxen of Geryones. They stated that Hercules on his return visited Italy, where he abolished human sacrifices among the Sabines, established the worship of fire, and slew Cacus, a robber, who had stolen his oxen. [Cacus.] The aborigines, and especially Evander, honoured Hercules with divine worship; and Hercules in return taught them the way in which he was to be worshipped, and entrusted the care of his worship to 2 distinguished families, the Potitii and Pinarii. [Pinaria Gens.] The Fabia gens traced its origin to Hercules; and Fauna and Acca Laurentia are called mistresses of Hercules. In this manner the Romans connected their earliest legends with Hercules. It should be observed that in the Italian traditions the hero bore the name of Recaranus, and this Recaranus was afterwards identified with the Greek Hercules. He had 2 temples at Rome. One was a small round temple of Hercules Victor, or Hercules Triumphalis, between the river and the Circus Maximus; in front of which was

the ara maxima, on which, after a triumph, the tenth of the booty was deposited for distribution among the citizens. The 2nd temple stood near the porta trigemina, and contained a bronze statue and the altar on which Hercules himself was believed to have once offered a sacrifice. Here the city praetor offered every year a young cow, which was consumed by the people within the sanctuary. At Rome Hercules was connected with the Muses, whence he is called *Musagetes*, and was represented with a lyre, of which there is no trace in Greece. —**III. Traditions of other nations.** The ancients themselves expressly mention several heroes of the name of Hercules, who occur among the principal nations of the ancient world. 1. *The Egyptian Hercules*, whose Egyptian name was Som, or Dsom, or Chon, or, according to Pausanias, Maceris, was a son of Amon or Nilus. He was placed by the Egyptians in the 2nd of the series of the evolutions of their gods. — 2. *The Cretan Hercules*, one of the Idaean Dactyls, was believed to have founded the temple of Zeus at Olympia, but to have come originally from Egypt. He was worshipped with funeral sacrifices, and was regarded as a magician, like other ancient daemones of Crete. — 3. *The Indian Hercules*, was called by the unintelligible name Dorsanes (Δορσάνης). The later Greeks believed that he was their own hero, who had visited India; and they related that in India he became the father of many sons and daughters by Pandaea, and the ancestral hero of the Indian kings. —4. *The Phoenician Hercules*, whom the Egyptians considered to be more ancient than their own, was worshipped in all the Phoenician colonies, such as Carthage and Gades, down to the time of Constantine, and it is said that children were sacrificed to him. — 5. *The Celtic and Germanic Hercules* is said to have founded Alesia and Nemausus, and to have become the father of the Celtic race. We become acquainted with him in the accounts of the expedition of the Greek Hercules against Geryones. We must either suppose that the Greek Hercules was identified with native heroes of those northern countries, or that the notions about Hercules had been introduced there from the E.

Hercŭles (Ἡρακλῆς), a son of Alexander the Great by Barsine, the widow of the Rhodian Memnon. In B.C. 310 he was brought forward by Polysperchon as a pretender to the Macedonian throne; but he was murdered by Polysperchon himself in the following year, when the latter became reconciled to Cassander.

Hercŭlis Columnae. [Abyla; Calpe.]
Hercŭlis Monoeci Portus. [Monoecus.]
Hercŭlis Portus. [Cosa.]
Hercŭlis Promontŏrium (*C. Spartivento*), the most S.ly point of Italy in Bruttium.
Hercŭlis Silva, a forest in Germany, sacred to Hercules, E. of the Visurgis.

Hercȳnĭa Silva, Hercynĭus Saltus, Hercynĭum Jugum, an extensive range of mountains in Germany, covered with forests, is described by Caesar (*B. G.* vi. 24) as 9 days' journey in breadth, and more than 60 days' journey in length, extending E. from the territories of the Helvetii, Nemetes, and Rauraci, parallel to the Danube. to the frontiers of the Dacians. Under this general name Caesar appears to have included all the mountains and forests in the S. and centre of Germany, the *Black Forest, Odenwald, Thüringerwald*, the *Harz*, the *Erzgebirge*, the *Riesengebirge*, &c. As the Romans became better acquainted with Germany, the name was confined to narrower limits. Pliny and Tacitus use it to indicate the range of mountains between the Thüringerwald and the Carpathian mountains The name is still preserved in the modern *Harz* and *Erz.*

Herdōnīa (Herdoniensis : *Ordona*), a town in Apulia, was destroyed by Hannibal, who removed its inhabitants to Thurii and Metapontum ; it was rebuilt by the Romans, but remained a place of no importance.

Herdōnīus. 1. **Turnus**, of Aricia in Latium, endeavoured to rouse the Latins against Tarquinius Superbus, and was in consequence falsely accused by Tarquinius, and put to death. — 2. **Applus**, a Sabine chieftain, who, in B. c. 460, with a band of outlaws and slaves, made himself master of the capitol. On the 4th day from his entry the capitol was re-taken, and Herdonius and nearly all his followers were slain.

Herennīa Gens, originally Samnite, and by the Samnite invasion established in Campania, became at a later period a plebeian house at Rome. The Herennii were a family of rank in Italy, and are frequently mentioned in the time of the Samnite and Punic wars. They were the hereditary patrons of the Marii.

Herennīus 1. **Modestinus.** [MODESTINUS.] — 2. **Pontīus.** [PONTIUS.] — 3. **Seneclo.** [SENECIO.]

Hērillus ("Ηριλλος), of Carthage, a Stoic philosopher, was the disciple of Zeno of Cittium. He did not, however, confine himself to the opinions of his master, but held some doctrines directly opposed to them. He held that the chief good consisted in knowledge (ἐπιστήμη). This notion is often attacked by Cicero.

Hermaeum, or, in Latin, **Mercurii Promontorium** ('Ερμαία ἄκρα). 1. (*Cape Bon*, Arab. *Ras Addar*), the headland which forms the E. extremity of the Sinus Carthaginiensis, and the extreme N.E. point of the Carthaginian territory (aft. the province of Africa) opposite to Lilybaeum, the space between the 2 being the shortest distance between Sicily and Africa. — 2. (*Ras el Ashan*), a promontory on the coast of the Greater Syrtis, 50 stadia W. of Leptis. — There were other promontories of the name on the coast of Africa.

Hermăgŏras ('Ερμαγόρας). 1. Of Temnos, a distinguished Greek rhetorician of the time of Cicero. He belonged to the Rhodian school of oratory, but is known chiefly as a teacher of rhetoric. He devoted particular attention to what is called the *invention*, and made a peculiar division of the parts of an oration, which differed from that adopted by other rhetoricians. — 2. Surnamed Carion, a Greek rhetorician, taught rhetoric at Rome in the time of Augustus. He was a disciple of Theodorus of Gadara.

Hermaphrōdītus ('Ερμαφρόδιτος), son of Hermes and Aphrodite, and consequently great-grandson of Atlas, whence he is called *Atlantiades* or *Atlantius.* (Ov. *Met.* iv. 368). He had inherited the beauty of both his parents, and was brought up by the nymphs of Mount Ida. In his 15th year he went to Caria. In the neighbourhood of Halicarnassus he laid down by the fountain of Salmacis. The nymph of the fountain fell in love with him, and tried in vain to win his affections. Once when he was bathing in the fountain, she embraced him, and prayed to the gods that she

might be united with him for ever. The gods granted the request, and the bodies of the youth and the nymph became united together, but retained the characteristics of each sex. Hermaphroditus, on becoming aware of the change, prayed that in future every one who bathed in the well might be metamorphosed in the same manner.

Hermarchus ('Ερμαρχος), of Mytilene, a rhetorician, became afterwards a disciple of Epicurus, who left to him his garden, and appointed him his successor in his school, about B. C. 270. He wrote several works, all of which are lost.

Hermas ('Ερμᾶς), a disciple of the Apostle Paul, and one of the apostolic fathers. He is supposed to be the same person as the Hermas who is mentioned in St. Paul's epistle to the Romans (xvi. 14). He wrote in Greek a work entitled *The Shepherd of Hermas*, of which a Latin translation is still extant. Its object is to instruct persons in the duties of the Christian life. Edited by Cotelier in his *Patres Apostol.* Paris, 1672.

Hermes ('Ερμῆς, 'Ερμείας, Dor. 'Ερμᾶς), called **Mercūrius** by the Romans. The Greek Hermes was a son of Zeus and Maia, the daughter of Atlas, and born in a cave of Mt. Cyllene in Arcadia, whence he is called *Atlantiades* or *Cyllenius.* A few hours after his birth, he escaped from his cradle, went to Pieria, and carried off some of the oxen of Apollo. In the Iliad and Odyssey this tradition is not mentioned, though Hermes is characterised as a cunning thief. That he might not be discovered by the traces of his footsteps, he put on sandals, and drove the oxen to Pylos, where he killed 2, and concealed the rest in a cave. The skins of the slaughtered animals were nailed to a rock ; and part of their flesh was cooked and eaten, and the rest burnt. Thereupon he returned to Cyllene, where he found a tortoise at the entrance of his native cave. He took the animal's shell, drew strings across it, and thus invented the lyre, on which he immediately played. Apollo, by his prophetic power, had meantime discovered the thief, and went to Cyllene to charge Hermes with the crime before his mother Maia. She showed to the god the child in its cradle ; but Apollo carried the boy before Zeus, and demanded back his oxen. Zeus commanded him to comply with the demand of Apollo, but Hermes denied that he had stolen the cattle. As, however, he saw that his assertions were not believed, he conducted Apollo to Pylos, and restored to him his oxen ; but when Apollo heard the sounds of the lyre, he was so charmed that he allowed Hermes to keep the animals. Hermes now invented the syrinx, and after disclosing his inventions to Apollo, the 2 gods concluded an intimate friendship with each other. Apollo presented his young friend with his own golden shepherd's staff, and taught him the art of prophesying by means of dice. Zeus made him his own herald, and likewise the herald of the gods of the lower world. — The principal feature in the traditions about Hermes consists in his being the herald of the gods, and in this capacity he appears even in the Homeric poems. His original character of an ancient Pelasgian, or Arcadian divinity of nature, gradually disappeared in the legends. As the herald of the gods, he is the god of eloquence, for the heralds are the public speakers in the assemblies and on other occasions. The gods especially employed him as messenger, when eloquence was required to attain the desired object. Hence the tongues of sacrificial animals were offered to aim. As heralds and messengers are usually men of prudence and circumspection, Hermes was also the god of prudence and skill in all the relations of social intercourse. These qualities were combined with similar ones, such as cunning, both in words and actions, and even fraud, perjury, and the inclination to steal ; but acts of this kind were committed by Hermes always with a certain skill, dexterity, and even gracefulness. — Being endowed with this shrewdness and sagacity, he was regarded as the author of a variety of inventions, and, besides the lyre and syrinx, he is said to have invented the alphabet, numbers, astronomy, music, the art of fighting, gymnastics, the cultivation of the olive tree, measures, weights, and many other things. The powers which he possessed himself he conferred upon those mortals and heroes who enjoyed his favour ; and all who possessed them were under his especial protection, or are called his sons. He was employed by the gods, and more especially by Zeus, on a variety of occasions which are recorded in ancient story. Thus he led Priam to Achilles to fetch the body of Hector ; tied Ixion to the wheel ; conducted Hera, Aphrodite, and Athena to Paris ; fastened Prometheus to Mt. Caucasus ; rescued Dionysus after his birth from the flames, or received him from the hands of Zeus to carry him to Athamas ; sold Hercules to Omphale ; and was ordered by Zeus to carry off Io, who was metamorphosed into a cow, and guarded by Argus, whom he slew. [ARGUS.] From this murder he is very commonly called Ἀργειφόντης. —In the Trojan war Hermes was on the side of the Greeks. His ministry to Zeus was not confined to the offices of herald and messenger, but he was also his charioteer and cupbearer. As dreams are sent by Zeus, Hermes conducts them to man, and hence he is also described as the god who had it in his power to send refreshing sleep, or take it away. Another important function of Hermes was to conduct the shades of the dead from the upper into the lower world, whence he is called ψυχοπομπός, νεκροπομπός, ψυχαγωγός, &c.—The idea of his being the herald and messenger of the gods, of his travelling from place to place and concluding treaties, necessarily implied the notion that he was the promoter of social intercourse and of commerce among men. In this capacity he was regarded as the maintainer of peace, and as the god of roads, who protected travellers, and punished those who refused to assist travellers who had mistaken their way. Hence the Athenian generals, on setting out on an expedition, offered sacrifices to Hermes, surnamed Hegemonius, or Agetor ; and numerous statues of the god were erected on roads, at doors and gates, from which circumstance he derived a variety of surnames and epithets. As the god of commerce he was called διέμπορος, ἐμπολαῖος, παλιγκάπηλος, κερδέμπορος, ἀγοραῖος, &c. As commerce is the source of wealth, he was also the god of gain and riches, especially of sudden and unexpected riches, such as are acquired by commerce. As the giver of wealth and good luck (πλουτοδότης), he also presided over the game of dice. — Hermes was believed to be the inventor of sacrifices. Hence he not only acts the part of a herald at sacrifices, but is also the protector of sacrificial animals, and was believed in particular to increase the fertility of sheep. For this reason he was especially worshipped by shepherds, and is mentioned in connection with Pan and the Nymphs. This

feature in the character of Hermes is a remnant of the ancient Arcadian religion, in which he was the fertilising god of the earth, who conferred his blessings on man. — Hermes was likewise the patron of all the gymnastic games of the Greeks. This idea seems to be of late origin, for in Homer no trace of it is found. Athens appears to have been the first place in which he was worshipped in this capacity. At a later time almost all gymnasia were under his protection ; and the Greek artists derived their ideal of the god from the gymnasium, and represented him as a youth whose limbs were beautifully and harmoniously developed by gymnastic exercises. — The most ancient seat of the worship of Hermes is Arcadia, the land of his birth, where Lycaon, the son of Pelasgus, is said to have built to him the first temple. From thence his worship was carried to Athens, and ultimately spread through all Greece. The festivals celebrated in his honour were called *Hermaea.* (*Dict. of Ant. s. v.*) His temples and statues (*Dict. of Ant. s. v. Hermae*) were extremely numerous in Greece. Among the things sacred to him were the palm tree, the tortoise, the number 4, and several kinds of fish ; and the sacrifices offered to him consisted of incense, honey, cakes, pigs, and especially lambs and young goats. — The principal attributes of Hermes are : 1. A travelling hat with a broad brim, which in later times was adorned with 2 small wings. 2. The staff (ῥάβδος or σκῆπτρον), which he bore as a herald, and had received from Apollo. In late works of art the white ribbons which surrounded the herald's staff were changed into 2 serpents. 3. The sandals (πέδιλα). They were beautiful and golden, and carried the god across land and sea with the rapidity of wind ; at the ankles of the god they were provided with wings, whence he is called πτηνοπέδιλος, or *alipes.* —The Roman MERCURIUS is spoken of separately.

Hermes Trismegistus (Ἑρμῆς Τρισμέγιστος), the reputed author of a variety of works, some of which are still extant. The Greek god Hermes was identified with the Egyptian Thot, or Theut, as early as the time of Plato. The New Platonists regarded the Egyptian Hermes as the source of all knowledge and thought, or the λόγος embodied, and hence called him Trismegistus. A vast number of works on philosophy and religion, written by the New Platonists, were ascribed to this Hermes ; from whom it was pretended that Pythagoras and Plato had derived all their knowledge. Most of these works were probably written in the 4th century of our era. The most important of them is entitled *Poemander* (from ποιμήν, a shepherd, pastor), apparently in imitation of the *Pastor* of Hermas. [HERMAS.] This work is in the form of a dialogue. It treats of nature, the creation of the world, the deity, his nature and attributes, the human soul, knowledge, &c.

Hermesianax (Ἑρμησιάναξ), of Colophon, a distinguished elegiac poet, lived in the time of Alexander the Great. His chief work was an elegiac poem, in 3 books, addressed to his mistress, Leontium, whose name formed the title of the poem. His fragments are edited by Rigler and Axt, Colon. 1828, and by Bailey, Lond. 1839.

Hermias or **Hermeias** (Ἑρμείας or Ἑρμίας). 1. Tyrant of Atarneus and Assos in Mysia, celebrated as the friend and patron of Aristotle. Aristotle remained with Hermias 3 years, from B. C. 347 to 344, in the latter of which years Hermias was seized by Mentor, the Greek general of the Persian king, and sent as a captive to the Persian court, where he was put to death. Aristotle married Pythias, the adopted daughter of Hermias, and celebrated the praises of his benefactor in an ode addressed to Virtue, which is still extant. — **2.** A Christian writer, who lived about A. D. 180, was the author of an extant work, entitled Διασυρμὸς τῶν ἔξω φιλοσόφων, in which the Greek philosophers are held up to ridicule. Edited with Tatianus by Worth, Oxon. 1700.

Herminia Gens, a very ancient patrician house at Rome, which appears in the first Etruscan war with the republic, B. C. 506, and vanishes from history in 448. T. Herminius was one of the 3 heroes who kept the Sublician bridge along with Horatius Cocles against the whole force of Porsena.

Herminius Mons (*Sierra de la Estrella*), the chief mountain in Lusitania, S. of the Durius, from 7000 to 8000 feet high, called in the middle ages *Hermeno* or *Arminha.*

Hermione ('Ἑρμιόνη), the beautiful daughter of Menelaus and Helena. She had been promised in marriage to Orestes before the Trojan war; but Menelaus after his return home married her to Neoptolemus (Pyrrhus). Thereupon Orestes claimed Hermione for himself; but Neoptolemus haughtily refused to give her up. Orestes, in revenge, incited the Delphians against him, and Neoptolemus was slain. Hermione afterwards married Orestes, whom she had always loved, and bore him a son Tisamenus. The history of Hermione is related with various modifications. According to some Menelaus betrothed her at Troy to Neoptolemus; but in the meantime her grandfather, Tyndareus, promised her to Orestes, and actually gave her in marriage to him. Neoptolemus, on his return, took possession of her by force, but was slain soon after either at Delphi or in his own home at Phthia.

Hermione ('Ἑρμιόνη: 'Ἑρμιονεύς: *Kastri*), a town of Argolis, but originally independent of Argos, was situated on a promontory on the E. coast, and on a bay of the sea, which derived its name from the town (Hermionicus Sinus). Its territory was called **Hermionis.** It was originally inhabited by the Dryopes; and, in consequence of its isolated position, it became a flourishing city at an early period. It contained several temples, and among them a celebrated one of Demeter Chthonia. At a later time it joined the Achaean League.

Hermiones. [GERMANIA.]

Hermippus ("Ἑρμιππος). 1. An Athenian poet of the old comedy, vehemently attacked Pericles and Aspasia. — **2.** Of Smyrna, a distinguished philosopher, was a disciple of Callimachus of Alexandria, and flourished about B. C. 200. He wrote a great biographical work (Βίοι), which is frequently referred to by later writers. — **3.** Of Berytus, a grammarian, who flourished under Trajan and Hadrian.

Hermisium, a town in the Tauric Chersonesus, on the Cimmerian Bosporus.

Hermocrates ('Ἑρμοκράτης), a Syracusan of rank, and an able statesman and orator, was chosen one of the Syracusan generals, B. C. 414, in order to oppose the Athenians. He afterwards served under Gylippus, when the latter took the command of the Syracusan forces; and after the destruction of the Athenian armament he attempted to save the lives of Nicias and Demosthenes. He then employed all his influence to induce his countrymen

to support with vigour the Lacedaemonians in the war in Greece itself. He was with two colleagues appointed to the command of a small fleet, which the Syracusans sent to the assistance of the Lacedaemonians. But during his absence from home, he was banished by the Syracusans (410). Having obtained support from the Persian satrap Pharnabazus, he returned to Sicily, and endeavoured to effect his restoration to his native city by force of arms, but was slain in an attack which he made upon Syracuse in 407.

Hermodorus ('Ἑρμόδωρος). 1. Of Ephesus, a person of distinction, was expelled by his fellow-citizens, and is said to have gone to Rome, and to have explained to the decemvirs the Greek laws, and thus assisted them in drawing up the laws of the 12 Tables, B. C. 451. — **2.** A disciple of Plato, is said to have circulated the works of Plato, and to have sold them in Sicily. He wrote a work on Plato. — **3.** Of Salamis, the architect of the temple of Mars in the Flaminian Circus.

Hermogenes ('Ἑρμογένης). 1. A son of Hipponicus, and a brother of the wealthy Callias, is introduced by Plato as one of the speakers in his "Cratylus," where he maintains that all the words of a language were formed by an agreement of men among themselves. — **2.** A celebrated Greek rhetorician, was a native of Tarsus, and lived in the reign of M. Aurelius, A. D. 161—180. At the age of 15 his eloquence excited the admiration of M. Aurelius. He was shortly afterwards appointed public teacher of rhetoric, and at the age of 17 he began his career as a writer; but unfortunately when he was 25, his mental powers gave way, and he never recovered their full use, although he lived to an advanced age. After his death his heart is said to have been found covered with hair. His works 5 in number, which are still extant, form together a complete system of rhetoric, and were for a long time used in all the rhetorical schools as manuals. They are: 1. Τέχνη ῥητορικὴ περὶ τῶν στάσεων. 2. Περὶ εὑρέσεως (*De Inventione*). 3. Περὶ ἰδεῶν (*De Formis Oratoriis*). 4. Περὶ μεθόδου δεινότητος (*De apto et solerti genere dicendi Methodus*). 5. Προγυμνάσματα, An abridgment of the latter work was made by Aphthonius, in consequence of which the original fell into oblivion. The works of Hermogenes are printed in Walz's *Rhetor. Graec.* — **3.** An architect of Alabanda, in Caria who invented what was called the pseudodipterus, that is, a form of a temple, with *apparently* two rows of columns. His great object as an architect was to increase the taste for the Ionic form of temples, in preference to Doric temples.

Hermogenes, M. Tigellius, a notorious detractor of Horace, who calls him (*Sat.* i. 3. 129) however *optimus cantor et modulator.* He was opposed to Satires altogether, was a man without talent, but yet had a foolish fancy for trying his hand at literature. It is conjectured that, under the fictitious name of Pantolabus (*Sat.* i. 8. 11, ii. 1. 21.), Horace alludes to Hermogenes, for the prosody of the 2 names is the same, so that one may be substituted for the other.

Hermogenianus, the latest Roman jurist from whom there is an extract in the Digest, lived in the time of Constantine the Great. It is probable that he was the compiler of the Codex Hermogenianus, but so many persons of the same name lived nearly at the same time, that this cannot be affirmed with certainty.

Hermŏlāus ('Ερμόλαος), a Macedonian youth, and a page of Alexander the Great. During a hunting party in Bactria, B. c. 327, he slew a wild boar, without waiting to allow Alexander the first blow, whereupon the king ordered him to be flogged. Incensed at this indignity, Hermolaus formed a conspiracy against the king's life; but the plot was discovered, and Hermolaus and his accomplices were stoned to death by the Macedonians.

Hermonassa. 1. A town of the Sindi at the entrance of the Cimmerian Bosporus, founded by the Mytilenaeans, called after Hermonassa, the wife of the founder, who died during its foundation, and left to her the sovereignty. — 2. A town on the coast of Pontus, near Trapezus.

Hermonthis ('Ερμωνθις: Erment, Ru.), the chief city of the Nomos Hermonthites, in Upper Egypt, on the W. bank of the Nile, a little above Thebes.

Hermŏpŏlis ('Ερμόπολις, Ἕρμου πόλις). 1. Parva (ἡ μικρά: Damanhour), a city of Lower Egypt, the capital of the Nomos of Alexandria, stood upon the canal which connected the Canopic branch of the Nile with the Lake Mareotis. — 2. Magna (ἡ μεγάλη: nr. Eshmounein, Ru.), the capital of the Nomos Hermopolites, in the Heptanomis, or Middle Egypt, and one of the oldest cities in the land, stood on the W. bank of the Nile, a little below the confines of Upper Egypt. At the boundary line itself was a military station, or custom house, called 'Ερμοπολιτικὴ φυλακή, for collecting a toll on goods entering the Heptanomis. Hermopolis was a chief seat of the worship of Anubis (Cynocephalus); and it was the sacred burial-place of the Ibis.

Hermŏtimus ('Ερμότιμος). 1. A mathematician of Colophon, was one of the immediate predecessors of Euclid, and the discoverer of several geometrical propositions. — 2. Of Clazomenae, an early Greek philosopher of uncertain date, belonged to the Ionic school. Some traditions represent him as a mysterious person, gifted with supernatural power, by which his soul, apart from the body, wandered from place to place, bringing tidings of distant events in incredibly short spaces of time. At length his enemies burned his body, in the absence of the soul, which put an end to his wanderings.

Hermundūri, one of the most powerful nations of Germany, belonged to the Suevic race, dwelt between the Main and the Danube, and were bounded by the Sudeti mountains in the N., the Agri Decumates of the Romans in the W. and S., the Narisci on the E., the Cherusci on the N.E., and the Catti on the N.W. They were for a long time the allies of the Romans; but along with the other German tribes they assisted the Marcomanni in the great war against the Romans in the reign of M. Aurelius. After this time they are rarely mentioned as a separate people, but are included under the general name of Suevi.

Hermus (τὸ Ἕρμος: Ἕρμειος), a demus in Attica, belonging to the tribe Acamantis, on the road from Athens to Eleusis.

Hermus (Ἕρμος; Ghiediz-Chai), a considerable river of Asia Minor, rises in Mt. Dindymene (Morad-Dagh) in Phrygia; flows through Lydia, watering the plain N. of Sardis, which was hence called Ἕρμου πεδίον; passes by Magnesia and Temnus; and falls into the Gulf of Smyrna, between Smyrna and Phocaea. It formed the boundary between Aeolia and Ionia. Its chief tributaries were the Hyllus, Cogamus, Pactolus, and Phryguus.

Hernĭci, a people in Latium, belonged to the Sabine race, and are said to have derived their name from the Marsic (Sabine) word herna, "rock." According to this etymology their name would signify "mountaineers." They inhabited the mountains of the Apennines between the lake Fucinus and the river Trerus, and were bounded on the N. by the Marsi and Aequi, and on the S. by the Volsci. Their chief town was ANAGNIA. They were a brave and warlike people, and long offered a formidable resistance to the Romans. The Romans formed a league with them on equal terms in the 3rd consulship of Sp. Cassius, B. c. 486. They were finally subdued by the Romans, 306.

Hērō. [LEANDER.]

Hērō (Ἥρων). 1. The Elder, a celebrated mathematician, was a native of Alexandria, and lived in the reigns of the Ptolemies Philadelphus and Evergetes (B. c. 285—222.) He is celebrated on account of his mechanical inventions, of which one of the best known is the common pneumatic experiment, called *Hero's fountain*, in which a jet of water is maintained by condensed air. We also find in his works a description of a *steam engine*, and of a double forcing pump used for a fire-engine. The following works of Hero are extant, though not in a perfect form: — 1. Χειροβαλλίστρας κατασκευὴ καὶ συμμετρία, *de Constructione et Mensura Manubalistae*. 2. Βελοποιϊκά, on the manufacture of darts. 3. Πνευματικά, or *Spiritalia*, the most celebrated of his works. 4. Περὶ αὐτοματοποιητικῶν, *de Automatorum Fabrica Libri duo*. All these works are published in the *Mathematici Veteres*, Paris, 1693. — 2. The Younger, a mathematician, is supposed to have lived under Heraclius (A. D. 610—641). The principal extant works assigned to him are: — 1. *De Machinis bellicis*. 2. *Geodaesia*, on practical geometry. 3. *De Obsidione repellenda*. Published in the *Mathematici Veteres*.

Hērōdes I. ('Ηρώδης), commonly called Herod. 1. Surnamed the Great, king of the Jews, was the second son of Antipater, and consequently of Idumaean origin. [ANTIPATER, No. 3.] When his father was appointed by Caesar procurator of Judaea, in B. c. 47, Herod, though only 25 years of age, obtained the government of Galilee. In 46 he obtained the government of Coele-Syria. After the death of Caesar (44), Herod first supported Cassius; but upon the arrival of Antony in Syria, in 41, he exerted himself to secure his favour, and completely succeeded in his object. In 40 he went to Rome, and obtained from Antony and Octavian a decree of the senate, constituting him king of Judaea. He supported Antony in the civil war against Octavian; but after the battle of Actium (31) he was pardoned by Octavian and confirmed in his kingdom. During the remainder of his reign he cultivated with assiduity the friendship of Augustus and his counsellor Agrippa, and enjoyed the highest favour both of the one and the other. He possessed a jealous temper and ungovernable passions. He put to death his beautiful wife Mariamne, whom he suspected without cause of adultery, and with whom he was violently in love; and at a later period he also put to death his two sons by Mariamne, Alexander and Aristobulus. His government, though cruel and tyrannical, was vigorous; and he was both feared and respected by his subjects and the surrounding nations. He especially loved to display his power and magnificence by costly and splendid public works. He commenced rebuilding the temple of Jerusalem; he rebuilt the city of Samaria, and bestowed on it the name of Sebaste; while he converted a small town on the sea-coast into a magnificent city, to which he gave the name of Caesarea. He adorned these new cities with temples, theatres, gymnasia, and other buildings in the Greek style; and he even ventured to erect a theatre at Jerusalem itself, and an amphitheatre without the walls, in which he exhibited combats of wild beasts and gladiators. In the last year of his reign Jesus Christ was born; and it must have been on his deathbed that he ordered that massacre of the children at Bethlehem which is recorded by the Evangelist. (Matth. ii. 16.) He died in the 37th year of his reign, and the 70th of his age, B. C. 4.[*] — 2. **Herodes Antipas**, son of Herod the Great, by Malthace, a Samaritan, obtained the tetrarchy of Galilee and Peraea, on his father's death, while the kingdom of Judaea devolved on his elder brother Archelaus. He married Herodias, the wife of his half-brother, Herod Philip, she having, in defiance of the Jewish law, divorced her first husband. He had been previously married to a daughter of the Arabian prince Aretas, who quitted him in disgust at this new alliance. Aretas thereupon invaded the dominions of Antipas, and defeated the army which was opposed to him. In A. D. 38, after the death of Tiberius, Antipas went to Rome to solicit from Caligula the title of king, which had just been bestowed upon his nephew, Herod Agrippa; but through the intrigues of Agrippa, who was high in the favour of the Roman emperor, Antipas was deprived of his dominions, and sent into exile at Lyons (39); he was subsequently removed to Spain, where he died. It was Herod Antipas who imprisoned and put to death John the Baptist, who had reproached him with his unlawful connexion with Herodias. It was before him also that Christ was sent by Pontius Pilate at Jerusalem, as belonging to his jurisdiction, on account of his supposed Galilean origin. — 3. **Herodes Agrippa.** [AGRIPPA.] — 4. Brother of Herod Agrippa I., obtained the kingdom of Chalcis from Claudius at the request of Agrippa, 41. After the death of Agrippa (44), Claudius bestowed upon him the superintendence of the temple at Jerusalem, together with the right of appointing the high priests. He died in 48, when his kingdom was bestowed by Claudius upon his nephew, Herod Agrippa II. — 5. **Herodes Atticus**, the rhetorician. [ATTICUS.]

Hĕrōdĭānus ('Ηρωδιανός). 1. An historian, who wrote in Greek a history of the Roman empire in 8 books, from the death of M. Aurelius to the commencement of the reign of Gordianus III. (A. D. 180—238). He himself informs us that the events of this period had occurred in his own lifetime; but beyond this we know nothing respecting his life. He appears to have had Thucydides before him as a model, both for style and for the general composition of his work, like him, introducing here and there speeches wholly or in part imaginary. In spite of occasional inaccuracies in chronology and geography, his narrative is in the main truthful and impartial. Edited by Irmisch, Lips. 1789—1805, 5 vols., and by Bekker, Berlin, 1826. — 2. **Aelius Herodiānus**, one of the most celebrated grammarians of antiquity, was the son of Apollonius Dyscolus [APOLLONIUS, No. 4], and was born at Alexandria. From that place he removed to Rome, where he gained the favour of the emperor M. Aurelius, to whom he dedicated his work on prosody. This work seems to have embraced not merely prosody, but most of those subjects now included in the etymological portion of grammar. The estimation in which he was held by subsequent grammarians was very great. Priscian styles him *maximus auctor artis grammaticae.* He was a very voluminous writer; but none of his works have come down to us complete, though several extracts from them are preserved by later grammarians.

Hĕrōdĭcus ('Ηρόδικος). 1. Of Babylon, a grammarian, was one of the immediate successors of Crates of Mallus, and an opponent of the followers of Aristarchus, against whom he wrote an epigram, which is still extant and included in the Greek Anthology. — 2. A celebrated physician of Selymbria in Thrace, lived in the 5th century B. C., and was one of the tutors of Hippocrates.

Hĕrōdōrus ('Ηρόδωρος), of Heraclea, in Pontus, a contemporary of Hecataeus and Pherecydes, about B. C. 510, wrote a work on Hercules and his exploits.

Hĕrōdŏtus ('Ηρόδοτος). 1. A Greek historian, and the father of history, was born at Halicarnassus, a Doric colony in Caria, B. C. 484. He belonged to a noble family at Halicarnassus. He was the son of Lyxes and Dryo; and the epic poet Panyasis was one of his relations. Herodotus left his native city at an early age, in order to escape from the oppressive government of Lygdamis, the tyrant of Halicarnassus, who put to death Panyasis. He probably settled at Samos for some time, and there became acquainted with the Ionic dialect; but he spent many years in his extensive travels in Europe, Asia, and Africa, of which we shall speak presently. At a later time he returned to Halicarnassus, and took a prominent part in expelling Lygdamis from his native city. In the contentions which followed the expulsion of the tyrant, Herodotus was exposed to the hostile attacks of one of the political parties, whereupon he again left Halicarnassus, and settled at Thurii, in Italy, where he died. Whether he accompanied the first colonists to Thurii in 443, or followed them a few years afterwards, is a disputed point, and cannot be determined with certainty; though it appears probable from a passage in his work that he was at Athens at the commencement of the Peloponnesian war (431). It is also disputed where Herodotus wrote his history. Lucian relates that Herodotus read his work to the assembled Greeks at Olympia, which was received with such universal applause, that the 9 books of the work were in consequence honoured with the names of the 9 muses. The same writer adds that the young Thucydides was present at this recitation and was moved to tears. But this celebrated story, which rests upon the authority of Lucian alone, must be rejected for many reasons. Nor is there sufficient evidence in favour of the tradition that Herodotus read his work at the Panathenaea at Athens in 446 or 445, and received from the Athenians a reward of 10 talents. It is far more probable that he wrote his

---

[*] The death of Herod took place in the same year with the actual birth of Christ, as is mentioned above, but it is well known that this is to be placed 4 years before the date in general use as the Christian era.

work at Thurii, when he was advanced in years; and it appears that he was engaged upon it, at least in the way of revision, when he was 77 years of age, since he mentions the revolt of the Medes against Darius Nothus, and the death of Amyrtaeus, events which belong to the years 409 and 408. Though the work of Herodotus was probably not written till he was advanced in years, yet he was collecting materials for it during a great part of his life. It was apparently with this view that he undertook his extensive travels through Greece and foreign countries; and his work contains on almost every page the results of his personal observations and inquiries. There was scarcely a town of any importance in Greece Proper and on the coasts of Asia Minor with which he was not perfectly familiar; and at many places in Greece, such as Samos, Athens, Corinth, and Thebes, he seems to have staid some time. The sites of the great battles between the Greeks and barbarians, as Marathon, Thermopylae, Salamis, and Plataeae, were well known to him; and on Xerxes' line of march from the Hellespont to Athens, there was probably not a place which he had not seen with his own eyes. He also visited most of the Greek islands, not only in the Aegean, but even in the W. of Greece, such as Zacynthus. In the N. of Europe he visited Thrace and the Scythian tribes on the Black Sea. In Asia he travelled through Asia Minor and Syria, and visited the cities of Babylon, Ecbatana, and Susa. He spent some time in Egypt, and travelled as far S. as Elephantine. He saw with his own eyes all the wonders of Egypt, and the accuracy of his observations and descriptions still excites the astonishment of travellers in that country. From Egypt he appears to have made excursions to the E. into Arabia, and to the W. into Libya, at least as far as Cyrene, which was well known to him. — The object of his work is to give an account of the struggles between the Greeks and Persians. He traces the enmity between Europe and Asia to the mythical times. He passes rapidly over the mythical ages to come to Croesus, king of Lydia, who was known to have committed acts of hostility against the Greeks. This induces him to give a full history of Croesus and of the kingdom of Lydia. The conquest of Lydia by the Persians under Cyrus then leads him to relate the rise of the Persian monarchy, and the subjugation of Asia Minor and Babylon. The nations which are mentioned in the course of this narrative are again discussed more or less minutely. The history of Cambyses and his expedition into Egypt induce him to enter into the details of Egyptian history. The expedition of Darius against the Scythians causes him to speak of Scythia and the N. of Europe. In the meantime the revolt of the Ionians breaks out, which eventually brings the contest between Persia and Greece to an end. An account of this insurrection is followed by the history of the invasion of Greece by the Persians; and the history of the Persian war now runs in a regular channel until the taking of Sestos by the Greeks, B. C. 478, with which event his work concludes. It will be seen from the preceding sketch that the history is full of digressions and episodes; but those do not impair the unity of the work, for one thread, as it were, runs through the whole, and the episodes are only like branches of the same tree. The structure of the work thus bears

a strong resemblance to a grand epic poem. The whole work is pervaded by a deep religious sentiment. Herodotus shows the most profound reverence for everything which he conceives as divine, and rarely ventures to express an opinion on what he considers a sacred or religious mystery. — In order to form a fair judgment of the historical value of the work of Herodotus, we must distinguish between those parts in which he speaks from his own observations and those in which he merely repeats what he was told by priests and others. In the latter case he was undoubtedly often deceived; but whenever he speaks from his own observations, he is a real model of truthfulness and accuracy; and the more the countries which he describes have been explored by modern travellers, the more firmly has his authority been established. Many things which used to be laughed at as impossible or paradoxical are found now to be strictly in accordance with truth. — The dialect in which he wrote is the Ionic, intermixed with epic or poetical expressions, and sometimes even with Attic and Doric forms. The excellencies of his style consist in its antique and epic colouring, its transparent clearness, and the lively flow of the narrative. But notwithstanding all the merits of Herodotus, there were certain writers in antiquity who attacked him, both in regard to the form and the substance of his work; and there is still extant a work ascribed to Plutarch, entitled "On the Malignity of Herodotus," full of the most futile accusations of every kind. The best editions of Herodotus are by Schweighäuser, Argentor. 1806, often reprinted; by Gaisford, Oxon. 1824; and by Bähr. Lips. 1830. — 2. A Greek physician, who practised at Rome with great reputation, about A. D. 100. He wrote some medical works, which are several times quoted by Galen. — 3. Also a Greek physician, a native either of Tarsus or Philadelphia, taught Sextus Empiricus.

Heroöpŏlis or Hero ('Hρώων πόλις, 'Hρώ: O. T. Raamses or Rameses ?: Ru. nr. Abou-Keshid ?), the capital of the Nomos Heroöpolites or Arsinoïtes in Lower Egypt, stood on the border of the Desert E. of the Delta, upon the canal connecting the Nile with the W. head of the Red Sea, which was called from it Sinus Heroöpoliticus (κόλπος 'Hρώων, 'Hρωσπολίτης or -ιτικός). The country about it is supposed to be the Goshen of Scripture.

Hēröphilus ('Hρόφιλος), one of the most celebrated physicians of antiquity, was born at Chalcedon in Bithynia, was a pupil of Praxagoras, and lived at Alexandria, under the first Ptolemy, who reigned B. C. 323—285. Here he soon acquired a great reputation, and was one of the founders of the medical school in that city. He seems to have given his chief attention to anatomy and physiology, which he studied not merely from the dissection of animals, but also from that of human bodies. He is even said to have carried his ardour in his anatomical pursuits so far as to have dissected criminals alive. He was the author of several medical and anatomical works, of which nothing but the titles and a few fragments remain. These have been collected and published by Marx, De Herophili Vita, &c. Gotting. 1840.

Hērostrātus ('Hρόστρατος), an Ephesian, set fire to the temple of Artemis at Ephesus, on the same night that Alexander the Great was born, B. C. 356. He was put to the torture, and confessed that he had fired the temple to immortalise himself. The Ephesians passed a decree condemning his name to oblivion; but it has been, as might have been expected, handed down by history.

Hersē ('Ερση), daughter of Cecrops and sister of Agraulos, was beloved by Hermes, by whom she became the mother of Cephalus. Respecting her story, see AGRAULOS. At Athens sacrifices were offered to her, and the maidens who carried the vessels containing the libation (ἔρση) were called ἐδρηφόροι.

Hersilia, the wife of Romulus, was the only married woman carried off by the Romans in the rape of the Sabine maidens. As Romulus after death became Quirinus, so Hersilia his wife became a goddess, Hora or Horta. Some writers, however, made Hersilia the wife of Hostus, grandfather of Tullus Hostilius.

Hertha (containing probably the same elements as the words *earth*, *erde*), the goddess of the earth, among the ancient Germans.

Hērūli or **Eruli**, a powerful German race, are said to have come originally from Scandinavia, but they appear on the shores of the Black Sea in the reign of Gallienus (A. D. 262), when in conjunction with the Goths, they invaded the Roman empire. They were conquered by the Ostrogoths, and afterwards formed part of the great army of Attila, with which he invaded Gaul and Italy. After the death of Attila (453) a portion of the Heruli united with other German tribes; and under the command of Odoacer, who is said to have been an Herulian, they destroyed the Western Empire, 476. Meantime the remainder of the nation formed a powerful kingdom on the banks of the Theiss and the Danube, which was eventually destroyed by the Langobardi or Lombards. Some of the Heruli were allowed by Anastasius to settle in Pannonia, and they served with great distinction in the armies of Justinian.

Hēsiŏdus ('Ησίοδος), one of the earliest Greek poets, of whose personal history we possess little authentic information. He is frequently mentioned along with Homer; as Homer represents the Ionic school of poetry in Asia Minor, so Hesiod represents the Boeotian school of poetry, which spread over Phocis and Euboea. The only points of resemblance between the 2 schools consist in their versification and dialect. In other respects they entirely differ. The Homeric school takes for its subjects the restless activity of the heroic age, while the Hesiodic turns its attention to the quiet pursuits of ordinary life, to the origin of the world, the gods and heroes. Hesiod lived about a century later than Homer, and is placed about B. C. 735. We learn from his own poem on *Works and Days*, that he was born in the village of Ascra in Boeotia, whither his father had emigrated from the Aeolian Cyme in Asia Minor. After the death of his father, he was involved in a dispute with his brother Perses about his small patrimony, which was decided in favour of his brother. He then emigrated to Orchomenos, where he spent the remainder of his life. This is all that can be said with certainty about the life of Hesiod. Many of the stories related about him refer to his school of poetry, and not to the poet personally. In this light we may regard the tradition, that Hesiod had a poetical contest with Homer, which is said to have taken place at Chalcis during the funeral solemnities of king Amphidamas, or, according to others, at Aulis or

Delos. The story of this contest gave rise to a composition still extant under the title of 'Αγὼν 'Ομήρου καὶ 'Ησιόδου, the work of a grammarian who lived towards the end of the first century of our era, in which the 2 poets are represented as engaged in the contest, and answering one another. The following works were attributed to Hesiod in antiquity : — 1. 'Εργα or 'Εργα καὶ ἡμέραι, *Opera et Dies*, *Works and Days*. It is written in the most homely style, with scarcely any poetical imagery or ornament, and must be looked upon as the most ancient specimen of didactic poetry. It contains ethical, political, and economical precepts, the last of which constitute the greater part of the work, consisting of rules about choosing a wife, the education of children, agriculture, commerce, and navigation. It would further seem that 3 distinct poems have been inserted in it ; viz. 1. The fable of Prometheus and Pandora (47—105) ; 2. On the ages of the world, which are designated by the names of metals (109—201) ; and, 3. A description of winter (504—558). 2. Θεογονία, a *Theogony*, was not considered by Hesiod's countrymen to be a genuine production of the poet. This work gives an account of the origin of the world and the birth of the gods, explaining the whole order of nature in a series of genealogies, for every part of physical as well as moral nature there appears personified in the character of a distinct being. The whole concludes with an account of some of the most illustrious heroes. 3. 'Ηοῖαι or ἠοῖαι μεγάλαι, also called κατάλογοι γυναικῶν, *Catalogue of Women*, This work is lost. It contained accounts of the women who had been beloved by the gods, and had thus become the mothers of the heroes in the various parts of Greece, from whom the ruling families derived their origin. 4. 'Ασπὶς 'Ηρακλέους, *Shield of Hercules*, which is extant, probably formed part of the work last mentioned. It contains a description of the shield of Hercules, and is an imitation of the Homeric description of the shield of Achilles. The best edition of Hesiod is by Göttling, Gotha and Erfurt, 1843, 2d ed.

Hēsiŏnē ('Ησιόνη), daughter of Laomedon, king of Troy, was chained by her father to a rock, in order to be devoured by a sea-monster, that he might thus appease the anger of Apollo and Poseidon. Hercules promised to save her, if Laomedon would give him the horses which he had received from Zeus as a compensation for Ganymedes. Hercules killed the monster, but Laomedon refused to keep his promise. Thereupon Hercules took Troy, killed Laomedon, and gave Hesione to his friend and companion Telamon, by whom she became the mother of Teucer. Her brother Priam sent Antenor to claim her back, and the refusal on the part of the Greeks is mentioned as one of the causes of the Trojan war.

Hespēria ('Εσπερία), the Western land (from ἕσπερος, *vesper*), the name given by the Greek poets to Italy, because it lay W. of Greece. In imitation of them, the Roman poets gave the name of Hesperia to Spain, which they sometimes called *ultima Hesperia* (Hor. *Carm.* i. 36. 4) to distinguish it from Italy, which they occasionally called *Hesperia Magna* (Virg. *Aen.* i. 569).

Hespērides ('Εσπερίδες), the celebrated guardians of the golden apples which Ge (Earth) gave to Hera at her marriage with Zeus. Their parentage is differently related. They are called the daughters either of Night or Erebus, or of Phorcys and Ceto, or of Atlas and Hesperis (whence their names Atlantides or Hesperides), or of Hesperus, or of Zeus and Themis. Some traditions mentioned 3 Hesperides, viz. *Aegle, Arethusa,* and *Hesperia ;* others 4, *Aegle, Crytheia, Hestia,* and *Arethusa ;* and others again 7. The poets describe them as possessing the power of sweet song. In the earliest legends, these nymphs are described as living on the river Oceanus, in the extreme W. ; but the later attempts to fix the geographical position of their gardens led poets and geographers to different parts of . Libya, as the neighbourhood of Cyrene, Mount Atlas, or the islands on the W. coast of Libya, or even to the N. extremity of the earth, beyond the wind Boreas, among the Hyperboreans. They were assisted in watching the golden apples by the dragon Ladon. It was one of the labours of Hercules to obtain possession of these apples. (See p. 310, a.)

Hesperīdum Insŭlae. [HESPERIUM.]

Hespĕris. [BERENICE, No. 4, p. 120.]

Hespĕrĭum ('Εσπέριον, 'Εσπέρου κέρας : *C. Verde* or *C. Roxo*), a headland on the W. coast of Africa, was one of the furthest points to which the knowledge of the ancients extended along that coast. Near it was a bay called Sinus Hesperius ; and a day's journey from it a group of islands called **Hesperīdum Insŭlae,** wrongly identified by some with the Fortunatae Insulae ; they are either the *Cape de Verde* islands, or, more probably, the *Bissagos,* at the mouth of the *Rio Grande.*

Hespĕrus ('Εσπερος), the evening star, is called by Hesiod a son of Astraeus and Eos. He was also regarded as the same as the morning star, whence both Homer and Hesiod call him the bringer of light (ἑωσφόρος). A later account makes him a son of Atlas, who was fond of astronomy, and who disappeared, after ascending Mount Atlas to observe the stars. He was worshipped with divine honours, and was regarded as the fairest star in the heavens. The Romans designated him by the names Lucifer and Hesperus, to characterise him as the morning or evening star.

Hestĭa ('Εστία, Ion. 'Ιστίη), called **Vesta** by the Romans, the goddess of the hearth, or rather of the fire burning on the hearth, was one of the 12 great divinities of the Greeks. She was a daughter of Cronus and Rhea, and, according to common tradition, was the first-born of Rhea, and consequently the first of the children swallowed by Cronus. She was a maiden divinity, and when Apollo and Poseidon sued for her hand, she swore by the head of Zeus to remain a virgin for ever. As the hearth was looked upon as the centre of domestic life, so Hestia was the goddess of domestic life and the giver of all domestic happiness: as such she was believed to dwell in the inner part of every house, and to have invented the art of building houses. In this respect she often appears together with Hermes, who was likewise a *deus penetralis.* Being the goddess of the sacred fire of the altar, Hestia had a share in the sacrifices offered to all the gods. Hence, when sacrifices were offered, she was invoked first, and the first part of the sacrifice was presented to her. Solemn oaths were sworn by the goddess of the hearth ; and the hearth itself was the sacred asylum where suppliants implored the protection of the inhabitants of the house. A town or city is only an extended family, and therefore had likewise its sacred hearth. This public hearth

usually existed in the prytaneum of a town, where the goddess had her especial sanctuary (θάλαμος), under the name of *Prytanītis* (Πρυτανῖτις), with a statue and the sacred hearth. There, as at a private hearth, Hestia protected the suppliants. When a colony was sent out, the emigrants took the fire which was to burn on the hearth of their new home from that of the mother town. If ever the fire of her hearth became extinct, it was not allowed to be lighted again with ordinary fire, but either by fire produced by friction, or by burning glasses drawing fire from the sun. The mystical speculations of later times took their origin from the simple ideas of the ancients, and assumed a sacred hearth not only in the centre of the earth, but even in that of the universe, and confounded Hestia in various ways with other divinities, such as Cybele, Gaea, Demeter, Persephone, and Artemis. There were but few special temples of Hestia in Greece, since every prytaneum was in reality a sanctuary of the goddess, and since a portion of the sacrifices, to whatever divinity they were offered, belonged to her. The worship of the Roman Vesta is spoken of under VESTA.

Hestĭaeōtis ('Εστιαιῶτις) 1. The N.W. part of Thessaly [THESSALIA.] — **2.** Or **Histiaea,** a district in Euboea. [EUBOEA.]

Hesychĭus ('Ησύχιος). **1.** An Alexandrine grammarian, under whose name a large Greek dictionary has come down to us. Respecting his personal history nothing is known, but he probably lived about A.D. 380. The work is based, as the writer himself tells us, upon the lexicon of Diogenianus. Hesychius was probably a pagan : the Christian glosses and the references to Christian writers in the work are interpolations by a later hand. The work is one of great importance, not only on account of its explaining the words of the Greek language, but also from its containing much literary and archaeological information, derived from earlier grammarians and commentators, whose works are lost. The arrangement of the work however is very defective. The best edition is by Alberti, completed after Alberti's death by Ruhnken, Lugd. Bat. 1746—1766, 2 vols. fol. — **2.** Of Miletus, surnamed *Illustris,* from some office which he held, lived about A.D. 540, and wrote : 1. An *Onomasticon,* or account of illustrious men, published by Orelli, Lips. 1820. 2. A *Chronicon* or synoptical view of universal history, in 6 parts, from the reign of Belus, the reputed founder of the Assyrian empire, to the death of the Byzantine emperor, Anastasius I., A. D. 518. The work itself is lost, but an account of it is preserved by Photius.

Hetrĭcŭlum, a town of the Bruttii.

Hibernĭa, also called **Ierne, Iverna** or **Juverna** ('Ιέρνη, Ιερνίς νῆσος, 'Ιουερνία), the island of *Ireland,* appears to have derived its name from the inhabitants of its S. coast, called Juverni ('Ιουερνοι) by Ptolemy, but its original name was probably *Bergion* or *Vergion.* It is mentioned by Caesar, and is frequently spoken of by subsequent writers; but the Romans never made any attempt to conquer the island, though they obtained some knowledge of it from the commercial intercourse which was carried on between it and Britain. We have no account of the island except from Ptolemy, who must have derived his information from the statements of the British merchants, who visited its coasts. Ptolemy gives rather a long list of its promontories, rivers, tribes and towns.

Hicesia. [AEOLIAE INSULAE.]

Hicetas ('Ικέτας or 'Ικέτης). 1. A Syracusan, contemporary with the younger Dionysius and Timoleon. He was at first a friend of Dion, after whose death (B. C. 353) his wife Arete, and his sister Aristomache placed themselves under the care of Hicetas; but he was persuaded notwithstanding to consent to their destruction. A few years later he became tyrant of Leontini. He carried on war against the younger Dionysius, whom he defeated, and had made himself master of the whole city, except the island citadel, when Timoleon landed in Sicily, 344. Hicetas then opposed Timoleon and called in the aid of the Carthaginians, but he was defeated and put to death by Timoleon, 339 or 338. — 2. Tyrant of Syracuse, during the interval between the reign of Agathocles and that of Pyrrhus. He defeated Phintias, tyrant of Agrigentum, and was himself defeated by the Carthaginians. After a reign of 9 years (288—279), he was expelled from Syracuse. — 3. Of Syracuse, one of the earlier Pythagoreans.

Hiempsal. 1. Son of Micipsa, king of Numidia, and grandson of Masinissa, was murdered by Jugurtha, soon after the death of Micipsa, B. C. 118. — 2. King of Numidia, grandson or great-grandson of Masinissa, and father of Juba, appears to have received the sovereignty of part of Numidia after the Jugurthine war. He was expelled from his kingdom by Cn. Domitius Ahenobarbus, the leader of the Marian party in Africa, but was restored by Pompey in 81. Hiempsal wrote some works in the Punic language, which are cited by Sallust (*Jug.* 17).

Hiera. 1. [AEOLIAE.] — 2. [AEGATES.]

Hierapolis ('Ιεράπολις). 1. A city of Great Phrygia, near the Maeander, celebrated for its hot springs and its temple of Cybele. Like the neighbouring cities of Colossae and Laodicea, it was an early seat of Christianity, and it is mentioned in St. Paul's *Epistle to the Colossians* (iv. 13). — 2. Formerly **Bambyce** (Βαμβύκη : *Bambuch*, or *Membij*), a city in the N.E. of Syria, one of the chief seats of the worship of Astarte.

Hierocles ('Ιεροκλῆς). 1. A Greek rhetorician of Alabanda in Caria, lived about B.C. 100, and was distinguished, like his brother Menecles, by the Asiatic style of oratory. — 2. Governor of Bithynia, and afterwards of Alexandria, is said to have been one of the chief instigators of the persecution of the Christians under Diocletian. He wrote a work against the Christians, entitled Λόγοι φιλαλήθεις πρὸς τοὺς Χριστιανούς, of which we may form an idea from the account of Lactantius and the refutation which Eusebius wrote against it. We see from these writers that Hierocles attacked the character of Jesus Christ and his apostles, and put him on an equality with Apollonius of Tyana. — 3. A New Platonist, who lived at Alexandria about the middle of the 5th century. He wrote: 1. A commentary on the golden verses of Pythagoras, in which he endeavours to give an intelligible account of the philosophy of Pythagoras. Published by Needham, Cambridge, 1709; and by Warren, London, 1742. 2. A work on Providence, Fate, and the reconciliation of man's free will with the divine government of the world, in 7 books. The work is lost, but some extracts from it preserved in Photius. 3. An ethical work on justice, on reverence towards the gods, parents, relations, &c., which bore the title Τὰ φιλοσοφού-

μενα. This work is also lost, but there are several extracts from it in Stobaeus. The extant work, entitled 'Αστεῖα, a collection of ludicrous tales, is erroneously ascribed to Hierocles, the New Platonist. The work is of no merit. — 4. A Greek grammarian, the author of an extant work, entitled Συνέκδημος, that is, The Travelling Companion, intended as a handbook for travellers through the provinces of the Eastern empire. It was perhaps written at the beginning of the 6th century of our era. It contains a list of 64 eparchiae or provinces of the Eastern empire, and of 935 different towns, with brief descriptions. Published by Wesseling, in *Veterum Romanorum Itineraria*, Amsterdam, 1735.

Hieron ('Ιέρων). 1. Tyrant of Syracuse (B. C. 478—467), was son of Dinomenes and brother of Gelon, whom he succeeded in the sovereignty. In the early part of his reign he became involved in a war with Theron of Agrigentum, who had espoused the cause of his brother Polyzelus, with whom he had quarrelled. But Hieron afterwards concluded a peace with Theron, and became reconciled to his brother Polyzelus. After the death of Theron, in 472, he carried on war against his son Thrasydaeus, whom he defeated in a great battle, and expelled from Agrigentum. But by far the most important event of his reign was the great victory which he obtained over the Etruscan fleet near Cumae (474), and which appears to have effectually broken the naval power of that nation. Hieron died at Catana in the 12th year of his reign, 467. His government was much more despotic than that of his brother Gelon. He maintained a large guard of mercenary troops, and employed numerous spies and informers. He was however a liberal and enlightened patron of men of letters; and his court became the resort of the most distinguished poets and philosophers of the day. Aeschylus, Pindar, and Bacchylides took up their abode with him, and we find him associating in friendly intercourse with Xenophanes, Epicharmus, and Simonides. His intimacy with the latter was particularly celebrated, and has been made the subject by Xenophon of an imaginary dialogue, entitled the *Hieron*. His love of magnificence was especially displayed in the great contests of the Grecian games, and his victories at Olympia and Delphi have been immortalised by Pindar. — 2. King of Syracuse (B. C. 270—216), was the son of Hierocles, a noble Syracusan, descended from the great Gelon, but his mother was a female servant. When Pyrrhus left Sicily (275), Hieron, who had distinguished himself in the wars of that monarch, was declared general by the Syracusan army. He strengthened his power by marrying the daughter of Leptines, at that time the most influential citizen at Syracuse; and after his defeat of the Mamertines, he was saluted by his fellow-citizens with the title of king, 270. It was the great object of Hieron to expel the Mamertines from Sicily; and accordingly when the Romans, in 264, interposed in favour of that people, Hieron concluded an alliance with the Carthaginians, and, in conjunction with them, carried on war against the Romans. But having been defeated by the Romans, he concluded a peace with them in the following year (263), in virtue of which he retained possession of the whole S. E. of Sicily, and the E. side of the island as far as Tauromenium. From this time till his death, a period of little less than half a century, Hieron continued the stedfast

Hephaestus (Vulcanus). (From an
Altar in the Vatican.) Page 304.

Hephaestus (Vulcan). (From a Gem in the Royal
Cabinet at Paris.) Page 304.

Hecate. (Causei, Museum Romanum, vol.[1,
tav. 21.) Page 399.

Hera (Juno). (Visconti, Mus. Pio.
Clem., vol. 4, tav. 3.) Pages 304, 305.

Hera (Juno) seated on a Throne, with Mercury behind.
(Museo Borbonico.) Pages 304, 305.

A Harpy. (British Museum. From a
Tomb at Xanthus.) Pages 297, 298.

[To face p. 390.

Gela in Sicily. Page 278.

Halesa in Sicily. Page 292.

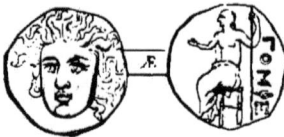

Gomphi in Thessaly. Page 284.

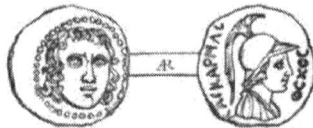

Halicarnassus. Page 292.

Gortyna in Sicily. Page 280.

Heraclea in Lucania. Page 305.

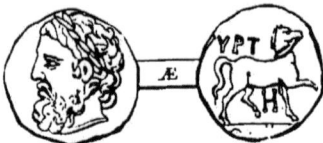

Gyrton in Thessaly. Page 290.

Heraclea Sintica in Macedonia. Page 305.

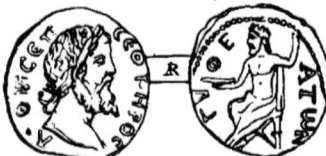

Gythium, in Laconia. Page 290.

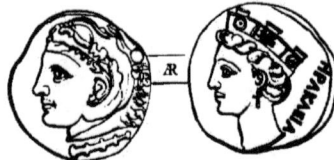

Heraclea Pontica in Bithynia. Page 305.

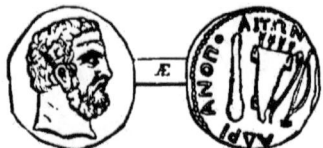

Hadrianopolis in Thrace. Page 291.

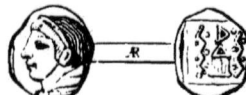

Heraea in Arcadia. Page 307.

To face p. 321.]

friend and ally of the Romans, a policy of which his subjects as well as himself reaped the benefits, in the enjoyment of a state of uninterrupted tranquillity and prosperity. Even the heavy losses which the Romans sustained in the first 3 years of the 2nd Punic war did not shake his fidelity; and after their great defeats, he sent them large supplies of corn and auxiliary troops. He died in 216 at the age of 92. His government was mild and equitable: though he did not refuse the title of king, he avoided all external display of the insignia of royalty, and appeared in public in the garb of a private citizen. The care he bestowed upon the financial department of his administration is attested by the laws regulating the tithes of corn and other agricultural produce, which, under the name of *Leges Hieronicae*, were retained by the Romans when they reduced Sicily to a province. He adorned the city of Syracuse with many public works. His power and magnificence were celebrated by Theocritus in his 16th Idyll. Hieron had only one son, Gelon, who died shortly before his father. He was succeeded by his grandson, Hieronymus.

Hieronymus ('Ιερώνυμος). 1. Of Cardia, probably accompanied Alexander the Great to Asia, and after the death of that monarch (B. C. 323) served under his countryman Eumenes. In the last battle between Eumenes and Antigonus (316) Hieronymus fell into the hands of Antigonus, who treated him with kindness, and to whose service he henceforth attached himself. After the death of Antigonus (301), Hieronymus continued to follow the fortunes of his son Demetrius, and was appointed by the latter governor of Boeotia, after his first conquest of Thebes, 292. He continued unshaken in his attachment to Demetrius and to his son, Antigonus Gonatas, after him. It appears that he survived Pyrrhus, and died at the advanced age of 104. Hieronymus wrote a history of the events from the death of Alexander to that of Pyrrhus, if not later. This work has not come down to us, but it is frequently cited by later writers as one of the chief authorities for the history of Alexander's successors. We are told that Hieronymus displayed partiality to Antigonus and Demetrius, and in consequence treated Pyrrhus and Lysimachus with great injustice. — 2. King of Syracuse, succeeded his grandfather, Hieron II., B. C. 216, at 15 years of age. He was persuaded by the Carthaginian party to renounce the alliance with the Romans, which his grandfather had maintained, for so many years. He was assassinated after a short reign of only 13 months. — 3. Of Rhodes, commonly called a peripatetic, though Cicero questions his right to the title, was a disciple of Aristotle, and appears to have lived down to the time of Ptolemy Philadelphus. He held the highest good to consist in freedom from pain and trouble, and denied that pleasure was to be sought for its own sake. — 4. Commonly known as **Saint Jerome**, one of the most celebrated of the Christian fathers, was born at Stridon, a town upon the confines of Dalmatia and Pannonia, about A. D. 340. His father sent him to Rome for the prosecution of his studies, where he devoted himself with great ardour and success to the Greek and Latin languages, to rhetoric, and to the different branches of philosophy, enjoying the instructions of the most distinguished preceptors of that era, among whom was Aelius Donatus. [DONATUS.] After completing his studies he went to Gaul, where he remained

some time, and subsequently travelled through various countries in the E. At Antioch he was attacked by a dangerous malady, and on his recovery he resolved to withdraw from the world. In 374 he retired to the desert of Chalcis, lying between Antioch and the Euphrates, where he passed 4 years, adhering strictly to the most rigid observances of monkish ascetism, but at the same time pursuing the study of Hebrew. In 379 he was ordained a presbyter at Antioch by Paulinus. Soon after he went to Constantinople, where he lived for 3 years, enjoying the instructions and friendship of Gregory of Nazianzus. In 382 he accompanied Paulinus to Rome, where he formed a close friendship with the Pope Damasus. He remained at Rome 3 years, and there laboured in proclaiming the glory and merit of a contemplative life and monastic discipline. He had many enthusiastic disciples among the Roman ladies, but the influence which he exercised over them excited the hatred of their relations, and exposed him to attacks against his character. Accordingly he left Rome in 385, having lost his patron Damasus in the preceding year; and accompanied by the rich widow Paula, her daughter Eustochium, and a number of devout maidens, he made a tour of the Holy Land, and finally settled at Bethlehem, where Paula erected 4 monasteries, 3 for nuns and 1 for monks. Here he passed the remainder of his life. He died A. D. 420.—Jerome wrote a great number of works, most of which have come down to us. Of these the most celebrated are his Commentaries on the various books of the Scriptures. He also translated into Latin the Old and New Testaments: his translation is in substance the Latin version of the Scriptures, known by the name of the Vulgate. The translation of the Old Testament was made by Jerome directly from the Hebrew; but the translation of the New Testament was formed by him out of the old translations carefully corrected from the original Greek. Jerome likewise translated from the Greek the Chronicle of Eusebius, which he enlarged, chiefly in the department of Roman history, and brought down to A. D. 378. Jerome was the most learned of the Latin fathers. His profound knowledge of the Latin, Greek, and Hebrew languages, his familiarity with ancient history and philosophy, and his personal acquaintance with the manners and scenery of the East, enabled him to throw much light upon the Scriptures. In his controversial works he is vehement and dogmatical. His language is exceedingly pure, bearing ample testimony to the diligence with which he must have studied the choicest models. The best editions of the works of Jerome are the Benedictine, Par. 5 vols. fol. 1693—1706, and that by Vallarsi, Veron. 11 vols. fol. 1734—1742; reprinted Venet. 11 vols. 4to. 1766.

Hierosolyma. [JERUSALEM.]

Hilarius. 1. A Christian writer, was born of pagan parents at Poitiers. He afterwards became a Christian, and was elected bishop of his native place, A. D. 350. From this time he devoted all his energies to check the progress of Arianism, which was making rapid strides in Gaul. He became so troublesome to the Arians, that they induced the emperor Constantius in 356 to banish him to Phrygia. He was allowed to return to Gaul about 361, and died in his diocese in 368. Several of his works have come down to us. They consist chiefly of polemical treatises against the Arians

Y

and addresses to the emperor Constantius. The best edition of his works is by Coustant, Paris, 1693, forming one of the Benedictine series, and reprinted by Scipio Maffei, Veron., 1730.—2. Bishop of Arles, succeeded his master Honoratus in that diocese, A.D. 429, and died in 449. He wrote the life of Honoratus and a few other works.

Hilleviōnes. [GERMANIA, p. 282, a.]

Himēra ('Ιμέρα) 1. (*Fiume Salso*), one of the principal rivers in the S. of Sicily, at one time the boundary between the territories of the Carthaginians and Syracusans, receives near Enna the water of a salt spring, and hence has salt water as far as its mouth. — 2. A smaller river in the N. of Sicily, flows into the sea between the towns of Himera and Thermae. — 3. ('Ιμεραῖος), a celebrated Greek city on the N. coast of Sicily, W. of the mouth of the river Himera [No. 2.], was founded by the Chalcidians of Zancle, B. c. 648, and afterwards received Dorian settlers, so that the inhabitants spoke a mixed dialect, partly Ionic (Chalcidian) and partly Doric. About 560 Himera, being threatened by its powerful neighbours, placed itself under the protection of Phalaris, tyrant of Agrigentum, in whose power it appears to have remained till his death. At a later time (500) we find Himera governed by a tyrant Terillus, who was expelled by Theron of Agrigentum. Terillus thereupon applied for assistance to the Carthaginians, who, anxious to extend their influence in Sicily, sent a powerful army into Sicily under the command of Hamilcar. The Carthaginians were defeated with great slaughter at Himera by the united forces of Theron and Gelon of Syracuse on the same day as the battle of Salamis was fought (480). Himera was now governed by Thrasydaeus, the son of Theron, in the name of his father ; but the inhabitants having attempted to revolt, Theron put to death or drove into exile a considerable part of the population, and repeopled the city with settlers from all quarters, but especially of Dorian origin. After the death of Theron (472), Himera recovered its independence, and for the next 60 years was one of the most flourishing cities in Sicily. It assisted Syracuse against the Athenians in 415. In 409 it was taken by Hannibal, the son of Gisgo, who, to revenge the great defeat which the Carthaginians had suffered before this town, levelled it to the ground and destroyed almost all the inhabitants. Himera was never rebuilt ; but on the opposite bank of the river Himera, the Carthaginians founded a new town, which, from a warm medicinal spring in its neighbourhood, was called Thermae (Θέρμαι: Θερμίτης, Thermitanus: *Termini*.) Here the remains of the unfortunate inhabitants of Himera were allowed to settle. The Romans, who highly prized the warm springs of Thermae, permitted the town to retain its own constitution; and Augustus made it a colony.—The poet Stesichorus was born at the ancient Himera, and the tyrant Agathocles at Thermae.

Himěrius ('Ιμέριος), a celebrated Greek sophist, was born at Prusa in Bithynia, and studied at Athens. He was subsequently appointed professor of rhetoric at Athens, where he gave instruction to Julian, afterwards emperor, and the celebrated Christian writers, Basil and Gregory Nazianzen. In 362 the emperor Julian invited him to his court at Antioch, and made him his secretary. He returned to Athens in 368, and there passed the remainder of his life. Himerius was a pagan ; but

he does not manifest in his writings any animosity against the Christians. There were extant in the time of Photius 71 orations by Himerius ; but of these only 24 have come down to us complete. Edited by Wernsdorf, Göttingen, 1790.

Himilco ('Ιμίλκων). 1. A Carthaginian, who conducted a voyage of discovery from Gades towards the N., along the W. shores of Europe, at the same time that Hanno undertook his voyage to the S. along the coast of Africa. [HANNO, No. 10.] Himilco represented that his further progress was prevented by the stagnant nature of the sea, loaded with sea weed, and by the absence of wind. His voyage is said to have lasted 4 months, but it is impossible to judge how far it was extended. Perhaps it was intentionally wrapt in obscurity by the commercial jealousy of the Carthaginians. — 2. Son of Hanno, commanded, together with Hannibal, son of Gisco [HANNIBAL, No. 1.], a Carthaginian army in Sicily, and laid siege to Agrigentum, B. c. 406. Hannibal died before Agrigentum of a pestilence, which broke out in the camp ; and Himilco, now left sole general, succeeded in taking the place, after a siege of nearly 8 months. At a later period he carried on war against Dionysius of Syracuse. In 395 he defeated Dionysius, and laid siege to Syracuse ; but, while pressing the siege of the city, a pestilence carried off a great number of his men. In this weakened condition, Himilco was attacked and defeated by Dionysius, and was obliged to purchase his safety by an ignominious capitulation. Such was his grief and disappointment at this termination to the campaign, that, on his return to Carthage, he put an end to his life by voluntary abstinence. — 3. The Carthaginian commander at Lilybaeum, which he defended with skill and bravery, when it was attacked by the Romans, 250. — 4. Commander of the Carthaginian forces in Sicily during a part of the 2nd Punic war, 214—212. — 5. Surnamed PHAMAEAS, commander of the Carthaginian cavalry in the 3rd Punic war. He deserted to the Romans, by whom he was liberally rewarded.

Hippāna (τὰ "Ιππανα), a town in the N. of Sicily near Panormus.

Hipparchĭa ('Ιππαρχία), wife of Crates the Cynic. [For details, see CRATES, No. 3.]

Hipparchus ('Ιππαρχος). 1. Son of Pisistratus. [PISISTRATIDAE.] — 2. A celebrated Greek astronomer, was a native of Nicaea in Bithynia, and flourished B. c. 160—145. He resided both at Rhodes and Alexandria. He was the true father of astronomy, which he raised to that rank among the applications of arithmetic and geometry which it has always since preserved. He was the first who gave and demonstrated the means of solving all triangles, rectilinear and spherical. He constructed a table of chords, of which he made the same sort of use as we make of our sines. He made more observations than his predecessors, and understood them better. He invented the planisphere, or the mode of representing the starry heavens upon a plane, and of producing the solutions of problems of spherical astronomy. He is also the father of true geography, by his happy idea of marking the position of spots on the earth, as was done with the stars, by circles drawn from the pole perpendicularly to the equator ; that is, by latitudes and longitudes. His method of eclipses was the only one by which differences of meridians could be determined. The catalogue which Hipparchus constructed of the stars is preserved in the Almagest of Ptolemy. Hipparchus wrote numerous works, which are all lost with the exception of his commentary on the phenomena of Aratus.

Hipparīnus ('Ιππαρῖνος). 1. A Syracusan, father of Dion and Aristomache, supported the elder Dionysius, who married his daughter Aristomache. — 2. Son of Dion, and grandson of the preceding, threw himself from the roof of a house, and was killed on the spot, when his father attempted, by restraint, to cure him of the dissolute habits which he had acquired while under the power of Dionysius. — 3. Son of the elder Dionysius by Aristomache, daughter of No. 1, succeeded Callippus in the tyranny of Syracuse, B. C. 352. He was assassinated, after reigning only 2 years.

Hippāris ('Ιππαρίς: Camarina), a river in the S. of Sicily, which flows into the sea near Camarina.

Hippāsus ('Ιππασος), of Metapontum or Croton, in Italy, one of the elder Pythagoreans, held the element of fire to be the cause of all things. In consequence of his making known the sphere, consisting of 12 pentagons, which was regarded by the Pythagoreans as a secret, he is said to have perished in the sea as an impious man.

Hippīa and Hippīus ('Ιππία and 'Ιππιος, or 'Ιππειος), in Latin Equester and Equestris, surnames of several divinities, as of Hera and Athena, of Poseidon and of Ares; and at Rome also of Fortuna and Venus.

Hippīas ('Ιππίας). 1. Son of Pisistratus. [PISISTRATIDAE.] — 2. The Sophist, was a native of Elis, and the contemporary of Socrates. His fellow-citizens availed themselves of his abilities in political matters, and sent him on a diplomatic mission to Sparta. But he was in every respect like the other sophists of the time. He travelled through Greece for the purpose of acquiring wealth and celebrity, by teaching and public speaking. His character as a sophist, his vanity, and his boastful arrogance, are well described in the 2 dialogues of Plato, Hippias major and Hippias minor. Though his knowledge was superficial, yet it appears that he had paid attention not only to rhetorical, philosophical, and political studies, but also to poetry, music, mathematics, painting and sculpture; and he must even have acquired some practical skill in the mechanical arts, as he used to boast of wearing on his body nothing that he had not made with his own hands, such as his seal-ring, his cloak, and shoes. He possessed great facility in extempore speaking; and once his vanity led him to declare that he would travel to Olympia, and there deliver before the assembled Greeks an oration on any subject that might be proposed to him.

Hippo ('Ιππών), in Africa. 1. H. Regius ('I. βασιλικός: nr. Bonah, Ru.), a city on the coast of Numidia, W. of the mouth of the Rubricatus; once a royal residence, and afterwards celebrated as the bishopric of St. Augustine. — 2. H. Diarrhytus or Zaritus ('I. διάῤῥυτος: Bizerta), a city on the N. coast of the Carthaginian territory (Zeugitana), W. of Utica, at the mouth of the Sinus Hipponensis. — 3. A town of the Carpetani in Hispania Tarraconensis, S. of Toletum.

Hippocentauri. [CENTAURI.]

Hippocŏon ('Ιπποκόων), son of Oebalus and Batea. After his father's death, he expelled his brother Tyndareus, in order to secure the kingdom to himself; but Hercules led Tyndareus back, and slew Hippocoon and his sons. Ovid (Met. viii.

314) mentions the sons of Hippocoon among the Calydonian hunters.

Hippocrātes ('Ιπποκράτης). 1. Father of Pisistratus, the tyrant of Athens. — 2. An Athenian, son of Megacles, was brother of Clisthenes, the legislator, and grandfather, through his daughter Agariste, of the illustrious Pericles. — 3. An Athenian, son of Xanthippus and brother of Pericles. He had 3 sons who, as well as their father, are alluded to by Aristophanes, as men of a mean capacity, and devoid of education. — 4. An Athenian, son of Ariphron, commanded the Athenians, B. C. 424, when he was defeated and slain by the Boeotians at the battle of Delium.—5. A Lacedaemonian, served under Mindarus on the Asiatic coast in 410, and after the defeat of Mindarus at Cyzicus, became commander of the fleet. — 6. A Sicilian, succeeded his brother Cleander, as tyrant of Gela, 498. His reign was prosperous; and he extended his power over several other cities of Sicily. He died in 491, while besieging Hybla.— 7. A Sicilian, brother of EPICYDES. — 8. The most celebrated physician of antiquity. He was born in the island of Cos about B. C. 460. He belonged to the family of the Asclepiadae, and was the son of Heraclides, who was also a physician. His mother's name was Phaenarete, who was said to be descended from Hercules. He was instructed in medical science by his father and by Herodicus, and he is said to have been also a pupil of Gorgias of Leontini. He wrote, taught, and practised his profession at home; travelled in different parts of the continent of Greece; and died at Larissa in Thessaly, about 357, at the age of 104. He had 2 sons, Thessalus and Dracon, and a son-in-law, Polybus, all of whom followed the same profession, and who are supposed to have been the authors of some of the works in the Hippocratic collection. These are the only certain facts which we know respecting the life of Hippocrates; but to these later writers have added a large collection of stories, many of which are clearly fabulous. Thus he is said to have stopped the plague at Athens by burning fires throughout the city, by suspending chaplets of flowers, and by the use of an antidote. It is also related that Artaxerxes Longimanus, king of Persia, invited Hippocrates to come to his assistance during a time of pestilence, but that Hippocrates refused his request, on the ground of his being the enemy of his country.—The writings which have come down to us under the name of Hippocrates were composed by several differen' persons, and are of very different merit. They are more than 60 in number, but of these only a few are certainly genuine. They are : — 1. Προγνωστικόν, Praenotiones or Prognosticon. 2. Ἀφορισμοί, Aphorismi. 3. Ἐπιδημίων Βιβλία, De Morbis Popularibus (or Epidemiorum). 4. Περὶ Διαίτης Ὀξέων, De Ratione Victus in Morbis Acutis, or De Diaeta Acutorum. 5. Περὶ Ἀέρων, Ὑδάτων, Τόπων, De Aëre, Aquis, et Locis. 6. Περὶ τῶν ἐν Κεφαλῇ Τρωμάτων, De Capitis Vulneribus. Some of the other works were perhaps written by Hippocrates; but the great majority of them were composed by his disciples and followers, many of whom bore the name of Hippocrates. The ancient physicians wrote numerous commentaries on the works in the Hippocratic collection. Of these the most valuable are the commentaries of Galen.—Hippocrates divided the causes of disease into 2 principal classes; the one comprehending the influence

Y 2

of seasons, climates, water, situation, &c., and the other the influence of food, exercise, &c. He considered that while heat and cold, moisture and dryness, succeeded one another throughout the year, the human body underwent certain analogous changes, which influenced the diseases of the period. He supposed that the 4 fluids or humours of the body (blood, phlegm, yellow bile, and black bile) were the primary seat of disease ; that health was the result of the due combination (or *crasis*) of these, and that, when this crasis was disturbed, disease was the consequence ; that, in the course of a disorder that was proceeding favourably, these humours underwent a certain change in quality (or *coction*), which was the sign of returning health, as preparing the way for the expulsion of the morbid matter, or *crisis ;* and that these crises had a tendency to occur at certain stated periods, which were hence called " critical days." — Hippocrates 'was evidently a person who not only had had great experience, but who also knew how to turn it to the best account ; and the number of moral reflections and apophthegms that we meet with in his writings, some of which (as, for example, " Life is short, and Art is long ") have acquired a sort of proverbial notoriety, show him to have been a profound thinker. His works are written in the Ionic dialect, and the style is so concise as to be sometimes extremely obscure. — The best edition of his works is by Littré, Paris, 1839, seq., with a French translation.

Hippocrēnē ('Ιπποκρήνη), the " Fountain of the Horse," called by Persius *Fons Caballinus*, was a fountain in Mt. Helicon in Boeotia, sacred to the Muses, said to have been produced by the horse Pegasus striking the ground with his feet.

Hippŏdămīa ('Ιπποδάμεια). 1. Daughter of Oenomaus, king of Pisa in Elis. For details see OENOMAUS and PELOPS. — 2. Wife of Pirithous, at whose nuptials took place the celebrated battle between the Centaurs and Lapithae. For details see PIRITHOUS. — 3. See BRISEIS.

Hippŏdămus ('Ιππόδαμος), a distinguished Greek architect, a native of Miletus, and the son of Euryphon or Eurycoön. His fame rests on his construction, not of single buildings, but of whole cities. His first great work was the town of Piraeus, which he built under the auspices of Pericles. When the Athenians founded their colony of Thurii (B. c. 443), Hippodamus went out with the colonists, and was the architect of the new city. Hence he is often called a Thurian. He afterwards built Rhodes (408—407).

Hippŏlŏchus ('Ιππόλοχος), son of Bellerophontes and Philonoë or Anticlea, and father of Glaucus, the Lycian prince.

Hippŏlÿtē ('Ιππολύτη). 1. Daughter of Ares and Otrera, was queen of the Amazons, and sister of Antiope and Melanippe. She wore a girdle given to her by her father ; and when Hercules came to fetch this girdle, she was slain by Hercules. [See p. 309, b.] According to another tradition, Hippolyte, with an army of Amazons, marched into Attica, to take vengeance on Theseus for having carried off Antiope ; but being conquered by Theseus, she fled to Megara, where she died of grief, and was buried. In some accounts Hippolyte, and not Antiope, is said to have been married to Theseus. — 2. Or Astydamia, wife of Acastus, fell in love with Peleus. See ACASTUS.

Hippŏlÿtus ('Ιππόλυτος). 1. Son of Theseus by Hippolyte, queen of the Amazons, or her sister Antiope. Theseus afterwards married Phaedra, who fell in love with Hippolytus ; but as her offers were rejected by her step-son, she accused him to his father of having attempted her dishonour. Theseus thereupon cursed his son, and requested his father (Aegeus or Poseidon) to destroy him. Accordingly, as Hippolytus was riding in his chariot along the sea-coast, Poseidon sent forth a bull from the water. The horses were frightened, upset the chariot, and dragged Hippolytus along the ground till he was dead. Theseus afterwards learned the innocence of his son, and Phaedra, in despair, made away with herself. Artemis induced Aesculapius to restore Hippolytus to life again ; and, according to Italian traditions, Artemis (Diana) placed him, under the name of Virbius, under the protection of the nymph Egeria, in the grove of Aricia, in Latium, where he was honoured with divine worship. Horace, following the more ancient tradition, says that Diana could not restore Hippolytus to life (*Carm.* iv. 7. 25). — 2. An early ecclesiastical writer of considerable eminence, but whose real history is very uncertain. He appears to have lived early in the 3rd century ; and is said to have suffered martyrdom under Alexander Severus, being drowned in a ditch or pit full of water. Others suppose that he perished in the Decian persecution. He is said to have been a disciple of Irenaeus and a teacher of Origen.—His works, which are written in Greek, are edited by Fabricius, Hamb. 1716—1718, 2 vols. fol.

Hippŏmĕdon ('Ιππομέδων), son of Aristomachus, or, according to Sophocles, of Talaus, was one of the Seven against Thebes, where he was slain during the siege by Hyperbius or Ismarus.

Hippŏmĕnes ('Ιππομένης). 1. Son of Megareus, and great-grandson of Poseidon, conquered Atalanta in the foot-race. For details see ATALANTA, No. 2. — 2. A descendant of Codrus, the 4th and last of the decennial archons. Incensed at the barbarous punishment which he inflicted on his daughter, the Attic nobles deposed him.

Hippon ('Ιππων), of Rhegium, a philosopher of uncertain date, belonging to the Ionian school. He was accused of Atheism, and so got the surname of the Melian, as agreeing in sentiment with Diagoras. He held water and fire to be the principles of all things, the latter springing from the former, and developing itself by generating the universe.

Hippōnax ('Ιππώναξ). Of Ephesus, son of Pytheus and Protis, was, after Archilochus and Simonides, the 3rd of the Iambic poets of Greece. He flourished B. c. 546—520. He was distinguished for his love of liberty, and having been expelled from his native city by the tyrants, he took up his abode at Clazomenae, for which reason he is sometimes called a Clazomenian. In person, Hipponax was little, thin, and ugly, but very strong. The 2 brothers Bupalus and Athenis, who were sculptors of Chios, made statues of Hipponax, in which they caricatured his natural ugliness ; and he in return directed all the power of his satirical poetry against them, and especially against Bupalus. (Hor. *Epod.* vi. 14.) Later writers add that the sculptors hanged themselves in despair. Hipponax was celebrated in antiquity for the severity of his satires. He severely chastised the effeminate luxury of his Ionian brethren ; he did not spare his own parents ; and he ventured even to ridicule the gods. — In his satires he introduced a spondee x a trochee in the last foot, instead of an iambus. This change made the verse irregular in its rhythm, and gave it a sort of halting movement, whence it was called the Choliambus (χωλίαμβός, *lame iambic*), or Iambus Scazon (σκάζων, *limping*). He also wrote a parody on the Iliad. He may be said to occupy a middle place between Archilochus and Aristophanes. He is as bitter, but not so earnest, as the former, while in lightness and jocoseness he more resembles the latter. The fragments of Hipponax are edited by Welcker, Gotting. 1817, 8vo, and by Bergk, in the *Poetae Lyrici Graeci.*

Hippŏnĭcus. [CALLIAS AND HIPPONICUS.]

Hippŏnĭum. [VIBO.]

Hippŏnŏus. [BELLEROPHON.]

Hippŏtădes ('Iπποτάδης), son of Hippotes, that is, Aeolus. [AEOLUS, No. 2.] Hence the Aeoliae Insulae are called *Hippotadas regnum.* (Ov. *Met.* xiv. 86.)

Hippŏtes ('Iππότης). 1. Father of Aeolus. [AEOLUS, No. 2.] — 2. Son of Phylas by a daughter of Iolaus, great-grandson of Hercules, and father of Aletes. When the Heraclidae invaded Peloponnesus, Hippotes killed the seer Carnus. The army in consequence began to suffer very severely, and Hippotes by the command of an oracle was banished for 10 years.

Hippŏthŏon ('Iπποθόων), an Attic hero, son of Poseidon and ALOPE, the daughter of Cercyon. He had a heroum at Athens; and one of the Attic phylae, or tribes, was called after him Hippothoontis.

Hippŏthŏus ('Iππόθοος). 1. Son of Cercyon, and father of Aepytus, succeeded Agapenor as king in Arcadia. — 2. Son of Lethus, grandson of Teutamus, and brother of Pylaeus, led a band of Pelasgians from Larissa to the assistance of the Trojans. He was slain by the Telamonian Ajax.

Hirpīni, a Samnite people, whose name is said to come from the Sabine word *hirpus*, "a wolf," dwelt in the S. of Samnium between Apulia, Lucania and Campania. Their chief town was AECULANUM.

A. Hirtĭus, belonged to a plebeian family, which came probably from Ferentinum in the territory of the Hernici. He was the personal and political friend of Caesar the dictator. In B. C. 58 he was Caesar's legatus in Gaul, and during the Civil War his name constantly appears in Cicero's correspondence. He was one of the 10 praetors nominated by Caesar for 46, and during Caesar's absence in Africa he lived principally at his Tusculan estate, which was contiguous to Cicero's villa. Though politically opposed, they were on friendly terms, and Cicero gave Hirtius lessons in oratory. In 44 Hirtius received Belgic Gaul for his province, but he governed it by deputy, and attended Caesar at Rome, who nominated him and Vibius Pansa, consuls for 43. After Caesar's assassination (44) Hirtius first joined Antony, but being disgusted by the despotic arrogance of the latter, he retired to Puteoli, where he renewed his intercourse with Cicero. Later in the year he resided at his Tusculan villa, where he was attacked by a dangerous illness, from which he never perfectly recovered. On the 1st of January, 43, Hirtius and Pansa entered on their consulship, according to Caesar's arrangement. The 2 consuls were sent along with Octavian, against Antony, who was besieging Dec. Brutus at Mutina. Pansa was defeated by Antony, and died of a wound which he had received in the battle. Hirtius retrieved this disaster by defeating Antony, but he also fell on the 27th of April, in leading an assault on the besieger's camp. Octavian sent the bodies of the slain consuls to Rome, where they were received with extraordinary honours, and publicly buried in the Field of Mars. To Octavian their removal from the scene was so timely, that he was accused by many of murdering them. Hirtius divides with Oppius the claim to the authorship of the 8th book of the Gallic war, as well as that of the Alexandrian, African, and Spanish. It is not impossible that he wrote the 3 first, but he certainly did not write the Spanish war.

Hirtuleius, a distinguished general of Sertorius in Spain. In B. C. 78 he was routed and slain near Italica in Baetica by Metellus.

Hispălis, more rarely **Hispal** (*Seville*), a town of the Turdetani in Hispania Baetica, founded by the Phoenicians, was situated on the left bank of the Baetis, and was in reality a seaport, for, although 500 stadia from the sea, the river is navigable for the largest vessels up to the town. Under the Romans Hispalis was the 3rd town in the province, Corduba and Gades being the 2 first. It was patronised by Caesar, because Corduba had espoused the side of Pompey. He made it a Roman colony, under the name of *Julia Romula* or *Romulensis*, and a conventus juridicus or town of assize. Under the Goths and Vandals Hispalis was the chief town in the S. of Spain, and under the Arabs was the capital of a separate kingdom.

Hispānĭa or **Ibērĭa** ('Iσπανία, 'Iβηρία: Hispānus, Ibērus: *Spain*), a peninsula in the S.W. of Europe, is connected with the land only on the N.E., where the Pyrenees form its boundary, and is surrounded on all other sides by the sea, on the E. and S. by the Mediterranean, on the W. by the Atlantic, and on the N. by the Cantabrian sea. The Greeks and Romans had no accurate knowledge of the country till the time of the Roman invasion in the 2nd Punic war. It was first mentioned by Hecataeus (about B. C. 500) under the name of *Iberia*; but this name originally indicated only the E. coast: the W. coast beyond the pillars of Hercules was called *Tartessis* (Ταρτησσίς); and the interior of the country *Celtica* (ἡ Κελτική). At a later time the Greeks applied the name of *Iberia*, which is usually derived from the river Iberus, to the whole country. The name *Hispania*, by which the Romans call the country, first occurs at the time of the Roman invasion. It is usually derived from the Punic word *Span*, "a rabbit," on account of the great number of rabbits which the Carthaginians found in the Peninsula; but others suppose the name to be of native origin, and to be the same as the Basque *Expaña*, an edge or border. The poets also called it *Hesperia*, or, to distinguish it from Italy, *Hesperia Ultima*. Spain is a very mountainous country. The principal mountains are, in the N.E. the Pyrenees [PYRENAEUS M.], and in the centre of the country the IDUBEDA, which runs parallel with the Pyrenees from the land of the Cantabri to the Mediterranean, and the OROSPEDA or ORTOSPEDA, which begins in the centre of the Idubeda, runs S.W. throughout Spain, and terminates at Calpe. The rivers of Spain are numerous. The 6 most important are the IBERUS (*Ebro*), BAETIS (*Guadalquiver*), and ANAS (*Guadiana*), in the E. and S.; and the TAGUS, DURIUS (*Douro*), and MINIUS (*Minho*), in the W. Spain was considered by the ancients very fertile, but more especially the S. part of the country, Baetica and Lusitania, which were also praised for their splendid climate. The central and N. parts of the country were less productive, and the climate in these districts was very cold in winter. In the S. there were numerous flocks of excellent sheep, the wool of which was very celebrated in foreign countries. The Spanish horses and asses were also much valued in antiquity; and on the coast there was abundance of fish. The country produced a great quantity of corn, oil, wine, flax, figs, and other fruits. But the principal riches of the country consisted in its mineral productions, of which the greatest quantity was found in Turdetania. Gold was found in abundance in various parts of the country; and there were many silver mines, of which the most celebrated were near Carthago Nova, Ilipa, Sisapon, and Castulo. The precious stones, copper, lead, tin, and other metals, were also found in more or less abundance. — The most ancient inhabitants of Spain were the Iberi, who, as a separate people, must be distinguished from the Iberi, a collective name of all the inhabitants of Spain. The Iberi dwelt on both sides of the Pyrenees, and were found in the S. of Gaul, as far as the Rhone. Celts afterwards crossed the Pyrenees, and became mingled with the Iberi, whence arose the mixed race of the Celtiberi, who dwelt chiefly in the high table land in the centre of the country. [CELTIBERI.] But besides this mixed race of the Celtiberi, there were also several tribes, both of Iberians and Celts, who were never united with one another. The unmixed Iberians, from whom the modern Basques are descended, dwelt chiefly in the Pyrenees and on the coasts, and their most distinguished tribes were the ASTURES, CANTABRI, VACCAEI, &c. The unmixed Celts dwelt chiefly on the river Anas, and in the N.W. corner of the country or Gallaecia. Besides these inhabitants, there were Phoenician and Carthaginian settlements on the coasts, of which the most important were GADES and CARTHAGO NOVO; there were likewise Greek colonies, such as EMPORIAE and SAGUNTUM; and lastly the conquest of the country by the Romans introduced many Romans among the inhabitants, whose customs, civilisation, and language, gradually spread over the whole peninsula, and effaced the national characteristics of the ancient population. The spread of the Latin language in Spain seems to have been facilitated by the schools, established by Sertorius, in which both the language and literature of Greece and Rome were taught. Under the empire some of the most distinguished Latin writers were natives of Spain, such as the 2 Senecas, Lucan, Martial, Quintilian, Silius Italicus, Pomponius Mela, Prudentius, and others. The ancient inhabitants of Spain were a proud, brave, and warlike race; easily excited and ready to take offence; inveterate robbers; moderate in the use of food and wine; fond of song and of the dance; lovers of their liberty, and ready at all times to sacrifice their lives rather than submit to a foreign master. The Cantabri and the inhabitants of the mountains in the N. were the fiercest and most uncivilised of all the tribes; the Vaccaei and the Turdetani were the most civilised; and the latter people were not only acquainted with the alphabet, but possessed a literature which contained records of their history, poems, and collections of laws composed in verse. — The history of Spain begins with the invasion of the country by the Carthaginians,

B. C. 238; for up to that time hardly any thing was known of Spain except the existence of 2 powerful commercial states in the W., TARTESSUS and GADES. After the 1st Punic war Hamilcar, the son of Hannibal, formed the plan of conquering Spain, in order to obtain for the Carthaginians possessions which might indemnify them for the loss of Sicily and Sardinia. Under his command (238—229), and that of his son-in-law and successor, Hasdrubal (228—221), the Carthaginians conquered the greater part of the S.E. of the peninsula as far as the Iberus; and Hasdrubal founded the important city of Carthago Nova. These successes of the Carthaginians excited the jealousy of the Romans; and a treaty was made between the 2 nations about 228, by which the Carthaginians bound themselves not to cross the Iberus. The town of Saguntum, although on the W. side of the river, was under the protection of the Romans; and the capture of this town by Hannibal in 219, was the immediate cause of the 2nd Punic war. In the course of this war the Romans drove the Carthaginians out of the peninsula, and became masters of their possessions in the S. of the country. But many tribes in the centre of the country, which had been only nominally subject to Carthage, still retained their virtual independence; and the tribes in the N. and N.W. of the country had been hitherto quite unknown both to the Carthaginians and Romans. There now arose a long and bloody struggle between the Romans and the various tribes in Spain, and it was nearly 2 centuries before the Romans succeeded in subduing entirely the whole of the peninsula. The Celtiberians were conquered by the elder Cato (195), and Tib. Gracchus, the father of the 2 tribunes (179). The Lusitanians, who long resisted the Romans under their brave leader Viriathus, were obliged to submit, about the year 137, to D. Brutus, who penetrated as far as Gallaecia; but it was not till Numantia was taken by Scipio Africanus the younger, in 133, that the Romans obtained the undisputed sovereignty over the various tribes in the centre of the country, and of the Lusitanians to the S. of the Tagus. Julius Caesar, after his praetorship, subdued the Lusitanians N. of the Tagus (60). The Cantabri, Astures, and other tribes in the mountains of the N., were finally subjugated by Augustus and his generals. The whole peninsula was now subject to the Romans; and Augustus founded in it several colonies, and caused excellent roads to be made throughout the country. The Romans had, as early as the end of the 2nd Punic war, divided Spain into 2 provinces, separated from one another by the Iberus, and called *Hispania Citerior* and *Hispania Ulterior*, the former being to the E., and the latter to the W. of the river. In consequence of there being 2 provinces, we frequently find the country called *Hispaniae*. The provinces were governed by 2 proconsuls or 2 propraetors, the latter of whom also frequently bore the title of proconsuls. Augustus made a new division of the country, and formed 3 provinces *Tarraconensis, Baetica*, and *Lusitania*. The province *Tarraconensis*, which derived its name from Tarraco, the capital of the province, was by far the largest of the 3, and comprehended the whole of the N., W., and centre of the peninsula. The province *Baetica*, which derived its name from the river Baetis, was separated from Lusitania on the N. and W. by the river Anas, and from Tarracosensis on the E. by a line drawn from the river Anas to the promontory Charidemus in the Mediterranean. The province *Lusitania*, which corresponded very nearly in extent to the modern Portugal, was separated from Tarraconensis on the N. by the river Durius, from Baetica on the E. by the Anas, and from Tarraconensis on the E. by a line drawn from the Durius to the Anas, between the territories of the Vettones and Carpetani. Augustus made Baetica a senatorial province, but reserved the government of the 2 others for the Caesar; so that the former was governed by a proconsul appointed by the senate, and the latter by imperial legati. In Baetica, Corduba or Hispalis was the seat of government; in Tarraconensis Tarraco; and in Lusitania Augusta Emerita. On the reorganisation of the empire by Constantine, Spain, together with Gaul and Britain, was under the general administration of the *Praefectus Praetorio Galliae*, one of whose 3 vicarii had the government of Spain, and usually resided at Hispalis. At the same time the country was divided into 7 provinces: *Baetica, Lusitania, Gallaecia, Turraconensis, Carthaginiensis, Baleáres, r.nd Mauritania Tingitana* in Africa (which was then reckoned part of Spain). The capitals of these 7 provinces were respectively *Hispalis, Augusta Emerita, Bracara, Caesaraugusta, Carthago Nova, Palma,* and *Tingis.* In A. D. 409 the Vandals and Suevi, together with other barbarians, invaded Spain, and obtained possession of the greater part of the country. In 414 the Visigoths, as allies of the Roman empire, attacked the Vandals, and in the course of 4 years (414—418) compelled a great part of the peninsula to submit again to the Romans. In 429 the Vandals left Spain, and crossed over into Africa under their king Genseric; after which time the Suevi established a powerful kingdom in the S. of the peninsula. Soon afterwards the Visigoths again invaded Spain, and after many years' struggle, succeeded in conquering the whole peninsula, which they kept for themselves, and continued the masters of the country for 2 centuries, till they were in their turn conquered by the Arabs, A. D. 712.

Hispellum (Hispellas, -ātis: Hispellensis: *Spello*), a town in Umbria, and a Roman colony, with the name of Colonia Julia Hispellum.

Histiaea. [HESTIAEOTIS.]

Histiaeus ('Ιστιαῖος), tyrant of Miletus, was left with the other Ionians to guard the bridge of boats over the Danube, when Darius invaded Scythia (B. C. 513). He opposed the proposal of Miltiades, the Athenian, to destroy the bridge, and leave the Persians to their fate, and was in consequence rewarded by Darius with the rule of Mytilene, and with a district in Thrace, where he built a town called Myrcinus, apparently with a view of establishing an independent kingdom. This excited the suspicions of Darius, who invited Histiaeus to Susa, where he treated him kindly, but prohibited him from returning. Tired of the restraint in which he was kept, he induced his kinsman Aristagoras to persuade the Ionians to revolt, hoping that a revolution in Ionia might lead to his release. His design succeeded. Darius allowed Histiaeus to depart (496) on his engaging to reduce Ionia. The revolt however was nearly put down when Histiaeus reached the coast. Here Histiaeus threw off the mask, and after raising a small fleet carried on war against the Persians for 2 years, and obtained pos-

session of Chios. In 494 he made a descent upon the Ionian coast, but was defeated and taken prisoner by Harpagus. Artaphernes, the satrap of Ionia, caused him to be put to death by impalement, and sent his head to the king.

Histonium (Histoniensis: *Vasto d'Ammone*), a town of the Frentani on the coast, and subsequently a Roman colony.

Homeritae ('Ομηρῖται), a people of Arabia Felix, who migrated from the interior to the S. part of the W. coast, and established themselves in the territory of the Sabaei (in *El. Yemen*), where they founded a kingdom, which lasted more than 5 centuries.

Homerus ("Ομηρος). 1. The great epic poet of Greece. His poems formed the basis of Greek literature. Every Greek who had received a liberal education was perfectly well acquainted with them from his childhood, and had learnt them by heart at school; but nobody could state any thing certain about their author. His date and birthplace were equally matters of dispute. Seven cities claimed Homer as their countryman (Smyrna, Rhodus, Colophon, Salamis, Chios, Argos, Athenae); but the claims of Smyrna and Chios are the most plausible, and between these 2 we have to decide. It is supposed by the best modern writers that Homer was an Ionian, who settled at Smyrna, at the time when the Achaeans and Aeolians formed the chief part of the population. We can thus explain how Homer became so well acquainted with the traditions of the Trojan war, which had been waged by Achaeans and Aeolians, but in which the Ionians had not taken part. We know that the Ionians were subsequently driven out of Smyrna; and it is further supposed either that Homer himself fled to Chios, or his descendants or disciples settled there, and formed the famous family of Homerids. According to this account the time of Homer would be a few generations after the Ionian migration. But with the exception of the simple fact of his being an Asiatic Greek, all other particulars respecting his life are purely fabulous. The common tradition related that he was the son of Maeon (hence called *Maeonides vates*), and that in his old age he was blind and poor. Homer was universally regarded by the ancients as the author of the 2 great poems of the Iliad and the Odyssey. Other poems were also attributed to Homer, the genuineness of which was disputed by some; but the Iliad and Odyssey were ascribed to him by the concurrent voice of antiquity. Such continued to be the prevalent belief in modern times, till 1795, when F. A. Wolf wrote his famous Prolegomena, in which he endeavoured to show that the Iliad and Odyssey were not two complete poems, but small, separate, independent epic songs, celebrating single exploits of the heroes, and that these lays were *for the first time* written down and united, as the Iliad and Odyssey, by Pisistratus, the tyrant of Athens. This opinion gave rise to a long and animated controversy respecting the origin of the Homeric poems, which is not yet settled, and which probably never will be. The following, however, may be regarded as the most probable conclusion. An abundance of heroic lays preserved the tales of the Trojan war. Europe must necessarily have been the country where these songs originated, both because the victorious heroes dwelt in Europe, and because so many traces in the poems still point to these regions

These heroic lays were brought to Asia Minor by the Greek colonies, which left the mother-country about 3 ages after the Trojan war. These unconnected songs were, for the first time, united by a great genius, called Homer, and he was the *one individual* who conceived in his mind the lofty idea of that poetical unity which we must acknowledge and admire in the Iliad and Odyssey. But as writing was not known, or at least little practised, in the age in which Homer lived, it naturally followed that in such long works many interpolations were introduced, and that they gradually became more and more dismembered, and thus returned into their original state of separate independent songs. They were preserved by the rhapsodists, who were minstrels, and who sung lays at the banquets of the great and at public festivals. A class of rhapsodists at Chios, the Homerids, who called themselves the descendants of the poet, made it their especial business to sing the lays of the Iliad and Odyssey, and to transmit them to their disciples by oral teaching, and not by writing. These rhapsodists preserved the knowledge of the unity of the Homeric poems ; and this knowledge was never entirely lost, although the public recitation of the poems became more and more fragmentary, and the time at festivals and musical contests formerly occupied by epic rhapsodists exclusively, was encroached upon by the rising lyrical performances. Solon directed the attention of his countrymen towards the unity of the Homeric poems ; but the unanimous voice of antiquity ascribed to Pisistratus the merit of having collected the disjointed poems of Homer, and of having first committed them to writing. From the time of Pisistratus, the Greeks had a written Homer, a regular text, which was the source and foundation of all subsequent editions. — We have already stated that the ancients attributed many other poems to Homer besides the Iliad and the Odyssey ; but the claims of none of these to this honour can stand investigation. The hymns, which still bear the name of Homer, probably owe their origin to the rhapsodists. They exhibit such a diversity of language and poetical tone, that in all probability they contain fragments from every century from the time of Homer to the Persian war. The *Batrachomyomachia*, the Battle of the Frogs and Mice, an extant poem, and the *Margites*, a poem which is lost, and which ridiculed a man who was said to know many things and who knew all badly, were both frequently ascribed by the ancients to Homer, but were clearly of later origin. — The Odyssey was evidently composed after the Iliad ; and many writers maintain that they are the works of 2 different authors. But it has been observed in reply that there is not a greater difference in the 2 poems than we often find in the productions of the same man in the prime of life and in old age ; and the chief cause of difference in the 2 poems is owing to the difference of the subject. — We must add a few words on the literary history of the Iliad and Odyssey. From the time of Pisistratus to the establishment of the Alexandrine school, we read of 2 new editions (διορθώσεις) of the text, one made by the poet Antimachus, and the other by Aristotle, which Alexander the Great used to carry about with him in a splendid ca-e (νάρθηξ) on all his expeditions. But it was not till the foundation of the Alexandrine school, that the Greeks possessed a really critical edition of Homer. Zenodotus was the first who directed his attention to the study and criticism of Homer. He was followed by Aristophanes and Aristarchus ; and the edition of Homer by the latter has been the basis of the text to the present day. Aristarchus was the prince of grammarians, and did more for the text and interpretation of Homer than any other critic in modern times. He was opposed to Crates of Mallus, the founder of the Pergamene school of grammar. [ARISTARCHUS ; CRATES.] In the time of Augustus the great compiler, Didymus, wrote comprehensive commentaries on Homer, copying mostly the works of preceding Alexandrine grammarians, which had swollen to an enormous extent. Under Tiberius, Apollonius Sophista lived, whose lexicon Homericum is very valuable (ed. Bekker, 1833). The most valuable scholia on the Iliad are those which were published by Villoison from a MS. of the 10th century in the library of St. Mark at Venice, 1788, fol. These scholia were reprinted with additions, edited by I. Bekker, Berlin, 1825, 2 vols. 4to. The most valuable scholia to the Odyssey are those published by Buttmann, Berl. 1821. The extensive commentary of Eustathius contains much valuable information from sources which are now lost. [EUSTATHIUS, No. 3.] The best critical editions of Homer are by Wolf, Lips. 1804, seq. ; by Bothe, Lips. 1832, seq. ; and by Bekker, Berlin, 1843. There is a very good edition of the Iliad by Spitzner, Gotha, 1832, seq. ; and a valuable commentary on the Odyssey by Nitzsch, Hannov. 1825, seq.—2. A grammarian and tragic poet of Byzantium, in the time of Ptolemy Philadelphus (about B. C. 280), was the son of the grammarian Andromachus and the poetess Myro. He was one of the 7 poets who formed the tragic Pleiad.

HŎMŎLĒ ('Ομόλη). 1. A lofty mountain in Thessaly, near Tempe, with a sanctuary of Pan. — 2. Or HŎMŎLIUM ('Ομόλιον: 'Ομαλιεύς : *Lamina*), a town in Magnesia in Thessaly, at the foot of Mt. Ossa, near the Peneus.

HŎNOR or HŎNOS, the personification of honour at Rome. Marcellus had vowed a temple, which was to belong to Honor and Virtus in common ; but as the pontiffs refused to consecrate one temple to 2 divinities, he built 2 temples, one of Honor and the other of Virtus, close together. C. Marius also built a temple to Honor, after his victory over the Cimbri and Teutones. There was also an altar of Honor outside the Colline gate, which was more ancient than either of the temples. Honor is represented on coins as a male figure in armour, and standing on a globe, or with the cornucopia in his left and a spear in his right hand.

HŎNORIA. [GRATA.]

HŎNORIUS, FLĀVĬUS, Roman emperor of the West, A. D. 395—423, was the 2nd son of Theodosius the Great, and was born 384. On the death of Theodosius, in 395, Honorius succeeded peaceably to the sovereignty of the West, which he had received from his father in the preceding year ; while his elder brother Arcadius obtained possession of the East. During the minority of Honorius, the government was entirely in the hands of the able and energetic Stilicho, whose daughter Maria the young emperor married. Stilicho for a time defended Italy against the attacks of the Visigoths under Alaric (402, 403), and the ravages of other barbarians under Radagaisus ; but after Honorius had put to death Stilicho, on a charge of treason (408), Alaric again invaded Italy, and took and plundered Rome

410). Honorius meantime lived an inglorious life at Ravenna, where he continued to reside till his death, in 423.

Hŏrae ("Ωραι), originally the goddesses of the order of nature and of the seasons, but in later times the goddesses of order in general and of justice. In Homer, who neither mentions their parents nor their number, they are the Olympian divinities of the weather and the ministers of Zeus. In this capacity they guard the doors of Olympus, and promote the fertility of the earth, by the various kinds of weather which they give to mortals. As the weather, generally speaking, is regulated according to the seasons, they are further described as the goddesses of the seasons. The course of the seasons is symbolically described as the dance of the Horae. At Athens 2 Horae, *Thallo* (the Hora of spring) and *Carpo* (the Hora of autumn), were worshipped from very early times. The Hora of spring accompanied Persephone every year on her ascent from the lower world; and the expression of "The chamber of the Horae opens" is equivalent to "The spring is coming." The attributes of spring — flowers, fragrance, and graceful freshness — are accordingly transferred to the Horae. Thus they adorned Aphrodite as she rose from the sea, and made a garland of flowers for Pandora. Hence they bear a resemblance to and are mentioned along with the Charites, and both are frequently confounded or identified. As they were conceived to promote the prosperity of every thing that grows, they appear also as the protectresses of youth and newly-born gods. Even in early times ethical notions were attached to the Horae; and the influence which these goddesses originally exercised on nature was subsequently transferred to human life in particular. Hesiod describes them as giving to a state good laws, justice, and peace; he calls them the daughters of Zeus and Themis, and gives them the significant names of *Eunomia, Dice,* and *Irene.* The number of the Horae is different in the different writers, though the most ancient number seems to have been 2, as at Athens; but afterwards their common number was 3, like that of the Moerae and Charites. In works of art the Horae were represented as blooming maidens, carrying the different products of the seasons.

Horapollo (Ὡραπόλλων), the name prefixed to an extant work on hieroglyphics, which purports to be a Greek translation, made by one Philippus from the Egyptian. The writer was a native of Egypt, and probably lived about the beginning of the 5th century. The best edition is by Leemans, Amsterdam, 1835.

Hŏrātĭa Gens, one of the most ancient patrician gentes at Rome. 3 brothers of this race fought with the Curiatii, 3 brothers from Alba, to determine whether Rome or Alba was to exercise the supremacy. The battle was long undecided. 2 of the Horatii fell; but the 3 Curiatii, though alive, were severely wounded. Seeing this, the surviving Horatius, who was still unhurt, pretended to fly, and vanquished his wounded opponents, by encountering them severally. He returned in triumph, bearing his threefold spoils. As he approached the Capene gate his sister Horatia met him, and recognised on his shoulders the mantle of one of the Curiatii, her betrothed lover. Her importunate grief drew on her the wrath of Horatius, who stabbed her, exclaiming "so perish every

Roman woman who bewails a foe." For this murder he was adjudged by the duumviri to be scourged with covered head, and hanged on the accursed tree. Horatius appealed to his peers, the burghers or populus; and his father pronounced him guiltless, or he would have punished him by the paternal power. The populus acquitted Horatius, but prescribed a form of punishment. With veiled head, led by his father, Horatius passed under a yoke or gibbet — *tigillum sororium,* "sister's gibbet."

Horātĭus Cocles. [COCLES.]

Q. Horātĭus Flaccus, the poet, was born December 8th, B. C. 65, at Venusia in Apulia. His father was a libertinus or freedman. He had received his manumission before the birth of the poet, who was of ingenuous birth, but who did not altogether escape the taunt, which adhered to persons even of remote servile origin. His father's occupation was that of collector (*coactor*), either of the indirect taxes farmed by the publicans, or at sales by auction. With the profits of his office he had purchased a small farm in the neighbourhood of Venusia, where the poet was born. The father, either in his parental fondness for his only son, or discerning some hopeful promise in the boy, determined to devote his whole time and fortune to the education of the future poet. Though by no means rich, he declined to send the young Horace to the common school, kept in Venusia by one Flavius, to which the children of the rural aristocracy resorted. Probably about his 12th year, his father carried him to Rome, to receive the usual education of a knight's or senator's son. He frequented the best schools in the capital. One of these was kept by Orbilius, a retired military man, whose flogging propensities have been immortalised by his pupil. (*Epist.* ii 1. 71.) The names of his other teachers are not recorded by the poet. He was instructed in the Greek and Latin languages: the poets were the usual school books, Homer in the Greek, and the old tragic writer, Livius Andronicus, in the Latin. In his 18th year Horace proceeded to Athens, in order to continue his studies at that seat of learning. He seems chiefly to have attached himself to the opinions which he heard in the Academus, though later in life he inclined to those of Epicurus. When Brutus came to Athens after the death of Caesar, Horace joined his army, and received at once the rank of a military tribune, and the command of a legion. He was present at the battle of Philippi, and shared in the flight of the republican army. In one of his poems he playfully alludes to his flight, and throwing away his shield. (*Carm.* ii. 7. 9.) He now resolved to devote himself to more peaceful pursuits, and having obtained his pardon, he ventured at once to return to Rome. He had lost all his hopes in life; his paternal estate had been swept away in the general forfeiture; but he was enabled, however, to obtain sufficient money to purchase a clerkship in the quaestor's office; and on the profits of that place he managed to live with the utmost frugality. Meantime some of his poems attracted the notice of Varius and Virgil, who introduced him to Maecenas (B. C. 39). Horace soon became the friend of Maecenas, and this friendship quickly ripened into intimacy. In a year or two after the commencement of their friendship (37), Horace accompanied his patron on that journey to Brundusium, so agreeably described in the 5th Satire of the 1st book. About the year 34 Maecenas bestowed upon the poet a Sabine farm, sufficient to maintain him in ease, comfort, and even in content (*satis beatus unicis Sabinis*), during the rest of his life. The situation of this Sabine farm was in the valley of Ustica, within view of the mountain Lucretilis, and near the Digentia, about 15 miles from Tibur (*Tivoli*). A site exactly answering to the villa of Horace, and on which were found ruins of buildings, has been discovered in modern times. Besides this estate, his admiration of the beautiful scenery in the neighbourhood of Tibur inclined him either to hire or to purchase a small cottage in that romantic town; and all the later years of his life were passed between these two country residences and Rome. He continued to live on the most intimate terms with Maecenas; and this intimate friendship naturally introduced Horace to the notice of the other great men of his period, and at length to Augustus himself, who bestowed upon the poet substantial marks of his favour. Horace died on November 17th, B. C. 8, aged nearly 57. His death was so sudden, that he had not time to make his will; but he left the administration of his affairs to Augustus, whom he instituted as his heir. He was buried on the slope of the Esquiline Hill, close to his friend and patron Maecenas, who had died before him in the same year.—Horace has described his own person. He was of short stature, with dark eyes and dark hair, but early tinged with grey. In his youth he was tolerably robust, but suffered from a complaint in his eyes. In more advanced life he grew fat, and Augustus jested about his protuberant belly. His health was not always good, and he seems to have inclined to be a valetudinarian. When young he was irascible in temper, but easily placable. In dress he was rather careless. His habits, even after he became richer, were generally frugal and abstemious; though on occasions, both in youth and maturer age, he seems to have indulged in conviviality. He liked choice wine, and in the society of friends scrupled not to enjoy the luxuries of his time. He was never married.— The philosophy of Horace was that of a man of the world. He playfully alludes to his Epicureanism, but it was practical rather than speculative Epicureanism. His mind, indeed, was not in the least speculative. Common life wisdom was his study, and to this he brought a quickness of observation and a sterling common sense, which have made his works the delight of practical men.— The *Odes* of Horace want the higher inspirations of lyric verse. His amatory verses are exquisitely graceful, but they have no strong ardour, no deep tenderness, nor even much of light and joyous gaiety. But as works of refined art, of the most skilful felicities of language and of measure, of translucent expression, and of agreeable images, embodied in words which imprint themselves indelibly on the memory, they are unrivalled. According to Quintilian, Horace was almost the only Roman lyric poet worth reading.— In the *Satires* of Horace there is none of the lofty moral indignation, the fierce vehemence of invective, which characterised the later satirists. It is the folly rather than the wickedness of vice, which he touches with such playful skill. Nothing can surpass the keenness of his observation, or his ease of expression: it is the finest comedy of manners, in

a descriptive instead of a dramatic form. — In the *Epodes* there is bitterness provoked, it should seem, by some personal hatred, or sense of injury, and the ambition of imitating Archilochus; but in these he seems to have exhausted all the malignity and violence of his temper. — But the *Epistles* are the most perfect of the Horatian poetry, the poetry of manners and society, the beauty of which consists in a kind of ideality of common sense and practical wisdom. The Epistles of Horace are with the Poem of Lucretius, the Georgics of Virgil, and perhaps the Satires of Juvenal, the most perfect and most original form of Roman verse. The title of the *Art of Poetry* for the Epistle to the Pisos is as old as Quintilian, but it is now agreed that it was not intended for a complete theory of the poetic art. It is conjectured with great probability that it was intended to dissuade one of the younger Pisos from devoting himself to poetry, for which he had little genius, or at least to suggest the difficulties of attaining to perfection.—The chronology of the Horatian poems is of great importance, as illustrating the life, the times, and the writings of the poet. There has been great dispute upon this subject, but the following view appears the most probable. The 1st book of Satires, which was the first publication, appeared about B. C. 35, in the 30th year of Horace. — The 2nd book of Satires was published about 33, in the 32nd year of Horace.—The Epodes appeared about 31, in the 34th year of Horace.— The 3 first books of the Odes were published about 24 or 23 in the 41st or 42nd year of Horace. — The 1st book of the Epistles was published about 20 or 19 in the 45th or 46th year of Horace. — The Carmen Seculare appeared in 17 in the 48th year of Horace. — The 4th book of the Odes was published in 14 or 13 in his 51st or 52nd year.— The dates of the 2nd book of Epistles, and of the *Ars Poetica*, are admitted to be uncertain, though both appeared before the poet's death, B. C. 8. One of the best editions of Horace is by Orelli, Turici, 1843.

Hordeōnĭus Flaccus. [FLACCUS.]

Hormisdas. [SASSANIDAE.]

Horta or **Hortānum** (Hortanus: *Orte*), a town in Etruria, at the junction of the Nar and the Tiber, so called from the Etruscan goddess Horta, whose temple at Rome always remained open.

Hortensĭus. 1. **Q.**, the orator, was born in B. C. 114, eight years before Cicero. At the early age of 19 he spoke with great applause in the forum, and at once rose to eminence as an advocate. He served two campaigns in the Social war (90, 89). In the civil wars he joined Sulla, and was afterwards a constant supporter of the aristocratical party. His chief professional labours were in defending men of this party, when accused of maladministration and extortion in their provinces, or of bribery and the like in canvassing for public honours. He had no rival in the forum, till he encountered Cicero, and he long exercised an undisputed sway over the courts of justice. In 81 he was quaestor; in 75 aedile; in 72 praetor; and in 69 consul with Q. Caecilius Metellus.— It was in the year before his consulship that the prosecution of Verres commenced. Hortensius was the advocate of Verres, and attempted to put off the trial till the next year, when he would be able to exercise all the consular authority in favour of his client. But Cicero, who accused Verres, baffled all the schemes of Hortensius; and the issue of this contest was to dethrone Hortensius from the seat which had been already tottering, and to establish his rival, the despised provincial of Arpinum, as the first orator and advocate of the Roman forum. After his consulship, Hortensius took a leading part in supporting the optimates against the rising power of Pompey. He opposed the Gabinian law, which invested Pompey with absolute power on the Mediterranean, in order to put down the pirates of Cilicia (67); and the Manilian, by which the conduct of the war against Mithridates was transferred from Lucullus to Pompey (66). Cicero in his consulship (63) deserted the popular party, with whom he had hitherto acted, and became one of the supporters of the optimates. Thus Hortensius no longer appears as his rival. We first find them pleading together for C. Rabirius, for L. Muraena, and for P. Sulla. After the coalition of Pompey with Caesar and Crassus in 60, Hortensius drew back from public life, and confined himself to his advocate's duties. He died in 50. The eloquence of Hortensius was of the florid or (as it was termed) "Asiatic" style, fitter for hearing than for reading. His voice was soft and musical, his memory so ready and retentive, that he is said to have been able to come out of a saleroom and repeat the auction-list backwards. His action was very elaborate, so that sneerers called him Dionysia — the name of a well-known dancer of the day; and the pains he bestowed in arranging the folds of his toga have been recorded by ancient writers. But in all this there must have been a real grace and dignity, for we read that Aesopus and Roscius, the tragedians, used to follow him into the forum to take a lesson in their own art. He possessed immense wealth, and was keenly alive to all the enjoyments which wealth can give. He had several villas, the most splendid of which was the one near Laurentum. Here he laid up such a stock of wine, that he left 10,000 casks of Chian to his heir. Here he had a park full of all sorts of animals; and it was customary, during his sumptuous dinners, for a slave, dressed like Orpheus, to issue from the woods with these creatures following the sound of his cithara. At his villa at Bauli he had immense fish-ponds, into which the sea came: the fish were so tame that they would feed from his hand; and he was so fond of them, that he is said to have wept for the death of a favourite muraena. He was also very curious in trees: he is said to have fed them with wine, and we read that he once begged Cicero to change places in speaking, that he might perform this office for a favourite plane-tree at the proper time. It is a characteristic trait, that he came forward from his retirement (55) to oppose the sumptuary law of Pompey and Crassus, and spoke so eloquently and wittily as to procure its rejection. He was the first person at Rome who brought peacocks to table. — 2. Q., surnamed Hortalus, son of the preceding, by Lutatia, the daughter of Catulus. In youth he lived a low and profligate life, and appears to have been at last cast off by his father. On the breaking out of the civil war in 49, he joined Caesar, and fought on his side in Italy and Greece. In 44 he held the province of Macedonia, and Brutus was to succeed him. After Caesar's assassination, M. Antony gave the province to his brother Caius. Brutus, however, had already taken possession, with the assistance of Hortensius.

When the proscription took place, Hortensius was in the list; and in revenge he ordered C. Antonius, who had been taken prisoner, to be put to death. After the battle of Philippi, he was executed on the grave of his victim.

Hôrus (Ὧρος), the Egyptian god of the sun, whose worship was also established in Greece, and afterwards at Rome. He was compared with the Greek Apollo, and identified with Harpocrates, the last-born and weakly son of Osiris. Both were represented as youths, and with the same attributes and symbols. He was believed to have been born with his finger on his mouth, as indicative of secrecy and mystery. In the earlier period of his worship at Rome he seems to have been particularly regarded as the god of quiet life and silence.

Hostilia (Ostiglia), a small town in Gallia Cisalpina, on the Po, and on the road from Mutina to Verona; the birthplace of Cornelius Nepos.

Hostilius Mancinus. [MANCINUS.]

Hostilius Tullus. [TULLUS HOSTILIUS.]

Hostius, the author of a poem on the Istrian war (B.C. 178), which is quoted by the grammarians. He was probably a contemporary of Julius Caesar.

Hunneric, king of the Vandals in Africa, A.D. 477—484, was the son of Genseric, whom he succeeded. His reign was chiefly marked by his savage persecution of the Catholics.

Hunni (Οὖννοι), an Asiatic race, who dwelt for some centuries in the plains of Tartary, and were formidable to the Chinese empire, long before they were known to the Romans. It was to repel the inroads of the Huns that the Chinese built their celebrated wall, 1500 miles in length. A portion of the nation afterwards migrated W., conquered the Alani, a warlike race between the Volga and the Tanais, and then crossed into Europe about A.D. 375. The appearance of these new barbarians excited the greatest terror, both among the Romans and Germans. They are described by the Greek and Roman historians as hideous and repulsive beings, resembling apes, with broad shoulders, flat noses, and small black eyes deeply buried in their head; while their manners and habits were savage to the last degree. They destroyed the powerful monarchy of the Ostrogoths, who were obliged to retire before them, and were allowed by Valens to settle in Thrace, A.D. 376. The Huns now frequently ravaged the Roman dominions. They were joined by many other barbarian nations, and under their king Attila (A.D. 434—453), they devastated the fairest portions of the empire, both in the E. and the W. [ATTILA.] On the death of Attila, the various nations which composed his army, dispersed, and his sons were unable to resist the arms of the Ostrogoths. In a few years after the death of Attila, the empire of the Huns was completely destroyed. The remains of the nation became incorporated with other barbarians, and never appear again as a separate people.

Hyäcinthus (Ὑάκινθος). 1. Son of the Spartan king Amyclas and Diomede, or of Pierus and Clio, or of Oebalus or Eurotas. He was a youth of extraordinary beauty, and was beloved by Apollo and Zephyrus. He returned the love of Apollo; and as he was once playing at quoit with the god, Zephyrus, out of jealousy, drove the quoit of Apollo with such violence against the head of the youth, that he fell down dead. From the blood of Hyacinthus there sprang the flower of the same name (hyacinth), on the leaves of which appeared the exclamation of woe AI, AI, or the letter Υ, being the initial of Ὑάκινθος. According to other traditions, the hyacinth sprang from the blood of Ajax. Hyacinthus was worshipped at Amyclae as a hero, and a great festival, Hyacinthia, was celebrated in his honour. (*Dict. of Antiq. s. v.*)—2. A Lacedaemonian, who is said to have gone to Athens, and to have sacrificed his daughters for the purpose of delivering the city from a famine and plague, under which it was suffering during the war with Minos. His daughters were known in the Attic legends by the name of the *Hyacinthides*, which they derived from their father. Some traditions make them the daughters of Erechtheus, and relate that they received their name from the village of Hyacinthus, where they were sacrificed at the time when Athens was attacked by the Eleusinians and Thracians, or Thebans.

Hÿădes (Ὑάδες), that is, the Rainy, the name of nymphs, whose parentage, number and names are described in various ways by the ancients. Their parents were Atlas and Aethra, or Atlas and Pleione, or Hyas and Boeotia: others call their father Oceanus, Meliseus, Cadmilus, or Erechtheus. Their number differs in various legends; but their most common number is 7, as they appear in the constellation which bears their name, viz., *Ambrosia*, *Eudora*, *Pedile*, *Coronis*, *Polyxo*, *Phyto*, and *Thyene* or *Dione*. They were entrusted by Zeus with the care of his infant son Dionysus, and were afterwards placed by Zeus among the stars. The story which made them the daughters of Atlas relates that their number was 12 or 15, and that at first 5 of them were placed among the stars as Hyades, and the 7 (or 10) others afterwards under the name of Pleiades, to reward them for the sisterly love they had evinced after the death of their brother Hyas, who had been killed in Libya by a wild beast. Their name, Hyades, is derived by the ancients from their father, Hyas, or from Hyes, a mystic surname of Dionysus; or according to others, from their position in the heavens, where they formed a figure resembling the Greek letter Υ. The Romans, who derived it from ὗς, a pig, translated the name by *Suculae*. The most natural derivation is from ὕειν, to rain, as the constellation of the Hyades, when rising simultaneously with the sun, announced rainy weather. Hence Horace speaks of the *tristes Hyades* (*Carm.* i, 3. 14).

Hyampĕa. [PARNASSUS.]

Hyampŏlis (Ὑάμπολις: Ὑαμπολίτης), a town in Phocis, E. of the Cephissus, near Cleonae, was founded by the Hyantes, when they were driven out of Boeotia by the Cadmeans; was destroyed by Xerxes; afterwards rebuilt; and again destroyed by Philip and the Amphictyons.—Cleonae, from its vicinity to Hyampolis, is called by Xenophon (*Hell.* vi. 4. § 2) Ὑαμπολιτῶν τὸ προάστειον. — Strabo speaks of 2 towns of the name of Hyampolis in Phocis; but it is doubtful whether his statement is correct.

Hyantes (Ὑάντες), the ancient inhabitants of Boeotia, from which country they were expelled by the Cadmeans. Part of the Hyantes emigrated to Phocis [HYAMPOLIS], and part to Aetolia. The poets use the adjective *Hyantius* as equivalent to Boeotian.

Hÿas (Ὑας), the name of the father and the brother of the Hyades. The father was married to Boeotia, and was looked upon as the ancestor of the ancient Hyantes. His son, the brother of the Hyades, was killed in Libya by a serpent, a boar, or a lion.

Hybla (Ὑβλη: Ὑβλαῖος, Hyblensis), 3 towns in Sicily. 1. Major (ἡ μείζων or μεγάλη), on the S. slope of Mt. Aetna and on the river Symaethus, was originally a town of the Siculi.—2. Minor (ἡ μικρά), afterwards called Megara. [MEGARA.] — 3. Heraea, in the S. of the island, on the road from Syracuse to Agrigentum.—It is doubtful from which of these 3 places the Hyblaean honey came, so frequently mentioned by the poets.

Hybrĕas (Ὑβρέας), of Mylasa in Caria, a celebrated orator, contemporary with the triumvir Antonius.

Hyccăra (τὰ Ὕκκαρα: Ὑκκαρεύς: *Muro di Carini*), a town of the Sicani on the N. coast of Sicily, W. of Panormus, said to have derived its name from the sea fish ὕκκαι. It was taken by the Athenians, and plundered, and its inhabitants sold as slaves, B. C. 415. Among the captives was the beautiful Timandra, the mistress of Alcibiades and the mother of Lais.

Hydarnes (Ὑδάρνης), one of the 7 Persians who conspired against the Magi in B. C. 521.

Hydaspes (Ὑδάσπης: *Jelum*), the N.most of the 5 great tributaries of the Indus, which, with the Indus itself, water the great plain of N. India, which is bounded on the N. by the *Himalaya* range, and which is now called the *Punjab*, i. e. 5 *rivers*. The Hydaspes falls into the Acesines (*Chenab*), which also receives, from the S., first the Hydraotes (*Ravee*), and then the Hyphasis (*Beeas*, and lower down, *Gharra*), which has previously received, on the S. side, the Hesidrus or Zaradrus (*Sutlej* or *Hesudru*); and the Acesines itself falls into the Indus. These 5 rivers all rise on the S.W. side of the Emodi M. (*Himalaya*), except the *Sutlej*, which, like the Indus, rises on the N. E. side of the range. They became known to the Greeks by Alexander's campaign in India: his great victory over Porus (B. C. 327) was gained on the left side of the Hydaspes, near, or perhaps upon, the scene of the recent battle of *Chilianwallah*; and the Hyphasis formed the limit of his progress. The epithet "fabulosus," which Horace applies to the Hydaspes (*Carm.* i. 22. 7) refers to the marvellous stories current among the Romans, who knew next to nothing about India; and the "*Medus* Hydaspes" of Virgil (*Georg.* iv. 211) is merely an example of the vagueness with which the Roman writers, especially the poets, refer to the countries beyond the E. limit of the empire.

Hydra. [HERCULES, p. 308, b.]

Hydraōtes (Ὑδραώτης, Strab. Ὑάρωτις: *Ravee*), a river of India, falling into the Acesines. [HYDASPES.]

Hydrĕa (Ὑδρέα: Ὑδρεάτης: *Hydra*), a small island in the gulf of Hermione off Argolis, of no importance in antiquity, but the inhabitants of which in modern times played a distinguished part in the war of Greek independence, and are some of the best sailors in Greece.

Hydruntum or Hydrūs (Ὑδροῦς: Hydruntīnus: *Otranto*), one of the most ancient towns of Calabria, situated on the S. E. coast, with a good harbour, and near a mountain Hydrus, was in later times a municipium. Persons frequently crossed over to Epirus from this port.

Hyettus ('Υηττός: 'Υήττιος), a small town in Boeotia on the lake Copais, and near the frontiers of Locris.

Hygiēa ('Υγίεια), also called **Hygēa** or **Hygia**, the goddess of health, and a daughter of Aesculapius; though some traditions make her the wife of the latter. She was usually worshipped in the temples of Aesculapius, as at Argos, where the 2 divinities had a celebrated sanctuary, at Athens, at Corinth, &c. At Rome there was a statue of her in the temple of Concordia. In works of art she is represented as a virgin dressed in a long robe, and feeding a serpent from a cup. — Although she was originally the goddess of physical health, she is sometimes conceived as the giver or protectress of mental health, that is, she appears as ὑγίεια φρενῶν (Aeschyl. Eum. 522), and was thus identified with Athena, surnamed Hygiea.

Hygīnus. 1. C. Jūlĭus, a Roman grammarian, was a native of Spain, and lived at Rome in the time of Augustus, whose freedman he was. He wrote several works, all of which have perished. — **2. Hygīnus Gromătĭcus**, so called from gruma, an instrument used by the Agrimensores. He lived in the time of Trajan, and wrote works on land surveying and castrametation, of which considerable fragments are extant. — **3. Hygīnus**, the author of 2 extant works; 1. *Fabularum Liber*, a series of short mythological legends, with an introductory genealogy of divinities. Although the larger portion of these narratives has been copied from obvious sources, they occasionally present the tales under new forms or with new circumstances. 2. *Poeticon Astronomicon Libri IV*. We know nothing of the author of these 2 works. He is sometimes identified with C. Julius Hyginus, the freedman of Augustus, but he must have lived at a much later period. Both works are included in the *Mythographi Latini* of Muncker, Amst. 1681, and of Van Staveren, Lug. Bat. 1742.

Hylaea ('Υλαίη, Herod.), a district in Scythia, covered with wood, is the peninsula adjacent to Taurica on the N.W., between the rivers Borysthenes and Hypacyris.

Hylaeus ('Υλαῖος), that is, the Woodman, the name of an Arcadian centaur, who was slain by Atalante, when he pursued her. According to some legends, Hylaeus fell in the fight against the Lapithae, and others again said that he was one of the centaurs slain by Hercules.

Hylas ("Υλας), son of Theodamas, king of the Dryopes, by the nymph Menodice; or, according to others, son of Hercules, Euphemus, or Ceyx. He was beloved by Hercules, whom he accompanied in the expedition of the Argonauts. On the coast of Mysia, Hylas went on shore to draw water from a fountain; but his beauty excited the love of the Naiads, who drew him down into the water, and he was never seen again. Hercules endeavoured in vain to find him; and when he shouted out to the youth, the voice of Hylas was heard from the bottom of the well only like a faint echo, whence some say that he was actually metamorphosed into an echo. While Hercules was engaged in seeking his favourite, the Argonauts sailed away, leaving him and his companion, Polyphemus, behind.

Hylē ("Υλη, also 'Υλαι), a small town in Boeotia, situated on the **Hyllice**, which was called after this town, and into which the river Ismenus flows.

Hyllas, a river in Bruttium, separating the territories of Sybaris and Croton.

Hyllce (ἡ 'Υλικὴ λίμνη), a lake in Boeotia, S. of the lake Copais. See **Hyle**.

Hyllcus ("Υλικος, "Υλλικος), a small river in Argolis, near Troezen.

Hyllus ("Υλλος), son of Hercules by Deianira. For details see **Heraclidae**.

Hyllus ("Υλλος: *Demirji*), a river of Lydia, falling into the Hermus on its N. side.

Hymēn or **Hymēnaeus** ('Υμήν or 'Υμέναιος), the god of marriage, was conceived as a handsome youth, and invoked in the hymeneal or bridal song. The names originally designated the bridal song itself, which was subsequently personified. He is described as the son of Apollo and a Muse, either Calliope, Urania, or Terpsichore. Others describe him only as the favourite of Apollo or Thamyris, and call him a son of Magnes and Calliope, or of Dionysus and Aphrodite. The ancient traditions, instead of regarding the god as a personification of the hymeneal song, speak of him as originally a mortal, respecting whom various legends were related. The Attic legends described him as a youth of such delicate beauty, that he might be taken for a girl. He fell in love with a maiden, who refused to listen to him; but in the disguise of a girl he followed her to Eleusis to the festival of Demeter. The maidens, together with Hymenaeus, were carried off by robbers into a distant and desolate country. On their landing, the robbers laid down to sleep, and were killed by Hymenaeus, who now returned to Athens, requesting the citizens to give him his beloved in marriage, if he restored to them the maidens who had been carried off by the robbers. His request was granted, and his marriage was extremely happy. For this reason he was invoked in the hymeneal songs. According to others he was a youth, who was killed by the fall of his house on his wedding-day, whence he was afterwards invoked in bridal songs, in order to be propitiated. Some related that at the wedding of Dionysus and Ariadne he sang the bridal hymn, but lost his voice. He is represented in works of art as a youth, but taller and with a more serious expression than Eros, and carrying in his hand a bridal torch.

Hymettus ('Υμηττός), a mountain in Attica, celebrated for its marble (*Hymettiae trabes*, Hor. Carm. ii. 18. 3), and more especially for its honey. It is about 3 miles S. of Athens, and forms the commencement of the range of mountains which runs S. through Attica. It is now called *Telovuni*, and by the Franks *Monte Matto*; the part of the mountain near the promontory Zoster, which was called in ancient times **Anhydrus** (ὁ "Ανυδρος, sc. 'Υμηττός), or the Dry Hymettus, is now called *Mavrovuni*.

Hypacÿris, Hypacăris, or Pacăris (*Kamilshak*), a river in European Sarmatia, which flows through the country of the nomad Scythians, and falls into the Sinus Carcinites in the Euxine sea.

Hypaea. [STOECHADES.]

Hypaepa ('Υπαιπα: *Tapaya*), a city of Lydia, on the S. slope of Mt. Tmolus, near the N. bank of the Caïster.

Hypāna ('Υπάνη: τὰ "Υπανα: 'Υπανεύς), a town in Triphylian Elis, belonging to the Pentapolis.

Hypănis (*Bog*), a river in European Sarmatia, rises, according to Herodotus, in a lake, flows parallel to the Borysthenes, has at first sweet, then bitter water, and falls into the Euxine sea W. of the Borysthenes.

Hypăta (τὰ Ὕπατα, ἡ Ὑπάτη: Ὑπαταῖος, Ὑπατεύς: *Neopatra*, Turk. *Batrajik*), a town of the Aenianes in Thessaly, S. of the Spercheus, belonged in later times to the Aetolian league. The inhabitants of this town were notorious for witchcraft.

Hypatia (Ὑπατία), daughter of Theon, by whom she was instructed in philosophy and mathematics. She soon made such immense progress in these branches of knowledge, that she is said to have presided over the Neoplatonic school of Plotinus at Alexandria, where she expounded the principles of his system to a numerous auditory. She appears to have been most graceful, modest, and beautiful, but nevertheless to have been a victim to slander and falsehood. She was accused of too much familiarity with Orestes, prefect of Alexandria, and the charge spread among the clergy, who took up the notion that she interrupted the friendship of Orestes with their archbishop, Cyril. In consequence of this, a number of them seized her in the street, and dragged her into one of the churches, where they tore her to pieces, A. D. 415.

Hypatŏdŏrus (Ὑπατόδωρος), a statuary of Thebes, flourished B. C. 372.

Hyperbŏlus (Ὑπέρβολος), an Athenian demagogue in the Peloponnesian war, was of servile origin, and was frequently satirised by Aristophanes and the other comic poets. In order to get rid either of Nicias or Alcibiades, Hyperbolus called for the exercise of the ostracism. But the parties endangered combined to defeat him, and the vote of exile fell on Hyperbolus himself: an application of that dignified punishment by which it was thought to have been so debased that the use of it was never recurred to. Some years afterwards he was murdered by the oligarchs at Samos, B. C. 411.

Hyperbŏrĕi or -ĕi (Ὑπερβόρεοι, Ὑπερβόρειοι), a fabulous people, the earliest mention of whom seems to have been in the sacred legends connected with the worship of Apollo, both at Delos and at Delphi. In the earliest Greek conception of the Hyperboreans, as embodied by the poets, they were a blessed people, *living beyond the N. wind* (ὑπερβόρεοι, fr. ὑπέρ and βορέας), and therefore not exposed to its cold blasts, in a land of perpetual sunshine, which produced abundant fruits, on which the people lived, abstaining from animal food. In innocence and peace, free from disease and toil and care, ignorant of violence and war, they spent a long and happy life, in the due and cheerful observance of the worship of Apollo, who visited their country soon after his birth, and spent a whole year among them, dancing and singing, before he returned to Delphi. The poets related further how the sun only rose once a year and set once a year, upon the Hyperboreans, whose year was thus divided, at the equinoxes, into a 6 months' day and a 6 months' night, and they were therefore said to sow in the morning, to reap at noon, to gather their fruits in the evening, and to store them up at night: how, too, their natural life lasted 1000 years, but if any of them was satiated with its unbroken enjoyment, he threw himself, crowned and anointed, from a sacred rock into the sea. The Delian legends told of offerings sent to Apollo by the Hyperboreans, first by the hands of virgins named Arge and Opis (or Hecaërge), and then by Laodice and Hyperoche, escorted by 5 men called Perpherees; and lastly, as their messengers did not return, they sent the offerings packed in wheat-straw, and the sacred package was forwarded from

people to people till it reached Delos. If these legends are based on any geographical relations at all, the most probable explanation is that which regards them as pointing to regions N. of Greece (the N. part of Thessaly especially) as the chief original seat of the worship of Apollo. Naturally enough, as the geographical knowledge of the Greeks extended, they moved back the Hyperboreans further and further into the unknown parts of the earth; and, of those who sought to fix their precise locality, some placed them in the extreme W. of Europe, near the Pyrenaean mountains and the supposed sources of the Ister, and thus they came to be identified with the Celtae; while others placed them in the extreme N. of Europe, on the shores of the Hyperboreus Oceanus, beyond the fabulous Grypes and Arimaspi, who themselves lived beyond the Scythians. The latter opinion at length prevailed; and then, the religious aspect of the fable being gradually lost sight of, the term *Hyperborean* came to mean only *most northerly*, as when Virgil and Horace speak of the "Hyperboreae orae" and "Hyperborei campi." The fable of the Hyperboreans may probably be regarded as one of the forms in which the tradition of an original period of innocence, happiness, and immortality, existed among the nations of the ancient world.

Hyperbŏrĕi Montes was originally the mythical name of an imaginary range of mountains in the N. of the earth [HYPERBOREI], and was afterwards applied by the geographers to various chains, as, for example, the Caucasus, the Rhipaei Montes, and others.

Hyperīdes (Ὑπερείδης or Ὑπερίδης), one of the 10 Attic orators, was the son of Glaucippus, and belonged to the Attic demus of Collytus. He was a pupil of Plato in philosophy, and of Demosthenes in oratory. He was a friend of Demosthenes, and with him and Lycurgus was at the head of the anti-Macedonian party. He is first mentioned about B. C. 358, when he and his son equipped 2 triremes at their own expense in order to serve against Euboea, and from this time to his death he continued a stedfast friend to the patriotic cause. After the death of Alexander (323) Hyperides took an active part in organising that confederacy of the Greeks against Antipater, which produced the Lamian war. Upon the defeat of the confederates at the battle of Crannon in the following year (322), Hyperides fled to Aegina, where he was slain by the emissaries of Antipater. The number of orations attributed to Hyperides was 77; but none of them have come down to us. His oratory was graceful and powerful, holding a middle place between that of Lysias and Demosthenes.

Hyperīon (Ὑπερίων), a Titan, son of Uranus and Ge, and married to his sister Thia, or Euryphaessa, by whom he became the father of Helios, Selene, and Eos. Homer uses the name as a patronymic of Helios, so that it is equivalent to *Hyperionion* or *Hyperionides*; and Homer's example is imitated also by other poets. [HELIOS.]

Hypermnestra (Ὑπερμνήστρα). 1. Daughter of Thestius and Eurythemis, wife of Oicles, and mother of Amphiaraus. — 2. One of the daughters of Danaus, and wife of Lynceus. [DANAUS; LYNCEUS.]

Hyphăsis or **Hypăsis** or **Hypănis** (Ὕφασις, Ὕπασις, Ὕπανις: *Beeas*, and *Gharra*), a river of India. [HYDASPES.]

Hypius ("Υπιος), a river and mountain in Bithynia.

Hypsas ("Υψας), 2 rivers on the S. coast of Sicily, one between Selinus and Thermae Selinuntiae (now *Belici*) and the other near Agrigentum (now *Fiume drago*).

Hypseus ('Υψεύς), son of Peneus and Creusa, was king of the Lapithae, and father of Cyrene.

Hypsicles ('Υψικλῆς), of Alexandria, a Greek mathematician, who is usually said to have lived about A. D. 160, but who ought not to be placed earlier than A. D. 550. The only work of his extant, is entitled Περὶ τῆς τῶν ζωδίων ἀναφορᾶς, published with the Optics of Heliodorus at Paris, 1567. He is supposed however to have added the 14th and 15th books to the Elements of Euclid.

Hypsipyle ('Υψιπύλη), daughter of Thoas, king of Lemnos. When the Lemnian women killed all the men in the island, because they had taken some female Thracian slaves to their beds, Hypsipyle saved her father. [THOAS.] She then became queen of Lemnos ; and when the Argonauts landed there shortly afterwards, she bore twin sons to Jason, Euneus and Nebrophonus, also called Deiphilus or Thoas. The Lemnian women subsequently discovered that Thoas was alive, whereupon they compelled Hypsipyle to quit the island. On her flight she was taken prisoner by pirates and sold to the Nemean king Lycurgus, who entrusted to her care his son Archemorus or Opheltes. [ARCHEMORUS.]

Hypsus ('Υψοῦς, -οῦντος), a town in Arcadia, on a mountain of the same name.

Hyrcania ('Υρκανία : 'Υρκάνιος, Hyrcānus: *Mazanderan*), a province of the ancient Persian Empire, on the S. and S.E. shores of the Caspian or Hyrcanian Sea, and separated by mountains on the W., S., and E., from Media, Parthia, and Margiana. Its valleys were very fertile ; and it flourished most under the Parthians, whose kings often resided in it during the summer.

Hyrcanum or **-ium Mare.** [CASPIUM MARE.]

Hyrcanus ('Υρκανός). 1. Joannes, prince and high-priest of the Jews, was the son and successor of Simon Maccabaeus, the restorer of the independence of Judaea. He succeeded to his father's power B. C. 135. He was at first engaged in war with Antiochus VII. Sidetes, who invaded Judaea, and laid siege to Jerusalem. In 133 he concluded a peace with Antiochus, on the condition of paying an annual tribute. Owing to the civil wars in Syria between the several claimants to the throne, the power of Hyrcanus steadily increased ; and at length he took Samaria, and rased it to the ground (109), notwithstanding the army which Antiochus IX. Cyzicenus had sent to the assistance of the city. Hyrcanus died in 106. Although he did not assume the title of king, he may be regarded as the founder of the monarchy of Judaea, which continued in his family till the accession of Herod. — 2. High-priest and king of the Jews, was the eldest son of Alexander Jannaeus, and his wife, Alexandra. On the death of Alexander (78) the royal authority devolved upon Alexandra, who appointed Hyrcanus to the high-priesthood. Alexandra reigned 9 years ; and upon her death in 69, Hyrcanus succeeded to the sovereignty, but was quickly attacked by his younger brother Aristobulus, who possessed more energy and ambition than Hyrcanus. In the following year (68) Hyrcanus was driven from the throne, and took refuge with Aretas, king of Arabia Petraea. That monarch

assembled an army, with which he invaded Judaea in order to restore Hyrcanus. He defeated Aristobulus, and blockaded him in the temple of Jerusalem. Aristobulus, however, gained over by bribes and promises Pompey's lieutenant, M. Scaurus, who had arrived at Damascus, and who now ordered Aretas and Hyrcanus to withdraw from Judaea (64). The next year Pompey himself arrived in Syria : he reversed the decision of Scaurus, carried away Aristobulus as a prisoner to Rome, and reinstated Hyrcanus in the high-priesthood, with the authority, though not the name, of royalty. Hyrcanus, however, did not long enjoy his newly recovered sovereignty in quiet. Alexander, the son of Aristobulus, and subsequently Aristobulus himself, escaped from Rome, and excited dangerous revolts, which were only quelled by the assistance of the Romans. The real government was now in the able hands of Antipater, the father of Herod, who rendered such important services to Caesar during the Alexandrian war (47), that Caesar made him procurator of Judaea, leaving to Hyrcanus the title of high-priest. Although Antipater was poisoned by the contrivance of Hyrcanus (43), the latter was a man of such feeble character, that he allowed Herod to take vengeance on the murderer of his father, and to succeed to his father's power and influence. The Parthians, on their invasion of Syria, carried away Hyrcanus as prisoner (40). He was treated with much liberality by the Parthian king, and allowed to live in perfect freedom at Babylon. Here he remained for some years ; but having at length received an invitation from Herod, who had meanwhile established himself on the throne of Judaea, he returned to Jerusalem, with the consent of the Parthian king. He was treated with respect by Herod till the battle of Actium ; when Herod, fearing lest Augustus might place Hyrcanus on the throne, accused him of a treasonable correspondence with the king of Arabia, and on this pretext put him to death (30).

Hyria ('Υρία : 'Υριεύς, 'Υριάτης). 1. A town in Boeotia near Tanagra, was in the earliest times a place of importance, but afterwards sunk into insignificance. — 2. A town in Apulia. [URIA.]

Hyrieus ('Υριεύς), son of Poseidon and Alcyone, king of Hyria in Boeotia, husband of Clonia, and father of Nycteus, Lycus, and Orion. Respecting his treasures see AGAMEDES.

Hyrmina ('Υρμίνη), a town in Elis, mentioned by Homer, but of which all trace had disappeared in the time of Strabo. Near it was the promontory Hyrmina or Hormina (*C. Chiarensa*).

Hyrmine ('Υρμίνη), daughter of Neleus, or Nycteus, wife of Phorbas, and mother of Aetor.

Hyrtacus ("Υρτακος), a Trojan, to whom Priam gave his first wife Arisbe, when he married Hecuba. Homer makes him the father of Asius, hence called *Hyrtacides*. — In Virgil Nisus and Hippocoon are also represented as sons of Hyrtacus.

Hysiae ('Υσίαι). 1. ('Υσιάτης), a town in Argolis, S. of Argos, destroyed by the Spartans in the Peloponnesian war. — 2. ('Υσιεύς), a town in Boeotia, E. of Plataeae, called by Herodotus (v. 74) a demus of Attica, but probably belonging to Plataeae.

Hystaspes ('Υστάσπης ; in Persian, Goshtasp, Gustasp, Histasp, or Wistasp). 1. Son of Arsames, and father of Darius I., was a member of the Persian royal house of the Achaemenidae. He was satrap of Persis under Cambyses, and probably under Cyrus also. — 2. Son of Darius I. and Atossa, commanded the Bactrians and Sacae in the army of his brother Xerxes.

I.

Iacchus ('Ιακχος), the solemn name of Bacchus in the Eleusinian mysteries, whose name was derived from the boisterous song, called Iacchus. In these mysteries Iacchus was regarded as the son of Zeus and Demeter, and was distinguished from the Theban Bacchus (Dionysus), the son of Zeus and Semele. In some traditions Iacchus is even called a son of Bacchus, but in others the 2 are identified. On the 6th day of the Eleusinian festival (the 20th of Boëdromion) the statue of Iacchus was carried from the temple of Demeter across the Thriasian plain to Eleusis, accompanied by a numerous and riotous procession of the initiated, who sang the Iacchus, carried mystic baskets, and danced to the sound of cymbals and trumpets.

Iādēra or Iadēr (Iaderīnus: *Old Zara*), a town on the coast of Illyricum, with a good harbour, and a Roman colony under the name of " Colonia Claudia Augusta Felix."

Ialēmus ('Ιάλεμος), a similar personification to that of Linus, and hence called a son of Apollo and Calliope, and the inventor of the song Ialemus, which was a kind of dirge, and is only mentioned as sung on most melancholy occasions.

Ialmēnus ('Ιάλμενος), son of Ares and Astyoche, and brother of Ascalaphus, was a native of the Boeotian Orchomenos. He was one of the Argonauts and a suitor of Helena. After the destruction of Troy, he wandered about with the Orchomenians, and founded colonies in Colchis.

Ialȳsus (Ιάλυσος), one of the 3 very ancient Dorian cities in the island of Rhodes, and one of the 6 original members of the Dorian Hexapolis [Doris], stood on the N.W. coast of the island, about 60 stadia S.W. of Rhodes. It is said to have derived its name from the mythical Ialysus, son of Cercaphus, and grandson of Helios.

Iambē ('Ιάμβη), a Thracian woman, daughter of Pan and Echo, and a slave of Metanira. When Demeter, in search of her daughter, arrived in Attica, and visited the house of Metanira, Iambe cheered the mournful goddess by her jokes.

Iamblichus ('Ιάμβλιχος). 1. A Syrian who lived in the time of the emperor Trajan, wrote a romance in the Greek language, entitled *Babylonica*. The work itself is lost, but an epitome of it is preserved by Photius. — 2. A celebrated Neo-Platonic philosopher, was born at Chalcis in Coele-Syria. He resided in Syria during the greater part of his life, and died in the reign of Constantine the Great, probably before A. D. 333. He was inferior in judgment and learning to the earlier Neo-Platonists, Plotinus and Porphyry ; and he introduced into his system many of the superstitions and mysteries of the E., by means of which he endeavoured to check the progress of Christianity. The extant works of Iamblichus are: 1. Περὶ Πυθαγόρου αἱρέσεως, on the philosophy of Pythagoras. It was intended as a preparation for the study of Plato, and consisted originally of 10 books, of which 5 only are extant. 1. The 1st book contains an account of the life of Pythagoras, and though compiled without care, it is yet of value, as the other works, from which it is taken, are lost.

Edited by Kuster, Amsterd. 1707 ; and by Kiess, ling, Lips. 1815. 2. Προτρεπτικοὶ λόγοι εἰς φιλοσοφίαν, forms a sort of introduction to the study of Plato. Edited by Kiessling, Lips. 1813, 8vo. 3. Περὶ κοινῆς μαθηματικῆς ἐπιστήμης, contains many fragments of the works of early Pythagoreans. Edited by Fries, Copenhagen, 1790. 4. Περὶ τῆς Νικομάχου ἀριθμητικῆς εἰσαγωγῆς. Edited by Tennulius, Deventer and Arnheim, 1668. 5. Τὰ Θεολογούμενα τῆς ἀριθμητικῆς. Edited by Ast, Lips. 1817. — II. Περὶ μυστηρίων, written to prove the divine origin of the Egyptian and Chaldaean theology. Edited by Gale, Oxon. 1678. Iamblichus wrote other works which are lost. — 3. A later Neo-Platonic philosopher of Apamea, a contemporary of the emperor Julian and of Libanius.

Iamīdae. [Iamus.]

Iamnīa ('Ιάμνεια ; 'Ιαμνία; 'Ιαμνείτης : O. T. Jabneel, Jabneh : *Ibneh* or *Gabneh*), a considerable city of Palestine, between Diospolis and Azotus, near the coast, with a good harbour, was taken by King Uzziah from the Philistines. Pompey united it to the province of Syria. After the destruction of Jerusalem it became the seat of the Sanhedrim, and of a celebrated school of Jewish learning.

Iamus ('Ίαμος), son of Apollo and Evadne, received the art of prophecy from his father, and was regarded as the ancestor of the famous family of seers, the Iamidae at Olympia.

Ianīra ('Ιάνειρα), one of the Nereids.

Ianthē ('Ιάνθη). 1. Daughter of Oceanus and Tethys, and one of the playmates of Persephone. — 2. Daughter of Telestes of Crete, beloved by Iphis.

Iapētus ('Ιαπετός), one of the Titans, son of Uranus and Ge, married Asia or Clymene, the daughter of his brother Oceanus, and became by her the father of Atlas, Prometheus, Epimetheus, and Menoetius. He was imprisoned with Cronus in Tartarus. Being the father of Prometheus, he was regarded by the Greeks as the ancestor of the human race. His descendants, Prometheus, Atlas, and others, are often designated by the patronymics *Iapetidae (es)*, *Iapetionidae (es)*, and the feminine *Iapetionis*.

Iapȳdes ('Ιάπυδες or 'Ιάποδες), a warlike and barbarous people in the N. of Illyricum, between the rivers Arsia and Tedanius, were a mixed race, partly Illyrian and partly Celtic, who tattooed their bodies. They were subdued by Augustus. Their country was called Iapydia.

Iapȳgia ('Ιαπυγία : 'Ιάπυγες), the name given by the Greeks to the S. of Apulia, from Tarentum and Brundusium to the Prom. Iapygium (*C. Leuca*) ; though it is sometimes applied to the whole of Apulia. [Apulia.] The name is derived from the mythical Iapyx.

Iapyx ('Ιάπυξ). 1. Son of Lycaon and brother of Daunius and Peucetius, who went as leaders of a colony to Italy. According to others, he was a Cretan, and a brother of Icadius, or a son of Daedalus and a Cretan woman, from whom the Cretans who migrated to Italy derived the name of Iapyges. — 2. The W.N.W. wind, blowing off the coast of Iapygia (Apulia), in the S. of Italy, and consequently favourable to persons crossing over to Greece. It was the same as the ἀργέστης of the Greeks.

Iarbas or Hiarbas, king of the Gaetulians, and son of Jupiter Ammon by a Libyan nymph, sued

Hermes (Mercury). (Pitture e Bronzi
d'Ercolano, vol. 4, tav. 31.) Page 313.

Hermes (Mercury). (Museo Borbonico,
tom. 6, tav. 2.) Page 313.

Hermes (Mercury) making a Lyre.
(Osterley, Denk. der alt. Kunst, theil 2, tav. 9.) Page 313.

Horae (Seasons).
(From a Coin of Commodus.) Page 329.

Horae (Seasons). (From a Bas-relief at Rome.) Page 329.

[To face p. 316.

Helena, wife of Julian. Page 301.

Hicetas, Tyrant of Syracuse. Page 320, No. 2.

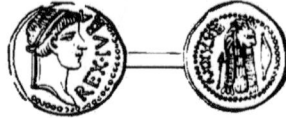

Hieron II., King of Syracuse, B.C. 270—216. Page 320.

Hieronymus, King of Syracuse, B.C. 216. Page 321, No. 2.

Honorius, Roman Emperor, A.D. 395—423. Page 328.

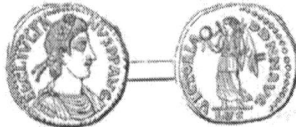

Idrieus, King of Caria, A.D. 344. Page 339.

To face p. 337.]

Juba I., King of Numidia, ob. B.C. 46. Page 355.

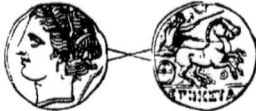

Juba II., King of Mauretania, ob. A.D. 19. Page 355.

Julia, daughter of Augustus, ob. A.D. 29. Page 356, No. 5.

Julia, daughter of Titus. Page 357, No. 9.

Julian, Roman Emperor, A.D. 361—363. Page 357.

Justinian, Roman Emperor, A.D. 527—565. Page 359.

sn vain for the hand of Dido in marriage. For details see DIDO.

Iardănes ('Ιαρδάνης), a king of Lydia, and father of Omphale, who is hence called *Iardanis.*

Iardănes or **Iardănus** ('Ιαρδάνης, 'Ιάρδανος). 1. (*Jardan*), a river in Elis. — 2. A river in the N. of Crete, which flowed near the town Cydonia.

Iăsion or **Iăsius** ('Ιασίων, 'Ιάσιος), son of Zeus and Electra, the daughter of Atlas, or son of Corythus and Electra. At the wedding of his sister Harmonia, Demeter fell in love with him, and in a thrice-ploughed field (τρίπολος) she became by him the mother of Pluton or Plutus in Crete ; Zeus in consequence killed Iasion with a flash of lightning. Others represent him as living to an advanced age as the husband of Demeter. In some traditions Iasion and his brother Dardanus are said to have carried the palladium to Samothrace, and there to have been instructed in the mysteries of Demeter by Zeus. Others relate that Iasion, being inspired by Demeter and Cora (Proserpina), travelled about in Sicily and many other countries, and everywhere taught the people the mysteries of Demeter.

Iăsis, i. e. Atalante, the daughter of Iasius.

Iăso ('Ιασώ), i. e. Recovery, a daughter of Aesculapius, or Amphiaraus, and sister of Hygiea, was worshipped as the goddess of recovery.

Iassius or **Iassīous Sinus** ('Ιασικὸς κόλπος : *Gulf of Mandeliyeh*), a large gulf on the W. coast of Caria, between the peninsulae of Miletus and Myndus ; named after the city of Iassus, and called Bargylieticus Sinus (Βαργυλιητικὸς κόλπος) from another city which stood upon it, namely, Bargylia.

Iassus or **Iăsus** ('Ιασσος, 'Ιασος : 'Ιασεύς : *Asyn-Kalessi*, Ru.), a city of Caria, on the Iassius Sinus, founded by Argives and further colonised by Milesians.

Iasus ('Ιασος). 1. An Arcadian, son of Lycurgus and Cleophile or Eurynome, brother of Ancaeus, husband of Clymene, the daughter of Minyas, and father of Atalante. He is likewise called Iasius and Iasion. — 2. Father of Amphion, and king of the Minyans.

Iăzyges ('Ιάζυγες), a powerful Sarmatian people, who originally dwelt on the coast of the Pontus Euxinus and the Palus Maeotis, but in the reign of Claudius settled near the Quadi in Dacia, in the country bounded by the Danube, the Theiss, and the Sarmatian mountains. They are generally called *Sarmatae Iazyges* or simply *Sarmatae*, but Ptolemy gives them the name of *Iazyges Metanastae*, on account of their migration. The Iazyges were in close alliance with the Quadi, along with whom they frequently attacked the Roman dominions, especially Moesia and Pannonia. In the 5th century they were conquered by the Goths.

Ibēria ('Ιβηρία : S. part of *Georgia*), a country of Asia, in the centre of the isthmus between the Black and Caspian Seas, was bounded on the N. by the Caucasus, on the W. by Colchis, on the E. by Albania, and on the S. by Armenia. It was surrounded on every side by mountains, through which there were only 4 passes. Sheltered by these mountains and watered by the Cyrus (*Kour*) and its upper tributaries, it was famed for a fertility of which its modern name (trom Γέωργος) remains a witness. Its inhabitants, **Ibēres** ('Ιβηρες) or **Ibēri**, were, and are still, among the most perfect specimens of the Caucasian race. The ancients believed them to be of the same family as the

Assyrians and Medes, whom they were thought to resemble in their customs. They were more civilised than their neighbours in Colchis and Albania, and were divided into 4 castes : 1. the nobles, from whom 2 kings were chosen ; 2. the priests, who were also the magistrates ; 3. the soldiers and husbandmen ; 4. the slaves, who performed all public and mechanical work. The chief employment of the Iberians was agriculture. The Romans first became acquainted with the country through the expedition of Pompey, in B. C. 65 ; and under Trajan it was subjected to Rome. In the 5th century it was conquered by the Persian king, Sapor.— No connection can be traced between the Iberians of Asia and those of Spain.

Ibērus ('Ιβηρος or 'Ιβηρ : *Ebro*), the principal river in the N.E. of Spain, rises among the mountains of the Cantabri near Juliobriga, flows S.E. through a great plain between the Pyrenees and the M. Idubeda, and falls into the Mediterranean, near Dertosa, after forming a Delta.

Ibycus ('Ιβυκος), a Greek lyric poet, was a native of Rhegium, and spent the best part of his life at Samos, at the court of Polycrates, about B. C. 540. It is related that travelling through a desert place near Corinth, he was murdered by robbers, but before he died he called upon a flock of cranes that happened to fly over him to avenge his death. Soon afterwards, when the people of Corinth were assembled in the theatre, the cranes appeared ; and one of the murderers, who happened to be present, cried out involuntarily, " Behold the avengers of Ibycus : " and thus were the authors of the crime detected. The phrase *αἱ Ἰβύκου γέρανοι* passed into a proverb. The poetry of Ibycus was chiefly erotic, and partook largely of the impetuosity of his character. In his dialect there was a mixture of the Doric and Aeolic. In antiquity there were 7 books of his lyric poems, of which only a few fragments now remain.

Icăria or **Icărius** ('Ικαρία, 'Ικάριος : 'Ικαριεύς), a mountain and a demus in Attica, belonging to the tribe Aegeis, where Dionysus is said to have taught Icarius the cultivation of the vine.

Icărius ('Ικάριος), also called **Icărus** or **Icărion**. 1. An Athenian, who lived in the reign of Pandion, and hospitably received Dionysus on his arrival in Attica. The god in return taught him the cultivation of the vine. Icarius made a present of some wine to peasants, who became intoxicated by it, and thinking that they were poisoned by Icarius, slew him, and threw his body into a well, or buried it under a tree. His daughter Erigone, after a long search, found his grave, to which she was conducted by his faithful dog Maera. From grief she hung herself on the tree under which he was buried. Zeus or Dionysus placed her and Icarius among the stars, making Erigone the *Virgin*, Icarius *Boötes* or *Arcturus*, and Maera *Procyon* or the little dog. Hence the latter is called *Icarius canis*. The god then punished the ungrateful Athenians with madness, in which condition the Athenian maidens hung themselves as Erigone had done. The Athenians propitiated Icarius and Erigone by the institution of the festival of the *Aeora*. (See *Dict. of Antiq. s. v.*) — 2. A Lacedaemonian, son of Perieres and Gorgophône, and brother of Tyndareus. Others called him grandson of Perieres, and son of Oebalus. When Icarius and Tyndareus were expelled from Lacedaemon by their half-brother Hippocoon, Icarius

z

went to Acarnania, and there became the father of Penelope, and of several other children. He afterwards returned to Lacedaemon. Since there were many suitors for the hand of Penelope, he promised to give her to the hero who should conquer in a foot-race. Ulysses won the prize, and was betrothed to Penelope. Icarius tried to persuade his daughter to remain with him, and not accompany Ulysses to Ithaca. Ulysses allowed her to do as she pleased, whereupon she covered her face with her veil to hide her blushes, and thus intimated that she would follow her husband. Icarius then desisted from further entreaties, and erected a statue of Modesty on the spot.

Icărus ('Ίκαρος), son of Daedalus. [DAEDALUS.]

Icărus or **Icăria** ('Ίκαρος, 'Ικαρία: *Nikaria*), an island of the Aegean Sea ; one of the Sporades ; W. of Samos; called also Doliche (δολιχή, i.e. *long island*). Its common name, and that of the surrounding sea, **Icarium Mare**, were derived from the myth of ICARUS. It was first colonised by the Milesians, but afterwards belonged to the Samians, who fed their herds on its rich pastures.

Iccius, a friend of Horace, who addressed to him an ode (*Carm.* i. 29), and an epistle (*Ep.* i. 12). The ode was written in B. C. 25, when Iccius was preparing to join Aelius Gallus in his expedition to Arabia. The epistle was composed about 10 years afterwards, when Iccius had become Vipsanius Agrippa's steward in Sicily. In both poems Horace reprehends pointedly, but delicately, in Iccius an inordinate desire for wealth.

Iceni, called **Simeni** (Σιμενοί) by Ptolemy, a numerous and powerful people in Britain, who dwelt N. of the Trinobantes, in the modern counties of Suffolk and Norfolk. Their revolt from the Romans, under their heroic queen Boadicēa, is celebrated in history. [BOADICEA.] Their chief town was **Venta Icenorum** (*Caister*), about 3 miles from Norwich.

Ichnae ('Ίχναι: 'Ιχναῖος). **1.** A town in Bottiaea in Macedonia, near the mouth of the Axius. — **2.** A town in Phthiotis in Thessaly, celebrated for its worship of Themis, who was hence surnamed *Ichnaea*.

Ichnae or **Ischnae** ('Ίχναι, 'Ίσχναι), a Greek city in the N. of Mesopotamia, founded by the Macedonians, was the scene of the first battle between Crassus and the Parthians, in which the former gained the victory. According to Appian, the Parthians soon after defeated the Romans near the same spot.

Ichthyŏphăgi ('Ίχθυοφάγοι, i.e. *Fish-eaters*), was a vague descriptive name given by the ancients to various peoples on the coasts of Asia and Africa, of whom they knew but little. Thus we find Ichthyophagi: 1. in the extreme S. E. of Asia, in the country of the Sinae: 2. on the coast of GEDROSIA: 3. on the N.E. coast of Arabia Felix: 4. in Africa, on the coast of the Red Sea, above Egypt: 5. on the W. coast of Africa.

Icilius. 1. Sp., was one of the 3 envoys sent by the plebeians, after their secession to the Sacred Mount, to treat with the senate, B.C. 494. He was thrice elected tribune of the plebs, namely, in 492, 481, and 471. — **2.** L., a man of great energy and eloquence, was tribune of the plebs, 456, when he claimed for the tribunes the right of convoking the senate, and also carried the important law for the assignment of the Aventine (*de Aventino publicando*) to the plebs. In the following year (455),

he was again elected tribune. He was one of the chief leaders in the outbreak against the decemvirs, 449. Virginia had been betrothed to him, and he boldly defended her cause before App. Claudius ; and when at length she fell by her father's hand, Icilius hurried to the army which was carrying on the war against the Sabines, and prevailed upon them to desert the government.

Icŏnĭum ('Ικόνιον: 'Ικονιεύς: *Koniyeh*), the capital of Lycaonia, in Asia Minor, was, when visited by St. Paul, a flourishing city, with a mixed population of Jews and Greeks: under the later emperors, a colony: and in the middle ages, one of the greatest cities of Asia Minor, and important in the history of the crusades.

Ictinus ('Ικτῖνος), a contemporary of Pericles, was the architect of two of the most celebrated of the Greek temples, namely, the great temple of Athene, in the acropolis of Athens, called the Parthenon, and the temple of Apollo Epicurius, near Phigalia in Arcadia. Callicrates was associated with Ictinus in building the Parthenon.

Ida ('Ίδη, Dor. 'Ίδα). 1. (*Ida*, or *Kas-Dagh*), a mountain range of Mysia, in Asia Minor, which formed the S. boundary of the Troad; extending from Lectum Pr. in the S. W. corner of the Troad, E. wards along the N. side of the Gulf of Adramyttium, and further E. into the centre of Mysia. Its highest summits were Cotylus on the N. and Gargara on the S. : the latter is about 5000 feet high, and is often capped with snow. Lower down, the slopes of the mountain are well-wooded ; and lower still, they form fertile fields and valleys. The sources of the Scamander and the Aesepus, besides other rivers and numerous brooks, are on Ida. The mountain is celebrated in mythology, as the scene of the rape of Ganymede, whom Ovid (*Fast.* ii. 145) calls *Idaeus puer* and of the judgment of Paris, who is called *Idaeus Judex* by Ovid (*Fast.* vi. 44), and *Idaeus pastor* by Cicero (*ad Att.* i. 18). In Homer, too, its summit is the place from which the gods watch the battles in the plain of Troy. Ida was also an ancient seat of the worship of Cybele, who obtained from it the name of *Idaea Mater*. 2. (*Psiloriti*), a mountain in the centre of Crete, belonging to the mountain range which runs through the whole length of the island. Mt. Ida is said to be 7674 feet above the level of the sea. It was closely connected with the worship of Zeus, who is said to have been brought up in a cave in this mountain.

Idaea Mater. [IDA.]

Idaei Dactyli. [DACTYLI.]

Idalium ('Ιδάλιον), a town in Cyprus, sacred to Venus, who hence bore the surname *Idalia*.

Idas ('Ίδας), son of Aphareus and Arene, the daughter of Oebalus, brother of Lynceus, husband of Marpessa, and father of Cleopatra or Alcyone. From the name of their father, Idas and Lynceus are called *Apharetidae* or *Apharīdae*. Apollo was in love with Marpessa, the daughter of Evenus, but Idas carried her off in a winged chariot which Poseidon had given him. Evenus could not overtake Idas, but Apollo found him in Messene, and took the maiden from him. The lovers fought for her possession, but Zeus separated them, and left the decision with Marpessa, who chose Idas, from fear lest Apollo should desert her if she grew old. The Apharetidae also took part in the Calydonian hunt, and in the expedition of the Argonauts. But the most celebrated part of their story is their battle with the Dioscuri, Castor and Pollux, which is related elsewhere [p. 228, b.].

Idistavisus Campus, a plain in Germany near the Weser, probably in the neighbourhood of the Porta Westphalica, between *Rinteln* and *Hausberge*, memorable for the victory of Germanicus over the Cherusci, A. D. 16.

Idmon ('Ίδμων), son of Apollo and Asteria, or Cyrene, was a soothsayer, and accompanied the Argonauts, although he knew beforehand that death awaited him. He was killed in the country of the Mariandynians by a boar or a serpent ; or, according to others, he died there of a disease.

Idomeneus ('Ίδομενεύς). 1. Son of the Cretan Deucalion, and grandson of Minos and Pasiphae, was king of Crete. He is sometimes called *Lyctius* or *Cnossius*, from the Cretan towns of Lyctus and Cnossus. He was one of the suitors of Helen; and in conjunction with Meriones, the son of his half-brother Molus, he led the Cretans in 80 ships against Troy. He was one of the bravest heroes in the Trojan war, and distinguished himself especially in the battle near the ships. According to Homer, Idomeneus returned home in safety after the fall of Troy. Later traditions relate that once in a storm he vowed to sacrifice to Poseidon whatever he should first meet on his landing, if the god would grant him a safe return. This was his own son, whom he accordingly sacrificed. As Crete was thereupon visited by a plague, the Cretans expelled Idomeneus. He went to Italy, where he settled in Calabria, and built a temple to Athena. From thence he is said to have migrated again to Colophon, on the coast of Asia. His tomb, however, was shown at Cnosus, where he and Meriones were worshipped as heroes. — 2. Of Lampsacus, a friend and disciple of Epicurus, flourished about B. C. 310—270. He wrote several philosophical and historical works, all of which are lost. The latter were chiefly devoted to an account of the private life of the distinguished men of Greece.

Idothea (Εἰδοθέα), daughter of Proteus, taught Menelaus how he might secure her father, and compel him to declare in what manner he might reach home in safety.

Idrieus or Hidrieus ('Ίδριεύς, 'Ίδριεύς), king of Caria, 2nd son of Hecatomnus, succeeded to the throne on the death of Artemisia, the widow of his brother Maussolus, in B. C. 351. He died in 344, leaving the kingdom to his sister ADA, whom he had married.

Idubeda (*Sierra de Oca* and *Lorenzo*), a range of mountains in Spain, begins among the Cantabri, forms the S. boundary of the plain of the Ebro, and runs S.E. to the Mediterranean.

Idumaea ('Ίδουμαία), is the Greek form of the scriptural name Edom, but the terms are not precisely equivalent. In the O. T., and in the time before the Babylonish captivity of the Jews, Edom is the district of Mt. Seir, that is, the mountainous region extending N. and S. from the Dead Sea to the E. head of the Red Sea, peopled by the descendants of Esau, and added by David to the Israelitish monarchy. The decline of the kingdom of Judaea, and at last its extinction by Nebuchadnezzar, enabled the Edomites to extend their power to the N.W. over the S. part of Judaea as far as Hebron, while their original territory was taken possession of by the Nabathaean Arabs. Thus the Idumaea of the later Jewish, and of the Roman, history is the S. part of Judaea, and a small portion of the N. of Arabia Petraea, extending N.W. and S. E. from the Mediterranean to the W. side of Mt. Seir. Under the Maccabees, the Idumaeans were again subjected to Judaea (B. C. 129), and governed, under them, by prefects (στρατηγοί), who were very probably descended from the old princes of Edom; but the internal dissensions in the Asmonaean family led at last to the establishment of an Idumaean dynasty on the Jewish throne. [ANTIPATER, Nos. 3, 4; HERODES.] The Roman writers of the Augustan age and later use Idumaea and Judaea as equivalent terms. Soon after the destruction of Jerusalem the name of Idumaea disappears from history, and is merged in that of Arabia. Both the old Edomites and the later Idumaeans were a commercial people, and carried on a great part of the traffic between the East and the shores of the Mediterranean.

Idyia ('Ίδυῖα), daughter of Oceanus and Tethys, and wife of the Colchian king AEETES.

Ierne. [HIBERNIA.]

Ietae ('Ίεται : 'Ίετῖνος : *Jato*), a town in the interior of Sicily, on a mountain of the same name, S.W. of Macella.

Igilium (*Giglio*), a small island off the Etruscan coast, opposite Cosa.

Ignatius ('Ίγνάτιος), one of the Apostolical Fathers, was a hearer of the Apostle John, and succeeded Evodius as bishop of Antioch in A.D. 69. He was condemned to death by Trajan at Antioch, and was taken to Rome, where he was thrown to the wild beasts in the amphitheatre. The date of his martyrdom is uncertain. Some place it in 107, but others as late as 116. On his way from Antioch to Rome, Ignatius wrote several epistles in Greek to various churches. There are extant at present 15 epistles ascribed to Ignatius, but of these only 7 are considered to be genuine ; and even these 7 are much interpolated. The ancient Syriac version of some of these epistles, which has been recently discovered, is free from many of the interpolations found in the present Greek text, and was evidently executed when the Greek text was in a state of greater purity than it is at present. The Greek text has been published in the *Patres Apostolici* by Cotelerius, Amsterd. 1724, and by Jacobson, Oxon. 1838 ; and the Syriac version, accompanied with the Greek text, by Cureton, Lond. 1849.

Iguvium (Iguvinus, Iguvinas, -Atis : *Gubbio* or *Eugubio*), an important town in Umbria, on the S. slope of the Apennines. On a mountain in the neighbourhood of this town was a celebrated temple of Jupiter, in the ruins of which were discovered, 4 centuries ago, 7 brazen tables, covered with Umbrian inscriptions, and which are still preserved at Gubbio. These tables, frequently called the *Eugubian Tables*, contain more than 1000 Umbrian words, and are of great importance for a knowledge of the ancient languages of Italy. They are explained by Grotefend, *Rudimenta Linguae Umbricae*, &c., Hannov. 1835, seq., and by Lepsius, *Inscriptiones Umbricae et Oscae*, Lips. 1841.

Ilaira ('Ίλάειρα), daughter of Leucippus and Philodice, and sister of Phoebe. The 2 sisters are frequently mentioned by the poets under the name of *Leucippidae*. Both were carried off by the Dioscuri, and Ilaira became the wife of Castor.

Ileracones, Ilercaonenses, or Illurgavonenses, a people in Hispania Tarraconensis on the W. coast between the Iberus and M. Idubeda. Their chief town was DERTOSA.

Ilerda (*Lerida*), a town of the Ilergētes in Hispania Tarraconensis, situated on a height above the river Sicoris (*Segre*), which was here crossed by a stone bridge. It was afterwards a Roman colony, but in the time of Ausonius had ceased to be a place of importance. It was here that Afranius and Petreius, the legates of Pompey, were defeated by Caesar (B. C. 49).

Ilergētes, a people in Hispania Tarraconensis, between the Iberus and the Pyrenees.

Ilia or **Rhea Silvia**. [ROMULUS.]

Ilici or **Illice** (*Elche*), a town of the Contestani on the E. coast of Hispania Tarraconensis, on the road from Carthago Nova to Valentia, was a colonia immunis. The modern *Elche* lies at a greater distance from the coast than the ancient town.

Ilienses, an ancient people in SARDINIA.

Iliona ('Ιλιόνη), daughter of Priam and Hecuba, wife of Polymnestor or Polymestor, king of the Thracian Chersonesus, to whom she bore a son Deipylus. At the beginning of the Trojan war her brother Polydorus was intrusted to her care, and she brought him up as her own son. For details see POLYDORUS. Iliona was the name of one of the tragedies of Pacuvius. (Hor. *Sat.* ii. 3, 61.)

Ilioneus ('Ιλιονεύς), a son of Niobe, whom Apollo would have liked to save, because he was praying; but the arrow was no longer under the control of the god. [NIOBE.]

Ilipa (*Pennaflor*), a town in Hispania Baetica, on the right bank of the Baetis, which was navigable to this place with small vessels.

Ilissus ('Ιλισσός, more rarely Ειλισσός), a small river in Attica, rises on the N. slope of Mt. Hymettus, receives the brook Eridanus near the Lyceum outside the walls of Athens, then flows through the E. side of Athens, and loses itself in the marshes in the Athenian plain. The Ilissus is now usually dry, as its waters are drawn off to supply the city.

Ilithyia (Ειλείθυια), also called Elithyia, Ilethyia, or Eleutho, the goddess of birth, who came to the assistance of women in labour. When she was kindly disposed, she furthered the birth; but when she was angry, she protracted the labour. In the Iliad the Ilithyiae (in the plural) are called the daughters of Hera. But in the Odyssey and Hesiod, and in the later poets in general, there is only one goddess of this name. Ilithyia was the servant of Hera, and was employed by the latter to retard the birth of Hercules. [HERCULES.] — The worship of Ilithyia appears to have been first established among the Dorians in Crete, where she was believed to have been born in a cave in the territory of Cnossus. From thence her worship spread over Delos and Attica. According to a Delian tradition Ilithyia was not born in Crete, but had come to Delos from the Hyperboreans, for the purpose of assisting Leto. In an ancient hymn attributed to Olen, which was sung in Delos, Ilithyia was called the mother of Eros (Love). It is probable that Ilithyia was originally a goddess of the moon, and hence became identified with Artemis or Diana. The moon was supposed to exercise great influence over growth in general, and consequently over that of children.

Ilium. [TROAS.]

Iliberis ('Ιλλιβέρις). 1. (*Tech*), called **Tichis** or **Techum** by the Romans, a river in Gallia Narbonensis in the territory of the Sardones, rises in the Pyrenees and falls, after a short course, into the

Mare Gallicum. — 2. (*Elne*), a town of the Santones, on the above-mentioned river, at the foot of the Pyrenees, was originally a place of importance, but afterwards sunk into insignificance. It was restored by Constantine, who changed its name into Heléna, whence the modern *Elne*.

Illiturgis or **Illiturgi** (*Andujar*), an important town of the Turduli in Hispania Baetica, situated on a steep rock near the Baetis, and on the road from Corduba to Castulo; it was destroyed by Scipio B. C. 210, but was rebuilt, and received the name of Forum Julium.

Illyricum or **Illyris**, more rarely **Illyria** (τὸ 'Ιλλυρικόν, 'Ιλλυρίς, 'Ιλλυρία), included, in its widest signification, all the land W. of Macedonia and E. of Italy and Rhaetia, extending S. as far as Epirus, and N. as far as the valleys of the Savus and Dravus, and the junction of these rivers with the Danube. This wide extent of country was inhabited by numerous Illyrian tribes, all of whom were more or less barbarous. They were probably of the same origin as the Thracians, but some Celts were mingled with them. The country was divided into 2 parts: 1. **Illyris Barbara** or **Romana**, the Roman province of Illyricum, extended along the Adriatic sea from Italy (Istria), from which it was separated by the Arsia, to the river Drilo, and was bounded on the E. by Macedonia and Moesia Superior, from which it was separated by the Drinus, and on the N. by Pannonia, from which it was separated by the Dravus. It thus comprehended a part of the modern *Croatia*, the whole of *Dalmatia*, almost the whole of *Bosnia*, and a part of *Albania*. It was divided in ancient times into 3 districts, according to the tribes by which it was inhabited: — Iapydia, the interior of the country on the N., from the Arsia to the Tedanius [IAPYDES]; Liburnia, along the coast from the Arsia to the Titius [LIBURNI]; and Dalmatia, S. of Liburnia, along the coast from the Titius to the Drilo. [DALMATIA.] The Liburnians submitted at an early time to the Romans; but it was not till after the conquest of the Dalmatians in the reign of Augustus, that the entire country was organised as a Roman province. From this time the Illyrians, and especially the Dalmatians, formed an important part of the Roman legions. — 2. **Illyris Graeca**, or **Illyria** proper, also called **Epirus Nova**, extended from the Drilo, along the Adriatic, to the Cerannian mountains, which separated it from Epirus proper: it was bounded on the E. by Macedonia. It thus embraced the greater part of the modern *Albania*. It was a mountainous country, but possessed some fertile land on the coast. Its principal rivers were the AOUS, APSUS, GENUSUS, and PANYASUS. In the interior was an important lake, the LYCHNITIS. On the coast there were the Greek colonies of Epidamnus, afterwards DYRRHACHIUM, and APOLLONIA. It was at these places that the celebrated Via Egnatia commenced, which ran through Macedonia to Byzantium. The country was inhabited by various tribes, ATINTANES, TAULANTII, PARTHINI, DASSARETAE, &c. In early times they were troublesome and dangerous neighbours to the Macedonian kings. They were subdued by Philip, the father of Alexander the Great, who defeated and slew in battle their king Bardylis, B. C. 359. After the death of Alexander the Great, most of the Illyrian tribes recovered their independence. At a later time the injury which the Roman trade suffered from their piracies brought against them the arms of the republic. The forces of their queen Teuta were easily defeated by the Romans, and she was obliged to purchase peace by the surrender of part of her dominions and the payment of an annual tribute, 229. The 2nd Illyrian war was finished by the Romans with the same ease. It was commenced by Demetrius of Pharos, who was guardian of Pineus, the son of Agron, but he was conquered by the consul Aemilius Paulus, 219. Pineus was succeeded by Pleuratus, who cultivated friendly relations with the Romans. His son Gentius formed an alliance with Perseus, king of Macedonia, against Rome ; but he was conquered by the praetor L. Anicius, in the same year as Perseus, 168 ; whereupon Illyria, as well as Macedonia, became subject to Rome. — In the new division of the empire under Constantine, Illyricum formed one of the great provinces of the empire. It was divided into **Illyricum Occidentale**, which included Illyricum proper, Pannonia, and Noricum, and **Illyricum Orientale**, which comprehended Dacia, Moesia, Macedonia, and Thrace.

Ilus ('Ἶλος). 1. Son of Dardanus by Batea, the daughter of Teucer. Ilus died without issue, and left his kingdom to his brother, Erichthonius. — 2. Son of Tros and Callirhoë, grandson of Erichthonius, and great-grandson of Dardanus ; whence he is called *Dardanides*. He was the father of Laomedon and the grandfather of Priam. He was believed to be the founder of Ilion, which was also called Troy, after his father. Zeus gave him the palladium, a statue of 3 cubits high, with its feet close together, holding a spear in its right hand, and a distaff in its left, and promised that as long as it remained in Troy, the city should be safe. The tomb of Ilus was shown in the neighbourhood of Troy. — 3. Son of Mermerus, and grandson of Jason and Medea. He lived at Ephyra, between Elis and Olympia ; and when Ulysses came to him to fetch the poison for his arrows, Ilus refused it, from fear of the vengeance of the gods.

Ilva. [AETHALIA.]

Ilvätes, a people in Liguria, S. of the Po, in the modern *Montferrat*.

Imachära (Imacharensis : *Maccara*), a town in Sicily, in the Heraean mountains.

Imäus (τὸ Ἴμαον ὄρος), the name of a great mountain range of Asia, is one of those terms which the ancient geographers appear to have used indefinitely, for want of exact knowledge. In its most definite application, it appears to mean the W. part of the *Himalaya*, between the Paropamisus and the Emodi Montes ; but when it is applied to some great chain, extending much further to the N. and dividing Scythia into 2 parts, Scythia intra Imaum and Scythia extra Imaum, it must either be understood to mean the *Moussour* or *Altai* mountains, or else some imaginary range, which cannot be identified with any actually existing mountains.

Imbräsus ('Ἴμβρασος), a river in the island of Samos, formerly called Parthenius, flowing into the sea not far from the city of Samos. The celebrated temple of Hera ('Ηραιον) stood near it, and it gave the epithet of Imbrasia both to Hera and to Artemis.

Imbrus ('Ἴμβρος : 'Ἴμβριος : *Embro* or *Imbrus*), an island in the N. of the Aegean sea, near the Thracian Chersonesus, about 18 miles S. E. of Samothrace, and about 22 N. E. of Lemnos. It is about 25 miles in circumference, and is hilly but

contains many fertile valleys. Imbros, like the neighbouring island of Samothrace, was in ancient times one of the chief seats of the worship of the Cabiri and Hermes. There was a town of the same name on the E. of the island, of which there are still some ruins.

Inächis ('Ἰναχίς), a surname of Io, the daughter of Inachus. The goddess Isis is also called *Inachis*, because she was identified with Io ; and sometimes *Inachis* is used as synonymous with an Argive or Greek woman. — *Inachides* in the same way was used as a name of Epaphus, a grandson of Inachus, and also of Perseus, because he was born at Argos, the city of Inachus.

Inächus ('Ἴναχος), son of Oceanus and Tethys, and father of Phoroneus and Aegialeus, to whom others add Io, Argos Panoptes, and Phegeus or Pegeus. He was the first king and the most ancient hero of Argos, whence the country is frequently called the land of Inachus ; and he is said to have given his name to the river Inachus. The ancients made several attempts to explain the stories about Inachus : sometimes they looked upon him as a native of Argos, who, after the flood of Deucalion, led the Argives from the mountains into the plains ; and sometimes they regarded him as the leader of an Egyptian or Libyan colony, which settled on the banks of the Inachus.

Inächus ('Ἴναχος). 1. (*Banitza*), the chief river in Argolis, rises in the mountain Lyrceus on the borders of Arcadia, flows in a S.E.-ly direction, receives near Argos the Charadrus, and falls into the Sinus Argolicus S. of Argos. — 2. A river in Acarnania, which rises in Mt. Lacmon in the range of Pindus, and falls into the Achelous.

Inärimē. [AENARIA.]

Inäros ('Ἰνάρως, occasionally 'Ἴναρος), son of Psammitichus, a chief of some Libyan tribes to the W. of Egypt, commenced hostilities against the Persians, which ended in a revolt of the whole of Egypt, B.C. 461. In 460 Inaros called in the Athenians, who, with a fleet of 200 galleys, were then off Cyprus : the ships sailed up to Memphis, and, occupying two parts of the town, besieged the third. In the same year Inaros defeated the Persians in a great battle, in which Achaemenes, the brother of the king Artaxerxes, was slain. But a new army, under a new commander, Megabyzus, was more successful. The Egyptians and their allies were defeated ; and Inaros was taken by treachery and crucified, 455.

India (ἡ 'Ἰνδία : 'Ἰνδός, Indus), was a name used by the Greeks and Romans, much as the modern term *East Indies*, to describe the whole of the S.E. part of Asia, to the E., S. and S.E. of the great ranges of mountains now called the *Soliman* and *Himalaya Mountains*, including the 2 peninsulas of *Hindustan*, and of *Burmah, Cochin-China, Siam,* and *Malacca*, and also the islands of the *Indian Archipelago*. There is ample evidence that commercial intercourse was carried on, from a very early time, between the W. coast of *Hindustan* and the W. parts of Asia, by the way of the Persian Gulf, the Euphrates, and across the Syrian Desert to Phoenicia, and also by way of the Red Sea and Idumaea, both to Egypt and to Phoenicia ; and so on from Phoenicia to Asia Minor and Europe. The direct acquaintance of the western nations with India dates from the reign of Darius, the son of Hystaspes, who added to the Persian empire a part of its N.W. regions, perhaps only as far as the Indus, certainly not beyond the limits of the *Punjab;* and the slight knowledge of the country thus obtained by the Persians was conveyed to the Greeks through the inquiries of travellers, especially Herodotus, and afterwards by those Greeks who resided for some time in the Persian empire, such as CTESIAS, who wrote a special work on India ('Ινδικά). The expedition of ALEXANDER into India first brought the Greeks into actual contact with the country ; but the conquests of Alexander only extended within *Scinde,* and the *Punjab,* as far as the river HYPHASIS, down which he sailed into the Indus, and down the Indus to the sea. The Greek king of Syria, Seleucus Nicator, crossed the Hyphasis, and made war with the Prasii, a people dwelling on the banks of the upper Ganges, to whom he afterwards sent ambassadors, named Megasthenes and Daimachus, who lived for several years at Palibothra, the capital of the Prasii, and had thus the opportunity of obtaining much information respecting the parts of India about the Ganges. Megasthenes composed a work on India, which appears to have been the chief source of all the accurate information contained in the works of later writers. After the death of Seleucus Nicator, B. C. 281, the direct intercourse of the western nations with India, except in the way of commerce, ceased almost entirely ; and whatever new information the later writers obtained was often very erroneous. Meanwhile, the foundation of Alexandria had created an extensive commerce between India and the West, by way of the Indian Ocean, the Red Sea, and Egypt, which made the Greeks better acquainted with the W. coast of the peninsula, and extended their knowledge further into the eastern seas ; but the information they thus obtained of the countries beyond *Cape Comorin* was extremely vague and scanty. Another channel of information, however, was opened, during this period, by the establishment of the Greek kingdom of Bactria, to which a considerable part of N. India appears to have been subject. The later geographers made two great divisions of India, which are separated by the Ganges, and are called India intra Gangem, and India extra Gangem, the former including the peninsula of *Hindustan,* the latter the *Burmese* peninsula. They were acquainted with the division of the people of *Hindustan* into castes, of which they enumerate 7. It is not necessary, for the object of this work, to mention the other particulars which they relate concerning India and its people.

Indibilis and Mandonius, 2 brothers, and chiefs of the Spanish tribe of the Ilergetes, who played an important part in the war between the Romans and Carthaginians in Spain during the 2nd Punic war. For some years they were faithful allies of the Carthaginians ; but in consequence of the generous treatment which the wife of Mandonius and the daughters of Indibilis received from P. Scipio, when they fell into his hands, the 2 brothers deserted the Carthaginian cause, and joined Scipio in 209 with all the forces of their nation. But in 206 the illness and reported death of Scipio gave them hopes of shaking off the yoke of Rome, and they excited a general revolt not only among their own subjects, but the neighbouring Celtiberian tribes also. They were defeated by Scipio, and upon suing for forgiveness were pardoned. But when Scipio left Spain in the next year (205), they

again revolted. The Roman generals whom Scipio had left in Spain forthwith marched against them ; Indibilis was slain in battle, and Mandonius was taken soon afterwards and put to death.

Indicētae or Indigetes, a people in the N.E. corner of Hispania Tarraconensis, close upon the Pyrenees. Their chief town was EMPORIUM.

Indicus Oceanus. [ERYTHRAEUM MARE.]

Indigetes, the name of those indigenous gods and heroes at Rome, who once lived on earth as mortals, and were worshipped after their death as gods, such as Janus, Picus, Faunus, Aeneas, Evander, Hercules, Latinus, Romulus, and others. Thus Aeneas, after his disappearance on the banks of the Numicus, became a *deus Indiges, pater Indiges,* or *Jupiter Indiges;* and in like manner Romulus became *Quirinus,* and Latinus *Jupiter Latiaris.* The Indigetes are frequently mentioned together with the Lares and Penates ; and many writers connect the Indigetes with those divinities to whom a share in the foundation of the Latin and Roman state is ascribed, such as Mars, Venus, Vesta, &c.

Indus or Sindus ('Ινδός : *Indus, Sind*), a great river of India, rises in the table land of *Thibet,* N. of the *Himalaya* mountains, flows nearly parallel to the great bend of that chain on its N. side, till it breaks through the chain a little E. of *Attock,* in the N.W. corner of the *Punjab,* and then flows S.W. through the great plain of the *Punjab,* into the Erythraeum Mare (*Indian Ocean*), which it enters by several mouths, 2 according to the earlier Greek writers, 6 according to the later. Its chief tributaries are the Cophen (*Cabul*), which enters it from the N.W. at *Attock,* and the Acesines on the E. side. [HYPHASIS.] Like the Nile, the Indus overflows its banks, but with a much less fertilising result, as the country about its lower course is for the most part a sandy desert, and the deposit it brings down is much less rich than that of the Nile. The erroneous notions of the early Greeks respecting the connection between the S.E. parts of the continents of Africa and Asia, led to a confusion between the Indus and the Nile ; but this and other mistakes were corrected by the voyage of Alexander's fleet down the Hyphasis and the Indus. The ancient name of India was derived from the native name of the Indus (*Sind*).

Indus ('Ινδός : *Dollomon-Chai*), a considerable river of Asia Minor, rising in the S.W. of Phrygia, and flowing through the district of Cibyratis and the S. E. corner of Caria into the Mediterranean, opposite to Rhodes.

Indutiomārus, or Induciomārus, one of the leading chiefs of the Treviri in Gaul. As he was opposed to the Romans, Caesar induced the leading men of the nation to side with Cingetorix, the son-in-law but rival of Indutiomarus, B. C. 54. Indutiomarus in consequence took up arms against the Romans, but was defeated and slain by Labienus.

Inessa. [AETNA, No. 2.]

Inferi, the gods of the Nether World, in contradistinction from the *Superi,* or the gods of heaven. In Greek the *Inferi* are called οἱ κάτω, οἱ χθόνιοι, οἱ ὑπὸ γαῖαν, οἱ ἔνερθε, or οἱ ὑπένερθε θεοί ; and the *Superi,* οἱ ἄνω, ὕπατοι and οὐράνιοι. But the word *Inferi* is also frequently used to designate the dead, in contradistinction from those living upon the earth ; so that *apud inferos* is equivalent to " in Hades," or " in the lower world." The Inferi therefore comprise all the inhabitants of the lower world, the gods, viz. Hades or Pluto, his wife Persephone (Proserpina), the Erinnyes or Furies, and others, as well as the souls of departed men. The gods of the lower world are treated of in separate articles.

Inferum Mare. [ETRURIA.]

Ingaevōnes. [GERMANIA, pp. 281, b., 282, a.]

Ingauni, a people in Liguria on the coast, whose chief town was ALBIUM INGAUNUM.

Ingenŭus, one of the Thirty Tyrants, was governor of Pannonia when Valerian set out upon his campaign against the Persians A. D. 258. He assumed the purple in his province, but was defeated and slain by Gallienus.

Ino ('Ινώ), daughter of Cadmus and Harmonia, and wife of Athamas. For details see ATHAMAS.

Inŏus, a name both of Melicertes and of Palaemon, because they were the sons of Ino.

Insubres, a Gallic people, who crossed the Alps and settled in Gallia Transpadana in the N. of Italy. Their chief town was MEDIOLANUM. Next to the Boii, they were the most powerful and warlike of the Gallic tribes in Cisalpine Gaul. They were conquered by the Romans, shortly before the commencement of the 2nd Punic war.

Intaphernes ('Ινταφέρνης), one of the 7 conspirators against the 2 Magi in Persia, B.C. 522. He was afterwards put to death by Darius.

Intĕmĕlĭi, a people in Liguria on the coast, whose chief town was ALBIUM INTEMELIUM.

Interamna (Interamnas), the name of several towns in Italy, so called from their lying between 2 streams. — 1. (*Terni*), an ancient municipium in Umbria, situated on the Nar, and surrounded by a canal flowing into this river, whence its inhabitants were called *Interamnates Nartes*. It was the birthplace of the historian Tacitus, as well as of the emperor of the same name. — 2. A town in Latium on the Via Latina, and at the junction of the Casinus with the Liris, whence its inhabitants are called *Interamnates Lirinates*. It was made a Roman colony, B. C. 312, but subsequently sunk into insignificance.

Intercatĭa, an important town of the Vaccaei in Hispania Tarraconensis, on the road from Asturica to Caesaraugusta.

Intercisa or **Petra Pertusa,** a town in Umbria, so called because a road was here cut through the rocks by order of Vespasian. An ancient inscription on the spot still commemorates this work.

Internum Mare, the *Mediterranean Sea,* extended on the W. from the Straits of Hercules, which separated it from the Atlantic, to the coasts of Syria and Asia Minor on the E. In the N.E. it was usually supposed to terminate at the Hellespont. From the Straits of Hercules to the furthest shores of Syria it is 2000 miles in length; and, including the islands, it occupies an area of 734,000 square miles. It was called by the Romans *Mare Internum* or *Intestinum*; by the Greeks ἡ ἔσω θάλαττα or ἡ ἐντὸς θάλαττα, or, more fully, ἡ ἐντὸς 'Ηρακλείων στηλῶν θάλαττα, and by Herodotus ἥδε ἡ θάλαττα; and from its washing the coasts both of Greece and Italy, it was also called both by Greeks and Romans *Our Sea* (ἡ ἡμετέρα θάλαττα, ἡ καθ' ἡμᾶς θάλαττα, *Mare Nostrum*). The term *Mare Mediterraneum* is not used by the best classical writers, and occurs first in Solinus. Most of the ancients believed that the Mediterranean received its waters from the Atlantic, and poured them through the Hellespont and the Propontis into the Euxine; but others, on the contrary,

maintained that the waters came from the Euxine into the Mediterranean. The ebb and flow of the tide are perceptible in only a few parts of the Mediterranean, such as in the Syrtes on the coast of Africa, in the Adriatic, &c. The different parts of the Mediterranean are called by different names, which are spoken of in separate articles. See MARE TYRRHENUM or INFERUM, ADRIA or M. ADRIATICUM or M. SUPERUM, M. SICULUM, M. AEGAEUM, &c.

Intonsus, the Unshorn, a surname of Apollo and Bacchus, in allusion to the eternal youth of these gods, since the Greek youths allowed their hair to grow until they attained manhood.

Inŭi Castrum. [CASTRUM, No. 1.]

Inycum ('Ινυκον or -os : 'Ινυκῖνος : *Calda Belota ?*), a small town in the S. of Sicily, not far from Selinus, on the river Hypsas.

Io ('Ιώ), daughter of Inachus, the first king of Argos, or, according to others, of Iasus or Piren. Zeus loved Io, but on account of Hera's jealousy, he metamorphosed her into a white heifer. The goddess, who was aware of the change, obtained the heifer from Zeus, and placed her under the care of Argus Panoptes; but Zeus sent Hermes to slay Argus and deliver Io. [ARGUS.] Hera then tormented Io with a gad-fly, and drove her in a state of phrensy from land to land over the whole earth, until at length she found rest on the banks of the Nile. Here she recovered her original form, and bore a son to Zeus, called Epaphus. [EPAPHUS.] This is the common story, which appears to be very ancient, since Homer constantly gives the epithet of *Argiphontes* (the slayer of Argus) to Hermes. The wanderings of Io were very celebrated in antiquity, and were extended and embellished with the increase of geographical knowledge. Of these there is a full account in the Prometheus of Aeschylus. The Bosporus is said to have derived its name from her swimming across it. According to some traditions Io married Telegonus, king of Egypt, and was afterwards identified with Isis. The legend of Io is difficult to explain. It appears that Io was identical with the moon; which is probably signified by her being represented as a woman, with the horns of a heifer. Her connection with Egypt seems to be an invention of later times, and was probably suggested by the resemblance which was found to exist between the Argive Io and the Egyptian Isis.

Iobătes, king of Lycia. [BELLEROPHON.]

Iol. [CAESAREA, No. 4.]

Iolaenses. [IOLAUS.]

Iŏlăus ('Ιόλαος), son of Iphicles and Automedusa. Iphicles was the half-brother of Hercules, and Iolaus was the faithful companion and charioteer of the hero. [HERCULES.] He assisted Hercules in slaying the Lernaean Hydra. After Hercules had instituted the Olympic games, Iolaus won the victory with the horses of his master. Hercules sent him to Sardinia at the head of his sons whom he had by the daughters of Thespius. He introduced civilisation among the inhabitants of that island, and was worshipped by them. From Sardinia he went to Sicily, and then returned to Hercules shortly before the death of the latter. After the death of the hero, Iolaus was the first who offered sacrifices to him as a demigod. According to Pausanias, Iolaus died in Sardinia, whereas, according to others, he was buried in the tomb of his grandfather, Amphitryon. His descendants in

z 4

Sardinia were called Ἰολαεῖς and *Iolaenses*. [SAR-DINIA.] Iolaus after his death obtained permission from the gods of the Nether World to come to the assistance of the children of Hercules. He slew Eurystheus, and then returned to the shades.

Iolcus (Ἰωλκός, Ep. Ἰαωλκός, Dor. Ἰαλκός : Ἰόλκιος), an ancient town in Magnesia in Thessaly at the top of the Pagasaean gulf, 7 stadia from the sea. It is said to have been founded by the mythical Cretheus, and to have been colonised by Minyans from Orchomenus. It was celebrated in mythology as the residence of Pelias and Jason, and as the place from which the Argonauts sailed in quest of the golden fleece. At a later time it fell into decay, and its inhabitants were removed to the neighbouring town of Demetrias, which was founded by Demetrius Poliorcetes.

Iölë (Ἰόλη), daughter of Eurytus of Oechalia, was beloved by Hercules. For details see p. 310. After the death of Hercules, she married his son Hyllus.

Iollas or Ioläus (Ἰόλλας or Ἰόλαος). 1. Son of Antipater, and brother of Cassander, king of Macedonia. He was cup-bearer to Alexander at the period of his last illness. Those writers who adopt the idea of the king having been poisoned, represent Iollas as the person who actually administered the fatal draught.—2. Of Bithynia, a writer on materia medica, flourished in the 3rd century B.C.

Ion (Ἴων). 1. The fabulous ancestor of the Ionians, is described as the son of Apollo by Creusa, the daughter of Erechtheus and wife of Xuthus. The most celebrated story about Ion is the one which forms the subject of the *Ion* of Euripides. Apollo had visited Creusa in a cave below the Propylaea, at Athens ; and when she gave birth to a son, she exposed him in the same cave. The god, however, had the child conveyed to Delphi, where he was educated by a priestess. Some time afterwards Xuthus and Creusa came to consult the oracle about the means of obtaining an heir. They received for answer that the first human being which Xuthus met on leaving the temple should be his son. Xuthus met Ion, and acknowledged him as his son ; but Creusa, imagining him to be a son of her husband by a former mistress, caused a cup to be presented to the youth, which was filled with the poisonous blood of a dragon. However, her object was discovered, for as Ion, before drinking, poured out a libation to the gods, a pigeon which drank of it died on the spot. Creusa thereupon fled to the altar of the god. Ion dragged her away, and was on the point of killing her, when a priestess interfered, explained the mystery, and showed that Ion was the son of Creusa. Mother and son thus became reconciled, but Xuthus was not let into the secret. — Among the inhabitants of the Aegialus, i. e. the N. coast of Peloponnesus, who were Ionians, there was another tradition current. Xuthus, when expelled from Thessaly, came to the Aegialus. After his death Ion was on the point of marching against the Aegialeans, when their king Selinus gave him his daughter Helice in marriage. On the death of Selinus, Ion succeeded to the throne, and thus the Aegialeans received the name of Ionians, and the town of Helice was built in honour of Ion's wife. — Other traditions represent Ion as king of Athens between the reigns of Erechtheus and Cecrops ; for it is said that his assistance was called in by the Athenians in their war with the Eleusinians, that he conquered Eu-

molpus, and then became king of Athens. He there became the father of 4 sons, Geleon, Aegicores, Argades, and Hoples, whose names were given to the 4 Athenian classes. After his death he was buried at Potamus. —2. Of Chios, son of Orthomenes, was a celebrated tragic poet. He went to Athens when young, and there enjoyed the society of Aeschylus and Cimon. The number of his tragedies is variously stated at 12, 30, and 40. We have the titles and a few fragments of 11. Ion also wrote other kinds of poetry, and prose works both in history and philosophy. —3. Of Ephesus, a rhapsodist in the time of Socrates, from whom one of Plato's dialogues is named.

Ionia (Ἰωνία: Ἴωνες) and Iōnis (Rom. poet.), a district on the W. coast of Asia Minor, so called from the Ionian Greeks who colonized it at a time earlier than any distinct historical records. The mythical account of "the great Ionic migration" relates that in consequence of the disputes between the sons of Codrus, king of Athens, about the succession to his government, his younger sons, Neleus and Androclus, resolved to seek a new home beyond the Aegean Sea. Attica was at the time overpeopled by numerous exiles, whom the great revolution, known as "the return of the Heraclidae," had driven out of their own states, the chief of whom were the Ionians who had been expelled from Peloponnesus by the Dorian invaders. A large portion of this superfluous population went forth as Athenian colonists, under the leadership of Androclus and Neleus, and of other chieftains of other races, and settled on that part of the W. shores of Asia Minor which formed the coast of Lydia and part of Caria, and also in the adjacent islands of Chios and Samos, and in the Cyclades. The mythical chronology places this great movement 140 years after the Trojan war, or 60 years after the return of the Heraclidae, that is in B.C. 1060 or 1044, according to the 2 chief dates imagined for the Trojan war. Passing from mythology to history, the earliest authentic records show us the existence of 12 great cities on the above-named coast, claiming to be (though some of them only partially) of Ionic origin, and all united into one confederacy, similar to that of the 12 ancient Ionian cities on the N. coast of the Peloponnesus. The district they possessed formed a narrow strip of coast, extending between, and somewhat beyond, the mouths of the rivers Maeander, on the S., and Hermus, on the N. The names of the 12 cities, going from S. to N. were MILETUS, MYUS, PRIENE, SAMOS (city and island), EPHESUS, COLOPHON, LEBEDJA, TEOS, ERYTHRAE, CHIOS (city and island), CLAZOMENAE, and PHOCAEA ; the first 3 on the coast of Caria, the rest on that of Lydia: the city of Smyrna, which lay within this district, but was of Aeolic origin, was afterwards (about B.C. 700) added to the Ionian confederacy. The common sanctuary of the league was the Panionium (Πανιώνιον), a sanctuary of Poseidon Heliconius, on the N. side of the promontory of Mycale, opposite to Samos ; and here was held the great national assembly (πανήγυρις) of the confederacy, called Panionia (Πανιώνια: see *Dict. of Antiq. s. v.*). It is very important to observe that the inhabitants of these cities were very far from being exclusively and purely of Ionian descent. The traditions of the original colonization and the accounts of the historians agree in representing them as peopled by a great mixture, not only of Hellenic races, but also of these with the earlier inhabitants, such as Carians, Leleges, Lydians, Cretans, and Pelasgians ; their dialects, Herodotus expressly tells us, were very different, and nearly all of them were founded on the sites of pre-existing native settlements. The religious rites, also, which the Greeks of Ionia observed, in addition to their national worship of Poseidon, were borrowed in part from the native peoples ; such were the worship of Apollo Didymaeus at Branchidae near Miletus, of Artemis at Ephesus, and of Apollo Clarius at Colophon. All these facts point to the conclusion, that the Greek colonization of this coast was effected, not by one, but by successive emigrations from different states, but chiefly of the Ionic race. The central position of this district, its excellent harbours, and the fertility of its plains, watered by the Maeander, the Cayster, and the Hermus, combined with the energetic character of the Ionian race to confer a high degree of prosperity upon these cities ; and it was not long before they began to send forth colonies to many places on the shores of the Mediterranean and the Euxine, and even to Greece itself. During the rise of the Lydian empire, the cities of Ionia preserved their independence until the reign of Croesus, who subdued those on the mainland, but relinquished his design of attacking the islands. When Cyrus had overthrown Croesus, he sent his general Harpagus to complete the conquest of the Ionic Greeks, B. C. 545. Under the Persian rule, they retained their political organization, subject to the government of the Persian satraps, and of tyrants who were set up in single cities, but they were required to render tribute and military service to the king. In B. C. 500 they revolted from Darius Hystaspis, under the leadership of HISTIAEUS, the former tyrant of Miletus, and his brother-in-law ARISTAGORAS, and supported by aid from the Athenians. The Ionian army advanced as far as Sardis, which they took and burnt, but they were driven back to the coast, and defeated near Ephesus B. C. 499. The reconquest of Ionia by the Persians was completed by the taking of Miletus, in 496, and the Ionians were compelled to furnish ships, and to serve as soldiers, in the 2 expeditions against Greece. After the defeat of Xerxes, the Greeks carried the war to the coasts of Asia, and effected the liberation of Ionia by the victories of Mycale (479), and of the Eurymedon (469). In 387 the peace of Antalcidas restored Ionia to Persia ; and after the Macedonian conquest, it formed part, successively, of the kingdom of Pergamus, and of the Roman province of Asia. For the history of the several cities, see the respective articles. In no country inhabited by the Hellenic race, except at Athens, were the refinements of civilisation, the arts, and literature, more highly cultivated than in Ionia. The restless energy and free spirit of the Ionic race, the riches gained by commerce, and the neighbourhood of the great seats of Asiatic civilisation, combined to advance with rapidity the intellectual progress and the social development of its people ; but these same influences, unchecked by the rigid discipline of the Doric race, or the simple earnestness of the Aeolic, imbued their social life with luxury and licence, and invested their works of genius with the hues of enchanting beauty at the expense of severe good taste and earnest purpose. Out of

the long list of the authors and artists of Ionia, we may mention Mimnermus of Colophon, the first poet of the amatory elegy ; Anacreon of Teos, who sang of love and wine to the music of the lyre ; Thales of Miletus, Anaxagoras of Clazomenae, and several other early philosophers ; the early annalists, Cadmus, Dionysius, and Hecataeus, all of Miletus ; and, in the fine arts, besides being the home of that exquisitely beautiful order of architecture, the Ionic, and possessing many of the most magnificent temples in the world, Ionia was the native country of that refined school of painting, which boasted the names of Zeuxis, Apelles, and Parrhasius. The most flourishing period in the history of Ionia is that during which it was subject to Persia ; but its prosperity lasted till the decline of the Roman empire, under which its cities were among the chief resorts of the celebrated teachers of rhetoric and philosophy. The important place which some of the chief cities of Ionia occupy in the early history of Christianity, is attested by the *Acts of the Apostles*, and the epistles of St. Paul to the Ephesians, and of St. John to the 7 churches of Asia.

IŎNĬUM MARE ('Ιόνιος πόντος, 'Ιόνιον πέλαγος, 'Ιονίη θάλαττα, 'Ιόνιος πόρος), a part of the Mediterranean Sea between Italy and Greece, was S. of the Adriatic, and began on the W. at Hydruntum in Calabria, and on the E. at Oricus in Epirus, or at the Ceraunian mountains. In more ancient times the Adriatic was called 'Ιόνιος μυχὸς or 'Ιόνιος κόλπος ; while at a later time the Ionium Mare itself was included in the Adriatic. In its widest signification the Ionium Mare included the *Mare Siculum*, *Creticum* and *Icarium*. Its name was usually derived by the ancients from the wanderings of Io, but it was more probably so called from the Ionian colonies, which settled in Cephallenia and the other islands off the W. coasts of Greece.

IŎPHON ('Ιοφῶν), son of Sophocles, by Nicostrate, was a distinguished tragic poet. He brought out tragedies during the life of his father, and was still flourishing in B. C. 405, the year in which Aristophanes brought out the *Frogs*. For the celebrated story of his undutiful charge against his father, see SOPHOCLES.

IPHĬAS ('Ιφιάς), i. e. Evadne, a daughter of Iphis, and wife of Capaneus.

IPHĬCLES or IPHĬCLUS ('Ιφικλῆς, 'Ιφικλος or 'Ιφικλεύς). 1. Son of Amphitryon and Alcmene of Thebes, was one night younger than his half-brother Hercules. He was first married to Automedusa, the daughter of Alcathous, by whom he became the father of Iolaus, and afterwards to the youngest daughter of Creon. He accompanied Hercules on several of his expeditions, and also took part in the Calydonian hunt. He fell in battle against the sons of Hippocoon, or, according to another account, was wounded in the battle against the Molionidae, and was carried to Pheneus, where he died. — 2. Son of Thestius by Laophonte or Deïdamia or Eurythemis or Leucippe. He took part in the Calydonian hunt and the expedition of the Argonauts. — 3. Son of Phylacus, and grandson of Deion and Clymene, or son of Cephalus and Clymene, the daughter of Minyas. He was married to Diomedia or Astyoche, and was the father of Podarces and Protesilaus. He was also one of the Argonauts ; and he possessed large herds of oxen, which he gave to the seer Melampus. He was also celebrated for his swiftness in running.

Iphicrătes ('Iφικράτης), the famous Athenian general, was the son of a shoemaker. He distinguished himself at an early age by his gallantry in battle ; and in B. C. 394, when he was only 25 years of age, he was appointed by the Athenians to the command of the forces which they sent to the aid of the Boeotians after the battle of Coronea. In 393 he commanded the Athenian forces at Corinth, and at the same time introduced an important improvement in military tactics — the formation of a body of targeteers (πελτασταί) possessing, to a certain extent, the advantages of heavy and light-armed forces. This he effected by substituting a small target for the heavy shield, adopting a longer sword and spear, and replacing the old coat of mail by a linen corslet. At the head of his targeteers he defeated and nearly destroyed a Spartan Mora in the following year (392), an exploit which became very celebrated throughout Greece. In the same year he was succeeded in the command at Corinth by Chabrias. In 389 he was sent to the Hellespont to oppose Anaxibius, who was defeated by him and slain in the following year. On the peace of Antalcidas, in 387, Iphicrates went to Thrace to assist Seuthes, king of the Odrysae, but he soon afterwards formed an alliance with Cotys, who gave him his daughter in marriage. In 377 Iphicrates was sent by the Athenians, with the command of a mercenary force, to assist Pharnabazus, in reducing Egypt to subjection ; but the expedition failed through a misunderstanding between Iphicrates and Pharnabazus. In 373 Iphicrates was sent to Corcyra, in conjunction with Callistratus and Chabrias, in the command of an Athenian force, and he remained in the Ionian sea till the peace of 371 put an end to hostilities. About 367, he was sent against Amphipolis, and after carrying on the war against this place for 3 years, was superseded by Timotheus. Shortly afterwards, he assisted his father-in-law Cotys, in his war against Athens for the possession of the Thracian Chersonesus. But his conduct in this matter was passed over by the Athenians. After the death of Chabrias (357) Iphicrates, Timotheus, and Menestheus were joined with Chares as commanders in the Social War, and were prosecuted by their unscrupulous colleague, because they had refused to risk an engagement in a storm. Iphicrates was acquitted. From the period of his trial he seems to have lived quietly at Athens. He died before 348. Iphicrates has been commended for his combined prudence and energy as a general. The worst words, he said, that a commander could utter were, " I should not have expected it." His services were highly valued by the Athenians, and were rewarded by them with almost unprecedented honours.

Iphigĕnĭa ('Iφίγενεια), according to the most common tradition, a daughter of Agamemnon and Clytaemnestra, but according to others, a daughter of Theseus and Helena, and brought up by Clytaemnestra as a foster-child. Agamemnon had once killed a stag in the grove of Artemis ; or he had boasted that the goddess herself could not hit better ; or he had vowed in the year in which Iphigenia was born to sacrifice the most beautiful production of that year, but had afterwards neglected to fulfil his vow. One of these circumstances is said to have been the cause of the calm which detained the Greek fleet in Aulis, when the Greeks wanted to sail against Troy. The seer Calchas

declared that the sacrifice of Iphigenia was the only means of propitiating Artemis. Agamemnon was obliged to yield, and Iphigenia was brought to Chalcis under the pretext of being married to Achilles. When Iphigenia was on the point of being sacrificed, Artemis carried her in a cloud to Tauris, where she became the priestess of the goddess, and a stag was substituted for her by Artemis. While Iphigenia was serving Artemis as priestess in Tauris, her brother Orestes and his friend Pylades came to Tauris to carry off the image of the goddess at this place, which was believed to have fallen from heaven. As strangers they were to be sacrificed in the temple of Artemis ; but Iphigenia recognised her brother, and fled with him and the statue of the goddess. In the meantime Electra, another sister of Orestes, had heard that he had been sacrificed in Tauris by the priestess of Artemis. At Delphi she met Iphigenia, whom she supposed had murdered Orestes. She therefore resolved to deprive Iphigenia of her sight, but was prevented by the interference of Orestes ; and a scene of recognition took place. All now returned to Mycenae ; but Iphigenia carried the statue of Artemis to the Attic town of Brauron near Marathon. She there died as priestess of the goddess. — As a daughter of Theseus Iphigenia was connected with the heroic families of Attica, and after her death the veils and most costly garments which had been worn by women who had died in childbirth were dedicated to her. According to some traditions Iphigenia never died but was changed by Artemis into Hecate, or was endowed by the goddess with immortality and eternal youth, and under the name of Orilochia became the wife of Achilles in the island of Leuce. — The Lacedaemonians maintained that the image of Artemis, which Iphigenia and Orestes had carried away from Tauris, was preserved in Sparta and not in Attica, and was worshipped in the former place under the name of Artemis Orthia. Both in Attica and in Sparta human sacrifices were offered to Iphigenia in early times. In place of these human sacrifices the Spartan youths were afterwards scourged at the festival of Artemis Orthia. It appears probable that Iphigenia was originally the same as Artemis herself.

Iphimĕdĭa or Iphimĕdē ('Iφιμέδεια, 'Iφιμέδη), daughter of Triopa, and wife of Aloeus. Being in love with Poseidon, she often walked on the sea-shore, and collected its waters in her lap, whence she became, by Poseidon, the mother of the Aloïdae, Otus and Ephialtes. While Iphimedia and her daughter, Pancratis, were celebrating the orgies of Dionysus on Mount Drius, they were carried off by Thracian pirates to Naxos or Strongyle ; but they were delivered by the Aloïdae.

Iphis ('Iφις). 1. Son of Alector, and father of Eteoclus and Evadne, the wife of Capaneus, was king of Argos. He advised Polynices to give the celebrated necklace of Harmonia to Eriphyle, that she might persuade her husband Amphiaraus to take part in the expedition against Thebes. He lost his two children, and therefore left his kingdom to Sthenelus, son of Capaneus. — 2. Son of Sthenelus, and brother of Eurystheus, was one of the Argonauts who fell in the battle with Aeetes. — 3. A youth in love with Anaxarete. [ANAXARETE.] — 4. Daughter of Ligdus and Telethusa, of Phaestus in Crete. She was brought up as a boy, on the advice of Isis, because her father, previous to her birth, had ordered the child to be killed, if it should be a girl. When Iphis had grown up, and was to be betrothed to Ianthe, she was metamorphosed by Isis into a youth.

Iphitus (Ἴφιτος). 1. Son of Eurytus of Oechalia, one of the Argonauts, was afterwards killed by Hercules. (For details, see p. 310, a.) — 2. Son of Naubolus, and father of Schedius, Epistrophus, and Eurynome, in Phocis, likewise one of the Argonauts. — 3. Son of Haemon, or Praxonides, or Iphitus, king of Elis, restored the Olympic games, and instituted the cessation of all war during their celebration, B. c. 884.

Ipsus (Ἴψος), a small town in Great Phrygia, celebrated in history as the scene of the decisive battle which closed the great contest between the generals of Alexander for the succession to his empire, and in which Antigonus was defeated and slain, B. c. 301. [ANTIGONUS.] The site is unknown, but it appears to have been about the centre of Phrygia, not far from SYNNADA.

Ira (Εἶρα, Ἰρά), a mountain fortress in Messenia, memorable as the place where Aristomenes defended himself for 11 years against the Spartans. Its capture by the Spartans in B. c. 668 put an end to the 2nd Messenian war. It is doubtful whether it is the same as Ira (Il. ix. 150), one of the 7 cities, which Agamemnon promised to Achilles.

Irenaeus (Εἰρηναῖος), one of the early Christian fathers, was probably born at Smyrna between A. D. 120 and 140. In his early youth he heard Polycarp. He afterwards went to Gaul, and in 177 succeeded Pothinus as bishop of Lyon. He made many converts from heathenism, and was most active in opposing the Gnostics, especially the Valentinians. He seems to have lived till about the end of the 2nd century. The only work of Irenaeus now extant, *Adversus Haereses*, is intended to refute the Gnostics. The original Greek is lost, with the exception of a few fragments, but the work exists in a barbarous, but ancient Latin version. Edited by Grabe, Oxon. 1702.

Irene (Εἰρήνη), called **Pax** by the Romans, the goddess of peace, was, according to Hesiod, a daughter of Zeus and Themis, and one of the Horae. [HORAE.] After the victory of Timotheus over the Lacedaemonians, altars were erected to her at Athens at the public expense. Her statue at Athens stood by the side of that of Amphiaraus, carrying in its arms Plutus, the god of wealth, and another stood near that of Hestia in the Prytaneum. At Rome, where peace was also worshipped as a goddess, she had a magnificent temple, which was built by the emperor Vespasian. Pax is represented on coins as a youthful female, holding in her left arm a cornucopia, and in her right hand an olive branch or the staff of Mercury. Sometimes she appears in the act of burning a pile of arms, or carrying corn-ears in her hand or upon her head.

Iris (Ἶρις), daughter of Thaumas (whence she is called *Thaumantias*) and of Electra, and sister of the Harpies. In the Iliad she appears as the messenger of the gods, especially of Zeus and Hera. In the Odyssey, Hermes is the messenger of the gods, and Iris is never mentioned. Iris appears to have been originally the personification of the rainbow, for this brilliant phenomenon in the skies, which vanishes as quickly as it appears, was regarded as the swift messenger of the gods. Some poets describe Iris as the rainbow itself, but other writers represent the rainbow as only the road on which Iris travels, and which therefore appears whenever the goddess wants it, and vanishes when it is no longer needed. In the earlier poets, Iris appears as a virgin goddess; but in the later, she is the wife of Zephyrus, and the mother of Eros. Iris is represented in works of art dressed in a long and wide tunic, over which hangs a light upper garment, with wings attached to her shoulders, carrying the herald's staff in her left hand, and sometimes also holding a pitcher.

Iris (Ἶρις: *Yeshil-Irmak*), a considerable river of Asia Minor, rises on the N. side of the N.most range of the Anti-Taurus, in the S. of Pontus, and flows first W. past Comana Pontica, then N. to Amasia, where it turns to the E. to Eupatoria (Megalopolis), where it receives the Lycus, and then flows N. through the territory of Themiscyra into the Sinus Amisenus. Xenophon states its breadth at 3 plethra.

Irus (Ἶρος). 1. Son of Actor, and father of Eurydamus and Eurytion. He purified Peleus, when the latter had murdered his brother; but during the chase of the Calydonian boar, Peleus unintentionally killed Eurytion, the son of Irus. Peleus endeavoured to soothe him by offering him his flocks; but Irus would not accept them, and at the command of an oracle, Peleus allowed them to run wherever they pleased. A wolf devoured the sheep, but was thereupon changed into a stone, which was shown, in later times, on the frontier between Locris and Phocis. — 2. The well-known beggar of Ithaca. His real name was Arnaeus, but he was called Irus because he was the messenger of the suitors of Penelope. He was slain by Ulysses.

Is (Ἴς: *Hit*), a city in the S. of Mesopotamia, 8 days' journey from Babylon, on the W. bank of the Euphrates, and upon a little river of the same name. In its neighbourhood were the springs of asphaltus, from which was obtained the bitumen that was used, instead of mortar, in the walls of Babylon.

Isaeus (Ἰσαῖος). 1. One of the 10 Attic orators, was born at Chalcis, and came to Athens at an early age. He was instructed in oratory by Lysias and Isocrates. He was afterwards engaged in writing judicial orations for others, and established a rhetorical school at Athens, in which Demosthenes is said to have been his pupil. It is further said that Isaeus composed for Demosthenes the speeches against his guardians, or at least assisted him in the composition. We have no particulars of his life. He lived between B. c. 420 and 348. Isaeus is said to have written 64 orations, but of these only 11 are extant. They all relate to questions of inheritance, and afford considerable information respecting this branch of the Attic law. The style of Isaeus is clear and concise, and at the same time vigorous and powerful. His orations are contained in the collections of the Greek orators. [DEMOSTHENES.] There is a good separate edition by Schömann, Greifswald, 1831. — 2. A sophist and rhetorician, a native of Assyria, taught at Rome in the time of the younger Pliny.

Isagoras (Ἰσαγόρας), the leader of the oligarchical party at Athens, in opposition to Clisthenes, B. c. 510. He was expelled from Athens by the popular party, although supported by Cleomenes and the Spartans.

Isander (Ἴσανδρος), son of Bellerophon, killed by Ares in the fight with the Solymi.

Isăra (*Isère*), a river in Gallia Narbonensis, descends from the Graian Alps, flows W. with a rapid stream, and flows into the Rhone N. of Valentia. At its junction with the Rhone Fabius Aemilianus defeated the Allobroges and Arverni, B. C. 121.

Isauria (ἡ Ἰσαυρία, ἡ Ἰσαυρική), a district of Asia Minor, on the N. side of the Taurus, between Pisidia and Cilicia, of which the ancients knew little beyond the troublesome fact, that its inhabitants, the Isauri (Ἰσαυροι) were daring robbers, whose incursions into the surrounding districts received only a temporary check from the victory over them, which gained for L. Servilius the surname of Isauricus (B. C. 75). Their chief city was called Isaura.

Isca. 1. (*Axminster* or *Bridport* or *Exeter*), the capital of the Damnonii or Dumnonii in the S.W. of Britain. — 2. (*Caer Leon*, at the mouth of the Usk), a town of the Silures in Britain, and the head quarters of the Legio II. There are many Roman remains at *Caer Leon*. The word *Leon* is a corruption of Legio: *Caer* is the old Celtic name.

Ischys. [AESCULAPIUS.]

Isidōrus (Ἰσίδωρος). 1. Of Aegae, a Greek poet of uncertain age, 5 of whose epigrams are contained in the Greek Anthology.—2. Of Charax, a geographical writer, who probably lived under the early Roman emperors. His work, Σταθμοὶ Παρθικοί, is printed in the edition of the minor geographers, by Hudson, Oxon. 1703.—3. Of Gaza, a Neo-Platonic philosopher, the friend of Proclus and Marinus, whom he succeeded as chief of the school.—4. Of Pelusium, a Christian exegetical writer, a native of Alexandria, who spent his life in a monastery near Pelusium, of which he was the abbot. He died about A. D. 450. As many as 2013 of his letters are extant. They are almost all expositions of Scripture. Published at Paris, 1638.—5. Bishop of Hispalis (*Seville*) in Spain, from A. D. 600 to 636, one of the most learned men of his age, and an ardent cultivator of ancient literature. A great number of his works is still extant, but by far the most important of them is his *Originum s. Etymologiarum Libri XX.* This work is an Encyclopaedia of Arts and Sciences, and treats of all subjects in literature, science, and religion, which were studied at that time. It was much used in the middle ages. Published in the Corpus Grammaticorum Veterum, Lindemann, Lips. 1833. A complete collection of the works of Isidorus was published by Arevali, Rom., 1797–1803, 7 vols. 4to.—6. Of Miletus, the elder and younger, were eminent architects in the reign of Justinian.

Isigŏnus (Ἰσίγονος), a Greek writer, of uncertain date, but who lived before the time of Pliny, wrote a work entitled Ἄπιστα, a few fragments of which are extant. Published in Westermann's *Paradoxographi,* Brunswick, 1839.

Isionda (Ἰσιόνδα: Ἰσιονδεύς, Isiondensis), a city of Pisidia in Asia Minor, E. of the district of Cibyra, and 5 Roman miles N.W. of Termessus. Mr. Fellows lately discovered considerable ruins 12 miles from Perge, which he supposes to be those of Isionda.

Isis (Ἴσις), one of the principal Egyptian divinities. The ideas entertained about her underwent very great changes in antiquity. She is described as the wife of Osiris and the mother of Horus. As Osiris, the god of the Nile, taught the people the use of the plough, so Isis invented the culti-

vation of wheat and barley, which were carried about in the processions at her festival. She was the goddess of the earth, which the Egyptians called their mother: whence she and Osiris were the only divinities that were worshipped by *all* the Egyptians. This simple and primitive notion of the Egyptians was modified at an early period through the influence of the East, with which Egypt came into contact, and at a later time through the influence of the Greeks. Thus Osiris and Isis came gradually to be considered as divinities of the sun and the moon. The Egyptian priests represented that the principal religious institutions of Greece came from Egypt; and after the time of Herodotus, this belief became established among the learned men in Greece. Hence Isis was identified with Demeter, and Osiris with Dionysus, and the sufferings of Isis were accordingly modified to harmonise with the mythus of the unfortunate Demeter. As Isis was the goddess of the moon, she was also identified with Io. [Io.] —The worship of Isis prevailed extensively in Greece. It was introduced into Rome in the time of Sulla; and though the senate made many attempts to suppress her worship, and ordered her temples to be destroyed, yet the new religious rites took deep root at Rome, and became very popular. In B. C. 43 the triumvirs courted the popular favour by building a new temple of Isis and Serapis. Augustus forbade any temples to be erected to Isis in the city; but this command was afterwards disregarded; and under the early Roman emperors the worship of Isis and Serapis became firmly established. The most important temple of Isis at Rome stood in the Campus Martius, whence she was called Isis Campensis. The priests and servants of the goddess wore linen garments, whence she herself is called *linigera.* Those initiated in her mysteries wore in the public processions masks representing the heads of dogs. In works of art Isis appears in figure and countenance like Hera: she wears a long tunic, and her upper garment is fastened on her breast by a knot: her head is crowned with a lotus flower, and her right hand holds the sistrum. Her son Horus is often represented with her as a fine naked boy, holding the fore-finger on the mouth, with a lotus flower on his head, and a cornucopia in his left hand. The German goddess Isis mentioned by Tacitus is probably the same as Hertha.

Ismărus (Ἴσμαρος: Ἰσμάριος), a town in Thrace, near Maronēa, situated on a mountain of the same name, which produced excellent wine. It is mentioned in the Odyssey as a town of the Cicones. Near it was the lake Ismăris (Ἰσμαρίς). The poets frequently use the adjective *Ismarius* as equivalent to Thracian. Thus Ovid calls Tereus, king of Thrace, *Ismarius tyrannus* (*Am.* ii. 6. 7), and Polymnestor, king of Thrace, *Ismarius rex* (*Met.* xiii. 530).

Ismēnē (Ἰσμήνη). 1. Daughter of Asopus, wife of Argus, and mother of Isaus and Io. —2. Daughter of Oedipus and Jocasta, and sister of Antigone.

Ismēnus (Ἰσμηνός), a small river in Boeotia, which rises in Mt. Cithaeron, flows through Thebes, and falls into the lake Hylica. The brook Dirce, so celebrated in Theban story, flowed into the Ismenus. From this river Apollo was called *Ismenius.* His temple, the *Ismenium,* at which the festival of the Daphnephoria was celebrated, was situated outside the city. The river is said to have been originally called Ladon, and to have derived its subsequent name from Ismenus, a son of Asopus and Metope. According to other traditions, Ismenus was a son of Amphion and Niobe, who when struck by the arrow of Apollo leaped into a river near Thebes, which was hence called Ismenus.

Isocrates ('Ισοκράτης), one of the 10 Attic orators, was the son of Theodorus, and was born at Athens B.C. 436. Theodorus was a man of wealth, and educated his son with the greatest care. Among his teachers were Tisias, Gorgias, Prodicus, and also Socrates. Since Isocrates was naturally timid, and of a weakly constitution, he did not come forward as a public speaker himself, but devoted himself to giving instruction in oratory, and writing orations for others. He first taught rhetoric in Chios, and afterwards at Athens. At the latter place he met with great success, and gradually acquired a large fortune by his profession. He had 100 pupils, every one of whom paid him 1000 drachmae. He also derived a large income from the orations which he wrote for others; thus, he received 20 talents for the speech which he composed for Nicocles, king of Cyprus. Although Isocrates took no part in public affairs, he was an ardent lover of his country; and, accordingly, when the battle of Chaeronea had destroyed the last hopes of freedom, he put an end to his life, B.C. 338, at the age of 98. — The school of Isocrates exercised the greatest influence upon the development of public oratory at Athens. No other rhetorician had so many disciples of celebrity. The language of Isocrates forms a great contrast with the natural simplicity of Lysias, as well as with the sublime power of Demosthenes. His style is artificial. The carefully-rounded periods, and the frequent application of figurative expressions, are features which remind us of the sophists. The immense care he bestowed upon the composition of his orations may be inferred from the statement, that he was engaged for 10, or, according to others, 15 years, upon his Panegyric oration alone. There were in antiquity 60 orations which went under the name of Isocrates, but they were not all recognised as genuine. Only 21 have come down to us. Of these 8 were written for the courts; all the others are political discourses, intended to be read by a large public. The most celebrated is his Panegyric oration, in which he shows what services Athens had rendered to Greece in every period of her history, and contends that she, and not Sparta, deserves the supremacy in Greece. The orations are printed in the collections of the Greek orators. The best separate edition is by Baiter and Sauppe, Turici, 1839.

Issa ('Ίσσα), daughter of Macareus of Lesbos, and beloved by Apollo, from whom the Lesbian town of Issa is said to have received its name.

Issa (Issaeus: *Lissa*), a small island in the Adriatic sea, with a town of the same name, off the coast of Dalmatia, was colonised at an early period by Greeks. It was inhabited by a hardy race of sailors, whose barks (*lembi Issaei*) were much prized. The Issaei placed themselves under the protection of the Romans, when they were attacked by the Illyrian queen, Teuta, B.C. 229; and their town is spoken of as a place of importance in Caesar's time.

Issedones ('Ίσσηδόνες), a Scythian tribe, in Scythia extra Imaum, the E.most people with

whom the Greeks of the time of Herodotus had any intercourse. Their country was in *Great Tartary*, near the Massagetae, whom they resembled in their manners. They are represented as extending as far as the borders of Serica.

Issicus Sinus (ὁ 'Ισσικὸς κόλπος: *Gulf of Iskenderoon*), the deep gulf at the N.E. corner of the Mediterranean, between Cilicia and Syria, named after the town of Issus. The width is about 8 miles. The coast is much altered since ancient times.

Issoria ('Ισσωρία), a surname of Artemis, derived from Mt. Issorion, in Laconia, on which she had a sanctuary.

Issus ('Ισσός, also 'Ισσοί, Xen.: 'Ισσαΐοι), a city in the S.E. extremity of Cilicia, near the head of the Issicus Sinus, and at the N. foot of the pass of M. Amanus called the Syrian Gates; memorable for the great battle in which Alexander defeated Darius Codomannus (B.C. 333), which was fought in a narrow valley near the town. It was at that time large and flourishing, but its importance was much diminished by the foundation of Alexandria in its neighbourhood. Its exact site is doubtful.

Istaevones. [GERMANIA, pp. 281, b, 282, a.]
Ister. [DANUBIUS.]

Ister, a Greek historian, was at first a slave of Callimachus, and afterwards his friend, and accordingly lived in the reign of Ptolemy Evergetes (B.C. 247—222). He wrote a large number of works, the most important of which was an *Attis*, or history of Attica. His fragments are published by C. and Th. Müller, *Fragmenta Histor. Graec.*

Istria or **Histria**, a peninsula at the N. extremity of the Adriatic, between the Sinus Tergestinus on the W. and the Sinus Flanaticus on the E. It was separated from Venetia on the N.W. by the river Timavus, and from Illyricum on the E. by the river Arsia. Its inhabitants, the **Istri** or **Histri**, a warlike Illyrian race, who carried on several wars with the Romans, till their final subjugation by the consul C. Claudius Pulcher, B.C. 177. Their chief towns were TERGESTE and POLA. Istria was originally reckoned part of Illyricum, but from the time of Augustus it formed one of the divisions of Upper Italy. In consequence of its name it was believed at one time that a branch of the river Ister (Danube) flowed into the Adriatic.

Istropolis, Istros or **Istria** ('Ιστρόπολις, 'Ίστρος, 'Ιστρίη, Herod. ii. 33: *Istere*), a town in Lower Moesia, not far from the mouth of the Danube, and at a little distance from the coast, was a colony from Miletus.

Italia ('Ιταλία), signified, from the time of Augustus, the country which we call *Italy*. It was bounded on the W. by the Mare Ligusticum and Tyrrhenum, Tuscum or Inferum; on the S. by the Mare Siculum or Ausonium; on the E. by the Mare Adriaticum or Superum; and on the N, by the Alps, which sweep round it in a semicircle, the river Varus (*Var, Varo*) separating it on the N.W. from Transalpine Gaul, and the river Arsia (*Arsa*) on the N.E. from Illyricum. The name Italia, however, was originally used to indicate a much more limited extent of country. Most of the ancients, according to their usual custom, derived the name from an ancient king Italus; but others, still more absurdly, connected it with the old Italian word *Italus* (in Oscan, *vitlu* or *vitelu*), an ox, because the country was rich in oxen! But there can be no doubt that *Italia*, or *Vitalia*, as it was also called, was the land of the *Itali*, *Vitali*, *Vitelli*, or *Vituli*, an ancient race, who are better known under the name of *Siculi*. This race was widely spread over the S. half of the peninsula, and may be said to have been bounded on the N. by a line drawn from Mt. Garganus on the E. to Terracina on the W. The Greeks were ignorant of this wide extent of the name. According to them Italia was originally only the S.most part of what was afterwards called Bruttium, and was bounded on the N. by a line drawn from the Lametic to the Scylletic gulf. They afterwards extended the name to signify the whole country S. of Posidonia on the W. and Tarentum on the E. After the Romans had conquered Tarentum and the S. part of the peninsula, about B. C. 272, the name Italia had a still further extension given to it. It then signified the whole country subject to the Romans, from the Sicilian straits as far N. as the Arnus and the Rubico. The country N. of these rivers continued to be called Gallia Cisalpina and Liguria down to the end of the republic. Augustus was the first who extended the name of Italia, so as to comprehend the whole of the basin of the Po and the S. part of the Alps, from the Maritime Alps to Pola in Istria, both inclusive. In the later times of the empire, when Maximian had transferred the imperial residence to Milan, the name Italia was again used in a narrower compass. As it had originally signified only the S. of the country, so now it was restricted to the N., comprising the 5 provinces of Aemilia, Liguria, Flaminia, Venetia, and Istria. — Besides Italia, the country was called by various other names, especially by the poets. These were Hesperia, a name which the Greeks gave to it, because it lay to the W. of Greece, or **Hesperia Magna**, to distinguish it from Spain [HESPERIA], and Saturnia, because Saturn was said to have once reigned in Latium. The names of separate parts of Italy were also applied by the poets to the whole country. Thus it was called Oenotria, originally the land of the Oenotri, in the country afterwards called Bruttium and Lucania; Ausonia, or Opica, or Opicia, originally the land of the Ausones or Ausonii, Opici or Osci, on the W. coast, in the country afterwards called Campania; Tyrrhenia, properly the land of the Tyrrheni, also on the W. coast, N. of Ausonia or Opica, and more especially in the country afterwards called Etruria; Iapygia, properly the land of the Iapyges on the E. coast, in the country afterwards called Calabria; and Ombrica, the land of the Umbri on the E. coast, alongside of Etruria. — Italy was never inhabited by one single race. It contained a great number of different races, who had migrated into the country at a very early period. The most ancient inhabitants were Pelasgians or Oenotrians, a branch of the same great race who originally inhabited Greece and the coasts of Asia Minor. They were also called Aborigines and Siculi, who, as we have already seen, were the same as the Vituli or Itali. At the time when Roman history begins, Italy was inhabited by the following races. From the mouth of the Tiber, between its right bank and the sea, dwelt the Etruscans, who extended as far N. as the Alps. Alongside of these, between the left bank of the Tiber and the Adriatic, dwelt the Umbrians. To the S. of the Etruscans were the Sacrani, Casci, or Prisci, Oscan tribes,

who had been driven out of the mountains by the Sabines, had overcome the Pelasgian tribes of the Siculi, Aborigines, or Latins, and, uniting with these conquered people, had formed the people called Prisci Latini, subsequently simply Latini. S. of these again, as far as the river Laus, were the Opici, who were also called Ausones or Aurunci, and to whom the Volsci, Sidicini, Saticuli, and Aequi, also belonged. The S. of the peninsula was inhabited by the Oenotrians, who were subsequently driven into the interior by the numerous Greek colonies founded along the coasts. S. of the Umbrians, extending as far as Mt. Garganus, dwelt the various Sabellian or Sabine tribes, the Sabines proper, the Peligni, Marsi, Marrucini, Vestini, and Hernici, from which tribes the warlike race of the Samnites subsequently sprung. From Mt. Garganus to the S. E. extremity of the peninsula, the country was inhabited by the Daunians or Apulians, Peucetii, Messapii, and Sallentini. An account of these people is given in separate articles. They were all eventually subdued by the Romans, who became the masters of the whole of the peninsula. At the time of Augustus the following were the chief divisions of Italy, an account of which is also given in separate articles :
I. **Upper Italy**, which extended from the Alps to the rivers Macra on the W. and Rubico on the E. It comprehended, 1. LIGURIA. 2. GALLIA CISALPINA. 3. VENETIA, including *Carnia*. 4. ISTRIA.
II. **Central Italy**, sometimes called Italia Propria (a term not used by the ancients), to distinguish it from Gallia Cisalpina or Upper Italy, and Magna Graecia or Lower Italy, extended from the rivers Macra on the W. and Rubico on the E., to the rivers Silarus on the W. and Frento on the E. It comprehended, 1. ETRURIA. 2. UMBRIA. 3. PICENUM. 4. SAMNIUM, including the country of the Sabini, Vestini, Marrucini, Marsi, Peligni, &c. 5. LATIUM. 6. CAMPANIA. III. **Lower Italy**, or **Magna Graecia**, included the remaining part of the peninsula, S. of the rivers Silarus and Frento. It comprehended, 1. APULIA, including Calabria. 2. LUCANIA. 3. BRUTTIUM. — Augustus divided Italy into the following 11 Regiones. 1. Latium and Campania. 2. The land of the Hirpini, Apulia and Calabria. 3. Lucania and Bruttium. 4. The land of the Frentani, Marrucini, Peligni, Marsi, Vestini, and Sabini, together with Samnium. 5. Picenum. 6. Umbria and the district of Ariminum, in what was formerly called Gallia Cisalpina. 7. Etruria. 8. Gallia Cispadana. 9. Liguria. 10. The E. part of Gallia Transpadana, Venetia, Carnia, and Istria. 11. The W. part of Gallia Transpadana. — The leading features of the physical geography of Italy are so well described by a modern writer, that we cannot do better than quote his words. "The mere plangeography of Italy gives us its shape and the position of its towns ; to these it may add a semicircle of mountains round the N. boundary, to represent the Alps ; and another long line stretching down the middle of the country, to represent the Apennines. But let us carry this on a little further, and give life and harmony to what is at present at once lifeless and confused. Observe, in the first place, how the Apennine line, beginning from the S. extremity of the Alps, runs across Italy to the very edge of the Adriatic, and thus separates naturally the Italy proper of the Romans from Cisalpine Gaul. Observe again, how the Alps after

running N. and S. where they divide Italy from France, turn then away to the E.ward, running almost parallel to the Apennines, till they too touch the head of the Adriatic, on the confines of Istria. Thus between these 2 lines of mountains there is enclosed one great basin or plain ; enclosed on 3 sides by mountains, open only on the E. to the sea. Observe how widely it spreads itself out, and then see how well it is watered. One great river (the Po) flows through it in its whole extent ; and this is fed by streams almost unnumbered, descending towards it on either side, from the Alps on one side, and from the Apennines on the other. Then, descending into Italy proper, we find the complexity of its geography quite in accordance with its manifold political divisions. It is not one simple central ridge of mountains, having a broad belt of level country on either side between it and the sea ; nor yet is it a chain rising immediately from the sea on one side, like the Andes in S. America, and leaving room therefore on the other side for wide plains of table land, and for rivers with a sufficient length of course to become at last great and navigable. It is a back-bone, thickly set with spines of unequal length, some of them running out at regular distances parallel to each other, but others twisted so strangely that they often run for a long way parallel to the back-bone, or main ridge, and interlace with one another in a mass almost inextricable. And, as if to complete the disorder, in those spots where the spines of the Apennines, being twisted round, run parallel to the sea and to their own central chain, and thus leave an interval of plain between their bases and the Mediterranean, volcanic agency has broken up the space thus left with other and distinct groups of hills of its own creation, as in the case of Vesuvius and of the Alban hills near Rome. Speaking generally, then, Italy is made up of an infinite multitude of valleys pent in between high and steep hills, each forming a country to itself, and cut off by natural barriers from the others. Its several parts are isolated by nature, and no art of man can thoroughly unite them. Hence arises the romantic character of Italian scenery: the constant combination of a mountain outline, and all the wild features of a mountain country, with the wild vegetation of a southern climate in the valleys." More minute details respecting the physical features of the different parts of Italy are given in the articles on the separate provinces into which it is divided.

Itălĭca. 1. (*Sevilla la vieja* nr. *Santiponce*), a municipium in Hispania Baetica, on the W. bank of the Baetis, N. W. of Hispalis, was founded by Scipio Africanus in the 2nd Punic war, who settled here some of his veterans. It was the birthplace of the emperors Trajan and Hadrian. — 2. The name given to Corfinium by the Italian Socii during their war with Rome. [CORFINIUM.]

Itălĭcus, Silĭus. [SILIUS.]

Itălus ('Iταλός), an ancient king of the Pelasgians, Siculians, or Oenotrians, from whom Italy was believed to have derived its name. Some call him a son of Telegonus by Penelope.

Itănus ('Iτανος), a town on the E. coast of Crete, near a promontory of the same name, founded by the Phoenicians.

Ithāca ('Iθάκη: Iθακήσιος: *Thiaki*), a small island in the Ionian Sea, celebrated as the birthplace of Ulysses, lies off the coast of Epirus, and is separated from Cephalonia by a channel about 3 or

4 miles wide. The island is about 12 miles long, and 4 in its greatest breadth. It is divided into 2 parts, which are connected by a narrow isthmus, not more than half a mile across. In each of these parts there is a mountain-ridge of considerable height ; the one in the N. called *Neritum* (Nήριτον, now *Anoi*), and the one in the S. *Neium* (Nήιον, now *Stefano*). The city of Ithaca, the residence of Ulysses, was situated on a precipitous, conical hill, now called *Aeto*, or "eagle's cliff," occupying the whole breadth of the isthmus mentioned above. The acropolis, or castle of Ulysses, crowned the extreme summit of the mountain, and is described by a modern traveller as "about as bleak and dreary a spot as can well be imagined for a princely residence." Hence Cicero (*de Orat.* i. 44) describes it, *in asperrimis saxulis tanquam nidulus affixa.* It is at the foot of Mt. Neium, and is hence described by Telemachus as "Under-Neïum" ('Iθάκης 'Yπονήιου, Hom. *Od.* iii. 81). The walls of the ancient city are in many places well preserved. — Ithaca is now one of the 7 Ionian islands under the protection of Great Britain.

Ithōmē (Iθώμη: 'Iθωμήτης, 'Iθωμαῖος). 1. A strong fortress in Messenia, situated on a mountain of the same name, which afterwards formed the citadel of the town of Messene. On the summit of the mountain stood the ancient temple of Zeus, who was hence surnamed *Ithometas* ('Iθωμήτης, Dor. 'Iθωμάτας). Ithome was taken by the Spartans, B. C. 723, at the end of the last Messenian war, after an heroic defence by Aristodemus, and again in 455, at the end of the 3rd Messenian war. — 2. A mountain fortress in Pelasgiotis, in Thessaly, near Metropolis, also called Thome.

Itĭus Portus, a harbour of the Morini, on the N. coast of Gaul, from which Caesar set sail for Britain. The position of this harbour is much disputed. It used to be identified with Gesoriacum, or *Boulogne*, but it is now usually supposed to be some harbour near Calais, probably *Vissant*, or *Witsand.*

Iton. [ITONIA.]

Itōnĭa, Itōnĭas, or Itōnis ('Iτωνία, 'Iτωνιάς, or 'Iτωνίς), a surname of Athena, derived from the town of Iton, in the S. of Phthiotis in Thessaly. The goddess there had a celebrated sanctuary and festivals, and hence is called *Incola Itoni.* From Iton her worship spread into Boeotia and the country about lake Copais, where the Pambœotia was celebrated, in the neighbourhood of a temple and grove of Athena. According to another tradition, Athena received the surname of Itonia from Itonus, a king or priest.

Itŭci ('Iτύκκη, App.), a town in Hispania Baetica, in the district of Hispalis, and a Roman colony under the name of Virtus Julia.

Itūna (*Solway Frith*), an aestuary on the W. coast of Britain, between England and Scotland.

Itūraea, Itўraea ('Iτουραία: 'Iτουραῖοι, Ituraei, Ityraei: *El-Jeidur*), a district on the N.E. borders of Palestine, bounded on the N. by the plain of Damascus, on the W. by the mountain-chain (*Jebel-Heish*), which forms the E. margin of the valley of the Jordan, on the S.W. and S. by Gaulanitis, and on the E. by Auranitis and Trachonitis. It occupied a part of the elevated plain into which Mt. Hermon sinks down on the S.E., and was inhabited by an Arabian people, of warlike and predatory habits, which they exercised upon the caravans from Arabia to Damascus, whose great road lay through their country. In the wars between the Syrians and Israelites, they are found acting as allies of the kings of Damascus. They are scarcely heard of again till B.C. 105, when they were conquered by the Asmonaean king of Judah, Aristobulus, who compelled them to profess Judaism. Restored to independence by the decline of the Asmonaean house, they seized the opportunity offered, on the other side, by the weakness of the kings of Syria, to press their predatory incursions into Coele-Syria, and even beyond Lebanon, to Byblos, Botrys, and other cities on the coast of Phoenice. Pompey reduced them again to order, and many of their warriors entered the Roman army, in which they became celebrated for their skill in horsemanship and archery. They were not, however, reduced to complete subjection to Rome until after the civil wars. Augustus gave Ituraea, which had been hitherto ruled by its native princes, to the family of Herod. During the ministry of our Saviour, it was governed by Philip, the brother of Herod Antipas, as tetrarch. Upon Philip's death, in A. D. 37, it was united to the Roman province of Syria, from which it was presently again separated, and assigned partly to Herod Agrippa I., and partly to Soaemus, the prince of Emesa. In A.D. 50, it was finally reunited by Claudius to the Roman province of Syria, and there are inscriptions which prove that the Ituraeans continued to serve with distinction in the Roman armies. There were no cities or large towns in the country, a fact easily explained by the unsettled character of the people, who lived in the Arab fashion, in unwalled villages and tents, and even, according to some statements, in the natural caves with which the country abounds.

Itys. [TEREUS.]

Iūlis ('Ιουλίς: 'Ιουλιήτης, 'Ιουλιεύς), the chief town in Ceos; the birthplace of Simonides. [CEOS.]

Iūlus. 1. Son of Aeneas, usually called Ascanius. [ASCANIUS.] — 2. Eldest son of Ascanius, who claimed the government of Latium, but was obliged to give it up to his brother Silvius.

Ixion ('Ιξίων), son of Phlegyas, or of Antion and Perimela, or of Pasion, or of Ares. According to the common tradition, his mother was Dia, a daughter of Deïoneus. He was king of the Lapithae or Phlegyes, and the father of Pirithous. When Deïoneus demanded of Ixion the bridal gifts he had promised, Ixion treacherously invited him to a banquet, and then contrived to make him fall into a pit filled with fire. As no one purified Ixion of this treacherous murder, Zeus took pity upon him, purified him, carried him to heaven, and caused him to sit down at his table. But Ixion was ungrateful to the father of the gods, and attempted to win the love of Hera. Zeus thereupon created a phantom resembling Hera, and by it Ixion became the father of a Centaur. [CENTAURI.] Ixion was fearfully punished for his impious ingratitude. His hands and feet were chained by Hermes to a wheel, which is said to have rolled perpetually in the air or in the lower world. He is further said to have been scourged, and compelled to exclaim, "Benefactors should be honoured."

Ixīonĭdes, i. e. Pirithous, the son of Ixion. — The Centaurs are also called *Ixionidae.*

Ixĭus ('Ιξιος), a surname of Apollo, derived from a district of the island of Rhodes which was called Ixiae or Ixia.

Iynx ('Ιυγξ), daughter of Peitho and Pan, or of Echo. She endeavoured to charm Zeus, or make him fall in love with Io; but she was metamorphosed by Hera into the bird called Iynx.

J.

Jaccĕtāni, a people in Hispania Tarraconensis between the Pyrenees and the Iberus.

Jana. [JANUS.]

Janĭcŭlum. [ROMA.]

Jānus and **Jāna,** a pair of ancient Latin divinities, who were worshipped as the sun and moon. The names *Janus* and *Jana* are only other forms of *Dianus* and *Diana,* which words contain the same root as *dies,* day. Janus was worshipped both by the Etruscans and Romans, and occupied an important place in the Roman religion. He presided over the beginning of everything, and was therefore always invoked first in every undertaking, even before Jupiter. He opened the year and the seasons, and hence the first month of the year was called after him. He was the porter of heaven, and therefore bore the surnames *Patulcus* or *Patulcius,* the "opener," and *Clusius* or *Clusivius,* the "shutter." In this capacity he is represented with a key in his left hand, and a staff or sceptre in his right. On earth also he was the guardian deity of gates, and hence is commonly represented with 2 heads, because every door looks 2 ways. (*Janus bifrons.*) He is sometimes represented with 4 heads (*Janus quadrifrons*), because he presided over the 4 seasons. Most of the attributes of this god, which are very numerous, are connected with his being the god who opens and shuts; and this latter idea probably has reference to his original character as the god of the sun, in connection with the alternations of day and night. At Rome, Numa is said to have dedicated to Janus the covered passage bearing his name, which was opened in times of war, and closed in times of peace. This passage is commonly, but erroneously, called a temple. It stood close by the forum. It appears to have been left open in war, to indicate symbolically that the god had gone out to assist the Roman warriors, and to have been shut in time of peace that the god, the safeguard of the city, might not escape. A temple of Janus was built by C. Duilius in the time of the first Punic war: it was restored by Augustus, and dedicated by Tiberius. On new year's day, which was the principal festival of the god, people gave presents to one another, consisting of sweetmeats and copper coins, showing on one side the double head of Janus and on the other a ship. The general name for these presents was *strenae.* The sacrifices offered to Janus consisted of cakes (called *janual*), barley, incense, and wine.

Jāson ('Ιάσων). 1. The celebrated leader of the Argonauts, was a son of Aeson and Polymede or Alcimede, and belonged to the family of the Aeolidae, at Iolcus in Thessaly. Cretheus, who had founded Iolcus, was succeeded by his son Aeson; but the latter was deprived of the kingdom by his half-brother Pelias, who attempted to take the life of the infant Jason. He was saved by his friends, who pretended that he was dead, and intrusted him to the care of the centaur Chiron. Pelias was now warned by an oracle to be on his guard against the *one-sandaled* man. When Jason had grown up, he came to claim the throne. As he entered the

Hestia (Vesta). (From an ancient Statue.) Page 319.

Honos et Virtus.
(Coin of Galba, British Museum.) Page 328.

Laocoon. (Group in the Vatican.) Page 365.

Iris. (From an ancient Vase.) Page 347.

Janus. (From a Coin of Sex. Pompeius, in the
British Museum.) Page 352.

Leto (Latona). (From a Painted Vase.) Page 379.

Lycurgus infuriate. (Osterley, Denk. der alt. Kunst,
part 2, tav. 37.) Page 397.

[To face p. 358.

Hierapolis in Phrygia. Page 320.

Ilipa in Spain. Page 340.

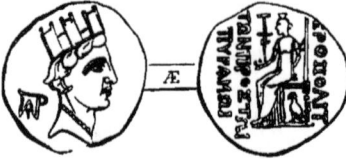

Hierapolis in Cilicia. Page 320.

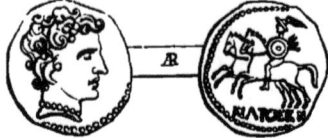

Illiberis in Spain. Page 340.

Himera in Sicily. Page 322.

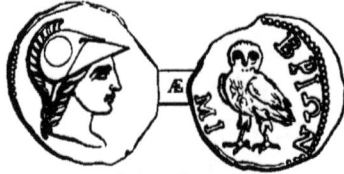

Imbros. Page 341.

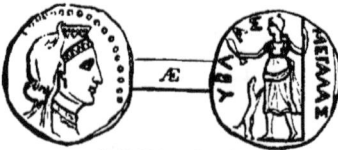

Hybla Major. Page 332.

Issa. Page 349.

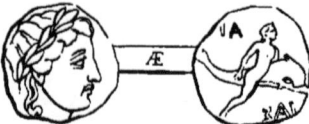

Iassus in Caria. Page 337.

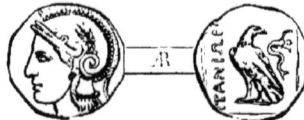

Itanus in Crete. Page 351.

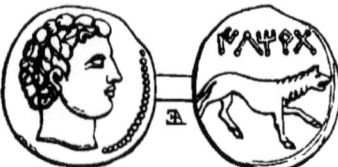

Ilerda in Spain. Page 340.

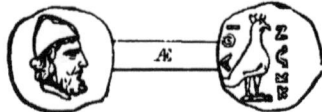

Ithaca. Page 351.

To face p. 353.]

market-place, Pelias, perceiving he had only one sandal, asked him who he was; whereupon Jason declared his name, and demanded the kingdom. Pelias consented to surrender it to him, but persuaded him to remove the curse which rested on the family of the Aeolidae, by fetching the golden fleece, and soothing the spirit of Phrixus. Another tradition related that Pelias, once upon a time, invited all his subjects to a sacrifice, which he intended to offer to Poseidon. Jason came with the rest, but, on his journey to Iolcus, he lost one of his sandals in crossing the river Anaurus. Pelias, remembering the oracle about the *one-sandaled* man, asked Jason what he would do if he were told by an oracle that he should be killed by one of his subjects? Jason, on the suggestion of Hera, who hated Pelias, answered, that he would send him to fetch the golden fleece. Pelias accordingly ordered Jason to fetch the golden fleece, which was in the possession of king Aeëtes in Colchis, and was guarded by an ever-watchful dragon. Jason willingly undertook the enterprize, and set sail in the ship Argo, accompanied by the chief heroes of Greece. He obtained the fleece with the assistance of Medea, whom he made his wife, and along with whom he returned to Iolcus. The history of his exploits on this memorable enterprize, and his adventures on his return home, are related elsewhere. [ARGONAUTAE.] On his arrival at Iolcus, Jason, according to one account, found his aged father Aeson still alive, and Medea made him young again ; but according to the more common tradition, Aeson had been slain by Pelias, during the absence of Jason, who accordingly called upon Medea to take vengeance on Pelias. Medea thereupon persuaded the daughters of Pelias to cut their father to pieces and boil him, in order to restore him to youth and vigour, as she had before changed a ram into a lamb, by boiling the body in a cauldron. But Pelias was never restored to life, and his son Acastus expelled Jason and Medea from Iolcus. They then went to Corinth, where they lived happily for several years, until Jason deserted Medea, in order to marry Glauce or Creusa, daughter of Creon, the king of the country. Medea fearfully revenged this insult. She sent Glauce a poisoned garment, which burnt her to death when she put it on. Creon likewise perished in the flames. Medea also killed her children by Jason, viz. Mermerus and Pheres, and then fled to Athens in a chariot drawn by winged dragons. Later writers represent Jason as becoming in the end reconciled to Medea, returning with her to Colchis, and there restoring Aeëtes to his kingdom, of which he had been deprived. The death of Jason is related differently. According to some, he made away with himself from grief, according to others, he was crushed by the poop of the ship Argo, which fell upon him as he was lying under it. — 2. Tyrant of Pherae and Tagus of Thessaly (*Dict. of Antiq.* art. *Tagus*), was probably the son of Lycophron, who established a tyranny on the ruins of aristocracy at Pherae. He succeeded his father as tyrant of Pherae soon after B. C. 395, and in a few years extended his power over almost the whole of Thessaly. Pharsalus was the only city in Thessaly which maintained its independence under the government of Polydamas ; but even this place submitted to him in 375. In the following year (374) he was elected Tagus or generalissimo of Thessaly. His power was strengthened by the weakness of the other Greek states, and by the exhausting contest in which Thebes and Sparta were engaged. He was now in a position which held out to him every prospect of becoming master of Greece ; but when at the height of his power, he was assassinated at a public audience, 370. — Jason had an insatiable appetite for power, which he sought to gratify by any and every means. With the chief men in the several states of Greece, as e. g. with Timotheus and Pelopidas, he cultivated friendly relations. He is represented as having all the qualifications of a great general and diplomatist — as active, temperate, prudent, capable of enduring much fatigue, and skilful in concealing his own designs and penetrating those of his enemies. He was an admirer of the rhetoric of Gorgias ; and Isocrates was one of his friends. — 3. Of Argos, an historian, lived under Hadrian, and wrote a work on Greece in 4 books.

Javolēnus Priscus, an eminent Roman jurist, was born about the commencement of the reign of Vespasian (A. D. 79), and was one of the council of Antoninus Pius. He was a pupil of Caelius Sabinus, and a leader of the Sabinian or Cassian school. [See p. 144, b.] There are 206 extracts from Javolenus in the Digest.

Jaxartes ('Ιαξάρτης: *Syr, Syderia,* or *Syhoun),* a great river of Central Asia, about which the ancient accounts are very different and confused. It rises in the Comēdi Montes (*Moussour),* and flows N.W. into the *Sea of Aral :* the ancients supposed it to fall into the N. side of the Caspian, not distinguishing between the 2 seas. It divided Sogdiana from Scythia. On its banks dwelt a Scythian tribe called Jaxartae.

Jericho or **Hiěrichus** ('Ιεριχώ, 'Ιεριχοῦς: *Er-Riha ?* Ru.), a city of the Canaanites, in a plain on the W. side of the Jordan near its mouth, was destroyed by Joshua, rebuilt in the time of the Judges, and formed an important frontier fortress of Judaea. It was again destroyed by Vespasian, rebuilt under Hadrian, and finally destroyed during the crusades.

Jerom. [HIERONYMUS.]

Jerusalem or **Hiěrosŏlyma** ('Ιερουσάλημ, 'Ιεροσόλυμα: 'Ιεροσολυμίτης: *Jerusalem,* Arab. *El-Kuds,* i. e. *the Holy City),* the capital of Palestine, in Asia. At the time of the Israelitish conquest of Canaan, under Joshua, Jerusalem, then called Jebus, was the chief city of the Jebusites, a Canaanitish tribe, who were not entirely driven out from it till B. C. 1050, when David took the city, and made it the capital of the kingdom of Israel. It was also established as the permanent centre of the Jewish religion, by the erection of the temple by Solomon. After the division of the kingdom, under Rehoboam, it remained the capital of the kingdom of Judah, until it was entirely destroyed, and its inhabitants were carried into captivity by Nebuchadnezzar, king of Babylon, B. C. 588. In B. C. 536, the Jewish exiles, having been permitted by Cyrus to return, began to rebuild the city and temple ; and the work was completed in about 24 years. In B. C. 332, Jerusalem quietly submitted to Alexander. During the wars which followed his death, the city was taken by Ptolemy, the son of Lagus (B. C. 320), and remained subject to the Greek kings of Egypt, till the conquest of Palestine by Antiochus III. the Great, king of Syria, B. C. 198. Up to this time the Jews had been allowed the free enjoyment of their religion and their own internal government, and Antiochus confirmed them in these privileges ; but the altered government of his son, Antiochus IV. Epiphanes, provoked a rebellion, which was at first put down when Antiochus took Jerusalem and polluted the temple (B. c. 170) ; but the religious persecution which ensued drove the people to despair, and led to a new revolt under the Maccabees, by whom Jerusalem was retaken, and the temple purified in B. c. 163 [MACCABAEI]. In B. c. 133, Jerusalem was retaken by Antiochus VII. Sidetes, and its fortifications dismantled, but its government was left in the hands of the Maccabee, John Hyrcanus, who took advantage of the death of Antiochus in Parthia (B. c. 128) to recover his full power. His son Aristobulus assumed the title of king of Judaea, and Jerusalem continued to be the capital of the kingdom till B. c. 63, when it was taken by Pompey, and the temple was again profaned. For the events which followed, see HYRCANUS, HERODES, and PALAESTINA. In A. D. 70, the rebellion of the Jews against the Romans was put down, and Jerusalem was taken by Titus, after a siege of several months, during which the inhabitants endured the utmost horrors ; the survivors were all put to the sword or sold as slaves, and the city and temple were utterly razed to the ground. In consequence of a new revolt of the Jews, the emperor Hadrian resolved to destroy all vestiges of their national and religious peculiarities ; and, as one means to this end, he established a new Roman colony, on the ground where Jerusalem had stood, by the name of Aelia Capitolina, and built a temple of Jupiter Capitolinus, on the site of the temple of Jehovah, A. D. 135. The establishment of Christianity as the religion of the Roman empire restored to Jerusalem its sacred character, and led to the erection of several churches ; but the various changes which have taken place in it, since its conquest by the Arabs under Omar in A. D. 638, have left very few vestiges even of the Roman city. Jerusalem stands due W. of the head of the *Dead Sea*, at the distance of about 20 miles (in a straight line) and about 35 miles from the Mediterranean, on an elevated platform, divided, by a series of valleys, from hills which surround it on every side. This platform has a general slope from W. to E. its highest point being the summit of Mt. Zion, in the S. W. corner of the city on which stood the original " city of David." The S. E. part of the platform is occupied by the hill called Moriah, on which the temple stood, and the E. part by the hill called Acra ; but these two summits are now hardly distinguishable from the general surface of the platform, probably on account of the gradual filling up of the valleys between. The height of Mt. Zion is 2535 feet above the level of the Mediterranean, and about 300 feet above the valley below. The extent of the platform is 5400 feet from N. to S., and 1100 feet from E. to W.

Jŏcastē ('Ιοκάστη), called Epicaste in Homer, daughter of Menoeceus, and wife of the Theban king Laius, by whom she became the mother of Oedipus. She afterwards married Oedipus, not knowing that he was her son ; and when she discovered the crime she had unwittingly committed, she put an end to her life. For details see OEDIPUS.

Joppē, Joppa ('Ιόππη: O. T. Japho: *Jaffa*), a very ancient maritime city of Palestine, and,

before the building of Caesarea, the only sea-port of the whole country, and therefore called by Strabo the port of Jerusalem, lay just S. of the boundary between Judaea and Samaria, S.W. of Antipatris, and N.W. of Jerusalem.

Jordānes ('Ιορδάνης, 'Ιόρδανος: *Jordan*, Arab. *Esh-Sheriah el-Kebir*, or *el-Urdun*), has its source at the S. foot of M. Hermon (the S.most part of Anti-Libanus), near Paneas (aft. Caesarea Philippi), whence it flows S. into the little lake Semechonitis, and thence into the Sea of Galilee (Lake of Tiberias), and thence through a narrow plain, depressed below the level of the surrounding country into the lake Asphaltites (*Dead Sea*), where it is finally lost. [PALAESTINA.] Its course, from the lake Semechonitis to the Dead Sea, is about 60 miles ; the depression through which it runs consists, first, of a sandy valley, from 5 to 10 miles broad, within which is a lower valley, in width about half a mile, and, for the most part, beautifully clothed with grass and trees ; and, in some places, there is still a lower valley within this. The average width of the river itself is calculated at 30 yards, and its average depth at 9 feet. It is fordable in many places in summer. but in spring it becomes much deeper, and often overflows its banks. Its bed is considerably below the level of the Mediterranean.

Jornandes, or Jordānes, an historian, lived in the time of Justinian, or in the 6th century of our era. He was a Goth by birth ; was secretary to the king of the Alani, adopted the Christian religion, took orders, and was made a bishop in Italy. There is not sufficient evidence for the common statement that he was bishop of Ravenna. He wrote 2 historical works in the Latin language. 1. *De Getarum* (*Gothorum*) *Origine et Rebus Gestis*, containing the history of the Goths, from the earliest times down to their subjugation by Belisarius in 541. The work is abridged from the lost history of the Goths by Cassiodorus, to which Jornandes added various particulars ; but it is compiled without judgment, and is characterised by partiality to the Goths. 2. *De Regnorum ac Temporum Successione*, a short compendium of history from the creation down to the victory obtained by Narses, in 552, over king Theodatus. It is only valuable for some accounts of the barbarous nations of the North, and the countries which they inhabited. Edited by Lindenbrog, Hamburg, 1611.

Josĕphus, Flăvius, the Jewish historian, was born at Jerusalem, A. D. 37. On his mother's side he was descended from the Asmonaean princes, while from his father, Matthias, he inherited the priestly office. He enjoyed an excellent education ; and at the age of 26 he went to Rome to plead the cause of some Jewish priests whom Felix, the procurator of Judaea, had sent thither as prisoners. After a narrow escape from death by shipwreck, he safely landed at Puteoli ; and being introduced to Poppaea, he not only effected the release of his friends, but received great presents from the empress. On his return to Jerusalem he found his countrymen eagerly bent on a revolt from Rome, from which he used his best endeavours to dissuade them ; but failing in this, he professed to enter into the popular designs. He was chosen one of the generals of the Jews, and was sent to manage affairs in Galilee. When Vespasian and his army entered Galilee, Josephus threw himself into Iotapata, which he defended for 47 days.

When the place was taken, the life of Josephus was spared by Vespasian through the intercession of Titus. Josephus thereupon assumed the character of a prophet, and predicted to Vespasian that the empire should one day be his and his son's. Vespasian treated him with respect, but did not release him from captivity, till he was proclaimed emperor nearly 3 years afterwards (A. D. 70). Josephus was present with Titus at the siege of Jerusalem, and afterwards accompanied him to Rome. He received the freedom of the city from Vespasian, who assigned him, as a residence, a house formerly occupied by himself, and treated him honourably to the end of his reign. The same favour was extended to him by Titus and Domitian as well. He assumed the name of Flavius, as a dependant of the Flavian family. His time at Rome appears to have been employed mainly in the composition of his works. He died about 100. — The works of Josephus are written in Greek. They are : — 1. *The History of the Jewish War* (Περὶ τοῦ Ἰουδαικοῦ πολέμου ἢ Ἰουδαϊκῆς ἱστορίας περὶ ἀλώσεως), in 7 books, published about A. D. 75. Josephus first wrote it in Hebrew, and then translated it into Greek. It commences with the capture of Jerusalem by Antiochus Epiphanes in B. C. 170, runs rapidly over the events before Josephus's own time, and gives a detailed account of the fatal war with Rome. — 2. *The Jewish Antiquities* (Ἰουδαϊκὴ ἀρχαιολογία), in 20 books, completed about A. D. 93, and addressed to Epaphroditus. The title as well as the number of books may have been suggested by the Ῥωμαϊκὴ ἀρχαιολογία of Dionysius of Halicarnassus. It gives an account of Jewish History from the creation of the world to A. D. 66, the 12th year of Nero, in which the Jews were goaded to rebellion by Gessius Florus. In this work Josephus seeks to accommodate the Jewish religion to heathen tastes and prejudices. Thus he speaks of Moses and his law in a tone which might be adopted by any disbeliever in his divine legation. He says that Abraham went into Egypt (Gen. xii.), intending to adopt the Egyptian views of religion, should he find them better than his own. He speaks doubtfully of the preservation of Jonah by the whale. He intimates a doubt of there having been any miracle in the passage of the Red Sea, and compares it with the passage of Alexander the Great along the shore of the sea of Pamphylia. He interprets Exod. xxii. 28, as if it conveyed a command to respect the idols of the heathen. Many similar instances might be quoted from his work. — 3. *His own life*, in one book. This is an appendage to the Archaeologia, and is addressed to the same Epaphroditus. It was not written earlier than A. D. 97, since Agrippa II. is mentioned in it as no longer living. — 4. *A treatise on the Antiquity of the Jews*, or *Against Apion*, in 2 books, also addressed to Epaphroditus. It is in answer to such as impugned the antiquity of the Jewish nation, on the ground of the silence of Greek writers respecting it. [APION.] The treatise exhibits extensive acquaintance with Greek literature and philosophy. — 5. Εἰς Μακκαβαίους ἢ περὶ αὐτοκράτορος λογισμοῦ, in 1 book. Its genuineness is doubtful. It is a declamatory account of the martyrdom of Eleazar (an aged priest), and of 7 youths and their mother, in the persecution under Antiochus Epiphanes. The best editions of Josephus are by Hudson, Oxon. 1720 ; and by Havercamp, Amst. 1726.

Jovianus, Flavius Claudius, was elected emperor by the soldiers, in June A. D. 363, after the death of Julian [JULIANUS], whom he had accompanied in his campaign against the Persians. In order to effect his retreat in safety, Jovian surrendered to the Persians the Roman conquests beyond the Tigris, and several fortresses in Mesopotamia. He died suddenly at a small town on the frontiers of Bithynia and Galatia, February 17th, 364, after a reign of little more than 7 months. Jovian was a Christian ; but he protected the heathens.

Juba (Ἰόβας). 1. King of Numidia, was son of Hiempsal, who was re-established on the throne by Pompey. On the breaking out of the civil war between Caesar and Pompey, he actively espoused the cause of the latter ; and, accordingly, when Caesar sent Curio into Africa (B. C. 49), he supported the Pompeian general Attius Varus with a large body of troops. Curio was defeated by their united forces, and fell in the battle. In 46 Juba fought along with Scipio against Caesar himself, and was present at the decisive battle of Thapsus. After this defeat he wandered about for some time, and then put an end to his own life. — 2. King of Mauretania, son of the preceding, was a mere child at his father's death (46), was carried a prisoner to Rome by Caesar, and compelled to grace the conqueror's triumph. He was brought up in Italy, where he received an excellent education, and applied himself with such diligence to study, that he turned out one of the most learned men of his day. After the death of Antony (30), Augustus conferred upon Juba his paternal kingdom of Numidia, and at the same time gave him in marriage Cleopatra, otherwise called Selene, the daughter of Antony and Cleopatra. At a subsequent period (25), Augustus gave him Mauretania in exchange for Numidia, which was reduced to a Roman province. He continued to reign in Mauretania till his death, which happened about A. D. 19. He was beloved by his subjects, among whom he endeavoured to introduce the elements of Greek and Roman civilisation ; and, after his death, they even paid him divine honours. — Juba wrote a great number of works in almost every branch of literature. They are all lost, with the exception of a few fragments. They appear to have been all written in Greek. The most important of them were : — 1. *A History of Africa* (Λιβυκά), in which he made use of Punic authorities. — 2. *On the Assyrians*. — 3. *A History of Arabia*. — 4. *A Roman History* (Ῥωμαϊκὴ ἱστορία). — 5. Θεατρικὴ ἱστορία, a general treatise on all matters connected with the stage. — 6. Περὶ γραφικῆς, or περὶ ζωγράφων, seems to have been a general history of painting. He also wrote some treatises on botany and on grammatical subjects.

Judaea, Judaei. [PALAESTINA.]

Jugunthi, a German people, sometimes described as a Gothic, and sometimes as an Alemannic tribe.

Jugurtha (Ἰουγούρθας or Ἰογόρθας), king of Numidia, was an illegitimate son of Mastanabal, and a grandson of Masinissa. He lost his father at an early age, but was adopted by his uncle Micipsa, who brought him up with his own sons, Hiempsal and Adherbal. Jugurtha quickly distinguished himself both by his abilities and his skill in all bodily exercises, and rose to so much favour and popularity with the Numidians, that he began to excite the jealousy of Micipsa. In order to remove him to a distance, Micipsa sent him, in B. C. 134, with an auxiliary force, to assist Scipio against Numantia. Here his zeal, courage, and ability, gained for him the favour and commendation of Scipio, and of all the leading nobles in the Roman camp. On his return to Numidia he was received with honour by Micipsa, who was obliged to dissemble the fears which he entertained of his ambitious nephew. Micipsa died in 118, leaving the kingdom to Jugurtha and his 2 sons, Hiempsal and Adherbal, in common. Jugurtha soon showed that he aspired to the sole sovereignty of the country. In the course of the same year he found an opportunity to assassinate Hiempsal at Thirmida, and afterwards defeated Adherbal in battle. Adherbal fled to Rome to invoke the assistance of the senate; but Jugurtha, by a lavish distribution of bribes, counteracted the just complaints of his enemy. The senate decreed that the kingdom of Numidia should be equally divided between the 2 competitors; but the senators entrusted with the execution of this decree were also bribed by Jugurtha, who thus succeeded in obtaining the W. division of the kingdom, adjacent to Mauretania, by far the larger and richer portion of the two (117). But this advantage was far from contenting him. Shortly afterwards he invaded the territories of Adherbal with a large army, and defeated him. Adherbal made his escape to the strong fortress of Cirta, where he was closely blockaded by Jugurtha. The Romans commanded Jugurtha to abstain from further hostilities; but he paid no attention to their commands, and at length gained possession of Cirta, and put Adherbal to death, 112. War was now declared against Jugurtha at Rome, and the consul, L. Calpurnius Bestia, was sent into Africa. 111. Jugurtha had recourse to his customary arts; and by means of large sums of money given to Bestia and M. Scaurus, his principal lieutenant, he purchased from them a favourable peace. The conduct of Bestia excited the greatest indignation at Rome; and Jugurtha was summoned to the city under a safe conduct, the popular party hoping to be able to convict the nobility by means of his evidence. The scheme, however, failed; since one of the tribunes who had been gained over by the friends of Bestia and Scaurus forbade the king to give evidence. Soon afterwards Jugurtha was compelled to leave Italy, in consequence of his having ventured on the assassination of Massiva, whose counter influence he regarded with apprehension. [MASSIVA.] The war was now renewed; but the consul, Sp. Postumius Albinus, who arrived to conduct it (110), was able to effect nothing against Jugurtha. When the consul went to Rome to hold the comitia, he left his brother Aulus in command of the army. Aulus was defeated by Jugurtha; great part of his army was cut to pieces, and the rest only escaped a similar fate by the ignominy of passing under the yoke. But this disgrace at once roused all the spirit of the Roman people: the treaty concluded by Aulus was instantly annulled; and the consul Q. Caecilius Metellus was sent into Africa at the head of a new army (109). Metellus was an able general and an upright man, whom Jugurtha was unable to cope with in the field, or to seduce by bribes. In the course of 2 years Metellus frequently defeated Jugurtha, and at length drove him to take refuge among the Gaetulians. In 107 Metellus

was succeeded in the command by Marius; but the cause of Jugurtha had meantime been espoused by his father-in-law Bocchus, king of Mauretania, who had advanced to his support with a large army. The united forces of Jugurtha and Bocchus were defeated in a decisive battle by Marius; and Bocchus purchased the forgiveness of the Romans by surrendering his son-in-law to Sulla, the quaestor of Marius (106). Jugurtha remained in captivity till the return of Marius to Rome, when, after adorning the triumph of his conqueror (Jan. 1, 104), he was thrown into a dungeon, and there starved to death.

JÚLIA. 1. Aunt of Caesar the dictator, and wife of C. Marius the elder. She died B. C. 68, and her nephew pronounced her funeral oration. — 2. Mother of M. Antonius, the triumvir. In the proscription of the triumvirate (43) she saved the life of her brother, L. Caesar [CAESAR, No. 5.]— 3. Sister of Caesar the dictator, and wife of M. Atius Balbus, by whom she had Atia, the mother of Augustus [ATIA]. — 4. Daughter of Caesar the dictator, by Cornelia, and his only child in marriage, was married to Cn. Pompey in 59. She was a woman of beauty and virtue, and was tenderly attached to her husband, although 23 years older than herself. She died in childbed in 54. — 5. Daughter of Augustus by Scribonia, and his only child, was born in 39. She was educated with great strictness, but grew up one of the most profligate women of her age. She was thrice married: —1. to M. Marcellus, her first cousin in 25: 2. after his death (23) without issue, to M. Agrippa, by whom she had 3 sons, C. and L. Caesar, and Agrippa Postumus, and 2 daughters, Julia and Agrippina: 3. after Agrippa's death in 12, to Tiberius Nero, the future emperor. In B. C. 2 Augustus at length became acquainted with the misconduct of his daughter, whose notorious adulteries had been one reason why her husband Tiberius had quitted Italy 4 years before. Augustus was incensed beyond measure, and banished her to Pandataria, an island off the coast of Campania. At the end of 5 years she was removed to Rhegium, but she was never suffered to quit the bounds of the city. Even the testament of Augustus showed the inflexibility of his anger. He bequeathed her no legacy, and forbade her ashes to repose in his mausoleum. Tiberius on his accession (A. D. 14) deprived her of almost all the necessaries of life; and she died in the course of the same year. — 6. Daughter of the preceding, and wife of L. Aemilius Paulus. She inherited her mother's licentiousness, and was in consequence banished by her grandfather Augustus to the little island Tremerus, on the coast of Apulia, A. D. 9, where she lived nearly 20 years. She died in 28. It was probably this Julia whom Ovid celebrated as Corinna in his elegies and other erotic poems; and his intrigues with her appear to have been the cause of the poet's banishment in A. D. 9. — 7. Youngest child of Germanicus and Agrippina, was born A. D. 18; was married to M. Vinicius in 33; and was banished in 37 by her brother Caligula, who was believed to have had an incestuous intercourse with her. She was recalled by Claudius, but was afterwards put to death by this emperor at Messalina's instigation. The charge brought against her was adultery, and Seneca, the philosopher, was banished to Corsica as the partner of her guilt. — 8. Daughter of Drusus and Livia, the sister of Germanicus. She was married, A. D.

20, to her first cousin, Nero, son of Germanicus and Agrippina; and after Nero's death, to Rubellius Blandus, by whom she had a son, Rubellius Plautus. She, too, was put to death by Claudius, at the instigation of Messalina, 59. — 9. Daughter of Titus, the son of Vespasian, married Flavius Sabinus, a nephew of the emperor Vespasian. Julia died of abortion, caused by her uncle Domitian, with whom she lived in criminal intercourse. — 10. Domna [DOMNA]. — 11. Drusilla [DRUSILLA]. — 12. Maesa [MAESA].

Julia Gens, one of the most ancient patrician houses at Rome, was of Alban origin, and was removed to Rome by Tullus Hostilius upon the destruction of Alba Longa. It claimed descent from the mythical Iulus, the son of Venus and Anchises. The most distinguished family in the gens is that of CAESAR. Under the empire we find an immense number of persons of the name of Julius, the most important of whom are spoken of under their surnames.

Juliānus Didĭus. [DIDIUS.]

Juliānus, Flavĭus Claudĭus, usually called Julian, and surnamed the Apostate, Roman emperor, A. D. 361—363. He was born at Constantinople, A. D. 331, and was the son of Julius Constantius by his second wife, Basilina, and the nephew of Constantine the Great. Julian and his elder brother, Gallus, were the only members of the imperial family whose lives were spared by the sons of Constantine the Great, on the death of the latter in 337. The 2 brothers were educated with care, and were brought up in the principles of the Christian religion ; but as they advanced to manhood, they were watched with jealousy and suspicion by the emperor Constantius. After the execution of Gallus in 354 [GALLUS], the life of Julian was in great peril; but he succeeded in pacifying the suspicions of the emperor, and was allowed to go to Athens in 355 to pursue his studies. Here he devoted himself with ardour to the study of Greek literature and philosophy, and attracted universal attention both by his attainments and abilities. Among his fellow-students were Gregory of Nazianzus and Basil, both of whom afterwards became so celebrated in the Christian church. Julian had already abandoned Christianity in his heart and returned to the pagan faith of his ancestors; but fear of Constantius prevented him from making an open declaration of his apostacy. Julian did not remain long at Athens. In November, 355, he received from Constantius the title of Caesar, and was sent into Gaul to oppose the Germans, who had crossed the Rhine, and were ravaging some of the fairest provinces of Gaul. During the next 5 years (356—360) Julian carried on war against the 2 German confederacies of the Alemanni and Franks with great success, and gained many victories over them. His internal administration was distinguished by justice and wisdom ; and he gained the goodwill and affection of the provinces intrusted to his care. His growing popularity awakened the jealousy of Constantius, who commanded him to send some of his best troops to the East, to serve against the Persians. His soldiers refused to leave their favourite general, and proclaimed him emperor at Paris in 360. After several fruitless negotiations between Julian and Constantius, both parties prepared for war. In 361 Julian marched along the valley of the Danube towards Constantinople; but Constantius, who had

set out from Syria to oppose his rival, died on his march in Cilicia. His death left Julian the undisputed master of the empire. On the 11th of December Julian entered Constantinople. He lost no time in publicly avowing himself a pagan, but he proclaimed that Christianity would be tolerated equally with paganism. He did not, however, act impartially towards the Christians. He preferred pagans as his civil and military officers, forbade the Christians to teach rhetoric and grammar in the schools, and, in order to annoy them, allowed the Jews to rebuild the temple at Jerusalem. In the following year (362) Julian went to Syria in order to make preparations for the war against the Persians. He spent the winter at Antioch, where he made the acquaintance of the orator Libanius ; and in the spring of 363 he set out against the Persians. He crossed the Euphrates and the Tigris; and after burning his fleet on the Tigris, that it might not fall into the hands of the enemy, he boldly marched into the interior of the country in search of the Persian king. His army suffered much from the heat, want of water, and provisions ; and he was at length compelled to retreat. The Persians now appeared and fearfully harassed his rear. Still the Romans remained victorious in many a bloody engagement ; but in the last battle fought on the 26th of June, Julian was mortally wounded by an arrow, and died in the course of the day. Jovian was chosen emperor in his stead, on the field of battle. [JOVIANUS.] Julian was an extraordinary character. As a monarch he was indefatigable in his attention to business, upright in his administration, and comprehensive in his views; as a man, he was virtuous, in the midst of a profligate age, and did not yield to the luxurious temptations to which he was exposed. In consequence of his apostacy he has been calumniated by Christian writers; but for the same reason he has been unduly extolled by heathen authors. He wrote a large number of works, many of which are extant. He was a man of reflection and thought, but possessed no creative genius. He did not however write merely for the sake of writing, like so many of his contemporaries ; his works show that he had his subjects really at heart, and that in literature as well as in business his extraordinary activity arose from the wants of a powerful mind, which desired to improve itself and the world. The style of Julian is remarkably pure, and is a close imitation of the style of the classical Greek writers. The following are his most important works:—1. Letters, most of which were intended for public circulation, and are of great importance for the history of the time. Edited by Heyler, Mainz,1828.—2. Orations, on various subjects, as for instance, On the emperor Constantius, On the worship of the sun, On the mother of the gods (Cybele), On true and false Cynicism, &c. — 3. The Caesars or the Banquet (Καῖσαρες ἢ Συμπόσιον), a satirical composition, which is one of the most agreeable and instructive productions of ancient wit. Julian describes the Roman emperors approaching one after the other to take their seat round a table in the heavens ; and as they come up, their faults, vices, and crimes, are censured with a sort of bitter mirth by old Silenus, whereupon each Caesar defends himself as well as he can. Edited by Heusinger, Gotha, 1736, and by Harless, Erlangen, 1785. — 4. Misopogon or the Enemy of the Beard (Μισοπώγων), a severe satire on the licentious and effeminate manners of the

A A 3

inhabitants of Antioch, who had ridiculed Julian, when he resided in the city, on account of his austere virtues, and had laughed at his allowing his beard to grow in the ancient fashion. — 5. *Against the Christians* (Κατὰ Χριστιανῶν). This work is lost, but some extracts from it are given in Cyrill's reply to it, which is still extant.—The best edition of the collected works of Julian is by Spanheim, Lips. 1696.

Juliānus, Salvǐus, an eminent Roman jurist, who flourished under Hadrian and the Antonines. He was praefectus urbi, and twice consul, but his name does not appear in the Fasti. By the order of Hadrian, he drew up the *edictum perpetuum*, which forms an epoch in the history of Roman jurisprudence. His work appears to have consisted in collecting and arranging the clauses which the praetors were accustomed to insert in their annual edict, in condensing the materials, and in omitting antiquated provisions. He was a voluminous legal writer, and his works are cited in the Digest.

Juliǎs ('Ιουλίας : Bib. Bethsaida : *Et-Tell*, Ru.), a city of Palestine on the E. side of the Jordan, N. of the Lake of Tiberias, so called by the tetrarch Philip, in honour of Julia, the daughter of Augustus.

Juliobrīga (*Retortillo*, nr. *Reynosa*), a town of the Cantabri in Hispania Tarraconensis, near the sources of the Iberus.

Juliomăgus. [ANDECAVI.]

Juliŏpŏlis ('Ιουλιόπολις). [GORDIUM ; TARSUS.]

Jūlius. [JULIA GENS.]

Juncārĭa (*Junquera*), a town of the Indigetes in Hispania Tarraconensis, on the road from Barcino to the frontiers of Gaul, in a plain covered with rushes ('Ιουγκάριον πεδίον).

Jūnǐa. 1. Half-sister of M. Brutus, the murderer of Caesar, and wife of M. Lepidus, the triumvir. — 2. **Tertĭa**, or **Tertulla**, own sister of the preceding, was the wife of C. Cassius, one of Caesar's murderers. She survived her husband a long while, and did not die till A. D. 22.

Jūnǐa Gens, an ancient patrician house at Rome, to which belonged the celebrated M. Junius Brutus, who took such an active part in expelling the Tarquins. But afterwards the gens appears as only a plebeian one. Under the republic the chief families were those of BRUTUS, BUBULCUS, GRACCHANUS, NORBANUS, PULLUS, SILANUS. The Junii who lived under the empire, are likewise spoken of under their various surnames.

Jūno, called Hera by the Greeks. The Greek goddess is spoken of in a separate article. [HERA.] The word *Ju-no* contains the same root as *Ju-piter*. As Jupiter is the king of heaven and of the gods, so Juno is the queen of heaven, or the female Jupiter. She was worshipped at Rome as the queen of heaven, from early times, with the surname of *Regina*. At a later period her worship was solemnly transferred from Veii to Rome, where a sanctuary was dedicated to her on the Aventine. As Jupiter was the protector of the male sex, so Juno watched over the female sex. She was supposed to accompany every woman through life, from the moment of her birth to her death. Hence she bore the special surnames of *Virginalis* and *Matrona*, as well as the general ones of *Opigena* and *Sospita*, and under the last mentioned name she was worshipped at Lanuvium. On their birthday women offered sacrifices to Juno surnamed *Natalis*, just as men sacrificed to their genius natalis.

The great festival, celebrated by all the women, in honour of Juno, was called *Matronalia* (*Dict. of Ant. s. v.*), and took place on the 1st of March. Her protection of women, and especially her power of making them fruitful, is further alluded to in the festival *Populifugia* (*Dict. of Ant. s. v.*), as well as in the surname of *Februlis*, *Februata*, *Februta*, or *Februalis*. Juno was further, like Saturn, the guardian of the finances, and under the name of Moneta she had a temple on the Capitoline hill, which contained the mint. The most important period in a woman's life is that of her marriage, and she was therefore believed especially to preside over marriage. Hence she was called *Juga* or *Jugalis*, and had a variety of other names, such as *Pronuba*, *Cinxia*, *Lucina*, &c. The month of June, which is said to have been originally called Junonius, was considered to be the most favourable period for marrying. Women in childbed invoked Juno Lucina to help them, and newly-born children were likewise under her protection : hence she was sometimes confounded with the Greek Artemis or Ilithyia. In Etruria she was worshipped under the name of *Cupra*. She was also worshipped at Falerii, Lanuvium, Aricia, Tibur, Praeneste, and other places. In the representations of the Roman Juno that have come down to us, the type of the Greek Hera is commonly adopted.

Jūpiter, called Zeus by the Greeks. The Greek god is spoken of in a separate article [ZEUS.] Jupiter was originally an elemental divinity, and his name signifies the father or lord of heaven, being a contraction of *Diovis pater*, or *Diespiter*. Being the lord of heaven, he was worshipped as the god of rain, storms, thunder, and lightning, whence he had the epithets of *Pluvius*, *Fulgurator*, *Tonitrualis*, *Tonans*, and *Fulminator*. As the pebble or flint stone was regarded as the symbol of lightning, Jupiter was frequently represented with such a stone in his hand instead of a thunderbolt. In concluding a treaty, the Romans took the sacred symbols of Jupiter, viz. the sceptre and flint stone, together with some grass from his temple, and the oath taken on such an occasion was expressed by *per Jovem Lapidem jurare*. In consequence of his possessing such powers over the elements, and especially of his always having the thunderbolt at his command, he was regarded as the highest and most powerful among the gods. Hence he is called the Best and Most High (*Optimus Maximus*). His temple at Rome stood on the lofty hill of the Capitol, whence he derived the surnames of Capitolinus and Tarpeius. He was regarded as the special protector of Rome. As such he was worshipped by the consuls on entering upon their office ; and the triumph of a victorious general was a solemn procession to his temple. He therefore bore the surnames of *Imperator*, *Victor*, *Invictus*, *Stator*, *Opitulus*, *Feretrius*, *Praedator*, *Triumphator*, and the like. Under all these surnames he had temples or statues at Rome ; and 2 temples, viz. those of Jupiter Stator and of Jupiter Feretrius, were believed to have been built in the time of Romulus. Under the name of *Jupiter Capitolinus*, he presided over the great Roman games ; and under the name of *Jupiter Latialis* or *Latiaris*, over the Feriae Latinae. Jupiter, according to the belief of the Romans, determined the course of all human affairs. He foresaw the future, and the events happening in it were the results of his will. He revealed the future to man through signs in the heavens and the flight of birds, which are hence called the messengers of Jupiter, while the god himself is designated as *Prodigialis*, that is, the sender of prodigies. For the same reason the god was invoked at the beginning of every undertaking, whether sacred or profane, together with Janus, who blessed the beginning itself. Jupiter was further regarded as the guardian of law, and as the protector of justice and virtue. He maintained the sanctity of an oath, and presided over all transactions which were based upon faithfulness and justice. Hence Fides was his companion on the Capitol, along with Victoria ; and hence a traitor to his country, and persons guilty of perjury, were thrown down from the Tarpeian rock. — As Jupiter was the lord of heaven, and consequently the prince of light, the white colour was sacred to him, white animals were sacrificed to him, his chariot was believed to be drawn by 4 white horses, his priests wore white caps, and the consuls were attired in white when they offered sacrifices in the Capitol the day they entered on their office. The worship of Jupiter at Rome was under the special care of the *Flamen Dialis*, who was the highest in rank of all the flamens. (*Dict. of Ant.* art. *Flamen.*) The Romans, in their representations of the god, adopted the type of the Greek Zeus.

Jura or **Jurassus Mons** (*Jura*), a range of mountains, which run N. of the lake Lemanus as far as Augusta Rauracorum (*August* near *Basle*), on the Rhine, forming the boundary between the Sequani and Helvetii.

Justiniāna. 1. **Prima**, a town in Illyria, near Tauresium, was the birthplace of Justinian, and was built by that emperor ; it became the residence of the archbishop of Illyria, and, in the middle ages, of the Servian kings. — 2. **Secunda**, also a town in Illyria, previously called Ulpiana, was enlarged and embellished by Justinian.

Justiniānus, surnamed the Great, emperor of Constantinople, A.D. 527—565. He was born near Tauresium in Illyria, A.D. 483 ; was adopted by his uncle, the emperor Justinus, in 520 ; succeeded his uncle in 527 ; married the beautiful but licentious actress, Theodora, who exercised great influence over him ; and died in 565, leaving the crown to his nephew, Justin II. He was, during the greater part of his reign, a firm supporter of orthodoxy, and thus has received from ecclesiastical writers the title of Great ; but towards the end of his life, he became a heretic, being one of the adherents of Nestorianism. His foreign wars were glorious, but all his victories were won by his generals. The empire of the Vandals in Africa was overthrown by Belisarius, and their king Gelimer led a prisoner to Constantinople ; and the kingdom of the Ostrogoths in Italy was likewise destroyed, by the successive victories of Belisarius and Narses. [BELISARIUS ; NARSES.] Justinian adorned Constantinople with many public buildings of great magnificence ; but the cost of their erection, as well as the expenses of his foreign wars, obliged him to impose many new taxes, which were constantly increased by the natural covetousness and rapacity of the emperor.—The great work of Justinian is his legislation. He resolved to establish a perfect system of written legislation for all his dominions ; and, for this end, to make 2 great collections, one of the imperial constitutions, the other of all that was valuable in the works of jurists. His first work was the collection of the imperial constitutions. This he commenced in 528, in the 2nd year of his reign. The task was entrusted to a commission of 10, who completed their labours in the following year (529) ; and their collection was declared to be law under the title of *Justinianeus Codex*. — In 530 Tribonian, who had been one of the commission of 10 employed in drawing up the Code, was authorised by the emperor to select fellow-labourers to assist him in the other division of the undertaking. Tribonian selected 16 coadjutors ; and this commission proceeded at once to lay under contribution the works of those jurists who had received from former emperors "auctoritatem conscribendarum interpretandique legum." They were ordered to divide their materials into 50 Books, and to subdivide each Book into Titles (*Tituli*). Nothing that was valuable was to be excluded, nothing that was obsolete was to be admitted, and neither repetition nor inconsistency was to be allowed. This work was to bear the name *Digesta* or *Pandectae*. The work was completed, in accordance with the instructions that had been given, in the short space of 3 years ; and on the 30th of Dec. 533, it received from the imperial sanction the authority of law. It comprehends upwards of 9000 extracts, in the selection of which the compilers made use of nearly 2000 different books, containing more than 3,000,000 lines.—The Code and the Digest contained a complete body of law ; but as they were not adapted to elementary instruction, a commission was appointed, consisting of Tribonian, Theophilus, and Dorotheus, to compose an institutional work, which should contain the elements of the law (*legum incunabula*), and should not be encumbered with useless matter. Accordingly they produced a treatise under the title of *Institutiones*, which was based on elementary works of a similar character, but chiefly on the Institutiones of Gaius. [GAIUS.] The Institutiones consisted of 4 books, and were published with the imperial sanction, at the same time as the Digest. —After the publication of the Digest and the Institutiones, 50 decisiones and some new constitutiones also were promulgated by the emperor. This rendered a revision of the Code necessary ; and accordingly a new Code was promulgated at Constantinople, on the 16th of November, 534, and the use of the decisiones, of the new constitutiones, and of the first edition of the Code, was forbidden. The 2nd edition (*Codex Repetitae Praelectionis*) is the Code that we now possess, in 12 books, each of which is divided into titles. — Justinian subsequently published various new constitutiones, to which he gave the name of *Novellae Constitutiones*. These Constitutiones form a kind of supplement to the Code, and were published at various times from 535 to 565, but most of them appeared between 535 and 539. It does not seem, however, that any official compilation of these *Novellae* appeared in the lifetime of Justinian. — The 4 legislative works of Justinian, the *Institutiones*, *Digesta* or *Pandectae, Codex*, and *Novellae*, are included under the general name of *Corpus Juris Civilis*, and form the Roman law, as received in Europe. — The best editions of the Corpus for general use are by Gothofredus and Van Leeuwen, Amst. 1663, 2 vols. fol. ; by Gebauer and Spangenberg, Gotting. 1776—1797, 2 vols. 4to. ; and by Beck, Lips. 1836, 2 vols. 4to.

Justīnus. 1. The historian, of uncertain date,

but who did not live later than the 4th or 5th century of our aera, is the author of an extant work entitled *Historiarum Philippicarum Libri XLIV.* This work is taken from the *Historiae Philippicae* of Trogus Pompeius, who lived in the time of Augustus. The title *Philippicae* was given to it, because its main object was to give the history of the Macedonian monarchy, with all its branches; but in the execution of this design, Trogus permitted himself to indulge in so many excursions, that the work formed a kind of universal history from the rise of the Assyrian monarchy to the conquest of the East by Rome. The original work of Trogus, which was one of great value, is lost. The work of Justin is not so much an abridgment of that of Trogus, as a selection of such parts as seemed to him most worthy of being generally known. Edited by Graevius, Lug. Bat. 1683; by Gronovius, Lug. Bat. 1719 and 1760; and by Frotscher, Lips. 1827, 3 vols. — **2.** Surnamed the **Martyr,** one of the earliest of the Christian writers, was born about A. D. 103, at Flavia Neapolis, the Shechem of the Old Testament, a city in Samaria. He was brought up as a heathen, and in his youth studied the Greek philosophy with zeal and ardour. He was afterwards converted to Christianity. He retained as a Christian the garb of a philosopher, but devoted himself to the propagation, by writing and otherwise, of the faith which he had embraced. He was put to death at Rome in the persecution under M. Antoninus, about 165. Justin wrote a large number of works in Greek, several of which have come down to us. Of these the most important are: — 1. *An Apology for the Christians,* addressed to Antoninus Pius, about 139; 2. *A Second Apology for the Christians,* addressed to the emperors M. Aurelius and L. Verus; 3. *A Dialogue with Tryphon the Jew,* in which Justin defends Christianity against the objections of Tryphon. The best edition of the collected works of Justin is by Otto, Jena, 1842—1844, 2 vols. 8vo.

Justus, a Jewish historian of Tiberias in Galilaea, was a contemporary of the historian Josephus, who was very hostile to him.

Jūturna, the nymph of a fountain in Latium, famous for its healing qualities. Its water was used in nearly all sacrifices; a chapel was dedicated to its nymph at Rome in the Campus Martius by Lutatius Catulus; and sacrifices were offered to her on the 11th of January. A pond in the forum, between the temples of Castor and Vesta, was called Lacus Juturnae, whence we must infer that the name of the nymph Juturna is not connected with *jugis,* but probably with *juvare.* She is said to have been beloved by Jupiter, who rewarded her with immortality and the rule over the waters. Some writers call her the wife of Janus and mother of Fontus, but in the Aeneid she appears as the affectionate sister of Turnus.

Juvāvum or **Juvāvia** (*Salzburg*), a town in Noricum, on the river Jovavus or Isonta (*Salza*), was a Roman colony founded by Hadrian, and the residence of the Roman governor of the province. It was destroyed by the Heruli in the 5th century, but was afterwards rebuilt.

Jŭvēnālis, Dēcimus Jūnius, the great Roman satirist, but of whose life we have few authentic particulars. His ancient biographers relate that he was either the son or the "alumnus" of a rich freedman; that he occupied himself, until he had nearly reached the term of middle life, in declaiming; that, having subsequently composed some clever lines upon Paris the pantomime, he was induced to cultivate assiduously satirical composition; and that in consequence of his attacks upon Paris becoming known to the court, the poet, although now an old man of 80, was appointed to the command of a body of troops, in a remote district of Egypt, where he died shortly afterwards. It is supposed by some that the Paris, who was attacked by Juvenal, was the contemporary of Domitian, and that the poet was accordingly banished by this emperor. But this opinion is clearly untenable. 1. We know that Paris was killed in A. D. 83, upon suspicion of an intrigue with the empress Domitia. 2. The 4th satire, as appears from the concluding lines, was written after the death of Domitian, that is, not earlier than 96. 3. The 1st satire, as we learn from the 49th line, was written after the condemnation of Marius Priscus, that is, not earlier than 100. These positions admit of no doubt; and hence it is established that Juvenal was alive at least 17 years after the death of Paris, and that some of his satires were composed after the death of Domitian. — The only facts with regard to Juvenal upon which we can implicitly rely are, that he flourished towards the close of the first century, that Aquinum, if not the place of his nativity, was at least his chosen residence (*Sat.* iii. 319), and that he is in all probability the friend whom Martial addresses in 3 epigrams. There is, perhaps, another circumstance which we may admit. We are told that he declaimed for many years of his life; and every page in his writings bears evidence to the accuracy of this assertion. Each piece is a finished rhetorical essay, energetic, glowing, and sonorous. He denounces vice in the most indignant terms; but the obvious tone of exaggeration which pervades all his invectives leaves us in doubt how far this sustained passion is real, and how far assumed for show. The extant works of Juvenal consist of 16 satires, the last being a fragment of very doubtful authenticity, all composed in heroic hexameters. Edited by Ruperti, Lips. 1819; and by Heinrich, Bonn, 1839.

Juventas. [HEBE.]

Juventius. 1. Celsus. [CELSUS.] — **2.** Laterensis. [LATERENSIS.] — **3.** Thalna. [THALNA.]

L.

Labda (Λάβδα), daughter of the Bacchiad Amphion, and mother of Cypselus, by Eëtion [CYPSELUS.]

Labdacīdae. [LABDACUS.]

Labdăcus (Λάβδακος), son of the Theban king, Polydorus, by Nycteïs, daughter of Nycteus. Labdacus lost his father at an early age, and was placed under the guardianship of Nycteus, and afterwards under that of Lycus, a brother of Nycteus. When Labdacus had grown up to manhood, Lycus surrendered the government to him; and on the death of Labdacus, which occurred soon after, Lycus undertook the guardianship of his son Laius, the father of Oedipus. — The name *Labdacïdae* is frequently given to the descendants of Labdacus, — Oedipus, Polynices, Eteocles and Antigone.

Labdălum. [SYRACUSAE.]

Labeātes, a warlike people in Dalmatia, whose chief town was Scodra, and in whose territory was the **Labeatis Palus** (*Lake of Scutari*), through which the river Barbana (*Bogana*) runs.

Lăbĕo, Antistĭus. 1. A Roman jurist, was one of the murderers of Julius Caesar, and put an end to his life after the battle of Philippi, B. C. 42. — 2. Son of the preceding, and a still more eminent jurist. He adopted the republican opinions of his father, and was in consequence disliked by Augustus. It is probable that the *Labeone insanior* of Horace (*Sat.* i. 3. 80) was a stroke levelled against the jurist, in order to please the emperor. Labeo wrote a large number of works, which are cited in the Digest. He was the founder of one of the 2 great legal schools, spoken of under CAPITO.

Lăbĕo, Q. Fabĭus, quaestor urbanus B. C. 196; praetor 189, when he commanded the fleet in the war against Antiochus ; and consul 183.

Lăbĕrĭus, Decĭmus, a Roman eques, and a distinguished writer of mimes, was born about B. C. 107, and died in 43 at Puteoli, in Campania. At Caesar's triumphal games in October, 45, P. Syrus, a professional mimus, seems to have challenged all his craft to a trial of wit in extemporaneous farce, and Caesar offered Laberius 500,000 sesterces to appear on the stage. Laberius was 60 years old, and the profession of a mimus was infamous, but the wish of the dictator was equivalent to a command, and he reluctantly complied. He had however revenge in his power, and took it. His prologue awakened compassion, and perhaps indignation : and during the performance he adroitly availed himself of his various characters to point his wit at Caesar. In the person of a beaten Syrian slave he cried out, — "Marry ! Quirites, but we lose our freedom," and all eyes were turned upon the dictator ; and in another mime he uttered the pregnant maxim " Needs must he fear, who makes all else adread." Caesar, impartially or vindictively, awarded the prize to Syrus. The prologue of Laberius has been preserved by Macrobius (*Sat.* ii. 7) ; and if this may be taken as a specimen of his style, he would rank above Terence, and second only to Plautus, in dramatic vigour. Laberius evidently made great impression on his contemporaries, although he is depreciated by Horace (*Sat.* i. 10. 6).

Labicum, Labici, Lavicum, Lavici (Labicānus : *Colonna*), an ancient town in Latium on one of the hills of the Alban mountain, 15 miles S.E. of Rome, W. of Praeneste, and N.E. of Tusculum. It was an ally of the Aequi ; it was taken and was colonised by the Romans, B. C. 418.

Labĭēnus. 1. T., tribune of the plebs B. C. 63, the year of Cicero's consulship. Under pretence of avenging his uncle's death, who had joined Saturninus (100), and had perished along with the other conspirators, he accused Rabirius of perduellio or high treason. Rabirius was defended by Cicero. [RABIRIUS] In his tribuneship Labienus was entirely devoted to Caesar's interests. Accordingly when Caesar went into Transalpine Gaul in 58, he took Labienus with him as his legatus. Labienus continued with Caesar during the greater part of his campaigns in Gaul, and was the ablest officer he had. On the breaking out of the civil war in 49, he deserted Caesar and joined Pompey. His defection caused the greatest joy among the Pompeian party ; but he disappointed the expectations of his new friends, and never performed any thing of importance. He fought against his old commander at the battle of Pharsalia in Greece, 48, at the battle of Thapsus in Africa, 46, and at the battle of Munda in Spain, 45. He was slain in the last of these battles. — 2. Q., son of the preceding, joined the party of Brutus and Cassius after the murder of Caesar, and was sent by them into Parthia to seek aid from Orodes, the Parthian king. Before he could obtain any definite answer from Orodes, the news came of the battle of Philippi, 42. Two years afterwards he persuaded Orodes to entrust him with the command of a Parthian army; and Pacorus, the son of Orodes, was associated with him in the command. In 40 they crossed the Euphrates and met with great success. They defeated Decidius Saxa, the lieutenant of Antony, obtained possession of the two great towns of Antioch and Apamea, and penetrated into Asia Minor. But in the following year, 39, P. Ventidius, the most able of Antony's legates, defeated the Parthians. Labienus fled in disguise into Cilicia, where he was apprehended, and put to death. — 3. T., a celebrated orator and historian in the reign of Augustus, either son or grandson of No. 1. He retained all the republican feelings of his family, and never became reconciled to the imperial government, but took every opportunity to attack Augustus and his friends. His enemies obtained a decree of the senate that all his writings should be burnt; whereupon he shut himself up in the tomb of his ancestors, and thus perished, about A. D. 12.

Labranda (τὰ Λάβρανδα : Λαβρανδεύς, Λαβρανδηνός, Labrandēnus), a town in Caria, 68 stadia N. of Mylasa, celebrated for its temple of Zeus Stratios or Labrandenus, on a hill near the city. Mr. Fellowes considers some ruins at *Jakli* to be those of the temple ; but this is doubtful.

Labro, a sea-port in Etruria, mentioned by Cicero along with Pisae, and supposed by some to be the Liburnum, mentioned by Zosimus, and the modern *Livorno* or *Leghorn.* Others however maintain that the ancient Portus Pisanus corresponds to Leghorn.

Labus or **Labūtas** (Λάβος or Λαβούτας : *Sobad Koh,* part of the *Elburz*), a mountain of Parthia, between the Coronus and the Sariphi Montes.

Labynētus (Λαβύνητος), a name common to several of the Babylonian monarchs, seems to have been a title rather than a proper name. The Labynetus, mentioned by Herodotus (i. 74) as mediating a peace between Cyaxares and Alyattes, is the same with Nebuchadnezzar. The Labynetus who is mentioned by Herodotus (i. 77) as a contemporary of Cyrus and Croesus, is the same with the Belshazzar of the prophet Daniel. By other writers he is called Nabonadius or Nabonidus. He was the last king of Babylon. [CYRUS.]

Labyrinthus. [See *Dict. of Antiq. s. v.*]

Lacedaemon (Λακεδαίμων), son of Zeus and Taygete, was married to Sparta, the daughter of Eurotas, by whom he became the father of Amyclas, Eurydice, and Asine. He was king of the country which he called after his own name, Lacedaemon, while he called the capital Sparta after the name of his wife. [SPARTA.]

Lacedaemŏnĭus (Λακεδαιμόνιος), son of Cimon, so named in honour of the Lacedaemonians.

Lacēdas (Λακήδας), or **Leocēdes** (Herod. vi. 127) king of Argos, and father of Melas.

Lacetāni, a people in Hispania Tarraconensis at the foot of the Pyrenees.

Lachāres (Λαχάρης). 1. An Athenian demagogue, made himself tyrant of Athens, B. C. 296, when the city was besieged by Demetrius. When Athens was on the point of falling into the hands of Demetrius, Lachares made his escape to Thebes. — 2. An eminent Athenian rhetorician, who flourished in the 5th century of our era.

Lāchēs (Λάχης), an Athenian commander in the Peloponnesian war, is first mentioned in B. C. 427. He fell at the battle of Mantinea, 418. In the dialogue of Plato which bears his name, he is represented as not over-acute in argument, and with temper on a par with his acuteness.

Lāchēsis, one of the Fates. [MOERAE.]

Lacia or **Laciadae** (Λακία, Λακιάδαι : Λακιάδης, Λακιεύς), a demus in Attica, belonging to the tribe Oeneis, W. of, and near to Athens.

Lacinium (Λακίνιον ἄκρον), a promontory on the E. coast of Bruttium, a few miles S. of Croton, and forming the W. boundary of the Tarentine gulf. It possessed a celebrated temple of Juno, who was worshipped here under the surname of Lacinia. The remains of this temple are still extant, and have given the modern name to the promontory, *Capo delle Colonne* or *Capo di Nao* (ναός). Hannibal dedicated in this temple a bilingual inscription (in Punic and Greek), which recorded the history of his campaigns, and of which Polybius made use in writing his history.

Lacippo (*Alecippe*), a town in Hispania Baetica not far from the sea, and W. of Malaca.

Lacmon or **Lacmus** (Λάκμων, Λάκμος), the N. part of Mt. Pindus, in which the river Aous takes its origin.

Lacobrīga. 1. (*Lobera*), a town of the Vaccaei in the N. of Hispania Tarraconensis on the road from Asturica to Tarraco. — 2. (*Lagoa*), a town on the S.W. of Lusitania, E. of the Prom. Sacrum.

Lacōnica (Λακωνική), sometimes called **Lacōnia** by the Romans, a country of Peloponnesus, was bounded on the N. by Argolis and Arcadia, on the W. by Messenia, and on the E. and S. by the sea. Laconica was a long valley, running southwards to the sea, and was inclosed on 3 sides by mountains. On the N. it was separated by Mt. Parnon from Argolis, and by Mt. Sciritis from Arcadia. It was bounded by Mt. Taygetus on the W. and by Mt. Parnon on the E., which are 2 masses of mountains extending from Arcadia to the S. extremities of the Peloponnesus, Mt. Taygetus terminating at the Prom. Taenarum, and Mt. Parnon, continued under the names of Thornax and Zarex, terminating at the Prom. Malea. The river Eurotas flows through the valley lying between these mountain masses, and falls into the Laconian gulf. In the upper part of its course the valley is narrow, and near Sparta the mountains approach so close to each other as to leave little more than room for the channel of the river. It is for this reason that we find the vale of Sparta called the *hollow Lacedaemon*. Below Sparta the mountains recede, and the valley opens out into a plain of considerable extent. The soil of this plain is poor, but on the slopes of the mountains there is land of considerable fertility. There were valuable marble quarries near Taenarus. Off the coast shell-fish were caught, which produced a purple dye inferior only to the Tyrian. Laconica is well described by Euripides as difficult of access to an enemy. On the N. the country could only be invaded by the valleys of the Eurotas and the Oenus ; the range of Taygetus formed an almost insuperable barrier on the W.; and the want of good harbours on the E. coast protected it from invasion by sea on that side. Sparta was the only town of importance in the country [SPARTA].—The most ancient inhabitants of the country are said to have been Cynurians and Leleges. They were expelled or conquered by the Achaeans, who were the inhabitants of the country in the heroic age. The Dorians afterwards invaded Peloponnesus and became the ruling race in Laconica. Some of the old Achaean inhabitants were reduced to slavery ; but a great number of them became subjects of the Dorians under the name of *Perioeci* (Περίοικοι). The general name for the inhabitants is **Lacōnes** (Λάκωνες) or **Lacedaemonii** (Λακεδαιμόνιοι) ; but the *Perioeci* are frequently called Lacedaemonii, to distinguish them from the Spartans.

Lacōnicus Sinus (κόλπος Λακωνικὸς), a gulf in the S. of Peloponnesus, into which the Eurotas falls, beginning W. at the Prom. Taenarum and E. at the Prom. Malea.

Lactantius, a celebrated Christian Father, but his exact name, the place of his nativity, and the date of his birth, are uncertain. In modern works we find him denominated *Lucius Coelius Firmianus Lactantius ;* but the 2 former appellations, in the 2nd of which *Caecilius* is often substituted for *Coelius*, are omitted in many MSS., while the 2 latter are frequently presented in an inverted order. Since he is spoken of as far advanced in life about A. D. 315, he must have been born not later than the middle of the 3rd century, probably in Italy, possibly at Firmum, on the Adriatic, and certainly studied in Africa, where he became the pupil of Arnobius, who taught rhetoric at Sicca. His fame became so widely extended, that about 301 he was invited by Diocletian to settle at Nicomedia, and there to practise his art. At this period he appears to have become a Christian. He was summoned to Gaul, about 312—318, when now an old man, to superintend the education of Crispus, son of Constantine, and he probably died at Treves some 10 or 12 years afterwards (325—330.) — The extant works of Lactantius are : — 1. *Divinarum Institutionum Libri VII.*, a sort of introduction to Christianity, intended to supersede the less perfect treatises of Minucius Felix, Tertullian, and Cyprian. Each of the 7 books bears a separate title : (1.) *De Falsa Religione.* (2.) *De Origine Erroris.* (3.) *De Falsa Sapientia.* (4.) *De Vera Sapientia et Religione.* (5.) *De Justitia.* (6.) *De Vero Cultu.* (7.) *De Vita Beata.* — 2. An *Epitome* of the Institutions. — 3. *De Ira Dei.* — 4. *De Opificio Dei* s. *De Formatione Hominis.* — 5. *De Mortibus Persecutorum.* — 6. Various *Poems*, most of which were probably not written by Lactantius. — The style of Lactantius, formed upon the model of the great orator of Rome, has gained for him the appellation of the *Christian Cicero*, and not undeservedly. The best edition of Lactantius is by Le Brun and Lenglet du Fresnoy, Paris, 1748.

Lactarius Mons or **Lactis Mons**, a mountain in Campania, belonging to the Apennines, 4 miles E. of Stabiae, so called because the cows which grazed upon it produced excellent milk. Here Narses gained a victory over the Goths, A. D. 553.

Lacȳdes (Λακύδης), a native of Cyrene, succeeded Arcesilaus as president of the Academy at

Athens. The place where his instructions were delivered was a garden, named the Lacydeum (Λακύδειον), provided for the purpose by his friend Attalus Philometor, king of Pergamus. This alteration in the locality of the school seems at least to have contributed to the rise of the name of the *New Academy.* He died about 215, from the effects, it is said, of excessive drinking.

Ladé (Λάδη), an island off the W. coast of Caria, opposite to Miletus and to the bay into which the Maeander falls.

Ladon (Λάδων), the dragon who guarded the apples of the Hesperides, was the offspring of Typhon and Echidna, or of Ge, or of Phorcys and Ceto. He was slain by Hercules, and the representation of the battle was placed by Zeus among the stars.

Ladon (Λάδων). 1. A river in Arcadia, which rose near Clitor, and fell into the Alphéus between Heraea and Phrixa. In mythology Ladon is the husband of Stymphalis, and the father of Daphne and Metope. — 2. A small river in Elis, which rose on the frontiers of Achaia and fell into the Penéus.

Laeëtāni, a people on the E. coast of Hispania Tarraconensis, near the mouth of the river Rubricatus (Llobregat), probably the same as the Laletani, whose country, Laletānĭa produced good wine, and whose chief town was BARCINO.

Laelaps (Λαῖλαψ), i. e. the storm wind, personified in the legend of the dog of Procris which bore this name. Procris had received this swift animal from Artemis, and gave it to her husband Cephalus. When the Teumessian fox was sent to punish the Thebans, Cephalus sent the dog Laelaps against the fox. The dog overtook the fox, but Zeus changed both animals into a stone, which was shown in the neighbourhood of Thebes.

Laeliānus, one of the 30 tyrants, emperor in Gaul after the death of POSTUMUS, A. D. 267, was slain, after a few months, by his own soldiers, who proclaimed VICTORINUS in his stead.

Laelius. 1. C., was from early manhood the friend and companion of Scipio Africanus the elder, and fought under him in almost all his campaigns. He was consul B. C. 190, and obtained the province of Cisalpine Gaul. — 2. C., surnamed Sapiens, son of the preceding. His intimacy with Scipio Africanus the younger was as remarkable as his father's friendship with the elder, and it obtained an imperishable monument in Cicero's treatise *Laelius sive de Amicitia.* He was born about 186, was tribune of the plebs 151 ; praetor 145 ; and consul 140. Though not devoid of military talents, as his campaign against the Lusitanian Viriathus proved, he was more of a statesman than a soldier, and more of a philosopher than a statesman. From Diogenes of Babylon, and afterwards from Panaetius, he imbibed the doctrines of the stoic school ; his father's friend Polybius was his friend also ; the wit and idiom of Terence were pointed and polished by his and Scipio's conversation ; and the satirist Lucilius was his familiar companion. The political opinions of Laelius were different at different periods of his life. He endeavoured, probably during his tribunate, to procure a re-division of the public land, but he desisted from the attempt, and for his forbearance received the appellation of the *Wise* or the *Prudent.* He afterwards became a strenuous supporter of the aristocratical party. Several of his orations were extant in the

time of Cicero, but were characterised more by smoothness (*lenitas*) than by power. — Laelius is the principal interlocutor in Cicero's dialogue *De Amicitia*, and is one of the speakers in the *De Senectute*, and in the *De Republica.* His two daughters were married, the one to Q. Mucius Scaevola, the augur, the other to C. Fannius Strabo. The opinion of his worth seems to have been universal, and it is one of Seneca's injunctions to his friend Lucilius " to live like Laelius."

Laenas, Popillius, plebeians. The family was unfavourably distinguished, even among the Romans, for their sternness, cruelty, and haughtiness of character. 1. M., 4 times consul B. C. 359, 356, 350, 348. In his 3rd consulship (350) he won a hard-fought battle against the Gauls, for which he celebrated a triumph—the first ever obtained by a plebeian. — 2. M., praetor 176, consul 172, and censor 159. In his consulship he defeated the Ligurian mountaineers ; and when the remainder of the tribe surrendered to him, he sold them all as slaves. — 3. C., brother of No. 2, was consul 172. He was afterwards sent as ambassador to Antiochus, king of Syria, whom the senate wished to abstain from hostilities against Egypt. Antiochus was just marching upon Alexandria, when Popilius gave him the letter of the senate, which the king read and promised to take into consideration with his friends. Popilius straightway described with his cane a circle in the sand round the king, and ordered him not to stir out of it before he had given a decisive answer. This boldness so frightened Antiochus, that he at once yielded to the demand of Rome. — 4. P., consul 132, the year after the murder of Tib. Gracchus. He was charged by the victorious aristocratical party with the prosecution of the accomplices of Gracchus ; and in this odious task he showed all the hardheartedness of his family. He subsequently withdrew himself, by voluntary exile, from the vengeance of C. Gracchus, and did not return to Rome till after his death.

Laertes (Λαέρτης), king of Ithaca, was son of Acrisius and Chalcomedusa, and husband of Anticléa, by whom he became the father of Ulysses and Ctimene. Some writers call Ulysses the son of Sisyphus. [ANTICLEA.] Laertes took part in the Calydonian hunt, and in the expedition of the Argonauts. He was still alive when Ulysses returned to Ithaca after the fall of Troy.

Laertius, Diogenes. [DIOGENES.]

Laestrygŏnes (Λαιστρυγόνες), a savage race of cannibals, whom Ulysses encountered in his wanderings. They were governed by ANTIPHATES and LAMUS. They belong however to mythology rather than to history. The modern interpreters of Homer place them on the N. W. coast of Sicily. The Greeks themselves placed them on the E. coast of the island in the plains of Leontini, which are therefore called *Laestrygonii Campi.* The Romans however, and more especially the Roman poets, who regarded the prom. Circeium as the Homeric island of Circe, transplanted the Laestrygones to the S. coast of Latium in the neighbourhood of Formiae, which they supposed to have been built by Lamus, the king of this people. Hence Horace (*Carm.* iii. 16. 34) speaks of *Laestrygonia Bacchus in amphora*, that is, Formian wine ; and Ovid (*Met.* xiv. 233) calls Formiae, *Laestrygonis Lami Urbs.*

Laevi or Levi, a Ligurian people in Gallia Transpadana on the river Ticinus, who, in conjunction with the Marici, built the town of Ticinum (*Pavia*).

Laevinus, Valerius. 1. P., consul B.C. 280, had the conduct of the war against Pyrrhus. The king wrote to Laevinus, offering to arbitrate between Rome and Tarentum ; but Laevinus bluntly bade him mind his own business, and begone to Epirus. An Epirot spy having been taken in the Roman lines, Laevinus showed him the legions under arms, and bade him tell his master, if he was curious about the Roman men and tactics, to come and see them himself. In the battle which followed, Laevinus was defeated by Pyrrhus on the banks of the Siris. — 2. M., praetor 215, crossed over to Greece and carried on war against Philip. He continued in the command in Greece till 211, when he was elected consul in his absence. In his consulship (210) he carried on the war in Sicily, and took Agrigentum. He continued as proconsul in Sicily for several years, and in 208 made a descent upon the coast of Africa. He died 200, and his sons Publius and Marcus honoured his memory with funeral games and gladiatorial combats, exhibited during 4 successive days in the forum. — 3. C., son of No. 2, was by the mother's side brother of M. Fulvius Nobilior, consul 189. Laevinus was himself consul in 176, and carried on war against the Ligurians.

Lagos, a city in great Phrygia.

Lagus (Λάγος), a Macedonian of obscure birth, was the father, or reputed father, of Ptolemy, the founder of the Egyptian monarchy. He married Arsinoë, a concubine of Philip of Macedon, who was said to have been pregnant at the time of their marriage, on which account the Macedonians generally looked upon Ptolemy as the son of Philip.

Lais (Λαΐς), the name of 2 celebrated Grecian Hetaerae, or courtesans. — 1. The elder, a native probably of Corinth, lived in the time of the Peloponnesian war, and was celebrated as the most beautiful woman of her age. She was notorious also for her avarice and caprice. — 2. The younger, was the daughter of Timandra, and was probably born at Hyccara in Sicily. According to some accounts she was brought to Corinth when 7 years old, having been taken prisoner in the Athenian expedition to Sicily, and bought by a Corinthian. This story, however, involves numerous difficulties, and seems to have arisen from a confusion between this Lais and the elder one of the same name. She was a contemporary and rival of Phryne. She became enamoured of a Thessalian named Hippolochus, or Hippostratus, and accompanied him to Thessaly. Here, it is said, some Thessalian women, jealous of her beauty, enticed her into a temple of Aphrodite, and there stoned her to death.

Laius (Λάϊος), son of Labdacus, lost his father at an early age, and was brought up by Lycus. [LABDACUS.] When Lycus was slain by Amphion and Zethus, Laius took refuge with Pelops in Peloponnesus. After the death of Amphion and Zethus, Laius returned to Thebes, and ascended the throne of his father. He married Jocasta, and became by her the father of Oedipus, by whom he was slain. For details see OEDIPUS.

Lalage, a common name of courtesans, from the Greek λαλαγή, prattling, used as a term of endearment. " little prattler."

Laletani. [LAEETANI.]

Lamachus (Λάμαχος), an Athenian, son of

Xenophanes, was the colleague of Alcibiades and Nicias, in the great Sicilian expedition, B.C. 415. He fell under the walls of Syracuse, in a sally of the besieged. He appears amongst the dramatis personae of Aristophanes, as the brave and somewhat blustering soldier, delighting in the war, and thankful, moreover, for its pay. Plutarch describes him as brave, but so poor, that on every fresh appointment he used to beg for money from the government to buy clothing and shoes.

Lametus (*Lamato*), a river in Bruttium, near Croton, which falls into the **Lameticus Sinus.** Upon it was the town **Lametini** (*St. Eufemia*).

Lamia (Λαμία). 1. A female phantom. [EMPUSA.] — 2. A celebrated Athenian courtezan ; was a favourite mistress for many years of Demetrius Poliorcetes.

Lamia, Aelius. This family claimed a high antiquity, and pretended to be descended from the mythical hero, LAMUS. — 1. L., a Roman eques, supported Cicero in the suppression of the Catilinarian conspiracy, B.C. 63, and was accordingly banished by the influence of the consuls Gabinius and Piso in 58. He was subsequently recalled from exile, and during the civil wars espoused Caesar's party. — 2. L., son of the preceding, and the friend of Horace, was consul A.D. 3. He was made praefectus urbi in 32, but he died in the following year. — 3. L., was married to Domitia Longina, the daughter of Corbulo: but during the lifetime of Vespasian he was deprived of her by Domitian, who first lived with her as his mistress, and subsequently married her. Lamia was put to death by Domitian after his accession to the throne.

Lamia (Λαμία : Λαμιεύς, Λαμιώτης : Zeitun or Zeituni), a town in Phthiotis in Thessaly, situated on the small river Achelous, and 50 stadia inland from the Maliac gulf, on which it possessed a harbour, called Phalara. It has given its name to the war which was carried on by the confederate Greeks against Antipater after the death of Alexander, B.C. 323. The confederates under the command of Leosthenes, the Athenian, defeated Antipater, who took refuge in Lamia, where he was besieged for some months. Leosthenes was killed during the siege ; and the confederates were obliged to raise it in the following year (322), in consequence of the approach of Leonnatus. The confederates under the command of Antiphilus defeated Leonnatus, who was slain in the action. Soon afterwards Antipater was joined by Craterus; and thus strengthened he gained a decisive victory over the confederates at the battle of Cranon, which put an end to the Lamian war.

Laminium (Laminitanus), a town of the Carpetani in Hispania Tarraconensis, 95 miles S.E. of Toletum.

Lampa or **Lappa** (Λάμπη, Λάππη : Λαμπαῖος, Λαμπεύς), a town in the N. of Crete, a little inland, S. of Hydramum, said to have been built by Agamemnon, but to have been called after Lampus.

Lampea (ἡ Λάμπεια) or **Lampeus Mons,** a part of the mountain range of Erymanthus, on the frontiers of Achaia and Elis.

Lampetia (Λαμπετίη), daughter of Helios by the nymph Neaera. She and her sister Phaetusa tended the flocks of their father in Sicily. In some legends she appears as one of the sisters of Phaethon.

Lampon (Λάμπων), an Athenian, a celebrated

soothsayer and interpreter of oracles. In conjunction with Xenocritus, he led the colony which founded Thurii in Italy, B.C. 443.

Lamponia, or -**ium** (Λαμπώνεια, -όνιον), an important city of Mysia, in the interior of the Troad, near the borders of Aeolia.

Lampra, Lamprae, or **Lamptrae** (Λαμπρά, Λαμπραί, Λαμπτραί: Λαμπρεύς: Lamorica), a demus on the W. coast of Attica, near the promontory Astypalaea, belonging to the tribe Erechtheis. It was divided into an upper and a lower city.

Lampridius, Aelius, one of the *Scriptores Historiae Augustae*, lived in the reigns of Diocletian and Constantine, and wrote the lives of the emperors :—1. Commodus ; 2. Antoninus Diadumenus ; 3. Elagabalus, and 4. Alexander Severus. It is not improbable that Lampridius is the same as Spartianus, and that the name of the author in full was Aelius Lampridius Spartianus. For the editions of Lampridius, see CAPITOLINUS.

Lampsacus (Λάμψακος: Λαμψακηνός: Lapsaki, Ru.), an important city of Mysia, in Asia Minor, on the coast of the Hellespont ; possessed a good harbour. It was celebrated for its wine ; and hence it was one of the cities assigned by Xerxes to Themistocles for his maintenance. It was the chief seat of the worship of Priapus ; and the birthplace of the historian Charon, the philosophers Adimantus and Metrodorus, and the rhetorician Anaximenes. Lampsacus was a colony of the Phocaeans : the name of the surrounding district, Berbrycia, connects its old inhabitants with the Thracian BEBRYCES.

Lamus (Λάμος), son of Poseidon, and king of the Laestrygones, was said to have founded Formiae, in Italy. [FORMIAE.]

Lamus (Λάμος: Lamas), a river of Cilicia, the boundary between Cilicia Aspera and Cilicia Campestris ; with a town of the same name.

Lancia (Lancienses). 1. (Sollanco or Sollancia, near Leon), a town of the Astures in Hispania Tarraconensis, 9 miles E. of Legio, was destroyed by the Romans. — 2. Surnamed **Oppidana**, a town of the Vettones in Lusitania, not far from the sources of the river Munda.

Langobardi or **Longobardi,** corrupted into **Lombards,** a German tribe of the Suevic race. They dwelt originally on the left bank of the Elbe, near the river Saale ; but they afterwards crossed the Elbe, and dwelt on the E. bank of the river, where they were for a time subject to Maroboduus in the reign of Tiberius. After this they disappear from history for 4 centuries. Like most of the other German tribes, they migrated southwards; and in the 2nd half of the 5th century we find them again on the N. bank of the Danube, in Upper Hungary. Here they defeated and almost annihilated the Heruli. In the middle of the 6th century they crossed the Danube, at the invitation of Justinian, and settled in Pannonia. Here they were engaged for 30 years in a desperate conflict with the Gepidae, which only ended with the extirmination of the latter people. In A.D. 568, Alboin, the king of the Lombards, under whose command they had defeated the Gepidae, led his nation across the Julian Alps, and conquered the plains of N. Italy, which have ever since received the name of Lombardy. Here he founded the celebrated kingdom of the Lombards, which existed for upwards of 2 centuries, till its overthrow by Charlemagne.— Paulus Diaconus, who was a Lombard by birth

derives their name of Langobardi from their long beards ; but modern critics reject this etymology, and suppose the name to have reference to their dwelling on the banks of the Elbe, inasmuch as *Börde* signifies in low German a fertile plain on the bank of a river, and there is still a district in Magdeburg called the *lange Börde*. Paulus Diaconus also states that the Lombards came originally from Scandinavia, where they were called *Vinili*, and that they did not receive the name of *Langobardi* or *Long-Beards*, till they settled in Germany ; but this statement ought probably to be rejected.

Lanice (Λανίκη), nurse of Alexander the Great, and sister of Clitus.

Lanuvium (Lanuvinus: Lavigna), an ancient city in Latium, situated on a hill of the Alban Mount, not far from the Appia Via, and subsequently a Roman municipium. It possessed an ancient and celebrated temple of Juno Sospita. Under the empire it obtained some importance as the birthplace of Antoninus Pius. Part of the walls of Lanuvium and the substructions of the temple of Juno are still remaining.

Laöcoon (Λαοκόων), a Trojan, who plays a prominent part in the post-Homeric legends, was a son of Antenor or Acoëtes, and a priest of the Thymbraean Apollo. He tried to dissuade his countrymen from drawing into the city the wooden horse, which the Greeks had left behind them when they pretended to sail away from Troy ; and, to show the danger from the horse, he hurled a spear into its side. The Trojans, however, would not listen to his advice ; and as he was preparing to sacrifice a bull to Poseidon, suddenly 2 fearful serpents were seen swimming towards the Trojan coast from Tenedos. They rushed towards Laocoon, who, while all the people took to flight, remained with his 2 sons standing by the altar of the god. The serpents first coiled around the 2 boys, and then around the father, and thus all 3 perished. The serpents then hastened to the acropolis of Troy, and disappeared behind the shield of Tritonia. The reason why Laocoon suffered this fearful death is differently stated. According to some, it was because he had run his lance into the side of the horse ; according to others, because, contrary to the will of Apollo, he had married and begotten children ; or, according to others again, because Poseidon, being hostile to the Trojans, wanted to show to the Trojans in the person of Laocoon what fate all of them deserved. — The story of Laocoon's death was a fine subject for epic and lyric as well as tragic poetry, and was therefore frequently related by ancient poets, such as by Bacchylides, Sophocles, Euphorion, Virgil, and others. His death also formed the subject of many ancient works of art ; and a magnificent group, representing the father and his 2 sons entwined by the 2 serpents, is still extant, and preserved in the Vatican. [AGESANDER.]

Laödamas (Λαοδάμας). 1. Son of Alcinous, king of the Phaeacians, and Arete. — 2. Son of Eteocles, and king of Thebes, in whose reign the Epigoni marched against Thebes. In the battle against the Epigoni, he slew their leader Aegialeus, but was himself slain by Alcmaeon. Others related, that after the battle was lost, Laodamas fled to the Encheleans in Illyricum.

Laödamia (Λαοδάμεια). 1. Daughter of Acastus, and wife of Protesilaus. When her husband was slain before Troy, she begged the gods to be allowed to converse with him for only 3 hours. The request was granted. Hermes led Protesilaus back to the upper world, and when Protesilaus died a second time, Laodamia died with him. A later tradition states, that after the second death of Protesilaus, Laodamia made an image of her husband, to which she payed divine honours ; but as her father Acastus interfered, and commanded her to burn the image, she herself leaped into the fire. — 2. Daughter of Bellerophontes, became by Zeus the mother of Sarpedon, and was killed by Artemis while she was engaged in weaving. — 3. Nurse of Orestes, usually called ARSINOE.

Laŏdíčē (Λαοδίκη). 1. Daughter of Priam and Hecuba, and wife of Helicaon. Some relate that she fell in love with Acamas, the son of Theseus, when he came with Diomedes as ambassador to Troy, and that she became by Acamas the mother of Munitus. On the death of this son, she leaped down a precipice, or was swallowed up by the earth. — 2. Daughter of Agamemnon and Clytaemnestra (Hom. *Il.* ix. 146), called Electra by the tragic poets. [ELECTRA.] — 3. Mother of Seleucus Nicator, the founder of the Syrian monarchy. — 4. Wife of Antiochus II. Theos, king of Syria, and mother of Seleucus Callinicus. For details, see p. 55. a. — 5. Wife of Seleucus Callinicus, and mother of Seleucus Ceraunus and Antiochus the Great. — 6. Wife of Antiochus the Great, was a daughter of Mithridates IV. king of Pontus, and granddaughter of No. 4. — 7. Wife of Achaeus, the cousin and adversary of Antiochus the Great, was a sister of No. 6. — 8. Daughter of Antiochus the Great by his wife Laodice [No. 6]. She was married to her eldest brother Antiochus, who died in his father's lifetime, 195. — 9. Daughter of Seleucus IV. Philopator, was married to Perseus, king of Macedonia. — 10. Daughter of Antiochus IV. Epiphanes, was married to the impostor Alexander Balas. — 11. Wife and also sister of Mithridates Eupator (commonly called the Great), king of Pontus. During the absence of her husband, and deceived by a report of his death, she gave free scope to her amours ; and, alarmed for the consequences, on his return attempted his life by poison. Her designs were, however, betrayed to Mithridates, who immediately put her to death. — 12. Another sister of Mithridates Eupator, married to Ariarathes VI., king of Cappadocia. After the death of her husband she married Nicomedes, king of Bithynia.

Laŏdíčēa (Λαοδίκεια: Λαοδικεύς, Laodicensis, Laodicēnus), the name of 6 Greek cities in Asia, 4 of which (besides another now unknown) were founded by Seleucus I. Nicator, and named in honour of his mother Laodice, the other 2 by Antiochus II. and Antiochus I. or III. (See Nos. 1. & 5). — 1. L. ad Lycum (Λ. πρὸς τῷ Λύκῳ, *Eski-Hissar*, Ru.), a city of Asia Minor, stood on a ridge of hills near the S. bank of the river Lycus (*Choruk-Su*), a tributary of the Maeander, a little to the W. of Colossae, and to the S. of Hierapolis, on the borders of Lydia, Caria, and Phrygia, to each of which it is assigned by different writers ; but, after the definitive division of the provinces, it is reckoned as belonging to Great Phrygia, and under the later Roman emperors it was the capital of Phrygia Pacatiana. It was founded by Antiochus II. Theos, on the site of a previously existing town, and named in honour of his wife Laodice. It passed from the

kings of Syria to those of Pergamus, and from them to the Romans, to whom Attalus III. bequeathed his kingdom. Under the Romans it belonged to the province of Asia. At first it was comparatively an insignificant place, and it suffered much from the frequent earthquakes to which its site seems to be more exposed than that of any other city of Asia Minor, and also from the Mithridatic War. Under the later Roman republic and the early emperors, it rose to importance ; and, though more than once almost destroyed by earthquakes, it was restored by the aid of the emperors and the munificence of its own citizens, and became, next to Apamea, the greatest city in Phrygia, and one of the most flourishing in Asia Minor. In an inscription it is called " the most splendid city of Asia," a statement confirmed by the magnificent ruins of the city, which comprise an aqueduct, a gymnasium, several theatres, a stadium almost perfect, besides remains of roads, porticoes, pillars, gates, foundations of houses, and sarcophagi. This great prosperity was owing partly to its situation, on the high road for the traffic between the E. and W. of Asia, and partly to the fertility and beauty of the country round it. Already in the apostolic age it was the seat of a flourishing Christian Church, which, however, became very soon infected with the pride and luxury produced by the prosperity of the city, as we learn from St. John's severe Epistle to it. (*Revel.* iii. 14—22). St. Paul also addresses it in common with the nighbouring church of Colossae (*Coloss.* ii. 1 ; iv. 13. 16). — 2. L. Combusta (Λ. ἡ κατακεκαυμένη or κεκαυμένη, i. e. *the burnt*; the reason of the epithet is doubtful : *Ladik*, Ru.), a city of Lycaonia, N. of Iconium, on the high road from the W. coast of Asia Minor to the Euphrates. — 3. L. ad Mare (Λ. ἐπὶ τῇ θαλάττῃ: *Ladikiyeh*), a city on the coast of Syria, about 50 miles S. of Antioch, was built by Seleucus I. on the site of an earlier city, called Ramitha or Λευκὴ 'Ακτή. It had the best harbour in Syria, and the surrounding country was celebrated for its wine and fruits, which formed a large part of the traffic of the city. In the civil contests during the later period of the Syrian kingdom, Laodicea obtained virtual independence, in which it was confirmed probably by Pompey, and certainly by Julius Caesar, who greatly favoured the city. In the civil wars, after Caesar's death, the Laodiceans were severely punished by Cassius for their adherence to Dolabella, and the city again suffered in the Parthian invasion of Syria, but was recompensed by Antony with exemption from taxation. Herod the Great built the Laodiceans an aqueduct, the ruins of which still exist. It is mentioned occasionally as an important city under the later Roman empire ; and, after the conquest of Syria by the Arabs, it was one of those places on the coast which still remained in the hands of the Greek emperors, and with a Christian population. It was taken and destroyed by the Arabs in 1188. It is now a poor Turkish village, with very considerable ruins of the ancient city, the chief of which are a triumphal arch, the remains of the mole of the harbour, of a portico near it, of catacombs on the sea-coast, of the aqueducts and cisterns, and of pillars where the Necropolis is supposed to have stood. — 4. L. ad Libănum (Λ. Λιβανοῦ, πρὸς Λιβάνῳ), a city of Coele-Syria, at the N. entrance to the narrow valley (αὐλάων), between

Libanus and Antilibanus, appears to have been, through its favourable situation, a place of commercial importance. During the possession of Coele-Syria by the Greek kings of Egypt, it was the S. W. border fortress of Syria. It was the chief city of a district called Laodicene.—5. A city in the S. E. of Media, near the boundary of Persia, founded either by Antiochus I., Soter, or Antiochus II. the Great: site unknown.— 6. In Mesopotamia: site unknown.

Laŏdŏcus (Λαοδόκος). 1. Son of Bias and Pero and brother of Talaus, took part in the expeditions of the Argonauts, and of the Seven against Thebes.—2. Son of Antenor.

Laŏmĕdon (Λαομέδων). 1. King of Troy, son of Ilus and Eurydice, and father of Priam, Hesione, and other children. His wife is called Strymo, Rhoeo, Placia, Thoosa, Zeuxippe, or Leucippe. Poseidon and Apollo, who had displeased Zeus, were doomed to serve Laomedon for wages. Accordingly, Poseidon built the walls of Troy, while Apollo tended the king's flocks on Mount Ida. When the two gods had done their work, Laomedon refused them the reward he had promised them, and expelled them from his dominions. Thereupon Poseidon in wrath let loose the sea over the lands, and also sent a marine monster to ravage the country. By the command of an oracle, the Trojans were obliged, from time to time, to sacrifice a maiden to the monster; and on one occasion it was decided by lot that Hesione, the daughter of Laomedon himself, should be the victim. But it happened that Hercules was just returning from his expedition against the Amazons, and he promised to save the maiden, if Laomedon would give him the horses which Tros had once received from Zeus as a compensation for Ganymedes. Laomedon promised them to Hercules, but again broke his word, when Hercules had killed the monster and saved Hesione. Hereupon Hercules sailed with a squadron of 6 ships against Troy, killed Laomedon, with all his sons, except Podarces (Priam), and gave Hesione to Telamon. Hesione ransomed her brother Priam with her veil. — Priam, as the son of Laomedon, is called Laomedontiades; and the Trojans, as the subjects of Laomedon, are called Laomedontiadae. — 2. Of Mytilene, was one of Alexander's generals, and after the king's death (B.C. 323), obtained the government of Syria. He was afterwards defeated by Nicanor, the general of Ptolemy, and deprived of Syria.

Lapăthus or **Lapathus** (Λάπηθος, Λάπαθος: Λαπήθιος, Λαπηθεύς: Lapitho or Lapta), an important town on the N. coast of Cyprus, on a river of the same name, E. of the prom. Crommyon.

Laphrĭa (Λαφρία), a surname of Artemis among the Calydonians, from whom the worship of the goddess was introduced into Naupactus and Patrae, in Achaia. The name was traced back to a hero, Laphrius, son of Castalius, who was said to have instituted her worship at Calydon.

Laphystĭus (Λαφύστιος), a mountain in Boeotia, between Coronea, Lebadea, and Orchomenus, on which was a temple of Zeus, who hence bore the surname Laphystius.

Lapidĕi Campĭ. [CAMPI LAPIDEI.]

Lăpĭthes (Λαπίθης), son of Apollo and Stilbe, brother of Centaurus, and husband of Orsinome, the daughter of Eurynomus, by whom he became the father of Phorbas, Triopas, and Periphas. He was regarded as the ancestor of the Lapithae in

the mountains of Thessaly. The Lapithae were governed by Pirithous, who being a son of Ixion, was a half-brother of the Centaurs. The latter, therefore, demanded their share in their father's kingdom, and, as their claims were not satisfied, a war arose between the Lapithae and Centaurs, which, however, was terminated by a peace. But when Pirithous married Hippodamia, and invited the Centaurs to the marriage feast, the latter, fired by wine, and urged on by Ares, attempted to carry off the bride and the other women. Thereupon a bloody conflict ensued, in which the Centaurs were defeated by the Lapithae.—The Lapithae are said to have been the inventors of bits and bridles for horses. It is probable that they were a Pelasgian people, who defeated the less civilised Centaurs, and compelled them to abandon Mt. Pelion.

Lar or Lars, was an Etruscan praenomen, borne for instance by Porsena and Tolumnius. From the Etruscans it passed over to the Romans, whence we read of Lar Herminius, who was consul B. C. 448. This word signified lord, king, or hero in the Etruscan.

Lara. [LARUNDA.]

Laranda (τὰ Λάρανδα: Larenda or Caraman), a considerable town in the S. of Lycaonia, at the N. foot of M. Taurus, in a fertile district: taken by storm by Perdiccas, but afterwards restored. It was used by the Isaurian robbers as one of their strongholds.

Larentĭa. [ACCA LARENTIA.]

Lăres, inferior gods at Rome. Their worship was closely connected with that of the Manes, and was analogous to the hero worship of the Greeks. The Lares may be divided into 2 classes, the *Lares domestici* and *Lares publici*. The former were the Manes of a house raised to the dignity of heroes. The Manes were more closely connected with the place of burial, while the Lares were more particularly the divinities presiding over the hearth and the whole house. It was only the spirits of good men that were honoured as Lares. All the domestic Lares were headed by the Lar familiaris, who was regarded as the founder of the family. He was inseparable from the family; and when the latter changed their abode, he went with them. Among the *Lares publici* we have mention made of *Lares praestites* and *Lares compitales*, who are in reality the same, and differ only in regard to the place or occasion of their worship. Servius Tullius is said to have instituted their worship; and when Augustus improved the regulations of the city, he also renewed the worship of the public Lares. Their name, *Lares praestites*, characterises them as the protecting spirits of the city, in which they had a temple in the uppermost part of the Via Sacra, that is, near a compitum, whence they might be called Compitales. This temple (*Sacellum Larum* or *aedes Larum*) contained 2 images, which were probably those of Romulus and Remus. Now, while these Lares were the general protectors of the whole city, the *Lares compitales* must be regarded as those who presided over the several divisions of the city, which were marked by the compita or the points where two or more streets crossed each other, and where small chapels (*aediculae*) were erected to them. In addition to the Lares praestites and compitales, there are other Lares which must be reckoned among the public ones, viz., the *Lares rurales*, who were worshipped in the country; the *Lares viales*, who were worshipped on the high-roads by travellers ; and the *Lares marini* or *permarini*, to whom P. Aemilius dedicated a sanctuary in remembrance of his naval victory over Antiochus. —The worship of the domestic Lares, together with that of the Penates and Manes, constituted what are called the *sacra privata.* The images of the Lares, in great houses, were usually in a separate compartment, called *aediculae* or *lararia.* They were generally represented in the cinctus Gabinus. Their worship was very simple, especially in early times and in the country. The offerings were set before them in patellae, whence they themselves are called *patellarii.* Pious people made offerings to them every day ; but they were more especially worshipped on the calends, nones, and ides of every month. When the inhabitants of the house took heir meals, some portion was offered to the Lares, and on joyful family occasions they were adorned with wreaths, and the lararia were thrown open. When the young bride entered the house of her husband, her first duty was to offer a sacrifice to the Lares. Respecting the public worship of the Lares, and the festival of the Larentalia, see *Dict. of Ant.* art. *Larentalia, Compitalia.*

Lares (Λάρης : *Alarbous*), a city of N. Africa, in the Carthaginian territory (Byzacena), S. W. of Zama ; a place of some importance at the time of the war with Jugurtha.

Largus, Scribonius. [SCRIBONIUS.]

Larinum (Larīnaa, ātis : *Larino*), a town of the Frentani (whence the inhabitants are sometimes called Frentani Larinates), on the river Tifernus, and near the borders of Apulia, subsequently a Roman municipium, possessed a considerable territory extending down to the Adriatic sea. The town of Clitoria on the coast was subject to Larinum.

Larissa (Λάρισσα), the name of several Pelasgian places, whence Larissa is called in mythology the daughter of Pelasgus. I. *In Europe.* 1. (*Larissa* or *Larza*), an important town of Thessaly, in Pelasgiotis, situated on the Peneus, in an extensive plain. It was once the capital of the Pelasgi, and had a democratical constitution, but subsequently became subject to the Macedonians. It retained its importance under the Romans, and after the time of Constantine the Great, became the capital of the province of Thessaly. — 2. Surnamed **Cremaste** (ἡ Κρεμαστή), another important town of Thessaly, in Phthiotis, situated on a height, whence probably its name, and distant 20 stadia from the Maliac gulf. II. *In Asia.* 1. An ancient city on the coast of the Troad, near Hamaxitus ; ruined at the time of the Persian war. — 2. L. Phricōnis (Λ. ἡ Φρικωνίς, also *al* Λήρισσαι), a city on the coast of Mysia, near Cyme (hence called ἡ περὶ τὴν Κύμην), of Pelasgian origin, but colonised by the Aeolians, and made a member of the Aeolic confederacy. It was also called the Egyptian Larissa (ἡ Αιγυπτία), because Cyrus the Great settled in it a body of his Egyptian mercenary soldiers. — 3. L. Ephesia (Λ. ἡ Ἐφεσία), a city of Lydia, in the plain of the Cayster, on the N. side of M. Messogis, N.E. of Ephesus ; with a temple of Apollo Larissaeua. — 4. In Assyria, an ancient city on the E. bank of the Tigris, some distance N. of the mouth of the river Zabatas or Lycus, described by Xenophon (*Anab.* iii. 4). It was deserted when Xenophon saw it ; but its brick walls still stood, 25 feet thick, 100 feet high, and 2 parasangs (= 60 stadia = 6 geog. miles), in

circuit, and there was a stone pyramid near it. Xenophon relates the tradition that, when the empire passed from the Medes to the Persians, the city resisted all the efforts of the Persian king (i. e. Cyrus) to take it, until the inhabitants, terrified at an obscuration of the sun, deserted the city. Mr. Layard identifies the site of Larissa with that of the ruins near *Nimroud*, the very same site as that of Nineveh. The name Larissa is no doubt a corruption of some Assyrian name (perhaps Al-Assur), which Xenophon naturally fell into through his familiarity with the word as the name of cities in Greece. — 5. In Syria, called by the Syrians Sizara (Σίζαρα : *Kulat Seijar*), a city in the district of Apamese, on the W. bank of the Orontes, about half-way between Apamea and Epiphania.

Larissus or Larisus (Λάρισσος, Λάρισος : *Risso*), a small river forming the boundary between Achaia and Elis, rises in Mt. Scollis, and flows into the Ionian sea.

Lārius Lacus (*Lake of Como*), a beautiful lake in Gallia Transpadana, running from N. to S., through which the river Adda flows. After extending about 15 miles, it is divided into 2 branches, of which the one to the S.W. is about 18 miles in length, and the one to the S.E. about 12 miles. At the extremity of the S.W. branch is the town of Comum ; and at the extremity of the S.E. branch the river Adda issues out of the lake. The beauty of the scenery of this lake is praised by Pliny. He had several villas on the banks of the lake, of which he mentions 2 particularly ; one called *Comoedia,* and the other *Tragoedia.* (Plin. *Ep.* ix. 7.) Some believe Comoedia to have been situated at the modern *Bellagio,* on the promontory which divides the 2 branches of the lake ; and Tragoedia at *Lenno,* on the W. bank, where the scenery is more wild. The intermitting fountain, of which Pliny gives an account in another letter (*Ep.* iv. 30), is still called *Pliniana.*

Lars Tolumnius. [TOLUMNIUS.]

Lartia Gens, patrician, distinguished at the beginning of the republic through 2 of its members, T. Lartius, the first dictator, and Sp. Lartius, the companion of Horatius on the wooden bridge. The name soon after disappears entirely from the annals. The Lartii were of Etruscan origin, as is clearly shown by their name, which comes from the Etruscan word Lar or Lars. [LAR.]

Larunda, or Lāra, daughter of Almon, was a nymph who informed Juno of the connexion between Jupiter and Juturna ; hence her name is connected with λαλεῖν. Jupiter deprived her of her tongue, and ordered Mercury to conduct her into the lower world. On the way thither, Mercury fell in love with her, and she afterwards gave birth to 2 Lares.

Larvae. [LEMURES.]

Larymna (Λάρυμνα), the name of 2 towns on the river Cephissus, on the borders of Boeotia and Locris, and distinguished as Upper and Lower Larymna. The latter was at the mouth of the river and the former a little way inland.

Las (Λᾶς : Ep. Λάας : *Passava*), an ancient town of Laconia, on the E. side of the Laconian gulf, 10 stadia from the sea, and S. of Gytheum. It is said to have been once destroyed by the Dioscuri, who hence received the surname of *Lapersae,* or the Destroyers of Las. In the time of the Romans it had ceased to be a place of importance.

Lampsacus on the Hellespont. Page 365.

Locri Epizephyrii. Page 387.

Laodicea ad Mare. Page 396.

Locri Opuntii. Page 387.

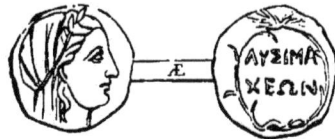

Larissa in Thessaly. Page 368.

Lysimachia in Thrace. Page 402.

Leontini in Sicily. Page 375.

Macedonia. Page 403.

Leucas. Page 379.

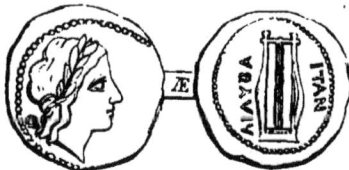

Magnesia ad Maeandrum. Page 409.

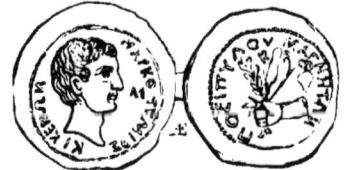

Lilybaeum in Sicily. Page 384.

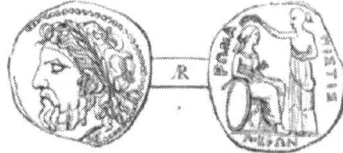

Magnesia ad Sipylum. Page 409.

[To face p. 368.

Q. Labienus, ob. B.C. 39.   Page 361, No. 2.

Macrianus Senior, one of the Thirty Tyrants, ob. A.D. 262.
Page 405.

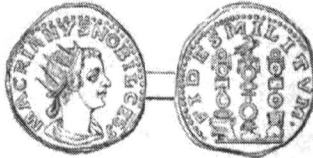

Laelianus, one of the Thirty Tyrants, ob. A.D. 267.   Page 363.

Macrianus Junior, one of the Thirty Tyrants, ob. A.D. 262.
Page 405.

Licinius, Roman Emperor, A.D. 307—324.   Page 383.

Macrinus, Roman Emperor, A.D. 217—218.   Page 405.

Livia, mother of the Emperor Tiberius, ob. A.D. 29.   Page 345.

Majorianus, Roman Emperor, A.D. 457—461.

Annia Lucilla, daughter of M. Aurelius, ob. A.D. 183.
Page 392.

Julia Mamaea, mother of Alexander Severus, ob. A.D. 235.

Lysimachus, King of Thrace, ob. B.C. 281.   Page 402.

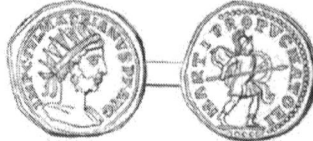

Marcellus, the Conqueror of Syracuse. The reverse represents him carrying the *spolia opima* to the Temple of Jupiter Feretrius.   Page 413, No. 1.

To face p. 389.]

Lasaea (Λασαία), a town in the E. of Crete, not far from the Prom. Samonium, mentioned in the *Acts of the Apostles* (xxvii. 8).

Lasion (Λασίων: Λασιώνιος: *Lala*), a fortified town in Elis, on the frontiers of Arcadia, and not far from the confluence of the Erymanthus and the Alpheus. The possession of this town was a constant source of dispute between the Eleans and Arcadians.

Lasthenes (Λασθένης) 1. An Olynthian, who, together with Euthycrates, betrayed his country to Philip of Macedon, by whom he had been bribed, B. C. 347. — 2. A Cretan, one of the principal leaders of his countrymen in their war with the Romans. He was defeated and taken prisoner by Q. Metellus, 67.

Lasus (Λάσος), one of the principal Greek lyric poets, was a native of Hermione, in Argolis. He is celebrated as the founder of the Athenian school of dithyrambic poetry, and as the teacher of Pindar. He was cotemporary with Simonides, like whom he lived at Athens, under the patronage of Hipparchus. It would appear that Lasus introduced a greater freedom, both of rhythm and of music, into the dithyrambic Ode ; that he gave it a more artificial and more mimetic character; and that the subjects of his poetry embraced a far wider range than had been customary.

Latera Stagnum (*Etang de Maguelone et de Perols*), a lake in the territory of Nemausus in Gallia Narbonensis, connected with the sea by a canal. On this lake was a fortress of the same name. (*Chateau de la Latte.*)

Laterensis, Juventius, was one of the accusers of Plancius, whom Cicero defended, B. C. 54. [PLANCIUS.] He was praetor in 51. He served as a legate in the army of M. Lepidus, and when the soldiers of Lepidus passed over to Antony, Laterensis put an end to his life.

Lathon, Lethon, Lethes, Lethaeus (Λάθων Doric, Λήθων, Ληθαῖος), a river of Cyrenaica in N. Africa, falling into a Lacus Hesperidum, near the city of Hesperis or Berenice, in the region which the early Greek navigators identified with the gardens of the Hesperides.

Latialis or **Latiaris**, a surname of Jupiter as the protecting divinity of Latium. The Latin towns and Rome celebrated to him every year the feriae Latinae, on the Alban mount, which were conducted by one of the Roman consuls. [LATINUS.]

Latinus. 1. King of Latium, son of Faunus and the nymph Marica, brother of Lavinius, husband of Amata, and father of Lavinia, whom he gave in marriage to Aeneas. [LAVINIA.] This is the common tradition ; but according to Hesiod he was a son of Ulysses and Circe, and brother of Agrius, king of the Tyrrhenians ; according to Hyginus he was a son of Telemachus and Circe; while others describe him as a son of Hercules, by an Hyperborean woman, who was afterwards married to Faunus, or as a son of Hercules by a daughter of Faunus. According to one account Latinus after his death became Jupiter Latiaris, just as Romulus became Quirinus. — 2. A celebrated player in the farces called mimes (*Dict. of Ant. s. v.*) in the reign of Domitian, with whom he was a great favourite, and whom he served as a delator. He frequently acted as mimus with Thymele as mima.

Latium (ἡ Λατίνη), a country in Italy, inhabited by the **Latini**. The origin of the name is uncertain. Most of the ancients derived it from a king Latinus, who was supposed to have been a cotemporary of Aeneas [LATINUS] ; but there can be no doubt that the name of the people was transferred to this fictitious king. Other ancient critics connected the name with the verb *latere*, either because Saturn had been hidden in the country, or because Italy is hidden between the Alps and the Apennines ! But neither of these explanations deserves a serious refutation. A modern writer derives *Latium* from *latus* (like *Campania* from *campus*), and supposes it to mean the "flat land ; " but the quantity of the ā in *lātus* is opposed to this etymology. — The boundaries of Latium varied at different periods. 1. In the most ancient times it reached only from the river Tiber on the N., to the river Numicus and the town of Ardea on the S., and from the sea-coast on the W. to the Alban Mt. on the E. 2. The territory of Latium was subsequently extended S.wards ; and long before the conquest of the Latins by the Romans, it stretched from the Tiber on the N., to the Prom. Circeium and Anxur or Tarracina on the S. Even in the treaty of peace made between Rome and Carthage in B. C. 509, we find Antium, Circeii, and Tarracina, mentioned as belonging to Latium. The name of *Latium antiquum* or *vetus* was subsequently given to the country from the Tiber to the Prom. Circeium. 3. The Romans still further extended the territories of Latium, by the conquest of the Hernici, Aequi, Volsci, and Aurunci, as far as the Liris on the S., and even beyond this river to the town Sinuessa and to Mt. Massicus. This new accession of territory was called *Latium novum* or *adjectum.* — Latium, therefore, in its widest signification was bounded by Etruria on the N., from which it was separated by the Tiber ; by Campania on the S., from which it was separated by the Liris ; by the Tyrrhene sea on the W. ; and by the Sabine and Samnite tribes on the E. The greater part of this country is an extensive plain of volcanic origin, out of which rise an isolated range of mountains known by the name of MONS ALBANUS, of which the Algidus and the Tusculan hills are branches. Part of this plain, on the coast between Antium and Tarracina, which was at one time well cultivated, became a marsh in consequence of the rivers Nymphaeus, Ufens, and Amasenus finding no outlet for their waters [POMPTINAE PALUDES] ; but the remainder of the country was celebrated for its fertility in antiquity. — The Latini were some of the most ancient inhabitants of Italy. They appear to have been a Pelasgian tribe, and are frequently called Aborigines. At a period long anterior to the foundation of Rome, these Pelasgians or Aborigines descended into the narrow plain between the Tiber and the Numicus, expelled or subdued the Siculi, the original inhabitants of that district, and there became known under the name of Latini. These ancient Latins, who were called *Prisci Latini*, to distinguish them from the later Latins, the subjects of Rome, formed a league or confederation, consisting of 30 states. The town of Alba Longa subsequently became the head of the league. This town, which founded several colonies, and among others Rome, boasted of a Trojan origin ; but the whole story of a Trojan settlement in Italy is probably an invention of later times. Although Rome was a colony from Alba, she became powerful enough in the reign of her 3rd king, Tullus Hostilius, to take Alba and raze it to the ground.

B B

In this war Alba seems to have received no assistance from the other Latin towns. Ancus Marcius and Tarquinius Priscus carried on war successfully with several other Latin towns. Under Servius Tullius Rome was admitted into the Latin League; and his successor Tarquinius Superbus compelled the other Latin towns to acknowledge Rome as the head of the league, and to become dependent upon the latter city. But upon the expulsion of the kings the Latins asserted their independence, and commenced a struggle with Rome, which, though frequently suspended and apparently terminated by treaties, was as often renewed, and was not brought to a final close till B.C. 340, when the Latins were defeated by the Romans at the battle of Mt. Vesuvius. The Latin league was now dissolved, and the Latins became the subjects of Rome. — The following were the most important institutions of the Latins during the time of their independence: — The towns of Latium were independent of one another, but formed a league for purposes of mutual protection. This league consisted, as we have already seen, of 30 cities, a number which could not be exceeded. Each state sent deputies to the meetings of the league, which were held in a sacred grove at the foot of the Alban Mt., by the fountain of Ferentina. On the top of the mountain was a temple of Jupiter Latiaris, and a festival was celebrated there in honour of this god from the earliest times. This festival, which was called the *Feriae Latinae*, is erroneously said to have been instituted by Tarquinius Superbus, in commemoration of the alliance between the Romans and Latins. It is true, however, that the festival was raised into one of much greater importance when Rome became the head of the league; for it was now a festival common both to Rome and Latium, and served to unite the 2 nations by a religious bond. Having thus become a Roman as well as a Latin festival, it continued to be celebrated by the Romans after the dissolution of the Latin league. (*Dict. of Ant.* art. *Feriae.*) — The chief magistrate in each Latin town appears to have borne the title of dictator. He was elected annually, but might be re-elected at the close of his year of office. Even in the time of Cicero we find dictators in the Latin towns, as for instance in Lanuvium. (Cic. *pro Mil.* 10.) In every Latin town there was also a senate and a popular assembly, but the exact nature of their powers is unknown. — The old Latin towns were built for the most part on isolated hills, the sides of which were made by art very steep and almost inaccessible. They were surrounded by walls built of great polygonal stones, the remains of which still excite our astonishment. — On the conquest of the Latins in 340, several of the Latin towns, such as Lanuvium, Aricia, Nomentum, Pedum, and Tusculum, received the Roman franchise. All the other towns became Roman Socii, and are mentioned in history under the general name of *Nomen Latinum* or *Latini*. The Romans, however, granted to them from time to time certain rights and privileges, which the other Socii did not enjoy; and in particular they founded many colonies, consisting of Latins, in various parts of Italy. These Latin colonies formed a part of the *Nomen Latinum*, although they were not situated in Latium. Thus the Latini came eventually to hold a certain status intermediate between that of Roman citizens and peregrini. (For details see *Dict. of Ant.* art. *Latini.*)

Latmīcus Sinus (ὁ Λατμικὸς κόλπος), a gulf on the coast of Ionia, in Asia Minor, into which the river Maeander fell, named from M. Latmus, which overhangs it. Its width from Miletus, which stood on its S. side, to Pyrrha, was about 30 stadia. Through the changes effected on this coast by the Maeander, the gulf is now an inland lake, called *Akess-Chai* or *Uffa-Bassi*.

Latmus (Λάτμος: *Monte di Palatia*), a mountain in Caria, extending in a S.E. direction from its commencement on the S. side of the Maeander, N.E. of Miletus and the Sinus Latmicus. It was the mythological scene of the story of Luna and Endymion, who is hence called by the Roman poets "Latmius heros" and "Latmius venator;" he had a temple on the mountain, and a cavern in its side was shown as his grave.

Latobrigi, a people in Gallia Belgica, who are mentioned, along with the Tulingi and Rauraci, as neighbours of the Helvetii. They probably dwelt near the sources of the Rhine, in Switzerland.

Latōna. [LETO.]

Latōpōlis (Λατόπολις: *Esneh*, Ru.), a city of Upper Egypt, on the W. bank of the Nile, between Thebes and Apollonopolis; the seat of the worship of the Nile-fish called latus, which was the symbol of the goddess Neith, whom the Greeks identified with Athena.

Latovĭci, a people in the S.W. of Pannonia on the river Savus, in the modern Illyria and Croatia.

Latro, M. Porcĭus, a celebrated Roman rhetorician in the reign of Augustus, was a Spaniard by birth, and a friend and contemporary of the elder Seneca, by whom he is frequently mentioned. His school was one of the most frequented at Rome, and he numbered among his pupils the poet Ovid. He died B.C. 4. Many modern writers suppose that he was the author of the Declamations of Sallust against Cicero, and of Cicero against Sallust.

Laureācum or Laurĭăcum (*Lorch* near *Ens*), a strongly fortified town on the Danube in Noricum Ripense, the head-quarters of the 2nd legion, and the station of a Roman fleet.

Laurentĭa, Acca. [ACCA LAURENTIA.]

Laurentĭus Lydus. [LYDUS.]

Laurentum (Laurens, -ntis: *Casale* of *Capocotta*, not *Paterno*), one of the most ancient towns of Latium, was situated on a height between Ostia and Ardea, not far from the sea, and was surrounded by a grove of laurels, from which the place was supposed to have derived its name. According to Virgil, it was the residence of king Latinus and the capital of Latium; and it is certain that it was a place of importance in the time of the Roman kings, as it is mentioned in the treaty concluded between Rome and Carthage in B.C. 509. The younger Pliny and the emperor Commodus had villas at Laurentum, which appears to have been a healthy place, notwithstanding the marshes in the neighbourhood. These marshes supplied the tables of the Romans with excellent boars. — In the time of the Antonines Laurentum was united with Lavinium, from which it was only 6 miles distant, so that the 2 formed only one town, which was called Laurolavinium, and its inhabitants were named Laurentes Lavinates.

Laurětānus Portus, a harbour of Etruria, on the road from Populonia to Cosa.

Laurĭăcum. [LAUREACUM.]

Laurium (Λαύριον, Λαύρειον), a mountain in the S. of Attica, a little N. of the Prom. Sunium, celebrated for its silver mines, which in early times were so productive that every Athenian citizen received annually 10 drachmae. On the advice of Themistocles, the Athenians applied this money to equip 200 triremes, shortly before the invasion of Xerxes. In the time of Xenophon the produce of the mines was 100 talents. They gradually became less and less productive, and in the ime of Strabo they yielded nothing.

Lauron (*Lawry*, W. of Xucar in Valencia), a town in the E. of Hispania Tarraconensis, near the sea and the river Sucro, celebrated on account of its siege by Sertorius, and as the place where Cn. Pompey, the Younger, was put to death after the battle of Munda.

Laus (Λᾶος: Λαῖνος), a Greek city in Lucania, situated near the mouth of the river Laus, which formed the boundary between Lucania and Bruttium. It was founded by the Sybarites, after their own city had been taken by the inhabitants of Croton, B. c. 510, but it had disappeared in the time of Pliny. — The gulf into which the river Laus flowed, was also called the gulf of Laus.

Laus Pompeii (*Lodi Vecchio*), a town in Gallia Cisalpina, N.W. of Placentia, and S.E. of Mediolanum. It was founded by the Boii, and was afterwards made a municipium by Pompeius Strabo, the father of Pompeius Magnus, whence it was called by his name.

Lausus. 1. Son of Mezentius, king of the Etruscans, slain by Aeneas.—2. Son of Numitor and brother of Ilia, killed by Amulius.

Lautulae, a village of the Volsci in Latium, in a narrow pass between Tarracina and Fundi.

Laverna, the Roman goddess of thieves and impostors. A grove was sacred to her on the via Salaria, and she had an altar near the porta Lavernalis, which derived its name from her.

Lavicum. [LABICUM.]

Lavinia, daughter of Latinus and Amata, was betrothed to Turnus [TURNUS], but was afterwards given in marriage to Aeneas, by whom she became the mother of Aeneas Silvius.

Lavinium (Laviniensis: *Pratica*), an ancient town of Latium, 3 miles from the sea and 6 miles E. of Laurentum, on the Via Appia, and near the river Numicus, which divided its territory from that of Ardea. It is said to have been founded by Aeneas, and to have been called Lavinium, in honour of his wife Lavinia, the daughter of Latinus. It possessed a temple of Venus, common to all the Latins, of which the inhabitants of Ardea had the oversight. It was at Lavinium that the king Titus Tatius was said to have been murdered. Lavinium was at a later time united with Laurentum; respecting which see LAURENTUM.

Lazae or Lazi (Λάζαι, Λαζοί), a people of Colchis, S. of the Phasis.

Leaena (Λέαινα), an Athenian hetaera, beloved by Aristogiton or Harmodius. On the murder of Hipparchus she was put to the torture; but she died under her sufferings, without making any disclosure, and, if we may believe one account, she bit off her tongue, that no secret might be wrung from her. The Athenians honoured her memory greatly, and in particular by a bronze statue of a lioness (Λέαινα) without a tongue, in the vestibule of the Acropolis.

Leander (Λείανδρος or Λέανδρος), the famous youth of Abydos, who was in love with Hero, the priestess of Aphrodite in Sestus, and swam every

night across the Hellespont to visit her, and returned before daybreak. Once during a stormy night he perished in the waves. Next morning his corpse was washed on the coast of Sestus, whereupon Hero threw herself into the sea. This story is the subject of the poem of Musaeus, entitled *De Amore Herois et Leandri* [MUSAEUS], and is also mentioned by Ovid (*Her.* xviii. 19), and Virgil. (*Georg.* iii. 258.)

Learchus (Λέαρχος). 1. [ATHAMAS.]—2. Of Rhegium, one of those Daedalian artists who stand on the confines of the mythical and historical periods, and about whom we have extremely uncertain information. One account made him a pupil of Daedalus, another of Dipoenus and Scyllis.

Lebadea (Λεβάδεια: *Livadhia*), a town in Boeotia, W. of the lake Copais, between Chaeronea and Mt. Helicon, at the foot of a rock from which the river Hercyna flows. In a cave of this rock, close to the town, was the celebrated oracle of Trophonius, to which the place owed its importance.

Lebedos (Λέβεδος: Λεβέδιος), one of the 12 cities of the Ionian confederacy, in Asia Minor, stood on the coast of Lydia, between Colophon and Teos, 90 stadia E. of the promontory of Myonnesus. It was said to have been built at the time of the Ionian migration, on the site of an earlier Carian city; and it flourished, chiefly by commerce, until Lysimachus transplanted most of its inhabitants to Ephesus. Near it were some mineral springs, which still exist near *Ekklesia*, but no traces remain of the city itself.

Leben or Lebena (Λεβήν, Λεβήνα), a town on the S. coast of Crete, 90 stadia S.E. of Gortyna, of which it was regarded as the harbour. It possessed a celebrated temple of Aesculapius.

Lebinthus (Λέβινθος: *Lebitha*), an island in the Aegaean sea, one of the Sporades, W. of Calymna, E. of Amorgos and N. of Astypalaea.

Lechaeum (τὸ Λεχαῖον: Λεχαῖος), one of the 2 harbours of Corinth, with which it was connected by 2 long walls. It was 12 stadia from Corinth, was situated on the Corinthian gulf, and received all the ships which came from Italy and Sicily. It possessed a temple of Poseidon, who was hence surnamed Lechaeus.

Lectum (τὸ Λεκτόν: *C. Baba* or *S. Maria*), the S. W. promontory of the Troad, is formed where the W. extremity of M. Ida juts out into the sea, opposite to the N. side of the island of Lesbos. It was the S. limit of the Troad; and, under the Byzantine emperors, the N. limit of the province of Asia. An altar was shown here in Strabo's time, which was said to have been erected by Agamemnon to the 12 chief gods of Greece.

Leda (Λήδα), daughter of Thestius, whence she is called *Thestias*, and wife of Tyndareus, king of Sparta. One night she was embraced both by her husband and by Zeus; by the former she became the mother of Castor and Clytaemnestra, by the latter of Pollux and Helena. According to Homer (*Od.* xi. 298), both Castor and Pollux were sons of Tyndareus and Leda, while Helena is described as a daughter of Zeus. Other traditions reverse the story, making Castor and Pollux the sons of Zeus, and Helena the daughter of Tyndareus. According to the common legend Zeus visited Leda in the form of a swan; and she brought forth 2 eggs, from the one of which issued Helena, and from the other Castor and Pollux. The visit of Zeus to Leda in the form of a swan was frequently represented by ancient artists. The Roman poets sometimes call Helena *Ledaea*, and Castor and Pollux *Ledaei Dii*.

Lēdon (Λέδων), a town in Phocis, N. W. of Tithorea ; the birth-place of Philomelus, the commander of the Phocians in the Sacred war ; it was destroyed in this war.

Ledus or **Ledum** (*Les* or *Lez*, near Montpellier), a small river in Gallia Narbonensis.

Lēgae (Λῆγαι or Λῆγες), a people on the S. shore of the Caspian Sea, belonging to the same race as the Cadusii. A branch of them was found by the Romans in the N. mountains of Albania, at the time of Pompey's expedition into those regions.

Legio Septima Gemina (*Leon*), a town in Hispania Tarraconensis, in the country of the Astures, which was originally the head-quarters of the legion so-called.

Lēĭtus (Λήϊτος), son of Alector or Alectryon, by Cleobule, and father of Peneleus, was one of the Argonauts, and commanded the Boeotians in the war against Troy.

Lelantus Campus (τὸ Λήλαντον πεδίον), a plain in Euboea, between Eretria and Chalcis, for the possession of which these two cities often contended. It contained warm springs and mines of iron and copper, but was subject to frequent earthquakes.

Lĕlĕges (Λέλεγες), an ancient race which inhabited Greece before the Hellenes. They are frequently mentioned along with the Pelasgians as the most ancient inhabitants of Greece. Some writers erroneously identify them with the Pelasgians, but their character and habits were essentially different: the Pelasgians were a peaceful and agricultural people, whereas the Leleges were a warlike and migratory race. They appear to have first taken possession of the coasts and the islands of Greece, and afterwards to have penetrated into the interior. Piracy was probably their chief occupation; and they are represented as the ancestors of the Teleboans and the Taphians, who sailed as far as Phoenicia, and were notorious for their piracies. The coasts of Acarnania and Aetolia appear to have been inhabited by Leleges at the earliest times ; and from thence they spread over other parts of Greece. Thus we find them in Phocis and Locris, in Boeotia, in Megaris, in Laconia, which is said to have been more anciently called Lelegia, in Elis, in Euboea, in several of the islands of the Aegaean sea, and also on the coasts of Asia Minor, in Caria, Ionia, and the S. of Troas. — The origin of the Leleges is uncertain. Many of the ancients connected them with the Carians, and according to Herodotus (i. 171), the Leleges were the same as the Carians ; but whether there was any real connection between these peoples cannot be determined. The name of the Leleges was derived, according to the custom of the ancients, from an ancestor Lelex, who is called king either of Megaris or of Lacedaemon. According to some traditions this Lelex came from Egypt, and was the son of Poseidon and Libya ; but the Egyptian origin of the people was evidently an invention of later times. — The Leleges must be regarded as a branch of the great Indo-Germanic race, who became gradually incorporated with the Hellenes, and thus ceased to exist as an independent people.

Lelex. [LELEGES.]

Lemannus or **Lemānus Lacus** (*Lake of Geneva*), a large lake formed by the river Rhodanus,

was the boundary between the old Roman province in Gaul and the land of the Helvetii. Its greatest length is 55 miles, and its greatest breadth 6 miles.

Lemnos (Λῆμνος : Λήμνιος, fem. Λημνιάς : *Stalimene, i. e. εἰς τὰν Λήμνον*), one of the largest islands in the Aegaean sea, was situated nearly midway between Mt. Athos and the Hellespont, and about 22 miles S. W. of Imbros. Its area is about 147 square miles. In the earliest times it appears to have contained only one town, which bore the same name as the island (Hom. *Il.* xiv. 230) ; but at a later period we read of 2 towns, Myrina (*Palaeo Castro*) on the W. of the island, and Hephaestia or Hephaestias (nr. *Rapanidi*) on the N. W., with a harbour. Lemnos was sacred to Hephaestus (Vulcan), who is said to have fallen here, when Zeus hurled him down from Olympus. Hence the workshop of the god is sometimes placed in this island. The legend appears to have arisen from the volcanic nature of Lemnos, which possessed in antiquity a volcano called *Mosychlus* (Μόσυχλος). The island still bears traces of having been subject to the action of volcanic fire, though the volcano has long since disappeared. — The most ancient inhabitants of Lemnos, according to Homer, were the Thracian *Sinties* ; a name, however, which probably only signifies robbers (Σίντιες from σίνομαι). When the Argonauts landed at Lemnos, they are said to have found it inhabited only by women, who had murdered all their husbands, and had chosen as their queen Hypsipyle, the daughter of Thoas, the king of the island. [HYPSIPYLE.] Some of the Argonauts settled here, and became by the Lemnian women the fathers of the *Minyae*, the later inhabitants of the island. The Minyae are said to have been driven out of the island by the Pelasgians, who had been expelled from Attica. These Pelasgians are further said to have carried away from Attica some Athenian women ; but as the children of these women despised their half-brothers, born of Pelasgian women, the Pelasgians murdered both them and their children. In consequence of this atrocity, and of the former murder of the Lemnian husbands by the wives, *Lemnian Deeds* became a proverb in Greece for all atrocious acts. Lemnos was afterwards conquered by one of the generals of Darius ; but Miltiades delivered it from the Persians, and made it subject to Athens, in whose power it remained for a long time. Pliny speaks of a remarkable labyrinth in Lemnos, but no traces of it have been discovered by modern travellers. The principal production of the island was a red earth called *terra Lemnia* or *sigillata*, which was employed by the ancient physicians as a remedy for wounds and the bites of serpents, and which is still much valued by the Turks and Greeks for its supposed medicinal virtues.

Lemonĭa, one of the country tribes of Rome, named after a village Lemonium, situated on the Via Latina before the Porta Capena.

Lemovĭces, a people in Gallia Aquitanica, between the Bituriges and Arverni, whose chief town was Augustoritum, subsequently called Lemovicae, the modern *Limoges*.

Lemovĭi, a people of Germany, mentioned along with the Rugii, who inhabited the shores of the Baltic in the modern Pommerania.

Lĕmūres, the spectres or spirits of the dead. Some writers describe Lemures as the common name for all the spirits of the dead, and divide them into 2 classes; the *Lares*, or the souls of good men, and the *Larvae*, or the souls of wicked men. But the common idea was that the *Lemures* and *Larvae* were the same. They were said to wander about at night as spectres, and to torment and frighten the living. In order to propitiate them the Romans celebrated the festival of the *Lemuralia* or *Lemuria*. (*Dict. of Antiq. s. v.*)

Lēnaeus (Ληναῖος), a surname of Dionysus, derived from ληνός, the wine-press or the vintage.

Lentia (*Linz*), a town in Noricum, on the Danube.

Lentienses, a tribe of the Alemanni, who lived on the N. shore of the Lacus Brigantinus (*Lake of Constance*), in the modern *Linzgau*.

Lento, Caesennius, a follower of M. Antony. He was one of Antony's 7 agrarian commissioners (*septemviratus*) in B. C. 44, for apportioning the Campanian and Leontine lands, whence Cicero terms him *divisor Italiae*.

Lentŭlus, Cornēlius, one of the naughtiest patrician families at Rome; so that Cicero coins the words *Appietas* and *Lentulitas* to express the qualities of the high aristocratic party (*ad Fam.* iii. 7). The name was derived from *lens*, like Cicero from *cicer.* — 1. L., consul B. C. 327; legate in the Caudine campaign, 321; and dictator 320, when he avenged the disgrace of the Furculae Caudinae. This was indeed disputed (Liv. ix. 15); but his descendants at least claimed the honour for him, by assuming the agnomen of Caudinus. — 2. L., surnamed Caudinus, pontifex maximus, and consul 237, when he triumphed over the Ligurians. He died 213. — 3. P., surnamed Caudinus, served with P. Scipio in Spain, 210; praetor 204; one of the 10 ambassadors sent to Philip of Macedon, 196. — 4. P., praetor in Sicily 214, and continued in his province for the 2 following years. In 189 he was one of 10 ambassadors sent into Asia after the submission of Antiochus. — 5. Cn., quaestor 212; curule aedile 204; consul 201; and proconsul in Hither Spain 199. — 6. L., praetor in Sardinia 211, succeeded Scipio as proconsul in Spain, where he remained for 11 years, and on his return was only allowed an ovation, because he only held proconsular rank. He was consul 199, and the next year proconsul in Gaul. — 7. L., curule aedile 163; consul 156; censor 147. — 8. P., curule aedile with Scipio Nasica 169, consul suffectus, with C. Domitius 162, the election of the former consuls being declared informal. He became princeps senatus, and must have lived to a good old age, since he was wounded in the contest with C. Gracchus in 121. — 9. P., surnamed Sura, the man of chief note in Catiline's crew. He was quaestor to Sulla in 81: before him and L. Triarius, Verres had to give an account of the monies he had received as quaestor in Cisalpine Gaul. He was soon after himself called to account for the same matter, but was acquitted. It is said that he got his cognomen of Sura from his conduct on this occasion; for when Sulla called him to account, he answered by scornfully putting out his *leg*, "like boys," says Plutarch, "when they make a blunder in playing at ball." Other persons, however, had borne the name before, one perhaps of the Lentulus family. In 75 he was praetor; and Hortensius, pleading before such a judge, had no difficulty in procuring the acquittal of Terentius Varro, when accused of extortion.

In 71 he was consul. But in the next year he was ejected from the senate, with 63 others, for infamous life and manners. It was this, probably, that led him to join Catiline and his crew. From his distinguished birth and high rank, he calculated on becoming chief of the conspiracy; and a prophecy of the Sibylline books was applied by flattering haruspices to him. Three Cornelii were to rule Rome, and he was the 3rd after Sulla and Cinna; the 20th year after the burning of the capitol, &c., was to be fatal to the city. To gain power, and recover his place in the senate, he became praetor again in 63. When Catiline quitted the city for Etruria, Lentulus was left as chief of the home conspirators, and his irresolution probably saved the city from being fired. For it was by his over-caution that the negotiation with the ambassadors of the Allobroges was entered into: these unstable allies revealed the secret to the consul Cicero, who directed them to feign compliance with the conspirators' wishes, and thus to obtain written documents which might be brought in evidence against them. The well-known sequel will be found under the life of Catiline. Lentulus was deposed from the praetorship, and was strangled in the Capitoline prison on the 5th of December. His step-son Antony pretended that Cicero refused to deliver up his corpse for burial. — 10. P., surnamed Spinther. He received this nickname from his resemblance to the actor Spinther. Caesar commonly calls him by this name: not so Cicero; but there could be no harm in it, for he used it on his coins when pro-praetor in Spain, simply to distinguish himself from the many of the same family; and his son bore it after him. He was curule aedile in 63, the year of Cicero's consulship, and was entrusted with the care of the apprehended conspirator, P. Sura [No. 9]. His games were long remembered for their splendour; but his toga, edged with Tyrian purple, gave offence. He was praetor in 60; and by Caesar's interest he obtained Hither Spain for his next year's province, where he remained into part of 58. In 57 he was consul, which dignity he also obtained by Caesar's support. In his consulship he moved for the immediate recall of Cicero, brought over his colleague Metellus Nepos to the same views; and his services were gratefully acknowledged by Cicero. Now, therefore, notwithstanding his obligations to Caesar, he had openly taken part with the aristocracy. He received Cilicia as his province, but he attempted in vain to obtain a decree of the senate, charging him with the office of restoring Ptolemy Auletes, the exiled king of Egypt. He remained as proconsul in Cilicia from 56 till July, 53, and obtained a triumph, though not till 51. On the breaking out of the civil war in 49, he joined the Pompeian party. He fell into Caesar's hands at Corfinium, but was dismissed by the latter uninjured. He then joined Pompey in Greece; and after the battle of Pharsalia, he followed Pompey to Egypt, and got safe to Rhodes. — 11. P., surnamed Spinther, son of No. 10, followed Pompey's fortunes with his father. He was pardoned by Caesar, and returned to Italy. In 45 he was divorced from his abandoned wife, Metella. (Comp. Hor., *Serm.* ii. 3. 239.) After the murder of Caesar (44) he joined the conspirators. He served with Cassius against Rhodes; with Brutus in Lycia. — 12. Cn., surnamed Clodianus, a Claudius adopted into the Lentulus family. He was consul in 72, with L. Gellius Publicola. In the war with Spartacus both he and his colleague were defeated — but after their consulship. With the same colleague he held the censorship in 70, and ejected 63 members from the senate for infamous life, among whom were Lentulus Sura [No. 9] and C. Antonius, afterwards Cicero's colleague in the consulship. Yet the majority of those expelled were acquitted by the courts, and restored; and Lentulus supported the Manilian law, appointing Pompey to the command against Mithridates. As an orator, he concealed his want of talent by great skill and art, and by a good voice. — 13. L., surnamed Crus, appeared in 61 as the chief accuser of P. Clodius, for violating the mysteries of the Bona Dea. In 58 he was praetor, and in 49 consul with C. Marcellus. He was raised to the consulship in consequence of his being a known enemy of Caesar. He did all he could to excite his wavering party to take arms and meet Caesar: he called Cicero cowardly; blamed him for seeking a triumph at such a time; urged war at any price, in the hope, says Caesar (B. C. i. 4), of retrieving his ruined fortunes, and becoming another Sulla. It was mainly at Lentulus' instigation that the violent measures passed the senate early in the year, which gave the tribunes a pretence for flying to Caesar at Ravenna. He himself fled from the city at the approach of Caesar, and afterwards crossed over to Greece. After the battle of Pharsalia, he fled to Egypt, and arrived there the day after Pompey's murder. On landing, he was apprehended by young Ptolemy's ministers, and put to death in prison. — 14. L., surnamed Niger, flamen of Mars. In 57, he was one of the priests to whom was referred the question whether the site of Cicero's house was consecrated ground. In 56 he was one of the judges in the case of P. Sextius, and he died in the same year, much praised by Cicero. — 15. L., son of the last, and also flamen of Mars. He defended M. Scaurus, in 54, when accused of extortion; he accused Gabinius of high treason, about the same time, but was suspected of collusion. In the Philippics he is mentioned as a friend of Antony's. — 16. Cossus, surnamed Gaetulicus, consul B. C. 1, was sent into Africa in A. D. 6, where he defeated the Gaetuli: hence his surname. On the accession of Tiberius, A. D. 14, he accompanied Drusus, who was sent to quell the mutiny of the legions in Pannonia. He died 25, at a very great age, leaving behind him an honourable reputation. — 17. Cn., surnamed Gaetulicus, son of the last, consul A. D. 26. He afterwards had the command of the legions of Upper Germany for 10 years, and was very popular among the troops. In 39 he was put to death by order of Caligula, who feared his influence with the soldiers. He was an historian and a poet; but we have only 3 lines of his poems extant, unless he is the author of 9 epigrams in the Greek Anthology, inscribed with the name of Gaetulicus.

Léo, or Léon (Λέων). 1. Also called Leonides (Λεωνίδης), of Heraclea on the Pontus, disciple of Plato, was one of the conspirators who, with their leader, Chion, assassinated Clearchus, tyrant of Heraclea, B. C. 353. — 2. Of Byzantium, a rhetorician and historical writer of the age of Philip and Alexander the Great. — 3. Diaconus or the Deacon, a Byzantine historian of the 10th century. His history, in 10 books, includes the period from the Cretan expedition of Nicephorus Phocas, in the reign of the emperor Romanus II., A. D. 959, to the death of Joannes I. Zimisces, 975. The style of Leo is vicious: he employs unusual and inappropriate words (many of them borrowed from Homer, Agathias the historian, and the Septuagint), in the place of simple and common ones; and he abounds in tautological phrases. His history, however, is a valuable contemporary record of a stirring time, honestly and fearlessly written. Edited for the first time by Hase, Paris, 1818. — 4. Grammaticus, one of the continuators of Byzantine history from the period when Theophanes leaves off. His work, entitled Chronographia, extends from the accession of Leo V. the Armenian, 813, to the death of Romanus Lecapenus, 944. Edited with Theophanes by Combéfis, Paris, 1655. — 5. Archbishop of Thessalonica, an eminent Byzantine philosopher and ecclesiastic of the 9th century. His works are lost, but he is frequently mentioned in terms of the highest praise by the Byzantine writers; especially for his knowledge of geometry and astronomy. — 6. Magentenus, a commentator on Aristotle, flourished during the 1st half of the 14th century. He was a monk, and afterwards archbishop of Mytilene. Several of his commentaries on Aristotle are extant, and have been published. — 7. Leo was also the name of 6 Byzantine emperors. Of these Leo VI., surnamed the philosopher, who reigned 886—911, is celebrated in the history of the later Greek literature. He wrote a treatise on Greek tactics, 17 oracles, 33 orations, and several other works, which are still extant. He is also celebrated in the history of legislation. As the Latin language had long ceased to be the official language of the Eastern empire, Basil, the father of Leo, had formed and partly executed the plan of issuing an authorised Greek version of Justinian's legislation. This plan was carried out by Leo. The Greek version is known under the title of Βασιλικαὶ Διατάξεις, or shortly, Βασιλικαί; in Latin, Basilica, which means "Imperial Constitutions," or "Laws." It is divided into 60 books, subdivided into titles, and contains the Institutes, the Digest, the Codex, and the Novellae; and likewise such constitutions as were issued by the successors of Justinian down to Leo VI. There are, however, many laws of the Digest omitted in the Basilica, which contain, on the other hand, a considerable number of laws or extracts from ancient jurists which are not in the Digest. The publication of this authorised body of law in the Greek language led to the gradual disuse of the original compilations of Justinian in the East. But the Roman law was thus more firmly established in Eastern Europe and Western Asia, where it has maintained itself among the Greek population to the present day. The best edition of the Basilica is the one now publishing by Heimbach, Lips. 1833, seq.

Leobōtes. [LABOTAS.]

Leochāres (Λεωχάρης), an Athenian statuary and sculptor, was one of the great artists of the later Athenian school, at the head of which were Scopas and Praxiteles. He flourished B. C. 352—338. The masterpiece of Leochares seems to have been his statue of the rape of Ganymede. The original work was in bronze. Of the extant copies in marble, the best is one, half the size of life, in the Museo Pio-Clementino.

Leocŏrĭum (Λεωκόριον), a shrine in Athens, in the Ceramicus, erected in honour of the daughters of Leos. Hipparchus was murdered here.

Leōdămas (Λεωδάμας), a distinguished Attic orator, was educated in the school of Isocrates, and is greatly praised by Aeschines.

Leonīca, a town of the Edetani in the W. of Hispania Tarraconensis.

Leōnĭdas (Λεωνίδας). 1. I. King of Sparta, B. C. 491—480, was one of the sons of Anaxandrides by his first wife, and, according to some accounts, was twin-brother to Cleombrotus. He succeeded his half-brother Cleomenes I., B. C. 491, his elder brother Dorieus also having previously died. When Greece was invaded by Xerxes, 480, Leonidas was sent with a small army to make a stand against the enemy at the pass of Thermopylae. The number of his army is variously stated: according to Herodotus, it amounted to somewhat more than 5000 men, of whom 300 were Spartans; in all probability, the regular band of (so called) knights (ἱππεῖς). The Persians in vain attempted to force their way through the pass of Thermopylae. They were driven back by Leonidas and his gallant band with immense slaughter. At length the Malian Ephialtes betrayed the mountain path of the Anopaea to the Persians, who were thus able to fall upon the rear of the Greeks. When it became known to Leonidas that the Persians were crossing the mountain, he dismissed all the other Greeks, except the Thespian and Theban forces, declaring that he and the Spartans under his command must needs remain in the post they had been sent to guard. Then, before the body of Persians, who were crossing the mountain under Hydarnes, could arrive to attack him in the rear, he advanced from the narrow pass and charged the myriads of the enemy with his handful of troops, hopeless now of preserving their lives, and anxious only to sell them dearly. In the desperate battle which ensued, Leonidas himself fell soon. His body was rescued by the Greeks, after a violent struggle. On the hillock in the pass, where the remnant of the Greeks made their last stand, a lion of stone was set up in his honour.—2. II. King of Sparta, was son of the traitor, Cleonymus. He acted as guardian to his infant relative, Areus II., on whose death he ascended the throne, about 256. Being opposed to the projected reforms of his contemporary Agis IV., he was deposed, and the throne was transferred to his son-in-law, Cleombrotus; but he was soon afterwards recalled, and caused Agis to be put to death, 240. He died about 236, and was succeeded by his son, Cleomenes III.—3. A kinsman of Olympias, the mother of Alexander the Great, was entrusted with the main superintendence of Alexander's education in his earlier years, before he became the pupil of Aristotle. Leonidas was a man of austere character, and trained the young prince in hardy and self-denying habits. There were 2 excellent cooks (said Alexander afterwards) with which Leonidas had furnished him,—a night's march to season his breakfast, and a scanty breakfast to season his dinner.—4. Of Tarentum, the author of upwards of 100 epigrams in the Doric dialect. His epigrams formed a part of the Garland of Meleager. They are chiefly inscriptions for dedicatory offerings and works of art, and, though not of a very high order of poetry, are usually

pleasing, ingenious, and in good taste. Leonidas probably lived in the time of Pyrrhus.—5. Of Alexandria, also an epigrammatic poet, flourished under Nero and Vespasian. In the Greek Anthology, 43 epigrams are ascribed to him: they are of a very low order of merit.

Leonnātus (Λεοννάτος), a Macedonian of Pella, one of Alexander's most distinguished officers. His father's name is variously given, as Anteas, Anthes, Onasus, and Eunus. He saved Alexander's life in India in the assault on the city of the Malli. After the death of Alexander (B. C. 323), he obtained the satrapy of the Lesser or Hellespontine Phrygia, and in the following year he crossed over into Europe, to assist Antipater against the Greeks; but he was defeated by the Athenians and their allies, and fell in battle.

Leontĭădes (Λεοντιάδης). 1. A Theban, commanded at Thermopylae the forces supplied by Thebes to the Grecian army, B. C. 480.—2. A Theban, assisted the Spartans in seizing the Cadmea, or citadel of Thebes, in 382. He was slain by Pelopidas in 379, when the Spartan exiles recovered possession of the Cadmea.

Leontīni (οἱ Λεοντῖνοι: Λεοντῖνος: Lentini), a town in the E. of Sicily, about 5 miles from the sea, N. W. of Syracuse, was situated upon the small river Lissus. It was built upon 2 hills, which were separated from one another by a valley, in which were the forum, the senate-house, and the other public buildings, while the temples and the private houses occupied the hills. The rich plains N. of the city, called Leontini Campi, were some of the most fertile in Sicily, and produced abundant crops of most excellent wheat. Leontini was founded by Chalcidians from Naxos, B. C. 730, only 6 years after the foundation of Naxos itself. It never attained much political importance in consequence of its proximity to Syracuse, to which it soon became subject, and whose fortunes it shared. At a later time it joined the Carthaginians, and was in consequence taken and plundered by the Romans. Under the Romans it sunk into insignificance. Gorgias was a native of Leontini.

Leontĭum (Λεόντιον), an Athenian hetaera, the disciple and mistress of Epicurus, wrote a treatise against Theophrastus. She had a daughter, Danë, who was also an hetaera of some notoriety.

Leontĭum (Λεόντιον), a town in Achaia, between Pharae and Aegium.

Leontŏpŏlis (Λεοντόπολις, Λεόντων πόλις). 1. A city in the Delta of Egypt, S. of Thmuïs, and N. W. of Athribis, was the capital of the Nomos Leontopolites, and probably of late foundation, as no writer before Strabo mentions it. Its site is uncertain.—2. [Nicephorium.]

Leoprepĭdes, i. e. Simonides, the son of Leoprepes.

Leos (Λεώς), one of the heroes eponymi of the Athenians, said to have been a son of Orpheus. The phyle or tribe of Leontis derived its name from him. Once, when Athens was suffering from famine or plague, the Delphic oracle demanded that the daughters of Leos should be sacrificed, and the father complied with the command of the oracle. The maidens were afterwards honoured by the Athenians, who erected the Leocorium (from Λεώς and κόραι) to them. Their names were Praxithea, Theope, and Eubule.

Leosthĕnes (Λεωσθένης), an Athenian commander of the combined Greek army in the Lamian war. In the year after the death of Alexander (B. c. 323), he defeated Antipater near Thermopylae ; Antipater thereupon threw himself into the small town of Lamia. Leosthenes pressed the siege with the utmost vigour, but was killed by a blow from a stone. His loss was mourned by the Athenians as a public calamity. He was honoured with a public burial in the Ceramicus, and his funeral oration was pronounced by Hyperides.

Leotychides (Λεωτυχίδης, Λευτυχίδης, Herod.). 1. King of Sparta, B. c. 491—469. He commanded the Greek fleet in 479, and defeated the Persians at the battle of Mycale. He was afterwards sent with an army into Thessaly to punish those who had sided with the Persians ; but in consequence of his accepting the bribes of the Aleuadae, he was brought to trial on his return home, and went into exile to Tegea, 469, where he died. He was succeeded by his grandson, Archidamus II.—2. Grandson of Archidamus II., and son of Agis II. There was, however, some suspicion that he was in reality the fruit of an intrigue of Alcibiades with Timaea, the queen of Agis ; in consequence of which he was excluded from the throne, mainly through the influence of Lysander, and his uncle, Agesilaus II., was substituted in his room.

Lepidus Aemilius, a distinguished patrician family. 1. M., aedile B. c. 192 ; praetor 191, with Sicily as his province ; consul 187, when he defeated the Ligurians ; pontifex maximus 180 ; censor 179 with M. Fulvius Nobilior ; and consul a second time 175. He was six times chosen by the censors princeps senatus, and he died 152, full of years and honours. Lepidus the triumvir is called by Cicero (Phil. xiii. 7) the pronepos of this Lepidus ; but he would seem more probably to have been his abnepos, or great-great-grandson.— 2. M., consul 137, carried on war in Spain against the Vaccaei, but unsuccessfully. Since he had attacked the Vaccaei in opposition to the express orders of the senate, he was deprived of his command, and condemned to pay a fine. He was a man of education and refined taste. Cicero, who had read his speeches, speaks of him as the greatest orator of his age. He helped to form the style of Tib. Gracchus and C. Carbo, who were accustomed to listen to him with great care.—3. M., the father of the triumvir, was praetor in Sicily in 81, where he earned a character by his oppressions only second to that of Verres. In the civil wars between Marius and Sulla he belonged at first to the party of the latter, but he afterwards came forward as a leader of the popular party. In his consulship, 78, he attempted to rescind the laws of Sulla, who had lately died, but he was opposed by his colleague Catulus, who received the powerful support of Pompey. In the following year (77) Lepidus took up arms, and marched against Rome. He was defeated by Pompey and Catulus, under the walls of the city, in the Campus Martius, and was obliged to take to flight. Finding it impossible to hold his ground in Italy, Lepidus sailed with the remainder of his forces to Sardinia ; but repulsed even in this island by the propraetor, he died shortly afterwards of chagrin and sorrow, which is said to have been increased by the discovery of his wife's infidelity.—4. Mam., surnamed Livianus, because he belonged originally to the Livia gens, consul 77, belonged to the aristocratical party, and was one of the influential persons who prevailed upon Sulla to spare the life of the

young Julius Caesar.—5. M., consul 66, with L. Volcatius Tullus, the same year in which Cicero was praetor. He belonged to the aristocratical party, but on the breaking out of the civil war in 49, he retired to his Formian villa to watch the progress of events.—6. L. Aemilius Paulus, son of No. 3, and brother of M. Lepidus, the triumvir. His surname of Paulus was probably given him by his father, in honour of the celebrated Aemilius Paulus, the conqueror of Macedonia. But since he belonged to the family of the Lepidi, and not to that of the Pauli, he is inserted in this place and not under Paulus. Aemilius Paulus did not follow the example of his father, but commenced his public career by supporting the aristocratical party. His first public act was the accusation of Catiline in 63. He was quaestor in Macedonia 59 ; aedile 55 ; praetor 53 ; and consul 50, along with M. Claudius Marcellus. Paulus was raised to the consulship, on account of his being one of the most determined enemies of Caesar, but Caesar gained him over to his side by a bribe of 1500 talents, which he is said to have expended on the completion of a magnificent basilica which he had commenced in his aedileship. After the murder of Caesar (44), Paulus joined the senatorial party. He was one of the senators who declared M. Lepidus a public enemy, on account of his having joined Antony ; and, accordingly, when the triumvirate was formed, his name was set down first in the proscription list by his own brother. The soldiers, however, who were appointed to kill him, allowed him to escape. He passed over to Brutus in Asia, and after the death of the latter repaired to Miletus. Here he remained, and refused to go to Rome, although he was pardoned by the triumvirs. —7. M. Aemilius Lepidus, the Triumvir, brother of the last. On the breaking out of the civil war (49), Lepidus, who was then praetor, joined Caesar's party ; and as the consuls had fled with Pompey from Italy, Lepidus, as praetor, was the highest magistrate remaining in Italy. During Caesar's absence in Spain, Lepidus presided at the comitia in which the former was appointed dictator. In the following year (48) he received the province of Nearer Spain. On his return to Rome in 47, Caesar granted him a triumph, and made him his magister equitum ; and in the next year (46), his colleague in the consulship. In 44 he received from Caesar the government of Narbonese Gaul and Nearer Spain, but had not quitted the neighbourhood of Rome at the time of the dictator's death. Having the command of an army near the city, he was able to render M. Antony efficient assistance ; and the latter in consequence allowed Lepidus to be chosen pontifex maximus, which dignity had become vacant by Caesar's death. Lepidus soon afterwards repaired to his provinces of Gaul and Spain. He remained neutral in the struggle between Antony and the senate ; but he subsequently joined Antony, when the latter fled to him in Gaul after his defeat at Mutina. This was in the end of May, 43 ; and when the news reached Rome, the senate proclaimed Lepidus a public enemy. In the autumn Lepidus and Antony crossed the Alps at the head of a powerful army. Octavian (afterwards Augustus) joined them ; and in the month of October the celebrated triumvirate was formed, by which the Roman world was divided between Octavian, Antony, and Lepidus. [See p. 108, a.] In 42 Lepidus remained in Italy as consul, while the two other triumvirs prosecuted the war against Brutus and Cassius. In the fresh division of the provinces after the battle of Philippi, Lepidus received Africa, where he remained till 36. In this year Octavian summoned him to Sicily to assist him in the war against Sex. Pompey. Lepidus obeyed, but tired of being treated as a subordinate, he resolved to make an effort to acquire Sicily for himself and to regain his lost power. He was easily subdued by Octavian, who spared his life, but deprived him of his triumvirate, his army, and his provinces, and commanded that he should live at Circeii, under strict surveillance. He allowed him, however, to retain his dignity of pontifex maximus. He died B. C. 13. Augustus succeeded him as pontifex maximus. Lepidus was fond of ease and repose, and it is not improbable that he possessed abilities capable of effecting much more than he ever did. — **8. Paulus Aemilius Lepidus,** son of No. 6, with whom he is frequently confounded. His name is variously given by the ancient writers *Aemilius Paulus,* or *Paulus Aemilius,* or *Aemilius Lepidus Paulus,* but *Paulus Aemilius Lepidus* seems to be the most correct form. He probably fled with his father to Brutus, but he afterwards made his peace with the triumvirs. He accompanied Octavian in his campaign against Sex. Pompey in Sicily in 36. In 34 he was consul suffectus. In 22 he was censor with L. Munatius Plancus, and died while holding this dignity. — **9. M. Aemilius Lepidus,** son of the triumvir [No. 7] and Junia, formed a conspiracy in 30, for the purpose of assassinating Octavian on his return to Rome after the battle of Actium. Maecenas, who had charge of the city, became acquainted with the plot, seized Lepidus, and sent him to Octavian in the East, who put him to death. His father was ignorant of the conspiracy, but his mother was privy to it. Lepidus was married twice : his first wife was Antonia, the daughter of the triumvir, and his 2nd Servilia, who put an end to her life by swallowing burning coals when the conspiracy of her husband was discovered. — 10. **Q. Aemilius Lepidus,** consul 21 with M. Lollius. (Hor. *Ep.* i. 20. 28.) — 11. **L. Aemilius Paulus,** son of No. 8 and Cornelia, married Julia, the granddaughter of Augustus. [JULIA, No. 6.] Paulus is therefore called the *progener* of Augustus. He was consul A. D. 1 with C. Caesar, his wife's brother. He entered into a conspiracy against Augustus, of the particulars of which we are not informed. — **12. M. Aemilius Lepidus,** brother of the last, consul A. D. 6 with L. Arruntius. He lived on the most intimate terms with Augustus, who employed him in the war against the Dalmatians in A. D. 9. After the death of Augustus, he was also held in high esteem by Tiberius. — **13. M. Aemilius Lepidus,** consul with T. Statilius Taurus in A. D. 11, must be carefully distinguished from the last. In A. D. 21 he obtained the province of Asia. — **14. Aemilius Lepidus,** the son of 11 and Julia, the granddaughter of Augustus, and consequently the great-grandson of Augustus. He was one of the minions of the emperor Caligula, with whom he had the most shameful connection. He married Drusilla, the favourite sister of the emperor ; but he was notwithstanding put to death by Caligula, A. D. 39.

Lepontii, a people inhabiting the Alps, in whose country Caesar places the sources of the Rhine, and Pliny the sources of the Rhone. They dwelt on the S. slope of the St. Gotthard and the Simplon, towards the Lago Maggiore, and their name is still retained in the *Val Leventina.* Their chief town was Oscela (*Domo d'Ossola*).

Leprea (Λέπρεα), daughter of Pyrgeus, from whom the town of Lepreum in Elis was said to have derived its name. [LEPREUM.] Another tradition derived the name from Lepreus, a son of Caucon, Glaucon, or Pyrgeus, by Astydamia. He was a grandson of Poseidon, and a rival of Hercules both in his strength and his powers of eating, but he was conquered and slain by the latter. His tomb was believed to exist at Phigalia.

Lepreum (Λέπρεον, Λέπρεος : Λεπρεάτης : *Strovitzi*), a town of Elis in Triphylia, situated 40 stadia from the sea, was said to have been founded in the time of Theseus by Minyans from Lemnos. After the Messenian wars it was subdued by the Eleans with the aid of Sparta ; but it recovered its independence in the Peloponnesian war, and was assisted by the Spartans against Elis. At the time of the Achaean league it was subject to Elis.

Q. Lepta, a native of Cales in Campania, and praefectus fabrûm to Cicero in Cilicia B.C. 51. He joined the Pompeian party in the civil war, and is frequently mentioned in Cicero's letters.

Leptines (Λεπτίνης). 1. A Syracusan, son of Hermocrates, and brother of Dionysius the elder, tyrant of Syracuse. He commanded his brother's fleet in the war against the Carthaginians B.C. 397, but was defeated by Mago with great loss. In 390 he was sent by Dionysius with a fleet to the assistance of the Lucanians against the Italian Greeks. Some time afterwards he gave offence to the jealous temper of the tyrant, by giving one of his daughters in marriage to Philistus, without any previous intimation to Dionysius, and on this account he was banished from Syracuse, together with Philistus. He thereupon retired to Thurii, but was subsequently recalled by Dionysius to Syracuse. Here he was completely reinstated in his former favour, and obtained one of the daughters of Dionysius in marriage. In 383, he again took an active part in the war against the Carthaginians, and commanded the right wing of the Syracusan army in the battle near Cronium ; in which he was killed. — **2.** A Syracusan, who joined with Calippus in expelling the garrison of the younger Dionysius from Rhegium, 351. Soon afterwards he assassinated Calippus, and then crossed over to Sicily, where he made himself tyrant of Apollonia and Engyum. He was expelled in common with the other tyrants by Timoleon ; but his life was spared and he was sent into exile at Corinth, 342. — **3.** An Athenian, known only as the proposer of a law taking away all special exemptions from the burden of public charges (ἀτέλειαι τῶν λειτουργιῶν), against which the celebrated oration of Demosthenes is directed, usually known as the oration against Leptines. This speech was delivered 355 : and the law must have been passed above a year before, as we are told that the lapse of more than that period had already exempted Leptines from all personal responsibility. Hence the efforts of Demosthenes were directed solely to the repeal of the law, not to the punishment of its proposer. His arguments were successful, and the law was repealed. — **4.** A Syrian Greek, who assassinated with his own hand at Laodicea, Cn. Octavius, the chief of the Roman deputies, who had been sent into Syria, 162. Demetrius caused Leptines to be seized, and sent as a prisoner to Rome; but the senate refused to receive him, being desirous to reserve this cause of complaint as a public grievance.

Leptis (Λεπτίς). 1. **Leptis Magna** or **Neapolis** (ἡ Λεπτὶς μεγάλη, Νεάπολις), a city on the coast of N. Africa, between the Syrtes, E. of Abrotonum, and W. of the mouth of the little river Cinyps, was a Phoenician colony, with a flourishing commerce, though it possessed no harbour. With Abrotonum and Oea it formed the African Tripolis. The Romans made it a colony: it was the birthplace of the emperor Septimius Severus: and it continued to flourish till A. D. 366, when it was almost ruined by an attack from a Libyan tribe. Justinian did something towards its restoration; but the Arabian invasion completed its destruction. Its ruins are still considerable. — 2. **Leptis Minor** or **Parva** (Λεπτὶς ἡ μικρὰ : *Lamta*, Ru.), usually called simply Leptis, a Phoenician colony on the coast of Byzacium, in N. Africa, between Hadrumetum and Thapsus: an important place under both the Carthaginians and the Romans.

Lerina (*St. Honorat*), an island off the coast of Gallia Narbonensis, opposite Antipolis (*Antibes*).

Lerna or **Lernê** (Λέρνη), a district in Argolis, not far from Argos, in which was a marsh and a small river of the same name. It was celebrated as the place where Hercules killed the Lernean Hydra. [See p. 308, b.]

Lero (*St. Marguerite*), a small island off the coast of Gallia Narbonensis.

Leros (Λέρος : Λέριος), a small island, one of the Sporades, opposite to the mouth of the Sinus Iassius, on the coast of Caria. Its inhabitants, who came originally from Miletus, bore a bad character. Besides a city of the same name, it had in it a temple of Artemis, where the transformation of the sisters of Meleager into guinea-fowls was said to have taken place, in memory of which guinea-fowls were kept in the court of that temple.

Lesbonax (Λεσβῶναξ). 1. Son of Potamon of Mytilene, a philosopher and sophist, in the time of Augustus. He was the father of Polemon, the teacher and friend of the emperor Tiberius. Lesbonax wrote several political orations, of which 2 have come down to us, one entitled περὶ τοῦ πολέμου Κορινθίων, and the other προτρεπτικὸς λόγος, both of which are not unsuccessful imitations of the Attic orators of the best times. They are printed in the collections of the Greek orators [DEMOSTHENES], and separately by Orelli, Lips. 1820. — 2. A Greek grammarian, of uncertain age, but later than No. 1, the author of an extant work on grammatical figures (περὶ σχημάτων), published by Valckenaer in his edition of Ammonius.

Lesbos (Λέσβος : Λέσβιος, Lesbius : *Mytilene*, *Metelin*), the largest, and by far the most important, of the islands of the Aegean along the coast of Asia Minor, lay opposite to the Gulf of Adramyttium, off the coast of Mysia, the direction of its length being N. W. and S. E. It is intersected by lofty mountains, and indented with large bays, the chief of which, on the W. side, runs more than half way across the island. It had 3 chief headlands, Argennum on the N. E., Sigrium on the W., and Malea on the S. Its vallies were very fertile, especially in the N. part, near Methymna; and it produced corn, oil, and wine renowned for its excellence. In early times it was called by various names, the chief of which were, Issa, Pelasgia, Mytania, and Macaria: the late Greek writers called it Mytilene, from its chief city, and this name has been preserved to modern times. The earliest reputed inhabitants were Pelasgians; the next, an Ionian colony, who were said to have settled in it 2 generations before the Trojan War; lastly, at the time of the great Aeolic migration ´130 years after the Trojan War, according to the mythical chronology), the island was colonised by Aeolians, who founded in it an Hexapolis, consisting of the 6 cities, Mytilene, Methymna, Eresus, Pyrrha, Antissa, and Arisbe, afterwards reduced to 5 through the destruction of Arisbe by the Methymnaeans. The Aeolians of Lesbos afterwards founded numerous settlements along the coast of the Troad and in the region of Mt. Ida, and at one time a great part of the Troad seems to have been subject to Lesbos. The chief facts in the history of the island are connected with its principal city, Mytilene, which was the scene of the struggles between the nobles and the commons, in which ALCAEUS and PITTACUS took part. At the time of the Peloponnesian War, Lesbos was subject to Athens. After various changes, it fell under the power of Mithridates, and passed from him to the Romans. The island is most important in the early history of Greece, as the native region of the Aeolian school of lyric poetry. It was the birthplace of the musician and poet TERPANDER, of the lyric poets ALCAEUS, SAPPHO, and others, and of the dithyrambic poet ARION. Other forms of literature and philosophy early and long flourished in it: the sage and statesman PITTACUS, the historians HELLANICUS and Theophanes, and the philosophers Theophrastus and Phanias, were all Lesbians.

Lesbothemis (Λεσβόθεμις), a statuary of ancient date, and a native of Lesbos.

Lesches or **Lescheus** (Λέσχης, Λέσχευς), one of the so-called cyclic poets, son of Aeschylinus, a native of Pyrrha, in the neighbourhood of Mytilene, and hence called a Mytilenean or a Lesbian. He flourished about B. C. 708, and was usually regarded as the author of the *Little Iliad* (Ἰλιὰς ἡ ἐλάσσων or Ἰλιὰς μικρά), though this poem was also ascribed to various other poets. It consisted of 4 books, and was intended as a supplement to the Homeric Iliad. It related the events after the death of Hector, the fate of Ajax, the exploits of Philoctetes, Neoptolemus, and Ulysses, and the final capture and destruction of Troy, which part of the poem was called The Destruction of Troy (Ἰλίου πέρσις). There was no unity in the poem, except that of historical and chronological succession. Hence Aristotle remarks that the little Iliad furnished materials for 8 tragedies, whilst only one could be based upon the Iliad or Odyssey of Homer.

Lethaeus (Ληθαῖος). 1. A river of Ionia, in Asia Minor, flowing S. past Magnesia into the Maeander. — 2. A river in the S. of Crete, flowing past Gortyna. — 3. [LATHON.]

Lethe (Λήθη), the personification of oblivion, called by Hesiod a daughter of Eris. A river in the lower world was likewise called Lethe. The souls of the departed drank of this river, and thus forgot all they had said or done in the upper world.

Lethes, a river in Spain. See LIMAEA.

Leto (Λητώ), called **Latona** by the Romans, is described by Hesiod as a daughter of the Titan Coeus and Phoebe, a sister of Asteria, and the mother of Apollo and Artemis by Zeus, to whom she was married before Hera. Homer likewise calls her the mother of Apollo and Artemis by Zeus; he mentions her in the story of Niobe, who paid so dearly for her conduct towards Leto [NIOBE], and he also describes her as the friend of the Trojans in the war with the Greeks. In later writers these elements of her story are variously embellished, for they do not describe her as the lawful wife of Zeus, but merely as his mistress, who was persecuted by Hera during her pregnancy. All the world being afraid of receiving Leto on account of Hera, she wandered about till she came to Delos, which was then a floating island, and bore the name of Asteria or Ortygia. When Leto arrived there, Zeus fastened it by adamantine chains to the bottom of the sea, that it might be a secure resting-place for his beloved, and here she gave birth to Apollo and Artemis. The tradition is also related with various other modifications. Some said that Zeus changed Leto into a quail (ὄρτυξ), and that in this state she arrived in the floating island, which was hence called Ortygia. Others related that Zeus was enamoured with Asteria, but that she being metamorphosed into a bird, flew across the sea; that she was then changed into a rock, which for a long time, lay under the surface of the sea; and that this rock arose from the waters and received Leto when she was pursued by Python. Leto was generally worshipped only in conjunction with her children. Delos was the chief seat of her worship. [APOLLO.]—It is probable that the name of Leto belongs to the same class of words as the Greek λήθη and the Latin *lateo*. Leto would therefore signify "the obscure" or "concealed," not as a physical power, but as a divinity yet quiescent and invisible, from whom issued the visible divinity with all his splendour and brilliancy. This view is supported by the account of her genealogy given by Hesiod.—From their mother Apollo is frequently *Letoïus* or *Latoïus*, and Artemis (Diana) *Letoïa, Letoïs, Latoïa,* or *Latoë.*

Leuca (τὰ Λευκά), a town at the extremity of the Iapygian promontory in Calabria, with a stinking fountain, under which the giants who were vanquished by Hercules are said to have been buried. The promontory is still called *Copo di Leuca.*

Leucae, Leuca (Λεῦκαι, Λεύκη : *Lefke*), a small town on the coast of Ionia, in Asia Minor, near Phocaea, built by the Persian general Tachos in B. C. 352, and remarkable as the scene of the battle between the consul Licinius Crassus and Aristonicus, in 131.

Leucas or **Leucadia** (Λευκάς, Λευκαδία : Λευκάδιος: *Santa Maura*), an island in the Ionian sea, off the W. coast of Acarnania, about 20 miles in length, and from 5 to 8 miles in breadth. It has derived its name from the numerous calcareous hills which cover its surface. It was originally united to the mainland at its N.E. extremity by a narrow isthmus. Homer speaks of it as a peninsula, and mentions its well fortified town *Nericus* (Νήρικος). It was at that time inhabited by the Teleboans and Leleges. Subsequently the Corinthians under Cypselus, between B. c. 665 and 625, founded a new town, called *Leucas* in the N. E. of the country near the isthmus, in which they settled 1000 of their citizens, and to which they removed the inhabitants of Nericus, which lay a little to the W. of the new town. The Corinthians also cut a

canal through the isthmus and thus converted the peninsula into an island. This canal was afterwards filled up by deposits of sand; and in the Peloponnesian war it was no longer available for ships, which during that period were conveyed across the isthmus on more than one occasion (Thuc. iii. 81, iv. 8). The canal was opened again by the Romans. At present the channel is dry in some parts, and has from 3 to 4 feet of water in others. The town of Leucas was a place of importance, and during the war between Philip and the Romans was at the head of the Acarnanian league, and the place where the meetings of the league were held. It was in consequence taken and plundered by the Romans, B.C. 197. The remains of this town are still to be seen. The other towns in the island were *Hellomĕnum* (Ἑλλόμενον) on the S. E. coast, and *Phara* (Φαρά), on the S.W. coast.—At the S. extremity of the island, opposite Cephallenia, was the celebrated promontory, variously called *Leucae, Leucătas, Leucătes,* or *Leucăte* (*C. Ducato*), on which was a temple of Apollo, who hence had the surname of Leucadius. At the annual festival of the god it was the custom to cast down a criminal from this promontory into the sea: to break his fall birds of all kinds were attached to him, and if he reached the sea uninjured, boats were ready to pick him up. This appears to have been an expiatory rite; and it gave rise to the well known story that lovers leaped from this rock, in order to seek relief from the pangs of love. Thus Sappho is said to have leapt down from this rock, when in love with Phaon; but this well known story vanishes at the first approach of criticism.

Lenos (Λευκή), an island in the Euxine sea, near the mouth of the Borysthenes, sacred to Achilles. [ACHILLEUS DROMOS.]

Leuci, a people in the S. E. of Gallia Belgica, S. of the Mediomatrici, between the Matrona and Mosella. Their chief town was Tullum (*Toul*).

Leuci Montes, called by the Romans Albi Montes, a range of mountains in the W. of Crete. [ALBI MONTES.]

Leucippe. [ALCATHOE.]

Leucippĭdes (Λευκιππίδες), i. e. *Phoebe* and *Hilaïra,* the daughters of Leucippus. They were priestesses of Athena and Artemis, and betrothed to Idas and Lynceus, the sons of Aphareus; but Castor and Pollux being charmed with their beauty carried them off and married them.

Leucippus (Λεύκιππος). 1. Son of Oenomaus. For details see DAPHNE.—2. Son of Perieres and Gorgophone, brother of Aphareus, and prince of the Messenians, was one of the Calydonian hunters. By his wife Philodice, he had 2 daughters, Phoebe and Hilaira, usually called LEUCIPPIDES.—3. A Grecian philosopher, the founder of the atomic theory of the ancient philosophy, which was more fully developed by Democritus. Where and when he was born we have no data for deciding. Miletus, Abdera, and Elis have been assigned as his birth-place; the 1st, apparently, for no other reason than that it was the birth-place of several natural philosophers; the 2nd, because Democritus came from that town; the 3rd, because he was looked upon as a disciple of the Eleatic school. The period when he lived is equally uncertain. He is called the teacher of Democritus the disciple of Parmenides, or, according to other accounts, of Zeno, of Melissus, nay even of Pythagoras. With regard to his philosophical system it is impossible to speak with certainty, since the writers who mention him, either mention him in conjunction with Democritus, or attribute to him doctrines which are in like manner attributed to Democritus. [DEMOCRITUS.]

Leucon (Λεύκων). 1. Son of Poseidon or Athamas and Themisto, and father of Erythrus and Evippe. — 2. A powerful king of Bosporus, who reigned B. C. 393—353. He was in close alliance with the Athenians, whom he supplied with corn in great abundance, and who, in return for his services, admitted him and his sons to the citizenship of Athens. — 3. An Athenian poet, of the old comedy, a contemporary and rival of Aristophanes.

Leuconium (Λευκώνιον), a place in the island of Chios. (Thuc. viii. 24.)

Leuconoë (Λευκονόη), daughter of Minyas, usually called Leucippe. [ALCATHOE.]

Leucopetra (Λευκόπετρα: C. dell' Armi), a promontory in the S.W. of Bruttium, on the Sicilian straits, and a few miles S. of Rhegium, to whose territory it belonged. It was regarded by the ancient writers as the termination of the Apennines, and it derived its name from the white colour of its rocks.

Leucophrys (Λευκόφρυς). 1. A city of Caria, in the plain of the Maeander, close to a curious lake of warm water, and having a renowned temple of Artemis Leucophryne. — 2. A name given to the island of TENEDOS, from its white cliffs.

Leucophryne. [LEUCOPHRYS.]

Leucosia or Leucasia (Piana), a small island in the S. of the gulf of Paestum, off the coast of Lucania, and opposite the promontory Posidium, said to have been called after one of the Sirens.

Leucosyri (Λευκόσυροι, i. e. White Syrians), was a name early applied by the Greeks to the inhabitants of Cappadocia, who were of the Syrian race, in contradistinction to the Syrian tribes of a darker colour beyond the Taurus. Afterwards, when Cappadoces came to be the common name for the people of S. Cappadocia, the word Leucosyri was applied specifically to the people in the N. of the country (aft. Pontus) on the coast of the Euxine, between the rivers Halys and Iris: these are the White Syrians of Xenophon (Anab. v. 6). After the Macedonian conquest, the name appears to have fallen into disuse.

Leucothea (Λευκοθέα), a marine goddess, was previously Ino, the wife of Athamas. For details see ATHAMAS.

Leucothoë (Λευκοθόη), daughter of the Babylonian king Orchamus and Eurynome, was beloved by Apollo. Her amour was betrayed by the jealous Clytia to her father, who buried her alive; whereupon Apollo metamorphosed her into an incense shrub. — Leucothoe is in some writers only another form for Leucothea.

Leuctra (τὰ Λεῦκτρα: Lefka or Leftra), a small town in Boeotia, on the road from Plataeae to Thespiae, memorable for the victory which Epaminondas and the Thebans here gained over Cleombrotus and the Spartans, B. C. 371.

Leuctrum (Λεῦκτρον). 1. Or Leuctra (Leftro), a town in Messenia, on the E. side of the Messenian gulf, between Cardamyle and Thalama, on the small river Pamisus. The Spartans and Messenians disputed for the possession of it. — 2. A small town in Achaia, dependent on Rhypae.

Lexovii or Lexobii, a people in Gallia Lugdunensis, on the Ocean, W. of the mouth of the Sequana. Their capital was Noviomagus. (Lisieux).

Liba (ἡ Λίβα), a city of Mesopotamia, between Nisibis and the Tigris.

Libanius (Λιβάνιος), a distinguished Greek sophist and rhetorician, was born at Antioch, on the Orontes, about A. D. 314. He studied at Athens, where he imbibed an ardent love for the great classical writers of Greece; and he afterwards set up a private school of rhetoric at Constantinople, which was attended by so large a number of pupils, that the classes of the public professors were completely deserted. The latter, in revenge, charged Libanius with being a magician, and obtained his expulsion from Constantinople about 346. He then went to Nicomedia, where he taught with equal success, but also drew upon himself an equal degree of malice from his opponents. After a stay of five years at Nicomedia, he was recalled to Constantinople. Eventually he took up his abode at Antioch, where he spent the remainder of his life. Here he received the greatest marks of favour from the emperor Julian, 362. In the reign of Valens, he was at first persecuted, but he afterwards succeeded in winning the favour of that monarch also. The emperor Theodosius likewise showed him marks of respect, but his enjoyment of life was disturbed by ill health, by misfortunes in his family, and more especially by the disputes in which he was incessantly involved, partly with rival sophists, and partly with the prefects. It cannot, however, be denied, that he himself was as much to blame as his opponents, for he appears to have provoked them by his querulous disposition, and by the pride and vanity which everywhere appear in his orations, and which led him to interfere in political questions which it would have been wiser to have left alone. He was the teacher of St. Basil and Chrysostom, with whom he always kept up a friendly connexion. The year of his death is uncertain, but from one of his epistles it is evident that he was alive in 391, and it is probable that he died a few years after, in the reign of Arcadius. The extant works of Libanius are: 1. Models for rhetorical exercises (Προγυμνασμάτων παραδείγματα). 2. Orations (Λόγοι), 67 in number. 3. Declamations (Μελέται), i. e. orations on fictitious subjects, and descriptions of various kinds, 50 in number. 4. A life of Demosthenes, and arguments to the speeches of the same orator. 5. Letters (Ἐπιστολαί), of which a very large number is still extant. Many of these letters are extremely interesting, being addressed to the most eminent men of his time, such as the emperor Julian, Athanasius, Basil, Gregory of Nyssa, Chrysostom, and others. The style of Libanius is superior to that of the other rhetoricians of the 4th century. He took the best orators of the classic age as his models, and we can often see in him the disciple and happy imitator of Demosthenes; but he is not always able to rise above the spirit of his age, and we rarely find in him that natural simplicity which constitutes the great charm of the best Attic orators. His diction is a curious mixture of the pure old Attic with what may be termed modern. Moreover it is evident that, like all other rhetoricians, he is more concerned about the form than the substance. As far as the history of his age is concerned, some of his orations, and still more his epistles are of great value, such as the oration in which he relates the events of his own life, the eulogies on Constantius and Constans, the orations on Julian, several orations describing the condition of Antioch, and those which he wrote against his professional and political opponents. There is no complete edition of all the works of Libanius. The best edition of the orations and declamations is by Reiske, Altenburg, 1791—97, 4 vols. 8vo., and the best edition of the epistles is by Wolf, Amsterdam, 1738, fol.

Libanus (ὁ Λίβανος, τὸ Λίβανον: Heb. Lebanon, i. e. *the White Mountain: Jebel Libnan*), a lofty and steep mountain range on the confines of Syria and Palestine, dividing Phoenice from Coele-Syria. It extends from above Sidon, about lat. 33½° N., in a direction N.N.E. as far as about lat. 34¼°. Its highest summits are covered with perpetual snow, its sides were in ancient times clothed with forests of cedars, of which only scattered trees now remain, and on its lower slopes grow vines, figs, mulberries, and other fruits: its wines were highly celebrated in ancient times. It is considerably lower than the opposite range of ANTILIBANUS. In the Scriptures the word Lebanon is used for both ranges, and for either of them; but in classical authors the names Libanus and Antilibanus are distinctive terms, being applied to the W. and E. ranges respectively.

Libarna or **Libarnum**, a town of Liguria on the Via Aurelia, N.W. of Genua.

Libentina, Lubentina, or **Lubentia**, a surname of Venus among the Romans, by which she is described as the goddess of sexual pleasure (*dea libidinis*).

Liber, or **Liber Pater**, a name frequently given by the Roman poets to the Greek Bacchus or Dionysus, who was accordingly regarded as identical with the Italian Liber. But the god Liber, and the goddess Libera were ancient Italian divinities, presiding over the cultivation of the vine and the fertility of the fields. Hence they were worshipped even in early times in conjunction with Ceres. A temple to these 3 divinities was vowed by the dictator, A. Postumius, in B.C. 496, and was built near the Circus Flaminius; it was afterwards restored by Augustus, and dedicated by Tiberius. The name Liber is probably connected with *liberare*. Hence Seneca says, *Liber dictus est quia liberat servitio curarum animi;* while others, who were evidently thinking of the Greek Bacchus, found in the name an allusion to licentious drinking and speaking. Poets usually called him *Liber Pater*, the latter word being very commonly added by the Italians to the names of gods. The female Libera was identified by the Romans with Cora or Proserpīna, the daughter of Demeter (Ceres); whence Cicero calls Liber and Libera children of Ceres; whereas Ovid calls Ariadne Libera. The festival of the Liberalia was celebrated by the Romans every year on the 17th of March.

Libera. [LIBER.]

Libertas, the personification of Liberty, was worshipped at Rome as a divinity. A temple was erected to her on the Aventine by Tib. Sempronius Gracchus. Another was built by Clodius on the spot where Cicero's house had stood. A third was erected after Caesar's victories in Spain. From these temples we must distinguish the Atrium Libertatis, which was in the N. of the forum, towards the Quirinal. This building under the republic served as an office of the censors, and also contained tables with laws inscribed upon them. It was rebuilt by Asinius Pollio, and then became the repository of the first public library at Rome

—Libertas is usually represented in works of art as a matron, with the pileus, the symbol of liberty or a wreath of laurel. Sometimes she appears holding the Phrygian cap in her hand.

Libethrides. [LIBETHRUM.]

Libethrius Mons (τὸ Λιβήθριον ὄρος), a mountain in Boeotia, a branch of Mt. Helicon, 40 stadia from Coronea, possessing a grotto of the Libethrian nymphs, adorned with their statues, and 2 fountains *Libethrias* and *Petra.*

Libethrum (Λείβηθρον, τὰ Λείβηθρα, τὰ Λίβηθρα), an ancient Thracian town in Pieria in Macedonia, on the slope of Olympus, and S.W. of Dium, where Orpheus is said to have lived. This town and the surrounding country were sacred to the Muses, who were hence called *Libethrides*; and it is probable that the worship of the Muses under this name was transferred from this place to Boeotia.

Libitīna, an ancient Italian divinity, who was identified by the later Romans sometimes with Persephone (Proserpina), on account of her connection with the dead and their burial, and sometimes with Aphrodite (Venus). The latter was probably the consequence of etymological speculations on the name Libitina, which people connected with libido. Her temple at Rome was a repository of everything necessary for burials, and persons might there either buy or hire those things. Hence a person undertaking the burial of a person (an undertaker) was called *libitinarius,* and his business *libitina;* hence the expressions *libitinam exercere,* or *facere,* and *libitina funeribus non sufficiebat,* i. e. they could not all be buried. It is related that king Servius Tullius, in order to ascertain the number of deaths, ordained that for every person who died, a piece of money should be deposited in the temple of Libitina.— Owing to this connection of Libitina with the dead, Roman poets frequently employ her name in the sense of death itself.

Libo, Scribonius, a plebeian family. 1. L., tribune of the plebs, B.C. 149, accused Ser. Sulpicius Galba on account of the outrages which he had committed against the Lusitanians. [GALBA, No. 6.] It was perhaps this Libo who consecrated the *Puteal Scribonianum* or *Puteal Libonis,* of which we so frequently read in ancient writers. The Puteal was an enclosed place in the forum, near the Arcus Fabianus, and was so called from its being open at the top, like a puteal or well. It appears that there was only one such puteal at Rome, and not two, as is generally believed. It was dedicated in very ancient times either on account of the whetstone of the augur Navius (comp. Liv. i. 36), or because the spot had been struck by lightning; it was subsequently repaired and re-dedicated by Libo, who erected in its neighbourhood a tribunal for the praetor, in consequence of which the place was frequented by persons who had law-suits, such as money lenders and the like. (Comp. Hor. *Sat.* ii. 6. 35, *Epist.* i. 19. 8.)—2. L., the father-in-law of Sex. Pompey, the son of Pompey the Great. On the breaking out of the civil war in 49, he naturally sided with Pompey, and was entrusted with the command of Etruria. Shortly afterwards he accompanied Pompey to Greece, and was actively engaged in the war that ensued. On the death of Bibulus (48) he had the chief command of the Pompeian fleet. In the civil wars which followed Caesar's death, he followed the fortunes of his son-in-law Sex. Pompey. In 40, Octavian married his sister Scribonia, and this marriage was followed by a peace between the triumvirs and Pompey (39). When the war was renewed in 36, Libo for a time continued with Pompey, but, seeing his cause hopeless, he deserted him in the following year. In 34, he was consul with M. Antony.

Libon (Λίβων), an Elean, the architect of the great temple of Zeus in the Altis at Olympia, flourished about B.C. 450.

Libui, a Gallic tribe in Gallia Cispadana, to whom the towns of Brixia and Verona formerly belonged, from which they were expelled by the Cenomani. They are probably the same people whom we afterwards find in the neighbourhood of Vercellae under the name of Lebecii or Libici.

Liburnia, a district of Illyricum, along the coast of the Adriatic sea, was separated from Istria on the N. W. by the river Arsia, and from Dalmatia on the S. by the river Titius, thus corresponding to the W. part of Croatia, and the N. part of the modern Dalmatia. The country is mountainous and unproductive, and its inhabitants, the **Liburni**, supported themselves chiefly by commerce and navigation. They were celebrated at a very early period as bold and skilful sailors, and they appear to have been the first people who had the sway of the waters of the Adriatic. They took possession of most of the islands of this sea as far as Corcyra, and had settlements even on the opposite coast of Italy. Their ships were remarkable for their swift sailing, and hence vessels built after the same model were called *Liburnicae* or *Liburnae naves*. It was to light vessels of this description that Augustus was mainly indebted for his victory over Antony's fleet at the battle of Actium. The Liburnians were the first Illyrian people who submitted to the Romans. Being hard pressed by the Iapydes on the N. and by the Dalmatians on the S., they sought the protection of Rome at a comparatively early period. Hence we find that many of their towns were immunes, or exempt from taxes. The islands off the coast were reckoned a part of Liburnia and are known by the general name of *Liburnides* or *Liburnicae Insulae*. [ILLYRICUM.]

Libya (Λιβύη), daughter of Epaphus and Memphis, from whom Libya (Africa) is said to have derived its name. By Poseidon she became the mother of Agenor, Belus, and Lelex.

Libya (Λιβύη: Λίβυες, Libyes). 1. The Greek name for the continent of Africa in general [AFRICA].—2. L. Interior (A. ἡ ἐντός), the whole interior of Africa, as distinguished from the well-known regions on the N. and N.E. coasts.— 3. Libya, specifically, or **Libyae Nomos** (Λιβύης νομός), a district of N. Africa, between Egypt and Marmarica, so called because it once formed an Egyptian Nomos. It is sometimes called Libya Exterior.

Libyci Montes (τὸ Λιβυκὸν ὄρος: Jebel Selseleh), the range of mountains which form the W. margin of the valley of the Nile. [AEGYPTUS.]

Libycum Mare (τὸ Λιβυκὸν πέλαγος), the part of the Mediterranean between the island of Crete and the N. coast of Africa.

Libyphoenices (Λιβυφοίνικες, Λιβοφοίνικες), a term applied to the people of those parts of N. Africa, in which the Phoenicians had founded colonies, and especially to the inhabitants of the Phoenician cities on the coast of the Carthaginian territory: it is derived from the fact that these people were a mixed race of the Libyan natives with the Phoenician settlers.

Libyssa (Λίβυσσα: Herekeh?), a town of Bithynia, in Asia Minor, on the N. coast of the Sinus Astacenus, W. of Nicomedia, celebrated as the place where the tomb of Hannibal was to be seen.

Licates or **Licatii**, a people of Vindelicia on the E. bank of the river Licus or Licia (Lech), one of the fiercest of the Vindelician tribes.

Lichades (Λιχάδες: Ponticonesi), 3 small islands between Euboea and the coast of Locris, called Scarphia, Caresa, and Phocaria. See LICHAS, No. 1.

Lichas (Λίχας). 1. An attendant of Hercules, brought his master the poisoned garment, which destroyed the hero. [See p. 310, b.] Hercules, in anguish and wrath, threw Lichas into the sea, and the Lichadian islands were believed to have derived their name from him. — 2. A Spartan, son of Arcesilaus, was proxenus of Argos, and is frequently mentioned in the Peloponnesian war. He was famous throughout Greece for his hospitality, especially in his entertainment of strangers at the Gymnopaedia.

Licia or **Licus**. [LICATES.]

Licinia. 1. A Vestal virgin, accused of incest, together with 2 other Vestals, Aemilia and Marcia, B.C. 114. L. Metellus, the pontifex maximus, condemned Aemilia, but acquitted Licinia and Marcia. The acquittal of the 2 last caused such dissatisfaction that the people appointed L. Cassius Longinus to investigate the matter; and he condemned both Licinia and Marcia.— 2. Wife of C. Sempronius Gracchus, the celebrated tribune. — 3. Daughter of Crassus the orator, and wife of the younger Marius.

Licinia Gens, a celebrated plebeian house, to which belonged C. Licinius Calvus Stolo, whose exertions threw open the consulship to the plebeians. Its most distinguished families at a later time were those of CRASSUS, LUCULLUS and MURENA. There were likewise numerous other surnames in the gens, which are also given in their proper places.

Licinius. 1. C. **Licinius Calvus**, surnamed Stolo, which he derived, it is said, from the care with which he dug up the shoots that sprang up from the roots of his vines. He brought the contest between the patricians and plebeians to a happy termination, and thus became the founder of Rome's greatness. He was tribune of the people from B.C. 376 to 367, and was faithfully supported in his exertions by his colleague L. Sextius. The laws which he proposed were: 1. That in future no more consular tribunes should be appointed, but that consuls should be elected, one of whom should always be a plebeian. 2. That no one should possess more than 500 jugera of the public land, or keep upon it more than 100 head of large and 500 of small cattle. 3. A law regulating the affairs between debtor and creditor. 4. That the Sibylline books should be entrusted to a college of ten men (decemviri), half of whom should be plebeians. These rogations were passed after a most vehement opposition on the part of the patricians, and L. Sextius was the first plebeian who obtained the consulship, 366. Licinius himself was elected twice to the consulship, 364 and 361. Some years later he was accused by M. Popilius Laenas of having transgressed his own law respecting the amount of public land which a person might possess. He was condemned and sentenced to pay a heavy fine.— 2. C. **Licinius Macer**, an annalist and an orator, was a man of praetorian dignity, who, when impeached (66) of extortion by Cicero, finding that the verdict was against him, forthwith committed suicide before the formalities of the trial were completed, and thus averted the dishonour and loss which would have been entailed upon his family by a public condemnation and by the confiscation of property which it involved. His *Annales* commenced with the very origin of the city, and extended to 21 books at least ; but how far he brought down his history, is unknown. — 3. C. Licinius Macer Calvus, son of the last, a distinguished orator and poet, was born in 82, and died about 47 or 46, in his 35th or 36th year. His most celebrated oration was delivered against Vatinius, who was defended by Cicero, when he was only 27 years of age. So powerful was the effect produced by this speech, that the accused started up in the midst of the pleading, and passionately exclaimed, " Rogo vos, judices, num, si iste disertus est, ideo me damnari oportest?" His poems were full of wit and grace, and possessed sufficient merit to be classed by the ancients with those of Catullus. His elegies, especially that on the untimely death of his mistress Quintilia, have been warmly extolled by Catullus, Propertius, and Ovid. Calvus was remarkable for the shortness of his stature, and hence the vehement action in which he indulged while pleading was in such ludicrous contrast with his insignificant person, that even his friend Catullus has not been able to resist a joke, and has presented him to us as the " Salaputium disertum," " the eloquent Tom Thumb."

Licinius, Roman emperor A. D. 307—324, whose full name was PUBLIUS FLAVIUS GALERIUS VALERIUS LICINIANUS LICINIUS. He was a Dacian peasant by birth, and the early friend and companion in arms of the emperor Galerius, by whom he was raised to the rank of Augustus, and invested with the command of the Illyrian provinces at Carmentum, on the 11th of November, A. D. 307. Upon the death of Galerius in 311, he concluded a peaceful arrangement with MAXIMINUS II., in virtue of which the Hellespont and the Bosporus were to form the boundary of the two empires. In 313 he married at Milan, Constantia, the sister of Constantine, and in the same year set out to encounter Maximinus, who had invaded his dominions. Maximinus was defeated by Licinius near Heraclea, and died a few months afterwards at Tarsus. Licinius and Constantine were now the only emperors, and each was anxious to obtain the undivided sovereignty. Accordingly war broke out between them in 315. Licinius was defeated at Cibalis in Pannonia, and afterwards at Adrianople, and was compelled to purchase peace by ceding to Constantine Greece, Macedonia, and Illyricum. This peace lasted about 9 years, at the end of which time hostilities were renewed. The great battle of Adrinople (July, 323), followed by the reduction of Byzantium, and a second great victory achieved near Chalcedon (September), placed Licinius at the mercy of Constantine, who, although he spared his life for the moment, and merely sentenced him to an honourable imprisonment at Thessalonica, soon found a convenient pretext for putting him to death, 324.

Licinus. 1. A Gaul by birth, was taken prisoner in war, and became a slave of Julius Caesar, whose confidence he gained so much as to be made his dispensator or steward. Caesar gave him his freedom. He also gained the favour of Augustus, who appointed him in B. C. 15, governor of his native country, Gaul. By the plunder of Gaul and by other means, he acquired enormous wealth, and hence his name is frequently coupled with that of Crassus. He lived to see the reign of Tiberius. — 2. The barber (*tonsor*) Licinius spoken of by Horace (*Ars Poët.* 301), must have been a different person from the preceding, although identified by the Scholiast. — 3. Clodius Licinus, a Roman annalist, who lived about the beginning of the first century B. C., wrote the history of Rome from its capture by the Gauls to his own time. This Clodius is frequently confounded with Q. Claudius Quadrigarius. [QUADRIGARIUS.] — 4. L. Porcius Licinus, plebeian aedile, 210, and praetor 207, when he obtained Cisalpine Gaul as his province. — 5. L. Porcius Licinus, praetor 193, with Sardinia as his province, and consul 184, when he carried on war against the Ligurians. — 6. Porcius Licinus, an ancient Roman poet, who probably lived in the latter part of the 2nd century B. C.

Licymnia, spoken of by Horace (*Carm.* ii. 12. 13, seq.), is probably the same as Terentia, the wife of Maecenas.

Licymnius (Λικύμνιος). 1. Son of Electryon and the Phrygian slave Midea, and consequently half-brother of Alcmene. He was married to Perimede, by whom he became the father of Oeonus, Argeus, and Melas. He was a friend of Hercules, whose son Tlepolemus slew him, according to some unintentionally, and according to others in a fit of anger. — 2. Of Chios, a distinguished dithyrambic poet, of uncertain date. Some writers place him before Simonides ; but it is perhaps more likely that he belonged to the later Athenian dithyrambic school about the end of the 4th century B. C. — 3. Of Sicily, a rhetorician, the pupil of Gorgias, and the teacher of Polus.

Lidē (Λίδη), a mountain of Caria, above Pedasus.

Q. Ligarius, was legate, in Africa, of C. Considius Longus, who left him in command of the province, B. C. 50. Next year (49) Ligarius resigned the government of the province into the hands of L. Attius Varus. Ligarius fought under Varus against Curio in 49, and against Caesar himself in 46. After the battle of Thapsus, Ligarius was taken prisoner at Adrumetum ; his life was spared, but he was banished by Caesar. Meantime, a public accusation was brought against Ligarius by Q. Aelius Tubero. The case was pleaded before Caesar himself in the forum. Cicero defended Ligarius in a speech still extant, in which he maintains that Ligarius had as much claims to the mercy of Caesar, as Tubero and Cicero himself. Ligarius was pardoned by Caesar, who was on the point of setting out for the Spanish war. The speech which Cicero delivered in his defence was subsequently published, and was much admired. Ligarius joined the conspirators, who assassinated Caesar in 44. Ligarius and his 2 brothers perished in the proscription of the triumvirs in 43.

Liger or Ligēris (*Loire*), one of the largest rivers in Gaul, rises in M. Cevenna, flows through the territories of the Arverni, Aedui, and Carnutes, and falls into the ocean between the territories of the Namnetes and Pictones.

Liguria (ἡ Λιγυστική, ἡ Λιγυστίνη), a district of Italy, was, in the time of Augustus, bounded on the W. by the river Varus, and the Maritime

Alps, which separated it from Transalpine Gaul, on the S. E. by the river Macra, which separated it from Etruria, on the N. by the river Po, and on the S. by the Mare Ligusticum. The country is very mountainous and unproductive, as the Maritime Alps and the Apennines run through the greater part of it. The mountains run almost down to the coast, leaving only space sufficient for a road, which formed the highway from Italy to the S. of Gaul. The chief occupation of the inhabitants was the rearing and feeding of cattle. The numerous forests on the mountains produced excellent timber, which, with the other products of the country, was exported from Genua, the principal town of the country. The inhabitants were called by the Greeks **Ligyes** (Λίγυες) and **Ligystini** (Λιγυστῖνοί) and by the Romans **Ligūres** (Sing. *Ligus*, more rarely *Ligur*). They were in early times a powerful and widely extended people; but their origin is uncertain, some writers supposing them to be Celts, others Iberians, and others again of the same race as the Siculians, or most ancient inhabitants of Italy. It is certain that the Ligurians at one time inhabited the S. coast of Gaul as well as the country afterwards called Liguria, and that they had possession of the whole coast from the mouth of the Rhone to Pisae in Etruria. The Greeks probably became acquainted with them first from the Samians and Phocaeans, who visited their coasts for the purposes of commerce; and so powerful were they considered at this time that Hesiod names them, along with the Scythians and Ethiopians, as one of the chief people of the earth. Tradition also related that Hercules fought with the Ligurians on the plain of stones near Massilia; and even a writer so late as Eratosthenes gave the name of Ligystice to the whole of the W. peninsula of Europe. So widely were they believed to be spread that the Ligyes in Germany and Asia were supposed to be a branch of the same people. The Ligurian tribes were divided by the Romans into *Ligures Transalpini* and *Cisalpini*. The tribes which inhabited the Maritime Alps were called in general *Alpini*, and also *Capillati* or *Comati*, from their custom of allowing their hair to grow long; the tribes which inhabited the Apennines were called *Montani*. The names of the principal tribes were:— on the W. side of the Alps, the SALYES or SALLUVII, OXYBII, and DECIATES; on the E. side of the Alps, the INTEMELII, INGAUNI and APUANI near the coast, the VAGIENNI, SALASSI and TAURINI on the upper course of the Po, and the LAEVI and MARISCI N. of the Po.—The Ligurians were small of stature, but strong, active, and brave. In early times they served as mercenaries in the armies of the Carthaginians, and subsequently they carried on a long and fierce struggle with the Romans. Their country was invaded for the first time by the Romans in B.C. 238; but it was not till after the termination of the 2nd Punic war and the defeat of Philip and Antiochus that the Romans were able to devote their energies to the subjugation of Liguria. It was many years however before the whole country was finally subdued. Whole tribes, such as the Apuani, were transplanted to Samnium, and their place supplied by Roman colonists. The country was divided between the provinces of Gallia Narbonensis and Gallia Cisalpina; and in the time of Augustus and of the succeeding emperors, the tribes in the mountains were placed under the government of an imperial procurator, called *Procurator* or *Praefectus Alpium Maritimarum*.

Ligustĭcum Mare, the name originally of the whole sea S. of Gaul and of the N.W. of Italy, but subsequently only the E. part of this sea, or the *Gulf of Genoa*, whence later writers speak only of a Sinus Ligusticus.

Lilaea (Λίλαια: Λιλαιεύς), an ancient town in Phocis, near the sources of the Cephissus.

Lilybaeum (Λιλύβαιον: *Marsala*), a town in the W. of Sicily, with an excellent harbour, situated on a promontory of the same name (*C. Boeo* or *di Marsala*), opposite to the Prom. Hermaeum or Mercurii (*C. Bon*) in Africa, the space between the 2 being the shortest distance between Sicily and Africa. The town of Lilybaeum was founded by the Carthaginians about B.C. 397, and was made the principal Carthaginian fortress in Sicily. It was surrounded by massive walls and by a trench 60 feet wide and 40 feet deep. On the destruction of Selinus in 249, the inhabitants of the latter city were transplanted to Lilybaeum, which thus became still more powerful. Lilybaeum was besieged by the Romans in the 1st Punic war, but they were unable to take it; and they only obtained possession of it by the treaty of peace. Under the Romans Lilybaeum continued to be a place of importance. At *Marsala*, which occupies only the S. half of the ancient town, there are the ruins of a Roman aqueduct, and a few other ancient remains.

Limaea, Limia, Limius, Belion (*Lima*), a river in Gallaecia in Spain, between the Durius and the Minius, which flowed into the Atlantic Ocean. It was also called the river of Forgetfulness (ὁ τῆς Λήθης, *Flumen Oblivionis*); and it is said to have been so called, because the Turduli and the Celts on one occasion lost here their commander, and forgot the object of their expedition. This legend was so generally believed that it was with difficulty that Brutus Callaicus could induce his soldiers to cross the river, when he invaded Gallaecia, B.C. 136. On the banks of this river dwelt a small tribe called Limici.

Limĭtes Romāni, the name of a continuous series of fortifications, consisting of castles, walls, earthern ramparts, and the like, which the Romans erected along the Rhine and the Danube, to protect their possessions from the attacks of the Germans.

Limnae (Λίμναι, Λιμναῖος). 1. A town in Messenia, on the frontiers of Laconia, with a temple of Artemis, who was hence surnamed Limnatis. This temple was common to the people of both countries; and the outrage which the Messenian youth committed against some Lacedaemonian maidens, who were sacrificing at this temple, was the occasion of the 1st Messenian war. Limnae was situated in the Ager Denthaliatis, which district was a subject of constant dispute between the Lacedaemonians and Messenians after the re-establishment of the Messenian independence by Epaminondas.—2. A town in the Thracian Chersonesus on the Hellespont, not far from Sestus, founded by the Milesians.—3. See SPARTA.

Limnaea (Λιμναία: Λιμναῖος), a town in the N. of Acarnania, on the road from Argos Amphilochicum to Stratos, and near the Ambracian gulf, on which it had a harbour.

Limnaea, Limnētes, Limnēgĕnes (Λιμναία (ος), Λιμνήτης (ις), Λιμνηγενής), i. e. inhabiting or born in a lake or marsh, a surname of several divinities who were believed either to have sprung from a lake, or who had their temples near a lake. Hence we find this surname given to Dionysus at Athens, and to Artemis at various places.

Limonum. [PICTONES.]

Limyra (τὰ Λίμυρα: Ru. N. of *Phineka ?*), a city in the S.E. of Lycia, on the river LIMYRUS, 20 stadia from its mouth.

Limyrus (Λίμυρος: *Phineka ?*), a river of Lycia, flowing into the bay W. of the Sacrum Promontorium (*Phineka Bay*): navigable as far up as LIMYRA. The recent travellers differ as to whether the present river *Phineka* is the Limyra or its tributary the Arycandus.

Lindum (*Lincoln*), a town of the Coritani, in Britain, on the road from Londinium to Eboracum, and a Roman colony. The modern name *Lincoln* has been formed out of Lindum Colonia.

Lindus (Λίνδος: Λίνδιος: *Lindo*, Ru.), on the E. side of the island of Rhodes, was one of the most ancient Dorian colonies on the Asiatic coast. It is mentioned by Homer (*Il.* ii. 656), with its kindred cities, Ialysus and Camirus. These 3 cities, with Cos, Cnidus, and Halicarnassus, formed the original Hexapolis, in the S.W. corner of Asia Minor. Lindus stood upon a mountain in a district abounding in vines and figs, and had 2 celebrated temples, one of Athena surnamed Λινδία, and one of Hercules. It was the birthplace of Cleobulus, one of the 7 wise men. It retained much of its consequence even after the foundation of Rhodes. Inscriptions of some importance have lately been found in its Acropolis.

Lingones. 1. A powerful people in Transalpine Gaul, whose territory extended from the foot of Mt. Vogesus and the sources of the Matrona and Mosa, N. as far as the Treviri, and S. as far as the Sequani, from whom they were separated by the river Arar. The emperor Otho gave them the Roman franchise. Their chief town was Andematurinum, afterwards Lingones (*Langres*).— 2. A branch of the above mentioned people, who migrated into Cisalpine Gaul along with the Boii, and shared the fortunes of the latter. [BOII.] They dwelt E. of the Boii as far as the Adriatic sea in the neighbourhood of Ravenna.

Linternum. [LITERNUM.]

Linus (Λίνος), the personification of a dirge or lamentation, and therefore described as a son of Apollo by a Muse (Calliope, or by Psamathe or Chalciope), or of Amphimarus by Urania. Both Argos and Thebes claimed the honour of his birth. An Argive tradition related, that Linus was exposed by his mother after his birth, and was brought up by shepherds, but was afterwards torn to pieces by dogs. Psamathe's grief at the occurrence betrayed her misfortune to her father, who condemned her to death. Apollo, indignant at the father's cruelty, visited Argos with a plague ; and, in obedience to an oracle, the Argives endeavoured to propitiate Psamathe and Linus by means of sacrifices. Matrons and virgins sang dirges which were called λίνοι. According to a Boeotian tradition Linus was killed by Apollo, because he had ventured upon a musical contest with the god ; and every year before sacrifices were offered to the Muses, a funeral sacrifice was offered to him, and dirges (λίνοι) were sung in his honour. His tomb was claimed by Argos and by Thebes, and likewise by Chalcis in Euboea. It is probably owing to the

difficulty of reconciling the different mythuses about Linus, that the Thebans thought it necessary to distinguish between an earlier and later Linus ; the latter is said to have instructed Hercules in music, but to have been killed by the hero. In the time of the Alexandrine grammarians Linus was considered as the author of apocryphal works, in which the exploits of Dionysus were described.

Lipăra and Liparenses Insulae. [AEOLIAE.]

Lipăris (Λίπαρις), a small river of Cilicia, flowing past Soloё.

Liquentia (*Livenza*), a river in Venetia in the N. of Italy between Altinum and Concordia, which flowed into the Sinus Tergestinus.

Liris (*Garigliano*), more anciently called **Clanis**, or **Glanis**, one of the principal rivers in central Italy, rises in the Apennines W. of lake Fucinus, flows first through the territory of the Marsi in a S. E.-ly direction, then turns S. W. near Sora, and at last flows S. E. into the Sinus Caietanus near Minturnae, forming the boundary between Latium and Campania. Its stream was sluggish, whence the " Liris *quieta* aqua " of Horace (*Carm.* i. 31).

Lissus (Λισσός: Λίσσιος, Λισσεύς). 1. (*Alessio*), a town in the S. of Dalmatia, at the mouth of the river Drilon, founded by Dionysius of Syracuse, B. C. 385. It was situated on a hill near the coast, and possessed a strongly fortified acropolis, called **Acrolissus**, which was considered impregnable. The town afterwards fell into the hands of the Illyrians, and was eventually colonized by the Romans.— 2. A small river in Thrace W. of the Hebrus.

Lista (*S. Anatoglia*), a town of the Sabines, S. of Reate, is said to have been the capital of the Aborigines, from which they were driven out by the Sabines, who attacked them in the night.

Lităna Silva (*Silva di Luge*), a large forest on the Apennines in Cisalpine Gaul, S. E. of Mutina, in which the Romans were defeated by the Gauls, B. C. 216.

Liternum or **Linternum** (*Patria*), a town on the coast of Campania, at the mouth of the river Clanius or Glania, which in the lower part of its course takes the name of **Liternus** (*Patria* or *Clanio*), and which flows through a marsh to the N. of the town called **Literna Palus.** The town was made a Roman colony B. C. 194, and was recolonized by Augustus. It was to this place that the elder Scipio Africanus retired, when the tribunes attempted to bring him to trial, and here he is said to have died. His tomb was shown at Liternum ; but some maintained that he was buried in the family sepulchre near the Porta Capena at Rome.

Livia. 1. Sister of M. Livius Drusus, the celebrated tribune, B. C. 91, was married first to M. Porcius Cato, by whom she had Cato Uticensis, and subsequently to Q. Servilius Caepio, by whom she had a daughter, Servilia, the mother of M. Brutus, who killed Caesar.— 2. Livia Drusilla, the daughter of Livius Drusus Claudianus [DRUSUS, No. 3], was married first to Tib. Claudius Nero ; and afterwards to Augustus, who compelled her husband to divorce her, B. C. 38. She had already borne her husband one son, the future emperor Tiberius, and at the time of her marriage with Augustus was 6 months pregnant with another, who subsequently received the name of Drusus. She never had any children by Augustus, but she retained his affections till his death. It was gene-

c c

rally believed that she caused C. Caesar and L. Caesar, the 2 grandsons of Augustus to be poisoned, in order to secure the succession for her own children ; and she was even suspected of having hastened the death of Augustus. On the accession of her son Tiberius to the throne, she at first attempted to obtain an equal share in the government ; but this the jealous temper of Tiberius would not brook. He commanded her to retire altogether from public affairs, and soon displayed even hatred towards her. When she was on her death-bed, he refused to visit her. She died in A. D. 29, at the age of 82 or 86. Tiberius took no part in the funeral rites, and forbade her consecration, which had been proposed by the senate. — 3. Or Livilla, the daughter of Drusus senior and Antonia, and the wife of Drusus junior, the son of the emperor Tiberius. She was seduced by Sejanus, who persuaded her to poison her husband, A. D. 23. Her guilt was not discovered till the fall of Sejanus, 8 years afterwards, 31. — 4. Julia Livilla, daughter of Germanicus and Agrippina. [JULIA, No. 7.]

Livia Gens, plebeian, but one of the most illustrious houses among the Roman nobility. The Livii obtained 8 consulships, 2 censorships, 3 triumphs, a dictatorship, and a mastership of the horse. The most distinguished families are those of DRUSUS and SALINATOR.

LIVIUS, T., the Roman historian, was born at Patavium (*Padua*), in the N. of Italy, B. C. 59. The greater part of his life appears to have been spent in Rome, but he returned to his native town before his death, which happened at the age of 76, in the 4th year of Tiberius, A. D. 17. We know that he was married, and that he had at least 2 children, a son and a daughter, married to L. Magius, a rhetorician. His literary talents secured the patronage and friendship of Augustus ; he became a person of consideration at court, and by his advice Claudius, afterwards emperor, was induced in early life to attempt historical composition ; but there is no ground for the assertion that Livy acted as preceptor to the young prince. Eventually his reputation rose so high and became so widely diffused, that a Spaniard travelled from Cadiz to Rome, solely for the purpose of beholding him, and having gratified his curiosity in this one particular, immediately returned home. The great and only extant work of Livy is a History of Rome, termed by himself *Annales* (xliii. 13), extending from the foundation of the city to the death of Drusus, B. C. 9, comprised in 142 books. Of these 35 have descended to us ; but of the whole, with the exception of 2, we possess *Epitomes*, which must have been drawn up by one who was well acquainted with his subject. By some they have been ascribed to Livy himself, by others to Florus ; but there is nothing in the language or context to warrant either of these conclusions ; and external evidence is altogether wanting. From the circumstance that a short introduction or preface is found at the beginning of books 1, 21, and 31, and that each of these marks the commencement of an important epoch, the whole work has been divided into *decades*, containing 10 books each ; but the grammarians Priscian and Diomedes, who quote repeatedly from particular books, never allude to any such distribution. The commencement of book xli. is lost, but there is certainly no remarkable crisis at this place which invalidates one part of the argument in favour of the antiquity

of the arrangement. The 1st decade (bks. i—x.) is entire. It embraces the period from the foundation of the city to the year B. C. 294, when the subjugation of the Samnites may be said to have been completed. The 2nd decade (bks. xi—xx.) is altogether lost. It embraced the period from 294 to 219, comprising an account, among other matters, of the invasion of Pyrrhus and of the first Punic war. The 3rd decade (bks. xxi—xxx.) is entire. It embraces the period from 219 to 201, comprehending the whole of the 2nd Punic war. The 4th decade (bks. xxxi—xl.) is entire, and also one half of the 5th (bks. xli—xlv.). These 15 books embrace the period from 201 to 167, and develope the progress of the Roman arms in Cisalpine Gaul, in Macedonia, Greece and Asia, ending with the triumph of Aemilius Paulus. Of the remaining books nothing remains except inconsiderable fragments, the most notable being a few chapters of the 91st book, concerning the fortunes of Sertorius. The composition of such a vast work necessarily occupied many years ; and we find indications which throw some light upon the epochs when different sections were composed. Thus in book first (c. 19) it is stated that the temple of Janus had been closed twice only since the reign of Numa, for the first time in the consulship of T. Manlius (B. C. 235), a few years after the termination of the first Punic war ; for the second time by Augustus Caesar, after the battle of Actium, in 29. But we know that it was shut again by Augustus after the conquest of the Cantabrians, in 25 ; and hence it is evident that the first book must have been written between the years 29 and 25. Moreover, since the last book contained an account of the death of Drusus, it is evident that the task must have been spread over 17 years, and probably occupied a much longer time. — The style of Livy may be pronounced almost faultless. The narrative flows on in a calm, but strong current ; the diction displays richness without heaviness, and simplicity without tameness. There is, moreover, a distinctness of outline and a warmth of colouring in all his delineations, whether of living men in action, or of things inanimate, which never fail to call up the whole scene before our eyes. — In judging of the merits of Livy as an historian, we are bound to ascertain, if possible, the end which he proposed to himself. No one who reads Livy with attention can suppose that he ever conceived the project of drawing up a critical history of Rome. His aim was to offer to his countrymen a clear and pleasing narrative, which, while it gratified their vanity, should contain no startling improbabilities nor gross amplifications. To effect this purpose he studied with care the writings of some of his more celebrated predecessors on Roman history. Where his authorities were in accordance with each other, he generally rested satisfied with this agreement ; where their testimony was irreconcileable, he was content to point out their want of harmony, and occasionally to offer an opinion on their comparative credibility. But, in no case did he ever dream of ascending to the fountain head. He never attempted to test the accuracy of his authorities by examining monuments of remote antiquity, of which not a few were accessible to every inhabitant of the metropolis. Thus, it is perfectly clear that he had never read the Leges Regiae, nor the Commentaries of Servius Tullius, nor even the Licinian Rogations ; and that he had never consulted the vast collection of decrees of the senate, ordinances of the plebs, treaties and other state papers, which were preserved in the city. Nay more, he did not consult even all the authors to whom he might have resorted with advantage, such as the Annals and Antiquities of Varro, and the Origines of Cato. And even those writers whose authority he followed, he did not use in the most judicious manner. He seems to have performed his task piecemeal. A small section was taken in hand, different accounts were compared, and the most plausible was adopted; the same system was adhered to in the succeeding portions, so that each considered by itself, without reference to the rest, was executed with care; but the witnesses who were rejected in one place were admitted in another, without sufficient attention being paid to the dependence and the connection of the events. Hence the numerous contradictions and inconsistencies which have been detected by sharp-eyed critics. Other mistakes also are found in abundance, arising from his want of anything like practical knowledge of the world, from his never having acquired even the elements of the military art, of jurisprudence, or of political economy, and above all, from his singular ignorance of geography. But while we fully acknowledge these defects in Livy, we cannot admit that his general good faith has ever been impugned with any show of justice. We are assured (Tacit. *Ann.* iv. 34) that he was fair and liberal upon matters of contemporary history; we know that he praised Cassius and Brutus, that his character of Cicero was a high eulogium, and that he spoke so warmly of the unsuccessful leader in the great civil war, that he was sportively styled a Pompeian by Augustus. It is true that in recounting the domestic strife which agitated the republic for nearly two centuries, he represents the plebeians and their leaders in the most unfavourable light. But this arose, not from any wish to pervert the truth, but from ignorance of the exact relation of the contending parties. It is manifest that he never can separate in his own mind the spirited plebeians of the infant commonwealth from the base and venal rabble which thronged the forum in the days of Marius and Cicero; while in like manner he confounds those bold and honest tribunes, who were the champions of liberty, with such men as Saturninus or Sulpicius, Clodius or Vatinius.—There remains one topic to which we must advert. We are told by Quintilian (i. 5. § 56, viii. 1. § 3) that Asinius Pollio had remarked a certain *Patavinity* in Livy. Scholars have given themselves a vast deal of trouble to discover what this term may indicate, and various hypotheses have been propounded; but if there is any truth in the story, it is evident that Pollio must have intended to censure some provincial peculiarities of expression, which we, at all events, are in no position to detect. The best edition of Livy is by Drakenborch, Lugd. Bat. 1738—46, 7 vols. 4to. There is also a valuable edition, now in course of publication, by Alchefski, Berol. 8vo. 1841, seq.

Livius Andronicus. [ANDRONICUS.]

Lix, Lixa, Lixus (*Λίξ, Λίξα, Λίξος; Al-Arrish*), a city on the W. coast of Mauretania Tingitana, in Africa, at the mouth of a river of the same name: it was a place of some commercial importance.

Locri, sometimes called **Locrenses** by the Romans, the inhabitants of Locris (*ἡ Λοκρίς*),

were an ancient people in Greece, descended from the Leleges, with which some Hellenic tribes were intermingled at a very early period. They were, however, in Homer's time regarded as Hellenes; and according to tradition even Deucalion, the founder of the Hellenic race, was said to have lived in Locris in the town of Opus or Cynos. In historical times the Locrians were divided into 2 distinct tribes, differing from one another in customs, habits and civilization. Of these the Eastern Locrians, called Epicnemidii and Opuntii, who dwelt on the E. coast of Greece opposite the island of Euboea, were the more ancient and more civilized; while the Western Locrians, called Ozolae, who dwelt on the Corinthian gulf, were a colony of the former, and were more barbarous. Homer mentions only the E. Locrians. At a later time there was no connexion between the Eastern and Western Locrians; and in the Peloponnesian war we find the former siding with the Spartans, and the latter with the Athenians. — 1. **Eastern Locris**, extended from Thessaly and the pass of Thermopylae along the coast to the frontiers of Boeotia, and was bounded by Doris and Phocis on the W. It was a fertile and well cultivated country. The N. part was inhabited by the **Locri Epicnemidii** (*Ἐπικνημίδιοι*), who derived their name from Mt. Cnemis. The S. part was inhabited by the **Locri Opuntii** (*Ὀπούντιοι*), who derived their name from their principal town, Opus. The two tribes were separated by Daphnus, a small slip of land, which at one time belonged to Phocis. These two tribes are frequently confounded with one another; and ancient writers sometimes use the name either of Epicnemidii or of Opuntii alone, when both tribes are intended. The Epicnemidii were for a long time subject to the Phocians, and were included under the name of the latter people; whence the name of the Opuntii occurs more frequently in Greek history. — 2. **Western Locris**, or the country of the **Locri Ozolae** (*Ὀζόλαι*), was bounded on the N. by Doris, on the W. by Aetolia, on the E. by Phocis, and on the S. by the Corinthian gulf. The origin of the name of Ozolae is uncertain. The ancients derived it either from the undressed skins worn by the inhabitants, or from *ὄζειν* "to smell," on account of the great quantity of asphodel that grew in their country, or from the stench arising from mineral springs, beneath which the centaur Nessus is said to have been buried. The country is mountainous, and for the most part unproductive. Mt. Corax from Aetolia, and Mt. Parnassus from Phocis, occupy the greater part of it. The Locri Ozolae resembled their neighbours, the Aetolians, both in their predatory habits and in their mode of warfare. They were divided into several tribes, and are described by Thucydides as a rude and barbarous people, even in the time of the Peloponnesian war. From B. C. 315 they belonged to the Aetolian League. Their chief town was AMPHISSA.

Locri Epizephyrii (*Λοκροὶ Ἐπιζεφύριοι: Motta di Burzano*), one of the most ancient Greek cities in Lower Italy, was situated in the S. E. of Bruttium. N. of the promontory of Zephyrium, from which it was said to have derived its surname Epizephyrii, though others suppose this name given to the place, simply because it lay to the W. of Greece. It was founded by the Locrians from Greece, B. C. 683. Strabo expressly says that it was founded by the Ozolae, and not by the Opuntii, as most writers related; but his statement is not so probable as the common one. The inhabitants regarded themselves as descendants of Ajax Oileus; and as he resided at the town of Naryx among the Opuntii, the poets gave the name of *Narycia* to Locris (Ov. *Met.* xv. 705), and called the founders of the town the *Narycii Locri* (Virg. *Aen.* iii. 399). For the same reason the pitch of Bruttium is frequently called *Narycia* (Virg. *Georg.* ii. 438). Locri was celebrated for the excellence of its laws, which were drawn up by Zaleucus soon after the foundation of the city. [ZALEUCUS.] The town enjoyed great prosperity down to the time of the younger Dionysius, who resided here for some years after his expulsion from Syracuse, and committed the greatest atrocities against the inhabitants. It suffered much in the wars against Pyrrhus, and in the 2nd Punic war. The Romans allowed it to retain its freedom and its own constitution, which was democratical; but it gradually sunk in importance, and is rarely mentioned in later times. Near the town was an ancient and wealthy temple of Proserpina.

Locusta, or, more correctly, **Lucusta**, a woman celebrated for her skill in concocting poisons. She was employed by Agrippina in poisoning the emperor Claudius, and by Nero for despatching Britannicus. She was rewarded by Nero with ample estates; but under the emperor Galba she was executed with other malefactors of Nero's reign.

Lollia Paulina, granddaughter of M. Lollius, mentioned below, and heiress of his immense wealth. She was married to C. Memmius Regulus; but on the report of her grandmother's beauty, the emperor Caligula sent for her, divorced her from her husband, and married her, but soon divorced her again. After Claudius had put to death his wife Messalina, Lollia was one of the candidates for the vacancy, but she was put to death by means of Agrippina.

Lollianus (Λολλιανός), a celebrated Greek sophist in the time of Hadrian and Antoninus Pius, was a native of Ephesus, and taught at Athens.

Lollius. 1. **M. Lollius Palicanus**, tribune of the plebs, B. C. 71, and an active opponent of the aristocracy. — 2. **M. Lollius**, consul 21, and governor of Gaul in 16. He was defeated by some German tribes who had crossed the Rhine. Lollius was subsequently appointed by Augustus as tutor to his grandson, C. Caesar, whom he accompanied to the East, B. C. 2. Here he incurred the displeasure of C. Caesar, and is said in consequence to have put an end to his life by poison. Horace addressed an Ode (iv. 9) to Lollius, and 2 Epistles (i. 2, 18) to the eldest son of Lollius.

Londinium, also called **Oppidum Londiniense Lundinium** or **Londinum** (*London*), the capital of the Cantii in Britain, was situated on the S. bank of the Thames in the modern *Southwark*, though it afterwards spread over the other side of the river. It is not mentioned by Caesar, probably because his line of march led him in a different direction; and its name first occurs in the reign of Nero, when it is spoken of as a flourishing and populous town, much frequented by merchants, although neither a Roman colony nor a municipium. On the revolt of the Britons under Boadicea, A. D. 62, the Roman governor Suetonius Paulinus abandoned Londinium to the enemy, who massacred the inhabitants and plun-

dered the town. From the effects of this devastation it gradually recovered, and it appears again as an important place in the reign of Antoninus Pius. It was surrounded with a wall and ditch by Constantine the Great or Theodosius, the Roman governor of Britain; and about this time it was distinguished by the surname of *Augusta*, whence some writers have conjectured that it was then made a colony. Londinium had now extended so much on the N. bank of the Thames, that it was called at this period a town of the Trinobantes, from which we may infer that the new quarter was both larger and more populous than the old part on the S. side of the river. The wall built by Constantine or Theodosius was on the N. side of the river, and is conjectured to have commenced at a fort near the present site of the tower, and to have been continued along the Minories, to Cripplegate, Newgate and Ludgate. London was the central point, from which all the Roman roads in Britain diverged. It possessed a *Milliarium Aureum*, from which the miles on the roads were numbered; and a fragment of this Milliarium, the celebrated London Stone, may be seen affixed to the wall of St. Swithin's Church in Cannon Street. This is almost the only monument of the Roman Londinium still extant, with the exception of coins, tessellated pavements, and the like, which have been found buried under the ground.

Longanus (*St. Lucia*), a river in the N. E. of Sicily between Mylae and Tyndaris, on the banks of which Hieron gained a victory over the Mamertines.

Longinus, a distinguished Greek philosopher and grammarian of the 3rd century of our era. His original name seems to have been Dionysius; but he also bore the name of *Dionysius Longinus, Cassius Longinus*, or *Dionysius Cassius Longinus*, probably because either he or one of his ancestors had received the Roman franchise through the influence of some Cassius Longinus. The place of his birth is uncertain; he was brought up with care by his uncle Fronto, who taught rhetoric at Athens, whence it has been conjectured that he was a native of that city. He afterwards visited many countries, and became acquainted with all the illustrious philosophers of his age, such as Ammonius Saccas, Origen the disciple of Ammonius, not to be confounded with the Christian writer, Plotinus, and Amelius. He was a pupil of the 2 former, and was an adherent of the Platonic philosophy; but instead of following blindly the system of Ammonius, he went to the fountainhead, and made himself thoroughly familiar with the works of Plato. On his return to Athens he opened a school, which was attended by numerous pupils, among whom the most celebrated was Porphyry. He seems to have taught philosophy and criticism, as well as rhetoric and grammar; and the extent of his information was so great, that he was called "a living library" and "a walking museum." After spending a considerable part of his life at Athens he went to the East, where he became acquainted with Zenobia, of Palmyra, who made him her teacher of Greek literature. On the death of her husband Odenathus Longinus became her principal adviser. It was mainly through his advice that she threw off her allegiance to the Roman empire. On her capture by Aurelian in 273, Longinus was put to death by the emperor. Longinus was unquestionably the greatest philosopher of his age. He was a man of excellent sense, sound judgment, and extensive knowledge. His work *on the Sublime* (Περὶ ὕψους), a great part of which is still extant, surpasses in oratorical power every thing written after the time of the Greek orators. There is scarcely any work in the range of ancient literature which, independent of its excellence of style, contains so many exquisite remarks upon oratory, poetry, and good taste in general. The best edition of this work is by Weiske, Lips. 1809, 8vo., reprinted in London, 1820. Longinus wrote many other works, both rhetorical and philosophical, all of which have perished.

Longīnus, Cassĭus. [CASSIUS.]

Longobardi. [LANGOBARDI.]

Longūla (Longulānus : *Buon Riposo*), a town of the Volsci in Latium, not far from Corioli, and belonging to the territory of Antium, but destroyed by the Romans at an early period.

Longus (Λόγγος), a Greek sophist, of uncertain date, but not earlier than the 4th or 5th century of our era, is the author of an erotic work, entitled Ποιμενικῶν τῶν κατὰ Δάφνιν καὶ Χλόην, or *Pastoralia de Daphnide et Chloe*, written in pleasing and elegant prose. The best editions are by Villoison, Paris, 1778 ; Schaefer, Lips. 1803 ; and Passow, Lips. 1811.

Lŏpădūsa (Λοπαδοῦσα : *Lampedusa*), an island in the Mediterranean, between Melita (*Malta*) and the coast of Byzacium in Africa.

Lorĭum or **Lorĭi**, a small place in Etruria with an imperial villa, 12 miles N. W. of Rome on the Via Aurelia, where Antoninus Pius was brought up, and where he died.

Lŏrўma (τὰ Λώρυμα : *Aplotheki*, Ru.), a city on the S. coast of Caria, close to the promontory of Cynossema (*C. Aloupo*), opposite to Ialysus in Rhodes, the space between the two being about the shortest distance between Rhodes and the coast of Caria.

Lŏtis, a nymph, who, to escape the embraces of Priapus, was metamorphosed into a tree, called after her Lotus. (Ov. *Met.* ix. 347.)

Lŏtŏphăgi (Λωτοφάγοι, i. e. *lotus-eaters*). Homer, in the *Odyssey*, represents Ulysses as coming in his wanderings to a coast inhabited by a people who fed upon a fruit called lotus, the taste of which was so delicious that every one who eat it lost all wish to return to his native country, but desired to remain there with the Lotophagi, and to eat the lotus (*Od.* ix. 94). Afterwards, in historical times, the Greeks found that the people on the N. coast of Africa, between the Syrtes, and especially about the Lesser Syrtis, used to a great extent, as an article of food, the fruit of a plant, which they identified with the lotus of Homer, and they called these people Lotophagi. To this day, the inhabitants of the same part of the coast of *Tunis* and *Tripoli* eat the fruit of the plant which is supposed to be the lotus of the ancients, and drink a wine made from its juice, as the ancient Lotophagi are also said to have done. This plant, the *Zizyphus Lotus* of the botanists (or *jujube-tree*), is a prickly branching shrub, with fruit of the size of a wild-plum, of a saffron colour and a sweetish taste. The ancient geographers also place the Lotophagi in the large island of Meninx or Lotophagitis (*Jerbah*), adjacent to this coast. They carried on a commercial intercourse with Egypt and with the interior of Africa, by the very same caravan routes which are used to the present day.

Loxīas (Λοξίας), a surname of Apollo, derived by some from his intricate and ambiguous oracles (λόξα), but better from λέγειν, as the prophet or interpreter of Zeus.

Loxo (Λοξώ), daughter of Boreas, one of the Hyperborean maidens, who brought the worship of Artemis to Delos, whence the name is also used as a surname of Artemis herself.

Lua, also called **Lua mater** or **Lua Saturni**, one of the early Italian divinities, whose worship was forgotten in later times. It may be that she was the same as Ops, the wife of Saturn ; but all we know of her is, that sometimes the arms taken from a defeated enemy were dedicated to her, and burnt as a sacrifice, with a view of averting calamity.

Luca (Lucensis : *Lucca*), a Ligurian city in Upper Italy, at the foot of the Apennines and on the river Ausus, N. E. of Pisae. It was included in Etruria by Augustus ; but in the time of Julius Caesar it was the most S.-ly city in Liguria, and belonged to Cisalpine Gaul. It was made a Roman colony, B. C. 177. The amphitheatre of Lucca may still be seen at the modern town in a state of tolerable preservation, and its great size proves the importance and populousness of the ancient city.

Lucānĭa (Lucānus), a district in Lower Italy, was bounded on the N. by Campania and Samnium, on the E. by Apulia and the gulf of Tarentum, on the S. by Bruttium, and on the W. by the Tyrrhene sea, thus corresponding for the most part to the modern provinces of *Principato, Citeriore* and *Basilicata*, in the kingdom of Naples. It was separated from Campania by the river Silarus, and from Bruttium by the river Laus, and it extended along the gulf of Tarentum from Thurii to Metapontum. The country is mountainous, as the Apennines run through the greater part of it ; but towards the gulf of Tarentum there is an extensive and fertile plain. Lucania was celebrated for its excellent pastures (Hor. *Ep.* i. 28) ; and its oxen were the finest and largest in Italy. Hence, the elephant was at first called by the Romans a Lucanian ox (*Lucas bos*). The swine also were very good ; and a peculiar kind of sausages was celebrated at Rome under the name of *Lucanica*. The coast of Lucania was inhabited chiefly by Greeks, whose cities were numerous and flourishing. The most important were METAPONTUM, HERACLEA, THURII, BUXENTUM, ELEA or VELIA, POSIDONIA or PAESTUM. The interior of the country was originally inhabited by the Chones and Oenotrians. The Lucanians proper were Samnites, a brave and warlike race, who left their mother-country and settled both in Lucania and Bruttium. They not only expelled or subdued the Oenotrians, but they gradually acquired possession of most of the Greek cities on the coast. They are first mentioned in B. C. 396 as the allies of the elder Dionysius in his war against Thurii. They were subdued by the Romans after Pyrrhus had left Italy. Before the 2nd Punic war their forces consisted of 30,000 foot and 3000 horse ; but in the course of this war their country was repeatedly laid waste, and never recovered its former prosperity.

Lucānus, M. Annaeus, usually called **Lucan**, a Roman poet, was born at Corduba in Spain, A. D. 39. His father was L. Annaeus Mella, a brother of M. Seneca, the philosopher. Lucan was carried to Rome at an early age, where his education was superintended by the most eminent preceptors of the day. His talents developed themselves at a very early age, and excited such general admiration as to awaken the jealousy of Nero, who, unable to brook competition, forbade him to recite in public. Stung to the quick by this prohibition Lucan embarked in the famous conspiracy of Piso, was betrayed, and, by a promise of pardon, was induced to turn informer. He began by denouncing his own mother Acilia (or Atilia), and then revealed the rest of his accomplices without reserve. But he received a traitor's reward. After the more important victims had been despatched, the emperor issued the mandate for the death of Lucan who, finding escape hopeless, caused his veins to be opened. When, from the rapid effusion of blood, he felt his extremities becoming chill, he began to repeat aloud some verses which he had once composed, descriptive of a wounded soldier perishing by a like death, and, with these lines upon his lips, expired A. D. 65, in the 26th year of his age. Lucan wrote various poems, the titles of which are preserved, but the only extant production is an heroic poem, in 10 books, entitled *Pharsalia*, in which the progress of the struggle between Caesar and Pompey is fully detailed, the events, commencing with the passage of the Rubicon, being arranged in regular chronological order. The 10th book is imperfect, and the narrative breaks off abruptly in the middle of the Alexandrian war, but we know not whether the conclusion has been lost, or whether the author ever completed his task. The whole of what we now possess was certainly not composed at the same time, for the different parts do not by any means breathe the same spirit. In the earlier portions we find liberal sentiments expressed in very moderate terms, accompanied by open and almost fulsome flattery of Nero; but, as we proceed, the blessings of freedom are loudly proclaimed, and the invectives against tyranny are couched in language the most offensive, evidently aimed directly at the emperor. The work contains great beauties and great defects. It is characterised by copious diction, lively imagination, and a bold and masculine tone of thought; but it is at the same time disfigured by extravagance, far-fetched conceits, and unnatural similes. The best editions are by Oudendorp, Lug. Bat. 1728; by Burmann, 1740; and by Weber, Lips 1821—1831.

Lucānus, Ocellus. [OCELLUS.]

Lucceius. 1. L., an old friend and neighbour of Cicero. His name frequently occurs at the commencement of Cicero's correspondence with Atticus, with whom Lucceius had quarrelled. Cicero attempted to reconcile his two friends. In B.C. 63 Lucceius accused Catiline; and in 60 he became a candidate for the consulship, along with Julius Caesar, who agreed to support him; but he lost his election in consequence of the aristocracy bringing in Bibulus, as a counterpoise to Caesar's influence. Lucceius seems now to have withdrawn from public life and to have devoted himself to literature. He was chiefly engaged in the composition of a contemporaneous history of Rome, commencing with the Social or Marsic war. In 55 he had nearly finished the history of the Social and of the first Civil war, when Cicero wrote a most urgent letter to his friend, pressing him to suspend the thread of his history, and to devote a separate work to the period from Catiline's conspiracy to Cicero's recall from banishment (*ad Fam.* v. 12).

Lucceius promised compliance with his request, but he appears never to have written the work. On the breaking out of the civil war in 49, he espoused the side of Pompey. He was subsequently pardoned by Caesar and returned to Rome, where he continued to live on friendly terms with Cicero. — **2. C.**, surnamed **Hirrus**, of the Pupinian tribe, tribune of the plebs 53, proposed that Pompey should be created dictator. In 52 he was a candidate with Cicero for the augurship, and in the following year a candidate with M. Caelius for the aedileship, but he failed in both. On the breaking out of the civil war in 49, he joined Pompey. He was sent by Pompey as ambassador to Orodes, king of Parthia, but he was thrown into prison by the Parthian king. He was pardoned by Caesar after the battle of Pharsalia, and returned to Rome.

Lucenses Callaici, one of the 2 chief tribes of the Callaici or Gallaeci on the N. coast of Hispania Tarraconensis, derived their name from their town Lucus Augusti.

Lucentum (*Alicante*), a town of the Contestani, on the coast of Hispania Tarraconensis.

Lucěrīa (Lucerīnus: *Lucera*), sometimes called **Nucěrīa**, a town in Apulia on the borders of Samnium, S. W. of Arpi, was situated on a steep hill, and possessed an ancient temple of Minerva. In the war between Rome and Samnium, it was first taken by the Samnites (B. C. 321), and next by the Romans (319); but having revolted to the Samnites in 314, all the inhabitants were massacred by the Romans, and their place supplied by 2500 Roman colonists. Having thus become a Roman colony, it continued faithful to Rome in the 2nd Punic war. In the time of Augustus it had greatly declined in prosperity; but it was still of sufficient importance in the 3rd century to be the residence of the praetor of Apulia.

Lucianus (Λουκιανός), usually called **Lucian**, a Greek writer, born at Samosata, the capital of Commagene, in Syria. The date of his birth and death is uncertain; but it has been conjectured, with much probability, that he was born about A. D. 120, and he probably lived till towards the end of this century. We know that some of his more celebrated works were written in the reign of M. Aurelius. Lucian's parents were poor, and he was at first apprenticed to his maternal uncle, who was a statuary. He afterwards became an advocate, and practised at Antioch. Being unsuccessful in this calling, he employed himself in writing speeches for others, instead of delivering them himself. But he did not remain long at Antioch; and at an early period of his life he set out upon his travels, and visited the greater part of Greece, Italy, and Gaul. At that period it was customary for professors of the rhetorical art to proceed to different cities, where they attracted audiences by their displays, much in the same manner as musicians or itinerant lecturers in modern times. He appears to have acquired a good deal of money as well as fame. On his return to his native country, probably about his 40th year, he abandoned the rhetorical profession, the artifices of which, he tells us, were foreign to his temper, the natural enemy of deceit and pretension. He now devoted most of his time to the composition of his works. He still, however, occasionally travelled; for it appears that he was in Achaia and Ionia about the close of the Parthian war, 160—165; on which occasion, too, he seems to have visited Olympia, and beheld the self-immolation of Peregrinus. About the year 170, or a little previously, he visited the false oracle of the impostor Alexander, in Paphlagonia. Late in life he obtained the office of procurator of part of Egypt, which office was probably bestowed upon him by the emperor Commodus. The nature of Lucian's writings inevitably procured him many enemies, by whom he has been painted in very black colours. According to Suidas he was surnamed *the Blasphemer*, and was torn to pieces by dogs, as a punishment for his impiety ; but on this account no reliance can be placed. Other writers state that Lucian apostatised from Christianity ; but there is no proof in support of this charge ; and the dialogue entitled *Philopatris*, which would appear to prove that the author had once been a Christian, was certainly not written by Lucian, and was probably composed in the reign of Julian the Apostate. — As many as 82 works have come down to us under the name of Lucian ; but some of these are spurious. The most important of them are his *Dialogues*. They are of very various degrees of merit, and are treated in the greatest possible variety of style, from seriousness down to the broadest humour and buffoonery. Their subjects and tendency, too, vary considerably ; for while some are employed in attacking the heathen philosophy and religion, others are mere pictures of manners without any polemic drift. Our limits only allow us to mention a few of the more important of these Dialogues : — The *Dialogues of the Gods*, 26 in number, consist of short dramatic narratives of some of the most popular incidents in the heathen mythology. The reader, however, is generally left to draw his own conclusions from the story, the author only taking care to put it in the most absurd point of view.—In the *Jupiter Convicted* a bolder style of attack is adopted ; and the cynic proves to Jupiter's face, that every thing being under the dominion of fate, he has no power whatever. As this dialogue shows Jupiter's want of power, so the *Jupiter the Tragedian* strikes at his very existence, and that of the other deities. — The *Vitarum Auctio*, or *Sale of the Philosophers*, is an attack upon the ancient philosophers. In this humourous piece the heads of the different sects are put up to sale, Hermes being the auctioneer. — The *Fisherman* is a sort of apology for the preceding piece, and may be reckoned among Lucian's best dialogues. The philosophers are represented as having obtained a day's life for the purpose of taking vengeance upon Lucian, who confesses that he has borrowed the chief beauties of his writings from them. — *The Banquet*, or *the Lapithae*, is one of Lucian's most humourous attacks on the philosophers. The scene is a wedding feast, at which a representative of each of the principal philosophic sects is present. A discussion ensues, which sets all the philosophers by the ears, and ends in a pitched battle. — The *Nigrinus* is also an attack on philosophic pride ; but its main scope is to satirise the Romans, whose pomp, vain-glory, and luxury, are unfavourably contrasted with the simple habits of the Athenians. — The more miscellaneous class of Lucian's dialogues, in which the attacks upon mythology and philosophy are not direct but incidental, or which are mere pictures of manners, contains some of his best. At the head must be placed *Timon*, which may perhaps be regarded as Lucian's masterpiece. — The *Dialogues of the Dead* are

perhaps the best known of all Lucian's works. The subject affords great scope for moral reflection, and for satire on the vanity of human pursuits. Wealth, power, beauty, strength, not forgetting the vain disputations of philosophy, afford the materials. Among the moderns these dialogues have been imitated by Fontenelle and Lord Lyttelton. — The *Icaro-Menippus* is in Lucian's best vein, and a master-piece of Aristophanic humour. Menippus, disgusted with the disputes and pretensions of the philosophers, resolves on a visit to the stars, for the purpose of seeing how far their theories are correct. By the mechanical aid of a pair of wings he reaches the moon, and surveys thence the miserable passions and quarrels of men. Hence he proceeds to Olympus, and is introduced to the Thunderer himself. Here he is witness of the manner in which human prayers are received in heaven. They ascend by enormous ventholes, and become audible when Jupiter removes the covers. Jupiter himself is represented as a partial judge, and as influenced by the largeness of the rewards promised to him. At the end he pronounces judgment against the philosophers, and threatens in 4 days to destroy them all. — *Charon* is a very elegant dialogue, but of a graver turn than the preceding. Charon visits the earth to see the course of life there, and what it is that always makes men weep when they enter his boat. Mercury acts as his Cicerone. — Lucian's merits as a writer consist in his knowledge of human nature ; his strong common sense ; the fertility of his invention ; the raciness of his humour ; and the simplicity and Attic grace of his diction. There was abundance to justify his attacks, in the systems against which they were directed. Yet he establishes nothing in their stead. His aim is only to pull down ; to spread a universal scepticism. Nor were his assaults confined to religion and philosophy, but extended to every thing old and venerated, the poems of Homer and Hesiod, and the history of Herodotus. — The best editions of Lucian are by Hemsterhuis and Reitz, Amst. 1743, 4 vols. 4to. ; by Lehman, Lips. 1821—1831, 9 vols. 8vo. ; and by Dindorf, with a Latin version, but without notes, Paris, 1840, 8vo.

Lucifer or **Phosphŏrus** (Φωσφόρος, also by the poets Ἑωσφόρος or Φαεσφόρος), that is, the bringer of light, is the name of the planet Venus, when seen in the morning before sunrise. The same planet was called *Hesperus, Vesperugo, Vesper, Noctifer*, or *Nocturnus*, when it appeared in the heavens after sunset. Lucifer as a personification is called a son of Astraeus and Aurora or Eos, of Cephalus and Aurora, or of Atlas. By Philonis he is said to have been the father of Ceyx. He is also called the father of Daedalion and of the Hesperides. Lucifer is also a surname of several goddesses of light, as Artemis, Aurora, and Hecate.

Lucilius. 1. C., was born at Suessa of the Aurunci, B. C. 148. He served in the cavalry under Scipio in the Numantine war ; lived upon terms of the closest familiarity with Scipio and Laelius; and was either the maternal grand-uncle, or, which is less probable, the maternal grandfather of Pompey the Great. He died at Naples, 103, in the 46th year of his age. Ancient critics agree that, if not absolutely the inventor of Roman satire, he was the first to mould it into that form which afterwards received full developement in the hands of Horace, Persius, and Juvenal. The first of these 3 great masters, while he censures the harsh versification and the slovenly haste with which Lucilius threw off his compositions, acknowledges with admiration the fierceness and boldness of his attacks upon the vices and follies of his contemporaries. The *Satires* of Lucilius were divided into 30 books. Upwards of 800 fragments from these have been preserved, but the greatest number consist of isolated couplets, or single lines. It is clear from these fragments that his reputation for caustic pleasantry was by no means unmerited, and that in coarseness and broad personalities he in no respect fell short of the licence of the old comedy, which would seem to have been, to a certain extent, his model. The fragments were published separately, by Franciscus Dousa, Lug. Bat. 4to. 1597, reprinted by the brothers Volpi, 8vo. Patav. 1735; and, along with Censorinus, by the two sons of Havercamp, Lug. Bat. 8vo. 1743. — 2. **Lucilius Junior**, probably the author of an extant poem in 640 hexameters, entitled *Aetna*, which exhibits throughout great command of language, and contains not a few brilliant passages. Its object is to explain upon philosophical principles, after the fashion of Lucretius, the causes of the various physical phenomena presented by the volcano. Lucilius Junior was the procurator of Sicily, and the friend to whom Seneca addresses his Epistles, his Natural Questions, and his tract on Providence, and whom he strongly urges to select this very subject of Aetna as a theme for his muse.

Lucilla, Annia, daughter of M. Aurelius and the younger Faustina, was born about A. D. 147. She was married to the emperor, L. Verus, and after his death (169) to Claudius Pompeianus. In 183 she engaged in a plot against the life of her brother Commodus, which, having been detected, she was banished to the island of Capreae, and there put to death.

Lucina, the goddess of light, or rather the goddess that brings to light, and hence the goddess that presides over the birth of children. It was therefore used as a surname of Juno and Diana. Lucina corresponded to the Greek goddess ILITHYIA.

Lucretia, the wife of L. Tarquinius Collatinus, whose rape by Sex. Tarquinius led to the dethronement of Tarquinius Superbus and the establishment of the republic. For details see TARQUINIUS.

Lucretia Gens, originally patrician, but subsequently plebeian also. The surname of the patrician Lucretii was *Triciptinus*, one of whom, Sp. Lucretius Triciptinus, the father of Lucretia, was elected consul, with L. Junius Brutus, on the establishment of the republic, B. C. 509. The plebeian families are known by the surnames of *Gallus*, *Ofella*, and *Vespillo*, but none of them is of sufficient importance to require notice.

Lucretilis, a pleasant mountain in the country of the Sabines, overhanging Horace's villa, a part of the modern *Monte Gennaro*.

T. Lucretius Carus, the Roman poet, respecting whose personal history, our information is both scanty and suspicious. The Eusebian Chronicle fixes B. C. 95 as the date of his birth, adding that he was driven mad by a love potion, that during his lucid intervals he composed several works which were revised by Cicero, and that he perished by his own hand in his 44th year, B. C. 52 or 51. Another ancient authority places his death in 55. From what source the tale about the philtre may have been derived we know not; but it is not im-

probable that the whole story was an invention of some enemy of the Epicureans. Not a hint is to be found anywhere which corroborates the assertion with regard to the editorial labours of Cicero. — The work, which has immortalised the name of Lucretius, is a philosophical didactic poem, composed in heroic hexameters, divided into 6 books, containing upwards of 7400 lines, addressed to C. Memmius Gemellus, who was praetor in 58, and is entitled *De Rerum Natura*. It was probably published about 57 or 56; for, from the way in which Cicero speaks of it in a letter to his brother, written in 55, we may conclude that it had only recently appeared. The poem has been sometimes represented as a complete exposition of the religious, moral, and physical doctrines of Epicurus, but this is far from being a correct description. Epicurus maintained that the unhappiness and degradation of mankind arose in a great degree from the slavish dread which they entertained of the power of the gods, and from terror of their wrath; and the fundamental doctrine of his system was, that the gods, whose existence he did not deny, lived in the enjoyment of absolute peace, and totally indifferent to the world and its inhabitants. To prove this position Epicurus adopted the atomic theory of Leucippus, according to which the material universe was not created by the Supreme Being, but was formed by the union of elemental particles which had existed from all eternity, governed by certain simple laws. He further sought to show that all those striking phaenomena which had been regarded by the vulgar as direct manifestations of divine power, were the natural results of ordinary processes. To state clearly and develope fully the leading principle of this philosophy, in such a form as might render the study attractive to his countrymen, was the object of Lucretius, his work being simply an attempt to show that there is nothing in the history or actual condition of the world which does not admit of explanation without having recourse to the active interposition of divine beings. The poem of Lucretius has been admitted by all modern critics to be the greatest of didactic poems. The most abstruse speculations are clearly explained in majestic verse; while the subject, which in itself was dry and dull, is enlivened by digressions of matchless power and beauty.—The best editions are by Wakefield, London, 1796, 3 vols. 4to., reprinted at Glasgow, 1813, 4 vols. 8vo.; and by Forbiger, Lips. 1828, 12mo.

Lucrinus Lacus, was properly the inner part of the Sinus Cumanus or Puteolanus, a bay on the coast of Campania, between the promontory Misenum and Puteoli, running a considerable way inland. But at a very early period the Lucrine lake was separated from the remainder of the bay by a dike 8 stadia in length, which was probably formed originally by some volcanic change, and was subsequently rendered more complete by the work of man. Being thus separated from the rest of the sea, it assumed the character of an inland lake, and is therefore called Lacus by the Romans. Its waters still remained salt, and were celebrated for their oyster beds. Behind the Lucrine lake was another lake called LACUS AVERNUS. In the time of Augustus, Agrippa made a communication between the lake Avernus and the Lucrine lake, and also between the Lucrine lake and the Sinus Cumanus, thus forming out of the 3 the celebrated Julian Harbour. The Lucrine lake was filled up by a volcanic eruption in 1538. when a conical mountain rose in its place, called *Monte Nuovo.* The Avernus has thus become again a separate lake, and no trace of the dike is to be seen in the Gulf of Pozzuoli.

Lucullus, Licinius, a celebrated plebeian family. 1. L., the grandfather of the conqueror of Mithridates, was consul a. c. 151, together with A. Postumius Albinus, and carried on war in Spain against the Vaccaei. — 2. L., son of the preceding, was praetor 103, and carried on war unsuccessfully against the slaves in Sicily. On his return to Rome he was accused, condemned, and driven into exile. — 3. L., son of the preceding, and celebrated as the conqueror of Mithridates. He was probably born about 110. He served with distinction in the Marsic or Social war, and accompanied Sulla as his quaestor into Greece and Asia, 88. When Sulla returned to Italy after the conclusion of peace with Mithridates in 84, Lucullus was left behind in Asia, where he remained till 80. In 79 he was curule aedile with his younger brother Marcus. So great was the favour at this time enjoyed by Lucullus with Sulla, that the dictator, on his death-bed, not only confided to him the charge of revising and correcting his Commentaries, but appointed him guardian of his son Faustus, to the exclusion of Pompey; a circumstance which is said to have first given rise to the enmity and jealousy that ever after subsisted between the two. In 77 Lucullus was praetor, and at the expiration of this magistracy obtained the government of Africa, where he distinguished himself by the justice of his administration. In 74 he was consul with M. Aurelius Cotta. In this year the war with Mithridates was renewed, and Lucullus received the conduct of it. He carried on this war for 8 years with great success. The details are given under MITHRIDATES, and it is only necessary to mention here the leading outlines. Lucullus defeated Mithridates with great slaughter, and drove him out of his hereditary dominions, and compelled him to take refuge in Armenia with his son-in-law Tigranes (71). He afterwards invaded Armenia, defeated Tigranes, and took his capital Tigranocerta (69). In the next campaign (68) he again defeated the combined forces of Mithridates, and laid siege to Nisibis; but in the spring of the following year (67), a mutiny among his troops compelled him to raise the siege of Nisibis, and return to Pontus. Mithridates had already taken advantage of his absence to invade Pontus, and had defeated his lieutenants Fabius and Triarius in several successive actions. But Lucullus on his arrival was unable to effect any thing against Mithridates, in consequence of the mutinous disposition of his troops. The adversaries of Lucullus availed themselves of so favourable an occasion, and a decree was passed to transfer to Acilius Glabrio, one of the consuls for the year, the province of Bithynia and the command against Mithridates. But Glabrio was wholly incompetent for the task assigned him: on arriving in Bithynia, he made no attempt to assume the command, but remained quiet within the confines of the Roman province. Mithridates meanwhile ably availed himself of this position of affairs, and Lucullus had the mortification of seeing Pontus and Cappadocia occupied by the enemy before his eyes, without being able to stir a step in their defence. But it was still more galling to his feelings when, in 66, he was called upon to resign the

command to his old rival Pompey, who had been appointed by the Manilian law to supersede both him and Glabrio. Lucullus did not obtain his triumph till 63, in consequence of the opposition of his enemies. He was much courted by the aristocratical party, who sought in Lucullus a rival and antagonist to Pompey; but, instead of putting himself prominently forward as the leader of a party, he soon began to withdraw gradually from public affairs, and devote himself more and more to a life of indolence and luxury. He died in 57 or 56. Previous to his death he had fallen into a state of complete dotage, so that the management of his affairs was confided to his brother Marcus. The name of Lucullus is almost as celebrated for the luxury of his latter years as for his victories over Mithridates. He amassed vast treasures in Asia; and these supplied him the means, after his return to Rome, of gratifying his natural taste for luxury, together with an ostentatious display of magnificence. His gardens in the immediate suburbs of the city were laid out in a style of extraordinary splendour; but still more remarkable were his villas at Tusculum, and in the neighbourhood of Neapolis. In the construction of the latter, with its parks, fish-ponds, &c., he had laid out vast sums in cutting through hills and rocks, and throwing out advanced works into the sea. So gigantic indeed was the scale of these labours for objects apparently so insignificant, that Pompey called him, in derision, the Roman Xerxes. His feasts at Rome itself were celebrated on a scale of inordinate magnificence: a single supper in the hall, called that of Apollo, was said to cost the sum of 50,000 denarii. Even during his campaigns the pleasures of the table had not been forgotten; and it is well known that he was the first to introduce cherries into Italy, which he had brought with him from Cerasus in Pontus. Lucullus was an enlightened patron of literature, and had from his earliest years devoted much attention to literary pursuits. He collected a valuable library, which was opened to the free use of the literary public; and here he himself used to associate with the Greek philosophers and literati, and would enter warmly into their metaphysical and philosophical discussions. Hence the picture drawn by Cicero at the commencement of the Academics was probably to a certain extent taken from the reality. His constant companion from the time of his quaestorship had been Antiochus of Ascalon, from whom he imbibed the precepts of the Academic school of philosophy, to which he continued through life to be attached. His patronage of the poet Archias is well known. He composed a history of the Marsic war in Greek. — 4. L. or M., son of the preceding and of Servilia, half-sister of M. Cato, was a mere child at his father's death. His education was superintended by Cato and Cicero. After Caesar's death, he joined the republican party, and fell at the battle of Philippi, 42. — 5. M., brother of No. 3, was adopted by M. Terentius Varro, and consequently bore the names of M. TERENTIUS VARRO LUCULLUS. He fought under Sulla in Italy, 82; was curule aedile with his brother 79; praetor 77; and consul 73. After his consulship he obtained the province of Macedonia. He carried on war against the Dardanians and Bessi, and penetrated as far as the Danube. On his return to Rome he obtained a triumph, 71. He was a strong supporter of the aristocratical party. He pronounced the funeral oration of his brother, but died before the commencement of the civil war, 49.

Lucŭmo. [TARQUINIUS.]

Ludĭas. [LYDIAS.]

Lugdunensis Gallia. [GALLIA.]

Lugdŭnum (Lugdunensis). 1. (*Lyon*), the chief town of Gallia Lugdunensis, situated at the foot of a hill at the confluence of the Arar (*Saône*) and the Rhodanus (*Rhone*), is said to have been founded by some fugitives from the town of Vienna, further down the Rhone. In the year after Caesar's death (B. C. 43) Lugdunum was made a Roman colony by L. Munatius Plancus, and became under Augustus the capital of the province and the residence of the Roman governor. Being situated on two navigable rivers, and being connected with the other parts of Gaul by roads, which met at this town as their central point, it soon became a wealthy and populous place, and is described by Strabo as the largest city in Gaul next to Narbo. It received many privileges from the emperor Claudius ; but it was burnt down in the reign of Nero. It was, however, soon rebuilt, and continued to be a place of great importance till A. D. 197, when it was plundered and the greater part of it destroyed by the soldiers o Septimius Severus, after his victory over his rival Albinus in the neighbourhood of the town. From this blow it never recovered, and was more and more thrown into the shade by Vienna. Lugdunum possessed a vast aqueduct, of which the remains may still be traced for miles, and and an imperial palace, in which Claudius was born, and in which many of the other Roman emperors resided. At the tongue of land between the Rhone and the Arar stood an altar dedicated to Augustus by the different states of Gaul ; and here Caligula instituted contests in rhetoric, prizes being given to the victors, but the most ridiculous punishments inflicted on the vanquished. (Comp. Juv. i. 44.) Lugdunum is memorable in the history of the Christian church as the seat of the bishopric of Irenaeus, and on account of the persecutions which the Christians endured here in the 2nd and 3rd centuries. — 2. L. Batavŏrum (*Leyden*), the chief town of the Batavi. [BATAVI.] — 3. Convenărum (*St. Bertrand de Comminges*), the chief town of the Convenae in Aquitania. [CONVENAE.]

Lūna. [SELENE.]

Lūna (Lunensis: *Luni*), an Etruscan town, situated on the left bank of the Macra, about 4 miles from the coast, originally formed part of Liguria, but became the most N.ly city of Etruria, when Augustus extended the boundaries of the latter country as far as the Macra. The town itself was never a place of importance, but it possessed a large and commodious harbour at the mouth of the river, called Lunae Portus (*Gulf of Spezzia*). In B. C. 177 Luna was made a Roman colony, and 2000 Roman citizens were settled there. In the civil war between Caesar and Pompey it had sunk into utter decay, but was colonised a few years afterwards. Luna was celebrated for its white marble, which now takes its name from the neighbouring town of Carrara. The quarries, from which this marble was obtained, appear not to have been worked before the time of Julius Caesar ; but it was extensively employed in the public buildings erected in the reign of Augustus The wine and the cheeses of Luna also

enjoyed a high reputation : some of these cheeses are said to have weighed 1000 pounds. The ruins of Luna are few and unimportant, consisting of the vestiges of an amphitheatre, fragments of columns, &c.

Lūnae Montes (τὸ τῆς Σελήνης ὄρος), a range i f mountains, which some of the ancient geographers *believed* to exist in the interior of Africa, covered with perpetual snow, and containing the sources of the Nile. Their actual existence is neither proved nor disproved.

Lŭperca, or Lŭpa, an ancient Italian divinity, the wife of Lupercus, who, in the shape of a shewolf, performed the office of nurse to Romulus and Remus. In some accounts she is identified with ACCA LAURENTIA, the wife of Faustulus.

Lŭpercus, an ancient Italian divinity, who was worshipped by shepherds as the protector of their flocks against wolves. On the N. side of the Palatine hill there had been in ancient times a cave, the sanctuary of Lupercus, surrounded by a grove, containing an altar of the god and his figure clad in a goatskin, just as his priests, the Luperci. The Romans sometimes identified Lupercus with the Arcadian Pan. Respecting the festival celebrated in honour of Lupercus and his priests, the Luperci, see *Dict. of Ant.* art. *Lupercalia* and *Luperci.*

Lupia. [LUPPIA.]

Lupiae or Luppiae, a town in Calabria, between Brundusium and Hydruntum.

Lupodŭnum (*Ladenburg?*), a town in Germany, on the river Nicer (*Neckar*).

Luppia or Lupia (*Lippe*), a navigable river in the N. W. of Germany, which falls into the Rhine at *Wesel* in *Westphalia*, and on which the Romans built a fortress of the same name. The river Eliso (*Alme*) was a tributary of the Luppia, and at the confluence of these 2 rivers was the fortress of Aliso.

Lŭpus, Rutilĭus. 1. P., consul, with L. Julius Caesar, in B.C. 90, was defeated by the Marsi, and slain in battle. — 2. P., tribune of the plebs, 56, and a warm partisan of the aristocracy. He was praetor in 49, and was stationed at Terracina with 3 cohorts. He afterwards crossed over to Greece. — 3. Probably a son of the preceding, the author of a rhetorical treatise in 2 books, entitled *De Figuris Sententiarum et Elocutionis*, which appears to have been originally an abridgement of a work by Gorgias of Athens, one of the preceptors of young M. Cicero, but which has evidently undergone many changes. Its chief value is derived from the numerous translations which it contains, of striking passages from the works of Greek orators now lost. — Edited by Ruhnken along with Aquila and Julius Ruffinianus, Lug. Bat. 1768, reprinted by Frotscher, Lips. 1831.

Lurco, M. Aufidĭus, tribune of the plebs, B.C. 61, the author of a law on bribery (*de Ambitu*). He was the maternal grandfather of the empress Livia, wife of Augustus. He was the first person in Rome who fattened peacocks for sale, and he derived a large income from this source.

Luscĭnus, Fabricĭus. [FABRICIUS.]

Lusitanĭa, Lusitāni. [HISPANIA.]

Lusŏnes, a tribe of the Celtiberi in Hispania Tarraconensis, near the sources of the Tagus.

Lutātĭus Catŭlus. [CATULUS.]

Lutātĭus Cerco. [CERCO.]

Lutētĭa, or, more commonly, Lutetĭa Parisiōrum (*Paris*), the capital of the Parisii in

Gallia Lugdunensis, was situated on an island in the Sequana (*Seine*), and was connected with the banks of the river by 2 wooden bridges. Under the emperors it became a place of importance, and the chief naval station on the Sequana. Here Julian was proclaimed emperor, A. D. 360.

Lycabettus (Λυκαβηττός: *St. George*), a mountain in Attica, belonging to the range of Pentelicus, close to the walls of Athens on the N. E. of the city, and on the left of the road leading to Marathon. It is commonly, but erroneously, supposed that the small hill N. of the Pnyx is Lycabettus, and that *St. George* is the ancient Anchesmus.

Lycaeus (Λυκαῖος), or **Lyceus**, a lofty mountain in Arcadia, N. W. of Megalopolis, from the summit of which a great part of the country could be seen. It was one of the chief seats of the worship of Zeus, who was hence surnamed *Lycaeus*. Here was a temple of this god; and here also was celebrated the festival of the *Lycaea* (*Dict. of Ant.* s. v.). Pan was likewise called *Lycaeus*, because he was born and had a sanctuary on this mountain.

Lycambes. [ARCHILOCHUS.]

Lycaon (Λυκάων), king of Arcadia, son of Pelasgus by Meliboea or Cyllene. The traditions about Lycaon represent him in very different lights. Some describe him as the first civiliser of Arcadia, who built the town of Lycosura, and introduced the worship of Zeus Lycaeus. But he is more usually represented as an impious king, with a large number of sons as impious as himself. Zeus visited the earth in order to punish them. The god was recognised and worshipped by the Arcadian people. Lycaon resolved to murder him; and in order to try if he were really a god, served before him a dish of human flesh. Zeus pushed away the table which bore the horrible food, and the place where this happened was afterwards called Trapezus. Lycaon and all his sons, with the exception of the youngest (or eldest), Nyctimus, were killed by Zeus with a flash of lightning, or according to others, were changed into wolves.—Callisto, the daughter of Lycaon, is said to have been changed into the constellation of the Bear, whence she is called by the poets *Lycaonis Arctos*, *Lycaonia Arctos*, or *Lycaonia Virgo*, or by her patronymic *Lycaonis*.

Lycaonia (Λυκαονία: Λυκάονες: part of *Karaman*), a district of Asia Minor, assigned, under the Persian Empire, to the satrapy of Cappadocia, but considered by the Greek and Roman geographers the S.E. part of Phrygia; bounded on the N. by Galatia, on the E. by Cappadocia, on the S. by Cilicia Aspera, on the S.W. by Isauria (which was sometimes reckoned as a part of it) and by Phrygia Paroreios, and on the N.W. by Great Phrygia. Its boundaries, however, varied much at different times. — It was a long narrow strip of country, its length extending in the direction of N.W. and S.E. ; Xenophon, who first mentions it, describes its width as extending E. of Iconium (its chief city) to the borders of Cappadocia, a distance of 30 parasangs, about 110 miles. It forms a table land between the Taurus and the mountains of Phrygia, deficient in good water, but abounding in flocks of sheep. The people were, so far as can be traced, an aboriginal race, speaking a language which is mentioned in the *Acts of the Apostles* as a distinct dialect: they were warlike, and especially skilled in archery. After the overthrow of Antiochus the Great by the Romans, Lycaonia, which had belonged successively to Persia and to Syria, was partly assigned to Eumenes, and partly governed by native chieftains, the last of whom, Antipater, a contempory of Cicero, was conquered by Amyntas, king of Galatia, at whose death in B. C. 25 it passed, with Galatia, to the Romans, and was finally united to the province of Cappadocia. Lycaonia was the chief scene of the labours of the Apostle Paul on his first mission to the Gentiles. (*Acts*, xiv.)

Lyceum (τὸ Λύκειον), the name of one of the 3 ancient gymnasia at Athens, called after the temple of Apollo Lyceus, in its neighbourhood. It was situated S. E. of the city, outside the walls, and just above the river Ilissus. Here the Polemarch administered justice. It is celebrated as the place where Aristotle and the Peripatetics taught.

Lyceus (Λύκειος), a surname of Apollo, the meaning of which is not quite certain. Some derive it from λύκος, a wolf, so that it would mean " the wolf-slayer;" others from λύκη, light, according to which it would mean " the giver of light;" and others again from the country of Lycia.

Lychnitis. [LYCHNIDUS.]

Lychnidus, more rarely **Lychnidium** or **Lychnis** (Λύχνιδος, Λυχνίδιον, Λυχνίς: Λυχνίδιος; *Achrita*, *Ochrida*), a town of Illyricum, was the ancient capital of the Dessaretii, but was in the possession of the Romans as early as their war with king Gentius. It was situated in the interior of the country, on a height on the N. bank of the lake **Lychnitis** (Λυχνῖτις, or ἡ Λυχνιδία λίμνη), from which the river Drilo rises. The town was strongly fortified, and contained many springs within its walls. In the middle ages it was the residence of the Bulgarian kings, and was called *Achris* or *Achrita*, whence its modern name.

Lycia (Λυκία: Λύκιος, Lycius: *Meis*), a small, but most interesting, district on the S. side of Asia Minor, jutting out into the Mediterranean in a form approaching to a rough semicircle, adjacent to parts of Caria and Pamphylia on the W. and E., and on the N. to the district of Cibyratis in Phrygia, to which, under the Byzantine emperors, it was considered to belong. It was bounded on the N.W. by the little river Glaucus and the gulf of the same name, on the N.E. by the mountain called CLIMAX (the N. part of the same range as that called Solyma), and on the N. its natural boundary was the Taurus, but its limits in this direction were not strictly defined. The N. parts of Lycia and the district of Cibyratis form together a high table land, which is supported on the N. by the Taurus ; on the E. by the mountains called Solyma (*Taktalu-Dagh*), which run from N. to S. along the E. coast of Lycia, far out into the sea, forming the S.E. promontory of Lycia, called Sacrum Pr. (*C. Khelidonia*) ; the summit of this range is 7800 feet high, and is covered with snow * : the S.W. and S. sides of this table land are formed by the range called Massicytus (*Aktar Dagh*), which runs S.E. from the E. side of the upper course of the river Xanthus: its summits are about 4000 feet high ; and its S. side descends towards the sea in a succession of terraces, terminated by bold cliffs. The mountain system of Lycia is completed by the Cragus, which fills up the space between the W. side of the Xanthus and the Gulf of Glaucus, and forms the S.W. promontory of Lycia : its summits are nearly 6000 feet high. The chief rivers are

---

* According to many of the ancients the Taurus began at this range.

the Xanthus (*Echen-Chai*), which has its sources in the table-land S. of the Taurus, and flows from N. to S. between the Cragus and Massicytus, and the Limyrus, which flows from N. to S. between the Massicytus and the Solyma mountains. The vallies of these and the smaller rivers, and the terraces above the sea in the S. of the country were fertile in corn, wine, oil, and fruits, and the mountain slopes were clothed with splendid cedars, firs, and plane-trees : saffron also was one chief product of the land. The total length of the coast, from Telmissus on the W. to Phaselis on the E., including all windings, is estimated by Strabo at 1720 stadia (172 geog. miles), while a straight line drawn across the country, as the chord of this arc, is about 80 geog. miles in length. The general geographical structure of the peninsula of Lycia, as connected with the rest of Asia Minor, bears no little resemblance to that of the peninsula of Asia Minor itself, as connected with the rest of Asia. According to the tradition preserved by Herodotus, the most ancient name of the country was Milyas (ἡ Μιλυάς), and the earliest inhabitants (probably of the Syro-Arabian race) were called Milyae, and afterwards Solymi : subsequently the Termilae, from Crete, settled in the country : and lastly, the Athenian Lycus, the son of Pandion, fled from his brother Aegeus to Lycia, and gave his name to the country. Homer, who gives Lycia a prominent place in the Iliad, represents its chieftains, Glaucus and Sarpedon, as descended from the royal family of Argos (Aeolids) : he does not mention the name of Milyas ; and he speaks of the Solymi as a warlike race, inhabiting the mountains, against whom the Greek hero Bellerophontes is sent to fight, by his relative the king of Lycia. Besides the legend of Bellerophon and the chimaera, Lycia is the scene of another popular Greek story, that of the Harpies and the daughters of Pandarus ; and memorials of both are preserved on the Lycian monuments now in the British Museum. On the whole, it is clear that Lycia was colonized by the Hellenic race (probably from Crete) at a very early period, and that its historical inhabitants were Greeks, though with a mixture of native blood. The earlier names were preserved in the district in the N. of the country called Milyas, and in the mountains called Solyma. The Lycians always kept the reputation they have in Homer, as brave warriors. They and the Cilicians were the only people W. of the Halys whom Croesus did not conquer, and they were the last who resisted the Persians. [XANTHUS.] Under the Persian empire they must have been a powerful maritime people, as they furnished 50 ships to the fleet of Xerxes. After the Macedonian conquest, Lycia formed part of the Syrian kingdom, from which it was taken by the Romans after their victory over Antiochus III. the Great, and given to the Rhodians. It was soon restored to independence, and formed a flourishing federation of cities, each having its own republican form of government. and the whole presided over by a chief magistrate, called Λυκιάρχης. There was a federal council, composed of deputies from the 23 cities of the federation, in which the 6 chief cities, Xanthus, Patara, Pinara, Olympus, Myra, and Tlos, had 3 votes each, certain lesser cities 2 each, and the rest 1 each : this assembly determined matters relating to the general government of the country, and elected the Lyciarches, as well as the judges

and the inferior magistrates. Internal dissensions at length broke up this constitution, and the country was united by the emperor Claudius to the province of Pamphylia, from which it was again separated by Theodosius, who made it a separate province, with Myra for its capital. Its cities were numerous and flourishing (see the articles), and its people celebrated for their probity. Their customs are said to have resembled those both of the Carians and of the Cretans. Respecting the works of art found by Mr. Fellows in Lycia, and now in the British Museum, see XANTHUS.

Lycius (Λύκιος). 1. The *Lycian*, a surname of Apollo, who was worshipped in several places of Lycia, especially at Patara, where he had an oracle. Hence the *Lyciae sortes* are the responses of the oracle at Patara (Virg. *Aen.* iv. 346). — 2. Of Eleutherae, in Boeotia, a distinguished statuary, the disciple or son of Myron, flourished about B.C. 428.

Lycomedes (Λυκομήδης). 1. A king of the Dolopians, in the island of Scyros, near Euboea. It was to his court that Achilles was sent disguised as a maiden by his mother Thetis, who was anxious to prevent his going to the Trojan war. Here Achilles became by Deidamia, the daughter of Lycomedes, the father of Pyrrhus or Neoptolemus. Lycomedes treacherously killed Theseus by thrusting him down a rock. — 2. A celebrated Arcadian general, was a native of Mantinea and one of the chief founders of Megalopolis B.C. 370. He afterwards showed great jealousy of Thebes, and formed a separate alliance between Athens and Arcadia, in 366. He was murdered in the same year on his return from Athens, by some Arcadian exiles.

Lycon (Λύκων). 1. An orator and demagogue at Athens, was one of the 3 accusers of Socrates and prepared the case against him. When the Athenians repented of their condemnation of Socrates, they put Meletus to death and banished Anytus and Lycon. — 2. Of Troas, a distinguished Peripatetic philosopher, and the disciple of Straton, whom he succeeded as the head of the Peripatetic school, B.C. 272. He held that post for more than 44 years, and died at the age of 74. He enjoyed the patronage of Attalus and Eumenes. He was celebrated for his eloquence and for his skill in educating boys. He wrote on the boundaries of good and evil (*De Finibus*).

Lycophron (Λυκόφρων). 1. Younger son of Periander, tyrant of Corinth, by his wife Melissa. For details see PERIANDER. — 2. A citizen of Pherae, where he put down the government of the nobles and established a tyranny about B.C. 405. He afterwards endeavoured to make himself master of the whole of Thessaly, and in 404 he defeated the Larissaeans and others of the Thessalians, who opposed him. He was probably the father of JASON of Pherae. — 3. A son, apparently, of Jason, and one of the brothers of Thebe, wife of Alexander, the tyrant of Pherae, in whose murder he took part together with his sister and his 2 brothers, Tisiphonus and Pitholaus, 367. On Alexander's death the power appears to have been wielded mainly by Tisiphonus, though Lycophron had an important share in the government. Lycophron succeeded to the supreme power on the death of Tisiphonus, but in 352 he was obliged to surrender Pherae to Philip, and withdraw from Thessaly. — 4. A grammarian and poet, was a native of Chalcis in Euboea, and lived at Alexandria, under Ptolemy Philadelphus (B.C. 285—247), who entrusted to him the arrangement of the works of the comic poets in the Alexandrian library. In the execution of this commission Lycophron drew up an extensive work on comedy. Nothing more is known of his life. Ovid (*Ibis*, 533) states that he was killed by an arrow.—As a poet, Lycophron obtained a place in the Tragic Pleiad. He also wrote a satyric drama. But the only one of his poems which has come down to us is the *Cassandra* or *Alexandra*. This is neither a tragedy nor an epic poem, but a long iambic monologue of 1474 verses, in which Cassandra is made to prophesy the fall of Troy, the adventures of the Grecian and Trojan heroes, with numerous other mythological and historical events, going back as early as the fables of Io and Europa, and ending with Alexander the Great. The work has no pretensions to poetical merit. It is simply a cumbrous store of traditional learning. Its obscurity is proverbial. Its author obtained the epithet of the *Obscure* (σκοτεινός). Its stores of learning and its obscurity alike excited the efforts of the ancient grammarians, several of whom wrote commentaries on the poem. The only one of these works which survives, is the *Scholia* of Isaac and John Tzetzes, which are far more valuable than the poem itself.—The best editions are by Potter, Oxon. 1697, fol.; Reichard, Lips. 1788, 2 vols. 8vo.; and Bachmann, Lips. 1828, 2 vols. 8vo.

Lycōpŏlis (ἡ Λύκων πόλις: *Sioul*, Ru.), a city of Upper Egypt, on the W. bank of the Nile, between Hermopolis and Ptolemais, said to have derived its name from the circumstance, that an Aethiopian army was put to flight near it by a pack of wolves.

Lycorēa (Λυκώρεια: Λυκωρεύς, Λυκώριος, Λυκωρείτης), an ancient town at the foot of Mt. Lycorea (*Liakura*), which was the southern of the 2 peaks of Mt. Parnassus. [PARNASSUS.] Hence Apollo derived the surname of Lycoreus. The town Lycorea is said to have been the residence of Deucalion, and Delphi is also reported to have been colonised by it.

Lyctŏris. [CYTHERIS.]

Lycortas (Λυκόρτας), of Megalopolis, was the father of Polybius, the historian, and the close friend of Philopoemen, whose policy he always supported. He is first mentioned in B.C. 189, as one of the ambassadors sent to Rome; and his name occurs for the last time in 168.

Lycostūra (Λυκόσουρα: Λυκοσουρεύς: *Palaeo-krambavos* or *Sidhirokastro* near *Stala*), a town in the S. of Arcadia, and on the N. W. slope of Mt. Lycaeus, and near the small river Plataniston, said by Pausanias to have been the most ancient town in Greece, and to have been founded by Lycaon, the son of Pelasgus.

Lyctus (Λύκτος: Λύκτιος), sometimes called Lyttus (Λύττος), an important town in the E. of Crete, S. E. of Cnossus, was situated on a height of Mt. Argaeus, 80 stadia from the coast. Its harbour was called Chersonesus. It was one of the most ancient cities in the island, and is mentioned in the Iliad. It was generally considered to be a Spartan colony, and its inhabitants were celebrated for their bravery. At a later time it was conquered and destroyed by the Cnossians, but it was afterwards rebuilt, and was extant in the 7th century of our era.

Lycurgus (Λυκοῦργος). 1. Son of Dryas, and king of the Edones in Thrace. He is famous for his persecution of Dionysus (Bacchus) and his worship in Thrace. Homer relates that, in order to escape from Lycurgus, Dionysus leaped into the sea, where he was kindly received by Thetis; and that Zeus thereupon blinded the impious king, who died soon afterwards, hated by the immortal gods. This story has received many additions from later poets and mythographers. Some relate that Dionysus, on his expeditions, came to the kingdom of Lycurgus; but was expelled by the impious king. Thereupon the god drove Lycurgus mad, in which condition he killed his son Dryas, and also hewed off one of his legs, supposing that he was cutting down vines. The country now produced no fruit; and the oracle declaring that fertility should not be restored unless Lycurgus were killed,' the Edonians carried him to mount Pangaeum, where he was torn to pieces by horses. According to Sophocles (*Antig.* 955), Lycurgus was entombed in a rock.—2. King in Arcadia, son of Aleus and Neaera, brother of Cepheus and Auge, husband of Cleophile, Eurynome, or Antinoe, and father of Ancaeus, Epochus, Amphidamas, and Iasus. Lycurgus killed Areïthous, who used to fight with a club. Lycurgus bequeathed this club to his slave Ereuthalion, his sons having died before him.—3. Son of Pronax and brother of Amphithea, the wife of Adrastus. He took part in the war of the Seven against Thebes, and fought with Amphiaraus. He is mentioned among those whom Aesculapius called to life again after their death.—4. King of Nemea, son of Pheres and Periclymene, brother of Admetus, husband of Eurydice or Amphithea, and father of Opheltes.

Lycurgus. 1. The Spartan legislator. Of his personal history we have no certain information; and there are such discrepancies respecting him in the ancient writers, that many modern critics have denied his real existence altogether. The more generally received account about him was as follows:—Lycurgus was the son of Eunomus, king of Sparta, and brother of Polydectes. The latter succeeded his father as king of Sparta, and afterwards died, leaving his queen with child. The ambitious woman proposed to Lycurgus to destroy her offspring if he would share the throne with her. He seemingly consented; but when she had given birth to a son (Charilaus), he openly proclaimed him king; and as next of kin, acted as his guardian. But to avoid all suspicion of ambitious designs, with which the opposite party charged him, Lycurgus left Sparta, and set out on his celebrated travels, which have been magnified to a fabulous extent. He is said to have visited Crete, and there to have studied the wise laws of Minos. Next he went to Ionia and Egypt, and is reported to have penetrated into Libya, Iberia, and even India. In Ionia he is said to have met either with Homer himself, or at least with the Homeric poems, which he introduced into the mother country. The return of Lycurgus to Sparta was hailed by all parties. Sparta was in a state of anarchy and licentiousness, and he was considered as the man who alone could cure the growing diseases of the state. He undertook the task; yet before he set to work, he strengthened himself with the authority of the Delphic oracle, and with a strong party of influential men at Sparta. The reform seems not to have been carried altogether peaceably. The new division of the land among the citizens must have violated many existing interests. But all opposition was overborne, and the whole constitution, military and civil, was remodelled. After Lycurgus had obtained for his institutions an approving oracle of the national god of Delphi, he exacted a promise from the people not to make any alterations in his laws before his return. And now he left Sparta to finish his life in voluntary exile, in order that his countrymen might be bound by their oath to preserve his constitution inviolate for ever. Where and how he died nobody could tell. He vanished from the earth like a god, leaving no traces behind but his spirit; and he was honoured as a god at Sparta with a temple and yearly sacrifices down to the latest times. The date of Lycurgus is variously given, but it is impossible to place it later than B. C. 825.—Lycurgus was regarded through all subsequent ages as the legislator of Sparta, and therefore almost all the Spartan institutions were ascribed to him as their author. We therefore propose to give here a sketch of the Spartan institution, referring for details to the *Dict. of Antiq.*; though we must not imagine that this constitution was entirely the work of Lycurgus. The Spartan constitution was of a mixed nature: the monarchical principle was represented by the kings, the aristocracy by the senate, and the democratical element by the assembly of the people, and subsequently by their representatives, the ephors. The kings had originally to perform the common functions of the kings of the heroic age. They were high priests, judges, and leaders in war; but in all of these departments they were in course of time superseded more or less. As judges they retained only a particular branch of jurisdiction, that referring to the succession of property. As military commanders they were restricted and watched by commissioners sent by the senate; the functions of high priest were curtailed least, perhaps because least obnoxious. In compensation for the loss of power, the kings enjoyed great honours, both during their life and after their death. Still the principle of monarchy was very weak among the Spartans.—The powers of the senate were very important: they had the right of originating and discussing all measures before they could be submitted to the decision of the popular assembly; they had, in conjunction with the ephors, to watch over the due observance of the laws and institutions; and they were judges in all criminal cases, without being bound by any written code. For all this they were not responsible, holding their office for life.—But with all these powers, the elders formed no real aristocracy. They were not chosen either for property qualification or for noble birth. The senate was open to the poorest citizen, who, during 60 years, had been obedient to the laws and zealous in the performance of his duties.—The mass of the people, that is, the Spartans of pure Doric descent, formed the sovereign power of the state. The popular assembly consisted of every Spartan of 30 years of age, and of unblemished character; only those were excluded who had not the means of contributing their portion to the syssitia. They met at stated times, to decide on all important questions brought before them, after a previous discussion in the senate. They had no right of amendment, but only that of simple approval or rejection, which was given in the rudest form possible, by shouting. The popular assembly, however, had neither frequent nor very important occasions for directly exerting their sovereign power.

Their chief activity consisted in delegating it; hence arose the importance of the ephors, who were the representatives of the popular element of the constitution. The ephors answer in every characteristic feature to the Roman tribunes of the people. Their origin was lost in obscurity and insignificance; but at the end they engrossed the whole power of the state.—With reference to their subjects, the few Spartans formed a most decided aristocracy. On the conquest of Peloponnesus by the Dorians, part of the ancient inhabitants of the country, under name of the *Perioici*, were allowed indeed to retain their personal liberty, but lost all civil rights, and were obliged to pay to the state a rent for the land that was left them. But a great part of the old inhabitants were reduced to a state of perfect slavery, different from that of the slaves of Athens and Rome, and more similar to the villanage of the feudal ages. These were called *Helots.* They were allotted with patches of land, to individual members of the ruling class. They tilled the land, and paid a fixed rent to their *masters*, not, as the perioici, to the state. The number of these miserable creatures was large. They were treated with the utmost cruelty by the Spartans, and were frequently put to death by their oppressors. — The Spartans formed, as it were, an army of invaders in an enemy's country, their city was a camp, and every man a soldier. At Sparta, the citizen only existed for the state; he had no interest but the state's, and no property but what belonged to the state. It was a fundamental principle of the constitution, that all citizens were entitled to the enjoyment of an equal portion of the common property. This was done in order to secure to the commonwealth a large number of citizens and soldiers, free from labour for their sustenance, and able to devote their whole time to warlike exercises, in order thus to keep up the ascendancy of Sparta over her perioici and helots. The Spartans were to be warriors and nothing but warriors. Therefore, not only all mechanical labour was thought to degrade them; not only was husbandry despised and neglected, and commerce prevented, or at least impeded, by prohibitive laws and by the use of iron money; but also the nobler arts and sciences were so effectually stifled, that Sparta is a blank in the history of the arts and literature of Greece. The state took care of a Spartan from his cradle to his grave, and superintended his education in the minutest points. This was not confined to his youth, but extended throughout his whole life. The syssitia, or, as they were called at Sparta, phiditia, the common meals, may be regarded as an educational institution; for at these meals subjects of general interest were discussed and political questions debated. The youths and boys used to eat separately from the men, in their own divisions. — 2. A Lacedaemonian, who, though not of the royal blood, was chosen king, in B. C. 220, together with Agesipolis III., after the death of Cleomenes. It was not long before he deposed his colleague and made himself sole sovereign, though under the control of the Ephori. He carried on war against Philip V. of Macedon, and the Achaeans. He died about 210, and Machanidas then made himself tyrant. — 3. An Attic orator, son of Lycophron, who belonged to the noble family of the Eteobutadae, was born at Athens, about B. C. 396. He was a disciple of Plato and Isocrates. In public life he was a warm supporter of the policy of Demosthenes, and was universally admitted to be one of the most virtuous citizens and upright statesmen of his age. He was thrice appointed *Tamias* or manager of the public revenue, and held this office each time for five years, beginning with 337. He discharged the duties of this office with such ability and integrity, that he raised the public revenue to the sum of 1200 talents. One of his laws enacted that bronze statues should be erected to Aeschylus, Sophocles, and Euripides, and that copies of their tragedies should be preserved in the public archives. He often appeared as a successful accuser in the Athenian courts, but he himself was as often accused by others, though he always succeeded in silencing his enemies. He died while holding the office of President of the theatre of Dionysus, in 323. A fragment of an inscription, containing an account of his administration of the finances, is still extant. There were 15 orations of Lycurgus extant in antiquity; but only one has come down to us entire, the oration against Leocrates, which was delivered in 330. The style is noble and grand, but neither elegant nor pleasing. The oration is printed in the various collections of the Attic orators. [DEMOSTHENES.]

Lжcus (Λύκος). 1. Son of Poseidon and Celaeno, who was transferred by his father to the islands of the blessed. By Alcyone, the sister of Celaeno, Poseidon begot Hyrieus, the father of the following.—2. Son of Hyrieus and Clonia, and brother of Nycteus. Polydorus, king of Thebes, married the daughter of Nycteus, by whom he had a son Labdacus; and on his death he left the government of Thebes and the guardianship of Labdacus to his father-in-law. Nycteus afterwards fell in battle against Epopeus, king of Sicyon, who had carried away his beautiful daughter Antiope. Lycus succeeded his brother in the government of Thebes, and in the guardianship of Labdacus. He surrendered the kingdom to Labdacus when the latter had grown up. On the death of Labdacus soon afterwards, Lycus again succeeded to the government of Thebes, and undertook the guardianship of Laius, the son of Labdacus. Lycus marched against Epopeus, whom he put to death (according to other accounts Epopeus fell in the war with Nycteus), and he carried away Antiope to Thebes. She was treated with the greatest cruelty by Dirce, the wife of Lycus; in revenge for which her sons by Zeus, Amphion and Zethus, afterwards put to death both Lycus and Dirce. [AMPHION.]—3. Son of No. 2, or, according to others, son of Poseidon, was also king of Thebes. In the absence of Hercules, Lycus attempted to kill his wife Megara and her children, but was afterwards put to death by Hercules.—4. Son of Pandion, and brother of Aegeus, Nisus, and Pallas. He was expelled by Aegeus, and took refuge in the country of the Termili, which was called Lycia after him. He was honoured at Athens as a hero, and the Lyceum derived its name from him. He is said to have introduced the Eleusinian mysteries into Andania in Messenia. He is sometimes also described as an ancient prophet, and the family of the Lycomedae, at Athens, traced their name and origin from him.—5. Son of Dascylus, and king of the Mariandynians, who received Hercules and the Argonauts with hospitality.—6. Of Rhegium, the father, real or adoptive, of the poet Lycophron, was an historical writer in the time of Demetrius Phalereus.

Lжcus (Λύκος), the name of several rivers, which are said to be so called from the impetuosity of their current. 1. (*Kilij*), a little river of Bithynia, falling into the sea S. of Heraclea Pontica.—2. (*Germeneh-Chai*), a considerable river of Pontus, rising in the mountains on the N. of Armenia Minor, and flowing W. into the Iris at Eupatoria.—3. (*Choruk-Su*), a considerable river of Phrygia, flowing from E. to W. past Colossae and Laodicea into the Maeander.—4. (*Nahr-el-Kelb*), a river of Phoenicia, falling into the sea N. of Berytus.—5. (*Great Zab* or *Ulu-Su*), a river of Assyria, rising in the mountains on the S. of Armenia, and flowing S. W. into the Tigris, just below Larissa (*Nimroud*). It is undoubtedly the same as the Zabatus of Xenophon.

Lydda (τὰ Λύδδα, ἡ Λύδδη: *Lud*), a town of Palestine, S. E. of Joppa, and N. W. of Jerusalem, at the junction of several roads which lead from the sea-coast, was destroyed by the Romans in the Jewish War, but soon after rebuilt, and called Diospolis.

Lydia (Λυδία: Λυδός, Lydus), a district of Asia Minor, in the middle of the W. side of the peninsula, between Mysia on the N. and Caria on the S., and between Phrygia on the E. and the Aegean Sea on the W. Its boundaries varied so much at different times, that they cannot be described with any approach to exactness till we come to the time of the Roman rule over W. Asia. At that time the N. boundary, towards Mysia, was the range of mountains which form the N. margin of the valley of the Hermus, called Sardene, a S. W. branch of the Phrygian Olympus: the E. boundary towards Phrygia was an imaginary line: and the S. boundary towards Caria was the river Maeander, or, according to some authorities, the range of mountains which, under the name of Messogis (*Kastane Dagh*) forms the N. margin of the valley of the Maeander, and is a N. W. prolongation of the Taurus. From the E. part of this range, in the S. E. corner of Lydia, another branches off to the N. W., and runs to the W. far out into the Aegean Sea, where it forms the peninsula opposite to the island of Chios. This chain, which is called Tmolus (*Kisilja Musa Dagh*), divides Lydia into 2 unequal vallies; of which the S. and smaller is watered by the river CAYSTER, and the N. forms the great plain of the HERMUS: these vallies are very beautiful and fertile, and that of the Hermus especially is one of the most delicious regions of the earth. The E. part of Lydia, and the adjacent portion of Phrygia, about the upper course of the Hermus and its tributaries, is an elevated plain, showing traces of volcanic action, and hence called Catacecaumēne (κατακεκαυμένη). In the boundaries of Lydia, as just described, the strip of coast belonging to IONIA is included, but the name is sometimes used in a narrower signification, so as to exclude Ionia. In early times the country had another name, Maeonia (Μηονίη, Μαιονία), by which alone it is known to Homer; and this name was afterwards applied specifically to the E. and S. part of Lydia, and then, in contradistinction to it, the name Lydia was used for the N.W. part. In the mythical legends the common name of the people and country, Lydi and Lydia, is derived from Lydus, the son of Atys, the first king. The Lydians appear to have been a race closely connected with the Carians and the Mysians, with whom they observed a common worship in the temple of Zeus Carius at Mylasa: they also practised the worship of Cybele, and other Phrygian customs. Amidst the uncertainties of the early legends, it is clear that Lydia was a very early seat of Asiatic civilization, and that it exerted a very important influence on the Greeks. The Lydian monarchy, which was founded at Sardis, before the time of authentic history, grew up into an empire, under which the many different tribes of Asia Minor W. of the river Halys were for the first time united. Tradition mentioned 3 dynasties of kings ; the Atyădae, which ended (according to the backward computations of chronologers) about B. C. 1221 ; the Heraclīdae, which reigned 505 years, down to 716 ; and the Mermnădae, 160 years, down to 556. Only the last dynasty can be safely regarded as historical, and the fabulous element has a large place in the details of their history : their names and computed dates were : — (1) Gyges, B. c. 716—678 ; (2) Ardys, 678—629 ; (3) Sadyattes, 629—617 ; (4) Alyattes, 617—560 ; (5) Croesus, 560 (or earlier)—546 ; under whose names an account is given of the rise of the Lydian empire in Asia Minor, and of its overthrow by the Persians under Cyrus. Under these kings, the Lydians appear to have been a highly civilised, industrious, and wealthy people, practising agriculture, commerce, and manufactures, and acquainted with various arts ; and exercising, through their intercourse with the Greeks of Ionia, an important influence on the progress of Greek civilisation. Among the inventions, or improvements, which the Greeks are said to have derived from them, were the weaving and dyeing of fine fabrics ; various processes of metallurgy ; the use of gold and silver money, which the Lydians are said first to have coined, the former from the gold found on Tmolus and from the golden sands of the Pactolus ; and various metrical and musical improvements, especially the scale or *mode* of music called the *Lydian*, and the form of the lyre called the *magadis*. (See *Dict. of Antiq., Musica*). The Lydians had also public games similar to those of the Greeks. Their high civilisation, however, was combined with a lax morality, and, after the Persian conquest, when they were forbidden by Cyrus to carry arms, they sank gradually into a bye-word for effeminate luxuriousness, and their very name and language had almost entirely disappeared by the commencement of our era. Under the Persians, Lydia and Mysia formed the 2nd satrapy : after the Macedonian conquest, Lydia belonged first to the kings of Syria, and next (after the defeat of Antiochus the Great by the Romans) to those of Pergamus, and so passed, by the bequest of Attalus III., to the Romans, under whom it formed part of the province of Asia.

Lydīădes (Λυδιάδης), a citizen of Megalopolis, who, though of an obscure family, raised himself to the sovereignty of his native city, about B. c. 244. In 234 he voluntarily abdicated the sovereignty, and permitted Megalopolis to join the Achaean League as a free state. He was elected several times general of the Achaean League, and became a formidable rival to Aratus. He fell in battle against Cleomenes, 226.

Lydĭas or Ludias (Λυδίας, Ion. Λυδίης, Λουδίας : *Karasmak* or *Mavronero*), a river in Macedonia, rises in Eordaea, passes Edessa, and after flowing through the lake on which Pella is situated, falls into the Axius, a short distance from the Thermaic gulf. In the upper part of its course

it is called the Eordaean river (Ἐορδαϊκὸς ποταμὸς) by Arrian. Herodotus (vii. 127) by mistake makes the Lydias unite with the Haliacmon, the latter of which is W. of the former.

Lydus (Λῦδος), son of Atys and Callithea, and brother of Tyrrhenus, said to have been the mythical ancestor of the Lydians.

Lydus, Joannes Laurentius, was born at Philadelphia, in Lydia (whence he is called Lydus or the Lydian), in a. d. 490. He held various public offices, and lived to an advanced age. He wrote : 1. Περὶ μηνῶν συγγραφή, *De Mensibus Liber*, of which there are two epitomae, or summaries, and a fragment extant. 2. Περὶ ἀρχῶν κ. τ. λ. *De Magistratibus Reipublicae Romanae*. 3. Περὶ διοσημειῶν, *De Ostentis*. The work *De Mensibus* is an historical commentary on the Roman calendar, with an account of the various festivals, derived from a great number of authorities, most of which have perished. Of the two summaries of this curious work, the larger one is by an unknown hand, the shorter one by Maximus Planudes. The work *De Magistratibus* was thought to have perished, but was discovered by Villoison in the suburbs of Constantinople, in 1785. The best edition of these works is by Bekker, Bonn, 1837.

Lygdămis (Λύγδαμις). 1. Of Naxos, a distinguished leader of the popular party of the island in the struggle with the oligarchy. He conquered the latter, and obtained thereby the chief power in the state. He assisted Pisistratus in his third return to Athens ; but during his absence his enemies seem to have got the upper hand again ; for Pisistratus afterwards subdued the island, and made Lygdamis tyrant of it, about B. c. 540. In 532 he assisted Polycrates in obtaining the tyranny of Samos. — 2. Father of Artemisia, queen of Halicarnassus, the contemporary of Xerxes. — 3 Tyrant of Halicarnassus, the son of Pisindelis, and the grandson of Artemisia. The historian Herodotus is said to have taken an active part in delivering his native city from the tyranny of this Lygdamis.

Lygii or Ligii, an important people in Germany, between the Viadus (*Oder*) and the Vistula, in the modern *Silesia* and *Posen*, were bounded by the Burgundiones on the N., the Goths on the E., the Bastarnae and Osi on the W., and the Marsingi, Silingae and Semnones on the S. They were divided into several tribes, the chief of which were the Manimi, Duni, Elysii, Burii, Arii, Naharvali and Helveconae. They first appear in history as members of the great Marcomannic league formed by Maroboduus in the reigns of Augustus and Tiberius. In the 3rd century some of the Lygii migrated with the Burgundians W.-wards, and settled in the country bordering on the Rhine.

Lyncestis (Λυγκηστίς), a district in the S. W. of Macedonia, N. of the river Erigon, and upon the frontiers of Illyria. Its inhabitants, the Lyncestae, were Illyrians, and were originally an independent people, who were governed by their own princes, said to be descended from the family of the Bacchiadae. The Lyncestae appear to have become subject to Macedonia by a marriage between the royal families of the 2 countries. The ancient capital of the country was Lyncus (ἡ Λύγκος), though Heraclea at a later time became the chief town in the district. Near Lyncus was a river, the waters of them are said to have been as intoxicating as wine. (Ov. *Met.* xv. 329.)

Lynceus (Λυγκεύς). 1. One of the 50 sons of Aegyptus, whose life was saved by his wife Hypermnestra, when all his other brothers were murdered by the daughters of Danaus on their wedding night. [AEGYPTUS.] Danaus thereupon kept Hypermnestra in strict confinement, but was afterwards prevailed upon to give her to Lynceus, who succeeded him on the throne of Argos. According to a different legend, Lynceus slew Danaus and all the sisters of Hypermnestra, in revenge for his brothers. Lynceus was succeeded as king of Argos by his son ABAS. — 2. Son of Aphareus and Arene, and brother of Idas, was one of the Argonauts and famous for his keen sight. He is also mentioned among the Calydonian hunters, and was slain by Pollux. For details respecting his death. see p. 228, b. — 3. Of Samos, the disciple of Theophrastus, and the brother of the historian Duris, was a contemporary of Menander, and his rival in comic poetry. He survived Menander, upon whom he wrote a book. He seems to have been more distinguished as a grammarian and historian than as a comic poet.

Lyncus, king of Scythia, or, according to others, of Sicily, endeavoured to murder Triptolemus, who came to him with the gifts of Ceres, but he was metamorphosed by the goddess into a lynx.

Lyroëa or **Lyroëum** (Λυρκεία, Λύρκειον), a small town in Argolis, situated on a mountain of the same name.

Lyrnessus (Λυρνησσός), a town in the interior of Mysia, in Asia Minor, frequently mentioned by Homer: destroyed before the time of Strabo.

Lysander (Λύσανδρος), a Spartan, was of servile origin, or at least the offspring of a marriage between a freeman and a woman of inferior condition. He obtained the citizenship, and became one of the most distinguished of the Spartan generals and diplomatists. In B. C. 407, he was sent out to succeed Cratesippidas in the command of the fleet, off the coasts of Asia Minor. He fixed his head-quarters at Ephesus, and soon obtained great influence, not only with the Greek cities, but also with Cyrus, who supplied him with large sums of money to pay his sailors. Next year, 406, he was succeeded by Callicratidas. In one year the reputation and influence of Lysander had become so great, that Cyrus and the Spartan allies in Asia requested the Lacedaemonians to appoint Lysander again to the command of the fleet. The Lacedaemonian law, however, did not allow the office of admiral to be held twice by the same person; and, accordingly, Aracus was sent out in 405, as the nominal commander-in-chief, while Lysander, virtually invested with the supreme direction of affairs, had the title of vice-admiral (ἐπιστολεύς). In this year he brought the Peloponnesian war to a conclusion, by the defeat and capture of the Athenian fleet off Aegos-potami. Only 8 Athenian ships made their escape under the command of Conon. He afterwards sailed to Athens, and in the spring of 404 the city capitulated; the long walls and the fortifications of the Piraeus were destroyed, and an oligarchical form of government established, known by the name of the 30 Tyrants. Lysander was now by far the most powerful man in Greece, and he displayed more than the usual pride and haughtiness which distinguished the Spartan commanders in foreign countries. He was passionately fond of praise, and took care that his exploits should be celebrated

by the most illustrious poets of his time. He always kept the poet Choerilus in his retinue; and his praises were also sung by Antilochus, Antimachus of Colophon, and Niceratus of Heraclea. He was the first of the Greeks to whom Greek cities erected altars as to a god, offered sacrifices, and celebrated festivals. His power and ambition caused the Spartan government uneasiness, and accordingly the Ephors recalled him from Asia Minor, to which he had again repaired, and for some years kept him without any public employment. On the death of Agis II. in 397, he secured the succession for Agesilaus, the brother of Agis, in opposition to Leotychides, the reputed son of the latter. He did not receive from Agesilaus the gratitude he had expected. He was one of the members of the council, 30 in number, which was appointed to accompany the new king in his expedition into Asia in 396. Agesilaus purposely thwarted all his designs, and refused all the favours which he asked. On his return to Sparta, Lysander resolved to bring about the change he had long meditated in the Spartan constitution, by abolishing hereditary royalty, and making the throne elective. He is said to have attempted to obtain the sanction of the gods in favour of his scheme, and to have tried in succession the oracles of Delphi, Dodona, and Zeus Ammon, but without success. He does not seem to have ventured upon any overt act, and his enterprise was cut short by his death in the following year. On the breaking out of the Boeotian war in 395, Lysander was placed at the head of one army, and the king Pausanias at the head of another. Lysander marched against Haliartus and perished in battle under the walls, 395.

Lysandra (Λύσανδρα), daughter of Ptolemy Soter and Eurydice, the daughter of Antipater. She was married first to Alexander, the son of Cassander, king of Macedonia, and after his death to Agathocles, the son of Lysimachus. After the murder of her 2nd husband, B. C. 284 [AGATHOCLES, No. 3], she fled to Asia, and besought assistance from Seleucus. The latter in consequence marched against Lysimachus, who was defeated and slain in battle 281.

Lysanias (Λυσανίας). 1. Tetrarch of Abilene, was put to death by Antony, to gratify Cleopatra, B. C. 36. — 2. A descendant of the last, who was tetrarch of Abilene at the time when our Saviour entered upon his ministry. (Luke, iii. 1.)

Lysias (Λυσίας), an Attic orator, was born at Athens, B. C. 458. He was the son of Cephalus, who was a native of Syracuse, and had taken up his abode at Athens, on the invitation of Pericles. At the age of 15, Lysias and his brothers joined the Athenians who went as colonists to Thurii in Italy, 443. He there completed his education under the instruction of two Syracusans, Tisias and Nicias. He afterwards enjoyed great esteem among the Thurians, and seems to have taken part in the administration of the city. After the defeat of the Athenians in Sicily, he was expelled by the Spartan party from Thurii, as a partisan of the Athenians. He now returned to Athens, 411. During the rule of the 30 Tyrants (404), he was looked upon as an enemy of the government, his large property was confiscated, and he was thrown into prison; but he escaped, and took refuge at Megara. He joined Thrasybulus and the exiles, and in order to render them effectual assistance, he sacrificed all that remained

of his fortune. He gave the patriots 2000 drachmas
and 200 shields, and engaged a band of 300 mercenaries. Thrasybulus procured him the Athenian
franchise, which he had not possessed hitherto,
since he was the son of a foreigner ; but he was
afterwards deprived of this right, because it had
been conferred without a probuleuma. Henceforth
he lived at Athens as an isoteles, occupying himself,
as it appears, solely with writing judicial speeches
for others, and died in 378, at the age of 80. —
Lysias wrote a great number of orations ; and
among those which were current under his name,
the ancient critics reckoned 230 as genuine. Of
these 35 only are extant ; and even some of these
are incomplete, and others are probably spurious.
Most of these orations were composed after his
return from Thurii to Athens.   The only one
which he delivered himself is that against Eratosthenes, 403. The language of Lysias is perfectly
pure, and may be regarded as one of the best specimens of the Attic idiom. All the ancient writers
agreed that his orations were distinguished by
grace and elegance. His style is always clear and
lucid ; and his delineations of character striking
and true to life. The orations of Lysias are contained in the collections of the Attic orators. [DE-
MOSTHENES.]   The best separate editions are by
Foertsch, Lips. 1829 : and by Franz, Monac. 1831.

Lysimachia or -ea (Λυσιμαχία, Λυσιμάχεια :
Λυσιμαχεύς). 1. (Eksemil), an important town
on the N. E. of the gulf of Melas, and on the
isthmus connecting the Thracian Chersonesus with
the mainland, was founded B. C. 309 by Lysimachus, who removed to his new city the greater
part of the inhabitants of the neighbouring town
of Cardia. It was subsequently destroyed by the
Thracians, but was restored by Antiochus the
Great. Under the Romans it greatly declined ;
but Justinian built a strong fortress on the spot,
which he called Hexamilium ('Εξαμίλιον), doubtless, from the width of the isthmus, under which
name it is mentioned in the middle ages. —
2. A town in the S. W. of Aetolia, near Pleuron,
situated on a lake of the same name, which was
more anciently called Hydra.

Lysimachus (Λυσίμαχος), king of Thrace, was
a Macedonian by birth, and one of Alexander's generals, but of mean origin, his father Agathocles
having been originally a Penest or serf in Sicily.
He was early distinguished for his undaunted
courage, as well as for his great activity and
strength of body. We are told by Q. Curtius that
Lysimachus, when hunting in Syria, had killed a
lion of immense size single-handed ; and this circumstance that writer regards as the origin of a
fable gravely related by many authors, that on
account of some offence, Lysimachus had been shut
up by order of Alexander in the same den with a
lion ; but though unarmed, had succeeded in destroying the animal, and was pardoned by the king
in consideration of his courage. In the division of
the provinces, after the death of Alexander (B. c.
323), Thrace and the neighbouring countries as
far as the Danube were assigned to Lysimachus.
For some years he was actively engaged in war
with the warlike barbarians that bordered his province on the N. At length, in 315, he joined the
league which Ptolemy, Seleucus, and Cassander
had formed against Antigonus ; but he did not
take any active part in the war for some time. In
306 he took the title of king, when it was as-

sumed by Antigonus, Ptolemy, Seleucus, and Cassander.   In 302 Lysimachus crossed over into
Asia Minor to oppose Antigonus, while Seleucus
also advanced against the latter from the East. In
301 Lysimachus and Seleucus effected a junction,
and gained a decisive victory at Ipsus over Antigonus and his son Demetrius. Antigonus fell on
the field, and Demetrius became a fugitive. The
conquerors divided between them the dominions of
the vanquished ; and Lysimachus obtained for his
share all that part of Asia Minor extending from
the Hellespont and the Aegaean to the heart of
Phrygia. In 291 Lysimachus crossed the Danube
and penetrated into the heart of the country of
the Getae ; but he was reduced to the greatest
distress by want of provisions, and was ultimately
compelled to surrender with his whole army. Dromichaetes, king of the Getae, treated him with the
utmost generosity, and restored him to liberty. In
288 Lysimachus united with Ptolemy, Seleucus, and
Pyrrhus, in a common league against Demetrius,
who had for some years been in possession of Macedonia, and was now preparing to march into
Asia. Next year, 287, Lysimachus and Pyrrhus
invaded Macedonia. Demetrius was abandoned by
his own troops, and was compelled to seek safety in
flight. Pyrrhus for a time obtained possession of
the Macedonian throne, but he was expelled by
Lysimachus in 286. Lysimachus was now in possession of all the dominions in Europe that had
formed part of the Macedonian monarchy, as well
as of the greater part of Asia Minor. He remained
in undisturbed possession of these vast dominions
till shortly before his death. His downfall was
occasioned by a dark domestic tragedy. His wife
Arsinoë, daughter of Ptolemy Soter, had long hated
her step-son Agathocles, and at length, by false
accusations, induced Lysimachus to put his son to
death. This bloody deed alienated the minds of his
subjects ; and many cities of Asia broke out into
open revolt. Lysandra, the widow of Agathocles,
fled with her children to the court of Seleucus, who
forthwith invaded the dominions of Lysimachus.
The two monarchs met in the plain of Corus (Co-
rupedion) ; and Lysimachus fell in the battle that
ensued, B. c. 281. He was in his 80th year at
the time of his death. — Lysimachus founded Ly-
SIMACHIA, on the Hellespont, and also enlarged and
rebuilt many other cities.

Lysimelia (ἡ Λυσιμέλεια λίμνη), a marsh near
Syracuse in Sicily, probably the same as the marsh
more anciently called Syraco from which the town
of Syracuse is said to have derived its name.

Lysinoë (Λυσινόη : Agelan ?), a town in Pisidia, S. of the lake Ascania.

Lysippus (Λύσιππος), of Sicyon, one of the
most distinguished Greek statuaries, was a contemporary of Alexander the Great. Originally a
simple workman in bronze (faber aerarius), he rose
to the eminence which he afterwards obtained by
the direct study of nature. He rejected the last
remains of the old conventional rules which the
early artists followed. In his imitation of nature
the ideal appears almost to have vanished, or
perhaps it should rather be said that he aimed to
idealise merely human beauty. He made statues
of gods, it is true ; but even in this field of art his
favourite subject was the human hero Hercules ;
while his portraits seem to have been the chief
foundation of his fame. The works of Lysippus
are said to have amounted to the enormous number

of 1500. They were almost all, if not all, in bronze ; in consequence of which none of them are extant. He made statues of Alexander at all periods of life, and in many different positions. Alexander's edict is well known, that no one should paint him but Apelles, and no one make his statue but Lysippus. The most celebrated of these statues was that in which Alexander was represented with a lance, which was considered as a sort of companion to the picture of Alexander wielding a thunderbolt, by Apelles.

Lysis (Λῦσις), an eminent Pythagorean philosopher, who, driven out of Italy in the persecution of his sect, betook himself to Thebes, and became the teacher of Epaminondas, by whom he was held in the highest esteem.

Lysis, a river of Caria, only mentioned by Livy (xxxviii. 15).

Lysistratus, of Sicyon, the brother of Lysippus, was a statuary, and devoted himself to the making of portraits. He was the first who took a cast of the human face in gypsum ; and from this mould he produced copies by pouring into it melted wax.

Lystra (ἡ Λύστρα, τὰ Λύστρα: prob. *Karadagh*, Ru.), a city of Lycaonia, on the confines of Isauria, celebrated as one chief scene of the preaching of Paul and Barnabas. (*Acts*, xiv.)

M.

Macae (Μάκαι). 1. A people on the E. coast of Arabia Felix, probably about *Muscat.*—2. An inland people of Libya, in the Regio Syrtica, that is, the part of N. Africa between the Syrtes.

Macalla, a town on the E. coast of Bruttium, which was said to possess the tomb and a sanctuary of Philoctetes.

Macar or **Macareus** (Μάκαρ or Μακαρεύς). 1. Son of Helios (or Crinacus) and Rhodos, fled from Rhodes to Lesbos after the murder of Tenages.— 2. Son of Aeolus, who committed incest with his sister Canace. [CANACE.]—3. Son of Jason and Medea, also called Mermerus or Mormorus.

Macaria (Μακαρία), daughter of Hercules and Deïanira.

Macaria (Μακαρία). 1. A poetical name of several islands, such as Lesbos, Rhodes, and Cyprus.—2. An island in the S. part of the Sinus Arabicus (*Red Sea*), off the coast of the Troglodytae.

Maccabaei (Μακκαβαῖοι), the descendants of the family of the heroic Judas Maccabi or Maccabaeus, a surname which he obtained from his glorious victories. (From the Hebrew *makkab*, "a hammer.") They were also called *Asmonaei* ('Ασαμωναῖοι), from Asamonaeus. or Chasmon, the great-grandfather of Mattathias, the father of Judas Maccabaeus, or, in a shorter form, *Asmonaei* or *Hasmonaei*. This family first obtained distinction from the attempts which were made by Antiochus IV. Epiphanes, king of Syria, to root out the worship of Jehovah, and introduce the Greek religion among the inhabitants of Judaea. Antiochus published an edict, which enjoined uniformity of worship throughout his dominions. At Modin, a town not far from Lydda, lived Mattathias, a man of the priestly line and of deep religious feeling, who had 5 sons in the vigour of their days, John, Simon, Judas, Eleazar, and Jonathan. When the officer of the Syrian king visited Modin, to enforce obedience to the royal edict, Mattathias not only refused to desert the religion of his forefathers, but with his own hand struck dead the first renegade who attempted to offer sacrifice on the heathen altar. He then put to death the king's officer, and retired to the mountains with his 5 sons (B. C. 167). Their numbers daily increased ; and as opportunities occurred, they issued from their mountain fastnesses, cut off detachments of the Syrian army, destroyed heathen altars, and restored in many places the synagogues and the open worship of the Jewish religion. Within a few months the insurrection at Modin had grown into a war for national independence. But the toils of such a war were too much for the aged frame of Mattathias, who died in the 1st year of the revolt, leaving the conduct of it to Judas, his 3rd son. 1. **Judas**, who assumed the surname of Maccabaeus, as has been mentioned above, carried on the war with the same prudence and energy with which it had been commenced. After meeting with great success, he at length fell in battle against the forces of Demetrius I Soter, 160. He was succeeded in the command by his brother, — 2. **Jonathan**, who maintained the cause of Jewish independence with equal vigour and success, and became recognised as high-priest of the Jews. He was put to death by Tryphon, the minister of Antiochus VI., who treacherously got him into his power, 144. Jonathan was succeeded in the high-priesthood by his brother, — 3. **Simon**, who was the most fortunate of the sons of Mattathias, and under whose government the country became virtually independent of Syria. He was murdered by his son-in-law Ptolemy, the governor of Jericho, together with 2 of his sons, Judas and Mattathias, 135. His other son Joannes Hyrcanus escaped, and succeeded his father. — 4. **Joannes Hyrcanus I.** was high-priest 135—106. He did not assume the title of king, but was to all intents and purposes an independent monarch. [HYRCANUS.] He was succeeded by his son Aristobulus I. — 5. **Aristobulus I.**, was the first of the Maccabees who assumed the kingly title, which was henceforth borne by his successors. His reign lasted only a year 106—105. [ARISTOBULUS.] He was succeeded by his brother, —6. **Alexander Jannaeus**, who reigned 105—78. [ALEXANDER, p. 35, a.] He was succeeded by his widow, — 7. **Alexandra**, who appointed her son Hyrcanus II. to the priesthood, and held the supreme power 78 —69. On her death in the latter year her son.— 8. **Hyrcanus II.**, obtained the kingdom, 69, but was supplanted almost immediately afterwards by his brother, — 9. **Aristobulus II.**, who obtained the throne 68. [ARISTOBULUS.] For the remainder of the history of the house of the Maccabees see HYRCANUS II. and HERODES I.

Macedonia (Μακεδονία: Μακεδόνες), a country in Europe, N. of Greece, which is said to have derived its name from an ancient king Macedon, a son of Zeus and Thyia, a daughter of Deucalion. The name first occurs in Herodotus, but its more ancient form appears to have been *Macetia* (Μακετία) ; and accordingly the Macedonians are sometimes called *Macetae*. The country is said to have been originally named Emathia. The boundaries of Macedonia differed at different periods. In the time of Herodotus the name *Macedonis* designated only the country to the S. and W. of the river Lydias. The boundaries of the ancient Macedonian monarchy, before the time of

Philip, the father of Alexander, were on the S Olympus and the Cambunian mountains, which separated it from Thessaly and Epirus, on the E. the river Strymon, which separated it from Thrace, and on the N. and W. Illyria and Paeonia, from which it was divided by no well defined limits. Macedonia was greatly enlarged by the conquests of Philip. He added to his kingdom Paeonia on the N., so that the mountains Scordus and Orbelus now separated it from Moesia; a part of Thrace on the E. as far as the river Nestus, which Thracian district was usually called *Macedonia adjecta*; the peninsula Chalcidice on the S.; and on the W. a part of Illyria, as far as the lake Lychnitis. On the conquest of the country by the Romans, B.C. 158, Macedonia was divided into 4 districts, which were quite independent of one another:—1. The country between the Strymon and the Nestus, with a part of Thrace E. of the Nestus, as far as the Hebrus, and also including the territory of Heraclea Sintica and Bisaltice, W. of the Strymon; the capital of this district was Amphipolis. 2. The country between the Strymon and the Axius, exclusive of those parts already named, but including Chalcidice; the capital Thessalonica. 3. The country between the Axius and Peneus; the capital Pella. 4. The mountainous country in the W.; the capital Pelagonia. After the conquest of the Achaeans, in 146, Macedonia was formed into a Roman province, and Thessaly and Illyria were incorporated with it; but at the same time the district E. of the Nestus was again assigned to Thrace. The Roman province of Macedonia accordingly extended from the Aegaean to the Adriatic seas, and was bounded on the S. by the province of Achaia. It was originally governed by a proconsul; it was made by Tiberius one of the provinces of the Caesar; but it was restored to the senate by Claudius. — Macedonia may be described as a large plain, surrounded on 3 sides by lofty mountains. Through this plain, however, run many smaller ranges of mountains, between which are wide and fertile valleys, extending from the coast far into the interior. The chief mountains were SCORDUS, or SCARDUS, on the N.W. frontier, towards Illyria and Dardania; further E. ORBELUS and SCOMIUS, which separated it from Moesia; and RHODOPE, which extended from Scomius in a S.E. direction, forming the boundary between Macedonia and Thrace. On the S. frontier were the CAMBUNII MONTES and OLYMPUS. The chief rivers were in the direction of E. to W., the NESTUS, the STRYMON, the AXIUS, the largest of all, the LUDIAS or LYDIAS, and the HALIACMON.—The great bulk of the inhabitants of Macedonia consisted of Thracian and Illyrian tribes. At an early period some Greek tribes settled in the S. part of the country. They are said to have come from Argos, and to have been led by Gauanes, Aëropus, and Perdiccas, the 3 sons of Temenus, the Heraclid. Perdiccas, the youngest of the brothers, was looked upon as the founder of the Macedonian monarchy. A later tradition, however, regarded Caranus, who was also a Heraclid from Argos, as the founder of the monarchy. These Greek settlers intermarried with the original inhabitants of the country. The dialect which they spoke was akin to the Doric, but it contained many barbarous words and forms; and the Macedonians were accordingly never regarded

by the other Greeks as genuine Hellenes. Moreover, it was only in the S. of Macedonia that the Greek language was spoken; in the N. and N.W. of the country the Illyrian tribes continued to speak their own language and to preserve their ancient habits and customs. Very little is known of the history of Macedonia till the reign of Amyntas I., who was a contemporary of Darius Hystaspis; but from that time their history is more or less intimately connected with that of Greece, till at length Philip, the father of Alexander the Great, became the virtual master of the whole of Greece. The conquests of Alexander extended the Macedonian supremacy over a great part of Asia; and the Macedonian kings continued to exercise their sovereignty over Greece, till the conquest of Perseus by the Romans, 168, brought the Macedonian monarchy to a close. The details of the Macedonian history are given in the lives of the separate kings.

Macella (*Macellaro*), a small fortified town in the W. of Sicily, S.E. of Segesta.

Macer, Aemilius. 1. A Roman poet, a native of Verona, died in Asia, B.C. 16. He wrote a poem or poems upon birds, snakes, and medicinal plants, in imitation, it would appear, of the Theriaca of Nicander. (Ov. *Trist.* iv. 10. 44.) The work now extant, entitled "Aemilius Macer de Herbarum Virtutibus," belongs to the middle ages.—**2.** We must carefully distinguish from Aemilius Macer of Verona, a poet Macer, who wrote on the Trojan war, and who must have been alive in A.D. 12, since he is addressed by Ovid in that year (*ex Pont.* ii. 10. 2.) —**3.** A Roman jurist, who lived in the reign of Alexander Severus. He wrote several works, extracts from which are given in the Digest.

Macer, Clodius, was governor of Africa at Nero's death A.D. 68, when he laid claim to the throne. He was murdered at the instigation of Galba by the procurator, Trebonius Garucianus.

Macer, Licinius. [LICINIUS.]

Macestus (Μάκηστος: *Simaul-Su*, and lower *Susugherli*), a considerable river of Mysia, rises in the N.W. of Phrygia, and flows N. through Mysia into the Rhyndacus. It is probably the same river which Polybius (v. 77) calls Megistus (Μέγιστος).

Machaerus (Μαχαιροῦς: Μαχαιρίτης), a strong border fortress in the S. of Peraea, in Palestine, on the confines of the Nabathaei: a stronghold of the Sicarii in the Jewish war. A tradition made it the place where John the Baptist was beheaded.

Machanidas, tyrant of Lacedaemon, succeeded Lycurgus about B.C. 210. Like his predecessor, he had no hereditary title to the crown, but ruled by the swords of his mercenaries alone. He was defeated and slain in battle by Philopoemen, the general of the Achaean league in 207.

Machaon (Μαχάων), son of Aesculapius, was married to Anticlea, the daughter of Dioclea, by whom he became the father of Gorgasus, Nicomachus, Alexanor, Sphyrus, and Polemocrates. Together with his brother Podalirius he went to Troy with 30 ships, commanding the men who came from Tricca, Ithome, and Oechalia. In this war he acted as the surgeon of the Greeks, and also distinguished himself in battle. He was himself wounded by Paris, but was carried from the field by Nestor. Later writers mention him as one of the Greek heroes who were concealed in the wooden horse, and he is said to have cured Philoctetes. He was killed by Eurypylus, the son of Telephus, and he received divine honours at Gerenia, in Messenia.

Machlyes (Μάχλυες), a people of Libya, near the Lotophagi, on the W. side of the lake Triton, in what was afterwards called Africa Propria.

Machon (Μάχων), of Corinth or Sicyon, a comic poet, flourished at Alexandria, where he gave instructions respecting comedy to the grammarian Aristophanes of Byzantium.

Macistus or **Macistum** (Μάκιστος, Μάκιστον: Μακίστιος), an ancient town of Elis in Triphylia, N.E. of Lepreum, originally called Platanistus (Πλατανιστοῦς), and founded by the Caucones.

Macoraba (Μακοράβα: Mecca), a city in the W. of Arabia Felix ; probably the sacred city of the Arabs, even before the time of Mohammed, and the seat of the worship of Alitat or Alitta under the emblem of a meteoric stone.

Macra (Magra), a small river rising in the Apennines and flowing into the Ligurian sea near Luna, which, from the time of Augustus, formed the boundary between Liguria and Etruria.

Macrianus, one of the 30 tyrants, a distinguished general, who accompanied Valerian in his expedition against the Persians, A. D. 260. On the capture of that monarch, Macrianus was proclaimed emperor, together with his 2 sons Macrianus and Quietus. He assigned the management of affairs in the East to Quietus, and set out with the younger Macrianus for Italy. They were encountered by Aureolus on the confines of Thrace and Illyria, defeated and slain, 262. Quietus was shortly afterwards slain in the East by Odenathus.

Macri Campi. [CAMPI MACRI.]

Macrinus, M. Opilius Severus, Roman emperor, April, A. D. 217—June, 218. He was born at Caesarea in Mauretania, of humble parents, A. D. 164, and rose at length to be praefect of the praetorians under Caracalla. He accompanied Caracalla in his expedition against the Parthians, and was proclaimed emperor after the death of Caracalla, whom he had caused to be assassinated. He conferred the title of Caesar upon his son Diadumenianus, and at the same time gained great popularity by repealing some obnoxious taxes. But in the course of the same year he was defeated with great loss by the Parthians, and was obliged to retire into Syria. While here his soldiers, with whom he had become unpopular by enforcing among them order and discipline, were easily seduced from their allegiance, and proclaimed Elagabalus as emperor. With the troops which remained faithful to him, Macrinus marched against the usurper, but was defeated, and fled in disguise. He was shortly afterwards seized in Chalcedon, and put to death, after a reign of 14 months.

Macro, Naevius Sertorius, a favourite of the emperor Tiberius, was employed to arrest the powerful Sejanus in A. D. 31. On the death of the latter he was made praefect of the praetorians, an office which he continued to hold for the remainder of Tiberius's reign and during the earlier part of Caligula's. Macro was as cruel as Sejanus. He laid informations ; he presided at the rack ; and he lent himself to the most savage caprices of Tiberius during the last and worst period of his government. During the lifetime of Tiberius he paid court to the young Caligula ; and he promoted an intrigue between his wife Ennia and the young prince. It was rumoured that Macro shortened the last moments of Tiberius by stifling him with the bedding

as he recovered unexpectedly from a swoon. But Caligula soon became jealous of Macro, and compelled him to kill himself with his wife and children, 38.

Macrobii (Μακρόβιοι, i. e. Long-lived), an Aethiopian people in Africa, placed by Herodotus (iii. 17) on the shores of the S. Ocean. It is in vain to attempt their accurate identification with any known people.

Macrobius, the grammarian, whose full name was Ambrosius Aurelius Theodosius Macrobius. All we know about him is that he lived in the age of Honorius and Theodosius, that he was probably a Greek, and that he had a son named Eustathius. He states in the preface to his Saturnalia that Latin was to him a foreign tongue, and hence we may fairly conclude that he was a Greek by birth, more especially as we find numerous Greek idioms in his style. He was probably a pagan. His extant works are :— 1. *Saturnaliorum Conviviorum Libri VII.*, consisting of a series of dissertations on history, mythology, criticism, and various points of antiquarian research, supposed to have been delivered during the holidays of the Saturnalia at the house of Vettius Praetextatus, who was invested with the highest offices of state under Valentinian and Valens. The form of the work is avowedly copied from the dialogues of Plato, especially the Banquet: in substance it bears a strong resemblance to the Noctes Atticae of A. Gellius. The 1st book treats of the festivals of Saturnus and Janus, of the Roman calendar, &c. The 2nd book commences with a collection of bon mots, ascribed to the most celebrated wits of antiquity ; to these are appended a series of essays on matters connected with the pleasures of the table. The 4 following books are devoted to criticisms on Virgil. The 7th book is of a more miscellaneous character than the preceding.— 2. *Commentarius ex Cicerone in Somnium Scipionis*, a tract much studied during the middle ages. The Dream of Scipio, contained in the 6th book of Cicero's De Republica is taken as a text, which suggests a succession of discourses on the physical constitution of the universe, according to the views of the New Platonists, together with notices of some of their peculiar tenets on mind as well as matter.—3. *De Differentiis et Societatibus Graeci Latinique Verbi*, a treatise purely grammatical, of which only an abridgment is extant, compiled by a certain Joannes.—The best editions of the works of Macrobius are by Gronovius, Lug. Bat. 1670, and by Zeunius, Lips. 1774.

Macrones (Μάκρωνες) a powerful and warlike Caucasian people on the N. E. shore of the Pontus Euxinus.

Mactorium (Μακτόριον: Μακτωρῖνος), a town in the S. of Sicily, near Gela.

Macynia (Μακυνία: Μακυνεύς), a town in the S. of Aetolia, near the mountain Taphiassus, E. of Calydon and the Evenus.

Madianitae (Μαδιανῖται, Μαδιηναῖοι, Μαδιηνοί: O. T. Midianim), a powerful nomad people in the S. of Arabia Petraea, about the head of the Red Sea. They carried on a caravan trade between Arabia and Egypt, and were troublesome enemies of the Israelites until they were conquered by Gideon. They do not appear in history after the Babylonish captivity.

Madytus (Μάδυτος: Μαδύτιος: Maito), a seaport town on the Thracian Chersonesus.

Maeander (Μαίανδρος: Menderoh or Meinder,

or *Buyuk-Mendereh,* i. e. *the Great Mendereh,* in contradistinction to *the Little Mendereh,* the ancient *Caÿster*), has its source in the mountain called Aulocrenae, above Celaenae, in the S. of Phrygia, close to the source of the Marsyas, which immediately joins it. [CELAENAE.] It flows in a general W. direction, with various changes of direction, but on the whole with a slight inclination to the S. After leaving Phrygia, it flows parallel to Mt. Messogis, on its S. side, forming the boundary between Lydia and Caria, and at last falls into the Icarian Sea between Myus and Priene. Its whole length is above 170 geographical miles. The Maeander is deep, but narrow, and very turbid; and therefore not navigable far up. Its upper course lies chiefly through elevated plains, and partly in a deep rocky valley: its lower course, for the last 110 miles, is through a beautiful wide plain, through which it flows, in those numerous windings that have made its name a descriptive verb (*to meander*), and which it often inundates. The alteration made in the coast about its mouth by its alluvial deposit was observed by the ancients, and it has been continually going on. [See LATMICUS SINUS and MILETUS.] The tributaries of the Maeander were, on the right or N. side, the Marsyas, Cludrus, Lethaeus, and Gaeson, and, on the left or S. side, the Obrimas, Lycus, Harpasus, and another Marsyas. — As a god Maeander is described as the father of the nymph Cyane, who was the mother of Caunus. Hence the latter is called by Ovid (*Met.* ix. 573) *Maeandrius juvenis.*

Maecēnas, C. Cilnĭus, was born some time between B.C. 73 and 63; and we learn from Horace (*Carm.* iv. 11) that his birth-day was the 13th of April. His family, though belonging wholly to the equestrian order, was of high antiquity and honour, and traced its descent from the *Lucumones* of Etruria. His paternal ancestors the *Cilnii,* are mentioned by Livy (x. 3, 5) as having attained great power and wealth at Arretium about B.C. 301. The maternal branch of the family was likewise of Etruscan origin, and it was from them that the name of Maecenas was derived, it being customary among the Etruscans to assume the mother's as well as the father's name. It is in allusion to this circumstance that Horace (*Sat.* i. 6. 3) mentions both his *avus maternus atque paternus* as having been distinguished by commanding numerous legions; a passage, by the way, from which we are not to infer that the ancestors of Maecenas had ever led the Roman legions. Although it is unknown where Maecenas received his education, it must doubtless have been a careful one. We learn from Horace that he was versed both in Greek and Roman literature; and his taste for literary pursuits was shown, not only by his patronage of the most eminent poets of his time, but also by several performances of his own, both in verse and prose. It has been conjectured that he became acquainted with Augustus at Apollonia before the death of Julius Caesar; but he is mentioned for the first time in B.C. 40, and from this year his name constantly occurs as one of the chief friends and ministers of Augustus. Thus we find him employed in B.C. 37, in negotiating with Antony; and it was probably on this occasion that Horace accompanied him to Brundisium, a journey which he has described in the 5th satire of the 1st book. During the war with Antony, which was brought to a close by the battle of Actium, Maecenas remained

at Rome, being entrusted with the administration of the civil affairs of Italy. During this time he suppressed the conspiracy of the younger Lepidus. Maecenas was not present at the battle of Actium, as some critics have supposed; and the 1st epode of Horace probably does not relate at all to Actium, but to the Sicilian expedition against Sext. Pompeius. On the return of Augustus from Actium, Maecenas enjoyed a greater share of his favour than ever, and in conjunction with Agrippa, had the management of all public affairs. It is related that Augustus at this time took counsel with Agrippa and Maecenas respecting the expediency of restoring the republic; that Agrippa advised him to pursue that course, but that Maecenas strongly urged him to establish the empire. For many years Maecenas continued to preserve the uninterrupted favour of Augustus; but between B.C. 21 and 16, a coolness, to say the least, had sprung up between the emperor and his faithful minister, and after the latter year he retired entirely from public life. The cause of this estrangement is enveloped in doubt. Dion Cassius positively attributes it to an intrigue carried on by Augustus with Terentia, Maecenas's wife. Maecenas died B.C. 8, and was buried on the Esquiline. He left no children, and he bequeathed his property to Augustus. — Maecenas had amassed an enormous fortune. He had purchased a tract of ground on the Esquiline hill, which had formerly served as a burial-place for the lower orders. (Hor. *Sat.* i. 8. 7.) Here he had planted a garden, and built a house, remarkable for its loftiness, on account of a tower by which it was surmounted, and from the top of which Nero is said to have afterwards contemplated the burning of Rome. In this residence he seems to have passed the greater part of his time, and to have visited the country but seldom. His house was the *rendezvous* of all the wits of Rome; and whoever could contribute to the amusement of the company was always welcome to a seat at his table. But his really intimate friends consisted of the greatest geniuses and most learned men of Rome; and if it was from his universal inclination towards men of talent that he obtained the reputation of a literary patron, it was by his friendship for such poets as Virgil and Horace that he deserved it. Virgil was indebted to him for the recovery of his farm, which had been appropriated by the soldiery in the division of lands, in B.C. 41; and it was at the request of Maecenas that he undertook the *Georgics,* the most finished of all his poems. To Horace he was a still greater benefactor. He presented him with the means of comfortable subsistence, a farm in the Sabine country. If the estate was but a moderate one, we learn from Horace himself that the bounty of Maecenas was regulated by his own contented views, and not by his patron's want of generosity. (*Carm.* ii. 18. 14, *Carm.* iii. 16. 38.) — Of Maecenas's own literary productions only a few fragments exist. From these, however, and from the notices which we find of his writings in ancient authors, we are led to think that we have not suffered any great loss by their destruction; for, although a good judge of literary merit in others, he does not appear to have been an author of much taste himself. In his way of life Maecenas was addicted to every species of luxury. We find several allusions in the ancient authors to the effeminacy of his dress. He was fond of theatrical entertainments, especially pantomimes; as may be inferred from his patronage of Bathyllus, the celebrated dancer, who was a freedman of his. That moderation of character which led him to be content with his equestrian rank, probably arose from his love of ease and luxury, or it might have been the result of more prudent and political views. As a politician, the principal trait in his character was fidelity to his master, and the main end of all his cares was the consolidation of the empire. But at the same time he recommended Augustus to put no check on the free expression of public opinion; and above all to avoid that cruelty, which, for so many years, had stained the Roman annals with blood.

Maecius Tarpa. [TARPA.]

Maedica (Μαιδική), the country of the Maedi, a powerful people in the W. of Thrace, on the W. bank of the Strymon, and the S. slope of Mt. Scomius. They frequently made inroads into the country of the Macedonians, till at length they were conquered by the latter people, and their land incorporated with Macedonia, of which it formed the N.E. district.

Maelius, Sp., the richest of the plebeian knights, employed his fortune in buying up corn in Etruria in the great famine at Rome in B.C. 440. This corn he sold to the poor at a small price, or distributed it gratuitously. Such liberality gained him the favour of the plebeians, but at the same time exposed him to the hatred of the ruling class. Accordingly in the following year he was accused of having formed a conspiracy for the purpose of seizing the kingly power. Thereupon Cincinnatus was appointed dictator, and C. Servilius Ahala, the master of the horse. Maelius was summoned to appear before the tribunal of the dictator; but as he refused to go, Ahala, with an armed band of patrician youths, rushed into the crowd, and slew him. His property was confiscated, and his house pulled down; its vacant site, which was called the *Aequimaelium*, continued to subsequent ages a memorial of his fate. Later ages fully believed the story of Maelius's conspiracy, and Cicero repeatedly praises the glorious deed of Ahala. But his guilt is very doubtful. None of the alleged accomplices of Maelius were punished; and Ahala was brought to trial, and only escaped condemnation by a voluntary exile.

Maenaca (Μαινάκη), a town in the S. of Hispania Baetica on the coast, the most W.-ly colony of the Phocaeans.

Maenades (Μαινάδες), a name of the Bacchantes, from μαίνομαι, "to be mad," because they were frensied in the worship of Dionysus or Bacchus.

Maenalus (τὸ Μαίναλον or Μαινάλιον ὅρος: *Roïnon*), a mountain in Arcadia, which extended from Megalopolis to Tegea, was celebrated as the favourite haunt of the god Pan. From this mountain the surrounding country was called *Maenalia* (Μαιναλία); and on the mountain was a town *Maenalus*. The mountain was so celebrated that the Roman poets frequently use the adjectives *Maenalius* and *Maenalis* as equivalent to Arcadian.

Maenius. 1. C., consul, B.C. 338, with L. Furius Camillus. The 2 consuls completed the subjugation of Latium; they were both rewarded with a triumph; and equestrian statues were erected to their honour in the forum. The statue of Maenius was placed upon a column, which is spoken of by later writers, under the name of *Columna Maenia*, and which appears to have stood near the end of the forum, on the Capitoline. Maenius was dictator in 320, and censor in 318. In his censorship he allowed balconies to be added to the various buildings surrounding the forum, in order that the spectators might obtain more room for beholding the games which were exhibited in the forum; and these balconies were called after him *Maeniana* (sc. *aedificia*). — **2.** The proposer of the law, about 286, which required the patres to give their sanction to the election of the magistrates before they had been elected, or in other words to confer, or agree to confer, the imperium on the person whom the comitia should elect. — **3.** A contemporary of Lucilius, was a great spendthrift, who squandered all his property, and afterwards supported himself by playing the buffoon. He possessed a house in the forum, which Cato in his censorship (184) purchased of him, for the purpose of building the basilica Porcia. Some of the scholiasts on Horace ridiculously relate, that when Maenius sold his house, he reserved for himself one column, the Columna Maenia, from which he built a balcony, that he might thence witness the games. The true origin of the Columna Maenia, and of the balconies called Maeniana, has been explained above. (Hor. *Sat.* i. 1. 101, i. 3. 21, *Epist.* i. 15. 26.)

Maenoba, a town in the S.E. of Hispania Baetica, near the coast, situated on a river of the same name, and 12 miles E. of Malaca.

Maeon (Μαίων). **1.** Son of Haemon of Thebes. He and Lycophontes were the leaders of the band that lay in ambush against Tydeus, in the war of the Seven against Thebes. Maeon was the only one whose life was spared by Tydeus. Maeon in return buried Tydeus, when the latter was slain. — **2.** Husband of Dindyme, the mother of Cybele.

Maeonia. [LYDIA.]

Maeonides (Μαιονίδης), i. e. Homer, either because he was a son of Maeon, or because he was a native of Maeonia, the ancient name of Lydia. Hence he is also called *Maeonius senex*, and his poems the *Maeoniae chartae*, or *Maeonium carmen*. — *Maeonis*, also occurs as a surname of Omphale, and of Arachne, because both were Lydians.

Maeotae. [MAEOTIS PALUS.]

Maeotis Palus (ἡ Μαιῶτις λίμνη: *Sea of Azov*), an inland sea on the borders of Europe and Asia, N. of the Pontus Euxinus (*Black Sea*), with which it communicates by the BOSPORUS CIMMERIUS. Its form may be described roughly as a triangle, with its vertex at its N.E. extremity, where it receives the waters of the great river Tanaïs (*Don*): it discharges its superfluous water by a constant current into the Euxine. The ancients had very vague notions of its true form and size: the earlier geographers thought that both it and the Caspian Sea were gulfs of the great N. Ocean. The Scythian tribes on its banks were called by the collective name of Maeōtae or Maeōtici (Μαιῶται, Μαιωτικοί). The sea had also the names of Cimmerium or Bosporicum Mare. Aeschylus (*Prom.* 731) applies the name of Maeotic Strait to the Cimmerian Bosporus (αὐλῶν' Μαιωτικόν).

Maera (Μαῖρα). **1.** The dog of Icarius, the father of Erigone. [ICARIUS, No. 1.] — **2.** Daughter of Proetus and Antea, a companion of Artemis, by whom she was killed, after she had become by Zeus the mother of Locrus. Others state that she died a virgin. — **3.** Daughter of Atlas, was married to Tegeates, the son of Lycaon. Her tomb was shown both at Tegea and Mantinea in Arcadia.

Maesa, Julia, sister-in-law of Septimius Severus, aunt of Caracalla, and grandmother of Elagabalus and Alexander Severus. She was a native of Emesa in Syria, and seems, after the elevation of Septimius Severus, the husband of her sister Julia Domna, to have lived at the imperial court until the death of Caracalla, and to have accumulated great wealth. She contrived and executed the plot which transferred the supreme power from Macrinus to her grandson ELAGABALUS. When she foresaw the downfall of the latter, she prevailed on him to adopt his cousin ALEXANDER SEVERUS. By Severus she was always treated with the greatest respect ; she enjoyed the title of Augusta during her life, and received divine honours after her death.

Maevius. [BAVIUS.]

Magaba, a mountain in Galatia, 10 Roman miles E. of Ancyra.

Magas (Μάγας), king of Cyrene, was a step-son of Ptolemy Soter, being the offspring of Berenice by a former marriage. He was a Macedonian by birth; and he seems to have accompanied his mother to Egypt, where he soon rose to a high place in the favour of Ptolemy. In B. C. 308 he was appointed by that monarch to the command of the expedition destined for the recovery of Cyrene after the death of Ophellas. The enterprise was completely successful, and Magas obtained from his step-father the government of the province. At first he ruled over the province only as a dependency of Egypt, but after the death of Ptolemy Soter he not only assumed the character of an independent monarch, but even made war on the king of Egypt. He married Apama, daughter of Antiochus Soter, by whom he had a daughter, Berenice, afterwards the wife of Ptolemy Euergetes. He died 258.

Magdolum (Μάγδολον, Μάγδωλον: O.T. Migdol), a city of Lower Egypt, near the N. E. frontier, about 12 miles S. W. of Pelusium: where Pharaoh Necho defeated the Syrians, according to Herodotus (ii. 159).

Magetobria (Moigte de Broie, on the Saone), a town on the W. frontiers of the Sequani, near which the Gauls were defeated by the Germans shortly before Caesar's arrival in Gaul.

Magi (Μάγοι), the name of the order of priests and religious teachers among the Medes and Persians, is said to be derived from the Persian word mag, mog, or mugh, i. e. a priest. There is strong evidence that a class similar to the Magi, and in some cases bearing the same name, existed among other Eastern nations, especially the Chaldaeans of Babylon ; nor is it at all probable that either the Magi, or their religion, were of strictly Median or Persian origin : but, in classical literature, they are presented to us almost exclusively in connection with Medo-Persian history. Herodotus represents them as one of the 6 tribes into which the Median people were divided. Under the Median empire, before the supremacy passed to the Persians, they were so closely connected with the throne, and had so great an influence in the state, that they evidently retained their position after the revolution ; and they had power enough to be almost successful in the attempt they made to overthrow the Persian dynasty after the death of Cambyses, by putting forward one of their own number as a pretender to the throne, alleging that he was Smerdis, the son of Cyrus, who had been put to death by his brother Cambyses. It is clear that this was a plot to re-store the Median supremacy ; but whether it arose from mere ambition, or from any diminution of the power of the Magi under the vigorous government of Cyrus, cannot be said with certainty. The defeat of this Magian conspiracy by Darius the son of Hystaspes and the other Persian nobles was followed by a general massacre of the Magi, which was celebrated by an annual festival (τὰ Μαγοφόνια), during which no Magian was permitted to appear in public. Still their position as the only ministers of religion remained unaltered. The breaking up of the Persian empire must have greatly altered their condition ; but they still continue to appear in history down to the time of the later Roman empire. The "wise men" who came from the East to Jerusalem at the time of our Saviour's birth were Magi (μάγοι is their name in the original, Matt. ii. 1). Simon, who had deceived the people of Samaria before Philip preached to them (Acts, viii.), and Elymas, who tried to hinder the conversion of Sergius Paulus at Cyprus (Acts, xiii.), are both called Magians ; but in these cases the words μάγος and μαγεύων are used in a secondary sense, for a person who pretends to the wisdom, or practises the arts, of the Magi. This use of the name occurs very early among the Greeks, and from it we get our word magic (ἡ μαγική, i. e. the art or science of the Magi). — The constitution of the Magi as an order is ascribed by tradition to Zoroastres, or Zoroaster as the Greeks and Romans called him, the Zarathustra of the Zendavesta (the sacred books of the ancient Persians), and the Zerdusht of the modern Persians ; but whether he was their founder, their reformer, or the mythical representative of their unknown origin, cannot be decided. He is said to have restored the true knowledge of the supreme good principle (Ormuzd), and to have taught his worship to the Magi, whom he divided into 3 classes, learners, masters, and perfect scholars. They alone could teach the truths and perform the ceremonies of religion, foretell the future, interpret dreams and omens, and ascertain the will of Ormuzd by the arts of divination. They had 3 chief methods of divination, by calling up the dead, by cups or dishes, and by waters. The forms of worship and divination were strictly defined, and were handed down among the Magi by tradition. Like all early priesthoods, they seem to have been the sole possessors of all the science of their age. To be instructed in their learning was esteemed the highest of privileges, and was permitted, with rare exceptions, to none but the princes of the royal family. Their learning became celebrated at an early period in Greece, by the name of μάγεια, and was made the subject of speculation by the philosophers, whose knowledge of it seems, however, to have been very limited ; while their high pretensions, and the tricks by which their knowledge of science enabled them to impose upon the ignorant, soon attached to their name among the Greeks and Romans that bad meaning which is still commonly connected with the words derived from it. — Besides being priests and men of learning, the Magi appear to have discharged judicial functions.

Magna Graecia. [GRAECIA.]

Magna Mater. [RHEA.]

Magnentius, Roman emperor in the West, A. D. 350—353, whose full name was FLAVIUS POPILIUS MAGNENTIUS. He was a German by birth, and after serving as a common soldier was eventually intrusted by Constans, the son of Constantine the Great, with the command of the Jovian and Herculian battalions who had replaced the ancient praetorian guards when the empire was remodelled by Diocletian. He availed himself of his position to organise a conspiracy against the weak and profligate Constans, who was put to death by his emissaries. Magnentius thereupon was acknowledged as emperor in all the Western provinces, except Illyria, where Vetranio had assumed the purple. Constantius hurried from the frontier of Persia to crush the usurpers. Vetranio submitted to Constantius at Sardica in December, 350. Magnentius was first defeated by Constantius at the sanguinary battle of Mursa on the Drave, in the autumn of 351, and was obliged to fly into Gaul. He was defeated a second time in the passes of the Cottian Alps, and put an end to his own life about the middle of August, 353. Magnentius was a man of commanding stature and great bodily strength; but not one spark of virtue relieved the blackness of his career as a sovereign. The power which he obtained by treachery and murder he maintained by extortion and cruelty.

Magnes (Μάγνης), one of the most important of the earlier Athenian comic poets of the old comedy, was a native of the demus of Icaria or Icarius, in Attica. He flourished B. C. 460, and onwards, and died at an advanced age, shortly before the representation of the *Knights* of Aristophanes, that is, in 423. (Aristoph. *Equit.* 524.) His plays contained a great deal of coarse buffoonery.

Magnesia (Μαγνησία: Μάγνης, pl. Μάγνητες). 1. The most E.-ly district of Thessaly, was a long narrow slip of country, extending from the Peneus on the N. to the Pagasaean gulf on the S., and bounded on the W. by the great Thessalian plain. It was a mountainous country, as it comprehended the Mts. Ossa and Pelion. Its inhabitants, the Magnetes, are said to have founded the 2 cities in Asia mentioned below. — 2. **M. ad Sipylum** (M. πρὸς Σιπύλῳ or ὑπὸ Σιπύλῳ: *Manissa*, Ru.), a city in the N.W. of Lydia, in Asia Minor, at the foot of the N.W. declivity of Mt. Sipylus, and on the S. bank of the Hermus, is famous in history as the scene of the victory gained by the 2 Scipios over Antiochus the Great, which secured to the Romans the empire of the East, B. C. 190. After the Mithridatic war, the Romans made it a libera civitas. It suffered, with other cities of Asia Minor, from the great earthquake in the reign of Tiberius; but it was still a place of importance in the 5th century. — 3. **M. ad Maeandrum** (M. ἡ πρὸς Μαιάνδρῳ, M. ἐπὶ Μαιάνδρῳ: *Inek-bazar*, Ru.), a city in the S.W. of Lydia, in Asia Minor, was situated on the river Lethaeus, a N. tributary of the Maeander. It was destroyed by the Cimmerians (probably about B. C. 700) and rebuilt by colonists from Miletus, so that it became an Ionian city by race as well as position. It was one of the cities given to Themistocles by Artaxerxes. It was celebrated for its temple of Artemis Leucophryene, one of most beautiful in Asia Minor, the ruins of which still exist.

Magnopolis (Μαγνόπολις), or **Eupatoria Magnopolis**, a city of Pontus, in Asia Minor, near the confluence of the rivers Lycus and Iris, begun by Mithridates Eupator and finished by Pompey, but probably destroyed before very long.

Mago (Μάγων). 1. A Carthaginian, said to have been the founder of the military power of that city, by introducing a regular discipline and organisation into her armies. He flourished from B. C. 550 to 500, and was probably the father of Hasdrubal, who was slain in the battle against Gelo at Himera [HAMILCAR, No. 1.] — 2. Commander of the Carthaginian fleet under Himilco in the war against Dionysius, 396. When Himilco returned to Africa after the disastrous termination of the expedition, Mago appears to have been invested with the chief command in Sicily. He carried on the war with Dionysius, but in 392 was compelled to conclude a treaty of peace, by which he abandoned his allies the Sicilians to the power of Dionysius. In 383 he again invaded Sicily, but was defeated by Dionysius and slain in the battle. — 3. Commander of the Carthaginian army in Sicily in 344. He assisted Hicetas in the war against Timoleon; but becoming apprehensive of treachery, he sailed away to Carthage. Here he put an end to his own life, to avoid a worse fate at the hands of his countrymen, who, nevertheless, crucified his lifeless body. — 4. Son of Hamilcar Barca, and youngest brother of the famous Hannibal. He accompanied Hannibal to Italy, and after the battle of Cannae (216) carried the news of this great victory to Carthage. But instead of returning to Italy, he was sent into Spain with a considerable force to the support of his other brother Hasdrubal, who was hard pressed by the 2 Scipios (215). He continued in this country for many years; and after his brother Hasdrubal quitted Spain in 208, in order to march to the assistance of Hannibal in Italy, the command in Spain devolved upon him and upon Hasdrubal, the son of Gisco. After their decisive defeat by Scipio at Silpia in 206, Mago retired to Gades, and subsequently passed the winter in the lesser of the Balearic islands, where the memory of his sojourn is still preserved, in the name of the celebrated harbour, Portus Magonis, or *Port Mahon*. Early in the ensuing summer (205) Mago landed in Liguria, where he surprised the town of Genoa. Here he maintained himself for 2 years, but in 203 he was defeated with great loss in Cisalpine Gaul, by Quintilius Varus, and was himself severely wounded. Shortly afterwards he embarked his troops in order to return to Africa, but he died of his wound before reaching Africa. Cornelius Nepos, in opposition to all other authorities, represents Mago as surviving the battle of Zama, and says that he perished in a shipwreck, or was assassinated by his slaves. — 5. Surnamed the Samnite, was one of the chief officers of Hannibal in Italy, where he held for a considerable time the chief command in Bruttium. — 6. Commander of the garrison of New Carthage when that city was taken by Scipio Africanus, 209. Mago was sent a prisoner to Rome. — 7. A Carthaginian of uncertain date, who wrote a work upon agriculture in the Punic language, in 28 books. So great was the reputation of this work even at Rome, that after the destruction of Carthage, the senate ordered that it should be translated into Latin by competent persons, at the head of whom was D. Silanus. It was subsequently translated into Greek, though with some abridgment and alteration, by Cassius Dionysius of Utica. Mago's precepts on agricultural matters are continually cited by the Roman writers on those subjects in terms of the highest commendation.

Magonis Portus. [MAGO, No. 4.]

Magontiacum. [MOGONTIACUM.]

Maharbal (Μαάρβας), son of Himilco, and one of the most distinguished officers of Hannibal in the 2nd Punic war. He is first mentioned at the siege of Saguntum. After the battle of Cannae he urged Hannibal to push on at once with his cavalry upon Rome itself ; and on the refusal of his commander, he is said to have observed, that Hannibal knew indeed how to gain victories, but not how to use them.

Maia (Μαῖα or Μαιάς), daughter of Atlas and Pleione, was the eldest of the Pleiades, and the most beautiful of the 7 sisters. In a grotto of Mt. Cyllene in Arcadia she became by Zeus the mother of Hermes. Arcas, the son of Zeus by Callisto, was given to her to be reared. [PLEIADES.]—Maia was likewise the name of a divinity worshipped at Rome, who was also called Majesta. She is mentioned in connection with Vulcan, and was regarded by some as the wife of that god, though it seems for no other reason but because a priest of Vulcan offered a sacrifice to her on the 1st of May. In the popular superstition of later times she was identified with Maia, the daughter of Atlas.

Majoriānus, Jūlius Vălērius, Roman emperor in the West, A. D. 457—461, was raised to the empire by Ricimer. His reign was chiefly occupied in making preparations to invade the Vandals in Africa ; but the immense fleet which he had collected for this purpose in the harbour of New Carthage in Spain was destroyed by the Vandals in 460. Thereupon he concluded a peace with Genseric. His activity and popularity excited the jealousy of Ricimer, who compelled him to abdicate and then put an end to his life.

Majūma. [CONSTANTIA, No. 3.]

Malăca (*Malaga*), an important town on the coast of Hispania Baetica, and on a river of the same name (*Guadalmedina*), was founded by the Phoenicians, and has always been a flourishing place of commerce from the earliest times to the present day.

Malalas. [MALELAS.]

Malanga (Μαλάγγα), a city of India, probably the modern *Madras.*

Malchus (Μάλχος), of Philadelphia in Syria, a Byzantine historian and rhetorician, wrote a history of the empire from A. D. 474 to 480, of which we have some extracts, published along with Dexippus by Bekker and Niebuhr, Bonn, 1829.

Malĕa (Μαλέα ἄκρα: *C. Maria*), the S. promontory of the island of Lesbos.

Malĕa (Μαλέα or Μαλέαι: *C. St. Angelo* or *Malio di St. Angelo*), a promontory on the S.E. of Laconia, separating the Argolic and Laconic gulfs ; the passage round it was much dreaded by sailors. Here was a temple of Apollo, who hence bore the surname *Maleates.*

Malĕlas, or **Malălas, Joannes** ('Ιωάννης ὁ Μαλέλα or Μαλάλα), a native of Antioch, and a Byzantine historian, lived shortly after Justinian the Great. The word *Malalas* signifies in Syriac an orator. He wrote a chronicle of universal history from the creation of the world to the reign of Justinian inclusive. Edited by Dindorf, Bonn, 1831.

Malĕnĕ (Μαλήνη), a city of Mysia, only mentioned by Herodotus (vi. 29).

Maliacus Sinus (Μαλιακὸς κόλπος: *Bay of Zeitun*), a narrow bay in the S. of Thessaly, running W. from the N.W. point of the island of Euboea. On one side of it is the pass of Thermopylae. It derived its name from the Malienses,

who dwelt on its shores. It is sometimes called the *Lamiacus Sinus,* from the town of Lamia in its neighbourhood.

Malis (Μαλίς γῆ, Ionic and Att. Μηλὶς γῆ: Μαλιεύς or Μηλιεύς, Maliensis), a district in the S. of Thessaly, on the shores of the Maliacus Sinus, and opposite the N.W. point of the island of Euboea. It extended as far as the pass of Thermopylae. Its inhabitants, the Malians, were Dorians, and belonged to the Amphictyonic league.

Malli (Μαλλοί), an Indian people on both sides of the HYDRAOTES : their capital is supposed to have been on the site of the celebrated fortress of *Mooltan.*

Mallus (Μαλλός), a very ancient city of Cilicia, on a hill a little E. of the mouth of the river Pyramus, was said to have been founded at the time of the Trojan War by Mopsus and Amphilochus. It had a port called Magarsa.

Maluginensis, a celebrated patrician family of the Cornelia gens in the early ages of the republic, the members of which frequently held the consulship. It disappears from history before the time of the Samnite wars.

Malva. [MULUCHA.]

Mamaea, Julia, a native of Emesa in Syria, was daughter of Julia Maesa, and mother of Alexander Severus. She was a woman of integrity and virtue, and brought up her son with the utmost care. She was put to death by the soldiers along with her son, A. D. 235.

Mamercus. 1. Son of king Numa, according to one tradition, and son of Mars and Silvia, according to another.— 2. Tyrant of Catana, when Timoleon landed in Sicily, B.C. 344. After his defeat by Timoleon he fled to Messana, and took refuge with Hippon, tyrant of that city. But when Timoleon laid siege to Messana, Hippon took to flight, and Mamercus surrendered, stipulating only for a regular trial before the Syracusans. But as soon as he was brought into the assembly of the people there, he was condemned by acclamation, and executed like a common malefactor.

Mamercus or **Mamercinus, Aemilius,** a distinguished patrician family which professed to derive its name from Mamercus in the reign of Numa. 1. L., thrice consul, namely, B. C. 484, 478, 473.— 2. Tib., twice consul, 470 and 467. — 3. Mam., thrice dictator, 437, 433, and 426. In his first dictatorship he carried on war against the Veientines and Fidenae. Lar Tolumnius, the king of Veii, is said to have been killed in single combat in this year by Cornelius Cossus. In his 2nd dictatorship Aemilius carried a law limiting to 18 months the duration of the censorship, which had formerly lasted for 5 years. This measure was received with great approbation by the people; but the censors then in office were so enraged at it, that they removed him from his tribe, and reduced him to the condition of an aerarian.— 4. L., a distinguished general in the Samnite wars, was twice consul 341 and 329, and once dictator 335. In his 2nd consulship he took Privernum, and hence received the surname of Privernas.

Mamers, the Oscan name of the god MARS.

Mamertini. [MESSANA.]

Mamertium (Mamertini), a town in Bruttium, of uncertain site, founded by a band of Samnites, who had left their mother country under the protection of Mamers or Mars, to seek a new home.

Mamilia Gens, plebeian, was originally a distinguished family in Tusculum. They traced their name and origin to Mamilia, the daughter of Telegonus, the founder of Tusculum, and the son of Ulysses and the goddess Circe. It was to a member of this family, Octavius Mamilius, that Tarquinius betrothed his daughter ; and on his expulsion from Rome, he took refuge with his son-in-law, who, according to the beautiful lay preserved by Livy, roused the Latin people against the infant republic, and perished in the great battle at the lake Regillus. In B.C. 458, the Roman citizenship was given to L. Mamilius the dictator of Tusculum, because he had 2 years before marched to the assistance of the city when it was attacked by Herdonius. The gens was divided into 3 families, *Limetanus, Turrinus,* and *Vitulus,* but none of them became of much importance.

Mammŭla, the name of a patrician family of the Cornelia gens, which never became of much importance in the state.

Māmurĭus Veturĭus. [VETURIUS.]

Māmurra, a Roman eques, born at Formiae, was the commander of the engineers (*praefectus fabrum*) in Julius Caesar's army in Gaul. He amassed great riches, the greater part of which, however, he owed to Caesar's liberality. He was the first person at Rome who covered all the walls of his house with layers of marble, and also the first, all of the columns in whose house were made of solid marble. He was violently attacked by Catullus in his poems, who called him *decoctor Formianus.* Mamurra seems to have been alive in the time of Horace, who calls Formiae, in ridicule, *Mamurrarum urbs (Sat.* i. 5. 37), from which we may infer that his name had become a byword of contempt.

Mancĭa, Helvĭus, a Roman orator, about B.C. 90, who was remarkably ugly, and whose name is recorded chiefly in consequence of a laugh being raised against him on account of his deformity by C. Julius Caesar Strabo, who was opposed to him on one occasion in some lawsuit.

Mancīnus, Hostilĭus. 1. A., was praetor urbanus B.C. 180, and consul 170, when he had the conduct of the war against Perseus, king of Macedonia. He remained in Greece for part of the next year (169) as proconsul. — **2. L.,** was legate of the consul L. Calpurnius Piso (148) in the siege of Carthage, in the 3rd Punic war. He was consul 145. — **3. C.,** consul 137, had the conduct of the war against Numantia. He was defeated by the Numantines, and purchased the safety of the remainder of his army by making a peace with the Numantines. The senate refused to recognise it, and went through the hypocritical ceremony of delivering him over to the enemy, by means of the fetiales. This was done with the consent of Mancinus, but the enemy refused to accept him. On his return to Rome Mancinus took his seat in the senate, as heretofore, but was violently expelled from it by the tribune P. Rutilius, on the ground that he had lost his citizenship. As the enemy had not received him, it was a disputed question whether he was a citizen or not by the *Jus Postliminii* (see *Dict. of Ant. s. v. Postliminium*), but the better opinion was that he had lost his civic rights, and they were accordingly restored to him by a lex.

Mandānē. [CYRUS.]

Mandŏnĭus. [INDIBILIS.]

Mandrŭpĭum, Mandropus, or **Mandrŭpŏlis**

(Μανδρουπολις), a town in the S. of Phrygia, on the lake Caralitis.

Mandubĭi, a people in Gallia Lugdunensis, in the modern *Burgundy,* whose chief town was ALESIA.

Mandurĭa (Μανδύριον in Plut. : *Casal Nuovo*), a town in Calabria, on the road from Tarentum to Hydruntum, and near a small lake, which is said to have been always full to the edge, whatever water was added to or taken from it. Here Archidamus III., king of Sparta, was defeated and slain in battle by the Messapians and Lucanians, B. c. 338.

Mānēs, the general name by which the Romans designated the souls of the departed ; but as it is a natural tendency to consider the souls of departed friends as blessed spirits, the Manes were regarded as gods, and were worshipped with divine honours. Hence on Roman sepulchres we find D. M. S., that is, *Dis Manibus Sacrum.* [LARES.] At certain seasons, which were looked upon as sacred days (*feriae denicales*), sacrifices were offered to the spirits of the departed. An annual festival, which belonged to all the Manes in general, was celebrated on the 19th of February, under the name of *Feralia* or *Parentalia,* because it was the duty of children and heirs to offer sacrifices to the shades of their parents and benefactors.

Mănĕtho (Μανεθώς or **Μανεθών),** an Egyptian priest of the town of Sebennytus, who lived in the reign of the first Ptolemy. He was the first Egyptian who gave in the Greek language an account of the religion and history of his country. He based his information upon the ancient works of the Egyptians themselves, and more especially upon their sacred books. The work in which he gave an account of the theology of the Egyptians and of the origin of the gods and the world, bore the title of Τῶν Φυσικῶν Ἐπιτομή. His historical work was entitled a *History of Egypt.* It was divided into 3 parts or books. The first contained the history of the country previous to the 30 dynasties, or what may be termed the mythology of Egypt, and also of the first dynasties. The 2nd opened with the 11th, 12th, and concluded with the 19th dynasty. The 3rd gave the history of the remaining 11 dynasties, and concluded with an account of Nectanebus, the last of the native Egyptian kings. The work of Manetho is lost ; but a list of the dynasties is preserved in Julius Africanus and Eusebius (most correct in the Armenian version), who, however, has introduced various interpolations. According to the calculation of Manetho, the 30 dynasties, beginning with Menes, filled a period of 3555 years. The lists of the Egyptian kings and the duration of their several reigns were undoubtedly derived by him from genuine documents, and their correctness, so far as they are not interpolated, is said to be confirmed by the hieroglyphic inscriptions on the monuments. There exists an astrological poem, entitled Ἀποτελεσματικά, in 6 books, which bears the name of Manetho ; but this poem is spurious, and cannot have been written before the 5th century of our era. Edited by Axt and Rigler, Cologne, 1832.

Manĭa, a formidable Italian, probably Etruscan, divinity of the lower world, called the mother of the Manes or Lares. The festival of the Compitalia was celebrated as a propitiation to Mania in common with the Lares.

Mānīlīa. 1. M., was consul B.C. 149, the first year of the 3rd Punic war, and carried on war against Carthage. He was celebrated as a jurist, and is one of the speakers in Cicero's *De Re Publica* (i. 12).—2. C., tribune of the plebs, B.C. 66, proposed the law, granting to Pompey the command of the war against Mithridates and Tigranes, and the government of the provinces of Asia, Cilicia, and Bithynia. This bill was warmly opposed by Q. Catulus, Q. Hortensius, and the leaders of the aristocratical party, but was supported by Cicero, in an oration which has come down to us. At the end of his year Manilius was brought to trial for the aristocratical party, and was condemned ; but we do not know of what offence he was accused.—3. Also called **Manlius** or **Mallius**, a Roman poet of uncertain age, but is conjectured to have lived in the time of Augustus. He is the author of an astrological poem in 5 books, entitled *Astronomica.* The style of this poem is extremely faulty, being harsh and obscure, and abounding in repetitions and in forced metaphors. But the author seems to have consulted the best authorities, and to have adopted their most sagacious views. The best edition is by Bentley, Lond. 1739.

Manlia Gens, an ancient and celebrated patrician gens at Rome. The chief families were those of ACIDINUS, TORQUATUS and VULSO.

Manliāna (Μανλίανα: *Miliana*, Ru.), a city of importance in Mauretania Caesariensis, where one of Pompey's sons died.

M. Manlīus, consul B.C. 392, took refuge in the Capitol when Rome was taken by the Gauls in 390. One night, when the Gauls endeavoured to ascend the Capitol, Manlius was roused from his sleep by the cackling of the geese ; collecting hastily a body of men, he succeeded in driving back the enemy, who had just reached the summit of the hill. From this heroic deed he is said to have received the surname of **Capitolinus.** In 385, he defended the cause of the plebeians, who were suffering severely from their debts and from the harsh and cruel treatment of their patrician creditors. The patricians accused him of aspiring to royal power, and he was thrown into prison by the dictator Cornelius Cossus. The plebeians put on mourning for their champion, and were ready to take up arms in his behalf. The patricians in alarm liberated Manlius ; but this act of concession only made him bolder, and he now did not scruple to instigate the plebeians to open violence. In the following year the patricians charged him with high treason, and brought him before the people assembled in the campus Martius ; but as the Capitol which had once been saved by him could be seen from this place, the court was removed to the Poetelinian grove outside the porta Nomentana. Here Manlius was condemned, and the tribunes threw him down the Tarpeian rock. The members of the Manlia gens accordingly resolved that none of them should ever bear in future the praenomen of Marcus.

Mannus, a son of Tuisco, was regarded by the ancient Germans, along with his father, as the founders of their race. They further ascribed to Mannus 3 sons, from whom the 3 tribes of the Ingaevones, Hermiones, and Istaevones derived their names.

Mantiāna Palus. [ARSISSA PALUS.]

Mantinēa (Μαντίνεια: Μαντινεύς: *Paleopoli*),

one of the most ancient and important towns in Arcadia, situated on the small river Ophis, near the centre of the E. frontier of the country. It is celebrated in history for the great battle fought under its walls between the Spartans and Thebans, in which Epaminondas fell, B.C. 362. According to tradition, Mantinea was founded by Mantineus, the son of Lycaon, but it was formed in reality out of the union of 4 or 5 hamlets. Till the foundation of Megalopolis, it was the largest city in Arcadia, and it long exercised a kind of supremacy over the other Arcadian towns ; but in the Peloponnesian war the Spartans attacked the city, and destroyed it by turning the waters of the Ophis against its walls, which were built of bricks. After the battle of Leuctra the city recovered its independence. At a later period it joined the Achaean league, but notwithstanding formed a close connection with its old enemy Sparta, in consequence of which it was severely punished by Aratus, who put to death its leading citizens and sold the rest of its inhabitants as slaves. It never recovered the effects of this blow. Its name was now changed into *Antigonīa*, in honour of Antigonus Doson, who had assisted Aratus in his campaign against the town. The emperor Hadrian restored to the place its ancient appellation, and rebuilt part of it in honour of his favourite Antinous, the Bithynian, who derived his family from Mantinea.

Mantius (Μάντιος), son of Melampus, and brother of Antiphates. [MELAMPUS.]

Manto (Μαντώ,-οῦς). 1. Daughter of the Theban soothsayer Tiresias, was herself prophetess of the Ismenian Apollo at Thebes. After the capture of Thebes by the Epigoni, she was sent to Delphi with other captives, as an offering to Apollo, and there became the prophetess of this god. Apollo afterwards sent her and her companions to Asia, where they founded the sanctuary of Apollo near the place where the town of Colophon was afterwards built. Rhacius, a Cretan, who had settled there, married Manto, and became by her the father of Mopsus. According to Euripides, she had previously become the mother of Amphilochus and Tisiphone, by Alcmaeon, the leader of the Epigoni. Being a prophetess of Apollo, she is also called *Daphne*, i. e. the laurel virgin.—2. Daughter of Hercules, was likewise a prophetess, and the person from whom the town of Mantua received its name. (Virg. *Aen.* x. 199.)

Mantŭa (Mantuānus: *Mantua*), a town in Gallia Transpadana, on an island in the river Mincius, was not a place of importance, but is celebrated because Virgil, who was born at the neighbouring village of Andes, regarded Mantua as his birthplace. It was originally an Etruscan city, and is said to have derived its name from Manto, the daughter of Hercules.

Maracanda (τὰ Μαράκανδα: *Samarkand*), the capital of the Persian province of Sogdiana, in the N. part of the country, was 70 stadia (7 geog. miles) in circuit. It was here that Alexander the Great killed his friend CLITUS.

Maraphīi (Μαράφιοι), one of the 3 noblest tribes of the Persians, standing, with the Maspii, next in honour to the Pasargadae.

Marathēsium (Μαραθήσιον), a town on the coast of Ionia, between Ephesus and Neapolis : it belonged to the Samians, who exchanged it with the Ephesians for Neapolis, which lay nearer to their island. The modern *Scala Nova* marks the site of one of these towns, but it is doubtful which.

Maráthon (Μαραθών: Μαραθώνιος), a demus in Attica, belonging to the tribe Leontis, was situated near a bay on the E. coast of Attica, 22 miles from Athens by one road, and 26 miles by another. It originally belonged to the Attic tetrapolis, and is said to have derived its name from the hero Marathon. This hero, according to one account, was the son of Epopeus, king of Sicyon, who having been expelled from Peloponnesus by the violence of his father, settled in Attica ; while, according to another account, he was an Arcadian who took part in the expedition of the Tyndaridae against Attica, and devoted himself to death before the battle. The site of the ancient town of Marathon was probably not at the modern village of *Marathon*, but at a place called *Vrana*, a little to the S. of Marathon. Marathon was situated in a plain, which extends along the sea-shore, about 6 miles in length, and from 3 miles to one mile and a half in breadth. It is surrounded on the other three sides by rocky hills and rugged mountains. Two marshes bound the extremity of the plain ; the northern is more than a square mile in extent, but the southern is much smaller, and is almost dry at the conclusion of the great heats. Through the centre of the plain runs a small brook. In this plain was fought the celebrated battle between the Persians and Athenians, B. C. 490. The Persians were drawn up on the plain, and the Athenians on some portion of the high ground above the plain ; but the exact ground occupied by the 2 armies cannot be identified, notwithstanding the investigations of modern travellers. The tumulus, raised over the Athenians who fell in the battle, is still to be seen.

Maráthus (Μάραθος), an important city on the coast of Phoenicia, opposite to Aradus and near Antaradus : it was destroyed by the people of Aradus in the time of the Syrian king, Alexander Balas, a little before B. C. 150.

Marcella. 1. Daughter of C. Marcellus and Octavia, the sister of Augustus. She was thrice married : 1st to M. Vipsanius Agrippa, who separated from her in B. C. 21, in order to marry Julia, the daughter of Augustus ; 2ndly to Julus Antonius, the son of the triumvir, by whom she had a son Lucius ; 3rdly to Sext. Appuleius, consul A. D. 14, by whom she had a daughter, Appuleia Varilia. — 2. Wife of the poet Martial, to whom he has addressed 2 epigrams (xii. 21, 31). She was a native of Spain, and brought him as her dowry an estate. As Martial was married previously to Cleopatra, he espoused Marcella probably after his return to Spain about A. D. 96.

Marcellinus, the author of the life of Thucydides. [THUCYDIDES.]

Marcellus, Claudius, an illustrious plebeian family. 1. M., celebrated as 5 times consul, and the conqueror of Syracuse. In his first consulship, B. C. 222, Marcellus and his colleague conquered the Insubrians in Cisalpine Gaul, and took their capital Mediolanum. Marcellus distinguished himself by slaying in battle with his own hand Britomartus or Viridomarus, the king of the enemy, whose spoils he afterwards dedicated as *spolia opima* in the temple of Jupiter Feretrius. This was the 3rd and last instance in Roman history in which such an offering was made. — In 216 Marcellus was appointed praetor, and rendered impor-

tant service to the Roman cause in the S. of Italy after the disastrous battle of Cannae. In 215 he remained in the S of Italy, with the title of proconsul. In the course of the same year he was elected consul in the place of Postumius Albinus, who had been killed in Cisalpine Gaul ; but as the senate declared that the omens were unfavourable, Marcellus resigned the consulship. In 214 Marcellus was consul a 3rd time, and still continued in the S. of Italy, where he carried on the war with ability, but without obtaining any decisive results. In the summer of this year he was sent into Sicily, since the party favourable to the Carthaginians had obtained the upper hand in many of the cities in the island. After taking Leontini, he proceeded to lay siege to Syracuse, both by sea and land. His attacks were vigorous and unremitting ; but though he brought many powerful military engines against the walls, these were rendered wholly unavailing by the superior skill and science of Archimedes, who directed those of the besieged. Marcellus was at last compelled to give up all hopes of carrying the city by open force, and to turn the siege into a blockade. It was not till 212 that he obtained possession of the place. It was given up to plunder, and Archimedes was one of the inhabitants slain by the Roman soldiers. The booty found in the captured city was immense ; and Marcellus also carried off many of the works of art with which the city had been adorned, to grace the temples at Rome. This was the first instance of a practice which afterwards became so general. In 210 he was consul a 4th time, and again had the conduct of the war against Hannibal. He fought a battle with the Carthaginian general near Numistro in Lucania, but without any decisive result. In 209 he retained the command of his army with the rank of proconsul. In 208 he was consul for the 5th time. He and his colleague were defeated by Hannibal near Venusia, and Marcellus himself was slain in the battle. He was buried with all due honours by order of Hannibal. — Marcellus appears to have been a rude stern soldier, brave and daring to excess, but harsh, unyielding, and cruel. The great praises bestowed upon Marcellus by the Roman historians are certainly undeserved, and probably found their way into history from his funeral oration by his son, which was used as an authority by some of the earlier annalists. — 2. M., son of the preceding, accompanied his father as military tribune, in 208, and was present with him at the time of his death. In 204 he was tribune of the people ; in 200 curule aedile ; in 198 praetor ; and in 196 consul. In his consulship he carried on the war against the Insubrians and Boii in Cisalpine Gaul. He was censor in 189. — 3. M., consul 183, carried on the war against the Ligurians. — 4. M., son of No. 2, was thrice consul, 1st in 166, when he gained a victory over the Alpine tribes of the Gauls ; 2ndly in 155, when he defeated the Ligurians ; and 3rdly in 152, when he carried on the war against the Celtiberians in Spain. In 148 he was sent ambassador to Masinissa, king of Numidia, but was shipwrecked on the voyage, and perished. — 5. M., an intimate friend of Cicero, is first mentioned as curule aedile with P. Clodius in 56. He was consul in 51, and showed himself a bitter enemy to Caesar. Among other ways in which he displayed his enmity, he caused a citizen of Comum to be scourged, in order to show his contempt for the privileges lately bestowed by Caesar upon that colony. But the animosity of Marcellus did not blind him to the imprudence of forcing on a war for which his party was unprepared; and at the beginning of 49 he in vain suggested the necessity of making levies of troops, before any open steps were taken against Caesar. His advice was overruled, and he was among the first to fly from Rome and Italy. After the battle of Pharsalia (48) he abandoned all thoughts of prolonging the contest, and withdrew to Mytilene, where he gave himself up to the pursuits of rhetoric and philosophy. Marcellus himself was unwilling to sue to the conqueror for forgiveness, but his friends at Rome were not backward in their exertions for that purpose. At length, in 46, in a full assembly of the senate, C. Marcellus, the cousin of the exile, threw himself at Caesar's feet to implore the pardon of his kinsman, and his example was followed by the whole body of the assembly. Caesar yielded to this demonstration of opinion, and Marcellus was declared to be forgiven. Cicero thereupon returned thanks to Caesar, in the oration *Pro Marcello*, which has come down to us. Marcellus set out on his return; but he was murdered at the Piraeus, by one of his own attendants, P. Magius Chilo. — 6. C., brother of the preceding, was consul 49. He is constantly confounded with his cousin, C. Marcellus [No. 8], who was consul in 50. He accompanied his colleague, Lentulus, in his flight from Rome, and eventually crossed over to Greece. In the following year (48) he commanded part of Pompey's fleet; but this is the last we hear of him. — 7. C., uncle of the 2 preceding, was praetor in 80, and afterwards succeeded M. Lepidus in the government of Sicily. His administration of the province is frequently praised by Cicero in his speeches against Verres, as affording the most striking contrast to that of the accused. Marcellus himself was present on that occasion, as one of the judges of Verres. — 8. C., son of the preceding, and first cousin of M. Marcellus [No. 5], whom he succeeded in the consulship, 50. He enjoyed the friendship of Cicero from an early age, and attached himself to the party of Pompey, notwithstanding his connection with Caesar by his marriage with Octavia. In his consulship he was the advocate of all the most violent measures against Caesar; but when the war actually broke out, he displayed the utmost timidity and helplessness. He could not make up his mind to join the Pompeian party in Greece; and after much hesitation he at length determined to remain in Italy. He readily obtained the forgiveness of Caesar, and thus was able to intercede with the dictator in favour of his cousin, M. Marcellus [No. 5]. He must have lived till near the close of 41, as his widow, Octavia, was pregnant by him when betrothed to Antony in the following year.—9. M., son of the preceding and of Octavia, the daughter of C. Octavius and sister of Augustus, was born in 43. As early as 39 he was betrothed in marriage to the daughter of Sex. Pompey; but the marrrage never took place, as Pompey's death, in 35, removed the occasion for it. Augustus, who had probably destined the young Marcellus as his successor, adopted him as his son in 25, and at the same time gave him his daughter Julia in marriage. In 23 he was curule aedile, but in the autumn of the same year he was attacked by the disease of which he died shortly after at Baiae, notwithstanding all the skill and care of the celebrated

physician Antonius Musa. He was in the 20th year of his age, and was thought to have given so much promise of future excellence, that his death was mourned as a public calamity; and the grief of Augustus, as well as that of his mother Octavia, was for a time unbounded. Augustus himself pronounced the funeral oration over his remains, which were deposited in the mausoleum lately erected for the Julian family. At a subsequent period (14) Augustus dedicated in his name the magnificent theatre near the Forum Olitorium, of which the remains are still visible. But the most durable monument to the memory of Marcellus is to be found in the well-known passage of Virgil (*Aen.* vi. 860—886), which must have been recited to Augustus and Octavia before the end of 22.—10. M., called by Cicero, for distinction's sake, the father of Aeserninus (*Brut.* 36), served under Marius in Gaul in 102, and as one of the lieutenants of L. Julius Caesar in the Marsic war, 90. — 11. M. Claudius Marcellus Aeserninus, son or grandson of No. 10, quaestor in Spain in 48, under Q. Cassius Longinus, took part in the mutiny of the soldiers against Cassius.—12. P. Cornelius Lentulus Marcellinus, son of No. 10, must have been adopted by one of the Cornelii Lentuli. He was one of Pompey's lieutenants in the war against the pirates, B. C. 67. — 13. Cn. Cornelius Lentulus Marcellinus, son of the preceding, was praetor 59, after which he governed the province of Syria for nearly 2 years, and was consul 56, when he showed himself a friend of the aristocratical party, and opposed all the measures of the triumvirate.

Marcellus, Eprius, born of an obscure family at Capua, rose by his oratorical talents to distinction at Rome in the reigns of Claudius, Nero, and Vespasian. He was one of the principal delators under Nero, and accused many of the most distinguished men of his time. He was brought to trial in the reign of Vespasian, but was acquitted, and enjoyed the patronage and favour of this emperor as well. In A. D. 69, however, he was convicted of having taken part in the conspiracy of Alienus Caecina, and therefore put an end to his own life.

Marcellus, Nonius, a Latin grammarian, the author of an important treatise, entitled *De Compendiosa Doctrina per Litteras ad Filium*, sometimes but erroneously called *De Proprietate Sermonis.* He must have lived between the 2nd and 6th centuries of the Christian era. His work is divided into 18 chapters, but of these the first 12 are in reality separate treatises on different grammatical subjects. The last 6 are in the style of the Onomasticon of Julius Pollux, each containing a series of technical terms in some one department. The whole work contains numerous quotations from the earlier Latin writers. The best edition is by Gerlach and Roth, Basil. 1842.

Marcellus Sidētes, a native of Side in Pamphylia, lived in the reigns of Hadrian and Antoninus Pius, A. D. 117—161. He wrote a long medical poem in Greek hexameter verse, consisting of 42 books, of which 2 fragments remain.

Marcellus, Ulpius, a jurist, lived under Antoninus Pius and M. Aurelius. He is often cited in the Digest.

Marcia. 1. Wife of M. Regulus, who was taken prisoner by the Carthaginians. — 2. Wife of M. Cato Uticensis, daughter of L. Marcius Philippus, consul B. c. 56. It was about 56 that Cato is related to have ceded her to his friend Q. Hortensius,

with the approbation of her father. She continued
to live with Hortensius till the death of the latter,
in 50, after which she returned to Cato. — 3. Wife
of Fabius Maximus, the friend of Augustus, learnt
from her husband the secret visit of the emperor to
his grandson Agrippa, and informed Livia of it, in
consequence of which she became the cause of her
husband's death, A. D. 13 or 14. She is mentioned
on 2 or 3 occasions by Ovid. — 4. Daughter of
Cremutius Cordus. [CORDUS.] — 5. The favourite
concubine of Commodus, organised the plot by
which the emperor perished. [COMMODUS.] She
subsequently became the wife of Eclectus, his
chamberlain, also a conspirator, and was eventually
put to death by Julianus, along with Laetus, who
also had been actively engaged in the plot.

Marcia Gens, claimed to be descended from
Ancus Marcius, the 4th king of Rome. [ANCUS
MARCIUS.] Hence one of its families subsequently
assumed the name of Rex, and the heads of Numa
Pompilius and Ancus Marcius were placed upon
the coins of the Marcii. But notwithstanding these
claims to such high antiquity, no patricians of this
name, with the exception of Coriolanus, are mentioned in the early history of the republic [CORIO-
LANUS] ; and it was not till after the enactment
of the Licinian laws that any member of the gens
obtained the consulship. The names of the most
distinguished families are CENSORINUS, PHILIPPUS,
REX, and RUTILUS.

Marciāna, the sister of Trajan, and mother of
Matidia, who was the mother of Sabina, the wife
of the emperor Hadrian.

Marciānopŏlis (Μαρκιανούπολις), an important
city in the interior of Moesia Inferior, W. of
Odessus, founded by Trajan, and named, after his
sister Marciana. It was situated on the high
road from Constantinople to the Danube. It subsequently became the capital of the Bulgarians,
who called it Pristhlava (Πρισθλάβα), whence its
modern name Presthlaw, but the Greeks still call
it Marcenopoli.

Marciānus. 1. Emperor of the East A. D. 450
—457, was a native of Thrace or Illyricum, and
served for many years as a common soldier in the
imperial army. Of his early history we have only
a few particulars ; but he had attained such distinction at the death of Theodosius II. in 450, that
the widow of the latter, the celebrated Pulcheria,
offered her hand and the imperial title to Marcian,
who thus became emperor of the East. Marcian
was a man of resolution and bravery ; and when
Attila sent to demand the tribute which the
younger Theodosius had engaged to pay annually,
the emperor sternly replied, " I have iron for Attila,
but no gold." Attila swore vengeance ; but he
first invaded the Western Empire, and his death,
2 years afterwards, saved the East. In 451 Marcian assembled the council of Chalcedon, in which
the doctrines of the Eutychians were condemned.
He died in 457, and was succeeded by Leo.—2. Of
Heraclea in Pontus, a Greek geographer, of uncertain date, but who perhaps lived in the 5th century
of the Christian era. He wrote a work in prose,
entitled, " A Periplus of the External Sea, both
eastern and western, and of the largest Islands in
it." The External Sea he used in opposition to
the Mediterranean. This work was in 2 books ;
of which the former, on the E. and S. seas, has come
down to us entire ; but of the latter, which treated
of the W. and N. seas, we possess only the 3 last

chapters on Africa, and a mutilated one on the
distance from Rome to the principal cities in the
world. In this work he chiefly follows Ptolemy.
He also made an epitome of the Periplus of Arte-
miodorus of Ephesus [ARTEMIODORUS, No. 4],
of which we possess the introduction, and the periplus of Pontus, Bithynia, and Paphlagonia. Marcianus likewise published an edition of Menippus
with additions and corrections. [MENIPPUS.] The
works of Marcianus are edited by Hudson, in the
Geographi Graeci Minores, and separately by Hoffmann, Marciani Periplus, &c., Lips. 1841.

Marciānus, Aellus, a Roman jurist, who lived
under Caracalla and Alexander Severus. His
works are frequently cited in the Digest.

Marciānus Capella. [CAPELLA.]

Marcius, an Italian seer, whose prophetic verses
(Carmina Marciana) were first discovered by M.
Atilius, the praetor, in B. C. 213. They were
written in Latin, and 2 extracts from them are
given by Livy, one containing a prophecy of the
defeat of the Romans at Cannae, and the 2nd, commanding the institution of the Ludi Apollinares.
The Marcian prophecies were subsequently preserved in the Capitol with the Sibylline books.
Some writers mention only one person of this name,
but others speak of 2 brothers, the Marcii.

Marcius. [MARCIA GENS.]

Marcomanni, that is, men of the mark or
border, a powerful German people of the Suevic
race, originally dwelt in the S.W. of Germany,
between the Rhine and the Danube, on the banks
of the Main ; but under the guidance of their
chieftain Maroboduus, who had been brought up
at the court of Augustus, they migrated into the
land of the Boii, a Celtic race, who inhabited
Bohemia and part of Bavaria. Here they settled
after subduing the Boii, and founded a powerful
kingdom, which extended S. as far as the Danube.
[MAROBODUUS.] At a later time, the Marcomanni, in conjunction with the Quadi and other
German tribes, carried on a long and bloody war
with the emperor M. Aurelius, which lasted
during the greater part of his reign, and was only
brought to a conclusion by his son Commodus
purchasing peace of the barbarians as soon as he
ascended the throne, A. D. 180.

Mardēnē or Mardyēnē (Μαρδηνή, Μαρδυηνή),
a district of Persia, extending N. from Taocene to
the W. frontier and to the sea-coast. It seems to
have taken its name from some branch of the great
people called Mardi or Amardi, who are found in
various parts of W. and central Asia ; for example,
in Armenia, Media, Margiana, and, under the
same form of name as those in Persis, in Sogdiana.

Mardi. [AMARDI ; MARDENE.]

Mardŏnius (Μαρδόνιος), a distinguished Persian,
was the son of Gobryas, and the son-in-law of
Darius Hystaspis. In B. C. 492 he was sent by
Darius, with a large armament, to punish Eretria
and Athens for the aid they had given to the
Ionians. But his expedition was an entire failure.
His fleet was destroyed by a storm off Mt. Athos,
and the greater part of his land forces was destroyed
on his passage through Macedonia, by the Brygians,
a Thracian tribe. In consequence of his failure he
was superseded in the command by Datis and Artaphernes, 490. On the accession of Xerxes, Mardonius was one of the chief instigators of the expedition against Greece, with the government of
which he hoped to be invested after its conquest ;

and he was appointed one of the generals of the land army. After the battle of Salamis (480), he became alarmed for the consequences of the advice he had given, and persuaded Xerxes to return home with the rest of the army, leaving 300,000 men under his command for the subjugation of Greece. He was defeated in the following year (479), near Plataeae, by the combined Greek forces under the command of Pausanias, and was slain in the battle.

Mardus. [AMARDUS.]

Mardyene, Mardyeni. [MARDENE.]

Marea, -ea, -ia (Μαρέη, Μαρεία, Μαρία· Μαρεώτης, Mareōta: *Mariouth,* Ru.), a town of Lower Egypt, in the district of Mareotis, on the S. side of the lake Mareotis, at the mouth of a canal.

Mareōtis (Μαρεῶτις). 1. Also called Μαρεώτης Νομός, a district of Lower Egypt, on the extreme N.W., on the borders of the Libyae Nomos: it produced good wine. — 2. A town in the interior of the Libyae Nomos, between the Oasis of Ammon and the Oasis Minor.

Mareōtis or **Marea** or (-ia) **Lacus** (ἡ Μαρεῶτις, Μαρεία, Μαρία λίμνη: *Birket-Mariouth,* or *El-Kreit*), a considerable lake in the N.W. of Lower Egypt, separated from the Mediterranean by the neck of land on which Alexandria stood, and supplied with water by the Canopic branch of the Nile, and by canals. It was less than 300 stadia (30 geog. miles) long, and more than 150 wide. It was surrounded with vines, palms, and papyrus. It served as the port of Alexandria for vessels navigating the Nile.

Mares (Μάρες), a people of Asia, on the N. coast of the Euxine, who served in the army of Xerxes, being equipped with helmets of wickerwork, leathern shields, and javelins.

Maresa, Marescha (Μαρησά, Μαρισά, Μαρισσά, Μαρεσχά: prob. Ru. S. E. of *Beit Jibrin*), an ancient fortress of Palestina, in the S. of Judaea, of some importance in the history of the early kings of Judah and of the Maccabees. The Parthians had destroyed it before the time of Eusebius; and it is probable that its ruins contributed to the erection of the city of Eleutheropolis (*Beit Jibrin*), which was afterwards built on the site of the ancient Baetogabra, 2 Roman miles N.W. of Maresa.

Marescha. [MARESA.]

Margiana (ἡ Μαργιανή: the S. part of *Khiva,* S.W. part of *Bokhara,* and N.E. part of *Khorassan*), a province of the ancient Persian empire, and afterwards of the Greco-Syrian, Parthian, and Persian kingdoms, in Central Asia, N. of the mountains called Sariphi (*Ghoor*), a part of the chain of the Indian Caucasus, which divided it from Aria; and bounded on the E. by Bactriana, on the N.E. and N. by the river Oxus, which divided it from Sogdiana and Scythia, and on the W. by Hyrcania. It received its name from the river Margus (*Moorghab*), which flows through it, from S.E. to N.W., and is lost in the sands of the *Desert of Khiva.* On this river, near its termination, stood the capital of the district, Antiochia Margiana (*Meru*). With the exception of the districts round this and the minor rivers, which produced excellent wine, the country was for the most part a sandy desert. Its chief inhabitants were the Derbices, Parni, Tapuri, and branches of the great tribes of the Massagetae, Dahae, and Mardi. The country became known to the Greeks by the expeditions of Alexander and Antiochus I., the first of whom founded, and the second rebuilt, Antiochia; and the

Romans of the age of Augustus obtained further information about it from the returned captives who had been taken by the Parthians and had resided at Antiochia.

Margites. [HOMERUS, p. 328, a.]

Margum or **Margus,** a fortified place in Moesia Superior, W. of Viminacium, situated on the river Margus (*Morava*) at its confluence with the Danube. Here Diocletian gained a decisive victory over Carinus. The river Margus, which is one of the most important of the southern tributaries of the Danube, rises in Mt. Orbelus.

Margus. [MARGIANA.]

Maria. [MAREA, MAREOTIS.]

Mariaba. [SABA.]

Mariamma (Μαριάμμη, -άμη, -άμνη), a city of Coele-Syria, some miles W. of Emesa, assigned by Alexander the Great to the territory of Aradus.

Mariamne. [HERODES.]

Mariamne Turris, a tower at Jerusalem, built by Herod the Great.

Marianae Fossae. [FOSSA.]

Mariandyni (Μαριανδυνοί), an ancient people of Asia Minor, on the N. coast, E. of the river Sangarius, in the N.E. part of Bithynia. With respect to their ethnical affinities, it seems doubtful whether they were connected with the Thracian tribes (the Thyni and Bithyni) on the W., or the Paphlagonians on the E.; but the latter appears the more probable.

Marianus Mons (*Sierra Morena*), a mountain in Hispania Baetica, properly only a western offshoot of the Orospeda. The eastern part of it was called Saltus Castulonensis, and derived its name from the town of Castulo.

Marica, a Latin nymph, the mother of Latinus by Faunus, was worshipped by the inhabitants of Minturnae in a grove on the river Liris. Hence the country round Minturnae is called by Horace (*Carm.* iii. 17. 7) *Maricae litora.*

Marinus (Μαρῖνος) 1. Of Tyre, a Greek geographer, who lived in the middle of the 2nd century of the Christian era, and was the immediate predecessor of Ptolemy. Marinus was undoubtedly the founder of mathematical geography in antiquity; and Ptolemy based his whole work upon that of Marinus. [PTOLEMAEUS.] The chief merit of Marinus was, that he put an end to the uncertainty that had hitherto prevailed respecting the positions of places, by assigning to each its latitude and longitude. — 2. Of Flavia Neapolis, in Palestine, a philosopher and rhetorician, was the pupil and successor of Proclus, whose life he wrote, a work which is still extant, edited by Boissonade, Lips. 1814.

Marisus (*Marosch*), called **Maris** (Μάρις) by Herodotus, a river of Dacia, which, according to the ancient writers, falls into the Danube, but which in reality falls into the *Theiss,* and, along with this river, into the Danube.

Maritima, a sea-port town of the Avatici, and a Roman colony in Gallia Narbonensis.

Marius. 1. C., the celebrated Roman, who was 7 times consul, was born in B.C. 157, near Arpinum, of an obscure and humble family. His father's name was C. Marius, and his mother's Fulcinia; and his parents, as well as Marius himself, were clients of the noble plebeian house of the Herennii. So indigent, indeed, is the family represented to have been, that young Marius is said to have worked as a common peasant for

Minoa. Nisaea. Megara. Page 429.

Gate of the Lions at Mycenae. Page 461.

Ithome, from the Stadium of Messene. Page 441.

Roman Aqueduct near Nemausus, now called the Pont du Gard. Page 471.

[To face p. 416.

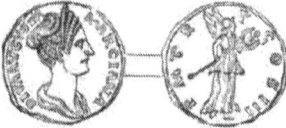

Marciana, sister of Trajan. Page 415.

Maximianus I., Roman Emperor, A.D. 235—238.

Marcianus, Roman Emperor, A.D. 450—457. Page 415.

Maximianus II., Roman Emperor, A.D. 306—311.

Aurelius Marius, one of the Thirty Tyrants. Page 418, No. 4.

Maximinus I., Roman Emperor, A.D. 235—238. Page 424.

Martinianus, Roman Caesar, ob. A.D. 323. Page 421.

Maximinus II., Roman Emperor, A.D. 305—314. Page 425.

Mausolus, King of Caria, B.C. 377—353. Page 473.

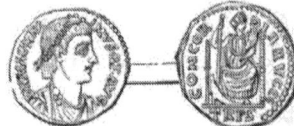

Maximus Magnus, Roman Emperor, A.D. 383—388. Page 426.

Maxentius, Roman Emperor, A.D. 306—312. Page 424.
To face p. 417.]

Mithridates VI., King of Pontus, B.C. 120—63. Page 451.

wages, before he entered the ranks of the Roman army. (Comp. Juv. viii. 246.) The meanness of his origin has probably been somewhat exaggerated; and at all events he distinguished himself so much by his valour at the siege of Numantia in Spain (134), as to attract the notice of Scipio Africanus, who is said to have foretold his future greatness. His name does not occur again for 15 years; but in 119 he was elected tribune of the plebs, when he was 38 years of age. In this office he came forward as a popular leader, and proposed a law to give greater freedom to the people at the elections; and when the senate attempted to overawe him, he commanded one of his officers to carry the consul Metellus to prison. He now became a marked man, and the aristocracy opposed him with all their might. He lost his election to the aedileship, and with difficulty obtained the praetorship; but he acquired influence and importance by his marriage with Julia, the sister of C. Julius Caesar, who was the father of the future ruler of Rome. In 109 Marius crossed over into Africa as legate of the consul Q. Metellus. Here, in the war against Jugurtha, the military genius of Marius had ample opportunity of displaying itself, and he was soon regarded as the most distinguished officer in the army. He also ingratiated himself with the soldiers, who praised him in the highest terms in their letters to their friends at Rome. His popularity became so great that he resolved to return to Rome, and become at once a candidate for the consulship; but it was with great difficulty that he obtained from Metellus permission to leave Africa. On his arrival at Rome he was elected consul with an enthusiasm which bore down all opposition before it; and he received from the people the province of Numidia, and the conduct of the war against Jugurtha (107). On his return to Numidia he carried on the war with great vigour; and in the following year (106) Jugurtha was surrendered to him by the treachery of Bocchus, king of Mauretania. [JUGURTHA.] Marius sent his quaestor Sulla to receive the Numidian king from Bocchus. This circumstance sowed the seeds of the personal hatred which afterwards existed between Marius and Sulla, since the enemies of Marius claimed for Sulla the merit of bringing the war to a close by obtaining possession of the person of Jugurtha. Meantime Italy was threatened by a vast horde of barbarians, who had migrated from the N. of Germany. The 2 leading nations of which they consisted were called Cimbri and Teutoni, the former of whom are supposed to have been Celts, and the latter Gauls. To these two great races were added the Ambrones, and some of the Swiss tribes, such as the Tigurini. The whole host is said to have contained 300,000 fighting men, besides a much larger number of women and children. They had defeated one Roman army after another, and it appeared that nothing could check their progress. The utmost alarm prevailed throughout Italy; all party quarrels were hushed. Every one felt that Marius was the only man capable of saving the state, and he was accordingly elected consul a 2nd time during his absence in Africa. Marius entered Rome in triumph on the 1st of January, 104, the first day of his 2nd consulship. Meanwhile, the threatened danger was for a while averted. Instead of crossing the Alps, the Cimbri

marched into Spain, which they ravaged for the next 2 or 3 years. But as the return of the barbarians was constantly expected, Marius was elected consul a 3rd time in 103, and a 4th time in 102. In the latter of these years the Cimbri returned into Gaul. The barbarians now divided their forces. The Cimbri marched round the northern foot of the Alps, in order to enter Italy by the N. E., crossing the Tyrolese Alps by the defiles of Tridentum (Trent). The Teutoni and Ambrones, on the other hand, marched against Marius, who had taken up a position in a fortified camp on the Rhone. The decisive battle was fought near Aquae Sextiae (Aix). The carnage was dreadful. The whole nation was annihilated, for those who did not fall in the battle put an end to their own lives. The Cimbri, meantime, had forced their way into Italy. Marius was elected consul a 5th time (101), and joined the proconsul Catulus in the N. of Italy. The 2 generals gained a great victory over the enemy on a plain called the Campi Raudii, near Vercellae (Vercelli). The Cimbri met with the same fate as the Teutoni; the whole nation was destroyed. Marius was received at Rome with unprecedented honours. He was hailed as the saviour of the state; his name was coupled with the gods in the libations at banquets, and he received the title of 3rd founder of Rome. Hitherto the career of Marius had been a glorious one; but the remainder of his life is full of horrors, and brings out the worst features of his character. In order to secure the consulship a 6th time, he entered into close connection with two of the worst demagogues that ever appeared at Rome, Saturninus and Glaucia. He gained his object, and was consul a 6th time in 100. In this year he drove into exile his old enemy Metellus; and shortly afterwards, when Saturninus and Glaucia took up arms against the state, Marius crushed the insurrection by command of the senate. [SATURNINUS.] His conduct in this affair was greatly blamed by the people, who looked upon him as a traitor to his former friends. For the next few years Marius took little part in public affairs. He possessed none of the qualifications which were necessary to maintain influence in the state during a time of peace, being an unlettered soldier, rude in manners, and arrogant in conduct. The Social war again called him into active service (90). He served as legate of the consul P. Rutilius Lupus; and after the latter had fallen in battle, he defeated the Marsi in 2 successive engagements. Marius was now 67, and his body had grown stout and unwieldy; but he was still as greedy of honour and distinction as he had ever been. He had set his heart upon obtaining the command of the war against Mithridates, which the senate had bestowed upon the consul Sulla at the end of the Social war (88). In order to gain his object, Marius allied himself to the tribune, P. Sulpicius Rufus, who brought forward a law for distributing the Italian allies, who had just obtained the Roman franchise, among all the Roman tribes. As those new citizens greatly exceeded the old citizens in number, they would of course be able to carry whatever they pleased in the comitia. The law was carried notwithstanding the violent opposition of the consuls; and the tribes, in which the new citizens now had the majority, appointed Marius to the command of the war against Mithridates. Sulla fled to his army, which was stationed at

Nola ; and when Marius sent thither 2 military tribunes, to take the command of the troops, Sulla not only refused to surrender the command, but marched upon Rome at the head of his army. Marius was now obliged to take to flight. After wandering along the coast of Latium, and encountering terrible sufferings and privations, which he bore with unflinching fortitude, he was at length taken prisoner in the marshes formed by the river Liris, near Minturnae. The magistrates of this place resolved to put him to death, in accordance with a command which Sulla had sent to all the towns in Italy. A Gallic or Cimbrian soldier undertook to carry their sentence into effect, and with a drawn sword entered the apartment where Marius was confined. The part of the room in which Marius lay was in the shade ; and to the frightened barbarian the eyes of Marius seemed to dart out fire, and from the darkness a terrible voice exclaimed — "Man, durst thou murder C. Marius?" The barbarian immediately threw down his sword, and rushed out of the house. Straightway there was a revulsion of feeling among the inhabitants of Minturnae. They got ready a ship, and placed Marius on board. He reached Africa in safety, and landed at Carthage ; but he had scarcely put his foot on shore before the Roman governor sent an officer to bid him leave the country. This last blow almost unmanned Marius : his only reply was—"Tell the praetor that you have seen C. Marius a fugitive sitting on the ruins of Carthage." Soon afterwards Marius was joined by his son, and they took refuge in the island of Cercina. During this time a revolution had taken place at Rome, in consequence of which Marius was enabled to return to Italy. The consul Cinna (87) who belonged to the Marian party, had been driven out of Rome by his colleague Octavius, and had subsequently been deprived by the senate of the consulate. Cinna collected an army, and resolved to recover his honours by force of arms. As soon as Marius heard of these changes he left Africa, and joined Cinna in Italy. Marius and Cinna now laid siege to Rome. The failure of provisions compelled the senate to yield, and Marius and Cinna entered Rome as conquerors. The most frightful scenes followed. The guards of Marius stabbed every one whom he did not salute, and the streets ran with the blood of the noblest of the Roman aristocracy. Among the victims of his vengeance, were the great orator M. Antonius and his former colleague Q. Catulus. Without going through the form of an election, Marius and Cinna named themselves consuls for the following year (86). But he did not long enjoy the honour : he was now in his 71st year; his body was worn out by the fatigues and sufferings he had recently undergone; and on the 18th day of his consulship he died of an attack of pleurisy, after 7 days' illness. — 2. C., the son of the preceding, but only by adoption. He followed in the footsteps of his father, and was equally distinguished by merciless severity against his enemies. He was consul in 82, when he was 27 years of age. In this year he was defeated by Sulla near Sacriportus on the frontiers of Latium, whereupon he took refuge in the strongly fortified town of Praeneste. Here he was besieged for some time ; but after Sulla's great victory at the Colline gate of Rome over Pontius Telesinus, Marius put an end to his own life, after making an unsuccessful attempt to escape. —

3. The false Marius. [AMATIUS.]—**4. M. Aurelius Marius,** one of the 30 tyrants, was the 4th of the usurpers who in succession ruled Gaul, in defiance of Gallienus. He reigned only 2 or 3 days, but there are coins of his extant. — **5. Marius Celsus.** [CELSUS.]—**6. Marius Maximus,** a Roman historian, who is repeatedly cited by the Augustan historians. He probably flourished under Alexander Severus, and appears to have written the biographies of the Roman emperors, beginning with Trajan and ending with Elagabalus. — **7. Marius Mercator,** an ecclesiastical writer, distinguished as a zealous antagonist of the Pelagians and the Nestorians. He appears to have commenced his literary career during the pontificate of Zosimus, A. D. 418, at Rome, and he afterwards repaired to Constantinople. Mercator seems undoubtedly to have been a layman, but we are ignorant of every circumstance connected with his origin and personal history. The works of Mercator refer exclusively to the Pelagian and Nestorian heresies, and consist, for the most part, of passages extracted and translated from the chief Greek authorities. The best edition is by Baluze, Par. 1684.

Marmarica (ἡ Μαρμαρικὴ Μαρμαρίδαι : E. part of Tripoli and N.W. part of Egypt), a district of N. Africa, between Cyrenaica and Egypt, but by some ancient geographers reckoned as a part of Cyrenaica, and by others as a part of Egypt ; while others, again, call only the W. part of it, from the borders of Cyrenaica to the Catabathmus Magnus, by the name of Marmarica, and the E. part, from the Catabathmus Magnus to the Sinus Plinthinetes, Libyae Nomos. Inland it extended as far as the Oasis of Ammon. It was, for the most part, a sandy desert, intersected with low ranges of hills. — Its inhabitants were called by the general name of Marmaridae. Their chief tribes were the Adyrmachidae and Giligammae, on the coast, and the Nasamones and Augilae, in the interior.

Marmarium (Μαρμάριον : Μαρμάριος : Marmari), a place on the S. W. coast of Euboea, with a temple of Apollo Marmarius, and celebrated marble quarries, which belonged to Carystus.

Maro, Virgilius. [VIRGILIUS.]

Maroboduus, the Latinised form of the German Marbod, king of the Marcomanni, was a Suevian by birth, and was born about B. C. 18. He was sent in his boyhood with other hostages to Rome, where he attracted the notice of Augustus, and received a liberal education. After his return to his native country, he succeeded in establishing a powerful kingdom in central Germany, along the N. bank of the Danube, from Regensberg nearly to the borders of Hungary, and which stretched far into the interior. His power excited the jealousy of Augustus, who had determined to send a formidable army to invade his dominions ; but the revolt of the Pannonians and Dalmatians (A. D. 6) prevented the emperor from carrying his design into effect. Maroboduus eventually became an object of suspicion to the other German tribes, and was at length expelled from his dominions by Catualda, a chief of the Gothones, about A. D. 19. He took refuge in Italy, where Tiberius allowed him to remain, and he passed the remainder of his life at Ravenna. He died in 35 at the age of 53 years.

Maron (Μάρων), son of Evanthes, and grandson of Dionysus and Ariadne, priest of Apollo at Maro-aea in Thrace. He was the hero of sweet wine, and is mentioned among the companions of Dionysus.

Maronēa (Μαρώνεια: Μαρωνείτης: *Marogna*), a town on the S. coast of Thrace, situated on the N. bank of the lake Ismaris and on the river Sthenas, more anciently called Ortagurea. It belonged originally to the Cicones, but afterwards received colonists from Chios. It was celebrated for its excellent wine, which even Homer mentions.

Marpessa (Μάρπησσα), daughter of Evenus and Alcippe. For details see IDAS.

Marpessa (Μάρπησσα), a mountain in Paros, from which the celebrated Parian marble was obtained. Hence Virgil (*Aen.* vi. 471) speaks of *Marpēsia cautes*.

Marrucini, a brave and warlike people in Italy of the Sabellian race, occupying a narrow slip of country along the right bank of the river Aternus, and bounded on the N. by the Vestini, on the W. by the Peligni and Marsi, on the S. by the Frentani, and on the E. by the Adriatic sea. Their chief town was TEATE, and at the mouth of the Aternus, they possessed, in common with the Vestini, the seaport ATERNUM. Along with the Marsi, Peligni, and the other Sabellian tribes they fought against Rome; and together with them they submitted to the Romans in B. C. 304, and concluded a peace with the republic.

Marruvium or **Maruvium**. 1. (*S. Benedetto*), the chief town of the Marsi (who are therefore called *gens Maruvia*, Virg. *Aen.* vii. 750), situated on the E. bank of the lake Fucinus, and on the road between Corfinium and Alba Fucentia. — 2. (*Morro*), an ancient town of the Aborigines in the country of the Sabines, not to be confounded with the Marsic Marruvium.

Mars, an ancient Roman god, who was at an early period identified by the Romans with the Greek Ares, or the god delighting in bloody war. [ARES.] The name of the god in the Sabine and Oscan was Mamers; and Mars itself is a contraction of Mavers or Mavors. Next to Jupiter, Mars enjoyed the highest honours at Rome. He is frequently designated as *father Mars*, whence the forms *Marspiter* and *Maspiter*, analogous to Jupiter. Jupiter, Mars, and Quirinus were the 3 tutelary divinities of Rome, to each of whom king Numa appointed a flamen. He was worshipped at Rome as the god of war, and war itself was frequently designated by the name of Mars. His priests, the Salii, danced in full armour, and the place dedicated to warlike exercises was called after his name (*Campus Martius*). But being the father of the Romans, Mars was also the protector of the most honourable pursuit, i. e. agriculture; and under the name of Silvanus, he was worshipped as the guardian of cattle. Mars was also identified with Quirinus, who was the deity watching over the Roman citizens in their civil capacity as Quirites. Thus Mars appears under 3 aspects. As the warlike god, he was called *Gradivus*; as the rustic god, he was called *Silvanus*; while, in his relation to the state, he bore the name of *Quirinus*. His wife was called *Neria* or *Neriene*, the feminine of *Nero*, which in the Sabine language signified " strong." The wolf and the woodpecker (*picus*) were sacred to Mars. Numerous temples were dedicated to him at Rome, the most important of which was that outside the Porta Capena, on the Appian road, and that of Mars Ultor, which was built by Augustus in the forum.

Marsi. 1. A brave and warlike people of the Sabellian race, dwelt in the centre of Italy, in the high land surrounded by the mountains of the Apennines, in which the lake Fucinus is situated. Along with their neighbours the Peligni, Marrucini, &c., they concluded a peace with Rome, B. C. 304. Their bravery was proverbial; and they were the prime movers of the celebrated war waged against Rome by the Socii or Italian allies in order to obtain the Roman franchise, and which is known by the name of the Marsic or Social war. Their chief town was MARRUVIUM. — The Marsi appear to have been acquainted with the medicinal properties of several of the plants growing upon their mountains, and to have employed them as remedies against the bites of serpents, and in other cases. Hence they were regarded as magicians, and were said to be descended from a son of Circe. Others again derived their origin from the Phrygian Marsyas, simply on account of the resemblance of the name. — 2. A people in Germany, appear to have dwelt originally on both banks of the Ems, and to have been only a tribe of the Cherusci, although Tacitus makes them one of the most ancient peoples in Germany. They joined the Cherusci in the war against the Romans, which terminated in the defeat of Varus, but they were subsequently driven into the interior of the country by Germanicus.

Marsigni, a people in the S. E. of Germany, of Suevic extraction.

Marsus, Domitius, a Roman poet of the Augustan age. He wrote poems of various kinds, but his epigrams were the most celebrated of his productions. Hence he is frequently mentioned by Martial, who speaks of him in terms of the highest admiration. He wrote a beautiful epitaph on Tibullus, which has come down to us.

Marsyas (Μαρσύας). 1. A mythological personage, connected with the earliest period of Greek music. He is variously called the son of Hyagnis, or of Oeagrus, or of Olympus. Some make him a satyr, others a peasant. All agree in placing him in Phrygia. The following is the outline of his story : — Athena having, while playing the flute, seen the reflection of herself in water, and observed the distortion of her features, threw away the instrument in disgust. It was picked up by Marsyas, who no sooner began to blow through it, than the flute, having once been inspired by the breath of a goddess, emitted of its own accord the most beautiful strains. Elated by his success, Marsyas was rash enough to challenge Apollo to a musical contest, the conditions of which were that the victor should do what he pleased with the vanquished. The Muses, or, according to others, the Nysaeans, were the umpires. Apollo played upon the cithara, and Marsyas upon the flute; and it was not till the former added his voice to the music of his lyre that the contest was decided in his favour. As a just punishment for the presumption of Marsyas, Apollo bound him to a tree, and flayed him alive. His blood was the source of the river Marsyas, and Apollo hung up his skin in the cave out of which that river flows. His flutes (for, according to some, the instrument on which he played was the double flute) were carried by the river Marsyas into the Maeander, and again emerging in the Asopus, were thrown on land by it in the Sicyonian territory, and were dedicated to Apollo in his temple at Sicyon. The fable evidently refers to the struggle between the citharoedic and auloedic styles of music, of which the former was connected with the worship of Apollo among the Dorians, and the latter with the orgiastic rites of Cybele in Phrygia. In the fora of ancient cities there was frequently placed a statue of Marsyas, which was probably intended to hold forth an example of the severe punishment of arrogant presumption. The statue of Marsyas in the forum of Rome is well known by the allusions of Horace (*Sat.* i. 6. 120), Juvenal (ix. 1, 2), and Martial (ii. 64. 7). — **2.** A Greek historian, was the son of Periander, a native of Pella in Macedonia, a contemporary of Alexander, with whom he is said to have been educated. His principal work was a history of Macedonia, in 10 books, from the earliest times to the wars of Alexander. He also wrote other works, the titles of which are given by Suidas. — **3.** Of Philippi, commonly called the Younger, to distinguish him from the preceding, was also a Greek historian. The period at which ne flourished is uncertain : the earliest writers by whom he is cited are Pliny and Athenaeus.

Marsyas (Μαρσύας). 1. A small and rapid river of Phrygia, a tributary of the Maeander, took its rise, according to Xenophon, in the palace of the Persian kings at Celaenae, beneath the Acropolis, and fell into the Maeander, outside of the city. Pliny, however, states that its source was in the valley called Aulocrene, about 10 miles from Apamea Cibotus (which city was on or near the site of Celaenae), and that after a subterraneous course, it first came out to light at Apamea. Colonel Leake reconciles these statements by the natural explanation that the place where the river first broke forth from its subterraneous course, was regarded as its true origin. Tradition ascribed its name to the fable of MARSYAS. — **2.** (*Chinar-Chai*), a considerable river of Caria, having its source in the district called Idrias, flowing N.W. and N. through the middle of Caria, past Stratonicea and Alabanda, and falling into the S. side of the Maeander, nearly opposite to Tralles. — **3.** In Syria, a small tributary of the Orontes, into which it falls on the E. side, near Apamea. — **4.** A name given to the extensive plain in Syria, through which the upper course of the Orontes flows, lying between the ranges of Casius and Lebanon, and reaching from Apamea on the N. to Laodicea ad Libanum on the S.

Martialis. 1. **M. Valĕrĭus**, the epigrammatic poet, was born at Bilbilis in Spain, in the 3rd year of Claudius, A. D. 43. He came to Rome in the 13th year of Nero, 66; and after residing in the metropolis 35 years, he returned to the place of his birth, in the 3rd year of Trajan, 100. He lived there for upwards of 3 years at least, on the property of his wife, a lady named Marcella, whom he seems to have married after his return to Bilbilis. His death cannot have taken place before 104. His fame was extended and his books were eagerly sought for, not only in the city, but also in Gaul, Germany, and Britain ; he secured the patronage of the emperors Titus and Domitian, obtained by his influence the freedom of the state for several of his friends, and received for himself, although apparently without family, the privileges accorded to those who were the fathers of three children (*jus trium liberorum*). together with the rank of tribunus and the rights of the equestrian order. His circumstances appear to have been easy during his residence at Rome, for he had a mansion in the city whose situation he describes, and a suburban villa near Nomentum, to which he frequently alludes with pride.—The extant works of Martial consist of a collection of short poems, all included under the general appellation *Epigrammata*, upwards of 1500 in number, divided into 14 books. Those which form the 2 last books, usually distinguished respectively as *Xenia* and *Apophoreta*, amounting to 350, consist of distichs, descriptive of a vast variety of small objects, chiefly articles of food or clothing, such as were usually sent as presents among friends during the Saturnalia, and on other festive occasions. In addition to the above, nearly all the printed copies include 33 epigrams, forming a book apart from the rest, which has been commonly known as *Liber de Spectaculis*, because the contents relate to the shows exhibited by Titus and Domitian, but there is no ancient authority for the title. The different books were collected and published by the author, sometimes singly and sometimes several at one time. The *Liber de Spectaculis* and the first 9 books of the regular series involve a great number of historical allusions, extending from the games of Titus (80) down to the return of Domitian from the Sarmatian expedition, in January, 94. All these books were composed at Rome, except the 3rd, which was written during a tour in Gallia Togata. The 10th book was published twice : the first edition was given hastily to the world ; the second, that which we now read (x. 2), celebrates the arrival of Trajan at Rome, after his accession to the throne (99). The 11th book seems to have been published at Rome, early in 100, and at the close of the year he returned to Bilbilis. After keeping silence for 3 years (xii. procem.), the 12th book was despatched from Bilbilis to Rome (xii. 3, 18), and must therefore be assigned to 104. Books xiii. and xiv., *Xenia* and *Apophoreta*, were written chiefly under Domitian, although the composition may have been spread over the holidays of many years. It is well known that the word *Epigram*, which originally denoted simply *an inscription*, was, in process of time, applied to any brief metrical effusion, whatever the subject might be, or whatever the form under which it was presented. Martial, however, first placed the epigram upon the narrow basis which it now occupies, and from his time the term has been in a great measure restricted to denote a short poem, in which all the thoughts and expressions converge to one sharp point, which forms the termination of the piece. Martial's epigrams are distinguished by singular fertility of imagination, prodigious flow of wit, and delicate felicity of language ; and from no source do we derive more copious information on the national customs and social habits of the Romans during the first century of the empire. But, however much we may admire the genius of the author, we feel no respect for the character of the man. The servility of adulation with which he loads Domitian, proves that he was a courtier of the lowest class ; and his works are defiled by the most cold-blooded filth, too clearly denoting habitual impurity of thought, combined with habitual impurity of expression. The best edition is by Schneidewinn, Grem. 1842. — **2. Gargillus**, a Roman historian, and a contemporary of Alexander Severus, who is cited by Vopiscus. There is extant a short fragment on veterinary surgery, bearing the name of Gargilius Martialis ; and Angelo Mai discovered on a palimpsest in the royal library at Naples, part of a work *De Hortis*, also ascribed to Gargilius Martialis. But whether Gargilius Martialis the historian, Gargilius Martialis the horticulturist, and Gargilius Martialis the veterinarian, are all, or any two of them, the same, or all different personages, cannot be determined.

Martiniānus, was elevated to the dignity of Caesar, by Licinius, when he was making preparations for the last struggle against Constantine. After the defeat of Licinius, Martinianus was put to death by Constantine, A. D. 323.

Martius Campus. [CAMPUS MARTIUS.]

Martyröpölis (Μαρτυρόπολις: *Meia Farekin*), a city of Sophene, in Armenia Major, on the river Nymphus, a tributary of the Tigris ; under Justinian, a strong fortress, and the residence of the first Dux Armeniae.

Marullus, C. Epidīus, tribune of the plebs, B. C. 44, removed, in conjunction with his colleague L. Caesetius Flavus, the diadem which had been placed upon the statue of C. Julius Caesar, and attempted to bring to trial the persons who had saluted the dictator as king. Caesar, in consequence, deprived him of the tribunate, and expelled him from the senate.

Marūvium. [MARRUVIUM.]

Mascas (Μάσκας, Μασκᾶς: *Wady-el-Selxa*), an E. tributary of the Euphrates, in Mesopotamia, mentioned only by Xenophon (*Anab.* i. 5), who describes it as surrounding the city of Corsote, and as being 35 parasangs from the Chaboras. It appears to be the same river as the Saocoras of Ptolemy.

Mases (Μάσης: Μασήτιος), a town on the S. coast of Argolis, the harbour of Hermione.

Mäsinissa (Μασσανάσσης), king of the Numidians, was the son of Gala, king of the Massylians, the easternmost of the 2 great tribes into which the Numidians were at that time divided; but he was brought up at Carthage, where he appears to have received an education superior to that usual among his countrymen. In B. C. 213 the Carthaginians persuaded Gala to declare war against Syphax, king of the neighbouring tribe of the Massaesylians, who had lately entered into an alliance with Rome. Masinissa was appointed by his father to command the invading force, with which he attacked and totally defeated Syphax. In the next year (212) Masinissa crossed over into Spain, and supported the Carthaginian generals there with a large body of Numidian horse. He fought on the side of the Carthaginians for some years; but after their great defeat by Scipio in 206, he secretly promised the latter to support the Romans as soon as they should send an army into Africa. In his desertion of the Carthaginians he is said to have been also actuated by resentment against Hasdrubal, who had previously betrothed to him his beautiful daughter Sophonisba, but violated his engagement, in order to bestow her hand upon Syphax. — During the absence of Masinissa in Spain, his father Gala had died, and the throne had been seized by an usurper; but Masinissa on his return soon expelled the usurper and obtained possession of the kingdom. He was now attacked by Syphax and the Carthaginians, who were anxious to crush him before he could receive assistance from Rome. He was repeatedly defeated by Syphax and his generals, and with difficulty escaped falling into the hands of his enemies. But

the arrival of Scipio in Africa (204) soon changed the posture of affairs. He instantly joined the Roman general, and rendered the most important services to him during the remainder of the war. He took a prominent part in the defeat of the combined forces of Syphax and Hasdrubal, and in conjunction with Laelius he reduced Cirta, the capital of Syphax. Among the captives that fell into their hands on this occasion was Sophonisba, the wife of Syphax, and the same who had been formerly promised in marriage to Masinissa himself. The story of his hasty marriage with her, and its tragical termination, is related elsewhere. [SOPHONISBA.] In the decisive battle of Zama (202), Masinissa commanded the cavalry of the right wing, and contributed in no small degree to the successful result of the day. On the conclusion of the final peace between Rome and Carthage, he was rewarded with the greater part of the territories which had belonged to Syphax, in addition to his hereditary dominions. For the next 50 years Masinissa reigned in peace, though constantly making aggressions upon the Carthaginian territory. At length in 150 he declared open war against Carthage, and these hostilities led to the outbreak of the 3rd Punic war. Masinissa died in the 2nd year of the war, 148. From this time till the commencement of the 3rd Punic war there elapsed an interval of more than 50 years, during the whole of which period Masinissa continued to reign with undisputed authority over the countries thus subjected to his rule. On his deathbed he had sent for Scipio Africanus the younger, at that time serving in Africa as a military tribune, but he expired before his arrival, leaving it to the young officer to settle the affairs of his kingdom. He died at the advanced age of 90, having retained in an extraordinary degree his bodily strength and activity to the last, so that in the war against the Carthaginians, only 2 years before, he not only commanded his army in person, but was able to go through all his military exercises with the agility and vigour of a young man. His character has been extolled by the Roman writers far beyond his true merits. He possessed indeed unconquerable energy and fortitude ; but he was faithless to the Carthaginians as soon as fortune began to turn against them; and though he afterwards continued steady to the cause of the Romans, it was because he found it uniformly his interest to do so. He was the father of a very numerous family; but it appears that 3 only of his legitimate sons survived him, Micipsa, Mastanabal, and Gulussa. Between these 3 the kingdom was portioned out by Scipio, according to the dying directions of the old king.

Masīus Mons (τὸ Μάσιον ὄρος: *Karajeh Dagh*), a mountain chain in the N. of Mesopotamia, between the upper course of the Tigris and the Euphrates, running from the main chain of the Taurus S.E. along the border of Mygdonia.

Maso, C. Papirīus, consul B. C. 231, carried on war against the Corsicans, whom he subdued ; and from the booty obtained in this war, he dedicated a temple to Fons. Maso was the maternal grandfather of Scipio Africanus the younger, his daughter Papiria marrying Aemilius Paulus.

Massa, Baebīus, or Bebīus, was accused by Pliny the younger and Herennius Senecio, of plundering the province of Baetica, of which he had been governor, A. D. 93. He was condemned, but escaped punishment by the favour of Domitian and from this time he became one of the informers and favourites of the tyrant.

Massaesýli or -**ii**. [MAURETANIA: NUMIDIA.]

Massăga (τὰ Μάσσαγα), the capital city of the Indian people ASSACENI.

Massăgĕtae (Μασσαγέται), a wild and warlike people of Central Asia, in Scythia intra Imaüm, N. of the Jaxartes (the Araxes of Herodotus) and the *Sea of Aral*, and on the peninsula between this lake and the Caspian. Their country corresponds to that of the *Kirghiz Tartars* in the N. of *Independent Tartary*. Some of the ancient geographers give them a greater extent towards the S.E., and Herodotus appears to include under the name all the nomad tribes of Asia E. of the Caspian. They appear to have been of the Turkoman race; their manners and customs resembled those of the Scythians in general; but they had some peculiarities, such as the killing and eating of their aged people. Their chief appearance in ancient history is in connection with the expedition undertaken against them by Cyrus the Great, in which Cyrus was defeated and slain. [CYRUS.]

Massăni (Μασσανοί), a people of India intra Gangem, on the lower course of the Indus, near the Island of Pattalene.

Massicus Mons, a mountain in the N. W. of Campania near the frontiers of Latium, celebrated for its excellent wine, the produce of the vineyards on the southern slope of the mountain. The celebrated Falernian wine came from the eastern side of this mountain.

Massicytus or **Massicytes** (Μασικύτης), one of the principal mountain chains of LYCIA.

Massilia (Μασσαλία: Μασσαλιώτης, Massiliensis: *Marseilles*), a Greek city in Gallia Narbonensis, on the coast of the Mediterranean, in the country of the Salyes. It was situated on a promontory, which was connected with the mainland by a narrow isthmus, and was washed on 3 sides by the sea. Its excellent harbour, called *Lacydon*, was formed by a small inlet of the sea, about half a mile long, and a quarter of a mile broad. This harbour had only a narrow opening, and before it lay an island, where ships had good anchorage. Massilia was founded by the Phocaeans of Asia Minor about B. C. 600, and soon became a very flourishing city. It extended its dominion over the barbarous tribes in its neighbourhood, and planted several colonies on the coast of Gaul and Spain, such as ANTIPOLIS, NICAEA and EMPORIUM. Its naval power and commercial greatness soon excited the jealousy of the Carthaginians, who made war upon the city, but the Massilians not only maintained their independence, but defeated the Carthaginians in a sea-fight. At an early period they cultivated the friendship of the Romans, to whom they always continued faithful allies. Accordingly when the S. E. corner of Gaul was made a Roman province, the Romans allowed Massilia to retain its independence and its own constitution. This constitution was aristocratic. The city was governed by a senate of 600 persons called Timuchi. From these were selected 15 presidents, who formed a sort of committee for carrying on the ordinary business of the government, and 3 of these were intrusted with the executive power. The inhabitants retained the religious rites of their mother country, and they cultivated with especial reverence the worship of the Ephesian Artemis or Diana. Massilia was for

many centuries one of the most important commercial cities in the ancient world. In the civil war between Caesar and Pompey (B. C. 49), it espoused the cause of the latter, but after a protracted siege, in which it lost its fleet, it was obliged to submit to Caesar. From the effects of this blow it never fully recovered. Its inhabitants had long paid attention to literature and philosophy; and under the early emperors it became one of the chief seats of learning, to which the sons of many illustrious Romans resorted to complete their studies. —The modern *Marseilles* occupies the site of the ancient town, but contains no remains of ancient buildings.

Massiva. **1**. A Numidian, grandson of Gala, king of the Massylians, and nephew of Masinissa, whom he accompanied into Spain. —**2**. Son of Gulussa, and grandson of Masinissa, was assassinated at Rome by order of Jugurtha, because he had put in his claim to the kingdom of Numidia.

Massūrius Sabinus. [SABINUS.]

Massýli or -**ii**. [MAURETANIA: NUMIDIA.]

Mastanăbal or **Manastăbal**, the youngest of the 3 legitimate sons of Masinissa, between whom the kingdom of Numidia was divided by Scipio after the death of the aged king (B. C. 148). He died before his brother Micipsa, and left 2 sons, Jugurtha and Gauda.

Mastaura (τὰ Μάσταυρα: *Mastaura-Kalesi*, Ru.), a city of Lydia on the borders of Caria, near Nysa.

Mastramēla, a town on the S. coast of Gallia Narbonensis, E. of the Rhone, and a lake of the same name, called by Mela *Avaticorum stagnum*.

Mastūsia. **1**. The S. W. point of the Thracian Chersonesus, opposite Sigeum. —**2**. A mountain of Lydia, on the S. slope of which Smyrna lay.

Maternus, Curiatius, a Roman rhetorician and tragic poet, one of the speakers in the *Dialogus de Oratoribus* ascribed to Tacitus.

Maternus Firmicus. [FIRMICUS.]

Mătho. **1**. One of the leaders of the Carthaginian mercenaries in their war against Carthage, after the conclusion of the 1st Punic war, B. C. 241. He was eventually taken prisoner, and put to death. — **2**. A pompous blustering advocate, ridiculed by Juvenal and Martial.

Mătho, Pomponius. **1**. M'., consul B. C. 233, carried on war against the Sardinians, whom he defeated. In 217 he was magister equitum; in 216 praetor; and in 215 propraetor in Cisalpine Gaul. — **2**. M., brother of the preceding, consul 231, also carried on war against the Sardinians. He was likewise praetor in 217. He died in 204. — **3**. M., probably son of No. 2., aedile 206, and praetor 204, with Sicily as his province.

Matiăna (Ματιανή, Ματιανοί, -ηνή, -ηνοί, Herod.), the S.W.-most district of Media Atropatene, along the mountains separating Media from Assyria, which were also called Matiani. The great salt lake of Spauta (Ματιανή λίμνη: *Lake of Urmi*) was in this district. Herodotus also mentions a people on the Halys in Asia Minor by the name of Matieni.

Matīnus, a mountain in Apulia, running out into the sea, was one of the offshoots of Mt. Garganus, and is frequently mentioned by Horace in consequence of his being a native of Apulia.

Matisco (*Mâcon*), a town of the Aedui in Gallia Lugdunensis on the Arar, and on the road from Lugdunum to Augustodunum.

Matius Calvēna, C., a Roman eques, and a friend of Caesar and Cicero. After Caesar's death he espoused the side of Octavianus, with whom he became very intimate.

Matron (Μάτρων), of Pitana, a celebrated writer of parodies upon Homer, probably lived a little before the time of Philip of Macedon.

Matrōna (Marne), a river in Gaul, which formed the boundary between Gallia Lugdunensis and Bolgica, and which falls into the Sequana, a little S. of Paris.

Mattiāci, a people in Germany, who dwelt on the E. bank of the Rhine, between the Main and the Lahn, and were a branch of the Chatti. They were subdued by the Romans, who, in the reign of Claudius, had fortresses and silver-mines in their country. After the death of Nero they revolted against the Romans and took part with the Chatti and other German tribes in the siege of Moguntiacum. From this time they disappear from history; and their country was subsequently inhabited by the Alemanni. Their chief towns were Aquae Mattiacae (Wiesbaden), and Mattiacum (Marburg), which must not be confounded with Mattium, the capital of the Chatti.

Mattium (Maden), the chief town of the Chatti, situated on the Adrana (Eder), was destroyed by Germanicus.

Matūta, commonly called **Mater Matūta,** is usually considered as the goddess of the dawn of morning, and her name is considered to be connected with maturus or matutinus. It seems, however, to be well attested that Matuta was only a surname of Juno; and it is probable that the name is connected with mater, so that Mater Matuta is an analogous expression with Hostus Hostilius, Faunus Fatuus, Aius Locutius, and others. Her festival, the Matralia, was celebrated on the 11th of June (Dict. of Ant. art. Matralia). The Romans identified Matuta with the Greek Leucothea. A temple was dedicated to Matuta at Rome by king Servius, and was restored by the dictator Camillus, after the taking of Veii. There was also a temple of Matuta at Satricum.

Maurētānĭa or **Maurĭtānĭa** (ἡ Μαυρουσία: Μαυρούσιοι, Μαῦροι, Mauri), the W.-most of the principal divisions of N. Africa, lay between the Atlantic on the W., the Mediterranean on the N., Numidia on the E., and Gaetulia on the S.; but the districts embraced under the names of Mauretania and Numidia respectively were of very different extent at different periods. The earliest known inhabitants of all N. Africa W. of the Syrtes were the Gaetulians, who were displaced and driven inland by peoples of Asiatic origin, who are found, in the earliest historical accounts, settled along the N. coast under various names; their chief tribes being the Mauri or Maurusii, W. of the river Malva or Malucha (Mulvia or Mohalow); thence the Massaesylii to (or nearly to) the river Ampsaga (Wady-el-Kebir), and the Massylii between the Ampsaga and the Tusca (Wady-Zain), the W. boundary of the Carthaginian territory. Of these people, the Mauri, who possessed a greater breadth of fertile country between the Atlas and the coasts, seem to have applied themselves more to the settled pursuits of agriculture than their kindred neighbours on the E., whose unsettled warlike habits were moreover confirmed by their greater exposure to the intrusions of the Phoenician settlers. Hence arose

a difference, which the Greeks marked by applying the general name of Νομάδες to the tribes between the Malva and the Tusca; whence came the Roman names of Numidia for the district, and Numidae for its people. [NUMIDIA.] Thus Mauretania was at first only the country W. of the Malva, and corresponded to the later district of Mauretania Tingitana, and to the modern empire of Marocco, except that the latter extends further S.; the ancient boundary on the S. was the Atlas. The Romans first became acquainted with the country during the war with Jugurtha, B. C. 106; of their relations with it, till it became a Roman province, about 33, an account is given under BOCCHUS. During this period the kingdom of Mauretania had been increased by the addition of the W. part of Numidia, as far as Saldae, which Julius Caesar bestowed on Bogud, as a reward for his services in the African war. A new arrangement was made about 25, when Augustus gave Mauretania to Juba II., in exchange for his paternal kingdom of Numidia. Upon the murder of Juba's son, Ptolemaeus, by Caligula (A. D. 40), Mauretania became finally a Roman province, and was formally constituted as such by Claudius, who added to it nearly half of what was still left of Numidia, namely, as far as the Ampsaga, and divided it into 2 parts, of which the W. was called Tingitana, from its capital Tingis (Tangier), and the E. Caesariensis from its capital Julia Caesarea (Zershell), the boundary between them being the river Malva, the old limit of the kingdom of Bocchus I. The latter corresponded to the W. and central part of the modern regency (and now French colony) of Algiers. These "Mauretaniae duae" were governed by an equestrian procurator. In the later division of the empire under Diocletian and Constantine, the E. part of M. Caesariensis, from Saldae to the Ampsaga, was erected into a new province, and called M. Sitifensis from the inland town of Sitifi (Setif); at the same time the W. province, M. Tingitana, seems to have been placed under the same government as Spain, so that we still find mention of the "Mauretaniae duae," meaning now, however, Caesariensis and Sitifensis. From A. D. 429 to 534 Mauretania was in the hands of the Vandals, and in 650 and the following years it was conquered by the Arabs. Its ancient inhabitants still exist as powerful tribes in Marocco and Algier, under the names of Berbers, Schillus, Kalyles, and Twariks. Its chief physical features are described under AFRICA and ATLAS. Under the later Roman emperors it was remarkable for the great number of its episcopal sees.

Mauri. [MAURETANIA.]

Mauriciānus, Junius, a Roman jurist, lived under Antonius Pius (A. D. 138—161). His works are cited a few times in the Digest.

Mauricus, Junius, an intimate friend of Pliny, was banished by Domitian, but recalled from exile by Nerva.

Mauritania. [MAURETANIA.]

Maurus, Terentiānus. [TERENTIANUS.]

Maurusii. [MAURETANIA.]

Mausōlus (Μαύσωλος or Μαύσσωλος), king of Caria, was the eldest son of Hecatomnus, whom he succeeded in the sovereignty, B. C. 377. In 362 he took part in the general revolt of the satraps against Artaxerxes Mnemon, and availed himself of that opportunity to extend his dominions. In 358 he joined with the Rhodians and others in the war waged by them against the Athenians, known by the name of the Social war. He died in 353, leaving no children, and was succeeded by his wife and sister Artemisia. The extravagant grief of the latter for his death, and the honours she paid to his memory — especially by the erection of the costly monument, which was called from him the Mausoleum — are related elsewhere. [ARTEMISIA.]

Mavors. [MARS.]

Maxentius, Roman emperor A. D. 306—312, whose full name was **M. Aurelius Valerius Maxentius.** He was the son of Maximianus and Eutropia, and received in marriage the daughter of Galerius ; but he was passed over in the division of the empire which followed the abdication of his father and Diocletian in A. D. 305. Maxentius, however, did not tamely acquiesce in this arrangement, and, being supported by the praetorian troops, who had been recently deprived of their exclusive privileges, he was proclaimed emperor at Rome in 306. He summoned his father, Maximianus, from his retirement in Lucania, who again assumed the purple. The military abilities of Maximianus were of great service to his son, who was of indolent and dissolute habits. Maximianus compelled the Caesar Severus, who had marched upom Rome, to retreat in haste to Ravenna, and soon afterwards put the latter to death when he had treacherously got him into his power (307). The emperor Galerius now marched in person against Rome, but Maximianus compelled him likewise to retreat. Maxentius, relieved from these imminent dangers, proceeded to disentangle himself from the control which his father sought to exercise, and succeeded in driving him from his court. Soon afterwards Maxentius crossed over to Africa, which he ravaged with fire and sword, because it had submitted to the independent authority of a certain Alexander. Upon his return to Rome Maxentius openly aspired to dominion over all the Western provinces ; and soon afterwards declared war against Constantine, alleging, as a pretext, that the latter had put to death his father Maximianus. He began to make preparations to pass into Gaul ; but Constantine anticipated his movements, and invaded Italy. The struggle was brought to a close by the defeat of Maxentius at Saxa Rubra near Rome, October 27th, 312. Maxentius tried to escape over the Milvian bridge into Rome, but perished in the river. Maxentius is represented by all historians as a monster of rapacity, cruelty, and lust. The only favoured class was the military, upon whom he depended for safety ; and in order to secure their devotion and to gratify his own passions, all his other subjects were made the victims of the most revolting licentiousness, and ruined by the most grinding exactions.

Maxilūa, a town in Hispania Baetica, where bricks were made so light as to swim upon water. See CALENTUM.

Maxima Caesariensis. [BRITANNIA, p. 126.]

Maximianopōlis, previously called **Porsulae,** a town in Thrace on the Via Egnatia, E. of Abdera, probably the same place as the town called Mosynopolis (Μοσυνούπολις) by the Byzantine writers.

Maximiānōpōlis (Μαξιμιανούπολις : O.T. Hadad Rimmon), a city of Palestine, in the valley of Megiddo, a little to the S.W. of Megiddo.

Maximiānus. I. Roman emperor, A. D. 286—305, whose full name was **M. Aurelius Valerius**

Maximianus. He was born of humble parents in Pannonia, and had acquired such fame by his services in the army, that Diocletian selected this rough soldier for his colleague, as one whose abilities were likely to prove valuable in the disturbed state of public affairs, and accordingly created him first Caesar (285), and then Augustus (286), conferring at the same time the honorary appellation of *Herculius,* while he himself assumed that of *Jovius.* The subsequent history of Maximian has been fully detailed in former articles. [DIOCLETIANUS : CONSTANTINUS I.: MAXENTIUS.] It is sufficient to relate here, that after having been reluctantly compelled to abdicate, at Milan (305), he was again invested with the imperial title by his son Maxentius, in the following year (306), to whom he rendered the most important services in the war with Severus and Galerius. Having been expelled from Rome shortly afterwards by his son, he took refuge in Gaul with Constantine, to whom he had previously given his daughter Fausta in marriage. Here he again attempted to resume the imperial throne, but was easily deposed by Constantine (308). Two years afterwards, he endeavoured to induce his daughter Fausta to destroy her husband, and was in consequence compelled by Constantine to put an end to his own life. — **II.,** Roman emperor, A. D. 305—311, usually called **Galerius.** His full name was **Galerius Valerius Maximianus.** He was born near Sardica in Dacia, and was the son of a shepherd. He rose from the ranks to the highest commands in the army, and was appointed Caesar by Diocletian, along with Constantius Chlorus, in 292. At the same time he was adopted by Diocletian, whose daughter Valeria he received in marriage, and was entrusted with the command of Illyria and Thrace. In 297 he undertook an expedition against the Persian monarch Narses, in which he was unsuccessful, but in the following year (298) he defeated Narses with great slaughter, and compelled him to conclude a peace. Upon the abdication of Diocletian and Maximian (305), Galerius became Augustus or emperor. In 307 he made an unsuccessful attempt to recover Italy, which had owned the authority of the usurper Maxentius. [MAXENTIUS.] He died in 311, of the disgusting disease, known in modern times by the name of morbus pediculosus. He was a cruel persecutor of the Christians ; and it was at his instigation that Diocletian issued the fatal ordinance (303), which for so many years deluged the world with innocent blood.

Maximīnus. I., Roman emperor A. D. 235—238, whose full name was **C. Julius Verus Maximinus.** He was born in a village on the confines of Thrace, of barbarian parentage, his father being a Goth, and his mother a German from the tribe of the Alani. Brought up as a shepherd, he attracted the attention of Septimius Severus, by his gigantic stature and marvellous feats of strength, and was permitted to enter the army. He eventually rose to the highest rank in the service ; and, on the murder of Alexander Severus by the mutinous troops in Gaul (235), he was proclaimed emperor. He immediately bestowed the title or Caesar on his son Maximus. During the 3 years of his reign he carried on war against the Germans with success ; but his government was characterised by a degree of oppression and sanguinary excess hitherto unexampled. The Roman world became at length tired of this monster. The senate and the provinces gladly acknowledged the 2 Gordiani, who had been proclaimed emperors in Africa; and after their death the senate itself proclaimed Maximus and Balbinus emperors (238). As soon as Maximinus heard of the elevation of the Gordians, he hastened from his winter-quarters as Sirmium. Having crossed the Alps he laid siege to Aquileia, and was there slain by his own soldiers along with his son Maximus, in April. The most extraordinary tales are related of the physical powers of Maximinus, which seem to have been almost incredible. His height exceeded 8 feet. The circumference of his thumb was equal to that of a woman's wrist, so that the bracelet of his wife served him for a ring. It is said, that he was able single-handed to drag a loaded waggon, could with his fist knock out the grinders, and with a kick break the leg of a horse; while his appetite was such, that in one day he could eat 40 pounds of meat, and drink an amphora of wine. — II., Roman emperor 305—314, originally called Daza, and subsequently **Galerius Valerius Maximinus.** He was the nephew of Galerius by a sister, and in early life followed the occupation of a shepherd in his native Illyria. Having entered the army, he rose to the highest rank in the service; and upon the abdication of Diocletian in 305, he was adopted by Galerius and received the title of Caesar. In 308 Galerius gave him the title of Augustus; and on the death of the latter in 311, Maximinus and Licinius divided the East between them. In 313 Maximinus attacked the dominions of Licinius, who had gone to Milan, for the purpose of receiving in marriage the sister of Constantine. He was, however, defeated by Licinius near Heraclea, and fled to Tarsus, where he soon after died. Maximinus possessed no military talents. He owed his elevation to his family connection. He surpassed all his contemporaries in the profligacy of his private life, in the general cruelty of his administration, and in the furious hatred with which he persecuted the Christians.

Maximus. 1. Of Ephesus or Smyrna, one of the teachers of the emperor Julian, to whom he was introduced by Aedesius. Maximus was a philosopher of the New Platonic school, and, like many others of that school, both believed in and practised magic. It is said that Julian through his persuasion was induced to abjure Christianity. On the accession of Julian, Maximus was held in high honour at the court, and accompanied the emperor on his fatal expedition against the Persians, which he had prophesied would be successful. In 364 he was accused of having caused by sorcery the illness of the emperors Valens and Valentinian, and was thrown into prison, where he was exposed to cruel tortures. He owed his liberation to the philosopher Themistius. In 371 Maximus was accused of taking part in a conspiracy against Valens, and was put to death. — 2. Of Epirus, or perhaps of Byzantium, was also an instructor of the emperor Julian in philosophy and heathen theology. He wrote in Greek, *De insolubilibus Oppositionibus,* published by H. Stephanus, Paris, 1554, appended to the edition of Dionysius Halicarnassus, as well as other works.

Maximus, Fabius. — 1. Q. **Fabius Maximus Rullianus,** was the son of M. Fabius Ambustus, consul B. C. 360. Fabius was master of the horse to the dictator L. Papirius Cursor in 325, whose anger he incurred by giving battle to the Samnites

during the dictator's absence, and contrary to his orders. Victory availed Fabius nothing in exculpation. A hasty flight to Rome, where the senate, the people, and his aged father interceded for him with Papirius, barely rescued his life, but could not avert his degradation from office. In 322 Fabius obtained his first consulship. It was the 2nd year of the 2nd Samnite war, and Fabius was the most eminent of the Roman generals in that long and arduous struggle for the empire of Italy. Yet nearly all authentic traces are lost of the seat and circumstances of his numerous campaigns. His defeats have been suppressed or extenuated; and the achievements of others ascribed to him alone. In 315 he was dictator, and was completely defeated by the Samnites at Lautulae. In 310 he was consul for the 2nd time, and carried on the war against the Etruscans. In 308 he was consul a 3rd time, and is said to have defeated the Samnites and Umbrians. He was censor in 304, when he seems to have confined the libertini to the 4 city tribes, and to have increased the political importance of the equites. In 297 he was consul for the 5th time, and in 296 for the 6th time. In the latter year he commanded at the great battle of Sentinum, when the combined armies of the Samnites, Gauls, Etruscans, and Umbrians, were defeated by the Romans. — 2. Q. **Fabius Maximus Gurges,** or the Glutton, from the dissoluteness of his youth, son of the last. His mature manhood atoned for his early irregularities. He was consul 292, and was completely defeated by the Pentrian Samnites. He escaped degradation from the consulate, only through his father's offer to serve as his lieutenant for the remainder of the war. In a 2nd battle the consul retrieved his reputation, and was rewarded with a triumph of which the most remarkable feature was old Fabius riding beside his son's chariot. He was consul the 2nd time 276. Shortly afterwards he went as legatus from the senate to Ptolemy Philadelphus, king of Egypt. He was consul a 3rd time, 265. — 3. Q. **Fabius Maximus,** with the agnomens **Verrucosus,** from a wart on his upper lip, **Ovicula,** or the Lamb, from the mildness or apathy of his temper, and **Cunctator,** from his caution in war, was the grandson of Fabius Gurges. He was consul for the 1st time 233, when Liguria was his province; censor 230; consul a 2nd time 228; opposed the agrarian law of C. Flaminius 227; was dictator for holding the comitia in 221; and in 218 was legatus from the senate to Carthage, to demand reparation for the attack on Saguntum. In 217, immediately after the defeat at Thrasymenus, Fabius was appointed dictator. From this period, so long as the war with Hannibal was merely defensive. Fabius became the leading man at Rome. On taking the field he laid down a simple and immutable plan of action. He avoided all direct encounter with the enemy; moved his camp from highland to highland, where the Numidian horse and Spanish infantry could not follow him; watched Hannibal's movements with unrelaxing vigilance, and cut off his stragglers and foragers. His enclosure of Hannibal in one of the upland valleys between Cales and the Vulturnus, and the Carthaginian's adroit escape by driving oxen with blazing faggots fixed to their horns, up the hill-sides, are well-known facts. But at Rome and in his own camp the caution of Fabius was misinterpreted; and the people in consequence divided the command between him **and M. Minu-**

cius Rufus, his master of the horse. Minucius was speedily entrapped, and would have been destroyed by Hannibal, had not Fabius generously hastened to his rescue. Fabius was consul for the 3rd time in 215, and for the 4th time in 214. In 213 he served as legatus to his own son, Q. Fabius, consul in that year, and an anecdote is preserved which exemplifies the strictness of the Roman discipline. On entering the camp at Suessula, Fabius advanced on horseback to greet his son. He was passing the lictors when the consul sternly bade him dismount. " My son," exclaimed the elder Fabius alighting, " I wished to see whether you would remember that you were consul." Fabius was consul for the 5th time in 209, in which year he retook Tarentum. In the closing years of the 2nd Punic war Fabius appears to less advantage. The war had become aggressive under a new race of generals. Fabius disapproved of the new tactics; he dreaded the political supremacy of Scipio, and was his uncompromising opponent in his scheme of invading Africa. He died in 203. — 4. Q. Fabius Maximus, elder son of the preceding, was praetor 214 and consul 213. He was legatus to the consul M. Livius Salinator 207. He died soon after this period, and his funeral oration was pronounced by his father.—5. Q. Fabius Maximus Aemilianus, was by birth the eldest son of L. Aemilius Paulus, the conqueror of Perseus, and was adopted by No. 3. Fabius served under his father (Aemilius) in the Macedonian war, 168, and was despatched by him to Rome with the news of his victory at Pydna. He was praetor in Sicily 149—148, and consul in 145. Spain was his province, where he encountered, and at length defeated Viriathus. Fabius was the pupil and patron of the historian Polybius.—6. Q. Fabius Maximus Allobrogicus, son of the last. He was consul 121; and he derived his surname from the victory which he gained in this year over the Allobroges and their ally, Bituitus, king of the Arverni in Gaul. He was censor in 108. He was an orator and a man of letters. — 7. Q. Fabius Maximus Servilianus, was adopted from the gens Servilia, by No. 5. He was uterine brother of Cn. Servilius Caepio, consul in 141. He himself was consul in 142, when he carried on war with Viriathus.

Maximus, Magnus Clemens, Roman emperor, A. D. 383—388, in Gaul, Britain, and Spain, was a native of Spain. He was proclaimed emperor by the legions in Britain in 383, and forthwith crossed over to Gaul to oppose Gratian, who was defeated by Maximus, and was shortly afterwards put to death. Theodosius found it expedient to recognise Maximus as emperor of Gaul, Britain, and Spain, in order to secure Valentinian in the possession of Italy. Maximus however aspired to the undivided empire of the West, and accordingly in 387 he invaded Italy at the head of a formidable army. Valentinian was unable to resist him, and fled to Theodosius in the East. Theodosius forthwith prepared to avenge his colleague. In 388 he forced his way through the Noric Alps, which had been guarded by the troops of Maximus, and shortly afterwards took the city of Aquileia by storm and there put Maximus to death. Victor, the son of Maximus, was defeated and slain in Gaul by Arbogastes, the general of Theodosius.

Maximus, Petronius, Roman emperor, A. D. 455, belonged to a noble Roman family, and enjoyed some of the highest offices of state under Honorius and Valentinian III. In consequence of the violence offered to his wife by Valentinian, Maximus formed a conspiracy against this emperor, who was assassinated, and Maximus himself proclaimed emperor in his stead. His reign however lasted only 2 or 3 months. Having forced Eudoxia, the widow of Valentinian, to marry him, she resolved to avenge the death of her former husband, and accordingly Genseric was invited to invade Italy. When Genseric landed at the mouth of the Tiber, Maximus prepared to fly from Rome, but was slain by a band of Burgundian mercenaries, commanded by some old officers of Valentinian.

Maximus Planudes. [PLANUDES.]

Maximus Tyrius, a native of Tyre, a Greek rhetorician and Platonic philosopher, lived during the reigns of the Antonines and of Commodus. Some writers suppose that he was one of the tutors of M. Aurelius; but it is more probable that he was a different person from Claudius Maximus, the Stoic, who was the tutor of this emperor. Maximus Tyrius appears to have spent the greater part of his life in Greece, but he visited Rome once or twice. There are extant 41 Dissertations (Διαλέξεις or Λόγοι) of Maximus Tyrius on theological, ethical, and other philosophical subjects, written in an easy and pleasing style, but not characterised by much depth of thought. The best edition is by Reiske, Lips. 1774—5, 2 vols. 8vo.

Maximus, Valerius. [VALERIUS.]

Maxula. [ADES.]

Maxyes (Μάξυες), a people of N. Africa, on the coast of the Lesser Syrtis, on the W. bank of the river Triton, who claimed descent from the Trojans. They allowed their hair to grow only on the left side of the head, and they painted their bodies with vermilion ; customs still preserved by some tribes in the same regions.

Mazaca. [CAESAREA, No. 1.]

Mazara (Μαζάρα; Μαζαραῖος: Mazzara), a town on the W. coast of Sicily, situated on a river of the same name. between Lilybaeum and Selinus, and founded by the latter city, was taken by the Romans in the 1st Punic war.

Maxices (Μάξικες), a people of N. Africa, in Mauretania Caesariensis, on the S. slope of M. Zalacus. They, as well as the MAXYES, are thought to be the ancestors of the Amazirghs.

Mecyberna (Μηκύβερνα: Μηκυβερναῖος: Molivo), a town of Macedonia in Chalcidice, at the head of the Toronaic gulf, E. of Olynthus, of which it was the seaport. From this town part of the Toronaic gulf was subsequently called Sinus Mecybernaeus.

Medaba (Μήδαβα), a city of Peraea in Palestine.

Medama, Medma, or Mesma, a Greek town on the W. coast of Bruttium, founded by the Locrians, with a celebrated fountain and a harbour, called Emporium.

Medaura, Ad Medera, or Amedera (Ayedrah, Ru.), a flourishing city of N. Africa, on the borders of Numidia and Byzacena, between Lares and Theveste ; a Roman colony ; and the birthplace of Appuleius.

Medea (Μήδεια), daughter of Aeëtes, king of Colchis, by the Oceanid Idyia, or, according to others, by Hecate, the daughter of Perses. She was celebrated for her skill in magic. The principal parts of her story are given under ABSYRTUS, ARGONAUTAE, and JASON. It is sufficient to state here that, when Jason came to Colchis to fetch the golden fleece, she fell in love with the hero, assisted him in accomplishing the object for which he had visited Colchis, and afterwards fled with him as his wife to Greece ; that having been deserted by Jason for the youthful daughter of Creon, king of Corinth, she took fearful vengeance upon her faithless spouse by murdering the two children which she had had by him, and by destroying his young wife by a poisoned garment ; and that she then fled to Athens in a chariot drawn by winged dragons. So far her story has been related elsewhere. At Athens she is said to have married king Aegeus, or to have been beloved by Sisyphus. Zeus himself is said to have sued for her, but in vain, because Medea dreaded the anger of Hera ; and the latter rewarded her by promising inmortality to her children. Her children are, according to some accounts, Mermerus, Pheres, or Thessalus, Alcimenes, and Tisander ; according to others, she had 7 sons and 7 daughters, while others mention only 2 children, Medus (some call him Polyxenus) and Eriopis, or one son Argus. Respecting her flight from Corinth, there are different traditions. Some say, as we remarked above, that she fled to Athens and married Aegeus, but when it was discovered that she had laid snares for Theseus, she escaped and went to Asia, the inhabitants of which were called after her Medes. Others relate that she first fled from Corinth to Hercules at Thebes, who had promised her his assistance while yet in Colchis, in case of Jason being unfaithful to her. She cured Hercules, who was seized with madness ; and as he could not afford her the assistance he had promised, she went to Athens. She is said to have given birth to her son Medus after her arrival in Asia, where she had married a king ; whereas others state that her son Medus accompanied her from Athens to Colchis, where her son slew Perses, and restored her father Aeëtes to his kingdom. The restoration of Aeëtes, however, is attributed by some to Jason, who accompanied Medea to Colchis. At length Medea is said to have become immortal, to have been honoured with divine worship, and to have married Achilles in Elysium.

Mĕdĕŏn (Μεδεών: Μεδεώνιοσ). 1. Or **Medion** (*Katuna*), a town in the interior of Acarnania, near the road which led from Limnaea to Stratos. — 2. A town on the coast of Phocis near Anticyra, destroyed in the sacred war, and never rebuilt. — 3. An ancient town in Boeotia, mentioned by Homer, situated at the foot of Mt. Phoenicus, near Onchestus and the lake Copaïs. — 4. A town of the Labeates in Dalmatia, near Scodra.

Mĕdĭa (ἡ Μηδία: Μῆδος, Mēdus), an important country of W. Asia, occupying the extreme W. of the great table-land of *Iran*, and lying between Armenia on the N. and N.W., Assyria and Susiana on the W. and S.W., Persis on the S., the great desert of Aria on the E., and Parthia, Hyrcania, and the Caspian on the N.E. Its boundaries were, on the N. the Araxes, on the W. and S.W. the range of mountains called Zagros and Parachoatras (*Mts. of Kurdistan and Louristan*), which divided it from the Tigris and Euphrates valley, on the E. the Desert, and on the N.E. the Caspii Montes (*Elburz M.*), the country between which and the Caspian, though reckoned as a part of Media, was possessed by the Gelae, Mardi, and other independent tribes. Media thus corresponded nearly to the modern province of *Irak-Ajemi*. It was for the most part

a fertile country, producing wine, figs, oranges and citrons, and honey, and supporting an excellent breed of horses. It was well peopled, and was altogether one of the most important provinces of the ancient Persian empire. After the Macedonian conquest, it was divided into 2 parts, Great Media (ἡ μεγάλη Μηδία), and Atropatēne. [ATROPATENE.] The earliest history of Media is involved in much obscurity. Herodotus and Ctesias (in Diodorus) give different chronologies for its early kings. Ctesias makes ARBACES the founder of the monarchy, about B.C. 842, and reckons 8 kings from him to the overthrow of the kingdom by Cyrus. Herodotus reckons only 4 kings of Media, namely : 1. DEIOCES, B.C. 710—657 ; 2. PHRAORTES, 657—635 ; 3. CYAXARES, 635 —595 ; 4. ASTYAGES, 595—560. The last king was dethroned by a revolution, which transferred the supremacy to the Persians, who had formerly been the subordinate people in the united Medo-Persian empire. [CYRUS.] The Medes made more than one attempt to regain their supremacy ; the usurpation of the Magian Pseudo-Smerdis was no doubt such an attempt [MAGI] ; and another occurred in the reign of Darius II., when the Medes revolted, but were soon subdued (B.C. 408). With the rest of the Persian Empire, Media fell under the power of Alexander ; it next formed a part of the kingdom of the Seleucidae, from whom it was conquered by the Parthians, in the 2nd century B.C., from which time it belonged to the Parthian, and then to the later Persian empire. The people of Media were a branch of the Indo-Germanic family, and nearly allied to the Persians ; their language was a dialect of the Zend, and their religion the Magian. They called themselves **Arii**, which, like the native name of the Persians (Artaei) means *noble*. They were divided, according to Herodotus, into 6 tribes, the Buzae, Parataceni, Struchates, Arizanti, Budii, and Magi. In the early period of their history, they were eminent warriors, especially as horse-archers ; but the long prevalence of peace, wealth, and luxury reduced them to a by-word for effeminacy.— It is important to notice the use of the names **Medus** and **Medi** by the Roman poets, for the nations of Asia E. of the Tigris in general, and the Parthians in particular.

Mediae Murus (τὸ Μηδίας καλούμενον τεῖχος), an artificial wall, which ran from the Euphrates to the Tigris, at the point where they approach nearest, a little above 33° N. lat. and divided Mesopotamia from Babylonia. It is described by Xenophon (*Anab.* ii. 4), as being 20 parasangs long, 100 feet high, and 20 thick, and as built of baked bricks, cemented with asphalt. Its erection was ascribed to Semiramis, and hence it was also called τὸ Σεμιράμιδος διατείχισμα.

Mĕdĭŏlānum (Mediolanensis), more frequently called by Greek writers **Mediolānĭum** (Μεδιολάνιον), the name of several cities founded by the Celts. 1. (*Milan*), the capital of the Insubres in Gallia Transpadana, was situated in an extensive plain between the rivers Ticinus and Addua. It was taken by the Romans B.C. 222, and afterwards became both a municipium and a colony. On the new division of the empire made by Diocletian, it became the residence of his colleague Maximianus, and continued to be the usual residence of the emperors of the West, till the irruption of Attila, who took and plundered the town, induced them to transfer the seat of government to the more strongly fortified town of Ravenna. Mediolanum was at this time one of the first cities of the empire ; it possessed an imperial mint, and was the seat of an archbishopric. It is celebrated in ecclesiastical history as the see of St. Ambrose. On the fall of the Western empire, it became the residence of Theodoric the Great and the capital of the Ostrogothic kingdom, and surpassed even Rome itself in populousness and prosperity. It received a fearful blow in A. D. 539, when, in consequence of having sided with Belisarius, it was taken by the Goths under Vitiges, a great part of it destroyed, and its inhabitants put to the sword. It however gradually recovered from the effects of this blow, and was a place of importance under the Lombards, whose capital, however, was Pavia. The modern Milan contains no remains of antiquity, with the exception of 16 handsome fluted pillars near the church of S. Lorenzo. — 2. (Saintes), a town of the Santones in Aquitania, N. E. of the mouth of the Garumna ; subsequently called Santones after the people, whence its modern name. — 3. (Château Meillan), a town of the Bituriges Cubi in Aquitania, N. E. of the town last mentioned.— 4. (Evreux), a town of the Aulerci Eburovices in the N. of Gallia Lugdunensis, S. of the Sequana, on the road from Rotomagus to Lutetia Parisiorum ; subsequently called Civitas Ebroicorum, whence its modern name. — 5. A town of the Segusiani in the S. of Gallia Lugdunensis. — 6. A town in Gallia Belgica, on the road from Colonia Trajana to Colonia Agrippina.

Mediomatrici, a people in the S.E. of Gallia Belgica on the Mosella, S. of the Treviri. Their territory originally extended to the Rhine, but in the time of Augustus they had been driven from the banks of this river by the Vangiones, Nemetes, and other German tribes. Their chief town was Divodūrum (Metz).

Mediterrānĕum Mare. [INTERNUM MARE.]

Meditrīna, a Roman divinity of the art of healing, in whose honour the festival of the Meditrinalia was celebrated in the month of October. (Dict. of Ant. art. Meditrinalia.)

Medma. [MEDAMA.]

Medŏācus or **Medŭācus**, a river in Venetia in the N. of Italy, formed by the union of 2 rivers, the Medoacus Major (Brenta) and Medoacus Minor (Bacchiglione), which falls into the Adriatic sea near Edron, the harbour of Patavium.

Medobriga (Marvao, on the frontiers of Portugal), a town in Lusitania, on the road from Emerita to Scalabis.

Medŏcus. [AMADOCUS.]

Medŏn (Μέδων). 1. Son of Oileus, and brother of the lesser Ajax, fought against Troy, and was slain by Aeneas. — 2. Son of Codrus. [CODRUS.]

Medŭli, a people in Aquitania on the coast of the Ocean, S. of the mouth of the Garumna, in the modern Medoc. There were excellent oysters found on their shores.

Medulli, a people on the E. frontier of Gallia Narbonensis and in the Maritime Alps, in whose country the Druentia (Durance) and Duria (Doria Minor) took their rise.

Medullīa (Medullīnus : St. Angelo), a colony of Alba, in the land of the Sabines, was situated between the Tiber and the Anio, in the neighbourhood of Corniculum and Ameriola. Tarquinius Priscus incorporated their territory with the Roman state.

Medullīnus, Furius, an ancient patrician family at Rome, the members of which held the highest offices of state in the early times of the republic.

Medullus, a mountain in Hispania Tarraconensis, near the Minius.

Mĕdus, a son of Medea. [MEDEA.]

Mĕdus (Μῆδος), a small river of Persis, flowing from the confines of Media, and falling into the Araxes (Bend-Emir) near Persepolis.

Medūsa. [GORGONES.]

Megabāzus or **Megabȳzus.** 1. One of the 7 Persian nobles who conspired against the Magian Smerdis, B. C. 521. Darius left him behind with an army in Europe, when he himself recrossed the Hellespont, on his return from Scythia, 506. Megabazus subdued Perinthus and the other cities on the Hellespont and along the coast of Thrace. — 2. Son of Zopyrus, and grandson of the above, was one of the commanders in the army of Xerxes, 480. He afterwards commanded the army sent against the Athenians in Egypt, 458.

Megācles (Μεγακλῆς). 1. A name borne by several of the Athenian family of the Alcmaeonidae. The most important of these was the Megacles who put to death Cylon and his adherents, after they had taken refuge at the altar of Athena, B. c. 612. [CYLON.] — 2. A Syracusan, brother of Dion, and brother-in-law of the elder Dionysius. He accompanied Dion in his flight from Syracuse, 358, and afterwards returned with him to Sicily.

Megaera. [EUMENIDES.]

Megālla or **Megāris**, a small island in the Tyrrhene sea, opposite Neapolis.

Megalŏpŏlis (ἡ Μεγάλη πόλις, Μεγαλόπολις: Μεγαλοπολίτης). 1. (Sinano or Sinanu), the most recent, but the most important of the cities of Arcadia, was founded on the advice of Epaminondas, after the battle of Leuctra, B. C. 371, and was formed out of the inhabitants of 38 villages. It was situated in the district Maenalia, near the frontiers of Messenia, on the river Helisson, which flowed through the city, dividing it into nearly 2 equal parts. It stood on the site of the ancient town Orestion or Orestia ; was 50 stadia (6 miles) in circumference ; and contained, when it was besieged by Polysperchon, about 15,000 men capable of bearing arms, which would give us a population of about 70,000 inhabitants. Megalopolis was for a time subject to the Macedonians ; but soon after the death of Alexander the Great, it was governed by a series of native tyrants, the last of whom, Lydiades, voluntarily resigned the government, and united the city to the Achaean league, B. C. 234. It became in consequence opposed to Sparta, and was taken and plundered by Cleomenes, who either killed or drove into banishment all its inhabitants, and destroyed a great part of the city, 222. After the battle of Sellasia in the following year, it was restored by Philopoemen, who again collected its inhabitants ; but it never recovered its former prosperity, and gradually sunk into insignificance. Philopoemen and the historian Polybius were natives of Megalopolis. The ruins of its theatre, once the largest in Greece, are the only remains of the ancient town to be seen in the village of Sinano. — 2. A town in Caria. [APHP DISIAS.] — 3. A town in Pontus. [SEBASTIA] — 4. A town in the N. of Africa, was a Carthaginian city in the interior of Byzacena, in a beautiful situation ; it was taken and destroyed by the troops of Agathocles.

Meganira (Μεγάνειρα), wife of Celeus, usually called METANIRA.

Megapenthes (Μεγαπένθης). 1. Son of Proetus, father of Anaxagoras and Iphianira, and king of Argos. He exchanged his dominion for that of Perseus, so that the latter received Tiryns instead of Argos.—2. Son of Menelaus by an Aetolian slave, Pieris or Teridaë. Menelaus brought about a marriage between Megapenthes and a daughter of Alector. According to a Rhodian tradition, Megapenthes, after the death of his father, expelled Helen from Argos, who thereupon fled to Polyxo at Rhodes.

Megara (Μεγάρα), daughter of Creon, king of Thebes, and wife of Hercules. See p. 308.

Megara (τὰ Μέγαρα, in Lat. Megara, -ae, and pl. Megara, -orum: Μεγαρεύς, Megarensis). 1. (*Megara*), the capital of MEGARIS, was situated 8 stadia (1 mile) from the sea opposite to Salamis, about 26 miles from Athens and 31 miles from Corinth. It consisted of 3 parts: 1. The ancient Pelasgian citadel, called *Caria*, said to have been built by Car, the son of Phoroneus, which was situated on a hill N. W. of the later city. This citadel contained the ancient and celebrated *Megaron* (μέγαρον) or temple of Demeter, from which the town is supposed to have derived its name. 2. The modern citadel, situated on a lower hill to the S.W. of the preceding, and called *Alcathous*, from its reputed founder Alcathous, son of Pelops. 3. The town properly so called, situated at the foot of the two citadels, said to have been founded by the Pelopidae under Alcatheus, and subsequently enlarged by a Doric colony under Alethes and Athemenes at the time of Codrus. It appears to have been originally called *Polichne* (Πολίχνη). The town contained many public buildings which are described at length by Pausanias. Its seaport was *Nisaea* (Νίσαια), which was connected with Megara by 2 walls, 8 stadia in length, built by the Athenians when they had possession of Megara, B. C. 461—445. Nisaea is said to have been built by Nisus, the son of Pandion ; and the inhabitants of Megara are sometimes called Nisaean Megarians (οἱ Νισαῖοι Μεγαρεῖς) to distinguish them from the Hyblaean Megarians (οἱ Ὑβλαῖοι Μεγαρεῖς) in Sicily. In front of Nisaea lay the small island *Minoa* (Μίνωα), which added greatly to the security of the harbour. —In the most ancient times Megara and the surrounding country was inhabited by Leleges. It subsequently became annexed to Attica ; and Megaris formed one of the 4 ancient divisions of Attica. It was next conquered by the Dorians, and was for a time subject to Corinth ; but it finally asserted its independence, and rapidly became a wealthy and powerful city. To none of these events can any date be assigned with certainty. Its power at an early period is attested by the flourishing colonies which it founded, of which Selymbria, Chalcedon, and Byzantium, and the Hyblaean Megara in Sicily, were the most important. Its navy was a match for that of Athens, with which it contested the island of Salamis ; and it was not till after a long struggle that the Athenians succeeded in obtaining possession of this island. The government was originally an aristocracy as in most of the Doric cities ; but Theagenes, who put himself at the head of the popular party, obtained the supreme power about B. C. 620. Theagenes was afterwards expelled ; and a democratical

form of government established. After the Persian wars, Megara was for some time at war with Corinth, and was thus led to form an alliance with Athens, and to receive an Athenian garrison into the city, 461 ; but the oligarchical party having got the upper hand the Athenians were expelled, 441. Megara is not often mentioned after this period. It was taken and its walls destroyed by Demetrius Poliorcetes ; it was taken again by the Romans under Q. Metellus ; and in the time of Augustus it had ceased to be a place of importance. —Megara is celebrated in the history of philosophy, as the seat of a philosophical school, usually called the Megarian, which was founded by Euclid, a native of the city, and a disciple of Socrates. [EUCLIDES, No. 2.]—There are no remains of any importance of the ancient city of Megara.— 2. A town in Sicily on the E. coast, N. of Syracuse, founded by Dorians from Megara in Greece, B. C. 728, on the site of a small town Hybla, and hence called **Megara Hyblaea**, and its inhabitants Megarenses Hyblaei (Μεγαρεῖς Ὑβλαῖοι). From the time of Gelon it belonged to Syracuse. It was taken and plundered by the Romans in the 2nd Punic war, and from that time sunk into insignificance, but it is still mentioned by Cicero under the name of Megaris.

Megareus (Μεγαρεύς), son of Onchestus, also called a son of Poseidon and Oenope, of Hippomenes, of Apollo, or of Aegeus. He was a brother of Abrote, the wife of Nisus, king of Megara, and the father of Evippus, Timalcus, Hippomenes, and Evaechme. Megara is said to have derived its name from him.

Megaris (ἡ Μεγαρίς or ἡ Μεγαρική, sc. γῆ), a small district in Greece between the Corinthian and Saronic gulfs, originally reckoned part of Hellas proper, but subsequently included in the Peloponnesus It was bounded on the N. by Boeotia, on the E. and N.E. by Attica, and on the S. by the territory of Corinth. It contained about 143 square miles. The country was very mountainous ; and its only plain was the one in which the city of Megara was situated. It was separated from Boeotia by Mt. Cithaeron, and from Attica by the mountains called the Horns (τὰ κέρατα) on account of their 2 projecting summits. The Geranean mountains extended through the greater part of the country, and formed its S. boundary towards Corinth. There were 2 roads through these mountains from Corinth, one called the Scironian pass, which ran along the Saronic gulf, passed by Crommyon and Megara, and was the direct road from Corinth to Athens ; the other ran along the Corinthian gulf, passed by Geranëa and Pegae, and was the road from Corinth into Boeotia. The only town of importance in Megaris was its capital Megara. [MEGARA.]

Megasthenes (Μεγασθένης), a Greek writer, who was sent by Seleucus Nicator as ambassador to Sandracottus, king of the Prasii, where he resided some time. He wrote a work on India, in 4 books, entitled *Indica* (τὰ Ἰνδικά), to which later Greek writers were chiefly indebted for their accounts of the country.

Meges (Μέγης), son of Phyleus, and grandson of Augeas, was one of the suitors of Helen, and led his bands from Dulichium and the Echinades against Troy.

Megiddo (Μαγεδδώ, Μαγεδώ: *Lejjun* ?), a considerable city of Palestine, on the river Kishon, in a valley of the same name, which formed a part of the great plain of Jezreel or Esdraelon, on the confines of Galilee and Samaria. It was a residence of the Canaanitish kings before the conquest of Palestine by the Jews. It was fortified by Solomon. It was probably the same place which was called Legio under the Romans.

Megistāni, a people of Armenia, in the district of Sophene, near the Euphrates.

Mēla, river. [MELLA.]

Mela, Fabius, a Roman jurist, who is often cited in the Digest, probably lived in the time of Antoninus Pius.

Mela, or Mella, M. Annaeus, the youngest son of M. Annaeus Seneca, the rhetorician, and brother of L. Seneca the philosopher, and Gallio. By his wife Acilia he had at least one son, the celebrated Lucan. After Lucan's death, A.D. 65, Mela laid claim to his property; and as he was rich, he was accused of being privy to Piso's conspiracy, and anticipated a certain sentence by suicide.

Mela, Pomponius, the first Roman author who composed a formal treatise upon Geography, was a native of Spain, and probably flourished under the emperor Claudius. His work is entitled *De Situ Orbis Libri III.* It contains a brief description of the whole world as known to the Romans. The text is often corrupt, but the style is simple, and the Latinity is pure; and although every thing is compressed within the narrowest limits, we find the monotony of the catalogue occasionally diversified by animated and pleasing pictures. The best edition is by Tzschuckius, 7 parts, 8vo. Lips. 1807.

Melaena Acra (ἡ Μέλαινα ἄκρα). 1. (*Kara Burnu*, which means the same as the Greek name, i. e. *the Black Cape*), the N.W. promontory of the great peninsula of Ionia: formed by Mt. Mimas; celebrated for the millstones hewn from it.—2. (*C. St. Nicolo*), the N.W. promontory of the island of Chios.—3. (*Kara Burnu*) a promontory of Bithynia, a little E. of the Bosporus, between the rivers Rhebas and Artanes; also called Καλίνακρον and Βιθυνίας ἄκρον.

Melaenae (Μελαιναί: Μελαινεύς). 1. Or **Melaeneae** (Μελαινεαί), a town in the W. of Arcadia on the Alpheus, N.W. of Buphagium, and S.E. of Hernea.—2. A demus in Attica, on the frontiers of Boeotia, belonging to the tribe Antiochis.

Melambium (Μελάμβιον), a town of Thessaly in Pelasgiotis, belonging to the territory of Scotussa.

Melampus (Μελάμπους). 1. Son of Amythaon by Idomene, or, according to others, by Aglaia or Rhodope, and a brother of Bias. He was looked upon by the ancients as the first mortal who had been endowed with prophetic powers, as the person who first practised the medical art, and who established the worship of Dionysus in Greece. He is said to have been married to Iphianassa (others call her Iphianira or Cyrianassa), by whom he became the father of Mantius and Antiphates. Abas, Bias, Manto, and Pronoe are also named by some writers as his children. Before his house there stood an oak tree containing a serpent's nest. The old serpents were killed by his servants, but Melampus took care of the young ones and fed them carefully. One day, when he was asleep, they cleaned his ears with their tongues. On his waking he perceived, to his astonishment, that he now understood the language of birds, and that with their assistance he could foretell the future. In addition to this he acquired the power of pro-

phesying from the victims that were offered to the gods; and, after having an interview with Apollo on the banks of the Alpheus, he became a most renowned soothsayer. During his residence at Pylos his brother Bias was one of the suitors for the hand of Pero, the daughter of Neleus. The latter promised his daughter to the man who should bring him the oxen of Iphiclus, which were guarded by a dog whom neither man nor animal could approach. Melampus undertook the task of procuring the oxen for his brother, although he knew that the thief would be caught and kept in imprisonment for a year, after which he was to come into possession of the oxen. Things turned out as he had said; Melampus was thrown into prison, and in his captivity he learned from the wood-worms that the building in which he was imprisoned would soon break down. He accordingly demanded to be let out, and as Phylacus and Iphiclus thus became acquainted with his prophetic powers, they asked him in what manner Iphiclus, who had no children, was to become father. Melampus, on the suggestion of a vulture, advised Iphiclus to take the rust from the knife with which Phylacus had once cut his son, and drink it in water during ten days. This was done, and Iphiclus became the father of Podarces. Melampus now received the oxen as a reward for his good services, drove them to Pylos, and thus gained Pero for his brother. Afterwards Melampus obtained possession of a third of the kingdom of Argos in the following manner:— In the reign of Anaxagoras, king of Argos, the women of the kingdom were seized with madness, and roamed about the country in a frantic state. Melampus cured them of their frenzy, on condition that he and his brother Bias should receive an equal share with Anaxagoras in the kingdom of Argos. Melampus and Bias married the two daughters of Proetus, and ruled over two-thirds of Argos.—2. The author of 2 little Greek works still extant, entitled *Divinatio ex Palpitationes* and *De Naevis Oleaceis in Corpore.* He lived probably in the 3rd century B. C. at Alexandria. Both the works are full of superstitions and absurdities. Edited by Franz, in his *Scriptores Physiognomias Veteres*, Altenburg, 1780.

Melanchlaeni (Μελάγχλαινοι), a people in the N. of Sarmatia Asiatica, about the upper course of the river Tanaïs (*Don*), resembling the Scythians in manners, though of a different race. Their Greek name was derived from their dark clothing.

Melanippe (Μελανίππη), daughter of Chiron, also called Evippe. Being with child by Aeolus, she fled to mount Pelion; and in order that her condition might not become known, she prayed to be metamorphosed into a mare. Artemis granted her prayer, and in the form of a horse she was placed among the stars. Another account describes her metamorphosis as a punishment for having despised Artemis or for having divulged the counsels of the gods.

Melanippides (Μελανιππίδης), of Melos, a celebrated lyric poet in the department of the dithyramb. He flourished about B.C. 440, and lived for some time at the court of Perdiccas, of Macedonia, and there died. His high reputation as a poet is intimated by Xenophon, who makes Aristodemus give him the first place among dithyrambic poets, by the side of Homer, Sophocles, Polycletus, and Zeuxis, as the chief masters in their respective arts; and by Plutarch, who mentions aim, with Simonides and Euripides, as among the most distinguished masters of music. Several verses of his poetry are still preserved. See Bergk, *Poët. Lyr. Graec.* pp. 847—850. Some writers, following the authority of Suidas, make 2 poets of this name.

Mělănippus (Μελάνιππος), son of Astacus of Thebes, who, in the attack of the Seven on his native city, slew Tydeus and Mecisteus. His tomb was shown in the neighbourhood of Thebes on the road to Chalcis.

Melanogaetūli. [GAETULIA.]

Mělanthīus (Μελάνθιος). 1. Also called Melantheus, son of Dolius, was a goat-herd of Ulysses, who sided with the suitors of Penelope, and was killed by Ulysses.—2. An Athenian tragic poet, of whom little is known beyond the attacks made on him by Aristophanes and the other comic poets. The most important passage respecting him is in the *Peace* of Aristophanes (796, &c.). He was celebrated for his wit, of which several specimens are preserved by Plutarch.— 3. Or Melanthius, an eminent Greek painter of the Sicyonian school, was contemporary with Apelles (B. C. 332), with whom he studied under Pamphilus. He was one of the best colourist of all the Greek painters.

Mělanthīus (Μελάνθιος, prob. *Melet-Irma*), a river of Pontus, in Asia Minor, E. of the Prom. Jasonium ; the boundary between Pontus Polemoniacus and Pontus Cappadocius.

Mělanthus or **Mělanthīus** (Μέλανθος), one of the Nelidae, and king of Messenia, whence he was driven out by the Heraclidae, on their conquest of the Peloponnesus ; and, following the instructions of the Delphic oracle, took refuge in Attica. In a war between the Athenians and Boeotians, Xanthus, the Boeotian king, challenged Thymoetes, king of Athens and the last of the Thesidae, to single combat. Thymoetes declined the challenge on the ground of age and infirmity. So ran the story, which strove afterwards to disguise the violent change of dynasty; and Melanthus undertook it on condition of being rewarded with the throne in the event of success. He slew Xanthus, and became king, to the exclusion of the Thesidae. According to Pausanias, the conqueror of Xanthus was Andropompus, the father of Melanthus ; according to Aristotle, it was Codrus, his son.

Mělas (Μέλας), the name of several rivers, whose waters were of a dark colour. 1. (*Mauro Nero* or *Mauro Potamo*), a small river in Boeotia, which rises 7 stadia N. of Orchomenus, becomes navigable almost from its source, flows between Orchomenus and Aspledon, and loses the greater part of its waters in the marshes connected with lake Copais. A small portion of its waters fell in ancient times into the river Cephissus. — 2. A river of Thessaly in the district Malis, flows near Heraclea and Trachis, and falls into the Maliac gulf. — 3. A river of Thessaly in Phthiotis, falls into the Apidanus. — 4. A river of Thrace, flows first S.W., then N.W., and falls N. of Cardia into the Melas Sinus. — 5. A river in the N. E. of Sicily, which flows into the sea between Mylae and Naulochus, through excellent meadows, in which the oxen of the sun are said to have fed. — 6. (*Manaugat-Su*), a navigable river, 50 stadia (5 geog. miles) E. of Side, was the boundary between Pamphylia and Cilicia. — 7. (*Kara-Su*, i. e. *the Black River*), in Cappadocia, rises in M. Argaeus, flows past Masaca, and, after forming a succession of morasses,

falls into the Halys, and not (as Strabo says) into the Euphrates.

Mělas Sinus (Μέλας κόλπος : *Gulf of Saros*), a gulf of the Aegaean sea, between the coast of Thrace on the N.W. and the Thracian Chersonesus on the S. E., into which the river Melas flows.

Meldi or **Meldae**, a people in Gallia Lugdnnensis on the borders of Belgica, and upon the river Sequana (*Seine*), in whose territory Caesar built 40 ships for his expedition against Britain.

Mělěăger (Μελέαγρος). 1. Son of Oeneus and Althaea, the daughter of Thestius, husband of Cleopatra, and father of Polydora. Others call him a son of Ares and Althaea. He was one of the most famous Aetolian heroes of Calydon, and distinguished himself by his skill in throwing the javelin. He took part in the Argonautic expedition. On his return home, the fields of Calydon were laid waste by a monstrous boar, which Artemis had sent against the country as a punishment, because Oeneus, the king of the place, once neglected to offer up a sacrifice to the goddess. No one dared encounter the terrible animal, till at length Meleager, with a band of other heroes, went out to hunt the boar. He slew the animal ; but the Calydonians and Curetes quarrelled about the head and hide, and at length waged open war against each other. The Calydonians were always victorious, so long as Meleager went out with them. But when his mother Althaea pronounced a curse upon him, enraged at the death of her brother who had fallen in the fight, Meleager stayed at home with his wife Cleopatra. The Curetes now began to press Calydon very hard. It was in vain that the old men of the town made him the most brilliant promises if he would again join in the fight, and that his father, his sisters, and his mother supplicated him. At length, however, he yielded to the prayers of his wife, Cleopatra : he put the Curetes to flight, but he never returned home, for the Erinnys, who had heard the curse of his mother, overtook him. Such is the more ancient form of the legend, as we find it in Homer. (*Il.* ix. 527, seq.) In the later traditions Meleager collects the heroes from all parts of Greece to join him in the hunt. Among others was the fair maiden Atalanta ; but the heroes refused to hunt with her, until Meleager, who was in love with her, overcame their opposition. Atalanta gave the animal the first wound, which was at length slain by Meleager. He presented the hide to Atalanta, but the sons of Thestius took it from her, whereupon Meleager in a rage slew them. This, however, was the cause of his own death which came to pass in the following way. When he was 7 days old the Moerae appeared, declaring that the boy would die as soon as the piece of wood which was burning on the hearth should be consumed. Althaea, upon hearing this, extinguished the firebrand, and concealed it in a chest. Meleager himself became invulnerable ; but after he had killed the brothers of his mother, she lighted the piece of wood, and Meleager died. Althaea, too late repenting of what she had done, put an end to her life ; and Cleopatra died of grief. The sisters of Meleager wept unceasingly after his death, until Artemis changed them into guinea-hens (μελεαγρίδες), which were transferred to the island of Leros. Even in this condition they mourned during a certain part of the year for their brother. Two of them, Gorge and Deïanira, through the mediation of Dionysus, were not meta-morphosed.—2. Son of Neoptolemus, a Macedonian officer in the service of Alexander the Great. After the death of Alexander the Great (B.C. 323) Meleager resisted the claims of Perdiccas to the regency, and was eventually associated with the latter in this office. Shortly afterwards, however, he was put to death by order of Perdiccas.—3. Son of Eucrates, the celebrated writer and collector of epigrams, was a native of Gadara in Palestine, and lived about B. C. 60. There are 131 of his epigrams in the Greek Anthology, written in a good Greek style, though somewhat affected, and distinguished by sophistic acumen and amatory fancy. An account of his collection of epigrams is given under PLANUDES.

Mělětus or **Melitus** (Μέλητος: Μέλιτος), an obscure tragic poet, but notorious as one of the accusers of Socrates, was an Athenian, of the Pitthean demus. He is represented by Plato and Aristophanes and their scholiasts as a frigid and licentious poet, and a worthless and profligate man. In the accusation of Socrates it was Meletus who laid the indictment before the Archon Basileus; but in reality he was the most insignificant of the accusers; and according to one account he was bribed by Anytus and Lycon to take part in the affair. Soon after the death of Socrates, the Athenians repented of their injustice, and Meletus was stoned to death as one of the authors of their folly.

Mělia (Μελία), a nymph, daughter of Oceanus, became by Inachus the father of Phoroneus and Aegialeus or Pegeus; and by Silenus the mother of the centaur, Pholus; and by Poseidon of Amy-cus. She was carried off by Apollo, and became by him the mother of Ismenius, and of the seer Tenerus. She was worshipped in the Ismenium, the sanctuary of Apollo, near Thebes. In the plural form, the *Meliae* or *Meliades* (Μελίαι, Μελιάδες) are the nymphs, who, along with the Gigantes and Erinnyes, sprang from the drops of blood that fell from Uranus and were received by Gaea. The nymphs that nursed Zeus are likewise called Meliae.

Měliboea (Μελίβοια: Μελιβοεύς). 1. A town on the coast of Thessaly in Magnesia, between Mt. Ossa and Mt. Pelion, is said to have been built by Magnes, and to have been named Meliboea in honour of his wife. It is mentioned by Homer as belonging to the dominions of Philoctetes, who is hence called by Virgil (*Aen.* iii. 401) *dux Meliboeus.* It was celebrated for its purple dye. (Lucret. ii. 499; Virg. *Aen.* v. 251.)—2. A small island at the mouth of the river Orontes in Syria.

Mělicertes. [PALAEMON.]

Mělissa (Μέλισσα). 1. A nymph said to have discovered the use of honey, and from whom bees were believed to have received their name (μέλισσαι). There can be no doubt, however, that the name really came from μέλι, honey, and was hence given to nymphs. According to some traditions bees were nymphs metamorphosed. Hence the nymphs who fed the infant Zeus with honey are called Melissae.—2. The name of priestesses in general, but more especially of the priestesses of Demeter, Persephone, Apollo, and Artemis.—3. Wife of Periander, tyrant of Corinth, and daughter of Procles, tyrant of Epidaurus, was slain by her husband. [PERIANDER.]

Mělissus (Μέλισσος). 1. Of Samos, a Greek philosopher, the son of Ithagenes, was, according to

the common account, the commander of the fleet opposed to Pericles, B. C. 440. But he is not mentioned by Thucydides, and ought probably to be placed much earlier, as he is said to have been connected with Heraclitus, and to have been a disciple of Parmenides. It appears from the fragments of his work, which was written in prose, and in the Ionic dialect, that he adopted the doctrines of the Eleatics.—2. A Latin grammarian and a comic poet, was a freedman of Maecenas, and was entrusted by Augustus with the arrangement of the library in the portico of Octavia.

Mělita or **Mělite** (Μελίτη: Μελιταῖος, Melitensis). 1. (*Malta*), an island in the Mediterranean sea, situated 58 miles from the nearest point of Sicily, and 179 miles from the nearest point of Africa. Its greatest length is 17½ miles, and its greatest breadth 9½ miles. The island was first colonised by the Phoenicians, who used it as a place of refuge for their ships, on account of its excellent harbours. It afterwards passed into the hands of the Carthaginians, but was taken possession of by the Romans in the 2nd Punic war, and annexed to the province of Sicily. The Romans however appear to have neglected the island, and it is mentioned by Cicero as a frequent resort of pirates. It contained a town of the same name founded by the Carthaginians, and 2 celebrated temples, one of Juno on a promontory near the town, and another of Hercules in the S. E. of the island. It is celebrated in sacred history as the island on which the Apostle Paul was shipwrecked; though some writers erroneously suppose that the apostle was shipwrecked on the island of the same name off the Illyrian coast. The inhabitants manufactured fine cloth, which was in much request at Rome. They also exported a considerable quantity of honey; and from this island, according to some authorities, came the *catuli Melitaei*, the favourite lapdogs of the Roman ladies, though other writers make them come from the island off the Illyrian coast.—2. (*Meleda*), a small island in the Adriatic sea off the coast of Illyria (Dalmatia), N. W. of Epidaurus.—3. A demus in Attica, which also formed part of the city of Athens, was situated S. of the inner Ceramicus, and probably included the hill of the Museum. It was said to have derived its name from a nymph Melite, with whom Hercules was in love, and it therefore contained a temple of this god. One of the gates of Athens was called the Melitian gate, because it led to this demus. [See p. 103, a.]—4. A lake in Aetolia near the mouth of the Achelous, belonging to the territory of the town Oeniadae.

Mělitaea, Mělitēs. or **Mělitia** (Μελιταία, Μελίτεια, Μελιτία: Μελιταιεύς), a town of Thessaly in Phthiotis, on the N. slope of Mt. Othrys, and near the river Enipeus. It is said to have been called Pyrrha in more ancient times, and the sepulchre of Hellen was shown in its market-place.

Mělitě (Μελίτη), a nymph, one of the Nereides, a daughter of Nereus and Doris.

Mělitēnē (Μελιτηνή), a district of Armenia Minor, between the Anti-Taurus and the Euphrates, celebrated for its fertility, and especially for its fruit-trees, oil, and wine. It possessed no great town until the 1st century of our era, when a city, also called Melitene (now *Malatiyah*) was built on a tributary of the Euphrates, and near that river itself, probably on the site of a very ancient fort. This became a place of considerable

Marsyas. (Osterley, Denk. der alt. Kunst, part 2, tav. 14.) Page 419.

Meleager.
(From a Painting at Pompeii.) Page 431.

Althaea and the Fates. (Zoëga, Bassirilievi, tav. 46.) Page 431.

Medea and her Children.
(Museo Borbonico, vol. 5, tav. 33.) Page 427.

Medea boiling a Ram, in order to persuade the daughters of Pelias to put him to death. (From a Vase in the British Museum.) See art. JASON, p. 353.

[To face p. 432.

Maronea in Thrace. Page 419.

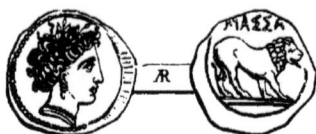

Menaenum in Sicily. Page 434.

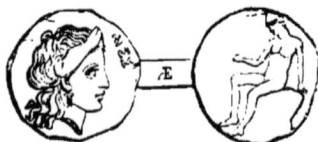

Massilia. Page 422.

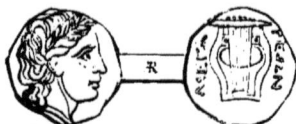

Mende. Page 435.

Medama, or Medma, in Bruttium. Page 426.

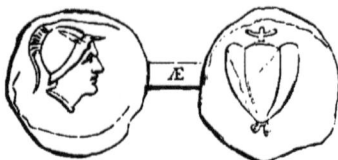

Mesembria. Page 436.

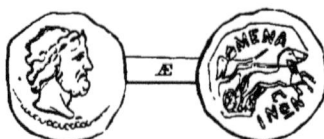

Megara. Page 429.

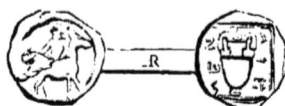

Messana in Sicily. Page 440.

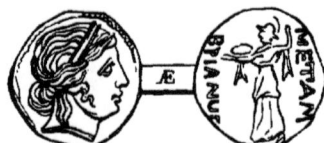

Melita. Page 432.

Messenia. Page 441.

Melos. Page 433.

Metapontum. Page 442.

To face p. 433.]

importance; the centre of several roads; the station, under Titus, of the 12th legion; and, in the later division of the provinces, the capital of Armenia Secunda. In A.D. 577, it was the scene of a victory gained by the Romans over the Persians under Chosroes I.

Melito (Μελίτων), a Christian writer of considerable eminence, was bishop of Sardes in the reign of M. Aurelius, to whom he presented an Apology for the Christians. Of his numerous works only fragments are extant.

Mella or **Mela** (*Mella*), a river in Gallia Transpadana, which flows by Brixia and falls into the Ollius (*Oglio*).

Mellaria. 1. A town of the Bastuli in Hispania Baetica between Belon and Calpe, on the road from Gades to Malaca. — 2. A town in the same province, considerably N. of the former, on the road from Corduba to Emerita.

Melodunum (*Melun*), a town of the Senones in Gallia Lugdunensis, on an island of the Sequana (*Seine*), and on the road from Agendicum to Lutetia Parisiorum.

Melos (Μῆλος: Μήλιος: *Milo*), an island in the Aegaean sea, and the most W.-ly of the group of the Cyclades, whence it was called *Zephyria* by Aristotle. It is about 70 miles N. of the coast of Crete, and 65 E. of the coast of Peloponnesus. Its length is about 14 miles from E. to W., and its breadth about 8 miles. It contains on the N. a deep bay, which forms an excellent harbour, and on which was situated a town, bearing the same name as the island. The island is of volcanic origin; it contains hot springs, and mines of sulphur and alum. Its soil is very fertile, and it produced in antiquity, as it does at present, abundance of corn, oil, wine, &c. It was first colonised by the Phoenicians, who are said to have called it *Byblus* or *Byblis*, after the Phoenician town Byblus. It was afterwards colonised by Lacedaemonians, or at least by Dorians; and consequently in the Peloponnesian war it embraced the side of Sparta. In B.C. 426 the Athenians made an unsuccessful attack upon the island; but in 416 they obtained possession of the town after a siege of several months, whereupon they killed all the adult males, sold the women and children as slaves, and peopled the island by an Athenian colony.—Melos was the birthplace of Diagoras, the atheist, whence Aristophanes calls Socrates also the Melian.

Melpomene (Μελπομένη), i. e. the singing goddess, one of the 9 Muses, who presided over Tragedy. See MUSAE.

Memini, a people in Gallia Narbonensis, on the W. bank of the Durentia, whose chief town was Carpentoracte (*Carpentras*).

Memmia Gens, a plebeian house at Rome, whose members do not occur in history before B.C. 173, but who pretended to be descended from the Trojan Mnestheus. (Virg. *Aen.* v. 117.)

Memmius. 1. C., tribune of the plebs B.C. 111, was an ardent opponent of the oligarchical party at Rome during the Jugurthine war. Among the nobles impeached by Memmius were L. Calpurnius Bestia and M. Aemilius Scaurus. Memmius was slain by the mob of Saturninus and Glaucia, while a candidate for the consulship in 100. — 2. C. **Memmius Gemellus**, tribune of the plebs 66, curule aedile 60, and praetor 58. He belonged at that time to the Senatorian party, since he impeached P. Vatinius, opposed P. Clodius, and was vehe-

ment in his invectives against Julius Caesar. But before he competed for the consulship, 54, he had been reconciled to Caesar, who supported him with all his interest. Memmius, however, again offended Caesar by revealing a certain coalition with his opponents at the comitia. He was impeached for ambitus, and, receiving no aid from Caesar, withdrew from Rome to Mytilene, where he was living in the year of Cicero's proconsulate. Memmius married Fausta, a daughter of the dictator Sulla, whom he divorced after having by her at least one son C. Memmius. [No. 3.] He was eminent both in literature and in eloquence. Lucretius dedicated his poem, *De Rerum Natura*, to him. He was a man of profligate character, and wrote indecent poems. — 3. C. **Memmius**, son of the preceding, was tribune of the plebs 54, when he prosecuted A. Gabinius for malversation in his province of Syria, and Domitius Calvinus for ambitus at his consular comitia. Memmius was step-son of T. Annius Milo who married his mother Fausta after her divorce. He was consul suffectus 34. — 4. P. **Memmius Regulus**, consul suffectus A.D. 31, afterwards praefect of Macedonia and Achaia. He was the husband of Lollia Paulina, and was compelled by Caligula to divorce her.

Memnon (Μέμνων). 1. The beautiful son of Tithonus and Eos (Aurora), and brother of Emathion. He is rarely mentioned by Homer, and must be regarded essentially as a post-Homeric hero. According to these later traditions, he was a prince of the Ethiopians, who came to the assistance of his uncle Priam, for Tithonus and Priam were half-brothers, being both sons of Laomedon by different mothers. Respecting his expedition to Troy there are different legends. According to some Memnon the Ethiopian first went to Egypt, thence to Susa, and thence to Troy. At Susa, which had been founded by Tithonus, Memnon built the acropolis, which was called after him the Memnonium. According to others Tithonus was the governor of a Persian province, and the favourite of Teutamus; and Memnon obtained the command of a large host of Ethiopians and Susans to succour Priam. Memnon came to the war in armour made for him by Hephaestus. He slew Antilochus, the son of Nestor, but was himself slain by Achilles, after a long and fierce combat. While the two heroes were fighting, Zeus weighed their fates, and the scale containing Memnon's sank. His mother was inconsolable at his death. She wept for him every morning; and the dew-drops of the morning are the tears of Eos. To soothe the grief of his mother, Zeus caused a number of birds to issue out of the funeral pile, on which the body of Memnon was burning, which, after flying thrice around the burning pile, divided into two separate bodies, which fought so fiercely, that half of them fell down upon the ashes of the hero, and thus formed a funeral sacrifice for him. These birds were called *Memnonides*, and according to a story current on the Hellespont, they visited every year the tomb of the hero. At the entreaties of Eos, Zeus conferred immortality upon Memnon. At a comparatively late period, the Greeks gave the name of Memnon to the colossal statue in the neighbourhood of Thebes, which was said to give forth a sound like the snapping asunder of a chord, when it was struck by the first rays of the rising sun. Although the Greeks gave this name to the statue, they were well aware that the Egyptians

F F

did not call the statue Memnon, but Amenophis. This figure was made of black stone, in a sitting posture, with its feet close together, and the hands leaning on the seat. Several very ingenious conjectures have been propounded respecting the alleged meaning of the so-called statue of Memnon. Some have asserted that it served for astronomical purposes, and others that it had reference to the mystic worship of the sun and light, but there can be little doubt that the statue represented nothing else than the Egyptian king Amenophis. — 2. A native of Rhodes, joined Artabazus, satrap of Lower Phrygia, who had married his sister, in his revolt against Darius Ochus. When fortune deserted the insurgents they fled to the court of Philip. Mentor, the brother of Memnon, being high in favour with Darius, interceded on behalf of Artabazus and Memnon, who were pardoned and again received into favour. On the death of Mentor, Memnon, who possessed great military skill and experience, succeeded him in his authority, which extended over all the W. coast of Asia Minor (about B. C. 336). When Alexander invaded Asia, Memnon defended Halicarnassus against Alexander, until it was no longer possible to hold out. He then collected an army and a fleet, with the design of carrying the war into Greece, but died at Mytilene in 333, before he could carry his plan into execution. His death was an irreparable loss to the Persian cause; for several Greek states were prepared to join him, had he carried the war into Greece. — 3. A native of Heraclea Pontica, wrote a large work on the history of that city. Of how many books it consisted we do not know. Photius had read from the 9th to the 16th inclusive, of which portion he has made a tolerably copious abstract. The first 8 books he had not read, and he speaks of other books after the 16th. The 9th book began with an account of the tyrant Clearchus, the disciple of Plato and Isocrates, and the 16th book came down to the time of Julius Caesar, after the latter had obtained the supreme power. The work was probably written in the time of Augustus, and certainly not later than the time of Hadrian or the Antonines. The Excerpta of Photius are published separately, by Orelli, Lips. 1816.

Memnonium and **-ia** (Μεμνόνειον, Μεμνόνεια), were names applied by the Greeks to certain very ancient buildings and monuments in Egypt and Asia, which they supposed to have been erected by or in honour of MEMNON. 1. The most celebrated of these was a great temple at Thebes, described by Strabo, and commonly identified by modern travellers with the magnificent ruins of the temple of Remeses the Great, at W. Thebes, or, as it is usually called, the tomb of Osymandyas, from its agreement with the description of that monument given by Diodorus. There are, however, strong grounds for supposing that the true Memnonium, described by Strabo, stood behind the 2 colossal sitting statues on the plain of Thebes, one of which is clearly the celebrated vocal statue of Memnon, and that it has entirely disappeared. — 2. [ABYDOS, No. 2.] — 3. The citadel of Susa was so called, and its erection was ascribed to the Memnon who appears in the legends of the Trojan war; but there is no reason to suppose that this connection of Memnon with the Persian capital existed before the Persian conquest of Egypt.

Memphis (Μέμφις, Μενφ: O. T. Moph: Μεμφίτης, Memphltes: *Menf* and *Metrahenny*, Ru.), a great city of Egypt, second in importance only to Thebes, after the fall of which it became the capital of the whole country, a position which it had previously shared with Thebes. It was of unknown antiquity, its foundation being ascribed to Menes. It stood on the left (W.) bank of the Nile, about 10 miles above the pyramids of *Jizeh*, near the N. limit of the Heptanomis, or Middle Egypt, a nome of which (Μεμφίτης) was named after the city. It was connected by canals with the lakes of Moeris and Mareotis, and was the great centre of the commerce of Egypt until the Persian conquest (B. C. 524), when Cambyses partially destroyed the city. After the foundation of Alexandria, it sank into insignificance, and was finally destroyed at the Arab conquest in the 7th century. In the time of its splendour it is said to have been 150 stadia in circumference, and half a day's journey in every direction. Of the splendid buildings with which it was adorned, the chief were the palace of the Pharaohs; the temple-palace of the god-bull Apis; the temple of Serapia, with its avenue of sphinxes, now covered by the sand of the desert; and the temple of Hephaestus, the Egyptian Phtha, of whose worship Memphis was the chief seat. The ruins of this temple and of other buildings, still cover a large portion of the plain between the Nile and the W. range of hills which skirt its valley.

Menaenum or **Menae** (Menenius Cic., Menaninus Plin., but on coins Menaenus: *Mineo*), a town on the E. coast of Sicily, S. of Hybla, the birthplace and residence of the Sicel chief Ducetius, who was long a formidable enemy of the Greek cities in Sicily. [DUCETIUS.] On his fall the town lost all its importance.

Menalippus. [MELANIPPUS.]

Menander (Μένανδρος), of Athens, the most distinguished poet of the New Comedy, was the son of Diopithes and Hegesistrate, and flourished in the time of the successors of Alexander. He was born B. C. 342. His father, Diopithes, commanded the Athenian forces on the Hellespont in the year of his son's birth. Alexis, the comic poet, was the uncle of Menander, on the father's side; and we may naturally suppose that the young Menander derived from his uncle his taste for the comic drama, and was instructed by him in its rules of composition. His character must have been greatly influenced by his intimacy with Theophrastus and Epicurus, of whom the former was his teacher and the latter his intimate friend. His taste and sympathies were altogether with the philosophy of Epicurus; and in an epigram he declared that "as Themistocles rescued Greece from slavery, so Epicurus from unreason." From Theophrastus, on the other hand, he must have derived much of that skill in the discrimination of character which we so much admire in the *Characteres* of the philosopher, and which formed the great charm of the comedies of Menander. His master's attention to external elegance and comfort he not only imitated, but, as was natural in a man of an elegant person, a joyous spirit, and a serene and easy temper, he carried it to the extreme of luxury and effeminacy. The moral character of Menander is defended by modern writers against the aspersions of Suidas and others. Thus much is certain, that his comedies contain nothing ofsensive, at least to the taste of his own and the following ages, none of the purest, it must be admitted, as they were frequently acted at private banquets. Of the actual events of his life we know but little. He enjoyed the friendship of Demetrius Phalereus, whose attention was first drawn to him by admiration of his works. Ptolemy, the son of Lagus, was also one of his admirers; and he invited the poet to his court at Alexandria; but Menander seems to have declined the proffered honour He died at Athens B. c. 291, at the age of 52, and is said to have been drowned while swimming in the harbour of Piraeus. Notwithstanding Menander's fame as a poet, his public dramatic career was not eminently successful; for, though he composed upwards of 100 comedies, he only gained the prize 8 times. His preference for elegant exhibitions of character above coarse jesting may have been the reason why he was not so great a favourite with the common people as his principal rival, Philemon, who is said, moreover, to have used unfair means of gaining popularity. Menander appears to have borne the popular neglect very lightly, in the consciousness of his superiority; and once, when he happened to meet Philemon, he is said to have asked him, " Pray, Philemon, do not you blush when you gain a victory over me?" The neglect of Menander's contemporaries has been amply compensated by his posthumous fame. His comedies retained their place on the stage down to the time of Plutarch, and the unanimous consent of antiquity placed him at the head of the New Comedy, and on an equality with the great masters of the various kinds of poetry. His comedies were imitated by the Roman dramatists, particularly by Terence, who was little more than a translator of Menander. But we cannot form, from any one play of Terence, a fair notion of the corresponding play of Menander, as the Roman poet frequently compressed two of Menander's plays into one. It was this mixing up of different plays that Caesar pointed to by the phrase *O dimidiate Menander*, in the epigram which he wrote upon Terence. Of Menander's comedies only fragments are extant. The best edition of them is by Meineke, in his *Fragmenta Comicorum Graecorum*, Berol. 1841.

Menapia (Μεναπία), a city of Bactriana, on the river Zariaspis.

Menapii, a powerful people in the N. of Gallia Belgica, originally dwelt on both banks of the Rhine, but were afterwards driven out of their possessions on the right bank by the Usipetes and Tenchteri, and inhabited only the left bank near its mouth, and W. of the Mosa. Their country was covered with forests and swamps. They had a fortress on the Mosa called Castellum Menapiorum (*Kessel*).

Menas (Μηνᾶς), also called **Menodōrus** (Μηνόδωρος) by Appian, a freedman of Pompey the Great, was one of the principal commanders of the fleet of Sext. Pompey in his war against Octavian and Antony, B. c. 40. In 39 he tried in vain to dissuade his master from concluding a peace with Octavian and Antony; and, at an entertainment given to them by Sextus on board his ship at Misenum, Menas suggested to him to cut the cables of the vessel, and, running it out to sea, despatch both his rivals. The treacherous proposal, however, was rejected by Pompey. On the breaking out of the war again in 38, Menas

deserted Pompey and went over to Octavian. In 36 he returned to his old master's service; but in the course of the same year he again played the deserter, and joined Octavian. In 35 he accompanied Octavian, in the Pannonian campaign, and was slain at the siege of Siscia. According to the old scholiasts, this Menas is the person so vehemently attacked by Horace in his 4th epode. This statement has been called in question by many modern commentators; but their arguments are far from satisfactory.

Mendē or **Mendae** (Μένδη, Μενδαῖος), a town on the W. coast of the Macedonian peninsula Pellene and on the Thermaic gulf, was a colony of the Eretrians, and was celebrated for its wine. It was for some time a place of considerable importance, but was ruined by the foundation of Cassandrea.

Mendes (Μένδης: Μενδήσιος: Rn. near *Mataricà*), a considerable city of the Delta of Egypt, on the S. side of the lake of Tanis (*Menzaleh*), and on the bank of one of the lesser arms of the Nile, named after it Μενδήσιον στόμα: the chief seat of the worship of MENDES.

Menecles (Μενεκλῆς). 1. Of Barca in Cyrene, an historian of uncertain date.—2. Of Alabanda, a celebrated rhetorician. He and his brother Hierocles taught rhetoric at Rhodes, where the orator M. Antonius heard them, about B. c. 94.

Menecrates (Μενεκράτης). 1. A Syracusan physician at the court of Philip, king of Macedon, B. c. 359—336. He made himself ridiculous by calling himself "Jupiter," and assuming divine honours. There is a tale that he was invited one day by Philip to a magnificent entertainment, where the other guests were sumptuously fed, while he himself had nothing but incense and libations, as not being subject to the human infirmity of hunger. He was at first pleased with his reception, but afterwards perceiving the joke, and finding that no more substantial food was offered him, he left the party in disgust.—2. Tiberius Claudius Menecrates, a physician mentioned by Galen, composed more than 150 medical works, of which only a few fragments remain.

Menedēmus (Μενέδημος), a Greek philosopher, was a native of Eretria, and though of noble birth was poor, and worked for a livelihood either as a builder or as a tent-maker. According to one story he seized the opportunity afforded by his being sent on some military service to Megara to hear Plato, and abandoned the army to addict himself to philosophy; but it may be questioned whether he was old enough to have heard Plato before the death of the latter. According to another story, he and his friend Asclepiades got their livelihood as millers, working during the night, that they might have leisure for philosophy in the day. The 2 friends afterwards became disciples of Stilpo at Megara. From Megara they went to Elis, and placed themselves under the instruction of some disciples of Phaedo. On his return to Eretria Menedemus established a school of philosophy, which was called the Eretrian. He did not, however, confine himself to philosophical pursuits, but took an active part in the political affairs of his native city, and came to be the leading man in the state. He went on various embassies to Lysimachus, Demetrius, and others; but being suspected of the treacherous intention of betraying Eretria into the power of Antigonus, he quitted his native city secretly, and took refuge with Antigonus in Asia. Here he starved himself to death in the 74th year of his age, probably about B.C. 277. Of the philosophy of Menedemus little is known, except that it closely resembled that of the Megarian school. [EUCLIDES, No. 2.]

Mĕnĕlăi, or -us, **Portus** (Μενελάϊος λίμην, Μενέλαος: *Marsa-Toubrouk*, or *Ras-el-Milh* ?), an ancient city on the coast of Marmarica, in N. Africa, founded, according to tradition, by Menelaus. It is remarkable in history as the place where Agesilaus died.

Mĕnĕlăĭum (Μενελάϊον), a mountain in Laconia, S. E. of Sparta near Therapne, on which the heroum of Menelaus was situated, the foundations of which temple were discovered in the year 1834.

Mĕnĕlăus (Μενέλαος, Μενέλεως, or Μενέλας). 1. Son of Plisthenes or Atreus, and younger brother of Agamemnon. His early life is related under AGAMEMNON. He was king of Lacedaemon, and married to the beautiful Helen, by whom he became the father of Hermione. When Helen had been carried off by Paris, Menelaus and Ulysses sailed to Troy in order to demand her restitution. Menelaus was hospitably treated by Antenor, but the journey was of no avail; and the Trojan Antimachus even advised his fellow-citizens to kill Menelaus and Ulysses. Thereupon Menelaus and his brother Agamemnon resolved to march against Troy with all the forces that Greece could muster. Agamemnon was chosen the commander-in-chief. In the Trojan war Menelaus was under the special protection of Hera and Athena, and distinguished himself by his bravery in battle. He killed many illustrious Trojans, and would have slain Paris also in single combat, had not the latter been carried off by Aphrodite in a cloud. Menelaus was one of the heroes concealed in the wooden horse; and as soon as Troy was taken he and Ulysses hastened to the house of Deiphobus, who had married Helen after the death of Paris, and put him to death in a barbarous manner. Menelaus is said to have been secretly introduced into the chamber of Deiphobus by Helen, who thus became reconciled to her former husband. He was among the first that sailed away from Troy, accompanied by his wife Helen and Nestor; but he was 8 years wandering about the shores of the Mediterranean, before he reached home. He arrived at Sparta on the very day on which Orestes was engaged in burying Clytaemnestra and Aegisthus. Henceforward he lived with Helen at Sparta in peace and wealth, and his palace shone in its splendour like the sun or the moon. When Telemachus visited Sparta to inquire after his father, Menelaus was solemnising the marriage of his daughter Hermione with Neoptolemus, and of his son Megapenthes with a daughter of Alector. In the Homeric poems Menelaus is described as a man of an athletic figure; he spoke little, but what he said was always impressive; he was brave and courageous, but milder than Agamemnon, intelligent and hospitable. According to the prophecy of Proteus in the Odyssey, Menelaus and Helen were not to die, but the gods were to conduct them to Elysium. According to a later tradition, he and Helen went to the Taurians, where they were sacrificed by Iphigenia to Artemis. Menelaus was worshipped as a hero at Therapne, where his tomb and that of Helen were shown. Respecting the tale that Helen never went to Troy, but was detained in Egypt, see HELENA.—**2.** Son of Lagus, and brother of Ptolemy Soter, held possession of Cyprus for his brother, but was defeated and driven out of the island by Demetrius Poliorcetes, B.C. 306.—**3.** A Greek mathematician, a native of Alexandria, the author of an extant treatise in 3 books, on the Sphere. He made some astronomical observations at Rome in the 1st year of the emperor Trajan, A.D. 98.

Mĕnĕlāus (Μενέλαος), a city of Lower Egypt, on the Canopic branch of the Nile, named after the brother of Ptolemy the son of Lagus. It was made the capital of the district between the lakes of Moeris and Mareotis (νομὸς Μενελαΐτης).

Mĕnēnĭus Lanātus. 1. Agrippa, consul, B.C. 503, conquered the Sabines. It was owing to his mediation that the first great rupture between the patricians and plebeians, when the latter seceded to the Sacred Mount, was brought to a happy and peaceful termination in 493; and it was upon this occasion he is said to have related to the plebeians his well-known fable of the belly and its members.—**2. T.,** consul 477, was defeated by the Etruscans. He had previously allowed the Fabii to be destroyed by the Etruscans, although he might have assisted them with his army. For this act of treachery he was brought to trial by the tribunes and condemned to pay a fine. He took his punishment so much to heart, that he shut himself up in his house and died of grief.

Mĕnes (Μήνης), first king of Egypt, according to the traditions of the Egyptians themselves. Herodotus records of him that he built Memphis on a piece of ground which he had rescued from the river by turning it from its former course, and erected therein a magnificent temple to Hephaestus (Pthah). Diodorus tells us that he introduced into Egypt the worship of the gods and the practice of sacrifices, as well as a more elegant and luxurious style of living. That he was a conqueror, like other founders of kingdoms, we learn from an extract from Manetho preserved by Eusebius. By Marsham and others he has been identified with the Mizraim of Scripture. According to some accounts he was killed by a hippopotamus.

Mĕnesthĕi Portus (*Puerto de S. Maria*), a harbour in Hispania Baetica, not far from Gades, with an oracle of Menestheus, who is said in some legends to have settled in Spain.

Mĕnestheus (Μενεσθεύς). 1. Son of Peteus, an Athenian king, who led the Athenians against Troy, and surpassed all other mortals in arranging the war-steeds and men for battle. With the assistance of the Tyndarids, he is said to have driven Theseus from his kingdom.—**2.** Son of Iphicrates, the famous Athenian general, by the daughter of Cotys, king of Thrace. He married the daughter of Timotheus; and in 356 was chosen commander in the Social war. his father and his father-in-law being appointed to aid him with their counsel and experience. They were all three impeached by their colleague, CHARES, for alleged misconduct and treachery in the campaign; but Iphicrates and Menestheus were acquitted.

Mĕninx or **Lotophagītis,** aft. **Girba** (Μῆνιγξ, Λωτοφαγῖτις, Λωτοφάγων νῆσος: *Jerbah*), a considerable island, close to the coast of Africa Propria, at the S.E. extremity of the Lesser Syrtis, with 2 cities, Meninx (*Menax*) on the N.E., and Girba, or Gerra, on the S.W. It was the birthplace of the emperors Vibius Gallus and Volusianus.

Mĕnippe (Μενίππη), daughter of Orion and sister of Metioche. These 2 sisters put themselves to death of their own accord in order to propitiate the 2 Erinnyes, who had visited Aonia with a plague. They were metamorphosed by Persephone and Hades into comets, and the Aonians erected to them a sanctuary near Orchomenos.

Mĕnippus (Μένιππος), a cynic philosopher, and originally a slave, was a native of Gadara in Coele-Syria. He seems to have been a hearer of Diogenes, and flourished about B. C. 60. He amassed great wealth as a usurer (ἡμεροδανειστής), but was cheated out of it all, and committed suicide. We are told that he wrote nothing serious, but that his books were full of jests ; whence it would appear that he was one of those cynic philosophers who threw all their teaching into a satirical form. In this character he is several times introduced by Lucian. His works are now entirely lost; but we have considerable fragments of Varro's *Saturae Menippeae*, written in imitation of Menippus.

Mennis, a city of Adiabene, in Assyria, only mentioned by Curtius (v. 1).

Menŏdŏtus (Μηνόδοτος), a physician of Nicomedia in Bithynia, who was a pupil of Antiochus, of Laodicea, and tutor to Herodotus of Tarsus ; he belonged to the medical sect of the Empirici, and lived probably about the beginning of the 2nd century after Christ.

Menoeceus (Μενοικεύς). 1. A Theban, grandson of Pentheus, and father of Hipponome, Jocasta, and Creon. — 2. Grandson of the former, and son of Creon. He put an end to his life because Tiresias had declared that his death would bring victory to his country, when the 7 Argive heroes marched against Thebes. His tomb was shown at Thebes near the Neitian gate.

Menoetius (Μενοίτιος). 1. Son of Iapetus and Clymene or Asia, and brother of Atlas, Prometheus, and Epimetheus. He was killed by Zeus with a flash of lightning, in the battle with the Titans, and was hurled into Tartarus. — 2. Son of Actor and Aegina, husband of Polymele or Sthenele, and father of Patroclus, who is hence called *Menoetiades*. After Patroclus had slain the son of Amphidamas, Menoetius fled with him to Peleus in Phthia, and had him educated there.

Mĕnon (Μένων), a Thessalian adventurer, was one of the generals of the Greek mercenaries in the army of Cyrus the Younger when the latter marched into Upper Asia against his brother Artaxerxes, B. C. 401. After the death of Cyrus he was apprehended along with the other Greek generals by Tissaphernes, and was put to death by lingering tortures, which lasted for a whole year. His character is drawn in the blackest colours by Xenophon. He is the same as the Menon introduced in the dialogue of Plato, which bears his name.

Mens, a personification of mind, worshipped by the Romans. She had a sanctuary on the Capitol ; and the object of her worship was, that the citizens might always be guided by a right spirit.

Mentĕsa (Mentesanus). 1. Surnamed **Bastia**, a town of the Oretani in Hispania Tarraconensis, on the road from Castulo to Carthago Nova. — 2. A small town of the Bastuli in the S. of Hispania Baetica.

Mentor (Μέντωρ). 1. Son of Alcimus and a faithful friend of Ulysses, frequently mentioned in the Odyssey. — 2. A Greek of Rhodes, who, with his brother Memnon, rendered active assistance to Artabazus. When the latter found himself compelled to take refuge at the court of Philip, Mentor entered the service of Nectanabis, king of Egypt. He was sent to the assistance of Tennes, king of Sidon, in his revolt against Darius Ochus; and when Tennes went over to the Persians, Mentor was taken into the service of Darius. He rose rapidly in the favour of Darius, and eventually received a satrapy, including all the western coast of Asia Minor. His influence with Darius enabled him to procure the pardon of his brother Memnon. He died in possession of his satrapy, and was succeeded by his brother Memnon. [MEMNON.]— 3. The most celebrated silver-chaser among the Greeks, who must have flourished before B. C. 356. His works were vases and cups, which were most highly prized by the Romans.

Mercurii Promontorium. [HERMAEUM.]

Mercurĭus, a Roman divinity of commerce and gain. The character of the god is clear from his name, which is connected with *merx* and *mercari*. A temple was built to him as early as B. C. 495 near the Circus Maximus ; an altar of the god existed near the Porta Capena, by the side of a well ; and in later times a temple seems to have been built on the same spot. Under the name of the ill-willed (*malevolus*), he had a statue in what was called the *vicus sobrius*, or the sober street, in which no shops were allowed to be kept, and milk was offered to him there instead of wine. This statue had a purse in its hand, to indicate his functions. His festival was celebrated on the 25th of May, and chiefly by merchants, who also visited the well near the Porta Capena, to which magic powers were ascribed ; and with water from that well they used to sprinkle themselves and their merchandise, that they might be purified, and yield a large profit. The Romans of later times identified Mercurius, the patron of merchants and tradespeople, with the Greek Hermes, and transferred all the attributes and myths of the latter to the former. The Fetiales, however, never recognised the identity ; and instead of the *caduceus* used a sacred branch as the emblem of peace. The resemblance between Mercurius and Hermes is indeed very slight ; and their identification is a proof of the thoughtless manner in which the Romans acted in this respect. [HERMES.]

Mercurĭus Trismegistus. [HERMES TRISMEGISTUS.]

Mērĭŏnes (Μηριόνης), a Cretan hero, son of Molus, who, conjointly with Idomeneus, led the Cretans in 80 ships against Troy. He was one of the bravest heroes in the Trojan war, and usually acted together with his friend Idomeneus. Later traditions relate, that on his way homeward he was thrown on the coast of Sicily, where he was received by the Cretans who had settled there ; whereas, according to others, he returned safely to Crete, and was buried and worshipped as a hero, together with Idomeneus, at Cnossus.

Mermĕrus (Μέρμερος). 1. Son of Jason and Medea, also called Macareus or Mormorus, was murdered, together with his brother Pheres, by his mother at Corinth. — 2. Son of Pheres, and grandson of Jason and Medea.

Mermessus or **Myrmessus** (Μερμηνσούός, Μυρμησσός), also written **Marmessus** and **Marpessus**, a town of Mysia, in the territory of Lampsacus, not far from Polichna ; the native place of a sibyl.

Merobaudes, Flavĭus, a general and a poet.

whose merits are recorded in an inscription on the base of a statue dug up in the Ulpian forum at Rome in the year 1812 or 1813. We learn from the inscription that the statue was erected in A. D. 435. Some fragments of the poems of Merobaudes were discovered by Niebuhr upon a palimpsest belonging to the monastery of St. Gall, and were published by him at Bonn, 1823.

Měroě (Μερόη: pts. of *Nubia* and *Sennar*), the island, so-called, and almost an island in reality, formed by the rivers Astapus (*Blue Nile*) and Astaboras (*Atbarah*), and the portion of the Nile between their mouths, was a district of Ethiopia. Its capital, also called Meroë, stood near the N. point of the island, on the E. bank of the Nile, below the modern *Shendy*, where the plain, near the village of *Assour*, is covered with ruins of temples, pyramids, and other works, in a style closely resembling the Egyptian. Standing in a fertile district, rich in timber and minerals, at the foot of the highlands of *Abyssinia*, and at the junction of 2 great rivers, Meroë became at a very early period a chief emporium for the trade between Egypt, N. Africa, Ethiopia, Arabia, and India, and the capital of a powerful state. The government was a hierarchical monarchy, entirely in the hands of a ruling caste of priests, who chose a king from among themselves, bound him to govern according to their laws, and put him to death when they chose; until king Ergamenes (about B. c. 300) threw off the yoke of the priests, whom he massacred, and converted his kingdom into an absolute monarchy. The priests of Meroë were closely connected in origin and customs with those of Egypt; and, according to some traditions, the latter sprang from the former, and they from India; but the settlement of this point involves an important ethnical question, which lies beyond the limits of this book. For further details respecting the kingdom of Meroë, see AETHIOPIA. Meroë had a celebrated oracle of Ammon.

Merom Lacus. [SEMECHONITIN.]

Měropě (Μερόπη). 1. One of the Heliades or sisters of Phaëthon. — 2. Daughter of Atlas, one of the Pleiades, and wife of Sisyphus of Corinth, by whom she became the mother of Glaucus. In the constellation of the Pleiades she is the 7th and the least visible star, because she is ashamed of having had intercourse with a mortal man. — 3. Daughter of Cypselus, wife of Cresphontes, and mother of Aepytus. For details, see AEPYTUS.

Měrops (Μέροψ). 1. King of the island of Cos, husband of the nymph Ethemea, and father of Eumelus. His wife was killed by Artemis, because she had neglected to worship that goddess. Merops, in order to rejoin his wife, wished to make away with himself, but Hera changed him into an eagle, whom she placed among the stars. — 2. King of the Ethiopians, by whose wife, Clymene, Helios became the father of Phaëthon. — 3. King of Rhyndacus, on the Hellespont, also called Macar or Macareus, was a celebrated soothsayer, and father of Clite, Arisbe, Amphius, and Adrastus.

Merula, L. Cornēlius, was flamen dialis, and, on the deposition of L. Cinna in B. c. 87, was elected consul in his place. On the capture of Rome by Marius and Cinna at the close of the same year, Merula put an end to his own life, in order to escape the hands of the executioner.

Mesambria (Μεσαμβρίη: *Bushehr*), a peninsula on the coast of Persia, near the river Padargus.

Meschěla (Μεσχέλα: prob. near *Bonak*), a large city on the coast of N. Africa, said to have been founded by Greeks returning from the Trojan war. It was taken by Eumachus, the lieutenant of Agathocles.

Mesembria (Μεσημβρία, Herod. Μεσαμβρίη: Μεσημβριανός). 1. (*Missivria* or *Messuri*), a celebrated town of Thrace on the Pontus Euxinus, and at the foot of Mt. Haemus, founded by the inhabitants of Chalcedon and Byzantium in the time of Darius Hystaspis, and hence called a colony of Megara, since those 2 towns were founded by the Megarians. — 2. A town in Thrace, but of much less importance, on the coast of the Aegaean sea, and in the territory of the Cicones, near the mouth of the Lissus, and the most W.-ly of the Samothracian settlements on the mainland.

Měsěně (Μεσηνή, i. e. *Midland*), a name given to that part of Babylonia which consisted of the great island formed by the Euphrates, the Tigris, and the Royal Canal; and contained, therefore, the greater part of Babylonia.

Mesŏa or **Messŏa.** [SPARTA.]

Mesōgis. [MESSOGIS.]

Mesōmēdes (Μεσομήδης), a lyric and epigrammatic poet under Hadrian and the Antonines, was a native of Crete, and a freedman of Hadrian, whose favourite Antinous he celebrated in a poem. A salary, which he had received from Hadrian, was diminished by Antoninus Pius. Three poems of his are preserved in the Greek Anthology.

Měsŏpŏtāmia (Μεσοποταμία, Μέση τῶν ποταμῶν: O. T. Aram Naharaim, i. e. *Syria between the Rivers*: LXX. Μεσοποταμία Συρίας: *Al-Jesira*, i. e. *The Island*), a district of W. Asia, named from its position between the Euphrates and the Tigris, of which rivers the former divided it from Syria and Arabia on the W., the latter from Assyria on the E.: on the N. it was separated from Armenia by a branch of the Taurus, called Masius, and on the S. from Babylonia, by the Median Wall. The name was first used by the Greeks in the time of the Seleucidae. In earlier times the country was reckoned a part, sometimes of Syria, and sometimes of Assyria. Nor in the division of the Persian empire was it recognised as a distinct country, but it belonged to the satrapy of Babylonia. Excepting the mountainous region on the N. and N.E. formed by the chain of MASIUS, and its prolongation parallel to the Tigris, the country formed a vast plain, broken by few hills, well watered by rivers and canals, and very fertile, except in the S. part. which was more like the Arabian Desert, on the opposite side of the Euphrates. Besides corn, and fruits, and spices (e. g. the *amomum*), it produced fine timber, and supported large herds of cattle; in the S., or desert part, there were numerous wild animals, such as wild asses, gazelles, ostriches, and lions. Its chief mineral products were naphtha and jet. The N. part of Mesopotamia was divided into the districts of MYGDONIA and OSROËNE. It belonged successively to the Assyrian, Babylonian, Persian, Macedonian, Syro-Grecian, Parthian, and later Persian empires. In a wider sense, the name is sometimes applied to the whole country between the Euphrates and the Tigris.

Mespila (ἡ Μέσπιλα: Ru. at *Kouyounjik*, opp. to *Mosul*, Layard: others give different sites for it), a city of Assyria, on the E. side of the Tigris, which Xenophon (*Anab.* iii. 4) mentions as having been formerly a great city, inhabited by Medes, but in his time fallen to decay. It had a wall 6 parasangs in circuit, composed of 2 parts; namely, a base 50 feet thick and 50 high, of polished stone full of shells (the limestone of the country), upon which was built a brick wall 50 feet thick and 100 high. It had served, according to tradition, as the refuge for the Median queen, when the Persians overthrew the empire of the Medes, and it resisted all the efforts of the Persian king to take it, until a thunder storm frightened the inhabitants into a surrender.

Messa (Μέσσα, Μέσση: Mezapo), a town and harbour in Laconia near C. Taenarum.

Messabatēnē or -loē (Μεσσαβατηνή, Μεσσαβατική: Μεσσαβάται), a small district on the S.E. margin of the Tigris and Euphrates valley, on the borders of Media, Persis, and Susiana, reckoned sometimes to Persis and sometimes to Susiana. The name seems to be derived from the mountain passes in the district.

Messāla or **Messalla**, the name of a distinguished family of the Valeria gens at Rome. They appear for the first time on the consular Fasti in B. C. 263, and for the last in A. D. 506.—1. **M'. Valerius Maximus Corvinus Messala**, was consul B. C. 263, and, in conjunction with his colleague M. Otacilius, carried on the war with success against the Carthaginians in Sicily. The 2 consuls concluded a peace with Hieron. In consequence of his relieving Messana he obtained the cognomen of Messala. His triumph was distinguished by two remarkable monuments of his victory—by a pictorial representation of a battle with the Sicilian and Punic armies, which he placed in the Curia Hostilia, and by a sun-dial (Horologium), from the booty of Catana, which was set up on a column behind the rostra, in the forum. Messala was censor in 252.—2. **M. Valerius Messala**, consul 226.—3. **M. Valerius Messala**, praetor peregrinus 194, and consul 188, when he had the province of Liguria.—4. **M. Valerius Messala**, consul 161, and censor 154.—5. **M. Valerius Messala Niger**, praetor 63; consul 61; and censor 55. He belonged to the aristocratical party. He married a sister of the orator Q. Hortensius, by whom he had at least one son.—6. **M. Valerius Messala**, son of the preceding; consul 53; belonged, like his father, to the aristocratical party; but in consequence probably of his enmity to Pompey, he joined Caesar in the civil war, and served under him in Africa. He was in high repute for his skill in augury, on which science he wrote.—7. **M. Valerius Messala Corvinus**, son of the preceding, was partly educated at Athens, where probably began his intimacy with Horace and L. Bibulus. After Caesar's death (44) he joined the republican party, and attached himself especially to Cassius, whom, long after, when he had become the friend of Augustus, he was accustomed to call "my general." Messala was proscribed; but since his kinsmen proved his absence from Rome at the time of Caesar's assassination, the triumvirs erased his name from the list, and offered him security for his person and property. Messala, however, rejected their offers, followed Cassius into Asia, and at Philippi, in the first day's battle, turned Augustus's flank, stormed his camp, and narrowly missed taking him prisoner. After the death of Brutus and Cassius, Messala, with a numerous body of fugitives, took refuge

in the island of Thasos. His followers, though defeated, were not disorganised, and offered him the command. But he induced them to accept honourable terms from Antony, to whom he attached himself until Cleopatra's influence made his ruin certain and easy to be foreseen. Messala then again changed his party, and served Augustus effectively in Sicily, 36; against the Salassians, a mountain tribe lying between the Graian and the Pennine Alps, 34; and at Actium, 31. A decree of the senate had abrogated Antony's consulship for 31, and Messala was appointed to the vacant place. He was proconsul of Aquitania in 28—27, and obtained a triumph for his reduction of that province. Shortly before or immediately after his administration of Aquitania, Messala held a prefecture in Asia Minor. He was deputed by the senate, probably in 30, to greet Augustus with the title of "Pater Patriae;" and the opening of his address on that occasion is preserved by Suetonius. During the disturbances at the comitia in 27, Augustus nominated Messala to the revived office of warden of the city; but he resigned it in a few days. Messala soon afterwards withdrew from all public employments except his augurship, to which Augustus had specially appointed him, although, at the time of his admission, there was no vacancy in the augural college. About 2 years before his death, which happened about the middle of Augustus's reign, B. C. 3—A. D. 3, Messala's memory failed him, and he often could not recall his own name. His tomb was of remarkable splendour. Messala was as much distinguished in the literary as in the political world of Rome. He was a patron of learning and the arts, and was himself an historian, a poet, a grammarian, and an orator. He wrote commentaries on the civil wars after Caesar's death, and a genealogical work, *De Romanis Familiis*. The treatise, however, *De Progenie Augusti*, which sometimes accompanies Eutropius and the minor Roman historians, is the forgery of a much later age. Messala's poems were of a satirical or even licentious character. His writings as a grammarian were numerous and minute, comprising treatises on collocation and lexicography, and on the powers and uses of single letters. His eloquence reflected the character of his age. More smooth and correct than vigorous or original, he persuaded rather than convinced, and conciliated rather than persuaded. His health was feeble, and the prooemia of his speeches generally pleaded indisposition and solicited indulgence. He mostly took the defendant's side, and was frequently associated in causes with C. Asinius Pollio. He recommended and practised translation from the Greek orators; and his version of the *Phryne* of Hyperides was thought to exhibit remarkable skill in either language. His political eminence, the wealth he inherited or acquired in the civil wars, and the favour of Antony and Augustus, rendered Messala one of the principal persons of his age, and an effective patron of its literature. His friendship for Horace and his intimacy with Tibullus are well known. In the elegies of the latter poet, the name of Messala is continually introduced. The dedication of the *Ciris*, a doubtful work, is not sufficient proof of his friendship with Virgil; but the companion of "Plotius and Varius, of Maecenas and Octavius" (Hor. *Sat.* i. 10. 81), cannot well have been unknown to the author of the Eclogues and Georgics. He directed

Ovid's early studies (*ex Pont.* iv. 16), and Tiberius sought his acquaintance in early manhood, and took him for his model in eloquence. — 8. **M. Valerius Messala Barbatus Appianus**, was consul B. C. 12, and died in his year of office. He was the father (or grandfather) of the empress Messalina. — 9. **L. Valerius Messala Volesus**, consul A. D. 5, and afterwards proconsul of Asia, where his cruelties drew on him the anger of Augustus and a condemnatory decree from the senate. — 10. **L. Vipstanus Messala**, legionary tribune in Vespasian's army, A. D. 70, was brother of Aquilius Regulus, the notorious delator in Domitian's reign. He is one of Tacitus' authorities for the history of the civil wars after Galba's death, and a principal interlocutor in the dialogue *De Oratoribus*, ascribed to Tacitus.

Messalina. 1. **Statilla**, granddaughter of T. Statilius Taurus, cos. A. D. 11, was the 3rd wife of the emperor Nero, who married her in A. D. 66. She had previously espoused Atticus Vestinus, whom Nero put to death without accusation or trial, merely that he might marry Messalina. — 2. **Valeria**, daughter of M. Valerius Messala Barbatus and of Domitia Lepida, was the 3rd wife of the emperor Claudius. She married Claudius, to whom she was previously related, before his accession to the empire. Her profligacy and licentiousness were notorious; and the absence of virtue was not concealed by a lingering sense of shame or even by a specious veil of decorum. She was as cruel as she was profligate; and many members of the most illustrious families of Rome were sacrificed to her fears or her hatred. She long exercised an unbounded empire over her weak husband, who alone was ignorant of her infidelities. For some time she was supported in her career of crime by the freedmen of Claudius; but when Narcissus, the most powerful of the emperor's freedmen, perceived that he should probably fall a victim to Messalina's intrigues, he determined to get rid of her. The insane folly of Messalina furnished the means of her own destruction. Having conceived a violent passion for a handsome Roman youth, C. Silius, she publicly married him with all the rites of a legal connubium during the absence of Claudius at Ostia, A. D. 48. Narcissus persuaded the emperor that Silius and Messalina would not have dared such an outrage had they not determined also to deprive him of empire and life. Claudius wavered long, and at length Narcissus himself issued Messalina's death-warrant. She was put to death by a tribune of the guards in the gardens of Lucullus.

Messana (Μεσσάνα Dor., Μεσσήνη: Μεσσάνιος: *Messina*), a celebrated town on the N. E. coast of Sicily, on the straits separating Italy from this island, which are here about 4 miles broad. The Romans called the town *Messana*, according to its Doric pronunciation, but *Messene* was its more usual name among the Greeks. It was originally a town of the Siceli, and was called Zancle (Ζάγκλη), or a sickle, on account of the shape of its harbour, which is formed by a singular curve of sand and shells. The first Greek colonists were, according to Thucydides, pirates from the Chalcidian town of Cumae in Italy, who were joined by Chalcidians from Euboea, and, according to Strabo, by Naxians: but these 2 accounts are not contradictory, for since Naxos in Sicily was also a colony from Chalcis, we may easily suppose that the

Naxians joined the other Chalcidians in the foundation of the town. Zancle soon became so powerful that it founded the town of Himera, about B. C. 648. After the capture of Miletus by the Persians, the inhabitants of Zancle invited the Ionians, who had been expelled from their native country, to settle on their "beautiful coast" (καλὴ ἀκτή, Herod. vi. 22.); and a number of Samians and other Ionic Greeks accepted their offer. On landing in the S. of Italy, they were persuaded by Anaxilas, tyrant of Rhegium, to take possession of Zancle during the absence of Scythes, the tyrant of the city, who was engaged in the siege of some other Sicilian town. But their treachery was soon punished; for Anaxilas himself shortly afterwards drove the Samians out of Zancle, and made himself master of the town, the name of which he changed into *Messana* or *Messene*, both because he was himself a Messenian, and because he transferred to the place a body of Messenians from Rhegium. Anaxilas died 476; and about 10 years afterwards (466) his sons were driven out of Messana and Rhegium, and republican governments established in these cities. Messana now enjoyed great prosperity for several years, and in consequence of its excellent harbour and advantageous position, it became a place of great commercial importance. But in 396 it was taken by the Carthaginians, who destroyed the town because they saw that they should be unable to maintain so distant a possession against the power of Dionysius of Syracuse. Dionysius began to rebuild it in the same year, and besides collecting the remains of the former population, he added a number of Locrians, Messenians, and others, so that its inhabitants were of a very mixed kind. After the banishment of the younger Dionysius, Messana was for a short time free, but it fell into the power of Agathocles about 312. Among the mercenaries of this tyrant were a number of Mamertini, an Oscan people from Campania, who had been sent from home under the protection of the god Mamers or Mars to seek their fortune in other lands. These Mamertini were quartered in Messana; and after the death of Agathocles (282) they made themselves masters of the town, killed the male inhabitants, and took possession of their wives, their children, and their property. The town was now called **Mamertina**, and the inhabitants **Mamertini**; but its ancient name of Messana continued to be in more general use. The new inhabitants could not lay aside their old predatory habits, and in consequence became involved in a war with Hieron of Syracuse, who defeated them in several battles, and would probably have conquered the town, had not the Carthaginians come in to the aid of the Mamertini, and, under the pretext of assisting them, taken possession of their citadel. The Mamertini had at the same time applied to the Romans for help, who gladly availed themselves of the opportunity to obtain a footing in Sicily. Thus Messana was the immediate cause of the 1st Punic war, 264. The Mamertini expelled the Carthaginian garrison, and received the Romans, in whose power Messana remained till the latest times. There are scarcely any remains of the ancient city at *Messina*.

Messapia (Μεσσαπία). 1. The Greek name of CALABRIA. — 2. (*Messagna*), a town in Calabria, between Uria and Brundusium.

Messapium (τὸ Μεσσάπιον ὄρος), a mountain in Boeotia on the E. coast, near the town Anthedon, from which Messapus is said to have sailed to the S. of Italy.

Messāpus (Μέσσαπος), a Boeotian, from whom Messapia in the S. of Italy was believed to have derived its name.

Messēnē (Μεσσήνη), daughter of Triopas, and wife of Polycaon, whom she induced to take possession of the country which was called after her, Messenia. She is also said to have introduced there the worship of Zeus and the mysteries of the great goddess of Eleusis.

Messēnē (Μεσσήνη: Μεσσήνιος). 1. (*Mavromati*), the later capital of Messenia, was founded by Epaminondas B. c. 369, and completed and fortified within the space of 85 days. It was situated at the foot of the steep hill of Ithome, which was so celebrated as a fortress in the history of the Messenian wars, and which now formed the acropolis of the new city. Messene was one of the most strongly fortified cities of Greece. It was surrounded by massive walls built entirely of stone and flanked with numerous towers. There are still considerable remains of some of these towers, as well as the foundations of the walls, and of several public buildings. They are described by a modern traveller as "built of the most regular kind of masonry, and formed of large stones fitted together with great accuracy." The northern gate of the city is also extant, and opens into a circular court, 62 feet in diameter. The city was supplied with water from a fountain called *Clepsydra*, which is still a fine spring, from which the modern village of *Mavromati* derives its name, meaning Black Spring, or literally, Black Eye.—2. See **MESSANA**.

Messēnia (Μεσσηνία: Μεσσήνιος), a country in Peloponnesus, bounded on the E. by Laconia, on the N. by Elis and Arcadia, and on the S. and W. by the sea. It was separated from Laconia by Mt. Taygetus; but part of the W. slope of Taygetus belonged to Laconia; and it is difficult to determine the exact boundaries between the 2 countries, as they were different at different periods. In the most ancient times the river Nedon formed the boundary between Messenia and Laconia towards the sea; but Pausanias places the frontier line further E. at a woody hollow called Choerius, 20 stadia S. of Abia. The river Neda formed the N. frontier between Messenia and Elis. The area of Messenia is about 1162 square miles. It was for the most part a mountainous country, and contained only 2 plains of any extent, in the N. the plain of *Stenyclerus*, and in the S. a still larger plain, through which the Pamisus flowed, and which was called *Macaria* or the Blessed, on account of its great fertility. There were, however, many smaller valleys among the mountains; and the country was much less rugged and far more productive than the neighbouring Laconia. Hence Messenia is described by Pausanias as the most fertile country in Peloponnesus; and it is praised by Euripides on account of its climate, which was neither too cold in winter nor too hot in summer. The most ancient inhabitants of Messenia were Leleges, intermingled with Argives. According to tradition Polycaon, the younger son of Lelex, married the Argive Messene, a daughter of Triopas, and named the country Messene in honour of his wife. This is the name by which it is called in Homer, who does not use the form Messenia. Five generations afterwards Aeolians settled in the country, under the guidance of Perieres, a son

of Aeolus. His son Aphareus gave a home to Neleus, who had been driven out of Thessaly, and who founded the town of Pylos, which became the capital of an independent sovereignty. For a long time there was properly no Messenian kingdom. The western part of the land belonged to the dominions of the Neleid princes of Pylos, of whom Nestor was the most celebrated, and the eastern to the Lacedaemonian monarchy. Thus it appears to have remained till the conquest of Peloponnesus by the Dorians, when Messenia fell to the share of Cresphontes, who destroyed the kingdom of Pylos, and united the whole country under his sway. The ruling class were now Dorians, and they continued to speak the purest Doric down to the latest times. The Spartans soon coveted the more fertile territory of their brother Dorians; and after many disputes between the 2 nations, and various inroads into each other's territories, open war at length broke out. This war, called the 1st Messenian war, lasted 20 years, B. c. 743—723; and notwithstanding the gallant resistance of the Messenian king, Aristodemus, the Messenians were obliged to submit to the Spartans after the capture of their fortress Ithome, and to become their subjects. [ARISTODEMUS.] After bearing the yoke 38 years, the Messenians again took up arms under their heroic leader Aristomenes. [ARISTOMENES.] The 2nd Messenian war lasted 17 years, B. c. 685—668, and terminated with the conquest of Ira and the complete subjugation of the country. Most of the Messenians emigrated to foreign countries, and those who remained behind were reduced to the condition of Helots or serfs. In this state they remained till 464, when the Messenians and other Helots took advantage of the devastation occasioned by the great earthquake at Sparta, to rise against their oppressors. This 3rd Messenian war lasted 10 years, 464—455, and ended by the Messenians surrendering Ithome to the Spartans on condition of their being allowed a free departure from Peloponnesus. They settled at Naupactus on the Corinthian gulf opposite Peloponnesus, which town the Athenians had lately taken from the Locri Ozolae, and gladly granted to such deadly enemies of Sparta. At the conclusion of the Peloponnesian war (404), the unfortunate Messenians were obliged to leave Naupactus and take refuge in Italy, Sicily, and other countries; but when the supremacy of Sparta was overthrown by the battle of Leuctra, Epaminondas resolved to restore the independence of Messenia. He accordingly gathered together the Messenian exiles from the various lands in which they were scattered; and in the summer of 369 he founded the town of Messene at the foot of Mt. Ithome. [MESSENE.] Messenia was never again subdued by the Spartans, and it maintained its independence till the conquest of the Achaeans and the rest of Greece by the Romans, 146.

Mestlēta (Μεστλῆτα), a city of Iberia, in Asia probably on the river Cyrus.

Mestra (Μήστρα), daughter of Erysichthon, and granddaughter of Triopas, whence she is called *Triopeïs* by Ovid. She was sold by her hungry father, that he might obtain the means of satisfying his hunger. In order to escape from slavery, she prayed to Poseidon, who loved her, and who conferred upon her the power of metamorphosing herself whenever she was sold.

Mesyla, a town of Pontus, in Asia Minor, on the road from Tavium to Comana.

METETLLUS.

Metagōnītis (Μεταγωνῖτις: Μεταγωνῖται, Metagonītae), a name applied to the N. coast of Mauretania Tingitana (Marocco), between the Fretum Gaditanum and the river Mulucha; derived probably from the Carthaginian colonies (μεταγόνια) settled along it. There was at some point of this coast a promontory called Metagonium or Metagonites, probably the same as Russadir (Rasud-Dir, or C. Tres Forcas).

Metagōnium. [METAGONITIS.]

Metallinum or **Metellinum** (Metallinensis: Medellin), a Roman colony in Lusitania on the Anas, not far from Augusta Emerita.

Metānīra (Μετάνειρα), wife of Celeus, and mother of Triptolemus, received Demeter on her arrival in Attica. Pausanias calls her Meganaera. For details see CELEUS.

Metaphrastes, Symēon (Συμεὼν ὁ Μεταφράστης), a celebrated Byzantine writer, lived in the 9th and 10th centuries, and held many high offices at the Byzantine court. His surname Metaphrastes was given to him on account of his having composed a celebrated paraphrase of the lives of the saints. Besides his other works, he wrote a Byzantine history, entitled Annales, beginning with the emperor Leo Armenus, A. D. 813, and finishing with Romanus, the son of Constantine Porphyrogenitus, 963. Edited by Bekker, Bonn, 1838.

Metapontium called **Metapontum** by the Romans (Μεταπόντιον: Μεταπόντιος, Metapontīnus: Torre di Mare), a celebrated Greek city in the S. of Italy, on the Tarentine gulf, and on the E. coast of Lucania, is said to have been originally called Metabum (Μέταβον). There were various traditions respecting its foundation, all of which point to its high antiquity, but from which we cannot gather any certain information on the subject. It is said to have been afterwards destroyed by the Samnites, and to have been repeopled by a colony of Achaeans, who had been invited for that purpose by the inhabitants of Sybaris. Hence it is called by Livy an Achaean town, and is regarded by some writers as a colony from Sybaris. It fell into the hands of the Romans with the other Greek cities in the S. of Italy in the war against Pyrrhus; but it revolted to Hannibal after the battle of Cannae. From the time of the 2nd Punic war it disappears from history, and was in ruins in the time of Pausanias.

Metaurum. [METAURUS, No. 2.]

Metaurus. 1. (Metaro), a small river in Umbria, flowing into the Adriatic sea, but rendered memorable by the defeat and death of Hasdrubal, the brother of Hannibal, on its banks, B. C. 207. — 2. (Marro), a river on the E. coast of Bruttium, at whose mouth was the town of Metaurum.

Metella. [CAECILIA.]

Metellus, a distinguished plebeian family of the Caecilia gens at Rome. 1. **L. Caecilius Metellus**, consul B. C. 251, carried on the war in Sicily against the Carthaginians. In the following year he gained a great victory over Hasdrubal, the Carthaginian general. The elephants which he took in this battle were exhibited in his triumph at Rome. Metellus was consul a 2nd time in 249, and was elected pontifex maximus in 243, and held this dignity for 22 years. He must, therefore, have died shortly before the commencement of the 2nd Punic war. In 241 he rescued the Palladium when the temple of Vesta was on fire, but lost his sight in consequence. He

was dictator in 224, for the purpose of holding the comitia. — 2. Q. Caecilius Metellus, son of the preceding, was plebeian aedile 209; curule aedile 208; served in the army of the consul Claudius Nero 207, and was one of the legates sent to Rome to convey the joyful news of the defeat and death of Hasdrubal; and was consul with L. Veturius Philo, 206. In his consulship he and his colleague carried on the war against Hannibal in Bruttium, where he remained as proconsul during the following year. In 205 he was dictator for the purpose of holding the comitia. Metellus survived the 2nd Punic war many years, and was employed in several public commissions. — 3. Q. Caecilius Metellus Macedonicus, son of the last, was praetor 148, and carried on war in Macedonia against the usurper Andriscus, whom he defeated and took prisoner. He next turned his arms against the Achaeans, whom he defeated at the beginning of 146. On his return to Rome in 146, he triumphed, and received the surname of Macedonicus. Metellus was consul in 143, and received the province of Nearer Spain, where he carried on the war with success for 2 years against the Celtiberi. He was succeeded by Q. Pompeius in 141. Metellus was censor 131. He died 115, full of years and honours. He is frequently quoted by the ancient writers as an extraordinary instance of human felicity. He had filled all the highest offices of the state with reputation and glory, and was carried to the funeral pile by 4 sons, 3 of whom had obtained the consulship in his lifetime, while the 4th was a candidate for the office at the time of his death. — 4. L. Caecilius Metellus Calvus, brother of the last, consul 142. — 5. Q. Caecilius Metellus Balearicus, eldest son of No. 3, was consul 123, when he subdued the inhabitants of the Balearic islands, and received in consequence the surname of Balearicus. He was censor 120. — 6. L. Caecilius Metellus Diadematus, 2nd son of No. 3, has been frequently confounded with Metellus Dalmaticus, consul 119 [No. 9.]. Metellus Diadematus received the latter surname from his wearing for a long time a bandage round his forehead, in consequence of an ulcer. He was consul 117. — 7. M. Caecilius Metellus, 3rd son of No. 3, was consul 115, the year in which his father died. In 114 he was sent into Sardinia as proconsul, and suppressed an insurrection in the island, in consequence of which he obtained a triumph in 113 on the same day as his brother Caprarius. — 8. C. Caecilius Metellus Caprarius, 4th son of No. 3. The origin of his surname is quite uncertain. He was consul 113, and carried on war in Macedonia against the Thracians, whom he subdued. He obtained a triumph in consequence in the same year and on the same day with his brother Marcus. He was censor 102 with his cousin Metellus Numidicus.— 9. L. Caecilius Metellus Dalmaticus, elder son of No. 4, and frequently confounded, as has been already remarked, with Diadematus [No. 5], was consul 119, when he subdued the Dalmatians, and obtained in consequence the surname Dalmaticus. He was censor with Cn. Domitius Ahenobarbus in 115; and he was also pontifex maximus. He was alive in 100, when he is mentioned as one of the senators of high rank, who took up arms against Saturninus. — 10. Q. Caecilius Metellus Numidicus, younger son of No. 4, was one of the most distinguished members of his family. The character of Metellus stood very high among his contemporaries; in an age of growing corruption his personal integrity remained unsullied; and he was distinguished for his abilities in war and peace. He was one of the chief leaders of the aristocratical party at Rome. He was consul 109, and carried on the war against Jugurtha in Numidia with great success. [JUGURTHA.] He remained in Numidia during the following year as proconsul; but as he was unable to bring the war to a conclusion, his legate C. Marius industriously circulated reports in the camp and the city that Metellus designedly protracted the war, for the purpose of continuing in the command. These rumours had the desired effect. Marius was raised to the consulship. Numidia was assigned to him as his province, and Metellus saw the honour of finishing the war snatched from his grasp. [MARIUS.] On his return to Rome in 107 he was received with the greatest honour. He celebrated a splendid triumph, and received the surname of Numidicus. In 102 he was censor with his cousin Metellus Caprarius. In 100 the tribune Saturninus and Marius resolved to ruin Metellus. Saturninus proposed an agrarian law, to which he added the clause, that the senate should swear obedience to it within 5 days after its enactment, and that whosoever should refuse to do so should be expelled the senate, and pay a heavy fine. Metellus refused to take the oath, and was therefore expelled the senate; but Saturninus, not content with this, brought forward a bill to punish him with exile. The friends of Metellus were ready to take up arms in his defence; but Metellus quitted the city, and retired to Rhodes, where he bore his misfortune with great calmness. He was however recalled to Rome in the following year (99) on the proposition of the tribune Q. Calidius. The orations of Metellus are spoken of with praise by Cicero, and they continued to be read with admiration in the time of Fronto. — **11. Q. Caecilius Metellus Nepos**, son of Balearicus [No. 5], and grandson of Macedonicus [No. 3], appears to have received the surname of Nepos, because he was the eldest grandson of the latter. Metellus Nepos exerted himself in obtaining the recall of his kinsman Metellus Numidicus from banishment in 99, and was consul in 98, with T. Didius. In this year the 2 consuls carried the lex Caecilia Didia. — **12. Q. Caecilius Metellus Pius**, son of Numidicus [No. 10], received the surname of Pius on account of the love which he displayed for his father when he besought the people to recall him from banishment in 99. He was praetor 89, and was one of the commanders in the Marsic or Social war. He was still in arms in 87, prosecuting the war against the Samnites, when Marius landed in Italy and joined the consul Cinna. The senate, in alarm, summoned Metellus to Rome; but as he was unable to defend the city against Marius and Cinna, he crossed over to Africa. After remaining in Africa 3 years he returned to Italy, and joined Sulla, who also returned to Italy in 83. In the war which followed against the Marian party, Metellus was one of the most successful of Sulla's generals, and gained several important victories both in Umbria, and in Cisalpine Gaul. In 80, Metellus was consul with Sulla himself; and in the following year (79) he went as proconsul into Spain, in order to prosecute the war against Sertorius, who adhered to the Marian party. Here he remained

for the next 8 years, and found it so difficult to obtain any advantages over Sertorius, that the senate sent Pompey to his assistance with proconsular power and another army. Sertorius, however, was a match for them both, and would probably have continued to defy all the efforts of Metellus and Pompey, if he had not been murdered by Perperna and his friends in 72. [SERTORIUS.] Metellus was pontifex maximus, and, as he was succeeded in this dignity by Julius Caesar in 63, he must have died either in this year or at the end of the preceding. — **13. Q. Caecilius Metellus Celer**, elder son of Nepos [No. 11.]. In 66 he served as legate in the army of Pompey in Asia; and was praetor in 63, the year in which Cicero was consul. During his year of office he afforded warm and efficient support to the aristocratical party. He prevented the condemnation of C. Rabirius by removing the military flag from the Janiculum. He co-operated with Cicero in opposing the schemes of Catiline; and, when the latter left the city to make war upon the republic, Metellus had the charge of the Picentine and Senonian districts. By blocking up the passes he prevented Catiline from crossing the Apennines and penetrating into Gaul, and thus compelled him to turn round and face Antonius, who was marching against him from Etruria. In the following year, 62, Metellus went with the title of proconsul into the province of Cisalpine Gaul, which Cicero had relinquished because he was unwilling to leave the city. In 60, Metellus was consul with L. Afranius, and opposed all the efforts of his colleague to obtain the ratification of Pompey's acts in Asia, and an assignment of lands for his soldiers. He died in 59, and it was suspected that he had been poisoned by his wife Clodia, with whom he lived on the most unhappy terms, and who was a woman of the utmost profligacy. — **14. Q. Caecilius Metellus Nepos**, younger son of the elder Nepos [No. 11.]. He served as legate of Pompey in the war against the pirates and in Asia from 67 to 64. He returned to Rome in 63 in order to become a candidate for the tribunate, that he might thereby favour the views of Pompey. His election was opposed by the aristocracy, but without success. His year of office was a stormy one. One of his first acts in entering upon his office on the 10th of December, 63, was a violent attack upon Cicero. He maintained that the man who had condemned Roman citizens without a hearing ought not to be heard himself, and accordingly prevented Cicero from addressing the people on the last day of his consulship, and only allowed him to take the usual oath, whereupon Cicero swore that he had saved the state. In the following year (62) Metellus brought forward a bill to summon Pompey, with his army, to Rome, in order to restore peace, but on the day on which the bill was to be read, the two parties came to open blows; and Metellus was obliged to take to flight. He repaired to Pompey, with whom he returned to Rome in 61. He was praetor in 60, and consul in 57 with P. Lentulus Spinther. Notwithstanding his previous enmity with Cicero, he did not oppose his recall from exile. In 56 Metellus administered the province of Nearer Spain, where he carried on war against the Vaccaei. He died in 55. Metellus did not adhere strictly to the political principles of his family. He did not support the aristocracy, like his brother; nor, on the other hand, can he be said to have been a leader of the democracy. He was in fact little more than a servant of Pompey, and according to his bidding at one time opposed, and at another supported Cicero. — 15. Q. Caecilius Metellus Pius Scipio, the adopted son of Metellus Pius [No. 12.]. He was the son of P. Scipio Nasica, praetor 94. Hence his name is given in various forms. Sometimes he is called P. Scipio Nasica, sometimes Q. Metellus Scipio, and sometimes simply Scipio or Metellus. He was tribune of the plebs in 59, and was a candidate for the consulship along with Plautius Hypsaeus and Milo in 53. He was supported by the Clodian mob, since he was opposed to Milo, but in consequence of the disturbances in the city, the comitia could not be held for the election of consuls. After the murder of Clodius at the beginning of 52, Pompey was elected sole consul. In the course of the same year Pompey married Cornelia, the daughter of Scipio, and on the 1st of August he made his father-in-law his colleague in the consulship. Scipio showed his gratitude by using every effort to destroy the power of Caesar and strengthen that of Pompey. He took an active part in all the proceedings, which led to the breaking out of the civil war in 49; and in the division of the provinces, made among the Pompeian party, he obtained Syria to which he hastened without delay. After plundering the province in the most unmerciful manner, he crossed over into Greece in 48 to join Pompey. He commanded the centre of the Pompeian army at the battle of Pharsalia. After the loss of the battle he fled, first to Corcyra and then to Africa, where he received the chief command of the Pompeian troops. He was defeated by Caesar at the decisive battle of Thapsus in 46. He attempted to escape by sea, but his squadron having been overpowered by P. Sittius, he put an end to his own life. Metellus Scipio never exhibited any proofs of striking abilities either in war or in peace. In public, he showed himself cruel, vindictive, and oppressive; in private, he was mean, avaricious, and licentious, even beyond most of his contemporaries. — 16. Q. Caecilius Metellus Creticus, was consul 69, and carried on war against Crete, which he subdued in the course of 3 years. He returned to Rome in 66, but was unable to obtain a triumph in consequence of the opposition of Pompey, to whom he had refused to surrender his command in Crete, which Pompey had claimed in virtue of the Gabinian law, which had given him the supreme command in the whole of the Mediterranean. Metellus, however, would not relinquish his claim to a triumph, and accordingly resolved to wait in the neighbourhood of the city till more favourable circumstances. He was still before the city in 63, when the conspiracy of Catiline broke out. He was sent into Apulia to prevent an apprehended rising of the slaves; and in the following year, 62, after the death of Catiline, he was at length permitted to make his triumphal entrance into Rome, and received the surname of Creticus. Metellus, as was to be expected, joined the aristocracy in their opposition to Pompey, and succeeded in preventing the latter from obtaining the ratification of his acts in Asia. — 17. L. Caecilius Metellus, brother of the last, was praetor 71, and as propraetor succeeded Verres in the government of Sicily in 70. He defeated the pirates, and compelled them to leave the island. His administration is praised by Cicero; but he

nevertheless attempted, in conjunction with his brothers, to shield Verres from justice. He was consul 68 with Q. Marcius Rex, but died at the beginning of the year. — 18. M. Caecilius Metellus, brother of the 2 last, was praetor 69, in the same year that his eldest brother was consul. The lot gave him the presidency in the court *de pecuniis repetundis*, and Verres was very anxious that his trial should come on before Metellus. — 19. L. Caecilius Metellus Creticus, was tribune of the plebs, 49, and a warm supporter of the aristocracy. He did not fly from Rome with Pompey and the rest of his party; and he attempted to prevent Caesar from taking possession of the sacred treasury, and only gave way upon being threatened with death.

METHANA. [METHONE, No. 4.]

METHARME (Μεθάρμη), daughter of king Pygmalion, and wife of Cinyras. See CINYRAS.

METHONE (Μεθώνη: Μεθωναῖος). 1. Or MOTHONE (Μοθώνη: *Modon*), a town at the S. W. corner of Messenia, with an excellent harbour, protected from the sea by a reef of rocks, of which the largest was called Mothon. The ancients regarded Methone as the Pedasus of Homer. After the conquest of Messenia, it became one of the Lacedaemonian harbours, and is mentioned as such in the Peloponnesian war. The emperor Trajan conferred several privileges upon the city. — 2. (*Eleutherokhori*,) a Greek town in Macedonia on the Thermaic gulf, 40 stadia N. E. of Pydna, was founded by the Eretrians, and is celebrated from Philip having lost an eye at the siege of the place. After its capture by Philip it was destroyed, but was subsequently rebuilt, and is mentioned by Strabo as one of the towns of Macedonia. — 3. A town in Thessaly mentioned by Homer, but does not occur in historical times. The ancients placed it in Magnesia. — 4. Or METHANA (Μέθανα: *Methana* or *Mitone*), an ancient town in Argolis, situated on a peninsula of the same name, opposite the island of Aegina. The peninsula runs a considerable way into the sea, and is connected with the mainland by a narrow isthmus, lying between the towns of Troezen and Epidaurus. The town of Methana lay at the foot of a mountain of volcanic origin.

METHORA (Μέθορα, Μόδουρα ἡ τῶν Θεῶν: *Matra*, the sacred city of Krishna), a city of India intra Gangem, on the river Jomanes (*Jumna*), was a great seat of the worship of the Indian god whom the Greeks identified with Hercules.

METHYDRIUM, (Μεθύδριον: Μεθυδριεύς), a town in central Arcadia, 170 stadia N. of Megalopolis.

METHYMNA (ἡ Μήθυμνα, Μέθυμνα, the former generally in the best writers; also on coins the Aeolic form Μάθυμνα: Μηθυμναῖος, Μεθυμναῖος: *Molivo*), the second city of LESBOS, stood at the north extremity of the island, and had a good harbour. It was the birthplace of the musician and dithyrambic poet Arion, and of the historian Hellanicus. The celebrated Lesbian wine grew in its neighbourhood. In the Peloponnesian war it remained faithful to Athens, even during the great Lesbian revolt [MYTILENE]: afterwards it was sacked by the Spartans (B. C. 406) and never quite recovered its prosperity.

METION (Μητίων), son of Erechtheus and Praxithea, and husband of Alcippe. His sons, the Metionidae, expelled their cousin Pandion from his kingdom of Athens, but were themselves afterwards expelled by the sons of Pandion.

METIS (Μῆτις), the personification of prudence,

to described as a daughter of Oceanus and Tethys, and the 1st wife of Zeus. Afraid lest she should give birth to a child wiser and more powerful than himself, Zeus devoured her in the first month of her pregnancy. Afterwards he gave birth to Athena, who sprang from his head. [See p. 101, a.]

Mĕtĭus. [METTIUS.]

Mĕton (Μέτων), an astronomer of Athens, who, in conjunction with **Euctemon**, introduced the cycle of 19 years, by which he adjusted the course of the sun and moon, since he had observed that 235 lunar months correspond very nearly to 19 solar years. The commencement of this cycle has been placed B. C. 432. We have no details of Meton's life, with the exception that his father's name was Pausanias, and that he feigned insanity to avoid sailing for Sicily in the ill-fated expedition of which he is stated to have had an evil presentiment.

Metrŏdōrus (Μητρόδωρος). 1. Of Cos, son of Epicharmus, and grandson of Thyrsus. Like several of that family, he addicted himself partly to the study of the Pythagorean philosophy, partly to the science of medicine. He wrote a treatise upon the works of Epicharmus. He flourished about B. C. 460. — **2.** Of Lampsacus, a contemporary and friend of Anaxagoras. He wrote on Homer, the leading feature of his system of interpretation being that the deities and stories in Homer were to be understood as allegorical modes of representing physical powers and phenomena. He died 464. — **3.** Of Chios, a disciple of Democritus, or, according to other accounts, of Nessus of Chios, flourished about 330. He was a philosopher of considerable reputation, and professed the doctrine of the sceptics in their fullest sense. He also studied, if he did not practise, medicine, on which he wrote a good deal. He was the instructor of Hippocrates and Anaxarchus. — **4.** A native of Lampsacus or Athens, was the most distinguished of the disciples of Epicurus, with whom he lived on terms of the closest friendship. He died 277, in the 53rd year of his age, 7 years before Epicurus, who would have appointed him his successor had he survived him. The philosophy of Metrodorus appears to have been of a more grossly sensual kind than that of Epicurus. Perfect happiness, according to Cicero's account, he made to consist in having a well-constituted body. He found fault with his brother Timocrates for not admitting that the belly was the test and measure of every thing that pertained to a happy life. He was the author of several works, quoted by the ancient writers. — **5.** Of Scepsis, a philosopher, who was raised to a position of great influence and trust by Mithridates Eupator, being appointed supreme judge without appeal even to the king. Subsequently he was led to desert his allegiance, when sent by Mithridates on an embassy to Tigranes, king of Armenia. Tigranes sent him back to Mithridates, but he died on the road. According to some accounts he was despatched by order of the king; according to others he died of disease. He is frequently mentioned by Cicero; he seems to have been particularly celebrated for his powers of memory. In consequence of his hostility to the Romans he was surnamed the *Roman-hater.* — **6.** Of Stratonice in Caria, was at first a disciple of the school of Epicurus, but afterwards attached himself to Carneades. He flourished about 110.

Mĕtrŏpŏlis (Μητρόπολις). 1. The most ancient capital of Phrygia, but in historical times an inconsiderable place. Its position is doubtful. Some identify it with *Afioum-Kara-Hisar* near the centre of Great Phrygia, which agrees well enough with the position of the Campus Metropolitanus of Livy (xxxviii. 15), while others find it in the ruins at *Pismesh-Kalessi* in the N. of Phrygia, and suppose a second Metropolis in the S., as that to which the Campus Metropolitanus belonged.—**2.** In Lydia (*Turbali*, Ru.), a city in the plain of the Cayster, between Ephesus and Smyrna, 120 stadia from the former and 200 from the latter.—There were other cities of Asia so called ; but they are either unimportant, or better known by other names, such as Ancyra, Bostra, Caesarea in Palestine, Edessa, and others.— **3.** (*Kastri*), a town in Thessaly in Histiaeotis, near the Peneus, and between Gomphi and Pharsalus, formed by the union of several small towns, to which Ithome also belonged. — **4.** A town of Acarnania in the district Amphilochia, between the Ambracian gulf and the river Achelous.

Mĕtrōüm aft. **Aulia** (Μητρῷον, on coins Μῆτρος, Αὐλία, Αὐλαία), a city of Bithynia.

Mettĭus or **Metĭus.** 1. **Curtius.** [CURTIUS.] — **2. Fuffetĭus,** dictator of Alba in the reign of Tullus Hostilius, third king of Rome. After the combat between the Horatii and Curiatii had determined the supremacy of the Romans, Mettius was summoned to aid them in a war with Fidenae and the Veientines. On the field of battle Mettius drew off his Albans to the hills, and awaited the issue of the battle. On the following day the Albans were all deprived of their arms, and Mettius himself, as the punishment of his treachery, was torn asunder by chariots driven in opposite directions.

Metŭlum, the chief town of the Iapydes in Illyricum, was near the frontiers of Liburnia, and was situated on 2 peaks of a steep mountain. Augustus nearly lost his life in reducing this place, the inhabitants of which fought against him with the most desperate courage.

Mĕvānĭa (Mevānas, ātis: *Beragna*), an ancient city in the interior of Umbria on the river Tinea, was situated on the road from Rome to Ancona in a very fertile country, and was celebrated for its breed of beautiful white oxen. It was a strongly fortified place, though its walls were built only of brick. According to some accounts Propertius was a native of this place.

Mĕzentĭus (Μεσέντιος), king of the Tyrrhenians or Etruscans, at Caere or Agylla, was expelled by his subjects on account of his cruelty, and took refuge with Turnus, king of the Rutulians, whom he assisted in the war against Aeneas and the Trojans. Mezentius and his son Lausus were slain in battle by Aeneas. This is the account of Virgil. Livy and Dionysius, however, say nothing about the expulsion of Mezentius from Caere, but represent him as an ally of Turnus, and relate that Aeneas disappeared during the battle against the Rutulians and Etruscans at Lanuvium. Dionysius adds, that Ascanius was besieged by Mezentius and Lausus ; that the besieged in a sally by night slew Lausus, and then concluded a peace with Mezentius, who from henceforth continued to be their ally.

Mĭcipsa (Μικίψας), king of Numidia, the eldest of the sons of Masinissa. After the death of the latter (B. C. 148), the sovereign power was divided by Scipio between Micipsa and his two brothers, Gulussa and Mastanabal, in such a manner that the possession of Cirta, the capital of Numidia, together with the financial administration of the kingdom, fell to the share of Micipsa. It was not long, however, before the death of both his brothers left him in possession of the undivided sovereignty of Numidia, which he held from that time without interruption till his death. He died in 118, leaving the kingdom to his 2 sons, Adherbal and Hiempsal, and their adopted brother JUGURTHA.

Micon (Μίκων), of Athens, son of Phanochus, was a very distinguished painter and statuary, contemporary with Polygnotus, about B. C. 460.

Midaëum (Μιδάειον), a city of Phrygia Epictetus, between Dorylaeum and Pessinus ; the place where Sextus Pompeius was captured by the troops of Antony, B. C. 35.

Midas (Μίδας), son of Gordius and Cybele, is said to have been a wealthy but effeminate king of Phrygia, a pupil of Orpheus, and a great patron of the worship of Dionysus. His wealth is alluded to in a story connected with his childhood, for it is said that while a child, ants carried grains of wheat into his mouth, to indicate that one day he should be the richest of all mortals. Midas was introduced into the Satyric drama of the Greeks, and was represented with the ears of a satyr, which were afterwards lengthened into the ears of an ass. He is said to have built the town of Ancyra, and as king of Phrygia he is called *Berecynthius heros* (Ov. *Met.* xi. 106). There are several stories connected with Midas, of which the following are the most celebrated. 1. Silenus, the companion and teacher of Dionysus, had gone astray in a state of intoxication, and was caught by country people in the rose gardens of Midas. He was bound with wreaths of flowers and led before the king. These gardens were in Macedonia, near Mount Bermion or Bromion, where Midas was king of the Briges, with whom he afterwards emigrated to Asia, where their name was changed into Phryges. Midas received Silenus kindly ; and, after treating him with hospitality, he led him back to Dionysus, who allowed Midas to ask a favour of him. Midas in his folly desired that all things which he touched should be changed into gold. The request was granted ; but as even the food which he touched became gold, he implored the god to take his favour back. Dionysus accordingly ordered him to bathe in the source of Pactolus near Mount Tmolus. This bath saved Midas, but the river from that time had an abundance of gold in its sand.—2. Midas, who was himself related to the race of Satyrs, once had a visit from a Satyr, who indulged in all kinds of jokes at the king's expence. Thereupon Midas mixed wine in a well ; and when the Satyr had drunk of it, he fell asleep and was caught. This well of Midas was at different times assigned to different localities. Xenophon (*Anab.* i. 2. § 13) places it in the neighbourhood of Thymbrium and Tyraeum, and Pausanias at Ancyra.— 3. Once when Pan and Apollo were engaged in a musical contest on the flute and lyre, Midas was chosen to decide between them. The king decided in favour of Pan, whereupon Apollo changed his ears into those of an ass. Midas contrived to conceal them under his Phrygian cap, but the servant who used to cut his hair discovered them. The secret so much harassed this man,

that as he could not betray it to a human being, he dug a hole in the earth, and whispered into it. "King Midas has ass's ears." He then filled the hole up again, and his heart was released. But on the same spot a reed grew up, which in its whispers betrayed the secret. Midas is said to have killed himself by drinking the blood of an ox.

Midëa or **Midëa** (Μίδεια, Μιδέα : Μιδεάτης), a town in Argolis, of uncertain site, is said to have been originally called Persepolis, because it had been fortified by Perseus. It was destroyed by the Argives.

Midianïtae. [MADIANITAE].

Midias (Μειδίας), an Athenian of wealth and influence, was a violent enemy of Demosthenes, the orator. In B. C. 354 Midias assaulted Demosthenes when he was discharging the duties of Choregus, during the celebration of the great Dionysia. Demosthenes brought an accusation against Midias ; but the speech, which he wrote for the occasion, and which is extant, was never published, since Demosthenes dropped the accusation, in consequence of his receiving the sum of 30 minae.

Mieza (Μίεζα : Μιεζεύς), a town of Macedonia in Emathia, S. W. of Pella, and not far from the frontiers of Thessaly.

Milanïon (Μειλανίων), son of Amphidamas, and husband of Atalanta. For details, see ATALANTA.

Milëtopölis (Μιλητόπολις : *Muhalich*, or *Hamamli?* Ru.), a city of Mysia, in Asia Minor, at the confluence of the river Rhyndacus and Macestus, and somewhat E. of the lake which was named after it, Lacus Miletopolitis (Μιλητοπολῖτις λίμνη : *Lake of Maniyas*). This lake, which was also called Artynia, lies some miles W. of the larger lake of Apollonia (*Abullionte*).

Miletopolis. [BORYSTHENES].

Milëtus (Μίλητος), son of Apollo and Aria of Crete. Being beloved by Minos and Sarpedon, he attached himself to the latter, and fled from Minos to Asia, where he built the city of Miletus. Ovid (*Met.* ix. 442) calls him a son of Apollo and Deïone, and hence Deïonides.

Milëtus (Μίλητος, Dor. Μίλατος : Μιλήσιος, and on inscriptions, Μειλήσιος : Milesius), one of the greatest cities of Asia Minor, belonged territorially to Caria and politically to Ionia, being the S.-most of the 12 cities of the Ionian confederacy. It is mentioned by Homer as a Carian city ; and one of its early names, Lelegeïs, is a sign that the Leleges also formed a part of its population. Its first Greek colonists were said to have been Cretans who were expelled by Minos ; the next were led to it by Neleus at the time of the so-called Ionic migration. Its name was derived from the mythical leader of the Cretan colonists, Miletus : it was also called Pityusa (Πιτυοῦσα), and Anactoria ('Ανακτορία). The city stood upon the S. headland of the Sinus Latmicus, opposite to the mouth of the Maeander, and possessed 4 distinct harbours, protected by a group of islets, called Lade, Dromiscus, and Perne. The city wall enclosed two distinct towns, called the outer and the inner ; the latter, which was also called Old Miletus, stood upon an eminence overhanging the sea, and was of great strength. Its territory extended on both sides of the Maeander, as far apparently as the promontories of Mycale on the N. and Posidium on the S. It was rich in flocks ; and the city was celebrated for its woollen fabrics, the *Milesia vellera*. At a very early period it became a great maritime state, extending its commerce throughout the Mediterranean, and even beyond the Pillars of Hercules, but more especially in the direction of the Euxine, along the shore of which the Milesians planted several important colonies, such as Cyzicus, Sinope, Abydos, Istropolis, Tomi, Olbia or Borysthenes, Apollonia, Odessus, and Panticapaeum. Naucratis in Egypt was also a colony of Miletus. It also occupies a high place in the early history of Greek literature, as the birthplace of the philosophers Thales, Anaximander, and Anaximenes, and of the historians Cadmus and Hecataeus. After the rise of the Lydian monarchy, Miletus, by its naval strength, resisted the attacks of Alyattes and Sadyattes for 11 years, but fell before Croesus, whose success may perhaps be ascribed to the intestine factions which for a long period weakened the city. With the rest of Ionia, it was conquered by Harpagus, the general of Cyrus, in B.C. 557; and under the dominion of the Persians it still retained its prosperity till the great Ionian revolt, of which Miletus was the centre [ARISTAGORAS, HISTIAEUS], and after the suppression of which it was destroyed by the Persians (B.C. 494). It recovered sufficient importance to oppose a vain resistance to Alexander the Great, which brought upon it a second ruin. Under the Roman empire it still appears as a place of some consequence, until its final destruction by the Turks. — Its ruins are difficult to discover, on account of the great change made in the coast by the river Maeander. [MAEANDER.] They are usually supposed to be those at the wretched village of *Palatia*, on the S. bank of the *Mendereh*, a little above its present mouth; but Forbiger has shown that these are more probably the ruins of MYUS, and that those of Miletus are buried in a lake formed by the *Mendereh* at the foot of Mt. Latmus.

MILICHUS, a Phoenician god, represented as the son of a satyr and of the nymph Myrice, and with horns on his head. (Sil. Ital. iii. 103.)

MILICHUS (Μείλιχος), a small river in Achaia, which flowed by the town of Patrae, and is said to have been originally called *Amilichus* ('Αμείλιχος) on account of the human victims sacrificed on its banks to Artemis.

MILO or **MILON** (Μίλων). 1. Of Crotona, son of Diotimus, an athlete, famous for his extraordinary bodily strength. He was 6 times victor in wrestling at the Olympic games, and as often at the Pythian; but having entered the lists at Olympia a 7th time, he was worsted by the superior agility of his adversary. By these successes he obtained great distinction among his countrymen, so that he was even appointed to command the army which defeated the Sybarites, B.C. 511. Many stories are related by ancient writers of Milo's extraordinary feats of strength; such as his carrying a heifer of four years old on his shoulders through the stadium at Olympia, and afterwards eating the whole of it in a single day. The mode of his death is thus related: as he was passing through a forest when enfeebled by age, he saw the trunk of a tree which had been partially split open by woodcutters, and attempted to rend it further, but the wood closed upon his hands, and thus held him fast, in which state he was attacked and devoured by wolves. — 2. A general in the service

of Pyrrhus king of Epirus, who sent him forward with a body of troops to garrison the citadel of Tarentum, previous to his own arrival in Italy. When Pyrrhus finally quitted that country and withdrew into Epirus, he still left Milo in charge of the citadel of Tarentum, together with his son Helenus. — 3. T. **ANNIUS MILO PAPINIANUS**, was the son of C. Papius Celsus and Annia, and was adopted by his maternal grandfather T. Annius Luscus. He was born at Lanuvium, of which place he was in B.C. 53 dictator or chief magistrate. Milo was a man of a daring and unscrupulous character; and as he was deeply in debt, he resolved to obtain a wealthy province. For this purpose he connected himself with the aristocracy. As tribune of the plebs, B.C. 57, he took an active part in obtaining Cicero's recall from exile, and from this time he carried on a fierce and memorable contest with P. Clodius. In 53 Milo was candidate for the consulship, and Clodius for the praetorship of the ensuing year. Each of the candidates kept a gang of gladiators, and there were frequent combats between the rival ruffians in the streets of Rome. At length, on the 20th of January, 52, Milo and Clodius met apparently by accident at Bovillae on the Appian road. An affray ensued between their followers, in which Clodius was slain. At Rome such tumults followed upon the burial of Clodius, that Pompey was appointed sole consul in order to restore order to the state. Pompey immediately brought forward various laws in connection with the late disturbances. As soon as these were passed, Milo was formally accused. All Pompey's influence was directed against him; but Milo was not without hope, since the higher aristocracy, from jealousy of Pompey, supported him, and Cicero undertook his defence. His trial opened on the 4th of April, 52. He was impeached on 3 counts — *de Vi, de Ambitu*, or bribery, and *de Sodalitiis*, or illegal interference with the freedom of elections. L. Domitius Ahenobarbus, a consular, was appointed quaesitor by a special law of Pompey's, and all Rome and thousands of spectators from Italy thronged the forum and its avenues. But Milo's chances of acquittal were wholly marred by the virulence of his adversaries, who insulted and obstructed the witnesses, the process, and the conductors of the defence. Pompey availed himself of these disorders to line the forum and its encompassing hills with soldiers. Cicero was intimidated, and Milo was condemned. Had he even been acquitted on the 1st count, *de Vi*, the two other charges of bribery and conspiracy awaited him. He therefore went into exile. Cicero, who could not deliver, re-wrote and expanded the defence of Milo — the extant oration — and sent it to him at Marseilles. Milo remarked, "I am glad this was not spoken, since I must have been acquitted, and then had never known the delicate flavour of these Marseilles-mullets." Caesar refused to recall Milo from exile in 49, when he permitted many of the other exiles to return. In the following year (48) M. Caelius, the praetor, had, during Caesar's absence, promulgated a bill for the adjustment of debts. Needing desperate allies, Caelius accordingly invited Milo to Italy, as the fittest tool for his purposes. At the head of a band of criminals and run-away slaves, Milo appeared in the S. of Italy, but was opposed by the praetor Q. Pedius, and slain under the walls of an obscure fort in the district of Thurii. Milo, in 57, married Fausta, a daughter of the dictator Sulla. She proved a faithless wife, and Sallust, the historian, was soundly scourged by Milo for an intrigue with her.

Miltiades (Μιλτιάδης). 1. Son of Cypselus, was a man of considerable distinction in Athens in the time of Pisistratus. The Doloncians, a Thracian tribe dwelling in the Chersonesus, being hard pressed in war by the Absinthians, applied to the Delphic oracle for advice, and were directed to admit a colony led by the man who should be the first to entertain them after they left the temple. This was Miltiades, who, eager to escape from the rule of Pisistratus, gladly took the lead of a colony under the sanction of the oracle, and became tyrant of the Chersonesus, which he fortified by a wall built across its isthmus. In a war with the people of Lampsacus he was taken prisoner, but was set at liberty on the demand of Croesus. He died without leaving any children, and his sovereignty passed into the hands of Stesagoras, the son of his half-brother Cimon. Sacrifices and games were instituted in his honour, in which no Lampsacene was suffered to take part.—2. Son of Cimon and brother of Stesagoras, became tyrant of the Chersonesus on the death of the latter, being sent out by Pisistratus from Athens to take possession of the vacant inheritance. By a stratagem he got the chief men of the Chersonesus into his power and threw them into prison, and took a force of mercenaries into his pay. In order to strengthen his position still more, he married Hegesipyla, the daughter of a Thracian prince named Olorus. He joined Darius Hystaspis on his expedition against the Scythians, and was left with the other Greeks in charge of the bridge over the Danube. When the appointed time had expired, and Darius had not returned, Miltiades recommended the Greeks to destroy the bridge and leave Darius to his fate. Some time after the expedition of Darius an inroad of the Scythians drove Miltiades from his possessions; but after the enemy had retired the Doloncians brought him back. It appears to have been between this period and his withdrawal to Athens, that Miltiades conquered and expelled the Pelasgian inhabitants of Lemnos and Imbros and subjected the islands to the dominion of Attica. Lemnos and Imbros belonged to the Persian dominions; and it is probable that this encroachment on the Persian possessions was the cause which drew upon Miltiades the hostility of Darius, and led him to fly from the Chersonesus, when the Phoenician fleet approached, after the subjugation of Ionia. Miltiades reached Athens in safety, but his eldest son Metiochus fell into the hands of the Persians. At Athens Miltiades was arraigned, as being amenable to the penalties enacted against tyranny, but was acquitted. When Attica was threatened with invasion by the Persians under Datis and Artaphernes, Miltiades was chosen one of the ten generals. Miltiades by his arguments induced the polemarch Callimachus to give the casting vote in favour of risking a battle with the enemy, the opinions of the ten generals being equally divided. Miltiades waited till his turn came, and then drew his army up in battle array on the ever memorable field of Marathon. [MARATHON.] After the defeat of the Persians Miltiades endeavoured to urge the Athenians to measures of retaliation, and induced them to entrust to him an armament of 70 ships, without knowing the purpose for which they were designed. He proceeded to attack the island of Paros, for the purpose of gratifying a private enmity. His attacks, however, were unsuccessful; and after receiving a dangerous hurt in the leg, while penetrating into a sacred enclosure on some superstitious errand, he was compelled to raise the siege and return to Athens, where he was impeached by Xanthippus for having deceived the people. His wound had turned into a gangrene, and being unable to plead his cause in person, he was brought into court on a couch, his brother Tisagoras conducting his defence for him. He was condemned; but on the ground of his services to the state the penalty was commuted to a fine of 50 talents, the cost of the equipment of the armament. Being unable to pay this, he was thrown into prison, where he not long after died of his wound. The fine was subsequently paid by his son Cimon.

Milvius Pons. [ROMA.]

Milyas (ἡ Μιλυάς: Μιλύαι, Milyae), was originally the name of all Lycia; but it was afterwards applied to the high table land in the N. of Lycia, between the Cadmus and the Taurus, and extending considerably into Pisidia. Its people seem to have been the descendants of the original inhabitants of Lycia. It contained a city of the same name. After the defeat of Antiochus the Great, the Romans gave it to Eumenes, king of Pergamus, but its real government seems to have been in the hands of Pisidian princes.

Mimallon (Μιμαλλών), the Macedonian name of the Bacchantes, or, according to others, of Bacchic Amazons. Ovid (Ars Am. i. 541) uses the form Mimallonides.

Mimas (Μίμας), a giant, said to have been killed by Ares, or by Zeus, with a flash of lightning. The island of Prochyte, near Sicily, was believed to rest upon his body.

Mimnermus (Μίμνερμος), a celebrated elegiac poet, was generally called a Colophonian, but was properly a native of Smyrna, and was descended from those Colophonians who reconquered Smyrna from the Aeolians. He flourished from about B. c. 634 to 600. He was a contemporary of Solon, who, in an extant fragment of one of his poems, addresses him as still living. Only a few fragments of the compositions of Mimnermus have come down to us. They belong chiefly to a poem entitled *Nanno*, and are addressed to the flute-player of that name. The compositions of Mimnermus form an epoch in the history of elegiac poetry. Before his time the elegy had been devoted chiefly either to warlike or national, or to convivial and joyous subjects. Archilochus had, indeed, occasionally employed the elegy for strains of lamentation, but Mimnermus was the first who systematically made it the vehicle for plaintive, mournful, and erotic strains. The instability of human happiness, the helplessness of man, the cares and miseries to which life is exposed, the brief season that man has to enjoy himself in, the wretchedness of old age, are plaintively dwelt upon by him, while love is held up as the only consolation that men possess, life not being worth having when it can no longer be enjoyed. The latter topic was most frequently dwelt upon, and as an erotic poet he was held in high estimation in antiquity. (Hor. *Epist.* ii. 2, 100.) The fragments are published separately by Bach, Lips. 1826.

Minaei (Μιναῖοι), one of the chief peoples of

The Moirae or Parcae (Fates) and Prometheus.
(Visconti, Mus. Pio Clem., vol. 4, tav. 31.) Pages 454, 455.

1. Clio, the Muse of History.
(From a Statue now in Sweden.) Page 460.

2. Euterpe, the Muse of Lyric Poetry.
(From a Statue in the Vatican.) Page 460.

3. Thalia, the Muse of Comedy.
(From a Statue in the Vatican.) Page 460.

4. Melpomene, the Muse of Tragedy.
(From a Statue in the Vatican. Page 460.

[To face p. 448.

6. Erato, the Muse of Erotic Poetry.
(From a Statue in the Vatican.) Page 460.

7. Polymnia, the Muse of the Sublime Hymn.
(From a Statue in the Louvre.) Page 460.

8. Urania, the Muse of Astronomy.
(From a Statue now in Sweden.) Page 460.

9. Calliope, the Muse of Epic Poetry.
(From a Statue in the Vatican.) Page 460.

Niobe and her Children.
(Visconti, Mus. Pio Clem., vol. 4, tav. 17.) Page 482. See Illustrations opposite p. 484.

Arabia, dwelt on the W. coast of Arabia Felix, and in the interior of the peninsula, and carried on a large trade in spices, incense, and the other products of the land.

Minas Sabbatha (Μείνας Σαβατθά), a fort in Babylonia, built in the time of the later Roman empire, on the site of Seleucia, which the Romans had destroyed.

Mincius (*Mincio*), a river in Gallia Transpadana, flows through the lake Benacus (*Lago di Garda*), and falls into the Po, a little below Mantua.

Mindarus (Μίνδαρος), a Lacedaemonian, succeeded Astyochus in the command of the Lacedaemonian fleet, B.C. 411. He was defeated and slain in battle by the Athenians near Cyzicus in the following year.

Minerva, called Athena by the Greeks. The Greek goddess is spoken of in a separate article. [ATHENA.] Minerva was one of the great Roman divinities. Her name seems to be of the same root as *mens;* and she is accordingly the thinking, calculating, and inventive power personified. Jupiter was the 1st, Juno the 2nd, and Minerva the 3rd in the number of the Capitoline divinities. Tarquin, the son of Demaratus, was believed to have united the 3 divinities in one common temple, and hence, when repasts were prepared for the gods, these 3 always went together. She was the daughter of Jupiter, and is said to have sometimes wielded the thunderbolts of her father. As Minerva was a virgin divinity, and her father the supreme god, the Romans easily identified her with the Greek Athena, and accordingly all the attributes of Athena were gradually transferred to the Roman Minerva. But we confine ourselves at present to those which were peculiar to the Roman goddess. Being a maiden goddess, her sacrifices consisted of calves which had not borne the yoke. She is said to have invented numbers; and it is added that the law respecting the driving in of the annual nail was for this reason attached to the temple of Minerva. She was worshipped as the patroness of all the arts and trades, and at her festival she was particularly invoked by all who desired to distinguish themselves in any art or craft, such as painting, poetry, the art of teaching, medicine, dyeing, spinning, weaving, and the like. This character of the goddess may be perceived also from the proverbs " to do a thing *pingui Minerva,*" i. e. to do a thing in an awkward or clumsy manner; and *sus Minervam,* of a stupid person who presumed to set right an intelligent one. Minerva, however, was the patroness, not only of females, on whom she conferred skill in sewing, spinning, weaving, &c., but she also guided men in the dangers of war, where victory is gained by cunning, prudence, courage, and perseverance. Hence she was represented with a helmet, shield, and a coat of mail; and the booty gained in war was frequently dedicated to her. Minerva was further believed to be the inventor of musical instruments, especially wind instruments, the use of which was very important in religious worship, and which were accordingly subjected to a sort of purification every year on the last day of the festival of Minerva. This festival lasted 5 days, from the 10th to the 23rd of March, and was called *Quinquatrus,* because it began on the 5th day after the ides of the month. This number of days was not accidental, for we are told that the number 5 was sacred to Minerva.

The most ancient temple of Minerva at Rome was probably that on the Capitol; another existed on the Aventine; and she had a chapel at the foot of the Caelian hill, where she bore the surname of Capta.

Minervae Arx or **Minervium** (*Castro*), a hill on the coast of Calabria, where Aeneas is said to have landed.

Minervae Promontorium (*Punta della Campanella* or *della Minerva*), a rocky promontory in Campania, running out a long way into the sea, 6 miles S.E. of Surrentum, on whose summit was a temple of Minerva, which was said to have been built by Ulysses, and which was still standing in the time of Seneca. Here the Sirens are reported to have dwelt. The Greeks regarded it as the N.W. boundary of Oenotria.

Minio (*Mignone*), a small river in Etruria, which rises near Satrium, and falls into the Tyrrhene sea between Graviscae and Centum Cellae.

Minius (*Minho*), a river in the N.W. of Spain, rises in the Cantabrian mountains in the N. of Gallaecia, and falls into the ocean. It was also called Baenis, and derived its name of Minius from the *minium* or vermilion carried down by its waters.

Minoa (Μινώα). **1.** A small island in the Saronic gulf, off the coast of Megaris, and opposite a promontory of the same name, was united to the mainland by a bridge, and formed, with the promontory, the harbour of Nisaea. [See p. 429.] —**2.** A town on the E. coast of Laconia, and on a promontory of the same name, N.E. of Epidaurus Limera.—**3.** A town on the W. part of the N. coast of Crete, between the promontories Drepanum and Psacum.—**4.** A town on the E. part of the N. coast of Crete, belonging to the territory of Lyctus, and situated on the narrowest part of the island.—**5.** A town in Sicily. See HERACLEA MINOA.

Minos (Μίνως). **1.** Son of Zeus and Europa, brother of Rhadamanthus, was the king and legislator of Crete. After his death he became one of the judges of the shades in Hades. He was the father of Deucalion and Ariadne; and, according to Apollodorus, the brother of Sarpedon. Some traditions relate that Minos married Itone, daughter of Lyctius, by whom he had a son, Lycastus, and that the latter became, by Ida, the daughter of Corybas, the father of another Minos. But it should be observed, that Homer and Hesiod know only of one Minos, the ruler of Cnossus, and the son and friend of Zeus; and that they relate nearly the same things about him which later traditions assign to a second Minos, the grandson of the former. In this case, as in many other mythical traditions, a rationalistic criticism attempted to solve contradictions and difficulties in the stories about a person, by assuming that the contradictory accounts must refer to two different personages. —**2.** Grandson of the former, and a son of Lycastus and Ida, was likewise a king and lawgiver of Crete. He is described as the husband of Pasiphaë, a daughter of Helios; and as the father of Catreus, Deucalion, Glaucus, Androgeus, Acalle, Xenodice, Ariadne, and Phaedra. After the death of Asterius, Minos aimed at the supremacy of Crete, and declared that it was destined to him by the gods; in proof of which, he asserted that the gods always answered his prayers. Accordingly, as he was offering up a sacrifice to Poseidon, he prayed that a bull might come forth from the sea,

G G

and promised to sacrifice the animal. The bull appeared, and Minos became king of Crete. (Others say that Minos disputed the government with his brother, Sarpedon, and conquered.) But Minos, who admired the beauty of the bull, did not sacrifice him, and substituted another in his place. Poseidon therefore rendered the bull furious, and made Pasiphaë conceive a passion for the animal. Daedalus enabled Pasiphaë to gratify her passion, and she became by the bull the mother of the Minotaurus, a monster with a human body and a bull's head, or, according to others, with a bull's body and a human head. The monster was kept in the labyrinth at Cnossus, constructed by Daedalus. Daedalus fled from Crete to escape the wrath of Minos and took refuge in Sicily. Minos followed him to Sicily, and was there slain by Cocalus and his daughters. —Minos is further said to have divided Crete into 3 parts, and to have ruled 9 years. The Cretans traced their legal and political institutions to Minos. He is said to have been instructed in the art of lawgiving by Zeus himself; and the Spartan, Lycurgus, was believed to have taken the legislation of Minos as his model. In his time Crete was a powerful maritime state; and Minos not only checked the piratical pursuits of his contemporaries, but made himself master of the Greek islands of the Aegean. The most ancient legends describe Minos as a just and wise law-giver, whereas the later accounts represent him as an unjust and cruel tyrant. In order to avenge the wrong done to his son Androgeus [ANDROGEUS] at Athens, he made war against the Athenians and Megarians. He subdued Megara, and compelled the Athenians either every year or every 9 years, to send him as a tribute 7 youths and 7 maidens, who were devoured in the labyrinth by the Minotaurus. The monster was slain by Theseus.

Minotaurus. [MINOS.]

Mintha (Μίνθη), a daughter of Cocytus, beloved by Hades, was metamorphosed by Demeter or Persephone into a plant called after her *mintha*, or mint. In the neighbourhood of Pylos there was a hill called after her, and at its foot there was a temple of Pluto, and a grove of Demeter.

Minthē (Μίνθη: *Vunuka*), a mountain of Elis in Triphylia, near Pylos.

Minturnae (Minturnensis: *Trajetta*), an important town in Latium, on the frontiers of Campania, was situated on the Appia Via, and on both banks of the Liris, and near the mouth of this river. It was an ancient town of the Ausones or Aurunci, but surrendered to the Romans of its own accord, and received a Roman colony B.C. 296. It was subsequently recolonised by Julius Caesar. In its neighbourhood was a grove sacred to the nymph Marica, and also extensive marshes (*Paludes Minturnenses*), formed by the overflowing of the river Liris, in which Marius was taken prisoner. [See p. 418, a.] The neighbourhood of Minturnae produced good wine. There are the ruins of an amphitheatre and of an aqueduct at the modern *Trajetta*.

Minuciānus (Μινουκιανός). 1. A Greek rhetorician, was a contemporary of the celebrated rhetorician Hermogenes of Tarsus (fl. A.D. 170), with whom he was at variance.—2. An Athenian, the son of Nicagoras, was also a Greek rhetorician, and lived in the reign of Gallienus (A.D. 260—

268). He was the author of several rhetorical works, and a portion of his Τέχνη ῥητορική is extant, and is published in the 9th volume of Walz's *Rhetores Graeci.*

Minucius Augurīnus. [AUGURINUS.]

Minucius Basilus. [BASILUS.]

Minucius Rufus. 1. M., consul B.C. 221, when he carried on war against the Istrians. In 217 he was magister equitum to the dictator Q. Fabius Maximus. The cautious policy of Fabius displeased Minucius; and accordingly when Fabius was called away to Rome, Minucius disobeyed the positive commands of the dictator, and risked a battle with a portion of Hannibal's troops. He was fortunate enough to gain a victory; in consequence of which he became so popular at Rome, that a bill was passed, giving him equal military power with the dictator. The Roman army was now divided, and each portion encamped separately under its own general. Anxious for distinction, Minucius eagerly accepted a battle which was offered him by Hannibal, but was defeated, and his troops were only saved from total destruction by the timely arrival of Fabius, with all his forces. Thereupon Minucius generously acknowledged his error, gave up his separate command, and placed himself again under the authority of the dictator. He fell at the battle of Cannae in the following year.—2. Q., plebeian aedile 201, praetor 200, and consul 197, when he carried on war against the Boii with success. In 189 he was one of the 10 commissioners sent into Asia after the conquest of Antiochus the Great; and in 183 he was one of the 3 ambassadors sent into Gaul.—3. M., praetor 197.—4. M., tribune of the plebs 121, brought forward a bill to repeal the laws of C. Gracchus. This Marcus Minucius and his brother Quintus are mentioned as arbiters between the inhabitants of Genua and the Viturii, in a very interesting inscription, which was discovered in the year 1506, about 10 miles from the modern city of Genoa.—5. Q., consul 110, obtained Macedonia as his province, carried on war with success against the barbarians in Thrace, and triumphed on his return to Rome. He perpetuated the memory of his triumph by building the Porticus Minucia, near the Circus Flaminius.

Minucius Felix. [FELIX.]

Minyae (Μινύαι), an ancient Greek race, who originally dwelt in Thessaly. Iolcos, in Thessaly, was one of their most ancient seats. Their ancestral hero, Minyas, is said to have migrated from Thessaly into the N. of Boeotia, and there to have established the empire of the Minyae, with the capital of Orchomenos. [ORCHOMENOS.] As the greater part of the Argonauts were descended from the Minyae, they are themselves called Minyae. The descendants of the Argonauts founded a colony in Lemnos, called Minyae. Thence they proceeded to Elis Triphylia, and to the island of Thera.

Minyas (Μινύας), son of Chryses, and the ancestral hero of the race of the Minyae. The accounts of his genealogy vary very much in the different traditions, for some call him a son of Orchomenus or Eteocles, others of Poseidon, Aleus, Ares, Sisyphus, or Halmus. He is further called the husband of Tritogenia, Clytodora, or Phanosyra. Orchomenus, Presbon, Athamas, Diochthondas, Eteoclymene, Periclymene, Leucippe, Arsinoë, and Alcathoë or Alcithoë, are mentioned as his children. His tomb was shown at Orchomenos in Boeotia. A daughter of Minyas was called *Minyeias* (*-ădis*) or *Minēis* (*-ĭdis*). (See Ov. *Met.* iv. 1. 32.)

Mirobriga. 1. A town of the Celtici in Lusitania, on the coast of the ocean. — 2. A Roman municipium in the territory of the Turduli, in Hispania Baetica, on the road from Emerita to Caesaraugusta.

Misēnum (*Punta di Miseno*), a promontory in Campania, S. of Cumae, said to have derived its name from Misenus, the companion and trumpeter of Aeneas, who was drowned and buried here. The bay formed by this promontory was converted by Augustus into an excellent harbour, and was made the principal station of the Roman fleet on the Tyrrhene sea. A town sprung up around the harbour, and here the admiral of the fleet usually resided. The inhabitants were called Misenates and Misenenses. The Roman nobles had previously built villas on the coast. Here was the villa of C. Marius, which was purchased by Lucullus, and which afterwards passed into the hands of the emperor Tiberius, who died at this place.

Misitheus, the father-in-law of the emperor Gordian III., who married his daughter Sabinia Tranquillina in A. D. 241. Misitheus was a man of learning, virtue, and ability. He was appointed by his son-in-law praefect of the praetorians, and effected many important reforms in the royal household. He accompanied Gordian in his expedition against the Persians, whom he defeated ; but in the course of this war he was cut off either by disease, or by the treachery of his successor Philippus, 243.

Mithras (Μίθρας), the god of the sun among the Persians. About the time of the Roman emperors his worship was introduced at Rome, and thence spread over all parts of the empire. The god is commonly represented as a handsome youth, wearing the Phrygian cap and attire, and kneeling on a bull which is thrown on the ground, and whose throat he is cutting. The bull is at the same time attacked by a dog, a serpent, and a scorpion. This group appears frequently among ancient works of art, and a fine specimen is preserved in the British Museum.

Mithridates or **Mithradates** (Μιθριδάτης or Μιθραδάτης), a common name among the Medes and Persians, derived from *Mitra* or *Mithra*, the Persian name for the sun, and the root *da*, signifying "to give." Mithridates would therefore mean, "given by the sun." 1. I. King, or, more properly, satrap of Pontus, was son of Ariobarzanes I., and was succeeded by Ariobarzanes II., about B. C. 363. The kings of Pontus claimed to be lineally descended from one of the 7 Persians who had conspired against the Magi, and who was subsequently established by Darius Hystaspis in the government of the countries bordering on the Euxine sea. Very little is known of their history until after the fall of the Persian empire. — 2. II. King of Pontus (337—302), succeeded his father Ariobarzanes II., and was the founder of the independent kingdom of Pontus. After the death of Alexander the Great, he was for a time subject to Antigonus ; but during the war between the successors of Alexander, he succeeded in establishing his independence. He died at the age of 84. — 3. III. King of Pontus (302—266), son and successor of the preceding. He enlarged his paternal dominions by the acquisition of great part

of Cappadocia and Paphlagonia. He was succeeded by his son Ariobarzanes III. — 4. IV King of Pontus (about 240—190), son and successor of Ariobarzanes III. He gave his daughter Laodice in marriage to Antiochus III. He was succeeded by his son Pharnaces I. — 5. V. King of Pontus (about 156—120), surnamed Euergetes, son and successor of Pharnaces I. He was the first of the kings of Pontus who made an alliance with the Romans, whom he assisted in the 3rd Punic war and in the war against Aristonicus (131—129). He was assassinated at Sinope by a conspiracy among his own immediate attendants. — 6. VI. King of Pontus (120—63), surnamed Eupator, also Dionysus, but more commonly the Great, was the son and successor of the preceding, and was only 11 years old at the period of his accession. We have very imperfect information concerning the earlier years of his reign, and much of what has been transmitted to us wears a very suspicious aspect. We are told that immediately on ascending the throne he found himself assailed by the designs of his guardians, but that he succeeded in eluding all their machinations, partly by displaying a courage and address in warlike exercises beyond his years, partly by the use of antidotes against poison, to which he began thus early to accustom himself. In order to evade the designs formed against his life, he also devoted much of his time to hunting, and took refuge in the remotest and most unfrequented regions, under pretence of pursuing the pleasures of the chase. Whatever truth there may be in these accounts, it is certain that when he attained to manhood, he was not only endowed with consummate skill in all martial exercises, and possessed of a bodily frame inured to all hardships, as well as a spirit to brave every danger, but his naturally vigorous intellect had been improved by careful culture. As a boy he had been brought up at Sinope, where he had probably received the elements of a Greek education ; and so powerful was his memory, that he is said to have learnt not less than 25 languages, and to have been able in the days of his greatest power to transact business with the deputies of every tribe subject to his rule in their own peculiar dialect. The first steps of his career were marked by blood. He is said to have murdered his mother, to whom a share in the royal authority had been left by Mithridates Euergetes ; and this was followed by the assassination of his brother. In the early part of his reign he subdued the barbarian tribes between the Euxine and the confines of Armenia, including the whole of Colchis and the province called Lesser Armenia, and even extended his conquests beyond the Caucasus. He assisted Parisades, king of the Bosporus, against the Sarmatians and Roxolani, and rendered the whole of the Tauric Chersonese tributary to his kingdom. After the death of Parisades, the kingdom of Bosporus itself was incorporated with his dominions. He was now in possession of such great power, that he began to deem himself equal to a contest with Rome itself. Many causes of dissension had already arisen between them, but Mithridates had hitherto submitted to the mandates of Rome. Even after expelling Ariobarzanes from Cappadocia, and Nicomedes from Bithynia in 90, he offered no resistance to the Romans when they restored these monarchs to their kingdom. But when Nicomedes, urged by the Roman legates, invaded the territories of Mithridates, the latter made preparations for immediate hostilities. His success was rapid and striking. In 88, he drove Ariobarzanes out of Cappadocia, and Nicomedes out of Bithynia, defeated the Roman generals who had supported the latter, made himself master of Phrygia and Galatia, and at last of the Roman province of Asia. During the winter he issued the sanguinary order to all the cities of Asia to put to death, on the same day, all the Roman and Italian citizens who were to be found within their walls. So hateful had the Romans rendered themselves, that these commands were obeyed with alacrity by almost all the cities of Asia, and 80,000 Romans and Italians are said to have perished in this fearful massacre. Meantime Sulla had received the command of the war against Mithridates, and crossed over into Greece in 87. Mithridates, however, had resolved not to await the Romans in Asia, but had already sent his general Archelaus into Greece, at the head of a powerful army. The war proved unfavourable to the king. Archelaus was twice defeated by Sulla with immense loss, near Chaeronea and Orchomenos in Boeotia (86). About the same time Mithridates was himself defeated in Asia by Fimbria. [Fim-BRIA.] These disasters led him to sue for peace, which Sulla was willing to grant, because he was anxious to return to Italy, which was entirely in the hands of his enemies. Mithridates consented to abandon all his conquests in Asia, to pay a sum of 2000 talents, and to surrender to the Romans a fleet of 70 ships. Thus terminated the 1st Mithridatic war (84). — Shortly afterwards Murena, who had been left in command of Asia by Sulla, invaded the dominions of Mithridates (83), under the flimsy pretext that the king had not yet evacuated the whole of Cappadocia. In the following year (82) Murena renewed his hostile incursions, but was defeated by Mithridates on the banks of the river Halys. But shortly afterwards Murena received peremptory orders from Sulla to desist from hostilities ; in consequence of which peace was again restored. This is usually called the 2nd Mithridatic war. — Mithridates, however, was well aware that the peace between him and Rome was in fact a mere suspension of hostilities ; and that the republic would never suffer the massacre of her citizens in Asia to remain ultimately unpunished. No formal treaty was ever concluded between Mithridates and the Roman senate ; and the king had in vain endeavoured to obtain the ratification of the terms agreed on between him and Sulla. The death of Nicomedes III., king of Bithynia, at the beginning of 74, brought matters to a crisis. That monarch left his dominions by will to the Roman people ; and Bithynia was accordingly declared a Roman province : but Mithridates asserted that the late king had left a legitimate son by his wife Nysa, whose pretensions he immediately prepared to support by his arms. He had employed the last few years in forming a powerful army, armed and disciplined in the Roman manner ; and he now took the field with 120,000 foot soldiers, 16,000 horse, and a vast number of barbarian auxiliaries. This was the commencement of the 3rd Mithridatic war. The two Roman consuls, Lucullus and Cotta, were unable to oppose his first irruption. He traversed Bithynia without encountering any resistance ; and when at length Cotta ventured to give him battle under the walls of Chalcedon, the

consul was totally defeated both by sea and land. Mithridates then proceeded to lay siege to Cyzicus both by sea and land. Lucullus marched to the relief of the city, cut off the king's supplies, and eventually compelled him to raise the siege, early in 73. On his retreat Mithridates suffered great loss, and eventually took refuge in Pontus. Hither Lucullus followed him in the next year. The new army, which the king had collected, was entirely defeated by the Roman general ; and Mithridates, despairing of opposing the farther progress of Lucullus, took refuge in the dominions of his son-in-law Tigranes, the king of Armenia. Tigranes at first showed no disposition to attempt the restoration of his father-in-law ; but being offended at the haughty conduct of Appius Claudius, whom Lucullus had sent to demand the surrender of Mithridates, the Armenian king not only refused this request, but determined to prepare for war with the Romans. Accordingly in 69 Lucullus marched into Armenia, defeated Tigranes and Mithridates near Tigranocerta, and in the next year (68) again defeated the allied monarchs near Artaxata. The Roman general then turned aside into Mesopotamia, and laid siege to Nisibis. Here the Roman soldiers broke out into open mutiny, and demanded to be led home ; and Lucullus was obliged to raise the siege, and return to Asia Minor. Meanwhile Mithridates had taken advantage of the absence of Lucullus to invade Pontus at the head of a large army. He defeated Fabius and Triarius, to whom the defence of Pontus had been committed ; and when Lucullus returned to Pontus, he was unable to resume the offensive in consequence of the mutinous spirit of his own soldiers. Mithridates was thus able before the close of 67 to regain possession of the greater part of his hereditary dominions. In the following year (66) the conduct of the war was entrusted to Pompey. Hostilities were resumed with greater vigour than ever. Mithridates was obliged to retire before the Romans, but was surprised and defeated by Pompey ; and as Tigranes now refused to admit him into his dominions, he resolved to plunge with his small army into the heart of Colchis, and thence make his way to the Palus Maeotis and the Cimmerian Bosporus. Arduous as this enterprise appeared it was successfully accomplished ; and he at length established himself without opposition at Panticapaeum, the capital of Bosporus. He had now nothing to fear from the pursuit of Pompey, who turned his arms first against Tigranes, and afterwards against Syria. Unable to obtain peace from Pompey, except he would come in person to make his submission, Mithridates conceived the daring project of marching round the N. and W. coasts of the Euxine, through the wild tribes of the Sarmatians and Getae, and having gathered round his standard all these barbarian nations, to penetrate into Italy itself. But meanwhile disaffection had made rapid progress among his followers. His son Pharnaces at length openly rebelled against him. He was joined both by the whole army and the citizens of Panticapaeum, who unanimously proclaimed him king ; and Mithridates, who had taken refuge in a strong tower, saw that no choice remained to him but death or captivity. Hereupon he took poison, which he constantly carried with him ; but his constitution had been so long inured to antidotes, that it did not produce the desired effect, and he was compelled to call in the assistance of one of his Gaulish mercenaries to despatch him with his sword. He died in 63. His body was sent by Pharnaces to Pompey at Amisus, as a token of his submission ; but the conqueror caused it to be interred with regal honours in the sepulchre of his forefathers at Sinope. He was 68 or 69 years old at the time of his death, and had reigned 57 years, of which 25 had been occupied, with only a few brief intervals, in one continued struggle against the Roman power. The estimation in which he was held by his adversaries is the strongest testimony to his great abilities : Cicero calls him the greatest of all kings after Alexander, and in another passage says that he was a more formidable opponent than any other monarch whom the Roman arms had yet encountered.—7. Kings of Parthia. [ARSACES, 6, 9, 13.]—8. Of Pergamus, son of Menodotus ; but his mother having had an amour with Mithridates the Great, he was generally looked upon as in reality the son of that monarch. The king himself bestowed great care on his education ; and he appears as early as 64 to have exercised the chief control over the affairs of his native city. At a subsequent period he served under Julius Caesar in the Alexandrian war (48) ; and after the defeat of Pharnaces in the following year (47), Caesar bestowed upon Mithridates the kingdom of the Bosporus, and also the tetrarchy of the Galatians. But the kingdom of the Bosporus still remained to be won, for Asander, who had revolted against Pharnaces, was in fact master of the whole country, and Mithridates having attempted to expel Asander, was defeated and slain.

Mithridátis Régio (Μιθριδάτου χώρα), a district of Sarmatia Asiatica, on the W. side of the river Rha (*Wolga*), so called because it was the place of refuge of the last Mithridates, in the reign of Claudius.

Mitylēnē. [MYTILENE.]

Mnaséas (Μνασέας), of Patara in Lycia, not of Patrae in Achaia, was a pupil of Eratosthenes, and a grammarian of considerable celebrity. He wrote 2 works, one of a chorographical description, entitled *Periplus* (Περίπλους), and the other a collection of oracles given at Delphi.

Mnēmē (Μνήμη), i. e. memory, one of the 3 Muses who were in early times worshipped at Ascra in Boeotia. There seems to have been also a tradition that Mneme was the mother of the Muses, for Ovid (*Met.* v. 268) calls them Mnemonides ; unless this be only an abridged form for the daughters of Mnemosyne. [MUSAE.]

Mnemosynē (Μνημοσύνη), i. e. memory, daughter of Uranus, and one of the Titanides, became by Zeus the mother of the Muses.

Mnesarchus (Μνήσαρχος). 1. Son of Euphron or Euthyphron, and father of Pythagoras. He was generally believed not to have been of purely Greek origin. According to some accounts, he belonged to the Tyrrhenians of Lemnos and Imbros, and is said to have been an engraver of rings. According to other accounts, the name of the father of Pythagoras was Marmacus, whose father Hippasus came from Phlius. — 2. Grandson of the preceding, and son of Pythagoras and Theano. According to some accounts he succeeded Aristaeus as president of the Pythagorean school. — 3. A Stoic philosopher, a disciple of Panaetius, flourished about B. c. 110, and taught at Athens. Among his pupils was Antiochus of Ascalon.

Mnesicles (Μνησικλῆς), one of the great Athenian artists of the age of Pericles, was the architect of the *Propylaea* of the Acropolis, the building of which occupied 5 years, B. C. 437—433. It is said that, during the progress of the work, he fell from the summit of the building, and was supposed to be mortally injured. but was cured by a herb which Athena showed to Pericles in a dream.

Mnesithēus (Μνησίθεος), a physician, was a native of Athens, and lived probably in the 4th century B. C., as he is quoted by the comic poet Alexis. He enjoyed a great reputation, and is frequently mentioned by Galen, and others.

Mnester (Μνήστηρ), a celebrated pantomime actor in the reigns of Caligula and Claudius, was also one of the lovers of the empress Messalina, and was put to death upon the ruin of the latter.

Mnestheus, a Trojan, who accompanied Aeneas to Italy, and is said to have been the ancestral hero of the Memmii.

Moábitis (Μωαβῖτις, Μόβα: Μωαβῖται, Moabitae : O. T. Moab, for both country and people), a district of Arabia Petraea, E. of the Dead Sea, from the river Arnon (*Wady-el-Mojib*, the boundary between Palestine and Arabia) on the N., to Zoar, near the S. end of the Dead Sea, on the S., between the Amorites on the N., the Midianites on the E., and the Edomites on the S., that is, before the Israelitish conquest of Canaan. At an earlier period, the country of Moab had extended N.-wards, beyond the N. end of the Dead Sea, and along the E. bank of the Jordan, as far as the river Jabbok, but it had been wrested from them by the Amorites. The plains E. of the Jordan were, however, still called the plains of Moab. The Moabites were left undisturbed by the Israelites on their march to Canaan ; but Balak, king of Moab, through fear of the Israelites, did what he could to harm them, first by his vain attempt to induce the prophet Balaam to curse the people whom a divine impulse forced him to bless, and then by seducing them to worship Baal-peor. Hence the hereditary enmity between the Israelites and Moabites, and the threatenings denounced against Moab by the Hebrew prophets. In the time of the Judges they subdued the S. part of the Jewish territory, with the assistance of the Ammonites and Amalekites, and held it for 18 years (Judges iii. 12 foll.). They were conquered by David, after the partition of whose kingdom they belonged to the kingdom of Israel. They revolted after the death of Ahab (B. C. 896) and appear to have become virtually independent ; and after the 10 tribes had been carried into captivity, the Moabites seem to have recovered the N. part of their original territory. They were subdued by Nebuchadnezzar, with other nations bordering on Palestine, very soon after the Babylonian conquest of Judaea, after which they scarcely appear as a distinct nation, but, after a few references to them, they disappear in the general name of the Arabians. The name Moabitis, however, was still applied to the district of Arabia, between the Arnon (the S. frontier of Peraea, or Palestine E. of the Jordan), and the Nabathaei, in the mountains of Seir. The Moabites were a kindred race with the Hebrews, being descended from Moab, the son of Lot. They worshipped Baal-Peor and Chemosh with most licentious rites, and they sometimes offered human sacrifices. Their government was monarchical. They were originally a pastoral people ; but the excessive fertility of their country, which is a mountainous tract intersected with rich valleys and numerous streams, led them to diligence and success in agriculture. The frequent ruins of towns and traces of paved roads, which still cover the face of the country, show how populous and prosperous it was. The chief city, Ar or Rabbath-Moab, aft. Areopolis (*Rabba*, Ru.), was about 25 miles S. of the Arnon.

Modestinus, Herennius, a Roman jurist, and a pupil of Ulpian, flourished in the reigns of Alexander Severus, Maximinus and the Gordians, A. D. 222—244. He taught law to the younger Maximinus. Though Modestinus is the latest of the great Roman jurists, he ranks among the most distinguished. There are 345 excerpts in the Digest from his writings, the titles of which show the extent and variety of his labours.

Modestus, a military writer, the author of a *Libellus de Vocabulis Rei Militaris*, addressed to the emperor Tacitus, A. D. 275. It is very brief, and presents no features of interest. Printed in all the chief collections of *Scriptores de Re Militari*.

Modicia (*Monza*). a town in Gallia Transpadana, on the river Lambrus, N. of Mediolanum (*Milan*), where Theodoric built a palace, and Theodolinda, queen of the Langobards, a splendid church, which still contains many of the precious gifts of this queen.

Modin (Μοδείν, -εείν, or ιείμ), a little village on a mountain N. of Lydda or Diospolis, on the extreme N.W. of Judaea, celebrated as the native place of the Maccabaean family. Its exact site is uncertain.

Moenus, Moenis, Maenus, or **Menus** (*Main*), a river in Germany, which rises in the Sudeti Montes, flows through the territory of the Hermunduri and the Agri decumates of the Romans, and falls into the Rhine opposite Mogontiacum.

Moeris or **Myris** (Μοίρις, Μύρις), a king of Egypt, who, Herodotus tells us, reigned some 900 years before his own visit to that country, which seems to have been about B. C. 450. We hear of Moeris that he formed the lake known by his name, and joined it by a canal to the Nile, in order to receive the waters of the river when they were superabundant, and to supply the defect when they did not rise sufficiently. In the lake he built 2 pyramids on each of which was a stone statue, seated on a throne, and intended to represent himself and his wife.

Moeris (Μοίρις), commonly called **Moeris Atticista,** a distinguished grammarian, the author of a work still extant, entitled Λέξεις 'Αττικαί, though the title varies somewhat in different manuscripts. Of the personal history of the author nothing is known. He is conjectured to have lived about the end of the 2nd century after Christ. His treatise is a sort of comparison of the Attic with other Greek dialects ; consisting of a list of Attic words and expressions, which are illustrated by those of other dialects, especially the common Greek. Edited by Pierson, Lugd. Bat. 1759.

Moeris Lacus (Μοίριος or Μοίριδος λίμνη : *Birket-el-Keroun*), a great lake on the W. side of the Nile, in Middle Egypt, used for the reception and subsequent distribution of a part of the overflow of the Nile. It was believed by the ancients to have been dug by king Moeris ; but it is really a natural, and not an artificial lake.

Moero (Μοιρώ), or **Myro** (Μυρώ), a poetess of

Byzantium, wife of Andromachus surnamed Philologus, and mother of the grammarian and tragic poet Homerus. lived about B. C. 300. She wrote epic, elegiac, and lyric poems.

Moerocles (Μοιροκλῆς), an Athenian orator, a native of Salamis, was a contemporary of Demosthenes, and like him an opponent of Philip and Alexander.

Moesia, called by the Greeks **Mysia** (Μυσία, also M. ἡ ἐν Εὐρώπῃ, to distinguish it from Mysia in Asia), a country of Europe, was bounded on the S. by M. Haemus, which separated it from Thrace, and by M. Orbelus and Scordus, which separated it from Macedonia, on the W. by M. Scordus and the rivers Drinus and Savus, which separated it from Illyricum and Pannonia, on the N. by the Danube, which separated it from Dacia, and on the E. by the Pontus Euxinus, thus corresponding to the present *Servia* and *Bulgaria*. This country was subdued in the reign of Augustus, but does not appear to have been formally constituted a Roman province till the commencement of the reign of Tiberius. It was originally only one province, but was afterwards formed into 2 provinces (probably after the conquest of Dacia by Trajan), called *Moesia Superior* and *Moesia Inferior*, the former being the western, and the latter the eastern half of the country, and separated from each other by the river Cebrus or Ciabrus, a tributary of the Danube. When Aurelian surrendered Dacia to the barbarians, and removed the inhabitants of that province to the S. of the Danube, the middle part of Moesia was called *Dacia Aureliani ;* and this new province was divided into *Dacia Ripensis*, the district along the Danube, and *Dacia Interior*, the district S. of the latter as far as the frontiers of Macedonia. In the reign of Valens, some of the Goths crossed the Danube and settled in Moesia. These Goths are sometimes called Moeso-Goths, and it was for their use that Ulphilas translated the Scriptures into Gothic about the middle of the 4th century. The original inhabitants of the country, called **Moesi** by the Romans, and **Mysi** (Μυσοί) by the Greeks, were a Thracian race, and were divided into several tribes, such as the TRIBALLI, PEUCINI, &c.

Mogontiacum, Moguntiacum or **Magontiacum** (*Mainz* or *Mayence*), a town on the left bank of the Rhine, opposite the mouth of the river Moenus (*Main*), was situated in the territory of the Vangiones, and was subsequently the capital of the province of Germania Prima. It was a Roman municipium, and was founded, or at least enlarged and fortified, by Drusus. It was always occupied by a strong Roman garrison, and continued to the downfall of the empire to be one of the chief Roman fortresses on the Rhine.

Moirae (Μοῖραι) called **Parcae** by the Romans, the Fates. *Moira* properly signifies " a share," and as a personification " the deity who assigns to every man his fate or his share." Homer usually speaks of one Moira, and only once mentions the *Moirae* in the plural. (*Il.* xxiv. 29.) In his poems Moira is fate personified, which, at the birth of man, spins out the thread of his future life, follows his steps, and directs the consequences of his actions according to the counsel of the gods. But the personification of his Moira is not complete; for he mentions no particular appearance of the goddess, no attributes, and no parentage. His

Moira is therefore quite synonymous with *Aisa* (Αἶσα). — In Hesiod the personification of the Moirae is complete. He calls them daughters of Zeus and Themis, and makes them 3 in number, viz. Clotho, or the spinning fate; Lachesis, or the one who assigns to man his fate; and Atropos, or the fate that cannot be avoided. Later writers differ in their genealogy of the Moirae from that of Hesiod; thus they are called children of Erebus and Night, of Cronos and Night, of Ge and Oceanus, or lastly of Ananke or Necessity. — The character and nature of the Moirae are differently described at different times and by different authors. Sometimes they appear as divinities of fate in the strict sense of the term, and sometimes only as allegorical divinities of the duration of human life. — In the former character they take care that the fate assigned to every being by eternal laws may take its course without obstruction; and Zeus, as well as the other gods and men, must submit to them. They assign to the Erinnyes, who inflict the punishment for evil deeds, their proper functions; and with them they direct fate according to the laws of necessity, whence they are sometimes called the sisters of the Erinnyes. These grave and mighty goddesses were represented by the earliest artists with staffs or sceptres, the symbol of dominion.—The Moirae, as the divinities of the duration of human life, which is determined by the two points of birth and of death, are conceived either as goddesses of birth or as goddesses of death, and hence their number was 2, as at Delphi, and was subsequently increased to 3. The distribution of the functions among the 3 was not strictly observed, for we sometimes find all 3 described as spinning, although this should be the function of Clotho alone, who is moreover often mentioned alone as the representative of all. As goddesses of birth, who spin the thread of the beginning of life, and even prophesy the fate of the newly born, they are mentioned along with Ilithyia, who is called their companion. The symbol with which they, or rather Clotho alone, are represented to indicate this function, is a spindle, and the idea implied in it was carried out so far, that sometimes we read of their breaking or cutting off the thread when life is to end. Being goddesses of fate, they must necessarily know the future, which at times they reveal, and thus become prophetic divinities. As goddesses of death, they appear together with the Keres and the infernal Erinnyes, with whom they are even confounded. For the same reason they, along with the Charites, lead Persephone out of the lower world into the regions of light. The various epithets which poets apply to the Moirae generally refer to the severity, inflexibility, and sternness of fate. They had sanctuaries in many parts of Greece. The poets sometimes describe them as aged and hideous women, and even as lame, to indicate the slow march of fate; but in works of art they are represented as grave maidens, with different attributes, viz., Clotho with a spindle or a roll (the book of fate); Lachesis pointing with a staff to the globe; and Atropos with a pair of scales, or a sun-dial, or a cutting instrument.

Moliōne. [MOLIONES.]

Moliōnes or **Moliōnĭdae** (Μολίονες, Μολίονε, Μολιονίδαι), that is, Eurytus and Cteatus, so called after their mother Molione. They are also called *Actoridae* or *Actoriōne* (᾽Ακτορίωνε) after their reputed father Actor, the husband of Molione,

though they were generally regarded as the sons of Poseidon. According to a late tradition, they were born out of an egg; and it is further stated, that their bodies grew together, so that they had only one body, but 2 heads, 4 arms, and 4 legs. Homer mentions none of these extraordinary circumstances; and, according to him, the Moliones, when yet boys, took part in an expedition of the Epeans against Neleus and the Pylians. They are represented as nephews of Augeas, king of the Epeans. When Hercules marched against Augeas, the latter entrusted the conduct of the war to the Moliones; but as Hercules was taken ill, he concluded peace with Augeas, whereupon his army was attacked and defeated by the Molionidae. In order to take vengeance, he afterwards slew them near Cleonae, on the frontiers of Argolis, when they had been sent from Elis to sacrifice at the Isthmian games, on behalf of the town. —The Moliones are mentioned as conquerors of Nestor in the chariot race, and as having taken part in the Calydonian hunt. Cteatus was the father of Amphimachus by Theronice; and Eurytus, of Thalpius by Theraphone. Their sons Amphimachus and Thalpius led the Epeans to Troy.

Molo, surname of Apollonius, the rhetorician of Rhodes. [APOLLONIUS, No. 2.]

Molochath. [MULUCHA.]

Mŏlossi (Μολοσσοί), a people in Epirus, who inhabited a narrow slip of country, called after them **Molossia** (Μολοσσία) or **Molossis,** which extended from the Aous, along the W. bank of the Arachthus, as far as the Ambracian gulf. The Molossi were a Greek people, who claimed descent from Molossus, the son of Pyrrhus (Neoptolemus) and Andromache, and are said to have emigrated from Thessaly into Epirus, under the guidance of Pyrrhus himself. In their new abodes they intermingled with the original inhabitants of the land and with the neighbouring Illyrian tribes, in consequence of which they were regarded by the other Greeks as half barbarians. They were, however, by far the most powerful people in Epirus, and their kings gradually extended their dominion over the whole of the country. The first of their kings, who took the title of king of Epirus, was Alexander, who perished in Italy B. c. 326. [EPIRUS.] The ancient capital of the Molossi was PASSARON, but AMBRACIA afterwards became their chief town, and the residence of their kings. The Molossian hounds were celebrated in antiquity, and were much prized for hunting.

Molycrĭum (Μολύκρειον, also Μολύκρεια, Μολυκρία: Μολύκριος, Μολυκριεύς, Μολυκραῖος), a town in the most S.-ly part of Aetolia, at the entrance of the Corinthian gulf, gave the name of Rhium Molycrium (᾽Ρίον Μολύκριον) to the neighbouring promontory of Antirrhium. It was founded by the Corinthians, but was afterwards taken possession of by the Aetolians.

Mŏmemphis (Μόμεμφις: *Panouf-Khet,* or *Manouf-el-Seffti,* i. e. *Lower Memphis*), the capital of the Nomos Momemphites in Lower Egypt, stood on the E. side of the lake Mareotis.

Mŏmus (Μῶμος), the god of mockery and censure, is not mentioned by Homer, but is called in Hesiod the son of night. Thus he is said to have censured in the man formed by Hephaestus, that a little door had not been left in his breast, so as to enable one to look into his secret thoughts.

Mona (*Anglesey*), an island off the coast of the Ordovices in Britain, was one of the chief seats of the Druids. It was invaded by Suetonius Paulinus A. D. 61, and was conquered by Agricola, 78. Caesar (*B. G.* v. 13), erroneously describes this island as half way between Britannia and Hibernia. Hence it has been supposed by some critics that the Mona of Caesar is the *Isle of Man;* but it is more probable that he received a false report respecting the real position of Mona, especially since all other ancient writers give the name of Mona to the *Isle of Anglesey*, and the name of the latter island is likely to have been mentioned to Caesar on account of its celebrity in connection with the Druids.

Mönaeses. 1. A Parthian general mentioned by Horace (*Carm.* iii. 6. 9) is probably the same as Surenas, the general of Orodes, who defeated Crassus. — **2.** A Parthian noble, who deserted to Antony and urged him to invade Parthia, but soon afterwards returned to the Parthian king Phraates. — **3.** A general of the Parthian king, Vologeses I., in the reign of Nero.

Monapía or **Monarína** (*Isle of Man*), an island between Britannia and Hibernia.

Monda or **Munda** (*Mondego*), a river on the W. coast of Spain, which flows into the ocean between the Tagus and Durius.

Mönéta, a surname of Juno among the Romans, by which she was characterised as the protectress of money. Under this name she had a temple on the Capitoline, in which there was at the same time the mint, just as the public treasury was in the temple of Saturn. The temple had been vowed by the dictator L. Furius in a battle against the Aurunci, and was erected on the spot where the house of M. Manlius Capitolinus had stood. Moneta signifies the mint; but some writers found such a meaning too plain. Thus Livius Andronicus used Moneta as a translation of *Mnemosyne* (*Μνημοσύνη*), and thus made her the mother of the Muses or Camenae. Cicero relates, that during an earthquake, a voice was heard issuing from the temple of Juno on the Capitol, and admonishing (*monens*) that a pregnant sow should be sacrificed. A somewhat more probable reason for the name is given by Suidas, though he assigns it to too late a time. In the war with Pyrrhus and the Tarentines, he says, the Romans being in want of money, prayed to Juno, and were told by the goddess, that money would not be wanting to them, so long as they would fight with the arms of justice. As the Romans by experience found the truth of the words of Juno, they called her Juno Moneta. Her festival was celebrated on the 1st of June.

Monīma (*Μονίμη*), a Greek woman, either of Stratonicea, in Ionia, or of Miletus, was the wife of Mithridates, but was put to death by order of this monarch, when he fled into Armenia, B. C. 72.

Monoeci Portus, also **Herculis Monoeci Portus** (*Monaco*), a port-town on the coast of Liguria, between Nicaea and Album Intemelium, founded by the Massilians, was situated on a promontory (hence the *arx Monoeci* of Virg. *Aen.* vi. 801), and possessed a temple of Hercules Monoecus, from whom the place derived its name. The harbour, though small and exposed to the S.E. wind, was of importance, as it was the only one on this part of the coast of Liguria.

Montānus, Curtíus, was exiled by Nero, A. D. 67; but was soon afterwards recalled at his father's petition. On the accession of Vespasian, he vehemently attacked in the senate the notorious delator, Aquilius Regulus. If the same person with the Curtius Montanus satirised by Juvenal (iv. 107, 131, xi. 34), Montanus in later life sullied the fair reputation he enjoyed in youth; for Juvenal describes him as a corpulent epicure, a parasite of Domitian, and a hackneyed declaimer.

Montānus, Voltiënus, an orator and declaimer in the reign of Tiberius. From his propensity to refine upon thought and diction, he was named the "Ovid" of the rhetorical schools. He was convicted on a charge of majestas, and died an exile in the Balearic islands, A. D. 25.

Mopsia or **Mopsopia**, an ancient name of Pamphylia, derived from Mopsus, the mythical leader of certain Greeks who were supposed to have settled in Pamphylia, as also in Cilicia and Syria, after the Trojan war, and whose name appears more than once in the geographical names in Cilicia. (See e. g. MOPSUCRENE, MOPSUESTIA.)

Mopsīum (*Μόψιον : Μόψιος*), a town of Thessaly in Pelasgiotis, situated on a hill of the same name between Tempe and Larissa.

Mopsucrēnē (*Μόψου κρήνη* or *κρῆναι*, i. e. *the Spring of Mopsus*), a city of Cilicia Campestria, on the S. slope of the Taurus, and 12 Roman miles from Tarsus, was the place where the emperor Constantius died, A. D. 364.

Mopsuestia, (*Μόψου ἑστία, Μοψουεστία*, i. e. *the Hearth of Mopsus*, also *Μόψου πόλις* and *Μόψος :* *Μοψεάτης :* Mamistra, in the Middle Ages : *Messis*), an important city of Cilicia Campestria, on both banks of the river Pyramus, 12 Roman miles from its mouth, on the road from Tarsus to Issus, in the beautiful plain called *τὸ Ἀλήϊον πεδίον*, was a *civitas libera* under the Romans. The 2 parts of the city were connected by a handsome bridge built by Constantius over the Pyramus. In ecclesiastical history, it is notable as the birthplace of Theodore of Mopsuestia.

Mopsus (*Μόψος*). **1.** Son of Ampyx or Ampycus by the nymph Chloris. Being a seer, he was also called a son of Apollo by Himantis. He was one of the Lapithae of Oechalia or Titaeron (Thessaly), and took part in the combat at the wedding of Pirithous. He was one of the Calydonian hunters, and also one of the Argonauts, and was a famous prophet among the Argonauts. He died in Libya of the bite of a snake, and was buried there by the Argonauts. He was afterwards worshipped as an oracular hero.—**2.** Son of Apollo and Manto, the daughter of Tiresias, and also a celebrated seer. He contended in prophecy with Calchas at Colophon, and showed himself superior to the latter in prophetic power. [CALCHAS.] He was believed to have founded Mallos in Cilicia, in conjunction with the seer Amphilochus. A dispute arose between the two seers respecting the possession of the town, and both fell in combat by each other's hand. Mopsus had an oracle at Mallos, which existed as late as the time of Strabo.

Morgantium, Morgantina, Murgantia, Morgentia (*Μοργάντιον, Μοργαντίνη : Μοργαντῖνος, Murgentinus*), a town in Sicily founded by the Morgetes, after they had been driven out of Italy by the Oenotrians. According to Livy (xxiv. 27) this city was situated on the E. coast, probably at the mouth of the Symaethus; but according to other writers it was situated in the interior of the island, S. E. of Agyrium, and near the Symaethus. The neighbouring country produced good wine.

Morgëtes (Μόργητες), an ancient people in the S. of Italy. According to Strabo they dwelt in the neighbourhood of Rhegium, but being driven out of Italy by the Oenotrians crossed over to Sicily and there founded the town of Morgantium. According to Dionysius of Halicarnassus, Morges was the successor of the Oenotrian king Italus, and hospitably received Siculus, who had been driven out of Latium by the Aborigines, in consequence of which the earlier Oenotrians were called *Italietes*, *Morgetes* and *Siculi:* according to this account, the Morgetes ought to be regarded as a branch of the Oenotrians.

Moria or **Morija** (Μώριον ὄρος), a mountain of Judaea, within the city of Jerusalem, on the summit of which the temple was built. [JERU-SALEM.]

Moriměnê (Μοριμενή), the N.W. district of Cappadocia, on the banks of the Halys, assigned under the Romans to Galatia. Its meadows were entirely devoted to the feeding of cattle.

Mörïni, a people in Gallia Belgica, W. of the Nervii and Menapii, and the most N.-ly people in all Gaul, whence Virgil calls them *extremi hominum* (*Aen.* viii. 727). They dwelt on the coast, opposite Britain, and at the narrowest part of the channel between Gaul and Britain, which is hence some-times called *Fretum Morinorum* or *Morinum.* They were a brave and warlike people. Their country was covered with woods and marshes. Their principal town was GESORIACUM.

Morïus (Μώριος), a small river in Boeotia, a S. tributary of the Cephissus, at the foot of Mt. Thurion near Chaeronëa.

Mormo (Μορμώ, also Μορμολύκη, Μορμολυκείον), a female spectre, with which the Greeks used to frighten children.

Morpheus (Μορφεύς,), the son of Sleep, and the god of dreams. The name signifies the fashioner or moulder, because he shaped or formed the dreams which appeared to the sleeper.

Mors, called **Thanátos** (Θάνατος) by the Greeks, the god of death. In the Homeric poems Death does not appear as a distinct divinity, though he is described as the brother of Sleep, together with whom he carries the body of Sar-pedon from the field of battle to the country of the Lycians. In Hesiod he is a son of Night and a brother of Ker and Sleep, and Death and Sleep reside in the lower world. In the Alcestis of Euripides, where Death comes upon the stage, he appears as an austere priest of Hades in a dark robe and with the sacrificial sword, with which he cuts off a lock of a dying person, and devotes it to the lower world. On the whole, later poets describe Death as a sad or terrific being (Horat. *Carm.* i. 4. 13 ; *Sat.* ii. 1. 57) ; but the best artists of the Greeks, avoiding any thing that might be displeasing, abandoned the idea suggested to them by the poets, and represented Death under a more pleasing aspect. On the chest of Cypselus, Night was represented with two boys, one black and the other white ; and at Sparta there were statues of both Death and Sleep. Both were usually re-presented as slumbering youths, or as genii with torches turned upside down. There are traces of sacrifices having been offered to Death, but no temples are mentioned anywhere.

Morÿchus (Μόρυχος), a tragic poet, a con-

temporary of Aristophanes, noted especially for his gluttony and effeminacy.

Mösa (*Maas* or *Meuse*), a river in Gallia Bel-gica, rises in Mt. Vogesus, in the territory of the Lingones, flows first N.E. and then N.W , and falls into the Vahalis or W. branch of the Rhine.

Moscha (Μόσχα: *Muscat*), an important sea-port on the N. E. coast of Arabia Felix, N.W. of Syagrus, the E.-most promontory of the peninsula (*Ras el-Hud*) ; a chief emporium for the trade be-tween India and Arabia.

Moschi (Μόσχοι), a people of Asia, whose ter-ritory (ἡ Μοσχική, Moschorum Tractus) formed originally the S. part of Colchis, but, at the time of Augustus, was divided between Colchis, Iberia, and Armenia.

Moschici Montes, or -**Icus Mons** (τὰ Μοσχικὰ ὄρη : *Mesjidi*), a range of mountains extending S. and S.W. from the main chain of the Caucasus to that of the Anti-Taurus, and forming the boundary between Colchis and Iberia : named after the MOSCHI, who dwelt among them. Though lofty, they were well wooded to the summit, and their lower slopes were planted with vines.

Moschion (Μοσχίων), a Greek physician, the author of a short Greek treatise "On Female Dis-eases," is supposed to have lived in the begin-ning of the 2nd century after Christ. The work is edited by Dewez, Vienn. 1793.

Moschus (Μόσχος), of Syracuse, a grammarian and bucolic poet, lived about B. C. 250. Suidas says that he was acquainted with Aristarchus. According to this statement his date ought to be placed later ; but he calls himself a pupil of Bion, in the idyl in which he bewails the death of the latter [BION]. There are 4 of his idyls extant. He writes with elegance and liveliness ; but he is inferior to Bion, and comes still further behind Theocritus. His style labours under an excess of polish and ornament. For editions see BION.

Mösella (*Mosel* or *Moselle*), a river in Gallia Belgica, rises in Mt. Vogesus, flows N.E. through the territories of the Treviri, and falls into the Rhine at Confluentes (*Coblenz*). This river forms the subject of a descriptive poem by Ausonius.

Mostëni (Μοστηνοί, Μόστινα, Μουστήνη, Μυσ-τήνη), a city of Lydia, in the Hyrcanian plain, S.E. of Thyatira, was one of the cities of Asia Minor destroyed by the great earthquake of A. D. 17. Its coins are numerous.

Mosychlus. [LEMNOS.]

Mosynoeci (Μοσύνοικοι, Μοσσύνοικοι), or **Mo-syni** or **Mossyni** (Μοσυνοί, Μοσσυνοί), a people on the N. coast of Asia Minor, in Pontus, E. of the Chalybes and the city of Cerasus, celebrated for their warlike spirit and savage customs, which are described by Xenophon (*Anab.* iv. 4, v. 4). Their name was derived from the conical wooden houses in which they dwelt. Their government was very curious : a king chosen by them was strictly guarded in a house higher than the rest, and maintained at the public cost ; but as soon as he displeased the commons, they literally stopped the supplies, and starved him to death.

Mothönê. [METHONE.]

Motüca (Μότουκα: Mutycensis: *Modica*), a town in the S. of Sicily, W. of the promontory Pachynus and near the sources of the river Moty-chanus (*Fiume di Ragusa*). Since both Cicero and Pliny call the inhabitants Mutycenses, it is pro-bable that *Mutyca* is the more correct form of the name. This town must not be confounded with the more celebrated MOTYA.

Motya (Μοτύη: Μοτυαῖος), an ancient town in the N.W. of Sicily, situated on a small island (*Isola di Mezzo*) only 6 stadia from the coast, with which it was connected by a mole. It was founded by the Phoenicians in the territory of the Elymi. It possessed a good harbour, and was in early times one of the most flourishing cities of Sicily. It afterwards passed into the hands of the Carthaginians, was taken from them by Dionysius of Syracuse, and was finally captured by the Carthaginian general Himilco, who transplanted all its inhabitants to the town of Lilybaeum, which he had founded in its neighbourhood, B. C. 397. From this time it disappears from history.

Motychānus. [MOTUCA.]

Mūcia, daughter of Q. Mucius Scaevola, the augur, consul B. C. 95, married Cn. Pompey, by whom she had 2 sons, Cneius and Sextus, and a daughter, Pompeia. She was divorced by Pompey in 62. She next married M. Aemilius Scaurus a step-son of the dictator Sulla. In 39, Mucia went to Sicily to mediate between her son Sex. Pompey and Augustus. She was living at the time of the battle of Actium, 31. Augustus treated her with great respect.

Muciānus. 1. P. Licinius Crassus Dives Mucianus, was the son of P. Mucius Scaevola, and was adopted by P. Licinius Crassus Dives. He was consul B. C. 131, and carried on the war against Aristonicus in Asia, but was defeated by the latter. He succeeded Scipio Nasica as pontifex maximus. He was distinguished both as an orator and a lawyer.—2. Licinius Mucianus, three times consul in A. D. 52, 70, and 75. On Nero's death in 68, Mucianus had the command of the province of Syria ; and he rendered efficient aid to Vespasian, when the latter resolved to seize the imperial throne. As soon as Vespasian was proclaimed emperor, Mucianus set out for Europe to oppose Vitellius ; but the Vitellians were entirely defeated by Antonius Primus [PRIMUS], before Mucianus entered Italy. Antonius however had to surrender all power into the hands of Mucianus, upon the arrival of the latter at Rome. Mucianus was an orator and an historian. His powers of oratory are greatly praised by Tacitus. He made a collection of the speeches of the republican period, which he published in 11 books of *Acta* and 3 of *Epistolae*. The subject of his history is not mentioned ; but it appears to have treated chiefly of the East.

Mucius Scaevola. [SCAEVOLA.]

Mugilla (Mugillanus), a town in Latium near Corioli, from which a family of the Papirii probably derived their name Mugillanus.

Mulciber, a surname of Vulcan, which seems to have been given to him as an euphemism, that he might not consume the habitations and property of men, but might kindly aid them in their pursuits. It occurs frequently in the Latin poets.

Mulucha, Malva, or Molochath (Μόλοχαθ: *Wad el Mulwia* or *Mohalou*, or *Sourb-ou-Herb*), the largest river of Mauretania, rising in the Atlas, and flowing N. by E. into the *Gulf of Melillah*, has been successively the boundary between the Mauri and the Massaesylii, Mauretania and Numidia, Mauretania Tingitana and Mauretania Caesariensis, *Marocco* and *Algier*. [Comp. MAURETANIA.]

Mummius. 1. L., tribune of the plebs, B. C. 187, and praetor 177.—2. L., surnamed ACHAICUS, son of the last, was praetor 154, when he carried on the war successfully in further Spain, against the Lusitanians. He was consul in 146, when he won for himself the surname of Achaicus, by the conquest of Greece, and the establishment of the Roman province of Achaia. After defeating the army of the Achaean league at the Isthmus of Corinth, he entered Corinth without opposition. The city was burnt, rased, and abandoned to pillage : the native Corinthians were sold for slaves, and the rarest specimens of Grecian art were given up to the rapacity of an ignorant conqueror. Polybius the historian saw Roman soldiers playing at draughts upon the far-famed picture of Dionysus by Aristides ; and Mummius himself was so unconscious of the real value of his prize, that he sold the rarer works of painting, sculpture, and carving, to the king of Pergamus, and exacted securities from the masters of vessels who conveyed the remainder to Italy, to replace by equivalents any picture or statue lost or injured in the passage. He remained in Greece during the greater part of 145 with the title of proconsul. He arranged the fiscal and municipal constitution of the newly acquired province, and won the confidence and esteem of the provincials by his integrity, justice, and equanimity. He triumphed in 145. He was censor in 142 with Scipio Africanus the younger. The political opinions of Mummius inclined to the popular side.—3. Sp., brother of the preceding, and his legatus at Corinth in 146—145, was an intimate friend of the younger Scipio Africanus. In political opinions Spurius was opposed to his brother Lucius, and was a high aristocrat. He composed ethical and satirical epistles, which were extant in Cicero's age, and were probably in the style which Horace afterwards cultivated so successfully.

Munātius Plancus. [PLANCUS.]

Munda. 1. A Roman colony and an important town in Hispania Baetica, situated on a small river, and celebrated on account of 2 battles fought in its neighbourhood, the victory of Cn. Scipio over the Carthaginians in B. C. 216, and the important victory of Julius Caesar over the sons of Pompey in 45. The town had fallen into decay as early as the time of Pliny. The site of the ancient town is usually supposed to be the modern village of *Monda*, S.W. of Malaga ; but Munda was more probably in the neighbourhood of Cordova, and there are ruins of ancient walls and towers between Martos, Alcandete, Espejo and Baena, which are conjectured to be the remains of Munda.—2. A river. See MONDA.

Munychia (Μουνυχία), a hill in the peninsula of Piraeus, which formed the citadel of the ports of Athens. It was strongly fortified, and is frequently mentioned in Athenian history. At its foot lay the harbour of Munychia, one of the 3 harbours in the peninsula of Piraeus, fortified by Themistocles. The names of these 3 harbours were Piraeus, Zea, and Munychia. The last was the smallest and the most E.-ly of the 3, and is called at the present day *Phanari* : Zea was situated between Piraeus and Munychia. Most topographers have erroneously supposed *Phanari* to be Phaleron, and Zea to be Munychia. The entrance to the harbour of Munychia was very narrow, and could be closed by a chain. The hill at Munychia contained several public buildings. Of these the most important were: —(1) a temple of Artemis Munychia, in which persons accused of crimes against the state took refuge: (2) The Bendideum, the sanctuary of the Thracian Artemis Bendis, in whose honour the festival of the Bendidea was celebrated: (3) The theatre on the N.W. slope of the hill, in which the assemblies of the people were sometimes held.

Murcia, Murtea, or Murtia, a surname of Venus at Rome, where she had a chapel in the circus, with a statue. This surname, which is said to be the same as Myrtea (from *myrtus*, a myrtle), was believed to indicate the fondness of the goddess for the myrtle tree. In ancient times there is said to have been a myrtle grove in the front of her chapel at the foot of the Aventine.

Murcus, L. Statius, was Caesar's legatus, B.C. 48, and praetor 45. He went into Syria after his year of office expired; and after Caesar's death became an active supporter of the republican party. Cassius appointed him prefect of the fleet. After the ruin of the republican party at Philippi, in 42, Murcus went over to Sex. Pompey in Sicily. Here he was assassinated by Pompey's order at the instigation of his freedman Menas, to whom Murcus had borne himself loftily.

Murēna, Licinius. The name Murena, which is the proper way of writing the word, not Muraena, is said to have been given in consequence of one of the family having a great liking for the lamprey (murena), and building tanks (vivaria) for them.— **1.** P., a man of some literary knowledge, lost his life in the wars of Marius and Sulla, B. C. 82. — **2.** L., brother of the preceding, served under Sulla in Greece, in the Mithridatic war. After Sulla had made peace with Mithridates (84), Murena was left as propraetor in Asia. Anxious for distinction, Murena sought a quarrel with Mithridates; and after carrying on the war for 2 years, was at length compelled by the strict orders of Sulla to stop hostilities. [See p. 452, a.] Murena returned to Rome, and had a triumph in 81. He probably died soon after.— **3.** L., son of the last, served under his father in the 2nd Mithridatic war, and also under Lucullus in the 3rd Mithridatic war. In 65 he was praetor, in 64 propraetor of Gallia Cisalpina, and in 63 was elected consul with D. Junius Silanus. Serv. Sulpicius, an unsuccessful candidate, instituted a prosecution against Murena for bribery (*ambitus*), and he was supported in the matter by M. Porcius Cato, Cn. Postumius, and Serv. Sulpicius the younger. Murena was defended by Q. Hortensius, M. Tullius Cicero, who was then consul, and M. Licinius Crassus. The speech of Cicero, which is extant, was delivered in the latter part of November. The orator handled his subject skilfully, by making merry with the formulae and the practice of the lawyers, to which class Sulpicius belonged, and with the paradoxes of the Stoics, to which sect Cato had attached himself. Murena was acquitted, and was consul in the following year, 62. — **4.** A. Terentius Varro Murena, probably the son of the preceding, was adopted by A. Terentius Varro, whose name he took, according to the custom in such cases. In the civil wars he is said to have lost his property, and C. Proculeius, a Roman eques, is said to have given him a share of his own property. This Proculeius is called the brother of Varro, but, if we take the words of

Horace literally (*Carm.* ii. 2), Proculeius had more than one brother. It is conjectured that this Proculeius was a son of the brother of No. 3, who had been adopted by one Proculeius. This would make Proculeius the cousin of Varro. It was common enough among the Romans to call cousins by the name of brothers (*frater patruelis* and *frater*). In 25 Murena subdued the Salassi in the Alps, and founded the town of Augusta (*Aosta*) in their territory. He was consul suffectus in 23. In 22 he was involved in the conspiracy of Fannius Caepio, and was condemned to death and executed, notwithstanding the intercession of Proculeius and Terentia, the sister of Murena. Horace (*Carm.* ii. 10) addresses Murena by the name of Licinius, and probably intended to give him some advice as to being more cautious in his speech and conduct.

Murgantia. 1. See MORGANTIUM.— **2.** A town in Samnium of uncertain site.

Murgis, a town in Hispania Baetica, on the frontiers of Tarraconensis, and on the road from Acci to Malaga.

Muridūnum or **Moridūnum** (*Dorchester*), called **Dunium** by Ptolemy, the capital of the Durotriges in the S. of Britain. At *Dorchester* there are remains of the walls and the amphitheatre of the ancient town.

Mursa or **Mursia** (*Essek*, capital of Slavonia), an important town in Pannonia Inferior, situated on the Dravus, not far from its junction with the Danube, was a Roman colony founded by the emperor Hadrian, and was the residence of the governor of Lower Pannonia. Here Magnentius was defeated by Constantius II., A.D. 351.

Mursella, or **Mursa Minor,** a town in Pannonia Inferior, only 10 miles W. of the great Mursa.

Mus, Decius. [DECIUS.]

Musa, Antonius, a celebrated physician at Rome about the beginning of the Christian era. He was brother to Euphorbus, the physician to king Juba, and was himself the physician to the emperor Augustus. He had been originally a slave. When the emperor was seriously ill, and had been made worse by a hot regimen and treatment, B. C. 23, Antonius Musa succeeded in restoring him to health by means of cold bathing and cooling drinks, for which service he received from Augustus and the senate a large sum of money and the permission to wear a gold ring, and also had a statue erected in his honour near that of Aesculapius by public subscription. He seems to have been attached to this mode of treatment, to which Horace alludes (*Epist.* i. 15. 3), but failed when he applied it to the case of M. Marcellus, who died under his care a few months after the recovery of Augustus, 23. He wrote several pharmaceutical works, which are frequently quoted by Galen, but of which nothing except a few fragments remain. There are, however, 2 short Latin medical works ascribed to Antonius Musa, but these are universally considered to be spurious.

Musa or **Muza** (Μοῦσα, Μοῦζα: prob. *Moushid*, N. of *Mokha*), a celebrated port of Arabia Felix, on the W. coast, near its S. extremity, or in other words on the E. shore of the *Red Sea*, near the *Straits of Bab-el-Mandeb*.

Musae (Μοῦσαι), the Muses, were, according to the earliest writers, the inspiring goddesses of song, and, according to later notions, divinities presiding over the different kinds of poetry, and over the arts and sciences. They were originally regarded as the nymphs of inspiring wells, near which they were worshipped, and they bore different names in different places, until the Thraco-Boeotian worship of the *nine* Muses spread from Boeotia over other parts of Greece, and ultimately became generally established.— 1. *Genealogy of the Muses.* The most common notion was that they were the daughters of Zeus and Mnemosyne, and born in Pieria, at the foot of Mt. Olympus. Some call them the daughters of Uranus and Gaea, and others daughters of Pierus and Antiope, or of Apollo, or of Zeus and Plusia, or of Zeus and Moneta, probably a mere translation of Mnemosyne or Mneme, whence they are called *Mnemonides,* or of Zeus and Minerva, or, lastly, of Aether and Gaea.— 2. *Number of the Muses.* Originally there were 3 Muses worshipped on Mt. Helicon in Boeotia, namely, *Melete* (meditation), *Mneme* (memory), and *Aoide* (song). Three Muses also were recognised at Sicyon and at Delphi. As daughters of Zeus and Plusia we find mention of 4 Muses, viz. *Thelxinoe* (the heart delighting), *Aoide* (song), *Arche* (beginning), and *Melete.* Some accounts, in which they are called daughters of Pierus, mention 7 Muses, viz. *Nilo, Tritone, Asopo, Heptapora, Achelois, Tipoplo,* and *Rhodia ;* and others, lastly, mention 8, which is also said to have been the number recognised at Athens. At length, however, the number 9 became established throughout all Greece. Homer sometimes mentions Musa only in the singular, and sometimes Musae in the plural, and once only he speaks of 9 Muses, though without mentioning any of their names. Hesiod is the first who states the names of all the 9, and these 9 names became the usual ones. They are *Clio, Euterpe, Thalia, Melpomene, Terpsichore, Erato, Polymnia* or *Polyhymnia, Urania,* and *Calliope.*— 3. *Nature and character of the Muses.* In Homer's poems, they are the goddesses of song and poetry, and live in Olympus. There they sing the festive songs at the repasts of the immortals. They bring before the mind of the mortal poet the events which he has to relate, and confer upon him the gift of song. The earliest poets in their invocation of the Muse or Musae were perfectly sincere, and actually believed in their being inspired by the goddesses; but in later times the invocation of the Muses was a mere formal translation of the early poets. Thamyris, who presumed to excel the Muses, was deprived by them of the gift they had bestowed on him, and punished with blindness. The Sirens, who likewise ventured upon a contest with them, were deprived of the feathers of their wings, and the Muses put them on their own persons as ornaments. The 9 daughters of Pierus, who presumed to rival the Muses, were metamorphosed into birds. Since poets and bards derived their power from the Muses, they are frequently called either their disciples or sons. Thus Linus is called a son of Amphimarus and Urania, or of Apollo and Calliope, or Terpsichore; Hyacinthus a son of Pierus and Clio; Orpheus a son of Calliope or Clio, and Thamyris a son of Erato. These and a few others are the cases in which the Muses are described as mothers; but the more general idea was, that, like other nymphs, they were virgin divinities. Being goddesses of song, they were naturally connected with Apollo, the god of the lyre, who like them instructs the bards, and is

mentioned along with them even by Homer. In later times Apollo is placed in very close connection with the Muses, for he is described as the leader of the choir of the Muses by the surname *Musagetes* (Μουσαγέτης). A further feature in the character of the Muses is their prophetic power, which belongs to them, partly because they were regarded as inspiring nymphs, and partly because of their connection with the prophetic god of Delphi. Hence, they instructed, for example, Aristaeus in the art of prophecy. As the Muses loved to dwell on Mt. Helicon, they were naturally associated with Dionysus and dramatic poetry, and hence they are described as the companions, playmates, or nurses of Dionysus. The worship of the Muses points originally to Thrace and Pieria about Mt. Olympus, whence it was introduced into Boeotia; and the names of mountains, grottoes, and wells, connected with their worship in the N., were likewise transferred to the S. Near Mt. Helicon, Ephialtes and Otus are said to have offered the first sacrifices to them. In the same place there was a sanctuary with their statues, the sacred wells Aganippe and Hippocrene, and on Mt. Libethrion, which is connected with Helicon, there was a sacred grotto of the Muses. Pierus, a Macedonian, is said to have been the first who introduced the worship of the *nine* Muses, from Thrace to Thespiae, at the foot of Mt. Helicon. There they had a temple and statues, and the Thespians celebrated a solemn festival of the Muses on Mt. Helicon, called *Musea.* Mt. Parnassus was likewise sacred to them, with the Castalian spring, near which they had a temple. The sacrifices offered to the Muses consisted of libations of water or milk, and of honey. The various surnames by which they are designated by the poets are for the most part derived from the places which were sacred to them or in which they were worshipped, while some are descriptive of the sweetness of their songs.— 4. *Representations of the Muses in works of art.* In the most ancient works of art we find only 3 Muses, and their attributes are musical instruments, such as the flute, the lyre, or the barbiton. Later artists gave to each of the 9 sisters different attributes as well as different attitudes. 1. *Calliope,* the Muse of epic poetry, appears with a tablet and stylus, and sometimes with a roll of paper; 2. *Clio,* the Muse of history, appears in a sitting attitude, with an open roll of paper, or an open chest of books; 3. *Euterpe,* the Muse of lyric poetry, with a flute; 4. *Melpomene,* the Muse of tragedy, with a tragic mask, the club of Hercules, or a sword, her head is surrounded with vine leaves, and she wears the cothurnus; 5. *Terpsichore,* the Muse of choral dance and song, appears with the lyre and the plectrum; 6. *Erato,* the Muse of erotic poetry and mimic imitation, sometimes also has the lyre; 7. *Polymnia,* or *Polyhymnia,* the Muse of the sublime hymn, usually appears without any attribute in a pensive or meditating attitude; 8. *Urania,* the Muse of astronomy, with a staff pointing to a globe; 9. *Thalia,* the Muse of comedy and of merry or idyllic poetry, appears with a comic mask, a shepherd's staff, or a wreath of ivy. Sometimes the Muses are seen with feathers on their heads, alluding to their contest with the Sirens.

Musaeus (Μουσαῖος). 1. A semi-mythological personage, to be classed with Olen, Orpheus, and Pamphus. He was regarded as the author

of various poetical compositions, especially as connected with the mystic rites of Demeter at Eleusis,
over which the legend represented him as presiding in the time of Hercules. He was reputed
to belong to the family of the Eumolpidae, being
the son of Eumolpus and Selene. In other variations of the myth he was less definitely called a
Thracian. According to other legends he was the
son of Orpheus, of whom he was generally considered as the imitator and disciple. Some accounts
gave him a wife Deioce and a son Eumolpus.
There was a tradition that the Museum in Piraeus
bore that name from having been the place where
Musaeus was buried. Among the numerous compositions attributed to him by the ancients the
most celebrated were his *Oracles*. Onomacritus,
in the time of the Pisistratidae, made it his business to collect and arrange the oracles that passed
under the name of Musaeus, and was banished by
Hipparchus for interpolating in the collection oracles
of his own making. — 2. A grammarian, the author
of the celebrated poem on the loves of Hero and
Leander. Nothing is known of the personal history of the writer; but it is certain that the poem
is a late production. Some critics suppose that the
author did not live earlier than the 5th century of
our era. Edited by Passow, Lips. 1810; and by
Schaefer, Lips. 1825.

Mûsagĕtĕs. [MUSAE.]

C. Mūsŏnĭus Rŭfus, a celebrated Stoic philosopher, was the son of a Roman eques, and was
banished by Nero to the island of Gyaros, in
A. D. 66, under the pretext of his having been
privy to the conspiracy of Piso. He returned
from exile on the accession of Galba, and seems
to have been held in high estimation by Vespasian,
as he was allowed to remain at Rome when the
other philosophers were banished from the city.
Musonius wrote various philosophical works, all
of which have perished.

Musti (Μούστη), a town in the Carthaginian
territory (Zeugitana), near the river Bagradas, on
the road from Carthage to Sicca Veneria. Here
Regulus killed an enormous serpent.

Muthul, a river of Numidia, the boundary between the kingdoms of Jugurtha and Adherbal.
It is probably the same as the RUBRICATUS.

Mutĭlus, C. Papĭus, one of the principal Samnite
generals in the Marsic war, B. C. 90—89.

Mutĭna (Mutinensis : *Modena*), an important
town in Gallia Cispadana, on the high road from
Mediolanum to the S. of Italy, was originally a
Celtic town, and was the first place which the
Romans took away from the Boii. It is mentioned
at the beginning of the 2nd Punic war (B. C. 218)
under the name of *Motina*, as a fortified place
inhabited by the Romans ; but it was not till 183
that it was made a Roman colony. Mutina is
celebrated in the history of the civil war after
Caesar's death. Decimus Brutus was besieged here
by M. Antonius from December, 44, to April, 43;
and under its walls the battles were fought, in
which the consuls Hirtius and Pansa perished.
Hence this war was called the *Bellum Mutinense.*
The best wool in all Italy came from the neighbourhood of Mutina.

Mutunus or **Mutinus,** was among the Romans
the same as the phallus, or Priapus, among the
Greeks, and was believed to be the most powerful
averter of demons, and of all evil that resulted
from pride, boastfulness, and the like.

Mўcăle (Μυκάλη: *Samsun*), a mountain in the
S. of Ionia in Asia Minor, N. of the mouth of the
Maeander. It forms the W. extremity of M. Messogis, and runs far out into the sea, opposite to
Samos, forming a sharp promontory, which was
called Mycale or Trogilium (Τρωγίλιον, Τρωγύ-
λιον : *C. S. Maria*). This cape and the S. E. promontory of Samos (Posidonium) overlap one another, and the 2 tongues of land are separated by
a strait only 7 stadia (little more than 3-4ths of a
mile) in width, which is renowned in Greek history
as the scene of the victory gained over the Persian
fleet by Leotychides and Xanthippus, B. C. 479.
There seems to have been a city of the same name
on or near the promontory. On the N. side of the
promontory, near Priene, was the great temple of
Poseidon, which was the place of meeting for the
Panionic festival and Amphictyony.

Mycalessus (Μυκαλησσός : Μυκαλήσσιος), an
ancient and important city in Boeotia, mentioned
by Homer, was situated on the road from Aulis to
Thebes. In B. C. 413 some Thracian mercenaries
in the pay of Athens surprised and sacked the
town, and butchered the inhabitants. From this
blow it never recovered, and was in ruins in the
time of Pausanias. It possessed a celebrated temple
of Demeter, who was hence surnamed **Mycalessia.**

Mycēnae sometimes **Mycēnē** (Μυκῆναι, Μυκήνη: Μυκηναῖος : *Karvata*), an ancient town in
Argolis, about 6 miles N. E. of Argos, is situated
on a hill at the head of a narrow valley, and is
hence described by Homer as " in a recess (μυχῷ)
of the Argive land ": hence the etymology of the
name. Mycenae is said to have been founded by
Perseus, and was subsequently the favourite residence of the Pelopidae. During the reign of
Agamemnon it was regarded as the first city in all
Greece ; but after the conquest of Peloponnesus by
the Dorians, it ceased to be a place of importance.
It still, however, continued an independent town
till B. C. 468, when it was attacked by the Argives,
whose hatred the Mycenaeans are said to have
incurred by the part they took in the Persian war
in favour of the Greek cause. The massive walls
of Mycenae resisted all the attacks of the Argives;
but the inhabitants were at length compelled by
famine to abandon their town. They effected their
escape without a surrender, and took refuge, some
at Cleonae, some in Achaia, and others in Macedonia. Mycenae was now destroyed by the Argives
and was never rebuilt; but there are still numerous
remains of the ancient city, which on account of
their antiquity and grandeur are some of the most
interesting in all Greece. Of these the most remarkable are the subterranean vault, commonly
called the " Treasury of Athens," but which was
more probably a sepulchre, and the Gate of Lions,
so called from 2 lions sculptured over the gate.

Mycēnē (Μυκήνη), daughter of Inachus and
wife of Arestor, from whom the town of Mycenae
was believed to have derived its name : the true
etymology of the name is given above.

Mycerĭnus, or **Mecherinus** (Μυκερῖνος, Μεχε-
ρῖνος), son of Cheops, king of Egypt, succeeded
his uncle Chephren on the throne. His conduct
formed a strong contrast to that of his father and
uncle, being as mild and just as theirs had been tyrannical. On the death of his daughter, he placed
her corpse within the hollow body of a wooden
cow, which was covered with gold. Herodotus
tells us that it was still to be seen at Saïs in his

time. We further hear of Mycerinus that, being warned by an oracle that he should die at the end of 6 years, because he had been a gentle ruler and had not wreaked the vengeance of the gods on Egypt, he gave himself up to revelry, and strove to double his allotted time by turning night into day. He began to build a pyramid, but died before it was finished. It was smaller than those of Cheops and Chephren, and, according to Herodotus, was wrongly ascribed by some to the Greek hetaera Rhodopis.

Myconus (Μύκονος: Μυκόνιος: *Mycono*), a small island in the Aegaean sea, one of the Cyclades, S.E. of Tenos and E. of Delos, never attained any importance in history, but is celebrated in mythology as one of the places where the giants were defeated by Hercules. The island was poor and unproductive, and its inhabitants were rapacious. It contained 2 towns, a promontory, called *Phorbia*, and a mountain named *Dimastus*. The large number of bald persons in this island was considered worthy of record by several ancient writers.

Mygdon (Μύγδων), son of Acmon, a Phrygian king, who fought with Otreus and Priam against the Amazons, and from whom some of the Phrygians are said to have been called Mygdonians. He had a son Coroebus, who is hence called *Mygdonides*.

Mygdonia (Μυγδονία: Μύγδονες). 1. A district in the E. of Macedonia, bordering on the Thermaic Gulf and the Chalcidic peninsula. Its people were of Thracian origin. — 2. A district in the N. of Asia Minor, between M. Olympus and the coast, in the E. of Mysia and the W. of Bithynia, named after the Thracian people, Mygdones, who formed a settlement here, but were afterwards subdued by the Bithyni. — 3. The N.E. district of Mesopotamia, between M. Masius and the Chaboras, which divided it from Osroëne. From its great fertility, it was also called Anthemusia (Ἀνθεμουσία). The name of Mygdonia was first introduced after the Macedonian conquests: in the passage of Xenophon (*Anab.* iv. 3), sometimes cited to prove the contrary, the true reading is Μαρδόνιοι, not Μυγδόνιοι.

Myia (Μυῖα), daughter of Pythagoras and Theano, and wife of Milon of Crotona. A letter, addressed to a certain Phyllis, is extant under her name.

Mylae (Μυλαί: Μυλαῖος, Μυλαΐτης). 1. (*Melazzo*), a town on the E. part of the N. coast of Sicily, situated on a promontory running out far into the sea, with a harbour and a citadel. It was founded by Zancle (Messana), and continued subject to the latter city. It was off Mylae that Agrippa defeated the fleet of Sex. Pompeius, B. C. 36. — 2. A town of Thessaly in Magnesia, of uncertain site.

Mylasa or **Mylassa** (τὰ Μύλασα, Μύλασσα: Μυλασεύς: *Melasso*, Ru.), a very ancient and flourishing inland city of Caria, lay 80 stadia (8 geog. miles) from the coast at the Gulf of Iassus, in a fertile plain, on and at the foot of an isolated rock of beautiful white marble, which furnished the material for the splendid temples and other public buildings of the city. The most important of these buildings was the great national temple of Zeus Carius or Osagon. [CARIA.] Mylasa was the birthplace and capital of HECATOMNUS. Under the Romans it was made a free city. In the civil wars, it was taken and partly destroyed by La-

bienus. Its remains are very extensive, and the ruins of the temple of Zeus are supposed to have been found on the rock which formed the Acropolis of the ancient city.

Myndus (Μύνδος: Μυνδιος: prob. *Port Gamishia*, Ru.), a Dorian colony on the coast of Caria, in Asia Minor, founded by settlers from Troezene, probably on the site of an old town of the Leleges, which continued to exist under the name of Palaemyndus. Myndus stood at the W. extremity of the same peninsula on which Halicarnassus stood. It was not one of the cities of the Dorian Hexapolis, but never became a place of much importance.

Myon or **Myonia** (Μύων, Μυονία: Μυονεύς), a town of the Locri Ozolae, situated on a considerable height 30 stadia from Amphissa, and in one of the passes which led from Aetolia into Phocis.

Myonnesus (Μυόννησος: *C. Hypsili*) a promontory of Ionia, with a town and a little island of the same name, S. of Teos and W. of Lebedus, and forming the N. headland of the Gulf of Ephesus. Here the Romans, under the praetor L. Aemilius, gained a great naval victory over Antiochus the Great, B. C. 190.

Myos Hormos (ὁ Μυὸς ὅρμος, i. e. *Muscle-port*, rather than *Mouse-port*, for μῦς is the Greek for *muscle*, and this shell-fish is very common on the W. coast of the Red Sea), aft. **Veneris Portus** (Ἀφροδίτης ὅρμος), an important sea-port town of Upper Egypt, built by Ptolemy II. Philadelphus on a promontory of the same name, 6 or 7 days' journey from Coptos. Some of the best modern geographers identify the port with *Kosseir* (lat. 26° 10'), which is still an important port of the Red Sea, and the place of embarkation for the caravan to Mecca. *Kosseir* lies due E. of Coptos, and is connected with it by a valley, which contains traces of an ancient road, and which still forms the route of the Mecca caravan. At the village of *Abu-Shaar*, near *Cosseir*, are extensive ruins, which are supposed to be the remains of the town of Myos Hormos. Others, however, place it a degree further N., in lat. 26° 10, opposite the *Jaffatine* islands.

Myra or **Myron** (τὰ and ἡ Μύρα, ἡ Μύρων: Μυρεύς: *Myra*, Grk., *Dembre*, Turk., Ru.), one of the chief cities of Lycia, and, under the later Roman empire, the capital of the province, was built on a rock 20 stadia (2 geog. miles) from the sea, and had a port called Andriaca (Ἀνδριακή). St. Paul touched here on his voyage as a prisoner to Rome, and the passage where this is mentioned (*Acts*, xxvii. 5, 6), affords incidental proof that the place was then an important sea-port. There are still magnificent ruins of the city, in great part hewn out of the rock.

Myriandrus (Μυρίανδρος), a Phoenician colony in Syria, on the E. side of the Gulf of Issus, a day's journey from the Cilician Gates. It probably stood a little S. of Alexandria, at a spot where there are ruins. Herodotus calls the Gulf of Issus ὁ Μαριανδικὸς κόλπος, a name evidently derived from this place, with a slight variation of form.

Myriotus (Μυρικοῦς), a city on the coast of Troas, opposite to Tenedos.

Myrina (ἡ Μυρίνα, or Μύρινα, Μύριννα, Μυρίνη: Μυριναῖος). 1. (*Sandarlik?*), a very ancient and strongly fortified city on the W. coast of Mysia, founded, according to mythical tradition, by Myrinus or by the Amazon Myrina, and colonized by the Aeolians, of whose confederacy it formed a member. It was also called Smyrna, and, under the Roman empire, Sebastopolis: it was made by the Romans a *civitas libera*. It was destroyed by earthquakes under Tiberius and Trajan, but each time rebuilt. It was the birthplace of the epigrammatic poet Agathias. — 2. [See LEMNOS.]

Myrlēa (Μύρλεια: Μυρλεᾶνός: *Amapoli*, Ru., a little distance inland from *Mudanich*), a city of Bithynia, not far from Prusa, founded by the Colophonians, and almost rebuilt by Prusias I., who called it **Apamea** after his wife. The Romans colonized it under Julius Caesar and Augustus.

Myrmĕcĭdes (Μυρμηκίδης), a sculptor and engraver, of Miletus or Athens, is generally mentioned in connection with Callicrates, like whom he was celebrated for the minuteness of his works. [CALLICRATES.] His works in ivory were so small that they could scarcely be seen without placing them on black hair.

Myrmēcĭum (Μυρμήκιον), a Scythian or Cimmerian town of the Chersonesus Taurica, situated on a promontory of the same name at the narrowest part of the Bosporus, opposite the Achilleum in Asia.

Myrmĭdon (Μυρμιδών), son of Zeus and Eurymedusa, daughter of Clitos, whom Zeus deceived in the disguise of an ant. Her son was for this reason called Myrmidon (from μύρμηξ, an ant), and was regarded as the ancestor of the Myrmidons in Thessaly. He was married to Pisidice, by whom he became the father of Antiphus and Actor.

Myrmĭdŏnes (Μυρμιδόνες), an Achaean race in Phthiotis in Thessaly, whom Achilles ruled over and who accompanied this hero to Troy. They are said to have inhabited originally the island of Aegina, and to have emigrated with Peleus into Thessaly; but modern critics on the contrary suppose that a colony of them emigrated from Thessaly into Aegina. The Myrmidones disappear from history at a later period. The ancients derived their name either from a mythical ancestor MYRMIDON, or from the ants (μύρμηκες) in Aegina, which were supposed to have been metamorphosed into men in the time of Aeacus. [AEACUS.]

Myrōn (Μύρων). 1. Tyrant of Sicyon, the father of Aristonymus, and grandfather of Clisthenes. He gained the victory at Olympia in the chariot-race in B. C. 648. — 2. One of the most celebrated of the Greek statuaries, and also a sculptor and engraver, was born at Eleutherae, in Boeotia, about 480. He is also called an Athenian, because Eleutherae had been admitted to the Athenian franchise. He was the disciple of Ageladas, the fellow-disciple of Polycletus, and a younger contemporary of Phidias. He flourished about 431, the time of the beginning of the Peloponnesian war. The chief characteristic of Myron seems to have been his power of expressing a great variety of forms. Not content with the human figure in its most difficult and momentary attitudes, he directed his art towards various other animals, and he seems to have been the first great artist who did so. His great works were nearly all in bronze. The most celebrated of his statues were his *Discobolus* and his Cow. Of his *Discobolus* there are several marble copies in existence. It is true that we cannot prove by testimony that any of these alleged copies were really taken from Myron's work, or from imitations of it; but the resemblance between them, the fame of the original, and the well-known

frequency of the practice of making such marble copies of celebrated bronzes, all concur to put the question beyond reasonable doubt. Of these copies we possess one in the Townley Gallery of the British Museum, which was found in the grounds of Hadrian's Tiburtine Villa, in 1791. The Cow of Myron appears to have been a perfect work of its kind. It was celebrated in many popular verses, and the Greek Anthology still contains no less than 36 epigrams upon it. The Cow was represented as lowing, and the statue was placed on a marble base, in the centre of the largest open place in Athens, where it still stood in the time of Cicero. In the time of Pausanias it was no longer there; it must have been removed to Rome, where it was still to be seen in the temple of Peace, in the time of Procopius. — 3. Of Priene, the author of an historical account of the first Messenian war, probably lived not earlier than the 3rd century B. C.

Myrōnĭdes (Μυρωνίδης), a skilful and successful Athenian general. In B. C. 457, he defeated the Corinthians, who had invaded Megara; and in 456 he defeated the Boeotians at Oenophyta.

Myrrha (Μύρρα) or **Smyrna**, daughter of Cinyras and mother of Adonis. For details see ADONIS.

Myrrhĭnūs (Μυρρινοῦς: Μυρρινούσιος), a demus on the E. coast of Attica, belonging to the tribe Pandionis, a little S. of the promontory Cynosura. It is said to have been built by a hero Colaenus, and it contained a temple of Artemis Colaenis.

Myrsĭlus (Μύρσιλος). 1. [CANDAULES.] — 2. A Greek historical writer of uncertain date, a native of Lesbos, from whom Dionysius of Halicarnassus borrowed a part of his account of the Pelasgians.

Myrsīnus. [MYRTUNTIUM.]

Myrtĭlis, a town of the Turdetani on the Anas in Lusitania, possessing the Jus Latii.

Myrtĭlus (Μυρτίλος), son of Hermes by Cleobule, Clytia, Phaetusa or Myrto. He was the charioteer of Oenomaus king of Elis, whom he betrayed, when Pelops contended with his master in the chariot-race. He was afterwards thrown into the sea by Pelops near Geraestus in Euboea; and that part of the Aegean is said to have thenceforth been called after him the Myrtoan sea. [OENOMAUS; PELOPS.] At the moment he expired, he pronounced a curse upon the house of Pelops, which was henceforward tormented by the Erinnyes. His father placed him among the stars as *auriga*.

Myrtis (Μύρτις), a lyric poetess, a native of Anthedon, in Boeotia. She was reported to have been the instructress of Pindar, and to have contended with him for the palm of superiority. This is alluded to in an extant fragment of Corinna. There were statues in honour of her in various parts of Greece.

Myrtōum Mare (τὸ Μυρτῷον πέλαγος), the part of the Aegaean sea, S. of Euboea, Attica and Argolis, which derived its name from the small island Myrtus, though others suppose it to come from Myrtilus, whom Pelops threw into this sea, or from the maiden Myrto.

Myrtuntĭum (Μυρτούντιον: Μυρτούσιος), called **Myrsīnus** (Μύρσινος) in Homer, a town of the Epeans in Elis, on the road from Elis to Dyme.

Myrtus. [MYRTOUM MARE.]

Mȳs (Μῦς), an artist in the toreutic department, engraved the battle of the Lapithae and the Centaurs and other figures on the shield of

Phidias's colossal bronze statue of Athena Promachos, in the Acropolis of Athens. He is mentioned as one of the most distinguished engravers by several ancient writers.

Myscelus (Μύσκελος, or Μύσκελλος), a native of Achaia, and, according to Ovid (*Metam.* xv. 1), an Heraclid, and the son of an Argive named Alemon. He founded Croton in Italy, B. C. 710, in accordance with the Delphic oracle. The oracle had commanded him to build a city, where he should find rain with fine weather. For a long time he thought it impossible to fulfil the command of the oracle, till at length he found in Italy a beautiful woman in tears ; whereupon he perceived that the oracle was accomplished, and straightway founded Croton on the spot.

Mysi (Μυσοί), one of the Thracian peoples, who seem to have crossed over from Europe into Asia Minor before recorded history begins. They appear to be the same people as the Moesi (in Greek also Μυσοί), on the banks of the Danube. [MOESIA.] They stand in close connection with the Teucri. These 2 peoples appear to have moved from the banks of the Strymon to the S.E. of Thrace, forcing the Bithyni over the Thracian Bosporus into Asia, and then to have crossed over into Asia themselves, by way of the Thracian Bosporus, and to have settled on the S.E. shore of the Propontis, as far W. as the river Rhyndacus (the rest of the Asiatic coast of the Propontis and the Hellespont being occupied by Phrygians), and also in the E. and S. parts of the district afterwards called MYSIA, in the mountains called Olympus and Temnus, and on the S. side of Ida. The Teucrians obtained a permanent footing also on the N. side of Ida, in the Troad. Being afterwards driven W.-ward over the Rhyndacus by the Bithynians, and hemmed in on the W. and N. by the Aeolian colonies, the Mysians may be regarded as about shut up within the ranges of Ida and Olympus on the N. and N.E. and Temnus on the S. They were a simple pastoral people, low in the scale of civilization. Their language and religion bore a strong resemblance to those of their neighbours, the Phrygians and Lydians, who were of the same Thracian origin as themselves ; and hence arose the error, which is found in Herodotus, of deriving them directly from the Lydians.

Mysia (ἡ Μυσία, poet. Μυσὶς αἶα : Μυσός, Mysus and Mysius : *Chan Karasi*, the N.W. district of *Anadoli*), a district of Asia Minor, called also the Asiatic Mysia (Μυσία ἡ 'Ασιανή), in contradistinction to Moesia on the banks of the Danube. Originally it meant of course the territory of the Mysi, but in the usual division of Asia Minor, as settled under Augustus, it occupied the whole of the N.W. corner of the peninsula, between the Hellespont on the N.W. ; the Propontis on the N. ; the river Rhyndacus and M. Olympus on the E., which divided it from Bithynia and Phrygia ; M. Temnus, and an imaginary line drawn from Temnus to the S. side of the Elaïtic Gulf, on the S., where it bordered upon Lydia ; and the Aegean Sea on the W. It was subdivided into 5 parts : (1.) **Mysia Minor** (M. ἡ μικρά), along the N. coast. (2.) **Mysia Major** (M. ἡ μεγάλη), the S.E. inland region, with a small portion of the coast between the Troad and the Aeolic settlements about the Elaïtic Gulf. (3.) **Troas** (ἡ Τρωάς), the N.W. angle, between the Aegean and Hellespont and the S. coast along the foot of Ida. (4.) **Aeolis**

or **Aeolia** (ἡ Αἰολίς or Αἰολία), the S. part of the W. coast, around the Elaïtic Gulf, where the chief cities of the Aeolian confederacy were planted ; but applied in a wider sense to the W. coast in general ; and (5.) **Teuthrania** (ἡ Τευθρανία), the S.W. angle, between Temnus and the borders of Lydia, where, in very early times, Teuthras was said to have established a Mysian kingdom, which was early subdued by the kings of Lydia ; this part was also called Pergamene, from the celebrated city of PERGAMUS, which stood in it. This account applies to the time of the early Roman empire ; the extent of Mysia, and its subdivisions, varied greatly at other times. In the heroic ages we find the great Teucrian monarchy of Troy in the N.W. of the country, and the Phrygians along the Hellespont : as to the Mysians, who appear as allies of the Trojans, it is not clear whether they are Europeans or Asiatics. The Mysia of the legends respecting Telephus is the Teuthranian kingdom in the S., only with a wider extent than the later Teuthrania. Under the Persian empire, the N.W. portion, which was still occupied in part by Phrygians, but chiefly by Aeolian settlements, was called Phrygia Minor, and by the Greeks HELLESPONTUS. Mysia was the region S. of the chain of Ida ; and both formed, with Lydia, the second satrapy. In the division of the empire of Alexander the Great, Mysia fell, with Thrace, to the share of Lysimachus, B. C. 311, after whose defeat and death, in 281, it became a part of the Greco-Syrian kingdom, with the exception of the S.W. portion, where Philetaerus founded the kingdom of PERGAMUS (280), to which kingdom the whole of Mysia was assigned, together with Lydia, Phrygia, Caria, Lycia, Pisidia, and Pamphylia, after the defeat of Antiochus the Great by the Romans in 190. With the rest of the kingdom of Pergamus, Mysia fell to the Romans in 133, by the bequest of Attalus III., and formed part of the province of Asia. Under the later empire, Mysia formed a separate proconsular province, under the name of Hellespontus. The country was for the most part mountainous ; its chief chains being those of IDA, OLYMPUS, and TEMNUS, which are terminal branches of the N.W. part of the Taurus chain, and the union of which forms the elevated land of S. E. Mysia. Their prolongations into the sea form several important bays and capes ; namely, among the former, the great gulf of Adramyttium (*Adramytti*), which cuts off Lesbos from the continent, and the Sinus Elaïticus (*G. of Chandeli*) ; and, among the latter, Sigeum (*C. Yenicheri*) and Lectum (*G. Baba*), at the N.W. and S.W. extremities of the Troad, and Cane (*C. Coloni*) and Hydria (*Fokia*), the N. and S. headlands of the Elaïtic Gulf. Its rivers are numerous ; some of them considerable, in proportion to the size of the country ; and some of first-rate importance in history and poetry : the chief of them, beginning on the E., were RHYNDACUS and MACESTUS, TARSIUS, AESEPUS, GRANICUS, RHODIUS, SIMOIS and SCAMANDER, SATNOÏS, EVENUS, and CAÏCUS. The peoples of the country, besides the general appellations mentioned above, were known by the following distinctive names : the Olympiëni or Olympëni ('Ολυμπιηνοί, 'Ολυμπηνοί), in the district of Olympëne at the foot of M. Olympus ; next to them, on the S. and W., and occupying the greater part of Mysia Proper, the Abrettëni, who had a native divinity called by

Nemesis and Elpis.
(From the Chigi Vase.) Page 471.

Nereid.
(Museo Borbonico, vol. vi. tav. xxxiv.) Page 473.

Nereus. (Panofka Musée Blacas, pl. 20.) Page 473.

The Group of Niobe.
(Zannoni, Gal. di Firenze, série 4, vol. i.) Page 482. See illustrations opposite p. 449.

[To face p. 464.

Methymna. Page 444.

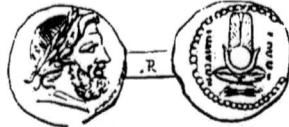

Myndus. Page 462.

Miletus. Page 446.

Myrina. Page 462.

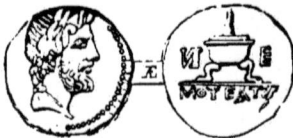

Mopsuestia in Cilicia. Page 456.

Mytilene. Page 465.

Morgantium. Page 456.

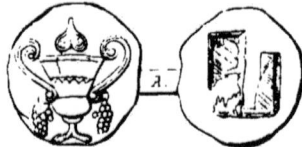

The Island of Naxos. Page 469.

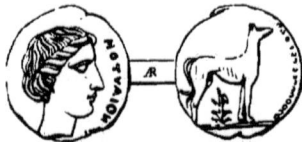

Motya. Page 456.

Naxos in Sicily. Page 469.

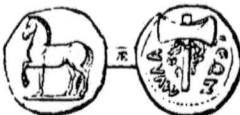

Mylasa. Page 462.

Neapolis in Campania. Page 469.

To face p. 465.]

the Greeks Ζεὺς Ἀβρεττηνός; the Trimenthurîtae, the Pentademîtae, and the Mysomacedônes, all in the region of M. Temnus.

Mysius (*Bergama*), a tributary of the river Caïcus in Mysia, or rather the upper part of the Caïcus itself, had its source in M. Temnus.

Myson (Μύσων), of Chenae, a village either in Laconia or on Mt. Oeta, is enumerated by Plato as one of the 7 sages, in place of Periander.

Mystia, a town in the S.E. of Bruttium, a little above the Prom. Cocintum.

Mytilene or **Mitylene** (Μυτιλήνη, Μιτυλήνη: the former is the ancient form, and the one usually found on coins and inscriptions; the latter is sometimes found on inscriptions, and is the commoner form in MSS.: Μυτιληναῖος: Mitylenaeus: *Mytilene* or *Metelin*), the chief city of LESBOS, stood on the E. side of the island opposite the coast of Asia, upon a promontory which was once an island, and both sides of which formed excellent harbours. Its first foundation is ascribed to Carians and Pelasgians. It was early colonised by the Aeolians. [LESBOS.] Important hints respecting its political history are furnished by the fragments of the poetry of Alcaeus, whence (and from other sources) it seems that, after the rule and overthrow of a series of tyrants, the city was nearly ruined by the bitter hatred and conflicts of the factions of the nobles and the people, till Pittacus was appointed to a sort of dictatorship, and the nobles were expelled. [ALCAEUS; PITTACUS.] Meanwhile, the city had grown to great importance as a naval power, and had founded colonies on the coasts of Mysia and Thrace. At the beginning of the 7th century B. C., the possession of one of these colonies, Sigeum at the mouth of the Hellespont, was disputed in war between the Mytilenaeans and Athenians, and assigned to the latter by the award of Periander, tyrant of Corinth. Among the other colonies of Mytilene were Achilleum, Assos, Antandrus, &c. Mytilene submitted to the Persians after the conquest of Ionia and Aeolis, and furnished contingents to the expeditions of Cambyses against Egypt and of Darius against Scythia. It was active in the Ionian revolt, after the failure of which it again became subject to Persia, and took part in the expedition of Xerxes against Greece. After the Persian war, it formed an alliance with Athens, and remained one of the most important members of the Athenian confederacy, retaining its independence till the 4th year of the Peloponnesian War, B. C. 428, when it headed a revolt of the greater part of Lesbos, the progress and suppression of which forms one of the most interesting episodes in the history of the Peloponnesian War. (See the Histories of Greece.) This event destroyed the power of Mytilene. Its subsequent fortunes cannot be related in detail here. It fell under the power of the Romans after the Mithridatic War. Respecting its important position in Greek literary history, see LESBOS.

Myttistratum. [AMESTRATUS.]

Myus (Μυοῦς: Μυούσιος: *Palatia*, Ru.), the least city of the Ionian confederacy, stood in Caria, on the S. side of the Maeander, 30 stadia from its mouth, and very near Miletus. Its original site was probably at the mouth of the river; but its site gradually became an unhealthy marsh; and by the time of Augustus it was so deserted by its inhabitants that the few who remained were reckoned as citizens of Miletus.

N.

Naarda (Νάαρδα), a town of Babylonia, chiefly inhabited by Jews, and with a Jewish academy.

Naarmalcha or **Nahrmalcha** (Νααρμάλχας, Ναρμάλχας, i. e. *the King's Canal*: ὁ Βασίλειος ποταμός, ἡ βασιλικὴ διῶρυξ, flumen regium: *Nahr-al-Malk* or *Ne Gruel Melek*), the greatest of the canals connecting the Euphrates and the Tigris, was situated near the N. limit of Babylonia, a little S. of the Median Wall, in lat. 33° 5′ about. Its formation was ascribed to a governor named Gobares. It was repaired upon the building of Seleucia at its junction with the Tigris by Seleucus Nicator, and again under the Roman emperors, Trajan, Severus, and Julian.

Naballa. [NAVALIA.]

Nabarzanes (Ναβαρζάνης), a Persian, conspired along with Bessus, against Darius, the last king of Persia. He was pardoned by Alexander.

Nabataei, Nabathae (Ναβαταῖοι, Ναβάται: O. T. Nebaioth), an Arabian people, descended from the eldest son of Ishmaël, had their original abodes in the N.W. part of the Arabian peninsula, E. and S.E. of the Moabites and Edomites, who dwelt on the E. of the Dead Sea and in the mountains reaching from it to the Persian Gulf. In the changes effected among the peoples of these regions by the Babylonian conquest of Judaea, the Nabathaeans extended W. into the Sinaïtic peninsula and the territory of the Edomites, while the latter took possession of the S. of Judaea [IDUMAEI]; and hence the Nabathaeans of Greek and Roman history occupied nearly the whole of Arabia Petraea, along the N.E. coast of the Red Sea, on both sides of the Aelanitic Gulf, and in the Idumaean mountains (M. of Seir), where they had their celebrated rock-hewn capital, PETRA. At first they were a roving pastoral people; but, as their position gave them the command of the trade between Arabia and the W., they, prosecuted that trade with great energy, establishing regular caravans between Leuce Come, a port of the Red Sea, in the N.W. part of Arabia, and the port of Rhinocolura (*El-Arish*) on the Mediterranean, upon the frontiers of Palestine and Egypt. Sustained by this traffic a powerful monarchy grew up, which resisted all the attacks of the Greek kings of Syria, and which, sometimes at least, extended its power as far N. as Syria. Thus, in the reign of Caligula, even after the Nabathaeans had nominally submitted to Rome, we find even Damascus in possession of an ethnarch of "Aretas the king," i. e. of the Nabathaean Arabs: the usual names of these kings were Aretas and Obodas. Under Augustus the Nabathaeans are found, as nominal subjects of the Roman empire, assisting Aelius Gallus in his expedition into Arabia Felix, through which, and through the journey of Athenodorus to Petra, Strabo derived important information. Under Trajan the Nabathaeans were conquered by A. Cornelius Palma, and Arabia Petraea became a Roman province, A. D. 105—107. In the 4th century it was considered a part of Palestine, and formed the diocese of a metropolitan, whose see was at Petra. The Mohamedan conquest finally overthrew the power of the Nabathaeans, which had been long declining: their country soon became a haunt of the wandering Arabs of the Desert; and their very name disappeared.

Nabis (Νάβις), succeeded in making himself tyrant of Lacedaemon on the death of Machanidas, B.C. 207. He carried the licence of tyranny to the furthest possible extent. All persons possessed of property were subjected to incessant exactions, and the most cruel tortures if they did not succeed in satisfying his rapacity. One of his engines of torture resembled the *maiden* of more recent times ; it was a figure resembling his wife Apega, so constructed as to clasp the victim and pierce him to death with the nails with which the arms and bosom of the figure were studded. The money which he got by these means and by the plunder of the temples enabled him to raise a large body of mercenaries, whom he selected from among the most abandoned and reckless villains. With these forces he was able to extend his sway over a considerable part of Peloponnesus ; but his further progress was checked by Flaminius, who after a short campaign compelled him to sue for peace (195). The tyrant, however, was allowed to retain the sovereignty of Sparta, and soon after the departure of Flamininus from Greece, he resumed hostilities. He was opposed by Philopoemen, the general of the Achaean league ; and though Nabis met at first with some success, he was eventually defeated by Philopoemen, and was soon afterwards assassinated by some Aetolians who had been sent to his assistance (192).

Nabonassar (Ναβονάσαρος), king of Babylon, whose accession to the throne was fixed upon by the Babylonian astronomers as the era from which they began their calculations. This era is called the *Era of Nabonassar*. It commenced on the 26th of February, B.C. 747.

Nabrissa or **Nebrissa**, surnamed Veneria, a town of the Turdetani in Hispania Baetica, near the mouth of the Baetis.

Nacolia (Νακόλεια, or -ία, or Νακώλεια: *Sidighasi*), a town of Phrygia Epictetus, on the W. bank of the river Thymbrius, between Dorylaeum and Cotyaeum, was the place where the emperor Valens defeated his rival Procopius, A. D. 366.

Naenia, i. e. a dirge or lamentation, chaunted at funerals, was personified at Rome and worshipped as a goddess. She had a chapel outside the walls of the city, near the porta Viminalis.

Naevius, Cn., an ancient Roman poet, of whose life few particulars have been recorded. He was probably a native of Campania, and was born somewhere between B.C. 274 and 264. He appears to have come to Rome early, and he produced his first play in 235. He was attached to the plebeian party; and, with the licence of the old Attic comedy, he made the stage a vehicle for his attacks upon the aristocracy. He attacked Scipio and the Metelli ; but he was indicted by Q. Metellus and thrown into prison, to which circumstance Plautus alludes in his *Miles Gloriosus* (ii. 2. 56). Whilst in prison he composed two plays, the *Hariolus* and *Leon*, in which he recanted his previous imputations, and thereby obtained his release through the tribunes of the people. His repentance, however, did not last long, and he was soon compelled to expiate a new offence by exile. He retired to Utica ; and it was here, probably, that he wrote his poem on the first Punic war ; and here it is certain that he died, either in 204 or 202. Naevius was both an epic and a dramatic poet. Of his epic poem on the first Punic war a few fragments are still extant. It was written in the old Saturnian metre ; for Ennius, who introduced the hexameter among the Romans, was not brought to Rome till after the banishment of Naevius. The poem appears to have opened with the story of Aeneas's flight from Troy, his visit to Carthage and amour with Dido, together with other legends connected with the early history both of Carthage and of Rome. It was extensively copied both by Ennius and Virgil. The latter author took many passages from it; particularly the description of the storm in the first Aeneïd, the speech with which Aeneas consoles his companions, and the address of Venus to Jupiter. His dramatic writings comprised both tragedies and comedies, most of which were taken from the Greek. Even in the Augustan age Naevius was still a favourite with the admirers of the genuine old school of Roman poetry ; and the lines of Horace (*Ep.* ii. 1. 53) show that his works, if not so much read as formerly, were still fresh in the memories of men. The best edition of the fragments of Naevius is by Klussman, 8vo. Jena, 1843.

Naevius Sertorius Macro. [MACRO.]

Naharvali, a tribe of the Lygii in Germany, probably dwelt on the banks of the Vistula. In their country was a grove sacred to the worship of 2 divinities called Alces, whom Tacitus compares with Castor and Pollux.

Nahrmalcha [NAARMALCHA].

Naïades. [NYMPHAE.]

Nain (Ναΐν: *Nain*), a city of Galilee, S. of M. Tabor. (*Luke*, vii. 11.)

Naisus, Naissus, or **Naesus** (Ναϊσός, Ναϊσσός. Ναΐσσος: *Nissa*), an important town of Upper Moesia, situated on an E. tributary of the Margus, and celebrated as the birthplace of Constantine the Great. It was enlarged and beautified by Constantine, was destroyed by Attila, but was rebuilt and fortified by Justinian.

Namnětae or **Namnētes**, a people on the W. coast of Gallia Lugdunensis, on the N. bank of the Liger, which separated them from Aquitania. Their chief town was Condivincum, afterwards Namnetes (*Nantes*).

Namusa, Aufidius, a Roman jurist, one of the numerous pupils of Serv. Sulpicius.

Nantuātae or **Nantuātes**, a people in the S. E. of Gallia Belgica between the Rhodanus and the Rhenus, and at the E. extremity of the Lacus Lemanus.

Napaeae. [NYMPHAE.]

Naparis, a northern tributary of the Danube : its modern name is uncertain.

Napata (Νάπατα: prob. *El-Kab*, Ru., at the great bend of the Nile to the S.W., between the 4th and 5th cataracts), the capital of an Aethiopian kingdom N. of that of Meroë, was the S.-most point reached by Petronius, under Augustus. Its sovereigns were females, bearing the title of Candace ; and through a minister of one of them Christianity was introduced into Aethiopia in the apostolic age (Acts viii. 27). This custom of female government has been continued to our own times in the neighbouring kingdom of *Shendy*. In the reign of Nero, Napata was only a small town.

Napoca or **Napuca** (Napocensis or Napucensis), a Roman colony in Dacia, on the high road leading through the country, between Patavissa and Optatiana.

Nar (*Nera*), a river in central Italy, rises in M. Fiscellus, on the frontiers of Umbria and Picenum, flows in a S. W.-ly direction, forming the boundary between Umbria and the land of the Sabini, and after receiving the Velinus (*Velino*) and Tolenus (*Turano*), and passing by Interamna and Narnia, falls into the Tiber, not far from Ocriculum. It was celebrated for its sulphureous waters and white colour (*sulphurea Nar albus aqua,* Virg. *Aen.* vii. 517).

Naraggăra (Ναράγαρα: *Kassir Jebir*, Ru.) one of the most important inland cities of Numidia, between Thagura and Sicca Venena, was the scene of Scipio's celebrated interview with Hannibal before the battle of Zama.

Narbo Martius, at a later time **Narbona** (Narbonensis: *Narbonne*), a town in the S. of Gaul and the capital of the Roman province of Gallia Narbonensis, was situated on the river Atax (*Aude*), also called Narbo, and at the head of the lake Rubresus or Rubrensis (also called Narbonitis), which was connected with the sea by a canal. By this means the town, which was 12 miles from the coast, was made a sea-port. It was a very ancient place, and is supposed to have been originally called Atax. It was made a Roman colony by the consul Q. Marcius or Martius, B. C. 118, and hence received the surname Martius; and it was the first colony founded by the Romans in Gaul. Julius Caesar also settled here the veterans of his 10th legion, whence it received the name of Colonia Decumanorum. It was a handsome and populous town; the residence of the Roman governor of the province; and a place of great commercial importance. The coast was celebrated for its excellent oysters. There are scarcely any vestiges of the ancient town; but there are still remains of the canal.

Narbonensis Gallia. [GALLIA.]

Narcissus (Νάρκισσος). 1. A beautiful youth, son of the river god Cephissus and the nymph Liriope of Thespiae. He was wholly inaccessible to the feeling of love; and the nymph Echo, who was enamoured of him, died of grief. [ECHO.] One of his rejected lovers, however, prayed to Nemesis to punish him for his unfeeling heart. Nemesis accordingly caused Narcissus to see his own image reflected in a fountain, and to become enamoured of it. But as he could not approach this object, he gradually pined away, and his corpse was metamorphosed into the flower which bears his name.—2. A freedman and secretary of the emperor Claudius, over whom he possessed unbounded influence. He long connived at the irregularities of Messalina; but fearing that the empress meditated his death, he betrayed to Claudius her marriage with C. Silius, and obtained the order for her execution, A. D. 48. After the murder of Claudius, Narcissus was put to death by command of Agrippina, 54. He had amassed an enormous fortune, amounting, it is said, to 400,000,000 sesterces, equivalent to 3,125,000*l.* of our money. —3. A celebrated athlete, who strangled the emperor Commodus, 192. He was afterwards exposed to the lions by the emperor Severus.

Narisci, a small but brave people in the S. of Germany, of the Suevic race, dwelt W. of the Marcomanni and E. of the Hermunduri, and extended from the Sudeti Montes on the N. to the Danube on the S., thus inhabiting part of the Upper Palatinate and the country of the *Fichtelgebirge.*

Narmalcha. [NAARMALCHA.]

Narnia (Narniensis: *Narni*), a town in Umbria, situated on a lofty hill, on the S. bank of the river Nar, originally called **Nequinum,** was made a Roman colony B. C. 299, when its name was changed into Narnia, after the river. This town was strongly fortified by nature, being accessible only on the E. and W. sides. On the W. side it could only be approached by a very lofty bridge which Augustus built over the river.

Naro, sometimes **Nar** (*Narenta*), a river in Dalmatia, which rises in M. Albius, and falls into the Adriatic sea.

Narôna, a Roman colony in Dalmatia, situated on the river Naro, some miles from the sea, and on the road to Dyrrhachium.

Narses, king of Persia. [SASSANIDAE.]

Narses (Ναρσῆς), a celebrated general and statesman in the reign of Justinian, was an eunuch. He put an end to the Gothic dominion in Italy by two brilliant campaigns, A. D. 552, 553, and annexed Italy again to the Byzantine empire. He was rewarded by Justinian with the government of the country, which he held for many years. He was deprived of this office by Justin, the successor of Justinian, whereupon he invited the Langobards to invade Italy. His invitation was eagerly accepted by their king Alboin; but it is said that Narses soon after repented of his conduct, and died of grief at Rome shortly after the Langobards had crossed the Alps (568). Narses was 95 years of age at the time of his death.

Narthacĭum (Ναρθάκιον), a town in Thessaly, on M. Narthacius, S.W. of Pharsalus.

Naryx, also **Narycus** or **Narycĭum** (Νάρυξ, Νάρυκος, Ναρύκιον: Ναρύκιος, Ναρυκαῖος: *Talanda* or *Talanti*), a town of the Locri Opuntii on the Euboean sea, the reputed birthplace of Ajax, son of Oileus, who is hence called *Narycius heros.* Since Locri Epizephyrii in the S. of Italy claimed to be a colony from Naryx in Greece, we find the town of Bruttium called *Narycia* by the poets, and the pitch of Bruttium also named *Narycia.*

Nasămônes (Νασαμῶνες), a powerful but savage Libyan people, who dwelt originally on the shores of the Great Syrtis, but were driven inland by the Greek settlers of Cyrenaica, and afterwards by the Romans. An interesting account of their manners and customs is given by Herodotus (iv. 172), who also tells (ii. 32) a curious story respecting an expedition beyond the Libyan Desert, undertaken by 5 Nasamonian youths, the result of which was certain important information concerning the interior of Africa. [NIGEIR.]

Nasica, Scipio. [SCIPIO.]

Nasidiēnus, a wealthy (*beatus*) Roman, who gave a supper to Maecenas, which Horace ridicules in the 8th satire of his 2nd book. It appears from v. 58, that Rufus was the cognomen of Nasidienus.

Nasidius, Q. or **L.,** was sent by Pompey, in B. C. 49, with a fleet of 16 ships to relieve Massilia, when it was besieged by D. Brutus. He was defeated by Brutus, and fled to Africa, where he had the command of the Pompeian fleet. He served in Sicily under Sex. Pompey, whom he deserted in 35. He joined Antony, and commanded part of his fleet in the war with Octavian, 31.

Naso, Ovidius. [OVIDIUS.]

Nasus or **Nesus.** [OENIADAE.]

Natiso (*Natisone*), a small river in Venetia in the N. of Italy, which flows by Aquileia, and falls into the Sinus Tergestinus.

Natta or **Nacca**, "a fuller," the name of an ancient family of the Pinaria gens. The Natta satirised by Horace (*Sat.* i. 6. 124) for his dirty meanness, was probably a member of the noble Pinarian family, and therefore attacked by the poet for such conduct.

Naucrătes (Ναυκράτης), of Erythrae, a Greek rhetorician, and a disciple of Isocrates, is mentioned among the orators who competed (B.C. 352) for the prize offered by Artemisia for the best funeral oration delivered over Mausolus.

Naucrătis (Ναύκρατις: Ναυκρατίτης: *Sa-el-Hadjar*, Ru.), a city in the Delta of Egypt, in the Nomus of Saïs, on the E. bank of the Canopic branch of the Nile, which was hence called also Naucraticum Ostium. It was a colony of the Milesians, founded probably in the reign of Amasis, about B.C. 550, and remained a pure Greek city. It was the only place in Egypt, where Greeks were permitted to settle and trade. After the Greek and Roman conquests it continued a place of great prosperity and luxury, and was celebrated for its worship of Aphrodite. It was the birthplace of Athenaeus, Lyceas, Phylarchus, Polycharmus, and Julius Pollux.

Naucydes (Ναυκύδης), an Argive statuary, son of Mothon, and brother and teacher of Polycletus II. of Argos, flourished B.C. 420.

Naulŏchus (Ναύλοχος), that is, a place where ships can anchor. 1. A naval station on the E. part of the N. coast of Sicily between Mylae and the promontory Pelorus.—2. A small island off Crete, near the promontory Sammonium.—3. A naval station belonging to Mesembria in Thrace.

Naumachius (Ναυμάχιος), a Gnomic poet, of uncertain age, some of whose verses are preserved by Stobaeus.

Naupactus (Ναύπακτος: Ναυπάκτιος: *Lepanto*), an ancient and strongly fortified town of the Locri Ozolae near the promontory Antirrhium, possessing the largest and best harbour on the whole of the N. coast of the Corinthian gulf. It is said to have derived its name from the Heraclidae having here built the fleet, with which they crossed over to the Peloponnesus. After the Persian wars it fell into the power of the Athenians, who settled here the Messenians who had been compelled to leave their country at the end of the 3rd Messenian war, B.C. 455; and during the Peloponnesian war it was the head-quarters of the Athenians in all their operations against the W. of Greece. At the end of the Peloponnesian war the Messenians were obliged to leave Naupactus, which passed into the hands first of the Locrians and afterwards of the Achaeans. It was given by Philip with the greater part of the Locrian territory to Aetolia, but it was again assigned to Locris by the Romans.

Nauplia (Ναυπλία: Ναυπλιεύς: *Nauplia*), the port of Argos, situated on the Saronic gulf, was never a place of importance in antiquity, and was in ruins in the time of Pausanias. The inhabitants had been expelled by the Argives as early as the 2nd Messenian war on suspicion of favouring the Spartans, who in consequence settled them at Methone in Messenia. At the present day Nauplia is one of the most important cities in Greece.

Nauplius (Ναύπλιος). 1. Of Argos, son of Poseidon and Amymone, a famous navigator, and the founder of the town of Nauplia. —2. Son of Clytoneus, was one of the Argonauts and a de-

scendant of the preceding.—3. King of Euboea, and father of Palamedes, Oeax, and Nausimedon, by Clymene. Catreus had given his daughter Clymene and her sister Aërope to Nauplius, to be carried to a foreign land; but Nauplius married Clymene, and gave Aërope to Plisthenes, who became by her the father of Agamemnon and Menelaus. His son Palamedes had been condemned to death by the Greeks during the siege of Troy; and as Nauplius considered his condemnation to be an act of injustice, he watched for the return of the Greeks, and as they approached the coast of Euboea he lighted torches on the dangerous promontory of Caphareus. The sailors thus misguided suffered shipwreck, and perished in the waves or by the sword of Nauplius.

Nauportus (*Ober* or *Upper Laibach*), an ancient and important commercial town of the Taurisci, situated on the river Nauportus (*Laibach*), a tributary of the Savus, in Pannonia Superior. The town fell into decay after the foundation of Aemona (*Laibach*), which was only 15 miles from it. The name of Nauportus is said to have been derived from the Argonauts having sailed up the Danube and the Savus to this place and here built the town; and it is added that they afterwards carried their ships across the Alps to the Adriatic sea, where they again embarked. This legend, like many others, probably owes its origin to a piece of bad etymology.

Nausicăa (Ναυσικάα), daughter of Alcinous, king of the Phaeacians, and Arete, who conducted Ulysses to the court of her father, when he was shipwrecked on the coast.

Nausithŏus (Ναυσίθοος), son of Poseidon and Periboea, the daughter of Eurymedon, was the father of Alcinous and Rhexenor, and king of the Phaeacians, whom he led from Hyperia in Thrinacia to the island of Scheria, in order to escape from the Cyclopes.

Nautaca (Ναύτακα: *Naksheb* or *Kesh*), a city of Sogdiana, near the Oxus, towards the E. part of its course.

Nautes. [NAUTIA GENS.]

Nautia Gens, an ancient patrician gens, claimed to be descended from Nautes, one of the companions of Aeneas, who was said to have brought with him the Palladium from Troy, which was placed under the care of the Nautii at Rome. The Nautii, all of whom were surnamed *Rutili*, frequently held the highest offices of state in the early times of the republic, but like many of the other ancient gentes they disappear from history about the time of the Samnite wars.

Nava (*Nahe*), a W. tributary of the Rhine in Gaul, which falls into the Rhine at the modern *Bingen*.

Navalia or **Naballa**, a river on the N. coast of Germany, mentioned by Tacitus, probably the E. arm of the Rhine.

Navius, Attus, a renowned augur in the time of Tarquinius Priscus. This king proposed to double the number of the equestrian centuries, and to name the three new ones after himself and two of his friends, but was opposed by Navius, because Romulus had originally arranged the equites under the sanction of the auspices, and consequently no alteration could be made in them without the same sanction. The tale then goes on to say that Tarquinius thereupon commanded him to divine whether what he was thinking of in his mind could be done, and that when Navius, after consulting the heavens, declared that it could, the king held out a whetstone and a razor to cut it with. Navius immediately cut it. His statue was placed in the comitium, on the steps of the senate-house, the place where the miracle had been wrought, and beside the statue the whetstone was preserved. Attus Navius seems to be the best orthography, making Attus an old praenomen, though we frequently find the name written Attius.

Naxos (Ná£os: Ná£ios). 1. (*Naxia*), an island in the Aegaean sea, and the largest of the Cyclades, is situated nearly half way between the coasts of Greece and Asia Minor. It is about 18 miles in length and 12 in breadth. It was very fertile in antiquity, as it is in the present day, producing an abundance of corn, wine, oil, and fruit. It was especially celebrated for its wine, and hence plays a prominent part in the legends about Dionysus. Here the god is said to have found Ariadne after she had been deserted by Theseus. The marble of the island was also much prized, and was considered equal to the Parian.—Naxos is frequently called *Dia* (Δία) by the poets, which was one of its ancient names. It was likewise called *Strongyle* (Στρογγύλη) on account of its round shape, and *Dionysias* (Διονυσιάς) from its connection with the worship of Dionysus. It is said to have been originally inhabited by Thracians and then by Carians, and to have derived its name from a Carian chief, Naxos. In the historical age it was inhabited by Ionians, who had emigrated from Athens. Naxos was conquered by Pisistratus, who established Lygdamis as tyrant of the island about B.C. 540. The Persians in 501 attempted, at the suggestion of Aristagoras, to subdue Naxos ; and upon the failure of their attempt, Aristagoras, fearing punishment, induced the Ionian cities to revolt from Persia. In 490 the Persians, under Datis and Artaphernes, conquered Naxos, and reduced the inhabitants to slavery. The Naxians recovered their independence after the battle of Salamis (480). They were the first of the allied states whom the Athenians reduced to subjection (471), after which time they are rarely mentioned in history. The chief town of the island was also called Naxos ; and we also have mention of the small towns of Tragaea and Lestadae.—2. A Greek city on the E. coast of Sicily, S. of Mt. Taurus, was founded B.C. 735 by the Chalcidians of Euboea, and was the first Greek colony established in the island. It grew so rapidly in power that in only 5 or 6 years after its foundation it sent colonies to Catana and Leontini. It was for a time subject to Hieronymus, tyrant of Gela ; but it soon recovered its independence, carried on a successful war against Messana, and was subsequently an ally of the Athenians against Syracuse. In 403 the town was taken by Dionysius of Syracuse and destroyed. Nearly 50 years afterwards (358) the remains of the Naxians scattered over Sicily were collected by Andromachus, and a new city was founded on Mt. Taurus, to which the name of Tauromenium was given. [TAUROMENIUM.]

Naxuana (Na£ουάνα: Nakshivan), a city of Armenia Major, on the Araxes, near the confines of Media.

Nazareth, Nazara (Na£αρέθ, or -έτ, or -ά: Na£αραῖος, Na£ωραῖος, Nazarēnus, Nazarēus: en-*Nasirah*), a city of Palestine, in Galilee, S. of Cana, on a hill in the midst of the range of mountains N. of the plain of Esdraëlon.

Nazianzus (Na£ιανζός: Na£ιαν(ηνός), a city of Cappadocia, on the road from Archelaïs to Tyana, celebrated as the diocese of the Father of the Church, Gregory Nazianzen. Its site is doubtful.

Neaera (Néαιρα), the name of several nymphs, and also of several maidens mentioned by the poets.

Neaethus (Néαιθος : *Nieto*), a river in Bruttium in the S. of Italy, falling into the Tarentine gulf a little N. of Croton. Here the captive Trojan women are said to have burnt the ships of the Greeks.

Nealces (Néάλκης), a painter who flourished in the time of Aratus, B.C. 245.

Neandria (Νεάνδρεια: Νεανδρεῖς, pl.), a town of the Troad, upon the Hellespont, probably an Aeolian colony. By the time of Augustus it had disappeared.

Neanthes (Νεάνθης), of Cyzicum, lived about B.C. 241, and was a disciple of the Milesian Philiscus, who himself had been a disciple of Isocrates. He was a voluminous writer, principally of history.

Neapolis (Νεάπολις: Νεαπολίτης, Neapolitanus). I. *In Europe*. 1. (*Napoli* or *Naples*), a city in Campania in Italy, on the W. slope of Mt. Vesuvius and on the river Sebethus, was founded by the Chalcidians of Cumae, on the site of an ancient place called **Parthenope** (Παρθενόπη), after the Siren of that name. Hence we find the town called Parthenope by Virgil and Ovid. The year of the foundation of Neapolis is not recorded. It was called the "New City," because it was regarded simply as a new quarter of the neighbouring city of Cumae. When the town is first mentioned in Roman history, it consisted of 2 parts, divided from each other by a wall, and called respectively Palaeopolis and Neapolis. This division probably arose after the capture of Cumae by the Samnites, when a large number of the Cumaeans took refuge in the city they had founded ; whereupon the old quarter was called Palaeopolis, and the new quarter, built to accommodate the new inhabitants, was named Neapolis. There has been a dispute respecting the site of these 2 quarters ; but it is probable that Palaeopolis was situated on the W. side near the harbour, and Neapolis on the E. side near the river Sebethus. In B.C. 327 the town was taken by the Samnites, and in 290 it passed into the hands of the Romans, who allowed it however to retain its Greek constitution. At a later period it became a municipium, and finally a Roman colony. Under the Romans the 2 quarters of the city were united, and the name of Palaeopolis disappeared. It continued to be a prosperous and flourishing place till the time of the empire ; and its beautiful scenery, and the luxurious life of its Greek population, made it a favourite residence with many of the Romans. In the reign of Titus the city was destroyed by an earthquake, but was rebuilt by this emperor in the Roman style. The modern city of Naples does not stand on exactly the same site as Neapolis. The ancient city extended further E. than the modern city, since the former was situated on the Sebethus, whereas the latter does not reach so far as the *Fiume della Madalena;* but the modern city on the other hand extends further N. and W. than the ancient one, since the island of Megaria, on which the *Castel del Ovo* now stands, was situated in ancient times between Pausilypum and Neapolis. In the neighbourhood of Neapolis there were warm baths, the celebrated villa of Lucullus, and the villa Pausilypi or Pausilypum, bequeathed by Vedius Pollio to Augustus, and which has given its name to the celebrated grotto of Posilippo between Naples and Puzzuoli, at the entrance of which the tomb of Virgil is still shown.—2. A part of Syracuse. [SYRACUSAE.] —3. (*Napoli*), a town on the W. coast of the island of Sardinia, celebrated for its warm baths.—4. (*Kavallo*), a sea-port town in Thrace, subsequently Macedonia adjecta, on the Strymonic gulf, between the Strymon and Nessus.—II. *In Asia and Africa*. 1. (*Scala Nuova*, or near it), a small Ionian city, on the coast of Lydia, N. of Mycale and S.W. of Ephesus. The Ephesians, to whom it at first belonged, exchanged it with the Samians for MARATHESIUM. — 2, 3. Two towns of Caria, the one near Harpasa, the other on the coast, perhaps the new town of Myndus. —4. (*Tutinek ?* Rn.), in Pisidia S. of Antioch; afterwards reckoned to Galatia. — 5. In Palestine, the Sychem or Sychar of Scripture (Συχέμ, Συχάρ, Σικίμα, Joseph.: *Nablous*), one of the most ancient cities of Samaria, stood in the narrow valley between Mts. Ebal and Gerizim, and was the religious capital of the Samaritans, whose temple was built upon Mt. Gerizim. This temple was destroyed by John Hyrcanus, B.C. 129. Its full name, under the Romans, was Flavia Neapolis. It was the birthplace of Justin Martyr. — 6. A small town of Babylonia, on the W. bank of the Euphrates, opposite to the opening of the King's Canal. — 7. In Egypt. [CAENE]. — 8. In N. Africa on the W. coast of the Great Syrtis, by some identified with Leptis Magna, by others with the modern *Tripoli*. — 9. (*Nabal*), a very ancient Phoenician colony, on the E. coast of Zeugitana, near the N. extremity of the great gulf which was called after it Sinus Neapolitanus (*Gulf of Hammamet*). Under the Romans it was a libera civitas, and, according to Ptolemy, a colony.

Nearchus (Νέαρχος), a distinguished friend and officer of Alexander, was a native of Crete, but settled at Amphipolis. He appears to have occupied a prominent position at the court of Philip, by whom he was banished for participating in the intrigues of Alexander. After the death of Philip he was recalled, and treated with the utmost distinction by Alexander. He accompanied the king to Asia; and in B.C. 325, he was entrusted by Alexander with the command of the fleet which he had caused to be constructed on the Hydaspes. Upon reaching the mouth of the Indus, Alexander resolved to send round his ships by sea from thence to the Persian gulf, and he gladly accepted the offer of Nearchus to undertake the command of the fleet during this long and perilous navigation. Nearchus set out on the 21st of September, 326, and arrived at Susa in safety in February, 325. He was rewarded with a crown of gold for his distinguished services, and at the same time obtained in marriage a daughter of the Rhodian Mentor and of Barsine, to whom Alexander himself had been previously married. In the division of the provinces after the death of Alexander, he received the government of Lycia and Pamphylia, which he held as subordinate to Antigonus. In 317 he accompanied Antigonus in his march against Eumenes, and in 314 he is mentioned again as one of the generals of Antigonus.—Nearchus left a history of the voyage, the substance of which has been preserved to us by Arrian, who has derived from it the whole of the latter part of his "Indica."

Nebo, a mountain of Palestine, on the E. side of the Jordan, opposite to Jericho, was in the S. part of the range called Abarim. It was on a summit of this mountain, called Pisgah, that Moses died.

Nebrodes Montes, the principal chain of mountains in Sicily, running through the whole of the island, and a continuation of the Apennines.

Neco or **Necho** (Νεκώς, Νέχως, Νεκαῦς, Νεχαώς, Νεχαώ), son of Psammetichus, whom he succeeded on the throne of Egypt in B.C. 617. His reign was marked by considerable energy and enterprise. He began to dig the canal intended to connect the Nile with the Arabian Gulf; but he desisted from the work, according to Herodotus, on being warned by an oracle that he was constructing it only for the use of the barbarian invader. But the greatest and most interesting enterprise with which his name is connected, is the circumnavigation of Africa by the Phoenicians, in his service, who set sail from the Arabian Gulf, and accomplishing the voyage in somewhat more than 2 years, entered the Mediterranean, and returned to Egypt through the Straits of Gibraltar. His military expeditions were distinguished at first by brilliant success, which was followed, however, by the most rapid and signal reverses. On his march against the Babylonians and Medes, whose joint forces had recently destroyed Nineveh, he was met at Magdolus (Megiddo) by Josiah, king of Judah, who was a vassal of Babylon. In the battle which ensued, Josiah was defeated and mortally wounded, and Necho advanced to the Euphrates, where he conquered the Babylonians and took Carchemish or Circesium, where he appears to have established a garrison. After the battle at Megiddo, he took the town of Cadytis, probably Jerusalem. In 606, Nebuchadnezzar attacked Carchemish, defeated Necho, and would appear also to have invaded Egypt itself. In 601 Necho died after a reign of 16 years, and was succeeded by his son Psammis or Psammuthis.

Nectanabis, Nectanebus, or **Nectanebes** (Νεκτάναβις, Νεκτάνεβος, Νεκτανέβης). 1. King of Egypt, the 1st of the 3 sovereigns of the Sebennite dynasty, succeeded Nepherites on the throne about B.C. 374, and in the following year successfully resisted the invasion of the Persian force under Pharnabazus and Iphicrates. He died after a reign of 10 years, and was succeeded by Tachos. — 2. The nephew of Tachos, deprived the latter of the sovereignty in 361, with the assistance of Agesilaus. For some time he defeated all the attempts of Artaxerxes III. (Ochus) to recover Egypt, but he was at length defeated himself, and despairing of making any further resistance, he fled into Aethiopia, 350. Nectanabis was the 3rd king of the Sebennite dynasty, and the last native sovereign who ever ruled in Egypt.

Neda (Νέδα: *Busi*), a river in Peloponnesus, rises in Arcadia in Mt. Cerausion, a branch of Mt. Lycaeus, and falls into the Ionian sea after forming the boundary between Arcadia and Messenia, and between Messenia and Elis.

Negra or **Negrana** (τὰ Νέγρανα: *El-Nokra*, N. of *Mareb*), a city of Arabia Felix, destroyed by Aelius Gallus.

Neleus (Νηλεύς). 1. Son of Tyro, the daughter of Salmoneus. Poseidon once visited Tyro in the form of the river-god Enipeus, and she became by him the mother of Pelias and Neleus. To conceal her shame she exposed the two boys.

but they were found and reared by some countrymen. They subsequently learnt their parentage; and after the death of Cretheus, king of Iolcos, who had married their mother, they seized the throne of Iolcos, excluding Aeson, the son of Cretheus and Tyro. But Pelias soon afterwards expelled his brother, and thus became sole king. Thereupon Neleus went with Melampus and Bias to Pylos, which his uncle Aphareus gave to him, and of which he thus became king. Several towns of this name claimed the honour of being the city of Neleus or of his son Nestor, such as Pylos in Messenia, Pylos in Elis, and Pylos in Triphylia; the last of which is probably the one mentioned by Homer in connection with Neleus and Nestor. Neleus was married to Chloris, a daughter of Amphion of Orchomenos, according to Homer, and a Theban woman according to others. By her he became the father of Nestor, Chronius, Periclymenus, and Pero, though he had in all 12 sons. When Hercules had killed Iphitus, he went to Neleus to be purified; but Neleus, who was a friend of Eurytus, the father of Iphitus, refused to grant the request of Hercules. In order to take vengeance, Hercules afterwards marched against Pylos, and slew all the sons of Neleus, with the exception of Nestor: some later writers add that Neleus himself was also killed. Neleus was now attacked, and his dominions plundered by Augeas, king of the Epeans; but the attacks of the latter were repelled by Nestor. The descendants of Neleus, the Nelïdae, were eventually expelled from their kingdom by the Heraclidae, and migrated for the most part to Athens.—2. The younger son of Codrus, disputed the right of his elder brother Medon to the crown on account of his lameness, and when the Delphic oracle declared in favour of Medon, he placed himself at the head of the colonists who migrated to Ionia, and himself founded Miletus. His son of Aepytus headed the colonists who settled in Priene. Another son headed a body of settlers who reinforced the inhabitants of Iasus, after they had lost a great number of their citizens in a war with the Carians.—3. Of Scepsis, the son of Coriscus, was a disciple of Aristotle and Theophrastus, the latter of whom bequeathed to him his library, and appointed him one of his executors. The history of the writings of Aristotle as connected with Neleus and his heirs, is related elsewhere [p. 86, a].

Nelïdes, Nelëïades, and **Nelëïus** (Νηλείδης, Νηληϊάδης, Νηλήϊος), patronymics of Neleus, by which either Nestor, the son of Neleus, or Antilochus, his grandson, is designated.

Nemausus (Nemausensis: *Nismes*), one of the most important towns of Gallia Narbonensis, was the capital of the Arecomici and a Roman colony. It was situated inland E. of the Rhone on the highroad from Italy to Spain, and on the S. slope of M. Cevenna. It was celebrated as the place from which the family of the Antonines came. Though rarely mentioned by ancient writers, the Roman remains at *Nismes*, which are some of the most perfect N. of the Alps, prove that the ancient Nemausus was a large and flourishing city. Of these remains the most important are the amphitheatre, the *Maison Carrée*, a name given to a beautiful Corinthian temple, and the magnificent aqueduct, now called *Pont du Gard*, consisting of 3 rows of arches, raised one above the other, and 180 feet in height.

Nĕmĕa (Νεμέα, Ion. Νεμέη), a valley in Argolis between Cleonae and Phlius, celebrated in mythical story as the place where Hercules slew the Nemean lion. [See p. 308, b.] In this valley there was a splendid temple of Zeus Nemëus surrounded by a sacred grove, in which the Nemean games were celebrated every other year. (See *Dict. of Antiq.* art. *Nemea*.)

Nemesiānus, M. Aurelïus Olympïus, a Roman poet, probably a native of Africa, flourished at the court of the emperor Carus (A. D. 283), carried off the prize in all the poetical contests of the day, and was esteemed second to the youthful prince Numerianus alone, who honoured him so far as to permit him to dispute, and to yield to the palm of verse. We are told that Nemesianus was the author of poems upon fishing, hunting, and aquatics; all of which have perished, with the exception of a fragment of the *Cynegetica*, extending to 325 hexameter lines, which, in so far as neatness and purity of expression are concerned, in some degree justifies the admiration of his contemporaries. The best edition of this fragment is by Stern, published along with Gratius Faliscus, Hal. Sax. 1832.

Nĕmĕsis (Νέμεσις), a Greek goddess, is most commonly described as a daughter of Night, though some call her a daughter of Erebus or of Oceanus. She is a personification of the moral reverence for law, of the natural fear of committing a culpable action, and hence of conscience. In later writers, as Herodotus and Pindar, Nemesis measures out happiness and unhappiness to mortals; and he who is blessed with too many or too frequent gifts of fortune, is visited by her with losses and sufferings, in order that he may become humble. This notion arose from a belief that the gods were envious of excessive human happiness. Nemesis was thus a check upon extravagant favours conferred upon man by Tyche or Fortune; and from this idea lastly arose that of her being an avenging and punishing fate, who, like Justice (Dike) and the Erinnyes, sooner or later overtakes the reckless sinner. She is frequently mentioned under the surnames Adrastia [ADRASTIA, No. 2], and Rhamnusia or Rhamnusia, the latter of which she derived from the town of Rhamnus in Attica, where she had a celebrated sanctuary. She was usually represented in works of art as a virgin divinity: in the more ancient works she seems to have resembled Aphrodite, whereas in the later ones she was more grave and serious. But there is an allegorical tradition that Zeus begot by Nemesis at Rhamnus an egg, which Leda found, and from which Helena and the Dioscuri sprang, whence Helena herself is called Rhamnusis.

Nĕmĕsïus (Νεμέσιος), the author of a Greek treatise *On the Nature of Man*, is called bishop of Emesa, in Syria, and probably lived at the end of the 4th or beginning of the 5th century after Christ. His treatise is an interesting philosophical work, which has generally been highly praised by all who have read it. Edited by Matthaei, Halae, 8vo. 1802.

Nemetacum. [NEMETOCENNA.]

Nemĕtes or **Nemĕtae,** a people in Gallia Belgica on the Rhine, whose chief town was Noviomagus, subsequently Nemetae (*Speyer* or *Spires*).

Nemetocenna or **Nemetacum** (*Arras*), the chief town of the Atrebates in Gallia Belgica, subsequently Atrebati, whence its modern name.

Nemorensis Lacus. [ARICIA.]

Nemossus. [ARVERNI.]

Neobūlē. [ARCHILOCHUS.]

Neōcaesarēa (Νεοκαισαρεία; Νεοκαισαρεύς, Neo-caesariensis). 1. (*Niksar*), the capital, under the Roman empire, of Pontus Polemoniacus, in Asia Minor, stood on the river Lycus, 63 Roman miles E. of Amasia. It was a splendid city, and is famous in ecclesiastical history for the council held there in A. D. 314. — 2. (*Kulat-en-Nejur?* Ru.), a fortress established by Justinian, on the Euphrates, in the district of Syria called Chalybonitis.

Neōn (Νέων: Νεώνιος, Νεωναῖος), an ancient town in Phocis at the E. foot of Mt. Tithorea, a branch of Mt. Parnassus, was 80 stadia from Delphi across the mountains. Neon was destroyed by the Persians under Xerxes, but was subsequently rebuilt and named **Tithōrēa** (Τιθορέα: Τιθορεύς) after the mountain on which it was situated. The new town however was not on exactly the same site as the ancient one. Tithorea was situated at the modern *Velitza*, and Neon at *Palea-Fiva*, between 4 and 5 miles N. of Velitza. Tithorea was destroyed in the Sacred war, and was again rebuilt, but remained an unimportant, though fortified place.

Neontīchos (Νέον τεῖχος, i. e. *New Wall*). 1. (*Ainadzjik*), one of the 12 cities of Aeolis on the coast of Mysia, in Asia Minor, stood on the N. side of the Hermus, on the slope of M. Sardene, 30 stadia inland from Larissa. One tradition makes it older than Cyme; but the more probable account is that it was built by the Aeolians of Cyme as a fortress against the Pelasgians of Larissa. — 2. A fort on the coast of Thrace, near the Chersonesus.

Neoptŏlēmus (Νεοπτόλεμος). 1. Also called **Pyrrhus**, son of Achilles and Deidamīa, the daughter of Lycomedes; according to some he was a son of Achilles and Iphigenia, and after the sacrifice of his mother was carried by his father to the island of Scyros. The name of Pyrrhus is said to have been given to him by Lycomedes, because he had fair (πυῤῥός) hair, or because Achilles, while disguised as a girl, had borne the name of Pyrrha. He was called Neoptolemus, that is, young or late warrior, either because he had fought in early youth or because he had come late to Troy. From his father he is sometimes called *Achillīdes*, and from his grandfather or great-grandfather, *Pelīdes* and *Aeacīdes*. Neoptolemus was brought up in Scyros in the palace of Lycomedes, and was fetched from thence by Ulysses to join the Greeks in the war against Troy, because it had been prophesied by Helenus that Neoptolemus and Philoctetes were necessary for the capture of Troy. At Troy Neoptolemus showed himself worthy of his great father. He was one of the heroes concealed in the wooden horse. At the capture of the city he killed Priam at the sacred hearth of Zeus, and sacrificed Polyxena to the spirit of his father. When the Trojan captives were distributed among the conquerors, Andromache, the widow of Hector, was given to Neoptolemus, and by her he became the father of Molossus, Pielus, Pergamus, and Amphialus. Respecting his return from Troy and the subsequent events of his life the traditions differ. It is related that Neoptolemus returned home by land, because he had been forewarned by Helenus of the dangers which the Greeks would have to encounter at sea. According to Homer Neoptolemus lived in Phthia,

the kingdom of his father, and here he married Hermione, whom her father Menelaus sent to him from Sparta. According to others Neoptolemus himself went to Sparta to receive Hermione, because he had heard a report that she was betrothed to Orestes. Most writers relate that he abandoned his native kingdom of Phthia, and settled in Epirus, where he became the ancestor of the Molossian kings. Shortly after his marriage with Hermione, Neoptolemus went to Delphi, where he was murdered; but the reason of his visiting Delphi, as well as the person by whom he was slain, are differently related. Some say he went to plunder the temple of Apollo, others to present part of the Trojan booty as an offering to the god, and others again to consult the god about the means of obtaining children by Hermione. Some relate that he was slain at the instigation of Orestes, who was angry at being deprived of Hermione, and others, by the priest of the temple, or by Machaereus, the son of Daetas. His body was buried at Delphi; and he was worshipped there as a hero.— 2. I. King of Epirus, was son of Alcetas I., and father of Alexander I., and of Olympias, the mother of Alexander the Great. Neoptolemus reigned in conjunction with his brother Arymbas or Arrybas till his death, about B. C. 360. — 3. II. King of Epirus, son of Alexander I. and grandson of the preceding. At his father's death in 326, he was probably a mere infant, and his pretensions to the throne were passed over in favour of Aeacides. It was not till 302 that the Epirots, taking advantage of the absence of Pyrrhus, the son of Aeacides, rose in insurrection against him, and set up Neoptolemus in his stead. The latter reigned for the space of 6 years, but was obliged to share the throne with Pyrrhus in 296. He was shortly afterwards assassinated by Pyrrhus. — 4. A Macedonian officer of Alexander the Great, after whose death he obtained the government of Armenia. In 321 he revolted from Perdiccas, and joined Craterus, but he was defeated by Eumenes, and was slain in battle by the hands of the latter.—5. A general of Mithridates, and brother of Archelaus. — 6. An Athenian tragedian, who performed at the games in which Philip of Macedon was slain, 336. — 7. Of Paros, a Greek grammarian of uncertain date, wrote several works quoted by Athenaeus and the Scholiasts.

Nĕpēte, Nepe or **Nepet** (Nepesinus: *Nepi*), an ancient town of Etruria, but not one of the 12 cities, was situated near the saltus Ciminius and was regarded as one of the keys and gates of Etruria (*claustra portaeque Etruriae*, Liv. vi. 9) It appears as an ally of the Romans at an early period, soon after the capture of Rome by the Gauls, and was subsequently made a Roman colony. There are still remains at *Nepi* of the walls of the ancient city.

Nĕphĕlē (Νεφέλη), wife of Athamas and mother of Phrixus and Helle. Hence Helle is called *Nephelēis* by Ovid. For details see ATHAMAS.

Nĕphēlis (Νεφελίς), a small town and promontory on the coast of Cilicia Aspera, between Anemurium and Antiochia.

Nĕphēris (Νέφερις), a fortified town in the immediate neighbourhood of Carthage, on a rock near the coast.

Nĕpos, Cornēlīus, the contemporary and friend of Cicero, Atticus, and Catullus, was probably a native of Verona, or of some neighbouring village, and died during the reign of Augustus. No other particulars, with regard to his personal history, have been transmitted to us. He is known to have written the following pieces, all of which are now lost. 1. *Chronica*, an Epitome of Universal History, probably in 3 books, to which Catullus appears to allude in dedicating his poems to Cornelius Nepos. 2. *Exemplorum Libri*, probably a collection of remarkable sayings and doings. 3. *De Viris Illustribus*, perhaps the same work as the preceding, quoted under a different title. 4. *Vita Ciceronis*. 5. *Epistolae ad Ciceronem*. 6. *De Historicis*.—There is still extant a work entitled *Vitae Excellentium Imperatorum*, containing biographies of several distinguished commanders, which is supposed by many critics to have been the production of Cornelius Nepos. In all MSS., however, this work is ascribed to an unknown Aemilius Probus, living under Theodosius at the end of the 4th century of the Christian aera, with the exception however of the life of Atticus, and the fragment of a life of Cato the Censor, which are expressly attributed to Cornelius Nepos. These 2 lives may safely be assigned to Cornelius Nepos; but the Latinity of the other biographies is such that we cannot suppose them to have been written by a learned contemporary of Cicero. At the same time their style presents a striking contrast to the meretricious finery of the later empire; and hence it may be conjectured that Probus abridged the work of Nepos, and that the biographies, as they now exist, are in reality epitomes of lives actually written by Nepos. The most useful editions of these lives are by Van Staveren, 8vo. Lug. Bat. 1773; by Tzschucke, 8vo. Gotting. 1804; by Bremi, 8vo. Zurich, 1820; and by Roth, Basil. 8vo. 1841.

Nepos, Jūlĭus, last emperor but one of the West, A. D. 474—475, was raised to the throne by Leo, the emperor of the East. Nepos easily deposed Glycerius, who was regarded at Constantinople as an usurper [GLYCERIUS]; but he was in his turn deposed in the next year by Orestes, who proclaimed his son Romulus. Nepos fled into Dalmatia, where he was killed in 480.

Nepotĭānus, Flavĭus Popĭlĭus, son of Eutropia, the half-sister of Constantine the Great, was proclaimed emperor at Rome in A. D. 350, but was slain by Marcellinus, the general of the usurper Magnentius, after a reign of 28 days.

Neptūnus, called Poseidon by the Greeks. The Greek god is spoken of in a separate article. [POSEIDON.] Neptunus was the chief marine divinity of the Romans. As the early Romans were not a maritime people, the marine divinities are rarely mentioned, and we scarcely know with certainty what day in the year was set apart as the festival of Neptunus, though it seems to have been the 23rd of July (*X. Kal. Sext.*). His temple stood in the Campus Martius, not far from the *septa*. At his festival the people formed tents (*umbrae*) of the branches of trees, in which they enjoyed themselves in feasting and drinking. (*Dict. of Ant.* art. *Neptunalia*). When a Roman commander set sail with a fleet, he first offered up a sacrifice to Neptunus, which was thrown into the sea. In the Roman poets Neptunus is completely identified with the Greek Poseidon, and accordingly all the attributes of the latter are transferred by them to the former.

Nerātĭus Priscus, a Roman jurist, who lived under Trajan and Hadrian. It is said that Trajan sometimes had the design of making Neratius his

successor in place of Hadrian. He enjoyed a high reputation under Hadrian, and was one of his consiliarii. His works are cited in the Digest.

Nērēis or **Nērēĭs** (Νηρείς, in Hom. Νηρηΐς), a daughter of Nereus and Doris, and used especially in the plural, **Nereides** (Νηρείδες, Νηρηΐδες) to indicate the 50 daughters of Nereus and Doris. The *Nereides* were the marine nymphs of the Mediterranean, in contradistinction from the *Naiades*, or the nymphs of fresh water, and the *Oceanides*, or the nymphs of the great ocean. Their names are not the same in all writers; one of the most celebrated was Thetis, the mother of Achilles. They are described as lovely divinities, dwelling with their father at the bottom of the sea, and were believed to be propitious to all sailors, and especially to the Argonauts. They were worshipped in several parts of Greece, but more especially in seaport towns. The epithets given them by the poets refer partly to their beauty and partly to their place of abode. They are frequently represented in works of art, and commonly as youthful, beautiful, and naked maidens; and they are often grouped with Tritons and other marine beings. Sometimes they appear on gems as half maidens and half fishes.

Nērēĭus, a name given by the poets to a descendant of Nereus, such as Phocus and Achilles.

Nerētum or **Neritum** (Neretinus: *Narbo*), a town of the Salentini in Calabria in the S. of Italy.

Nēreus (Νηρεύς), son of Pontus and Gaea, and husband of Doris, by whom he became the father of the 50 Nereides. He is described as the wise and unerring old man of the sea, at the bottom of which he dwelt. His empire is the Mediterranean or more particularly the Aegean sea, whence he is sometimes called the Aegean. He was believed, like other marine divinities, to have the power of prophesying the future and of appearing to mortals in different shapes; and in the story of Hercules he acts a prominent part, just as Proteus in the story of Ulysses, and Glaucus in that of the Argonauts. Virgil (*Aen.* ii. 418) mentions the trident as his attribute, and the epithets given him by the poets refer to his old age, his kindliness, and his trustworthy knowledge of the future. In works of art, Nereus, like other sea-gods, is represented with pointed sea-weeds taking the place of hair in the eyebrows, the chin, and the breast.

Nērĭcus. [LEUCAS.]

Nērĭnē, equivalent to Nereis, a daughter of Nereus. [NEREIS.]

Nerĭo, Nerĭēne, or **Nerĭēnis**. [MARS.]

Nērĭtum, a mountain in Ithaca. [ITHACA.]

Nērĭtus, a small rocky island near Ithaca, erroneously supposed by some to be Ithaca itself.

Nerĭum, also called Celtĭcum (*C. Finisterre*), a promontory in the N. W. corner of Spain, and in the territory of the Nerii, a tribe of the Celtic Artabri, whence the promontory is also called Artabrum.

Nēro, Claudĭus. Nero is said to have signified "brave" in the Sabine tongue. 1. **Tĭb.**, son of the 4 sons of App. Claudius Caecus, censor B. C. 312, from whom all the Claudii Nerones were descended. — 2. **C.**, a celebrated general in the 2nd Punic war. He was praetor 212, and was sent into Spain to oppose Hasdrubal, who eluded his attack, and he was succeeded by Scipio Africanus. Nero was consul in 207 with M. Livius Salinator. Nero marched into the S. of Italy against Hannibal, whom he defeated. He then marched into the N. of Italy, effected a junction with his colleague M. Livius in Picenum, and proceeded to crush Hasdrubal before his brother Hannibal could come to his assistance. Hasdrubal was defeated and slain on the river Metaurus. This great battle, which probably saved Rome, gave a lustre to the name of Nero, and consecrated it among the recollections of the Romans.

> Quid debeas, o Roma, Neronibus,
> Testis Metaurum flumen et Hasdrubal
> Devictus.   Horat. *Carm.* iv. 4.

Nero was censor, 204, with M. Livius. — **3.** Tib., praetor, 204, with Sardinia for his province ; and consul 202, when he obtained Africa as his province, but his fleet suffered so much at sea, that he was unable to join Scipio in Africa. — **4. Tib.**, served under Pompey in the war against the pirates, B.C. 67. He is probably the Tib. Nero who recommended that the members of the conspiracy of Catiline, who had been seized, should be kept confined till Catiline was put down. — **5.** Tib., father of the emperor Tiberius, was probably the son of the last. He served as quaestor under Caesar (48) in the Alexandrine war. He sided with L. Antonius in the war of Perusia (41) ; and when this town surrendered, he passed over to Sex. Pompey in Sicily, and subsequently to M. Antony in Achaea. On a reconciliation being effected between Antony and Octavian at the close of the year (40), he returned with his wife to Rome. Livia, who possessed great beauty, excited the passion of Octavian, to whom she was surrendered by her husband, being then 6 months gone with child of her second son Drusus. Nero died shortly after, and left Octavian the tutor of his two sons.

Nero. 1. Roman emperor, A. D. 54—68, was the son of Cn. Domitius Ahenobarbus, and of Agrippina, daughter of Germanicus Caesar, and sister of Caligula. Nero's original name was *L. Domitius Ahenobarbus*, but after the marriage of his mother with her uncle, the emperor Claudius, he was adopted by Claudius (A. D. 50), and was called *Nero Claudius Caesar Drusus Germanicus.* Nero was born at Antium, on the 15th of December, A. D. 37. Shortly after his adoption by Claudius, Nero, being then 16 years of age, married Octavia, the daughter of Claudius and Messalina (53). Among his early instructors was Seneca. Nero had some talent and taste. He was fond of the arts, and made verses ; but he was indolent and given to pleasure, and had no inclination for laborious studies. On the death of Claudius (54), Agrippina secured the succession for her son, to the exclusion of Britannicus, the son of Claudius. His mother wished to govern in the name of her son, and her ambition was the cause of Nero's first crime. Jealousy thus arose between Nero and his mother, which soon broke out into a quarrel, and Agrippina threatened to join Britannicus and raise him to his father's place ; whereupon Nero caused Britannicus to be poisoned, at an entertainment where Agrippina and Octavia were present (55). During the early part of Nero's reign, the government of Rome was in the hands of Seneca, and of Burrhus, the praefect of the praetorians, who opposed the ambitious designs of Agrippina. Meantime the young emperor indulged his licentious inclinations without restraint. He neglected his wife for the beautiful, but dissolute Poppaea Sa

bina, the wife of Otho. This abandoned woman aspired to become the emperor's wife ; but since she had no hopes of succeeding in her design while Agrippina lived, she used all her arts to urge Nero to put his mother to death. Accordingly in 59, Agrippina was assassinated by Nero's order, with the approbation at least of Seneca and Burrhus, who saw that the time was come for the destruction either of the mother or the son. Though Nero had no longer any one to oppose him, he felt the punishment of his guilty conscience, and said that he was haunted by his mother's spectre. He attempted to drown his reflections in fresh riot, in which he was encouraged by a band of flatterers. He did not, however, immediately marry Poppaea, being probably restrained by fear of Burrhus and Seneca. But the death of Burrhus in 62, and the retirement of Seneca from public affairs, which immediately followed, left Nero more at liberty. Accordingly he divorced his wife Octavia, and in 18 days married Poppaea. Not satisfied with putting away his wife, he falsely charged her with adultery, and banished her to the island of Pandataria, where she was shortly after put to death.—In 64 the great fire at Rome happened. Its origin is uncertain, for it is hardly credible that the city was fired by Nero's order, as some ancient writers assert. Out of the 14 regiones of Rome into which Rome was divided, 3 were totally destroyed, and in 7 others only a few half-burnt houses remained. The emperor set about rebuilding the city on an improved plan, with wider streets. He found money for his purposes by acts of oppression and violence, and even temples were robbed of their wealth. With these means he began to erect his sumptuous golden palace, on a scale of magnitude and splendour which almost surpasses belief. The vestibule contained a colossal statue of himself 120 feet high. The odium of the conflagration which the emperor could not remove from himself, he tried to throw on the Christians, who were then numerous in Rome, and many of them were put to a cruel death. — The tyranny of Nero at last (65) led to the organisation of a formidable conspiracy against him, usually called Piso's conspiracy, from the name of one of the principal accomplices. The plot was discovered, and many distinguished persons were put to death, among whom was Piso himself, the poet Lucan, and the philosopher Seneca, though the latter appears to have taken no part in the plot. In the same year, Poppaea died of a kick, which her brutal husband gave her in a fit of passion when she was with child. Nero now married Statilia Messallina. The history of the remainder of Nero's reign is a catalogue of his crimes. Virtue in any form was the object of his fear ; and almost every month was marked by the execution or banishment of some distinguished man. Among his other victims were Thrasea Paetus and Barea Soranus, both men of high rank, but of spotless integrity. In 67 Nero paid a visit to Greece, and took part in the contests of both the Olympic and Pythian games. He commenced a canal across the Isthmus of Corinth, but the works were afterwards suspended by his own orders. While in Greece he sent orders to put to death his faithful general Domitius Corbulo, which the old soldier anticipated by stabbing himself. The Roman world had long been tired of its oppressor ; and the storm at length broke out in Gaul, where Julius Vindex, the governor, openly raised the standard of revolt. His example was followed by Galba, who was governor of Hispania Tarraconensis. Galba was proclaimed emperor by his troops, but he only assumed the title of legatus of the senate and the Roman people. Soon after these news reached Rome, Nymphidius Sabinus, who was praefectus praetorio along with Tigellinus, persuaded the troops to proclaim Galba. Nero was immediately deserted. He escaped from the palace at night with a few freedmen, and made his way to a house about 4 miles from Rome, which belonged to his freedman Phaon. Here he gave himself a mortal wound, when he heard the trampling of the horses on which his pursuers were mounted. The centurion on entering attempted to stop the flow of blood, but Nero saying, "It is too late. Is this your fidelity?" expired with a horrid stare. Nero's progress in crime is easily traced, and the lesson is worth reading. Without a good education, and with no talent for his high station, he was placed in a position of danger from the first. He was sensual, and fond of idle display, and then he became greedy of money to satisfy his expenses; he was timid, and by consequence he became cruel when he anticipated danger; and, like other murderers, his first crime, the poisoning of Britannicus, made him capable of another. But, contemptible and cruel as he was, there are many persons who, in the same situation, might run the same guilty career. He was only in his 31st year when he died, and he had held the supreme power for 13 years and 8 months. He was the last of the descendants of Julia, the sister of the dictator Caesar. — The most important external events in the reign of Nero were the conquest of Armenia by Domitius Corbulo [CORBULO], and the insurrection of the Britons under Boadicea, which was quelled by Suetonius Paulinus. [PAULINUS]. — 2. Eldest son of Germanicus and Agrippina, fell a victim to the ambition of Sejanus, who resolved to get rid of the sons of Germanicus in order to obtain the imperial throne for himself. Drusus, the brother of Nero, was persuaded to second the designs of Sejanus, in hopes that the death of his elder brother would secure him the succession to the throne. There was no difficulty in exciting the jealousy of Tiberius; and accordingly in A. D. 29, Nero was declared an enemy of the state, was removed to the island of Pontia, and was there either starved to death or perished by his own hands.

Nertobriga. 1. (*Valera la vieja*), a town in Hispania Baetica, with the surname Concordia Julia, probably the same place which Polybius calls (xxxv. 2) Ercobrica (Ἐρκόβρικα). — 2. (*Almuna*), a town of the Celtiberi in Hispania Tarraconensis on the road from Emerita to Caesaraugusta.

Nertilum, a fortified place in Lucania on the Via Popilia.

Nerva, Cocceius. 1. M., consul B. C. 36, brought about the reconciliation between M. Antonius and Octavianus, 40, and is the same as the Cocceius mentioned by Horace (*Sat.* i. 5. 28). — 2. M., probably the son of the preceding, and grandfather of the emperor Nerva. He was consul A. D. 22. In 33, he resolutely starved himself to death, notwithstanding the intreaties of Tiberius, whose constant companion he was. He

was a celebrated jurist and is often mentioned in the Digest. — 3. M., the son of the last, and probably father of the emperor, was also a celebrated jurist, and is often cited in the Digest under the name of Nerva Filius. — 4. M., Roman emperor, A. D. 96-98, was born at Narnia, in Umbria, A. D. 32. He was consul with Vespasian, 71, and with Domitian, 90. On the assassination of Domitian, in September, 96, Nerva, who had probably been privy to the conspiracy, was declared emperor at Rome by the people and the soldiers, and his administration at once restored tranquillity to the state. He stopped proceedings against those who had been accused of treason (majestas), and allowed many exiled persons to return to Rome. The class of informers were suppressed by penalties, and some were put to death. At the commencement of his reign, Nerva swore that he would put no senator to death; and he kept his word, even when a conspiracy had been formed against his life by Calpurnius Crassus. Though Nerva was virtuous and humane, he did not possess much energy and vigour; and his feebleness was shown by a mutiny of the Praetorian soldiers. The soldiers demanded the punishment of the assassins of Domitian, which the emperor refused. Though his body was feeble, his will was strong, and he offered them his own neck, and declared his readiness to die. However, it appears that the soldiers effected their purpose, and Nerva was obliged to put Petronius Secundus and Parthenius to death, or to permit them to be massacred by the soldiers. Nerva felt his weakness, but he showed his noble character and his good sense by appointing as his successor a man who possessed both vigour and ability to direct public affairs. He adopted as his son and successor, without any regard to his own kin, M. Ulpius Trajanus, who was then at the head of an army in Germany. Nerva died suddenly on the 27th of January, A. D. 98, at the age of 65 years.

Nervii, a powerful and warlike people in Gallia Belgica, whose territory extended from the river Sabis (*Sambre*) to the Ocean, and part of which was covered by the wood Arduenna. They were divided into several smaller tribes, the Centrones, Grudii, Levaci, Pleumoxii and Geiduni. In B. C. 58 they were defeated by Caesar with such slaughter that out of 60,000 men capable of bearing arms only 500 were left.

Nesactium, a town in Istria on the river Arsia, taken by the Romans, B. C. 177.

Nesis (*Nisita*), a small island off the coast of Campania between Puteoli and Neapolis, and opposite Mt. Pausilypus. This island was a favourite residence of some of the Roman nobles.

Nessonis (Νεσσωνίς), a lake in Thessaly, a little S. of the river Peneus, and N. E. of Larissa, is in summer merely a swamp, but in winter is not only full of water, but even overflows its banks. Nessonis and the neighbouring lake Boebeis were regarded by the ancients as remains of the vast lake, which was supposed to have covered the whole of Thessaly, till an outlet was made for its waters through the rocks of Tempe.

Nessus (Νέσσος), a centaur, who carried Deianira across the river Evenus, but, attempting to run away with her, was shot by Hercules with a poisoned arrow, which afterwards became the cause of the death of Hercules. See pp. 310, 311.

Nestor (Νέστωρ), king of Pylos, son of Neleus

and Chloris, husband of Eurydice and father of Pisidice, Polycaste, Perseus, Stratius, Aretus, Echephron, Pisistratus, Antilochus, and Thrasymedes. Some relate that, after the death of Eurydice, Nestor married Anaxibia, the daughter of Atreus, and sister of Agamemnon ; but this Anaxibia is elsewhere described as the wife of Strophius, and the mother of Pylades. When Hercules invaded the country of Neleus, and slew his sons, Nestor alone was spared, either because he was absent from Pylos, or because he had taken no part in carrying off from Hercules the oxen of Geryones. In his youth and early manhood, Nestor was a distinguished warrior. He defeated both the Arcadians and Eleans. He took part in the fight of the Lapithae against the Centaurs, and he is mentioned among the Calydonian hunters and the Argonauts. Although far advanced in age, he sailed with the other Greek heroes against Troy. Having ruled over three generations of men, his advice and authority were deemed equal to that of the immortal gods, and he was renowned for his wisdom, his justice, and his knowledge of war. After the fall of Troy he returned home, and arrived safely in Pylos, where Zeus granted to him the full enjoyment of old age, surrounded by intelligent and brave sons. Various towns in Peloponnesus, of the name of Pylos, laid claim to being the city of Nestor. On this point see p. 471, a.

Nestŏrĭdes (Νεστορίδης), i. e. a son of Nestor, as Antilochus and Pisistratus.

Nestŏrĭus, a celebrated Haeresiarch, was appointed patriarch of Constantinople A. D. 428, but in consequence of his heresy was deposed at the council of Ephesus, 431. His great opponent was Cyril. Nestorius was subsequently banished to one of the Oases in Egypt, and he died in exile probably before 450. Nestorius carefully distinguished between the divine and human nature attributed to Christ, and refused to give to the Virgin Mary the title of *Theotocus* (Θεοτόκος) or "Mother of God." The opinions of Nestorius are still maintained by the Nestorian Christians.

Nestus, sometimes **Nessus** (Νέστος: *Mesto* by the Greeks, *Karasu* by the Turks), a river in Thrace, which rises in Mt. Rhodope, flows S. E., and falls into the Aegaean sea W. of Abdera and opposite the island of Thasos. The Nestus formed the E. boundary of Macedonia from the time of Philip and Alexander the Great.

Nesus. [ORNIADAE.]

Nētum (Netinus: *Noto Antiquo* near *Noto*), a town in Sicily S. W. of *Syracuse*, and a dependency of the latter.

Neuri (Νεύροι, Νευροί), a people of Sarmatia Europaea, whom Herodotus describes as not of Scythian race, though they followed Scythian customs. Having been driven out from their earlier abodes by a plague of serpents, they settled to the N.W. of the sources of the Tyras (*Dniester*). They were esteemed skilful in enchantment.

Nevirnum. [NOVIODUNUM, No. 2.]

Nicaea (Νίκαια: Νικαιεύς, Νικαεύς, Nicaeensis, Nicensis). 1. (*Iznik*, Ru.), one of the most celebrated cities of Asia, stood on the E. side of the lake Ascania (*Iznik*) in Bithynia. Its site appears to have been occupied in very ancient times by a town called Attaea, and afterwards by a settlement of the Bottineans, called Ancore or Helicore, which was destroyed by the Mysians. Not long after the death of Alexander the Great, Antigonus built on the same spot a city which he named after himself. Antigonea; but Lysimachus soon after changed the name into Nicaea, in honour of his wife. Under the kings of Bithynia it was often the royal residence, and it long disputed with Nicomedia the rank of capital of Bithynia. The Roman emperors bestowed upon it numerous honours and benefits, which are recorded on its coins. Its position, at the junction of several of the chief roads leading through Asia Minor to Constantinople, made it the centre of a large traffic. It is very famous in ecclesiastical history as the seat of the great Oecumenical Council, which Constantine convoked in A. D. 325, chiefly for the decision of the Arian controversy, and which drew up the Nicene Creed; that is to say, the first part of the well known creed so called, the latter part of which was added by the Council of Constantinople, in the year 381. The Council of Nice (as we commonly call it) also settled the time of keeping Easter. A second council held here in 787 decided in favour of the worship of images. In the very year of the great Council, Nicaea was overthrown by an earthquake, but it was restored by the emperor Valens in 368. Under the later emperors of the East, Nicaea long served as the bulwark of Constantinople against the Arabs and Turks : it was taken by the Seljuks in 1078, and became the capital of the Sultan Soliman; it was retaken by the First Crusaders in 1097. After the taking of Constantinople by the Venetians and the Franks, and the foundation of the Latin empire there in 1204, the Greek emperor Theodorus Lascaris made Nicaea the capital of a separate kingdom ; in which his followers maintained themselves with various success against the Latins of Constantinople on the one side, and the Seljuks of Iconium on the other, and in 1261 regained Constantinople. At length, in 1330, Nicaea was finally taken by Orchan the son of the founder of the Ottoman empire, Othman. *Isnik*, the modern Nicaea, is a poor village of about 100 houses ; but the double walls of the ancient city still remain almost complete, exhibiting 4 large and 2 small gates. There are also the remains of the 2 moles which formed the harbour on the lake, of an aqueduct, of the theatre, and of the gymnasium ; in this last edifice, we are told, there was a point from which all the 4 gates were visible, so great was the regularity with which the city was built. — 2. (*Nilab*) a city of India, on the borders of the Paropamisadae, on the W. of the river Cophen. — 3. (Prob. *Darapoor*, Ru.), a city of India, on the river Hydaspes (*Jelum*) built by Alexander to commemorate his victory over Porus. — 4. A fortress of the Epicnemidian Locrians on the sea, near the pass of Thermopylae, which it commanded. From its important position, it is often mentioned in the wars of Greece with Macedonia and with the Romans. In the former, its betrayal to Philip by the Thracian dynast Phalaecus led to the decision of the Sacred War, B. C. 346; and after various changes, it is found, at the time of the wars with Rome, in the hands of the Aetolians. — 5. In Illyria. [NICIA]. — 6. An ancient name of Mariana in Corsica. — 7. (*Nizza, Nice*), a city on the coast of Liguria, a little E. of the river Var; a colony of Massilia, and subject to that city; hence it was considered as belonging to Gaul, though it was just beyond the frontier. It first became important as a stronghold of the Christian religion, which was preached there by Nazarius at an early period.

Nicander (Νίκανδρος). 1. King of Sparta, son of Charilaus, and father of Theopompus, reigned about B.C. 809—770. — 2. A Greek poet, grammarian and physician, was a native of Claros near Colophon in Ionia, whence he is frequently called a Colophonian. He succeeded his father as one of the hereditary priests of Apollo Clarius. He appears to have flourished about B.C. 185—135. Of the numerous works of Nicander only two poems are extant, one entitled *Theriaca* (Θηριακά), which consists of nearly 1000 hexameter lines, and treats of venomous animals and the wounds inflicted by them, and another entitled *Alexipharmaca* ('Αλεξιφάρμακα), which consists of more than 600 hexameter lines, and treats of poisons and their antidotes. Among the ancients his authority in all matters relating to toxicology seems to have been considered high. His works are frequently quoted by Pliny, Galen, and other ancient writers. His style is harsh and obscure; and his works are now scarcely ever read as *poems*, and are only consulted by those who are interested in points of zoological and medical antiquities. The best edition is by Schneider, who published the *Alexipharmaca* in 1792 Halae; and the *Theriaca* in 1816, Lips.

Nicanor (Νικάνωρ). 1. Son of Parmenion, a distinguished officer in the service of Alexander, died during the king's advance into Bactria, B. C. 330. — 2. A Macedonian officer, who, in the division of the provinces after the death of Perdiccas, (321), obtained the government of Cappadocia. He attached himself to the party of Antigonus, who made him governor of Media and the adjoining provinces, which he continued to hold until 312, when he was deprived of them by Seleucus. — 3. A Macedonian officer under Cassander, by whom he was secretly despatched, immediately on the death of Antipater, 319, to take the command of the Macedonian garrison at Munychia. Nicanor arrived at Athens before the news of Antipater's death, and thus readily obtained possession of the fortress. Soon afterwards he surprised the Piraeus also, and placed both fortresses in the hands of Cassander on the arrival of the latter in Attica in 318. Nicanor was afterwards despatched by Cassander with a fleet to the Hellespont, where he gained a victory over the admiral of Polysperchon. On his return to Athens he incurred the suspicion of Cassander, and was put to death.

Nicarchus (Νίκαρχος), the author of 38 epigrams in the Greek Anthology, appears to have lived at Rome near the beginning of the 2nd century of the Christian era.

Nicator, Seleucus. [SELEUCUS.]

Nice (Νίκη), called Victoria by the Romans, the goddess of victory, is described as a daughter of Pallas and Styx, and as a sister of Zelus (zeal), Cratos (strength), and Bia (force). When Zeus commenced fighting against the Titans, and called upon the gods for assistance, Nice and her 2 sisters were the first who came forward, and Zeus was so pleased with their readiness, that he caused them ever after to live with him in Olympus. Nice had a celebrated temple on the acropolis at Athens, which is still extant and in excellent preservation. She is often seen represented in ancient works of art, especially with other divinities, such as Zeus and Athena, and with conquering heroes whose horses she guides. In her appearance she resembles Athena, but has wings, and carries a palm or a wreath, and is engaged in raising a trophy, or in inscribing the victory of the conqueror on a shield.

Nicephorium (Νικηφόριον). 1. (*Rakkah*), a fortified town of Mesopotamia, on the Euphrates, near the mouth of the river Bilecha (*el Belikh*), and due S. of Edessa, built by order of Alexander, and probably completed under Seleucus. It is doubtless the same place as the **Callinicus** or **Callinicum** (Καλλίνικος or ον), the fortifications of which were repaired by Justinian. Its name was again changed to **Leontopolis**, when it was adorned with fresh buildings by the emperor Leo. — 2. A fortress on the Propontis, belonging to the territory of Pergamus.

Nicephorius (Νικηφόριος), a river of Armenia Major, on which Tigranes built his residence TIGRANOCERTA. It was a tributary of the Upper Tigris; probably identical with the CENTRITES, or a small tributary of it.

Nicephorus (Νικηφόρος). 1. Callistus Xanthopulus, the author of the Ecclesiastical History, was born in the latter part of the 13th century, and died about 1450. His Ecclesiastical history was originally in 23 books, of which there are 18 extant, extending from the birth of Christ down to the death of the tyrant Phocas, in 610. Although Nicephorus compiled from the works of his predecessors, he entirely remodelled his materials, and his style is vastly superior to that of his contemporaries. Edited by Ducaeus, Paris, 1630, 2 vols. fol. — 2. Gregoras. [GREGORAS.] — 3. Patriarcha, originally the notary or chief secretary of state to the emperor Constantine V. Copronymus, subsequently retired into a convent, and was raised to the patriarchate of Constantinople in 806. He was deposed in 815, and died in 828. Several of his works have come down to us, of which the most important is entitled *Breviarium Historicum*, a Byzantine history, extending from 602 to 770. This is one of the best works of the Byzantine period. Edited by Petavius, Paris, 1616.

Nicer (*Neckar*), a river in Germany falling into the Rhine at the modern *Mannheim*.

Niceratus (Νικήρατος). 1. Father of Nicias, the celebrated Athenian general. — 2. Son of Nicias, put to death by the 30 tyrants, to whom his great wealth was no doubt a temptation. — 3. A Greek writer on plants, one of the followers of Asclepiades of Bithynia.

Nicetas (Νικήτας). 1. Acominatus, also called Choniates, because he was a native of Chonae, formerly Colossae, in Phrygia, one of the most important Byzantine historians, lived in the latter half of the 12th, and the former half of the 13th centuries. He held important public offices at Constantinople, and was present at the capture of the city by the Latins in 1204, of which he has given us a faithful description. He escaped to Nicaea, where he died about 1216. The history of Nicetas consists of 10 distinct works, each of which contains one or more books, of which there are 21, giving the history of the emperors from 1118 to 1206. The best edition is by Bekker, Bonn, 1835. — 2. Eugenianus, lived probably towards the end of the 12th century, and wrote "The History of the Lives of Drusilla and Charicles," which is the worst of all the Greek romances that have come down to us. It was published for the first time by Boissonade, Paris, 1819, 2 vols.

Nicia (*Enza*?), a tributary of the Po in Gallia Cisalpina.

Nicias (Νικίας). 1. A celebrated Athenian general during the Peloponnesian war, was the son of Niceratus, from whom he inherited a large fortune. His property was valued at 100 talents. From this cause, combined with his unambitious character, and his aversion to all dangerous innovations, he was naturally brought into connection with the aristocratical portion of his fellow-citizens. He was several times associated with Pericles, as strategus; and his great prudence and high character gained for him considerable influence. On the death of Pericles he came forward more openly as the opponent of Cleon, and the other demagogues of Athens; but from his military reputation, the mildness of his character, and the liberal use which he made of his great wealth, he was looked upon with respect by all classes of the citizens. His timidity led him to buy off the attacks of the sycophants. He was a man of strong religious feeling, and Aristophanes ridicules him in the *Equites* for his timidity and superstition. His characteristic caution was the distinguishing feature of his military career; and his military operations were almost always successful. He frequently commanded the Athenian armies during the earlier years of the Peloponnesian war. After the death of Cleon (B. C. 422) he exerted all his influence to bring about a peace, which was concluded in the following year (421). For the next few years Nicias used all his efforts to induce the Athenians to preserve the peace, and was constantly opposed by Alcibiades, who had now become the leader of the popular party. In 415, the Athenians resolved on sending their great expedition to Sicily, and appointed Nicias, Alcibiades and Lamachus to the command. Nicias disapproved of the expedition altogether, and did all that he could to divert the Athenians from this course. But his representations produced no effect; and he set sail for Sicily with his colleagues. Alcibiades was soon afterwards recalled [ALCIBIADES]; and the sole command was thus virtually left in the hands of Nicias. His early operations were attended with success. He defeated the Syracusans in the autumn, and employed the winter in securing the co-operation of several of the Greek cities, and of the Sicel tribes in the island. In the spring of next year he renewed his attacks upon Syracuse; he seized Epipolae, in which he was successful, and commenced the circumvallation of Syracuse. About this time Lamachus was slain, in a skirmish under the walls. All the attempts of the Syracusans to stop the circumvallation failed. The works were nearly completed, and the doom of Syracuse seemed sealed, when Gylippus, the Spartan, arrived in Sicily. [GYLIPPUS.] The tide of success now turned; and Nicias found himself obliged to send to Athens for reinforcements, and requested at the same time that another commander might be sent to supply his place, as his feeble health rendered him unequal to the discharge of his duties. The Athenians voted reinforcements, which were placed under the command of Demosthenes and Eurymedon; but they would not allow Nicias to resign his command. Demosthenes, upon his arrival in Sicily (413), made a vigorous effort to recover Epipolae, which the Athenians had lost. He was nearly successful, but was finally driven back with severe loss. Demosthenes now deemed any further attempts against the city hopeless, and therefore proposed to abandon the siege and return to Athens.

To this Nicias would not consent. He professed to stand in dread of the Athenians at home; but he appears to have had reasons for believing that a party amongst the Syracusans themselves were likely in no long time to facilitate the reduction of the city. But meantime fresh succours arrived for the Syracusans; sickness was making ravages among the Athenian troops, and at length Nicias himself saw the necessity of retreating. Secret orders were given that every thing should be in readiness for departure, when an eclipse of the moon happened. The credulous superstition of Nicias led to the total destruction of the Athenian armament. The soothsayers interpreted the event as an injunction from the gods that they should not retreat before the next full moon, and Nicias resolutely determined to abide by their decision. The Syracusans resolved to bring the enemy to an engagement, and, in a decisive naval battle, defeated the Athenians. They were now masters of the harbour, and the Athenians were reduced to the necessity of making a desperate effort to escape. The Athenians were again decisively defeated; and having thus lost their fleet, they were obliged to retreat by land. They were pursued by the enemy, and were finally compelled to surrender. Both Nicias and Demosthenes were put to death by the Syracusans. — 2. The physician of Pyrrhus, king of Epirus, who offered to the Roman consul to poison the king, for a certain reward. Fabricius not only rejected his base offer with indignation, but immediately sent him back to Pyrrhus with notice of his treachery. He is sometimes, but erroneously, called Cineas. — 3. A Coan grammarian, who lived at Rome in the time of Cicero, with whom he was intimate. — 4. A celebrated Athenian painter, flourished about B. C. 320. He was the most distinguished disciple of Euphranor. His works seem to have been all painted in encaustic. One of his greatest paintings was a representation of the infernal regions as described by Homer. He refused to sell this picture to Ptolemy, although the price offered for it was 60 talents.

Nicochares (Νικοχάρης), an Athenian poet of the Old Comedy, the son of Philonides, was contemporary with Aristophanes.

Nicocles (Νικοκλῆς). 1. King of Salamis in Cyprus, son of Evagoras, whom he succeeded B. C. 374. Isocrates addressed him a long panegyric upon his father's virtues, for which Nicocles rewarded the orator with the magnificent present of 20 talents. Scarcely any particulars are known of the reign of Nicocles. — He is said to have perished by a violent death, but neither the period nor circumstances of this event are recorded. — 2. Prince or ruler of Paphos, in Cyprus, during the period which followed the death of Alexander. He was at first one of those who took part with Ptolemy against Antigonus; but having subsequently entered into secret negotiations with Antigonus, he was compelled by Ptolemy to put an end to his own life, 310. — 3. Tyrant of Sicyon, was deposed by Aratus, after a reign of only 4 months, 251.

Nicocreon (Νικοκρέων), king of Salamis in Cyprus, at the time of Alexander's expedition into Asia. After the death of Alexander he took part with Ptolemy against Antigonus, and was entrusted by Ptolemy with the chief command over the whole island. Nicocreon is said to have ordered the philosopher Anaxarchus to be pounded to death in a stone mortar, in revenge for an insult which the latter had offered the king, when he visited Alexander at Tyre.

Nicolāus Chalcocondyles. [CHALCOCONDYLES.]

Nicolāus Damascēnus, a Greek historian, and an intimate friend both of Herod the Great and of Augustus. He was, as his name indicates, a native of Damascus, and a son of Antipater and Stratonice. He received an excellent education, and he carried on his philosophical studies in common with Herod, at whose court he resided. In B. C. 13 he accompanied Herod on a visit to Augustus at Rome ; on which occasion Augustus made Nicolaus a present of the finest fruit of the palm-tree, which the emperor called *Nicolai*, — a name by which it continued to be known down to the Middle Ages. Nicolaus rose so high in the favour of Augustus, that he was on more than one occasion of great service to Herod, when the emperor was incensed against the latter. Nicolaus wrote a large number of works, of which the most important were : — 1. A life of himself, of which a considerable portion is still extant. 2. An universal history, which consisted of 144 books, of which we have only a few fragments. 3. A life of Augustus, from which we have some extracts made by command of Constantine Porphyrogenitus. He also wrote commentaries on Aristotle, and other philosophical works, and was the author of several tragedies and comedies : Stobaeus has preserved a fragment of one of his comedies, extending to 44 lines. The best edition of his fragments is by Orelli, Lips. 1804.

Nicomāchus (Νικόμαχος). 1. Father of Aristotle. See p. 84, a. — 2. Son of Aristotle by the slave Herpyllis. He was himself a philosopher, and wrote some philosophical works. A portion of Aristotle's writings bears the name of *Nicomachean Ethics*, but why we cannot tell ; whether the father so named them, as a memorial of his affection for his young son, or whether they derived their title from being afterwards edited and commented on by Nicomachus. — 3. Called *Gerasenus*, from his native place, Gerasa in Arabia, was a Pythagorean, and the writer of a life of Pythagoras, now lost. His date is inferred from his mention of Thrasyllus, who lived under Tiberius. He wrote on arithmetic and music ; and 2 of his works on these subjects are still extant. The work on arithmetic was printed by Wechel, Paris, 1538 ; also, after the *Theologumena Arithmeticae*, attributed to Iamblichus, Lips. 1817. The work on music was printed by Meursius, in his collection, Lugd. Bat. 1616, and in the collection of Meibomius, Amst. 1652. — 4. Of Thebes, a celebrated painter, was the elder brother and teacher of the great painter Aristides. He flourished B. C. 360, and onwards. He was an elder contemporary of Apelles and Protogenes. He is frequently mentioned by the ancient writers in terms of the highest praise. Cicero says that in his works, as well as in those of Echion, Protogenes, and Apelles, every thing was already perfect. (*Brutus*, 18.)

Nicomēdes (Νικομήδης). 1. I. King of Bithynia, was the eldest son of Zipoetes, whom he succeeded, B. C. 278. With the assistance of the Gauls, whom he invited into Asia, he defeated and put to death his brother Zipoetes, who had for some time held the independent sovereignty of a considerable part of Bithynia. The rest of his reign appears to have been undisturbed, and under his sway Bithynia rose to a high degree of power and prosperity. He founded the city of Nicomedia,

which he made the capital of his kingdom. The length of his reign is uncertain, but he probably died about 250. He was succeeded by his son ZIELAS. — 2. II. Surnamed EPIPHANES, king of Bithynia, reigned B. C. 149—91. He was the son and successor of Prusias II., and 4th in descent from the preceding. He was brought up at Rome, where he succeeded in gaining the favour of the senate. Prusias, in consequence, became jealous of his son, and sent secret instructions for his assassination. The plot was revealed to Nicomedes, who thereupon returned to Asia, and declared open war against his father. Prusias was deserted by his subjects, and was put to death by order of his son, 149. Of the long and tranquil reign of Nicomedes few events have been transmitted to us. He courted the friendship of the Romans, whom he assisted in the war against Aristonicus, 131. He subsequently obtained possession of Paphlagonia, and attempted to gain Cappadocia, by marrying Laodice, the widow of Ariarathes VI. He was, however, expelled from Cappadocia by Mithridates ; and he was also compelled by the Romans to abandon Paphlagonia, when they deprived Mithridates of Cappadocia. — 3. III. Surnamed PHILOPATOR, king of Bithynia (91—74), son and successor of Nicomedes II. Immediately after his accession, he was expelled by Mithridates, who set up against him his brother Socrates ; but he was restored by the Romans in the following year (90). At the instigation of the Romans, Nicomedes now proceeded to attack the dominions of Mithridates, who expelled him a second time from his kingdom (88). This was the immediate occasion of the 1st Mithridatic war ; at the conclusion of which (84) Nicomedes was again reinstated in his kingdom. He reigned nearly 10 years after this second restoration. He died at the beginning of 74, and having no children, by his will bequeathed his kingdom to the Roman people.

Nicomēdia (Νικομήδεια: Νικομηδεύς, fem. Νικομήδισσα: *Izmid* or *Iznikmid*, Ru.), a celebrated city of Bithynia, in Asia Minor, built by king Nicomedes I. (B. C. 264), at the N.E. corner of the Sinus Astacenus (*Gulf of Izmid* : comp. ASTACUS). It was the chief residence of the kings of Bithynia, and it soon became one of the most splendid cities of the then known world. Under the Romans, it was a colony, and a favourite residence of several of the later emperors, especially of Diocletian and Constantine the Great. Though repeatedly injured by earthquakes, it was always restored by the munificence of the emperors. Like its neighbour and rival, NICAEA, it occupies an important place in the wars against the Turks ; but it is still more memorable in history as the scene of Hannibal's death. It was the birthplace of the historian Arrian.

Nicōnia or **Nicōnium**, a town in Scythia on the right bank of the Tyras (*Dniester*).

Nicŏphon and **Nicŏphron** (Νικοφῶν, Νικόφρων), an Athenian comic poet, son of Theron, and a contemporary of Aristophanes at the close of his career.

Nicŏpŏlis (Νικόπολις: Νικοπολίτης, Nicopolitānus). 1. (*Paleoprevysa*, Ru.), a city at the S.W. extremity of Epirus, on the point of land which forms the N. side of the entrance to the Gulf of Ambracia, opposite to Actium. It was built by Augustus in memory of the battle of Actium, and was peopled from Ambracia, Anactorium, and ether neighbouring cities, and also with settlers from Aetolia. Augustus also built a temple of Apollo on a neighbouring hill, and founded games in honour of the god, which were held every 5th year. The city was received into the Amphictyonic league in place of the Dolopes. It is spoken of both as a libera civitas, and as a colony. It had a considerable commerce and extensive fisheries. It was made the capital of Epirus by Constantine, and its buildings were restored both by Julian and by Justinian. — 2. (*Nicopoli*), a city of Moesia Inferior, on the Danube, built by Trajan in memory of a victory over the Dacians, and celebrated as the scene of the great defeat of the Hungarians and Franks by the sultan Bajazet, on Sept. 28, 1396. — 3. (*Enderez*, or *Devrigni?*), a city of Armenia Minor, on or near the Lycus, and not far from the sources of the Halys, founded by Pompey on the spot where he gained his first victory over Mithridates: a flourishing place in the time of Augustus: restored by Justinian. — 4. A city in the N. E. corner of Cilicia, near the junction of the Taurus and Amanus. — 5. (*Kara, Kiassera*, or *Caesar's Castle*, Ru.), a city of Lower Egypt, about 2 or 3 miles E. of Alexandria, on the canal between Alexandria and Canopus, was built by Augustus in memory of his last victory over Antonius. Here also, as at Nicopolis opposite to Actium, Augustus founded a temple of Apollo, with games every 5th year. Not being mentioned after the time of the first Caesars, it would seem to have become a mere suburb of Alexandria.

Nicostrātus (Νικόστρατος), the youngest of the 3 sons of Aristophanes, was himself a comic poet. His plays belonged both to the middle and the new comedy.

Nigeir, Nigir, or **Nigris** (Νίγειρ, Νίγιρ, a compounded form of the word *Geir* or *Gir*, which seems to be a native African term for a river in general), changed, by a confusion which was the more easily made on account of the colour of the people of the region, into the Latin word **Niger**, a great river of Aethiopia Interior, which modern usage has identified with the river called *Joli-ba* (i. e. *Great River*) and *Quorra* (or rather *Kowara*), in W. Africa. As early as the time of Herodotus, we find an authentic statement concerning a river of the interior of Libya, which is evidently identical both with the Nigir of most of the ancient geographers, and with the *Quorra*. He tells us (ii. 32) that 5 young men of the Nasamones, a Libyan people on the Great Syrtis, on the N. coast of Africa, started to explore the desert parts of Libya ; that, after crossing the inhabited part, and the region of the wild beasts, they journeyed many days through the Desert towards the W., till they came to a plain where fruit trees grew ; and as they eat the fruit, they were seized by some little black men, whose language they could not understand, who led them through great marshes to a city, inhabited by the same sort of little black men, who were all enchanters ; and a great river flowed by the city from W. to E., and in it there were crocodiles. Herodotus, like his informants, inferred from the course of the river, and from the crocodiles in it, that it was the Nile ; but it can hardly be any river but the *Quorra ;* and that the city was Timbuctoo is far more probable than not. The opinion, that the Niger was a W. branch of the Nile, prevailed very generally in ancient times ; but by no means universally. Pliny gives

the same account in a very confused manner, and makes the Nigris (as he calls it) the boundary between N. Africa and Aethiopia. Ptolemy, however, who evidently had new sources of information respecting the interior of Africa, makes the Nigeir rise not far from its real source (allowing for the imperfect observations on which his numerical latitudes and longitudes are founded) and follow a direction not very different from what that of the *Joli-ba* and *Quorra* would be if we suppose that the *Zirmi, Koji,* and *Yeo,* form an unbroken communication between the *Quorra* and the lake *Tchad.* But Ptolemy adds, what the most recent discoveries render a very remarkable statement, that a branch of the Nigeir communicates with the lake Libya (Λιβύη), which he places in 16° 30' N. lat. and 35° E. long. (i. e. from the Fortunate I.=17° from Greenwich). This is *almost exactly* the position of lake *Tchad ;* and, if the *Tchadda* really flows out of this lake, it will represent the branch of the Nigeir spoken of by Ptolemy, whose informants, however, seem to have inverted the *direction* of its stream. It is further remarkable that Ptolemy places on the Nigeir a city named Thamondocana in the *exact* position of *Timbuctoo,* and that the length of the river, computed from his position, agrees very nearly with its real length. The error of connecting the Niger and the Nile revived after the time of Ptolemy, and has only been exploded by very recent discoveries.

Niger, C. Pescennius, was governor of Syria during the latter end of the reign of Commodus, on whose death he was saluted emperor by the legions in the East, A. D. 193. But in the following year he was defeated and put to death by Septimius Severus. Many anecdotes have been preserved of the firmness with which Niger enforced the most rigid discipline among his troops ; but he preserved his popularity by the impartiality which he displayed, and by the example of frugality, temperance, and hardy endurance of toil which he exhibited in his own person.

Nigīra (Νίγειρα, Ptol.: *Jennah?*), a city on the N. side of the river Nigir, and the capital of the NIGRITAE.

Nigrītae or **-ētes** (Νιγρῖται, Νιγρῖται Αἰθίοπες, Νίγρητες), the N.-most of the Ethiopian (i. e. Negro) peoples of Central Africa, dwelt about the Nigir, in the great plain of *Soudan.*

Nigrītis Lacus (Νιγρῖτις λίμνη), a lake in the interior of Africa, out of which Ptolemy represents the river Nigir as flowing. He places it about at the true source of the Nigir (i. e. the *Joli-ba*) ; but it is not yet discovered whether the river has its source in a lake. Some modern geographers identify it with the lake *Debo,* S. W. of *Timbuctoo.*

Nilūpŏlis or **Nilus** (Νείλου πόλις, Νεῖλος), a city of the Heptanomis, or Middle Egypt, in the Nomos Heracleopolites, was built on an island in the Nile, 20 geographical miles N. E. of Heracleopolis. There was a temple here in which, as throughout Egypt, the river Nile was worshipped as a god.

Nilus (' Νεῖλος, derived probably from a word which still exists in the old dialects of India, *Nilas,* i. e. *black,* and sometimes called Μέλας by the Greeks: Νεῖλος occurs first in Hesiod ; Homer calls the river Αἴγυπτός : *Nile,* Arab. *Bahr-Nil,* or simply *Bahr,* i. e. *the River :* the modern names of its upper course, in Nubia and Abyssinia, are various). This river, one of the most important in

Orpheus. (From a Mosaic.) Pages 504, 505.

Pan. (From a Bronze Relief found at Pompeii.) Page 518.

Temple of Niké Apteros (the Wingless Victory), on the Acropolis at Athens.

Niké (Victory).
(From an ancient Gem.) Page 477.

Omphale and Hercules.
(Farnese Group, now at Naples.) Page 498.

[To face p. 480.

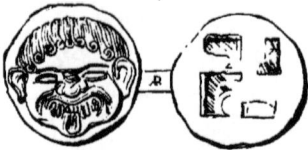

Neapolis in Thrace.   Page 470.

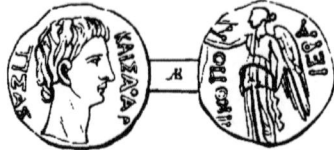

Nicopolis in Epirus.   Page 479.

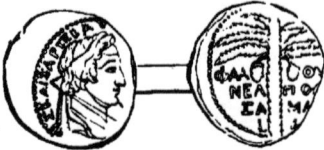

Neapolis in Palestine.   Page 470.

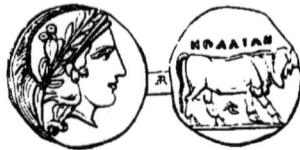

Nola.   Page 484.

Nemausus.   Page 471.

Nuceria in Campania.   Page 485.

Nuceria in Bruttium.   Page 485.

Nicaea in Bithynia.   Page 476.

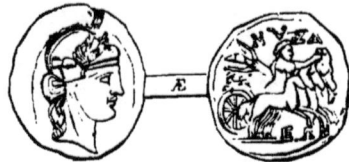

Nysa in Caria.   Page 486.

Nicomedia.   Page 479.

Obulco in Spain.   Page 489.

To face p. 481.]

the world, flows through a channel which forms a part of cleft extending N. and S. through the high rocky and sandy land of N.E. Africa. Its W. or main branch has not yet been traced to its source, but it has been followed up to a point in 4° 42' N. lat. and 30° 58' E. long., where it is a rapid mountain stream, running at the rate of 6 knots an hour over a rocky bed, free from alluvial soil. After a course in the general direction of N. N. E. as far as a place called *Khartum*, in 15° 34' N. lat. and 32° 30' E. long., this river, which is called the *Bahr-el-Abiad*, i. e. *White River*, receives another large river, the *Bahr-el-Azrek*, i. e. *Blue River*, the sources of which are in the highlands of *Abyssinia*, about 11° N. lat. and 37 E. long: this is the middle branch of the Nile system, the ASTAPUS of the ancients. The third, or E. branch, called *Tacazze*, the ASTABORAS of the ancients, rises also in the highlands of *Abyssinia*, in about 11° 40' N. lat., and 39° 40' E. long., and joins the Nile (i. e. the main stream formed by the union of the *Abiad* and the *Azrek*), in 17° 45' N. lat., and about 34° 5' E. long.: the point of junction was the apex of the island of MEROE. Here the united river is about 2 miles broad. Hence it flows through *Nubia*, in a magnificent rocky valley, falling over 6 cataracts, the N.-most of which, called the *First cataract* (i. e. to a person going up the river), is and has always been the S. boundary of Egypt. Of its course from this point, to its junction with the Mediterranean, a sufficient general description has been given under AEGYPTUS (p. 14). The branches into which it parted at the S. point of the Delta were, in ancient times, 3 in number, and these again parted into 7, of which, Herodotus tells us, 5 were natural and 2 artificial. These 7 mouths were nearly all named from cities which stood upon them : they were called, proceeding from E. to W., the Pelusiac, the Tanitic or Saïtic, the Mendesian, the Phatnitic or Pathmetic or Bucolic, the Sebennytic, the Bolbitic or Bolbitine, and the Canobic or Canopic. Through the alterations caused by the alluvial deposits of the river, they have now all shifted their positions, or dwindled into little channels, except 2, and these are much diminished ; namely, the *Damiat* mouth on the E. and the *Rosetta* mouth on the W. Of the canals connected with the Nile in the Delta, the most celebrated were the Canobic, which connected the Canobic mouth with the lake Mareotis and with Alexandria, and that of Ptolemy (afterwards called that of Trajan) which connected the Nile at the beginning of the Delta with the bay of Heroöpolis at the head of the Red Sea : the formation of the latter is ascribed to king Necho, and its repair and improvement successively to Darius the son of Hystaspes, Ptolemy Philadelphus and Trajan. That the Delta, and indeed the whole alluvial soil of Egypt has been created by the Nile, cannot be doubted ; but the present small rate of deposit proves that the formation must have been made long before the historical period. The periodical rise of the river has been spoken of under AEGYPTUS. It is caused by the tropical rains on the highlands in which it rises. The best ancient accounts, preserved by Ptolemy, place its source in a range of mountains in Central Africa, called the Mountains of the Moon ; and the most recent information points to a range of mountains, a little N. of the Equator, called *Jebel-el-Kumri*, or the *Blue Mountain*, as containing the

probable sources of the *Bahr Abiad*. The ancient Egyptians deified the Nile, and took the utmost care to preserve its water from pollution.

Ninus, the reputed founder of the city of Ninus or Nineveh. An account of his exploits is given under Semiramis, his wife, whose name was more celebrated. [SEMIRAMIS.]

Ninus, Ninīvē (*Nίνος*, or less correctly *Nίνος*: O. T. Nineveh, LXX. *Nινευή, Nινευί*; *Nίνιος*, Ninivītae, pl.), the capital of the great Assyrian monarchy, and one of the most ancient cities in the world, stood on the E. side of the Tigris, at the upper part of its course, in the district of Aturia. The accounts of its foundation and history are as various as those respecting the Assyrian monarchy in general [ASSYRIA]. The Greek and Roman writers ascribe its foundation to Ninus ; but in the book of Genesis (x. 11) we are told, immediately after the mention of the kingdom of Nimrod and his foundation of Babel and other cities in Shinar (i. e. Babylonia), that "out of that land went forth Asshur" (or otherwise, "he — i. e. Nimrod — went forth into Assyria "), "and builded Nineveh." There is no further mention of Nineveh in Scripture till the reign of Jeroboam II., about B. C. 825, when the prophet Jonah was commissioned to preach repentance to its inhabitants. It is then described as "an exceeding great city, of 3 days' journey," and as containing "more than 120,000 persons that cannot discern between their right hand and their left hand," which, if this phrase refers to children, would represent a population of 600,000 souls. The other passages, in which the Hebrew prophets denounce ruin against it, bear witness to its size, wealth, and luxury, and the latest of them (*Zeph.* ii. 13) is dated only a few years before the final destruction of the city, which was effected by the Medes and Babylonians about B. C. 606. It is said by Strabo to have been larger than Babylon, and Diodorus describes it as an oblong quadrangle of 150 stadia by 90, making the circuit of the walls 480 stadia (more than 55 statute miles) : if so, the city was twice as large as London together with its suburbs. In judging of these statements, not only must allowance be made for the immense space occupied by palaces and temples, but also for the Oriental mode of building a city, so as to include large gardens and other open spaces within the walls. The walls of Nineveh are described as 100 feet high, and thick enough to allow 3 chariots to pass each other on them ; with 1500 towers, 200 feet in height. The city is said to have been entirely destroyed by fire when it was taken by the Medes and Babylonians, about B. C. 606 ; and frequent allusions occur to its desolate state. Under the Roman empire, however, we again meet with a city Nineve, in the district of Adiabene, mentioned by Tacitus, and again by Ammianus Marcellinus, and a medieval historian of the 13th century mentions a fort of the same name : but statements like these must refer to some later place built among or near the ruins of the ancient Nineveh. Thus, of all the great cities of the world, none was thought to have been more utterly lost than the capital of the most ancient of the great monarchies. Tradition pointed out a few shapeless mounds opposite *Mosul* on the Upper Tigris, as all that remained of Nineveh ; and a few fragments of masonry were occasionally dug up there, and elsewhere in Assyria, bearing inscriptions in an almost unknown character, called, from its shape, cuneiform or arrow-headed. Within the last 10 years, however, those shapeless mounds have been shown to contain the remains of great palaces, on the walls of which the scenes of Assyrian life and the records of Assyrian conquests are sculptured ; while the efforts which had long been made to decipher the cuneiform inscriptions found in Persia and Babylonia, as well as Assyria, have been so far successful as to make it probable that we may soon read the records of Assyrian history from her own monuments. It is as yet premature to form definite conclusions to any great extent. The results of Major Rawlinson's study of the cuneiform inscriptions of Assyria are only in process of publication. The excavations conducted by Dr. Layard and M. Botta have brought to light the sculptured remains of immense palaces, not only at the traditional site of Nineveh, namely *Kouyunjik* and *Nebbi-Yunus*, opposite to *Mosul*, and at *Khorsabad*, about 10 miles to the N.N.E., but also in a mound, 18 miles lower down the river, in the tongue of land between the Tigris and the *Great Zab*, which still bears the name of *Nimroud ;* and it is clear that their remains belong to different periods, embracing the records of two distinct dynasties, extending over several generations ; none of which *can* be later than B. c. 606, while some of them probably belong to a period at least as ancient as the 13th, and perhaps even the 15th century B. c. There are other mounds of ruins as yet unexplored. Which of these ruins correspond to the true site of Nineveh, or whether (as Dr. Layard suggests) that vast city may have extended all the way along the Tigris from *Kouyunjik* to *Nimroud*, and to a corresponding breadth N. E. of the river, as far as *Khorsabad*, are questions still under discussion. Meanwhile, the study of the monuments and inscriptions thus discovered must soon throw fresh light on the whole subject. Some splendid fragments of sculpture, obtained by Dr. Layard from *Nimroud*, are now to be seen in the British Museum.

Ninyas (Νινύας), son of Ninus and Semiramis. See SEMIRAMIS.

Niŏbē (Νιόβη). 1. Daughter of Phoroneus, and by Zeus the mother of Argus and Pelasgus. — 2. Daughter of Tantalus by the Pleiad Taygete or the Hyad Dione. She was the sister of Pelops, and the wife of Amphion, king of Thebes, by whom she became the mother of 6 sons and 6 daughters. Being proud of the number of her children, she deemed herself superior to Leto, who had given birth to only 2 children. Apollo and Artemis, indignant at such presumption, slew all her children with their arrows. For 9 days their bodies lay in their blood without any one burying them, for Zeus had changed the people into stones ; but on the 10th day the gods themselves buried them. Niobe herself, who had gone to Mt. Sipylus, was metamorphosed into stone, and even thus continued to feel the misfortune with which the gods had visited her. This is the Homeric story, which later writers have greatly modified and enlarged. The number and names of the children of Niobe vary very much in the different accounts ; for while Homer states that their number was 12, Hesiod and others mentioned 20, Alcman only 6, Sappho 18, and Herodotus 14 ; but the most commonly received number in later times appears to have been 14, namely 7 sons and 7 daughters. According to Homer all the children of Niobe fell by the arrows of Apollo and Artemis ; but later writers state that one of her sons. Amphion or Amyclas, and one of her daughters, Meliboea, were saved, but that Meliboea, having turned pale with terror at the sight of her dying brothers and sisters, was afterwards called Chloris. The time and place at which the children of Niobe were destroyed are likewise stated differently. According to Homer, they perished in their mother's house. According to Ovid, the sons were slain while they were engaged in gymnastic exercises in a plain near Thebes, and the daughters during the funeral of their brothers. Others, again, transfer the scene to Lydia, or make Niobe, after the death of her children, go from Thebes to Lydia, to her father Tantalus on Mt. Sipylus, where Zeus, at her own request, metamorphosed her into a stone, which during the summer always shed tears. In the time of Pausanias people still fancied they could see the petrified figure of Niobe on Mt. Sipylus. The tomb of the children of Niobe, however was shown at Thebes. The story of Niobe and her children was frequently taken as a subject by ancient artists. One of the most celebrated of the ancient works of art still extant is the group of Niobe and her children, which filled the pediment of the temple of Apollo Sosianus at Rome, and which was discovered at Rome in the year 1583. This group is now at Florence, and consists of the mother, who holds her youngest daughter on her knees, and 13 statues of her sons and daughters, besides a figure usually called the paedagogus of the children. The Romans themselves were uncertain whether the group was the work of Scopas or Praxiteles.

Niphătes (ό Νιφάτης, i. e. *Snow-mountain : Balan*), a mountain chain of Armenia, forming an E. prolongation of the Taurus from where it is crossed by the Euphrates towards the Lake of *Van*, before reaching which it turns to the S., and approaches the Tigris below Tigranocerta ; thus surrounding on the N. and E. the basin of the highest course of the Tigris (which is enclosed on the S. and S.W. by Mt. Masius), and dividing it from the valley of the Arsanias (*Murad*) or S. branch of the Euphrates. The continuation of Mt. Niphates to the S.E. along the E. margin of the Tigris valley is formed by the mountains of the Carduchi (*Mts. of Kurdistan*).

Nireus (Νιρεύς), son of Charopus and Aglaia, was, next to Achilles, the handsomest among the Greeks at Troy. He came from the island of Syme (between Rhodes and Cnidus). Later writers relate that he was slain by Eurypylus or Aeneas.

Nisaea.   [MEGARA.]

Nisaea, Nisaei, Nisaeus Campus (Νίσαια, Νισαῖοι, τὸ Νίσαιον πεδίον), these names are found in the Greek and Roman writers used for various places on the S. and S.E. of the Caspian : thus one writer mentions a city Nisaea in Margiana, and another a people Nisaei in the N. of Aria ; but most apply the term Nisaean Plain to a plain in the N. of Great Media, near Rhagae, the pasture ground of a great number of horses of the finest breed, which supplied the studs of the king and nobles of Persia. It seems not unlikely that this breed of horses was called Nisaean from their original home in Margiana (a district famous for its horses) and that the Nisaean plain received its name from the horses kept in it.

Nisĭbis (Νίσιβις : Νισιβηνός). 1. Also **Antiochia Mygdoniae** (O. T. Aram Zoba ? Ru. nr. *Nisi-*

bia), a celebrated city of Mesopotamia, and the capital of the district of Mygdonia, stood on the river Mygdonius (*Nahr-al-Huali*) 37 Roman miles S.W. of Tigranocerta, in a very fertile district. It was the centre of a considerable trade, and was of great importance as a military post. In the successive wars between the Romans and Tigranes, the Parthians, and the Persians, it was several times taken and retaken, until at last it fell into the hands of the Persians in the reign of Jovian. — **2.** A city of Aria at the foot of M. Paropamisus.

Nisus (Νῖσος). **1.** King of Megara, was son of Pandion and Pylia, brother of Aegeus, Pallas, and Lycus, and husband of Abrote, by whom he became the father of Scylla. When Megara was besieged by Minos, Scylla, who had fallen in love with Minos, pulled out the purple or golden hair which grew on the top of her father's head, and on which his life depended. Nisus thereupon died, and Minos obtained possession of the city. Minos, however, was so horrified at the conduct of the unnatural daughter, that he ordered Scylla to be fastened to the poop of his ship, and afterwards drowned her in the Saronic gulf. According to others, Minos left Megara in disgust ; Scylla leapt into the sea, and swam after his ship ; but her father, who had been changed into a sea-eagle (*haliaeëtus*), pounced down upon her, whereupon she was metamorphosed into either a fish or a bird called Ciris. — Scylla, the daughter of Nisus, is sometimes confounded by the poets with Scylla, the daughter of Phorcus. Hence the latter is sometimes erroneously called *Nisëia Virgo*, and *Nisëis*. [SCYLLA.] — Nisaea, the port town of Megara, is supposed to have derived its name from Nisus, and the promontory of Scyllaeum from his daughter. — **2.** Son of Hyrtacus, and a friend of Euryalus. The two friends accompanied Aeneas to Italy, and perished in a night attack against the Rutulian camp.

Nisyrus (Νίσουρος : *Nikero*), a small island in the Carpathian Sea, a little distance off the promontory of Caria called Triopium, of a round form, 80 stadia (8 geog. miles) in circuit, and composed of lofty rocks, the highest being 2271 feet high. Its volcanic nature gave rise to the fable respecting its origin, that Poseidon tore it off the neighbouring island of Cos to hurl it upon the giant Polybotes. It was celebrated for its warm springs, wine, and mill-stones. Its capital, of the same name, stood on the N.W. of the island, where considerable ruins of its Acropolis remain. Its first inhabitants are said to have been Carians ; but already in the heroic age it had received a Dorian population, like other islands near it, with which it is mentioned by Homer as sending troops to the Greeks. It received other Dorian settlements in the historical age. At the time of the Persian War, it belonged to the Carian queen Artemisia : it next became a tributary ally of Athens : though transferred to the Spartan alliance by the issue of the Peloponnesian War, it was recovered for Athens by the victory at Cnidus, B. C. 394. After the victory of the Romans over Antiochus the Great, it was assigned to Rhodes ; and, with the rest of the Rhodian republic, was united to the Roman empire about B. C. 70.

Nitiobriges, a Celtic people in Gallia Aquitanica between the Garumna and the Liger, whose fighting force consisted of 5000 men. Their chief town was AGINNUM (*Agen*).

Nitocris (Νίτωκρις). **1.** A queen of Babylon, mentioned by Herodotus, who ascribes to her many important works at Babylon and its vicinity. It is supposed by most modern writers that she was the wife of Nebuchadnezzar, and the mother or grandmother of Labynetus or Belshazzar, the last king of Babylon. — **2.** A queen of Egypt, was elected to the sovereignty in place of her brother, whom the Egyptians had killed. In order to take revenge upon the murderers of her brother, she built a very long chamber under ground, and when it was finished invited to a banquet in it those of the Egyptians who had had a principal share in the murder. While they were engaged in the banquet she let in upon them the waters of the Nile by means of a large concealed pipe, and drowned them all, and then, in order to escape punishment, threw herself into a chamber full of ashes. This is the account of Herodotus. We learn from other authorities that she was a celebrated personage in Egyptian legends. She is said to have built the third pyramid, by which we are to understand, that she finished the third pyramid, which had been commenced by Mycerinus. Modern writers make her the last sovereign of the 6th dynasty, and state that she reigned 6 years in place of her murdered husband (not her brother, as Herodotus states), whose name was Menthuôphis. The latter is supposed to be the son or grandson of the Moeris of the Greeks and Romans.

Nitriae, Nitrariae (Νιτρίαι, Νίτρια, Νίτραιαι: *Birket-el-Dwarah*), the celebrated natron lakes in Lower Egypt, which lay in a valley on the S.W. margin of the Delta, and gave to the surrounding district the name of the Νομὸς Νιτριῶτις or Νιτριώτης, and to the inhabitants, whose chief occupation was the extraction of the natron from the lakes, the name of Νιτριῶται. This district was the chief seat of the worship of Serapis, and the only place in Egypt where sheep were sacrificed.

Nixi Dii, a general term, applied by the Romans to those divinities who were believed to assist women in child-birth.

Nobilior, Fulvius, plebeians. This family was originally called **Paetinus**, and the name of Nobilior was first assumed by No. 1, to indicate that he was more noble than any others of this name. **1. Ser.**, consul B. C. 255, with M. Aemilius Paulus, about the middle of the 1st Punic war. The 2 consuls were sent to Africa, to bring off the survivors of the army of Regulus. On their way to Africa they gained a naval victory over the Carthaginians ; but on their return to Italy, they were wrecked off the coast of Sicily, and most of their ships were destroyed. — **2. M.**, grandson of the preceding, curule aedile 195 ; praetor 193, when he defeated the Celtiberi in Spain, and took the town of Toletum ; and consul 189, when he received the conduct of the war against the Aetolians. He took the town of Ambracia, and compelled the Aetolians to sue for peace. On his return to Rome in 187, he celebrated a most splendid triumph. In 179 he was censor with M. Aemilius Lepidus, the pontifex maximus. Fulvius Nobilior had a taste for literature and art ; he was a patron of the poet Ennius, who accompanied him in his Aetolian campaign ; and he belonged to that party among the Roman nobles who were introducing into the city a taste for Greek literature and refinement. He was, therefore, attacked by Cato the censor, who made merry with his name, calling him *mo-*

bilior instead of *nobilior*. Fulvius, in his censorship, erected a temple to Hercules and the Muses in the Circus Flaminius, as a proof that the state ought to cultivate the liberal arts ; and he adorned it with the paintings and statues which he had brought from Greece upon his conquest of Aetolia. — 3. M., son of No. 2, tribune of the plebs 171 ; curule aedile 166, the year in which the Andria of Terence was performed ; and consul 159.—4., Q., also son of No. 2, consul 153, when he had the conduct of the war against the Celtiberi in Spain, by whom he was defeated with great loss. He was censor in 136. He inherited his father's love for literature : he presented the poet Ennius with the Roman franchise when he was a triumvir for founding a colony.

Nōla (Nolānus : *Nola*), one of the most ancient towns in Campania, 21 Roman miles S. E. of Capua, on the road from that place to Nuceria, was founded by the Ausonians, but afterwards fell into the hands of the Tyrrheni (Etruscans), whence some writers call it an Etruscan city. In B. C. 327 Nola was sufficiently powerful to send 2000 soldiers to the assistance of Neapolis. In 313 the town was taken by the Romans. It remained faithful to the Romans even after the battle of Cannae, when the other Campanian towns revolted to Hannibal ; and it was allowed in consequence to retain its own constitution as an ally of the Romans. In the Social war it fell into the hands of the confederates, and when taken by Sulla it was burnt to the ground by the Samnite garrison. It was afterwards rebuilt, and was made a Roman colony by Vespasian. The emperor Augustus died at Nola. In the neighbourhood of the town some of the most beautiful Campanian vases have been found in modern times. According to an ecclesiastical tradition, church bells were invented at Nola, and were hence called *Campanae.*

Nomentānus, mentioned by Horace as proverbially noted for extravagance and a riotous mode of living. The Scholiasts tell us that his full name was L. Cassius Nomentanus.

Nōmentum (Nomentanus : *La Mentana*), originally a Latin town founded by Alba, but subsequently a Sabine town, 14 (Roman) miles from Rome, from which the *Via Nomentana* (more anciently Via Ficulensis) and the *Porta Nomentana* at Rome derived their name. The neighbourhood of the town was celebrated for its wine.

Nōmia (τὰ Νόμια), a mountain in Arcadia on the frontiers of Laconia, is said to have derived its name from a nymph Nomia.

Nōmīus (Νόμιος), a surname of divinities protecting the pastures and shepherds, such as Apollo, Pan, Hermes, and Aristaeus.

Nōnācris (Νώνακρις : Νωνακριάτης, Νωνακριεύς), a town in the N. of Arcadia, N.W. of Pheneus, was surrounded by lofty mountains, in which the river Styx took its origin. The town is said to have derived its name from Nonacris, the wife of Lycaon. From this town Hermes is called *Nonacriates,* Evander *Nonacrius,* Atalanta *Nonacria,* and Callisto *Nonacrina Virgo,* in the general sense of Arcadian.

Nōnius Marcellus. [MARCELLUS.]
Nōnius Sufēnas. [SUFENAS.]
Nonnus (Νόννος). 1. A Greek poet, was a native of Panopolis in Egypt, and lived in the 6th century of the Christian era. Respecting his life nothing is known, except that he was a Christian.

He is the author of an enormous epic poem, which has come down to us under the name of *Diony-siaca* or *Bassarica* (Διονυσιακά or Βασσαρικά), and which consists of 48 books. The work has no literary merit ; the style is bombastic and inflated ; and the incidents are patched together with little or no coherence. Edited by Graefe, Lips. 1819—1826, 2 vols. 8vo. Nonnus also made a paraphrase of the gospel of St. John in Hexameter verse, which is likewise extant. Edited by Heinsius, Lugd. Bat. 1627. — 2. **Theophanes Nonnus,** a Greek medical writer who lived in the 10th century after Christ. His work is entitled a " Compendium of the whole Medical art," and is compiled from previous writers. Edited by Bernard, Gothae et Amstel. 1794, 1795, 2 vols.

Nōra (τὰ Νῶρα : Νωρανός, Norensis). 1. (*Torre Foroadixo*), one of the oldest cities of Sardinia, founded by Iberian settlers under Norax, stood on the coast of the Sinus Caralitanus, 32 Roman miles S.W. of Caralis. — 2. A mountain fortress of Cappadocia, on the borders of Lycaonia, on the N. side of the Taurus, noted for the siege sustained in it by Eumenes against Antigonus for a whole winter. In the time of Strabo, who calls it Νηρασσός, it was the treasury of Sisinas, a pretender to the throne of Cappadocia.

Norba (Norbanensis, Norbanus). 1. (*Norma*), a strongly fortified town in Latium on the slope of the Volscian mountains and near the sources of the Nymphaeus, originally belonged to the Latin and subsequently to the Volscian league. As early as B. C. 492 the Romans founded a colony at Norba. It espoused the cause of Marius in the civil war, and was destroyed by fire by its own inhabitants, when it was taken by one of Sulla's generals. There are still remains of polygonal walls, and a subterraneous passage, at Norma. — 2. Surnamed **Caesarea** (*Alcantara*), a Roman colony in Lusitania on the left bank of the Tagus, N.W. of Augusta Emerita. The bridge built by order of Trajan over the Tagus at this place is still extant. It is 600 feet long by 28 wide, and contains 6 arches.

Norbānus, C., tribune of the plebs, B. C. 95, when he accused Q. Servilius Caepio of majestas, but was himself accused of the same crime in the following year, on account of disturbances which took place at the trial of Caepio. In 90 or 89, Norbanus was praetor in Sicily during the Marsic war ; and in the civil wars he espoused the Marian party. He was consul in 83, when he was defeated by Sulla near Capua. In the following year, 82, he joined the consul Carbo in Cisalpine Gaul, but their united forces were entirely defeated by Metellus Pius. Norbanus escaped from Italy, and fled to Rhodes, where he put an end to his life, when his person was demanded by Sulla.

Norbānus Flaccus. [FLACCUS.]

Noreia (Νωρήεια : *Neumarkt* in *Styria*), the ancient capital of the Taurisci or Norici in Noricum, from which the whole country probably derived its name. It was situated in the centre of Noricum, a little S. of the river Murius, and on the road from Virunum to Ovilaba. It is celebrated as the place where Carbo was defeated by the Cimbri, B. C. 113. It was besieged by the Boii in the time of Julius Caesar. (Caes. *B. G.* i. 5.)

Nōrĭcum, a Roman province S. of the Danube, which probably derived its name from the town of NOREIA, was bounded on the N. by the Danube, on the W. by Rhaetia and Vindelicia, on the E. by Pannonia, and on the S. by Pannonia and Italy. It was separated from Rhaetia and Vindelicia by the river Aenus (*Inn*), from Pannonia on the E. by M. Cetius, and from Pannonia and Italy on the S. by the river Savus, the Alpes Carnicae, and M. Ocra. It thus corresponds to the greater part of Styria and Carinthia, and a part of Austria, Bavaria, and Salzburg. Noricum was a mountainous country, for it was not only surrounded on the S. and E. by mountains, but one of the main branches of the Alps, the ALPES NORICAE (in the neighbourhood of Salzburg), ran right through the province. In those mountains a large quantity of excellent iron was found; and the Noric swords were celebrated in antiquity. Gold also is said to have been found in the mountains in ancient times. The inhabitants of the country were Celts, divided into several tribes, of which the Taurisci, also called Norici, after their capital Noreia, were the most important. They were conquered by the Romans towards the end of the reign of Augustus, after the subjugation of Raetia by Tiberius and Drusus, and their country was formed into a Roman province. In the later division of the Roman empire into smaller provinces, Noricum was formed into 2 provinces, *N. Ripense*, along the bank of the Danube, and *N. Mediterraneum*, separated from the former by the mountains, which divide Austria and Styria: they both belonged to the diocese of Illyricum and the prefecture of Italy.

Nortia or **Nurtia**, an Etruscan divinity, worshipped at Volsinii, where a nail was driven every year into the wall of her temple, for the purpose of marking the number of years.

Nossis, a Greek poetess, of Locri in Italy, lived about B. C. 310, and is the author of 12 epigrams of considerable beauty in the Greek Anthology.

Notus. [AUSTER.]

Novaria (Novarensis: *Novara*), a town in Gallia Transpadana, situated on a river of the same name (*Gogna*), and on the road from Mediolanum to Vercellae, subsequently a Roman municipium.

Novatiānus, a heretic, who insisted upon the perpetual exclusion from the Church of all Christians, who had fallen away the faith under the terrors of persecution. On the election of Cornelius to the see of Rome, A. D. 251, Novatianus was consecrated bishop by a rival party, but was condemned by the council held in the autumn of the same year. After a vain struggle to maintain his position, he was obliged to give way, and became the founder of a new sect, who from him derived the name of Novatians. It should be observed that the individual who first proclaimed these doctrines was not Novatianus, but an African presbyter under Cyprian, named Novatus. Hence much confusion has arisen between *Novatus* and *Novatianus*, who ought, however, to be carefully distinguished. A few of the works of Novatianus are extant. The best edition of them is by Jackson, Lond. 1728.

Novātus. [NOVATIANUS.]

Novensiles or **Novensides Dii**, Roman gods whose name is probably composed of *novus* and *insides*, and therefore signifies the new gods in opposition to the *Indigetes*, or old native divinities. It was customary among the Romans, after the conquest of a neighbouring town, to carry its gods to Rome, and there establish their worship.

Novesium (*Neuss*), a fortified town of the Ubii on the Rhine, and on the road leading from Colonia Agrippina (*Cologne*), to Castra Vetern (*Xanten*). The fortifications of this place were restored by Julian in A. D. 359.

Noviodūnum, a name given to many Celtic places from their being situated on a hill (*dun*). 1. (*Nouan*), a town of the Bituriges Cubi in Gallia Aquitanica, E. of their capital Avaricum. — 2. (*Nevers*), a town of the Aedui in Gallia Lugdunensis, on the road from Augustodunum to Lutetia, and at the confluence of the Niveris and the Liger, whence it was subsequently called Nevirnum, and thus acquired its modern name. — 3. A town of the Suessones in Gallia Belgica, probably the same as Augusta Suessonum. [AUGUSTA, No. 6.] — 4. (*Nion*), a town of the Helvetii in Gallia Belgica, on the N. bank of the Lacus Lemanus, was made a Roman colony by Julius Caesar, B. C. 45, under the name of Colonia Equestris. — 5. (*Isaczi*), a fortress in Moesia Inferior on the Danube, near which Valens built his bridge of boats across the Danube in his campaign against the Goths.

Noviomagus or **Noeomagus.** 1. (*Castelnau de Medoc*), a town of the Bituriges Vivisci in Gallia Aquitanica, N. W. of Burdigala. — 2. A town of the Tricastini in Gallia Narbonensis, probably the modern *Nions*, though some suppose it to be the same place as Augusta Tricastinorum (*Aouste*). — 3. (*Spires*), the capital of the Nemetes. [NEMETES.] — 4. (*Neumagen*), a town of the Treviri in Gallia Belgica on the Mosella. — 5. (*Nimwegen*), a town of the Batavi.

Novius, Q., a celebrated writer of Atellane plays, a contemporary of the dictator Sulla.

Novum Comum. [COMUM.]

Nuba Palus (Νοῦβα λίμνη: prob. *L. Fittreh*, in *Dar Zaleh*), a lake in Central Africa, receiving the great river Gir, according to Ptolemy, who places it in 15° N. lat. and 40° E. long. (=22° from Greenwich.)

Nubae, Nubaei (Νοῦβαι, Νουβαῖοι), an African people, who are found in 2 places, namely about the lake NUBA, and also on the banks of the Nile N. of Meroë, that is, in the N. central part of *Nubia*: the latter were governed by princes of their own, independent of Meroë. By the reign of Diocletian they had advanced N.-wards as far as the frontier of Egypt.

Nuceria (Nucerinus.) 1. Surnamed **Alfaterna** (*Nocera*), a town in Campania on the Sarnus (*Sarno*), and on the Via Appia, S. E. of Nola, and 9 (Roman) miles from the coast, was taken by the Romans in the Samnite wars, and was again taken by Hannibal after the battle of Cannae, when it was burnt to the ground. It was subsequently rebuilt, and both Augustus and Nero planted here colonies of veterans. Pompeii was used as the harbour of Nuceria. — 2. Surnamed **Camellaria** (*Nocera*), a town in the interior of Umbria on the Via Flaminia. — 3. (*Luzzara*), a small town in Gallia Cispadana on the Po, N. E. of Brixellum. — 4. A town in Apulia, more correctly called LUCERIA.

Nuithones, a people of Germany, dwelling on the right bank of the Albis (*Elbe*), S. W. of the Saxones, and N. of the Langobardi, in the S. E. part of the modern *Mecklenburg*.

Numa, Marcius. 1. An intimate friend of Numa Pompilius, whom he is said to have accompanied to Rome, where Numa made him the 1st Pontifex Maximus. Marcius aspired to the kingly dignity on the death of Pompilius, and he starved himself to death on the election of Tullus Hostilius. — 2. Son of the preceding, is said to have married Pompilia, the daughter of Numa Pompilius, and to have become by her the father of Ancus Marcius. Numa Marcius was appointed by Tullus Hostilius praefectus urbi.

Numa Pompilius, the 2nd king of Rome, who belongs to legend and not to history. He was a native of Cures in the Sabine country, and was elected king one year after the death of Romulus, when the people became tired of the interregnum of the senate. He was renowned for his wisdom and his piety ; and it was generally believed that he had derived his knowledge from Pythagoras. His reign was long and peaceful, and he devoted his chief care to the establishment of religion among his rude subjects. He was instructed by the Camena Egeria, who visited him in a grove near Rome, and who honoured him with her love. He was revered by the Romans as the author of their whole religious worship. It was he who first appointed the pontiffs, the augurs, the flamens, the virgins of Vesta, and the Salii. He founded the temple of Janus, which remained always shut during his reign. The length of his reign is stated differently. Livy makes it 43 years ; Polybius and Cicero, 39 years. The sacred books of Numa, in which he prescribed all the religious rites and ceremonies, were said to have been buried near him in a separate tomb, and to have been discovered by accident, 500 years afterwards, in B. C. 181. They were carried to the city-praetor Petilius, and were found to consist of 12 or 7 books in Latin on ecclesiastical law, and the same number of books in Greek on philosophy : the latter were burnt on the command of the senate, but the former were carefully preserved. The story of the discovery of these books is evidently a forgery ; and the books, which were ascribed to Numa, and which were extant at a later time, were evidently nothing more than works containing an account of the ceremonial of the Roman religion.

Numana (*Umana Distrutta*), a town in Picenum, on the road leading from Ancona to Aternum along the coast, was founded by the Siculi, and was subsequently a municipium.

Numantia (Numantinus: nr. *Puente de Don Guarray* Ru.), the capital of the Arevacae or Arevaci in Hispania Tarraconensis, and the most important town in all Celtiberia, was situated near the sources of the Durius, on a small tributary of this river, and on the road leading from Asturica to Caesaraugusta. It was strongly fortified by nature, being built on a steep and precipitous, though not lofty, hill, and accessible by only one path, which was defended by ditches and palisades. It was 24 stadia in circumference, but was not surrounded by regular walls, which the natural strength of its position rendered unnecessary. It was long the head-quarters of the Celtiberians in their wars with the Romans ; and its protracted siege and final destruction by Scipio Africanus the younger (B. C. 133) is one of the most memorable events in the early history of Spain.

Numenius (Νουμήνιος), of Apamea in Syria, a Pythagoreo-Platonic philosopher, who was highly esteemed by Plotinus and his school, as well as by Origen. He probably belongs to the age of the Antonines. His object was to trace the doctrines of Plato up to Pythagoras, and at the same time to show that they were not at variance with the

dogmas and mysteries of the Brahmins, Jews, Magi, and Egyptians. Considerable fragments of his works have been preserved by Eusebius, in his *Praeparatio Evangelica.*

Numerianus, M. Aurelius, the younger of the 2 sons of the emperor Carus, who accompanied his father in the expedition against the Persians, A. D. 283. After the death of his father, which happened in the same year, Numerianus was acknowledged as joint emperor with his brother Carinus. The army, alarmed by the fate of Carus, who was struck dead by lightning, compelled Numerianus to retreat towards Europe. During the greater part of the march, which lasted for 8 months, he was confined to his litter by an affection of the eyes ; but the suspicions of the soldiers having become excited, they at length forced their way into the imperial tent, and discovered the dead body of their prince. Arrius Aper, praefect of the praetorians, and father-in-law of the deceased, was arraigned of the murder in a military council, held at Chalcedon, and, without being permitted to speak in his own defence, was stabbed to the heart by Diocletian, whom the troops had already proclaimed emperor. [DIOCLETIANUS.]

Numicius or **Numicus** (*Numico*), a small river in Latium flowing into the Tyrrhene sea near Ardea, on the banks of which was the tomb of Aeneas, whom the inhabitants called Jupiter Indiges.

Numidia (Νουμιδία, ἡ Νομαδία and Νομαδική: Νομάς, Νυμίδα, pl. Νομάδες or Νομάδες Αἴθνες, Νυμίδae: *Algier*), a country of N. Africa, which, in its original extent, was divided from Mauretania on the W. by the river Malva or Mulucha, and on the E. from the territory of Carthage (aft. the Roman Province of Africa) by the river Tusca: its N. boundary was the Mediterranean, and on the S. it extended indefinitely towards the chain of the Great Atlas and the country of the Gaetuli. Intersected by the chain of the Lesser Atlas, and watered by the streams running down from it, it abounded in fine pastures, which were early taken possession of by wandering tribes of Asiatic origin, who from their occupation as herdmen were called by the Greeks, here as elsewhere, Νομάδες, and this name was perpetuated in that of the country. A sufficient account of these tribes, and of their connection with their neighbours on the W., is given under MAURETANIA. The fertility of the country, inviting to agriculture, gradually gave a somewhat more settled character to the people ; and, at their first appearance in Roman history, we find their 2 great tribes, the Massylians and the Massaesylians, forming 2 monarchies, which were united into one under Masinissa, B. C. 201. (For the historical details, see MASINISSA.) On Masinissa's death in 148, his kingdom was divided, by his dying directions, between his 3 sons, Micipsa, Mastanabal, and Gulussa ; but it was soon reunited under MICIPSA, in consequence of the death of both his brothers. His death, in 118, was speedily followed by the usurpation of Jugurtha, an account of which and of the ensuing war with the Romans is given under JUGURTHA. On the defeat of Jugurtha in 106, the country became virtually subject to the Romans, but they permitted the family of Masinissa to govern it, with the royal title (see HIEMPSAL, No. 2 ; JUBA No. 1), until B. C. 46, when Juba, who had espoused the cause of Pompey in the Civil Wars, was defeated and dethroned by Julius Caesar, and Numidia was made a Roman province. It seems to have been about the same time or a little later, under Augustus, that the W. part of the country was taken from Numidia, and added to MAURETANIA, as far E. as Saldae. In B. C. 30 Augustus restored Juba II. to his father's kingdom of Numidia ; but in B. C. 25 he exchanged it for Mauretania, and Numidia, that is, the country between Saldae on the W. and the Tusca on the E., became a Roman province. It was again diminished by near a half, under Claudius (see MAURETANIA) ; and henceforth, until the Arab conquest, the senatorial province of Numidia denotes the district between the river Ampsaga on the W. and the Tusca on the E.: its capital was Cirta (*Constantineh*). The country, in its later restricted limits, is often distinguished by the name of New Numidia or Numidia Proper. The Numidians are celebrated in military history as furnishing the best light cavalry to the armies, first of Carthage, and afterwards of Rome.

Numidious Sinus (Νουμιδικὸς κόλπος: *Bay of Storak*), the great gulf E. of Pr. Tretum (*Seven Capes*), on the N. of Numidia.

Numistro (Numistrānus), a town in Lucania near the frontiers of Apulia.

Numitor. [ROMULUS.]

Nursia (Nursïnus : *Norcia*), a town in the N. of the land of the Sabines, situated near the sources of the Nar and amidst the Apennines, whence it is called by Virgil (*Aen.* vii. 716) *frigida Nursia.* It was the birthplace of Sertorius and of the mother of Vespasian.

Nyctēis (Νυκτηΐς), that is, Antiope, daughter of Nycteus, and mother of Amphion and Zethus. [ANTIOPE ; NYCTEUS.]

Nycteus (Νυκτεύς), son of Hyrieus by the nymph Clonia, and husband of Polyxo, by whom he became the father of Antiope ; though, according to others, Antiope was the daughter of the river-god Asopus. Antiope was carried off by Epopeus, king of Sicyon ; whereupon Nycteus, who governed Thebes, as the guardian of Labdacus, invaded Sicyon with a Theban army. Nycteus was defeated, and being severely wounded, he was carried back to Thebes, where, previous to his death, he appointed his brother Lycus guardian of Labdacus, and at the same time required him to take vengeance on Epopeus. [LYCUS.]

Nyctimēnē, daughter of Epopeus, king of Lesbos, or, according to others, of Nycteus. Pursued and dishonoured by her amorous father, she concealed herself in the shade of forests, where she was metamorphosed by Athena into an owl.

Nymphae (Νύμφαι), the name of a numerous class of female divinities of a lower rank, though they are designated by the title of Olympian, are called to the meetings of the gods in Olympus, and are described as the daughters of Zeus. They may be divided into 2 great classes. The 1st class embraces those who were recognised in the worship of nature. The early Greeks saw in all the phenomena of ordinary nature some manifestation of the deity ; springs, rivers, grottoes, trees, and mountains, all seemed to them fraught with life ; and all were only the visible embodiments of so many divine agents. The salutary and beneficent powers of nature were thus personified, and regarded as so many divinities. The 2nd class of nymphs are personifications of tribes, races, and

states, such as Cyrene, and many others. —I. The nymphs of the 1st class must again be subdivided into various species, according to the different parts of nature of which they are the representatives. 1. *Nymphs of the watery element.* To these belong first the nymphs of the ocean, *Oceanides* ('Ωκεανῖναι, 'Ωκεανῖδες, νύμφαι ἅλιαι), who were regarded as the daughters of Oceanus ; and next the nymphs of the Mediterranean or inner sea, who were regarded as the daughters of Nereus, and hence were called *Nereides* (Νηρεΐδες). The rivers were represented by the *Potameides* (Ποταμηῖδες), who, as local divinities, were named after their rivers, as Acheloides, Anigrides, Ismenides, Amnisiades, Pactolides. The nymphs of fresh water, whether of rivers, lakes, brooks, or springs, were also designated by the general name *Naiades* (Νηΐδες), though they had, in addition, specific names (Κρηναῖαι, Πηγαῖαι, Ἑλειονόμοι, Λιμνατίδες, or Λιμνάδες). Even the rivers of the lower regions were described as having their nymphs ; hence we read of *Nymphae infernae paludis* and *Avernales.* Many of these nymphs presided over waters or springs which were believed to inspire those who drank of them. The nymphs themselves were, therefore, thought to be endowed with prophetic power, and to inspire men with the same, and to confer upon them the gift of poetry. Hence all persons in a state of rapture, such as seers, poets, madmen, &c., were said to be caught by the nymphs (νυμφόληπτοι, in Lat. *lymphati, lymphatici*). As water is necessary to feed all vegetation as well as all living beings, the water-nymphs frequently appear in connection with higher divinities, as, for example, with Apollo, the prophetic god and the protector of herds and flocks ; with Artemis, the huntress and the protectress of game, who was herself originally an Arcadian nymph ; with Hermes, the fructifying god of flocks ; with Dionysus ; and with Pan, the Sileni and Satyrs, whom they join in their Bacchic revels and dances. — 2. *Nymphs of mountains and grottoes,* called *Oreades* ('Ορειάδες, 'Οροδεμνιάδες), but sometimes also by names derived from the particular mountains they inhabited (*e. g.* Κιθαιρωνίδες, Πηλιάδες, Κορύκιαι). — 3. *Nymphs of forests, groves, and glens,* were believed sometimes to appear to and frighten solitary travellers. They are designated by the names 'Αλσηΐδες, 'Υληωροί, Αὐλωνιάδες, and Ναπαῖαι. — 4. *Nymphs of trees,* were believed to die together with the trees which had been their abode, and with which they had come into existence. They were called *Dryades* and *Hamadryades* (Δρυάδες, 'Αμαδρυάδες or 'Αδρυάδες), from δρῦς, which signifies not only an oak, but any wild-growing lofty tree ; for the nymphs of fruit trees were called *Melides* (Μηλίδες, also Μηλιάδες, 'Επιμηλίδες, or 'Αμαμηλίδες). They seem to be of Arcadian origin, and never appear together with any of the great gods. — II. The 2nd class of nymphs, who were connected with certain races or localities (Νύμφαι χθόνιαι), usually have a name derived from the places with which they are associated, as Nysiades, Dodonides, Lemniae. — The sacrifices offered to nymphs usually consisted of goats, lambs, milk, and oil, but never of wine. They were worshipped in many parts of Greece, especially near springs, groves, and grottoes. They are represented in works of art as beautiful maidens, either quite naked or only half-covered. Later poets sometimes describe them as having sea-coloured hair.

114

Nymphaeum (Νυμφαῖον, i. e. *Nymph's* abode).
1. A mountain, with perhaps a village, by the river Aous, near Apollonia, in Illyricum. — **2.** A port and promontory on the coast of Illyricum, 3 Roman miles from Lissus.— **3.** (*C. Ghiorgi*), the S.W. promontory of Acte or Athos, in Chalcidice. — **4.** A sea-port town of the Chersonesus Taurica (*Crimea*) on the Cimmerian Bosporus, 25 stadia (2½ geog. miles) from Panticapaeum. — **5.** A place on the coast of Bithynia, 30 stadia (3 geog. miles) W. of the mouth of the river Oxines. — **6.** A place in Cilicia, between Celenderis and Soloë.

Nymphaeus (Νύμφαιος). 1. (*Ninfa* or *Nimpa*), a small river of Latium, falling into the sea above Astura; of some note as contributing to the formation of the Pomptine marshes. It now no longer reaches the sea, but falls into a little lake, called *Lago di Monaci.* — 2. A harbour on the W. side of the island of Sardinia, between the Prom. Mercurii and the town of Tillium. — 3. Also called **Nymphius** (*Basilimfu*), a small river of Sophene in Armenia, a tributary of the upper Tigris, flowing from N. to S. past Martyropolis, in the valley between M. Niphates and M. Masius.

Nymphidius Sabinus, commander of the praetorian troops, together with Tigellinus, towards the latter end of Nero's reign. On the death of Nero, A. D. 68, he attempted to seize the throne, but was murdered by the friends of Galba.

Nymphis (Νύμφις), son of Xenagoras, a native of the Pontic Heraclea, lived about B. C. 250. He was a person of distinction in his native land, as well as an historical writer of some note. He wrote a work on Alexander and his successors, in 24 books, and also a history of Heraclea in 13 books.

Nymphodōrus (Νυμφόδωρος). 1. A Greek historian of Amphipolis, of uncertain date, the author of a work on the Laws or Customs of Asia (Νόμιμα 'Ασίας). — 2. Of Syracuse, likewise an historian, seems to have lived about the time of Philip and Alexander the Great. He wrote a Periplus of Asia, and a work on Sicily.

Nysa or **Nyssa** (Νύσα, Νύσσα), was the legendary scene of the nurture of Dionysus, whence the name was applied to several places which were sacred to that god. 1. In India, in the district of Goryaea, at the N.W. corner of the *Punjab*, near the confluence of the rivers Cophen and Choaspes, probably the same place as Nagāra or Dionysopolis (*Nagar* or *Naggar*). Near it was a mountain of like name. — 2. A city or mountain in Aethiopia. — 3. (*Sultan-Hisar*, Ru., a little W. of *Nazeli*), a city of Caria, on the S. slope of M. Messogis, built on both sides of the ravine of the brook Eudon, which falls into the Maeander. It was said to have been named after the queen of one of the Antiochi, having been previously called Athymbra and Pythopolis. — 4. A city of Cappadocia, near the Halys, on the road from Caesarea to Ancyra: the bishopric of St. Gregory of Nyssa. — 5. A town in Thrace between the rivers Nestus and Strymon. — 6. A town in Boeotia near Mt. Helicon.

Nysaeus, Nysïus, Nyseus, or **Nysigēna,** a surname of Dionysus, derived from Nysa, a mountain or city (see above), where the god was said to have been brought up by nymphs.

Nysëïdes or **Nysïädes,** the nymphs of Nysa, who are said to have reared Dionysus, and whose names are Ciasseïs, Nysa, Erato, Eriphia, Bromia, and Polyhymno.

Nyx (Νύξ), called **Nox** by the Romans, was a personification of Night. Homer calls her the subduer of gods and men, and relates that Zeus himself stood in awe of her. In the ancient cosmogonies Night is one of the very first created beings, for she is described as the daughter of Chaos, and the sister of Erebus, by whom she became the mother of Aether and Hemera. She is further said to have given birth, without a husband, to Moros, the Keres, Thanatos, Hypnos, Dreams, Momus, Oizys, the Hesperides, Moerae, Nemesis, and similar beings. In later poets, with whom she is merely the personification of the darkness of night, she is sometimes described as a winged goddess, and sometimes as riding in a chariot, covered with a dark garment and accompanied by the stars in her course. Her residence was in the darkness of Hades.

O.

Oānus ("Ὤανος: *Frascolari*), a small river on the S. coast of Sicily near Camarina.

Oārus ("Ὤαρος), a considerable river mentioned by Herodotus as rising in the country of the Thyssagetae, and falling into the Palus Maeotis (*Sea of Azov*) E. of the Tanaïs (*Don*). As there is no river which very well answers this description, Herodotus is supposed to refer to one of the E. tributaries of the *Don*, such as the *Sal* or the *Manytch.*

Oāsis ("Ὄασις, Αὔασις, and in later writers "Ὤασις) is the Greek form of an Egyptian word (in Coptic *ouahé, an inhabited place*), which was used to denote *an island in the sea of sand* of the great Libyan Desert: the word has been adopted into our language. The Oases are depressions in the great table-land of Libya, preserved from the inroad of the shifting sands by steep hills of limestone round them, and watered by springs, which make them fertile and habitable. With the substitution of these springs for the Nile, they closely resemble that greater depression in the Libyan table-land, the valley of Egypt. The chief specific applications of the word by the ancient writers are to the 2 Oases on the W. of Egypt, which were taken possession of by the Egyptians at an early period. — 1. **Oasis Minor**, the Lesser or Second Oasis ("Ὄασις Μικρά, or ἡ δευτέρα: *Wah-el-Bahryeh* or *Wah-el-Behnesa*), lay W. of Oxyrynchus, and a good day's journey from the S.W. end of the lake Moeris. It was reckoned as belonging to the Heptanomis, or Middle Egypt; and formed a separate Nomos. — 2. **Oasis Major**, the Greater, Upper, or First Oasis ("Ο. μεγάλη, ἡ πρώτη, ἡ ἄνω "Ο., and, in Herodotus, πόλις "Ὄασις and νῆσος Μακάρων, *Wah-el-Khargeh*), is described by Strabo as 7 days' journey W. of Abydos, which applies to its N. end, as it extends over more than 1½° of latitude. It belonged to Upper Egypt, and, like the other, formed a distinct nome: these 2 nomes are mentioned together as " duo Oasitae " (αἱ δύο 'Ὀασῖται). When the ancient writers use the word Oasis alone, the Greater Oasis must generally be understood. The Greater Oasis contains considerable ruins of the ancient Egyptian and Roman periods. Between and near these were other Oases, about which we learn little or nothing from the ancient writers, though in one of them, the *Wah-el-Gharbee* or *Wah-el-Dakhleh*, 3 days W. of the Greater Oasis, there are the ruins of a Roman temple, inscribed with the names of Nero and of Titus. The Greater Oasis is about level with the valley of the Nile, the Lesser is about 200 feet higher than the Nile, in nearly the same latitude. — 3. A still more celebrated Oasis than either of these was that called Ammon, Hammon, Ammonium, Hammōnis Oraculum, from its being a chief seat of the worship and oracle of the god Ammon. It was called by the Arabs in the middle ages *Santariah*, and now *Siwah*. It is about 15 geog. miles long, and 12 wide: its chief town, *Siwah*, is in 29° 12′ N. lat., and 26° 17′ E. long.: its distance from Cairo is 12 days, and from the N. coast about 160 statute miles; the ancients reckoned it 12 days from Memphis, and 5 days from Paraetonium on the N. coast. It was inhabited by various Libyan tribes, but the ruling people were a race kindred to the Aethiopians above Egypt, who, at a period of unknown antiquity, had introduced, probably from Meroë, the worship of Ammon: the government was monarchical. The Ammonians do not appear to have been subject to the old Egyptian monarchy. Cambyses, after conquering Egypt in B. C. 525, sent an army against them, which was overwhelmed by the sands of the Desert. In B. C. 331, Alexander the Great visited the oracle, which hailed him as the son of Zeus Ammon. The oracle was also visited by Cato of Utica. Under the Ptolemies and the Romans, it was subject to Egypt, and formed part of the Nomos Libya. The most remarkable objects in the Oasis, besides the temple of Ammon, were the palace of the ancient kings, abundant springs of salt water (as well as fresh) from which salt was made, and a well, called Fons Solis, the water of which was cold at noon, and warm in the morning and evening. Considerable ruins of the temple of Ammon are still standing at the town of *Siwah*. In ancient times, the Oasis had no town, but the inhabitants dwelt in scattered villages. — 4. In other parts of the Libyan Desert, there were oases of which the ancients had some knowledge, but which they do not mention by the name of Oases, but by their specific names, such as AUGILA, PHAZANIA, and others.

Oaxes. [OAXUS.]

Oaxus (῎Οαξος: ᾽Οάξιος), called **Axus** (῎Αξος) by Herodotus, a town in the interior of Crete on the river Oaxes, and near Eleutherna, is said to have derived its name from Oaxes or Oaxus, who was, according to some accounts, a son of Acacallis, the daughter of Minos, and, according to others, a son of Apollo by Anchiale.

Obila (*Avila*), a town of the Vettones in Hispania Tarraconensis.

Obliviōnis Flumen. [LIMAEA.]

Obrimas (*Ko'ja-Chai* or *Sandukli-Chai*), an E. tributary of the Maeander, in Phrygia.

Obringa (*Aar*), a W. tributary of the Rhine, forming the boundary between Germania Superior and Inferior.

Obsěquens, Jūlius, the name prefixed to a fragment entitled *De Prodigiis* or *Prodigiorum Libellus*, containing a record of the phenomena classed by the Romans under the general designation of *Prodigia* or *Ostenta*. The series extends in chronological order from the consulship of Scipio and Laelius, B. C. 190, to the consulship of Fabius and Aelius, B. C. 11. The materials are derived in a great measure from Livy, whose very words are frequently employed. With regard to the com-

piler we know nothing. The style is tolerably pure, but does not belong to the Augustan age The best editions are by Scheffer, Amst. 1679, an by Oudendorp, Lng. Bat. 1720.

Obncŏla, Obncūla or **Obulcŭla** (*Monclova*), a town in Hispania Baetica on the road from Hispalis to Emerita and Corduba.

Obulco (*Porcuna*), surnamed **Pontificense,** a Roman municipium in Hispania Baetica, 300 stadia from Corduba.

Ocălěa (᾽Ωκαλέα, ᾽Ωκαλέη, also ᾽Ωκάλεια, ᾽Ωκαλέαι: ᾽Ωκαλεύς), an ancient town in Boeotia, between Haliartus and Alalcomenae, situated on a river of the same name falling into the lake Copais, and at the foot of the mountain Tilphusion.

Oceănĭdes. [NYMPHAE.]

Oceănus (᾽Ωκεανός), in the oldest Greek poets is the god of the water which was believed to surround the whole earth, and which was supposed to be the source of all the rivers and other waters of the world. This water-god, in the *Theogony* of Hesiod, is the son of Heaven and Earth (Οὐρανός and Γαῖα), the husband of Tethys, and the father of all the river-gods and water-nymphs of the whole earth. He is introduced in person in the Prometheus of Aeschylus. As to the physical idea attached by the early Greeks to the word, it seems that they regarded the earth as a flat circle, which was encompassed by a *river* perpetually flowing round it, and this *river* was Oceanus. (This notion is ridiculed by Herodotus.) Out of and into this river the sun and the stars were supposed to rise and set ; and on its banks were the abodes of the dead. From this notion it naturally resulted that, as geographical knowledge advanced, the name was applied to the great *outer* waters of the earth, in contradistinction to the *inner* seas, and especially to the *Atlantic*, or the sea without the Pillars of Hercules (ἡ ἔξω θάλαττα, Mare Exterius) as distinguished from the *Mediterranean*, or the Sea within that limit (ἡ ἐντὸς θάλαττα, Mare Internum); and thus the Atlantic is often called simply Oceanus. The epithet Atlantic (ἡ ᾽Ατλαντικὴ θάλασσα, Herod., ὁ ᾽Α. πόντος, Eurip.; ᾽Atlantĭcum Mare) was applied to it from the mythical position of ATLAS being on its shores. The other great waters which were denoted by the same term are described under their specific names.

Ocēlis (᾽Ωκηλις : *Ghela*), a celebrated harbour and emporium, at the S.W. point of Arabia Felix, just at the entrance to the Red Sea.

Ocellus Lucānus, a Pythagorean philosopher, was a native of some Greek city in Lucania, but we have no particulars of his life. We have still extant under his name a considerable fragment of a work, entitled, "On the Nature of the Whole," (περὶ τῆς τοῦ παντὸς φύσιος), written in the Ionic dialect ; but it is much disputed whether it is a genuine work. In this work the author maintains that the whole (τὸ πᾶν, or ὁ κόσμος) had no beginning, and will have no end. Edited by Rudolphi, Lips. 1801—8.

Ocēlum. 1. A town in the N. E. of Lusitania between the Tagus and the Durius, whose inhabitants, the Ocelenses, also bore the name of Lancienses. — **2.** (*Uxello* or *Uzeau*), a town in the Cottian Alps, was the last place in Cisalpine Gaul, before entering the territories of king Cottius.

Ocha (῎Οχη), the highest mountain in Euboea, was in the S. of the island near Carystus, running out into the promontory Caphareus.

Ochus. [Artaxerxes III.]

Ochus ("Ὦχος, 'Ωχος), a great river of Central Asia, flowing from the N. side of the Paropamisus (*Hindoo Koosh*), according to Strabo, through Hyrcania, into the Caspian; according to Pliny and Ptolemy, through Bactria, into the Oxus. Some suppose it to be only another name for the Oxus. In the Pehlvi dialect the word denotes a river in general.

Ocriculum (Ocriculānus: nr. *Otricoli* Ru.), an important municipium in Umbria, situated on the Tiber near its confluence with the Nar, and on the Via Flaminia, leading from Rome to Narnia, &c. There are ruins of an aqueduct, an amphitheatre and temples near the modern *Otricoli*.

Ocrisia. or **Oclisia,** mother of Servius Tullius. For details, see Tullius.

Octavia. 1. Sister of the emperor Augustus, was married first to C. Marcellus, consul, B. C. 50, and subsequently, upon the death of the latter, to Antony, the triumvir, in 40. This marriage was regarded as the harbinger of a lasting peace. Augustus was warmly attached to his sister, and she possessed all the charms and virtues likely to secure a lasting influence over the mind of a husband. Her beauty was universally allowed to be superior to that of Cleopatra, and her virtue was such as to excite admiration in an age of growing licentiousness and corruption. For a time Antony seemed to forget Cleopatra; but he soon became tired of his virtuous wife, and upon his return to the East, he forbade her to follow him. When at length the war broke out between Antony and Augustus, Octavia was divorced by her husband; but instead of resenting the insults she had received from him, she brought up with care his children by Fulvia and Cleopatra. She died B. C. 11. Octavia had 5 children, 3 by Marcellus, a son and 2 daughters, and 2 by Antony, both daughters. Her son, M. Marcellus, was adopted by Augustus, and was destined to be his successor, but died in 23. [Marcellus, No. 9.] The descendants of her 2 daughters by Antonius successively ruled the Roman world. The elder of them married L. Domitius Ahenobarbus, and became the grandmother of the emperor Nero; the younger of them married Drusus, the brother of the emperor Tiberius, and became the mother of the emperor Claudius, and the grandmother of the emperor Caligula. [Antonia.] — 2. The daughter of the emperor Claudius, by his 3rd wife, Valeria Messalina, was born about A. D. 42. She was at first betrothed by Claudius to L. Silanus, who put an end to his life, as Agrippina had destined Octavia to be the wife of her son, afterwards the emperor Nero. She was married to Nero in A. D. 53, but was soon deserted by her young and profligate husband for Poppaea Sabina. After living with the latter as his mistress for some time, he resolved to recognise her as his legal wife; and accordingly he divorced Octavia on the alleged ground of sterility, and then married Poppaea, A. D. 62. Shortly afterwards, Octavia was falsely accused of adultery, and was banished to the little island of Pandataria, where she was put to death. Her untimely end excited general commiseration. Octavia is the heroine of a tragedy, found among the works of Seneca, but the author of which was more probably Curiatius Maternus.

Octaviānus. [Augustus.]

Octavius. 1. Cn., surnamed Rufus, quaestor

about B. C. 230, may be regarded as the founder of the family. The Octavii originally came from the Volscian town of Velitrae, where a street and an altar bore the name of Octavius. — 2. Cn., son of No. 7, plebeian aedile 206, and praetor 205, when he obtained Sardinia as his province. He was actively employed during the remainder of the 2nd Punic war, and he was present at the battle of Zama. — 3. Cn., son of No. 2, was praetor 168, and had the command of the fleet in the war against Perseus. He was consul 165. In 162 he was one of 3 ambassadors sent into Syria, but was assassinated at Laodicea, by a Greek of the name of Leptines, at the instigation, as was supposed, of Lysias, the guardian of the young king Antiochus V. A statue of Octavius was placed on the rostra at Rome, where it was in the time of Cicero. — 4. Cn., son of No. 3, consul 128. — 5. M., perhaps younger son of No. 3, was the colleague of Tib. Gracchus in the tribunate of the plebs, 133, when he opposed his tribunitian veto to the passing of the agrarian law. He was in consequence deposed from his office by Tib. Gracchus. — 6. Cn., a supporter of the aristocratical party, was consul 87 with L. Cornelius Cinna. After Sulla's departure from Italy, in order to carry on the war against Mithridates, a vehement contest arose between the 2 consuls, which ended in the expulsion of Cinna from the city, and his being deprived of the consulship. Cinna soon afterwards returned at the head of a powerful army, and accompanied by Marius. Rome was compelled to surrender, and Octavius was one of the first victims in the massacres that followed. His head was cut off and suspended on the rostra. — 7. L., son of No. 6, consul 75, died in 74, as proconsul of Cilicia, and was succeeded in the command of the province by L. Lucullus. — 8. Cn., son of No. 7, consul 76. — 9. Cn., son of No. 8, was curule aedile 50, along with M. Caelius. On the breaking out of the civil war in 49, Octavius espoused the aristocratical party, and served as legate to M. Bibulus, who had the supreme command of the Pompeian fleet. After the battle of Pharsalia, Octavius sailed to Illyricum; but having been driven out of this country (47) by Caesar's legates, he fled to Africa. He was present at the battle of Actium (31), when he commanded part of Antony's fleet. — 10. C., younger son of No. 1, and the ancestor of Augustus, remained a simple Roman eques, without attempting to rise any higher in the state. — 11. C., son of No. 10, and great-grandfather of Augustus, lived in the time of the 2nd Punic war, in which he served as tribune of the soldiers. He was present at the battle of Cannae (216), and was one of the few who survived the engagement. — 12. C., son of No. 11, and grandfather of Augustus, lived quietly at his villa at Velitrae, without aspiring to the dignities of the Roman state. — 13. C., son of No. 12, and father of Augustus, was praetor 61, and in the following year succeeded C. Antonius in the government of Macedonia, which he administered with equal integrity and energy. He returned to Italy in 59, died the following year, 58, at Nola, in Campania, in the very same room in which Augustus afterwards breathed his last. By his 2nd wife Atia, Octavius had a daughter and a son, the latter of whom was subsequently the emperor Augustus. [Augustus.] — 14 L., a legate of Pompey in the war against the pirates, 67, was sent by Pompey into Crete to supersede Q. Metellus in the command of the island; but Metellus refused to surrender the command to him. [METELLUS, No. 16.]

Octāvius Balbus. [BALBUS.]

Octodūrus (Octodurensis: *Martigny*), a town of the Veragri in the country of the Helvetii, is situated in a valley surrounded by lofty mountains, and on the river *Dranœ* near the spot where it flows into the Rhone. The ancient town, like the modern one, was divided by the Drance into 2 parts. The inhabitants had the *Jus Latii.*

Octogēsa, a town of the Ilergetes in Hispania Tarraconensis near the Iberus, probably S. of the Sicoris.

Octolŏphus, a place of uncertain site, in the N. of Thessaly or the S. of Macedonia.

Ocўpētā. [HARPYIAE.]

Ocўrhŏē(Ὠκυρόη.) 1. One of the daughters of Oceanus and Tethys. — 2. Daughter of the centaur Chiron, possessed the gift of prophecy, and is said to have been changed into a mare.

Odenāthus, the ruler of Palmyra, checked the victorious career of the Persians after the defeat and capture of Valerian, A. D. 260, and drove Sapor out of Syria. In return for these services, Gallienus bestowed upon Odenathus the title of Augustus. Odenathus was soon afterwards murdered by some of his relations, not without the consent, it is said, of his wife Zenobia, 266. He was succeeded by ZENOBIA.

Odessus (Ὀδησσός: Ὀδησσίτης, Ὀδησσεύς). 1. (*Varna*), also called Odyssus and Odissus at a later time, a Greek town in Thracia (in the later Moesia Inferior) on the Pontus Euxinus nearly due E. of Marcianopolis, was founded by the Milesians in the territory of the Crobyzi in the reign of Astyages, king of Media (B. C. 594—559). The town possessed a good harbour, and carried on an extensive commerce. — 2. A seaport in Sarmatia Europaea, on the N. of the Pontus Euxinus and on the river Sangarius, W. of Olbia and the mouth of the Borysthenes. It was some distance N.E. of the modern *Odessa.*

Odoācer, usually called king of the Heruli, was the leader of the barbarians, who overthrew the Western empire, A. D. 476. He took the title of king of Italy, and reigned till his power was overthrown by Theodoric, king of the Goths. Odoacer was defeated in 3 decisive battles by Theodoric (489—490), and then took refuge in Ravenna, where he was besieged for 3 years. He at last capitulated on condition that he and Theodoric should be joint kings of Italy; but Odoacer was soon afterwards murdered by his rival.

Odomantiœ (Ὀδομαντική), a district in the N.E. of Macedonia between the Strymon and the Nestus, inhabited by the Thracian tribe of the Odomanti or Odomantes.

Odrȳsae (Ὀδρύσαι), the most powerful people in Thrace, dwelt, according to Herodotus, on both sides of the river Artiscus, a tributary of the Hebrus, but also spread further W. over the whole plain of the Hebrus. Soon after the Persian wars Teres, king of the Odrysae, obtained the sovereignty over several of the other Thracian tribes, and extended his dominions as far as the Black sea. He was succeeded by his son Sitalces, who became the master of almost the whole of Thrace. His empire comprised all the territory from Abdera to the mouths of the Danube, and from

Byzantium to the sources of the Strymon; and it is described by Thucydides as the greatest of all the kingdoms between the Ionian gulf and the Euxine, both in revenue and opulence. Sitalces assisted the Athenians in the Peloponnesian war against Perdiccas, king of Macedonia. [SITALCES.] He died B. C. 424, and was succeeded by his nephew Seuthes I. On the death of the latter about the end of the Peloponnesian war, the power of the Odrysae declined. For the subsequent history of the Odrysae, see THRACIA.

Odyssēa (Ὀδύσσεια), a town of Hispania Baetica, situated N. of Abdera amidst the mountains of Turdetania, with a temple of Athena, said to have been built by Odysseus (Ulysses). Its position is quite uncertain. Some of the ancients supposed it to be the same as OLISIPO.

Odysseus. [ULYSSES.]

Oea (Ἐόα, Ptol.: Oeensis: *Tripoli* ? Ru.), a city on the N. coast of Africa, in the Regio Syrtica (i. e. between the Syrtes), was one of the 3 cities of the African Tripolis, and, under the Romans, a colony by the name of Aelia Augusta Felix. It had a mixed population of Libyans and Sicilians.

Oea (Οἴα), a town in the island of Aegina, 20 stadia from the capital.

Oeagrus, or **Oeāger** (Οἴαγρος), king of Thrace, was the father, by the muse Calliope, of Orpheus and Linus. Hence the sisters of Orpheus are called *Oeagrides,* in the sense of the Muses. The adjective *Oeagrius* is also used by the poets as equivalent to Thracian. Hence *Oeagrius Haemus, Oeagrius Hebrus,* &c.

Oeanthē or **Oeanthīa** (Οἰάνθη, Οἰάνθεια: Οἰάνθεός: Galaxidhi), a town of the Locri Ozolae on the coast, near the entrance of the Crissaean gulf.

Oeāso or **Oeasso** (Οἴαρσων), a town of the Vascones on the N. coast of Hispania Tarraconensis situated on a promontory of the same name, and on the river Magrada.

Oeax (Οἴαξ), son of Nauplius and Clymene, and brother of Palamedes and Nausimedon.

Oebalus (Οἴβαλος). 1. Son of Cynortas, husband of Gorgophone, and father of Tyndareus, Pirene, and Arene, was king of Sparta, where he was afterwards honoured with a heroum. According to others he was son of Perieres and grandson of Cynortas, and was married to the nymph Batea, by whom he had several children. The patronymic *Oebalides* is not only applied to his descendants, but to the Spartans generally, as Hyacinthus, Castor, Pollux, &c. The feminine patronymic *Oebalis* and the adjective *Oebalius* are applied in the same way. Hence Helen is called by the poets *Oebalis,* and *Oebalia pellex;* the city of Tarentum is termed *Oebalia arx,* because it was founded by the Lacedaemonians; and since the Sabines were, according to one tradition, a Lacedaemonian colony, we find the Sabine king Titus Tatius named *Oebalius Titus,* and the Sabine women *Oebalides matres.* (Ov. *Fast.* i. 260, iii. 230.) — 2. Son of Telon by a nymph of the stream Sebethus, near Naples, ruled in Campania.

Oechālia (Οἰχαλία: Οἰχαλιεύς, Οἰχαλιώτης). 1. A town in Thessaly on the Peneus near Tricca. — 2. A town in Thessaly, belonging to the territory of Trachis. — 3. A town in Messenia on the frontier of Arcadia, identified by Pausanias with Carnasium, by Strabo with Andania. — 4. A town of Euboea in the district Eretria. — The ancients were divided in opinion which of these places was the residence of Eurytus, whom Hercules defeated and slew. The original legend probably belonged to the Thessalian Oechalia, and was thence transferred to the other towns.

Oecūmĕnĭus (Οἰκουμένιος), bishop of Tricca in Thessaly, a Greek commentator on various parts of the New Testament, probably flourished about A. D. 950. He has the reputation of a judicious commentator, careful in compilation, modest in offering his own judgment, and neat in expression. Most of his commentaries were published at Paris, 1631.

Oedĭpus (Οἰδίπους), son of Laius and Jocaste of Thebes. The tragic fate of this hero is more celebrated than that of any other legendary personage, on account of the frequent use which the tragic poets have made of it. In their hands it underwent various changes and embellishments; but the common story ran as follows. Laius, son of Labdacus, was king of Thebes, and husband of Jocaste, a daughter of Menoeceus and sister of Creon. An oracle had informed Laius that he was destined to perish by the hands of his own son. Accordingly, when Jocaste gave birth to a son, they pierced his feet, bound them together, and exposed the child on Mt. Cithaeron. There he was found by a shepherd of king Polybus of Corinth, and was called from his swollen feet Oedipus. Having been carried to the palace, the king and his wife Merope (or Periboea) brought him up as their own child. Once, however, Oedipus was taunted by a Corinthian with not being the king's son, whereupon he proceeded to Delphi to consult the oracle. The oracle replied that he was destined to slay his father and commit incest with his mother. Thinking that Polybus was his father, he resolved not to return to Corinth; but on his road between Delphi and Daulis he met his real father Laius. Polyphontes, the charioteer of Laius bade Oedipus make way for them; whereupon a scuffle ensued in which Oedipus slew both Laius and his charioteer. In the mean time the celebrated Sphinx had appeared in the neighbourhood of Thebes. Seated on a rock, she put a riddle to every Theban that passed by, and whoever was unable to solve it was killed by the monster. This calamity induced the Thebans to proclaim that whoever should deliver the country of the Sphinx, should be made king, and should receive Jocaste as his wife. Oedipus came forward, and when he approached the Sphinx she gave the riddle as follows: "A being with 4 feet has 2 feet and 3 feet, and only one voice; but its feet vary, and when it has most it is weakest." Oedipus solved the riddle by saying that it was man, who in infancy crawls upon all fours, in manhood stands erect upon 2 feet, and in old age supports his tottering legs with a staff. The Sphinx, enraged at the solution of the riddle, thereupon threw herself down from the rock. Oedipus now obtained the kingdom of Thebes, and married his mother, by whom he became the father of Eteocles, Polynices, Antigone, and Ismene. In consequence of this incestuous alliance of which no one was aware, the country of Thebes was visited by a plague. The oracle, on being consulted, ordered that the murderer of Laius should be expelled. Oedipus accordingly pronounced a solemn curse upon the unknown murderer, and declared him an exile; but when he endeavoured to discover him, he was informed by the seer Tiresias that he himself was both the parricide and the husband of his mother.

Jocaste now hung herself, and Oedipus put out his own eyes. From this point traditions differ, for according to some, Oedipus in his blindness was expelled from Thebes by his sons and brother-in-law, Creon, who undertook the government, and he was accompanied by Antigone in his exile to Attica; while according to others he was imprisoned by his sons at Thebes, in order that his disgrace might remain concealed from the eyes of the world. The father now cursed his sons, who agreed to rule over Thebes alternately, but became involved in a dispute, in consequence of which they fought in single combat, and slew each other. Hereupon Creon succeeded to the throne, and expelled Oedipus. After long wanderings Oedipus arrived in the grove of the Eumenides, near Colonus, in Attica; he was there honoured by Theseus in his misfortune, and, according to an oracle, the Eumenides removed him from the earth, and no one was allowed to approach his tomb. According to Homer, Oedipus, tormented by the Erinnyes of his mother, continued to reign at Thebes, after her death; he fell in battle, and was honoured at Thebes with funeral solemnities.

Oenĕōn (Οἰνεών: Οἰνεωνεύς), a seaport town of the Locri Ozolae, E. of Naupactus.

Oeneus (Οἰνεύς), son of Portheus, husband of Althaea, by whom he became the father of Tydeus and Meleager, and was thus the grandfather of Diomedes. He was king of Pleuron and Calydon in Aetolia. This is Homer's account; but according to later authorities he was the son of Porthaon and Euryte, and the father of Toxeus, whom he himself killed, Thyreus (Phereus), Clymenus, Periphas, Agelaus, Meleager, Gorge, Eurymede, Melanippe, Mothone, and Deianira. His second wife was Melanippe, the daughter of Hipponous, by whom he had Tydeus according to some accounts: though according to others Tydeus was his son by his own daughter Gorge. He is said to have been deprived of his kingdom by the sons of his brother Agrius, who imprisoned and ill used him. He was subsequently avenged by Diomedes, who slew Agrius and his sons, and restored the kingdom either to Oeneus himself, or to his son-in-law Andraemon, as Oeneus was too old. Diomedes took his grandfather with him to Peloponnesus, but some of the sons who lay in ambush, slew the old man, near the altar of Telephus in Arcadia. Diomedes buried his body at Argos, and named the town of Oenoe after him. According to others Oeneus lived to extreme old age with Diomedes at Argos, and died a natural death. Homer knows nothing of all this; he merely relates that Oeneus once neglected to sacrifice to Artemis, in consequence of which she sent a monstrous boar into the territory of Calydon, which was hunted by Meleager. The hero Bellerophon was hospitably entertained by Oeneus, and received from him a costly girdle as a present.

Oenĭădae (Οἰνιάδαι: *Trigardon* or *Trikhardo*), an ancient town of Acarnania, situated on the Achelous near its mouth, and surrounded by marshes caused by the overflowing of the river, which thus protected it from hostile attacks. It was called in ancient times **Erysiche** (Ἐρυσίχη), and its inhabitants **Erysichaei** (Ἐρυσιχαῖοι); and it probably derived its later name from the mythical Oeneus, the grandfather of Diomedes. Unlike the other cities of Acarnania, Oeniadae espoused the cause of the Spartans in the Peloponnesian war. At the time of Alexander the Great, the town was taken by the Aetolians, who expelled the inhabitants; but the Aetolians were expelled in their turn by Philip V., king of Macedonia, who surrounded the place with strong fortifications. The Romans restored the town to the Acarnanians. The fortress Nesus or Nasus belonging to the territory of Oeniadae was situated in a small lake near Oeniadae.

Oenĭdes, a patronymic from Oeneus, and hence given to Meleager, the son of Oeneus, and Diomedes, the grandson of Oeneus.

Oenoanda or **Oeneanda**, a town of Asia Minor, in the N.W. of Pisidia, or the district of Cabalia, subject to Cibyra.

Oenobaras (Οἰνοβάρας), a tributary of the Orontes, flowing through the plain of Antioch, in Syria.

Oenŏē (Οἰνόη : Οἰνοαῖος). 1. A demus of Attica, belonging to the tribe Hippothoontis, near Eleutherae on the frontiers of Boeotia, frequently mentioned in the Peloponnesian war.—2. A demus of Attica, near Marathon, belonging to the tribe Aiantis, and also to the Tetrapolis.—3. A fortress of the Corinthians, on the Corinthian gulf, between the promontory Olmiae and the frontier of Megaris.—4. A town in Argolis on the Arcadian frontier at the foot of Mt. Artemisium.—5. A town in Elis, near the mouth of the Selleis.—6. A town in the island Icarus or Icaria.

Oenŏmāus (Οἰνόμαος). 1. King of Pisa in Elis, was son of Ares and Harpinna, the daughter of Asopus, and husband of the Pleiad Sterope, by whom he became the father of Hippodamia. According to others he was a son of Ares and Sterope or a son of Alxion. An oracle had declared that he should perish by the hands of his son-in-law; and as his horses were swifter than those of any other mortal, he declared that 'all who came forward as suitors for Hippodamia's hand should contend with him in the chariot-race, that whoever conquered should receive her, and that whoever was conquered should suffer death. The race-course extended from Pisa to the altar of Poseidon, on the Corinthian isthmus. The suitor started with Hippodamia in a chariot, and Oenomaus then hastened with his swift horses after the lovers. He had overtaken and slain many a suitor, when Pelops, the son of Tantalus, came to Pisa. Pelops bribed Myrtilus, the charioteer of Oenomaus, to take out the linch-pins from the wheels of his master's chariot, and he received from Poseidon a golden chariot, and most rapid horses. In the race which followed, the chariot of Oenomaus broke down, and he fell out and was killed. Thus Pelops obtained Hippodamia and the kingdom of Pisa. There are some variations in this story, such as, that Oenomaus was himself in love with his daughter, and for this reason slew her lovers. Myrtilus also is said to have loved Hippodamia, and as she favoured the suit of Pelops, she persuaded Myrtilus to take the linch-pins out of the wheels of her father's chariot. As Oenomaus was breathing his last he pronounced a curse upon Myrtilus. This curse had its desired effect, for as Pelops refused to give to Myrtilus the reward he had promised, or as Myrtilus had attempted to dishonour Hippodamia, Pelops thrust him down from Cape Geraestus. Myrtilus, while dying, likewise pronounced a curse upon Pelops, which was the cause of all the calamities that afterwards befell his house. The tomb of Oenomaus was shown on the river Cladeus in Elis. His

house was destroyed by lightning, and only one pillar of it remained standing.—2. Of Gadara, a cynic philosopher, who flourished in the reign of Hadrian, or somewhat later, but before Porphyry. He wrote a work to expose the oracles, of which considerable fragments are preserved by Eusebius. —3. A tragic poet. [DIOGENES, No. 5.]

Oenŏnē (Οἰνώνη), daughter of the river-god Cebren, and wife of Paris, before he carried off Helen. [PARIS.]

Oenŏnē or **Oenopĭa**, the ancient name of AEGINA.

Oenŏphўta (τὰ Οἰνόφυτα : Inia), a town in Boeotia, on the left bank of the Asopus, and on the road from Tanagra to Oropus, memorable for the victory gained here by the Athenians over the Boeotians, B. C. 456.

Oenŏpĭdes (Οἰνοπίδης) of Chios, a distinguished astronomer and mathematician, perhaps a contemporary of Anaxagoras. Oenopides derived most of his astronomical knowledge from the priests and astronomers of Egypt, with whom he lived for some time. He obtained from this source his knowledge of the obliquity of the ecliptic, the discovery of which he is said to have claimed. The length of the solar year was fixed by Oenopides at 365 days, and somewhat less than 9 hours. He is said to have discovered the 12th and 23rd propositions of the 1st book of Euclid, and the quadrature of the meniscus.

Oenŏpion (Οἰνοπίων), son of Dionysus and husband of the nymph Helice, by whom he became the father of Thalus, Euanthes, Melas, Salagus, Athamas, and Merope, Aerope or Haero. Some writers call Oenopion a son of Rhadamanthus by Ariadne, and a brother of Staphylus. From Crete he migrated with his sons to Chios, which Rhadamanthus had assigned to him as his habitation. When king of Chios, the giant Orion sued for the hand of his daughter Merope. As Oenopion refused to give her to Orion, the latter violated Merope, whereupon Oenopion put out his eyes, and expelled him from the island. Orion went to Lemnos ; he was afterwards cured of his blindness, and returned to Chios to take vengeance on Oenopion. But the latter was not to be found in Chios, for his friends had concealed him in the earth, so that Orion, unable to discover him, went to Crete.

Oenŏtri, Oenōtrĭa. [ITALIA.]

Oenōtrĭdes, 2 small islands in the Tyrrhene sea, off the coast of Lucania, and opposite the town of Elea or Velia and the mouth of the Helos.

Oenōtrŏpae. [ANIUS.]

Oenōtrus (Οἴνωτρος), youngest son of Lycaon, emigrated with a colony from Arcadia to Italy, and gave the name of Oenotria to the district in which he settled.

Oenŭs (Οἰνοῦς : Kelesina), a river in Laconia, rising on the frontier of Arcadia, and flowing into the Eurotas, N. of Sparta. There was a town of the same name upon this river, celebrated for its wine.

Oenussae (Οἰνοῦσσαι, Οἰνοῦσαι). 1. A group of islands lying off the S. point of Messenia, opposite to the port of Phoenicus: the 2 largest of them are now called Sapienza and Cabrera.—2. (Spalmadori or Egonuses), a group of 5 islands between Chios and the coast of Asia Minor.

Oeōnus (Οἰωνός), son of Licymnius of Midea in Argolis, first victor at Olympia, in the foot-race. He is said to have been killed at Sparta by the sons of Hippocoon, but was avenged by Hercules, whose kinsman he was, and was honoured with a monument near the temple of Hercules.

Oërŏë ('Ωερόη), an island in Boeotia, formed by the river Asopus and opposite Plataeae.

Oescus (*Isker* or *Esker*) called Oscĭus ("Οσκιος) by Thucydides, and Scĭus (Σκίος) by Herodotus, a river in Moesia, which rises in Mt. Scomius according to Thucydides, or in Mt. Rhodope according to Pliny, but in reality on the W. slope of Mt. Haemus, and flows into the Danube near a town of the same name (*Orezzovitz*).

Oesyma (Οἰσύμη: Οἰσυμαῖος), called Aesyma (Αἰσύμη) by Homer (*Il.* viii. 304), an ancient town in Thrace between the Strymon and the Nestus, a colony of the Thasians.

Oeta (Οἴτη, τὰ Οἰταῖον οὔρεα: *Katavothra*), a rugged pile of mountains in the S. of Thessaly, an eastern branch of Mt. Pindus, extended S. of Mt. Othrys along the S. bank of the Sperchius to the Maliac gulf at Thermopylae, thus forming the N. barrier of Greece. Strabo and Livy give the name of Callidromus to the eastern part of Oeta, an appellation which does not occur in Herodotus and the earlier writers. Respecting the pass of Mt. Oeta, see THERMOPYLAE. Oeta was celebrated in mythology as the mountain on which Hercules burnt himself to death. From this mountain the S. of Thessaly bordering on Phocis was called Oetaea (Οἰταία) and its inhabitants Oetaei (Οἰταῖοι).

Oetylus (Οἴτυλος: Οἰτύλιος: *Vitylo*), also called Tylus (Τύλος), an ancient town in Laconia, on the Messenian gulf, S. of Thalama, called after an Argive hero of this name.

Ofella, a man of sound sense and of a straightforward character, whom Horace contrasts with the Stoic quacks of his time.

Ofella, Q. Lucrētĭus, originally belonged to the Marian party, but deserted to Sulla, who appointed him to the command of the army employed in the blockade of Praeneste, B. C. 82. Ofella became a candidate for the consulship in the following year, although he had not yet been either quaestor or praetor, thus acting in defiance of one of Sulla's laws. He was in consequence put to death by Sulla's orders.

Ofĭllus, a distinguished Roman jurist, was one of the pupils of Servius Sulpicius, and a friend of Cicero and Caesar. His works are often cited in the Digest.

Oglasa (*Monte Christo*), a small island off the coast of Etruria.

Ogulnĭi, Q. and Cn., 2 brothers, tribunes of the plebs, B. C. 300, carried a law by which the number of the pontiffs was increased from 4 to 8, and that of the augurs from 4 to 9, and which enacted that 4 of the pontiffs and 5 of the augurs should be taken from the plebs. Besides these 8 pontiffs there was the pontifex maximus, who is generally not included when the number of pontiffs is spoken of.

Ogygĭa ('Ωγυγία), the mythical island of Calypso, is placed by Homer in the navel or central point of the sea, far away from all lands. Later writers pretended to find it in the Ionian sea, near the promontory Lacinium, in Bruttium.

Ogȳgus or Ogȳges ('Ωγύγης), sometimes called a Boeotian autochthon, and sometimes son of Boeotus, and king of the Hectenes, is said to have been the first ruler of the territory of Thebes, which was called after him Ogygia. In his reign

the waters of lake Copais rose above its banks, and inundated the whole valley of Boeotia. This flood is usually called after him the Ogygian. The name of Ogyges is also connected with Attic story, for in Attica an Ogygian flood is likewise mentioned, and he is described as the father of the Attic hero Eleusis, and as the father of Daira, the daughter of Oceanus. In the Boeotian tradition he was the father of Alalcomenia, Thelxinoea and Aulis. — Bacchus is called *Ogygius deus*, because he is said to have been born at Thebes.

Ogyris ('Ωγυρις), an island of the Erythraean Sea (*Indian Ocean*), off the coast of Carmania, at a distance of 2000 stadia (20 geog. miles), noted as the alleged burial-place of the ancient king Erythras.

Oicles or Oicleus ('Οἰκλῆς, 'Οἰκλεύς), son of Antiphates, grandson of Melampus and father of Amphiaraus, of Argos. He is also called a son of Amphiaraus, or a son of Mantius, the brother of Antiphates. Oicles accompanied Hercules on his expedition against Laomedon of Troy, and was there slain in battle. According to other traditions he returned home from the expedition, and dwelt in Arcadia, where he was visited by his grandson Alcmaeon, and where his tomb was shown.

Oïleus ('Οιλεύς), son of Hodoedocus and Laonome, grandson of Cynna, and great-grandson of Opus, was a king of the Locrians, and married to Eriopis, by whom he became the father of Ajax, who is hence called Oïlīdes, Oïlīādes, and Ajax Oïlëi. Oïleus was also the father of Medon by Rhene. He is mentioned among the Argonauts.

Olba or Olbe ("Ολβη), an ancient inland city of Cilicia, in the mountains above Soloë, and between the rivers Lamus and Cydnus. Its foundation was ascribed by mythical tradition, to Ajax the son of Teucer, whose alleged descendants, the priests of the very ancient temple of Zeus, once ruled over all Cilicia Aspera. In later times it belonged to Isauria, and was the see of a bishop.

Olbĭasa ("Ολβασα). 1. A city of Cilicia Aspera, at the foot of the Taurus, N. of Selinus, and N.W. of Cafystrus; not to be confounded with OLBA.—2. A city in the S.E. of Lycaonia, S.W. of Cybistra, in the district called Antiochiana. — 3. A city in the N. of Pisidia, between Pednelissus and Selge Olbe. [OLBA.]

Olbe ("Ολβη). [OLBA.]

Olbĭa ('Ολβία). 1. (Prob. *Eoubes*, near *Hières*), a colony of Massilia, on the coast of Gallia Narbonensis, on a hill called Olbianus, E. of Telo Martius (*Toulon*). — 2. (Prob. *Terra Nova*), a very ancient city, near the N. end of the E. side of the island of Sardinia, with the only good harbour on this coast; and therefore the usual landing-place for persons coming from Rome. A mythical tradition ascribed its foundation to the Thespiadae.— 3. In Bithynia [ASTACUS]. The gulf of Astacus was also called from it, Sinus Olbianus. — 4. A fortress on the W. frontier of Pamphylia, on the coast, W. of the river Catarrharractes; not improbably on the same site as the later ATTALIA.—5. [BORYSTHENES.]

Olcădes, an ancient people in Hispania Tarraconensis, N. of Carthago Nova, near the sources of the Anas, in a part of the country afterwards inhabited by the Oretani. They are mentioned only in the wars of the Carthaginians with the inhabitants of Spain. Hannibal transplanted some of the Olcades to Africa. Their chief towns were Althaea and Carteia, the site of both of which is uncertain ; the latter place must not be confounded with the celebrated CARTEIA in Baetica.

Olcinium (Olciniātae : *Dulcigno*), an ancient town on the coast of Illyria, S. W. of Scodra, belonging to the territory of Gentius.

Olearus. [OLIARUS.]

Oleastrum. 1. A town of the Cosetani, in Hispania Tarraconensis, on the road from Dertosa to Tarraco, probably the place from which the *plumbum Oleastrense* derived its name. — 2. A town in Hispania Baetica, near Gades.

Olen ('Ωλήν), a mythical personage, who is represented as the earliest Greek lyric poet, and the first author of sacred hymns in hexameter verse. He is closely connected with the worship of Apollo, of whom, in one legend, he was made the prophet. His connection with Apollo is also marked by his being called Hyperborean, and one of the establishers of oracles ; though the more common story made him a native of Lycia. He is said to have settled at Delos. His name seems to signify simply the *flute-player*. Of the ancient hymns, which went under his name, Pausanias mentions those to Here, to Achaeïa, and to Ilithyia ; the last was in celebration of the birth of Apollo and Artemis.

Olěnus ('Ωλενος : 'Ωλένιος). 1. An ancient town in Aetolia, near New Pleuron, and at the foot of Mt. Aracynthus, is mentioned by Homer, but was destroyed by the Aetolians at an early period. — 2. A town in Achaia, between Patrae and Dyme, refused to join the Achaean league on its restoration, in B. C. 280. In the time of Strabo the town was deserted. The goat Amalthaea, which suckled the infant Zeus, is called *Olenia capella* by the poets, either because the goat was supposed to have been born near the town of Olenus, and to have been subsequently transferred to Crete, or because the nymph Amalthaea, to whom the goat belonged, was a daughter of Olenus.

Olgassys ('Ολγασσυς : *Al-Gez Dagh*), a lofty, steep, and rugged mountain chain of Asia Minor, extending nearly W. and E. through the E. of Bithynia, and the centre of Paphlagonia to the river Halys, nearly parallel to the chain of Olympus, of which it may be considered as a branch. Numerous temples were built upon it by the Paphlagonians.

Oliãrus ('Ωλίαρος, 'Ωλέαρος : 'Ωλίδριος : *Antiparos*), a small island in the Aegean sea, one of the Cyclades, W. of Paros, originally colonised by the Phoenicians, is celebrated in modern times for its stalactite grotto, which is not mentioned by ancient writers.

Oligyrtus ('Ολίγυρτος), a fortress in the N. E. of Arcadia on a mountain of the same name, between Stymphalus and Caphyae.

Olisipo (*Lisbon*), a town in Lusitania, on the right bank of the Tagus near its mouth, and a Roman municipium with the surname Felicitas Julia. It was celebrated for its swift horses. Its name is sometimes written **Ulyssippo**, because it was supposed by some to have been the town which Ulysses was said to have founded in Spain ; but the town to which this legend referred was situated in the mountains of Turdetania.

Olizōn ('Ολιζών), a town of Thessaly on the coast of Magnesia and on the Pagasaean gulf, mentioned by Homer.

Ollius (*Oglio*), a river in Gallia Transpadana, falls into the Po, S. W. of Mantua.

Olmiae ('Ολμιαί), a promontory in the territory of Corinth, which separated the Corinthian and Alcyonian gulfs.

Oloosson ('Ολοοσσόν : 'Ολοοσσόνιος : *Elassona*), a town of the Perrhaebi in Thessaly, in the district of Hestiaeotis. Homer (*Il.* ii. 739) calls it " white," an epithet which it obtained, according to Strabo, from the whiteness of its soil.

Olophyxus ('Ολόφυξος : 'Ολοφύξιος), a town of Macedonia, on the peninsula of Mt. Athos.

Olpae or **Olpe** ('Ολπαι, 'Ολπή : 'Ολπαῖος) 1. (*Arapi*), a town of the Amphilochi in Acarnania, on the Ambracian gulf, N. W. of Argos Amphilochicum. — 2. A town of the Locri Ozolae.

Olūrus ('Ολουρος : 'Ολούριος) 1. A town in Achaia, near Pellene, on the Sicyonian frontier. — 2. Also **Olŭris** ("Ολουρις), called **Dorium** (Δώριον) by Homer, a town in Messenia, S. of the river Neda.

Olūs ('Ολοῦς : 'Ολούντιος), a town and harbour on the E. coast of Crete, near the promontory of Zephyrium.

Olybrius, Anicius, Roman emperor A. D. 472, was raised to this dignity by Ricimer, who deposed Anthemius. He died in the course of the same year, after a reign of 3 months and 13 days. His successor was GLYCERIUS.

Olympēnā, and **Olympēni,** or **Olympiāni** ('Ολυμπηνή, 'Ολυμπηνοί, 'Ολυμπιηνοί), the names of the district about the Mysian Olympus, and of its inhabitants.

Olympia ('Ολυμπία), the name of a small plain in Elis, in which the Olympic games were celebrated. It was surrounded on the N. and N. E. by the mountains Cronion and Olympus, on the S. by the river Alphēus, and on the W. by the river Cladēus. In this plain was the sacred grove of Zeus, called *Altis* ("Αλτις, an old Elean form of ἄλσος, a grove), situated at the angle formed by the confluence of the rivers Alpheus and Cladeus, and 300 stadia distant from the town of Pisa. The Altis and its immediate neighbourhood were adorned with numerous temples, statues, and public buildings, to which the general appellation of Olympia was given ; but there was no town of this name. The Altis was surrounded by a wall. It contained the following temples : — 1. The *Olympiěum*, or temple of Zeus Olympius, which was the most celebrated of all the buildings at Olympia, and which contained the master-piece of Greek art, the colossal statue of Zeus by Phidias. The statue was made of ivory and gold, and the god was represented as seated on a throne of cedar wood, adorned with gold, ivory, ebony, and precious stones. [PHIDIAS.] 2. The *Heraeum*, or temple of Hera, which contained the celebrated chest of Cypselus, and was situated N. of the Olympiěum. 3. The *Metrōum*, or temple of the Mother of the gods. The other public buildings in the Altis most worthy of notice were, the *Thesauri*, or treasuries of the different states, which had sent dedicatory offerings to the Olympian Zeus, situated at the foot of Mt. Cronion : the *Zanes*, or statues of Zeus, which had been erected from fines imposed upon those who had been guilty of fraud or other irregularities in the Olympic contests, and which were placed on a stone platform near the Thesauri: the *Prytaneum*, in which the Olympic victors dined after the contests had been brought to a close : the *Bouleuterion*, in which all the regulations relating to the games were made, and which contained a statue of Zeus Horcius, before which the usual oaths were taken by the judges and the combatants: the *Philippeum*, a circular building of brick, surmounted with a dome, which was erected by Philip after the battle of Chaeronea, and which was situated near one of the gates of the Altis, close to the Prytaneum: the *Hippodamium*, a sacred enclosure erected in honour of Hippodamia; the *Pelopium*, a sacred enclosure, erected in honour of Pelops. The 2 chief buildings outside the Altis were the *Stadium* to the E. of Mt. Cronion, in which the gymnastic games were celebrated, and the *Hippodromus*, a little S. E. of the Stadium, in which the chariot races took place. At the place which formed the connection between the Stadium and Hippodromus, the Hellanodicae, or judges of the Olympic games had their seats. (For details see *Dict. of Antiq.* arts. *Hippodromus* and *Stadium.*) The Olympic games were celebrated from the earliest times in Greece, and their establishment was assigned to various mythical personages. There was an interval of 4 years between each celebration of the festival, which interval was called an Olympiad; but the Olympiads were not employed as a chronological aera till the victory of Coroebus in the foot-race, B. C. 776. An account of the Olympic games and of the Olympiads is given in the *Dict. of Antiq.* arts. *Olympia* and *Olympias*.

Olympias ('Ολυμπιάς), wife of Philip II., king of Macedonia, and mother of Alexander the Great, was the daughter of Neoptolemus I., king of Epirus. She was married to Philip B. C. 359. The numerous amours of Philip, and the passionate and jealous character of Olympias occasioned frequent disputes between them; and when Philip married Cleopatra, the niece of Attalus (337), Olympias withdrew from Macedonia, and took refuge at the court of her brother Alexander, king of Epirus. It was generally believed that she lent her support to the assassination of Philip, 336; but it is hardly credible that she evinced her approbation of that deed in the open manner asserted by some writers. After the death of Philip she returned to Macedonia, where she enjoyed great influence through the affection of Alexander. On the death of the latter (323), she withdrew from Macedonia, where her enemy Antipater had the undisputed control of affairs, and took refuge in Epirus. Here she continued to live, as it were, in exile, until the death of Antipater (319) presented a new opening to her ambition. She gave her support to the new regent Polysperchon, in opposition to Cassander, who had formed an alliance with Eurydice the wife of Philip Arrhidaeus, the nominal king of Macedonia. In 317 Olympias, resolving to obtain the supreme power in Macedonia, invaded that country, along with Polysperchon, defeated Eurydice in battle, and put both her and her husband to death. Olympias followed up her vengeance by the execution of Nicanor, the brother of Cassander, as well as of 100 of his leading partisans among the Macedonian nobles. Cassander, who was at that time in the Peloponnesus, hastened to turn his arms against Macedonia. Olympias on his approach threw herself (together with Roxana and the young Alexander) into Pydna, where she was closely blockaded by Cassander throughout the winter. At length in the spring of 316, she was compelled to surrender to Cassander, who caused her to be put to death. Olympias was not without something of the grandeur and loftiness of spirit

which distinguished her son, but her ungovernable passions led her to acts of sanguinary cruelty that must for ever disgrace her name.

Olympiŏdōrus ('Ολυμπιόδωρος). 1. A native of Thebes in Egypt, who lived in the 5th century after Christ. He wrote a work in 22 books (entitled 'Ιστορικοὶ λόγοι), which comprised the history of the Western empire under the reign of Honorius, from A. D. 407 to October, A. D. 425. Olympiodorus took up the history from about the point at which Eunapius had ended. [EUNAPIUS.] The original work of Olympiodorus is lost, but an abridgment of it has been preserved by Photius. After the death of Honorius Olympiodorus removed to Byzantium, to the court of the emperor Theodosius. Hierocles dedicated to this Olympiodorus his work on providence and fate [HIEROCLES]. Olympiodorus was a heathen. — 2. A peripatetic philosopher, who taught at Alexandria, where Proclus was one of his pupils. — 3. The last philosopher of celebrity in the Neo-Platonic school of Alexandria. He lived in the first half of the 6th century after Christ, in the reign of the emperor Justinian. His life of Plato, and commentaries on several of Plato's dialogues are still extant. — 4. An Aristotelic philosopher, the author of a commentary on the *Meteorologica* of Aristotle, which is still extant, lived at Alexandria, in the latter half of the 6th century after Christ. Like Simplicius, to whom, however, he is inferior, he endeavours to reconcile Plato and Aristotle.

Olympĭus ('Ολύμπιος), the Olympian, occurs as a surname of Zeus, Hercules, the Muses (*Olympiades*), and in general of all the gods who were believed to live in Olympus, in contradistinction from the gods of the lower world.

Olympĭus Nemesiānus. [NEMESIANUS.]

Olympŭs ("Ολυμπος), the name of 2 Greek musicians, of whom one is mythical, and the other historical. — 1. The elder Olympus belongs to the mythical genealogy of Mysian and Phrygian fluteplayers — Hyagnis, Marsyas, Olympus — to each of whom the invention of the flute was ascribed, under whose names we have the mythical representation of the contest between the Phrygian auletic and the Greek citharoedic music. Olympus was said to have been a native of Mysia, and to have lived before the Trojan war. Olympus not unfrequently appears on works of art, as a boy, sometimes instructed by Marsyas, and sometimes as witnessing and lamenting his fate. — 2. The true Olympus was a Phrygian, and perhaps belonged to a family of native musicians, since he was said to be descended from the first Olympus. He flourished about B. C. 660—620. Though a Phrygian by origin, Olympus must be reckoned among the Greek musicians; for all the accounts make Greece the scene of his artistic activity; and he may be considered as having naturalized in Greece the music of the flute, which had previously been almost peculiar to Phrygia.

Olympŭs ('Ολυμπος). I. *In Europe*. 1. (Grk. *Elymbo*, Turk. *Semavat-Evi*, i. e. *Abode of the Celestials*). The E. part of the great chain of mountains which extends W. and E. from the Acroceraunian promontory on the Adriatic, to the Thermaic Gulf, and which formed the N. boundary of ancient Greece proper. In a wide sense, the name is sometimes applied to all that part of this great chain which lies E. of the central range of Pindus, and which is usually called the Cambunian moun-

Panathenaic Procession. (From the Frieze of the Parthenon.) Page 527.

The Parthenon Restored. Page 527.

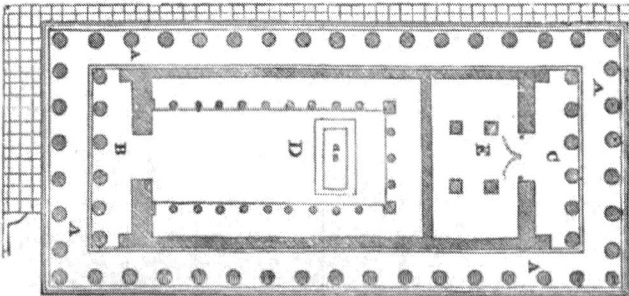

Ground Plan of the Parthenon. Page 527.

A. Peristylium.
B. Pronaos or Prodomus.
C. Opisthodomus or Posticum.

D. Hecatompedon.
   a. Statue of the Goddess.
E. Parthenon, afterwards Opisthodomus.

[To face p. 496.

Julius Nepos, Roman Emperor, A.D. 474—475. Page 473.

Nicomedes III., King of Bithynia, B.C. 91—74. Page 479.

Nepotianus, Roman Emperor, A.D. 350.

Pescennius Niger, Roman Emperor, A.D. 193. Page 480.

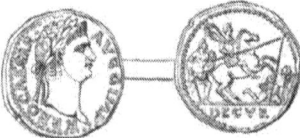

Nero, Roman Emperor, A.D. 54—68. Page 474.

Numerianus, Roman Emperor, A.D. 283. Page 486.

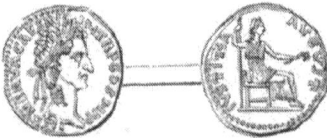

Nerva, Roman Emperor, A.D. 96—98. Page 475.

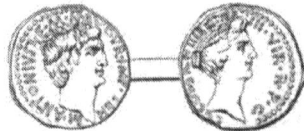

Octavia, the sister of Augustus, and wife of M. Antonius. The head of her husband is on the obverse. Page 490, No. 1.

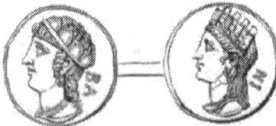

Nicocles, King of Salamis, B.C. 374. Page 478, No. 1.

Octavia, the wife of Nero. The head of her husband is on the obverse. Page 491, No. 2.

Nicomedes II., King of Bithynia, B.C. 149—91. Page 479.
To face p. 497.]

Otho, Roman Emperor, A.D. 69. Page 507.

...uns; but the more specific and ordinary use of the name Olympus is to denote the extreme E. part of the chain, which striking off from the Cambunian mountains to the S.E., skirts the S. end of the slip of coast called Pieria, and forms at its termination the N. wall of the vale of TEMPE. Its shape is that of a blunt cone, with its outline picturesquely broken by minor summits; its height is about 9700 feet; and its chief summit is covered with perpetual snow. From its position as the boundary between Thessaly and Macedonia, it is sometimes reckoned to the former, sometimes to the latter. — In the Greek mythology, Olympus was the chief seat of the third dynasty of gods, of which Zeus was the head. It was a really local conception with the early poets, to be understood literally, and not metaphorically, that these gods

" on the snowy top
Of cold Olympus ruled the middle air, ·
Their highest heaven."

Indeed, if Homer uses either of the terms Ὄλυμπος and οὐρανός metaphorically, it is the latter that is a metaphor for the former. Even the fable of the giants scaling heaven must be understood in this sense; not that they placed Pelion and Ossa upon the top of Olympus to reach the still higher heaven, but that they piled Pelion on the top of Ossa, and both on the lower slopes of Olympus, to scale the summit of Olympus itself, the abode of the gods. Homer describes the gods as having their several palaces on the summit of Olympus; as spending the day in the palace of Zeus, round whom they sit in solemn conclave, while the younger gods dance before them, and the Muses entertain them with the lyre and song. They are shut in from the view of men upon the earth by a wall of clouds, the gates of which are kept by the Hours. The same conceptions are found in Hesiod, and to a great extent in the later poets; with whom, however, even as early as the lyric poets and the tragedians, the idea becomes less material, and the real abode of the gods is gradually transferred from the summit of Olympus to the vault of heaven (i. e. the sky) itself. This latter is also the conception of the Roman poets, so far at least as any definite idea can be framed out of their compound of Homer's language with later notions. — 2. A hill in Laconia, near Sellasia, overhanging the river Oenus. — 3. Another name for Lycaeum in Arcadia. — II. In Asia. — 1. The Mysian Olympus (Ὄλυμπος ὁ Μύσιος: Keshish Dagh, Ala Dagh, Ishik Dagh, and Kush-Dagh), a chain of lofty mountains, in the N.W. of Asia Minor, forming, with Ida, the W. part of the N.-most line of the mountain system of that peninsula. It extends from W. to E. through the N. E. of Mysia and the S.W. of Bithynia, and thence, inclining a little N.-wards, it first passes through the centre of Bithynia, then forms the boundary between Bithynia and Galatia, and then extends through the S. of Paphlagonia to the river Halys. Beyond the Halys, the mountains in the N. of Pontus form a continuation of the chain. — 2. (Yanar Dagh), a volcano on the E. coast of Lycia, above the city of Phoenicus (Yanar). The names of the mountain and of the city are often interchanged. [Phoenicus.]

Olynthus (Ὄλυνθος: Ὀλύνθιος: Aio Mamas), a town of Macedonia in Chalcidice, at the head of the Toronaic gulf, and at a little distance from the coast, between the peninsulas of Pallene and Si-

thonia. It was the most important of the Greek cities on the coast of Macedonia, though we have no record of its foundation. It afterwards fell into the hands of the Thracian Bottiaei, when they were expelled from their own country by the Macedonians. [BOTTIAEI] It was taken by Artabazus, one of the generals of Xerxes, who peopled it with Chalcidians from Torone; but it owed its greatness to Perdiccas, who persuaded the inhabitants of many of the smaller towns in Chalcidice to abandon their own abodes and settle in Olynthus. This happened about the commencement of the Peloponnesian war; and from this time Olynthus appears as a prosperous and flourishing town, with a population of 5000 inhabitants capable of bearing arms. It became the head of a confederacy of all the Greek towns in this part of Macedonia, and it long maintained its independence against the attacks of the Athenians, Spartans and Macedonians; but in B.C. 379 it was compelled to submit to Sparta, after carrying on war with this state for 4 years. When the supremacy of Sparta was destroyed by the Thebans, Olynthus recovered its independence, and even received an accession of power from Philip, who was anxious to make Olynthus a counterpoise to the influence of Athens in the N. of the Aegean. With this view Philip gave Olynthus the territory of Potidaea, after he had wrested this town from the Athenians in 356. But when he had sufficiently consolidated his power to be able to set at defiance both Olynthus and Athens, he threw off the mask, and laid siege to the former city. The Olynthians earnestly besought Athens for assistance, and were warmly supported by Demosthenes in his Olynthiac orations; but as the Athenians did not render the city any effectual assistance, it was taken and destroyed by Philip, and all its inhabitants sold as slaves (347). Olynthus was never restored, and the remnants of its inhabitants were at a later time transferred by Cassander to Cassandrea. At the time of its prosperity Olynthus used the neighbouring town of MECYBERNA as its seaport.

Omana or Omanum (Ὄμανα, Ὄμανον). 1. A celebrated port on the N.E. coast of Arabia Felix, a little above the E.-most point of the peninsula, Pr. Syagros (Ras el Had), on a large gulf of the same name. The people of this part of Arabia were called Omanitae (Ὀμανῖται) or Omani, and the name is still preserved in that of the district, Oman. — 2. (Prob. Schaina), a sea-port town in the E. of Carmania; the chief emporium on that coast, for the trade between India, Persia, and Arabia.

Omanitae and Omanum. [OMANA.]

Ombi (Ὄμβοι: Ὀμβῖται: Koum Ombou, i. e. Hill of Ombos, Ru.), the last great city of Upper Egypt, except Syene, from which it was distant about 30 miles, stood on the E. bank of the Nile, in the Ombites Nomos, and was celebrated as one of the chief seats of the worship of the crocodile. Juvenal's 15th satire is founded on a religious war between the people of Ombi and those of Tentyra, who hated the crocodile; but, as Tentyra lies so much further down the Nile, with several intervening cities celebrated, as well as Ombi, for crocodile-worship, critics have suspected an error in the names, and some have proposed to read Coptos or Copton for Ombos in v. 35. It seems, however, better to suppose that Juvenal used the name without reference to topographical precision.

Opposite to Ombi, on the left bank, was the town of Contra-Ombos.

Omphāle ('Ομφάλη), daughter of the Lydian king Iardanus, and wife of Tmolus, after whose death she undertook the government herself. When Hercules, in consequence of the murder of Iphitus, was afflicted with a serious disease, and was informed by the oracle that he could only be cured by serving some one for wages for the space of 3 years, Hermes sold Hercules to Omphale. The hero became enamoured of his mistress, and to please her, he is said to have spun wool and put on the garments of a woman, while Omphale wore his lion's skin. She bore Hercules several children.

Omphalīum ('Ομφάλιον: 'Ομφαλίτης), a town in Crete in the neighbourhood of Cnossus.

On. [HELIOPOLIS.]

Onātas ('Ονάτας), of Aegina, the son of Micon, was a distinguished statuary and painter, contemporary with Polygnotus, Ageladas, and Hegias. He flourished down to about B. C. 460, that is, in the age immediately preceding that of Phidias.

Oncae ("Ογκαι), a village in Boeotia near Thebes, from which one of the gates of Thebes derived its name ('Ογκαῖαι), and which contained a sanctuary of Athena, who was hence called Athena Onca.

Onchesmus or Onchismus ("Ογχησμος, "Ογχισμος: Orchido), a seaport town of Epirus in Chaonia, opposite the W. extremity of Corcyra. The ancients derived its name from Anchises, whence it is named by Dionysius the "Harbour of Anchises" ('Αγχίσου λίμην). From this place Cicero calls the wind blowing from Epirus towards Italy Onchesmites.

Onchestus ('Ογχηστός: 'Ογχήστιος) 1. An ancient town of Boeotia, said to have been founded by Onchestus, son of Poseidon, was situated a little S. of the lake Copais near Haliartus. It contained a celebrated temple and grove of Poseidon, and was the place of meeting of the Boeotian Amphictyony. The ruins of this town are still to be seen on the S. W. slope of the mountain Faga.—2. A river in Thessaly, which rises in the neighbourhood of Eretria, and flows by Cynoscephalae, and falls into the lake Boebēis. It is perhaps the same as the river Onochōnus ('Ονόχωνος) mentioned by Herodotus.

Onesicrītus (Ονησίκριτος), a Greek historical writer, who accompanied Alexander on his campaigns in Asia, and wrote a history of them, which is frequently cited by later authors. He is called by some authorities a native of Astypalaea, and by others of Aegina. When Alexander constructed his fleet on the Hydaspes, he appointed Onesicritus chief pilot of the fleet, a post which he held not only during the descent of the Indus, but throughout the voyage from the mouth of that river to the Persian gulf, which was conducted under the command of Nearchus. Though an eye-witness of much that he described, it appears that he intermixed many fables and falsehoods with his narrative, so that he early fell into discredit as an authority.

Oningis or Oringis. [ORINGIS.]

Onīros ("Ονειρος), the Dream-God, was a personification of dreams. According to Homer Dreams dwell on the dark shores of the W. Oceanus, and the deceitful dreams come through an ivory gate, while the true ones issue from a gate made of horn. Hesiod calls dreams the children of night; and Ovid, who calls them children of Sleep, mentions 3 of them by name, viz. Morpheus, Icelus or Phobetor, and Phantasus. Euripides called them sons of Gaea, and conceived them as genii with black wings.

Onōba, surnamed Aestuāria (Huelva), a seaport town of the Turdetani in Hispania Baetica, between the mouths of the Baetis and Anas, on an aestuary formed by the river Luxia. There are remains of a Roman aqueduct at Huelva.

Onomacrītus ('Ονομάκριτος), an Athenian, who occupies an interesting position in the history of the early Greek religious poetry. He lived about B. C. 520—485. He enjoyed the patronage of Hipparchus, until he was detected by Lasus of Hermione (the dithyrambic poet) in making an interpolation in an oracle of Musaeus, for which Hipparchus banished him. He seems to have gone into Persia, where the Pisistratida, after their expulsion from Athens, took him again into favour, and employed him to persuade Xerxes to engage in his expedition against Greece, by reciting to him all the ancient oracles which seemed to favour the attempt. It appears that Onomacritus had made a collection and arrangement of the oracles ascribed to Musaeus. It is further stated that he made interpolations in Homer as well as in Musaeus, and that he was the real author of some of the poems which went under the name of Orpheus.

Onomarchus ('Ονόμαρχος), general of the Phocians in the Sacred war, succeeded his brother Philomelus in this command, B. C. 353. In the following year he was defeated in Thessaly by Philip, and perished in attempting to reach by swimming the Athenian ships, which were lying off the shore. His body fell into the hands of Philip, who caused it to be crucified, as a punishment for his sacrilege.

Onosander ('Ονόσανδρος), the author of a celebrated work on military tactics (entitled Στρατηγικὸς λόγος), which is still extant. All subsequent Greek and Roman writers on the same subject made this work their text-book, and it is still held in considerable estimation. He appears to have lived about A. D. 50. In his style he imitated Xenophon with some success. Edited by Schwebel, Nürnberg, 1761 ; and by Coraes, Paris, 1822.

Onu-gnathus ("Ονου γνάθος: Elaphonisi), an island and a promontory on the S. coast of Laconia, W. of C. Malea.

Onūphis ('Ονουφις), the capital of the Nomos Onuphites in the Delta of Egypt. Its site is uncertain; but it was probably near the middle of the Delta.

Ophēlion ('Ωφελίων), an Athenian comic poet, probably of the Middle Comedy, B. C. 380.

Ophellas ('Οφέλλας), of Pella in Macedonia, was one of the generals of Alexander the Great, after whose death he followed the fortunes of Ptolemy. In B. C. 322, he conquered Cyrene for Ptolemy, of which city he held the government on behalf of the Egyptian king for some years. But soon after 313 he threw off his allegiance to Ptolemy, and continued to govern Cyrene as an independent state for nearly 5 years. In 308 he formed an alliance with Agathocles, and marched against Carthage ; but he was treacherously attacked by Agathocles near this city, and was slain.

Opheltes ('Οφέλτης). 1. Also called Archemorus. [ARCHEMORUS.] — 2. One of the Tyrrhenian pirates, who attempted to carry off Dionysus, and were therefore metamorphosed into dolphins.

Ophion ('Οφίων). 1. One of the oldest of the Titans was married to Eurynome, with whom he ruled over Olympus, but being conquered by Cronos and Rhea, he and Eurynome were thrown into Oceanus or Tartarus.—2. A giant, who perished in the battle with Zeus.—3. Father of the centaur Amycus, who is hence called *Ophiōnĭdes*.

Ophionenses or Ophienses ('Οφιονεῖς, 'Οφιεῖς), a people in the N.E. of Aetolia.

Ophir (O. T. LXX. Σουφίρ, Σωφίρ, Σωφάρα), a place frequently referred to in the Old Testament, as proverbial for its gold, and to which Solomon, in conjunction with Hiram, king of Tyre, sent a fleet, which brought back gold and sandal-wood and precious stones. These ships were sent from Ezion-geber, at the head of the Red Sea, whence also king Jehoshaphat built ships to go to Ophir for gold, but this voyage was stopped by a shipwreck. It is clear, therefore, that Ophir was on the shores of the Erythraeum Mare of the ancients, or our Indian Ocean. Among the most plausible conjectures as to its site are: (1) that it was on the coast of India, or a name for India itself ; (2) that it was on the coast of Arabia, in which case it is not necessary to suppose that Arabia furnished all the articles of commerce which were brought from Ophir, for Ophir may have been a great emporium of the Indian and Arabian trade ; (3) that it is not the name of any specific place, but a general designation for the countries (or any of them) on the shores of the Indian Ocean, which supplied the chief articles of Indian and Arabian commerce.

Ophis (Ὄφις), a river in Arcadia, which flowed by Mantinēa.

Ophiūsa or Ophiussa ('Οφίεσσα, 'Οφιοῦσσα, 'Οφιοῦσα, i. e. *abounding in snakes*). 1. [PITYUSAE.]—2. Or Ophiussa (Perhaps *Palanea*), a town of European Scythia on the left bank of the Tyras (Dniester).—3. A little island near Crete.—4. (*Afsia* or *Rabbi*), a small island in the Propontis (*Sea of Marmara*), off the coast of Mysia, N.W. of Cyzicus and S.W. of Proconnesus. —5. [RHODUS.]—6. [TENOS.]

Ophrynium ('Οφρύνειον : prob. *Fren-Kevi*), a small town of the Troad, near the lake of Pteleos, between Dardanus and Rhoeteum, with a grove consecrated to Hector.

Opici. [OSCI.]

Opilius Macrinus. [MACRINUS.]

Opilius, Aurelius, the freedman of an Epicurean, taught at Rome, first philosophy, then rhetoric, and, finally, grammar. He gave up his school upon the condemnation of Rutilius Rufus (B. C. 92), whom he accompanied to Smyrna, and there the two friends grew old together in the enjoyment of each other's society. He composed several learned works, one of which, named *Musae*, is referred to by A. Gellius.

Opimius. 1. Q., consul B.C. 154, when he subdued some of the Ligurian tribes N. of the Alps, who had attacked Massilia. He was notorious in his youth for his riotous living.—2. L., son of the preceding, was praetor 125, in which year he took Fregellae, which had revolted against the Romans. He belonged to the high aristocratical party, and was a violent opponent of C. Gracchus. He was consul in 121, and took the leading part in the proceedings which ended in the murder of Gracchus. Opimius and his party abused their victory most savagely, and are said to have killed more than 300 persons. For details see p. 288, a. In the following year (120), he was accused of having put Roman citizens to death without trial ; but he was defended by the consul, C. Papirius Carbo, and was acquitted. In 112 he was at the head of the commission which was sent into Africa in order to divide the dominions of Micipsa between Jugurtha and Adherbal, and was bribed by Jugurtha, to assign to him the better part of the country. Three years after he was condemned under the law of the tribune, C. Mamilius Limetanus, by which an inquiry was made into the conduct of all those who had received bribes from Jugurtha. Opimius went into exile to Dyrrhachium in Epirus, where he lived for some years, hated and insulted by the people, and where he eventually died in great poverty. He richly deserved his punishment, and met with a due recompense for his cruel and ferocious conduct towards C. Gracchus and his party. Cicero, on the contrary, who, after his consulship, had identified himself with the aristocratical party, frequently laments the fate of Opimius. The year in which Opimius was consul (121) was remarkable for the extraordinary heat of the autumn, and thus the vintage of this year was of an unprecedented quality. This wine long remained celebrated as the *Vinum Opimianum*, and was preserved for an almost incredible space of time.

Opis ('Ωπις), an important commercial city of Assyria, in the district of Apolloniatis, at the confluence of the Physcus (*Odorneh*) with the Tigris; not mentioned later than the Christian era.

Opitergium (Opiterginus: *Oderzo*), a Roman colony in Venetia in the N. of Italy, on the river Liquentia near its source, and on the high road from Aquileia to Verona. In the Marcomannic war it was destroyed by the Quadi, but it was rebuilt, and afterwards belonged to the Exarchate. From it the neighbouring mountains were called *Montes Opitergini*.

Oppiānus ('Οππιανός), the author of 2 Greek hexameter poems still extant, one on fishing, entitled *Halieutica* ('Αλιευτικά), and the other on hunting, entitled *Cynegetica* (Κυνηγετικά). Modern critics, however, have shown that these 2 poems were written by 2 different persons of this name. 1. The author of the *Halieutica*, was born either at Corycus or at Anazarba, in Cilicia, and flourished about A. D. 180. The poem consists of about 3500 hexameter lines, divided into 5 books, of which the first 2 treat of the natural history of fishes, and the other 3 of the art of fishing.—2. The author of the *Cynegetica*, was a native of Apamea or Pella, in Syria, and flourished a little later than the other Oppianus, about A. D. 206. His poem, which is addressed to the emperor Caracalla, consists of about 2100 hexameter lines, divided into 4 books. The best edition of the 2 poems is by Schneider, Argent. 1776, and 2nd ed. Lips. 1813. There is also a prose paraphrase of a poem on hawking ('Ιξευτικά) attributed to Oppianus, but it is doubtful to which of the 2 authors of this name it belongs. Some critics think that the work was probably written by Dionysius.

Oppius. 1. C., tribune of the plebs B. C. 213, carried a law to curtail the expenses and luxuries of Roman women. It enacted that no woman should have more than half an ounce of gold, nor wear a dress of different colours, nor ride in a carriage in the city, or in any town, or within a mile of it, unless on account of public sacrifices. This law was repealed in 195, notwithstanding the vehement opposition of the elder Cato.— 2. Q., a Roman general in the Mithridatic war, B. C. 88, fell into the hands of Mithridates, but was subsequently surrendered by the latter to Sulla.—3. C., an intimate friend of C. Julius Caesar, whose private affairs he managed in conjunction with Cornelius Balbus. Oppius was the author of several works, referred to by the ancient writers, but all of which have perished. The authorship of the histories of the Alexandrine, African, and Spanish wars, was a disputed point as early as the time of Suetonius, some assigning them to Oppius and others to Hirtius. But the similarity in style and diction between the work on the Alexandrine war and the last book of the Commentaries on the Gallic war, leads to the conclusion that the former, at all events, was the work of Hirtius. The book on the African war was probably written by Oppius He also wrote the lives of several distinguished Romans, such as Scipio Africanus the elder, Marius, Pompey, and probably Caesar.

Ops, a female Roman divinity of plenty and fertility, as is indicated by her name, which is connected with *opimus, opulentus, inops,* and *copia.* She was regarded as the wife of Saturnus, and the protectress of every thing connected with agriculture. Her abode was in the earth, and hence those who invoked her used to touch the ground. Her worship was intimately connected with that of her husband Saturnus, for she had both temples and festivals in common with him ; but she had likewise a separate sanctuary on the Capitol, and in the vicus jugarius, not far from the temple of Saturnus, she had an altar in common with Ceres. The festivals of Ops are called *Opalia* and *Opiconsivia,* from her surname *Consiva,* connected with the verb *serere,* to sow.

Optātus, bishop of Milevi in Numidia, flourished under the emperors Valentinian and Valens. He wrote a work, still extant, against the errors of the Donatists, entitled, *De Schismate Donatistarum adversus Parmenianum.* Edited by Dupin, Paris fol. 1700.

Opus ('Οποῦς, contr. of "Οπόεις: 'Οπούντιος). 1. (*Talanda* or *Talanti* ?), the capital of the Opuntian Locrians, was situated, according to Strabo, 15 stadia (2 miles) from the sea, and 60 stadia from its harbour Cynos ; but, according to Livy, it was only 1 mile from the coast. It was the birthplace of Patroclus. The bay of the Euboean sea near this town was called Opuntius Sinus. [LOCRI.]— 2. A small town in Elis.

Ora. 1. ("Ορα) a city of Carmania, near the borders of Gedrosia.—2. ("Ωρα), a city in the N.W. of India, near the sources of the Indus.

Orae. [ORITAE.]

Orbēlus ('Ορβηλος), a mountain in the N.E. of Macedonia, on the borders of Thrace, extends from Mt. Rhodope along the Strymon to Mt. Pangaeus.

Orbilius Pupillus, a Roman grammarian and schoolmaster, best known to us from his having been the teacher of Horace, who gives him the epithet of *plagosus* from the severe floggings which his pupils received from him. (Hor. *Ep.* ii. 1. 71.) He was a native of Beneventum, and after serving as an apparitor of the magistrates, and also as a soldier in the army, he settled at Rome in the 50th

year of his age, in the consulship of Cicero, B.C. 63. He lived nearly 100 years, but had lost his memory long before his death.

Orbōna, a female Roman divinity, was invoked by parents who had been deprived of their children, and desired to have others, and also in dangerous maladies of children.

Orcădes Insūlae (*Orkney* and *Shetland Isles*), a group of several small islands off the N. coast of Britain, with which the Romans first became acquainted when Agricola sailed round the N. of Britain.

Orchŏmĕnus ('Ορχόμενος: 'Ορχομένιος). 1. (*Scripu*), an ancient, wealthy, and powerful city of Boeotia, the capital of the Minyean empire in the ante-historical ages of Greece, and hence called by Homer the Minyean Orchomenos ('Ορχ. Μινύειος). It was situated N.W. of the lake Copais, on the river Cephissus, and was built on the slope of a hill on the summit of which stood the acropolis. It is said to have been originally called *Andreis* ('Ανδρείς), from Andreus, the son of Peneus, who emigrated from the Peneus in Thessaly ; to have been afterwards called *Phlegya* (Φλεγύα), from Phlegyas, a son of Ares and Chryse ; and to have finally obtained its later name from Orchomenus, son of Zeus or Eteocles and the Danaid Hesione, and father of Minyas. This Orchomenus was regarded as the real founder of the Minyean empire, which before the time of the Trojan war extended over the whole of the W. of Boeotia. The cities of Coronea, Haliartus, Lebedea, and Chaeronea were subject to it ; and even Thebes at one time was compelled to pay it tribute. It lost, however, much of its power after its capture by Hercules, but in the time of the Trojan war it still appears as a powerful city. Sixty years after the Trojan war it was taken by the Boeotians ; its empire was completely destroyed ; and it became a member of the Boeotian league. All this belongs to the mythical period. In the historical age it continued to exist as an independent town till B.C. 367, when it was taken and destroyed by the Thebans, and its inhabitants murdered or sold as slaves. In order to weaken Thebes, it was rebuilt at the instigation of the Athenians, but was soon destroyed again by the Thebans ; and although it was again restored by Philip in 338, it never recovered its former prosperity ; and in the time of Strabo was in ruins. The most celebrated building in Orchomenos was the so-called treasury of Minyas, but which, like the similar monument at Mycenae, was more probably a family-vault of the ancient heroes of the place. It was a circular vault of massive masonry embedded in the hill, with an arched roof, and had a side door of entrance. The remains of this building are extant; and its form may still be traced, though the whole of the stonework of the vault has disappeared. Orchomenos possessed a very ancient temple of the Charites or Graces ; and here was celebrated in the most ancient times a musical festival, which was frequented by poets and singers from all parts of the Hellenic world. There was a temple of Hercules 7 stadia N. of the town, near the sources of the river Melas. Orchomenos is memorable on account of the great victory which Sulla gained in its neighbourhood over Archelaus, the general of Mithridates, 86.— 2. (*Kalpaki*), an ancient town of Arcadia, mentioned by Homer with the epithet πολύμηλος, to distinguish it from the Minyean Orchomenus, is said to have been founded by Orchomenus, son of Lycaon. It was situated on a hill N.W. of Mantinea, and its territory included the towns of Methydrium, Theisoa, Teuthis, and the Tripolis. In the Peloponnesian war Orchomenus sided with Sparta, and was taken by the Athenians. After the battle of Leuctra the Orchomenians did not join the Arcadian confederacy in consequence of its hatred against Mantinea. In the contests between the Achaeans and Aetolians, it was taken successively by Cleomenes and Antigonus Doson; but it eventually became a member of the Achaean League.—3. A town on the confines of Macedonia and Thessaly, and hence sometimes said to belong to the former, and sometimes to the latter country.

Orcus. [HADES.]

Ordessus ('Ορδησσός), a tributary of the Ister (Danube) in Scythia, mentioned by Herodotus, but which cannot be identified with any modern river.

Ordovices, a people in the W. of Britain, opposite the island Mona (Anglesey), occupying the N. portion of the modern Wales.

Oreädes. [NYMPHAE.]

Orestae ('Ορέσται), a people in the N. of Epirus on the borders of Macedonia, inhabiting the district named after them, Orestis or Orestias. They were originally independent, but were afterwards subject to the Macedonian monarchs. They were declared free by the Romans in their war with Philip. According to the legend, they derived their name from Orestes, who is said to have fled into this country after murdering his mother, and to have there founded the town of Argos Oresticum.

Orestes ('Ορέστης). 1. Son of Agamemnon and Clytaemnestra, and brother of Chrysothemis, Laodice (Electra), and Iphianassa (Iphigenia). According to the Homeric account, Agamemnon on his return from Troy was murdered by Aegisthus and Clytaemnestra before he had an opportunity of seeing him. In the 8th year after his father's murder Orestes came from Athens to Mycenae and slew the murderer of his father. This simple story of Orestes has been enlarged and embellished in various ways by the tragic poets. Thus it is said that at the murder of Agamemnon it was intended to despatch Orestes also, but that by means of Electra he was secretly carried to Strophius, king in Phocis, who was married to Anaxibia, the sister of Agamemnon. According to some, Orestes was saved by his nurse, who allowed Aegisthus to kill her own child, supposing it to be Orestes. In the house of Strophius, Orestes grew up with the king's son Pylades, with whom he had formed that close and intimate friendship which has become proverbial. Being frequently reminded by messengers from Electra of the necessity of avenging his father's death, he consulted the oracle of Delphi, which strengthened him in his plan. He therefore repaired in secret to Argos. Here he pretended to be a messenger of Strophius, who had come to announce the death of Orestes, and brought the ashes of the deceased. After visiting his father's tomb, and sacrificing upon it a lock of his hair, he made himself known to his sister Electra, and soon afterwards slew both Aegisthus and Clytaemnestra in the palace. Immediately after the murder of his mother he was seized with madness. He now fled from land to land, pursued by the Erinnyes of his mother. At length by Apollo's advice, he took refuge with Athena at Athens. The goddess af-

forded him protection, and appointed the court of the Areopagus to decide his fate. The Erinnyes brought forward their accusation, and Orestes made the command of the Delphic oracle his excuse. When the court voted, and was equally divided, Orestes was acquitted by the command of Athena. According to another modification of the legend, Orestes consulted Apollo how he could be delivered from his madness and incessant wandering. The god advised him to go to Tauris in Scythia, and to fetch from that country the image of Artemis, which was believed to have fallen there from heaven, and to carry it to Athens. Orestes and Pylades accordingly went to Tauris, where Thoas was king. On their arrival they were seized by the natives, in order to be sacrificed to Artemis, according to the custom of the country. But Iphigenia, the priestess of Artemis, was the sister of Orestes, and, after recognising each other, all three escaped with the statue of the goddess. After his return to Peloponnesus Orestes took possession of his father's kingdom at Mycenae, which had been usurped by Aletes or Menelaus. When Cylarabes of Argos died without leaving any heir, Orestes also became king of Argos. The Lacedaemonians likewise made him their king of their own accord, because they preferred him, the grandson of Tyndareus, to Nicostratus and Megapenthes, the sons of Menelaus by a slave. The Arcadians and Phocians increased his power by allying themselves with him. He married Hermione, the daughter of Menelaus, and became by her the father of Tisamenus. The story of his marriage with Hermione, who had previously been married to Neoptolemus, is related elsewhere. [HERMIONE; NEOPTOLEMUS.] He died of the bite of a snake in Arcadia, and his body, in accordance with an oracle, was afterwards carried from Tegea to Sparta, and there buried. His bones are said to have been found at a later time in a war between the Lacedaemonians and Tegeatans, and to have been conveyed to Sparta.— 2. Regent of Italy during the short reign of his infant son Romulus Augustulus, A.D. 475—476. He was born in Pannonia, and served for some years under Attila; after whose death he rose to eminence at the Roman court. Having been entrusted with the command of an army by Julius Nepos, he deposed this emperor, and placed his son Romulus Augustulus on the throne; but in the following year he was defeated by Odoacer and put to death. [ODOACER.]— 3. L. Aurelius Orestes, consul B.C. 126, received Sardinia as his province, where he remained upwards of 3 years. C. Gracchus was quaestor to Orestes in Sardinia.—4. Cn. Aufidius Orestes, originally belonged to the Aurelia gens, whence his surname of Orestes, and was adopted by Cn. Aufidius, the historian, when the latter was an old man. Orestes was consul, 71.

Orestēum, Oresthēum, or Oresthasīum (Ορέστειον, 'Ορέσθειον, 'Ορεσθάσιον), a town in the S. of Arcadia in the district Maenalia, not far from Megalopolis.

Orestīas. 1. The country of the Orestae. [ORESTAE.]—2. A name frequently given by the Byzantine writers to Hadrianopolis in Thrace.

Orestilla, Aurelia. [AURELIA.]

Orētāni, a powerful people in the S.W. of Hispania Tarraconensis, bounded on the S. by Baetica, on the N. by the Carpetani, on the W. by Lusitania, and on the E. by the Bastetani; their territory corresponded to the eastern part of Granada, the whole of *La Mancha*, and the western part of Murcia. Their chief town was CASTULO.

Orĕus ('Ωρεός: 'Ωρείτης), a town in the N. of Euboea, on the river Callas, at the foot of the mountain Telethrium, and in the district Hestiaeotis, was itself originally called Hestiaea or Histiaea. After the Persian wars Oreus, with the rest of Euboea, became subject to the Athenians; but on the revolt of the island, in B.C. 445, Oreus was taken by Pericles, its inhabitants expelled, and their p'ace supplied by 2000 Athenians. The site of Oreus made it an important place, and its name frequently occurs in the Grecian wars down to the dissolution of the Achaean league.

Orgetŏrix, the noblest and richest among the Helvetii, formed a conspiracy to obtain the royal power B.C. 61, and persuaded his countrymen to emigrate from their own country. Two years were devoted to making the necessary preparations; but the real designs of Orgetorix having meantime transpired, and the Helvetii having attempted to bring him to trial, he suddenly died, probably, as was suspected, by his own hands.

Oribasĭus ('Ορειβάσιος or 'Οριβάσιος), an eminent Greek medical writer, born about A. D. 325, either at Sardis in Lydia, or at Pergamus in Mysia. He early acquired a great professional reputation. He was an intimate friend of the emperor Julian, with whom he became acquainted several years before Julian's accession to the throne. He was almost the only person to whom Julian imparted the secret of his apostasy from Christianity. He accompanied Julian in his expedition against Persia, and was with him at the time of his death, 363. The succeeding emperors, Valentinian and Valens, confiscated the property of Oribasius and banished him. He was afterwards recalled from exile, and was alive at least as late as 395. Of the personal character of Oribasius we know little or nothing, but it is clear that he was much attached to paganism and to the heathen philosophy. He was an intimate friend of Eunapius, who praises him very highly, and wrote an account of his life. We possess at present 3 works of Oribasius: 1. *Collecta Medicinalia* (Συναγωγαί 'Ιατρικαί), or sometimes *Hebdomecontabiblos* ('Εβδομηκοντάβιβλος), which was compiled at the command of Julian, when Oribasius was still a young man. It contains but little original matter, but is very valuable on account of the numerous extracts from writers whose works are no longer extant. More than half of this work is now lost, and what remains is in some confusion. There is no complete edition of the work. 2. An abridgment (Σύνοψις) of the former work, in 9 books. It was written 30 years after the former. 3. *Euporista* or *De facile Parabilibus* (Εὐπόριστα), in 4 books. Both this and the preceding work were intended as manuals of the practice of medicine.

Orĭcum or Orĭcus ('Ωρικον, 'Ωρικος: 'Ωρίκιος: *Erĭcho*), an important Greek town on the coast of Illyria, near the Ceraunian mountains and the frontiers of Epirus. According to tradition it was founded by the Euboeans, who were cast here by a storm on their return from Troy; but, according to another legend, it was a Colchian colony. The town was strongly fortified, but its harbour was not very secure. It was destroyed in the civil wars, but was rebuilt by Herodes Atticus. The turpentine tree (*terebinthus*) grew in the neighbourhood of Oreus.

Orĭgĕnes ('Ωριγένης), usually called Origen, one of the most eminent of the early Christian writers, was born at Alexandria, A. D. 186. He received a careful education from his father, Leonides, who was a devout Christian; and he subsequently became a pupil of Clement of Alexandria. His father having been put to death in the persecution of the Christians in the 10th year of Severus (202), Origen was reduced to destitution; whereupon he became a teacher of grammar, and soon acquired a great reputation. At the same time he gave instruction in Christianity to several of the heathen; and though only in his 18th year, he was appointed to the office of Catechist, which was vacant through the dispersion of the clergy consequent on the persecution. The young teacher showed a zeal and self-denial beyond his years. Deeming his profession as teacher of grammar inconsistent with his sacred work, he gave it up; and he lived on the merest pittance. His food and his periods of sleep were restricted within the narrowest limits; and he performed a strange act of self-mutilation, in obedience to what he regarded as the recommendation of Christ. (Matth. xix. 12.) At a later time however he repudiated this literal understanding of our Lord's words. About 211 or 212 Origen visited Rome, where he made however a very short stay. On his return to Alexandria he continued to discharge his duties as Catechist, and to pursue his biblical studies. About 216 he paid a visit to Caesarea in Palestine, and about 230 he travelled into Greece. Shortly after his return to Alexandria, he had to encounter the open enmity of Demetrius, the bishop of the city. He was first deprived of his office of Catechist, and was compelled to leave Alexandria; and Demetrius afterwards procured his degradation from the priesthood and his excommunication. The charges brought against him are not specified; but his unpopularity appears to have arisen from the obnoxious character of some of his opinions, and was increased by the circumstance that even in his lifetime his writings were seriously corrupted. Origen withdrew to Caesarea in Palestine, where he was received with the greatest kindness. Among his pupils at this place was Gregory Thaumaturgus, who afterwards became his panegyrist. In 235 Origen fled from Caesarea in Palestine, and took refuge at Caesarea in Cappadocia, where he remained concealed 2 years. It was subsequent to this that he undertook a 2nd journey into Greece, the date of which is doubtful. In the Decian persecution (249—251), Origen was put to the torture; but though his life was spared, the sufferings which he underwent hastened his end. He died in 253 or 254, in his 69th year at Tyre, in which city he was buried.—The following are the most important of Origen's works: 1. The *Hexapla*, which consisted of 6 copies of the Old Testament, ranged in parallel columns. The 1st column contained the Hebrew text in Hebrew characters, the 2nd the same text in Greek characters. the 3rd the version of Aquila, the 4th that of Symmachus, the 5th the Septuagint, the 6th the version of Theodotion. Beside the compilation and arrangement of these versions, Origen added marginal notes, containing, among other things, an explanation of the Hebrew names. Only fragments of this valuable work are extant; the best edition of which is by Montfaucon, Paris, 1714. 2. *Exegetical works*, which comprehend 3 classes: (1.) *Tomi*, which Jerome renders *Volumina*, containing ample commentaries, in which he gave full scope to his intellect. (2.) *Scholia*, brief notes on detached passages. (3.) *Homiliae*, popular expositions, chiefly delivered at Caesarea. In his various expositions Origen sought to extract from the Sacred Writings their historical, mystical or prophetical, and moral significance. His desire of finding continually a mystical sense led him frequently into the neglect of the historical sense, and even into the denial of its truth. This capital fault has at all times furnished ground for depreciating his labours, and has no doubt materially diminished their value: it must not, however, be supposed that his denial of the historical truth of the Sacred Writings is more than occasional, or that it has been carried out to the full extent which some of his accusers have charged upon him. 3. *De Principiis* (Περὶ ἀρχῶν). This work was the great object of attack with Origen's enemies, and the source from which they derived their chief evidence of his various alleged heresies. It was divided into 4 books. Of this work some important fragments are extant; and the Latin version of Rufinus has come down to us entire; but Rufinus took great liberties with the original, and the unfaithfulness of his version is denounced in the strongest terms by Jerome. 4. *Exhortatio ad Martyrium* (Εἰς μαρτύριον προτρεπτικὸς λόγος), or *De Martyria* (Περὶ μαρτυρίου), written during the persecution under the emperor Maximin (235—238), and still extant. 5. *Contra Celsum Libri VIII.* (Κατὰ Κέλσου τόμοι η'), still extant. In this important work Origen defends the truth of Christianity against the attacks of Celsus. [CELSUS.]— There is a valuable work entitled *Philocalia* (Φιλοκαλία), which is a compilation by Basil of Caesarea and his friend Gregory of Nazianzus, made almost exclusively from the writings of Origen, of which many important fragments have been thus preserved. Few writers have exercised greater influence by the force of their intellect and the variety of their attainments than Origen, or have been the occasion of longer and more acrimonious disputes. Of his more distinctive tenets, several had reference to the doctrine of the Trinity, to the subject of the incarnation, and to the pre-existence of Christ's human soul, which, as well as the pre-existence of other human souls, he affirmed. He was charged also with holding the corporeity of angels, and with other errors as to angels and daemons. He held the freedom of the human will, and ascribed to man a nature less corrupt and depraved than was consistent with orthodox views of the operation of divine grace. He held the doctrine of the universal restoration of the guilty, conceiving that the devil alone would suffer eternal punishment. The best edition of his works is by Delarue, Paris, 1733—1759, 4 vols. fo.

ORINGIS or ONINGIS, probably the same place as **Aurinx,** a wealthy town in Hispania Baetica, with silver mines, near Munda.

ORION ('Ωρίων), son of Hyrieus, of Hyria, in Boeotia, a handsome giant and hunter, said to have been called by the Boeotians Candaon. Once he came to Chios (Ophiusa), and fell in love with Aero, or Merope, the daughter of Oenopion, by the nymph Helice. He cleared the island from wild beasts, and brought the spoils of the chase as presents to his beloved; but as Oenopion constantly deferred the marriage, Orion once when intoxicated offered violence to the maiden. Oenopion now

implored the assistance of Dionysus, who caused Orion to be thrown into a deep sleep by satyrs, in which state Oenopion deprived him of his sight. Being informed by an oracle that he should recover his sight, if he would go towards the east and expose his eye-balls to the rays of the rising sun, Orion followed the sound of a Cyclops' hammer, went to Lemnos, where Hephaestus gave to him Cedalion as his guide. Having recovered his sight, Orion returned to Chios to take vengeance on Oenopion; but as the latter had been concealed by his friends, Orion was unable to find him, and then proceeded to Crete, where he lived as a hunter with Artemis. The cause of his death, which took place either in Crete or Chios, is differently stated. According to some, Eos (Aurora), who loved Orion for his beauty, carried him off, but as the gods were angry at this, Artemis killed him with an arrow in Ortygia. According to others, he was beloved by Artemis, and Apollo, indignant at his sister's affection for him, asserted that she was unable to hit with her arrow a distant point which he showed her in the sea. She thereupon took aim, and hit it, but the point was the head of Orion, who had been swimming in the sea. A third account, which Horace follows (*Carm.* ii. 4. 72), states that he attempted to violate Artemis (Diana), and was killed by the goddess with one of her arrows. A fourth account, lastly, states that he boasted he would conquer every animal, and would clear the earth from all wild beasts; but the earth sent forth a scorpion which destroyed him. Aesculapius attempted to recall him to life, but was slain by Zeus with a flash of lightning. The accounts of his parentage and birth-place vary in the different writers, for some call him a son of Poseidon and Euryale, and others say that he was born of the earth, or a son of Oenopion. He is further called a Theban, or Tanagraean, but probably because Hyria, his native place, sometimes belonged to Tanagra, and sometimes to Thebes. After his death, Orion was placed among the stars where he appears as a giant with a girdle, sword, a lion's skin and a club. The constellation of Orion set at the commencement of November, at which time storms and rain were frequent; hence he is often called *imbrifer, nimbosus,* or *aquosus.*

ORION and ORUS ('Ωρίων and "Ωρος), names of several ancient grammarians, who are frequently confounded with each other. It appears, however, that we may distinguish 3 writers of these names. 1. **Orion,** a Theban grammarian, who taught at Caesarea, in the 5th century after Christ, and is the author of a lexicon, still extant, published by Sturz, Lips. 1820.—2. **Orus,** of Miletus, a grammarian, lived in the 2nd century after Christ, and was the author of the works mentioned by Suidas.— 3. **Orus,** an Alexandrine grammarian, who taught at Constantinople not earlier than the middle of the 4th century after Christ.

ORIPPO, a town in Hispania Baetica, on the road between Gades and Hispalis.

ORITAE, HORITAE, or ORAE ('Ωρεῖται, "Ωραι), a people of Gedrosia, who inhabited a district on the coast nearly 200 miles long, abounding in wine, corn, rice, and palm-trees, the modern *Urboo* on the coast of Beloochistan. Some of the ancient writers assert that they were of Indian origin, while others say that, though they resembled the Indians in many of their customs, they spoke a different language.

Orithȳia ('Ορείθυια), daughter of Erechtheus, king of Athens, and Praxithea. Once as she had strayed beyond the river Ilissus she was seized by Boreas, and carried off to Thrace, where she bore to Boreas Cleopatra, Chione, Zetes, and Calais.

Ormēnus ("Ορμενος), son of Cercaphus, grandson of Aeolus and father of Amyntor, was believed to have founded the town of Ormenium, in Thessaly. From him Amyntor is sometimes called *Ormenides*, and Astydamia, his grand-daughter, *Ormenis*.

Orŭĕae ('Ορνεαί: 'Ορνεάτης), an ancient town of Argolis, near the frontiers of the territory of Phlius, and 120 stadia from Argos. It was originally independent of Argos, but was subdued by the Argives in the Peloponnesian war, B. C. 415.

Orneus ('Ορνεύς), son of Erechtheus, father of Peteus, and grandfather of Menestheus; from him the town of Orneae was believed to have derived its name.

Oroanda ('Ορόανδα: 'Οροανδεύς, or -ικός, Oro-andensis), a mountain city of Pisidia, S. E. of Antiochia, from which the "Oroandicus tractus" obtained its name.

Oroātis ('Οροάτις: Tab), the largest of the minor rivers which flow into the Persian Gulf, formed the boundary between Susiana and Persis.

Orŏbīae ('Οροβίαι), a town on the coast of Euboea, not far from Aegae, with an oracle of Apollo.

Orōdes ('Ορώδης), the name of 2 kings of Parthia. [ARSACES XIV., XVII.]

Oroetes ('Οροίτης), a Persian, was made satrap of Sardis by Cyrus, which government he retained under Cambyses. In B. c. 522, he decoyed POLYCRATES into his power by specious promises, and put him to death. But being suspected of aiming at the establishment of an independent sovereignty, he was himself put to death by order of Darius.

Orontes ('Ορόντης). **1.** (Nahr-el-Asy), the largest river of Syria, has 2 chief sources in Coelesyria, the one in the Antilibanus, the other further N. in the Libanus; flows N. E. into a lake S. of Emesa, and thence N. past Epiphania and Apamea, till near Antioch, where it suddenly sweeps round to the S. W. and falls into the sea at the foot of M. Pieria. According to tradition its earlier name was Typhon (Τυφών), and it was called Orontes from the person who first built a bridge over it. — **2.** A mountain on the S. side of the Caspian, between Parthia and Hyrcania. — **3.** A people of Assyria, E. of Gaugamela.

Orōpus ('Ωρωπός: 'Ωρώπος: Oropo), a town on the eastern frontiers of Boeotia and Attica, near the Euripus, originally belonged to the Boeotians, but was at an early time seized by the Athenians, and was long an object of contention between the 2 peoples. At length, after being taken and retaken several times, it remained permanently in the hands of the Athenians, and is always reckoned by later writers as a town of Attica. Its seaport was Delphinium at the mouth of the Asopus, about 1½ mile from the town.

Orōsius, Paulus, a Spanish presbyter, a native of Tarragona, flourished under Arcadius and Honorius. Having conceived a warm admiration for St. Augustine, he passed over into Africa about A. D. 413. After remaining in Africa about 2 years, Augustine sent him into Syria, to counteract the influence of Pelagius, who had resided for some years in Palestine. Orosius found a warm friend in Jerome, but was unable to procure the condemnation of Pelagius, and was himself anathe-

matized by John, bishop of Jerusalem, when he brought a formal charge against Pelagius. Orosius subsequently returned to Africa, and there, it is believed, died, but at what period is not known. The following works by Orosius are still extant. 1. *Historiarum adversus Paganos Libri VII.*, dedicated to St. Augustine, at whose suggestion the task was undertaken. The pagans having been accustomed to complain that the ruin of the Roman empire must be ascribed to the wrath of the ancient deities, whose worship had been abandoned, Orosius, upon his return from Palestine, composed this history to demonstrate that from the earliest epoch the world had been the scene of calamities as great as the Roman empire was then suffering. The work, which extends from the Creation down to A. D. 417, is, with exception of the concluding portion, extracted from Justin, Eutropius, and inferior second-hand authorities. Edited by Havercamp, Lug. Bat. 1738. 2. *Liber Apologeticus de Arbitrii Libertate*, written in Palestine, A. D. 415, appended to the edition of the History by Havercamp. 3. *Commonitorium ad Augustinum*, the earliest of the works of Orosius, composed soon after his first arrival in Africa.

Orospĕda or **Ortospĕda** (Sierra del Mundo), the highest range of mountains in the centre of Spain, began in the centre of Mt. Idubeda, ran first W. and then S., and terminated near Calpe at the Fretum Herculeum. It contained several silver mines, whence the part in which the Baetis rises was called Mt. Argentarius or the Silver Mountain.

Orpheus ('Ορφεύς), a mythical personage, was regarded by the Greeks as the most celebrated of the early poets, who lived before the time of Homer. His name does not occur in the Homeric or Hesiodic poems; but it already had attained to great celebrity in the lyric period. There were numerous legends about Orpheus, but the common story ran as follows. Orpheus, the son of Oeagrus and Calliope, lived in Thrace at the period of the Argonauts, whom he accompanied in their expedition. Presented with the lyre by Apollo, and instructed by the Muses in its use, he enchanted with its music not only the wild beasts, but the trees and rocks upon Olympus, so that they moved from their places to follow the sound of his golden harp. The power of his music caused the Argonauts to seek his aid, which contributed materially to the success of their expedition: at the sound of his lyre the Argo glided down into the sea; the Argonauts tore themselves away from the pleasures of Lemnos; the Symplegadae, or moving rocks, which threatened to crush the ship between them, were fixed in their places; and the Colchian dragon, which guarded the golden fleece, was lulled to sleep: other legends of the same kind may be read in the *Argonautica*, which bears the name of Orpheus. After his return from the Argonautic expedition he took up his abode in a cave in Thrace, and employed himself in the civilisation of its wild inhabitants. There is also a legend of his having visited Egypt. The legends respecting the loss and recovery of his wife, and his own death, are very various. His wife was a nymph named Agriope or Eurydice. In the older accounts the cause of her death is not referred to. The legend followed in the well-known passages of Virgil and Ovid, which ascribes the death of Eurydice to the bite of a serpent, is no doubt of high antiquity; but the introduction of

Aristaeus into the legend cannot be traced to any writer older than Virgil himself. He followed his lost wife into the abodes of Hades, where the charms of his lyre suspended the torments of the damned, and won back his wife from the most inexorable of all deities ; but his prayer was only granted upon this condition, that he should not look back upon his restored wife, till they had arrived in the upper world: at the very moment when they were about to pass the fatal bounds, the anxiety of love overcame the poet ; he looked round to see that Eurydice was following him ; and he beheld her caught back into the infernal regions. His grief for the loss of Eurydice led him to treat with contempt the Thracian women, who in revenge tore him to pieces under the excitement of their Bacchanalian orgies. After his death, the Muses collected the fragments of his body, and buried them at Libethra at the foot of Olympus, where the nightingale sang sweetly over his grave. His head was thrown into the Hebrus, down which it rolled to the sea, and was borne across to Lesbos, where the grave in which it was interred was shown at Antissa. His lyre was also said to have been carried to Lesbos ; and both traditions are simply poetical expressions of the historical fact that Lesbos was the first great seat of the music of the lyre: indeed Antissa itself was the birth-place of Terpander, the earliest historical musician. The astronomers taught that the lyre of Orpheus was placed by Zeus among the stars, at the intercession of Apollo and the Muses. In these legends there are some points which are sufficiently clear. The invention of music, in connection with the services of Apollo and the Muses, its first great application to the worship of the gods, which Orpheus is therefore said to have introduced, its power over the passions, and the importance which the Greeks attached to the knowledge of it, as intimately allied with the very existence of all social order, — are probably the chief elementary ideas of the whole legend. But then comes in one of the dark features of the Greek religion, in which the gods envy the advancement of man in knowledge and civilisation, and severely punish any one who transgresses the bounds assigned to humanity. In a later age, the conflict was no longer viewed as between the gods and man, but between the worshippers of different divinities ; and especially between Apollo, the symbol of pure intellect, and Dionysus, the deity of the senses ; hence Orpheus, the servant of Apollo, falls a victim to the jealousy of Dionysus, and the fury of his worshippers.— *Orphic Societies and Mysteries.* About the time of the first development of Greek philosophy, societies were formed, consisting of persons called the *followers of Orpheus* (οἱ Ὀρφικοί), who, under the pretended guidance of Orpheus, dedicated themselves to the worship of Dionysus. They performed the rites of a mystical worship, but instead of confining their notions to the initiated, they published them to others, and committed them to literary works. The Dionysus, to whose worship the Orphic rites were annexed, was Dionysus Zagreus, closely connected with Demeter and Cora (Persephone). The Orphic legends and poems related in great part to this Dionysus, who was combined, as an infernal deity, with Hades ; and upon whom the Orphic theologers founded their hopes of the purification and ultimate immortality of the soul. But their mode of celebrating this worship was very different from the popular rites of Bacchus. The Orphic worshippers of Bacchus did not indulge in unrestrained pleasure and frantic enthusiasm, but rather aimed at an ascetic purity of life and manners. All this part of the mythology of Orpheus, which connects him with Dionysus, must be considered as a later invention, quite irreconcilable with the original legend, in which he is the servant of Apollo and the Muses : but it is almost hopeless to explain the transition. — Many poems ascribed to Orpheus were current as early as the time of the Pisistratids [ONOMACRITUS]. They are often quoted by Plato, and the allusions to them in later writers are very frequent. The extant poems, which bear the name of Orpheus, are the forgeries of Christian grammarians and philosophers of the Alexandrian school ; but among the fragments, which form a part of the collection, are some genuine remains of that Orphic poetry which was known to Plato, and which must be assigned to the period of Onomacritus, or perhaps a little earlier. The Orphic literature, which in this sense may be called genuine, seems to have included *Hymns*, a *Theogony*, *Oracles*, &c. The apocryphal productions which have come down to us are, 1. *Argonautica*, an epic poem in 1384 hexameters, giving an account of the expedition of the Argonauts. 2. *Hymns*, 87 or 88 in number, in hexameters, evidently the productions of the Neo-Platonic school. 3. *Lithica* (Λιθικά), treats of properties of stones, both precious and common, and their uses in divination. 4. Fragments, chiefly of the *Theogony*. It is in this class that we find the genuine remains of the literature of the early Orphic theology, but intermingled with others of a much later date. The best edition is by Hermann, Lips. 1805.

Orthia (Ὀρθία, Ὀρθίς, or Ὀρθωσία), a surname of the Artemis who is also called Iphigenia or Lygodesma, and must be regarded as the goddess of the moon. Her worship was probably brought to Sparta from Lemnos. It was at the altar of Artemis Orthia that Spartan boys had to undergo the flogging, called *diamastigosis.*

Orthosia (Ὀρθωσία). 1. A city of Caria, on the Maeander, with a mountain of the same name, where the Rhodians defeated the Carians, B.C. 167. — 2. A city of Phoenice, S. of the mouth of the Eleutherus, and 12 Roman miles from Tripolis.

Orthrus (Ὄρθρος), the two-headed dog of Geryones, who was begotten by Typhon and Echidna, and was slain by Hercules. [See p. 309, b.]

Ortospana or **-um** (Ὀρτόσπανα: *Cabul?*), a considerable city of the Paropamisadae, at the sources of a W. tributary of the river Coes, and at the junction of 3 roads, one leading N. into Bactria, and the others S. and E. into India. It was also called Carura or Cabura.

Ortygia (Ὀρτυγία). 1. The ancient name of Delos. Since Artemis (Diana) and Apollo were born at Delos, the poets sometimes call the goddess *Ortygia*, and give the name of *Ortygiae boves* to the oxen of Apollo. The ancients connected the name with *Ortyx* (Ὄρτυξ) a quail. [See p. 379, a.] — 2. An island near Syracuse. [SYRACUSAE]. — 3. A grove near Ephesus, in which the Ephesians pretended that Apollo and Artemis were born. Hence Propertius calls the Cayster, which flowed near Ephesus, *Ortygius Cayster.*

Orus. [HORUS ; ORION.]

Osca. 1. (*Huesca* in Arragonia), an important

town of the Ilergetes and a Roman colony in Hispania Tarraconensis, on the road from Tarraco to Ilerda, with silver mines; whence Livy speaks of *argentum Oscense*, though these words may perhaps mean silver money coined at Osca.—2. (W. of *Huescar* in Granada), a town of the Turdetani in Hispania Baetica.

Oscēla. [LEPONTII.]

Osci or **Opīci** ('Οσκοι, 'Οπικοι), one of the most ancient tribes of Italy, inhabited the centre of the peninsula, from which they had driven out the Siculi. Their principal settlement was in Campania, but we also find them in parts of Latium and Samnium. They were subdued by the Sabines and Tyrrhenians, and disappeared from history at a comparatively early period. They were called in their own language *Uskus*. They are identified by many writers with the Ausones or Aurunci; but others think that the latter is a collective name for all the people dwelling in the plain, and that the Osci were a branch of the Ausones. The Oscan language was closely connected with the other ancient Italian dialects, out of which the Latin language was formed; and it continued to be spoken by the people of Campania long after the Oscans had disappeared as a separate people. A knowledge of it was preserved at Rome by the Fabulae Atellanae, which were a species of farce or comedy written in Oscan.

Osi, a people in Germany, probably in the mountains between the sources of the Oder and the Gran, were, according to Tacitus, tributary to the Sarmatians, and spoke the Pannonian language.

Osicerda. [OSSIGERDA.]

Osīris ('Οσιρις), the great Egyptian divinity, and husband of Isis. According to Herodotus they were the only divinities who were worshipped by all the Egyptians. His Egyptian name is said to have been Hysiris, which is interpreted to mean "son of Isis;" though some said that it meant "many-eyed." He is said to have been originally king of Egypt, and to have reclaimed his subjects from a barbarous life by teaching them agriculture, and enacting wise laws. He afterwards travelled into foreign lands, spreading, wherever he went, the blessings of civilisation. On his return to Egypt, he was murdered by his brother Typhon, who cut his body into pieces, and threw them into the Nile. After a long search Isis discovered the mangled remains of her husband, and with the assistance of her son Horus defeated Typhon, and recovered the sovereign power, which Typhon had usurped. See ISIS.

Osismii, a people in Gallia Lugdunensis, at the N.W. extremity of the coast, and in the neighbourhood of the modern *Quimper* and *Brest*.

Oaroēnē ('Οσροηνή : 'Οσροηνοι, pl. : *Pashalik of Orfah*), the W. of the 2 portions into which N. Mesopotamia was divided by the river Chaboras (*Khabour*), which separated it from Mygdonia on the E. and from the rest of Mesopotamia on the S.: the Euphrates divided it, on the W. and N. W., from the Syrian districts of Chalybonitis, Cyrrhestice, and Commagene; and on the N. it was separated by M. Masius from Armenia. Its name was said to be derived from Osroës, an Arabian chieftain, who, in the time of the Seleucidae, established over it a petty principality, with EDESSA for its capital, which lasted till the reign of Caracalla, and respecting the history of which, see ABGARUS.

Ossa ('Οσσα : *Kissavo*, i. e. *ivy-clad*), a celebrated mountain in the N. of Magnesia, in Thessaly, connected with Pelion on the S. E., and divided from Olympus on the N. W. by the vale of TEMPE. It is one of the highest mountains in Greece, but much less lofty than Olympus. It is mentioned by Homer, in the legend of the war of the Giants, respecting which see OLYMPUS.

Osset, with the surname *Constantia Julia*, a town in Hispania Baetica, on the right bank of the Baetis, opposite Hispalis.

Ossigerda or **Osicerda** (Ossigerdensis), a town of the Edetani in Hispania Tarraconensis, and a Roman municipium.

Ossīgi (*Maquiz*), a town of the Turduli in Hispania Baetica, on the spot where the Baetis first enters Baetica.

Ossonōba (*Estoy* N. of *Faro*), a town of the Turdetani in Lusitania, between the Tagus and Anas.

Osteōdes ('Οστεώδης νῆσος : *Alicur*), an island at some distance from the N. coast of Sicily, opposite the town of Soli.

Ostia (Ostiensis: *Ostia*), a town at the mouth of the river Tiber, and the harbour of Rome, from which it was distant 16 miles by land, was situated on the left bank of the left arm of the river. It was founded by Ancus Martius, the 4th king of Rome, was a Roman colony, and eventually became an important and flourishing town. In the civil wars it was destroyed by Marius, but it was soon rebuilt with greater splendour than before. The emperor Claudius constructed a new and better harbour on the right arm of the Tiber, which was enlarged and improved by Trajan. This new harbour was called simply *Portus Romanus* or *Portus Augusti*, and around it there sprang up a flourishing town, also called *Portus* (the inhabitants Portuenses). The old town of Ostia, whose harbour had been already partly filled up by sand, now sank into insignificance, and only continued to exist through its salt-works (*salinae*), which had been established by Ancus Martius. The ruins of Ostia are between 2 and 3 miles from the coast, as the sea has gradually receded in consequence of the accumulation of sand deposited by the Tiber.

Ostia Nili. [NILUS.]

Ostorius Scapula. [SCAPULA.]

Ostra (Ostrānus), a town in Umbria in the territory of the Senones.

T. Otacilius Crassus, a Roman general during the 2nd Punic war, was praetor B. C. 217, and subsequently pro-praetor in Sicily. In 215 he crossed over to Africa, and laid waste the Carthaginian coast. He was praetor for the 2nd time, 214, and his command was prolonged during the next 3 years. He died in Sicily, 211.

L. Otacilius Pilitus, a Roman rhetorician, who opened a school at Rome B. C. 81, was originally a slave; but having exhibited talent, and a love of literature, he was manumitted by his master. Cn. Pompeius Magnus was one of his pupils, and he wrote the history of Pompey, and of his father likewise.

Otānes ('Οτάνης). 1. A Persian, son of Pharnaspes, was the first who suspected the imposture of Smerdis the Magian, and took the chief part in organizing the conspiracy against the pretender (B. C. 521). After the accession of Darius Hystaspis, he was placed in command of the Persian force which invaded Samos for the purpose of placing Syloson, brother of Polycrates, in the government. — 2. A Persian, son of Sisamnes, succeeded Megabyzus (B. C. 506) in the command of the forces on the sea-coast, and took Byzantium, Chalcedon, Antandrus, and Lamponium, as well as the islands of Lemnos and Imbros. He was probably the same Otanes who is mentioned as a son-in-law of Darius Hystaspis, and as a general employed against the revolted Ionians in 499.

Otho, L. Roscius, tribune of the plebs B. C. 67, was a warm supporter of the aristocratical party. He opposed the proposal of Gabinius to bestow upon Pompey the command of the war against the pirates ; and in the same year he proposed and carried the law which gave to the equites a special place at the public spectacles, in fourteen rows or seats (*in quattuordecim gradibus sive ordinibus*), next to the place of the senators, which was in the orchestra. This law was very unpopular ; and in Cicero's consulship (63) there was such a riot occasioned by the obnoxious measure, that it required all his eloquence to allay the agitation.

Otho, Salvius. 1. M., grandfather of the emperor Otho, was descended from an ancient and noble family of the town of Ferentinum, in Etruria. His father was a Roman eques ; his mother was of low origin, perhaps even a freedwoman. Through the influence of Livia Augusta, in whose house he had been brought up, Otho was made a Roman senator, and eventually obtained the praetorship, but was not advanced to any higher honour. — 2. L., son of the preceding, and father of the emperor Otho, stood so high in the favour of Tiberius and resembled this emperor so strongly in person, that it was supposed by most that he was his son. He was consul suffectus in A. D. 33; was afterwards proconsul in Africa ; and in 42 was sent into Illyricum, where he restored discipline among the soldiers, who had lately rebelled against Claudius. At a later time he detected a conspiracy which had been formed against the life of Claudius. — 3. L., surnamed Titianus, elder son of No. 2, was consul 52, and proconsul in Asia 63, when he had Agricola for his quaestor. It is related to the honour of the latter that he was not corrupted by the example of his superior officer, who indulged in every kind of rapacity. On the death of Galba in January 69, Titianus was a second time made consul, with his brother Otho, the emperor. On the death of the latter, he was pardoned by Vitellius. — 4. M., Roman emperor from January 15th to April 16th, A. D. 69, was the younger son of No. 2. He was born in the early part of 32. He was of moderate stature, ill-made in the legs, and had an effeminate appearance. He was one of the companions of Nero in his debaucheries ; but when the emperor took possession of his wife, the beautiful but profligate Poppaea Sabina, Otho was sent as governor to Lusitania, which he administered with credit during the last 10 years of Nero's life. Otho attached himself to Galba when he revolted against Nero, in the hope of being adopted by him and succeeding to the empire. But when Galba adopted L. Piso, on the 10th of January, 69, Otho formed a conspiracy against Galba, and was proclaimed emperor by the soldiers at Rome, who put Galba to death. Meantime Vitellius had been proclaimed emperor at Cologne by the German troops on the 3rd of January ; and his generals forthwith set out for Italy to place their master on the throne. When these news reached Otho, he marched into the N. of Italy to oppose the generals of Vitellius. The fortune of war was at first in his favour. He defeated Caecina, the general of Vitellius, in more than one engagement ; but his army was subsequently defeated in a decisive battle near Bedriacum by the united forces of Caecina and Valens, whereupon he put an end to his own life at Brixellum in the 37th year of his age.

Othryades ('Οθρυάδης). 1. A patronymic given to Panthous or Panthus, the Trojan priest of Apollo, as the son of Othrys. — 2. ? Spartan, one of the 300 selected to fight with an equal number of Argives for the possession of Thyrea. Othryades was the only Spartan who survived the battle, and was left for dead. He spoiled the dead bodies of the enemy, and remained at his post, while Alcenor and Chromius, the two survivors of the Argive party, hastened home with the news of victory, supposing that all their opponents had been slain. As the victory was claimed by both sides, a general battle ensued, in which the Argives were defeated. Othryades slew himself on the field, being ashamed to return to Sparta as the one survivor of her 300 champions.

Othrys (Οθρυς), a lofty range of mountains in the S. of Thessaly, which extended from Mt. Tymphrestus, or the most S.-ly part of Pindus, to the E. coast and the promontory between the Pagasaean gulf and the N. point of Euboea. It shut in the great Thessalian plain on the S.

Otus, and his brother, Ephialtes, are better known by their name of the *Aloïdae*. [Aloeus.]

P. Ovidius Naso, the Roman poet, was born at Sulmo, in the country of the Peligni, on the 20th March, B. C. 43. He was descended from an ancient equestrian family, but possessing only moderate wealth. He, as well as his brother Lucius, who was exactly a year older than himself, was destined to be a pleader, and received a careful education to qualify him for that calling. He studied rhetoric under Arellius Fuscus and Porcius Latro, and attained to considerable proficiency in the art of declamation. But the bent of his genius showed itself very early. The hours which should have been spent in the study of jurisprudence were employed in cultivating his poetical talent. The elder Seneca, who had heard him declaim, tells us that his oratory resembled a *solutum carmen*, and that any thing in the way of argument was irksome to him. His father denounced his favourite pursuit as leading to inevitable poverty ; but the death of his brother, at the early age of 20, probably served in some degree to mitigate his father's opposition, for the patrimony which would have been scanty for two might amply suffice for one. Ovid's education was completed at Athens, where he made himself thoroughly master of the Greek language. Afterwards he travelled with the poet Macer, in Asia and Sicily. It is a disputed point whether he ever actually practised as an advocate after his return to Rome. The picture Ovid himself draws of his weak constitution and indolent temper prevents us from thinking that he ever followed his profession with perseverance, if indeed at all. The same causes deterred him from entering the senate, though he had put on the *latus clavus* when he assumed the *toga virilis*, as being by birth entitled to aspire to the senatorial dignity. (*Trist.* iv. 10. 29.) He became, however, one of the *Triumviri Capitales;* and he was subsequently made one of the *Centumviri*, or judges who tried testamentary and even

criminal causes; and in due time he was promoted
to be one of the *Decemviri*, who assembled and
presided over the court of the Centumviri. — Such
is all the account that can be given of Ovid's business life. He married twice in early life at the
desire of his parents, but he speedily divorced
each of his wives in succession. The restraint of
a wife was irksome to a man like Ovid, who was
devoted to gallantry and licentious life. His chief
mistress in the early part of his life was the one
whom he celebrates in his poems under the name
of Corinna. If we may believe the testimony of
Sidonius Apollinaris, Corinna was no less a personage than Julia, the accomplished, but abandoned
daughter of Augustus. There are several passages
in Ovid's *Amores* which render the testimony of
Sidonius highly probable. Thus it appears that
his mistress was a married woman, of high rank,
but profligate morals; all which particulars will
suit Julia. How long Ovid's connection with Corinna lasted there are no means of deciding; but it
probably ceased before his marriage with his 3rd
wife, whom he appears to have sincerely loved. We
can hardly place his 3rd marriage later than his 30th
year, since a daughter, Perilla, was the fruit of it
(*Trist.* iii. 7. 3), who was grown up and married
at the time of his banishment. Perilla was twice
married, and had a child by each husband. Ovid
was a grandfather before he lost his father at the
age of 90; soon after whose decease his mother
also died. Till his 50th year Ovid continued to
reside at Rome, where he had a house near the
Capitol, occasionally taking a trip to his Pelignan
farm. He not only enjoyed the friendship of a
large circle of distinguished men, but the regard
and favour of Augustus and the imperial family.
But in A. D. 9 Ovid was suddenly commanded by
an imperial edict to transport himself to Tomi, a
town on the Euxine, near the mouths of the
Danube, on the very border of the empire. He
underwent no trial, and the sole reason for his
banishment stated in the edict was his having
published his poem on the Art of Love (*Ars Amatoria*). It was not, however, an *exsilium*, but a
relegatio; that is, he was not utterly cut off from
all hope of return, nor did he lose his citizenship.
The real cause of his banishment has long exercised the ingenuity of scholars. The publication
of the *Ars Amatoria* was certainly a mere pretext.
The poem had been published nearly 10 years previously; and moreover, whenever Ovid alludes to
that, the ostensible cause, he invariably couples with
it another which he mysteriously conceals. According to some writers, the real cause was his intrigue
with Julia. But this is sufficiently refuted by the
fact that Julia had been an exile since B. C. 2.
Other writers suppose that he had been guilty of
an intrigue with the younger Julia, the daughter
of the elder one; and the remarkable fact that the
younger Julia was banished in the same year with
Ovid leads very strongly to the inference that his
fate was in some way connected with hers. But
Ovid states himself that his fault was an involun-
tary one; and the great disparity of years between
the poet and the younger Julia renders it improbable that there had been an intrigue between
them. He may more probably have become acquainted with Julia's profligacy by accident, and
by his subsequent conduct, perhaps, for instance,
by concealing it, have given offence to Livia, or
Augustus, or both. Ovid draws an affecting pic-

ture of the miseries to which he was exposed in
his place of exile. He complains of the inhospitable soi', of the severity of the climate, and of
the perils to which he was exposed, when the
barbarians plundered the surrounding country, and
insulted the very walls of Tomi. In the most
abject terms he supplicated Augustus to change his
place of banishment, and besought his friends to
use their influence in his behalf. In the midst of
all his misfortunes he sought some relief in the
exercise of his poetical talents. Not only did he
finish his *Fasti* in his exile, besides writing the
Ibis, the *Tristia*, *Ex Ponto*, &c., but he likewise
acquired the language of the Getae, in which he
composed some poems in honour of Augustus.
These he publicly recited, and they were received
with tumultuous applause by the Tomitae. With
his new fellow-citizens, indeed, he had succeeded
in rendering himself highly popular, insomuch that
they honoured him with a decree, declaring him
exempt from all public burthens. He died at
Tomi in the 60th year of his age, A. D. 18. — The
following is a list of Ovid's works, arranged, as far
as possible, in chronological order: — 1. *Amorum
Libri III.*, the earliest of the poet's works. According to the epigram prefixed, the work, as we
now possess it, is a 2nd edition, revised and
abridged, the former one having consisted of 5
books. 2. *Epistolae Heroïdum*, 21 in number.
3. *Ars Amatoria*, or *De Arte Amandi*, written
about B. C. 2. At the time of Ovid's banishment
this poem was ejected from the public libraries by
command of Augustus. 4. *Remedia Amoris*, in 1
book. 5. *Nux*, the elegiac complaint of a nut-
tree respecting the ill-treatment it receives from
wayfarers, and even from its own master. 6.
Metamorphoseon Libri XV. This, the greatest
of Ovid's poems in bulk and pretensions, appears
to have been written between the age of 40 and
50. It consists of such legends or fables as involved a transformation, from the Creation to the
time of Julius Caesar, the last being that emperor's
change into a star. It is thus a sort of cyclic poem
made up of distinct episodes, but connected into
one narrative thread, with much skill. 7. *Fasto-
rum Libri XII.*, of which only the first 6 are
extant. This work was incomplete at the time of
Ovid's banishment. Indeed he had perhaps done
little more than collect the materials for it; for
that the 4th book was written in Pontus appears
from ver. 88. The *Fasti* is a sort of poetical
Roman calendar, with its appropriate festivals and
mythology, and the substance was probably taken
in a great measure from the old Roman annalists.
The work shows a good deal of learning, but it has
been observed that Ovid makes frequent mistakes
in his astronomy, from not understanding the books
from which he took it. 8. *Tristium Libri V.*, elegies
written during the first 4 years of Ovid's banishment. They are chiefly made up of descriptions
of his afflicted condition, and petitions for mercy.
The 10th elegy of the 4th book is valuable, as
containing many particulars of Ovid's life. 9.
Epistolarum ex Ponto Libri IV., are also in the
elegiac metre, and much the same in substance as
the *Tristia*, to which they were subsequent. It
must be confessed that age and misfortune seem
to have damped Ovid's genius both in this and the
preceding work. Even the versification is more
slovenly, and some of the lines very prosaic. 10.
Ibis, a satire of between 600 and 700 elegiac

verses, also written in exile. The poet inveighs in it against an enemy who had traduced him. Though the variety of Ovid's imprecations displays learning and fancy, the piece leaves the impression of an impotent explosion of rage. The title and plan were borrowed from Callimachus. 11. *Consolatio ad Liviam Augustam*, is considered by most critics not to be genuine, though it is allowed on all hands to be not unworthy of Ovid's genius. 12. The *Medicamina Faciei* and *Halieuticon* are mere fragments, and their genuineness not altogether certain. — Of his lost works, the most celebrated was his tragedy, *Medea*, of which only two lines remain. That Ovid possessed a great poetical genius is unquestionable; which makes it the more to be regretted that it was not always under the control of a sound judgment. He possessed great vigour of fancy, warmth of colouring, and facility of composition. Ovid has himself described how spontaneously his verses flowed; but the facility of composition possessed more charms for him than the irksome, but indispensable labour of correction and retrenchment. Ovid was the first to depart from that pure and correct taste which characterises the Greek poets, and their earlier Latin imitators. His writings abound with those false thoughts and frigid conceits which we find so frequently in the Italian poets; and in this respect he must be regarded as unantique. The best edition of Ovid's complete works is by Burmann, Amsterdam, 1727, 4 vols. 4to.

Oxia Palus, is first mentioned distinctly by Ammianus Marcellinus as the name of the *Sea of Aral*, which the ancients in general did not distinguish from the Caspian. When Ptolemy, however, speaks of the Oxiana Palus (ἡ Ὀξειανὴ λίμνη) as a small lake in the steppes of Sogdiana, he is perhaps following some vague account of the separate existence of the *Sea of Aral*, and the same remark may be applied to Pliny's account that the *source* (instead of the *termination*) of the river Oxus was in a lake of the same name.

Oxiani (Ὀξιανοί, Οὐξιανοί), a people of Sogdiana, on the N. of the Oxus.

Oxii Montes (τὰ Ὀξεια, or Οὔξεια, ὄρη: prob. *Ak-tagh*), a range of mountains between the rivers Oxus and Jaxartes; the N. boundary of Sogdiana towards Scythia.

Oxus or Oaxus (Ὦξος, Ὦξος: *Jihoun* or *Amou*), a great river of Central Asia, rose, according to some of the ancient geographers, on the N. side of the Paropamisus M. (*Hindoo Koosh*), and, according to others, in the Emodi M., and flowed N. W., forming the boundary between Sogdiana on the N. and Bactria and Margiana on the S., and then, skirting the N. of Hyrcania, it fell into the Caspian. The *Jihoun* now flows into the S. W. corner of the *Sea of Aral*; but there are still distinct traces of a channel extending in a S. W. direction from the *Sea of Aral* to the Caspian, by which at least a portion, and probably the whole, of the waters of the Oxus found their way into the Caspian; and very probably the *Sea of Aral* itself was connected with the Caspian by this channel. The ancient geographers mention, as important tributaries of the Oxus, the Ochus, the Margus, and the Bactrus, which are now intercepted by the sands of the Desert. The Oxus is a broad and rapid river, navigable through a considerable portion of its course. It formed, in ancient times, a channel of commercial intercourse

between India and W. Asia, goods being brought down it to the Caspian, and thence up the Oxus and across Armenia, into Asia Minor. It occupies also an important place in history, having been in nearly all ages the extreme boundary between the great monarchies of S. W. Asia and the hordes which wander over the central steppes. Cyrus and Alexander both crossed it; but the former effected no permanent conquests on its N. side; and the conquests of the latter in Sogdiana, though for a time preserved under the Bactrian kings, were always regarded as lying beyond the limits of the civilised world, and were lost at the fall of the Bactrian kingdom. — Herodotus does not mention the Oxus by name, but it is supposed to be the river which he calls Araxes.

Oxybii, a Ligurian people on the coast of Gallia Narbonensis, W. of the Alps, and between the Flumen Argenteum (*Argens*) and Antipolis (*Antibes*). They were neighbours of the Sulluvii and Deciates.

Oxydracae (Ὀξυδράκαι), a warlike people of India intra Gangem, in the *Punjab*, between the rivers Hydaspes (*Jhelum*) and Acesines (*Chenab*), in whose capital Alexander was wounded. They called themselves descendants of Dionysus.

Oxylus (Ὄξυλος), the leader of the Heraclidae in their invasion of Peloponnesus, and subsequently king of Elis. [See p. 306, b.]

Oxyrhynchus (Ὀξύρυγχος: *Behnesch*, Ru.), a city of Middle Egypt, on the W. bank of the canal which runs parallel to the Nile on its W. side (*Bahr Yussuf*). It was the capital of the Nomos Oxyrhynchites, and the chief seat of the worship of the fish called oxyrynchus.

Ozogardana, a city of Mesopotamia on the Euphrates, the people of which preserved a lofty throne or chair of stone, which they called Trajan's judgment-seat.

P.

Pacaris. [HYPACYRIS.]

Pacatiana. [PHRYGIA.]

Paccius or Paccius Antiochus, a physician about the beginning of the Christian era, who was a pupil of Philonides of Catana, and lived probably at Rome. He made a large fortune by the sale of a certain medicine of his own invention, the composition of which he kept a profound secret. At his death he left his prescription as a legacy to the emperor Tiberius, who, in order to give it as wide a circulation as possible, ordered a copy of it to be placed in all the public libraries.

Paches (Πάχης), an Athenian general in the Peloponnesian war, took Mytilene and reduced Lesbos, B.C. 427. On his return to Athens he was brought to trial on some charge, and, perceiving his condemnation to be certain, drew his sword and stabbed himself in the presence of his judges.

Pachymeres, Georgius, an important Byzantine writer, was born about A.D. 1242 at Nicaea, but spent the greater part of his life at Constantinople. He was a priest, and opposed the union of the Greek and Latin churches. Pachymeres wrote several works, the most important of which is a *Byzantine History*, containing an account of the emperors Michael Palaeologus and Andronicus

Palaeologus the elder, in 13 books. The style is remarkably good and pure for the age. Edited by Possinus, Rome, 1666—1669, 2 vols. fol., and by Bekker, Bonn, 1835, 2 vols. 8vo.

Pachȳnus or Pachȳnum (*Capo Passaro*), a promontory at the S. E. extremity of Sicily, and one of the 3 promontories which give to Sicily its triangular figure, the other 2 being Pelorum and Lilybaeum. By the side of Pachynus was a bay, which was used as a harbour, and which is called by Cicero Portus Pachyni (*Porto di Palo*).

Pacīlus, the name of a family of the patrician Furia gens, mentioned in the early history of the republic.

Pacōrus. 1. Son of Orodes I., king of Parthia. His history is given under ARSACES XIV.— 2. King of Parthia. [ARSACES XXIV.]

Pactōlus (Πακτωλός: *Sarabat*), a small but celebrated river of Lydia, rose on the N. side of Mt. Tmolus, and flowed N. past Sardis into the Hermus, which it joined 30 stadia below Sardis. The golden sands of Pactolus have passed into a proverb. Lydia was long the California of the ancient world, its streams forming so many gold "washings;" and hence the wealth of the Lydian kings, and the alleged origin of gold money in that country. But the supply of gold was only on the surface, and by the beginning of our era, it was so far exhausted as not to repay the trouble of collecting it.

Pactȳas (Πακτύας), a Lydian, who on the conquest of Sardis (B.C. 546), was charged by Cyrus with the collection of the revenue of the province. When Cyrus left Sardis on his return to Ecbatana, Pactyas induced the Lydians to revolt against Cyrus; but when an army was sent against him he first fled to Cyme, then to Mytilene, and eventually to Chios. He was surrendered by the Chians to the Persians.

Pactȳē (Πακτύη: *St. George*), a town in the Thracian Chersonesus, on the Propontis, 36 stadia from Cardia, to which Alcibiades retired when he was banished by the Athenians, B.C. 407.

Pactyīca (Πακτυϊκή), the country of the Pactyes (Πάκτυες), in the N.W. of India, W. of the Indus, and in the 13th satrapy of the Persian Empire, is most probably the N.E. part of *Afghanistan*, about *Jellalabad*.

M. Pācūvius, one of the early Roman tragedians, was born about B.C. 220, at Brundisium, and is said to have been the son of the sister of Ennius. Pacuvius appears to have been brought up at Brundisium, but he afterwards repaired to Rome. Here he devoted himself to painting and poetry, and obtained so much distinction in the former art, that a painting of his in the temple of Hercules, in the forum boarium, was regarded as only inferior to the celebrated painting of Fabius Pictor. After living many years at Rome, for he was still there in his 80th year, he returned to Brundisium, on account of the failure of his health, and died in his native town, in the 90th year of his age, B.C. 130. We have no further particulars of his life, save that his talents gained him the friendship of Laelius, and that he lived on the most intimate terms with his younger rival Accius. Pacuvius was universally allowed by the ancient writers to have been one of the greatest of the Latin tragic poets. (Hor. *Ep.* ii. 1. 56.) He is especially praised for the loftiness of his thoughts, the vigour of his language, and the extent of his

knowledge. Hence we find the epithet *doctus* frequently applied to him. He was also a favourite with the people, with whom his verses continued to be esteemed in the time of Julius Caesar. His tragedies were taken from the great Greek writers; but he did not confine himself, like his predecessors, to a mere translation of the latter, but worked up his materials with more freedom and independent judgment. Some of the plays of Pacuvius were not based upon the Greek tragedies, but belonged to the class called *Praetextatae*, in which the subjects were taken from Roman story. One of these was entitled *Paulus*, which had as its hero L. Aemilius Paulus, the conqueror of Perseus, king of Macedonia. The fragments of Pacuvius are published by Bothe, *Poët. Lat. Scenic. Fragm.* Lips. 1834.

Pādus (*Po*), the chief river of Italy, whose name is said to have been of Celtic origin, and to have been given it on account of the pine trees (in Celtic *padi*) which grew on its banks. In the Ligurian language it was called *Bodencus* or *Bodincus*. Almost all later writers identified the Padus with the fabulous Eridanus, from which amber was obtained; and hence the Roman poets frequently give the name of Eridanus to the Padus. The reason of this identification appears to have been, that the Phoenician vessels received at the mouths of the Padus the amber which had been transported by land from the coasts of the Baltic to those of the Adriatic. The Padus rises from 2 springs on the E. side of Mt. Vesula (*Monte Viso*) in the Alps, and flows with a general E.-ly direction through the great plain of Cisalpine Gaul, which it divides into 2 parts, Gallia Cispadana and Gallia Transpadana. It receives numerous affluents, which drain the whole of this vast plain, descending from the Alps on the N. and the Apennines on the S. These affluents, increased in the summer by the melting of the snow on the mountains, frequently bring down such a large body of water as to cause the Padus to overflow its banks. The whole course of the river, including its windings, is about 450 miles. About 20 miles from the sea the river divides itself into 2 main branches, of which the N. one was called Padoa (*Maestra, Po Grande*, or *Po delle Fornaci*) and the S. one Olana (*Po d'Ariano*); and each of these now falls into the Adriatic by several mouths. The ancient writers enumerate 7 of these mouths, some of which were canals. They lay between Ravenna and Altinum, and bore the following names, according to Pliny, beginning with the S. and ending with the N. 1. Padusa, also called Augusta Fossa, was a canal dug by Augustus, which connected Ravenna with the Po. 2. Vatrenus, also called Eridanum Ostium or Spineticum Ostium (*Po di Primaro*), from the town of Spina at its mouth. 3. Ostium Caprasiae (*Porto Interito di bell' Occhio*). 4. Ostium Sagis (*Porto di Magnuvacca*). 5. Olane or Volane, the S. main branch of the river, mentioned above. 6. Padoa, the N. main branch, subdivided into several small branches called Ostia Carbonaria. 7. Fossae Philistinae, connecting the river, by means of the Tartarus, with the Athesis.

Padūsa. [PADUS.]

Paean (Παιάν, Παιήων or Παιών), that is, "the healing," is according to Homer the designation of the physician of the Olympian gods, who heals, for example, the wounded Ares and Hades. After the time of Homer and Hesiod, the word *Paeon* became a surname of Aesculapius, the god who had the power of healing. The name was, however, used also in the more general sense of deliverer from any evil or calamity, and was thus applied to Apollo and Thanatos, or Death, who are conceived as delivering men from the pains and sorrows of life. With regard to Apollo and Thanatos, however, the name may at the same time contain an allusion to παίειν, to strike, since both are also regarded as destroyers. From Apollo himself the name Paean was transferred to the song dedicated to him, that is, to hymns chaunted to Apollo for the purpose of averting an evil, and to warlike songs, which were sung before or during a battle.

Paeānīa (Παιανία: Παιανιεύς), a demus in Attica, on the E. slope of Mt. Hymettus, belonging to the tribe Pandionis. It was the demus of the orator Demosthenes.

Paemāni, a people of German origin in Gallia Belgica.

Paeōnes (Παίονες), a powerful Thracian people, who in early times were spread over a great part of Macedonia and Thrace. According to a legend preserved by Herodotus, they were of Teucrian origin ; and it is not impossible that they were a branch of the great Phrygian people, a portion of which seems to have settled in Europe. In Homer the Paeonians appear as allies of the Trojans, and are represented as having come from the river Axius. In historical times they inhabited the whole of the N. of Macedonia, from the frontiers of Illyria to some little distance E. of the river Strymon. Their country was called **Paeōnīa** (Παιονία). The Paeonians were divided into several tribes, independent of each other, and governed by their own chiefs ; though at a later period they appear to have owned the authority of one king. The Paeonian tribes on the lower course of the Strymon were subdued by the Persians, B. c. 513, and many of them were transplanted to Phrygia ; but the tribes in the N. of the country maintained their independence. They were long troublesome neighbours to the Macedonian monarchs, whose territories they frequently invaded and plundered ; but they were eventually subdued by Philip, the father of Alexander the Great, who allowed them nevertheless to retain their own monarchs. They continued to be governed by their own kings till a much later period ; and these kings were often virtually independent of the Macedonian monarchy. Thus we read of their king Audoleon, whose daughter Pyrrhus married. After the conquest of Macedonia by the Romans, 168, the part of Paeonia E. of the Axius formed the 2nd, and the part of Paeonia W. of the Axius formed the 3rd, of the 4 districts into which Macedonia was divided by the Romans.

Paeōnius (Παιώνιος). 1. Of Ephesus, an architect, probably lived between B. c. 420 and 380. In conjunction with Demetrius, he finally completed the great temple of Artemis, at Ephesus, which Chersiphron had begun ; and, with Daphnis the Milesian, he began to build at Miletus a temple of Apollo, of the Ionic order. The latter was the famous *Didymaeum*, or temple of Apollo Didymus, the ruins of which are still to be seen near Miletus. The former temple, in which the Branchidae had an oracle of Apollo, was burnt at the capture of Miletus by the army of Darius, 498. The new temple, which was on a scale only in-

ferior to that of Artemis, was never finished. — **2.** Of Mende, in Thrace, a statuary and sculptor, flourished about 435.

Paeoplae (Παιόπλαι), a Paeonian people on the lower course of the Strymon and the Angites, who were subdued by the Persians, and transplanted to Phrygia by order of Darius, B. c. 513. They returned to their native country with the help of Aristagoras, 500 ; and we find them settled N. of Mt. Pangaeus in the expedition of Xerxes, 480.

Paerisādes or **Parisādes** (Παιρισάδης or Παρισάδης), the name of 2 kings of Bosporus. 1. Son of Leucon, succeeded his brother Spartacus B. C. 349, and reigned 38 years. He continued the same friendly relations with the Athenians which were begun by his father Leucon. — **2.** The last monarch of the first dynasty that ruled in Bosporus. The pressure of the Scythian tribes induced Paerisades to cede his sovereignty to Mithridates the Great. The date of this event cannot be placed earlier than 112, nor later than 88.

Paestānus Sinus. [PAESTUM.]

Paestum (Paestanus), called **Posīdōnīa** (Ποσειδωνία: Ποσειδωνιάτης) originally, was a city in Lucania, situated between 4 and 5 miles S. E. of the mouth of the Silarus, and near the bay which derived its name from the town (Ποσειδωνιάτης κόλπος, Paestanus Sinus: *G. of Salerno*). Its origin is uncertain, but it was probably in existence before it was colonised by the Sybarites about B. c. 524. It soon became a powerful and flourishing city ; but after its capture by the Lucanians (between 438 and 424), it gradually lost the characteristics of a Greek city, and its inhabitants at length ceased to speak the Greek language. Its ancient name of Posidonia was probably changed into that of Paestum at this time. Under the supremacy of the Romans, who founded a Latin colony at Paestum about B. c. 274, the town gradually sank in importance ; and in the time of Augustus it is only mentioned on account of the beautiful roses grown in its neighbourhood. The ruins of Paestum are striking and magnificent. They consist of the remains of walls, of an amphitheatre, of 2 fine temples, and of another building. The 2 temples are in the Doric style, and are some of the most remarkable ruins of antiquity.

Paesus (Παισός), a town in the Troad, mentioned by Homer, but destroyed before the time of Strabo, its population having been transplanted to Lampsacus. Its site was on a river of the same name (*Beiram-Dere*) between Lampsacus and Parium.

Paetīnus, the name of a family of the Fulvia Gens, which was eventually superseded by the name of Nobilior. [NOBILIOR.]

Paetus, a cognomen in many Roman gentes, signified a person who had a slight cast in the eye.

Paetus, Aelīus. 1. P., probably the son of Q. Aelius Paetus, a pontifex, who fell in the battle of Cannae. He was plebeian aedile B. c. 204; praetor 203; magister equitum 202; and consul 201. In his consulship he fought a battle with the Boii, and made a treaty with the Ingauni Ligures. In 199, he was censor with P. Scipio Africanus. He afterwards became an augur, and died 174, during a pestilence at Rome. He is mentioned as one of the Roman jurists. — 2. **Sex.**, brother of the last, curule aedile 200; consul 198; and censor 193 with Cn. Cethegus. He was a jurist of eminence, and a prudent man, whence he got the cognomen Catus. He is described in a line of Ennius as "Egregie cordatus homo Catus Aelius Sextus." He is enumerated among the old jurists who collected or arranged the matter of law, which he did in a work entitled *Tripartita* or *Jus Aelianum*. This was a work on the Twelve Tables, which contained the original text, an interpretation, and the *Legis actio* subjoined. It was probably the first commentary written on the Twelve Tables. — 3. Q., son of No. 1., was elected augur 174, in place of his father, and was consul 167, when he laid waste the territory of the Ligurians.

Paetus, P. Autrōnius, was elected consul for B.C. 65 with P. Cornelius Sulla; but he and Sulla were accused of bribery by L. Aurelius Cotta and L. Manlius Torquatus, and condemned. Their election was accordingly declared void: and their accusers were chosen consuls in their stead. Enraged at his disappointment Paetus conspired with Catiline to murder the consuls Cotta and Torquatus; and this design is said to have been frustrated solely by the impatience of Catiline, who gave the signal prematurely before the whole of the conspirators had assembled. [CATILINA.] Paetus afterwards took an active part in the Catilinarian conspiracy, which broke out in Cicero's consulship, 63. After the suppression of the conspiracy Paetus was brought to trial for the share he had had in it; he was condemned, and went into exile to Epirus, where he was living when Cicero himself went into banishment in 58. Cicero was then much alarmed lest Paetus should make an attempt upon his life.

Paetus, C. Caesennius, sometimes called Caesonius, consul A. D. 61, was sent by Nero in 63 to the assistance of Domitius Corbulo in Armenia. He was defeated by Vologeses, king of Parthia, and purchased peace of the Parthians on the most disgraceful terms. After the accession of Vespasian, he was appointed governor of Syria, and deprived Antiochus IV., king of Commagene, of his kingdom.

Paetus Thrasēa. [THRASEA.]

Pāgae or Pēgae (Παγαί, Att. Πηγαί: Παγαῖος: *Psatho*), a town in Megaris, a colony from Megara, was situated at the E. extremity of the Alcyonian sea, and was the most important town in the country after Megara. It possessed a good harbour.

Pagāsae, called by the Romans Pāgāsa -ae (Παγασαί: *Volo*), a town of Thessaly, on the coast of Magnesia, and on the bay called after it Sinus Pagasaeus or Pagasicus (Παγασητικὸς κόλπος: *G. of Volo*). It was the port of Iolcos, and afterwards of Pherae, and is celebrated in mythology as the place where Jason built the ship Argo. Hence some of the ancients derived its name from πήγνυμι; but others connected the name with the fountains (πηγαί) in the neighbourhood. — The adjective *Pagasaeus* is applied to Jason on account of his building the ship Argo, and to Apollo because he had a sanctuary at Pagasae. The adjective is also used in the general sense of Thessalian; thus Alcestis, the wife of Admetus, is called by Ovid *Pagasaea conjux*.

Pagrae (Πάγραι: *Pagras, Bagras, Bargus*), a city of Syria, on the E. side of Mt. Amanus, at the foot of the pass called by Ptolemy the Syrian Gates, on the road between Antioch and Alexandria: the scene of the battle between Alexander Balas and Demetrius Nicator, B. c. 145.

Pagus (Πάγος), a remarkable conical hill, about 500—600 feet high, a little N. of Smyrna in Ionia. It was crowned with a shrine of Nemesis, and had a celebrated spring.

Palaemon (Παλαίμων). 1. Son of Athamas and Ino, was originally called Melicertes. When his mother, who was driven mad by Hera, had thrown herself, with her boy, into the sea, both were changed into marine divinities, Ino becoming Leucothea, and Melicertes Palaemon. [For details see ATHAMAS.] According to some, Melicertes after his apotheosis was called Glaucus, whereas, according to another version, Glaucus is said to have leaped into the sea from his love of Melicertes. The body of Melicertes, according to the common tradition, was washed by the waves, or carried by dolphins into the port Schoenus on the Corinthian isthmus, or to that spot on the coast where the altar of Palaemon subsequently stood. There the body was found by his uncle Sisyphus, who ordered it to be carried to Corinth, and on the command of the Nereides he instituted the Isthmian games and sacrifices of black bulls in honour of the deified Palaemon. In the island of Tenedos, it is said that children were sacrificed to him, and the whole worship seems to have had something gloomy about it. The Romans identified Palaemon with their own god Portunus, or Portumnus. [PORTUNUS.] — 2. Q. Remmius Palaemon, a grammarian in the reigns of Tiberius, Caligula, and Claudius. He was a native of Vicentia (*Vicenza*), in the north of Italy, and was originally a slave; but having been manumitted, he opened a school at Rome, where he became the most celebrated grammarian of his time, though his moral character was infamous. He is twice mentioned by Juvenal (vi. 451, vii. 251). He was the master of Quintilian.

Palaeopŏlis. [NEAPOLIS.]

Palaephātus (Παλαίφατος). 1. Of Athens, a mythical epic poet of the ante-Homeric period. The time at which he lived is uncertain, but he appears to have been usually placed after Phemonoe [PHEMONOE], though some writers assigned him even an earlier date. — 2. Of Paros, or Priene, lived in the time of Artaxerxes. Suidas attributes to him the work "On Incredible Tales," spoken of below. — 3. Of Abydus, an historian, lived in the time of Alexander the Great, and is stated to have been loved by the philosopher Aristotle. — 4. An Egyptian or Athenian, and a grammarian. His most celebrated work was entitled *Troica* (Τρωϊκά), which is frequently referred to by the ancient grammarians. — There is extant a small work in 51 sections, entitled Παλαίφατος περὶ ἀπίστων, or " On Incredible Tales," giving a brief account of some of the most celebrated Greek legends. It is an abstract of a much larger work, which is lost. It was to the original work to which Virgil refers (*Ciris*, 88): " Docta Palaephatia testatur voce papyrus." It is doubtful who was the author of this work; but as he adopts the rationalistic interpretation of the myths, he must be looked upon as a disciple of Evemerus [EVEMERUS], and may thus have been an Alexandrine Greek, and the same person as No. 4. The best edition is by Westermann, in the *Mythographi*, Brunswick, 1843.

Palaerus (Παλαιρός: Παλαιρεύς), a town on the coast of Acarnania near Leucas.

Palaestē (*Palasa*), a town of Epirus, on the

Peleus and Thetis.
(From a painted Vase.) Page 535.

Pegasus and Bellerophon. (From an Antique.) Page 531.
See also illustrations opposite p. 128.

Paris. (Aegina Marbles.)
Page 523. See also illustrations opposite p. 32.

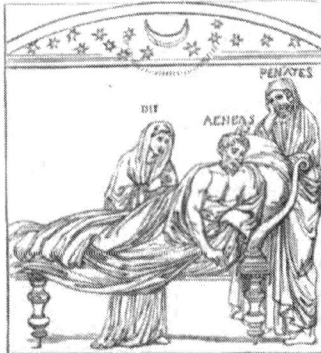

Penates.
(From the Vatican Virgil.) Page 539.

Judgment of Paris. (From a painted Vase.) Page 523.

[To face p. 512.

Odessus. Page 491.

Oeniadae. Page 492.

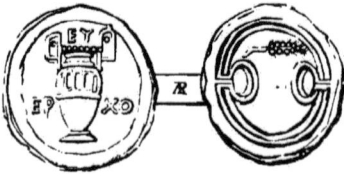

Orchomenus in Boeotia. Page 500.

Orippo in Spain. Page 503.

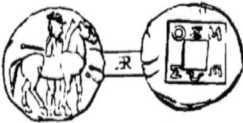

Ossa. Page 505.

Osset in Spain. Page 506.

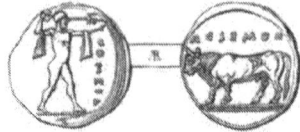

Paestum in Lucania. Page 511.

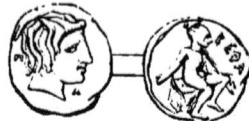

Pale in Cephallenia. Page 514.

Panormus in Sicily. Page 520.

Panticapaeum in the Tauric Chersonesus. Page 521.

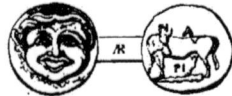

Parium in Mysia. Page 524.

Paros. Page 526.

To face p. 513.]

coast of Chaonia, and a little S. of the Acroceraunian mountains: here Caesar landed his forces
when he crossed over to Greece to carry on the
war against Pompey.

Palaestina (Παλαιστίνη, ἡ Παλαιστίνη Συρίη:
Παλαιστινός, Palaestinus, and rarely Palaestinensis:
Palestine, or *the Holy Land*), is the Greek and
Roman form of the Hebrew word which was used
to denote the country of the Philistines, and which
was extended to the whole country. In the Scrip-
tures it is called **Canaan**, from Canaan, the son of
Ham, whose descendants were its first inhabitants ;
the **Land of Israel**, the **Land of Promise**, the
Land of Jehovah, and the **Holy Land**. The
Romans usually called it **Judaea**, extending to the
whole country the name of its S. part. It was
regarded by the Greeks and Romans as a part of
Syria. Its extent is pretty well defined by natural
boundaries ; namely, the Mediterranean on the
W. ; the mountains of Lebanon on the N. ; the
Jordan and its lakes on the E., in the original
extent of the country as defined in the O. T.,
but in the wider and usual extent of the country, the Arabian Desert was its boundary on
the E. ; and on the S. and S.W. the deserts
which stretch N. of the head of the Red Sea
as far as the Dead Sea and the Mediterranean :
here it was separated from Egypt by the small
stream called in Scripture the River of Egypt
(prob. the brook *El-Arish*), which fell into the
Mediterranean at Rhinocolura (*El-Arish*), the
frontier town of Egypt. The S. boundary of the
territory E. of Jordan was the river Arnon (*Wady-
el-Mojib*). The extent of country within these
limits was about 11,000 square miles. The political boundaries varied at different periods. By
the covenant of God with Abraham (Gen. xv. 18),
the whole land was given to his descendants, *from
the river of Egypt to the Euphrates* ; but the Israelites never had the faith or courage to take
permanent possession of this their lot ; the nearest
approach made to the realisation of the promise
was in the reigns of David and Solomon, when the
conquests of the former embraced a large part of
Syria, and the latter built Tadmor (aft. Palmyra)
in the Syrian Desert ; and, for a time, the Euphrates seems to have been the border of the kingdom on the N.E. (See 2 Sam. viii. 3, 1 Chron.
xviii. 3). On the W. again, the Israelites never had
full possession of the Mediterranean coast, a strip of
which, N. of Mt.Carmel, was always retained by the
Phoenicians [PHOENICE] ; and another portion in
the S. W. was held by the Philistines, who were independent, except during brief intervals. On the S.
and E. again, portions of the land were frequently
subjugated by the neighbouring peoples of Ama-
lek, Edom, Midian, Moab, Ammon, &c. On the
N., except during the reigns of David and Solomon,
Palestine ceased at the S. entrance of the valley of
Coelesyria, and at M. Hermon in Antilibanus.—
In the physical formation of Palestine, the most
remarkable feature is the depression which forms
by the valley of the Jordan and its lakes [JOR-
DANES], between which and the Mediterranean
the country is intersected by mountains, chiefly
connected with the Lebanon system, and running
N. and S. Between these ranges, and between
the central range and the W. coast, are some
comparatively extensive plains, such as those of
Esdraelon and Sharon, and several smaller valleys ;
in the S. of the country the mountains gradually

subside into the rocky deserts of Arabia Petraea.
The valleys and slopes of the hills are extremely
fertile, and were much more so in ancient times,
when the soil on the mountain sides was preserved
by terraces which are now destroyed through neglect
or wantonness. This division of the country has
only a few small rivers (besides mountain streams),
which fall into the Mediterranean : the chief of
them are the Belus, just S. of Ptolemaïs (*Acre*),
the Kishon, flowing from M. Tabor, through the
plain of Esdraelon, and falling into the *Bay of
Acre* N. of M. Carmel, the Chorseus, N. of Caesarea,
the Kanah, W. of Sebaste (Samaria), the Jarkon,
N. of Joppa, the Eshcol, near Askelon, and the
Besor, near Gaza. On the E. of the Jordan, the
land rises towards the rocky desert of the *Hauran*
(the ancient Auranitis), and the hills bordering the
Syrian Desert, its lower portion, near the river,
forming rich pastures, watered by the E. tributaries of the Jordan, the chief of which are the
Hieromax, the Jabbok, and the Arnon, the last
flowing into the Dead Sea.—The earliest inhabitants
of Palestine were the several tribes of Canaanites.
It is unnecessary to recount in detail those events
with which we are familiar through the sacred history : the divine call of Abraham from Mesopotamia
to live as a stranger in the land which God promised
to his descendants, and the story of his and his
son's and his grandson's residence in it, till Israel
and his family removed to Egypt : their return
and conquest of the land of Canaan and of the
portion of territory E. of the Jordan, and the partition of the whole among the 12 tribes : the contests
with the surrounding nations, and the government
by Judges, till the establishment of the monarchy
under Saul : the conquests of David, the splendid
reign of Solomon, and the division of the kingdom under Rehoboam into the kingdom of Israel,
including 2-3rds of the country W. of Jordan, and
all E. of it, and the kingdom of Judah, including
the S. portion which was left, between the Mediterranean on the W. and the Dead Sea and a small
extent of Jordan on the E. : and the histories of
these 2 monarchies down to their overthrow by
the Assyrians and Babylonians respectively. The
former of these conquests made an important
change in the population of Palestine, by the
removal of the greater part of the inhabitants of
the kingdom of Israel, and the settlement in their
place of heathen peoples from other parts of the
Assyrian empire, thus restricting the country occupied by the genuine Israelites within the limits of
the kingdom of Judah. Hence the names of Judaea
and Jews applied to the country and the people in
their subsequent history. Between these last and
the mixed people of N. Palestine a deadly enmity
arose ; the natural dislike of the pure race of Israel
to heathen foreigners being aggravated by the
wrongs they suffered from them, especially at their
return from the Babylonish captivity, and still
more by the act of religious usurpation of which
the remnant of the N. Israelites were guilty at a
later period, in setting up a temple for themselves
on M. Gerizim [SAMARIA]. The date assigned
to the Assyrian conquest of the kingdom of Israel
is B. C. 721. The remainder of the history of the
kingdom of Judah (passing over its religious history, which is most important during this period)
consists of alternate contests with, and submissions
to, the kings of Assyria, Egypt, and Babylon, till
the conquest of the country by Nebuchadnezzar

and the removal of a part of its people to Babylonia, in 598, and the destruction of Jerusalem and the temple, after the rebellion of Zedekiah, in 588, when a still larger portion of the people were carried captive to Babylon, while others escaped to Egypt. In 584, during the siege of Tyre, Nebuchadnezzar sent a further portion of the Jews into captivity ; but there was still a considerable remnant left in the land, and (what is very important) foreign settlers were not introduced ; so that, when Cyrus, after overthrowing the Babylonian empire, issued his edict for the return of the Jews to their own land (B.C. 536), there was no great obstacle to their quiet settlement in it. They experienced some trouble from the jealousy and attacks of the Samaritans, and the changeful dispositions of the Persian court ; but at length, by the efforts of Zerubbabel and Joshua, and the preaching of Haggai and Zechariah, the new temple was finished and dedicated, in 516, and Jerusalem was rebuilt. Fresh bands of Jewish exiles returned under Ezra, 458, and Nehemiah, 445 ; and, between this time and that of the Macedonian conquest, Judaea was repeopled by the Jews, and through the tolerance of the Persian kings, it was governed virtually by the high-priests. In B.C. 332, after Alexander had taken Tyre and Gaza, he visited Jerusalem, and received the quiet submission of the Jews, paying the most marked respect to their religion. Under the successors of Alexander, Palestine belonged alternately to Egypt and Syria, the contests between whose kings for its possession are too complicated to recount here ; but its internal government seems to have been pretty much in the hands of the high-priests, until the tyranny of Antiochus Epiphanes provoked the successful revolt under the Maccabees, or Asmonaeans, whose history is given under MACCABAEI, and the history of the Idumaean dynasty, who succeeded them, is given under ANTIPATER, HERODES, and ARCHELAUS. The later Asmonaean princes had regained the whole of Palestine, including the districts of Judaea, Samaria, and Galilee (besides Idumaea), W. of the Jordan, and the several districts of Peraea, Batanea, Gaulonitis, Ituraea, and Trachonitis or Auranitis, E. of it ; and this was the extent of Herod's kingdom. But, from B.C. 63, when Pompey took Jerusalem, the country was really subject to the Romans. At the death of Herod, his kingdom was divided between his sons as tetrarchs, under the sanction of Augustus, Archelaus receiving Judaea, Samaria, and Idumaea, Herod Antipas Galilee and Peraea, and Philip Batanaea, Gaulonitis, and Trachonitis ; all standing to the Roman empire in a relation of virtual subjection, which successive events converted into an integral union. First, A.D. 7, Archelaus was deposed by Augustus, and Judaea was placed under a Roman procurator : next, about 31, Philip died, and his government was united to the province of Syria, and was in 37 again conferred on Herod Agrippa I., with the title of king, and with the addition of Abilene, the district round Damascus. In 39, Herod Antipas was banished to Gaul, and his tetrarchy was added to the kingdom of Herod Agrippa ; and 2 years later he received from Claudius the government of Judaea and Samaria, and thus Palestine was reunited under a nominal king. On his death, in 44, Palestine again became a part of the Roman province of Syria under the name of Judaea, which was governed by a procurator. The Jews were, however, most turbulent subjects of the Roman empire, and at last they broke out into a general rebellion, which, after a most sanguinary war, was crushed by Vespasian and Titus ; and the latter took and destroyed Jerusalem in A.D. 70. Under Constantine, Palestine was divided afresh into the three provinces of P. Prima in the centre, P. Secunda in the N., and P. Tertia, the S. of Judaea, with Idumaea.

Palamēdēs (Παλαμήδης). 1. Son of Nauplius and Clymene. He joined the Greeks in their expedition against Troy ; but Agamemnon, Diomedes, and Ulysses, envious of his fame, caused a captive Phrygian to write to Palamedes a letter in the name of Priam, and bribed a servant of Palamedes to conceal the letter under his master's bed. They then accused Palamedes of treachery ; upon searching his tent they found the letter which they themselves had dictated ; and thereupon they caused him to be stoned to death. When Palamedes was led to death, he exclaimed, " Truth, I lament thee, for thou hast died even before me." According to some traditions, it was Ulysses alone who hated and persecuted Palamedes. The cause of this hatred is also stated differently. According to some, Ulysses hated him because he had been compelled by him to join the Greeks against Troy ; according to others, because he had been severely censured by Palamedes for returning with empty hands from a foraging excursion into Thrace. The manner in which Palamedes perished is likewise related differently. Some say that Ulysses and Diomedes induced him to descend into a well, where they pretended they had discovered a treasure, and when he was below they cast stones upon him, and killed him ; others state that he was drowned by them whilst fishing ; and others that he was killed by Paris with an arrow. The place where he was killed is either Colonae in Troas, or in Tenedos, or at Geraestus. The story of Palamedes, which is not mentioned by Homer, seems to have been first related in the Cypria, and was afterwards developed by the tragic poets, especially by Euripides, and lastly by the sophists, who liked to look upon Palamedes as their pattern. The tragic poets and sophists describe him as a sage among the Greeks, and as a poet ; and he is said to have invented light-houses, measures, scales, the discus, dice, the alphabet, and the art of regulating sentinels. — 2. A Greek grammarian, was a contemporary of Athenaeus, who introduces him as one of the speakers in his work.

Palātīnus Mons. [ROMA.]

Palatīum. [ROMA.]

Palē (Πάλη : Παλεῖς, Ion. Παλέες, Att. Παλῆς, in Polyb. Παλαιεῖς: nr. *Lixuri*, Ru.), one of the 4 cities of Cephallenia, situated on a height opposite Zacynthus.

Palēs, a Roman divinity of flocks and shepherds, is described by some as a male, and by others as a female divinity. Hence some modern writers have inferred that Pales was a combination of both sexes ; but such a monstrosity is altogether foreign to the religion of the Romans. Some of the rites performed at the festival of Pales, which was celebrated on the 21st of April, the birth-day of the city of Rome, would seem to indicate, that the divinity was a female ; but besides the express statements to the contrary, there are also other reasons for believing that Pales was a male divinity. The name seems to be connected with Palatinus, the centre of all the earliest legends of Rome, and the god himself was with the Romans the embodiment of the same idea as Pan among the Greeks. Respecting the festival of the Palilia see *Dict. of Antiq. s. v.*

Palicānus, Lollīus. [LOLLIUS.]

Pălĭci (Παλικοί), were Sicilian gods, twin sons of Zeus and the nymph Thalia, the daughter of Hephaestus. Sometimes they are called sons of Hephaestus by Aetna, the daughter of Oceanus. Thalia, from fear of Hera, prayed to be swallowed up by the earth ; her prayer was granted ; but in due time she sent forth from the earth twin boys, who, according to the absurd etymology of the ancients, were called Παλικοί, from τοῦ πάλιν ἱκέσθαι. They were worshipped in the neighbourhood of Mt. Aetna, near Palice ; and in the earliest times human sacrifices were offered to them. Their sanctuary was an asylum for runaway slaves, and near it there gushed forth from the earth two sulphureous fountains, called Deilloi, or brothers of the Palici ; at which solemn oaths were taken. The oaths were written on tablets, and thrown into one of the fountains ; if the tablet swam on the water, the oath was considered to be true, but if it sank down, the oath was regarded as a perjury, and was believed to be punished instantaneously by blindness or death.

Palinūrum (*C. Palinuro*), a promontory on the W. coast of Lucania, which was said to have derived its name from Palinurus, the son of Jasus, and pilot of the ship of Aeneas, who fell into the sea, and was murdered on the coast by the natives.

Pallacŏpas (Παλλακόπας), a canal in Babylonia, cut from the Euphrates, at a point 800 stadia (80 geog. miles) S. of Babylon, W.-ward to the edge of the Arabian Desert, where it lost itself in marshes.

Pallădas (Παλλάδας), the author of a large number of epigrams in the Greek Anthology, was a pagan and an Alexandrian grammarian. He lived at the beginning of the 5th century of the Christian era, for in one of his epigrams he speaks of Hypatia, the daughter of Theon, as still alive. Hypatia was murdered in A. D. 415.

Pallădĭum (Παλλάδιον), properly any image of Pallas Athena (Minerva), but generally applied to an ancient image of this goddess, which was kept hidden and secret, and was revered as a pledge of the safety of the town, where it existed. Among these ancient images of Pallas none is more celebrated than the Trojan Palladium, concerning which there was the following tradition. Athena was brought up by Triton; and when his daughter, Pallas, and Athena were once wrestling together for the sake of exercise, Zeus interfered in the struggle, and suddenly held the aegis before the face of Pallas. Pallas, while looking up to Zeus, was wounded by Athena, and died. Athena in her sorrow caused an image of the maiden to be made, round which she hung the aegis. When Electra had come as a suppliant to the Palladium, Zeus hurled it down from heaven upon the earth, because it had been sullied by the hands of one, who was no longer a pure maiden. The image fell upon the earth at Troy, when Ilus was just beginning to build the city. Ilus erected a sanctuary to it. According to some, the image was dedicated by Electra, and according to others it was given by Zeus to Dardanus. The image itself is said to have been 3

cubits in height, with its legs close together, and holding in its right hand a spear, and in the left a spindle and a distaff. This Palladium remained at Troy until Ulysses and Diomedes contrived to carry it away, because the city could not be taken so long as it was in the possession of that sacred treasure. According to some accounts Troy contained two Palladia, one of which was carried off by Ulysses and Diomedes, while the other was conveyed by Aeneas to Italy, or the one taken by the Greeks was a mere imitation, while that which Aeneas brought to Italy was the genuine image. But this twofold Palladium was probably a mere invention to account for its existence in more than one place. Several towns both in Greece and Italy claimed the honour of possessing the genuine Trojan Palladium ; as for example, Argos and Athens, where it was believed that Demophon took it from Diomedes on his return from Troy. [DEMOPHON.] This Palladium at Athens, however, was different from another image of Pallas there, which was also called Palladium, and stood on the acropolis. In Italy the cities of Rome, Lavinium, Luceria, and Siris likewise pretended to possess the Trojan Palladium.

Pallădĭus (Παλλάδιος). — 1. Of Methone, a sophist or rhetorician, who lived in the reign of Constantine the Great.—2. Bishop of Helenopolis, in Bithynia, to which he was raised A. D. 400. He was ordained by Chrysostom; and on the banishment of the latter, Palladius was accused of holding the opinions of Origen, and, fearful of the violence of his enemies, he fled to Rome, 405. Shortly afterwards he ventured to return to the East, but was arrested and banished to the extremity of Upper Egypt. He was afterwards restored to his bishopric of Helenopolis, from which he was translated to that of Aspona or Aspuna in Galatia, perhaps about 419 or 420. Three works in Greek have come down to us under the name of Palladius ; but there has been considerable dispute, whether they were written by one individual or more : — (1.) *Historia Lausiaca*, " *the Lausiac History*," so called from its being dedicated to Lausus, a chamberlain at the imperial court. This work contains internal proofs of having been written by the bishop of Helenopolis. It gives biographical notices or characteristic anecdotes of a number of ascetics, with whom Palladius was personally acquainted, or concerning whom he received information from those who had known them personally. Edited by Meursius, Lugd. Bat. 1616. (2.) *The Life of Chrysostom*, was probably written by a different person from the bishop of Helenopolis. Edited by Bigotius, Paris, 1680. (3.) *De Gentibus Indiae et Bragmanibus (Brahmans).* The authorship of this work is uncertain. It appears that the writer himself had visited India. Edited by Camerarius in *Liber Gnomologicus*, 8vo. Lips. without date ; and by Bissaeus, London, 1665. — 3. Surnamed *Iatrosophista*, a Greek medical writer, of whose life nothing is known. He lived after Galen. We possess 3 works commonly attributed to him: namely, 2 books of commentaries on Hippocrates, and a short treatise on Fevers, all of which are taken chiefly from Galen. — 4. Pallădĭus Rutīlĭus Taurus Aemilĭānus, the author of a treatise *De Re Rustica*, in the form of a Farmer's Calendar, the various operations connected with agriculture and a rural life being arranged in regular order, according to the seasons in which they ought to be performed. It is comprised in 14 books: the first is introductory, the 12 following contain the duties of the 12 months in succession, commencing with January; the last is a poem, in 85 elegiac couplets, upon the art of grafting (*De Insitione*). A considerable portion of the work is taken from Columella. The date of the author is uncertain; but it is most probable that he lived in the middle of the 4th century of the Christian aera. The work was very popular in the middle ages. Edited in the *Scriptores Rei Rusticae* by Gesner, Lips. 1735; reprinted by Ernesti in 1773, and by Schneider, Lips. 1794.

Pallantia (Pallantinus: *Palencia*), the chief town of the Vaccaei in the N. of Hispania Tarraconensis, and on a tributary of the Durius.

Pallantias and **Pallantis**, patronymics, given to Aurora, the daughter of the giant Pallas.

Pallantium (Παλλάντιον: Παλλαντιεύς), an ancient town of Arcadia, near Tegea, said to have been founded by Pallas, the son of Lycaon. Evander is said to have come from this place, and to have called the town, which he founded on the banks of the Tiber, *Pallantēum* (afterwards *Palantium* and *Palatium*), after the Arcadian town. On the foundation of Megalopolis, most of the inhabitants of Pallantium settled in the new city; and the town remained almost deserted, till it was restored by Antoninus Pius, and exempted from taxes on account of its supposed connection with the imperial city.

Pallas (Πάλλας).—**1.** One of the Titans, son of Crius and Eurybia, husband of Styx, and father of Zelus, Cratos, Bia, and Nice.—**2.** A giant, slain by Athena in the battle with the gods.—**3.** According to some traditions, the father of Athena, who slew him when he attempted to violate her. —**4.** Son of Lycaon, and grandfather of Evander, is said to have founded the town of Pallantium in Arcadia. Hence Evander is called by the poets *Pallantius heros.*—**5.** Son of Evander, and an ally of Aeneas, was slain by the Rutulian Turnus.—**6.** Son of the Athenian king Pandion, and father of Clytus and Butes. His 2 sons were sent with Cephalus to implore assistance of Aeacus against Minos. Pallas was slain by Theseus. The celebrated family of the Pallantidae at Athens traced their origin from this Pallas.

Pallas (Παλλάς), a surname of **Athena**. In Homer this name always appears united with that of Athena, as Παλλὰς Ἀθήνη or Παλλὰς Ἀθηναίη; but in later writers we also find Pallas alone instead of Athena. Some ancient writers derive the name from πάλλειν, to brandish, in reference to the goddess brandishing the spear or aegis, others derive it from the giant Pallas, who was slain by Athena. But it is more probable that Pallas is the same word as πάλλαξ, i. e. a virgin or maiden.

Pallas, a favourite freedman of the emperor Claudius. In conjunction with another freedman, Narcissus, he administered the affairs of the empire. After the death of Messalina, Pallas persuaded the weak emperor to marry Agrippina; and as Narcissus had been opposed to this marriage, he now lost his former power, and Pallas and Agrippina became the rulers of the Roman world. It was Pallas who persuaded Claudius to adopt the young Domitius (afterwards the emperor Nero), the son of Agrippina; and it was doubtless with the assistance of Pallas that Agrippina poisoned her husband. Nero soon after his accession became tired of his mother's control, and as one step towards emancipating himself from her authority, he deprived Pallas of all his public offices, and dismissed him from the palace in 56. He was suffered to live unmolested for some years, till at length his immense wealth excited the rapacity of Nero, who had him removed by poison in 63. His enormous wealth, which was acquired during the reign of Claudius, had become proverbial, as we see from the line in Juvenal (i. 107), *ego possideo plus Pallante et Licinio.* The brother of Pallas was Antonius or Claudius Felix, who was appointed by Claudius procurator of Judaea [FELIX, ANTONIUS.]

Pallas Lacus. [TRITON.]

Pallēnē (Παλλήνη). 1. (Παλληναῖος, Παλλήνιος), the most W.-ly of the 3 peninsulas running out from Chalcidice in Macedonia. It is said to have been formerly called Phlegra (Φλέγρα), and on the narrow isthmus, which connected it with the main land, stood the important town of Potidaea.—**2.** (Παλληνεύς, rarely Παλληναῖος), a demus in Attica belonging to the tribe Antiochis, was situated on one of the slopes of Pentelicus, a few miles S. W. of Marathon. It possessed a temple of Athena, surnamed *Pallenis* (Παλληνίς) from the place; and in its neighbourhood took place the contest between Pisistratus and the party opposed to him.

Palma (*Palma*), a Roman colony on the S.W. coast off the island Balearis Major (*Majorca*).

Palmaria (*Palmaruola*), a small uninhabited island off the coast of Latium and the promontory Circeium.

Palmyra (Πάλμυρα: Παλμυρηνός, Palmyrēnus. O. T. Tadmor: *Tadmor*, Ru.), a celebrated city of Syria, stood in an oasis of the great Syrian Desert, which from its position must have been in the earliest times a halting place for the caravans between Syria and Mesopotamia. Here Solomon built a city, which was called in Hebrew Tadmor, that is, *the city of palm-trees;* and of this name the Greek Πάλμυρα is a translation. It lies in 34° 18' N. lat. and 38° 14' E. long., and was reckoned 237 Roman miles from the coast of Syria, 176 N.E. of Damascus, 80 E. of Emesa, and 113 S.E. of Apamea. With the exception of a tradition that it was destroyed by Nebuchadnezzar, we hear nothing of it till the time of the government of the East by M. Antonius, who marched to surprise it, but the inhabitants retreated with their moveable property beyond the Euphrates. Under the early Roman emperors it was a free city and a great commercial emporium. Its position on the border between the Parthian and Roman dominions gave it the command of the trade of both, but also subjected it to the injuries of war. Under Hadrian and the Antonines it was highly favoured and reached its greatest splendour. The history of its temporary elevation to the rank of a capital, in the 3rd century, is related under ODENATHUS and ZENOBIA. On its capture by Aurelian, in 270, it was plundered, and soon afterwards an insurrection of its inhabitants led to its partial destruction. It was fortified by Justinian, but never recovered from its fall. In the Arabian conquest it was one of the first cities taken; but it was still inhabited by a small population, chiefly of Jews, till it was taken and plundered by Timour (Tamerlane) in

1400. It has long been entirely deserted, except when a horde of Bedouins pitch their tents among its splendid ruins. Those ruins, which form a most striking object in the midst of the Desert, are of the Roman period, and decidedly inferior in the style of architecture, as well as in grandeur of effect, to those of Baalbek [HELIOPOLIS], the sister deserted city of Syria. The finest remains are those of the temple of the Sun ; the most interesting are the square sepulchral towers of from 3 to 5 stories. The streets and the foundations of the houses are traceable to some extent ; and there are several inscriptions in Greek and in the native Palmyrene dialect, besides one in Hebrew and one or two in Latin. The surrounding district of **Palmyrēne** contained the Syrian Desert from the E. border of Coelesyria to the Euphrates.

Pamisus (Πάμισος). 1. A southern tributary of the Peneus in Thessaly. — 2. (Pirnatza), the chief river of Messenia, rises in the E. part of the country, 40 stadia E. of Ithome, flows first S. W., and then S. through the Messenian plain, and falls into the Messenian gulf. — 3. A small river in Laconia, falls into the Messenian gulf near Leuctra. It was at one time the ancient boundary between Laconia and Messenia.

Pamphia or **Pamphium** (Παμφία, Πάμφιον), a village of Aetolia, destroyed by the Macedonians.

Pamphila (Παμφίλη), a female historian of considerable reputation, who lived in the reign of Nero. She is described by some writers as a native of Epidaurus, by others as an Egyptian. Her principal work, of which Photius has given some extracts, was a kind of Historical Miscellany (entitled συμμίκτων ἱστορικῶν ὑπομνημάτων λόγοι). It was not arranged according to subjects or according to any settled plan, but it was more like a common-place book, in which each piece of information was set down as it fell under the notice of the writer. Modern scholars are best acquainted with the name of Pamphila, from a statement in her work, preserved by A. Gellius (xv. 23), by which is ascertained the year of the birth of Hellanicus, Herodotus, and Thucydides respectively.

Pamphilus (Πάμφιλος). 1. A disciple of Plato, who is only remembered by the circumstance that Epicurus, when a young man, heard him at Samos. Epicurus used to speak of him with great contempt, that he might not be thought to owe anything to his instruction ; for it was the great boast of Epicurus, that he was the sole author of his own philosophy. — 2. An Alexandrian grammarian, of the school of Aristarchus, and the author of a lexicon, which is supposed by some scholars to have formed the foundation of the lexicon of Hesychius. He appears to have lived in the 1st century of our era. — 3. A philosopher or grammarian of Nicopolis, the author of a work on agriculture, of which there are considerable fragments in the Geoponica. — 4. Presbyter of Caesarea, in Palestine, saint and martyr, and celebrated for his friendship with Eusebius, who, as a memorial of this intimacy, assumed the surname of Pamphilus. [EUSEBIUS.] He suffered martyrdom A. D. 307. The life of Pamphilus seems to have been entirely devoted to the cause of biblical literature. He was an ardent admirer and follower of Origen. He formed, at Caesarea, an important public library chiefly of ecclesiastical authors. Perhaps the most valuable of the contents of this library were the Tetrapla and Hexapla of Origen,

from which Pamphilus, in conjunction with Eusebius, formed a new recension of the Septuagint, numerous copies of which were put into circulation. — 5. Of Amphipolis, one of the most distinguished of the Greek painters, flourished about B. C. 390—350. He was the disciple of Eupompus, the founder of the Sicyonian school of painting, for the establishment of which, however, Pamphilus seems to have done much more than even Eupompus himself. Of his own works we have most scanty accounts ; but as a teacher of his art he was surpassed by none of the ancient masters. According to Pliny, he was the first artist who possessed a thorough acquaintance with all branches of knowledge, especially arithmetic and geometry, without which he used to say that the art could not be perfected. All science, therefore, which could in any way contribute to form the perfect artist, was included in his course of instruction, which extended over ten years, and for which the fee was no less than a talent. Among those who paid this price for his tuition were Apelles and Melanthius. Not only was the school of Pamphilus remarkable for the importance which the master attached to general learning, but also for the minute attention which he paid to accuracy in drawing.

Pamphôs (Πάμφως), a mythical poet, who is placed by Pausanias later than Olen, and much earlier than Homer. His name is connected particularly with Attica.

Pamphylia (Παμφυλία: Πάμφῦλος, Παμφύλιος, Pamphylius), in its original and more restricted sense, was a narrow strip of the S. coast of Asia Minor, extending in a sort of arch along the **Sinus Pamphylius** (G. of Adalia), between Lycia on the W., and Cilicia on the E., and on the N. bordering on Pisidia. Its boundaries, as commonly stated, were Mt. Climax on the W., the river Melas on the E., and the foot of Mt. Taurus on the N. ; but the statements are not very exact : Strabo gives to the coast of Pamphylia a length of 640 stadia, from Olbia on the W. to Ptolemaïs, some distance E. of the Melas, and he makes its width barely 2 miles ; and there are still other different accounts. It was a belt of mountain coast land, intersected by rivers flowing down from the Taurus in a short course, but several of them with a considerable body of water : the chief of them, going from W. to E., were the CATARRHACTES, CESTRUS, EURYMEDON, and MELAS [No. 6], all navigable for some distance from their mouths. The inhabitants were a mixture of races, whence their name Πάμφυλοι, of all races (the genuine old form, the other in -ιοι is later). Besides the aboriginal inhabitants, of the Semitic (Syro-Arabian) family, and Cilicians, there were very early Greek settlers and later Greek colonies in the land. Tradition ascribed the first Greek settlements to MOPSUS, after the Trojan War, from whom the country was in early times called **Mopsopia**. It was successively a part of the Persian, Macedonian, Greco-Syrian, and Pergamene kingdoms, and passed by the will of Attalus III. to the Romans (B. C. 130), under whom it was made a province ; but this province of Pamphylia included also Pisidia and Isauria, and afterwards a part of Lycia. Under Constantine Pisidia was again separated from Pamphylia.

Pamphylium Mare, Pamphylius Sinus (τὸ Παμφύλιον πέλαγος, Παμφύλιος κόλπος: Gulf of

Adalia), the great gulf formed in the S. coast of Asia Minor by the direction of th Taurus chain and by Mt. Solyma, between the Pr. Sacrum or Chelidonium (*C. Khelidonia*), the S.E. point of Lycia, and Pr. Anemurium (*C. Anemour*), the S. point of Cilicia. Its depth from N. to S., from Pr. Sacrum to Olbia, is reckoned by Strabo at 367 stadia (36·7 geog. miles), which is too little.

Pamphylus (Πάμφυλος), son of Aegimius and brother of Dymas, was king of the Dorians at the foot of Mt. Pindus, and along with the Heraclidae invaded Peloponnesus.

Pan (Πάν), the great god of flocks and shepherds among the Greeks. He is usually called a son of Hermes by the daughter of Dryops ; but he is also described as a son of Hermes by Callisto, by Oeneis or Thymbris, or by Penelope, whom the god visited in the shape of a ram, or as a son of Penelope by Ulysses, or by all her suitors in common. He was perfectly developed from his birth ; and when his mother saw him, she ran away through fear ; but Hermes carried him to Olympus, where all the gods were delighted with him, and especially Dionysus. From his delighting *all* the gods, the Homeric hymn derives his name. He was originally only an Arcadian god ; and Arcadia was always the principal seat of his worship. From this country his name and worship afterwards spread over other parts of Greece ; but at Athens his worship was not introduced till the time of the battle of Marathon. In Arcadia he was the god of forests, pastures, flocks, and shepherds, and dwelt in grottoes, wandered on the summits of mountains and rocks, and in valleys, either amusing himself with the chase, or leading the dances of the nymphs. As the god of flocks, both of wild and tame animals, it was his province to increase and guard them ; but he was also a hunter, and hunters owed their success or failure to him. The Arcadian hunters used to scourge the statute of the god, if they had been disappointed in the chase. During the heat of mid-day he used to slumber, and was very indignant when any one disturbed him. As the god of flocks, bees also were under his protection, as well as the coast where fishermen carried on their pursuit. As the god of every thing connected with pastoral life, he was fond of music, and the inventor of the syrinx or shepherd's flute, which he himself played in a masterly manner, and in which he instructed others also, such as Daphnis. He is thus said to have loved the poet Pindar, and to have sung and danced his lyric songs, in return for which Pindar erected to him a sanctuary in front of his house. Pan, like other gods who dwelt in forests, was dreaded by travellers to whom he sometimes appeared, and whom he startled with sudden awe or terror. Thus when Phidippides, the Athenian, was sent to Sparta to solicit its aid against the Persians, Pan accosted him, and promised to terrify the barbarians, if the Athenians would worship him. Hence sudden fright without any visible cause was ascribed to Pan, and was called a Panic fear. He is further said to have had a terrific voice, and by it to have frightened the Titans in their fight with the gods. It seems that this feature, namely, his fondness of noise and riot, was the cause of his being considered the minister and companion of Cybele and Dionysus. He was at the same time believed to be possessed of prophetic powers, and to have even instructed Apollo

in this art. While roaming in his forests he fell in love with Echo, by whom or by Pitho he became the father of Iynx. His love of Syrinx, after whom he named his flute, is well known from Ovid (*Met.* i. 691, seq.). Fir-trees were sacred to him, since the nymph Pitys, whom he loved, had been metamorphosed into that tree ; and the sacrifices offered to him consisted of cows, rams, lambs, milk, and honey. Sacrifices were also offered to him in common with Dionysus and the nymphs. The various epithets which are given him by the poets refer either to his singular appearance, or are derived from the names of the places in which he was worshipped. The Romans identified with Pan their own god Inuus, and also Faunus, which name is merely another form of Pan. In works of art Pan is represented as a voluptuous and sensual being, with horns, puck-nose, and goat's feet, sometimes in the act of dancing, and sometimes playing on the syrinx.

Panacea (Πανάκεια), i. e. "the all-healing," a daughter of Aesculapius, who had a temple at Oropus.

Panachaicus Mons (τὸ Παναχαϊκὸν ὄρος), a mountain in Achaia, 6300 feet high, immediately behind Patrae.

Panacra (Πάνακρα), a mountain in Crete, a branch of Mt. Ida.

Panactum (Πάνακτον), a town on the frontiers of Attica and Boeotia, originally belonged to Boeotia, and after being a frequent object of contention between the Athenians and Boeotians, at length became permanently annexed to Attica.

Panaenus (Πάναινος), a distinguished Athenian painter, who flourished B. C. 448. He was the nephew of Phidias, whom he assisted in decorating the temple of Zeus, at Olympia. He was also the author of a series of paintings, of the battle of Marathon, in the Poecile at Athens.

Panaetius (Παναίτιος), a native of Rhodes, and a celebrated Stoic philosopher, studied first at Pergamum under the grammarian Crates, and subsequently at Athens under the stoic Diogenes, of Babylon, and his disciple Antipater of Tarsus. He afterwards went to Rome, where he became an intimate friend of Laelius and of Scipio Africanus the younger. In B. C. 144 he accompanied Scipio on the embassy which he undertook to the kings of Egypt and Asia in alliance with Rome. Panaetius succeeded Antipater, as head of the stoic school, and died at Athens, at all events before 111. The principal work of Panaetius was his treatise on the theory of moral obligation (περὶ τοῦ καθήκοντος), in 3 books, from which Cicero took the greater part of his work *De Officiis.* Panaetius had softened down the harsh severity of the older stoics, and, without giving up their fundamental definitions, had modified them so as to make them applicable to the conduct of life, and had clothed them in the garb of eloquence.

Panaetolium, a mountain in Aetolia near Thermon, in which town the Panaetolium or general assembly of the Aetolians was held.

Panda, a river in the country of the Siraces in the interior of Sarmatia Asiatica (Tac. *Ann.* xii. 16).

Pandareos (Πανδάρεως), son of Merops of Miletus, is said to have stolen from the temple of Zeus in Crete the golden dog which Hephaestus had made, and to have carried it to Tantalus. When Zeus sent Hermes to Tantalus to claim the dog back, Tantalus declared that it was not in his possession. The god, however, took the animal by force, and threw mount Sipylus upon Tantalus. Pandareos fled to Athens, and thence to Sicily, where he perished with his wife Harmothoe. The story of Pandareos derives more interest from that of his 3 daughters. Aëdon, the eldest of them, was married to Zethus, the brother of Amphion, by whom she became the mother of Itylus. From envy of Amphion, who had many children, she determined to murder one of his sons, Amaleus, but in the night she mistook her own son for her nephew, and killed him. The 2 other daughters of Pandareos, Merope and Cleodora (according to Pausanias, Camira and Clytia), were, according to Homer, deprived of their parents by the gods, and remained as helpless orphans in the palace. Aphrodite, however, fed them with milk, honey, and wine. Hera gave them beauty and understanding far above other women. Artemis gave them dignity, and Athena skill in the arts. When Aphrodite went up to Olympus to arrange the nuptials for her maidens, they were carried off by the Harpies.

Pandárus (Πάνδαρος.) 1. A Lycian, son of Lycaon, commanded the inhabitants of Zelea on Mt. Ida, in the Trojan war. He was distinguished in the Trojan army as an archer, and was said to have received his bow from Apollo. He was slain by Diomedes, or, according to others, by Sthenelus. He was afterwards honoured as a hero at Pinara in Lycia. — 2. Son of Alcanor, and twin-brother of Bitias, was one of the companions of Aeneas, and was slain by Turnus.

Pandátaria (*Vendutene*), a small island in the Tyrrhenian sea off the coast of Campania, to which Julia, the daughter of Augustus, was banished.

Pandēmos (Πάνδημος), i. e. "common to all the people," a surname of Aphrodite, used in a twofold sense: 1. as the goddess of low sensual pleasures as *Venus vulgivaga* or *popularis*, in opposition to Venus Urania, or the heavenly Aphrodite; 2. as the goddess uniting all the inhabitants of a country into one social or political body. Under the latter view she was worshipped at Athens along with Peitho (persuasion), and her worship was said to have been instituted by Theseus at the time when he united the scattered townships into one great body of citizens. The sacrifices offered to her consisted of white goats.

Pandīon (Πανδίων). 1. I. King of Athens, son of Erichthonius, by the Naiad Pasithea, was married to Zeuxippe, by whom he became the father of Procne and Philomela, and of the twins Erechtheus and Butes. In a war against Labdacus, king of Thebes, he called upon Tereus of Daulis in Phocis, for assistance, and afterwards rewarded him by giving him his daughter Procne in marriage. [TEREUS.] It was in his reign that Dionysus and Demeter were said to have come to Attica. — 2. II. King of Athens, son of Cecrops and Metinduss. Being expelled from Athens by the Metionidae, he fled to Megara, and there married Pylia, the daughter of king Pylas. When the latter, in consequence of a murder, migrated into Peloponnesus, Pandion obtained the government of Megara. He became the father of Aegeus, Pallas, Nisus, Lycus, and a natural son, Oeneus, and also of a daughter, who was married to Sciron. After his death his 4 sons, called the *Pandīonidae* (Πανδιονίδαι), returned from Megara to Athens, and expelled the Metionidae.

Aegeus obtained Athens, Lycus the E. coast of Attica, Nisus Megaris, and Pallas the S. coast.

Pandōra (Πανδώρα), the name of the first woman on earth. When Prometheus had stolen the fire from heaven, Zeus in revenge caused Hephaestus to make a woman out of earth, who by her charms and beauty should bring misery upon the human race. Aphrodite adorned her with beauty; Hermes bestowed upon her boldness and cunning; and the gods called her Pandora, or *Allgifted*, as each of the gods had given her some power by which she was to work the ruin of man. Hermes took her to Epimetheus, who made her his wife, forgetting the advice of his brother Prometheus that he should not receive any gifts from Zeus. In the house of Epimetheus was a closed jar, which he had been forbidden to open. But the curiosity of a woman could not resist the temptation to know its contents; and when she opened the lid all the evils incident to man poured out. She had only time to shut down the lid, and prevent the escape of hope. Later writers relate that Pandora brought with her from heaven a box (and not a jar), containing all human ills, upon opening which all escaped and spread over the earth, Hope alone remaining. At a still later period, the box is said to have contained all the blessings of the gods, which would have been preserved for the human race, had not Pandora opened the vessel, so that the winged blessings escaped.

Pandōsia (Πανδοσία). 1. (*Kastri*), a town of Epirus in the district Thesprotia, on the river Acheron, and in the territory of the Cassopaei. — 2. (*Castel Franco* ?), a town in Bruttium near the frontiers of Lucania, situated on the river Acheron, and also either upon or at the foot of 3 hills, was originally a residence of native Oenotrian chiefs. It was here that Alexander of Epirus fell, B. C. 326, in accordance with an oracle.

Pandrōsos (Πάνδροσος), i.e. "the all-bedewing," or "refreshing," was a daughter of Cecrops and Agraulos, and a sister of Erysichthon, Herse, and Aglauros. She was worshipped at Athens, along with Thallo, and had a sanctuary there near the temple of Athena Polias.

Panēas. [CAESAREA, No. 2.]

Panēum or -**ium** (Πάνειον, Πάνιον, i. e. *Pan's-abode*), the Greek name of the cave, in a mountain at the S. extremity of the range of Antilibanus, out of which the river Jordan takes its rise, a little above the town of Paneas or Caesarea Philippi. The mountain, in whose S. side the cave is, was called by the same name; and the surrounding district was called Paneas.

Pangaeum or **Pangaeus** (Παγγαῖον, Πάγγαιος: *Pangea*), a celebrated range of mountains in Macedonia, between the Strymon and the Nestus, and in the neighbourhood of Philippi, with gold and silver mines, and with splendid roses.

Panhellēnius (Πανελλήνιος), i. e. the god worshipped by all the Hellenes. This surname is said to have been given to Zeus by Aeacus, when he offered a propitiatory sacrifice on behalf of all the Greeks, for the purpose of averting a famine. In Aegina there was a sanctuary of Zeus Panhellenius, which was said to have been founded by Aeacus; and a festival, Panhellenia, was celebrated there.

Paniōnium. [MYCALE: and *Dict. of Ant. s. v. Panionia.*]

Panium (Πάνιον), a town on the coast of Thrace near Heraclea.

Pannŏnĭa, one of the most important of the Roman provinces between the Danube and the Alps, was separated on the W. from Noricum by the Mons Cetius, and from Upper Italy by the Alpes Juliae, on the S. from Illyria by the Savus, on the E. from Dacia by the Danube, and on the N. from Germany by the same river. It thus corresponded to the eastern part of *Austria*, *Styria*, *Carinthia*, *Carniola*, the whole of *Hungary* between the Danube and the Save, *Slavonia*, and a part of *Croatia* and *Bosnia*. The mountains in the S. and W. of the country on the borders of Illyria, Italy, and Noricum, belonged to the Alps, and are therefore called by the general name of the Alpes Panno-nicae, of which the separate names are Ocra, Car-vancas, Cetius, and Albii or Albani Montes. The principal rivers of Pannonia, besides the Danube, were the Dravus (*Drave*), Savus (*Save*), and Arrabo (*Raab*), all of which flow into the Danube. — The Pannonians (Pannonii), sometimes called Paeonians by the Greek writers, were probably of Illyrian origin, and were divided into numerous tribes. They were a brave and warlike people, but are described by the Roman writers as cruel, faithless, and treacherous. They maintained their independence of Rome, till Augustus, after his conquest of the Illyrians (B. C. 35), turned his arms against the Pannonians, who were shortly after-wards subdued by his general Vibius. In A. D. 7 the Pannonians joined the Dalmatians and the other Illyrian tribes in their revolt from Rome, and were with difficulty conquered by Tiberius, after a desperate struggle, which lasted 3 years (A. D. 7—9). It was after the termination of this war that Pannonia appears to have been reduced to the form of a Roman province, and was garrisoned by several Roman legions. The dangerous mutiny of these troops after the death of Augustus (A. D. 14) was with difficulty quelled by Drusus. From this time to the end of the empire, Pannonia always contained a large number of Roman troops, on ac-count of its bordering on the Quadi and other powerful barbarous nations. We find at a later time that Pannonia was the regular quarters of 7 legions. In consequence of this large number of troops always stationed in the country, several towns were founded and numerous fortresses were erected along the Danube. Pannonia originally formed only one province, but was soon divided into 2 provinces, called *Pannonia Superior* and *Pannonia Inferior*. These were separated from one another by a straight line drawn from the river Arrabo S. as far as the Savus, the country W. of this line being *P. Superior*, and the part E. *P. Inferior*. Each of the provinces was governed by a separate propraetor ; but they were fre-quently spoken of in the plural under the name of *Pannoniae*. In the 4th century the part of P. Inferior between the Arrabo, the Danube, and the Dravus, was formed into a separate province by Galerius, who gave it the name of *Valeria* in honour of his wife. But as P. Inferior had thus lost a great part of its territory, Constantine added to it a portion of P. Superior, comprising the upper part of the course of the Dravus and the Savus. P. Superior was now called *Pannonia I.*, and P. In-ferior *Pannonia II.*; and all 3 Pannonian pro-vinces (together with the 2 Noric provinces and Dalmatia) belonged to the 6 Illyrian provinces of the Western Empire. In the middle of the 5th century Pannonia was taken possession of by the

Huns. After the death of Attila it passed into the hands of the Ostrogoths, and subsequently into those of the Langobards.

Panomphaeus (Πανομφαῖος), i. e. the author of all signs and omens, a surname of Zeus, who had a sanctuary on the Hellespont between capes Rhoe-teum and Sigeum.

Pănŏpe (Πανόπη), a nymph of the sea, daughter of Nereus and Doris.

Pănŏpeus (Πανοπεύς), son of Phocus and Aste-ropaea, accompanied Amphitryon on his expedition against the Taphians or Teleboans, and took an oath not to embezzle any part of the booty ; but having broken his oath, he was punished by his son Epeus becoming unwarlike. He is also men-tioned among the Calydonian hunters.

Pănŏpeus (Πανοπεύς, Hom.), **Pănŏpēae** (Πανο-πέαι), or **Pănŏpe** (Πανόπη, Thuc. ; ethnic Πανο-πεύς, *Agio Vlasi*), an ancient town in Phocis on the Cephissus and near the frontiers of Boeotia, 20 stadia W. of Chaeronea, said to have been founded by Panopeus, son of Phocus.

Panŏpŏlis. [Chemmis.]

Panoptes. [Argus.]

Panormus (Πάνορμος), that is, " All-Port," or a place always fit for landing, the name of several harbours. **1.** (Πανορμίτης, Panormīta, Panormi-tanus : *Palermo*), an important town on the N. coast of Sicily and at the mouth of the river Ore-thus, was founded by the Phoenicians, and at a later time received its Greek name from its ex-cellent harbour. From the Phoenicians it passed into the hands of the Carthaginians, in whose power it remained for a long time, and who made it one of the chief stations for their fleet. It was taken by the Romans in the 1st Punic war, B. C. 254, and was subsequently made a Roman colony. — **2.** (*Porto Raphti*), the principal harbour on the E. coast of Attica, near the demus Prasiae, and opposite the S. extremity of Euboea. — **3.** (*Tekieh*), a harbour in Achaia, 15 stadia E. of the promon-tory Rhium. — **4.** A harbour in Epirus in the middle of the Acroceraunian rocks. — **5.** (Nr. *Mylo-potamo* Rn.), a town and harbour on the N. coast of Crete. — **6.** The outer harbour of Ephesus formed by the mouth of the river Cayster. [See p. 242, a.]

Pansa, C. Vibĭus, a friend and partisan of Caesar, was tribune of the plebs B. C. 51, and was appointed by Caesar in 46 to the government of Cisalpine Gaul as successor to M. Brutus. Caesar subsequently nominated him and Hirtius, consuls for 43. Pansa was consul in that year along with Hirtius, and fell before Mutina in the month of April. The details are given under Hirtius.

Pantăcy̆as, Pantăgĭas, or **Pantăgĭes** (Παν-τακύας : *Fiume di Porcari*), a small river on the E. coast of Sicily, which flowed into the sea be-tween Megara and Syracuse.

Pantălĕŏn (Πανταλέων), son of Omphalion, king or tyrant of Pisa in Elis at the period of the 34th Olympiad (B. C. 644), assembled an army, with which he made himself master of Olympia, and assumed by force the sole presidency of the Olympic games. The Eleans on this account would not reckon this as one of the regular Olympiads. Pantaleon assisted the Messenians in the 2nd Messenian war.

Panthĕa. [Abradatas.]

Panthĕum (Πάνθειον), a celebrated temple at Rome in the Campus Martius, which is still extant and used as a Christian church. It is in a circular form, surmounted by a dome, and contains a noble Corinthian portico of 16 pillars. In its general form it resembles the Colosseum in the Regent's Park. It was built by M. Agrippa in his 3rd consulship, B. C. 27, as the inscription on the portico still testifies. All the ancient authors call it a temple, and there is no reason for supposing, as some modern writers have done, that it was originally an entrance to the public baths. The name is commonly derived from its being supposed to be sacred to all the gods; but Dion Cassius expressly states that it was dedicated to Mars and Venus. The temple of Julius Caesar was erected by Augustus in the interior of the temple, and that of Augustus in the pronaos. It was restored by the emperor Septimius Severus, A. D. 202. Between 608 and 610 it was consecrated as a Christian church by the pope Boniface IV., with the approbation of the emperor Phocas. In 655, the plates of gilded-bronze that covered the roof were carried to Constantinople by command of Constans II. The Pantheon is the largest circular building of antiquity; the interior diameter of the rotunda is 142 feet, and the height from the pavement to the summit about 148 feet. The portico is 103 feet wide, and the columns 47 feet high.

Panthŏus contr. **Panthūs** (Πάνθοος, Πάνθους), one of the elders at Troy, husband of Phrontis, and father of Euphorbus, Polydamas, and Hyperenor. Hence both Euphorbus and Polydamas are called *Panthoides*. He is said to have been originally a priest of Apollo at Delphi, and to have been carried to Troy by Antenor, on account of his beauty. He continued to be a priest of Apollo, and is called by Virgil (*Aen.* ii. 319) *Othryades*, or son of Othryas.

Panticapaeum (Παντικάπαιον: Παντικαπαίος, Παντικαπαιεύς, Παντικαπιάτης: *Kertsch*), a town in the Tauric Chersonesus, was situated on a hill 20 stadia in circumference on the Cimmerian Bosporus, and opposite the town of Phanagoria in Asia. It derived its name from the river Panticapes. It was founded by the Milesians, about B. C. 541, and from its position and excellent harbour soon became a place of great commercial importance. It was the residence of the Greek kings of the Bosporus, and hence is sometime called Bosporus. Justinian caused it to be surrounded with new walls.

Panticapes (Παντικάπης), a river in European Sarmatia, which, according to Herodotus, rises in a lake, separates the agricultural and nomad Scythians, flows through the district Hylaea, and falls into the Borysthenes. It is usually identified with the modern *Somara*, but without sufficient grounds.

Panyasis (Πανύασις). 1. A Greek epic poet, was a native of Halicarnassus, and a relation of the historian Herodotus, probably his uncle. Panyasis began to be known about B. C. 489, continued in reputation till 467, and was put to death by Lygdamis, the tyrant of Halicarnassus, about 457. The most celebrated of the poems of Panyasis was his *Heraclea* or *Heracleas*, which gave a detailed account of the exploits of Hercules. It consisted of 14 books and 9000 verses. Another poem of Panyasis bore the name of *Ionica* ('Ιωνικά), and contained 7000 verses; it related the history of Neleus, Codrus, and the Ionic colonies. In later times the works of Panyasis were extensively read, and much admired; the Alexandrine grammarians ranked him with Homer, Hesiod, Pisander, and

Antimachus, as one of the 5 principal epic poets.— 2. A philosopher. also a native of Halicarnassus, who wrote 2 books "On Dreams" (Περὶ ὀνείρων), was perhaps a grandson of the poet.

Paphlăgŏnĭa (Παφλαγονία: Παφλαγών, pl. -όνες, Paphlăgo), a district on the N. side of Asia Minor, between Bithynia on the W. and Pontus on the E., being separated from the former by the river Parthenius, and from the latter by the Halys; on the S. it was divided by the chain of Mt. Olympus (according to others by Olgassys) from Phrygia, in the earlier times, but from Galatia afterwards; and on the N. it bordered on the Euxine. These boundaries, however, are not always exactly observed. Xenophon brings the Paphlagonians as far E. as Themiscyra and the Jasonian promontory. It appears to have been known to the Greeks in the mythical period. The Argonautic legends mentioned Paphlagon, the son of Phineus, as the hero eponymus of the country. In the Homeric Catalogue, Pylaemenes leads the Paphlagonians, as allies of the Trojans, from the land of the Heneti, about the river Parthenius, a region famed for its mules: and from this Pylaemenes the later princes of Paphlagonia claimed their descent, and the country itself was sometimes called **Pylaemenia**. Herodotus twice mentions the Halys as the boundary between the Paphlagonians and the Syrians of Cappadocia; but we learn also from him and from other authorities that the Paphlagonians were of the same race as the Cappadocians (i. e. the Semitic or Syro-Arabian) and quite distinct, in their language and their customs, from their Thracian neighbours on the W. They were good soldiers, especially as cavalry; but uncivilised and superstitious. The country had also other inhabitants, probably of a different race, namely the Heneti and the Caucones; and Greek settlements were established on the coast at an early period. The Paphlagonians were first subdued by Croesus. Under the Persian empire they belonged to the third satrapy, but their satraps made themselves independent and assumed the regal title; maintaining themselves in this position (with a brief interruption, during which Paphlagonia was subject to Eumenes) until the conquest of the country by Mithridates, who added the E. part of his own kingdom, and made over the W. part to Nicomedes, king of Bithynia, who gave it to his son Pylaemenes. After the fall of Mithridates the Romans added the N. of Paphlagonia, along the coast, to Bithynia; and the interior was left to the native princes, as tributaries to Rome; but, the race of these princes becoming soon extinct, the whole of Paphlagonia was made Roman, and Augustus made it a part of the province of Galatia. It was made a separate province under Constantine; but the E. part, from Sinope to the Halys, was assigned to Pontus, under the name of Hellespontus. Paphlagonia was a mountainous country, being intersected from W. to E. by 3 chains of the Olympus system, namely the Olympus itself on the S. border, Olgassys in the centre, and a minor chain with no specific name nearer to the coast. The belt of land between this last chain and the sea was very fertile, and the Greek cities of Amastris and Sinope brought a considerable commerce to its shore; but the inland parts were chiefly covered with native forests, which were celebrated as hunting grounds. The country was famed for its horses and mules, and in some parts there were extensive sheepwalks; and its rivers were particularly famous for their fish. The country was divided into 9 districts, the names of which are not of enough importance to be specified here.

Pāphus (Πάφος), son of Pygmalion by the statue into which life had been breathed by Aphrodite. From him the town of Paphus is said to have derived its name; and Pygmalion himself is called the Paphian hero. (Ov. Met. x. 290.)

Pāphus (Πάφος : Πάφιος), the name of 2 towns on the W. coast of Cyprus, near each other, and called respectively " Old Paphos " (Παλαίπαφος) and " New Paphos " (Πάφος νέα). Old Paphos was situated near the promontory Zephyrium on the river Bocarus 10 stadia from the coast, where it had a good harbour; while New Paphos lay more inland, in the midst of a fertile plain, 60 stadia from the former. Old Paphos was the chief seat of the worship of Aphrodite (Venus), who is said to have landed at this place after her birth among the waves, and who is hence frequently called the Paphian goddess (Paphia). Here she had a celebrated temple, the high priest of which exercised a kind of religious superintendence over the whole island. Every year there was a grand procession from New Paphos to the temple of the goddess in the old city. There were 2 legends respecting the foundation of Paphos, one describing the Syrian king Cinyras as its founder, and the other the Arcadian Agapenor on his return from Troy. These statements are reconciled by the supposition that Cinyras was the founder of Old Paphos and Agapenor of New Paphos. There can be no doubt of the Phoenician origin of Old Paphos, and that the worship of Aphrodite was introduced here from the East; but an Arcadian colony cannot be admitted. When Paphos is mentioned by later writers without any epithet, they usually mean the New City; but when the name occurs in the poets, we are generally to understand the Old City, as the poets, for the most part, speak of the place in connection with the worship of Aphrodite. Old Paphos was destroyed by an earthquake in the reign of Augustus, but was rebuilt by order of the emperor, and called Augusta. Under the Romans New Paphos was the capital of one of the 4 districts into which the island was divided. Old Paphos corresponds to the modern Kukla or Konuklia, and New Paphos to the modern Baffa.

Papīas (Παπίας), an early Christian writer, said to have been a hearer of the Apostle John, and a companion of Polycarp, was bishop of Hierapolis, on the border of Phrygia. He taught the doctrine of the Millennium, maintaining that there will be for 1000 years after the resurrection of the dead, a bodily reign of Christ on this earth. Only fragments of his works are extant.

Papiniānus, Aemilīus, a celebrated Roman jurist, was praefectus praetorio, under the emperor Septimius Severus, whom he accompanied to Britain. The emperor died at York A. D. 211, and is said to have commended his 2 sons Caracalla and Geta to the care of Papinian. On the death of his father, Caracalla dismissed Papinian from his office, and shortly afterwards put him to death. There are 595 excerpts from Papinian's works in the Digest. These excerpts are from the 37 books of Quaestiones, a work arranged according to the order of the Edict, the 19 books of Responsa, the 2 books of Definitiones,

the 2 books De Adulteriis, a single book De Adulteriis, and a Greek work or fragment, which probably treated of the office of Aedile both at Rome and in other towns. No Roman jurist had a higher reputation than Papinian. Nor is his reputation unmerited. It was not solely because of the high station that he filled, his penetration and his knowledge, that he left an imperishable name; his excellent understanding, guided by integrity of purpose, has made him the model of a true lawyer.

Pāpirius Statīus. [STATIUS.]

Pāpiria Gens, patrician and plebeian. The patrician Papirii were divided into the families of Crassus, Cursor, Maso, and Mugillanus; and the Plebeian Papirii into those of Carbo, Paetus, and Turdus. Of these the families of CARBO, CURSOR, MASO, and MUGILLANUS, alone require mention.

Papiriānae Fossae, a village in Etruria on the Via Aemilia, between Luna and Pisa.

Pāpirius, C. or Sex., the author of a supposed collection of the Leges Regiae, which was called Jus Papirianum, or Jus Civile Papirianum. He is said to have lived in the reign of Tarquinius Superbus.

Papius Mutīlus. [MUTILUS.]

Pappūa (Παππούα), a lofty rugged mountain on the extreme border of Numidia, perhaps the same as the Thammes of Ptolemy, and as the mountain abounding with wild cats, near the city of Melitene, to which Diodorus Siculus refers (xx. 58), but without mentioning its name.

Pappus (Πάππος), of Alexandria, one of the later Greek geometers, is said by Suidas to have lived under Theodosius (A. D. 379—395). Of the works of Pappus, the only one which has come down to us is his celebrated Mathematical Collections (Μαθηματικῶν συναγωγῶν βιβλία). This work, as we have it now in print, consists of the last 6 of 8 books. Only portions of these books have been published in Greek. There are 2 Latin editions of Pappus; the first, by Commandinus, Pisauri, 1588; and the second by Manolessius, Bononiae, 1660.

Paprēmis (Πάπρημις), a city of Lower Egypt, capital of the Nomos Papremites, and sacred to the Egyptian god whom the Greeks identified with Ares. It is only mentioned by Herodotus, and is perhaps the same as the Chois of later times.

Papus, Aemilīus. 1. M., dictator B. C. 321. — 2. Q., twice consul 282, and 278; and censor 275. In both his consulships and in his censorship he had as colleague C. Fabricius Luscinus. — 3. L., consul 225, defeated the Cisalpine Gauls with great slaughter. He was censor 220 with C. Flaminius.

Parachelōītis (Παραχελωῖτις), the name of the plain in Acarnania and Aetolia, near the mouth of the Achelous, and through which that river flows.

Parachoāthras (Παραχοάθρας, τὰ Παραχοάθρα : Mnts. of Louristan), a part of the chain of mountains forming the E. margin of the Tigris and Euphrates valley, was the boundary between Susiana and Media. The same name is given to an E. branch of the chain, which formed the boundary between Parthia and the desert of Carmania. Strabo places it too far N.

Paraetācēnē (Παραιτακηνή : Παραιτακαί, Παραιτακηνοί, Paraetīcae, Paraetacēni), the name of various mountainous regions in the Persian empire, is the Greek form of a Persian word, signifying mountainous. 1. The best known of those districts was on the borders of Media and Persia, and was inhabited by a people of Median origin, who are mentioned several times by the historians of Alexander and his successors. — 2. A district between the rivers Oxus and Jaxartes, on the borders of Bactria and Sogdiana. — 3. A district between Arachosia and Drangiana, also called Sacastana, from its inhabitants, the Scythian Sacae.

Paraetonium or Ammonia (Παραιτόνιον, ἡ 'Αμμωνία: El-Bareton or Marsa-Labeit), an important city on the N. coast of Africa, belonged to Marmarica in its widest sense, but politically to Egypt, namely to the Nomos Libya: hence this city on the W. and Pelusium on the E. are called "cornua Aegypti." It stood near the promontory Artos or Pythis (Ras-el-Hazeit); and was reckoned 200 Roman miles W. of Alexandria, between 70 and 80, or, according to Strabo, 900 stadia (all too small) E. of the Catabathmos Major, and 1300 stadia N. of Ammonium in the Desert (Siwah), which Alexander the Great visited by the way of Paraetonium. The city was 40 stadia in circuit. It was an important sea-port, a strong fortress, and a renowned seat of the worship of Isis. It was restored by Justinian, and continued a place of some consequence till its complete destruction by the late Pasha of Egypt, Mehemet Ali, in 1820.

Parāgon Sinus (Παραγων κόλπος: Gulf of Oman), a gulf of the Indicus Oceanus, on the coast of Gedrosia, namely, the gulf formed in the N. W. of the Indian Ocean by the approach of the N. E. coast of Arabia to that of Beloochistan and Persia, outside of the entrance to the Persian Gulf.

Parālia (Παραλία), the sea-coast district of Attica, around the promontory of Sunium, extending upwards as far as Halae Axonides on the W. coast and Prasiae on the E. coast. The inhabitants of this district, the Paralii (Παράλιοι), were one of the 3 political parties, into which Attica was divided at the time of Pisistratus, the other 2 being the Diacrii (Διάκριοι), or Highlanders, and the Pediasii (Πεδιάσιοι), or inhabitants of the plain.

Parālus (Πάραλος), the younger of the 2 legitimate sons of Pericles. He and his brother Xanthippus were educated by their father with the greatest care, but they both appear to have been of inferior capacity, which was anything but compensated by worth of character, though Paralus seems to have been a somewhat more hopeful youth than his brother. They both fell victims to the plague, B. c. 429.

Parapotāmii or Ia (Παραπόταμιοι, -αμία: Belissi), an ancient town in Phocis, situated on a steep hill, and on the left bank of the river Cephissus, from which it derives its name. It was near the frontiers of Boeotia, being only 40 stadia from Chaeronea and 60 stadia from Orchomenus. It is probably mentioned by Homer (Il. ii. 522). It was destroyed by Xerxes, but was rebuilt, and was destroyed a second time in the Sacred War.

Parasōpis (Παρασωπία), a district in the S. of Boeotia, on both banks of the Asopus, the inhabitants of which were called Parasōpii (Παρασώπιοι).

Parcae. [MOIRAE.]

Parentium (Parenzo), a town in Istria, with a good harbour, inhabited by Roman citizens, but not a Roman colony, 31 miles from Pola.

Pāris (Πάρις), also called Alexander ('Αλέξαν-

δρος), was the second son of Priam and Hecuba. Before his birth Hecuba dreamed that she had brought forth a firebrand, the flames of which spread over the whole city. Accordingly as soon as the child was born, he was given to a shepherd, who was to expose him on Mt. Ida. After the lapse of 5 days, the shepherd, on returning to Mt. Ida, found the child still alive, and fed by a she-bear. Thereupon he carried the boy home, and brought him up along with his own child, and called him Paris. When Paris had grown up, he distinguished himself as a valiant defender of the flocks and shepherds, and hence received the name of Alexander, i. e. the defender of men. He also succeeded in discovering his real origin, and was received by Priam as his son. He now married Oenone, the daughter of the river god Cebren, by whom, according to some, he became the father of Corythus. But the most celebrated event in the life of Paris was his abduction of Helen. This came to pass in the following way. Once upon a time, when Peleus and Thetis solemnized their nuptials, all the gods were invited to the marriage, with the exception of Eris, or Strife. Enraged at her exclusion, the goddess threw a golden apple among the guests, with the inscription, "to the fairest." Thereupon Hera, Aphrodite and Athena each claimed the apple for herself. Zeus ordered Hermes to take the goddesses to Mt. Gargarus, a portion of Ida, to the beautiful shepherd Paris, who was there tending his flocks, and who was to decide the dispute. The goddesses accordingly appeared before him. Hera promised him the sovereignty of Asia and great riches, Athena great glory and renown in war, and Aphrodite the fairest of women for his wife. Paris decided in favour of Aphrodite, and gave her the golden apple. This judgment called forth in Hera and Athena fierce hatred against Troy. Under the protection of Aphrodite, Paris now sailed to Greece, and was hospitably received in the palace of Menelaus at Sparta. Here he succeeded in carrying off Helen, the wife of Menelaus, who was the most beautiful woman in the world. — The accounts of this rape are not the same in all writers. According to the more usual account Helen followed her seducer willingly, owing to the influence of Aphrodite, while Menelaus was absent in Crete. Others relate that the goddess deceived Helen, by giving to Paris the appearance of Menelaus; and others again say that Helen was carried off by Paris by force, either during a festival or during the chase. — On his return to Troy, Paris passed through Egypt and Phoenicia, and at length arrived at Troy with Helen and the treasures which he had treacherously taken from the hospitable house of Menelaus. — In regard to this voyage the accounts again differ, for according to some Paris and Helen reached Troy 3 days after their departure; whereas, according to later traditions, Helen did not reach Troy at all, for Zeus and Hera allowed only a phantom resembling her to accompany Paris to Troy, while the real Helen was carried to Proteus in Egypt, and remained there until she was fetched by Menelaus. — The abduction of Helen gave rise to the Trojan war. Before her marriage with Menelaus, she had been wooed by the noblest chiefs in all parts of Greece. Her former suitors now resolved to revenge her abduction, and sailed against Troy. [AGAMEMNON.] Homer describes Paris as a handsome man, fond of the female sex and of music, and not ignorant of war, but as dilatory and cowardly, and detested by his own friends for having brought upon them the fatal war with the Greeks. He fought with Menelaus before the walls of Troy, and was defeated, but was carried off by Aphrodite. He is said to have killed Achilles, either by one of his arrows, or by treachery in the temple of the Thymbraean Apollo. [ACHILLES.] On the capture of Troy, Paris was wounded by Philoctetes with an arrow of Hercules, and then returned to his long abandoned wife Oenone. But she, remembering the wrongs she had suffered, or according to others being prevented by her father, refused to heal the wound. He then went back to Troy and died. Oenone quickly repented, and hastened after him with remedies, but came too late, and in her grief hung herself. According to others she threw herself from a tower, or rushed into the flames of the funeral pile on which the body of Paris was burning. Paris is represented in works of art as a beautiful youth, without a beard, with a Phrygian cap, and sometimes with an apple in his hand, which he presented to Aphrodite.

Păris, the name of two celebrated pantomimes. 1. The elder Paris lived in the reign of the emperor Nero, with whom he was a great favourite. He was originally a slave of Domitia, the aunt of the emperor, and he purchased his freedom by paying her a large sum of money. Paris was afterwards declared, by order of the emperor, to have been free-born (*ingenuus*), and Domitia was compelled to restore to him the sum which she had received for his freedom. When Nero attempted to become a pantomime, he put Paris to death as a dangerous rival. — 2. The younger Paris, and the more celebrated of the two, was a native of Egypt, and lived in the reign of Domitian, with whom he was also a great favourite. He was put to death by Domitian, because he had an intrigue with Domitia, the wife of the emperor.

Părisĭi. [LUTETIA PARISIORUM.]

Părĭum (τὸ Πάριον: Παριᾱνός, Παριηνός, Παριανεύς: *Kemer*, Ru.), a city of Mysia, on the N. coast of the Troad, on the Propontis, between Lampsacus and Priapus, was founded by a colony from Miletus, mingled with natives of Paros and Erythrae, and became a flourishing seaport, having a better harbour than that of Priapus. Under Augustus it was made a Roman colony, by the name of Colonia Pariana Julia Augusta. It was a renowned seat of the worship of Eros, Dionysus, and Apollo. The surrounding district was called ἡ Παριανή.

Parma (Parmensis: *Parma*), a town in Gallia Cispadana, situated on a river of the same name and on the Via Aemilia, between Placentia and Mutina, was originally a town of the Boii, but was made a Roman colony B.C. 183, along with Mutina, and from that time became a place of considerable importance. It suffered some injury in the civil war after Caesar's death, but was enlarged and embellished by Augustus, and received the name of Colonia Julia Augusta. After the fall of the Western Empire it was for a time called Chrysopolis, or the "Gold-City," but for what reason we do not know. The country around Parma was originally marshy; but the marshes were drained by the consul Scaurus, and converted into fertile land. The wool of Parma was particularly good.

Parmenĭdes (Παρμενίδης), a distinguished Greek philosopher, was a native of Elea in Italy. According to Plato, Parmenides, at the age of 65, came to Athens to the Panathenaea, accompanied by Zeno, then 40 years old, and became acquainted with Socrates, who at that time was quite young. Supposing Socrates to have been 19 or 20 years of age at the time, we may place the visit of Parmenides to Athens in B.C. 448, and consequently his birth in 513. Parmenides was regarded with great esteem by Plato and Aristotle; and his fellow-citizens thought so highly of him, that every year they bound their magistrates to render obedience to the laws which he had enacted for them. The philosophical opinions of Parmenides were developed in a didactic poem, in hexameter verse, entitled *On Nature*, of which only fragments remain. In this poem he maintained that the phaenomena of sense were delusive; and that it was only by mental abstraction that a person could attain to the knowledge of the only reality, a One and All, a continuous and self-existent substance, which could not be perceived by the senses. But although he believed the phaenomena of sense to be delusive, nevertheless he adopted 2 elements, Warm and Cold, or Light and Darkness. The best edition of the fragments of Parmenides is by Karsten, in *Philosophorum Graec. Veterum Oper. Reliquiae*, Amstelod. 1835.

Parmĕnĭon (Παρμενίων). 1. Son of Philotas, a distinguished Macedonian general in the service of Philip of Macedon and Alexander the Great. Philip held him in high esteem, and used to say of him, that he had never been able to find more than one general, and that was Parmenion. In Alexander's invasion of Asia, Parmenion was regarded as second in command. At the three great battles of the Granicus, Issus and Arbela, while the king commanded the right wing of the army, Parmenion was placed at the head of the left, and contributed essentially to the victory on all those memorable occasions. The confidence reposed in him by Alexander appears to have been unbounded, and he is continually spoken of as the most attached of the king's friends, and as holding, beyond all question, the second place in the state. But when Philotas, the only surviving son of Parmenion, was accused in Drangiana (B.C. 330) of being privy to the plot against the king's life, he not only confessed his own guilt, when put to the torture, but involved his father also in the plot. Whether the king really believed in the guilt of Parmenion, or deemed his life a necessary sacrifice to policy after the execution of his son, he caused his aged friend to be assassinated in Media before he could receive the tidings of his son's death. The death of Parmenion, at the age of 70 years, will ever remain one of the darkest stains upon the character of Alexander. It is questionable whether even Philotas was really concerned in the conspiracy, and we may safely pronounce that Parmenion had no connection with it. — 2. Of Macedonia, an epigrammatic poet, whose verses were included in the collection of Philip of Thessalonica; whence it is probable that he flourished in, or shortly before, the time of Augustus.

Parnassus (Παρνασσός, Παρνασός, Ion. Παρνησός), the name, in its widest signification, of a range of mountains, which extends from Oeta and Corax S. E. through Doris and Phocis, and under the name of Cirphis (Κίρφις) terminates at the Corinthian gulf between Cirrha and Anticyra.

But in its narrower sense, Parnassus indicates the highest part of the range a few miles N. of Delphi. Its 2 highest summits were called Tithorĕa (Τιθορέα: *Velitza*), and Lycorĕa (Λυκώρεια: *Liakura*), the former being N. W. and the latter N. E. of Delphi; and hence Parnassus is frequently described by the poets as double-headed. Immediately above Delphi the mountain forms a semi-circular range of lofty rocks, at the foot of which the town was built. These rocks were called *Phædriades* (Φαιδριάδες) or the " Resplendent," from their facing the S., and thus receiving the full rays of the sun during the most brilliant part of the day. The sides of Parnassus were well wooded ; at its foot grew myrtle, laurel and olive-trees, and higher up firs ; and its summit was covered with snow during the greater part of the year. It contained numerous caves, glens and romantic ravines. It is celebrated as one of the chief seats of Apollo and the Muses, and an inspiring source of poetry and song. On Mt. Lycorea was the Corycian cave, from which the Muses are sometimes called the Corycian nymphs. Just above Delphi was the far-famed Castalian spring, which issued from between 2 cliffs, called *Nauplia* and *Hyamplia*. These cliffs are frequently called by the poets the summits of Parnassus, though they are in reality only small peaks at the base of the mountain. The mountain also was sacred to Dionysus, and on one of its summits the Thyades held their Bacchic revels. Between Parnassus Proper and Mt. Cirphis was the valley of the Plistus, through which the sacred road ran from Delphi to Daulis and Stiris ; and at the point where the road branched off to these 2 places (called σχιστή), Oedipus slew his father Laius.— **2.** A town in the N. of Cappadocia, on a mountain of the same name (*Pascha Dagh*), probably on the river Halys, and on the road between Ancyra and Archelais.

Parnēs (Πάρνης, gen. Πάρνηθος: *Ozia* or *Nozia*), a mountain in the N. E. of Attica, in some parts as high as 4000 feet, was a continuation of Mt. Cithaeron, from which it extended E.-wards as far as the coast at Rhamnus. It was well wooded, abounded in game, and on its lower slopes produced excellent wine. It formed part of the boundary between Boeotia and Attica ; and the pass through it between these 2 countries was easy of access, and was therefore strongly fortified by the Athenians. On the summit of the mountain there was a statue of Zeus Parnethius, and there were likewise altars of Zeus Semaleos and Zeus Ombrius or Apemius.

Parnōn (Πάρνων: *Malevo*), a mountain 6335 feet high, forming the boundary between Laconia and the territory of Tegea in Arcadia.

Paropamisădae (Παροπαμισάδαι) or **Paropamisii**, the collective name of several peoples dwelling in the S. slopes of Mt. Paropamisus (see next article), and of the country they inhabited, which was not known by any other name. It was divided on the N. from Bactria by the Paropamisus ; on the W. from Aria, and o the S., from Drangiana and Arachosia, by indefinite boundaries ; and on the E. from India by the river Indus: thus corresponding to the E. part of *Afghanistan* and the strip of the *Punjab* W. of the Indus. Under the Persian empire it was the N.E.-most district of Ariana. It was conquered by Alexander, when he passed through it on his march to India ; but

the people soon regained their independence, though parts of the country were nominally included in the limits of the Greco-Syrian and Bactrian kingdoms. It is a rugged mountain region, intersected by branches of the Paropamisus. In the N. the climate is so severe that, according to the ancient writers, confirmed by modern travellers, the snow almost buries the houses ; but in the S. the valleys of the lower mountain slopes yield all the products of the warmer regions of Asia. In its N. was the considerable river Cophes or COPHEN (*Cabool*), flowing into the Indus, and having a tributary, Choäs, Choës, or CHOASPES (No. 2). The particular tribes, included under the general name of Paropamisadae, were the Cabolitae (Καβολῖται) in the N., whose name and position point to *Cabool*, the Parsii (Παρσιοί) in the S.W., the Ambautae (Ἀμβαῦται) in the E., on the river Choas, the Parsuëtae (Παρσυῆται) on the S., and the Ἀρισόφυλοι, probably a dominant tribe of a different race, on the W. At the time of the Macedonian conquest the people were little civilised, but quiet and inoffensive. The chief cities were Ortospana and Alexandria, the latter founded by Alexander the Great.

Paropamisus (Παροπάμισος, and several other forms, of which the truest is probably Παροπάνισος : *Hindoo-Koosh*), a word no doubt derived, as many other words beginning like it, from the Old Persian *puru, a mountain*, is the name of a part of the great mountain-chain which runs from W. to E. through the centre of the S. portion of the highlands of Central Asia, and divides the part of the continent, which slopes down to the Indian Ocean, from the great central table-land of *Tartary* and *Thibet*. It is a prolongation of the chain of Anti-Taurus. The name was applied to that part of the chain between the Sariphi M. (*M. of Kohistan*) on the W. and M. Imaus (*Himalaya*) on the E., or from about the sources of the river Margus on the W. to the point where the Indus breaks through the chain on the E. They were believed by the ancients to be among the highest mountains in the world (which they are), and to contain the sources of the Oxus and the Indus ; the last statement being an error which naturally arose from confounding the cleft by which the Indus breaks through the chain with its unknown source. When Alexander the Great crossed these mountains, his followers — regarding the achievement as equivalent to what a Greek considered as the highest geographical adventure, namely the passage of the Caucasus — conferred this glory on their chief by simply applying the name of Caucasus to the mountain chain which he had thus passed ; and then, for the sake of distinction, this chain was called Caucasus Indicus, and this name has come down to our times in the native form of *Hindoo-Koosh*, and in others also. The name Paropamisus is also applied sometimes to the great S. branch of this chain (*Soliman M.*) which skirts the valley of the Indus on the W., and which is more specifically called PARYETI or PARSYETAE.

Parŏpus (Paropinus), a small town in the interior of Sicily, N. of the Nebrodes Montes.

Parŏrĕa (Παρώρεια). **1.** A town in Thrace on the frontiers of Macedonia, whose inhabitants were the same people as the Paroraei of Pliny.— **2.** Or **Parŏrĭa** (Παρωρία), a town in the S. of Arcadia, N. of Megalopolis, said to have been founded by Paroreus, son of Tricolonus, and a grandson of Lycaon, the inhabitants of which took part in the building of Megalopolis.

Parŏrĕātae (Παρωρεᾶται), the most ancient inhabitants of the mountains in Triphylia in Elis, who were expelled by the Minyae.

Parorios. [PHRYGIA.]

Păros (Πάρος: Πάριος: Paro), an island in the Aegean sea, one of the larger of the Cyclades, was situated S. of Delos and W. of Naxos, being separated from the latter by a channel 5 or 6 miles wide. It is about 36 miles in circumference. It is said to have been originally colonized by Cretans, but was afterwards inhabited by Ionians, and became so prosperous, even at an early period, as to send out colonies to Thasos and to Parium on the Propontis. In the first invasion of Greece by the generals of Darius, Paros submitted to the Persians; and after the battle of Marathon, Miltiades attempted to reduce the island, but failed in his attempt, and received a wound, of which he died. [MILTIADES.] After the defeat of Xerxes, Paros came under the supremacy of Athens and shared the fate of the other Cyclades. Its name rarely occurs in subsequent history. The most celebrated production of Paros was its marble, which was extensively used by the ancient sculptors. It was chiefly obtained from a mountain called *Marpessa.* The Parian figs were also highly prized. The chief town of Paros was situated on the W. coast, and bore the same name as the island. The ruins of it are still to be seen at the modern *Paroikia.* Paros was the birthplace of the poet Archilochus. — In Paros was discovered the celebrated inscription called the *Parian Chronicle,* which is now preserved at Oxford. The inscription is cut on a block of marble, and in its perfect state contained a chronological account of the principal events in Greek history from Cecrops, B. C. 1582 to the archonship of Diognetus, 264.

Parrhăsĭa (Παῤῥασία: Παῤῥάσιοι), a district in the S. of Arcadia, to which, according to Pausanias, the towns Lycosura, Thocnia, Trapezus, Proseis, Acacesium, Acontium, Macaria, and Dasea belonged. The Parrhasii are said to have been one of the most ancient of the Arcadian tribes. At the time of the Peloponnesian war they were under the supremacy of Mantinea, but were rendered independent of that city by the Lacedaemonians. Homer (*Il.* ii. 608) mentions a town Parrhasia, said to have been founded by Parrhasus, son of Lycaon, or by Pelasgus, son of Arestor. — The adjective *Parrhasius* is frequently used by the poets as equivalent to Arcadian.

Parrhăsĭus (Παῤῥάσιος), one of the most celebrated Greek painters, was a native of Ephesus, the son and pupil of Evenor. He practised his art chiefly at Athens: and by some writers he is called an Athenian, probably because the Athenians had bestowed upon him the right of citizenship. He flourished about B. c. 400. Parrhasius did for painting, at least in pictures of gods and heroes, what had been done for sculpture by Phidias in divine subjects, and by Polycletus in the human figure: he established a canon of proportion, which was followed by all the artists that came after him. Several interesting observations on the principles of art which he followed are made in a dialogue with Socrates, as reported by Xenophon (*Mem.* iii. 10). The character of Parrhasius was marked in the highest degree by that arrogance which often accompanies the consciousness of pre-

eminent ability. In epigrams inscribed on his works he not only made a boast of his luxurious habits, but he also claimed the honour of having assigned with his own hand the precise limits of the art, and fixed a boundary which never was to be transgressed. Respecting the story of his contest with Zeuxis, see ZEUXIS. Of the works of Parrhasius, the most celebrated seems to have been his picture of the Athenian People.

Parsii. [PAROPAMISADAE.]

Parsĭci Montes (τὰ Παρσικὰ ὄρη, *Bushkurd M.* in the W. of *Beloochistan*), a chain of mountains running N.E. from the Paragon Sinus (*G. of Oman*) and forming the boundary between Carmania and Gedrosia. At the foot of these mountains, in the W. of Gedrosia, were a people called **Parsidae,** with a capital **Parsis** (perhaps *Serbah*).

Parsyĕtae (Παρσυῆται), a people on the borders of Arachosia and the Paropamisadae, with a mountain of the same name, which is probably identical with the PARUETI M. and with the *Soliman* mountains.

Parthălis, the chief city of the Calingae, a tribe of the Gangaridae, in India intra Gangem, at the head of the Sinus Gangeticus (*Sea of Bengal*).

Partheni. [PARTHINI.]

Parthĕnĭas (Παρθενίας), also called **Parthĕnĭa,** a small river in Elis, which flows into the Alpheus E. of Olympia not far from Harpinna.

Parthĕnĭum (Παρθένιον). 1. A town in Mysia, S. of Pergamum. — 2. (*Felenk-burun*), a promontory in the Chersonesus Taurica, on which stood a temple of the Tauric Artemis, from whom it derived its name. It was in this temple that human sacrifices were offered to the goddess.

Parthĕnĭum Mare (τὸ Παρθενικὸν πέλαγος), the S.E. part of the Mediterranean, between Egypt and Cyprus.

Parthĕnĭus (Παρθένιος), of Nicaea, or according to others, of Myrlea, a celebrated grammarian, is said by Suidas to have been taken prisoner by Cinna, in the Mithridatic war, to have been manumitted on account of his learning, and to have lived to the reign of Tiberius. If this statement is true, Parthenius must have attained a great age, since there were 77 years from the death of Mithridates to the accession of Tiberius. Parthenius taught Virgil Greek; and he seems to have been very popular among the distinguished Romans of his time. The emperor Tiberius imitated his poems, and placed his works and statues in the public libraries, along with the most celebrated ancient writers. Parthenius wrote many poems, but the only one of his works which has come down to us is in prose, and entitled Περὶ ἐρωτικῶν παθημάτων. It contains 36 brief love-stories, which ended in an unfortunate manner. It is dedicated to Cornelius Gallus, and was compiled for his use, that he might avail himself of the materials in the composition of epic and elegiac poems. The best edition is by Westermann, in the *Mythographi,* Brunswick, 1843.

Parthĕnĭus (Παρθένιος). 1. A mountain on the frontiers of Argolis and Arcadia, through which was an important pass leading from Argolis to Tegea. This pass is still called *Partheni,* but the mountain itself, which rises to the height of 3993 feet, bears the name of *Roino.* It was on this mountain that Telephus, the son of Hercules and Auge, was said to have been suckled by a hind; and it was here also that the god Pan is said to have appeared to Phidippides, the Athenian courier, shortly before the battle of Marathon.—2. (also Παρθένης : *Chati-Su* or *Bartun-Su*), the chief river of Paphlagonia, rises in Mt. Olgassys, and flows N.W. into the Euxine 90 stadia W. of Amastris, forming in the lower part of its course the boundary between Bithynia and Paphlagonia.

Parthĕnŏn (ὁ Παρθενών, i. e. *the virgin's chamber*), was the usual name of one of the finest and, in its influence upon art, one of the most important edifices ever built, the temple of Athena Parthenos on the Acropolis of Athens. It was also called **Hecatompĕdon** (Ἑκατόμπεδον) or **Hecatompĕdos** (Ἑκατόμπεδος, sc. νεώς) from its being 100 feet in one of its chief dimensions, probably in the breadth of the top step on which the front pillars stand. It was erected, under the administration of Pericles, on the site of the older temple of Athena, burnt during the Persian invasion, and was completed by the dedication of the statue of the goddess, B.C. 438. Its architects were Ictinus and Callicrates, but all the works were under the superintendence of Phidias. It was built entirely of Pentelic marble : its dimensions were, 227 English feet long, 101 broad, and 65 high : it was 50 feet longer than the edifice which preceded it. Its architecture was of the Doric order, and of the purest kind. It consisted of an oblong central building (the *cella* or νεώς), surrounded on all sides by a peristyle of pillars, 46 in number, 8 at each end and 17 at each side (reckoning the corner pillars twice), elevated on a platform, which was ascended by 3 steps all round the building. Within the porticoes at each end was another row of 6 pillars, standing on a level with the floor of the *cella*, and 2 steps higher than that of the peristyle. The cella was divided into 2 chambers of unequal size, the *prodomus* or *pronaos* (πρόδομος, πρόναος), and the *opisthodomus* (ὀπισθόδομος) or *posticum ;* the former, which was the larger, contained the statue of the goddess, and was the true sanctuary, the latter being probably used as a treasury and vestry. Both these chambers had inner rows of pillars (in 2 stories, one over the other), 16 in the former and 4 in the latter, supporting the partial roof, for the large chamber, at least, had its centre open to the sky. Technically, the temple is called *peripteral octastyle hypaethral.* It was adorned, within and without, with colours and gilding, and with sculptures which are regarded as the masterpieces of ancient art. The colossal chryselephantine (ivory and gold) statue of Athena, which stood at the end of the *prodomus,* opposite to the entrance, was the work of Phidias himself, and surpassed every other statue in the ancient world, except that of Zeus at Olympia by the same artist. The other sculptures were executed under the direction of Phidias by different artists, as may still be seen by differences in their style ; but the most important of them were doubtless from the hand of Phidias himself. (1.) *The tympana of the pediments* (i. e. the inner flat portion of the triangular gable-ends of the roof above the 2 end porticoes), were filled with groups of detached colossal statues, those of the E. or principal front representing the birth of Athena, and those of the W. front the contest between Athena and Poseidon for the land of Attica. (2.) In the *frieze of the entablature* (i. e. the upper of the 2 portions into which the surface between the columns and the roof is divided), the *metopes between the triglyphs* (i. e.

the square spaces between the projections answering to the ends of beams if the roof had been of wood) were filled with sculptures in high relief, 92 in all, 14 on each front, and 32 on each side, representing subjects from the Attic mythology, among which the battle of the Athenians with the Centaurs forms the subject of the 15 metopes from the S. side, which are now in the British Museum. (3.) Along the top of the external wall of the *cella,* under the ceiling of the peristyle, ran a frieze sculptured with a representation of the Panathenaic procession, in very low relief. A large number of the slabs of this frieze were brought to England by Lord Elgin, with the 15 metopes just mentioned, and a considerable number of other fragments, including some of the most important, though mutilated, statues from the pediments ; and the whole collection was purchased by the nation in 1816, and deposited in the British Museum, where may also be seen excellent models of the ruins of the Parthenon and of the temple as conjecturally restored. The worst of the injuries which it has suffered from war and pillage was inflicted in the siege of Athens by the Venetians in 1687, when a bomb exploded in the very centre of the Parthenon, and threw down much of both the side walls. Its ruins are still, however, in sufficient preservation to give a good idea of the construction of all its principal parts.

Parthĕnŏpaeus (Παρθενοπαῖος), one of the 7 heroes who accompanied Adrastus in his expedition against Thebes. He is sometimes called a son of Ares or Milanion and Atalanta, sometimes of Meleager and Atalanta, and sometimes of Talaus and Lysimache. His son, by the nymph Clymene, who marched against Thebes as one of the Epigoni, is called Promachus, Stratolaus, Thesimenes, or Tlesimenes. Parthenopaeus was killed at Thebes by Asphodicus, Amphidicus or Periclymenus.

Parthĕnŏpŏlis (Παρθενόπολις), a town in Moesia Inferior near the Pontus Euxinus, and between Calatis and Tomi.

Parthĭa, Parthÿaea, Parthiĕnĕ (Παρθία, Παρθυαία, Παρθυηνή : Πάρθοι, Παρθυαῖοι, Parthi, Parthieni : *Khorassan*), a country of Asia, to the S.E. of the Caspian. Its extent was different at different times ; but, as the term was generally understood by the ancient geographers, it denoted the partly mountainous and partly desert country on the S. of the mountains which hem in the Caspian on the S.E. (M. Labuta), and which divided Parthia on the N. from Hyrcania. On the N.E. and E., a branch of the same chain, called Masdoranus, divided it from Aria ; on the S. the deserts of Parthia joined those of Carmania, and further W.-ward the M. Parachoathras divided Parthia from Persis and Susiana : on the W. and N.W. it was divided from Media by boundaries which cannot be exactly marked out. Of this district, only the N. part, in and below the mountains of Hyrcania, seems to have formed the proper country of the Parthi, who were a people of Scythian origin. The ancient writers tell us that the name means *exiles ;* but this is uncertain. They were a very warlike people, and were especially celebrated as horse-archers. Their tactics, of which the Romans had fatal experience in their first wars with them, became so celebrated as to pass into a proverb. Their mail-clad horsemen spread like a cloud round the hostile army, and poured in a shower of darts; and then evaded any closer conflict by a rapid flight, during which they still shot their arrow backwards upon the enemy. Under the Persian empire, the Parthians, with the Chorasmii, Sogdii, and Arii, formed the 16th satrapy: under Alexander and the Greek kings of Syria, Parthia and Hyrcania together formed a satrapy. About B.C. 250 they revolted from the Seleucidae, under a chieftain named Arsaces, who founded an independent monarchy, the history of which is given under ARSACES. During the period of the downfall of the Syrian kingdom, the Parthians overran the provinces E. of the Euphrates, and about B.C. 130 they overthrew the kingdom of Bactria, so that their empire extended over Asia from the Euphrates to the Indus, and from the Indian Ocean to the Paropamisus, or even to the Oxus; but on this N. frontier they had to maintain a continual conflict with the nomad tribes of Central Asia. On the W. their progress was checked by Mithridates and Tigranes, till those kings fell successively before the Romans, who were thus brought into collision with the Parthians. After the memorable destruction of Crassus and his army, B.C. 53 [CRASSUS], the Parthians threatened Syria and Asia Minor; but their progress was stopped by 2 signal defeats, which they suffered from Antony's legate Ventidius, in 39 and 38. The preparations for renewing the war with Rome were rendered fruitless by the contest for the Parthian throne between Phraates IV. and Tiridates, which led to an appeal to Augustus, and to the restoration of the standards of Crassus, B.C. 20; an event to which the Roman poets often allude in terms of flattery to Augustus, almost as if he had conquered the Parthian empire. It is to be observed that the poets of the Augustan age use the names Parthi, Persae, and Medi indifferently. The Parthian empire had now begun to decline, owing to civil contests and the defection of the governors of provinces, and had ceased to be formidable to the Romans. There were, however, continual disputes between the 2 empires for the protectorate of the kingdom of Armenia. In consequence of one of these disputes Trajan invaded the Parthian empire, and obtained possession for a short time of Mesopotamia; but his conquests were surrendered under Hadrian, and the Euphrates again became the boundary of the 2 empires. There were other wars at later periods, which resulted in favour of the Romans, who took Seleucia and Ctesiphon, and made the district of Osroëne a Roman province. The exhaustion which was the effect of these wars at length gave the Persians the opportunity of throwing off the Parthian yoke. Led by Artaxerxes (Ardshir) they put an end to the Parthian kingdom of the Arsacidae, after it had lasted 476 years, and established the Persian dynasty of the Sassanidae, A.D. 226. [ARSACES: SASSANIDAE.]

Parthíni or Parthêni (Παρθινοί, Παρθηνοί), an Illyrian people in the neighbourhood of Dyrrhachium.

Parthiscus or Parthissus, a river in Dacia, probably the same as the Tibiscus. [TIBISCUS.]

Paryadres (Παρυάδρης: Kara-bel Dagh, or Kut-Tagh), a mountain chain of W. Asia, running S.W. and N.E. from the E. of Asia Minor into the centre of Armenia, and forming the chief connecting link between the Taurus and the mountains of Armenia. It was considered as the boundary between Cappadocia (i. e. Pontus Cappadocius) and Armenia (i. e. Armenia Minor). In a wide sense the name seems sometimes to extend so far N.E as to include M. Abus (Ararat) in Armenia.

Paryêti Montes (τὰ Παρυητῶν ὄρη, from the Indian word paruta, i. e. a mountain: Soliman M.), the great mountain chain which runs N. and S. on the W. side of the valley of the Indus, and forms the connecting link between the mountains which skirt the N. coast of the Persian Gulf and the Indian Ocean, and the parallel chain, further N., called the Paropamisus or Indian Caucasus; or, between the E. extensions of the Taurus and Anti-Taurus systems, in the widest sense. This chain formed the boundary between Arachosia and the Paropamisadae: it now divides Beloochistan and Afghanistan on the W. from Scinde and the Punjab on the E., and it meets the Hindoo-Koosh in the N.E. corner of Afghanistan, between Cabool and Peshawur. Its ancient inhabitants were called Paryêtae (Παρυῆται); and the name Paruta is found in old Persian inscriptions and in the Zend-avesta (the old Persian sacred book), as that of a people.

Parysatis (Παρύσατις or Παρυσάτις), daughter of Artaxerxes I. Longimanus, king of Persia, was given by her father in marriage to her own brother Darius, surnamed Ochus, who in B.C. 424 succeeded Xerxes II. on the throne of Persia. The feeble character of Darius threw the chief power into the hands of Parysatis; whose administration was little else than a series of murders. Four of her sons grew up to manhood. The eldest of these, Artaxerxes Mnemon, was born before Darius had obtained the sovereign power, and on this pretext Parysatis sought to set aside his claims to the throne in favour of her second son Cyrus. Failing in this attempt, she nevertheless interposed after the death of Darius, 405, to prevent Artaxerxes from putting Cyrus to death; and prevailed with the king to allow him to return to his satrapy in Asia Minor. After the death of Cyrus at the battle of Cunaxa (401), she did not hesitate to display her grief for the death of her favourite son, by bestowing funeral honours on his mutilated remains; and she subsequently succeeded in getting into her power all the authors of the death of Cyrus, whom she put to death by the most cruel tortures. She afterwards poisoned Statira, the wife of Artaxerxes. The feeble and indolent king was content to banish her to Babylon; and it was not long before he recalled her to his court, where she soon recovered all her former influence. Of this she availed herself to turn his suspicions against Tissaphernes, whom she had long hated as having been the first to discover the designs of Cyrus to his brother, and who was now put to death by Artaxerxes at her instigation, 396. She appears to have died soon afterwards.

Pasargāda or -ae (Πασαργάδα, Πασαργάδαι), the older of the 2 capitals of Persis (the other and later being Persepolis), is said to have been founded by Cyrus the Great, on the spot where he gained his great victory over Astyages. The tomb of Cyrus stood here in the midst of a beautiful park. The exact site is doubtful. Strabo describes it as lying in the hollow part of Persis, on the river Cyrus, S.E. of Persepolis, and near the borders of Carmania. Most modern geographers identify it with Murghab, N.E. of Persepolis, where there are the remains of a great sepulchral monument of the

Persephone (Proserpine) enthroned.   (Gerhard, Archäolog. Zeit., tav. 11.)   Page 545.

Penelope.
(British Museum.)   Page 539.

Perseus and Medusa.
(From a Terra-cotta in the British Museum.)   Page 546.

Phaethon.   (Zannoni, Gal. di Firenze, serie 4, vol, 2.)   Page 551.

[To face p. 538.

Pausanias, King of Macedonia, B.C. 394. Page 533, No. 3.

Perdiccas III., King of Macedonia, B.C. 364—359. Page 541.

Perseus, King of Macedonia, B.C. 178—168. Page 547.

Pertinax, Roman Emperor, A.D. 193. Page 549.

Philetaerus, founder of the kingdom of Pergamus, ob. B.C. 263. Page 558.

Philippus II., King of Macedonia, B.C. 359—336. Page 559.

To face p. 579.

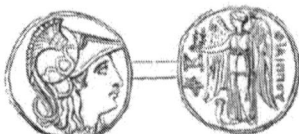

Philippus III. Arrhidaeus, King of Macedonia, ob. B.C. 317. Pages 561 and 84.

Philippus V., King of Macedonia, B.C. 220—178. Page 561.

M. Julius Philippus I., Roman Emperor, A.D. 244—249. Page 562.

M. Julius Philippus II., Roman Emperor, ob. A.D. 249. Page 562.

Phintias, Tyrant of Agrigentum, B.C. 289. Page 567.

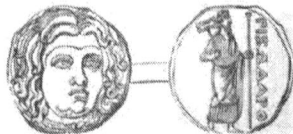

Pixodarus, Prince of Caria, B.C. 340—335. Page 564.

ancient **Persians.** Others place it at *Farsa* or at *Darab-ghord*, both S.E. of Persepolis, but not answering Strabo's description in other respects so well as *Murghab.* Others identify it with Persepolis; which is almost certainly an error

Pasargădae (Πασαργάδαι), the most noble of the 3 chief tribes of the ancient Persians, the other 2 being the Maraphii and Maspii. The royal house of the Achaemenidae were of the race of the Pasargadae. They had their residence chiefly in and about the city of PASARGADA.

Pasĭas, a Greek painter, belonged to the Sicyonian school, and flourished about B. C. 220.

Pasĭon (Πασίων), a wealthy banker at Athens, was originally a slave of Antisthenes and Archestratus, who were also bankers. In their service he displayed great fidelity as well as aptitude for business, and was manumitted as a reward. He afterwards set up a banking concern on his own account, by which, together with a shield manufactory, he greatly enriched himself, while he continued all along to preserve his old character for integrity, and his credit stood high throughout Greece. He did not however escape an accusation of fraudulently keeping back some money which had been entrusted to him by a foreigner from the Euxine. The plaintiff's case is stated in an oration of Isocrates (τραπεζιτικός), still extant. Pasion did good service to Athens with his money on several occasions. He was rewarded with the freedom of the city, and was enrolled in the demus of Acharnae. He died at Athens in B. C. 370, after a lingering illness, accompanied with failure of sight. Towards the end of his life his affairs were administered to a great extent by his freedman Phormion, to whom he let his banking shop and shield manufactory, and settled in his will that he should marry his widow Archippe, with a handsome dowry, and undertake the guardianship of his younger son Pasicles. His elder son, Apollodorus, grievously diminished his patrimony by extravagance and law-suits.

Pāsĭphăĕ (Πασιφάη), daughter of Helios (the Sun) and Perseis, and a sister of Circe and Aeetes, was the wife of Minos, by whom she became the mother of Androgeos, Catreus, Deucalion, Glaucus, Acalle, Xenodice, Ariadne, and Phaedra. Hence Phaedra is called *Pasiphaëia* (Ov. Met. xv. 500.) Respecting the passion of Pasiphaë for the beautiful bull, and the birth of the Minotaurus, see p. 450, a.

Pasĭtĕles (Πασιτέλης). 1. A statuary, who flourished about B. C. 468, and was the teacher of Colotes, the contemporary of Phidias. — 2. A statuary, sculptor, and silver-chaser, of the highest distinction, was a native of Magna Graecia, and obtained the Roman franchise with his countrymen in B. C. 90. He flourished at Rome from about 60 to 30. Pasiteles also wrote a treatise in 5 books upon celebrated works of sculpture and chasing.

Pasĭthĕa (Πασιθέα). 1. One of the Charites, or Graces, also called Aglaia. — 2. One of the Nereids.

Pasitigris (Πασιτίγρης or Πασιτίγρις: prob. *Karoon*), a considerable river of Asia, rising in the mountains E. of Mesobatene, on the confines of Media and Persia, and flowing first W. by N. to M. Zagros or Parachoathras, then, breaking through this chain, it turns to the S., and flows through Susiana into the head of the Persian Gulf, after receiving the Eulaeus on its W. side. Some geo-

graphers make the Pasitigris a tributary of the Tigris.

Passărŏn (Πασσάρων: near *Dhramisius* S.W. of *Joannina*), a town of Epirus in Molossia, and the ancient capital of the Molossian kings. It was destroyed by the Romans, together with 70 other towns of Epirus, after the conquest of Macedonia, B. C. 168.

Passĭēnus Crispus. [CRISPUS.]

Passĭēnus Paulus. [PAULUS.]

Pataeci (Πάταικοι), Phoenician divinities whose dwarfish figures were attached to Phoenician ships.

Pătăla, Patalēne. [PATTALA, PATTALENE.]

Patăra (τὰ Πάταρα: Παταρεύς: *Patara*, Ru.), one of the chief cities of Lycia, was a flourishing sea-port, on a promontory of the same name (ἡ Παταρῶν ἄκρα), 60 stadia (6 geog. miles) E. of the mouth of the Xanthus. It was early colonised by Dorians from Crete, and became a chief seat of the worship of Apollo, who had here a very celebrated oracle, which uttered responses in the winter only, and from whose son Patarus the name of the city was mythically derived. It was restored and enlarged by Ptolemy Philadelphus, who called it Arsinoë, but it remained better known by its old name.

Pătăvĭum (Patavīnus: *Padova* or *Padua*), an ancient town of the Veneti in the N. of Italy, on the Medoacus Minor, and on the road from Mutina to Altinum, was said to have been founded by the Trojan Antenor. It became a flourishing and important town in early times, and was powerful enough in B. C. 302 to drive back the Spartan king Cleomenes with great loss, when he attempted to plunder the surrounding country. Under the Romans Patavium was the most important city in the N. of Italy, and, by its commerce and manufactures (of which its woollen stuffs were the most celebrated), it attained great opulence. According to Strabo it possessed 500 citizens, whose fortune entitled them to the equestrian rank. It was plundered by Attila; and, in consequence of a revolt of its citizens, it was subsequently destroyed by Agilolf, king of the Langobards, and razed to the ground; hence the modern town contains few remains of antiquity. — Patavium is celebrated as the birth-place of the historian Livy. — In its neighbourhood were the *Aquae Patavinae*, also called *Aponi Fons*, respecting which, see p. 65, b.

Patercŭlus, C. Velleius, a Roman historian, was probably born about B. C. 19, and was descended from a distinguished Campanian family. He adopted the profession of arms; and, soon after he had entered the army, he accompanied C. Caesar in his expedition to the East, and was present with the latter at his interview with the Parthian king, in A. D. 2. Two years afterwards, A. D. 4, he served under Tiberius in Germany, succeeding his father in the rank of Praefectus Equitum, having previously filled in succession the offices of tribune of the soldiers and tribune of the camp. For the next 8 years Paterculus served under Tiberius, either as praefectus or legatus, in the various campaigns of the latter in Germany, Pannonia, and Dalmatia, and, by his activity and ability, gained the favour of the future emperor. He was quaestor A. D. 7, but he continued to serve as legatus under Tiberius. He accompanied his commander on his return to Rome in 12, and took a prominent part in the triumphal procession of Tiberius, along with

M M

his brother Magius Celer. The 2 brothers were praetors in 15. Paterculus was alive in 30, as he drew up his history in that year for the use of M. Vinicius, who was then consul; and it is conjectured, with much probability, that he perished in the following year (31), along with the other friends of Sejanus. The favourable manner in which he had so recently spoken in his history of this powerful minister would be sufficient to ensure his condemnation on the fall of the latter. The work of Paterculus, which has come down to us, is a brief historical compendium in two books, and bears the title *C. Velleii Paterculi Historiae Romanae ad M. Vinicium Cos. Libri II.* The beginning of the work is wanting, and there is also a portion lost after the 8th chapter of the first book. The object of this compendium was to give a brief view of universal history, but more especially of the events connected with Rome, the history of which occupies the main portion of the book. It commenced apparently with the destruction of Troy, and ended with the year 30. In the execution of his work, Velleius has shown great skill and judgment. He does not attempt to give a consecutive account of all the events of history; he seizes only upon a few of the more prominent facts, which he describes at sufficient length to leave them impressed upon the recollection of his hearers. His style, which is a close imitation of Sallust's, is characterised by clearness, conciseness, and energy. In his estimate of the characters of the leading actors in Roman history he generally exhibits both discrimination and judgment; but he lavishes the most indiscriminate praises, as might have been expected, upon his patron Tiberius. Only one manuscript of Paterculus has come down to us; and as this manuscript abounds with errors, the text is in a very corrupt state. The best editions are by Ruhnken, Lugd. Bat. 1789; by Orelli, Lips. 1835; and by Bothe, Turici, 1837.

Paternus, Tarruntēnus, a jurist, is probably the same person who was praefectus praetorio under Commodus, and was put to death by the emperor on a charge of treason. He was the author of a work in 4 books, entitled *De Re Militari* or *Militarium*, from which there are two excerpts in the Digest.

Patmos (Πάτμος: *Patmo*), one of the islands called Sporades, in the Icarian Sea, at about equal distances S. of Samos, and W. of the Prom. Posidium on the coast of Caria, celebrated as the place to which the Apostle John was banished, and in which he wrote the Apocalypse. The natives still affect to show the cave where St. John saw the apocalyptic visions (τὸ σπήλαιον τῆς ἀποκαλύψεως). On the E. side of the island was a city with a harbour.

Patrae (Πάτραι, Πατρέες Herod.: Πατρεύς: *Patras*), one of the 12 cities of Achaia, was situated W. of Rhium, near the opening of the Corinthian gulf. It is said to have been originally called Aroe ('Αρόη), and to have been founded by the autochthon Eumelus; and after the expulsion of the Ionians to have been taken possession of by Patreus, from whom it derived its name. The town is rarely mentioned in early Greek history, and was chiefly of importance as the place from which the Peloponnesians directed their attacks against the opposite coast of Aetolia. Patrae was one of the 4 towns which took the leading part in

founding the 2nd Achaean league. In consequence of assisting the Aetolians against the Gauls in B.C. 279, Patrae became so weakened that most of the inhabitants deserted the town and took up their abodes in the neighbouring villages. Under the Romans it continued to be an insignificant place till the time of Augustus, who rebuilt the town after the battle of Actium, again collected its inhabitants, and added to them those of Rhypae. Augustus further gave Patrae dominion over the neighbouring towns, and even over Locris, and also bestowed upon it the privileges of a Roman colony: hence we find it called on coins *Colonia Augusta Aroe Patrensis.* Strabo describes Patrae in his time as a flourishing and populous town with a good harbour; and it was frequently the place at which persons landed sailing from Italy to Greece. The modern *Patras* is still an important place, but contains few remains of antiquity.

Patrocles (Πατροκλῆς), a Macedonian general in the service of Seleucus I. and Antiochus I., kings of Syria. Patrocles held, both under Seleucus and Antiochus, an important government over some of the E. provinces of the Syrian empire. During the period of his holding this position, he collected accurate geographical information, which he afterwards published to the world; but though he is frequently cited by Strabo, who placed the utmost reliance on his accuracy, neither the title nor exact subject of his work is mentioned. It seems clear, however, that it included a general account of India, as well as of the countries on the banks of the Oxus and the Caspian Sea. Patrocles regarded the Caspian Sea as a gulf or inlet of the ocean, and maintained the possibility of sailing thither by sea from the Indian Ocean.

Patrocli Insŭla (Πατρόκλου νῆσος: *Gadaronesi* or *Gaidronisi*), a small island off the S.W. coast of Attica, near Sunium.

Patroclus (Πάτροκλος or Πατροκλῆς), the celebrated friend of Achilles, was son of Menoetius of Opus, and grandson of Actor and Aegina, whence he is called *Actorides*. His mother is commonly called Sthenele, but some mention her under the name of Periapis or Polymele. Aeacus, the grandfather of Achilles, was a brother of Menoetius, so that Achilles and Patroclus were kinsmen as well as friends. While still a boy Patroclus involuntarily slew Clysonymus, son of Amphidamas. In consequence of this accident he was taken by his father to Peleus at Phthia, where he was educated together with Achilles. He is said to have taken part in the expedition against Troy on account of his attachment to Achilles. He fought bravely against the Trojans, until his friend withdrew from the scene of action, when Patroclus followed his example. But when the Greeks were hard pressed, he begged Achilles to allow him to put on his armour, and with his men to hasten to the assistance of the Greeks. Achilles granted the request, and Patroclus succeeded in driving back the Trojans and extinguishing the fire which was raging among the ships. He slew many enemies, and thrice made an assault upon the walls of Troy; but on a sudden he was struck by Apollo, and became senseless. In this state Euphorbus ran him through with his lance from behind, and Hector gave him the last and fatal blow. Hector also took possession of his armour. A long struggle now ensued between the Greeks and Trojans for the body of Patroclus ; but the former obtained possession of it, and brought it to Achilles, who was deeply grieved, and vowed to avenge the death of his friend. Thetis protected the body with ambrosia against decomposition, until Achilles had leisure solemnly to burn it with funeral sacrifices. His ashes were collected in a golden urn which Dionysus had once given to Thetis, and were deposited under a mound, where the remains of Achilles were subsequently buried. Funeral games were celebrated in his honour. Achilles and Patroclus met again in the lower world ; or, according to others, they continued after their death to live together in the island of Leuce.

Patron, an Epicurean philosopher, lived for some time in Rome, where he became acquainted with Cicero and others. From Rome he removed to Athens, and there succeeded Phaedrus as president of the Epicurean school, B. C. 52.

Pattăla. [PATTALENE.]

Pattălêne or Patalêne (Παττάληνή, Παταληνή: *Lower Scinde*), the name of the great delta formed by the 2 principal arms by which the Indus falls into the sea. At the apex of the delta stood the city Pattăla or Patăla (prob. *Hyderabad*). The name is probably a native Indian word, namely the Sanscrit *patăla*, which means *the W. country*, and is applied to the W. part of N. India about the Indus, in contradistinction to the E. part about the Ganges.

Patulcĭus, a surname of Janus. [JANUS.]

Patūmus (Πάτουμος : O. T. Pithom : prob. near *Habascyh*, or *Belbeïs*), an Egyptian city in the Arabian Desert, on the E. margin of the Delta, near Bubastis, and near the commencement of Necho's canal from the Nile to the Red Sea ; built by the Israelites during their captivity (Exod. i. 11).

Paulîna or Paullîna. 1. Lollia. [LOLLIA.] — 2. Pompeia, wife of Seneca the philosopher, and probably the daughter of Pompeius Paulinus, who commanded in Germany in the reign of Nero. When her husband was condemned to death, she opened her veins along with him. After the blood had flowed some time, Nero commanded her veins to be bound up ; she lived a few years longer, but with a paleness which testified how near she had been to death.

Paulînus. 1. Pompeius, commanded in Germany along with L. Antistius Vetus in A. D. 58, and completed the dam to restrain the inundations of the Rhine, which Drusus had commenced 63 years before. Seneca dedicated to him his treatise *De Brevitate Vitae* ; and the Pompeia Paulina, whom the philosopher married, was probably the daughter of this Paulinus.—2. C. Suetōnius, propraetor in Mauretania, in the reign of the emperor Claudius, A. D. 42, when he conquered the Moors who had revolted, and advanced as far as Mt. Atlas. He had the command of Britain in the reign of Nero, from 59 to 62. For the first 2 years all his undertakings were successful ; but during his absence on an expedition against the island of Mona (*Anglesey*), the Britons rose in rebellion under Boadicea (61). They at first met with great success, but were conquered by Suetonius on his return from Mona. [BOADICEA.] In 66 he was consul ; and after the death of Nero in 68 he was one of Otho's generals in the war against Vitellius. It was against his advice that Otho fought the battle at Bedriacum. He was pardoned

by Vitellius after Nero's death.—3. Of Milan(*Mediolanensis*), was the secretary of St. Ambrose, after whose death he became a deacon, and repaired to Africa, where, at the request of St. Augustine, he composed a biography of his former patron. This biography, and 2 other small works by Paulinus, are still extant. — 4. Meropius Pontius Anicius Paulinus, bishop of Nola, and hence generally designated *Paulinus Nolanus*, was born at Bourdeaux, or at a neighbouring town, which he calls Embromagum, about A. D. 353. His parents were wealthy and illustrious, and he received a careful education, enjoying in particular the instructions of the poet Ausonius. After many years spent in worldly honours he withdrew from the world, and was eventually chosen bishop of Nola in 409. He died in 431. The works of Paulinus are still extant, and consist of *Epistolae* (51 in. number), *Carmina* (32 in number, composed in a great variety of metres), and a short tract entitled *Passio S. Genesii Arelatensis*. Edited by Le Brun, 4to. Paris, 1685, reprinted at Veron. 1736.

Paullus or Paulus, a Roman cognomen in many gentes, but best known as the name of a family of the Aemilia gens. The name was originally written with a double *l*, but subsequently with only one *l*.

Paulus (Παῦλος), Greek writers. 1. Aeginēta, a celebrated medical writer, of whose personal history nothing is known except that he was born in Aegina, and that he travelled a good deal, visiting, among other places, Alexandria. He probably lived in the latter half of the 7th century after Christ. He wrote several medical works in Greek, of which the principal one is still extant, with no exact title, but commonly called *De Re Medica Libri Septem*. This work is chiefly a compilation from former writers. The Greek text has been twice published, Venet. 1528, and Basil. 1538. There is an excellent English translation by Adams, London, 1834, seq. — 2. Of Alexandria, wrote, in A. D. 378, an *Introduction to Astrology* (Εἰσαγωγὴ εἰς τὴν ἀποτελεσματικήν), which has come down to us, edited by Schatus or Schato, Wittenberg, 1586.— 3. Of Samosata, a celebrated heresiarch of the 3rd century, was made bishop of Antioch, about A. D. 260. He was condemned and deposed by a council held in 269. Paulus denied the distinct personality of the Son of God, and maintained that the Word came and dwelt in the man Jesus. — 4. Silentiarius, so called, because he was chief of the *silentiarii*, or secretaries of the emperor Justinian. He wrote various poems, of which the following are extant : — (1.) *A Description of the Church of St. Sophia* (Ἔκφρασις τοῦ ναοῦ τῆς ἁγίας Σοφίας), consisting of 1029 verses, of which the first 134 are iambic, the rest hexameter. This poem gives a clear and graphic description of the superb structure which forms its subject, and was recited by its author at the second dedication of the church (A. D. 562), after the restoration of the dome, which had fallen in. Edited by Graefe, Lips. 1822, and by Bekker, Bonn, 1837, in the Bonn edition of the Byzantine historians. (2.) *A Description of the Pulpit* (Ἔκφρασις τοῦ ἄμβωνος), consisting of 304 verses, is a supplement to the former poem. It is printed in the editions mentioned above. (3.) *Epigrams*, 83 in all, given in the *Anthologia*. Among these is a poem *On the Pythian Baths* (Εἰς τὰ ἐν Πυθίοις θέρμα).

Paulus, Aemilius. 1. M., consul B. C. 302, and magister equitum to the dictator Q. Fabius Maximus Rullianus, 301. — **2. M.**, consul 255 with Ser. Fulvius Paetinus Nobilior, about the middle of the 1st Punic war. See NOBILIOR, No. 1. — **3. L.**, son of No. 2., consul 219, when he conquered Demetrius of the island of Pharos in the Adriatic, and compelled him to fly for refuge to Philip, king of Macedonia. He was consul a 2nd time in 216 with C. Terentius Varro. This was the year of the memorable defeat at Cannae. [HANNIBAL.] The battle was fought against the advice of Paulus ; and he was one of the many distinguished Romans who perished in the engagement, refusing to fly from the field, when a tribune of the soldiers offered him his horse. Hence we find in Horace (*Carm.* i. 12) : "animaeque magnae prodigum Paulum superante Poeno." Paulus was a staunch adherent of the aristocracy, and was raised to the consulship by the latter party to counterbalance the influence of the plebeian Terentius Varro. — **4. L.**, afterwards surnamed MACEDONICUS, son of No. 3, was born about 230 or 229, since at the time of his 2nd consulship, 168, he was upwards of 60 years of age. He was one of the best specimens of the high Roman nobles. He would not condescend to flatter the people for the offices of the state, maintained with strictness severe discipline in the army, was deeply skilled in the law of the augurs, to whose college he belonged, and maintained throughout life a pure and unspotted character. He was elected curule aedile 192 ; was praetor 191, and obtained Further Spain as his province, where he carried on war with the Lusitani ; and was consul 181, when he conquered the Ingauni, a Ligurian people. For the next 13 years he lived quietly at Rome, devoting most of his time to the education of his children. He was consul a 2nd time in 168, and brought the war against Perseus to a conclusion by the defeat of the Macedonian monarch near Pydna, on the 22nd of June. Perseus shortly afterwards surrendered himself to Paulus. [PERSEUS.] Paulus remained in Macedonia during the greater part of the following year as proconsul, and arranged the affairs of Macedonia, in conjunction with 10 Roman commissioners, whom the senate had despatched for the purpose. Before leaving Greece, he marched into Epirus, where, in accordance with a cruel command of the senate, he gave to his soldiers 70 towns to be pillaged, because they had been in alliance with Perseus. The triumph of Paulus, which was celebrated at the end of November, 167, was the most splendid that Rome had yet seen. It lasted three days. Before the triumphal car of Aemilius walked the captive monarch of Macedonia and his children, and behind it were his two illustrious sons, Q. Fabius Maximus and P. Scipio Africanus the younger, both of whom had been adopted into other families. But the glory of the conqueror was clouded by family misfortune. At this very time he lost his two younger sons; one, 12 years of age, died only 5 days before his triumph, and the other, 14 years of age, only 3 days after his triumph. The loss was all the severer, since he had no son left to carry his name down to posterity. In 164 Paulus was censor with Q. Marcius Philippus, and died in 160, after a long and tedious illness. The fortune he left behind him was so small as scarcely to be sufficient to pay his wife's dowry. The Adelphi of Terence

was brought out at the funeral games exhibited in his honour. Aemilius Paulus was married twice. By his first wife, Papiria, the daughter of C. Papirius Maso, consul 231, he had 4 children, 2 sons, one of whom was adopted by Fabius Maximus and the other by P. Scipio, and 2 daughters, one of whom was married to Q. Aelius Tubero, and the other to M. Cato, son of Cato the censor. He afterwards divorced Papiria ; and by his 2nd wife, whose name is not mentioned, he had 2 sons, whose death has been mentioned above, and a daughter, who was a child at the time that her father was elected to his 2nd consulship.

Paulus, Julius, one of the most distinguished of the Roman jurists, has been supposed, without any good reason, to be of Greek origin. He was in the auditorium of Papinian, and consequently was acting as a jurist in the reign of Septimius Severus. He was exiled by Elagabalus, but he was recalled by Alexander Severus when the latter became emperor, and was made a member of his consilium. Paulus also held the office of praefectus praetorio : he survived his contemporary Ulpian. Paulus was perhaps the most fertile of all the Roman law writers, and there is more excerpted from him in the Digest than from any other jurist, except Ulpian. Upwards of 70 separate works by Paulus are quoted in the Digest. Of these his greatest work was *Ad Edictum*, in 80 books.

Paulus, Passiēnus, a contemporary and friend of the younger Pliny, was a distinguished Roman eques, and was celebrated for his elegiac and lyric poems He belonged to the same municipium (Mevania in Umbria) as Propertius, whom he numbered among his ancestors.

Pausanias (Παυσανίας). 1. A Spartan of the Agid branch of the royal family, the son of Cleombrotus and nephew of Leonidas. Several writers incorrectly call him king ; but he only succeeded his father Cleombrotus in the guardianship of his cousin Plistarchus, the son of Leonidas, for whom he exercised the functions of royalty from B. C. 479 to the period of his death. In 479, when the Athenians called upon the Lacedaemonians for aid against the Persians, the Spartans sent a body of 5000 Spartans, each attended by 7 Helots, under the command of Pausanias. At the Isthmus Pausanias was joined by the other Peloponnesian allies, and at Eleusis by the Athenians, and forthwith took the command of the combined forces, the other Greek generals forming a sort of council of war. The allied forces amounted to nearly 110,000 men. Near Plataeae in Boeotia, Pausanias defeated the Persian army under the command of Mardonius. This decisive victory secured the independence of Greece. Pausanias received as his reward a tenth of the Persian spoils. In 477 the confederate Greeks sent out a fleet under the command of Pausanias, to follow up their success by driving the Persians completely out of Europe and the islands. Cyprus was first attacked, and the greater part of it subdued. From Cyprus Pausanias sailed to Byzantium, and captured the city. The capture of this city afforded Pausanias an opportunity for commencing the execution of the design which he had apparently formed even before leaving Greece. Dazzled by his success and reputation, his station as a Spartan citizen had become too restricted for his ambition. His position as regent was one which must terminate when the king became of age. He therefore aimed at becoming tyrant over the whole of Greece, with the assistance of the Persian king. Among the prisoners taken at Byzantium were some Persians connected with the royal family. These he sent to the king, with a letter, in which he offered to bring Sparta and the rest of Greece under his power, and proposed to marry his daughter. His offers were gladly accepted, and whatever amount of troops and money he required for accomplishing his designs. Pausanias now set no bounds to his arrogant and domineering temper. The allies were so disgusted by his conduct, that they all, except the Peloponnesians and Aeginetans, voluntarily offered to transfer to the Athenians that pre-eminence of rank which Sparta had hitherto enjoyed.' In this way the Athenian confederacy first took its rise. Reports of the conduct and designs of Pausanias reached Sparta, and he was recalled and put upon his trial; but the evidence respecting his meditated treachery was not yet thought sufficiently strong. Shortly afterwards he returned to Byzantium, without the orders of the ephors, and renewed his treasonable intrigues. He was again recalled to Sparta, was again put on his trial, and again acquitted. But even after this second escape he still continued to carry on his intrigues with Persia. At length a man, who was charged with a letter to Persia, having his suspicions awakened by noticing that none of those sent previously on similar errands had returned, counterfeited the seal of Pausanias and opened the letter, in which he found directions for his own death. He carried the letter to the ephors, who prepared to arrest Pausanias: but he took refuge in the temple of Athena Chalcioecus. The ephors stripped off the roof of the temple and built up the door; the aged mother of Pausanias is said to have been among the first who laid a stone for this purpose. When he was on the point of expiring, the ephors took him out lest his death should pollute the sanctuary. He died as soon as he got outside, B. C. 470. He left 3 sons behind him, Plistoanax, afterwards king, Cleomenes and Aristocles. — **2.** Son of Plistoanax, and grandson of the preceding, was king of Sparta from B. C. 408 to 394. In 403 he was sent with an army into Attica, and secretly favoured the cause of Thrasybulus and the Athenian exiles, in order to counteract the plans of Lysander. In 395 Pausanias was sent with an army against the Thebans; but in consequence of the death of Lysander, who was slain under the walls of Haliartus, on the day before Pausanias reached the spot, the king agreed to withdraw his forces from Boeotia. On his return to Sparta he was impeached, and seeing that a fair trial was not to be hoped for, went into voluntary exile, and was condemned to death. He was living at Tegea in 385, when Mantinea was besieged by his son Agesipolis, who succeeded him on the throne. — **3.** King of Macedonia, the son and successor of Aeropus. He was assassinated in the year of his accession by Amyntas II., 394. — **4.** A pretender to the throne of Macedonia, made his appearance in 367, after Alexander II. had been assassinated by Ptolemaeus. Eurydice, the mother of Alexander, sent to request the aid of the Athenian general, Iphicrates, who expelled Pausanias from the kingdom. — **5.** A Macedonian youth of distinguished family, from the province of Orestis. Having been shamefully treated by Attalus, he complained of the outrage to Philip; but as Philip

took no notice of his complaints, he directed his vengeance against the king himself. He shortly afterwards murdered Philip at the festival held at Aegae, 336, but was slain on the spot by some officers of the king's guard. Suspicion rested on Olympias and Alexander of having been privy to the deed; but with regard to Alexander at any rate the suspicion is probably totally unfounded. There was a story that Pausanias, while meditating revenge, having asked the sophist Hermocrates which was the shortest way to fame, the latter replied, that it was by killing the man who had performed the greatest achievements. — **6.** The traveller and geographer, was perhaps a native of Lydia. He lived under Antoninus Pius and M. Aurelius, and wrote his celebrated work in the reign of the latter emperor. This work, entitled Ἑλλάδος Περιήγησις, a *Periegesis* or *Itinerary of Greece*, is in 10 books, and contains a description of Attica and Megaris (i.), Corinthia, Sicyonia, Phliasia, and Argolis (ii.), Laconica (iii.), Messenia (iv.), Elis (v. vi.), Achaea (vii.), Arcadia (viii.), Boeotia (ix.), Phocis (x.). The work shows that Pausanias visited most of the places in these divisions of Greece, a fact which is clearly demonstrated by the minuteness and particularity of his description. The work is merely an Itinerary. Pausanias gives no general description of a country or even of a place, but he describes the things as he comes to them. His account is minute; but it mainly refers to objects of antiquity, and works of art, such as buildings, temples, statues, and pictures. He also mentions mountains, rivers, and fountains, and the mythological stories connected with them, which indeed are his chief inducements to speak of them. His religious feeling was strong, and his belief sure, for he tells many old legends in true good faith and seriousness. His style has been much condemned by modern critics; but if we except some corrupt passages, and if we allow that his order of words is not that of the best Greek writers, there is hardly much obscurity to a person who is competently acquainted with Greek, except that obscurity which sometimes is owing to the matter. With the exception of Herodotus, there is no writer of antiquity, and perhaps none of modern times, who has comprehended so many valuable facts in a small volume. The best editions are by Siebelis, Lips. 1822—1828, 5 vols. 8vo. and by Schubart and Walz, Lips. 1838—40, 3 vols. 8vo.

Pausias (Παυσίας), one of the most distinguished Greek painters, was a contemporary of Aristides, Melanthius, and Apelles (about B. C. 360—330), and a disciple of Pamphilus. He had previously been instructed by his father Brietes, who lived at Sicyon, where also Pausias passed his life. The department of the art which Pausias most practised was painting in encaustic with the *cestrum*. His favourite subjects were small panel-pictures, chiefly of boys. One of his most celebrated pictures was the portrait of Glycera, a flower-girl of his native city, of whom he was enamoured when a young man. Most of his paintings were probably transported to Rome with the other treasures of Sicyonian art, in the aedileship of Scaurus, when the state of Sicyon was compelled to sell all the pictures which were public property, in order to pay its debts.

Pausilypum (τὸ Παυσίλυπον), that is, the "grief-assuaging," was the name of a splendid villa near Neapolis in Campania, which Vedius

Pollio bequeathed to Augustus. The name was transferred to the celebrated grotto (now *Posilippo*) between Naples and Puzzuoli, which was formed by a tunnel cut through the rock by the architect Cocceius, by command of Agrippa. At its entrance the tomb of Virgil is still shown.

Pauson (Παύσων), a Greek painter, who appears from the description of Aristotle (*Poet.* 2. § 2.) to have lived somewhat earlier than the time of this philosopher.

Paustilae (Pausulānus: *Monte dell' Olmo*), a town in the interior of Picenum, between Urbs Salvia and Asculum.

Pāvor. [PALLOR.]

Pax, the goddess of Peace, called **Irēne** by the Greeks. [IRENE.]

Pax Jūlia or **Pax Augusta** (*Beja*), a Roman colony in Lusitania, and the seat of a Conventus juridicus, N. of Julia Myrtilis.

Paxi (*Paxo* and *Antipaxo*), the name of 2 small islands off the W. coast of Greece, between Corcyra and Leucas.

Pĕdaeum or **Pedaeus** (Πήδαιον, accus., Hom. *Il.* xiii. 172), a town of the Troad.

Pĕdālĭum (Πηδάλιον). 1. (*C. Ghinazi*), a promontory of Caria, on the W. side of the Sinus Glaucus, called also Artemisium from a temple of Artemis upon it.—2. (*Capo della Grega*) a promontory on the E. side of Cyprus.

Pĕdāsa (Πήδασα: Πηδασεύς, pl. Πηδασέες, Herod.), a very ancient city of Caria, was originally a chief abode of the Leleges. Alexander assigned it to Halicarnassus. At the time of the Roman empire it had entirely vanished, though its name was preserved in that of the district around its site, namely **Pedāsis** (Πηδασίς). Its locality is only known thus far, that it must have stood somewhere in the triangle formed by Miletus, Halicarnassus, and Stratonicea.

Pĕdāsus (Πήδασος), a town of Mysia on the Satnioïs, mentioned several times by Homer. It was destroyed by the time of Strabo, who says that it was a settlement of the Leleges on M. Ida.

Pĕdiānus, Asconīus. [ASCONIUS.]

Pedius. 1. **Q.**, the great-nephew of the dictator C. Julius Caesar, being the grandson of Julia, Caesar's eldest sister. He served under Caesar in Gaul as his legatus, B. C. 57. In 55, he was a candidate for the curule aedileship with Cn. Plancius and others, but he lost his election. In the civil war he fought on Caesar's side. He was praetor in 48, and in that year he defeated and slew Milo in the neighbourhood of Thurii. In 45, he served against the Pompeian party in Spain. In Caesar's will Pedius was named one of his heirs along with his two other great-nephews, C. Octavius and L. Pinarius, Octavius obtaining 3-4ths of the property, and the remaining 1-4th being divided between Pinarius and Pedius: the latter resigned his share of the inheritance to Octavius. After the fall of the consuls, Hirtius and Pansa, at the battle of Mutina in April, 43, Octavius marched upon Rome at the head of an army, and in the month of August he was elected consul along with Pedius. The latter forthwith proposed a law, known by the name of the *Lex Pedia*, by which all the murderers of Julius Caesar were punished with *aquae et ignis interdictio*. Pedius was left in charge of the city, while Octavius marched into the N. of Italy. He died towards the end of the year shortly after the news of the proscription had reached Rome.—2

Sextus, a Roman jurist, frequently cited by Paulus and Ulpian, lived before the time of Hadrian.

Pednēlissus (Πεδνηλισσός), a city in the interior of Pisidia, and apparently on the Eurymedon, above Aspendus and Selge. It formed an independent state; but was almost constantly at war with Selge. Mr. Fellowes supposes its site to be marked by the ruins of the Roman period near. *Bolkas-Koi* on the E. bank of the Eurymedon.

Pĕdo Albinovānus. [ALBINOVANUS.]

Peducaeus, Sex. 1. Propraetor in Sicily, B. C. 76 and 75, in the latter of which years Cicero served under him as quaestor.—2. Son of the preceding, and an intimate friend of Atticus and Cicero. In the civil war Peducaeus sided with Caesar, by whom he was appointed in 48 to the government of Sardinia. In 39, he was propraetor in Spain.

Pedum (Pedānus: *Gallicano*), an ancient town of Latium on the Via Lavicana, which fell into decay at an early period.

Pegae. [PAGAE.]

Pēgāsis (Πηγασίς), i. e. sprung from Pegasus, was applied to the fountain Hippocrene, which was called forth by the hoof of Pegasus. The Muses are also called *Pegasides*, because the fountain Hippocrene was sacred to them.

Pēgāsus (Πήγασος). 1. The celebrated winged horse, whose origin is thus related. When Perseus struck off the head of Medusa, with whom Poseidon had had intercourse in the form of a horse or a bird, there sprang from her Chrysaor and the horse Pegasus. The latter received this name because he was believed to have made his appearance near the sources (πηγαί) of Oceanus. He ascended to the seats of the immortals, and afterwards lived in the palace of Zeus, for whom he carried thunder and lightning. According to this view, which is apparently the most ancient, Pegasus was the thundering horse of Zeus; but later writers describe him as the horse of Eos (Aurora), and place him among the stars.—Pegasus also acts a prominent part in the combat of Bellerophon against the Chimaera. In order to kill the Chimaera, it was necessary for Bellerophon to obtain possession of Pegasus. For this purpose the soothsayer Polyidus at Corinth advised him to spend a night in the temple of Athena. As Bellerophon was asleep in the temple, the goddess appeared to him in a dream, commanding him to sacrifice to Poseidon, and gave him a golden bridle. When he awoke he found the bridle, offered the sacrifice, and caught Pegasus, while he was drinking at the well Pirene. According to some Athena herself tamed and bridled Pegasus, and surrendered him to Bellerophon. After he had conquered the Chimaera, he endeavoured to rise up to heaven upon his winged horse, but fell down upon the earth. [BELLEROPHON.] Pegasus however continued his flight to heaven. — Pegasus was also regarded as the horse of the Muses, and in this connection is more celebrated in modern times than in antiquity; for with the ancients he had no connection with the Muses, except producing with his hoof the inspiring fountain Hippocrene. The story about this fountain runs as follows. When the 9 Muses engaged in a contest with the 9 daughters of Pierus on Mt. Helicon, all became darkness when the daughters of Pierus began to sing; whereas during the song of the Muses, heaven, the sea, and all the rivers stood still to listen, and Helicon rose heavenward with delight, antil Pegasus, on the advice of Poseidon, stopped its ascent by kicking it with his hoof. From this kick there arose Hippocrene, the inspiring well of the Muses, on Mt. Helicon, which, for this reason, Persius calls *fons caballinus*. Others again relate that Pegasus caused the well to gush forth because he was thirsty. Pegasus is often seen represented in ancient works of art along with Athena and Bellerophon. — **2.** A Roman jurist, one of the followers or pupils of Proculus and praefectus urbi under Domitian (Juv. iv. 76). The Senatusconsultum Pegasianum, which was passed in the time of Vespasian, when Pegasus was consul suffectus with Pusio, probably took its name from him.

Peiso Lacus. [PELSO LACUS.]

Pelagius, probably a native of Britain, celebrated as the propagator of those heretical opinions, which have derived their name from him, and which were opposed with great energy by his contemporaries Augustine and Jerome. He first appears in history about the beginning of the 5th century, when we find him residing at Rome. In the year 409 or 410, when Alaric was threatening the metropolis, Pelagius accompanied by his disciple and ardent admirer Coelestius, passed over to Sicily, from thence proceeded to Africa, and leaving Coelestius at Carthage, sailed for Palestine. The fame of his sanctity had preceded him, for upon his arrival he was received with great warmth by Jerome and many other distinguished fathers of the church. Soon afterwards the opinions of Pelagius were denounced as heretical; and in A. D. 417 Pelagius and Coelestius were anathematized by Pope Innocentius. A very few only of the numerous treatises of Pelagius have descended to us. They are printed with the works of Jerome.

Pelagonia (Πελαγονία: Πελάγονες, pl.). **1.** A district in Macedonia. The Pelagones were an ancient people, probably of Pelasgic origin, and seem originally to have inhabited the valley of the Axius, since Homer calls Pelagon, a son of Axius. The Pelagones afterwards migrated W.-wards to the Erigon, the country around which received the name of Pelagonia, which thus lay S. of Paeonia. The chief town of this district was also called Pelagonia (now *Vitolia* or *Monastir*), which was under the Romans the capital of the 4th division of Macedonia. It was situated on the Via Egnatia not far from the narrow passes leading into Illyria. — **2.** A district in Thessaly, called the Pelagonian Tripolis, because it consisted of the 3 towns of Azôrus, Pythium, and Doliche. It was situated W. of Olympus in the upper valley of the Titaresius, and belonged to Perrhaebia, whence these 3 towns are sometimes called the Perrhaebian Tripolis. Some of the Macedonian Pelagonians, who had been driven out of their homes by the Paeonians, migrated into this part of Thessaly, which was originally inhabited by Dorians.

Pelasgi (Πελασγοί), the earliest inhabitants of Greece who established the worship of the Dodonaean Zeus, Hephaestus, the Cabiri, and other divinities that belong to the earliest inhabitants of the country. They claimed descent from a mythical hero Pelasgus, of whom we have different accounts in the different parts of Greece inhabited by Pelasgians. The nation was widely spread over Greece and the islands of the Grecian archipelago; and the name of *Pelasgia* was given at one time to

Greece. One of the most ancient traditions represented Pelasgus, as a descendant of Phoroneus, king of Argos; and it seems to have been generally believed by the Greeks that the Pelasgi spread from Argos to the other countries of Greece. Arcadia, Attica, Epirus and Thessaly, were, in addition to Argos. some of the principal seats of the Pelasgi. They were also found on the coasts of Asia Minor, and according to some writers in Italy as well. Of the language, habits, and civilisation of this people, we possess no certain knowledge. Herodotus says they spoke a barbarous language, that is, a language not Greek; but from the facility with which the Greek and Pelasgic languages coalesced in all parts of Greece, and from the fact that the Athenians and Arcadians are said to have been of pure Pelasgic origin, it is probable that the 2 languages had a close affinity. The Pelasgi are further said to have been an agricultural people, and to have possessed a considerable knowledge of the useful arts. The most ancient architectural remains of Greece, such as the treasury or tomb of Atheus at Mycenae, are ascribed to the Pelasgians, and are cited as specimens of Pelasgian architecture, though there is no positive authority for these statements.

Pelasgia (Πελασγία), an ancient name of the islands of Delos and Lesbos, referring, of course, to their having been early seats of the Pelasgians.

Pelasgiôtis(Πελασγιῶτις), a district in Thessaly, between Hestiaeotis and Magnesia. [THESSALIA.]

Pelasgus. [PELASGI.]

Pelendônes, a Celtiberian people in Hispania Tarraconensis between the sources of the Durius and the Iberus.

Pelethrônium (Πελεθρόνιον), a mountainous district in Thessaly, part of Mt. Pelion, where the Lapithae dwelt, and which is said to have derived its name from Pelethronius, king of the Lapithae, who invented the use of the bridle and the saddle.

Pēleus (Πηλεύς), son of Aeacus and Endeis, was king of the Myrmidons at Phthia in Thessaly. He was a brother of Telamon, and step-brother of Phocus, the son of Aeacus, by the Nereid Psamathe. Peleus and Telamon resolved to get rid of Phocus, because he excelled them in their military games, and Telamon, or, according to others, Peleus, murdered their step-brother. The 2 brothers concealed their crime by removing the body of Phocus, but were nevertheless found out, and expelled by Aeacus from Aegina. Peleus went to Phthia in Thessaly, where he was purified from the murder by Eurytion, the son of Actor, married his daughter Antigone, and received with her a 3rd of Eurytion's kingdom. Others relate that he went to Ceyx at Trachis; and as he had come to Thessaly without companions, he prayed to Zeus for an army; and the god, to please Peleus, metamorphosed the ants (μύρμηκες) into men, who were accordingly called Myrmidons. Peleus accompanied Eurytion to the Calydonian hunt, and involuntarily killed him with his spear, in consequence of which he fled from Phthia to Iolcus, where he was again purified by Acastus, the king of the place. While residing at Iolcus, Astydamia, the wife of Acastus, fell in love with him; but as her proposals were rejected by Peleus, she accused him to her husband of having attempted her virtue. Acastus, unwilling to stain his hand with the blood of the man whom he had hospitably received, and whom he had purified from his guilt, took him to Mt. Pelion, where they hunted wild beasts; and when Peleus, overcome with fatigue, had fallen asleep, Acastus left him alone, and concealed his sword, that he might be destroyed by the wild beasts. When Peleus awoke and sought his sword, he was attacked by the Centaurs, but was saved by Chiron, who also restored to him his sword. There are some modifications of this account in other writers: instead of Astydamia, some mention Hippolyte, the daughter of Cretheus ; and others relate that after Acastus had concealed the sword of Peleus, Chiron or Hermes brought him another, which had been made by Hephaestus. While on Mt. Pelion, Peleus married the Nereid Thetis, by whom he became the father of Achilles, though some regarded this Thetis as different from the marine divinity, and called her a daughter of Chiron. The gods took part in the marriage solemnity ; Chiron presented Peleus with a lance, Poseidon with the immortal horses, Balius and Xanthus, and the other gods with arms. Eris or Strife was the only goddess who was not invited to the nuptials, and she revenged herself by throwing an apple among the guests, with the inscription " to the fairest." [PARIS.] Homer mentions Achilles as the only son of Peleus and Thetis, but later writers state that she had already destroyed by fire 6 children, of whom she was the mother by Peleus, and that she attempted to make away with Achilles, her 7th child, she was prevented by Peleus. After this Peleus, who is also mentioned among the Argonauts, in conjunction with Jason and the Dioscuri, besieged Acastus and Iolcus, slew Astydamia, and over the scattered limbs of her body led his warriors into the city. The flocks of Peleus were at one time worried by a wolf, which Psamathe had sent to avenge the murder of her son Phocus, but she herself afterwards, on the request of Thetis, turned the animal into stone. Peleus, who had in former times joined Hercules in his expedition against Troy, was too old to accompany his son Achilles against that city: he remained at home and survived the death of his son.

Pĕlīădes (Πελιάδες), the daughters of Pelias. See PELIAS.

Pĕlĭas (Πελίας), son of Poseidon and Tyro, a daughter of Salmoneus. Poseidon once visited Tyro in the form of the river-god Enipeus, with whom she was in love, and she became by him the mother of Pelias and Neleus. To conceal her shame, their mother exposed the 2 boys, but they were found and reared by some countrymen. They subsequently learnt their parentage ; and after the death of Cretheus, king of Iolcos, who had married their mother, they seized the throne of Iolcos, to the exclusion of Aeson, the son of Cretheus and Tyro. Pelias soon afterwards expelled his own brother Neleus, and thus became sole ruler of Iolcos. After Pelias had long reigned over Iolcos, Jason, the son of Aeson, came to Iolcos and claimed the kingdom as his right. In order to get rid of him, Pelias sent him to Colchis to fetch the golden fleece. Hence arose the celebrated expedition of the Argonauts. After the return of Jason, Pelias was cut to pieces and boiled by his own daughters (the Peliades), who had been told by Medea that in this manner they might restore their father to vigour and youth. His son Acastus held funeral games in his honour at Iolcus, and expelled Jason and Medea from the country. [For details, see JASON ; MEDEA ; ARGONAUTAE.] The names of several of the daughters of Pelias

are recorded. The most celebrated of them was Alcestis, the wife of Admetus, who is therefore called by Ovid Peliae gener.

Pēlīdes (Πηλείδης, Πηλείων), a patronymic from Peleus, generally given to his son Achilles, more rarely to his grandson Neoptolemus.

Pĕligni, a brave and warlike people of Sabine origin in central Italy, bounded S.E. by the Marsi, N. by the Marrucini, S. by Samnium and the Frentani, and E. by the Frentani likewise. The climate of their country was cold (Hor. Carm. iii., 19. 8.) ; but it produced a considerable quantity of flax and was celebrated for its honey. The Peligni, like their neighbours, the Marsi, were regarded as magicians. Their principal towns were CORFINIUM and SULMO. They offered a brave resistance to the Romans, but concluded a peace with the republic along with their neighbours the Marsi, Marrucini and Frentani in B. C. 304. They took an active part in the Social war (90, 89), and their chief town Corfinium was destined by the allies to be the new capital of Italy in place of Rome. They were subdued by Pompeius Strabo, after which time they are rarely mentioned.

Pĕlinaeus Mons (τὸ Πελιναῖον ὄρος, or Πελληναῖον : M. Elias), the highest mountain of the island of Chios, a little N. of the city of Chios, with a celebrated temple of Zeus Πελιναῖος.

Pelinna, or more commonly **Pelinnaeum** (Πελίννα, Πελινναῖον : Gardhiki), a town of Thessaly in Hestiaeotis, on the left bank of the Peneus, was taken by the Romans in their war with Antiochus.

Pēlīon, more rarely **Pēlĭos** (τὸ Πήλιον ὄρος : Plessidhi or Zagora), a lofty range of mountains in Thessaly in the district of Magnesia, was situated between the lake Boebëis and the Pagasaean gulf, and formed the promontories of Sepias and Aeantium. Its sides were covered with wood, and on its summit was a temple of Zeus Actaeus, where the cold was so severe, that the persons who went in procession to this temple once a year wore thick skins to protect themselves. Mt. Pelion was celebrated in mythology. The giants in their war with the gods are said to have attempted to heap Ossa and Olympus on Pelion, or Pelion and Ossa on Olympus in order to scale heaven. Near the summit of this mountain was the cave of the Centaur Chiron, whose residence was probably placed here on account of the number of the medicinal plants which grew upon the mountain, since he was celebrated for his skill in medicine. On Pelion also the timber was felled, with which the ship Argo was built, whence Ovid applies the term Pelias arbor to this ship.

Pella (Πέλλα : Πελλαῖος, Pellaeus). 1. (Alaklisi), an ancient town of Macedonia in the district Bottiaea, was situated upon a hill, and upon a lake formed by the river Lydias, 120 stadia from its mouth. It continued to be a place of small importance till the time of Philip, who made it his residence and the capital of the Macedonian monarchy, and adorned it with many public buildings. It is frequently mentioned by subsequent writers on account of its being the birth-place of Alexander the Great. It was the capital of one of the 4 districts into which the Romans divided Macedonia [see p. 404, a.], and was subsequently made a Roman colony under the name of Col. Jul. Aug. Pella. — 2. (El-Bujeh ?), the S.-most of the 10 cities which composed the Decapolis in Peraea, that is in Palestine E. of the Jordan, stood 5 Roman miles S.E.

of Scythopolis, and was also called Βοῦτις. It was taken by Antiochus the Great, in the wars between Syria and Egypt, and was held by a Macedonian colony, till it was destroyed by Alexander Jannaeus on account of the refusal of its inhabitants to embrace the Jewish religion. It was restored and given back to its old inhabitants by Pompey. It was the place of refuge of the Christians who fled from Jerusalem before its capture by the Romans. The exact site of Pella is very uncertain. — 3. A city of Syria on the Orontes, formerly called Pharnace, was named Pella by the Macedonians, and afterwards APAMEA (No. 1.) — 4. In Phrygia. [PELTAE.]

Pellaeus Pagus was the name given by Alexander, after Pella in Macedonia, to the district of Susiana about the mouths of the Tigris; in which he built the city of Alexandria, afterwards called Charax.

Pellāna. [PELLENE, No. 2.]

Pellēnē (Πελλήνη, Dor. Πελλάνα: Πελληνεύς). 1. A city in Achaia bordering on Sicyonia, the most E.-ly of the 12 Achaean cities, was situated on a hill 60 stadia from the city, and was strongly fortified. Its port-town was Aristonautae. The ancients derived its name from the giant Pallas, or from the Argive Pellen, the son of Phorbas. It is mentioned in Homer; and the inhabitants of Scione in the peninsula of Pallene in Macedonia professed to be descended from the Pellenaeans in Achaia, who were shipwrecked on the Macedonian coast on their return from Troy. In the Peloponnesian war Pellene sided with Sparta. In the later wars of Greece between the Achaean and Aetolian leagues, the town was several times taken by the contending parties. — Between Pellene and Aegae there was a smaller town of the same name, where the celebrated Pellenian cloaks (Πελληνιακαὶ χλαῖναι) were made, which were given as prizes to the victors in the games at this place. — 2. Usually called Pellana, a town in Laconia on the Eurotas, about 50 stadia N.W. of Sparta, belonging to the Spartan Tripolis.

Pēlōdēs (Πηλώδης λιμήν, in App. Παλόεις: Armyro), a port-town belonging to Buthrotum in Epirus, and on a bay which probably bore the same name.

Pēlŏpēa or Pelopīa (Πελόπεια), daughter of Thyestes, dwelt at Sicyon, where her father offered her violence, without knowing that she was his daughter. While pregnant by her father, she married her uncle Atreus. Shortly afterwards she bore a son Aegisthus, who eventually murdered Atreus. [For details, see AEGISTHUS.]

Pelŏpīdas (Πελοπίδας), the Theban general and statesman, son of Hippoclus, was descended from a noble family and inherited a large estate, of which he made a liberal use. He lived always in the closest friendship with Epaminondas, to whose simple frugality, as he could not persuade him to share his riches, he is said to have assimilated his own mode of life. He took a leading part in expelling the Spartans from Thebes, B.C. 379; and from this time until his death there was not a year in which he was not entrusted with some important command. In 371 he was one of the Theban commanders at the battle of Leuctra, so fatal to the Lacedaemonians, and joined Epaminondas in urging the expediency of immediate action. In 369, he was also one of the generals in the 1st invasion of Peloponnesus by the Thebans.

Respecting his accusation on his return from this campaign, see p. 241, b. In 368 Pelopidas was sent again into Thessaly, on 2 separate occasions, in consequence of complaints against Alexander of Pherae. On his 1st expedition Alexander of Pherae sought safety in flight; and Pelopidas advanced into Macedonia to arbitrate between Alexander II. and Ptolemy of Alorus. Among the hostages whom he took with him from Macedonia was the famous Philip, the father of Alexander the Great. On his 2nd visit to Thessaly, Pelopidas went simply as an ambassador, not expecting any opposition, and unprovided with a military force. He was seized by Alexander of Pherae, and was kept in confinement at Pherae till his liberation in 367, by a Theban force under Epaminondas. In the same year in which he was released he was sent as ambassador to Susa, to counteract the Lacedaemonian and Athenian negotiations at the Persian court. In 364, the Thessalian towns again applied to Thebes for protection against Alexander, and Pelopidas was appointed to aid them. His forces, however, were dismayed by an eclipse of the sun (June 13), and, therefore, leaving them behind, he took with him into Thessaly only 300 horse. On his arrival at Pharsalus he collected a force which he deemed sufficient, and marched against Alexander, treating lightly the great disparity of numbers, and remarking that it was better as it was, since there would be more for him to conquer. At Cynoscephalae a battle ensued, in which Pelopidas drove the enemy from their ground, but he himself was slain as, burning with resentment, he pressed rashly forward to attack Alexander in person. The Thebans and Thessalians made great lamentations for his death, and the latter, having earnestly requested leave to bury him, celebrated his funeral with extraordinary splendour.

Pĕlŏponnēsus (ἡ Πελοπόννησος: Morea), the S. part of Greece or the peninsula, which was connected with Hellas proper by the isthmus of Corinth. It is said to have derived its name Peloponnesus or the "island of Pelops," from the mythical Pelops. [PELOPS.] This name does not occur in Homer. In his time the peninsula was sometimes called Apia, from Apis, son of Phoroneus, king of Argos, and sometimes Argos; which names were given to it on account of Argos being the chief power in Peloponnesus at that period. Peloponnesus was bounded on the N. by the Corinthian gulf, on the W. by the Ionian or Sicilian sea, on the S. by the Libyan, and on the W. by the Cretan and Myrtoan seas. On the E. and S. there are 3 great gulfs, the Argolic, Laconian, and Messenian. The ancients compared the shape of the country to the leaf of a plane tree; and its modern name, the Morea (ὁ Μωρέος), which first occurs in the 12th century of the Christian aera, was given it on account of its resemblance to a mulberry-leaf. Peloponnesus was divided into various provinces, all of which were bounded on one side by the sea, with the exception of ARCADIA, which was in the centre of the country. These provinces were ACHAIA in the N., ELIS in the W., MESSENIA in the W. and S., LACONIA in the S. and E., and CORINTHIA in the E. and N. An account of the geography of the peninsula is given under these names. The area of Peloponnesus is computed to be 7779 English miles; and it probably contained a population of upwards of a million in the flourishing period of

Greek history. — Peloponnesus was originally inhabited by Pelasgians. Subsequently the Achaeans, who belonged to the Aeolic race, settled in the E. and S. parts of the peninsula, in Argolis, Laconia, and Messenia ; and the Ionians in the N. part, in Achaia ; while the remains of the original inhabitants of the country, the Pelasgians, collected chiefly in the central part, in Arcadia. Eighty years after the Trojan war, according to mythical chronology, the Dorians, under the conduct of the Heraclidae, invaded and conquered Peloponnesus, and established Doric states in Argolis, Laconia, and Messenia, from whence they extended their power over Corinth, Sicyon, and Megara. Part of the Achaean population remained in these provinces as tributary subjects to the Dorians under the name of Perioeci ; while others of the Achaeans passed over to the N. of Peloponnesus, expelled the Ionians, and settled in this part of the country, which was called after them Achaia. The Aetolians, who had invaded Peloponnesus along with the Dorians, settled in Elis and became intermingled with the original inhabitants. The peninsula remained under Doric influence during the most important period of Greek history, and opposed to the great Ionic city of Athens. After the conquest of Messenia by the Spartans, it was under the supremacy of Sparta, till the overthrow of the power of the latter by the Thebans at the battle of Leuctra, B. C. 371.

Pělops (Πέλοψ), grandson of Zeus, and son of Tantalus and Dione, the daughter of Atlas. Some writers call his mother Euryanassa or Clytia. He was married to Hippodamia, by whom he became the father of Atreus, Thyestes, Dias, Cynosurus, Corinthius, Hippalmus (Hippalcmus or Hippalcimus), Hippasus, Cleon, Argius, Alcathous, Aelius, Pittheus, Troezen, Nicippe, and Lysidice. By Axioche or the nymph Danais he is said to have been the father of Chrysippus. Pelops was king of Pisa in Elis, and from him the great southern peninsula of Greece was believed to have derived its name Peloponnesus. According to a tradition which became very general in later times, Pelops was a Phrygian, who was expelled by Ilus from Phrygia (hence called by Ovid, Met. viii. 622, Pelopeïa arva), and thereupon migrated with his great wealth to Pisa. Others describe him as a Paphlagonian, and call the Paphlagonians themselves Πελοπήιοι. Others again represent him as a native of Greece ; and there can be little doubt that in the earliest traditions Pelops was described as a native of Greece and not as a foreign immigrant; and in them he is called the tamer of horses and the favourite of Poseidon. The legends about Pelops consist mainly of the story of his being cut to pieces and boiled, of his contest with Oenomaus and Hippodamia, and of his relation to his sons; to which we may add the honours paid to his remains. 1. Pelops cut to pieces and boiled (Κρεουργία Πέλοπος). Tantalus, the favourite of the gods, once invited them to a repast, and on that occasion killed his own son, and having boiled him set the flesh before them that they might eat it. But the immortal gods, knowing what it was, did not touch it ; Demeter alone, being absorbed by grief for her lost daughter, consumed the shoulder of Pelops. Hereupon the gods ordered Hermes to put the limbs of Pelops into a cauldron, and thereby restore him to life. When the process was over, Clotho took him out of the cauldron, and as the shoulder consumed by Demeter

was wanting, the goddess supplied its place by one made of ivory ; his descendants (the Pelopidae) as a mark of their origin, were believed to have one shoulder as white as ivory. 2. Contest with Oenomaus and Hippodamia. As an oracle had declared to Oenomaus that he should be killed by his son-in-law, he refused giving his fair daughter Hippodamia in marriage to any one. But since many suitors appeared, Oenomaus declared that he would bestow her hand upon the man who should conquer him in the chariot-race, but that he should kill all who were defeated by him. Among other suitors Pelops also presented himself, but when he saw the heads of his conquered predecessors stuck up above the door of Oenomaus, he was seized with fear, and endeavoured to gain the favour of Myrtilus, the charioteer of Oenomaus, promising him half the kingdom if he would assist him in conquering his master. Myrtilus agreed, and left out the linch-pins of the chariot of Oenomaus. In the race the chariot of Oenomaus broke down, and he was thrown out and killed. Thus Hippodamia became the wife of Pelops. But as Pelops had now gained his object, he was unwilling to keep faith with Myrtilus ; and accordingly as they were driving along a cliff he threw Myrtilus into the sea. As Myrtilus sank, he cursed Pelops and his whole race. Pelops returned with Hippodamia to Pisa in Elis, and soon also made himself master of Olympia, where he restored the Olympian games with greater splendour than they had ever been celebrated before. 3. The sons of Pelops. Chrysippus was the favourite of his father, and was in consequence envied by his brothers. The two eldest among them, Atreus and Thyestes, with the connivance of Hippodamia, accordingly murdered Chrysippus, and threw his body into a well. Pelops, who suspected his sons of the murder, expelled them from the country. Hippodamia, dreading the anger of her husband, fled to Midea in Argolis, from whence her remains were afterwards conveyed by Pelops to Olympia. Pelops, after his death, was honoured at Olympia above all other heroes. His tomb with an iron sarcophagus existed on the banks of the Alpheus, not far from the temple of Artemis near Pisa. The spot on which his sanctuary (Πελόπιον) stood in the Altis, was said to have been dedicated by Hercules, who also offered to him the first sacrifices. The magistrates of the Eleans likewise offered to him there an annual sacrifice, consisting of a black ram, with special ceremonies. The name of Pelops was so celebrated that it was constantly used by the poets in connection with his descendants and the cities they inhabited. Hence we find Atreus, the son of Pelops, called Pelopeïus Atreus, and Agamemnon, the grandson or great-grandson of Atreus, called Pelopeïus Agamemnon. In the same way Iphigenia, the daughter of Agamemnon, and Hermione, the wife of Menelaus, are each called by Ovid Pelopeïa virgo. Virgil (Aen. ii. 193) uses the phrase Pelopēa moenia to signify the cities in Peloponnesus, which Pelops and his descendants ruled over ; and in like manner Mycenae is called by Ovid Pelopeïades Mycenae.

Pelōris, Pelōrïas, or Pelōrus (Πελωρίς, Πελωριάς, Πέλωρος: C. Faro), the N.E. point of Sicily, was N.E. of Messana on the Fretum Siculum, and one of the 3 promontories which formed the triangular figure of the island. According to the usual story it derived its name from

Pelorus, the pilot of Hannibal's ship, who was buried here after being killed by Hannibal in a fit of anger; but the name was more ancient than Hannibal's time, being mentioned by Thucydides. On the promontory there was a temple of Poseidon, and a tower, probably a light-house, from which the modern name of the Cape (*Faro*) appears to have come.

Pelōrus (Πέλωρος : prob. *Lori or Luri*), a river of Iberia in Asia, appears to have been a S. tributary of the Cyrus (*Kour.*)

Pelso or Peiso (*Plattensee*), a great lake in Pannonia, the waters of which were conducted into the Danube by the emperor Galerius, who thus gained a great quantity of fertile land for his newly formed province of Valeria.

Peltae (Πέλται : Πελτηνός), an ancient and flourishing city of Asia Minor, in the N. of Phrygia, 10 parasangs from Celaenae (Xenoph.), and no doubt the same place as the Pella of the Roman writers, 25 Roman miles N. or N.E. of Apamea Cibotus, to the *conventus* of which it belonged. The surrounding district is called by Strabo τὸ Πελτηνὸν πέδιον. Its site is uncertain. Some identify it with the ruins 8 miles S. of *Sandakli*; others with those near *Ishekli*.

Peltuinum (Peltuīnas, -ātis : *Monte Bello*), a town of the Vestini in central Italy.

Pelūsium (Πηλούσιον : Egypt. Peremoun or Peromi ; O. T. Sin.: all these names are derived from nouns meaning *mud :* Πηλουσιώτης ; Pelusiōta : *Tineh*, Ru.), also called Abaris in early times, a celebrated city of Lower Egypt, stood on the E. side of the E.-most mouth of the Nile, which was called after it the Pelusiac mouth, 20 stadia (2 geog. miles) from the sea, in the midst of morasses, from which it obtained its name. As the key of Egypt on the N. E., and the frontier city towards Syria and Arabia, it was strongly fortified, and was the scene of many battles and sieges, in the wars of Egypt with Assyria, Persia, Syria, and Rome, from the defeat of Sennacherib near it by Sethon, down to its capture by Octavianus after the battle of Actium. In later times it was the capital of the district of Augustamnica. It was the birth-place of the geographer Claudius Ptolemaeus.

Penātes, the household gods of the Romans, both those of a private family and of the state, as the great family of citizens. Hence we have to distinguish between private and public Penates. The name is connected with *penus ;* and the images of those gods were kept in the *penetralia*, or the central part of the house. The Lares were included among the Penates ; both names, in fact, are often used synonymously. The Lares, however, though included in the Penates, were not the only Penates ; for each family had usually no more than one Lar, whereas the Penates are always spoken of in the plural. Since Jupiter and Juno were regarded as the protectors of happiness and peace in the family, these divinities were worshipped as Penates. Vesta was also reckoned among the Penates, for each hearth, being the symbol of domestic union, had its Vesta. All other Penates, both public and private, seem to have consisted of certain sacred relics connected with indefinite divinities, and hence Varro says that the number and names of the Penates were indefinite. Most ancient writers believe that the Penates of the state were brought by Aeneas from Troy

into Italy, and were preserved first at Lavinium, afterwards at Alba Longa, and finally at Rome At Rome they had a chapel near the centre of the city, in a place called *sub Velia*. As the public Lares were worshipped in the central part of the city, and at the public hearth, so the private Penates had their place at the hearth of every house ; and the table also was sacred to them. On the hearth a perpetual fire was kept up in their honour, and the table always contained the salt-cellar and the firstlings of fruit for these divinities. Every meal that was taken in the house thus resembled a sacrifice offered to the Penates, beginning with a purification and ending with a libation which was poured either on the table or upon the hearth. After every absence from the hearth, the Penates were saluted like the living inhabitants of the house ; and whoever went abroad prayed to the Penates and Lares for a happy return, and when he came back to his house, he hung up his armour, staff, and the like by the side of their images.

Peneïs, that is, Daphne, daughter of the river-god Peneus.

Penēlēos (Πηνέλεως), son of Hippalcmus and Asterope, and one of the Argonauts. He was the father of Opheltes, and is also mentioned among the suitors of Helen. He was one of the leaders of the Boeotians in the war against Troy, where he slew Ilioneus and Lycon, and was wounded by Polydamas. He is said to have been slain by Eurypylus, the son of Telephus.

Penēlŏpē (Πηνελόπη, Πενελόπη, Πηνελόπεια), daughter of Icarius and Periboea of Sparta, married Ulysses, king of Ithaca. [Respecting her marriage, see ICARIUS, No. 2.] By Ulysses she had an only child, Telemachus, who was an infant when her husband sailed against Troy. During the long absence of Ulysses she was beleaguered by numerous and importunate suitors, whom she deceived by declaring that she must finish a large robe which she was making for Laërtes, her aged father-in-law, before she could make up her mind. During the daytime she accordingly worked at the robe, and in the night she undid the work of the day. By this means she succeeded in putting off the suitors. But at length her stratagem was betrayed by her servants ; and when, in consequence, the faithful Penelope was pressed more and more by the impatient suitors, Ulysses at length arrived in Ithaca, after an absence of 20 years. Having recognised her husband by several signs, she heartily welcomed him, and the days of her grief and sorrow were at an end. [ULYSSES.] While Homer describes Penelope as a most chaste and faithful wife, some later writers charge her with the very opposite vice, and relate that by Hermes or by all the suitors together she became the mother of Pan. They add that Ulysses on his return repudiated her, whereupon she went to Sparta, and thence to Mantinea, where her tomb was shown in after-times. According to another tradition, she married Telegonus, after he had killed his father Ulysses.

Penēus (Πηνειός), 1. (*Salambria* or *Salamria*), the chief river of Thessaly, and one of the most important in all Greece, rises near Alalcomenae in Mt. Lacmon, a branch of Mt. Pindus, flows first S.E. and then N.E., and after receiving many affluents, of which the most important were the Enipeus, the Lethaeus, and the Titaresius, forces its way through the vale of Tempe between Mts.

Ossa and Olympus into the sea. [TEMPE.] As a god Peneus was called a son of Oceanus and Tethys. By the Naiad Creusa he became the father of Hypseus, Stilbe, and Daphne. Cyrene also is called by some his wife, and by others his daughter; and hence Peneus is described as the genitor of Aristaeus.— **2.** (*Gastuni*), a river in Elis, which rises on the frontiers of Arcadia, flows by the town of Elis, and falls into the sea between the promontory Chelonatas and Ichthys.

Pēnĭus, a little river of Pontus falling into the Euxine. (Ovid, *Ex Ponto*, iv. 10.)

Pennīnae Alpes. [ALPES.]

Pentăpŏlis (Πεντάπολις), the name for any association of 5 cities, was applied specifically to —1. The 5 chief cities of Cyrenaïca in N. Africa, Cyrene, Berenice, Arsinoë, Ptolemaïs, and Apollonia, from which, under the Ptolemies, Cyrenaica received the name of Pentapolis, or Pentapolis Libyae, or, in the Roman writers, Pentapolitana Regio. When the name occurs alone, this is its usual meaning; the other applications of it are but rare.—**2.** The 5 cities of the Philistines in the S. W. of Palestine, namely, Gaza, Ashdod (Azotus), Askalon, Gath, and Ekron.—**3.** In the apocryphal *Book of the Wisdom of Solomon* (x. 6.) the name is applied to the 5 "cities of the plain" of the southern Jordan, Sodom, Gomorrha, Adama, Zeboïm, and Zoar, all of which (except the last, which was spared at the intercession of Lot) were overthrown by fire from heaven, and the valley in which they stood was buried beneath the waters of the Dead Sea.

Pentelēum (Πεντέλειον), a fortified place in the N. of Arcadia near Pheneus.

Pentĕlĭcus Mons (τὸ Πεντελικὸν ὄρος: *Pentéli*), a mountain in Attica, celebrated for its marble, which derived its name from the demus of Pentéle (Πεντέλη), lying on its S. slope. It is a branch of Mt. Parnes, from which it runs in a S.E.-ly direction between Athens and Marathon to the coast. It is probably the same as the mountain called Brilessus (Βριλησσός) by Thucydides and others.

Penthĕsĭlēa (Πενθεσίλεια), daughter of Ares and Otrera, and queen of the Amazons. After the death of Hector, she came to the assistance of the Trojans, but was slain by Achilles, who mourned over the dying queen on account of her beauty, youth and valour. Thersites ridiculed the grief of Achilles, and was in consequence killed by the hero. Thereupon Diomedes, a relative of Thersites, threw the body of Penthesilea into the river Scamander; but, according to others, Achilles himself buried it on the banks of the Xanthus.

Pentheus (Πενθεύς), son of Echion and Agâve, the daughter of Cadmus. He succeeded Cadmus as king of Thebes; and having resisted the introduction of the worship of Dionysus into his kingdom, he was driven mad by the god, his palace was hurled to the ground, and he himself was torn to pieces by his own mother and her two sisters, Ino and Autonoe, who in their Bacchic frenzy believed him to be a wild beast. The place where Pentheus suffered death, is said to have been Mt. Cithaeron or Mt. Parnassus. It is related that Pentheus got upon a tree, for the purpose of witnessing in secret the revelry of the Bacchic women, but on being discovered by them was torn to pieces. According to a Corinthian tradition, the women were afterwards commanded by an oracle to discover that tree, and to worship it like the god Dionysus; and accordingly out of the tree two carved images of the god were made. The tragic fate of Pentheus forms the subject of the *Bacchae* of Euripides.

Penthĭlus(Πένθιλος), son of Orestes and Erigone, is said to have led a colony of Aeolians to Thrace. He was the father of Echelatus and Damasias.

Pentri, one of the most important of the tribes in Samnium, were conquered by the Romans along with the other Samnites, and were the only one of the Samnite tribes who remained faithful to the Romans when the rest of the nation revolted to Hannibal in the 2nd Punic war. Their chief town was BOVIANUM.

Peor, a mountain of Palestine, in the land of Moab, only mentioned in the Pentateuch. It was probably one of the summits of the mountains called Abarim, which ran N. and S. through Moabitis, along the E. side of the valley of the southern Jordan and the Dead Sea.

Pēos Artĕmĭdos (Πέος, probably corrupted from Σπέος, *cave*, Ἀρτεμίδος: *Beni Hassan*, Ru.), a city of the Heptanomis, or Middle Egypt, on the E. bank of the Nile, nearly opposite to Hermopolis the Great on the W. bank. It is remarkable as the site of the most extensive rock-hewn catacombs in all Egypt, the walls of which are covered with sculptures and paintings of the greatest importance for elucidating Egyptian antiquities.

Pĕparēthus (Πεπάρηθος: Πεπαρήθιος: *Piperi*), a small island in the Aegaean sea, off the coast of Thessaly, and E. of Halonesus, with a town of the same name upon it and 2 other small places. It produced a considerable quantity of wine. It is mentioned in connection with Halonesus in the war between Philip and the Athenians. [HALONESUS.]

Pephrēdo (Πεφρηδώ). [GRAEAE.]

Pepūza (Πέπουζα: Ru. near *Bash-Shehr*), a city in the W. of Phrygia, of some note in ecclesiastical history.

Pĕraea (ἡ Περαία, sc. γῆ or χώρα, *the country on the opposite side*), a general name for any district belonging to or closely connected with a country, from the main part of which it was separated by a sea or river, was used specifically for—**1.** The part of Palestine E. of the Jordan in general, but usually, in a more restricted sense, for a part of that region, namely, the district between the rivers Hieromax on the N., and Arnon on the S. Respecting its political connections with the rest of the country, see PALAESTINA.—**2. Peraea Rhodiorum** (ἡ Περαία τῶν Ῥοδίων), also called the Rhodian Chersonese, a district in the S. of Caria, opposite to the island of Rhodes, from Mt. Phoenix on the W. to the frontier of Lycia on the E. This strip of coast, which was reckoned 1500 stadia in length (by sea), and was regarded as one of the finest spots on the earth, was colonised by the Rhodians at an early period, and was always in close political connection with Rhodes even under the successive rulers of Caria; and, after the victory of the Romans over Antiochus the Great, B.C. 190, it was assigned, with the whole of Carian Doris, to the independent republic of the Rhodians. [RHODUS.]—**3.** P. Tenediōrum (περαία Τενεδίων), a strip of the W. coast of Mysia, opposite to the island of Tenedos, between C. Sigeum on the N., and Alexandria Troas on the S.—**4.** A city on the W. coast of Mysia, near Adramyttium, one of the colonies of the Mytilenaeans, and not improbably preserving in its name that of a district once called Peraea Mytilenaeorum; for the people of Mytilene are known to have had many settlements on this coast.

Percōtē (Περκώτη, formerly Περκώτη, according to Strabo: *Boryas* or *Burgas*, Turk., and *Percate*, Grk.), a very ancient city of Mysia, between Abydos and Lampsacus, near the Hellespont, on a river called Percates, in a beautiful situation. It is mentioned by Homer.

Perdiccas (Περδίκκας) 1. I. The founder of the Macedonian monarchy, according to Herodotus, though later writers represent Caranus as the 1st king of Macedonia, and make Perdiccas only the 4th. [CARANUS.] According to Herodotus, Perdiccas and his two brothers, Gauanes and Aëropus, were Argives of the race of Temenus, who settled near Mt. Bermius, from whence they subdued the rest of Macedonia (Herod. viii. 137, 138). It is clear, however, that the dominions of Perdiccas and his immediate successors, comprised but a very small part of the country subsequently known under that name. Perdiccas was succeeded by his son Argaeus. — 2. II. King of Macedonia, from about B. C. 454 to 413, was the son and successor of Alexander I. Shortly before the commencement of the Peloponnesian war Perdiccas was at war with the Athenians, who sent a force to support his brother Philip, and Derdas, a Macedonian chieftain, against the king, while the latter espoused the cause of Potidaea, which had shaken off the Athenian yoke, B. C. 432. In the following year peace was concluded between Perdiccas and the Athenians, but it did not last long, and he was during the greater part of his reign on hostile terms with the Athenians. In 429 his dominions were invaded by Sitalces, king of the powerful Thracian tribe of the Odrysians, but the enemy was compelled, by want of provisions, to return home. It was in great part at his instigation that Brasidas in 424 set out on his celebrated expedition to Macedonia and Thrace. In the following year (423) however a misunderstanding arose between him and Brasidas; in consequence of which he abandoned the Spartan alliance, and concluded peace with Athens. Subsequently we find him at one time in alliance with the Spartans, and at another time with the Athenians; and it is evident that he joined one or other of the belligerent parties according to the dictates of his own interest at the moment. — 3. III. King of Macedonia, B. C. 364—359, was the second son of Amyntas II., by his wife Eurydice. On the assassination of his brother Alexander II., by Ptolemy of Alorus, 367, the crown of Macedonia devolved upon him by hereditary right, but Ptolemy virtually enjoyed the sovereign power as guardian of Perdiccas till 364, when the latter caused Ptolemy to be put to death, and took the government into his own hands. Of the reign of Perdiccas we have very little information. We learn only that he was at one time engaged in hostilities with Athens on account of Amphipolis, and that he was distinguished for his patronage of men of letters. He fell in battle against the Illyrians, 359. — 4. Son of Orontes, a Macedonian of the province of Orestis, was one of the most distinguished of the generals of Alexander the Great. He accompanied Alexander throughout his campaigns in Asia; and the king on his death-bed is said to have taken the royal signet ring from

his finger and given it to Perdiccas. After the death of the king (323), Perdiccas had the chief authority entrusted to him under the command of the new king Arrhidaeus, who was a mere puppet in his hands, and he still further strengthened his power by the assassination of his rival Meleager. [MELEAGER.] The other generals of Alexander regarded him with fear and suspicion; and at length his ambitious schemes induced Antipater, Craterus, and Ptolemy, to unite in a league and declare open war against Perdiccas. Thus assailed on all sides, Perdiccas determined to leave Eumenes in Asia Minor, to make head against their common enemies in that quarter, while he himself marched into Egypt against Ptolemy. He advanced without opposition as far as Pelusium, but found the banks of the Nile strongly fortified and guarded by Ptolemy, and was repulsed in repeated attempts to force the passage of the river; in the last of which, near Memphis, he lost great numbers of men. Thereupon his troops, who had long been discontented with Perdiccas, rose in mutiny and put him to death in his own tent.

Perdix (Πέρδιξ), the sister of Daedalus, and mother of Talos, or according to others, the sister's son of Daedalus, figures in the mythological period of Greek art, as the inventor of various implements, chiefly for working in wood. Perdix is sometimes confounded with Talos or Calos, and it is best to regard the various legends respecting Perdix, Talos, and Calos, as referring to one and the same person, namely, according to the mythographers, a nephew of Daedalus. The inventions ascribed to him are: the saw, the idea of which is said to have been suggested to him by the back-bone of a fish, or the teeth of a serpent; the chisel; the compasses; the potter's wheel. His skill excited the jealousy of Daedalus, who threw him headlong from the temple of Athena on the Acropolis, but the goddess caught him in his fall, and changed him into the bird which was named after him, *perdix*, the partridge.

Peregrīnus Proteus, a cynic philosopher, born at Parium, on the Hellespont, flourished in the reign of the Antonines. After a youth spent in debauchery and crimes, he visited Palestine, where he turned Christian, and by dint of hypocrisy attained to some authority in the Church. He next assumed the cynic garb, and returned to his native town, where, to obliterate the memory of his crimes, he divided his inheritance among the populace. He again set out on his travels, and after visiting many places, and adopting every method to make himself conspicuous, he at length resolved on publicly burning himself at the Olympic games; and carried his resolution into effect in the 236th Olympiad, A. D. 165. Lucian, who knew Peregrinus, and who was present at his strange self immolation, has left us an account of his life.

Pĕrenna, Anna. [ANNA.]

Perennis, succeeded Paternus in A. D. 183, as sole praefect of the praetorians, and Commodus being completely sunk in debauchery and sloth, virtually ruled the empire. Having, however, rendered himself obnoxious to the soldiery, he was put to death by them in 186 or 187. Dion Cassius represents Perennis as a man of a pure and upright life; but the other historians charge him with having encouraged the emperor in all his excesses, and urged him on in his career of profligacy.

Perga (Πέργη: Περγαῖος: *Murtana*, Ru.), an ancient and important city of Pamphylia, lay a

542	PERGAMA.

PERIANDER.

little inland, N. E. of Attalia, between the rivers Catarrhactes and Cestrus, 60 stadia (6 geog. miles) from the mouth of the former. It was a celebrated seat of the worship of Artemis. On an eminence near the city stood a very ancient and renowned temple of the goddess, at which a yearly festival was celebrated; and the coins of Perga bear images of the goddess and her temple. Under the later Roman empire, it was the capital of Pamphylia Secunda. It was the first place in Asia Minor visited by the apostle Paul on his first missionary journey (Acta, xiii. 13.; see also xiv. 25). Splendid ruins of the city are still visible about 16 miles N. E. of *Adalia*.

Pergăma and Pergămĭa [PERGAMON, No. 1].

Pergămon or -um, Pergămos or -us (τὸ Πέργαμον, ἡ Πέργαμος: the former by far the most usual form in the classical writers, though the latter is more common in English, probably on account of its use in our version of the Bible, *Rev.* ii. 13.; in Latin it seldom occurs in the nominative, but, when used, the form is Pergamum: Περγαμηνός, Pergamēnus. The word is significant, connected with πύργος, *a tower;* it is used in the plural form, πέργαμα, as a common noun by Aeschylus, *Prom.* 956; Euripides, *Phoen.* 1098, 1176). —1. The citadel of Troy, and used poetically for Troy itself: the poets also use the forms Pergăma (τὰ Πέργαμα) and Pergamĭa (ἡ Περγαμία, sc. πόλις): the king of Troy, Laomedon, is called Περγαμίδης, and the Romans are spoken of by Silius Italicus as "sanguis Pergameus." — 2. (*Bergama* or *Pergamo,* Ru.), a celebrated city of Asia Minor, the capital of the kingdom of Pergamus, and afterwards of the Roman province of Asia, was situated in the district of S. Mysia called Teuthrania, in one of the most beautiful and fertile vallies in the world. It stood on the N. bank of the river Caïcus, at a spot where that river receives the united waters of 2 small tributaries, the Selinus, which flowed through the city, and the Cetius, which washed its walls. The navigable river Caïcus connected it with the sea, at the Elaïtic Gulf, from which its distance was somewhat less than 20 miles. It was built at the foot, and on the lowest slopes, of 2 steep hills, on one of which the ruins of the acropolis are still visible, and in the plain below are the remains of the Asclepieum and other temples, of the stadium, the theatre, and the amphitheatre, and of other buildings. The origin of the city is lost in mythical traditions, which ascribed its foundation to a colony from Arcadia under the Heracleid Telephus, and its name to Pergamus, a son of Pyrrhus and Andromache, who made himself king of Teuthrania by killing the king Arius in single combat. There is also a tradition, that a colony of Epidaurians settled here under Asclepius. At all events, it was already, in the time of Xenophon, a very ancient city, with a mixed population of Teuthranians and Greeks; but it was not a place of much importance until the time of the successors of Alexander. After the defeat of Antigonus at Ipsus, in 301, the N.W. part of Asia Minor was united to the Thracian kingdom of LYSIMACHUS, who enlarged and beautified the city of Pergamus, and used it as a treasury on account of its strength as a fortress. The command of the fortress was entrusted to PHILETAERUS, who, towards the end of the reign of Lysimachus, revolted to Seleucus, king of Syria, retaining,

however, the fortress of Pergamus in his own hands; and upon the death of Seleucus, in 280, Philetaerus established himself as an independent ruler. This is the date of the commencement of the kingdom of Pergamus, though the royal title was only assumed by the second successor of Philetaerus, ATTALUS I., after his great victory over the Gauls. The successive kings of Pergamus were: PHILETAERUS, 280—263; EUMENES I., 263—241; ATTALUS I., 241—197; EUMENES II., 197—159; ATTALUS II. PHILADELPHUS, 159—138; ATTALUS III. PHILOMETOR, 138—133. For the outline of their history, see the articles. The kingdom reached its greatest extent after the defeat of Antiochus the Great by the Romans, in B.C. 190, when the Romans bestowed upon Eumenes II. the whole of Mysia, Lydia, both Phrygias, Lycaonia, Pisidia and Pamphylia. It was under the same king that Pergamus reached the height of its splendour, and that the celebrated library was founded, which for a long time rivalled that of Alexandria, and the formation of which occasioned the invention of parchment, *charta Pergamena.* This library was afterwards united to that of Alexandria, having been presented by Antony to Cleopatra. During its existence at Pergamus, it formed the centre of a great school of literature, which rivalled that of Alexandria. On the death of Attalus III. in B.C. 133, the king dom, by a bequest in his will, passed to the Romans, who took possession of it in 130 after a contest with the usurper Aristonicus, and erected it into the province of Asia, with the city of Pergamus for its capital, which continued in such prosperity, that Pliny calls it "longe clarissimum Asiae." The city was an early seat of Christianity, and is one of the Seven Churches of Asia, to whom the apocalyptic epistles are addressed. St. John describes it as the scene of a persecution of Christianity, and the seat of gross idolatry, which had even infected the Church. The expression "where Satan's seat is" is thought by some to refer to the worship of the serpent, as the symbol of Asclepius, the patron god of the city. Under the Byzantine emperors, the capital of the province of Asia was transferred to Ephesus, and Pergamus lost much of its importance. Among the celebrated natives of the city were the rhetorician Apollodorus and the physician Galen. — 2. A very ancient city of Crete, the foundation of which was ascribed to the Trojans who survived their city. The legislator Lycurgus was said to have died here, and his grave was shown. The site of the city is doubtful. Some place it at *Perama,* others at *Platania.*

Pergămus. [PERGAMON.]

Pergă. [PERGA.]

Pĕriander (Περίανδρος). 1. Son of Cypselus, whom he succeeded as tyrant of Corinth, B.C. 625, and reigned 40 years, to B.C. 585. His rule was mild and beneficent at first, but afterwards became oppressive. According to the common story this change was owing to the advice of Thrasybulus, tyrant of Miletus, whom Periander had consulted on the best mode of maintaining his power, and who is said to have taken the messenger through a corn-field, cutting off, as he went, the tallest ears, and then to have dismissed him without committing himself to a verbal answer. The action, however, was rightly interpreted by Periander, who proceeded to rid himself of the most powerful nobles in the state. He made his power respected abroad as well as at home; and besides his conquest of Epidaurus, mentioned below, he kept Corcyra in subjection. He was, like many of the other Greek tyrants, a patron of literature and philosophy; and Arion and Anacharsis were in favour at his court. He was very commonly reckoned among the Seven Sages, though by some he was excluded from their number, and Myson of Chenae in Laconia was substituted in his room. The private life of Periander was marked by misfortune and cruelty. He married Melissa, daughter of Procles, tyrant of Epidaurus. She bore him two sons, Cypselus and Lycophron, and was passionately beloved by him; but he is said to have killed her by a blow during her pregnancy, having been roused to a fit of anger by a false accusation brought against her. His wife's death embittered the remainder of his days, partly through the remorse which he felt for the deed, partly through the alienation of his younger son Lycophron, inexorably exasperated by his mother's fate. The young man's anger had been chiefly excited by Procles, and Periander in revenge attacked Epidaurus, and, having reduced it, took his father-in-law prisoner. Periander sent Lycophron to Corcyra; but when he was himself advanced in years, he summoned Lycophron back to Corinth to succeed to the tyranny, seeing that Cypselus, his elder son, was unfit to hold it, from deficiency of understanding. Lycophron refused to return to Corinth, as long as his father was there. Thereupon Periander offered to withdraw to Corcyra, if Lycophron would come home and take the government. To this he assented; but the Corcyraeans, not wishing to have Periander among them, put Lycophron to death. Periander shortly afterwards died of despondency, at the age of 80, and after a reign of 40 years, according to Diogenes Laërtius. He was succeeded by a relative, Psammetichus, son of Gordias. — 2. Tyrant of Ambracia, was contemporary with his more famous namesake of Corinth, to whom he was also related, being the son of Gorgus, who was son or brother to Cypselus. Periander was deposed by the people, probably after the death of the Corinthian tyrant (585).

PERIBOEA (Περίβοια). 1. Wife of Icarius, and mother of Penelope. [ICARIUS, No. 2.] — 2. Daughter of Alcathous, and wife of Telamon, by whom she became the mother of Ajax and Teucer. Some writers call her Eriboea. — 3. Daughter of Hipponous, and wife of Oeneus, by whom she became the mother of Tydeus. [OENEUS.] — 4. Wife of king Polybus of Corinth.

PERICLES (Περικλῆς). 1. The greatest of Athenian statesmen, was the son of Xanthippus, and Agariste, both of whom belonged to the noblest families of Athens. The fortune of his parents procured for him a careful education, which his extraordinary abilities and diligence turned to the best account. He received instruction from Damon, Zeno of Elea, and Anaxagoras. With Anaxagoras he lived on terms of the most intimate friendship, till the philosopher was compelled to retire from Athens. From this great and original thinker Pericles was believed to have derived not only the cast of his mind, but the character of his eloquence, which, in the elevation of its sentiments, and the purity and loftiness of its style, was the fitting expression of the force and dignity of his character and the grandeur of his conceptions. Of

the oratory of Pericles no specimens remain to us, but it is described by ancient writers as characterised by singular force and energy. He was described as thundering and lightning when he spoke, and as carrying the weapons of Zeus upon his tongue. — In B. c. 469, Pericles began to take part in public affairs, 40 years before his death, and was soon regarded as the head of the more democratical part in the state, in opposition to Cimon. He gained the favour of the people by the laws which he got passed for their benefit. Thus it was enacted through his means that the citizens should receive from the public treasury the price of their admittance to the theatre, amounting to 2 oboli apiece; that those who served in the courts of the Heliaea should be paid for their attendance; and that those citizens who served as soldiers should likewise be paid. It was at his instigation that his friend Ephialtes proposed in 461 the measure by which the Areopagus was deprived of those functions which rendered it formidable as an antagonist to the democratical party. This success was followed by the ostracism of Cimon, who was charged with Laconism; and Pericles was thus placed at the head of public affairs at Athens. Pericles was distinguished as a general as well as a statesman, and frequently commanded the Athenian armies in their wars with the neighbouring states. In 454 he commanded the Athenians in their campaigns against the Sicyonians and Acarnanians; in 448 he led the army which assisted the Phocians in the Sacred War; and in 445 he rendered the most signal service to the state by recovering the island of Euboea, which had revolted from Athens. Cimon had been previously recalled from exile, without any opposition from Pericles, but had died in 449. On his death the aristocratical party was headed by Thucydides, the son of Melesias, but on the ostracism of the latter in 444, the organized opposition of the aristocratical party was broken up, and Pericles was left without a rival. Throughout the remainder of his political course no one appeared to contest his supremacy; but the boundless influence which he possessed was never perverted by him to sinister or unworthy purposes. So far from being a mere selfish demagogue, he neither indulged nor courted the multitude. The next important event in which Pericles was engaged was the war against Samos, which had revolted from Athens, and which he subdued after an arduous campaign, 440. The poet Sophocles was one of the generals who fought with Pericles against Samos. For the next 10 years till the outbreak of the Peloponnesian war, the Athenians were not engaged in any considerable military operations. During this period Pericles devoted especial attention to the Athenian navy, as her supremacy rested on her maritime superiority, and he adopted various judicious means for consolidating and strengthening her empire over the islands of the Aegaean. The funds derived from the tribute of the allies and from other sources were to a large extent devoted by him to the erection of those magnificent temples and public buildings which rendered Athens the wonder and admiration of Greece. Under his administration the Propylaea, and the Parthenon, and the Odeum were erected, as well as numerous other temples and public buildings. With the stimulus afforded by these works architecture and sculpture reached their highest perfection, and some of the greatest artists of antiquity were employed in erecting or adorning the buildings. The chief direction and oversight of the public edifices was entrusted to Phidias. [PHIDIAS.] These works calling into activity almost every branch of industry and commerce at Athens, diffused universal prosperity while they proceeded, and thus contributed in this, as well as in other ways, to maintain the popularity and influence of Pericles. But he still had many enemies, who were not slow to impute to him base and unworthy motives. From the comic poets Pericles had to sustain numerous attacks. They exaggerated his power, spoke of his party as Pisistratids, and called upon him to swear that he was not about to assume the tyranny. His high character and strict probity, however, rendered all these attacks harmless. But as his enemies were unable to ruin his reputation by these means, they attacked him through his friends. His friends Phidias and Anaxagoras, and his mistress Aspasia were all accused before the people. Phidias was condemned and cast into prison [PHIDIAS]; Anaxagoras was also sentenced to pay a fine and quit Athens [ANAXAGORAS]; and Aspasia was only acquitted through the entreaties and tears of Pericles. — The Peloponnesian war has been falsely ascribed to the ambitious schemes of Pericles. It is true that he counselled the Athenians not to yield to the demands of the Lacedaemonians, and he pointed out the immense advantages which the Athenians possessed in carrying on the war; but he did this because he saw that war was inevitable; and that as long as Athens retained the great power which she then possessed, Sparta would never rest contented. On the outbreak of the war in 431 a Peloponnesian army under Archidamus invaded Attica; and upon his advice the Athenians conveyed their moveable property into the city, and their cattle and beasts of burden to Euboea, and allowed the Peloponnesians to desolate Attica without opposition. Next year (430), when the Peloponnesians again invaded Attica, Pericles pursued the same policy as before. In this summer the plague made its appearance in Athens. The Athenians, being exposed to the devastation of the war and the plague at the same time, began to turn their thoughts to peace, and looked upon Pericles as the author of all their distresses, inasmuch as he had persuaded them to go to war. Pericles attempted to calm the public ferment; but such was the irritation against him, that he was sentenced to pay a fine. The ill feeling of the people having found this vent, Pericles soon resumed his accustomed sway, and was again elected one of the generals for the ensuing year (429). Meantime Pericles had suffered in common with his fellow-citizens. The plague carried off most of his near connections. His son Xanthippus, a profligate and undutiful youth, his sister, and most of his intimate friends died of it. Still he maintained unmoved his calm bearing and philosophic composure. At last his only surviving legitimate son, Paralus, a youth of greater promise than his brother, fell a victim. The firmness of Pericles then at last gave way; as he placed the funeral garland on the head of the lifeless youth he burst into tears and sobbed aloud. He had one son remaining, his child by Aspasia; and he was allowed to enrol this son in his own tribe and give him his own name. In the autumn of 429 Pericles himself died of a lingering sickness. When at the point of death, as his friends were gathered round his bed, recalling his virtues and enumerating his triumphs, Pericles overhearing their remarks, said that they had forgotten his greatest praise: that no Athenian through his means had been made to put on mourning. He survived the commencement of the war 2 years and 6 months. The name of the wife of Pericles is not mentioned. She had been the wife of Hipponicus, by whom she was the mother of Callias. She bore two sons to Pericles, Xanthippus and Paralus. She lived unhappily with Pericles, and a divorce took place by mutual consent, when Pericles connected himself with Aspasia. Of his strict probity he left the decisive proof in the fact that at his death he was found not to have added a single drachma to his hereditary property. — 2. Son of the preceding, by Aspasia, was one of the generals at the battle of Arginusae, and was put to death by the Athenians with the other generals, 406.

Periclymenus (Περικλύμενος). 1. One of the Argonauts, was son of Neleus and Chloris, and brother of Nestor. Poseidon gave him the power of changing himself into different forms, and conferred upon him great strength, but he was nevertheless slain by Hercules at the capture of Pylos. — 2. Son of Poseidon and Chloris, the daughter of Tiresias, of Thebes. In the war of the Seven against Thebes he was believed to have killed Parthenopaeus; and when he pursued Amphiaraus, the latter by the command of Zeus was swallowed up by the earth.

Perieres (Περιήρης), son of Aeolus and Enarete, king of Messene, was the father of Aphareus and Leucippus by Gorgophone. In some traditions Perieres was called a son of Cynortas, and besides the sons above mentioned he is said to have been the father of Tyndareos and Icarius.

Perilaus (Περίλαος), son of Icarius and Periboea, and a brother of Penelope.

Perillus (Περίλλος), a statuary, was the maker of the bronze bull of the tyrant Phalaris, respecting which see further under PHALARIS. Like the makers of other instruments of death, Perillus is said to have become one of the victims of his own handiwork.

Perinthus (Πέρινθος: Περίνθιος: Eski Eregli), an important town in Thrace on the Propontis, was founded by the Samians about B. c. 559. It was situated 22 miles W. of Selymbria on a small peninsula, and was built on the slope of a hill with rows of houses rising above each other like seats in an amphitheatre. It is celebrated for the obstinate resistance which it offered to Philip of Macedon, at which time it was a more powerful place than Byzantium. Under the Romans it still continued to be a flourishing town, being the point at which most of the roads met leading to Byzantium. The commercial importance of the town is attested by its numerous coins which are still extant. At a later time, but not earlier than the 4th century of the Christian aera, we find it called Heraclea, which occurs sometimes alone without any addition and sometimes in the form of Heraclea Thraciae or Heraclea Perinthus.

Periphas (Περίφας), an Attic autochthon, previous to the time of Cecrops, was a priest of Apollo, and on account of his virtues was made king of the country. In consequence of the honours paid to him, Zeus wished to destroy him; but at the request of Apollo he was metamorphosed by Zeus into an eagle, and his wife into a bird.

Bird's-eye View of the Forum of Pompeii.   See page 601.

A. Temple of Jupiter.
B. Temple of Venus.
C. Temple of Mercury.
D. Basilica.
E. Edifice of Eumachia.
F. Thermae.
G. Pantheon or Temple of Augustus.
I, K, L. Tribunals or Courts of Justice.

N. Granaries.
P. Curia or Senaculum.
R. Part not yet excavated.
S. Street of the Dried Fruits.
T. Street leading to the Temple of Fortune.
V. Triumphal Arch.
W. Pedestals.
Y. Street of the Silversmiths.

[To face p. 541.

Patrae in Achaia. Page 530.

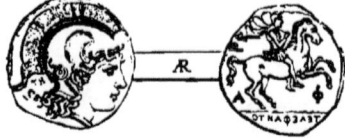

Pella in Macedonia. Page 536.

Pellene in Achaia. Page 537.

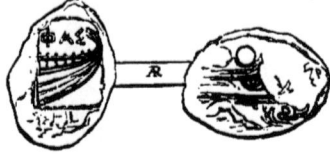

Perga in Pamphylia. Page 541.

Perinthus in Thrace. Page 544.

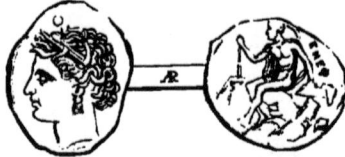

Phaestus in Crete. Page 551.

Pharsalus. Page 554.

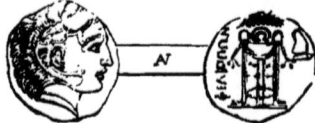

Phaselis in Lycia. Page 554.

Pheneus in Arcadia. Page 555.

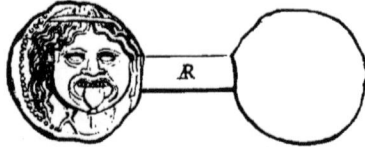

Philippi in Macedonia. Page 559.

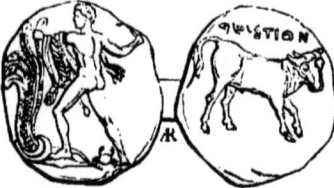

Populonia in Etruria. Page 607.

Praesus in Crete. Page 611.

To face p. 545.]

Pĕrĭphĕtes (Περιφήτης), son of Hephaestus and Anticlĕa, surnamed Corynetes, that is, Club-bearer, was a robber at Epidaurus, who slew travellers with an iron club. Theseus at last killed him and took his club for his own use.

Permessus (Περμησσός: Kefalari), a river in Boeotia, which descends from Mt. Helicon, unites with the Olmius, and falls into the lake Copais near Haliartus.

Pernē (Πέρνη), a little island off the coast of Ionia, opposite to the territory of Miletus, to which an earthquake united it.

Pēro (Πηρώ), daughter of Neleus and Chloris, was married to Bias, and celebrated for her beauty.

Perperēna (Περπερήνα, and other forms), a small town of Mysia, S. of Adramyttium, in the neighbourhood of which there were copper-mines and celebrated vineyards. It was said to be the place at which Thucydides died.

Perperna or Perpenna (the former is the pre-ferable form). 1. M., praetor B.C. 135, when he carried on war against the slaves in Sicily; and consul 130, when he defeated Aristonicus in Asia, and took him prisoner. He died near Pergamum on his return to Rome in 129. — 2. M., son of the last, consul 92, and censor 86. He is mentioned by the ancient writers as an extraordinary instance of longevity. He attained the age of 98 years, and died in 49, the year in which the civil war broke out between Caesar and Pompey. He took no prominent part in the agitated times in which he lived. — 3. M. Perperna Vento, son of the last, joined the Marian party in the civil war, and was raised to the praetorship. After the conquest of Italy by Sulla, in 82, Perperna fled to Sicily, which he quitted however upon the arrival of Pom-pey shortly afterwards. On the death of Sulla, in 78, Perperna joined the consul M. Lepidus in his attempt to overthrow the new aristocratical consti-tution, and retired with him to Sardinia on the failure of this attempt. Lepidus died in Sardinia in the following year, 77, and Perperna with the remains of his army crossed over to Spain and joined Sertorius. Perperna was jealous of the ascendancy of Sertorius, and after serving under him some years he and his friends assassinated Sertorius at a banquet in 72. His death soon brought the war to a close. Perperna was de-feated by Pompey, was taken prisoner, and was put to death.

Perrhaebi (Περραιβοί or Περαιβοί), a powerful and warlike Pelasgic people, who, according to Strabo, migrated from Euboea to the mainland, and settled in the districts of Hestiaeotis and Pe-lasgiotis in Thessaly. Hence the northern part of this country is frequently called Perrhaebia (Περ-ραιβία, Περαιβία), though it never formed one of the regular Thessalian provinces. Homer places the Perrhaebi in the neighbourhood of the Thes-salian Dodona and the river Titaresius; and at a later time the name of Perrhaebia was applied to the district bounded by Macedonia and the Cam-bunian mountains on the N., by Pindus on the W., by the Peneus on the S. and S.E., and by the Peneus and Ossa on the E. The Perrhaebi were members of the Amphictyonic league. At an early period they were subdued by the Lapithae; at the time of the Peloponnesian war they were subject to the Thessalians, and subsequently to Philip of Macedon; but at the time of the Roman wars in Greece they appear independent of Macedonia.

Perrhidae (Περρίδαι), an Attic demus near Aphidna, belonging to the tribe Antiochis.

Persabŏra or Perisabŏra (Περσαβώρα: Anbar), a strongly fortified city of Babylonia, on the W. side of the Euphrates, at the point where the canal called Maarsares left the river.

Persae. [PERSIS.]

Persaeus (Περσαῖος), a Stoic philosopher, was a native of Cittium in Crete, and a disciple of Zeno. He lived for some years at the court of Antigonus Gonatas, with whom he seems to have been in high favour. Antigonus appointed him to the chief command in Corinth, where he was slain, when the city was taken by Aratus, B.C. 243.

Persē (Πέρση), daughter of Oceanus, and wife of Helios (the Sun), by whom she became the mother of Aeëtes and Circe. She is further called the mother of Pasiphaë and Perses. Homer and Apollonius Rhodius call her Perse, while others call her Perseis or Persea.

Persēis, a name given to Hecate, as the daughter of Perses by Asteria.

Persēphŏnē (Περσεφόνη), called Proserpina by the Romans, the daughter of Zeus and Deme-ter. In Homer she is called Persephonīa (Περσε-φόνεια); the form Persephone first occurs in He-siod. But besides these forms of the name, we also find Persephassa, Phersephassa, Persephatta, Phersephatta, Pherrephassa, Pherephatta, and Pher-sephonīa, for which various etymologies have been proposed. The Latin Proserpina is probably only a corruption of the Greek. In Attica she was worshipped under the name of Cora (Κόρη, Ion. Κούρη), that is, the Daughter, namely, of Demeter; and the two were frequently called The Mother and the Daughter (ἡ Μητὴρ καὶ ἡ Κόρη). Being the infernal goddess of death, she is also called a daughter of Zeus and Styx. In Arcadia she was worshipped under the name of Despoena, and was called a daughter of Poseidon Hippius and Deme-ter, and said to have been brought up by the Titan Anytus. Homer describes her as the wife of Hades, and the formidable, venerable, and majestic queen of the Shades, who rules over the souls of the dead, along with her husband. Hence she is called by later writers Juno Inferna, Averna, and Stygia; and the Erinnyes are said to have been her daughters by Pluto. Groves sacred to her are placed by Homer in the western extremity of the earth, on the frontiers of the lower world, which is itself called the house of Persephone. The story of her being carried off by Hades or Pluto against her will is not mentioned by Homer, who simply describes her as the wife and queen of Hades. Her abduction is first mentioned by Hesiod. The ac-count of her abduction, which is the most celebrated part of her story, and the wanderings of her mother in search of her, and the worship of the 2 goddesses in Attica at the festival of the Eleusinia, are related under DEMETER. In the mystical theories of the Orphics, Persephone is described as the all-per-vading goddess of nature, who both produces and destroys every thing; and she is therefore men-tioned along, or identified with, other mystic divi-nities, such as Isis, Rhea, Ge, Hestia, Pandora, Artemis, Hecate. This mystic Persephone is fur-ther said to have become by Zeus the mother of Dionysus, Iacchus, Zagreus or Sabazius. — Perse-phone frequently appears in works of art. She is represented either with the grave and severe cha-racter of an infernal Juno, or as a mystical divinity

N N

with a sceptre and a little box, in the act of being carried off by Pluto.

Persĕpŏlĭs (Περσέπολις, Περσαίπολις: in the middle ages, *Istakhar*: now *Takhti-Jemshid*, i. e. *Throne of Jemshid*, or *Chil-Minar*, i. e. *Forty Pillars*: large Ru.) is the Greek name, probably translated from the Persian name, which is not recorded, of the great city which succeeded Pasargada as the capital of Persis and of the Persian empire. From the circumstance, however, of the conquest of the Babylonian empire taking place about the time when Persepolis attained this dignity, it appears to have been seldom used as the royal residence. Neither Herodotus, Xenophon, Ctesias, nor the sacred writers during the Persian period, mention it at all; though they often speak of Babylon, Susa, and Ecbatana, as the capitals of the empire. It is only from the Greek writers after the Macedonian conquest that we learn its rank in the empire, which appears to have consisted chiefly in its being one of the 2 burial places of the kings (the other being Pasargada), and also a royal treasury; for Alexander found in the palace immense riches, which were said to have accumulated from the time of Cyrus. Its foundation is sometimes ascribed to Cyrus the Great, but more generally to his son Cambyses. It was greatly enlarged and adorned by Darius I. and Xerxes, and preserved its splendour till after the Macedonian conquest, when it was burnt; Alexander, as the story goes, setting fire to the palace with his own hand, at the end of a revel, by the instigation of the courtezan Thaïs, B. c. 331. It was not, however, so entirely destroyed as some historians represent. It appears frequently in subsequent history, both ancient and medieval. It is now deserted, but its ruins are considerable, though too dilapidated to give any good notion of Persian architecture, and they are rich in cuneiform inscriptions. It was situated in the heart of Persis, in the part called Hollow Persis (κοίλη Πέρσις), not far from the border of the Carmanian Desert, in a beautiful and healthy valley, watered by the river Araxes (*Bend-Emir*), and its tributaries the Medus and the Cyrus. The city stood on the N. side of the Araxes, and had a citadel (the ruins of which are still seen) built on the levelled surface of a rock, and enclosed by triple walls rising one above the other to the heights of 16, 48, and 60 cubits, within which was the palace, with its royal sepulchres and treasuries.

Perses (Πέρσης). 1. Son of the Titan Crius and Eurybia, and husband of Asteria, by whom he became the father of Hecate. — 2. Son of Perseus and Andromeda, described by the Greeks as the founder of the Persian nation. — 3. Son of Helios (the Sun) and Perse, and brother of Aeëtes and Circe.

Perseus (Περσεύς), the famous Argive hero, was a son of Zeus and Danaë, and a grandson of Acrisius. An oracle had told Acrisius that he was doomed to perish by the hands of Danaë's son; and he therefore shut up his daughter in an apartment made of brass or stone. But Zeus having metamorphosed himself into a shower of gold, came down through the roof of the prison, and became by her the father of Perseus. From this circumstance Perseus is sometimes called *aurigena*. As soon as Acrisius discovered that Danaë had given birth to a son, he put both mother and son into a chest, and threw them into the sea; but

Zeus caused the chest to land in the island of Seriphos, one of the Cyclades, where Dictys, a fisherman, found them, and carried them to Polydectes, the king of the country. They were treated with kindness by Polydectes; but the latter having afterwards fallen in love with Danaë, who finding it impossible to gratify his desires in consequence of the presence of Perseus, who had meantime grown up to manhood, he sent Perseus away to fetch the head of Medusa, one of the Gorgons. Guided by Hermes and Athena, Perseus first went to the Graeae, the sisters of the Gorgons, took from them their one tooth and their one eye, and would not restore them until they showed him the way to the nymphs, who possessed the winged sandals, the magic wallet, and the helmet of Hades, which rendered the wearer invisible. Having received from the Nymphs these invaluable presents, from Hermes a sickle, and from Athena a mirror, he mounted into the air, and arrived at the Gorgons, who dwelt near Tartessus on the coast of the Ocean, whose heads were covered, like those of serpents, with scales, and who had large tusks like boars, brazen hands, and golden wings. He found them asleep, and cut off the head of Medusa, looking at her figure through the mirror, for a sight of the monster herself would have changed him into stone. Perseus put her head into the wallet which he carried on his back, and as he went away he was pursued by 2 other Gorgons; but his helmet, which rendered him invisible, enabled him to escape in safety. Perseus then proceeded to Aethiopia, where he saved and married Andromeda. [ANDROMEDA.] Perseus is also said to have come to the Hyperboreans, by whom he was hospitably received, and to Atlas, whom he changed into the mountain of the same name by the Gorgon's head. On his return to Seriphos, he found his mother with Dictys in a temple, whither they had fled from the violence of Polydectes. Perseus then went to the palace of Polydectes, and metamorphosed him and all his guests, and, some say, the whole island, into stone. He then presented the kingdom to Dictys. He gave the winged sandals and the helmet to Hermes, who restored them to the nymphs and to Hades, and the head of Gorgon to Athena, who placed it in the middle of her shield or breastplate. Perseus then went to Argos, accompanied by Danaë and Andromeda. Acrisius, remembering the oracle, escaped to Larissa, in the country of the Pelasgians; but Perseus followed him, in order to persuade him to return. Some writers state that Perseus, on his return to Argos, found Proetus, who had expelled his brother Acrisius, in possession of the kingdom; and that Perseus slew Proetus, and was afterwards killed by Megapenthes, the son of Proetus. The more common tradition, however, relates that when Teutamidas, king of Larissa, celebrated games in honour of his guest Acrisius, Perseus, who took part in them, accidentally hit the foot of Acrisius with the discus, and thus killed him. Acrisius was buried outside the city of Larissa, and Perseus, leaving the kingdom of Argos to Megapenthes, the son of Proetus, received from him in exchange the government of Tiryns. According to others, Perseus remained in Argos, and successfully opposed the introduction of the Bacchic orgies. Perseus is said to have founded the towns of Midea and Mycenae. By Andromeda he became the father of Perses,

Alcaeus, Sthenelus, Heleus, Mestor, Electryon, Gorgophone, and Autochthe. Perseus was worshipped as a hero in several places.

Perseus or Perses (Περσεύς), the last king of Macedonia, was the eldest son of Philip V., and reigned 11 years from B. C. 178 to 168. Before his accession he persuaded his father to put to death his younger brother Demetrius, whom he suspected that the Roman senate intended to set up as a competitor for the throne on the death of Philip. Immediately after his accession he began to make preparations for war with the Romans, which he knew to be inevitable, though 7 years elapsed before actual hostilities commenced. The war broke out in 171. The 1st year of the war was marked by no striking action. The consul P. Licinius Crassus first suffered a defeat in Thessaly in an engagement between the cavalry of the 2 armies, but subsequently gained a slight advantage over the king's troops. — The 2nd year of the war (170), in which the consul A. Hostilius Mancinus commanded, also passed over without any important battle, but was on the whole favourable to Perseus. — The 3rd year (169), in which the consul Q. Marcius Philippus commanded, again produced no important results. The length to which the war had been unexpectedly protracted, and the ill success of the Roman arms, had by this time excited a general feeling in favour of the Macedonian monarch; but the ill-timed avarice of Perseus, who refused to advance the sum of money which Eumenes, king of Pergamus, demanded, deprived him of this valuable ally; and the same unseasonable niggardliness likewise deprived him of the services of 20,000 Gaulish mercenaries, who had actually advanced into Macedonia to his support, but retired on failing to obtain their stipulated pay. He was thus led to carry on the contest against Rome single-handed. — The 4th year of the war (168) was also the last. The new consul, L. Aemilius Paulus, defeated Perseus with great loss in a decisive battle fought near Pydna on June 22, 168. Perseus took refuge in the island of Samothrace, where he shortly afterwards surrendered with his children to the praetor Cn. Octavius. When brought before Aemilius, he is said to have degraded himself by the most abject supplications: but he was treated with kindness by the Roman general. The following year he was carried to Italy, where he was compelled to adorn the splendid triumph of his conqueror (Nov. 30, 167), and afterwards cast into a dungeon, from whence, however, the intercession of Aemilius procured his release, and he was permitted to end his days in an honourable captivity at Alba. He survived his removal thither a few years, and died, according to some accounts, by voluntary starvation, while others — fortunately with less probability — represent him as falling a victim to the cruelty of his guards, who deprived him of sleep. Perseus had been twice married; the name of his first wife, whom he is said to have killed with his own hand in a fit of passion, is not recorded; his second, Laodice, was the daughter of Seleucus IV. Philopator. He left two children; a son, Alexander, and a daughter, both apparently by his second marriage, as they were mere children when carried to Rome. Besides these, he had adopted his younger brother Philip, who appears to have been regarded by him as the heir to his throne, and became the partner of his captivity

Persis. [PERSIS.]
Persici Montes. [PARSICI MONTES.]
Persicus Sinus, Persicum Mare (ὁ Περσικὸς κόλπος, ἡ Περσικὴ θάλασσα, and other forms: the Persian Gulf), is the name given by the later geographers to the great gulf of the Mare Erythraeum (Indian Ocean), extending in a S.E. direction from the mouths of the Tigris, between the N.E. coast of Arabia and the opposite coast of Susiana, Persia, and Karmania, to the narrow strait formed by the long tongue of land which projects from the N. side of Oman in Arabia, by which strait it is connected with the more open gulf of the Indian Ocean called Paragon Sinus (Gulf of Oman). The earlier Greek writers know nothing of it. Herodotus does not distinguish it from the Erythraean Sea. The voyage of Alexander's admiral Nearchus from the Indus to the Tigris made it better known, but still the ancient geographers in general give very inaccurate statements of its size and form.

Persides (Περσείδης, Περσηϊάδης), a patronymic given to the descendants of Perses.

Persis, and very rarely Persia (ἡ Πέρσις, and ἡ Περσική, sc. γῆ, the fem. adjectives, the masc. being Περσικός, from the ethnic noun Πέρσης, pl. Πέρσαι, fem. Πέρσις, Latin Persa and Perses, pl. Persae: in modern Persian and Arabic, Fars or Farsistan, i. e. stan, land of, Fars = old Persian pars, horse or horseman: Eng. Persia), originally a small mountainous district of W. Asia, lying on the N.E. side of the Persian Gulf, and surrounded on the other sides by mountains and deserts. On the N.W. and N. it was separated from Susiana, Media, and Parthia, by the little river Oroatis or Orosis, and by M. Parachoathras; and on the E. from Carmania by no definite boundaries in the Desert. The only level part of the country was the strip of sea-coast called Persis Paralia: the rest was intersected with branches of M. Parachoathras, the valleys between which were watered by several rivers, the chief of which were the ARAXES, CYRUS, and MEDUS: in this part of the country, which was called Koile Persis, stood the capital cities PASARGADA and PERSEPOLIS. The country has a remarkable variety of climate and of products; the N. mountainous regions being comparatively cold, but with good pastures, especially for camels; the middle slopes having a temperate climate and producing abundance of fruit and wine; and the S. strip of coast being intensely hot, and sandy, with little vegetation except the palm-tree. The inhabitants were a collection of nomad peoples of the Indo-European stock, who called themselves by a name which is given in Greek as Artaei (Ἀρταῖοι), and which, like the kindred Median name of Arii (Ἄριοι), signifies noble or honourable, and is applied especially to the true worshippers of Ormuzd and followers of Zoroaster: it was in fact rather a title of honour than a proper name; the true collective name of the people seems to have been Pâracæ. According to Herodotus, they were divided into 3 classes or castes: 1st, the nobles or warriors, containing the 3 tribes of the PASARGADAE, who were the most noble, and to whom the royal family of the Achaemenidae belonged, the Maraphii and the Maspii; 2ndly, the agricultural and other settled tribes, namely, the Panthialaei, Derusiaei, and Germanii; 3rdly, the tribes which remained nomadic, namely, the Daae, Mardi, Dropici, and Sagartii, names common to other parts of W. and Central Asia. The

Persians had a close ethnical affinity to the Medes, and followed the same customs and religion [MAGI; ZOROASTER]. The simple and warlike habits, which they cultivated in their native mountains, preserved them from the corrupting influences which enervated their Median brethren; so that from being, as we find them at the beginning of their recorded history, the subject member of the Medo-Persian kingdom, they obtained the supremacy under CYRUS, the founder of the great Persian Empire, B.C. 559. Of the Persian history before this date, we know but little: the native poetical annalists of a later period are perfectly untrustworthy: the additional light lately obtained from the Persian inscriptions is, so far as it goes, confirmatory of the Greek writers, from whom, and from some small portions of Scripture, all our knowledge of ancient Persian history is derived. According to these accounts, the Persians were first subjected by the Medes under Phraortes, about B.C. 688, at the time of the formation of the Great Median Empire; but they continued to be governed by their own princes, the Achaemenidae. An account of the revolution, by which the supremacy was transferred to the Persians, is given under CYRUS. At this time there existed in W. Asia two other great kingdoms, the Lydian, which comprised nearly the whole of Asia Minor, W. of the river Halys, which separated it from the Medo-Persian territories; and the Babylonian, which, besides the Tigris and Euphrates valley, embraced Syria and Palestine. By the successive conquest of these kingdoms, the dominions of Cyrus were extended on the W. as far as the coasts of the Euxine, the Aegean, and the Mediterranean, and to the frontier of Egypt. Turning his arms in the opposite direction, he subdued Bactria, and effected some conquests beyond the Oxus, but fell in battle with the Massagetae. [CYRUS.] His son Cambyses added Egypt to the empire. [CAMBYSES.] Upon his death the Magian priesthood made an effort to restore the supremacy to the Medes [MAGI; SMERDIS], which was defeated by the conspiracy of the 7 Persian chieftains, whose success conferred the crown upon Darius, the son of Hystaspes. This king was at first occupied with crushing rebellions in every part of the empire, and with the two expeditions against Scythia and Cyrenaïca, of which the former entirely failed, and the latter was only partially successful. He conquered Thrace; and on the E. he added the valley of the Indus to the kingdom; but in this quarter the power of Persia seems never to have been much more than nominal. The Persian Empire had now reached its greatest extent, from Thrace and Cyrenaïca on the W. to the Indus on the E., and from the Euxine, the Caucasus (or rather a little below it), the Caspian, and the Oxus and Jaxartes on the N. to Aethiopia, Arabia, and the Erythraean Sea on the S., and it embraced, in Europe, Thrace and some of the Greek cities N. of the Euxine; in Africa, Egypt and Cyrenaïca; in Asia, on the W., Palestine, Phoenicia, Syria, the several districts of Asia Minor, Armenia, Mesopotamia, Assyria, Babylonia, Susiana, Atropatene, Great Media; on the N., Hyrcania, Margiana, Bactriana, and Sogdiana; on the E., the Paropamisus, Arachosia, and India (i. e. part of the Punjab and Scinde); on the S. Persis, Carmania and Gedrosia; and in the centre of the E. part, Parthia, Aria, and Drangiana. The capital cities of the empire were Babylon, Susa, Ecbatana in Media, and, though these were seldom, if ever, used as residences, Pasargada and Persepolis in Persis. (See the several articles.) Of this vast empire Darius undertook the organisation, and divided it into 20 satrapies, of which a full account is given by Herodotus. For the other details of his reign, and especially the commencement of the wars with Greece, see DARIUS. Of the remaining period of the ancient Persian history, till the Macedonian conquest, a sufficient abstract will be found under the names of the several kings, a list of whom is now subjoined:—(1) CYRUS, B.C. 559—529: (2) CAMBYSES, 529—522: (3) Usurpation of the pseudo-SMERDIS, 7 months, 522—521: (4) DARIUS I., son of Hystaspes, 521—485: (5) XERXES I. 485—465: (6) Usurpation of ARTABANUS, 7 months, 465—464: (7) ARTAXERXES I. LONGIMANUS, 464—425: (8) XERXES II., 2 months: (9) SOGDIANUS, 7 months, 425—424: (10) Ochus, or DARIUS II. Nothus, 424—405: (11) ARTAXERXES II. Mnemon, 405—359: (12) Ochus, or ARTAXERXES III., 359—338: (13) ARSES, 338 —336: (14) DARIUS III. Codomannus, 336— 331 [ALEXANDER]. Here the ancient history of Persia ends, as a kingdom; but, as a people, the Persians proper, under the influence especially of their religion, preserved their existence, and at length regained their independence on the downfall of the Parthian Empire [SASSANIDAE].—In reading the Roman poets it must be remembered that they constantly use *Persae*, as well as *Medi*, as a general term for the peoples E. of the Euphrates and Tigris, and especially for the Parthians.

A. **Persius Flaccus**, the poet, was a Roman knight connected by blood and marriage with persons of the highest rank, and was born at Volaterrae in Etruria on the 4th of December, A.D. 34. He received the first rudiments of education in his native town, remaining there until the age of 12, and then removed to Rome, where he studied grammar under the celebrated Remmius Palaemon, and rhetoric under Verginius Flavius. He was afterwards the pupil of Cornutus the Stoic, who became the guide, philosopher, and friend of his future life, and to whom he attached himself so closely that he never quitted his side. While yet a youth he was on familiar terms with Lucan, with Caesius Bassus the lyric poet, and with several other persons of literary eminence. He was tenderly beloved by the high-minded Paetus Thrasea, and seems to have been well worthy of such affection, for he is described as a virtuous and pleasing youth. He died of a disease of the stomach, on the 24th of November, A.D. 62, before he had completed his 28th year. The extant works of Persius, who, we are told, wrote seldom and slowly, consist of 6 short satires, extending in all to 650 hexameter lines, and were left in an unfinished state. They were slightly corrected after his death by Cornutus, while Caesius Bassus was permitted, at his own earnest request, to be the editor. In boyhood Persius had written some other poems, which were destroyed by the advice of Cornutus. Few productions have ever enjoyed more popularity than the Satires; but it would seem that Persius owes not a little of his fame to a cause which naturally might have produced an effect directly the reverse, we mean the multitude of strange terms, proverbial phrases, far-fetched metaphors, and abrupt transitions which every where embarrass our progress. The difficulty experienced in removing these impediments necessarily impresses both the words and the ideas upon every one who has carefully studied his pages, and hence no author clings more closely to our memory. The first satire is superior both in plan and execution to the rest; and those passages in the 5th, where Persius describes the process by which his own moral and intellectual faculties were expanded, are remarkable for their grace and beauty. The best editions are by Jahn, Lips. 1843, and by Heinrich, Lips. 1844.

Pertinax, Helvius, Roman emperor from January 1st to March 28th, A. D. 193, was of humble origin, and rose from the post of centurion both to the highest military and civil commands in the reigns of M. Aurelius and Commodus. On the murder of Commodus on the last day of December, 192, Pertinax, who was then 66 years of age, was reluctantly persuaded to accept the empire. He commenced his reign by introducing extensive reforms into the civil and military administration of the empire; but the troops, who had been accustomed both to ease and license under Commodus, were disgusted with the discipline which he attempted to enforce upon them, and murdered their new sovereign after a reign of 2 months and 27 days. On his death the praetorian troops put up the empire to sale, which was purchased by M. Didius Salvius Julianus. [See p. 219, b.]

Perūsia (Perusīnus: *Perugia*), an ancient city in the E. part of Etruria between the lake Trasimenus and the Tiber, and one of the 12 cities of the Etruscan confederacy. It was situated on a hill, and was strongly fortified by nature and by art. In conjunction with the other cities of Etruria, it long resisted the power of the Romans, and at a later period it was made a Roman colony. It is memorable in the civil wars as the place in which L. Antonius, the brother of the triumvir took refuge, when he was no longer able to oppose Octavianus in the field, and where he was kept closely blockaded by Octavianus for some months, from the end of B. C. 41 to the spring of 40. Famine compelled it to surrender; but one of its citizens having set fire to his own house, the flames spread, and the whole city was burnt to the ground. The war between L. Antonius and Octavianus is known from the long siege of this town by the name of the *Bellum Perusinum*. It was rebuilt and colonised anew by Augustus, from whom it received the surname of *Augusta*. In the later time of the empire it was the most important city in all Etruria, and long resisted the Goths. Part of the walls and some of the gates of Perusia still remain. The best preserved of the gates is now called *Arco d'Augusta*, from the inscription AVGVSTA PERVVSIA over the arch: the whole structure is at least 60 or 70 feet high. Several interesting tombs with valuable remains of Etruscan art have been discovered in the neighbourhood of the city.

Pescennius Niger. [NIGER.]

Pessinūs or **Pěsinūs** (Πεσσινοῦς, Πεσινοῦς: Πεσσινούντιος, fem. Πεσσινουντίς: *Bala-Hisar* Ru.), a city of Asia Minor, in the S.W. corner of Galatia, on the S. slope of M. Dindymus or Agdistis, was celebrated as a great seat of the worship of Cybele, under the surname of Agdistis, whose temple, crowded with riches, stood on a hill outside the city. In this temple was a wooden (Livy says stone) image of the goddess, which was removed to Rome, to satisfy an oracle in the Sibyl-

line books. Under Constantine the city was made the capital of the province of Galatia Salutaris, but it gradually declined until the 6th century, after which it is no more mentioned.

Petālia or **Petāliae** (*Petaliae*), an uninhabited and rocky island off the S.W. coast of Euboea at the entrance into the Euripus.

Petēlia or **Petilia** (Πετηλία: Petelīnus: *Strongoli*), an ancient Greek town on the E. coast of Bruttium, founded, according to tradition, by Philoctetes. (Virg. *Aen.* iii. 402.) It was situated N. of Croton, to whose territory it originally belonged, but it was afterwards conquered by the Lucanians. It remained faithful to the Romans, when the other cities of Bruttium revolted to Hannibal, and it was not till after a long and desperate resistance that it was taken by one of Hannibal's generals. It was repeopled by Hannibal with Bruttians; but the Romans subsequently collected the remains of the former population, and put them again in possession of the town.

Petēōn (Πετεών: Πετεώνιος), a small town in Boeotia, of uncertain site, dependent upon Haliartus, according to some, and upon Thebes, according to others.

Petēōs (Πετεώς), son of Orneus, and father of Menestheus, was expelled from Athens by Aegeus, and went to Phocis, where he founded Stiris.

Petīllus or **Petillius.** 1. **Capitolīnus.** [CAPITOLINUS.]—2. **Cereālis.** [CEREALIS.]—3. **Spurīnus.** [SPURINUS.]

Petosīris (Πετόσιρις), an Egyptian priest and astrologer, generally named along with Nechepsos, an Egyptian king. The two are said to be the founders of astrology. Some works on astrology were extant under his name. Like our own Lilly, Petosiris became the common name for an astrologer. (Juv. vi. 580.)

Petovio or **Poetovio** (*Pettau*), a town in Pannonia Superior, on the frontiers of Noricum, and on the Dravus (*Drave*), was a Roman colony with the surname *Ulpia*, having been probably enlarged and made a colony by Trajan or Hadrian. It was one of the chief towns of Pannonia, had an imperial palace, and was the head-quarters of a Roman legion. The ancient town was probably on the right bank of the Drave, opposite the modern *Pettau*, as it is only on the former spot that inscriptions, coins, and other antiquities have been found.

Petra (ἡ Πέτρα: Πετραῖος, Petraeus, later Petrensis), the name of several cities built on rocks, or in rocky places.—**1.** A small place in the Corinthian territory, probably on the coast, near the borders of Argolis.—**2.** A place in Elis, not far from the city of Elis, of which some suppose it to have been the Acropolis. The sepulchral monument of the philosopher Pyrrho was shown here. —**3.** (*Casa della Pietra*), also called **Petraea** and **Petrīne** (the people Πετρῖνοι and Petrīni), an inland town of Sicily, on the road from Agrigentum to Panormus.—**4.** A town on the coast of Illyricum, with a bad harbour.—**5.** A city of Pieria in Macedonia.—**6.** A fortress of the Maedi, in Thrace.—**7.** (Pl. neut.), a place in Dacia, on one of the 3 great roads which crossed the Danube.—**8.** In Pontus, a fortress built by Justinian, on a precipice on the sea-coast, between the rivers Bathys and Acinasis.—**9.** In Sogdiana, near the Oxus (Q. Curt. vii. 11).—**10.** By far the most celebrated of all the places of this name was **Petra**

or **Petrae** (*Wady-Musa*), in Arabia Petraea, the capital, first of the Idumaeans, and afterwards of the Nabathaeans. It is probably the same place which is called Selah (which means. like πέτρα, *a rock*) and Joktheel, in the O. T. It lies in the midst of the mountains of Seir, at the foot of Mt. Hor, just half-way between the Dead Sea and the head of the Aelanitic Gulf of the Red Sea, in a valley, or rather ravine, surrounded by almost inaccessible precipices, which is entered by a narrow gorge on the E., the rocky walls of which approach so closely as sometimes hardly to permit 2 horsemen to ride abreast. On the banks of the river which runs through this ravine stood the city itself, a mile in length, and half-a-mile in breadth between the sides of the valley, and some fine ruins of its public buildings still remain. But this is not all: the rocks which surround, not only the main valley, but all its lateral ravines, are completely honeycombed with excavations, some of which were tombs, some temples, and some private houses, at the entrances to which the surface of the rock is sculptured into magnificent architectural façades, and other figures, whose details are often so well preserved as to appear but just chiselled, while the effect is wonderfully heightened by the brilliant variegated colours of the rock, where red, purple, yellow, sky-blue, black, and white, are seen in distinct layers. These ruins are chiefly of the Roman period, when Petra had become an important city as a centre of the caravan traffic of the Nabathaeans. At the time of Augustus, as Strabo learnt from a friend who had resided there, it contained many Romans and other foreigners, and was governed by a native prince. It had maintained its independence against the Greek kings of Syria, and retained it under the Romans, till the time of Trajan, by whom it was taken. It was the chief city of the whole country of Arabia Petraea, which probably derived its name from Petra; and under the later empire, it was the capital of Palaestina Tertia.

M. Petreius, a man of great military experience, is first mentioned in B. C. 62, when he served as legatus to the proconsul C. Antonius, and commanded the army in the battle in which Catiline perished. He belonged to the aristocratical party; and in 55 he was sent into Spain along with L. Afranius as legatus of Pompey, to whom the provinces of the two Spains had been granted. Soon after the commencement of the civil war in 49, Caesar defeated Afranius and Petreius in Spain, whereupon the latter joined Pompey in Greece. After the loss of the battle of Pharsalia (48) Petreius crossed over to Africa, and took an active part in the campaign in 46, which was brought to an end by the decisive defeat of the Pompeian army at the battle of Thapsus. Petreius then fled with Juba, and despairing of safety they fell by each other's hands.

Petrinus (*Rocca di monti Ragoni*), a mountain near Sinuessa on the confines of Latium and Campania, on which good wine was grown.

Petrocŏrii, a people in Gallia Aquitanica, in the modern *Perigord*. Their country contained iron-mines, and their chief town was Vesunna (*Perigueux*).

Petrŏnius, C., or T., an accomplished voluptuary at the court of Nero. He was one of the chosen companions of Nero, and was regarded as director-in-chief of the imperial pleasures, the judge whose decision upon the merits of any proposed scheme of enjoyment was held as final (*Elegantiae arbiter*). The influence thus acquired excited the jealous suspicions of Tigellinus: he was accused of treason; and believing that destruction was inevitable, he resolved to die as he had lived, and to excite admiration by the frivolous eccentricity of his end. Having caused his veins to be opened, he from time to time arrested the flow of blood by the application of bandages. During the intervals he conversed with his friends, and even showed himself in the public streets of Cumae, where these events took place; so that at last, when he sunk from exhaustion, his death (A. D. 66), although compulsory, appeared to be the result of natural and gradual decay. He is said to have despatched in his last moments a sealed document to the prince, taunting him with his brutal excesses. — A work has come down to us bearing the title *Petronii Arbitri Satyricon*, which, as it now exists, is composed of a series of fragments, chiefly in prose, but interspersed with numerous pieces of poetry. It is a sort of comic romance, in which the adventures of a certain Encolpius and his companions in the S. of Italy, chiefly in Naples or its environs, are made a vehicle for exposing the false taste and vices of the age. Unfortunately the vices of the personages introduced are depicted with such fidelity that we are perpetually disgusted by the obscenity of the descriptions. The longest section is generally known as the *Supper of Trimalchio*, presenting us with a detailed account of a fantastic banquet, such as the gourmands of the empire were wont to exhibit on their tables. Next in interest is the well-known tale of the Ephesian Matron. — A great number of conflicting opinions have been formed by scholars with regard to the author of the *Satyricon*. Many suppose that he is the same person as the C. or T. Petronius mentioned above; and though there are no proofs in favour of this hypothesis, yet there is good reason to believe that the work belongs to the first century, or, at all events, is not later than the reign of Hadrian. The best edition is by P. Burmannus, 4to. Traj. ad Rhen. 1709, and again Amst. 1743.

Peuce (Πεύκη: *Piczina*), an island in Moesia Inferior formed by the 2 southern mouths of the Danube, of which the most southernly was also called Peuce, but more commonly the Sacred Mouth. This island is of a triangular form, and is said by the ancients to be as large as Rhodes. It was inhabited by the Peucini, who were a tribe of the Bastarnae, and took their name from the island.

Peucĕla, Peucelaŏtis (Πευκέλα, Πευκελαῶτις: *Pekheli* or *Pakholi*), a city and district in the N.W. of India intra Gangem, between the rivers Indus and Suastus.

Peucestas (Πευκέστας), a Macedonian, and a distinguished officer of Alexander the Great. He had the chief share in saving the life of Alexander in the assault on the city of the Malli in India, and was afterwards appointed by the king to the satrapy of Persia. In the division of the provinces after the death of Alexander (B. C. 323) he obtained the renewal of his government of Persia. He fought on the side of Eumenes against Antigonus (317—316), but displayed both arrogance and insubordination in these campaigns. Upon the surrender of Eumenes by the Argyraspids, Peucestas fell into the hands of Antigonus, who deprived him of his satrapy.

Peucĕtia. [APULIA.]

Peucini. [PEUCE.]

Phacĭum (Φάκιον: Φακιεύς: *Alifaka*), a mountain fortress of Thessaly in the district Hestiaeotis on the right bank of the Peneus, N.E. of Limnaea.

Phacussa (Φακοῦσσα: *Fecussa*), an island in the Aegaean sea, one of the Sporades.

Phaea (Φαιά), the name of the sow of Crommyon in Megaris, which ravaged the neighbourhood, and was slain by Theseus.

Phaeāces (Φαίακες, Φαίηκες), a fabulous people immortalised by the Odyssey, who inhabited the island **Scheria** (Σχερία), situated at the extreme western part of the earth, and who were governed by king Alcinous. [ALCINOUS.] They are described by Homer as a people fond of the feast, the lyre, and the dance, and hence their name passed into a proverb to indicate persons of luxurious and sensual habits. Thus a glutton is called *Phaeax* by Horace (*Ep.* i. 15. 24).—The ancients identified the Homeric Scheria with Corcyra, whence the latter is called by the poets *Phaeacia tellus*; but there is no sound argument in favour of the identity of the 2 islands, and it is better to regard Scheria as altogether fabulous.

Phaeax (Φαίαξ), an Athenian orator and statesman, and a contemporary of Nicias and Alcibiades. Some critics maintain that the extant speech against Alcibiades, commonly attributed to Andocides was written by Phaeax.

Phaedon (Φαίδων), a Greek philosopher, was a native of Elis, and of high birth, but was taken prisoner, probably about B. C. 400, and was brought to Athens. It is said that he ran away from his master to Socrates, and was ransomed by one of the friends of the latter. Phaedon was present at the death of Socrates, while he was still quite a youth. He appears to have lived in Athens some time after the death of Socrates, and then returned to Elis, where he became the founder of a school of philosophy. He was succeeded by Plistanus, after whom the Elean school was merged in the Eretrian. The dialogue of Plato, which contains an account of the death of Socrates, bears the name of Phaedon.

Phaedra (Φαίδρα), daughter of Minos by Pasiphaë or Crete, and the wife of Theseus. She was the stepmother of Hippolytus, the son of Theseus, with whom she fell in love; but having been repulsed by Hippolytus, she accused him to Theseus of having attempted her dishonour. After the death of Hippolytus, his innocence became known to his father, and Phaedra made away with herself. For details see HIPPOLYTUS.

Phaedriădes. [PARNASSUS.]

Phaedrĭas (Φαιδρίας), a town in the S. of Arcadia, S.W. of Megalopolis, 15 stadia from the Messenian frontier.

Phaedrus (Φαῖδρος.) 1. An Epicurean philosopher, and the president of the Epicurean school during Cicero's residence in Athens, B. C. 80. He died in 70, and was succeeded by Patron. He was the author of a work on the gods (Περὶ Θεῶν), of which an interesting fragment was discovered at Herculaneum in 1806, and published, by Petersen, Hamb. 1833. Cicero was largely indebted to this work for the materials of the first book of the *De Natura Deorum*.—2. The Latin Fabulist, of whom we know nothing but what is collected or inferred from his fables. He was originally a slave, and was brought from Thrace or Macedonia to Rome,

where he learned the Latin language. As the title of his work is *Phaedri Aug. Liberti Fabulae Aesopiae*, we must conclude that he had belonged to Augustus, who manumitted him. Under Tiberius he appears to have undergone some persecution from Sejanus. The fables extant under the name of Phaedrus are 97 in number, written in iambic verse, and distributed into 5 books. Most of the fables are transfusions of the Aesopian fables, or those which pass as such, into Latin verse. The expression is generally clear and concise, and the language, with some few exceptions, as pure and correct as we should expect from a Roman writer of the Augustan age. But Phaedrus has not escaped censure, when he has deviated from his Greek model, and much of the censure is just. The best fables are those in which he has kept the closest to his original. Many of the fables, however, are not Aesopian, as the matter clearly shows, for they refer to historical events of a much later period (v. 1, 8, iii. 10); and Phaedrus himself, in the prologue to the 5th book, intimates that he had often used the name of Aesop only to recommend his verses.—There is also another collection of 32 fables, attributed to Aesop, and entitled *Epitome Fabularum*, which was first published at Naples, in 1809, by Cassitti. Opinions are much divided as to the genuineness of this collection. The probability is, that the *Epitome* is founded on genuine Roman fables, which, in the process of transcription during many centuries, have undergone considerable changes. — The last and only critical edition of Phaedrus is by Orelli, Zürich, 1831.

Phaenarĕtē. [SOCRATES.]

Phaenĭas. [PHANIAS.]

Phaestus (Φαιστός: Φαίστιος). 1. A town in the S. of Crete near Gortyna, 20 stadia from the sea, with a port-town Matala or Matalia, said to have been built by the Heraclid Phaestus, who came from Sicyon to Crete. The town is mentioned by Homer, but was destroyed at an early period by Gortyna. It was the birth-place of Epimenides, and its inhabitants were celebrated for their wit and sarcasm. — 2. A town of Thessaly in the district Thessaliotis.

Phăĕthon (Φαέθων), that is, "the shining," occurs in Homer as an epithet or surname of Helios (the Sun), and is used by later writers as a proper name for Helios; but it is more commonly known as the name of a son of Helios by the Oceanid Clymene, the wife of Merops. The genealogy of Phaethon, however, is not the same in all writers, for some call him a son of Clymenus, the son of Helios, by Merope, or a son of Helios by Prote, or, lastly, a son of Helios by the nymph Rhode or Rhodos. He received the significant name of Phaethon from his father, and was afterwards presumptuous and ambitious enough to request his father to allow him for one day to drive the chariot of the sun across the heavens. Helios was induced by the entreaties of his son and of Clymene to yield, but the youth being too weak to check the horses, they rushed out of their usual track, and came so near the earth, as almost to set it on fire. Thereupon Zeus killed him with a flash of lightning, and hurled him down into the river Eridanus. His sisters, the *Heliades* or *Phaethontiades*, who had yoked the horses to the chariot, were metamorphosed into poplars, and their tears into amber. [HELIADAE.]

Phaethontiădes. [HELIADAE.]

Phaethūsa. [HELIADAE.]

Phagres (Φάγρης : *Orfan* or *Orfana*), an ancient and fortified town of the Pierians in Macedonia at the foot of Mt. Pangaeon.

Phălaecus (Φάλαικος). 1. Son of Onomarchus, succeeded his uncle Phayllus as leader of the Phocians in the Sacred War, B. C. 351. In order to secure his own safety, he concluded a treaty with Philip, by which he was allowed to withdraw into the Peloponnesus with a body of 8000 mercenaries, leaving the unhappy Phocians to their fate, 346. Phalaecus now assumed the part of a mere leader of mercenary troops, in which character we find him engaging in various enterprises. He was slain at the siege of Cydonia in Crete. — 2. A lyric and epigrammatic poet, from whom the metre called *Phalaecian* took its name. Five of his epigrams are preserved in the Greek Anthology. His date is uncertain ; but he was probably one of the principal Alexandrian poets.

Phalaesīae (Φαλαισίαι), a town in Arcadia, S. of Megalopolis on the road to Sparta, 20 stadia from the Laconian frontier.

Phalanna (Φάλαννα : Φαλανναῖος : *Karadjoli*), a town of the Perrhaebi in the Thessalian district of Hestiaeotis on the left bank of the Peneus, not far from Tempe.

Phălanthus (Φάλανθος), son of Aracus, was one of the Lacedaemonian Partheniae, or the offspring of some marriages of disparagement, which the necessity of the first Messenian war had induced the Spartans to permit. (See *Dict. of Antiq.* art. *Partheniae.*) As the Partheniae were looked down upon by their fellow-citizens, they formed a conspiracy under Phalanthus, against the government. Their design having been detected, they went to Italy under the guidance of Phalanthus, and founded the city of Tarentum, about B. C. 708. Phalanthus was afterwards driven out from Tarentum by a sedition, and ended his days at Brundisium.

Phalăra (τὰ Φάλαρα : Φαλαρεύς), a town in the Thessalian district of Phthiotis on the Sinus Maliacus, served as the harbour of Lamia.

Phălāris (Φάλαρις), ruler of Agrigentum in Sicily, has obtained a proverbial celebrity as a cruel and inhuman tyrant ; but we have scarcely any real knowledge of his life and history. His reign probably commenced about B. C. 570, and is said to have lasted 16 years. He was a native of Agrigentum, and appears to have been raised by his fellow-citizens to some high office in the state, of which he afterwards availed himself to assume a despotic authority. He was engaged in frequent wars with his neighbours, and extended his power and dominion on all sides, though more frequently by stratagem than open force. He perished by a sudden outbreak of the popular fury, in which it appears that Telemachus, the ancestor of Theron, must have borne a conspicuous part. No circumstance connected with Phalaris is more celebrated than the brazen bull in which he is said to have burnt alive the victims of his cruelty, and of which we are told that he made the first experiment upon its inventor Perillus. This latter story has much the air of an invention of later times; but the fame of this celebrated engine of torture was inseparably associated with the name of Phalaris as early as the time of Pindar. (Pind. *Pyth.* i. 185.) That poet also speaks of Phalaris himself in terms which clearly prove that his reputation as a barbarous

tyrant was then already fully established, and all subsequent writers, until a very late period, allude to him in terms of similar import. But in the later ages of Greek literature, there appears to have existed or arisen a totally different tradition concerning Phalaris, which represented him as a man of a naturally mild and humane disposition, and only forced into acts of severity or occasional cruelty, by the pressure of circumstances and the machinations of his enemies. Still more strange is it that he appears at the same time as an admirer of literature and philosophy, and the patron of men of letters. Such is the aspect under which his character is presented to us in 2 declamations commonly ascribed to Lucian, and still more strikingly in the well-known epistles which bear the name of Phalaris himself. These epistles are now remembered chiefly on account of the literary controversy to which they gave rise, and the masterly dissertation in which Bentley exposed their spuriousness. They are evidently the composition of some sophist ; though the period at which this forgery was composed cannot now be determined. The first author who refers to them is Stobaeus. The best edition is by Schaefer, Lips. 1823.

Phalarīum (Φαλάριον), a fortress named after Phalaris near the S. coast of Sicily, situated on a hill 40 stadia E. of the river Himera.

Phalasarna (τὰ Φαλάσαρνα), a town on the N.W. coast of Crete.

Phalērum (Φάληρον : Φαληρεύς), the most E.-ly of the harbours of Athens, and the one chiefly used by the Athenians before the time of the Persian wars. Phalerum is usually described as the most E.-ly of the 3 harbours in the peninsula of Piraeus; but this appears to be incorrect. The names of the 3 harbours in the peninsula were Piraeus, Zea, and Munychia ; while Phalerum lay S.E. of these 3, nearer the city at *Hagios Georgios* After the establishment by Themistocles of the 3 harbours in the peninsula of Piraeus, Phalerum was not much used; but it was connected with the city by means of a wall called the *Phalerian Wall* (Φαληρικὸν τεῖχος). Paleron or Phalerus was also an Attic demus, containing temples of Zeus, Demeter, and other deities.

Phalōrīa (Φαλωρία), a fortified town of Thessaly in Hestiaeotis, N. of Tricca on the left bank of the Peneus.

Phănae (Φάναι, ἡ Φαναία ἄκρα : *C. Mastico*), the S. point of the island of Chios, celebrated for its temple of Apollo, and for its excellent wine

Phanagorīa (Φαναγόρεια, and other forms : *Phanagori*, Ru., near *Taman*, on the E. side of the *Straits of Kaffa*), a Greek city, founded by a colony of Teians under Phanagoras, on the Asiatic coast of the Cimmerian Bosporus. It became the great emporium for all the traffic between the coasts of the Palus Maeotis and the countries on the S. side of the Caucasus, and was chosen by the kings of Bosporus as their capital in Asia. It had a temple of Aphrodite Apaturos, and its neighbourhood was rich in olive yards. In the 6th century of our era, it was destroyed by the surrounding barbarians.

Phanaroea (Φανάροια), a great plain of Pontus in Asia Minor, enclosed by the mountain chains of Paryadres on the E., and Lithrus and Ophlimus on the W., was the most fertile part of Pontus.

Phanīas or **Phaenīas** (Φανίας, Φαινίας), of Eresos in Lesbos, a distinguished Peripatetic philosopher, the immediate disciple of Aristotle, and the contemporary, fellow-citizen, and friend of Theophrastus. He flourished about B. C. 336. Phanias does not seem to have founded a distinct school of his own, but he was a most diligent writer upon every department of philosophy, as it was studied by the Peripatetics, especially logic, physics, history, and literature. His works, all of which are lost, are frequently quoted by later writers. One of his works most frequently cited was a sort of chronicle of his native city, bearing the title of Πρυτάνεις 'Ερέσιοι.

Phanŏcles (Φανοκλῆς), one of the best of the later Greek elegiac poets, probably lived in the time of Philip and Alexander the Great. He seems only to have written one poem, which was entitled "Ερωτες ἢ Καλοί. The work was upon paederasteia; but the subject was so treated as to exhibit the retribution which fell upon those who addicted themselves to the practice. We still possess a considerable fragment from the opening of the poem, which describes the love of Orpheus for Calaïs, and the vengeance taken upon him by the Thracian women. The fragments of Phanocles are edited by Bach, Philetae, Hermesianactis, atque Phanoclis Reliquiae ; and by Schneidewin, Delectus Poet. Graec. p. 158.

Phanodēmus (Φανόδημος), the author of one of those works on the legends and antiquities of Attica, known under the name of Atthides. His age and birthplace are uncertain, but we know that he lived before the time of Augustus, as he is cited by Dionysius of Halicarnassus.

Phanote (Garthiki), a fortified town of Epirus in Chaonia near the Illyrian frontier.

Phantasia (Φαντασία), one of those numerous mythical personages, to whom Homer is said to have been indebted for his poems. She is said to have been an Egyptian, the daughter of Nicarchus, an inhabitant of Memphis, and to have written an account of the Trojan war, and the wanderings of Ulysses.

Phāŏn (Φάων), a boatman at Mytilene, is said to have been originally an ugly old man; but in consequence of his carrying Aphrodite across the sea without accepting payment, the goddess gave him youth and beauty. After this Sappho is said to have fallen in love with him, and to have leapt from the Leucadian rock, when he slighted her; but this well-known story vanishes at the first approach of criticism. [SAPPHO.]

Phārae (Φαραί or Φῆραι). 1. (Φαραιεύς or Φαρεύς), an ancient town in the W. part of Achaea, and one of the 12 Achaean cities, was situated on the river Pierus, 70 stadia from the sea, and 150 from Patrae. It was one of the states which took an active part in reviving the Achaean League in B. C. 281. Augustus included it in the territory of Patrae. — 2. (Φαραίτης, Φαραιδρης, Φαράτης : Kalamata), an ancient town in Messenia mentioned by Homer, on the river Nedon, near the frontiers of Laconia, and about 6 miles from the sea. In B. C. 180 Pharae joined the Achaean League together with the neighbouring towns of Thuria and Abia. It was annexed by Augustus to Laconia. — 3. Originally Pharis (Φαρις: Φαρίτης, Φαριδρης), a town in Laconia in the valley of the Eurotas, S. of Sparta. — 4. A town in Crete, founded by the Messenian Pharae.

Pharbaethus (Φάρβαιθος: Horbeyt ? Ru.), the capital of the Nomos Pharbaethites in Lower Egypt, lay S. of Tanis, on the W. side of the Pelusiac branch of the Nile.

Pharcādōn (Φαρκαδών), a town of Thessaly, in the E. part of Hestiaeotis.

Phāris. [PHARAE, No. 3.]

Pharmacussae (Φαρμακοῦσσαι). 1. Two small islands off the coast of Attica, near Salamis, in the bay of Eleusis, now called Kyradhes or Megali and Mikri Kyra : on one of them was shown the tomb of Circe — 2. Pharmacussa (Φαρμακοῦσα), an island off the coast of Asia Minor, 120 stadia from Miletus, where king Attalus died, and where Julius Caesar was taken prisoner by pirates, when a very young man. The whole adventure is related by Plutarch (Caes. 1, 2).

Pharnabāzus (Φαρνάβαζος), son of Pharnaces, succeeded his father as satrap of the Persian provinces near the Hellespont. In B. C. 411 and the following years, he rendered active assistance to the Lacedaemonians in their war against the Athenians. When Dercyllidas, and subsequently Agesilaus, passed over into Asia, to protect the Asiatic Greeks against the Persian power, we find Pharnabazus connecting himself with Conon to resist the Lacedaemonians. In 374 Pharnabazus invaded Egypt in conjunction with Iphicrates, but the expedition failed, chiefly through the dilatory proceedings and the excessive caution of Pharnabazus. The character of Pharnabazus is eminently distinguished by generosity and openness. He has been charged, it is true, with the murder of Alcibiades ; but the latter probably fell by the hands of others. [ALCIBIADES.]

Pharnāces (Φαρνάκης). 1. King of Pontus, was the son of Mithridates IV., whom he succeeded on the throne, about B. C. 190. He carried on war for some years with Eumenes, king of Pergamus, and Ariarathes, king of Cappadocia, but was obliged to conclude with them a disadvantageous peace in 179. The year of his death is uncertain ; it is placed by conjecture in 156. — 2. King of Pontus, or more properly of the Bosporus, was the son of Mithridates, the Great, whom he compelled to put an end to his life in 63. [MITHRIDATES VI.] After the death of his father, Pharnaces hastened to make his submission to Pompey, who granted him the kingdom of the Bosporus with the titles of friend and ally of the Roman people. In the civil war between Caesar and Pompey, Pharnaces seized the opportunity to reinstate himself in his father's dominions, and made himself master of the whole of Colchis and the lesser Armenia. He defeated Domitius Calvinus, the lieutenant of Caesar in Asia, but was shortly afterwards defeated by Caesar himself in a decisive action near Zela (47). The battle was gained with such ease by Caesar, that he informed the senate of his victory by the words, Veni, vidi, vici. In the course of the same year, Pharnaces was again defeated and was slain by Asander, one of his generals, who hoped to obtain his master's kingdom. [ASANDER.]

Pharnacia (Φαρνακία: Kheresoun or Kerasunda), a flourishing city of Asia Minor, on the coast of Pontus Polemoniacus, was built near (some think on) the site of Cerasus, probably by Pharnaces, the grandfather of Mithridates the Great, and peopled by the transference to it of the inhabitants of Cotyora. It had a large commerce and extensive fisheries ; and in its neighbourhood were the iron mines of the Chalybes. It was strongly fortified.

and was used by Mithridates, in the war with Rome, for the place of refuge of his harem.

Pharsālus (Φάρσαλος, Ion. Φάρσηλος: Φαρσάλιος: *Pharsa* or *Fersala*), a town in Thessaly in the district Thessaliotis, not far from the frontiers of Phthiotis, W. of the river Enipeus, and on the N. slope of Mt. Narthacius. It was divided into an old and new city, and contained a strongly fortified acropolis. In its neighbourhood, N.E. of the town and on the other side of the Enipeus was a celebrated temple of Thetis, called *Thetidium*. Near Pharsalus was fought the decisive battle between Caesar and Pompey, B. C. 48, which made Caesar master of the Roman world. It is frequently called the battle of Pharsalia, which was the name of the territory of the town.

Phărus (Φάρος). 1. (*Pharos* or *Raudhat-el-tin*, i. e. *Fig-garden*), a small island off the Mediterranean coast of Egypt, mentioned by Homer, who describes it as a whole day's sail distant from Aegyptus, meaning probably, not Egypt itself, but the river Nile. When Alexander the Great planned the city of Alexandria, on the coast opposite to Pharos, he caused the island to be united to the coast by a mole 7 stadia in length, thus forming the 2 harbours of the city. [ALEXANDRIA.] The island was chiefly famous for the lofty tower built upon it by Ptolemy II. Philadelphus, for a light-house, whence the name of *pharus* was applied to all similar structures. It was in this island too that, according to the common story, the 70 translators of the Greek version of the Old Testament, hence called the Septuagint, were confined till their work was finished. The island was well peopled, according to Julius Caesar, but soon afterwards Strabo tells us that it was inhabited only by a few fishermen.—2. (*Lesina* or *Hvar*), an island of the Adriatic, off the coast of Dalmatia, E. of Issa, with a Greek city of the same name (*Civita Vecchia*, Ru.), which was taken and destroyed by the Romans under Aemilius Paulus, but probably rebuilt, as it is mentioned by Ptolemy under the name of Pharia.

Phartsii (Φαρούσιοι), a people in the interior (prob. nr. the W. coast) of N. Africa, who carried on a considerable traffic with Mauritania.

Phasaëlis (Φασαηλίς: prob. *Ain-el-Fusail*), a city of Palestine, in the valley of the Jordan, N. of Jericho, built by Herod the Great.

Phasēlis (Φασηλίς, Φασηλίτης: *Tekrova*, Ru.), an important sea-port town of Lycia, near the borders of Pamphylia, stood on the gulf of Pamphylia, at the foot of Mt. Solyma, in a narrow pass between the mountains and the sea. It was founded by Dorian colonists, and from its position, and its command of 3 fine harbours, it soon gained an extensive commerce. It did not belong to the Lycian confederacy, but had an independent government of its own. It became afterwards the head-quarters of the pirates who infested the S. coasts of Asia Minor, and was therefore destroyed by P. Servilius Isauricus; and though the city was restored, it never recovered its importance. Phaselis is said to have been the place at which the light quick vessels called φάσηλοι were first built, and the figure of such a ship appears on its coins.

Phāsis (Φᾶσις). 1. (*Fas* or *Rioni*), a renowned river of the ancient world, rose in the Moschici M. (or according to others in the Caucasus, where, in fact, its chief tributaries rise), and flowed W.-ward

through the plain of Colchis into the E. end of the Pontus Euxinus (*Black Sea*), after receiving several affluents, the chief of which were the Glaucus and the Rion: the name of the latter was sometimes transferred, as it now is, to the main river. It was navigable about 38 miles above its mouth for large vessels, and for small ones further up, as far as Sarapana (*Sharapan*), whence goods were conveyed in 4 days across the Moschici M. to the river Cyrus, and so to the Caspian. It was spanned by 120 bridges, and had many towns upon its banks. Its waters were celebrated for their purity and for various other supposed qualities, some of a very marvellous nature; but it was most famous in connection with the story of the Argonautic expedition. [ARGONAUTAE.] Some of the early geographers made it the boundary between Europe and Asia; it was afterwards the N.E. limit of the kingdom of Pontus, and, under the Romans, it was regarded as the N. frontier of their empire in W. Asia. Another notable circumstance connected with it, is that it has given name to the *pheasant* (phasianus, φασιανός, φασιανικὸς ὄρνις), which is said to have been first brought to Greece from its banks, where the bird is still found in great numbers.—When the geography of these regions was comparatively unknown, it was natural that there should be a doubt as to the identification of certain celebrated names; and thus the name Phasia, like Araxes, is applied to different rivers. The most important of these variations is Xenophon's application of the name Phasis to the river Araxes in Armenia. (*Anab.* iv. 6.)—2. Near the mouth of the river, on its S. side, was a town of the same name, founded and fortified by the Milesians as an emporium for their commerce, and used under the Kings of Pontus, and under the Romans, as a frontier fort, and now a Russian fortified station, under the name of *Poti*. Some identify it with Sebastopolis, but most likely incorrectly.—3. There was a river of the same name in the island of Taprobane (*Ceylon*).

Phavorīnus. [FAVORINUS.]

Phayllus (Φάϋλλος). 1. A celebrated athlete of Crotona, who had thrice gained the victory at the Pythian games. He fought at the battle of Salamis, B. C. 480, in a ship fitted out at his own expense.—2. A Phocian, brother of Onomarchus, whom he succeeded as general of the Phocians in the Sacred War, 352. He died in the following year after a long and painful illness. Phayllus made use of the sacred treasures of Delphi with a far more lavish hand than either of his brothers, and he is accused of bestowing the consecrated ornaments upon his wife and mistresses.

Phasania (*Fezzan*), a district of Libya Interior. [GARAMANTES.]

Phazēmon (Φαζημόν: prob. *Marsivan*), a city of Pontus in Asia Minor, N.W. of Amasia, and the capital of the W. district of Pontus, called Phazemonītis (Παζημονῖτις), which lay on the E. side of the Halys, S. of Gazelonitis, and was celebrated for its warm mineral springs. Pompey changed the name of the city to Neapolis, and the district was called Neapolitis; but these names seem to have been soon dropt.

Phea (Φειά, Φεά, Φεαί: Φεαῖος), a town on the frontiers of Elis and Pisatis with a harbour situated on a promontory of the same name, and on the river Iardanus. In front of the harbour was a small island called Phēas (Φείας.)

Pheca or Phecadum, a fortress in Thessaly in the district Hestiaeotis.

Phēgeus (Φηγεύς), king of Psophis in Arcadia, father of Alphesiboea or Arsinoe, of Pronous and Agenor, or of Temenus and Axion. He purified Alcmaeon after he had killed his mother, and gave him his daughter Alphesiboea in marriage. Alcmaeon presented Alphesiboea with the celebrated necklace and peplus of Harmonia ; but when Alcmaeon afterwards wished to obtain them again for his new wife Callirhoë, he was murdered by the sons of Phegeus, by their father's command. Phegeus was himself subsequently put to death by the sons of Alcmaeon. For details see ALCMAEON.

Phellus (Φελλος or Φελλός: Φελλίτης: Ru. near Saaret), an inland city of Lycia, on a mountain between Xanthus and Antiphellus ; the latter having been at first the port of Phellus, but afterwards eclipsing it.

Phellūsa, a small island near Lesbos.

Phēmīus (Φήμιος), a celebrated minstrel, son of Terpius, who entertained with his song the suitors in the palace of Ulysses in Ithaca.

Phēmŏnŏē (Φημονόη), a mythical Greek poetess of the ante-Homeric period, was said to have been the daughter of Apollo, and his first priestess at Delphi, and the inventor of the hexameter verse. There were poems which went under the name of Phemonoë, like the old religious poems which were ascribed to Orpheus, Musaeus, and the other mythological bards.

Phēnĕus (Φένεος or Φενεός: Φενεάτης: Fonia), a town in the N.E. of Arcadia, at the foot of Mt. Cyllene, and on the river Aroanius. Its territory was called Phenēātis (Φενεᾶτις). There were extensive marshes in the neighbourhood, the waters of which were partly carried off by a subterraneous emissary, which was supposed to have been made by Hercules. The town was of great antiquity. It is mentioned by Homer, and was said to have been built by an autochthon Pheneus. It contained a strongly fortified acropolis with a temple of Athena Tritonia ; and in the town itself were the tombs of Iphicles and Myrtilus, and temples of Hermes and Demeter.

Phērae (Φεραί: Φεραῖος: Valestino), an ancient town of Thessaly in the S.E. of the Pelasgian plain, W. of Mt. Pelion, S.W. of the lake Boebeis, and 90 stadia from its port-town Pagasae on the Pagasaean gulf. Pherae is celebrated in mythology as the residence of Admetus, and in history on account of its tyrants who extended their power over nearly the whole of Thessaly. Of these the most powerful was Jason, who was made Tagus or generalissimo of Thessaly about B.C. 374. Jason was succeeded in 370 by his 2 brothers Polydorus and Polyphron. The former was soon after assassinated by Polyphron. The latter was murdered in his turn in 369 by his nephew Alexander, who was notorious for his cruelty, and who was put to death in 367 by his wife Thebe and her 3 brothers. At a later period we read that Pherae was surrounded by a number of gardens and country houses.

Phērae. [PHARAE.]

Phĕrĕcrātes (Φερεκράτης), of Athens, one of the best poets of the Old Comedy, was contemporary with the comic poets Cratinus, Crates, Eupolis, Plato, and Aristophanes, being somewhat younger than the first two, and somewhat older than the others. He gained his first victory B.C. 438, and

he imitated the style of Crates, whose actor he had been. Crates and Pherecrates very much modified the coarse satire and vituperation of which this sort of poetry had previously been the vehicle, and constructed their comedies on the basis of a regular plot, and with more dramatic action. Pherecrates did not, however, abstain altogether from personal satire, for we see by the fragments of his plays that he attacked Alcibiades, the tragic poet Melanthius, and others. He invented a new metre, which was named, after him, the Pherecratean. The system of the verse is ∠ _ ∠̈ ∨ ∨ ∠ _ which may be best explained as a choriambus, with a spondee for its base, and a long syllable for its termination. The metre is very frequent in the choruses of the Greek tragedians, and in Horace, as, for example — Grato Pyrrha sub antro. The extant titles of the plays of Pherecrates are 18.

Phĕrĕcȳdes (Φερεκύδης). 1. Of Syros, an island in the Aegean, an early Greek philosopher or rather theologian. He flourished about B.C. 544. He is said to have obtained his knowledge from the secret books of the Phoenicians, and to have travelled in Egypt. Almost all the ancient writers who speak of him state that he was the teacher of Pythagoras. According to a common tradition he died of the lousy disease or Morbus Pediculosus ; though others give different accounts of his death. The most important subject which he is said to have taught was the doctrine of the Metempsychosis, or, as it is put by other writers, the doctrine of the immortality of the soul. He gave an account of his views in a work, which was extant in the Alexandrian period. It was written in prose, which he is said to have been the first to employ in the explanation of philosophical questions. — 2. Of Athens, one of the most celebrated of the early Greek logographers. He lived in the former half of the 5th century B.C., and was a contemporary of Hellanicus and Herodotus. His principal work was a mythological history in 10 books. It began with a theogony, and then proceeded to give an account of the heroic age and of the great families of that time. His fragments have been collected by Sturtz, Pherecydis Fragmenta, Lips. 1824, 2nd ed. ; and by C. and T. Müller in Fragmenta Historicum Graecorum, vol. i.

Phĕres (Φέρης). 1. Son of Cretheus and Tyro, and brother of Aeson and Amythaon; he was married to Periclymene, by whom he became the father of Admetus, Lycurgus, Idomene, and Periapis. He was believed to have founded the town of Pherae in Thessaly. — 2. Son of Jason and Medea.

Phĕrētĭădes (Φερητιαδης), i. e. a son of Pheres, is especially used as the name of Admetus.

Phĕrĕtīma (Φερετίμα), wife of Battus III., and mother of Arcesilaus III., successive kings of Cyrene. After the murder of her son by the Barcaeans [BATTIADAE, No. 6], Pheretima fled into Egypt to Aryandes, the viceroy of Darius Hystaspis, and representing that the death of Arcesilaus had been the consequence of his submission to the Persians, she induced him to avenge it. On the capture of Barca by the Persian army, she caused those who had the principal share in her son's murder to be impaled, and ordered the breasts of their wives to be cut off. Pheretima then returned to Egypt, where she soon after died of a painful and loathsome disease.

Phĕron or Phĕros (Φέρων, Φερῶς), king of

Egypt, and son of Sesostris. He was visited with blindness, an hereditary complaint, though, according to the legend preserved in Herodotus, it was a punishment for his presumptuous impiety in throwing a spear into the waters of the Nile when it had overflowed the fields. By attending to the directions of an oracle he was cured; and he dedicated an obelisk at Heliopolis in gratitude for his recovery. Pliny tells us that this obelisk, together with another also made by him but broken in its removal, was to be seen at Rome in the Circus of Caligula and Nero at the foot of the Vatican hill. Pliny calls the Pheron of Herodotus Nuncoreus, or Nencoreus, a name corrupted, perhaps, from Menophtheus. Diodorus gives him his father's name, Sesoosis. Pheron is of course the same word as Pharaoh.

PHIDIAS (Φειδίας), the greatest sculptor and statuary of Greece. Of his personal history we possess but few details. He was a native of Athens, and the son of Charmides, and was born about the time of the battle of Marathon, B. C. 490. He began to work as a statuary about 464, and one of his first great works was the statue of Athena Promachus, which may be assigned to about 460. This work must have established his reputation; but it was surpassed by the splendid productions of his own hand, and of others working under his direction, during the administration of Pericles. That statesman not only chose Phidias to execute the principal statues which were to be set up, but gave him the oversight of all the works of art which were to be erected. Of these works the chief were the Propylaea of the Acropolis, and, above all, the temple of Athena on the Acropolis, called the *Parthenon*, on which, as the central point of the Athenian polity and religion, the highest efforts of the best of artists were employed. There can be no doubt that the sculptured ornaments of this temple, the remains of which form the glory of the British Museum, were executed under the immediate superintendence of Phidias; but the colossal statue of the divinity made of ivory and gold, which was enclosed within that magnificent shrine, was the work of the artist's own hand. The statue was dedicated in 438. Having finished his great work at Athens, he went to Elis and Olympia, which he was now invited to adorn. He was there engaged for about 4 or 5 years from 437 to 434 or 433, during which time he finished his statue of the Olympian Zeus, the greatest of all his works. On his return to Athens, he fell a victim to the jealousy against his great patron, Pericles, which was then at its height. The party opposed to Pericles, thinking him too powerful to be overthrown by a direct attack, aimed at him in the persons of his most cherished friends, Phidias, Anaxagoras, and Aspasia. [PERICLES.] Phidias was first accused of peculation, but this charge was at once refuted, as, by the advice of Pericles, the gold had been affixed to the statue of Athena, in such a manner that it could be removed and the weight of it examined. The accusers then charged Phidias with impiety, in having introduced into the battle of the Amazons, on the shield of the goddess, his own likeness and that of Pericles. On this latter charge Phidias was thrown into prison, where he died from disease, in 432.—Of the numerous works executed by Phidias for the Athenians the most celebrated was the statue of Athena in the Parthenon, to which reference has

already been made. This statue was of that kind of work which the Greeks called *chryselephantine*, that is, the statue was formed of plates of ivory laid upon a core of wood or stone, for the flesh parts, while the drapery and other ornaments were of solid gold. The statue stood in the foremost and larger chamber of the temple (*prodomus*). It represented the goddess standing, clothed with a tunic reaching to the ancles, with her spear in her left hand and an image of Victory 4 cubits high in her right: she was girded with the aegis, and had a helmet on her head, and her shield rested on the ground by her side. The height of the statue was 26 cubits, or nearly 40 feet, including the base. The eyes were of a kind of marble, nearly resembling ivory, perhaps painted to imitate the iris and pupil; there is no sufficient authority for the statement which is frequently made, that they were of precious stones. The weight of the gold upon the statue, which, as above stated, was removable at pleasure, is said by Thucydides to have been 40 talents (ii. 13). — Still more celebrated than his statue of Athena was the colossal ivory and gold statue of Zeus, which Phidias made for the great temple of this god, in the *Altis* or sacred grove at Olympia. This statue was regarded as the masterpiece, not only of Phidias, but of the whole range of Grecian art; and was looked upon not so much as a statue, but rather as if it were the actual manifestation of the present deity. It was placed in the *prodomus* or front chamber of the temple, directly facing the entrance. It was only visible, however, on great festivals, at other times it was concealed by a magnificent curtain. The god was represented as seated on a throne of cedar wood, adorned with gold, ivory, ebony, stones, and colours, crowned with a wreath of olive, holding in his right hand an ivory and gold statue of Victory, and in his left hand supporting a sceptre, which was ornamented with all sorts of metals, and surmounted by an eagle. The throne was brilliant both with gold and stones, and with ebony and ivory, and was ornamented with figures both painted and sculptured. The statue almost reached to the roof, which was about 60 feet in height. The idea which Phidias essayed to embody in this, his greatest work, was that of the supreme deity of the Hellenic nation, no longer engaged in conflicts with the Titans and the Giants, but having laid aside his thunderbolt, and enthroned as a conqueror, in perfect majesty and repose, ruling with a nod the subject world. It is related that when Phidias was asked what model he meant to follow in making his statue, he replied that of Homer (*Il.* i. 528—530). The imitation of this passage by Milton gives no small aid to the comprehension of the idea (*Paradise Lost*, iii. 135—137):

' Thus while God spake, ambrosial fragrance fill'd

All heaven, and in the blessed spirits elect Sense of new joy ineffable diffused."

The statue was removed by the emperor Theodosius I. to Constantinople, where it was destroyed by a fire in A. D. 475.—The distinguishing character of the art of Phidias was *ideal beauty*, and that of the *sublimest* order, especially in the representation of divinities. and of subjects connected with their worship. While on the one hand he set himself free from the stiff and unnatural forms which, by a sort of religious precedent, had fettered his prodecessors of the archaic or hieratic school, he never, on the other hand, descended to the exact imitation of any human model, however beautiful; nor did he ever approach to that almost meretricious grace, by which some of his greatest followers, if they did not corrupt the art themselves, gave the occasion for its corruption in the hands of their less gifted and spiritual imitators.

Phidippides or Philippides (Φειδιππίδης, Φιλιππίδης), a courier, was sent by the Athenians to Sparta in B. C. 490, to ask for aid against the Persians, and arrived there on the 2nd day from his leaving Athens. On his return to Athens, he related that on his way to Sparta he had fallen in with Pan on Mt. Parthenium, near Tegea, and that the god had bid him ask the Athenians why they paid him no worship, though he had been hitherto their friend, and ever would be so. In consequence of this revelation, they dedicated a temple to Pan after the battle of Marathon, and honoured him thenceforth with annual sacrifices and a torch-race.

Phidon (Φείδων). 1. Son of Aristodamidas, and king of Argos, restored the supremacy of Argos over Cleonae, Phlius, Sicyon, Epidaurus, Troezen, and Aegina, and aimed at extending his dominions over the greater part of the Peloponnesus. The Pisans invited him, in the 8th Olympiad (B. C. 748), to aid them in excluding the Eleans from their usurped presidency at the Olympic games, and to celebrate them jointly with themselves. The invitation quite fell in with the ambitious pretensions of Phidon, who succeeded in dispossessing the Eleans and celebrating the games along with the Pisans; but the Eleans not long after defeated him, with the aid of Sparta, and recovered their privilege. Thus apparently fell the power of Phidon; but as to the details of the struggle we have no information. The most memorable act of Phidon was his introduction of copper and silver coinage, and a new scale of weights and measures, which, through his influence, became prevalent in the Peloponnesus, and ultimately throughout the greater portion of Greece. The coinage of Phidon is said to have been struck in Aegina.—2. An ancient Corinthian legislator of uncertain date.

Phigalia (Φιγαλία, Φιγάλεια, Φιγαλία: Φιγαλεύς: Paolitza), at a later time called Phialia, a town in the SW. corner of Arcadia on the frontiers of Messenia and Elis, and upon the river Lymax. It was taken by the Spartans B. C. 559, but was afterwards recovered by the Phigalians with the help of the Oresthasians. It is frequently mentioned in the later wars of the Achaean and Aetolian Leagues.—Phigalia however owes its celebrity in modern times to the remains of a splendid temple in its territory, situated about 6 miles NE. of the town at Bassae on Mt. Cotylum. This temple was built by Ictinus, the contemporary of Pericles and Phidias, and the architect, along with Callicrates, of the Parthenon at Athens. It was dedicated to Apollo Epicurius, or the Deliverer, because the god had delivered the country from the pestilence during the Peloponnesian war. Pausanias describes this temple as the most beautiful one in all Peloponnesus after the temple of Athena at Tegea. Most of the columns are still standing. In 1812 the frieze round the interior of the inner cella was discovered, containing a series of sculptures in alto-relievo, representing the combat of the Centaurs and the Lapithae, and of

the Greeks and the Amazons. Their height is a little more than 2 feet, and their total length is 100 feet. They were found on the ground under the spot which they originally occupied, and were much injured by their fall, and by the weight of the ruins lying upon them. They were purchased for the British Museum in 1814, where they are still preserved, and are usually known by the name of the *Phigalian Marbles.* They are some of the most interesting and beautiful remains of ancient art in this country.

Phila (Φίλα), daughter of Antipater, the regent of Macedonia, was married to Craterus in B. C. 322, and after the death of Craterus, who survived his marriage with her scarcely a year, she was again married to the young Demetrius, the son of Antigonus. When Demetrius was expelled from Macedonia in 287, she put an end to her own life at Cassandrea. She left 2 children by Demetrius; Antigonus, surnamed Gonatas, and a daughter, Stratonice, married first to Seleucus, and afterwards to his son Antiochus.

Phila (Φίλα: Φιλαῦος, Φιλάτης). 1. A town of Macedonia in the province Pieria, situated on a steep hill on the Peneus between Dium and Tempe and at the entrance into Thessaly, built by Demetrius II. and named after his mother Phila.—2. An island off the S. coast of Gaul, one of the Stoechades.

Philadelphia (Φιλαδέλφεια: Φιλαδελφεύς.) 1. (*Allah Shehr,* Ru.), a city of Lydia, at the foot of M. Tmolus, on the little river Cogamus, S.E. of Sardis. It was built by Attalus Philadelphus, king of Pergamus. It suffered greatly from earthquakes; so that in Strabo's time (under Augustus) it had greatly declined. In the reign of Tiberius, it was almost destroyed by one of these visitations. It was an early seat of Christianity, and its church is one of the 7 to which the Apocalypse is addressed. (Rev. iii. 7.)—2. A city of Cilicia Aspera, on the Calycadnus, above Aphrodisias.—3. In Palestine. [RABBATAMANA.]

Philadelphus (Φιλάδελφος), a surname of Ptolemaeus II. king of Egypt [PTOLEMAEUS] and of Attalus II. king of Pergamum [ATTALUS].

Philae (Φιλαί: *Jesiret-el-Birbeh,* i. e. the Island of Temples), an island in the Nile, just below the First Cataract, on the S. boundary of the country towards Aethiopia. It was inhabited by Egyptians and Ethiopians jointly, and was covered with magnificent temples, whose splendid ruins still remain. It was celebrated in Egyptian mythology as the burial-place of Osiris and Isis.

Philaeni (Φίλαινοι); 2 brothers, citizens of Carthage, of whom the following story is told. A dispute having arisen between the Carthaginians and Cyrenaeans about their boundaries, it was agreed that deputies should start at a fixed time from each of the cities, and that the place of their meeting, wherever it might be, should thenceforth form the limit of the 2 territories. The Philaeni were appointed for this service on the part of the Carthaginians, and advanced much further than the Cyrenaean party. The Cyrenaeans accused them of having set forth before the time agreed upon, but at length consented to accept the spot which they had reached as a boundary-line, if the Philaeni would submit to be buried alive there in the sand. Should they decline the offer, they were willing, they said, on their side, if permitted to advance as far as they pleased, to purchase for Cyrene an ex-

tension of territory by a similar death. The Philaeni accordingly then and there devoted themselves
for their country, in the way proposed. The Carthaginians paid high honours to their memory, and
erected altars to them where they had died ; and
from these, even long after all traces of them had
vanished, the place still continued to be called
" The Altars of the Philaeni." Our main authority
for this story is Sallust, who probably derived his
information from African traditions during the
time that he was proconsul of Numidia, and at
least 300 years after the event. We cannot, therefore, accept it unreservedly. The Greek name by
which the heroic brothers have become known to
us — Φίλαινοι, or lovers of praise — seems clearly
to have been framed to suit the tale.

Philagrius (Φιλάγριος), a Greek medical writer,
born in Epirus, lived after Galen and before Oribasius, and therefore probably in the 3rd century
after Christ. He wrote several works, of which,
however, only a few fragments remain.

Philammon (Φιλάμμων), a mythical poet and
musician of the ante-Homeric period, was said to
have been the son of Apollo and the nymph Chione,
or Philonis, or Leuconoë. By the nymph Agriope,
who dwelt on Parnassus, he became the father of
Thamyris and Eumolpus. He is closely associated
with the worship of Apollo at Delphi, and with
the music of the cithara. He is said to have established the choruses of girls, who, in the Delphian
worship of Apollo, sang hymns in which they
celebrated the births of Latona, Artemis, and
Apollo. Pausanias relates that in the most ancient
musical contests at Delphi, the first who conquered
was Chrysothemis of Crete, the second was Philammon, and the next after him his son Thamyris.

Philargyrius Junius, or Philargyrus, or Ju-
nilius Flagrius, an early commentator upon Virgil, who wrote upon the Bucolics and Georgics.
His observations are less elaborate than those of
Servius, and have descended to us in a mutilated
condition. The period when he flourished is altogether uncertain. They are printed in the edition
of Virgil by Burmann.

Phile or Philes, Manuel (Μανουήλ ὁ Φιλῆς), a
Byzantine poet, and a native of Ephesus, was born
about A. D. 1275, and died about 1340. His poem,
De Animalium Proprietate, chiefly extracted from
Aelian, is edited by De Paw, Traj. Rhen. 1739 ;
and his other poems on various subjects are edited
by Wernsdorf, Lips. 1768.

Philéas (Φιλέας), a Greek geographer of Athens,
whose time cannot be determined with certainty,
but who probably belonged to the older period of
Athenian literature. He was the author of a Periplus, which was divided into 2 parts, one on Asia,
and the other on Europe.

Philemon (Φιλήμων). 1. An aged Phrygian
and husband of Baucis. Once upon a time, Zeus
and Hermes, assuming the appearance of ordinary
mortals, visited Phrygia ; but no one was willing
to receive the strangers, until the hospitable hut of
Philemon and Baucis was opened to them, where
the two gods were kindly treated. Zeus rewarded
the good old couple by taking them to an eminence,
while all the neighbouring district was visited with
a sudden inundation. On that eminence Zeus appointed them the guardians of his temple, and
allowed them both to die at the same moment, and
then metamorphosed them into trees. — 2. An
Athenian poet of the New Comedy, was the son

of Damon, and a native of Soli in Cilicia, but at
an early age went to Athens, and there received
the citizenship. He flourished in the reign of
Alexander, a little earlier than Menander, whom.
however, he long survived. He began to exhibit
about B. C. 330. He was the first poet of the
New Comedy in order of time, and the second
in celebrity ; and he shares with Menander
the honour of its invention, or rather of reducing
it to a regular form. Philemon lived nearly
100 years. The manner of his death is differently related ; some ascribing it to excessive
laughter at a ludicrous incident ; others to joy at
obtaining a victory in a dramatic contest ; whil
another story represents him as quietly called
away by the goddesses whom he served, in the
midst of the composition or representation of his
last and best work. Although there can be no
doubt that Philemon was inferior to Menander as
a poet, yet he was a greater favourite with the
Athenians, and often conquered his rival in the
dramatic contests. [MENANDER.] The extant
fragments of Philemon display much liveliness,
wit, elegance, and practical knowledge of life
His favourite subjects seem to have been love intrigues, and his characters were the standing ones
of the New Comedy, with which Plautus and
Terence have made us familiar. The number of
his plays was 97 ; the number of extant titles,
after the doubtful and spurious ones are rejected,
amounts to about 53 ; but it is very probable that
some of these should be assigned to the younger
Philemon. The fragments of Philemon are printed
with those of Menander by Meineke, in his Fragmenta Comicorum Graecorum, Berol. 1841. —
3. The younger Philemon, also a poet of the New
Comedy, was a son of the former, in whose fame
nearly all that belongs to him has been absorbed ;
so that, although he was the author of 54 dramas,
there are only 2 short fragments, and not one title,
quoted expressly under his name. — 4. The author
of a Λεξικὸν τεχνολογικόν, the extant portion of
which was first edited by Burney, Lond. 1812,
and afterwards by Osann, Berlin, 1821. The au
thor informs us that his work was intended to take
the place of a similar Lexicon by the Grammarian
Hyperechius. The work of Hyperechius was arranged in 8 books, according to the 8 different
parts of speech. Philemon's lexicon was a meagre
epitome of this work ; and the part of it which is
extant consists of the 1st book and the beginning
of the 2nd. Hyperechius lived about the middle
of the 5th century of our era, and Philemon may
probably be placed in the 7th.

Philetaerus (Φιλέταιρος). 1. Founder of the
kingdom of Pergamus, was a native of Tieium in
Paphlagonia, and an eunuch. He is first mentioned in the service of Docimus, the general
of Antigonus, from which he passed into that
of Lysimachus, who entrusted him with the charge
of the treasures which he had deposited in the
strong fortress of Pergamus. Towards the end of
the reign of Lysimachus he declared in favour of
Seleucus ; and, after the death of the latter (B. C.
280), he took advantage of the disorders in Asia
to establish himself in virtual independence. At
his death he transmitted the government of Pergamus, as an independent state, to his nephew Eumenes. He lived to the age of 80, and died apparently in 263. — 2. An Athenian poet of the
Middle Comedy. Some said he was the third son

of Aristophanes, but others maintained that it was Nicostratus. He wrote 21 plays.

Philĕtas (Φιλητᾶς), of Cos, the son of Telephus, a distinguished Alexandrian poet and grammarian, flourished during the reign of the first Ptolemy, who appointed him tutor of his son, Ptolemy II. Philadelphus. His death may be placed about B. C. 280. Philetas seems to have been naturally of a very weak constitution, which at last broke down under excessive study. He was so remarkably thin as to become an object for the ridicule of the comic poets, who represented him as wearing leaden soles to his shoes, to prevent his being blown away by a strong wind. His poetry was chiefly elegiac. Of all the writers in that department he was esteemed the best after Callimachus ; to whom a taste less pedantic than that of the Alexandrian critics would probably have preferred him ; for, to judge by his fragments, he escaped the snare of cumbrous learned affectation. These 2 poets formed the chief models for the Roman elegy : nay, Propertius expressly states, in one passage, that he imitated Philetas in preference to Callimachus. The elegies of Philetas were chiefly amatory, and a large portion of them was devoted to the praises of his mistress Bittis, or, as the Latin poets give the name, Battis. Besides his poems, Philetas wrote in prose on grammar and criticism. His most important grammatical work was entitled Ἄτακτα. The fragments of Philetas have been collected by Bach, with those of Hermesianax and Phanocles, Halis Sax. 1829.

Phileus, an eminent Ionian architect, built the Mausoleum, in conjunction with Satyrus, and the temple of Athena Polias, at Priene. The date of the erection of the Mausoleum was soon after B. C. 353, the year in which Mausolus died ; that of the temple at Priene must have been about 20 years later.

Philīnus (Φιλῖνος). 1. A Greek of Agrigentum, accompanied Hannibal in his campaigns against Rome, and wrote a history of the Punic wars, in which he exhibited much partiality towards Carthage. — 2. An Attic orator, a contemporary of Demosthenes and Lycurgus. He is mentioned by Demosthenes in his oration against Midias, who calls him the son of Nicostratus, and says that he was trierarch with him. Three orations of Philinus are mentioned by the grammarians. — 3. A Greek physician, born in the island of Cos, and the reputed founder of the sect of the Empirici, probably lived in the 3rd century B. C. He wrote a work on part of the Hippocratic collection, and also one on botany.

Philippi (Φίλιπποι: Φιλιππεύς, Φιλιππήσιος, Φιλιππηνός: Filibah or Felibejik), a celebrated city in Macedonia adjecta [see p. 404, a], was situated on a steep height of Mt. Pangaeus, and on the river Gangas or Gangites, between the rivers Nestus and Strymon. It was founded by Philip on the site of an ancient town Crenides (Κρηνίδες), a colony of the Thasians, who settled here on account of the valuable gold mines in the neighbourhood. Philippi is celebrated in history in consequence of the victory gained here by Octavianus and Antony over Brutus and Cassius, B. C. 42, and as the place where the Apostle Paul first preached the gospel in Europe, A.D. 53. The church at Philippi soon became one of the most important of the early Christian churches : one of St. Paul's Epistles is addressed to it. It was made a Roman colony by Octavianus after the victory over Brutus and Cassius, under the name of Col. Augusta Julia Philippensis ; and it continued to be under the empire a flourishing and important city. Its seaport was Datum or Datus on the Strymonic gulf.

Philippĭdes (Φιλιππίδης). 1. See Phidippides. — 2. Of Athens, the son of Philocles, is mentioned as one of the 6 principal comic poets of the New Comedy by the grammarians. He flourished about B. C. 323. Philippides seems to have deserved the rank assigned to him, as one of the best poets of the New Comedy. He attacked the luxury and corruptions of his age, defended the privileges of his art, and made use of personal satire with a spirit approaching to that of the Old Comedy. His death is said to have been caused by excessive joy at an unexpected victory : similar tales are told of the deaths of other poets, as for example, Sophocles, Alexis, and Philemon. The number of his dramas is stated at 45. There are 15 titles extant.

Philippŏpŏlis (Φιλιππόπολις : Philippopoli), an important town in Thrace founded by Philip of Macedon on the site of a place previously called Eumolpias or Poneropolis. It was situated in a large plain S.E. of the Hebrus on a hill with 3 summits, whence it was sometimes called Trimontium. Under the Roman empire it was the capital of the province of Thracia in its narrower sense, and one of the most important towns in the country.

Philippus (Φίλιππος). I. Minor historical persons. 1. Son of Alexander I. of Macedonia, and brother of Perdiccas II., against whom he rebelled in conjunction with Derdas. The rebels were aided by the Athenians, B. C. 432. — 2. Son of Herod the Great, king of Judea, by his wife Cleopatra, was appointed by his father's will tetrarch of Ituraea and Trachonitis, the sovereignty of which was confirmed to him by the decision of Augustus. He continued to reign over the dominions thus entrusted to his charge for 37 years (B. C. 4 — A. D. 34). He founded the city of Caesarea, surnamed Paneas, but more commonly known as Caesarea Philippi, near the sources of the Jordan, which he named in honour of Augustus. [Caesarea, No. 2.] — 3. Son of Herod the Great, by Mariamne, whose proper name was Herodes Philippus. He must not be confounded with the preceding Philip. He was the first husband of Herodias, who afterwards divorced him, contrary to the Jewish law, and married his half-brother, Herod Antipas. It is Herod Philip, and not the preceding, who is meant by the Evangelists (Matt. xiv. 3 ; Mark, vi. 17 ; Luke, iii. 19), when they speak of Philip, the brother of Herod.

II. Kings of Macedonia.

I. Son of Argaeus, was the 3rd king, according to Herodotus and Thucydides, who, not reckoning Caranus and his two immediate successors (Coenus and Thurimas or Turimmas), look upon Perdiccas I. as the founder of the monarchy. Philip left a son, named Aëropus, who succeeded him. — II. Youngest son of Amyntas II. and Eurydice, reigned B. C. 359—336. He was born in 382, and was brought up at Thebes, whither he had been carried as a hostage by Pelopidas, and where he received a most careful education. Upon the death of his brother Perdiccas III., who was slain in battle against the Illyrians, Philip obtained the government of Macedonia, at first merely as regent and guardian to his infant nephew Amyntas ; but at the end of a few months he was enabled to set aside the claims of the young prince, and to assume for himself the title of king. Macedonia was beset by dangers on every side. Its territory was ravaged by the Illyrians on the W., and the Paeonians on the N., while Pausanias and Argaeus took advantage of the crisis to put forward their pretensions to the throne. Philip was fully equal to the emergency. By his tact and eloquence he sustained the failing spirits of the Macedonians, while at the same time he introduced among them a stricter military discipline, and organised their army on the plan of the phalanx. He first turned his arms against Argaeus, the most formidable of the pretenders, since he was supported by the Athenians. He defeated Argaeus in battle, and then concluded a peace with the Athenians. He next attacked the Paeonians, whom he reduced to subjection, and immediately afterwards defeated the Illyrians in a decisive battle, and compelled them to accept a peace, by which they lost a portion of their territory. Thus in the short period of one year, and at the age of 24, had Philip delivered himself from his dangerous position, and provided for the security of his kingdom. But energy and talents such as his were not satisfied with mere security, and henceforth his views were directed, not to defence, but to aggrandisement. His first efforts were directed to obtain possession of the various Greek·cities upon the Macedonian coast. Soon after his accession he had withdrawn his garrison from Amphipolis, and had declared it a free city, because the Athenians had supported Argaeus with the hope of recovering Amphipolis, and his continuing to hold the place would have interposed difficulties in the way of a peace with Athens, which was at that time an object of great importance to him. But he had never meant seriously to abandon this important town ; and accordingly having obtained pretexts for war with the Amphipolitans, he laid siege to the town and gained possession of it in 358. The Athenians had sent no assistance to Amphipolis, because Philip in a secret negotiation with the Athenians, led them to believe that he was willing to restore the city to them when he had taken it, and would do so on condition of their making him master of Pydna. After the capture of Amphipolis, he proceeded at once to Pydna, which seems to have yielded to him without a struggle, and the acquisition of which, by his own arms, and not through the Athenians, gave him a pretext for declining to stand by his secret engagement with them. The hostile feeling which such conduct necessarily excited against him at Athens, made it most important for him to secure the good will of the powerful town of Olynthus, and to detach the Olynthians from the Athenians. Accordingly he gave to the Olynthians the town of Potidaea, which he took from the Athenians in 356. Soon after this, he attacked and took a settlement of the Thasians, called Crenides, and, having introduced into the place a number of new colonists, he named it Philippi after himself. One great advantage of this acquisition was, that it put him in possession of the gold mines of the district. From this point there is for some time a pause in the active operations of Philip. In 352 he took Methone after a lengthened siege, in the course of which he himself lost an eye. The capture of this

place was a necessary preliminary in any movement towards the S., lying as it did between him and the Thessalian border. He now marched into Thessaly to aid the Aleuadae against Lycophron, the tyrant of Pherae. The Phocians sent a force to support Lycophron, but they were defeated by Philip, and their general Onomarchus slain. This victory gave Philip the ascendancy in Thessaly. He established at Pherae what he wished the Greeks to consider a free government, and then advanced S.-ward to ·Thermopylae. The pass, however, he found guarded by a strong Athenian force, and he was compelled, or at least thought it expedient to retire. He now turned his arms against Thrace, and succeeded in establishing his ascendancy in that country also. Meanwhile Philip's movements in Thessaly had opened the eyes of Demosthenes to the real danger of Athens and Greece, and his first Philippic (delivered in 352) was his earliest attempt to rouse his countrymen to energetic efforts against their enemy; but he did not produce much effect upon the Athenians. In 349 Philip commenced his attacks on the Chalcidian cities. Olynthus, in alarm, applied to Athens for aid, and Demosthenes, in his 3 Olynthiac orations, roused the people to efforts against the common enemy, not very vigorous at first and fruitless in the end.· In the course of 3 years Philip gained possession of all the Chalcidian cities, and the war was brought to a conclusion by the capture of Olynthus itself in 347. In the following year (346) he concluded peace with the Athenians, and straightway marched into Phocis, and brought the Phocian war to an end. The Phocian cities were destroyed, and their place in the Amphictyonic council was made over to the king of Macedonia, who was appointed also, jointly with the Thebans and Thessalians, to the presidency of the Pythian games. Ruling as he did over a barbaric nation, such a recognition of his Hellenic character was of the greatest value to him, especially as he looked forward to an invasion of the Persian empire in the name of Greece, united under him in a great national confederacy. During the next few years Philip steadily pursued his ambitious projects. From 342 to 340 he was engaged in an expedition in Thrace, and attempted to bring under his power all the Greek cities in that country. In the last of these years he laid siege to Perinthus and Byzantium; but the Athenians, who had long viewed Philip's aggrandisement with fear and alarm, now resolved to send assistance to these cities. Phocion was appointed to the command of the armament destined for this service, and succeeded in compelling Philip to raise the siege of both the cities (339). Philip now proceeded to carry on war against his northern neighbours, and seemed to give himself no further concern about the affairs of Greece. But meanwhile his hirelings were treacherously promoting his designs against the liberties of Greece. In 339 the Amphictyons declared war against the Locrians of Amphissa for having taken possession of a district of the sacred land ; but as the general they had appointed to the command of the Amphictyonic army was unable to effect any thing against the enemy, the Amphictyons at their next meeting in 338 conferred upon Philip the command of their army. Philip straightway marched through Thermopylae and seized Elatea. The Athenians heard of his approach with alarm; they succeeded, mainly through the influence of Demosthenes in forming an alliance with the Thebans; but their united army was defeated by Philip in the month of August, 338, in the decisive battle of Chaeronea, which put an end to the independence of Greece. Thebes paid dear for her resistance, but Athens was treated with more favour than she could have expected. Philip now seemed to have within his reach the accomplishment of the great object of his ambition, the invasion and conquest of the Persian empire. In a congress held at Corinth, which was attended by deputies from every Grecian state with the exception of Sparta, war with Persia was determined on, and the king of Macedonia was appointed to command the forces of the national confederacy. In 337 Philip's marriage with Cleopatra, the daughter of Attalus, one of his generals, led to the most serious disturbances in his family. Olympias and Alexander withdrew in great indignation from Macedonia; and though they returned home soon afterwards, they continued to be on hostile terms with Philip. Meanwhile, his preparations for his Asiatic expedition were not neglected, and early in 336 he sent forces into Asia, under Parmenion, to draw over the Greek cities to his cause. But in the summer of this year he was murdered at a grand festival which he held at Aegae, to solemnise the nuptials of his daughter with Alexander of Epirus. His murderer was a youth of noble blood, named Pausanias, who stabbed him as he was walking in the procession. The assassin was immediately pursued and slain by some of the royal guards. His motive for the deed is stated by Aristotle to have been private resentment against Philip, to whom he had complained in vain of a gross outrage offered to him by Attalus. Olympias and Alexander, however, were suspected of being implicated in the plot. [OLYMPIAS.] Philip died in the 47th year of his age and the 24th of his reign, and was succeeded by Alexander the Great. Philip had a great number of wives and concubines. Besides Olympias and Cleopatra, we may mention, 1. his first wife Audata, an Illyrian princess, and the mother of Cynane; 2. Phila, sister of Derdas and Machatas, a princess of Elymiotis; 3. Nicesipolis of Pherae, the mother of Thessalonica; 4. Philinna of Larissa, the mother of Arrhidaeus; 5. Meda, daughter of Cithelas, king of Thrace; 6. Arsinoë, the mother of Ptolemy I., king of Egypt, with whom she was pregnant when she married Lagus. To these numerous connections temperament as well as policy seems to have inclined him. He was strongly addicted, indeed, to sensual enjoyment of every kind; but his passions, however strong, were always kept in subjection to his interests and ambitious views. He was fond of science and literature, in the patronage of which he appears to have been liberal; and his appreciation of great minds is shown by his connection with Aristotle. In the pursuit of his political objects he was, as we have seen, unscrupulous, and ever ready to resort to duplicity and corruption; but when we consider his humanity and generous clemency, we may admit that he does not appear to disadvantage, even morally speaking, by the side of his fellow-conquerors of mankind. — III. The name of Philip was bestowed by the Macedonian army upon Arrhidaeus, the bastard son of Philip II., when he was raised to the throne after the death of Alexander the Great. He accordingly appears in the list of Macedonian kings as Philip III. For his

life and reign see ARRHIDAEUS. — IV. Eldest son of Cassander, whom he succeeded on the throne, B. C. 296. He reigned only a few months, and was carried off by a consumptive disorder. — V. Son of Demetrius II., reigned B. C. 220—178. He was only 8 years old at the death of his father Demetrius (229); and the sovereign power was consequently assumed by his uncle Antigonus Doson, who, though he certainly ruled as king rather than merely as guardian of his nephew, was faithful to the interests of Philip, to whom he transferred the sovereignty at his death in 220, to the exclusion of his own children. Philip was only 17 years old at the time of his accession, but he soon showed that he possessed ability and wisdom superior to his years. In consequence of the defeat of the Achaeans and Aratus by the Aetolians, the former applied for aid to Philip. This was granted; and for the next 3 years Philip conducted with distinguished success the war against the Aetolians. This war, usually called the Social war, was brought to a conclusion in 217, and at once gained for Philip a distinguished reputation throughout Greece, while his clemency and moderation secured him an equal measure of popularity. But a change came over his character soon after the close of the Social war. He became suspicious and cruel; and having become jealous of his former friend and counsellor Aratus, he caused him to be removed by a slow and secret poison in 213. Meantime he had become engaged in war with the Romans. In 215 he concluded an alliance with Hannibal; but he did not prosecute the war with any activity against the Romans, who on their part were too much engaged with their formidable adversary in Italy to send any powerful armament against the Macedonian king. In 211 the war assumed a new character in consequence of the alliance entered into by the Romans with the Aetolians. It was now carried on with greater vigour and alternate success; but as Philip gained several advantages over the Aetolians, the latter people made peace with Philip in 205. In the course of the same year the Romans likewise concluded a peace with Philip, as they were desirous to give their undivided attention to the war in Africa. It is probable that both parties looked upon this peace as little more than a suspension of hostilities. Such was clearly the view with which the Romans had accepted it; and Philip not only proceeded to carry out his views for his own aggrandisement in Greece, without any regard to the Roman alliances in that country, but he even sent a body of auxiliaries to the Carthaginians in Africa, who fought at Zama under Hannibal. As soon as the Romans had brought the 2nd Punic war to an end, they again declared war against Philip, 200. This war lasted between 3 and 4 years, and was brought to an end by the defeat of Philip by the consul Flamininus at the battle of Cynoscephalae in the autumn of 197. [FLAMININUS.] By the peace finally granted to Philip (196), the king was compelled to abandon all his conquests, both in Europe and Asia, surrender his whole fleet to the Romans, and limit his standing army to 5000 men, besides paying a sum of 1000 talents. Philip was now effectually humbled, and endeavoured to cultivate the friendship of the all-powerful republic. But towards the end of his reign he determined to try once more the fortune of war, and began to make active preparations for this purpose. His declining years were embittered by the disputes between his sons Perseus and Demetrius ; and the former by forged letters at length persuaded the king that Demetrius was plotting against his life, and induced him to consent to the execution of the unhappy prince. Philip was struck with the deepest grief and remorse, when he afterwards discovered the deceit that had been practised upon him. He believed himself to be haunted by the avenging spirit of Demetrius, and died shortly after, imprecating curses upon Perseus. His death took place in 179, in the 59th year of his age, after a reign of nearly 42 years.

III. *Family of the Marcii Philippi.*

1. **Q. Marcius Philippus**, praetor 188, with Sicily as his province, and consul 186, when he carried on war in Liguria with his colleague Sp. Postumius Albinus. He was defeated by the enemy in the country of the Apuani, and the recollection of his defeat was preserved by the name of the *saltus Marcius.* In 169 Philippus was consul a 2nd time, and carried on the war in Macedonia against Perseus, but accomplished nothing of importance. [PERSEUS.] In 164, Philippus was censor with L. Aemilius Paulus, and in his censorship he set up in the city a new sun-dial.— **2. L. Marcius Philippus**, was a tribune of the plebs, 104, when he brought forward an agrarian law, and was consul in 91 with Sex. Julius Caesar. In this year Philippus, who belonged to the popular party, opposed with the greatest vigour the measures of the tribune Drusus, who at first enjoyed the full confidence of the senate. But his opposition was all in vain; the laws of the tribune were carried. Soon afterwards Drusus began to be regarded with mistrust and suspicion ; Philippus became reconciled to the senate, and on his proposition a senatus consultum was passed, declaring all the laws of Drusus to be null and void, as having been carried against the auspices [DRUSUS.] In the civil wars between Marius and Sulla, Philippus took no part. He survived the death of Sulla ; and he is mentioned afterwards as one of those who advocated sending Pompey to conduct the war in Spain against Sertorius. Philippus was one of the most distinguished orators of his time (Hor. *Epist.* i. 7. 46). As an orator he was reckoned only inferior to Crassus and Antonius. He was a man of luxurious habits, which his wealth enabled him to gratify: his fish-ponds were particularly celebrated for their magnificence and extent, and are mentioned by the ancients along with those of Lucullus and Hortensius. Besides his son, L. Philippus, who is spoken of below, he had a step-son Gellius Publicola [PUBLICOLA].— **3. L. Marcius Philippus**, son of the preceding, was consul in 56. Upon the death of C. Octavius, the father of Augustus, Philippus married his widow Atia, and thus became the step-father of Augustus. Philippus was a timid man. Notwithstanding his close connection with Caesar's family, he remained neutral in the civil wars ; and after the assassination of Caesar, he endeavoured to dissuade his step-son, the young Octavius, from accepting the inheritance which the dictator had left him. He lived till his step-son had acquired the supremacy of the Roman world. He restored the temple of Hercules and the Muses, and surrounded it with a colonnade, which is frequently mentioned under the name of *Porticus*

Philippi. (*Clara monimenta Philippi,* Ov. *Fast.* vi. 801.)

IV. *Emperors of Rome.*

1. **M. Julius Philippus I.**, Roman emperor A. D. 244—249, was an Arabian by birth, and entered the Roman army, in which he rose to high rank. He accompanied Gordianus III. in his expedition against the Persians ; and upon the death of the excellent Misitheus [MISITHEUS] he was promoted to the vacant office of praetorian praefect. He availed himself of the influence of his high office to excite discontent among the soldiers, who at length assassinated Gordian, and proclaimed Philippus emperor, 244. Philippus proclaimed his son Caesar, concluded a disgraceful peace with Sapor, founded the city of Philippopolis, and then returned to Rome. In 245 he was engaged in prosecuting a successful war against the Carpi, on the Danube. In 248, rebellions, headed by Iotapinus and Marinus, broke out simultaneously in the East and in Moesia. Both pretenders speedily perished, but Decius having been despatched to recall the legions on the Danube to their duty, was himself forcibly invested with the purple by the troops, and compelled by them to march upon Italy. Philippus having gone forth to encounter his rival, was slain near Verona either in battle or by his own soldiers. The great domestic event of the reign of Philippus was the exhibition of the secular games, which were celebrated with even more than the ordinary degree of splendour, since Rome had now, according to the received tradition, attained the thousandth year of her existence (A. D. 248).— **2. M. Julius Philippus II.**, son of the foregoing, was a boy of 7 at the accession (244) of his father, by whom he was proclaimed Caesar, and 3 years afterwards (247) received the title of Augustus. In 249 he was slain, according to Zosimus, at the battle of Verona, or murdered, according to Victor, at Rome by the praetorians, when intelligence arrived of the defeat and death of the emperor.

V. *Literary.*

1. Of Medma, in the S. of Italy, a Greek astronomer, and a disciple of Plato. His observations, which were made in the Peloponnesus and in Locris, were used by the astronomers Hipparchus, Geminus the Rhodian, and Ptolemy.— **2.** Of Thessalonica, an epigrammatic poet, who, besides composing a large number of epigrams himself, compiled one of the ancient Greek Anthologies. The whole number of epigrams ascribed to him in the Greek Anthology is nearly 90 ; but of these, 6 (Nos. 36—41) ought to be ascribed to Lucillius, and a few others are manifestly borrowed from earlier poets, while others are mere imitations. The *Anthology* ('Ανθολογία) of Philip, in imitation of that of Meleager, and as a sort of supplement to it, contains chiefly the epigrams of poets who lived in, or shortly before, the time of Philip. The earliest of these poets seems to be Philodemus, the contemporary of Cicero, and the latest Automedon, who probably flourished under Nerva. Hence it is inferred that Philip flourished under Trajan.

Philiscus (Φίλισκος). 1. An Athenian poet of the Middle Comedy, of whom little is known. He must have flourished about B. C. 400, or a little later, as his portrait was painted by Parrhasius.— **2.** Of Miletus, an orator or rhetorician, and the disciple of Isocrates, wrote a life of the orator Lycurgus, and an epitaph on Lysias.—3. Of Aegina, a cynic philosopher, was the disciple of Diogenes the Cynic, and the teacher of Alexander in grammar.—4. Of Corcyra, a distinguished tragic poet, and one of the 7 who formed the Tragic Pleiad at Alexandria, was also a priest of Dionysus, and in that character he was present at the coronation procession of Ptolemy Philadelphus in B.C. 284. He wrote 42 dramas.—5. Of Rhodes, a sculptor, several of whose works were placed in the temple of Apollo, adjoining the portico of Octavia at Rome. One of these statues was that of the god himself: the others were Latona and Diana, the 9 Muses, and another statue of Apollo, without drapery. He probably lived about B.C. 146. The group of Muses, found in the villa of Cassius at Tivoli, is supposed by some to be a copy of that of Philiscus. Others take the beautiful statue at Florence, known as the Apollino, for the naked Apollo of Philiscus.

Philistinae Fossae. [PADUS.]

Philistion (Φιλιστίων). 1. Of Nicaea or Magnesia, a mimographer, who flourished in the time of Augustus, about A.D. 7. He was an actor, as well as a writer of mimes, and is said to have died of excessive laughter.—2. A physician, born either at one of the Greek towns in Sicily, or at Locri Epizephyrii in Italy, was tutor to the physician Chrysippus of Cnidos and the astronomer and physician Eudoxus, and therefore must have lived in the 4th century B.C.

Philistus (Φίλιστος), a Syracusan, son of Archonides or Archomenides, was born probably about B.C. 435. He assisted Dionysius in obtaining the supreme power, and stood so high in the favour of the tyrant, that the latter entrusted him with the charge of the citadel of Syracuse. But at a later period he excited the jealousy of the tyrant by marrying, without his consent, one of the daughters of his brother Leptines, and was in consequence banished from Sicily. He at first retired to Thurii, but afterwards established himself at Adria, where he composed the historical work which has given celebrity to his name. He was recalled from exile by the younger Dionysius soon after his accession, and quickly succeeded in establishing his influence over the mind of the latter. He exerted all his efforts to alienate Dionysius from his former friends, and not only caused Plato to be sent back to Athens, but ultimately succeeded in effecting the banishment of Dion also. Philistus was unfortunately absent from Sicily, when Dion first landed in the island, and made himself master of Syracuse, B.C. 356. He afterwards raised a powerful fleet, with which he gave battle to the Syracusans, but having been defeated, and finding himself cut off from all hopes of escape, he put an end to his own life to avoid falling into the hands of his enraged countrymen. Philistus wrote a history of Sicily, which was one of the most celebrated historical works of antiquity, though unfortunately only a few fragments of it have come down to us. It consisted of 2 portions, which might be regarded either as 2 separate works, or as parts of one great whole, a circumstance which explains the discrepancies in the statements of the number of books of which it was composed. The first 7 books comprised the general history of Sicily, commencing from the earliest times, and ending with the capture of Agrigentum by the Carthaginians, B.C. 406. The 2nd part, which formed a sequel to the 1st, contained the history of the elder Dionysius in 4 books, and that of the younger in 2: the latter was necessarily imperfect. In point of style Philistus is represented by the concurrent testimony of antiquity as imitating and even closely resembling Thucydides, though still falling far short of his great model. The fragments of Philistus have been collected by Goeller in an appendix to his work, *De Situ et Origine Syracusarum*, Lips. 1818, and by C. Muller, in the *Fragmenta Historicorum Graecorum*, Paris, 1841.

Philo (Φίλων). 1. An **Academic** philosopher, was a native of Larissa and a disciple of Clitomachus. After the conquest of Athens by Mithridates he removed to Rome, where he settled as a teacher of philosophy and rhetoric, and had Cicero as one of his hearers.—2. **Byblius**, also called HERENNIUS BYBLIUS, a Roman grammarian, and a native of Byblus in Phoenicia, as his patronymic indicates, was born about the time of Nero, and lived to a good old age, having written of the reign of Hadrian. He wrote many works, which are cited by Suidas and others; but his name is chiefly memorable by his translation of the writings of the Phoenician Sanchuniathon, of which considerable fragments have been preserved by Eusebius. [SANCHUNIATHON.]—3. Of **Byzantium**, a celebrated mechanician, and a contemporary of Ctesibius, flourished about B.C. 146. He wrote a work on military engineering, of which the 4th and 5th books have come down to us, and are printed in the *Veterum Mathematicorum Opera*, of Thevenot, Paris, 1693. There is also attributed to this Philo a work *On the Seven Wonders of the World*; but this work must have been written at a later time. The 7 wonders are the Hanging Gardens, the Pyramids, the statue of Jupiter Olympius, the Walls of Babylon, the Colossus of Rhodes, the Temple of Artemis at Ephesus, and, we may presume, from the prooemium, the Mausoleum; but the last is entirely wanting, and we have only a fragment of the Ephesian temple. Edited by Orelli, Lips. 1816.—4. **Judaeus**, the Jew, was born at Alexandria, and was descended from a priestly family of distinction. He had already reached an advanced age, when he went to Rome (A.D. 40) on an embassy to the emperor Caligula, in order to procure the revocation of the decree which exacted from the Jews divine homage to the statue of the emperor. We have no other particulars of the life of Philo worthy of record. His most important works treat of the books of Moses, and are generally cited under different titles. His great object was to reconcile the Sacred Scriptures with the doctrines of the Greek philosophy, and to point out the conformity between the two. He maintained that the fundamental truths of Greek philosophy were derived from the Mosaic revelation; and in order to make the latter agree more perfectly with the former, he had recourse to an allegorical interpretation of the books of Moses. Philo may therefore be regarded as a precursor of the Neo-Platonic philosophy. The best edition of his works is by Mangey, Lond. 1742, 2 vols. fo.—5. A **Megarian** philosopher, was a disciple of Diodorus Cronus, and a friend of Zeno.—6. Of **Tarsus** in Cilicia, a celebrated physician, frequently quoted by Galen and others.—7. **Artists.** (1). Son of Antipater, a statuary who lived in the time of Alexander the Great, and made the statue of Hephaestion, and also the statue of Zeus Ourios, which stood on the shore of the Black Sea, at the entrance of the Bosporus, near Chalcedon, and formed an important landmark for sailors. It was still perfect in the time of Cicero (*in Verr.* iv. 58), and the base has been preserved to modern times, bearing an inscription of 8 elegiac verses. — (2.) A very eminent architect at Athens in the time of the immediate successors of Alexander. He built for Demetrius Phalereus, about B.C. 318, the portico of 12 Doric columns to the great temple at Eleusis. He also constructed for the Athenians, under the administration of Lycurgus, a basin (*armamentarium*) in the Piraeus, in which 1000 ships could lie. This work, which excited the greatest admiration, was destroyed in the taking of Athens by Sulla.

Philo, Q. Publilius, a distinguished general in the Samnite wars, and the author of one of the great reforms in the Roman constitution. He was consul B.C. 339, with Ti. Aemilius Mamercinus, and defeated the Latins, over whom he triumphed. In the same year he was appointed dictator by his colleague Aemilius Mamercinus, and, as such, proposed the celebrated *Publilias Leges*, which abolished the power of the patrician assembly of the curiae, and elevated the plebeians to an equality with the patricians for all practical purposes. (*Dict. of Antiq.* art. *Publilias Leges.*) In 337 Philo was the 1st plebeian praetor, and in 332 he was censor with Sp. Postumius Albinus. In 327 he was consul a 2nd time, and carried on war in the S. of Italy. He was continued in the command for the following year with the title of proconsul, the 1st instance in Roman history in which a person was invested with proconsular power. He took Palaepolis in 326. In 320 he was consul a 3rd time, with L. Papirius Cursor, and carried on the war with success against the Samnites.

Philo, L. Veturius. 1. L., consul B.C. 220, with C. Lutatius Catulus; dictator 217 for the purpose of holding the comitia; and censor 210 with P. Licinius Crassus Dives, and died while holding this office. — 2. L., praetor 209 with Cisalpine Gaul as his province. In 207 he served under Claudius Nero and Livius Salinator in the campaign against Hasdrubal. In 206 he was consul with Q. Caecilius Metellus, and in conjunction with his colleague carried on the war against Hannibal in Bruttium. He accompanied Scipio to Africa, and after the battle of Zama, 202, was sent to Rome to announce the news of Hannibal's defeat.

Philochares (Φιλοχάρης), a distinguished painter, mentioned by Pliny, is supposed by the modern writers on art to be the same person as the brother of Aeschines, of whose artistic performances Demosthenes speaks contemptuously, but whom Ulpian ranks with the most distinguished painters.

Philochorus (Φιλόχορος), a celebrated Athenian writer, chiefly known by his *Atthis*, or work on the legends, antiquities, and history of Attica. He was a person of considerable importance in his native city, and was put to death by Antigonus Gonatas when the latter obtained possession of Athens, about B.C. 260. His *Atthis* consisted of 17 books, and related the history of Attica, from the earliest times to the reign of Antiochus Theos, B.C. 261. The work is frequently quoted by the scholiasts, lexicographers, as well as other later authors. He also wrote many other works, the

titles of which are preserved by Suidas and the grammarians. The fragments of Philochorus have been published by Siebelis, Lips. 1811, and by Müller, Paris, 1841.

Philocles (Φιλοκλῆς), an Athenian tragic poet, the sister's son of Aeschylus; his father's name was Philopithes. He is said to have composed 100 tragedies. In the general character of his plays he was an imitator of Aeschylus; and that he was not unworthy of his great master, may be inferred from the fact that he gained a victory over Sophocles, when the latter exhibited his *Oedipus Tyrannus*, B.C. 429. Philocles was frequently ridiculed by the comic poets.

Philocrates (Φιλοκράτης), an Athenian orator, was one of the venal supporters of Philip in opposition to Demosthenes.

Philoctetes (Φιλοκτήτης), a son of Poeas (whence he is called *Poeantiades*, Ov. *Met.* xiii. 313) and Demonassa, the most celebrated archer in the Trojan war. He led the warriors from Methone, Thaumacia, Meliboea, and Olizon, against Troy, in 7 ships. But on his voyage thither he was left behind by his men in the island of Lemnos, because he was ill of a wound which he had received from the bite of a snake; and Medon, the son of Oïleus and Rhene, undertook the command of his troops. This is all that the Homeric poems relate of Philoctetes, with the addition that he returned home in safety; but the cyclic and tragic poets have added numerous details to the story. Thus they relate that he was the friend and armour-bearer of Hercules, who instructed him in the use of the bow, and who bequeathed to him his bow, with the poisoned arrows. These presents were a reward for his having erected and set fire to the pile on Mt. Oeta, where Hercules burnt himself. Philoctetes was also one of the suitors of Helen, and thus took part in the Trojan war. On his voyage to Troy, while staying in the island of Chryse, he was bitten by a snake. This misfortune happened to him when he was showing to the Greeks the altar of Athena Chryse, or while he was looking at the tomb of Troilus in the temple of Apollo Thymbraeus, or as he was pointing out to his companions the altar of Hercules. According to some accounts, the wound in his foot was not inflicted by a serpent, but by his own poisoned arrows. The wound is said to have become ulcerated, and to have produced such an intolerable stench that the Greeks, on the advice of Ulysses, abandoned Philoctetes and left him alone on the solitary coast of Lemnos. He remained in this island till the 10th year of the Trojan war, when Ulysses and Diomedes came to fetch him to Troy, as an oracle had declared that the city could not be taken without the arrows of Hercules. He accompanied these heroes to Troy, and on his arrival Apollo sent him into a deep sleep, during which Machaon (or Podalirius, or both, or Aesculapius himself) cut out the wound, washed it with wine, and applied healing herbs to it. Philoctetes was thus cured, and soon after slew Paris, whereupon Troy fell into the hands of the Greeks. On his return from Troy he is said to have been cast upon the coast of Italy, where he settled, and built Petelia and Crimissa. In the latter place he founded a sanctuary of Apollo Alaeus, to whom he dedicated his bow.

Philodemus (Φιλόδημος) of Gadara, in Palestine, an Epicurean philosopher and epigrammatic poet, contemporary with Cicero. The Greek Anthology contains 34 of his Epigrams, which are chiefly of a light and amatory character, and which quite bear out Cicero's statements concerning the licentiousness of his matter and the elegance of his manner. (Cic. *in Pis.* 28, 29.) Philodemus is also mentioned by Horace (*Sat.* i. 2. 121.)

Philolaus (Φιλόλαος), a distinguished Pythagorean philosopher, was a native of Croton or Tarentum. He was a contemporary of Socrates, and the instructor of Simmias and Cebes at Thebes, where he appears to have lived many years. Pythagoras and his earliest successors did not commit any of their doctrines to writing ; and the first publication of the Pythagorean doctrines is pretty uniformly attributed to Philolaus. He composed a work on the Pythagorean philosophy in 3 books, which Plato is said to have procured at the cost of 100 minae through Dion of Syracuse, who purchased it from Philolaus, who was at the time in deep poverty. Other versions of the story represent Plato as purchasing it himself from Philolaus or his relatives when in Sicily. Plato is said to have derived from this work the greater part of his Timaeus.

Philomela (Φιλομήλα), daughter of king Pandion in Attica, who, being dishonoured by her brother-in-law Tereus, was metamorphosed into a nightingale. The story is given under TEREUS.

Philomelium or Philomelum (Φιλομήλιον, or in the Pisidian dialect Φιλομηδή: Φιλομηλεύς, Philomelensis or Philomeliensis: prob. *Ak-Shehr*, Ru.), a city of Phrygia Parorios, on the borders of Lycaonia and Pisidia, said to have been named from the numbers of nightingales in its neighbourhood. It is mentioned several times by Cicero. According to the division of the provinces under Constantine, it belonged to Pisidia. It is still found mentioned at the time of the Crusades, by the name of Philomene.

Philomelus (Φιλόμηλος), a general of the Phocians in the Phocian or Sacred war, was the person who persuaded his countrymen to seize the temple of Delphi, and to apply the riches of the temple to the purpose of defending themselves against the Amphictyonic forces, B.C. 357. He commanded the Phocians during the early years of the war, but was slain in battle in 353. He was succeeded in the command by his brother Onomarchus.

Philonides (Φιλωνίδης), an Athenian poet of the Old Comedy, who is, however, better known on account of his connection with the literary history of Aristophanes. It is generally stated that Philonides was an actor of Aristophanes, who is said to have committed to him and to Callistratus his chief characters; but the best modern critics have shown that this is an erroneous statement, and that the true state of the case is, that several of the plays of Aristophanes were brought out in the names of Callistratus and Philonides. We learn from Aristophanes himself, not only the fact that he brought out his early plays in the names of other poets, but also his reasons for so doing. In the *Parabasis* of the Knights (v. 514), he states that he had pursued this course, not from want of thought, but from a sense of the difficulty of his profession, and from a fear that he might suffer from that fickleness of taste which the Athenians had shown towards other poets, as Magnes, Crates, and Cratinus. It appears that Aristophanes used the name of Philonides, probably, for the *Clouds*,

and certainly for the *Wasps*, the *Proagon*, the *Amphiaraus*, and the *Frogs*. The *Daetaleis*, the *Babylonians*, the *Acharnians*, the *Birds*, and the *Lysistrata*, were brought out in the name of Callistratus. Of the extant plays of Aristophanes, the only ones which he is known to have brought out in his own name are the *Knights*, the *Peace*, and the *Plutus*.

Philonome. [TENES.]

Philopoemen (Φιλοποίμην), of Megalopolis in Arcadia, one of the few great men that Greece produced in the decline of her political independence. The great object of his life was to infuse among the Achaeans a military spirit, and thereby to establish their independence on a firm and lasting basis. He was the son of Craugis, a distinguished man at Megalopolis, and was born about B.C. 252. He lost his father at an early age, and was brought up by Cleander, an illustrious citizen of Mantinea, who had been obliged to leave his native city, and had taken refuge at Megalopolis. He received instruction from Ecdemus and Demophanes, both of whom had studied the Academic philosophy under Arcesilaus. At an early age he became distinguished by his love of arms and his bravery in war. His name, however, first occurs in history in B.C. 222, when Megalopolis was taken by Cleomenes, and in the following year (221) he fought with conspicuous valour at the battle of Sellasia, in which Cleomenes was completely defeated. In order to gain additional military experience, he soon afterwards sailed to Crete, and served for some years in the wars between the cities of that island. On his return to his native country, in 210, he was appointed commander of the Achaean cavalry; and in 208 he was elected strategus, or general of the Achaean league. In this year he defeated Machanidas, tyrant of Lacedaemon, and slew him in battle with his own hand. In 201 he was again elected general of the league, when he defeated Nabis, who had succeeded Machanidas as tyrant of Lacedaemon. Soon afterwards Philopoemen took another voyage to Crete, and assumed the command of the forces of Gortyna. He did not return to Peloponnesus till 194. He was made general of the league in 192, when he again defeated Nabis, who was slain in the course of the year by some Aetolian mercenaries. Philopoemen was reelected general of the league several times afterwards; but the state of Greece did not afford him much further opportunity for the display of his military abilities. The Romans were now in fact the masters of Greece, and Philopoemen clearly saw that it would be an act of madness to offer open resistance to their authority. At the same time as the Romans still recognised in words the independence of the league, Philopoemen offered a resolute resistance to all their encroachments upon the liberties of his country, whenever he could do so without affording them any pretext for war. In 188, when he was general of the league, he took Sparta, and treated it with the greatest severity. He razed the walls and fortifications of the city, abolished the institutions of Lycurgus, and compelled the citizens to adopt the Achaean laws in their stead. In 183 the Messenians revolted from the Achaean league. Philopoemen, who was general of the league for the 8th time, hastily collected a body of cavalry, and pressed forward to Messene. He fell in with a large body of Messenian troops, by whom he was taken prisoner, and carried to Messene. Here he was thrown into a dungeon, and was compelled by Dinocrates to drink poison. The news of his death filled the whole of Peloponnesus with grief and rage. An assembly was immediately held at Megalopolis; Lycortas was chosen general; and in the following year, he invaded Messenia, which was laid waste far and wide ; Dinocrates and the chiefs of his party were obliged to put an end to their lives. The remains of Philopoemen were conveyed to Megalopolis in solemn procession; and the urn which contained the ashes was carried by the historian Polybius. His remains were then interred at Megalopolis with heroic honours ; and soon afterwards statues of him were erected in most of the towns belonging to the Achaean league.

Philostephanus (Φιλοστέφανος), of Cyrene, an Alexandrian writer of history and geography, the friend or disciple of Callimachus, flourished under Ptolemy II. Philadelphus, about B.C. 249.

Philostorgius (Φιλοστόργιος), a native of Borissus in Cappadocia, was born about A.D. 358. He wrote an ecclesiastical history, from the heresy of Arius in 300, down to 425. Philostorgius was an Arian, which is probably the reason why his work has not come down to us. It was originally in 12 books; and we still possess an abstract of it, made by Photius.

Philostratus (Φιλόστρατος), the name of a distinguished family of Lemnos, of which there are mentioned 3 persons in the history of Greek literature. 1. Son of Verus, taught at Athens ; but we know nothing about him, with the exception of the titles of his works, given by Suidas. He could not however have lived in the reign of Nero, according o the statement of Suidas, since his son was not b rn till the latter part of the 2nd century. —2. **Flavius Philostratus**, son of the preceding, and the most eminent of the 3, was born about A.D. 182. He studied and taught at Athens, and is usually called the Athenian to distinguish him from the younger Philostratus [No. 3], who more usually bears the surname of the Lemnian. Flavius afterwards removed to Rome, where we find him a member of the circle of literary men, whom the philosophic Julia Domna, the wife of Severus, had drawn around her. It was at her desire that he wrote the life of Apollonius. He was alive in the reign of the emperor Philippus (244—249). The following works of Philostratus have come down to us : — 1. *The Life of Apollonius of Tyana* (τὰ ἐς τὸν Τυανέα 'Απολλώνιον), in 8 books, [See APOLLONIUS, No. 7.] — 2. *Lives of the Sophists* (Βίοι Σοφιστῶν), in 2 books, contains the history of philosophers who had the character of being sophists, and of those who were in reality sophists. It begins with the life of Gorgias, and comes down to the contemporaries of Philostratus in the reign of Philippus. 3. *Heroica* or *Heroicus* ('Ηρωικά, 'Ηρωικὸς), is in the form of a dialogue, and gives an account of the heroes engaged in the Trojan war. 4. *Imagines* ('Εικόνες), in 2 books, contains an account of various paintings. This is the author's most pleasing work, exhibiting great richness of fancy, power and variety of delineation, and a rich exuberance of style. 5. *Epistolae* ('Επιστολαί), 73 in number, chiefly amatory. The best editions of the collected works of Philostratus are by Olearius, Lips. 1709, and by Kayser, Turic. 1844. — 3. **Philostratus**, the younger, usually called the Lemnian, as men-

tioned above, was a son of Nervianus and of a daughter of Flavius Philostratus, but is erroneously called by Suidas a son-in-law of the latter. He enjoyed the instructions of his grandfather and of the sophist Hippodromus, and had obtained sufficient distinction at the early age of 24 to receive exemption from taxes. He visited Rome, but he taught at Athens, and died in Lemnos. He wrote several works, and among others one entitled *Imagines*, in imitation of his grandfather's work with the same title, of which a portion is still extant.

Philotas (Φιλώτας), son of Parmenion, enjoyed a high place in the friendship of Alexander, and in the invasion of Asia obtained the chief command of the ἑταῖροι, or native Macedonian cavalry. He served with distinction in the battles of the Granicus and Arbela, and also on other occasions; but in B.C. 330, while the army was in Drangiana, he was accused of being privy to a plot which had been formed by a Macedonian, named Dimnus, against the king's life. There was no proof of his guilt; but a confession was wrung from him by the torture, and he was stoned to death by the troops after the Macedonian custom. [PARMENION.]

Philotimus (Φιλότιμος), an eminent Greek physician, pupil of Praxagoras, and fellow-pupil of Herophilus, lived in the 4th and 3rd centuries B.C.

Philoxenus (Φιλόξενος). 1. A Macedonian officer of Alexander the Great, received the government of Cilicia from Perdiccas in 321.—2. Of Cythera, one of the most distinguished dithyrambic poets of Greece, was born B.C. 435 and died 380, at the age of 55. He was reduced to slavery in his youth, and was bought by the lyric poet Melanippides, by whom he was educated in dithyrambic poetry. After residing some years at Athens, he went to Syracuse, where he speedily obtained the favour of Dionysius, and took up his abode at his court. But soon afterwards he offended Dionysius, and was cast into prison; an act of oppression which most writers ascribe to the wounded vanity of the tyrant, whose poems Philoxenus not only refused to praise, but, on being asked to revise one of them, said that the best way of correcting it would be to draw a black line through the whole paper. Another account ascribes his disgrace to too close an intimacy with the tyrant's mistress Galatea; but this looks like a fiction, arising out of a misunderstanding of the object of his poem entitled Cyclops or Galatea. After some time he was released from prison, and restored outwardly to the favour of Dionysius; but he finally left his court, and is said to have spent the latter part of his life in Ephesus. — Of the dithyrambs of Philoxenus by far the most important was his *Cyclops* or *Galatea*, the loss of which is greatly to be lamented. Philoxenus also wrote another poem, entitled *Deipnon* (Δεῖπνον) or the *Banquet*, which appears to have been the most popular of his works, and of which we have more fragments than of any other. This poem was a most minute and satirical description of a banquet, and the subject of it was furnished by the luxury of the court of Dionysius. Philoxenus was included in the attacks which the comic poets made on all the musicians of the day, for their corruptions of the simplicity of the ancient music; but we have abundant testimony to the high esteem in which he was held both during his life and after his death. — 3. The Leucadian, lived at Athens about the same time as Philoxenus of Cythera, with whom he is frequently confounded by the grammarians. Like his more celebrated namesake, the Leucadian was ridiculed by the poets of the Old Comedy, and seems to have spent a part of his life in Sicily. The Leucadian was a most notorious parasite, glutton, and effeminate debauchee; but he seems also to have had great wit and good-humour, which made him a favourite at the tables which he frequented. — 4. A celebrated Alexandrian grammarian, who taught at Rome, and wrote on Homer, on the Ionic and Laconian dialects, and several other grammatical works, among which was a *Glossary*, which was edited by H. Stephanus, Paris, 1573. — 5. An Aegyptian surgeon, who wrote several valuable volumes on surgery. He must have lived in or before the first century after Christ. — 6. A painter of Eretria, the disciple of Nicomachus, who painted for Cassander a battle of Alexander with Darius.

Philus, Furius. 1. P., was consul B.C. 223 with C. Flaminius, and accompanied his colleague in his campaign against the Gauls in the N. of Italy. He was praetor 216, when he commanded the fleet, with which he proceeded to Africa. In 214 he was censor with M. Atilius Regulus, but died at the beginning of the following year. — **2.** L., consul 136, received Spain as his province, and was commissioned by the senate to deliver up to the Numantines C. Hostilius Mancinus, the consul of the preceding year. Philus, like his contemporaries Scipio Africanus the younger and Laelius, was fond of Greek literature and refinement. He is introduced by Cicero as one of the speakers in his dialogue *De Republica.*

Philyllius (Φιλύλλιος), an Athenian comic poet, belongs to the latter part of the Old Comedy, and the beginning of the Middle.

Philyreis (Φιλυρηίς: prob. the little island off C. Zefreh, E. of Kerassunt-Ada), an island off the N. coast of Asia Minor (Pontus), E. of the country of the Mosynoeci, and near the promontory of Zephyrium (Zefreh), where CHIRON was nurtured by his mother Philyra.

Philyres (Φίλυρες), a people on the coast of Pontus, in the neighbourhood of the island PHILY-REIS.

Phineus (Φινεύς). **1.** Son of Belus and Anchinoe, and brother of Cepheus. He was slain by Perseus. For details see ANDROMEDA and PERSEUS. — **2.** Son of Agenor, and king of Salmydessus in Thrace. He was first married to Cleopatra, the daughter of Boreas and Orithyia, by whom he had 2 children, Oryithus (Oarthus) and Crambis; but their names are different in the different legends: Ovid calls them Polydectus and Polydorus. Afterwards he was married to Idaea (some call her Dia, Eurytia, or Idothea), by whom he again had 2 sons, Thynus and Mariandynus. — Phineus was a blind soothsayer, who had received his prophetic powers from Apollo; but the cause of his blindness is not the same in all accounts. He is most celebrated on account of his being tormented by the Harpies, who were sent by the gods to punish him on account of his cruelty towards his sons by the first marriage. His second wife falsely accused them of having made an attempt upon her virtue, whereupon Phineus put out their eyes, or, according to others, exposed them to be devoured by wild beasts, or ordered them to be half buried in the earth, and then to be scourged.

Whenever a meal was placed before Phineus, the Harpies darted down from the air and carried it off; later writers add that they either devoured the food themselves, or rendered it unfit to be eaten. When the Argonauts visited Thrace, Phineus promised to instruct them respecting their voyage, if they would deliver him from the monsters. This was done by Zetes and Calais, the sons of Boreas, and brothers of Cleopatra. [See p. 76, a.] Phineus now explained to the Argonauts the further course they had to take, and especially cautioned them against the Symplegades. According to another story the Argonauts, on their arrival at Thrace, found the sons of Phineus half buried, and demanded their liberation, which Phineus refused. A battle thereupon ensued, in which Phineus was slain by Hercules. The latter also delivered Cleopatra from her confinement, and restored the kingdom to the sons of Phineus; and on their advice he also sent the second wife of Phineus back to her father, who ordered her to be put to death. Some traditions, lastly, state that Phineus was killed by Boreas, or that he was carried off by the Harpies into the country of the Bistones or Milchessians. Those accounts in which Phineus is stated to have put out the eyes of his sons, add that they had their sight restored to them by the sons of Boreas, or by Aesculapius.

Phinopolis (Φινόπολις), a town in Thrace on the Pontus Euxinus near the entrance to the Bosporus.

Phintias (Φιντίας). **1.** A Pythagorean, the friend of Damon, who was condemned to die by Dionysius the elder. For details see DAMON. — **2.** Tyrant of Agrigentum, who established his power over that city during the period of confusion which followed the death of Agathocles (B.C. 289.) He founded a new city on the S. coast of Sicily, to which he gave his own name, and whither he removed all the inhabitants from Gela, which he razed to the ground.

Phintonis Insula (*Isola di Figo*), an island between Sardinia and Corsica.

Phlegethon (Φλεγέθων), i. e. the flaming, a river in the lower world, in whose channel flowed flames instead of water.

Phlegon (Φλέγων), a native of Tralles in Lydia, was a freedman of the emperor Hadrian, whom he survived. The only 2 works of Phlegon which have come down to us, are a small treatise on wonderful events (Περὶ θαυμασίων), and another short treatise on long-lived persons (Περὶ μακροβίων), which gives a list of persons in Italy who had attained the age of a hundred years and upwards. Besides these 2 works Phlegon wrote many others, of which the most important was an account of the Olympiads in 17 books, from Ol. 1 to Ol. 229 (A. D. 137). The best edition of Phlegon is by Westermann in his *Paradoxographi*, Brunsvig. 1839.

Phlegra. [PALLENE.]

Phlegraei Campi (τὰ Φλεγραῖα πεδία, or ἡ Φλέγρα: *Solfatara*), the name of the volcanic plain extending along the coast of Campania from Cumae to Capua, so called because it was believed to have been once on fire. It was also named Laboriae or Laborinus Campus, either on account of its great fertility, which occasioned its constant cultivation, or on account of the frequent earthquakes and internal convulsions to which it was exposed.

Phlegyas (Φλεγύας) son of Ares and Chryse,

the daughter of Halmus, succeeded Eteocles in the government of Orchomenos in Boeotia, which he called after himself Phlegyantis. He was the father of Ixion and Coronis, the latter of whom became by Apollo the mother of Aesculapius. Enraged at this, Phlegyas set fire to the temple of the God, who killed him with his arrows, and condemned him to severe punishment in the lower world. Phlegyas is represented as the mythical ancestor of the race of the Phlegyae, a branch of the Minyae, who emigrated from Orchomenos in Boeotia and settled in Phocis.

Phliasia. [PHLIUS.]

Phlius (Φλιούς, -οῦντος: Φλιάσιος), the chief town of a small province in the N.E. of Peloponnesus, whose territory Phliasia (Φλιασία), was bounded on the N. by Sicyonia, on the W. by Arcadia, on the E. by the territory of Cleonae, and on the S. by that of Argos. The greater part of this country was occupied by mountains, called Coelossa, Carneates, Arantinus and Tricaranon. According to Strabo the most ancient town in the country was Araethyrēa, which the inhabitants deserted, and afterwards founded Phlius; while Pausanias says nothing about a migration, but relates that the town was first called Arantia from its founder Aras, an autochthon, afterwards Araethyrea from the daughter of Aras, and finally Phlius, from Phlias, a grandson of Temenus. Phlius was originally inhabited by Argives. It afterwards passed into the hands of the Dorians, with whom part of the Argive population intermingled, while part migrated to Samos and Clazomenae. During the greater part of its history it remained faithful to Sparta.

Phlygonium (Φλυγόνιον), a small town in Phocis, destroyed in the Phocian war.

Phocaea (Φώκαια: Φωκαεύς, Phocaeënsis: the Ru. called Karaja-Fokia, i. e. Old Fokia, S.W. of Fouges or New Fokia), the N.-most of the Ionian cities on the W. coast of Asia Minor, stood at the W. extremity of the tongue of land which divides the Sinus Elaiticus (G. of Fouges), on the N. from the Sinus Hermaeus (G. of Smyrna), on the S. It was said to have been founded by Phocian colonists under Philogenes and Damon. It was originally within the limits of Aeolis, in the territory of Cyme; but the Cymaeans voluntarily gave up the site for the new city, which was soon admitted into the Ionian confederacy on the condition of adopting oecists of the race of Codrus. Admirably situated, and possessing 2 excellent harbours, Naustathmus and Lampter, Phocaea became celebrated as a great maritime state, and especially as the founder of the most distant Greek colonies towards the W., namely MASSILIA in Gaul, and the still more distant, though far less celebrated, city of Maenaca in Hispania Baetica. After the Persian conquest of Ionia, Phocaea had so declined, that she could only furnish 3 ships to support the great Ionian revolt; but the spirit of her people had not been extinguished; when the common cause was hopeless, and their city was besieged by Harpagus, they embarked, to seek new abodes in the distant W., and bent their course to their colony of Aleria in Corsica. During the voyage, however, a portion of the emigrants resolved to return to their native city, which they restored, and which recovered much of its prosperity, as is proved by the rich booty gained by the Romans, when they plundered it under the

praetor Aemilius, after which it does not appear as a place of any consequence in history.—Care must be taken not to confound Phocaea with Phocis, as the ethnic adjectives of the former Φωκαεύς and Phocaeënsis, with those of the latter, Φωκεύς and Phocensis: some of the ancient writers themselves have fallen into such mistakes. It should be observed also that the name of Phocaean is often used with reference to Massilia; and, by an amusing affectation, the people of Marseille still call themselves Phocaeans.

Phocion (Φωκίων), the Athenian general and statesman, son of Phocus, was a man of humble origin, and appears to have been born in B. C. 402. He studied under Plato and Xenocrates. He distinguished himself for the first time under his friend Chabrias, in 376, at the battle of Naxos; but he was not employed prominently in any capacity for many years afterwards. In 354 (according to others in 350), he was sent into Euboea in the command of a small force, in consequence of an application from Plutarchus, tyrant of Eretria; and he was subsequently employed on several occasions in the war between the Athenians and Philip of Macedon. He frequently opposed the measures of Demosthenes, and recommended peace with Philip; but he must not be regarded as one of the mercenary supporters of the Macedonian monarch. His virtue is above suspicion, and his public conduct was always influenced by upright motives. When Alexander was marching upon Thebes, in 335, Phocion rebuked Demosthenes for his invectives against the king; and after the destruction of Thebes he advised the Athenians to comply with Alexander's demand for the surrender of Demosthenes and other chief orators of the anti-Macedonian party. This proposal was indignantly rejected by the people, and an embassy was sent to Alexander, which succeeded in deprecating his resentment. According to Plutarch, there were two embassies, the first of which Alexander refused to receive, but to the second he gave a gracious audience, and granted its prayer, chiefly from regard to Phocion, who was at the head of it. Alexander ever continued to treat Phocion with the utmost consideration, and to cultivate his friendship. He also pressed upon him valuable presents; but Phocion persisted in refusing his presents, begging the king to leave him no less honest than he found him, and only so far availed himself of the royal favour as to request the liberty of certain prisoners at Sardis, which was immediately granted to him. After Alexander's death, Phocion opposed vehemently, and with all the caustic bitterness which characterised him, the proposal for war with Antipater. Thus, to Hyperides, who asked him tauntingly when he would advise the Athenians to go to war, he answered, "When I see the young willing to keep their ranks, the rich to contribute of their wealth, and the orators to abstain from pilfering the public money." When the Piraeus was seized by Alexander, the son of Polysperchon in 318, Phocion was suspected of having advised Alexander to take this step; whereupon, being accused of treason by Agnonides, he fled, with several of his friends, to Alexander, who sent them with letters of recommendation to his father Polysperchon. The latter, willing to sacrifice them as a peace-offering to the Athenians, sent them back to Athens for the people to deal with them as they would. Here Phocion was sentenced to death. To the last, he maintained his calm, and dignified, and somewhat contemptuous bearing. When some wretched man spat upon him as he passed to the prison, "Will no one," said he, "check this fellow's indecency?" To one who asked him whether he had any message to leave for his son Phocus, he answered, "Only that he bear no grudge against the Athenians." And when the hemlock which had been prepared was found insufficient for all the condemned, and the jailer would not furnish more until he was paid for it, "Give the man his money," said Phocion to one of his friends, "since at Athens one cannot even die for nothing." He perished in 317, at the age of 85. The Athenians are said to have repented of their conduct. A brazen statue was raised to the memory of Phocion, and Agonides was condemned to death. Phocion was twice married, and his 2nd wife appears to have been as simple and frugal in her habits as himself; but he was less fortunate in his son Phocus, who, in spite of his father's lessons and example, was a thorough profligate. As for Phocion himself, our commendation of him must be almost wholly confined to his private qualities. His fellow-citizens may have been degenerate, but he made no effort to elevate them.

Phōcis (ἡ Φωκίς: Φωκῆες Hom., Φωκέες Herod., Φωκεῖς Attic, Phocenses by the Romans), a country in Northern Greece, was bounded on the N. by the Locri Epicnemidii and Opuntii, on the E. by Boeotia, on the W. by the Locri Ozolae and Doris, and on the S. by the Corinthian gulf. At one time it possessed a narrow strip of country on the Euboean sea with the seaport Daphnus, between the territory of the Locri Ozolae and Locri Opuntii. It was a mountainous and unproductive country, and owes its chief importance in history to the fact of its possessing the Delphic oracle. Its chief mountain was PARNASSUS, situated in the interior of the country, to which however CNEMIS on its N. frontier, CIRPHIS S. of Delphi, and HELICON on the S.E. frontier all belonged. The principal river in Phocis was the CEPHISSUS, the valley of which contained almost the only fertile land in the country, with the exception of the celebrated Crissaean plain in the S.E. on the borders of the Locri Ozolae.—Among the earliest inhabitants of Phocis we find mentioned Leleges, Thracians, Abantes and Hyantes. Subsequently, but still in the antihistorical period, the Phlegyae, an Achaean race, a branch of the Minyae at Orchomenos, took possession of the country; and from this time the main bulk of the population continued to be Achnean, although there were Dorian settlements at Delphi and Bulis. The Phocians are said to have derived their name from an eponymous ancestor Phocus [PHOCUS], and they are mentioned under this name in the Iliad. The Phocians played no conspicuous part in Greek history till the time of Philip of Macedon; but at this period they became involved in a war, called the Phocian or Sacred War, in which the principal states of Greece took part. The Thebans had long been inveterate enemies of the Phocians; and as the latter people had cultivated a portion of the Crissaean plain, which the Amphictyons had declared in B. c. 585 should lie waste for ever, the Thebans availed themselves of this pretext to persuade the Amphictyons to impose a fine upon the Phocians, and upon their refusal to pay it, the Thebans further induced the council to declare the Phocian land forfeited to the god at Delphi. Thus threatened by the Amphictyonic council, backed by the whole power of Thebes, the Phocians were persuaded by Philomelus, one of their citizens, to seize Delphi, and to make use of the treasures of the temple for the purpose of carrying on the war. They obtained possession of the temple in B. c. 357. The war which ensued lasted 10 years, and was carried on with various success on each side. The Phocians were commanded first by PHILOMELUS, B. c. 357—353, afterwards by his brother ONOMARCHUS, 353—352, then by PHAYLLUS, the brother of the 2 preceding, 352—351, and finally by PHALAECUS, the son of Onomarchus, 351 - - 346. The Phocians received some support from Athens, but their chief dependence was upon their mercenary troops, which the treasures of the Delphic temple enabled them to hire. The Amphictyons and the Thebans, finding at length that they were unable with their own resources to subdue the Phocians, called in the assistance of Philip of Macedon, who brought the war to a close in 346. The conquerors inflicted the most signal punishment upon the Phocians, who were regarded as guilty of sacrilege. All their towns were razed to the ground with the exception of Abae ; and the inhabitants distributed in villages, containing not more than 50 inhabitants. The 2 votes which they had in the Amphictyonic council were taken away and given to Philip.

Phocra (Φόκρα), a mountain of N. Africa, in Mauretania Tingitana, apparently on the W. bank of the Mulucha, between the chains of the Great and Little Atlas.

Phōcus (Φῶκος). 1. Son of Ornytion of Corinth, or according to others of Poseidon, is said to have been the leader of a colony from Corinth into the territory of Tithorea and Mt. Parnassus, which derived from him the name of Phocis.—2. Son of Aeacus and the Nereid Psamathe, husband of Asteria or Asterodia, and father of Panopeus and Crissus. He was murdered by his half-brothers Telamon and Peleus. [PELEUS.] According to some accounts the country of Phocis derived its name from him.—3. Son of Phocion. [PHOCION.]

Phocylides (Φωκυλίδης), of Miletus, an Ionian poet, contemporary with Theognis, was born B. c. 560. His poetry was chiefly gnomic; and the few fragments of it which we possess display that contempt for birth and station, and that love for substantial enjoyment, which always marked the Ionian character. These fragments, which are 18 in number, are included in all the chief collections of the lyric and gnomic poets. Some of these collections contain a didactic poem, in 217 hexameters, entitled ποίημα νουθετικόν, to which the name of Phocylides is attached, but which is undoubtedly a forgery, made since the Christian era.

Phoebē (Φοίβη). 1. Daughter of Uranus and Ge, became by Coeus the mother of Asteria and Leto (Latona).—2. A surname of Artemis (Diana) in her capacity as the goddess of the moon (Luna), the moon being regarded as the female Phoebus or sun.—3. Daughter of Tyndareos and Leda, and a sister of Clytaemnestra.—4. Daughter of Leucippus, and sister of Hilaira, a priestess of Athena, was carried off with her sister by the Dioscuri, and became by Pollux the mother of Mnesileos.

Phoebidas (Φοιβίδας), a Lacedaemonian, who, in B. C. 382, was appointed to the command of the troops destined to reinforce his brother Eudamidas, who had been sent against Olynthus. On his way Phoebidas halted at Thebes, and treacherously made himself master of the Cadmea. The Lacedaemonians fined Phoebidas 100,000 drachmas, but nevertheless kept possession of the Cadmea. In 378 he was left by Agesilaus as harmost at Thespiae, and was slain in battle by the Thebans.

Phoebus (Φοῖβος), the *Bright* or *Pure*, occurs in Homer as an epithet of Apollo, and is used to signify the brightness and purity of youth. At a later time when Apollo became connected with the Sun, the epithet Phoebus was also applied to him as the Sun-god.

Phoenice (Φοινίκη: Phoenicia is only found in a doubtful passage of Cicero: Φοῖνιξ, pl. Φοίνικες, fem. Φοίνισσα, Phoenix, Phoenices: also, the adj. Punica, though used specifically in connection with Carthago, is etymologically equivalent to Φοῖνιξ, by the well-known interchange of οι and ῡ: parts of the Pashalicks of *Acre and Aleppo*), a country of Asia, on the coast of Syria, extending from the river Eleutherus (*Nahr-el-Kebir*) on the N. to below Mt. Carmel on the S., and bounded on the E. by Coelesyria and Palestine. (Sometimes, though rarely, the name is extended to the whole W. coast of Syria and Palestine). It was a mountainous strip of coast land, not more than 10 or 12 miles broad, hemmed in between the Mediterranean and the chain of Lebanon, whose lateral branches, running out into the sea in bold promontories, divided the country into valleys, which are well watered by rivers flowing down from Lebanon, and are extremely fertile. Of these rivers, the most important are, to one going from N. to S., the Eleutherus (*Nahr-el-Kebir*) ; the Sabbaticus (*Arka*) ; the river of Tripolis (*Kadisha*) ; the Adonis (*Nahr-Ibrahim*), S. of Byblus ; the Lycus (*Nahr-el-Kelb*) N. of Berytus ; the Magoras (*Nahr-Beirut*), by Berytus ; the Tamyras (*Nahr-el-Damur*), between Berytus and Sidon ; the Leo, or Boatrenus (*Nahr-el-Auly*), N. of Sidon ; the great river (*Litany and Kasimiyeh*) which flows from Heliopolis S.S.W. through Coele-Syria, and then, turning W.wards, falls into the sea N. of Tyre, and which some call, but without sufficient authority, the Leontes ; the Belus, or Pagida (*Numan* or *Rahwin*) by Ptolemaïs, and the Kishon (*Kishon*), N. of Mt. Carmel. Of the promontories referred to, omitting a number of less important ones, the chief were, Theu-prosōpon (*Rasesh-Shukah*), between Tripolis and Byblus, Pr. Album (*Ras-el-Abiad*, i. e. *White Cape*), S. of Tyre, and Mt. Carmel, besides those occupied by the cities of Tripolis, Byblus, Berytus, Sidon, Tyrus, and Ptolemaïs. This conformation of the coast and the position of the country rendered it admirably suited for the home of great maritime states ; and accordingly we find the cities of Phoenicia at the head, both in time and importance, of all the naval enterprise of the ancient world. For the history of those great cities, see SIDON, TYRUS, and the other articles upon them. As to the country in general, there is some difficulty about the origin of the inhabitants and of their name. In the O. T. the name does not occur ; the people seem to be included under the general designation of Canaanites, and they are also named specifically after their several cities, as the Sidonians, Giblites (from Gebal, *i. e.* Byblus),

Sinites, Arkites, Arvadites, &c. The name Φοινίκη is first found in Greek writers, as early as Homer, and is derived by some from the abundance of palm trees in the country (φοῖνιξ, *the date-palm*), and by others from the purple-red (φοῖνιξ), which was obtained from a fish on the coasts, and was a celebrated article of Phoenician commerce ; besides the mythical derivation from Phoenix, the brother of Cadmus. The people were of the Semitic (Syro-Arabian) race, and closely allied to the Hebrews ; and they are said to have dwelt originally on the shores of the Erythraean sea. Their language was a dialect of the Aramaic, closely related to the Hebrew and Syriac. Their written characters were the same as the Samaritan or Old Hebrew ; and from them the Greek alphabet, and through it most of the alphabets of Europe, were undoubtedly derived ; hence they were regarded by the Greeks as the inventors of letters. Other inventions in the sciences and arts are ascribed to them ; such as arithmetic, astronomy, navigation, the manufacture of glass, and the coining of money. That, at a very early time, they excelled in the fine arts, is clear from the aid which Solomon received from Hiram, king of Tyre, in the building and the sculptured decorations of the temple at Jerusalem, and from the references in Homer to Sidonian artists. Respecting Phoenician literature, we know of little beyond the celebrated work of SANCHUNIATHON. In the sacred history of the Israelitish conquest of Canaan, in that of the Hebrew monarchy, and in the earliest Greek poetry, we find the Phoenicians already a great maritime people. Early formed into settled states, supplied with abundance of timber from Lebanon, and placed where the caravans from Arabia and the E. came upon the Mediterranean, they carried over to the coasts of this sea the products of those countries, as well as of their own, which was rich in metals, and on the shores of which furnished the materials of glass and the purple-fish already mentioned. Their voyages and their settlements extended beyond the Pillars of Hercules, to the W. coasts of Africa and Spain, and even as far as our own islands. [BRITANNIA, p. 126, a.] Within the Mediterranean they planted numerous colonies, on its islands, on the coast of Spain, and especially on the N. coast of Africa, the chief of which was CARTHAGO ; they had also settlements on the Euxine and in Asia Minor. In the E. seas, we have records of their voyages to OPHIR, in connection with the navy of Solomon, and to the coasts of Africa under the kings of Egypt. [AFRICA, p. 22, b.] They were successively subdued by the Assyrians, Babylonians, Persians, Macedonians, and Romans ; but neither these conquests, nor the rivalry of Carthage, entirely ruined their commerce, which was still considerable at the Christian era ; on the contrary, their ships formed the fleet of Persia and the Syrian kings, and partly of the Romans. [SIDON, TYRUS, &c.] Under the Romans, Phoenice formed a part of the province of Syria ; and, under the E. empire, it was erected, with the addition of Coele-Syria, into the province of Phoenice Libanesia or Libanensia.

Phoenice (Φοινίκη). 1. (*Finiki*), an important commercial town on the coast of the Epirus in the district Chaonia, 56 miles N.W. of Buthrotum, in the midst of a marshy country. It was strongly fortified by Justinian.—2. A small island off Gallia Narbonensis, belonging to the Stoechades.

Phoenicium Mare (τὸ Φοινίκιον πέλαγος: Σιδονίη Θάλασσα), the part of the Mediterranean which washes the coast of Phoenice.

Phoenicus (Φοινικοῦς: Φοινικούντιος, Φοινικούσιος). 1. Also **Phoenix** (Φοῖνιξ). a harbour on the S. of Crete, visited by St. Paul during his voyage to Rome. (Acts, xxvii. 12.)—2. The harbour of the city of Colone, in Messenia.—3. A sea-port of the island of Cythera.—4. (Chesmeh or Egri Liman?), a harbour of Ionia, in Asia Minor, at the foot of Mt. Mimas. —5. (Deliktash, Ru.), a flourishing city in the S. of Lycia, on Mt. Olympus, with a harbour below it. It is often called **Olympus**. Having become, under the Romans, one of the head-quarters of the pirates, who celebrated here the festival and mysteries of Mithras, it was destroyed by Servilius Isauricus.

Phoenicussa. [AEOLIAE INSULAE.]

Phoenix (Φοῖνιξ). 1. Son of Agenor by Agriope or Telephassa, and brother of Europa, but Homer makes him the father of Europa. Being sent by his father in search of his sister, who was carried off by Zeus, he settled in the country, which was called after him Phoenicia.—2. Son of Amyntor by Cleobule or Hippodamia, and king of the Dolopes, took part in the Calydonian hunt. His father Amyntor neglected his legitimate wife, and attached himself to a mistress; whereupon Cleobule persuaded her son to seduce her rival. When Amyntor discovered the crime, he cursed Phoenix, who shortly afterwards fled to Peleus. Peleus received him kindly, made him the ruler of the country of the Dolopes, on the frontiers of Phthia, and entrusted to him his son Achilles, whom he was to educate. He afterwards accompanied Achilles on his expedition against Troy. According to another tradition, Phoenix did not dishonour his father's mistress, but she merely accused him of having made improper overtures to her, in consequence of which his father put out his eyes. But Peleus took him to Chiron, who restored to him his sight. Phoenix moreover is said to have called the son of Achilles Neoptolemus, after Lycomedes had called him Pyrrhus. Neoptolemus was believed to have buried Phoenix at Eion in Macedonia or at Trachis in Thessaly.—3. A fabulous bird Phoenix, which, according to a tale related to Herodotus (ii. 73) at Heliopolis in Egypt, visited that place once in every 500 years, on his father's death, and buried him in the sanctuary of Helios. For this purpose the Phoenix was believed to come from Arabia, and to make an egg of myrrh as large as possible; this egg he then hollowed out and put into it his father, closing it up carefully, and the egg was believed then to be of exactly the same weight as before. This bird was represented as resembling an eagle, with feathers partly red and partly golden. It is further related, that when his life drew to a close, he built a nest for himself in Arabia, to which he imparted the power of generation, so that after his death a new phoenix rose out of it. As soon as the latter was grown up, he, like his predecessor, proceeded to Heliopolis in Egypt, and burned and buried his father in the temple of Helios. — According to a story which has gained more currency in modern times, the Phoenix, when he arrived at a very old age (some say 500 and others 1461 years), committed himself to the flames.—Others, again, state that only one Phoenix lived at a time, and that when he died a worm crept forth from his body, and was developed into a new Phoenix by

the heat of the sun. His death, further, took place in Egypt after a life of 7006 years. — Another modification of the same story relates, that when the Phoenix arrived at the age of 500 years, he built for himself a funeral pile, consisting of spices, settled upon it, and died. Out of the decomposing body he then rose again, and having grown up, he wrapped the remains of his old body up in myrrh, carried them to Heliopolis, and burnt them there. Similar stories of marvellous birds occur in many parts of the East, as in Persia, the legend of the bird Simorg, and in India that of the bird Semendar.

Phoenix (Φοῖνιξ), a small river in the S.E. of Thessaly, flowing into the Asopus near Thermopylae.

Phoenix. [PHOENICUS, No. 1.]

Phoetiae or **Phytia** (Φοιτεῖαι, Φοιτίαι, Φυτία, Thuc.), a town in Acarnania on a hill, W. of Stratus.

Pholegandros (Φολέγανδρος: Polykandro), an island in the Aegaean sea, one of the smaller Cyclades, situated between Melos and Sicinos.

Pholoe (Φολόη: Olono), a mountain forming the boundary between Arcadia and Elis; being a S. continuation of Mt. Erymanthus, in which the rivers Selleïs and Ladon took their origin. It is mentioned as one of the seats of the Centaurs. [PHOLUS.]

Pholus (Φόλος), a Centaur. a son of Silenus and the nymph Melia. He was accidentally slain by one of the poisoned arrows of Hercules. The mountain, between Arcadia and Elis, where he was buried, was called Pholoe after him. The details of his story are given on p. 309, a.

Phorbantia. [AEGATES.]

Phorbas (Φόρβας). 1. Son of Lapithes and Orsinome, and brother of Periphas. The Rhodians, in pursuance of an oracle, are said to have invited him into their island to deliver it from snakes, and afterwards to have honoured him with heroic worship. From this circumstance he was called Ophiuchus, and is said by some to have been placed among the stars. According to another tradition, Phorbas went from Thessaly to Olenos, where Alector, king of Elis, made use of his assistance against Pelops, and shared his kingdom with him. Phorbas then gave his daughter Diogenia in marriage to Alector, and he himself married Hyrmine, a sister of Alector, by whom be became the father of Augeas and Actor. He is also described as a bold boxer, and is said to have plundered the temple of Delphi along with the Phlegyae, but to have been defeated by Apollo.

Phorcides, Phorcydes, or **Phorcynides,** that is, the daughters of Phorcus and Ceto, or the Gorgons and Graeae. [GORGONES and GRAEAE.]

Phorcus, Phorcys, or **Phorcyn** (Φόρκος, Φόρκυς, Φόρκυν), 1. A sea-deity, is described by Homer as "the old man of the sea," to whom a harbour in Ithaca was dedicated, and is called the father of the nymph Thoosa. Later writers call him a son of Pontus and Ge, and a brother of Thaumas, Nereus, Eurybia, and Ceto. By his sister Ceto he became the father of the Graeae and Gorgones, the Hesperian dragon, and the Hesperides; and by Hecate or Cratais, he was the father of Scylla. — 2. Son of Phaenops, commander of the Phrygians of Ascania, assisted Priam in the Trojan war, but was slain by Ajax.

Phormion (Φορμίων). 1. A celebrated Athenian general, the son of Asopius. He distinguished

himself particularly in the command of an Athenian fleet in the Corinthian gulf, where with far inferior forces he gained some brilliant victories over the Peloponnesian fleet in B.C. 429. In the ensuing winter he landed on the coast of Acarnania, and advanced into the interior, where he also gained some successes. He was a man of remarkably temperate habits, and a strict disciplinarian.—
2. A peripatetic philosopher of Ephesus, of whom is told the story that he discoursed for several hours before Hannibal on the military art and the duties of a general. When his admiring auditory asked Hannibal what he thought of him, the latter replied, that of all the old blockheads whom he had seen, none could match Phormion.

Phormis or Phormus (Φόρμις, Φόρμος), a native of Maenalus in Arcadia, removed to Sicily, where he became intimate with Gelon, whose children he educated. He distinguished himself as a soldier, both under Gelon and Hieron his brother. In gratitude for his martial successes, he dedicated gifts to Zeus at Olympia, and to Apollo at Delphi. He is associated with Aristotle with Epicharmus, as one of the originators of comedy, or of a particular form of it.

Phŏrōneus (Φορωνεύς), son of Inachus and the Oceanid Melia or Archia, was a brother of Aegialeus and the ruler of Argos. He was married to the nymph Laodice, by whom he became the father of Niobe, Apis, and Car. According to other writers his sons were Pelasgus, Iasus, and Agenor, who, after their father's death, divided the kingdom of Argos among themselves. Phoroneus is said to have been the first who offered sacrifices to Hera at Argos, and to have united the people, who until then had lived in scattered habitations, into a city which was called after him ἄστυ Φορωνικόν. The patronymic Phoronides is sometimes used for Argives in general, and especially to designate Amphiaraus and Adrastus.

Phŏrōnĭs (Φορωνίς), a surname of Io, being according to some a descendant, and according to others a sister of Phoroneus.

Phōtĭus (Φώτιος), patriarch of Constantinople in the 9th century, played a distinguished part in the political and religious history of his age. After holding various high offices in the Byzantine court, he was, although previously a layman, elected patriarch of Constantinople in A.D. 858, in place of Ignatius, who had been deposed by Bardas, who was all-powerful at the court of his nephew Michael III., then a minor. The patriarchate of Photius was a stormy one, and full of vicissitudes. The cause of Ignatius was espoused by the Romish church; and Photius thus became one of the great promoters of the schism between the Eastern and Western Churches. In 867 Photius was himself deposed by the emperor Basil I., and Ignatius was restored; but on the death of Ignatius in 877, Photius, who had meantime gained the favour of Basil, was again elevated to the patriarchate. On the death of Basil in 886, Photius was accused of a conspiracy against the life of the new emperor Leo VI., and was banished to a monastery in Armenia, where he seems to have remained till his death. Photius was one of the most learned men of his time, and in the midst of a busy life found time for the composition of numerous works, several of which have come down to us. Of these the most important is entitled *Myriobiblion* seu *Bibliotheca* (Μυριόβιβλον ἢ Βιβλιοθήκη). It may

be described as an extensive review of ancient Greek literature by a scholar of immense erudition and sound judgment. It is an extraordinary monument of literary energy, for it was written while the author was engaged in an embassy to Assyria, at the request of Photius' brother Tarasius, who desired an account of the books which Photius had read in his absence. It contains the analyses of or extracts from 280 volumes ; and many valuable works are only known to us from the account which Photius has given of them. The best edition of this work is by Bekker, Berlin, 1824—1825. Photius was also the author of a *Nomocanon*, and of a *Lexicon* or Glossary, which has reached us in a very imperfect state. It was first published by Hermann, Lips. 1808, and subsequently at London, 1822, from the papers of Porson. Photius likewise wrote many theological works, some of which have been published, and others still remain in MS.

Phraăta (τὰ Φράατα, and other forms), a great city of Media Atropatene, the winter residence of the Parthian kings, especially as a refuge in time of war, lay S.E. of Gaza, near the river Amardus. The mountain fortress of Vera (Οὐέρα), which was besieged by Antony, was probably the same place.

Phraataces, king of Parthia. [ARSACES XVI.]

Phraātes, the name of 4 kings of Parthia. [ARSACES, V. VII. XII. XV.]

Phranza or Phranzes (Φραντζῆ or Φραντζῆς), the last and one of the most important Byzantine historians, was frequently employed on important public business by Constantine XIII., the last emperor of Constantinople. On the capture of Constantinople by the Turks, in 1453, Phranza was reduced to slavery, but succeeded in making his escape. He subsequently retired to a monastery, where he wrote his *Chronicon*. This work extends from 1259 to 1477, and is the most valuable authority for the history of the author's time, especially for the capture of Constantinople. It is edited by Alter, Vienna, 1796, and by Bekker, Bonn, 1838.

Phraortes (Φραόρτης), 2nd king of Media, and son of Deioces, whom he succeeded, reigned from B.C. 656 to 634. He first conquered the Persians, and then subdued the greater part of Asia, but was at length defeated and killed while laying siege to Ninus (Nineveh), the capital of the Assyrian empire. He was succeeded by his son Cyaxares.

Phrĭcĭum (Φρίκιον), a mountain in the E. of Locris near Thermopylae.

Phricōnis. [CYME: LARISSA, II. 2.]

Phrixa (Φρίξα, Φρίξαι, Θρίξαι: Paleofanaro), a town of Elis in Triphylia on the borders of Pisatis, was situated upon a steep hill on the river Alpheus, and was 30 stadia from Olympia. It was founded by the Minyae, and is said to have derived its name from Phrixus.

Phrixus (Φρίξος), son of Athamas and Nephele, and brother of Helle. In consequence of the intrigues of his stepmother, Ino, he was to be sacrificed to Zeus ; but Nephele rescued her 2 children, who rode away through the air upon the ram with the golden fleece, the gift of Hermes. Between Sigeum and the Chersonesus, Helle fell into the sea which was called after her the Hellespont ; but Phrixus arrived in safety in Colchis, the kingdom of Aeetes, who gave him his daughter Chalciope in marriage. Phrixus sacrificed the ram which had carried him, to Zeus Phyxius or Laphystius, and gave its fleece to Aeetes, who fast ened it to an oak tree in the grove of Ares. This fleece was afterwards carried away by Jason and the Argonauts. [JASON.] By Chalciope Phrixus became the father of Argus, Melas, Phrontis, Cytissorus, and Presbon. Phrixus either died of old age in the kingdom of Aeetes, or was killed by Aeetes in consequence of an oracle, or returned to Orchomenus, in the country of the Minyans.

Phrixus (Φρίξος), a river in Argolis, which flows into the Argolic gulf between Temenium and Lerna.

Phrygia Mater, a name frequently given to Cybele, because she was especially worshipped in Phrygia.

Phrygia (Φρυγία: Φρύξ, pl. Φρύγες, Phryx, Phryges), a country of Asia Minor, which was of very different extent at different periods. According to the division of the provinces under the Roman empire, Phrygia formed the E. part of the province of Asia, and was bounded on the W. by Mysia, Lydia, and Caria, on the S. by Lycia and Pisidia, on the E. by Lycaonia (which is often reckoned as a part of Phrygia) and Galatia (which formerly belonged to Phrygia), and on the N. by Bithynia. With reference to its physical geography, it formed the W. part (as Cappadocia did the E.) of the great central table-land of Asia Minor, supported by the chains of Olympus on the N. and Taurus on the S., and breaking on the W. into the ridges which separate the great valleys of the HERMUS, the MAEANDER, &c., and which form the headlands of the W. coast. This table-land itself was intersected by mountain-chains, and watered by the upper courses and tributaries of the rivers just mentioned in its W. part, and in its N. part by those of the RHYNDACUS and SANGARIUS. These parts of the country were very fertile, especially in the valley of the Sangarius, but in the S. and E. the streams which descend from Taurus lose themselves in extensive salt marshes and salt lakes, some of which are still famous, as in ancient times, for their manufactures of salt. The Phrygians were a distinct and remarkable people, whose origin is one of the most difficult problems of antiquity. They claimed a very high antiquity; and according to the amusing account given by Herodotus of the absurd experiment of Psammetichus, king of Egypt, on the first spontaneous speech of children, they were thought to have been proved the most ancient of people. Elsewhere, Herodotus mentions a Macedonian tradition, that the Phryges formerly dwelt in Macedonia, under the name of Briges; and later writers add, that they passed over into Asia Minor 100 years after the Trojan war. They are, however, mentioned by Homer as already settled on the banks of the Sangarius, where later writers tell us of the powerful Phrygian kingdom of GORDIUS and MIDAS. Although any near approach to certainty is hopeless, it would seem that they were a branch of the great Thracian family, settled, in times of unknown antiquity, in the N.W. of Asia Minor, as far as the shores of the Hellespont and Propontis, and perhaps of the Euxine, and that the successive migrations of other Thracian peoples, as the Thyni, Dithyni, Mysians, and Teucrians, drove them further inland, till, from this cause, and perhaps too by the conquests of the Phrygian kings in the opposite direction, they reached the Halys on the E. and the Taurus on the S. They were not, however, entirely displaced by the Mysians and Teu-

crians from the country between the shores of the Hellespont and Propontis and Mts. Ida and Olympus, where they continued side by side with the Greek colonies, and where their name was preserved in that of the district under all subsequent changes, namely Phrygia Minor or Phrygia Hellespontus The kingdom of Phrygia was conquered by Croesus, and formed part of the Persian, Macedonian, and Syro-Grecian empires; but, under the last, the N.E. part, adjacent to Paphlagonia and the Halys, was conquered by the Gauls, and formed the W. part of GALATIA; and a part W. of this, containing the richest portion of the country, about the Sangarius, was subjected by the kings of Bithynia: this last portion was the object of a contest between the kings of Bithynia and Pergamus, but at last, by the decision of the Romans, it was added, under the name of Phrygia Epictetus (Φ. ἐπίκτητος, i. e. the acquired Phrygia), to the kingdom of Pergamus, to which the whole of Phrygia was assigned by the Romans, after the overthrow of Antiochus the Great in B.C. 190. With the rest of the kingdom of Pergamus, Phrygia passed to the Romans by the testament of Attalus III., and thus became a part of the province of Asia, B.C. 130. As to the distinctive names: the inland district usually understood by the name of Phrygia, when it occurs alone, was also called Great Phrygia or Phrygia Proper, in contradistinction to the Lesser Phrygia or Phrygia on the Hellespont; and of this Great or Proper Phrygia, the N. part was called, as just stated, Phrygia Epictetus, and the S. part, adjacent to the Taurus, was called, from its position, Phrygia Parorios (Φ. παρόριος). At the division of the provinces in the 4th century, the last mentioned part, also called Phrygia Pisidica, was assigned to Pisidia; and the S.W. portion, about the Maeander, to Caria: and the remainder was divided into Phrygia Salutaris, on the E., with Synnada for its capital, and Phrygia Pacatiana on the W., extending N. and S. from Bithynia to Pamphylia.—Phrygia was rich in products of every kind. Its mountains furnished gold and marble; its valleys oil and wine; the less fertile hills in the W. afforded pasture for sheep, whose wool was highly celebrated; and even the marshes of the S.E. furnished abundance of salt.—In connection with the early intellectual culture of Greece, Phrygia is highly important. The earliest Greek music, especially that of the flute, was borrowed in part, through the Asiatic colonies, from Phrygia, and one of the three musical modes was called the Phrygian. With this country also were closely associated the orgies of Dionysus, and of Cybele, the Mother of the Gods, the Phrygia Mater of the Roman poets. After the Persian conquest, however, the Phrygians seem to have lost all intellectual activity, and they became proverbial among the Greeks and Romans for submissiveness and stupidity.—It should be observed that the Roman poets constantly use the epithet Phrygian as equivalent to Trojan.

Phryne (Φρύνη), one of the most celebrated Athenian hetairae, was a native of Thespiae in Boeotia. Her beauty procured for her so much wealth that she is said to have offered to rebuild the walls of Thebes, after they had been destroyed by Alexander, if she might be allowed to put up this inscription on the walls:—" Alexander destroyed them, but Phryne, the hetaira, rebuilt them." She had among her admirers many of the most celebrated men of the age of Philip and Alexander, and the beauty of her form gave rise to some of the greatest works of art. The most celebrated picture of Apelles, his "Venus Anadyomene" [APELLES], is said to have been a representation of Phryne, who, at a public festival at Eleusis, entered the sea with dishevelled hair. The celebrated Cnidian Venus of Praxiteles, who was one of her lovers, was taken from her.

Phrynichus (Φρύνιχος). 1. An Athenian, and one of the early tragic poets, is said to have been the disciple of Thespis. He gained his first tragic victory in B.C. 511, 24 years after Thespis (535), 12 years after Choerilus (523), and 12 years before Aeschylus (499), and his last in 476, on which occasion Themistocles was his *choragus*, and recorded the event by an inscription. Phrynichus probably went, like other poets of the age, to the court of Hiero, and there died. In all the accounts of the rise and development of tragedy, the chief place after Thespis is assigned to Phrynichus; and the improvements which he introduced in the internal poetical character of the drama, entitle him to be considered as the real inventor of tragedy. For the light, ludicrous, Bacchanalian stories of Thespis, he substituted regular and serious subjects, taken either from the heroic age, or the heroic deeds which illustrated the history of his own time. In these he aimed, not so much to amuse the audience as to move their passions; and so powerful was the effect of his tragedy on the capture of Miletus, that the audience burst into tears, and fined the poet 1000 drachmae, because he had exhibited the sufferings of a kindred people, and even passed a law that no one should ever again make use of that drama. To the light mimetic chorus of Thespis he added the sublime music of dithyrambic choruses. Aristophanes more than once contrasts these ancient and beautiful melodies with the involved refinements of later poets. Phrynichus was the first poet who introduced masks, representing female persons in the drama. He also paid particular attention to the dances of the chorus. In the drama of Phrynichus, however, the chorus still retained the principal place, and it was reserved for Aeschylus and Sophocles to bring the dialogue and action into their due position.—2. A distinguished comic poet of the Old Comedy, was a contemporary of Eupolis, and flourished B.C. 429.—3. A Greek sophist and grammarian, described by some as an Arabian, and by others as a Bithynian, lived under M. Aurelius and Commodus. His great work was entitled Σοφιστικὴ Παρασκευή in 37 books, of which we still possess a fragment, published by Bekker, in his *Anecdota Graeca*, Berol. 1814, vol. i. He also wrote a Lexicon of Attic words ('Εκλογὴ ῥημάτων καὶ ὀνομάτων Ἀττικῶν), which is extant: the best edition is by Lobeck, Lips. 1830.

Phrynnis (Φρύννις), or **Phrynis** (Φρῦνις), a celebrated dithyrambic poet, of the time of the Peloponnesian war, was a native of Mytilene, but flourished at Athens. His innovations, effeminacies, and frigidness, are repeatedly attacked by the comic poets. Among the innovations which he is said to have made, was the addition of 2 strings to the heptachord. He was the first who gained the victory in the musical contests established by Pericles, in connection with the Panathenaic festival, probably in B.C. 445.

Phthia. [PHTHIOTIS.]

Phthiotis (Φθιῶτις; Φθιώτης), a district in the S.E. of Thessaly, bounded on the S. by the Maliac gulf, and on the E. by the Pagasaean gulf, and inhabited by Achaeans. [THESSALIA.] Homer calls it **Phthia** (Φθίη), and mentions a city of the same name, which was celebrated as the residence of Achilles. Hence the poets call Achilles *Phthius hero*, and his father Peleus *Phthius rex*.

Phthira (τὰ Φθίρα, Φθειρῶν ὄρος), a mountain of Caria, forming a part or a branch of Latmus, inhabited by a people called Φθίρες.

Phthirophagi (Φθειρόφαγοι, i. e. *eaters of lice*), a Scythian people near the Caucasus, or, according to some, beyond the river Rha, in Sarmatia Asiatica.

Phya. [PISISTRATUS.]

Phycus (Φυκοῦς: *Ras-Sem* or *Ras-el-Kasat*), a promontory on the coast of Cyrenaica, a little W. of Apollonia and N.W. of Cyrene. It is the N.-most headland of Libya E. of the Lesser Syrtis, and the nearest point of this coast to that of Europe, the distance from Phycus to Taenarum, the S. promontory of Peloponnesus, being 208 miles. There was a small town of the same name on the headland.

Phylaсe (Φυλάκη). 1. A small town of Thessaly in Phthiotis, S.E. of Eretria, and E. of Enipeus, on the N. slope of Mt. Othrys. It was the birthplace of Protesilaus.—2. A town of Epirus in Molossia.—3. A town in Arcadia near the sources of the Alpheus, on the frontiers of Tegea and Laconia.

Phylacus (Φύλακος), son of Deion and Diomede, and husband of Periclymene or Clymene, the daughter of Minyas, by whom he became the father of Iphiclus and Alcimede. He was believed to be the founder of the town of Phylace, in Thessaly. Either from his name or that of the town, his descendants, Phylacus, Iphiclus, and Protesilaus, are called *Phylacidae*.

Phylarchus (Φύλαρχος), a Greek historical writer, and a contemporary of Aratus, was probably a native of Naucratis in Egypt, but spent the greater part of his life at Athens. His great work was a history in 28 books, which embraced a period of 52 years, from the expedition of Pyrrhus into Peloponnesus, B.C. 272, to the death of Cleomenes, 220. Phylarchus is vehemently attacked by Polybius, who charges him with falsifying history through his partiality to Cleomenes, and his hatred against Aratus and the Achaeans. The accusation is probably not unfounded, but it might be retorted with equal justice upon Polybius, who has fallen into the opposite error of exaggerating the merits of Aratus and his party, and depreciating Cleomenes. The style of Phylarchus appears to have been too oratorical and declamatory; but it was at the same time lively and attractive. The fragments of Phylarchus have been collected by Lucht. Lips. 1836; by Brückner, Vratisl. 1838; and by Müller, *Fragm. Histor. Graec.* Paris, 1840.

Phylas (Φύλας). 1. King of the Dryopes, was attacked and slain by Hercules, because he had violated the sanctuary of Delphi. By his daughter Midea, Hercules became the father of Antiochus.—2. Son of Antiochus, and grandson of Hercules and Midea, was married to Deiphile, by whom he had 2 sons, Hippotas and Thero.—3. King of Ephyra in Thesprotia, and the father of Polymele and Astyoche, by the latter of whom Hercules was the father of Tlenolemus.

Phylē (Φυλή: Φυλάσιος: *Fili*), a demus in Attica, and a strongly fortified place, belonging to the tribe Oeneis, was situated on the confines of Boeotia, and on the S.W. slope of Mt. Parnes. It is memorable as the place which Thrasybulus and the Athenian patriots seized, soon after the end of the Peloponnesian war, B. c. 404, and from which they directed their operations against the 30 Tyrants at Athens.

Phyleus (Φυλεύς), son of Augeas, was expelled by his father from Ephyra, because he gave evidence in favour of Hercules. [See p. 309, a.] He then emigrated to Dulichium. By Ctimene or Timandra he became the father of Meges, who is hence called Phylïdes.

Phyllis. [DEMOPHON, No. 2.]

Phyllis (Φύλλις), a district in Thrace S. of the Strymon, near Mt. Pangaeus.

Phyllus (Φύλλος: *Petrino*), a town of Thessaly in the district Thessaliotis, N. of Metropolis.

Physca (Φύσκα), a town of Macedonia in the district Eordaea.

Physcon. [PTOLEMAEUS.]

Physcus (Φύσκος). 1. A city of the Ozolian Locrians in N. Greece. — 2. (*Paitchshis*), a town on the S. coast of Caria, in the Rhodian territory, with an excellent harbour, which was used as the port of Mylasa, and was the landing-place for travellers coming from Rhodes. — 3. (*Odorneh*), an E. tributary of the Tigris in Lower Assyria. The town of Opis stood at its junction with the Tigris.

Phytaeum (Φύταιον: Φυταῖος), a town in Aetolia, S.E. of Thermum, on the lake Trichonis.

Piceni. [PICENUM.]

Picentes. [PICENUM.]

Picentia (Picentinus: *Vicenza*), a town in the S. of Campania at the head of the Sinus Paestanus, and between Salernum and the frontiers of Lucania, the inhabitants of which were compelled by the Romans, in consequence of their revolt to Hannibal, to abandon their town and live in the neighbouring villages. Between the town and the frontiers of Lucania, there was an ancient temple of the Argive Juno, said to have been founded by Jason, the Argonaut.—The name of Picentini was not confined to the inhabitants of Picentia, but was given to the inhabitants of the whole coast of the Sinus Paestanus, from the promontory of Minerva to the river Silarus. They were a portion of the Sabine Picentes, who were transplanted by the Romans to this part of Campania after the conquest of Picenum, B. c. 268, at which time they founded the town of Picentia.

Picentini. [PICENTIA.]

Picenum (Picentes sing. Picens, more rarely Picentini and Piceni), a country in central Italy, was a narrow strip of land along the N. coast of the Adriatic, and was bounded on the N. by Umbria, from which it was separated by the river Aesis, on the W. by Umbria and the territory of the Sabines, and on the S. by the territory of the Marsi and Vestini, from which it was separated by a range of hills and by the river Matrinus. It is said to have derived its name from the bird *picus*, which directed the Sabine immigrants into the land, or from a mythical leader Picus; some modern writers connect the name with the Greek πεύκη, a pine-tree, on account of the pine-trees growing in the country on the slopes of the Apennines; but none of these etymologies can be received. Picenum formed the 5th region in the division of Italy made by Augustus. The country was traversed by a number of hills of moderate height, eastern offshoots of the Apennines, and was drained by several small rivers flowing into the Adriatic through the valleys between these hills. The country was upon the whole fertile, and was especially celebrated for its apples; but the chief employment of the inhabitants was the feeding of cattle and swine. — The Picentes, as already remarked, were Sabine immigrants; but the population of the country appears to have been of a mixed nature. The Umbrians were in possession of the land, when it was conquered by the Sabine Picentes, and some of the Umbrian population became intermingled with their Sabine conquerors. In addition to this the S. part of the country was for a time in possession of the Liburnians, and Ancona was occupied by Greeks from Syracuse. In B. c. 299 the Picentes made a treaty with the Romans; but having revolted in 269, they were defeated by the consul Sempronius Sophus in the following year, and were obliged to submit to the Roman supremacy. A portion of the people was transplanted to the coast of the Sinus Paestanus, where they founded the town Picentia. [PICENTIA.] Two or three years afterwards the Romans sent colonies to Firmum and Castrum Novum in Picenum, in order to secure their newly conquered possession. The Picentes fought with the other Socii against Rome in the Social or Marsic war (90—89), and received the Roman franchise at the close of it.

Picti, a people inhabiting the northern part of Britain. appear to have been either a tribe of the Caledonians, or the same people as the Caledonians, though under another name. They were called Picti by the Romans from their practice of painting their bodies. They are first mentioned by the rhetorician Eumenius in an oration addressed to Constantius Chlorus, A. D. 296; and after this time their name frequently occurs in the Roman writers, and often in connection with that of the Scoti. In the next century we find them divided into 2 tribes, the Dicaledonae or Dicaledones, and the Vecturiones or Vecturones. At a still later period their principal seat was in the N.E. of Scotland.

Pictones, subsequently **Pictavi,** a powerful people on the coast of Gallia Aquitanica, whose territory extended N. as far as the Liger (*Loire*), and E. probably as far as the river *Creuse*. Their chief town was Limonum, subsequently Pictavi (*Poitiers*).

Pictor, Fabius. 1. C., painted the temple of Salus, which the dictator C. Junius Brutus Bubulcus contracted for in his censorship, B. c. 307, and dedicated in his dictatorship, 302. This painting, which must have been on the walls of the temple, was probably a representation of the battle which Bubulus had gained against the Samnites. This is the earliest Roman painting of which we have any record. It was preserved till the reign of Claudius, when the temple was destroyed by fire. In consequence of this painting C. Fabius received the surname of Pictor, which was borne by his descendants. — 2. C., son of No. 1, consul 269. — 3. N., (i. e. Numerius), also son of No. 1, consul, 266. — 4. Q., son of No. 2, was the most ancient writer of Roman history in prose. He served in the Gallic war, 225, and also in the 2nd Punic war. His history, which was written in Greek, began with the arrival of Aeneas in Italy, and came down to his own time. Hence, Polybius speaks of him as one of the historians of the 2nd Punic war. — 5. Q., praetor 189, and flamen Quirinalis. — 6. Ser., is said by Cicero to have been well skilled in law, literature, and antiquity. He lived about B. C. 150. He appears to be the same as the Fabius Pictor who wrote a work *De Jure Pontificio*, in several books. He probably wrote *Annals* likewise in the Latin language, since Cicero (*de Orat.* ii. 12) speaks of a Latin annalist, Pictor, whom he places after Cato, but before Piso; which corresponds with the time at which Ser. Pictor lived, but could not apply to Q. Pictor, who lived in the time of the 2nd Punic war.

Picumnus and **Pilumnus**, 2 Roman divinities, were regarded as 2 brothers, and as the beneficent gods of matrimony in the rustic religion of the ancient Romans. A couch was prepared for them in the house in which there was a newly-born child. Pilumnus was believed to ward off all sufferings from the infant with his *pilum*, with which he taught to pound the grain; and Picumnus, who, under the name of Sterquilinius, was believed to have discovered the use of manure for the fields, conferred upon the infant strength and prosperity. Hence both were also looked upon as the gods of good deeds, and were identified with Castor and Pollux. When Danaë landed in Italy, Picumnus is said to have built with her the town of Ardea, and to have become by her the father of Daunus.

Picus (Πῖκος), a Latin prophetic divinity, is described as a son of Saturnus or Sterculus, as the husband of Canens, and the father of Faunus. In some traditions he was called the first king of Italy. He was a famous soothsayer and augur, and as he made use in his prophetic art of a *picus* (a wood-pecker), he himself was also called Picus. He was represented in a rude and primitive manner as a wooden pillar with a wood-pecker on the top of it, but afterwards as a young man with a wood-pecker on his head. The whole legend of Picus is founded on the notion that the wood-pecker is a prophetic bird, sacred to Mars. Pomona, it is said, was beloved by him, and when Circe's love for him was not requited, she changed him into a wood-pecker, who, however, retained the prophetic powers which he had formerly possessed as a man.

Pieria (Πιερία: Πιερες). 1. A narrow slip of country on the S.E. coast of Macedonia, extending from the mouth of the Peneus in Thessaly to the Haliacmon, and bounded on the W. by Mt. Olympus and its offshoots. A portion of these mountains was called by the ancient writers Pierus, or the Pierian mountain. The inhabitants of this country, the Pieres, were a Thracian people, and are celebrated in the early history of Greek poetry and music, since their country was one of the earliest seats of the worship of the Muses, and Orpheus is said to have been buried there. After the establishment of the Macedonian kingdom in Emathia in the 7th century B. C. Pieria was conquered by the Macedonians, and the inhabitants were driven out of the country. — 2. A district in Macedonia E. of the Strymon near Mt. Pangaeum, where the Pierians settled, who had been driven out of their original abodes by the Macedonians, as already related. They possessed in this district the fortified towns of Phagres and Pergamus.— 3. A district on the N. coast of Syria, so called from the mountain Pieria, a branch of the Amanus, a name

given to it by the Macedonians after their conquest of the East. In this district was the city of Seleucia, which is distinguished from other cities of the same name, as Seleucia in Pieria.

Pierides (Πιερίδες). 1. A surname of the Muses, which they derived from Pieria, near Mt. Olympus, where they were first worshipped among the Thracians. Some derived the name from an ancient king Pierus, who is said to have emigrated from Thrace into Boeotia, and to have established their worship at Thespiae. Pieris also occurs in the singular.— 2. The nine daughters of Pierus, king of Emathia (Macedonia), whom he begot by Euippe or Antiope, and to whom he gave the names of the 9 Muses. They afterwards entered into a contest with the Muses, and, being conquered, they were metamorphosed into birds called Colymbas, Iynx, Cenchris, Cissa, Chloris, Acalanthis, Nessa, Pipo, and Dracontis.

Pierus (Πίερος). 1. Mythological. [PIERIDES.] — 2. A mountain. [PIERIA, No. 1.]

Pietas, a personification of faithful attachment, love, and veneration among the Romans. At first she had only a small sanctuary at Rome, but in B. C. 191 a larger one was built. She is represented on Roman coins, as a matron throwing incense upon an altar, and her attributes are a stork and children. She is sometimes represented as a female figure offering her breast to an aged parent.

Pietas Julia. [POLA.]

Pigres (Πίγρης), of Halicarnassus, either the brother or the son of the celebrated Artemisia, queen of Caria. He is said to have been the author of the Margites, and the Batrachomyomachia.

Pilia, the wife of T. Pomponius Atticus, to whom she was married on the 12th of February, B. C. 56. In the summer of the following year, she bore her husband a daughter, who subsequently married Vipsanius Agrippa.

Pilorus (Πίλωρος), a town of Macedonia in Chalcidice, at the head of the Singitic gulf.

Pilumnus. [PICUMNUS.]

Pimplea (Πίμπλεια), a town in the Macedonian province of Pieria, sacred to the Muses, whence called *Pimpleïdes*. Horace (*Carm.* i. 26. 9) uses the form *Pimplea* in the singular, and not *Pimpleïs*.

Pinara (τὰ Πίναρα: Πιναρεύς: *Pinara* or *Minara*, Ru.), an inland city of Lycia, some distance W. of the river Xanthus, at the foot of Mt. Cragus. Here Pandarus was worshipped as a hero.

Pinaria Gens, one of the most ancient patrician gentes at Rome, traced its origin to a time long previous to the foundation of the city. The legend related that when Hercules came into Italy he was hospitably received on the spot, where Rome was afterwards built, by the Potitii and the Pinarii, two of the most distinguished families in the country. The hero, in return, taught them the way in which he was to be worshipped; but as the Pinarii were not at hand when the sacrificial banquet was ready, and did not come till the entrails of the victim were eaten, Hercules, in anger, determined that the Pinarii should in all future time be excluded from partaking of the entrails of the victims, and that in all matters relating to his worship they should be inferior to the Potitii. These two families continued to be the hereditary priests of Hercules till the censorship of App. Claudius (B. C. 312), who purchased from the Potitii the knowledge of the sacred rites, and entrusted them to public slaves; whereat the god was so angry, that the whole Potitia gens, containing 12 families and 30 grown up men, perished within a year, or according to other accounts within 30 days, and Appius himself became blind. The Pinarii did not share in the guilt of communicating the sacred knowledge, and therefore did not receive the same punishment as the Potitii, but continued in existence to the latest times. It appears that the worship of Hercules by the Potitii and Pinarii was a *sacrum gentilitium* belonging to these gentes, and that in the time of App. Claudius these *sacra privata* were made *sacra publica*. The Pinarii were divided into the families of *Mamercinus*, *Natta*, *Posca*, *Rusca*, and *Scarpus*, but none of them obtained sufficient importance to require a separate notice.

Pinārīus, L., the great-nephew of the dictator C. Julius Caesar, being the grandson of Julia, Caesar's eldest sister. In the will of the dictator, Pinarius was named one of his heirs along with his two other great-nephews, C. Octavius and L. Pinarius, Octavius obtaining three-fourths of the property, and the remaining fourth being divided between Pinarius and Pedius.

Pinārus (Πίναρος), a river of Cilicia, rising in M. Amanus, and falling into the gulf of Issus near Issus, between the mouth of the Pyramus and the Syrian frontier.

Pindārus (Πίνδαρος), the greatest lyric poet of Greece, was born either at Thebes or at Cynoscephalae, a village in the territory of Thebes, about B. C. 522. His family was one of the noblest in Thebes, and seems also to have been celebrated for its skill in music. The father or uncle of Pindar was a flute-player, and Pindar at an early age received instruction in the art from the flute-player Scopelinus. But the youth soon gave indications of a genius for poetry, which induced his father to send him to Athens to receive more perfect instruction in the art. Later writers tell us that his future glory as a poet was miraculously foreshadowed by a swarm of bees which rested upon his lips while he was asleep, and that this miracle first led him to compose poetry. At Athens Pindar became the pupil of Lasus of Hermione, the founder of the Athenian school of dithyrambic poetry. He returned to Thebes before he completed his 20th year, and is said to have received instruction there from Myrtis and Corinna of Tanagra, two poetesses, who then enjoyed great celebrity in Boeotia. With both these poetesses Pindar contended for the prize in the musical contests at Thebes; and he is said to have been defeated five times by Corinna. Pindar commenced his professional career as a poet at an early age, and was soon employed by different states and princes in all parts of the Hellenic world to compose for them choral songs for special occasions. He received money and presents for his works; but he never degenerated into a common mercenary poet, and he continued to preserve to his latest days the respect of all parts of Greece. He composed poems for Hieron, tyrant of Syracuse, Alexander, son of Amyntas, king of Macedonia, Theron, tyrant of Agrigentum, Arcesilaus, king of Cyrene, as well as for many free states and private persons. He was courted especially by Alexander, king of Macedonia, and Hieron, tyrant of Syracuse; and the praises which he bestowed upon the former are said to have been the chief reason which led his

descendant, Alexander, the son of Philip, to spare the house of the poet, when he destroyed the rest of Thebes. Pindar's stated residence was at Thebes, though he frequently left home in order to witness the great public games, and to visit the states and distinguished men who courted his friendship and employed his services. Thus about B. C. 473 he visited the court of Hieron at Syracuse, where he remained 4 years. He probably died in his 80th year in 442.—The only poems of Pindar which have come down to us entire are his *Epinicia*, or *triumphal odes*. But these were but a small portion of his works. Besides his triumphal odes he wrote hymns to the gods, paeans, dithyrambs, odes for processions (προσόδια), songs of maidens (παρθένεια), mimic dancing songs (ὑπορχήματα), drinking-songs (σκόλια), dirges (Δρῆνοι), and encomia (ἐγκώμια), or panegyrics on princes. Of these we have numerous fragments. Most of them are mentioned in the well-known lines of Horace (*Carm.* iv. 2):

" Seu per audaces nova dithyrambos
　Verba devolvit, numerisque fertur
　　　　Lege solutis:
Seu deos (*hymns and paeans*) regesve (*encomia*)
　　　　canit, deorum
Sanguinem : . . .
Sive quos Elea domum reducit
Palma caelestes (*the Epinicia*) : . . .
Flebili sponsae juvenemve raptum
Plorat " (*the dirges*).

In all of these varieties Pindar equally excelled, as we see from the numerous quotations made from them by the ancient writers, though they are generally of too fragmentary a kind to allow us to form a judgment respecting them. Our estimate of Pindar as a poet must be formed almost exclusively from his *Epinicia*, which were composed in commemoration of some victory in the public games. The *Epinicia* are divided into 4 books, celebrating respectively the victories gained in the Olympian, Pythian, Nemean, and Isthmian games. In order to understand them properly we must bear in mind the nature of the occasion for which they were composed, and the object which the poet had in view. A victory gained in one of the 4 great national festivals conferred honour not only upon the conqueror and his family, but also upon the city to which he belonged. It was accordingly celebrated with great pomp and ceremony. Such a celebration began with a procession to a temple, where a sacrifice was offered, and it ended with a banquet and the joyous revelry, called by the Greeks *comus* (κῶμος). For this celebration a poem was expressly composed, which was sung by a chorus. The poems were sung either during the procession to the temple or at the comus at the close of the banquet. Those of Pindar's Epinician odes which consist of strophes without epodes were sung during the procession, but the majority of them appear to have been sung at the comus. In these odes Pindar rarely describes the victory itself, as the scene was familiar to all the spectators, but he dwells upon the glory of the victor, and celebrates chiefly either his wealth (ὄλβος) or his skill (ἀρετή),—his *wealth*, if he had gained the victory in the chariot-race, since it was only the wealthy that could contend for the prize in this contest; his *skill*, if he had been exposed to peril in the contest.—The metres of Pindar are too extensive and

difficult a subject to admit of explanation in the
present work. No two odes possess the same
metrical structure. The Doric rhythm chiefly pre-
vails, but he also makes frequent use of the Aeolian
and Lydian as well. The best editions of Pindar
are by Böckh, Lips. 1811—1821, 2 vols. 4to., and
by Dissen, of which there is a 2nd edition by
Schneidewin, Gotha, 1843, seq.

Pindāsus (Πίνδασος), a S. branch of M. Temnus in Mysia, extending to the Elaïtic Gulf, and
containing the sources of the river Cetius.

Pindus (Πίνδος). 1. A lofty range of mountains in northern Greece, a portion of the great
back bone, which runs through the centre of Greece
from N. to S. The name of Pindus was confined
to that part of the chain which separates Thessaly
and Epirus ; and its most N.-ly and also highest
part was called LACMON.—2. One of the 4 towns
in Doria, near the sources of a small river of the
same name which flowed through Locris into the
Cephissus.

Pinna (Pinnensis: Civitá di Penna), the chief
town of the Vestini at the foot of the Apennines,
surrounded by beautiful meadows.

Pinnes, Pinneus, or Pineus, was the son of
Agron, king of Illyria, by his first wife, Triteuta.
At the death of Agron (B.C. 231), Pinnes, who was
then a child, was left in the guardianship of his
step-mother Teuta, whom Agron had married after
divorcing Triteuta. When Teuta was defeated by
the Romans, the care of Pinnes devolved upon
Demetrius of Pharos ; but when Demetrius in his
turn made war against the Romans and was defeated, Pinnes was placed upon the throne by the
Romans, but was compelled to pay tribute.

Pintuaria (Πιντουαρία: Teneriffe), one of the
INSULAE FORTUNATAE (Canary Is.) off the W.
coast of Africa, also called Convallis, and, from
the perpetual snow on its peak, Nivaria.

Piraeeus or Piraeus (Πειραιεύς: Porto Leone or
Porto Dracone), the most important of the harbours
of Athens, was situated in the peninsula about 5
miles S.W. of Athens. This peninsula, which is
sometimes called by the general name of Piraeeus,
contained 3 harbours, Piraeeus proper on the W.
side, by far the largest of the 3, Zea on the E. side
separated from Piraeeus by a narrow isthmus, and
Munychia (Pharnari) still further to the E. The
position of Piraeeus and of the Athenian harbours has been usually misunderstood. In consequence of a statement in an ancient Scholiast, it
was generally supposed that the great harbour of
Piraeeus was divided into 3 smaller harbours, Zea
for corn-vessels, Aphrodisium for merchant-ships in
general, and Cantharus for ships of war ; but this
division of the Piraeeus is now rejected by the
best topographers. Zea was a harbour totally distinct from the Piraeeus, as is stated above ; the N.
portion of the Piraeeus seems to have been used
by the merchant vessels, and the Cantharus, where
the ships of war were stationed, was on the S. side
of the harbour near the entrance. It was through
the suggestion of Themistocles that the Athenians
were induced to make use of the harbour of Piraeeus. Before the Persian wars their principal
harbour was Phalerum, which was not situated in
the Piraean peninsula at all, but lay to the E. of
Munychia. [PHALERUM.] At the entrance of
the harbour of Piraeeus there were 2 promontories,
the one on the right-hand called Alcimus ("Αλκι-
μος), on which was the tomb of Themistocles, and

the other on the left called Eetionēa ("Ηετιώνεια),
on which the Four Hundred erected a fortress.
The entrance of the harbour, which was narrow
by nature, was rendered still narrower by two
mole-heads, to which a chain was attached to prevent the ingress of hostile ships. The town or
demus of Piraeeus was surrounded with strong
fortifications by Themistocles, and was connected
with Athens by means of the celebrated Long
Walls under the administration of Pericles. [See
p. 102, b.] The town possessed a considerable
population, and many public and private buildings.
The most important of its public buildings were:
the Agora Hippodamia, a temple of Zeus Soter,
a large stoa, a theatre, the Phreattys or tribunal
for the admirals, the arsenal, the docks, &c.

Pīrēnē (Πειρήνη), a celebrated fountain at Corinth, which, according to tradition, took its origin
from Pirene, a daughter of Oebalus, who here
melted away into tears through grief for the loss
of her son Cenchrias. At this fountain Bellerophon
is said to have caught the horse Pegasus. It
gushed forth from the rock in the Acrocorinthus,
was conveyed down the hill by subterraneous con-
duits, and fell into a marble basin, from which
the greater part of the town was supplied with
water. The fountain was celebrated for the purity
and salubrity of its water, and was so highly valued
that the poets frequently employed its name as
equivalent to that of Corinth itself.

Pīrēsīae (Πειρεσίαι), probably the same as the
Iresiae of Livy, a town of Thessaly in the district
Thessaliotis, on the left bank of the Peneus.

Pīrithŏus (Πειρίθοος), son of Ixion or Zeus by
Dia, was king of the Lapithae in Thessaly, and
married to Hippodamia, by whom he became the
father of Polypoetes. When Pirithoüs was celebrating his marriage with Hippodamia, the intoxicated Centaur Eurytion or Eurytus carried her off,
and this act occasioned the celebrated fight between
the Centaurs and Lapithae, in which the Centaurs
were defeated. Pirithoüs once invaded Attica, but
when Theseus came forth to oppose him, he conceived a warm admiration for the Athenian king ;
and from this time a most intimate friendship
sprung up between the 2 heroes. Theseus was
present at the wedding of Pirithoüs, and assisted
him in his battle against the Centaurs. Hippodamia afterwards died, and each of the two friends
resolved to wed a daughter of Zeus. With the
assistance of Pirithoüs, Theseus carried off Helen
from Sparta, and placed her at Aethra under the care
of Phaedra. Pirithoüs was still more ambitious,
and resolved to carry off Persephone (Proserpina),
the wife of the king of the lower world. Theseus
would not desert his friend in the enterprise,
though he knew the risk which they ran. The 2
friends accordingly descended to the lower world,
but they were seized by Pluto and fastened to a
rock, where they both remained till Hercules
visited the lower world. Hercules delivered
Theseus, who had made the daring attempt only
to please his friend, but Pirithoüs remained for ever
in torment (amatorem trecentas Pirithoum cohibent
catenae, Hor. Carm, iii. 4. 80). Pirithoüs was
worshipped at Athens, along with Theseus, as a
hero.

Pīrus (Πεῖρος), Pierus (Πίερος), or Achelous,
the chief river of Achaia, which falls into the gulf
of Patrae, near Olenus.

Pirustae, a people in Illyria, exempted from

taxes by the Romans, because they deserted Gentius and passed over to the Romans.

Pisa (Πῖσα : Πισάτης), the capital of **Pisatis** (Πισᾶτις), the middle portion of the province of Elis in Peloponnesus. [ELIS.] In the most ancient times Pisatis formed an union of 8 states, of which, in addition to Pisa, we find mention of Salmone, Heraclea, Harpinna, Cycesium and Dyspontium. Pisa itself was situated N. of the Alpheus, at a very short distance E. of Olympia, and, in consequence of its proximity to the latter place, was frequently identified by the poets with it. The history of the Pisatae consists of their struggle with the Eleans, with whom they contended for the presidency of the Olympic games. The Pisatae obtained this honour in the 8th Olympiad (B. C. 748) with the assistance of Phidon, tyrant of Argos, and also a 2nd time in the 34th Olympiad (644) by means of their own king Pantaleon. In the 52nd Olympiad (572) the struggle between the 2 peoples was brought to a close by the conquest and destruction of Pisa by the Eleans. So complete was the destruction of the city, that not a trace of it was left in later times ; and some persons, as we learn from Strabo, even questioned whether it had ever existed, supposing that by the name of Pisa, the kingdom of the Pisatae was alone intended. The existence, however, of the city does not admit of dispute. Even after the destruction of the city, the Pisatae did not relinquish their claims ; and in the 104th Olympiad (364), they had the presidency of the Olympic games along with the Arcadians, when the latter people were making war with the Eleans.

Pisa, more rarely **Pisa** (Pisanus : *Pisa*), one of the most ancient and important of the cities of Etruria, was situated at the confluence of the Arnus and Ausar (*Serchio*), about 6 miles from the sea ; but the latter river altered its course in the 12th century, and now flows into the sea by a separate channel. According to some traditions, Pisae was founded by the companions of Nestor, the inhabitants of Pisa in Elis, who were driven upon the coast of Italy on their return from Troy ; whence the Roman poets give the Etruscan town the surname of Alphea. This legend, however, like many others, probably arose from the accidental similarity of the names of the 2 cities. It would seem that Pisa was originally a Pelasgic town, that it afterwards passed into the hands of the Ligyae, and from them into those of the Etruscans. It then became one of the 12 cities of Etruria, and was down to the time of Augustus the most N.-ly city in the country. Pisa is frequently mentioned in the Ligurian wars as the head-quarters of the Roman legions. In B.C. 180 it was made a Latin colony, and appears to have been colonised again in the time of Augustus, since we find it called in inscriptions *Colonia Julia Pisana.* Its harbour, called *Portus Pisanus,* at the mouth of the Arnus, was much used by the Romans ; and in the time of Strabo the town of Pisa was still a place of considerable importance on account of the marble-quarries in its neighbourhood, and the quantity of timber which it yielded for ship-building. About 3 miles N. of the town were mineral springs, called *Aquae Pisanae,* which were less celebrated in antiquity than they are at the present day. There is scarcely a vestige of the ancient city in the modern *Pisa.*

Pisander (Πείσανδρος). 1. Son of Polyctor,

and one of the suitors of Penelope. — 2. An Athenian, of the demus of Acharnae, lived in the time of the Peloponnesian war, and was attacked by the comic poets for his rapacity and cowardice. In 412 he comes before us as the chief ostensible agent in effecting the revolution of the Four Hundred. In all the measures of the new government, of which he was a member, he took an active part ; and when Theramenes and others withdrew from it, he sided with the more violent aristocrats, and was one of those who, on the counter-revolution, took refuge with Agis at Decelea. His property was confiscated, and it does not appear that he ever returned to Athens. — 3. A Spartan, brother-in-law of Agesilaus II., who made him admiral of the fleet in 395. In the following year he was defeated and slain in the sea-fight off Cnidus, against Conon and Pharnabazus. — 4. A poet of Camirus in Rhodes, flourished about B. c. 648—645. He was the author of a poem in 2 books on the exploits of Hercules, called *Heraclēa* ('Ἡράκλεια). The Alexandrian grammarians thought so highly of the poem that they received Pisander, as well as Antimachus and Panyasis, into the epic canon together with Homer and Hesiod. Only a few lines of it have been preserved. In the Greek Anthology we find an epigram attributed to Pisander of Rhodes, perhaps the poet of Camirus. — 5. A poet of Laranda, in Lycia or Lycaonia, was the son of Nestor, and flourished in the reign of Alexander Severus (A. D. 222—235). He wrote a poem, called 'Ἡρωικαὶ Θεογαμίαι, which probably treated of the marriages of gods and goddesses with mortals, and of the heroic progeny thus produced.

Pisatis. [PISA.]

Pisaurum (Pisaurensis : *Pesaro*), an ancient town of Umbria, near the mouth of the river **Pisaurus** (*Foglia*), on the road to Ariminum. It was colonised by the Romans in B. C. 186, and probably colonised a 2nd time by Augustus, since it is called in inscriptions *Colonia Julia Felix*

Pisaurus. [PISAURUM.]

Pisgah. [NEBO.]

Pisidia (ἡ Πισιδική : Πισίδης, pl. Πισίδαι, also Πεισίδαι, Πισίδαι and Πισιδικοί, **Pisida** pl. Pisidae, anc. **Peisidae**), an inland district of Asia Minor, bounded by Lycia and Pamphylia on the S. ; Cilicia on the S. E. ; Lycaonia and Isauria (the latter often reckoned a part of Pisidia) on the E. and N. E. ; Phrygia Parorios on the N., where the boundary varied at different times, and was never very definite ; and Caria on the W. It was a mountainous region, formed by that part of the main chain of Mt. Taurus which sweeps round in a semicircle parallel to the shore of the Pamphylian gulf ; the strip of shore itself, at the foot of the mountains, constituting the district of PAMPHYLIA. The inhabitants of the mountains were a warlike aboriginal people, related apparently to the Isaurians and Cilicians. They maintained their independence, under petty chieftains, against all the successive rulers of Asia Minor. The Romans never subdued the Pisidians in their mountain fortresses, though they took some of the towns on the outskirts of their country ; for example, Antiochia, which was made a colony with the Jus Italicum. In fact the N. part, in which Antiochia stood, had originally belonged to Phrygia, and was more accessible and more civilised than the mountains which formed the proper country of the

Pisidians. Nominally, the country was considered a part of Pamphylia, till the new sub-division of the empire under Constantine, when Pisidia was made a separate province. The country is still inhabited by wild tribes, among whom travelling is dangerous; and it is therefore little known. Ancient writers say that it contained, amidst its rugged mountains, some fertile valleys, where the olive flourished; and it also produced the gum storax, some medicinal plants, and salt. On the S. slope of the Taurus, several rivers flowed through Pisidia and Pamphylia, into the Pamphylian gulf, the chief of which were the Cestrus and the Catarrhactes; and on the N. the mountain streams form some large salt lakes, namely, Ascania (*Hoiran* and *Egerdir*) S. of Antiochia, Caralius or Pusgusa (*Bei Shehr* or *Kereli*) S. E. of the former, and Trogitis (*Soghla*) further to the S. E., in Isauria. Special names were given to certain districts, which are sometimes spoken of as parts of Pisidia, sometimes as distinct countries; namely, Cibyrātis, in the S. W. along the N. of Lycia, and Cabalia, the S. W. corner of Cibyratis itself; Milyas, the district E. of Cibyratis, N. E. of Lycia, and N. W. of Pamphylia, and Isauria, in the E. of Pisidia, on the borders of Lycaonia.

Pisistratīdae (Πεισιστρατίδαι), the legitimate sons of Pisistratus. The name is used sometimes to indicate only Hippias and Hipparchus, and sometimes in a wider application, embracing the grandchildren and near connections of Pisistratus (as by Herod. viii. 52. referring to a time when both Hippias and Hipparchus were dead).

Pisistrātus (Πεισίστρατος), the youngest son of Nestor and Anaxibia, was a friend of Telemachus, and accompanied him on his journey from Pylos to Menelaus at Sparta.

Pisistrātus (Πεισίστρατος), an Athenian, son of Hippocrates, was so named after Pisistratus, the youngest son of Nestor, since the family of Hippocrates was of Pylian origin, and traced their descent to Neleus, the father of Nestor. The mother of Pisistratus (whose name we do not know) was cousin-german to the mother of Solon. Pisistratus grew up equally distinguished for personal beauty and for mental endowments. The relationship between him and Solon naturally drew them together, and a close friendship sprang up between them. He assisted Solon by his eloquence in persuading the Athenians to renew their struggle with the Megarians for the possession of Salamis, and he afterwards fought with bravery in the expedition which Solon led against the island. When Solon, after the establishment of his constitution, retired for a time from Athens, the old rivalry between the parties of the Plain, the Highlands and the Coast broke out into open feud. The party of the Plain, comprising chiefly the landed proprietors, was headed by Lycurgus; that of the Coast, consisting of the wealthier classes not belonging to the nobles, by Megacles, the son of Alcmaeon; the party of the Highlands, which aimed at more of political freedom and equality than either of the two others, was the one at the head of which Pisistratus placed himself, because they seemed the most likely to be useful in the furtherance of his ambitious designs. His liberality, as well as his military and oratorical abilities, gained him the support of a large body of citizens. Solon, on his return, quickly saw through the designs of Pisistratus, who listened with re-

spect to his advice, though he prosecuted his schemes none the less diligently. When Pisistratus found his plans sufficiently ripe for execution, he one day made his appearance in the agora with his mules and his own person exhibiting recent wounds, pretending that he had been nearly assassinated by his enemies as he was riding into the country. An assembly of the people was forthwith called, in which one of his partisans proposed that a body-guard of 50 citizens, armed with clubs, should be granted to him. It was in vain that Solon opposed this; the guard was given him. Through the neglect or connivance of the people Pisistratus took this opportunity of raising a much larger force, with which he seized the citadel, B. c. 560, thus becoming, what the Greeks called *Tyrant* of Athens. Having secured to himself the substance of power, he made no further change in the constitution, or in the laws, which he administered ably and well. His first usurpation lasted but a short time. Before his power was firmly rooted, the factions headed by Megacles and Lycurgus combined, and Pisistratus was compelled to evacuate Athens. He remained in banishment 6 years. Meantime the factions of Megacles and Lycurgus revived their old feuds, and Megacles made overtures to Pisistratus, offering to reinstate him in the tyranny if he would connect himself with him by receiving his daughter in marriage. The proposal was accepted by Pisistratus, and the following stratagem was devised for accomplishing his restoration, according to the account of Herodotus. A damsel named Phya, of remarkable stature and beauty, was dressed up as Athena in a full suit of armour, and placed in a chariot, with Pisistratus by her side. The chariot was then driven towards the city, heralds being sent on before to announce that Athena in person was bringing back Pisistratus to her Acropolis. The report spread rapidly, and those in the city believing that the woman was really their tutelary goddess, worshipped her, and admitted Pisistratus. Pisistratus nominally performed his part of the contract with Megacles; but in consequence of the insulting manner in which he treated his wife, Megacles again made common cause with Lycurgus, and Pisistratus was a second time compelled to evacuate Athens. He retired to Eretria in Euboea, and employed the next 10 years in making preparations to regain his power. At the end of that time he invaded Attica, with the forces he had raised, and also supported by Lygdamis of Naxos with a considerable body of troops. He defeated his opponents near the temple of Athena at Pallene, and then entered Athens without opposition. Lygdamis was rewarded by being established as tyrant of Naxos, which island Pisistratus conquered. [LYGDAMIS.] Having now become tyrant of Athens for the third time, Pisistratus adopted measures to secure the undisturbed possession of his supremacy. He took a body of foreign mercenaries into his pay, and seized as hostages the children of several of the principal citizens, placing them in the custody of Lygdamis, in Naxos. He maintained at the same time the form of Solon's institutions, only taking care, as his sons did after him, that the highest offices should always be held by some member of the family. He not only exacted obedience to the laws from his subjects and friends, but himself set the example of submitting to them. On one occasion he even appeared before the Areopagus to answer

a charge of murder, which however was not prosecuted. Athens was indebted to him for many
stately and useful buildings. Among these may
be mentioned a temple to the Pythian Apollo, and
a magnificent temple to the Olympian Zeus, which
remained unfinished for several centuries, and was
at length completed by the emperor Hadrian. Besides these, the Lyceum, a garden with stately
buildings a short distance from the city, was the
work of Pisistratus, as also the fountain of the
Nine Springs. Pisistratus also encouraged literature in various ways. It was apparently under
his auspices that Thespis introduced at Athens his
rude form of tragedy (B. c. 535), and that dramatic
contests were made a regular part of the Attic
Dionysia. It is to Pisistratus that we owe the
first written text of the whole of the poems of
Homer, which, without his care, would most likely
now exist only in a few disjointed fragments.
[HOMERUS.] Pisistratus is also said to have been
the first person in Greece who collected a library,
to which he generously allowed the public access.
By his first wife Pisistratus had 2 sons, Hippias
and Hipparchus. By his 2nd wife, Timonassa, he
had also 2 sons, Iophon and Thessalus, who are
rarely mentioned. He had also a bastard son,
Hegesistratus, whom he made tyrant of Sigeum,
after taking that town from the Mytilenaeans.
Pisistratus died at an advanced age in 527, and
was succeeded in the tyranny by his eldest son
Hippias: but Hippias and his brother Hipparchus
appear to have administered the affairs of the state
with so little outward distinction, that they are
frequently spoken of as though they had been joint
tyrants. They continued the government on the
same principles as their father. Thucydides (vi.
54) speaks in terms of high commendation of the
virtue and intelligence with which their rule was
exercised till the death of Hipparchus. Hipparchus inherited his father's literary tastes. Several
distinguished poets lived at Athens under the
patronage of Hipparchus, as, for example, Simonides of Ceos, Anacreon of Teos, Lasus of Hermione, and Onomacritus. After the murder of
Hipparchus in 514, an account of which is given
under HARMODIUS, a great change ensued in the
character of the government. Under the influence
of revengeful feelings and fears for his own safety
Hippias now became a morose and suspicious
tyrant. He put to death great numbers of the
citizens, and raised money by extraordinary imposts.
His old enemies the Alcmaeonidae, to whom Megacles belonged, availed themselves of the growing
discontent of the citizens; and after one or two
unsuccessful attempts they at length succeeded,
supported by a large force under Cleomenes, in
expelling the Pisistratidae from Attica. Hippias
and his connections retired to Sigeum, 510. The
family of the tyrants was condemned to perpetual
banishment, a sentence which was maintained even
in after-times, when decrees of amnesty were
passed. Hippias afterwards repaired to the court
of Darius, and looked forward to a restoration to
his country by the aid of the Persians. He accompanied the expedition sent under Datis and
Artaphernes, and pointed out to the Persians the
plain of Marathon, as the most suitable place for their
landing. He was now (490) of great age. According to some accounts he fell in the battle of
Marathon; according to others he died at Lemnos
on his return. Hippias was the only one of the

legitimate sons of Pisistratus who had children;
but none of them attained distinction.

PISO, CALPURNIUS, the name of a distinguished
plebeian family. The name of Piso, like many
other Roman cognomens, is connected with agriculture, the noblest and most honourable pursuit
of the ancient Romans: it comes from the verb
pisere or *pinsere*, and refers to the pounding or
grinding of corn. — 1. Was taken prisoner at the
battle of Cannae, B. c. 216; was praetor urbanus
211, and afterwards commanded as propraetor in
Etruria, 210. Piso in his praetorship proposed to
the senate, that the Ludi Apollinares, which had
been exhibited for the first time in the preceding
year (212), should be repeated, and should be
celebrated in future annually. The senate passed
a decree to this effect. The establishment of these
games by their ancestor was commemorated on
coins by the Pisones in later times. — 2. C., son of
No. 1, was praetor 186, and received Further
Spain as his province. He returned to Rome in
184, and obtained a triumph for a victory he had
gained over the Lusitani and Celtiberi. He was
consul in 180, and died during his consulship.

Pisones with the agnomen Caesoninus.

3. L., received the agnomen Caesoninus, because
he originally belonged to the Caesonia gens. He
was praetor in 154, and obtained the province
of Further Spain, but was defeated by the
Lusitani. He was consul in 148, and was sent
to conduct the war against Carthage; he was
succeeded in the command in the following year
by Scipio. — 4. L., son of No. 3, consul 112 with
M. Livius Drusus. In 107 he served as legatus
to the consul, L. Cassius Longinus, who was sent
into Gaul to oppose the Cimbri and their allies,
and he fell together with the consul in the battle,
in which the Roman army was utterly defeated by
the Tigurini in the territory of the Allobroges.
This Piso was the grandfather of Caesar's father-
in-law, a circumstance to which Caesar himself
alludes in recording his own victory over the Tigurini at a later time. (Caes. *B. G.* i. 7, 12.) — 5. L.,
son of No. 4, never rose to any of the offices of
state, and is only known from the account given of
him by Cicero in his violent invective against his
son. He married the daughter of Calventius,
a native of Cisalpine Gaul, who came from
Placentia and settled at Rome; and hence Cicero
calls his son in contempt a semi-Placentian. —
6. L., son of No. 5, was an unprincipled debauchee and a cruel and corrupt magistrate.
He is first mentioned in 59, when he was brought
to trial by P. Clodius for plundering a province,
of which he had the administration after his
praetorship, and he was only acquitted by throwing himself at the feet of the judges. In the
same year Caesar married his daughter Calpurnia; and through his influence Piso obtained
the consulship for 58, having for his colleague A.
Gabinius, who was indebted for the honour to
Pompey. Both consuls supported Clodius in his
measures against Cicero, which resulted in the
banishment of the orator. The conduct of Piso in
support of Clodius produced that extreme resentment in the mind of Cicero, which he displayed
against Piso on many subsequent occasions. At
the expiration of his consulship Piso went to his
province of Macedonia, where he remained during
2 years (57 and 56), plundering the province in the

most shameless manner. In the latter of these years the senate resolved that a successor should be appointed ; and in the debate in the senate which led to his recall, Cicero attacked him in the most unmeasured terms in an oration which has come down to us (*De Provinciis Consularibus*). Piso on his return (55) complained in the senate of the attack of Cicero, and justified the administration of his province, whereupon Cicero reiterated his charges in a speech which is likewise extant (*In Pisonem*). Cicero, however, did not venture to bring to trial the father-in-law of Caesar. In 50 Piso was censor with Ap. Claudius Pulcher. On the breaking out of the civil war (49) Piso accompanied Pompey in his flight from the city ; and although he did not go with him across the sea, he still kept aloof from Caesar. He subsequently returned to Rome, and remained neutral during the remainder of the civil war. After Caesar's death (44) Piso at first opposed Antony, but is afterwards mentioned as one of his partisans. —**7. L.**, son of No. 6, was consul 15, and afterwards obtained the province of Pamphylia ; from thence he was recalled by Augustus in 11, in order to make war upon the Thracians, who had attacked the province of Macedonia. He was appointed by Tiberius praefectus urbi. While retaining the favour of the emperor, without condescending to servility, he at the same time earned the good-will of his fellow-citizens by the integrity and justice with which he governed the city. He died in A. D. 32, at the age of 80, and was honoured by a decree of the senate, with a public funeral. It was to this Piso and his 2 sons that Horace addressed his epistle on the Art of Poetry.

Pisones with the agnomen Frugi.

8. L., received from his integrity and conscientiousness the surname of Frugi, which is perhaps nearly equivalent to our " man of honour." He was tribune of the plebs, 149, in which year he proposed the first law for the punishment of extortion in the provinces. He was consul in 133, and carried on war against the slaves in Sicily. He was a staunch supporter of the aristocratical party, and offered a strong opposition to the measures of C. Gracchus. Piso was censor, but it is uncertain in what year. He wrote Annals, which contained the history of Rome from the earliest period to the age in which Piso himself lived.—**9. L.**, son of No. 8, served with distinction under his father in Sicily in 133, and died in Spain about 111, whither he had gone as propraetor.—**10. L.**, son of No. 9, was a colleague of Verres in the praetorship, 74, when he thwarted many of the unrighteous schemes of the latter.—**11. C.**, son of No. 10, married Tullia, the daughter of Cicero, in 63, but was betrothed to her as early as 67. He was quaestor in 58, when he used every exertion to obtain the recall of his father-in-law from banishment ; but he died in 57 before Cicero's return to Rome. He is frequently mentioned by Cicero in terms of gratitude on account of the zeal which he had manifested in his behalf during his banishment.

Pisones without an agnomen.

12. C., consul 67, belonged to the high aristocratical party ; and in his consulship opposed with the utmost vehemence the law of the tribune Gabinius, for giving Pompey the command of the war against the pirates. In 66 and 65, Piso ad-

ministered the province of Narbonese Gaul as proconsul, and while there suppressed an insurrection of the Allobroges. In 63 he was accused of plundering the province, and was defended by Cicero. The latter charge was brought against Piso at the instigation of Caesar ; and Piso, in revenge, implored Cicero, but without success, to accuse Caesar as one of the conspirators of Catiline.—**13. M.**, usually called **M. Pupius Piso**, because he was adopted by M. Pupius, when the latter was an old man. He retained, however, his family-name Piso, just as Scipio, after his adoption by Metellus, was called Metellus Scipio. [METELLUS, No. 15.] On the death of L. Cinna, in 84, Piso married his wife Annia. In 83 he was appointed quaestor to the consul L. Scipio ; but he quickly deserted this party, and went over to Sulla, who compelled him to divorce his wife on account of her previous connection with Cinna. After his praetorship, the year of which is uncertain, he received the province of Spain with the title of proconsul, and on his return to Rome in 69, enjoyed the honour of a triumph. He served in the Mithridatic war as a legatus of Pompey. He was elected consul for 61 through the influence of Pompey. In his consulship Piso gave great offence to Cicero, by not asking the orator first in the senate for his opinion, and by taking P. Clodius under his protection after his violation of the mysteries of the Bona Dea. Cicero revenged himself on Piso, by preventing him from obtaining the province of Syria, which had been promised him. Piso, in his younger days, had so high a reputation as an orator, that Cicero was taken to him by his father, in order to receive instruction from him. He belonged to the Peripatetic school in philosophy, in which he received instructions from Staseas.—**14. Cn.**, a young noble who had dissipated his fortune by his extravagance and profligacy, and therefore joined Catiline in what is usually called his first conspiracy (66). [For details see p. 155, b.] The senate anxious to get rid of Piso sent him into Nearer Spain as quaestor, but with the rank and title of propraetor. His exactions in the province soon made him so hateful to the inhabitants, that he was murdered by them. It was, however, supposed by some that he was murdered at the instigation of Pompey or of Crassus.—**15. Cn.**, fought against Caesar in Africa (46), and after the death of the dictator, joined Brutus and Cassius. He was subsequently pardoned, and returned to Rome ; but he disdained to ask Augustus for any of the honours of the state, and was, without solicitation, raised to the consulship in 23.—**16. Cn.**, son of No. 15, inherited all the pride and haughtiness of his father. He was consul B. C. 7, and was sent by Augustus as legate into Spain, where he made himself hated by his cruelty and avarice. Tiberius after his accession was chiefly jealous of Germanicus, his brother's son ; and accordingly, when the eastern provinces were assigned to Germanicus in A. D. 18, Tiberius conferred upon Piso the command of Syria, in order that the latter might do every thing in his power to thwart and oppose Germanicus. Plancina, the wife of Piso, was also urged on by Livia, the mother of the emperor, to vie with and annoy Agrippina. Germanicus and Agrippina were thus exposed to every species of insult and opposition from Piso and Plancina ; and when Germanicus fell ill in the autumn of 19, he believed that he had been poisoned by them. Piso on his return to Rome

(20) was accused of murdering Germanicus; the matter was investigated by the senate; but before the investigation came to an end, Piso was found one morning in his room with his throat cut, and his sword lying by his side. It was generally supposed that, despairing of the emperor's protection, he had put an end to his own life; but others believed that Tiberius dreaded his revealing his secrets, and accordingly caused him to be put to death. The powerful influence of Livia secured the acquittal of Plancina. — 17. C., the leader of the well-known conspiracy against Nero in A. D. 65. Piso himself did not form the plot; but as soon as he had joined it, his great popularity gained him many partizans. He possessed most of the qualities which the Romans prized, high birth, an eloquent address, liberality and affability; and he also displayed a sufficient love of magnificence and luxury to suit the taste of the day, which would not have tolerated austerity of manner or character. The conspiracy was discovered by Milichus, a freedman of Flavius Scevinus, one of the conspirators. Piso thereupon opened his veins, and thus died. There is extant a poem in 261 lines, containing a panegyric on a certain Calpurnius Piso, who is probably the same person as the leader of the conspiracy against Nero. — 18. L., surnamed Licinianus, was the son of M. Licinius Crassus Frugi, and was adopted by one of the Pisones. On the accession of Galba to the throne, he adopted as his son and successor Piso Licinianus; but the latter only enjoyed the distinction 4 days, for Otho, who had hoped to receive this honour, induced the praetorians to rise against the emperor. Piso fled for refuge into the temple of Vesta, but was dragged out by the soldiers, and despatched at the threshold of the temple, A. D. 69.

Pistor, that is, the baker, a surname of Jupiter at Rome, which is said to have arisen in the following manner. When the Gauls were besieging Rome, the god suggested to the besieged the idea of throwing loaves of bread among the enemies, to make them believe that the Romans had plenty of provisions, and thus caused them to give up the siege.

Pistoria or **Pistorium** (Pistoriensis: *Pistoia*), a small place in Etruria, on the road from Luca to Florentia, rendered memorable by the defeat of Catiline in its neighbourhood.

Pitana. [Sparta.]

Pitana (Πιτάνη: *Sanderli*), a seaport town of Mysia, on the coast of the Elaitic gulf, at the mouth of the Evenus or, according to some, of the Caïcus; almost destroyed by an earthquake under Titus. It was the birthplace of the Academic philosopher Arcesilaus.

Pithecusa. [Aenaria.]

Pitho (Πειθώ), called **Suada** or **Suadela** by the Romans, the personification of Persuasion. She was worshipped as a divinity at Sicyon, where she was honoured with a temple in the agora. Pitho also occurs as a surname of Aphrodite, whose worship was said to have been introduced at Athens by Theseus, when he united the country communities into towns. At Athens the statues of Pitho and Aphrodite Pandemos stood close together; and at Megara the statue of Pitho stood in the temple of Aphrodite; so that the 2 divinities must be conceived as closely connected, or the one, perhaps, merely as an attribute of the other.

Pithon (Πίθων also Πείθων and Πόθων). 1. Son of Agenor, a Macedonian officer of Alexander the Great. He received from Alexander the government of part of the Indian provinces, in which he was confirmed after the king's death. In B.C. 316, he received from Antigonus the satrapy of Babylon. He afterwards fought with Demetrius against Ptolemy, and was slain at the battle of Gaza, 312. — 2. Son of Crateuas or Crateas, a Macedonian officer of Alexander, who is frequently confounded with the preceding. After Alexander's death he received from Perdiccas the satrapy of Media. He accompanied Perdiccas on his expedition to Egypt, (321), but he took part in the mutiny against Perdiccas, which terminated in the death of the latter. Pithon rendered important service to Antigonus in his war against Eumenes; but after the death of Eumenes, he began to form schemes for his own aggrandisement, and was accordingly put to death by Antigonus, 316.

Pitinum (Pitinas, -atis). 1. (*Pitino*), a municipium in the interior of Umbria on the river Pisaurus, whence its inhabitants are called in inscriptions *Pitinates Pisaurenses*. The town also bore the surname Mergens. — 2. A town in Picenum, on the road from Castrum Novum to Prifernum.

Pittacus (Πιττακός), one of those early cultivators of letters, who were designated as "the Seven Wise Men of Greece," was a native of Mytilene in Lesbos, and was born about B. c. 652. He was highly celebrated as a warrior, a statesman, a philosopher, and a poet. He is first mentioned, in public life, as an opponent of the tyrants of Mytilene. In conjunction with the brothers of Alcaeus, he overthrew and killed the tyrant Melanchrus, B. c. 612. In 606, he commanded the Mytilenaeans, in their war with the Athenians for the possession of Sigeum, on the coast of the Troad, and signalized himself by killing in single combat Phrynon, the commander of the Athenians. This feat Pittacus performed by entangling his adversary in a net, and then despatching him with a trident and a dagger, exactly after the fashion in which the gladiators called *retiarii* long afterwards fought at Rome. This war was terminated by the mediation of Periander, who assigned the disputed territory to the Athenians; but the internal troubles of Mytilene still continued. The supreme power was fiercely disputed between a succession of tyrants, and the aristocratic party, headed by Alcaeus and his brother Antimenidas; and the latter were driven into exile. As the exiles tried to effect their return by force of arms, the popular party chose Pittacus as their ruler, with absolute power, under the title of *Aesymnetes* (αἰσυμνήτης). He held this office for 10 years (589—579) and then voluntarily resigned it, having by his administration restored order to the state, and prepared it for the safe enjoyment of a republican form of government. He lived in great honour at Mytilene for 10 years after the resignation of his government; and died in 569, at an advanced age. Of the proverbial maxims of practical wisdom, which were current under the names of the seven wise men of Greece, two were ascribed to Pittacus, namely, Χαλεπὸν ἐσθλὸν ἔμμεναι, and Καιρὸν γνῶθι.

Pittheus (Πιτθεύς), king of Troezene, was son of Pelops and Dia, father of Aethra, and grandfather and instructor of Theseus. When Theseus married Phaedra, Pittheus took Hippolytus into his house. His tomb and the chair on which he had sat in judgment were shown at Troezene down to a late time. He is said to have taught the art of speaking, and even to have written a book upon it. Aethra as his daughter is called *Pittheïs*.

Pityïa (Πιτύεια: prob. *Shamelik*), a town mentioned by Homer, in the N. of Mysia, between Parium and Priapus, evidently named from the pine forests in its neighbourhood.

Pityonēsus (Πιτυόνησος: *Anghistri*), an island off the coast of Argolis.

Pityūs (Πιτυοῦς: prob. *Pitzunda*), a Greek city, in Sarmatia Asiatica, on the N. E. coast of the Euxine, 360 stadia N. W. of Dioscurias. In the time of Strabo, it was a considerable city and port. It was afterwards destroyed by the neighbouring tribe of the Heniochi, but it was restored, and long served as an important frontier fortress of the Roman Empire.

Pityūssa, Pityussa (Πιτυοῦσα, Πιτυοῦσσα, contracted from πιτυόεσσα fem. of πιτυόεις), i. e. abounding in pine-trees. 1. The ancient name of Lampsacus, Salamis, and Chios. — 2. A small island in the Argolic gulf. — 3. The name of 2 islands off the S. coast of Spain, W. of the Baleares. The larger of them was called Ebusus (*Iviza*), the smaller Ophiussa (*Formentera*): the latter was uninhabited.

Pixōdărus (Πιξώδαρος), prince or king of Caria, was the youngest of the 3 sons of Hecatomnus, all of whom successively held the sovereignty of Caria. Pixodarus obtained possession of the throne by the expulsion of his sister ADA, the widow and successor of her brother IDRIEUS, and held it without opposition for 5 years, B. C. 340—335. He was succeeded by his son-in-law Orontobates.

Placentia (Placentinus: *Piacenza*), a Roman colony in Cisalpine Gaul, founded at the same time as Cremona, B. C. 219. It was situated in the territory of the Anamares, on the right bank of the Po, not far from the mouth of the Trebia, and on the road from Mediolanum to Parma. It was taken and destroyed by the Gauls in 200, but was soon rebuilt by the Romans, and became an important place. It continued to be a flourishing town down to the time of the Goths.

Placīa (Πλακίη, Ion.: Πλακιηνός), an ancient Pelasgian settlement, in Mysia, E. of Cyzicus, at the foot of Mt. Olympus, seems to have been early destroyed.

Placīdīa, Galla. [GALLA.]

Placĭtus, Sex., the author of a short Latin work, entitled *De Medicina* (or *Medicamentis*) *ex Animalibus*, consisting of 34 chapters, each of which treats of some animal whose body was supposed to possess certain medical properties. As might be expected, it contains numerous absurdities, and is of little or no value or interest. The date of the author is uncertain, but he is supposed to have lived in the 4th century after Christ. The work is printed by Stephanus in the *Medicae Artis Principes*, Paris, fol. 1567, and elsewhere.

Plācus (Πλάκος), a mountain of Mysia, above the city of Thebe: *not* in the neighbourhood of PLACIA, as the resemblance of the names had led some to suppose.

Planārīa (prob. *Canaria, Canary*), one of the islands in the Atlantic, called FORTUNATAE.

Planasīa. 1. (*Pianosa*), an island between Corsica and the coast of Etruria, to which Augustus banished his grandson Agrippa Postumus. —

2. An island off the S. coast of Gaul, E. of the Stoechades.

Planciădes, Fulgentĭus. [FULGENTIUS.]

Plancīna, Munātĭa, the wife of Cn. Piso, who was appointed governor of Syria in A. D. 18. While her husband used every effort to thwart Germanicus, she exerted herself equally to annoy and insult Agrippina. She was encouraged in this conduct by Livia, the mother of the emperor, who saved her from condemnation by the senate when she was accused along with her husband in 20. [PISO, No. 16.] She was brought to trial again in 33, a few years after the death of Livia; and having no longer any hope of escape, she put an end to her own life.

Plancĭus, Cn., first served in Africa under the propraetor A. Torquatus, subsequently in B. C. 68 under the proconsul Q. Metellus in Crete, and next in 62 as military tribune in the army of C. Antonius in Macedonia. In 58 he was quaestor in Macedonia under the propraetor L. Appuleius, and here he showed great kindness to Cicero, when the latter came to this province during his banishment. He was tribune of the plebs in 56; and was elected curule aedile with A. Plotius in 54. But before Plancius and Plotius entered upon their office they were accused by Juventius Laterensis, and L. Cassius Longinus, of the crime of *sodalitium*, or the bribery of the tribes by means of illegal associations, in accordance with the Lex Licinia, which had been proposed by the consul Licinius Crassus in the preceding year. Cicero defended Plancius in an oration still extant, and obtained his acquittal. Plancius espoused the Pompeian party in the civil wars, and after Caesar had gained the supremacy lived in exile in Corcyra.

Plancus, Munātĭus, the name of a distinguished plebeian family. The surname Plancus signified a person having flat splay feet without any bend in them. 1. L., was a friend of Julius Caesar, and served under him both in the Gallic and the civil wars. Caesar shortly before his death nominated him to the government of Transalpine Gaul for B. C. 44, with the exception of the Narbonese and Belgic portions of the province, and also to the consulship for 42, with D. Brutus as his colleague. After Caesar's death Plancus hastened into Gaul, and took possession of his province. Here he prepared at first to support the senate against Antony; but when Lepidus joined Antony, and their united forces threatened to overwhelm Plancus, the latter was persuaded by Asinius Pollio to follow his example, and to unite with Antony and Lepidus. Plancus during his government of Gaul founded the colonies of Lugdunum and Raurica. He was consul in 42 according to the arrangement made by Caesar, and he subsequently followed Antony to Asia, where he remained for some years, and governed in succession the provinces of Asia and Syria. He deserted Antony in 32 shortly before the breaking out of the civil war between the latter and Octavian. He was favourably received by Octavian, and continued to reside at Rome during the remainder of his life. It was on his proposal that Octavian received the title of Augustus in 27; and the emperor conferred upon him the censorship in 22 with Paulus Aemilius Lepidus. Both the public and private life of Plancus was stained by numerous vices. One of Horace's odes (*Carm.* i. 7) is addressed to him. — 2. T., surnamed Bursa, brother of the former, was tribune of the plebs

B. c. 52, when he supported the views of Pompey, who was anxious to obtain the dictatorship. With this object he did every thing in his power to increase the confusion which followed upon the death of Clodius. At the close of the year, as soon as his tribunate had expired, Plancus was accused by Cicero of *Vis* and was condemned. After his condemnation Plancus went to Ravenna in Cisalpine Gaul, where he was kindly received by Caesar. Soon after the beginning of the civil war he was restored to his civic rights by Caesar ; but he appears to have taken no part in the civil war. After Caesar's death Plancus fought on Antony's side in the campaign of Mutina. He was driven out of Pollentia by Pontius Aquila, the legate of D. Brutus, and in his flight broke his leg. — 3. **Cn.**, brother of the two preceding, praetor elect 44, was charged by Caesar in that year with the assignment to his soldiers of lands at Buthrotum in Epirus. As Atticus possessed property in the neighbourhood, Cicero commended to Plancus with much earnestness the interests of his friend. He was praetor in 43 and was allowed by the senate to join his brother Lucius [No. 1] in Transalpine Gaul. — 4. **L. Plautius Plancus**, brother of the 3 preceding, was adopted by a L. Plautius, and therefore took his praenomen as well as nomen, but retained his original cognomen, as was the case with Metellus Scipio [METELLUS, No. 15], and Pupius Piso. [PISO, No. 13.] Before his adoption his praenomen was Caius. He was included in the proscription of the triumvirs, 43, with the consent of his brother Lucius, and was put to death.

Planudes Maximus, was one of the most learned of the Constantinopolitan monks of the last age of the Greek empire, and was greatly distinguished as a theologian, grammarian, and rhetorician; but his name is now chiefly interesting as that of the compiler of the latest of those collections of minor Greek poems, which were known by the names of *Garlands* or *Anthologies* (Στέφανοι, 'Ανθολογίαι). Planudes flourished at Constantinople in the first half of the 14th century, under the emperors Andronicus II. and III. Palaeologi. In A. D. 1327 he was sent by Andronicus II. as ambassador to Venice. As the *Anthology* of Planudes was not only the latest compiled, but was also that which was recognised as *The Greek Anthology*, until the discovery of the Anthology of Constantinus Cephalas, this is chosen as the fittest place for an account of the *Literary History of the Greek Anthology*. 1. *Materials*. The various collections, to which their compilers gave the name of *Garlands* and *Anthologies*, were made up of short poems, chiefly of an epigrammatic character, and in the elegiac metre. The earliest examples of such poetry were furnished by the inscriptions on monuments, such as those erected to commemorate heroic deeds, the statues of distinguished men, especially victors in the public games, sepulchral monuments, and dedicatory offerings in temples (ἀναθήματα); to which may be added oracles and proverbial sayings. At an early period in the history of Greek literature, poets of the highest fame cultivated this species of composition, which received its most perfect development from the hand of Simonides. Thenceforth, as a set form of poetry, it became a fit vehicle for the brief expression of thoughts and sentiments on any subject; until at last the form came to be cultivated for its own sake, and the *literati* of Alexandria and Byzantium deemed the

ability to make epigrams an essential part of the character of a scholar. Hence the mere trifling, the stupid jokes, and the wretched personalities, which form so large a part of the epigrammatic poetry contained in the Greek Anthology. — 2. *The Garland of Meleager*. At a comparatively early period in the history of Greek literature, various persons collected epigrams of particular classes, and with reference to their use as historical authorities; but the first person who made such a collection solely for its own sake, and to preserve epigrams of all kinds, was MELEAGER, a cynic philosopher of Gadara, in Palestine, about B. c. 60. His collection contained epigrams by 46 poets, of all ages of Greek poetry, up to the most ancient lyric period. He entitled it *The Garland* (Στέφανος), with reference to the common comparison of small beautiful poems to flowers. The same idea is kept up in the word *Anthology* (ἀνθολογία), which was adopted by the next compiler as the title of his work. The *Garland* of Meleager was arranged in alphabetical order, according to the initial letters of the first line of each epigram. — 3. *The Anthology of Philip of Thessalonica*, was compiled in the time of Trajan, avowedly in imitation of the *Garland* of Meleager, and chiefly with the view of adding to that collection the epigrams of more recent writers. — 4. *Diogenianus, Straton, and Diogenes Laërtius*. Shortly after Philip, in the reign of Hadrian, the learned grammarian, Diogenianus of Heraclea, compiled an Anthology, which is entirely lost. It might have been well if the same fate had befallen the very polluted collection of his contemporary, Straton of Sardis. About the same time Diogenes Laërtius collected the epigrams which are interspersed in his lives of the philosophers, into a separate book. — 5. *Agathias Scholasticus*, who lived in the time of Justinian, made a collection entitled Κύκλος ἐπιγραμμάτων. It was divided into 7 books, according to subjects. The poems included in it were those of recent writers, and chiefly those of Agathias himself and of his contemporaries, such as Paulus Silentiarius and Macedonius. — 6. *The Anthology of Constantinus Cephalas, or the Palatine Anthology*. Constantinus Cephalas appears to have lived about 4 centuries after Agathias, and to have flourished in the 10th century, under the emperor Constantinus Porphyrogenitus. The labours of preceding compilers may be viewed as merely supplementary to the *Garland* of Meleager; but the *Anthology* of Constantinus Cephalas was an entirely new collection from the preceding Anthologies and from original sources. Nothing is known of Constantine himself. The MS. of the Anthology was discovered by Salmasius in 1606, in the library of the Electors Palatine at Heidelberg. It was afterwards removed to the Vatican, with the rest of the Palatine library (1623), and has become celebrated under the names of the *Palatine Anthology* and the *Vatican Codex of the Greek Anthology*. This MS. was restored to its old home at Heidelberg after the peace of 1815.— 7. *The Anthology of Planudes* is arranged in 7 books, each of which, except the 5th and 7th, is divided into chapters according to subjects, and these chapters are arranged in alphabetical order. The contents of the books are as follows: — 1. Chiefly ἐπιδεικτικά, that is, displays of skill in this species of poetry, in 91 chapters. 2. Jocular or satiric (σκωπτικά), chaps. 53. 3. Sepulchral (ἐπιτύμβια), chaps. 32. 4. Inscriptions on statues of athletes and other works of art, descriptions of places, &c. chaps. 33. 5. The *Ecphrasis* of Christodorus, and epigrams on statues of charioteers in the Hippodrome at Constantinople. 6. Dedicatory (ἀναθηματικά), chaps. 27. 7. Amatory (ἐρωτικά). Planudes did little more than abridge and rearrange the Anthology of Constantinus Cephalas. Only a few epigrams are found in the Planudean Anthology, which are not in the Palatine.—The best editions of the Greek Anthology are by Brunck and Jacobs. Brunck's edition, which appeared under the title of *Analecta Veterum Poetarum Graecorum*, Argentorati, 1772—1776, 3 vols. 8vo, contains the whole of the Greek Anthology, besides some poems which are not properly included under that title. Brunck adopted a new arrangement : he discarded the books and chapters of the early Anthology, placed together all the epigrams of each poet, and arranged the poets themselves in chronological order, placing those epigrams, the authors of which were unknown, under the separate head of ἀδέσποτα. Jacobs' edition is founded upon Brunck's, but is much superior, and ranks as the standard edition of the Greek Anthology. It is in 13 vols. 8vo, namely, 4 vols. of the Text, one of Indices, and 3 of Commentaries, divided into 8 parts, Lips. 1795—1814. After the restoration of the MS. of the Palatine Anthology to the University of Heidelberg, Jacobs published a separate edition of the Palatine Anthology, Lips. 1813—1817, 3 vols.

Plataea, more commonly Plataeae (Πλάταια, Πλάταιαί : Πλαταιεύς), an ancient city of Boeotia, on the N. slope of Mt. Cithaeron, not far from the sources of the Asopus, and on the frontiers of Attica. It was said to have been founded by Thebes ; and its name was commonly derived from Plataea, a daughter of Asopus. The town, though not large, played an important part in Greek history, and experienced many striking vicissitudes of fortune. At an early period the Plataeans deserted the Boeotian confederacy and placed themselves under the protection of Athens ; and when the Persians invaded Attica, in B.C. 490, they sent 1000 men to the assistance of the Athenians, and had the honour of fighting on their side at the battle of Marathon. Ten years afterwards (480) their city was destroyed by the Persian army under Xerxes at the instigation of the Thebans ; and the place was still in ruins in the following year (479), when the memorable battle was fought in their territory, in which Mardonius was defeated, and the independence of Greece secured. In consequence of this victory, the territory of Plataea was declared inviolable, and Pausanias and the other Greeks swore to guarantee its independence. The sanctity of the city was still further secured by its being selected as the place in which the great festival of the Eleutheria was to be celebrated in honour of those Greeks who had fallen in the war. (See *Dict. of Antiq.* art. *Eleutheria.*) The Plataeans further received from the Greeks the large sum of 80 talents. Plataea now enjoyed a prosperity of 50 years ; but in the 3rd year of the Peloponnesian war (429) the Thebans persuaded the Spartans to attack the town, and after a siege of 2 years at length succeeded in obtaining possession of the place (427). Plataea was now razed to the ground, but was again rebuilt after the peace of Antalcidas (387). It was destroyed the 3rd time by its inveterate enemies the Thebans in 374. It was once more restored under the Macedonian supremacy, and continued in existence till a very late period. Its walls were rebuilt by Justinian.

Platamōdes (Πλαταμώδης : *Aja Kyriaki*), a promontory in the W. of Messenia.

Plătăna, -um, -us (Πλατάνη, Πλάτανον, Πλάτανος), a fortress in Phoenicia, in a narrow pass between Lebanon and the sea, near the river Damuras or Tamyras (*Damur*).

Plătĕa (Πλατέα, also -εία, -ειαί, -αία), an island on the coast of Cyrenaica, in N. Africa, the first place taken possession of by the Greek colonists under Battus. [CYRENAICA.]

Plăto (Πλάτων). 1. The comic poet, was a native of Athens, contemporary with Aristophanes, Phrynichus, Eupolis, and Pherecrates, and flourished from B.C. 428 to 389. He ranked among the very best poets of the Old Comedy. From the expressions of the grammarians, and from the large number of fragments which are preserved, it is evident that his plays were only second in popularity to those of Aristophanes. Purity of language, refined sharpness of wit, and a combination of the vigour of the Old Comedy with the greater elegance of the Middle and the New, were his chief characteristics. Suidas gives the titles of 30 of his dramas.—2. The philosopher, was the son of Ariston and Perictione or Potone, and was born at Athens either in B.C. 429 or 428. According to others, he was born in the neighbouring island of Aegina. His paternal family boasted of being descended from Codrus ; his maternal ancestors of a relationship with Solon. Plato himself mentions the relationship of Critias, his maternal uncle, with Solon. Originally, we are told, he was named after his grandfather Aristocles, but in consequence of the fluency of his speech, or, as others have it, the breadth of his chest, he acquired that name under which alone we know him. One story made him the son of Apollo ; another related that bees settled upon the lips of the sleeping child. He is also said to have contended, when a youth, in the Isthmian and other games, as well as to have made attempts in epic, lyric, and dithyrambic poetry, and not to have devoted himself to philosophy till a later time, probably after Socrates had drawn him within the magic circle of his influence. Plato was instructed in grammar, music, and gymnastics by the most distinguished teachers of that time. At an early age he had become acquainted, through Cratylus, with the doctrines of Heraclitus, and through other instructors with the philosophical dogmas of the Eleatics and of Anaxagoras. In his 20th year he is said to have betaken himself to Socrates, and became one of his most ardent admirers. After the death of Socrates (399) he withdrew to Megara, where he probably composed several of his dialogues, especially those of a dialectical character. He next went to Cyrene through friendship for the mathematician Theodorus ; and is said to have visited afterwards Egypt, Sicily, and the Greek cities in Lower Italy, through his eagerness for knowledge. The more distant journeys of Plato into the interior of Asia, to the Hebrews, Babylonians, and Assyrians, to the Magi and Persians, are mentioned only by writers on whom no reliance can be placed. That Plato, during his residence in Sicily, became acquainted, through Dion, with the elder Dionysius, but very soon fell out with the tyrant, is asserted by credible witnesses. But more doubt attaches to the story, which relates that he was given up by the tyrant to the Spartan ambassador Pollis, by him sold into Aegina, and set at liberty by the Cyrenian Anniceris. Plato is said to have visited Sicily when 40 years old, consequently in 389. After his return he began to teach, partly in the gymnasium of the Academy and its shady avenues, near the city, between the exterior Ceramicus and the hill Colonus Hippius, and partly in his garden, which was situated at Colonus. He taught gratuitously, and without doubt mainly in the form of lively dialogue ; yet on the more difficult parts of his doctrinal system he probably delivered also connected lectures. The more narrow circle of his disciples assembled themselves in his garden at common simple meals, and it was probably to them alone that the inscription said to have been set up over the vestibule of the house, " let no one enter who is unacquainted with geometry," had reference. From this house came forth his nephew Speusippus, Xenocrates of Chalcedon, Aristotle, Heraclides Ponticus, Hestiaeus of Perinthus, Philippus the Opuntian, and others, men from the most different parts of Greece. To the wider circle of those who, without attaching themselves to the more narrow community of the school, sought instruction and incitement from him, such distinguished men as Chabrias, Iphicrates, Timotheus, Phocion, Hyperides, Lycurgus, and Isocrates, are said to have belonged. Whether Demosthenes was of the number is doubtful. Even women are said to have attached themselves to him as his disciples. Plato's occupation as an instructor was twice interrupted by his voyages to Sicily; first when Dion, probably soon after the death of the elder Dionysius, persuaded him to make the attempt to win the younger Dionysius to philosophy ; the 2nd time, a few years later (about 360), when the wish of his Pythagorean friends, and the invitation of Dionysius to reconcile the disputes which had broken out between him and his step-uncle Dion, brought him back to Syracuse. His efforts were both times unsuccessful, and he owed his own safety to nothing but the earnest intercession of Archytas. That Plato cherished the hope of realising through the conversion of Dionysius his idea of a state in the rising city of Syracuse, was a belief pretty generally spread in antiquity, and which finds some confirmation in the expressions of the philosopher himself, and of the 7th Platonic letter, which, though spurious, is written with the most evident acquaintance with the matters treated of. With the exception of these 2 visits to Sicily, Plato was occupied from the time when he opened the school in the Academy in giving instruction and in the composition of his works. He died in the 82nd year of his age, B.C. 347. According to some he died while writing, according to others at a marriage feast. According to his last will his garden remained the property of the school, and passed, considerably increased by subsequent additions, into the hands of the Neo-Platonists, who kept as a festival his birth-day as well as that of Socrates. Athenians and strangers honoured his memory by monuments. Still he had no lack of enemies and enviers. He was attacked by contemporary comic poets, as Theopompus, Alexis, Cratinus the younger, and others, by one-sided Socratics, as Antisthenes, Diogenes, and the later Megarics, and also by the Epicureans, Stoics, cer-

tain Peripatetics, and later writers eager for detraction. Thus even Antisthenes and Aristoxenus charged him with sensuality, avarice, and sycophancy ; and others with vanity, ambition, and envy towards other Socratics, Protagoras, Epicharmus, and Philolaus. — **The Writings of Plato.** These writings have come down to us complete, and have always been admired as a model of the union of artistic perfection with philosophical acuteness and depth. They are in the form of dialogue ; but Plato was not the first writer who employed this style of composition for philosophical instruction. Zeno the Eleatic had already written in the form of question and answer. Alexamenus the Teian and Sophron in the mimes had treated ethical subjects in the form of dialogue. Xenophon, Aeschines, Antisthenes, Euclides, and other Socratics also had made use of the dialogical form ; but Plato has handled this form not only with greater mastery than any one who preceded him, but, in all probability, with the distinct intention of keeping by this very means true to the admonition of Socrates, not to communicate instruction, but to lead to the spontaneous discovery of it. The dialogues of Plato are closely connected with one another, and various arrangements of them have been proposed. Schleiermacher divides them into 3 series or classes. In the 1st he considers that the germs of dialectic and of the doctrine of ideas begin to unfold themselves in all the freshness of youthful inspiration ; in the 2nd those germs develop themselves further by means of dialectic investigations respecting the difference between common and philosophical acquaintance with things, respecting notion and knowledge (δόξα and ἐπιστήμη) ; in the 3rd they receive their completion by means of an objectively scientific working out, with the separation of ethics and physics. The 1st series embraces, according to Schleiermacher, the *Phaedrus, Lysis, Protagoras, Laches, Charmides, Euthyphron,* and *Parmenides;* to which may be added as an appendix the *Apologia, Crito, Ion, Hippias Minor, Hipparchus, Minos* and *Alcibiades II.* The 2nd series contains the *Gorgias, Theaetetus, Meno, Euthydemus, Cratylus, Sophistes, Politicus, Symposium, Phaedo,* and *Philebus;* to which may be added as an appendix the *Theages, Erastae, Alcibiades I., Menexenus, Hippias Major,* and *Clitophon.* The 3rd series comprises the *Republic, Timaeus, Critias,* and the *Laws.* This arrangement is perhaps the best that has hitherto been made of the dialogues, though open to exception in several particulars. The genuineness of several of the dialogues has been questioned, but for the most part on insufficient grounds. The *Epinomis,* however, is probably to be assigned to a disciple of Plato, the *Minos* and *Hipparchus* to a Socratic. The *2nd Alcibiades* was attributed by ancient critics to Xenophon. The *Anterastae* and *Clitophon* are probably of much later origin. The Platonic letters were composed at different periods ; the oldest of them, the 7th and 8th, probably by disciples of Plato. The dialogues *Demodocus, Sisyphus, Eryxias, Axiochus,* and those on justice and virtue, were with good reason regarded by ancient critics as spurious, and, with them may be associated the *Hipparchus, Theages,* and the *Definitions.* The genuineness of the 1st *Alcibiades* seems doubtful. The *smaller Hippias,* the *Ion,* and the *Menexenus,* on the other hand, which are assailed by many modern cities, may very well maintain their ground as occasional compositions of Plato.—The Philosophy of Plato. The nature of this work will allow only a few brief remarks upon this subject. The attempt to combine poetry and philosophy (the two fundamental tendencies of the Greek mind), gives to the Platonic dialogues a charm, which irresistibly attracts us, though we may have but a deficient comprehension of their subject-matter. Plato, like Socrates, was penetrated with the idea that wisdom is the attribute of the Godhead; that philosophy, springing from the impulse *to know*, is the necessity of the intellectual man, and the greatest of the blessings in which he participates. When once we strive after Wisdom with the intensity of a lover, she becomes the true consecration and purification of the soul, adapted to lead us from the night-like to the true day. An approach to wisdom, however, presupposes an original communion with *Being*, truly so called; and this communion again presupposes the divine nature or immortality of the soul, and the impulse to become like the Eternal. This impulse is the love which generates in Truth, and the development of it is termed *Dialectics*. Out of the philosophical impulse which is developed by *Dialectics* not only correct knowledge, but also correct action springs forth. Socrates' doctrine respecting the unity of virtue, and that it consists in true, vigorous, and practical knowledge, is intended to be set forth in a preliminary manner in the Protagoras and the smaller dialogues attached to it. They are designed, therefore, to introduce a foundation for ethics, by the refutation of the common views that were entertained of morals and of virtue. For although not even the words ethics and physics occur in Plato, and even dialectics are not treated of as a distinct and separate province, yet he must rightly be regarded as the originator of the threefold division of philosophy, inasmuch as he had before him the decided object to develop the Socratic method into a scientific system of dialectics, that should supply the grounds of our knowledge as well as of our moral action (physics and ethics), and therefore he separates the general investigations on knowledge and understanding, at least relatively, from those which refer to physics and ethics. Accordingly, the Theaetetus, Sophistes, Parmenides, and Cratylus, are principally dialectical; the Protagoras, Gorgias, Politicus, Philebus, and the Politics, principally ethical; while the Timaeus is exclusively physical. Plato's dialectics and ethics, however, have been more successful than his physics.—Plato's doctrine of *ideas* was one of the most prominent parts of his system. He maintained that the existence of things, cognisable only by means of conception, is their true essence, their *idea*. Hence he asserts that to deny the reality of ideas is to destroy all scientific research. He departed from the original meaning of the word idea (namely, that of form or figure), inasmuch as he understood by it the unities (ἑνάδες, μονάδες) which lie at the basis of the visible, the changeable, and which can only be reached by pure thinking. He included under the expression *idea* every thing stable amidst the changes of mere phenomena, all really existing and unchangeable definitudes, by which the changes of things and our knowledge of them are conditioned, such as the ideas of genus and species, the laws and ends of nature, as also the principles of cognition, and of moral action, and the essences

of individual, concrete, thinking souls. His system of ethics was founded upon his dialectica, as is remarked above. Hence he asserted that not being in a condition to grasp the idea of the good with full distinctness, we are able to approximate to it only so far as we elevate the power of thinking to its original purity. — The best editions of the collected works of Plato are by Bekker, Berol. 1816—1818, by Stallbaum, Gotha, 1827, seq., and by Orelli and others, Turic. 1839.

Plautia Gens, a plebeian gens at Rome. The name is also written *Plotius*, just as we have both *Clodius* and *Claudius*. The gens was divided into the families of *Hypsaeus, Proculus, Silvanus, Veino, Venox*; and although several members of these families obtained the consulship, none of them are of sufficient importance to require a separate notice.

Plautiānus, Fulvius, an African by birth, the fellow-townsman of Septimius Severus. He served as praefect of the praetorium under this emperor, who loaded him with honours and wealth, and virtually made over much of the imperial authority into his hands. Intoxicated by these distinctions, Plautianus indulged in the most despotic tyranny, and perpetrated acts of cruelty almost beyond belief. In A. D. 202 his daughter Plautilla was married to Caracalla; but having discovered the dislike cherished by Caracalla towards both his daughter and himself, and looking forward with apprehension to the downfall which awaited him upon the death of the sovereign, he formed a plot against the life both of Septimius and Caracalla. His treachery was discovered, and he was immediately put to death, 203. His daughter Plautilla was banished first to Sicily, and subsequently to Lipara, where she was treated with the greatest harshness. After the murder of Geta, in 212, Plautilla was put to death by order of her husband.

Plautilla. [PLAUTIANUS.]

Plautius. 1. A., a man of consular rank, who was sent by the emperor Claudius in A. D. 43 to subdue Britain. He remained in Britain 4 years, and subdued the S. part of the island. He obtained an ovation on his return to Rome in 47. — 2. A Roman jurist, who lived about the time of Vespasian, and is cited by subsequent jurists.

Plautus, the most celebrated comic poet of Rome, was a native of Sarsina, a small village in Umbria. He is usually called *M. Accius Plautus*, but his real name, as an eminent modern scholar has shown, was T. **Maccius Plautus**. The date of his birth is uncertain, but it may be placed about B. C. 254. He probably came to Rome at an early age, since he displays such a perfect mastery of the Latin language, and an acquaintance with Greek literature, which he could hardly have acquired in a provincial town. Whether he ever obtained the Roman franchise is doubtful. When he arrived at Rome he was in needy circumstances, and was first employed in the service of the actors. With the money he had saved in this inferior station he left Rome and set up in business: but his speculations failed; he returned to Rome, and his necessities obliged him to enter the service of a baker, who employed him in turning a handmill. While in this degrading occupation he wrote 3 plays, the sale of which to the managers of the public games enabled him to quit his drudgery, and begin his literary career. He was then probably about 30 years of age (224), and accordingly commenced writing comedies a few years before the breaking out of the 2nd Punic war. He continued his literary occupation for about 40 years, and died in 184, when he was 70 years of age. His contemporaries at first were Livius Andronicus and Naevius, afterwards Ennius and Caecilius: Terence did not rise into notice till almost 20 years after his death. . During the long time that he held possession of the stage, he was always a great favourite of the people; and he expressed a bold consciousness of his own powers in the epitaph which he wrote for his tomb, and which has come down to us : —

" Postquam est mortem aptus Plautus, comoedia luget
  Scena deserta, dein risus, ludus jocusque
  Et numeri innumeri simul omnes collacrumarunt."

Plautus wrote a great number of comedies, and in the last century of the republic there were 130 plays, which bore his name. Most of these however were not considered genuine by the best Roman critics. There were several works written upon the subject; and of these the most celebrated was the treatise of Varro, entitled *Quaestiones Plautinae*. Varro limited the undoubted comedies of the poet to 21, which were hence called the *Fabulae Varronianae*. These Varronian comedies are the same as those which have come down to our own time, with the loss of one. At present we possess only 20 comedies of Plautus ; but there were originally 21 in the manuscripts, and the *Vidularia*, which was the 21st, and which came last in the collection, was torn off from the manuscript in the middle ages. The titles of the 21 Varronian plays are : 1. *Amphitruo*. 2. *Asinaria*. 3. *Aulularia*. 4. *Captivi*. 5. *Curculio*. 6. *Casina*. 7. *Cistellaria*. 8. *Epidicus*. 9. *Bacchides*. 10. *Mostellaria*. 11. *Menaechmi*. 12. *Miles*. 13. *Mercator*. 14. *Pseudolus*. 15. *Poenulus*. 16. *Persa*. 17. *Rudens*. 18. *Stichus*. 19. *Trinummus*. 20. *Truculentus*. 21. *Vidularia*. This is the order in which they occur in the manuscripts, though probably not the one in which they were originally arranged by Varro. The present order is evidently alphabetical ; the initial letter of the title of each play is alone regarded, and no attention is paid to those which follow: hence we find *Captivi*, *Curculio*, *Casina*, *Cistellaria : Mostellaria*, *Menaechmi*, *Miles*, *Mercator : Pseudolus*, *Poenulus*, *Persa*. The play of the *Bacchides* forms the only exception to the alphabetical order. It was probably placed after the *Epidicus* by some copyist, because he had observed that Plautus, in the *Bacchides* (ii. 2. 36), referred to the *Epidicus* as an earlier work. The names of the comedies are either taken from some leading character in the play, or from some circumstance which occurs in it: those titles ending in *aria* are adjectives, giving a general description of the play: thus *Asinaria* is the " Ass-Comedy." The comedies of Plautus enjoyed unrivalled popularity among the Romans, and continued to be represented down to the time of Diocletian. The continued popularity of Plautus through so many centuries was owing, in a great measure, to his being a national poet. Though he founds his plays upon Greek models, the characters in them act, speak, and joke like genuine Romans, and he thereby secured the sympathy of his audience more completely than Terence could ever have done. Whether Plautus borrowed the plan of all his plays from Greek mo-

dels, it is impossible to say. The *Cistellaria*, *Bacchides*, *Poenulus*, and *Stichus*, were taken from Menander, the *Casina* and *Rudens* from Diphilus, and the *Mercator* and the *Trinummus* from Philemon, and many others were undoubtedly founded upon Greek originals. But in all cases Plautus allowed himself much greater liberty than Terence; and in some instances he appears to have simply taken the leading idea of the play from the Greek, and to have filled it up in his own fashion. It has been inferred from a well-known line of Horace (*Epist.* ii. 1. 58), " Plautus ad exemplar Siculi properare Epicharmi," that Plautus took great pains to imitate Epicharmus. But there is no correspondence between any of the existing plays of Plautus and the known titles of the comedies of Epicharmus; and the verb *properare* probably has reference only to the liveliness and energy of Plautus's style, in which he bore a resemblance to the Sicilian poet. It was, however, not only with the common people that Plautus was a favourite; educated Romans read and admired his works down to the latest times. Cicero (*de Off.* i. 29) places his wit on a par with that of the old Attic comedy, and ' St. Jerome used to console himself with the perusal of the poet after spending many nights in tears, on account of his past sins. The favourable opinion which the ancients entertained of the merits of Plautus has been confirmed by the judgment of the best modern critics, and by the fact that several of his plays have been imitated by many of the best modern poets. Thus the *Amphitruo* has been imitated by Molière and Dryden, the *Aulularia* by Molière in his *Avare* the *Mostellaria* by Regnard, Addison, and others, the *Menaechmi* by Shakspere in his *Comedy of Errors*, the *Trinummus* by Lessing in his *Schatz*, and so with others. Horace (*De Arte Poët.* 270), indeed, expresses a less favourable opinion of Plautus ; but it must be recollected that the taste of Horace had been formed by a different school of literature, and that he disliked the ancient poets of his country. Moreover, it is probable that the censure of Horace does not refer to the general character of Plautus's poetry, but merely to his inharmonious verses and to some of his jests. The text of Plautus has come down to us in a very corrupt state. It contains many lacunae and interpolations. Thus the *Aulularia* has lost its conclusion, the *Bacchides* its commencement, &c. Of the present complete editions the best are by Bothe, Lips. 1834, 2 vols. 8vo., and by Weise, Quedlinb. 1837—1838, 2 vols. 8vo. ; but Ritschl's edition, of which the 1st volume has only yet appeared (Bonn, 1849), will far surpass all others.

Plavis (*Piave*), a river in Venetia in the N. of Italy, which fell into the Sinus Tergestinus.

Pleiades (Πλειάδες or Πελειάδες), the Pleiads, are usually called the daughters of Atlas and Pleïone, whence they bear the name of the *Atlantides*. They were called *Vergiliae* by the Romans. They were the sisters of the Hyades, and 7 in number, 6 of whom are described as visible, and the 7th as invisible. Some call the 7th Sterope, and relate that she became invisible from shame, because she alone among her sisters had had intercourse with a mortal man ; others call her Electra, and make her disappear from the choir of her sisters on account of her grief at the destruction of the house of Dardanus. The Pleiades are said to have made away with themselves from grief at the death of their sisters, the Hyades, or at the fate of their father Atlas, and were afterwards placed as stars at the back of Taurus, where they formed a cluster resembling a bunch of grapes, whence they were sometimes called βότρυς. According to another story, the Pleiades were virgin companions of Artemis, and, together with their mother Pleione, were pursued by the hunter Orion in Boeotia; their prayer to be rescued from him was heard by the gods, and they were metamorphosed into doves (πελ ιάδες), and placed among the stars. The rising of the Pleiades in Italy was about the beginning of May, and their setting about the beginning of November. Their names are Electra, Maia, Taygete, Alcyone, Celaeno, Sterope, and Merope.

Plemmyrium (Πλεμμύριον : *Punta di Gigante*), a promontory on the S. coast of Sicily, immediately S. of Syracuse.

Plēīōnē (Πληίόνη), a daughter of Oceanus, and mother of the Pleiades by Atlas. [ATLAS; PLEIADES]

Pleumoxīī, a small tribe in Gallia Belgica, subject to the Nervii.

Pleuratus (Πλεύρατος), king of Illyria, was the son of Scerdilaīdas. His name occurs as an ally of the Romans in the 2nd Punic war, and in their subsequent wars in Greece.

Pleurōn (Πλευρών : Πλευρώνιος), an ancient city in Aetolia, and along with Calydon the most important in the country, was situated at a little distance from the coast, N.W. of the mouth of the Evenus, and on the S. slope of Mt. Aracynthus or Curius. It was originally inhabited by the Curetes. This ancient city was abandoned by its inhabitants, when Demetrius II. King of Macedon, laid waste the surrounding country, and a new city was built under the same name to the W. of the ancient one. The 2 cities are distinguished by geographers under the names of Old Pleuron and New Pleuron respectively.

Plīnīus. 1. C. Plīnīus Secundus, the celebrated author of the *Historia Naturalis*, and frequently called Pliny the Elder, was born A. D. 23, either at Verona or Novum Comum (*Como*) in the N. of Italy. But whichever was the place of his birth, it is certain that his family belonged to Novum Comum, since the estates of the elder Pliny were situated there, the younger Pliny was born there, and several inscriptions found in the neighbourhood relate to various members of the family. He came to Rome while still young, and being descended from a family of wealth and distinction, he had the means at his disposal for availing himself of the instruction of the best teachers to be found in the imperial city. At the age of about 23 he went to Germany, where he served under L. Pomponius Secundus, of whom he afterwards wrote a memoir, and was appointed to the command of a troop of cavalry (*praefectus ulae*). It appears from notices of his own that he travelled over most of the frontier of Germany, having visited the Cauci, the sources of the Danube, &c. It was in the intervals snatched from his military duties that he composed his treatise *de Jaculatione equestri*. At the same time he commenced a history of the Germanic wars, which he afterwards completed in 20 books. He returned to Rome with Pomponius (52), and applied himself to the study of jurisprudence. He practised for some time as a pleader, but does not seem to have distinguished himself very greatly in that capacity. The greater part of the reign of Nero he spent in retirement, chiefly, no doubt, at his native place. It may have been with a view to the education of his nephew that he composed the work entitled *Studiosus*, an extensive treatise in 3 books, occupying 6 volumes, in which he marked out the course that should be pursued in the training of a young orator, from the cradle to the completion of his education and his entrance into public life. During the reign of Nero he wrote a grammatical work in 8 books, entitled *Dubius Sermo ;* and towards the close of the reign of this emperor he was appointed procurator in Spain. He was here in 71, when his brother-in-law died, leaving his son, the younger Pliny, to the guardianship of his uncle, who, on account of his absence, was obliged to entrust the care of him to Virginius Rufus. Pliny returned to Rome in the reign of Vespasian, shortly before 73, when he adopted his nephew. He had known Vespasian in the Germanic wars, and the emperor received him into the number of his most intimate friends. It was at this period of his life that he wrote a continuation of the history of Aufidius Bassus, in 31 books, carrying the narrative down to his own times. Of his manner of life at this period an interesting account has been preserved by his nephew (*Epist.* iii. 5). It was his practice to begin to spend a portion of the night in studying by candle-light, at the festival of the Vulcanalia (towards the end of August), at first at a late hour of the night, in winter at 1 or 2 o'clock in the morning. Before it was light he betook himself to the emperor Vespasian, and after executing such commissions as he might be charged with, returned home and devoted the time which he still had remaining to study. After a slender meal he would, in the summer-time, lie in the sunshine while some one read to him, he himself making notes and extracts. He never read anything without making extracts in this way, for he used to say that there was no book so bad but that some good might be got out of it. He would then take a cold bath, and after a slight repast sleep a very little, and then pursue his studies till the time of the coena. During this meal some book was read to, and commented on by him. At table, as might be supposed, he spent but a short time. Such was his mode of life when in the midst of the bustle and confusion of the city. When in retirement in the country, the time spent in the bath was nearly the only interval not allotted to study, and that he reduced to the narrowest limits ; for during all the process of scraping and rubbing he had some book read to him, or himself dictated. When on a journey he had a secretary by his side with a book and tablets. By this incessant application, persevered in throughout life, he amassed an enormous amount of materials, and at his death left to his nephew 160 volumina of notes (*electorum commentarii*), written extremely small on both sides. With some reason might his nephew say that, when compared with Pliny, those who had spent their whole lives in literary pursuits seemed as if they had spent them in nothing else than sleep and idleness. From the materials which he had in this way collected he compiled his celebrated *Historia Naturalis*, which he published about 77. The details of Pliny's death are given in a letter of the younger Pliny to Tacitus (*Ep.* vi. 16). He perished in the celebrated eruption of Vesuvius, which overwhelmed Herculaneum and Pompeii, in 79 being 56 years of age. He was at the time stationed at Misenum in the command of the Roman fleet; and it was his anxiety to examine more closely the extraordinary phaenomenon, which led him to sail to Stabiae, where he landed and perished. The only work of Pliny which has come down to us is his *Historia Naturalis*. By Natural History the ancients understood more than modern writers would usually include in the subject. It embraced astronomy, meteorology, geography, mineralogy, zoology, botany,—in short, every thing that does not relate to the results of human skill or the products of human faculties. Pliny, however, has not kept within even these extensive limits. He has broken in upon the plan implied by the title of the work, by considerable digressions on human inventions and institutions (book vii.), and on the history of the fine arts (xxxv.—xxxvii.) Minor digressions on similar topics are also interspersed in various parts of the work, the arrangement of which in other respects exhibits but little scientific discrimination. It comprises, as Pliny says in the preface, 20,000 matters of importance, drawn from about 2000 volumes. It is divided into 37 books, the 1st of which consists of a dedicatory epistle to Titus, followed by a table of contents of the other books. When it is remembered that this work was not the result of the undistracted labour of a life, but written in the hours of leisure secured from active pursuits, and that too by the author of other extensive works, it is, to say the least, a wonderful monument of human industry. It may easily be supposed that Pliny, with his inordinate appetite for accumulating knowledge out of books, was not the man to produce a scientific work of any value. He was not even an original observer. The materials which he worked up into his huge encyclopaedic compilation were almost all derived at second-hand, though doubtless he has incorporated the results of his own observation in a larger number of instances than those in which he indicates such to be the case. Nor did he, as a compiler, show either judgment or discrimination in the selection of his materials, so that in his accounts the true and the false are found intermixed. His love of the marvellous, and his contempt for human nature, lead him constantly to introduce what is strange or wonderful, or adapted to illustrate the wickedness of man, and the unsatisfactory arrangements of Providence. His work is of course valuable to us from the vast number of subjects treated of, with regard to many of which we have no other sources of information. But what he tells us is often unintelligible, from his retailing accounts of things with which he was himself personally unacquainted, and of which he in consequence gives no satisfactory idea to the reader. Though a writer on zoology, botany, and mineralogy, he has no pretensions to be called a naturalist. His compilations exhibit scarcely a trace of scientific arrangement; and frequently it can be shown that he does not give the true sense of the authors whom he quotes and translates, giving not uncommonly wrong Latin names to the objects spoken of by his Greek authorities. The best editions of Pliny's Natural History, with a commentary, are by Hardouin (Paris, 1685, 5 vols. 4to.; 2nd edit. 1723, 3 vols. fol.), and by Panckoucke (Paris, 1829—1833, 20 vols.), with a French translation and notes by Cuvier and other eminent scientific

and literary men of France. The most valuable critical edition of the text of Pliny is by Sillig (Lips. 1831—1836, 5 vols. 12mo.).—2. C. Plinius Caecilius Secundus, frequently called Pliny the younger, was the son of C. Caecilius, and of Plinia, the sister of the elder Pliny. He was born at Comum in A. D. 61; and having lost his father at an early age, he was adopted by his uncle, as has been mentioned above. His education was conducted under the care of his uncle, his mother, and his tutor, Virginius Rufus. From his youth he was devoted to letters. In his 14th year he wrote a Greek tragedy. He studied eloquence under Quintilian. His acquirements finally gained him the reputation of being one of the most learned men of the age; and his friend Tacitus, the historian, had the same honourable distinction. He was also an orator. In his 19th year he began to speak in the forum, and he was frequently employed as an advocate before the court of the Centumviri and before the Roman senate. He filled numerous offices in succession. While a young man he served in Syria as tribunus militum, and was there a hearer of the stoic Euphrates and of Artemidorus. He was subsequently quaestor Caesaris, praetor in or about 93, and consul 100, in which year he wrote his *Panegyricus*, which is addressed to Trajan. In 103 he was appointed propraetor of the province Pontica, where he did not stay quite 2 years. Among his other functions he also discharged that of curator of the channel and the banks of the Tiber. He was twice married. His 2nd wife was Calpurnia, the granddaughter of Calpurnius Fabatus, and an accomplished woman: she was considerably younger than her husband, who has recorded her kind attentions to him. He had no children by either wife born alive. The life of Pliny is chiefly known from his letters. So far as this evidence shows, he was a kind and benevolent man, fond of literary pursuits, and of building on and improving his estates. He was rich, and he spent liberally. He was a kind master to his slaves. His body was feeble, and his health not good. Nothing is known as to the time of his death. The extant works of Pliny are his *Panegyricus* and the 10 books of his *Epistolae*. The *Panegyricus* is a fulsome eulogium on Trajan; it is of small value for the information which it contains about the author himself and his times. Pliny collected his own letters, as appears from the 1st letter of the 1st book, which looks something like a preface to the whole collection. It is not an improbable conjecture that he may have written many of his letters with a view to publication, or that when he was writing some of them the idea of future publication was in his mind. However, they form a very agreeable collection, and make us acquainted with many interesting facts in the life of Pliny and that of his contemporaries. The letters from Pliny to Trajan and the emperor's replies are the most valuable part of the collection: they form the whole of the 10th book. The letter on the punishment of the Christians (x. 97), and the emperor's answer (x. 98), have furnished matter for much remark. The fact of a person admitting himself to be a Christian was sufficient for his condemnation; and the punishment appears to have been death. The Christians, on their examination, admitted nothing further than their practice of meeting on a fixed day before it was light, and singing a hymn to

Christ, as God (*quasi Deo*); their oath (whatever Pliny may mean by *sacramentum*) was not to bind them to any crime, but to avoid theft, robbery, adultery, breach of faith, and denial of a deposit. Two female slaves, who were said to be deaconesses (*ministrae*), were put to the torture by Pliny, but nothing unfavourable to the Christians could be got out of them: the governor could detect nothing except a perverse and extravagant superstition (*superstitionem pravam et immodicam*). Hereupon he asked the emperor's advice, for the contagion of the superstition was spreading; yet he thought that it might be stopped. The emperor in his reply approves of the governor's conduct, as explained in his letter, and observes that no general rule can be laid down. Persons supposed to be Christians are not to be sought for: if they are accused and the charge is proved, they are to be punished; but if a man denied the charge, and could prove its falsity by offering his prayers to the heathen gods (*diis nostris*), however suspected he may have been, he shall be excused in respect of his repentance. Charges of accusation (*libelli*) without the name of the informant or accuser, were not to be received, as they had been: it was a thing of the worst example, and unsuited to the age. One of the best editions of the *Epistolae* and *Panegyricus* is by Schaefer, Lips. 1805. The best editions of the *Epistolae* are by Cortius and Longolius, Amsterdam, 1734, and by Gierig, Lips. 1800.

Plinthine (Πλινθίνη), a city of Lower Egypt, on the bay called from it **Sinus Plinthinetes** (Πλινθινήτης κόλπος), was the W.-most city of Egypt (according to its narrower limits) on the frontier of Marmarica. It stood a little N. of Taposiris (*Aboussir*).

Plistarchus (Πλείσταρχος), king of Sparta, was the son and successor of Leonidas, who was killed at Thermopylae, B.C. 480. He reigned from 480 to 458, but being a mere child at the time of his father's death, the regency was assumed by his cousin Pausanias. It appears that the latter continued to administer affairs in the name of the young king till his own death, about 467.

Plisthenes (Πλεισθένης), son of Atreus, and husband of Aërope or Eriphyle, by whom he became the father of Agamemnon, Menelaus, and Anaxibia; but Homer makes the latter the children of Atreus. See AGAMEMNON, ATREUS.

Plistia (*Prestia*), a village in Samnium in the valley between M. Tifata and Taburnus.

Plistoanax or **Plistonax** (Πλεισ τοάναξ, Πλεισ τώναξ), king of Sparta, was the eldest son of the Pausanias who conquered at Plataea, B.C. 479. On the death of Plistarchus, in 458, without issue, Plistoanax succeeded to the throne, being yet a minor. He reigned from 458 to 408. In 445 he invaded Attica; but the premature withdrawal of his army from the enemy's territory exposed him to the suspicion of having been bribed by Pericles. He was punished by a heavy fine, which he was unable to pay, and was therefore obliged to leave his country. He remained 19 years in exile, taking up his abode near the temple of Zeus on Mt. Lycaeus in Arcadia, and having half his house within the sacred precincts that he might enjoy the benefit of the sanctuary. During this period his son Pausanias, a minor, reigned in his stead. The Spartans at length recalled him in 426, in obedience to the injunctions of the Delphic oracle. But

he was accused of having tampered with the Pythian priestess to induce her to interpose for him, and his alleged impiety in this matter was continually assigned by his enemies as the cause of all Sparta's misfortunes in the war; and therefore it was that he used all his influence to bring about peace with Athens in 421. He was succeeded by his son Pausanias.

Plistus (Πλεῖστός: *Xeropotamo*), a small river in Phocis, which rises in Mt. Parnassus, flows past Delphi, where it receives the small stream Castalia, and falls into the Crissaean gulf near Cirrha.

Plotina, Pompeia, the wife of the emperor Trajan, and a woman of extraordinary merit and virtue. As she had no children, she persuaded her husband to adopt Hadrian. She died in the reign of Hadrian, who honoured her memory by mourning for her 9 days, by building a temple in her honour, and by composing hymns in her praise.

Plotinopolis (Πλωτινόπολις), a town in Thrace on the road from Trajanopolis to Hadrianopolis, founded by Trajan, and named in honour of his wife Plotina.

Plotinus (Πλωτῖνος), the originator of the Neo-Platonic system, was born at Lycopolis in Egypt, about A.D. 203. The details of his life have been preserved by his disciple Porphyry in a biography which has come down to us. From him we learn that Plotinus began to study philosophy in his 28th year, and remained 11 years under the instruction of Ammonius Saccas. In his 39th year he joined the expedition of the emperor Gordian (242) against the Persians, in order to become acquainted with the philosophy of the Persians and Indians. After the death of Gordian he fled to Antioch, and from thence to Rome (244). For the first 10 years of his residence at Rome he gave only oral instructions to a few friends; but he was at length induced in 254 to commit his instructions to writing. In this manner when, 10 years later (264) Porphyry came to Rome and joined himself to Plotinus, 21 books of very various contents had been already composed by him. During the 6 years that Porphyry lived with Plotinus at Rome, the latter, at the instigation of Amelius and Porphyry, wrote 23 books on the subjects which had been discussed in their meetings, to which 9 books were afterwards added. Of the 54 books of Plotinus, Porphyry remarks, that the first 21 books were of a lighter character, that only the 23 following were the production of the matured powers of the author, and that the other 9, especially the 4 last, were evidently written with diminished vigour. The correction of these 54 books was committed to Plotinus himself to the care of Porphyry. On account of the weakness of his sight, Plotinus never read them through a second time, to say nothing of making corrections; intent simply upon the *matter*, he was alike careless of orthography, of the division of the syllables, and the clearness of his handwriting. The 54 books was divided by Porphyry into 6 *Enneads*, or sets of 9 books. Plotinus was eloquent in his oral communications, and was said to be very clever in finding the appropriate word, even if he failed in accuracy on the whole. Besides this, the beauty of his person was increased when discoursing; his countenance was lighted up with genius, and covered with small drops of perspiration. He lived on the scantiest fare, and his hours of sleep were restricted

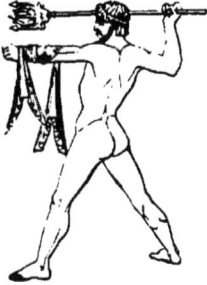

Poseidon (Neptune). (From a Medal of
Demetrius Poliorcetes.) Page 609.

Poseidon (Neptune).
(Coin of Hadrian.) Page 9.

Priapus. Visconti, Mus. Pio. Clem., vol. I, pl. 50. Page 613.

Psyche. (From an ancient Gem.) Page 621.

The Cyclops Polyphemus. (Zoega, Bassirilievi, tav. 37.) Pages 600, 601

[To face p. 592.]

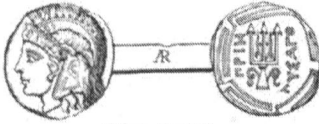

Priene. Page 613.

Saguntum. Page 665.

Ressina. Page 641.

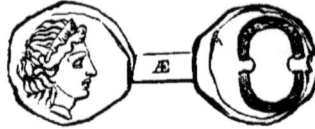

Salamis. Page 665.

Rhegium. Page 648.

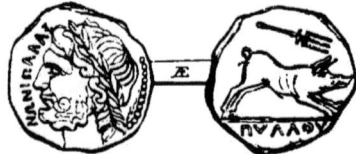

Salapia in Apulia. Page 666.

Rhodus. Page 645.

Salmantica. Page 668.

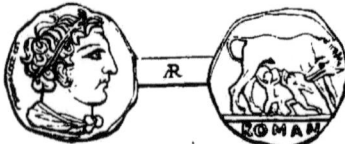

Roma. Page 647.

Samos. Page 670.

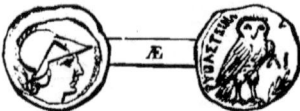

Rubi in Apulia. Page 650.

Samosata in Syria. Page 671.

to the briefest time possible. He was regarded with admiration and respect not only by men of science like the philosophers Amelius, Porphyry, the physicians Paulinus, Eustochius, and Zethus the Arab, but even by senators and other statesmen. He enjoyed the favour of the emperor Gallienus, and the empress Salonina, and almost obtained from them the rebuilding of two destroyed towns in Campania, with the view of their being governed according to the laws of Plato. He died at Puteoli in 262. The philosophical system of Plotinus is founded upon Plato's writings, with the addition of various tenets drawn from the Oriental philosophy and religion. He appears however to avoid studiously all reference to the Oriental origin of his tenets ; he endeavours to find them all under the veil of the Greek mythology, and points out here the germ of his own philosophical and religious convictions. Plotinus is not guilty of that commixture and falsification of the Oriental mythology and mysticism, which is found in Iamblichus, Proclus, and others of the Neo-Platonic school. The best edition of the Enneads of Plotinus is by Kreuzer, Oxonii, 1835, 3 vols. 4to.

PLŌTIUS, whose full name was MARIUS PLOTIUS SACERDOS, a Latin grammarian, the author of De Metris Liber, who probably lived in the 5th or 6th century of the Christian aera. His work is published by Putschius in the Grammaticae Latinae Auctores, Hannov. 1605, and by Gaisford in the Scriptores Latini Rei Metricae, Oxon. 1837.

Plutarchus (Πλούταρχος). 1. Tyrant of Eretria in Euboea, whom the Athenians assisted in B. C. 354 against his rival, Callias of Chalcis. The Athenian army was commanded by Phocion, who defeated Callias at Tamynae ; but Phocion having suspected Plutarchus of treachery, expelled him from Eretria.—2. The biographer and philosopher, was born at Chaeronea in Boeotia. The year of his birth is not known; but we learn from Plutarch himself, that he was studying philosophy under Ammonius at the time when Nero was making his progress through Greece, in A. D. 66 ; from which we may assume that he was a youth or a young man at that time. He spent some time at Rome, and in other parts of Italy; but he tells us that he did not learn the Latin language in Italy, because he was occupied with public commissions, and in giving lectures on philosophy; and it was late in life before he busied himself with Roman literature. He was lecturing at Rome during the reign of Domitian, but the statement of Suidas that Plutarch was the preceptor of Trajan, ought to be rejected. Plutarch spent the later years of his life at Chaeronea, where he discharged various magisterial offices, and held a priesthood. The time of his death is unknown.—The work which has immortalised Plutarch's name is his Parallel Lives (Βίοι Παράλληλοι) of 46 Greeks and Romans. The 46 Lives are arranged in pairs; each pair contains the life of a Greek and a Roman, and is followed by a comparison of the two men : in a few pairs the comparison is omitted or lost. He seems to have considered each pair of Lives and the Parallel as making one book (Βιβλίον). The 46 Lives are the following :— 1. Theseus and Romulus; 2. Lycurgus and Numa ; 3. Solon and Valerius Publicola ; 4. Themistocles and Camillus ; 5. Pericles and Q. Fabius Maximus ; 6. Alcibiades and Coriolanus ; 7. Timoleon and Aemilius Paulus ; 8. Pelopidas and Marcellus ; 9. Aristides and Cato the Elder ;

10. Philopoemen and Flamininus; 11. Pyrrhus and Marius ; 12. Lysander and Sulla ; 13. Cimon and Lucullus ; 14. Nicias and Crassus ; 15. Eumenes and Sertorius ; 16. Agesilaus and Pompeius ; 17. Alexander and Caesar; 18. Phocion and Cato the Younger ; 19. Agis and Cleomenes, and Tiberius and Caius Gracchi ; 20. Demosthenes and Cicero ; 21. Demetrius Poliorcetes and M. Antonius ; 22. Dion and M. Junius Brutus. There are also the Lives of Artaxerxes Mnemon, Aratus, Galba, and Otho, which are placed in the editions after the 46 Lives. Perhaps no work of antiquity has been so extensively read in modern times as Plutarch's Lives. The reason of their popularity is that Plutarch has rightly conceived the business of a biographer: his biography is true portraiture. Other biography is often a dull, tedious enumeration of facts in the order of time, with perhaps a summing up of character at the end. The reflections of Plutarch are neither impertinent, nor trifling : his sound good sense is always there : his honest purpose is transparent : his love of humanity warms the whole. His work is and will remain, in spite of all the fault that can be found with it by plodding collectors of facts, and small critics, the book of those who can nobly think, and dare and do. The best edition of the Lives is by Sintenis, Lips. 1839—1846, 4 vols. 8vo. — Plutarch's other writings, above 60 in number, are placed under the general title of Moralia or Ethical works, though some of them are of an historical and anecdotical character, such as the essay on the malignity (κακοήθεια) of Herodotus, which neither requires nor merits refutation, and his Apophthegmata, many of which are of little value. Eleven of these essays are generally classed among Plutarch's historical works: among them, also, are his Roman Questions or Inquiries, his Greek Questions, and the Lives of the Ten Orators. But it is likely enough that several of the essays which are included in the Moralia of Plutarch, are not by him. At any rate, some of them are not worth reading. The best of the essays included among the Moralia are of a different stamp. There is no philosophical system in these essays: pure speculation was not Plutarch's province. His best writings are practical; and their merits consist in the soundness of his views on the ordinary events of human life, and in the benevolence of his temper. His " Marriage Precepts " are a sample of his good sense, and of his happiest expression. He rightly appreciated the importance of a good education, and he gives much sound advice on the bringing up of children. The best edition of the Moralia is by Wyttenbach: it consists of 6 volumes of text (Oxon. 1795—1800), and 2 volumes of notes (Oxon. 1810—1821). The best editions of all the works of Plutarch are by Reiske, Lips. 1774— 1782, 12 vols. 8vo., and by Hutten, 1791—1805, 14 vols. 8vo. — 3. The younger, was a son of the last, and is supposed by some to have been the author of several of the works which pass usually for his father's, as e. g. the Apophthegmata. — 4. An Athenian, son of Nestorius, presided with distinction over the Neo-Platonic school at Athens in the early part of the 5th century, and was surnamed the Great. He numbered among his disciples Syrianus of Alexandria, who succeeded him as head of the school, and Proclus of Lycia. He wrote commentaries, which are lost, on the " Timaeus " of Plato, and on Aristotle's treatise

Q Q

" On the Soul." He died at an advanced age, about A. D. 430.

Plūto or Plūton (Πλούτων), the giver of wealth, at first a surname of Hades, the god of the lower world, and afterwards used as the real name of the god. In the latter sense it first occurs in Euripides. An account of the god is given under HADES.

Plūtus (Πλοῦτος), sometimes called Pluton, the personification of wealth, is described as a son of Iasion and Demeter. [IASION.] Zeus is said to have deprived him of sight, that he might not bestow his favours on righteous men exclusively, but that he might distribute his gifts blindly and without any regard to merit. At Thebes there was a statue of Tyche or Fortune, at Athens one of Irene or Peace, and at Thespiae one of Athena Ergane; and in each of these cases Plutus was represented as the child of those divinities, symbolically expressing the sources of wealth. He seems to have been commonly represented as a boy with a Cornucopia.

Pluviālia (Πλουιτάλια, Ptol.: prob. Ferro), one of the islands in the Atlantic, called FORTUNATAE.

Plūvius, i. e. the sender of rain, a surname of Jupiter among the Romans, to whom sacrifices were offered during long protracted droughts.

Pnytagōras (Πνυταγόρας). 1. Eldest son of Evagoras, king of Salamis in Cyprus, was assassinated along with his father, B. C. 374. — 2. King of Salamis in Cyprus, probably succeeded Nicocles, though we have no account of his accession, or his relation to the previous monarchs. He submitted to Alexander in 332, and served with a fleet under that monarch at the siege of Tyre.

Podalīrius (Ποδαλείριος), son of Aesculapius and Epione or Arsinoe, and brother of Machaon, along with whom he led the Thessalians of Tricca against Troy. He was, like his brother, skilled in the medical art. On his return from Troy he was cast by a storm on the coast of Syros in Caria, where he is said to have settled. He was worshipped as a hero on Mt. Dria.

Pŏdarcēs (Ποδάρκης). 1. The original name of Priam. [PRIAMUS.] — 2. Son of Iphiclus and grandson of Phylacus, was a younger brother of Protesilaus, and led the Thessalians of Phylace against Troy.

Pŏdargē. [HARPYIAE.]

Poeas (Ποίας), son of Phylacus or Thaumacus, husband of Methone, and the father of Philoctetes, who is hence called Poeantiades, Poeantius heros, Poeantia proles, and Poeante satus. Poeas is mentioned among the Argonauts, and is said to have killed with an arrow, Talaus, in Crete. Poeas set fire to the pile on which Hercules burnt himself, and was rewarded by the hero with his arrows. [HERCULES; PHILOCTETES.]

Poemander (Ποίμανδρος), son of Chaeresilaus and Stratonice, was the husband of Tanagra, a daughter of Aeolus or Aesopus, by whom he became the father of Ephippus and Leucippus. He was the reputed founder of the town of Tanagra in Boeotia which was hence called Poemandria. When Poemander had inadvertently killed his own son, he was purified by Elephenor.

Poemanēnus (Ποιμανηνός; ethnic, the same: prob. Manias), a fortified place in Mysia, S. of Cyzicus, with a celebrated temple of Aesculapius.

Poena (Ποινή), a personification of retaliation, sometimes mentioned as one being, and sometimes

in the plural. The Poenae belonged to the train of Dice, and are akin to the Erinnyes.

Poetovio. [PETOVIO.]

Pōgōn (Πώγων), the harbour of Troezen in Argolis.

Pola (Pola), an ancient town in Istria, situated on the W. coast, and near the promontory Polaticum, which was the most S.-ly point in the country. According to tradition Pola was founded by the Colchians, who had been sent in pursuit of Medea. It was subsequently a Roman colony, with the surname Pietas Julia, and became an important commercial town, being united by good roads with Aquileia and the principal towns of Illyria. Its importance in antiquity is attested by its magnificent ruins, of which the principal are those of an amphitheatre, of a triumphal arch (Porta aurea), erected to L. Sergius by his wife Salvia Postuma, and of several temples.

Pōlēmōn (Πολέμων). 1. I. King of Pontus and the Bosporus, was the son of Zenon, the orator of Laodicea. As a reward for the services rendered by his father as well as himself he was appointed by Antony in B. C. 39 to the government of a part of Cilicia; and he subsequently obtained in exchange the kingdom of Pontus. He accompanied Antony in his expedition against the Parthians in 36. After the battle of Actium he was able to make his peace with Octavian, who confirmed him in his kingdom. About the year 16 he was intrusted by Agrippa with the charge of reducing the kingdom of Bosporus, of which he was made king after conquering the country. His reign after this was long and prosperous; he extended his dominions as far as the river Tanaïs; but having engaged in an expedition against the barbarian tribe of the Aspurgians he was not only defeated by them, but taken prisoner, and put to death. By his 2nd wife Pythodoris, who succeeded him on the throne, he left 2 sons, Polemon II., and Zenon, king of Armenia, and 1 daughter who was married to Cotys king of Thrace. — 2. II. Son of the preceding and of Pythodoris, was raised to the sovereignty of Pontus and Bosporus by Caligula in A. D. 39. Bosporus was afterwards taken from him by Claudius, who assigned it to Mithridates, while he gave Polemon a portion of Cilicia in its stead, 41. In 62 Polemon was induced by Nero to abdicate the throne, and Pontus was reduced to the condition of a Roman province. — 3. Of Athens, an eminent Platonic philosopher, was the son of Philostratus, a man of wealth and political distinction. In his youth, Polemon was extremely profligate; but one day, when he was about 30, on his bursting into the school of Xenocrates, at the head of a band of revellers, his attention was so arrested by the discourse which chanced to be upon temperance, that he tore off his garland and remained an attentive listener, and from that day he adopted an abstemious course of life, and continued to frequent the school, of which, on the death of Xenocrates, he became the head, B. C. 315. He died in 273 at a great age. He esteemed the object of philosophy to be, to exercise men in things and deeds, not in dialectic speculation. He placed the summum bonum in living according to the laws of nature. — 4. Of Athens by citizenship, but by birth either of Ilium, or Samos, or Sicyon, a Stoic philosopher and an eminent geographer, surnamed Periegetes (ὁ περιηγήτης), lived in the time of Ptolemy Epiphanes, at the beginning of the 2nd century B.C. In philosophy he was a disciple of Panaetius. He made extensive journeys through Greece, to collect materials for his geographical works, in the course of which he paid particular attention to the inscriptions on votive offerings and on columns. As the collector of these inscriptions, he was one of the earlier contributors to the *Greek Anthology.* Athenaeus and other writers make very numerous quotations from his works. They were chiefly descriptions of different parts of Greece; some were on the paintings preserved in various places, and several are controversial, among which is one against Eratosthenes. — 5. **Antonius**, a celebrated sophist and rhetorician, flourished under Trajan, Hadrian, and the first Antoninus, and was in high favour with the 2 former emperors. He was born of a consular family, at Laodicea, but spent the greater part of his life at Smyrna. His most celebrated disciple was Aristides. Among his imitators in subsequent times was Gregory Nazianzen. His style of oratory was imposing rather than pleasing; and his character was haughty and reserved. During the latter part of his life he was so tortured by the gout, that he resolved to put an end to his existence; he had himself shut up in the tomb of his ancestors at Laodicea, where he died of hunger, at the age of 65. The only extant work of Polemon is the funeral orations for Cynaegirus and Callimachus, the generals who fell at Marathon, which are supposed to be pronounced by their fathers. These orations are edited by Orelli, Lips. 1819.—6. The author of a short Greek work on Physiognomy, which is still extant. He must have lived in or before the 3rd century after Christ, as he is mentioned by Origen, and from his style he cannot be supposed to have lived much earlier than this time. His work consists of 2 books: in the 1st, which contains 23 chapters, after proving the utility of physiognomy, he lays down the general principles of the science; in the 2nd book, which consists of 27 chapters, he goes on to apply the principles he had before laid down, and describes in a few words the characters of the courageous man, the timid, the impudent, the passionate, the talkative, &c. The best edition of it is by Franz in his " Scriptores Physiognomoniae Veteres," Altenburg. 1780.

Pŏlĕmōnĭum (Πολεμώνιον: Πολεμώνιος, and Πολεμωνιεύς: *Polemon*), a city on the coast of Pontus in Asia Minor, built by King Polemon (probably the 2nd), on the site of the older city of Side, at the mouth of the river Sidenus (*Polemon Chai*), and at the bottom of a deep gulf, with a good harbour. It was the capital of the kingdom of Polemon, comprising the central part of Pontus, E. of the Iris, which was hence called Pontus Polemoniacus.

Pŏlĭas (Πολιάς), i. e. " the goddess protecting the city," a surname of Athena at Athens, where she was worshipped as the protecting divinity of the acropolis.

Pŏlĭchna (Πολίχνη, Dor. Πολίχνα: Πολιχνίτης), a town: — 1. In the N.W. of Messenia, W. of Andania. — 2. In the N.E. of Laconia. — 3. In Chios. — 4. In Crete, whose territory bordered on that of Cydonia. — 5. In Mysia, in the district Troas, on the left bank of the Aesepus near its source.

Pŏlĭeus (Πολιεύς), " the protector of the city," a surname of Zeus, under which he had an altar on the acropolis at Athens.

Pŏlĭorcētēs, Demetrius. [DEMETRIUS.]

Pŏlis (Πόλις), a village of the Locri Opuntii, subject to Hyle.

Pŏlītēs (Πολίτης), son of Priam and Hecuba, and father of Priam the younger, was a valiant warrior, but was slain by Pyrrhus.

Pŏlītōrĭum, a town in the interior of Latium, destroyed by Ancus Martius.

Pŏlĭūchus (Πολιοῦχος), i. e. " protecting the city," occurs as a surname of several divinities, such as Athena Chalcioecus at Sparta, and of Athena at Athens.

Polla, Argentārĭa, the wife of the poet Lucan.

Pollentĭa (Pollentinus). 1. (*Polenza*), a town of the Statielli in Liguria at the confluence of the Sturia and the Tanarus, and subsequently a Roman municipium. It was celebrated for its wool. In its neighbourhood Stilicho gained a victory over the Goths under Alaric. — 2. A town in Picenum probably identical with Urbs Salvia. — 3. (*Pollenza*), a Roman colony on the N.E. point of the Balearis Major.

Pollĭo, Annīus, was accused of treason (*majestas*) towards the end of the reign of Tiberius, but was not brought to trial. He was subsequently one of Nero's intimate friends, but was accused of taking part in Piso's conspiracy against that emperor in A. D. 63, and was in consequence banished.

Pollĭo, C. Asĭnĭus, a distinguished orator, poet and historian of the Augustan age. He was born at Rome in B. C. 76, and became distinguished as an orator at an early age. On the breaking out of the civil war he joined Caesar, and in 49 he accompanied Curio to Africa. After the defeat and death of Curio, he crossed over to Greece, and fought on Caesar's side at the battle of Pharsalia (48). He also accompanied Caesar in his campaigns against the Pompeian party in Africa (46) and Spain (45). He returned with Caesar to Rome, but was shortly afterwards sent back to Spain, with the command of the Further Province, in order to prosecute the war against Sex. Pompey. He was in his province at the time of Caesar's death (44). He took no part in the war between Antony and the senate; but when Antony was joined by Lepidus and Octavian in 43, Pollio espoused their cause, and persuaded L. Plancus in Gaul to follow his example. In the division of the provinces among the triumvirs, Antony received the Gauls. The administration of the Transpadane Gaul was committed to Pollio by Antony, and he had accordingly the difficult task of settling the veterans in the lands which had been assigned to them in this province. It was upon this occasion that he saved the property of the poet Virgil at Mantua from confiscation, whom he took under his protection from his love of literature. In 40 Pollio took an active part in effecting the reconciliation between Octavian and Antony at Brundusium. In the same year he was consul; and it was during his consulship that Virgil addressed to him his 4th Eclogue. In 39, Antony went to Greece, and sent Pollio with a part of his army against the Parthini, an Illyrian people. Pollio defeated the Parthini and took the Dalmatian town of Salonae; and in consequence of his success obtained the honour of a triumph on the 25th of October in this year. He gave his son Asinius Gallus the agnomen of Saloninus after the town which he had taken. It was during his Illyrian campaign that Virgil addressed to him the 8th Eclogue. From this time Pollio withdrew altogether from political life, and devoted himself to the study of literature. He still continued however to exercise his oratorical powers, and maintained his reputation for eloquence by his speeches both in the senate and the courts of justice. He died at his Tusculan villa, A. D. 4, in the 80th year of his age, preserving to the last the full enjoyment of his health and of all his faculties. — Pollio deserves a distinguished place in the history of Roman literature, not so much on account of his works, as of the encouragement which he gave to literature. He was not only a patron of Virgil, Horace (see *Carm.* ii. 1), and other great poets and writers, but he has the honour of having been the first person to establish a public library at Rome, upon which he expended the money he had obtained in his Illyrian campaign. None of Pollio's own works have come down to us, but they possessed sufficient merit to lead his contemporaries and successors to class his name with those of Cicero, Virgil and Sallust, as an orator, a poet and an historian. It was however as an orator that he possessed the greatest reputation. Catullus describes him in his youth (*Carm.* xii. 9) as " leporum disertus puer et facetiarum," and Horace speaks of him in the full maturity of his powers (*Carm.* ii. 1. 13) as " Insigne maestis praesidium reis et consulenti, Pollio, curiae ; " and we have also the more impartial testimony of Quintilian, the two Senecas and the author of the Dialogue on Orators to the greatness of his oratorical powers. —Pollio wrote the history of the civil wars in 17 books. It commenced with the consulship of Metellus and Afranius, B. C. 60, in which year the first triumvirate was formed, and appears to have come down to the time when Augustus obtained the undisputed supremacy of the Roman world.— As a poet Pollio was best known for his tragedies, which are spoken of in high terms by Virgil and Horace, but which probably did not possess any great merit, as they are hardly mentioned by subsequent writers. The words of Virgil (*Ecl.* iii. 86), " Pollio et ipse facit *nova* carmina," probably refer to tragedies of a new kind, namely, such as were not borrowed from the Greek, but contained subjects entirely new, taken from Roman story.—Pollio also enjoyed great reputation as a critic, but he is chiefly known in this capacity for the severe judgment which he passed upon his great contemporaries. Thus he pointed out many mistakes in the speeches of Cicero, censured the Commentaries of Caesar for their want of historical fidelity, and found fault with Sallust for affectation in the use of antiquated words and expressions. He also complained of a certain *Patavinity* in Livy, respecting which some remarks are made in the life of Livy. [p. 387, a.] Pollio had a son, C. Asinius Gallus Saloninus. [See p. 276.] Asinius Gallus married Vipsania, the former wife of Tiberius, by whom he had several children : namely, 1. Asinius Saloninus. 2. Asinius Gallus. 3. Asinius Pollio, consul A. D. 23. 4. Asinius Agrippa, consul A. D. 25. 5. Asinius Celer.

Pollio, Vedius, a Roman eques and a friend of Augustus, was by birth a freedman, and has obtained a place in history on account of his riches and his cruelty. He was accustomed to feed his lampreys with human flesh, and whenever a slave displeased him, the unfortunate wretch was forthwith thrown into the pond as food for the fish. On one occasion Augustus was supping with him, when a slave had the misfortune to break a crystal

goblet, and his master immediately ordered him to be thrown to the fishes. The slave fell at the feet of Augustus, praying for mercy ; and when the emperor could not prevail upon Pollio to pardon him, he dismissed the slave of his own accord, and commanded all Pollio's crystal goblets to be broken and the fish-pond to be filled up. Pollio died B. C. 15, leaving a large part of his property to Augustus. It was this Pollio, who built the celebrated villa of Pausilypum near Naples.

Pollux or Polydeuces. [DIOSCURI.]

Pollux, Jūlīus ('Ιούλιος Πολυδεύκης). 1. Of Naucratis in Egypt, was a Greek sophist and grammarian. He studied rhetoric at Athens under the sophist Adrian, and afterwards opened a private school in this city, where he gave instruction in grammar and rhetoric. At a later time he was appointed by the emperor Commodus to the chair of rhetoric at Athens. He died during the reign of Commodus at the age of 58. We may therefore assign A. D. 183 as the year in which he flourished. He seems to have been attacked by many of his contemporaries on account of the inferior character of his oratory, and especially by Lucian in his 'Ρητόρων διδάσκαλος. Pollux was the author of several works, all of which have perished, with the exception of the *Onomasticon.* This work is divided into 10 books, each of which contains a short dedication to the *Caesar* Commodus : it was therefore published before A. D. 177, since Commodus became Augustus in that year. Each book forms a separate treatise by itself, containing the most important words relating to certain subjects, with short explanations of the meanings of the words. The alphabetical arrangement is not adopted, but the words are given according to the subjects treated of in each book. The best editions are by Lederlin and Hemsterhuis, Amsterdam, 1706; by Dindorf, Lips. 1824; and by Imm. Bekker, Berol. 1846.— 2. A Byzantine writer, the author of a Chronicon, which treats at some length of the creation of the world, and is therefore entitled 'Ιστορία φυσική. Like most other Byzantine histories, it is an universal history, beginning with the creation of the world and coming down to the time of the writer. The two manuscripts from which this work is published end with the reign of Valens, but the Paris manuscript is said to come down as low as the death of Romanus, A. D. 963. The best edition is by Hardt, Munich, 1792.

Pōlus (Πῶλος). 1. A sophist and rhetorician, a native of Agrigentum. He was a disciple of Gorgias, and wrote a treatise on rhetoric, as well as other works mentioned by Suidas. He is introduced by Plato as an interlocutor in the Gorgias. —2. A celebrated tragic actor, the son of Charicles of Sunium, and a disciple of Archias of Thurii. It is related of him, that at the age of 70, shortly before his death, he acted in 8 tragedies on 4 successive days.

Pŏlyaegos (Πολύαιγος: *Polybos* or *Antimelos*), an uninhabited island in the Aegaean sea, near Melos.

Pŏlyaenus (Πολύαινος). 1. Of Lampsacus, a mathematician and a friend of Epicurus, adopted the philosophical system of his friend, and, although he had previously acquired great reputation as a mathematician, he now maintained with Epicurus the worthlessness of geometry.—2. Of Sardis, a sophist, lived in the time of Julius Caesar. He is the author of 4 epigrams in the Greek Anthology.

His full name was *Julius Polyaenus*. — 3. The Macedonian, the author of the work on Stratagems in war (Στρατηγήματα), which is still extant, lived about the middle of the 2nd century of the Christian aera. Suidas calls him a rhetorician, and we learn from Polyaenus himself that he was accustomed to plead causes before the emperor. He dedicated his work to M. Aurelius and Verus, while they were engaged in the Parthian war, about A. D. 163, at which time, he says, he was too old to accompany them in their campaigns. This work is divided into 8 books, of which the first 6 contain an account of the stratagems of the most celebrated Greek generals, the 7th of those of barbarous or foreign people, and the 8th of the Romans, and illustrious women. Parts, however, of the 6th and 7th books are lost, so that of the 900 stratagems which Polyaenus described, only 833 have come down to us. The work is written in a clear and pleasing style, though somewhat tinged with the artificial rhetoric of the age. It contains a vast number of anecdotes respecting many of the most celebrated men in antiquity ; but its value as an historical authority is very much diminished by the little judgment which the author evidently possessed, and by our ignorance of the sources from which he took his statements. The best editions are by Maasvicius, Leyden, 1690 ; by Mursinna, Berlin, 1756 ; and by Coray, Paris, 1809.

Pŏlўbĭus (Πολύβιος). 1. The historian, the son of Lycortas, and a native of Megalopolis, in Arcadia, was born about B. C. 204. His father Lycortas was one of the most distinguished men of the Achaean league ; and Polybius received the advantages of his father's instruction in political knowledge and the military art. He must also have reaped great benefit from his intercourse with Philopoemen, who was a friend of his father's, and on whose death, in 182, Polybius carried the urn in which his ashes were deposited. In the following year Polybius was appointed one of the ambassadors to Egypt, but he did not leave Greece, as the intention of sending an embassy was abandoned. From this time he probably began to take part in public affairs, and he appears to have soon obtained great influence among his countrymen. After the conquest of Macedonia, in 168, the Roman commissioners, who were sent into the S. of Greece, commanded, at the instigation of Callicrates, that 1000 Achaeans should be carried to Rome, to answer the charge of not having assisted the Romans against Perseus. This number included all the best and noblest part of the nation, and among them was Polybius. They arrived in Italy in B. C. 167, but, instead of being put upon their trial, they were distributed among the Etruscan towns. Polybius was more fortunate than the rest of his countrymen. He had probably become acquainted in Greece with Aemilius Paulus, or his sons Fabius and Scipio, and the two young men now obtained permission from the praetor for Polybius to reside at Rome in the house of their father Paulus. Scipio was then 18 years of age, and soon became warmly attached to Polybius. Scipio was accompanied by his friend in all his military expeditions, and received much advantage from his experience and knowledge. Polybius, on the other hand, besides finding a liberal patron and protector in Scipio, was able by his means to obtain access to public documents, and to accumulate materials for his great historical work. After

remaining in Italy 17 years, Polybius returned to Peloponnesus in 151, with the surviving Achaean exiles, who were at length allowed by the senate to revisit their native land. He did not, however, remain long in Greece. He joined Scipio in his campaign against Carthage, and was present at the destruction of that city in 146. Immediately afterwards he hurried to Greece, where the Achaeans were waging a mad and hopeless war against the Romans. He appears to have arrived in Greece soon after the capture of Corinth ; and he exerted all his influence to alleviate the misfortunes of his countrymen, and to procure favourable terms for them. His grateful fellow-countrymen acknowledged the great services he had rendered them, and statues were erected to his honour at Megalopolis, Mantinea, Pallantium, Tegea, and other places. Polybius seems now to have devoted himself to the composition of the great historical work, for which he had long been collecting materials. At what period of his life he made the journeys into foreign countries for the purpose of visiting the places which he had to describe in his history, it is impossible to determine. He tells us (iii. 59) that he undertook long and dangerous journeys into Africa, Spain, Gaul, and even as far as the Atlantic, on account of the ignorance which prevailed respecting those parts. Some of these countries he visited while serving under Scipio, who afforded him every facility for the prosecution of his design. At a later period of his life he visited Egypt likewise. He probably accompanied Scipio to Spain in 134, and was present at the fall of Numantia, since Cicero states (*ad Fam.* v. 12) that Polybius wrote a history of the Numantine war. He died at the age of 82, in consequence of a fall from his horse, about 122. — The history of Polybius consisted of 40 books. It began B. C. 220, where the history of Aratus left off, and ended at 146, in which year Corinth was destroyed, and the independence of Greece perished. It consisted of 2 distinct parts, which were probably published at different times and afterwards united into one work. The first part comprised a period of 35 years, beginning with the 2nd Punic war, and the Social war in Greece, and ending with the conquest of Perseus and the downfal of the Macedonian kingdom, in 168. This was in fact the main portion of his work, and its great object was to show how the Romans had in this brief period of 53 years conquered the greater part of the world ; but since the Greeks were ignorant for the most part of the early history of Rome, he gives a survey of Roman history from the taking of the city by the Gauls to the commencement of the 2nd Punic war, in the first 2 books, which thus form an introduction to the body of the work. With the fall of the Macedonian kingdom the supremacy of the Roman dominion was decided, and nothing more remained for the other nations of the world than to yield submission to the Romans. The second part of the work, which formed a kind of supplement to the former part, comprised the period from the conquest of Perseus in 168, to the fall of Corinth in 146. The history of the conquest of Greece seems to have been completed in the 39th book ; and the 40th book probably contained a chronological summary of the whole work. The history of Polybius is one of the most valuable works that has come down to us from antiquity. He had a clear apprehension of the knowledge which an historian must possess; and his preparatory studies were carried on with the greatest energy and perseverance. Thus he not only collected with accuracy and care an account of the events that he intended to narrate, but he also studied the history of the Roman constitution, and made distant journeys to become acquainted with the geography of the countries that he had to describe in his work. In addition to this, he had a strong judgment and a striking love of truth, and, from having himself taken an active part in political life, he was able to judge of the motives and actions of the great actors in history in a way that no mere scholar or rhetorician could possibly do. But the characteristic feature of his work, and the one which distinguishes it from all other histories which have come down to us from antiquity, is its *didactic* nature. He did not, like other historians, write to afford amusement to his readers; his object was to teach by the past a knowledge of the future, and to deduce from previous events lessons of practical wisdom. Hence he calls his work a *Pragmateia* (πραγματεία), and not a *History* (ἱστορία). The value of history consisted, in his opinion, in the instruction that might be obtained from it. Thus the narrative of events became in his view of secondary importance; they formed only the text of the political and moral discourses which it was the province of the historian to deliver. Excellent, however, as these discourses are, they materially detract from the merits of the history as a work of art; their frequent occurrence interrupts the continuity of the narrative, and destroys, to a great extent, the interest of the reader in the scenes which are described. Moreover he frequently inserts long episodes, which have little connection with the main subject of his work, because they have a didactic tendency. Thus we find that one whole book (the 6th) was devoted to a history of the Roman constitution; and the 34th book seems to have been exclusively a treatise on geography. The style of Polybius bears the impress of his mind; and, as instruction and not amusement was the great object for which he wrote, he did not seek to please his readers by the choice of his phrases or the composition of his sentences. Hence the later Greek critics were severe in their condemnation of his style. The greater part of the history of Polybius has perished. We possess the first 5 books entire, but of the rest we have only fragments and extracts, some of which, however, are of considerable length, such as the account of the Roman army, which belonged to the 6th book. There have been discovered at different times 4 distinct collections of extracts from the lost books. The first collection, discovered soon after the revival of learning in a MS. brought from Corfu, contained the greater part of the 6th book, and portions of the following 11. In 1582 Ursinus published at Antwerp a 2nd collection of Extracts, entitled *Excerpta de Legationibus*, which were made in the 10th century of the Christian era. In 1634, Valesius published a 3rd collection of extracts from Polybius, also taken from the Excerpta of Constantinus, entitled *Excerpta de Virtutibus et Vitiis*. The 4th collection of extracts was published at Rome in 1827 by Angelo Mai, who discovered in the Vatican library at Rome the section of the Excerpta of Constantinus Porphyrogenitus, entitled *Excerpta de Sententiis*. The best edition of Polybius with a commentary is by Schweighæuser, Lips. 1789—

1795, 8 vols. 8vo. The best edition of the text alone is by Bekker (Berol. 1844, 2 vols. 8vo.), who has added the Vatican fragments. Livy did not use Polybius till he came to the 2nd Punic war, but from that time he followed him very closely. Cicero likewise chiefly followed Polybius in the account which he gives of the Roman constitution in his *De Republica*. The history of Polybius was continued by Posidonius and Strabo. [POSIDONIUS; STRABO.] Besides the great historical work of which we have been speaking, Polybius wrote, 2. *The Life of Philopoemen* in 3 books. 3. A treatise on *Tactics*. 4. *A History of the Numantine War.* — **2.** A freedman of the emperor Augustus, read in the senate the will of the emperor after his decease. — **3.** A favourite freedman of the emperor Claudius. He was the companion of the studies of Claudius; and on the death of his brother. Seneca addressed to him a *Consolatio*, in which he bestows the highest praises upon his literary attainments. Polybius was put to death through the intrigues of Messalina, although he had been one of her paramours.

Polybotes (Πολυβώτης), one of the giants who fought against the gods, was pursued by Poseidon across the sea as far as the island of Cos. There Poseidon tore away a part of the island, which was afterwards called Nisyrion, and throwing it upon the giant buried him under it.

Polybotus (Πολύβοτος: *Bulawadin*, Ru.), a city of Great Phrygia, E. of Synnada.

Polybus (Πόλυβος). 1. King of Corinth, by whom Oedipus was brought up. [OEDIPUS.] He was the husband of Periboea or Merope. Pausanias makes him king of Sicyon, and describes him as a son of Hermes and Chthonophyle, and as the father of Lysianassa, whom he gave in marriage to Talaus, king of the Argives. — **2.** A Greek physician, was one of the pupils of Hippocrates, who was also his son-in-law, and lived in the island of Cos, in the 4th century B.C. With his brothers-in-law, Thessalus and Dracon, Polybus was one of the founders of the ancient medical sect of the Dogmatici. He was sent abroad by Hippocrates, with his fellow-pupils, during the time of the plague, to assist different cities with his medical skill, and he afterwards remained in his native country. He has been supposed, both by ancient and modern critics, to be the author of several treatises in the Hippocratic collection.

Polycarpus (Πολύκαρπος), one of the apostolical fathers, was a native of Smyrna. The date of his birth and of his martyrdom are uncertain. He is said to have been a disciple of the apostle John, and to have been consecrated by this apostle bishop of the church at Smyrna. It has been conjectured that he was the angel of the church of Smyrna to whom Jesus Christ directed the letter in the Apocalypse (ii. 8—11); and it is certain that he was bishop of Smyrna at the time when Ignatius of Antioch passed through that city on his way to suffer death at Rome, some time between 107 and 116. Ignatius seems to have enjoyed much this intercourse with Polycarp, whom he had known in former days, when they were both hearers of the apostle John. The martyrdom of Polycarp occurred in the persecution under the emperors Marcus Aurelius and Lucius Verus. As he was led to death the proconsul offered him his life, if he would revile Christ. "Eighty and six years have I served him," was

.he reply, "and he never did me wrong: how then can I revile my King and my Saviour?" We have remaining only one short piece of Polycarp, his *Letter to the Philippians*, which is published along with Ignatius and the other apostolical writers. [IGNATIUS.]

Pŏlÿclēs (Πολυκλῆς), the name of 2 artists. The elder Polycles was probably an Athenian, and flourished about B. C. 370. He appears to have been one of the artists of the later Athenian school, who obtained great celebrity by the sensual charms exhibited in their works. One of his chief works was a celebrated statue of an Hermaphrodite. The younger Polycles is placed by Pliny in 155, and is said to have made a statue of Juno, which was placed in the portico of Octavia at Rome, when that portico was erected by Metellus Macedonicus. But since most of the works of art, with which Metellus decorated his portico, were not the original productions of living artists, but the works of former masters, it has been conjectured that this Polycles may be no other than the Athenian artist already mentioned.

Pŏlyclētus (Πολύκλειτος). 1. The Elder, of Argos, probably by citizenship, and of Sicyon, probably by birth, was one of the most celebrated statuaries of the ancient world ; he was also a sculptor, an architect, and an artist in toreutic. He was the pupil of the great Argive statuary Ageladas, under whom he had Phidias and Myron for his fellow-disciples. He was somewhat younger than Phidias, and about the same age as Myron. He flourished about B. C. 452—412. Of his personal history we know nothing further. As an artist, he stood at the head of the schools of Argos and Sicyon, and approached more nearly than any other to an equality with Phidias, the great head of the Athenian school. The essential difference between these artists was that Phidias was unsurpassed in making the images of the gods, Polycletus in those of men. One of the most celebrated works of Polycletus was his *Doryphorus* or *Spear-bearer*, a youthful figure, but with the full proportions of a man. This was the statue which became known by the name of *Canon*, because in it the artist had embodied a perfect representation of the ideal of the human figure. Another of his great works was his ivory and gold statue of Hera in her temple between Argos and Mycenae. This work was executed by the artist in his old age, and was doubtless intended by him to rival Phidias's chryselephantine statues of Athena and of Zeus, though it was surpassed by them in costliness and size. The goddess was seated on a throne, her head crowned with a garland, on which were worked the Graces and the Hours, the one hand holding the symbolical pomegranate, and the other a sceptre, surmounted by a cuckoo. a bird sacred to Hera, on account of her having been once changed into that form by Zeus. This statue remained always the ideal model of Hera. In the department of toreutic, the fame of Polycletus no doubt rested chiefly on the golden ornaments of his statue of Hera ; but he also made small bronzes (*sigilla*), and drinking-vessels (*phialae*). As an architect Polycletus obtained great celebrity by the theatre, and the circular building (*tholus*), which he built in the sacred enclosure of Aesculapius at Epidaurus.—2. The Younger, also a statuary of Argos, of whom very little is known, because his fame was eclipsed by that of his more

celebrated namesake, and, in part, contemporary. The younger Polycletus may be placed about 400. — 3. Of Larissa, a Greek historian, and one of the numerous writers of the history of Alexander the Great.—4. A favourite freedman of Nero, who sent him into Britain to inspect the state of the island.

Polycrātes (Πολυκράτης). 1. Of Samos, one of the most fortunate, ambitious, and treacherous of the Greek tyrants. With the assistance of his brothers Pantagnotus and Syloson, he made himself master of the island towards the latter end of the reign of Cyrus. At first he shared the supreme power with his brothers ; but he shortly afterwards put Pantagnotus to death, and banished Syloson. Having thus become sole despot, he raised a powerful fleet, and extended his sway over several of the neighbouring islands, and even conquered some towns on the mainland. He had formed an alliance with Amasis, king of Egypt, who, however, finally renounced it through alarm at the amazing good fortune of Polycrates, which never met with any check or disaster, and which therefore was sure, sooner or later, to incur the envy of the gods. Such, at least, is the account of Herodotus, who has narrated the story of the rupture between Amasis and Polycrates in his most dramatic manner. In a letter which Amasis wrote to Polycrates, the Egyptian monarch advised him to throw away one of his most valuable possessions, in order that he might thus inflict some injury upon himself. In accordance with this advice Polycrates threw into the sea a seal-ring of extraordinary beauty ; but in a few days it was found in the belly of a fish, which had been presented to him by a fisherman. In the reign of Cambyses, the Spartans and Corinthians sent a powerful force to Samos, in order to depose the tyrant ; but their expedition failed, and after besieging the city 40 days, they left the island. The power of Polycrates now became greater than ever. The great works which Herodotus saw at Samos were probably executed by him. He lived in great pomp and luxury, and, like others of the Greek tyrants, was a patron of literature and the arts. The most eminent artists and poets found a ready welcome at his court ; and his friendship for Anacreon is particularly celebrated. But in the midst of all his prosperity he fell by the most ignominious fate. Oroetes, the satrap of Sardis, had formed a deadly hatred against Polycrates. By false pretences, the satrap contrived to allure him to the mainland, where he was arrested soon after his arrival, and crucified, 522. — 2. An Athenian rhetorician and sophist of some repute, a contemporary of Socrates and Isocrates, taught first at Athens and afterwards at Cyprus. He was the teacher of Zoilus. He wrote, 1. An accusation of Socrates, which was a declamation on the subject composed some years after the death of the philosopher. 2. A defence of Busiris. The oration of Isocrates, entitled *Busiris*, is addressed to Polycrates, and points out the faults which the latter had committed in his oration on this subject. 3. An obscene poem, which he published under the name of the poetess Philaenis, for the purpose of injuring her reputation.

Pŏlÿdāmas (Πολυδάμας). 1. Son of Panthous and Phrontis, was a Trojan hero, a friend of Hector, and brother of Euphorbus.—2. Of Scotussa in Thessaly, son of Nicias, conquered in the Pancratium at the Olympic games, in Ol. 93, B. C.

408. His size was immense, and the most marvellous stories are related of his strength, how he killed without arms a huge and fierce lion on Mt. Olympus, how he stopped a chariot at full gallop, &c. His reputation led the Persian king, Darius Ochus, to invite him to his court, where he performed similar feats. — 3. Of Pharsalus in Thessaly, was entrusted by his fellow-citizens about B.C. 375, with the supreme government of their native town. He afterwards entered into a treaty with Jason of Pherae. On the murder of Jason in 370, his brother Polyphron put to death Polydamas.

Pŏlÿdectēs (Πολυδέκτης). 1. King of the island of Seriphos, was son of Magnes, and brother of Dictys. He received kindly Danaë and Perseus, when the chest, in which they had been exposed by Acrisius, floated to the island of Seriphos. His story is related under PERSEUS. — 2. King of Sparta, was the eldest son of Eunomus, the brother of Lycurgus the lawgiver, and the father of Charilaüs, who succeeded him. Herodotus, contrary to the other authorities, makes Polydectes the father of Eunomus.

Pŏlÿdeucēs (Πολυδεύκης), one of the Dioscuri, and the twin-brother of Castor, called by the Romans Pollux. [DIOSCURI.]

Pŏlÿdōrus (Πολύδωρος). 1. King of Thebes, son of Cadmus and Harmonia, husband of Nycteïs, and father of Labdacus. — 2. The youngest among the sons of Priam and Laotoë, was slain by Achilles. This is the Homeric account ; but later traditions make him a son of Priam and Hecuba, and give a different account of his death. One tradition relates, that when Ilium was on the point of falling into the hands of the Greeks, Priam entrusted Polydorus and a large sum of money to Polymestor or Polymnestor, king of the Thracian Chersonesus. After the destruction of Troy, Polymestor killed Polydorus for the purpose of getting possession of his treasures, and cast his body into the sea. His body was afterwards washed upon the coast, where it was found and recognised by his mother Hecuba, who, together with other Trojan captives, took vengeance upon Polymestor by killing his two children, and putting out his eyes. Another tradition stated that Polydorus was entrusted to his sister Iliona, who was married to Polymestor. She brought him up as her own son, while she made every one else believe that her own son Deïphilus or Deïpylus was Polydorus. The Greeks, anxious to destroy the race of Priam, promised to Polymestor Electra for his wife, and a large amount of gold, if he would kill Polydorus. Polymestor was prevailed upon, and he accordingly slew his own son. Polydorus, thereupon, persuaded his sister Iliona to kill Polymestor. — 3. King of Sparta, was the son of Alcamenes and the father of Eurycrates, who succeeded him. He assisted in bringing the 1st Messenian war to a conclusion, B.C. 724. He was murdered by Polemarchus, a Spartan of high family ; but his name was precious among his people on account of his justice and kindness. Crotona and the Epizephyrian Locri were founded in his reign. — 4. Brother of Jason of Pherae, obtained the supreme power along with his brother Polyphron, on the death of Jason in B.C. 370, but was shortly afterwards assassinated by the latter. — 5. A sculptor of Rhodes, one of the associates of Agesander, in the execution of the celebrated group of the Laocoon. [AGESANDER.]

Pŏlÿeuctus (Πολύευκτος), an Athenian orator

of the demus Sphettus, was a political friend of Demosthenes, with whom he worked in resisting the Macedonian party,

Pŏlÿgnōtus (Πολύγνωτος), one of the most celebrated Greek painters, was a native of the island of Thasos, and was honoured with the citizenship of Athens, on which account he is sometimes called an Athenian. His father, Aglaophon, was his instructor in his art ; and he had a brother, named Aristophon, who was also a painter. Polygnotus lived on intimate terms with Cimon and his sister Elpinice ; and he probably came to Athens in B.C. 463, after the subjugation of Thasos by Cimon. He appears to have been at that time an artist of some reputation, and he continued to exercise his art almost down to the beginning of the Peloponnesian war (431). The period of his greatest artistic activity at Athens seems to have been that which elapsed from his removal to Athens (463) to the death of Cimon (449), who employed him in the pictorial decoration of the public buildings with which he began to adorn the city, such as the temple of Theseus, the Anacēum, and the Poecile. He afterwards went to Delphi, when he was employed with other artists in decorating the buildings connected with the temple. He appears to have returned to Athens about 435, where he executed a series of paintings in the Propylaea of the Acropolis. The Propylaea were commenced in 437, and completed in 432. The subjects of the pictures of Polygnotus were almost invariably taken from Homer and the other poets of the epic cycle. They appear to have been mostly painted on panels, which were afterwards let into the walls where they were to remain.

Pŏlÿhymnīa. [POLYMNIA.]

Pŏlÿidus (Πολύιδος). 1. Son of Coeranus, grandson of Abas and great-grandson of Melampus. He was, like his ancestor Melampus, a celebrated soothsayer at Corinth, and is described as the father of Euchenor, Astycratīa, and Manto. When Alcathous had murdered his own son Callipolis at Megara, he was purified by Polyidus, who erected at Megara a sanctuary to Dionysus, and a statue of the god. — 2. A dithyrambic poet of the most flourishing period of the later Athenian dithyramb, and also skilful as a painter, was contemporary with Philoxenus, Timotheus, and Telestes, about B.C. 400.

Pŏlÿmestor or Polymnestor. [POLYDORUS.]

Pŏlÿmnestus, or Polymnastus (Πολύμνηστος), the son of Meles of Colophon, was an epic, elegiac, and lyric poet, and a musician. He flourished B.C. 675–644. He belongs to the school of Dorian music, which flourished at this time at Sparta, where he carried on the improvements of Thaletas. The Attic comedians attacked his poems for their erotic character. As an elegiac poet, he may be regarded as the predecessor of his fellow-countryman, Mimnermus.

Pŏlÿmnīa or Polyhymnīa (Πολύμνια), daughter of Zeus, and one of the 9 Muses. She presided over lyric poetry, and was believed to have invented the lyre. In works of art she was usually represented in a pensive attitude. [MUSAE.]

Pŏlÿnīcēs (Πολυνείκης), son of Oedipus and Jocasta, and brother of Eteocles and Antigone. His story is given under ETEOCLES and ADRASTUS.

Pŏlÿphēmus (Πολύφημος). 1. Son of Poseidon, and the nymph Thoosa, was one of the Cyclopes in Sicily. [CYCLOPES.] He is represented as a gigantic monster, having only one eye in the centre of his forehead, caring nought for the gods, and devouring human flesh. He dwelt in a cave near Mt. Aetna, and fed his flocks upon the mountain. He fell in love with the nymph Galatea, but as she rejected him for Acis, he destroyed the latter by crushing him under a huge rock. When Ulysses was driven upon Sicily, Polyphemus devoured some of his companions ; and Ulysses would have shared the same fate, had he not put out the eye of the monster, while he was asleep. [ULYSSES.] — 2. Son of Elatus or Poseidon and Hippea, was one of the Lapithae at Larissa in Thessaly. He was married to Laonoᴇ .·, a sister of Hercules. He was also one of the Argonauts, but being left behind by them in Mysia, he founded Cios, and fell against the Chalybes.

Pŏlyphron (Πολύφρων), brother of Jason of Pherae, succeeded to the supreme power with his brother Polydorus on the death of Jason in B. c. 370. Shortly afterwards he murdered Polydorus. He exercised his power with great cruelty, and was murdered in his turn, 369, by his nephew Alexander, who proved a still greater tyrant.

Pŏlypoetes (Πολυποίτης), son of Pirithous and Hippodamia, was one of the Lapithae, and joined the Greeks in the Trojan war.

Polyrrhēnĭa or -ĭum (Πολυῤῥηνία: Πολυῤῥήνιος), a town in Crete, whose territory embraced the whole western corner of the island. It possessed a sanctuary of Dictynna, and is said to have been colonised by Achaeans and Lacedaemonians.

Pŏlysperchon (Πολυσπέρχων), a Macedonian, and a distinguished officer of Alexander the Great. In B. c. 323 he was appointed by Alexander 2nd in command of the army of invalids and veterans, which Craterus had to conduct home to Macedonia. He afterwards served under Antipater in Europe, and so great was the confidence which the latter reposed in him, that Antipater on his death-bed (319) appointed Polysperchon to succeed him as regent and guardian of the king, while he assigned to his own son Cassander the subordinate station of Chiliarch. Polysperchon soon became involved in war with Cassander, who was dissatisfied with this arrangement. It was in the course of this war that Polysperchon basely surrendered Phocion to the Athenians, in the hope of securing the adherence of Athena. Although Polysperchon was supported by Olympias, and possessed great influence with the Macedonian soldiers, he proved no match for Cassander, and was obliged to yield to him possession of Macedonia about 316. For the next few years Polysperchon is rarely mentioned, but in 310, he again assumed an important part by reviving the long-forgotten pretensions of Hercules, the son of Alexander and Barsine to the throne of Macedonia. Cassander marched against him, but distrusting the fidelity of his own troops, he entered into secret negotiations with Polysperchon, and persuaded the latter, by promises and flatteries, to murder Hercules. From this time he appears to have served under Cassander ; but the period of his death is not mentioned.

Pŏlӯtimētus (Πολυτίμητος: Sogd or Kohik in Bokhara), a considerable river of Sogdiana, which, according to Strabo, vanished underground near Maracanda (Samarkand), or, as Arrian says, was lost in the sands of the steppes.

Pŏlyxēna (Πολυξένη), daughter of Priam and Hecuba, was beloved by Achilles. When the Greeks, on their voyage home, were still lingering on the coast of Thrace, the shade of Achilles appeared to them, demanding that Polyxena should be sacrificed to him. Neoptolemus accordingly sacrificed her on the tomb of his father. It was related that Achilles had promised Priam to bring about a peace with the Greeks, if the king would give him his daughter Polyxena in marriage ; and that when Achilles had gone to the temple of the Thymbraean Apollo, for the purpose of negotiating the marriage, he was treacherously killed by Paris. Another tradition stated that Achilles and Polyxena fell in love with each other when Hector's body was delivered up to Priam ; and that Polyxena fled to the Greeks after the death of Achilles, and killed herself on the tomb of her beloved with a sword.

Pŏlyxo (Πολυξώ). 1. The nurse of queen Hypsipyle in Lemnos, was celebrated as a prophetess. — 2. An Argive woman, married to Tlepolemus, son of Hercules, followed her husband to Rhodes, where, according to some traditions, she is said to have put to death the celebrated Helen. [HELENA.]

Pŏlyzēlus (Πολύζηλος). 1. Brother of Hieron, the tyrant of Syracuse. [HIERON.] — 2. Of Rhodes, an historian, of uncertain date, wrote a history of his native country. — 3. An Athenian comic poet, belonging to the last period of the Old Comedy and the beginning of the Middle.

Pōmōna, the Roman divinity of the fruit of trees, hence called Pomorum Patrona. Her name is evidently derived from Pomum. She is represented by the poets as beloved by several of the rustic divinities, such as Silvanus, Picus, Vertumnus, and others. Her worship must originally have been of considerable importance, since a special priest, under the name of flamen Pomonalis, was appointed to attend to her service.

Pompēĭa. 1. Daughter of Q. Pompeius Rufus, son of the consul of B. c. 88, and of Cornelia, the daughter of the dictator Sulla. She married C. Caesar, subsequently the dictator, in 67, but was divorced by him in 61, because she was suspected of intriguing with Clodius, who stealthily introduced himself into her husband's house while she was celebrating the mysteries of the Bona Dea. — 2. Sister of Cn. Pompey, the triumvir, married C. Memmius, who was killed in the war against Sertorius, in 75. — 3. Daughter of the triumvir by his third wife Mucia. She married Faustus Sulla, the son of the dictator, who perished in the African war, 46. She afterwards married L. Cornelius Cinna, and her son by this marriage, Cn. Cinna Magnus, entered into a conspiracy against Augustus. As her brother Sextus survived her, she must have died before 35. — 4. Daughter of Sex. Pompey, the son of the triumvir and of Scribonia. At the peace of Misenum in 39 she was betrothed to M. Marcellus, the son of Octavia, the sister of Octavian, but was never married to him. She accompanied her father in his flight to Asia, 36. — 5. Paulīna. [PAULINA.]

Pompeiānus, Tib. Claudĭus, son of a Roman knight originally from Antioch, rose to the highest dignities under M. Aurelius. This emperor gave him his daughter Lucilla in marriage. He lived to the reign of Severus.

Pompēĭi (Πομπήϊοι, Πομπαία, Πομπηΐα: Pompeianus), a city of Campania, was situated on the coast, at the mouth of the river Sarnus, and at the foot of Mt. Vesuvius ; but in consequence of the physical changes which the surrounding country has undergone, the ruins of Pompeii are found at present about 2 miles from the sea. Pompeii was first in the hands of the Oscans, afterwards of the Tyrrhenians, and finally became a Roman municipium. It was partly destroyed by an earthquake in A. D. 63, but was overwhelmed in 79, along with Herculaneum and Stabiae, by the great eruption of Mt. Vesuvius. The lava did not reach Pompeii, but the town was covered with successive layers of ashes and other volcanic matter, on which a soil was gradually formed. Thus a great part of the city has been preserved with its market-places, theatres, baths, temples, and private houses; and the excavation of it in modern times has thrown great light upon many points of antiquity, such as the construction of Roman houses, and in general all subjects connected with the private life of the ancients. The first traces of the ancient city were discovered in 1689, rising above the ground; but it was not till 1721 that the excavations were commenced. These have been continued with various interruptions to the present day; and now about half the city is exposed to view. It was surrounded by walls, which were about 2 miles in circumference, surmounted at intervals by towers, and containing 6 gates.

Pompeiopŏlis (Πομπηϊούπολις), the name of several cities founded or enlarged by Pompey. 1. (*Tash Köprü*), an inland city of Cappadocia, S.W. of Sinope, on the river Amnias (*Gök Irmak*), a W. tributary of the Halys. — 2. [POMPELON.] — 3. [SOLOÏ.]

Pompēius. 1. Q. Pompeius, said to have been the son of a flute-player, was the first of the family, who rose to dignity in the state. He was consul in 141, when he carried on war against the Numantines in Spain. Having been defeated by the enemy in several engagements, he concluded a peace with them; but on the arrival of his successor in the command, he disowned the treaty, which was declared invalid by the senate. He was censor in 131 with Q. Metellus Macedonicus.—2. Q. Pompeius Rufus, either son or grandson of the preceding, was a zealous supporter of the aristocratical party. He was tribune of the plebs, 100; praetor, 91; and consul, 88, with L. Sulla. When Sulla set out for the East to conduct the war against Mithridates, he left Italy in charge of Pompeius Rufus, and assigned to him the army of Cn. Pompeius Strabo, who was still engaged in carrying on war against the Marsi. Strabo, however, who was unwilling to be deprived of the command, caused Pompeius Rufus to be murdered by the soldiers. Cicero mentions Pompeius Rufus among the orators whom he had heard in his youth. — 3. Q. Pompeius Rufus, son of No. 2, married Sulla's daughter, and was murdered by the party of Sulpicius and Marius in the forum, during the consulship of his father, 88. — 4. Q. Pompeius Rufus, son of No. 3 and grandson of the dictator Sulla, was tribune of the plebs 52, when he distinguished himself as the great partizan of the triumvir Pompey, and assisted the latter in obtaining the sole consulship. Rufus however on the expiration of his office was accused of Vis, was condemned, and went into exile at Bauli in Campania. — 5. Q. Pompeius Rufus, praetor 63, was sent to Capua to watch over Campania and Apulia during Catiline's conspiracy. In 61 he obtained the province of Africa, with the title of proconsul. — 6. Sex.

Pompeius, married Lucilia, a sister of the poet C. Lucilius. — 7. Sex. Pompeius, elder son of No. 6, never obtained any of the higher offices of the state, but acquired great reputation as a man of learning, and is praised by Cicero for his accurate knowledge of jurisprudence, geometry, and the Stoic philosophy. — 8. Sex. Pompeius, a descendant of No. 7, consul A. D. 14, with Sex. Appuleius, in which year the emperor Augustus died. He seems to have been a patron of literature. Ovid addressed him several letters during his exile; and it was probably this same Sex. Pompeius, whom the writer Valerius Maximus accompanied to Asia, and of whom he speaks as his Alexander. — 9. Cn. Pompeius Strabo, younger son of No. 6, and father of the triumvir. He was quaestor in Sardinia 103, praetor 94, and propraetor in Sicily in the following year. He was consul 89, when he carried on war with success against the allies, subduing the greater number of the Italian people who were still in arms. Towards the end of the year he brought forward the law (*lex Pompeia*), which gave to all the towns of the Transpadani the Jus Latii or Latinitas. He continued in the S. of Italy as proconsul in the following year (88), and when Pompeius Rufus [No. 2.] was appointed to succeed him in the command of the army, Strabo caused him to be assassinated by the troops. Next year (87) the Marian party obtained the upper hand. Strabo was summoned by the aristocratical party to their assistance; and though not active in their cause, he marched to the relief of the city, and fought a battle near the Colline Gate with Cinna and Sertorius. Shortly afterwards, he was killed by lightning. His avarice and cruelty had made him hated by the soldiers to such a degree, that they tore his corpse from the bier and dragged it through the streets. Cicero describes him (*Brut.* 47) "as worthy of hatred on account of his cruelty, avarice, and perfidy." He possessed some reputation as an orator, and still more as a general. He left behind him a considerable property, especially in Picenum. — 10. Cn. Pompeius Magnus, the Triumvir, son of No. 9, was born on the 30th of September, B. C. 106, in the consulship of Atilius Serranus and Servilius Caepio, and was consequently a few months younger than Cicero, who was born on the 3d of January in this year, and 6 years older than Caesar. He fought under his father in 89 against the Italians, when he was only 17 years of age, and continued with him till his death two years afterwards. For the next few years the Marian party had possession of Italy; and accordingly Pompey, who adhered to the aristocratical party, was obliged to keep in the back ground. But when it became known in 84, that Sulla was on the point of returning from Greece to Italy, Pompey hastened into Picenum, where he raised an army of 3 legions. Although only 23 years of age, Pompey displayed great military abilities in opposing the Marian generals by whom he was surrounded; and when he succeeded in joining Sulla in the course of the year (83), he was saluted by the latter with the title of Imperator. During the remainder of the war in Italy Pompey distinguished himself as one of the most successful of Sulla's generals; and when the war in Italy was brought to a close, Sulla sent Pompey against the Marian party in Sicily and Africa. Pompey first proceeded to Sicily, of which he easily made himself master (82): here he put Carbo to death. In 81 Pompey crossed over to Africa, where he defeated Cn. Domitius Ahenobarbus and the Numidian king Hiarbas, after a hard fought battle. On his return to Rome, in the same year, he was received with enthusiasm by the people, and was greeted by Sulla with the surname of MAGNUS, a name which he bore ever afterwards, and handed down to his children. Pompey, however, not satisfied with this distinction, sued for a triumph, which Sulla at first refused ; but at length overcome by Pompey's importunity, he allowed him to have his own way. Accordingly Pompey, who had not yet held any public office, and was still a simple eques, entered Rome in triumph in September 81, and before he had completed his 25th year. Pompey continued faithful to the aristocracy after Sulla's death (78), and supported the consul Catulus in resisting the attempts of his colleague Lepidus to repeal the laws of Sulla ; and when Lepidus had recourse to arms in the following year (77), Pompey took an active part in the war against him, and succeeded in driving him out of Italy. — The aristocracy, however, now began to fear the young and successful general ; but since Sertorius in Spain had for the last three years successfully opposed Metellus Pius, one of the ablest of Sulla's generals, and it had become necessary to send the latter some effectual assistance, the senate, with considerable reluctance, determined to send Pompey to Spain, with the title of proconsul, and with equal powers to Metellus. Pompey remained in Spain between 5 and 6 years (76—71); but neither he nor Metellus was able to gain any decisive advantage over Sertorius. But when Sertorius was treacherously murdered by his own officer Perperna, in 82, the war was speedily brought to a close. Perperna was easily defeated by Pompey in the first battle, and the whole of Spain was subdued by the early part of the following year (71). Pompey then returned to Italy at the head of his army. In his march towards Rome he fell in with the remains of the army of Spartacus, which M. Crassus had previously defeated. Pompey cut to pieces these fugitives, and therefore claimed for himself, in addition to all his other exploits, the glory of finishing the Servile war. Pompey was now a candidate for the consulship ; and although he was ineligible by law, inasmuch as he was absent from Rome, had not yet reached the legal age, and had not held any of the offices of the state, still his election was certain. His military glory had charmed the people ; and as it was known that the aristocracy looked upon Pompey with jealousy, they ceased to regard him as belonging to this party, and hoped to obtain, through him, a restoration of the rights and privileges of which they had been deprived by Sulla. Pompey was accordingly elected consul, along with M. Crassus ; and on the 31st of December, 71, he entered the city a second time in his triumphal car, a simple eques. — In his consulship (70), Pompey openly broke with the aristocracy, and became the great popular hero. He proposed and carried a law, restoring to the tribunes the power of which they had been deprived by Sulla. He also afforded his all-powerful aid to the Lex Aurelia, proposed by the praetor L. Aurelius Cotta, by which the judices were to be taken in future from the senatus, equites, and tribuni aerarii, instead of from the senators exclusively, as Sulla

had ordained. In carrying both these measures Pompey was strongly supported by Caesar, with whom he was thus brought into close connection. — For the next two years (69 and 68) Pompey remained in Rome. In 67 the tribune A. Gabinius brought forward a bill, proposing to confer upon Pompey the command of the war against the pirates with extraordinary powers. This bill was opposed by the aristocracy with the utmost vehemence, but was notwithstanding carried. The pirates were at this time masters of the Mediterranean, and had not only plundered many cities on the coasts of Greece and Asia, but had even made descents upon Italy itself. As soon as Pompey received the command, he began to make his preparations for the war, and completed them by the end of the winter. His plans were formed with great skill and judgment, and were crowned with complete success. In 40 days he cleared the western sea of pirates, and restored communication between Spain, Africa, and Italy. He then followed the main body of the pirates to their strongholds on the coast of Cilicia ; and after defeating their fleet, he induced a great part of them, by promises of pardon, to surrender to him. Many of these he settled at Soli, which was henceforward called Pompeiopolis. The 2nd part of the campaign occupied only 49 days, and the whole war was brought to a conclusion in the course of 3 months ; so that, to adopt the panegyric of Cicero (pro Leg. Man. 12) " Pompey made his preparations for the war at the end of the winter, entered upon it at the commencement of spring, and finished it in the middle of the summer." Pompey was employed during the remainder of this year and the beginning of the following in visiting the cities of Cilicia and Pamphylia, and providing for the government of the newly-conquered districts. — During his absence from Rome, Pompey was appointed to succeed Lucullus in the command of the war against Mithridates (66). The bill, conferring upon him this command, was proposed by the tribune C. Manilius, and was supported by Cicero, in an oration which has come down to us (Pro Lege Manilia). Like the Gabinian law, it was opposed by the whole weight of the aristocracy, but was carried triumphantly. The power of Mithridates had been broken by the previous victories of Lucullus, and it was only left to Pompey to bring the war to a conclusion. On the approach of Pompey, Mithridates retreated towards Armenia, but he was defeated by the Roman general ; and as Tigranes now refused to receive him into his dominions, Mithridates resolved to plunge into the heart of Colchis, and from thence make his way to his own dominions in the Cimmerian Bosporus. Pompey now turned his arms against Tigranes ; but the Armenian king submitted to him without a contest, and was allowed to conclude a peace with the republic. In 65 Pompey set out in pursuit of Mithridates, but he met with much opposition from the Iberians and Albanians ; and after advancing as far as the river Phasis (Fas), he resolved to leave these savage districts. He accordingly retraced his steps, and spent the winter at Pontus, which he reduced to the form of a Roman province. In 64 he marched into Syria, deposed the king Antiochus Asiaticus, and made that country also a Roman province. In 63 he advanced further south, in order to establish the Roman supremacy in Phoenicia, Coele-Syria, and

Palestine. The Jews refused to submit to him, and shut the gates of Jerusalem against him; and it was not till after a siege of 3 months that the city was taken. Pompey entered the Holy of Holies, the first time that any human being, except the high-priest, had dared to penetrate into this sacred spot. It was during the war in Palestine that Pompey received intelligence of the death of Mithridates. [MITHRIDATES VI.] Pompey spent the next winter in Pontus; and after settling the affairs of Asia, he returned to Italy in 62. He disbanded his army almost immediately after landing at Brundisium, and thus calmed the apprehensions of many, who feared that, at the head of his victorious troops, he would seize upon the supreme power. He did not, however, return to Rome till the following year (61), and he entered the city in triumph on the 30th of September. He had just completed his 45th year, and this was the third time that he had enjoyed the honour of a triumph. With this triumph the first and most glorious part of Pompey's life may be said to have ended. Hitherto his life had been an almost uninterrupted succession of military glory. But now he was called upon to play a prominent part in the civil commotions of the commonwealth, a part for which neither his natural talents nor his previous habits had in the least fitted him. It would seem, that on his return to Rome, Pompey hardly knew what part to take in the politics of the city. He had been appointed to the command against the pirates and Mithridates in opposition to the aristocracy, and they still regarded him with jealousy and distrust. At the same time he was not disposed to unite himself to the popular party, which had risen into importance during his absence in the East, and over which Caesar possessed unbounded influence. The object, however, which engaged the immediate attention of Pompey was to obtain from the senate a ratification for all his acts in Asia, and an assignment of lands which he had promised to his veterans. The senate, however, glad of an opportunity to put an affront upon a man whom they both feared and hated, resolutely refused to sanction his measures in Asia. This was the unwisest thing the senate could have done. If they had known their real interests, they would have sought to win Pompey over to their side, as a counterpoise to the growing and more dangerous influence of Caesar. But their short-sighted policy threw Pompey into Caesar's arms, and thus sealed the downfal of their party. Caesar promised to obtain for Pompey the ratification of his acts; and Pompey, on his part, agreed to support Caesar in all his measures. That they might be more sure of carrying their plans into execution, Caesar prevailed upon Pompey to become reconciled to Crassus, with whom he was at variance, but who, by his immense wealth, had great influence at Rome. The 3 agreed to assist one another against their mutual enemies; and thus was first formed the first triumvirate. — This union of the 3 most powerful men at Rome crushed the aristocracy for the time. Supported by Pompey and Crassus, Caesar was able in his consulship (59) to carry all his measures. Pompey's acts in Asia were ratified; and Caesar's agrarian law, which divided the rich Campanian land among the poorer citizens, enabled Pompey to fulfil the promises he had made to his veterans. In order to cement their union more closely, Caesar gave to Pompey his daughter Julia

in marriage. Next year (58) Caesar went to his province in Gaul, but Pompey remained in Rome. While Caesar was gaining glory and influence in Gaul, Pompey was gradually losing the confidence of all parties at Rome. The senate hated and feared him; the people had deserted him for their favourite Clodius; and he had no other resource left but to strengthen his connection with Caesar. Thus he came to be regarded as the second man in the state, and was obliged to abandon the proud position which he had occupied for so many years. According to an arrangement made with Caesar, Pompey and Crassus were consuls for a second time in 55. Pompey received as his provinces the two Spains, Crassus obtained Syria, while Caesar's government was prolonged for 5 years more, namely from the 1st of January, 53, to the end of the year 49. At the end of his consulship Pompey did not go in person to his provinces, but sent his legates, L. Afranius and M. Petreius to govern the Spains, while he himself remained in the neighbourhood of the city. His object now was to obtain the dictatorship, and to make himself the undisputed master of the Roman world. Caesar's increasing power and influence had at length made it clear to Pompey that a struggle must take place between them, sooner or later. The death of his wife Julia, in 54, to whom he was tenderly attached, broke one link which still connected him with Caesar; and the fall of Crassus in the following year (53), in the Parthian expedition, removed the only person who had the least chance of contesting the supremacy with them. In order to obtain the dictatorship, Pompey secretly encouraged the civil discord with which the state was torn asunder; and such frightful scenes of anarchy followed the death of Clodius at the beginning of 52, that the senate had now no alternative but calling in the assistance of Pompey, who was accordingly made sole consul in 52, and succeeded in restoring order to the state. Soon afterwards Pompey became reconciled to the aristocracy, and was now regarded as their acknowledged head. The history of the civil war which followed is related in the life of CAESAR. It is only necessary to mention here, that after the battle of Pharsalia (48) Pompey sailed to Egypt, where he hoped to meet with a favourable reception, since he had been the means of restoring to his kingdom the father of the young Egyptian monarch. The ministers of the latter, however, dreading Caesar's anger if they received Pompey, and likewise Pompey's resentment if they forbade him to land, resolved to release themselves from their difficulties by putting him to death. They accordingly sent out a small boat, took Pompey on board, and rowed for the shore. His wife and friends watched him from the ship, anxious to see in what manner he would be received by the king, who was standing on the edge of the sea with his troops; but just as the boat reached the shore, and Pompey was in the act of rising from his seat, in order to step on land, he was stabbed in the back by Septimius, who had formerly been one of his centurions, and was now in the service of the Egyptian monarch. Pompey was killed on the 29th of September, B.C. 48, and had just completed his 58th year. His head was cut off, and his body, which was thrown out naked on the shore, was buried by his freedman Philippus, who had accompanied him from the ship. The head was

brought to Caesar when he arrived in Egypt soon afterwards, but he turned away from the sight, shed tears at the melancholy death of his rival, and put his murderers to death. Pompey's untimely death excites pity; but no one, who has well studied the state of parties at the close of the Roman commonwealth, can regret his fall. There is abundant evidence to prove, that had Pompey's party gained the mastery, a proscription far more terrible than Sulla's would have taken place, and Italy and the provinces been divided as booty among a few profligate and unprincipled nobles. From such horrors the victory of Caesar saved the Roman world. Pompey was married 5 times. The names of his wives were 1. Antistia. 2. Aemilia. 3. Mucia. 4. Julia. 5. Cornelia. —
11. **Cn. Pompeius Magnus**, elder son of the triumvir by his third wife Mucia. In the civil war in 48, he commanded a squadron of the fleet in the Adriatic Sea. After his father's death, at Pharsalia, he crossed over to Africa, and after remaining there a short time, he sailed to Spain in 47. In Spain he was joined by his brother Sextus and others of his party, who had fled from Africa after their defeat at Thapsus. Here the 2 brothers collected a powerful army, but were defeated by Caesar himself at the battle of Munda, fought on the 17th of March, 45. Cneius escaped from the field of battle, but was shortly afterwards taken prisoner, and put to death. — **12. Sex. Pompeius Magnus**, younger son of the triumvir by his third wife Mucia, was born 75. After the battle of Pharsalia he accompanied his father to Egypt, and saw him murdered before his eyes. After the battle of Munda and the death of his brother, Sextus lived for a time in concealment in the country of the Lacetani, between the Iberus and the Pyrenees; but when Caesar quitted Spain, he collected a body of troops, and emerged from his lurking-place. In the civil wars, which followed Caesar's death, the power of Sextus increased. He obtained a large fleet, became master of the sea, and eventually took possession of Sicily. His fleet enabled him to stop all the supplies of corn which were brought to Rome from Egypt and the eastern provinces; and such scarcity began to prevail in the city, that the triumvirs were compelled by the popular discontent to make peace with Pompey. This peace was concluded at Misenum in 39, but the war was renewed in the following year. Octavian made great efforts to collect a large and powerful fleet, which he placed under the command of Agrippa. In 36 Pompey's fleet was defeated off Naulochus, with great loss. Pompey himself fled from Sicily to Lesbos and from Lesbos to Asia. Here he was taken prisoner by a body of Antony's troops, and carried to Miletus, where he was put to death (35), probably by command of Antony, though the latter sought to throw the responsibility of the deed upon his officers.

Pompeius Festus. [FESTUS.]

Pompeius Trogus. [JUSTINUS.]

· **Pompelon** (*Pamplona*), which name is equivalent to Pompeiopolis, so called by the sons of Pompey, was the chief town of the Vascones in Hispania Tarraconensis, on the road from Asturica to Burdigala.

Pomponia. 1. Sister of T. Pomponius Atticus, was married to Q. Cicero, the brother of the orator, B. C. 68. The marriage proved an extremely unhappy one. Q. Cicero, after leading a miserable

life with his wife for almost 24 years, at length divorced her at the end of 45, or in the beginning of the following year. — 2. Daughter of T. Pomponius Atticus. She is also called Caecilia, because her father was adopted by Q. Caecilius, and likewise Attica. She was born in 51, and she was still quite young when she was married to M. Vipsanius Agrippa. Her daughter Vipsania Agrippina married Tiberius, the successor of Augustus.

Pomponiana. [STOECHADES.]

Pomponius, Sextus, a distinguished Roman jurist, who lived under Antoninus Pius and M. Aurelius. Some modern writers think that there were 2 jurists of this name. The works of Pomponius are frequently cited in the Digest.

Pomponius Atticus. [ATTICUS.]

Pomponius Bononiensis, the most celebrated writer of Fabulae Atellanae, was a native of Bononia (*Bologna*) in northern Italy, as his surname shows, and flourished B. C. 91.

Pomponius Mela. [MELA.]

Pomptinae Paludes (Πόντιναι λίμναι: *Palude Pontine*, in English the *Pontine Marshes*), the name of a low marshy plain on the coast of Latium between Circeii and Terracina, said to have been so called after an ancient town Pontia, which disappeared at an early period. The plain is about 24 miles long, and from 8 to 10 miles in breadth. The marshes are formed chiefly by the rivers Nymphaeus, Ufens, and Amasenus, and some other small streams, which, instead of finding their way into the sea, spread over this plain. Hence the plain is turned into a vast number of marshes, the miasmas arising from which are exceedingly unhealthy in the summer. At an early period, however, they appear not to have existed at all, or at any rate to have been confined to a narrow district. We are told that originally there were 23 towns situated in this plain; and in B. C. 432 the *Pomptinus Ager* is mentioned as yielding a large quantity of corn. Even as late as 312, the greater part of the plain must still have been free from the marshes, since the censor Appius Claudius conducted the celebrated Via Appia in that year through the plain, which must then have been sufficiently strong to bear the weight of this road. In the course of a century and a half after this, the marshes had spread to a great extent; and accordingly attempts were made to drain them by the consul Cethegus in 160, by Julius Caesar and by Augustus. It is usually said that Augustus caused a navigable canal to be dug along side of the Via Appia from Forum Appii to the grove of Feronia, in order to carry off a portion of the waters of the marshes: but this canal must have been dug before the time of Augustus, since Horace embarked upon it on his celebrated journey from Rome to Brundisium in 37, at which time Octavian, as he was then called, could not have undertaken any of his public works. Subsequently the marshes again spread over the whole plain, and the Via Appia entirely disappeared; and it was not until the pontificate of Pius VI. that any serious attempt was made to drain them. The works were commenced in 1778, and the greater part of the marshes was drained; but the plain is still unhealthy in the great heats of the summer.

C. Pomptinus, was praetor B. C. 63, when he was employed by Cicero in apprehending the ambassadors of the Allobroges. He afterwards obtained the province of Gallia Narbonensis, and in 61 defeated the Allobroges, who had invaded the province. He triumphed in 54, after suing in vain for this honour for some years.

Pons, a common name for stations on the Roman roads at the passage of rivers, some of which stations on the more important roads grew into villages or towns. **1.** P. **Aeni** (*Pfünzen*), in Vindelicia, at the passage of the Inn, was a fortress with a Roman garrison.—**2.** P. **Aureoli** (*Pontirolo*), in Gallia Transpadana on the road from Bergamum to Mediolanum, derived its name from one of the 30 Tyrants, who was defeated and slain by Claudius in this place.—**3.** P. **Campanus**, in Campania between Sinuessa and Urbana on the Savo.—Respecting the bridges of Rome, see ROMA.

Pontia (*Ponza*), a rocky island off the coast of Latium opposite Formiae, which was taken by the Romans from the Volscians, and colonised, B. C. 313. Under the Romans it was used as a place of banishment for state criminals. There is a group of smaller islands round Pontia, which are sometimes called Insulae Pontiae.

Pontinus (Ποντῖνος), a river and mountain in Argolis near Lerna, with a sanctuary of Athena Saitis.

C. **Pontius**, son of **Herennius Pontius**, the general of the Samnites in B. C. 321, defeated the Roman army under the two consuls T. Veturius Calvinus and Sp. Postumius Albinus in one of the mountain passes in the neighbourhood of Caudium. The survivors, who were completely at the mercy of the Samnites, were dismissed unhurt by Pontius. They had to surrender their arms, and to pass under the yoke; and as the price of their deliverance, the consuls and the other commanders swore, in the name of the republic, to a humiliating peace. The Roman state however refused to ratify the treaty. Nearly 30 years afterwards, Pontius was defeated by Q. Fabius Gurges (292), was taken prisoner, and was put to death after the triumph of the consul.

Pontius Aquila. [AQUILA.]

Pontius Pilatus, was the sixth procurator of Judaea, and the successor of Valerius Gratus. He held the office for 10 years in the reign of Tiberius, from A. D. 26 to 36, and it was during his government that Christ taught, suffered, and died. By his tyrannical conduct he excited an insurrection at Jerusalem, and at a later period commotions in Samaria also, which were not put down without the loss of life. The Samaritans complained of his conduct to Vitellius, the governor of Syria, who deprived him of his office, and sent him to Rome to answer before the emperor the accusations that were brought against him. Eusebius states that Pilatus put an end to his own life at the commencement of the reign of Caligula, worn out by the many misfortunes he had experienced. The early Christian writers refer frequently to an official report, made by Pilatus to the emperor Tiberius, of the condemnation and death of Christ. It is very doubtful whether this document was genuine; and it is certain that the acts of Pilate, as they are called, which are extant in Greek, as well as his two Latin letters to the emperor, are the productions of a later age.

Pontius Telesinus. 1. A Samnite, and commander of a Samnite army, with which he fought against Sulla. He was defeated by Sulla in a

hard-fought battle near the Colline gate, B. C. 82. He fell in the fight; his head was cut off, and carried under the walls of Praeneste, to let the younger Marius know that his last hope of succour was gone.—**2.** Brother of the preceding, was shut up in Praeneste with the younger Marius, when his brother was defeated by Sulla. After the death of the elder Pontius, Marius and Telesinus, finding it impossible to escape from Praeneste, resolved to die by one another's hands. Telesinus fell first, and Marius put an end to his own life, or was slain by his slave.

Pontus (ὁ Πόντος), the N.E.-most district of Asia Minor, along the coast of the Euxine, E. of the river Halys, having originally no specific name, was spoken of as the country ἐν Πόντῳ, *on the Pontus* (*Euxinus*), and hence acquired the name of Pontus, which is first found in Xenophon's *Anabasis*. The term, however, was used very indefinitely, until the settlement of the boundaries of the country as a Roman province. Originally it was regarded as a part of CAPPADOCIA; but its parts were best known by the names of the different tribes who dwelt along the coast, and of whom some account is given by Xenophon, in the *Anabasis*. We learn from the legends of the Argonauts, who are represented as visiting this coast, and the Amazons, whose abodes are placed about the river Thermodon, E. of the Iris, as well as from other poetical allusions, that the Greeks had some knowledge of these S. E. shores of the Euxine at a very early period. A great accession to such knowledge was made by the information gained by Xenophon and his comrades, when they passed through the country in their famous retreat: and long afterwards the Romans became well acquainted with it by means of the Mithridatic war, and Pompey's subsequent expedition through Pontus into the countries at the foot of the Caucasus. The name first acquired a *political* rather than a *territorial* importance, through the foundation of a new kingdom in it, about the beginning of the 4th century B. C., by ARIOBARZANES I. The history of the gradual growth of this kingdom until, under Mithridates VI., it threatened the Roman empire in Asia, is given under the names of its kings, of whom the following is the list:— (1) ARIOBARZANES I., exact date unknown: (2) MITHRIDATES I., to B. C. 363: (3) ARIOBARZANES II., 363—337: (4) MITHRIDATES II., 337—302: (5) MITHRIDATES III., 302—266: (6) ARIOBARZANES III., 266—240? (7) MITHRIDATES IV., 240—190? (8) PHARNACES I., 190—156? (9) MITHRIDATES V. EUERGETES, 156—120? (10) MITHRIDATES VI. EUPATOR, 120—63: (11) PHARNACES II., 63—47. After the death of Pharnaces, the reduced kingdom retained a nominal existence under his son Darius, who was made king by Antony in B. C. 39, but was soon deposed; and under POLEMON I. and POLEMON II., till about A. D. 62, when the country was constituted by Nero a Roman province. Of this province the W. boundary was the river Halys, which divided it from Paphlagonia; the furthest E. limit was the Phasis, which separated it from Colchis; but others carry it only as far as Trapezus, and others to an intermediate point, at the river Acampsis: on the S. it was divided from Galatia, Cappadocia, and Armenia Minor by the great chain of the Paryadres and by its branches. It was divided into the 3 districts of **Pontus Galaticus**, in the W., bordering on Galatıa, P. **Polemoniacus** in the centre, so called from its capital POLEMONIUM, and P. **Cappadocius** in the E. bordering on Cappadocia (Armenia Minor). In the new division of the provinces under Constantine, these 3 districts were reduced to 2, **Helenopontus** in the W., so called in honour of the emperor's mother, Helena, and **Pontus Polemoniacus** in the E. The country was also divided into smaller districts, named from the towns they surrounded and the tribes who peopled them. Pontus was a mountainous coúntry; wild and barren in the E., where the great chains approach the Euxine; but in the W. watered by the great rivers HALYS and IRIS and their tributaries, the valleys of which, as well as the land along the coast, are extremely fertile. Besides corn and olives, it was famous for its fruit trees, and some of the best of our common fruits are said to have been brought to Europe from this quarter; for example, the cherry (see CERASUS). The sides of the mountains were covered with fine timber, and their lower slopes with box and other shrubs. The E. part was rich in minerals, and contained the celebrated iron mines of the CHALYBES. Pontus was peopled by numerous tribes, belonging probably to very different races, though the Semitic (Syro-Arabian) race appears to have been the prevailing one, and hence the inhabitants were included under the general name of LEUCOSYRI. The chief of these peoples are spoken of in separate articles.

Pontus Euxinus, or simply **Pontus** (ὁ Πόντος, Πόντος Εὔξεινος: τὸ Ποντικὸν πέλαγος, Mare Euxīnum : *the Black Sea*, Turk. *Kara Deniz*, Grk. *Maurethalassa*, Russ. *Tcheriago More* or *Czarne-More*, all names of the same meaning, and supposed to have originated from the terror with which it was at first regarded by the Turkish mariners, as the first wide expanse of sea with which they became acquainted), the great inland sea enclosed by Asia Minor on the S., Colchis on the E., Sarmatia on the N., and Dacia and Thracia on the W., and having no other outlet than the narrow BOSPORUS THRACIUS in its S.W. corner. It lies between 28° and 41° 30′ E. long., and between 41° and 46° 40′ N. lat., its length being about 700 miles, and its breadth varying from 400 to 160. Its surface contains more than 180,000 square miles. It receives the drainage of an immense extent of country in Europe and in Asia; but much the greater portion of its waters flows from the former continent by the following rivers : the Ister or Danubius (*Danube*), whose basin contains the greater part of central Europe ; the Tyras or Damaster (*Dniester*), Hypanis or Bogus (*Boug*), Borysthenes (*Dnieper*), and Tanaïs (*Don*), which drain the immense plains of *S. Russia*, and flow into the N. side of the Euxine, the last of them (i. e. the Tanaïs) through the Palus Mneotis (*Sea of Azov*). The space thus drained is calculated at above 860,000 square miles, or nearly 1-5th of the whole surface of Europe. In Asia, the basin of the Euxine contains, first, the triangular piece of Sarmatia Asiatica between the Tanaïs on the N., the Caucasus on the S., and on the E. the Hippici M., which form the watershed dividing the tributaries of the Euxine from those of the Caspian ; the waters of this space flow into the Tanaïs and the Palus Maeotis, and the largest of them is the Hypanis or Vardanes (*Kuban*), which comes down to the Palus Maeotis and the Euxine

at their junction, and divides its waters between them : next we have the narrow strip of land between the Caucasus and the N.E. coast of the sea, then on the E., Colchis, hemmed in between the Caucasus and Moschici M., and watered by the Phasis ; and lastly, on the S., the whole of that part of Asia Minor which lies between the Paryadres and Antitaurus on the E. and S.E., the Taurus on the S., and the highlands of Phrygia on the W., the chief rivers of this portion being the Iris (*Yeshil Irmak*), the Halys (*Kizil Irmak*), and the Sangarius (*Sakariyeh*). The whole of the Asiatic basin of the Euxine is estimated at 100,000 square miles. As might be expected from this vast influx of fresh water, the water is much less salt than that of the Ocean. The waters which the Euxine receives from the rivers that flow directly into it, and also from the Palus Maeotis (*Sea of Azov*) through the Bosporus Cimmerius (*Straits of Kaffa* or *Yenikaleh*), find their exit at the S.W. corner, through the Bosporus Thracius (*Channel of Constantinople*), into the Propontis (*Sea of Marmara*), and thence in a constant rapid current through the Hellespontus (*Straits of Gallipoli* or *Dardanelles*) into the Aegeum Mare (*Archipelago*). — The Argonautic and other legends show that the Greeks had some acquaintance with this sea at a very early period. It is said that they at first called it *Ἄξενος* (*inhospitable*), from the savage character of the peoples on its coast, and from the supposed terrors of its navigation, and that afterwards, on their favourite principle of *euphemism* (i. e. abstaining from words of evil omen) they changed its name to Εὔξενος, Ion. Εὔξεινος, *hospitable*. The Greeks of Asia Minor, especially the people of Miletus, founded many colonies and commercial emporiums on its shores, and as early as the Persian wars we find Athens carrying on a regular trade with these settlements in the corn grown in the great plains on its N. side (the *Ukraine*) and in the Chersonesus Taurica (*Crimea*), which have ever since supplied W. Europe with large quantities of grain. The history of the settlements themselves will be found under their several names. The Romans had a pretty accurate knowledge of the sea. An account of its coasts exists in Greek, entitled "Periplus Maris Euxini," ascribed to Arrian, who lived in the reign of Hadrian. [ARRIANUS.]

Popillius Laenas. [LAENAS.]
Poplicola. [PUBLICOLA.]
Poppaea Sabina. [SABINA.]
Poppaeus Sabinus. [SABINUS.]

Populōnia, or -**ium** (Populoniensis: *Populonia*), an ancient town of Etruria, situated on a lofty hill, sinking abruptly to the sea, and forming a peninsula. According to one tradition it was founded by the Corsicans ; but according to another it was a colony from Volaterrae, or was taken from the Corsicans by the Volaterrani. It was not one of the 12 Etruscan cities, and was never a place of political importance ; but it carried on an extensive commerce, and was the principal seaport of Etruria. It was destroyed by Sulla in the civil wars, and was in ruins in the time of Strabo. There are still remains of the walls of the ancient Populonia, showing that the city was only about 1¼ mile in circumference.

Porcia. 1. Sister of Cato Uticensis, married L. Domitius Ahenobarbus, consul B. C. 54, who was slain in the battle of Pharsalia. She died in

46. — 2. Daughter of Cato Uticensis by his first wife Atilia. She was married first to M. Bibulus, consul 59, to whom she bore three children. Bibulus died in 48; and in 45 she married M. Brutus, the assassin of Julius Caesar. She inherited all her father's republican principles, and likewise his courage and firmness of will. She induced her husband on the night before the 15th of March to disclose to her the conspiracy against Caesar's life, and she is reported to have wounded herself in the thigh in order to show that she had a courageous soul and could be trusted with the secret. She put an end to her own life after the death of Brutus in 42. The common tale was, that her friends, suspecting her design, had taken all weapons out of her way, and that she therefore destroyed herself by swallowing live coals. The real fact may have been that she suffocated herself by the vapour of a charcoal fire, which we know was a frequent means of self-destruction among the Romans.

Porcĭus Cato. [CATO.]
Porcĭus Festus. [FESTUS.]
Porcĭus Latro. [LATRO.]
Porcĭus Licĭnus. [LICINUS.]

Porphȳrĭo, Pompōnĭus, the most valuable among the ancient commentators on Horace. He lived after Festus and Acro.

Porphȳrĭon (Πορφυρίων), one of the giants who fought against the gods. When he attempted to offer violence to Hera, or to throw the island of Delos against the gods, Zeus hurled a thunderbolt at him, and Hercules completed his destruction with his arrows.

Porphȳris (Πορφυρίς), an earlier name of the island of NISYRUS.

Porphȳrĭus (Πορφύριος), usually called Porphyry, the celebrated antagonist of Christianity, was a Greek philosopher of the Neo-Platonic school. He was born A. D. 233 either in Batanea in Palestine or at Tyre. His original name was *Malchus*, the Greek form of the Syrophoenician *Meloch*, a word which signified king. The name *Porphyrius* (in allusion to the usual colour of royal robes) was subsequently devised for him by his preceptor Longinus. After studying under Origen at Caesarea, and under Apollonius and Longinus at Athens, he settled at Rome in his 30th year, and there became a diligent disciple of Plotinus. He soon gained the confidence of Plotinus, and was entrusted by the latter with the difficult and delicate duty of correcting and arranging his writings. [PLOTINUS.] After remaining in Rome 6 years, Porphyry fell into an unsettled state of mind, and began to entertain the idea of suicide, in order to get free from the shackles of the flesh; but on the advice of Plotinus he took a voyage to Sicily, where he resided for some time. It was during his residence in Sicily that he wrote his treatise against the Christian religion, in 15 books. Of the remainder of his life we know very little. He returned to Rome, where he continued to teach until his death, which took place about 305 or 306. Late in life he married Marcella, the widow of one of his friends, and the mother of 7 children, with the view, as he avowed, of superintending their education. As a writer Porphyry deserves considerable praise. His style is tolerably clear, and not unfrequently exhibits both imagination and vigour. His learning was most extensive. A great degree of critical and philosophical acumen was not to be expected in one so ardently attached to the enthusiastic and somewhat fanatical system of Plotinus. His attempt to prove the identity of the Platonic and Aristotelic systems would alone be sufficient to show this. Nevertheless, his acquaintance with the authors whom he quotes was manifestly far from superficial. His most celebrated work was his treatise against the Christian religion ; but of its nature and merits we are not able to judge, as it has not come down to us. It was publicly destroyed by order of the emperor Theodosius. The attack was sufficiently vigorous to call forth replies from above 30 different antagonists, the most distinguished of whom were Methodius, Apollinaris, and Eusebius. A large number however of his works has come down to us; of which his Life of Pythagoras and Life of Plotinus are some of the best known.

Porphȳrĭus, Publĭlĭus Optatiānus, a Roman poet, who lived in the age of Constantine the Great. He wrote a Panegyric upon Constantine ; 3 Idyllia, namely, 1. *Ara Pythia*, 2. *Syrinx*, 3. *Organon*, with the lines so arranged as to represent the form of these objects ; and 5 Epigrams.

Porsena* or Porsenna, Lars, king of the Etruscan town of Clusium, marched against Rome at the head of a vast army, in order to restore Tarquinius Superbus to the throne. He took possession of the hill Janiculum, and would have entered the city by the bridge which connected Rome with the Janiculum, had it not been for the superhuman prowess of Horatius Cocles, who kept the whole Etruscan army at bay, while his comrades broke down the bridge behind him. [COCLES.] The Etruscans proceeded to lay siege to the city, which soon began to suffer from famine. Thereupon a young Roman, named C. Mucius, resolved to deliver his country by murdering the invading king. He accordingly went over to the Etruscan camp, but ignorant of the person of Porsena, killed the royal secretary instead. Seized, and threatened with torture, he thrust his right hand into the fire on the altar, and there let it burn, to show how little he heeded pain. Astonished at his courage, the king bade him depart in peace ; and Scaevola, as he was henceforward called, told him, out of gratitude, to make peace with Rome, since 300 noble youths had sworn to take the life of the king, and he was the first upon whom the lot had fallen. Porsena thereupon made peace with the Romans, and withdrew his troops from the Janiculum after receiving 20 hostages from the Romans. Such was the tale by which Roman vanity concealed one of the earliest and greatest disasters of the city. The real fact is, that Rome was completely conquered by Porsena. This is expressly stated by Tacitus (*Hist.* iii. 72.), and is confirmed by other writers. Pliny tells us that so thorough was the subjection of the Romans that they were expressly prohibited from using iron for any other purpose but agriculture. The Romans, however, did not long remain subject to the Etruscans. After the conquest of Rome, Aruns, the son of Porsena, proceeded to attack Aricia, but was defeated before the city by the united forces of the Latin cities, assisted by the Greeks of Cumae. The Etruscans appear, in con-

---

* The quantity of the penultimate is doubtful. It is short in Horace and Martial, but long in Virgil.

sequence, to have been confined to their own territory on the right bank of the Tiber, and the Romans to have availed themselves of the opportunity to recover their independence.

Porthāon (Πορθάων), son of Agenor and Epicaste, was king of Pleuron and Calydon in Aetolia, and married to Euryte, by whom he became the father of Oeneus, Agrius, Alcathous, Melas, Leucopeus, and Sterope.

Porthmus (Πόρθμος), a harbour in Euboea, belonging to Eretria, opposite the coast of Attica.

Portūnus or Portumnus, the protecting genius of harbours among the Romans. He was invoked to grant a happy return from a voyage. Hence a temple was erected to him at the port of the Tiber, from whence the road descended to the port of Ostia. At his temple an annual festival, the Portunalia, was celebrated on the 17th of August. When the Romans became familiar with Greek mythology, Portunus was identified with the Greek Palaemon. [PALAEMON.]

Pŏrus (Πῶρος). 1. King of the Indian provinces E. of the river Hydaspes, offered a formidable resistance to Alexander, when the latter attempted to cross this river, B. C. 327. The battle which he fought with Alexander was one of the most severely contested which occurred during the whole of Alexander's campaigns. Porus displayed great personal courage in the battle; and when brought before the conqueror, he proudly demanded to be treated in a manner worthy of a king. This magnanimity at once conciliated the favour of Alexander, who not only restored to him his dominions, but increased them by large accessions of territory. From this time Porus became firmly attached to his generous conqueror, whom he accompanied to the Hyphasis. In 321 Porus was treacherously put to death by Eudemus, who commanded the Macedonian troops in the adjacent province. We are told that Porus was a man of gigantic stature — not less than five cubits in height; and his personal strength and prowess in war were not less conspicuous than his valour. — 2. Another Indian monarch who, at the time of Alexander's expedition, ruled over the district termed Gandaris, E. of the river Hydraotes. His dominions were subdued by Hephaestion, and annexed to those of the preceding Porus, who was his kinsman.

Poseidon (Ποσειδῶν), called Neptūnus by the Romans, was the god of the Mediterranean sea. His name seems to be connected with πότος, πόντος and ποταμός, according to which he is the god of the fluid element. He was a son of Cronos and Rhea (whence he is called Cronius and by Latin poets Saturnius). He was accordingly a brother of Zeus, Hades, Hera, Hestia and Demeter, and it was determined by lot that he should rule over the sea. Like his brothers and sisters, he was, after his birth, swallowed by his father Cronos, but thrown up again. According to others, he was concealed by Rhea, after his birth, among a flock of lambs, and his mother pretended to have given birth to a young horse, which she gave to Cronos to devour. In the Homeric poems Poseidon is described as equal to Zeus in dignity, but less powerful. He resents the attempts of Zeus to intimidate him; he even threatens his mightier brother, and once conspired with Hera and Athena to put him into chains; but on other occasions we find him submissive to Zeus. The palace of Poseidon was in the depth of the sea near Aegae in Euboea, where he kept his horses with brazen hoofs and golden manes. With these horses he rides in a chariot over the waves of the sea, which become smooth as he approaches, and the monsters of the deep recognise him and play around his chariot. Generally he yoked his horses to his chariot himself, but sometimes he was assisted by Amphitrite. Although he generally dwelt in the sea, still he also appears in Olympus in the assembly of the gods. — Poseidon in conjunction with Apollo is said to have built the walls of Troy for Laomedon, whence Troy is called Neptunia Pergama. Laomedon refused to give these gods the reward which had been stipulated, and even dismissed them with threats. Poseidon in consequence sent a marine monster, which was on the point of devouring Laomedon's daughter, when it was killed by Hercules; and he continued to bear an implacable hatred against the Trojans. He sided with the Greeks in the war against Troy, sometimes witnessing the contest as a spectator from the heights of Thrace, and sometimes interfering in person, assuming the appearance of a mortal hero and encouraging the Greeks, while Zeus favoured the Trojans. In the Odyssey, Poseidon appears hostile to Ulysses, whom he prevents from returning home in consequence of his having blinded Polyphemus, a son of Poseidon by the nymph Thoosa. — Being the ruler of the sea (the Mediterranean), he is described as gathering clouds and calling forth storms, but at the same time he has it in his power to grant a successful voyage and save those who are in danger; and all other marine divinities are subject to him. As the sea surrounds and holds the earth, he himself is described as the god who holds the earth (γαιήοχος), and who has it in his power to shake the earth (ἐνοσίχθων, κινητὴρ γᾶς). — He was further regarded as the creator of the horse. It is said that when Poseidon and Athena disputed as to which of them should give the name to the capital of Attica, the gods decided, that it should receive its name from the deity who should bestow upon man the most useful gift. Poseidon then created the horse, and Athena called forth the olive tree, in consequence of which the honour was conferred upon the goddess. According to others, however, Poseidon did not create the horse in Attica, but in Thessaly, where he also gave the famous horses to Peleus. Poseidon was accordingly believed to have taught men the art of managing horses by the bridle, and to have been the originator and protector of horse races. Hence he was also represented on horseback, or riding in a chariot drawn by two or four horses, and is designated by the epithets Ἵππιος, Ἵππειος, or Ἵππιος ἄναξ. He even metamorphosed himself into a horse, for the purpose of deceiving Demeter. — The symbol of Poseidon's power was the trident, or a spear with three points, with which he used to shatter rocks, to call forth or subdue storms, to shake the earth, and the like. — Herodotus states, that the name and worship of Poseidon were brought into Greece from Libya; but he was probably a divinity of Pelasgian origin, and originally a personification of the fertilising power of water, from which the transition to regarding him as the god of the sea was not difficult. — The following legends respecting Poseidon deserve to be mentioned. In conjunction with Zeus he fought against Cronos and the Titans;

and in the contest with the Giants he pursued Polybotes across the sea as far as Coa, and there killed him by throwing the island upon him. He further crushed the Centaurs when they were pursued by Hercules, under a mountain in Leucosia, the island of the Sirens. He sued together with Zeus for the hand of Thetis; but he withdrew when Themis prophesied that the son of Thetis would be greater than his father. When Ares had been caught in the wonderful net by Hephaestus, the latter set him free at the request of Poseidon; but the latter god afterwards brought a charge against Ares before the Areopagus, for having killed his son Halirrhothius. At the request of Minos, king of Crete, Poseidon caused a bull to rise from the sea, which the king promised to sacrifice; but when Minos treacherously concealed the animal among a herd of oxen, the god punished Minos by causing his daughter Pasiphaë to fall in love with the bull. —Poseidon was married to Amphitrite, by whom he had three children, Triton, Rhode, and Benthesicyme; but he had also a vast number of children by other divinities and mortal women. His worship extended over all Greece and southern Italy, but he was more especially revered in Peloponnesus and in the Ionic towns on the coast. The sacrifices offered to him generally consisted of black and white bulls; but wild boars and rams were also sacrificed to him. Horse and chariot races were held in his honour on the Corinthian isthmus. The Panionia, or the festival of all the Ionians near Mycale, was celebrated in honour of Poseidon. In works of art, Poseidon may be easily recognised by his attributes, the dolphin, the horse, or the trident, and he was frequently represented in groups along with Amphitrite, Tritons, Nereids, dolphins, the Dioscuri, Palaemon, Pegasus, Bellerophontes, Thalassa, Ino, and Galene. His figure does not present the majestic calm which characterises his brother Zeus; but as the state of the sea is varying, so also is the god represented sometimes in violent agitation, and sometimes in a state of repose. The Roman god Neptunus is spoken of in a separate article.

Posidippus (Ποσείδιππος, Ποσίδιππος). 1. An Athenian comic poet of the New Comedy, was a native of Cassandrea in Macedonia. He was reckoned one of the 6 most celebrated poets of the New Comedy. In time, he was the last of all the poets of the New Comedy. He began to exhibit dramas in the third year after the death of Menander, that is, in B. C. 289. —2. An epigrammatic poet, who was probably a different person from the comic poet, though he seems to have lived about the same time. His epigrams formed a part of the *Garland* of *Meleager*, and 22 of them are preserved in the Greek Anthology.

Posidium (Ποσείδιον), the name of several promontories sacred to Poseidon. 1. (*Punta della Licosa*), in Lucania, opposite the island Leucosia, the S. point of the gulf of Paestum. — 2. In Epirus, opposite the N.E. point of Corcyra. — 3. (*C. Stavros*), in Thessaly, forming the W. point of the Sinus Pagasaeus, perhaps the same as the promontory which Livy (xxxi. 46.) calls Zelasium.— 4. (*C. Helene*), the S.W. point of Chios. — 5. On the W. coast of Caria, between Miletus and the Iassius Sinus, with a town of the same name upon it. — 6. On the W. coast of Arabia, with an altar dedicated to Poseidon by Aristor., whom Ptolemy

had sent to explore the Arabian gulf. — 7. (*Posseda*), a seaport town in Syria in the district Cassiotis.

Posidonia. [PAESTUM.]

Posidonium (Ποσειδώνιον: *C. Possidhi* or *Kassandhrea*), a promontory on the W. coast of the peninsula Pallene in Macedonia, not far from Mende.

Posidonius (Ποσειδώνιος), a distinguished Stoic philosopher, was a native of Apamea in Syria. The date of his birth is not known with any exactness, but it may be placed about B. C. 135. He studied at Athens under Panaetius, after whose death (112) Posidonius set out on his travels. After visiting most of the countries on the coast of the Mediterranean, he fixed his abode at Rhodes, where he became the president of the Stoic school. He also took a prominent part in the political affairs of Rhodes, and was sent as ambassador to Rome in 86. Cicero, when he visited Rhodes, received instruction from Posidonius. Pompey also had a great admiration for Posidonius, and visited him twice, in 67 and 62. To the occasion of his first visit probably belongs the story that Posidonius, to prevent the disappointment of his distinguished visitor, though severely afflicted with the gout, had a long discourse on the topic that pain is not an evil. In 51 Posidonius removed to Rome, and appears to have died soon after at the age of 84. Posidonius was a man of extensive and varied acquirements in almost all departments of human knowledge. Cicero thought so highly of his powers, that he requested him to write an account of his consulship. As a physical investigator he was greatly superior to the Stoics generally, attaching himself in this respect rather to Aristotle. His geographical and historical knowledge was very extensive. He cultivated astronomy with considerable diligence. He also constructed a planetary machine, or revolving sphere, to exhibit the daily motions of the sun, moon and planets. His calculation of the circumference of the earth differed widely from that of Eratosthenes. He made it only 180,000 stadia, and his measurement was pretty generally adopted. None of the writings of Posidonius has come down to us entire. His fragments are collected by Bake, Lugd. Bat. 1810.

Postumia Castra (*Salado*), a fortress in Hispania Baetica, on a hill near the river Salsum (*Salado*).

Postumia Gens, patrician, was one of the most ancient patrician gentes at Rome. Its members frequently held the highest offices of the state, from the banishment of the kings to the downfall of the republic. The most distinguished family in the gens was that of ALBUS or ALBINUS; but we also find at the commencement of the republic families of the names of *Megellus* and *Tubertus*.

Postumus, whose full name was *M. Cassianus Latinius Postumus*, stands 2nd in the list of the so-called 30 Tyrants. Being nominated by Valerian governor of Gaul, he assumed the title of emperor in A. D. 258, while Valerian was prosecuting his campaign against the Persians. Postumus maintained a strong and just government, and preserved Gaul from the devastation of the warlike tribes upon the eastern border. After reigning nearly 10 years, he was slain by his soldiers in 267, and Laelianus proclaimed emperor in his stead.

Postverta or **Postvorta**, properly a surname of Carmenta, describing her as turning backward and looking to the past, which she revealed to poets and other mortals. In like manner the prophetic power, with which she looked into the future, is indicated by the surnames *Antevorta, Prorsa* (i. e. *Proversa*), and *Porrima*. Poets, however, have personified these attributes of Carmenta, and thus describe them as the companions of the goddess.

Pŏtămi, or **Pŏtămus** (Ποταμοί, Ποταμός: Ποτάμιος: *Keratia*), a demus in the S. of Attica, belonging to the tribe Leontis, where the tomb of Ion was shown.

Pŏtămon (Ποτάμων). 1. A rhetorician of Mytilene, lived in the time of Tiberius Caesar, whose favour he enjoyed. — 2. A philosopher of Alexander, who is said to have introduced at Rome an eclectic sect of philosophy. He appears to have lived at Rome a little before the time of Plotinus, and to have entrusted his children to the guardianship of the latter.

Potentia (Potentinus). 1. A town of Picenum on the river Flosis, between Ancona and Castellum Firmanum, was made a Roman colony in B.C. 186. — 2. (*Potenza*), a town of Lucania on the Via Popilia, E. of Forum Popilii.

Pŏthīnus, an eunuch, the guardian of the young king Ptolemy, recommended the assassination of Pompey, when the latter fled to Egypt, B.C. 48. Pothinus plotted against Caesar when he came to Alexandria shortly afterwards, and was put to death by Caesar's order.

Pŏtidaea (Ποτίδαια: Ποτιδαιάτης: *Pinaka*), a town in Macedonia on the narrow isthmus of the peninsula Pallene, was a strongly fortified place and one of considerable importance. It was a colony of the Corinthians, and must have been founded before the Persian wars, though the time of its foundation is not recorded. It afterwards became tributary to Athens, and its revolt from the latter city in B.C. 432 was one of the immediate causes of the Peloponnesian war. It was taken by the Athenians in 429 after a siege of more than 2 years, its inhabitants expelled, and their place supplied by Athenian colonists. In 356 it was taken by Philip, who destroyed the city and gave its territory to the Olynthians. Cassander, however, built a new city on the same site, to which he gave the name of **Cassandrēa** (Κασσάνδρεια: Κασσανδρεύς), and which he peopled with the remains of the old population and with the inhabitants of Olynthus and the surrounding towns, so that it soon became the most flourishing city in all Macedonia. It was taken and plundered by the Huns, but was restored by Justinian.

Potidania, a fortress in the N.E. of Aetolia, near the frontiers of Locris.

Pŏtītii. [PINARIA GENS.]

Pŏtītus, the name of an ancient and celebrated family of the Valeria Gens. This family disappears about the time of the Samnite wars; but the name was revived at a later period by the Valeria gens, as a praenomen: thus we find mention of a Potitus Valerius Messala, who was consul suffectus in B.C. 29.

Potniae (Ποτνιαί: Ποτνιεύς), a small town in Boeotia on the Asopus, 10 stadia S. of Thebes, on the road to Plataea. The adjective *Potniades* (sing. *Potnias*) is an epithet frequently given to the mares which tore to death Glaucus of Potniae. [GLAUCUS, No. 1.]

Praaspa. [PHRAATA.]

Practius (Πράκτιος: *Borgas* or *Muskukn-Su*), a river of the Troad, rising in M. Ida, and flowing into the Hellespont, N. of Abydus.

Praenestě (Praenestinus: *Palestrina*), one of the most ancient towns of Latium, was situated on a steep and lofty hill, about 20 miles S.E. of Rome, with which it was connected by a road, called Via Praenestina. It was probably a Pelasgic city, but it claimed a Greek origin, and was said to have been founded by Telegonus, the son of Ulysses. It was strongly fortified by nature and by art, and frequently resisted the attacks of the Romans. Together with the other Latin towns, it became subject to Rome, and was at a later period made a Roman colony. It was here that the younger Marius took refuge, and was for a considerable time besieged by Sulla's troops. Praeneste possessed a very celebrated and ancient temple of Fortuna, with an oracle, which is often mentioned under the name of Praenestinae *sortes.* It also had a temple of Juno. In consequence of its lofty situation Praeneste was a cool and healthy residence in the great heats of summer (*frigidum Praeneste*, Hor. *Carm.* iii. 4. 22), and was therefore much frequented at that season by the wealthy Romans. The remains of the ancient walls and some other antiquities are still to be seen at *Palestrina.*

Praesus (Πραῖσος: Πραίσιος), an inland town in the E. of Crete, belonging to the Eteocretes, which was destroyed by the neighbouring town of Hierapytna.

Praetōria Augusta. [AUGUSTA, No. 4.]

Priā (Πρᾶς, gen. Πραντός: Πράντες), a town of Thessaly, in the W. of the district Phthiotis, on the N.E. slope of Mt. Narthacius.

Prasiae (Πρασιαί: Πρασιεύς). 1. Or **Prasia** (Πρασία), a town of the Eleuthero-lacones, on the E. coast of Laconia, was taken and destroyed by the Athenians in the 2nd year of the Peloponnesian war. — 2. (*Prassa*), a demus in Attica, S. of Stiria, belonging to the tribe Pandionis, with a temple of Apollo.

Prasias Lacus (Πρασιὰς λίμνη: *Takino*), a lake in Thrace between the Strymon and Nestus, and near the Strymonic gulf with silver mines in the neighbourhood.

Prasii, Praesii, and **Parrhasii** (Πράσιοι: Sanscrit, Prachinas, i. e. *people of the E. country*), a great and powerful people of India on the Ganges, governed at the time of Seleucus I. by king SANDROCOTTUS. Their capital city was Palibothra (*Patna*); and the extent of the kingdom seems to have embraced the whole valley of the upper Ganges, at least as far down as that city. At a later time the monarchy declined, so that in Ptolemy we only find the name as that of the inhabitants of a small district, called Prasiaca (Πρασιακή) about the river Soa.

Prasōdis Mare (Πρασώδης θάλασσα or κόλπος), the S.W. part of the Indian Ocean, about the promontory PRASUM.

Prasum (Πράσον ἀκρωτήριον: *C. Delgado*), a promontory on the E. coast of Africa in 10¼° S. lat., appears to have been the S.-most point to which the ancient knowledge of this coast extended.

Pratīnas (Πρατίνας), one of the early tragic poets at Athens, whose combined efforts brought the art to its perfection. was a native of Phlius, and was therefore by birth a Dorian. It is not stated at what time he went to Athens; but he was older than Choerilus and younger than Aeschylus, with both of whom he competed for the prize, about B. C. 500. The step in the progress of the art, which was ascribed to Pratinas, was the separation of the satyric from the tragic drama. His plays were much esteemed. Pratinas also ranked high among the lyric, as well as the dramatic poets of his age. He may perhaps be considered to have shared with his contemporary Lasus the honour of founding the Athenian school of dithyrambic poetry.

Praxagŏras (Πραξαγόρας), a celebrated physician, was a native of the island of Cos, and lived in the 4th century B. C. He belonged to the medical sect of the Dogmatici, and was celebrated for his knowledge of medical science in general, and especially for his attainments in anatomy and physiology.

Praxĭas (Πραξίας), an Athenian sculptor of the age of Phidias, but of the more archaic school of Calamis, commenced the execution of the statues in the pediments of the great temple of Apollo at Delphi, but died while he was still engaged upon the work. His date may be placed about B. C. 448, and onwards.

Praxidĭcē (Πραξιδίκη), i. e. the goddess who carries out the objects of justice, or watches that justice is done to men. When Menelaus arrived in Laconia, on his return from Troy, he set up a statue of Praxidice near Gytheum, not far from the spot where Paris, in carrying off Helen, had founded a sanctuary of Aphrodite Migonitis. Near Haliartus, in Boeotia, we meet with the worship of Praxidicae, in the plural: they were here called daughters of Oxyges, and their names were Alalcomenia, Thelxinoea, and Aulis. In the Orphic poets Praxidice seems to be a surname of Persephone.

Praxilla (Πράξιλλα), of Sicyon, a lyric poetess, who flourished about B. C. 450, and was one of the 9 poetesses who were distinguished as the Lyric Muses. Her scolia were among the most celebrated compositions of that species. She belonged to the Dorian school of lyric poetry, but there were also traces of Aeolic influence in her rhythms, and even in her dialect.

Praxiphănes (Πραξιφάνης), a Peripatetic philosopher, a native either of Mytilene or of Rhodes, was a pupil of Theophrastus, and lived about B. C. 322. Epicurus is said to have been one of his pupils. Praxiphanes paid especial attention to grammatical studies, and is hence named along with Aristotle as the founder and creator of the science of grammar.

Praxĭtĕles (Πραξιτέλης), one of the most distinguished artists of ancient Greece, was both a statuary in bronze and a sculptor in marble. We know nothing of his personal history, except that he was a citizen, if not a native, of Athens, and that his career as an artist was intimately connected with that city. He probably flourished about B. C. 364 and onwards. Praxiteles stands, with Scopas, at the head of the later Attic school, so called in contradistinction to the earlier Attic school of Phidias. Without attempting those sublime impersonations of divine majesty, in which Phidias had been so inimitably successful, Praxiteles was unsurpassed in the exhibition of the softer beauties of the human form, especially in the female figure. The most celebrated work of Pra-

xiteles was his marble statue of Aphrodite (Venus), which was distinguished from other statues of the goddess by the name of the Cnidians, who purchased it. It was always esteemed the most perfectly beautiful of the statues of the goddess. Many made the voyage to Cnidus expressly to behold it. So highly did the Cnidians themselves esteem their treasure, that when King Nicomedes offered them, as the price of it, to pay off the whole of their heavy public debt, they preferred to endure any suffering rather than part with the work which gave their city its chief renown. It was afterwards carried to Constantinople, where it perished by fire in the reign of Justinian. Praxiteles modelled it from a favourite courtezan named Phryne, of whom also he made more than one portrait statue. Another of the celebrated works of Praxiteles was his statue of Eros. It was preserved at Thespiae, where it was dedicated by Phryne; and an interesting story is told of the manner in which she became possessed of it. Praxiteles had promised to give Phryne whichever of his works she might choose, but he was unwilling to tell her which of them, in his own opinion, was the best. To discover this, she sent a slave to tell Praxiteles that a fire had broken out in his house, and that most of his works had already perished. On hearing this message, the artist rushed out, exclaiming that all his toil was lost, if the fire had touched his Satyr or his Eros. Upon this Phryne confessed the stratagem, and chose the Eros. This statue was removed to Rome by Caligula, restored to Thespiae by Claudius, and carried back by Nero to Rome, where it stood in Pliny's time in the schools of Octavia, and it finally perished in the conflagration of that building in the reign of Titus. Praxiteles had 2 sons, who were also distinguished sculptors, Timarchus and Cephisodotus.

Praxĭthĕa (Πραξιθέα), daughter of Phrasimus and Diogenia, was the wife of Erechtheus, and mother of Cecrops, Pandorus, Metion, Orneus, Procris, Creusa, Chthonia, and Orithyia.

Preciăni, a people in Gallia Aquitanica at the foot of the Pyrenees.

Prellĭus Lacus (*Lago di Castiglione*), a lake in Etruria near the coast, near the N. end of which was a small island.

Prĕpĕsinthus (Πρεπέσινθος), one of the smaller Cyclades, between Oliaros and Siphnos.

Priămĭdes, that is, a son of Priam, by which name Hector, Paris, Helenus, Deiphobus, and the other sons of Priam, are frequently called.

Priămus (Πρίαμος), the famous king of Troy, at the time of the Trojan war. He was a son of Laomedon and Strymo or Placia. His original name is said to have been Podarces, i. e. "the swift-footed," which was changed into Priamus, "the ransomed" (from πρίαμαι), because he was the only surviving son of Laomedon and was ransomed by his sister Hesione, after he had fallen into the hands of Hercules. He is said to have been first married to Arisbe, the daughter of Merops, by whom he became the father of Aesacus; but afterwards he gave up Arisbe to Hyrtacus, and married Hecuba, by whom he had the following children: Hector, Alexander or Paris, Deïphobus, Helenus, Pammon, Polites, Antiphus, Hipponous, Polydorus, Troïlus, Creusa, Laodice, Polyxena, and Cassandra. By other women he had a great many children besides. According to the Homeric tradition, he was the father of 50 sons, 19 of whom were children of Hecuba, to whom others add an equal number of daughters. In the earlier part of his reign, Priam is said to have supported the Phrygians in their war against the Amazons. When the Greeks landed on the Trojan coast Priam was already advanced in years, and took no active part in the war. Once only did he venture upon the field of battle, to conclude the agreement respecting the single combat between Paris and Menelaus. After the death of Hector, Priam, accompanied by Hermes, went to the tent of Achilles to ransom his son's body for burial and obtained it. His death is not mentioned by Homer, but is related by later poets. When the Greeks entered Troy, the aged king put on his armour, and was on the point of rushing against the enemy, but he was prevailed on by Hecuba to take refuge with herself and her daughters, as a suppliant at the altar of Zeus. While he was tarrying in the temple, his son Polites, pursued by Pyrrhus, rushed into the sacred spot, and expired at the feet of his father, whereupon Priam, overcome with indignation, hurled his spear with feeble hand against Pyrrhus, but was forthwith killed by the latter. — Virgil mentions (*Aen.* v. 564) another Priam, a son of Polites, and a grandson of king Priam.

Priansus (Πρίανσος: Πριάνσιος, Πριανσιεύς), a town in Crete on the S. coast, S. of Lyctus, confounded by Strabo with Praesus.

Priāpus (Πρίαπος), son of Dionysus and Aphrodite. It is said that Aphrodite, who was in love with Dionysus, went to meet the god on his return from India, but soon abandoned him, and proceeded to Lampsacus on the Hellespont, to give birth to the child of the god. Hera, who was dissatisfied with her conduct, caused her to give birth to a child of extreme ugliness, who was named Priapus. The earliest Greek poets, such as Homer and Hesiod, do not mention this divinity; and it was only in later times that he was honoured with divine worship. He was worshipped more especially at Lampsacus on the Hellespont, whence he is sometimes called *Hellespontiacus*. He was regarded as the promoter of fertility both in vegetation and in all animals connected with an agricultural life ; and in this capacity he was worshipped as the protector of flocks of sheep and goats, of bees, of the vine, of all garden produce, and even of fishing. Like other divinities presiding over agricultural pursuits, he was believed to be possessed of prophetic powers, and is sometimes mentioned in the plural. As Priapus had many attributes in common with other gods of fertility, the Orphics identified him with their mystic Dionysus, Hermes, Helios, &c. The Attic legends connect Priapus with such sensual and licentious beings as Conisalus, Orthanes, and Tychon. In like manner he was confounded by the Italians with Mutunus or Muttunus, the personification of the fructifying power in nature. The sacrifices offered to him consisted of the firstfruits of gardens, vineyards, and fields, of milk, honey, cakes, rams, asses, and fishes. He was represented in carved images, mostly in the form of hermae, carrying fruit in his garment, and either a sickle or cornucopia in his hand. The hermae of Priapus in Italy, like those of other rustic divinities, were usually painted red, whence the god is called *ruber* or *rubicundus*.

Priāpus (Πρίαπος, Ion. Πρίηπος: Πριαπηνός:

Karabuki, Ru.), a city of Mysia, on the Propontis, E. of Parium, with a small but excellent harbour. It was a colony of the Milesians, and a chief seat of the worship of PRIAPUS. The surrounding district was called **Priāpis** (Πριαπίς) and **Priapēnē** (Πριαπηνή).

Priēnē (Πριήνη: Πριηνεύς, Πριήνιος: Priēneus, pl. Priēnenses: *Samsun*, Ru.), one of the 12 Ionian cities on the coast of Asia Minor, stood in the N.W. corner of Caria, at the S. foot of M. Mycale, and on the N. side of the Sinus Latinicus. Its foundation was ascribed mythically to the Neleid Aepytus, in conjunction with Cadmeans, from whom it was also called Καδμή. It stood originally on the seashore, and had 2 harbours and a small fleet, but the change in the coast by the alluvial deposits of the Maeander left it some distance inland. It was of much religious importance in connection with the Panionian festival on M. Mycale, at which the people of Priene took precedence in virtue of their being the supposed descendants of those of Helice in Greece Proper. The city was also celebrated as the birthplace of BIAS.

Prifernum, a town of the Vestini on the E. coast of central Italy.

Primus, M. Antōnius, a native of Tolosa in Gaul, was condemned of forgery (*falsum*) in the reign of Nero, was expelled the senate of which he was a member, and was banished from the city. After the death of Nero (68), he was restored to his former rank by Galba, and appointed to the command of the 7th legion, which was stationed in Pannonia. He was one of the first generals in Europe who declared in favour of Vespasian ; and he rendered him the most important services. In conjunction with the governors of Moesia and Pannonia, he invaded Italy, gained a decisive victory over the Vitellian army at Bedriacum, and took Cremona, which he allowed his soldiers to pillage and destroy. He afterwards forced his way into Rome, notwithstanding the obstinate resistance of the Vitellian troops, and had the government of the city till the arrival of Mucianus from Syria. [MUCIANUS, No. 2.] We learn from Martial, who was a friend of Antonius Primus, that he was alive at the accession of Trajan.

Priscianus, a Roman grammarian, surnamed *Caesariensis*, either because he was born at Caesarea, or educated there. He flourished about A. D. 450, and taught grammar at Constantinople. He was celebrated for the extent and depth of his grammatical knowledge, of which he has left the evidence in his work on the subject, entitled *Commentariorum grammaticorum Libri XVIII.*, addressed to his friend and patron, the consul Julianus. Other titles are, however, frequently given to it. The first 16 books treat upon the eight parts of speech recognised by the ancient grammarians, letters, syllables, &c. The last 2 books are on syntax. This treatise soon became the standard work on Latin grammar, and in the epitome of Rabanus Maurus obtained an extensive circulation. The other works of Priscianus still extant are : — 1. A grammatical catechism on 12 lines of the Aeneid, manifestly intended as a school book. 2. A treatise on accents. 3. A treatise on the symbols used to denote numbers and weights, and on coins and numbers. 4. On the metres of Terence. 5. A translation of the Προγυμνάσματα (*Praeexercitamenta*) of Hermogenes. 6. On the declensions of nouns.

R R 3

7. A poem on the emperor Anastasius in 312 hexameters, with a preface in 22 iambic lines. 8. A piece *De Ponderibus et Mensuris*, in verse. 9. An *Epitome phaenomenōn*, or *De Sideribus*, in verse. 10. A free translation of the Periegesis of Dionysius in 1427 lines, manifestly made for the instruction of youth. 11. A couple of epigrams. The best edition of Priscianus is by Krehl, Lips. 1819—20, 2 vols. 8vo.

Prisciānus, Theodōrus, a physician, and a pupil of Vindicianus, lived in the 4th century after Christ. He is supposed to have lived at the court of Constantinople, and to have attained the dignity of Archiater. He is the author of a Latin work, entitled, *Rerum Medicarum Libri Quatuor*, published in 1532, both at Strasburg and at Basel.

Priscus (Πρίσκος), a Byzantine historian, was a native of Panium in Thrace, and was one of the ambassadors sent by Theodosius the Younger to Attila, A. D. 445. He died about 471. Priscus wrote an account of his embassy to Attila, enriched by digressions on the life and reign of that king. The work was in 8 books, but only fragments of it have come down to us. Priscus was an excellent and trustworthy historian, and his style was remarkably elegant and pure. The fragments are published with those of Dexippus and others, by Bekker and Niebuhr, in the Bonn Collection of the Byzantines, 1829, 8vo.

Priscus, Helvīdius, son-in-law of Thrasea Paetus, and, like him, distinguished by his love of virtue, philosophy, and liberty. He was quaestor in Achaia during the reign of Nero, and tribune of the plebs A. D. 56. When Thrasea was put to death by Nero (66), Priscus was banished from Italy. He was recalled to Rome by Galba (68); but in consequence of his freedom of speech and love of independence, he was again banished by Vespasian, and was shortly afterwards put to death by order of this emperor. His life was written by Herennius Senecio at the request of his widow Fannia ; and the tyrant Domitian, in consequence of this work, subsequently put Senecio to death, and sent Fannia into exile. Priscus left a son, Helvidius, who was put to death by Domitian.

Priscus, Servilius. The Prisci were an ancient family of the Servilia gens, and filled the highest offices of the state during the early years of the republic. They also bore the agnomen of Structus, which is always appended to their name in the Fasti, till it was supplanted by that of Fidenas, which was first obtained by Q. Servilius Priscus Structus, who took Fidenae in his dictatorship, B. C. 435, and which was also borne by his descendants.

Priscus, Tarquinĭus. [TARQUINIUS.]

Privernum (Privernas, -ātis : *Piperno*), an ancient town of Latium on the river Amasenus, belonged to the Volscians. It was conquered by the Romans at an early period, and was subsequently made a colony.

Proaerēsĭus (Προαιρέσιος), a teacher of rhetoric, was a native of Armenia, and was born about A. D. 276. He first studied at Antioch under Ulpian, and afterwards at Athens under Julianus. He became at a later time the chief teacher of rhetoric at Athens, and enjoyed a very high reputation. He died 368, in his 92nd year.

Probalinthus (Προβάλινθος : Προβαλίσιος), a demus in Attica, S. of Marathon, belonging to the tribe Pandionis.

Probatīa (Προβατία), a river of Boeotia, which, after passing through the territory of Trachin, and receiving its tributary the Hercyna, flowed into the lake Copais.

Probus, Aemilĭus. [NEPOS, CORNELIUS.]

Probus, M. Aurēlĭus, Roman emperor A. D. 276—282, was a native of Sirmium in Pannonia, and rose to distinction by his military abilities. He was appointed by the emperor Tacitus governor of the whole East, and, upon the death of that sovereign, the purple was forced upon his acceptance by the armies of Syria. The downfall of Florianus speedily removed his only rival [FLORIANUS], and he was enthusiastically hailed by the united voice of the senate, the people, and the legions. The reign of Probus presents a series of the most brilliant achievements. He defeated the barbarians on the frontiers of Gaul and Illyricum, and in other parts of the Roman empire, and put down the rebellions of Saturninus at Alexandria, and of Proculus and Bonosus in Gaul. But, after crushing all external and internal foes, he was killed at Sirmium by his own soldiers, who had risen in mutiny against him, because he had employed them in laborious public works. Probus was as just and virtuous as he was warlike, and is deservedly regarded as one of the greatest and best of the Roman emperors.

Probus, Vălērĭus. 1. Of Berytus, a Roman grammarian, who lived in the time of Nero. To this Probus we may assign those annotations on Terence, from which fragments are quoted in the Scholia on the dramatist.—2. A Roman grammarian, flourished some years before A. Gellius, and therefore about the beginning of the 2nd century. He was the author of commentaries on Virgil, and possessed a copy of a portion at least of the Georgics, which had been corrected by the hand of the poet himself. These are the commentaries so frequently cited by Servius ; but the *Scholia in Bucolica et Georgica*, now extant, under the name of Probus, belong to a much later period. This Probus was probably the author of the life of Persius, commonly ascribed to Suetonius.—There is extant a work upon grammar, in 2 books, entitled *M. Valerii Probi Grammaticae Institutiones* ; but this work was probably not written by either of the preceding grammarians. It is published in the collections of Putschius, Hannov. 1605, and of Lindemann, Lips. 1831.

Prŏcas, one of the fabulous kings of Alba Longa, succeeded Aventinus, and reigned 23 years : he was the father of Numitor and Amulius.

Prŏchўta (*Procida*), an island off the coast of Campania near the promontory Misenum, is said to have been torn away by an earthquake either from this promontory or from the neighbouring island of Pithecusa or Aenaria.

Procles (Προκλῆς), one of the twin sons of Aristodemus. For details see EURYSTHENES.

Proclus (Πρόκλος), surnamed *Diadochus* (Διάδοχος), the successor, from his being regarded as the genuine successor of Plato in doctrine, was one of the most celebrated teachers of the Neoplatonic school. He was born at Byzantium A. D. 412, but was brought up at Xanthus in Lycia, to which city his parents belonged, and which Proclus himself regarded as his native place. He studied at Alexandria under Olympiodorus, and afterwards at Athens under Plutarchus and Syrianus. At an early age his philosophical attainments attracted the attention and admiration of his contemporaries. He had written his commentary on the Timaeus of Plato, as well as many other treatises by his 28th year. On the death of Syrianus Proclus succeeded him in his school, and inherited from him the house in which he resided and taught.   Marinus in his life of Proclus records, with intense admiration, the perfection to which his master attained in all virtues. The highest of these virtues were, in the estimation of Marinus, those of a purifying and ascetic kind. From animal food he almost totally abstained ; fasts and vigils he observed with scrupulous exactitude. The reverence with which he honoured the sun and moon would seem to have been unbounded. He celebrated all the important religious festivals of every nation, himself composing hymns in honour not only of Grecian deities, but of those of other nations also. Nor were departed heroes and philosophers excepted from this religious veneration ; and he even performed sacred rites in honour of the departed spirits of the entire human race. It was of course not surprising that such a man should be favoured with various apparitions and miraculous interpositions of the gods. He used to tell how a god had once appeared and proclaimed to him the glory of the city. But the still higher grade of what, in the language of the school, was termed the theurgic virtue, he attained by his profound meditations on the oracles, and the Orphic and Chaldaic mysteries, into the profound secrets of which he was initiated by Asclepigenia, the daughter of Plutarchus, who alone was in complete possession of the theurgic knowledge and discipline, which had descended to her from the great Nestorius. He profited so much by her instructions, as to be able, according to Marinus, to call down rain in a time of drought, to stop an earthquake, and to procure the immediate intervention of Aesculapius to cure the daughter of his friend Archiadas. Proclus died A. D. 485. During the last 5 years of his life he had become superannuated, his strength having been exhausted by his fastings and other ascetic practices. As a philosopher Proclus enjoyed the highest celebrity among his contemporaries and successors ; but his philosophical system is characterised by vagueness, mysticism, and want of good sense. He professed that his design was not to bring forward views of his own, but simply to expound Plato, in doing which he proceeded on the idea that everything in Plato must be brought into accordance with the mystical theology of Orpheus. He wrote a separate work on the coincidence of the doctrines of Orpheus, Pythagoras, and Plato. It was in much the same spirit that he attempted to blend together the logical method of Aristotle and the fanciful speculations of Neoplatonic mysticism. Several of the works of Proclus are still extant. The most important of them consist of Commentaries on Plato, a treatise on various theological and philosophical subjects. There is no complete edition of Proclus. The edition of Cousin (Paris, 6 vols. 8vo. 1820—1827) contains the following treatises of Proclus : — On Providence and Fate ; On Ten Doubts about Providence ; On the Nature of Evil ; a Commentary on the Alcibiades, and a Commentary on the Parmenides. The other principal works of Proclus are : — On the Theology of Plato, in 6 books ; Theological Elements ; a Commentary on the Timaeus of Plato ; five Hymns of an Orphic character. Several of these have been

translated into English by Thomas Taylor. Proclus was also a distinguished mathematician and grammarian. His Commentaries on the first book of Euclid, and on the Works and Days of Hesiod are still extant.

Procne (Πρόκνη), daughter of king Pandion of Athens, and wife of Tereus. Her story is given under TEREUS.

Proconnesus (Προκόννησος, or Προικόννησος i. e. Fawn-island, Marmara), an island of the Propontis which takes from it its modern name (Sea of Marmara) off the N. coast of Mysia, N.W. of the peninsula of Cyzicus or Dolionis. The latter was also called Proconnesus from πρόξ (fawn) because it was a favourite resort of deer in the fawning season, whence it was also called **Elaphonnesus** ('Ελαφόννησος, i. e. deer-island) ; and the two were distinguished by the names of Old and New Proconnesus. The island was celebrated for its marble ; and hence its modern name. It was the native place of the poet ARISTEAS.

Procopius (Προκόπιος). 1. A native of Cilicia, and a relative of the emperor Julian, served with distinction under Constantius II. and Julian. Having incurred the suspicions of Jovian and of his successor Valens, Procopius remained in concealment for about 2 years ; but in A. D. 365 he was proclaimed emperor at Constantinople, while Valens was staying at Caesarea in Cappadocia. Both parties prepared for war. In the following year (366) the forces of Procopius were defeated in 2 great battles. Procopius himself was taken prisoner, and put to death by order of Valens. — **2.** An eminent Byzantine historian, was born at Caesarea in Palestine about A. D. 500. He went to Constantinople when still a young man, and there obtained so much distinction as an advocate and a professor of eloquence, that he attracted the attention of Belisarius, who appointed him his secretary in 527. In this capacity Procopius accompanied the great hero on his different wars in Asia, Africa, and Italy, being frequently employed in state business of importance, or in conducting military expeditions. Procopius returned with Belisarius to Constantinople a little before 542. His eminent talents were appreciated by the emperor Justinian, who conferred upon him the title of illustris, made him a senator, and in 562 created him prefect of Constantinople. Procopius died about the same time as Justinian, 565. As an historian Procopius deserves great praise. His style is good, formed upon classic models, often elegant, and generally full of vigour. His works are : — 1. Histories ('Ιστορίαι), in 8 books ; viz. 2 On the Persian War, containing the period from 408—553, and treating more fully of the author's own times ; 2 On the War with the Vandals, 395—545 ; 4 On the Gothic War, or properly speaking, only 3 books, the 4th (8th) being a sort of supplement containing various matters, and going down to the beginning of 553. It was continued by Agathias till 559. The work is extremely interesting ; the descriptions of the habits, &c. of the barbarians are faithful and done in a masterly style. — 2. On the Public Buildings erected by Justinian (Κτίσματα), in 6 books. A work equally interesting and valuable in its kind, though apparently too much seasoned with flattery of the emperor. — 3. Anecdota ('Ανέκδοτα), a collection of anecdotes, some of them witty and pleasant, but others most indecent, reflecting upon Justinian, the empress Theodora, Belisarius, and other eminent persons. It is a complete *Chronique Scandaleuse* of the court of Constantinople, from 549 till 562. — 4. *Orationes*, probably extracts from the "History," which is rather overstocked with harangues and speeches. The best edition of the collected works of Procopius is by Dindorf, Bonn, 3 vols. 8vo. 1833—1838.

Procris (Πρόκρις), daughter of Erechtheus and wife of Cephalus. For details see CEPHALUS.

Procrustes (Προκρούστης), that is, "the Stretcher," a surname of the famous robber Polypemon or Damastes. He used to tie all travellers who fell into his hands upon a bed : if they were shorter than the bed, he stretched their limbs till they were of the same length ; if they were longer than the bed, he made them of the same size by cutting off some of their limbs. He was slain by Theseus, on the Cephissus in Attica. The bed of Procrustes is used proverbially even at the present day.

C. Proculeīus, a Roman eques, one of the friends of Augustus, was sent by the latter, after the victory at Actium, to Antony and Cleopatra. It is of this Proculeius that Horace speaks (*Carm.* ii. 2). He is said to have divided his property with his brothers (perhaps cousins) Caepio and Murena, who had lost their property in the civil wars. Proculeius put an end to his life by taking gypsum, when suffering from a disease in the stomach.

Prŏcŭlus, the jurist, was the contemporary of the jurist Nerva the younger, who was probably the father of the emperor Nerva. The fact that Proculus gave his name to the school or sect (*Proculiani* or *Proculeiani*, as the name is also written), which was opposed to that of the Sabiniani, shows that he was a jurist of note. Proculus is often cited, and there are 37 extracts from him in the Digest from his 8 books of Epistolae. He appears to have written notes on Labeo. Some writers suppose that Proculus is the Licinius Proculus, who was Praefectus Praetorio under Otho.

Procŭlus, Julius, a Roman senator, is said in the legend of Romulus to have informed the sorrowing Roman people, after the strange departure of their king from the world, that Romulus had descended from heaven and appeared to him, bidding him tell the people to honour him in future as a god under the name of Quirinus.

Prŏdĭcus (Πρόδικος), the celebrated sophist, was a native of Iulis in the island of Ceos. He lived in the time of the Peloponnesian war and subsequently ; but the date cannot be determined either of his birth or of his death. Prodicus came frequently to Athens on the public business of his native city. He was brought forward in the *Clouds* and the *Birds* of Aristophanes, which belong respectively to B. C. 423 and 414. Prodicus is mentioned as one of the teachers of Isocrates, and he was alive at the time of the death of Socrates (399). Suidas relates that Prodicus was put to death by the Athenians as a corrupter of the youth, but this statement sounds very suspicious. He is mentioned both by Plato and Xenophon with more respect than the other sophists. Like Protagoras and others he travelled through Greece, delivering lectures for money, and in this way he amassed a large fortune. He paid especial attention to the correct use of words. We have the substance of one of his lec-

tures preserved by Xenophon in the well-known fable, called "The Choice of Hercules." When Hercules, as he entered upon manhood, was upon the point of choosing between virtue and vice, there appeared to him two women, the one of dignified beauty, adorned with purity, modesty, and discretion, the other of a voluptuous form, and meretricious look and dress. The latter promised to lead him by the shortest road, without any toil, to the enjoyment of every pleasure. The other, while she reminded him of his ancestors and his noble nature, did not conceal from him that the gods have granted nothing really beautiful and good without toil and labour. The former sought to deter him from the path of virtue by urging its difficulties ; the latter impressed upon him the emptiness of pleasure, and the honour and happiness flowing from a life of virtue. Thereupon Hercules decided in favour of virtue.

Prŏerna (Πρόερνα), a town of Thessaly in the W. part of the district Phthiotis, on the W. slope of M. Narthacius, and near the sources of the Apidanus.

Proetides. [PROETUS.]

Proetus (Προῖτος), son of Abas and Ocalea, and twin-brother of Acrisius. In the dispute between the 2 brothers for the kingdom of Argos, Proetus was expelled, whereupon he fled to Iobates in Lycia, and married Antea or Stheneboea, the daughter of the latter. With the assistance of Iobates, Proetus was restored to his kingdom, and took Tiryns, which was now fortified by the Cyclopes. Acrisius then shared his kingdom with his brother, surrendering to him Tiryns, Midea and the coast of Argolis. By his wife, Proetus became the father of 3 daughters, Lysippe, Iphinoë, and Iphianassa, who are often mentioned under the general name of **Proetides.** When these daughters arrived at the age of maturity, they were stricken with madness, the cause of which is differently related. Some say that it was a punishment inflicted upon them by Dionysus, because they had despised his worship ; others relate that they were driven mad by Hera, because they presumed to consider themselves more handsome than the goddess, or because they had stolen some of the gold of her statue. The frenzy spread to the other women of Argos ; till at length Proetus agreed to divide his kingdom between Melampus and his brother Bias, upon the former promising that he would cure the women of their madness. Melampus then chose the most robust among the young men, gave chase to the mad women, amid shouting and dancing, and drove them as far as Sicyon. During this pursuit, Iphinoë died, but the 2 other daughters were cured by Melampus by means of purifications, and were then married to Melampus and Bias. The place where the cure was effected upon his daughters is not the same in all traditions, some mentioning the well Anigros, others the fountain Clitor in Arcadia, or Lusi in Arcadia. Besides these daughters, Proetus had a son, Megapenthes. When Bellerophon came to Proetus to be purified of a murder which he had committed, the wife of Proetus fell in love with him ; but, as Bellerophon declined her advances, she charged him before Proetus with having made improper proposals to her. Proetus then sent Bellerophon to Iobates in Lycia, with a letter desiring the latter to murder Bellerophon. [BELLEROPHON.] — According to

Ovid (*Met* v. 238) Acrisius was expelled from his kingdom by Proetus ; and Perseus, the grandson of Acrisius, avenged his grandfather by turning Proetus into stone by means of the head of Medusa.

Prŏmētheus (Προμηθεύς), son of the Titan Iapetus and Clymene, and brother of Atlas, Menoetius, and Epimetheus. His name signifies "forethought," as that of his brother Epimetheus denotes "afterthought." Once in the reign of Zeus, when gods and men were disputing with one another at Mecone (afterwards Sicyon), Prometheus, with a view of deceiving Zeus, cut up a bull and divided it into two parts: he wrapped up the best parts and the intestines in the skin, and at the top he placed the stomach, which is one of the worst parts, while the second heap consisted of the bones covered with fat. When Zeus pointed out to him how badly he had made the division, Prometheus desired him to choose, but Zeus, in his anger, and seeing through the stratagem of Prometheus, chose the heap of bones covered with the fat. The father of the gods avenged himself by withholding fire from mortals, but Prometheus stole it in a hollow tube (νάρθηξ, *ferula*). Zeus thereupon chained Prometheus to a pillar, where an eagle consumed in the daytime his liver, which was restored in each succeeding night. Prometheus was thus exposed to perpetual torture ; but Hercules killed the eagle and delivered the sufferer, with the consent of Zeus, who in this way had an opportunity of allowing his son to gain immortal fame. Further in order to punish men Zeus gave Pandora as a present to Epimetheus, in consequence of which diseases and sufferings of every kind befell mortals. [For details, see PANDORA.] This is an outline of the legend about Prometheus, as contained in the poems of Hesiod. — Aeschylus, in his trilogy *Prometheus*, added various new features to this legend. Although Prometheus belonged to the Titans, he is nevertheless represented by Aeschylus as having assisted Zeus against the Titans. But when Zeus wanted to extirpate the whole race of man, whose place he proposed to fill by an entirely new race of beings, Prometheus prevented the execution of the scheme, and saved mankind from destruction. Prometheus further deprived them of their knowledge of the future, and gave them hope instead. He taught them the use of fire, made them acquainted with architecture, astronomy, mathematics, writing, the treatment of domestic animals, navigation, medicine, the art of prophecy, working in metal, and all the other arts. But, as he had acted in all these things contrary to the will of Zeus, the latter ordered Hephaestus to chain him to a rock in Scythia, which was done in the presence of Cratos and Bia, two ministers of Zeus. Prometheus, however, still continued to defy Zeus, and declared that it was the decree of fate, by which Zeus was destined to be dethroned by his own son. As Prometheus steadfastly refused to give any explanation of this decree, Zeus hurled him into Tartarus, together with the rock to which he was chained. After the lapse of a long time, Prometheus returned to the upper world, to endure a fresh course of suffering, for he was now fastened to Mt. Caucasus, and his liver devoured by an eagle, as related in the Hesiodic legend. This state of suffering was to last until some other god, of his own accord, should take his place, and descend into Tartarus for him. This came to pass when Chiron, who

had been incurably wounded by an arrow of Hercules, desired to go into Hades ; and Zeus allowed him to supply the place of Prometheus. According to others, however, Zeus himself delivered Prometheus, when the Titan was at length prevailed upon to reveal to Zeus the decree of fate, which was that, if he should become by Thetis the father of a son, that son should deprive him of the sovereignty. There was also a legend, which related that Prometheus had created man out of earth and water, either at the very beginning of the human race, or after the flood of Deucalion, when Zeus is said to have ordered him and Athena to make men out of the mud, and the winds to breathe life into them. Prometheus is said to have given to men a portion of all the qualities possessed by the other animals (Hor. *Carm.* i. 16. 13). The kind of earth out of which Prometheus formed men was shown in later times near Panopeus in Phocis. — In the legend of Prometheus, he often appears in connection with Athena. Thus he is said to have been punished on Mt. Caucasus for the criminal love he entertained for her: and he is further said, with her assistance, to have ascended into heaven, and there secretly to have lighted his torch at the chariot of Helios, in order to bring down the fire to man. At Athens Prometheus had a sanctuary in the Academy, from whence a torch-race took place in honour of him.

Prŏmōna (Προμόνα: *Petrovacs* on Mt. *Promina*), a mountain fortress in the interior of Dalmatia.

Prŏnapĭdes (Προναπίδης), an Athenian, is said to have been the teacher of Homer. He is enumerated among those who used the Pelasgic letters, before the introduction of the Phoenician, and is characterised as a graceful composer of song.

Prōnax (Πρῶναξ), son of Talaus and Lysimache, brother of Adrastus and Eriphyle, and father of Lycurgus and Amphithea. According to some traditions the Nemean games were instituted in honour of Pronax.

Pronni (Πρόννοι: Προνναῖος), a town on the E. coast of Cephallenia, and one of the 4 towns of the island.

Prŏnŏmus (Πρόνομος), of Thebes, son of Oeniadas, was one of the most distinguished auletic musicians of Greece at the time of the Peloponnesian war. He was the instructor of Alcibiades in flute-playing. He invented a new sort of flute, the compass of which was such, that melodies could be played upon it in all the 3 modes of music, the Dorian, the Phrygian, and the Lydian, for each of which, before this invention, a separate flute had been necessary.

Prōnŏus (Πρόνοος), son of Phegeus, and brother of Agenor, in conjunction with whom he slew Alcmaeon. [For details, see AGENOR and ALCMAEON.]

Prŏnŭba, a surname of Juno among the Romans, describing her as the deity presiding over marriage.

Prŏpertius, Sex. Aurēlius, the Roman poet, was probably born about B.C. 51. He tells us that he was a native of Umbria, where it borders on Etruria, but nowhere mentions the exact spot. He was not descended from a family of any distinction (ii. 24. 37), and he was deprived of his paternal estate by an agrarian division, probably that in 36, after the Sicilian war. At the time of this misfortune he had not yet assumed the *toga virilis*, and was therefore under 16 years of age. He had already lost his father, who, it has been conjectured, was one of the victims sacrificed after the taking of Perusia; but this notion does not rest on any satisfactory grounds. We have no account of Propertius's education; but from one of his elegies (iv. 1) it would seem that he was destined to be an advocate, but abandoned the profession for that of poetry. The history of his life, so far as it is known to us, is the history of his amours, nor can it be said how much of this is fiction. He began to write poetry at a very early age, and the merit of his productions soon attracted the attention and patronage of Maecenas. This was most probably shortly after the death of Antony in 30, when Propertius was about 21. It was probably in 32 or 31, that Propertius first became acquainted with his Cynthia. She was a native of Tibur, and her real name was Hostia. As Propertius (iii. 20. 8) alludes to her *doctus avus*, it is probable that she was a grand-daughter of Hostius, who wrote a poem on the Histric war. [HOSTIUS.] She seems to have inherited a considerable portion of the family talent, and was herself a poetess, besides being skilled in music, dancing, and needlework. It appears that Propertius subsequently married, probably after Cynthia's death, and left legitimate issue, since the younger Pliny twice mentions Passiennus Paulus as descended from him. This must have been through the female line. The year of Propertius's death is altogether unknown. — Propertius resided on the Esquiline, near the gardens of Maecenas. He seems to have cultivated the friendship of his brother poets, as Ponticus, Bassus, Ovid, and others. He mentions Virgil (ii. 34. 63) in a way that shows he had heard parts of the Aeneid privately recited. But though he belonged to the circle of Maecenas, he never once mentions Horace. He is equally silent about Tibullus. His not mentioning Ovid is best explained by the difference in their ages; for Ovid alludes more than once to Propertius, and with evident affection. — As an elegiac poet, a high rank must be awarded to Propertius, and among the ancients it was a disputed point whether the preference should be given to him or to Tibullus. To the modern reader, however, the elegies of Propertius are not nearly so attractive as those of Tibullus. This arises partly from their obscurity, but in a great measure also from a certain want of nature in them. The fault of Propertius was too pedantic an imitation of the Greeks. His whole ambition was to become the Roman Callimachus (iv. 1. 63), whom, as well as Philetas and other of the Greek elegiac poets, he made his model. He abounds with obscure Greek myths, as well as Greek forms of expression, and the same pedantry infects even his versification. Tibullus generally, and Ovid almost invariably, close their pentameter with a word contained in an iambic foot; Propertius, especially in his first book, frequently ends with a word of 3, 4, or even 5 syllables. The best editions of Propertius are by Burmann, Utrecht, 1780; by Kuinoel, Leipzig, 1804; by Lachmann, Leipzig, 1816; and by Hertzberg, Halle, 1844, 1845.

Prophthasia (Προφθασία: prob. *Peshawurun*, Ru.), the N.-most city of Drangiana, on the borders of Asia, was probably the place where PHILOTAS was put to death.

Propontis (ἡ Προποντίς: *Sea of Marmara*), so called from its position with reference to the Pontus (Euxinus), and thus more fully described as ἡ πρὸ τοῦ Πόντου τοῦ Εὐξείνου θάλασσα, and "Vestibulum Ponti," is the small sea which united the Euxine and the Aegean [PONTUS EUXINUS] and divides Europe (Thracia) from Asia (Mysia and Bithynia). It is of an irregular oval shape, running out on the E. into 2 deep gulfs, the Sinus Astacenus (*G. of Ismid*) and the Sinus Cianus (*G. of Modonia*), and containing several islands. It received the waters of the RHYNDACUS and other rivers of E. Mysia and W. Bithynia, flowing from M. Ida and Olympus; and several important Greek cities stood on its shores, the chief of which were BYZANTIUM and HERACLEA PERINTHUS on the N., and CYZICUS on the S. Its length is calculated by Herodotus at 1400 stadia (140 geog. miles) and its greatest breadth at 500 stadia (50 g. m.) which is very near the truth.

Proschium. [PYLENE.]

Proserpina. [PERSEPHONE.]

Prospalta (τὰ Πρόσπαλτα: Προσπάλτιος), a demus in the S. of Attica, belonging to the tribe Acamantis.

Prosper, a celebrated ecclesiastical writer, was a native of Aquitania, and flourished during the first half of the 5th century. He distinguished himself by his numerous writings in defence of the doctrines of Augustin against the attacks of the Semipelagians. Many of his theological works are extant; and there are also 2 Chronicles bearing his name: — 1. *Chronicon Consulare*, extending from A.D. 379, the date at which the chronicle of Jerome ends, down to 455, the events being arranged according to the years of the Roman consuls. We find short notices with regard to the Roman emperors, the Roman bishops, and political occurrences in general, but the troubles of the Church are especially dwelt upon, and above all the Pelagian heresy. 2. *Chronicon Imperiale*, comprehended within the same limits as the preceding (379–455), but the computations proceed according to the years of the Roman emperors, and not according to the consuls. While it agrees with the Chronicon Consulare in its general plan, it differs from it in many particulars, especially in the very brief allusions to the Pelagian controversy, and in the slight, almost disrespectful notices of Augustine. The 2nd of these Chronicles was probably not written by Prosper of Aquitania, and is assigned by most critics to Prosper Tiro, who, it is imagined, flourished in the 6th century. There are likewise several poems, which have come down to us under the name of Prosper. The best edition of Prosper's works is the Benedictine, Paris, 1711.

Prosymna (Πρόσυμνα: Προσυμναῖος), an ancient town of Argolis, with a temple of Hera, N. of Argos.

Prote (Πρῶτα: *Prote*), an island in the Propontis near Chalcedon.

Protagoras (Πρωταγόρας), a celebrated sophist, was born at Abdera, in Thrace, probably about B.C. 480, and died about 411, at the age of nearly 70 years. It is said that Protagoras was once a poor porter, and that the skill with which he had fastened together, and poised upon his shoulders, a large bundle of wood, attracted the attention of Democritus, who conceived a liking for him, took him under his care, and instructed him in philosophy. This well-known story, however, appears to have arisen out of the statement of Aristotle, that Protagoras invented a sort of porter's knot for the more convenient carrying of burdens. In addition to which, Protagoras was about 20 years older than Democritus. Protagoras was the first who called himself a sophist, and taught for pay; and he practised his profession for the space of 40 years. He must have come to Athens before B. C. 445, since he drew up a code of laws for the Thurians, who left Athens for the first time in that year. Whether he accompanied the colonists to Thurii, we are not informed; but at the time of the plague (430) we find him again in Athens. Between his first and second visit to Athens, he had spent some time in Sicily, where he had acquired great fame; and he brought with him to Athens many admirers out of other Greek cities through which he had passed. His instructions were so highly valued that he sometimes received 100 minae from a pupil; and Plato says that Protagoras made more money than Phidias and 10 other sculptors. In 411 he was accused of impiety by Pythodorus, one of the Four Hundred. His impeachment was founded on his book on the gods, which began with the statement: "Respecting the gods, I am unable to know whether they exist or do not exist." The impeachment was followed by his banishment. or, as others affirm, only by the burning of his book. Protagoras wrote a large number of works, of which the most important were entitled *Truth* ('Αλήθεια), and *On the Gods* (Περὶ Θεῶν). The first contained the theory refuted by Plato in the Theaetetus. Plato gives a vivid picture of the teaching of Protagoras in the dialogue that bears his name. Protagoras was especially celebrated for his skill in the rhetorical art. By way of practice in the art he was accustomed to make his pupils discuss Theses (*communes loci*); an exercise which is also recommended by Cicero. He also directed his attention to language. and endeavoured to explain difficult passages in the poets.

Prŏtĕsĭlāus (Πρωτεσίλαος), son of Iphiclus and Astyoche, belonged to Phylace in Thessaly. He is called *Phylacius* and *Phylacides*, either from his native place, or from his being a grandson of Phylacus. He led the warriors of several Thessalian places against Troy, and was the first of all the Greeks who was killed by the Trojans, being the first who leaped from the ships upon the Trojan coast. According to the common tradition he was slain by Hector. Protesilaus is most celebrated in ancient story for the strong affection existing between him and his wife Laodamia, the daughter of Acastus. [For details see LAODAMIA.] His tomb was shown near Eleus, in the Thracian Chersonesus, where a magnificent temple was erected to him. There was a belief that nymphs had planted elm-trees around his grave, which died away when they had grown sufficiently high to see Troy, and that fresh shoots then sprang from the roots. There was also a sanctuary of Protesilaus at Phylace, at which funeral games were celebrated.

Proteus (Πρωτεύς), the prophetic old man of the sea, is described in the earliest legends as a subject of Poseidon, whose flocks (the seals) he tended. According to Homer he resided in the island of Pharos, at the distance of one day's journey from the river Aegyptus (Nile); whereas Virgil places his residence in the island of Car-

pathos, between Crete and Rhodes. At midday Proteus rose from the sea, and slept in the shadow of the rocks of the coast, with the monsters of the deep lying around him. Any one wishing to learn from him the future, was obliged to catch hold of him at that time: as soon as he was seized, he assumed every possible shape, in order to escape the necessity of prophesying. but whenever he saw that his endeavours were of no avail, he resumed his usual form, and told the truth. After finishing his prophecy he returned into the sea. Homer ascribes to him a daughter Idothea. — Another set of traditions describes Proteus as a son of Poseidon, and as a king of Egypt, who had two sons, Telegonus and Polygonus or Tmolus. His Egyptian name is said to have been Cetes, for which the Greeks substituted that of Proteus. His wife is called Psamathe or Torone, and, besides the above mentioned sons, Theoclymenus and Theonoë are likewise called his children. He is said to have hospitably received Dionysus during his wanderings. Hermes brought to him Helena after her abduction, or, according to others, Proteus himself took her from Paris, gave to the lover a phantom, and restored the true Helen to Menelaus after his return from Troy.

Prŏtŏgĕnĕs (Πρωτογένης), a celebrated Greek painter. He was a native of Caunus, in Caria, a city subject to the Rhodians, and flourished B. C. 332 —300. He resided at Rhodes almost entirely; the only other city of Greece which he is said to have visited is Athens, where he executed one of his great works in the Propylaea. Up to his 50th year he is said to have lived in poverty and in comparative obscurity, supporting himself by painting ships, which at that period used to be decorated with elaborate pictorial devices. His fame had, however, reached the ears of Apelles, who, upon visiting Rhodes, made it his first business to seek out Protogenes. As the surest way of making the merits of Protogenes known to his fellow-citizens, Apelles offered him, for his finished works the enormous sum of 50 talents *apiece*, and thus led the Rhodians to understand what an artist they had among them. Protogenes was distinguished by the care with which he wrought up his pictures. His masterpiece was the picture of Ialysus, the tutelary hero of Rhodes, on which he is said to have spent 7 years, or even, according to another statement, 11; and to have painted it 4 times over. This picture was so highly prized even in the artist's lifetime that when Demetrius Poliorcetes was using every effort to subdue Rhodes, he refrained from attacking the city at its most vulnerable point, lest he should injure this picture, which had been placed in that quarter. There is a celebrated story about this picture, relating to the accidental production of one of the most effective parts of it, the foam at the mouth of a tired hound. The artist, it is said, dissatisfied with his repeated attempts to produce the desired effect, at last, in his vexation, dashed the sponge, with which he had repeatedly effaced his work, against the faulty place; and the sponge charged as it was by repeated use with the necessary colours, left a mark in which the painter recognised the very foam which his art had failed to produce.

Prŏtŏgĕnĭa (Πρωτογένεια), daughter of Deucalion and Pyrrha, and wife of Locrus; but Zeus carried her off, and became by her the father of Opus.

Prŏxĕnus (Πρόξενος), a Boeotian, was a disciple of Gorgias, and a friend of Xenophon. Being connected by the ties of hospitality with the younger Cyrus, the latter engaged him in his service. He was seized by Tissaphernes and put to death, with the other Greek generals. It was at the invitation of Proxenus that Xenophon was induced to enter the service of Cyrus.

Prŭdentĭus, Aurēlĭus Clemens, the earliest of the Christian poets of any celebrity, was a native of Spain, and was born A. D. 348. After practising as an advocate, and discharging the duties of a civil and criminal judge in 2 important cities, he received from the emperor Theodosius, or Honorius, a high military appointment at court; but as he advanced in years, he became sensible of the emptiness of worldly honour, and earnest in the exercises of religion. His poems are composed in a great variety of metres, but possess little merit either in expression or in substance. The Latinity is impure, abounding both in words altogether barbarous, and in classical words employed in a barbarous sense; and the author is totally ignorant or regardless of the common laws of prosody. The best editions of Prudentius are by Arevalus, Rom. 1788 and 1789, 2 vols. 4to. and by Obbarius, Tubing. 1845, 8vo.

Prūsa or **Prūsĭas** (Προῦσα: Προυσιεύς). **1. P. ad Olympum** (Π. ἡ ἐπὶ τῷ Ὀλύμπῳ: *Brusa*), a great city of Bithynia, on the N. side of M. Olympus, 15 Roman miles from Cius and 25 from Nicaea, was built by Prusias king of Bithynia, or, according to some, by Hannibal. — **2.** Some writers distinguish from this a smaller city, called **P. ad Hypium** or **Hyppium** (πρὸς τῷ Ὑπίῳ ποταμῷ, Ptol.; sub Hypio monte, Plin.), which stood N.W. of the former, and was originally called **Ciĕrus** (Κίερος) and belonged to the territory of Heraclea, but was conquered by Prusias, who named it after himself. It stood N.W. of the former. Perhaps it is only another name for Cius.

Prūsĭas (Προυσίας). **1. I.** King of Bithynia from about B. C. 228 to 180, though the date neither of his accession nor of his death is exactly known. He was the son of Zielas, whom he succeeded. He appears to have been a monarch of vigour and ability, and raised his kingdom of Bithynia to a much higher pitch of power and prosperity than it had previously attained. It was at his court that Hannibal took refuge; and when the Romans demanded the surrender of the Carthaginian general, the king basely gave his consent, and Hannibal only escaped falling into the hands of his enemies by a voluntary death. — **2. II.** King of Bithynia, son and successor of the preceding, reigned from about 180 to 149. He courted assiduously the alliance of the Romans. He carried on war with Attalus, king of Pergamus, with whom, however, he was compelled by the Romans to conclude peace in 154. He was slain in 149 by order of his son Nicomedes, as is related in the life of the latter. [NICOMEDES II.] Prusias is described to us as a man in whom personal deformity was combined with a character the most vicious and degraded. His passion for the chase is attested by the epithet of the "Huntsman" (Κυνηγός).

Prymnēsĭa or **Prymnēsus** (Πρυμνησία, Πρυμνησός, Πρυμνησσός: *Seid-el-Ghazi*, Ru.), a city in the N. of Phrygia, which appears, from its coins, to have been a chief seat of the worship of Midas as a hero.

Prytănis (Πρύτανις), king of Sparta, of the Proclid line, was the son of Eurypon, and 4th king of that race.

Psamăthūs (Ψαμαθοῦς, -οῦντος: Ψαμαθοῦντιος, Ψαμμαθούσιος), a seaport town in Laconia near the promontory Taenarum.

Psammenĭtus (Ψαμμήνιτος), king of Egypt, succeeded his father Amasis in B. C. 526, and reigned only 6 months. He was conquered by Cambyses in 525, and his country made a province of the Persian empire. His life was spared by Cambyses, but as he was detected shortly afterwards in endeavouring to excite a revolt among the Egyptians, he was compelled to put an end to his life by drinking bull's blood.

Psammis (Ψάμμις), king of Egypt, succeeded his father Necho, and reigned from B. C. 601 to 595. He carried on war against Ethiopia, and died immediately after his return from the latter country. He was succeeded by his son Apries.

Psammitĭchus or **Psammetĭchus** (Ψαμμίτιχος or Ψαμμήτιχος), the Greek form of the Egyptian PSAMETIK, a king of Egypt, and founder of the Saitic dynasty, reigned from B. C. 671 to 617. He was originally one of the 12 kings, who obtained an independent sovereignty in the confusion which followed the death of Setho. Having been driven into banishment by the other kings, he took refuge in the marshes: but shortly afterwards with the aid of some Ionian and Carian pirates, he conquered the other kings, and became sole ruler of Egypt. He provided a settlement for his Greek mercenaries on the Pelusiac or eastern branch of the Nile, a little below Bubastis, and he appears to have mainly relied upon them for the maintenance of his power. In order to facilitate intercourse between the Greeks and his other subjects, he ordered a number of Egyptian children to live with them, that they might learn the Greek language; and from them sprung the class of interpreters. The employment of foreign mercenaries by Psammitichus gave great offence to the military caste in Egypt; and being indignant at other treatment which they received from him, they emigrated in a body of 240,000 men, into Ethiopia, where settlements were assigned to them by the Ethiopian king. It must, therefore, have been chiefly with his Ionian and Carian troops that Psammitichus carried on his wars against Syria and Phoenicia. He laid siege to the city of Azotus (the Ashod of Scripture) for 29 years, till he took it. As Psammitichus had displeased a large portion of his subjects by the introduction of foreigners, he seems to have paid especial court to the priesthood. He built the southern propylaea of the temple of Hephaestus at Memphis, and a splendid aula, with a portico round it, for the habitation of Apis, in front of the temple.

Pselcis (Ψελκίς: *Dakke*, or *Dekkeh*, Ru.), the chief city in the Dodecaschoenus, that is, the N. part of Aethiopia, which was adjacent to Egypt, to which it was regarded by the Romans as belonging. The city stood on the W. bank of the Nile, between Syene and Tachompso, the latter of which was so far eclipsed by Pselcis as to acquire the name of Contrapselcis. Under the later empire, Pselcis was garrisoned by a body of German horsemen.

Psellus (Ψέλλος). **1. Michael Psellus,** the elder, of Andros, flourished in the 9th century after Christ. He was a learned man, and an eager student of the Alexandrian philosophy. He was probably the author of some of the works which are ascribed to the younger Psellus. — 2. **Michael Constantius Psellus**, the younger, a far more celebrated person, flourished in the 11th century of our era. He was born at Constantinople 1020, and lived at least till 1105. He taught philosophy, rhetoric, and dialectics, at Constantinople, where he stood forth as almost the last upholder of the falling cause of learning. The emperors honoured him with the title of Prince of the Philosophers. His works are both in prose and poetry, on a vast variety of subjects, and distinguished by an eloquence and taste which are worthy of a better period. They are too numerous to be mentioned in this place.

Psophis (Ψωφίς: Ψωφίδιος: *Khan of Tripotamo*), a town in the N. W. of Arcadia, on the river Erymanthus, is said to have been originally called **Phegia**. It sided with the Aetolians against the Achaeans, but was taken B. c. 219 by Philip, king of Macedonia, who was then in alliance with the Achaeans.

Psyche (Ψυχή), " the soul," occurs in the later times of antiquity, as a personification of the human soul. Psyche was the youngest of the 3 daughters of a king, and excited by her beauty the jealousy and envy of Venus. In order to avenge herself, the goddess ordered Cupid or Amor to inspire Psyche with a love for the most contemptible of all men : but Cupid was so stricken with her beauty that he himself fell in love with her. He accordingly conveyed her to a charming spot, where unseen and unknown he visited her every night, and left her as soon as the day began to dawn. Psyche might have continued to enjoy this state of happiness, if she had attended to the advice of her lover, who told her never to give way to her curiosity, or to inquire who he was. But her jealous sisters made her believe that in the darkness of night she was embracing some hideous monster, and accordingly once, while Cupid was asleep, she drew near to him with a lamp, and, to her amazement, beheld the most handsome and lovely of the gods. In her excitement of joy and fear, a drop of hot oil fell from her lamp upon his shoulder. This awoke Cupid, who censured her for her mistrust, and escaped. Psyche's happiness was now gone, and after attempting in vain to throw herself into a river, she wandered about from temple to temple, inquiring after her lover, and at length came to the palace of Venus. There her real sufferings began, for Venus retained her, treated her as a slave, and imposed upon her the hardest and most humiliating labours. Psyche would have perished under the weight of her sufferings, had not Cupid, who still loved her in secret, invisibly comforted and assisted her in her toils. With his aid she at last succeeded in overcoming the jealousy and hatred of Venus: she became immortal, and was united to him for ever. It is not difficult to recognise in this lovely story the idea of which it is merely the mythical embodiment ; for Psyche is evidently the human soul, which is purified by passions and misfortunes, and is thus prepared for the enjoyment of true and pure happiness. In works of art Psyche is represented as a maiden with the wings of a butterfly, along with Cupid in the different situations described in the allegory.

Psychium (Ψύχιον), a town on the S. coast of Crete.

Psylli (Ψύλλοι), a Libyan people, the earliest known inhabitants of the district of N. Africa called Cyrenaica.

Psyra (τὰ Ψυρά: Ψύριος: *Ipsara*), a small island of the Aegean Sea, 40 stadia (4 geog. miles) in circuit, lying 50 stadia (5 geog. miles) W. off the N.W. point of Chios. It had a city of the same name.

Psyttalëa. [SALAMIS.]

Ptelëos (Πτελέως), a small lake in Mysia, near Ophrynium on the coast of the Hellespont.

Ptelëum (Πτελεόν: Πτελεάτης, Πτελεούσιος). 1. (*Ftelia*), an ancient seaport town of Thessaly in the district Phthiotis, at the S. W. extremity of the Sinus Pagasaeus, was destroyed by the Romans. — 2. A town in Elis Triphylia, said to have been a colony from the preceding. — 3. A fortress of Ionia, on the coast of Asia Minor, belonging to Erythrae.

Ptolemaeus (Πτολεμαῖος) usually called **Ptolemy**. I. *Minor historical persons.* 1. Nephew of Antigonus, king of Asia. He carried on war in Greece on behalf of Antigonus, but in 310 he abandoned the cause of his uncle and concluded a treaty with Cassander and Ptolemy the son of Lagus. He soon gave offence to the Egyptian king, and was in consequence compelled to put an end to his life by poison, B. c. 309. — 2. Son of Lysimachus, king of Thrace. He was the eldest of the 3 sons of that monarch by his last wife Arsinoë, and the only one who escaped falling into the hands of Ptolemy Ceraunus. — 3. Son of Pyrrhus, king of Epirus, by his wife Antigone, the stepdaughter of Ptolemy Lagi. When only 15 years of age he was left by his father in charge of his hereditary dominions, when Pyrrhus himself set out on his expedition to Italy, 280. At a later time he fought under his father in Greece, and was slain in the course of Pyrrhus's campaign in the Peloponnesus, 272. — 4. Surnamed PHILADELPHUS, son of M. Antony, the Triumvir, by Cleopatra. After the death of Antony, 30, his life was spared by Augustus, at the intercession of Juba and Cleopatra, and he was brought up by Octavia with her own children.

II. *Kings of Egypt.*

I. Surnamed **Soter**, the Preserver, but more commonly known as the son of Lagus, reigned B. c. 323—285. His father Lagus was a Macedonian of ignoble birth, but his mother Arsinoë had been a concubine of Philip of Macedon, on which account it seems to have been generally believed that Ptolemy was in reality the offspring of that monarch. Ptolemy is mentioned among the friends of the young Alexander before the death of Philip. He accompanied Alexander throughout his campaigns in Asia, and was always treated by the king with the greatest favour. On the division of the empire which followed Alexander's death (323), Ptolemy obtained the government of Egypt. In 321 his dominions were invaded by Perdiccas, the regent; but the assassination of Perdiccas by his mutinous soldiers soon delivered Ptolemy from this danger. In the following year Ptolemy enlarged his dominions by seizing upon the important satrapy of Phoenicia and Coele-Syria. It was probably during this expedition that he made himself master of Jerusalem, by attacking the city on the Sabbath day. A few years afterwards (316) Ptolemy entered into an alliance with Cassander and Lysimachus against Antigonus, whose growing power had excited their common apprehensions. In the war which followed, Antigonus conquered Coele-Syria and Phoenicia (315, 314); but Ptolemy recovered these provinces by the defeat of Demetrius, the son of Antigonus, in 312. In 311 hostilities were suspended by a general peace. This peace, however, was of short duration, and Ptolemy appears to have been the first to recommence the war. He crossed over to Greece, where he announced himself as the liberator of the Greeks, but he effected little. In 306 Ptolemy was defeated by Demetrius in a great sea-fight off Salamis in Cyprus. In consequence of this defeat, Ptolemy lost the important island of Cyprus, which had previously been subject to him. Antigonus was so much elated by this victory as to assume the title of king, an example which Ptolemy, notwithstanding his defeat, immediately followed. Antigonus and Demetrius followed up their success by the invasion of Egypt, but were compelled to return to Syria without effecting any thing. Next year (305) Ptolemy rendered the most important assistance to the Rhodians, who were besieged by Demetrius; and when Demetrius was at length compelled to raise the siege (304), the Rhodians paid divine honours to the Egyptian monarch as their saviour and preserver (Σωτήρ), a title which appears to have been now bestowed upon Ptolemy for the first time. Ptolemy took comparatively little part in the contest, which led to the decisive battle of Ipsus, in which Antigonus was defeated and slain (301). The latter years of Ptolemy's reign appear to have been devoted almost entirely to the arts of peace, and to promoting the internal prosperity of his dominions. In 285 Ptolemy abdicated in favour of his youngest son Ptolemy Philadelphus, the child of his latest and most beloved wife, Berenice, excluding from the throne his two eldest sons Ptolemy Ceraunus and Meleager, the offspring of Eurydice. The elder Ptolemy survived this event 2 years, and died in 283. His reign is variously estimated at 38 or 40 years, according as we include or not these 2 years which followed his abdication. — The character of Ptolemy has been generally represented in a very favourable light by historians, and there is no doubt that if we compare him with his contemporary and rival potentates he appears to deserve the praises bestowed upon his mildness and moderation. But it is only with this important qualification that they can be admitted: for there are many evidences, that he did not shrink from any measure that he deemed requisite in order to carry out the objects of his ambition. But as a ruler Ptolemy certainly deserves the highest praise. By his able and vigorous administration he laid the foundations of the wealth and prosperity which Egypt enjoyed for a long period. Under his fostering care Alexandria quickly rose to the place designed for it by its founder, that of the greatest commercial city of the world. Not less eminent were the services rendered by Ptolemy to the advancement of literature and science. In this department indeed it is not always easy to distinguish the portion of credit due to the father from that of his son: but it seems certain that to the elder monarch belongs the merit of having originated those literary institutions which assumed a more definite and regular form, as well as a more prominent place, under his successor. Such appears

to have been the case with the two most celebrated of all, the Library and the Museum of Alexandria. The first suggestion of these important foundations is ascribed by some writers to Demetrius of Phalerus, who spent all the latter years of his life at the court of Ptolemy. But many other men of literary eminence were also gathered around the Egyptian king: among whom may be especially noticed the great geometer Euclid, the philosophers Stilpo of Megara, Theodorus of Cyrene, and Diodorus surnamed Cronus; as well as the elegiac poet Philetas of Cos, and the grammarian Zenodotus. To the two last we are told Ptolemy confided the literary education of his son Philadelphus. Many anecdotes sufficiently attest the free intercourse which subsisted between the king and the men of letters by whom he was surrounded, and prove that the easy familiarity of his manners corresponded with his simple and unostentatious habits of life. We also find him maintaining a correspondence with Menander, whom he in vain endeavoured to attract to his court, and sending overtures probably of a similar nature to Theophrastus. Nor were the fine arts neglected: the rival painters Antiphilus and Apelles both exercised their talents at Alexandria, where some of their most celebrated pictures were produced.— Ptolemy was himself an author: he composed a history of the wars of Alexander, which is frequently cited by later writers, and is one of the chief authorities which Arrian made the groundwork of his own history. — **II. Philadelphus** (B. C. 285—247), the son of Ptolemy I. by his wife Berenice, was born in the island of Cos, 309. His long reign was marked by few events of a striking character. He was engaged in war with his half-brother Magas, who had governed Cyrene as viceroy under Ptolemy Soter, but on the death of that monarch not only asserted his independence, but even attempted to invade Egypt. Magas was supported by Antiochus II., king of Syria; and the war was at length terminated by a treaty, which left Magas in undisputed possession of the Cyrenaïca, while his infant daughter Berenice was betrothed to Ptolemy, the son of Philadelphus. Ptolemy also concluded a treaty with the Romans. He was frequently engaged in hostilities with Syria, which were terminated towards the close of his reign by a treaty of peace, by which Ptolemy gave his daughter Berenice in marriage to Antiochus II. Ptolemy's chief care, however, was directed to the internal administration of his kingdom, and to the patronage of literature and science. The institutions of which the foundations had been laid by his father quickly rose under his fostering care to the highest prosperity. The Museum of Alexandria became the resort and abode of all the most distinguished men of letters of the day, and in the library attached to it were accumulated all the treasures of ancient learning. Among the other illustrious names which adorned the reign of Ptolemy, may be mentioned those of the poets Philetas and Theocritus, the philosophers Hegesias and Theodorus, the mathematician Euclid, and the astronomers Timocharis, Aristarchus of Samos, and Aratus. Nor was his patronage confined to the ordinary cycle of Hellenic literature. By his interest in natural history he gave a stimulus to the pursuit of that science, which gave birth to many important works, while he himself formed collections of rare animals within the precincts of the royal palace. It was during his reign also, and perhaps at his desire, that Manetho gave to the world in a Greek form the historical records of the Egyptians ; and according to a well-known tradition, it was by his express command that the Holy Scriptures of the Jews were translated into Greek. The new cities or colonies founded by Philadelphus in different parts of his dominions were extremely numerous. On the Red Sea alone we find at least two bearing the name of Arsinoë, one called after another of his sisters Philotera, and two cities named in honour of his mother Berenice. The same names occur also in Cilicia and Syria : and in the latter country he founded the important fortress of Ptolemaïs in Palestine. All authorities concur in attesting the great power and wealth, to which the Egyptian monarchy was raised under Philadelphus. He possessed at the close of his reign a standing army of 200,000 foot, and 40,000 horse, besides war-chariots and elephants ; a fleet of 1500 ships ; and a sum of 740,000 talents in his treasury ; while he derived from Egypt alone an annual revenue of 14,800 talents. His dominions comprised, besides Egypt itself, and portions of Ethiopia, Arabia, and Libya, the important provinces of Phoenicia and Coele-Syria, together with Cyprus, Lycia, Caria, and the Cyclades : and during a great part at least of his reign, Cilicia and Pamphylia also. Before his death Cyrene was reunited to the monarchy by the marriage of his son Ptolemy with Berenice, the daughter of Magas. The private life and relations of Philadelphus do not exhibit his character in as favourable a light as we might have inferred from the splendour of his administration. He put to death 2 of his brothers ; and he banished his first wife Arsinoë, the daughter of Lysimachus, to Coptos in Upper Egypt on a charge of conspiracy. After her removal Ptolemy married his own sister Arsinoë, the widow of Lysimachus ; a flagrant violation of the religious notions of the Greeks, but which was frequently imitated by his successors. He evinced his affection for Arsinoë, not only by bestowing her name upon many of his newly-founded colonies, but by assuming himself the surname of Philadelphus, a title which some writers referred in derision to his unnatural treatment of his 2 brothers. By this 2nd marriage Ptolemy had no issue : but his first wife had borne him 2 sons — Ptolemy, who succeeded him on the throne, and Lysimachus ; and a daughter, Berenice, whose marriage to Antiochus II., king of Syria, has been already mentioned. — III. Euergetes (B.C. 247 — 222), eldest son and successor of Philadelphus. Shortly after his accession he invaded Syria, in order to avenge the death of his sister Berenice. [BERENICE, No. 2.] He met with the most striking success. He advanced as far as Babylon and Susa, and after reducing all Mesopotamia, Babylonia, and Susiana, received the submission of all the upper provinces of Asia as far as the confines of Bactria and India. From this career of conquest he was recalled by the news of seditions in Egypt, and returned to that country, carrying with him an immense booty, comprising, among other objects, all the statues of the Egyptian deities which had been carried off by Cambyses to Babylon or Persia. These he restored to their respective temples, an act by which he earned the greatest popularity with his native Egyptian sub-

jecta, who bestowed on him in consequence the title of Euergetes (the Benefactor), by which he is generally known. While the arms of the king himself were thus successful in the East, his fleets reduced the maritime provinces of Asia, including Cilicia, Pamphylia, and Ionia, as far as the Hellespont, together with Lysimachia and other important places on the coast of Thrace which continued for a long period subject to the Egyptian rule. Concerning the events which followed the return of Euergetes to his own dominions (probably in 243) we are almost wholly in the dark ; but it appears that the greater part of the eastern provinces speedily fell again into the hands of Seleucus, while Ptolemy retained possession of the maritime regions and a great part of Syria itself. He soon obtained a valuable ally in the person of Antiochus Hierax, the younger brother of Seleucus, whom he supported in his wars against his elder brother. We find Euergetes maintaining the same friendly relations as his father with Rome. During the latter years of his reign he subdued the Ethiopian tribes on his southern frontier, and advanced as far as Adule, a port on the Red Sea, where he established an emporium, and set up an inscription commemorating the exploits of his reign. To a copy of this, accidentally preserved to us by an Egyptian monk, Cosmas Indicopleustes, we are indebted for much of the scanty information we possess concerning his reign. Ptolemy Euergetes is scarcely less celebrated than his father for his patronage of literature and science : he added so largely to the library at Alexandria that he has been sometimes erroneously deemed its founder. Eratosthenes, Apollonius Rhodius, and Aristophanes, the grammarian, flourished at Alexandria during his reign, — sufficient to prove that the literature and learning of the Alexandrian school still retained their former eminence. By his wife Berenice, who survived him, Euergetes left three children : 1. Ptolemy, his successor ; 2. Magas and 3. Arsinoë, afterwards married to her brother Ptolemy Philopator. — IV. Philopator (B.C. 222–205), eldest son and successor of Euergetes. He was very far from inheriting the virtues or abilities of his father : and his reign was the commencement of the decline of the Egyptian kingdom, which had been raised to such a height of power and prosperity by his three predecessors. Its first beginning was stained with crimes of the darkest kind. He put to death his mother, Berenice, and his brother, Magas, and his uncle Lysimachus, the brother of Euergetes. He then gave himself up without restraint to a life of indolence and luxury, while he abandoned to his minister Sosibius the care of all political affairs. The latter seems to have been as incapable as his master : and the kingdom was allowed to fall into a state of the utmost disorder, of which Antiochus the Great, king of Syria, was not slow to avail himself. In the first 2 campaigns (219, 218), Antiochus conquered the greater part of Coele-Syria and Palestine, but in the 3rd year of the war (217), he was completely defeated by Ptolemy in person at the decisive battle of Raphia, and was glad to conclude a peace with the Egyptian monarch. On his return from his Syrian expedition, Ptolemy gave himself up more and more to every species of vice and debauchery. His mistress Agathoclea, and her brother Agathocles, divided with Sosibius the patronage and distribution of all places of honour or profit. Towards the close of his reign Ptolemy put to death his wife Arsinoë. His debaucheries shortened his life. He died in 205, leaving only one son, a child of 5 years old. We find Ptolemy following up the policy of his predecessors, by cultivating the friendship of the Romans, to whom he furnished large supplies of corn during their struggle with Carthage. Plunged as he was in vice and debauchery, Philopator appears to have still inherited something of the love of letters for which his predecessors were so conspicuous. We find him associating on familiar terms with philosophers and men of letters, and especially patronising the distinguished grammarian Aristarchus. — V. Epiphanes (B. C. 205—181), son and successor of Ptolemy IV. He was a child of 5 years old at the death of his father, 205. Philip king of Macedonia and Antiochus III. of Syria, determined to take advantage of the minority of Ptolemy, and entered into a league to divide his dominions between them. In pursuance of this arrangement Antiochus conquered Coele-Syria, while Philip reduced the Cyclades and the cities in Thrace which had still remained subject to Egypt. In this emergency the Egyptian ministers had recourse to the powerful intervention of the Romans, who commanded both monarchs to refrain from further hostilities, and restore all the conquered cities. In order to evade this demand without openly opposing the power of Rome, Antiochus concluded a treaty with Egypt, by which it was agreed that the young king should marry Cleopatra, the daughter of Antiochus, and receive back the Syrian provinces as her dower. This treaty took place in 199, but the marriage was not actually solemnised until 6 years after. The administration of Egypt was placed in the hands of Aristomenes, a man who was every way worthy of the charge. As early, however, as 196 the young king was declared of full age, and the ceremony of his Anacleteria, or coronation, was solemnised with great magnificence. It was on this occasion that the decree was issued which has been preserved to us in the celebrated inscription known as the Rosetta stone, a monument of great interest in regard to the internal history of Egypt under the Ptolemies, independent of its importance as having afforded the key to the discovery of hieroglyphics. In 193 the marriage of Ptolemy with the Syrian princess Cleopatra was solemnised at Raphia. Ptolemy, however, refused to assist his father-in-law in the war against the Romans, which was at this time on the eve of breaking out, and he continued steadfast in his alliance with Rome. But he derived no advantage from the treaty which concluded it, and Antiochus still retained possession of Coele-Syria and Phoenicia. As long as Ptolemy continued under the guidance and influence of Aristomenes, his administration was equitable and popular. Gradually, however, he became estranged from his able and virtuous minister, and threw himself more and more into the power of flatterers and vicious companions, until at length he was induced to rid himself of Aristomenes, who was compelled to take poison. Towards the close of his reign Ptolemy conceived the project of recovering Coele-Syria from Seleucus, the successor of Antiochus, and had assembled a large mercenary force for that purpose: but having, by an unguarded expression, excited the apprehensions of some of his friends, he was cut off by poison in the 24th year of his reign and the 29th of his age, 181. He left 2 sons, both named Ptolemy, who subsequently ascended the throne, under the names of Ptolemy Philometor and Euergetes II. and a daughter, who bore her mother's name of Cleopatra. His reign was marked by the rapid decline of the Egyptian monarchy, for the provinces and cities wrested from it during his minority by Antiochus and Philip were never recovered, and at his death Cyprus and the Cyrenaïca were almost the only foreign possessions still attached to the crown of Egypt.—VI. Philometor (B. C. 181—146), eldest son and successor of Ptolemy V. He was a child at the death of his father in 181, and the regency was assumed during his minority by his mother Cleopatra, who, by her able administration, maintained the kingdom in a state of tranquillity. But after her death, in 173, the chief power fell into the hands of Eulaeus and Lenaeus, ministers as corrupt as they were incapable; who had the rashness to engage in war with Antiochus Epiphanes, king of Syria, in the vain hope of recovering the provinces of Coele-Syria and Phoenicia. But their army was totally defeated by Antiochus, near Pelusium, and Antiochus was able to advance without opposition as far as Memphis, 170. The young king himself fell into his hands, but was treated with kindness and distinction, as Antiochus hoped by his means to make himself the master of Egypt. On learning the captivity of his brother, the younger Ptolemy, who was then at Alexandria with his sister Cleopatra, assumed the title of king, under the name of Euergetes II., and prepared to defend the capital to the utmost. Antiochus hereupon laid siege to Alexandria; but he was unable to take the city, and withdrew into Syria, after establishing Philometor as king at Memphis, but retaining in his hands the frontier fortress of Pelusium. This last circumstance, together with the ravages committed by the Syrian troops, awakened Philometor, who had hitherto been a mere puppet in the hands of the Syrian king, to a sense of his true position, and he hastened to make overtures of peace to his brother and sister at Alexandria. It was agreed that the two brothers should reign together, and that Philometor should marry his sister Cleopatra. But this arrangement did not suit the views of Antiochus, who immediately renewed hostilities. The two brothers were unable to offer any effectual opposition, and he had advanced a second time to the walls of Alexandria, when he was met by a Roman embassy, headed by M. Popillius Laenas, who haughtily commanded him instantly to desist from hostilities. Antiochus did not venture to disobey, and withdrew to his own dominions, 168. Dissensions soon broke out between the 2 brothers, and Euergetes expelled Philometor from Alexandria. Hereupon Philometor repaired in person to Rome, 164, where he was received by the senate with the utmost honour, and deputies were appointed to reinstate him in the sovereign power. This they effected with little opposition; but they settled that Euergetes should obtain Cyrene as a separate kingdom. Euergetes, however, shortly afterwards laid claim to Cyprus as well, in which he was supported by the Romans; but Philometor refused to surrender the island to him, and in the war which ensued, Euergetes was taken prisoner by his brother, who not only spared his life, but sent him back to Cyrene on condition that he should thenceforth content himself with that king

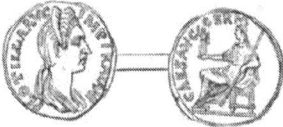

Plotina, wife of Trajan. Page 592.

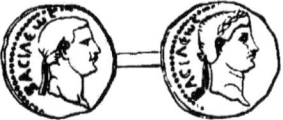

Prusias II., King of Bithynia, ob. A.D. 149. Page 620.

Polemon II., King of Pontus and the Bosporus, A.D. 39-63. Page 594.

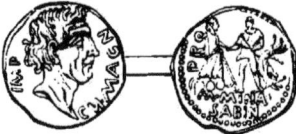

Ptolemaeus I. Soter, King of Egypt, B.C. 323—283. Page 621.

Cn. Pompeius Magnus, the Triumvir, ob. B.C. 48. This coin was struck by his son. Pages 602—605.

Ptolemaeus II. Philadelphus, King of Egypt, B.C. 285—247. Page 622.

Postumus, one of the Thirty Tyrants, A.D. 258—267. Page 610.

Ptolemaeus III. Euergetes, King of Egypt, B.C. 247—222. Page 623.

Probus, Roman Emperor, A.D. 276—282. Page 614.

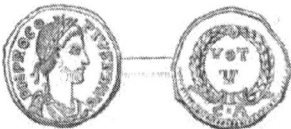

Ptolemaeus IV. Philopator, King of Egypt, B.C. 222—205. Page 623.

Procopius, Roman Emperor, A.D. 365—366. Page 615.

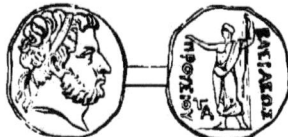

Ptolemaeus V. Epiphanes, King of Egypt, B.C. 205—181. Page 624.

[To face p. 624.

Ptolemaeus VI. Philometor, King of Egypt, B.C. 181—146.
Page 634.

Ptolemaeus VII. Euergetes II. or Physcon, King of Egypt,
B.C. 146—117. Page 635.

Ptolemaeus VIII. Lathyrus, King of Egypt, B.C. 117—107
and 89—81. Page 635.

Ptolemaeus IX. Alexander I., King of Egypt, B.C. 107—90.
Page 636.

Ptolemaeus XI. Dionysus, or Auletes, King of Egypt,
B.C. 80—51. Page 636.

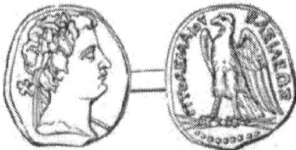

Ptolemaeus XII. King of Egypt, ob. B.C. 47. Page 636.

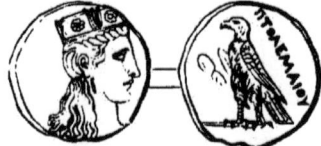

To face p. 635.]

Ptolemaeus, King of Epirus, about B.C. 239—229.
Page 627, No. 6.

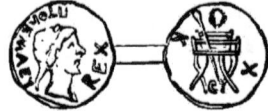

Ptolemaeus, King of Mauretania, ob. A.D. 40. Page 627, No. 7.

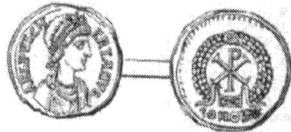

Pulcheria, Roman Empress, A.D. 453. Page 639.

Pupienus Maximus, Roman Emperor, A.D. 238. Page 29.

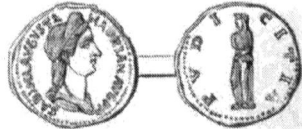

Sabina, the wife of Hadrian. Page 662.

Poppaea Sabina, the wife of Nero. Page 662.

dom. The attention of Philometor appears to have been, from this time, principally directed to the side of Syria. Demetrius Soter having sought during the dissensions between the two brothers to make himself master of Cyprus, Ptolemy now supported the usurper Alexander Balas, to whom he gave his daughter Cleopatra in marriage, 150. But when Ptolemy advanced with an army to the assistance of his son-in-law, Ammonius, the favourite and minister of Alexander, formed a plot against the life of Ptolemy; whereupon the latter took away his daughter Cleopatra from her faithless husband, and bestowed her hand on Demetrius Nicator, the son of Soter, whose cause he now espoused. In conjunction with Demetrius, Ptolemy carried on war against Alexander, whom he defeated in a decisive battle; but he died a few days afterwards in consequence of an injury which he had received from a fall from his horse in this battle, 146. He had reigned 35 years from the period of his first accession, and 18 from his restoration by the Romans. Philometor is praised for the mildness and humanity of his disposition. Polybius even tells us that not a single citizen of Alexandria was put to death by him for any political or private offence. On the whole, if not one of the greatest, he was at least one of the best of the race of the Ptolemies. He left three children: 1. A son, Ptolemy, who was proclaimed king after his father's death, under the name Ptolemy Eupator, but was put to death almost immediately after by his uncle Euergetes. 2. A daughter, Cleopatra, married first to Alexander Balas, then to Demetrius II. king of Syria; and 3. Another daughter, also named Cleopatra, who was afterwards married to her uncle Ptolemy Euergetes. — VII. Euergetes II. or Physcon (Φύσκων), that is Big-Belly, reigned B. C. 146 — 117. His history down to the death of his brother has been already given. In order to secure undisputed possession of the throne, he married his sister Cleopatra, the widow of his brother Philometor, and put to death his nephew Ptolemy, who had been proclaimed king under the surname of Eupator. A reign thus commenced in blood was continued in a similar spirit. Many of the leading citizens of Alexandria, who had taken part against him on the death of his brother, were put to death, while the populace were given up to the cruelties of his mercenary troops, and the streets of the city were repeatedly deluged with blood. Thousands of the inhabitants fled from the scene of such horrors, and the population of Alexandria was so greatly thinned that the king found himself compelled to invite foreign settlers from all quarters to re-people his deserted capital. At the same time that he thus incurred the hatred of his subjects by his cruelties, he rendered himself an object of their aversion and contempt by abandoning himself to the most degrading vices. In consequence of these, he had become bloated and deformed in person, and enormously corpulent, whence the Alexandrians gave him the nickname of Physcon, by which appellation he is more usually known. His union with Cleopatra was not of long duration. He became enamoured of his niece Cleopatra (the offspring of his wife by her former marriage with Philometor), and he did not hesitate to divorce the mother, and receive her daughter instead, as his wife and queen. By this proceeding he alienated still more the minds of his Greek subjects; and his vices and cruelties at length produced an insurrection at Alexandria.

Thereupon he fled to Cyprus, and the Alexandrians declared his sister Cleopatra queen (130). Enraged at this, Ptolemy put to death Memphitis, his son by Cleopatra, and sent his head and hands to his unhappy mother. But Cleopatra having been shortly afterwards expelled from Alexandria in her turn, Ptolemy found himself unexpectedly reinstated on the throne (127). His sister Cleopatra fled to the court of her elder sister Cleopatra, the wife of Demetrius II., king of Syria, who espoused the cause of the fugitive. Ptolemy, in revenge, set up against him a pretender named Zabinas or Zebina, who assumed the title of Alexander II. But the usurper behaved with such haughtiness to Ptolemy, that the latter suddenly changed his policy, became reconciled to his sister Cleopatra, whom he permitted to return to Egypt, and gave his daughter Tryphaena in marriage to Antiochus Grypus, the son of Demetrius. Ptolemy died after reigning 29 years from the death of his brother Philometor; but he himself reckoned the years of his reign from the date of his first assumption of the regal title in 170. Although the character of Ptolemy Physcon was stained by the most infamous vices, and by the most sanguinary cruelty, he still retained that love of letters which appears to have been hereditary in the whole race of the Ptolemies. He had in his youth been a pupil of Aristarchus, and not only courted the society of learned men, but was himself the author of a work called Ὑπομνήματα, or memoirs, which extended to 24 books. He left two sons; Ptolemy, afterwards known as Soter II., and Alexander, both of whom subsequently ascended the throne of Egypt; and 3 daughters: 1. Cleopatra, married to her brother Ptolemy Soter; 2. Tryphaena, the wife of Antiochus Grypus, king of Syria; and 3. Selene, who was unmarried at her father's death. To his natural son Ptolemy, surnamed Apion, he bequeathed by his will the separate kingdom of Cyrene. — VIII., Soter II., and also Philometor, but more commonly called Lathyrus or Lathurus (Λάθουρος), reigned B. C. 117—107, and also 89—81. Although he was of full age at the time of his father's death (117), he was obliged to reign jointly with his mother, Cleopatra, who had been appointed by the will of her late husband to succeed him on the throne. She was indeed desirous of associating with herself her younger son, Ptolemy Alexander; but since Lathyrus was popular with the Alexandrians, she was obliged to give way, and sent Alexander to Cyprus. After declaring Lathyrus king, she compelled him to repudiate his sister Cleopatra, of whose influence she was jealous, and to marry his younger sister Selene in her stead. After reigning 10 years jointly with his mother, he was expelled from Alexandria by an insurrection of the people which she had excited against him (107). His brother Alexander now assumed the sovereignty of Egypt, in conjunction with his mother, while Lathyrus was able to establish himself in the possession of Cyprus. Cleopatra indeed attempted to dispossess him of that island also, but without success, and Ptolemy held it as an independent kingdom for the 18 years during which Cleopatra and Alexander reigned in Egypt. After the death of Cleopatra and the expulsion of Alexander in 89, Ptolemy Lathyrus was recalled by the Alexandrians, and established anew on the throne of Egypt, which he occupied thenceforth without interruption till his death in 81. The most important event of this period was the revolt of Thebes, in Upper Egypt, which was still powerful enough to hold out for nearly 3 years against the arms of Ptolemy, but at the end of that time was taken and reduced to the state of ruin in which it has ever since remained. Lathyrus reigned in all 35½ years; 10 in conjunction with his mother (117—107), 18 in Cyprus (107—89), and 7½ as sole ruler of Egypt. He left only one daughter Berenice, called also Cleopatra, who succeeded him on the throne: and 2 sons, both named Ptolemy, who, though illegitimate, became severally kings of Egypt and Cyprus.—**IX. Alexander I.**, youngest son of Ptolemy VII., reigned conjointly with his mother Cleopatra from the expulsion of his brother Lathyrus, B. C. 107 to 90. In this year he assassinated his mother; but he had not reigned alone a year, when he was compelled by a general sedition of the populace and military to quit Alexandria. He, however, raised fresh troops, but was totally defeated in a sea-fight by the rebels; whereupon Lathyrus was recalled by the Alexandrians to Egypt, as has been already related. Alexander now attempted to make himself master of Cyprus, and invaded that island, but was defeated and slain. He left a son, Alexander, who afterwards ascended the throne of Egypt.—**X. Alexander II.**, son of the preceding, was at Rome at the death of Ptolemy Lathyrus in 81. Sulla, who was then dictator, nominated the young Alexander (who had obtained a high place in his favour) king of Egypt, and sent him to take possession of the crown. It was, however, agreed, in deference to the claims of Cleopatra Berenice, the daughter of Lathyrus, whom the Alexandrians had already placed on the throne, that Alexander should marry her, and admit her to share the sovereign power. He complied with the letter of this treaty by marrying Cleopatra, but only 19 days afterwards caused her to be assassinated. The Alexandrians, thereupon, rose against their new monarch, and put him to death.—**XI. Dionysus**, but more commonly known by the appellation of **Auletes**, the flute-player, was an illegitimate son of Ptolemy Lathyrus. When the assassination of Berenice and the death of Alexander II. had completed the extinction of the legitimate race of the Lagidae, Ptolemy was proclaimed king by the Alexandrians, B. C. 80. He was anxious to obtain from the Roman senate their ratification of his title to the crown, but it was not till the consulship of Caesar (59) that he was able to purchase by vast bribes the desired privilege. He had expended immense sums in the pursuit of this object, which he was compelled to raise by the imposition of fresh taxes, and the discontent thus excited combining with the contempt entertained for his character, led to his expulsion by the Alexandrians, in 58. Thereupon he proceeded in person to Rome to procure from the senate his restoration. His first reception was promising; and he procured a decree from the senate, commanding his restoration, and entrusting the charge of effecting it to P. Lentulus Spinther, then proconsul of Cilicia. Meanwhile, the Alexandrians sent an embassy of 100 of their leading citizens to plead their cause with the Roman senate; but Ptolemy had the audacity to cause the deputies, on their arrival in Italy, to be waylaid, and the greater part of them murdered. The indignation excited at Rome by this proceed-

ing produced a reaction: the tribunes took up the matter against the nobility; and an oracle was produced from the Sibylline books, forbidding the restoration of the king by an armed force. The intrigues and disputes thus raised were protracted throughout the year 56, and at length Ptolemy, despairing of a favourable result, quitted Rome in disgust, and withdrew to Ephesus. But in 55, A. Gabinius, who was proconsul in Syria, was induced, by the influence of Pompey, aided by the enormous bribe of 10,000 talents from Ptolemy himself, to undertake his restoration. The Alexandrians had in the meantime placed on the throne of Egypt, Berenice, the eldest daughter of Ptolemy, who had married Archelaus, the son of the general of Mithridates, and they opposed Gabinius with an army on the confines of the kingdom. They were, however, defeated in 3 successive battles, Archelaus was slain, and Ptolemy once more established on the throne, 55. One of his first acts was to put to death his daughter Berenice, and many of the leading citizens of Alexandria. He survived his restoration only 3½ years, during which time he was supported by a large body of Roman soldiers who had been left behind by Gabinius for his protection. He died in 51, after a reign of 29 years from the date of his first accession. He left 2 sons, both named Ptolemy, and 2 daughters, Cleopatra and Arsinoë.—**XII.** Eldest son of the preceding. By his father's will the sovereign power was left to himself and his sister Cleopatra jointly, and this arrangement was carried into effect without opposition, 51. Auletes had also referred the execution of his will to the Roman senate, and the latter accepted the office, confirmed its provisions and bestowed on Pompey the title of guardian of the young king. But the approach of the civil war prevented them from taking any active part in the administration of affairs, which fell into the hands of an eunuch named Pothinus. It was not long before dissensions broke out between the latter and Cleopatra, which ended in the expulsion of the princess, after she had reigned in conjunction with her brother about 3 years, 48. Hereupon she took refuge in Syria, and assembled an army, with which she invaded Egypt. The young king, accompanied by his guardians, met her at Pelusium, and it was while the two armies were there encamped opposite to one another, that Pompey landed in Egypt, to throw himself as a suppliant on the protection of Ptolemy; but he was assassinated by the orders of Pothinus, before he could obtain an interview with the king himself. Shortly after, Caesar arrived in Egypt, and took upon himself to settle the dispute between Ptolemy and his sister. But as Cleopatra's charms gained for her the support of Caesar, Pothinus determined to excite an insurrection against Caesar. Hence arose what is usually called the Alexandrian war. Ptolemy, who was at first in Caesar's hands, managed to escape, and put himself at the head of the insurgents, but he was defeated by Caesar, and was drowned in an attempt to escape by the river (47).—**XIII.** Youngest son of Ptolemy Auletes, was declared king by Caesar in conjunction with Cleopatra, after the death of his elder brother Ptolemy XII., 47: and although he was a mere boy, it was decreed that he should marry his sister, with whom he was thus to share the power. Both his marriage and regal title were, of course, purely nominal; and in 43 Cleopatra put him to death.

III. Kings of other Countries.

1. Surnamed **Alorites**, that is, of Alorus, regent, or, according to some authors, king of Macedonia. He obtained the supreme power by the assassination of Alexander II., the eldest son of Amyntas, B. c. 367, but was, in his turn, assassinated by Perdiccas III., 364. — **2.** Surnamed **Apion**, king of Cyrene (117—96) was an illegitimate son of Ptolemy Physcon, king of Egypt, who left him by his will the kingdom of the Cyrenaïca. At his death in 96, Apion bequeathed his kingdom by his will to the Roman people. The senate, however, refused to accept the legacy, and declared the cities of the Cyrenaïca free. They were not reduced to the condition of a province till near 30 years afterwards. — **3.** Surnamed **Ceraunus**, king of Macedonia, was the son of Ptolemy I. king of Egypt, by his 2nd wife Eurydice. When his father in 285 set aside the claim of Ceraunus to the throne, and appointed his younger son, Ptolemy Philadelphus, his successor, Ceraunus repaired to the court of Lysimachus. After Lysimachus had perished in battle against Seleucus (281) Ptolemy Ceraunus was received by the latter in the most friendly manner; but shortly afterwards (280) he basely assassinated Seleucus, and took possession of the Macedonian throne. After reigning a few months he was defeated in battle by the Gauls, taken prisoner and put to death. — **4.** Tetrarch of Chalcis in Syria, the son of Mennaeus. He appears to have held the cities of Heliopolis and Chalcis as well as the mountain district of Ituraea, from whence he was in the habit of infesting Damascus and the more wealthy parts of Coele-Syria with predatory incursions. He reigned from about 70 to 40, when he was succeeded by his son Lysanias. — **5.** King of **Cyprus**, was the younger brother of Ptolemy Auletes, king of Egypt, being like him an illegitimate son of Ptolemy Lathyrus. He was acknowledged as king of Cyprus at the same time that his brother Auletes obtained possession of the throne of Egypt, 80. He had offended P. Clodius, by neglecting to ransom him when he had fallen into the hands of the Cilician pirates; and accordingly Clodius, when he became tribune (58), brought forward a law to deprive Ptolemy of his kingdom, and reduce Cyprus to a Roman province. Cato, who had to carry into execution this nefarious decree, sent to Ptolemy, advising him to submit, and offering him his personal safety, with the office of high-priest at Paphos, and a liberal maintenance. But the unhappy king refused these offers, and put an end to his own life, 57. — **6.** King of **Epirus**, was the 2nd son of Alexander II., king of Epirus, and Olympias, and grandson of the great Pyrrhus. He succeeded to the throne on the death of his elder brother, Pyrrhus II., but reigned only a very short time. The date of his reign cannot be fixed with certainty, but as he was contemporary with Demetrius II. king of Macedonia, it may be placed between 239—229. — **7.** King of **Mauretania**, was the son and successor of Juba II. By his mother Cleopatra he was descended from the kings of Egypt, whose name he bore. The period of his accession cannot be determined with certainty, but we know that he was on the throne in A. D. 18. He continued to reign without interruption till A. D. 40, when he was summoned to Rome by Caligula, and shortly after put to death, his great riches having excited the cupidity of the emperor.

IV. Literary.

1. **Claudius Ptolemaeus**, a celebrated mathematician, astronomer, and geographer. Of Ptolemy himself we know absolutely nothing but his date. He certainly observed in A. D. 139, at Alexandria; and since he survived Antoninus he was alive A. D. 161. His writings are as follows: — 1. Μεγάλη Σύνταξις τῆς Ἀστρονομίας, usually known by its Arabic name of *Almagest.* Since the *Tetrabiblus*, the work on astrology, was also entitled σύνταξις, the Arabs to distinguish the two, probably called the greater work μεγάλη, and afterwards μεγίστη: the title *Almagest* is a compound of this last adjective and the Arabic article. The Almagest is divided into 13 books. It treats of the relations of the earth and heaven; the effect of position upon the earth; the theory of the sun and moon, without which that of the stars cannot be undertaken; the sphere of the fixed stars, and those of the five stars called *planets.* The 7th and 8th books are the most interesting to the modern astronomer as they contain a catalogue of the stars. This catalogue gives the longitudes and latitudes of 1022 stars, described by their positions in the constellations. It seems that this catalogue is in the main really that of Hipparchus, altered to Ptolemy's own time by assuming the value of the precession of the equinoxes given by Hipparchus as the least which could be; some changes having also been made by Ptolemy's own observations. Indeed the whole work of Ptolemy appears to have been based upon the observations of Hipparchus, whom he constantly cites as his authority. The best edition of the Almagest is by Halma, Paris, 1813, 1816, 2 vols. 4to. There are also 2 other volumes by Halma (1819—1820), which contain some of the other writings of Ptolemy.—2. Τετράβιβλος σύνταξις, generally called *Tetrabiblon*, or *Quadripartitum de Apotelesmatibus et Judiciis Astrorum.* With this goes another small work, called καρπὸς, or *Fructus Librorum Suorum*, often called *Centiloquium*, from its containing a hundred aphorisms. Both of these works are astrological, and it has been doubted by some whether they be genuine. But the doubt merely arises from the feeling that the contents are unworthy of Ptolemy. —3. Κανὼν Βασιλέων, a catalogue of Assyrian, Persian, Greek, and Roman sovereigns, with the length of their reigns, several times referred to by Syncellus.—4. Φάσεις ἀπλανῶν ἀστέρων καὶ συναγωγὴ ἐπισημασειῶν, *De Apparentiis et Significationibus inerrantium*, an annual list of sidereal phaenomena. — 5, 6. *De Analemmate* and *Planisphaerium.* These works are obtained from the Arabic. The *Analemma* is a collection of graphical processes for facilitating the construction of sun-dials. The *Planisphere* is a description of the stereographic projection, in which the eye is at the pole of the circle on which the sphere is projected. — 7. Περὶ ὑποθέσεων τῶν πλανωμένων, *De Planetarum Hypothesibus.* This is a brief statement of the principal hypotheses employed in the Almagest for the explanation of the heavenly motions. — 8. Ἁρμονικῶν βιβλία γ'., a treatise on the theory of the musical scale. — 9. Περὶ κριτηρίου καὶ ἡχεμονικοῦ, *De Judicandi Facultate et Animi Principatu*, a metaphysical work, attributed to Ptolemy. — 10. Γεωγραφικὴ Τφήγησις, in 8 books, the great geographical work of Ptolemy. This work was the last attempt made by the ancients to form a com-

plete geographical system ; it was accepted as the text-book of the science ; and it maintained that position during the middle ages, and until the 15th century, when the rapid progress of maritime discovery caused it to be superseded. It contains, however, very little information respecting the objects of interest connected with the different countries and places ; for with the exception of the introductory matter in the first book, and the latter part of the work, it is a mere catalogue of the names of places, with their longitudes and latitudes, and with a few incidental references to objects of interest. The latitudes of Ptolemy are tolerably correct ; but his longitudes are very wide of the truth, his length of the known world, from east to west, being much too great It is well worthy, however, of remark in passing, that the modern world owes much to this error ; for it tended to encourage that belief in the practicability of a western passage to the Indies, which occasioned the discovery of America by Columbus. The 1st book is introductory. The next 6¼ books (ii—vii. 4) are occupied with the description of the known world, beginning with the West of Europe, the description of which is contained in book ii. ; next comes the East of Europe, in book iii. ; then Africa, in book iv. ; then Western or Lesser Asia, in book v. ; then the Greater Asia, in book vi. ; then India, the Chersonesus Aurea, Serica, the Sinae, and Taprobane, in book vii. cc. 1—4. The form in which the description is given is that of lists of places with their longitudes and latitudes, arranged under the heads, first, of the three continents, and then of the several countries and tribes. Prefixed to each section is a brief general description of the boundaries and divisions of the part about to be described ; and remarks of a miscellaneous character are interspersed among the lists, to which, however, they bear but a small proportion. The remaining part of the 7th, and the whole of the 8th book, are occupied with a description of a set of maps of the known world. These maps are still extant. The best edition of the *Geographia* of Ptolemy is by Petrus Bertius, Lugd. Bat. 1619, fol. ; reprinted Antwerp, 1624, fol.— 2. Of Megalopolis, the son of Agesarchus, wrote a history of king Ptolemy IV. Philopator.— 3. An Egyptian priest, of Mendes, who wrote on the ancient history of Egypt. He probably lived under the first Roman emperors.— 4. Surnamed **Chemnis**, a grammarian of Alexandria, flourished under Trajan and Hadrian. An epitome of one of his works is preserved by Photius.

Ptŏlĕmăïs (Πτολεμαΐς : Πτολεμαΐτης and Πτολεμαεύς). **1.** Also called **Ace** ('Ακή, a corruption of the native name **Acco**, O. T. : Arab. *Akka*, Fr. *St. Jean d'Acre*, Eng. *Acre*), a celebrated city on the coast of Phoenicia, S. of Tyre, and N. of M. Carmel, lies at the bottom of a bay surrounded by mountains, in a position marked out by nature as a key of the passage between Coele-Syria and Palestine. It is one of the oldest cities of Phoenicia, being mentioned in the Book of Judges (i. 31). Under the Persians, it was made the headquarters of the expeditions against Egypt ; but it was not till the decline of Tyre that it acquired its great importance as a military and commercial city. The Ptolemy who enlarged and strengthened it, and from whom it obtained its Greek name, is supposed to have been Ptolemy I. the son of Lagus. After the change of its name, its citadel continued

to be called Ace. Under the Romans, it was a colony, and belonged to Galilee. To recount its great celebrity in medieval and modern history does not fall within the province of this work.— 2. (At or near *El-Lahun*), a small town of Middle Egypt, in the Nomos Arsinoïtes, between Arsinoë and Heracleopolis the Great.— 3. P. Hermii (Π. ἡ 'Ερμείου, Πτολεμαϊκὴ πόλις : *Menshieh*, Ru.), a city of Upper Egypt, on the W. bank of the Nile, below Abydos, was a place of great importance under the Ptolemies, who enlarged and adorned it, and made it a purely Greek city, exempt from all peculiarly Egyptian laws and customs. — 4. P. Thērōn, or Ĕpĭthēras (Π. Θηρῶν, ἡ ἐπὶ Θήρας), a port on the Red Sea, on the coast of the Troglodytae, an emporium for the trade with India and Arabia; but chiefly remarkable in the history of mathematical geography, inasmuch as, the sun having been observed to be directly over it 45 days before and after the summer solstice, the place was taken as one of the fixed points for determining the length of a degree of a great circle on the earth's surface.— 5. (*Tolmeïta*, or *Tolomeïa*, Ru.), on the N.W. coast of Cyrenaica, one of the 5 great cities of the Libyan Pentapolis, was at first only the port of BARCA, which lay 100 stadia (10 geog. miles) inland, but which was so entirely eclipsed by Ptolemaïs that, under the Romans, even the name of Barca was transferred to the latter city. From which of the Ptolemies it took its name, we are not informed. Its magnificence is attested by its splendid ruins, which are now partly covered by the sea. They are 4 miles in circumference, and contain the remains of several temples, 3 theatres, and an aqueduct.

Ptŏon (Πτῶον : *Palea* and *Strutsina*), a mountain in Boeotia, an offshoot of Helicon, which extends from the S. E. side of the lake Copais S.-wards to the coast.

Publĭcŏla, or **Poplĭcŭla**, or **Poplĭcŏla**, a Roman cognomen, signified " one who courts the people " (from *populus* and *colo*), and thus " a friend of the people." The form *Poplicola* or *Poplicola* was the more ancient, but *Publicola* was the one usually employed by the Romans in later times.

Publĭcŏla, Gellĭus. 1. L., consul with Cn. Lentulus Clodianus, B. c. 72. Both consuls carried on war against Spartacus, but were defeated by the latter. In 70, Gellius was censor, and in 67 and 66 he served as one of Pompey's legates in the war against the pirates. He belonged to the aristocratical party. In 63 he warmly supported Cicero in the suppression of the Catilinarian conspiracy. In 59 he opposed the agrarian law of Caesar, and in 57 he spoke in favour of Cicero's recall from exile. He was alive in 55, when Cicero delivered his speech against Piso, but he probably died soon afterwards. He was married twice. He must have reached a great age, since he is mentioned as the contubernalis of C. Papirius Carbo, who was consul in 120.— 2. L., son of the preceding by his first wife. He espoused the republican party after Caesar's death (44), and went with M. Brutus to Asia. After plotting against the lives of both Brutus and Cassius, he deserted to the triumvirs, Octavian and Antony. He was rewarded for his treachery by the consulship in 36. In the war between Octavian and Antony, he espoused the side of the latter, and commanded the right wing of Antony's fleet at the battle of

Actium.— 3. Brother probably of No. 1, is called step-son of L. Marcius Philippus, consul 91, and brother of L. Marcius Philippus, consul 56. According to Cicero's account he was a profligate and a spendthrift, and having dissipated his property, united himself to P. Clodius.

Publicōla, P. Valērius, took an active part in expelling the Tarquins from the city, and was thereupon elected consul with Brutus (B. C. 509). He secured the liberties of the people by proposing several laws, one of the most important of which was that every citizen who was condemned by a magistrate should have the right of appeal to the people. He also ordered the lictors to lower the fasces before the people, as an acknowledgment that their power was superior to that of the consuls. Hence he became so great a favourite with the people, that he received the surname of *Publicola.* He was consul 3 times again, namely in 508, 507 and 504. He died in 503. He was buried at the public expense, and the matrons mourned for him 10 months, as they had done for Brutus.— The descendants of Publicola bore the same name, and several of them held the highest offices of state during the early years of the republic.

Publilia, the 2nd wife of M. Tullius Cicero, whom he married, B. C. 46. As Cicero was then 60 years of age, and Publilia quite young, the marriage occasioned great scandal. It appears that Cicero was at the time in great pecuniary embarrassments ; and after the divorce of Terentia, he was anxious to contract a new marriage for the purpose of obtaining money to pay his debts. Publilia had a large fortune, which had been left to Cicero in trust for her. The marriage proved an unhappy one, as might have been expected ; and Cicero divorced her in 45.

Publīlius Philo. [PHILO.]

Publilius, Volēro, tribune of the plebs, B. C. 472, and again 471, effected an important change in the Roman constitution. In virtue of the laws which he proposed, the tribunes of the plebs and the aediles, were elected by the comitia tributa, instead of by the comitia centuriata, as had previously been the case, and the tribes obtained the power of deliberating and determining in all matters affecting the whole nation, and not such only as concerned the plebs. Some said that the number of the tribunes was now for the first time raised to 5, having been only 2 previously.

Publius Syrus. [SYRUS.]

Pucinum (Πούκινον), a fortress in Istria in the N. of Italy, on the road from Aquileia to Pola, was situated on a steep rock, which produced wine, mentioned by Pliny under the name of *Vinum Pucinum.*

Pudicitia (Αἰδώς), a personification of modesty, was worshipped both in Greece and at Rome. At Athens an altar was dedicated to her. At Rome two sanctuaries were dedicated to her, one under the name of *Pudicitia patricia,* and the other under that of *Pudicitia plebeia.* The former was in the forum Boarium near the temple of Hercules. When the patrician Virginia was driven from this sanctuary by the other patrician women, because she had married the plebeian consul L. Volumnius, she built a separate sanctuary to *Pudicitia plebeia* in the Vicus Longus.

Pulcher, Claudius. [CLAUDIUS.]

Pulchēria, eldest daughter of the emperor Ar-

cadius, was born A. D. 399. In 414, when she was only 15 years of age, she became the guardian of her brother Theodosius, and was declared Augusta or empress. She had the virtual government in her hands during the whole lifetime of her brother, who died in 450. On his death she remained at the head of affairs, and shortly afterwards she married Marcian, with whom she continued to reign in common till her death in 453. Pulcheria was a woman of ability, and was celebrated for her piety, and her public and private virtues.

Pulchrum Promontorium (καλὸν ἀκρωτήριον), a promontory on the N. coast of the Carthaginian territory in N. Africa, where the elder Scipio Africanus landed ; probably identical with the APOLLINIS PROMONTORIUM.

Pullus, L. Jūnius, consul B. C. 249, in the first Punic war. His fleet was destroyed by a storm, on account, it was said, of his neglecting the auspices. In despair he put an end to his own life.

Pupiēnus Maximus, M. Clōdius, was elected emperor with Balbinus, in A. D. 238 when the senate received intelligence of the death of the two Gordians in Africa ; but the new emperors were slain by the soldiers at Rome in the same year.

Pupius, a Roman dramatist, whose compositions are characterised by Horace, as the " lacrymosa poemata Pupi."

Pūra (Πούρα : prob. *Bumpur*), the capital of Gedrosia, in the interior of the country, on the borders of Carmania.

Purpurāriae Insūlae (prob. the *Madeira* group), a group of islands in the Atlantic Ocean, off the N. W. coast of Africa, which are supposed to have derived their name from the purple muscles which abound on the opposite coast of Africa (Gaetulia). The islands of Hera (Ἥρα) and Autolala (Αὐτολάλα), mentioned by Ptolemy, appear to belong to the group.

Purpurēo, L. Furius, praetor B. C. 200, obtained Cisalpine Gaul as his province, and gained a brilliant victory over the Gauls, who had laid siege to Cremona. He was consul 196, when he defeated the Boii.

Puteōlānum, a country-house of Cicero near Puteoli, where he wrote his *Quaestiones Academicae,* and where the emperor Hadrian was buried.

Puteōlānus Sinus (*Bay of Naples*), a bay of the sea on the coast of Campania between the promontory Misenum and the promontory of Minerva, which was originally called Cumanus, but afterwards Puteolanus from the town Puteoli. The N. W. corner of it was separated by a dike 8 stadia in length from the rest of the bay, thus forming the LUCRINUS LACUS.

Puteōli (Puteolānus : *Pozzuoli*), originally named Dicaearchia (Δικαιαρχία, Δικαιάρχεια : Δικαιαρχεύς, Δικαιαρχείτης, -χίτης), a celebrated seaport town of Campania, situated on a promontory on the E. side of the Puteolanus Sinus, and a little to the E. of Cumae, was founded by the Greeks of Cumae, B. C. 521, under the name of Dicaearchia. In the 2nd Punic war it was fortified by the Romans, who changed its name into that of Puteoli, either from its numerous wells or from the stench arising from the mineral springs in its neighbourhood. The town was indebted for its importance to its excellent harbour, which was protected by an extensive mole formed from the celebrated reddish earth of the neighbouring hills. This earth, called *Pozzolana*, when mixed with chalk, forms an excellent cement, which in course of time becomes as hard in water as stone. The mole was built on arches like a bridge, and 17 of the piers are still visible projecting above the water. To this mole Caligula attached a floating bridge, which extended as far as Baiae, a distance of 2 miles. Puteoli was the chief emporium for the commerce with Alexandria and with the greater part of Spain. The town was colonised by the Romans in B. c. 194, and also anew by Augustus, Nero, and Vespasian. It was destroyed by Alaric in A. D. 410, by Genseric in 455, and also by Totilas in 545, but was on each occasion speedily rebuilt. There are still many ruins of the ancient town at the modern Pozzuoli. Of these the most important are the remains of the temple of Serapis, of the amphitheatre, and of the mole already described.

Putput (prob. *Hamamet*), a seaport town of Africa Propria (Zeugitana) on the gulf of Neapolis (G. of *Hamamet*). Its name is evidently Phoenician.

Pydna (Πύδνα: Πυδναῖος: *Kitron*), a town of Macedonia in the district Pieria, was situated at a small distance W. of the Thermaic gulf, on which it had a harbour. It was originally a Greek colony, but it was subdued by the Macedonian kings, from whom, however, it frequently revolted. Towards the end of the Peloponnesian war it was taken after a long siege by Archelaus, and its inhabitants removed 20 stadia inland ; but at a later period we still find the town situated on the coast. It again revolted from the Macedonians, and was subdued by Philip, who enlarged and fortified the place. It was here that Olympias sustained a long siege against Cassander, B. c. 317 —316. It is especially memorable on account of the victory gained under its walls by Aemilius Paulus over Perseus, the last king of Macedonia, 168. Under the Romans it was also called Citrum or Citrus.

Pygēla or **Phygēla** (Πύγελα, Φύγελα), a small town of Ionia, on the coast of Lydia, with a temple of Artemis Munychia. Tradition ascribed its foundation to Agamemnon, on his return from Troy.

Pygmaei (Πυγμαῖοι, i. e. *men of the height of a* πυγμή, i. e. 13½ inches), a fabulous people, first mentioned by Homer (*Il.* iii. 5), as dwelling on the shores of Ocean, and attacked by cranes in spring time. The fable is repeated by numerous writers, in various forms, especially as to the locality. Some placing them in Aethiopia, others in India, and others in the extreme N. of the earth. The story is referred to by Ovid and Juvenal, and forms the subject of several works of art.

Pygmālĭon (Πυγμαλίων). 1. King of Cyprus and father of Metharme. He is said to have fallen in love with the ivory image of a maiden which he himself had made, and therefore to have prayed to Aphrodite to breathe life into it. When the request was granted, Pygmalion married the maiden, and became by her the father of Paphus. — 2. Son of Belus and brother of Dido, who murdered Sichaeus, Dido's husband. For details see DIDO.

Pylādes (Πυλάδης). 1. Son of Strophius and Anaxibia, a sister of Agamemnon. His father was king of Phocis ; and after the death of Agamemnon, Orestes was secretly carried to his father's court. Here Pylades contracted that friendship with Orestes, which became proverbial. He assisted Orestes in murdering his mother Clytaemnestra, and also accompanied him to the Tauric Chersonesus ; and he eventually married his sister Electra, by whom he became the father of Hellanicus, Medon, and Strophius. For details see ORESTES. — 2. A pantomime dancer in the reign of Augustus, spoken of under BATHYLLUS.

Pȳlae (Πύλαι, *Gates*). 1. A general name for any narrow pass, such as THERMOPYLAE, Pylae Albaniae, Caspiae, &c. (See the several specific names). — 2. Two small islands at the entrance into the Arabicus Sinus (*Red Sea*) from the Erythraean Sea.

Pylaemĕnes (Πυλαιμένης), appears to have been the name of many kings of Paphlagonia, so as to have become a kind of hereditary appellation, like that of Ptolemy in Egypt, and Arsaces in Parthia. We have, however, very little definite information concerning them.

Pylas (Πύλας), son of Cteson, and king of Megara, who, after slaying Bias, his own father's brother, founded the town of Pylos in Peloponnesus, and gave Megara to Pandion who had married his daughter Pylia, and accordingly was his son-in-law.

Pȳlēnē (Πυλήνη), an ancient town of Aetolia on the S. slope of Mt. Aracynthus, on whose site Proschium was subsequently built.

Pȳlos (Πύλος), the name of 3 towns on the W. coast of Peloponnesus. 1. In Elis, at the foot of Mt. Scollis, and about 70 or 80 stadia from the city of Elis on the road to Olympia, near the confluence of the Ladon and the Peneus. It is said to have been founded by Pylon or Phylas of Megara, to have been destroyed by Hercules, and to have been afterwards rebuilt by the Eleans. — 2. In Triphylia, about 30 stadia from the coast, on the river Mamaus, W. of the mountain Minthe, and N. of Lepreum. — 3. In the S. W. of Messenia, was situated at the foot of Mt. Aegaleos on a promontory at the N. entrance of the basin, now called the *Bay of Navarino*, the largest and safest harbour in all Greece. This harbour was fronted and protected by the small island of Sphacteria (*Sphagia*), which stretched along the coast about 1½ mile, leaving only 2 narrow entrances at each end. In the 2nd Messenian war the inhabitants of Pylos offered a long and brave resistance to the Spartans ; but after the capture of Ira, they were obliged to quit their native country with the rest of the Messenians. Pylos now remained in ruins, but again became memorable in the Peloponnesian war, when the Athenians under Demosthenes built a fort on the promontory Coryphasium a little S. of the ancient city, and just within the N. entrance to the harbour (B. c. 425). The attempts of the Spartans to dislodge the Athenians proved unavailing ; and the capture by Cleon of the Spartans, who had landed in the island of Sphacteria, was one of the most important events in the whole war.—There has been much controversy, which of these 3 places was the Pylos founded by Neleus, and governed by Nestor and his descendants. The town in Elis has little or no claim to the honour, and the choice lies between the towns in Triphylia and Messenia. The ancients usually decided in favour of the Messenian Pylos ; but some modern critics, without sufficient grounds, support the claims of the Triphylian city.

Pyramĭa (τὰ Πυράμια), a town of Argolis, in the district Thyreatis, where Danaus is said to have landed.

Pyramon. [CYCLOPES.]

Pyrămus. [THISBE.]

Pyrămus (Πύραμος : Jihan), one of the largest rivers of Asia Minor, rises in the Anti-Taurus range, near Arabissus in Cataonia (the S. E. part of Cappadocia), and after running S. E., first underground, and then as a navigable river, breaks through the Taurus chain by a deep and narrow ravine, and then flows S. W. through Cilicia, in a deep and rapid stream, about 1 stadium (606 feet) in width, and falls into the sea near Mallus. Its ancient name is said to have been Leucosyrus, from the LEUCOSYRI, who dwelt on its banks.

Pyrēnē or Pyrenaei Montes (Πυρήνη, τὰ Πυρηναῖα ὄρη : Pyrenees), a range of mountains, extending from the Atlantic to the Mediterranean, and forming the boundary between Gaul and Spain. The length of these mountains is about 270 miles in a straight line ; their breadth varies from about 40 miles to 20 ; their greatest height is between 11,000 and 12,000 feet. The Romans first became acquainted with these mountains by their campaigns against the Carthaginians in Spain in the 2nd Punic war. Their name however had travelled E.-ward at a much earlier period, since Herodotus (ii. 33) speaks of a city Pyrene belonging to the Celts, near which the Ister rises. The ancient writers usually derived the name from πῦρ, "fire," and then, according to a common practice, invented a story to explain the false etymology, relating that a great fire once raged upon the mountains. The name, however, is probably connected with the Celtic Byrin or Bryn, "a mountain." The continuation of the mountains along the Mare Cantabricum was called Saltus Vasconum, and still further W. Mons Vindius or Vinnius. The Romans were acquainted with only 3 passes over the Pyrenees, the one on the W. near Carasae (Garis) not far from the Mare Cantabricum, the one in the middle leading from Caesaraugusta to Beneharnum (Baréges), and the one on the E., which was most frequently used, near the coast of the Mediterranean by Juncaria (Junquera).

Pyrēnēs Promontorĭum, or Prom. Venēris (C. Creus), the S.E. extremity of the Pyrenees in Spain, on the frontiers of Gaul, derived its 2nd name from a temple of Venus on the promontory.

Pyrgi. 1. (Πύργοι or Πύργος : Πυργίτης), the most S.-ly town of Triphylia in Elis, near the Messenian frontier, said to have been founded by the Minyae.—2. (Pyrgensis : Santa Severa), an ancient Pelasgic town on the coast of Etruria, was used as the port of Caere or Agylla, and was a place of considerable importance as a commercial emporium. It was at an early period the headquarters of the Tyrrhenian pirates. It possessed a very wealthy temple of Ilithyia, which Dionysius of Syracuse plundered in B.C. 384. Pyrgi is mentioned at a later time as a Roman colony, but lost its importance under the Roman dominion. There are still remains at Sta Severa of the ancient polygonal walls of Pyrgi.

Pyrgotĕles (Πυργοτέλης), one of the most celebrated gem-engravers of ancient Greece, was a contemporary of Alexander the Great, who placed him on a level with Apelles and Lysippus, by naming him as the only artist who was permitted to engrave seal-rings for the king.

Pyricus, a Greek painter, who probably lived soon after the time of Alexander the Great. He devoted himself entirely to the production of small pictures of low and mean subjects.

Pyriphlĕgĕthon (Πυριφλεγέθων), that is, flaming with fire, the name of one of the rivers in the lower world.

Pyromăchus, the name of 2 artists. The name occurs in 4 different forms, namely, Phyromachus, Phylomachus, Philomachus, and Pyromachus. — 1. An Athenian sculptor, who executed the bas-reliefs on the frieze of the temple of Athena Polias, about B.C. 415. The true form of his name appears to have been Phyromachus.—2. An artist who flourished B.C. 295—240, is mentioned by Pliny (xxxiv. 8. s. 19) as one of those statuaries who represented the battles of Attalus and Eumenes against the Gauls. Of these battles the most celebrated was that which obtained for Attalus I. the title of king, about 241. It is supposed by the best writers on ancient art that the celebrated statue of a dying combatant, popularly called the Dying Gladiator, is a copy from one of the bronze statues in the works mentioned by Pliny. It is evidently the statue of a Celt.

Pyrrha (Πύρρα : Πυρραῖος). 1. A town on the W. coast of the island of Lesbos, on the inner part of the deep bay named after it, and consequently on the narrowest part of the island.—2. A town and promontory of Phthiotis in Thessaly, on the Pagasaean gulf and near the frontiers of Magnesia. Off this promontory there were 2 small islands, named Pyrrha and Deucalion.—3. A small Ionic town in Caria on the N. side of the Sinus Latmicus and 50 stadia from the mouth of the Maeander.

Pyrrhi Castra (Πύρρου χάραξ), a fortified place in the N. of Laconica, where Pyrrhus probably encamped in his invasion of the country in B.C. 272.

Pyrrhichus (Πύρριχος), a town of the Eleuthero-lacones in the S.W. of Laconica.

Pyrrho (Πύρρων), the founder of the Sceptical or Pyrrhonian school of philosophy, was a native of Elis in Peloponnesus. He is said to have been poor, and to have followed, at first, the profession of a painter. He is then said to have been attracted to philosophy by the books of Democritus, to have attended the lectures of Bryson, a disciple of Stilpon, to have attached himself closely to Anaxarchus, and with him to have joined the expedition of Alexander the Great. During the greater part of his life he lived in retirement, and endeavoured to render himself independent of all external circumstances. His disciple Timon extolled with admiration his divine repose of soul, and his indifference to pleasure or pain. So highly was he valued by his fellow-citizens that they made him their high priest, and erected a monument to him after his death. The Athenians conferred upon him the rights of citizenship. We know little respecting the principles of his sceptical philosophy ; and the ridiculous tales told about him by Diogenes Laertius are probably the invention of his enemies. He asserted that certain knowledge on any subject was unattainable ; and that the great object of man ought to be to lead a virtuous life. Pyrrho wrote no works, except a poem addressed to Alexander, which was rewarded by the latter in a royal manner. His philosophical system was first reduced to writing by his disciple Timon. He reached the age of 90 years, but we have no mention of the year either of his birth or of his death.

Pyrrhus (Πύρρος). 1. Mythological. [NEO-PTOLEMUS.]. — 2. I. King of Epirus, son of Aeacides and Phthia, was born B. C. 318. His ancestors claimed descent from Pyrrhus, the son of Achilles, who was said to have settled in Epirus after the Trojan war, and to have become the founder of the race of Molossian kings. On the deposition of his father by the Epirots [AEACIDES], Pyrrhus, who was then a child of only two years old, was saved from destruction by the faithful adherents of the king, who carried him to Glaucias, the king of the Taulantians, an Illyrian people. Glaucias took the child under his care, and brought him up with his own children. He not only refused to surrender Pyrrhus to Cassander, but about 10 years afterwards he marched into Epirus at the head of an army, and placed Pyrrhus on the throne, leaving him, however, under the care of guardians, as he was then only 12 years of age. In the course of 4 or 5 years, however, Cassander, who had regained his supremacy in Greece, prevailed upon the Epirots to expel their young king. Pyrrhus, who was still only 17 years of age, joined Demetrius, who had married his sister Deïdama, accompanied him to Asia, and was present at the battle of Ipsus, 301, in which he gained great renown for his valour. Antigonus fell in the battle, and Demetrius became a fugitive; but Pyrrhus did not desert his brother-in-law in his misfortunes, and shortly afterwards went for him as a hostage into Egypt. Here he was fortunate enough to win the favour of Berenice, the wife of Ptolemy, and received in marriage Antigone, her daughter by her first husband. Ptolemy now supplied him with a fleet and forces, with which he returned to Epirus. Neoptolemus, who had reigned from the time that Pyrrhus had been driven from the kingdom, agreed to share the sovereignty with Pyrrhus. But such an arrangement could not last long; and Pyrrhus anticipated his own destruction by putting his rival to death. This appears to have happened in 295, in which year Pyrrhus is said to have begun to reign. He was now 23 years old, and he soon became one of the most popular princes of his time. His daring courage made him a favourite with his troops, and his affability and generosity secured the love of his people. He seems at an early age to have taken Alexander as his model, and to have been fired with the ambition of imitating his exploits and treading in his footsteps. His eyes were first directed to the conquest of Macedonia. By assisting Alexander, the son of Cassander, against his brother Antipater, he obtained possession of the whole of the Macedonian dominions on the western side of Greece. But the Macedonian throne itself fell into the hands of Demetrius, greatly to the disappointment of Pyrrhus. The two former friends now became the most deadly enemies, and open war broke out between them in 291. After the war had been carried on with great vigour and various vicissitudes for 4 years, Pyrrhus joined the coalition formed in 287 by Seleucus, Ptolemy, and Lysimachus against Demetrius. Lysimachus and Pyrrhus invaded Macedonia; Demetrius was deserted by his troops, and obliged to fly in disguise; and the kingdom was divided between Lysimachus and Pyrrhus. But the latter did not long retain his portion; the Macedonians preferred the rule of their old general Lysimachus; and Pyrrhus was accordingly driven out of the country after a reign of 7 months (286).

For the next few years Pyrrhus reigned quietly in Epirus without embarking in any new enterprize. But a life of inactivity was insupportable to him; and accordingly he readily accepted the invitation of the Tarentines to assist them in their war against the Romans. He crossed over to Italy early in 280, in the 38th year of his age. He took with him 20,000 foot, 3000 horse, 2000 archers, 500 slingers, and either 50 or 20 elephants, having previously sent Milo, one of his generals, with a detachment of 3000 men. As soon as he arrived at Tarentum, he began to make vigorous preparations for carrying on the war; and as the giddy and licentious inhabitants of Tarentum complained of the severity of his discipline, he forthwith treated them as their master rather than as their ally, shut up the theatre and all other public places, and compelled their young men to serve in his ranks. In the 1st campaign (280) the Roman consul M. Valerius Laevinus was defeated by Pyrrhus near Heraclea, on the bank of the river Siris. The battle was long and bravely contested, and it was not till Pyrrhus brought forward his elephants, which bore down every thing before them, that the Romans took to flight. The loss of Pyrrhus, though inferior to that of the Romans, was still very considerable. A large proportion of his officers and best troops had fallen; and he said, as he viewed the field of battle, "Another such victory, and I must return to Epirus alone." He therefore availed himself of his success to send his minister Cineas to Rome with proposals of peace, while he himself marched slowly towards the city. His proposals, however, were rejected by the senate. He accordingly continued his march, ravaging the Roman territory as he went along. He advanced within 24 miles of Rome; but as he found it impossible to compel the Romans to accept the peace, he retraced his steps and withdrew into winter-quarters to Tarentum. As soon as the armies were quartered for the winter, the Romans sent an embassy to Pyrrhus, to endeavour to obtain the ransom of the Roman prisoners. The ambassadors were received by Pyrrhus in the most distinguished manner; and his interviews with C. Fabricius, who was at the head of the embassy, form one of the most celebrated stories in Roman history. [FABRICIUS.] In the 2nd campaign (279) Pyrrhus gained another victory near Asculum over the Romans, who were commanded by the consuls P. Decius Mus and P. Sulpicius Saverrio. The battle, however, was followed by no decisive results, and the brunt of it had again fallen, as in the previous year, almost exclusively on the Greek troops of the king. He was therefore unwilling to hazard his surviving Greeks by another campaign with the Romans, and accordingly he lent a ready ear to the invitations of the Greeks in Sicily, who begged him to come to their assistance against the Carthaginians. The Romans were likewise anxious to get rid of so formidable an opponent that they might complete the subjugation of southern Italy without further interruption. When both parties had the same wishes, it was not difficult to find a fair pretext for bringing the war to a conclusion. This was afforded at the beginning of the following year (278), by one of the servants of Pyrrhus deserting to the Romans and proposing to the consuls to poison his master. The consuls Fabricius and Aemilius sent back the deserter to the king, stating that they abhorred a victory gained by treason.

Thereupon Pyrrhus, to show his gratitude, sent Cineas to Rome with all the Roman prisoners without ransom and without conditions; and the Romans granted him a truce, though not a formal peace, as he had not consented to evacuate Italy. Pyrrhus now crossed over into Sicily, where he remained upwards of 2 years, from the middle of 478 to the latter end of 476. At first he met with brilliant success, defeated the Carthaginians and took Eryx; but having failed in an attempt upon Lilybaeum, he lost his popularity with the Greeks, who began to form cabals and plots against him. This led to retaliation on the part of Pyrrhus, and to acts which were deemed both cruel and tyrannical by the Greeks. His position in Sicily at length became so uncomfortable and dangerous, that he soon became anxious to abandon the island. Accordingly, when his Italian allies again begged him to come to their assistance, he gladly complied with their request. Pyrrhus returned to Italy in the autumn of 276. In the following year (275) the war was brought to a close. Pyrrhus was defeated with great loss near Beneventum by the Roman consul Curius Dentatus, and was obliged to leave Italy. He brought back with him to Epirus only 8000 foot and 500 horse, and had not money to maintain even these without undertaking new wars. Accordingly, in 272, he invaded Macedonia, of which Antigonus Gonatas, the son of Demetrius, was then king. His only object at first seems to have been plunder; but his success far exceeded his expectations. Antigonus was deserted by his own troops, and Pyrrhus thus became king of Macedonia a second time. But scarcely had he obtained possession of the kingdom before his restless spirit drove him into new enterprises. On the invitation of Cleonymus he turned his arms against Sparta, but was repulsed in an attack upon this city. From Sparta he marched towards Argos in order to support Aristeas, one of the leading citizens at Argos, against his rival Aristippus, whose cause was espoused by Antigonus. In the night-time Aristeas admitted Pyrrhus into the city; but the alarm having been given, the citadel and all the strong places were seized by the Argives of the opposite faction. On the dawn of day Pyrrhus saw that it would be necessary for him to retreat; and as he was fighting his way out of the city, an Argive woman hurled down from the house-top, a ponderous tile, which struck Pyrrhus on the back of his neck. He fell from his horse stunned with the blow, and being recognised by some of the soldiers of Antigonus, was quickly despatched. His head was cut off and carried to Antigonus, who turned away from the sight, and ordered the body to be interred with becoming honours. Pyrrhus perished in 272, in the 46th year of his age, and in the 23rd of his reign. He was the greatest warrior and one of the best princes of his time. With his daring courage, his military skill, and his kingly bearing, he might have become the most powerful monarch of his day, if he had steadily pursued the immediate object before him. But he never rested satisfied with any acquisition, and was ever grasping at some fresh object: hence Antigonus compared him to a gambler, who made many good throws with the dice, but was unable to make the proper use of the game. Pyrrhus was regarded in subsequent times as one of the greatest generals that had ever lived. Hannibal said that of all generals Pyrrhus was the first, Scipio the

second, and himself the third; or, according to another version of the story, Alexander was the first, Pyrrhus the second, and himself the third. Pyrrhus wrote a work on the art of war, which was read in the time of Cicero; and his commentaries are quoted both by Dionysius and Plutarch. Pyrrhus married 4 wives. 1. Antigone, the daughter of Berenice. 2. A daughter of Audoleon, king of the Paeonians. 3. Bircenna, a daughter of Bardylis, king of the Illyrians. 4. Lanassa, a daughter of Agathocles of Syracuse. His children were: — 1. Ptolemy, born 295; killed in battle, 272. 2. Alexander, who succeeded his father as king of Epirus. 3. Helenus. 4. Nereis, who married Gelon of Syracuse. 5. Olympias, who married her own brother Alexander. 6. Deidamia or Laodamia. — 3. II. King of Epirus, son of Alexander II. and Olympias, and grandson of Pyrrhus I. was a child at the time of his father's death (between 262 and 258). During his minority the kingdom was governed by his mother Olympias. According to one account Olympias survived Pyrrhus, who died soon after he had grown up to manhood; according to another account Olympias had poisoned a maiden to whom Pyrrhus was attached, and was herself poisoned by him in revenge.

PYTHAGORAS (Πυθαγόρας). 1. A celebrated Greek philosopher, was a native of Samos, and the son of Mnesarchus, who was either a merchant, or, according to others, an engraver of signets. The date of his birth is uncertain; but all authorities agree that he flourished in the times of Polycrates and Tarquinius Superbus (B. C. 540—510). He studied in his own country under Creophilus, Pherecydes of Syros, and others, and is said to have visited Egypt and many countries of the East for the purpose of acquiring knowledge. We have not much trustworthy evidence, either as to the kind and amount of knowledge which he acquired, or as to his definite philosophical views. It is certain however that he believed in the transmigration of souls; and he is said to have pretended that he had been Euphorbus, the son of Panthus, in the Trojan war, as well as various other characters. He is further said to have discovered the propositions that the triangle inscribed in a semi-circle is right-angled, that the square on the hypotenuse of a right-angled triangle is equal to the sum of the squares on the sides. There is a celebrated story of his having discovered the arithmetical relations of the musical scale by observing accidentally the various sounds produced by hammers of different weights striking upon an anvil, and suspending by strings weights equal to those of the different hammers. The retailers of the story of course never took the trouble to verify the experiment, or they would have discovered that different hammers do not produce different sounds from the same anvil, any more than different clappers do from the same bell. Discoveries in astronomy are also attributed to Pythagoras. There can be little doubt that he paid great attention to arithmetic, and its application to weights, measures, and the theory of music. Apart from all direct testimony, however, it may safely be affirmed, that the very remarkable influence exerted by Pythagoras, and even the fact that he was made the hero of so many marvellous stories, prove him to have been a man both of singular capabilities and of great acquirements. It may also be affirmed with safety that the religious element was the predominant one in the character of Pythagoras, and that religious ascendancy in connection with a certain mystic religious system was the object which he chiefly laboured to secure. It was this religious element which made the profoundest impression upon his contemporaries. They regarded him as standing in a peculiarly close connection with the gods. The Crotoniates even identified him with the Hyperborean Apollo. And without viewing him as an impostor, we may easily believe that he himself to some extent shared the same views. He pretended to divination and prophecy; and he appears as the revealer of a mode of life calculated to raise his disciples above the level of mankind, and to recommend them to the favour of the gods. — No certainty can be arrived at as to the length of time spent by Pythagoras in Egypt or the East, or as to his residence and efforts in Samos or other Grecian cities, before he settled at Crotona in Italy. He probably removed to Crotona because he found it impossible to realise his schemes in his native country, while under the tyranny of Polycrates. The reason why he selected Crotona as the sphere of his operations, it is impossible to ascertain; but soon after his arrival in that city he attained extensive influence, and gained over great numbers to enter into his views. His adherents were chiefly of the noble and wealthy classes. Three hundred of these were formed into a select brotherhood or club, bound by a sort of vow to Pythagoras and each other, for the purpose of cultivating the religious and ascetic observances enjoyed by their master, and of studying his religious and philosophical theories. Every thing that was done and taught among the members was kept a profound secret from all without its pale. It was an old Pythagorean maxim, that every thing was not to be told to every body. There were also gradations among the members themselves. In the admission of candidates Pythagoras is said to have placed great reliance on his physiognomical discernment. If admitted, they had to pass through a period of probation, in which their powers of maintaining silence were especially tested, as well as their general temper, disposition, and mental capacity. As regards the nature of the esoteric instruction to which only the most approved members of the fraternity were admitted, some have supposed that it had reference to the political views of Pythagoras. Others have maintained, with greater probability, that it related mainly to the *orgia*, or secret religious doctrines and usages, which undoubtedly formed a prominent feature in the Pythagorean system, and were peculiarly connected with the worship of Apollo. There were some outward peculiarities of an ascetic kind in the mode of life to which the members of the brotherhood were subjected. Some represent him as forbidding all animal food; but all the members cannot have been subjected to this prohibition, since the athletic Milo, for instance, could not possibly have dispensed with animal food. According to some ancient authorities, he allowed the use of all kinds of animal food except the flesh of oxen used for ploughing, and rams. There is a similar discrepancy as to the prohibition of fish and beans. But temperance of all kinds seems to have been strictly enjoined. It is also stated that they had common meals, resembling the Spartan sys-

sitia, at which they met in companies of ten. Considerable importance seems to have been attached to music and gymnastics in the daily exercises of the disciples. Their whole discipline is represented as tending to produce a lofty serenity and self-possession, regarding the exhibition of which various anecdotes were current in antiquity. Among the best ascertained features of the brotherhood are the devoted attachment of the members to each other, and their sovereign contempt for those who did not belong to their ranks. It appears that they had some secret conventional symbols, by which members of the fraternity could recognise each other, even if they had never met before. Clubs similar to that at Crotona were established at Sybaris, Metapontum, Tarentum, and other cities of Magna Graecia. — The institutions of Pythagoras were certainly not intended to withdraw those who adopted them from active exertion, that they might devote themselves exclusively to religious and philosophical contemplations. He rather aimed at the production of a calm bearing and elevated tone of character, through which those trained in the discipline of the Pythagorean life should exhibit in their personal and social capacities a reflection of the order and harmony of the universe. Whether he had any distinct political designs in the foundation of his brotherhood, is doubtful; but it was perfectly natural, even without any express design on his part, that a club such as the Three Hundred of Crotona should gradually come to mingle political with other objects, and by the facilities afforded by their secret and compact organisation should speedily gain extensive political influence. That this influence should be decisively on the side of aristocracy or oligarchy, resulted naturally both from the nature of the Pythagorean institutions, and from the rank and social position of the members of the brotherhood. Through them, of course, Pythagoras himself exercised a large amount of indirect influence over the affairs both of Crotona and of other Italian cities. This Pythagorean brotherhood or order resembled in many respects the one founded by Loyola. It is easy to understand how this aristocratical and exclusive club would excite the jealousy and hostility not only of the democratical party in Crotona, but also of a considerable number of the opposite faction. The hatred which they had excited speedily led to their destruction. The populace of Crotona rose against them; and an attack was made upon them while assembled either in the house of Milo, or in some other place of meeting. The building was set on fire, and many of the assembled members perished; only the younger and more active escaped. Similar commotions ensued in the other cities of Magna Graecia in which Pythagorean clubs had been formed. As an active and organised brotherhood the Pythagorean order was everywhere suppressed; but the Pythagoreans still continued to exist as a sect, the members of which kept up among themselves their religious observances and scientific pursuits, while individuals, as in the case of Archytas, acquired now and then great political influence. Respecting the fate of Pythagoras himself, the accounts varied. Some say that he perished in the temple with his disciples, others that he fled first to Tarentum, and that, being driven thence, he escaped to Metapontum, and there starved himself to death. His tomb was shown at Metapontum in the time of

Cicero.— According to some accounts Pythagoras married Theano, a lady of Crotona, and had a daughter Damo, and a son Telauges, or, according to others, two daughters, Damo and Myia; while other notices seem to imply that he had a wife and a daughter grown up, when he came to Crotona. — When we come to inquire what were the philosophical or religious opinions held by Pythagoras himself, we-are met at the outset by the difficulty that even the authors from whom we have to draw possessed no authentic records bearing upon the age of Pythagoras himself. If Pythagoras ever wrote any thing, his writings perished with him, or not long after. The probability is that he wrote nothing. Every thing current under his name in antiquity was spurious. It is all but certain that Philolaus was the first who *published* the Pythagorean doctrines, at any rate in a written form [PHILOLAUS]. Still there was so marked a peculiarity running through the Pythagorean philosophy, that there can be little question as to the germs of the system at any rate having been derived from Pythagoras himself. Pythagoras resembled the philosophers of the Ionic school, who undertook to solve by means of a single primordial principle the vague problem of the origin and constitution of the universe as a whole. His predilection for mathematical studies led him to trace the origin of all things to *number*, his theory being suggested, or at all events confirmed, by the observation of various numerical relations, or analogies to them, in the phenomena of the universe. — Musical principles likewise played almost as important a part in the Pythagorean system as mathematical or numerical ideas. We find running through the entire system the idea that order, or harmony of relation, is the regulating principle of the whole universe. The intervals between the heavenly bodies were supposed to be determined according to the laws and relations of musical harmony. Hence arose the celebrated doctrine of the harmony of the spheres; for the heavenly bodies in their motion could not but possess a certain sound or note, depending on their distances and velocities; and as these were determined by the laws of harmonical intervals, the notes altogether formed a regular musical scale or harmony. This harmony, however, we do not hear, either because we have been accustomed to it from the first, and have never had an opportunity of contrasting it with stillness, or because the sound is so powerful as to exceed our capacities for hearing. The ethics of the Pythagoreans consisted more in ascetic practice, and maxims for the restraint of the passions, especially of anger, and the cultivation of the power of endurance, than in scientific theory. What of the latter they had was, as might be expected, intimately connected with their number-theory. Happiness consisted in the science of the perfection of the virtues of the soul, or in the perfect science of numbers. Likeness to the Deity was to be the object of all our endeavours, man becoming better as he approaches the gods, who are the guardians and guides of men. Great importance was attached to the influence of music in controlling the force of the passions. Self-examination was strongly insisted on. The transmigration of souls was viewed apparently in the light of a process of purification. Souls under the dominion of sensuality either passed into the bodies of animals, or, if incurable, were thrust down into Tartarus, to meet with expiation, or condign punishment. The pure were exalted to higher modes of life, and at last attained to incorporeal existence. As regards the fruits of this system of training or belief, it is interesting to remark, that wherever we have notices of distinguished Pythagoreans, we usually hear of them as men of great uprightness, conscientiousness, and self-restraint, and as capable of devoted and enduring friendship. [See ARCHYTAS; DAMON and PHINTIAS.]— 2. Of Rhegium, one of the most celebrated statuaries of Greece, probably flourished B. C. 480—430. His most important works appear to have been his statues of athletes.

Pytheas (Πυθέας). 1. An Athenian orator, distinguished by his unceasing animosity against Demosthenes. He had no political principles, made no pretensions to honesty, and changed sides as often as suited his convenience or his interest. Of the part that he took in political affairs only two or three facts are recorded. He opposed the honours which the Athenians proposed to confer upon Alexander, but he afterwards espoused the interests of the Macedonian party. He accused Demosthenes of having received bribes from Harpalus. In the Lamian war, B. c. 322, he joined Antipater, and had thus the satisfaction of surviving his great enemy Demosthenes. He is said to have been the author of the well-known saying, that the orations of Demosthenes smelt of the lamp. — 2. Of Massilia, in Gaul, a celebrated Greek navigator, who sailed to the western and northern parts of Europe, and wrote a work containing the results of his discoveries. He probably lived in the time of Alexander the Great, or shortly afterwards. He appears to have undertaken voyages, one in which he visited Britain and Thule, and of which he probably gave an account in his work *On the Ocean*; and a second, undertaken after his return from his first voyage, in which he coasted along the whole of Europe from Gadira (*Cadiz*) to the Tanais, and the description of which probably formed the subject of his *Periplus*. Pytheas made Thule a 6 days' sail from Britain; and said that the day and the night were each 6 months long in Thule. Hence some modern writers have supposed that he must have reached Iceland; while others have maintained that he advanced as far as the Shetland Islands. But either supposition is very improbable, and neither is necessary; for reports of the great length of the day and night in the northern parts of Europe had already reached the Greeks, before the time of Pytheas. There has been likewise much dispute as to what river we are to understand by the Tanais. The most probable conjecture is that upon reaching the Elbe, Pytheas concluded that he had arrived at the Tanais, separating Europe from Asia. — 3. A silver-chaser, who flourished at Rome in the age immediately following that of Pompey, and whose productions commanded a remarkably high price.

Pythias (Πυθιάς). 1. The sister or adopted daughter of Hermias, and the wife of Aristotle. — 2. Daughter of Aristotle and Pythias.

Pythium (Πύθιον). 1. A place in Attica, not far from Eleusis. — 2. A town of Thessaly in the E. part of the district Hestiaeotis, which with Azorus and Doliche formed a Tripolis.

Pythius (Πύθιος), a Lydian, the son of Atys, was a man of enormous wealth, which he derived from his gold mines in the neighbourhood of Celaenae in Phrygia. When Xerxes arrived at Celaenae, Pythius banqueted him and his whole army. His five sons accompanied Xerxes. Pythius, alarmed by an eclipse of the sun which happened, came to Xerxes, and begged that the eldest might be left behind. This request so enraged the king that he had the young man immediately killed and cut in two, and the two portions of his body placed on either side of the road, and then ordered the army to march between them.

Pythoclides (Πυθοκλείδης), a celebrated musician of the time of Pericles, was a native of Ceos, and flourished at Athens, under the patronage of Pericles, whom he instructed in his art.

Pythodoris (Πυθοδωρίς), wife of Polemon I. king of Pontus. After the death of her husband she retained possession of the government. She subsequently married Archelaus, king of Cappadocia, but after his death (A. D. 17) returned to her own kingdom, of which she continued to administer the affairs herself until her decease, which probably did not take place until A. D. 38. Of her two sons, the one, Zenon, became king of Armenia, while the other, Polemon, succeeded her on the throne of Pontus.

Python (Πύθων). 1. The celebrated serpent, which was produced from the mud left on the earth after the deluge of Deucalion. He lived in the caves of Mt. Parnassus, but was slain by Apollo, who founded the Pythian games in commemoration of his victory, and received in consequence the surname Pythius. — 2. Of Catana, a dramatic poet of the time of Alexander, whom he accompanied into Asia, and whose army he entertained with a satyric drama, when they were celebrating the Dionysia on the banks of the Hydaspes. The drama was in ridicule of Harpalus and the Athenians.

Pyxites (Πυξίτης : Vitzeh), a river of Pontus, falling into the Euxine near Trapezus.

Pyxus. [BUXENTUM.]

Q.

Quadi, a powerful German people of the Suevic race, dwelt in the S.E. of Germany, between Mt. Gabreta, the Hercynian forest, the Sarmatian mountains, and the Danube. They were bounded on the W. by the Marcomanni, with whom they were always closely united, on the N. by the Gothini and Osi, on the E. by the Iazyges Metanastae, from whom they were separated by the river Granuas (Gran), and on the S. by the Pannonians, from whom they were divided by the Danube. They probably settled in this district at the same time as the Marcomanni made themselves masters of Bohemia [MARCOMANNI]; but we have no account of the earlier settlements of the Quadi. When Maroboduus, and shortly afterwards his successor Catualda, had been expelled from their dominions and had taken refuge with the Romans in the reign of Tiberius, the Romans assigned to the barbarians, who had accompanied these monarchs, and who consisted chiefly of Marcomanni and Quadi, the country between the Marus (March? Morava? or Marosch?) and Cusus (Waag?), and gave to them as king Vannius, who belonged to the Quadi. Vannius was expelled by his nephews Vangio and Sido, but this new kingdom of the Quadi continued for a long time afterwards under Roman protection In the reign of M. Aurelius, however, the Quadi joined the Marcomanni and other German tribes in the long and bloody war against the empire, which lasted during the greater part of that emperor's reign. The independence of the Quadi and Marcomanni was secured by the peace which Commodus made with them in A. D. 180. Their name is especially memorable in the history of this war by the victory which M. Aurelius gained over them in 174, when his army was in great danger of being destroyed by the barbarians, and was said to have been saved by a sudden storm, which was attributed to the prayers of his Christian soldiers. [See p. 111, a.] The Quadi disappear from history towards the end of the 4th century. They probably migrated with the Suevi further W.

Quadratus, one of the Apostolic Fathers, and an early apologist for the Christian religion. He passed the early part of his life in Asia Minor, and was afterwards bishop of the Church at Athens. He presented his Apology to Hadrian, in the 10th year of his reign (A. D. 126). This apology has been long lost.

Quadratus, Asinius, lived in the times of Philippus I. and II., emperors of Rome (A. D. 244 —249), and wrote two historical works in the Greek language. 1. A history of Rome, in 15 books, in the Ionic dialect, called Χιλιετηρίς, because it related the history of the city, from its foundation to the 1000th year of its nativity (A. D. 248), when the Ludi Saeculares were performed with extraordinary pomp. 2. A history of Parthia.

Quadratus, Fannius, a contemporary of Horace, was one of those envious Roman poets who tried to depreciate Horace, because his writings threw their own into the shade.

Quadratus, L. Ninnius, tribune of the plebs B. C. 58, distinguished himself by his opposition to the measures of his colleague P. Clodius against Cicero.

Quadratus, Ummidius. 1. Governor of Syria during the latter end of the reign of Claudius, and the commencement of the reign of Nero, from about A. D. 51 to 60. — 2. A friend and admirer of the younger Pliny, whom he took as his model in oratory.

Quadrifrons, a surname of Janus. It is said that after the conquest of the Faliscans an image of Janus was found with 4 foreheads. Hence a temple of Janus Quadrifrons was afterwards built in the Forum transitorium, which had 4 gates. The fact of the god being represented with 4 heads is considered by the ancients to be an indication of his being the divinity presiding over the year with its 4 seasons.

Quadrigarius, Q. Claudius, a Roman historian who flourished B. C. 100—78. His work, which contained at least 23 books, commenced immediately after the destruction of Rome by the Gauls, and must in all probability have come down to the death of Sulla, since the 7th consulship of Marius was commemorated in the 19th book. By Livy he is uniformly referred to simply as Claudius or Clodius. By other authors he is cited as Quintius, as Claudius, as Q. Claudius, as Claudius Quadrigarius, or as Quadrigarius. From the caution evinced by Livy in making use of him as an authority, especially in matters relating to numbers, it would appear that he was disposed to indulge, although in a less degree, in those exaggertions which disfigured the productions of his contemporary Valerius Antias. It is somewhat remarkable that he is nowhere noticed by Cicero. By A. Gellius, on the other hand, he is quoted repeatedly, and praised in the warmest terms.

Quariates, a people in Gallia Narbonensis, on the W. slope of the Alpes Cottiae, in the valley of *Queiras.*

Quies, the personification of tranquillity, was worshipped as a divinity by the Romans. She had one sanctuary on the Via Lavicana, probably a pleasant resting-place for the weary traveller; and another outside the Porta Collina.

Quiētus, Q. Lusīus, an independent Moorish chief, served with distinction under Trajan both in the Dacian and Parthian wars. Trajan made him governor of Judaea, and raised him to the consulship in A. D. 116 or 117. After Trajan's death he returned to his native country, but he was suspected by Hadrian of fomenting the disturbances which then prevailed in Mauretania, and was shortly afterwards put to death by order of Hadrian.

Quintīlius Varus. [VARUS.]

Quintia, or Quinctia Gens, an ancient patrician gens at Rome, was one of the Alban houses removed to Rome by Tullus Hostilius, and enrolled by him among the patricians. Its members often held throughout the whole history of the republic the highest offices of the state. Its 3 most distinguished families bore the names of *Capitolinus, Cincinnatus,* and *Flamininus.*

Quintīliānus, M. Fabius, the most celebrated of Roman rhetoricians, was born at Calagurris (*Calahorra*), in Spain, A. D. 40. If not reared at Rome, he must at least have completed his education there, for he himself informs us that, while yet a very young man, he attended the lectures of Domitius Afer, who died in 59. Having revisited Spain, he returned from thence (68) in the train of Galba, and forthwith began to practise at the bar, where he acquired considerable reputation. But he was chiefly distinguished as a teacher of eloquence, bearing away the palm in this department from all his rivals, and associating his name, even to a proverb, with pre-eminence in the art. Among his pupils were numbered Pliny the younger and the two grand-nephews of Domitian. By this prince he was invested with the insignia and title of consul (*consularia ornamenta*), and is, moreover, celebrated as the first public instructor, who, in virtue of the endowment by Vespasian, received a regular salary from the imperial exchequer. After having devoted 20 years, commencing probably with 69, to the duties of his profession, he retired into private life, and is supposed to have died about 118. The great work of Quintilian is a complete system of rhetoric in 12 books, entitled *De Institutione Oratoria Libri XII.,* or sometimes, *Institutiones Oratoriae,* dedicated to his friend Marcellus Victorius, himself a celebrated orator, and a favourite at court. It was written during the reign of Domitian, while the author was discharging his duties as preceptor to the sons of the emperor's niece. In a short preface to his bookseller Trypho, he acquaints us that he commenced this undertaking after he had retired from his labours as a public instructor (probably in 89), and that he finished his task in little more than 2 years. The 1st book contains a dissertation on the preliminary training requisite before a youth can enter directly upon the studies necessary to mould an accom-

plished orator, and presents us with a carefully sketched outline of the method to be pursued in educating children, from the time they leave the cradle until they pass from the hands of the grammarian. In the 2nd book we find an exposition of the first principles of rhetoric, together with an investigation into the nature or essence of the art. The 5 following are devoted to invention and arrangement (*inventio, dispositio*); the 8th, 9th, 10th, and 11th to composition (including the proper use of the figures of speech) and delivery, comprised under the general term *elocutio;* and the last is occupied with what the author considers by far the most important portion of his project, an inquiry, namely, into various circumstances not included in a course of scholastic discipline, but essential to the formation of a perfect public speaker; such as his manners — his moral character, — the principles by which he must be guided in undertaking, in preparing, and in conducting causes, — the peculiar style of eloquence which he may adopt with greatest advantage — the collateral studies to be pursued — the age at which it is most suitable to commence pleading — the necessity of retiring before the powers begin to fail — and various other kindred topics. This production bears throughout the impress of a clear, sound judgment, keen discrimination, and pure taste, improved by extensive reading, deep reflection, and long practice. The diction is highly polished, and very graceful. The sections which possess the greatest interest for general readers are those chapters in the first book which relate to elementary education, and the commencement of the 10th book, which furnishes us with a compressed but spirited history of Greek and Roman literature. There are also extant 164 declamations under the name of Quintilian, 19 of considerable length; the remaining 145, which form the concluding portion only of a collection which originally extended to 388 pieces, are mere skeletons or fragments. No one believes these to be the genuine productions of Quintilian, and few suppose that they proceeded from any one individual. They apparently belong not only to different persons, but to different periods, and neither in style nor in substance do they offer any thing which is either attractive or useful. Some scholars suppose that the anonymous *Dialogus de Oratoribus,* usually printed among the works of Tacitus, ought to be assigned to Quintilian. The best editions of Quintilian are, by Burmann, 2 vols. 4to., Lug. Bat. 1720; by Gesner, 4to. Gott. 1738; and by Spalding and Zumpt, 6 vols. 8vo. Lips. 1798—1829.

Quintillus, M. Aurēlius, the brother of the emperor M. Aurelius Claudius, was elevated to the throne by the troops whom he commanded at Aquileia, in A. D. 270. But as the army at Sirmium, where Claudius died, had proclaimed Aurelian emperor, Quintillus put an end to his own life, seeing himself deserted by his own soldiers, to whom the rigour of his discipline had given offence.

T. Quintius Capitolīnus Barbātus, a celebrated general in the early history of the republic, and equally distinguished in the internal history of the state. He frequently acted as mediator between the patricians and plebeians, with both of whom he was held in the highest esteem. He was six times consul, namely, in B. C. 471, 468, 465, 446, 443, 439. — Several of his descendants held the consulship, but none of these require mention except **T. Quintius Pennus Capitolinus Crispinus**, who was consul 208, and was defeated by Hannibal.

Quintus, an eminent physician at Rome, in the former half of the 2nd century after Christ. He was so much superior to his medical colleagues that they grew jealous of his eminence, and formed a sort of coalition against him, and forced him to quit the city by charging him with killing his patients. He died about A. D. 148.

Quintus Curtius. [CURTIUS.]

Quintus Smyrnaeus (Κόϊντος Σμυρναῖος), commonly called **Quintus Calaber**, from the circumstance that the first copy through which his poem became known was found in a convent at Otranto in Calabria. He was the author of an epic poem in 14 books, entitled τὰ μεθ' Ὅμηρον, or παραλειπόμενα Ὁμήρῳ. Scarcely any thing is known of his personal history; but it appears most probable that he lived towards the end of the 4th century after Christ. The matters treated of in his poem are the events of the Trojan war from the death of Hector to the return of the Greeks. In phraseology, similes, and other technicalities, Quintus closely copied Homer. The materials for his poem he found in the works of the earlier poets of the epic cycle. But not a single poetical idea of his own seems ever to have inspired him. His gods and heroes are alike devoid of all character: every thing like pathos or moral interest was quite beyond his powers. With respect to chronology his poem is as punctual as a diary. His style, however, is clear, and marked on the whole by purity and good taste, without any bombast or exaggeration. There can be little doubt that his work is nothing more than an amplification or remodelling of the poems of Arctinus and Lesches. He appears to have also made diligent use of Apollonius. The best edition is by Tychsen, Strasburg, 1807.

Quirīnālis Mons. [ROMA.]

Quirīnus, a Sabine word, perhaps derived from *quiris*, a lance or spear. It occurs first of all as the name of Romulus, after he had been raised to the rank of a divinity; and the festival celebrated in his honour bore the name of *Quirinalia*. It is also used as a surname of Mars, Janus, and even of Augustus.

Quirīnus, P. Sulpicius, was a native of Lanuvium, and of obscure origin, but was raised to the highest honours by Augustus. He was consul B. C. 12, and subsequently carried on war against some of the robber tribes dwelling in the mountains of Cilicia. In B. C. 1, Augustus appointed him to direct the counsels of his grandson C. Caesar, then in Armenia. Some years afterwards, but not before A. D. 5, he was appointed governor of Syria, and while in this office he took a census of the Jewish people. This is the statement of Josephus, and appears to be at variance with that of Luke, who speaks as if the census or enrolment of Cyrenius (i. e. Quirinus) was made at the time of the birth of Christ. Quirinus had been married to Aemilia Lepida, whom he divorced; but in A. D. 20, twenty years after the divorce, he brought an accusation against her. The conduct of Quirinus met with general disapprobation as harsh and revengeful. He died in A. D. 21, and was honoured with a public funeral.

Quiza (Κούϊζα: *Giza* near *Oran*), a municipium on the coast of Mauretania Caesarensis in N. Africa, 40 Roman miles W. of Arsenaria.

R.

Raamses or **Rameses** (LXX. Ῥαμεσσῆ), a city of Lower Egypt, built as a treasure city by the captive Israelites under the oppression of the Pharaoh " who knew not Joseph " (Exod. i. 11); and usually identified with HEROOPOLIS.

Rabathmōba (Ῥαβαθμώβα, i. e. Rabbath-Moab, O. T., also called Rabbah, Ar, Ar.-Moab and aft. Areopŏlis: *Rabbah*), the ancient capital of the Moabites, lay in a fertile plain, on the E. side of the Dead Sea, and S. of the river Arnon, in the district of Moabitis in Arabia Petraea, or, according to the later division of the provinces, in Palaestina Tertia.

Rabbatamāna (Ῥαβατάμανα, i. e. Rabbath-Ammon, O. T.: *Ammon*, Ru.), the ancient capital of the Ammonites, lay in Peraea on a S. tributary of the Jabbok, N.E. of the Dead Sea. Ptolemy II. Philadelphus gave it the name of **Philadelphia**; and it long continued a flourishing and splendid city.

Rabīrius. 1. C., an aged senator, was accused in B. C. 63, by T. Labienus, tribune of the plebs, of having put to death the tribune L. Appuleius Saturninus in 100, nearly 40 years before. [SATURNINUS.] The accusation was set on foot at the instigation of Caesar, who judged it necessary to deter the senate from resorting to arms against the popular party. To make the warning still more striking, Labienus did not proceed against him on the charge of *majestas*, but revived the old accusation of *perduellio*, which had been discontinued for some centuries, since persons found guilty of the latter crime were given over to the public executioner and hanged on the accursed tree. The *Duumviri Perduellionis* appointed to try Rabirius were C. Caesar himself and his relative L. Caesar. With such judges the result could not be doubtful; Rabirius was forthwith condemned; and the sentence of death would have been carried into effect, had he not availed himself of his right of appeal to the people in the comitia of the centuries. The case excited the greatest interest; since it was not simply the life or death of Rabirius, but the power and authority of the senate, which were at stake. Rabirius was defended by Cicero; but the eloquence of his advocate was of no avail, and the people would have ratified the decision of the duumvirs, had not the meeting been broken up by the praetor, Q. Metellus Celer, who removed the military flag which floated on the Janiculum. This was in accordance with an ancient custom, which was intended to prevent the Campus Martius from being surprised by an enemy, when the territory of Rome scarcely extended beyond the boundaries of the city. — 2. **C. Rabirius Postumus**, was the son of the sister of the preceding. He was born after the death of his father, whence his surname Postumus; and he was adopted by his uncle, whence his name C. Rabirius. He had lent large sums of money to Ptolemy Auletes; and after the restoration of Ptolemy to his kingdom by means of Gabinius, in B. C. 55, Rabirius repaired to Alexandria, and was invested by the king with the office of *Dioecetes*, or chief treasurer. In this office he had to amass money both for himself and for Gabinius; but his extortions were so terrible that Ptolemy had him apprehended, either to secure him against the wrath of the people, or to satisfy their indignation, lest they should drive him again from his kingdom. Rabirius escaped from prison, probably through the connivance of the king, and returned to Rome. Here a trial awaited him. Gabinius had been sentenced to pay a heavy fine on account of his extortions in Egypt ; and as he was unable to pay this fine, a suit was instituted against Rabirius, who was liable to make up the deficiency, if it could be proved that he had received any of the money of which Gabinius had illegally become possessed. Rabirius was defended by Cicero, and was probably condemned. He is mentioned at a later time (46) as serving under Caesar, who sent him from Africa into Sicily, in order to obtain provisions for his army.—3. A Roman poet, who lived in the last years of the republic, and wrote a poem on the Civil Wars. A portion of this poem was found at Herculaneum, and was edited by Kreyssig, under the title "Carminis Latini de bello Actiaco a. Alexandrino fragmenta," 4to. Schneeberg, 1814.

L. Racilius, tribune of the plebs, B. C. 56, and a warm friend of Cicero and of Lentulus Spinther. In the civil war Racilius espoused Caesar's party, and was with him in Spain in 48. There he entered into the conspiracy formed against the life of Q. Cassius Longinus, the governor of that province, and was put to death, with the other conspirators, by Longinus.

Radagaisus, a Scythian, invaded Italy at the head of a formidable host of barbarians, in the reign of the emperor Honorius. He was defeated by Stilicho, near Florence, in A. D. 408, and was put to death after the battle, although he had capitulated on condition that his life should be saved.

Rama or **Arimathaea** ('Ραμά, 'Αριμαθαία : Er-Ram), a town of Judaea, N. of Jerusalem, in the mountains of Ephraim, frequently mentioned both in the O. and N. T.

Rambacia ('Ραμβακία), the chief city of the Oritae, on the coast of Gedrosia, colonised by Alexander the Great.

Ramitha. [LAODICEA, No. 3.]

Ramses, the name of many kings of Egypt of the 18th, 19th, and 20th dynasties. It was during this era that most of the great monuments of Egypt were erected, and the name is consequently of frequent occurrence on these monuments, where it appears under the form of Ramessu. In Julius Africanus and Eusebius it is written Ramses, Rameses, or Ramesses. The most celebrated of the kings of this name is, however, usually called Sesostris by the Greek writers. [SESOSTRIS.]

Raphana or **Raphaneae** ('Ραφανέαι: Rafaniat, Ru.), a city of Syria, in the district of Cassiotis, at the N. extremity of Lebanon.

Raphia or **Raphaa** ('Ραφία, 'Ράφεια: Repha), a sea-port town in the extreme S.W. of Palestine, beyond Gaza, on the edge of the desert. It was restored by Gabinius.

Rasenae. [ETRURIA.]

Ratiaria (Arzer Palanka), an important town in Moesia Superior on the Danube, the headquarters of a Roman legion, and the station of one of the Roman fleets on the Danube.

Ratomagus or **Rotomagus** (Rouen), the chief town of the Vellocasses in Gallia Ludgunensis.

Raudii Campi. [CAMPI RAUDII.]

Rauraci, a people ·in Gallia Belgica, bounded on the S. by the Helvetii, on the W. by the Sequani, on the N. by the Tribocci, and on the F.

by the Rhine. They must have been a people of considerable importance, as 23,000 of them are said to have emigrated with the Helvetii in B. C. 58, and they possessed several towns, of which the most important were Augusta (Augst) and Basilia (Basel or Bâle).

Rauranum (Rom or Raum nr. Chenay), a town of the Pictones in Gallia Aquitanica, S. of Limonum.

Rausium or **Rausia** (Ragusa), a town on the coast of Dalmatia, is not mentioned till a late period, and only rose into importance after the destruction of Epidaurus.

Ravenna (Ravennas, -atis: Ravenna), an important town in Gallia Cisalpina, on the river Bedesis and about a mile from the sea, though it is now about 5 miles in the interior in consequence of the sea having receded all along this coast. Ravenna was situated in the midst of marshes, and was only accessible in one direction by land, probably by the road leading from Ariminum. The town laid claim to a high antiquity. It was said to have been founded by Thessalians (Pelasgians), and afterwards to have passed into the hands of the Umbrians, but it long remained an insignificant place, and its greatness does not begin till the time of the empire, when Augustus made it one of the 2 chief stations of the Roman fleet. This emperor not only enlarged the town, but caused a large harbour to be constructed on the coast, capable of containing 240 triremes, and he connected this harbour with the Po by means of a canal called Padusa or Augusta Fossa. This harbour was called Classes, and between it and Ravenna a new town sprung up, to which the name of Caesarea was given. All three were subsequently formed into one town, and were surrounded by strong fortifications. Ravenna thus suddenly became one of the most important places in the N. of Italy. The town itself however was mean in appearance. In consequence of the marshy nature of the soil, most of the houses were built of wood, and since an arm of the canal was carried through some of the principal streets, the communication was carried on to a great extent by gondolas, as in modern Venice. The town also was very deficient in a supply of good drinking-water ; but it was not considered unhealthy, since the canals drained the marshes to a great extent, and the ebb and flow of the tide prevented the waters from stagnating. In the neighbourhood good wine was grown, notwithstanding the marshy nature of the soil. When the Roman empire was threatened by the barbarians, the emperors of the West took up their residence at Ravenna, which on account of its situation and its fortifications was regarded as impregnable. After the downfall of the Western empire, Theodoric also made it the capital of his kingdom ; and after the overthrow of the Gothic dominion by Narses, it became the residence of the Exarchs or the governors of the Byzantine empire in Italy, till the Lombards took the town, A. D. 752. The modern Ravenna stands on the site of the ancient town ; the village Porto di Fuori on the site of Caesarea ; and the ancient harbour is called Porto Vecchio del Caudiano.

Reate (Reatinus: Rieti), an ancient town of the Sabines in central Italy, said to have been founded by the Aborigines or Pelasgians, was situated on the Lacus Velinus and the Via Salaria. It was the chief place of assembly for the Sabines, and was subsequently a praefectura or a municipium. The valley, in which Reate was situated, was so beautiful that it received the name of *Tempe*; and in its neighbourhood is the celebrated waterfall, which is now known under the name of the fall of *Terni* or the *Cascade delle Marmore*. This waterfall owed its origin to a canal constructed by M'. Curius Dentatus, in order to carry off the superfluous waters from the lake Velinus into the river Nar. It falls into this river from a height of 140 feet. By this undertaking, the Reatini gained a large quantity of land, which was called *Rosea Rura*. — Reate was celebrated for its mules and asses.

Rebĭlus, C. Canĭnĭus one of Caesar's legates in Gaul and in the civil war. On the last day of December in B. c. 45, on the sudden death of the consul Q. Fabius Maximus, Caesar made Rebilus consul for the few remaining hours of the day.

Redicŭlus, a Roman divinity, who had a temple near the Porta Capena, and who was believed to have received his name from having induced Hannibal, when he was near the gates of the city, to return (*redire*) southward. A place on the Appian road, near the 2nd mile-stone from the city, was called Campus Rediculi. This divinity was probably one of the Lares of the city of Rome.

Redŏnes, a people in the interior of Gallia Lugdunensis, whose chief town was Condate (*Rennes*).

Redux, i. e. "the divinity who leads the traveller back to his home in safety," occurs as a surname of Fortuna.

Regaliänus, Regalliänus or Regilliänus, a Dacian, who served with distinction under the emperors Claudius and Valerian. The Moesians, terrified by the cruelties inflicted by Gallienus on those who had taken part in the rebellion of Ingenuus, suddenly proclaimed Regalianus emperor, and quickly, with the consent of the soldiers, in a new fit of alarm, put him to death, A. D. 263. Hence he is enumerated among the 30 Tyrants.

Regiäna (*Villa de Rayna*), a town in Hispania Baetica on the road from Hispalis to Emerita.

Regillum, a small place in the Sabine territory, from which Appius Claudius migrated to Rome. Its site is uncertain, as it disappeared at an early period.

Regillus, Aemilĭus. 1. M., had been declared consul, with T. Otacilius, for B. c. 214, by the centuria praerogativa, and would have been elected, had not Q. Fabius Maximus, who presided at the comitia, pointed out that there was need of generals of more experience to cope with Hannibal. Regillus died in 205, at which time he is spoken of as Flamen Martialis. — **2. L.,** son of the preceding, was praetor 190, when he received the command of the fleet in the war against Antiochus.

Regillus Lacus, a lake in Latium, memorable for the victory gained on its banks by the Romans over the Latins, B. c. 498. It was E. of Rome in the territory of Tusculum, and between Lavicum and Gabii; but it cannot be identified with certainty with any modern lake. It perhaps occupied the site of the valley of Isidoro, which is now dry.

Regīnum or Castra Regīna (*Regensburg*), a Roman fortress in Vindelicia on the Danube, and on the road leading to Vindobona, was the head-quarters of a Roman legion.

Regium Flumen. [NAARMALCHA.]

Regium Lepĭdi, Regium Lepĭdum, or simply **Regium,** also **Forum Lepidi** (*Regienses a Lepido*:

Reggio), a town of the Boii in Gallia Cisalpina between Mutina and Tarentum, which was probably made a colony by the consul M. Aemilius Lepidus, when he constructed the Aemilia Via through Cisalpine Gaul, though we have no record of the foundation of the colony.

Regŭlus, M. Aquillus, was one of the delatores or informers in the time of Nero, and thus rose from poverty to great wealth. Under Domitian he resumed his old trade, and became one of the instruments of that tyrant's cruelty. He survived Domitian, and is frequently spoken of by Pliny with the greatest detestation and contempt. Martial, on the contrary, who flattered all the creatures of Domitian, celebrates the virtues, the wisdom, and the eloquence of Regulus.

Regŭlus, Atilĭus. 1. M., consul B. c. 335, carried on war against the Sidicini. — **2. M.,** consul 294, carried on war against the Samnites. — **3. M.,** consul 267, conquered the Sallentini, took the town of Brundusium, and obtained in consequence the honour of a triumph. In 256, he was consul a 2nd time with L. Manlius Vulso Longus. The 2 consuls defeated the Carthaginian fleet, and afterwards landed in Africa with a large force. They met with great and striking success; and after Manlius returned to Rome with half of the army, Regulus remained in Africa with the other half and prosecuted the war with the utmost vigour. The Carthaginian generals Hasdrubal, Bostar, and Hamilcar avoided the plains, where their cavalry and elephants would have given them an advantage over the Roman army, and withdrew into the mountains. There they were attacked by Regulus, and defeated with great loss; 15,000 men are said to have been killed in battle, and 5000 men with 18 elephants to have been taken. The Carthaginian troops retired within the walls of the city, and Regulus now overran the country without opposition. Numerous towns fell into the power of the Romans, and among others Tunis, at the distance of only 20 miles from the capital. The Carthaginians in despair sent a herald to Regulus to solicit peace. But the Roman general would only grant it on such intolerable terms that the Carthaginians resolved to continue the war, and hold out to the last. In the midst of their distress and alarm, success came to them from an unexpected quarter. Among the Greek mercenaries who had lately arrived at Carthage, was a Lacedaemonian of the name of Xanthippus. He pointed out to the Carthaginians that their defeat was owing to the incompetency of their generals, and not to the superiority of the Roman arms; and he inspired such confidence in the people, that he was forthwith placed at the head of their troops. Relying on his 4000 cavalry and 100 elephants, Xanthippus boldly marched into the open country to meet the enemy. In the battle which ensued, Regulus was totally defeated; 30,000 of his men were slain; scarcely 2000 escaped to Clypea; and Regulus himself was taken prisoner with 500 more (255). Regulus remained in captivity for the next 5 years, till 250, when the Carthaginians, after their defeat by the proconsul Metellus, sent an embassy to Rome to solicit peace, or at least an exchange of prisoners. They allowed Regulus to accompany the ambassadors on the promise that he would return to Rome if their proposals were declined, thinking that he would persuade his countrymen to agree to an exchange of prisoners in order to obtain his own liberty. This embassy of Regulus is one of the most celebrated stories in Roman history. The orators and poets related how Regulus at first refused to enter the city as a slave of the Carthaginians; how afterwards he would not give his opinion in the senate, as he had ceased by his captivity to be a member of that illustrious body; how, at length, when he was allowed by the Romans to speak, he endeavoured to dissuade the senate from assenting to a peace, or even to an exchange of prisoners, and when he saw them wavering, from their desire of redeeming him from captivity, how he told them that the Carthaginians had given him a slow poison, which would soon terminate his life; and how, finally, when the senate through his influence refused the offers of the Carthaginians, he firmly resisted all the persuasions of his friends to remain in Rome, and returned to Carthage, where a martyr's death awaited him. On his arrival at Carthage he is said to have been put to death with the most excruciating tortures. It was related that he was placed in a chest covered over in the inside with iron nails, and thus perished; and other writers stated in addition, that after his eyelids had been cut off, he was first thrown into a dark dungeon, and then suddenly exposed to the full rays of a burning sun. When the news of the barbarous death of Regulus reached Rome, the senate is said to have given Hamilcar and Bostar, 2 of the noblest Carthaginian prisoners, to the family of Regulus, who revenged themselves by putting them to death with cruel torments. This celebrated tale, however, has not been allowed to pass without question in modern times. Many writers supposed that it was invented in order to excuse the cruelties perpetrated by the family of Regulus on the Carthaginian prisoners committed to their custody. Regulus was one of the favourite characters of early Roman story. Not only was he celebrated on account of his heroism in giving the senate advice which secured him a martyr's death, but also on account of his frugality and simplicity of life. Like Fabricius and Curius he lived on his hereditary farm which he cultivated with his own hands; and subsequent ages loved to tell how he petitioned the senate for his recall from Africa when he was in the full career of victory, as his farm was going to ruin in his absence, and his family was suffering from want. — 4. C. surnamed Serranus, consul 257, when he defeated the Carthaginian fleet off the Liparaean islands, and obtained possession of the islands of Lipara and Melite. He was consul a 2nd time in 250, with L. Manlius Vulso. The 2 consuls undertook the siege of Lilybaeum; but they were foiled in their attempts to carry the place by storm, and after losing a great number of men, were obliged to turn the siege into a blockade. This Regulus is the first Atilius who bears the surname Serranus, which afterwards became the name of a distinct family in the gens. The origin of this name is spoken of under SERRANUS. — 5. M., son of No. 3. was consul 227, and again 217, in the latter of which years he was elected to supply the place of C. Flaminius, who had fallen in the battle of the Trasimene lake. He was censor in 214. — 6. C., consul 225, conquered the Sardinians, who had revolted. On his return to Italy he fought against the Gauls, and fell in the battle.

Reii Apollinares (Riex), a Roman colony in Gallia Narbonensis, with the surname Julia Au-

gusta, E. of the river Druentia, N. of Forum Voconii and N.W. of Forum Julii.

Remesiäna or Romesiäna (Mustapha Palanka), a town in Moesia Superior, between Naisus and Serdica.

Remi or Rhemi, one of the most powerful people in Gallia Belgica, inhabited the country through which the Axona flowed, and were bounded on the S. by the Nervii, on the S. E. by the Veromandui, on the E. by the Suessiones and Bellovaci, and on the W. by the Nervii. They formed an alliance with Caesar, when the rest of the Belgae made war against him, B.C. 57. Their chief town was Durocortorum, afterwards called Remi (Rheims).

Remmius Palaemon. [PALAEMON.]

Rēmus. [ROMULUS.]

Resaina, Ressaena, Resina ('Ρέσαινα, 'Ρέσινα: Ras-el-Ain), a city of Mesopotamia, near the sources of the Chaboras, on the road from Carrae to Nisibis. After its restoration and fortification by Theodosius, it was called Theodosiopolis (Θεοδοσιούπολις). Whether it is the same as the Resen of the O. T. (Gen. x. 12) seems very doubtful.

Restio, Antius. 1. The author of a sumptuary law of uncertain date, but passed after the sumptuary law of the consul Aemilius Lepidus, B.C. 78, and before the one of Caesar. — 2. Probably a son of the preceding, proscribed by the triumvirs in 43, but preserved by the fidelity of a slave.

Reudigni, a people in the N. of Germany on the right bank of the Albis, N. of the Langobardi.

Rex, Marcius. 1. Q., praetor B.C. 144, built the aqueduct, called Aqua Marcia, which was one of the most important at Rome (Dict. of Antiq. art. Aquaeductus). — 2. Q., consul 118, founded in this year the colony of Narbo Martius in Gaul, and carried on war against the Stoeni, a Ligurian people at the foot of the Alps. — 3. Q., consul 68, and proconsul in Cilicia in the following year. On his return to Rome in 66 he sued for a triumph, but as obstacles were thrown in the way by certain parties, he remained outside the city to prosecute his claims, and was still there when the Catilinarian conspiracy broke out in 63. The senate sent him to Faesulae, to watch the movements of C. Mallius or Manlius, Catiline's general.

Rha ('Ρά: Volga), a great river of Asia, first mentioned by Ptolemy, who describes it as rising in the N. of Sarmatia, in 2 branches, Rha Occidentalis and Rha Orientalis (the Volga and the Kama), after the junction of which it flowed S.W., forming the boundary between Sarmatia Asiatica and Scythia, till near the Tanaïs (Don), where it suddenly turns to the S.E., and falls into the N.W part of the Caspian.

Rhadamanthus ('Ραδάμανθος), son of Zeus and Europa, and brother of king Minos of Crete. From fear of his brother he fled to Ocalea in Boeotia, and there married Alcmene. In consequence of his justice throughout life, he became, after his death, one of the judges in the lower world.

Rhaetia, a Roman province S. of the Danube, was originally distinct from Vindelicia, and was bounded on the W. by the Helvetii, on the E. by Noricum, on the N. by Vindelicia, and on the S. by Cisalpine Gaul, thus corresponding to the Grisons in Switzerland, and to the greater part of the Tyrol. Towards the end of the first century, however, Vindelicia was added to the province of Rhaetia, whence Tacitus speaks of Augusta Vindelicorum as situated in Rhaetia. At a later time Rhaetia was subdivided into 2 provinces *Rhaetia Prima* and *Rhaetia Secunda*, the former of which answered to the old province of Rhaetia, and the latter to that of Vindelicia. The boundaries between the 2 provinces are not accurately defined, but it may be stated in general that they were separated from each other by the Brigantinus Lacus (*Lake of Constance*) and the river Oenus (*Inn*). Vindelicia is spoken of in a separate article. [VINDELICIA.] Rhaetia was a very mountainous country, since the main chain of the Alps ran through the greater part of the province. These mountains were called Alpes Rhaeticae, and extended from the St. Gothard to the Orteler by the pass by the Stelvio; and in them rose the Oenus (*Inn*) and most of the chief rivers in the N. of Italy, such as the Athesis (*Adige*), and the Addua (*Adda*). The valleys produced corn and excellent wine, the latter of which was much esteemed in Italy. Augustus drank Rhaetian wine in preference to all others. The original inhabitants of the country, the **Rhaeti**, are said by most ancient writers to have been Tuscans, who were driven out of the N. of Italy by the invasion of the Celts, and who took refuge in this mountainous district under a leader called Rhaetus. Many modern writers suppose the Rhaeti and the Etruscans to have been the same people, only they invert the ancient tradition, and believe that the Rhaeti descended from their original abodes on the Alps, and settled first in the N. of Italy and next in the country afterwards called Etruria. They support this view by the fact that the Etruscans were called in their own language Rasena, which seems merely another form of Rhaeti, as well as by other arguments, into which it is unnecessary to enter in this place. It is impossible to arrive at any certain conclusion respecting the original population of the country. In the time of the Romans the country was inhabited by various Celtic tribes. The Rhaeti are first mentioned by Polybius. They were a brave and warlike people, and caused the Romans much trouble by their marauding incursions into Gaul and the N. of Italy. They were not subdued by the Romans till the reign of Augustus, and they offered a brave and desperate resistance against both Drusus and Tiberius, who finally conquered them. Rhaetia was then formed into a Roman province, to which Vindelicia was afterwards added, as has been already stated. The victories of Drusus and Tiberius were celebrated by Horace (*Carm.* iv. 14.) The Rhaeti were divided into several tribes, such as the LEPONTII, VENNONES, TRIDENTINI, &c. The only town in Rhaetia of any importance was TRIDENTINUM (*Trent*).

Rhāgae ('Ῥάγαι, 'Ῥάγα, 'Ῥαγειά: 'Ῥαγηνός: *Rai*, Ru. S. E. of *Tehran*). the greatest city of Media, lay in the extreme N. of Great Media, at the S. foot of the mountains (Caspius M.), which border the S. shores of the Caspian Sea, and on the W. side of the great pass through those mountains called the Caspiae Pylae. It was therefore the key of Media towards Parthia and Hyrcania. Having been destroyed by an earthquake, it was restored by Seleucus Nicator, and named **Eurōpus** (Εὑρωπός). In the Parthian wars it was again destroyed, but it was rebuilt by Arsaces, and called **Arsacia** ('Αρσακία). In the middle ages it was still a great city under its original name, slightly

altered (*Rai*); and it was finally destroyed by the Tartars in the 12th century. The surrounding district, which was a rugged volcanic region, subject to frequent earthquakes, was called 'Ῥαγιανή.

Rhamnūs ('Ῥαμνοῦς, — οὗντος : 'Ῥαμνούσιος: *Obrio Kastro*), a demus in Attica, belonging to the tribe Aeantis, which derived its name from the *rhamnus*, a kind of prickly shrub. ('Ῥαμνοῦς is an adjective, a contraction of ῥαμνόεις, which comes from ῥάμνος.) Rhamnus was situated on a small rocky peninsula on the E. coast of Attica, 60 stadia from Marathon. It possessed a celebrated temple of Nemesis, who is hence called by the Latin poets *Rhamnusia dea* or *virgo*. In this temple there was a colossal statue of the goddess made by Agoracritus, the disciple of Phidias. Another account, but less trustworthy, relates that the statue was the work of Phidias, and was made out of the block of Parian marble, which the Persians brought with them for the purpose of setting up a trophy, when they were defeated at Marathon. There are still remains of this temple, as well as of a smaller one to the same goddess.

Rhampsinītus ('Ῥαμψίνιτος), one of the ancient kings of Egypt, succeeded Proteus, and was succeeded by Cheops. This king is said to have possessed immense wealth; and in order to keep it safe he had a treasury built of stone, respecting the robbery of which Herodotus (ii. 121) relates a romantic story, which bears a great resemblance to the one told about the treasury built by the 2 brothers Agamedes and Trophonius of Orchomenus. [AGAMEDES.] Rhampsinitus belongs to the 20th dynasty, and is known in inscriptions by the name of *Ramessu Neter-kek-pen*.

Rhapta (τὰ 'Ῥαπτά), the S.-most sea-port known to the ancients, the capital of the district of Barbaria, or Azania, on the E. coast of Africa. It stood on a river called **Rhaptus** (*Doara*), and near a promontory called **Rhaptum** (*Formosa*), and the people of the district were called 'Ῥάψιοι Αἰθίοπες.

Rhěa ('Ῥέα, Epic and Ion. 'Ῥεία, 'Ῥείη, or 'Ῥέη), an ancient Greek goddess, appears to have been a goddess of the earth. She is represented as a daughter of Uranus and Ge, and the wife of Cronos, by whom she became the mother of Hestia, Demeter, Hera, Hades, Poseidon and Zeus. Cronos devoured all his children by Rhea, but when she was on the point of giving birth to Zeus, she went to Lyctus in Crete, by the advice of her parents. When Zeus was born she gave to Cronos a stone wrapped up like an infant, which the god swallowed supposing it to be his child. Crete was undoubtedly the earliest seat of the worship of Rhea; though many other parts of Greece laid claim to the honour of being the birth-place of Zeus. Rhea was afterwards identified by the Greeks in Asia Minor with the Great Asiatic goddess, known under the name of " the Great Mother," or the " Mother of the Gods," and also bearing other names such as Cybele, Agdistis, Dindymene, &c. Hence her worship became of a wild and enthusiastic character, and various Eastern rites were added to it, which soon spread throughout the whole of Greece. From the orgiastic nature of these rites, her worship became closely connected with that of Dionysus. Under the name of Cybele her worship was universal in Phrygia. Under the name of Agdistis, she was worshipped with great solemnity at Pessinus in Galatia, which town was regarded as the principal seat of her worship. Under different names we might trace the worship of Rhea even much further east, as far as the Euphrates and even Bactriana. She was, in fact, the great goddess of the Eastern world, and we find her worshipped there under a variety of forms and names. As regards the Romans, they had from the earliest times worshipped Jupiter and his mother Ops, the wife of Saturn. During the war with Hannibal the Romans fetched the image of the Mother of the Gods from Pessinus; but the worship then introduced was quite new to them, and either maintained itself as distinct from the worship of Ops, or became united with it. A temple was built to her on the Palatine, and the Roman matrons honoured her with the festival of the Megalesia. In all European countries Rhea was conceived to be accompanied by the Curetes, who are inseparably connected with the birth and bringing up of Zeus in Crete, and in Phrygia by the Corybantes, Atys, and Agdistis. The Corybantes were her enthusiastic priests, who with drums, cymbals, horns, and in full armour, performed their orgiastic dances in the forests and on the mountains of Phrygia. In Rome the Galli were her priests. The lion was sacred to her. In works of art she is usually represented seated on a throne, adorned with the mural crown, from which a veil hangs down. Lions appear crouching on the right and left of her throne, and sometimes she is seen riding in a chariot drawn by lions.

Rhea Silvia. [ROMULUS.]

Rhebas ('Ρήβας, 'Ρήβαιος: *Riva*), a river of Bithynia, in Asia Minor, falling into the Euxine N. E. of Chalcedon; very small and insignificant in itself, but much celebrated in the Argonautic legends.

Rhedones. [REDONES.]

Rhegium ('Ρήγιον: Rheginus: *Reggio*), a celebrated Greek town on the coast of Bruttium in the S. of Italy, was situated on the Fretum Siculum, or the Straits which separate Italy and Sicily. The ancients derived its name from the verb ῥήγνυμι (" break "), because it was supposed that Sicily was at this place torn asunder from Italy. Rhegium was founded about the beginning of the first Messenian war, B. C. 743, by Aeolian Chalcidians from Euboea and by Doric Messenians, who had quitted their native country on the commencement of hostilities between Sparta and Messenia. At the end of the 2nd Messenian war, 668, a large body of Messenians, under the conduct of the sons of Aristomenes settled at Rhegium, which now became a flourishing and important city, and extended its authority over several of the neighbouring towns. Even before the Persian wars Rhegium was sufficiently powerful to send 3000 of its citizens to the assistance of the Tarentines, and in the time of the elder Dionysius it possessed a fleet of 80 ships of war. The government was an aristocracy, but in the beginning of the 5th century B. C., Anaxilaus, who was of a Messenian family, made himself tyrant of the place. In 494 this Anaxilaus conquered Zancle in Sicily, the name of which he changed into Messana. He ruled over the 2 cities, and on his death in 476 he bequeathed his power to his sons. About 10 years afterwards (466) his sons were driven out of Rhegium and Messana, and republican governments were established in both cities, which now became independent of one another.

At a later period Rhegium incurred the deadly enmity of the elder Dionysius in consequence of a personal insult which the inhabitants had offered him. It is said that when he asked the Rhegians to give him one of their maidens for his wife, they replied that they could only grant him the daughter of their public executioner. Dionysius carried on war against the city for a long time, and after two or three unsuccessful attempts he at length took the place, which he treated with the greatest severity. Rhegium never recovered its former greatness, though it still continued to be a place of considerable importance. The younger Dionysius gave it the name of *Phoebia*, but this name never came into general use, and was speedily forgotten. The Rhegians having applied to Rome for assistance when Pyrrhus was in the S. of Italy, the Romans placed in the town a garrison of 4000 soldiers, who had been levied among the Latin colonies in Campania. These troops seized the town in 279, killed or expelled the male inhabitants, and took possession of their wives and children. The Romans were too much engaged at the time with their war against Pyrrhus to take notice of this outrage; but when Pyrrhus was driven out of Italy, they took signal vengeance upon these Campanians, and restored the surviving Rhegians to their city. Rhegium suffered greatly from an earthquake shortly before the breaking out of the Social war, 90; but its population was augmented by Augustus, who settled here a number of veterans from his fleet, whence the town bears in Ptolemy the surname *Julium*. Rhegium was the place from which persons usually crossed over to Sicily, but the spot, at which they embarked, was called **Columna Rhegina** ('Ρηγίνων στηλίς: *Torre di Carallo*), and was 100 stadia N. of the town. The Greek language continued to be spoken at Rhegium till a very late time, and the town was subject to the Byzantine court long after the downfall of the Western empire.

Rhenea ('Ρήνεια, also 'Ρήνη, 'Ρηναία), formerly called *Ortygia* and *Celadussa*, an island in the Aegaean sea and one of the Cyclades, W. of Delos, from which it was divided by a narrow strait only 4 stadia in width. When Polycrates took the island, he dedicated it to Apollo, and united it by a chain to Delos; and Nicias connected the 2 islands by means of a bridge. When the Athenians purified Delos in B. C. 426, they removed all the dead from the latter island to Rhenea.

Rhenus. 1. (*Rhein* in German, *Rhine* in English), one of the great rivers in Europe, forming in ancient times the boundary between Gaul and Germany, rises in Mons Adula (*St. Gothard*) not far from the sources of the Rhone, and flows first in a W.-ly direction, passing through the Lacus Brigantinus (*Lake of Constance*), till it reaches Basilia (*Basle*), where it takes a N.-ly direction and eventually flows into the Ocean by several mouths. The ancients spoke of 2 main arms, into which the Rhine was divided in entering the territory of the Batavi, of which the one on the E. continued to bear the name of Rhenus, while that on the W., into which the Mosa (*Maas* or *Meuse*) flowed, was called Vahalis (*Waal*). After Drusus in B. C. 12 had connected the Flevo Lacus (*Zuyder-See*) with the Rhine by means of a canal, in making which he probably made use of the bed of the Yssel, we find mention of 3 mouths of the Rhine. Of these the names, as given by Pliny, are on the

W. Helium (the Vahalis of other writers), in the centre Rhenus, and on the E. Flevum; but at a later time we again find mention of only 2 mouths. The Rhine is described by the ancients as a broad, rapid and deep river. It receives many tributaries, of which the most important were the Mosella (*Moselle*) and Mosa (*Maas* or *Mense*) on the left, and the Nicer (*Neckar*), Moenus (*Main*) and Luppia (*Lippe*) on the right. It passed through various tribes, of which the principal on the W. were the Nantuates, Helvetii, Sequani, Mediomatrici, Tribocci, Treviri, Ubii, Batavi, and Canninefates, and the principal on the E. were the Rhaeti, Vindelici, Mattiaci, Sigambri, Tencteri, Usipetes, Bructeri, and Frisii. The length of the Rhine is stated differently by the ancient writers. Its whole course amounts to about 950 miles. The inundations of the Rhine near its mouth are mentioned by the ancients. Caesar was the first Roman general who crossed the Rhine. He threw a bridge of boats across the river, probably in the neighbourhood of Cologne. — The etymology of the name is doubtful; some connect it with *rinnen* or *rinnan*, according to which it would mean the "current" or "stream;" others with *rhen* or *rein*, that is, the "clear" river. — 2. (*Reno*), a tributary of the Padus (*Po*) in Gallia Cisalpina near Bononia, on a small island of which Octavian, Antony and Lepidus formed the celebrated triumvirate. The small river Lavinius (*Lavino*) flows into the Rhenus; and Appian places in the Lavinius the island on which the triumvirate was formed.

Rhephāim, a valley of Judaea, continuous with the valley of Hinnom, S.W. of Jerusalem. Rhephaïm was also the name of a very ancient people of Palestine.

Rhēsus ('Ρῆσος). 1. A river-god in Bithynia, one of the sons of Oceanus and Tethys. — 2. Son of king Eïoneus in Thrace, marched to the assistance of the Trojans in their war with the Greeks. An oracle had declared that Troy would never be taken, if the snow-white horses of Rhesus should once drink the water of the Xanthus, and feed upon the grass of the Trojan plain. But as soon as Rhesus had reached the Trojan territory and had pitched his tents late at night, Ulysses and Diomedes penetrated into his camp, slew Rhesus himself, and carried off his horses. In later writers Rhesus is described as a son of Strymon and Euterpe, or Calliope, or Terpsichore.

Rhiānus ('Ριανός), of Crete, a distinguished Alexandrian poet and grammarian, flourished B. C. 222. He wrote several epic poems, one of which was on the Messenian wars. He also wrote epigrams, 10 of which are preserved in the Palatine Anthology, and one by Athenaeus. His fragments are printed in Gaisford's *Poetae Minores Graeci*; and separately edited by Nic. Saal. Bonn, 1831.

Rhidagus, a tributary of the river Zioberis in Parthia.

Rhinocolūra or **Rhinocorūra** (τὰ 'Ρινοκόλουρα or 'Ρινοκόρουρα, and ἡ 'Ρινοκολούρα or 'Ρινοκορούρα: *Kulat-el-Arish*), the frontier town of Egypt and Palestine, lay in the midst of the desert, at the mouth of the brook (*El-Arish*), which was the boundary between the countries, and which is called in Scripture the river of Egypt. It was sometimes reckoned to Syria, sometimes to Egypt. Its name "*The-cut-off-noses*," is derived from its having been the place of exile of criminals who

had first been so mutilated, under the Ethiopian dynasty of kings of Egypt.

Rhinthōn ('Ρίνθων), of Syracuse or Tarentum, said to have been the son of a potter, was a dramatic poet, of that species of burlesque tragedy, which was called φλυακογραφία or ἱλαροτραγῳδία, and flourished in the reign of Ptolemy I. king of Egypt. When he is placed at the head of the composers of this burlesque drama, we are not to suppose that he actually invented it, but that he was the first to develope in a written form, and to introduce into Greek literature, a species of dramatic composition, which had already long existed as a popular amusement among the Greeks of southern Italy and Sicily, and especially at Tarentum. The species of drama which he cultivated may be described as an exhibition of the subjects of tragedy, in the spirit and style of comedy. A poet of this description was called φλύαξ. This name, and that of the drama itself, φλυακογραφία, seem to have been the genuine terms used at Tarentum. Rhinthon wrote 38 dramas.

Rhipaei Montes (τὰ 'Ριπαῖα ὄρη, also 'Ρίπαι), the name of a lofty range of mountains in the northern part of the earth, respecting which there are diverse statements in the ancient writers. The name seems to have been given by the Greek poets quite indefinitely to all the mountains in the northern parts of Europe and Asia. Thus the Rhipaei Montes are sometimes called the Hyperborei Montes. [HYPERBOREI.] The later geographical writers place the Rhipaean mountains N. E. of M. Alaunus on the frontiers of Asiatic Sarmatia, and state that the Tanais rises in these mountains. According to this account the Rhipaean mountains may be regarded as a western branch of the Ural Mountains.

Rhium ('Ρίον: *Castello di Morea*), a promontory in Achaia, opposite the promontory of Antirrhium (*Castello di Romelia*), on the borders of Aetolia and Locris, with which it formed the narrow entrance to the Corinthian gulf, which Straits are now called the *Little Dardanelles*. It is sometimes called 'Αχαϊκὸν 'Ρίον, to distinguish it from the opposite promontory, which was surnamed Μολυκρικὸν or Αἰτωλικὸν. On the promontory of Rhium there was a temple of Poseidon.

Rhizōn or **Rhizinium** ('Ρίζων: 'Ριζωνίτης: *Risano*), an ancient town in Dalmatia, situated at the upper end of the gulf, called after it Rhizonaeus Sinus (*G. of Cattaro*).

Rhōda or **Rhōdus** ('Ρόδη, 'Ρόδος: *Rosas*), a Greek emporium on the coast of the Indigetae in Hispania Tarraconensis, founded by the Rhodians, and subsequently occupied by the inhabitants of Massilia.

Rhōdānus (*Rhône*), one of the chief rivers of Gaul, rises in M. Adula on the Pennine Alps, not far from the sources of the Rhine, flows first in a westerly direction, and after passing through the Lacus Lemanus, turns to the S., passes by the towns of Lugdunum, Vienna, Avenio and Arelate, receives several tributaries, and finally falls by several mouths into the Sinus Gallicus in the Mediterranean. The number of the mouths of the Rhone is stated differently by the ancient writers; which is not surprising, as the river has frequently altered its course near the sea. Pliny mentions 3 mouths, of which the most important was called Os Massalioticum, while the 2 others bore the general name of *Libyca ora*, being distinguished from each other as the *Os Hispaniense* and the *Os Metapinum*. Besides these mouths there was a canal to the E. of the *Os Massalioticum*, called *Fossae Marianae*, which was dug by order of Marius during his war with the Cimbri, in order to make an easier connection between the Rhone and the Mediterranean, as the mouths of the river were frequently choked up with sand. The Rhone is a very rapid river, and its upward navigation is therefore difficult, though it is navigable for large vessels as high as Lugdunum, and by means of the Arar still further N.

Rhŏdĕ. [RHODOS.]

Rhŏdïa and **Rhŏdïŏpŏlis** ('Ροδία, 'Ροδιόπολος : 'Ροδιεύς, 'Ροδιοπολίτης : *Eski-Hissar*, Ru.), a mountain city of Lycia, near Corydallus, with a temple of Asclepius.

Rhŏdïus ('Ρόδιος : prob. *the brook of the Dardanelles*), a small river of the Troad, mentioned both by Homer and Hesiod. It rose on the lower slopes of Mt. Ida, and flowed N. W. into the Hellespont, between Abydus and Dardanus, after receiving the Selleïs from the W. It is identified by some with the river Πόθιος, which Thucydides mentions, between Cynossema and Abydus. Some made it erroneously a tributary of the Aesepus. It is found mentioned on the coins of Dardanus.

Rhŏdŏpē ('Ροδόπη), one of the highest range of mountains in Thrace, extending from Mt. Scomius, E. of the river Nestus and the boundaries of Macedonia, in a S. E.-ly direction almost down to the coast. It is highest in its northern part, and is thickly covered with wood. Rhodope, like the rest of Thrace, was sacred to Dionysus (Bacchus), and is frequently mentioned by the poets in connection with the worship of this god.

Rhŏdŏpis ('Ροδῶπις), a celebrated Greek courtezan, of Thracian origin, was a fellow-slave with the poet Aesop, both of them belonging to the Samian Iadmon. She afterwards became the property of Xanthes, another Samian, who carried her to Naucratis in Egypt, in the reign of Amasis, and at this great sea-port she carried on the trade of an hetaera for the benefit of her master. While thus employed, Charaxus, the brother of the poetess Sappho, who had come to Naucratis as a merchant, fell in love with her, and ransomed her from slavery for a large sum of money. She was in consequence attacked by Sappho in a poem. She continued to live at Naucratis, and with the tenth part of her gains she dedicated at Delphi 10 iron spits, which were seen by Herodotus. She is called Rhodopis by Herodotus, but Sappho in her poem spoke of her under the name of Doricha. It is therefore probable that Doricha was her real name, and that she received that of Rhodopis, which signifies the " rosy-cheeked," on account of her beauty. There was a tale current in Greece that Rhodopis built the third pyramid. It has been conjectured, with great probability, that in consequence of her name Rhodopis, the " rosy-cheeked," she was confounded with Nitocris, the beautiful Egyptian queen, and the heroine of many an Egyptian legend, who is said by the ancient chronologers to have built the third pyramid.

Rhŏdos ('Ρόδος), sometimes called Rhŏdē, daughter of Poseidon and Halia, or of Helios and Amphitrite, or of Poseidon and Aphrodite, or lastly of Oceanus. From her the island of Rhodes is said to have derived its name ; and in this island she bore to Helios 7 sons.

Rhŏdus (ἡ 'Ρόδος : 'Ρόδιος, Rhodius : *Rhodos, Rhodes*), the E.-most island of the Aegaean, or more specifically, of the Carpathian Sea, lies off the S. coast of Caria, due S. of the promontory of Cynossema (*C. Aloupo*), at the distance of about 12 geog. miles. Its length, from N. E. to S. W. is about 45 miles ; its greatest breadth about 20 to 25. In early times it was called Aethraea and Ophiussa, and several other names. The earliest Greek records make mention of it. Mythological stories ascribed its origin to the power of Apollo, who raised it from beneath the waves ; and its first peopling to the Telchines, children of Thalatta (*the Sea*), upon whose destruction by a deluge, the Heliadae were planted in the island by Helios, where they formed 7 tribes, and founded a kingdom, which soon became flourishing by their skill in astronomy and navigation, and other sciences and arts. These traditions appear to signify the early peopling of the island by some of the civilised races of W. Asia, probably the Phoenicians. After other alledged migrations into the island, we come to its Hellenic colonisation, which is ascribed to Tlepolemus, the son of Hercules, before the Trojan war, and after that war to Althaemenes. Homer mentions the 3 Dorian settlements in Rhodes, namely, Lindus, Ialysus, and Camirus ; and these cities, with Cos, Cnidus, and Halicarnassus, formed the Dorian Hexapolis, which was established, from a period of unknown antiquity, in the S. W. corner of Asia Minor. Rhodes soon became a great maritime state, or rather confederacy, the island being parcelled out between the 3 cities above mentioned. The Rhodians made distant voyages, and founded numerous colonies, of which the chief were, Rhoda in Iberia ; Gela, in Sicily ; Parthenope, Salacia, Siris, and Sybaris, in Italy ; settlements in the Balearic islands ; and, in their own neighbourhood, Soli in Cilicia, and Gagae and Corydalla in Lycia. During this early period the government of each of the 3 cities seems to have been monarchical ; but about B. C. 660 the whole island seems to have been united in an oligarchical republic, the chief magistrates of which, called prytanes, were taken from the family of the Eratidae, who had been the royal family of Ialysus. [DIAGORAS: DORIEUS.] At the beginning of the Peloponnesian war, Rhodes was one of those Dorian maritime states which were subject to Athens ; but in the 20th year of the war, 412, it joined the Spartan alliance, and the oligarchical party, which had been depressed and their leaders, the Eratidae, expelled, recovered their former power, under Dorieus. In 408, the new capital, called **Rhŏdus**, was built, and peopled from the 3 ancient cities of Ialysus, Lindus, and Camirus. The history of the island now presents a series of conflicts between the democratical and oligarchical parties, and of subjection to Athens and Sparta in turn, till the end of the Social war, 355, when its independence was acknowledged. Then followed a conflict with the princes of Caria, during which the island was for a time subject to Artemisia, and, nominally at least, to Idrieus. During this period there were great internal dissensions, which were at length composed by a mixed form of government, uniting the elements of aristocracy and democracy. At the Macedonian conquest, they submitted to Alexander ; but, upon his death, they expelled the Macedonian garrison. In the ensuing wars they formed an alliance with Ptolemy, the son of Lagus, and their city, Rhodes, successfully endured a most famous siege by the forces of De-metrius Poliorcetes, who at length, in admiration of the valour of the besieged, presented them with the engines he had used against the city, from the sale of which they defrayed the cost of the cele-brated Colossus, which is described under the name of its artist, CHARES. The state now for a long time flourished, with an extensive commerce, and with such a maritime power, that it compelled the Byzantines to remit the toll which they levied on ships passing the Bospofus. At length they came into connection with the Romans, whose alliance they joined, with Attalus, king of Perga-mus, in the war against Philip III. of Macedon. In the ensuing war with Antiochus, the Rhodians gave the Romans great aid with their fleet ; and, in the subsequent partition of the Syrian posses-sions of Asia Minor, they were rewarded by the supremacy of S. Caria, where they had had settle-ments from an early period. [PERAEA RHODIO-RUM.] A temporary interruption of their alliance with Rome was caused by their espousing the cause of Perseus, for which they were severely punished, 168 ; but they recovered the favour of Rome by the important naval aid they rendered in the Mithridatic war. In the Civil wars, they took part with Caesar, and suffered in consequence from Cassius, 42, but were afterwards compensated for their losses by the favour of Antonius. They were at length deprived of their independence by Claudius ; and their prosperity received its final blow from an earthquake, which laid the city of Rhodes in ruins, in the reign of Antoninus Pius, A. D. 155. The celebrated medieval history of the island, as the seat of the Knights of St. John, does not belong to this work. The island is of great beauty and fertility, with a delicious climate. It was further celebrated as the home of distinguished schools of Greek art and of Greek oratory. The city of Rhodes was famous for the beauty and re-gularity of its architecture, and the number of statues which adorned it ; it was designed by Hippodamus of Miletus. [Comp. IALYSUS, LINDUS, and CA-MIRUS.]

Rhoecus ('Ροῖκος). 1. A Centaur, who, in con-junction with Hylaeus, pursued Atalanta in Ar-cadia, but was killed by her with an arrow. The Roman poets call him Rhoetus, and relate that he was wounded at the nuptials of Pirithous. — 2. Son of Phileas or Philaeus, of Samos, an architect and statuary, belonging to the earliest period in the history of Greek art, is mentioned as the head of a family of Samian artists. He flourished about B. C. 640. He was the first architect of the great temple of Hera at Samos, which Theodorus com-pleted. In conjunction with Smilis and Theodorus, he constructed the labyrinth at Lemnos ; and he, and the members of his family who succeeded him, invented the art of casting statues in bronze and iron.

Rhoetēum (τὸ 'Ροίτειον ἄκρον, ἡ 'Ροιτειὰς ἀκτή, 'Ροιτηίαι ἀκταί : Virg. Rhoetea litora : C. Intepeh or Barbieri), a promontory, or a strip of rocky coast, breaking into several promontories, in Mysia, on the Hellespont, near Aeantium, with a town of the same name (prob. Paleo Castro).

Rhoetus. 1. A centaur. [RHOECUS.] — 2. One of the giants, who was slain by Dionysus ; he is usually called Eurytus.

Rhoxolāni or **Roxolāni**, a warlike people in European Sarmatia, on the coast of the Palus

Maeotis, and between the Borysthenes and the Tanais, usually supposed to be the ancestors of the modern Russians. They frequently attacked and plundered the Roman provinces S. of the Danube ; and Hadrian was even obliged to pay them tribute. They are mentioned as late as the 11th century. They fought with lances and with long swords wielded with both hands ; and their armies were composed chiefly of cavalry.

Rhyndācus ('Ρυνδακός : Edrenos), or **Lycus**, a considerable river of Asia Minor. Rising in Mt. Dindymene, opposite to the sources of the Hermus, it flows N. through Phrygia, then turns N. W. then W. and then N. through the lake Apollo-niatis, into the Propontis. From the point where it left Phrygia, it formed the boundary of Mysia and Bithynia. Its chief tributary, which joins it from the W. below the lake Apolloniatis, was called MACESTUS. On the banks of the Rhynda-cus, Lucullus gained a great victory over Mithri-dates, B. C. 73.

Rhypes ('Ρύπες and other forms : 'Ρυπαῖος), one of the 12 cities of Achaia, situated between Ae-gium and Patrae. It was destroyed by Augustus and its inhabitants removed to Patrae.

Rhytium ('Ρύτιον), a town in Crete, mentioned by Homer, which is identified by modern writers, but without any sufficient reasons, with the later Ritymna.

Ricimer, the Roman "King-Maker," was the son of a Suevian chief, and was brought up at the court of Valentinian III. He served with distinc-tion under Aëtius, in the reign of Valentinian III. In A. D. 456 he commanded the fleet of the emperor Avitus, with which he gained a great vic-tory over the Vandals, and in the same year he deposed Avitus ; but as he was a barbarian by birth, he would not assume the title of emperor, but gave it to Majorian, intending to keep the real power in his own hands. But as Majorian proved more able and energetic than Ricimer had ex-pected, he was put to death in 461 by order of Ricimer, who now raised Libius Severus to the throne. On the death of Severus in 465, Ricimer kept the government in his own hands for the next 18 months ; but in 467 Anthemius was appointed emperor of the West by Leo, emperor of the East. Ricimer acquiesced in the appointment, and re-ceived the daughter of Anthemius in marriage ; but in 472 he made war against his father-in-law, and took Rome by storm. Anthemius perished in the assault, and Olybrius was proclaimed emperor by Ricimer, who died however only 40 days after the sack of Rome.

Ricina. 1. (Ricinensis), a town in Picenum, colonised by the emperor Severus. Its mines are on the river Potenza near Macerata. — 2. One of the Ebudae Insulae, or the Hebrides.

Rigodūlum (Reol), a town of the Treviri in Gallia Belgica, distant 3 days' march from Mo-gontiacum.

Robigus, or **Robigo**, is described by some Latin writers as a divinity worshipped for the pur-pose of averting blight or too great heat from the young cornfields. The festival of the Robigalia was celebrated on the 25th of April, and was said to have been instituted by Numa. But consider-ing the uncertainty of the ancients themselves as to whether the divinity was masculine or feminine, and that the Romans did not pay divine honours to any evil demon, it is probable that the divinity

MAP OF ANCIENT ROME, SHOWING THE WALLS OF SERVIUS AND
THOSE OF AURELIAN.

(*To face p. 657.*)

Gates in the Walls of Servius.

1 Porta Collina.
2 P.   Viminalis.
3 P.   Esquilina.
4 P.   Querquetulana?
5 P.   Caelimontana.
6 P.   Capena.
7 P.   Raudusculana?
8 P.   Naevia.
9 P.   Minucia.
10 P.   Trigemina.
11 P.   Flumentana.
12 P.   Carmentalis.
13 P.   Ratumena?
14 P.   Fontinalis.

Gates in the Walls of Aurelian.

15 Porta Flaminia.
16 P.   Pinciana.
17 P.   Salaria.
18 P.   Nomentana.
19 P.   Clausa.

20 Porta Tiburtina (S. Lorenzo).
21 P.   Praenestina (Maggiore).
22 P.   Asinaria.
23 P.   Metrovia?
24 P.   Latina.
25 P.   Appia (S. Sebastiano).
26 P.   Ardeatina?
27 P.   Ostiensis.
28 P.   Portuensis.
29 P.   Aurelia (S. Pancrazio).
30 P.   Septimiana.
31 P.   Aurelia of Procopius.

Bridges.

32 Pons Aelius (Ponte S. Angelo).
33 P.   Vaticanus?
34 P.   Janiculensis?
35 P.   Fabricius.
36 P.   Cestius.
37 P.   Palatinus (Aemilius?).
38 P.   Supposed remains of the Sublician
         Bridge.

Robigus, or **Robigo**, is only an abstraction of the later Romans from the festival of the Robigalia.

Robus, a fortress in the territory of the Rauraci in Gallia Belgica, which was built by Valentinian near Basilia, A. D. 374.

Roma (Romanus: *Rome*), the capital of Italy and of the world, was situated on the left bank of the river Tiber, on the N.W. confines of Latium, about 16 miles from the sea. — **A. History of the City.** Rome is said to have been a colony from Alba Longa, and to have been founded by Romulus, about B. c. 753. [Romulus.] All traditions agree that the original city comprised only the *Mons Palatinus* or *Palatium* and some portion of the ground immediately below it. It was surrounded by walls, which followed the line of the *Pomoerium* (see *Dict. of Antiq. s. v.*), and was built in a square form, whence it was called *Roma Quadrata*. This city on the Palatine was inhabited only by Latins. On the neighbouring hills there also existed from the earliest times settlements of Sabines and Etruscans. The Sabine town, probably called *Quirium*, and inhabited by *Quirites*, was situated on the hills to the N. of the Palatine, that is, the *Quirinalis* and *Capitolinus*, or *Capitolium*, on the latter of which hills was the Sabine Arx or citadel. These Latin and Sabine towns afterwards became united, according to tradition, in the reign of Romulus, and the 2 peoples formed one collective body, known under the name of " Populus Romanus (et) Quirites." The Etruscans were settled on *Mons Caelius*, and extended over *Mons Cispius* and *Mons Oppius*, which are part of the Esquiline. These Etruscans were at an early period incorporated in the Roman state, but were compelled to abandon their seats on the hills, and to take up their abode in the plains between the Caelius and the Esquiline, whence the *Vicus Tuscus* derived its name. Under the kings the city rapidly grew in population and in size. Ancus Martius added the *Mons Aventinus* to the city. The same king also built a fortress on the *Janiculus*, a hill on the other side of the Tiber, as a protection against the Etruscans, and connected it with the city by means of the Pons Sublicius. Rome was still further improved and enlarged by Tarquinius Priscus and Servius Tullius. The former of these kings constructed the vast sewers (*cloacae*), by which the lower part of the city between the Palatine and Capitol was drained, and which still remain without a stone displaced. He also laid out the Circus Maximus and the forum, and, according to some traditions, commenced the erection of the Capitoline temple, which was finished by Tarquinius Superbus. The completion of the city however was ascribed to Servius Tullius. This king added the *Mons Viminalis* and *Mons Esquilinus*, and surrounded the whole city with a line of fortifications, which comprised all the seven hills of Rome (*Palatinus, Capitolinus, Quirinalis, Caelius, Aventinus, Viminalis, Esquilinus*). Hence Rome was called *Urbs Septicollis*. These fortifications were about 7 miles in circumference. At the same time Servius extended the pomoerium so as to make the sacred enclosure of the city identical with its walls. In B. C. 390 Rome was entirely destroyed by the Gauls, with the exception of a few houses on the Palatine. On the departure of the barbarians it was rebuilt in great haste and confusion, without any attention to regularity, and with narrow and crooked streets.

After the conquest of the Carthaginians and of the monarchs of Macedonia and Syria, the city began to be adorned with many public buildings and handsome private houses; and it was still further embellished by Augustus, who introduced great improvements into all parts of the city, and both erected many public buildings himself and induced all the leading nobles of his court to follow his example. So greatly had the appearance of the city improved during his long and prosperous reign that he used to boast that he had found the city of brick, and had left it of marble. Still the main features of the city remained the same; and the narrow streets and mean houses formed a striking and disagreeable contrast to the splendid public buildings and magnificent palaces which had been recently erected. The great fire at Rome in the reign of Nero (A. D. 64) destroyed two-thirds of the city. Nero availed himself of this opportunity to indulge his passion for building; and the city now assumed a more regular and stately appearance. The new streets were made both wide and straight; the height of the houses was restricted; and a certain part of each was required to be built of Gabian or Alban stone, which was proof against fire. Rome had long since extended beyond the walls of Servius Tullius; but down to the 3rd century of the Christian aera the walls of this monarch continued to mark the limits of the city properly so called. These walls however had long since been rendered quite useless, and the city was therefore left without any fortifications. Accordingly the emperor Aurelian determined to surround Rome with new walls, which embraced the city of Servius Tullius and all the suburbs which had subsequently grown up around it, such as the *M. Janiculus* on the right bank of the Tiber, and the *Collis Hortulorum* or *Mons Pincianus* on the left bank of the river to the N. of the Quirinalis. The walls of Aurelian were commenced by this emperor before he set out on his expedition against Zenobia (A. D. 271), and were terminated by his successor Probus. They were about 11 miles in circumference. They were restored by Honorius, and were also partly rebuilt by Belisarius. — **B. Divisions of the City.** Rome was divided by Servius Tullius into 4 *Regiones* or districts, corresponding to the 4 city tribes. Their names were : 1. *Suburana*, comprehending the space from the Subura to the Caelius, both inclusive. 2. *Esquilina*, comprehending the Esquiline hill. 3. *Collina*, extending over the Quirinal and Viminal. 4. *Palatina*, comprehending the Palatine hill. The Capitoline, as the seat of the gods, and the Aventine, were not included in these Regiones. These Regiones were again subdivided into 27 Sacella Argaeorum, which were probably erected where two streets (*compita*) crossed each other. It is probable that each of the 4 Regiones contained 6 of these sacella, and that the remaining 3 belonged to the Capitoline. The division of Servius Tullius into 4 Regiones remained unchanged till the time of Augustus; but this emperor made a fresh division of the city into 14 Regiones, which comprised both the ancient city of Servius Tullius and all the suburbs which had been subsequently added. This division was made by Augustus to facilitate the internal government of the city. The names of the Regiones were : — 1. *Porta Capena*, at the S. E. corner of the city by the Porta Capena. 2. *Caelimontium*, N. E. of the preceding, embracing

M. Caelius. 3. *Isis et Serapis*, N.W. of No. 2, in the valley between the Caelius, the Palatine and Esquiline. 4. *Via Sacra*, N.W. of No. 3, embracing the valley between the Esquiline, Viminal and Quirinal towards the Palatine. 5. *Esquilina cum Colle Viminali*, N.E. of No. 4, comprehending the whole of the Esquiline and Viminal. 6. *Alta Semita*, N.W. of No. 5, comprising the Quirinal. 7. *Via Lata*, W. of No. 6, between the Quirinal and Campus Martius. 8. *Forum Romanum*, S. of No. 7, comprehending the Capitoline and the valley between it and the Palatine. 9. *Circus Flaminius*, N.W. of No. 8, extending as far as the Tiber, and comprehending the whole of the Campus Martius. 10. *Palatium*, S.E. of No. 8, containing the Palatine. 11. *Circus Maximus*, S.W. of No. 10, comprehending the plain between the Palatine, Aventine and Tiber. 12. *Piscina Publica*, S.E. of No. 11. 13. *Aventinus*, N.W. of No. 12, embracing the Aventine. 14. *Trans Tiberim*, the only region on the right bank of the river, containing the *Insula Tiberina*, the valley between the river and the Janiculus, and a part of this mountain. Each of these Regiones was subdivided into a certain number of *Vici*, analogous to the *sacella* of Servius Tullius. The houses were divided into 2 different classes, called respectively *domus* and *insulae*. The former were the dwellings of the Roman nobles, corresponding to the modern palazzi ; the latter were the habitations of the middle and lower classes. Each insula contained several apartments or sets of apartments, which were let to different families, and it was frequently surrounded with shops. The insulae contained several stories ; and as the value of ground increased in Rome, they were frequently built of a dangerous height. Hence Augustus restricted the height of all new houses to 70 feet, and Trajan to 60 feet. No houses of any description were allowed to be built close together at Rome, and it was provided by the 12 Tables that a space of at least 5 feet should be left between every house. The number of insulae of course greatly exceeded that of the domi. It is stated that there were 46,602 insulae at Rome, but only 1790 domus.—
C. Size and Population of the City. It has been already stated that the circumference of the walls of Servius Tullius was about 7 miles ; but a great part of the space included within these walls was at first not covered with buildings. Subsequently, as we have seen, the city greatly extended beyond these limits ; and a measurement has come down to us, made in the reign of Vespasian, by which it appears to have been about 13 miles in circumference. It was probably about this time that Rome reached its greatest size. The walls of Aurelian were only about 11 miles in circuit. It is more difficult to determine the population of the city at any given period. We learn however from the Monumentum Ancyranum, that the plebs urbana in the time of Augustus was 320,000. This did not include the women nor the senators nor knights ; so that the free population could not have been less than 650,000. To this number we must add the slaves, who must have been at least as numerous as the free population. Consequently the whole population of Rome in the time of Augustus must have been at least 1,300,000, and in all probability greatly exceeded that number. Moreover, as we know that the city continued to increase in size and population down to the time of

Vespasian and Trajan, we shall not be far wrong in supposing that the city contained nearly 2 millions of inhabitants in the reigns of those emperors.
—D. Walls and Gates. I. Wall of Romulus. The direction of this wall is described by Tacitus. Commencing at the Forum Boarium, the site of which is marked by the arch erected there to Septimius Severus, it ran along the foot of the Palatine, having the valley afterwards occupied by the Circus Maximus on the right, as far as the altar of Consus, nearly opposite to the extremity of the Circus ; thence it turned round the southern angle of the Palatine, followed the foot of the hill nearly in a straight line to the Curiae Veteres, which stood not far from the site of the Arch of Constantine ; thence ascended the steep slope, at the summit of which stands the Arch of Titus, and descended again on the other side to the angle of the Forum, which was then a morass. In this wall there were 3 gates, the number prescribed by the rules of the Etruscan religion. 1. *Porta Mugonia* or *Mugionis*, also called *Porta vetus Palatii*, at the northern slope of the Palatine, at the point where the Via Sacra and the Via Nova met. 2. *Porta Romanula*, at the western angle of the hill near the temple of Victory, and between the modern churches of S. Teodoro and Santa Anastasia. 3. The name and position of the 3rd gate is not mentioned, for the *Porta Janualis* appears to be identical with the *Janus* or archway, commonly known as the temple of Janus, which stood on the other side of the forum, and could have had no connection with the original city of Romulus.—**II. Walls of Servius Tullius.** It is stated that this king surrounded the whole city with a wall of hewn stone ; but there are many reasons for questioning this statement. The 7 hills on which Rome was built, were most of them of great natural strength, having sides actually precipitous, or easily rendered so by cutting away the soft tufo rock. Instead, therefore, of building a wall around the whole circuit of the city, Servius Tullus appears only to have connected the several hills by walls or trenches drawn across the narrow valleys which separated them. The most formidable part of these fortifications was the Agger or mound, which extended across the broad table-land formed by the junction of the Quirinal, Esquiline, and Viminal, since it was on this side that the city was most open to the attacks of the enemy. The agger was a great rampart or mound of earth, 50 feet wide and above 60 high, faced with flagstones and flanked with towers, and at its foot was a moat 100 feet broad and 30 deep. There are still traces of this work. Starting from the southern extremity of this mound at the Porta Esquilina, the fortifications of Servius ran along the outside edge of the Caelian and Aventine hills to the river Tiber by the Porta Trigemina. From this point to the Porta Flumentana near the S.W. extremity of the Capitoline hill, there appears to have been no wall, the river itself being considered a sufficient defence. At the Porta Flumentana the fortifications again commenced ; and ran along the outside edge of the Capitoline and Quirinal hills, till they reached the northern extremity of the agger at the Porta Collina. The number of the gates in the walls of Servius is uncertain, and the position of many of them is doubtful. Pliny, indeed, states that their number was 37 ; but it is almost certain that this number includes many mere openings made through

Insula Tiberina, with the Pons Fabricius and Pons Cestius. Page 649. Bridges, Nos. 4, 5.

The Forum in its Present State. Pages 649 and 267.

[*To face* p. 648.

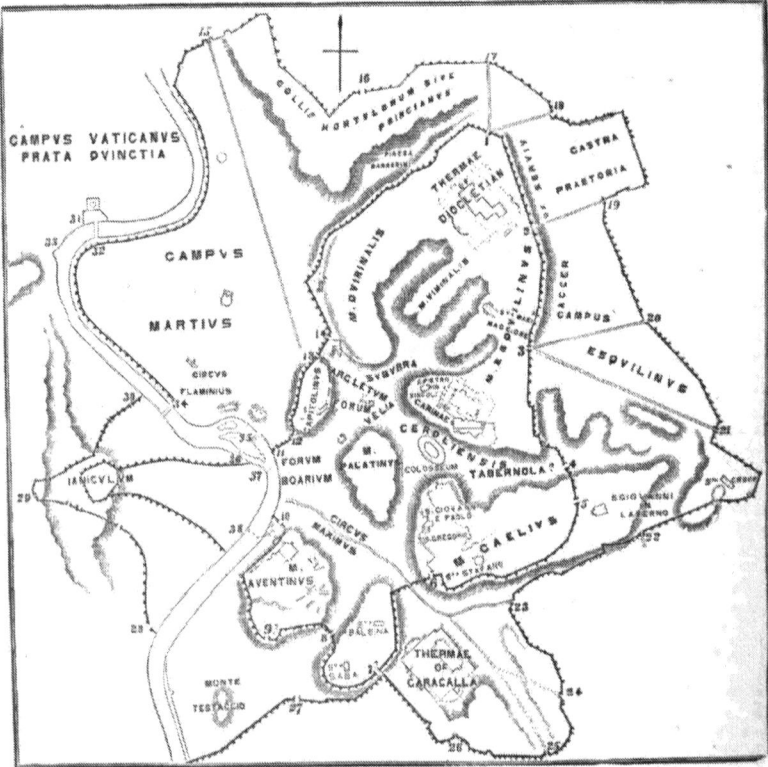

Map of Ancient Rome, showing the Walls of Servius and those of Aurelian.

the walls to connect different parts of the city with the suburbs, since the walls of Servius had long since ceased to be regarded. The following is a list of the gates as far as they can be ascertained : — 1. *Porta Collina*, at the N. extremity of the agger, and the most N.-ly of all the gates, stood at the point of junction of the Via Salaria and Via Nomentana, just above the N. angle of the Vigna dei Certosini. 2. *P. Viminalis*, S. of No. 1, and in the centre of the agger. 3. *P. Esquilina*, S. of No. 2, on the site of the arch of Gallienus, which probably replaced it ; the Via Praenestina and Labicana began here. 4. *P. Querquetulana*, S. of No. 3. 5. *P. Caeliomontana*, S. of No. 4, on the heights of M. Caelius, behind the hospital of S. Giovanni in Laterano, at the point of junction of the 2 modern streets which bear the name of S. Stefano Rotondo, and the SS. Quattro Coronati. 6. *P. Capena*, one of the most celebrated of all the Roman gates, from which issued the Via Appia. It stood S.W. of No. 5, and at the S. W. foot of the Caelian, on the spot now occupied by the grounds of the Villa Mattei. 7, 8, 9. *P. Lavernalis, P. Raudusculana*, and *P. Naevia*, 3 of the most S.-ly gates of Rome, lying between the Caelian and the Aventine. The walls of Servius probably here took a great bend to the S., inclosing the heights of Sta Balbina and Sta Saba. 10. *P. Minucia*, probably W. of the 3 preceding, and on the S. of the Aventine. 11. *P. Trigemina*, on the N.W. of the Aventine, near the Tiber and the great salt-magazines. 12. *P. Flumentana*, N. of the preceding, near the S.W. slope of the Capitol and close to the Tiber. 13. *P. Carmentalis*, N. of No. 12, and at the foot of the S. W. slope of the Capitoline, near the altar of Carmenta, and leading to the Forum Olitorium and the Theatre of Marcellus. This gate contained 2 passages, of which the right hand one was called Porta Scelerata from the time that the 300 Fabii passed through it, and was always avoided. 14. *P. Ratumenalis*, N. of No. 13, and at the N. W. slope of the Capitoline, leading from the Forum of Trajan to the Campus Martius. 15. *P. Fontinalis*, N. of No. 4 on the W. slope of the Quirinal, also leading to the Campus Martius. 16. *P. Sanqualis*, N. of No. 15, also on the W. slope of the same hill. 17. *P. Salutaris*, N. of No. 16, on the N. W. slope of the same hill, near the temple of Salus. 18. *P. Triumphalis*. The position of this gate is quite uncertain, except that it led, more or less directly, to the Campus Martius.—III. **Walls of Aurelian.** These walls are essentially the same as those which surround the modern city of Rome, with the exception of the part beyond the Tiber. The Janiculus and the adjacent suburb was the only portion beyond the Tiber which was included within the fortifications of Aurelian; for the Vatican was not surrounded with walls till the time of Leo IV. in the 9th century. On the left bank of the Tiber the walls of Aurelian embraced on the N. the Collis Hortulorum or Pincianus, on the W. the Campus Martius, on the E. the Campus Esquilinus, and on the S. the Mons Testaceus. There were 14 gates in the Aurelian walls, most of which derived their names from the roads issuing from them. These were, on the N. side : 1. *P. Aurelia*, on the Tiber in front of the Pons Aelius. 2. *P. Pinciana*, on the hill of the same name. 3. *P. Salaria*, extant under the same name, but restored in modern times. 4. *P. No-*

mentana, leading to the ancient P. Collina. On the E. side: 5. *P. Tiburtina*, leading to the old P. Esquilina, now Porta S. Lorenzo. 6. *P. Praenestina*, now Porta Maggiore. On the S. side: 7. *P. Asinaria*, on the site of the modern Porta S. Giovanni. 8. *P. Metronis*, or *Metronii*, or *Metrovia*, which has now disappeared, probably at the entrance to the Caelian, between S. Stefano Rotondo and the Villa Mattei. 9. *P. Latina*, now walled up. 10. *P. Appia*, now Porta S. Pancrazio. The roads through this gate and through No. 9, both led to the old Porta Capena. 11. *P. Ostiensis*, leading to Ostia, now Porta S. Paolo. On the W. side: 12. *P. Portuensis*, on the other side of the Tiber near the river, from which issued the road to Portus. 13. A second *P. Aurelia*, on the W. slope of the Janiculus, now Porta S. Pancrazio. 14. *P. Septimiana*, near the Tiber, which was destroyed by Alexander VI.—**E. Bridges.** There were 8 bridges across the Tiber, which probably ran in the following order from N. to S:— 1. *Pons Aelius*, which was built by Hadrian, and led from the city to the mausoleum of that emperor, now the bridge and castle of St. Angelo. 2. *Pons Neronianus*, or *Vaticanus*, which led from the Campus Martius to the Vatican and the gardens of Caligula and Nero. The remains of its piers may still be seen, when the waters of the Tiber are low, at the back of the Hospital of Sat. Spirito. 3. *P. Aurelius*, sometimes, but erroneously, called *Janiculensis*, which led to the Janiculus and the Porta Aurelia. It occupied the site of the present "Ponte Sisto," which was built by Sistus IV. upon the ruins of the old bridge. 4, 5. *P. Fabricius* and *P. Cestius*, the two bridges which connected the Insula Tiberina with the opposite sides of the river, the former with the city, the latter with the Janiculus. Both are still remaining. The P. Fabricius, which was built by one L. Fabricius, curator viarum, a short time before the conspiracy of Catiline, now bears the name of "Ponte Quattro Capi." The P. Cestius, which was built at a much later age, is now called "Ponte S. Bartolommeo." 6. *P. Senatorius*, or *Palatinus*, below the island of the Tiber, formed the communication between the Palatine and its neighbourhood and the Janiculus. 7. *P. Sublicius*, the oldest of the Roman bridges, said to have been built by Ancus Martius, when he erected a fort on the Janiculus. It was built of wood, whence its name, which comes from *sublices*, "wooden beams." It was carried away several times by the river, but from a feeling of religious respect was always rebuilt of wood down to the latest times. 8. *P. Milvius*, or *Mulvius*, now "Ponte Molle," was situated outside the city, N. of the P. Aelius, and was built by Aemilius Scaurus the censor.—**F. Interior of the City. I. Fora and Campi.** The Fora were open spaces of ground, paved with stones, surrounded by buildings, and used as market places, or for the transaction of public business. An account of the Fora is given elsewhere. [FORUM.] The Campi were also open spaces of ground, but much larger, covered with grass, planted with trees, and adorned with works of art. They were used by the people as places of exercise and amusement, and may be compared with the London parks. These Campi were: 1. *Campus Martius*, the open plain lying between the city walls and the Tiber, of which the southern part, in the neighbourhood of the Circus Flaminius, was called *Campus Flaminius*, or *Prata Flaminia*. This plain, which was by far the most celebrated of all, is spoken of separately. [CAMPUS MARTIUS.] 2. *Campus Sceleratus*, close to the Porta Collina and within the walls of Servius, where the vestals who had broken their vows of chastity were entombed alive. 3. *Campus Agrippae*, probably on the S. W. slope of the Pincian hill, E. of the Campus Martius, on the right of the Corso, and N. of the Piazza degli Apostoli. 4. *Campus Esquilinus*, outside of the agger of Servius and near the Porta Esquilina, where criminals were executed, and the lower classes were buried. The greater part of this plain was afterwards converted into pleasure grounds belonging to the palace of Maecenas. 5. *Campus Viminalis*, on the E. slope of the Viminal near the Villa Negroni.—II. **Streets and Districts.** There are said to have been in all 215 streets in Rome. The broad streets were called *Viae* and *Vici****; the narrow streets *Angiportus*. The chief streets were: 1. *Via Sacra*, the principal street in Rome. It began near the Sacellum Streniae, in the valley between the Caelian and the Esquiline, and leaving the Flavian Amphitheatre (Colosseum) on the left ran along the N. slope of the Palatine, passing under the arch of Titus, and past the Forum Romanum, till it reached the Capitol. 2. *Via Lata*, led from the N. side of the Capitol and the Porta Ratumena to the Porta Flaminia, whence the N. part of it was called *Via Flaminia*. 3. *Via Nova*, by the side of the W. slope of the Palatine, led from the ancient Porta Romanula and the Velabrum to the Forum, and was connected by a side street with the Via Sacra. 4. *Vicus Jugarius*, led from the Porta Carmentalis under the Capitol to the Forum Romanum, which it entered near the Basilica Julia and the Lacus Servilius. 5. *Vicus Tuscus*, connected the Velabrum with the Forum, running W. of, and nearly parallel with, the Via Nova. It contained a great number of shops, where articles of luxury were sold, and its inhabitants did not possess the best of characters (*Tusci turba impia vici*, Hor. *Sat.* ii. 3. 228). 6. *Vicus Cyprius*, ran from the Forum to the Esquiline. The upper part of it, turning on the right to the Urbius Clivus, was called *Sceleratus Vicus*, because Tullia here drove her chariot over the corpse of her father Servius. 7. *Vicus Patricius*, in the valley between the Esquiline and the Viminal in the direction of the modern Via Urbana and Via di S. Pudenziana. 8. *Vicus Africus*, in the district of Esquiline, but the exact situation of which cannot be determined, said to have been so called, because African hostages were kept here during the first Punic war. 9. *Vicus Sandalarius*, also in the district of the Esquiline, extending as far as the heights of the Carinae. Besides the shops of the shoemakers, from whom it derived its name, it contained several booksellers' shops. 10. *Vicus Vitriarius* or *Vitrarius*, in the S.E. part of the city, near the Porta Capena. 11. *Vicus Longus*, in the Vallis Quirini between the Quirinal and Viminal, now S. Vitale. 12. *Caput Africae*, near the Colosseum, the modern Via de S. Quattro Coronati. 13. *Subura* or *Suburra*, a district, through which a street of the same name ran, was the whole valley between the Esquiline, Quirinal and Viminal. It was one of the most frequented parts of the town

and contained a great number of shops and brothels. 14. *Velia*, a height near the forum, which extended from the Palatine near the Arch of Titus, to the Esquiline, and which separated the valley of the forum from that of the Colosseum. On the Velia were situated the Basilica of Constantine and the temple of Venus and Rome. 15. *Carinae*, a district on the S.W. part of the Esquiline, or the modern height of S. Pietro in Vincoli, where Pompey, Cicero and many other distinguished Romans lived. 16. *Velabrum*, a district on the W. slope of the Palatine between the Vicus Tuscus and the Forum Boarium, was originally a morass. 17. *Aequimelium*, a place at the E. foot of the Capitol and by the side of the Vicus Jugarius, where the house of Sp. Maelius once stood. [See p. 407. a.] 18. *Argiletum*, a district of uncertain site, but probably at the S. extremity of the Quirinal between the Subura, the Forum of Nerva and the Temple of Peace. The etymology of the name is uncertain; some of the ancients derived it from *argilla* " white clay "; others from a hero Argus, a friend of Evander, who is said to have been buried here. 19. *Lautumiae*, a district near the Argiletum and the Forum Piscatorium, on which subsequently the Basilica Porcia was built. In this district was one of the state prisons, called *Lautumiae* or *Carcer Lautumiarum*. —III. **Temples.** There are said to have been 400 temples in Rome. Of these the following, enumerated for the most part in chronological order, were the principal:—1. *Templum Jovis Feretrii*, on the Capitoline, the oldest of all the Roman temples, built, according to tradition, by Romulus, and restored by Augustus. 2. *T. Fidei*, likewise on the Capitoline, built by Numa, and restored successively by A. Atilius Collatinus and M. Aemilius Scaurus. 3. *T. Jani*, also called *Janus Bifrons* or *Biformis*, *Janus Geminus* and *Janus Quirinus*, also built by Numa, was, properly speaking, not a temple, but a passage with an entrance at each end, the gates of which were opened during war and closed in times of peace. It was situated N.E. of the forum towards the Quirinal. There were also other temples of Janus at Rome, of which one was near the Theatre of Marcellus, and the other near the forum of Nerva. 4. *Aedes Vestae*, a round temple built by Numa, in the S. part of the forum or on the slope of the Palatine, adjoining the *Regia Numae*, probably near Sta Maria Liberatice. The *Atrium Vestae*, also called *Atrium Regium*, probably formed a part of the Regia Numae, which may be regarded as forming a portion of the building sacred to Vesta. 5. *T. Dianae*, on the Aventine, which hill is hence called by Martial *Collis Dianae*, built by Servius Tullius, as the place of meeting for the Romans and the members of the Latin league, and restored by Augustus, probably near the modern church S. Prisca. 6. *T. Lunae*, frequently confounded with the preceding, also built by Servius Tullius, and on the Aventine, probably on the side adjoining the Circus. 7. *T. Jovis*, usually called the *Capitolium*, situated on the S. summit of the Capitoline hill, was vowed by Tarquinius Priscus and built by Tarquinius Superbus. It was the most magnificent of all the temples in Rome, and is described elsewhere. [CAPITOLIUM.] 8. *T. Saturni*, which was also used as the Aerarium, on the Clivus Capitolinus and by the Forum, to which it is supposed that the 3 pillars in the forum belong. It was built by Tarquinius Superbus and restored successively by L. Munatius Plancus and Septimius Severus. 9.

---

* *Vicus*, properly signified a quarter of the city, but the principal street in a vicus was frequently called by the name of the Vicus to which it belonged.

Temple of Trajan.

Basilica Ulpia.

Temple of Vesta. (From a Coin.)
Page 650. Temples, No. 4.

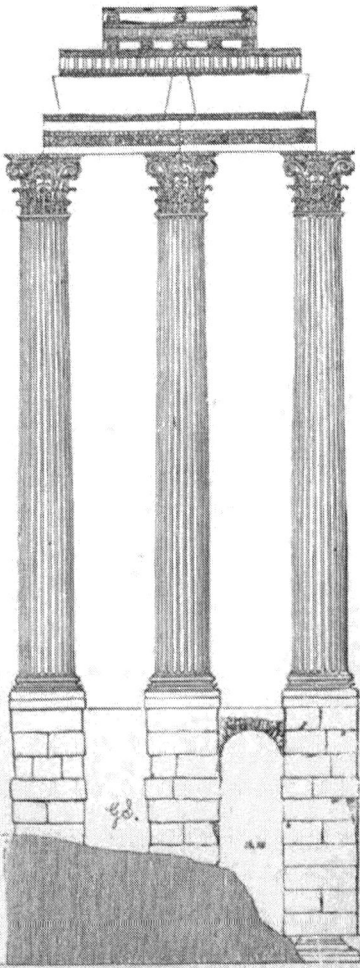

Columns of the Temple of Castor and Pollux, supposed by some
to belong to the Temple of Saturn. Pages 650, 651. Temples,
Nos. 8, 9.

Theatre of Marcellus. Page 652.
Theatres, No. 2.

[To face p. 650.

Pantheon of Agrippa. Page 651. Temples, No. 41.

Temple of Antoninus and Faustina. Page 651.
Temples, No. 46.

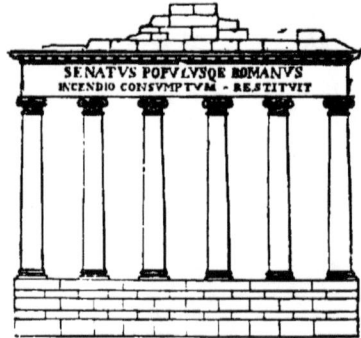

Temple of Saturn. Page 650.
Temples, No. 8.

Tabularium and Temples of Vespasian, Saturn, and Concord.
Page 650. Temples, Nos. 8, 17.

To face p. 651.]

Aedes Castoris or *T. Castoris et Pollucis*, by the Forum, near the fountain of Juturna, in which the senate frequently assembled. It was vowed by the dictator A. Postumius in the great battle with the Latins near the lake Regillus, and was successively restored by L. Metellus Dalmaticus, Tiberius, Caligula and Claudius. 10. *T. Mercurii*, between the Circus Maximus and the Aventine. 11. *T. Cereris*, on the slope of the Aventine near the Circus. 12. *T. Apollinis*, between the Circus Maximus and the Theatre of Marcellus near the Porticus Octaviae, where the senate often assembled. 13. *T. Junonis Reginae*, on the Aventine. 14. *T. Martis Extramuranei*, before the Porta Capena on the Via Appia. 15. *T. Junonis Monetae*, on the area of the Capitoline, where the house of M. Manlius had stood. 16. *T. Junonis Lucinae*, on the W. summit of the Esquiline. 17. *T. Concordiae*, on the slope of the Capitoline above the forum in which the senate frequently assembled. There were probably two temples of Concordia, both by the forum, of which the more ancient was consecrated by Camillus, and the other by L. Opimius after the death of C. Gracchus. The remains of the ancient temple of Concordia are to be seen behind the arch of Septimius Severus. 18. *T. Salutis*, on the slope of the Quirinal near the Porta Salutaris, adorned with paintings by Fabius Pictor, burnt down in the reign of Claudius. 19. *T. Bellonae*, before the Circus Flaminius, and near the confines of the Campus Martius, in which the senate assembled, in order to give audience to foreign ambassadors and to receive applications from generals who solicited the honour of a triumph. 20. *T. Jovis Victoris*, on the Palatine, between the Domus Augusti and the Curia Vetus. 21. *T. Victoriae*, on the summit of the Palatine, or the Clivus Victoriae above the Porta Romanula and the circus, in which the statue of the mother of the gods was at first preserved. 22. *T. Magnae Matris Idueae*, near the preceding and the Casa Romuli, in which the above named statue of the goddess was placed 13 years after its arrival in Rome. 23. *T. Jovis Statoris*, near the arch of Titus on the Via Sacra, where the senate frequently assembled. 24. *T. Quirini*, on the Quirinal, where also the senate frequently assembled, enlarged and adorned by Augustus. 25. *T. Fortunae*, built by Servius Tullius in the Forum Boarium. 26. *T. Aesculapii* in the island of the Tiber, which was called after it Insula Aesculapii. 27. *T. Mentis* and *Veneris Erycinae*, both of which were built at the same time and close to one another on the Capitoline. There was also another temple of Venus Erycina before the Porta Collina. 28. *T. Honoris* and *Virtutis*, which were built, close to one another, near the Porta Capena and Via Appia, by Marcellus, and adorned with Greek works of art brought from Syracuse. 29. *T. Jovis*, in the island of the Tiber, near the temple of Aesculapius. 30. *T. Fauni*, in the island of the Tiber. 31. *T. Spei*, in the Forum Olitorium. 32. *T. Junonis Sospitae* or *Matutae*, in the Forum Olitorium near the Theatre of Marcellus. 33. *T. Pietatis*, in the Forum Olitorium, which was pulled down in order to make room for the Theatre of Marcellus. 34. *Aedes Fortunae Equestris*, in the Campus Flaminius near the theatre of Pompey, built by Fulvius Flaccus, the roof of which, made of marble, was brought from a temple of Juno Lucina in Bruttium. It was probably burnt down in the reign of Augustus or Tiberius, since in A.D. 22 we are told there was no temple of Fortuna

Equestris at Rome. There were other temples of Fortuna on the Palatine, Quirinal, &c. 35. *Aedes Herculis Musarum*, close to the Porticus Octaviae, and between the Theatre of Marcellus and the Circus Flaminius, built by M. Fulvius Nobilior and adorned with the statues of the Muses brought from Ambracia. 36. *T. Honoris et Virtutis*, built by Marius, but of uncertain site: some modern writers suppose it to have been on the Esquiline, others on the Capitoline. 37. *T. Martis*, in the Campus Martius near the Circus Flaminius, built by D. Brutus Callaicus, and adorned with a colossal statue of the god. 38. *T. Veneris Genetricis*, in the forum of Caesar, before which Caesar's equestrian statue was placed. 39. *T. Martis Ultoris*, in the forum of Augustus, to which belong the 3 splendid Corinthian pillars near the convent S. Annunziata. 40. *T. Apollinis*, on the Palatine, surrounded by a porticus in which was the celebrated Palatine library. 41. *Pantheon*, a celebrated temple in the Campus Martius, built by Agrippa: it is described in a separate article. [PANTHEON.] 42. *T. Augusti*, founded by Tiberius and completed by Caligula, on the slope of the Palatine towards the Via Nova. It stood before the temple of Minerva, from which it was probably separated by the Via Nova. 43. *T. Pacis*, one of the most splendid temples in the city, built by Vespasian on the Velia. 44. *T. Isidis et Serapidis* in the 3rd Regio, which was named after the temple. 45. *T. Vespasiani et Titi*, in the forum, alongside of the temple of Concordia. 46. *T. Antonini et Faustinae*, at the further end of the N. side of the forum under the Velia. The remains of this temple are in the modern church of S. Lorenzo in Miranda. 47. *T. Minervae*, on the S. side of the forum, behind the temple of Augustus, built by Domitian. 48. *T. Bonae Deae*, a very ancient temple on a spot of the Aventine, which was called Saxum Sacrum, but removed by Hadrian, undoubtedly on the S. E. side of the hill, opposite the heights of S. Sabba and S. Balbina. 49. *T. Romae et Veneris*, subsequently called *T. Urbis*, a large and splendid temple, built by Hadrian, between the Esquiline and Palatine, N. E. of the Colosseum. It was burnt down in the reign of Maxentius, but was subsequently restored. Its remains are between the Colosseum and the church of S. Maria Nuova or S. Francesca Romana. 50. *T. Solis*, at the upper end of the Circus Maximus. 51. *T. Herculis*, in the forum Boarium, probably the round temple still extant of S. Maria del Sole, which used to be erroneously regarded as the temple of Vesta. There was another temple of Hercules by the Circus Maximus, near the Porta Trigemina. 52. *T. Solis*, a splendid temple built by Aurelian, E. of the Quirinal. 53. *T. Florae*, an ancient temple on the S. point of the Quirinal ; but the time of its foundation is not recorded. 54. *Vulcanale*, was not a temple, but only an Area dedicated to the god with an altar, on the N. side of the forum above the Comitium ; it was so large that not only were the Curia Hostilia and the Aedes Concordiae built there, but also a fish-market was held in the place. — IV. Circi. The Circi were places for chariot-races and horse-races. 1. *Circus Maximus*, frequently called simply *the Circus*, was founded by Tarquinius Priscus, in the plain between the Palatine and Aventine, and was successively enlarged by Julius Caesar and Trajan. Under the emperors it contained seats for 385,000 persons. It was restored by Constantine the Great, and games were celebrated in it as late as the 6th century. 2. *C. Flaminius*, erected by Flaminius in B.C. 221 in the Prata Flaminia before the Porta Carmentalis ; it was not sufficiently large for the population of Rome, and was therefore seldom used. 3. *C. Neronis*, erected by Caligula in the gardens of Agrippina on the other side of the Tiber. There was also another *C. Neronis*, on the other side of the Tiber, near the Moles Hadriani, in the gardens of Domitia. 4. *C. Palatinus*, on the Palatine in which the Ludi Palatini were celebrated. There are traces of it in the Orto Roncioni on the S. part of the hill. 5. *C. Heliogabali*, in the gardens of this emperor, behind the Amphitheatrum Castrense, at the E. point of the Aurelian walls. 6. *C. Maxentii*, commonly called Circo di Caracalla, before the Porta Appia in the S. part of the city. Among the Circi we may also reckon : 7. The *Stadium*, likewise called *C. Agonalis* and *C. Alexandri*, in the Campus Martius, erected by Domitian in place of the wooden Stadium built by Augustus. It contained seats for 33,888 persons. Its remains still exist in the Piazza Navona. — **V. Theatres.** Theatres were not built at Rome till a comparatively late period, and long after the Circi. At first they were only made of wood for temporary purposes, and were afterwards broken up ; but many of these wooden theatres were notwithstanding constructed with great magnificence. The splendid wooden theatre of M. Aemilius Scaurus was capable of containing 80,000 spectators. 1. *Theatrum Pompeii*, the first permanent stone theatre, was erected by Cn. Pompey, B.C. 55, in the Campus Martius, N. E. of the Circus Flaminius, after the model of the theatre of Mytilene. It contained seats for 40,000 spectators. It was restored successively by Augustus, Tiberius, Caligula, Diocletian, and Theodorich. Its ruins are by the Palazzo Pio, not far from the Campo di Fiore. 2. *Th. Cornelii Balbi*, S. E. of the preceding, near the Tiber, on the site of the Palazzo Cenci. It was dedicated by Cornelius Balbus in B.C. 13, was partly burnt down under Titus, but was subsequently restored. It contained seats for 11,600 persons. 3. *Th. Marcelli*, in the forum Olitorium, W. of the preceding, between the slope of the Capitoline and the island of the Tiber, on the site of the temple of Pietas. It was begun by Julius Caesar, and dedicated by Augustus in B.C. 13, to the memory of his nephew Marcellus. It was restored by Vespasian, and perhaps also by Alexander Severus. It contained seats for 20,000 spectators. The remains of its Cavea exist near the Piazza Montanara. These were the only 3 theatres at Rome, whence Ovid speaks of *terna theatra*. There was, however, an Odeum or concert-house, which may be classed among the theatres. 4. *Odeum*, in the Campus Martius, built by Domitian, though some writers attribute its erection to Trajan : it contained seats for about 11,000 persons. — **VI. Amphitheatres.** The amphitheatres, like the theatres, were originally made of wood for temporary purposes. They were used for the shows of gladiators and wild beasts. The first wooden amphitheatre was built by C. Scribonius Curio (the celebrated partisan of Caesar), and the next by Julius Caesar during his perpetual dictatorship, B.C. 46. 1. *Amph. Statilii Tauri*, in the Campus Martius, was the first stone amphi-

theatre in Rome, and was built by Statilius Taurus, B.C. 30. This edifice was the only one of the kind until the building of the Flavian amphitheatre. It did not satisfy Caligula, who commenced an amphitheatre near the Septa ; but the work was not continued by Claudius. Nero too, A.D. 57, erected a vast amphitheatre of wood, but this was only a temporary building. The amphitheatre of Taurus was destroyed in the burning of Rome, A.D. 64, and was probably not restored, as it is not again mentioned. 2. *Amph. Flavium*, or, as it has been called since the time of Bede, the *Colosseum* or *Colisaeum*, a name said to be derived from the Colossus of Nero, which stood close by. It was situated in the valley between the Caelius, the Esquiline and the Velia on the marshy ground which was previously the pond of Nero's palace. It was commenced by Vespasian, and was completed by Titus, who dedicated it in A.D. 80, when 5000 animals of different kinds were slaughtered. This wonderful building, of which there are still extensive remains, covered nearly 6 acres of ground, and furnished seats for 87,000 spectators. In the reign of Macrinus it was struck by lightning, and so much damage was done to it that the games were for some years celebrated in the Stadium. Its restoration was commenced by Elagabalus and completed by Alexander Severus. 3. *Amph. Castrense*, at the S. E. of the Aurelian walls. — **VII. Naumachiae.** These were buildings of a kind similar to the amphitheatres. They were used for representations of sea-fights, and consisted of artificial lakes or ponds, with stone seats around them to accommodate the spectators. 1. *Naumachia Julii Caesaris*, in the middle part of the Campus Martius, called the "Lesser Codeta." This lake was filled up in the time of Augustus, so that we find in later writers mention of only 2 Naumachiae. 2. *N. Augusti*, constructed by Augustus on the other side of the Tiber under the Janiculus and near the Porta Portuensis. It was subsequently called the *Vetus Naumachia*, to distinguish it from the following one. 3. *N. Domitiani*, constructed by the emperor Domitian, probably on the other side of the Tiber under the Vatican and the Circus Neronis. — **VIII. Thermae.** The Thermae were some of the most magnificent buildings of imperial Rome. They were distinct from the *Balneae*, or common baths, of which there were a great number at Rome. In the Thermae the baths constituted a small part of the building. They were, properly speaking, a Roman adaptation of the Greek gymnasia ; and besides the baths they contained places for athletic games and youthful sports, exedrae or public halls, porticoes and vestibules for the idle, and libraries for the learned. They were decorated with the finest objects of art, and adorned with fountains, and shaded walks and plantations. 1. *Thermae Agrippae*, in the Campus Martius, erected by M. Agrippa. The Pantheon, still existing, is supposed by some, but without sufficient reason, to have served originally as a vestibule to these *Thermae*. 2. *Th. Neronis*, erected by Nero in the Campus Martius alongside of the Thermae of Agrippa : they were restored by Alexander Severus, and were from that time called *Th. Alexandrinae*. 3. *Th. Titi*, on the Esquiline, near the amphitheatre of this emperor, of which there are still considerable remains. 4. *Th. Trajani*, also on the Esquiline, immediately behind the

Temple of Pudicitia Patricia.

Temple of Vespasian.

[To face p. 682.

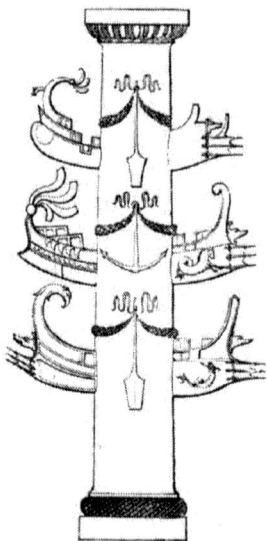

Columna Duilia.
Page 657. Columns, No. 2.

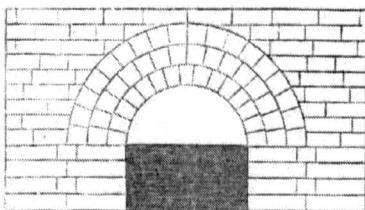

Cloaca Maxima. Pages 655, 656.

Pedestal of Column of Antoninus Pius.
Page 657. Columns, No. 4.

Colosseum. Page 652.

Elevation of Colosseum. Page 652.

two preceding, towards the N. E. 5. *Th. Commodianae* and *Th. Severianae*, close to one another, near S. Balbina, in the S. E. part of the city. 6. *Th. Antoninianae*, also in the S. E. part of the city, behind the two preceding, one of the most magnificent of all the Thermae, in which 2,300 men could bathe at the same time. The greater part of it was built by Caracalla, and it was completed by Heliogabalus and Alexander Severus. There are still extensive remains of this immense building below S. Balbina. 7. *Th. Diocletiani,* in the N. E. part of the city between the Agger of Servius and the Viminal and Quirinal. It was the most extensive of all the Thermae, containing a library, picture gallery, Odeum, &c., and such immense baths that 3,000 men could bathe in them at the same time. There are still extensive remains of this building near S. Maria d'Angeli. 8. *Th. Constantini,* on the Quirinal, on the site of the modern Palazzo Rospigliosi, but of which all traces have disappeared. The following Thermae were smaller and less celebrated. 9. *Th. Decianae,* on the Aventine. 10. *Th. Suranae,* erected by Trajan to the memory of his friend Sulpicius Sura, also in the neighbourhood of the Aventine, probably the same as the *Th. Varianae.* 11. *Th. Philippi,* near S. Matteo in Merulana. 12. *Th. Agrippinae,* on the Viminal behind S. Lorenzo. 13. *Th. Caii et Lucii,* on the Esquiline, called in the middle ages the Terme di Galluccio. — **IX. Basilicae.** The Basilicae were buildings which served as courts of law, and exchanges or places of meeting for merchants and men of business. 1. *Basilica Porcia,* erected by M. Porcius Cato, in the forum adjoining the Curia, B. C. 184. It was burnt down along with the Curia in the riots which followed the death of Clodius, 52. 2. *B. Fulvia,* also called *Aemilia et Fulvia,* because it was built by the censors L. Aemilius Lepidus and M. Fulvius Nobilior in 179. It was situated in the forum near the preceding one. It was restored by Aemilius Paulus in the time of Caesar, and was hence called *B. Aemilia* or *Pauli.* It was dedicated by his son Paulus Aemilius Lepidus in his consulship, 34. It was burnt down 20 years afterwards (14), and was rebuilt nominally by Paulus Lepidus, but in reality by Augustus and the friends of Paulus. The new building was a most magnificent one ; its columns of Phrygian marble were especially celebrated. It was repaired by another Lepidus in the reign of Tiberius, A. D. 22. 3. *B. Sempronia,* built by Ti. Sempronius Gracchus, B. C. 171, in the forum at the end of the Vicus Tuscus. 4. *B. Opimia,* in the forum near the temple of Concordia. 5. *B. Julia,* commenced by Julius Caesar and finished by Augustus, in the forum between the temples of Castor and Saturn, probably on the site of the B. Sempronia mentioned above. Some writers suppose that Aemilus Paulus built two Basilicae, and that the B. Julia occupied the site of one of them. 6. *B. Argentaria,* in the forum near the Clivus Argentarius and before the temple of Concordia, probably the same as the one mentioned under the name of B. Vascularia. The remains of this building are behind S. Martina, along side of the Salita di Marforio. 7. *B. Ulpia,* in the middle of the forum of Trajan, of which there are still considerable remains. 8. *B. Constantiana,* between the temple of Peace and the temple of Rome and Venus. — **X. Porticoes.** The Porticoes (*Porticus*)

were covered walks, supported by columns, and open on one side. There were several public porticoes at Rome, many of them of great size, which were used as places of recreation, and for the transaction of business. 1. *Porticus Pompeii,* adjoining the theatre of Pompey, and erected to afford shelter to the spectators in the theatre during a shower of rain. It was restored by Diocletian, and was hence called *P. Jovia.* 2. *P. Argonautarum,* or *Neptuni* or *Agrippae,* erected by Agrippa in the Campus Martius around the temple of Neptune, and adorned with a celebrated painting of the Argonauts. 3. *P. Philippi,* by the side of the T. Herculis Musarum and the Porticus Octaviae, built by M. Philippus the father-in-law of Augustus, and adorned with splendid works of art. 4. *P. Minucii* in the Campus Martius, near the Circus Flaminius, built by Q. Minucius Rufus in B. C. 109, to commemorate his victories over the Scordisci and Triballi in the preceding year. There appear to have been 2 porticos of this name, since we find mention of a *Minucia Vetus et Frumentaria.* It appears that the tesserae, or tickets, which entitled persons to a share in the public distributions of corn were given to them in the P. Minucia. 5. *P. Metelli,* built by Q. Metellus, after his triumph over Perseus, king of Macedonia, B. C. 146. It was situated in the Campus Martius between the Circus Flaminius and the theatre of Marcellus, and surrounded the 2 temples of Jupiter Stator and Juno Regina. 6. *P. Octaviae,* built by Augustus on the site of the P. Metelli just mentioned, in honour of his sister Octavia. It was a magnificent building, containing a vast number of works of art, and a public library, in which the senate frequently assembled ; hence it is sometimes called *Curia Octavia.* It was burnt down in the reign of Titus. Its ruins are near the church of S. Angelo in Pescaria. 7. *P. Octavia,* which must be carefully distinguished from the P. Octaviae just mentioned, was built by Cn. Octavius, who commanded the Roman fleet in the war against Perseus, king of Macedonia. It was situated in the Campus Martius between the theatre of Pompey and the Circus Flaminius. It was rebuilt by Augustus, and contained 2 rows of columns of the Corinthian order, with brazen capitals, whence it was also called *P. Corinthia.* 8. *P. Europae,* probably at the foot of the Pincius, in which foot-races took place. 9. *P. Polae,* built by the sister of Agrippa in the Campus Agrippae, in which also foot-races took place. 10. *P. Livia,* on the Esquiline, surrounding a temple of Concordia. 11. *P. Julia,* or *P. Caii et Lucii,* built by Julia in honour of these 2 sons of Agrippa, was probably also situated on the Esquiline near the Thermae Caii et Lucii. The following Porticoes were less celebrated : 12. *P. Vipsania,* supposed by some writers to be only a later name of the P. Agrippae. 13. *P. Claudia,* on the Esquiline. — **XI. Triumphal Arches.** The Triumphal Arches (*Arcus*) were structures peculiar to the Romans, and were erected by victorious generals in commemoration of their victories. They were built across the principal streets of the city, and, according to the space of their respective localities, consisted either of a single arch-way or of a central one for carriages, with 2 smaller ones on each side for foot passengers. Ancient writers mention 21 arches in the city of Rome. Of these the most important were : 1. *Arcus Fabianus,* also called

Fornix Fabianus, near the beginning of the Via Sacra, built by Fabius Maximus in B. C. 121, in commemoration of his victory over the Allobroges. 2. *A. Drusi*, erected by the senate in B. C. 9, in honour of Nero Claudius Drusus. It was situated on the Via Appia, and still exists, forming the inner gate of the Porta di S. Sebastiano. 3. *A. Augusti*, in the forum near the house of Julius Caesar. 4. *A. Tiberii*, near the temple of Saturn on the Clivus Capitolinus erected by Tiberius, A. D. 16, in honour of the victories of Germanicus in Germany. 5. *A. Claudii*, in the plain E. of the Quirinal, erected A. D. 51, to commemorate the victories of Claudius in Britain. Remains of it have been dug up at the beginning of the Piazza di Sciarra, by the Via di Pietra. 6. *A. Titi*, In the middle of the Via Sacra at the foot of the Palatine, which still exists. It was erected to the honour of Titus, after his conquest of Judaea, but was not finished till after his death; since in the inscription upon it he is called "Divus," and he is also represented as being carried up to heaven upon an eagle. The bas-reliefs of this arch represent the spoils from the temple of Jerusalem carried in triumphal procession. 7. *A. Trajani*, in the forum of this emperor, at the point where you enter it from the forum of Augustus. 8. *A. Veri*, on the Via Appia, erected to the honour of Verus after his victory over the Parthians. 9. *A. Marci Aurelii*, in the 7th Regio, probably erected to commemorate the victory of this emperor over the Marcomanni. It existed under different names near the Piazzo Fiano down to 1662, when it was broken up by order of Alexander VII. 10. *A. Septimii Severi*, in the forum at the end of the Via Sacra and the Clivus Capitolinus before the temple of Concordia, and still extant near the church of SS. Sergio e Bacco, was erected by the senate, A. D. 203, in honour of Septimius Severus and his 2 sons, Caracalla and Geta, on account of his victories over the Parthians and Arabians. 11. *A. Gordiani*, on the Esquiline. 12. *A. Gallieni*, erected to the honour of Gallienus by a private individual, M. Aurelius Victor, also on the Esquiline, S. E. of the Porta Esquilina. It is still extant near the church of S. Vito. 12. *A. Diocletiani*, probably identical with the *A. Novus*, in the 7th Regio. 13. *A. Constantini*, at the entrance to the valley between the Palatine and the Coelius, is still extant. It was erected by the senate in honour of Constantine after his victory over Maxentius, A. D. 312. It is profusely ornamented, and many of the bas-reliefs which adorn it were taken from one of the arches erected in the time of Trajan. 13. *A. Theodosiani, Gratiani et Valentiniani*, opposite the Pons Aelius and the Moles Hadriani. — **XII. Curiae** or **Senate-Houses**. 1. *Curia Hostilia*, frequently called *Curia* simply, was built by Tullus Hostilius, and was used as the ordinary place of assembly for the senate down to the time of Julius Caesar. It stood in the Forum on the N. side of the Comitium. It was burnt to the ground in the riots which followed the death of Clodius, B. C. 52. It was however soon rebuilt, the direction of the work being entrusted to Faustus, the son of the dictator Sulla; but scarcely had it been finished, when the senate, at the suggestion of Caesar, decreed that it should be destroyed, and a temple of Fortune erected on its site, while a new Curia should be erected, which should bear the name of Julia. (See below.) 2.

C. Pompeia or *Pompeii*, attached to the Portico of Pompey in the Campus Martius. It was in this Curia that Caesar was assassinated on the Ides of March. 3. *C. Julia*, the decree for the erection of which has been mentioned above, was finished and consecrated by Augustus. It did not stand on the site of the Curia Hostilia, as many modern writers have supposed, but at the S.W. angle of the Comitium, between the temple of Vesta and that of Castor and Pollux. 4. *C. Pompiliana*, built by Domitian and restored by Diocletian, was the usual place of the senate's meeting from the time of Domitian. It was situated alongside of the temple of Janus, which was said to have been built by Numa Pompilius, whence this curia was called Pompiliana. — **XII. Prisons.** There were 2 public prisons (*carceres*) in Rome. The more ancient one, called *Carcer Mamertinus* (a name however which does not occur in any ancient author), was built by Ancus Martius on the slope of the Capitoline overhanging the Forum. It was enlarged by Servius Tullius, who added to it a dismal subterranean dungeon, called from him *Tullianum*, where the conspirators of Catiline were put to death. This dungeon was 12 feet under ground, walled on each side, and arched over with stone-work. It is still extant, and serves as a subterranean chapel to a small church built on the spot called S. Pietro in Carcere. Near this prison were the *Scalae Gemoniae* or steps, down which the bodies of those who had been executed were thrown into the Forum, to be exposed to the gaze of the Roman populace. The other state prison was called *Lautumiae*, and was probably situated towards the N. side of the Forum, near the Curia Hostilia and Basilica Porcia. Some writers however suppose Lautumiae to be only another name of the Carcer Mamertinus. — **XIII. Castra** or **Barracks.** 1. *Castra Praetoria*, in the N.E. corner of the city on the slope of the Quirinal and Viminal, and beyond the Thermae of Diocletian, were built by the emperor Tiberius in the form of a Roman camp. Here the Praetorian troops or imperial guards were always quartered. 2. *Castra Peregrina*, on the Caelius, probably built by Septimius Severus for the use of the foreign troops, who might serve as a counterpoise against the Praetorians. — **XIV. Aqueducts.** The Aqueducts (*Aquaeductus*) supplied Rome with an abundance of pure water from the hills which surround the Campagna. The Romans at first had recourse to the Tiber and to wells sunk in the city. It was not till B. C. 313 that the first aqueduct was constructed, but their number was gradually increased till they amounted to 14 in the time of Procopius, that is, the 6th century of the Christian era. 1. *Aqua Appia*, was begun by the censor Appius Claudius Caecus in B. C. 313. Its sources were near the Via Praenestina, between the 7th and 8th milestones, and its termination was at the Salinae by the Porta Trigemina. Its length was 11,190 passus; for 11,130 of which it was carried under the earth, and for the remaining 60 passus, within the city, from the Porta Capena to the Porta Trigemina, it was on arches. No traces of it remain. 2. *Anio Vetus*, commenced B. C. 273, by the censor M'. Curius Dentatus, and finished by M. Fulvius Flaccus. The water was derived from the river Anio, above Tibur, at a distance of 20 Roman miles from the city; but, on account of its windings its actual length was 43 miles, of which length

Arch of Sept'mius Severus. Page 654. Arches, No. 10.

Arch of Constantine. Page 651. Arches, No. 13.

Arch of Drusus. Page 651. Arches, No. 2.

Arch of Titus restored. Page 654. Arches, No. 6.

Arch of Aurelius. Page 664. Arches, No. 9.

[To face p. 654.

The Septizonium. Page 656, col. 1.

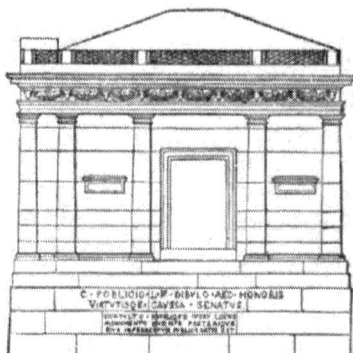

Tomb of Caius Bibulus.

Mausoleum of Hadrian restored. Page 656, col. 2.

Tomb of Caecilia Metella. Page 656, col. 2.

less than a quarter of a mile only (viz. 221 passus) was above the ground. There are considerable remains of this aqueduct on the Aurelian wall, near the Porta Maggiore, and also in the neighbourhood of Tivoli. 3. *Aqua Marcia*, which brought the coldest and most wholesome water to Rome, was built by the praetor Q. Marcius Rex, by command of the senate, in B. C. 144. It commenced at the side of the Via Valeria, 36 miles from Rome; its length was 61,710½ passus, of which only 7463 were above ground; namely, 528 on solid substructions, and 6935 on arches. It was high enough to supply water to the summit of the Capitoline mount. It was repaired by Agrippa in his aedileship, B. C. 33 (see below No. 5), and the volume of its water was increased by Augustus, by means of the water of a spring 800 passus from it: the short aqueduct which conveyed this water was called *Aqua Augusta*, but is never enumerated as a distinct aqueduct. Several arches of the Aqua Marcia are still standing. 4. *Aqua Tepula*, which was built by the censors Cn. Servilius Caepio and L. Cassius Longinus in B. C. 127, began in a spot in the Lucullan or Tusculan land, 2 miles to the right of the 10th milestone on the Via Latina. It was afterwards connected with, — 5. *Aqua Julia*. Among the splendid public works executed by Agrippa in his aedileship, B. C. 33, was the formation of a new aqueduct, and the restoration of all the old ones. From a source 2 miles to the right of the 12th milestone of the Via Latina, he constructed his aqueduct (the *Aqua Julia*) first to the Aqua Tepula, in which it was merged as far as the reservoir (*piscina*) on the Via Latina, 7 miles from Rome. From the reservoir, the water was carried along 2 distinct channels, on the same substructions (which were probably the original substructions of the Aqua Tepula newly restored), the lower channel being called the *Aqua Tepula*, and the upper the *Aqua Julia*; and this double aqueduct again was united with the *Aqua Marcia*, over the watercourse of which the other two were carried. The monument erected at the junction of these 3 aqueducts is still to be seen close to the Porta S. Lorenzo. It bears an inscription referring to the repairs under Caracalla. The whole course of the Aqua Julia, from its source, amounted to 15,426 passus, partly on massive substructions and partly on arches. 6. *Aqua Virgo*, built by Agrippa to supply his baths. Its water was as highly esteemed for bathing as that of the Aqua Marcia was for drinking. It commenced by the 8th milestone on the Via Collatina, and was conducted by a very circuitous route, chiefly under the ground, to the M. Pincius, whence it was carried on arches to the Campus Martius: its length was 14,105 passus, of which 12,865 were under ground. 7. *Aqua Alsietina*, sometimes called also *Aqua Augusta*, on the other side of the Tiber, was constructed by Augustus from the Lacus Alsietinus (Lago di Martignano) which lay 6500 passus to the right of the 14th milestone, on the Via Claudia, and was brought to the part of the Regio Transtiberina below the Janiculum. Its length was 22,172 passus, of which only 358 were on arches; and its water was so bad that it could only have been intended for the supply of Augustus's Naumachia, and for watering gardens. 8, 9. *Aqua Claudia* and *Anio Novus* (or *Aqua Aniena Nova*), the 2 most magnificent of all the aqueducts, both commenced by Caligula in A. D. 36, and finished by Claudius in A. D. 50. The *Aqua Claudia* com-

menced near the 38th milestone on the Via Sublacensis. Its water was reckoned the best after the Marcia. Its length was 46,406 passus (nearly 45½ miles) of which 9567 were on arches. The *Anio Novus* began at the 42nd milestone on the Via Sublacensis. Its length was 58,700 passus (nearly 59 miles) and some of its arches were 109 feet high. In the neighbourhood of the city, these two aqueducts were united, forming two channels on the same arches, the Claudia below and the Anio Novus above. An interesting monument connected with these aqueducts is the gate now called Porta Maggiore, which was originally a magnificent double arch, by means of which the aqueduct was carried over the Via Labicana and the Via Praenestina. Over the double arch are three inscriptions, which record the names of Claudius as the builder, and of Vespasian and Titus as the restorers of the aqueduct. By the side of this arch the aqueduct passes along the wall of Aurelian for some distance, and then it is continued upon the Arcus Neroniani or Caelimontani, which were added by Nero to the original structure, and which terminated at the temple of Claudius, which was also built by Nero, on the Caelius, where the water was probably conveyed to a castellum already built for the Aqua Julia, and for a branch of the Aqua Marcia, which had been at some previous time continued to the Caelius. 10. *Aqua Crabra*, which had its source near that of the Julia, and which was originally carried right through the Circus Maximus; but the water was so bad, that Agrippa would not bring it into the Júlia, but abandoned it to the people of the Tusculan land. Hence it was called *Aqua Damnata*. At a later period, part of the water was brought into the Aqua Julia. Considerable traces of it remain. 11. *Aqua Trajana*, was brought by Trajan from the Lacus Sabatinus (now Bracciano) to supply the Janiculus and the Regio Transtiberina. 12. *Aqua Alexandrina*, constructed by Alexander Severus; its source was in the lands of Tusculum, about 14 miles from Rome, between Gabii and the lake Regillus. Its small height shows that it was intended for the baths of Severus, which were in one of the valleys of Rome. 13. *Aqua Septimiana*, built by Septimius Severus, was perhaps only a branch of the Aqua Julia, formed by the emperor to bring water to his baths. 14. *Aqua Algentia* had its source at M. Algidus by the Via Tusculana. Its builder is unknown. Three of these aqueducts still supply the modern city of Rome with water. (1) The *Acqua Vergine*, the ancient *Aqua Virgo*, which was restored by Pope Pius IV. and further embellished by Benedict XIV. and Clement XIII. The chief portion of its waters gush out through the beautiful Fontana di Trevi, but it also supplies 12 other public fountains and the greater part of the lower city. (2) The *Acqua Felice*, named after the conventual name of its restorer Sixtus V. (Fra Felice), is, probably, a part of the ancient *Aqua Claudia*, though some take it for the *Alexandrina*. It supplies 27 public fountains and the eastern part of the city. (3) The *Acqua Paola*, the ancient Alsietina, supplies the Transtevere and the Vatican, and feeds, among others, the splendid fountains before St. Peter's. — XV. *Sewers.* Of these the most celebrated was the *Cloaca Maxima*, constructed by Tarquinius Priscus, which was formed to carry off the waters brought down from the adjacent hills into the Velabrum and valley of the Forum. It empties itself into the Tiber nearly opposite one extremity of the Tusula Tiberina. This cloaca was formed by 3 arches, one within the other, the innermost of which is a semicircular vault about 14 feet in diameter. It is still extant in its original state, with not a stone displaced.— **XVI. Palaces.** 1. *Palatium*, or the imperial palace, was situated on the N.E. side of the Palatine between the arch of Titus and the sanctuary of Vesta ; its front was turned towards the Forum, and the approach to it was from the Via Sacra close by the arch of Titus. It was originally the house of the orator Hortensius, and was enlarged by Augustus, who made it the imperial residence. A part of the Palatium was called *Domus Tiberiana*, which was originally a separate house of Tiberius on the Palatine, and was afterwards united to the palace of Augustus. It was on the side of the hill turned towards the Circus and the Velabrum, and is sometimes called *Postica Pars Palatii.* It was through this part of the palace that the emperor Otho fled into the Velabrum. We read of the Domus Tiberiana even after the imperial palace had been burnt to the ground in the reign of Nero; whence it follows that when the palace was rebuilt a portion of it still continued to bear this name. The Palatium was considerably enlarged by Caligula ; but it did not satisfy Nero's love of pomp and splendour. Nero built 2 magnificent palaces which must be distinguished from one another. The first, called the *Domus Transitoria Neronis*, covered the whole of the Palatine, and extended as far as the Esquiline to the gardens of Maecenas. This palace was burnt to the ground in the great fire of Rome, whereupon Nero commenced a new palace known by the name of *Domus Aurea*, which embraced the whole of the Palatine, the Velia, the valley of the Colosseum and the heights of the Thermae of Titus, extended near the Esquiline gate, and was cut through not only by the Via Sacra but also by other streets. The whole building however was not finished at the time of Nero's death ; and Vespasian confined the imperial palace to the Palatine, converting the other parts of the Domus Aurea into public or private buildings. The palace itself was not finished till the time of Domitian, who adorned it with numerous works of art. The emperor Septimius Severus added on the S. side of the Palatine a building called the Septizonium, which was probably intended as an Atrium. There were considerable remains of this Septizonium down to the end of the 16th century, when Sixtus V. caused them to be destroyed, and the pillars brought to the Vatican. Among the numerous private palaces at Rome the following were some of the most important. 2. *Domus Ciceronis*, close to the Porticus Catuli, probably on the N.E. edge of the Palatine, was built by M. Livius Drusus, and purchased by Cicero of one of the Crassi. It was destroyed by Claudius after the banishment of Cicero, but was subsequently rebuilt at the public expense. 3. *D. Pompeii*, the palace of Pompey was situated in the Carinae near the temple of Tellus. It was afterwards the residence of M. Antonius. 4. *D. Crassi*, the palace of L. Crassus the orator, on the Palatine. 5. *D. Scauri* also on the Palatine, celebrated for its magnificence, subsequently belonged to Clodius. 6. *D. Lateranorum*, on the E. confines of the Caelius, was a palace originally belonging to the distinguished family of the Plautii Laterani ; but after the execution of Plautius Lateranus under Nero,

it became imperial property. It was given by Septimius Severus to his friend Lateranus, and was subsequently the palace of Constantine, who adorned it with great magnificence. The modern palace of the Lateran occupies its site.—**XVII. Horti.** The Horti were parks or gardens, which were laid out by wealthy Roman nobles, on the hills around the city, and were adorned with beautiful buildings and works of art. 1. *Horti Luculliani*, on M. Pincius, which hill was hence called Collis Hortorum. They were laid out by Lucullus the conqueror of Mithridates. In the reign of Claudius they belonged to Valerius Asiaticus, who was put to death through the influence of Messalina, chiefly because she coveted the possession of these gardens. From this time they appear to have belonged to the imperial house. 2. *H. Sallustiani*, laid out by the historian Sallust, on his return from Numidia, in the valley between the Quirinal and the Pincius. 3. *H. Caesaris*, bequeathed by Julius Caesar to the people, were situated on the right bank of the Tiber at the foot of the Janiculus, probably on the spot where Augustus afterwards constructed his great Naumachia. 4. *H. Maecenatis*, in the Campus Esquilinus, bequeathed by Maecenas to Augustus and frequently used by the imperial family. 5. *H. Agrippinae*, on the right bank of the Tiber, in which Caligula built his Circus. It was here that Nero burnt the Christians to serve as lights for his nocturnal games, after previously wrapping them up in pitch. 6. *H. Domitiae*, also on the right bank of the Tiber, in which Hadrian built his Mausoleum. 7. *H. Pallantiani*, on the Esquiline, laid out by Pallas, the powerful freedman of Claudius. 8. *H. Getae*, on the other side of the Tiber, laid out by Septimius Severus.—**XVIII. Sepulchral Monuments.** 1. *Mausoleum Augusti*, was situated in the Campus Martius and was built by Augustus as the burial-place of the imperial family. It was surrounded with an extensive garden or park, and was considered one of the most magnificent buildings of his reign ; but there are only some insignificant ruins of it still extant. 2. *Mausoleum Hadriani*, was commenced by Hadrian in the gardens of Domitia on the right bank of the Tiber, and was connected with the city by the Pons Aelius ; it was finished and dedicated by Antoninus Pius, A. D. 140. Here were buried Hadrian, Antoninus Pius, L. Verus, Commodus, and probably also Septimius Severus, Geta, and Caracalla. This building, stripped of its ornaments, still forms the fortress of modern Rome (the castle of S. Angelo). 3. *Mausoleum Helenae*, a round building on the Esquiline, of considerable extent, erected by Constantine as the sepulchre of his mother. Its remains, situated in the street on the right of the Porta Maggiore, are now called Torre Pignattara. 4. *Sepulcrum Scipionum*, the burial-place of the Scipios, was situated, left of the Via Appia, near the Porta Capena. Most of the tombs of the distinguished Roman families during the Republican period lay on the Via Appia. The tomb of the Scipios was discovered in 1780, about 400 paces within the modern Porta S. Sebastiano. It contained many interesting monuments and inscriptions, which are now deposited in the Museo Pio-Clementino. 5. *Sepulcrum Caeciliae Metellae*, erected to the memory of Caecilia Metella, the daughter of Metellus Creticus, not far from the Circus Maxentii. This imposing monument is still extant and known

Column of Trajan.
Page 657. Columns, No. 3.

Antonine Column. (Column of M. Aurelius.)
Page 657. Columns, No. 5.

DIVO MARCO AVG
ANTONINO

Pons Sublicius, restored by Canina. Page 649. Bridges, No. 7.

[To face p. 656.

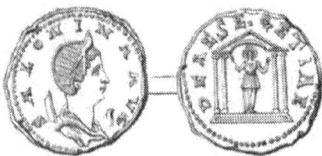

Salonina, wife of Gallienus, and mother of Saloninus.
Page 664.

Saloninus, Roman Caesar, A.D. 259. Page 668.

Seleucus I. Nicator, King of Syria, B.C. 312—280. Page 693.

Seleucus II. Callinicus, King of Syria, B.C. 246—7.6.
Page 693.

Seleucus III. Ceraunus, King of Syria, B.C. 226—213.
Page 694.

Seleucus IV. Philopator, King of Syria, B.C. 187—175.
Page 694.

To face p. 657.]

Seleucus VI. Epiphane, B.C. 15—93. Page 694.

Alexander Severus, Roman Emperor, A.D. 222—235.
Page 701.

Flavius Valerius Severus, Roman Emperor, A.D. 306—307.
Page 701.

Libius Severus, Roman Emperor, A.D. 461—465. Page 602.

Septimius Severus, Roman Emperor, A.D. 193—211.
Page 707.

Soemis or Sosemias, mother of Elagabalus, ob. A.D. 222.
Page 715.

by the name of Capo di Bove. 6. *Sepulcrum Cestii*, situated S. of the Aventine, near the Porta Ostiensis, being partly within and partly without the walls of Aurelian. This monument, which is still extant, is in the form of a pyramid, and was built in the time of Augustus for a certain C. Cestius. 7. *Sepulcrum Septimii Severi*, on the Via Appia, built by Septimius Severus in his lifetime, after the model of his Septizonium. [See above, XVI., No. 1.].—**XIX. Columns.** Columns (*Columnae*) were frequently erected at Rome to commemorate persons and events. 1. *Columna Maenia*, near the end of the Forum, towards the Capitol, was erected to the honour of the consul C. Maenius, who conquered the Latins and took the town of Antium, B. C. 338. 2. *Col. Rostrata*, also in the Forum, erected in honour of the consul C. Duilius, to commemorate his victory over the Carthaginian fleet, B. C. 260. The name of Rostrata was given to it from its being adorned with the beaks of the conquered ships. The inscription upon this column, written in obsolete Latin, is still preserved. 3. *Col. Trajani* in the Forum, in which the ashes of the emperor Trajan were deposited. This column is still extant, and is one of the most interesting monuments of ancient Rome. It is, including the pedestal, 117 feet high. The top was originally crowned with the statue of the emperor; it is now surmounted by that of the apostle Peter. A spiral bas-relief is folded round the pillar, which represents the emperor's wars against Decebalus and the Dacians, and is one of the most valuable authorities for archaeological inquiries. 4. *Col. Antonini Pii*, erected in honour of Antoninus Pius after his death, consisted of a column of red granite on a pediment of white marble, and was situated in the Campus Martius, near the temple dedicated to this emperor. It stood at an earlier period not far from the Curia Innocenziana on Monte Citorio, in the garden of the Casa della Missione. At present the basis only is extant, and is preserved in the garden of the Vatican. 5. *Col. M. Aurelii Antonini*, generally called the Antonine Column, erected to the memory of the emperor M. Aurelius, also in the Campus Martius, and still extant. It is an imitation of the Column of Trajan, and contains bas-reliefs representing the wars of M. Aurelius against the Marcomanni.—**XX. Obelisks.** The Obelisks (*Obelisci*) at Rome were mostly works of Egyptian art, which were transported from Egypt to Rome in the time of the emperors. Augustus caused 2 obelisks to be brought to Rome, one of which was erected in the Circus and another in the Campus Martius. The former was restored in 1589, and is called at present the Flaminian Obelisk. Its whole height is about 116 feet, and without the base about 78 feet. The obelisk in the Campus Martius was set up by Augustus as a sun-dial. It stands at present on the Monte Citorio, where it was placed in 1792. Its whole height is about 110 feet, and without the base about 71 feet. Another obelisk was brought to Rome by Caligula, and placed on the Vatican in the Circus of Caligula. It stands at present in front of St. Peter's, where it was placed in 1586, and its whole height is about 132 feet, and without the base and modern ornaments at top about 83 feet. But the largest obelisk at Rome is that which was originally transported from Heliopolis to Alexandria by Constantine, and conveyed to Rome by his son Constantius,

who placed it in the Circus Maximus. Its present position is before the north portico of the Lateran church, where it was placed in 1588. Its whole height is about 149 feet, and without the base about 105 feet. There are 8 other obelisks at Rome, besides those mentioned above, but none of them are of historical importance. — **G. Roads leading out of Rome.** Of these the most important were: 1. *Via Latina*, the most ancient of the south roads, which issued at first from the Porta Capena, and after the time of Aurelian from the Porta Latina. It joined the Via Appia at Beneventum. 2. *Via Appia*, the Great South Road, also issued from the Porta Capena, and was the most celebrated of all the Roman roads. It was commenced by Appius Claudius, when censor, and was eventually carried to Brundusium. [APPIA VIA.] 3. *Via Ostiensis*, originally passed through the Porta Trigemina, afterwards through the Porta Ostiensis, and kept the left bank of the Tiber to Ostia. 4. *Via Portuensis*, issued from the same gate as the Via Ostiensis, and kept the right bank of the Tiber to Portus, the new harbour founded by Claudius, near Ostia. 5. *Via Labicana*, issued from the Porta Esquilina, and passing Labicum fell into the Via Latina at the station ad Bivium, 30 miles from Rome. 6. *Via Praenestina*, originally the *Via Gabina*, issued at first from the Porta Esquilina, and subsequently from the Porta Praenestina. Passing through Gabii and Praeneste, it joined the Via Latina just below Anagnia. 7. *Via Tiburtina*, issued originally from the Porta Esquilina, or from the Porta Viminalis, and subsequently from the Porta Tiburtina, and proceeded to Tibur, from which it was continued under the name of the Via Valeria, past Corfinium to Adria. 8. *Via Nomentana*, anciently *Ficulnensis*, ran from the Porta Collina, subsequently from the Porta Nomentana, across the Anio to Nomentum, and a little beyond fell into the Via Salaria at Eretrum. 9. *Via Salaria*, ran from the Porta Collina, subsequently from the Porta Salaria, past Fidenae to Reate and Asculum Picenum. At Castrum Truentinum it reached the coast, which it followed until it joined the Via Flaminia at Ancona. 10. *Via Flaminia*, the Great North Road, commenced in the censorship of C. Flaminius, issued from the Porta Flaminia, and proceeded past Ocriculum, Narnia and Pisaurum to Ariminum, from which town it was continued under the name of the Via Aemilia to Placentia and Aquileia. 11. *Via Aurelia*, the Great Coast Road, issued originally from the Porta Janiculensis. It reached the coast at Alsium, and followed the shore of the Lower Sea along Etruria and Liguria by Genoa, as far as Forum Julii in Gaul.

Romulêa, an ancient town of the Hirpini in Samnium, on the road from Beneventum to Tarentum, destroyed at an early period by the Romans.

Rômŭlus, the founder of the city of Rome, must not be regarded as a real personage. The stories about him are mythical, and represent the traditional belief of the Roman people respecting their origin. Romulus, which is only a lengthened form of Romus, is the Roman people represented as an individual. The common legend about Romulus ran as follows:—At Alba Longa there reigned a succession of kings, descended from Iulus, the son of Aeneas. One of the last of these kings left two sons, Numitor and Amulius. The latter, who was the younger, deprived Numitor of the kingdom, but allowed him to live in the enjoyment of his private fortune. Fearful, however, lest the heirs of Numitor might not submit so quietly to his usurpation, he caused his only son to be murdered, and made his daughter Silvia, or Rhea Silvia, one of the Vestal virgins. Silvia was violated by Mars, and in course of time gave birth to twins. Amulius doomed the guilty Vestal and her babes to be drowned in the river. In the Anio Silvia exchanged her earthly life for that of a goddess, and became the wife of the river god. The stream carried the cradle in which the children were lying into the Tiber, which had overflowed its banks far and wide. It was stranded at the foot of the Palatine, and overturned on the root of a wild fig-tree, which, under the name of the Ficus Rumi-nalis, was preserved and held sacred for many ages after. ' A she-wolf, which had come to drink of the stream, carried them into her den hard by, and suckled them; where they were discovered by Faustulus, the king's shepherd, who took the children to his own house, and gave them to the care of his wife, Acca Larentia. They were called Romulus and Remus, and were brought up with the other shepherds on the Palatine hill. As they grew up, they became distinguished by the beauty of their person and the bravery of their deeds, and fought boldly against wild beasts and robbers. A quarrel having arisen between these shepherds and the herdsmen of Numitor, who stalled their cattle on the neighbouring hill of the Aventine, Remus was taken by a stratagem, during the absence of his brother, and carried off to Numi-tor. This led to the discovery of the parentage both of Romulus and Remus, who now slew Amu-lius, and placed their grandfather Numitor on the throne.—Romulus and Remus loved their old abode, and therefore left Alba to found a city on the banks of the Tiber. A strife arose between the brothers where the city should be built, and after whose name it should be called. Romulus wished to build it on the Palatine, Remus on the Aven-tine. It was agreed that the question should be decided by augury; and each took his station on the top of his chosen hill. The night passed away, and as the day was dawning Remus saw 6 vultures; but at sun-rise, when these tidings were brought to Romulus, 12 vultures flew by him. Each claimed the augury in his own favour; but the shepherds decided for Romulus, and Remus was obliged to yield. Romulus now proceeded to mark out the *pomoerium* of his city (see *Dict. of Antiq. s. v.*), and to raise the wall. Remus, who still resented the wrong he had suffered, leapt over the wall in scorn, whereupon he was slain by his brother. As soon as the city was built, Romulus found his people too few in numbers. He therefore set apart, on the Capitoline hill, an asylum, or a sanctuary, in which homicides and runaway slaves might take refuge. The city thus became filled with men, but they wanted women. Romulus, therefore, tried to form treaties with the neighbouring tribes, in order to obtain *connubium*, or the right of legal marriage with their citizens; but his offers were treated with disdain, and he accordingly resolved to obtain by force what he could not gain by en-treaty. In the fourth month after the foundation of the city, he proclaimed that games were to be celebrated in honour of the god Consus, and invited his neighbours, the Latins and Sabines, to the

festival. Suspecting no treachery, they came in numbers, with their wives and children. But the Roman youths rushed upon their guests, and car-ried off the virgins. The parents of the virgins returned home and prepared for vengeance. The inhabitants of 3 of the Latin towns, Caenina, An-temnae, and Crustumerium, took up arms one after the other, and were successively defeated by the Romans. Romulus slew with his own hand Acron, king of Caenina, and dedicated his arms and armour, as spolia opima, to Jupiter At last the Sabine king, Titus Tatius, advanced with a powerful army against Rome. The fortress of the Saturnian, afterwards called the Capitoline hill, was surrendered to the Sabines, by the treachery of Tarpeia, the daughter of the commander of the fortress. [TARPEIA.] On the next day the Romans endeavoured to recover the hill; and a long and desperate battle was fought in the valley between the Palatine and the Capitoline. At length, when both parties were exhausted with the struggle, the Sabine women rushed in between them, and prayed their husbands and fathers to be reconciled. Their prayer was heard; the two people not only made peace, but agreed to form only one nation. The Romans continued to dwell on the Palatine under their king Romulus; the Sabines built a new town on the Capitoline and Quirinal hills, where they lived under their king Titus Tatius. The two kings and their senates met for deliberation in the valley between the Palatine and Capitoline hills, which was hence called *comi-tium*, or the place of meeting. But this union did not last long. Titus Tatius was slain at a festival at Lavinium by some Laurentines, to whom he had refused satisfaction for outrages which had been committed by his kinsmen. Henceforward Romu-lus ruled alone over both Romans and Sabines. After reigning 37 years, he was at length taken away from the world. One day as he was review-ing his people in the Campus Martius, near the Goat's Pool, the sun was suddenly eclipsed, dark-ness overspread the earth, and a dreadful storm dispersed the people. When daylight had re-turned Romulus had disappeared, for his father Mars had carried him up to heaven in a fiery chariot. (*Quirinus Martis equis Acheronta fugit.* Hor. *Carm.* iii. 3.) Shortly afterwards he ap-peared in more than mortal beauty to Proculus Julius, and bade him tell the Romans to worship him as their guardian god under the name of Quirinus. Such was the glorified end of Romulus in the genuine legend. But as it staggered the faith of a later age, a tale was invented to account for his mysterious disappearance. It was related that the senators, discontented with the tyrannical rule of their king, murdered him during the gloom of a tempest, cut up his body, and car-ried home the mangled pieces under their robes. — As Romulus was regarded as the founder of Rome, its most ancient political institutions and the organisation of the people were ascribed to him. Thus he is said to have divided the people into 3 tribes, which bore the names Ram-nes, Tities, and Luceres. The Ramnes were sup-posed to have derived their name from Romu-lus, the Tities from Titus Tatius the Sabine king, and the Luceres from Lucumo, an Etruscan chief who had assisted Romulus in the war against the Sabines. Each tribe contained 10 curiae, which received their names from the 30 Sabine women who had brought about the peace between the Romans and their own people. Further, each curia contained 10 gentes, and each gens 100 men. Thus the people, according to the general belief, were divided originally into 3 tribes, 30 curiae, and 300 gentes, which mustered 3000 men, who fought on foot, and were called a legion. Besides those there were 300 horsemen, called Celeres, the same body as the Equites of a later time. To assist him in the government of the people Romulus is said to have selected a number of the aged men in the state, who were called Patres, or Senatores. The council itself, which was called the senatus, originally consisted of 100 members; but this number was increased to 200 when the Sabines were incorporated in the state. In addition to the senate, there was another assembly, consisting of the members of the gentes, which bore the name of comitia curiata, because they voted in it according to their division into curiae.

Rŏmŭlus Augustŭlus. [AUGUSTULUS.]
Rŏmŭlus Silvius. [SILVIUS.]
Rosciānum (*Rossano*), a fortress on the E. coast of Bruttium between Thurii and Paternum.
Roscillus [AEGUS.]
Roscius. 1. L., a Roman ambassador sent to Fidenae in B. C. 438. He and his three colleagues were killed by the inhabitants of Fidenae, at the instigation of Lar Tolumnius, king of the Veientes. The statues of all four were erected in the Rostra at Rome. — 2. **Sex.**, of Ameria, a town in Umbria. The father of this Roscius had been murdered at the instigation of 2 of his relations and fellow-townsmen, T. Roscius Magnus and T. Roscius Capito, who coveted the wealth of their neighbour. These two Roscii struck a bargain with Chrysogonus, the freedman and favourite of Sulla, to divide the property of the murdered man between them. But as the proceeding excited the utmost indignation at Ameria, and the magistrates of the town made an effort to obtain from Sulla the restitution of the property to the son, the robbers accused young Roscius of the murder of his father, and hired witnesses to swear to the fact. Roscius was defended by Cicero (B. C. 80) in an oration which is still extant, and was acquitted. Cicero's speech was greatly admired at the time, and though at a later period he found fault with it himself, as bearing marks of youthful exaggeration, it displays abundant evidence of his great oratorical powers. — 3. **Q.**, the most celebrated comic actor at Rome, was a native of Solonium, a small place in the neighbourhood of Lanuvium. His histrionic powers procured him the favour of many of the Roman nobles, and, among others, of the dictator Sulla, who presented him with a gold ring, the symbol of equestrian rank. Roscius enjoyed the friendship of Cicero, who constantly speaks of him in terms both of admiration and affection. Roscius was considered by the Romans to have reached such perfection in his own profession, that it became the fashion to call every one who became particularly distinguished in his own art, by the name of Roscius. In his younger years Cicero received instruction from Roscius; and at a later time he and Roscius often used to try which of them could express a thought with the greatest effect, the orator by his eloquence, or the actor by his gestures. These exercises gave Roscius so high an opinion of his art, that he wrote a work in which he compared eloquence and acting. Like

his celebrated contemporary, the tragic actor Aesopus, Roscius realized an immense fortune by his profession. He died in 62. — One of Cicero's extant orations is entitled *Pro Q. Roscio Comoedo.* It was delivered before the judex C. Piso, probably in 68, and relates to a claim for 50,000 sesterces, which one C. Fannius Chaerea brought against Roscius. — 4. **Fabātus.** [FABATUS.] — 5. **Otho.** [OTHO.]
Rotomāgus. [RATOMAGUS.]
Roxāna ('Ρωξάνη), daughter of Oxyartes the Bactrian, fell into the hands of Alexander on his capture of the hill-fort in Sogdiana, named "the rock," B. C. 327. Alexander was so captivated by her charms, that he married her. Soon after Alexander's death (323), she gave birth to a son (Alexander Aegus), who was admitted to share the nominal sovereignty with Arrhidaeus, under the regency of Perdiccas. Before the birth of the boy she had drawn Statira, or Barsine, to Babylon by a friendly letter, and there caused her to be murdered. Roxana afterwards crossed over to Europe with her son, and placed herself under the protection of Olympias. She shared the fortunes of Olympias, and threw herself into Pydna along with the latter, where they were besieged by Cassander. In 316 Pydna was taken by Cassander; Olympias was put to death; and Roxana and her son were placed in confinement in Amphipolis. Here they were detained under the charge of Glaucias till 311, in which year, soon after the general peace then concluded, they were murdered in accordance with orders from Cassander.
Roxolāni. [RHOXOLANI]
Rŭbi (Rubustinus: *Ruvo*), a town in Apulia on the road from Canusium to Brundusium.
Rŭbicŏ, a small river in Italy, falling into the Adriatic a little N. of Ariminum, formed the boundary in the republican period between the province of Gallia Cisalpina and Italia proper. It is celebrated in history on account of Caesar's passage across it at the head of his army, by which act he declared war against the republic. A papal decree, issued in 1756, declared the modern *Lusa* to be the ancient Rubico, but the *Pisatello*, a little further N., has better claims to this honour.
Rubra Saxa, called Rubrae breves (sc. petrae) by Martial, a small place in Etruria only a few miles from Rome, near the river Cremera, and on the Via Flaminia. It was near this spot that the great battle was fought, in which Maxentius was defeated by Constantine, A. D. 312.
Rubrēsus Lacus. [NARBO.]
Rubricātus. 1. Or **Ubus** (*Seibous*), a considerable river of Numidia in N. Africa, rising in the mountains S. E. of Cirta (*Constantineh*), flowing N. E., and falling into the Mediterranean E. of Hippo Regius (*Bonah*). — 2. (*Llobregat*), a small river of Hispania Tarraconensis, flowing into the sea W. of Barcino.
Rubrum Mare. [ERYTHRAEUM MARE.]
Rŭdiae (Rudinus: *Rotigliano* or *Ruge*), a town of the Peucetii in Apulia, on the road from Brundusium to Venusia, was originally a Greek colony, and afterwards a Roman municipium. Rudiae is celebrated as the birth-place of Ennius.
Ruesium, a town of the Vellavi or Velauni, hence called simply Civitas Vellavorum, in Gallia Aquitanica (in the modern *Velay*), probably the modern *St. Paulien* or *Paulhan* on the frontiers of Auvergne.

Rufīnus. 1. P. Cornēlius Rufīnus, was consul B. C. 290, with M'. Curius Dentatus, and in conjunction with his colleague brought the Samnite war to a conclusion, and obtained a triumph in consequence. He was consul a second time in 277, and carried on the war against the Samnites and the Greeks in Southern Italy. The chief event of his second consulship was the capture of the important town of Croton. In 275, Rufinus was expelled from the senate by the censors C. Fabricius and Q. Aemilius Papus, on account of his possessing 10 pounds of silver plate. The dictator Sulla was descended from this Rufinus. His grandson was the first of the family who assumed the surname of Sulla. — 2. Licinīus Rufīnus, a jurist, who lived under Alexander Severus. There are in the Digest 17 excerpts from 12 books of *Regulae* by Rufinus. — 3. The chief minister of state under Theodosius the Great, was an able, but at the same time a treacherous and dangerous man. He instigated Theodosius to those cruel measures which brought ruin upon Antioch, A. D. 390. After the death of Theodosius in 395, Rufinus exercised paramount influence over the weak Arcadius; but towards the end of the year a conspiracy was formed against him by Eutropius and Stilicho, who induced Gainas, the Gothic ally of Arcadius, to join in the plot. Rufinus was in consequence slain by the troops of Gainas. — 4. Surnamed Tyrannius or Turranius, or Toranus, a celebrated ecclesiastical writer, was probably born about A. D. 345 in Italy. He was at first an inmate of the monastery at Aquileia, and he afterwards resided many years at a monastery in Palestine, where he became very intimate with St. Jerome. The two friends afterwards quarrelled; and Jerome attacked Rufinus with the utmost vehemence on account of his supporting the tenets of Origen. After remaining in the East for about 26 years, Rufinus returned to Italy in 397, where he published a Latin translation of the Apology for Origen by Pamphilus, and of the books of Origen *De Principiis*, together with an original tract *De Adulteratione Librorum Origenis*. In the preface to the *De Principiis*, he quoted a panegyric, which Jerome had at an earlier period pronounced upon Origen. This led to a bitter correspondence between the 2 former friends, which was crowned by the *Apologia* of the one *adversus Hieronymum*, and the *Apologia* of the other *adversus Rufinum*. Rufinus died in Sicily in 410, to which island he had fled upon the invasion of Italy by Alaric. Several of his works are extant, but there is no complete edition of them. — 5. The author of a little poem in 22 lines, *Pasiphaes Fabula ex omnibus Metris Horatianis*, which, as the name imports, contains an example of each of the different metres employed by Horace. His date is quite uncertain, but he may be the same person with the following. — 6. A grammarian of Antioch, whose treatise *De Metris Comicis*, or rather extracts from it, is contained in the *Grammaticae Latinae Auctores Antiqui* of Putschius, Hannov. 1605. — 7. The author of 38 epigrams in the Greek Anthology. His date is uncertain; but there can be no doubt that he was a Byzantine. His verses are of the same light amatory character as those of Agathias, Paulus, Macedonius, and others.

Rufrae, a town in Campania, frequently confounded with Rufrium.

Rufrium, a town of the Hirpini in Samnium.

Rūfus, Curtĭus. [Curtius.]

Rūfus Ephesĭus, so called from the place of his birth, a celebrated Greek physician, lived in the reign of Trajan (A. D. 98—117), and wrote several medical works, some of which are still extant.

Rūfus, L. Caecilĭus, brother of P. Sulla by the same mother, but not by the same father. He was tribune of the plebs, B. C. 63, when he rendered warm support to Cicero, and in particular opposed the agrarian law of Rullus. In his praetorship, 57, he joined most of the other magistrates in proposing the recall of Cicero from banishment.

Rūfus, M. Caelĭus, a young Roman noble, distinguished as an elegant writer and eloquent speaker, but equally conspicuous for his profligacy and extravagance. Notwithstanding his vices he lived on intimate terms with Cicero, who defended him in B. C. 56 in an oration still extant. The accusation was brought against him by Sempronius Atratinus, at the instigation of Clodia Quadrantaria, whom he had lately deserted. Clodia charged him with having borrowed money from her in order to murder Dion, the head of the embassy sent by Ptolemy Auletes to Rome; and with having made an attempt to poison her. In 52 Caelius was tribune of the plebs, and in 50 aedile. During the years 51 and 50 he carried on an active correspondence with Cicero, who was then in Cilicia, and many of the letters which he wrote to Cicero at that time are preserved in the collection of Cicero's Letters. On the breaking out of the civil war in 49 he espoused Caesar's side, and was rewarded for his services by the praetorship, in 48. Being at this time overwhelmed with debt, he availed himself of Caesar's absence from Italy to bring forward a law for the abolition of debts. He was, however, resisted by the other magistrates and deprived of his office; whereupon he went into the S. of Italy to join Milo, whom he had secretly sent for from Massilia. Milo was killed near Thurii before Caelius could join him [Milo]; and Caelius himself was put to death shortly afterwards at Thurii.

Rūfus, Sextus. [Sextus Rufus.]

Rūgĭi, an important people in Germany, originally dwelt on the coast of the Baltic between the Viadus (*Oder*) and the Vistula. After disappearing a long time from history, they are found at a later time in Attila's army; and after Attila's death they founded a new kingdom on the N. bank of the Danube in Austria and Hungary, the name of which is still preserved in the modern *Rugiland.* They have left traces of their name in the country which they originally inhabited in the modern *Rügen, Rügenwalde, Rega, Regenwalde.*

Rullus, P. Servilĭus, tribune of the plebs, B. C. 63, proposed an agrarian law, which Cicero attacked in 3 orations which have come down to us. It was the most extensive agrarian law that had ever been brought forward; but as it was impossible to carry such a sweeping measure, it was withdrawn by Rullus himself.

P. Rupilĭus, consul B. C. 132, prosecuted with the utmost vehemence all the adherents of Tib. Gracchus, who had been slain in the preceding year. In his consulship he was sent into Sicily against the slaves, and brought the servile war to a close. He remained in the island as proconsul in the following year; and, with 10 commissioners appointed by the senate, he made various regulations for the government of the province, which were known by the name of Leges Rupiliae. Rupilius was condemned in the tribunate of C. Gracchus, 123, on account of his illegal and cruel acts in the prosecution of the friends of Tib. Gracchus. He was an intimate friend of Scipio Africanus the younger, who obtained the consulship for him, but who failed in gaining the same honour for his brother Lucius. He is said to have taken his brother's failure so much to heart as to have died in consequence.

Ruscino, a town of the Sordones or Sordi in the S.E. part of Gallia Narbonensis, at the foot of the Pyrenees, on the river Ruscino (*Tet*), and on the road from Spain to Narbo. A tower of the ancient town is still extant near Perpignan, called *la Tour de Roussillon.*

Rusellae (Rusellanus: nr. *Grosseto* Ru.), one of the most ancient cities of Etruria, situated on an eminence E. of the lake Prelius and on the Via Aurelia. It is first mentioned in the time of Tarquinius Priscus. It was taken by the Romans in B. c. 294, when 2000 of its inhabitants were slain, and as many more made prisoners. It was subsequently a Roman colony, and continued in existence till 1138, when its inhabitants were removed to Grosseto. The walls of Rusellae still remain, and are some of the most ancient in Italy. They are formed of enormous masses of travertine, piled up without regard to form, with small stones inserted in the interstices. The masses vary from 6 to 8 feet in length, and from 4 to 8 in height. The area enclosed by the walls forms an irregular quadrangle, between 10,000 and 11,000 feet, or about 2 miles in circuit.

Rusicada (S. E. of *Storah* Ru.), a sea-port and Roman colony in Numidia, used especially as the port of Cirta.

Ruspinum, a town of Africa Propria (Byzacium), 2 miles from the sea, between Leptis Parva and Hadrumetur.

Russadir (*Ras-ud-Dir*, or *C. di Tres Forcas*: *Rus* in ancient Punic, and *Ras* in Arabic, alike mean *cape*), a promontory of Mauretania Tingitana, in N. Africa, on the coast of the Metagonitae. S. E. of it was a city of the same name (prob. *Melillah*).

Rusticus, Fabius, a Roman historian, and a contemporary of Claudius and Nero.

Rusticus, L. Junius Arulenus, more usually called Arulenus Rusticus, but sometimes Junius Rusticus. He was a friend and pupil of Paetus Thrasea, and an ardent admirer of the Stoic philosophy. He was put to death by Domitian, because he had written a panegyric upon Thrasea.

Rusucurrum (*Coleah*, opposite *Algier*), a considerable sea-port in the E. part of Mauretania Caesariensis, constituted a Roman colony under Claudius.

Ruteni, a people in Gallia Aquitanica on the frontiers of Gallia Narbonensis in the modern *Rovergne.* Their chief town was Segodunum, afterwards Civitas Rutenorum (*Rodez*). The country of the Ruteni contained silver mines, and produced excellent flax.

Rutilius Lupus. [LUPUS.]

Rutilius Numatianus, Claudius, a Roman poet, and a native of Gaul, lived at the beginning of the 5th century of the Christian aera. He resided at Rome a considerable time, where he attained the dignity of praefectus urbi, about A. D. 413 or 414. He afterwards returned to his native country, and has described his return to Gaul in an elegiac poem, which bears the title of *Itinerarium*, or *De Reditu.* Of this poem the first book, consisting of 644 lines, and a small portion of the second, have come down to us. It is superior both in poetical colouring and purity of language to most of the productions of the age; and the passage in which he celebrates the praises of Rome is not unworthy of the pen of Claudian. Rutilius was a heathen, and attacks the Jews and monks with no small severity. The best edition is by A. W. Zumpt, Berlin, 1840.

P. Rutilius Rufus, a Roman statesman and orator. He was military tribune under Scipio in the Numantine war, praetor B. c. 111, consul 105, and legatus in 95 under Q. Mucius Scaevola, proconsul of Asia. While acting in this capacity he displayed so much honesty and firmness in repressing the extortions of the publicani, that he became an object of fear and hatred to the whole body. Accordingly, on his return to Rome, he was impeached of malversation (*de repetundis*), found guilty, and compelled to withdraw into banishment, 92. He retired first to Mytilene, and from thence to Smyrna, where he fixed his abode, and passed the remainder of his days in tranquillity, having refused to return to Rome, although recalled by Sulla. Besides his orations, Rutilius wrote an autobiography, and a History of Rome in Greek, which contained an account of the Numantine war, but we know not what period it embraced.

Rutilus, C. Marcius, was consul B. c. 357, when he took the town of Privernum. In 356 he was appointed dictator, being the first time that a plebeian had attained this dignity. In his dictatorship he defeated the Etruscans with great slaughter. In 352 he was consul a second time; and in 351, he was the first plebeian censor. He was consul for the third time in 344, for the fourth time in 342. The son of this Rutilus took the surname of Censorinus, which in the next generation entirely supplanted that of Rutilus, and became the name of the family. [CENSORINUS.]

Rutuba (*Roya*), a river on the coast of Liguria, which flows into the sea near Albium Intemelium.

Rutuli, an ancient people in Italy, inhabiting a narrow slip of country on the coast of Latium a little to the S. of the Tiber. Their chief town was Ardea. which was the residence of Turnus. They were subdued at an early period by the Romans, and disappear from history.

Rutupae or Rutupiae (*Richborough*), a port town of the Cantii in the S. E. of Britain, from which persons frequently crossed over to the harbour of Gessoriacum in Gaul. Excellent oysters were obtained in the neighbourhood of this place (*Rutupino edita fundo ostrea*, Juv. iv. 141). There are still several Roman remains at *Richborough.*

S.

Saba (Σάβα). 1. (O. T. Sheba), the capital of the SABAEI in Arabia Felix, lay on a high woody mountain, and was pointed out, by an Arabian tradition, as the residence of the "Queen of Sheba," who went to Jerusalem to hear the wisdom of Solomon. Its exact site is doubtful. — 2. There was another city of the same name in the interior of Arabia Felix, where a place *Sabea* is still found, about in the centre of *El-Yemen.*—3. A seaport town of Aethiopia, on the Red Sea, S. of Ptolemaïs Theron. A town called Σαβάτ and Σάββατα is mentioned by Ptolemy, who places it on the Sinus Adulitanus; and about in the same position Strabo mentions a town *Sabae* (Σάβαι) as distinct from Saba. The sites of these places (if they are really different) are sought by geographers at *Nowarat,* or *Port Mornington,* in the S.-part of the coast of *Nubia,* and *Massawah* on *Foul Bay,* on the N.E. coast of *Abyssinia.*

Sabacon (Σαβακῶν), a king of Ethiopia, who invaded Egypt in the reign of the blind king Anysis, whom he dethroned and drove into the marshes. The Ethiopian conqueror then reigned over Egypt for 50 years, but at length quitted the country in consequence of a dream, whereupon Anysis regained his kingdom. This is the account which Herodotus received from the priests (ii. 137—140); but it appears from Manetho, that there were 3 Ethiopian kings who reigned over Egypt, named *Sabacon, Sebichus,* and *Taracus,* whose collective reigns amount to 40 or 50 years, and who form the 25th dynasty of that writer. The account of Manetho is to be preferred to that of Herodotus. It appears that this Ethiopian dynasty reigned over Egypt in the latter half of the 8th century before the Christian era. They are mentioned in the Jewish records. The *So,* king of Egypt, with whom Hosea, king of Israel, made an alliance about B.C. 722 (2 Kings, xvii. 4), was probably the same as Sebichus; and the *Tirhakah,* king of the Ethiopians, who was preparing to make war against Sennacherib, in 711 (Is. xxxvii. 9), is the same as Taracus.

Sabaei or **Sabae** (Σαβαῖοι, Σάβαι: O.T. Shebaïïn), one of the chief peoples of Arabia, dwelt in the S.W. corner of the peninsula, in the most beautiful part of Arabia Felix, the N. and centre of the province of *El-Yemen.* So, at least, Ptolemy places them; but the earlier geographers give them a wider extent, quite to the S. of *El-Yemen.* The fact seems to be that they are the chief representatives of a race which, at an early period, was widely spread on both sides of the S. part of the Red Sea, where Arabia and Aethiopia all but joined at the narrow strait of *Bab-el-Mandeb;* and hence, probably, the confusion often made between the *Sheba* and *Seba* of Scripture, or between the *Shebaïm* of Arabia and the *Sebaïm* of Aethiopia. Another proof of the wide extent of this race is furnished by the mention, in the book of Job, of Sabeans as far N., probably, as Arabia Deserta (Job, i. 15). The Sabeans of *El-Yemen* were celebrated for their wealth and luxury. Their country produced all the most precious spices and perfumes of Arabia, and they carried on an extensive trade with the East. Their capital was at SABA, where we are told that their king was kept a close prisoner in his palace. The monarchy was not hereditary, but descended according to an order of succession arranged among the chief families of the country.

Sabate, a town of Etruria on the road from Cosa to Rome, and on the N.W. corner of a lake, which was named after it *Lacus Sabatinus* (*Lago di Bracciano*).

Sabatini, a people in Campania, who derived their name from the river Sabatus (*Sabbato*), a tributary of the *Calor,* which flows into the Vulturnus.

Sabazius (Σαβάζιος), a Phrygian divinity, commonly described as a son of Rhea or Cybele. In later times he was identified with the mystic Dionysus, who hence is sometimes called Dionysus Sabazius. For the same reason Sabazius is called a son of Zeus by Persephone, and is said to have been reared by a nymph Nyssa; though others, by philosophical speculations, were led to consider him a son of Cabiros, Dionysus, or Cronos. He was torn by the Titans into 7 pieces. The connection of Sabazius with the Phrygian mother of the gods accounts for the fact that he was identified, to a certain extent, with Zeus himself, who is mentioned as Zeus Sabazius, both Zeus and Dionysus having been brought up by Cybele or Rhea. His worship and festivals (*Sabazia*) were also introduced into Greece; but, at least in the time of Demosthenes, it was not thought reputable to take part in them, for they were celebrated at night by both sexes in a licentious manner. Serpents, which were sacred to him, acted a prominent part at the Sabazia and in the processions; the god himself was represented with horns, because, it is said, he was the first that yoked oxen to the plough for agriculture.

Sabelli. [SABINI.]

Sabellius, an heresiarch of the 3rd century, of whose personal history hardly anything is known. He broached his heresies in the Libyan Pentapolis, of which he appears to have been a native. His characteristic dogma related to the Divine Nature, in which he conceived that there was only one hypostasis or person, identifying with each other the Father, the Son, and the Spirit, "so that in one *hypostasis* there are three *designations*" (ὡς εἶναι ἐν μιᾷ ὑποστάσει τρεῖς ὀνομασίας).

Sabina, the wife of the emperor Hadrian, was the grand-niece of Trajan, being the daughter of Matidia, who was the daughter of Marciana, the sister of Trajan. Sabina was married to Hadrian about A.D. 100 through the influence of Plotina, the wife of Trajan. The marriage did not prove a happy one. Sabina at length put an end to her life, and there was a report that she had even been poisoned by her husband. She was certainly alive in 136, and probably did not die till 138, a few months before Hadrian. She was enrolled among the gods after her decease.

Sabina, Poppaea, a woman of surpassing beauty, but licentious morals, was the daughter of T. Ollius, but assumed the name of her maternal grandfather Poppaeus Sabinus, who had been consul in A.D. 9. She was first married to Rufius Crispinus, and afterwards to Otho, who was one of the boon companions of Nero. The latter soon became enamoured of her; and in order to get Otho out of the way Nero sent him to govern the province of Lusitania (58). Poppaea now became the acknowledged mistress of Nero, over whom she exercised absolute sway. Anxious to become the wife of the emperor, she persuaded Nero first to murder his mother Agrippina (59), who was opposed to such a disgraceful union, and next to divorce and shortly afterwards put to death his innocent and virtuous wife Octavia (62). Immediately after the divorce of Octavia, Poppaea became the wife of Nero. In the following year she gave birth to a daughter at Antium; but the infant died at the age of 4 months. In 65 Poppaea was pregnant again, but was killed by a kick trom her brutal husband in a fit of passion. She was enrolled among the gods, and a magnificent temple was dedicated to her by Nero. Poppaea was inordinately fond of luxury and pomp, and took immense pains to preserve the beauty of her person. Thus we are told that all her mules were shod with gold, and that 500 asses were daily milked to supply her with a bath.

Sabini, one of the most ancient and powerful of the peoples of central Italy. The ancients usually derived their name from Sabinus, a son of the native god Sancus. The different tribes of the Sabine race were widely spread over the whole of central Italy, and were connected with the Opicans, Umbrians, and those other peoples whose languages were akin to the Greek. The earliest traces of the Sabines are found in the neighbourhood of Amiternum at the foot of the main chain of the Apennines, whence they spread as far S. as the confines of Lucania and Apulia. The Sabines may be divided into 3 great classes, called by the names of Sabini, Sabelli, and Samnites respectively. The **Sabini** proper inhabited the country between the Nar, the Anio and the Tiber, between Latium, Etruria, Umbria and Picenum. This district was mountainous, and better adapted for pasturage than corn. The chief towns were Amiternum, Reate, Nursia, Cutiliae, Cures, Eretrum and Nomentum. The **Sabelli** were the smaller tribes who issued from the Sabines. To these belong the Vestini, Marsi, Marrucini, Peligni, Frentani and Hirpini. In addition to these peoples, to whom the name of Sabellians is usually restricted, the Picentes in Picenum, the Picentini, who were transplanted from the latter country to Campania, and the Lucani, were also of Sabine origin. The **Samnites**, who were by far the most powerful of all the Sabine peoples, are treated of in a separate article. [SAMNIUM.] There were certain national characteristics which distinguished the whole Sabine race. They were a people of simple and virtuous habits, faithful to their word, and imbued with deep religious feeling. Hence we find frequent mention of omens and prodigies in their country. They were a migratory race, and adopted a peculiar system of emigration. In times of great danger and distress they vowed a *Ver Sacrum*, or Sacred Spring; and all the children born in that spring were regarded as sacred to the god, and were compelled, at the end of 20 years, to leave their native country and seek a new home in foreign lands. The form of government among the Sabines was republican, but in war they chose a sovereign ruler (*Embratur*), whom the Romans sometimes call dictator, and sometimes king. With the exception of the Sabines in Lucania and Campania, they never attained any high degree of civilisation or mental culture; but they were always distinguished by their love of freedom, which they maintained with the greatest bravery. Of this the Samnites were the most striking example. After the decline of the Etruscan power, the Sabines were for a long time the greatest people in Italy; and if they had remained united, they might have conquered the whole peninsula. The Sabines formed one of the elements of which the Roman people was composed. In the time of Romulus, a portion of the Sabines, after the rape of their wives and daughters, became incorporated with the Romans, and the 2 peoples were united into one under the general name of Quirites. The remainder of the Sabini proper, who were less warlike than the Samnites and Sabellians, were finally subdued by M'. Curius Dentatus, B. C. 290, and received the Roman franchise, *sine suffragio*. The Sabellian tribes concluded a treaty with the Romans at an early period, namely, the Vestini in 328, and the Marsi, Marrucini, Peligni and Frentani in 304; but these peoples again took up arms against the Romans in the Social War (90—88), which ended in the complete subjugation of all the Sabellian tribes. The history of the wars between the Samnites and the Romans is given under SAMNIUM.

Sabinus. 1. A contemporary poet and a friend of Ovid. Ovid informs us that Sabinus had written answers to six of the *Epistolae Heroidum* of Ovid. Three answers enumerated by Ovid in this passage are printed in many editions of the poet's works as the genuine poems of Sabinus; but they were written by a modern scholar, Angelus Sabinus, about the year 1467. — **2. M. Caelius**, a Roman jurist, who succeeded Cassius Longinus, was consul A. D. 69. He was not the Sabinus from whom the Sabiniani took their name. He wrote a work, *Ad Edictum Aedilium Curulium*. There are no extracts from Caelius in the Digest, but he is often cited, sometimes as Caelius Sabinus, sometimes by the name of Sabinus only. — **3. C. Calvisius**, one of Caesar's legates in the civil war, B. C. 48. In 45 he received the province of Africa from Caesar. Having been elected praetor in 44, he obtained from Antony the province of Africa again; but he did not return to Africa, as the senate, after the departure of Antony for Mutina, conferred it upon Q. Cornificius. Sabinus was consul 39, and in the following year commanded the fleet of Octavian in the war with Sex. Pompey. He was superseded by Agrippa in the command of the fleet. He is mentioned too at a later time as one of the friends of Octavian. — **4. T. Flavius**, father of the emperor Vespasian, was one of the farmers of the taxes in Asia, and afterwards carried on business as a money-lender among the Helvetians. — **5. Flavius**, elder son of the preceding, and brother of the emperor Vespasian. He governed Moesia for 7 years during the reign of Claudius, and held the important office of praefectus urbis during the last 11 years of Nero's reign. He was removed from this office by Galba, but was replaced in it on the accession of Otho, who was anxious to conciliate Vespasian, who commanded the Roman legions in the East. He continued to retain the dignity under Vitellius; but when Vespasian was proclaimed general by the legions in the East, and Antonius Primus and his other generals in the West, after the defeat of the troops of Vitellius, were marching upon Rome, Vitellius, despairing of success, offered to surrender the empire, and to place the supreme power in the hands of Sabinus till the arrival of his brother. The German soldiers of Vitellius, however, refused submission to this arrangement, and resolved to support their sovereign by arms. Sabinus thereupon took refuge in the Capitol, where he was attacked by the Vitellian troops. In the assault the Capitol was burnt to the ground, Sabinus was taken prisoner, and put to death by the soldiers in the presence of Vitellius, who endeavoured in vain to save his life. Sabinus was a man of distinguished reputation, and of unspotted character. He left 2 sons, Flavius Sabinus, and Flavius

Clemens. [CLEMENS.] — 6. **Flavius**, son of the preceding, married Julia, the daughter of his cousin Titus. He was consul 82, with his cousin Domitian, but was afterwards slain by the latter. — 7. **Massurius**, a hearer of Ateius Capito, was a distinguished jurist in the time of Tiberius. This is the Sabinus from whom the school of the Sabiniani took its name. [CAPITO.] There is no direct excerpt from Sabinus in the Digest, but he is often cited by other jurists, who commented upon his *Libri tres Juris Civilis*. It is conjectured that Persius means to refer to this work (*Sat.* v. 90), when he says, " Excepto si quid Masuri rubrica vetavit." Massurius also wrote numerous other works, which are cited by name in the Digest. — 8. **Nymphidius**. [NYMPHIDIUS.] — 9. **Poppaeus**, consul A. D. 9, was appointed in the lifetime of Augustus governor of Moesia, and was not only confirmed in this government by Tiberius, but received from the latter the provinces of Achaia and Macedonia in addition. He continued to hold these provinces till his death in 35, having ruled over Moesia for 24 years. He was the maternal grandfather of Poppaea Sabina, the mistress, and afterwards the wife of Nero. — 10. **Q. Titurius**, one of Caesar's legates in Gaul, who perished along with L. Aurunculeius Cotta in the attack made upon them by Ambiorix in B. C. 54.

Sabis (*Sambre*) 1. A broad and deep river in Gallia Belgica and in the territory of the Ambiani, falling into the river Mosa. — 2. A small river on the coast of Carmania. — 3. See SAPIS.

Sabrata. [ABROTONUM.]

Sabrina, also called **Sabriāna** (*Severn*), a river in the W. of Britain, which flowed by Venta Silurum into the ocean.

Sacādas (Σακάδας), of Argos, an eminent Greek musician, was one of the masters who established at Sparta the second great school of music, of which Thaletas was the founder, as Terpander had been of the first. He gained the prize for flute-playing at the first of the musical contests which the Amphictyons established in connection with the Pythian games (B. C. 590), and also at the next two festivals in succession (586, 582). Sacadas was a composer of elegies, as well as a musician.

Sacae (Σάκαι), one of the most numerous and most powerful of the Scythian nomad tribes, had their abodes E. and N. E. of the Massagetae, as far as Serica, in the steppes of Central Asia, which are now peopled by the *Kirghiz Khasaks*, in whose name that of their ancestors is traced by some geographers. They were very warlike, and excelled especially as cavalry, and as archers both on horse and foot. Their women shared in their military spirit; and, if we are to believe Aelian, they had the custom of settling before marriage, whether the man or woman should rule the house, by the result of a combat between them. In early times they extended their predatory incursions as far W. as Armenia and Cappadocia. They were made tributary to the Persian empire, to the army of which they furnished a large force of cavalry and archers, who were among the best troops that the kings of Persia had. It should be remembered that the name of the Sacae is often used loosely for other Scythian tribes, and sometimes for the Scythians in general.

Sacasēnē (Σακασηνή), a fertile district of Armenia Major, on the river Cyrus and the confines of Albania, so called from its having been at one period conquered by the Sacae. A district of Drangiana bore the same name for a similar reason.

Sacer Mons. 1. An isolated hill in the country of the Sabines, on the right bank of the Anio and W. of the Via Nomentana, 3 miles from Rome, to which the plebeians repaired in their celebrated secessions. The hill is not called by any special name at the present day, but there is upon its summit the *Torre di Specchio*. — 2. A mountain in Hispania Tarraconensis near the Minius, probably the modern *Puerto de Rabanon* near Ponferrada.

Sacili, with the surname Martialium, a town of the Turduli in Hispania Baetica.

Sacra Via. [ROMA, p. 650, a.]

Sacraria, a town in Umbria on the road between Treba and Spoletium, supposed by some to be identical with Clitumni Fanum on the river Clitumnus.

Sacriportus, a small place in Latium, of uncertain site, memorable for the victory of Sulla over the younger Marius, B. C. 82.

Sacrum Flumen. 1. (*Uras*), a river on the W. coast of Sardinia. — 2. (*Tavignano*), a river on the E. coast of Corsica, which flowed into the sea at Aleria.

Sacrum Promontōrium. 1. (*C. St. Vincent*), on the W. coast of Spain, said by Strabo to be the most W.-ly point in the whole earth. — 2. (*C. Corso*), the N. E. point of Corsica. — 3. (*C. Iria*, also *Makri*, *Esfa Kavi* or *Jedi Burun*, i. e. the 7 points), the extreme point of the mountain Cragus in Lycia, between Xanthus and Telmissus. — 4. (*C. Khelidoni*), another promontory in Lycia, near the confines of Pamphylia, and opposite the Chelidonian islands, whence it is also called, **Prom Chelidonium.**

Sadyattes (Σαδυάττης), king of Lydia, succeeded his father Ardys, and reigned B. C. 629—617. He carried on war with the Milesians for 6 years, and at his death bequeathed the war to his son and successor, Alyattes. [ALYATTES.]

Saepinum or **Sepinum** (Sepinas, -ātis: *Sepino*), a municipium in Samnium on the road from Allifae to Beneventum.

Saetābis. 1. (*Alcoy?*), a river on the S. coast of Hispania Tarraconensis, W. of the Sucro. — 2. Or **Setābis** (Setabitanus : *Jativa*), an important town of the Contestani in Hispania Tarraconensis, and a Roman municipium, was situated on a hill S. of the Sucro, and was celebrated for its manufacture of linen.

Sagalassus (Σαγαλασσός: *Allahsun*, Ru.), a large fortified city of Pisidia, near the Phrygian border, a day's journey S. E. of Apamea Cibotus. It lay, as its large ruins still show, in the form of an amphitheatre on the side of a hill, and had a citadel on a rock 30 feet high. Its inhabitants were reckoned the bravest of the Pisidians, and seem, from the word Λακεδαίμων on their coins, to have claimed a Spartan origin. Among the ruins of the city are the remains of a very fine temple, of an amphitheatre, and of 52 other large buildings.

Saganus (Σαγανός), a small river on the coast of Carmania.

Sagapa, one of the mouths of the Indus.

Sagaris, (Ovid. *Ex Pont.* iv. 10, 47) a river of Sarmatia Europaea, falling into a bay in the N.W. of the Euxine, which was called after it **Sagaricus Sinus,** and which also received the river **Axiaces.**

The bay appears to be that on which *Odessa* now stands, and the rivers the *Bol-Kowialnik* and the *Mal-Kowialnik*.

Sagartii (Σαγάρτιοι), according to Herodotus, a nomad people of Persia. Afterwards, they are found, on the authority of Ptolemy, in Media and the passes of M. Zagros.

Sagra, a small river in Magna Graecia on the S. E. coast of Bruttium, falling into the sea between Caulonia and Locri, on the banks of which a memorable victory was gained by 10,000 Locrians over 120,000 Crotoniates. This victory appeared so extraordinary, that it gave rise to the proverbial expression, " It is truer than what happened on the Sagra," when a person wished to make any strong asseveration.

Saguntia. 1. (*Xigonza* or *Gigonza*, N. W. of Medina Sidonia), a town in the W. part of Hispania Baetica, S. of the Baetis.—**2.** A town of the Arevaci in Hispania Tarraconensis, S. W. of Bilbilis near the Mons Solarius.

Saguntum, more rarely **Saguntus** (Saguntinus: *Murviedro*), a town of the Edetani or Sedetani in Hispania Tarraconensis, S. of the Iberus on the river Palantias, about 3 miles from the coast. It is said to have been founded by Greeks from Zacynthus, with whom Rutulians from Ardea were intermingled, whence it is sometimes called *Ausonia Saguntus*. It was situated on an eminence in the midst of a fertile country, and became a place of great commercial importance. Although S. of the Iberus it had formed an alliance with the Romans; and its siege by Hannibal, B. C. 219, was the immediate cause of the 2nd Punic war. The inhabitants defended their city with the utmost bravery against Hannibal, who did not succeed in taking the place till after a siege of nearly 8 months. The greater part of the city was destroyed by Hannibal; but it was rebuilt by the Romans 8 years afterwards, and made a colony. Saguntum was celebrated for its manufacture of beautiful drinking-cups; and the figs of the surrounding country were much valued in antiquity. The ruins of the ancient town, consisting of a theatre and a temple of Bacchus, are extant at *Murviedro*, which is a corruption of *Muri veteres*.

Sais (Σαῖς, Σαΐτης: *Sa-el-Hajjar*, Ru.), a great city of Egypt, in the Delta, on the E. side of the Canopic branch of the Nile. It was the ancient capital of Lower Egypt, and contained the palace and burial place of the Pharaohs, as well as the tomb of Osiris. It was the chief seat of the worship of the Egyptian goddess Neith (also called Saïs), who had here a splendid temple in the middle of an artificial lake, where a great feast of lamps was celebrated yearly by worshippers from all parts of Egypt. The city gave its name to the Saïtes Nomos.

Saitis (Σαῖτις), a surname of Athena, under which she had a sanctuary on Mount Pontinus, near Lerna in Argolis. The name was traced by the Greeks to the Egyptians, among whom Athena was said to have been called Saïs.

Sala. 1. (*Saale*), a river of Germany, between which and the Rhine Drusus died. It was a tributary of the Albis.—**2.** (*Saale*), also a river of Germany and a tributary of the Moenus, which formed the boundary between the Hermunduri and Chatti, with great salt springs in its neighbourhood, for the possession of which these 2 peoples frequently contended.—**3.** (*Burargag*), a

river in the N. part of the W. coast of Mauretania Tingitana, rises in the Atlas Minor, and falls into the Atlantic, N. of a town of the same name. — **4.** A river in the same province, S. of the one last mentioned, rises in the Atlas Major and falls into the Atlantic near the S. boundary of Mauretania. —**5.** A Samothracian town in Thrace on the coast of the Aegaean sea, W. of the mouth of the Hebrus. — **6.** A town in Pannonia on the road from Sabaria to Poetovio. — **7.** (*Shella*), a town in the N. part of the W. coast of Mauretania Tingitana, S. of the mouth of the river of the same name mentioned under No. 3. This town was the furthest place in Mauretania towards the S. possessed by the Romans; for although the province nominally extended further S., the Romans never fully subdued the nomad tribes beyond this point.

Salacia, the female divinity of the sea among the Romans, and the wife of Neptune. The name is evidently connected with *sal* (ἅλς), and accordingly denotes the wide, open sea.

Salacia (*Alcacer do Sal*), a municipium of Lusitania in the territory of the Turdetani, N. W. of Pax Julia and S. W. of Ebora, with the surname of Urbs Imperatoria, celebrated for its woollen manufactures.

Salamis (Σαλαμίς: Σαλαμίνιος). 1. (*Koluri*), an island off the W. coast of Attica, from which it is separated by a narrow channel. It forms the S. boundary of the bay of Eleusis. Its form is that of an irregular semicircle towards the W., with many small indentations along the coast. Its greatest length, from N. to S., is about 10 miles, and its width, in its broadest part, from E. to W., is a little more. In ancient times it is said to have been called *Pityussa*, from the pines which grew in it, and also *Sciras* and *Cychrēa*, from the names of 2 native heroes. It is further said to have been called Salamis from a daughter of Asopus of this name. It was colonised at an early time by the Aeacidae of Aegina. Telamon, the son of Aeacus, fled thither after the murder of his half-brother Phocus, and became sovereign of the island. His son Ajax accompanied the Greeks with 12 Salaminian ships to the Trojan war. Salamis continued an independent state till about the beginning of the 40th Olympiad (B. C. 620), when a dispute arose for its possession between the Megarians and the Athenians. After a long struggle it first fell into the hands of the Megarians, but was finally taken possession of by the Athenians through a stratagem of Solon [SOLON], and became one of the Attic demi. It continued to belong to Athens till the time of Cassander, when its inhabitants voluntarily surrendered it to the Macedonians, 318. The Athenians recovered the island in 232 through means of Aratus, and punished the Salaminians for their desertion to the Macedonians with great severity. The old city of Salamis stood on the S. side of the island opposite Aegina; but this was afterwards deserted, and a new city of the same name built on the E. coast opposite Attica, on a small bay now called *Ambelakia*. Even this new city was in ruins in the time of Pausanias. At the extremity of the S. promontory forming this bay was the small island of **Psyttalia** (*Lypsokutali*), which is about a mile long, and from 200 to 300 yards wide.— Salamis is chiefly memorable on account of the great battle fought off its coast, in which the Persian fleet of Xerxes was defeated by the

Greeks, 430. The battle took place in the strait between the E. part of the island and the coast of Attica, and the Greek fleet was drawn up in the small bay in front of the town of Salamis. The battle was witnessed by Xerxes from the Attic coast, who had erected for himself a lofty throne on one of the projecting declivities of Mt. Aegaleos. — 2. A city of Cyprus, situated in the middle of the E. coast a little N. of the river Pediaeus. It is said to have been founded by Teucer, the son of Telamon, who gave it the name of his native island, from which he had been banished by his father. Salamis possessed an excellent harbour, and was by far the most important city in the whole of Cyprus. It became subject to the Persians with the rest of the island ; but it recovered its independence about 385 under Evagoras, who extended his sovereignty over the greater part of the island. [CYPRUS.] Under the Romans the whole of the E. part of the island formed part of the territory of Salamis. In the time of Trajan a great part of the town was destroyed in an insurrection of the Jews ; and under Constantine it suffered still more from an earthquake, which buried a large portion of the inhabitants beneath its ruins. It was, however. rebuilt by Constantine, who gave it the name of Constantia, and made it the capital of the island. There are still a few ruins of this town.

Salapia (Salapinus : *Sulpi*), an ancient town of Apulia in the district Daunia, was situated S. of Sipontum on a lake named after it. According to the common tradition it was founded by Diomedes, though others ascribe its foundation to the Rhodian Elpias. It is not mentioned till the 2nd Punic war, when it revolted to Hannibal after the battle of Cannae, but it subsequently surrendered to the Romans, and delivered to the latter the Carthaginian garrison stationed in the town. The original site of Salapia was at some distance from the coast ; but in consequence of the unhealthy exhalations arising from the lake above mentioned, the inhabitants removed to a new town on the sea coast, which was built by M. Hostilius with the approbation of the Roman senate, about B. c. 200. This new town served as the harbour of Arpi. The ruins of the ancient town still exist at some distance from the coast at the village of *Salpi*.

Salāpīna Palus (*Lago di Sulpi*), a lake of Apulia, between the mouths of the Cerbalus and Aufidus, which derived its name from the town of Salapia situated upon it, and which M. Hostilius connected with the Adriatic by means of a canal.

Salāria, a town of the Bastetani in Hispania Tarraconensis and a Roman colony.

Salāria Via. [ROMA, p. 657, b.]

Salassi, a brave and warlike people in Gallia Transpadana, in the valley of the Duria at the foot of the Graian and Pennine Alps, whom some regarded as a branch of the Salyes or Salluvii in Gaul. They defended the passes of the Alps in their territory with such obstinacy and courage that it was long before the Romans were able to subdue them. At length in the reign of Augustus the country was permanently occupied by Terentius Varro with a powerful Roman force ; the greater part of the Salassi were destroyed in battle, and the rest amounting to 36,000 were sold as slaves. Their chief town was Augusta Praetoria (*Aosta*), which Augustus colonised with soldiers of the Praetorian cohorts

Saldae (Σάλδαι: *Boujayah*, Ru. or *Dellys*, Ru?. a large seaport town of N. Africa, originally the E. frontier town of the kingdom of Mauretania, afterwards in Mauretania Caesariensis, and, after the division of that province, the W. frontier town of Mauretania Sitifensis. Augustus made it a colony.

Saldūba, 1. (*Rio Verde*), a river in the territory of the Turduli in Hispania Baetica, at the mouth of which was situated a town of the same name. — 2. See CAESARAUGUSTA.

Salē (Σάλη), a town on the coast of Thrace.

Salebro, a place in Etruria between Cosa and Populonium.

Saleius Bassus. [BASSUS.]

Salem, i. e. *peace*, the original name of JERUSALEM (Gen. xiv. 18).

Salentini or Sallentini, a people in the S. part of Calabria, who dwelt around the promontory Iapygium, which is hence called Salentinum or Salentina. They laid claim to a Greek origin and pretended to have come from Crete into Italy under the guidance of Idomeneus. They were subdued by the Romans at the conclusion of their war with Pyrrhus, and having revolted in the 2nd Punic war were again easily reduced to subjection.

Salernum (Salernitanus : *Salerno*), an ancient town in Campania at the innermost corner of the Sinus Paestanus, was situated on a height not far from the coast, and possessed a harbour at the foot of the hill. It was made a Roman colony at the same time as Puteoli, B. c. 194; but it attained its greatest prosperity in the middle ages, after it had been fortified by the Lombards.

Salganeus or Salganēa (Σαλγανεύς: Σαλγάδνιος, Σαλγανείτης), a small town of Boeotia on the Euripus, and on the road from Anthedon to Chalcis.

Salīnae, salt-works, the name of several towns which possessed salt-works in their vicinity. 1. A town in Britain on the E. coast, in the S. part of Lincolnshire. — 2. A town of the Suetrii in the Maritime Alps in Gallia Narbonensis, E. of Reii. — 3. (*Torre delle Saline*), a place on the coast of Apulia near Salapia. — 4. A place in Picenum on the river Sannus (*Salino*). — 5. (*Torda*), a place in Dacia. — 6. Salinae Herculeae, near Herculanum in Campania.

Salinātor, Livius. 1. M., consul B. c. 219, with L. Aemilius Paulus, carried on war along with his colleague against the Illyrians. On their return to Rome, both consuls were brought to trial on the charge of having unfairly divided the booty among the soldiers. Paulus escaped with difficulty, but Livius was condemned. The sentence seems to have been an unjust one, and Livius took his disgrace so much to heart that he left the city and retired to his estate in the country, where he lived some years without taking any part in public affairs. In 210 the consuls compelled him to return to the city, and in 207 he was elected consul a 2nd time with C. Claudius Nero. He shared with his colleague in the glory of defeating Hasdrubal on the Metaurus. [For details, see NERO, CLAUDIUS, No. 2.] Next year (206) Livius was stationed in Etruria, as proconsul, with an army, and his imperium was prolonged for 2 successive years. In 204 he was censor with his former colleague in the consulship, Claudius Nero. The two censors had long been enemies ; and their long-smothered resentment now burst forth, and occasioned no small scandal in the state. Livius, in his censorship, imposed a tax upon salt, in consequence of which he received the surname of *Salinator*, which seems to have been given him in derision, but which became, notwithstanding, hereditary in his family. — 2. C., curule aedile 203, and praetor 202, in which year he obtained Bruttii as his province. In 193 he fought under the consul against the Boii, and in the same year was an unsuccessful candidate for the consulship. — 3. C., praetor 191, when he had the command of the fleet in the war against Antiochus. He was consul 188, and obtained Gaul as his province.

Sallentini. [SALLENTINI.]

Sallustius or **Salustius** (Σαλούστιος). 1. Praefectus Praetorio under the emperor Julian, with whom he was on terms of friendship. Sallustius was a heathen, but dissuaded the emperor from persecuting the Christians. He was probably the author of a treatise Περὶ θεῶν καὶ κόσμου, which is still extant. If so, he was attached to the doctrines of the Neo-Platonists. The best edition of this treatise is by Orellius, Turici, 1821. — 2. A Cynic philosopher of some note, who lived in the latter part of the 5th century after Christ. He was a native of Emesa in Syria, and studied successively at Emesa, Alexandria, and Athens. Sallustius was suspected of holding somewhat impious opinions regarding the gods. He seems at least to have been unsparing in his attacks upon the fanatical theology of the Neo-Platonists.

C. Sallustius Crispus, or **Salustius.** 1. The Roman historian, belonged to a plebeian family, and was born B. c. 86, at Amiternum, in the country of the Sabines. He was quaestor about 59, and tribune of the plebs in 52, the year in which Clodius was killed by Milo. In his tribunate he joined the popular party, and took an active part in opposing Milo. It is said that he had been caught by Milo in the act of adultery with his wife Fausta, the daughter of the dictator Sulla; that he had received a sound whipping from the husband; and that he had been only let off on payment of a sum of money. In 50 Sallust was expelled from the senate by the censors, probably because he belonged to Caesar's party, though some give as the ground of his ejection from the senate the act of adultery already mentioned. In the civil war he followed Caesar's fortune. In 47 we find him praetor elect, by obtaining which dignity he was restored to his rank. He nearly lost his life in a mutiny of some of Caesar's troops in Campania, who had been led thither to pass over into Africa. He accompanied Caesar in his African war, 46, and was left by Caesar as the governor of Numidia, in which capacity he is charged with having oppressed the people, and enriched himself by unjust means. He was accused of maladministration before Caesar, but it does not appear that he was brought to trial. The charge is somewhat confirmed by the fact of his becoming immensely rich, as was shown by the expensive gardens which he formed (*horti Sallustiani*) on the Quirinalis. He retired into privacy after he returned from Africa, and he passed quietly through the troublesome period after Caesar's death. He died 34, about 4 years before the battle of Actium. The story of his marrying Cicero's wife, Terentia, ought to be rejected. It was probably not till after his return from Africa that Sallust wrote his historical works. 1. The *Catilina*, or *Bellum Catilinarium*, is a history of the

conspiracy of Catiline during the consulship of Cicero, 63. The introduction to this history, which some critics admire, is only a feeble and rhetorical attempt to act the philosopher and moralist. The history, however, is valuable. Sallust was a living spectator of the events which he describes, and considering that he was not a friend of Cicero, and was a partisan of Caesar, he wrote with fairness. The speeches which he has inserted in his history are certainly his own composition; but we may assume that Caesar's speech was extant, and that he gave the substance of it. 2. The *Jugurtha*, or *Bellum Jugurthinum*, contains the history of the war of the Romans against Jugurtha, king of Numidia, which began 111, and continued until 106. It is likely enough that Sallust was led to write this work from having resided in Africa, and that he collected some materials there. He cites the Punic Books of King Hiempsal, as authority for his general geographical description (*Jug.* c. 17). The Jugurthine war has a philosophical introduction of the same stamp as that to the *Catilina*. As a history of the campaign, the Jugurthine war is of no value: there is a total neglect of geographical precision, and apparently not a very strict regard to chronology. 3. Sallustius also wrote *Historiarum Libri Quinque*, which were dedicated to Lucullus, a son of L. Licinius Lucullus. The work is supposed to have comprised the period from the consulship of M. Aemilius Lepidus and Q. Lutatius Catulus, 78, the year of Sulla's death, to the consulship of L. Vulcatius Tullus and M. Aemilius Lepidus, 66, the year in which Cicero was praetor. This work is lost, with the exception of fragments which have been collected and arranged. The fragments contain, among other things, several orations and letters. Some fragments belonging to the 3rd book, and relating to the war with Spartacus, have been published from a Vatican MS. in the present century. 4. *Duae Epistolae de Re Publica ordinanda*, which appear to be addressed to Caesar at the time when he was engaged in his Spanish campaign (49) against Petreius and Afranius, and are attributed to Sallust; but the opinions of critics on their authenticity are divided. 5. The *Declamatio in Sallustium*, which is attributed to Cicero, is generally admitted to be the work of some rhetorician, the matter of which is the well-known hostility between the orator and the historian. The same opinion is generally maintained as to the *Declamatio in Ciceronem*, which is attributed to Sallust.—Some of the Roman writers considered that Sallustius imitated the style of Thucydides. His language is generally concise and perspicuous: perhaps his love of brevity may have caused the ambiguity that is sometimes found in his sentences. He also affected archaic words. Though he has considerable merit as a writer, his art is always apparent. He had no pretensions to great research or precision about facts. His reflections have often something of the same artificial and constrained character as his expressions. One may judge that his object was to obtain distinction as a writer; that style was what he thought of more than matter. He has, however, probably the merit of being the first Roman who wrote what is usually called history. He was not above his contemporaries as a politician; he was a party man, and there are no indications of any comprehensive views, which had a whole nation for their object. He hated the nobility, as a man may do, without loving the people. The best editions of Sallust are by Corte, Lips. 1724; Gerlach, Basil. 1823—1831, 3 vols.; and by Kritz, Lips. 1828—1834, 2 vols.— **2.** The grandson of the sister of the historian, was adopted by the latter, and inherited his great wealth. In imitation of Maecenas, he preferred remaining a Roman eques. On the fall of Maecenas he became the principal adviser of Augustus. He died in A. D. 20, at an advanced age. One of Horace's odes (*Carm.* ii. 2) is addressed to him.

Salmantica (*Salamanca*), called **Helmantica** or **Hermandica** by Livy, and **Elmantica** by Polybius, an important town of the Vettones in Lusitania, S. of the Durius, on the road from Emerita *v*: Caesaraugusta. It was taken by Hannibal. A bridge was built here by Trajan, of which the piers still exist.

Salmōna or **Salmōnīa** (Σαλμώνη, Σαλμωνία), a town of Elis in the district Pisatia, on the river Enipeus, said to have been founded by Salmoneus.

Salmōneus (Σαλμωνεύς), son of Aeolus and Enarete, and brother of Sisyphus. He was first married to Alcidice and afterwards to Sidero; by the former of whom he became the father of Tyro. He originally lived in Thessaly, but emigrated to Elis, where he built the town of Salmone. His presumption and arrogance were so great that he deemed himself equal to Zeus, and ordered sacrifices to be offered to himself; nay, he even imitated the thunder and lightning of Zeus, but the father of the gods killed him with his thunderbolt, destroyed his town, and punished him in the lower world. His daughter Tyro bears the patronymic *Salmonis*.

Salmōnium or **Salmōna** (Σαλμώνιον, Σαλμώνη: *C. Salmon*), the most E.-ly promontory of Crete.

Salmydessus, called **Halmydessus** also in later times (Σαλμυδησσός, Ἁλμυδησσός: Σαλμυδήσσιος: *Midja* or *Midjeh*), a town of Thrace on the coast of the Euxine, S. of the promontory Thynias. The name was originally applied to the whole coast from this promontory to the entrance of the Bosporus; and it was from this coast that the Black Sea obtained the name of Pontus *Axenos* ("Αξενος), or inhospitable. The coast itself was rendered dangerous by shallows and marshes, and the inhabitants were accustomed to plunder any ships that were driven upon them.

Sālo (*Xalon*), a tributary of the Iberus in Celtiberia, which flowed by Bilbilis, the birth-place of Martial, who accordingly frequently mentions it in his poems.

Sālōna, **Salōnae**, or **Salon** (*Salona*), an important town of Illyria and the capital of Dalmatia, was situated on a small bay of the sea. It was strongly fortified by the Romans after their conquest of the country, and was at a later time made a Roman colony, and the seat of a conventus juridicus. The emperor Diocletian was born at the small village Dioclea near Salona; and after his abdication he retired to the neighbourhood of this town, and here spent the rest of his days. The remains of his magnificent palace are still to be seen at the village of *Spalatro*, the ancient **Spolatum**, 3 miles S. of Salona.

Sālōnina, **Cornēlīa**, wife of Gallienus and mother of Saloninus. She witnessed with her own eyes the death of her husband before Milan, in A. D. 268.

Sālōnīnus, P. Licinīus Cornēlīus Valerīānus,

son of Gallienus and Salonina, grandson of the emperor Valerian. When his father and grandfather assumed the title of Augustus, in A. D. 253, the youth received the designation of Caesar. Some years afterwards he was left in Gaul, and was put to death upon the capture of Colonia Agrippina by Postumus in 259, being about 17 years old.

Salordūrum (*Soleure* or *Solothurn*), a town of the Helvetii on the road from Aventicum to Vindonissa, was fortified by the Romans about A. D. 350.

Salsum Flumen, a tributary of the Baetis in Hispania Baetica, between Attegua and Attubis.

Salviānus, an accomplished ecclesiastical writer of the 5th century, was born in the vicinity of Treves, and passed the latter part of his life as a presbyter of the church at Marseilles. The following works of Salvianus are still extant: — 1. *Adversus Avaritiam Libri IV. ad Ecclesiam Catholicam*, published under the name of Timotheus, about A. D. 440. 2. *De Providentia s. de Gubernatione Dei et de Justo Dei praesentique Judicio Libri*, written during the inroads by the barbarians upon the Roman empire, 451—455. 3. *Epistolae IX.*, addressed to friends upon familiar topics. The best edition of these works is by Balusius, 8vo. Paris, 1684.

Q. Salvidiēnus Rufus, one of the early friends of Octavian (Augustus), whose fleet he commanded in the war against Sex. Pompeius, B. C. 42. In the Perusinian war (41—40) he took an active part as one of Octavian's legates against L. Antonius and Fulvia. He was afterwards sent into Gallia Narbonensis, from whence he wrote to M. Antonius, offering to induce the troops in his province to desert from Octavian. But Antonius, who had just been reconciled to Octavian, betrayed the treachery of Salvidienus. The latter was forthwith summoned to Rome on some pretext, and on his arrival was accused by Augustus in the senate, and condemned to death, 40.

Salvius, the leader of the revolted slaves in Sicily, better known by the name of Tryphon, which he assumed. [TRYPHON.]

Salvius Juliānus. [JULIANUS.]

Salvius Otho. [OTHO.]

Sālus, a Roman goddess, the personification of health, prosperity, and the public welfare. In the first of these three senses she answers closely to the Greek Hygieia, and was accordingly represented in works of art with the same attributes as the Greek goddess. In the second sense she represents prosperity in general. In the third sense she is the goddess of the public welfare (*Salus publica* or *Romana*). In this capacity a temple had been vowed to her in the year B. C. 307, by the censor C. Junius Bubulcus on the Quirinal hill, which was afterwards decorated with paintings by C. Fabius Pictor. She was worshipped publicly on the 30th of April, in conjunction with Pax, Concordia, and Janus. It had been customary at Rome every year, about the time when the consuls entered upon their office, for the augurs and other high-priests to observe the signs for the purpose of ascertaining the fortunes of the republic during the coming year; this observation of the signs was called *augurium Salutis*. In the time of Cicero, this ceremony had become neglected; but Augustus restored it, and the custom afterwards remained as long as paganism was the religion of the state. Salus was represented, like Fortuna, with a rudder, a globe at her feet, and sometimes in a sitting posture, pouring from a patera a libation upon an altar, around which a serpent is winding.

Salustīus. [SALLUSTIUS.]

Salyes or **Salluvii,** the most powerful and most celebrated of all the Ligurian tribes, inhabited the S. coast of Gaul from the Rhone to the Maritime Alps. They were troublesome neighbours to Massilia, with which city they frequently carried on war. They were subdued by the Romans in B. C. 123 after a long and obstinate struggle, and the colony of Aquae Sextiae was founded in their territory by the consul Sextius.

Samachonītis Lacus [SEMECHONITIS LACUS].

Samāra. [SAMAROBRIVA.]

Sāmārīa (Σαμάρεια: Heb. Shomron, Chaldee, Shamraïn: Σαμαρεύς, Σαμαρείτης, Samarītes, pl. Σαμαρεῖς, Σαμαρεῖται, Samarītae), aft. **Sĕbaste** (Σεβαστή: Sebustieh, Ru.), one of the chief cities of Palestine, was built by Omri, king of Israel (about B. C. 922), on a hill in the midst of a plain surrounded by mountains, just in the centre of Palestine W. of the Jordan. Its name was derived from Shemer, the owner of the hill which Omri purchased for its site. It was the capital of the kingdom of Israel, and the chief seat of the idolatrous worship to which the ten tribes were addicted, until it was taken by Shalmaneser, king of Assyria (about B. C. 720), who carried away the inhabitants of the city and of the surrounding country, which is also known in history as Samaria (see below), and replaced them by heathen peoples from the E. provinces of his empire. These settlers, being troubled with the wild beasts who had become numerous in the depopulated country, sought to propitiate the god of the land; and Esarhaddon sent them a priest of the tribe of Levi, who resided at Bethel, and taught them the worship of the true God. The result was a strange mixture of religions and of races. When the Jews returned from the Babylonish captivity, those of the Samaritans who worshipped Jehovah offered to assist them in rebuilding the temple at Jerusalem; but their aid was refused, and hence arose the lasting hatred between the Jews and the Samaritans. This religious animosity reached its height when, in the reign of Darius Nothus, the son of the Jewish high-priest, having married the daughter of Sanballat, governor of Samaria, went over to the Samaritans and became high-priest of a temple which his father-in-law built for him, on Mt. Gerizim, near Sichem. The erection of this temple had also the effect of diminishing the importance of the city of Samaria. Under the Syrian kings and the Maccabean princes, we find the name of Samaria used distinctly as that of a province, which consisted of the district between Galilee on the N. and Judaea on the S. In the persecution of Antiochus Epiphanes, the Samaritans escaped by conforming to the king's edicts and dedicating the temple on Mt. Gerizim to Zeus Hellenius, B. C. 167. As the power of the Asmonean princes increased, they attacked the Samaritans; and, about B. C. 129, John Hyrcanus took and destroyed the temple on Mt. Gerizim and the city of Samaria. The latter seems to have been soon rebuilt. Pompey assigned the district to the province of Syria, and Gabinius fortified the city anew. Augustus gave the district to Herod, who greatly renovated the city of Samaria, which he called Sebaste in honour of his patron. Still, as the Samaritans continued to worship on Mt. Gerizim, even after their temple had been destroyed, the neighbouring city of Sichem was regarded as their capital, and, as it grew, Samaria declined; and, by the 4th century of our era it had become a place of no importance. Its beautiful site is now occupied by a poor village, which bears the Greek name of the city, slightly altered, viz. *Sebustieh.* — As a district of Palestine, Samaria extended from Ginaea (*Jenin*) on the N. to Bethhoron, N. W. of Gibeon on the S. , or, along the coast, from a little S. of Caesarea on the N. to a little N. of Joppa on the S. It was intersected by the Mountains of Ephraim, running N. and S. through its middle, and by their lateral branches, which divide the country into beautiful and fertile valleys. For its political history after the time of Herod the Great, see PALAESTINA. — A remnant of the ancient Samaritans have remained in the country to the present day, especially at *Nablous* (the ancient Sichem), and have preserved their ancient version of the Five Books of Moses, the only part of the Old Testament which they acknowledge. This version is known as the Samaritan Pentateuch, and is of vast importance in biblical criticism.

Samarobrīva, afterwards **Ambiāni** (*Amiens*), the chief town of the Ambiani in Gallia Belgica, on the river Samara; whence its name, which signifies Samara-Bridge.

Sambana (Σάμβανα), a city of Assyria, 2 days' journey N. of Sittace. In its neighbourhood dwelt the people called Sambatae (Σαμβάται).

Sambastae (Σαμβάσται), a people of India intra Gangem, on the Lower Indus, near the island Pattalene. The fort of *Sevistan* or *Sehwan* in the same neighbourhood has been thought to preserve their name, and is by some identified with the Brahman city taken by Alexander.

Sāmē or **Sāmos** (Σάμη, Σάμος), the ancient name of Cephallenia. [CEPHALLENIA.] It was also the name of one of the 4 towns of Cephallenia. The town Same or Samos was situated on the E. coast, opposite Ithaca, and was taken and destroyed by the Romans, B. C. 189.

Samīa (Σαμία: *Khaiaffa*), a town of Elis in the district Triphylia, S. of Olympia, between Lepreum and the Alpheus, with a citadel called Samīcum (Σαμικόν), the same as the Homeric Arene.

Saminthus (Σάμινθος: nr. *Phiklia*), a place in Argolis, on the W. edge of the Argive plain, opposite Mycenae.

Samnīum (Samnītes, more rarely Samnītae, pl.), a country in the centre of Italy, bounded on the N. by the Marsi, Peligni, and Marrucini, on the W. by Latium and Campania, on the S. by Lucania, and on the E. by the Frentani and Apulia. The Samnites were an offshoot of the Sabines, who emigrated from their country between the Nar, the Tiber, and the Anio, before the foundation of Rome, and settled in the country afterwards called Samnium. [SABINI.] This country was at the time of their migration inhabited by Opicans, whom the Samnites conquered, and whose language they adopted; for we find at a later time that the Samnites spoke Opican or Oscan. Samnium is a country marked by striking physical features. The greater part of it is occupied by a huge mass of mountains, called at the present day the *Matese*, which stands out from the central line of the Apennines. The circumference of the Matese is between 70 and 80 miles, and its greatest height is 6000 feet.

The 2 most important tribes of the Samnites were the Caudīni and Pentri, of whom the former occupied the S. side, and the latter the N. side of the Matese. To the Caudini belonged the towns of Allifae, Telesia, and Beneventum : to the Pentri, those of Aesernia, Bovianum, and Sepinum. Besides these 2 chief tribes, we find mention of the Caraceni, who dwelt N. of the Pentri, and to whom the town of Aufidena belonged; and of the Hirpini, who dwelt SE. of the Caudini, but who are sometimes mentioned as distinct from the Samnites. The Samnites were distinguished for their bravery and love of freedom. Issuing from their mountain fastnesses, they overran a great part of Campania ; and it was in consequence of Capua applying to the Romans for assistance against the Samnites, that war broke out between the 2 peoples in B. C. 343. The Romans found the Samnites the most warlike and formidable enemies whom they had yet encountered in Italy ; and the war, which commenced in 343, was continued with few interruptions for the space of 53 years. It was not till 290, when all their bravest troops had fallen, and their country had been repeatedly ravaged in every direction by the Roman legions, that the Samnites sued for peace and submitted to the supremacy of Rome. They never, however, lost their love of freedom ; and accordingly they not only joined the other Italian allies in the war against Rome (90), but, even after the other allies had submitted, they still continued in arms. The civil war between Marius and Sulla gave them hopes of recovering their independence ; but they were defeated by Sulla before the gates of Rome (82), the greater part of their troops fell in battle, and the remainder were put to death. Their towns were laid waste, the inhabitants sold as slaves, and their place supplied by Roman colonists.

Sămos or Sămus (Σάμος: Σάμιος, Samius : Grk. Samo, Turk. Susam Adassi), one of the principal islands of the Aegean Sea, lying in that portion of it called the Icarian Sea, off the coast of Ionia, from which it is separated only by a narrow strait formed by the overlapping of its E. promontory Posidium (C. Colonna) with the W.-most spur of M. Mycale, Pr. Trogilium (C. S. Maria). This strait, which is little more than 3-4ths of a mile wide, was the scene of the battle of Mycale. The island is formed by a range of mountains extending from E. to W., whence it derived its name ; for Σάμος was an old Greek word signifying a mountain : and the same root is seen in Same, the old name of Cephallenia, and Samothrace, i. e. the Thracian Samos. The circumference of the island is about 80 miles. It was and is very fertile ; and some of its products are indicated by its ancient names, Dryusa, Anthemura, Melamphyllus and Cyparissia. According to the earliest traditions, it was a chief seat of the Carians and Leleges, and the residence of their first king, Ancaeus ; and was afterwards colonised by Aeolians from Lesbos, and by Ionians from Epidaurus. In the earliest historical records, we find Samos decidedly Ionian, and a powerful member of the Ionic confederacy. Thucydides tells us that the Samians were the first of the Greeks, after the Corinthians, who paid great attention to naval affairs. They early acquired such power at sea, besides obtaining possession of parts of the opposite coast of Asia, they founded many colonies ; among which were, Bisanthe and Perinthus, in Thrace ; Celenderis and Nagidus, in

Cilicia ; Cydonia, in Crete ; Dicaearchia (Puteoli), in Italy ; and Zancle (Messana), in Sicily. After a transition from the state of an heroic monarchy, through an aristocracy, to a democracy, the island became subject to the most distinguished of the so-called tyrants, Polycrates (B. C. 532), under whom its power and splendour reached their highest pitch, and Samos would probably have become the mistress of the Aegean, but for the murder of Polycrates. At this period the Samians had extensive commercial relations with Egypt, and they obtained from Amasis the privilege of a separate temple at Naucratis. Their commerce extended into the interior of Africa, partly through their relations with Cyrene, and also by means of a settlement which they effected in one of the Oases, 7 days' journey from Thebes. The Samians now became subject to the Persian empire, under which they were governed by tyrants, with a brief interval at the time of the Ionic revolt, until the battle of Mycale, which made them independent, B. C. 479. They now joined the Athenian confederacy, of which they continued independent members until B. C. 440, when an opportunity arose for reducing them to entire subjection and depriving them of their fleet, which was effected by Pericles after an obstinate resistance of 9 months' duration. (For the details see the histories of Greece.) In the Peloponnesian war, Samos held firm to Athens to the last ; and, in the history of the latter part of that war, the island becomes extremely important as the head-quarters of the exiled democratical party of the Athenians. Transferred to Sparta after the battle of Aegospotami, 405, it was soon restored to Athens by that of Cnidus, 394 ; but went over to Sparta again in 390. Soon after, it fell into the hands of the Persians, being conquered by the satrap Tigranes ; but it was recovered by Timotheus for Athens. In the Social war, the Athenians successfully defended it against the attacks of the confederated Chians, Rhodians, and Byzantines, and placed in it a body of 2000 cleruchi, B. C. 352. After Alexander's death, it was taken from the Athenians by Perdiccas, 323 ; but restored to them by Polysperchon, 319. In the subsequent period, it seems to have been rather nominally than really a part of the Greco-Syrian kingdom : we find it engaged in a long contest with Priene on a question of boundary, which was referred to Antiochus II., and afterwards to the Roman senate. In the Macedonian war, Samos was taken by the Rhodians, then by Philip, and lastly by the Rhodians again, B. C. 200. In the Syrian war, the Samians took part with Antiochus the Great against Rome. Little further mention is made of Samos till the time of Mithridates, with whom it took part in his first war against Rome, on the conclusion of which it was finally united to the province of Asia, B. C. 84. Meanwhile it had greatly declined, and during the war it had been wasted by the incursions of pirates. Its prosperity was partially restored under the propraetorship of Q. Cicero, B. C. 62, but still more by the residence in it of Antony and Cleopatra, 32, and afterwards of Octavianus, who made Samos a free state. It was favoured by Caligula, but was deprived of its freedom by Vespasian, and it sank into insignificance as early as the 2nd century, although its departed glory is found still recorded, under the emperor Decius, by the inscription on its coins, Σαμίων πρώτων Ἰωνίας. — Samos may be regarded as almost the chief centre of Ionian manners, energies, luxury, science, and art. In very early times, there was a native school of statuary, at the head of which was Rhoecus, to whom tradition ascribed the invention of casting in metal. [RHOECUS, TELECLES, THEODORUS.] In the hands of the same school architecture flourished greatly; the Heraeum, one of the finest of Greek temples, was erected in a marsh, on the W. side of the city of Samos; and the city itself, especially under the government of Polycrates, was furnished with other splendid works, among which was an aqueduct pierced through a mountain. Samian architects became famous also beyond their own island; as, for example, Mandrocles, who constructed Darius's bridge over the Bosporus. In painting, the island produced Calliphon, Theodorus, Agatharchus, and Timanthes. Its pottery was celebrated throughout the ancient world. In literature, Samos was made illustrious by the poets Asius, Choerilus, and Aeschrion; by the philosophers Pythagoras and Melissus; and by the historians Pagaeus and Duris.—The capital city, also called Samos, stood on the S. E. side of the island, opposite Pr. Trogilium, partly on the shore, and partly rising on the hills behind in the form of an amphitheatre. It had a magnificent harbour, and numerous splendid buildings, among which, besides the Heraeum and other temples, the chief were the senate-house, the theatre, and a gymnasium dedicated to Eros. In the time of Herodotus, Samos was reckoned one of the finest cities of the world. Its ruins are so considerable as to allow its plan to be traced: there are remains of its walls and towers, and of the theatre and aqueduct. The Heraeum already mentioned, celebrated as one of the best early specimens of the Doric order of architecture, and as the chief centre of the worship of Hera among the Ionian Greeks, stood about 2 miles W. of the city. Its erection is ascribed to Rhoecus and his sons. It was burnt by the Persians, but soon rebuilt, probably in the time of Polycrates. This second temple was of the Ionic order, decastyle dipteral, 346 feet long by 189 wide, and is spoken of by Herodotus as the largest temple that he knew. It was gradually filled with works of sculpture and painting, of which it was plundered, first by the pirates in the Mithridatic War, then by Verres, and lastly by M. Antonius. Nothing is left of it but traces of the foundations and a single capital and base.

Sămŏsăta (τὰ Σαμόσατα: Σαμοσατεύς, Samosatensis: *Semeisat*), the capital of the province, and afterwards kingdom, of Commagene, in the N. of Syria, stood on the right bank of the Euphrates, N.W. of Edessa. It was strongly fortified as a frontier post against Osroëne. In the 1st century of our era, it was the capital of the kings of Commagene. It is celebrated, in literary history, as the birthplace of Lucian, and, in church history, as that of the heretic Paul, bishop of Antioch, in the 3rd century. Nothing remains of it but a heap of ruins on an artificial mound.

Sămŏthrācē (Σαμοθράκη, Σαμοθρᾳκία, Ep. ἡ Σάμος Θρηϊκίη: Σαμόθρᾳκες: *Samothraki*), a small island in the N. of the Aegaean sea, opposite the mouth of the Hebrus in Thrace, from which it was 38 miles distant. It is about 32 miles in circumference, and contains in its centre a lofty mountain, called Saôce, from which Homer says that Troy could be seen. Samothrace bore various names in ancient times. It is said to have been called Melite, Saonnesus, Leucosia, and more frequently Dardania, from Dardanus, the founder of Troy, who is reported to have settled here. Homer calls the island simply Samos; sometimes the Thracian Samos, because it was colonised, according to some accounts, from Samos on the coast of Asia Minor. Samothrace was the chief seat of the worship of the Cabiri [CABIRI], and was celebrated for its religious mysteries, which were some of the most famous in the ancient world. Their origin dates from the time of the Pelasgians, who are said to have been the original inhabitants of the island; and they enjoyed great celebrity down to a very late period. Both Philip of Macedon and his wife Olympias were initiated in them. The political history of Samothrace is of little importance. The Samothracians fought on the side of Xerxes at the battle of Salamis; and at this time they possessed on the Thracian mainland a few places, such as Sale, Serrhion, Mesambria, and Tempyra. In the time of the Macedonian kings, Samothrace appears to have been regarded as a kind of asylum, and Perseus accordingly fled thither after his defeat by the Romans at the battle of Pydna.

Sampsiceramus, the name of a petty prince of Emesa in Syria, a nickname given by Cicero to Cn. Pompeius.

Sanchuniathon (Σαγχουνιάθων), said to have been an ancient Phoenician writer, whose works were translated into Greek by Philo Byblius, who lived in the latter half of the first century of the Christian era. A considerable fragment of the translation of Philo is preserved by Eusebius in the first book of his *Praeparatio Evangelica.* The most opposite opinions have been held by the learned respecting the authenticity and value of the work of Sanchuniathon; but it is now generally agreed among modern scholars, that the work was a forgery of Philo. Nor is it difficult to see with what object the forgery was executed. Philo was one of the many adherents of the doctrine of Euhemerus, that all the gods were originally men, who had distinguished themselves in their lives as kings, warriors, or benefactors of man, and became worshipped as divinities after their death. This doctrine Philo applied to the religious system of the Oriental nations, and especially of the Phoenicians; and in order to gain more credit for his statements, he pretended that they were taken from an ancient Phoenician writer. Sanchuniathon, he says, was a native of Berytus, lived in the time of Semiramis, and dedicated his work to Abibalus, king of Berytus. The fragments of this work have been published separately by J. C. Orelli, Lips. 1826. In 1835 a manuscript, purporting to be the entire translation of Philo Byblius, was discovered in a convent in Portugal. The Greek text was published by Wagenfeld, Bremae, 1837. It was at first regarded as genuine, but is now universally agreed to have been the forgery of a later age.

Sancus, Sangus, or **Semo Sancus,** a Roman divinity, said to have been originally a Sabine god, and identical with Hercules and Dius Fidius. The name, which is etymologically the same as *Sanctus,* and connected with *Sancire,* seems to justify this belief, and characterises Sancus as a divinity presiding over oaths. Sancus also had a temple at Rome, on the Quirinal, opposite that of Quirinus, and close by the gate which derived from him the name of *Sanqualis porta*. This sanctuary was the same as that of Dius Fidius, which was consecrated B. C. 465 by Sp. Postumius, but was said to have been founded by Tarquinius Superbus.

Sandröcottus (Σανδρόκοττος), an Indian king at the time of Seleucus Nicator, ruled over the powerful nation of the Gangaridae and Prasii on the banks of the Ganges. He was a man of mean origin, and was the leader of a band of robbers, before he obtained the supreme power. In the troubles which followed the death of Alexander, he extended his dominions over the greater part of northern India, and conquered the Macedonians, who had been left by Alexander in the Panjab. His dominions were invaded by Seleucus, who did not however succeed in the object of his expedition; for, in the peace concluded between the two monarchs, Seleucus ceded to Sandrocottus not only his conquests in the Panjab, but also the country of the Paropamisus. Seleucus in return received 500 war elephants. Megasthenes subsequently resided for, many years at the court of Sandrocottus as the ambassador of Seleucus. [MEGASTHENES.] Sandrocottus is probably the same as the *Chandragupta* of the Sanscrit writers. The history of Chandragupta forms the subject of a Hindu drama, entitled *Mudra Rakshasa*, which has been translated from the Sanscrit by Prof. Wilson.

Sangārius, **Sangäris**, or **Sägäris** (Σαγγάριος, Σάγγαρις, Σάγγαρος: *Sakariyeh*), the largest river of Asia Minor after the Halys, had its source in a mountain called Adoreus, near the little town of Sangia, on the borders of Galatia and Phrygia, whence it flowed first N. through Galatia, then W. and N. W. through the N.E. part of Phrygia, and then N. through Bithynia, of which it originally formed the E. boundary. It fell at last into the Euxine, about half way between the Bosporus and Heraclea. It was navigable in the lower part of its course. Its chief tributaries were the Thymbres or Thymbrus, the Bathys, and the Gallus, flowing into it from the W.

Sangia. [SANGARIUS.]

Sannio, a name of the buffoon in the mimes, derived from *sanna*, whence comes the Italian *Zanni* (hence our *Zany*).

Sannyrion (Σαννυρίων), an Athenian comic poet, belonging to the latter years of the Old Comedy, and the beginning of the Middle. He flourished B.C. 407, and onwards. We know nothing of his personal history, except that his excessive leanness was ridiculed by Strattis and Aristophanes.

Santönes or **Santöni**, a powerful people in Gallia Aquitanica, dwelt on the coast of the ocean, N. of the Garumna. Under the Romans they were a free people. Their chief town was Mediolanum, afterwards Santones (*Saintes*). Their country produced a species of wormwood which was much valued.

Saöoras. [MASCAS.]

Säpaei (Σαπαῖοι, Σάπαιοι), a people in Thrace, dwelt on Mt. Pangaeus, between the lake Bistonis and the coast.

Saphar, **Sapphar**, or **Taphar** (Σάφαρ or Ἄφαρ, Σάπφαρ, Τάφαρον, *Dhafar*, Ru.), one of the chief cities of Arabia, stood on the S. coast of Arabia Felix, opposite to the Aromata Pr. in Africa (*C. Guardafui*). It was the capital of the Homeritae, a part of which tribe bore the name of Sapharitae or Sapphharitae (Σαπφαρῖται).

Säpis (*Savio*), a small river in Gallia Cisalpina, rising in the Apennines, and flowing into the Adriatic S. of Ravenna, between the Po and the Aternus.

Saper. [SASSANIDAE.]

Sappho (Σαπφώ, or, in her own Aeolic dialect, Ψάπφα), one of the two great leaders of the Aeolian school of lyric poetry (Alcaeus being the other), was a native of Mytilene, or, as some said, of Eresos in Lesbos. Her father's name was Scamandronymus, who died when she was only 6 years old. She had 3 brothers, Charaxus, Larichus, and Eurigius. Charaxus was violently upbraided by his sister in a poem, because he became so enamoured of the courtezan Rhodopis at Naucratis in Egypt, as to ransom her from slavery at an immense price. [CHARAXUS.] Sappho was contemporary with Alcaeus, Stesichorus, and Pittacus. That she was not only contemporary, but lived in friendly intercourse, with Alcaeus, is shown by existing fragments of the poetry of both. Of the events of her life we have no other information than an obscure allusion in the Parian Marble, and in Ovid (*Her.* xv. 51), to her flight from Mytilene to Sicily, to escape some unknown danger, between 604 and 592; and the common story that being in love with Phaon, and finding her love unrequited, she leapt down from the Leucadian rock. This story however seems to have been an invention of later times. The name of Phaon does not occur in one of Sappho's fragments, and there is no evidence that it was mentioned in her poems. As for the leap from the Leucadian rock, it is a mere metaphor, which is taken from an expiatory rite connected with the worship of Apollo, which seems to have been a frequent poetical image. At Mytilene Sappho appears to have been the centre of a female literary society, most of the members of which were her pupils in poetry, fashion and gallantry. Modern writers have indeed attempted to prove that the moral character of Sappho was free from all reproach; but it is impossible to read the fragments which remain of her poetry without being forced to come to the conclusion that a female, who could write such poetry, could not be the pure and virtuous woman, which her modern apologists pretend. Of her poetical genius however there cannot be a question. The ancient writers agree in expressing the most unbounded admiration for her poetry. Already in her own age the recitation of one of her poems so affected Solon, that he expressed an earnest desire to learn it before he died. Her lyric poems formed 9 books, but of these only fragments have come down to us. The most important is a splendid ode to Aphrodite (Venus), of which we perhaps possess the whole. The best separate edition of the fragments is by Neue. Berol, 1827.

Sarancae, **Sarangae** or **es** (Σαράγγαι, Σαραγγέες, Herod.), a people of Sogdiana.

Särävus (*Saar*), a small river in Gaul, flowing into the Mosella on its right bank.

Sardänäpälus (Σαρδανάπαλος), the last king of the Assyrian empire of Ninus or Nineveh, noted for his luxury, licentiousness and effeminacy. He passed his time in his palace unseen by any of his subjects, dressed in female apparel, and surrounded by concubines. At length Arbaces, satrap of Media, and Belesys, the noblest of the Chaldaean priests, resolved to renounce allegiance to such a worthless monarch, and advanced at the head of a formidable army against Nineveh. But all of a sudden the effeminate prince threw off his luxurious habits, and appeared an undaunted warrior. Placing himself at the head of his troops, he twice defeated the rebels, but was at length worsted and obliged to shut himself up in Nineveh. Here he sustained a siege for two years, till at length, finding it impossible to hold out any longer, he collected all his treasures, wives, and concubines, and placing them on an immense pile which he had constructed, set it on fire, and thus destroyed both himself and them. The enemies then obtained possession of the city. This is the account of Ctesias, which has been preserved by Diodorus Siculus and which has been followed by most subsequent writers and chronologists. The death of Sardanapalus and the fall of the Assyrian empire is placed B. C. 876. Modern writers however have shown that the whole narrative of Ctesias is mythical, and must not be received as a genuine history. The legend of Sardanapalus, who so strangely appears at one time sunk in the lowest effeminacy, and immediately afterwards an heroic warrior, has probably arisen from his being the same with the god Sandon, who was worshipped extensively in Asia, both as an heroic and a female divinity. The account of Ctesias is also in direct contradiction to Herodotus and the writers of the Old Testament. Herodotus places the revolt of the Medes from the Assyrians about 710, but relates that an Assyrian kingdom still continued to exist, which was not destroyed till the capture of Nineveh by the Median king Cyaxares, about 606. Further, the writers of the Old Testament represent the Assyrian empire in its glory in the 8th century before the Christian era. It was during this period that Pul, Tiglath-pileser, Shalmaneser, and Sennacherib, appear as powerful kings of Assyria, who, not contented with their previous dominions, subdued Israel, Phoenicia, and the surrounding countries. In order to reconcile these statements with those of Ctesias, modern writers have invented two Assyrian kingdoms at Nineveh, one which was destroyed on the death of Sardanapalus, and another which was established after that event, and fell on the capture of Nineveh by Cyaxares. But this is a purely gratuitous assumption, unsupported by any evidence. We have only records of one Assyrian empire, and of one destruction of Nineveh.

Sardemisus, a branch of M. Taurus, extending S.-wards on the borders of Pisidia and Pamphylia, as far as Phaselis in Lycia, whence it was continued in the chain called Climax. It divided the district of Milyas from Pisidia Proper.

Sardēnē (Σαρδένη), a mountain of Mysia, N. of the Hermus, near Cyme. The town of Neontichos was built on its side.

Sardi. [SARDINIA.]

Sardinia (ἡ Σαρδώ or Σαρδών, G. Σαρδόνος, D. Σαρδοῖ, A. Σαρδώ: subsequently Σαρδωνία, Σαρδανία, or Σαρδηνία: Σαρδῷος, Σαρδόνιος, Σαρδώνιος, Sardus: Sardinia), a large island in the Mediterranean, is in shape in the form of a parallelogram, upwards of 140 nautical miles in length from N. to S. with an average breadth of 60. It was regarded by the ancients as the largest of the Mediterranean islands, and this opinion, though usually considered an error, is now found to be correct ; since it appears by actual admeasurement that Sardinia is a little larger than Sicily. Sardinia lies in almost a central position between Spain, Gaul,

Italy, and Africa. The ancients derived its name from Sardus, a son of Hercules, who was worshipped in the island under the name of *Sardus pater*. The Greeks called it *Ichnusa* (Ἰχνοῦσα) from its resemblance to the print of a foot, and *Sandaliotis* (Σανδαλιῶτις) from its likeness to a sandal. A chain of mountains runs along the whole of the E. side of the island from N. to S. occupying about 1-3rd of its surface. These mountains were called by the ancients Insani Montes, a name which they probably derived from their wild and savage appearance, and from their being the haunt of numerous robbers. In the W. and S. parts of Sardinia there are numerous plains, intersected by ranges of smaller hills ; but this part of the island was in antiquity, as in the present day, exceedingly unhealthy. The principal rivers are the Termus (*Termo*) in the N., the Thyrsus (*Oristano*) on the W. (the largest river in the island), and the Flumen Sacrum (*Uras*) and the Saeprus (*Flumendoso*) on the E. The chief towns in the island were : on the N. coast, Tibula (*Porte Pollo*) and Turris Libyssonis ; on the S. coast, Sulci and Caralis (*Cagliari*); on the E. coast, Olbia ; and in the interior, Cornua (*Corneto*) and Nora (*Nurri*). — Sardinia was very fertile, but was not extensively cultivated, in consequence of the uncivilised character of its inhabitants. Still the plains in the W. and S. parts of the island produced a great quantity of corn, of which a large quantity was exported to Rome every year. Among the products of the island one of the most celebrated was the *Sardonica herba*, a poisonous plant, which was said to produce fatal convulsions in the person who ate of it. These convulsions agitated and distorted the mouth, so that the person appeared to laugh, though in excruciating pain ; hence the well-known *risus Sardonicus*. No plant possessing these properties is found at present in Sardinia ; and it is not impossible that the whole tale may have arisen from a piece of bad etymology, since we find mention in Homer of the Σαρδάνιος γέλως, which cannot have any reference to Sardinia, but is probably connected with the verb σαίρειν, "to grin." Another of the principal productions of Sardinia was its wool, which was obtained from a breed of domestic animals between a sheep and a goat, called *musmones*. The skins of these animals were used by the inhabitants as clothes, whence we find them often called *Pelliti* and *Mastrucati*. Sardinia also contained a large quantity of the precious metals, especially silver, the mines of which were worked in antiquity to a great extent. There were likewise numerous mineral springs ; and large quantities of salt were manufactured on the W. and S. coasts. — The population of Sardinia was of a very mixed kind. To what race the original inhabitants belonged we are not informed ; but it appears that Phoenicians, Tyrrhenians, and Carthaginians settled in the island at different periods. The Greeks are also said to have planted colonies in the island, but this account is very suspicious. The first Greek colony is said to have been led by Iolaus, a son of Hercules ; and from him a tribe in the island, called *Iolai* (Ἰόλαοι, Ἰολάειοι, Ἰολαεῖς), or *Ilienses* (Ἰλιεῖς), derived their name. These were some of the most ancient inhabitants of Sardinia, and were probably not of Greek, but Tyrrhenian origin. Their name is still preserved in the modern town of *Iliola*, in the middle of the W. coast. We also find in the island *Corsi*, who had crossed over from Corsica, and *Balari*, who were probably descendants of the Iberian and Libyan mercenaries of the Carthaginians, who revolted from the latter in the first Punic war, and settled in the mountains. At a later time all these names became merged under the general appellation of **Sardi**, although, even in the Roman period, we still find mention of several tribes in the island under distinct names. The Sardi are described as a rude and savage people, addicted to thievery and lying. — Sardinia was known to the Greeks as early as B. C. 500, since we find that Histiaeus of Miletus promised Darius that he would render the island of Sardo tributary to his power. It was conquered by the Carthaginians at an early period, and continued in their possession till the end of the first Punic war. Shortly after this event, the Romans availed themselves of the dangerous war which the Carthaginians were carrying on against their mercenaries in Africa, to take possession of Sardinia, B. C. 238. It was now formed into a Roman province under the government of a praetor; but a large portion of it was only nominally subject to the Romans; and it was not till after many years and numerous revolts, that the inhabitants submitted to the Roman dominion. It was after one of these revolts that so many Sardinians were thrown upon the slave market as to give rise to the proverb, "Sardi venales," to indicate any cheap and worthless commodity. In fact, the inhabitants of the mountains in the E. side of the island, were never completely subdued, and gave trouble to the Romans even in the time of Tiberius. Sardinia continued to belong to the Roman empire till the 5th century, when it was taken possession of by the Vandals.

Sardis or **Sardes** (αἱ Σάρδεις, Ion. Σάρδιες, contracted Σάρδῖς: Σάρδιος, Σαρδιανός, Ion. Σαρδιηνός, Sardiānus: *Sart*, Ru.), one of the most ancient and famous cities of Asia Minor, and the capital of the great Lydian monarchy, stood on the S. edge of the rich valley of the Hermus, at the N. foot of M. Tmolus, on the little river Pactolus, 30 stadia (3 geog. miles) S. of the junction of that river with the Hermus. On a lofty precipitous rock, forming an outpost of the range of Tmolus, was the almost impregnable citadel, which some suppose to be the Hyde of Homer, who, though he never mentions the Lydians or Sardis by name, speaks of M. Tmolus and the lake of Gyges. The erection of this citadel was ascribed to Meles, an ancient king of Lydia. It was surrounded by a triple wall, and contained the palace and treasury of the Lydian kings. At the downfall of the Lydian empire, it resisted all the attacks of Cyrus, and was only taken by surprise. The story is told by Herodotus, who relates other legends of the fortress. The rest of the city, which stood in the plain on both sides of the Pactolus, was very slightly built, and was repeatedly burnt down, first by the Cimmerians, then by the Greeks in the great Ionic revolt, and again, in part at least, by Antiochus the Great; but on each occasion it was restored. For its history, as the capital of the Lydian monarchy, see LYDIA. Under the Persian and Greco-Syrian empires, it was the residence of the satrap of Lydia. The rise of Pergamus greatly diminished its importance; but under the Romans it was still a considerable city, and the seat of a conventus juridicus. In the reign of Tiberius, it was almost entirely destroyed

by an earthquake, but it was restored by the emperor's aid. It was one of the earliest seats of the Christian religion, and one of the 7 churches of the province of Asia, to which St. John addressed the Apocalype; but the apostle's language implies that the church at Sardis had already sunk into almost hopeless decay (Rev. iii. 1, foll.). In the wars of the middle ages the city was entirely destroyed, and its site now presents one of the most melancholy scenes of desolation to be found among the ruins of ancient cities. Though its remains extend over a large surface on the plain, they scarcely present an object of importance, except two or three Ionic columns, belonging probably to a celebrated temple of Cybele. The chief of the other remains are those of a theatre, stadium, and a building supposed to be the senate-house. The triple wall of the acropolis can still be traced, and some of its lofty towers are standing. The necropolis of the city stood on the banks of the lake of Gyges [GYGAEUS LACUS], near which the sepulchre of Alyattes may still be seen. [ALYATTES.]

Sardōum or **Sardonicum Mare** (τὸ Σαρδῷον or Σαρδώνιον πέλαγος), the part of the Mediterranean sea on the W. and S. of Sardinia, separated from the Libyan sea by a line drawn from the promontory Lilybaeum in Sicily.

Sarepta or **Sarephtha** (Σάρεφθα, Σάρεπτα, Σάραπτα: O. T. Zarephath: *Surafend*, *Serphant*, or *Tzarphand*), a city of Phoenicia, about 10 miles S. of Sidon, to the territory of which it belonged; well known as the scene of 2 miracles of Elijah. (1 Kings xvii.) It was celebrated for its wine.

Sargētia (*Strel* or *Strey*, a tributary of the Marosch), a river in Dacia, on which was situated the residence of Decebalus.

Sariphi Montes (τὰ Σάριφα ὄρη: *Hazareh Mountains*), a mountain-range of Central Asia, separating Margiana on the N. from Aria on the S., and forming a W. part of the great chain of the Indian Caucasus, which may be regarded as a prolongation through Central Asia of the chain of Anti-Taurus.

Sarmātae or **Saurŏmātae** (Σαρμάται, Strabo; Σαυρομάται, Herod.), a people of Asia, dwelling on the N. E. of the Palus Maeotis (*Sea of Azov*), E. of the river Tanaïs (*Don*) which separated them from the Scythians of Europe. This is the account of Herodotus, who tells us that the Sarmatians were allied to the Scythians, and spoke a corrupted form of the Scythian language; and that their origin was ascribed to the intercourse of Scythians with Amazons. Strabo also places the Sauromatae between the Tanaïs and the Caspian; but he elsewhere uses the word in the much more extended sense, in which it was used by the Romans, and by the later geographers. [SARMATIA.]

Sarmātia (ἡ Σαρματία: Σαρμάται, Σαυρομάται: the E. part of *Poland*, and S. part of *Russia in Europe*), a name first used by Mela for the part of N. Europe and Asia extending from the Vistula (*Wisla*) and the SARMATICI MONTES on the W., which divided it from Germany, to the Rha (*Volga*) on the E., which divided it from Scythia; bounded on the S. W. and S. by the rivers Ister (*Danube*), Tibiscus (*Theiss*), and Tyras (*Dniester*), which divided it from Pannonia and Dacia, and, further, by the Euxine, and beyond it by M. Caucasus, which divided it from Colchis, Iberia, and Albanis; and extending on the N. as far as the *Baltic* and the unknown regions of N. Europe. The part of this country which lies in Europe just corresponds to the Scythia of Herodotus. The people from whom the name of Sarmatia was derived inhabited only a small portion of the country. [SARMATAE.] The greater part of it was peopled by Scythian tribes; but some of the inhabitants of its W. part seem to have been of German origin, as the VENEDI on the *Baltic*, and the IAZYGES, RHO-LOXANI, and HAMAXOBII in *S. Russia:* the chief of the other tribes W. of the Tanaïs were the Alauni or Alani Scythae, a Scythian people who came out of Asia and settled in the central parts of *Russia.* [ALANI.] The people E. of the Tanaïs were not of sufficient importance in ancient history to require specific mention. The whole country was divided by the river Tanaïs (*Don*) into 2 parts, called respectively Sarmatia Europaea and Sarmatia Asiatica (ἡ ἐν Εὐρώπῃ and ἡ ἐν Ἀσίᾳ Σαρματία); but it should be observed that, according to the modern division of the continent, the whole of Sarmatia belongs to Europe. It should also be noticed that the Chersonesus Taurica (*Crimea*), though falling within the specified limits, was not considered as a part of Sarmatia, but as a separate country.

Sarmăticae Portae (αἱ Σαρματικαὶ πύλαι: *Pass of Dariel*), the central pass of the Caucasus, leading from Iberia to Sarmatia. It was more commonly called Caucasiae Portae. [CAUCASUS.] It was also called Caspiae Portae, apparently through a confusion with the pass of that name at the E. end of the Caucasus. [CASPIAE PORTAE.] The remains of an ancient wall are still seen in the pass.

Sarmătĭci Montes (τὰ Σαρματικὰ ὄρη: part of the *Carpathian Mountains*), a range of mountains in central Europe, extending from the sources of the Vistula to the Danube, between Germany on the W. and Sarmatia on the E.

Sarmătĭcus Oceanus and **Pontus, Sarmătĭcum Mare** (Σαρματικὸς ὠκεανός: *Baltic*), a great sea, washing the N. coast of European Sarmatia.

Sarmizegethusa (nr. *Vachely*, also called *Gradischte*, Ru.), one of the most important towns of Dacia, and the residence of its kings, was situated on the river Sargetia (*Strel* or *Strey*). It was subsequently a Roman colony under the name of *Col. Ulpia Trajana Aug.*, and the capital of the province in which a legion had its head-quarters.

Sarnus (*Sarno*), a river in Campania, flowing by Nuceria, and falling into the Sinus Puteolanus near Pompeii. Its course was changed by the great eruption of Vesuvius, A. D. 79. On its banks dwelt a people named Sarrastes, who are said to have migrated from Peloponnesus.

Barŏn (Σάρων: O. T. Sharon), a most beautiful and fertile plain of Palestine, extending along the coast N. of Joppa towards Caesarea; celebrated for its pastures and its flowers.

Barŏnĭcus Sinus (Σαρωνικὸς κόλπος, also πόρος, πέλαγος, and πόντος: *G. of Egina*), a bay of the Aegaean sea lying between Attica and Argolis, and commencing between the promontory of Sunium in Attica and that of Scyllaeum in Argolis. It contains within it the islands of Aegina and Salamis. Its name was usually derived from Saron, king of Troezene, who was supposed to have been drowned in this part of the sea while swimming in pursuit of a stag.

Sarpēdon (Σαρπηδών). 1. Son of Zeus and Europa, and brother of Minos and Rhadamanthus. Being involved in a quarrel with Minos about Miletus, he took refuge with Cilix, whom he assisted against the Lycians. [MILETUS.] He afterwards became king of the Lycians, and Zeus granted him the privilege of living 3 generations. — 2. Son of Zeus and Laodamia, or, according to others, of Evander and Deidamia, and a brother of Clarus and Themon. He was a Lycian prince, and a grandson of No. 1. In the Trojan war he was an ally of the Trojans, and distinguished himself by his valour, but was slain by Patroclus. Apollo, by the command of Zeus, cleansed Sarpedon's body from blood and dust, covered it with ambrosia, and gave it to Sleep and Death to carry into Lycia, there to be honourably buried.

Sarpēdon Promontorium (Σαρπηδονία ἄκρα: *C. Lissan el Kapeh*), a promontory of Cilicia, in long. 34° E., 80 stadia W. of the mouth of the Calycadnus. In the peace between the Romans and Antiochus the Great, the W. boundary of the Syrian kingdom was fixed here.

Sarpēdonĭum Prom. (ἡ Σαρπηδονίη ἄκρα), a promontory of Thrace between the mouths of the rivers Melas and Erginus, opposite the island of Imbros.

Sarrastes. [SARNUS.]

Sars (*Sar*), a small river on the W. coast of Hispania Tarraconensis, between the Prom. Nerium and the Minius.

Sarsĭna (Sarsinas, -ātis: *Sarsina*), an ancient town of Umbria, on the river Sapis, S.W. of Ariminum, and subsequently a Roman municipium, celebrated as the birthplace of the comic poet Plautus.

Sarus (ὁ Σάρος: *Seihan*), a considerable river in the S. E. of Asia Minor. Rising in the Anti-Taurus, in the centre of Cappadocia, it flows S. past Comana to the borders of Cilicia, where it receives a W. branch that has run nearly parallel to it; and thence, flowing through Cilicia Campestris in a winding course, it falls into the sea a little E. of the mouth of the Cydnus, and S. E. of Tarsus. Xenophon gives 3 plethra (303 feet) for its width at its mouth.

Sāso or **Sasonis Insula** (*Saseno, Sassono, Sassa*), a small rocky island off the coast of Illyria, N. of the Acroceraunian promontory, much frequented by pirates.

Saspīres, or -i, or **Sapīres** (Σάσπειρες, Σασπείροι, Σάπειρες, Σάππειρες), a Scythian people of Asia, S. of Colchis and N. of Media, in an inland position (*i. e.* in Armenia) according to Herodotus, but, according to others, on the coast of the Euxine.

Sassanīdae, the name of a dynasty which reigned in Persia from A. D. 226 to A. D. 651. 1. **Artaxerxes** (the **Ardshir** or **Ardshir** of the Persians), the founder of the dynasty of the Sassanidae, reigned A. D. 226—240. He was a son of one Babek, an inferior officer, who was the son of Sassan, perhaps a person of some consequence, since his royal descendants chose to call themselves after him. Artaxerxes had served with distinction in the army of Artabanus, the king of Parthia, was rewarded with ingratitude, and took revenge in revolt. He obtained assistance from several grandees, and having met with success, claimed the throne on the plea of being descended from the ancient kings of Persia, the progeny of the great

Cyrus. The people warmly supported his cause, as he declared himself the champion of the ancient Persian religion. In 226 Artabanus was defeated, in a decisive battle ; and Artaxerxes thereupon assumed the pompous, but national title of " King of Kings." One of his first legislative acts was the restoration of the pure religion of Zoroaster and the worship of fire. The reigning branch of the Parthian Arsacidae was exterminated, but some collateral branches were suffered to live and to enjoy the privileges of Persian grandees, who, along with the Magi, formed a sort of senate. Having succeeded in establishing his authority at home, Artaxerxes demanded from the emperor Alexander Severus the immediate cession of all those portions of the Roman empire that had belonged to Persia in the time of Cyrus and Xerxes, that is, the whole of the Roman possessions in Asia, as well as Egypt. An immediate war between the two empires was the direct consequence. After a severe contest, peace was restored, shortly after the murder of Alexander in 237, each nation retaining the possessions which they held before the breaking out of the war. — 2. Sapor I. (Shapur), the son and successor of Artaxerxes I., reigned 240—273. He carried on war first against Gordian, and afterwards against Valerian. The latter emperor was defeated by Sapor, taken prisoner, and kept in captivity for the remainder of his life. After the capture of Valerian, Sapor conquered Syria, destroyed Antioch, and having made himself master of the passes in the Taurus, laid Tarsus in ashes, and took Caesarea. His further progress was stopt by Odenathus and Zenobia, who drove the king back beyond the Euphrates, and founded a new empire, over which they ruled at Palmyra. In his reign lived the celebrated Mani. who, endeavouring to amalgamate the Christian and Zoroastrian religions, gave rise to the famous sect of the Manichaeans, who spread over the whole East, exposing themselves to most sanguinary persecutions from both Christians and fire-worshippers. — 3. Hormisdas I. (Hormus), son of the preceding, who reigned only one year, and died 274. — 4. Varanes or Vararanes I. (Bahram or Baharam), son of Hormisdas I., reigned 274—277. He carried on unprofitable wars against Zenobia, and, after her captivity, was involved in a contest with Aurelian, which, however, was not attended with any serious results on account of the sudden death of Aurelian in 275. In his reign the celebrated Mani was put to death. —5. Varanes II. (Bahram), son of Varanes I., reigned 277—294. He was defeated by Carus, who took both Seleucia and Ctesiphon, and his dominions were only saved from further conquests by the sudden death of Carus (283). — 6. Varanes III. (Bahram), elder son of Varanes II., died after a reign of 8 months, 294. — 7. Narses (Narsi), younger son of Varanes II., reigned 294 —303. He carried on a formidable war against the emperor Diocletian. The Roman army was commanded by Galerius Caesar, who in the first campaign (296) sustained most signal defeats in Mesopotamia, and fled in disgrace to Antioch. In the second campaign Narses was defeated with great loss, and was obliged to conclude a peace with the Romans, by which he ceded to Diocletian Mesopotamia, five small provinces beyond the Tigris, the kingdom of Armenia, some adjacent Median districts, and the supremacy over Iberia, the kings

of which were henceforth under the protection of Rome. In 303 Narses abdicated in favour of his son, and died soon afterwards. — 8. Hormisdas II. (Hormus), son of Narses, reigned 303—310. During his reign nothing of importance happened regarding Rome. — 9. Sapor II. Postumus (Shapur), son of Hormisdas II., was born after the death of his father, and was crowned in his mother's womb, the Magi placing the diadem with great solemnity upon the body of his mother. He reigned 310—381. His reign was signalised by a cruel persecution of the Christians. He carried on war for many years against Constantius II. and his successors. The armies of Constantius were repeatedly defeated ; Julian, as is related elsewhere [JULIANUS], perished in battle; and the war was at length brought to a conclusion by Jovian ceding to the Persians the five provinces beyond the Tigris, and the fortresses of Nisibis, Singara, &c. Iberia and Armenia were left to their fate ; and were completely reduced by Sapor in 365, and the following year. Sapor has been surnamed the Great, and no Persian king had ever caused such terror to Rome as this monarch. — 10. Artaxerxes II. (Ardishir), the successor of Sapor II., reigned 381—385. He was a prince of royal blood, but was not a son of Sapor. — 11. Sapor III. (Shapur), reigned 385—390. He sent an embassy to Theodosius the Great, with splendid presents, which was returned by a Greek embassy headed by Stilicho going to Persia. Owing to these diplomatic transactions, an arrangement was made in 384, according to which Armenia and Iberia recovered their independence. — 12. Varanes IV. (Bahram), reigned A.D. 390—404, or perhaps not so long. He was the brother of Sapor III., and founded Kermanshah, still a flourishing town. — 13. Yesdigerd I. (Yesdijird), surnamed ULATHIM, or the SINNER, son or brother of the preceding, reigned 404—420 or 421. He was on friendly terms with the emperor Arcadius, who is said to have appointed him the guardian of his infant son and successor, Theodosius the Younger. He concluded a peace with Arcadius for 100 years. — 14. Varanes V. (Bahram), son of Yesdigerd I., surnamed GOUR, or the "WILD ASS," on account of his passion for the chase of that animal, reigned 420 or 421—448. He persecuted his Christian subjects with such severity that thousands of them took refuge within the Roman dominions. He carried on war with Theodosius, which was terminated by a peace for 100 years, which peace lasted till the 12th year of the reign of the emperor Anastasius. During the latter part of his reign Varanes carried on wars against the Huns, Turks, and Indians, in which he is said to have achieved those valorous deeds for which he has ever since continued to be a favourite hero in Persian poetry. He was accidentally drowned in a deep well together with his horse, and neither man nor beast ever rose again from the fathomless pit. — 15. Yesdigerd II., son of the preceding, reigned 448—458. The persecutions against the Christians were renewed by him with unheard of cruelty. His relations with Rome were peaceful. — 16. Hormisdas III. (Hormuz), and 17. Peroses (Firoze), sons of the preceding, claimed the succession, and rose in arms against each other. Peroses gained the throne by the assistance of the White Huns, against whom he turned his sword in after years. He perished in a great battle with them in 484, together with all of his sons except Pallas and Cobades. — 18. **Pallas (Pallash)**, who reigned 484—488, had to contest the throne with Cobades. He perished in a battle with his brother Cobades in 488. — 19. **Cobades (Kobad)**, reigned 488—498, and again 501 or 502—531. The years from 498 till 502 were filled up by the short reign of, 20. **Zames (Jamaspes)**. The latter was the brother of Cobades, whom he dethroned, and compelled to fly to the Huns, with whose assistance Cobades recovered his throne about 502. He carried on war with success against the emperor Anastasius; but in consequence of the Huns, who had previously been his auxiliaries, turning their arms against him, he made peace with Anastasius in 505, on receiving 11,000 pounds of gold as an indemnity. He also restored Mesopotamia and his other conquests to the Romans, being unable to maintain his authority there on account of the protracted war with the Huns. About this time the Romans constructed the fortress of Dara, the strongest bulwark against Persia, and situated in the very face of Ctesiphon. The war with Constantinople was renewed in 521, in the reign of the emperor Justin I. — 21. **Chosroes I. (Khosru or Khosrew)**, surnamed NUSHIRWAN, or "the generous mind," reigned 531—579. He carried on several wars against the Romans. The first war was finished in 532 or 533, Justinian having purchased peace by an annual tribute of 440,000 pieces of gold. One of the conditions of Chosroes was, that 7 Greek, but Pagan, philosophers who had resided some time at the Persian court, should be allowed to live in the Roman empire without being subject to the imperial laws against Pagans. The 2nd war lasted from 540 to 561. Peace was concluded on condition of Justinian promising an annual tribute of 40,000 pieces of gold, and receiving in return the cession of the Persian claims upon Colchis and Lazica. The third war broke out in 571, in the reign of Justin II., but Chosroes died before it was concluded. Chosroes was one of the greatest kings of Persia. In his protracted wars with the Romans he disputed the field with the conquerors of Africa and Italy, and with those very generals, Tiberius and Mauricius, who brought Persia to the brink of ruin but a few years after his death. His empire extended from the Indus to the Red Sea, and large tracts in Central Asia, perhaps a portion of eastern Europe, recognised him for a time as their sovereign. He received embassies and presents from the remotest kings of Asia and Africa. His internal government was despotic and cruel, but of that firm description which pleases Orientals, so that he still lives in the memory of the Persians as a model of justice. He provided for all the wants of his subjects; and agriculture, trade, and learning were equally protected by him. He caused the best Greek, Latin, and Indian works to be translated into Persian. — 22. **Hormisdas IV. (Hormuz)**, son of Chosroes, reigned 579—590. He continued the war with the Romans, which had been bequeathed him by his father, but was defeated successively by Mauricius and Heraclius. Hormisdas was deprived of his sight, and subsequently put to death by the Persian aristocracy. — 23. **Varanes VI. (Bahram) Shubin**, a royal prince, usurped the throne on the death of Hormisdas, and reigned 590—591. Unable to maintain the throne against Chosroes, who

was supported by the emperor Mauricius, he fled to the Turks. — 24. **Chosroes II. (Khosru) Purwiz**, reigned 590 or 591—628. He was the son of Hormisdas IV., and recovered his father's throne with the assistance of the emperor Mauricius. After the murder of Mauricius, Chosroes declared war against the tyrant Phocas, and met with extraordinary success. In several successive campaigns he conquered Mesopotamia, Syria, Palestine, Egypt, Asia Minor, and finally pitched his camp at Chalcedon, opposite Constantinople. At length Heraclius saved the empire from the brink of ruin, and in a series of splendid campaigns not only recovered the provinces which the Romans had lost, but carried his victorious arms into the heart of the Persian empire. Borne down by his misfortunes, and worn out by age and fatigue, Chosroes resolved, in 628, to abdicate in favour of his son Merdaza; but Shirweh, or Siroes, his eldest son, anticipated his design, and at the head of a band of conspirators seized upon the person of his father, deposed him, and put him to death. The Orientals say that Chosroes reigned 6 years too long. No Persian king lived in such splendour as Chosroes; and however fabulous the Eastern accounts respecting his magnificence may be, they are true in the main, as is attested by the Western writers. — 25. **Siroes (Shirweh)**, reigned only 8 months, 628. He concluded peace with the emperor Heraclius. The numerous captives were restored on both sides. Siroes also restored the holy cross which had been taken at the conquest of Jerusalem. — 26. **Artaxerxes III. (Ardishir)**, the infant son of Siroes, was murdered a few days after the death of his father. He was the last male Sassanid. After him the throne was disputed by a host of candidates of both sexes and doubtful descent, who had no sooner ascended the throne than they were hurried from it into death or captivity. — The last king was **Yesdigerd III.**, who was defeated and slain in 651 by Kaleb, the general of the khalif Abu-Bekr. Persia now became a Mohammedan country.

Sassüla, a town in Latium, belonging to the territory of Tiber.

Sātăla (τὰ Σάταλα, ἡ Σατάλα), a considerable town in the N. E. of Armenia Minor, important as the key of the mountain passes into Pontus. It stood at the junction of 4 roads leading to places on the Euxine, a little N. of the Euphrates, in a valley surrounded by mountains, 325 Roman miles from Caesarea in Cappadocia, and 135 from Trapezus. Under the later Roman empire, it was the station of the 15th legion. Notwithstanding the above indications, its site has not yet been identified with certainty.

Sătarchae, a Scythian tribe on the E. coast of the Tauric Chersonesus.

Săticŭla (Saticulanus), a town of Samnium, situated upon a mountain on the frontiers of Campania, probably upon one of the furthest heights of the mountain chain of *Cujazzo*. It was conquered by the Romans and colonised B.C. 313.

Satnīŏis (Σατνιόεις: *Tuzla*), a river in the S. of the Troad, rising in M. Ida, and flowing W. into the Aegean N. of Prom. Lectum, between Larissa and Hamaxitus.

Satrĭcum (Satricanus: *Casale di Conca*), a town in Latium, near Antium, to the territory of which it belonged. It was destroyed by the Romans.

Sătūrae Palus (*Lago di Paola*), a lake or marsh

in Latium, formed by the river Nymphaeus, and near the promontory Circeium.

Satūrium or **Satureium** (*Saturo*), a town in the S. of Italy near Tarentum, celebrated for its horses. (Hor. *Sat.* i. 6. 59.)

Satúrnia. 1. An ancient name of Italy [ITALIA]. — **2.** (Saturninus: *Saturnia*), formerly called **Aurinia**, an ancient town of Etruria, said to have been founded by the Pelasgians, was situated in the territory of Caletra, on the road from Rome to Cosa, about 20 miles from the sea. It was colonised by the Romans, B. C. 183. The ancient town was rather more than 2 miles in circuit, and there are still remains of its walls and tombs.

Saturninus I., one of the Thirty Tyrants, was a general of Valerian, by whom he was much beloved. Disgusted by the debauchery of Gallienus, he accepted from the soldiers the title of emperor, but was put to death by the troops, who could not endure the sterness of his discipline. The country, however, in which these events took place, is not mentioned. — II., a native of Gaul, and an able officer, was appointed by Aurelian commander of the Eastern frontier, and was proclaimed emperor at Alexandria during the reign of Probus. He was eventually slain by the soldiers of Probus, although the emperor would willingly have spared his life.

Saturninus, L. Antōnius, governor of Upper Germany in the reign of Domitian, raised a rebellion against that emperor, A. D. 91, but was defeated and put to death by Appius Maximus, the general of Domitian.

Saturninus, L. Appuleius, the celebrated demagogue, was quaestor, B. C. 104, and tribune of the plebs for the first time, 102. He entered into a close alliance with Marius and his friends, and soon acquired great popularity. He became a candidate for the tribunate for the 2nd time, 100. At the same time Glaucia, who next to Saturninus was the greatest demagogue of the day, offered himself as a candidate for the praetorship, and Marius for the consulship. Marius and Glaucia carried their elections; but A. Nonius, a partizan of the aristocracy, was chosen tribune instead of Saturninus Nonius, however, was murdered on the same evening by the emissaries of Glaucia and Saturninus; and early the following morning, Saturninus was chosen to fill up the vacancy. As soon as he had entered upon his tribunate, he brought forward an agrarian law, which led to the banishment of Metellus Numidicus, as is related elsewhere. [METELLUS, No. 10.] Saturninus proposed other popular measures, such as a Lex Frumentaria, and a law for founding new colonies in Sicily, Achaia, and Macedonia. In the comitia for the election of the magistrates for the following year, Saturninus obtained the tribunate for the third time, and along with him there was chosen a certain Equitius, a runaway slave, who pretended to be a son of Tib. Gracchus. Glaucia was at the same time a candidate for the consulship; the two other candidates were M. Antonius and C. Memmius. The election of M. Antonius was certain, and the struggle lay between Glaucia and Memmius. As the latter seemed likely to carry his election, Saturninus and Glaucia hired some ruffians who murdered him openly in the comitia. This last act produced a complete reaction against Saturninus and his associates. The senate declared them public enemies, and ordered the

consuls to put them down by force. Marius was unwilling to act against his friends, but he had no alternative, and his backwardness was compensated by the zeal of others. Driven out of the forum, Saturninus, Glaucia, and the quaestor Saufeius took refuge in the Capitol, but the partisans of the senate cut off the pipes which supplied the Capitol with water. Unable to hold out any longer, they surrendered to Marius. The latter did all he could to save their lives: as soon as they descended from the Capitol, he placed them for security in the Curia Hostilia, but the mob pulled off the tiles of the senate-house, and pelted them with the tiles till they died. The senate gave their sanction to these proceedings by rewarding with the citizenship a slave of the name of Scaeva, who claimed the honour of having killed Saturninus. Nearly 40 years after these events, the tribune T. Labienus accused an aged senator Rabirius, of having been the murderer of Saturninus. An account of this trial is given elsewhere. [RABIRIUS.]

Saturninus, Claudius, a jurist from whose *Liber Singularis de Poenis Paganorum* there is a single excerpt in the Digest. He was praetor under Antoninus Pius.

Saturninus, Pompēius, a contemporary of the younger Pliny, is praised by the latter as a distinguished orator, historian, and poet. Several of Pliny's letters are addressed to him.

Saturninus, C. Sentius. 1. Propraetor of Macedonia during the Social war, and probably for some time afterwards. He defeated the Thracians, who had invaded his province. — **2.** One of the persons of distinguished rank who deserted Sex. Pompeius in B. C. 35, and passed over to Octavian. He was consul in 19, and was afterwards appointed to the government of Syria. Three sons of Saturninus accompanied him as legati to Syria, and were present with their father at the trial of Herod's sons at Berytus in B. C. 6.

Saturninus, Venulēius, a Roman jurist, is said to have been a pupil of Papinianus, and a consiliarius of Alexander Severus. There are 71 excerpts from his writings in the Digest.

Saturnius, that is, a son of Saturnus, and accordingly used as a surname of Jupiter, Neptune, and Pluto. For the same reason the name of **Saturnia** is given both to Juno and Vesta.

Saturnus, a mythical king of Italy to whom was ascribed the introduction of agriculture and the habits of civilised life in general. The name is connected with the verb *sero, sevi, satum.* The Romans invariably identified Saturnus with the Greek Cronos, and hence made the former the father of Jupiter, Neptune, Pluto, Juno, &c. [CRONOS]; but there is in reality no resemblance between the attributes of the two deities, except that both were regarded as the most ancient divinities in their respective countries. The resemblance is much stronger between Demeter and Saturn, for all that the Greeks ascribe to their Demeter is ascribed by the Italians to Saturn. Saturnus, then, deriving his name from sowing, is justly called the introducer of civilisation and social order, both of which are inseparably connected with agriculture. His reign is conceived for the same reason to have been the golden age of Italy, and more especially of the Aborigines, his subjects. As agricultural industry is the source of wealth and plenty, his wife was Ops, the representative of plenty. The story ran that the god came to

Italy, in the reign of Janus, by whom he was hospitably received, and that he formed a settlement on the Capitoline hill, which was hence called the Saturnian hill. At the foot of that hill, on the road leading up to the Capitol, there stood in aftertimes the temple of Saturn. Saturn then taught the people agriculture, suppressed their savage mode of life, and introduced among them civilization and morality. The result was that the whole country was called Saturnia or the land of plenty. Saturn was suddenly removed from earth to the abodes of the gods, whereupon Janus erected an altar to him in the forum. It is further related that Latium received its name (from *lateo*) from this disappearance of Saturn, who for the same reason was regarded by some as a divinity of the nether world. Respecting the festival solemnized by the Romans in honour of Saturn, see *Dict. of Antiq. s. v. Saturnalia.* The statue of Saturnus was hollow and filled with oil, probably to denote the fertility of Latium in olives ; in his hand he held a crooked pruning knife, and his feet were surrounded with a woollen riband. In the pediment of the temple of Saturn were seen two figures resembling Tritons, with horns, and whose lower extremities grew out of the ground ; the temple itself was used as the treasury of the state, and many laws also were deposited in it.

Sätyri (Σάτυροι), the name of a class of beings in Greek mythology, who are inseparably connected with the worship of Dionysus, and represent the luxuriant vital powers of nature. Homer does not mention the Satyrs. Hesiod describes them as a race good for nothing and unfit for work. They are commonly said to be the sons of Hermes and Iphthima, or of the Naiads. The Satyrs are represented with bristly hair, the nose round and somewhat turned upwards, the ears pointed at the top like those of animals, with 2 small horns growing out of the top of the forehead, and with a tail like that of a horse or goat. In works of art they are represented at different stages of life ; the older ones were commonly called Sileni, and the younger ones are termed Satyrisci. The Satyrs are always described as fond of wine, (whence they often appear either with a cup or a thyrsus in their hand), and of every kind of sensual pleasure, whence they are seen sleeping, playing musical instruments, or engaged in voluptuous dances with nymphs. Like all the gods dwelling in forests and fields, they were greatly dreaded by mortals. Later writers, especially the Roman poets, confound the Satyrs with the Italian Fauni, and accordingly represent them with larger horns and goats' feet, although originally they were quite distinct kinds of beings. Satyrs usually appear with flutes, the thyrsus, syrinx, the shepherd's staff, cups or bags filled with wine ; they are dressed with the skins of animals, and wear wreaths of vine, ivy or fir. Representations of them are still very numerous, but the most celebrated in antiquity was the Satyr of Praxiteles at Athens.

Satÿrus (Σάτυρος). 1. I. King of Bosporus, was a son of Spartacus I., and reigned B. C. 407 or 406-393. He maintained friendly relations with Athens. He was slain at the siege of Theudosia in 393, and was succeeded by his son Leucon. — 2. II., king of Bosporus, was the eldest of the sons of Paerisades I., whom he succeeded in 311, but reigned only 9 months. — 3. A distinguished comic actor at Athens, is said to have given instructions

to Demosthenes in the art of giving full effect to his speeches by appropriate action. — 4. A distinguished Peripatetic philosopher and historian, who lived in the time of Ptolemy Philopator, if not later. He wrote a collection of biographies, among which were lives of Philip and Demosthenes, and which is frequently cited by ancient writers. — 5. A physician in the 2nd century after Christ, who wrote some works, which are no longer extant.

Sauconna. [ARAR.]

Saufeius. 1. C., quaestor B. C. 100, was one of the partisans of Saturninus, took refuge with him in the capitol, and was slain along with his leader, when they were obliged to surrender to Marius. — 2. L., a Roman eques, was an intimate friend of Atticus, and a warm admirer of the Epicurean philosophy. He had very valuable property in Italy, which was confiscated by the triumvirs, but was restored to him through the exertions of Atticus.

Saulöë Parthaunisa (Σαυλώη Παρθαύνισα), the later capital of Parthia, called by the Greeks Nisaea. Its site is not known.

Saurŏmătae. [SARMATAE.]

Saurŏmătes (Σαυρομάτης), the name of several kings of Bosporus, who are for the most part known only from their coins. We find kings of this name reigning over Bosporus from the time of Augustus to that of Constantine.

Saverrĭo, P. Sulpicius. 1. Consul B. C. 304, when he carried on the war against the Samnites. He was censor in 229 with Sempronius Sophus, his former colleague in the consulship. In their censorship 2 new tribes were formed, the Aniensis and Terentina. — 2. Son of the preceding, consul 279 with P. Decius Mus, commanded, with his colleague, against Pyrrhus.

Sävŏ (*Saone*), a river in Campania, which flows into the sea S. of Sinuessa.

Sävus (*Save* or *Sau*), a navigable tributary of the Danube, which rises in the Carnic Alps, forms first the boundary between Noricum and Italy, and afterwards between Pannonia and Illyria, and falls into the Danube near Singidunum.

Saxa, Decidius, a native of Celtiberia, was originally one of Caesar's common soldiers. He was tribune of the plebs in 44, and after Caesar's death in this year he took an active part in supporting the friends of his murdered patron. He served under M. Antonius in the siege of Mutina, and subsequently under both Antonius and Octavianus in their war against Brutus and Cassius. After the battle of Philippi Saxa accompanied Antony to the East, and was made by the latter governor of Syria. Here he was defeated by the younger Labienus and the Parthians, and was slain in the flight after the battle (40).

Saxa, Q. Voconius, tribune of the plebs, B. C. 169, proposed the Voconia lex, which was supported by the elder Cato, who spoke in its favour, when he was 65 years of age. Respecting this lex, see *Dict. of Antiq. s. v.*

Saxa Rubra. [RUBRA SAXA.]

Saxŏnes, a powerful people in Germany, who originally dwelt in the S. part of the Cimbric Chersoneaus, between the rivers Albis and Chalusus (*Trave*), consequently in the modern Holstein. They are not mentioned by Tacitus and Pliny, since these writers appear to have comprehended all the inhabitants of the Cimbric Chersonesus under the general name of Cimbri. The Saxones first occur in history in A. D. 286, when they are mentioned as brave and skilful sailors, who often joined the Chauci in piratical expeditions against the coast of Gaul. The Saxones afterwards appear at the head of a powerful confederacy of German peoples, who became united under the general name of Saxons, and who eventually occupied the country between the Elbe, the Rhine, the Lippe, and the German ocean. A portion of the Saxons, in conjunction with the Angli, led by Hengist and Horsa, conquered Briton, as is well known, about the middle of the 5th century. The Romans never came into close contact with the Saxons.

Scaeva, Cassius, a centurion in Caesar's army, who distinguished himself by his extraordinary feats of valour at the battle of Dyrrhachium. He survived the battle, and is mentioned as one of the partisans of Caesar, after the death of the latter.

Scaevŏla, Q. Cervidĭus, a Roman jurist, lived under Antoninus Pius. He wrote several works, and there are 307 excerpts from him in the Digest.

Scaevŏla, Mucĭus. 1. C., the hero of a celebrated story in early Roman history. When King Porsenna was blockading Rome, C. Mucius, a young man of the patrician class, resolved to rid his country of the invader. He went out of the city, with a dagger hid beneath his dress, and approached the place where Porsenna was sitting, with a secretary by his side, dressed nearly in the same style as the king himself. Mistaking the secretary for the king, Mucius killed him on the spot. He was seized by the king's guards, and brought before the royal seat, when he declared his name, and his design to kill the king himself, and told him that there were many more Romans ready to attempt his life. The king in his passion and alarm ordered him to be burnt alive, unless he explained more clearly what he meant by his vague threats, upon which Mucius thrust his right hand into a fire which was already lighted for a sacrifice, and held it there without flinching. The king, who was amazed at his firmness, ordered him to be removed from the altar, and bade him go away free and uninjured. To make some return to the king for his generous behaviour, Mucius told him that there were 300 of the first youths of Rome who had agreed with one another to kill the king, that the lot fell on him to make the first attempt, and that the rest would do the same when their turn came. Mucius received the name of Scaevola, or left-handed, from the circumstance of the loss of his right hand. Porsenna being alarmed for his life, which he could not secure against so many desperate men, made proposals of peace to the Romans, and evacuated the territory. The patricians gave Mucius a tract of land beyond the Tiber, which was thenceforth called *Mucia Prata*. The Mucius of this story was a patrician; but the Mucii of the historical period were plebeians. — **2. Q.**, praetor B. C. 215, had Sardinia for his province, where he remained for the next 3 years. He was decemvir sacrorum, and died 209. — **3. Q.**, probably son of No. 2, was praetor 179, with Sicily for his province, and consul 174. — **4. P.**, brother of No. 3, was praetor with his brother 179, and consul 175. In his consulship he gained a victory over the Ligurians. — **5. P.**, probably son of No. 4, was tribune of the plebs 141; praetor urbanus 136; and consul 133, the year in which Tib. Gracchus lost his life. In 131 he succeeded

his brother Mucianus [MUCIANUS] as Pontifex Maximus. Scaevola was distinguished for his knowledge of the *Jus Pontificium*. He was also famed for his skill in playing at ball, as well as at the game called Duodecim Scripta. His fame as a lawyer is recorded by Cicero in several passages. There is no excerpt from his writings in the Digest, but he is cited several times by the jurists whose works were used for that compilation. — **6. Q.**, called the AUGUR, was son of No. 3, and married the daughter of C. Laelius, the friend of Scipio Africanus the younger. He was tribune of the plebs 128, plebeian aedile 125, and as praetor was governor of the province of Asia in 121, the year in which C. Gracchus lost his life. He was prosecuted after his return from his province for the offence of Repetundae, in 120, by T. Albucius, but was acquitted. He was consul 117. He lived at least to the tribunate of P. Sulpicius Rufus 88. Cicero, who was born 106, informs us, that after he had put on the toga virilis, his father took him to Scaevola, who was then an old man, and that he kept as close to him as he could, in order to profit by his remarks. After his death Cicero became a hearer of Q. Mucius Scaevola, the pontifex. The Augur was distinguished for his knowledge of the law; but none of his writings are recorded.—Mucia, the Augur's daughter, married L. Licinius Crassus, the orator, who was consul 95, with Q. Mucius Scaevola, the pontifex maximus; whence it appears that the Q. Mucius, who is one of the speakers in the treatise *de Oratore*, is not the pontifex and the colleague of Crassus, but the Augur, the father-in-law of Crassus. He is also one of the speakers in the *Laelius sive de Amicitia* (c. 1), and in the *de Republica* (i. 12). — **7. Q.**, PONTIFEX MAXIMUS, was son of No. 5, and is quoted by Cicero as an example of a son who aimed at excellence in that which had given his father distinction. He was tribune of the plebs in 106, curule aedile in 104, and consul 95, with Licinius Crassus, the orator, as his colleague. After his consulship Scaevola was the governor (proconsul) of the province of Asia, in which capacity he gained the esteem of the people who were under his government. Subsequently he was made pontifex maximus, by which title he is often distinguished from Q. Mucius the Augur. He lost his life in the consulship of C. Marius the younger and Cn. Papirius Carbo (82), having been proscribed by the Marian party from which we may conclude that he belonged to Sulla's party. His body was thrown into the Tiber. The virtues of Scaevola are recorded by Cicero, who, after the death of the Augur, became an attendant (auditor) of the pontifex. The purity of his moral character, his exalted notions of equity and fair dealing, his abilities as an administrator, an orator, and a jurist, place him among the first of the illustrious men of all ages and countries. He was, says Cicero, the most eloquent of jurists, and the most learned jurist among orators. Q. Scaevola the pontifex is the first Roman to whom we can attribute a scientific and systematic handling of the Jus Civile, which he accomplished in a work in 18 books. He also wrote a *Liber Singularis* περὶ ὅρων, a work on Definitions, or perhaps, rather, short rules of law, from which there are 4 excerpts in the Digest. This is the oldest work from which there are any excerpts in the Digest, and even these may have been taken at second hand.

Scalăbis (*Santarem*), a town in Lusitania, on

the road from Olisipo to Emerita and Bracara, also a Roman colony with the surname Praesidium Julium, and the seat of one of the 3 Conventus Juridici of the province. The town is erroneously called Scalabiscus by Ptolemy.

Scaldis (*Scheldt*), an important river in the N. of Gallia Belgica, flowing into the ocean, but which Caesar erroneously makes a tributary of the Mosa. Ptolemy calls this river *Tabudas* or *Tabullas*, which name it continued to bear in the middle ages under the form of *Tabul* or *Tabula*.

Scămander (Σκάμανδρος). 1. A river in the W. part of the N. coast of Sicily, falling into the sea near Segesta. — 2. The celebrated river of the Troad. [TROAS.] As a mythological personage, the river-god was called Xanthus by the gods. His contest with Achilles is described by Homer (*Il.* xxi. 136, foll.).

Scamandrĭus (Σκαμάνδριος), son of Hector and Andromache, whom the people of Troy called Astyanax, because his father was the protector of the city of Troy.

Scambōnĭdae (Σκαμβωνίδαι), a demus in Attica, between Athens and Eleusis, belonging to the tribe Leontis.

Scampa (Σκάμπα: *Skumbi* or *Iscampi*), a town in the interior of Greek Illyria, on the Via Egnatia between Clodiana and Lychnidus.

Scandēa (Σκάνδεια), a port-town on the E. side of the island Cythera, forming the harbour of the town of Cythera, from which it was 10 stadia distant.

Scandĭa or **Scandinavĭa**, the name given by the ancients to Norway, Sweden, and the surrounding islands. Even the later Romans had a very imperfect knowledge of the Scandinavian peninsula. They supposed it to have been surrounded by the ocean, and to have been composed of several islands called by Ptolemy Scandiae. Of these the largest bore especially the name of Scandia or Scandinavia, by which the modern Sweden was undoubtedly indicated. This country was inhabited by the Hilleviones, of whom the Suiones and Sitones appear to have been tribes.

Scandĭla (*Scandole*), a small island in the N.E. of the Aegaean sea, between Peparethos and Scyros.

Scantĭa Silva, a wood in Campania, in which were probably the Aquae Scantiae mentioned by Pliny.

Scaptē Hȳlē (Σκαπτὴ ὕλη), also called, but less correctly, **Scaptesyle** (Σκαπτησύλη), a small town on the coast of Thrace opposite the island of Thasos. It contained celebrated gold mines, which were originally worked by the Thasians. Thucydides, who had some property in these mines, retired to this place after his banishment from Athens, and here arranged the materials for his history.

Scaptĭa (Scaptiensis or Scaptius), an ancient town in Latium, which gave its name to a Roman tribe, but which disappeared at an early period.

Scaptĭla, P. Ostorĭus, succeeded A. Plautius as governor of Britain, about A. D. 50. He defeated the powerful tribe of the Silures, took prisoner their king Caractacus, and sent him in chains to Rome. In consequence of this success he received the insignia of a triumph, but died soon afterwards in the province.

Scarabantĭa (*Oedenburg*), a town in Pannonia Superior on the road from Vindobona to Poetovio, and a municipium with the surname Flavia Augusta.

Scardōna (Σκαρδῶνα or Σκάρδων). 1. (*Skar-*

dona or *Skardin*), the chief town of Liburnia in Illyria on the right bank of the Titius, 12 miles from its mouth, the seat of a Conventus Juridicus. — 2. (*Arbe*), a small island off the coast of Liburnia, also called Arba, which was the name of its principal town.

Scardus or **Scordus Mons** (τὸ Σκάρδον ὄρος), a range of lofty mountains, forming the boundary between Moesia and Macedonia.

Scarphē, Scarphēa or **Scarphĭa** (Σκάρφη, Σκάρφεια, Σκαρφεία: Σκαρφεύς, Σκαρφιεύς, Σκαρφαῖος, Σκάρφιος), a town of the Epicnemidii Locri, 10 stadia from the coast, at which the roads united leading through Thermopylae. It possessed a harbour on the coast, probably at the mouth of the river Boagrius.

Scarponna (*Charpeigne*), a town in Gallia Belgica on the Mosella, and on the road from Tullum to Divodurum.

Scato or **Cato, Vettĭus**, one of the Italian generals in the Marsic war, B. C. 90. He defeated the consuls, L. Julius Caesar and P. Rutilius Lupus, in 2 successive battles. He was afterwards taken prisoner, and was stabbed to death by his own slave as he was being dragged before the Roman general, being thus delivered from the ignominy and punishment that awaited him.

Scaurus, Aemilĭus. 1. M., raised his family from obscurity to the highest rank among the Roman nobles. He was born in B. C. 163. His father, notwithstanding his patrician descent, had been obliged, through poverty, to carry on the trade of a coal-merchant, and left his son a very slender patrimony. The latter had thought at first of carrying on the trade of a money-lender; but he finally resolved to devote himself to the study of eloquence, with the hope of rising to the honours of the state. He likewise served in the army, where he appears to have gained some distinction. He was curule aedile in 123. He obtained the consulship in 115, when he carried on war with success against several of the Alpine tribes. In 112 he was sent at the head of an embassy to Jugurtha; and in 111 he accompanied the consul L. Calpurnius Bestia, as one of his legates, in the war against Jugurtha. The Numidian king bestowed large sums of money upon both Bestia and Scaurus, in consequence of which the consul granted the king most favourable terms of peace. This disgraceful transaction excited the greatest indignation at Rome; and C. Mamilius, the tribune of the plebs, 110, brought forward a bill, by which an inquiry was to be instituted against all those who had received bribes from Jugurtha. Although Scaurus had been one of the most guilty, such was his influence in the state that he contrived to be appointed one of the three quaesitores, who were elected under the bill, for the purpose of prosecuting the criminals. But though he thus secured himself, he was unable to save any of his accomplices. Bestia and many others were condemned. In 109, Scaurus was censor with M. Livius Drusus. In his consulship he restored the Milvian bridge, and constructed the Aemilian road, which ran by Pisae and Luna as far as Dertona. In 107, he was elected consul a second time, in place of L. Cassius Longinus, who had fallen in battle against the Tigurini. In the struggles between the aristocratical and popular parties, Scaurus was always a warm supporter of the former. He was several times accused of different offences, chiefly by his private enemies; but such was his influence in the state, that he was always acquitted. He died about 89. By his wife Caecilia Scaurus had three children, 2 sons mentioned below, and a daughter Aemilia, first married to M'. Glabrio, and next to Cn. Pompey, subsequently the triumvir. — 2. M., eldest son of the preceding, and stepson of the dictator Sulla, whom his mother Caecilia married after the death of his father. In the third Mithridatic war he served under Pompey as quaestor. The latter sent him to Damascus with an army, and from thence he marched into Judaea, to settle the disputes between the brothers Hyrcanus and Aristobulus. Scaurus was left by Pompey in the command of Syria with two legions. During his government of Syria he made a predatory incursion into Arabia Petraea, but withdrew on the payment of 300 talents by Aretas, the king of the country. He was curule aedile in 58, when he celebrated the public games with extraordinary splendour. The temporary theatre which he built accommodated 80,000 spectators, and was adorned in the most magnificent manner. 360 pillars decorated the stage, arranged in 3 stories, of which the lowest was made of white marble, the middle one of glass, and the highest of gilt wood. The combats of wild beasts were equally astonishing. 150 panthers were exhibited in the circus, and 5 crocodiles and a hippopotamus were seen for the first time at Rome. In 56 he was praetor, and in the following year governed the province of Sardinia, which he plundered without mercy. On his return to Rome he was accused of the crime of repetundae. He was defended by Cicero, Hortensius, and others, and was acquitted, notwithstanding his guilt. He was accused again in 52, under Pompey's new law against ambitus, and was condemned. He married Mucia, who had been previously the wife of Pompey, and by her he had one son [No. 4].—3. Younger son of No. 1, fought under the proconsul, Q. Catulus, against the Cimbri at the Athesis, and having fled from the field, was indignantly commanded by his father not to come into his presence; whereupon the youth put an end to his life. — 4. M., son of No. 2, and Mucia, the former wife of Pompey the triumvir, and consequently the half-brother of Sex. Pompey. He accompanied the latter into Asia, after the defeat of his fleet in Sicily, but betrayed him into the hands of the generals of M. Antonius, in 35. After the battle of Actium, he fell into the power of Octavian, and escaped death, to which he had been sentenced, only through the intercession of his mother, Mucia.—5. Mamercus, son of No. 5, was a distinguished orator and poet, but of a dissolute character. He was a member of the senate at the time of the accession of Tiberius, A. D. 14, when he offended this suspicious emperor by some remarks which he made in the senate. Being accused of majestas in 34, he put an end to his own life.

Scaurus, M. Aurelius, consul suffectus B. C. 108, was 3 years afterwards consular legate in Gaul, where he was defeated by the Cimbri, taken prisoner, and put to death.

Scaurus, Q. Terentius, a celebrated grammarian who flourished under the emperor Hadrian, and whose son was one of the preceptors of the emperor Verus. He was the author of an *Ars Grammatica* and of commentaries upon Plautus,

Virgil, and the *Ars Poëtica* of Horace, which are known to us from a few scattered notices only, for the tract entitled *Q. Terentii Scauri de Orthographia ad Theseum* included in the "Grammaticae Latinae Auctores Antiqui " of Putschius (Hannov. 1605) is not believed to be a genuine production of this Scaurus.

Sceleratus Campus. [ROMA, p. 650, a.]

Scenae (Σκηναί, i. e. *the tents*), a town of Mesopotamia, on the borders of Babylonia, on a canal of the Euphrates, 25 days' journey below Zeugma. It belonged to the SCENITAE, and was evidently only a collection of tents or huts.

Scenitae (Σκηνῖται, i. e. *dwellers in tents*), the general name used by the Greeks for the Bedawee (Bedouin) tribes of Arabia Deserta. It was also applied to nomad tribes in Africa, who likewise lived in tents.

Scepsis (Σκῆψις: prob. *Eski-Upski*, or *Eski-Shupshe*, Ru.), an ancient city in the interior of the Troad, S. E. of Alexandria, in the mountains of Ida. Its inhabitants were removed by Antigonus to Alexandria; but being permitted by Lysimachus to return to their homes, they built a new city, called ἡ νέα κώμη, and the remains of the old town were then called Παλαισκῆψις. Scepsis is celebrated in literary history as the place where certain MSS. of Aristotle and Theophrastus were buried, to prevent their transference to Pergamus. When dug up again, they were found nearly destroyed by mould and worms, and in this condition they were removed by Sulla to Athens. The philosopher Metrodorus and the grammarian Demetrius were natives of Scepsis.

Scerdilaidas, or Scerdilaedus (Σκερδιλαΐδας or Σκερδίλαιδος), king of Illyria, was in all probability a son of Pleuratus, and younger brother of Agron, both of them kings of that country. After the defeat and abdication of Teuta (B. C. 229), he probably succeeded to a portion of her dominions, but did not assume the title of king, till after the death of his nephew Pinnes. He carried on war for some years against Philip, king of Macedonia, and thus appears as an ally of the Romans. He probably died about 205, and was succeeded by his son Pleuratus.

Schedius (Σχέδιος). 1. Son of Iphitus and Hippolyte, commanded the Phocians in the war against Troy, along with his brother Epistrophus. He was slain by Hector, and his remains were carried from Troy to Anticyra in Phocis. — 2. Son of Perimedes, likewise a Phocian who was killed at Troy by Hector.

Schera (Scherinus), a town in the interior of Sicily in the S.W. part of the island.

Scheria. [PHAEACES.]

Schoenus (Σχοῖνος: Σχοινιεύς), a town of Boeotia, on a river of the same name, and on the road from Thebes to Anthedon.

Schoenus (Σχοινοῦς -οῦντος) 1. A harbour of Corinth, N. of Cenchreae, at the narrowest part of the isthmus. — 2. A place in the interior of Arcadia near Methydrium.

Sciathus (Σκίαθος: Σκιάθιος: Skiatho), a small island in the Aegaean sea, N. of Euboea and E. of the Magnesian coast of Thessaly, with a town of the same name upon it. It is said to have been originally colonised by Pelasgians from Thrace. It is frequently mentioned in the history of the invasion of Greece by Xerxes, since the Persian and Grecian fleets were stationed near its coasts.

It subsequently became one of the subject allies of Athens, but attained such little prosperity that it only had to pay the small tribute of 200 drachmae yearly. Its chief town was destroyed by the last Philip of Macedonia. At a later time it was restored by Antonius to the Athenians. Sciathus produced good wine.

Scidrus (Σκίδρος), a place in the S. of Italy of uncertain site, in which some of the Sybarites settled after the destruction of their own city.

Scillūs (Σκιλλοῦς -οῦντος: Σκιλλούντιος, Σκιλλούσιος), a town of Elis in the district Triphylia, on the river Selinus, 20 stadia S. of Olympia. It was destroyed by the Eleans in the war which they carried on against the Pisaeans, whose cause had been espoused by the inhabitants of Scillus. The Lacedaemonians subsequently took possession of the territory of Scillus ; and, although the Eleans still laid claim to it, they gave it to Xenophon after his banishment from Athens. Xenophon resided at this place during the remainder of his life, and erected here a sanctuary to Artemis, which he had vowed during the retreat of the Ten Thousand.

Scingomăgus, a small place in the S. E. part of Gallia Transpadana, in the kingdom of Cottius, W. of Segusio, at the pass across the Alps.

Sciōnē (Σκιώνη: Σκιωναῖος, Σκιωνεύς), the chief town in the Macedonian peninsula of Pallene, on the W. coast. It is said to have been founded by some Pellenians of Achaia, who settled here after their return from Troy. It revolted from the Athenians in the Peloponnesian war, but was retaken by Cleon ; whereupon all the men were put to death, the women and children sold as slaves, and the town given to the Plataeans.

Scipio, the name of an illustrious patrician family of the Cornelia gens. This name, which signifies a stick or staff, is said to have been given to the founder of the family, because he served as a staff in directing his blind father. This family produced some of the greatest men in Rome, and to them she was more indebted than to any others for the empire of the world. The family-tomb of the Scipios was discovered in 1780, on the left of the Appia Via, about 400 paces within the modern Porta S. Sebastiano. The inscriptions and other curiosities are now deposited in the Museo Pio-Clementino, at Rome. — 1. P. Cornelius Scipio, magister equitum, B. c. 396, and consular tribune 395, and 394. — 2. L. Corn. Scipio, consul 350. — 3. P. Corn. Scipio Barbatus, consul 328, and dictator, 306. He was also pontifex maximus. — 4. L. Corn. Scipio Barbatus, consul 298, when he carried on war against the Etruscans, and defeated them near Volaterrae. He also served under the consuls in 297, 295, and 293 against the Samnites. This Scipio was the great great-grandfather of the conqueror of Hannibal. The genealogy of the family can be traced with more certainty from this time.— 5. Cn. Corn. Scipio Asina, son of No. 4, was consul 260, in the 1st Punic war. In an attempt upon the Liparaean islands, he was taken prisoner with 17 ships. He probably recovered his liberty when Regulus invaded Africa ; for he was consul a 2nd time in 254. In this year he and his colleague A. Atilius Calatinus crossed over into Sicily, and took the town of Panormus. — 6. L. Corn. Scipio, also son of No. 4, was consul 259. He drove the Carthaginians out of Sardinia and Corsica, defeating Hanno, the Carthaginian commander. He was

censor in 258. — 7. P. Corn. Scipio Asina, son of No. 5, was consul 221, and carried on war, with his colleague M. Minucius Rufus, against the Istri, who were subdued by the consuls. He is mentioned again in 211, when he recommended that the senate should recall all the generals and armies from Italy for the defence of the capital, because Hannibal was marching upon the city. — 8. P. Corn. Scipio, son of No. 6. was consul, with Ti. Sempronius Longus, in 218, the first year of the 2nd Punic War. He sailed with an army to Gaul, in order to encounter Hannibal before crossing the Alps ; but finding that Hannibal had crossed the Rhone, and had got the start of him by a 3 days' march, he resolved to sail back to Italy, and await Hannibal's arrival in Cisalpine Gaul. But as the Romans had an army of 25,000 men in Cisalpine Gaul, under the command of 2 praetors, Scipio sent into Spain the army which he had brought with him, under the command of his brother Cn. Scipio. On his return to Italy, Scipio took the command of the army in Cisalpine Gaul, and hastened to meet Hannibal. An engagement took place between the cavalry and light-armed troops of the 2 armies. The Romans were defeated ; the consul himself received a severe wound, and was only saved from death by the courage of his young son, Publius, the future conqueror of Hannibal. Scipio now retreated across the Ticinus, crossed the Po also, first took up his quarters at Placentia, and subsequently withdrew to the hills on the left bank of the Trebia, where he was joined by the other consul, Sempronius Longus. The latter resolved upon a battle, in opposition to the advice of his colleague. The result was the complete defeat of the Roman army, which was obliged to take refuge within the walls of Placentia. In the following year 217, Scipio, whose imperium had been prolonged, crossed over into Spain. He and his brother Cneius continued in Spain till their death in 211; but the history of their campaigns, though important in their results, is full of confusions and contradictions. They gained several victories over the enemy, and they felt themselves so strong by the beginning of 212, that they resolved to cross the Iberus, and to make a vigorous effort to drive the Carthaginians out of Spain. They accordingly divided their forces, but they were defeated and slain in battle by the Carthaginians.— 9. Cn. Corn. Scipio Calvus, son of No. 6, and brother of No. 8, was consul 222, with M. Claudius Marcellus. In conjunction with his colleague he carried on war against the Insubrians. In 218 he carried on war as the legate of his brother Publius for 8 years in Spain, as has been related above. — 10. P. Corn. Scipio Africanus Major, son of No. 8. was born in 234. He was unquestionably one of the greatest men of Rome, and he acquired at an early age the confidence and admiration of his countrymen. His enthusiastic mind led him to believe that he was a special favourite of the gods ; and he never engaged in any public or private business without first going to the Capitol, where he sat some time alone, enjoying communication from the gods. For all he proposed or executed he alleged the divine approval; and the Roman people gave credit to his assertions, and regarded him as a being almost superior to the common race of men. There can be no doubt that Scipio believed himself in the divine revelations, which he asserted to have been vouchsafed to him, and the extraordinary success which attended all his enterprises must have deepened this belief. He is first mentioned in 218 at the battle of the Ticinus, when he saved the life of his father as has been already related. He fought at Cannae two years afterward (216), when he was already a tribune of the soldiers, and was one of the few Roman officers who survived that fatal day. He was chosen along with Appius Claudius to command the remains of the army, which had taken refuge at Canusium; and it was owing to his youthful heroism and presence of mind, that the Roman nobles, who had thought of leaving Italy in despair, were prevented from carrying their rash project into effect. He had already gained the favour of the people to such an extent, that he was elected aedile in 212, although he had not yet reached the legal age. In 210, after the death of his father and uncle in Spain, the Romans resolved to increase their army in that country, and to place it under the command of a proconsul. But when the people assembled to elect a proconsul, none of the generals of experience ventured to sue for so dangerous a command. At length Scipio, who was then barely 24, offered himself as a candidate, and was chosen with enthusiasm to take the command. His success in Spain was striking and rapid. In the first campaign (210) he took the important city of Carthago Nova, and in the course of the next 3 years he drove the Carthaginians entirely out of Spain, and became master of that country. He returned to Rome in 206, and was elected consul for the following year (205), although he had not yet filled the office of praetor, and was only 30 years of age. He was anxious to cross over at once to Africa, and bring the contest to an end at the gates of Carthage; but the oldest members of the senate, and among them Q. Fabius Maximus, opposed his project, partly through timidity and partly through jealousy of the youthful conqueror. All that Scipio could obtain was the province of Sicily, with permission to cross over to Africa; but the senate refused him an army, thus making the permission of no practical use. But the allies had a truer view of the interests of Italy than the Roman senate; and from all the towns of Italy volunteers flocked to join the standard of the youthful hero. The senate could not refuse to allow him to enlist volunteers; and such was the enthusiasm in his favour, that he was able to cross over to Sicily with an army and a fleet contrary to the expectations and even the wishes of the senate. After spending the winter in Sicily, and completing all his preparations for the invasion of Africa, he crossed over to the latter country in the course of the following year. Success again attended his arms. The Carthaginians and their ally Syphax were defeated with great slaughter; and the former were compelled to recall Hannibal from Italy as the only hope of saving their country. The long struggle between the 2 peoples was at length brought to a close by the battle fought near the city of Zama on the 19th of October, 202, in which Scipio gained a decisive and brilliant victory over Hannibal. Carthage had no alternative but submission; but the final treaty was not concluded till the following year (201). Scipio returned to Italy in 201, and entered Rome in triumph. He was received with universal enthusiasm, and the surname of Africanus was conferred upon him. The people wished to make him consul and dic-

tator for life, and to erect his statue in the comitia, the rostra, the curia, and even in the Capitol, but he prudently declined all these invidious distinctions. As he did not choose to usurp the supreme power, and as he was an object of suspicion and dislike to the majority of the senate, he took no prominent part in public affairs during the next few years. He was censor in 199 with P. Aelius Paetus, and consul a second time in 194 with Ti. Sempronius Longus. In 193, he was one of the 3 commissioners who were sent to Africa to mediate between Masinissa and the Carthaginians; and in the same year he was one of the ambassadors sent to Antiochus at Ephesus, at whose court Hannibal was then residing. The tale runs that he had there an interview with the great Carthaginian, who declared him the greatest general that ever lived. The compliment was paid in a manner the most flattering to Scipio. The latter had asked, "Who was the greatest general?" "Alexander the Great," was Hannibal's reply. "Who was the second?" "Pyrrhus." "Who the third?" "Myself," replied the Carthaginian. "What would you have said, then, if you had conquered me?" asked Scipio, in astonishment. "I should then have placed myself before Alexander, before Pyrrhus, and before all other generals." — In 190 Africanus served as legate under his brother Lucius in the war against Antiochus the Great. Shortly after his return, he and his brother Lucius were accused of having received bribes from Antiochus to let the monarch off too leniently, and of having appropriated to their own use part of the money which had been paid by Antiochus to the Roman state. The details of the accusation are related with such discrepancies by the ancient authorities, that it is impossible to determine with certainty the true history of the affair, or the year in which it occurred. It appears, however, that there were two distinct prosecutions, and the following is perhaps the most probable history of the transaction. In 187, 2 tribunes of the people of the name of Petillii, instigated by Cato and the other enemies of the Scipios, required L. Scipio to render an account of all the sums of money which he had received from Antiochus. L. Scipio accordingly prepared his accounts, but as he was in the act of delivering them up, the proud conqueror of Hannibal indignantly snatched them out of his hands, and tore them up in pieces before the senate. But this haughty conduct appears to have produced an unfavourable impression, and his brother, when brought to trial in the course of the same year, was declared guilty, and sentenced to pay a heavy fine. The tribune C. Minucius Augurinus ordered him to be dragged to prison and there detained till the money was paid; whereupon Africanus rescued his brother from the hands of the tribune's officer. The contest would probably have been attended with fatal results had not Tib. Gracchus, the father of the celebrated tribune, and then tribune himself, had the prudence to release Lucius from the sentence of imprisonment. The successful issue of the prosecution of Lucius emboldened his enemies to bring the great Africanus himself before the people. His accuser was M. Naevius, the tribune of the people, and the accusation was brought in 185. When the trial came on, and Africanus was summoned, he proudly reminded the people that this was the anniversary of the day on which he had defeated Hannibal at Zama, and called upon them to follow him to the Capitol, in order there to return thanks to the immortal gods, and to pray that they would grant the Roman state other citizens like himself. Scipio struck a chord which vibrated on every heart, and was followed by crowds to the Capitol. Having thus set all the laws at defiance, Scipio immediately quitted Rome, and retired to his country seat at Liternum. The tribunes wished to renew the prosecution, but Gracchus wisely persuaded them to let it drop. Scipio never returned to Rome. He passed his remaining days in the cultivation of his estate at Liternum; and at his death is said to have requested that his body might be buried there, and not in his ungrateful country. The year of his death is equally uncertain; but he probably died in 183. Scipio married Aemilia, the daughter of L. Aemilius Paulus, who fell at the battle of Cannae, and by her he had 4 children, 2 sons [Nos. 12, 13], and 2 daughters, the elder of whom married P. Scipio Nasica Corculum [No. 17.], and the younger Tib. Gracchus, and thus became the mother of the two celebrated tribunes. [Cornelia.] — **11. L. Corn. Scipio Asiaticus**, also called **Asiagenes** or **Asiagenus**, was the son of No. 8, and the brother of the great Africanus. He served under his brother in Spain; was praetor in 193, when he obtained the province of Sicily; and consul in 190, with C. Laelius. The senate had not much confidence in his abilities, and it was only through the offer of his brother Africanus to accompany him as a legate that he obtained the province of Greece and the conduct of the war against Antiochus. He defeated Antiochus at Mt. Sipylus, in 190, entered Rome in triumph in the following year, and assumed the surname of Asiaticus. The history of his accusation and condemnation has been already related in the life of his brother. He was a candidate for the censorship in 184, but was defeated by the old enemy of his family, M. Porcius Cato, who deprived Asiaticus of his horse at the review of the equites. It appears, therefore, that even as late as this time an eques did not forfeit his horse by becoming a senator. — **12. P. Corn. Scipio Africanus**, elder son of the great Africanus, was prevented by his weak health from taking any part in public affairs. Cicero praises his oratiunculae and his Greek history, and remarks that, with the greatness of his father's mind he possessed a larger amount of learning. He had no son of his own, but adopted the son of L. Aemilius Paulus [see below, No. 15]. — **13. L. or Cn. Corn. Scipio Africanus**, younger son of the great Africanus. He accompanied his father into Asia in 190, and was taken prisoner by Antiochus. This Scipio was a degenerate son of an illustrious sire, and only obtained the praetorship, in 174, through Cicereius, who had been a scriba of his father, giving way to him. In the same year he was expelled from the senate by the censors. — **14. L. Corn. Scipio Asiaticus**, a descendant of No. 11, belonged to the Marian party, and was consul 83 with C. Norbanus. In this year Sulla returned to Italy: Scipio was deserted by his troops, and taken prisoner in his camp along with his son Lucius, but was dismissed by Sulla uninjured. He was, however, included in the proscription in the following year (82), whereupon he fled to Massilia, and passed there the remainder of his life. His daughter was married to P. Sestius. — **15. P. Corn. Scipio Aemilianus Africanus Minor**, was the younger son of L. Aemilius Paulus, the conqueror of Macedonia, and was adopted by P. Scipio [No. 12], the son of the conqueror of Hannibal. He was born about 185. In his 17th year he accompanied his father Paulus to Greece, and fought under him at the battle of Pydna, 168. Scipio devoted himself with ardour to the study of literature, and formed an intimate friendship with Polybius, when the latter came to Rome along with the other Achaean exiles in 167. [Polybius.] At a later period he also cultivated the acquaintance of the philosopher Panaetius, and he likewise admitted the poets Lucilius and Terence to his intimacy, and is said to have assisted the latter in the composition of his comedies. His friendship with Laelius, whose tastes and pursuits were so congenial to his own, has been immortalised by Cicero's celebrated treatise entitled "Laelius sive de Amicitia." Although thus devoted to the study of polite literature, Scipio is said to have cultivated the virtues which distinguished the older Romans, and to have made Cato the model of his conduct. If we may believe his panegyrists, he possessed all the simple virtues of an old Roman, mellowed by the refining influences of Greek civilisation. Scipio first served in Spain with great distinction as military tribune under the consul L. Lucullus in 151. On the breaking out of the 3rd Punic war in 149 he accompanied the Roman army to Africa, again with the rank of military tribune. Here he gained still more renown. By his personal bravery and military skill he repaired, to a great extent, the mistakes of the consul Manilius, whose army on one occasion he saved from destruction. He returned to Rome in 148, and had already gained such popularity that when he became a candidate for the aedileship for the following year (147) he was elected consul, although he was only 37, and had not therefore attained the legal age. The senate assigned to him Africa as his province, to which he forthwith sailed, accompanied by his friends Polybius and Laelius. He prosecuted the siege of Carthage with the utmost vigour. The Carthaginians defended themselves with the courage of despair, and the Romans were unable to force their way into the city till the spring of the following year (146). The inhabitants fought from street to street, and from house to house, and the work of destruction and butchery went on for days. The fate of this once magnificent city moved Scipio to tears, and anticipating that a similar catastrophe might one day befall Rome, he repeated the lines of the Iliad (vi. 448), in which Hector bewails the approaching fall of Troy. After reducing Africa to the form of a Roman province, Scipio returned to Rome in the same year, and celebrated a splendid triumph on account of his victory. The surname of Africanus, which he had inherited by adoption from the conqueror of Hannibal, had been now acquired by him by his own exploits. In 142 Scipio was censor, and in the administration of the duties of his office he attempted to repress the growing luxury and immorality of his contemporaries. His efforts, however, were thwarted by his colleague Mummius, who had himself acquired a love for Greek and Asiatic luxuries. In 139 Scipio was accused by Ti. Claudius Asellus of majestas. Asellus attacked him out of private animosity, because he had been deprived of his horse, and reduced to the condition of an aerarian by Scipio in his censorship. Scipio was acquitted, and the speeches which he delivered on the occasion obtained great celebrity, and were held in high esteem in a later age. It appears to have been after this event that Scipio was sent on an embassy to Egypt and Asia to attend to the Roman interests in those countries. The long continuance of the war in Spain again called Scipio to the consulship. He was appointed consul in his absence, and had the province of Spain assigned to him in 134. His operations were attended with success; and in 133 he brought the war to a conclusion by the capture of the city of Numantia after a long siege. He now received the surname of Numantinus in addition to that of Africanus. During his absence in Spain Tib. Gracchus had been put to death. Scipio was married to Sempronia, the sister of the fallen tribune, but he had no sympathy with his reforms, and no sorrow for his fate. Upon his return to Rome in 132, he did not disguise his sentiments, and when asked in the assembly of the tribes by C. Papirius Carbo, the tribune, what he thought of the death of Tib. Gracchus, he boldly replied that he was justly slain (*jure caesum*). The people loudly expressed their disapprobation; whereupon Scipio proudly bad them be silent. He now took the lead in opposing the popular party, and endeavoured to prevent the agrarian law of Tib. Gracchus from being carried into effect. In order to accomplish this object, he proposed in the senate (129), that all disputes respecting the lands of the allies should be taken out of the hands of the commissioners appointed under the law of Tib. Gracchus, and should be committed to other persons. This would have been equivalent to an abrogation of the law; and accordingly Fulvius Flaccus, Papirius Carbo and C. Gracchus, the 3 commissioners, offered the most vehement opposition to his proposal. In the forum he was accused by Carbo with the bitterest invectives as the enemy of the people, and upon his again expressing his approval of the death of Tib. Gracchus, the people shouted out, "Down with the tyrant." In the evening he went home with the intention of composing a speech for the following day; but next day he was found dead in his room. The most contradictory rumours were circulated respecting his death, but it was generally believed that he was murdered. Suspicion fell upon various persons; his wife Sempronia and her mother Cornelia were suspected by some; Carbo, Fulvius, and C. Gracchus by others. Of all these Carbo was most generally believed to have been guilty, and is expressly mentioned as the murderer by Cicero. The general opinion entertained by the Romans of a subsequent age respecting Scipio is given by Cicero in his work on the Republic, in which Scipio is introduced as the principal speaker. — 16. P. Corn. Scipio Nasica, that is, "Scipio with the pointed nose," was the son of Cn. Scipio Calvus, who fell in Spain in 211. [No. 9.] He is first mentioned in 204 as a young man who was judged by the senate to be the best citizen in the state, and was therefore sent to Ostia along with the Roman matrons to receive the statue of the Idaean Mother, which had been brought from Pessinus. He was curule aedile 196; praetor in 194, when he fought with success in Further Spain; and consul

191, when he defeated the Boii, and triumphed over them on his return to Rome. Scipio Nasica was a celebrated jurist, and a house was given him by the state in the Via Sacra, in order that he might be more easily consulted. — 17. P. Corn. Scipio Nasica Corculum, son of No. 16, inherited from his father a love of jurisprudence, and became so celebrated for his discernment and for his knowledge of the pontifical and civil law, that he received the surname of *Corculum*. He married a daughter of Scipio Africanus the elder. He was consul for the first time 162, but abdicated, together with his colleague, almost immediately after they had entered upon their office, on account of some fault in the auspices. He was censor 159 with M. Popillius Laenas, and was consul a 2nd time in 155, when he subdued the Dalmatians. He was a firm upholder of the old Roman habits and manners, and in his 2nd consulship he induced the senate to order the demolition of a theatre, which was near completion, as injurious to public morals. When Cato repeatedly expressed his desire for the destruction of Carthage, Scipio, on the other hand, declared that he wished for its preservation, since the existence of such a rival would prove a useful check upon the licentiousness of the multitude. He was elected pontifex maximus in 150. — 18. P. Corn. Scipio Nasica Serapio, son of No. 17, is chiefly known as the leader of the senate in the murder of Tib. Gracchus. He was consul in 138, and in consequence of the severity with which he and his colleague conducted the levy of troops, they were thrown into prison by C. Curiatius, the tribune of the plebs. It was this Curiatius who gave Nasica the nickname of Serapio, from his resemblance to a person of low rank of this name; but though given him in derision, it afterwards became his distinguishing surname. In 133, when the tribes met to re-elect Tib. Gracchus to the tribunate, and the utmost confusion prevailed in the forum, Nasica called upon the consuls to save the republic; but as they refused to have recourse to violence, he exclaimed, "As the consul betrays the state, do you who wish to obey the laws follow me," and so saying he rushed forth from the temple of Fides, where the senate was sitting, followed by the greater number of the senators. The people gave way before them, and Gracchus was assassinated as he attempted to escape. In consequence of his conduct on this occasion Nasica became an object of such detestation to the people, that the senate found it advisable to send him on a pretended mission to Asia, although he was pontifex maximus, and ought not, therefore, to have quitted Italy. He did not venture to return to Rome, and after wandering about from place to place, died soon afterwards at Pergamum. — 19. P. Corn. Scipio Nasica, son of No. 18, was consul 111, and died during his consulship. — 20. P. Corn. Scipio Nasica, son of No. 19, praetor 94, is mentioned by Cicero as one of the advocates of Sex. Roscius of Ameria. He married Licinia, the 2nd daughter of L. Crassus, the orator. He had 2 sons, both of whom were adopted, one by his maternal grandfather L. Crassus in his testament, and is therefore called L. Licinius Crassus Scipio; and the other by Q. Caecilius Metellus Pius, consul 80, and is therefore called Q. Caecilius Metellus Pius Scipio. This Scipio became the father-in-law of Cn. Pompey the triumvir, and fell in Africa in 46. His life is given under METELLUS, No. 15. — 21. Cn. Corn.

Scipio Hispallus, son of L. Scipio who is only known as a brother of the 2 Scipios who fell in Spain. Hispallus was praetor 179, and consul 171. — 22. Cn. Corn. Scipio Hispallus, son of No. 21, was praetor, 139, when he published an edict that all Chaldaeans (i. e. astrologers) should leave Rome and Italy within 10 days.

Sciras or Sclērias (Σκίρας, Σκληρίας), of Tarentum, was one of the followers of Rhinthon in that peculiar sort of comedy, or rather burlesque tragedy, which was cultivated by the Dorians of Magna Graecia, and especially at Tarentum. [RHINTHON.]

Sciras (Σκιράς), a surname of Athena, under which she had a temple in the Attic port of Phaleron, and in the island of Salamis. The foundation of the temple at Phaleron is ascribed by Pausanias to a soothsayer, Scirus of Dodona, who is said to have come to Attica at the time when the Eleusinians were at war with Erechtheus.

Sciritis (Σκιρῖτις), a wild and mountainous district in the N. of Laconia, on the borders of Arcadia, with a town called Scirus (Σκῖρος), which originally belonged to Arcadia. Its inhabitants, the Sciritae (Σκιρῖται), formed a special division of the Lacedaemonian army. This body, which in the time of the Peloponnesian war, was 600 in number, was stationed in battle at the extreme left of the line, formed on march the vanguard, and was usually employed on the most dangerous kinds of service.

Sciron (Σκίρων or Σκείρων), a famous robber who infested the frontier between Attica and Megaris. He not only robbed the travellers who passed through the country, but compelled them, on the Scironian rock to wash his feet, and kicked them into the sea, while they were thus employed. At the foot of the rock there was a tortoise, which devoured the bodies of the robber's victims. He was slain by Theseus.

Scirōnia Saxa (Σκιρωνίδες πέτραι, also Σκιράδες: Derveni Bouno), large rocks on the E. coast of Megaris, between which and the sea there was only a narrow dangerous pass, called the Scironian road (ἡ Σκιρώνη or Σκιρωνὶς ὁδός: Kaki Skala). This road was afterwards enlarged by the emperor Hadrian. The name of the rocks was derived from the celebrated robber Sciron.

Scirri or Sciri, a people in European Sarmatia, on the N. coast, immediately E. of the Vistula, in the modern Curland and Samogitien. The Sciri afterwards joined the Huns; and to this people belonged Odoacer, the conqueror of Italy.

Scirtōnium (Σκιρτώνιον), a town in the S. of Arcadia, belonging to the district Aegytis, the inhabitants of which removed to Megalopolis, upon the foundation of the latter.

Scirtus (Σκίρτος: Jüllab), a river in Mesopotamia, flowing past Edessa into a small lake near Charrae. Its name, which signifies leaping, was derived from its rapid descent in a series of small cascades.

Sclērias. [SCIRAS.]

Scodra (Scodrensis: Scodar or Scutari), one of the most important towns in Illyricum, on the left bank of the river Barbana, at the S. E. corner of the Lacus Labeatis, and about 17 miles from the coast. It was strongly fortified, and was the residence of the Illyrian king Gentius. It subsequently contained many Roman inhabitants.

Scodrus. [SCARDUS.]

Scoedises, Scydisses, or Scordiscus (Σκοιδίσης, Σκυδίσσης, Σκορδίσκος: Dassim Dagh, or Chambu-Bel Dagh), a mountain in the N. E. of Asia Minor, dividing Pontus Cappadocius from Armenia Minor, and forming a part of the same range as M. Paryades.

Scollis (Σκόλλις: Sandameri), a rocky mountain between Elis and Achaia, 3333 feet high, which joins on the E. the mountain Lampēa.

Scolōti (Σκόλοτοι), the native name of the Scythians, according to Herodotus, is in all probability the Greek form of Slave-nie or Slove-nie, the generic name of the Slavonian race. [SCYTHIA.] The later Greek writers call them Σκλαβηνοί.

Scolus (Σκῶλος: Σκώλιος, Σκωλιεύς). 1. An ancient town in Boeotia, on the road from Thebes to Aphidna in Attica, was situated on the N. slope of Mt. Cithaeron and 40 stadia S. of the river Asopus. — 2. A small place in Macedonia, near Olynthus.

Scombraria (Islote), an island in front of the bay, on the S. E. coast of Spain, which formed the harbour of Carthago Nova. It received its name from the scombri, or mackerel, taken off its coast, from which the Romans prepared their garum.

Scŏmius Mons (τὸ Σκόμιον ὄρος), a mountain in Macedonia, which runs E. of Mt. Scardus, in the direction of N. to S. towards Mt. Haemus.

Scopas (Σκόπας). 1. An Aetolian, who held a leading position among his countrymen at the period of the outbreak of the war with Philip and the Achaeans, B. C. 220. He commanded the Aetolian army in the first year of the war; and he is mentioned again as general of the Aetolians, when the latter people concluded an alliance with the Romans to assist them against Philip (211). After the close of the war with Philip, Scopas and Dorimachus were appointed to reform the Aetolian constitution (204). Scopas had only undertaken the charge from motives of personal ambition; on finding himself disappointed in this object, he withdrew to Alexandria. Here he was received with the utmost favour by the ministers of the young king, Ptolemy V., and appointed to the chief command of the army against Antiochus the Great. At first he was successful, but was afterwards defeated by Antiochus at Panium, and reduced to shut himself up within the walls of Sidon, where he was ultimately compelled by famine to surrender. Notwithstanding this ill success he continued in high favour at the Egyptian court; but having formed a plot in 296 to obtain by force the chief administration of the kingdom, he was arrested and put to death. — 2. A distinguished sculptor, was a native of Paros, and appears to have belonged to a family of artists in that island. He flourished from B. C. 395 to 350. He was probably somewhat older than Praxiteles, with whom he stands at the head of that second period of perfected art which is called the later Attic school (in contradistinction to the earlier Attic school of Phidias), and which arose at Athens after the Peloponnesian war. Scopas was an architect and a statuary as well as a sculptor. He was the architect of the temple of Athena Alea, at Tegea, in Arcadia, which was commenced soon after B. C. 394. He was one of the artists employed in executing the bas-reliefs, which decorated the frieze of the Mausoleum at Halicarnassus in Caria. A portion of these bas-reliefs is now deposited in the British Museum. Among the single statues and groups of Scopas, the best known in modern times is his group of figures representing the destruction of the sons and daughters of Niobe. In Pliny's time the statues stood in the temple of Apollo Sosianus. The remaining statues of this group, or copies of them, are all in the Florence Gallery, with the exception of the so-called Ilioneus, at Munich, which some suppose to have belonged to the group. There is a head of Niobe in the collection of Lord Yarborough, which has some claim to be considered as the original. But the most esteemed of all the works of Scopas, in antiquity, was his group which stood in the shrine of Cn. Domitius in the Flaminian circus, representing Achilles conducted to the island of Leuce by the divinities of the sea. It consisted of figures of Neptune, Thetis, and Achilles, surrounded by Nereids, and attended by Tritons, and by an assemblage of sea monsters.

Scopas (Σκόπας: *Aladan*), a river of Galatia, falling into the Sangarius, from the E., at Juliopolis.

Soordisci, a people in Pannonia Superior, are sometimes classed among the Illyrians, but were the remains of an ancient and powerful Celtic tribe. They dwelt between the Savus and Dravus.

Soordisous. [SCORDISCA.]

Sooti, a people mentioned, together with the PICTI, by the later Roman writers as one of the the chief tribes of the ancient Caledonians. They dwelt in the S. of Scotland and in Ireland ; and from them the former country has derived its name.

Scotitas (Σκοτίτας), a woody district in the N. of Laconia on the frontiers of Tegeatis.

Sootussa (Σκότουσσα: Σκοτουσσαῖος), a very ancient town of Thessaly, in the district Pelasgiotis, near the source of the Onchestus, and not far from the hills Cynoscephalae, where Flamininus gained his celebrated victory over Philip, B. C. 197.

Scribonia, wife of Octavianus, afterwards the emperor Augustus, had been married twice before. By one of her former husbands, P. Scipio, she had two children, P. Scipio, who was consul, B. C. 16, and a daughter, Cornelia, who was married to Paulus Aemilius Lepidus, censor B. C. 22. Scribonia was the sister of L. Scribonius Libo, who was the father-in-law of Sex. Pompey. Augustus married her in 40, on the advice of Maecenas, because he was then afraid that Sex. Pompey would form an alliance with Antony to crush him ; but having renewed his alliance with Antony, Octavian divorced her in the following year (39), in order to marry Livia on the very day on which she had borne him a daughter, Julia. Scribonia long survived her separation from Octavian. In A. D. 2 she accompanied, of her own accord, her daughter Julia into exile, to the island of Pandateria.

Scribonius Curio. [CURIO.]
Scribonius Largus. [LARGUS.]
Scribonius Libo. [LIBO.]
Scribonius Proculus. [PROCULUS.]

Scultenna (*Panaro*), a river in Gallia Cispadana, rising in the Apennines, and flowing to the E. of Mutina into the Po.

Scupi (*Uskub*), a town in Moesia Superior on the Axius, and the capital of Dardania. It was the residence of the archbishop of Illyricum, and in the middle ages of the Servian kings.

Scydisses. [SCORDISES.]

Scylaeu (Σκυλάκη), or **Scylaceion**, an ancient city on the coast of Mysia Minor, at the foot of M. Olympus, said to have been founded by the Pelasgians.

Scylacium, also **Scylaceum**, or **Scylletium** (Σκυλάκιον, Σκυλακεῖον, Σκυλλήτιον : *Squillace*), a Greek town on the E. coast of Bruttium, was situated on 2 adjoining hills at a short distance from the coast, between the rivers Caecinus and Carcines. It is said to have been founded by the Athenians. It belonged to the territory of Croton, but was subsequently given by the elder Dionysius to the Locrians, and came eventually into the possession of the Romans. It had no harbour, whence Virgil (*Aen. iii.* 553) speaks of it as *navifragum Scylaceum*. From this town the **Scylacius** or **Scylleticus Sinus** (Σκυλλητικὸς κόλπος) derived its name. The isthmus which separated this bay from the Sinus Hipponiatus on the W. coast of Bruttium, was only 20 miles broad, and formed the ancient boundary of Oenotria.

Scylax (Σκύλαξ). 1. Of Caryanda in Caria, was sent by Darius Hystaspis on a voyage of discovery down the Indus. Setting out from the city of Caspatyrus and the Pactyican district, Scylax reached the sea, and then sailed W. through the Indian Ocean to the Red Sea, performing the whole voyage in 30 months.—2. Of Halicarnassus, a friend of Panaetius, distinguished for his knowledge of the stars, and for his political influence in his own state.—There is still extant a *Periplus*, containing a brief description of certain countries in Europe, Asia, and Africa, and bearing the name of Scylax of Caryanda. This work has been ascribed by some writers to the Scylax mentioned by Herodotus, and by others to the contemporary of Panaetius and Polybius ; but most modern scholars suppose the writer to have lived in the first half of the reign of Philip, the father of Alexander the Great, about B. C. 350. It is clear from internal evidence that the Periplus must have been composed long after the time of Herodotus ; whilst, from its omitting to mention any of the cities founded by Alexander, such as Alexandria in Egypt, we may conclude that it was drawn up before the reign of Alexander. It is probable that the author prefixed to his work the name of Scylax of Caryanda, on account of the celebrity of this navigator. This *Periplus* is printed by Hudson, in his *Geographi Graeci Minores*, and by Klausen, attached to his fragments of Hecataeus, Berlin, 1831.

Scylax (Σκύλαξ: *Choterlek-Irmak*), a river in the S. W. of Pontus, falling into the Iris, between Amasia and Gaziura.

Scylitzes or **Scylitza, Joannes**, a Byzantine historian, surnamed, from his office, Curopalates, flourished A. D. 1081. His work extends from the death of Nicephorus I. (811), down to the reign of Nicephorus Botaniotes (1078—1081). The portion of the history of Cedrenus, which extends from the death of Nicephorus I. (811) to the close of the work (1057), is found almost verbatim in the history of Scylitzes. Hence it has been supposed that Scylitzes copied from Cedrenus, and consequently the entire work of Scylitzes has not been published separately, but only the part extending from 1057 to 1080, which has been printed as an appendix to Cedrenus. [CEDRENUS.] It is now, however, generally admitted that Cedrenus copied from Scylitzes.

Satyr.
(From a Statue in the Louvre.) Page 679.

Silenus.
(From a Bronze Statue found at Pompeii.) Page 707.

Sisyphus, Ixion, and Tantalus. Bartoli, Sepolc. Ant. tav. 56.) Page 711.

COS III

Rhea, or Cybele.
(From a Medallion of Hadrian.) Pages 642, 643.

Rhea, or Cybele.
(From a Roman Lamp.) Pages 642, 643.

[To face p. 688.

Sardis. Page 674.

Segesta. Page 691.

Segobriga. Page 691.

Seleucia in Syria. Page 691. No. 2.

Seleucia in Cilicia. Page 692, No. 4.

Selge. Page 694.

Selinus. Page 694.

Sicily. Page 703.

Sicyon. Page 704.

Sida in Pamphylia. Page 705.

Scylla (Σκύλλα) and **Charybdis**, the names of two rocks between Italy and Sicily, and only a short distance from one another. In the one of these rocks which was nearest to Italy, there was a cave, in which dwelt Scylla, a daughter of Crataeis, a fearful monster, barking like a dog, with 12 feet, and 6 long necks and heads, each of which contained 3 rows of sharp teeth. The opposite rock, which was much lower, contained an immense fig-tree, under which dwelt Charybdis, who thrice every day swallowed down the waters of the sea, and thrice threw them up again: both were formidable to the ships which had to pass between them. This is the Homeric account. Later traditions give different accounts of Scylla's parentage. Some describe her as a monster with 6 heads of different animals, or with only 3 heads. One tradition relates that Scylla was originally a beautiful maiden, who often played with the nymphs of the sea, and was beloved by the marine god Glaucus. The latter applied to Circe for means to make Scylla return his love; but Circe, jealous of the fair maiden, threw magic herbs into the well in which Scylla was wont to bathe, by means of which the lower part of her body was changed into the tail of a fish or serpent, surrounded by dogs, while the upper part remained that of a woman. Another tradition related that Scylla was beloved by Poseidon, and that Amphitrite, from jealousy, metamorphosed her into a monster. Hercules is said to have killed her, because she stole some of the oxen of Geryon; but Phorcys is said to have restored her to life. Virgil (*Aen.* vi. 286) speaks of several Scyllae, and places them in the lower world. Charybdis is described as a daughter of Poseidon and Gaea, and a voracious woman, who stole oxen from Hercules, and was hurled by the thunderbolts of Zeus into the sea.

Scylla, daughter of king Nisus of Megara, who fell in love with Minos. For details see NISUS, and MINOS.

Scyllaeum (Σκύλλαιον). 1. (*Sciglio*), a promontory on the coast of Bruttium, at the N. entrance to the Sicilian straits, where the monster Scylla was supposed to live [SCYLLA].—**2.** (*Scilla* or *Sciglio*), a town in Bruttium, on the above-named promontory. There are still remains of the ancient citadel.—**3.** A promontory in Argolis on the coast of Troezen, forming, with the promontory of Sunium in Attica, the entrance to the Saronic gulf. It is said to have derived its name from Scylla, the daughter of Nisus. [NISUS.]

Scyllēticus Sinus. [SCYLACIUM.]

Scyllētium. [SCYLACIUM.]

Scyllis. [DIPOENUS.]

Scymnus (Σκύμνος), of Chios, wrote a *Periegesis*, or description of the earth, which is referred to by later writers. This work was in prose, and consequently different from the Periegesis in Iambic metre, which has come down to us, and which many modern writers have erroneously ascribed to Scymnus of Chios. The poem is dedicated to king Nicomedes, whom some modern writers suppose to be the same as Nicomedes III., king of Bithynia, who died B. C. 74; but this is quite uncertain. The best edition of the poem is by Meineke, Berlin, 1846.

Scyros (Σκῦρος: Σκύριος: *Scyro*), an island in the Aegaean sea, E. of Euboea, and one of the Sporades. It contained a town of the same name, and a river called Cephissus. Its ancient inhabitants are said to have been Pelasgians, Carians, and Dolopians. The island is frequently mentioned in the stories of the mythical period. Here Thetis concealed her son Achilles in woman's attire among the daughters of Lycomedes, in order to save him from the fate which awaited him under the walls of Troy. It was here also that Pyrrhus, the son of Achilles by Deidamīa, was brought up, and it was from this island that Ulysses fetched him to the Trojan war. According to another tradition, the island was conquered by Achilles, in order to revenge the death of Theseus, who is said to have been treacherously destroyed in Scyros by Lycomedes. The bones of Theseus were discovered by Cimon in Scyros, after his conquest of the island in B. C. 476, and were conveyed to Athens, where they were preserved in the Theseum. From this time Scyros continued subject to Athens till the period of the Macedonian supremacy; but the Romans compelled the last Philip to restore it to Athens in 196. The soil of Scyros was unproductive; but it was celebrated for its breed of goats, and for its quarries of variegated marble.

Scythia (ἡ Σκυθική, ἡ Σκυθία, Ion. Σκυθίη, ἡ τῶν Σκυθέων χώρῃ, Herod.: Σκύθης, Scythes, Scȳtha, pl. Σκύθαι, Scȳthae; fem. Σκυθίς, Scȳthis, Scythissa), a name applied to very different countries at different times. The Scythia of Herodotus comprises, to speak generally, the S. E. parts of Europe, between the Carpathian mountains and the river Tanaïs (*Don*). The Greeks became acquainted with this country through their settlements on the Euxine; and Herodotus, who had himself visited the coasts of the Euxine, collected all the information he could obtain about the Scythians and their country, and embodied the results in a most interesting digression, which forms the first part of his 4th book. The details, for which there is not room in this article, must be read in Herodotus. He describes the country as a square of 4000 stadia (400 geog. miles) each way, the W. boundary being the Ister (*Danube*) and the mountains of the Agathyrsi; the S. the shores of the Euxine and Palus Maeotis, from the mouth of the Ister to that of the Tanaïs, this side being divided into 2 equal parts, of 2000 stadia each, by the mouth of the Borysthenes (*Dnieper*); the E. boundary was the Tanaïs, and on the N. Scythia was divided by deserts from the Melanchlaeni, Androphagi, and Budini. It corresponded to the S. part of *Russia in Europe*. The people who inhabited this region were called by the Greeks Σκύθαι, a word of doubtful origin, which first occurs in Hesiod; but, in their own language, Σκόλοτοι, *i. e.* Slavonians. They were believed by Herodotus to be of Asiatic origin; and his account of them, taken in connection with the description given by Hippocrates of their physical peculiarities, leaves no doubt that they were a part of the great Mongol race, who have wandered from unknown antiquity, over the steppes of Central Asia. Herodotus says further that they were driven out of their abodes in Asia, N. of the Araxes, by the Massagetae; and that, migrating into Europe, they drove out the Cimmerians. If this account be true, it can hardly but have some connection with the irruption of the Cimmerians into Asia Minor, in the reign of the Lydian king Ardys, about B. C. 640. The Scythians were a nomad people, that is, shepherds or herdsmen, who had no fixed habitations, but roamed over a vast tract of country at their pleasure, and according to the wants of their cattle. They lived in a kind of covered waggons, which Aeschylus describes as " lofty houses of wickerwork, on well-wheeled chariots." They kept large troops of horses, and were most expert in cavalry exercises and archery ; and hence, as the Persian king Darius found, when he invaded their country (B. C. 507), it was almost impossible for an invading army to act against them. They simply retreated, waggons and all, before the enemy, harassing him with their light cavalry, and leaving famine and exposure, in their bare steppes, to do the rest. Like all the Mongol race, they were divided into several hordes, the chief of whom were called the Royal Scythians ; and to these all the rest owned some degree of allegiance. Their government was a sort of patriarchal monarchy or chieftainship. An important modification of their habits had, however, taken place, to a certain extent, before Herodotus described them. The fertility of the plains on the N. of the Euxine, and the influence of the Greek settlements at the mouth of the Borysthenes, and along the coast, had led the inhabitants of this part of Scythia to settle down as cultivators of the soil, and had brought them into commercial and other relations with the Greeks. Accordingly, Herodotus mentions 2 classes or hordes of Scythians, who had thus abandoned their nomad life ; first, on the W. of the Borysthenes, 2 tribes of Hellenized Scythians, called Callipidae and Alazones ; then, beyond these, " the Scythians who are ploughers (Σκύθαι ἀροτῆρες), who do not grow their corn for food, but for sale ;" these dwelt about the river Hypanis (Boug) in the region now called the Ukraine, which is still, as it was to the Greeks, a great corn exporting country. Again, on the E. of the Borysthenes were " the Scythians who are husbandmen " (Σκύθαι γεωργοί), i. e. who grew corn for their own consumption : these were called Borysthenītae by the Greeks : their country extended 3 days' journey E. of the Borysthenes to the river PANTICAPES. Beyond these, to the E., dwelt " the nomad Scythians (νομάδες Σκύθαι), who neither sow nor plough at all." Herodotus expressly states that the tribes E. of the Borysthenes were not Scythian. Of the history of these Scythian tribes there is little to state, beyond the tradition already mentioned, that they migrated from Asia, and expelled the Cimmerians ; their invasion of Media, in the reign of Cyaxares, when they held the supremacy of W. Asia for 28 years ; and the disastrous expedition of Darius into their country. In later times, they were gradually overpowered by the neighbouring people, especially the Sarmatians, who gave their name to the whole country. [SARMATIA.] Meanwhile, the conquests of Alexander and his successors in Central Asia had made the Greeks acquainted with tribes beyond the Oxus and the Jaxartes, who resembled the Scythians, and belonged, in fact, to the same great Mongol race, and to whom, accordingly, the same name was applied. Hence, in writers of the time of the Roman empire, the name of Scythia denotes the whole of N. Asia, from the river Rha (Volga) on the W., which divided it from Asiatic Sarmatia, to Serica on the E., extending to India on the S. It was divided, by M. Imaus, into 2 parts, called respectively Scythia intra Imaum,

i. e. on the N. W. side of the range, and Scythia extra Imaum, on its S. E. side. Of the people of this region nothing was known except some names; but the absence of knowledge was supplied by some marvellous and not uninteresting fables.

Scythini (Σκυθινοί), a people on the W. border of Armenia, through whose country the Greeks under Xenophon marched 4 days' journey. Their territory was bounded on the E. by the river Harpasus, and on the W. by the river Apsarus.

Scythīnus (Σκυθῖνος), of Teos, an iambic poet, turned into verse the great work of the philosopher Heraclitus, of which a considerable fragment is preserved by Stobaeus.

Scythŏpŏlis (Σκυθόπολις : O. T. Bethshean: Beisan, Ru.), an important city of Palestine, in the S. E. of Galilee, according to the usual division, but sometimes also reckoned to Samaria, sometimes to Decapolis, and sometimes to Coele-Syria. It stood on a hill in the Jordan valley, W. of the river, and near one of its fords. Its site was fertilised by numerous springs ; and to this advantage, as well as to its being the centre of several roads, it owed its great prosperity and its importance in the history of Palestine. It is often mentioned in O. T. history, in the time of the Maccabees, and under the Romans. It had a mixed population of Canaanites, Philistines, and Assyrian settlers; Josephus adds Scythians, but this is perhaps an error, founded on a false etymology of the name. Under the later Roman empire, it became the seat of the archbishop of Palaestina Secunda, and it continued a flourishing city to the time of the first Crusade.

Scythŏtauri, Tauri Scythae, or Tauroscythae, a people of Sarmatia Europaea, just without the Chersonesus Taurica, between the rivers Carcinites and Hypanis, as far as the tongue of land called Dromos Achilleos.

Sĕbastē (Σεβαστή = Augusta : Σεβαστηνός). 1. (Ayash, Ru.), a city on the coast of Cilicia Aspera, built for a residence by Archelaus, king of Cappadocia, to whom the Romans had granted the sovereignty of Cilicia, and named in honour of Augustus. It stood W. of the river Lamus, on a small island called Eleousa, the name of which appears to have been afterwards transferred to the city. — 2. (Segikler), a city of Phrygia, N. W. of Eumenia. — 3. [CABIRA.] This city was also called Σεβάστεια. — 4. [SAMARIA.]

Sĕbastŏpŏlis (Σεβαστόπολις : Turkhal), a city of Pontus, on the Iris, S. E. of Amasia, by some identified with GAZIURA. There were some other places of the name, which do not require particular notice.

Sebennytus (Σεβέννυτος, ἡ Σεβεννυτικὴ πόλις : Semennout, Ru.), a considerable city of Lower Egypt, in the Delta, on the W. side of the branch of the Nile called after it the Sebennytic Mouth, just at the fork made by this and the Phatnitic Mouth, and S. of Busiris. It was the capital of the Nomos Sebennytes or Sebennyticus.

Sebēthus (Maddalena), a small river in Campania, flowing round Vesuvius, and falling into the Sinus Puteolanus at the E. side of Neapolis.

Sebīnus Lacus (Lago Seo or Iseo), a lake in Gallia Cisalpina, formed by the river Ollius between the lakes Larius and Benacus.

Secundus, Pompōnĭus, a distinguished poet in the reigns of Tiberius, Caligula, and Claudius. He was one of the friends of Sejanus, and on the fall of that minister in A. D. 31 was thrown into prison, where he remained till the accession of Caligula in 37, by whom he was released. He was consul in 41, and in the reign of Claudius commanded in Germany, when he defeated the Chatti. Secundus was an intimate friend of the elder Pliny, who wrote his life in 2 books. His tragedies were the most celebrated of his literary compositions.

Sedëtäni. [EDETANI.]

Sedigïtus, Volcätius, from whose work *De Poëtis* A. Gellius (xv. 24) has preserved 13 Iambic senarians, in which the principal Latin comic dramatists are enumerated in the order of merit. In this "Canon," as it has been termed, the 1st place is assigned to Caecilius Statius, the 2nd to Plautus, the 3rd to Naevius, the 4th to Licinius, the 5th to Attilius, the 6th to Terentius, the 7th to Turpilius, the 8th to Trabea, the 9th to Luscius, the 10th, " causa antiquitatis," to Ennius.

Sêdülïus, Coelius, of Seville, a Christian poet, flourished about A. D. 450. Of his personal history we know nothing. His works are : — 1. *Puschale Carmen* s. *Mirabilium Divinorum Libri V.*, in heroic measure. 2. *Veteris et Novi Testamenti Collatio*, a sort of hymn containing a collection of texts from the Old and New Testaments, arranged in such a manner as to enable the reader to compare the two dispensations. 3. *Hymnus de Christo*, an account of the life and miracles of Christ. 4. *De Verbi Incarnatione*, a Cento Virgilianus. The best editions are by Cellarius, Hal. 1704 and 1739; by Arntzenius, Leovard. 1761; and by Arevalus, Rom. 1794.

Sedûni, an Alpine people in Gallia Belgica, E. of the lake of Geneva, in the valley of the Rhone, in the modern *Vallais.* Their chief town was called Civitas Sedunorum, the modern *Sion.*

Sedusii, a German people, forming part of the army of Ariovistus, when he invaded Gaul, B. C. 58. They are not mentioned at a later period, and consequently their site cannot be determined.

Segësäma or **Segïsämo** (Segisamonensis : *Sasamo*), a town of the Murbogi or Turmodigi in Hispania Tarraconensis, on the road from Tarraco to Asturica.

Segesta. (Segestanus : nr. *Alcamo* Ru.), the later Roman form of the town, called by the Greeks **Egesta** or **Aegesta** ('Εγεστα, Αἴγεστα, in Virg. Acesta: 'Εγεσταῖος, Αἰγεστανός, Acestaeus), situated in the N. W. of Sicily, near the coast between Panormus and Drepanum. It is said to have been founded by the Trojans on 2 small rivers, to which they gave the names of Simois and Scamander; hence the Romans made it a colony of Aeneas. One tradition, indeed, ascribed to it a Greek origin ; but in later times it was never regarded as a Greek city. Its inhabitants were constantly engaged in hostilities with Selinus ; and it was at their solicitation that the Athenians were led to embark in their unfortunate expedition against Sicily. The town was taken by Agathocles, who destroyed or sold as slaves all its inhabitants, peopled the city with a body of deserters, and changed its name into that of Dicaeopolis ; but after the death of this tyrant, the remains of the ancient inhabitants returned to the city and resumed their former name. In the neighbourhood of the city, on the road to Drepanum, were celebrated mineral springs, called *Aquae Segestanae* or *Aquae Pintianae.*

Segestes, a Cheruscan chieftain, the opponent

of Arminius. Private injuries embittered their political feud, for Arminius carried off and forcibly married the daughter of Segestes. In A. D. 9 Segestes warned Quintilius Varus of the conspiracy of Arminius, and other Cheruscan chiefs against him ; but his warning was disregarded, and Varus perished. In 14 Segestes was forced by his tribesmen into a war with Rome ; but he afterwards made his peace with the Romans, and was allowed to reside at Narbonne.

Segetïa, a Roman divinity, who, together with Setia or Seja and Semonia, was invoked by the early Italians at seed time, for Segetia, like the two other names, is connected with *sero* and *segos.*

Segni, a German people in Gallia Belgica, between the Treveri and Eburones, the name of whom is still preserved in the modern town of *Sinei* or *Signei.*

Segobrïga, the chief town of the Celtiberi, in Hispania Tarraconensis, S.W. of Caesaraugusta, probably in the neighbourhood of the modern *Priego.*

Segontïa or **Seguntïa,** a town of the Celtiberi, in Hispania Tarraconensis, 16 miles from Caesaraugusta.

Segovïa. 1. (*Segovia*), a town of the Arevaci, on the road from Emerita to Caesaraugusta. A magnificent Roman aqueduct is still extant at Segovia. — 2. A town in Hispania Baetica on the Flumen Silicense, near Sacili.

Segusiäni, one of the most important peoples in Gallia Lugdunensis, bounded by the Allobroges on the S., by the Sequani on the E., by the Aedui on the N., and by the Arverni on the W. In the time of Caesar they were dependent on the Aedui. In their territory was the town of Lugdunum, the capital of the province.

Segusïo (*Susa*), the capital of the Segusini and the residence of king Cottius, was situated in Gallia Transpadana, at the foot of the Cottian Alps The triumphal arch, erected at this place by Cottius in honour of Augustus, is still extant.

Seius Strabo. [SEJANUS.]

Sejänus, Aelïus, was born at Vulsinii, in Etruria, and was the son of Seius Strabo, who was commander of the praetorian troops at the close of the reign of Augustus, A. D. 14. In the same year Sejanus was made the colleague of his father in the command of the praetorian bands; and upon his father being sent as governor to Egypt, he obtained the sole command of these troops. He ultimately gained such influence over Tiberius, that this suspicious man, who was close and reserved to all mankind, opened his bosom to Sejanus, and made him his confidant. For many years he governed Tiberius ; but not content with this high position, he formed the design of obtaining the imperial power. With this view he sought to make himself popular with the soldiers, and gave posts of honour and emolument to his creatures and favourites. With the same object he resolved to get rid of all the members of the imperial family. He debauched Livia, the wife of Drusus, the son of Tiberius ; and by promising her marriage and a participation in the imperial power, he was enabled to poison Drusus with her connivance and assistance (23). An accident increased the credit of Sejanus, and confirmed the confidence of Tiberius. The emperor, with Sejanus and others, was feasting in a natural cave, between Amyclae, which was on the sea coast, and the hills of Fundi. The entrance of the cave suddenly fell in, and crushed some of the slaves; and all the guests, in alarm, tried to make their escape. Sejanus, resting his knees on the couch of Tiberius, and placing his shoulders under the falling rock, protected his master, and was discovered in this posture by the soldiers who came to their relief. After Tiberius had shut himself up in the island of Capreae, Sejanus had full scope for his machinations; and the death of Livia, the mother of Tiberius (29), was followed by the banishment of Agrippina and her sons Nero and Drusus. Tiberius at last began to suspect the designs of Sejanus, and felt that it was time to rid himself of a man who was almost more than a rival. To cover his schemes and remove Sejanus from about him, Tiberius made him joint consul with himself, in 31. He then sent Sertorius Macro to Rome, with a commission to take the command of the praetorian cohorts. Macro, after assuring himself of the troops, and depriving Sejanus of his usual guard, produced a letter from Tiberius to the senate, in which the emperor expressed his apprehensions of Sejanus. The consul Regulus conducted him to prison, and the people loaded him with insult and outrage. The senate on the same day decreed his death, and he was immediately executed. His body was dragged about the streets, and finally thrown into the Tiber. Many of the friends of Sejanus perished at the same time; and his son and daughter shared his fate.

Selene (Σελήνη), called **Luna** by the Romans, was the goddess of the moon, or the moon personified as a divine being. She is called a daughter of Hyperion and Thia, and accordingly a sister of Helios (Sol) and Eos (Aurora); but others speak of her as a daughter of Hyperion by Euryphaessa, or of Pallas, or of Zeus and Latona. She is also called Phoebe, as the sister of Phoebus, the god of the sun. By Endymion, whom she loved, and whom she sent to sleep in order to kiss him, she became the mother of 50 daughters; and to Zeus she bore Pandia, Ersa, and Nemea. Pan also is said to have had connexion with her in the shape of a white ram. Selene is described as a very beautiful goddess, with long wings and a golden diadem. She rode, like her brother Helios, across the heavens in a chariot drawn by two white horses. In later times Selene was identified with Artemis or Diana, and the worship of the two became amalgamated. In works of art, however, the two divinities are usually distinguished; the face of Selene being more full and round, her figure less tall, and always clothed in a long robe; her veil forms an arch over her head, and above it there is the crescent. At Rome Luna had a temple on the Aventine.

Selene. [CLEOPATRA, No. 9.]

Seleucia, and rarely **Seleucea** (Σελεύκεια: Σελευκεύς: Seleucensis, Seleucenus), the name of several cities in Asia, built by Seleucus I., king of Syria. 1. **S. ad Tigrin** (ἡ ἐπὶ τοῦ Τίγρητος ποταμοῦ, πρὸς Τίγρει, ἀπὸ Τίγριος), also called **S. Babylonia** (Σ. ἡ ἐν Βαβυλῶνι), **S. Assyriae**, and **S. Parthorum**, a great city on the confines of Assyria and Babylonia, and for a long time the capital of W. Asia, until it was eclipsed by CTESIPHON. Its exact site has been disputed; but the most probable opinion is that it stood on the W. bank of the Tigris, N. of its junction with the Royal Canal, opposite to the mouth of the river Delas or Silla (Diala), and to the spot where Ctesiphon

was afterwards built by the Parthians. It was a little to the S. of the modern city of Bagdad. Perhaps a better site could not be found in W. Asia. It commanded the navigation of the Tigris and Euphrates, and the whole plain of those two rivers; and it stood at the junction of all the chief caravan roads by which the traffic between E. and W. Asia was carried on. In addition to these advantages, its people had, by the gift of Seleucus, the government of their own affairs. It was built in the form of an eagle with expanded wings, and was peopled by settlers from Assyria, Mesopotamia, Babylonia, Syria, and Judaea. It rapidly rose, and eclipsed Babylon in wealth and splendour. Even after the Parthian kings had become masters of the banks of the Tigris, and had fixed their residence at Ctesiphon, Seleucia, though deprived of much of its importance, remained a very considerable city. In the reign of Titus, it had, according to Pliny, 600,000 inhabitants. It was burned by Trajan in his Parthian expedition, and again by L. Verus, the colleague of M. Aurelius Antoninus, when its population is given by different authorities as 300,000 or 400,000. It was again taken by Severus; and from this blow it never recovered. In Julian's expedition it was found entirely deserted. — 2. **S. Pieria** (Σ. Πιερία, ἡ ἐν Πιερίᾳ, ἡ πρὸς Ἀντιοχείᾳ, ἡ πρὸς θαλάσσῃ, ἡ ἐπιθαλασσία, Ru., called Seleukeh or Kepse, near Swaderiah), a great city and fortress of Syria, founded by Seleucus in April, B. C. 300, one month before the foundation of Antioch. It stood on the site of an ancient fortress, on the rocks overhanging the sea, at the foot of M. Pieria, about 4 miles N. of the Orontes, and 12 miles W. of Antioch. Its natural strength was improved by every known art of fortification, to which were added all the works of architecture and engineering required to make it a splendid city and a great seaport, while it obtained abundant supplies from the fertile plain between the city and Antioch. The remains of Seleucus I. were interred at Seleucia, in a mausoleum surrounded by a grove. In the war with Egypt, which ensued upon the murder of Antiochus II., Seleucia surrendered to Ptolemy III. Energetes (B. C. 246). It was afterwards recovered by Antiochus the Great (219). In the war between Antiochus VIII. and IX. the people of Seleucia made themselves independent (109 or 108). Afterwards, having successfully resisted the attacks of Tigranes for 14 years (84—70), they were confirmed in their freedom by Pompey. The city had fallen entirely into decay by the 6th century of our era. There are considerable ruins of the harbour and mole, of the walls of the city, and of its necropolis. The surrounding district was called SELEUCIS. — 3. **S. ad Belum**, a city of Syria, in the valley of the Orontes near Apamea. Its site is doubtful.—4. **S. Tracheotis** (Selefkeh Ru.), an important city of Cilicia Aspera, was built by Seleucus I. on the W. bank of the river Calycadnus, about 4 miles from its mouth, and peopled with the inhabitants of several neighbouring cities. It had an oracle of Apollo, and annual games in honour of Zeus Olympius. It vied with Tarsus in power and splendour, and was a free city under the Romans. It has remarkable claims to renown both in political and literary history: in the former, as the place where Trajan and Frederick Barbarossa died; in the latter, as the birthplace of the philosophers Athenaeus and

Xenarchus, of the sophist Alexander, the secretary of M. Aurelius Antoninus, and of other learned men. On its site are still seen the ruins of temples, porticoes, aqueducts, and tombs. — 5. 8. in Mesopotamia (Bir), on the left bank of the Euphrates, opposite to the ford of Zeugma, was a fortress of considerable importance in ancient military history. — 6. A considerable city of Margiana, built by Alexander the Great, in a beautiful situation, and called Alexandria ; destroyed by the barbarians, and rebuilt by Antiochus I., who named it Seleucia after his father Seleucus I. The Roman prisoners taken at the defeat of Crassus by the Parthians were settled here by king Orodes.— 7. 8. in Caria [TRALLES]. — There were other cities of the name, of less importance, in Pisidia, Pamphylia, Palestine, and Elymaïs.

Sĕleucis (Σελευκίς). 1. The most beautiful and fertile district of Syria, containing the N.W. part of the country, between M. Amanus on the N., the Mediterranean on the W., the districts of Cyrrhestice and Chalybonitis on the N.E., the desert on the E., and Coelesyria and the mountains of Lebanon on the S. It included the valley of the lower Orontes, and contained the 4 great cities of Antioch, Seleucia, Laodicea, and Apamea, whence it was also called Tetrapolis. In later times, the name was confined to the small district N. of the Orontes; the S. part of the former Seleucis being divided into Cassiotis, W. of the Orontes, and Apamene, E. of the river. — 2. A district of Cappadocia. — 3. A name which Seleucus I. endeavoured to give to the Caspian Sea, in memory of a voyage of exploration made round it by his command.

Sĕleucus (Σέλευκος), the name of several kings of Syria. I. Surnamed Nicator, the founder of the Syrian monarchy, reigned B. C. 312—280. He was the son of Antiochus, a Macedonian of distinction among the officers of Philip II., and was born about 358. He accompanied Alexander on his expedition to Asia, and distinguished himself particularly in the Indian campaigns. After the death of Alexander (323) he espoused the side of Perdiccas, whom he accompanied on his expedition against Egypt ; but he took a leading part in the mutiny of the soldiers, which ended in the death of Perdiccas (321). In the 2nd partition of the provinces which followed, Seleucus obtained the wealthy and important satrapy of Babylonia. In the war between Antigonus and Eumenes, Seleucus afforded efficient support to the former ; but after the death of Eumenes (316), Antigonus began to treat the other satraps as his subjects. Thereupon Seleucus fled to Egypt, where he induced Ptolemy to unite with Lysimachus and Cassander in a league against their common enemy. In the war that ensued Seleucus took an active part. At length, in 312, he recovered Babylon ; and it is from this period, that the Syrian monarchy is commonly reckoned to commence. This era of the Seleucidae, as it is termed, has been determined by chronologers to the 1st of October, 312. Soon afterwards Seleucus defeated Nicanor, the satrap of Media, and followed up his victory by the conquest of Susiana, Media, and some adjacent districts. For the next few years he gradually extended his power over all the eastern provinces which had formed part of the empire of Alexander, from the Euphrates to the banks of the Oxus and the Indus. In 306 Seleucus followed the example of Antigonus and Ptolemy, by

formally assuming the regal title and diadem. In 302 he joined the league formed for the second time by Ptolemy, Lysimachus, and Cassander, against their common enemy Antigonus. The united forces of Seleucus and Lysimachus gained a decisive victory over Antigonus at Ipsus (301), in which Antigonus himself was slain. In the division of the spoil, Seleucus obtained the largest share, being rewarded for his services with a great part of Asia Minor (which was divided between him and Lysimachus) as well as with the whole of Syria, from the Euphrates to the Mediterranean. The empire of Seleucus was now by far the most extensive and powerful of those which had been formed out of the dominions of Alexander. It comprised the whole of Asia, from the remote provinces of Bactria and Sogdiana to the coasts of Phoenicia, and from the Paropamisus to the central plains of Phrygia, where the boundary which separated him from Lysimachus is not clearly defined. Seleucus appears to have felt the difficulty of exercising a vigilant control over so extensive an empire, and accordingly, in 293, he consigned the government of all the provinces beyond the Euphrates to his son Antiochus, upon whom he bestowed the title of king, as well as the hand of his own youthful wife, Stratonice, for whom the prince had conceived a violent attachment. In 288, the ambitious designs of Demetrius (now become king of Macedonia) once more aroused the common jealousy of his old adversaries, and led Seleucus again to unite in a league with Ptolemy and Lysimachus against him. After Demetrius had been driven from his kingdom by Lysimachus, he transported the seat of war into Asia Minor, but he was compelled to surrender to Seleucus in 286. The Syrian king kept Demetrius in confinement till 3 years afterwards, but during the whole of that time treated him in a friendly and liberal manner. For some time jealousies had existed between Seleucus and Lysimachus ; but the immediate cause of the war between the 2 monarchs, which terminated in the defeat and death of Lysimachus (281), is related in the life of the latter. Seleucus now crossed the Hellespont in order to take possession of the throne of Macedonia, which had been left vacant by the death of Lysimachus ; but he had advanced no farther than Lysimachia, when he was assassinated by Ptolemy Ceraunus, to whom, as the son of his old friend and ally, he had extended a friendly protection. His death took place in the beginning of 280, only 7 months after that of Lysimachus, and in the 32nd year of his reign. He was in his 78th year. Seleucus appears to have carried out, with great energy and perseverance, the projects originally formed by Alexander himself, for the Hellenisation of his Asiatic empire ; and we find him founding, in almost every province, Greek or Macedonian colonies, which became so many centres of civilisation and refinement. Of these no less than 16 are mentioned as bearing the name of Antiochia after his father ; 5 that of Laodicea, from his mother ; 7 were called after himself Seleucia ; 3 from the name of his first wife, Apamea ; and one Stratonicea, from his second wife, the daughter of Demetrius. Numerous other cities, whose names attest their Macedonian origin — Beroea, Edessa, Pella, &c.—likewise owed their first foundation to Seleucus. — II. Surnamed Callinicus (246—226), was the eldest son of Antiochus II. by his first wife Laodice. The first measure of his administration, or rather that of his mother, was to put to death his stepmother Berenice, together with her infant son. This act of cruelty produced the most disastrous effects. In order to avenge his sister, Ptolemy Euergetes, king of Egypt, invaded the dominions of Seleucus, and not only made himself master of Antioch and the whole of Syria, but carried his arms unopposed beyond the Euphrates and the Tigris. During these operations Seleucus kept wholly aloof; but when Ptolemy had been recalled to his own dominions by domestic disturbances, he recovered possession of the greater part of the provinces which he had lost. Soon afterwards Seleucus became involved in a dangerous war with his brother Antiochus Hierax, who attempted to obtain Asia Minor as an independent kingdom for himself. This war lasted several years, but was at length terminated by the decisive defeat of Antiochus, who was obliged to quit Asia Minor and take refuge in Egypt. Seleucus undertook an expedition to the East, with the view of reducing the revolted provinces of Parthia and Bactria, which had availed themselves of the disordered state of the Syrian empire to throw off its yoke. He was, however, defeated by Arsaces, king of Parthia, in a great battle which was long after celebrated by the Parthians as the foundation of their independence. After the expulsion of Antiochus, Attalus, king of Pergamus, extended his dominions over the greater part of Asia Minor; and Seleucus appears to have been engaged in an expedition for the recovery of these provinces, when he was accidentally killed by a fall from his horse, in the 21st year of his reign, 226. He left 2 sons, who successively ascended the throne, Seleucus Ceraunus and Antiochus, afterwards surnamed the Great. His own surname of Callinicus was probably assumed after his recovery of the provinces that had been overrun by Ptolemy.—III. Surnamed **Ceraunus** (226—223), eldest son and successor of Seleucus II. The surname of Ceraunus was given him by the soldiery, apparently in derision, as he appears to have been feeble both in mind and body. He was assassinated by 2 of his officers, after a reign of only 3 years, and was succeeded by his brother, Antiochus the Great.—IV. Surnamed **Philopator** (187 —175), was the son and successor of Antiochus the Great. The defeat of his father by the Romans, and the ignominious peace which followed it, had greatly diminished the power of the Syrian monarchy, and the reign of Seleucus was in consequence feeble and inglorious, and was marked by no striking events. He was assassinated in 175 by one of his own ministers. He left 2 children: Demetrius, who subsequently ascended the throne; and Laodice, married to Perseus, king of Macedonia.—V. Eldest son of Demetrius II., assumed the royal diadem on learning the death of his father, 125; but his mother Cleopatra, who had herself put Demetrius to death, was indignant at hearing that her son had ventured to take such a step without her authority, and caused Seleucus also to be assassinated.—VI. Surnamed **Epiphanes**, and also **Nicator** (95—93) was the eldest of the 5 sons of Antiochus VIII. Grypus. On the death of his father, in 95, he ascended the throne, and defeated and slew in battle his uncle Antiochus Cyzicenus, who had laid claim to the kingdom. But shortly after Seleucus was in his turn defeated

by Antiochus Eusebes, the son of Cyzicenus, and expelled from Syria. He took refuge in Cilicia, where he established himself in the city of Mopsuestia; but in consequence of his tyranny, he was burned to death by the inhabitants in his palace.

Selgē (Σέλγη: Σελγεύς: Sürk? Ru.), one of the chief of the independent mountain cities of Pisidia, stood on the S. side of M. Taurus, on the Eurymedon, just where the river breaks through the mountain chain. On a rock above it was a citadel named Κεσβέδιον, in which was a temple of Hera. Its inhabitants, who were the most warlike of all the Pisidians, claimed descent from the Lacedaemonians, and inscribed the name Λακεδαίμων on their coins. They could bring an army of 20,000 men into the field, and, as late as the 5th century, we find them beating back a horde of Goths. In a valley near the city, in the heart of lofty mountains, grew wine and oil and other products of the most luxuriant vegetation.

Selinūs (Σελινοῦς -οῦντος, contraction of σελινόεις from σέλινον "parsley"). 1. A small river on the S.W. coast of Sicily, flowing by the town of the same name.—2. (Crestena), a river of Elis, in the district Triphylia, near Scillus, flowing into the Alpheus W. of Olympia.—3. (Vostitza), a river of Achaia, rising in Mt. Erymanthus.—4. A tributary of the Caicus in Mysia, flowing by the town of Pergamum.—4. (Σελινούντιος, Σελινούσιος: nr. Castel vetrano, Ru.), one of the most important towns in Sicily, situated upon a hill on the S.W. coast, and upon a river of the same name. It was founded by the Dorians from Megara Hyblaea on the E. coast of Sicily, B.C. 628. It soon attained great prosperity; but it was taken by the Carthaginians in 409, when most of its inhabitants were slain or sold as slaves, and the greater part of the city destroyed. The population of Selinus must at that time have been very considerable, since we are told that 16,000 men fell in the siege and conquest of the town, 5000 were carried to Carthage as slaves, 2600 fled to Agrigentum, and many others took refuge in the surrounding villages. The Carthaginians however allowed the inhabitants to return to Selinus in the course of the same year, and it continued to be a place of secondary importance till 249, when it was again destroyed by the Carthaginians and its inhabitants transferred to Lilybaeum. The surrounding country produced excellent wheat. East of Selinus on the road to Agrigentum, were celebrated mineral springs called *Aquae Selinuntiae*, subsequently *Aquae Labodae* or *Labodes*, the modern *Baths of Sciacca*. There are still considerable ruins of Selinus.—5. (*Selenti*), a town in Cilicia, situated on the coast and upon a rock which was almost entirely surrounded by the sea. In consequence of the death of the emperor Trajan in this town, it was for a long time called Trajanopolis.

Sellasia (Σελλασία or Σελασία), a town in Laconica, N. of Sparta, was situated near the river Oenus, and commanded one of the principal passes leading to Sparta. Here the celebrated battle was fought between Cleomenes III. and Antigonus Doson, B.C. 221, in which the former was defeated.

Sellēīs (Σελλήεις). 1. A river in Elis, on which the Homeric Ephyra stood, rising in mount Pholoë and falling into the sea, S. of the Peneus.—2. A river near Sicyon.—3. A river in Troas near Arisbe, and a tributary of the Rhodius.

Selli or **Helli.** [DODONA.]

Selymbria or **Selybria** (Σηλυμβρία, Σηλυβρία, Dor. Σαλαμβρία: Σηλυμβριανός: *Seliveria*), an important town in Thrace, situated on the Propontis. It was a colony of the Megarians, and was founded earlier than Byzantium. It perhaps derived its name from its founder Selys and the Thracian word *Bria*, a town. It continued to be a place of considerable importance till its conquest by Philip, the father of Alexander, from which time its decline may be dated. Under the later emperors it was called Eudoxiupolis, in honour of Eudoxia, the wife of Arcadius; but it afterwards recovered its ancient name.

Semechonitis or **Samachonitis Lacus** (Σεμεχωνῖτις, Σαμαχωνῖτις and ·ιτῶν λίμνη: O. T. Waters of Merom: *Nahr-el-Huleh*), a small lake in the N. of Palestine, the highest of the 3 formed by the Jordan, both branches of which fall into its N. end, while the river flows out of its S. end in one stream. The valley in which it lies is enclosed on the W. and E. by mountains belonging to the two ranges of Lebanon, forming a position which has been of military importance both in ancient and modern times, especially as the great Damascus road crosses the Jordan just below the lake. According to the division of Palestine under the Roman empire, it belonged to Galilee, but in earlier times, under the Syrian kings, it was reckoned to Coelesyria.

Semele (Σεμέλη), daughter of Cadmus and Harmonia, at Thebes, and accordingly sister of Ino, Agave, Autonoë, and Polydorus. She was beloved by Zeus. Hera, stimulated by jealousy, appeared to her in the form of her aged nurse Beroë, and induced her to ask Zeus to visit her in the same splendour and majesty with which he appeared to Hera. Zeus warned her of the danger of her request; but as he had sworn to grant whatever she desired, he was obliged to comply with her prayer. He accordingly appeared before her as the god of thunder, and Semele was consumed by the lightning; but Zeus saved her child Dionysus, with whom she was pregnant. Her son afterwards carried her out of the lower world, and conducted her to Olympus where she became immortal under the name of Thyone.

Semiramis (Σεμίραμις) and **Ninus** (Νίνος), the mythical founders of the Assyrian empire of Ninus or Nineveh. Ninus was a great warrior, who built the town of Ninus or Nineveh, about B. C. 2182, and subdued the greater part of Asia. Semiramis was the daughter of the fish-goddess Derceto of Ascalon in Syria by a Syrian youth; but being ashamed of her frailty, she made away with the youth, and exposed her infant daughter. But the child was miraculously preserved by doves, who fed her till she was discovered by the shepherds of the neighbourhood. She was then brought up by the chief shepherd of the royal herds, whose name was Simmas, and from whom she derived the name of Semiramis. Her surpassing beauty attracted the notice of Onnes, one of the king's friends and generals, who married her. He subsequently sent for his wife to the army, where the Assyrians were engaged in the siege of Bactra, which they had long endeavoured in vain to take. Upon her arrival in the camp she planned an attack upon the citadel of the town, mounted the walls with a few brave followers, and obtained possession of the place. Ninus was so charmed by her bravery and beauty, that he resolved to

make her his wife, whereupon her unfortunate husband put an end to his life. By Ninus Semiramis had a son, Ninyas, and on the death of Ninus she succeeded him on the throne. According to another account, Semiramis had obtained from her husband permission to rule over Asia for 5 days, and availed herself of this opportunity to cast the king into a dungeon, or, as is also related, to put him to death, and thus obtained the sovereign power. Her fame threw into the shade that of Ninus; and later ages loved to tell of her marvellous deeds and her heroic achievements. She built numerous cities, and erected many wonderful buildings; and several of the most extraordinary works in the East, which were extant in a later age, and the authors of which were unknown, were ascribed by popular tradition to this queen. In Nineveh she erected a tomb for her husband, 9 stadia high, and 10 wide; she built the city of Babylon, with all its wonders; and she constructed the hanging gardens in Media, of which later writers give us such strange accounts. Besides conquering many nations of Asia, she subdued Egypt and a great part of Ethiopia, but was unsuccessful in an attack which she made upon India. After a reign of 42 years she resigned the sovereignty to her son Ninyas, and disappeared from the earth, taking her flight to heaven in the form of a dove. The fabulous nature of this narrative is apparent. It is probable that Semiramis was originally a Syrian goddess, perhaps the same who was worshipped at Ascalon under the name of Astarte, or the Heavenly Aphrodite, to whom the dove was sacred. Hence the stories of her voluptuousness, which were current even in the time of Augustus (Ov. *Am.* i. 5. 11).

Semnones, more rarely **Sennones**, a German people, described by Tacitus as the most powerful tribe of the Suevic race, dwelt beween the rivers Viadus (*Oder*) and Albis (*Elbe*), from the Riesen gebirge in the S. as far as the country around Frankfurt on the Oder and Potsdam in the N.

Semo Sancus. [SANCUS.]

Sempronia. 1. Daughter of Tib. Gracchus, censor B. C. 169, and sister of the 2 celebrated tribunes, married Scipio Africanus minor. — **2.** Wife of D. Junius Brutus, consul 77, was a woman of great personal attractions and literary accomplishments, but of a profligate character. She took part in Catiline's conspiracy, though her husband was not privy to it.

Sempronia Gens, was of great antiquity, and one of its members, A. Sempronius Atratinus, obtained the consulship as early as B. C. 497, 12 years after the foundation of the republic. The Sempronii were divided into many families, of which those the ATRATINI were patrician, but all the others were plebeian: their names are ASELLIO, BLAESUS, GRACCHUS, SOPHUS, TUDITANUS.

Sena (Senensis). 1. (*Senigaglia*), surnamed **Gallica**, and sometimes called **Senogallia**, a town on the coast of Umbria, at the mouth of the small river Sena, was founded by the Senones, a Gallic people, and was made a colony by the Romans after the conquest of the Senones, B. C. 283. In the civil war it espoused the Marian party, and was taken and sacked by Pompey. — **2.** (*Siena*), a town in Etruria and a Roman colony, on the road from Clusium to Florentia, is only mentioned in the times of the emperors.

Seneca. 1. **M. Annaeus**, the rhetorician, was born at Corduba (*Cordova*) in Spain, about B.C. 61.

Seneca was at Rome in the early period of the power of Augustus, for he says that he had seen Ovid declaiming before Arellius Fuscus. He afterwards returned to Spain, and married Helvia, by whom he had 3 sons, L. Annaeus Seneca, L. Annaeus Mela or Mella, the father of the poet Lucan, and M. Novatus. Novatus was the eldest son, and took the name of Junius Gallio, upon being adopted by Junius Gallio. Seneca was rich, and he belonged to the equestrian class. At a later period Seneca returned to Rome, where he resided till his death, which probably occurred near the end of the reign of Tiberius. Two of Seneca's works have come down to us. 1. *Controversiarum Libri decem*, which he addressed to his 3 sons. The 1st, 2nd, 7th, 8th, and 10th books only are extant, and these are somewhat mutilated : of the other books only fragments remain. These Controversiae are rhetorical exercises on imaginary cases, filled with commonplaces, such as a man of large verbal memory and great reading carries about with him as his ready money. 2. *Suasoriarum Liber*, which is probably not complete. We may collect from its contents what the subjects were on which the rhetoricians of that age exercised their wits : one of them is, "Shall Cicero apologise to M. Antonius? Shall he agree to burn his Philippics, if Antonius requires it?" Another is, "Shall Alexander embark on the ocean?" If there are some good ideas and apt expressions in these puerile declamations, they have no value where they stand ; and probably most of them are borrowed. No merit of form can compensate for worthlessness of matter. The best edition of these works is by A. Schottus, Heidelberg, 1603, frequently reprinted. — 2. L. Annaeus, the philosopher, the son of the preceding, was born at Corduba, probably a few years B. c., and brought to Rome by his parents when he was a child. Though he was naturally of a weak body, he was a hard student from his youth, and he devoted himself with great ardour to rhetoric and philosophy. He also soon gained distinction as a pleader of causes, and he excited the jealousy and hatred of Caligula by the ability with which he conducted a case in the senate before the emperor. In the first year of the reign of Claudius (A. D. 41), Seneca was banished to Corsica, on account of his intimacy with Julia, the niece of Claudius, of whom Messalina was jealous. After 8 years' residence in Corsica, Seneca was recalled (49) by the influence of Agrippina, who had just married her uncle the emperor Claudius. He now obtained a praetorship, and was made the tutor of the young Domitius, afterwards the emperor Nero, who was the son of Agrippina by a former husband. On the accession of his pupil to the imperial throne (54) after the death of Claudius, Seneca became one of the chief advisers of the young emperor. He exerted his influence to check Nero's vicious propensities, but at the same time he profited from his position to amass an immense fortune. He supported Nero in his contests with his mother Agrippina, and was not only a party to the death of the latter (60), but he wrote the letter which Nero addressed to the senate in justification of the murder. After the death of his mother Nero abandoned himself without any restraint to his vicious propensities ; and the presence of Seneca soon became irksome to him, while the wealth of the philosopher excited the emperor's cupidity. Burrus, the praefect of the praetorian guards, who had always been a firm supporter of Seneca, died in 63. His death broke the power of Seneca ; and Nero now fell into the hands of persons who were exactly suited to his taste. Tigellinus and Fennius Rufus, who succeeded Burrus in the command of the praetorians, began an attack on Seneca. His enormous wealth, his gardens and villas, more magnificent than those of the emperor, his exclusive claims to eloquence, and his disparagement of Nero's skill in driving and singing, were all urged against him ; and it was time, they said, for Nero to get rid of a teacher. Seneca heard of the charges against him : he was rich, and he knew that Nero wanted money. He asked the emperor for permission to retire, and offered to surrender all that he had. Nero affected to be grateful for his past services, refused the proffered gift, and sent him away with perfidious assurances of his respect and affection. Seneca now altered his mode of life, saw little company, and seldom visited the city, on the ground of feeble health, or being occupied with his philosophical studies. The conspiracy of Piso (65) gave the emperor a pretext for putting his teacher to death, though there was not complete evidence of Seneca being a party to the conspiracy. Seneca was at the time returning from Campania, and had rested at a villa 4 miles from the city. Nero sent a tribune to him with the order of death. Without showing any sign of alarm, Seneca cheered his weeping friends by reminding them of the lessons of philosophy. Embracing his wife Pompeia Paulina, he prayed her to moderate her grief, and to console herself for the loss of her husband by the reflection that he had lived an honourable life. But as Paulina protested that she would die with him, Seneca consented, and the same blow opened the veins in the arms of both. Seneca's body was attenuated by age and meagre diet ; the blood would not flow easily, and he opened the veins in his legs. His torture was excessive ; and to save himself and his wife the pain of seeing one another suffer, he bade her retire to her chamber. His last words were taken down in writing by persons who were called in for the purpose, and were afterwards published. Seneca's torments being still prolonged, he took hemlock from his friend and physician, Statius Annaeus, but it had no effect. At last he entered a warm bath, and as he sprinkled some of the water on the slaves nearest to him, he said, that he made a libation to Jupiter the Liberator. He was then taken into a vapour stove, where he was quickly suffocated. Seneca died, as was the fashion among the Romans, with the courage of a stoic, but with somewhat of a theatrical affectation which detracts from the dignity of the scene. Seneca's great misfortune was to have known Nero ; and though we cannot say that he was a truly great or a truly good man, his character will not lose by comparison with that of many others who have been placed in equally difficult circumstances.—Seneca's fame rests on his numerous writings, of which the following are extant : — 1. *De Ira*, in 3 books, addressed to Novatus, probably the earliest of Seneca's works. In the 1st book he combats what Aristotle says of Anger in his Ethics. 2. *De Consolatione ad Helviam Matrem Liber*, a consolatory letter to his mother, written during his residence in Corsica. It is one of his best treatises. 3. *De Consolatione ad Polybium Liber*, also written in Corsica. If it is the work of Seneca, it does him no credit. Polybius was the powerful freedman of Claudius, and the *Consolatio* is intended to comfort him on the occasion of the loss of his brother. But it also contains adulation of the emperor, and many expressions unworthy of a true stoic, or of an honest man. 4. *Liber de Consolatione ad Marciam*, written after his return from exile, was designed to console Marcia for the loss of her son. Marcia was the daughter of A. Cremutius Cordus. 5. *De Providentia Liber*, or *Quare bonis viris mala accidant cum sit Providentia*, is addressed to the younger Lucilius, procurator of Sicily. The question that is here discussed often engaged the ancient philosophers: the stoical solution of the difficulty is that suicide is the remedy when misfortune has become intolerable. In this discourse Seneca says that he intends to prove " that Providence hath a power over all things, and that God is always present with us." 6. *De Animi Tranquillitate*, addressed to Serenus, probably written soon after Seneca's return from exile. It is in the form of a letter rather than a treatise: the object is to discover the means by which tranquillity of mind can be obtained. 7. *De Constantia Sapientis seu quod in sapientem non cadit injuria*, also addressed to Serenus, is founded on the stoical doctrine of the impassiveness of the wise man. 8. *De Clementia ad Neronem Caesarem Libri duo*, written at the beginning of Nero's reign. There is too much of the flatterer in this; but the advice is good. The 2nd book is incomplete. It is in the 1st chapter of this 2nd book that the anecdote is told of Nero's unwillingness to sign a sentence of execution, and his exclamation, " I would I could neither read nor write." 9. *De Brevitate Vitae ad Paulinum Liber*, recommends the proper employment of time and the getting of wisdom as the chief purpose of life. 10. *De Vita Beata ad Gallionem*, addressed to his brother, L. Junius Gallio, is probably one of the later works of Seneca, in which he maintains the stoical doctrine that there is no happiness without virtue; but he does not deny that other things, as health and riches, have their value. The conclusion of the treatise is lost. 11. *De Otio aut Secessu Sapientis*, is sometimes joined to No. 10. 12. *De Beneficiis Libri septem*, addressed to Aebucius Liberalis, is an excellent discussion of the way of conferring a favour, and of the duties of the giver and of the receiver. The handling is not very methodical, but it is very complete. It is a treatise which all persons might read with profit. 13. *Epistolae ad Lucilium*, 124 in number, are not the correspondence of daily life, like that of Cicero, but a collection of moral maxims and remarks without any systematic order. They contain much good matter, and have been favourite reading with many distinguished men. It is possible that these letters, and indeed many of Seneca's moral treatises, were written in the latter part of his life, and probably after he had lost the favour of Nero. That Seneca sought consolation and tranquillity of mind in literary occupation is manifest. 14. *Apocolocyntosis*, is a satire against the emperor Claudius. The word is a play on the term Apotheosis or deification, and is equivalent in meaning to Pumpkinification, or the reception of Claudius among the pumpkins. The subject was well enough, but the treatment has no great merit; and Seneca probably had no other object than to gratify his spite against the emperor. 15. *Quaestionum Naturalium Libri septem*, addressed to Lucilius Junior, is not a systematic

work, but a collection of natural facts from various writers, Greek and Roman, many of which are curious. The 1st book treats of meteors, the 2nd of thunder and lightning, the 3rd of water, the 4th of hail, snow, and ice, the 5th of winds, the 6th of earthquakes and the sources of the Nile, and the 7th of comets. Moral remarks are scattered through the work; and indeed the design of the whole appears to be to find a foundation for ethic, the chief part of philosophy, in the knowledge of nature (Physic). 16. *Tragoediae*, 10 in number. They are entitled *Hercules Furens, Thyestes, Thebais* or *Phoenissae, Hippolytus* or *Phaedra, Oedipus, Troades* or *Hecuba, Medea, Agamemnon, Hercules Oetaeus*, and *Octavia*. The titles themselves, with the exception of the *Octavia*, indicate sufficiently what the tragedies are, Greek mythological subjects treated in a peculiar fashion. They are written in Iambic sennrii, interspersed with choral parts, in anapaestic and other metres. The subject of the *Octavia* is Nero's ill-treatment of his wife, his passion for Poppaea, and the exile of Octavia. These tragedies are not adapted, and certainly were never intended for the stage. They were designed for reading or for recitation after the Roman fashion, and they bear the stamp of a rhetorical age. They contain many striking passages, and have some merit as poems. Moral sentiments and maxims abound, and the style and character of Seneca are as conspicuous here as in his prose works.—The judgments on Seneca's writings have been as various as the opinions about his character; and both in extremes. It has been said of him that he looks best in quotations; but this is an admission that there is something worth quoting, which cannot be said of all writers. That Seneca possessed great mental powers cannot be doubted. He had seen much of human life, and he knew well what man was. His philosophy, so far as he adopted a system, was the stoical, but it was rather an eclecticism of stoicism than pure stoicism. His style is antithetical, and apparently laboured; and when there is much labour, there is generally affectation. Yet his language is clear and forcible; it is not mere words: there is thought always. It would not be easy to name any modern writer who has treated on morality, and has said so much that is practically good and true, or has treated the matter in so attractive a way. The best editions of Seneca are by J. F. Gronovius, Leiden, 1649—1658, 4 vols. 12mo.; by Ruhkopf, Leipzig, 1797—1811, 5 vols. 8vo.; and the Bipont edition, Strassburg, 1809, 5 vols. 8vo.

Sĕnĕcĭo, Hĕrennĭus, was a native of Baetica in Spain, where he served as quaestor. He was put to death by Domitian on the accusation of Metius Carus, in consequence of his having written the life of Helvidius Priscus, which he composed at the request of Fannia, the wife of Helvidius.

Sĕnĭa (Senensis: *Segna* or *Zengg*), a Roman colony in Liburnia in Illyricum, on the coast, and on the road from Aquileia to Siscia.

Sĕnŏnes, a powerful people in Gallia Lugdunensis, dwelt along the upper course of the Sequana (*Seine*), and were bounded on the N. by the Parisii, on the W. by the Carnutes, on the S. by the Aedui, and on the E. by the Lingones and Mandubii. Their chief town was Agendicum, afterwards called Senones (*Sens*). A portion of this people crossed the Alps about B.C. 400, in order to settle in Italy; and as the greater part of Upper Italy was already occupied by other Celtic tribes, the Senones were obliged to penetrate a considerable distance to the S., and took up their abode on the Adriatic sea between the rivers Utis and Aesis (between Ravenna and Ancona), after expelling the Umbrians. In this country they founded the town of Sena. They extended their ravages into Etruria; and it was in consequence of the interference of the Romans while they were laying siege to Clusium, that they marched against Rome and took the city, B. C. 390. From this time we find them engaged in constant hostilities with the Romans, till they were at length completely subdued and the greater part of them destroyed by the consul Dolabella, 283.

Sentinum (Sentinas, Sentinatis: nr. *Sassoferrato*, Ru.), a fortified town in Umbria, not far from the river Aesis.

Sentius Saturninus. [SATURNINUS.]

Sepias (Σηπιάς: *St. George*), a promontory in the S.E. of Thessaly in the district Magnesia, on which a great part of the fleet of Xerxes was wrecked.

Seplasia, one of the principal streets in Capua, where perfumes and luxuries of a similar kind were sold.

Sepphoris (Σεπφωρίς: *Sefurieh*), a city of Palestine, in the middle of Galilee, about half-way between M. Carmel and the lake of Tiberias, was an insignificant place, until Herod Antipas fortified it, and made it the capital of Galilee, under the name of Diocaesarēa. It was the seat of one of the 5 Jewish Sanhedrim; and continued to flourish until the 4th century, when it was destroyed by the Caesar Gallus, on account of a revolt of its inhabitants.

Septem Aquae, a place in the territory of the Sabini, near Reate.

Septem Fratres ('Επτὰ ἀδελφοί: *Jebel Zatout*, i. e. *Apes' Hill*), a mountain on the N. coast of Mauretania Tingitana, at the narrowest part of the Fretum Gaditanum (*Straits of Gibraltar*), connected by a low tongue of land with the promontory of ABYLA, which is also included under the modern name.

Septem Maria, the name given by the ancients to the lagoons formed at the mouth of the Po by the frequent overflows of this river. Persons usually sailed through these lagoons from Ravenna to Altinum.

Septempēda (Septempedanus: *San Severino*), a Roman municipium in the interior of Picenum, on the road from Auximum to Urbs Salvia.

Septimius Geta. [GETA.]
Septimius Serēnus. [SERENUS.]
Septimius Sevērus. [SEVERUS.]

Septimius Titius, a Roman poet, whom Horace (i. 3. 9—14) represents as having ventured to quaff a draught from the Pindaric spring, and as having been ambitious to achieve distinction in tragedy. In this passage Horace speaks of him under the name of Titius; and he is probably the same individual with the *Septimius* who is addressed in the 6th ode of the 2nd book, and who is introduced in the 9th epistle of the 1st book.

Sequāna (*Seine*), one of the principal rivers of Gaul, rising in the central parts of that country, and flowing through the province of Gallia Lugdunensis into the ocean opposite Britain. It is 346 miles in length. Its principal affluents are the Matrona (*Marne*), Esia (*Oise*) with its tributary the Axona (*Aisne*) and Incaunus (*Yonne*). This

river has a slow current, and is navigable beyond Lutetia Parisiorum (*Paris*).

Sequāni, a powerful Celtic people in Gallia Belgica, separated from the Helvetii by Mons Jurassus, from the Aedui by the Arar, and from the province Narbonensis by the Rhone, inhabiting the country called *Franche Comté* and *Burgundy*. In the later division of the provinces of the empire, the country of the Sequani formed a special province under the name of Maxima Sequanorum. They derived their name from the river Sequana, which had its source in the N. W. frontiers of their territory; but their country was chiefly watered by the rivers Arar and Dubis. Their chief town was Vesontio (*Besançon*). They were governed by kings of their own, and were constantly at war with the Aedui.

Sequester, Vibius, the name attached to a glossary which professes to give an account of the geographical names contained in the Roman poets. The tract is divided into 7 sections:—1. *Flumina.* 2. *Fontes.* 3. *Lacus.* 4. *Nemora.* 5. *Paludes.* 6. *Montes.* 7. *Gentes.* To which in some MSS. an 8th is added, containing a list of the seven wonders of the world. Concerning the author personally we know nothing; and he probably lived not earlier than the middle of the 5th century. The best edition is by Oberlinus, Argent. 1778.

Sēra. [SERICA.]

Serapio, a surname of P. Cornelius Scipio Nasica, consul B. C. 138. [SCIPIO, No. 18.]

Serapion (Σεραπίων), a physician of Alexandria, who lived in the 3rd century B. C. He belonged to the sect of the Empirici, and so much extended and improved the system of Philinus, that the invention of it is by some authors attributed to him. Serapion wrote against Hippocrates with much vehemence; but neither this, nor any of his other works, are now extant. He is several times mentioned and quoted by Celsus, Galen, and others.

Serāpis or **Sarāpis** (Σάραπις), an Egyptian divinity, whose worship was introduced into Greece in the time of the Ptolemies. His worship was introduced into Rome with that of Isis. [ISIS.]

Serbōnis Lācus. [SIRBONIS LACUS.]

Serdica or **Sardica**, an important town in Upper Moesia, and the capital of Dacia Interior, situated in a fertile plain near the sources of the Oescus, and on the road from Naissus to Philippopolis. It was the birthplace of the emperor Maximianus; it was destroyed by Attila, but was soon afterwards rebuilt; and it bore in the middle ages the name of *Triaditza*. Its extensive ruins are to be seen S. of *Sophia*. Serdica derived its name from the Thracian people **Serdi**.

Serēna, niece of Theodosius the Great, foster-mother of the emperor Honorius, and wife of Stilicho.

Serēnus, Annaeus, one of the most intimate friends of the philosopher Seneca, who dedicated to him his work *De Tranquillitate* and *De Constantia*. He was praefectus vigilum under Nero, and died in consequence of eating a poisonous kind of fungus.

Serēnus, Q. Sammonicus (or *Samonicus*), enjoyed a high reputation at Rome, in the early part of the 3rd century after Christ, as a man of taste and varied knowledge. As the friend of Geta, by whom his compositions were studied with great pleasure, he was murdered while at supper, by command of Caracalla, A. D. 212, leaving behind him many learned works. His son, who bore the same name, was the preceptor of the younger Gordian, and bequeathed to his pupil the magnificent library which he had inherited from his father. A medical poem, extending to 115 hexameter lines, has descended to us under the title *Q. Sereni Sammonici de Medicina praecepta saluberrima*, or *Praecepta de Medicina parvo pretio parabili*, which is usually ascribed to the elder Sammonicus. It contains a considerable amount of information, extracted from the best authorities, on natural history and the healing art, mixed up with a number of puerile superstitions, the whole expressed in plain and almost prosaic language. The best edition is that of Burmann, in his *Poëtae Latini Minores* (4to. Leid. 1731, vol. ii. pp. 187—388).

Serēnus, A. Septimīus, a Roman lyric poet, who exercised his muse chiefly in depicting the charms of the country and the delight of rural pursuits. His works are lost, but are frequently quoted by the grammarians.

Sēres. [SERICA.]

Sergia Gens, patrician. The Sergii traced their descent from the Trojan Sergestus (Virg. *Aen.* v. 121). The Sergii were distinguished in the early history of the republic, and the first member of the gens who obtained the consulship was L. Sergius Fidenas, in B. C. 437. Catiline belonged to this gens. [CATILINA.] The Sergii bore also the surnames of *Esquilinus, Fidenas, Orata, Paulus, Plancus,* and *Silus;* but none of them are of sufficient importance to require a separate notice.

Sergius, a grammarian of uncertain date, but later than the 4th century after Christ, the author of 2 tracts; the 1st entitled *In primam Donati Editionem Commentarium;* the 2nd, *In secundam Donati Editionem Commentaria.* They are printed in the *Grammaticae Latinae auctores antiqui* of Putschius (Hannov. 1605, pp. 1816—1838).

Sērica (ἡ Σηρική, Σῆρες; Sēres, also rarely in the sing. Σὴρ, Sēr), a country in the extreme E. of Asia, famous as the native region of the silkworm, which was also called σήρ; and hence the adjective 'sericus' for *silken.* The name was known to the W. nations at a very early period, through the use of silk, first in W. Asia, and afterwards in Greece. It is clear, however, that, until some time after the commencement of our era, the name had no distinct geographical signification. Serica and Seres were simply the unknown country and people in the far East, from whom the article of commerce, silk, was obtained. At a later period, some knowledge of the country was obtained from the traders, the results of which are recorded by Ptolemy, who names several positions that can be identified with reasonable probability, but the detailed mention of which does not fall within the object of this work. The Serica of Ptolemy corresponds to the N. W. part of *China,* and the adjacent portions of *Thibet* and *Chinese Tartary.* The capital, **Sera,** is supposed by most to be *Singan,* on the *Hoang-ho,* but by some *Peking.* The country was bounded, according to Ptolemy, on the N. by unknown regions, on the W. by Scythia, on the S. and S. E. by India and the Sinae. The people were said by some to be of Indian, by others of Scythian, origin, and by others to be a mixed race. The Great Wall of China is mentioned by Ammianus Marcellinus under the name of Aggeres Serium.

Seriphus (Σέριφος: Σερίφιος: Serpho), an island in the Aegean sea, and one of the Cyclades,

lying between Cythnus and Siphnus. It was a small rocky island about 12 miles in circumference. It is celebrated in mythology as the island where Danaë and Perseus landed after they had been exposed by Acrisius, where Perseus was brought up, and where he afterwards turned the inhabitants into stone with the Gorgon's head. Seriphus was colonised by Ionians from Athens, and it was one of the few islands which refused submission to Xerxes. At a later time the inhabitants of Seriphus were noted for their poverty and wretchedness; and for this reason the island was employed by the Roman emperors as a place of banishment for state criminals. The ancient writers relate that the frogs in Seriphos were mute.

Sermyla (Σερμύλη: Σερμύλιος), a town in Macedonia on the isthmus of the peninsula Sithonia.

Serrānus, Atilius. Serranus was originally an agnomen of C. Atilius Regulus, consul B. c. 257 but afterwards became the name of a distinct family of the Atilia gens. Most of the ancient writers derive the name from *serere,* and relate that Regulus received the surname of Serranus, because he was engaged in sowing when the news was brought him of his elevation to the consulship (Virg. *Aen.* vi. 845). It appears, however, from coins, that *Saranus* is the proper form of the name, and some modern writers think that it is derived from Saranum, a town of Umbria.—1. C., praetor, B. c. 218, the 1st year of the 2nd Punic war, and was sent into northern Italy. At a later period of the year he resigned his command to the consul P. Scipio. He was an unsuccessful candidate for the consulship for 216.—2. C., curule aedile 193, with L. Scribonius Libo. They were the 1st aediles who exhibited the Megalesia as ludi scenici. He was praetor 185.—3. A., praetor 192, when he obtained, as his province, Macedonia and the command of the fleet. He was praetor a 2nd time in 173. He was consul in 170.—4. M., praetor 174, when he obtained the province of Sardinia.—5. M., praetor 152, in Further Spain, defeated the Lusitani.—6. Sex., consul 136.—7. C., consul 106 with Q. Servilius Caepio, the year in which Cicero and Pompey were born. Although a "stultissimus homo," according to Cicero, he was elected in preference to Q. Catulus. He was one of the senators who took up arms against Saturninus in 100.—8. Sex., surnamed **Gavianus,** because he originally belonged to the Gavia gens. He was quaestor in 63 in the consulship of Cicero, who treated him with distinguished favour; but in his tribunate of the plebs, 57, he took an active part in opposing Cicero's recal from banishment. After Cicero's return he once he put his veto upon the decree of the senate restoring to Cicero the site on which his house had stood, but he found it advisable to withdraw his opposition.

Serrhium (Σέρρειον), a promontory of Thrace in the Aegaean Sea, opposite the island of Samothrace, with a fortress of the same name upon it.

Q. Sertōrius, one of the most extraordinary men in the later times of the republic, was a native of Nursia, a Sabine village, and was born of obscure but respectable parents. He served under Marius in the war against the Teutones; and before the battle of Aquae Sextiae (*Aix*), B. c. 102, he entered the camp of the Teutones in disguise as a spy, for which hazardous undertaking his intrepid character and some knowledge of the Gallic language well qualified him. He also served as tribunus militum in Spain under T. Didius (97). He was quaestor in 91, and had before this time lost an eye in battle. On the outbreak of the civil war in 88, he declared himself against the party of the nobles, though he was by no means an admirer of his old commander, C. Marius, whose character he well understood. He commanded one of the 4 armies which besieged Rome under Marius and Cinna. He was however opposed to the bloody massacre which ensued after Marius and Cinna entered Rome; and he was so indignant at the horrible deeds committed by the slaves, whom Marius kept as guards, that he fell upon them in their camp, and speared 4000 of them. In 83 Sertorius was praetor, and either in this year or the following he went into Spain, which had been assigned to him as his province by the Marian party. After collecting a small body of troops in Spain, he crossed over to Mauretania, where he gained a victory over Paccianus, one of Sulla's generals. In consequence of his success in Africa, he was invited by the Lusitani, who were exposed to the invasion of the Romans, to become their leader. He gained great influence over the Lusitanians and the other barbarians in Spain, and soon succeeded in forming an army, which for some years successfully opposed all the power of Rome. He also availed himself of the superstitious character of the people among whom he was, to strengthen his authority over them. A fawn was brought to him by one of the natives as a present, which soon became so tame as to accompany him in his walks, and attend him on all occasions. After Sulla had become master of Italy, Sertorius was joined by many Romans who had been proscribed by the dictator; and this not only added to his consideration, but brought him many good officers. In 79 Metellus Pius was sent into Spain with a considerable force against Sertorius; but Metellus could effect nothing against the enemy. He was unable to bring Sertorius to any decisive battle, but was constantly harassed by the guerilla warfare of the latter. In 77 Sertorius was joined by M. Perperna with 53 cohorts [PERPERNA]. To give some show of form to his formidable power, Sertorius established a senate of 300, into which no provincial was admitted; but to soothe the more distinguished Spaniards, and to have some security for their fidelity, he established a school at Huesca (Osca), in Aragon, for the education of their children in Greek and Roman learning. The continued want of success on the part of Metellus induced the Romans to send Pompey to his assistance, but with an independent command. Pompey arrived in Spain in 76 with 30,000 infantry and 1000 cavalry, but even with this formidable force he was unable to gain any decisive advantages over Sertorius. For the next 5 years Sertorius kept both Metellus and Pompey at bay, and cut to pieces a large number of their forces. Sertorius was at length assassinated in 72 at a banquet by Perperna and some other Roman officers, who had long been jealous of the authority of their commander.

Servilia. 1. Daughter of Q. Servilius Caepio and the daughter of Livia, the sister of the celebrated M. Livius Drusus, tribune of the plebs, B. C. 91. Servilia was married twice; first to M. Junius Brutus, by whom she became the mother

of the murderer of Caesar, and secondly to D. Junius Silanus, consul 62. She was the favourite mistress of the dictator Caesar; and it is reported that Brutus was her son by Caesar. This tale however cannot be true, as Caesar was only 15 years older than Brutus, the former having been born in 100, and the latter in 85. She survived both her lover and her son. After the battle of Philippi, Antony sent her the ashes of her son.— 2. Sister of the preceding, was the 2nd wife of L. Lucullus, consul 74. She bore Lucullus a son, but, like her sister, she was faithless to her husband; and the latter, after putting up with her conduct for some time from regard to M. Cato Uticensis, her half-brother, at length divorced her.

Servilia Gens, was one of the Alban houses removed to Rome by Tullus Hostilius. This gens was very celebrated during the early ages of the republic, and it continued to produce men of influence in the state down to the imperial period. It was divided into numerous families, of which the most important bore the names of:—AHALA, CAEPIO, CASCA, GLAUCIA, RULLUS, VATIA.

Servius Maurus Honorātus, or **Servius Marius Honorātus,** a celebrated Latin grammarian, contemporary with Macrobius, who introduces him among the dramatis personae of the Saturnalia. His most celebrated production was an elaborate commentary upon Virgil. This is, nominally at least, still extant; but from the widely different forms which it assumes in different MSS. it is clear that it must have been changed and interpolated to such an extent by the transcribers of the middle ages, that it is impossible to determine how much belongs to Servius and how much to later hands. Even in its present condition, however, it is deservedly regarded as the most important and valuable of all the Latin Scholia. It is attached to many of the earlier editions of Virgil, but it will be found under its best form in the edition of Virgil by Burmann. We possess also the following treatises bearing the name of Servius:— 1. *In secundam Donati Editionem Interpretatio.* 2. *De Ratione ultimarum Syllabarum ad Aquilinum Liber.* 3. *Ars de centum Metris s. Centimetrum.*

Servius Tullius. [TULLIUS.]

Sēsămus (Σήσαμός), a little coast river of Paphlagonia, with a town of the same name: both called afterwards AMASTRIS.

Sĕsostris (Σέσωστρις), the name given by the Greeks to the great king of Egypt, who is called in Manetho and on the monuments Ramses or Ramesses. Ramses is a name common to several kings of the 18th, 19th, and 20th dynasties; but Sesostris must be identified with Ramses, the 3rd king of the 19th dynasty, the son of Seti, and the father of Menephthah. Sesostris was a great conqueror. He is said to have subdued Ethiopia, the greater part of Asia, and the Thracians in Europe; and in all the countries which he conquered he erected *stelae*, on which he inscribed his own name. He returned to Egypt after an absence of 9 years, and the countless captives whom he brought back with him were employed in the erection of numerous public works. Memorials of Ramses-Sesostris still exist throughout the whole of Egypt, from the mouth of the Nile to the south of Nubia. In the remains of his palace-temple at Thebes we see his victories and conquests represented on the walls, and we can still trace there some of the nations of Africa and Asia whom he subdued. The name of Sesostris is not found on monuments, and it was probably a popular surname given to the great hero of the 19th dynasty, and borrowed from Sesostris, one of the renowned kings of the 12th dynasty, or perhaps from Sesorthus, a king of the 3rd dynasty.

Sestiānae Arae (*C. Villano*), the most W.-ly promontory on the N. coast of Hispania Tarraconensis in Gallaecia, with 3 altars consecrated to Augustus.

Sestinum (Sestinas, -ātis: *Sestino*), a town in Umbria on the Apennines, near the sources of the Pisaurus.

Sestius. [SEXTIUS.]

Sestus (Σηστός: Σήστιος: *Ialova*), a town in Thrace, situated at the narrowest part of the Hellespont opposite Abydos in Asia, from which it was only 7 stadia distant. It was founded by the Aeolians. It was celebrated in Grecian poetry on account of the loves of Leander and Hero [LEANDER], and in history on account of the bridge of boats which Xerxes here built across the Hellespont. Sestus was always reckoned a place of importance in consequence of its commanding to a great extent the passage of the Hellespont. It was for some time in the possession of the Persians, but was retaken by the Greeks, B.C. 478, after a long siege. It subsequently formed part of the Athenian empire.

Setabis. [SAETABIS.]

Sethon (Σεθών), a priest of Hephaestus, made himself master of Egypt after the expulsion of Sabacon, king of the Ethiopians, and was succeeded by the Dodecarchia, or government of the 12 chiefs, which ended in the sole sovereignty of Psammitichus. Herodotus relates (ii. 141) that in Sethon's reign Sanacharibus, king of the Arabians and Assyrians, advanced against Egypt, at which Sethon was in great alarm, as he had insulted the warrior class, and deprived them of their lands, and they now refused to follow him to the war. But the god Hephaestus came to his assistance; for while the two armies were encamped near Pelusium, the field-mice in the night gnawed to pieces the bow-strings, the quivers, and the shield-handles of the Assyrians, who fled on the following day with great loss. The recollection of this miracle was perpetuated by a statue of the king in the temple of Hephaestus, holding a mouse in his hand, and saying, "Let every one look at me and be pious." This Sanacharibus is the Sennacherib of the Scriptures, and the destruction of the Assyrians at Pelusium is evidently only another version of the miraculous destruction of the Assyrians by the angel of the Lord, when they had advanced against Jerusalem in the reign of Hezekiah. According to the Jewish records, this event happened in B.C. 711.

Setia (Setinus: *Sexza* or *Sesse*), an ancient town of Latium in the E. of the Pontine Marshes, originally belonged to the Volscian confederacy, but was subsequently taken by the Romans and colonised. It was here that the Romans kept the Carthaginian hostages. It was celebrated for the excellent wine grown in the neighbourhood of the town, which was reckoned in the time of Augustus the finest wine in Italy.

Sevērus, M. Aurelius Alexander, usually called **Alexander Sevērus**, Roman emperor, A.D. 222—235, the son of Gessius Marcianus and Julia Mamaea, and first cousin of Elagabalus, was born

at Arce, in Phoenicia, in the temple of Alexander the Great, to which his parents had repaired for the celebration of a festival, the 1st of October, A.D. 205. His original name appears to have been *Alexianus Bassianus*, the latter appellation having been derived from his maternal grandfather. Upon the elevation of Elagabalus, he accompanied his mother and the court to Rome, a report having been spread abroad that he also, as well as the emperor, was the son of Caracalla. In 221 he was adopted by Elagabalus and created Caesar. The names *Alexianus* and *Bassianus* were laid aside, and those of *M. Aurelius Alexander* substituted; *M. Aurelius* in virtue of his adoption; *Alexander* in consequence, as was asserted, of a direct revelation on the part of the Syrian god. On the death of Elagabalus, on the 11th of March, A.D. 222, Alexander ascended the throne, adding *Severus* to his other designations, in order to mark more explicitly the descent which he claimed from the father of Caracalla. After reigning in peace some years, during which he reformed many abuses in the state, he was involved in a war with Artaxerxes, king of Persia, who had lately founded the new empire of the Sassanidae on the ruins of the Parthian monarchy. Alexander gained a great victory over Artaxerxes in 232; but he was unable to prosecute his advantage in consequence of intelligence having reached him of a great movement among the German tribes. He celebrated a triumph at Rome in 233, and in the following year (234) set out for Gaul, which the Germans were devastating; but before he had made any progress in the campaign, he was waylaid by a small band of mutinous soldiers, instigated, it is said, by Maximinus, and slain, along with his mother, in the early part of 235, in the 30th year of his age, and the 14th of his reign. Alexander Severus was distinguished by justice, wisdom, and clemency in all public transactions, and by the simplicity and purity of his private life.

Sevērus, A. Caecina. [CAECINA.]

Sevērus, Cassius, a celebrated orator and satirical writer in the time of Augustus and Tiberius, was born about B.C. 50 at Longula, in Latium. He was a man of low origin and dissolute character, but was much feared by the severity of his attacks upon the Roman nobles. He must have commenced his career as a public slanderer very early, if he is the person against whom the 6th epode of Horace is directed, as is supposed by many ancient and modern commentators. Towards the latter end of the reign of Augustus, Severus was banished by Augustus to the island of Crete on account of his libellous verses; but as he still continued to write libels, he was removed by Tiberius in A.D. 24 to the desert island of Seriphos, where he died in great poverty in the 25th year of his exile, A.D. 33.

Sevērus, Cornelius, the author of a poem entitled *Bellum Siculum*, was contemporary with Ovid, by whom he is addressed in one of the Epistles written from Pontus.

Sevērus, Flāvius Valerius, Roman emperor, A.D. 306—307. He was proclaimed Caesar by Galerius in 305; and on the death of Constantius Chlorus, in the following year, he was further proclaimed Augustus by Galerius. Soon afterwards he was sent against Maxentius, who had assumed the imperial title at Rome. The expedition however was unsuccessful; and Severus having surrendered at Ravenna, was taken prisoner to Rome and compelled to put an end to his life.

Sēvērus, Libĭus, Roman emperor A. D. 461—465, was a Lucanian by birth, and owed his accession to Ricimer, who placed him on the throne after the assassination of Majorian. During his reign the real government was in the hands of Ricimer. Severus died a natural death.

Sēvērus, L. Septīmĭus, Roman emperor A. D. 193—211, was born 146, near Leptis in Africa. After holding various important military commands under M. Aurelius and Commodus, he was at length appointed commander-in-chief of the army in Pannonia and Illyria. By this army he was proclaimed emperor after the death of Pertinax (193). He forthwith marched upon Rome, where Julianus had been made emperor by the praetorian troops. Julianus was put to death upon his arrival before the city. [JULIANUS.] Severus then turned his arms against Pescennius Niger, who had been saluted emperor by the eastern legions. The struggle was brought to a close by a decisive battle near Issus, in which Niger was defeated by Severus, and having been shortly afterwards taken prisoner was put to death by order of the latter (194). Severus then laid siege to Byzantium, which refused to submit to him even after the death of Niger, and which was not taken till 196. The city was treated with great severity by Severus. Its walls were levelled with the earth, its soldiers and magistrates put to death, and the town itself, deprived of all its political privileges, made over to the Perinthians. During the continuance of this siege, Severus had crossed the Euphrates (195) and subdued the Mesopotamian Arabians. He returned to Italy in 196, and in the same year proceeded to Gaul to oppose Albinus, who had been proclaimed emperor by the troops in that country. Albinus was defeated and slain in a terrible battle fought near Lyons on the 19th of February, 197. Severus returned to Rome in the same year ; but after remaining a short time in the capital, he set out for the East in order to repel the invasion of the Parthians, who were ravaging Mesopotamia. He crossed the Euphrates early in 198, and commenced a series of operations which were attended with brilliant results. Seleucia and Babylon were evacuated by the enemy ; and Ctesiphon was taken and plundered after a short siege. After spending 3 years in the East, and visiting Arabia, Palestine, and Egypt, Severus returned to Rome in 202. For the next 7 years he remained tranquilly at Rome ; but in 208 he went to Britain with his sons Caracalla and Geta. Here he carried on war against the Caledonians, and erected the celebrated wall, which bore his name, from the Solway to the mouth of the Tyne. After remaining 2 years in Britain he died at Eboracum (York) on the 4th of February, 211, in the 65th year of his age, and the 18th of his reign.

Sēvērus, Sulpĭcĭus, chiefly celebrated as an ecclesiastical historian, was a native of Aquitania, and flourished towards the close of the 4th century under Arcadius and Honorius. He was descended from a noble family, and was originally an advocate ; but he eventually became a presbyter of the church, and attached himself closely to St. Martin of Tours. The extant works of Severus are :— 1. *Historia Sacra*, an epitome of sacred history, extending from the creation of the world to the consulship of Stilicho and Aurelianus, A. D. 400. 2.

Vita S. Martini Turonensis. 3. *Tres Epistolae.* 4. *Dialogi duo*, containing a review of the dissensions which had arisen among ecclesiastics in the East regarding the works of Origen. 5. *Epistolae Sex.* The best edition of the complete works of Severus is by Hieronymus de Prato, 4to. 2 vols. Veron. 1741—1754.

Seuthes (Σεύθης), the name of several kings of the Odrysians in Thrace. Of these the most important was the nephew of Sitalces, whom he succeeded on the throne in 424. During a long reign he raised his kingdom to a height of power and prosperity, which it had never previously attained.

Sextĭa or **Sestĭa Gens**, plebeian, one of whose members, namely, L. Sextius Sextinus Lateranus, was the first plebeian who obtained the consulship, B. C. 366.

Sextĭae Aquae. [AQUAE SEXTIAE.]

Sextĭus or **Sestĭus.** 1. P., quaestor B. C. 63, and tribune of the plebs 57. In the latter year he took an active part in obtaining Cicero's recal from banishment. Like Milo, he kept a band of armed retainers to oppose P. Clodius and his partizans ; and in the following year (56) he was accused of *Vis* on account of his violent acts during his tribunate. He was defended by Cicero in an oration still extant, and was acquitted on the 14th of March, chiefly in consequence of the powerful influence of Pompey. In 53, Sextius was praetor. On the breaking out of the civil war in 49, Sextius first espoused Pompey's party, but he afterwards joined Caesar, who sent him, in 48, into Cappadocia. He was alive in 43, as appears from Cicero's correspondence.— 2. L., son of the preceding by his first wife, Postumia. He served under M. Brutus in Macedonia, but subsequently became the friend of Augustus. One of Horace's odes is addressed to him.— 3. T., one of Caesar's legates in Gaul, and afterwards governor of the province of Numidia, or New Africa, at the time of Caesar's death (44). Here he carried on war against Q. Cornificius, who held the province of Old Africa and whom he defeated and slew in battle.

Sextĭus Calvīnus. [CALVINUS.]

Sextus Empīrĭcus, was a physician, and received his name Empiricus from belonging to the school of the Empirici. He was a contemporary of Galen, and lived in the first half of the 3rd century of the Christian aera. Nothing is known of his life. He belonged to the Sceptical school of philosophy. Two of his works are extant :—1. Πυρρώνιαι Ὑποτυπώσεις ἢ σκεπτικὰ ὑπομνήματα, containing the doctrines of the Sceptics in 3 books. 2. Πρὸς τοὺς μαθηματικοὺς ἀντιρρητικοί, against the Mathematici, in 11 books, is an attack upon all positive philosophy. The first 6 books are a refutation of the 6 sciences of grammar, rhetoric, geometry, arithmetic, astrology, and music. The remaining 5 books are directed against logicians, physical philosophers, and ethical writers, and form, in fact, a distinct work, which may be viewed as belonging to the Ὑποτυπώσεις. The two works are a great repository of doubts ; the language is as clear and perspicuous as the subject will allow. Edited by Fabricius, Lips. 1718.

Sextus Rufus. 1. The name prefixed to a work entitled *De Regionibus Urbis Romae*, published by Onuphrius Panvinius at Frankfort in 1558. This work is believed by the best topographers to have been compiled at a late period, and is not regarded as a document of authority.— 2. **Sextus Rufus** is also the name prefixed to an abridgment of Roman History in 28 short chapters, entitled *Breviarium de Victoriis et Provinciis Populi Romani*, and executed by command of the emperor Valens, to whom it is dedicated. This work is usually printed with the larger editions of Eutropius, and of the minor Roman historians. There are no grounds for establishing a connexion between Sextus Rufus the historian and the author of the work *De Regionibus*.

Sibae or **Sibi** (Σίβαι, Σίβοι), a rude people in the N. W. of India (in the *Punjab*), above the confluence of the rivers Hydaspes (*Jelum*) and Acesines (*Chenab*), who were clothed in skins and armed with clubs, and whom therefore the soldiers of Alexander regarded, whether seriously or in jest, as descendants of Hercules.

Sibyllae (Σίβυλλαι), the name by which several prophetic women are designated. The first Sibyl, from whom all the rest are said to have derived their name, is called a daughter of Dardanus and Neso. Some authors mention only 4 Sibyls, the Erythraean, the Samian, the Egyptian, and the Sardian ; but it was more commonly believed that there were 10, namely, the Babylonian, the Libyan, the Delphian (an elder Delphian, who was a daughter of Zeus and Lamia, and a younger one), the Cimmerian, the Erythraean (also an elder and a younger one, the latter of whom was called Herophile), the Samian, the Cumaean (sometimes identified with the Erythraean), the Hellespontian, or Trojan, the Phrygian, and the Tiburtine. The most celebrated of these Sibyls is the Cumaean, who is mentioned under the names of Herophile, Demo, Phemonoë, Deiphobe, Demophile, and Amalthea. She was consulted by Aeneas before he descended into the lower world. She is said to have come to Italy from the East, and she is the one who, according to tradition, appeared before king Tarquinius, offering him the Sibylline books for sale. Respecting the Sibylline books, see *Dict. of Antiq.* art. *Sibyllini Libri.*

Sicambri. [SYGAMBRI.]

Sicāni, Sicĕli, Siceliōtae. [SICILIA.]

Sicārii (i. e. *assassins*), the name given by the Romans to certain savage mountain tribes of the Lebanon, who were, like the *Thugs* of India, avowed murderers by profession. In the same mountains there existed, at the time of the Crusades, a branch of the fanatic sect called *Assassins*, whose habits resembled those of the Sicarii, and whose name the Crusaders imported into Europe ; but these were of Arabian origin.

Sicca Veneria (prob. *Al-Kaff*), a considerable city of N. Africa, on the frontier of Numidia and Zeugitana, built on a hill near the river Bagradas. It derived its name from a temple of Venus, in which the goddess was worshipped with rites peculiar to the corresponding eastern deity Astarte, whence it may be inferred that the place was a Phoenician settlement.

Sichaeus, also called Acerbas. [ACERBAS.]

Sicilia (*Sicily*), one of the largest islands in the Mediterranean Sea. It was supposed by the ancients to be the same as the Homeric island *Thrinacia* (Θρινακία), and it was therefore frequently called **Thrinacia, Trinacia**, or **Trinacris**, a name which was believed to be derived from the triangular figure of the island. For the same reason the Roman poets called it **Triquetra**. Its more usual name came from its later inhabitants, the

Siceli, whence it was called **Sicelia** (Σικελία), which the Romans changed into **Sicilia**. As the Siceli also bore the name of Sicani, the island was also called **Sicania** (Σικανία). Sicily is separated from the S. coast of Italy by a narrow channel called **Fretum Siculum**, sometimes simply **Fretum** (Πορθμός) ; and also **Scyllaeum Fretum**, of which the modern name is *Faro di Messina*. The sea on the E. and S. of the island was also called Mare **Siculum**. The island itself is in the shape of a triangle. The N. and S. sides are about 175 miles each in length, not including the windings of the coast ; and the length of the E. side is about 115 miles. The N. W. point, the *Prom. Lilybaeum*, is about 90 miles from C. Bon on the coast of Africa ; the N. E. point, *Prom. Pelorus*, is about 3 miles from the coast of Calabria in Italy ; and the S. E. point, *Prom. Pachynus*, is 60 miles from the island of Malta. Sicily formed originally part of Italy, and was torn away from it by some volcanic eruption, as the ancients generally believed. A range of mountains, which are a continuation of the Apennines, extends throughout the island from E. to W. The general name of this mountain-range was Nebrodi Montes (*Madonia*), of which there were several offshoots known by different names. Of these the most important were, the celebrated volcano Aetna on the E. side of the island, Eryx (*St. Giuliano*) in the extreme W. near Drepanum, and the Heraei Montes (*Monti Sori*) in the S. running down to the promontory Pachynus. A large number of rivers flow down from the mountains, but most of them are dry, or nearly so, in the summer. The soil of Sicily was very fertile, and produced in antiquity an immense quantity of wheat, on which the population of Rome relied to a great extent for their subsistence. So celebrated was it even in early times on account of its corn, that it was represented as sacred to Demeter (Ceres), and as the favourite abode of this goddess. Hence it was in this island that her daughter Persephone (Proserpina) was carried away by Pluto. Besides corn the island produced excellent wine, saffron, honey, almonds, and the other southern fruits. The earliest inhabitants of Sicily are said to have been the savage Cyclôpes and Laestrygŏnes ; but these are fabulous beings, and the first inhabitants mentioned in history are the **Sicāni** (Σικανοί), or **Sicŭli** (Σικελοί), who crossed over into the island from Italy. Some writers, indeed, regard the Sicani and Siculi as two distinct peoples, supposing the latter only to have migrated from Italy, and the former to have been the aboriginal inhabitants of the country ; but there is no good reason for making any distinction between them. They appear to have been a Celtic people. According to Thucydides their original settlement was on the river Sicanus in Iberia ; but as Thucydides extends Iberia as far as the Rhone, it is probable that Sicanus was a river of Gaul, and it may have been the Sequana, as some modern writers suppose. The ancient writers relate that these Sicani, being hard pressed by the Ligyes (Ligures), crossed the Alps and settled in Latium ; that, being driven out of this country by the Aborigines with the help of Pelasgians, they migrated to the S. of the peninsula, where they lived for a considerable time along with the Oenotrians ; and that at last they crossed over to Sicily, to which they gave their name. They spread over the greater part of the island, but in later times were found chiefly in the interior and in the N. part; some of the most important towns belonging to them were Herbita, Agyrium, Adranum, and Enna. The next immigrants into the island were Cretans, who are said to have come to Sicily under their king, Minos, in pursuit of Daedalus, and to have settled on the S. coast in the neighbourhood of Agrigentum, where they founded Minoa (afterwards Heraclea Minoa). Then came the Elymaei, a small band of fugitive Trojans, who are said to have built Entella, Eryx, and Egesta. These Cretans and Elymaei, however, if indeed they ever visited Sicily, soon became incorporated with the Siculi. The Phoenicians likewise at an early period formed settlements, for the purposes of commerce, on all the coasts of Sicily, but more especially on the N. and N. W. parts. They were subsequently obliged to retire from the greater part of their settlements before the increasing power of the Greeks, and to confine themselves to Motya, Solûs, and Panormus. But the most important of all the immigrants into Sicily were the Greeks. The first body of Greeks who landed in the island were Chalcidians from Euboea, and Megarians led by the Athenian Thucles. These Greek colonists built the town of Naxos, B.C. 735. They were soon followed by other Greek colonists, who founded a number of very flourishing cities, such as Syracuse in 734, Leontini and Catana in 730, Megara Hybla in 726, Gela in 690, Selinus in 626, Agrigentum in 579, etc. The Greeks soon became the ruling race in the island, and received the name of Siceliôtae (Σικελιῶται) to distinguish them from the earlier inhabitants. At a later time the Carthaginians obtained a firm footing in Sicily. Their first attempt was made in 480; but they were defeated by Gelon of Syracuse, and obliged to retire with great loss. Their 2nd invasion in 409 was more successful. They took Selinus in this year, and 4 years afterwards (405) the powerful city of Agrigentum. They now became the permanent masters of the W. part of the island, and were engaged in frequent wars with Syracuse and the other Greek cities. The struggle between the Carthaginians and Greeks continued, with a few interruptions, down to the 1st Punic war; at the close of which (241) the Carthaginians were obliged to evacuate the island, the W. part of which now passed into the hands of the Romans, and was made a Roman province. The E. part still continued under the rule of Hieron of Syracuse as an ally of Rome; but after the revolt of Syracuse in the 2nd Punic war, and the conquest of that city by Marcellus, the whole island was made a Roman province, and was administered by a praetor. Under the Roman dominion more attention was paid to agriculture than to commerce; and consequently the Greek cities on the coast gradually declined in prosperity and in wealth. The inhabitants of the province received the *Jus Latii* from Julius Caesar; and Antony conferred upon them, in accordance, as it was said, with Caesar's will, the full Roman franchise. Augustus, after his conquest of Sex. Pompey, who had held the island for several years, founded colonies at Messana, Tauromenium, Catana, Syracuse, Thermae, and Panormus. On the downfal of the Roman empire, Sicily formed part of the kingdom of the Ostrogoths; but it was taken from them by Belisarius in A.D. 536, and annexed to the Byzantine empire. It continued a province of this empire till 828, when it was conquered by the Saracens. — Literature and the arts were cultivated with great success in the Greek cities of Sicily. It was the birthplace of the philosophers Empedocles, Epicharmus, and Dicaearchus; of the mathematician Archimedes; of the physicians Herodicus and Acron; of the historians Diodorus, Antiochus, Philistus, and Timaeus; of the rhetorician Gorgias; and of the poets Stesichorus and Theocritus.

Sicima. [Neapolis, No. 5.]

Sicinius. 1. L. Sicinius Bellutus, the leader of the plebeians in their secession to the Sacred Mount in B.C. 494. He was chosen one of the first tribunes. — 2. L. Sicinius Dentatus, called by some writers the Roman Achilles. He is said to have fought in 120 battles, to have slain 8 of the enemy in single combat, to have received 45 wounds on the front of his body, and to have accompanied the triumphs of 9 generals, whose victories were principally owing to his valour. He was tribune of the plebs in 454. He was put to death by the decemvirs in 450, because he endeavoured to persuade the plebeians to secede to the Sacred Mount. The persons sent to assassinate him fell upon him in a lonely spot, but he killed most of them before they succeeded in despatching him.

Sicinus (Σίκινος: Σικινίτης: *Sikino*), a small island in the Aegaean sea, one of the Sporades, between Pholegandrus and Ios, with a town of the same name. It is said to have been originally called Oenoë from its cultivation of the vine, but to have been named Sicinus after a son of Thoas and Oenoë. It was probably colonised by the Ionians. During the Persian war it submitted to Xerxes, but it afterwards formed part of the Athenian maritime empire.

Sicŏris (*Segre*), a river in Hispania Tarraconensis, which had its source in the territory of the Cerretani, divided the Ilergetes and Lacetani, flowed by Ilerda, and after receiving the river Cinga (*Cinca*), fell into the Iberus, near Octogesa.

Siculi. [Sicilia.]

Siculum Fretum, Siculum Mare. [Sicilia.]

Siculus Flaccus. [Flaccus.]

Sicyonia (Σικυωνία), a small district in the NE. of Peloponnesus, bounded on the E. by the territory of Corinth, on the W. by Achaia, on the S. by the territory of Phlius and Cleonae, and on the N. by the Corinthian gulf. The area of the country was probably somewhat less than 100 square miles. It consisted of a plain near the sea with mountains in the interior. Its rivers, which ran in a N.E.-ly direction, were Sythas on the frontier of Achaia, Helisson, Selleïs, and Asopus in the interior, and Nemea on the frontier of the territory of Corinth. The land was fertile, and produced excellent oil. Its almonds and its fish were also much prized. Its chief town was Sicyon (Σικυών: Σικυώνιος), which was situated a little to the W. of the river Asopus, and at the distance of 20, or, according to others, 12 stadia from the sea. The ancient city, which was situated in the plain, was destroyed by Demetrius Poliorcetes, and a new city, which bore for a short time the name of Demetrias, was built by him on the high ground close to the Acropolis. The harbour, which, according to some, was connected with the city by means of long walls, was well fortified, and formed a town of itself. Sicyon was one of the most ancient cities of Greece. It is said to have been originally called Aegialês or Aegiali (Αἰγιάλεια, Αἰγιαλοί), after an ancient king, Aegialeus; to have been subsequently named Mecōne (Μηκώνη), and to have been finally called Sicyon from an Athenian of this name. Sicyon is represented by Homer as forming part of the empire of Agamemnon; but on the invasion of Peloponnesus it became subject to Phalces, the son of Temenus, and was henceforward a Dorian state. The ancient inhabitants, however, were formed into a 4th tribe called Aegialeis, which possessed equal rights with the 3 tribes of the Hylleis, Pamphyli, and Dymanatae, into which the Dorian conquerors were divided. Sicyon, on account of the small extent of its territory, never attained much political importance, and was generally dependent either on Argos or Sparta. At the time of the 2nd Messenian war it became subject to a succession of tyrants, who administered their power with moderation and justice for 100 years. The first of these tyrants, was Andreas, who began to rule B.C. 676. He was followed in succession by Myron, Aristonymus, and Clisthenes, on whose death, about 576, a republican form of government was established. Clisthenes had no male children, but only a daughter, Agariste, who was married to the Athenian Megacles. In the Persian war the Sicyonians sent 15 ships to the battle of Salamis, and 300 hoplites to the battle of Plataea. In the interval between the Persian and the Peloponnesian wars, the Sicyonians were twice defeated and their country laid waste by the Athenians, first under Tolmides in 456, and again under Pericles in 454. In the Peloponnesian war they took part with the Spartans. From this time till the Macedonian supremacy their history requires no special mention; but in the middle of the 3rd century Sicyon took an active part in public affairs in consequence of its being the native town of Aratus, who united it to the Achaean league in 251. Under the Romans it gradually declined; and in the time of Pausanias, in the 2nd century of the Christian era, many of its public buildings were in ruins. — Sicyon was for a long time the chief seat of Grecian art. It gave its name to one of the great schools of painting, which was founded by Eupompus, and which produced Pamphilus and Apelles. It is also said to have been the earliest school of statuary in Greece, which was introduced into Sicyon by Dipoenus and Scyllis from Crete about 560; but its earliest native artist of celebrity was Canachus. Lysippus was also a native of Sicyon. The town was likewise celebrated for the taste and skill displayed in the various articles of dress made by its inhabitants, among which we find mention of a particular kind of shoe, which was much prized in all parts of Greece.

Sida, Sidē (Σίδη, Σιδίτης, and Σιδήτης, Sidītes and Sidētes). 1. (*Eski Adalia*, Ru.), a city of Pamphylia, on the coast, a little W. of the river Melas. It was an Aeolian colony from Cyme in Aeolis, and was a chief seat of the worship of Athena, who is represented on its coins holding a pomegranate (σίδη) as the emblem of the city. In the division of the provinces under Constantine, it was made the capital of Pamphylia Prima. — 2. The old name of **Polemonium**, from which a flat district in the N.E. of Pontus Polemoniacus, along the coast, obtained the name of Sidēne (Σιδηνή). Sidēnus. [POLEMONIUM.]

Sidicīni, an Ausonian people in the N. W. of

Campania and on the borders of Samnium, who, being hard pressed by the Samnites, united themselves to the Campanians. Their chief town was Teanum.

Sidon, gen. **onis** (Σιδών, gen. Σιδῶνος, Σιδόνος, O. T. Tsidon or, in the English form, Zidon: Σιδών, Σιδώνιος, Σιδόνιος, Sidonius: *Saida*, Ru.), for a long time the most powerful, and probably the most ancient, of the cities of Phoenice. As early as the conquest of Canaan by the Israelites, it is called 'Great Zidon' (Joshua, xi. 8.). It stood in a plain, about a mile wide, on the coast of the Mediterranean, 200 stadia (20 geog. miles) N. of Tyre, 400 stadia (40 geog. miles) S. of Berytus, 66 miles W. of Damascus, and a day's journey N. W. of the source of the Jordan at Paneas. It had a fine double harbour, now almost filled with sand; and was strongly fortified. It was the chief seat of the maritime power of Phoenice, until eclipsed by its own colony, Tyre [TYRUS]; and its power on the land side seems to have extended over all Phoenice, and at one period (in the time of the Judges) over at least a part of Palestine. In the time of David and Solomon, Sidon appears to have been subject to the king of Tyre. It probably regained its former rank, as the first of the Phoenician cities, by its submission to Shalmanezer at the time of the Assyrian conquest of Syria, for we find it governed by its own king under the Babylonians and the Persians. In the expedition of Xerxes against Greece, the Sidonians furnished the best ships in the whole fleet, and their king obtained the highest place, next to Xerxes, in the council, and above the king of Tyre. Sidon received the great blow to her prosperity in the reign of Artaxerxes III. Ochus, when the Sidonians, having taken part in the revolt of Phoenice and Cyprus, and being betrayed to Ochus by their own king, Tennes, burnt themselves with their city, B. C. 351. The city was rebuilt, but the fortifications were not restored, and the place was, therefore, of no further importance in military history. It shared the fortunes of the rest of PHOENICE, and under the Romans it retained much of its commercial importance, which it has not yet entirely lost. In addition to its commerce, Sidon was famed for its manufactures of glass, the invention of which was said to have been made in Phoenicia.

Sidonius Apollināris, whose full name was *C. Sollius Sidonius Apollinaris*, was born at Lugdunum (*Lyons*) about A. D. 431. At an early age he married Papianilla, the child of Flavius Avitus; and upon the elevation of his father-in-law to the imperial dignity (456), he accompanied him to Rome, and celebrated his consulship in a poem still extant. Avitus raised Sidonius to the rank of a senator, nominated him prefect of the city, and caused his statue to be placed among the effigies which graced the library of Trajan. The downfall of Avitus threw a cloud over the fortunes of Sidonius, who having been shut up in Lyons, and having endured the hardships of the siege, purchased pardon by a complimentary address to the victorious Majorian. The poet was not only forgiven, but was rewarded with a laurelled bust, and with the title of count. After passing some years in retirement during the reign of Severus, Sidonius was despatched to Rome (467) in the character of ambassador from the Arverni to Anthemius, and on this occasion delivered a third panegyric in

z z

honour of a third prince, which proved not less successful than his former efforts, for he was now raised to the rank of a patrician, again appointed prefect of the city, and once more honoured with a statue. But a still more remarkable tribute was soon afterwards rendered to his talents; for although not a priest, the vacant see of Clermont in Auvergne was forced upon his reluctant acceptance (472) at the death of the bishop Eparchius. During the remainder of his life he devoted himself to the duties of his sacred office, and especially resisted with energy the progress of Arianism. He died in 482, or, according to others, in 484. The extant works of Sidonius are :—1. *Carmina*, 24 in number, composed in various measures upon various subjects. Of these the most important are the 3 panegyrics already mentioned. 2. *Epistolarum Libri IX.*, containing 147 letters, many of them interspersed with pieces of poetry. They are addressed to a wide circle of relatives and friends upon topics connected with politics, literature, and domestic occurrences, but seldom touch upon ecclesiastical matters. The writings of Sidonius are characterised by great subtlety of thought, expressed in phraseology abounding with harsh and violent metaphors. Hence he is generally obscure; but his works throughout bear the impress of an acute, vigorous, and highly cultivated intellect. The best edition of his works is that of Sirmond, 4to. Paris, 1652.

Sidûs (Σιδοῦς, -οῦντος: Σιδοῦντιος), a fortified place in the territory of Corinth, on the bay of Cenchreae, and a little to the E. of Crommyon. It was celebrated for its apples.

Sidussa (Σιδοῦσσα), a small place in Lydia, belonging to the territory of the Ionian city of Erythra.

Sidyma (τὰ Σίδυμα: *Tortoorcar Hisar*, Ru.), a town in the interior of Lycia, on a mountain, N. of the mouth of Xanthus.

Siga (Σίγα), a considerable sea-port town of Mauretania Caesariensis, on a river of the same name, the mouth of which opened into a large bay, which formed the harbour of the town. Its site has not been identified with certainty.

Sigeum (*Yenisheri*), the N.W. promontory of the Troad, of Asia Minor, and of all Asia, and the S. headland at the entrance of the Hellespont, opposite to the Prom. Mastusium (*C. Helles*), at the extremity of the Thracian Chersonese. It is here that Homer places the Grecian fleet and camp during the Trojan war. Near it was a seaport town of the same name, which was the object of contention between the Aeolians and the Athenians, in the war in which Pittacus distinguished himself by his valour, and in which Alcaeus lost his shield. [PITTACUS: ALCAEUS.] It was afterwards the residence of the Pisistratidae, when they were expelled from Athens. It was destroyed by the people of Ilium soon after the Macedonian conquest.

Signia (Signinus: *Segni*), a town in Latium on the E. side of the Volscian mountains, founded by Tarquinius Priscus. It was celebrated for its temple of Jupiter Urius, for its astringent wine, for its pears, and for a particular kind of pavement for the floors of houses, called *opus Signinum*, consisting of plaster made of tiles beaten to powder and tempered with mortar. There are still remains of the polygonal walls of the ancient town.

Sigrium (Σίγριον: *Sigri*), the W. promontory of the island of Lesbos.

Sila Silva (*Sila*), a large forest in Bruttium on the Apennines, extending S. of Consentia to the Sicilian straits, a distance of 700 stadia. It was celebrated for the excellent pitch which it yielded.

Silanion (Σιλανίων), a distinguished Greek statuary in bronze, was an Athenian and a contemporary of Lysippus, and flourished 324. The statues of Silanion belonged to 2 classes, ideal and actual portraits. Of the former the most celebrated was his dying Jocasta, in which a deadly paleness was given to the face by the mixture of silver with the bronze. His statue of Sappho, which stood in the *prytaneum* at Syracuse in the time of Verres, is alluded to by Cicero in terms of the highest praise.

Silanus, Junius. 1. **M.**, was praetor 212. In 210 he accompanied P. Scipio to Spain, and served under him with great distinction during the whole of the war in that country. He fell in battle against the Boii in 196, fighting under the consul M. Marcellus.—2. **D.**, surnamed **Manlianus**, son of the jurist T. Manlius Torquatus, but adopted by a D. Junius Silanus. He was praetor 142, and obtained Macedonia as his province. Being accused of extortion by the inhabitants of the province, the senate referred the investigation of the charges to his own father Torquatus, who condemned his son, and banished him from his presence; and when Silanus hanged himself in grief, his father would not attend his funeral.—3. **M.**, consul 109, fought in this year against the Cimbri in Transalpine Gaul, and was defeated. He was accused in 104, by the tribune Cn. Domitius Ahenobarbus, in consequence of this defeat, but was acquitted.—4. **D.**, stepfather of M. Brutus, the murderer of Caesar, having married his mother Servilia. He was elected consul in 63 for the following year; and in consequence of his being consul designatus, he was first asked for his opinion by Cicero in the debate in the senate on the punishment of the Catilinarian conspirators. He was consul 62, with L. Licinius Murena, along with whom he proposed the Lex Licinia Julia.—5. **M.**, son of No. 4 and of Servilia, served in Gaul as Caesar's legatus in 53. After Caesar's murder in 44, he accompanied M. Lepidus over the Alps; and in the following year Lepidus sent him with a detachment of troops into Cisalpine Gaul, where he fought on the side of Antony. He was consul in 25. He had two sisters, one married to M. Lepidus, the triumvir, and the other to C. Cassius, one of Caesar's murderers.—6. **M.**, consul 19, with L. Norbanus Balbus. In 33 his daughter Claudia was married to C. Caesar, afterwards the emperor Caligula. Silanus was governor of Africa in the reign of Caligula, but was compelled by his father-in-law to put an end to his life. Julius Graecinus, the father of Agricola, had been ordered by Caligula to accuse Silanus, but he declined the odious task.—7. **App.**, consul A.D. 28 with P. Silius Nerva. Claudius soon after his accession gave to Silanus in marriage Domitia Lepida, the mother of his wife Messalina, and treated him otherwise with the greatest distinction. But shortly afterwards, having refused the embraces of Messalina, he was put to death by Claudius, on the accusations of Messalina and Narcissus. The first wife of Silanus was Aemilia Lepida, the *proneptis* or great-grand-daughter of Augustus.—8. **M.**, son of No. 7, consul 46. Silanus was proconsul of Asia at the succession of Nero in 54, and was poisoned by command of Agrippina, who feared that he might avenge the death of his brother [No. 9], and that his descent from Augustus might lead him to be preferred to the youthful Nero. — **9. L.**, also a son of No. 7, was betrothed to Octavia, the daughter of the emperor Claudius ; but when Octavia was married to Nero in 48, Silanus knew that his fate was sealed, and therefore put an end to his life. — **10. D. Junius Torquatus Silanus**, probably also a son of No. 7, was consul 53. He was compelled by Nero in 64 to put an end to his life, because he had boasted of being descended from Augustus. — **11. L. Junius Torquatus Silanus**, son of No. 8, and consequently the *atnepos*, or great-great-great grandson of Augustus. His descent from Augustus rendered him an object of suspicion to Nero. He was accordingly accused in 65 ; was sentenced to banishment ; and was shortly afterwards put to death at Barium in Apulia.

Silarus (*Silaro*), a river in lower Italy, forming the boundary between Lucania and Campania, rises in the Apennines, and, after receiving the Tanager (*Negri*) and Calor (*Calore*), falls into the Sinus Paestanus a little to the N. of Paestum. Its water is said to have petrified plants.

Silenus (Σειληνός). I. (Mythological). It is remarked in the article Satyri that the older Satyrs were generally termed Sileni ; but one of these Sileni is commonly *the* Silenus, who always accompanies the god, and whom he is said to have brought up and instructed. Like the other Satyrs he is called a son of Hermes ; but others make him a son of Pan by a nymph, or of Gaea. Being the constant companion of Dionysus, he is said, like the god, to have been born at Nysa. Moreover, he took part in the contest with the Giganta, and slew Enceladus. He is described as a jovial old man, with a bald head, a puck nose, fat and round like his wine bag, which he always carried with him, and generally intoxicated. As he could not trust his own legs, he is generally represented riding on an ass, or supported by other Satyrs. In every other respect he is described as resembling his brethren in their love of sleep, wine, and music. He is mentioned along with Marsyas and Olympus as the inventor of the flute, which he is often seen playing ; and a special kind of dance was called after him Silenus, while he himself is designated as the dancer. But it is a peculiar feature in his character that he was conceived also as an inspired prophet, who knew all the past and the most distant future, and as a sage who despised all the gifts of fortune. When he was drunk and asleep, he was in the power of mortals who might compel him to prophesy and sing by surrounding him with chains of flowers. — **2.** (Literary). A native of Calatia, and a writer upon Roman history. — **3.** It was probably a different writer from the last who is quoted several times by Athenaeus and others as the author of a work on foreign words.

Silicense Flumen, a river in Hispania Baetica in the neighbourhood of Corduba, probably the *Guadajoz*, or a tributary of the latter.

C. Silius Italicus, a Roman poet, was born about A. D. 25. The place of his birth is uncertain, as is also the import of his surname Italicus. From his early years he devoted himself to oratory and poetry, taking Cicero as his model in the former, and Virgil in the latter. He acquired great reputation as an advocate, and was afterwards one of the Centumviri. He was consul in 68, the year in which Nero perished ; he was admitted to familiar intercourse with Vitellius, and was subsequently

proconsul of Asia. His two favourite residences were a mansion near Puteoli, formerly the Academy of Cicero, and the house in the vicinity of Naples once occupied by Virgil ; and here he continued to reside until he had completed his 75th year, when, in consequence of the pain caused by an incurable disease, he starved himself to death. The great work of Silius Italicus was an heroic poem in 17 books, entitled *Punica*, which has descended to us entire. It contains a narrative of the events of the 2nd Punic war, from the capture of Saguntum to the triumph of Scipio Africanus. The materials are derived almost entirely from Livy and Polybius. It is a dull heavy performance, and hardly deserves the name of a poem. The best editions are by Drakenborch, 4to. Traj. ad Rhen. 1717 and Ruperti, 2 vols. 8vo. Goetting. 1795.

Silo, Q. Pompaedius, the leader of the Marsi in the Social War, and the soul of the whole undertaking. He fell in battle against Q. Metellus Pius, B. C. 88, and with his death the war came to an end.

Silo (Σιλώ, Σηλώ, Σηλών, Σιλοῦν: O. T. Shiloh and Shilon : *Seilun*, Ru.), a city of Palestine, in the mountains of Ephraim, in the district afterwards called Samaria ; important as the seat of the sacred ark and the tabernacle from the time of Joshua to the capture of the ark in the time of Eli, after which it seems to have fallen into insignificance, though it is occasionally mentioned in the O. T.

Siloah, Siloam (Σιλωά, Σιλωάμ : O. T. Shiloah : *Siloah*), a celebrated fountain in the S. E. of Jerusalem, just without the city, at the S. entrance of the valley called Tyropoeon, between the hills of Zion and Moriah. It is remarkable for the ebb and flow of its waters at the different seasons.

Silsilis (Σίλσιλις : *Hajjar Selseleh* or *Jebel Selseleh*, Ru.), a fortified station in Upper Egypt, on the W. bank of the Nile, S. of Apollinopolis the Great. The name signifies the *Rock* or *Hill of a Chain*, and is derived from the circumstance of the river flowing here in a ravine so narrow, that a chain can easily be stretched across it, to command the navigation.

Silures, a powerful people in Britain, inhabiting *South Wales*, long offered a formidable resistance to the Romans, and were the only people in the island who at a later time maintained their independence against the Saxons.

Silvanus, a Latin divinity of the fields and forests, to whom in the earliest times the Tyrrhenian Pelasgians are said to have dedicated a grove and a festival. He is also called the protector of the boundaries of fields. In connection with woods (*sylvestris deus*), he especially presided over plantations, and delighted in trees growing wild ; whence he is represented as carrying the trunk of a cypress. Respecting his connection with cypress, moreover, the following story is told. Silvanus, or, according to others, Apollo, once killed by accident a hind belonging to the youth Cyparissus, with whom the god was in love : the youth in consequence died of grief, and was metamorphosed into a cypress. Silvanus is further described as the divinity protecting the flocks of cattle, warding off wolves, and promoting their fertility. Being the god of woods and flocks, he is also described as fond of music ; the syrinx was sacred to him, and he is mentioned along with the Pans and Nymphs. Later writers even identified Silvanus with Pan, Faunus, Inuus, and Aegipan. In the Latin poets, as well as in works of art, he always appears as an old man, but as cheerful and in love with Pomona. The sacrifices offered to him consisted of grapes, corn-ears, milk, meat, wine, and pigs.

Silvium (Silvinus), a town of the Peucetii in Apulia on the borders of Lucania, 20 miles S. E. of Venusia.

Silvius, the son of Ascanius, is said to have been so called because he was born in a wood. All the succeeding kings of Alba bore the cognomen Silvius. The series of these mythical kings is given somewhat differently by Livy, Ovid, and Dionysius, as the following list will show : —

Livy.	*Ovid.*	*Dionysius.*
1. Aeneas.	Aeneas.	Aeneas.
2. Ascanius.	Ascanius.	Ascanius.
3. Silvius.	Silvius.	Silvius.
4. Aeneas Silvius.		Aeneas Silvius.
5. Latinus Silvius.	Latinus.	Latinus Silvius
6. Alba.	Alba.	Alba.
7. Atys.	Epytus.	Capetus.
8. Capys.	Capys.	Capys Silvius.
9. Capetus.	Capetus.	Calpetus.
10. Tiberinus.	Tiberinus.	Tiberinus.
11. Agrippa.	Remulus.	Agrippa.
12. Romulus Silvius.	Acrota.	Alladius.
13. Aventinus.	Aventinus.	Aventinus.
14. Proca.	Palatinus.	Procas.
15. Amulius.	Amulius.	Amulius.

Simmias (Σιμμίας). 1. Of Thebes, first the disciple of the Pythagorean philosopher Philolaüs, and afterwards the friend and disciple of Socrates, at whose death he was present, having come from Thebes, with his brother Cebes. The two brothers are the principal speakers, besides Socrates himself, in the *Phaedon*. Simmias wrote 23 dialogues on philosophical subjects, all of which are lost. — 2. Of Rhodes, a poet and grammarian of the Alexandrian school, flourished about B. C. 300. The Greek Anthology contains 6 epigrams ascribed to Simmias, besides 3 short poems of that fantastic species called *griphi* or *carmina figurata*, that is, pieces in which the lines are so arranged as to make the whole poem resemble the form of some object; those of Simmias are entitled, from their forms, the *Wings* (πτέρυγες), the *Egg* (ᾠόν), and the *Hatchet* (πέλεκυς).

Simoïs. [TROAS.] As a mythological personage, the river-god Simoïs is the son of Oceanus and Tethys, and the father of Astyochus and Hieromneme.

Simon (Σίμων). 1. One of the disciples of Socrates, and by trade a leather-cutter. Socrates was accustomed to visit his shop, and converse with him on various subjects. These conversations Simon afterwards committed to writing, in 33 dialogues, all of which are lost. — 2. Of Aegina, a celebrated statuary in bronze, who flourished about B. C. 475.

Simönides (Σιμωνίδης). 1. Of Amorgos, was the 2nd, both in time and in reputation, of the 3 principal iambic poets of the early period of Greek literature, namely, Archilochus, Simonides, and Hipponax. He was a native of Samos, whence he led a colony to the neighbouring island of Amorgos, where he founded 3 cities, Minoa, Aegialus, and Arcesine, in the first of which he fixed his own abode. He flourished about B. C. 664. Simonides was most celebrated for his iambic

poems, which were of 2 species, gnomic and satirical. The most important of his extant fragments is a satire upon women, in which he derives the various, though generally bad, qualities of women from the variety of their origin; thus the uncleanly woman is formed from the swine; the cunning woman, from the fox; the talkative woman, from the dog, and so on. The best separate edition of the fragments of Simonides of Amorgos is by Welcker, Bonn, 1835. — 2. Of Ceos, one of the most celebrated lyric poets of Greece, was the perfecter of the Elegy and Epigram, and the rival of Lasus and Pindar in the Dithyramb and the Epinician Ode. He was born at Iulis, in Ceos, B. C. 556, and was the son of Leoprepes. He appears to have been brought up to music and poetry as a profession. From his native island he proceeded to Athens, probably on the invitation of Hipparchus, who attached him to his society by great rewards. After remaining at Athens some time, probably even after the expulsion of Hippias, he went to Thessaly, where he lived under the patronage of the Aleuads and Scopads. He afterwards returned to Athens, and soon had the noblest opportunity of employing his poetic powers in the celebration of the great events of the Persian wars. In 489, he conquered Aeschylus in the contest for the prize which the Athenians offered for an elegy on those who fell at Marathon. Ten years later, he composed the epigrams which were inscribed upon the tomb of the Spartans who fell at Thermopylae, as well as an encomium on the same heroes; and he also celebrated the battles of Artemisium and Salamis, and the great men who commanded in them. He had completed his 80th year, when his long poetical career at Athens was crowned by the victory which he gained with the dithyrambic chorus (477), being the 56th prize which he had carried off. Shortly after this he was invited to Syracuse by Hiero, at whose court he lived till his death in 467. Simonides was a great favourite with Hiero, and was treated by the tyrant with the greatest munificence. He still continued, when at Syracuse, to employ his muse occasionally in the service of other Grecian states. Simonides is said to have been the inventor of the mnemonic art and of the long vowels and double letters in the Greek alphabet. He made literature a profession, and is said to have been the first who took money for his poems; and the reproach of avarice is too often brought against him by his contemporary and rival, Pindar, as well as by subsequent writers, to be altogether discredited. The chief characteristics of the poetry of Simonides were sweetness (whence his surname of *Melicertes*) and elaborate finish, combined with the truest poetic conception and perfect power of expression; though in originality and fervour he was far inferior, not only to the early lyric poets, such as Sappho and Alcaeus, but also to his contemporary Pindar. He was probably both the most prolific and the most generally popular of all the Grecian lyric poets. The general character of his dialect is the Epic, mingled with Doric and Aeolic forms. The best edition of his fragments in a separate form is by Schneidewin, Bruns. 1835.

Simplicius (Σιμπλίκιος), one of the last philosophers of the Neo-Platonic school, was a native of Cilicia and a disciple of Ammonius and Damascius. In consequence of the persecutions, to which the pagan philosophers were exposed in the reign of Justinian, Simplicius was one of the 7 philosophers who took refuge at the court of the Persian king Chosroës. These philosophers returned home about A. D. 533, in consequence of a treaty of peace concluded between Chosroes and Justinian, in which the former had stipulated that the philosophers should be allowed to return without risk, and to practise the rites of their paternal faith. Of the subsequent fortunes of the 7 philosophers we learn nothing ; nor do we know where Simplicius lived and taught. Simplicius wrote commentaries on several of Aristotle's works. His commentaries on the Categories, on the *De Coelo*, on the *Physica Auscultatio*, and on the *De Anima* are extant. In explaining Aristotle, Simplicius endeavours to show that Aristotle agrees with Plato even on those points which the former controverts ; but though he attaches himself too much to the Neo-Platonists, his commentaries are marked by sound sense and real learning. He also wrote a commentary on the Enchiridion of Epictetus, which is likewise extant.

Simyra (τὰ Σίμυρα: *Zamura* or *Sumore*), a fortress on the coast of Phoenice, between Orthasias and the mouth of the Eleutherus, of no importance except as being the point from which the N. part of Lebanon was usually approached.

Sinae (Σίναι), the E.-most people of Asia, of whom nothing but the name was known to the W. nations, till about the time of Ptolemy, who describes their country as bounded on the N. by Serica, and on the S. and W. by India extra Gangem. It corresponded to the S. part of China and the E. part of the *Burmese peninsula*. The detailed description of the knowledge of the ancient geographers concerning it does not fall within the province of this work.

Sinai or **Sina** (LXX. Σινᾶ: *Jebel-et-Tur*), a cluster of dark, lofty, rocky mountains in the S. angle of the triangular peninsula enclosed between the 2 heads of the Red Sea, and bounded on the N. by the deserts on the borders of Egypt and Palestine. The name, which signifies *a region of broken and cleft rocks*, is used in a wider sense for the whole peninsula, which formed a part of Arabia Petraea, and was peopled, at the time of the Exodus, by the Amalekites and Midianites, and afterwards by the Nabathaean Arabs. On the other hand, the name is applied, in a narrower sense, to one particular ridge in the Sinaïtic group of mountains running N. and S., and terminated by 2 summits, of which the one on the N. is called *Horeb*, and the one on the S. *Sinai* or *Jebel Musa*, i. e. *Moses' Mount*. From the latter name, assigned by tradition, it has usually, but too hastily, been inferred that the S. summit was that on which God gave the law to Moses. The fact seems, however, to be that Sinaï and Horeb in the O. T. are both general names for the whole group, the former being used in the first 4 books of Moses, and the latter in Deuteronomy ; and that the summit on which the law was given was probably that on the N., or the one usually called Horeb.

Sinda (Σίνδα: Σινδεύς, Sindensis). 1. A city of Pisidia, N. of Cibyra, near the river Caularis. — 2, 3. [SINDI.]

Sindi (Σινδοί). 1. A people of Asiatic Sarmatia, on the E. coast of the Euxine, and at the foot of the Caucasus. They probably dwelt in and about the peninsula of *Taman* (between the *Sea of Azov* and the *Black Sea*), and to the S. of

the river Hypanis (*Kouban*). They had a capital called **Sinda** (*Anapa?*) with a harbour (Σινδικὸς λιμήν). Their country is called Σινδική. They are also mentioned by the names of **Sindones** and **Sindiäni**. — 2. A people on the E. coast of India extra Gangem (in *Cochin China*), also called **Sindae** (Σίνδαι), and with a capital city, **Sinda**.

Sindicë. [SINDI.]

Sindomäna (*Sehwunt*), a city of India, on the lower course of the Indus, near the island of Pattalene.

Sindus (Σίνδος), a town in the Macedonian district of Mygdonia on the Thermaic gulf, and at the mouth of the Echedorus.

Singära (τὰ Σίγγαρα: *Sinjar?*), a strongly fortified city and Roman colony in the interior of Mesopotamia, 84 Roman miles S. of Nisibis. It lay in a dry plain, at the foot of M. Singaras (*Sinjar*), an E. prolongation of M. Masius. It was the scene of the defeat of Constantius by Sapor, through which the place was lost to the Romans.

Singidünum (*Belgrad*), a town in Moesia Superior at the confluence of the Savus and the Danube, was a strong fortress, and the head-quarters of a legion.

Singiticus Sinus. [SINGUS.]

Singus (Σίγγος: Σιγγαῖος), a town in Macedonia on the E. coast of the peninsula Sithonia, which gave its name to the Sinus Singiticus.

Sinis or **Sinnis** (Σίνις or Σίννις), son of Polypemon, Pemon or Poseidon by Sylea, the daughter of Corinthus. He was a robber, who frequented the isthmus of Corinth, and killed the travellers whom he captured, by fastening them to the top of a fir-tree, which he curbed, and then let spring up again. He himself was killed in this manner by Theseus. The name is connected with σίνομαι.

Sinon (Σίνων), son of Aesimus, or according to Virgil (*Aen.* ii. 79) of Sisyphus, and grandson of Autolycus, was a relation of Ulysses, whom he accompanied to Troy. After the Greeks had constructed the wooden horse, Sinon mutilated his person, in order to make the Trojans believe that he had been maltreated by the Greeks, and then allowed himself to be taken prisoner by the Trojans. He informed the Trojans that the wooden horse had been constructed as an atonement for the Palladium which had been carried off by the Greeks, and that if they would drag it into their own city, Asia would gain the supremacy over Greece. The Trojans believed the deceiver and dragged the horse into the city ; whereupon Sinon in the dead of night let the Greeks out of the horse, who thus took Troy.

Sinöpe (Σινώπη: Σινωπεύς, Sinopensis: *Sinope*, *Sinoub*, Ru.), the most important of all the Greek colonies on the shores of the Euxine, stood on the N. coast of Asia Minor, on the W. head-land of the great bay of which the delta of the river Halys forms the E. headland, and a little E. of the N.-most promontory of Asia Minor. Thus placed, and built on a peninsula, the neck of which formed 2 fine harbours, it had every advantage for becoming a great maritime city. Its foundation was referred mythically to the Argonaut Autolycus, who was worshipped in the city as a hero, and had an oracle ; but it appears in history as a very early colony of the Milesians. Having been destroyed in the invasion of Asia by the Cimmerians, it was restored by a new colony from

Miletus, B. C. 632, and soon became the greatest commercial city on the Euxine. Several colonies were established by the Sinopians on the adjacent coasts, the chief of which were Cotyora, Trapezus, and Cerasus. Its territory, called Sinōpis (Σι- νωπίς, also Σινωπῖτις), extended to the banks of the Halys. It remained an independent state till it was taken by Pharnaces I., king of Pontus. It was the birthplace and residence of Mithridates the Great, who enlarged and beautified it. After an obstinate resistance to the Romans under Lu- cullus, it was taken and plundered, and proclaimed a free city. Shortly before the murder of Julius Caesar, it was colonised by the name of Julia Caesarea Felix Sinope, and remained a flourishing city, though it never recovered its former import- ance. At the time of Constantine, it had declined so much as to be ranked second to Amasia. In addition to its commerce, Sinope was greatly enriched by its fisheries. It was the native city of the renowned cynic philosopher Diogenes, of the comic poet Diphilus, and of the historian Baton.

Sintĭca, a district in Macedonia, inhabited by the Thracian people **Sinti,** extended E. of Cres- tonia and N. of Bisaltia as far as the Strymon and the lake Prasias. Its chief town was Heraclea Sintica. The Sinti were spread over other parts of ancient Thrace, and are identified by Strabo with the Sintians (Σίντιες) of Homer, the ancient inhabitants of Lemnos.

Sinuessa (Sinuessanus : *Rocca di Mandragone*), the last city of Latium on the confines of Cam- pania, to which it originally belonged, was situated on the sea-coast and on the Via Appia, in the midst of a fertile country. It was colonised by the Romans, together with the neighbouring town of Minturnae, B. C. 296. It possessed a good har- bour, and was a place of considerable commercial importance. In its neighbourhood were celebrated warm baths, called **Aquae Sinuessanae.**

Sion. [JERUSALEM.]

Siphnus (Σίφνος : Σίφνιος : *Siphno*), an island in the Aegaean sea, forming one of the Cyclades, S. E. of Seriphus. It is of an oblong form, and about 40 miles in circumference. Its original name was Merope ; and it was colonised by Ionians from Athens. In consequence of their gold and silver mines, of which the remains are still visible, the Siphnians attained great prosperity, and were regarded in the time of Polycrates as the wealthiest of the islanders. Their treasury at Delphi, in which they deposited the tenth of the produce of their mines, was equal in wealth to that of any other Greek state. Their riches, however, exposed them to pillage ; and a party of Samian exiles in the time of Polycrates invaded the island, and compelled them to pay 100 talents. Siphnus was one of the few islands which refused tribute to Xerxes ; and one of its ships fought on the side of the Greeks at Salamis. At a later time the mines were less productive ; and Pausanias relates that in consequence of the Siphnians neglecting to send the tithe of their treasure to Delphi, the god destroyed their mines by an inundation of the sea. The moral character of the Siphnians stood low, and hence to act like a Siphnian (Σιφνιά(ειν) be- came a term of reproach.

Sipontum or **Sipuntum** (Sipontinus : *Siponto*), called by the Greeks **Sipûs** (Σιποῦς, -οῦντος), an ancient town in Apulia, in the district of Daunia,

on the S. slope of Mt. Garganus, and on the coast. It is said to have been founded by Diomede, and was of Greek origin. It was colonised by the Romans, under whom it became a place of some commercial importance. The inhabitants were re- moved from the town by king Manfred in the 13th century, in consequence of the unhealthy nature of the locality, and were settled in the neighbouring town of Manfredonia, founded by this monarch.

Sipўlus (Σίπυλος : *Sipuli-Dagh*), a mountain of Lydia, in Asia Minor, of volcanic formation, and rent and splinted by frequent earthquakes. It is a branch of the Tmolus, from the main chain of which it proceeds N. W. along the course of the river Hermus, as far as Magnesia and Sipylum. It is mentioned by Homer. The ancient capital of Maeonia was said to have been situated in the heart of the mountain chain, and to have been called by the same name ; but it was early swal- lowed up by an earthquake, and its site became a little lake called Sale or Saloë, near which was a tumulus, supposed to be the grave of Tantalus. The mountain was rich in metals, and many mines were worked in it.

Siracēnē (Σιρακηνή). 1. A district of Hyr- cania. — 2. A district of Armenia Major. — 3. [SIRACENI.]

Siracēni, Sirāci, Sirāces (Σιρακηνοί, Σιρακοί, Σίρακες), a powerful people of Sarmatia Asiatica, dwelt in the district of Siracene, E. of the Palus Maeotis, as far as the river Rha (*Volga*). The Romans were engaged in a war with them in A. D. 50.

Sirbōnis Lacus (Σιρβωνίδος λίμνη, aft. Σιρβω- νίς λίμνη and Σίρβων : *Sabakat Bardowal*), a large and deep lake on the coast of Lower Egypt, E. of M. Casius. Its circuit was 1000 stadia. It was strongly impregnated with asphaltus. A con- nection (called τὸ ἔκρεγμα) existed between the lake and the Mediterranean ; but this being stopped up, the lake grew continually smaller by evapo- ration, and it is now nearly dry.

Sirēnes (Σειρῆνες), sea-nymphs who had the power of charming by their songs all who heard them. When Ulysses came near the island on the beach of which the Sirens were sitting, and en- deavouring to allure him and his companions, he stuffed the ears of his companions with wax, and tied himself to the mast of his vessel, until he was so far off that he could no longer hear their song. According to Homer, the island of the Sirens was situated between Aeaea and the rock of Scylla, near the S. W. coast of Italy ; but the Roman poets place them on the Campanian coast. Homer says nothing of their names, but later writers mention both their names and number ; some state that they were 2, Aglaopheme and Thelxiepia ; and others, that there were 3, Pisinöe, Aglaope, and Thelxiepia, or Par- thenope, Ligia, and Leucosia. They are called daughters of Phorcus, of Achelous and Sterope, of Terpsichore, of Melpomene, of Calliope, or of Gaea. The Sirens are also connected with the legends of the Argonauts and the rape of Persephone. When the Argonauts sailed by the Sirens, the latter began to sing, but in vain, for Orpheus surpassed them ; and as it had been decreed that they should live only till some one hearing their song should pass by unmoved, they threw themselves into the sea, and were metamorphosed into rocks. Later poets represent them as provided with wings, which they are said to have received at their own request, in order to be able to search after Persephone, or as a punishment from Demeter for not having assisted Persephone, or from Aphrodite, because they wished to remain virgins. Once, however, they allowed themselves to be prevailed upon by Hera to enter into a contest with the Muses, and being defeated, were deprived of their wings.

Sirenusae, called by Virgil (*Aen.* v. 864) Sirenum scopuli, 3 small uninhabited and rocky islands near the S. side of the Prom. Misenum, off the coast of Campania, which were, according to tradition, the abode of the Sirens.

Siris. 1. (*Sinno*), a river in Lucania flowing into the Tarentine gulf, memorable for the victory which Pyrrhus gained on its banks over the Romans. — 2. (*Torre di Senna*), an ancient Greek town in Lucania at the mouth of the preceding river. Its locality was unhealthy; and after the foundation of the neighbouring town of Heraclea by the Tarentines, the inhabitants of Siris were removed to the new town, of which Siris now became the harbour.

Sirmio (*Sirmione*), a beautiful promontory on the S. shore of the Lacus Benacus (*Lago di Garda*), on which Catullus had an estate.

Sirmium (*Mitrovitz*), an important city in Pannonia Inferior, was situated on the left bank of the Savus. It was founded by the Taurisci, and under the Romans became the capital of Pannonia, and the head-quarters of all their operations in their wars against the Dacians and the neighbouring barbarians. It contained a large manufactory of arms, a spacious forum, an imperial palace, etc. It was the residence of the admiral of the first Flavian fleet on the Danube, and the birthplace of the emperor Probus.

Sisapon (*Almaden* in the Sierra Morena), an important town in Hispania Baetica N. of Corduba, between the Baetis and Anas, celebrated for its silver mines and cinnabar.

Siscia (*Sissek*), called Segesta by Appian, an important town in Pannonia Superior, situated upon an island formed by the rivers Savus, Colapis, and Odra, and on the road from Aemona to Sirmium. It was a strongly fortified place, and was conquered by Tiberius in the reign of Augustus, from which time it became the most important town in all Pannonia. It was probably made a colony by Tiberius, and was colonized anew by Septimius Severus. At a later time its importance declined, and Sirmium became the chief town in Pannonia.

Sisenna, L. Cornelius, a Roman annalist, was praetor in the year when Sulla died (B. c. 78), and probably obtained Sicily for his province in 77. From the local knowledge thus acquired he was enabled to render good service to Verres, whose cause he espoused. During the piratical war (67) he acted as the legate of Pompey, and having been despatched to Crete in command of an army, died in that island at the age of about 52. His great work, entitled *Historiae*, extended to at least 14 or 19 books, which contained the history of his own time. Cicero pronounces Sisenna superior as an historian to any of his predecessors. In addition to his *Historiae*, Sisenna translated the Milesian fables of Aristides, and he also composed a commentary upon Plautus.

Sisygambis (Σισύγαμβις), mother of Darius Codomannus, the last king of Persia, fell into the hands of Alexander, after the battle of Issus, B. c. 333, together with the wife and daughters of Darius. Alexander treated these captives with the greatest generosity and kindness, and displayed towards Sisygambis, in particular, a reverence and delicacy of conduct, which is one of the brightest ornaments of his character. On her part, Sisygambis became so strongly attached to her conqueror, that she felt his death as a blow not less severe than that of her own son; and overcome by this long succession of misfortunes, put an end to her own life by voluntary starvation.

Sisyphus (Σίσυφος), son of Aeolus and Enarete, whence he is called *Aeolides*. He was married to Merope, a daughter of Atlas or a Pleiad, and became by her the father of Glaucus, Ornytion (or Porphyrion), Thersander and Halmus. In later accounts he is also called a son of Autolycus, and the father of Ulysses by Anticlea [ANTICLEA]; whence we find Ulysses sometimes called *Sisyphides*. He is said to have built the town of Ephyra, afterwards Corinth. As king of Corinth he promoted navigation and commerce, but he was fraudulent, avaricious, and deceitful. His wickedness during life was severely punished in the lower world, where he had to roll up hill a huge marble block, which as soon as it reached the top always rolled down again. The special reasons for this punishment are not the same in all authors; some relate that it was because he had betrayed the designs of the gods; others because he attacked travellers, and killed them with a huge block of stone; and others again because he had betrayed to Asopus, that Zeus had carried off Aegina, the daughter of the latter. The more usual tradition related that Sisyphus requested his wife not to bury him, and that, when she complied with his request, Sisyphus in the lower world complained of this seeming neglect, and obtained from Pluto or Persephone, permission to return to the upper world to punish his wife. He then refused to return to the lower world, until Hermes carried him off by force; and this piece of treachery is said to have been the cause of his punishment.

Sitace or Sittace (Σιτάκη, Σιττάκη : *Eski-Bagdad*, Ru.), a great and populous city of Babylonia, near but not on the Tigris, and 8 parasangs within the Median wall. Its probable site is marked by a ruin called the Tower of Nimrod. It gave the name of Sittacene to the district on the lower course of the Tigris E. of Babylonia and N. W of Susiana.

Sitalces (Σιτάλκης), king of the Thracian tribe of the Odrysians, was a son of Teres, whom he succeeded on the throne. He increased his dominions by successful wars, so that they ultimately comprised the whole territory from Abdera to the mouths of the Danube, and from Byzantium to the sources of the Strymon. At the commencement of the Peloponnesian war he entered into an alliance with the Athenians, and in 429 he invaded Macedonia with a vast army, but was obliged to retire through failure of provisions.

Sithonia (Σιθωνία), the central one of the 3 peninsulas running out from Chalcidice in Macedonia, between the Toronaic and Singitic gulfs. The Thracians originally extended over the greater part of Macedonia; and the ancients derived the name of Sithonia from a Thracian king Sithon. We also find mention of a Thracian people, Sithonii, on the shores of the Pontus Euxinus; and the poets frequently use *Sithonis* and *Sithonius* in the general sense of Thracian.

Sitifi (Σίτιφα: *Setif*, Ru.), an inland city of Mauretania Caesariensis, on the borders of Numidia, stood upon a hill, in an extensive and beautiful plain. It first became an important place under the Romans, who made it a colony; and, upon the subdivision of M. Caesariensis into 2 provinces, it was made the capital of the eastern province, which was called after it Mauretania Sitifensis.

Sitones, a German tribe in Scandinavia, belonging to the race of the Suevi.

Sittace, Sittacēne. [SITACE.]

Sittius or **Sitius**, P., of Nuceria in Campania, was connected with Catiline, and went to Spain in B. C. 64, from which country he crossed over into Mauretania in the following year. It was said that P. Sulla had sent him into Spain to excite an insurrection against the Roman government; and Cicero accordingly, when he defended Sulla, in 62, was obliged to deny the truth of the charges that had been brought against Sittius. Sittius did not return to Rome. His property in Italy was sold to pay his debts, and he continued in Africa, where he fought in the wars of the kings of the country. He joined Caesar when the latter came to Africa, in 46, to prosecute the war against the Pompeian party. He was of great service to Caesar in this war, and at its conclusion was rewarded by Caesar with the western part of Numidia, where he settled down, distributing the land among his soldiers. After the death of Caesar, Arabio, the son of Masinissa, returned to Africa, and killed Sittius by stratagem.

Siuph (Σιοΰφ), a city of Lower Egypt, in the Saitic nome, only mentioned by Herodotus (ii. 172).

Smaragdus Mons (Σμάραγδος ὄρος: *Jebel Zaburuh*), a mountain of Upper Egypt, near the coast of the Red Sea, N. of Berenice. The extensive emerald mines, from which it obtained its name, were worked under the ancient kings of Egypt, under the Ptolemies, and under the Romans. They seem to have been exhausted, as only very few emeralds are now and then found in the neighbourhood.

Smerdis (Σμέρδις), the son of Cyrus, was murdered by order of his brother Cambyses. The death of Smerdis was kept a profound secret; and accordingly, when the Persians became weary of the tyranny of Cambyses, one of the Magians, named Patizithes, who had been left by Cambyses in charge of his palace and treasures, availed himself of the likeness of his brother to the deceased Smerdis, to proclaim this brother as king, representing him as the younger son of Cyrus. Cambyses heard of the revolt in Syria, but he died of an accidental wound in the thigh, as he was mounting his horse to march against the usurper. The false Smerdis was acknowledged as king by the Persians, and reigned for 7 months without opposition. The leading Persian nobles, however, were not quite free from suspicion; and this suspicion was increased by the king never inviting any of them to the palace, and never appearing in public. Among the nobles who entertained these suspicions was Otanes, whose daughter Phaedima had been one of the wives of Cambyses, and had been transferred to his successor. The new king had some years before been deprived of his ears

by Cyrus for some offence; and Otanes persuaded his daughter to ascertain whether her master had really lost his ears. Phaedima found out that such was the fact, and communicated the decisive information to her father. Otanes thereupon formed a conspiracy, and in conjunction with 6 other noble Persians, succeeded in forcing his way into the palace, where they slew the false Smerdis and his brother Patizithes in the 8th month of their reign, 521. The usurpation of the false Smerdis was an attempt on the part of the Medes, to whom the Magians belonged, to obtain the supremacy, of which they had been deprived by Cyrus. The assassination of the false Smerdis and the accession of Darius Hystaspis again gave the ascendancy to the Persians; and the anniversary of the day on which the Magians were massacred, was commemorated among the Persians by a solemn festival, called Magophonia, on which no Magian was allowed to show himself in public. The real nature of the transaction is also shown by the revolt of the Medes which followed the accession of Darius.

Smilis (Σμῖλις), son of Euclides, of Aegina, a sculptor of the legendary period, whose name appears to be derived from σμίλη, *a knife for carving wood*, and afterwards *a sculptor's chisel*. Smilis is the legendary head of the Aeginetan school of sculpture, just as Daedalus is the legendary head of the Attic and Cretan schools.

Smintheus (Σμινθεύς), a surname of Apollo, which is derived by some from σμίνθος, a mouse, and by others from the town of Sminthe in Troas. The mouse was regarded by the ancients as inspired by the vapours arising from the earth, and as the symbol of prophetic power. In the temple of Apollo at Chryse there was a statue of the god by Scopas, with a mouse under its foot, and on coins Apollo is represented carrying a mouse in his hands. Temples of Apollo Smintheus and festivals (Sminthia) existed in several parts of Greece.

Smyrna (Σμύρνα), or **Myrrha.** For details see ADONIS.

Smyrna and in many MSS. **Zmyrna** (Σμύρνα: Ion. Σμύρνη: Σμυρναῖος, Smyrnaeus: *Smyrna*, Turk. *Izmir*), one of the most ancient and flourishing cities of Asia Minor, and the only one of the great cities on its W. coast which has survived to this day, stood in a position alike remarkable for its beauty and for other natural advantages. Lying just about the centre of the W. coast of Asia Minor; on the banks of the little river Melea, at the bottom of a deep bay, the Sinus Hermaeus or Smyrnaeus (*G. of Smyrna*), which formed a safe and immense harbour for the largest ships up to the very walls of the city; at the foot of the rich slopes of Tmolus and at the entrance to the great and fertile valley of the Hermus, in which lay the great and wealthy city of Sardis; and in the midst of the Greek colonies on the E. shore of the Aegean; it was marked out by nature as one of the greatest emporiums for the trade between Europe and Asia, and has preserved that character to the present day. There are various accounts of its origin. The most probable is that which represents it as an Aeolian colony from Cyme. At an early period it fell, by a stratagem, into the hands of the Ionians of Colophon, and remained an Ionian city from that time forth: this appears to have happened before Ol. 23. (B.C. 688). As to the time when it became a member of the

Paniönic coufederacy, we have only a very un-trustworthy account, which refers its admission to the reign of Attalus, king of Pergamus. Its early history is also very obscure. There is an account in Strabo, that it was destroyed by the Lydian king Sadyattes, and that its inhabitants were compelled to live in scattered villages, until after the Macedonian conquest, when the city was rebuilt, 20 stadia from its former site, by Anti-gonus ; but this is inconsistent with Pindar's mention of Smyrna as a beautiful city. Thus much is clear, however, that, at some period the old city of Smyrna, which stood on the N. E. side of the Hermaean Gulf, was abandoned ; and that it was succeeded by a new city, on the S. E. side of the same gulf (the present site), which is said to have been built by Antigonus, and which was enlarged and beautified by Lysimachus. This new city stood partly on the sea-shore and partly on a hill called Mastusia. It had a magnificent harbour, with such a depth of water that the largest ships could lie alongside the quays. The streets were paved with stone, and crossed one another at right angles. The city soon became one of the greatest and most prosperous in the world. It was especially favoured by the Romans on account of the aid it rendered them in the Syrian and Mithridatic wars. It was the seat of a conventus juridicus. In the Civil Wars it was taken and partly destroyed by Dolabella, but it soon recovered. It occupies a distinguished place in the early history of Christianity, as one of the only two among the 7 churches of Asia which St. John addresses, in the Apocalypse, without any admix-ture of rebuke, and as the scene of the labours and martyrdom of Polycarp. In the years A. D. 178 —180, a succession of earthquakes, to which the city has always been much exposed, reduced it almost to ruins ; but it was restored by the em-peror M. Antoninus. In the successive wars under the Eastern empire it was frequently much injured, but always recovered ; and, under the Turks, it has survived repeated attacks of earth-quake, fire, and plague, and still remains the great-est commercial city of the Levant. There are but few ruins of the ancient city. In addition to all her other sources of renown Smyrna stood at the head of the cities which claimed the birth of Homer. The poet was worshipped as a hero in a magnificent building called the Homerēum ('Ομή-ρειον). Near the sea-shore there stood a magnifi-cent temple of Cybele, whose head appears on the coins of the city. The other divinities chiefly wor-shipped here were Nemesis and the nymph Smyrna, the heroine eponymus of the place, who had a shrine on the banks of the river Meles.

Smyrna Trachēa. [EPHESUS.]

Smyrnaeus Sinus (Σμυρναίων κόλπος, Σμυρ-ναϊκὸς κόλπος; G. of Ismir or Smyrna), the great gulf on the W. coast of Asia Minor, at the bottom of which Smyrna stands. Its entrance lies be-tween Pr. Melaena (C. Kara Burnu) on the W., and Phocaea (Fokia) on the E. Its depth was reckoned at 350 stadia. It received the river Hermus, whence it was called Hermēus Sinus ('Ερμαιος κόλπος). It is sometimes also called Μελήτου κόλπος, from the little river Meles, on which Old Smyrna stood.

Soānes (Σόανες), a powerful people of the Cau-casus, governed by a king who could bring 200,000 soldiers into the field. The mountain streams of

the country contained gold, which was separated by collecting the water in sheep-skins, whence the matter-of-fact interpreters derived the legend of the golden fleece. According to Strabo, the habits of the people were such that they stood in remark-able need of other "washings." They are also called **Suani** and **Suanocolchi** (Σούανοι, Σουανο-κόλχοι), and their land Suania (Σουανία).

Sŏcrătes (Σωκράτης). 1. The celebrated Athe-nian philosopher, was born in the demus Alopece, in the immediate neighbourhood of Athens, B. C. 469. His father Sophroniscus was a statuary ; his mother Phaenarete was a midwife. In his youth he followed the profession of his father, and attained sufficient proficiency to have executed the group of clothed Graces which was preserved in the Acropolis, and was shown as his work down to the time of Pausanias. The personal qualities of Socrates were marked and striking. His phy-sical constitution was healthy, robust, and en-during to an extraordinary degree. He was capable of bearing fatigue or hardship, and indifferent to heat or cold, in a measure which astonished all his companions. He went barefoot in all seasons of the year, even during the winter campaign at Po-tidaea, under the severe frosts of Thrace ; and the same homely clothing sufficed for him in winter as well as in summer. His ugly physiognomy ex-cited the jests both of his friends and enemies, who inform us that he had a flat nose, thick lips, and prominent eyes like a satyr or Silenus. Of the circumstances of his life we are almost wholly ignorant: he served as an hoplite at Potidaea, De-lium, and Amphipolis with great credit to himself. He seems never to have filled any political office until 406, in which year he was a member of the senate of Five Hundred, and one of the Prytanes, when he refused, on the occasion of the trial of the 6 generals, to put an unconstitutional question to the vote, in spite of all personal hazard. He dis-played the same moral courage in refusing to obey the order of the Thirty Tyrants for the apprehen-sion of Leon the Salaminian. — At what time Socrates relinquished his profession as a statuary we do not know ; but it is certain that all the middle and later part of his life at least was de-voted exclusively to the self-imposed task of teach-ing ; excluding all other business, public or pri-vate, and to the neglect of all means of fortune. But he never opened a school, nor did he, like the sophists of his time, deliver public lectures. Every-where, in the market-place, in the gymnasia, and in the workshops, he sought and found opportuni-ties for awakening and guiding, in boys, youth, and men, moral consciousness and the impulse after self-knowledge respecting the end and value of our actions. His object, however, was only to aid them in developing the germs of knowledge which were already present in them, not to communicate to them ready-made knowledge ; and he therefore professed to practise a kind of mental midwifery, just as his mother Phaenarete exercised the corresponding cor-poreal art. Unweariedly and inexorably did he fight against all false appearance and conceit of knowledge, in order to pave the way for correct knowledge. Consequently to the mentally proud and the mentally idle he appeared an intolerable bore, and often experienced their bitter hatred and calumny. This was probably the reason why he was selected by Aristophanes, and the other comic writers, to be attacked as a general representative of philosophical and rhetorical teaching ; the more so, as his marked and repulsive physiognomy admitted so well of being imitated in the mask which the actor wore. The audience at the theatre would more readily recognise the peculiar figure which they were accustomed to see every day in the market-place, than if Prodicus or Protagoras, whom most of them did not know by sight, had been brought on the stage ; nor was it of much importance either to them or to Aristophanes, whether Socrates was represented as teaching what he did really teach, or something utterly different. Attached to none of the prevailing parties, Socrates found in each of them his friends and his enemies. Hated and persecuted by Critias, Charicles, and others among the Thirty Tyrants, who had a special reference to him in the decree which they issued, forbidding the teaching of the art of oratory, he was impeached after their banishment and by their opponents. An orator named Lycon, and a poet (a friend of Thrasybulus) named Meletus, had united in the impeachment with the powerful demagogue Anytus, an embittered antagonist of the sophists and their system, and one of the leaders of the band which, setting out from Phyle, forced their way into the Piraeus, and drove out the Thirty Tyrants. The judges also are described as persons who had been banished, and who had returned with Thrasybulus. The chief articles of impeachment were, that Socrates was guilty of corrupting the youth, and of despising the tutelary deities of the state, putting in their place other new divinities. At the same time it had been made a matter of accusation against him, that Critias, the most ruthless of the Tyrants, had come forth from his school. Some expressions of his, in which he had found fault with the democratical mode of electing by lot, had also been brought up against him ; and there can be little doubt that use was made of his friendly relations with Theramenes, one of the most influential of the Thirty, with Plato's uncle Charmides, who fell by the side of Critias in the struggle with the popular party, and with other aristocrats, in order to irritate against him the party which at that time was dominant. The substance of the speech which Socrates delivered in his defence is probably preserved by Plato in the piece which goes under the name of the "Apology of Socrates." Being condemned by a majority of only 6 votes, he expresses the conviction that he deserved to be maintained at the public cost in the Prytaneum, and refuses to acquiesce in the adjudication of imprisonment, or a large fine, or banishment. He will assent to nothing more than a fine of 60 minae, on the security of Plato, Crito, and other friends. Condemned to death by the judges, who were incensed by this speech, by a majority of 80 votes, he departs from them with the protestation, that he would rather die after such a defence than live after one in which he should have endeavoured to excite their pity. The sentence of death could not be carried into execution until after the return of the vessel which had been sent to Delos on the periodical Theoric mission. The 30 days which intervened between its return and the condemnation of Socrates were devoted by him to poetic attempts (the first he had made in his life), and to his usual conversation with his friends. One of these conversations, on the duty of obedience to the laws, Plato has reported in the *Crito*, so called

after the faithful follower of Socrates, who had endeavoured without success to persuade him to make his escape. In another, imitated or worked up by Plato in the *Phaedo*, Socrates immediately before he drank the cup of hemlock developed the grounds of his immovable conviction of the immortality of the soul. He died with composure and cheerfulness in his 70th year, B.C. 399. Three peculiarities distinguished Socrates :— 1. His long life passed in contented poverty and in public dialectics, of which we have already spoken. 2. His persuasion of a special religious mission. He had been accustomed constantly to hear, even from his childhood, a divine voice — interfering, at moments when he was about to act, in the way of restraint, but never in the way of instigation. Such prohibitory warning was wont to come upon him very frequently, not merely on great, but ever on small occasions, intercepting what he was about to do or to say. Though later writers speak of this as the Daemon or Genius of Socrates, he himself does not personify it, but treats it merely as a "divine sign, a prophetic or supernatural voice." He was accustomed not only to obey it implicitly, but to speak of it publicly and familiarly to others, so that the fact was well known both to his friends and to his enemies. 3. His great intellectual originality, both of subject and of method, and his power of stirring and forcing the germ of inquiry and ratiocination in others. He was the first who turned his thoughts and discussions distinctly to the subject of ethics, and was the first to proclaim that "the proper study of mankind is man." With the philosophers who preceded him, the subject of examination had been Nature, or the Kosmos as one undistinguishable whole, blending together cosmogony, astronomy, geometry, physics, metaphysics, &c. In discussing ethical subjects Socrates employed the dialectic method, and thus laid the foundation of formal logic, which was afterwards expanded by Plato, and systematised by Aristotle. The originality of Socrates is shown by the results he achieved. Out of his intellectual school sprang, not merely Plato, himself a host, but all the other leaders of Grecian speculation for the next half-century, and all those who continued the great line of speculative philosophy down to later times. Euclid and the Megaric school of philosophers — Aristippus and the Cyrenaic Antisthenes and Diogenes, the first of those called the Cynics — all emanated more or less directly from the stimulus imparted by Socrates, though each followed a different vein of thought. Ethics continued to be what Socrates had first made them, a distinct branch of philosophy, alongside of which politics, rhetoric, logic, and other speculations relating to man and society, gradually arranged themselves ; all of them more popular, as well as more keenly controverted, than physics, which at that time presented comparatively little charm, and still less of attainable certainty. There can be no doubt that the individual influence of Socrates permanently enlarged the horizon, improved the method, and multiplied the ascendant minds, of the Grecian speculative world, in a manner never since paralleled. Subsequent philosophers may have had a more elaborate doctrine, and a larger number of disciples who imbibed their ideas ; but none of them applied the same stimulating method with the same efficacy, and none of them struck out of other minds that fire which sets light to original thought. — (A great part of this article is taken from Mr. Grote's account of Socrates in his *History of Greece*.) — 2. The ecclesiastical historian, was born at Constantinople about A. D. 379. He was a pupil of Ammonius and Helladius, and followed the profession of an advocate in his native city, whence he is surnamed Scholasticus. The *Ecclesiastical History* of Socrates extends from the reign of Constantine the Great, 306, to the end of the younger Theodosius, 439. He appears to have been a man of less bigotry than most of his contemporaries, and the very difficulty of determining from internal evidence some points of his religious belief, may be considered as arguing his comparative liberality. His history is divided into 7 books. His work is included in the editions of the ancient Greek ecclesiastical historians by Valesius, Paris, 1668 ; reprinted at Mentz, 1677 ; by Reading, Camb. 1720.

Sŏdŏma, gen. -orum and -ae, also -um, gen. -i, and -i, gen. -ōrum (τὰ Σόδομα : Σοδομίτης, Sodomita), a very ancient city of Canaan, in the beautiful valley of Siddim (ἡ Σοδομῖτις), closely connected with Gomorrha, over which and the other 3 "cities of the plain," the king of Sodom seems to have had a sort of supremacy. In the book of Genesis we find these cities as subject, in the time of Abraham, to the king of Elam and his allies (an indication of the early supremacy in W. Asia of the masters of the Tigris and Euphrates valley), and their attempt to cast off the yoke was the occasion of the first war on record. (Gen. xiv.) Soon afterwards, the abominable sins of these cities called down the divine vengeance, and they were all destroyed by fire from heaven, except Zoar, which was spared at the intercession of Lot. The beautiful valley in which they stood was overwhelmed by the Jordan and converted into the Dead Sea, whose bituminous waters still bear witness to the existence of the springs of asphaltus ("slime-pits " in our version) of which the valley of Siddim was full. It used to be assumed that, before the destruction of the cities of the plain, the Jordan flowed on into the Red Sea ; but this has been shown to be, if not physically impossible, most improbable. There was probably always a lake which received the waters both of the Jordan and the river which still flows into the S. end of the Dead Sea ; and the nature of the change seems to have consisted in the enlargement of this lake by a great depression of the whole valley. The site of Sodom was probably near the S. extremity of the lake.

Soemis or **Soaemias**, **Jūlia**, daughter of Julia Maesa, and mother of Elagabalus, either by her husband Sextus Varius Marcellus, or, according to the report industriously circulated with her own consent, by Caracalla. After the accession of her son, she became his chosen counsellor, and seems to have encouraged and shared his follies and enormities. She took a place in the senate, which then, for the first time, witnessed the intrusion of a woman, and was herself the president of a sort of female parliament, which held its sittings in the Quirinal, and published edicts for the regulation of all matters connected with the morals, dress, etiquette, and equipage of the matrons. She was slain by the praetorians, in the arms of her son, on the 11th of March, A. D. 222.

Sogdiāna (ἡ Σογδιανή or Σουγδιανή : Old Persian, Sughdâ : Σόγδιοι, Σογδιανοί, Σουγδιανοί : parts of *Turkestan* and *Bokhara*, including the district still called *Sogd*), the N.E. province of the ancient Persian Empire, separated on the S. from Bactriana and Margiana by the upper course of the Oxus (*Jihoun*) ; on the E. and N. from Scythia by the Sogdii Comedarum and Oscii M. (*Kara-Dagh, Alatan* and *Ak Tagh*) and by the upper course of the Jaxartes (*Sihoun*) ; and bounded on the N.W. by the great deserts E. of the *Sea of Aral*. The S. part of the country was fertile and populous. It was conquered by Cyrus, and afterwards by Alexander, both of whom marked the extreme limits of their advance by cities on the Jaxartes, Cyreschata and Alexandreschata. After the Macedonian conquest, it was subject to the kings, first of Syria, and then of Bactria, till it was overrun by the barbarians. The natives of the country were a wild warlike people of the great Arian race, resembling the Bactrians in their character and customs.

Sogdiānus (Σογδιανός), was one of the illegitimate sons of Artaxerxes I. Longimanus. The latter, on his death in B. C. 425, was succeeded by his legitimate son Xerxes II., but this monarch, after a reign of only 2 months, was murdered by Sogdianus, who now became king. Sogdianus, however, was murdered in his turn, after a reign of 7 months, by his brother Ochus. Ochus reigned under the name of Darius II.

Sogdii Montes. [Sogdiana].

Sol. [Helios.]

Sŏli or **Soloe** (Σόλοι). 1. (Ethnic, Σολεύς, Solensis : *Mezetlu*, Ru.), a city on the coast of Cilicia, between the rivers Lamus and Cydnus, said to have been colonised by Argives and Lydians from Rhodes. It was a flourishing city in the time of Alexander, who fined its people 200 talents for their adhesion to the Persians. The city was destroyed by Tigranes, who probably transplanted the inhabitants to Tigranocerta. Pompey restored the city after his war with the pirates, and peopled it with the survivors of the defeated bands ; and from this time forth it was called **Pompeiopolis** (Πομπηιούπολις). It was celebrated in literary history as the birthplace of the Stoic philosopher Chrysippus, of the comic poet Philemon, and of the astronomer and poet Aratus. Its name has been curiously perpetuated in the grammatical word *solecism* (soloecismus), which is said to have been first applied to the corrupt dialect of Greek spoken by the inhabitants of this city, or, as some say, of Soli in Cyprus. — 2. (Ethnic, Σόλιος : *Aligora*, in the valley of *Solea*, Ru.), a considerable sea-port town in the W. part of the N. coast of Cyprus, on a little river. According to some, it was a colony of the Athenians; while others ascribed its erection to a native prince acting under the advice of Solon, and others to Solon himself: the last account is doubtless an error. It had temples of Isis and Aphrodite, and there were mines in its vicinity.

Solicinīum, a town in Roman Germany (the Agri Decumates) on the mountain Pirus, where Valentinian gained a victory over the Alemanni in A. D. 369, probably in the neighbourhood of modern Heidelberg.

Solīnus, C. Jūlius, the author of a geographical compendium, divided into 57 chapters, containing a brief sketch of the world as known to the ancients, diversified by historical notices, remarks on the origin, habits, religious rites and social condition of various nations enumerated. The arrangement, and frequently the very words, are derived from the Natural History of Pliny, but little knowledge, care, or judgment, are displayed in the selection. We know nothing of Solinus himself, but he must have lived after the reign of Alexander Severus, and before that of Constantine. He may perhaps be placed about A. D. 238. We learn from the first of 2 prefatory addresses, that an edition of the work had already passed into circulation, in an imperfect state, without the consent or knowledge of the author, under the appellation *Collectanea Rerum Memorabilium*, while on the 2nd, revised, corrected, and published by himself, he bestowed the more ambitious title of *Polyhistor*; and hence we find the treatise designated in several MSS. as *C. Julii Solini Grammatici Polyhistor ab ipso editus et recognitus*. The most notable edition is that of Salmasius, published at Utrecht in 1689, prefixed to his "Plinianae Exercitationes," the whole forming 2 large folio volumes.

Sōlis Fons. [OASIS, No. 3.]

Sōlis Lacus (λίμνη 'Ηελίοιο), a lake in the far E., from which, in the old mythical system of the world, the sun arose to make his daily course through heaven. Some of the matter-of-fact expositors identified it with the Caspian Sea. Another lake of the same name was imagined by some of the poets in the far W., into which the sun sank at night.

Sōlis Mons. [SOLOIS.]

Sōlis Promontorium (ἄκρα 'Ηλίου ἱερά : *Ras Anfir*), a promontory of Arabia Felix, near the middle of the Persian Gulf.

Soloe. [SOLI].

Sōlōis (Σολόεις : *C. Cantin*, Arab. *Ras el Houdik*), a promontory running far out into the sea, in the S. part of the W. coast of Mauretania. Herodotus believed it to be the W.-most headland of all Libya. Upon it was a Phoenician temple of Poseidon. The later geographers under the Romans mention a **Mons Solis** ('Ηλίου ὄρος), which appears to be the same spot, its name being probably a corruption of the Greek name.

Sōlōn (Σόλων), the celebrated Athenian legislator, was born about B. C. 638. His father Execestides was a descendant of Codrus, and his mother was a cousin of the mother of Pisistratus. Execestides had seriously crippled his resources by a too prodigal expenditure; and Solon consequently found it either necessary or convenient in his youth to betake himself to the life of a foreign trader. It is likely enough that while necessity compelled him to seek a livelihood in some mode or other, his active and inquiring spirit led him to select that pursuit which would furnish the amplest means for its gratification. Solon early distinguished himself by his poetical abilities. His first effusions were in a somewhat light and amatory strain, which afterwards gave way to the more dignified and earnest purpose of inculcating profound reflections or sage advice. So widely indeed did his reputation spread, that he was ranked as one of the famous 7 sages, and his name appears in all the lists of the 7. The occasion which first brought Solon prominently forward as an actor on the political stage, was the contest between Athens and Megara respecting the possession of Salamis. The ill success of the attempts of the Athenians to make themselves masters of the island, had led to the enactment of a law forbidding the writing or saying anything to urge the Athenians to renew

the contest. Solon, indignant at this dishonourable renunciation of their claims, hit upon the device of feigning to be mad; and causing a report of his condition to be spread over the city, he rushed into the agora, and there recited a short elegiac poem of 100 lines, in which he called upon the Athenians to retrieve their disgrace and reconquer the *lovely island*. Pisistratus (who, however, must have been extremely young at the time) came to the support of his kinsman; the pusillanimous law was rescinded; war was declared; and Solon himself appointed to conduct it. The Megarians were driven out of the island, but a tedious war ensued, which was finally settled by the arbitration of Sparta. Both parties appealed, in support of their claim, to the authority of Homer; and it was currently believed in antiquity that Solon had surreptitiously inserted the line (*Il.* ii. 558) which speaks of Ajax as ranging his ships with the Athenians. The Spartans decided in favour of the Athenians, about B. C. 596. Solon himself, probably, was one of those who received grants of land in Salamis, and this may account for his being termed a Salaminian. Soon after these events (about 595) Solon took a leading part in promoting hostilities on behalf of Delphi against Cirrha, and was the mover of the decree of the Amphictyons by which war was declared. It does not appear, however, what active part he took in the war. According to a common story, which however rests only on the authority of a late writer, Solon hastened the surrender of the town by causing the waters of the Plistus to be poisoned. It was about the time of the outbreak of this war, that, in consequence of the distracted state of Attica, which was rent by civil commotions, Solon was called upon by all parties to mediate between them, and alleviate the miseries that prevailed. He was chosen archon 594, and under that legal title was invested with unlimited power for adopting such measures as the exigencies of the state demanded. In fulfilment of the task entrusted to him, Solon addressed himself to the relief of the existing distress. This he effected with the greatest discretion and success by his celebrated *disburdening ordinance* (σεισάχθεια), a measure consisting of various distinct provisions, calculated to relieve the debtors with as little infringement as possible on the claims of the wealthy creditors. The details of this measure, however, are involved in considerable uncertainty. We know that he depreciated the coinage, making the mina to contain 100 drachmae instead of 73; that is to say, 73 of the old drachmae produced 100 of the new coinage, in which obligations were to be discharged; so that the debtor saved rather more than a fourth in every payment. The success of the Seisachtheia procured for Solon such confidence and popularity that he was further charged with the task of entirely remodelling the constitution. As a preliminary step, he repealed all the laws of Draco except those relating to bloodshed. Our limits only allow us to glance at the principal features of the constitution established by Solon. This constitution was based upon the timocratic principle, that is, the title of citizens to the honours and offices of the state was regulated by their wealth. All the citizens were distributed into 4 classes. The 1st class consisted of those who had an annual income of at least 500 medimni of dry or liquid produce (equivalent to 500 drachmae, a medimnus being reckoned at a drachma), and were called *Pentacosiomedimni*. The 2nd class consisted of those whose incomes ranged between 300 and 500 medimni or drachmae, and were called *Hippeis* (Ἱππεῖς, Ἱππῆς), from their being able to keep a horse, and bound to perform military service as cavalry. The 3rd class consisted of those whose incomes varied between 200 and 300 medimni or drachmae, and were termed *Zeugitae* (Ζευγῖται). The 4th class included all whose property fell short of 200 medimni or drachmae, and bore the name of *Thetes*. The first 3 classes were liable to *direct* taxation, in the form of a graduated income tax. A *direct* tax, however, was an extraordinary, and not an annual payment. The 4th class were exempt from direct taxes, but of course they, as well as the rest, were liable to *indirect* taxes. To Solon was ascribed the institution of the *Boule* (βουλή), or deliberative assembly of Four Hundred, 100 members being elected from each of the 4 tribes. He greatly enlarged the functions of the *Ecclesia* (ἐκκλησία), which no doubt existed before his time, though it probably possessed scarcely more power than the assemblies which we find described in the Homeric poems. He gave it the right of electing the archons and other magistrates, and, what was even more important, made the archons and magistrates accountable directly to it when their year of office was expired. He also gave it what was equivalent to a veto upon any proposed measure of the Boule, though it could not itself originate any measure. Besides the arrangement of the general political relations of the people, Solon was the author of a great variety of special laws, which do not seem to have been arranged in any systematic manner. Those relating to debtors and creditors have been already referred to. Several had for their object the encouragement of trade and manufactures. Foreign settlers were not to be naturalised as citizens unless they carried on some industrial pursuit. If a father did not teach his son some trade or profession, the son was not liable to maintain his father in his old age. The council of Areopagus had a general power to punish idleness. Solon forbade the exportation of all produce of the Attic soil except olive oil. He was the first who gave to those who died childless the power of disposing of their property by will. He enacted several laws relating to marriage, especially with regard to heiresses. The rewards which he appointed to be given to victors at the Olympic and Isthmian games are for that age unusually large (500 drachmae to the former and 100 to the latter). One of the most curious of his regulations was that which denounced atimia against any citizen, who, on the outbreak of a sedition, remained neutral. The laws of Solon were inscribed on wooden rollers (ἄξονες) and triangular tablets (κύρβεις), and were set up at first in the Acropolis, afterwards in the Prytaneum. The Athenians were also indebted to Solon for some rectification of the calendar. It is said that Solon exacted from the people a solemn oath, that they would observe his laws without alteration for a certain space — 10 years according to Herodotus — 100 years according to other accounts. It is related that he was himself aware that he had been compelled to leave many imperfections in his system and code. He is said to have spoken of his laws as being not the best, but the best which the Athenians would have received. After he had completed his task, being,

we are told, greatly annoyed and troubled by those who came to him with all kinds of complaints, suggestions or criticisms about his laws, in order that he might not himself have to propose any change, he absented himself from Athens for ten years, after he had obtained the oath above referred to. He first visited Egypt; and from thence proceeded to Cyprus, where he was received with great distinction by Philocyprus, king of the little town of Aepea. Solon persuaded the king to remove from the old site, and build a new town on the plain. The new settlement was called Soli, in honour of the illustrious visitor. He is further said to have visited Lydia; and his interview with Croesus was one of the most celebrated stories in antiquity. [CROESUS.] During the absence of Solon the old dissensions were renewed, and shortly after his arrival at Athens, the supreme power was seized by Pisistratus. The tyrant, after his usurpation, is said to have paid considerable court to Solon, and on various occasions to have solicited his advice, which Solon did not withhold. Solon probably died about 558, two years after the overthrow of the constitution at the age of 80. There was a story current in antiquity that, by his own directions, his ashes were collected and scattered round the island of Salamis. Of the poems of Solon several fragments remain. They do not indicate any great degree of imaginative power, but their style is vigorous and simple. Those that were called forth by special emergencies appear to have been marked by no small degree of energy. The fragments of these poems are incorporated in the collections of the Greek gnomic poets; and there is also a separate edition of them by Bach, Lugd. Bat. 1825.

Sŏlūs (Σολοῦς, -οῦντος, contr. of Σολόεις: Σολεντῖνος), called **Soluntum** (Solentinus) by the Romans, an ancient town on the N. coast of Sicily between Panormus and Thermae.

Sŏlўma (τὰ Σόλυμα). 1. (*Taktalu-Dagh*), the mountain range which runs parallel to the E. coast of Lycia, and is a S. continuation of M. Climax. Sometimes the whole range is called Climax, and the name of Solyma is given to its highest peak.— 2. Another name of JERUSALEM.

Sŏlўmi. [LYCIA.]

Somnus (ὕπνος), the personification and god of sleep, is described as a brother of Death (θάνατος, *mors*), and as a son of Night. In works of art, Sleep and Death are represented alike as two youths, sleeping or holding inverted torches in their hands. [MORS.]

Sontĭus (*Isonzo*), a river in Venetia in the N. of Italy, rising in the Carnic Alps and falling into the Sinus Tergestinus E. of Aquileia.

Sŏpăter (Σώπατρος). 1. Of Paphos, a writer of parody and burlesque (φλυαρογράφος), who flourished from B.C. 323 to 283. — 2. Of Apamea, a distinguished sophist, the head for some time of the school of Plotinus, was a disciple of Iamblichus, after whose death (before A. D. 330) he went to Constantinople. Here he enjoyed the favour and personal friendship of Constantine, who afterwards, however, put him to death (between A. D. 330 and 337) from the motive, as was alleged, of giving a proof of the sincerity of his own conversion to Christianity. There are several grammatical and rhetorical works extant under the name of Sopater, but the best critics ascribe these to a younger Sopater, mentioned below. — 3. The younger sophist, of Apamea, or of Alexandria, is supposed to have lived about 200 years later than the former. Besides his extant works already alluded to, Photius has preserved an extract of a work, entitled the *Historical Extracts* (ἐκλογή), which contained a vast variety of facts and figments, collected from a great number of authors. The remains of his rhetorical works are contained in Walz's *Rhetores Graeci.*

Sŏphēnē (Σωφηνή, later Σωφανηνή) a district of Armenia Major, lying between the ranges of Antitaurus and Masius; separated from Melitene in Armenia Minor by the Euphrates, from Mesopotamia by the Antitaurus, and from the E. part of Armenia Major by the river Nymphius. In the time of the Greek kings of Syria, it formed, together with the adjacent district of Acilisene, an independent W. Armenian kingdom, which was subdued and united to the rest of Armenia by Tigranes.

Sŏphĭlus (Σώφιλος), a comic poet of the middle comedy, was a native of Sicyon or of Thebes, and flourished about B. C. 348.

Sŏphŏclēs (Σοφοκλῆς). 1. The celebrated tragic poet, was born at Colonus, a village little more than a mile to the N. W. of Athens, B. C. 495. He was 30 years younger than Aeschylus, and 15 years older than Euripides. His father's name was Sophilus, or Sophillus, of whose condition in life we know nothing for certain; but it is clear that Sophocles received an education not inferior to that of the sons of the most distinguished citizens of Athens. To both of the two leading branches of Greek education, music and gymnastics, he was carefully trained, and in both he gained the prize of a garland. Of the skill which he had attained in music and dancing in his 16th year, and of the perfection of his bodily form, we have conclusive evidence in the fact that, when the Athenians were assembled in solemn festival around the trophy which they had set up in Salamis to celebrate their victory over the fleet of Xerxes, Sophocles was chosen to lead, naked and with lyre in hand, the chorus which danced about the trophy, and sang the songs of triumph, 480. His first appearance as a dramatist took place in 468, under peculiarly interesting circumstances; not only from the fact that Sophocles, at the age of 27, came forward as the rival of the veteran Aeschylus, whose supremacy had been maintained during an entire generation, but also from the character of the judges. The solemnities of the Great Dionysia were rendered more imposing by the occasion of the return of Cimon from his expedition to Scyros, bringing with him the bones of Theseus. Public expectation was so excited respecting the approaching dramatic contest, and party feeling ran so high, that Apsephion, the Archon Eponymus, whose duty it was to appoint the judges, had not yet ventured to proceed to the final act of drawing the lots for their election, when Cimon, with his 9 colleagues in the command, having entered the theatre, the Archon detained them at the altar, and administered to them the oath appointed for the judges in the dramatic contests. Their decision was in favour of Sophocles, who received the first prize; the second only being awarded to Aeschylus, who was so mortified at his defeat that he left Athens and retired to Sicily. From this epoch Sophocles held the supremacy of the Athenian stage, until a formidable rival arose in Euri-

pides, who gained the first prize for the first time in 441. The year 440 is a most important era in the poet's life. In the spring of that year he brought out the earliest of his extant dramas, the *Antigone*, a play which gave the Athenians such satisfaction, especially on account of the political wisdom it displayed, that they appointed him one of the ten *strategi*, of whom Pericles was the chief, in the war against Samos. It would seem that in this war Sophocles neither obtained nor sought for any military reputation: he is represented as good-humouredly repeating the judgment of Pericles concerning him, that he understood the making of poetry, but not the commanding of an army. The family dissensions which troubled his last years, are connected with a well-known and beautiful story. His family consisted of two sons, Iophon, the offspring of Nicostrate, who was a free Athenian woman, and Ariston, his son by Theoris of Sicyon; and Ariston had a son named Sophocles, for whom his grandfather showed the greatest affection. Iophon, who was by the laws of Athens his father's rightful heir, jealous of his love for the young Sophocles, and apprehending that Sophocles purposed to bestow upon his grandson a large proportion of his property, is said to have summoned his father before the Phratores, who seem to have had a sort of jurisdiction in family affairs, on the charge that his mind was affected by old age. As his only reply, Sophocles exclaimed, " If I am Sophocles, I am not beside myself; and if I am beside myself, I am not Sophocles;" and then he read from his *Oedipus at Colonus*, which was lately written, but not yet brought out, the magnificent *parodos*, beginning—

Εὐίππου, ξένε, τᾶσδε χώρας,

whereupon the judges at once dismissed the case, and rebuked Iophon for his undutiful conduct. Sophocles forgave his son, and it is probable that the reconciliation was referred to in the lines of the *Oedipus at Colonus*, where Antigone pleads with her father to forgive Polynices, as other fathers had been induced to forgive their bad children (vv. 1192, foll.). Sophocles died soon afterwards in 406, in his 90th year. All the various accounts of his death and funeral are of a fictitious and poetical complexion. According to some writers he was choked by a grape; another writer related that in a public recitation of the *Antigone* he sustained his voice so long without a pause that, through the weakness of extreme age, he lost his breath and his life together; while others ascribed his death to excessive joy at obtaining a victory. By the universal consent of the best critics, both of ancient and of modern times, the tragedies of Sophocles are the perfection of the Greek drama. The subjects and style of Sophocles are human, while those of Aeschylus are essentially heroic. The latter excite terror, pity, and admiration, as we view them at a distance; the former bring those same feelings home to the heart, with the addition of sympathy and self-application. No individual human being can imagine himself in the position of Prometheus, or derive a personal warning from the crimes and fate of Clytemnestra; but every one can, in feeling, share the self-devotion of Antigone in giving up her life at the call of fraternal piety, and the calmness which comes over the spirit of Oedipus when he is reconciled to the gods. In Aeschylus, the sufferers are the victims of an inexorable destiny; but Sophocles brings more prominently into view those faults of their own, which form one element of the destiny of which they are the victims, and is more intent upon inculcating, as the lesson taught by their woes, that wise calmness and moderation, in desires and actions, in prosperity and adversity, which the Greek poets and philosophers celebrate under the name of σωφροσύνη. On the other hand, he never descends to that level to which Euripides brought down the art, the exhibition of human passion and suffering for the mere purpose of exciting emotion in the spectators, apart from a moral end. The difference between the 2 poets is illustrated by the saying of Sophocles, that " he himself represented men as they ought to be, but Euripides exhibited them as they are." The number of plays ascribed to Sophocles was 130. He contended not only with Aeschylus and Euripides, but also with Choerilus, Aristias, Agathon, and other poets, amongst whom was his own son Iophon ; and he carried off the first prize 20 or 24 times, frequently the 2nd, and never the 3rd. It is remarkable, as proving his growing activity and success, that, of his 113 dramas, 81 were brought out after his 54th year, and also that all his extant dramas, which of course in the judgment of the grammarians were his best, belong to this latter period of his life. The 7 extant tragedies were probably brought out in the following chronological order : — *Antigone, Electra, Trachiniae, Oedipus Tyrannus, Ajax, Philoctetes, Oedipus at Colonus :* the last of these was brought out, after the death of the poet, by his grandson. Of the numerous editions of Sophocles, the most useful one for the ordinary student is that by Wunder, Gothae et Erfurdt, 1831—1846, 2 vols. 8vo. — 2. Son of Ariston and grandson of the elder Sophocles, was also an Athenian tragic poet. The love of his grandfather towards him has been already mentioned. In 401 he brought out the *Oedipus at Colonus* of his grandfather ; but he did not begin to exhibit his own dramas till 396.

Sophonisba, daughter of the Carthaginian general, Hasdrubal, the son of Gisco. She had been betrothed by her father, at a very early age, to the Numidian prince Masinissa, but at a subsequent period Hasdrubal being desirous to gain over Syphax, the rival monarch of Numidia, to the Carthaginian alliance, offered him the hand of his daughter in marriage. The beauty and accomplishments of Sophonisba prevailed over the influence of Scipio : Syphax married her, and from that time became the zealous supporter and ally of Carthage. Sophonisba, on her part, was assiduous in her endeavours to secure his adherence to the cause of her countrymen. After the defeat of Syphax, and the capture of his capital city of Cirta by Masinissa, Sophonisba fell into the hands of the conqueror, upon whom, however, her beauty exercised so powerful an influence, that he determined to marry her himself. Their nuptials were accordingly celebrated without delay, but Scipio (who was apprehensive lest she should exercise the same influence over Masinissa which she had previously done over Syphax) refused to ratify this arrangement, and upbraiding Masinissa with his weakness, insisted on the immediate surrender of the princess. Unable to resist this command, the Numidian king spared her the humiliation of captivity, by sending her a bowl of poison, which she drank without hesitation, and thus put an end to her own life.

Sophron (Σώφρων) of Syracuse, was the principal writer of that pecies of composition called the *Mime* (μῖμος), which was one of the numerous varieties of the Dorian Comedy. He flourished about B. C. 460—420. When Sophron is called the inventor of mimes, the meaning is, that he reduced to the form of a literary composition a species of amusement which the Greeks of Sicily, who were pre-eminent for broad humour and merriment, had practised from time immemorial at their public festivals, and the nature of which was very similar to the performances of the Spartan *Deicelestae.* Such mimetic performances prevailed throughout the Dorian states under various names. One feature of the Mimes of Sophron, which formed a marked distinction between them and comic poetry, was the nature of their rhythm. There is, however, some difficulty in determining whether they were in mere prose, or in mingled poetry and prose, or in prose with a peculiar rhythmical movement but no metrical arrangement. With regard to the substance of these compositions, their character, so far as it can be ascertained, appears to have been *ethical ;* that is, the scenes represented were those of ordinary life, and the language employed was intended to bring out more clearly the characters of the persons exhibited in those scenes, not only for the amusement but also for the instruction of the spectators. Plato was a great admirer of Sophron ; and the philosopher is said to have been the first who made the Mimes known at Athens. The serious purpose which was aimed at in the works of Sophron was always, as in the Attic Comedy, clothed under a sportive form ; and it can easily be imagined that sometimes the latter element prevailed, even to the extent of obscenity, as the extant fragments and the parallel of the Attic Comedy combine to prove. The best collection of the fragments of Sophron is by Ahrens, *De Graecae Linguae Dialectis.*

Sophroniscus. [SOCRATES.]

Sophus, P. Semprönius, tribune of the plebs, B. C. 310, and consul 304, is mentioned as one of the earliest jurists, and is said to have owed his name of Sophus or Wise to his great merits.

Sopianae (*Fünfkirchen*), a town in Pannonia Inferior, on the road from Mursa to Vindobona, the birth-place of the emperor Maximinus.

Sora. 1. (Soranus: *Sora*), a town in Latium, on the right bank of the river Liris and N. of Arpinum, with a strongly fortified citadel. It was the most N.-ly town of the Volsci in Latium, and afterwards joined the Samnites ; but it was conquered by the Romans, and was twice colonised by them, since the inhabitants had destroyed the first body of colonists. There are still remains of the polygonal walls of the ancient town.—2. A town in Paphlagonia of uncertain site.

Soracte (*Monte di S. Oreste*), a celebrated mountain in Etruria, in the territory of the Falisci, near the Tiber, about 24 miles from Rome, but the summit of which, frequently covered with snow, was clearly visible from the city. (*Vides ut alta stet nive candi tum Soracte,* Hor. *Carm.* i. 9.) The whole mountain was sacred to Apollo, and on its summit was a temple of this god. At the festival of Apollo, celebrated on this mountain, the worshippers passed over burning embers without receiving any injury. (Virg. *Aen.* xi. 785, seq.)

Soranus. 1. A Sabine divinity, usually identified with Apollo, worshipped on Mt. Soracte.

[SORACTE.] — 2. The name of several physicians, of whom the most celebrated seems to have been a native of Ephesus, and to have practised his profession first at Alexandria, and afterwards at Rome, in the reigns of Trajan and Hadrian, A. D. 98—138. There are several medical works still extant under the name of Soranus, but whether they were written by the native of Ephesus cannot be determined.

Sordĭcē (*Etang de Leucate*), a lake in Gallia Narbonensis, at the foot of the Pyrenees, formed by the river Sordis.

Sordŏnes or **Sordi**, a small people in Gallia Narbonensis, at the foot of the Pyrenees, whose chief town was Ruscino.

Sosĭbĭus (Σωσίβιος), a distinguished Lacedaemonian grammarian, who flourished in the reign of Ptolemy Philadelphus (about B. C. 251), and was contemporary with Callimachus.

Sosĭgĕnes (Σωσιγένης), the peripatetic philosopher, was the astronomer employed by Julius Caesar to superintend the correction of the calendar (B. C. 46). He is called an Egyptian, but may be supposed to have been an Alexandrian Greek. (See *Dict. of Antiq.* art. *Calendarium*.)

Sosĭphănes (Σωσιφάνης), the son of Sosicles, of Syracuse, was one of the 7 tragedians who were called the Tragic Pleiad. He was born at the end of the reign of Philip, and flourished B. C. 284.

Sosĭthĕus (Σωσίθεος), of Syracuse or Athens, or Alexandria in the Troad, was a distinguished tragic poet, one of the Tragic Pleiad, and the antagonist of the tragic poet Homer. He flourished about B. C. 284.

Sosĭus. 1. C., quaestor B, C. 66, and praetor 49. He was afterwards one of Antony's principal lieutenants in the East. He was appointed by Antony, in 38, governor of Syria and Cilicia, in the place of Ventidius. Like his predecessor in the government, he carried on the military operations in his province with great success. In 37, he advanced against Jerusalem along with Herod, and after hard fighting became master of the city, and placed Herod upon the throne. In return for these services, Antony obtained for Sosius the honour of a triumph in 34, and the consulship in 32. Sosius commanded the left wing of Antony's fleet at the battle of Actium. He was afterwards pardoned by Octavian, at the intercession of L. Arruntius.—2. The name of two brothers (Sosii), booksellers at Rome in the time of Horace. They were probably freedmen, perhaps of the Sosius mentioned above.

Sospĭta, that is, the "saving goddess," was a surname of Juno at Lanuvium and at Rome, in both of which places she had a temple. Her worship was very ancient in Latium and was transplanted from Lanuvium to Rome.

Sosthĕnes (Σωσθένης), a Macedonian officer of noble birth, who obtained the supreme direction of affairs during the period of confusion which followed the invasion of the Gauls. He defeated the Gauls in 280. He is included by the chronologers among the kings of Macedonia ; but it is very doubtful whether he ever assumed the royal title.

Sostrătus (Σώστρατος), the name of at least 4, if not 5, Grecian artists, who have been frequently confounded with one another.—1. A statuary in bronze, the sister's son of Pythagoras of Rhegium, and his disciple, flourished about B. C. 424.—2. Of Chios, the instructor of Pantias, flourished about

B. C. 400.—3. A statuary in bronze, whom Pliny mentions as a contemporary of Lysippus, at OL 114, B. C. 323, the date of Alexander's death. It is probable, however, that he was identical with the following.—4. The son of Dexiphanes, of Cnidus, was one of the great architects who flourished during and after the life of Alexander the Great. He built for Ptolemy I., the son of Lagus, the celebrated Pharos of Alexandria. He also embellished his native city, Cnidus, with a work which was one of the wonders of ancient architecture, namely, a portico, or colonnade, supporting a terrace, which served as a promenade.—5. An engraver of precious stones, whose name appears on several very beautiful cameos and intaglios.

Sŏsus (Σῶσος), of Pergamus, a worker in mosaic, and, according to Pliny, the most celebrated of all who practised that art.

Sŏtădes (Σωτάδης). 1. An Athenian comic poet of the Middle Comedy, who must not be confounded with the more celebrated poet of Maronea.—2. A native of Maronea in Thrace, flourished at Alexandria about B. C. 280. He wrote lascivious poems (called φλύακες or κίναιδοι) in the Ionic dialect, whence they were also called Ἰωνικοὶ λόγοι. They were also called *Sotadean poems* (Σωτάδεια ᾄσματα). It would seem that Sotades carried his lascivious and abusive satire to the utmost lengths ; and the freedoms which he took at last brought him into trouble. According to Plutarch, he made a vehement and gross attack on Ptolemy Philadelphus, on the occasion of his marriage with his sister Arsinoë, and the king threw him into prison, where he remained for a long time According to Athenaeus, the poet attacked both Lysimachus and Ptolemy, and, having fled from Alexandria, he was overtaken at Caunus by Ptolemy's general Patroclus, who shut him up in a leaden chest and cast him into the sea.

Sŏtēr (Σωτήρ), i. e. "the Saviour" (Lat. *Servator* or *Sospes*), occurs as the surname of several divinities, especially of Zeus. It was also a surname of Ptolemaeus I., king of Egypt, as well as of several of the other later Greek kings.

Sŏtĭon (Σωτίων). 1. A philosopher, and a native of Alexandria, who flourished at the close of the third century B. C. He is chiefly remarkable as the author of a work (entitled Διαδοχαί) on the successive teachers in the different philosophical schools.—2. A philosopher, and also a native of Alexandria, who lived in the age of Tiberius. He was the instructor of Seneca, who derived from him his admiration of Pythagoras. It was perhaps this Sotion who was the author of a treatise on anger, quoted by Stobaeus. — 3. A Peripatetic philosopher, mentioned by A. Gellius, is probably a different person from either of the preceding.

Sottĭātes or **Sotĭātes**, a powerful and warlike people in Gallia Aquitanica, on the frontiers of Gallia Narbonensis, were subdued by P. Crassus, Caesar's legate, after a hard-fought battle. The modern *Sôs* probably represents the ancient town of this people.

Sozŏmĕnus (Σωζόμενος), usually called **Sozomen** in English, was a Greek ecclesiastical historian of the 5th century. He was probably a native of Bethelia or Bethel, a village near Gaza in Palestine. His parents were Christians. He practised as an advocate at Constantinople, whence he is surnamed *Scholasticus* ; and he was still engaged in his profession when he wrote his history. His

Theseus and Minotaur. (From a painted Vase.) Page 766.

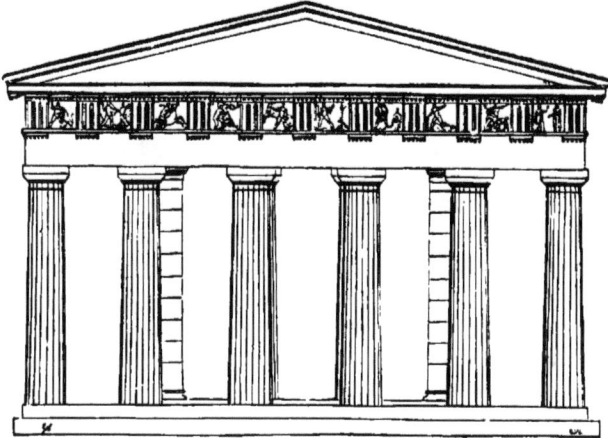

The Theseum at Athens. Page 767.

Statue of Theseus. (From the Pediment of the Parthenon.) Page 767.

[To face p. 790.

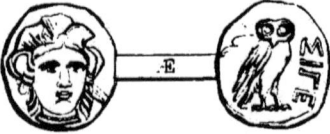

Sigeum in the Troad. Page 706.

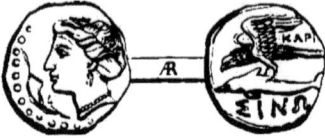

Snessa Aurunca. Page 728.

Sinope. Page 709.

Sybaris. Page 731.

Siphnus. Page 710.

Smyrna. Page 712.

Syracusae. Page 735.

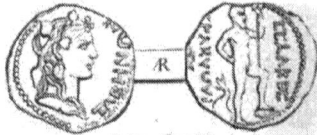

Soli. Page 715.

Tabae. Page 739.

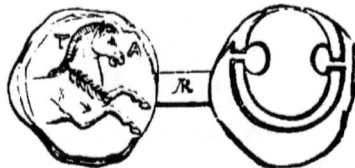

Solus. Page 717.

To face p. 781.

Tanagra. Page 741.

ecclesiastical history, which is extant, is in 9 books, and is dedicated to the emperor Theodosius II. It commences with the reign of Constantine, and comes down a little later than the death of Honorius, A. D. 423. The work is incomplete, and breaks off in the middle of a chapter. The author, we know, had proposed to bring it down to 439, the year in which the history of Socrates ends. Sozomen excels Socrates in style, but is inferior to the latter in soundness of judgment. The history of Sozomen is printed along with the other Greek ecclesiastical historians. [SOCRATES.]

Sozopölis, aft. **Susupölis** (Σωζόπολις, Σωζούπολις : *Susu,* Ru.), a considerable city of Pisidia, in a plain surrounded by mountains, N. of Termessus.

Sparta (Σπάρτη, Dor. Σπάρτα: Σπαρτιάτης, Spartiátes, Spartanus) also called **Lacedaemon** (Λακεδαίμων: Λακεδαιμόνιος, Lacedaemonius), the capital of Laconica and the chief city of Peloponnesus, was situated on the right bank of the Eurotas (*Iri*), about 20 miles from the sea. It stood on a plain which contained within it several rising grounds and hills. It was bounded on the E. by the Eurotas, on the N.W. by the small river Oenus (*Kelesina*), and on the S.E. by the small river Tisia (*Magula*), both of which streams fell into the Eurotas. The plain in which Sparta stood was shut in on the E. by Mt. Menelaium, and on the W. by Mt. Taygetus ; whence the city is called by Homer " the hollow Lacedaemon." It was of a circular form, about 6 miles in circumference, and consisted of several distinct quarters, which were originally separate villages, and which were never united into one regular town. Its site is occupied by the modern villages of *Magula* and *Psykhiko ;* and the principal modern town in the neighbourhood is *Mistra,* which lies about 2 miles to the W. on the slopes of Mt. Taygetus. During the flourishing times of Greek independence, Sparta was never surrounded by walls, since the bravery of its citizens, and the difficulty of access to it, were supposed to render such defences needless. It was first fortified by the tyrant Nabis ; but it did not possess regular walls till the time of the Romans. Sparta, unlike most Greek cities, had no proper Acropolis, but this name was only given to one of the steepest hills of the town, on the summit of which stood the temple of Athena Poliuchos, or Chalcioecus. Five distinct quarters of the city are mentioned : 1. *Pitane* (Πιτάνη : Ethnic Πιτανάτης), which appears to have been the most important part of the city, and in which was situated the Agora, containing the council-house of the senate, and the offices of the public magistrates. It was also surrounded by various temples and other public buildings. Of these, the most splendid was the Persian Stoa or portico, originally built of the spoils taken in the Persian war, and enlarged and adorned at later times. A part of the Agora was called the Chorus or dancing place, in which the Spartan youths performed dances in honour of Apollo. 2. *Limnae* (Λίμναι), a suburb of the city, on the banks of the Eurotas, N.E. of Pitane, was originally a hollow spot covered with water. 3. *Mesoa* or *Messoa* (Μεσόα, Μεσσόα: Eth. Μεσσοάτης), also by the side of the Eurotas, S.E. of the preceding, containing the Dromus and the Platanistas, which was a spot nearly surrounded with water, and so called from the plane-trees growing

there. 4. *Cynosūra* (Κυνόσουρα: Κυνοσουρεύς), in the S.W. of the city, and S. of Pitane. 5. *Aegidae* (Αἰγεῖδαι), in the N.W. of the city, and W. of Pitane. — The two principal streets of Sparta ran from the Agora to the extreme end of the city : these were, 1. *Aphetas* or *Aphetais* ('Αφέται, 'Αφεταῖς sc. ὁδός), extending in a S.E.-ly direction, past the temple of Dictynna, and the tombs of the Eurypontidae ; and 2. *Skias* (Σκιάς), running nearly parallel to the preceding one, but further to the E., and which derived its name from an ancient place of assembly, of a circular form, called Skias. The most important remains of ancient Sparta are the ruins of the theatre, which was near the Agora. — Sparta is said to have been founded by Lacedaemon, a son of Zeus and Taygete, who married Sparta, the daughter of Eurotas, and called the city after the name of his wife. His son Amyclas is said to have been the founder of Amyclae, which was for a long time a more important town than Sparta itself. In the mythical period, Argos was the chief city in Peloponnesus, and Sparta is represented as subject to it. Here reigned Menelaus, the younger brother of Agamemnon ; and by the marriage of Orestes, the son of Agamemnon, with Hermione, the daughter of Menelaus, the two kingdoms of Argos and Sparta became united. The Dorian conquest of Peloponnesus, which, according to tradition, took place 80 years after the Trojan war, made Sparta the capital of the country. Laconica fell to the share of the 2 sons of Aristodemus, Eurysthenes and Procles, who took up their residence at Sparta, and ruled over the kingdom conjointly. The old inhabitants of the country maintained themselves at Amyclae, which was not conquered for a long time. After the complete subjugation of the country we find three distinct classes in the population: the Dorian conquerors, who resided in the capital, and who were called Spartiatae or Spartans; the Perioeci or old Achaean inhabitants, who became tributary to the Spartans, and possessed no political rights; and the Helots, who were also a portion of the old Achaean inhabitants, but were reduced to a state of slavery. From various causes the Spartans became distracted by intestine quarrels, till at length Lycurgus, who belonged to the royal family, was selected by all parties to give a new constitution to the state. The date of Lycurgus is uncertain; but it is impossible to place it later than B. C. 825. The constitution of Lycurgus, which is described in a separate article [LYCURGUS], laid the foundation of Sparta's greatness. She soon became aggressive, and gradually extended her sway over the greater part of Peloponnesus. In B. C. 743 the Spartans attacked Messenia, and after a war of 20 years subdued this country, 723. In 685 the Messenians again took up arms, but at the end of 17 years were again completely subdued; and this country from this time forward became an integral portion of Laconia. [For details see MESSENIA.] After the close of the 2nd Messenian war the Spartans continued their conquests in Peloponnesus. They defeated the Tegeans, and wrested the district of Thyrea from the Argives. At the time of the Persian invasion, they were confessedly the first people in Greece ; and to them was granted by unanimous consent the chief command in the war. But after the final defeat of the Persians the haughtiness of Pausanias disgusted most of the Greek states, particularly the Ionians, and led them to transfer the supremacy to Athens (477). From this time the power of Athens steadily increased; and Sparta possessed little influence outside of the Peloponnesus. The Spartans, however, made several attempts to check the rising greatness of Athens; and their jealousy of the latter led at length to the Peloponnesian war (431). This war ended in the overthrow of Athens, and the restoration of the supremacy of Sparta over the rest of Greece (404). But the Spartans did not retain this supremacy more than 30 years. Their decisive defeat by the Thebans under Epaminondas at the battle of Leuctra (371) gave the Spartan power a shock from which it never recovered; and the restoration of the Messenians to their country 2 years afterwards completed the humiliation of Sparta. Thrice was the Spartan territory invaded by the Thebans; and the Spartan women saw for the first time the watch-fires of an enemy's camp. The Spartans now finally lost their supremacy over Greece, but no other Greek state succeeded to their power; and about 30 years afterwards the greater part of Greece was obliged to yield to Philip of Macedon. The Spartans, however, kept haughtily aloof from the Macedonian conqueror, and refused to take part in the Asiatic expedition of his son Alexander the Great. Under the later Macedonian monarchs the power of Sparta still further declined; the institutions of Lycurgus were neglected, luxury crept into the state, the number of citizens diminished, and the landed property became vested in a few families. Agis endeavoured to restore the ancient institutions of Lycurgus; but he perished in the attempt (240). Cleomenes III., who began to reign 236, was more successful. He succeeded in putting the Ephors to death, and overthrowing the existing government (225); and he then made a redistribution of the landed property, and augmented the number of the Spartan citizens by admitting some of the Perioeci to this honour. His reforms infused new blood into the state; and for a short time he carried on war with success against the Achaeans. But Aratus, the general of the Achaeans, called in the assistance of Antigonus Doson, the king of Macedonia, who defeated Cleomenes at the decisive battle of Sellasia (221), and followed up his success by the capture of Sparta. Sparta now sank into insignificance, and was ruled by a succession of native tyrants till at length it was compelled to abolish its peculiar institutions, and to join the Achaean league. Shortly afterwards it fell, with the rest of Greece, under the Roman power.

Spartācus, the name of several kings of the Cimmerian Bosporus. 1. Succeeded the dynasty of the Archeanactidae in B.C. 438, and reigned until 431. He was succeeded by his son Seleucus. — 2. Began to reign in 427 and reigned 20 years. He was succeeded in 407 by his son Satyrus. — 3. Succeeded his father Leucon in 353, and died, leaving his kingdom to his son Parysades, in 348. — 4. Son of Eumelus, began to reign in 304, and reigned 20 years.

Spartăcus, by birth a Thracian, was successively a shepherd, a soldier, and a chief of banditti. On one of his predatory expeditions he was taken prisoner, and sold to a trainer of gladiators. In 73 he was a member of the company of Lentulus, and was detained in his school at Capua, in readiness for the games at Rome. He persuaded his fellow-prisoners to make an attempt to gain their freedom. About

70 of them broke out of the school of Lentulus, and took refuge in the crater of Vesuvius. Spartacus was chosen leader, and was soon joined by a number of runaway slaves. They were blockaded by C. Claudius Pulcher at the head of 3000 men, but Spartacus attacked the besiegers and put them to flight. His numbers rapidly increased, and for 2 years (B.C. 73—71) he defeated one Roman army after another, and laid waste Italy, from the foot of the Alps to the southernmost corner of the peninsula. After both the consuls of 72 had been defeated by Spartacus, M. Licinius Crassus, the praetor, was appointed to the command of the war. Crassus carried on the contest, with vigour and success, and, after gaining several advantages over the enemy, at length defeated them on the river Silarus in a decisive battle, in which Spartacus was slain. The character of Spartacus has been maligned by the Roman writers. Cicero compares the vilest of his contemporaries to him: Horace speaks of him as a common robber; none recognise his greatness, but the terror of his name survived to a late period of the empire. Accident made Spartacus a shepherd, a freebooter, and a gladiator; nature formed him a hero. The excesses of his followers he could not always repress, and his efforts to restrain them often cost him his popularity. But he was in himself not less mild and just than he was able and valiant.

Spartārius Campus. [CARTHAGO NOVA.]

Sparti (Σπαρτοί from σπείρω), the Sown-Men, is the name given to the armed men who sprang from the dragon's teeth sown by Cadmus, and who were believed to be the ancestors of the 5 oldest families at Thebes.

Spartiānus, Aelius, one of the *Scriptores Historiae Augustae*, lived in the time of Diocletian and Constantine, and wrote the biographies of, 1. Hadrianus and Aelius Verus; 2. Didius Julianus; 3. Severus; 4. Pescennius Niger; 5. Caracalla; 6. Geta. For the editions of Spartianus see CAPITOLINUS.

Spartōlus (Σπάρτωλος), a town in the Macedonian peninsula of Chalcidice, N. of Olynthus.

Spauta (Σπαῦτα: *L. of Urmi*), a large salt-lake in the W. of Media, whose waters were singularly bitter and acrid. It was also called Matiāna (Ματιανὴ λίμνη) from the name of the people who dwelt around it.

Sperchēus (Σπερχειός: *Elladha*), a river in the S. of Thessaly, which rises in Mt. Tymphrestus, runs in an E.-ly direction through the territory of the Aenianes and through the district Malis, and falls into the innermost corner of the Sinus Maliacus. As a river-god Spercheus is a son of Oceanus and Ge, and the father of Menesthius by Polydora, the daughter of Peleus. To this god Peleus dedicated the hair of his son Achilles, in order that he might return in safety from the Trojan war.

Spes, the personification of Hope, was worshipped at Rome, where she had several temples, the most ancient of which had been built in B.C. 354, by the consul Atilius Calatinus, near the Porta Carmentalis. The Greeks also worshipped the personification of Hope, *Elpis*, and they relate the beautiful allegory, that when Epimetheus opened the vessel brought to him by Pandora, from which all manner of evils were scattered over the earth, Hope alone remained behind. Hope was represented in works of art as a youthful figure, lightly walking in full attire, holding in her right hand a flower, and with the left lifting up her garment.

Speusippus (Σπεύσιππος), the philosopher, was a native of Athens, and the son of Eurymedon and Potone, a sister of Plato. He accompanied his uncle Plato on his third journey to Syracuse, where he displayed considerable ability and prudence. He succeeded Plato as president of the Academy, but was at the head of the school for only 8 years (B. C. 347—339). He died, as it appears, of a lingering paralytic illness. He wrote several works, all of which are lost, in which he developed the doctrines of his great master.

Sphactēria. [PYLOS, No. 3.]

Sphaeria (Σφαιρία: Poros), an island off the coast of Troezen in Argolis, and between it and the island of Calauria, with the latter of which it was connected by means of a sand-bank. Here Sphaerus, the charioteer of Pelops, is said to have been buried.

Sphaerus (Σφαῖρος), a Stoic philosopher, studied first under Zeno of Citium, and afterwards under Cleanthes. He lived at Alexandria during the reigns of the first two Ptolemies. He also taught at Lacedaemon, and was believed to have had considerable influence in moulding the character of Cleomenes. He was in repute among the Stoics for the accuracy of his definitions. He was the author of several works, all of which are lost.

Sphendălē (Σφενδάλη: Σφενδαλεύς), a demus in Attica belonging to the tribe Hippothoontis, on the frontiers of Boeotia between Tanagra and Decelea.

Sphettus (Σφηττός: Σφήττιος), a demus in the S. of Attica, near the silver mines of Sunium, belonging to the tribe Acamantis.

Sphinx (Σφίγξ, gen. Σφιγγός), a she-monster, daughter of Orthus and Chimaera, born in the country of the Arimi, or of Typhon and Echidna, or lastly of Typhon and Chimaera. She is said to have proposed a riddle to the Thebans, and to have murdered all who were unable to guess it. Oedipus solved it, whereupon the Sphinx slew herself. [For details see OEDIPUS.] The legend appears to have come from Egypt, but the figure of the Sphinx is represented somewhat differently in Greek mythology and art. The Egyptian Sphinx is the figure of a lion without wings in a lying attitude, the upper part of the body being that of a human being. The Sphinxes appear in Egypt to have been set up in avenues forming the approaches to temples. The common idea of a Greek Sphinx, on the other hand, is that of a winged body of a lion, the breast and upper part being the figure of a woman. Greek Sphinxes, moreover, are not always represented in a lying attitude, but appear in different positions, as it might suit the fancy of the sculptor or poet. Thus they appear with the face of a maiden, the breast, feet, and claws of a lion, the tail of a serpent, and the wings of a bird. Sphinxes were frequently introduced by Greek artists, as ornaments of architectural works.

Spina. 1. (Spinaxxino), a town in Gallia Cispadana, in the territory of the Lingones, on the most S.-ly of the mouths of the Po, which was called after it Ostium Spineticum. It was a very ancient town, said to have been founded by the Greeks, but in the time of Strabo had ceased to be a place of any importance. — 2. (Spino), a town in Gallia Transpadana on the river Addua.

Spinthārus (Σπίνθαρος), of Heraclea on the

Pontus, a tragic poet, contemporary with Aristophanes, who designates him as a barbarian and a Phrygian. He was also ridiculed by the other comic poets.

Spolatum. [SALONA].

Spolētĭum or **Spolētum** (Spoletinus: Spoleto), a town in Umbria on the Via Flaminia, colonised by the Romans B. C. 242. It suffered severely in the civil wars between Sulla and Marius. At a later time it was taken by Totilas; but its walls, which had been destroyed by the Goths, were restored by Narses.

Spŏrădes (Σποράδες, sc. νῆσοι, from σπείρω), a group of scattered islands in the Aegaean sea off the island of Crete and the W. coast of Asia Minor, so called in opposition to the Cyclades, which lay in a circle around Delos. The division, however, between these 2 groups of islands was not well defined; and we find some of the islands at one time described as belonging to the Sporades, and at another time as belonging to the Cyclades.

Spurinna, Vestritĭus. 1. The haruspex who warned Caesar to beware of the Ides of March. It is related that, as Caesar was going to the senate-house on the fatal day, he said to Spurinna in jest, " Well, the Ides of March are come," upon which the seer replied, " Yes, they are come, but they are not past." — 2. A Roman general, who fought on the side of Otho against the Vitellian troops in the N. of Italy. In the reign of Trajan he gained a victory over the Bructeri. Spurinna lived upon terms of the closest friendship with the younger Pliny, from whom we learn that Spurinna composed lyric poems. There are extant 4 odes, or rather fragments of odes, in Choriambic measure, ascribed to Spurinna, and which were first published by Barthius in 1613. Their genuineness however is very doubtful.

Spurinus, Q. Petillĭus, praetor urbanus in B. C. 181, in which year the books of king Numa Pompilius are said to have been discovered upon the estate of one L. Petillius. Spurinus obtained possession of the books, and upon his representation to the senate that they ought not to be read and preserved, the senate ordered them to be burnt. [NUMA.] Spurinus was consul in 176, and fell in battle against the Ligurians.

Stăbĭae (Stabianus: Castell a Mare di Stabia), an ancient town in Campania between Pompeii and Surrentum, which was destroyed by Sulla in the Social War, but which continued to exist as a small place down to the great eruption of Vesuvius in A. D. 79, when it was overwhelmed along with Pompeii and Herculaneum. It was at Stabiae that the elder Pliny perished.

Stagĭrus, subsequently **Stagĭra** (Στάγειρος, τὰ Στάγειρα, ἡ Στάγειρα: Σταγειρίτης: Stavro), a town of Macedonia in Chalcidice, on the Strymonic gulf and a little N. of the isthmus which unites the promontory of Athos to Chalcidice. It was a colony of Andros, was founded B. C. 656, and was originally called Orthagoria. It is celebrated as the birth-place of Aristotle, and was in consequence restored by Philip, by whom it had been destroyed.

Staphylus (Στάφυλος), son of Dionysus and Ariadne, or of Theseus and Ariadne, and was one of the Argonauts. By Chrysothemis he became the father of 3 daughters, Molpadia, Rhoeo, and Parthenos.

Stasinus (Στασῖνος), of Cyprus, an epic poet,

to whom some of the ancient writers attributed the poem of the Epic Cycle, entitled *Cypria* (Κύπρια). In the earliest historical period of Greek literature the *Cypria* was accepted without question as a work of Homer ; and it is not till we come down to the times of Athenaeus and the grammarians, that we find any mention of Stasinus. Stasinus was said to be the son-in-law of Homer, who, according to one story, composed the *Cypria* and gave it to Stasinus as his daughter's marriage portion ; manifestly an attempt to reconcile the two different accounts, which ascribed it to Homer and Stasinus. The *Cypria* was the first, in the order of the events contained in it, of the poems of the Epic Cycle relating to the Trojan war. It embraced the period antecedent to the beginning of the Iliad, to which it was designed to form an introduction.

Statielli, Statiellātes, or **Statiellenses,** a small tribe in Liguria, S. of the Po, whose chief town was Statiellae Aquae (*Acqui*) on the road from Genua to Placentia.

Statilia Messalina.   [MESSALINA.]

Statilius Taurus.   [TAURUS.]

Statira (Στάτειρα). 1. Wife of Artaxerxes II., king of Persia, was poisoned by Parysatis, the mother of the king, who was a deadly enemy of Statira. — 2. Sister and wife of Darius III., celebrated as the most beautiful woman of her time. She was taken prisoner by Alexander, together with her mother-in-law Sisygambis and her daughters, after the battle of Issus, B. C. 333. They were all treated with the utmost respect by the conqueror, but Statira died shortly before the battle of Arbela, 331. — 3. Also called **Barsine,** elder daughter of Darius III. [BARSINE.]

Statius Murcus.   [MURCUS.]

Statius, P. Papinius, was born at Neapolis, about A. D. 61, and was the son of a distinguished grammarian. He accompanied his father to Rome, where the latter acted as the preceptor of Domitian, who held him in high honour. Under the skilful tuition of his father, the young Statius speedily rose to fame, and became peculiarly renowned for the brilliancy of his extemporaneous effusions, so that he gained the prize three times in the Alban contests ; but having, after a long career of popularity, been vanquished in the quinquennial games, he retired to Neapolis, the place of his nativity, along with his wife Claudia, whose virtues he frequently commemorates. He died about A. D. 96. It has been inferred from a passage in Juvenal (vii. 82), that Statius, in his earlier years at least, was forced to struggle with poverty ; but he appears to have profited by the patronage of Domitian (*Silv.* iv. 2), whom he addresses in strains of the most fulsome adulation. The extant works of Statius are : — 1. *Silvarum Libri V.,* a collection of 32 occasional poems, many of them of considerable length, divided into 5 books. To each book is prefixed a dedication in prose, addressed to some friend. The metre chiefly employed is the heroic hexameter, but four of the pieces (i. 6, ii. 7, iv. 3, 9), are in Phalaecian hendecasyllabics, one (iv. 5) in the Alcaic, and one (iv. 7) in the Sapphic stanza. 2. *Thebaidos Libri XII.,* an heroic poem in 12 books, embodying the ancient legends with regard to the expedition of the Seven against Thebes. 3. *Achilleidos Libri II.,* an heroic poem breaking off abruptly. According to the original plan, it would have comprised a complete history of the exploits of

Achilles, but was probably never finished. Statius may justly claim the praise of standing in the foremost rank among the heroic poets of the Silver Age. He is in a great measure free from extravagance and pompous pretensions ; but, on the other hand, in no portion of his works do we find the impress of high natural talent and imposing power. The pieces which form the Silvae, although evidently thrown off in haste, produce a much more pleasing effect than the ambitious poems of the Thebaid or the Achilleid. The best editions of the *Silvae* are by Markland, Lond. 1728, and by Sillig, Dresd. 1827. The best edition of the complete works of Statius is by Lemaire, 4 vols. 8vo., Paris, 1825—1830.

Statōnīa (Statoniensis), a town in Etruria, and a Roman Praefectura, on the river Albinia, and on the Lacus Statoniensis, in the neighbourhood of which were stone quarries, and excellent wine was grown.

Stător, a Roman surname of Jupiter, describing him as staying the Romans in their flight from an enemy, and generally as preserving the existing order of things.

Stectōrium (Στεκτόριον: *Afioum Kara-Hisar* ?), a city of Great Phrygia, between Peltae and Synnadia.

Stentor (Στέντωρ), a herald of the Greeks in the Trojan war, whose voice was as loud as that of 50 other men together. His name has become proverbial for any one shouting with an unusually loud voice.

Stentōris Lacus.   [HEBRUS.]

Stenyclērus (Στενύκληρος, Dor. Στενύκλαρος : Στενυκλήριος), a town in the N. of Messenia, which was the residence of the Dorian kings of the country. After the time of the 3rd Messenian war the town is no longer mentioned ; but its name continued to be given to an extensive plain in the N. of Messenia.

Stĕphănē or -**is** (Στεφάνη, Στεφανίς: *Stefanio*), a sea-port town of Paphlagonia, on the coast of the Mariandyni.

Stĕphănus (Στέφανος). 1. An Athenian comic poet of the New Comedy, was probably the son of Antiphanes, some of whose plays he is said to have exhibited. — 2. Of Byzantium, the author of the geographical lexicon, entitled *Ethnica* ('Εθνικά), of which unfortunately we only possess an epitome. Stephanus was a grammarian at Constantinople, and lived after the time of Arcadius and Honorius, and before that of Justinian II. His work was reduced to an epitome by a certain Hermolaus, who dedicated his abridgment to the emperor Justinian II. According to the title, the chief object of the work was to specify the gentile names derived from the several names of places and countries in the ancient world. But, while this is done in every article, the amount of information given went far beyond this. Nearly every article in the epitome contains a reference to some ancient writer, as an authority for the name of the place ; but in the original, as we see from the extant fragments, there were considerable quotations from the ancient authors, besides a number of very interesting particulars, topographical, historical, mythological, and others. Thus the work was not merely what it professed to be, a lexicon of a special branch of technical grammar, but a valuable dictionary of geography. How great would have been its value to us, if it had come down to us unmutilated, may be seen by any one who compares the extant fragments of the original with the corresponding articles in the epitome. These fragments, however, are unfortunately very scanty. The best editions of the Epitome of Stephanus are by Dindorf, Lips. 1825, &c., 4 vols.; by Westermann, Lips. 1839, 8vo.; and by Meineke, Berlin, 1849.

Sterculius, Stercutius, or **Sterqullinus,** a surname of Saturnus, derived from *Stercus*, manure, because he had promoted agriculture by teaching the people the use of manure. This seems to have been the original meaning, though some Romans state that Sterculius was a surname of Picumnus, the son of Faunus, to whom likewise improvements in agriculture are ascribed.

Stĕrŏpē (Στερόπη), one of the Pleiads, wife of Oenomaus, and daughter of Hippodamia.

Stĕrŏpes. [CYCLOPES.]

Stesichŏrus (Στησίχορος), of Himera in Sicily, a celebrated Greek poet, contemporary with Sappho, Alcaeus, Pittacus, and Phalaris, is said to have been born B. C. 632, to have flourished about 608, and to have died in 552 at the age of 80. Of the events of his life we have only a few obscure accounts. Like other great poets, his birth is fabled to have been attended by an omen; a nightingale sat upon the babe's lips, and sung a sweet strain. He is said to have been carefully educated at Catana, and afterwards to have enjoyed the friendship of Phalaris, the tyrant of Agrigentum. Many writers relate the fable of his being miraculously struck with blindness after writing an attack upon Helen, and recovering his sight when he had composed a Palinodia. He is said to have been buried at Catana by a gate of the city, which was called after him the Stesichorean gate. Stesichorus was one of the 9 chiefs of lyric poetry recognised by the ancients. He stands, with Alcman, at the head of one branch of the lyric art, the choral poetry of the Dorians. He was the first to break the monotony of the strophe and antistrophe by the introduction of the epode, and his metres were much more varied, and the structure of his strophes more elaborate, than those of Alcman. His odes contained all the essential elements of the perfect choral poetry of Pindar and the tragedians. The subjects of his poems were chiefly heroic; he transferred the subjects of the old epic poetry to the lyric form, dropping, of course, the continuous narrative, and dwelling on isolated adventures of his heroes. He also composed poems on other subjects. His extant remains may be classified under the following heads: — 1. Mythical Poems. 2. Hymns, Encomia, Epithalamia, Paeans. 3. Erotic Poems, and Scholia. 4. A pastoral poem, entitled *Daphnis.* 5. Fables. 6. Elegies. The dialect of Stesichorus was Dorian, with an intermixture of the epic. The best edition of his fragments is by Kleine, Berol. 1828.

Stēsimbrŏtus (Στησίμβροτος), of Thasos, a rhapsodist and historian in the time of Cimon and Pericles, who is mentioned with praise by Plato and Xenophon, and who wrote a work upon Homer, the title of which is not known. He also wrote some historical works.

Sthenebœa (Σθενέβοια), called **Antēa** by many writers, was a daughter of the Lycian king Iobates, and the wife of Proetus. Respecting her love for Bellerophon, see BELLEROPHONTES.

Sthĕnĕlus (Σθένελος). 1. Son of Perseus and Andromeda, king of Mycenae, and husband of Nicippe, by whom he became the father of Alcinoë, Medusa, and Eurystheus. The latter, as the great enemy of Hercules [HERCULES], is called by Ovid *Sthenelēius hostis.* — 2. Son of Androgeos and grandson of Minos. He accompanied Hercules from Paros on his expedition against the Amazons, and together with his brother Alcaeus he was appointed by Hercules ruler of Thasos. — 3. Son of Actor, likewise a companion of Hercules in his expedition against the Amazons; but he died and was buried in Paphlagonia, where he afterwards appeared to the Argonauts. — 4. Son of Capaneus and Evadne, belonged to the family of the Anaxagoridae in Argos, and was the father of Cylarabes; but, according to others, his son's name was Cometes. He was one of the Epigoni, by whom Thebes was taken, and he commanded the Argives under Diomedes, in the Trojan war, being the faithful friend and companion of Diomedes. He was one of the Greeks concealed in the wooden horse, and at the distribution of the booty, he was said to have received an image of a three-eyed Zeus, which was in after-times shown at Argos. His own statue and tomb also were believed to exist at Argos. — 5. Father of Cycnus, who was metamorphosed into a swan. Hence we find the swan called by Ovid *Stheneleis volucris* and *Stheneleia proles.* — 6. A tragic poet, contemporary with Aristophanes, who attacked him in the *Wasps.*

Sthĕno. [GORGONES.]

Stilicho, son of a Vandal captain under the emperor Valens, became one of the most distinguished generals of Theodosius I. On the death of Theodosius, A. D. 395, Stilicho became the real ruler of the West under the emperor Honorius; and his power was strengthened by the death of his rival Rufinus [RUFINUS]. and by the marriage of his daughter Maria to Honorius. His military abilities saved the Western empire; and after gaining several victories over the barbarians, he defeated Alaric at the decisive battle of Pollentia, 403, and compelled him to retire from Italy. In 405 he gained another great victory over Radagaisus, who had invaded Italy at the head of a formidable host of barbarians. These victories raised the ambition of Stilicho to so high a pitch, that he aspired to make himself master of the Roman empire; but he was apprehended and put to death at Ravenna in 408.

Stilo, L. Aelius Praeconinus, a celebrated Roman grammarian, one of the teachers of Varro and Cicero. He received the surname of Praeconinus, because his father had been a praeco, and that of Stilo on account of his compositions. He belonged to the aristocratical party, and accompanied Q. Metellus Numidicus into exile in B. C. 100. He wrote Commentaries on the Songs of the Salii and on the Twelve Tables, a work *De Proloquiis,* &c. He and his son-in-law, Ser. Claudius, may be regarded as the founders of the study of grammar at Rome. Some modern writers suppose that the work on Rhetoric ad C. Herennium, which is printed in the editions of Cicero, is the work of this Aelius, but this is mere conjecture.

Stilpo (Στίλπων), a celebrated philosopher, was a native of Megara, and taught philosophy in his native town. According to one account, he engaged in dialectic encounters with Diodorus Cronus at the court of Ptolemaeus Soter; while, according to another, he did not comply with the invitation of the king to visit Alexandria. He acquired a great reputation ; and so high was the esteem in which he was held, that Demetrius, the son of Antigonus, spared his house at the capture of Megara. He is said to have surpassed his contemporaries in inventive power and dialectic art, and to have inspired almost all Greece with a devotion to the Megarian philosophy. He seems to have made the idea of virtue the especial object of his consideration. He maintained that the wise man ought not only to overcome every evil, but not even to be affected by any.

Stimula, the name of Semele, according to the pronunciation of the Romans.

Stiria (Στειρία: Στειριεύς: Ru. on the bay *Porto Rafti*), a demus in Attica, S. E. of Brauron, belonging to the tribe Pandionis, to which there was a road from Athens called Στειριακὴ ὀδός. It was the birth-place of Theramenes and Thrasybulus.

Stobaeus, Joannes (Ἰωάννης ὁ Στοβαῖος), derived his surname apparently from being a native of Stobi in Macedonia. Of his personal history we know nothing. Even the age in which he lived cannot be fixed with accuracy ; but he must have been later than Hierocles of Alexandria, whom he quotes. Probably he did not live very long after him, as he quotes no writer of a later date. We are indebted to Stobaeus for a very valuable collection of extracts from earlier Greek writers. Stobaeus was a man of extensive reading, in the course of which he noted down the most interesting passages. The materials which he had collected in this way he arranged, in the order of subjects, for the use of his son Septimius. This collection of extracts has come down to us, divided into 2 distinct works, of which one bears the title of Ἐκλογαὶ φυσικαὶ διαλεκτικαὶ καὶ ἠθικαί (*Eclogae Physicae, etc.*), and the other the title of Ἀνθολόγιον (*Florilegium* or *Sermones*). The *Eclogae* consist for the most part of extracts conveying the views of earlier poets and prose writers on points of physics, dialectics, and ethics. The *Florilegium,* or *Sermones,* is devoted to subjects of a moral, political, and economical kind, and maxims of practical wisdom. Each chapter of the Eclogae and Sermones is headed by a title describing its matter. The extracts quoted in illustration begin usually with passages from the poets, after whom come historians, orators, philosophers and physicians. To Stobaeus we are indebted for a large proportion of the fragments that remain of the lost works of poets. Euripides seems to have been an especial favourite with him. He has quoted above 500 passages from him in the Sermones, 150 from Sophocles, and above 200 from Menander. In extracting from prose writers, Stobaeus sometimes quotes verbatim, sometimes gives only an epitome of the passage. The best edition of the Eclogae is by Heeren, Gotting. 1792—1801, 4 vols. 8vo., and of the Florilegium by Gaisford, Oxon. 1822, 4 vols. 8vo.

Stobi (Στόβοι: Στοβαῖοι), a town of Macedonia, and the most important place in the district Paeonia, was probably situated on the river Erigon, N. of Thessalonica and N. E. of Heraclea. It was made a Roman colony and a municipium, and under the later emperors was the capital of the province Macedonia II. or Salutaris. It was destroyed at the end of the 4th century by the Goths ; but it is still mentioned by the Byzantine

writers as a fortress under the name of Stypeum (Στύπειον). Its site is unknown ; for the modern *Istib,* which is usually supposed to stand upon the site of Stobi, lies too far to the N. E.

Stoechades Insulae (*I. d'Hières*), a group of 5 small islands in the Mediterranean, off the coast of Gallia Narbonensis and E. of Massilia, on which the Massiliotes kept an armed force to protect their trade against pirates. The 3 larger islands were called Prote, Mese or Pomponiana, and Hypaea, the modern *Porquerolle, Port Croz,* and *Isle de Levant* or *du Titan ;* the two smaller ones are probably the modern *Ratoneau* and *Promègne.*

Stoeni, a Ligurian people in the Maritime Alps, conquered by Q. Marcius Rex B. C. 118, before he founded the colony of Narbo Martius.

Strabo, a cognomen in many Roman gentes, signified a person who squinted, and is accordingly classed with *Paetus,* though the latter word did not indicate such a complete distortion of vision as Strabo.

Strabo, the geographer, was a native of Amasia in Pontus. The date of his birth is unknown, but may perhaps be placed about B. C. 54. He lived during the whole of the reign of Augustus, and during the early part, at least, of the reign of Tiberius. He is supposed to have died about A. D. 24. He received a careful education. He studied grammar under Aristodemus at Nysa in Caria, and philosophy under Xenarchus of Seleucia in Cilicia and Boethus of Sidon. He lived some years at Rome, and also travelled much in various countries. We learn from his own work that he was with his friend Aelius Gallus in Egypt in B. C. 24. He wrote an historical work (Ἱστορικὰ Ὑπομνήματα) in 43 books, which is lost. It began where the history of Polybius ended, and was probably continued to the battle of Actium. He also wrote a work on Geography (Γεωγραφικά), in 17 books, which has come down to us entire, with the exception of the 7th, of which we have only a meagre epitome. Strabo's work, according to his own expression, was not intended for the use of all persons. It was designed for all who had had a good education, and particularly for those who were engaged in the higher departments of administration. Consistently with this view, his plan does not comprehend minute description, except when the place or the object is of great interest or importance ; nor is his description limited to the physical characteristics of each country ; it comprehends the important political events of which each country has been the theatre, a notice of the chief cities and the great men who have illustrated them ; in short, whatever was most characteristic and interesting in every country. His work forms a striking contrast with the geography of Ptolemy, and the dry list of names, occasionally relieved by something added to them, in the geographical portion of the Natural History of Pliny. It is in short a book intended for reading, and it may be read ; a kind of historical geography. Strabo's language is generally clear, except in those passages where the text has been corrupted ; it is appropriate to the matter, simple and without affectation. The first 2 books of Strabo are an introduction to his Geography, and contain his views on the form and magnitude of the earth, and other subjects connected with mathematical geography. In the 3rd book he begins his description : he devotes 8 books to Europe ; 6 to

Asia; and the 17th and last to Egypt and Libya. The best editions of Strabo are by Casaubon, Geneva, 1587, and Paris, 1620, fol.,—reprinted by Almeloveen, Amsterdam, 1707, and by Falconer, Oxford, 1807, 2 vols. fol.—by Siebenkees, and Tzschucke, Lips. 1811, 7 vols. 8vo.; by Koray, Paris, 1815, seq. 4 vols. 8vo.; and by Krämer, Berlin, 1844. seq., of which only 2 vols. have yet appeared. This last is by far the best critical edition.

Strābo, Fannius. 1. C., consul B. C. 161 with M. Valerius Messala. In their consulship the rhetoricians were expelled from Rome. — 2. C., son of the preceding, consul 122. He owed his election to the consulship chiefly to the influence of C. Gracchus, who was anxious to prevent his enemy Opimius from obtaining the office. But in his consulship Fannius supported the aristocracy, and took an active part in opposing the measures of Gracchus. He spoke against the proposal of Gracchus, who wished to give the Roman franchise to the Latins, in a speech which was regarded as a master-piece in the time of Cicero. —3. C., son-in-law of Laelius, and frequently confounded with No. 2. He served in Africa, under Scipio Africanus, in 146, and in Spain under Fabius Maximus in 142. He is introduced by Cicero as one of the speakers both in his work *De Republica*, and in his treatise *De Amicitia*. He owed his celebrity in literature to his History, which was written in Latin, and of which Brutus made an abridgement.*

Strābo, Seius. [SEJANUS.]

Stratŏcles (Στρατοκλῆς), an Athenian orator, and a friend of the orator Lycurgus. He was a virulent opponent of Demosthenes, whom he charged with having accepted bribes from Harpalus. Stratocles especially distinguished himself by his extravagant flattery of Demetrius.

Strāton (Στράτων). 1. Son of Arcesilaus, of Lampsacus, was a distinguished peripatetic philosopher, and the tutor of Ptolemy Philadelphus. He succeeded Theophrastus as head of the school in B. C. 288, and, after presiding over it 18 years, was succeeded by Lycon. He devoted himself especially to the study of natural science, whence he obtained the appellation of *Physicus*. Cicero, while speaking highly of his talents, blames him for neglecting the most necessary part of philosophy, that which has respect to virtue and morals, and giving himself up to the investigation of nature. Straton appears to have held a pantheistic system, the specific character of which cannot, however, be determined. He seems to have denied the existence of any god out of the material universe, and to have held that every particle of matter has a plastic and seminal power, but without sensation or intelligence; and that life, sensation, and intellect, are but forms, accidents, and affections of matter. Some modern writers have regarded Straton as a forerunner of Spinoza, while others see in his system an anticipation of the hypothesis of monads. — 2. Of Sardis, an epigrammatic poet, and the compiler of a Greek Anthology, devoted to licentious subjects. [PLANUDES.]—3. A physician of Berytus in Phoenicia, one of whose medical formulae is quoted by Galen. — 4. Also a physician, and a pupil of Erasistratus in the 3rd century B. C., who appears to have lived on very intimate terms with his tutor.

Stratŏnice (Στρατονίκη). 1. Wife of Antigonus, king of Asia, by whom she became the mother of Demetrius Poliorcetes. — 2. Daughter of Demetrius Poliorcetes and Phila, the daughter of Antipater. In 300, at which time she could not have been more than 17 years of age, she was married to Seleucus, king of Syria. Notwithstanding the disparity of their ages, she lived in harmony with the old king for some years, when it was discovered that her step-son Antiochus was deeply enamoured of her, and Seleucus, in order to save the life of his son, which was endangered by the violence of his passion, gave up Stratonice in marriage to the young prince. She bore 3 children to Antiochus: 1. Antiochus II., surnamed Theos; 2. Apama, married to Magas, king of Cyrene; and 3. Stratonice. — 3. Daughter of the preceding and of Antiochus I., was married to Demetrius II., king of Macedonia. She quitted Demetrius in disgust, on account of his second marriage with Phthia, the daughter of Olympias, and retired to Syria. Here she was put to death by her nephew Seleucus II., against whom she had attempted to raise a revolt. — 4. Daughter of Antiochus II., king of Syria, married to Ariarathes III., king of Cappadocia. — 5. One of the favourite wives of Mithridates the Great.

Stratŏnicēa (Στρατονίκεια, Στρατονίκη: Στρατονικεύς, Stratonicēus, Stratonicensis: Eski-Hisar, Ru.), one of the chief inland cities of Caria, built by Antiochus I. Soter, who fortified it strongly, and named it in honour of his wife Stratonice. It stood E. of Mylasa and S. of Alabanda, near the river Marsyas, a S. tributary of the Maeander. Under the Romans it was a free city; and it was improved by Hadrian. Near it stood the great temple of Zeus Chrysaoreus, the centre of the national worship of the Carians. There is some reason to believe that Stratonicea stood on the site of a former city, called Idrias, and, still earlier, Chrysaoris.

Stratŏnis Turris. [CAESAREA, No. 3.]

Strattis (Στράττις or Στράτις), an Athenian poet of the Old Comedy, flourished from B. C. 412 to 380.

Stratus (Στράτος). 1. (Στράτιος: nr. *Lepenu* or *Lepanon* Ru.), the chief town in Acarnania, 10 stadia W. of the Achelous. Its territory was called **Stratice**. It was a strongly fortified town, and commanded the ford of the Achelous on the high road from Aetolia to Acarnania. Hence it was a place of military importance, and was at an early period taken possession of by the Aetolians. — 2. A town in Achaia, afterwards called DYME. —3. A town in the W. of Arcadia in the territory of Thelpusa, perhaps the same as the Homeric Stratia.

Strongÿlē. [NAXOS.]

Strongÿlion (Στρογγυλίων), a distinguished Greek statuary, flourished during the last 30 or 40 years of the 5th century B. C.

Strŏphādes Insūlae (Στροφάδες), formerly called **Plōtae** (Πλωταί: *Strofadia* and *Strivali*), 2 islands in the Ionian sea, off the coast of Messenia and S. of Zacynthus. The Harpies were pursued to these islands by the sons of Boreas; and it was from the circumstance of the latter *returning* from these islands after the pursuit, that they are supposed to have obtained the name of Strophades.

Strŏphĭus (Στρόφιος), king of Phocis, son of

Crissus and Antiphatia, and husband of Cydragora, Anaxibia or Astyochia, by whom he became the father of Astydamia and Pylades. See ORESTES.

Strŭchătes (Στρούχατες), a Median people, mentioned only by Herodotus (i. 101).

Strŷmon (Struma, by the Turks Karasu), an important river in Macedonia, forming the boundary between that country and Thrace down to the time of Philip. It rose in Mt. Scomius, flowed first S. and then S. E., passed through the lake Prasias, and, immediately S. of Amphipolis, fell into a bay of the Aegaean Sea, called after it Strymonicus Sinus. The numerous cranes on its banks are frequently mentioned by ancient writers.

Strȳmŏnii (Στρυμόνιοι), the old name, according to Herodotus, of the Bithynians, who migrated into Asia Minor from the banks of the river Strymon. Bithynia was sometimes called Strymonis.

Stubĕra, a town of Macedonia in the district Paeonia, probably on the river Erigon.

Stymphālīdes. [STYMPHALUS.]

Stymphālis (Στυμφαλίς). 1. A lake in Arcadia. [STYMPHALUS.] — 2. A district in Macedonia, between Atintania and Elimiotis.

Stymphālus (Στύμφαλος, Στύμφηλος: Στυμφάλιος), a town in the N. E. of Arcadia, the territory of which was bounded on the N. by Achaia, on the E. by Sicyonia and Phliasia, on the S. by the territory of Mantinea, and on the W. by that of Orchomenus and Pheneus. The district was one of military importance, since it commanded one of the chief roads from Arcadia to Argolis. Its name is said to have been derived from Stymphalus, a son of Elatus and grandson of Arcas. The town itself was situated on a mountain of the same name, and on the N. side of the lake Stymphālis (Στυμφαλίς: Zaraka), on which dwelt, according to tradition, the celebrated birds, called Stymphālīdes (Στυμφαλίδες), destroyed by Hercules. [For details, see p. 309, a.] From this lake issued the river Stymphalus, which after a short course disappeared under ground, and was supposed to appear again as the river Erasinus in Argolis.

Styra (τὰ Στύρα: Στυρεύς: Stura), a town in Euboea on the S. W. coast, not far from Carystus, and nearly opposite Marathon in Attica. The inhabitants were originally Dryopes, though they subsequently denied their descent from this people. They took an active part in the Persian war, and fought at Artemisium, Salamis and Plataea. They afterwards became subject to the Athenians, and paid a yearly tribute of 1200 drachmae. The town was destroyed in the Lamian war by the Athenian general Phaedrus ; and its territory was annexed to Eretria.

Styx (Στύξ), connected with the verb στυγέω, to hate or abhor, is the name of the principal river in the nether world, around which it flows 7 times. Styx is described as a daughter of Oceanus and Tethys. As a nymph she dwelt at the entrance of Hades, in a lofty grotto which was supported by silver columns. As a river Styx is described as a branch of Oceanus, flowing from its 10th source ; and the river Cocytus again is a branch of the Styx. By Pallas Styx became the mother of Zelus (zeal), Nice (victory), Bia (strength), and Cratos (power). She was the first of all the immortals who took her children to Zeus, to assist him against the Titans ; and, in return for this,

her children were allowed for ever to live with Zeus, and Styx herself became the divinity by whom the most solemn oaths were sworn. When one of the gods had to take an oath by Styx, Iris fetched a cup full of water from the Styx, and the god, while taking the oath, poured out the water.

Styx (Στύξ: Mavra-neria), a river in the N. of Arcadia, near Nonacris, descending from a high rock, and falling into the Crathis. The ancients believed that the water of this river was poisonous ; and according to one tale Alexander the Great was poisoned by it. It was said also to break all vessels made of glass, stone, metal and any other material, except of the hoof of a horse or a mule.

Suada, the Roman personification of persuasion, the Greek Pitho (Πειθώ), also called by the diminutive Suadela.

Stagēla (Σουάγγελα), an ancient city of Caria, near Myndus, was the burial-place of the old kings of the country.

Suasa (Suasanus: S. Lorenzo), a municipium in Umbria on the Sena.

Suastus. [CHOASPES, No. 2].

Subertum or Sudertum (Sudertanus: Soverette), a town in the interior of Etruria.

Sublaquĕum (Sublacensis: Subiaco), a small town of the Aequi in Latium, on the Anio near its source. Near it stood the celebrated villa of Claudius and Nero (Villa Sublacensis) ; and from it was derived the name of the Via Sublacensia, which was a branch of the Via Tiburtina.

Sublicius Pons. [ROMA, p. 649, b.]

Subur. 1. A town of the Laeëtani in Hispania Tarraconensis E. of Tarraco, described by some as a town of the Cosetani, and by others again as a town of the Ilergetes. — 2. (Subus or Cubu), a river in Mauretania Tingitana, flowing past the colony Banasa into the Atlantic ocean.

Subūra or Subŭrra. [ROMA, p. 650, a.]

Subsupara (Zarvi), a town in Thrace on the road from Philippopolis to Hadrianopolis.

Succabar (Σουχάβαρρι, Ptol.: Mazuna?), an inland city of Mauretania Caesariensis, S.E. of the mouth of the Chinalaph. It was a colonia, and is mentioned by Ammianus Marcellinus under the name of oppidum Sugar-baritanum.

Succi or Succorum Angustiae. [HAEMUS.]

Sucro. 1. (Xucar), a river in Hispania Tarraconensis, rising in a S. branch of Mt. Idubeda in the territory of the Celtiberi, and falling S. of Valentia into a gulf of the Mediterranean called after it Sinus Sucronensis (Gulf of Valencia). — 2. (Cullera), a town of the Edetani in Hispania Tarraconensis, on the preceding river, and between the Iberus and Carthago Nova.

Sudertum. [SUBERTUM.]

Sudēti Montes, a range of mountains in the S. E. of Germany, in which the Albis takes its rise.

Sual (Fuengirola), a town in Hispania Baetica on the road from Malaca to Gades.

Suessa Aurunca (Suessanus: Sessa), a town of the Aurunci in Latium, E. of the Via Appia, between Minturnae and Teanum, on the W. slope of Mons Massicus. It was situated in a beautiful district called Vescinus ager, whence it has been supposed that the town itself was at one time called Vescia. It was made a Roman colony in the Samnite wars, but must have been afterwards colonised afresh, since we find it called in inscriptions Col. Julia Felix. It was the birthplace of the poet Lucilius.

Suessa Pōmātia (Suessanus), also called Pōmātia simply, an ancient and important town of
the Volsci in Latium, S. of Forum Appii, conquered by the Romans under Tarquinius Priscus,
and taken a second time and sacked by the consul
Servilius. It was one of the 23 cities situated in
the plain afterwards covered by the Pomptine
Marshes, which are said indeed to have derived
their name from this town.

Suessetāni, a people in Hispania Tarraconensis,
mentioned in connection with the Sedetani.

Suessiōnes or **Suessōnes,** a powerful people in
Gallia Belgica, who were reckoned the bravest of
all the Belgic Gauls after the Bellovaci, and who
could bring 50,000 men into the field in Caesar's
time. Their king Divitiacus, shortly before Caesar's arrival in the country, was reckoned the
most powerful chief in all Gaul, and had extended
his sovereignty even over Britain. The Suessiones
dwelt in an extensive and fertile country E. of the
Bellovaci, S. of the Veromandui, and W. of the
Remi. They possessed 12 towns, of which the
capital was Noviodunum, subsequently Augusta
Suessonum or Suessones (*Soissons*).

Suessūla (Suessulanus: *Torre di Sessola*), a
town in Samnium, on the S. slope of Mt. Tifata.

Suetōnius Paulinus. [PAULINUS.]

C. **Suētōnius Tranquillus,** the Roman historian, was born about the beginning of the reign
of Vespasian. His father was Suetonius Lenis,
who was a tribune of the 13th legion in the battle
of Bedriacum, in which Otho was defeated. Suetonius practised as an advocate at Rome in the
reign of Trajan. He lived on intimate terms with
the younger Pliny, many of whose letters are addressed to him. At the request of Pliny Trajan
granted to Suetonius the *jus trium liberorum*, for
though he was married he had not 3 children,
which number was necessary to relieve him from
various legal disabilities. Suetonius was afterwards appointed private secretary (Magister Epistolarum) to Hadrian, but was deprived of this office
by the emperor, along with Septicius Clarus, the
Praefect of the Praetorians, on the ground of
associating with Sabina the emperor's wife, without his permission. Suetonius wrote many works,
of which the only ones extant are :— *Vitae Duodecim Caesarum*, or the 12 Emperors, of whom the
first is C. Julius Caesar and the last is Domitian;
*Liber de illustribus Grammaticis; Liber de claris
Rhetoribus; Vitae Terentii, Horatii, Persii, Lucani, Juvenalis, Plinii Majoris.* His chief work
is his Lives of the Caesars. Suetonius does not
follow the chronological order in his Lives, but he
groups together many things of the same kind.
His language is very brief and precise, sometimes
obscure, without any affectation of ornament. He
certainly tells a prodigious number of scandalous
anecdotes about the Caesars, but there was plenty
to tell about them; and if he did not choose to
suppress those anecdotes which he believed to be
true, that is no imputation on his veracity. As a
great collection of facts of all kinds, the work on
the Caesars is invaluable for the historian of this
period. His judgment and his honesty have both
been attacked by some modern critics; but we
are of opinion, that on both grounds a careful study
of his work will justify him. The friendship of
the younger Pliny is evidence in favour of his integrity. The treatise *De illustribus Grammaticis*
and that *De claris Rhetoribus* are probably only

parts of a larger work. They contain a few biographical and other notices, that are occasionally
useful. It has been conjectured that the few
scanty lives of the Latin poets, already enumerated,
belonged to a larger work De Poetis. If this
conjecture be true, the short notice of the elder
Pliny may not be by Suetonius. A work entitled
De Viris Illustribus, which has been attributed
both to Suetonius and the younger Plinius, is now
unanimously assigned to Aurelius Victor. The
best editions of Suetonius are by P. Burmann,
Amsterdam, 1736, 2 vols. 4to., and by Baum-
garten-Crusius, Lips. 1816, 3 vols. 8vo.

Suēvi, one of the greatest and most powerful
peoples of Germany, or, more properly speaking,
the collective name of a great number of German
tribes, who were grouped together on account of
their migratory mode of life, and spoken of in opposition to the more settled tribes, who went under
the general name of Ingaevones. The Suevi are
described by all the ancient writers as occupying
the greater half of all Germany; but the accounts
vary respecting the part of the country which they
inhabited. Caesar represents them as dwelling
E. of the Ubii and Sygambri, and W. of the Cherusci, and their country as divided into 100
cantons. Strabo makes them extend in an E.-ly
direction beyond the Albis, and in a S.-ly as far
as the sources of the Danube. Tacitus gives the
name of Suevia to the whole of the E. of Germany
from the Danube to the Baltic. At a later time
the collective name of the Suevi gradually disappeared; and the different tribes of the Suevic
race were each called by their distinctive names.
In the 2nd half of the 3rd century, however, we
again find a people called Suevi, dwelling between
the mouth of the Main and the Black Forest,
whose name is still preserved in the modern
Swabia; but this people was only a body of bold
adventurers from various German tribes, who assumed the celebrated name of the Suevi in consequence of their not possessing any distinguishing
appellation.

Sufēnas, M. Nonius, tribune of the plebs in
B. C. 56, fought on Pompey's side at the battle of
Pharsalia.

Sufes (*Sbiba*), a city of N. Africa, in the Carthaginian territory (Byzacena).

Sufetūla (*Sfaitla*), a city of Byzacena, S. of
Sufes, of which its name is a diminutive. It became, however, a much more important place, as a
chief centre of the roads in the interior of the
province of Africa. Its ruins are magnificent.

Suidas (Σουΐδας), a Greek lexicographer, of
whom nothing is known. No certain conclusions
as to the age of the compiler can be derived from
passages in the work, since it may have received
numerous interpolations and additions. Eustathius,
who lived about the end of the 12th century of
the Christian era, quotes the Lexicon of Suidas;
and there are passages in the Lexicon referring to
Michael Psellus, who lived at the close of the 11th
century. The Lexicon of Suidas is a dictionary of
words arranged in alphabetical order, with some
few peculiarities of arrangement; but it contains
both words which are found in dictionaries of languages, and also names of persons and places, with
extracts from ancient Greek writers, grammarians,
scholiasts, and lexicographers, and some extracts
from later Greek writers. The names of persons
comprehend both persons who are mentioned in

sacred and in profane history, which shows that if the work is by one hand, it is by a Christian. No well conceived plan has been the basis of this work : it is incomplete as to the number of articles, and exceedingly irregular and unequal in the execution. Some articles are pretty complete, others contain no information at all. As to the biographical notices it has been conjectured that Suidas or the compiler got them all from one source, which, it is further supposed, may be the Onomatologos or Pinax of Hesychius of Miletus. The Lexicon, though without merit as to its execution, is valuable both for the literary history of antiquity, for the explanation of words, and for the citations from many ancient writers. The best editions of the Lexicon are by Küster, Cambridge, 1705, 3 vols. fo.; by Gaisford, Oxford, 1834, 3 vols. fo.; and by Bernhardy, 4to. Halle, 1834.

Suiones, the general name of all the German tribes inhabiting Scandinavia.

Suismontium, a mountain in Liguria.

Sulci (Sulcitanus: *Sulci*), an ancient town in Sardinia, founded by the Carthaginians, and a place of considerable maritime and commercial importance. It was situated on a promontory on the S.W. corner of the island.

Sulgas (*Sorgue*), a river in Gaul, descending from the Alps, and flowing into the Rhone near Vindalum.

Sulla, Cornelius, the name of a patrician family. This family was originally called Rufinus [RUFINUS], and the first member of it who obtained the name of Sulla was P. Cornelius Sulla, mentioned below [No. 1.] The origin of the name is uncertain. Most modern writers suppose that it is a word of the same signification as Rufus or Rufinus, and refers simply to the red colour of the hair or the complexion; but it has been conjectured with greater probability that it is a diminutive of Sura, which was a cognomen in several Roman gentes. It would be formed from Sura on the same analogy as *puella* from *puera*, and *tenellus* from *tener*. There is no authority for writing the word Sylla, as is done by many modern writers. On coins and inscriptions we always find Sula or Sulla, never Sylla. **1. P.,** great grandfather of the dictator Sulla, and grandson of P. Cornelius Rufinus, who was twice consul in the Samnite wars. [RUFINUS, CORNELIUS.] His father is not mentioned. He was flamen dialis, and likewise praetor urbanus and peregrinus in B. C. 212, when he presided over the first celebration of the Ludi Apollinares. — **2. P.,** son of No. 1, and grandfather of the dictator Sulla, was praetor in 186.—**3. L.,** son of No. 2, and father of the dictator Sulla, lived in obscurity, and left his son only a slender fortune. **4. L.** surnamed **Felix,** the dictator, was born in 138. Although his father left him only a small property, his means were sufficient to secure for him a good education. He studied the Greek and Roman literature with diligence and success, and appears early to have imbibed that love for literature and art by which he was distinguished throughout life. At the same time he prosecuted pleasure with equal ardour, and his youth, as well as his manhood, was disgraced by the most sensual vices. Still his love of pleasure did not absorb all his time, nor did it emasculate his mind; for no Roman during the latter days of the republic, with the exception of Julius Caesar, had a clearer judgment, a keener discrimination of character, or a

firmer will. The slender property of Sulla was increased by the liberality of his step-mother and of a courtezan named Nicopolis, both of whom left him all their fortune. His means, though still scanty for a Roman noble, now enabled him to aspire to the honours of the state. He was quaestor in 107, when he served under Marius in Africa. Hitherto he had only been known for his profligacy; but he displayed both zeal and ability in the discharge of his duties, and soon gained the approbation of his commander, and the affections of the soldiers. It was to Sulla that Jugurtha was delivered by Bocchus; and the quaestor thus shared with the consul the glory of bringing this war to a conclusion. Sulla himself was so proud of his share in the success, that he had a seal ring engraved, representing the surrender of Jugurtha, which he continued to wear till the day of his death. Sulla continued to serve under Marius with great distinction in the campaigns against the Cimbri and Teutones; but Marius becoming jealous of the rising fame of his officer, Sulla left Marius in 102, and took a command under the colleague of Marius, Q. Catulus, who entrusted the chief management of the war to Sulla. Sulla now returned to Rome, where he appears to have lived quietly for some years. He was praetor in 93, and in the following year (92) was sent as propraetor into Cilicia, with special orders from the senate to restore Ariobarzanes to his kingdom of Cappadocia, from which he had been expelled by Mithridates. Sulla met with complete success. He defeated Gordius, the general of Mithridates, in Cappadocia, and placed Ariobarzanes on the throne. The enmity between Marius and Sulla now assumed a more deadly form. Sulla's ability and increasing reputation had already led the aristocratical party to look up to him as one of their leaders; and thus political animosity was added to private hatred. In addition to this Marius and Sulla were both anxious to obtain the command of the impending war against Mithridates; and the success which attended Sulla's recent operations in the East had increased his popularity, and pointed him out as the most suitable person for this important command. About this time Bocchus erected in the Capitol gilded figures, representing the surrender of Jugurtha to Sulla, at which Marius was so enraged that he could scarcely be prevented from removing them by force. The exasperation of both parties became so violent that they nearly had recourse to arms against each other; but the breaking out of the Social War hushed all private quarrels for the time. Marius and Sulla both took an active part in the war against the common foe. But Marius was now advanced in years; and he had the deep mortification of finding that his achievements were thrown into the shade by the superior energy of his rival. Sulla gained some brilliant victories over the enemy, and took Bovianum, the chief town of the Samnites. He was elected consul for 88, and received from the senate the command of the Mithridatic war. The events which followed, — his expulsion from Rome by Marius, his return to the city at the head of his legions, and the proscription of Marius and his leading adherents — are related in the life of Marius. Sulla remained at Rome till the end of the year, and set out for Greece at the beginning of 87, in order to carry on the war against Mithridates. He landed at Dyrrhachium, and forthwith marched against Athens, which had become the head-quarters of the Mithridatic cause in Greece. After a long and obstinate siege, Athens was taken by storm on the 1st of March in 86, and was given up to rapine and plunder. Sulla then marched against Archelaus, the general of Mithridates, whom he defeated in the neighbourhood of Chaeronea in Boeotia; and in the following year he again gained a decisive victory over the same general near Orchomenus. But while Sulla was carrying on the war with such success in Greece, his enemies had obtained the upper hand in Italy. The consul Cinna, who had been driven out of Rome by his colleague Octavius, soon after Sulla's departure from Italy, had entered it again with Marius at the close of the year. Both Cinna and Marius were appointed consuls 86, and all the regulations of Sulla were swept away. Sulla however would not return to Italy till he had brought the war against Mithridates to a conclusion. After driving the generals of Mithridates out of Greece, Sulla crossed the Hellespont, and early in 84 concluded a peace with the king of Pontus. He now turned his arms against Fimbria, who had been appointed by the Marian party as his successor in the command. But the troops of Fimbria deserted their general, who put an end to his own life. Sulla now prepared to return to Italy. After leaving his legate, L. Licinius Murena, in command of the province of Asia, with two legions, he set sail with his own army to Athens. While preparing for his deadly struggle in Italy, he did not lose his interest in literature. He carried with him from Athens to Rome the valuable library of Apellicon of Teos, which contained most of the works of Aristotle and Theophrastus. [APELLICON]. He landed at Brundusium in the spring of 83. The Marian party far outnumbered him in troops, and had every prospect of victory. By bribery and promises however Sulla gained over a large number of the Marian soldiers, and he persuaded many of the Italian towns to espouse his cause. In the field his efforts were crowned by equal success; and he was ably supported by several of the Roman nobles, who espoused his cause in different parts of Italy. Of these one of the most distinguished was the young Cn. Pompey, who was at the time only 23 years of age. [POMPEIUS, No. 10.] In the following year (82) the struggle was brought to a close by the decisive battle gained by Sulla over the Samnites and Lucanians under Pontius Telesinus before the Colline gate of Rome. This victory was followed by the surrender of Praeneste and the death of the younger Marius, who had taken refuge in this town. Sulla was now master of Rome and Italy; and he resolved to take the most ample vengeance upon his enemies, and to extirpate the popular party. One of his first acts was to draw up a list of his enemies who were to be put to death, called a *Proscriptio*. It was the first instance of the kind in Roman history. All persons in this list were outlaws who might be killed by any one with impunity, even by slaves; their property was confiscated to the state, and was to be sold by public auction; their children and grandchildren lost their votes in the comitia, and were excluded from all public offices. Further, all who killed a proscribed person, received two talents as a reward, and whoever sheltered such a person was punished with death. Terror now reigned, not only at Rome, but throughout

Italy. Fresh lists of the proscribed constantly appeared. No one was safe; for Sulla gratified his friends by placing in the fatal lists their personal enemies, or persons whose property was coveted by his adherents. The confiscated property, it is true, belonged to the state, and had to be sold by public auction, but the friends and dependents of Sulla purchased it at a nominal price, as no one dared to bid against them. The number of persons who perished by the proscriptions is stated differently, but it appears to have amounted to many thousands. At the commencement of these horrors Sulla had been appointed dictator for as long a time as he judged to be necessary. This was towards the close of 81. Sulla's chief object in being invested with the dictatorship was to carry into execution in a legal manner the great reforms which he meditated in the constitution and the administration of justice. He had no intention of abolishing the republic, and consequently he caused consuls to be elected for the following year, and was elected to the office himself in 80, while he continued to hold the dictatorship. The general object of Sulla's reforms was to restore, as far as possible, the ancient Roman constitution, and to give back to the senate and the aristocracy the power which they had lost. Thus he deprived the tribunes of the plebs of all real power, and abolished altogether the legislative and judicial functions of the comitia tributa. At the beginning of 81, he celebrated a splendid triumph on account of his victory over Mithridates. In a speech which he delivered to the people at the close of the ceremony, he claimed for himself the surname of *Felix*, as he attributed his success in life to the favour of the gods. In order to strengthen his power, Sulla established military colonies throughout Italy. The inhabitants of the Italian towns, which had fought against Sulla, were deprived of the full Roman franchise, and were only allowed to retain the commercium: their land was confiscated and given to the soldiers who had fought under him. 23 legions, or, according to another statement, 47 legions received grants of land in various parts of Italy. A great number of these colonies was settled in Etruria, the population of which was thus almost entirely changed. These colonies had the strongest interest in upholding the institutions of Sulla, since any attempt to invalidate the latter would have endangered their newly-acquired possessions. Sulla likewise created at Rome a kind of body-guard for his protection by giving the citizenship to a great number of slaves, who had belonged to persons proscribed by him. The slaves thus rewarded are said to have been as many as 10,000, and were called Cornelii after him as their patron. After holding the dictatorship till the beginning of 79, Sulla resigned this office, to the surprise of all classes. He retired to his estate at Puteoli, and there surrounded by the beauties of nature and art he passed the remainder of his life in those literary and sensual enjoyments in which he had always taken so much pleasure. His dissolute mode of life hastened his death. The immediate cause of his death was the rupture of a blood-vessel, but some time before he had been suffering from the disgusting disease, which is known in modern times by the name of Morbus Pediculosus or Phthiriasis. He died in 78 in the 60th year of his age. He was honoured with a public funeral, and a monument was erected to him in the Campus Martius the inscription on which had been composed by himself. It stated that none of his friends ever did him a kindness, and none of his enemies a wrong, without being fully repaid. — Sulla was married 5 times: — 1. To Ilia or Julia, who bore him a daughter, married to Q. Pompeius Rufus, the son of Sulla's colleague in the consulship in 88. 2. To Aelia. 3. To Coelia. 4. To Caecilia Metella, who bore him a son, who died before Sulla, and likewise twins, a son and a daughter. 5. Valeria, who bore him a daughter after his death. Sulla wrote a history of his own life and times, called *Memoirs* ('Ὑπομνήματα). It was dedicated to L. Lucullus, and extended to 22 books, the last of which was finished by Sulla a few days before his death. He also wrote Fabulae Atellanae, and the Greek Anthology contains a short epigram which is ascribed to him. — 5. Faustus, son of the dictator by his fourth wife Caecilia Metella, and a twin brother of Fausta, was born not long before 88, the year in which his father obtained his first consulship. He and his sister received the names of Faustus and Fausta respectively on account of the good fortune of their father. At the death of his father in 78, Faustus and his sister were left under the guardianship of L. Lucullus. Faustus accompanied Pompey into Asia, and was the first who mounted the walls of the temple of Jerusalem in 63. In 60 he exhibited the gladiatorial games which his father in his last will had enjoined upon him. In 54 he was quaestor. In 52 he received from the senate the commission to rebuild the Curia Hostilia, which had been burnt down in the tumults following the murder of Clodius, and which was henceforward to be called the Curia Cornelia, in honour of Faustus and his father. He married Pompey's daughter, and sided with his father-in-law in the civil war. He was present at the battle of Pharsalia, and subsequently joined the leaders of his party in Africa. After the battle of Thapsus in 46, he attempted to escape into Mauretania, but was taken prisoner by P. Sittius, and carried to Caesar. Upon his arrival in Caesar's camp he was murdered by the soldiers in a tumult. Faustus seems only to have resembled his father in his extravagance. We know from Cicero that he was overwhelmed with debt at the breaking out of the civil war. — 6. P., nephew of the dictator, was elected consul along with P. Autronius Paetus for the year 65, but neither he nor his colleague entered upon the office, as they were accused of bribery by L. Torquatus the younger, and were condemned. It was currently believed that Sulla was privy to both of Catiline's conspiracies, and he was accordingly accused of this crime by his former accuser, L. Torquatus, and by C. Cornelius. He was defended by Hortensius and Cicero, and the speech of the latter on his behalf is still extant. He was acquitted ; but, independent of the testimony of Sallust (*Cat.* 17), his guilt may almost be inferred from the embarrassment of his advocate. In the civil war Sulla espoused Caesar's cause. He served under him as legate in Greece, and commanded along with Caesar himself the right wing at the battle of Pharsalia (48). He died in 45. — 7. Serv., brother of No. 6, took part in both of Catiline's conspiracies. His guilt was so evident, that no one was willing to defend him ; but we do not read that he was put to death along with the other conspirators.

Sulmo (Sulmonensis). 1. (*Sulmona*), a town

of the Peligni in the country of the Sabines, 7 miles S. of Corfinium on the road to Capua, and situated on 2 small mountain streams, the water of which was exceedingly cold : hence we find the town called by the poets *gelidus Sulmo*. It is celebrated as the birthplace of Ovid. It was destroyed by Sulla, but was afterwards restored, and is mentioned as a Roman colony. — 2. (*Sermoneta*), an ancient town of the Volsci in Latium on the Ufens, which had disappeared in Pliny's time.

Sulpicia, a Roman poetess who flourished towards the close of the 1st century, celebrated for sundry amatory effusions, addressed to her husband Calenus. Their general character may be gathered from the expressions of Martial, Ausonius, and Sidonius Apollinaris, by all of whom they are noticed. There is extant a satirical poem, in 70 hexameters, on the edict of Domitian, by which philosophers were banished from Rome and from Italy, which is ascribed to Sulpicia by many modern critics. It is generally appended to the editions of Juvenal and Persius.

Sulpicia Gens, was one of the most ancient Roman gentes, and produced a succession of distinguished men, from the foundation of the republic to the imperial period. The chief families of the Sulpicii during the republican period bore the names of : — Camerinus, Galba, Gallus, Rufus (given below), Saverrio.

Sulpicius Apollināris, a contemporary of A. Gellius, was a learned grammarian. There are 3 poems in the Latin Anthology, purporting to be written by Sulpicius of Carthage, whom some identify with the above-named Sulpicius Apollinaris. One of these poems consists of 72 lines, giving the argument of the 12 books of Virgil's Aeneid, 6 lines being devoted to each book.

Sulpicius Rufus. 1. P., one of the most distinguished orators of his time, was born B. C. 124. He commenced public life as a supporter of the aristocratical party, and acquired great influence in the state by his splendid talents, while he was still young. In 93 he was quaestor, and in 89 he served as legate of the consul Cn. Pompeius Strabo in the Marsic war. In 88, he was elected to the tribunate ; but he deserted the aristocratical party, and joined Marius. The causes of this sudden change are not expressly stated ; but we are told that he was overwhelmed with debt ; and there can be little doubt that he was bought by Marius. Sulpicius brought forward a law in favour of Marius and his party, of which an account is given under Marius. When Sulla marched upon Rome at the head of his army, Marius and Sulpicius took to flight. Marius succeeded in making his escape to Africa, but Sulpicius was discovered in a villa, and put to death. — 2. P., probably son or grandson of the last, was one of Caesar's legates in Gaul and in the civil war. He was praetor in 48. Cicero addresses him in 45 as imperator. It appears that he was at that time in Illyricum, along with Vatinius. — 3. Serv., with the surname Lemonia, indicating the tribe to which he belonged, was a contemporary and friend of Cicero, and of about the same age. He first devoted himself to oratory, and he studied this art with Cicero in his youth. He afterwards studied law ; and he became one of the best jurists as well as most eloquent orators of his age. He was quaestor of the district of Ostia, in 74 ; curule aedile 69 ; praetor 65 ; and consul 51 with M.

Claudius Marcellus. He appears to have espoused Caesar's side in the civil war, and was appointed by Caesar proconsul of Achaia (46 or 45). He died in 43 in the camp of M. Antony, having been sent by the senate on a mission to Antony, who was besieging Dec. Brutus in Mutina. Sulpicius wrote a great number of legal works. He is often cited by the jurists whose writings are excerpted in the Digest; but there is no excerpt directly from him in the Digest. He had numerous pupils, the most distinguished of whom were A. Ofilius and Alfenus Varus. There are extant in the collection of Cicero's Epistles (ad Fam. iv.) two letters from Sulpicius to Cicero. one of which is the well-known letter of consolation on the death of Tullia, the daughter of the orator. The same book contains several letters from Cicero to Sulpicius. He is also said to have written some erotic poetry. — Sulpicius left a son Servius, who is frequently mentioned in Caesar's correspondence.

Summānus, a derivative form from *summus*, the highest, an ancient Roman or Etruscan divinity, who was equal or even of higher rank than Jupiter. In fact he may be regarded as the Jupiter of the night; for as Jupiter was the god of heaven in the bright day, so Summanus was the god of the nocturnal heaven, and hurled his thunderbolts during the night. Summanus had a temple at Rome near the Circus Maximus, and there was a representation of him in the pediment of the Capitoline temple.

Sūnĭum (Σούνιον: Σουνιεύς: C. Colonni), a celebrated promontory forming the S. extremity of Attica, with a town of the same name upon it. Here was a splendid temple of Athena, elevated 300 feet above the sea, the columns of which are still extant, and have given the modern name to the promontory. It was fortified by the Athenians in the Peloponnesian war, and remains of the ancient walls, with the temple of Athena, are still extant.

Sunonensis Lacus (L. Sabanjah), a lake in Bithynia, between the Ascania Palus and the river Sangarius, near Nicomedia.

Sŭperbus, Tarquinĭus. [TARQUINIUS.]

Sura, Lentŭlus. [LENTULUS, No. 9.]

Sūra, L. Licinĭus, an intimate friend of Trajan, and 3 times consul in A.D. 98, 102 and 10 . On the death of Sura, Trajan honoured him with a public funeral, and erected baths to perpetuate his memory. Two of Pliny's letters are addressed to him.

Sūra (Σοῦρα: Surie), a town of Syria, in the district Chalybonitis, on the Euphrates, a little W. of Thapsacus.

Surani or **Suarni** (Σουρανοί), a people of Sarmatia Asiatica, near the Portae Caucaseae and the river Rha. Their country contained many gold mines.

Surenas, the general of the Parthians, who defeated Crassus in B.C. 54. [CRASSUS.]

Sūrĭus (Σούριος), a tributary of the Phasis in Colchis, the water of which had the power of forming petrifactions. At its confluence with the Phasis stood a town named **Surĭum** (Σούριον). The plain through which it flows is still called *Surium*.

Surrentini Colles. [SURRENTUM.]

Surrentum (Surrentinus: Sorrento), an ancient town of Campania opposite Capreae, and situated on the promontory (Prom. Minervae) separating the Sinus Paestanus from the Sinus Puteolanus. It was subsequently a Roman colony; and on the hills (Surrentini Colles) in its neighbourhood was grown one of the best wines in Italy, which was strongly recommended to convalescents, on account of its thinness and wholesomeness.

Sūsa, gen. -orum (τὰ Σοῦσα: O. T. Shushan: Σοῦσιος, Susiānus: Shus, Ru.), the winter residence of the Persian kings, stood in the district Cissia of the province Susiana, on the E. bank of the river Choaspes. Its name in old Persian signifies *Lily*, and that flower is said to abound in the plain in which the city stood. It was of a quadrangular form, 120 (or, according to others, 200) stadia in circuit, and without fortifications; but it had a strongly fortified citadel, containing the palace and treasury of the Persian kings. The Greek name of this citadel, Memnonice or Memnonium, is perhaps a corruption of the Aramaic *Maaminon*, *a fortress*; and this easy confusion of terms gave rise to the fable that the city was founded by Tithonus, the father of Memnon. An historical tradition ascribes its erection to Darius the son of Hystaspes, but it existed already in the time of Daniel. (Dan. viii. 2.) (There is, however, a difficulty as to the identification of the Shushan of Daniel with the Susa of the Greeks, and as to the true position of the river Ulai or Eulaeus, which cannot be discussed within the limits of this article.) The climate of Susa was very hot, and hence the choice of it for the winter palace. It was here that Alexander and his generals celebrated their nuptials with the Persian princesses, B.C. 325. The site of Susa is now marked by extensive mounds, on which are found fragments of bricks and broken pottery, with cuneiform inscriptions.

Sūsărĭōn (Σουσαρίων), to whom the origin of the Attic Comedy is ascribed, was a native of Megara, whence he removed into Attica, to the village of Icaria, a place celebrated as a seat of the worship of Dionysus. This account agrees with the claim which the Megarians asserted to the invention of comedy, and which was generally admitted. Before the time of Susarion there was, no doubt, practised, at Icaria and the other Attic villages, that extempore jesting and buffoonery which formed a marked feature of the festivals of Dionysus; but Susarion was the first who so regulated this species of amusement, as to lay the foundation of Comedy, properly so called. The Megaric comedy appears to have flourished, in its full development, about B.C. 600 and onwards; and it was introduced by Susarion into Attica between 580—564.

Susĭāna, -e, or **Sūsis** (ἡ Σουσιανή, ἡ Σουσίς: nearly corresponding to Khuzistan), one of the chief provinces of the ancient Persian empire, lay between Babylonia and Persis, and between M. Parachoatras and the head of the Persian Gulf. In this last direction, its coast extended from the junction of the Euphrates with the Tigris, to about the mouth of the river Oroatis (Tab). It was divided from Persis on the S. E. and E. by a mountainous tract, inhabited by independent tribes, who made even the kings of Persia pay them for a safe passage. The chief pass through these mountains was called Susides or Persides Portae (Σουσίδες πύλαι, αἱ πύλαι αἱ Περσίδες, Σουσιάδες πέτραι): its position is uncertain; perhaps it was the pass of Kelahi Sefid, in the upper valley of the

Tab. On the N. it was separated from Great Media by M. Charbanus, an E. branch of M. Zagros ; which contained the sources of the chief rivers of Susiana, the CHOASPES, the COPRATES, and the EULAEUS (the PASITIGRIS came from the mountains on the E.). On the W. it was divided from Assyria by an imaginary line drawn S. from near the Median pass in M. Zagros to the Tigris ; and from Babylonia by the Tigris itself. The country was mountainous and cool in the N., and low and very hot in the S.; and the coast along the Persian Gulf was marshy. The mountains were inhabited by various wild and independent tribes ; and the plains by a quiet agricultural people, of the Semitic race, called Susii or Susiani.

Sutrium (Sutrĭnus : *Sutri*), an ancient town of Etruria on the E. side of the Saltus Ciminius, and on the road from Vulsinii to Rome. It was taken by the Romans at an early period; and in B.C. 383, or 7 years after the capture of Rome by the Gauls, it was made a Roman colony. It was celebrated for its fidelity to Rome, and was in consequence besieged several times by the Etruscans. On one occasion it was obliged to surrender to the Etruscans, but was retaken by Camillus in the same day, whence arose the proverb *ire Sutrium*. There are still remains of the walls and tombs of the ancient town.

Syager (Σύαγρος), one of the alleged ante-Homeric poets, is said to have flourished after Orpheus and Musaeus, and to have been the first who sang the Trojan War.

Syagrus (Σύαγρος ἄκρα), the greatest promontory of Arabia, is described differently by different ancient writers, but is most probably to be identified with the E.-most headland of the whole peninsula, *Ras-el-Had*.

Sybaris (Σύβαρις). 1. (*Coscile* or *Sibari*), a river in Lucania, flowing by the city of the same name, and falling into the Crathis. It derived its name from the fountain Sybaria, near Bura, in Achaia. — 2. (Συβαρίτης, Sybarīta), a celebrated Greek town in Lucania, was situated between the rivers Sybaris and Crathis at a short distance from the Tarentine gulf, and near the confines of Bruttium. It was founded B.C. 720 by Achaeans and Troezenians, and soon attained an extraordinary degree of prosperity and wealth. It carried on an extensive commerce with Asia Minor and other countries on the Mediterranean, and its inhabitants became so notorious for their love of luxury and pleasure, that their name was employed to indicate any voluptuary. At the time of their highest prosperity their city was 50 stadia, or upwards of 6 miles in circumference, and they exercised dominion over 25 towns, so that we are told they were able to bring into the field 300,000 men, a number however which appears incredible. But their prosperity was of short duration. The Achaeans having expelled the Troezenian part of the population, the latter took refuge at the neighbouring city of Croton, the inhabitants of which espoused their cause. In the war which ensued between the 2 states, the Sybarites were completely conquered by the Crotoniates, who followed up their victory by the capture of Sybaris, which they destroyed by turning the waters of the river Crathis against the town, B.C. 510. The greater number of the surviving Sybarites took refuge in other Greek cities in Italy; but a few remained near their ancient town, and their descendants

formed part of the population of Thurii, which was founded in 443 near Sybaris. [THURII]

Sybŏta (τὰ Σύβοτα : Συβότιος : *Syvota*), a number of small islands off the coast of Epirus, and opposite the promontory Leucimne in Corcyra, with a harbour of the same name on the main land. It was here that a naval battle was fought between the Corcyraeans and Corinthians, B.C. 432, just before the commencement of the Peloponnesian war.

Sychaeus or **Sichaeus**, also called **Acerbas**. [ACERBAS.]

Sychar, Sychem. [NEAPOLIS, No. 5.]

Syēnē (Συήνη : Συηνίτης and Συηνήτης, Syenites : *Assouan*, Ru.), a city of Upper Egypt, on the E. bank of the Nile, just below the First Cataract. It has been in all ages the S. frontier city of Egypt towards Aethiopia, and under the Romans it was kept by a garrison of 3 cohorts. From its neighbourhood was obtained the fine red granite called Syenites lapis. It was also an important point in the astronomy and geography of the ancients, as it lay just under the tropic of Cancer, and was therefore chosen as the place through which they drew their chief parallel of latitude. Of course the sun was vertical to Syene at the time of the summer solstice, and a well was shown in which the reflection of the sun was then seen at noon ; or, as the rhetorician Aristides expresses it, the disc of the sun covered the well as a vessel is covered by its lid.

Syennēsis (Συέννεσις), a common name of the kings of Cilicia. Of these the most important are : — 1. A king of Cilicia, who joined with Labynetus (Nebuchadnezzar) in mediating between Cyaxares and Alyattes, the kings respectively of Media and Lydia, probably in B.C. 610. — 2. Contemporary with Darius Hystaspis, to whom he was tributary. His daughter was married to Pixodarus. — 3. Contemporary with Artaxerxes II. (Mnemon), ruled over Cilicia, when the younger Cyrus marched through his country in his expedition against his brother Artaxerxes.

Sygambri, Sugambri, Sigambri, Sycambri, or **Sicambri,** one of the most powerful peoples of Germany at an early time, belonged to the Istaevones, and dwelt originally N. of the Ubii on the Rhine, from whence they spread towards the N. as far as the Lippe. The Sygambri are mentioned by Caesar, who invaded their territory. They were conquered by Tiberius in the reign of Augustus, and a large number of them were transplanted to Gaul, where they received settlements between the Maas and the Rhine as Roman subjects. The portion of the Sygambri who remained in Germany withdrew further S., probably to the mountainous country in the neighbourhood of the Taunus. Shortly afterwards they disappear from history, and are not mentioned again till the time of Ptolemy, who places them much further N. close to the Bructeri and the Langobardi, somewhere between the Vecht and the Yssel. At a still later period we find them forming an important part of the confederacy known under the name of Franci.

Sylla. [SULLA.]

Syllium (Σύλλιον : prob. Ru. near *Bolkasaku*, N. of *Legelahkoi*), a strongly fortified town of Pamphylia, on a mountain, 40 stadia (4 geog. miles) from the coast, between Side and Aspendus.

Sylvānus. [SILVANUS.]

Sylvius. [SILVIUS.]

Symaethus (Σύμαιθος: *Giaretta*), a river on the E. coast of Sicily and at the foot of Mt. Aetna, forming the boundary between Leontini and Catana, on which stood the town of Centuripae.

Syme (Σύμη: Συμαῖος, Συμεύς: *Symi*), a small island off the S.W. coast of Caria, lay in the mouth of the Sinus Doridis to the W. of the promontory of Cynossema. It was one of the early Dorian states, that existed in the S.W. of Asia Minor before the time of Homer. Its connection both with Cnidus and with Rhodes, between which it lay, is indicated by the tradition, that it was peopled by a colony from Cnidus led by Cthonius, the son of Poseidon and of Syme, the daughter of Ialysus. Some time after the Trojan war, the Carians are said to have obtained possession of the island, but to have deserted it again in consequence of a severe drought. Its final settlement by the Dorians is ascribed to the time of their great migration. The island was reckoned at 35 miles in circuit. It had 8 harbours and a town, which was also called Syme.

Symmachus, Q. Aurelius, a distinguished scholar, statesman, and orator in the latter half of the 4th century of the Christian aera. By his example and authority, he inspired for a time new life and vigour into the literature of his country. He was educated in Gaul; and having discharged the functions of quaestor and praetor, he was afterwards appointed (A. D. 365) Corrector of Lucania and the Bruttii; and in 373 he was proconsul of Africa. His zeal for the ancient religion of Rome checked for a while the prosperous current of his fortunes, and involved him in danger and disgrace. Having been chosen by the senate to remonstrate with Gratian on the removal of the altar of victory (382) from their council hall, and on the curtailment of the sums annually allowed for the maintenance of the Vestal Virgins, and for the public celebration of sacred rites, he was ordered by the indignant emperor to quit his presence, and to withdraw himself to a distance of 100 miles from Rome. Nothing daunted by this repulse, when appointed praefect of the city (384) after the death of his persecutor, he addressed an elaborate epistle to Valentinianus, again urging the restoration of the pagan deities to their former honours. This application was resisted by St. Ambrose, and was again unsuccessful. Symmachus afterwards espoused the cause of the usurper Maximus (387); but he was pardoned by Theodosius and raised to the consulship in 391. His personal character seems to have been unimpeachable, as he performed the duties of the high offices which he filled in succession with a degree of mildness, firmness, and integrity, seldom found among statesmen in that corrupt age. The extant works of Symmachus are:— 1. *Epistolarum Libri X.,* published after his death by his son. The last book contains his official correspondence, and is chiefly composed of the letters presented by him when praefect of the city to the emperors under whom he served. The remaining books comprise a multitude of epistles, addressed to a wide circle of relations, friends, and acquaintances. 2. *Novem Orationum Fragmenta,* published for the first time by Mai from a palimpsest in the Ambrosian library, Mediolan. 1815. The best editions of the epistles are by Juretus, Paris, 1604, and by Scioppius, Mogunt. 1608.

Synesius (Συνέσιος), one of the most elegant

of the ancient Christian writers, was a native of Cyrene, and devoted himself to the study of Greek literature, first in his own city, and afterwards at Alexandria, where he heard Hypatia. He became celebrated for his skill in eloquence and poetry, as well as in philosophy, in which he was a follower of Plato. About A. D. 397, he was sent by his fellow-citizens of Cyrene on an embassy to Constantinople, to present the emperor Arcadius with a crown of gold; on which occasion he delivered an oration on the government of a kingdom (περὶ βασιλείας), which is still extant. Soon after this he embraced Christianity, and in 410 was ordained bishop of Ptolemaïs, the chief city of the Libyan Pentapolis. He presided over his diocese with energy and success for about 20 years, and died about 430. His writings have been objects of admiration both to ancient and modern scholars, and have obtained for him the surname of Philosopher. The best edition of his works is by Morel, Paris, 1612: much improved and enlarged, Paris, 1633, ; reprinted, 1640.

Synnada, also **Synnas** (τὰ Συνναδα: Συνναδεύς, Synnadensis: prob. *Afioum-Kara-Hisar,* Ru.), a city in the N. of Phrygia Salutaris, at first inconsiderable, but afterwards a place of much importance, and, from the time of Constantine, the capital of Phrygia Salutaris. It stood in a fruitful plain, planted with olives, near a mountain from which was quarried the very celebrated Synnadic marble, which was of a beautiful white, with red veins and spots (Συνναδικὸς λίθος, Synnadicus lapis, called also Docimiticus, from a still nearer place, Docimia).

Syphax (Σύφαξ), king of the Massaesylians, the westernmost tribe of the Numidians. His history is related in the life of his contemporary and rival, MASINISSA. Syphax was taken prisoner by Masinissa, B. C. 203, and was sent by Scipio, under the charge of Laelius, to Rome. Polybius states that he was one of the captives who adorned the triumph of Scipio, and that he died in confinement shortly after. Livy, on the contrary, asserts that he was saved from that ignominy by a timely death at Tibur, whither he had been transferred from Alba.

Syraco. [SYRACUSAE.]

Syracusae (Συράκουσαι or Συράκοσσαι, Ion. Συρήκουσαι, also Συρακοῦσαι, Συρακούσαι: Συρακούσιος, Συρακόσιος, Syracusānus; *Siracusa* in Italian, *Syracuse* in English), the wealthiest and most populous town in Sicily, was situated on the S. part of the E. coast, 400 stadia N. of the promontory Plemmyrium, and 10 stadia N. E. of the mouth of the river Anapus, near the lake or marsh called *Syraco* (Συρακώ), from which it derived its name. It was founded B. C. 734, one year after the foundation of Naxos, by a colony of Corinthians and other Dorians, led by Archias the Corinthian. The town was originally confined to the island Ortygia lying immediately off the coast; but it afterwards spread over the neighbouring mainland, and at the time of its greatest extension under the elder Dionysius it consisted of 5 distinct towns, each surrounded by separate walls. Some writers indeed describe Syracuse as consisting of 4 towns, but this simply arises from the fact that Epipolae was frequently not reckoned a portion of the city. These 5 towns were, 1. Ortygia ('Ορτυγία, frequently called simply the **Island** (Νᾶσος or Νῆσος), an island of an oblong shape, about 2 miles in circumference, lying between the Great Harbour on the W. and the Little Harbour on the E. It was, as has been already remarked, the portion of the city first built, and it contained the citadel or Acropolis, surrounded by double walls, which Timoleon caused to be destroyed. In this island also was the celebrated fountain of Arethusa. It was originally separated from the mainland by a narrow channel, which was subsequently filled up by a causeway; but this causeway must at a still later time have been swept away, since we find in the Roman period that the island was connected with the mainland by means of a bridge. — 2 Achradina ('Αχραδίνη), occupied originally the high ground of the peninsula N. of Ortygia, and was surrounded on the N. and E. by the sea. The lower ground between Achradina and Ortygia was at first not included in the fortifications of either, but was employed partly for religious processions and partly for the burial of the dead. At the time of the siege of Syracuse by the Athenians in the Peloponnesian war (415), the city consisted only of the 2 parts already mentioned, Ortygia forming the inner and Achradina the outer city, but separated, as explained above, by the low ground between the two. — 3. Tyche (Τύχη), named after the temple of Tyche or Fortune, was situated N.W. of Achradina, in the direction of the port called Trogilus. At the time of the Athenian siege of Syracuse it was only an unfortified suburb, but it afterwards became the most populous part of the city. In this quarter stood the gymnasium. — 4. Neapolis (Νέα πόλις), nearly S. W. of Achradina, was also, at the time of the Athenian siege of Syracuse, merely a suburb and called Temenites, from having within it the statue and consecrated ground of Apollo Temenites. Neapolis contained the chief theatre of Syracuse, which was the largest in all Sicily, and many temples. — 5. Epipolae (αἱ 'Επιπολαί), a space of ground rising above the 3 quarters of Achradina, Tyche, and Neapolis, which gradually diminished in breadth as it rose higher, until it ended in a small conical mound. This rising ground was surrounded with strong walls by the elder Dionysius, and was thus included in Syracuse, which now became one of the most strongly fortified cities of the ancient world. The highest point of Epipolae was called Euryelus (Εὐρύηλος), on which stood the fort Labdalum (Λάβδαλον). After Epipolae had been added to the city, the circumference of Syracuse was 180 stadia or upwards of 22 English miles; and the entire population of the city is supposed to have amounted to 500,000 souls, at the time of its greatest prosperity. —Syracuse had 2 harbours. The Great Harbour, still called *Porto Maggiore*, is a splendid bay about 5 miles in circumference formed by the island Ortygia and the promontory Plemmyrium. The Small Harbour, also called *Laccius* (Λάκκιος), lying between Ortygia and Achradina, was capacious enough to receive a large fleet of ships of war. —There were several stone quarries (*lautumiae*) in Syracuse, which are frequently mentioned by ancient writers, and in which the unfortunate Athenian prisoners were confined. These quarries were partly in Achradina on the descent from the higher ground to the lower level towards Ortygia, and partly in Neapolis under the S. cliff of Epipolae. From them was taken the stone of which the city was built. On one side of these quarries is the remarkable excavation, called the Ear of

Dionysius, in which it is said that this tyrant confined the persons whom he suspected, and that he was able from a little apartment above to overhear the conversation of his captives. This tale however is clearly an invention. — The city was supplied with water from an aqueduct, which was constructed by Gelon and improved by Hieron. It was brought through Epipolae and Neapolis to Achradina and Ortygia.—The modern city of Syracuse is confined to the island. The remaining quarters of the ancient city are now uninhabited, and their position marked only by a few ruins. Of these the most important are the remains of the great theatre, and of an amphitheatre of the Roman period. — The government of Syracuse was originally an aristocracy; and the political power was in the hands of the landed proprietors called Geomori or Gamori. In course of time the people, having increased in numbers and wealth, expelled the Geomori and established a democracy. But this form of government did not last long. Gelon espoused the cause of the aristocratical party, and proceeded to restore them by force of arms; but on his approach the people opened the gates to him, and he was acknowledged without opposition tyrant or sovereign of Syracuse, B. C. 485. Under his rule and that of his brother Hieron, Syracuse was raised to an unexampled degree of wealth and prosperity. Hieron died in 467, and was succeeded by his brother Thrasybulus: but the rapacity and cruelty of the latter soon provoked a revolt among his subjects, which led to his deposition and the establishment of a democratical form of government. The next most important event in the history of Syracuse was the siege of the city by the Athenians, which ended in the total destruction of the great Athenian armament in 413. The democracy continued to exist in Syracuse till 406, when the elder Dionysius made himself tyrant of the city. After a long and prosperous reign he was succeeded in 367 by his son, the younger Dionysius, who was finally expelled by Timoleon in 343. A republican form of government was again established; but it did not last long; and in 317 Syracuse fell under the sway of Agathocles. This tyrant died in 289; and the city being distracted by factions, the Syracusans voluntarily conferred the supreme power upon Hieron II., with the title of king, in 270. Hieron cultivated friendly relations with the Romans; but on his death in 216, at the advanced age of 92, his grandson Hieronymus, who succeeded him, espoused the side of the Carthaginians. A Roman army under Marcellus was sent against Syracuse; and after a siege of 2 years, during which Archimedes assisted his fellow-citizens by the construction of various engines of war [ARCHIMEDES], the city was taken by Marcellus in 212. From this time Syracuse became a town of the Roman province of Sicily.

Syrgis (Σύργις), according to Herodotus, a great river of European Sarmatia, rising in the country of the Thyssagetae, and flowing through the land of the Maeotae into the Palus Maeotis. It has not been identified with certainty.

Syria Dea (Συρίη Θεός), "the Syrian goddess," a name by which the Syrian Astarte or Aphrodite is sometimes designated. This Astarte was a Syrian divinity, resembling in many points the Greek Aphrodite. It is not improbable that the latter was originally the Syrian Astarte; for there can be no doubt that the worship of Aphrodite came from the East to Cyprus, and thence was carried into the south of Greece.

Sȳria (ἡ Συρία, in Aramaean Surja: Σύρος, Sȳrus, and sometimes Σύριος, Sȳrius: Soristan, Arab. Esh-Sham, i. e. the land on the left, Syria), a country of W. Asia, lying along the E. end of the Mediterranean Sea, between Asia Minor and Egypt. In a wider sense the word was used for the whole tract of country bounded by the Tigris on the E., the mountains of Armenia and Cilicia on the N., the Mediterranean on the W., and the Arabian Desert on the S.; the whole of which was peopled by the Aramaean branch of the great Semitic (or Syro-Arabian) race, and is included in the O. T. under the name of Aram. This region may be well described physically as the great triangular depression of W. Asia encircled on the N. and N.E. by the Taurus and its prolongation to the S.E., or, in other words, by the highlands of Cilicia, Cappadocia, Armenia, and Aria; and subsiding on the S. and W. into the Mediterranean and the Great Desert of Arabia. Even a wider extent than this is often given to Syria, so as to include the E. part of Asia Minor, as far as the river Halys and the Euxine. The people were of the same races, and those of the N. of the Taurus in Cappadocia and Pontus are called White Syrians [Leucosyri] in contradistinction to the people of darker complexion in Syria Proper, who are sometimes even called Black Syrians (Σύριοι μέλανες). Even when the name of Syria is used in its ordinary narrower sense, it is often confounded with Assyria, which only differs from Syria by having the definite article prefixed. Again, in the narrower sense of the name, Syria still includes 2 districts which are often considered as not belonging to it, namely, Phoenice and Palestine, and a 3rd which is likewise often considered separate, namely, Coelesyria; but this last is generally reckoned a part of Syria. In this narrower sense, then, Syria was bounded on the W. (beginning from the S.) by M. Hermon, at the S. end of Antilibanus, which separated it from Palestine, by the range of Libanus, dividing it from Phoenice, by the Mediterranean, and by M. Amanus, which divided it from Cilicia; on the N. (where it bordered on Cappadocia) by the main chain of M. Taurus, almost exactly along the parallel of 38° N. lat., and striking the Euphrates just below Juliopolis, and considerably above Samosata : hence the Euphrates forms the E. boundary, dividing Syria, first from a very small portion of Armenia, and then from Mesopotamia, to about or beyond the 36th parallel of N. lat., whence the S.E. and S. boundaries, towards Babylonia and Arabia, in the Great Desert, are exceedingly indefinite. [Comp. Arabia.] The W. part of the S. boundary ran just below Damascus, being formed by the highlands of Trachonitis. The W. part of the country was intersected by a series of mountains, running S. from the Taurus, under the names of Amanus, Pieria, Casius, Bargylus, and Libanus, and Antilibanus ; and the N. part, between the Amanus and the Euphrates, was also mountainous. The chief river of Syria was the Orontes, and the smaller rivers Chalus and Chrysorrhoas were also of importance. The valleys among the mountains were fertile, especially in the N. part: even the E., which is now merged in the great desert of Arabia, appears to have had more numerous and more extensive spaces capable of culti-

vation, and supported great cities, the ruins of which now stand in the midst of sandy wastes. — In the earliest historical period, Syria contained a number of independent kingdoms, of which Damascus was the most powerful. These were subdued by David, but became again independent at the end of Solomon's reign ; from which time we find the kings of Damascus sometimes at war with the kings of Israel, and sometimes in alliance with them against the kings of Judah, till the reign of Tiglath-Pileser, king of Assyria, who, having been invited by Ahaz, king of Judah, to assist him against the united forces of Rezin, king of Syria, and Pekah, king of Israel, took Damascus and probably conquered all Syria, about B. c. 740. Having been a part successively of the Assyrian, Babylonian, Persian, and Macedonian empires, it fell, after the battle of Ipsus (B. c. 301), to the share of Seleucus Nicator, and formed a part of the great kingdom of the Seleucidae, whose history is given in the articles Seleucus, Antiochus, Demetrius, &c. In this partition, however, Coelesyria and Palestine went, not to Syria, but to Egypt, and the possession of those provinces became the great source of contention between the Ptolemies and the Seleucidae. By the irruptions of the Parthians on the E., and the unsuccessful war of Antiochus the Great with the Romans on the W., the Greek Syrian kingdom was reduced to the limits of Syria itself, and became weaker and weaker, until it was overthrown by Tigranes, king of Armenia, B. c. 79. Soon afterwards, when the Romans had conquered Tigranes as well as Mithridates, Syria was quietly added by Pompey to the empire of the republic and was constituted a province, B. c. 64; but its N. district, Commagene, was not included in this arrangement. As the E. province of the Roman empire, and with its great desert frontier, Syria was constantly exposed to the irruptions of the Parthians, and, after them, of the Persians ; but it long remained one of the most flourishing of the provinces. The attempt of Zenobia to make it the seat of empire is noticed under Palmyra and Zenobia. While the Roman emperors defended this precious possession against the attacks of the Persian kings with various success, a new danger arose, as early as the 4th century, from the Arabians of the Desert, who began to be known under the name of Saracens; and, when the rise of Mohammed had given to the Arabs that great religious impulse which revolutionised the E. World, Syria was the first great conquest that they made from the E. empire, A. D. 632—638. — In the time immediately succeeding the Macedonian conquest, Syria was regarded as consisting of 2 parts; the N., including the whole country down to the beginning of the Lebanon range, and the S., consisting of Coelesyria in its more extended sense. The former, which was called Syria Proper, or Upper Syria (ἡ ἄνω Συρία, Syria Superior), was divided into 4 districts or tetrarchies, which were named after their respective capitals, Seleucis, Antiochēne, Laodicēne, and Apamēne. Under the Romans it was divided into 10 districts, named (mostly after their capital cities) Commagēne, Cyrrhesticē, Pieria, Seleucis, Chalcidicē, Chalybonitis, Palmyrēne, Apamēne, Cassiōtis, and Laodicēne ; but the last is sometimes included under Cassiotis. (See the several articles.) Constantine the Great separated from Syria the 2 N. districts, namely, Commagene and Cyrrhestice, and erected them into a distinct province, called Euphratensis or Euphratesia; and the rest of Syria was afterwards divided by Theodosius II. into the 2 provinces of Syria Prima, including the sea-coast and the country N. of Antioch, and having that city for its capital; and Syria Secunda, the district along the Orontes, with Apamea for its capital: the E. districts no longer formed a part of Syria, but had fallen under the power of the Persians.

Syriae Portae (*al Συρίαι πύλαι: Pass of Beilan*), a most important pass between Cilicia and Syria, lying between the shore of the Gulf of Issus on the W., and M. Amanus on the E. Xenophon, who called the pass (or rather its fortifications) the *Gates of Cilicia and of Syria*, describes it as 3 stadia in length and very narrow, with walls built from the mountains to the sea at both ends (the Cilician and the Syrian), and gates in the walls (*Anab.* i. 4.). These walls and gates are not mentioned by the historians of Alexander.

Syriānus (Συριανός), a Greek philosopher of the Neo-Platonic school, was a native of Alexandria, and studied at Athens under Plutarchus, whom he succeeded as head of the Neo-Platonic school in the early part of the 5th century. The most distinguished of his disciples was Proclus, who regarded him with the greatest veneration, and gave directions that at his death he should be buried in the same tomb with Syrianus. Syrianus wrote several works, some of which are extant. Of these the most valuable are the commentaries on the Metaphysics of Aristotle.

Syrinx, an Arcadian nymph, who being pursued by Pan, fled into the river Ladon, and at her own request was metamorphosed into a reed, of which Pan then made his flute.

Syrinx (Σύριγξ), a great and strongly fortified city of Hyrcania, and the capital of the province under the Greek kings of Syria. Perhaps it is only the Greek name of the city called, in the native language, Zadrakarta.

Syros, or **Syrus** (Σῦρος, called Συρίη by Homer, and Σύρα by a few writers: Σύριος: *Syra*), an island in the Aegaean sea, and one of the Cyclades, lying between Rhenea and Cythnus. It is described by the ancients as 20 Roman miles in circumference, and as rich in pastures, wine, and corn. It contained 2 towns, one on the E. side, and one on the W. side of the island; of the latter there are still remains near the modern harbour of *Maria della Grazia*. The philosopher Pherecydes was a native of Syros.

Syrtes, gen. -ĭdos (Σύρτις, gen. -ιδος and -εως, Ion. -ιος), the Greek name for each of the 2 great gulfs in the E. half of the N. coast of Africa, is derived by ancient writers from σύρω, *to draw*, with reference to the quicksands by which, in the Greater Syrtis at least, ships were liable to be swallowed up; but modern scholars generally prefer the derivation from the Arabic *sert = a sandy desert*, which is at the present day applied to the country along this coast, the REGIO SYRTICA of the ancients. Both were proverbially dangerous, the Greater Syrtis from its sandbanks and quicksands, and its unbroken exposure to the N. winds, the Lesser from its shelving rocky shores, its exposure to the N.E. winds, and the consequent variableness of the tides in it. 1. **Syrtis Major** (ἡ μεγάλη Σύρτις: *Gulf of Sidra*), the E. of the 2, is a wide and deep gulf on the shores of Tripolita and Cyrenaica, exactly opposite to the Ionic

sea, or mouth of the Adriatic, between Sicily and Peloponnesus. Its greatest depth, from N. to S., is about 110 geographical miles; its width is about 230 geographical miles, between Cephalae Prom. (*Ras Kharra*) on the W., and Boreum Prom. (*Ras Teyonas*) on the E. (Strabo gives its width as 1500 stadia, its depth 1500 to 1800, and its circuit 4000 to 5000). The Great Desert comes down close to its shores, forming a sandy coast [SYRTICA REGIO]. The terror of being driven on shore in it is referred to in the narrative of St. Paul's voyage to Italy (Acts, xxvii. 17. "fearing lest they should fall *into the Syrtis*"); and the dangers of a march through the loose sand on its shores, sometimes of a burning heat, and sometimes saturated with sea-water, were scarcely less formidable. — **Syrtis Minor** (ἡ μικρὰ Σύρτις: *Gulf of Khabs*), lies in the S.W. angle of the great bend formed by the N. coast of Africa as it drops down to the S. from the neighbourhood of Carthage, and then bears again to the E.: in other words, in the angle between the E. coast of Zeugitana and Byzacena (*Tunis*) and the N coast of Tripolitana (*Tripoli*). Its mouth faces the E., between Caput Vada or Brachodes Prom. (*Ras Kapoudiah*) on the N., and the island called Meninx or Lotophagitis (*Jerbah*) on the S. In its mouth, near the N. extremity, lie the islands of Cercina and Cercinitis, which were often regarded as its N. extremity. Its dimensions are differently given, partly perhaps on account of the different points from which they were reckoned. The Greek geographers give the width as 600 stadia (60 geog. miles), and the circuit 1600 stadia: the Romans give 100 Roman miles for the width, and 300 for the circuit. The true width (between *Ras Kapoudiah* and the E. point of *Jerbah*) is about 80 geog. miles, and the greatest depth, measured W.-ward from the line joining those points, is about 65 geog. miles. In Herodotus, the word Syrtis occurs in a few passages, without any distinction between the Greater and the Less. It seems most probable that he means to denote by this term the Greater Syrtis, and that he included the Lesser in the lake TRITONIS.

Syrtĭca Regĭo (ἡ Συρτική: W. part of *Tripoli*), the special name of that part of the N. coast of Africa which lay between the 2 Syrtes, from the river Triton, at the bottom of the Syrtis Minor, on the W., to the Philaenorum Arae, at the bottom of the Syrtis Major, on the E. It was for the most part a very narrow strip of sand, interspersed with salt marshes, between the sea and a range of mountains forming the edge of the Great Desert (*Sahara*), with only here and there a few spots capable of cultivation, especially about the river Cinyps. It was peopled by Libyan tribes, the chief of whom were the Lotophagi, Macae, Psylli, and Nasamones; and several Egyptian and Phoenician colonies were settled on the coast at an early period. The Greeks of Cyrene disputed with the Carthaginians the possession of this district until it was secured to Carthage by the self-devotion of the PHILAENI. Under the Romans it formed a part of the province of Africa. It was often called Tripolitana, from its 3 chief cities, ABROTONUM, OEA, and LEPTIS MAGNA; and this became its usual name under the later empire, and has been handed down to our own time in the modern name of the Regency of *Tripoli*,

Syrus, a slave brought to Rome some years before the downfal of the republic, and designated, according to the usual practice, from the country of his birth. He attracted attention while yet a youth, by his accomplishment and wit, was manumitted by his master, who probably belonged to the Clodia gens, assumed the name of *Publius*, from his patron, and soon became highly celebrated as a mimographer. He may be said to have flourished B. C. 45. His mimes were committed to writing, and extensively circulated at an early period; and a collection of pithy moral sayings extracted from his works appears to have been used as a school-book in the boyhood of St. Jerome. A compilation of this description, extending to upwards of 1000 lines in iambic and trochaic measures, every apophthegm being comprised in a single line, and the whole ranged alphabetically, according to the initial letter of the first word in each, is now extant under the title *Publis Syri Sententiae*. These proverbs have been drawn from various sources, and are evidently the work of many different hands; but a considerable number may be ascribed to Syrus and his contemporaries. The best editions of the *Sententiae* are by Havercamp, Lug. Bat. 1708, 1727; by Orelli, Lips. 1822; and by Bothe, in his *Poetarum Latin. Scenicorum Fragmenta*, Lips. 1834.

Sythas (Σύθας), a river on the frontiers of Achaia and Sicyonia.

T.

Tabae (Τάβαι: Ταβηνός). **1.** (*Tavi*), a small inland town of Sicily.—**2.** (*Davas*), a city of Caria, on the borders of Phrygia.—**3.** A city of Persia, in the district of Paraetacene, on the road from Ecbatana to Persepolis.

Tabernae. [TRES TABERNAE.]

Taburnus (*Taburno*), a mountain belonging half to Campania and half to Samnium. Its S. side was very fertile, and was celebrated for its olive grounds. It shut in the Caudine pass on its S. side.

Tacape (Ταχάπη: *Khabs*, large Ru.), a city of N. Africa, in the Regio Syrtica, at the innermost angle of the Syrtis Minor, to which the modern town gives its name. Under the Romans, it at first belonged to Byzacena, but it was afterwards raised to a colony and made the W. town of Tripolitana. It had an indifferent harbour. A little to the W. was the bathing place, called, from its warm mineral springs, Aquae Tacipitanae (*El Hammat-el-Khabs*).

Tacfarinas, a Numidian in the reign of Tiberius, had originally served among the auxiliary troops in the Roman army, but he deserted; and, having collected a body of freebooters, he became at length the acknowledged leader of the Musulamii, a powerful people in the interior of Numidia, bordering on Mauretania. For some years he defied the Roman arms, but was at length defeated and slain in battle by Dolabella, A. D. 24.

Tachompso (Ταχομψώ, also Tacompsos, Plin., and Μετακομψώ, Ptol.), aft. Contrapselcis, a city in the Dodecaschoenus, that is, the part of Aethiopia immediately above Egypt, built on an island (*Derar?*) near the E. bank of the river, a little above Pselcis, which stood on the opposite bank. [PSELCIS.]

Tachos (Ταχώς), king of Egypt, succeeded Acoris, and maintained the independence of his country for a short time during the latter end of the reign of Artaxerxes II. He invited Chabrias, the Athenian, to take the command of his fleet, and Agesilaus to undertake the supreme command of all his forces. Both Chabrias and Agesilaus came to Egypt; but the latter was much aggrieved in having only the command of the mercenaries entrusted to him. Accordingly, when Nectanabis laid claim to the Egyptian crown, Agesilaus deserted Tachos, and espoused the cause of Nectanabis, who thus became king of Egypt, B. C. 361.

Tacitus. **1.** C. **Cornelius**, the historian. The time and place of his birth are unknown. He was a little older than the younger Pliny, who was born A. D. 61. His father was probably Cornelius Tacitus, a Roman eques, who is mentioned as a procurator in Gallia Belgica, and who died in 79. Tacitus was first promoted by the emperor Vespasian, and he received other favours from his sons Titus and Domitian. In 78 he married the daughter of C. Julius Agricola, to whom he had been betrothed in the preceding year, while Agricola was consul. In the reign of Domitian, and in 88, Tacitus was praetor, and he assisted as one of the quindecemviri at the solemnity of the Ludi Seculares which were celebrated in that year. Agricola died at Rome in 93, but neither Tacitus nor the daughter of Agricola was then with him. It is not known where Tacitus was during the last illness of Agricola. In the reign of Nerva, 97, Tacitus was appointed consul suffectus, in the place of T. Virginius Rufus, who had died in that year, and whose funeral oration he delivered. We know that Tacitus had attained oratorical distinction when the younger Pliny was commencing his career. He and Tacitus were appointed in the reign of Nerva (99) to conduct the prosecution of Marius, proconsul of Africa. Tacitus and Pliny were most intimate friends. In the collection of the letters of Pliny, there are 11 letters addressed to Tacitus. The time of the death of Tacitus is unknown, but he appears to have survived Trajan, who died 117. Nothing is recorded of any children of his, though the emperor Tacitus claimed a descent from the historian, and ordered his works to be placed in all (public) libraries. The following are the extant works of Tacitus: **1.** *Vita Agricolae*, the life of Agricola, which was written after the death of Domitian, 96, as we may probably conclude from the introduction, which was certainly written after Trajan's accession. This life is justly admired as a specimen of biography. It is a monument to the memory of a good man and an able commander and administrator, by an affectionate son-in-law, who has portrayed in his peculiar manner and with many masterly touches, the virtues of one of the most illustrious of the Romans. **2.** *Historiae*, which were written after the death of Nerva, 98, and before the Annales. They comprehended the period from the second consulship of Galba, 68, to the death of Domitian, 96, and the author designed to add the reigns of Nerva and Trajan. The first 4 books alone are extant in a complete form, and they comprehend only the events of about one year. The 5th book is imperfect, and goes no further than the commencement of the siege of Jerusalem by Titus, and the war of Civilis in Germany. It is not known how many books of the Historics there were, but it must have been a large work, if it was all written on the same scale as the first 5 books. — 3. *Annales*, which commence with the death of Augustus, 14, and comprise the period to the death of Nero, 68, a space of 54 years. The greater part of the 5th book is lost; and also the 7th, 8th, 9th, 10th, the beginning of the 11th, and the end of the 16th, which is the last book. These lost parts comprised the whole of Caligula's reign, the first 5 years of Claudius, and the 2 last of Nero. — 4. *De Moribus et Populis Germaniae*, a treatise describing the Germanic nations. It is of no value, as a geographical description; the first few chapters contain as much of the geography of Germany as Tacitus knew. The main matter is the description of the political institutions, the religion, and the habits, of the various tribes included under the denomination of Germani. The value of the information contained in this treatise has often been discussed, and its credibility attacked; but we may estimate its true character by observing the precision of the writer as to those Germans who were best known to the Romans from being near the Rhine. That the hearsay accounts of more remote tribes must partake of the defects of all such evidence, is obvious; and we cannot easily tell whether Tacitus embellished that which he heard obscurely told. But to consider the Germany as a fiction, is one of those absurdities which need only be recorded, not refuted. — 5. *Dialogus de Oratoribus*. If this dialogue is the work of Tacitus, and it probably is, it must be his earliest work, for it was written in the 6th year of Vespasian (c. 17). The style is more easy than that of the Annals, more diffuse, less condensed; but there is no obvious difference between the style of this Dialogue and the Histories, nothing so striking as to make us contend for a different authorship. Besides this, it is nothing unusual for works of the same author which are written at different times to vary greatly in style, especially if they treat of different matters. The old MSS. attribute this Dialogue to Tacitus. — The Annals of Tacitus, the work of a mature age, contain the chief events of the period which they embrace, arranged under their several years. There seems no peculiar propriety in giving the name of *Annales* to this work, simply because the events are arranged in the order of time. The work of Livy may just as well be called Annals. In the Annals of Tacitus the Princeps or Emperor is the centre about which events are grouped. Yet the most important public events, both in Italy and the provinces, are not omitted, though every thing is treated as subordinate to the exhibition of imperial power. The Histories, which were written before the Annals, are in a more diffuse style, and the treatment of the extant part is different from that of the Annals. Tacitus wrote the Histories as a contemporary; the Annals as not a contemporary. They are two distinct works, not parts of one; which is clearly shown by the very different proportions of the two works: the first 4 books of the Histories comprise about a year, and the first 4 books of the Annals comprise 14 years. The moral dignity of Tacitus is impressed upon his works; the consciousness of a love of truth, of the integrity of his purpose. His great power is in the knowledge of the human mind, his insight into the motives of human conduct; and he found materials for this study in the history of the emperors, and particularly Tiberius, the arch-hypocrite, and perhaps half madman. His Annals are filled with drama-

tic scenes and striking catastrophes. He laboured to produce effect by the exhibition of great personages on the stage; but as to the mass of the people we learn little from Tacitus. — The style of Tacitus is peculiar, though it bears some resemblance to Sallust. In the Annals it is concise, vigorous, and pregnant with meaning; laboured, but elaborated with art, and stripped of every superfluity. A single word sometimes gives effect to a sentence, and if the meaning of the word is missed, the sense of the writer is not reached. Such a work is probably the result of many transcriptions by the author. In the Annals Tacitus is generally brief and rapid in his sketches; but he is sometimes minute, and almost tedious, when he comes to work out a dramatic scene. Nor does he altogether neglect his rhetorical art when he has an opportunity for displaying it. The condensed style of Tacitus sometimes makes him obscure, but it is a kind of obscurity that is dispelled by careful reading. Yet a man must read carefully and often, in order to understand him; and we cannot suppose that Tacitus was ever a popular writer. His real admirers will perhaps always be few; his readers fewer still. The best editions of the complete works of Tacitus are by Oberlin, Lips. 1801, 2 vols. 8vo.; by Bekker, Lips. 1831, 2 vols. 8vo.; and by Orelli, Zürich, 1846 and 1848, 2 vols. 8vo. — 2. M. Claudius, Roman emperor from the 25th September, A. D. 275, until April, A. D. 276. He was elected emperor by the senate after the death of Aurelian, the army having requested the senate to nominate a successor to the imperial throne. Tacitus was at the time 70 years of age, and was with difficulty persuaded to accept the purple. The high character which he had borne before his elevation to the throne, he amply sustained during his brief reign. He endeavoured to repress the luxury and licentiousness of the age by various sumptuary laws, and he himself set an example to all around, by the abstemiousness, simplicity, and frugality of his own habits. The only military achievement of this reign was the defeat and expulsion from Asia Minor of a party of Goths, who had carried their devastation across the peninsula to the confines of Cilicia. He died either at Tarsus or at Tyana, about the 9th of April, 276.

Taenărum (*Ταίναρον*: *C. Matapan*), a promontory in Laconica, forming the S.-ly point of the Peloponnesus, on which stood a celebrated temple of Poseidon, possessing an inviolable asylum. A little to the N. of the temple and the harbour of Achilleus was a town also called **Taenarum** or **Taenarus**, and at a later time **Caenĕpŏlis**. It was situated 40 stadia from the extreme point of the promontory, and was said to have been built by Taenarus, a son of Zeus, or Icarius or Elatus. On this promontory was a cave, through which Hercules is said to have dragged Cerberus to the upper world. Here also was a statue of Arion seated on a dolphin, since he is said to have landed at this spot after his miraculous preservation by a dolphin. In the time of the Romans there were celebrated marble quarries on the promontory.

Tagae (*Ταγαί*: *Dameghan?*), a city mentioned by Polybius as in Parthia, on the border towards Hyrcania, apparently the same place which Strabo calls **Tapo** (*Τάπη*) and reckons to Hyrcania.

Tagaste (*Tagilt*, Ru.), an inland town of Numidia, on a tributary of the Bagradas, remarkable as the birthplace of St. Augustine.

Tages, a mysterious Etruscan being, who is described as a boy with the wisdom of an old man. Once when an Etruscan, of the name of Tarchon, was ploughing in the neighbourhood of Tarquinii, there suddenly rose out of the ground Tages, the son of a Genius Jovialis, and grandson of Jupiter. When Tages addressed Tarchon, the latter shrieked with fear, whereupon other Etruscans hastened to him, and in a short time all the people of Etruria were assembled around him. Tages now instructed them in the art of the haruspices, and died immediately after. The Etruscans, who had listened attentively to his instructions, afterwards wrote down all he had said, and thus arose the books of Tages, which, according to some, were 12 in number.

Tagus (Spanish *Tajo*, Portuguese *Tejo*, English *Tagus*), one of the chief rivers in Spain, rising in the land of the Celtiberians, between the mountains Orospeda and Idubeda, and, after flowing in a W.-ly direction, falling into the Atlantic. The whole course of the Tagus exceeds 550 English miles. At its mouth stood Olisippo (*Lisbon*). The ancient writers relate that much gold sand and precious stone were found in the Tagus.

Talabriga, a town in Lusitania, between Aeminium and Lagobriga.

Talassius or **Talasses**. [THALASSIUS.]

Talaura (τὰ Τάλαυρα : *Turkhal ?*), a fortress in Pontus, used by Mithridates the Great as a residence, and supposed by some to be identical with Gaziura.

Talaus (Τάλαος), son of Bias and Pero, and king of Argos. He was married to Lysimache (Eurynome, or Lysianassa), and was father of Adrastus, Parthenopaeus, Pronax, Mecisteus, Aristomachus, and Eriphyle. He occurs among the Argonauts, and his tomb was shown at Argos. The patronymic *Talaionides* (Ταλαϊονίδης) is given to his sons, Adrastus and Mecisteus.

Talmis (*El-Kalabsheh*, Ru.), a city of the Dodecaschoenus, that is, the district of Aethiopia immediately above Egypt, stood on the W. bank of the Nile, S. of Taphis, and N. of Tutzis. Its ruins consist of an ancient rock-hewn temple, with splendid sculptures, and of a later temple of the Roman period, in the midst of which stands the modern village. There was a place on the opposite bank called Contra Talmis.

Talna, Juventius. [THALNA.]

Talos (Τάλως). 1. Son of Perdix, the sister of Daedalus. For details see PERDIX. — 2. A man of brass, the work of Hephaestus. This wonderful being was given to Minos by Zeus or Hephaestus, and watched the island of Crete by walking round the island thrice every day. Whenever he saw strangers approaching, he made himself red hot in fire, and then embraced the strangers when they landed.

Talthybius (Ταλθύβιος), the herald of Agamemnon at Troy. He was worshipped as a hero at Sparta and Argos, where sacrifices also were offered to him.

Tamara. 1. Or **Tamaris** (*Tambre*), a small river in Hispania Tarraconensis, on the coast of Gallaecia, falling into the Atlantic between the Minius and the Prom. Nerium. — 2. (*Tamerton* near Plymouth), a town of the Damnonii in the S. of Britain, at the mouth of the Tamarus.

Tamarici, a people in Gallaecia, on the river Tamara.

Tamaris. [TAMARA.]

Tamarus (*Tamar*), a river in the S. of Britain.

Tamassus or **Tamāsus** (Ταμασσός, Τάμασος : Ταμασίτης, Ταμάσιος), probably the same as the Homeric **Temese** (Τεμέση), a town in the middle of Cyprus, N. W. of Olympus, and 29 miles S. E. of Soloë, on the road from the latter place to Tremithus, was situated in a fertile country and in the neighbourhood of extensive copper mines. Near it was a celebrated plain (*ager Tamaseus*), sacred to Venus. (Ov. *Met.* x. 644.)

Tambrax (Τάμβραξ), a great city of Hyrcania, on the N. side of Mt. Coronus, mentioned by Polybius. It is perhaps the same place which Strabo calls Ταλαβρόκη.

Tamesis or **Tamesa** (*Thames*), a river in Britain flowing into the sea on the E. coast, on which stood Londinium. Caesar crossed the Thames at the distance of 80 Roman miles from the sea, probably at Cowey Stakes, near Oatlands and the confluence of the Wey. There have been found in modern times in the ford of the river at this spot large stakes, which are supposed to have been the same as were fixed in the water by Cassivellaunus, when he attempted to prevent Caesar from crossing the river.

Tamna (Τάμνα), a very great city in the S.W. of Arabia Felix, the capital of the Catabani. It maintained a caravan traffic, in spices and other products of Arabia, with Gaza, from which its distance was reckoned 1436 Roman miles.

Tamos (Ταμώς), a native of Memphis in Egypt, was lieutenant-governor of Ionia under Tissaphernes. He afterwards attached himself to the service of the younger Cyrus ; upon whose death, he sailed to Egypt, where he hoped to find refuge with Psammetichus, on whom he had conferred an obligation. Psammetichus, however, put him to death, in order to possess himself of his money and ships.

Tamphilus or **Tampilus, Baebius.** 1. Cn., tribune of the plebs, B. C. 204 ; praetor 199, when he was defeated by the Insubrians ; and consul 182, when he fought against the Ligurians with success. — 2. M., brother of the last, was praetor 192, and served in Greece both in this year and the following, in the war against Antiochus. In 181 he was consul, when he defeated the Ligurians.

Tamynae (Ταμύναι), a town in Euboea, on Mt. Cotylaeum, in the territory of Eretria, with a temple of Apollo, said to have been built by Admetus. Here the Athenians under Phocion gained a celebrated victory over Callias of Chalcis, B. c 354.

Tamyraca, a town and promontory of European Sarmatia at the innermost corner of the Sinus Carcinites, which was also called from this town Sinus Tamyraces.

Tamyras or **Damuras** (Ταμύρας, Δαμούρας : *Damur*, or *Nahr-el-Kadi*), a little river of Phoenicia, rising on Mt. Libanus, and falling into the Mediterranean about half way between Sidon and Berytus.

Tanager (*Negro*), a river of Lucania, rising in the Apennines, which, after flowing in a N.E.-ly direction, loses itself under the earth near Polla for a space of about 2 miles, and finally falls into the Silarus near Forum Popilii.

Tanagra (Τάναγρα : Ταναγραῖος : *Grimadha* or *Grimala*), a celebrated town of Boeotia, situated on a steep ascent on the left bank of the Asopus, 13 stadia from Oropus, and 200 stadia from Platasae, in the district Tanagraea, which was also called Poemandris. Tanagra was supposed to be the same town as the Homeric Graea. The most ancient inhabitants are said to have been the Gephyraei, who came with Cadmus from Phoenicia; but it was afterwards taken possession of by the Aeolian Boeotians. It was a place of considerable commercial importance, and was celebrated, among other things, for its breed of fighting cocks. At a later time it belonged to the Boeotian confederacy. Being near the frontiers of Attica, it was frequently exposed to the attacks of the Athenians; and near it the Athenians sustained a celebrated defeat, B. C. 457.

Tănăĭs (Tάναῖς). **1.** (*Don*, i. e. *Water*), a great river, which rises in the N. of Sarmatia Europaea (about the centre of *Russia*), and flows to the S. E. till it comes near the *Volga*, when it turns to the S. W., and falls into the N. E. angle of the Palus Maeotis (*Sea of Azov*) by 2 principal mouths and several smaller ones. It was usually considered the boundary between Europe and Asia. Its chief tributary was the Hyrgis or Syrgis (prob. *Donets*). — **2.** (Ru. near *Kussatchei*), a city of Sarmatia Asiatica, on the N. side of the S. mouth of the Tanaïs, at a little distance from the sea. It was founded by a colony from Miletus, and became a very flourishing emporium. It reduced to subjection several of the neighbouring tribes, but in its turn it became subject to the kings of Bosporus. It was destroyed by Polemon on account of an attempted revolt, and, though afterwards restored, it never regained its former prosperity.

Tănăquil. [TARQUINIUS.]

Tanetum (Tanetanus: *Taneto*), a town of the Boii in Gallia Cispadana, between Mutina and Parma.

Tănis (Tάνις; O. T. Zoan: Tανίτης: *San*, Ru.), a very ancient city of Lower Egypt, in the E. part of the Delta, on the right bank of the arm of the Nile, which was called after it the Tanitic, and on the S. W. side of the great lake between this and the Pelusiac branch of the Nile, which was also called, after the city, Tanis (*Lake of Menzaleh*). It was one of the capitals of Lower Egypt under the early kings, and was said by tradition to have been the residence of the court in the time of Moses. It was the chief city of the Tanites Nomos.

Tantălus (Tάνταλος). **1.** Son of Zeus and Pluto. His wife is called by some Euryanassa, by others Taygete or Dione, and by others Clytia or Eupryto. He was the father of Pelops, Broteas, and Niobe. All traditions agree in stating that he was a wealthy king, but while some call him king of Lydia, others describe him as king of Argos or Corinth. Tantalus is particularly celebrated in ancient story for the terrible punishment inflicted upon him after his death in the lower world, the causes of which are differently stated by the ancient authors. According to the common account Zeus invited him to his table, and communicated his divine counsels to him. Tantalus divulged the secrets thus intrusted to him; and he was punished in the lower world by being afflicted with a raging thirst, and at the same time placed in the midst of a lake, the waters of which always receded from him as soon as he attempted to drink them. Over his head, moreover, hung branches of fruit, which receded in like manner when he stretched out his hand to reach

them. In addition to all this there was suspended over his head a huge rock ever threatening to crush him. Another tradition relates that, wishing to test the gods, he cut his son Pelops in pieces, boiled them and set them before the gods at a repast. A third account states that Tantalus stole nectar and ambrosia from the table of the gods and gave them to his friends; and a fourth lastly relates the following story. Rhea caused the infant Zeus and his nurse to be guarded in Crete by a golden dog, whom Zeus afterwards appointed guardian of his temple in Crete. Pandareus stole this dog, and, carrying him to Mount Sipylus in Lydia, gave him to Tantalus to take care of. But when Pandareus demanded the dog back, Tantalus took an oath that he had never received it. Zeus thereupon changed Pandareus into a stone, and threw Tantalus down from Mount Sipylus. Others again relate that Hermes demanded the dog of Tantalus, and that the perjury was committed before Hermes. Zeus buried Tantalus under Mount Sipylus as a punishment; and there his tomb was shown in later times. The punishment of Tantalus was proverbial in ancient times, and from it the English language has borrowed the verb "to tantalize," that is, to hold out hopes or prospects which cannot be realised. — The patronymic *Tantalides* is frequently given to the descendants of Tantalus. Hence we find not only his son Pelops, but also Atreus, Thyestes, Agamemnon, Menelaus, and Orestes called by this name. — **2.** Son of Thyestes, who was killed by Atreus. Others call him a son of Broteas. He was married to Clytaemnestra before Agamemnon, and is said by some to have been killed by Agamemnon. — **3.** Son of Amphion and Niobe.

Tanus or **Tanaus** (Tάνος or Tαναός: *Kani*), a river in the district of Thyreatis, on the E. coast of Peloponnesus, rising in Mt. Parnon, and falling into the Thyreatic gulf, after forming the boundary between Argolis and Cynuria.

Taŏĕ (Tαόκη: *Bunder-Reight*), a city on the coast of Persis, near the mouth of the river Granis, used occasionally as a royal residence. The surrounding district was called Tαοκηνή.

Taŏchi (Tάοχοι), a people of Pontus, on the borders of Armenia, frequently mentioned by Xenophon in the *Anabasis*.

Tapě. [TAGAE.]

Taphiae Insulae, a number of small islands in the Ionian sea, lying between the coasts of Leucadia and Acarnania. They were also called the islands of the Teleboae, and their inhabitants were in like manner named **Taphĭi** (Tάφιοι) or **Teleboae** (Tηλεβόαι). The largest of these islands is called **Taphus** (Tάφος) by Homer, but **Taphiûs** (Tαφιοῦς) or **Taphiûsa** (Tαφιοῦσα) by later writers. They are mentioned in Homer as the haunts of notorious pirates, and are celebrated in mythology on account of the war carried on between them and Electryon, king of Mycenae.

Taphiassus (Tαφιασσός: *Macrivoro* and *Rigani*), a mountain in Aetolia and Locris, properly only a S. W. continuation of Mts. Oeta and Corax.

Taphis (*Tapa*, Ru.), a city of the Dodecaschoenus, that is, the district of Aethiopia immediately above Egypt, stood on the W. bank of the Nile, S. of Tzitzis, and N. of Talmis. It is also called Tαθίς and Παγίς. There was a town on the opposite bank, called Contra Taphis.

Tāphrae or **Tāphros** (Τάφραι or Τάφρος : Τάφριος), a town on the isthmus of the Chersonesus Taurica, so called because a trench or ditch was cut across the isthmus at this point.

Taphus. [TAPHIAE.]

Taposiris (Ταπόσειρις, Ταπόσιρις, Ταφόσιρις, i. e. the tomb of Osiris : Abousir, Ru.), a city of Lower Egypt, on the N.W. frontier, in the Libya Nomos, near the base of the long tongue of land on which Alexandria stood, celebrated for its claim to be considered the burial-place of Osiris. Mention is also made of a Lesser Taposiris (ἡ μικρὰ Ταπόσειρις) near it.

Taprŏbănē (Ταπροβάνη : Ceylon), a great island of the Indian Ocean, opposite to the S. extremity of India intra Gangem. The Greeks first became acquainted with it through the researches of Onesicritus in the time of Alexander, and through information obtained by residents in India; and the Roman geographers acquired additional knowledge respecting the island through an embassy which was sent from it to Rome in the reign of Claudius. Of the accounts given of it by the ancients, it is only necessary here to state that Ptolemy makes it very much too large, while, on the other hand, he gives much too small a S.-ward extension to the peninsula of India.

Tāpŭri (Τάπουροι or Ταπουροί), a powerful people, apparently of Scythian origin, who dwelt in Media, on the borders of Parthia, S. of M. Coronus. They also extended into Margiana, and probably further N. on the E. side of the Caspian, where their original abodes seem to have been in the mountains called by their name. The men wore black clothes and long hair, and the women white clothes and hair cut close. They were much addicted to drunkenness.

Tāpŭri Montes (τὰ Τάπουρα ὄρη), a range of mountains on the E. of the Caspian sea, inhabited by the TAPURI.

Tăras. [TARENTUM.]

Tarbelli, one of the most important people in Gallia Aquitanica, between the Ocean (hence called Tarbellicum aequor and Tarbellus Oceanus) and the Pyrenees (hence called Tarbella Pyrene). Their country was sandy and unproductive, but contained gold and mineral springs. Their chief town was Aquae Tarbellicae or Augustae, on the Aturus (Dacqs on the Adour).

Tarchon, son of Tyrrhenus, who is said to have built the town of Tarquinii. [TARQUINII.] Virgil represents him as coming to the assistance of Aeneas against Turnus.

Tărentinus Sinus (Ταρεντῖνος κόλπος : G. of Tarentum), a great gulf in the S. of Italy, between Bruttium, Lucania, and Calabria, beginning W. near the Prom. Lacinium, and ending E. near the Prom. Iapygium, and named after the town of Tarentum. According to Strabo, it is 1920 stadia in circuit, and the entrance to it is 700 stadia wide.

Tărentum, called **Taras** by the Greeks (Τάρας, -αντος : Ταρεντῖνος, Tarentinus : Taranto), an important Greek city in Italy, situated on the W. coast of the peninsula of Calabria, and on a bay of the sea, about 100 stadia in circuit, forming an excellent harbour, and being a portion of the great Gulf of Tarentum. The city stood in the midst of a beautiful and fertile country, S. of Mt. Aulon and W. of the mouth of the Galaesus. It was originally built by the Iapygians, who are said to have been joined

by some Cretan colonists from the neighbouring town of Uria, and it derived its name from the mythical Taras, a son of Poseidon. The greatness of Tarentum, however, dates from B. C. 708, when the original inhabitants were expelled, and the town was taken possession of by a strong body of Lacedaemonian Partheniae under the guidance of Phalanthus [PHALANTHUS]. It soon became the most powerful and flourishing city in the whole of Magna Graecia, and exercised a kind of supremacy over the other Greek cities in Italy. It carried on an extensive commerce, possessed a considerable fleet of ships of war, and was able to bring into the field, with the assistance of its allies, an army of 30,000 foot and 3,000 horse. The city itself in its most flourishing period contained 22,000 men capable of bearing arms. The government of Tarentum was different at various periods. In the time of Darius Hystaspis, Herodotus speaks of a king (i. e. a tyrant) of Tarentum; but at a later period the government was a democracy. Archytas, who was born at Tarentum, and who lived about B. C. 400, drew up a code of laws for his native city. With the increase of wealth the citizens became luxurious and effeminate, and being hard pressed by the Lucanians and other barbarians in the neighbourhood, they were obliged to apply for aid to the mother-country. Archidamus, son of Agesilaus, was the first who came to their assistance in B. C. 338; and he fell in battle fighting on their behalf. The next prince whom they invited to succour them, was Alexander, king of Epirus, and uncle to Alexander the Great. At first he met with considerable success, but was eventually defeated and slain by the Bruttii in 326 near Pandosia on the banks of the Acheron. Shortly afterwards the Tarentines had to encounter a still more formidable enemy. Having attacked some Roman ships, and then grossly insulted the Roman ambassadors who had been sent to demand reparation, war was declared against the city by the powerful republic. The Tarentines were saved for a time by Pyrrhus, king of Epirus, who came to their help in 281; but two years after the defeat of this monarch and his withdrawal from Italy, the city was taken by the Romans (272). In the second Punic war Tarentum revolted from Rome to Hannibal (212); but it was retaken by the Romans in 207, and was treated by them with great severity. From this time Tarentum declined in prosperity and wealth. It was subsequently made a Roman colony, and it still continued to be a place of considerable importance in the time of Augustus. Its inhabitants retained their love of luxury and ease; and it is described by Horace as molle Tarentum and imbelle Tarentum. Even after the downfall of the Western Empire the Greek language was still spoken at Tarentum; and it was long one of the chief strongholds of the Byzantine empire in the S. of Italy. The town of Tarentum consisted of 2 parts, viz., of a peninsula or island at the entrance of the harbour, and of a town on the main land, which was connected with the island by means of a bridge. On the N.W. corner of the island, close to the entrance of the harbour, was the citadel: the principal part of the town was situated S. W. of the isthmus. The modern town is confined to the island or peninsula on which the citadel stood. The neighbourhood of Tarentum produced the best wool in all Italy, and was also celebrated for its excellent wine, figs, pears, and

3 s 4

other fruits. Its purple die was also much valued in antiquity.

Tarichēa or **-āae** (Ταρίχεια, -έαι, αἱαι: *El-Kereh*, Ru.), a town of Galilee, at the S. end of the lake of Tiberias, strongly fortified, and with a turbulent population, who gave the Romans much trouble during the Jewish War. It obtained its name from the quantities of the fish of the neighbouring lakes which were salted here.

Tarnē (Τάρνη), a city of Lydia, on M. Tmolus, mentioned by Homer. Pliny mentions simply a fountain of the name.

Tarpa, Sp. Maecius, was engaged by Pompeius to select the plays that were acted at his games exhibited in B. C. 55. Tarpa was likewise employed by Augustus as a dramatic censor.

Tarpēia, daughter of Sp. Tarpeius, the governor of the Roman citadel on the Saturnian hill, afterwards called the Capitoline, was tempted by the gold on the Sabine bracelets and collars to open a gate of the fortress to T. Tatius and his Sabines. As they entered, they threw upon her their shields, and thus crushed her to death. She was buried on the hill, and her memory was preserved by the name of the Tarpeian rock, which was given to a part of the Capitoline. A legend still exists at Rome which relates that the fair Tarpeia ever sits in the heart of the hill, covered with gold and jewels, and bound by a spell.

Tarphē (Τάρφη), a town in Locris on Mt. Oeta, mentioned by Homer, and subsequently called Pharygae.

Tarquinia. [TARQUINIUS.]

Tarquinii (Tarquiniensis: *Turchina* nr. *Corneto*), a city of Etruria, situated on a hill and on the river Marta, S. E. of Cosa and on a road leading from the latter town to Rome. It was one of the 12 Etruscan cities, and was probably regarded as the metropolis of the Confederation. It is said to have been founded by Tarchon, the son or brother of Tyrrhenus, who was the leader of the Lydian colony from Asia to Italy. It was in the neighbourhood of Tarquinii that the seer Tages appeared, from whom the Etruscans learnt their civil and religious polity. [TAGES.] According to one account Tarquinii was founded by Thessalians, that is, Pelasgians ; but there can be no doubt that it was an original Etruscan city, and that Tarchon is merely a personification of the race of the Tyrrhenians. It was at Tarquinii that Demaratus, the father of Tarquinius Priscus, settled ; and it was from this city that the Tarquinian family came to Rome. After the expulsion of Tarquinius Superbus from Rome, the Tarquinienses, in conjunction with the Veientes, espoused his cause, but they were defeated by the Romans. From this time the Tarquinienses were frequently engaged in war with the Romans ; but they were at length obliged to submit to Rome about B. C. 310. Tarquinii was subsequently made a Roman colony and a municipium ; but it gradually declined in importance ; and in the 8th or 9th century of the Christian era it was deserted by its inhabitants, who founded Corneto on the opposite hill. There are few remains of the ancient city itself ; but the cemetery of Tarquinii, consisting of a vast number of subterraneous caves in the hill on which Corneto stands, is still in a state of excellent preservation and contains numerous Etruscan paintings : here some of the most interesting remains of Etruscan art have been discovered in modern times.

Tarquinius, the name of a family in early Roman history, to which the 5th and 7th kings of Rome belonged. The legend of the Tarquins ran as follows. Demaratus, their ancestor, belonged to the noble family of the Bacchiadae at Corinth, and fled from his native city when the power of his order was overthrown by Cypselus. He settled at Tarquinii in Etruria, where he had mercantile connections. He married an Etruscan wife, by whom he had two sons, Lucumo and Aruns. The latter died in the lifetime of his father, leaving his wife pregnant ; but as Demaratus was ignorant of this circumstance, he bequeathed all his property to Lucumo, and died himself shortly afterwards. But, although Lucumo was thus one of the most wealthy persons at Tarquinii, and had married Tanaquil, who belonged to a family of the highest rank, he was excluded, as a stranger, from all power and influence in the state. Discontented with this inferior position, and urged on by his wife, he resolved to leave Tarquinii, and remove to Rome. He accordingly set out for Rome, riding in a chariot with his wife ; and accompanied by a large train of followers. When they had reached the Janiculus, an eagle seized his cap, and after carrying it away to a great height placed it again upon his head. Tanaquil, who was skilled in the Etruscan science of augury, bade her husband hope for the highest honour from this omen. Her predictions were soon verified. The stranger was received with welcome, and he and his followers were admitted to the rights of Roman citizens. He took the name of L. Tarquinius, to which Livy adds Priscus. His wealth, his courage, and his wisdom, gained him the love both of Ancus Marcius and of the people. The former appointed him guardian of his children ; and, when he died, the senate and the people unanimously elected Tarquinius to the vacant throne. The reign of Tarquinius was distinguished by great exploits in war, and by great works in peace. He defeated the Latins and Sabines ; and the latter people ceded to him the town of Collatia, where he placed a garrison under the command of Egerius, the son of his deceased brother Aruns, who took the surname of Collatinus. Some traditions relate that Tarquinius defeated the Etruscans likewise. Among the important works which Tarquinius executed in peace, the most celebrated are the vast sewers by which the lower parts of the city were drained, and which still remain, with not a stone displaced, to bear witness to his power and wealth. He is also said in some traditions to have laid out the Circus Maximus in the valley which had been redeemed from water by the sewers, and also to have instituted the Great or Roman Games, which were henceforth performed in the Circus. The Forum, with its porticoes and rows of shops, was also his work, and he likewise began to surround the city with a stone wall, a work which was finished by his successor Servius Tullius. The building of the Capitoline temple is moreover attributed to the elder Tarquinius, though most traditions ascribe this work to his son, and only the vow to the father. Tarquinius also made some changes in the constitution of the state. He added 100 new members to the senate, who were called *patres minorum gentium*, to distinguish them from the old senators, who were now called *patres majorum gentium*. He wished to add to the 3 centuries of equites established by Romulus 3 new centuries, and to call them after himself and two of his friends. His plan was opposed by the augur Attus Navius, who gave a convincing proof that the gods were opposed to his purpose. [NAVIUS.] Accordingly, he gave up his design of establishing new centuries, but to each of the former centuries he associated another under the same name, so that henceforth there were the first and second Ramnes, Tities, and Luceres. He increased the number of Vestal Virgins from 4 to 6. Tarquinius was murdered after a reign of 38 years at the instigation of the sons of Ancus Marcius. But the latter did not secure the reward of their crime, for Servius Tullius, with the assistance of Tanaquil, succeeded to the vacant throne. Tarquinius left two sons and two daughters. His two sons, L. Tarquinius and Aruns, were subsequently married to the two daughters of Servius Tullius. One of his daughters was married to Servius Tullius, and the other to M. Brutus, by whom she became the mother of the celebrated L. Brutus, the first consul at Rome. Servius Tullius, whose life is given under TULLIUS, was murdered after a reign of 44 years, by his son-in-law, L. Tarquinius, who ascended the vacant throne. — L. **Tarquinius Superbus** commenced his reign without any of the forms of election. One of the first acts of his reign was to abolish the rights which had been conferred upon the plebeians by Servius; and at the same time all the senators and patricians whom he mistrusted, or whose wealth he coveted, were put to death or driven into exile. He surrounded himself by a body-guard, by means of which he was enabled to do what he liked. His cruelty and tyranny obtained for him the surname of *Superbus*. But, although a tyrant at home, he raised Rome to great influence and power among the surrounding nations. He gave his daughter in marriage to Octavius Mamilius of Tusculum, the most powerful of the Latin chiefs ; and under his sway Rome became the head of the Latin confederacy. He defeated the Volscians, and took the wealthy town of Suessa Pometia, with the spoils of which he commenced the erection of the Capitol which his father had vowed. In the vaults of this temple be deposited the Sibylline books, which the king purchased from a sibyl or prophetess. She had offered to sell him 9 books for 300 pieces of gold. The king refused the offer with scorn. Thereupon she went away, and burned 3, and then demanded the same price for the 6. The king still refused. She again went away and burnt 3 more, and still demanded the same price for the remaining 3. The king now purchased the 3 books, and the sibyl disappeared. He next engaged in war with Gabii, one of the Latin cities, which refused to enter into the league. Unable to take the city by force of arms, Tarquinius had recourse to stratagem. His son, Sextus, pretending to be ill-treated by his father, and covered with the bloody marks of stripes, fled to Gabii. The infatuated inhabitants intrusted him with the command of their troops ; whereupon he sent a messenger to his father to inquire how he should deliver the city into his hands. The king, who was walking in his garden when the messenger arrived, made no reply, but kept striking off the heads of the tallest poppies with his stick. Sextus took the hint. He put to death or banished all the leading men of the place, and then had no difficulty in compelling it to submit to his father.

In the midst of his prosperity, Tarquinius fell through a shameful outrage committed by one of his sons. Tarquinius and his sons were engaged in besieging Ardea, a city of the Rutulians. Here, as the king's sons, and their cousin, Tarquinius Collatinus, the son of Egerius, were feasting together, a dispute arose about the virtue of their wives. As nothing was doing in the field, they mounted their horses to visit their homes by surprize. They first went to Rome, where they surprized the king's daughters at a splendid banquet. They then hastened to Collatia, and there, though it was late in the night, they found Lucretia, the wife of Collatinus, spinning amid her handmaids. The beauty and virtue of Lucretia had fired the evil passions of Sextus. A few days afterwards he returned to Collatia, where he was hospitably received by Lucretia as her husband's kinsman. In the dead of night he entered the chamber with a drawn sword : by threatening to lay a slave with his throat cut beside her, whom he would pretend to have killed in order to avenge her husband's honour, he forced her to yield to his wishes. As soon as Sextus had departed, Lucretia sent for her husband and father. Collatinus came, accompanied by L. Brutus ; Lucretius, with P. Valerius, who afterwards gained the surname of Publicola. They found her in an agony of sorrow. She told them what had happened, enjoined them to avenge her dishonour, and then stabbed herself to death. They all swore to avenge her. Brutus threw off his assumed stupidity, and placed himself at their head. They carried the corpse to Rome. Brutus, who was Tribunus Celerum, summoned the people, and related the deed of shame. All classes were inflamed with the same indignation. A decree was passed deposing the king, and banishing him and his family from the city. The army, encamped before Ardea, likewise renounced their allegiance to the tyrant. Tarquinius, with his two sons, Titus and Aruns, took refuge at Caere in Etruria. Sextus repaired to Gabii, his own principality, where he was shortly after murdered by the friends of those whom he had put to death. Tarquinius reigned 24 years. He was banished B. C. 510. The people of Tarquinii and Veii espoused the cause of the exiled tyrant, and marched against Rome. The two consuls advanced to meet them. A bloody battle was fought, in which Brutus and Aruns, the son of Tarquinius, slew each other. Tarquinius next repaired to Lars Porsena, the powerful king of Clusium, who marched against Rome at the head of a vast army. The history of this memorable expedition is related under PORSENA. After Porsena quitted Rome, Tarquinius took refuge with his son-in-law, Mamilius Octavius of Tusculum. Under the guidance of the latter, the Latin states espoused the cause of the exiled king, and declared war against Rome. The contest was decided by the celebrated battle of the lake Regillus, in which the Romans gained the victory by the help of Castor and Pollux. Tarquinius himself was wounded, but escaped with his life ; his son Sextus is said to have fallen in this battle, though, according to another tradition, as we have already seen, he was slain by the inhabitants of Gabii. Tarquinius Superbus had now no other state to whom he could apply for assistance. He had already survived all his family ; and he now fled to Aristobulus at Cumae, where he died a wretched and childless old man. Such is the story of the Tarquins according to the ancient writers; but this story must not be received as a real history. The narrative contains numerous inconsistencies and impossibilities. The following is only one instance out of many. We are told that the younger Tarquinius who was expelled from Rome in mature age, was the son of the king who ascended the throne 107 years previously in the vigour of life; and Servius Tullius, who married the daughter of Tarquinius Priscus, shortly before he ascended the throne, is represented immediately after his accession as the father of two daughters whom he marries to the brothers of his own wife!

Tarracina (Tarracinensis: *Terracina*), more anciently called **Anxur** (Anxurates Pl.), an ancient town of Latium situated 58 miles S.E. of Rome on the Via Appia and upon the coast, with a strongly fortified citadel upon a high hill, on which stood the temple of Jupiter Anxura. It was probably a Pelasgian town originally; but it afterwards belonged to the Volsci, by whom it was called Anxur. It was conquered by the Romans, who gave it the name of Tarracina, and it was made a Roman colony, B.C. 329. Three miles W. of the town stood the grove of Feronia, with a temple of this goddess. The ancient walls of the citadel of Tarracina are still visible on the slope of *Montecchio*.

Tarraco (Tarraconensis: *Tarragona*), an ancient town on the E. coast of Spain situated on a rock 760 ft. high, between the river Iberus and the Pyrenees on the river Tulcis. It was founded by the Massilians, and was made the head quarters of the 2 brothers P. and Cn. Scipio, in their campaigns against the Carthaginians in the 2nd Punic war. It subsequently became a populous and flourishing town; and Augustus, who wintered here (B. C. 26) after his Cantabrian campaign, made it the capital of one of the 3 Spanish provinces (*Hispania Tarraconensis*) and also a Roman colony. Hence we find it called *Colonia Tarraconensis*, also *Col. Victrix Togata* and *Col. Julia Victrix Tarraconensis*. The modern town of Tarragona is built to a great extent with the remains of the ancient city; and Roman inscriptions may frequently be seen embedded in the walls of the modern houses. The ancient Roman aqueduct, having been repaired in modern times, still supplies the modern city with water; and at a short distance to the N. W. of Tarragona, along the sea coast, is a Roman sepulchre called the tower of the Scipios, although the real place of the burial of the Scipios is quite unknown.

Tarruntēnus Paternus. [PATERNUS.]

Tarsia (Ταρσίη: *Ras Jird* or *C. Certes*), a promontory of Carmania, on the coast of the Persian Gulf, near the frontier of Persis. The neighbouring part of the coast of Carmania was called Tarsiäna.

Tarsius (ὁ Τάρσιος: *Tarza* or *Balikesri*), a river of Mysia, rising in M. Temnus, and flowing N. E., through the Miletopolites Lacus, into the Macestus.

Tarsus, Tarsos (Ταρσός, Ταρσοί, Τερσός, Θαρσός: Ταρσεύς, Tarsensis: *Tersus*, Ru.), the chief city of Cilicia, stood near the centre of Cilicia Campestris, on the river Cydnus, about 12 miles above its mouth, in a very large and fertile plain at the foot of M. Taurus, the chief pass through which (Pylae Ciliciae) led down to Tarsus. Its

position gave it the full benefit of the natural advantages of a fertile country, and the command of an important highway of commerce. It had also an excellent harbour, 12 miles from the city, which is filled up with sand. The city was of unknown antiquity. Some ascribed its foundation to the Assyrian king Sardanapalus; others to Perseus, in connection with whose legend the name of the city is fancifully derived from a hoof (ταρσός) which the winged horse Pegasus lost here; and others to the Argive chieftain Triptolemus, whose effigy appears on the coins of the city. All that can be determined with certainty seems to be that it was a very ancient city of the Syrians, who were the earliest known inhabitants of this part of Asia Minor, and that it received Greek settlers at an early period. In the time of Xenophon, who gives us the first historical notice of Tarsus, it was the capital of the Cilician prince Syennesis, and was taken by Cyrus. [Comp. CILICIA.] At the time of the Macedonian invasion, it was held by the Persian troops, who were about to burn it, when they were prevented by Alexander's arrival. After playing an important part as a military post in the wars of the successors of Alexander, and under the Syrian kings, it became, by the peace between the Romans and Antiochus the Great, the frontier city of the Syrian kingdom on the N. W. As the power of the Seleucidae declined, it suffered much from the oppression of its governors, and from the wars between the members of the royal family. At the time of the Mithridatic War, it suffered, on the one hand, from Tigranes, who overran Cilicia, and, on the other, from the pirates, who had their strongholds in the mountains of Cilicia Aspera, and made frequent incursions into the level country. From both these enemies it was rescued by Pompey, who made it the capital of the new Roman province of Cilicia, B. C. 66. In the Civil War, it took part with Caesar, and assumed, in his honour, the name of **Juliopolis**. For this the inhabitants were severely punished by Cassius, but were recompensed by Antony, who made Tarsus a free city. Under Augustus, the city obtained immunity from taxes, through the influence of the emperor's tutor, the Stoic Athenodorus, who was a native of the place. It enjoyed the favour, and was called by the names, of several of the later emperors. It was the scene of important events in the wars with the Persians, the Arabs, and the Turks, and also in the Crusades. The people of Tarsus were celebrated for their mental power, their readiness in repartee, and their fondness for the study of philosophy. Among the most distinguished natives of the place were: the Stoics, Antipater, Archedemus, Heraclides, Nestor, Zeno, and the 2 Athenodori; the Academic, Nestor; the Epicureans, Diogenes, celebrated for his powers of improvising, Lysias, who was for a time tyrant of the city, and Plutiades; the tragic poets, Dionysides and Bion; the satiric poets, Demetrius, and Boëthes, who was also a troublesome demagogue; the grammarians, Artemidorus, Diodorus, and Hermogenes; the historian Hermogenes; the physicians, Herodotus and Philo; and, above all, the apostle Paul, who belonged to one of several families of Jews, who had settled at Tarsus in considerable numbers, under the Persian and Syrian kings.

Tartărus (Τάρταρος), son of Aether and Ge, and by his mother Ge the father of the Gigantes,

Typhoeus and Echidna. In the Iliad Tartarus is a place beneath the earth, as far below Hades as Heaven is above the earth, and closed by iron gates. Later poets describe Tartarus as the place in the lower world in which the spirits of wicked men are punished for their crimes ; and sometimes they use the name as synonymous with Hades or the lower world in general.

Tartessus (Ταρτησσός: Ταρτήσσιος), an ancient town in Spain, and one of the chief settlements of the Phoenicians, probably the same as the *Tarshish* of Scripture. The position of this town has occasioned much dispute. Most of the ancient writers place it at the mouth of the river Baetis, which, they say, was originally called Tartessus. Others identify it, with more probability, with the city of Carteia on Mt. Calpe, the rock of Gibraltar. The whole country W. of Gibraltar was also called Tartessis.

Taruscon or Tarascon (Tarusconienses: *Tarascon*), a town of the Salyes in Gaul, on the E. bank of the Rhone, N. of Arelate, and E. of Nemausus.

Tarvisium (Tarvisanus: *Treviso*), a town of Venetia in the N. of Italy, on the river Silis, which became the seat of a bishopric, and a place of importance in the middle ages.

Tatianus (Τατιανός), a Christian writer of the 2nd century, was born in Assyria, and was originally a teacher of rhetoric. He was afterwards converted to Christianity, according to some accounts, by Justin Martyr, with whom at any rate he was very intimate. After Justin's death Tatian quitted Rome, where he had resided for some time, and returned into the East. There he imbibed and promulgated views of a Gnostic character, and gave rise to a new sect, called after him Tatiani. Tatian wrote numerous works, of which there is still extant an *Address to the Greeks* (Πρὸς Ἕλληνας), in which he points out the superiority of Christianity to the heathen religion. The best edition of this work is by Worth, Oxford, 1700.

T. Tatius, king of the Sabines. [ROMULUS.]

Tatta (ἡ Τάττα: *Tux-Göl*), a great salt lake in the centre of Asia Minor, on the Phrygian table-land, on the confines of Phrygia, Galatia, Cappadocia, and Lycaonia. It supplies the whole surrounding country with salt, as it doubtless did in ancient times.

Tauchira or Teuchira (Ταύχειρα, Τεύχειρα: *Taukra*, Ru.), a colony of Cyrene, on the N. W. coast of Cyrenaïca, in N. Africa. Under the Ptolemies, it was called Arsinoë, and was one of the 5 cities of the Libyan Pentapolis. It became a Roman colony, and was fortified by Justinian. It was a chief seat of the worship of Cybele, who had here a great temple and an annual festival.

Taulantii (Ταυλάντιοι), a people of Illyria, in the neighbourhood of Epidamnus, frequently mentioned by the Greek and Roman writers. One of their most powerful kings was Glaucias, a contemporary of Alexander the Great, who fought against the latter monarch, and at a later period afforded an asylum to the infant Pyrrhus, and refused to surrender him to Cassander.

Taunus (*Taunus*), a range of mountains in Germany, at no great distance from the confluence of the Moenus (*Main*) and the Rhine.

Taurasia. [TAURINI.]

Taurentum and Taurois (Ταυροέντιον, Ταυρόεις, -εντος), a fortress belonging to Massilia, and near the latter city, on the S. coast of Gaul.

Tauri, a wild and savage people in European Sarmatia, who sacrificed all strangers to a goddess whom the Greeks identified with Artemis. An account of this goddess is given elsewhere (p. 94 a). The Tauri dwelt in the peninsula which was called after them Chersonesus Taurica. [CHERSONESUS, No. 2.]

Taurianum (*Tauretto*), a town of Bruttium on the Via Popilia, 23 miles S. E. of Vibo.

Taurini, a people of Liguria dwelling on the upper course of the Po, at the foot of the Alps. Their chief town was Taurasia, afterwards colonised by Augustus, and called Augusta Taurinorum (*Turin*).

Tauris (*Torcola*), a small island off the coast of Illyria, between Pharus and Corcyra.

Taurisci, a Celtic people in Noricum, and probably the old Celtic name of the entire population of the country. They were subsequently called Norici by the Romans after their capital Noreia.

Taurois. [TAURENTUM.]

Tauromenium (Ταυρομένιον: Ταυρομενίτης, Tauromenitanus: *Taormina*), a city on the E. coast of Sicily, situated on Mt. Taurus, from which it derived its name, and founded B. C. 358 by Andromachus with the remains of the inhabitants of Naxos, whose town had been destroyed by Dionysius nearly 50 years before. [NAXOS, No. 2.] Tauromenium soon became a large and flourishing city; but in consequence of its espousing the side of Sex. Pompey against Augustus, most of its inhabitants were expelled from the city, and their place supplied by a colony of Roman veterans : hence we find the town called *Col. Augusta Tauromenitana*. From this time Tauromenium became a place of secondary importance. The hills in the neighbourhood produced excellent wine. There are still remains of the ancient town, of which the most important is a splendid theatre cut out of the rock, and capable of holding from 30,000 to 40,000 spectators, from which we may form some idea of the populousness of Tauromenium.

Tauroscythae [SCYTHOTAURI].

Taurunum (*Semlin*), a strongly fortified town in Pannonia at the confluence of the Savus and the Danube.

Taurus, Statilius, a distinguished general of Octavian. At the battle of Actium, B. C. 31, he commanded the land-forces of Octavian, which were drawn up on the shore. In 29 he defeated the Cantabri, Vaccaei, and Astures. He was consul in 26; and in 16, when the emperor went to Gaul, the government of the city and of Italy was left to Taurus, with the title of praefectus urbi. In the fourth consulship of Augustus, 30, Taurus built an amphitheatre of stone at his own expense. [ROMA, p. 652.]

Taurus (ὁ Ταῦρος, from the Aramaean Tur, a *high mountain* : *Taurus, Ala-Dagh*, and other special names), a great mountain chain of Asia. In its widest extent, the name was applied, by the later geographers, to the whole of the great chain, which runs through Asia from W. to E., forming the S. margin of the great table-land of Central Asia, which it divides from the Mediterranean coast of Asia Minor, from Syria and the Tigris and Euphrates valley, from the low lands on the N. shore of the Indian Ocean, and from the 2 great peninsulas of India. But this is not a common use of the name. In its usual signification, it denotes the mountain-chain in the S. of Asia Minor, which begins at the Sacrum or Chelidonium Prom. at the S. E. angle of Lycia, surrounds the gulf of Pamphylia, passing through the middle of Pisidia; then along the S. frontier of Lycaonia and Cappadocia, which it divides from Cilicia and Commagene; thence, after being broken through by the Euphrates, it proceeds almost due E. through the S. of Armenia, forming the water-shed between the sources of the Tigris on the S., and the streams which feed the upper Euphrates and the Araxes on the N.; thus it continues as far as the S. margin of the lake Arsissa, where it ceases to bear the name of Taurus, and is continued in the chain which, under the names of Niphates, Zagros, &c., forms the N. E. margin of the Tigris and Euphrates valley. This main chain sends off branches which are nearly as important as itself. In the middle of the frontier between Cilicia and Cappadocia, E. of the Cilician Gates, the ANTITAURUS branches off to the N. E. In the E. of Cilicia, the AMANUS goes off to the S. W. and S. Immediately E. of the Euphrates, a branch proceeds to the S. E., forming, under the name of MASIUS, the frontier between Armenia and Mesopotamia, and dividing the valley of the Upper Tigris from the waters which flow through Mesopotamia into the Euphrates. The Taurus is of moderate height, for the most part steep, and wooded to the summit. Its general character greatly resembles the mountains of central Germany.

Tāvĭum (Ταουίον, Ταύιον : prob. *Boghaz Kieni*, Ru.), the capital of the Trocmi, in Galatia, stood on the E. side of the Halys, but at some distance from the river, and formed the centre of meeting for roads leading to all parts of Asia Minor. It was therefore a place of considerable commercial importance. It had a temple and bronze colossus of Zeus.

Taxĭla or **Taxĭăla** (τὰ Τάξιλα, Ταξίαλα), an important city of India intra Gangem, stood in a large and fertile plain between the Indus and the Hydaspes, and was the capital of the Indian king Taxiles, in the time of Alexander. Its position has not been identified. It is not, as Major Rennell supposed, *Attock;* and there is no large city remaining which exactly answers to its position.

Taxīles (Ταξίλης). 1. An Indian prince or king, who reigned over the tract between the Indus and the Hydaspes, at the period of the expedition of Alexander, B.C. 327. His real name was Mophis, or Omphis, and the Greeks appear to have called him Taxiles or Taxilas, from the name of his capital city of Taxila, near the modern Attock. On the approach of Alexander he hastened to meet him with valuable presents, and was in consequence confirmed in his kingdom by the Macedonian monarch. — 2. A general in the service of Mithridates the Great, and one of those in whom he reposed the highest confidence.

Tāygĕtē (Ταϋγέτη), daughter of Atlas and Pleione, one of the Pleiades, from whom Mt. Taygetus in Laconia is said to have derived its name. By Zeus she became the mother of Lacedaemon and of Eurotas.

Tāygĕtus or **Taygĕtum** or **Taygĕta** (Ταΰγετος, Ταΰγετον, τὰ Ταΰγετα pl.), a lofty range of mountains of a wild and savage character, separating Laconica and Messenia, and extending from the frontiers of Arcadia down to the Prom. Taenarum.

Its highest points were called Talĕtus and Evōras, about 3 miles S. of Sparta. Taÿgetus is said to have derived its name from the nymph Taÿgete.

Teānum (Teanensis). 1. **Apŭlum** (nr. *Ponte Rotto*), a town of Apulia on the river Frento and the confines of the Frentani, 18 miles from Larinum. — 2. **Sidicīnum** (*Teano*), an important town of Campania, and the capital of the Sidicini, situated on the N. slope of Mt. Massicus and on the Via Praenestina, 6 miles W. of Cales. It was made a Roman colony by Augustus; and in its neighbourhood were some celebrated medicinal springs.

Teārus (Τέαρος : *Teara, Deara* or *Dere*), a river of Thrace, the waters of which were useful in curing cutaneous diseases. Herodotus relates that it rises from 38 fountains, all flowing from the same rock, some warm and others cold. It falls into the Contadesdus; this into the Agrianes; and the latter again into the Hebrus.

Teātĕ (Teatinus: *Chieti*), the capital of the Marrucini, situated on a steep hill on the river Aternus, and on the road from Aternum to Corfinium.

Tecmessa (Τέκμησσα), the daughter of the Phrygian king Teleutas, whose territory was ravaged by the Greeks during a predatory excursion from Troy. Tecmessa was taken prisoner, and was given to Ajax, the son of Telamon, by whom she had a son, Eurysaces.

Tecmōn (Τέκμων), a town of the Molossi in Epirus.

Tectaeus and **Angĕlīōn** (Τεκταῖος καὶ Ἀγγελίων), early Greek statuaries, who are always mentioned together. They were pupils of Dipoenus and Scyllis, and instructors of Callon of Aegina; and therefore they must have flourished about B.C. 548.

Tectŏsăges (Τεκτόσαγες). 1. In Gallia. [VOLCAE.] — 2. In Asia Minor. [GALATIA.]

Tecum or **Ticis** (*Tecli*), a river in Gallia Narbonensis in the territory of the Sardones, called Illiberis by the Greeks from a town of this name upon the river.

Tedanius, a river in Illyricum, separating Iapydia and Liburnia.

Tĕgĕa (Τεγέα). 1. (Τεγεάτης : *Piali*), an important city of Arcadia, and the capital of the district **Tegeātis** (Τεγεᾶτις), which was bounded on the E. by Argolis and Laconica, on the S. by Laconica, on the W. by Maenalia, and on the N. by the territory of Mantinea. It was one of the most ancient towns of Arcadia, and is said to have been founded by Tegeates, the son of Lycaon. It was formed out of 9 small townships, which were united into one city by Aleus, who was thus regarded as the real founder of the city. At a later time we find Tegea divided into 4 tribes, each of which possessed a statue of Apollo Agyieus, who was especially honoured in Tegea. The Tegeatae long resisted the supremacy of Sparta; and it was not till the Spartans discovered the bones of Orestes that they were enabled to conquer this people. The Tegeatae sent 3000 men to the battle of Plataea, in which they were distinguished for their bravery. They remained faithful to Sparta in the Peloponnesian war; but after the battle of Leuctra they joined the rest of the Arcadians in establishing their independence. During the wars of the Achaean league Tegea was taken both by Cleomenes, king of Sparta, and

Antigonus Doson, king of Macedonia, and the ally of the Achaeans. It continued to be a place of importance in the time both of Strabo and Pausanias. Its most splendid public building was the temple of Athena, which was the largest and most magnificent building in the Peloponnesus. It was erected soon after B. C. 394, in place of a more ancient temple of this goddess, which was burnt down in this year. The architect was Scopas, and the sculpture in the pediments were probably by the hand of Scopas himself. — 2. A town in Crete, said to have been founded by Agamemnon.

Telamon (Τελαμών), son of Aeacus and Endeïs, and brother of Peleus. Having assisted Peleus in slaying their half-brother Phocus [PELEUS], Telamon was expelled from Aegina, and came to Salamis. Here he was first married to Glauce, daughter of Cychreus, king of the island, on whose death Telamon became king of Salamis. He afterwards married Periboea or Eriboea, daughter of Alcathoüs, by whom he became the father of Ajax, who is hence frequently called *Telamoniades*, and *Telamonius heros*. Telamon himself was one of the Calydonian hunters and one of the Argonauts. He was also a great friend of Hercules, whom he joined in his expedition against Laomedon of Troy, which city he was the first to enter. He there erected an altar to Hercules Callinicus or Alexicacus. Hercules, in return, gave to him Theanira or Hesione, a daughter of Laomedon, by whom he became the father of Teucer and Trambelus. On this expedition Telamon and Hercules also fought against the Meropes in Cos, on account of Chalciope, the beautiful daughter of Eurypylus, the king of the Meropes, and against the giant Alcioneus, on the isthmus of Corinth. Telamon likewise accompanied Hercules on his expedition against the Amazons, and slew Melanippe.

Telamon (*Telamone*), a town and harbour of Etruria, a few miles S. of the river Umbro, said to have been founded by Telamon on his return from the Argonautic expedition. In its neighbourhood a great victory was gained over the Gauls in B. C. 225. It was here that Marius landed on his return from Africa in 87. Telamon was undoubtedly the port of the great Etruscan city recently discovered in its neighbourhood, which is supposed to be the ancient Vetulonia.

Telchines (Τελχῖνες), a family or a tribe, said to have been descended from Thalassa or Poseidon. They are represented in 3 different aspects : — 1. *As cultivators of the soil and ministers of the gods.* As such they came from Crete to Cyprus and from thence to Rhodes, where they founded Camirus, Ialysus, and Lindus. Rhodes, which was named after them *Telchinis*, was abandoned by them, because they foresaw that the island would be inundated. They then spread in different directions. Lycus went to Lycia, where he built the temple of the Lycian Apollo. This god had been worshipped by them at Lindus, and Hera at Ialysus and Camirus. Nymphs also are called after them Telchiniae. Poseidon was intrusted to them by Rhea, and they brought him up in conjunction with Caphira, a daughter of Oceanus. Rhea, Apollo and Zeus, however, are also described as hostile to the Telchines. Apollo is said to have assumed the shape of a wolf, and to have thus destroyed the Telchines, and Zeus to have overwhelmed them by an inundation. 2. *As sorcerers*

and *envious daemons*. Their very eyes and aspect are said to have been destructive. They had it in their power to bring on hail, rain, and snow, and to assume any form they pleased ; they further mixed Stygian water with sulphur, in order thereby to destroy animals and plants. 3. *As artists,* for they are said to have invented useful arts and institutions, and to have made images of the gods. They worked in brass and iron, made the sickle of Cronos and the trident of Poseidon. This last feature in the character of the Telchines seems to have been the reason of their being classed with the Idaean Dactyls ; and Strabo even states that those of the 9 Rhodian Telchines who accompanied Rhea to Crete, and there brought up the infant Zeus, were called Curetes.

Teleboae. [TAPHIAE.]

Teleboas (Τηλεβόας), a river of Armenia Major, falling into the Euphrates ; probably identical with the ARSANIAS.

Teleclides (Τηλεκλείδης), a distinguished Athenian comic poet of the Old Comedy, flourished about the same time as Crates and Cratinus, and a little earlier than Aristophanes. He was an earnest advocate of peace, and a great admirer of the ancient manners of the age of Themistocles.

Teleclus (Τήλεκλος), king of Sparta, 8th of the Agids, and son of Archelaus. He was slain by the Messenians, in a temple of Artemis Limnatis, on the borders. His death was the immediate occasion of the 1st Messenian war, B. C. 743.

Telegonus (Τηλέγονος), son of Ulysses and Circe. After Ulysses had returned to Ithaca, Circe sent out Telegonus in search of his father. A storm cast his ship on the coast of Ithaca, and being pressed by hunger, he began to plunder the fields. Ulysses and Telemachus being informed of the ravages caused by the stranger, went out to fight against him ; but Telegonus ran Ulysses through with a spear which he had received from his mother. At the command of Athena, Telegonus, accompanied by Telemachus and Penelope, went to Circe in Aeaea, there buried the body of Ulysses, and married Penelope, by whom he became the father of Italus. In Italy Telegonus was believed to have been the founder of the towns of Tusculum and Praeneste. He left a daughter Mamilia, from whom the family of the Mamilii traced their descent.

Telemachus (Τηλέμαχος), son of Ulysses and Penelope. He was still an infant when his father went to Troy ; and when the latter had been absent from home nearly 20 years, Telemachus went to Pylos and Sparta, to gather information concerning him. He was hospitably received by Nestor, who sent his own son to conduct Telemachus to Sparta. Menelaus also received him kindly, and communicated to him the prophecy of Proteus concerning Ulysses. From Sparta Telemachus returned home ; and on his arrival there he found his father, whom he assisted in slaying the suitors. According to some accounts, Telemachus became the father of Perseptolis either by Polycaste, the daughter of Nestor, or by Nausicaa, the daughter of Alcinous. Others relate that he was induced by Athena to marry Circe, and became by her the father of Latinus ; or that he married Cassiphone, a daughter of Circe, but in a quarrel with his mother-in-law slew her, for which he was in his turn killed by Cassiphone. One account makes Telemachus the founder of Clusium in Etruria.

Tĕlĕmus (Τήλεμος), son of Eurymus, and a celebrated soothsayer.

Tĕlĕphassa (Τηλέφασσα), wife of Agenor, and mother of Europa, Cadmus, Phoenix, and Cilix. She, with her sons, went out in search of Europa, who had been carried off by Zeus ; but she died on the expedition, and was buried by Cadmus.

Tĕlĕphus (Τήλεφος), son of Hercules and Auge, the daughter of king Aleus of Tegea. As soon as he was born he was exposed by his grandfather, but was reared by a hind (ἔλαφος), and educated by king Corythus in Arcadia. On reaching manhood, he consulted the Delphic oracle to learn his parentage, and was ordered to go to king Teuthras in Mysia. He there found his mother, and succeeded Teuthras on the throne of Mysia. He married Laodice or Astyoche, a daughter of Priam ; and he attempted to prevent the Greeks from landing on the coast of Mysia. Dionysus, however, caused him to stumble over a vine, whereupon he was wounded by Achilles. Being informed by an oracle that the wound could only be cured by him who had inflicted it, Telephus repaired to the Grecian camp ; and as the Greeks had likewise learnt from an oracle that without the aid of Telephus they could not reach Troy, Achilles cured Telephus by means of the rust of the spear by which he had been wounded. Telephus, in return, pointed out to the Greeks the road which they had to take.

Tĕleptĕ. [THALA.]

Telesia (Telesinus: *Telese*), a town in Samnium, on the road from Allifae to Beneventum, taken by Hannibal in the 2nd Punic war, and afterwards retaken by the Romans. It was colonised by Augustus with a body of veterans. It was the birthplace of Pontius, who fought against Sulla, and who was hence surnamed Telesinus.

Tĕlĕsilla (Τελέσιλλα), of Argos, a celebrated lyric poetess and heroine, flourished about B.C. 510. In the war of Argos against Sparta, she not only encouraged her countrymen by her lyre and song, but she took up arms at the head of a band of her countrywomen, and greatly contributed to the victory which they gained over the Spartans. In memory of this exploit, her statue was erected in the temple of Aphrodite at Argos, with the emblems of a poetess and a heroine ; Ares was worshipped in that city as a patron deity of women ; and the prowess of her female associates was commemorated by the annual festival called *Hybristica*. Only 2 complete verses of her poetry are extant.

Tĕlĕsĭnus, Pontĭus. [PONTIUS]

Tĕlestas or **Tĕlestĕs** (Τελέστας, Τελέστης), of Selinus, a distinguished poet of the later Athenian dithyramb, flourished B.C. 398. A few lines of his poetry are preserved by Athenaeus.

Tĕlĕthrĭus (Τελέθριος), a mountain in the N. of Euboea near Histiaea.

Tellenae, a town in Latium between the later Via Ostiensis and the Via Appia, destroyed by Ancus Martius.

Tellus. [GAEA.]

Telmessus or **Telmissus** (Τελμησσός, Τελμισσός: Τελμησσεύς, Τελμισσεύς). **1.** (*Méi*, the port of *Macri*, Ru.), a city of Lycia, near the borders of Caria, on a gulf called Telmissicus Sinus, and close to the promontory Telmissis.—**2.** A town of Caria, 60 stadia (6 geog. miles) from Halicarnassus, celebrated for the skill of its inhabitants in divination. It is often identified with the former place.

Telo Martius (*Toulon*), a port-town of Gallia Narbonensis on the Mediterranean, is rarely mentioned by the ancient writers, and did not become a place of importance till the downfal of the Roman empire.

Telos (Τήλος: Τήλιος: *Telos* or *Piskopi*), a small island of the Carpathian sea, one of the Sporades, lay off the coast of Caria S.W. of the mouth of the Sinus Doridis, between Rhodes and Nisyrus. It was also called Agathussa.

Telphussa. [THELPUSA.]

Temĕnīdae. [TEMENUS.]

Tĕmĕnītes (Τεμενίτης), a surname of Apollo, derived from his sacred temenus in the neighbourhood of Syracuse.

Tĕmĕnus (Τήμενος), son of Aristomachus, was one of the Heraclidae who invaded Peloponnesus. After the conquest of the peninsula, he received Argos as his share. His descendants, the Temenidae, being expelled from Argos, are said to have founded the kingdom of Macedonia, whence the kings of Macedonia called themselves Temenidae.

Tĕmĕsa or **Tempsa** (Temesaeus or Tempsanus: *Torre del Lupi*), a town in Bruttium on the Sinus Terinaeus, was one of the most ancient Ausonian towns in the S. of Italy, and is said to have been afterwards colonised by a body of Aetolians under Thoas. At a still later time it was successively in the possession of the Locrians, of the Bruttians, and finally of the Romans, who colonised it in B. C. 196. Some of the ancients identified this town with the Temese mentioned by Homer as celebrated for its copper mines ; but the Homeric town was probably in Cyprus.

Temnus. **1.** (τὸ Τῆμνον ὄρος: *Morad* or *Ak Dagh*), a mountain of Mysia, extending E.-ward from Ida to the borders of Phrygia, and dividing Mysia into 2 parts. It contains the sources of the Macestus, Mysius, Caïcus, and Evenus.—**2.** (*Menimen 9* or *Guzal-Hisar 9*), a city of Aeolis in the N.W. of Lydia (some say in Mysia), on the W. bank of the Hermus, 30 miles S. of Cyme. It was nearly destroyed by an earthquake in the reign of Tiberius, and in that of Titus (Pliny's time) it no longer existed.

Tempĕ (Τέμπη contr. of Τέμπεα), a beautiful and romantic valley in the N. of Thessaly between Mts. Olympus and Ossa, through which the Peneus escapes into the sea. The lovely scenery of this glen is frequently described by the ancient poets and declaimers ; and it was also celebrated as one of the favourite haunts of Apollo, who had transplanted his laurel from this spot to Delphi. The whole valley is rather less than 5 miles in length, and opens gradually to the E. into a spacious plain. Tempe is also of great importance in history, as it is the only pass through which an army can invade Thessaly from the N. In some parts the rocks on each side of the Peneus approach so close to each other as only to leave room between them for the stream ; and the road is obliged to be cut out of the rock in the narrowest point. Tempe is the only channel through which the waters of the Thessalian plain descend into the sea ; and it was the common opinion in antiquity that these waters had once covered the country with a vast lake, till an outlet was formed for them by some great convulsion in nature, which rent the rocks of Tempe asunder. So celebrated was the scenery of Tempe that its name was given to any beautiful valley. Thus we find a Tempe in the land of the Sabines near Reate, through which the river Velinus flowed; and also a Tempe in Sicily, through which the river Helorus flowed, hence called by Ovid *Tempe Heloria*.

TEMPȳRA, a town in Thrace at the foot of a narrow mountain pass between Mt. Rhodope and the coast.

TENCTĚRI or TENCHTĚRI, a people of Germany dwelling on the Rhine between the Ruhr and the Sieg, S. of the Usipetes, in conjunction with whom their name usually occurs. They crossed the Rhine together with the Usipetes, with the intention of settling in Gaul; but they were defeated by Caesar with great slaughter, and those who escaped took refuge in the territories of their S. neighbours, the Sygambri. The Tencteri afterwards belonged to the league of the Cherusci, and at a still later period they are mentioned as a portion of the confederacy of the Franks.

TĚNĚDOS or TĚNĚDUS (Tένεδος: Tενέδιος), a small island of the Aegean sea, off the coast of Troas, of an importance very disproportionate to its size, on account of its position near the mouth of the Hellespont, from which it is about 12 miles distant. Its distance from the coast of the Troad was 40 stadia (4 geog. miles), and from Lesbos 56 stadia: its circuit was 80 stadia. It was called, in early times, by the names of Calydna, Leucophrys, Phoenice, and Lyrnessus. The mythical derivation of its usual name is from Tenes, son of Cycnus. It had an Aeolian city of the same name, with 2 harbours. Its name appears in several proverbs, such as Tενέδιος πέλεκυς, T. ἄνθρωπος, T. αὐλητής, T. κακόν. It appears in the legend of the Trojan War as the station to which the Greeks withdrew their fleet, in order to induce the Trojans to think that they had departed, and to receive the wooden horse. In the Persian War it was used by Xerxes as a naval station. It afterwards became a tributary ally of Athens, and adhered to her during the whole of the Peloponnesian War, and down to the peace of Antalcidas, by which it was surrendered to the Persians. At the Macedonian conquest the Tenedians regained their liberty. In the war against Philip III., Attalus and the Romans used Tenedos as a naval station, and in the Mithridatic War Lucullus gained a naval victory over Mithridates off the island. About this time the Tenedians placed themselves under the protection of Alexandria Troas. The island was celebrated for the beauty of its women.

TENES or TENNES (Tέννης), son of Cycnus and Proclea, and brother of Hemithea. Cycnus was king of Colonae in Troas. His 2nd wife was Philonome, who fell in love with her stepson; but as he repulsed her advances, she accused him to his father, who threw both his son and daughter in a chest into the sea. But the chest was driven on the coast of the island of Leucophrys, of which the inhabitants elected him king, and which he called Tenedos, after his own name. Cycnus at length heard of the innocence of his son, killed Philonome, and went to his children in Tenedos. Here both Cycnus and Tenes were slain by Achilles. Tenes was afterwards worshipped as a hero in Tenedos.

TĚNOS (Tῆνος: Tήνιος: *Tino*), a small island in the Aegaean sea, S. E. of Andros and N. of Delos. It is about 15 miles in length. It was originally called *Hydrussa* ('Υδροῦσσα) because it was well watered, and *Ophiussa* ('Οφιοῦσσα) be-

cause it abounded in snakes. It possessed a town of the same name on the site of the modern *S. Nicolo*. It had also a celebrated temple of Poseidon, which is mentioned in the time of the emperor Tiberius. The wine of Tenos was celebrated in antiquity and is still valued at the present day.

TENTŷRA (τὰ Tέντυρα: Tεντυρίτης, Tentyrites: *Denderah*, Ru.), a city of Upper Egypt, on the W. bank of the Nile, between Abydos and Coptos, with celebrated temples of Athor (the Egyptian Venus), Isis, and Typhon. Its people were distinguished for their hatred of the crocodile; and upon this and the contrary propensities of the people of Ombi, Juvenal founds his 15th satire. [OMBI.] There are still magnificent remains of the temples of Athor and of Isis: in the latter was found the celebrated Zodiac, which is now preserved at Paris.

TĚŌS (ἡ Tέως: Tήϊος, Tēïus: *Sighajik*), one of the Ionian cities on the coast of Asia Minor, renowned as the birthplace of the lyric poet Anacreon. It stood on the S. side of the isthmus which connects the peninsula of M. Mimas with the mainland of Lydia, at the bottom of the bay between the promontories of Coryceum and Myonnesus. It was a flourishing seaport, until, to free themselves from the Persian yoke, most of its inhabitants retired to Abdera. It was still, however, a place of importance in the time of the Roman emperors. It had 2 harbours, and a celebrated temple of Dionysus.

TERĚDON (Tερηδών: prob. *Dorah*), a city of Babylonia, on the W. side of the Tigris, below its junction with the Euphrates, and not far from its mouth. It was a great emporium for the traffic with Arabia. It is no doubt the Diridotis (Διρίδωτις) of Arrian.

TĚRENTIA. 1. Wife of M. Cicero, the orator, to whom she bore 2 children, a son and daughter. She was a woman of sound sense and great resolution; and her firmness of character was of no small service to her weak and vacillating husband in some important periods of his life. On his banishment in B. C. 58, Tullia by her letters endeavoured to keep up Cicero's fainting spirits, and she vigorously exerted herself on his behalf among his friends in Italy. During the civil war however Cicero was offended with her conduct, and divorced her in 46. Shortly afterwards he married Publilia, a young girl of whose property he had the management. Terentia could not have been less than 50 at the time of her divorce, and therefore it is not probable that she married again. It is related, indeed, by Jerome, that she married Sallust the historian, and subsequently Messala Corvinus; but these marriages are not mentioned by any other writer, and may therefore be rejected. Terentia is said to have attained the age of 103. — 2. Also called Terentilla, the wife of Maecenas, and also one of the favourite mistresses of Augustus. The intrigue between Augustus and Terentia is said to have disturbed the good understanding which subsisted between the emperor and his minister, and finally to have occasioned the disgrace of the latter.

TERENTIĀNUS MAURUS, a Roman poet, probably lived at the end of the first or the beginning of the second century under Nerva and Trajan, and was a native of Africa, as his surname, Maurus, indicates. There is still extant a poem of Terentianus, intitled *De Literis, Syllabis, Pedibus, Metris*, which treats of prosody and the different kinds of metre with much elegance and skill. The work is printed by Santen and Van Lennep, Traj. ad Rhen. 1825, and by Lachmann, Berol. 1836.

P. Tĕrentĭus Afer, usually called Terence, the celebrated comic poet, was born at Carthage, B. C. 195. By birth or purchase he became the slave of P. Terentius Lucanus, a Roman senator. A handsome person and promising talents recommended Terence to his master, who afforded him the best education of the age and finally manumitted him. On his manumission, according to the usual practice, Terence assumed his patron's nomen, Terentius, having been previously called Publius or Publipor. The *Andria* was the first play offered by Terence for representation. The curule aediles referred the piece to Caecilius, then one of the most popular play-writers at Rome. Unknown and meanly clad, Terence began to read from a low stool his opening scene. A few verses showed the elder poet that no ordinary writer was before him, and the young aspirant, then in his 27th year, was invited to share the couch and supper of his judge. This reading of the *Andria*, however, must have preceded its performance nearly two years, for Caecilius died in 168, and it was not acted till 166. Meanwhile, copies were in circulation, envy was awakened, and Luscius Lavinius, a veteran, and not very successful play-writer, began his unwearied attacks on the dramatic and personal character of the author. The *Andria* was successful, and, aided by the accomplishments and good address of Terence himself, was the means of introducing him to the most refined and intellectual circles of Rome. His chief patrons were Laelius and the younger Scipio, both of whom treated him as an equal, and are said even to have assisted him in the composition of his plays. After residing some years at Rome, Terence went to Greece, and while there he translated 108 of Menander's comedies. He never returned to Italy, and we have various accounts of his death. According to one story, after embarking at Brundusium, he was never heard of more ; according to others, he died at Stymphalus in Arcadia, in Leucadia, or at Patrae in Achaia. One of his biographers said he was drowned, with all the fruits of his sojourn in Greece, on his home-passage. But the prevailing report was, that his translations of Menander were lost at sea, and that grief for their loss caused his death. He died in the 36th year of his age, in 159, or in the year following. He left a daughter, but nothing is known of his family. Six comedies are all that remain to us ; and they are probably all that Terence produced. His later versions of Menander were, in all likelihood, from their number and the short time in which they were made, merely studies for future dramas of his own. They were brought forward at the following seasons. 1. *Andria*, "the Woman of Andros," so called from the birth-place of Glycerium, its heroine, was first represented at the Megalesian Games, on the 4th of April, 166. 2. *Hecyra*, "the Step-Mother," produced at the Megalesian Games, in 165. 3. *Heauton-timorou-menos*, "the Self-Tormentor," performed at the Megalesian Games, 163. 4. *Eunuchus*, "the Eunuch," played at the Megalesian Games, 162. It was at the time the most popular of Terence's comedies. 5. *Phormio*, was performed in the same year with the preceding, at the Roman

Games on the 1st of October. 6. *Adelphi*, "the Brothers," was acted for the first time at the funeral games of L. Aemilius Paullus, 160. The comedies of Terence have been translated into most of the languages of modern Europe, and in conjunction with Plautus were, on the revival of the drama, the models of the most refined play-writers. The ancient critics are unanimous in ascribing to Terence immaculate purity and elegance of language, and nearly so in denying him *vis comica*. But it should be recollected that 4 of Terence's 6 plays are more or less sentimental comedies — in which *vis comica* is not a primary element. Moreover, Terence is generally contrasted with Plautus, with whom he had very little in common. Granting to the elder poet the highest genius for exciting laughter, and a natural force which his rival wanted, there will remain to Terence greater consistency of plot and character, closer observation of generic and individual distinctions, deeper pathos, subtler wit, more skill and variety in metre and in rhythm, and a wider command of the middle region between sport and earnest. It may be objected that Terence's superiority in these points arises from his copying his Greek originals more servilely. But no servile copy is an animated copy, and we have corresponding fragments enough of Menander to prove that Terence retouched and sometimes improved his model. In summing up his merits we ought not to omit the praise which has been universally accorded him — that, although a foreigner and a freedman, he divides with Cicero and Caesar the palm of pure Latinity. The best editions of Terence are by Bentley, Cantab. 1726, 4to., Amstel. 1727, 4to., Lips. 1791, 8vo. ; by Westerhovius, Hagae Com. 1727, 2 vols. 4to. ; and by Stallbaum, Lips. 1830, 8vo.

Terentĭus Cullĕo. [CULLEO.]

Terentĭus Varro. [VARRO.]

Tēres (Τήρης). 1. King of the Odrysae and father of SITALCES, was the founder of the great Odrysian monarchy. — 2. King of a portion of Thrace in the time of Philip of Macedon.

Tēreus (Τηρεύς), son of Ares, king of the Thracians in Daulis, afterwards Phocis. Pandion, king of Attica, who had 2 daughters, Philoméla and Procne, called in the assistance of Tereus against some enemy, and gave him his daughter Procne in marriage. Tereus became by her the father of Itys, and then concealed her in the country, that he might thus marry her sister Philomela whom he deceived by saying that Procne was dead. At the same time he deprived Philomela of her tongue. Ovid (*Met.* vi. 565) reverses the story by stating that Tereus told Procne that her sister Philomela was dead. Philomela, however, soon learned the truth, and made it known to her sister by a few words which she wove into a peplus. Procne thereupon killed her own son Itys, and served up the flesh of the child in a dish before Tereus. She then fled with her sister. Tereus pursued them with an axe, and when the sisters were overtaken they prayed to the gods to change them into birds. Procne, accordingly, became a nightingale, Philomela a swallow, and Tereus a hoopoo. According to some, Procne became a swallow, Philomela a nightingale, and Tereus a hawk.

Tergestĕ (Tergestinus : *Trieste*), a town of Istria, on a bay in the N. E. of the Adriatic guif, called after it Tergestinus Sinus. It was at first

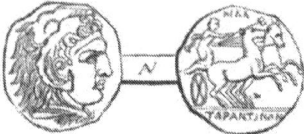

Tarentum. Page 743.

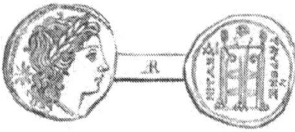

Tauromenium. Page 747.

Teanum Sidicinum. Page 748.

Teate. Page 748.

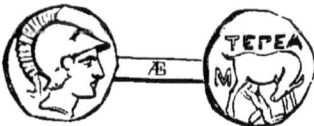

Tegea. Page 748.

Temnus in Aeolis. Page 750.

Tenedos. Page 751.

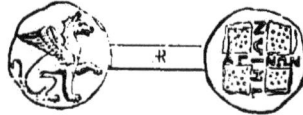

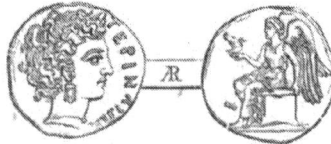

Teos in Ionia. Page 751.

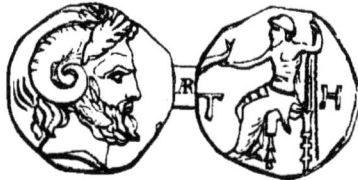

Tenos. Page 751.

Terina in Bruttium. Page 753.

Termessus in Pisidia. Page 753.

Thasos. Page 755.

[To face p. 752.

Thebes in Boeotia. Page 756.

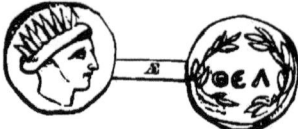

Thelpusa in Arcadia. Page 757.

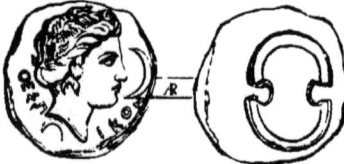

Thespiae in Boeotia. Page 757.

Thessalia. Page 757.

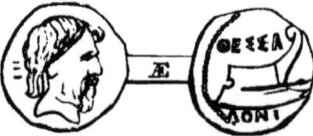

Thessalonica. Page 769.

Thurii. Page 774.

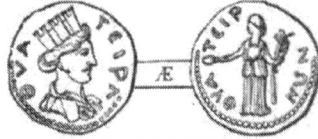

Thyatira. Page 774.

Tomi, or Tomis. Page 786.

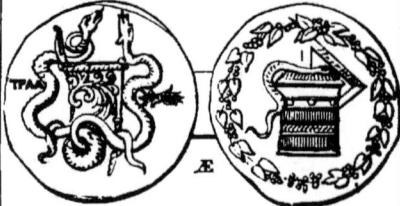

Tralles. Page 788.

Tripolis in Phoenicia. Page 790.

Troy, or Ilium. Page 792.

Tyre. Page 797.

To face p. 753.]

an insignificant place, with which the Romans became acquainted in their wars with the Iapydes; but under the Roman dominion it became a town of considerable commercial importance. It was made a Roman colony by Vespasian.

Teria (Τηρείης ὄρος αἰπύ, Hom.), a mountain of Mysia, probably in the neighbourhood of Cyzicus. Some identified it with a hill near Lampsacus, on which was a temple of Cybele.

Terias (*Guaralunga*), a river in Sicily near Leontini.

Teridates. [TIRIDATES.]

Terina (Terinaeus: *St. Eufemia*), a town on the W. coast of Bruttium, from which the Sinus Terinaeus derived its name. It was a Greek city founded by Croton, and was originally a place of some importance; but it was destroyed by Hannibal in the 2nd Punic war.

Teriolis or **Teriola Castra**, a fortress in Rhaetia, which has given its name to the country of the *Tyrol.* Its site is still occupied by the *Castle of Tyrol*, lying above Meran, to the N. of the road.

Termantia, Termes, or **Termesus** (Termestinus or Termesius: *Ermita de nuestra Señora de Tiermes*), a town of the Arevaci in Hispania Tarraconensis, originally situated on a steep hill, the inhabitants of which frequently resisted the Romans, who compelled them in consequence to abandon the town, and build a new one on the plain, B. C. 98.

Termera (τὰ Τέρμερα), a Dorian city in Caria, on the promontory Termerium (Τερμέριον), the N. W. headland of the Sinus Ceramicus. Under the Romans, it was a free city.

Termessus (Τερμησσός, and other forms: prob. *Skenet*, Ru.), a city of Pisidia, high up on the Taurus, in the pass through which the river Catarrhactes flowed. It was almost impregnable by nature and art, so that even Alexander did not attempt to take it.

Terminus, a Roman divinity presiding over boundaries and frontiers. His worship is said to have been instituted by Numa, who ordered that every one should mark the boundaries of his landed property by stones consecrated to Jupiter, and at these boundary-stones every year sacrifices should be offered at the festival of the Terminalia. The Terminus of the Roman state originally stood between the 5th and 6th milestone on the road towards Laurentum, near a place called Festi. Another public Terminus stood in the temple of Jupiter in the Capitol. It is said that when this temple was to be founded, all the gods gave way to Jupiter and Juno, with the exception of Terminus and Juventas, whose sanctuaries the auguries would not allow to be removed. This was taken as an omen that the Roman state would remain ever undiminished and young, and the chapels of the two divinities were inclosed within the walls of the new temple. It is however probable that the god Terminus is no other than Jupiter himself, in the capacity of protector of boundaries.

Terpander (Τέρπανδρος), the father of Greek music, and through it of lyric poetry. He was a native of Antissa in Lesbos, and flourished between B. C. 700 and 650. He removed from Lesbos to Sparta, and there introduced his new system of music, and established the first musical school or system that existed in Greece. He added 3 strings to the lyre, which before his time had only 4

strings, thus making it seven-stringed. His music produced a powerful effect upon the Spartans, and he was held in high honour by them, during his life and after his death. He was the first who obtained a victory in the musical contests at the festival of the Carnea (676). We have only 3 or 4 fragments of the remains of his poetry.

Terpsichore (Τερψιχόρα), one of the 9 Muses presided over the choral song and dancing. [MUSAE.]

Terra. [GAEA.]

Terracina, more usually written **Tarracina.** [TARRACINA.]

Tertullianus, Q. Septimius Florens usually called **Tertullian,** the most ancient of the Latin fathers now extant. Notwithstanding the celebrity which he has always enjoyed, our knowledge of his personal history is extremely limited, and is derived almost exclusively from a succinct notice by St. Jerome. From this we learn that Tertullian was a native of Carthage, the son of a proconsular centurion (an officer who appears to have acted as a sort of aide-de-camp to provincial governors); that he flourished chiefly during the reigns of Septimius Severus and of Caracalla; that he became a presbyter, and remained orthodox until he had reached the term of middle life, when, in consequence of the envy and ill-treatment which he experienced on the part of the Roman clergy, he went over to the Montanists, and wrote several books in defence of those heretics; that he lived to a great age, and was the author of many works. His birth may be placed about A. D. 160, and his death about 240. The most interesting of his numerous works is his *Apologia*, or defence of Christianity. It was written at Carthage, probably during the reign of Severus. The writings of Tertullian show that he was a man of varied learning; but his style is rough, abrupt, and obscure, abounding in far-fetched metaphors and extravagant hyperboles. The best editions of the complete works of Tertullian are the one printed at Venice, 1744, fo., and the one edited by Semler and by Schutz, 6 vols. 8vo. Hal. 1770. There is a good edition of the *Apologeticus*, by Havercamp, 8vo. Lug. Bat. 1710.

Testa, C. Trebatius, a Roman jurist, and a contemporary and friend of Cicero. He was recommended by Cicero to Julius Caesar during his proconsulship of Gaul, and he followed Caesar's party after the civil war broke out. Cicero dedicated to Trebatius his book of *Topica*, which he wrote to explain to him this book of Aristotle. Trebatius enjoyed considerable reputation under Augustus as a lawyer. Horace addressed to him the 1st Satire of the 2nd Book. Trebatius was a pupil of Q. Cornelius Maximus, and master of Labeo. He wrote some books *De Jure Civili*, and *De Religionibus*. He is often cited in the Digest, but there is no direct excerpt from his writings.

Tethys (Τηθύς), daughter of Uranus and Gaea, and wife of Oceanus, by whom she became the mother of the Oceanides and of the numerous river-gods. She also educated Hera, who was brought to her by Rhea.

Tetrica, a mountain on the frontiers of Picenum and the land of the Sabines, belonging to the great chain of the Apennines.

Tetricus, C. Pesuvius, one of the Thirty Tyrants, and the last of the pretenders who ruled Gaul during its separation from the empire under Gallienus and his successor. He reigned in Gaul from A. D. 267 to 274, and was defeated by Aurelian in 274, at the battle of Chalons, on which occasion he was believed to have betrayed his army to the emperor. It is certain that although Tetricus, along with his son, graced the triumph of the conqueror, he was immediately afterwards treated with the greatest distinction by Aurelian.

Teucer (Τεῦκρος). 1. Son of the river-god Scamander by the Nymph Idaea, was the first king of Troy, whence the Trojans are sometimes called *Teucri*. Dardanus of Samothrace came to Teucer, received his daughter Batea or Arisbe in marriage, and became his successor in the kingdom. According to others, Dardanus was a native prince of Troy, and Scamander and Teucer immigrated into Troas from Crete, bringing with them the worship of Apollo Smintheus. — **2.** Son of Telamon and Hesione, was a step-brother of Ajax, and the best archer among the Greeks at Troy. On his return from the Trojan war, Telamon refused to receive him in Salamis, because he had not avenged the death of his brother Ajax. Teucer thereupon sailed away in search of a new home, which he found in the island of Cyprus, which was given to him by Belus, king of Sidon. He there founded the town of Salamis, and married Eune, the daughter of Cyprus, by whom he became the father of Asteria.

Teucri. [MYSIA; TROAS.]

Teumessus (Τευμησσός), a mountain in Boeotia, near Hypatus, and close to Thebes, on the road from the latter place to Chalcis. It was from this mountain that Dionysus, enraged with the Thebans, sent the fox which committed such devastations in their territory.

Teuta (Τεῦτα), wife of Agron, king of the Illyrians, assumed the sovereign power on the death of her husband, B. C. 231. In consequence of the injuries inflicted by the piratical expeditions of her subjects upon the Italian merchants, the Romans sent two ambassadors to demand satisfaction, but she not only refused to comply with their demands, but caused the younger of the two brothers to be assassinated on his way home. War was now declared against her by the Romans. The greater part of her territory was soon conquered, and she was obliged to sue for peace, which was granted to her (B.C. 228), on condition of her giving up the greater part of her dominions.

Teuthrania. [MYSIA.]

Teuthras (Τεύθρας), an ancient king of Mysia, who married, or, according to other accounts, adopted as his daughter Auge, the daughter of Aleus. He also received with hospitality her son Telephus, when the latter came to Asia in search of his mother. He was succeeded in the kingdom of Mysia by Telephus. [TELEPHUS.] The 50 daughters of Teuthras, given as a reward to Hercules, are called by Ovid *Teuthrantia turba*.

Teuthras (Τεύθρας: prob. *Demirji-Dagh*), a mountain in the Mysian district of Teuthrania, a S.W. branch of Temnus. It contains a celebrated pass, called the *Iron Gates* (*Demir Kapu*), through which all caravans between Smyrna and Brusa (the ancient Prusias) must needs pass.

Teutoburgiensis Saltus, a range of hills in Germany covered with wood, extending N. of the Lippe, from Osnabrück to Paderborn, and known in the present day by the name of the *Teutoburger Wald* or *Lippische Wald*. It is celebrated on ac

count of the defeat and destruction of Varus and 3 Roman legions by the Germans under Arminius, A. D. 9.

Teutōnes or **Teutŏni**, a powerful people in Germany, who invaded Gaul and the Roman dominions along with the Cimbri, at the latter end of the 2nd century B. C. The history of their invasion is given under CIMBRI. The name Teutones is not a collective name of the whole people of Germany, as some writers have supposed, but only of one particular tribe, who probably dwelt on the coast of the Baltic, near the Cimbri.

Thabor, Tabor, or **Atabyrĭum** ('Αταβύριον LXX.: 'Ιταβύριον, Joseph.: *Jebel Tur*), an isolated mountain at the E. end of the plain of Esdraelon in Galilee, between 1700 and 1800 feet high. Its summit was occupied by a fortified town, under the Maccabees and the Romans. This is quite enough to prove that it cannot be, as a local tradition asserts, the lonely mountain on which our Saviour was transfigured; although the tradition has been bolstered up by a variation of the modern name of the mountain, which makes it *Jebel Nur*, i. e. the *Mountain of Light*.

Thabrāca or **Tabraca** (Θαβρακα, Τάβαθρα: *Tabarca*), a city of Numidia, at the mouth of the river Tusca, and on the frontier towards Zeugitana.

Thaïs (Θαΐς), a celebrated Athenian courtezan, who accompanied Alexander the Great on his expedition into Asia. Her name is best known from the story of her having stimulated the conqueror during a great festival at Persepolis, to set fire to the palace of the Persian kings: but this anecdote, immortalized as it has been by Dryden's famous ode, is in all probability a mere fable. After the death of Alexander, Thaïs attached herself to Ptolemy Lagi, by whom she became the mother of two sons, Leontiscus and Lagus, and of a daughter Irene.

Thala (Θάλα), a great city of Numidia, mentioned by Sallust and other writers, and probably identical with **Telepte** (Τελεπτή) or **Thelepte**, a city in the S. of Numidia, 71 Roman miles N.W. of Capsa. It was the S. W. frontier town towards the desert, and was connected by a road with Tacape on the Syrtis Minor. It is probably to be identified with *Ferianah*, or with the large ruins near it, called *Medinah el Kadima*.

Thalāmae (Θαλάμαι). 1. A fortified town in Elis, situated in the mountains above Pylos. — **2.** A town in Messenia, probably a little to the E. of the river Pamisus.

Thălassĭus, Tălassĭus, or **Tălassĭo**, a Roman senator of the time of Romulus. At the time of the rape of the Sabine women, when a maiden of surpassing beauty was carried off for Thalassius, the persons conducting her, in order to protect her against any assaults from others, exclaimed "for Thalassius." Hence, it is said, arose the wedding shout with which a bride at Rome was conducted to the house of her bridegroom.

Thălēs (Θαλῆς), the Ionic philosopher, and one of the Seven Sages, was born at Miletus about B. C. 636, and died about 546, at the age of 90, though the exact date neither of his birth nor of his death is known. He is said to have predicted the eclipse of the sun, which happened in the reign of the Lydian king Alyattes; to have diverted the course of the Halys in the time of Croesus; and later, in order to unite the Ionians when threatened by the Persians, to have instituted a federal council in Teos. In the lists of the Seven Sages his name seems to have stood at the head; and he displayed his wisdom both by political sagacity, and by prudence in acquiring wealth. He was also one of the founders in Greece of the study of philosophy and mathematics. In the latter science however we find attributed to him only proofs of propositions which belong to the first elements of geometry, and which could not possibly have enabled him to calculate the eclipses of the sun, and the course of the heavenly bodies. He may however have obtained his knowledge of the higher branches of mathematics from Egypt, which country he is said to have visited. Thales maintained that water is the origin of things, meaning thereby, that it is water, out of which every thing arises, and into which every thing resolves itself. Thales left no works behind him.

Thălĕs or **Thalētas** (Θαλῆς, Θαλήτας), the celebrated musician and lyric poet, was a native of Gortyna in Crete. On the invitation of the Spartans he removed to Sparta, where, by the influence of his music, he appeased the wrath of Apollo, who had visited the city with a plague, and composed the factions of the citizens, who were at enmity with each other. He founded the 2nd of the musical schools, which flourished at Sparta, the 1st having been established by Terpander. The date of Thaletas is uncertain, but he may probably be placed shortly after Terpander. [TERPANDER.]

Thălia (Θάλεια, Θαλία). 1. One of the 9 Muses and, at least in later times, the Muse of Comedy. [MUSAE.] — 2. One of the Nereides. — 3. One of the Charites or Graces.

Thallo. [HORAE.]

Thalna or **Talna, M'. Juventius**, was tribune of the plebs B. C. 170; praetor 167; and consul 163, when he subdued the Corsicans. The senate voted him the honour of a thanksgiving; and he was so overcome with joy at the intelligence, which he received as he was offering a sacrifice, that he dropt down dead on the spot.

Thambes (Θάμβης, Θάμμης, Θάμης), a mountain in the E. of Numidia, containing the source of the river Rubricatus.

Thamydēni or **Thamydītae** (Θαμυδηνοί, Θαμυδῖται), a people of Arabia Felix, on the coast of the Sinus Arabicus, in the neighbourhood of *Themond.*

Thamȳris or **Thamȳras** (Θάμυρις), an ancient Thracian bard, was a son of Philammon and the nymph Argiope. In his presumption he challenged the Muses to a trial of skill, and being overcome in the contest, was deprived by them of his sight and of the power of singing. He was represented with a broken lyre in his hand.

Thanătos. [MORS.]

Thapsa, a city of N. Africa, probably identical with RUSICADA.

Thapsăcus (Θάψακος: O. T. Thiphsach: an Aramean word signified a *ford*: Θαψακηνός: Ru. at the ford of *El-Hamman*, near *Rakkah*), a city of Syria, in the province of Chalybonitis, on the left bank of the Euphrates, 2000 stadia S. of Zeugma, and 15 parasangs from the mouth of the river Chaboras (the Araxes of Xenophon). At this place was the usual, and for a long time the only ford of the Euphrates, by which a passage was made between Upper and Lower Asia.

Thapsus (Θάψος: Θάψιος). 1. A city on the

E. coast of Sicily on a peninsula of the same name (*Isola degli Magnisi*), founded by Dorian colonists from Megara, who soon abandoned it in order to found Megara Hybla. — 2. (*Demas*, Ru.), a city on the E. coast of Byzacena, in Africa Propria, where Caesar finally defeated the Pompeian army, and finished the civil war, B. C. 46.

Thasos or **Thasus** (Θάσος: Θάσιος: *Thaso* or *Tasso*), an island in the N. of the Aegaean sea, off the coast of Thrace and opposite the mouth of the river Nestus. It was at a very early period taken possession of by the Phoenicians, on account of its valuable gold mines. According to tradition the Phoenicians were led by Thasus, son of Poseidon, or Agenor, who came from the East in search of Europa, and from whom the island derived its name. Thasos was afterwards colonised by the Parians, B. C. 708, and among the colonists was the poet Archilochus. Besides the gold mines in Thasos itself, the Thasians possessed still more valuable gold mines at Scapte Hyle on the opposite coast of Thrace. The mines in the island had been most extensively worked by the Phoenicians, but even in the time of Herodotus they were still productive. The clear surplus revenue of the Thasians before the Persian conquest amounted to 200, and sometimes even to 300 talents (46,000*l*., 66,000*l*.), of which sum the mines in Scapte Hyle produced 80 talents, and those in the island somewhat less. They possessed at this time a considerable territory on the coast of Thrace, and were one of the richest and most powerful peoples in the N. of the Aegaean. They were subdued by the Persians under Mardonius, and subsequently became part of the Athenian maritime empire. They revolted, however, from Athens in B. C. 465, and after sustaining a siege of 3 years, were subdued by Cimon in 463. They were obliged to surrender to the Athenians all their possessions in Thrace, to destroy their fortifications, to give up their ships, and to pay a large tribute for the future. They again revolted from Athens in 411, and called in the Spartans, but the island was again restored to the Athenians by Thrasybulus in 407. In addition to its gold mines, Thasos was celebrated for its marble and its wine. The soil, however, is otherwise barren, and merits even at the present day the description applied to it by the poet Archilochus, — "an ass's back-bone, overspread with wild wood." The principal town in the island, also called Thasos, was situated on the N. coast upon 8 eminences. There are still a few remains of the ancient town.

Thaumas (Θαύμας), son of Pontus and Ge, and by the Oceanid Electra, the father of Iris and the Harpies. Hence Iris is called *Thaumantias, Thaumantis*, and *Thaumantēa virgo*.

Theaetētus (Θεαίτητος), an Athenian, the son of Euphronius of Sunium, is introduced as one of the speakers in Plato's *Theaetetus* and *Sophistes*, in which dialogues he is spoken of as a noble and well-disposed youth; and ardent in the pursuit of knowledge, especially in the study of geometry.

Theagēnes (Θεαγένης). 1. Tyrant of Megara, obtained his power about B. C. 630, having espoused the part of the commonalty against the nobles. He was driven out before his death. He gave his daughter in marriage to Cylon. [CYLON.] — 2. A Thasian, the son of Timosthenes, renowned for his extraordinary strength and swiftness. He gained numerous victories at the Olympian, Pythian,

Nemean, and Isthmian games, and is said to have won 1300 crowns. He flourished B c. 480.

Thĕāno (Θεανώ), daughter of Cisseus, wife of Antenor, and priestess of Athena at Ilion.

Thĕāno (Θεανώ), the most celebrated of the female philosophers of the Pythagorean school, appears to have been the wife of Pythagoras, and the mother by him of Telanges, Mnesarchus, Myia, and Arignote; but the accounts respecting her were various. Several letters are extant under her name; and, though they are not genuine, they are valuable remains of a period of considerable antiquity.

Thĕbae (Θῆβαι), in the poets sometimes **Thebe** (Θήβη, Dor. Θήβα), aft. **Diospŏlis Magna** (Διόσπολις μεγάλη, i. e. *Great City of Jove*), in Scripture **No** or **No Ammon**, was the capital of Thebaïs, or Upper Egypt, and, for a long time, of the whole country. It was reputed the oldest city of the world. It stood in about the centre of the Thebaïd, on both banks of the Nile, above Coptos, and in the Nomos Coptites. It is said to have been founded by Aethiopians; but this is of course only a form of the tradition which represents the civilisation of Upper Egypt as having come down the Nile. Others ascribed its foundation to Osiris, who named it after his mother, and others to Busiris. It appears to have been at the height of its splendour, as the capital of Egypt, and as a chief seat of the worship of Ammon, about B. c. 1600. The fame of its grandeur had reached the Greeks as early as the time of Homer, who describes it, with poetical exaggeration, as having a hundred gates, from each of which it could send out 200 war chariots fully armed. Homer's epithet of "Hundred-Gated" (ἑκατόμπυλοι) is repeatedly applied to the city by later writers. Its real extent was calculated by the Greek writers at 140 stadia (14 geog. miles) in circuit; and in Strabo's time, when the long transference of the seat of power to Lower Egypt had caused it to decline greatly, it still had a circuit of 80 stadia. That these computations are not exaggerated, is proved by the existing ruins, which extend from side to side of the valley of the Nile, here about 6 miles wide; while the rocks which bound the valley are perforated with tombs. These ruins, which are perhaps the most magnificent in the world, enclose within their site the 4 modern villages of *Carnac, Luxor, Medinet Abou*, and *Gournos*; the 2 former on the E., and the 2 latter on the W. side of the river. They consist of temples, colossi, sphinxes, and obelisks, and, on the W. side, of tombs, many of which are cut in the rock and adorned with paintings, which are still as fresh as if just finished. These ruins are remarkable alike for their great antiquity, and for the purity of their style. It is most probable that the great buildings were all erected before the Persian invasion, when Thebes was taken by Cambyses, and the wooden habitations burnt; after which time it never regained the rank of a capital city; and thus its architectural monuments escaped that Greek influence which is so marked in the edifices of Lower Egypt. Among its chief buildings, the ancient writers mention the **Memnonium**, with the 2 colossi in front of it, the temple of Ammon, in which one of the 3 chief colleges of priests was established, and the tombs of the kings. To describe the ruins and discuss their identification, would far exceed the limits of this article.

Thēbae, in *Europe*. 1. (Θῆβαι, in Poetry Θήβη, Dor. Θήβα: Θηβαῖος, fem. Θηβαΐς, Thēbānus, fem. Thēbāis: *Theba*, Turkish *Stiva*), the chief city in Boeotia, was situated in a plain S. E. of the lake Hylice and N. E. of Plataeae. Its acropolis, which was an oval eminence of no great height, was called **Cadmēa** (Καδμεία), because it was said to have been founded by Cadmus, the leader of a Phoenician colony. On each side of this acropolis is a small valley, running up from the Theban plain into the low ridge of hills by which it is separated from that of Plataeae. Of these valleys, the one to the W. is watered by the Dirce; and the one to the E. by the Ismenus; both of which however are insignificant streamlets, though so celebrated in ancient story. The greater part of the city stood in these valleys, and was built some time after the acropolis. It is said that the fortifications of the city were constructed by Amphion and his brother Zethus; and that, when Amphion played his lyre, the stones moved of their own accord and formed the wall. The territory of Thebes was called **Thēbāis** (Θηβαΐς), and extended E.-wards as far as the Euboean sea. No city is more celebrated in the mythical ages of Greece than Thebes. It was here that the use of letters was first introduced from Phoenicia into W. Europe. It was the reputed birthplace of the 2 great divinities, Dionysus and Hercules. It was also the native city of the great seer Tiresias, as well as of the great musician Amphion. It was the scene of the tragic fate of Oedipus, and of one of the most celebrated wars in the mythical annals of Greece. Polynices, who had been expelled from Thebes by his brother Eteocles, induced 6 other heroes to espouse his cause, and marched against the city; but they were all defeated and slain by the Thebans, with the exception of Adrastus, Polynices and Eteocles falling by each other's hands. This is usually called the war of the "Seven against Thebes." A few years afterwards "The Epigoni," or descendants of the seven heroes, marched against Thebes to revenge their fathers' death; they took the city and rased it to the ground. Thebes is not mentioned by Homer in the catalogue of the Greek cities which fought against Troy, as it was probably supposed not yet to have recovered from its devastation by the Epigoni. It appears however at the earliest historical period as a large and flourishing city; and it is represented as possessing 7 gates, the number assigned to it in the ancient legends. Its government, after the abolition of monarchy, was an aristocracy, or rather an oligarchy, which continued to be the prevailing form of government for a long time, although occasionally exchanged for that of a democracy. Towards the end of the Peloponnesian war, however, the oligarchy finally disappears; and Thebes appears under a democratical form of government from this time, till it became with the rest of Greece subject to the Romans. The Thebans were from an early period inveterate enemies of their neighbours, the Athenians. Their hatred of the latter people was probably one of the reasons which induced them to desert the cause of Grecian liberty in the great struggle against the Persian power. In the Peloponnesian war the Thebans naturally espoused the Spartan side, and contributed not a little to the downfal of Athens. But, in common with the other Greek states, they soon became disgusted with the Spartan supremacy

and joined the confederacy formed against Sparta
in B. C. 394. The peace of Antalcidas in 387 put
an end to hostilities in Greece ; but the treacherous
seizure of the Cadmea by the Lacedaemonian general Phoebidas in 382, and its recovery by the
Theban exiles in 379, led to a war between Thebes
and Sparta, in which the former not only recovered
its independence, but for ever destroyed the Lacedaemonian supremacy. This was the most glorious
period in the Theban annals ; and the decisive
defeat of the Spartans at the battle of Leuctra in
371, made Thebes the first power in Greece. Her
greatness however was mainly due to the pre-
eminent abilities of her citizens, Epaminondas and
Pelopidas ; and with the death of the former at the
battle of Mantinea in 362, she lost the supremacy
which she had so recently gained. Soon afterwards Philip of Macedon began to exercise a paramount influence over the greater part of Greece.
The Thebans were induced, by the eloquence of
Demosthenes, to forget their old animosities against
the Athenians, and to join the latter in protecting
the liberties of Greece ; but their united forces
were defeated by Philip, at the battle of Chaeronea, in 338. Soon after the death of Philip and
the accession of Alexander, the Thebans made a
last attempt to recover their liberty, but were
cruelly punished by the young king. The city
was taken by Alexander in 336, and was entirely
destroyed, with the exception of the temples, and
the house of the poet Pindar ; 6000 inhabitants
were slain, and 30,000 sold as slaves. In 316 the
city was rebuilt by Cassander, with the assistance
of the Athenians. In 290 it was taken by Demetrius Poliorcetes, and again suffered greatly. Dicaearchus, who flourished about this time, has left
us an interesting account of the city. He describes
it as about 70 stadia (nearly 9 miles) in circumference, in form nearly circular, and in appearance
somewhat gloomy. He says that it is plentifully
provided with water, and contains better gardens
than any other city in Greece ; that it is most
agreeable in summer, on account of its plentiful
supply of cool and fresh water, and its large gardens ; but that in winter it is very unpleasant,
being destitute of fuel, exposed to floods and cold
winds, and frequently visited by heavy falls of
snow. He further represents the people as proud
and insolent, and always ready to settle disputes
by fighting, rather than by the ordinary course of
justice. It is supposed that the population of the
city at this time may have been between 50,000
and 60,000 souls. After the Macedonian period
Thebes rapidly declined in importance ; and it received its last blow from Sulla, who gave half of
its territory to the Delphians. Strabo describes
it as only a village in his time ; and Pausanias,
who visited it in the 2nd century of the Christian
era, says that the Cadmea alone was then inhabited. The modern town is also confined to
this spot, and the surrounding country is covered
with a confused heap of ruins — 2. Surnamed
Phthioticae (Θῆβαι αἱ Φθιώτιδες), an important
city of Thessaly in the district Phthiotis, at a short
distance from the coast, and with a good harbour.
— 3. A town in Lucania, rarely mentioned.

Thebais. [ΑΕΓΥΠΤΟΒ.]

Thebe (Θήβη Ὑποπλακίη), a city of Mysia, on
the wooded slope of M. Placus, destroyed by
Achilles. It was said to have been the birthplace
of Andromache and Chryseïs. It existed in the

historical period, but by the time of Strabo it had
fallen into ruin, and by that of Pliny it had vanished. Its site was near the head of the Gulf of
Adramyttium, where a beautiful tract of country
was named, after it, Thebanus campus (τὸ Θήβης
πεδίον).

Thecoa or Tekoa (Θεκόα, Joseph. : Θεκωέ LXX. :
Tekua, Ru.), a city of Judaea, on the edge of the
desert, 6 miles S. of Bethlehem, and 12 S. of Jerusalem, was the birthplace of the prophet Amos.
(See also 2 Chron. xi.) In the time of Jerome, it
was a mere village.

Thelpusa or Telphussa (Θέλπουσα, Τέλφουσσα·
Τελφούσιος : nr. Vanena Ru.), a town in Arcadia
on the river Ladon.

Theman, a city of the Edomites, in Arabia Petraea, whose people were celebrated for their
wisdom.

Themis (Θέμις), daughter of Uranus and Ge,
was married to Zeus, by whom she became the
mother of the Horae, Eunomia, Dice (Astraea),
Irene, and of the Moerae. In the Homeric poems,
Themis is the personification of the order of things
established by law, custom, and equity, whence
she is described as reigning in the assemblies of
men, and as convening, by the command of Zeus,
the assembly of the gods. She dwells in Olympus,
and is on friendly terms with Hera. She is also
described as a prophetic divinity, and is said to
have been in possession of the Delphic oracle as
the successor of Ge, and previous to Apollo.
Nymphs believed to be daughters of Zeus and
Themis lived in a cave on the river Eridanus, and
the Hesperides also are called daughters of Zeus
and Themis. She is often represented on coins
resembling the figure of Athena with a cornucopia
and a pair of scales.

Themiscyra (Θεμίσκυρα), a plain on the coast
of Pontus, extending E. of the river Iris beyond the
Thermodon, celebrated from very ancient times as
the country of the Amazons. It was well watered,
and rich in pasture. At the mouth of the Thermodon was a city of the same name, which had
been destroyed by the time of Augustus. It is
doubtful whether the present Thermeh occupies its
site. [THERMODON.]

Themison (Θεμίσων), a celebrated Greek physician, and the founder of the medical sect of the
Methodici, was a native of Laodicea in Syria, and
lived in the first century B. C. He wrote several
medical works, but of these only the titles and a
few fragments remain. The physician mentioned
by Juvenal was probably a contemporary of the
poet, and consequently a different person from the
founder of the Methodici.

Themistius (Θεμίστιος), a distinguished philosopher and rhetorician, was a Paphlagonian, and
flourished, first at Constantinople and afterwards
at Rome, in the reigns of Constantius, Julian,
Jovian, Valens, Gratian, and Theodosius. He
enjoyed the favour of all those emperors, and was
promoted by them to the highest honours of the
state. After holding various public offices, and
being employed on many important embassies, he
was made prefect of Constantinople by Theodosius,
A. D. 384. So great was the confidence reposed in
him by Theodosius, that, though Themistius was
a heathen, the emperor entrusted his son Arcadius
to the tutorship of the philosopher, 387. The life
of Themistius probably did not extend beyond
390. Besides the emperors, he numbered among

his friends the chief orators and philosophers of the age, Christian as well as heathen. Not only Libanius, but Gregory of Nazianzus also was his friend and correspondent, and the latter, in an epistle still extant, calls him the " king of arguments." The orations (πολιτικοὶ λόγοι) of Themistius, extant in the time of Photius, were 36 in number, of which 33 have come down to us in the original Greek, and one in a Latin version. The other two were supposed to be lost, until one of them was discovered by Cardinal Maio, in the Ambrosian Library at Milan, in 1816. The best edition of the Orations is by Dindorf, Lips.1832,8vo.

Thĕmistŏcles (Θεμιστοκλῆς), the celebrated Athenian, was the son of Neocles and Abrotonon, a Thracian woman, and was born about B. C. 514. In his youth he had an impetuous character ; he displayed great intellectual power combined with a lofty ambition and desire of political distinction. He began his career by setting himself in opposition to those who had most power, among whom Aristides was the chief. The fame which Miltiades acquired by his generalship at Marathon made a deep impression on Themistocles ; and he said that the trophy of Miltiades would not let him sleep. His rival Aristides was ostracized in 483, to which event Themistocles contributed ; and from this time he was the political leader in Athens. In 481 he was Archon Eponymus. It was about this time that he persuaded the Athenians to employ the produce of the silver mines of Laurium in building ships, instead of distributing it among the Athenian citizens. His great object was to draw the Athenians to the sea, as he was convinced that it was only by their fleet that Athens could repel the Persians and obtain the supremacy in Greece. Upon the invasion of Greece by Xerxes, Themistocles was appointed to the command of the Athenian fleet ; and to his energy, prudence, foresight, and courage the Greeks mainly owed their salvation from the Persian dominion. Upon the approach of Xerxes, the Athenians, on the advice of Themistocles, deserted their city, and removed their women, children, and infirm persons to Salamis, Aegina, and Troezen ; but as soon as the Persians took possession of Athens, the Peloponnesians were anxious to retire to the Corinthian isthmus. Themistocles used all his influence in inducing the Greeks to remain and fight with the Persians at Salamis, and with the greatest difficulty persuaded the Spartan commander Eurybiades to stay at Salamis. But as soon as the fleet of Xerxes made its appearance, the Peloponnesians were again anxious to sail away ; and when Themistocles saw that he should be unable to persuade them to remain, he sent a faithful slave to the Persian commanders, informing them that the Greeks intended to make their escape, and that the Persians had now the opportunity of accomplishing a noble enterprise, if they would only cut off the retreat of the Greeks. The Persians believed what they were told, and in the night their fleet occupied the whole of the channel between Salamis and the mainland. The Greeks were thus compelled to fight ; and the result was the great and glorious victory, in which the greater part of the fleet of Xerxes was destroyed. This victory, which was due to Themistocles, established his reputation among the Greeks. On his visiting Sparta, he was received with extraordinary honours by the Spartans, who gave Eurybiades the palm

of bravery, and to Themistocles the palm of wisdom and skill, with a crown of olive, and the best chariot that Sparta possessed. The Athenians began to restore their ruined city after the barbarians had left the country, and Themistocles advised them to rebuild the walls, and to make them stronger than before. The Spartans sent an embassy to Athens to dissuade them from fortifying their city, for which we can assign no motive except a miserable jealousy. Themistocles, however, went on an embassy to Sparta, where he amused the Spartans with lies, till the walls were far enough advanced to be in a state of defence. It was upon his advice also that the Athenians fortified the port of Piraeus. The influence of Themistocles does not appear to have survived the expulsion of the Persians from Greece and the fortification of the ports. He was probably justly accused of enriching himself by unfair means, for he had no scruples about the way of accomplishing an end. A story is told, that after the retreat of the fleet of Xerxes, when the Greek fleet was wintering at Pagasae, Themistocles told the Athenians in the public assembly that he had a scheme to propose which was beneficial to the state, but could not be expounded to the many. Aristides was named to receive the secret, and to report upon it. His report was that nothing could be more profitable than the scheme of Themistocles, but nothing more unjust ; and the Athenians abided by the report of Aristides. In 471 Themistocles was ostracised from Athens, and retired to Argos. After the discovery of the treasonable correspondence of Pausanias with the Persian king, the Lacedaemonians sent to Athens to accuse Themistocles of being privy to the design of Pausanias. Thereupon the Athenians sent off persons with the Lacedaemonians with instructions to arrest Themistocles (466). Themistocles, hearing of what was designed against him, first fled from Argos to Corcyra, and then to Epirus, where he took refuge in the house of Admetus, king of the Molossi, who happened to be from home. Admetus was no friend to Themistocles, but his wife told the fugitive that he would be protected if he would take their child in his arms, and sit on the hearth. The king soon came in, and respecting his suppliant attitude, raised him up, and refused to surrender him to the Lacedaemonian and Athenian agents. Themistocles finally reached the coast of Asia in safety. Xerxes was now dead (465), and Artaxerxes was on the throne. Themistocles went up to visit the king at his royal residence; and on his arrival he sent the king a letter, in which he promised to do the k ng a good service, and prayed that he might be allowed to wait a year, and then to explain personally what brought him there. In a year he made himself master of the Persian language and the Persian usages, and, being presented to the king, he obtained the greatest influence over him, and such as no Greek ever before enjoyed; partly owing to his high reputation and the hopes that he gave to the king of subjecting the Greeks to the Persians. The king gave him a handsome allowance, after the Persian fashion; Magnesia supplied him with bread nominally, but paid him annually fifty talents. Lampsacus supplied wine, and Myus the other provisions. Before he could accomplish any thing he died; some say that he poisoned himself, finding that he could not perform his promise to the king. A monument was erected to his memory in the Agora of Magnesia, which place was within his government. It is said that his bones were secretly taken to Attica by his relations, and privately interred there. Themistocles died in 449, at the age of 65. Themistocles undoubtedly possessed great talents as a statesman, great political sagacity, a ready wit, and excellent judgment: but he was not an honest man; and, like many other clever men with little morality, he ended his career unhappily and ingloriously, an xile and a traitor too. 21 letters attributed to Themistocles are spurious.

Themistŏgĕnes (Θεμιστογένης), of Syracuse, is said by Xenophon (*Hell.* iii. 1. § 2) to have written a work on the Anabasis of Cyrus; but most modern writers, following the statement of Plutarch, suppose that Xenophon really refers to his own work, to which he prefixed the name of Themistogenes.

Theŏcles (Θεοκλῆς), son of Hegylus, was a Lacedaemonian statuary, and one of the disciples of Dipoenus and Scyllis. He therefore flourished about B. C. 550.

Theoclўmĕnus (Θεοκλύμενος), son of Polyphides of Hyperasia, and a descendant of Melampus, was a soothsayer, and in consequence of a murder, was obliged to take to flight, and came to Telemachus when the latter quitted Sparta to return to Ithaca.

Theŏcosmus (Θεόκοσμος), of Megara, a statuary, flourished about B. C. 435—430.

Theŏcrĭtus (Θεόκριτος). 1. Of Chios, an orator, sophist, and perhaps an historian, in the time of Alexander the Great. He was contemporary with Ephorus and Theopompus; and the latter was his fellow-citizen and political opponent, Theopompus belonging to the aristocratic and Macedonian, and Theocritus to the democratic and patriotic party. Theocritus is said to have also given deep offence to Alexander by the sarcastic wit, which appears to have been the chief cause of his celebrity, and which at last cost him his life. He was put to death by Antigonus, in revenge for a jest upon the king's single eye. None of his works are extant with the exception of 2 or 3 epigrams, among which is a very bitter one upon Aristotle. — 2. The celebrated bucolic poet, was a native of Syracuse, and the son of Praxagoras and Philinna. He visited Alexandria during the latter end of the reign of Ptolemy Soter, where he received the instruction of Philetas and Asclepiades, and began to distinguish himself as a poet. His first efforts obtained for him the patronage of Ptolemy Philadelphus, who was associated in the kingdom with his father, Ptolemy Soter, in B. C. 285, and in whose praise, therefore, the poet wrote the 14th, 15th, and 17th Idyls. At Alexandria he became acquainted with the poet Aratus, to whom he addressed his 6th Idyl. Theocritus afterwards returned to Syracuse, and lived there under Hiero II. It appears from the 16th Idyl that Theocritus was dissatisfied, both with the want of liberality on the part of Hiero in rewarding him for his poems, and with the political state of his native country. It may therefore be supposed that he devoted the latter part of his life almost entirely to the contemplation of those scenes of nature and of country life, on his representations of which his fame chiefly rests. Theocritus was the creator of bucolic poetry as a branch of Greek,

and, through imitators, such as Virgil, of Roman literature. The bucolic idyls of Theocritus are of a dramatic and mimetic character. They are pictures of the ordinary life of the common people of Sicily; whence their name, εἶδη, εἰδύλλια. The pastoral poems and romances of later times are a totally different sort of composition from the bucolics of Theocritus, who knows nothing of the affected sentiment, the pure innocence, and the primeval simplicity, which have been ascribed to the imaginary shepherds of a fictitious Arcadia. He merely exhibits simple and faithful pictures of the common life of the Sicilian people, in a thoroughly objective, although truly poetical spirit. Dramatic simplicity and truth are impressed upon the pictures exhibited in his poems, into the colouring of which he has thrown much of the natural comedy which is always seen in the common life of a free people. The collection, which has come down to us under the name of Theocritus, consists of 30 poems, called by the general title of *Idyls*, a fragment of a few lines from a poem entitled *Berenice*, and 22 epigrams in the Greek Anthology. But these Idyls are not all bucolic, and were not all written by Theocritus. Those idyls, of which the genuineness is the most doubtful, are the 12th, 17th, 18th, 19th, 20th, 26th, 27th, 29th, and 30th. The dialect of Theocritus is a mixed or eclectic dialect, in which the new or softened Doric predominates. The best editions of Theocritus are by Kiessling, Lips. 1819, and by Wüstemann, Gothae, 1830.

Theŏdectes (Θεοδέκτης), of Phaselis, in Pamphylia, was a highly distinguished rhetorician and tragic poet in the time of Philip of Macedon. He was the son of Aristander, and a pupil of Isocrates and Aristotle. The greater part of his life was spent at Athens, where he died at the age of 41. The people of his native city honoured the memory of Theodectes with a statue in their agora, which Alexander, when he stopped at Phaselis on his march towards Persia, crowned with garlands, to show his respect for the memory of a man who had been associated with himself by means of Aristotle and philosophy. The passages of Aristotle, in which Theodectes is mentioned, show the strong regard and high esteem in which he was held by the philosopher. Theodectes devoted himself, during the first part of his life, entirely to rhetoric, and afterwards he turned his attention to tragic poetry. He was a professional teacher of rhetoric and composer of orations for others, and was in part dependent on this profession for his subsistence. None of the works of Theodectes have come down to us. He wrote 50 tragedies, which were very popular among his contemporaries. His treatise on rhetoric is repeatedly referred to by the ancient writers.

Theodŏrētus (Θεοδώρητος), an eminent ecclesiastic of the 5th century, was born at Antioch about A. D. 393, and was made bishop of Cyrus, or Cyrrhus, a small city near the Euphrates, in 420 or 423. He was accused of being a Nestorian, and was in consequence deposed at the second council of Ephesus in 449; but he was restored to his diocese at the council of Chalcedon, in 451, upon his anathematizing Nestorius and his doctrines. He appears to have died in 457 or 458. Theodoret was a man of learning and of sound judgment. The most important of his works are: 1. *Commentaries* on various books of the Old and New Testaments, in which he adopts the method, not of a continuous commentary, but of proposing and solving those difficulties which he thinks likely to occur to a thoughtful reader. 2. An *Ecclesiastical History*, in 5 books, intended as a continuation of the History of Eusebius. It begins with the history of Arianism, under Constantine the Great, and ends in 429. 3. An apologetic treatise, intended to exhibit the confirmations of the truth of Christianity contained in the Gentile philosophy. 4. Ten Orations on Providence. The complete editions of Theodoret are by Sirmond and Garnier, 5 vols. fo., Paris, 1642—1684, and by Schulze and Noesselt, Halae Sax. 1769—1774, 5 vols. in 10 parts 8vo.

Theodorias. [Vacca.]

Theodoricus or Theodoricus. 1. I. King of the Visigoths from A. D. 418 to 451, was the successor of Wallia, but appears to have been the son of the great Alaric. He fell fighting on the side of Aëtius and the Romans at the great battle of Chalons, in which Attila was defeated 451. — 2. II. King of the Visigoths A. D. 452—466, 2nd son of Theodoric I. He succeeded to the throne by the murder of his brother Thorismond. He ruled over the greater part of Gaul and Spain. He was assassinated in 466 by his brother Euric, who succeeded him on the throne. Theodoric II. was a patron of letters and learned men. The poet Sidonius Apollinaris resided for some time at his court. — 3. Surnamed the Great, king of the Ostrogoths, succeeded his father Theodemir, in 475. He was at first an ally of Zeno, the emperor of Constantinople, but was afterwards involved in hostilities with the emperor. In order to get rid of Theodoric, Zeno gave him permission to invade Italy, and expel the usurper Odoacer from the country. Theodoric entered Italy in 489, and after defeating Odoacer in 3 great battles, laid siege to Ravenna, in which Odoacer took refuge. After a siege of 3 years Odoacer capitulated on condition that he and Theodoric should rule jointly over Italy; but Odoacer was soon afterwards murdered by his more fortunate rival (493). Theodoric thus became master of Italy, which he ruled for 33 years, till his death in 526. His long reign was prosperous and beneficent, and under his sway Italy recovered from the ravages to which it had been exposed for so many years. Theodoric was also a patron of literature; and among his ministers were Cassiodorus and Boëthius, the two last writers who can claim a place in the literature of ancient Rome. But prosperous as had been the reign of Theodoric, his last days were darkened by disputes with the Catholics, and by the condemnation and execution of Boëthius and Symmachus, whom he accused of a conspiracy to overthrow the Gothic dominion in Italy. His death is said to have been hastened by remorse. It is related that one evening, when a large fish was served on the table, he fancied that he beheld the head of Symmachus, and was so terrified that he took to his bed, and died three days afterwards. Theodoric was buried at Ravenna, and a monument was erected to his memory by his daughter Amalasuntha. His ashes were deposited in a porphyry vase, which is still to be seen at Ravenna.

Theodoridas (Θεοδωρίδας), of Syracuse, a lyric and epigrammatic poet, who lived about B. C. 235. He had a place in the *Garland* of Meleager. There are 18 of his epigrams in the Greek Anthology.

Theodorus (Θεόδωρος). 1. Of Byzantium, a rhetorician, and a contemporary of Plato, who speaks of him somewhat contemptuously. Cicero describes him as excelling rather in the theory than the practice of his art. — 2. A philosopher of the Cyrenaic school, to one branch of which he gave the name of "Theodorians," Θεοδώρειοι. He is usually designated by ancient writers the Atheist. He was a disciple of the younger Aristippus, and was banished from Cyrene, but on what occasion is not stated. He then went to Athens, and only escaped being cited before the Areopagus, by the influence of Demetrius Phalereus. He was afterwards banished from Athens, probably with Demetrius (307), and went to Alexandria, where he was employed in the service of Ptolemy son of Lagus, king of the Macedonian dynasty in Egypt; it is not unlikely that he shared the overthrow and exile of Demetrius. While in the service of Ptolemy, Theodorus was sent on an embassy to Lysimachus, whom he offended by the freedom of his remarks. One answer which he made to a threat of crucifixion which Lysimachus had used has been celebrated by many ancient writers "Employ such threats to those courtiers of yours; for it matters not to Theodore whether he rots on the ground or in the air." He returned at length to Cyrene, where he appears to have ended his days. — 3. An eminent rhetorician of the age of Augustus, was a native of Gadara, in the country east of the Jordan. He settled at Rhodes, where Tiberius, afterwards emperor, during his retirement (B. C. 6—A. D. 2) to that island, was one of his hearers. He also taught at Rome; but whether his settlement at Rome preceded that at Rhodes is uncertain. Theodorus was the founder of a school of rhetoricians, called "Theodorei," as distinguished from the "Apollodorei," or followers of Apollodorus of Pergamus, who had been the tutor of Augustus Caesar at Apollonia. Theodorus wrote many works, all of which are lost. — 4. A Greek monk, surnamed *Prodromus*, who lived in the first half of the 12th century. He was held in great repute by his contemporaries as a scholar and philosopher, and wrote upon a great variety of subjects. Several of his works have come down to us, of which the following may be mentioned: 1. A metrical romance in 9 books, on the loves of Rhodanthe and Dosicles, written in iambic metre, and exhibiting very little ability. 2. A poem entitled *Galeomyomachia*, in iambic verse, on "the battle of the mice and cat," in imitation of the Homeric Batrachomyomachia. This piece is often appended to the editions of Aesop and Babrius. — 5. The name of 2 ancient Samian artists. (1.) The son of Rhoecus, and brother of Telecles, flourished about B. C. 600, and was an architect, a statuary in bronze, and a sculptor in wood. He wrote a work on the Heraeum at Samos, in the erection of which it may therefore be supposed that he was engaged as well as his father. Or, considering the time which such a building would occupy, the treatise may perhaps be ascribed to the younger Theodorus. He was also engaged with his father in the erection of the labyrinth of Lemnos; and he prepared the foundation of the temple of Artemis at Ephesus. In conjunction with his brother Telecles, he made the wooden statue of Apollo Pythius for the Samians, according to the fixed rules of the hieratic style. (2.) The son of Telecles, nephew of the elder Theodorus, and grandson of Rhoecus, flourished about 560, in the times of Croesus and Polycrates, and obtained such renown as a statuary in bronze, that the invention of that art was ascribed to him, in conjunction with his grandfather. He also practised the arts of engraving metals (τορευτική, caelatura), and of gem-engraving ; his works in those departments being celebrated gold and silver craters, and the ring of Polycrates.

Theodosiopōlis (Θεοδοσιούπολις : prob. Erzeroum), a city of Armenia Major, S. of the Araxes, and 42 stadia S. of the mountain which contains the sources of the Euphrates : built by Theodosius II. as a mountain fortress : enlarged and strengthened by Anastasius and Justinian. Its position made it a place of commercial importance. There were other cities of the name, but none of any great consequence.

Thĕŏdŏsĭus. I. Surnamed the Great, Roman emperor of the East, A. D. 378—395, was the son of the general Theodosius who restored Britain to the empire, and was beheaded at Carthage in the reign of Valens, 376. The future emperor was born in Spain about 346. He received a good education ; and he learned the art of war under his own father, whom he accompanied in his British campaigns. During his father's life-time he was raised to the rank of Duke (dux) of Moesia, where he defeated the Sarmatians (374), and saved the province. On the death of his father he retired before court intrigues to his native country. He acquired a considerable military reputation in the lifetime of his father; and after the death of Valens, who fell in battle against the Goths, he was proclaimed emperor of the East by Gratian, who felt himself unable to sustain the burden of the empire. The Roman empire in the East was then in a critical position ; for the Romans were disheartened by the bloody defeat which they had sustained, and the Goths were insolent in their victory. Theodosius, however, showed himself equal to the difficult position in which he was placed ; he gained two signal victories over the Goths, and concluded a peace with the barbarians in 382. In the following year (383) Maximus assumed the imperial purple in Britain, and invaded Gaul with a powerful army. In the war which followed Gratian was slain ; and Theodosius, who did not consider it prudent to enter into a contest with Maximus, acknowledged the latter emperor of the countries of Spain, Gaul, and Britain, but he secured to Valentinian, the brother of Gratian, Italy, Africa, and western Illyricum. But when Maximus expelled Valentinian from Italy in 387, Theodosius espoused the cause of the latter, and marched into the West at the head of a powerful army. After defeating Maximus in Pannonia, Theodosius pursued him across the Alps to Aquileia. Here Maximus was surrendered by his own soldiers to Theodosius and was put to death. Theodosius spent the winter at Milan, and in the following year (389) he entered Rome in triumph, accompanied by Valentinian and his own son Honorius. Two events in the life of Theodosius about this time may be mentioned as evidence of his uncertain character and his savage temper. In 387 a riot took place at Antioch, in which the statues of the emperor, of his father, and of his wife were thrown down ; but these idle demonstrations were quickly suppressed by an armed force. When Theodosius heard of these riots, he degraded Antioch from the rank of a city stripped it of its possessions and

privileges, and reduced it to the condition of a village dependent on Laodicea. But in consequence of the intercession of Antioch and the senate of Constantinople, he pardoned the city, and all who had taken part in the riot. The other event is an eternal brand of infamy on the name of Theodosius. In 390, while the emperor was at Milan, a serious riot broke out at Thessalonica, in which the imperial officer and several of his troops were murdered. Theodosius resolved to take the most signal vengeance upon the whole city. An army of barbarians was sent to Thessalonica ; the people were invited to the games of the Circus ; and as soon as the place was full, the soldiers received the signal for a massacre. For 3 hours the spectators were indiscriminately exposed to the fury of the soldiers, and 7000 of them, or, as some accounts say, more than twice that number, paid the penalty of the insurrection. St. Ambrose, the archbishop of Milan, represented to Theodosius his crime in a letter, and told him that penitence alone could efface his guilt. Accordingly, when the emperor proceeded to perform his devotions in the usual manner in the great church of Milan, the archbishop stopped him at the door, and demanded an acknowledgment of his guilt. The conscience-struck Theodosius humbled himself before the church, which has recorded his penance as one of its greatest victories. He laid aside the insignia of imperial power, and in the posture of a suppliant in the church of Milan entreated pardon for his great sin before all the congregation. After 8 months, the emperor was restored to communion with the church. Theodosius spent 3 years in Italy, during which he established Valentinian II. on the throne of the West. He returned to Constantinople towards the latter end of 391. Valentinian was slain in 392 by Arbogastes, who raised Eugenius to the empire of the West. This involved Theodosius in a new war ; but it ended in the defeat and death both of Eugenius and Arbogastes in 394. Theodosius died at Milan 4 months after the defeat of Eugenius, on the 17th of January 395. His 2 sons, Arcadius and Honorius, had already been elevated to the rank of Augusti, and it was arranged that the empire should be divided between them, Arcadius having the East, and Honorius the West. Theodosius was a firm Catholic, and a fierce opponent and persecutor of the Arians and all heretics. It was in his reign also that the formal destruction of paganism took place ; and we still possess a large number of the laws of Theodosius, prohibiting the exercise of the pagan religion, and forbidding the heathen worship under severe penalties, in some cases extending to death. —II. Roman emperor of the East, A. D. 408— 450, was born in 401, and was only 7 years of age at the death of his father Arcadius, whom he succeeded. Theodosius was a weak prince ; and his sister Pulcheria, who became his guardian in 414, possessed the virtual government of the empire during the remainder of his long reign. The principal external events in the reign of Theodosius were the war with the Persians, which only lasted a short time (421—422), and was terminated by a peace for 100 years, and the war with the Huns, who repeatedly defeated the armies of the emperor, and compelled him at length to conclude a disgraceful peace with them in 447 or 448. Theodosius died in 450, and was succeeded by his sister Pulcheria, who prudently took for her colleague in the empire the senator Marcian, and made him her husband. Theodosius had been married in 421 to the accomplished Athenais, the daughter of the sophist Leontius, who received at her baptism the name of Eudocia. Their daughter Eudoxia was married to Valentinian III., the emperor of the West. In the reign of Theodosius, and that of Valentinian III., was made the compilation called the *Codex Theodosianus*. It was published in 438. It consists of 16 books, which are divided into titles, with appropriate rubricae or headings; and the constitutions belonging to each title are arranged under it in chronological order. The first 5 books comprise the greater part of the constitution which relates to *Jus Privatum;* the 6th, 7th, and 8th books contain the law that relates to the constitution and administration; the 9th book treats of criminal law; the 10th and 11th treat of the public revenue and some matters relating to procedure; the 12th, 13th, 14th and 15th books treat of the constitution and the administration of towns and other corporations; and the 16th contains the law relating to ecclesiastical matters. The best edition of this Code with a commentary is that of J. Gothofredus, which was edited after his death by A. Marville, Lyon, 1665, 6 vols. fo.; and afterwards by Ritter, Leipzig, 1736—1745, fol. The best edition of the text alone is that by Hänel in the *Corpus Juris Antejustinianeum*, Bonn, 1837. — III. Literary. 1. Of Bithynia, a mathematician, mentioned by Strabo and by Vitruvius, the latter of whom speaks of him as the inventor of an universal sun-dial. — 2. Of Tripolis, a mathematician and astronomer of some distinction, who appears to have flourished later than the reign of Trajan. He wrote several works, of which the 3 following are extant, and have been published. 1. Σφαιρικὰ, a treatise on the properties of the sphere, and of the circles described on its surface. 2. Περὶ ἡμερῶν καὶ νυκτῶν. 3. Περὶ οἰκήσεων.

Theodóta (Θεοδότη), an Athenian courtezan, and one of the most celebrated persons of that class in Greece, is introduced as a speaker in Xenophon's *Memorabilia* (iii. 11.) She at last attached herself to Alcibiades, and, after his murder, she performed his funeral rites.

Theognis (Θέογνις). 1. Of Megara, an ancient elegiac and gnomic poet, is said to have flourished B. C. 548 or 544. He may have been born about 570, and would therefore have been 80 at the commencement of the Persian wars, 490, at which time we know from his own writings that he was alive. Theognis belonged to the oligarchical party in his native city, and in its fates he shared. He was a noble by birth; and all his sympathies were with the nobles. They are, in his poems, the ἀγαθοί and ἐσθλοί, and the commons the κακοί and δειλοί, terms which, in fact, at that period, were regularly used in this political signification, and not in their later ethical meaning. He was banished with the leaders of the oligarchical party, having previously been deprived of all his property; and most of his poems were composed while he was an exile. Most of his political verses are addressed to a certain Cyrnus, the son of Polypas. The other fragments of his poetry are of a social, most of them of a festive character. They place us in the midst of a circle of friends, who formed a kind of convivial society; all the members of this society belonged to the class whom

the poet calls "the good." The collection of gnomic poetry, which has come down to us under the name of Theognis, contains, however, many additions from later poets. The genuine fragments of Theognis contain much that is highly poetical in thought, and elegant as well as forcible in expression. The best editions are by Bekker, Lips. 1815, and 2d ed. 1827, 8vo.; by Welcker, Francof. 1826, 8vo.; and by Orellius, Turic. 1840, 4to. — 2. A tragic poet, contemporary with Aristophanes, by whom he is satirized.

Theon (Θέων). 1. The name of 2 mathematicians who are often confounded together. The first is Theon the elder, of Smyrna, best known as an arithmetician, who lived in the time of Hadrian. The second is Theon the younger, of Alexandria, the father of HYPATIA, best known as an astronomer and geometer, who lived in the time of Theodosius the elder. Both were heathens, a fact which the date of the second makes it desirable to state; and each held the Platonism of his period. Of Theon of Smyrna all that we have left is a portion of a work entitled, Τῶν κατὰ μαθηματικὴν χρησίμων εἰς τὴν τοῦ Πλάτωνος ἀνάγνωσιν. The portion which now exists is in 2 books, one on arithmetic, and one on music: there was a third on astronomy, and a fourth Περὶ τῆς ἐν κόσμῳ ἁρμονίας. The best edition is by Gelder, Leyden, 1827. Of Theon of Alexandria the following works have come down to us:— 1. Scholia on Aratus. 2. Edition of Euclid. 3. Commentary on the *Almagest* of Ptolemy, addressed to his son Epiphanius. 4. Commentary on the tables of Ptolemy. — 2. Aelius Theon, of Alexandria, a sophist and rhetorician of uncertain date, wrote several works, of which one entitled *Progymnasmata* (Προγυμνάσματα) is still extant. It is a useful treatise on the proper system of preparation for the profession of an orator, according to the rules laid down by Hermogenes and Aphthonius. One of the best editions is by Finckh, Stuttgard, 1834. — 3. Of Samos, a painter who flourished from the time of Philip onwards to that of the successors of Alexander. The peculiar merit of Theon was his prolific fancy.

Theonoë (Θεονόη), daughter of Proteus and Psammathe, also called Idothea. [IDOTHEA.]

Theophanes (Θεοφάνης). 1. Cn. Pompeius Theophanes, of Mytilene in Lesbos, a learned Greek, and one of the most intimate friends of Pompey. Pompey appears to have made his acquaintance during the Mithridatic war, and soon became so much attached to him that he presented to him the Roman franchise in the presence of his army, after a speech in which he eulogised his merits. This occurred about B. C. 62; and in the course of the same year Theophanes obtained from Pompey the privileges of a free state for his native city, although it had espoused the cause of Mithridates. Theophanes came to Rome with Pompey; and on the breaking out of the civil war he accompanied his patron to Greece. Pompey appointed him commander of the Fabri, and chiefly consulted him and Lucceius on all important matters in the war, much to the indignation of the Roman nobles. After the battle of Pharsalia Theophanes fled with Pompey from Greece, and it was owing to his advice that Pompey went to Egypt. After the death of his patron, Theophanes took refuge in Italy, and was pardoned by Caesar. After his death the Lesbians paid divine honours to his memory.

Theophanes wrote the history of Pompey's campaigns, in which he represented the exploits of his patron in the most favourable light. — 2. M. Pompeius Theophanes, son of the preceding, was sent to Asia by Augustus, in the capacity of procurator, and was at the time that Strabo wrote one of the friends of Tiberius. The latter emperor, however, put his descendants to death towards the end of his reign, A. D. 33, because their ancestor had been one of Pompey's friends, and had received after his death divine honours from the Lesbians. — 3. A Byzantine historian, flourished most probably in the latter part of the 6th century of our era. He wrote, in 10 books, the history of the Eastern Empire during the Persian war under Justin II., from A. D. 567 to 581. The work itself is lost, but some extracts from it are preserved by Photius. — 4. Also a Byzantine historian, lived during the second half of the 8th century, and the early part of the 9th. In consequence of his supporting the cause of image worship, he was banished by Leo the Armenian to the island of Samothrace, where he died, in 818. Theophanes wrote a Chronicon, which is still extant, beginning at the accession of Diocletian, in 277, and coming down to 811. It consists, like the *Chronica* of Eusebius and of Syncellus, of two parts, a history arranged according to years, and a chronological table, of which the former is very superior to the latter. It is published in the Collections of the Byzantine writers, Paris, 1655, fol., Venet. 1729, fol.

Theophilus (Θεόφιλος). 1. An Athenian comic poet, most probably of the Middle Comedy. — 2. An historian and geographer, quoted by Josephus, Plutarch, and Ptolemy. — 3. Bishop of Antioch, in the latter part of the 2nd century of our era, and the author of one of the early apologies for Christianity which have come down to us. This work is in the form of a letter to a friend, named Autolycus, who was still a heathen, but a man of extensive reading and great learning. It was composed A. D. 180 ; a year or two before the death of Theophilus. The best edition is that by Wolf, Hamb. 1724, 8vo. — 4. Bishop of Alexandria, in the latter part of the 4th and the beginning of the 5th centuries of our era, and distinguished for his persecutions of the Origenists and for his hostility to Chrysostom. He died A. D. 412. A few remains of his works have come down to us.—5. One of the lawyers of Constantinople who were employed by Justinian on his first Code, on the Digest, and on the composition of the Institutes. [JUSTINIANUS.] Theophilus is the author of the Greek translation or paraphrase of the Institutes of Justinian, which has come down to us. It is intitled 'Ἰνστιτοῦτα Θεοφίλου 'Αντικένσωρος, Instituta Theophili Antecensoris. It became the text for the Institutes in the East, where the Latin language was little known, and entirely displaced the Latin text. The best edition is by Reitz, Haag. 1751, 2 vols. 4to.—6. Theophilus Protospatharius, the author of several Greek medical works, which are still extant. *Protospatharius* was originally a military title given to the colonel of the body-guards of the emperor of Constantinople (*Spatharii*), but afterwards became also a high civil dignity. Theophilus probably lived in the 7th century after Christ. Of his works the 2 most important are: 1. Περὶ τῆς τοῦ 'Ανθρώπου Κατασκευῆς, *De Corporis Humani Fabrica*, an anatomical and physiological

treatise in 5 books. The best edition is by Greenhill, Oxon. 1842, 8vo. 2. Περὶ Οὔρων, *De Urinis*, of which the best edition is by Guidot, Lugd. Bat. 1703 (and 1731) 8vo.

Theophrastus (Θεόφραστος), the Greek philosopher, was a native of Eresus in Lesbos, and studied philosophy at Athens, first under Plato, and afterwards under Aristotle. He became the favourite pupil of Aristotle, who is said to have changed his original name of Tyrtamus to Theophrastus (or the Divine Speaker), to indicate the fluent and graceful address of his pupil ; but this tale is scarcely credible. Aristotle named Theophrastus his successor in the presidency of the Lyceum, and in his will bequeathed to him his library and the originals of his own writings. Theophrastus was a worthy successor of his great master, and nobly sustained the character of the school. He is said to have had 2000 disciples, and among them such men as the comic poet Menander. He was highly esteemed by the kings Philippus, Cassander, and Ptolemy, and was not the less the object of the regard of the Athenian people, as was decisively shown when he was impeached of impiety ; for he was not only acquitted, but his accuser would have fallen a victim to his calumny, had not Theophrastus generously interfered to save him. Nevertheless, when the philosophers were banished from Athens, in B. C. 305, according to the law of Sophocles, Theophrastus also left the city, until Philo, a disciple of Aristotle, in the very next year, brought Sophocles to punishment, and procured the repeal of the law. From this time Theophrastus continued to teach at Athens without any further molestation till his death. He died in 287, having presided over the Academy about 35 years. His age is differently stated. According to some accounts he lived 85 years, according to others 107 years. He is said to have closed his life with the complaint respecting the short duration of human existence, that it ended just when the insight into its problems was beginning. The whole population of Athens took part in his funeral obsequies. He bequeathed his library to Neleus of Scepsis. Theophrastus exerted himself to carry out the philosophical system of Aristotle, to throw light upon the difficulties contained in his books, and to fill up the gaps in them. With this view he wrote a great number of works, the great object of which was the development of the Aristotelian philosophy. Unfortunately most of these works have perished. The following are alone extant : 1. *Characteres* (ἠθικοὶ χαρακτῆρες), in 30 chapters, containing descriptions of vicious characters. 2. A treatise on sensuous perception and its objects (περὶ αἰσθήσεως [καὶ αἰσθητῶν]). 3. A fragment of a work on metaphysics (τῶν μετὰ τὰ φυσικά). 4. *On the History of Plants* (περὶ φυτῶν ἱστορίας), in 10 books, one of the earliest works on botany which have come down to us. 5. *On the Causes of Plants* (περὶ φυτῶν αἰτιῶν), originally in 8 books, of which 6 are still extant. 6. *Of Stones* (περὶ λίθων). The best editions of the complete works of Theophrastus are by Schneider, Lips. 1818—21, 5 vols., and by Wimmer, Vratislaviae, 1842, of which, however, the first volume has only yet appeared. The best separate edition of the *Characteres* is by Ast, Lips. 1816.

Theophylactus (Θεοφύλακτος). 1. Surnamed Simocatta, a Byzantine historian, lived at Constantinople, where he held some public offices under Heraclius, about A. D. 610—629. His chief work is a history of the reign of the emperor Maurice, in 8 books, from the death of Tiberius II. and the accession of Maurice, in 582, down to the murder of Maurice and his children by Phocas in 602. The best edition of this work is by Bekker, Bonn, 1834, 8vo. There is also extant another work of Theophylactus, entitled *Quaestiones Physicae*, of which the best edition is by Boissonade, Paris, 1835, 8vo. — 2. Archbishop of Bulgaria, flourished about A. D. 1070 and onwards, is celebrated for his commentaries on the Scriptures, which are founded on the commentaries of Chrysostom, and are of considerable value.

Theöpompus (Θεόπομπος). 1. King of Sparta, reigned about B. C. 770—720 He is said to have established the ephoralty, and to have been mainly instrumental in bringing the 1st Messenian war to a successful issue. — 2. Of Chios, a celebrated Greek historian, was the son of Damasistratus and the brother of Caucalus, the rhetorician. He was born about B. C. 378. He accompanied his father into banishment, when the latter was exiled on account of his espousing the interests of the Lacedaemonians, but he was restored to his native country in the 45th year of his age (333), in consequence of the letters of Alexander the Great, in which he exhorted the Chians to recal their exiles. In what year Theopompus quitted Chios with his father is uncertain ; but we know that before he left his native country, he attended the school of rhetoric which Isocrates opened at Chios, and that he profited so much by the lessons of his great master as to be regarded by the ancients as the most distinguished of all his scholars. Ephorus the historian was a fellow-student with him, but was of a very different character ; and Isocrates used to say of them, that Theopompus needed the bit and Ephorus the spur. In consequence of the advice of Isocrates, Theopompus did not devote his oratorical powers to the pleading of causes, but gave his chief attention to the study and composition of history. Like his master Isocrates, however, he composed many orations of the kind, called *Epideitic* by the Greeks, that is, speeches on set subjects delivered for display, such as eulogiums upon states and individuals. Thus in 352 he contended at Halicarnassus with Naucrates and his master Isocrates for the prize of oratory, given by Artemisia in honour of her husband, and gained the victory. On his return to Chios in 333, Theopompus, who was a man of great wealth as well as learning, naturally took an important position in the state ; but his vehement temper, and his support of the aristocratical party, soon raised against him a host of enemies. Of these one of the most formidable was the sophist Theocritus. As long as Alexander lived, his enemies dared not take any open proceedings against Theopompus ; and even after the death of the Macedonian monarch, he appears to have enjoyed for some years the protection of the royal house. Theopompus was supported by Alexander, and after his death by the royal house ; but he was eventually expelled from Chios as a disturber of the public peace, and fled to Egypt to Ptolemy, about 305, being at the time 75 years of age. We are informed that Ptolemy not only refused to receive Theopompus, but would even have put him to death as a dangerous busybody, had not some of

his friends interceded for his life. Of his further fate we have no particulars. None of the works of Theopompus have come down to us, but the following were his chief works: 1. Ἑλληνικαὶ ἱστορίαι or Σύνταξις Ἑλληνικῶν, *A History of Greece*, in 12 books, which was a continuation of the history of Thucydides. It commenced in B. C. 411, at the point where the history of Thucydides breaks off, and embraced a period of 17 years down to the death of Cnidus in 394. 2. Φιλιππικά, also called Ἱστορίαι (κατ' ἐξοχὴν), *The History of Philip*, father of Alexander the Great, in 58 books, from the commencement of his reign 360, to his death 336. This work contained numerous digressions, which in fact formed the greater part of the whole work ; so that Philip V., king of Macedonia, was able, by omitting them and retaining only what belonged to the proper subject, to reduce the work from 58 books to 16. 53 of the 58 books of the original work were extant in the 9th century of the Christian aera, and were read by Photius, who has preserved an abstract of the 12th book. 3. *Orationes*, which were chiefly Panegyrics, and what the Greeks called Συμβουλευτικοὶ λόγοι. Of the latter kind one of the most celebrated was addressed to Alexander on the state of Chios. Theopompus is praised by ancient writers for his diligence and accuracy ; but is at the same time said to have taken more pleasure in blaming than in commending ; and many of his judgments respecting events and characters were expressed with such acrimony and severity that several of the ancient writers speak of his malignity, and call him a reviler. The style of Theopompus was formed on the model of Isocrates, and possessed the characteristic merits and defects of his master. It was pure, clear, and elegant, but deficient in vigour, loaded with ornament, and in general too artificial. The best collections of the fragments of Theopompus are by Wichers, Lugd. Bat. 1829, and by C. and Theod. Müller in the *Fragmenta Historicorum Graecorum*, Paris, 1841. — 3. An Athenian comic poet, of the Old, and also of the Middle Comedy, was the son of Theodectes or Theodorus, or Tisamenus. He wrote as late as B. C. 380. His extant fragments contain examples of the declining purity of the Attic dialect.

Theoxenius (Θεοξένιος), a surname of Apollo and Hermes. Respecting the festival of the Theoxenia, see *Dict. of Antiq. s. v.*

Thera (Θήρα : Θηραῖος : Santorin), an island in the Aegaean sea, and the chief of the Sporades, distant from Crete 700 stadia, and 25 Roman miles S. of the island of Ios. It is described by Strabo as 200 stadia in circumference, but by modern travellers as 36 miles, and in figure exactly like a horse-shoe. Thera is clearly of volcanic origin. It is covered at the present day with pumice-stone ; and the rocks are burnt and scorched. It is said to have been formed by a clod of earth thrown from the ship Argo, and to have received the name of Calliste, when it first emerged from the sea. Therasia, a small island to the W., and called at the present day by the same name, was torn away from Thera by some volcanic convulsion. Thera is said to have been originally inhabited by Phoenicians, but was afterwards colonised by Lacedaemonians and Minyans of Lemnos under the guidance of the Spartan Theras, who gave his name to the island. In

B. C. 631 Battus conducted a colony from Thera to Africa, where he founded the celebrated city of Cyrene. Thera remained faithful to the Spartans, and was one of the few islands which espoused the Spartan cause at the commencement of the Peloponnesian war.

Thĕrambo (Θεράμβω, also Θράμβος), a town of Macedonia on the peninsula Pallene.

Theramĕnes (Θηραμένης), an Athenian, son of Hagnon, was a leading member of the oligarchical government of the 400 at Athens in B. C. 411. In this, however, he does not appear to have occupied as eminent a station as he had hoped to fill, while at the same time the declaration of Alcibiades and of the army at Samos against the oligarchy made it evident to him that its days were numbered. Accordingly he withdrew from the more violent aristocrats and began to cabal against them; and he subsequently took not only a prominent part in the deposition of the 400, but came forward as the accuser of Antiphon and Archeptolemus, who had been his intimate friends, but whose death he was now the mean and cowardly instrument in procuring. At the battle of Arginusae, in 406, Theramenes held a subordinate command in the Athenian fleet, and he was one of those who, after the victory, were commissioned by the generals to repair to the scene of action and save as many as possible of the disabled galleys and their crews. A storm, it is said, rendered the execution of the order impracticable; yet, instead of trusting to this as his ground of defence, Theramenes thought it safer to divert the popular anger from himself to others; and it appears to have been chiefly through his machinations that the 6 generals who had returned to Athens, were condemned to death. After the capture of Athens by Lysander, Theramenes was chosen one of the Thirty Tyrants (404). He endeavoured to check the tyrannical proceedings of his colleagues, foreseeing that their violence would be fatal to the permanence of their power. His opposition, however, had no effect in restraining them, but only induced the desire to rid themselves of so troublesome an associate, whose former conduct moreover had shown that no political party could depend on him, and who had earned, by his trimming, the nickname of Κόθορνος, — a boot which might be worn on either foot. He was therefore accused by Critias before the council as a traitor, and when his nominal judges, favourably impressed by his able defence, exhibited an evident disposition to acquit him, Critias introduced into the chamber a number of men armed with daggers, and declared that, as all who were not included in the privileged Three Thousand might be put to death by the sole authority of the Thirty, he struck the name of Theramenes out of that list, and condemned him with the consent of all his colleagues. Theramenes then rushed to the altar, which stood in the council-chamber, but was dragged from it and carried off to execution. When he had drunk the hemlock, he dashed out the last drops from the cup, exclaiming, "This to the health of the lovely Critias!" Both Xenophon and Cicero express their admiration of the equanimity which he displayed in his last hour; but surely such a feeling is sadly out of place when directed to such a man.

Thĕrapnae (Θεράπναι, also Θεράπνη, Dor. Θεράπνα: Θεραπναῖος). 1. A town in Laconica, on the left bank of the Eurotas, and a little above Sparta. It received its name from Therapne,

daughter of Lelex, and is celebrated in mythology as the birth-place of Castor and Pollux, and contained temples of these divinities as well as temples of Menelaus and Helen, both of whom were said to be buried here. — 2. A town in Boeotia, on the road from Thebes to the Asopus.

Thĕras. [THERA.]

Thĕrăsia. [THERA.]

Thĕrĭclēs (Θηρικλῆς), a Corinthian potter, whose works obtained such celebrity that they became known throughout Greece by the name of Θηρίκλεια (sc. ποτήρια) or κύλικες Θηρικλεῖαι (or -αι), and these names were applied not only to cups of earthenware, but also to those of wood, glass, gold, and silver. Some scholars make Thericles a contemporary of Aristophanes; but others deny the existence of Thericles altogether, and contend that the name of these vases is a descriptive one, derived from the figures of animals (θηρία) with which they were adorned.

Therma (Θέρμη: Θερμαῖος), a town in Macedonia, afterwards called Thessalonica [THESSALONICA], situated at the N. E. extremity of a great gulf of the Aegaean sea, lying between Thessaly and the peninsula Chalcidice, and called **Thermaĭcus** or **Thermaeus Sinus** (Θερμαῖος κόλπος), from the town at its head. This gulf was also called Macedonicus Sinus: its modern name is Gulf of Saloniki.

Thermae (Θέρμαι), a town in Sicily, built by the inhabitants of Himera, after the destruction of the latter city by the Carthaginians. For details see HIMERA.

Thermaĭcus Sinus. [THERMA.]

Thermōdon (Θερμώδων: Thermeh), a river of Pontus, in the district of Themiscyra, the reputed country of the Amazons, rises in a mountain called Amazonius M. (and still Mason Dagh), near Phanaroea, and falls into the sea about 30 miles E. of the mouth of the Iris, after a short course, but with so large a body of water, that its breadth, according to Xenophon, was 3 plethra (above 300 feet), and it was navigable. At its mouth was the city of Themiscyra; and there is still, on the W. side of the mouth of the Thermeh, a place of the same name, Thermeh.

Thermŏpylae, often called simply **Pylae** (Θερμοπύλαι, Πύλαι), that is, the Hot Gates or the Gates, a celebrated pass leading from Thessaly into Locris. It lay between Mt. Oeta and an inaccessible morass, forming the edge of the Malic Gulf. At one end of the pass, close to Anthela, the mountain approached so close to the morass as to leave room for only a single carriage between: this narrow entrance formed the W. gate of Thermopylae. About a mile to the E. the mountain again approached close to the sea, near the Locrian town of Alpeni, thus forming the E. gate of Thermopylae. The space between these 2 gates was wider and more open, and was distinguished by its abundant flow of hot springs, which were sacred to Hercules: hence the name of the place. Thermopylae was the only pass by which an enemy can penetrate from northern into southern Greece; whence its great importance in Grecian history. It is especially celebrated on account of the heroic defence of Leonidas and the 300 Spartans against the mighty host of Xerxes; and they only fell through the Persians having discovered a path over the mountains, and thus being enabled to attack the Greeks in the rear. This mountain path commenced from the neighbourhood of Trachis, ascended the gorge of the river Asopus and the hill called Anopaea, then crossed the crest of Oeta, and descended in the rear of Thermopylae near the town of Alpeni.

Thermum or Therma (Θέρμον or τὸ Θέρμα), a town of the Aetolians near Stratus, with warm mineral springs, was regarded for some time as the capital of the country, since it was the place of meeting of the Aetolian confederacy.

Thermus, Minucius. 1. Q., served under Scipio as tribunus militum in the war against Hannibal in Africa in B. c. 202; was tribune of the plebs 201; curule aedile 197; and praetor 196, when he carried on war with great success in nearer Spain. He was consul in 193, and carried on war against the Ligurians in this and the 2 following years. On his return to Rome in 190, a triumph was refused him, through the influence of M. Cato, who delivered on the occasion his two orations intitled *De decem Hominibus* and *De falsis Pugnis.* Thermus was killed in 188, while fighting under Cn. Manlius Vulso against the Thracians. — 2. M., propraetor in 81, accompanied L. Murena, Sulla's legate, into Asia. Thermus was engaged in the siege of Mytilene, and it was under him that Julius Caesar served his first campaign, and gained his first laurels. — 3. Q., propraetor 51 and 50 in Asia, where he received many letters from Cicero, who praises his administration of the province. On the breaking out of the civil war he espoused the side of Pompey.

Theron (Θήρων), tyrant of Agrigentum in Sicily, was the son of Aenesidemus, and descended from one of the most illustrious families in his native city. He obtained the supreme power about B. c. 488, and retained it till his death in 472. He conquered Himera in 482, and united this powerful city to his own dominions. He was in close alliance with Gelon, ruler of Syracuse and Gela, to whom he had given his daughter Demarete in marriage; and he shared with Gelon in the great victory gained over the Carthaginians in 480. On the death of Gelon in 478, Theron espoused the cause of Polyzelus, who had been driven into exile by his brother Hieron. Theron raised an army for the purpose of reinstating him, but hostilities were prevented, and a peace concluded between the two sovereigns.

Thersander (Θέρσανδρος), son of Polynices and Argia, and one of the Epigoni, was married to Demonassa, by whom he became the father of Tisamenus. He went with Agamemnon to Troy, and was slain in that expedition by Telephus. His tomb was shown at Elaea in Mysia, where sacrifices were offered to him. Virgil (*Aen.* ii. 261) enumerates Thersander among the Greeks concealed in the wooden horse. Homer does not mention him.

Thersites (Θερσίτης), son of Agrius, the most deformed and impudent talker among the Greeks at Troy. According to the later poets he was killed by Achilles, because he had ridiculed him for lamenting the death of Penthesilea, queen of the Amazons.

Theseus (Θησεύς), the great legendary hero of Attica, was the son of Aegeus, king of Athens, and of Aethra, the daughter of Pittheus, king of Troezen. He was brought up at Troezen; and when he reached maturity, he took, by his mother's directions, the sword and sandals, the tokens

which had been left by Aegeus, and proceeded to Athens. Eager to emulate Hercules, he went by land, displaying his prowess by destroying the robbers and monsters that infested the country. Periphetes, Sinis, Phaea the Crommyonian sow, Sciron, Cercyon, and Procrustes fell before him. At Athens he was immediately recognised by Medea, who laid a plot for poisoning him at a banquet to which he was invited. By means of the sword which he carried, Theseus was recognised by Aegeus, acknowledged as his son, and declared his successor. The sons of Pallas, thus disappointed in their hopes of succeeding to the throne, attempted to secure the succession by violence, and declared war; but, being betrayed by the herald Leos, were destroyed. The capture of the Marathonian bull, which had long laid waste the surrounding country, was the next exploit of Theseus. After this Theseus went of his own accord as one of the 7 youths, whom the Athenians were obliged to send every year, with 7 maidens, to Crete, in order to be devoured by the Minotaur. When they arrived at Crete, Ariadne, the daughter of Minos, became enamoured of Theseus, and provided him with a sword with which he slew the Minotaur, and a clue of thread by which he found his way out of the labyrinth. Having effected his object, Theseus sailed away, carrying off Ariadne. There were various accounts about Ariadne; but according to the general account Theseus abandoned her in the island of Naxos on his way home. [ARIADNE.] He was generally believed to have had by her two sons, Oenopion and Staphylus. As the vessel in which Theseus sailed approached Attica, he neglected to hoist the white sail, which was to have been the signal of the success of the expedition; whereupon Aegeus, thinking that his son had perished, threw himself into the sea. [AEGEUS.] Theseus thus became king of Athens. One of the most celebrated of the adventures of Theseus was his expedition against the Amazons. He is said to have assailed them before they had recovered from the attack of Hercules, and to have carried off their queen Antiope. The Amazons in their turn invaded Attica, and penetrated into Athens itself; and the final battle in which Theseus overcame them was fought in the very midst of the city. By Antiope Theseus was said to have had a son named Hippolytus or Demophoon, and after her death to have married Phaedra [HIPPOLYTUS, PHAEDRA]. Theseus figures in almost all the great heroic expeditions. He was one of the Argonauts (the anachronism of the attempt of Medea to poison him does not seem to have been noticed); he joined in the Calydonian hunt, and aided Adrastus in recovering the bodies of those slain before Thebes. He contracted a close friendship with Pirithous, and aided him and the Lapithae against the Centaurs. With the assistance of Pirithous he carried off Helen from Sparta while she was quite a girl, and placed her at Aphidnae, under the care of Aethra. In return he assisted Pirithous in his attempt to carry off Persephone from the lower world. Pirithous perished in the enterprise, and Theseus was kept in hard durance until he was delivered by Hercules. Meantime Castor and Pollux invaded Attica, and carried off Helen and Aethra, Academus having informed the brothers where they were to be found [ACADEMUS]. Menestheus also endeavoured to incite the people against Theseus, who on his return found himself unable to re-establish his authority, and retired to Scyros, where he met with a treacherous death at the hands of Lycomedes. The departed hero was believed to have appeared to aid the Athenians at the battle of Marathon. In 469 the bones of Theseus were discovered by Cimon in Scyros, and brought to Athens, where they were deposited in a temple (the *Theseum*) erected in honour of the hero. A considerable part of this temple still remains, forming one of the most interesting monuments of Athens. A festival in honour of Theseus was celebrated on the 8th day of each month, especially on the 8th of Pyanepsion.— There can be no doubt that Theseus is a purely legendary personage. Nevertheless, in later times the Athenians came to regard him as the author of a very important political revolution in Attica. Before his time Attica had been broken up into 12 petty independent states or townships, acknowledging no head, and connected only by a federal union. Theseus abolished the separate governments, and erected Athens into the capital of a single commonwealth. The festival of the Panathenaea was instituted to commemorate this important revolution. Theseus is said to have established a constitutional government, retaining in his own hands only certain definite powers and functions. He is further said to have distributed the Athenian citizens into the 3 classes of Eupatridae, Geomori, and Demiurgi. It would be a vain task to attempt to decide whether there is any historical basis for the legends about Theseus, and still more so to endeavour to separate the historical from the legendary in what has been preserved. The Theseus of the Athenians was a hero who fought the Amazons, and slew the Minotaur, and carried off Helen. A personage who should be nothing more than a wise king, consolidating the Athenian commonwealth, however *possible* his existence might be, would have no *historical* reality. The connection of Theseus with Poseidon, the national deity of the Ionic tribes, his coming from the Ionic town Troezen, forcing his way through the Isthmus into Attica, and establishing the Isthmia as an Ionic Panegyris, rather suggest that Theseus is, at least in part, the mythological representative of an Ionian immigration into Attica, which, adding perhaps to the strength and importance of Ionian settlers already in the country, might easily have led to that political aggregation of the disjointed elements of the state which is assigned to Theseus.

Thesmia or **Thesmŏphŏros** (Θεσμία, Θεσμοφόρος), that is, " the law-giver." a surname of Demeter and Persephone, in honour of whom the *Thesmophoria* were celebrated at Athens in the month of Pyanepsion.

Thespiae or **Thespia** (Θέσπεια, Θεσπίαι, Θέσπεια, Θέσπια : Θεσπιεύς, Θεσπιάδης, Thespiensis : *Eremo* or *Rimokastro*), an ancient town in Boeotia on the S. E. slope of Mt. Helicon, at no great distance from the Crissaean Gulf. Its inhabitants did not follow the example of the other Boeotian towns in submitting to Xerxes, and a number of them bravely fought under Leonidas at Thermopylae, and perished with the Spartans. Their city was burnt to the ground by the Persians, but was subsequently rebuilt. In the Peloponnesian war the Thebans made themselves masters of the town. At Thespiae was preserved the celebrated marble statue of Eros by Praxiteles, who had

given it to Phryne, by whom it was presented to her native town. [PRAXITELES.] From the vicinity of the town to Mt. Helicon the Muses are called *Thespiades*, and Helicon itself is named the *Thespia rupes.*

Thespis (Θέσπις), the celebrated father of Greek tragedy, was a contemporary of Pisistratus, and a native of Icarus, one of the demi in Attica, where the worship of Dionysus had long prevailed. The alteration made by Thespis, and which gave to the old tragedy a new and dramatic character, was very simple but very important. He introduced an actor, for the sake of giving rest to the chorus, and independent of it, in which capacity he probably appeared himself, taking various parts in the same piece, under various disguises, which he was enabled to assume by means of the linen masks, the invention of which is ascribed to him. The first representation of Thespis was in B. C. 535. For further details see *Dict. of Antiq.* art.*Tragoedia.*

Thespius (Θέσπιος), son of Erechtheus, who, according to some, founded the town of Thespiae in Boeotia. His descendants are called *Thespiadae.*

Thesprŏti (Θεσπρωτοί), a people of Epirus, inhabiting the district called after them **Thesprŏtia** (Θεσπρωτία) or **Thesprŏtis** (Θεσπρωτίς), which extended along the coast from the Ambracian gulf N.-wards as far as the river Thyamis, and inland as far as the territory of the Molossi. The S. E. part of the country on the coast, from the river Acheron to the Ambracian gulf, was called Cassopaea from the town Cassope, and is sometimes reckoned a distinct district. The Thesproti were the most ancient inhabitants of Epirus, and are said to have derived their name from Thesprotus, the son of Lycaon. They were Pelasgians, and their country was one of the chief seats of the Pelasgic nation. Here was the oracle of Dodona, the great centre of the Pelasgic worship. From Thesprotia issued the Thessalians, who took possession of the country afterwards called Thessaly. In the historical period the Thesprotians were a people of small importance, having become subject to the kings of the Molossians.

Thessalia (Θεσσαλία or Θετταλία : Θεσσαλός or Θετταλός), the largest division of Greece, was bounded on the N. by the Cambunian mountains, which separated it from Macedonia ; on the W. by Mt. Pindus, which separated it from Epirus ; on the E. by the Aegaean sea ; and on the S. by the Maliac gulf and Mt. Oeta, which separated it from Locris, Phocis and Aetolia. Thessaly Proper is a vast plain lying between the Cambunian mountains on the N. and Mt. Othrys on the S., Mt. Pindus on the W., and Mts. Ossa and Pelion on the E. It is thus shut in on every side by mountain barriers, broken only at the N. E. corner by the valley and defile of Tempe, which separates Ossa from Olympus, and is the only road through which an invader can enter Thessaly from the N. This plain is drained by the river Penëus and its affluents, and is said to have been originally a vast lake, the waters of which were afterwards carried off through the vale of Tempe by some sudden convulsion, which rent the rocks of this valley asunder. The lake of *Nessonis* at the foot of Mt. Ossa, and that of *Boebeis* at the foot of Mt. Pelion, are supposed to have been remains of this vast lake. In addition to the plain already described there were 2 other districts included under the general name of Thessaly : one called Magnesia, being a long narrow strip of country, extending along the coast of the Aegaean sea from Tempe to the Pagasaean gulf, and bounded on the W. by Mts. Ossa and Olympus ; and the other being a long narrow vale at the extreme S. of the country, lying between Mts. Othrys and Oeta, and drained by the river Spercheus. Thessaly is said to have been originally known by the names of *Pyrrha, Aemonia* and *Aeolis*. The two former appellations belong to mythology ; the latter refers to the period when the country was inhabited by Aeolians, who were afterwards expelled from the country by the Thessalians about 60 years after the Trojan war. The Thessalians are said to have come from Thesprotia ; but at what period their name became the name of the country cannot be determined. It does not occur in Homer, who only mentions the several principalities of which it was composed, and does not give any general appellation to the country. Thessaly was divided in very early times into 4 districts or tetrarchies, a division which we still find subsisting in the Peloponnesian war. These districts were *Hestiaeotis, Pelasgiotis, Thessaliotis* and *Phthiotis*. They comprised, however, only the great Thessalian plain ; and besides them, we find mention of 4 other districts, viz. *Magnesia, Dolopia, Oetaea,* and *Malis*. Thus there were 8 districts altogether. Perrhaebia was, properly speaking, not a district, since Perrhaebi was the name of a Pelasgic people settled in Hestiaeotis and Pelasgiotis. [PERRHAEBI.] 1. **Hestiaeōtis** ('Εστιαιῶτις or 'Εστιῶτις), inhabited by the *Hestiaeōtae* ('Εστιαιῶται or 'Εστιῶται), the N. W. part of Thessaly, bounded on the N. by Macedonia, on the W. by Epirus, on the E. by Pelasgiotis and on the S. by Thessaliotis : the Peneus may be said in general to have formed its S. limit. — **2. Pelasgiōtis** (Πελασγιῶτις) inhabited by the *Pelasgiōtae* (Πελασγιῶται), the E. part of the Thessalian plain, was bounded on the N. by Macedonia, on the W. by Hestiaeotis, on the E. by Magnesia and on the S. by the Sinus Pagasaeus and Phthiotis. The name shows that it was originally inhabited by Pelasgians ; and one of the chief towns in the district was Larissa, which was of Pelasgic origin. — **3. Thessaliōtis** (Θεσσαλιῶτις), the S. W. part of the Thessalian plain, so called because it was first occupied by the Thessalians who came from Thesprotia. It was bounded on the N. by Hestiaeotis, on the W. by Epirus, on the E. by Pelasgiotis, and on the S. by Dolopia and Phthiotis. — **4. Phthiōtis** (Φθιῶτις), inhabited by the *Phthiōtae* (Φθιῶται), the S. E. of Thessaly, bounded on the N. by Thessaliotis, on the W. by Dolopia, on the S. by the Sinus Maliacus, and on the E. by the Pagasaean gulf. Its inhabitants were Achaeans, and are frequently called the Achaean Phthiotae. It is in this district that Homer places Phthia and Hellas Proper, and the dominions of Achilles. — **5. Magnēsīa** [MAGNESIA]. — **6. Dōlŏpīa** (Δολοπία), inhabited by the *Dŏlŏpes* (Δόλοπες), a small district bounded on the E. by Phthiotis, on the N. by Thessaliotis, on the W. by Athamania, and on the S. by Oetaea. They were an ancient people, for they are not only mentioned by Homer as fighting before Troy, but they also sent deputies to the Amphictyonic assembly. — **7. Oetaea** (Οἰταία),

inhabited by the *Oetaei* (Οἰταῖοι) and *Aenianes* (Αἰνιᾶνες), a district in the upper valley of the Spercheus, lying between Mts. Othrys and Oeta, and bounded on the N. by Dolopia, on the S. by Phocis, and on the E. by Malia. — **8. Malis** [MALIS].—*History of Thessaly.* The Thessalians, as we have already seen, were a Thesprotian tribe. Under the guidance of leaders, who are said to have been descendants of Hercules, they invaded the W. part of the country, afterwards called Thessaliotis, and drove out or reduced to the condition of Penestae or bondsmen the ancient Aeolian inhabitants. The Thessalians afterwards spread over the other parts of the country, compelling the Perrhaebi, Magnetes, Achaean Phthiotae, etc., to submit to their authority and pay them tribute. The population of Thessaly, therefore, consisted, like that of Laconica, of 3 distinct classes. 1. The Penestae, whose condition was nearly the same as that of the Helots. 2. The subject people, corresponding to the Perioeci of Laconica. 3. The Thessalian conquerors, who alone had any share in the public administration, and whose lands were cultivated by the Penestae. For some time after the conquest, Thessaly was governed by kings of the race of Hercules ; but the kingly power seems to have been abolished in early times, and the government in the separate cities became oligarchical, the power being chiefly in the hands of a few great families descended from the ancient kings. Of these two of the most powerful were the Aleuadae and the Scopadae, the former of whom ruled at Larissa, and the latter at Cranon or Crannon. These nobles had vast estates cultivated by the Penestae ; they were celebrated for their hospitality and princely mode of life ; and they attracted to their courts many of the poets and artists of southern Greece. At an early period the Thessalians were united into a confederate body. Each of the 4 districts into which the country was divided probably regulated its affairs by some kind of provincial council ; and when occasion required, a chief magistrate was elected under the name of *Tagus* (Ταγός), whose commands were obeyed by all the 4 districts. His command was of a military rather than of a civil nature, and he seems to have been appointed only in case of war. We do not know the extent of his constitutional power nor the time for which he held his office ; probably neither was precisely fixed, and depended on the circumstances of the time and the character of the individual. This confederacy, however, was not of much practical benefit to the Thessalian people, and appears to have been only used by the Thessalian nobles as a means of cementing and maintaining their power. The Thessalians never became of much importance in Grecian history. They submitted to the Persians on their invasion of Greece, and they exercised no important influence on Grecian affairs till after the end of the Peloponnesian war. About this time the power of the aristocratical families began to decline, and Lycophron, who had established himself as tyrant at Pherae, offered a formidable opposition to the great aristocratical families, and endeavoured to extend his power over all Thessaly. His ambitious schemes were realized by Jason the successor, and probably the son of Lycophron, who caused himself to be elected Tagus about B. C. 374. While he lived the whole of Thessaly was united as one political power, and he began to aim at making himself master of all Greece, when he was assassinated in 370. The office of Tagus became a tyranny under his successors, Polydorus, Polyphron, Alexander, Tisiphon and Lycophron ; but at length the old aristocratical families called in the assistance of Philip of Macedonia, who deprived Lycophron of his power in 353, and restored the ancient government in the different towns. The country, however, only changed masters ; for a few years later (344) Philip made it completely subject to Macedonia, by placing at the head of the 4 divisions of the country governors devoted to his interests, and probably members of the ancient noble families, who had now become little better than his vassals. From this time Thessaly remained in a state of dependence upon the Macedonian kings, till the victory of T. Flamininus at Cynoscephalae in 197 again gave them a semblance of independence under the protection of the Romans

Thessalonica (Θεσσαλονίκη), daughter of Philip, the father of Alexander the Great, by his wife or concubine, Nicesipolis of Pherae. She was taken prisoner by Cassander along with Olympias on the capture of Pydna in B.C. 317 ; and Cassander embraced the opportunity to connect himself with the ancient royal house of Macedonia by marrying her. By Cassander she became the mother of 3 sons, Philip, Antipater, and Alexander ; and her husband paid her the honour of conferring her name upon the city of Thessalonica, which he founded on the site of the ancient Therma. [See below.] After the death of Cassander, Thessalonica was put to death by her son Antipater, 295.

Thessalonica (Θεσσαλονίκη, also Θεσσαλονίκεια : Θεσσαλονικεύς : Saloniki), more anciently **Therma** (Θέρμη : Θερμαῖος), an ancient city in Macedonia, situated at the N. E. extremity of the Sinus Thermaicus. Under the name of Therma it was not a place of much importance. It was taken and occupied by the Athenians a short time before the commencement of the Peloponnesian war (B.C. 432), but was soon after restored by them to Perdiccas. It was made an important city by Cassander, who collected in this place the inhabitants of several adjacent towns (about B.C. 315), and who gave it the name of Thessalonica, in honour of his wife, the daughter of Philip and sister of Alexander the Great. From this time it became a large and flourishing city. Its harbour was well situated for commercial intercourse with the Hellespont and the Aegaean ; and under the Romans it had the additional advantage of lying on the Via Egnatia, which led from the W. shores of Greece to Byzantium and the East. It was visited by the Apostle Paul about A. D. 53 ; and about 2 years afterwards he addressed from Corinth 2 epistles to his converts in the city. Thessalonica continued to be, under the empire, one of the most important cities of Macedonia ; and at a later time it became the residence of the prefect, and the capital, of the Illyrian provinces. It is celebrated at this period on account of the fearful massacre of its inhabitants by order of Theodosius, in consequence of a riot in which some of the Roman officers had been assassinated by the populace. [THEODOSIUS.]

Thessalus (Θεσσαλός). 1. A Greek physician, son of Hippocrates, passed some of his time at the court of Archelaus, king of Macedonia, who reigned B.C. 413—399. He was one of the founders of the sect of the Dogmatici, and is several times highly praised by Galen, who calls him the most eminent of the sons of Hippocrates. He was supposed by some of the ancient writers to be the author of several of the works that form part of the Hippocratic Collection, which he might have compiled from notes left by his father.— 2. Also a Greek physician, was a native of Tralles in Lydia, and one of the founders of the medical sect of the Methodici. He lived at Rome in the reign of the emperor Nero, A. D. 54—68, to whom he addressed one of his works ; and here he died and was buried, and his tomb was to be seen in Pliny's time on the Via Appia. He considered himself superior to all his predecessors ; he asserted that none of them had contributed any thing to the advance of medical science ; and boasted that he could himself teach the art of healing in 6 months. He is frequently mentioned by Galen, but always in terms of contempt and ridicule. None of his works are extant.

Thestius (Θέστιος), son of Ares and Demonice or Androdice, and, according to others, son of Agenor and grandson of Pleuron, the king of Aetolia. He was the father of Iphiclus, Euippus, Plexippus, Eurypylus, Leda, Althaea, and Hypermnestra. His wife is not the same in all traditions, some calling her Lycippe or Laophonte, a daughter of Pleuron, and others Deidamia. The patronymic **Thestiades** is given to his grandson Meleager, as well as to his sons, and the female patronymic **Thestias**, to his daughter Althaea, the mother of Meleager.

Thestor (Θέστωρ), son of Idmon and Laothoë, and father of Calchas, Theoclymenus, Leucippe, and Theonoë. The patronymic **Thestorides** is frequently given to his son Calchas.

Thetis (Θέτις), one of the daughters of Nereus and Doris, was the wife of Peleus, by whom she became the mother of Achilles. As a marine divinity, she dwelt like her sisters, the Nereids, in the depth of the sea, with her father Nereus. She there received Dionysus on his flight from Lycurgus, and the god, in his gratitude, presented her with a golden urn. When Hephaestus was thrown down from heaven, he was likewise received by Thetis. She had been brought up by Hera, and when she reached the age of maturity, Zeus and Hera gave her, against her will, in marriage to Peleus. Poseidon and Zeus himself are said by some to have sued for her hand ; but when Themis declared that the son of Thetis would be more illustrious than his father, both gods desisted from their suit. Others state that Thetis rejected the offers of Zeus, because she had been brought up by Hera ; and the god, to revenge himself, decreed that she should marry a mortal. Chiron then informed his friend Peleus how he might gain possession of her, even if she should metamorphose herself ; for Thetis, like Proteus, had the power of assuming any form she pleased ; and she had recourse to this means of escaping from Peleus, but the latter instructed by Chiron held the goddess fast till she again assumed her proper form, and promised to marry him. The wedding of Peleus was honoured with the presence of all the gods, with the exception of Eris or Discord, who was not invited, and who avenged herself by throwing among the assembled gods the apple, which was the source of so much misery. [PARIS.] After Thetis had become the mother of

3 D

Achilles, she bestowed upon him the tenderest care and love. [ACHILLES.]

Theūpŏlis (Θεούπολις), a later name given to the city of Antioch in Syria, on account of its eminence in the early history of Christianity.

Theūprŏsōpon (Θεοῦ πρόσωπον, i. e. *the face of a god: Ras-esh-Shukeh;* Arab. *Wejeh-el-Khiar,* i. e. *a face of stone*), a lofty rugged promontory on the coast of Phoenice, between Tripolis and Byblus, formed by a spur of Lebanon, and running far out to sea. Some travellers have fancied that they can trace in its side-view that resemblance to a human profile which its name implies.

Thĕvestē (Θεουέστη: *Tebessa,* Ru.), a considerable city of N. Africa, on the frontier of Numidia and Byzacena, at the centre of several roads. It was of comparatively late origin, and a Roman colony. Among its recently discovered ruins are a fine triumphal arch, and the old walls of the city, the circuit of which was large enough to have contained 40,000 inhabitants.

Thĭa (Θεία), daughter of Uranus and Ge, one of the female Titans, became by Hyperion the mother of Helios, Eos, and Selene, that is, she was regarded as the deity from whom all light proceeded.

Thilsaphata (prob. *Tell Afad,* between *Mosul* and *Sinjar*), a town of Mesopotamia, near the Tigris.

Thilutha, a fort in the S. of Mesopotamia, on an island in the Euphrates. Some identify it with Olabus, and that with the fort now called *Zobia* or *Juba* in about 34° N. lat.

Thinae or **Thina** (Θῖναι, Θῖνα), a chief city of the SINAE, and a great emporium for the silk and wool trade of the extreme E. Some seek it on the E. coast of China, others on the S. E. coast of *Cochin-China.*

Thĭŏdămas (Θειοδάμας), father of Hylas, and king of the Dryopes.

This (Θίς: Θινίτης), a great city of Upper Egypt, capital of the Thinites Nomos, and the seat of some of the ancient dynasties. It was either the same place as ABYDUS (No. 2.), or was so near it as to be entirely supplanted by Abydus.

Thisbē (Θίσβη), a beautiful Babylonian maiden, beloved by Pyramus. The lovers living in adjoining houses, often secretly conversed with each other through an opening in the wall, as their parents would not sanction their marriage. Once they agreed upon a rendezvous at the tomb of Ninus. Thisbe arrived first, and while she was waiting for Pyramus, she perceived a lioness which had just torn to pieces an ox, and took to flight. While running she lost her garment, which the lioness soiled with blood. In the mean time Pyramus arrived, and finding her garment covered with blood, he imagined that she had been murdered, and made away with himself under a mulberry tree, the fruit of which henceforth was as red as blood. Thisbe, who afterwards found the body of her lover, likewise killed herself.

Thisbe, afterwards **Thisbae** (Θίσβη, Θίσβαι: Θισβαῖος, Θισβεύς: *Kakosia*), a town of Boeotia, on the borders of Phocis, and between Mt. Helicon and the Corinthian gulf. It was famed for its number of wild pigeons, which are still found in abundance in the neighbourhood of Kakosia.

Thĭsŏa (Θεισόα: Θεισοάτης), a town in Arcadia on Mt. Lycaeus, called after a nymph of the same name.

Thmūis (Θμουΐς: *Tmaie,* Ru., near *Mansourah*), a city of Lower Egypt, on a canal on the E. side of the Mendesian mouth of the Nile. It was a chief seat of the worship of the god Mendes (the Egyptian Pan), under the symbol of a goat; and, according to Jerome, the word Thmuis signifies *goat.* It was the chief city of the Nomos Thmuites, which was afterwards united with the Mendesian Nomos.

Thŏantēa, a surname of the Taurian Artemis, derived from Thoas, king of Tauris.

Thŏas (Θόας). 1. Son of Andraemon and Gorge, was king of Calydon and Pleuron, in Aetolia, and sailed with 40 ships against Troy. — 2. Son of Dionysus and Ariadne, was king of Lemnos, and married to Myrina, by whom he became the father of Hypsipyle and Sicinus. When the Lemnian women killed all the men in the island, Hypsipyle saved her father Thoas, and concealed him. Afterwards, however, he was discovered by the other women, and killed; or, according to other accounts, he escaped to Taurus, or to the island of Oenoë near Euboea, which was henceforth called Sicinus. The patronymic **Thoantias** is given to Hypsipyle, as the daughter of Thoas. — 3. Son of Borysthenes, and king of Tauris, into whose dominions Iphigenia was carried by Artemis, when she was to have been sacrificed.

Thomas Magister, a rhetorician and grammarian, who flourished about A. D. 1310. He was a native of Thessalonica, and lived at the court of the emperor Andronicus Palaeologus I., where he held the offices of marshal (*Magister Officiorum*) and keeper of the archives (*Chartophylax*); but he afterwards retired to a monastery, where he assumed the name of *Theodulus,* and devoted himself to the study of the ancient Greek authors. His chief work, which has come down to us, is a *Lexicon of Attic Words* (κατὰ Ἀλφάβητον ὀνομάτων Ἀττικῶν Ἐκλογαί), compiled from the works of the elder grammarians, such as Phrynichus, Ammonius, Herodian, and Moeris. The work has some value on account of its containing much from the elder grammarians, which would otherwise have been lost; but, when Thomas deserts his guides, he often falls into the most serious errors. The best edition is by Ritschl, Halis Sax. 1831, 1832, 8vo.

Thŏrĭcus (Θόρικος or Θορικός: Θορίκιος, Θορικεύς: *Theriko*) one of the 12 ancient towns in Attica, and subsequently a demus belonging to the tribe Acamantis, was situated on the S. E. coast a little above Sunium, and was fortified by the Athenians towards the close of the Peloponnesian war. There are still extensive remains of the ancient town.

Thornax (Θόρναξ: *Paulaika*), a mountain in Laconica N. E. of Sparta, on which stood a celebrated temple of Apollo.

Thospītes Lacus (Θωσπῖτις λίμνη: *Goljik?*), a lake in Armenia Major, through which the Tigris flows. The lake, and the surrounding district, also called Thospitis, were both named from a city Thospia (Θωσπία) at the N. end of the lake.

Thrăcĭa (Θρᾴκη, Ion. Θρήκη, Θρηΐκη, Θρηΐκίη: Θρᾷξ, pl. Θρᾷκες, Ion. Θρῇξ and Θρηΐξ, pl. Θρῇκες, Θρηΐκες: Thrax, pl. Thraces), was in earlier times the name of the vast space of country bounded on the N. by the Danube, on the S. by the Propontis and the Aegaean, on the E. by the Pontus Euxinus, and on the W. by the river Strymon and the

E.-most of the Illyrian tribes. It was divided into 2 parts by Mt. Haemus (the *Balkan*), running from W. to E., and separating the plain of the lower Danube from the rivers which fall into the Aegaean. Two extensive mountain ranges branch off from the S. side of Mt. Haemus ; one running S. E. towards Constantinople ; and the other called Rhodope, E. of the preceding one, and also running in a S. E.-ly direction near the river Nestus. Between these two ranges there are many plains, which are drained by the Hebrus, the largest river in Thrace. At a later time the name Thrace was applied to a more limited extent of country. The district between the Strymon and the Nestus was added to Macedonia by Philip, and was usually called Macedonia Adjecta. [MACEDONIA.] Under Augustus the part of the country N. of the Haemus was made a separate Roman province under the name of Moesia [MOESIA] ; but the district between the Strymon and the Nestus had been previously restored to Thrace by the Romans. The Roman province of Thrace accordingly bounded on the W. by the river Nestus, which separated it from Macedonia, on the N. by Mt. Haemus, which divided it from Moesia, on the E. by the Euxine, and on the S. by the Propontis and Aegaean. — Thrace, in its widest extent, was peopled in the times of Herodotus and Thucydides by a vast number of different tribes ; but their customs and character were marked by great uniformity. Herodotus says that, next to the Indians, the Thracians were the most numerous of all races, and if united under one head would have been irresistible. He describes them as a savage, cruel, and rapacious people, delighting in blood, but brave and warlike. According to his account, which is confirmed by other writers, the Thracian chiefs sold their children for exportation to the foreign merchant ; they purchased their wives from their parents ; they punctured or tattooed their bodies and those of the women belonging to them, as a sign of noble birth ; they despised agriculture, and considered it most honourable to live by war and robbery. Deep drinking prevailed among them extensively, and their quarrels over their wine cups were notorious even in the time of Augustus. (Hor. *Carm.* i. 27.) They worshipped deities, whom the Greeks assimilated to Ares, Dionysus, and Artemis : the great sanctuary and oracle of their god Dionysus was in one of the loftiest summits of Mt. Rhodope. The tribes on the S. coast attained to some degree of civilisation, owing to the numerous Greek colonies which were founded in their vicinity ; but the tribes in the interior seem to have retained their savage habits, with little mitigation, down to the time of the Roman empire. In earlier times, however, some of the Thracian tribes must have been distinguished by a higher degree of civilisation than prevailed among them at a later period. The earliest Greek poets, Orpheus, Linus, Musaeus, and others, are all represented as coming from Thrace. Eumolpus, likewise, who founded the Eleusinian mysteries at Attica, is said to have been a Thracian, and to have fought against Erechtheus, king of Athens. We also find mention of the Thracians in other parts of southern Greece : thus they are said to have once dwelt both in Phocis and Boeotia. They were also spread over a part of Asia : the Thynians and Bithynians, and perhaps also the Mysians, were members of the great Thracian race. Even Xenophon speaks of Thrace

in Asia, which extended along the Asiatic side of the Bosporus, as far as Heraclea. — The principal Greek colonies along the coast, beginning at the Strymon and going E.-wards, were AMPHIPOLIS, at the mouth of the Strymon ; ABDERA, a little to the W. of the Nestus ; DICAEA or Dicaepolis, a settlement of Maronea ; MARONEA itself, colonised by the Chians ; STRYME, a colony of the Thasians ; MESEMBRIA, founded by the Samothracians ; and AENOS, a Lesbian colony at the mouth of the Hebrus. The Thracian Chersonesus was probably colonised by the Greeks at an early period, but it did not contain any important Greek settlement till the migration of the first Miltiades to the country, during the reign of Pisistratus at Athens. [CHERSONESUS.] On the Propontis the 2 chief Greek settlements were those of PERINTHUS and SELYMBRIA ; and on the Thracian Bosporus was the important town of BYZANTIUM. There were only a few Greek settlements on the S.W. coast of the Euxine ; the most important were those of APOLLONIA, ODESSUS, CALLATIS, TOMI, renowned as the place of Ovid's banishment, and ISTRIA, near the S. mouth of the Danube. — The Thracians are said to have been conquered by Sesostris, king of Egypt, and subsequently to have been subdued by the Teucrians and Mysians ; but the first really historical fact respecting them is their subjugation by Megabazus, the general of Darius. After the Persians had been driven out of Europe by the Greeks, the Thracians recovered their independence ; and at the beginning of the Peloponnesian war, almost all the Thracian tribes were united under the dominion of Sitalces, king of the Odrysae, whose kingdom extended from Abdera to the Euxine and the mouth of the Danube. In the 3rd year of the Peloponnesian war (B. C. 429), Sitalces, who had entered into an alliance with the Athenians, invaded Macedonia with a vast army of 150,000 men, but was compelled by the failure of provisions to return home, after remaining in Macedonia 30 days. Sitalces fell in battle against the Triballi in 424, and was succeeded by his nephew Seuthes, who during a long reign raised his kingdom to a height of power and prosperity which it had never previously attained, so that his regular revenues amounted to the annual sum of 400 talents, in addition to contributions of gold and silver in the form of presents, to a nearly equal amount. After the death of Seuthes, which appears to have happened a little before the close of the Peloponnesian war, we find his powerful kingdom split up into different parts ; and when Xenophon, with the remains of the 10,000 Greeks, arrived on the opposite coast of Asia, another Seuthes applied to him for assistance to reinstate him in his dominions. Philip, the father of Alexander the Great, reduced the greater part of Thrace ; and after the death of Alexander the country fell to the share of Lysimachus. It subsequently formed a part of the Macedonian dominions, but it continued to be governed by its native princes, and was only nominally subject to the Macedonian monarchs. Even under the Romans Thrace was for a long time governed by its own chiefs ; and we do not know at what period it was made into a Roman province.

P. Thrásĕa Paetus, a distinguished Roman senator, and Stoic philosopher, in the reign of Nero, was a native of Patavium and was probably born soon after the death of Augustus. He appears at an early period of his life to have made

3 D 2

the younger Cato his model, of whose life he wrote an account. He married Arria, the daughter of the heroic Arria, who showed her husband Caecina how to die; and his wife was worthy of her mother and her husband. At a later period he gave his own daughter in marriage to Helvidius Priscus, who trod closely in the footsteps of his father-in-law. After incurring the hatred of Nero by the independence of his character, and the freedom with which he expressed his opinions, he was condemned to death by the senate by command of the emperor, A. D. 66. By his execution and that of his friend Barea Soranus, Nero, says Tacitus, resolved to murder Virtue herself. The panegyric of Thrasea was written by Arulenus Rusticus, who was in consequence put to death by Domitian.

Thrasybulus (Θρασύβουλος). 1. Tyrant of Miletus, was a contemporary of Periander and Alyattes, the king of Lydia. He was intimately connected with Thrasybulus. The story of the mode in which Thrasybulus gave his advice to Periander as to the best means of securing his power, is given under PERIANDER. — 2. A celebrated Athenian, son of Lycus. He was zealously attached to the Athenian democracy, and took an active part in overthrowing the oligarchical government of the 400 in B. C. 411. This is the first occasion on which he is mentioned; but from this time he took a prominent part in the conduct of the war. On the establishment of the Thirty Tyrants at Athens he was banished, and was living in exile at Thebes when the rulers of Athens were perpetrating their excesses of tyranny. Being aided by the Thebans with arms and money, he collected a small band, and seized the fortress of Phyle. He next marched upon the Piraeus, which fell into his hands; and from this place he carried on war for several months against the Ten, who had succeeded to the government, and eventually he obtained possession of Athens, and restored the democracy, 403. In 390 he commanded the Athenian fleet in the Aegean, and was slain by the inhabitants of Aspendus. — 3. Brother of Gelon and Hieron, tyrants of Syracuse. He succeeded Hieron in the government, B. C. 467, and was soon afterwards expelled by the Syracusans, whom he had provoked by his rapacity and cruelty. He withdrew to Locri, in Italy, and there ended his days.

Thrasydaeus (Θρασυδαῖος), tyrant of Agrigentum, was the son and successor of Theron, B. C. 472. Shortly after his accession he was defeated by Hieron of Syracuse; and the Agrigentines immediately took advantage of this disaster to expel him from their city. He made his escape to Greece, but was arrested at Megara, and publicly executed.

Thrasyllus or Thrasylus (Θράσυλλος, Θράσυλος). 1. An Athenian, who actively assisted Thrasybulus in opposing the oligarchical revolution in B. C. 411. He was one of the commanders at the battle of Arginusae, and was among the 6 generals who returned to Athens and were put to death, 406. — 2. A celebrated astrologer at Rhodes, with whom Tiberius became acquainted during his residence in that island, and whom he ever after held in the highest honour. He died in A. D. 36, the year before Tiberius, and is said to have saved the lives of many persons whom Tiberius would otherwise have put to death, by falsely predicting for this very purpose that the

emperor would live ten years longer. The son of this Thrasyllus succeeded to his father's skill, and he is said to have predicted the empire to Nero.

Thrasymachus (Θρασύμαχος), a native of Chalcedon, was a sophist, and one of the earliest cultivators of the art of rhetoric. He was a contemporary of Gorgias. He is introduced by Plato as one of the interlocutors in the Politia, and is referred to several times in the Phaedrus.

Thrasymedes (Θρασυμήδης), son of the Pylian Nestor and Anaxibia, accompanied his father on the expedition against Troy, and returned with him to Pylos.

Thrasymenus. [TRASIMENUS.]

Thronium (Θρόνιον: Θρόνιος, Θρονιεύς: Romani), the chief town of the Locri Epicnemidii, on the river Bongrius, at a short distance from the sea, with a harbour upon the coast.

Thucydides (Θουκυδίδης). 1. An Athenian statesman, of the demus Alopece, son of Melesias. After the death of Cimon, in B. C. 449, Thucydides became the leader of the aristocratic party, which he concentrated and more thoroughly organised in opposition to Pericles. He was ostracised in 444, thus leaving the undisputed political ascendancy to Pericles. He left 2 sons, Melesias and Stephanus; and a son of the former of these, named Thucydides after his grandfather, was a pupil of Socrates. — 2. The great Athenian historian, of the demus Halimus, was the son of Olorus or Orolus and Hegesipyle. He is said to have been connected with the family of Cimon; and we know that Miltiades, the conqueror of Marathon, married Hegesipyle, the daughter of a Thracian king called Olorus, by whom she became the mother of Cimon; and it has been conjectured with much probability that the mother of Thucydides was a granddaughter of Miltiades and Hegesipyle. According to a statement of Pamphila [PAMPHILA], Thucydides was 40 years of age at the commencement of the Peloponnesian war or B. C. 431, and accordingly he was born in 471. There is a story in Lucian of Herodotus having read his History at the Olympic games to the assembled Greeks; and Suidas adds that Thucydides, then a boy, was present, and shed tears of emulation; a presage of his own future historical distinction. But this celebrated story ought probably to be rejected as a fable. Thucydides is said to have been instructed in oratory by Antiphon, and in philosophy by Anaxagoras; but whether these statements are to be received cannot be determined. It is certain, however, that being an Athenian, of a good family, and living in a city which was the centre of Greek civilisation, he must have had the best possible education: that he was a man of great ability and cultivated understanding his work clearly shows. He informs us that he possessed gold mines in that part of Thrace which is opposite to the island of Thasos, and that he was a person of the greatest influence among those in that part of Thrace. This property, according to some accounts, he had from his ancestors: according to other accounts he married a rich woman of Scaptesyle, and received them as a portion with her. Thucydides left a son, called Timotheus; and a daughter also is mentioned, who is said to have written the 8th book of the History of Thucydides. Thucydides (ii. 48) was one of those who suffered from the great plague of Athens, and one of the few who recovered. We have no trustworthy evidence of

Thucydides having distinguished himself as an orator, though it is not unlikely that he did, for his oratorical talent is shown by the speeches that he has inserted in his history. He was, however, employed in a military capacity, and he was in command of an Athenian squadron of 7 ships, at Thasus, B.C. 424, when Eucles, who commanded in Amphipolis, sent for his assistance against Brasidas, who was before that town with an army. Brasidas, fearing the arrival of a superior force, offered favourable terms to Amphipolis, which were readily accepted, for there were few Athenians in the place, and the rest did not wish to make resistance. Thucydides arrived at Eion, at the mouth of the Strymon, on the evening of the same day on which Amphipolis surrendered; and though he was too late to save Amphipolis, he prevented Eion from falling into the hand of the enemy. In consequence of this failure, Thucydides became an exile, probably to avoid a severer punishment; for Cleon, who was at this time in great favour with the Athenians, appears to have excited popular suspicion against him. There are various untrustworthy accounts as to his places of residence during his exile; but we may conclude that he could not safely reside in any place which was under Athenian dominion, and as he kept his eye on the events of the war, he must have lived in those parts which belonged to the Spartan alliance. His own words certainly imply that, during his exile, he spent much of his time either in the Peloponnesus or in places which were under Peloponnesian influence (v. 26); and his work was the result of his own experience and observations. His minute description of Syracuse and the neighbourhood leads to the probable conclusion that he was personally acquainted with the localities; and if he visited Sicily, it is probable that he also saw some parts of southern Italy. Thucydides says that he lived 20 years in exile (v. 26), and as his exile commenced in the beginning of 423, he may have returned to Athens in the beginning of 403, about the time when Thrasybulus liberated Athens. Thucydides is said to have been assassinated at Athens soon after his return; but other accounts place his death in Thrace. There is a general agreement, however, among the ancient authorities that he came to a violent end. His death cannot be placed later than 401. The time when he composed his work has been a matter of dispute. He informs us himself that he was busy in collecting materials all through the war from the beginning to the end (i. 22), and of course he would register them as he got them. Plutarch says that he wrote the work in Thrace; but the work in the shape in which we have it was certainly not finished until after the close of the war, and he was probably engaged upon it at the time of his death. A question has been raised as to the authorship of the 8th and last book of Thucydides, which breaks off in the middle of the 21st year of the war (411). It differs from all the other books in containing no speeches, and it has also been supposed to be inferior to the rest as a piece of composition. Accordingly, several ancient critics supposed that the 8th book was not by Thucydides: some attributed it to his daughter, and some to Xenophon or Theopompus, because both of them continued the history. The words with which Xenophon's *Hellenica* commence (μετὰ δὲ ταῦτα) may chiefly have led to the supposition that

he was the author, for his work is made to appear as a continuation of that of Thucydides: but this argument is in itself of little weight; and besides, both the style of the 8th book is different from that of Xenophon, and the manner of treating the subject, for the division of the year into summers and winters, which Thucydides has observed in his first 7 books, is continued in the 8th, but is not observed by Xenophon. The rhetorical style of Theopompus, which was the characteristic of his writing, renders it also improbable that he was the author of the 8th book. It seems the simplest supposition to consider Thucydides himself as the author of this book, since he names himself as the author twice (viii. 6, 60); but it is probable that he had not the opportunity of revising it with the same care as the first 7 books. It is stated by an ancient writer that Xenophon made the work of Thucydides known, which may be true, as he wrote the first 2 books of his *Hellenica*, or the part which now ends with the 2nd book, for the purpose of completing the history. The work of Thucydides, from the commencement of the 2nd book, is chronologically divided into winters and summers, and each summer and winter make a year (ii. 1). His summer comprises the time from the vernal to the autumnal equinox, and the winter comprises the period from the autumnal to the vernal equinox. The division into books and chapters was probably made by the Alexandrine critics. The history of the Peloponnesian war opens the 2nd book of Thucydides, and the 1st is introductory to the history. He begins his 1st book by observing that the Peloponnesian war was the most important event in Grecian history, which he shows by a rapid review of the history of the Greeks from the earliest period to the commencement of the war (i. 1—21). After his introductory chapters he proceeds to explain the alleged grounds and causes of the war: the real causes were, he says, the Spartan jealousy of the Athenian power. His narrative is interrupted (c. 89—118), after he has come to the time when the Lacedaemonians resolved on war, by a digression on the rise and progress of the power of Athens; a period which had been either omitted by other writers, or treated imperfectly, and with little regard to chronology, as by Hellanicus in his Attic history (c. 97). He resumes his narrative (c. 119) with the negotiations that preceded the war; but this leads to another digression of some length on the treason of Pausanias (c. 128—134), and the exile of Themistocles (c. 135—138). He concludes the book with the speech of Pericles, who advised the Athenians to refuse the demands of the Peloponnesians; and his subject, as already observed, begins with the 2nd book. A history which treats of so many events, which took place at remote spots, could only be written, in the time of Thucydides, by a man who took great pains to ascertain facts by personal inquiry. In modern times facts are made known by printing as soon as they occur; and the printed records of the time, newspapers and the like, are often the only evidence of many facts which become history. When we know the careless way in which facts are now reported and recorded by very incompetent persons, often upon very indifferent hearsay testimony, and compare with such records the pains that Thucydides took to ascertain the chief events of a war, with which he was contemporary, in which he took a share as a commander, the opportunities which his means allowed, his great abilities, and serious earnest character, it is a fair conclusion that we have a more exact history of a long eventful period by Thucydides than we have of any period in modern history, equally long and equally eventful. His whole work shows the most scrupulous care and diligence in ascertaining facts; his strict attention to chronology, and the importance that he attaches to it, are additional proof of his historical accuracy. His narrative is brief and concise: it generally contains bare facts expressed in the fewest possible words, and when we consider what pains it must have cost him to ascertain these facts, we admire the self-denial of a writer who is satisfied with giving facts in their naked brevity without ornament, without any parade of his personal importance, and of the trouble that his matter cost him. A single chapter must sometimes have represented the labour of many days and weeks. Such a principle of historical composition is the evidence of a great and elevated mind. The history of Thucydides only makes an octavo volume of moderate size; many a modern writer would have spun it out to a dozen volumes, and so have spoiled it. A work that is for all ages must contain much in little compass. He seldom makes reflections in the course of his narrative: occasionally he has a chapter of political and moral observations, animated by the keenest perception of the motives of action, and the moral character of man. Many of his speeches are political essays, or materials for them; they are not mere imaginations of his own for rhetorical effect; they contain the general sense of what was actually delivered as nearly as he could ascertain, and in many instances he had good opportunities of knowing what was said, for he heard some speeches delivered (i. 22). His opportunities, his talents, his character, and his subject, all combined to produce a work that stands alone, and in its kind has neither equal nor rival. His pictures are sometimes striking and tragic, an effect produced by severe simplicity and minute particularity. Such is the description of the plague of Athens. Such also is the incomparable history of the Athenian expedition to Sicily, and its melancholy termination. A man who thinks profoundly will have a form of expression which is stamped with the character of his mind; and the style of Thucydides is accordingly concise, vigorous, and energetic. We feel that all the words were intended to have a meaning, and have a meaning: none of them are idle. Yet he is sometimes harsh and obscure; and probably he was so, even to his own countrymen. Some of his sentences are very involved, and the connection and dependence of the parts are often difficult to seize. The best editions of Thucydides are by Bekker, Berlin, 1821, 3 vols. 8vo.; by Poppo, Leipzig, 10 vols. 8vo., 1821—1838, of which two volumes are filled with prolegomena; by Haack, with selections from the Greek Scholia and short notes, Leipzig, 1820, 2 vols. 8vo.; by Göller, 2 vols. 8vo., Leipzig, 1826; and by Arnold, 3 vols. 8vo., Oxford, 1830—1835.

Thūlē (Θούλη), an island in the N. part of the German Ocean, regarded by the ancients as the most N.-ly point in the whole earth. It is first mentioned by Pytheas, the celebrated Greek navigator of Massilia, who undertook a voyage to Britain and Thule, of which he gave a description in his work on the Ocean. All subsequent writers, who speak of Thule, appear to have taken their accounts from that of Pytheas. According to Pytheas, Thule was a six days' sail from Britain; and the day and night there were each 6 months long. He further stated that in Thule and those distant parts there was neither earth, sea, nor air, but a sort of mixture of all these, like to the mollusca, in which the earth and the sea and every thing else were suspended, and which could not be penetrated either by land or by sea. Many modern writers suppose the Thule of Pytheas to be the same as Iceland, while others regard it as a part of Norway. The Thule of Ptolemy, however, lay much further to the S., and should probably be identified with the largest of the Shetland islands.

Thūrii, more rarely **Thūrium** (Θούριοι, Θούριον: Θούριος, Θουριεύς, Thurius, Thurīnus: *Terra Nuova*), a Greek city in Lucania, founded B.C. 443, near the site of the ancient Sybaris, which had been destroyed more than 60 years before. [Sybaris.] It was built by the remains of the population of Sybaris, assisted by colonists from all parts of Greece, but especially from Athens. Among these colonists was the historian Herodotus and the orator Lysias, the latter of whom, however, was only a youth at the time and subsequently returned to Athens. The new city, from which the remains of the Sybarites were soon expelled, rapidly attained great power and prosperity, and became one of the most important Greek towns in the S. of Italy. Thus we are told that the Thurians were able to bring 14,000 foot soldiers and 1000 horse into the field against the Lucanians. In the Samnite wars Thurii received a Roman garrison; but it revolted to Hannibal in the 2nd Punic war. The Carthaginian general, however, at a later time, not trusting the Thurians plundered the town, and removed 3500 of its inhabitants to Croton. The Romans subsequently sent a Latin colony to Thurii, and changed its name into Copiae; but it continued to retain its original name, under which it is mentioned by Caesar in the civil war as a municipium.

Thyamis (Θύαμις: *Kalama*), a river in Epirus, flowing into the sea near a promontory of the same name.

Thyădes. [Thyia.]

Thyāmus (Θύαμος), a mountain in Acarnania, south of Argos Amphilochicum.

Thyatīra (τὰ Θυάτειρα: Θυατειρηνός), a city in the N. of Lydia, on the river Lycus, celebrated as one of the seven Churches in the Apocalypse (ii.18).

Thyestes (Θυέστης), son of Pelops and Hippodamia, was the brother of Atreus and the father of Aegisthus. See Atreus and Aegisthus.

Thyia (Θυία), a daughter of Castalius or Cephissus, became by Apollo the mother of Delphus. She is said to have been the first to have sacrificed to Dionysus, and to have celebrated orgies in his honour. From her the Attic women, who went yearly to Mt. Parnassus to celebrate the Dionysiac orgies with the Delphian Thyiades, received themselves the name of Thyiădes or Thyădes. This word, however, comes from θύω, and properly signifies the raging or frantic women.

Thymbra (Θύμβρη). 1. A city of the Troad, N. of Ilium Vetus, on a hill by the side of the river Thymbrius, with a celebrated temple of Apollo, who derived from this place the epithet

Thymbraeus. The surrounding plain still bears the same name. — **2.** A wooded district in Phrygia, no doubt connected with THYMBRIUM.

Thymbria (Θυμβρία), a place in Caria, on the Maeander, 4 stadia E. of Myus, with a Charonium, that is, a cave containing mephitic vapour.

Thymbrium (Θύμβριον: Thymbriäni), a small town of Phrygia, 10 parasangs W. of Tyriaeum, with the so-called fountain of Midas (Xen. *Anab.* i. 2.).

Thymbrius (Θύμβριος: *Thimbrek*), a river of the Troad, falling into the Scamander. At the present day, it flows direct into the Hellespont; and, on this and other grounds, some doubt whether the *Thimbrek* is the ancient river.

Thymělě, a celebrated mima or female actress in the reign of Domitian, with whom she was a great favourite. She frequently acted along with Latinus.

Thymoetes (Θυμοίτης), one of the elders of Troy. A soothsayer had predicted, that on a certain day a boy should be born, by whom Troy should be destroyed. On that day Paris was born to Priam, and Munippus to Thymoetes. Priam ordered Munippus and his mother Cylla to be killed. Hence Virgil (*Aen.* ii. 31) represents Aeneas saying, that it was doubtful whether Thymoetes advised the Trojans to draw the wooden horse into the city, in order to revenge himself.

Thyni (Θυνοί), a Thracian people, whose original abodes were near Salmydessus, but who afterwards passed over into BITHYNIA.

Thynia (Θυνία). 1. The land of the Thyni in Thrace. — **2.** Another name for BITHYNIA. — **3.** [THYNIAS].

Thynias or **Thynia** (Θυνιάς, Θυνία). 1. (*Inada*), a promontory on the coast of Thrace, N. W. of Salmydessus, with a town of the same name. — **2.** (*Kirpe*), a small island of the Euxine, on the coast of Bithynia, near the Prom. Calpe, also called Apollonia and Daphnusa.

Thyöně (Θυώνη), the name of Semele, under which Dionysus fetched her from Hades, and introduced her among the immortals. Hence Dionysus is also called **Thyöneus**. Both names are formed from ϑύειν, " to be inspired."

Thyrěa (Θυρέα, Ion. Θυρέη: Θυρεάτης), the chief town in Cynuria, the district on the borders of Laconia and Argolis, was situated upon a height on the bay of the sea called after it **Sinus Thyreates** (Θυρεάτης κόλποt). It was for the possession of Thyrea that the celebrated battle was fought between the 300 Spartans and 300 Argives. The territory of Thyrea was called **Thyreätis** (Θυρεᾶτις).

Thysdrus, Tisdrus, or **Tusdrus** (Θυσδρός: *El-Jemm*, Ru.), a large fortified city of Byzacena, N. W. of the promontory Brachodes (*Ras Kapoudiah*). Under the Romans, it was a free city. It was here that the emperor Gordian assumed the purple.

Thyssägětae (Θυσσαγέται), a people of Sarmatia Asiatica, on the E. shores of the Palus Maeotis.

Thyssus (Θύσσος or Θυσσός), a town of Macedonia on the peninsula of Acte.

Tiarantus, a river of Scythia and a tributary of the Danube.

Tibarēni or **Tibäri** (Τιβαρηνοί, Τίβαροι), a quiet agricultural people on the N. coast of Pontus, E. of the river Iris.

Tiběrias. 1. (Τιβεριάς: Τιβεριεύς), a city of Galilee, on the S.W. shore of the Lake of Tiberias, built by Herod Antipas in honour of the emperor Tiberius. After the destruction of Jerusalem, it became the seat of the Jewish sanhedrim. Near it were the warm baths of Emmaus. — **2.** (Τιβερίας, λίμνη ἡ Τιβερίων), or **Gennēsäret** (Γεννησαρέτ, ὕδωρ Γεννησάρ, ἡ Γεννησαρῖτις), also the **Sea of Galilee** (ἡ θάλασσα τῆς Γαλιλαίας), in the O. T. **Chinnereth** (*Bahr Tubariyeh*), the 2nd of the 3 lakes in Palestine, formed by the course of the Jordan. [JORDANES.] Its length is 11 or 12 geographical miles, and its breadth from 5 to 6. It lies deep among fertile hills, has very clear and sweet water, and is full of excellent fish. Its surface is 750 feet below the level of the Mediterranean. In the time of our Saviour, its shores were covered with populous villages, but they are now almost entirely deserted. Its E. coast belonged to the districts of Decapolis and Gaulonitis.

Tibĕrinus, one of the mythical kings of Alba, son of Capetus, and father of Agrippa, is said to have been drowned in crossing the river Alba, which was hence called Tiberis after him, and of which he became the guardian god.

Tiberiopŏlis (Τιβηριούπολις), a city of Great Phrygia, near Eumenia.

Tibĕris also **Tibris, Tybris, Thybris, Amnis Tiberinus** or simply **Tiberinus** (*Tiber* or *Tevere*), the chief river in central Italy, on which stood the city of Rome. It is said to have been originally called *Albula*, and to have received the name of *Tiberis* in consequence of Tiberinus, king of Alba, having been drowned in it. It has been supposed that *Albula* was the Latin and *Tiberis* the Etruscan name of the river. The Tiber rises from 2 springs of limpid water in the Apennines, near Tifernum, and flows in a S. W.-ly direction, separating Etruria from Umbria, the land of the Sabines, and Latium. After flowing about 110 miles it receives the Nar (*Nera*), and from its confluence with this river its regular navigation begins. Three miles above Rome, at the distance of nearly 70 miles. from the Nar, it receives the Anio (*Teverone*), and from this point becomes a river of considerable importance. Within the walls of Rome, the Tiber is about 300 feet wide and from 12 to 18 feet deep. After heavy rains the river in ancient times, as at the present day, frequently overflowed its banks, and did considerable mischief to the lower parts of the city. (Hor. *Carm.* i. 2.) At Rome the maritime navigation of the river begins; and at 18 miles from the city, and about 4 miles from the coast, it divides into 2 arms, forming an island, which was sacred to Venus, and called Insula Sacra (*Isola Sagra*). The left branch of the river runs into the sea by Ostia, which was the ancient harbour of Rome; but in consequence of the accumulation of sand at the mouth of the left branch, the right branch was widened by Trajan, and was made the regular harbour of the city under the name of *Portus Romanus, Portus Augusti,* or simply *Portus.* The whole length of the Tiber, with its windings, is about 200 miles. The waters of the river are muddy and yellowish, whence it is frequently called by the Roman poets *flavus Tiberis.* The poets also give it the epithets of *Tyrrhenus,* because it flowed past Etruria during the whole of its course, and of *Lydius,* because the Etruscans are said to have been of Lydian origin.

Tibĕrius. 1. Emperor of Rome, A. D. 14—37.

His full name was TIBERIUS CLAUDIUS NERO CAESAR. He was the son of T. Claudius Nero and of Livia, and was born on the 16th of November, B. C. 42, before his mother married Augustus. Tiberius was tall and strongly made, and his health was very good. His face was handsome, and his eyes were large. He was carefully educated, and became well acquainted with Greek and Latin literature. His master in rhetoric was Theodorus of Gadara. Though not without military courage, as his life shows, he had a great timidity of character, and was of a jealous and suspicious temper; and these qualities rendered him cruel after he had acquired power. In the latter years of his life, particularly, he indulged his lustful propensities in every way that a depraved imagination could suggest: lust and cruelty are not strangers. He affected a regard to decency and to externals. He was the prince of hypocrites; and the events of his reign are little more than the exhibition of his detestable character. In B. C. 11, Augustus compelled Tiberius, much against his will, to divorce his wife Vipsania Agrippina, and to marry Julia, the widow of Agrippa, and the emperor's daughter, with whom Tiberius however did not long live in harmony. Tiberius was thus brought into still closer contact with the imperial family; but as Caesar and L. Caesar, the grandsons of Augustus, were still living, the prospect of Tiberius succeeding to the imperial power seemed very remote. He was employed by Augustus on various military services. In 20 he was sent by Augustus to restore Tigranes to the throne of Armenia. It was during this campaign that Horace addressed one of his epistles to Julius Florus (i. 12), who was serving under Tiberius. In 15, Drusus and his brother Tiberius were engaged in warfare with the Rhaeti, and the exploits of the 2 brothers were sung by Horace (Carm. iv. 4, 14). In 13, Tiberius was consul with P. Quintilius Varus. In 11, while his brother Drusus was fighting against the Germans, Tiberius conducted the war against the Dalmatians and against the Pannonians. Drusus died in 9, owing to a fall from his horse. On the news of the accident, Tiberius was sent by Augustus to Drusus, whom he found just alive. Tiberius returned to the war in Germany, and crossed the Rhine. In 7 he was consul a second time. In 6 he obtained the tribunitia potestas for 5 years, but during this year he retired with the emperor's permission to Rhodes, where he spent the next 7 years. Tacitus says that his chief reason for leaving Rome was to get away from his wife, who treated him with contempt, and whose licentious life was no secret to her husband; probably, too, he was unwilling to stay at Rome when the grandsons of Augustus were attaining years of maturity, for there was mutual jealousy between them and Tiberius. He returned to Rome A. D. 2. He was relieved from one trouble during his absence, for his wife Julia was banished to the island of Pandataria (B. C. 2), and he never saw her again. After the deaths of L. Caesar (A. D. 2) and C. Caesar (A. D. 4), Augustus adopted Tiberius, with the view of leaving to him the imperial power; and at the same time he required Tiberius to adopt Germanicus, the son of his brother Drusus, though Tiberius had a son Drusus by his wife Vipsania. From the year of his adoption to the death of Augustus, Tiberius was in command of the Roman armies, though he visited Rome several

times. He was sent into Germany A. D. 4. He reduced all Illyricum to subjection A. D. 9; and in A. D. 12 he had the honour of a triumph at Rome for his German and Dalmatian victories. On the death of Augustus at Nola, on the 19th of August, A. D. 14, Tiberius, who was on his way to Illyricum, was immediately summoned home by his mother Livia. He took the imperial power without any opposition, affecting all the while a great reluctance. He began his reign by putting to death Postumus Agrippa, the surviving grandson of Augustus, and he alleged that it was done pursuant to the command of the late emperor. When he felt himself sure in his place, he began to exercise his craft. He took from the popular assembly the election of the magistrates, and transferred it to the senate. The news of the death of Augustus roused a mutiny among the legions in Pannonia, which was quelled by Drusus, the son of Tiberius. The armies on the Rhine under Germanicus showed a disposition to reject Tiberius, and if Germanicus had been inclined to try the fortune of a campaign, he might have had the assistance of the German armies against his uncle. But Germanicus restored discipline to the army by his firmness, and maintained his fidelity to the new emperor. The first year of his reign was marked by the death of Julia, whom Augustus had removed from Pandataria to Rhegium. The death of Germanicus in the East, in A. D. 19, relieved Tiberius from all fear of a rival claimant to the throne; and it was believed by many that Germanicus had been poisoned by order of Tiberius. From this time Tiberius began to indulge with less restraint in his love of tyranny, and many distinguished senators were soon put to death on the charge of treason against the emperor (laesa majestas). Notwithstanding his suspicious nature, Tiberius gave his complete confidence to Sejanus, who for many years possessed the real government of the state. This ambitious man aimed at the imperial power. In 23 Drusus, the son of Tiberius, was poisoned by the contrivance of Sejanus. Three years afterwards (26) Tiberius left Rome, and withdrew into Campania. He never returned to the city. He left on the pretext of dedicating temples in Campania, but his real motives were his dislike to Rome, where he heard a great deal that was disagreeable to him, and his wish to indulge his sensual propensities in private. In order to secure still greater retirement, he took up his residence (27) in the island of Capreae, at a short distance from the Campanian coast. The death of Livia (29), the emperor's mother, released Tiberius from one cause of anxiety. He had long been tired of her, because she wished to exercise authority, and one object in leaving Rome was to be out of her way. Livia's death gave Sejanus and Tiberius free scope, for Tiberius never entirely released himself from a kind of subjection to his mother, and Sejanus did not venture to attempt the overthrow of Livia's influence. The destruction of Agrippina and her children was now the chief purpose of Sejanus: he finally got from the tyrant (31) the reward that was his just desert, an ignominious death. [SEJANUS.] The death of Sejanus was followed by the execution of his friends; and for the remainder of the reign of Tiberius, Rome continued to be the scene of tragic occurrences. Tiberius died on the 16th of March, 37, at the villa of Lucullus, in Misenum. He was 78 years of age, and had reigned 22 years. He was succeeded by Caius (Caligula), the son of Germanicus, but he had himself appointed no successor. Tiberius did not die a natural death. It was known that his end was rapidly approaching, and having had a fainting fit, he was supposed to be dead. Thereupon Caius came forth and was saluted as emperor ; but he was alarmed by the intelligence that Tiberius had recovered and called for something to eat. Caius was so frightened that he did not know what to do ; but Macro, the praefect of the praetorians, with more presence of mind, gave orders that a quantity of clothes should be thrown on Tiberius, and that he should be left alone. — In the time of Tiberius lived Valerius Maximus, Velleius Paterculus, Phaedrus, Fenestella, and Strabo ; also the jurists Massurius Sabinus, M. Cocceius Nerva, and others. — Tiberius wrote a brief commentary of his own life, the only book that the emperor Domitian studied : Suetonius made use of it for his life of Tiberius. Tiberius also wrote Greek poems, and a lyric poem on the death of L. Caesar. — 2. A philosopher and sophist, of unknown time, the author of numerous works on grammar and rhetoric. One of his works, on the figures in the orations of Demosthenes (περὶ τῶν παρὰ Δημοσθένει σχημάτων), is still extant, and has been published.

Tibilis (*Hammam Miskouten?*), a town of Numidia, in N. Africa, on the road from Cirta to Carthage, with warm springs, called Aquae Tibilitanae.

Tibiscum, a town of Dacia and a Roman municipium on the river Tibiscus.

Tibiscus or Tibissus, probably the same as the Parthiscus or Parthissus (*Theiss*), a river of Dacia, forming the W. boundary of that country, rising in the Montes Carpates, and falling into the Danube.

Tibullus, Albius, the Roman poet, was of equestrian family. The date of his birth is uncertain ; but he died young, soon after Virgil. His birth is therefore placed by conjecture B. C. 54, and his death B. C. 18. Of his youth and education, absolutely nothing is known. The estate belonging to the equestrian ancestors of Tibullus was at Pedum, between Tibur and Praeneste. This property, like that of the other great poets of the day, Virgil and Horace, had been either entirely or partially confiscated during the civil wars ; yet Tibullus retained or recovered part of it, and spent there the better portion of his short, but peaceful and happy, life. His great patron was Messala, whom he accompanied in 31 into Aquitania, whither Messala had been sent by Augustus to suppress a formidable insurrection which had broken out in this province. Part of the glory of the Aquitanian campaign, which Tibullus celebrates in language of unwonted loftiness, redounds, according to the poet, to his own fame. He was present at the battle of Atax (*Aude* in Languedoc), which broke the Aquitanian rebellion. In the following year (30) Messala, having pacified Gaul, was sent into the East. Tibullus set out in his company, but was taken ill, and obliged to remain in Corcyra, from whence he returned to Rome. So ceased the active life of Tibullus ; his life is now the chronicle of his poetry and of those tender passions which were the inspiration of his poetry. The first object of his attachment is celebrated under the poetic name of Delia. To Delia are addressed the first 6 elegies of the 1st book. The poet's attachment to Delia

had begun before he left Rome for Aquitania. But Delia seems to have been faithless during his absence from Rome. On his return from Corcyra, he found her ill, and attended her with affectionate solicitude (*Eleg.* i. 5), and hoped to induce her to retire with him into the country. But first a richer lover appears to have supplanted him with the inconstant Delia ; and afterwards there appears a husband in his way. The 2nd book of Elegies is chiefly devoted to a new mistress named Nemesis. Besides these 2 mistresses Tibullus was enamoured of a certain Glycera. He wrote elegies to soften that cruel beauty, whom there seems no reason to confound either with Delia, the object of his youthful attachment, or with Nemesis. Glycera, however, is not known to us from the poetry of Tibullus, but from the ode of Horace, which gently reproves him for dwelling so long in his plaintive elegies on the pitiless Glycera. — The poetry of his contemporaries shows Tibullus as a gentle and singularly amiable man. To Horace especially he was an object of warm attachment. Besides the ode which alludes to his passion for Glycera (Hor. *Carm.* i. 33), the epistle of Horace to Tibullus gives the most full and pleasing view of his poetical retreat, and of his character : it is written by a kindred spirit. Horace does homage to that perfect purity of taste which distinguishes the poetry of Tibullus ; he takes pride in the candid but favourable judgment of his own satires. The time of Tibullus he supposes to be shared between the finishing his exquisite small poems, which were to surpass even those of Cassius of Parma, up to that time the models of that kind of composition, and the enjoyment of the country. Tibullus possessed, according to his friend's notions, all the blessings of life — a competent fortune, favour with the great, fame, health ; and he seemed to know how to enjoy all those blessings. — The 2 first books alone of the Elegies, under the name of Tibullus, are of undoubted authenticity. The 3rd is the work of another, a very inferior poet, whether Lygdamus be a real or fictitious name or not. This poet was much younger than Tibullus, for he was born in the year of the battle of Mutina, 43. The hexameter poem on Messala, which opens the 4th book, is so bad that, although a successful elegiac poet may have failed when he attempted epic verse, it cannot well be ascribed to a writer of the exquisite taste of Tibullus. The smaller elegies of the 4th book have all the inimitable grace and simplicity of Tibullus. With the exception of the 13th (of which some lines are hardly surpassed by Tibullus himself) these poems relate to the love of a certain Sulpicia, a woman of noble birth, for Cerinthus, the real or fictitious name of a beautiful youth. Nor is there any improbability in supposing that Tibullus may have written elegies in the name or by the desire of Sulpicia. If Sulpicia was herself the poetess, she approached nearer to Tibullus than any other writer of elegies. — The 1st book of Elegies alone seems to have been published during the author's life, probably soon after the triumph of Messala (27). The 2nd book no doubt did not appear till after the death of Tibullus. With it, according to our conjecture, may have been published the elegies of his imitator, perhaps his friend and associate in the society of Messala, Lygdamus (if that be a real name), i. e. the 3rd book : and likewise the 4th, made up of poems belonging, as it were, to this intimate society of Messala, the Panegyric by some nameless author, which, feeble as it is, seems to be of that age ; the poems in the name of Sulpicia, with the concluding one, the 13th, a fragment of Tibullus himself. The best editions of Tibullus are by Lachmann, Berol. 1829, and by Dissenus, Göttingen, 1835.

Tibur (Tibur, pl. Tiburtes, Tiburtinus: *Tivoli*), one of the most ancient towns of Latium, 16 miles N. E. of Rome, situated on the slope of a hill (hence called by Horace *supinum Tibur*), on the left bank of the Anio, which here forms a magnificent waterfall. It is said to have been originally built by the Siculi, and to have afterwards passed into the possession of the Aborigines and Pelasgi. According to tradition it derived its name from Tiburtus, son of Catillus, who emigrated from Greece with Evander. It was afterwards one of the chief towns of the Latin league, and became subject to Rome with the other Latin cities on the final subjugation of Latium in B.C. 338. Under the Romans Tibur continued to be a large and flourishing town, since the salubrity and beautiful scenery of the place led many of the most distinguished Roman nobles to build here magnificent villas. Of these the most splendid was the villa of the emperor Hadrian, in the extensive remains of which many valuable specimens of ancient art have been discovered. Here also the celebrated Zenobia lived after adorning the triumph of her conqueror Aurelian. Horace likewise had a country house in the neighbourhood of Tibur, which he preferred to all his other residences. The deity chiefly worshipped at Tibur was Hercules ; and in the neighbourhood was the grove and temple of the Sibyl Albunea, whose oracles were consulted from the most ancient times. [ALBUNEA.] The surrounding country produced excellent olives, and also contained some celebrated stone quarries. There was a road from Rome leading to Tibur, called Via Tiburtina, which was continued from the town under the name of the Via Valeria, past Corfinium to Adria.

Tichis or **Tecum**. [TECUM.]

Tichiussa (Τειχιοῦσσα), a fortress in the territory of Miletus.

Ticinum (Ticinensis: *Pavia*), a town of the Laevi, or, according to others, of the Insubres, in Gallia Cisalpina, on the left bank of the Ticinus. It was subsequently a Roman municipium ; but it owed its greatness to the Lombard kings, who made it the capital of their dominions. The Lombards gave it the name of Papia, which it still retains under the slightly changed form of Pavia.

Ticinus (*Tessino*), an important river in Gallia Cisalpina, rises in Mons Adula, and after flowing through Lacus Verbanus (*Lago Maggiore*), falls into the Po near Ticinum. It was upon the bank of this river that Hannibal gained his first victory over the Romans by the defeat of P. Scipio, B. C. 218.

Tifata, a mountain in Campania, E. of Capua, near which the Samnites defeated the Campanians, and where at a later time Sulla gained a victory over the proconsul Norbanus. On this mountain there was a temple of Diana and also one of Jupiter of some celebrity.

Tifernum. 1. **Tiberinum** (Tifernates Tiberini, pl. : *Citta di Castello*), a town of Umbria, near the sources of the river Tiber, whence its surname, and upon the confines of Etruria. Near this town the younger Pliny had a villa.— 2. **Metaurense** (Tifer-

nates Metaurenses : *S. Angelo in Vado*), a town in Umbria, E. of the preceding, on the river Metaurus, whence its surname. — 3. A town in Samnium, on the river Tifernus.

Tifernus (*Biferno*), a river of Samnium, rising in the Apennines, and flowing through the country of the Frentani into the Adriatic.

Tigellinus Sophonius, the son of a native of Agrigentum, owed his rise from poverty and obscurity to his handsome person and his unscrupulous character. He was banished to Scyllaceum in Bruttii (A. D. 39—40), for an intrigue with Agrippina and Julia Livilla, sisters of Caligula. He was probably among the exiles restored by Agrippina, after she became empress, since early in Nero's reign he was again in favour at court, and on the death of Burrus (63) was appointed praetorian prefect jointly with Fenius Rufus. Tigellinus ministered to Nero's worst passions, and of all his favourites was the most obnoxious to the Roman people. He inflamed his jealousy or his avarice against the noblest members of the senate and the most pliant dependants of the court. In 65, Tigellinus entertained Nero in his Aemilian gardens, with a sumptuous profligacy unsurpassed even in that age, and in the same year shared with him the odium of burning Rome, since the conflagration had broken out on the scene of the banquet. On Nero's fall he joined with Nymphidius Sabinus, who had succeeded Fenius Rufus as praetorian prefect, in transferring the allegiance of the soldiers to Galba. The people clamorously demanded his death. During the brief reign of Galba his life was spared ; but on the accession of Otho, he was compelled to put an end to his own life.

Tigellius Hermogenes. [HERMOGENES.]

Tigranes (Τιγράνης), kings of Armenia. 1. Reigned B. C. 96—56 or 55. He united under his sway not only all Armenia, but several of the neighbouring provinces, such as Atropatene and Gordyene, and thus raised himself to a degree of power far superior to that enjoyed by any of his predecessors. He assumed the pompous title of king of kings, and always appeared in public accompanied by some of his tributary princes as attendants. His power was also greatly strengthened by his alliance with Mithridates the Great, king of Pontus, whose daughter Cleopatra he had married at an early period of his reign. In consequence of the dissensions in the royal family of Syria, Tigranes was enabled in 83 to make himself master of the whole Syrian monarchy from the Euphrates to the sea. He was now at the summit of his power, and continued in the undisputed possession of these extensive dominions for nearly 14 years. At the instigation of his son-in-law Mithridates, he invaded Cappadocia in 74, and is said to have carried off into captivity no less than 300,000 of the inhabitants, a large portion of whom he settled in his newly founded capital of Tigranocerta. [TIGRANOCERTA.] In other respects he appears to have furnished little support to Mithridates in his war against the Romans ; but when the Romans haughtily demanded from him the surrender of Mithridates, who had taken refuge in his dominions, he returned a peremptory refusal, accompanied with an express declaration of war. Lucullus invaded Armenia in 69, defeated the mighty host which Tigranes led against him, and followed up his victory by the capture of Tigranocerta. In the following year (68) the united forces of

Tigranes and Mithridates were again defeated by Lucullus ; but the mutinous disposition of the Roman troops prevented Lucullus from gaining any further advantages over the Armenian king, and enabled the latter not only to regain his dominions, but also to invade Cappadocia. The arrival of Pompey (66) soon changed the face of events.. Mithridates, after his final defeat by Pompey, once more threw himself upon the support of his son-in-law : but Tigranes, who suspected him of abetting the designs of his son Tigranes, who had rebelled against his father, refused to receive him, while he himself hastened to make overtures of submission to Pompey. That general had already advanced into the heart of Armenia under the guidance of the young Tigranes, when the old king repaired in person to the Roman camp, and presenting himself as a suppliant before Pompey, laid his tiara at his feet. By this act of humiliation he at once conciliated the favour of the conqueror, who treated him in a friendly manner, and left him in possession of Armenia Proper with the title of king, depriving him only of the provinces of Sophene and Gordyene, which he erected into a separate kingdom for his son Tigranes. The elder monarch was so overjoyed at obtaining these unexpectedly favourable terms, that he not only paid the sum of 6000 talents demanded by Pompey, but added a large sum as a donation to his army, and continued ever after the steadfast friend of the Roman general. He died in 56 or 55, and was succeeded by his son Artavasdes.— 2. Son of Artavasdes, and grandson of the preceding. He was living an exile at Rome, when a party of his countrymen, discontented with the rule of his elder brother, Artaxias, sent to request that he should be placed on the throne. To this Augustus assented, and Tiberius was charged with the duty of accomplishing it, a task which he effected apparently without opposition (n. c. 20).

Tigranocerta (τὰ Τιγρανόκερτα and ἡ Τιγρ., i. e., in Armenian, the City of Tigranes : *Sert*, Ru.), the later capital of Armenia, built by Tigranes, on a height by the river Nicephorius, in the valley between M. Masius and Niphates. It was strongly fortified, and peopled chiefly with Macedonians and Greeks, forcibly removed from Cappadocia and Cilicia ; but, after the defeat of Tigranes by Lucullus under its walls, these people were permitted to return to their homes. The city was at the same time partially destroyed ; but it still remained a considerable place.

Tigris, gen. -ĭdos and -is (ὁ Τίγρις, gen. Τίγριδος and Τίγριος, also Τίγρης, gen. Τίγρητος : *Tigris*), a great river of W. Asia, rises from several sources on the S. side of that part of the Taurus chain called Niphates, in Armenia, and flows S. E., first through the narrow valley between M. Masius and the prolongation of M. Niphates, and then through the great plain which is bounded on the E. by the last-named chain, till it falls into the head of the Persian Gulf, after receiving the Euphrates from the W. [Comp. EUPHRATES.] Its other chief tributaries, all falling into its E. side, were the NICEPHORIUS or CENTRITES, the LYCUS, the CAPRUS, the PHYSCUS, the GORGUS, GILLAS, or DELAS, the GYNDES, and the CHOASPES. It divided Assyria and Susiana on the E., from Mesopotamia and Babylonia, and (at its mouth) Arabia, on the W. The name is sometimes applied to the PASITIGRIS.

Tigurīni, a tribe of the Helvetii, who joined the Cimbri in invading the country of the Allobroges in Gaul, where they defeated the consul L. Cassius Longinus, B. C. 107. They formed in the time of Caesar the most important of the 4 cantons (*pagi*) into which the Helvetii were divided. It was perhaps from this people that the town of Tigurum (*Zürich*) derived its name, though this name does not occur in any ancient writer.

Tilphūsĭum (Τιλφούσιον, Τιλφουσσιον, Dor. Τιλφώσσιον : Τιλφούσιος, Dor. Τιλφώσιος), a town in Boeotia, situated upon a mountain of the same name, S. of lake Copais, and between Coronea and Haliartus. It derived its name from the fountain Tilphūsa, which was sacred to Apollo, and where Tiresias is said to have been buried.

Timaeus (Τίμαιος). 1. The historian, was the son of Andromachus, tyrant of Tauromenium, in Sicily. Timaeus attained the age of 96 ; and though we do not know the exact date either of his birth or death, we cannot be far wrong in placing his birth in B. C. 352, and his death in 256. Timaeus received instruction from Philiscus, the Milesian, a disciple of Isocrates ; but we have no further particulars of his life, except that he was banished from Sicily by Agathocles, and passed his exile at Athens, where he had lived 50 years when he wrote the 34th book of his history. The great work of Timaeus was a history of Sicily from the earliest times to 264, in which year Polybius commences the introduction to his work. This history was one of great extent. We have a quotation from the 38th book, and there were probably many books after this. The value and authority of Timaeus as an historian have been most vehemently attacked by Polybius in many parts of his work. Most of the charges of Polybius appear to have been well founded ; but he has not only omitted to mention some of the peculiar excellencies of Timaeus, but has even regarded these excellencies as deserving the severest censure. Thus it was one of the great merits of Timaeus, for which he is loudly denounced by Polybius, that he attempted to give the myths in their simplest and most genuine form, as related by the most ancient writers. Timaeus also collected the materials of his history with the greatest diligence and care, a fact which even Polybius is obliged to admit. He likewise paid very great attention to chronology, and was the first writer who introduced the practice of recording events by Olympiads, which was adopted by almost all subsequent writers of Greek history. The fragments of Timaeus have been collected by Göller, in his *De Situ et Origine Syracusarum*, Lips. 1818, and by Car. and Theod. Müller, in the *Fragmenta Historic. Graec.*, Paris, 1841.—2. Of Locri, in Italy, a Pythagorean philosopher, is said to have been a teacher of Plato. There is an extant work, bearing his name, written in the Doric dialect, and entitled περὶ ψυχᾶς κόσμου καὶ φύσιος : but its genuineness is very doubtful, and it is in all probability nothing more than an abridgment of Plato's dialogue of *Timaeus*. The best edition is by Gelder, Leyden, 1836.—3. The Sophist, wrote a Lexicon to Plato, addressed to a certain Gentianus, which is still extant. The time at which he lived is quite uncertain. He is usually placed in the 3rd century of the Christian aera, which produced so many ardent admirers of the Platonic philosophy, such as Porphyry, Longinus,

Plotinus, &c. The Lexicon is very brief, and bears the title Τιμαίου σοφιστοῦ ἐκ τῶν τοῦ Πλάτωνος λέξεων. It is evident that the work has received several interpolations, especially in explanations of words occurring in Herodotus. But it is one of great value, and the explanations of words are some of the very best which have come down to us from the ancient grammarians. It has been edited by Ruhnken, Leyden, 1754, and again, Leyden, 1789 ; and by Koch, Leipzig, 1828, and 1833.

Tīmāgĕnĕs (Τιμαγένης), a rhetorician and a historian, was a native of Alexandria, from which place he was carried as a prisoner to Rome, where he was first employed as a slave in menial offices, but being liberated by Faustus Sulla, the son of the dictator, he opened a school of rhetoric, in which he taught with great success. (Comp. Hor. *Ep.* i. 19. 15.) The emperor Augustus induced him to write a history of his exploits ; but having offended Augustus by sarcastic remarks upon his family, he was forbidden the palace ; whereupon he burnt his historical works, gave up his rhetorical school, and retired from Rome to the house of his friend Asinius Pollio at Tusculum. He afterwards went to the East, and died at Dabanum in Mesopotamia.

Tīmanthēs (Τιμάνθης), a celebrated Greek painter at Sicyon, contemporary with Zeuxis and Parrhasius, about B.C. 400. The masterpiece of Timanthes was his celebrated picture of the sacrifice of Iphigenia, in which Agamemnon was painted with his face hidden in his mantle. The ancient critics tell us that the picture showed Iphigenia, standing by the altar, surrounded, among the assistants, by Calchas, whose prophetic voice had demanded her sacrifice, and whose hand was about to complete it ; Ulysses, who had brought her from her home, and Menelaus, her father's brother, all manifesting different degrees of grief, so that, when the artist had painted the sorrow of Calchas, and the deeper sorrow of Ulysses, and had added all his powers to express the woe of Menelaus, his resources were exhausted, and, unable to give a powerful expression to the agony of the father, he covered his head with a veil. But this is clearly not the reason why Timanthes hid the face of Agamemnon. The critics ascribe to impotence what was the forbearance of judgment. Timanthes felt like a father : he did not hide the face of Agamemnon because it was beyond the possibility, but because it was beyond the dignity, of expression. If he made Agamemnon bear his calamity as a man, he made him also feel it as a man. It became the leader of Greece to sanction the ceremony with his presence, but it did not become the father to see his daughter beneath the dagger's point.

Tīmāvus (*Timavo*), a small river in the N. of Italy, forming the boundary between Istria and Venetia, and falling into the Sinus Tergestinus in the Adriatic, between Tergeste and Aquileia. This river is frequently celebrated by the poets and other ancient writers, who speak of its numerous sources, its lake, and its subterraneous passage ; but these accounts seem, to a great extent, fabulous.

Timocles (Τιμοκλῆς), a distinguished Athenian comic poet of the Middle Comedy, who lived at a period when the revival of political energy, in consequence of the encroachments of Philip, restored to the Middle Comedy much of the vigour and real aim of the Old. He is conspicuous for the freedom with which he discussed public men and measures, as well as for the number of his dramas and the purity of his style. He flourished from about the middle of the 4th century B.C. till after 324, so that at the beginning of his career he was in part contemporary with Antiphanes, and at the end of it with Menander.

Timocrĕon (Τιμοκρέων), of Rhodes, a lyric poet, celebrated for the bitter and pugnacious spirit of his works, and especially for his attacks on Themistocles and Simonides. He was a native of Ialysus in Rhodes, whence he was banished on the then common charge of an inclination towards Persia (μηδισμός) ; and in this banishment he was left neglected by Themistocles, who had formerly been his friend, and his connection by the ties of hospitality. Timocreon was still flourishing after B.C. 471, since one of his poems, of which we have a fragment, was an attack upon Themistocles after the exile of the latter. It appears that Timocreon was a man of prodigious strength, which he sustained by great voracity.

Tīmōleon (Τιμολέων), son of Timodemus or Timaenetus and Demariste, belonged to one of the noblest families at Corinth. His early life was stained by a dreadful deed of blood. We are told that so ardent was his love of liberty, that when his brother Timophanes endeavoured to make himself tyrant of their native city, Timoleon murdered him rather than allow him to destroy the liberty of the state. The murder was perpetrated just before an embassy arrived from several of the Greek cities of Sicily, begging the Corinthians to send assistance to the island, which was distracted by internal dissensions, and was expecting an invasion of the Carthaginians. It is said that the Corinthians were at the very moment of the arrival of the Sicilians deliberating respecting Timoleon's act, and had not come to any decision respecting it ; and that they avoided the difficulty of a decision by appointing him to the command of the Sicilian expedition, with the singular provision, that if he conducted himself justly in the command, they would regard him as a tyrannicide, and honour him accordingly ; but if otherwise, they would punish him as a fratricide. To whatever causes Timoleon owed his appointment, his extraordinary success more than justified the confidence which had been reposed in him. His history reads almost like a romance; and yet of the main facts of the narrative we cannot entertain any reasonable doubt. Although the Corinthians had readily assented to the requests of the Sicilians in the appointment of a commander, they were not prepared to make many sacrifices in their favour ; and accordingly it was only with 10 triremes and 700 mercenaries that Timoleon sailed from Corinth to repel the Carthaginians, and restore order to the Sicilian cities. He reached Sicily in B.C. 344, and straightway marched against Syracuse, of 2 quarters of which he obtained possession. In the following spring (343) Dionysius, despairing of success, surrendered the citadel to Timoleon, on condition of his being allowed to depart in safety to Corinth. [DIONYSIUS.] Timoleon soon afterwards obtained possession of the whole of Syracuse. He destroyed the citadel, which had been for so many years the seat and bulwark of the power of the tyrants, and restored the democratical form of government. He then proceeded to expel the tyrants from the other Greek cities of Sicily, but was interrupted in this undertaking by a formidable invasion of the Carthaginians, who landed at Lilybaeum in 339, with an immense army, under the command of Hasdrubal and Hamilcar, consisting of 70,000 foot and 10,000 horse. Such an overwhelming force struck the Greeks with consternation and dismay. So great was their alarm that Timoleon could only induce 12,000 men to march with him against the Carthaginians. But with this small force he gained a brilliant victory over the Carthaginians on the river Crimissus (339). This victory justly ranks as one of the greatest gained by Greeks over barbarians. The booty which Timoleon acquired was prodigious; and some of the richest of the spoils he sent to Corinth and other cities in Greece, thus diffusing the glory of his victory throughout the mother country. Timoleon now resolved to carry into execution his project of expelling all the tyrants from Sicily. Of these, two of the most powerful, Hicetas of Leontini, and Mamercus of Catana, had recourse to the Carthaginians for assistance, who sent Gisco to Sicily with a fleet of 70 ships and a body of Greek mercenaries. Although Gisco gained a few successes at first, the war was upon the whole favourable to Timoleon, and the Carthaginians were therefore glad to conclude a treaty with the latter in 338, by which the river Halycus was fixed as the boundary of the Carthaginian and Greek dominions in Sicily. It was during the war with Gisco that Hicetas fell into the hands of Timoleon, and was massacred by his order. His wife and daughters were carried to Syracuse; where they were executed by the people, as a satisfaction to the manes of Dion, whose wife Arete and sister Aristomache had both been put to death by Hicetas. This is one of the greatest stains upon Timoleon's character, as he might easily have saved these unfortunate women if he had chosen. After the treaty between the Carthaginians and Timoleon, Mamercus, being unable to maintain himself in Catana, fled to Messana, where he took refuge with Hippon, tyrant of that city. Timoleon quickly followed, and besieged Messana so vigorously by sea and land, that Hippon, despairing of holding out, attempted to escape by sea, but was taken and put to death in the public theatre. Mamercus now surrendered, stipulating only for a public trial before the Syracusans, with the condition that Timoleon should not appear as his accuser. But as soon as he was brought into the assembly at Syracuse, the people refused to hear him, and unanimously condemned him to death. Thus almost all the tyrants were expelled from the Greek cities in Sicily, and a democratical form of government established in their place. Timoleon, however, was in reality the ruler of Sicily, for all the states consulted him on every matter of importance; and the wisdom of his rule is attested by the flourishing condition of the island for several years even after his death. He did not, however, assume any title or office, but resided as a private citizen among the Syracusans. Timoleon died in 337, having become blind a short time before his death. He was buried at the public expense in the market-place at Syracuse, where his monument was afterwards surrounded with porticoes and a gymnasium, which was called after him the *Timoleonteum*. Annual games were also instituted in his honour.

Tĭmŏmăchus (Τιμόμαχος), a distinguished

painter, of Byzantium, lived (according to Pliny) in the time of Julius Caesar, who purchased two of his pictures, the *Ajax* and *Medea*, for the immense sum of 80 Attic talents, and dedicated them in the temple of Venus Genitrix. It has been supposed, however, by some modern writers that Timomachus lived at an earlier period.

Tĭmōn (Τίμων). 1. The son of Timarchus of Phlius, a philosopher of the sect of the Sceptics, flourished in the reign of Ptolemy Philadelphus, about B. C. 279, and onwards. He first studied philosophy at Megara, under Stilpon, and then returned home and married. He next went to Elis with his wife, and heard Pyrrhon, whose tenets he adopted. Driven from Elis by straitened circumstances, he spent some time on the Hellespont and the Propontis, and taught at Chalcedon as a sophist with such success that he realised a fortune. He then removed to Athens, where he passed the remainder of his life, with the exception of a short residence at Thebes. He died at the age of almost 90. Timon appears to have been endowed by nature with a powerful and active mind, and with that quick perception of the follies of men which betrays its possessor into a spirit of universal distrust both of men and truths, so as to make him a sceptic in philosophy and a satirist in every thing. He wrote numerous works both in prose and poetry. The most celebrated of his poems were the satiric compositions called *Silli* (σίλλοι), a word of somewhat doubtful etymology, but which undoubtedly describes metrical compositions of a character at once ludicrous and sarcastic. The invention of this species of poetry is ascribed to Xenophanes of Colophon. [XENOPHANES.] The *Silli* of Timon were in 3 books, in the first of which he spoke in his own person, and the other 2 are in the form of a dialogue between the author and Xenophanes of Colophon, in which Timon proposed questions, to which Xenophanes replied at length. The subject was a sarcastic account of the tenets of all philosophers, living and dead; an unbounded field for scepticism and satire. They were in hexameter verse, and, from the way in which they are mentioned by the ancient writers, as well as from the few fragments of them which have come down to us, it is evident that they were very admirable productions of their kind. The fragments of his poems are collected by Wölke, *De Graecorum Syllis*, Varsav. 1820; and by Paul, *Dissertatio de Sillis*, Berol. 1821.—2. The Misanthrope (ὁ μισάνθρωπος), lived in the time of the Peloponnesian war. He was an Athenian, of the demos of Colyttus, and his father's name was Echecratides. In consequence of the ingratitude he experienced, and the disappointments he suffered, from his early friends and companions, he secluded himself entirely from the world, admitting no one to his society except Alcibiades, in whose reckless and variable disposition he probably found pleasure in tracing and studying an image of the world he had abandoned; and at last he is said to have died in consequence of refusing to suffer a surgeon to come to him to set a broken limb. One of Lucian's pieces bears his name.

Tĭmŏthĕus (Τιμόθεος). 1. Son of Conon, the famous general, was himself a distinguished Athenian general. He was first appointed to a public command in B. C. 378; and from this time his name frequently occurs as one of the Athenian generals down to 356. In this year he was associated with Iphicrates, Menestheus, and Chares in the command of the Athenian fleet. In consequence of his conduct in this war he was arraigned in 354, and condemned to the crushing fine of 100 talents (more than 24,000*l.*). Being unable to pay the fine, he withdrew to Chalcis in Euboea, where he died shortly after. The Athenians subsequently remitted nine-tenths of the penalty, and allowed his son Conon to expend the remainder on the repair of the walls, which the famous Conon had restored. — 2. Son of Clearchus, the tyrant of Heraclea on the Euxine, whom he succeeded in the sovereignty, B. c. 353. There is extant a letter addressed to him by Isocrates. — 3. A celebrated musician and poet of the later Athenian dithyramb, was a native of Miletus, and the son of Thersander. He was born B. c. 446, and died in 357, in the 90th year of his age. Of the details of his life we have very little information. He was at first unfortunate in his professional efforts. Even the Athenians, fond as they were of novelty, were offended at the bold innovations of Timotheus, and hissed off his performance. On this occasion it is said that Euripides encouraged Timotheus by the prediction that he would soon have the theatres at his feet. This prediction appears to have been accomplished in the vast popularity which Timotheus afterwards enjoyed. The Ephesians rewarded him, for his dedicatory hymn to Artemis, with the sum of 1000 pieces of gold; and the last accomplishment, by which the education of the Arcadian youth was finished, was learning the nomes of Timotheus and Philoxenus. Timotheus is said to have died in Macedonia. He delighted in the most artificial and intricate forms of musical expression, and he used instrumental music, without a vocal accompaniment, to a greater extent than any previous composer. Perhaps the most important of his innovations, as the means of introducing all the others, was his addition to the number of the strings of the *cithara*. Respecting the precise nature of that addition the ancient writers are not agreed; but it is most probable, from the whole evidence, that the lyre of Timotheus had 11 strings. It is said that, when Timotheus visited Sparta, and entered the musical contest at the Carnea, one of the ephors snatched away his lyre, and cut from it the strings, 4 in number, by which it exceeded the seven-stringed lyre of Terpander, and, as a memorial of this public vindication of the ancient simplicity of music, and for a warning to future innovators, the Lacedaemonians hung up the mutilated lyre of Timotheus in their Scias. With regard to the subjects of his compositions, and the manner in which he treated them, we have abundant evidence that he even went beyond the other musicians of the period in the liberties which he took with the ancient myths, in the attempt to make his music imitative as well as expressive, and in the confusion of the different subjects and departments of lyric poetry; in one word, in the application of that false principle, which also misled his friend Euripides, that pleasure is the end of poetry. — 4. A distinguished flute-player of Thebes, flourished under Alexander the Great, on whom his music made so powerful an impression that once in the midst of a performance by Timotheus, of an Orthian Nome to Athena, Alexander started from his seat, and seized his arms. — 5. A statuary and sculptor, whose country is not mentioned, but who belonged to the later Attic school of the time of

Scopas and Praxiteles. He was one of the artists who executed the bas-reliefs which adorned the frieze of the Mausoleum, about B. c. 352.

Tingis (ἡ Τίγγις: *Tangier*), a city of Mauretania, on the S. coast of the Fretum Gaditanum (*Straits of Gibraltar*), was a place of very great antiquity. It was made by Augustus a free city, and by Claudius a colony, and the capital of Mauretania Tingitana.

Tinia (*Timia*), a small river in Umbria, rising near Spoletium, and falling into the Tiber, after receiving the Clitumnus.

Tiresias (Τειρησίας), a Theban, son of Everes and Chariclo, was one of the most renowned soothsayers in all antiquity. He was blind from his seventh year, but lived to a very old age. It was believed that his blindness was occasioned by his having revealed to men things which they ought not to have known, or by his having seen Athena while she was bathing, on which occasion the goddess deprived him of sight by sprinkling water upon his face. Chariclo prayed to Athena to restore his sight, but as the goddess was unable to do this, she conferred upon him the power of understanding the voices of birds, and gave him a staff, with the help of which he could walk as safely as if he had his eyesight. Another tradition accounts for his blindness in the following manner. Once, when on Mount Cithaeron (others say Cyllene), he saw a male and a female serpent together; he struck at them with his staff, and as he happened to kill the female, he himself was metamorphosed into a woman. Seven years later he again saw 2 serpents, and now killing the male, he again became a man. It was for this reason that Zeus and Hera, when disputing whether a man or a woman had more enjoyments, referred the matter to Tiresias, who declared that women enjoyed more pleasure than men. Hera, indignant at the answer, deprived him of sight, but Zeus gave him the power of prophecy, and granted him a life which was to last for seven or nine generations. In the war of the Seven against Thebes, he declared that Thebes should be victorious, if Menoeceus would sacrifice himself; and during the war of the Epigoni, when the Thebans had been defeated, he advised them to commence negotiations of peace, and to avail themselves of the opportunity that would thus be afforded them, to take to flight. He himself fled with them (or, according to others, he was carried to Delphi as a captive), but on his way he drank from the well of Tilphossa and died. His daughter Manto (or Daphne) was sent by the victorious Argives to Delphi, as a present to Apollo. Even in the lower world Tiresias was believed to retain the powers of perception, while the souls of other mortals were mere shades, and there also he continued to use his golden staff. His tomb was shown in the neighbourhood of the Tilphusian well near Thebes, and in Macedonia likewise. The place near Thebes where he had observed the birds was pointed out as a remarkable spot even in later times. The blind seer Tiresias acts so prominent a part in the mythical history of Greece that there is scarcely any event with which he is not connected in some way or other; and this introduction of the seer in so many occurrences separated by long intervals of time, was facilitated by the belief in his long life.

Tiridates or **Teridates** (Τηριδάτης). 1. The second king of Parthia. [ARSACES II.] — 2,

King of Armenia, and brother of Vologeses I. (Arsaces XXIII.), king of Parthia. He was made king of Armenia by his brother, but was driven out of the kingdom by Corbulo, the Roman general, and finally received the Armenian crown from Nero at Rome in A. D. 63.

Tiro, M. Tullius, the freedman of Cicero, to whom he was an object of tender affection. He appears to have been a man of very amiable disposition, and highly cultivated intellect. He was not only the amanuensis of the orator, and his assistant in literary labour, but was himself an author of no mean reputation, and notices of several works from his pen have been preserved by ancient writers. It is supposed by many that Tiro was the chief agent in bringing together and arranging the works of his illustrious patron, and in preserving his correspondence from being dispersed and lost. After the death of Cicero, Tiro purchased a farm in the neighbourhood of Puteoli, where he lived until he reached his 100th year. It is usually believed that Tiro was the inventor of the art of short-hand writing among the Romans; and hence abbreviations of this description, which are common in MSS. from the 6th century downwards, have very generally been designated by the learned as *Notae Tironianae.*

Tiryns (Τίρυνς, -υνθος: Τιρύνθιος), an ancient town in Argolis, S. E. of Argos, and one of the most ancient in all Greece, is said to have been founded by Proetus, the brother of Acrisius, who built the massive walls of the city with the help of the Cyclopes. Proetus was succeeded by Perseus; and it was here that Hercules was brought up. Hence we find his mother Alcmena called *Tirynthia,* and the hero himself *Tirynthius.* Homer represents Tiryns as subject to Argos; the town was at a later time destroyed by the Argives, and most of the inhabitants were removed to Argos. Tiryns was built upon a hill of small extent, rising abruptly from the dead level of the surrounding country. The remains of the city are some of the most interesting in all Greece, and are, with those of Mycenae, the most ancient specimens of what is called Cyclopian architecture. They consist of masses of enormous stones, rudely piled in tiers above one another.

Tisamenus (Τισαμενός). 1. Son of Orestes and Hermione, was king of Argos, but was deprived of his kingdom when the Heraclidae invaded Peloponnesus. He was slain in a battle against the Heraclidae, and his tomb was afterwards shown at Helice, from which place his remains were subsequently removed to Sparta by command of an oracle. — 2. Son of Thersander and Demonassa, was king of Thebes, and the father of Autesion.— 3. An Elean soothsayer, of the family of the Clytiadae. He was assured by the Delphic oracle that he should be successful in 5 great conflicts. Supposing this to be a promise of distinction as an athlete, he devoted himself to gymnastic exercises; but the Spartans, understanding the oracle to refer, not to gymnastic, but to military victories, made great offers to Tisamenus to induce him to take with their kings the joint-command of their armies. This he refused to do on any terms short of receiving the full franchise of their city, which the Spartans eventually granted. He was present with the Spartans at the battle of Plataea, B.C. 379, which was the first of the 5 conflicts referred to by the oracle. The 2nd was with the Argives and Tegeans at Tegea; the 3rd, with the Arcadians at

Dipaea; the 4th was the 3rd Messenian War (465 —455); and the last was the battle of Tanagra, with the Athenians and their allies, in 457.

Tisia (Tisiates, pl.), a town in Bruttium in the Sila Silva, of uncertain site.

Tisicrates, an eminent Greek statuary, of the school of Lysippus, to whose works those of Tisicrates so nearly approached, that many of them were scarcely to be distinguished from the works of the master.

Tisiphone. [EUMENIDAE.]

Tissa (Tissiensis, Tissinensis), a town in Sicily N. of Mt. Aetna.

Tissaphernes (Τισσαφέρνης), a famous Persian, who was appointed satrap of lower Asia in B. C. 414. He espoused the cause of the Spartans in the Peloponnesian war, but he did not give them any effectual assistance, since his policy was not to allow either Spartans or Athenians to gain the supremacy, but to exhaust the strength of both parties by the continuance of the war. His plans, however, were thwarted by the arrival of Cyrus in Asia Minor in 407. This prince supplied the Lacedaemonians with cordial and effectual assistance. Tissaphernes and Cyrus were not on good terms; and after the death of Darius, they were engaged in continual disputes about the cities in the satrapy of the latter, over which Cyrus claimed dominion. The ambitious views of Cyrus towards the throne at length became manifest to Tissaphernes, who lost no time in repairing to the king with information of the danger. At the battle of Cunaxa, in 401, he was one of the 4 generals who commanded the army of Artaxerxes, and his troops were the only portion of the left wing that was not put to flight by the Greeks. When the 10,000 had begun their retreat, Tissaphernes professed his great anxiety to serve them, and promised to conduct them home in safety. In the course of the march he treacherously arrested Clearchus and 4 of the other generals, who were put to death. After this, Tissaphernes annoyed and harassed the Greeks in their march, without however seriously impeding it, till they reached the Carduchian Mountains, at which point he gave up the pursuit. Not long after, Tissaphernes, as a reward for his great services, was invested by the king, in addition to his own satrapy, with all the authority which Cyrus had enjoyed in western Asia. On his arrival he claimed dominion over the Ionian cities, which applied to Sparta for aid. Their request was granted, and the Spartans carried on war against Tissaphernes with success for some years under the command successively of Thimbron, Dercyllidas, and Agesilaus (400—395). The continued want of success on the part of Tissaphernes led to grievous complaints against him; and the charges were transmitted to court, where they were backed by all the influence of Parysatis, eager for revenge on the enemy of Cyrus, her favourite son. The result was that Tithraustes was commissioned by the king to put Tissaphernes to death and to succeed him in his government, which was accordingly done (395).

Titanes (Τιτᾶνες, sing. Τιτάν, Ion. Τιτήνες; Fem. Τιτανίδες, sing. Τιτανίς). 1. The sons and daughters of Uranus and Ge, originally dwelt in heaven, whence they are called Oὐρανίωνες or Oὐρανίδαι. They were 12 in number, 6 sons and 6 daughters, namely, Oceanus, Coeus, Crius, Hyperion, Iapetus, Cronus, Thia, Rhea, Themis, Mnemosyne,

Phoebe, and Tethys; but their names are different in other accounts. It is said that Uranus, the first ruler of the world, threw his sons, the Hecatoncheires (Hundred-Handed), — Briareus, Cottys, Gyes — and the Cyclopes, — Arges, Steropes, and Brontes — into Tartarus. Gaea, indignant at this, persuaded the Titans to rise against their father, and gave to Cronus an adamantine sickle. They did as their mother bade them, with the exception of Oceanus. Cronus, with his sickle, unmanned his father, and threw the part into the sea : from the drops of his blood there arose the Erinnyes, — Alecto, Tisiphone, and Megaera. The Titans then deposed Uranus, liberated their brothers who had been cast into Tartarus, and raised Cronus to the throne. But Cronus hurled the Cyclopes back into Tartarus, and married his sister Rhea. Having been foretold by Gaea and Uranus, that he should be dethroned by one of his own children, he swallowed successively his children Hestia, Demeter, Hera, Pluto, and Poseidon. Rhea therefore, when she was pregnant with Zeus, went to Crete, and gave birth to the child in the Dictaean Cave, where he was brought up by the Curetes. When Zeus had grown up he availed himself of the assistance of Thetis, the daughter of Oceanus, who gave to Cronus a potion which caused him to bring up the stone and the children he had swallowed. United with his brothers and sisters, Zeus now began the contest against Cronus and the ruling Titans. This contest (usually called the Titanomachia) was carried on in Thessaly, Cronus and the Titans occupying Mount Othrys, and the sons of Cronus Mount Olympus. It lasted 10 years, till at length Gaea promised victory to Zeus if he would deliver the Cyclopes and Hecatoncheires from Tartarus. Zeus accordingly slew Campe, who guarded the Cyclopes, and the latter furnished him with thunder and lightning. The Titans then were overcome, and hurled down into a cavity below Tartarus, and the Hecatoncheires were set to guard them. It must be observed that the fight of the Titans is sometimes confounded by ancient writers with the fight of the Gigantes. — 2. The name Titans is also given to those divine or semi-divine beings who were descended from the Titans, such as Prometheus, Hecate, Latona, Pyrrha, and especially Helios (the Sun) and Selene (the Moon) as the children of Hyperion and Thia, and even the descendants of Helios, such as Circe.

Titarēsius (Τιταρήσιος: *Elassonitiko* or *Xeraghi*), a river of Thessaly, also called Europus, rising in Mt. Titarus, flowing through the country of the Perrhaebi, and falling into the Peneus, S. E. of Phalanna. Its waters were impregnated with an oily substance, whence it was said to be a branch of the infernal Styx.

Tīthōnus (Τιθωνός), son of Laomedon and Strymo, and brother of Priam. By the prayers of Eos (Aurora), who loved him, he obtained from the gods immortality, but not eternal youth, in consequence of which he completely shrunk together in his old age, whence an old decrepit man was proverbially called Tithonus. As he could not die, Eos changed him into a cicada.

Tithŏrĕa. [NEON.]

Tithraustes (Τιθραύστης), a Persian, who succeeded Tissaphernes in his satrapy, and put him to death by order of Artaxerxes Mnemon, B. C. 395. Being unable to make peace with Agesilaus, he sent Timocrates, the Rhodian, into Greece with 50 talents, to distribute among the leading men in the several states, in order to induce them to excite a war against Sparta at home.

Titiānus, Jūlius, a Roman writer, was the father of the rhetorician Titianus, who taught the younger Maximinus. The elder Titianus may therefore be placed in the reigns of Commodus, Pertinax, and Severus. He was called the ape of his age, because he had imitated every thing. All his works are lost.

Titinius, a Roman dramatist whose productions belonged to the department of the *Comoedia Togata*, is commended by Varro on account of the skill with which he developed the characters of the personages whom he brought upon the stage. It appears that he was younger than Caecilius, but older than Terence, and flourished about B. C. 170. The names of upwards of 14 plays, together with a considerable number of short fragments, have been preserved by the grammarians.

Titius Septimius. [SEPTIMIUS.]

Titus Flavius Sabinus Vespasiānus, Roman emperor, A. D. 79—81, commonly called by his praenomen Titus, was the son of the emperor Vespasianus and his wife Flavia Domitilla. He was born on the 30th of December, A. D. 40. When a young man he served as tribunus militum in Britain and in Germany, with great credit. After having been quaestor, he had the command of a legion, and served under his father in the Jewish wars. Vespasian returned to Italy, after he had been proclaimed emperor on the 1st of July, A. D. 69 ; but Titus remained in Palestine to prosecute the siege of Jerusalem, during which he showed the talents of a general with the daring of a soldier. The siege of Jerusalem was concluded by the capture of the place, on the 8th of September, 70. Titus returned to Italy in the following year (71), and triumphed at Rome with his father. He also received the title of Caesar, and became the associate of Vespasian in the government. His conduct at this time gave no good promise, and the people looked upon him as likely to be another Nero. He was accused of being excessively addicted to the pleasures of the table, of indulging lustful passions in a scandalous way, and of putting suspected persons to death with very little ceremony. His attachment to Berenice, the sister of Agrippa II., also made him unpopular. Titus became acquainted with her when he was in Judaea, and after the capture of Jerusalem she followed him to Rome with her brother Agrippa, and both of them lodged in the emperor's residence. It was said that Titus had promised to marry Berenice, but as this intended union gave the Romans great dissatisfaction, he sent her away from Rome after he became emperor. Titus succeeded his father in 79, and his government proved an agreeable surprise to those who had anticipated a return of the times of Nero. His brother Domitian was accused of having entertained designs against Titus; but instead of punishing him, Titus endeavoured to win his affection, and urged him not to attempt to gain by criminal means that power which he would one day have in a legitimate way. During his whole reign Titus displayed a sincere desire for the happiness of the people, and he did all that he could to relieve them in times of distress. He assumed the office of Pontifex Maximus after the death of his father, and with the purpose, as he declared, of keeping his hands free from

Scylla. (From a Coin of Agrigentum.) Page 689.

Triton. (From a Roman Lamp.) Page 790.

Ulysses and the Sirens. (From a Vase in the British Museum.) Page 799.

Ulysses and Tiresias.
(Winckelmann Mon. Ined., No. 157.) Page 799.

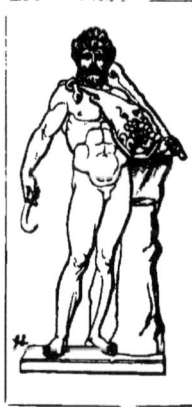

Vertumnus.
(Musée Bouillon, vol. 3, pl. 14.) Page 811.

[To face p. 784.

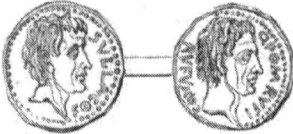

Sulla, the Dictator, ob. B.C. 78. Page 730.

Tiberius, Roman Emperor, A.D. 14—37. Pages 775—777.

M. Claudius Tacitus, Roman Emperor, A.D. 275—276.
Page 740.

Tigranes, King of Armenia, B.C. 96—56. Page 778.

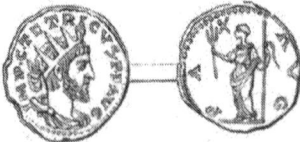

Tetricus Senior, Roman Emperor, A.D. 267—274. Page 754.

Titus, Roman Emperor, A.D. 79—81. Page 784.

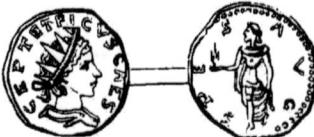

Tetricus Junior, Roman Caesar. Page 754.

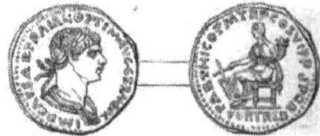

Trajan, Roman Emperor, A.D. 98—117. Page 787.

Theodosius I., Roman Emperor, A.D. 378—395. Page 761.

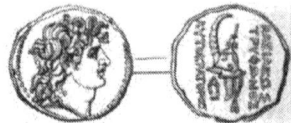

Tryphon, King of Syria, ob. B.C. 139. Page 792.

Theodosius II., Roman Emperor, A.D. 408—450. Page 761.

Valens, Roman Emperor, A.D. 364—378. Page 803.

To face p. 785.

blood; a resolution which he kept. Two patricians who were convicted by the senate of a conspiracy against him, were pardoned and treated with kindness and confidence. He checked all prosecutions for the crime of *laesa majestas*, and he severely punished all informers. The 1st year of his reign is memorable for the great eruption of Vesuvius, which desolated a large part of the adjacent country, and buried with lava and ashes the towns of Herculaneum and Pompeii. Titus endeavoured to repair the ravages of this great eruption: he sent two consulars with money to restore the ruined towns, and he applied to this purpose the property of those who had been destroyed, and had left no next of kin. At the beginning of the following year (80) there was a great fire at Rome, which lasted 3 days and 3 nights, and destroyed the Capitol, the library of Augustus, the theatre of Pompeius, and other public buildings, besides many houses. The emperor declared that he should consider all the loss as his own, and he set about repairing it with great activity: he took even the decorations of the imperial residences, and sold them to raise money. The eruption of Vesuvius was followed by a dreadful pestilence, which called for fresh exertions on the part of the benevolent emperor. In this year he completed the great amphitheatre called the Colosseum, which had been commenced by his father; and also the baths called the baths of Titus. The dedication of these two edifices was celebrated by spectacles which lasted 100 days; by a naval battle in the old naumachia, and fights of gladiators: on one day alone 5000 wild animals are said to have been exhibited, a number which we may reasonably suspect to be exaggerated. He died on the 13th of September, 81, after a reign of 2 years and 2 months, and 20 days. He was in the 41st year of his age. There were suspicions that he was poisoned by Domitian. There is a story that Domitian came before Titus was dead, and ordered him to be deserted by those about him: according to another story, he ordered him to be thrown into a vessel full of snow, under the pretext of cooling his fever. Titus was succeeded by his brother Domitian. His daughter Julia Sabina was married to Flavius Sabinus, his cousin, the son of Flavius Sabinus, the brother of Vespasian. Titus is said to have written Greek poems and tragedies; he was very familiar with Greek. He also wrote many letters in his father's name during Vespasian's life, and drew up edicta.

Tityus (Τιτυός), son of Gaea, or of Zeus and Elara, the daughter of Orchomenus, was a giant in Euboea. Instigated by Hera, he attempted to offer violence to Leto or Artemis (Latona), when she passed through Panopaeus to Pytho, but he was killed by the arrows of Artemis or Apollo; according to others, Zeus destroyed him with a flash of lightning. He was then cast into Tartarus, and there he lay outstretched on the ground, covering 9 acres, with 2 vultures or snakes devouring his liver. His destruction by the arrows of Artemis and Apollo was represented on the throne of Apollo at Amyclae.

Tius or **Tium** (Τίος, Τίον, also Τήϊον: Τίος or Τήϊος), a seaport town of Bithynia, on the river Billaeus; a colony from Miletus, and the native place of Philetaerus, the founder of the Pergamene kingdom. •

Tlepolemus (Τληπόλεμος), son of Hercules by

Astyoche, daughter of Phylas, or by Astydamia, daughter of Amyntor. He was king of Argos, but after slaying his uncle Licymnius, he was obliged to take to flight; and, in conformity with the command of an oracle, he settled in Rhodes, where he built the towns of Lindos, Ialysus, and Camirus. He joined the Greeks in the Trojan war with 9 ships, but was slain by Sarpedon.

Tlos (Τλῶς, gen. Τλῶ: Τλωεύς, Τλωΐτης: Ru. near *Doover*), a considerable city, in the interior of Lycia, about 2½ miles E. of the river Xanthus, on the road leading over M. Massicytus to Cibyra.

Tmarus. [TOMARUS.]

Tmolus (Τμῶλος), god of Mt. Tmolus in Lydia, is described as the husband of Pluto (or Omphale) and father of Tantalus, and is said to have decided the musical contest between Apollo and Pan.

Tmolus or **Timolus** (Τμῶλος: *Kisilja Musa Dagh*), a celebrated mountain of Asia Minor, running E. and W. through the centre of Lydia, and dividing the plain of the Hermus, on the N., from that of the Cayster, on the S. At its E. end it joins M. Messogis, thus entirely enclosing the valley of the Cayster. On the W., after throwing out the N.W. branch called Sipylus, it runs far out into the Aegean, forming, under the name of Mimas, the great Ionian peninsula, beyond which it is still further prolonged in the island of Chios. On its N. side are the sources of the Pactolus and the Cogamus; on its S. side those of the Cayster. It produced wine, saffron, zinc, and gold.

Togata, Gallia. [GALLIA.]

Tolbiacum (*Zulpich*), a town of Gallia Belgica, on the road from Colonia Agrippina to Treviri.

Tolentinum (Tolinas, -atis: *Tolentino*), a town of Picenum, on a height on the river Flusor (*Chiente*).

Tolenus or **Telonius** (*Turano*), a river in the land of the Sabines, rising in the country of the Marsi and Aequi, and falling into the Velinus.

Toletum (*Toledo*), the capital of the Carpetani in Hispania Tarraconensis, situated on the river Tagus, which nearly encompasses the town, and upon 7 hills. According to tradition it was founded by Jews, who fled thither when Jerusalem was taken by Nebuchadnezzar, and who called it *Toledoth*, or the "city of generations." It was taken by the Romans under the proconsul M. Fulvius, B. C. 192, when it is described as a small but fortified town. It was celebrated in ancient, as well as in modern times, for the manufactory of swords; but it owed its greatness to the Gothic kings, who made it the capital of their dominions. It still contains many Roman remains.

Tolistobogi, Tolistoboji (Τολιστοβόγιοι, Τολιστοβόϊοι, Τολιστοβώγιοι). [GALATIA.]

Tolophon (Τολοφών: Τολοφώνιος), also called **Colophon** (Κολοφών), a town of Locris, on the Corinthian gulf.

Tolosa (*Toulouse*), a town of Gallia Narbonensis, and the capital of the Tectosages, was situated on the Garumna, near the frontiers of Aquitania. It was subsequently made a Roman colony, and was surnamed *Palladia*. It was a large and wealthy town, and contained a celebrated temple, in which great riches were deposited. In this temple there is said to have been preserved a great part of the booty taken by Brennus from the temple at Delphi. The town and temple were plundered by the consul Q. Servilius Caepio, in B. C. 106; but the

3 B

subsequent destruction of his army and his own unhappy fate were regarded as a divine punishment for his sacrilegious act. Hence arose the proverb, *Aurum Tolosanum habet*. There are the ruins of a small amphitheatre, and some other Roman remains at the modern town.

Tŏlumnĭus, Lar, king of the Veientes, to whom Fidenae revolted in B. C. 438, and at whose instigation the inhabitants of Fidenae slew the 4 Roman ambassadors, who had been sent to Fidenae to inquire into the reasons of their recent conduct. Statues of these ambassadors were placed on the Rostra at Rome, where they continued till a late time. In the war which followed, Tolumnius was slain in single combat by Cornelius Cossus, who dedicated his spoils in the temple of Jupiter Feretrius, the 2nd of the 3 instances in which the spolia opima were won.

Tomeus (Τομεύς : *Kondoxoni*), a mountain in Messenia, E. of the promontory Coriphasium.

Tŏmī or **Tŏmĭs** (Τόμοι, Τόμις : Τομεύς, Tomita : *Tomiswar* or *Jegni Pangola*), a town of Thrace (subsequently Moesia), situated on the W. shore of the Euxine, and at a later time the capital of Scythia Minor. According to tradition it was called Tomi (from τέμνω, "cut"), because Medea here cut to pieces the body of her brother Absyrtus. It is said to have been a colony of the Milesians. It is renowned as the place of Ovid's banishment.

Tŏmŏrus or **Tmarus** (Τομορος, Τμάρος : *Tomaro*), a mountain in Epirus, in the district Molossia, between the lake Pambotis and the river Arachthus, near Dodona.

Tŏmȳris (Τόμυρις), a queen of the Massagetae, who dwelt south of the Araxes (Jaxartes), by whom Cyrus was slain in battle, B. C. 529.

Tornadotus. [PHYSCUS, No. 3.]

Tŏrōnē (Τορώνη : Τορωναῖος), a town of Macedonia, in the district Chalcidice, and on the S.W. side of the peninsula Sithonia, from which the gulf between the peninsulas Sithonia and Pallene was called Sinus Toronaicus.

Torquātus, the name of a patrician family of the Manlia Gens. **1. T. Manlius Imperiosus Torquatus**, the son of L. Manlius Capitolinus Imperiosus, dictator B. C. 363, was a favourite hero of Roman story. Manlius is said to have been dull of mind in his youth, and was brought up by his father in the closest retirement in the country. When the tribune M. Pomponius accused the elder Manlius in B. C. 362, on account of the cruelties he had practised in his dictatorship, he endeavoured to excite an odium against him, by representing him at the same time as a cruel and tyrannical father. As soon as the younger Manlius heard of this, he hurried to Rome, obtained admission to Pomponius early in the morning, and compelled the tribune, by threatening him with instant death if he did not take the oath, to swear that he would drop the accusation against his father. In 361 Manlius served under the dictator T. Quintius Pennus in the war against the Gauls, and in this campaign earned immortal glory by slaying in single combat a gigantic Gaul. From the dead body of the barbarian he took the chain (*torques*) which had adorned him, and placed it around his own neck; and from this circumstance he obtained the surname of Torquatus. He was dictator in 353, and again in 349. He was also three times consul, namely in 347, 344, and in 340. In the

last of these years Torquatus and his colleague P. Decius Mus gained the great victory over the Latins at the foot of Vesuvius, which established for ever the supremacy of Rome over Latium. [DECIUS.] Shortly before the battle, when the two armies were encamped opposite to one another, the consuls published a proclamation that no Roman should engage in single combat with a Latin on pain of death. Notwithstanding this proclamation, the young Manlius, the son of the consul, provoked by the insults of a Tusculan noble of the name of Mettius Geminus, accepted his challenge, slew his adversary, and bore the bloody spoils in triumph to his father. Death was his reward. The consul would not overlook this breach of discipline : and the unhappy youth was executed by the lictor in presence of the assembled army. This severe sentence rendered Torquatus an object of detestation among the Roman youths as long as he lived ; and the recollection of his severity was preserved in after ages by the expression *Manliana imperia*. — **2. T. Manlius Torquatus**, consul B. C. 235, when he conquered the Sardinians ; censor 231 ; and consul a 2nd time in 224. He possessed the hereditary sternness and severity of his family ; and we accordingly find him opposing in the senate the ransom of those Romans who had been taken prisoners at the fatal battle of Cannae. In 217 he was sent into Sardinia, where he carried on the war with success against the Carthaginians and the Sardinians. He was dictator in 210. — **3. T. Manlius Torquatus**, consul 165 with Cn. Octavius. He inherited the severity of his ancestors; of which an instance is related in the condemnation of his son, whom he had been adopted by D. Junius Silanus. [SILANUS, No. 1.] — **4. L. Manlius Torquatus**, consul B. C. 65 with L. Aurelius Cotta. Torquatus and Cotta obtained the consulship in consequence of the condemnation, on account of bribery, of P. Cornelius Sulla and P. Autronius Paetus, who had been already elected consuls. After his consulship Torquatus obtained the province of Macedonia. He took an active part in suppressing the Catilinarian conspiracy in 63; and he also supported Cicero when he was banished in 58. — **5. L. Manlius Torquatus**, son of No. 4, accused of bribery, in 66, the consuls elect, P. Cornelius Sulla and P. Autronius Paetus, and thus secured the consulship for his father. He was closely connected with Cicero during the praetorship (65) and consulship (63) of the latter. In 62 he brought a 2nd accusation against P. Sulla, whom he now charged with having been a party to both of Catiline's conspiracies. Sulla was defended by Hortensius and by Cicero in a speech which is still extant. Torquatus, like his father, belonged to the aristocratical party, and accordingly opposed Caesar on the breaking out of the civil war in 49. He was praetor in that year, and was stationed at Alba with 6 cohorts. He subsequently joined Pompey in Greece, and in the following year (48) he had the command of Oricum intrusted to him, but was obliged to surrender both himself and the town to Caesar, who, however, dismissed Torquatus uninjured. After the battle of Pharsalia Torquatus went to Africa, and upon the defeat of his party in that country in 46 he attempted to escape to Spain along with Scipio and others, but was taken prisoner by P. Sittius at Hippo Regius and slain together with his companions. Torquatus was well acquainted with Greek literature, and is praised by Cicero as a man well trained in every kind of learning. He belonged to the Epicurean school of philosophy, and is introduced by Cicero as the advocate of that school in his dialogue *De Finibus*, the first book of which is called *Torquatus* in Cicero's letters to Atticus.— 6. A. **Manlius** Torquatus, praetor in 52, when he presided at the trial of Milo for bribery. On the breaking out of the civil war he espoused the side of Pompey, and after the defeat of the latter retired to Athens, where he was living in exile in 45. He was an intimate friend of Cicero, who addressed 4 letters to him while he was in exile.

Torquātus Silānus. [SILANUS.]

Toxandri, a people in Gallia Belgica, between the Menapii and Morini, on the right bank of the Scaldis.

Trăbĕa, Q., a Roman comic dramatist who occupies the eighth place in the canon of Volcatius Sedigitus [SEDIGITUS]. The period when he flourished is uncertain, but he has been placed about B. C. 130. No portion of his works has been preserved with the exception of half a dozen lines quoted by Cicero.

Trachălus, Galerĭus, consul A. D. 68 with Silius Italicus, is frequently mentioned by his contemporary Quintilian, as one of the most distinguished orators of his age.

Trăchis or **Trăchin** (Τραχίς, Ion. Τρηχίς, Τραχίν: Τραχίνιος). 1. Also called **Heraclĕa Trachiniae,** or **Heraclĕa Phthiotidis,** or simply **Heraclĕa** (Ἡράκλεια ἡ ἐν Τραχίναις, or ʽΗ. ἡ ἐν Τραχῖνι), a town of Thessaly in the district Malis, celebrated as the residence of Hercules for a time. — 2. A town of Phocis, on the frontiers of Boeotia, and on the slope of Mt. Helicon in the neighbourhood of Lebadea.

Trachonītis or **Trachon** (Τραχωνῖτις, Τράχων), the N. district of Palestine beyond the Jordan, lay between Antilibanus and the mountains of Arabia, and was bounded on the N. by the territory of Damascus, on the E. by Auranitis, on the S. by Ituraea, and on the W. by Gaulanitis. It was for the most part a sandy desert, intersected by 2 ranges of rocky mountains, called Trachōnes (Τραχῶνες), the caves in which gave refuge to numerous bands of robbers. For its political relations under the Asmonaean and Idumaean princes, see PALAESTINA. Under the Romans, it belonged sometimes to the province of Judaea, and sometimes to that of Arabia. It forms part of the Hauran.

Tragïa, Tragïae, or **Tragïas** (Τραγία, Τραγίαι, Τραγίας), a small island (or more than one) in the Aegean sea, near Samos, probably between it and Pharmacussa, where Pericles gained a naval victory over the Samians, B. C. 439.

Tragurïum (*Trau* or *Troghie*), a town of Dalmatia in Illyricum, celebrated for its marble, and situated on an island connected with the main land by means of a dam.

Trajānŏpŏlis. 1. (*Orichovo*), a town in the interior of Thrace, on the Hebrus, founded by Trajan. — 2. A town of Cilicia. [SELINUS.] — 3. A town in Mysia on the borders of Phrygia.

Trajānus, M. Ulpĭus, Roman emperor A. D. 98 —117, was born at Italica, near Seville, the 18th of September, 52. He was trained to arms, and served with distinction in the East and in Germany. He was consul in 91, and at the close of 97 he was adopted by the emperor Nerva, who gave him the rank of Caesar and the names of Nerva and Germanicus, and shortly after the title of imperator, and the tribunitia potestas. His style and title after his elevation to the imperial dignity were *Imperator Caesar Nerva Trajanus Augustus.* He was the first emperor who was born out of Italy. Nerva died in January 98, and was succeeded by Trajan, who was then at Cologne. His accession was hailed with joy, and he did not disappoint the expectations of the people. He was a man adapted to command. He was strong and healthy, of a majestic appearance, laborious, and inured to fatigue. Though not a man of letters, he had good sense, a knowledge of the world, and a sound judgment. His mode of living was very simple, and in his campaigns he shared all the sufferings and privations of the soldiers, by whom he was both loved and feared. He was a friend to justice, and he had a sincere desire for the happiness of the people. Trajan did not return to Rome for some months, being employed in settling the frontiers on the Rhine and the Danube. He entered Rome on foot, accompanied by his wife Pompeia Plotina. This lady is highly commended by Pliny the younger for her modest virtues, and her affection to Marciana, the sister of Trajan. Trajan left Rome for his campaign against the Daci. Decebalus, king of the Daci, had compelled Domitian to purchase peace by an annual payment of money; and Trajan determined on hostilities. This war employed Trajan between 2 and 3 years; but it ended with the defeat of Decebalus, who sued for peace at the feet of the Roman emperor. Trajan assumed the name of Dacicus, and entered Rome in triumph (103). In the following year (104) Trajan commenced his second Dacian war against Decebalus, who, it is said, had broken the treaty. Decebalus was completely defeated, and put an end to his life (106). In the course of this war Trajan built (105) a permanent bridge across the Danube at a place called *Szerneez.* The piers were of stone and of an enormous size, but the arches were of wood. After the death of Decebalus Dacia was reduced to the form of a Roman province; strong forts were built in various places, and Roman colonies were planted. It is generally supposed that the column at Rome called the Column of Trajan was erected to commemorate his Dacian victories. On his return Trajan had a triumph, and he exhibited games to the people for 123 days. 11,000 animals were slaughtered during these amusements; and an army of gladiators, 10,000 men, gratified the Romans by killing one another. — About this time Arabia Petraea was subjected to the empire by A. Cornelius Palma, the governor of Syria; and an Indian embassy came to Rome. Trajan constructed a road across the Pomptine marshes, and built magnificent bridges across the streams. Buildings, probably mansiones, were constructed by the side of this road. In 114 Trajan left Rome to make war on the Armenians and the Parthians. He spent the winter of 114 at Antioch, and in the following year he invaded the Parthian dominions. The most striking and brilliant success attended his arms. In the course of 2 campaigns (115—116), he conquered the greater part of the Parthian empire, and took the Parthian capital of Ctesiphon. In 116 he descended the Tigris and entered the Erythraean Sea (the Persian Gulf). While he was thus engaged the Parthians rose against the Romans, but were again subdued by the generals

3 E 2

of Trajan. On his return to Ctesiphon, Trajan determined to give the Parthians a king, and placed the diadem on the head of Parthamaspates. In 117 Trajan fell ill, and as his complaint grew worse he set out for Italy. He lived to reach Selinus in Cilicia, afterwards called Trajanopolis, where he died in August, 117, after a reign of 19 years, 6 months and 15 days. His ashes were taken to Rome in a golden urn, carried in triumphal procession, and deposited under the column which bears his name. He left no children, and he was succeeded by Hadrian. Trajan constructed several great roads in the empire; he built libraries at Rome, one of which, called the *Ulpia Bibliotheca*, is often mentioned; and a theatre in the Campus Martius. His great work was the Forum Trajanum, in the centre of which was placed the column of Trajan.—Under the reign of Trajan lived Sextus Julius Frontinus, C. Cornelius Tacitus, the Younger Pliny, and various others of less note. Plutarch, Suetonius, and Epictetus survived Trajan. The jurists Juventius Celsus and Neratius Priscus were living under Trajan.

Trajānus Portus. [CENTUM CELLAE.]

Trajectum (*Utrecht*), a town of the Batavi on the Rhine, called at a later time *Trajectus Rheni*, or *Ad Rhenum*.

Tralles or **Trallis** (*al* Τραλλεῖς, *ἡ* Τράλλις : Τραλλιανός, Trallianus: *Ghiuzel-Hisar*, Ru., near *Aidin*), a flourishing commercial city of Asia Minor, reckoned sometimes to Ionia, and sometimes to Caria. It stood on a quadrangular height at the S. foot of M. Messogis (with a citadel on a higher point), on the banks of the little river Eudon, a N. tributary of the Maeander, from which the city was distant 80 stadia (8 geog. miles). The surrounding country was extremely fertile and beautiful, and hence the city was at first called Anthea (Ἄνθεια). Under the Seleucidae it bore the names of Seleucia and Antiochia. It was inhabited by a mixed population of Greeks and Carians. There was a less important city of the same name in Phrygia, if indeed it be not the same.

Tranquillus, Suetōnĭus. [SUETONIUS.]

Transcellensis Mons, a mountain of Mauretania Caesariensis, between Caesarea and the river Chinalaph.

Trapezopŏlis (Τραπεζούπολις), a town of Asia Minor, on the S. slope of M. Cadmus, on the confines of Caria and Phrygia. Its site is uncertain.

Trapĕzūs (Τραπεζοῦς : Τραπεζούντιος and -ούσιος). 1. (Near *Mauria*), a city of Arcadia, on the Alpheus, the name of which was mythically derived from the τράπεζα, or altar, on which Lycaon was said to have offered human sacrifices to Jove. At the time of the building of Megalopolis, the inhabitants of Trapezus, rather than be transferred to the new city, migrated to the shores of the Euxine, and their city fell to ruin. — 2. (*Tarabosan, Trabexun,* or *Trebizond*), a colony of Sinope, at almost the extreme E. of the N. shore of Asia Minor. After Sinope lost her independence, Trapezus belonged, first to Armenia Minor, and afterwards to the kingdom of Pontus. Under the Romans, it was made a free city, probably by Pompey, and, by Trajan, the capital of Pontus Cappadocius. Hadrian constructed a new harbour; and the city became a place of first-rate commercial importance. It was also strongly fortified. It was taken by the Goths in the reign of Valerian;

but it had recovered, and was in a flourishing state at the time of Justinian, who repaired its fortifications. In the middle ages it was for some time the seat of a fragment of the Greek empire, called the empire of Trebizond. It is now the second commercial port of the Black Sea, ranking next after Odessa.

Trāsĭmēnus Lacus (*Lago di Perugia*), sometimes, but not correctly, written **Thrasymēnus,** a lake in Etruria, between Clusium and Perusia, memorable for the victory gained by Hannibal over the Romans under Flaminius, B. C. 217.

Treba (Trebanus : *Trevi*), a town in Latium, near the sources of the Anio, N. E. of Anagnia.

Trebātĭus Testa. [TESTA.]

Trebellĭus Pollĭo, one of the 6 *Scriptores Historiae Augustae,* flourished under Constantine, and was anterior to Vopiscus. His name is prefixed to the biographies of, 1. The 2 Valeriani, father and son; 2. The Gallieni; 3. The Thirty Tyrants; 4. Claudius, the last-named piece being addressed to Constantine. We learn from Vopiscus that the lives written by Trebellius Pollio commenced with Philippus and extended down to Claudius. Of these, all as far as the Valeriani, regarding whom but a short fragment remains, have been lost.

Trebĭa (*Trebbia*), a small river in Gallia Cisalpina, falling into the Po near Placentia. It is memorable for the victory which Hannibal gained over the Romans, B. C. 218. This river is generally dry in summer, but is filled with a rapid stream in winter, which was the season when Hannibal defeated the Romans.

Trebōnĭus, C., played rather a prominent part in the last days of the republic. He commenced public life as a supporter of the aristocratical party, and in his quaestorship (B. C. 60) he attempted to prevent the adoption of P. Clodius into a plebeian family. He changed sides soon afterwards, and in his tribunate of the plebs (55) he was the instrument of the triumvirs in proposing that Pompey should have the 2 Spains, Crassus Syria, and Caesar the Gauls and Illyricum for another period of 5 years. This proposal received the approbation of the comitia, and is known by the name of the *Lex Trebonia.* For this service he was rewarded by being appointed one of Caesar's legates in Gaul, where he remained till the breaking out of the civil war in 49. In the course of the same year he was intrusted by Caesar with the command of the land forces engaged in the siege of Massilia. In 48 Trebonius was city-praetor, and in the discharge of his duties resisted the seditious attempts of his colleague M. Caelius Rufus to obtain by force the repeal of Caesar's law respecting the payment of debts. Towards the end of 47, Trebonius, as pro-praetor, succeeded Q. Cassius Longinus in the government of Further Spain, but was expelled from the province by a mutiny of the soldiers who espoused the Pompeian party. Caesar raised him to the consulship in October, 45, and promised him the province of Asia. In return for all these honours and favours, Trebonius was one of the prime movers in the conspiracy to assassinate Caesar, and after the murder of his patron (44) he went as proconsul to the province of Asia. In the following year (43) Dolabella, who had received from Antonius the province of Syria, surprised the town of Smyrna, where Trebonius was then residing, and slew him in his bed.

Trĕbŭla (Trebulanus). 1. (*Tregghia*), a town in Samnium situated in the S. E. part of the mountains of *Cajazzo*. — 2. **Mutusca**, a town of the Sabines of uncertain site. — 3. **Suffena**, also a town of the Sabines, and of uncertain site.

Trĕrus (*Sacco*), a river in Latium, and a tributary of the Liris.

Tres Tabernae. 1. A station on the Via Appia in Latium, between Aricia and Forum Appii. It is mentioned in the account of St. Paul's journey to Rome. — 2. (*Borghetto*), a station in Gallia Cisalpina, on the road from Placentia to Mediolanum.

Trĕtum (Τρητόν: *C. Bugiaroni*, or *Ras Seba Rous*, i. e. *Seven Capes*), a great promontory on the coast of Numidia, forming the W. headland of the Sinus Olcachites (*Bay of Storah*).

Treviri or **Treveri**, a powerful people in Gallia Belgica, who were faithful allies of the Romans, and whose cavalry was the best in all Gaul. The river Mosella flowed through their territory, which extended W.-ward from the Rhine as far as the Remi. Their chief town was made a Roman colony by Augustus, and was called **Augusta Trevirōrum** (*Trier* or *Treves*). It stood on the right bank of the Mosella, and became under the later empire one of the most flourishing Roman cities N. of the Alps. It was the capital of Belgica Prima; and after the division of the Roman world by Diocletian (A. D. 292) into 4 districts, it became the residence of the Caesar, who had the government of Britain, Gaul, and Spain. Here dwelt Constantius Chlorus and his son Constantine the Great, as well as several of the subsequent emperors. The modern city still contains many interesting Roman remains. They belong, however, to the latter period of the empire, and are consequently not in the best style of art. The most important of these remains is the *Porta Nigra* or *Black Gate*, a large and massive building in an excellent state of preservation. In addition to this, we have extensive remains of the Roman baths, of the amphitheatre, and of the palace of Constantine. The piers of the bridge over the Moselle are likewise Roman. At the village of Igel, about 6 miles from Treves, is a beautiful Roman structure, being a 4-sided obelisk, more than 70 feet high, covered with carvings, inscriptions, and bas-reliefs. There has been much dispute respecting the object for which this building was erected; but it appears to have been set up by 2 brothers, named Secundini; partly as a funeral monument to their deceased relatives, partly to celebrate their sister's marriage, which is represented on one of the bas-reliefs by the figures of a man and woman joining hands.

Triārius, Valĕrius. 1. L., quaestor urbanus B. C. 81; and propraetor in Sardinia 77, when he repulsed Lepidus, who had fled into that island after his unsuccessful attempt to repeal the laws of Sulla. Triarius served under Lucullus as one of his legates in the war against Mithridates, and at first gained considerable distinction by his zeal and activity. In 68 Triarius was despatched to the assistance of Fabius, who had been intrusted with the defence of Pontus, while Lucullus invaded Armenia, and who was now attacked by Mithridates with overwhelming numbers. Triarius compelled Mithridates to assume the defensive, and early in the following year he commenced active operations against the Pontic king. Anxious to gain the victory over Mithridates before the arrival of Lucullus, Triarius allowed himself to be attacked at a disadvantage, and was defeated with great slaughter near Zela. — 2. P., son of the preceding, accused M. Aemilius Scaurus, in 54, first of repetundae and next of ambitus. Scaurus was defended on both occasions by Cicero. — 3. C., a friend of Cicero, who introduces him as one of the speakers in his dialogue *De Finibus*, and praises his oratory in his *Brutus*. He fought on Pompey's side at the battle of Pharsalia. Triarius perished in the civil wars, probably in Africa, for Cicero speaks in 45 of his death, and adds, that Triarius had left him the guardian of his children.

Triballi, a powerful people in Thrace, a branch of the Getae dwelling along the Danube, who were defeated by Alexander the Great, B. C. 335, and obliged to sue for peace.

Tribocci, a German people, settled in Gallia Belgica, between M. Vogesus and the Rhine, in the neighbourhood of *Strasburg*.

Triboniānus, a jurist, commissioned by Justinianus, with 16 others, to compile the Digest or Pandect. For details see JUSTINIANUS.

Tricăla. [TRIOCALA.]

Tricarānon (Τρικάρανον: Τρικαρανεύς), a fortress in Phliasia, S. E. of Phlius, on a mountain of the same name.

Tricasses, Tricasii, or **Tricassini,** a people in Gallia Lugdunensis, E. of the Senones, whose chief town was Augustobona, afterwards Tricassae (*Troyes*).

Tricastini, a people in Gallia Narbonensis, between the Cavares and Vocontii, inhabiting a narrow slip of country between the Drome and the Isère. Their chief town was Augusta Tricastinorum, or simply Augustâ (*Aouste*).

Tricca, subsequently **Tricăla** (Τρίκκη, Τρίκαλα: *Trikkala*), an ancient town of Thessaly in the district Hestiaeotis, situated on the Lethaeus, N. of the Peneus. Homer represents it as governed by the sons of Aesculapius; and it contained in later times a celebrated temple of this god.

Trichōnis (Τριχωνίς: *Zygos* or *Vrakhori*), a large lake in Aetolia, E. of Stratos and N. of Mt. Aracynthus.

Trichōnīum (Τριχώνιον: Τριχωνιεύς), a town in Aetolia, E. of lake Trichonis.

Triciptīnus, Lucrētius. [LUCRETIA GENS.]

Tricŏlōni (Τρικόλωνοι: Τρικολωνεύς), a town of Arcadia, a little N. of Megalopolis, of which a temple of Poseidon alone remained in the time of Pausanias.

Tricorii, a Ligurian people in Gallia Narbonensis, a branch of the Sallyi, in the neighbourhood of Massilia and Aquae Sextiae.

Tricorȳthus (Τρικόρυθος: Τρικορύσιος), a demus in Attica, belonging to the tribe Aiantis, between Marathon and Rhamnus.

Tricrana (Τρίκρανα: *Trikhiri*), an island off the coast of Argolis near Hermione.

Tridentum (*Trent*, in Italian *Trento*), the capital of the **Tridentini**, and the chief town of Rhaetia, situated on the river Athesis (*Adige*), and on the pass of the Alps leading to Verona. Its greatness dates from the Middle Ages, and it is chiefly celebrated on account of the ecclesiastical council, which assembled within its walls, A. D. 1545.

Triĕres or **Triĕris** (Τριήρης: *Enfeh?*), a small fortress on the coast of Phoenicia, between Tripolis and the Prom. Theuprosopon.

Trifanum, a town in Latium of uncertain site, between Minturnae and Sinuessa.

Trinacria. [SICILIA.]

Trinemeis or **Trinemia** (Τρινεμεῖς, Τρινέμεια: Τρινεμεύς), a demus in Attica, belonging to the tribe Cecropia, on Mt. Parnes.

Trinobantes, one of the most powerful people of Britain, inhabiting the modern Essex. They are mentioned in Caesar's invasion of Britain, and they offered a formidable resistance to the invading force sent into the island by the emperor Claudius.

Triocala or **Tricala** (Τριόκαλα, Τρίκαλα: Τρικαλῖνος, Tricalīnus: nr. *Calata Bellota*), a mountain fortress in the interior of Sicily, near the Crimissus, was in the Servile War the head-quarters of the slaves, and the residence of their leader Tryphon.

Triopas (Τριόπας or Τρίοψ), son of Poseidon and Canace, a daughter of Aeolus, or of Helios and Rhodos, and the father of Iphimedia and Erysichthon. Hence, his son Erysichthon is called *Triopēïus*, and his granddaughter Mestra or Metra, the daughter of Erysichthon, *Triopēïs*. Triopas expelled the Pelasgians from the Dotian plain, but was himself obliged to emigrate, and went to Caria, where he founded Cnidus on the Triopian promontory. His son Erysichthon was punished by Demeter with insatiable hunger, because he had violated her sacred grove; but others relate the same of Triopas himself.

Triopia or **Triopion**, an early name of CNIDUS.

Triopium (Τριόπιον: *C. Krio*), the promontory which terminates the peninsula of Cnidus, forming the S.W. headland of Caria and of Asia Minor. Upon it was a temple of Apollo, surnamed Triopius, which was the centre of union for the states of DORIS. Hence it was also called the Sacred Promontory (ἀκρωτήριον ἱερόν).

Triphylia (Τριφυλία: Τριφύλιος), the S. portion of Elis, lying between the Alpheus and the Neda, is said to have derived its name from the 3 different tribes by which it was peopled. Its chief town was PYLOS.

Tripodiscus (Τριποδίσκος: Τριποδίσκιος nr. *Dervæni* Ru.), a town in the interior of Megaris, N. W. of Megara.

Tripolis (Τρίπολις: Τριπολίτης), is properly the name of a confederacy composed of 3 cities, or a district containing 3 cities, but it is also applied to single cities which had some such relation to others as to make the name appropriate. 1. In Arcadia, comprising the 3 cities of Callia, Dipoena, and Nonacris: its name is preserved in the modern town of *Tripolitza*. — 2. **T. Pelagonia**, in Thessaly, comprising the 3 towns of Azorus, Doliche, and Pythium. — 3. In Rhodes, comprising the 3 Dorian cities, Lindus, Ialysus, and Camirus. [RHODUS.] — 4. (*Kash Yeniji*), a city on the Maeander, 12 miles W. of Hierapolis, on the borders of Phrygia, Caria, and Lydia, to each of which it is assigned by different authorities. — 5. (*Tireboli*), a fortress on the coast of Pontus, on a river of the same name (*Tireboli Su*), 90 stadia E. of the Prom. Zephyrium (*C. Zefreh*). — 6. (*Tripoli, Tarabulus*), on the coast of Phoenicia, consisted of 3 distinct cities, 1 stadium (600 feet) apart, each having its own walls, but all united in a common constitution, having one place of assembly, and forming in reality one city. They were colonies of Tyre, Sidon, and Aradus respectively. Tripolis

stood about 30 miles S. of Aradus, and about the same distance N. of Byblus, on a bold headland, formed by a spur of M. Lebanon. It had a fine harbour, and a flourishing commerce. It is now a city of about 15,000 inhabitants, and the capital of one of the pachalicks of Syria, that of *Tripoli*. — 7. The district on the N. coast of Africa, between the 2 Syrtes, comprising the 3 cities of Sabrata (or Abrotonum), Oea, and Leptis Magna, and also called Tripolitana Regio. [SYRTICA.] Its name is preserved in that of the regency of *Tripoli*, the W. part of which answers to it, and in that of the city of *Tripoli*, probably the ancient Oea.

Tripolitana Regio. [SYRTICA: TRIPOLIS, No. 7.]

Triptolemus (Τριπτόλεμος), son of Celeus, king of Eleusis, and Metanira or Polymnia. Others describe him as son of king Eleusis by Cothonea, or of Oceanus and Gaea, or of Trochilus by an Eleusinian woman. Triptolemus was the favourite of Demeter, and the inventor of the plough and agriculture, and of civilisation, which is the result of it. He was the great hero in the Eleusinian mysteries. According to the common legend he hospitably received Demeter at Eleusis, when she was wandering in search of her daughter. The goddess, in return, wished to make his son Demophon immortal, and placed him in the fire in order to destroy his mortal parts; but Metanira screamed out at the sight, and the child was consumed by the flames. As a compensation for this bereavement, the goddess gave to Triptolemus a chariot with winged dragons and seeds of wheat. In this chariot Triptolemus rode over the earth, making man acquainted with the blessings of agriculture. On his return to Attica, Celeus endeavoured to kill him, but by the command of Demeter he was obliged to give up his country to Triptolemus, who now established the worship of Demeter, and instituted the Thesmophoria. Triptolemus is represented in works of art as a youthful hero, sometimes with the petasus, on a chariot drawn by dragons, and holding in his hand a sceptre and corn ears.

Tritaea (Τρίταια: Τριταιεύς). 1. A town of Phocis, N. W. of Cleonae, on the left bank of the Cephissus and on the frontiers of Locris. — 2. One of the 12 cities of Achaia, 120 stadia E. of Pharae and near the frontiers of Arcadia. Augustus made it dependent upon Patrae.

Trito or **Tritogenia** (Τριτώ or Τριτογένεια and Τριτογενής), a surname of Athena, which is explained in different ways. Some derive it from lake Tritonis in Libya, near which she is said to have been born; others from the stream Triton near Alalcomenae in Boeotia, where she was worshipped, and where according to some statements she was also born; the grammarians, lastly, derive the name from τριτώ, which, in the dialect of the Athamanians, is said to signify "head," so that it would be the goddess born out of the head of her father.

Triton (Τρίτων), son of Poseidon and Amphitrite (or Celaeno), who dwelt with his father and mother in a golden palace in the bottom of the sea, or, according to Homer, at Aegae. Later writers describe him as riding over the sea on horses or other sea-monsters. Sometimes we find mention of Tritons in the plural. Their appearance is differently described; though they are always conceived as having the human figure in the upper part of their bodies, and that of a fish in the lower part. The chief characteristic of Tritons in poetry as well as in works of art is a trumpet made out of a shell (*concha*), which the Tritons blow at the command of Poseidon, to soothe the restless waves of the sea.

Triton Fl., Tritōnis, or Tritonītis Palus (Τρίτων, Τριτωνίς, Τριτωνῖτις), a river and lake on the Mediterranean coast of Libya, which are mentioned in several old Greek legends, especially in the mythology of Athena, whom one account represented as born on the lake Tritonis, and as the daughter of the nymph of the same name, and of Poseidon: hence her surname of Τριτογένεια. When the Greeks first became acquainted geographically with the N. coast of Africa, they identified the gulf afterwards called the Lesser SYRTIS with the lake Tritonis. This seems to be the notion of Herodotus, in the story he relates of Jason (iv. 178, 179). A more exact knowledge of the coast showed them a great lake beyond the inmost recess of the Lesser Syrtis, to which the name Tritonis was then applied. This lake had an opening to the sea, as well as a river flowing into it, and accordingly the geographers represented the river Triton as rising in a mountain, called Zuchabari, and forming the lake Tritonis on its course to the Lesser Syrtis, into which it fell. The lake is undoubtedly the great salt lake, in the S. of *Tunis*, called *El-Sibkah;* but as this lake has no longer an opening to the sea, and the whole coast is much altered by the inroads of the sands of the *Sahara*, it seems impossible to identify the river: some suppose that it is represented by the *Wady-el-Khale.* Some of the ancient writers gave altogether a different locality to the legend, and identify the Triton with the river usually called LATHON, in Cyrenaïca; and Apollonius Rhodius even transfers the name to the Nile.

Trivīcus (*Trivico*), a small town in Samnium, situated among the mountains separating Samnium from Apulia.

Trōas (ἡ Τρωάς, sc. χώρα, the fem. of the adj. Τρώς: Τρωαδεύς: *Chun*), the territory of Ilium or Troy, formed the N. W. part of Mysia. It was bounded on the W. by the Aegean sea, from Pr. Lectum to Pr. Sigeum at the entrance of the Hellespont; on the N. W. by the Hellespont, as far as the river Rhodius, below Abydus; on the N. E. and E. by the mountains which border the valley of the Rhodius, and extend from its sources S.-wards to the main ridge of M. Ida, and on the S. by the N. coast of the Gulf of Adramyttium along the S. foot of Ida; but on the N. E. and E. the boundary is sometimes extended so far as to include the whole coast of the Hellespont and part of the Propontis, and the country as far as the river Granicus, thus embracing the district of Dardania, and somewhat more. Strabo extends the boundary still further E., to the river Aesepus, and also S. to the Caïcus; but this clearly results from his including in the territory of Troy that of her neighbouring allies. The Troad is for the most part mountainous, being intersected by M. IDA and its branches: the largest plain is that in which Troy stood. The chief rivers were the SATMOIS on the S., the RHODIUS on the N., and the Scamander and Simoïs in the centre. These 2 rivers, so renowned in the legends of the Trojan War, flow from 2 different points in the chain of

M. Ida, and unite in the plain of Troy, through which the united stream flows N.W. and falls into the Hellespont E. of the promontory of Sigeum. The Scamander, also called Xanthus, is usually identified with the *Menderek-Chai*, and the Simoïs with the *Gumbrek;* but this subject presents difficulties which cannot be discussed within the limits of the present article. The precise locality of the city of Troy, or, according to its genuine Greek name, Ilium, is also the subject still of much dispute. First, there is the question, whether the Ilium of Homer had any real existence; next, whether the **Ilium Vetus** of the historical period, which was visited by Xerxes and by Alexander the Great, was on the same site as the city of Priam. The most probable opinion seems to be that which places the original city in the upper part of the plain, on a moderate elevation at the foot of M. Ida, and its citadel (called Pergăma, Πέργαμα), on a loftier height, almost separated from the city by a ravine, and nearly surrounded by the Scamander. This city seems never to have been restored after its destruction by the Greeks. The Aeolian colonists subsequently built a new city, on the site, as they doubtless believed, of the old one, but really much lower down the plain; and this city is the **Trōja** or **Ilium Vetus** of most of the ancient writers. After the time of Alexander, this city declined, and a new one was built still further down the plain, below the confluence of the Simoïs and Scamander, and near the Hellespont, and this was called **Ilium Novum.** Under the Romans, this city was honoured with various immunities, as the only existing representative of the ancient Ilium. Its substantial importance, however, was entirely eclipsed by that of ALEXANDRIA TROAS.—For the general political history of the Troad, see MYSIA. The Teucrians, by whom it was peopled at a period of unknown antiquity, were a Thracian people. Settling in the plain of the Scamander, they founded the city of Ilium, which became the head of an extensive confederacy, embracing not only the N.W. of Asia Minor, but much of the opposite shores of Thrace, and with allies in Asia Minor even as far as Lycia, and evidently much in advance of the Greeks in civilisation. The mythical account of the origin of the kingdom is briefly as follows. Teucer, the first king in the Troad, had a daughter, who married Dardanus, the chieftain of the country N. E. of the Troad. [DARDANIA.] Dardanus had 2 sons, Ilus and Erichthonius; and the latter was the father of Tros, from whom the country and people derived the names of Troas and Troes. Tros was the father of Ilus, who founded the city, which was called after him Ilium, and also, after his father, **Trōja.** The next king was LAOMEDON, and after him Priam. [PRIAMUS.] In his reign the city was taken and destroyed by the confederated Greeks, after a 10 years' siege. [HELENA, ALEXANDER, AGAMEMNON, ACHILLES, HECTOR, AJAX, ULYSSES, NEOPTOLEMUS, AENEAS, &c. and HOMERUS.] To discuss the historical value of this legend is not the province of this work: it is enough to say that we have in it evidence of a great conflict, at a very early period, between the great Thracian empire in the N.W. of Asia Minor, and the rising power of the Achaeans in Greece, in which the latter were victorious; but their victory was fruitless, in consequence of their comparatively low civilisation, and especially of their want of maritime power. The chronologers assigned different dates for the capture of Troy : the calculation most generally accepted placed it in B. C. 1184. This date should be carefully remembered, as it forms the starting point of various computations; but it should also be borne in mind that the date is of no historical *authority*. (There is not space to explain this matter here.) The subsequent history of the Troad presents an entire blank, till we come to the period of the great Aeolic migration, when it merges in that of AEOLIS and MYSIA. — In writers of the Roman period, the name Troas is often used by itself for the city of ALEXANDRIA TROAS.

Trocmi or -ii. [GALATIA.]

Troës. [TROAS.]

Troesēn (Τροιζήν, more rarely Τροιζήνη : Τροιζήνιος : *Dhamala*), the capital of Troezēnĭa (Τροιζηνία), a district in the S. E. of Argolis on the Saronic gulf, and opposite the island of Aegina. The town was situated at some little distance from the coast, on which it possessed a harbour called Pōgŏn (Πώγων), opposite the island of Calauria. Troezen was a very ancient city, and is said to have been originally called Poseidonia, on account of its worship of Poseidon. It received the name of Troezen from Troezen, one of the sons of Pelops; and it is celebrated in mythology as the place where Pittheus, the maternal grandfather of Theseus, lived, and where Theseus himself was born. Troezen was for a long time dependent upon the kings of Argos ; but in the historical period it appears as an independent state. It was a city of some importance, for we read that the Troezenians sent 5 ships of war to Salamis and 1000 heavy-armed men to Plataea. When the Persians entered Attica the Troezenians distinguished themselves by the kindness with which they received the Athenians, who were obliged to abandon their city.

Trogīliae, 3 small islands, named Psilon, Argennon, and Sandalion, lying off the promontory of Trogilium. [MYCALE.]

Trogītis Lacus. [PISIDIA.]

Troglodȳtae (Τρωγλοδύται, i. e. *dwellers in caves*), the name applied by the Greek geographers to various uncivilised people, who had no abodes but caves, especially to the inhabitants of the W. coast of the Red Sea, along the shores of Upper Egypt and Aethiopia. The whole of this coast was called Troglodytĭce (Τρωγλοδυτική). There were also Troglodytae in Moesia, on the banks of the Danube.

Trogus, Pompeius. [JUSTINUS.]

Troīlum. [TROSSULUM.]

Troīlus (Τρωΐλος), son of Priam and Hecuba, or according to others son of Apollo. He fell by the hands of Achilles.

Trōja (Τροία, Ion. Τροίη, Ep. Τρυΐα: Τρώς, Τρωός, Ep. and Ion. Τρωΐος, fem. Τρωάς &c.: Trōs, Trōĭus, Trojānus, fem. Trōas, pl. Trōădes and Trōĭădea), the name of the city of Troy or Ilium, also applied to the country. [TROAS.]

Trophōnĭus (Τροφώνιος), son of Erginus, king of Orchomenus, and brother of Agamedes. He and his brother built the temple at Delphi and the treasury of king Hyrieus in Boeotia. For details see AGAMEDES. Trophonius after his death was worshipped as a hero, and had a celebrated oracle in a cave near Lebadea in Boeotia. (See *Dict. of Antiq.*, art. *Oraculum*.)

Trōs (Τρώς), son of Erichthonius and Astyoche, and grandson of Dardanus. He was married to Callirrhoë, by whom he became the father of Ilus, Assaracus, and Ganymedes, and was king of Phrygia. The country and people of Troy derived their name from him. He gave up his son Ganymedes to Zeus for a present of horses. [GANYMEDES.]

Trossŭlum (Trossulanus : *Trosso*), a town in Etruria, 9 miles from Volsinii, which is said to have been taken by some Roman equites without the aid of foot-soldiers ; whence the Roman equites obtained the name of Trossuli. Some writers identify this town with Troilium, which was taken by the Romans, B. C. 293; but they appear to have been different places.

Trōtĭlum (Τρώτιλον : *Trontello*), a town of Sicily, on the road from Syracuse to Leontini.

Truentum, a town of Picenum on the river Truentus or Truentinus (*Tronto*).

Trutulensis Portus, a harbour on the N. E. coast of Britain near the aestuary Taus (Tay), but of which the exact site is unknown.

Tryphiŏdōrus (Τρυφιόδωρος), a Greek grammarian and poet, was a native of Egypt ; but nothing is known of his personal history. He is supposed to have lived in the 5th century of the Christian era. Of his grammatical labours we have no record ; but one of his poems has come down to us, entitled 'Ιλίου ἅλωσις, the *Capture of Ilium*, consisting of 691 lines. From the small dimensions of it, it is necessarily little but a sketch. The best editions are by Northmore, Cambridge 1791, London 1804 ; by Schäfer, Leipzig 1808 ; and by Wernicke, Leipzig 1819.

Trȳphōn (Τρύφων). 1. Diodŏtus, a usurper of the throne of Syria during the reign of Demetrius II. Nicator. After the death of Alexander Balas in B. C. 146, Tryphon first set up Antiochus, the infant son of Balas, as a pretender against Demetrius ; but in 142 he murdered Antiochus and reigned as king himself. Tryphon was defeated and put to death by Antiochus Sidetes, the brother of Demetrius, in 139, after a reign of 3 years. — 2. Salvĭus, one of the leaders of the revolted slaves in Sicily, was supposed to have a knowledge of divination, for which reason he was elected king by the slaves in 103. He displayed considerable abilities, and in a short time collected an army of 20,000 foot and 2000 horse, with which he defeated the propraetor P. Licinius Nerva. After this victory Salvius assumed all the pomp of royalty, and took the surname of Tryphon, probably because it had been borne by Diodotus, the usurper of the Syrian throne. He chose the strong fortress of Triocala as the seat of his new kingdom. Tryphon was defeated by L. Lucullus in 102, and was obliged to take refuge in Triocala. But Lucullus failed in taking the place, and returned to Rome without effecting any thing more. Lucullus was succeeded by C. Servilius ; and on the death of Tryphon, about the same time, the kingdom devolved upon Athenion, who was not subdued till 101.

Tryphonīnus, Claudĭus, a Roman jurist, wrote under the reigns of Septimius Severus and Caracalla.

Tubantes, a people of Germany, allies of the Cherusci, originally dwelt between the Rhine and the Yssel ; in the time of Germanicus on the S. bank of the Lippe, between Paderborn, Hamm, and the Armsberger Wald ; and at a still later time in the neighbourhood of the Thüringer Wald between the Fulda and the Werra. Subsequently they are mentioned as a part of the great league of the Franci.

Tubĕro, Aellus. 1. Q., son-in-law of L. Aemilius Paulus, served under the latter in his war against Perseus, king of Macedonia. This Tubero, like the rest of his family, was so poor that he had not an ounce of silver plate, till his father-in-law gave him 5 pounds of plate from the spoils of the Macedonian monarch. — 2. Q., son of the preceding, was a pupil of Panaetius, and is called the Stoic. He had a reputation for talent and legal knowledge. He was praetor in 123, and consul suffectus in 118. He was an opponent of Tib. Gracchus, as well as of C. Gracchus, and delivered some speeches against the latter, 123. Tubero is one of the speakers in Cicero's dialogue *de Republica*. The passages in the Digest in which Tubero is cited do not refer to this Tubero, but to No. 4. — 3. L., an intimate friend of Cicero. He was a relation and a schoolfellow of the orator, had served with him in the Marsic war, and had afterwards served under his brother Quintus as legate in Asia. On the breaking out of the civil war, Tubero, who had espoused the Pompeian party, received from the senate the province of Africa ; but as Atius Varus and Q. Ligarius, who likewise belonged to the aristocratical party, would not surrender it to him, he passed over to Pompey in Greece. He was afterwards pardoned by Caesar, and returned with his son Quintus to Rome. Tubero cultivated literature and philosophy. He wrote a history, and the philosopher Aenesidemus dedicated to him his work on the sceptical philosophy of Pyrrhon. — 4. Q., son of the preceding. In 46 he made a speech before C. Julius Caesar against Q. Ligarius, who was defended by Cicero in a speech which is extant (*Pro Q. Ligario*). Tubero obtained considerable reputation as a jurist. He had a great knowledge both of Jus Publicum and Privatum, and he wrote several works on both these divisions of law. He married a daughter of Servius Sulpicius, and the daughter of Tubero was the mother of the jurist C. Cassius Longinus. Like his father, Q. Tubero wrote a history. Tubero the jurist, who is often cited in the Digest, is this Tubero ; but there is no excerpt from his writings.

Tucca, Plotius, a friend of Horace and Virgil. The latter poet left Tucca one of his heirs, and bequeathed his unfinished writings to him and Varius, who afterwards published the *Aeneid* by order of Augustus.

Tuder (Tuders, -tis : *Todi*), an ancient town of Umbria, situated on a hill near the Tiber, and on the road from Mevania to Rome. It was subsequently made a Roman colony. There are still remains of the polygonal walls of the ancient town.

Tuditanus, Sempronius. 1. M., consul B. C. 240, and censor 230. — 2. P., tribune of the soldiers at the battle of Cannae in 216, and one of the few Roman officers who survived that fatal day. In 214 he was curule aedile ; in 213 praetor, with Ariminum as his province, and was continued in the command for the two following years (212, 211). He was censor in 209 with M. Cornelius Cethegus, although neither he nor his colleague had yet held the consulship. In 205 he was sent into Greece with the title of proconsul, for the purpose of opposing Philip, with whom however he concluded a treaty, which was ratified by the Romans. Tuditanus was consul in 204, and received Bruttii as his province. He was at first defeated by Hannibal, but shortly afterwards he gained a decisive victory over the Carthaginian general. — 3. C., plebeian aedile 198, and praetor 197, when he obtained Nearer Spain as his province. He was defeated by the Spaniards with great loss, and died shortly afterwards of a wound which he had received in the battle. — 4. M., tribune of the plebs 193 ; praetor 189, when he obtained Sicily as his province ; and consul 185. In his consulship he carried on war in Liguria, and defeated the Apuani, while his colleague was equally successful against the Ingauni. He was carried off by the great pestilence which devastated Rome in 174. — 5. C., praetor 132, and consul 129. In his consulship he carried on war against the Iapydes in Illyricum, over whom he gained a victory chiefly through the military skill of his legate, D. Junius Brutus. Tuditanus was an orator and an historian, and in both obtained considerable distinction.

Tulcis, a river on the E. coast of Spain near Tarraco.

Tulingi, a people of Gaul of no great importance, who dwelt on the Rhine between the Rauraci and the Helvetii.

Tullia, the name of the 2 daughters of Servius Tullius, the 6th king of Rome. [TULLIUS.]

Tullia, frequently called by the diminutive Tulliola, was the daughter of M. Cicero and Terentia, and was probably born B. C. 79 or 78. She was betrothed in 67 to C. Calpurnius Piso Frugi, whom she married in 63 during the consulship of her father. During Cicero's banishment Tullia lost her first husband. She was married again in 56 to Furius Crassipes, a young man of rank and large property ; but she did not live with him long, though the time and the reason of her divorce are alike unknown. In 50 she was married to her 3rd husband, P. Cornelius Dolabella, who was a thorough profligate. The marriage took place during Cicero's absence in Cilicia, and, as might have been anticipated, was not a happy one. On the breaking out of the civil war in 49, the husband and the father of Tullia espoused opposite sides. While Dolabella fought for Caesar, and Cicero took refuge in the camp of Pompey, Tullia remained in Italy. On the 19th of May, 49, she was delivered of a 7 months' child, which died soon afterwards. After the battle of Pharsalia, Dolabella returned to Rome ; but he continued to lead a dissolute and profligate life, and at length (46) a divorce took place by mutual consent. At the beginning of 45 Tullia was delivered of a son. As soon as she was sufficiently recovered to bear the fatigues of a journey, she accompanied her father to Tusculum, but she died there in February. Her loss was a severe blow to Cicero. Among the many consolatory letters which he received on the occasion is the well-known one from the celebrated jurist Serv. Sulpicius (*ad Fam.* iv. 5). To dissipate his grief, Cicero drew up a treatise on Consolation.

Tullia Gens, patrician and plebeian. The patrician Tullii were one of the Alban houses, which were transplanted to Rome in the reign of Tullus Hostilius. The patrician branch of the gens appears to have become extinct at an early period ;

for after the early times of the republic no one of the name occurs for some centuries, and the Tullii of a later age are not only plebeians, but, with the exception of their bearing the same name, cannot be regarded as having any connection with the ancient gens. The first plebeian Tullius who rose to the honours of the state was M. Tullius Decula, consul B. C. 81, and the next was the celebrated orator M. Tullius Cicero. [CICERO.]

Tulliānum. [ROMA, p. 654, b.]

Tullus, Servius, the 6th king of Rome. The account of the early life and death of Servius Tullius is full of marvels, and cannot be regarded as possessing any title to a real historical narrative. His mother, Ocrisia, was one of the captives taken at Corniculum, and became a female slave of Tanaquil, the wife of Tarquinius Priscus. He was born in the king's palace, and notwithstanding his servile origin was brought up as the king's son, since Tanaquil by her powers of divination had foreseen the greatness of the child; and Tarquinius placed such confidence in him, that he gave him his daughter in marriage, and entrusted him with the exercise of the government. His rule was mild and beneficent; and so popular did he become, that the sons of Ancus Marcius, fearing lest they should be deprived of the throne which they claimed as their inheritance, procured the assassination of Tarquinius [TARQUINIUS]. They did not, however, reap the fruit of their crime, for Tanaquil, pretending that the king's wound was not mortal, told the people that Tarquinius would recover in a few days, and that he had commanded Servius meantime to discharge the duties of the kingly office. Servius forthwith began to act as king, greatly to the satisfaction of the people; and when the death of Tarquinius could no longer be concealed, he was already in firm possession of the royal power. The reign of Servius is almost as barren of military exploits as that of Numa. The only war which Livy mentions is one against Veii, which was brought to a speedy conclusion. The great deeds of Servius were deeds of peace; and he was regarded by the author of all their civil rights and institutions, just as Numa was of their religious rites and ordinances. Three important events are assigned to Servius by universal tradition. First, he gave a new constitution to the Roman state. The two main objects of this constitution were to give the plebs political independence, and to assign to property that influence in the state which had previously belonged to birth exclusively. In order to carry his purpose into effect, Servius made a two-fold division of the Roman people, one territorial, and the other according to property. For details, see Dict. of Antiq. art. Comitia. Secondly, he extended the pomoerium, or hallowed boundary of the city, and completed the city by incorporating with it the Quirinal, Viminal, and Esquiline hills. [ROMA.] Thirdly, he established an important alliance with the Latins, by which Rome and the cities of Latium became the members of one great league. By his new constitution Servius incurred the hostility of the patricians, who conspired with L. Tarquinius to deprive him of his life and of his throne. His death was the subject of a legend, which ran as follows. Servius, soon after his succession, gave his 2 daughters in marriage to the 2 sons of Tarquinius Priscus. L. Tarquinius the elder was married to a quiet and gentle wife; Aruns, the younger,

to an aspiring and ambitious woman. The character of the two brothers was the very opposite of the wives who had fallen to their lot; for Lucius was proud and haughty, but Aruns unambitious and quiet. The wife of Aruns, fearing that her husband would tamely resign the sovereignty to his elder brother, resolved to destroy both her father and her husband. She persuaded Lucius to murder his wife, and she murdered her own husband; and the survivors straightway married. Tullia now urged her husband to murder her father; and it was said that their design was hastened by the belief that Servius entertained the thought of laying down his kingly power, and establishing the consular form of government. The patricians were equally alarmed at this scheme. Their mutual hatred and fears united them closely together; and when the conspiracy was ripe, Tarquinius entered the forum arrayed in the kingly robes, seated himself in the royal chair in the senate-house, and ordered the senators to be summoned to him as their king. At the first news of the commotion, Servius hastened to the senate-house, and, standing at the door-way, ordered Tarquinius to come down from the throne. Tarquinius sprang forward, seized the old man, and flung him down the stone steps. Covered with blood, the king was hastening home; but, before he reached it, he was overtaken by the servants of Tarquinius, and murdered. Tullia drove to the senate-house, and greeted her husband as king; but her transports of joy struck even him with horror. He bade her go home; and as she was returning, her charioteer pulled up, and pointed out the corpse of her father lying in his blood across the road. She commanded him to drive on; the blood of her father spirted over the carriage and on her dress; and from that day forward the street bore the name of the Vicus Sceleratus, or Wicked Street. The body lay unburied, for Tarquinius said scoffingly, "Romulus too went without burial;" and this impious mockery is said to have given rise to his surname of Superbus. Servius had reigned 44 years. His memory was long cherished by the plebeians.

Tullius Tiro. [TIRO.]

Tullum (Toul), the capital of the Leuci, a people in the S. E. of Gallia Belgica between the Matrona and Mosella.

Tullus Hostilius, 3rd king of Rome, is said to have been the grandson of Hostus Hostilius, who fell in battle against the Sabines in the reign of Romulus. His legend ran as follows:— Tullus Hostilius departed from the peaceful ways of Numa, and aspired to the martial renown of Romulus. He made Alba acknowledge Rome's supremacy in the war wherein the 3 Roman brothers, the Horatii, fought with the 3 Alban brothers, the Curiatii, at the Fossa Cluilia. Next he warred with Fidenae and with Veii, and being straitly pressed by their joint hosts, he vowed temples to Pallor and Pavor—Paleness and Panic. And after the fight was won, he tore asunder with chariots Mettius Fufetius, the king or dictator of Alba, because he had desired to betray Rome; and he utterly destroyed Alba, sparing only the temples of the gods, and bringing the Alban people to Rome, where he gave them the Caelian hill to dwell on. Then he turned himself to war with the Sabines; and being again straitened in fight in a wood called the Wicked Wood, he vowed a yearly festival to Saturn and Ops, and to double the number of the Salii, or priests of Mamers. And when, by their help, he had vanquished the Sabines, he performed his vow, and its records were the feasts Saturnalia and Opalia. In his old age, Tullus grew weary of warring; and when a pestilence struck him and his people, and a shower of burning stones fell from heaven on Mt. Alba, and a voice as of the Alban gods came forth from the solitary temple of Jupiter on its summit, he remembered the peaceful and happy days of Numa, and sought to win the favour of the gods, as Numa had done, by prayer and divination. But the gods heeded neither his prayers nor his charms, and when he would inquire of Jupiter Elicius, Jupiter was wroth, and smote Tullus and his whole house with fire. Perhaps the only historical fact embodied in the legend of Tullus is the ruin of Alba.

Tunes or Tunis (Τύνης, Τοὔνις: Τυνησαῖος: Tunis), a strongly fortified city of N. Africa, stood at the bottom of the Carthaginian gulf, 10 miles S. W. of Carthage, at the mouth of the little river Catada. At the time of Augustus it had greatly declined, but it afterwards recovered, and is now the capital of the Regency of Tunis.

Tungri, a German people who crossed the Rhine, and settled in Gaul in the country formerly occupied by the Aduatici and the Eburones. Their chief town was called Tungri or Aduaca Tongrorum (Tongern), on the road from Castellum Morinorum to Colonia Agrippina.

Turdetani, the most numerous people in Hispania Baetica, dwelt in the S. of the province on both banks of the Baetis as far as Lusitania. They were regarded as the most civilised people in all Spain. Their country was called Turdetania.

Turduli, a people in Hispania Baetica, situated to the E. and S. of the Turdetani, with whom they were closely connected. The names, in fact, appear identical.

Turia or Turium (Guadalaviar), a river on the E. coast of Spain, flowing into the sea at Valentia, memorable for the battle fought on its banks between Pompey and Sertorius.

Turiasso (Turiassonensis: Tarrazona), a town of the Celtiberi in Hispania Tarraconensis, on the road from Caesaraugusta to Numantia. It possessed a fountain, the water of which was said to be very excellent for hardening iron.

Turnus (Τύρνος). 1. Son of Daunus and Venilia, and king of the Rutuli at the time of the arrival of Aeneas in Italy. He was a brother of Juturna, and related to Amata, the wife of king Latinus; and he fought against Aeneas, because Latinus had given to the Trojan hero his daughter Lavinia, who had been previously promised to Turnus. He appears in the Aeneid as a brave warrior; but in the end he fell by the hand of Aeneas.—2. A Roman satiric poet, was a native of Aurunca, and lived under Vespasian and Domitian. We possess 30 hexameters, forming a portion of, apparently, a long satiric poem, the subject being an enumeration of the crimes and abominations which characterised the reign of Nero. These lines are ascribed by some modern scholars to Turnus.

Turnus Herdonius. [HERDONIUS.]

Turones, Turoni or Turonii, a people in the interior of Gallia Lugdunensis between the Aulerci, Andes and Pictones. Their chief town was Caesarodunum, subsequently Turoni (Tours) on the Liger (Loire).

Turpilius, Sextus, a Roman dramatist, whose productions belonged to the department of Comoedia Palliata. The titles of 13 or 14 of his plays have been preserved, together with a few fragments. He died, when very old, at Sinuessa in B. C. 101. He stands 7th in the scale of Volcatius Sedigitus. [SEDIGITUS.]

Turpio, L. Ambivius, a very celebrated actor in the time of Terence, in most of whose plays he acted.

Turris Hannibalis (Bourj Salaktah, Ru.), a castle on the coast of Byzacena, between Thapsus and Acholla, belonging to Hannibal, who embarked here when he fled to Antiochus the Great.

Turris Stratonis. [CAESAREA, No. 3.]

Tuscania (Tuscaniensis: Toscanella), a town of Etruria on the river Marta, rarely mentioned by ancient writers, but celebrated in modern times, on account of the great number of Etruscan antiquities which have been discovered in its ancient tombs.

Tusci, Tuscia. [ETRURIA.]

Tusculum (Tusculanus: nr. Frascati, Ru.), an ancient town of Latium, situated about 10 miles S. E. of Rome, on a lofty summit of the mountains, which are called after the town Tusculani Montes, and which are a continuation of Mons Albanus. Tusculum was one of the most strongly fortified places in all Italy, both by nature and by art. It is said to have been founded by Telegonus, the son of Ulysses; and it was always one of the most important of the Latin towns. Its importance in the time of the Roman kings is shown by Tarquinius Superbus giving his daughter in marriage to Octavius Mamilius, the chief of Tusculum. At a later time it became a Roman municipium, and was the birth-place of several distinguished Roman families. Cato the Censor was a native of Tusculum. Its proximity to Rome, its salubrity, and the beauty of its situation made it a favourite residence of the Roman nobles during the summer. Cicero, among others, had a favourite villa at this place, which he frequently mentions under the name of Tusculanum. The site of this villa is not exactly known; some placing it near Grotta Ferrata, on the road from Frascati to the Alban lake; and others near La Rufinella. The ruins of ancient Tusculum are situated on the summit of the mountain about 2 miles above Frascati.

Tuticanus, a Roman poet and a friend of Ovid, who had translated into Latin verse a portion of the Odyssey.

Tutzis (Garshe or Guerfey Hassan, Ru.), a city in the Dodecaschoenus, that is, the part of Aethiopia immediately above Egypt. on the W. bank of the Nile, N. of Pselcis, and S. of Talmis.

Tyana (Τύανα: Τυανεύς: Kis Hisar, Ru.), a city of Asia Minor, stood in the S. of Cappadocia, at the N. foot of M. Taurus, on the high road to the Cilician Gates, 300 stadia from Cybistra, and 400 from Mazaca, in a position of great natural strength, which was improved by fortifications. Under Caracalla it was made a Roman colony. In B. C. 272 it was taken by Aurelian, in the war with Zenobia, to whose territory it then belonged. Valens made it the chief city of Cappadocia Secunda. In its neighbourhood was a great temple of Jupiter, by the side of a lake in a swampy plain; and near the temple was a remarkable effervescing spring called Asmabaeon. Tyana was the native place of Apollonius, the supposed worker of miracles. The S. district of Cappadocia, in which the city stood, was called Tyanītis.

Tychē. [FORTUNA.]

Tychē. [SYRACUSAE.]

Tўdeus (Τυδεύs), son of Oeneus, king of Calydon, and Periboea. He was obliged to leave Calydon in consequence of some murder which he had committed, but which is differently described by the different authors, some saying that he killed his father's brother, Melas, Lycopeus, or Alcathous; others that he slew Thoas or Aphareus, his mother's brother; others that he slew his brother Olenias; and others again that he killed the son of Melas, who had revolted against Oeneus. He fled to Adrastus at Argos, who purified him from the murder, and gave him his daughter Deïpyle in marriage, by whom he became the father of Diomedes, who is hence frequently called **Tydīdes.** He accompanied Adrastus in the expedition against Thebes, where he was wounded by Melanippus, who, however, was slain by him. When Tydeus lay on the ground wounded, Athena appeared to him with a remedy which she had received from Zeus, and which was to make him immortal. This, however, was prevented by a stratagem of Amphiaraus, who hated Tydeus, for he cut off the head of Melanippus and brought it to Tydeus, who divided it and ate the brain, or devoured some of the flesh. Athena, seeing this, shuddered, and left Tydeus to his fate, who consequently died, and was buried by Macon.

Tўlŏs or **Tyros** (Τύλος, Τύρος: *Bahrein*), an island in the Persian Gulf, off the coast of Arabia, celebrated for its pearl fisheries.

Tymbres or **Tembrogius** (*Pursek*), a river of Phrygia, rising in M. Dindymene, and flowing past Cotyaeum and Dorylaeum into the Sangarius. It was the boundary between Phrygia Epictetus and Phrygia Salutaris.

Tymnes (Τύμνης), an epigrammatic poet, whose epigrams were included in the *Garland* of Meleager, but respecting whose exact date we have no further evidence. There are 7 of his epigrams in the Greek Anthology.

Tymphaei (Τυμφαῖοι), a people of Epirus, on the borders of Thessaly, so called from Mt. **Tymphe** (Τύμφη), sometimes, but less correctly, written **Stymphe** (Στύμφη). Their country was called **Tymphaea** (Τυμφαία).

Tymphrestus (Τυμφρηστός: *Elladha*), a mountain in Thessaly, in the country of the Dryopes, in which the river Spercheus rises.

Tyndăreus (Τυνδάρεωs), not **Tyndărus,** which is not found in classical writers, was son of Perieres and Gorgophone, or, according to others, son of Oebalus, by the nymph Batïa or by Gorgophone. Tyndareus and his brother Icarius were expelled by their step-brother Hippocoon and his sons; whereupon Tyndareus fled to Thestius in Aetolia, and assisted him in his wars against his neighbours. In Aetolia Tyndareus married Leda, the daughter of Thestius, and was afterwards restored to Sparta by Hercules. By Leda, Tyndareus became the father of Timandra, Clytaemnestra, and Philonoë. One night Leda was embraced both by Zeus and Tyndareus, and the result was the birth of Pollux and Helena, the children of Zeus, and of Castor and Clytaemnestra, the children of Tyndareus. The patronymic **Tyndăridae** is frequently given to Castor and Pollux, and the female patronymic **Tyndăris** to Helen and Cly-

taemnestra. When Castor and Pollux had been received among the immortals, Tyndareus invited Menelaus to come to Sparta, and surrendered h' kingdom to him.

Tyndăris or **Tyndărĭum** (Τυνδαρίς, Τυνδάριον: Tyndaritānus: *Tindare*), a town on the N. coast of Sicily, with a good harbour, a little W. of Messana, near the promontory of the same name founded by the elder Dionysius, B. C. 396, which became an important place. It was the headquarters of Agrippa, the general of Octavian, in the war against Sex. Pompey. The greater part of the town was subsequently destroyed by an inundation of the sea.

Tўphŏn or **Typhŏeus** (Τυφάων, Τυφωεύς, contracted into Τυφώς), a monster of the primitive world, is described sometimes as a destructive hurricane, and sometimes as a fire-breathing giant. According to Homer, he was concealed in the earth in the country of the Arimi (Εἰν 'Αρίμοις, of which the Latin poets have made *Inarime*), which was lashed by Zeus with flashes of lightning. In Hesiod, Typhaon and Typhoeus are 2 distinct beings. Typhaon is represented as a son of Typhoeus, and a fearful hurricane, who by Echidna became the father of the dog Orthus, Cerberus, the Lernaean hydra, Chimaera, and the Sphynx. Typhoeus, on the other hand, is called the youngest son of Tartarus and Gaea, or of Hera alone, because she was indignant at Zeus having given birth to Athena. He is described as a monster with 100 heads, fearful eyes, and terrible voices; he wanted to acquire the sovereignty of gods and men, but was subdued, after a fearful struggle, by Zeus, with a thunderbolt. He begot the winds, whence he is also called the father of the Harpies; but the beneficent winds Notus, Boreas, Argestes, and Zephyrus, were not his sons. Aeschylus and Pindar describe him as living in a Cilician cave. He is further said to have at one time been engaged in a struggle with all the immortals, and to have been killed by Zeus with a flash of lightning; he was buried in Tartarus under Mount Aetna, the workshop of Hephaestus, which is hence called by the poets *Typhois Aetna.* The later poets frequently connect Typhoeus with Egypt. The gods, it is said, unable to hold out against him, fled to Egypt, where, from fear, they metamorphosed themselves into animals, with the exception of Zeus and Athena.

Tyragĕtae, Tyrigĕtae or **Tyrangetae,** a people in European Sarmatia, probably a branch of the Getae, dwelling E. of the river Tyras.

Tyrannion (Τυραννίων). 1. A Greek grammarian, a native of Amisus in Pontus, was originally called Theophrastus, but received from his instructor the name of Tyrannion on account of his domineering behaviour to his fellow disciples. In B. C. 72 he was taken captive by Lucullus, who carried him to Rome. He was given by Lucullus to Murena, who manumitted him. At Rome Tyrannion occupied himself in teaching. He was also employed in arranging the library of Apellicon, which Sulla brought to Rome. This library contained the writings of Aristotle, upon which Tyrannion bestowed considerable care and attention. Cicero speaks in the highest terms of the learning and ability of Tyrannion. Tyrannion amassed considerable wealth, and died at a very advanced age of a paralytic stroke. — 2. A native of Phoenicia, the son of Artemidorus, and a disciple of the preceding. His original name was Diocles. He was taken captive in the war between Antony and Octavian, and was purchased by Dymas, a freedman of the emperor. By him he was presented to Terentia, the wife of Cicero, who manumitted him. He taught at Rome, and wrote a great number of works, which are all lost.

Tyras (Τύρας, Τύρης: *Dniester*), subsequently called Danastris, a river in European Sarmatia, forming in the lower part of its course the boundary between Dacia and Sarmatia, and falling into the Pontus Euxinus, N. of the Danube. At its mouth there was a town of the same name, probably on the site of the modern *Ackjermann*.

Tyriaeum (Τυριαῖον: *Ilghun*), a city of Lycaonia, described by Xenophon (in the *Anabasis*) as 20 parasangs W. of Iconium. It lay due W. of Laodicea.

Tyro (Τυρώ), daughter of Salmoneus and Alcidice. She was wife of Cretheus, and beloved by the river-god Enipeus in Thessaly, in whose form Poseidon appeared to her, and became by her the father of Pelias and Neleus. By Cretheus she was the mother of Aeson, Pheres, and Amythaon.

Tyrrhēni, Tyrrhēnia. [ETRURIA.]

Tyrrhēnum Mare. [ETRURIA.]

Tyrrhēnus (Τυῤῥηνός or Τυρσηνός), son of the Lydian king Atys and Callithea, and brother of Lydus, is said to have led a Pelasgian colony from Lydia into Italy, into the country of the Umbrians, and to have given to the colonists his name, Tyrrhenians. Others call Tyrrhenus a son of Hercules by Omphale, or of Telephus and Hiera, and a brother of Tarchon. The name Tarchon seems to be only another form of Tyrrhenus.

Tyrrheus, a shepherd of king Latinus. As Ascanius was hunting, he killed a tame stag belonging to Tyrrheus, whereupon the country people took up arms, which was the first conflict in Italy between the natives and the Trojan settlers.

Tyrtaeus (Τυρταῖος or Τύρταιος), son of Archembrotus, of Aphidnae in Attica. According to the older tradition, the Spartans during the 2nd Messenian war were commanded by an oracle to take a leader from among the Athenians, and thus to conquer their enemies, whereupon they chose Tyrtaeus as their leader. Later writers embellish the story, and represent Tyrtaeus as a lame schoolmaster, of low family and reputation, whom the Athenians, when applied to by the Lacedaemonians in accordance with the oracle, purposely sent as the most inefficient leader they could select, being unwilling to assist the Lacedaemonians in extending their dominion in the Peloponnesus, but little thinking that the poetry of Tyrtaeus would achieve that victory which his physical constitution seemed to forbid his aspiring to. Many modern critics reject altogether the account of the Attic origin of Tyrtaeus, and maintain that the extant fragments of his poetry actually furnish evidence of his being a Lacedaemonian. But it is impossible to arrive at any positive decision upon the subject. It is certain, however, that the poems of Tyrtaeus exercised an important influence upon the Spartans, composing their dissensions at home, and animating their courage in the field. In order to appease their civil discords, he composed his celebrated elegy entitled " Legal Order " (Εὐνομία), which appears to have had a wondrous effect in stilling the excited passions of the Spartans. But still more celebrated were the poems by which he animated the courage of the Spartans in their conflict with the Messenians. These poems were of 2 kinds; namely, elegies, containing exhortations to constancy and courage, and descriptions of the glory of fighting bravely for one's native land ; and more spirited compositions, in the anapaestic measure, which were intended as marching songs, to be performed with the music of the flute. He lived to see the success of his efforts in the entire conquest of the Messenians, and their reduction to the condition of Helots. He therefore flourished down to B. C. 668, which was the last year of the 2nd Messenian war. The best separate edition of the fragments of his poems is by Bach, with the remains of the elegiac poets, Callinus and Asius, Lips. 1831.

Tyrus (Τύρος: Aram. Tura: O. T. Tsor: Τύριος, Tyrius: *Sur*, Ru.), one of the greatest and most famous cities of the ancient world, stood on the coast of Phoenice, about 20 miles S. of Sidon. It was a colony of the Sidonians, and is therefore called in Scripture " the daughter of Sidon." It gradually eclipsed the mother city, and came to be the chief place of all Phoenice for wealth, commerce, and colonising activity. In the time of Solomon, we find its king, Hiram, who was also king of Sidon, in close alliance with the Hebrew monarch, whom he assisted in building the temple and his palace, and in commercial enterprises. Respecting its colonies and maritime enterprise, see PHOENICE and CARTHAGO. The Assyrian king Shalmaneser laid siege to Tyre for 5 years, but without success. It was again besieged for 13 years by Nebuchadnezzar, and there is a tradition that he took it, but the matter is not quite certain. At the period when the Greeks began to be well acquainted with the city, its old site had been abandoned, and a new city erected on a small island about half a mile from the shore, and a mile in length, and a little N. of the remains of the former city, which was now called Old Tyre (Παλαίτυρος). With the additional advantage of its insular position, this new city soon rose to a prosperity scarcely less than that of its predecessor ; though, under the Persian kings, it seems to have ranked again below Sidon. [SIDON.] In B. C. 332 the Tyrians refused to open their gates to Alexander, who laid siege to the city for 7 months, and united the island on which it stood to the mainland by a mole constructed chiefly of the ruins of Old Tyre. This mole has ever since formed a permanent connection between the island and the mainland. After its capture and sack by Alexander, Tyre never regained its former consequence, and its commerce was for the most part transferred to Alexandria. It recovered, however, sufficiently to be mentioned as a strong fortress and flourishing port under the early Roman emperors. Septimius Severus made it a Roman colony. It was the see of a bishop, and Jerome calls it the most beautiful city of Phoenicia. It was a place of considerable importance in medieval history, especially as one of the last points held by the Christians on the coast of Syria. The wars of the Crusades completed its ruin, and its site is now occupied by a poor village ; and even its ruins are for the most part covered by the sea. Even the site of Babylon does not present a more striking fulfilment of prophecy.

Tzetzes (Τζέτζης). 1. Joannes, a Greek grammarian of Constantinople, flourished about A. D.

1150. His writings bear evident traces of the extent of his learning, and not less of the inordinate self-conceit with which they had filled him. He wrote a vast number of works, of which several are still extant. Of these the 2 following are the most important: 1. *Iliaca*, which consists properly of 3 poems, collected into one under the titles Τὰ πρὸ Ὁμήρου, τὰ Ὁμήρου, καὶ τὰ μεθ᾽ Ὅμηρον. The whole amounts to 1676 lines, and is written in hexameter metre. It is a very dull composition. Edited by Bekker, Berlin, 1816. 2. *Chiliades*, consisting in its present form of 12,661 lines. This name was given to it by the first editor, who divided it, without reference to the contents, into 13 divisions of 1000 lines, the last being incomplete. Its subject-matter is of the most miscellaneous kind, but embraces chiefly mythological and historical narratives, arranged under separate titles, and without any further connection. The following are a few of them, as they occur: Croesus, Midas, Gyges, Codrus, Alcmaeon, &c. It is written in bad Greek, in that abominable make-believe of a metre called *political verse*. Edited by Kiessling, Lips. 1826. — 2. **Isaac**, brother of the preceding, the author of a valuable commentary on the Cassandra of Lycophron. The commentary is printed in most of the editions of Lycophron.

Tzitzis or **Tzutzis** (Ru. S. of *Deboul*), a city in the N. of the Dodecaschoenus, that is, the part of Aethiopia immediately above Egypt, a little S. of Parembole, and considerably N. of Taphis.

U.

Ubii, a German people, who originally dwelt on the right bank of the Rhine, but were transported across the river by Agrippa in B.C. 37, at their own request, because they wished to escape the hostilities of the Suevi. They took the name of Agrippenses, from their town COLONIA AGRIPPINA.

Ucalegon (Οὐκαλέγων), one of the elders at Troy, whose house was burnt at the destruction of the city.

Ucubis, a town in Hispania Baetica near Corduba.

Ufens (*Uffente*), a river in Latium, flowing from Setia, and falling into the Amasenus.

Uffugum, a town in Bruttium, between Scyllacium and Rhegium.

Ugernum (*Beaucaire*), a town in Gallia Narbonensis, on the road from Nemausus to Aquae Sextiae, where Avitus was proclaimed emperor.

Ulia (*Montemayor*), a Roman municipium in Hispania Baetica, situated upon a hill and upon the road from Gades to Corduba.

Uliarus or **Olarionensis Insula** (*Oleron*), an island off the W. coast of Gaul, in the Aquitanian gulf.

Ulpianus. 1. Domitius Ulpianus, a celebrated jurist, derived his origin from Tyre in Phoenicia, but was probably not a native of Tyre himself. The time of his birth is unknown. The greater part of his juristical works were written during the sole reign of Caracalla, especially the 2 great works *Ad Edictum* and the *Libri ad Sabinum*. He was banished or deprived of his functions under Elagabalus, who became emperor 217; but on the accession of Alexander Severus 222, he became the emperor's chief adviser. The emperor conferred on

Ulpian the office of Scriniorum magister, and made him a consiliarius. He also held the office of Praefectus Annonae, and he was likewise made Praefectus Praetorio. Ulpian perished in the reign of Alexander by the hands of the soldiers, who forced their way into the palace at night, and killed him in the presence of the emperor and his mother, 228. His promotion to the office of praefectus praetorio was probably an unpopular measure. A great part of the numerous writings of Ulpian were still extant in the time of Justinian, and a much greater quantity is excerpted from him by the compilers of the Digest than from any other jurist. The number of excerpts from Ulpian is said to be 2462; and many of the excerpts are of great length, and altogether they form about one-third of the whole body of the Digest. The excerpts from Paulus and Ulpian together make about one half of the Digest. Ulpian's style is perspicuous, and presents fewer difficulties than that of many of the Roman jurists who are excerpted in the Digest. The great legal knowledge, the good sense, and the industry of Ulpian place him among the first of the Roman jurists; and he has exercised a great influence on the jurisprudence of modern Europe, through the copious extracts from his writings which have been preserved by the compilers of Justinian's Digest. We possess a fragment of a work under the title of *Domitii Ulpiani Fragmenta*; it consists of 29 titles, and is a valuable source for the history of the Roman law. The best editions are by Hugo, Berlin, 1834, and by Böcking, Bonn, 1836.—2. Of Antioch, a sophist, lived in the time of Constantine the Great, and wrote several rhetorical works. The name of Ulpianus is prefixed to extant Commentaries in Greek, on 18 of the orations of Demosthenes; and it is usually stated that they were written by Ulpianus of Antioch. But the Commentaries have evidently received numerous additions and interpolations from some grammarian of a very late period. They are printed in several editions of the Attic orators.

Ulpius Trajanus. [TRAJANUS.]

Ultor, "the avenger," a surname of Mars, to whom Augustus built a temple at Rome in the forum, after taking vengeance upon the murderers of his great-uncle, Julius Caesar.

Ulubrae (Ulubranus, Ulubrensis), a small town in Latium, of uncertain site, but in the neighbourhood of the Pontine Marshes.

Ulysses, Ulyxes, or **Ulixes,** called **Odysseus** (Ὀδυσσεύς) by the Greeks, one of the principal Greek heroes in the Trojan war. According to the Homeric account, he was a son of Laërtes and Anticlea, the daughter of Autolycus, and was married to Penelope, the daughter of Icarius, by whom he became the father of Telemachus. But according to a later tradition he was a son of Sisyphus and Anticlea, who, being with child by Sisyphus, was married to Laërtes, and thus gave birth to him either after her arrival in Ithaca, or on her way thither. Later traditions further state that besides Telemachus, Ulysses became by Penelope the father of Arcesilaus or Ptoliporthus; and, by Circe, the father of Agrius, Latinus, Telegonus, and Cassiphone; by Calypso of Nausithous and Nausinous or Auson, Telegonus, and Teledamus; and lastly, by Evippe of Leontophron, Doryclus or Euryalus. The name Odysseus is said to signify *the angry*. The story of Ulysses ran as follows:— When a young man, Ulysses went to see his grandfather Autolycus near Mt. Parnassus. There, while engaged in the chase, he was wounded by a boar in his knee, by the scar of which he was subsequently recognised by Euryclia. Even at that age he was distinguished for courage, for knowledge of navigation, for eloquence and for skill as a negotiator; and, on one occasion, when the Messenians had carried off some sheep from Ithaca, Laërtes sent him to Messene to demand reparation. He there met with Iphitus, who was seeking the horses stolen from him, and who gave him the famous bow of Eurytus. This bow Ulysses used only in Ithaca, regarding it as too great a treasure to be employed in the field, and it was so strong that none of the suitors was able to handle it. According to some accounts he went to Sparta as one of the suitors of Helen; and he is said to have advised Tyndareus to make the suitors swear, that they would defend the chosen bridegroom against any one who should insult him on Helen's account. Tyndareus, to show him his gratitude, persuaded his brother Icarius to give Penelope in marriage to Ulysses; or, according to others, Ulysses gained her by conquering his competitors in the footrace. Homer, however, mentions nothing of all this, and states that Agamemnon, who visited Ulysses in Ithaca, prevailed upon him only with great difficulty to join the Greeks in their expedition against Troy. Other traditions relate that he was visited by Menelaus and Agamemnon, and that Palamedes more especially induced him to join the Greeks. When Palamedes came to Ithaca, Ulysses pretended to be mad: he yoked an ass and ox to a plough, and began to sow salt. Palamedes, to try him, placed the infant Telemachus before the plough, whereupon the father could not continue to play his part. He stopped the plough, and was obliged to undertake the fulfilment of the promise he had made when he was one of the suitors of Helen. This occurrence is said to have been the cause of his hatred of Palamedes. Being now himself gained for the undertaking, he contrived to discover Achilles, who was concealed among the daughters of king Lycomedes. [ACHILLES.] Before, however, the Greeks sailed from home, Ulysses in conjunction with Menelaus went to Troy for the purpose of inducing the Trojans to restore Helen and her treasures. When the Greeks were assembled at Aulis, Ulysses joined them with 12 ships and men from Cephallene, Ithaca, Neriton, Crocylia, Zacynthus, Samos, and the coast of Epirus. During the siege of Troy he distinguished himself as a valiant and undaunted warrior, but more particularly as a cunning spy, and a prudent and eloquent negotiator. After the death of Achilles, Ulysses contended for his armour with the Telamonian Ajax, and gained the prize. He is said by some to have devised the stratagem of the wooden horse, and he was one of the heroes concealed within it. He is also said to have taken part in carrying off the palladium. — But the most celebrated part of his story consists of his adventures after the destruction of Troy, which form the subject of the Homeric poem called after him, the *Odyssey*. After the capture of Troy he set out on his voyage home, but was overtaken by a storm and thrown upon the coast of Ismarus, a 'town of the Cicones, in Thrace, N. of the island of Lemnos. He plundered the town, but several of his men were cut off by the Cicones. From thence he was driven by a N. wind towards Malea and to the Lotophagi on the

coast of Libya. Some of his companions were so much delighted with the taste of the lotus that they wanted to remain in the country, but Ulysses compelled them to embark again, and continued his voyage. In one day he reached the goat-island, situated N. of the country of the Lotophagi. He there left behind 11 ships, and with one he sailed to the neighbouring island of the Cyclopes (the western coast of Sicily), where with 12 companions he entered the cave of the Cyclops Polyphemus, a son of Poseidon and Thoosa. This giant devoured one after another 6 of the companions of Ulysses, and kept the unfortunate Ulysses and the 6 others as prisoners in his cave. In order to save himself Ulysses contrived to make the monster drunk with wine, and then with a burning pole deprived him of his one eye. He now succeeded in making his escape with his friends, by concealing himself and them under the bodies of the sheep which the Cyclops let out of his cave. In this way Ulysses reached his ship. The Cyclops implored his father Poseidon to take vengeance upon Ulysses, and henceforth the god of the sea pursued the wandering king with implacable enmity. Ulysses next arrived at the island of Aeolus; and the god on his departure gave him a bag of winds, which were to carry him home; but the companions of Ulysses opened the bag, and the winds escaped, whereupon the ships were driven back to the island of Aeolus, who indignantly refused all further assistance. After a voyage of 6 days, Ulysses arrived at Telepylos, the city of Lamus, in which Antiphates ruled over the Laestrygones, a sort of cannibals. This place must probably be sought somewhere in the N. of Sicily. Ulysses escaped from them with only one ship; and his fate now carried him to a western island, Aeaea, inhabited by the sorceress Circe. Part of his people were sent to explore the island, but they were changed by Circe into swine. Eurylochus alone escaped, and brought the sad news to Ulysses, who, when he was hastening to the assistance of his friends, was instructed by Hermes by what means he could resist the magic powers of Circe. He succeeded in liberating his companions, who were again changed into men, and were most hospitably treated by the sorceress. When at length Ulysses begged for leave to depart, Circe desired him to descend into Hades and to consult the seer Tiresias. He now sailed W right across the river Oceanus, and having landed on the other side in the country of the Cimmerians, where Helios does not shine, he entered Hades, and consulted Tiresias about the manner in which he might reach his native island. Tiresias informed him of the danger and difficulties arising from the anger of Poseidon, but gave him hope that all would yet turn out well, if Ulysses and his companions would leave the herds of Helios in Thrinacia uninjured. Ulysses now returned to Aeaea, where Circe again treated the strangers kindly, told them of the dangers that yet awaited them, and of the means of escaping. The wind which she sent with them carried them to the island of the Sirens, somewhere near the W. coast of Italy. The Sirens sat on the shore, and with their sweet voices attracted all that passed by, and then destroyed them. Ulysses, in order to escape the danger, filled the ears of his companions with wax, and fastened himself to the mast of his ship, until he was out of the reach of the Sirens' song. His ship next sailed between Scylla and Charybdis, two rocks between Thrinacia and Italy. As the ship passed between them, Scylla, the monster inhabiting the rock of the same name, carried off and devoured 6 of the companions of Ulysses. From thence he came to Thrinacia, the island of Helios, who there kept his sacred herds of oxen. Mindful of the advice of Tiresias and Circe, Ulysses wanted to sail past, but his companions compelled him to land. He made them swear not to touch any of the cattle; but as they were detained in the island by storms, and were hungry, they killed the finest of the oxen while Ulysses was asleep. After some days the storm abated, and they sailed away, but soon another storm came on, and their ship was destroyed by Zeus with a flash of lightning. All were drowned with the exception of Ulysses, who saved himself by means of the mast and planks, and after 10 days reached the island of Ogygia, inhabited by the nymph Calypso. She received him with kindness, and desired him to marry her, promising immortality and eternal youth, if he would consent, and forget Ithaca. But he could not overcome his longing after his own home. Athena, who had always protected Ulysses, induced Zeus to promise that her favourite hero, notwithstanding the anger of Poseidon, should one day return to his native island, and take vengeance on the suitors of Penelope. Hermes carried to Calypso the command of Zeus to dismiss Ulysses. The nymph obeyed, and taught him how to built a raft, on which, after remaining 8 years with her, he left the island. In 18 days he came in sight of Scheria, the island of the Phaeacians, when Poseidon sent a storm, which cast him off the raft. By the assistance of Leucothea and Athena he reached Scheria by dint of swimming. The exhausted hero slept on the shore, until he was awoke by the voices of maidens. He found Nausicaa, the daughter of king Alcinous and Arete, who conducted the hero to her father's court. He was there honoured with feasts and contests, and the minstrel Demodocus sang of the fall of Troy, which moved Ulysses to tears, and being questioned about the cause of his emotion, he related his whole history. At length he was sent home in a ship. One night as he had fallen asleep in his ship, it reached the coast of Ithaca; the Phaeacians who had accompanied him carried him on shore, and left him. He had now been away from Ithaca for 20 years, and when he awoke he did not recognise his native land, for Athena, that he might not be recognised, had enveloped him in a cloud. As he was lamenting his fate the goddess informed him where he was, and advised him how to take vengeance upon the enemies of his house. During his absence his father Laërtes, bowed down by grief and old age, had withdrawn into the country, his mother Anticlēa had died of sorrow, his son Telemachus had grown up to manhood, and his wife Penelope had rejected all the offers that had been made to her by the importunate suitors from the neighbouring islands. During the last few years more than a hundred nobles of Ithaca, Same, Dulichium, and Zacynthus had been suing for the hand of Penelope, and in their visits to her house had treated all that it contained as if it had been their own. That he might be able to take vengeance upon them, it was necessary that he should not be recognised. Athena accordingly metamorphosed him into an unsightly beggar, and he was kindly received by Eumaeus, the swine-

herd, a faithful servant of his house. While staying with Eumaeus, his son Telemachus returned from Sparta and Pylos, whither he had gone to obtain information concerning his father. Ulysses made himself known to him, and with him deliberated upon the plan of revenge. In the disguise of a beggar he accompanied Telemachus and Eumaeus to the town. The plan of revenge was now carried into effect. Penelope, with great difficulty, was made to promise her hand to him who should conquer the others in shooting with the bow of Ulysses. As none of the suitors was able to draw this bow, Ulysses himself took it up and then began to attack the suitors. He was supported by Athena and his son, and all fell by his hands. Ulysses now made himself known to Penelope, and went to see his aged father. In the meantime the report of the death of the suitors was spread abroad, and their relatives rose in arms against Ulysses; but Athena, who assumed the appearance of Mentor, brought about a reconciliation between the people and the king. It has already been remarked that in the Homeric poems Ulysses is represented as a prudent, cunning, inventive, and eloquent man, but at the same time as a brave, bold, and persevering warrior, whose courage no misfortune or calamity could subdue, but later poets describe him as a cowardly, deceitful, and intriguing personage. Respecting the last period of his life the Homeric poems give us no information, except the prophecy of Tiresias, who promised him a painless death in a happy old age; but later writers give us different accounts. According to one, Telegonus, the son of Ulysses by Circe, was sent out by his mother to seek his father. A storm cast him upon Ithaca, which he began to plunder in order to obtain provisions. Ulysses and Telemachus attacked him, but he slew Ulysses, and his body was afterwards carried to Aeaea. According to some, Circe recalled Ulysses to life again, or on his arrival in Tyrrhenia he was burnt on Mt. Perge. In works of art Ulysses is commonly represented as a sailor, wearing a semi-oval cap.

Umbria, called by the Greeks **Ombrĭca** ($\dot\eta$ 'Ομβρικ$\dot\eta$), a district of Italy, bounded on the N. by Gallia Cisalpina, from which it was separated by the river Rubicon; on the E. by the Adriatic sea; on the S. by Picenum, from which it was separated by the river Aesis, and by the land of the Sabines, from which it was separated by the river Nar; and on the W. by Etruria, from which it was separated by the Tiber. Under Augustus it formed the 6th Regio of Italy. The Apennines ran through the W. part of the country, but it contained many fertile plains on the coast. Its inhabitants, the **Umbri** (sing. Umber), called by the Greeks **Umbrĭci** ('Ομβρικοί), were one of the most ancient peoples of Italy, and were connected with the Opicans, Sabines, and those other tribes whose languages were akin to the Greek. The Umbri were at a very early period the most powerful people in central Italy, and extended across the peninsula from the Adriatic to the Tyrrhene seas. Thus they inhabited the country afterwards called Etruria; and we are expressly told that Crotona, Perusia, Clusium, and other Etruscan cities, were built by the Umbrians. They were afterwards deprived of their possessions W. of the Tiber by the Etruscans, and confined to the country between this river and the Adriatic. Their territories were still further diminished by the Senones a Gallic

Notus.

Boreas.

Horologium of Andronicus Cyrrhestes at Athens, commonly called the Temple of the Winds, from the Figures of the Winds upon its faces. Page 809.

Lips.

Zephyrus.

[To face p. 800.

Ulia in Spain. Page 794.

Venusia in Apulia. Page 810.

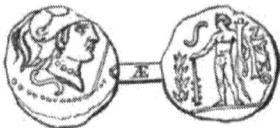

Uxentum in Calabria. Page 801.

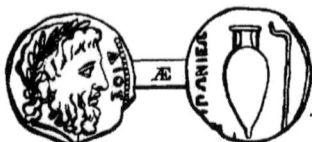

Vibo or Hipponium. Page 814.

Valentia in Spain. Page 802.

Zacynthus. Page 827.

Velia in Lucania. Page 80F.

Zeugma in Syria. Page 830.

View of the Fort Euryalus at Syracuse. Page 736, col. 1.

To face p. 801.]

people, who took possession of the whole country on the coast, from Ariminum to the Aesis. The Umbri were subdued by the Romans, B. c. 307 ; and after the conquest of the Senones by the Romans in 283, they again obtained possession of the country on the coast of the Adriatic. This district, however, continued to be called *Ager Gallicus* down to a late period. The chief towns of Umbria were ARIMINUM, FANUM FORTUNAE, MEVANIA, TUDER, NARNIA, and SPOLETIUM.

Umbro (*Ombrone*), one of the largest rivers in Etruria, falling into the Tyrrhene sea, near a town of the same name.

Ummĭdĭus Quadrātus. [QUADRATUS.]

Unelli, a people on the N. coast of Gaul, on a promontory opposite Britain (the modern *Cotantin*), belonging to the Armorici.

Upis (*Οὖπις*). 1. A surname of Artemis, as the goddess assisting women in child-birth. — 2. The name of a mythical being, who is said to have reared Artemis, and who is mentioned by Virgil as one of the nymphs in her train. The masculine Upis is mentioned by Cicero as the father of Artemis.

Ur. [EDESSA.]

Urānĭa (*Οὐρανία*). 1. One of the Muses, a daughter of Zeus by Mnemosyne. The ancient bard Linus is called her son by Apollo, and Hymenaeus also is said to have been a son of Urania. She was regarded, as her name indicates, as the Muse of Astronomy, and was represented with a celestial globe, to which she points with a small staff. — 2. Daughter of Oceanus and Tethys, who also occurs as a nymph in the train of Persephone. — 3. A surname of Aphrodite, describing her as " the heavenly," or spiritual, to distinguish her from Aphrodite Pandemos. Plato represents her as a daughter of Uranus, begotten without a mother. Wine was not used in the libations offered to her.

Urānus (*Οὐρανός*) or **Heaven,** sometimes called a son, and sometimes the husband of Gaea (Earth). By Gaea Uranus became the father of Oceanus, Coeus, Crius, Hyperion, Iapetus, Thia, Rhia, Themis, Mnemosyne, Phoebe, Tethys, Cronos ; of the Cyclopes, — Brontes, Steropes, Arges ; and of the Hecatoncheires — Cottus, Briareus, and Gyes. According to Cicero, Uranus also was the father of Mercury by Dia, and of Venus by Hemera. Uranus hated his children, and immediately after their birth he confined them in Tartarus, in consequence of which he was unmanned and dethroned by Cronos at the instigation of Gaea. Out of the drops of his blood sprang the Gigantes, the Melian nymphs, and according to some, Silenus, and from the foam gathering around his limbs in the sea sprang Aphrodite.

Urbĭgénus Pagus. [HELVETII.]

Urbīnum (Urbinas, -atis). 1. **Hortense** (*Urbeno*), a town in Umbria and a municipium, situated on a steep round rock. — 2. **Metaurense** (*Urbania*), a town in Umbria on the river Metaurus, and not far from its source.

Urbs Salvia. [POLLENTIA, No. 2.]

Urci, a town of the Bastetani in Hispania Tarraconensis, on the coast, and on the road from Castulo to Malaca.

Urcinĭum (*Orcine*), a town on the W. coast of Corsica.

Urgo or **Gorgon** (*Gorgona*), an island off the coast of Etruria, N. of Ilva.

Urĭa (Urias : *Oria*), called **Hyria** (*Ὑρίη*) by Herodotus, a town in Calabria on the road from Brundisium to Tarentum, was the ancient capital of Iapygia, and is said to have been founded by the Cretans under Minos.

Urĭum, a small town in Apulia, from which the Sinus Urias took its name, being the bay on the N. side of Mt. Garganus opposite the Diomedean islands.

Urseĭus Ferox. [FEROX.]

Ursus, a contemporary of Domitian, whom he dissuaded from killing his wife Domitia. Statius addressed to him a poem of consolation on the death of a favourite slave (*Silv.* ii. 6), and he also mentions him in the Preface to the 2d book of his *Silvae.*

Uscāna, a large town in Illyria, on a tributary of the Aous and in the district Penestiana.

Usĭpĕtes or **Usipĭi,** a German people, who, being driven out of their abodes by the Suevi, crossed the Rhine and penetrated into Gaul ; but they were defeated by Caesar, and compelled to recross the river. They were now received by the Sigambri, and allowed to dwell on the N. bank of the Lippe ; but we afterwards find them S. of the Lippe ; and at a still later time they become lost under the general name of Alemanni.

Ustĭca, a valley near the Sabine villa of Horace.

Utĭca (*ἡ Ἰτυκή* or *Οὐτίκη* : *Ἰτυκαῖος*, Uticensis : *Bou-Shater*, Ru.), the greatest city of ancient Africa, after Carthage, was a Phoenician colony, older (and, if the chronologers are to be trusted, much older) than Carthage. Like others of the very ancient Phoenician colonies in the territory of Carthage, Utica maintained a comparative independence, even during the height of the Punic power, and was rather the ally of Carthage than her subject. It stood on the shore of the N. part of the Carthaginian Gulf, a little W. of the mouth of the Bagradas, and 27 Roman miles N. W. of Carthage ; but its site is now inland, in consequence of the changes effected by the Bagradas in the coast-line. [BAGRADAS.] In the 3d Punic War, Utica took part with the Romans against Carthage, and was rewarded with the greatest part of the Carthaginian territory. It afterwards became renowned to all future time as the scene of the last stand made by the Pompeian party against Caesar, and of the glorious, though mistaken, self-sacrifice of the younger Cato. [CATO.]

Utus (*Vid*), a river in Moesia and a tributary of the Danube, falling into the latter river at the town Utus. It is perhaps the same river as the Artanes of Herodotus.

Uxăma (*Osma*), a town of the Arevaci in Hispania Tarraconensis, on the road from Asturica to Caesaraugusta, 50 miles W. of Numantia.

Uxantis (*Ushant*), an island off the N. W. coast of Gaul.

Uxellodūnum, a town of the Cadurci in Gallia Aquitanica, situated on a steep hill, rising out of the plain, at the foot of which a river flowed. It is probably the same as the modern *Capdenac* on the Lot.

Uxentum (Uxentinus : *Ugento*), a town in Calabria, N. W. of the Iapygian promontory.

Uxĭi (*Οὔξιοι*), a warlike people, of predatory habits, who had their strongholds in M. Parachoathras, on the N. border of Persis, in the district called **Uxĭa** (*Οὐξία*), but who also extended over a considerable tract of country in Media.

V.

Vacca, Vaga, or **Vaba** (Οὐάγα, Βάγα : *Beja*), a city of Zeugitana in N. Africa, on the borders of Numidia, on an E. tributary of the river Tusca, a good day's journey S. of Utica. It was a great emporium for the trade between Hippo, Utica, and Carthage, and the interior. It was destroyed by Metellus in the Jugurthine War, but was restored and colonised by the Romans. Its fortifications were renewed by Justinian, who named it Theodorias in honour of his wife.

Vaccaei, a people in the interior of Hispania Tarraconensis, occupying the modern *Toro, Palencia, Burgos,* and *Valladolid,* E. of the Astures, S. of the Cantabri, W. of the Celtiberi, and N. of the Cantabri. Their chief towns were PALLANTIA and INTERCATIA.

Vada. 1. A fortress of the Batavi in Gallia Belgica, E. of Batavodurum. — 2. **Vada Sabbatia** (*Vado*), a town of Liguria on the coast, which was the harbour of Sabbata or Savo. — 3. **Vada Volaterrana** (*Torre di Vado*), a small town on the coast of Etruria, in the territory of Volaterrae.

Vadicassii, a people in Gallia Belgica, near the sources of the Sequana.

Vadimonis Lacus (*Lago di Bassano*), a small lake of Etruria of a circular form, with sulphureous waters, and renowned for its floating islands, a minute description of which is given by the younger Pliny. It is celebrated in history for the defeat of the Etruscans in 2 great battles, first by the dictator Papirius Cursor, in B. C. 309, from the effects of which the Etruscans never recovered ; and again in 283, when the allied forces of the Etruscans and Gauls were routed by the consul Cornelius Dolabella. The lake has so shrunk in dimensions in modern times as to be only a small stagnant pond, almost lost in the tall reeds and bulrushes which grow in it.

Vagedrusa, a small river in Sicily, between Camarina and Gela.

Vagienni, a small people in Liguria, whose chief town was Augusta Vagiennorum. Their site is uncertain, but they perhaps dwelt near *Saluzzo.*

Vahalis. [RHENUS.]

Valens, emperor of the East A. D. 364—378, was born about A. D. 328, and was made emperor by his brother Valentinian. [VALENTINIANUS.] The greater part of Valens' reign is occupied by his wars with the Goths. At first he gained great advantages over the barbarians, and concluded a peace with them in 370, on the condition that they should not cross the Danube. In 376 the Goths were driven out of their country by the Huns, and were allowed by Valens to cross the Danube and settle in Thrace and the country on the borders of the Danube. Dissensions soon arose between the Romans and these dangerous neighbours ; and in 377 the Goths took up arms. Valens collected a powerful army, and marched against the Goths ; but he was defeated by them with immense slaughter, near Hadrianople, on the 9th of August, 378. Valens was never seen after the battle ; some say he died on the field ; and others relate that he was burnt to death in a peasant's house, to which he was carried, and which the barbarians set fire to without knowing who was in it. The reign of Valens is important in the history of the empire on account of the admission of the Goths into the countries S. of the Danube, the commencement of the decline of the Roman power. The furious contests between the rival creeds of the Catholics and the Arians also characterise this reign.

Valens, Aburnus, also called **Aburnius,** one of the jurists who are excerpted in the Digest, belonged to the school of the Sabinians. He flourished under Antoninus Pius.

Valens, Fabius, one of the principal generals of the emperor Vitellius in A. D. 69, marched into Italy through Gaul, and, after forming a junction with the forces of Caecina, defeated Otho in the decisive battle of Bedriacum, which secured for Vitellius the sovereignty of Italy. Vitellius raised Valens and Caecina to the consulship, and he left the whole government in their hands. Valens remained faithful to Vitellius, when Antonius Primus, the general of Vespasian, marched into Italy ; but as he had not sufficient forces to oppose Antonius after the capture of Cremona, he resolved to sail to Gaul and rouse the Gallic provinces to espouse the cause of Vitellius ; but he was taken prisoner at the islands of the Stoechadae (*Hières*), off Massilia, and was shortly afterwards put to death at Urbinum (*Urbino*).

Valentia. 1. (*Valencia*), the chief town of the Edetani on the river Turia, 3 miles from the coast, and on the road from Carthago Nova to Castulo. It was founded by Junius Brutus, who settled here the soldiers of Viriathus ; it was destroyed by Pompey, but it was soon afterwards rebuilt and made a Roman colony. It continued to be an important place down to the latest times. — 2. (*Valence*), a town in Gallia Narbonensis on the Rhone, and a Roman colony. Some writers call it a town of the Cavares, and others a town of the Segellauni. — 3. A town of Sardinia of uncertain site, but which some writers place on the E. coast between Portus Sulpicii and Sorabile. — 4. Or **Valentium,** a town in Apulia, 10 miles from Brundusium. — 5. A province in the N. of Britain, beyond the Roman wall, which existed only for a short time. [BRITANNIA.]

Valentinianus. I, Roman emperor A. D. 364 —375, was the son of Gratianus, and was born A. D. 321, at Cibalis in Pannonia. His first wife was Valeria Severa, by whom he became the father of the emperor Gratianus. He held important military commands under Julian and Jovian ; and on the death of the latter in February, 364, Valentinian was elected emperor by the troops at Nicaea. A few weeks after his elevation Valentinian elected his brother Valens emperor, and assigned to him the East, while he himself undertook the government of the West. Valentinian was a Catholic, though his brother Valens was an Arian ; but he did not persecute either Arians or heathens. He possessed good abilities, prudence, and vigour of character. He had a capacity for military matters, and was a vigilant, impartial, and laborious administrator ; but he sometimes punished with excessive severity. The greater part of Valentinian's reign was occupied by the wars against the Alemanni, and the other barbarians on the Roman frontiers. His operations were attended with success. He not only drove the Alemanni out of Gaul, but on more than one occasion crossed the Rhine, and carried the war into the enemy's country. His usual residence was Treviri (*Trèves*). In 375 he went to Carnuntum on the Danube, in order to repel the Quadi and Sarmatians, who had invaded Pannonia. After an indecisive campaign he took up his winter-quarters at Bregetio. In this place, while giving an audience to the deputies of the Quadi, and speaking with great heat, he fell down in a fit and expired suddenly on the 17th of November.—II., Roman emperor A. D. 375—392, younger son of the preceding, was proclaimed Augustus by the army after his father's death, though he was then only 4 or 5 years of age. His elder brother Gratianus, who had been proclaimed Augustus during the lifetime of their father, assented to the choice of the army, and a division of the West was made between the 2 brothers. Valentinian had Italy, Illyricum, and Africa. Gratian had the Gauls, Spain, and Britain. In 383 Gratian was defeated and slain by Maximus, who left Valentinian a precarious authority out of fear for Theodosius, the emperor of the East; but in 387, Valentinian was expelled from Italy by Maximus, and fled for refuge to Theodosius. In 388, Theodosius defeated Maximus, and restored Valentinian to his authority as emperor of the West. Theodosius returned to Constantinople in 391; and in the following year (392) Valentinian was murdered by the general Arbogastes, who raised Eugenius to the throne. Valentinian perished on the 15th of May, being only a few months above 20 years of age. His funeral oration was pronounced by St. Ambrose.—III., Roman emperor A. D. 425—455, was born 419, and was the son of Constantius III. by Placidia, the sister of Honorius, and the daughter of Theodosius I. He was declared Augustus in 425 by Theodosius II., and was placed over the West, but as he was only 6 years of age the government was intrusted to his mother Placidia. During his long reign the empire was repeatedly exposed to the invasions of the barbarians; and it was only the military abilities of Aëtius which saved the empire from ruin. In 429 the Vandals under Genseric crossed over into Africa, which they conquered, and of which they continued in possession till the reign of Justinian. The Goths likewise established themselves in Gaul; but Aëtius finally made peace with them (439), and with their assistance gained a great victory over Attila and the vast army of the Huns at Chalons in 451. The power and influence of Aëtius excited the jealousy and fears of Valentinian, who murdered his brave and faithful general in 454. In the following year the emperor himself was slain by Petronius Maximus, whose wife he had violated. He was a feeble and contemptible prince, and had all the vices that in a princely station disgrace a man's character.

Vălĕrĭa. 1. Sister of P. Valerius Publicola, advised the Roman matrons to ask Veturia, the mother of Coriolanus, to go to the camp of Coriolanus in order to deprecate his resentment.—2. The last wife of Sulla, was the daughter of M. Valerius Messala, and bore a daughter soon after Sulla's death. —3. **Galĕrĭa Valĕrĭa**, daughter of Diocletian and Prisca, was, upon the reconstruction of the empire in A. D. 292, united to Galerius, one of the new Caesars. After the death of her husband in 311 Valeria rejected the proposals of his successor Maximinus, who in consequence stripped her of her possessions, and banished her along with her mother. After the death of Maximinus, Valeria and her mother were executed by order of Licinius, 315.—4. **Messalina**. [MESSALINA.]

Vălĕrĭa Gens, one of the most ancient patrician houses at Rome. The Valerii were of Sabine origin, and their ancestor Volesus or Volusus is said to have settled at Rome with Titus Tatius. One of the descendants of this Volesus, P. Valerius, afterwards surnamed Publicola, plays a distinguished part in the story of the expulsion of the kings, and was elected consul in the first year of the republic, B. C. 509. From this time forward down to the latest period of the empire, for nearly 1000 years, the name occurs more or less frequently in the Fasti, and it was borne by the emperors Maximinus, Maximianus, Maxentius, Diocletian, Constantius, Constantine the Great, and others. The Valeria gens enjoyed extraordinary honours and privileges at Rome. Their house at the bottom of the Velia was the only one in Rome of which the doors were allowed to open back into the street. In the Circus a conspicuous place was set apart for them, where a small throne was erected, an honour of which there was no other example among the Romans. They were also allowed to bury their dead within the walls. The Valerii in early times were always foremost in advocating the rights of the plebeians, and the laws which they proposed at various times were the great charters of the liberties of the second order. (See *Dict. of Antiq. s. v. Leges Valeriae.*) The Valeria gens was divided into various families under the republic, the most important of which bore the names of CORVUS, FLACCUS, LAEVINUS, MESSALA, PUBLICOLA, and TRIARIUS.

Vălĕrĭa, a province in Pannonia formed by Galerius, and named in honour of his wife. [PANNONIA.]

Vălĕrĭānus. 1. Roman emperor, A. D. 253—260, whose full name was P. LICINIUS VALERIANUS. Valerian was proclaimed emperor by the troops whom he was leading against the usurper Aemilianus. Valerian proclaimed his son Gallienus Augustus, and first carried on war against the Goths, whom he defeated (257). But though the barbarians still threatened the Roman frontiers on the Danube and the Rhine, the conquests of the Persians, who had crossed the Euphrates and stormed Antioch, compelled him to hasten to the East. For a time his measures were both vigorous and successful. Antioch was recovered, and the Persian king Sapor was compelled to fall back behind the Euphrates; but the emperor, flushed by his good fortune, followed too rashly He was surrounded, in the vicinity of Edessa, by the countless horsemen of his active foe; he was entrapped into a conference, taken prisoner (260), and passed the remainder of his life in captivity, subjected to every insult which Oriental cruelty could devise. After death his skin was stuffed and long preserved as a trophy in the chief temple of the nation.—2. Son of the preceding, but not by the same mother as Gallienus. He perished along with Gallienus at Milan in 268. [GALLIENUS.]

Vălĕrĭus. [VALERIA GENS.]

Vălĕrĭus Volūsus Maxĭmus, M'., was a brother of P. Valerius Publicola, and was dictator in B. C. 494, when the dissensions between the burghers and commonalty of Rome *de Nexis* were at the highest. Valerius was popular with the plebs and induced them to enlist for the Sabine and Aequian wars, by promising that when the enemy was repulsed, the condition of the debtors (*nexi*) should be alleviated. He defeated and triumphed over the Sabines; but, unable to fulfil his promise to the commons, resigned his dictatorship. The plebs, seeing that Valerius at least had kept faith with them, escorted him honourably home. As he was advanced in life at the time of his dictatorship, he probably died soon after. — There were several descendants of this Valerius Maximus, but none of them are of sufficient importance to require special mention.

Vălĕrĭus Maxĭmus, is known to us as the compiler of a large collection of historical anecdotes, entitled *De Factis Dictisque Memorabilibus Libri IX.*, arranged under different heads, the sayings and doings of Roman worthies being, moreover, kept distinct in each division from those of foreigners. He lived in the reign of the emperor Tiberius, to whom he dedicated his work. Of his personal history we know nothing, except the solitary circumstance, recorded by himself, that he accompanied Sex. Pompeius into Asia (ii. 6. § 8), the Sextus Pompeius apparently who was consul A. D. 14, at the time when Augustus died. The subjects treated of in the work are of a character so miscellaneous, that it would be impossible, without transcribing the short notices placed at the head of each chapter, to convey a clear idea of the contents. In some books the topics selected for illustration are closely allied to each other, in others no bond of union can be traced. Thus the 1st book is entirely devoted to matters connected with sacred rites; the 2nd book relates chiefly to certain remarkable civil institutions; the 3rd, 4th, 5th, and 6th, to the more prominent social virtues; but in the 7th the chapters *De Strategematis, De Repulsis*, are abruptly followed by those *De Necessitate, De Testamentis Rescissis, De Ratis Testamentis et Insperatis*. In an historical point of view the work is by no means without value, since it preserves a record of many curious events not to be found elsewhere; but from the errors actually detected upon points where we possess more precise information, it is manifest that we must not repose implicit confidence in the statements unless where they are corroborated by collateral testimony. The work of Valerius Maximus became very popular in the later times of the empire and in the middle ages. It was frequently abridged, and we still possess an abridgment of it made by Julius Paris. The best editions of the original work are by Torrenius, Leid. 1726, and by Kappius, Lips. 1782.

Vălĕrĭus Flaccus. [FLACCUS.]

Valgius Rufus, C., a Roman poet, and a contemporary of Virgil and Horace, the latter of whom ranks him along with Varius, Maecenas, and Virgil, among those friends of genius whose approbation far more than compensated for the annoyance caused by the attacks of his detractors.

Vandăli, Vandălii, or Vindălii, a confederacy of German peoples, probably of the great Suevic race, to which the Burgundiones, Gothones, Gepidae, and Rugii belonged. They dwelt originally on the N. coast of Germany, but were afterwards settled N. of the Marcomanni in the Riesengebirge, which are hence called Vandalici Montes. They subsequently appear for a short time in Dacia and Pannonia; but at the beginning of the 5th century (A. D. 409) they traversed Germany and Gaul, and invaded Spain. In this country they subjugated the Alani, and founded a powerful kingdom, the name of which is still preserved in Andalusia

(Vandalusia). In A. D. 429 they crossed over into Africa, under their king Genseric, and conquered all the Roman dominions in that country. Genseric subsequently invaded Italy, and took and plundered Rome in 455. The Vandals continued masters of Africa till 535, when their kingdom was destroyed by Belisarius, and annexed to the Byzantine empire.

Vangĭŏnes, a German people, dwelling along the Rhine, in the neighbourhood of the modern *Worms*.

Varăgri. [VERAGRI.]

Vardŭli, a people in Hispania Tarraconensis, W. of the Vascones, in the modern *Guipuzcoa* and *Alava*.

Vargunteius, a senator and one of Catiline's conspirators, undertook, in conjunction with C. Cornelius, to murder Cicero in B. C. 63, but their plan was frustrated by information conveyed to Cicero through Fulvia. He was afterwards brought to trial, but could find no one to defend him.

Vărĭa (*Varea*), a town of the Berones in Hispania Tarraconensis on the Iberus, which was navigable from this town.

Varĭni, a people of Germany, on the right bank of the Albis, N. of the Langobardi.

Vărĭus. 1. Q. Varius Hybrida, tribune of the plebs, B. C. 90, was a native of Sucro in Spain, and received the surname of Hybrida, because his mother was a Spanish woman. In his tribuneship he carried a *lex de majestate*, in order to punish all those who had assisted or advised the Socii to take up arms against the Roman people. Under this law many distinguished senators were condemned; but in the following year Varius himself was condemned under his own law, and was put to death. — 2. L. Varius Rufus, one of the most distinguished poets of the Augustan age, the companion and friend of Virgil and Horace. By the latter he is placed in the foremost rank among the epic bards, and Quintilian has pronounced that his tragedy of Thyestes might stand a comparison with any production of the Grecian stage. He enjoyed the friendship of Maecenas, and it was to the recommendation of Varius in conjunction with that of Virgil, that Horace was indebted for an introduction to the minister, about B. C. 39. Virgil appointed Plotius Tucca and Varius his literary executors, and they revised the Aeneid. Hence Varius was alive subsequent to B. C. 19, in which year Virgil died. Only the titles of 3 works of Varius have been preserved: 1. *De Morte*. 2. *Panegyricus in Caesarem Octavianum*. 3. The tragedy *Thyestes*. Only a very few fragments of these poems are extant.

Varro, Atacĭnus. [See below, VARRO, No. 3.]

Varro, Cingŏnĭus, a Roman senator under Nero, supported the claims of Nymphidius to the throne on the death of Nero, and was put to death in consequence by Galba, being at the time consul designatus.

Varro, Terentĭus. 1. C., consul B. C. 216 with L. Aemilius Paulus. Varro is said to have been the son of a butcher, to have carried on business himself as a factor in his early years, and to have risen to eminence by pleading the causes of the lower classes in opposition to the opinion of all good men. Notwithstanding the strong opposition of the aristocracy, he was raised to the consulship by the people, who thought that it only needed a man of energy at the head of an overwhelming force to bring the war against Hannibal to a close. His colleague was L. Aemilius Paulus, one of the leaders of the aristocratical party. The 2 consuls were defeated by Hannibal at the memorable battle of Cannae. [HANNIBAL.] The battle was fought by Varro against the advice of Paulus. The Roman army was all but annihilated. Paulus and almost all the officers perished. Varro was one of the few who escaped and reached Venusia in safety, with about 70 horsemen. His conduct after the battle seems to have been deserving of high praise. He proceeded to Canusium, where the remnant of the Roman-army had taken refuge, and there adopted every precaution which the exigencies of the case required. His conduct was appreciated by the senate and the people, and his defeat was forgotten in the services he had lately rendered. On his return to the city all classes went out to meet him, and the senate returned him thanks because he had not despaired of the commonwealth. He continued to be employed in Italy for several successive years in important military commands till nearly the close of the Punic war. — 2. The celebrated writer, whose vast and varied erudition in almost every department of literature, earned for him the title of the "most learned of the Romans." He was born B.C.116, and was trained under the superintendence of L. Aelius Stilo Praeconinus, and he afterwards received instruction from Antiochus, a philosopher of the Academy. Varro held a high naval command in the wars against the pirates and Mithridates, and afterwards served as the legatus of Pompeius in Spain in the civil war, but was compelled to surrender his forces to Caesar. He then passed over into Greece, and shared the fortunes of the Pompeian party till after the battle of Pharsalia; when he sued for and obtained the forgiveness of Caesar, who employed him in superintending the collection and arrangement of the great library designed for public use. For some years after this period Varro remained in literary seclusion, passing his time chiefly at his country seats near Cumae and Tusculum, occupied with study and composition. Upon the formation of the 2nd triumvirate, his name appeared upon the list of the proscribed; but he succeeded in making his escape, and, after having remained for some time concealed, he obtained the protection of Octavian. The remainder of his career was passed in tranquillity, and he continued to labour in his favourite studies, although his magnificent library had been destroyed, a loss to him irreparable. His death took place B.C. 28, when he was in his 89th year. Not only was Varro the most learned of Roman scholars, but he was likewise the most voluminous of Roman authors. We have his own authority for the assertion that he had composed no less than 490 books; but of these only 2 works have come down to us, and one of them in a mutilated form. The following is a list of the principal works, both extant and lost: — 1. De Re Rustica Libri III., still extant, was written when the author was 80 years old, and is the most important of all the treatises upon ancient agriculture now extant, being far superior to the more voluminous production of Columella, with which alone it can be compared. The best editions are in the Scriptores Rei Rusticae veteres Latini by Gesner, 4to. 2 vols. Lips. 1735, and by Schneider, 8vo. 4 vols. Lips. 1794—1797. 2. De Lingua Latina, a grammatical treatise which extended to 24 books; but 6 only (v.—x.) have been

preserved, and these are in a mutilated condition. The remains of this treatise are particularly valuable, in so far as they have been the means of preserving many terms and forms which would otherwise have been altogether lost, and much curious information is here treasured up connected with the ancient usages, both civil and religious, of the Romans. The best editions are by Spengel, 8vo. Berol. 1826, and by Müller, 8vo. Lips. 1833. 3. Sententiae. 165 Sententiae, or pithy sayings, have been published by Devit under the name of Varro, Patav. 1843. It is manifest that these sayings were not strung together by Varro himself, but are scraps gleaned out of various works, probably at different times and by different hands. 4. Antiquitatum Libri, divided into 2 sections. Antiquitates Rerum humanarum, in 25 books, and Antiquitates Rerum divinarum, in 16 books. This was Varro's great work; and upon this chiefly his reputation for profound learning was based; but unfortunately only a few fragments of it have come down to us. With the 2nd section of the work we are, comparatively speaking, familiar, since Augustine drew very largely from this source in his "City of God." 5. Saturae, which were composed, not only in a variety of metres, but contained an admixture of prose also. Varro in these pieces copied to a certain extent the productions of Menippus the Gadarene [MENIPPUS], and hence designated them as Saturae Menippeae s. Cynicae. They appear to have been a series of disquisitions on a vast variety of subjects, frequently, if not uniformly, couched in the shape of dialogue, the object proposed being the inculcation of moral lessons and serious truths in a familiar, playful, and even jocular style. The best edition of the fragments of these Saturae is by Oehler, M. Terentii Varronis Saturarum Menippearum Reliquiae, Quedlingb. 1844. Of the remaining works of Varro we possess little except a mere catalogue of titles. — 3. P., a Latin poet of considerable celebrity, surnamed Atacinus, from the Atax, a river of Gallia Narbonensis his native province, was born B.C. 82. Of his personal history nothing further is known. He is believed to have been the composer of the following works, of which a few inconsiderable fragments only have come down to us; but some of them ought perhaps to be ascribed to his illustrious contemporary M. Terentius Varro:—1. Argonautica, probably a free translation of the well-known poem by Apollonius Rhodius. Upon this piece the fame of Varro chiefly rested. It is referred to by Propertius, by Ovid, and by Statius. 2. Chorographia s. Cosmographia, appears to have been a metrical system of astronomy and geography. 3. Libri Navales, appears to have been a poem upon navigation.

Varus, a cognomen in many Roman gentes, signified a person who had his legs bent inwards, and was opposed to Valgus, which signified a person having his legs turned outward.

Varus, Alfēnus. 1. A Roman jurist, was a pupil of Servius Sulpicius, and the only pupil of Servius from whom there are any excerpts in the Digest. The scholiast on Horace (Sat. i. 3. 130) tells us that the "Alfenus vafer" of Horace was the lawyer, and that he was a native of Cremona, where he carried on the trade of a barber or a botcher of shoes (for there are both readings, sutor and tonsor); that he came to Rome, where he became a pupil of Servius Sulpicius, attained the dignity of

3 F 3

the consulship, and was honoured with a public funeral.—2. A general of Vitellius, in the civil war in A. D. 69, and perhaps a descendant of the jurist.

Vārus, Atīus. 1. P., a zealous partisan of Pompey in the civil war, was stationed in Picenum on the breaking out of the civil war in B. C. 49. He subsequently crossed over into Africa, and took possession of the province, which was then governed by Q. Ligarius. [LIGARIUS.] In consequence of his having been propraetor of Africa a few years previously, Varus was well acquainted with the country and the people, and was thus able to raise 2 legions without much difficulty. Meantime, L. Aelius Tubero, who had received from the senate the province of Africa, arrived to take the command; but Varus would not even allow him to land, and compelled him to sail away. In the course of the same year Varus, assisted by king Juba, defeated Curio, Caesar's legate, who had crossed over from Sicily to Africa. [CURIO.] Varus fought with the other Pompeians in Africa against Caesar in 46; but after the battle of Thapsus he sailed away to Cn. Pompey in Spain. He fell at the battle of Munda, and his head was carried to Caesar.—**2. Q. Atius Varus,** commander of the cavalry under C. Fabius, one of Caesar's legates in Gaul, and probably the same as the Q. Varus, who commanded the cavalry under Domitius, one of Caesar's generals in Greece in the war with Pompey. It is supposed by many modern writers that he is the same person as the Varus to whom Virgil dedicated his 6th eclogue, and whose praises the poet also celebrates in the ninth (ix. 27), from which poems we learn that Varus had obtained renown in war.

Vārus, Quintilīus. 1. Sex., quaestor B. C. 49, belonged to the Pompeian party. He fell into Caesar's hands at the capture of Corfinium, but was dismissed by Caesar. He afterwards fought under Brutus and Cassius against the triumvirs; and after the loss of the battle of Philippi, he fell by the hands of his freedmen, who slew him at his own request.—**2. P.,** son of the preceding, was consul B. C. 13, and was subsequently appointed to the government of Syria, where he acquired enormous wealth. Shortly after his return from Syria he was made governor of Germany (probably about A. D. 7). Drusus had conquered a great part of central Germany as far as the Visurgis (*Weser*); and Varus received orders from Augustus to introduce the Roman jurisdiction into the newly conquered country. The Germans, however, were not prepared to submit thus tamely to the Roman yoke, and found a leader in Arminius, a noble chief of the Cherusci, who had previously served in the Roman army. Arminius organised a general revolt of all the German tribes between the Visurgis and the Weser, but kept his design a profound secret from Varus, with whom he continued to live on the most friendly terms. When he had fully matured his plans, he suddenly attacked Varus, at the head of a countless host of barbarians, as the Roman general was marching with his 3 legions through a pass of the *Saltus Teutoburgiensis*, a range of hills covered with wood, which extends N. of the Lippe from Osnabrück to Paderborn, and is known in the present day by the name of the Teutoburger-wald or Lippische Wald. The battle lasted 3 days, and ended with the entire destruction of the Roman army. Varus put an end to his own life.

His defeat was followed by the loss of all the Roman possessions between the Weser and the Rhine, and the latter river again became the boundary of the Roman dominions. When the news of this defeat reached Rome, the whole city was thrown into consternation; and Augustus, who was both weak and aged, gave way to the most violent grief, tearing his garments and calling upon Varus to give him back his legions. Orders were issued, as if the very empire was in danger; and Tiberius was despatched with a veteran army to the Rhine.

Vārus (Var, or Varo), a river in Gallia Narbonensis, forming the boundary between this province and Italy, rises in Mt. Cema in the Alps, and falls into the Mediterranean Sea, between Antipolis and Nicaea.

Vasātes, a people in Gallia Aquitanica, on the Garumna, whose chief town was Cossium (*Bazas*), on the road from Burdigala to Elusa.

Vascōnes, a powerful people on the N. coast of Hispania Tarraconensis, between the Iberus and the Pyrenees, in the modern *Navarre* and *Guipuzcoa*. Their chief towns were POMPELON and CALAGURRIS. They were a brave people, and fought in battle bare-headed. Under the empire they were regarded as skilful diviners and prophets. Their name is still retained in that of the modern Basques.

Vascōnum Saltus. [PYRENE.]

Vasīo (Vaison), a considerable town of the Vocontii in Gallia Narbonensis.

Vatīa Isauricus, P. Servilīus. 1. Consul in B. C. 79, was sent in the following year as proconsul to Cilicia, in order to clear the seas of the pirates, whose ravages now spread far and wide. He carried on the war with great ability and success, and from his conquest of the Isauri, he obtained the surname of Isauricus. After giving Cilicia the organisation of a Roman province, he entered Rome in triumph in 74. After his return Servilius took a leading part in public affairs. In 70 he was one of the judices at the trial of Verres; in 66 he supported the rogation of Manilius for conferring upon Pompey the command of the war against the pirates; in 63 he was a candidate for the dignity of pontifex maximus, but was defeated by Julius Caesar; in the same year he spoke in the senate in favour of inflicting the last penalty of the law upon the Catilinarian conspirators; in 57 he joined the other nobles in procuring Cicero's recall from banishment; in 56 he opposed the restoration of Ptolemy to his kingdom; and in 55 he was censor with M. Valerius Messala Niger. He took no part in the civil wars, probably on account of his advanced age, and died in 44.—**2.** Praetor 54, belonged originally to the aristocratical party, but espoused Caesar's side on the breaking out of the civil war, and was consul with Caesar in 48. In 46 he governed the province of Asia as proconsul, during which time Cicero wrote to him several letters. After the death of Caesar in 44, he supported Cicero and the rest of the aristocratical party, in opposition to Antony. But he soon changed sides again, became reconciled to Antony, and was made consul a second time in 41.

Vatīnius. 1. P., a political adventurer in the last days of the republic, who is described by Cicero as one of the greatest scamps and villains that ever lived. His personal appearance was unprepossessing; his face and neck were covered with swellings, to which Cicero alludes, calling him the

· *struma civitatis.* Vatinius was quaestor B. C. 63, and tribune of the plebs 59, when he sold his services to Caesar, who was then consul along with Bibulus. It was Vatinius who proposed the bill to the people, by which Caesar received the provinces of Cisalpine Gaul and Illyricum for 5 years. Vatinius continued to take an active part in political affairs. In 56 he appeared as a witness against Milo and Sestius, two of Cicero's friends, in consequence of which the orator made a vehement attack upon the character of Vatinius, in the speech which has come down to us. Vatinius was praetor in 55, and in the following year (54) he was accused by C. Licinius Calvus of having gained the praetorship by bribery. He was defended on this occasion by Cicero, in order to please Caesar, whom Cicero had offended by his former attack upon Vatinius. Soon afterwards Vatinius went to Gaul, where we find him serving in 51. He accompanied Caesar in the civil war, and was made consul suffectus for a few days, at the end of December 47. At the beginning of the following year, he was sent into Illyricum, where he carried on the war with success. After Caesar's death he was compelled to surrender Dyrrhachium and his army to Brutus who had obtained possession of Macedonia, because his troops declared in favour of Brutus. — 2. Of Beneventum, one of the vilest and most hateful creatures of Nero's court, equally deformed in body and in mind. He was originally a shoemaker's apprentice, next earned his living as one of the lowest kinds of *scurras* or buffoons, and finally obtained great power and wealth by accusing the most distinguished men in the state. A certain kind of drinking-cups, having *nasi* or nozzles, bore the name of Vatinius, probably because he brought them into fashion. Juvenal alludes (v. 46.) to a cup of this kind.

Vatrēnus. [PADUS.]

Vectis or **Vecta** (*Isle of Wight*), an island off the S. coast of Britain, with which the Romans became acquainted before their conquest of Britain, by means of the inhabitants of Massilia, who were accustomed to visit this island for the purpose of obtaining tin. It is related by Diodorus that at low water the space between Vectis and the coast of Britain was almost entirely dry, so that the Britons used to bring tin to the island in waggons. It was conquered by Vespasian in the reign of Claudius.

Vedius Pollio. [POLLIO.]

Vegetius, Flavius Renātus, the author of a treatise, *Rei Militaris Instituta*, or *Epitome Rei Militaris*, dedicated to the emperor Valentinian II. The materials were derived, according to the declaration of the writer himself, from Cato the Censor, *De Disciplina Militari*, from Cornelius Celsus, from Frontinus, from Paternus, and from the imperial constitutions of Augustus, Trajan, and Hadrian. The work is divided into 5 books. The 1st treats of the levying and training of recruits, including instructions for the fortification of a camp; the 2nd, of the different classes into which soldiers are divided, and especially of the organisation of the legion; the 3rd, of the operations of an army in the field; the 4th, of the attack and defence of fortresses; the 5th, of marine warfare. The value of this work is much diminished by the fact that the usages of periods the most remote from each other are mixed together into one confused mass, and not unfrequently, we have reason to suspect, are blended with arrangements which never existed, except in

the fancy of the author. The best edition is by Schwebelius, Norimberg, 1767; and by Oudendorp and Bessel, Argent. 1806.

Veiento, Fabricius, was banished in the reign of Nero, A. D. 62, in consequence of his having published several libels. He afterwards returned to Rome, and became in the reign of Domitian one of the most infamous informers and flatterers of that tyrant. He also enjoyed the friendship of Nerva.

Veii (Veiens, -entis, Veientanus: *Isola Farnese*), one of the most ancient and powerful cities of Etruria, situated on the river Cremēra, about 12 miles from Rome. It possessed a strongly fortified citadel, built on a hill rising precipitously from the deep glens which bound it, save at the single point where a narrow ridge unites it to the city. It was one of the 12 cities of the Etruscan Confederation, and apparently the largest of all. As far as we can judge from its present remains, it was about 7 miles in circumference, which agrees with the statement of Dionysius, that it was equal in size to Athens. Its territory (*Ager Veiens*) was extensive, and appears originally to have extended on the S. and E. to the Tiber; on the S.W. to the sea, embracing the salinae or salt-works, at the mouth of the river; and on the W. to the territory of Caere. The Ciminian forest appears to have been its N. W. boundary; on the E. it must have embraced all the district S. of Socrate and E.-ward to the Tiber. The cities of Capena and Fidenae were colonies of Veii. Veii was a powerful city at the time of the foundation of Rome, and the most formidable and dangerous of her neighbours. The Veientes were engaged in almost unceasing hostilities with Rome for more than 3 centuries and a half, and we have records of 14 distinct wars between the 2 peoples. Veii was at length taken by the dictator Camillus, after a siege which is said to have lasted 10 years. The city fell into his hands, according to the common story, by means of a cuniculus or mine, which was carried by Camillus from the Roman camp under the city into the citadel of Veii. So well built and spacious was Veii, that the Romans were anxious, after the destruction of their own city by the Gauls in 390, to remove to Veii, and are said to have been only prevented from carrying their purpose into effect by the eloquence of Camillus. From this time Veii was abandoned; but after the lapse of ages it was colonised afresh by Augustus, and made a Roman municipium. The new colony, however, occupied scarcely a 3rd of the ancient city, and had again sunk into decay in the reign of Hadrian. From this time Veii disappears entirely from history, and on the revival of letters, even its site was long an object of dispute. It is now settled, however, beyond a doubt, that it stood in the neighbourhood of the hamlet of *Isola Farnese*, where several remains of the ancient city have been discovered. Of these the most interesting is its cemetery; but there is now only one tomb remaining open, which was discovered in the winter of 1842-3, and contains many interesting remains of Etruscan art.

Veiovis, a Roman deity, whose name is explained by some to mean "little Jupiter;" while others interpret it "the destructive Jupiter," and identify him with Pluto. Veiovis was probably an Etruscan divinity of a destructive nature, whose fearful lightnings produced deafness in those who were to be struck by them, even before they were actually hurled. His temple at Rome stood between the Capitol and the Tarpeian rock; he was represented as a youthful god armed with arrows.

Vēlabrum. [ROMA, p. 650, b.]

Velauni or **Vellavi**, a people in Gallia Aquitanica, in the modern *Velay*, who were originally subject to the Arverni, but subsequently appear as an independent people.

Vělěda, a prophetic virgin, by birth belonged to the Bructeri, and was regarded as a divine being by most of the nations in central Germany in the reign of Vespasian. She inhabited a lofty tower in the neighbourhood of the river Luppia (Lippe). She encouraged Civilis in his revolt against the Romans, but she was afterwards taken prisoner and carried to Rome.

Vělïa or **Eléa**, also called **Hyěle** ('Ελέα, 'Τέλη, the different forms are owing to the word having originally the Aeolic digamma, which the Romans changed into V: Velienses or Eleātes, pl.: *Castell' a Mare della Brucca*), a Greek town of Lucania on the W. coast between Paestum and Buxentum, was founded by the Phocaeans, who had abandoned their native city to escape from the Persian sovereignty, about B. C. 543. It was situated about 3 miles E. of the river Hales, and possessed a good harbour. It is celebrated as the birthplace of the philosophers Parmenides and Zeno, who founded a school of philosophy usually known under the name of the Eleatic. It possessed a celebrated temple of Demeter (Ceres). Cicero, who resided at Velia at one time, frequently mentions it in his correspondence ; and it appears to have been reckoned a healthy place. (Hor. *Ep.* i. 15.) In the time of Strabo it had ceased to be a town of importance.

Vělīnus (*Velino*), a river in the territory of the Sabines, rising in the central Apennines, and falling into the Nar. This river in the neighbourhood of Reate overflowed its banks and formed several small lakes, the largest of which was called **Lacus Velinus** (*Piedi Lugo*, also *Lago delle Mormore*). In order to carry off these waters, a channel was cut through the rocks by Curius Dentatus, the conqueror of the Sabines, by means of which the waters of the Velinus were carried through a narrow gorge to a spot where they fall from a height of several hundred feet into the river Nar. This fall, which is one of the most celebrated in Europe, is known at the present day by the name of the fall of Terni, or the cascade delle Marmore.

Vělītrae (Veliternus: *Velletri*), an ancient town of the Volscians in Latium, but subsequently belonging to the Latin League. It was conquered by the Romans, and colonised at an early period, but it frequently revolted from Rome. It is chiefly celebrated as the birthplace of the emperor Augustus.

Vēllius Longus, a Latin grammarian, known to us from a treatise, *De Orthographia*, still extant, printed in the " Grammaticae Latinae Auctores Antiqui," of Putschius, 4to. Hanov. 1605. Velius also wrote a commentary on Virgil, which is mentioned by Macrobius.

Vellaunodūnum (*Beaume*), a town of the Senones in Gallia Lugdunensis.

Vellavi. [VELAUNI.]

Velleius Patercŭlus. [PATERCULUS.]

Vellocasses, a people in Gallia Lugdunensis, N.W. of the Parisii, extending along the Sequana as far as the ocean ; their chief town was RATOMAGUS.

Venăfrum (Venafranus: *Venafri*), a town in the N. of Samnium, near the river Vulturnus, and on the confines of Latium, celebrated for the excellence of its olives.

Venědi or **Venědae**, a people in European Sarmatia, dwelling on the Baltic E. of the Vistula. The **Sinus Venědĭcus** (*Gulf of Riga*), and the **Venědĭci Montes**, a range of mountains between Poland and East Prussia, were called after this people.

Věněris Promontorium. [PYRENES PROM.]

Veneris Portus or **Pyrenaei Portus**, a seaport town of the Indigetes in Hispania Tarraconensis, near the Prom. Veneris, and on the frontiers of Gaul.

Venětia. 1. A district in the N. of Italy, was originally included under the general name of Gallia Cisalpina, but was made by Augustus the 10th Regio of Italy. It was bounded on the W. by the river Athesis, which separated it from Gallia Cisalpina ; on the N. by the Carnic Alps ; on the E. by the river Timavus, which separated it from Istria ; and on the S. by the Adriatic Gulf. This country was, and is, very fertile ; and its inhabitants enjoyed great prosperity. The chief productions of the country were excellent wool, a sweet but much prized wine, and race-horses. Dionysius, the tyrant of Syracuse, is said to have kept a stud of race-horses in this country. — Its inhabitants, the **Veněti**, frequently called **Heněti** ('Ενετοί) by the Greeks, were commonly said to be descendants of the Paphlagonian Heneti, whom Antenor led into the country after the Trojan war ; but this tale, like so many others, has evidently arisen from the mere similarity of the name. Others supposed the Veneti to be a branch of the Celtic Veneti in Gaul ; but this supposition is disproved by the express testimony of Polybius, that they spoke a language entirely different from the Celtic: and that they had no connexion with the Celts, may be inferred from the fact that they were always on hostile terms with the Celtic tribes settled in Italy. Herodotus regards them as an Illyrian race ; and all writers are agreed that they did not belong to the original population of Italy. In consequence of their hostility to the Celtic tribes in their neighbourhood, they formed at an early period an alliance with Rome ; and their country was defended by the Romans against their dangerous enemies. On the conquest of the Cisalpine Gauls, the Veneti likewise became included under the Roman dominions ; and they were almost the only people in Italy who became the subjects of Rome without offering any resistance. The Veneti continued to enjoy great prosperity down to the time of the Marcomannic wars, in the reign of the emperor Aurelius ; but from this time their country was frequently devastated by the barbarians who invaded Italy ; and at length, in the 5th century, many of its inhabitants, to escape the ravages of the Huns under Attila, took refuge in the islands off their coast, on which now stands the city of Venice. The chief towns of Venetia in ancient times were, PATAVIUM, ALTINUM, and AQUILEIA. The 2 latter carried on an extensive commerce, and exported, among other things, large quantities of amber, which was brought from the Baltic through the interior of Europe to these cities. — 2. A district in the N. W. of Gallia Lugdunensis, inhabited by the Veneti, who were a brave people, and the best sailors in all Gaul. Off their coast was a group of islands called Insulae Venětïcae.

Venētus Lacus. [Brigantinus Lacus.]

Venīlia, a nymph, daughter of Pilumnus, sister of Amata, wife of king Latinus, and mother of Turnus and Juturna by Daunus.

Vennōnes, a people of Rhaetia, and according to Strabo the most savage of the Rhaetian tribes, inhabiting the Alps near the sources of the Athesis (*Adige*).

Venta. 1. **Belgārum** (*Winchester*), the chief town of the Belgae in Britain. The modern city still contains several Roman remains. — 2. **Icenōrum.** [Iceni.] — 3. **Silūrum** (*Caerwent*), a town of the Silures in Britain, in Monmouthshire.

Venti (ἄνεμοι), the winds. They appear personified, even in the Homeric poems, but at the same time they are conceived as ordinary phenomena of nature. The master and ruler of all the winds is Aeolus, who resides in the island Aeolia [Aeolus] ; but the other gods also, especially Zeus, exercise a power over them. Homer mentions by name Boreas (N. wind), Eurus (E. wind), Notus (S. wind), and Zephyrus (W. wind). When the funeral pile of Patroclus could not be made to burn, Achilles promised to offer sacrifices to the winds ; and Iris accordingly hastened to them, and found them feasting in the palace of Zephyrus in Thrace. Boreas and Zephyrus thereupon straightway crossed the Thracian sea into Asia, to cause the fire to blaze. According to Hesiod, the beneficial winds, Notus, Boreas, Argestes, and Zephyrus, were the sons of Astraeus and Eos; and the destructive ones, such as Typhon, are said to be the sons of Typhoeus. Later, especially philosophical, writers endeavoured to define the winds more accurately, according to their places in the compass. Thus Aristotle, besides the 4 principal winds (Boreas or Aparctias, Eurus, Notus, and Zephyrus), mentions 3, the Meses, Caicias, and Apeliotes, between Boreas and Eurus ; between Eurus and Notus he places the Phoenicias ; between Notus and Zephyrus he has only the Lips; and between Zephyrus and Boreas he places the Argestes (Olympias or Sciron) and the Thrascias. It must further be observed that, according to Aristotle, the Eurus is not due E. but S. E. In the Museum Pio-Clementinum there exists a marble monument upon which the winds are described with their Greek and Latin names, viz. Septentrio (Aparctias), Eurus (Euros or S. E.), and between these 2 Aquilo (Boreas), Vulturnus (Caicias) and Solanus (Apheliotes). Between Eurus and Notus (Notos) there is only one, the Euroauster (Euronotus) ; between Notus and Favonius (Zephyrus) are marked Austro-Africus (Libonotus), and Africus (Lips) ; and between Favonius and Septentrio we find Chrus (Iapyx) and Circius (Thrascius). The winds were represented by poets and artists in different ways ; the latter usually represented them as beings with wings at their heads and shoulders. The most remarkable monument representing the winds is the octagonal tower of Andronicus Cyrrhestes at Athens. Each of the 8 sides of the monument represents one of the 8 principal winds in a flying attitude. A moveable Triton in the centre of the cupola pointed with his staff to the wind blowing at the time. All these 8 figures have wings at their shoulders, all are clothed, and the peculiarities of the winds are indicated by their bodies and various attributes. Black lambs were offered as sacrifices to the destructive winds, and white

ones to favourable or good winds. Boreas had a temple on the river Ilissus in Attica ; and Zephyrus had an altar on the sacred road to Eleusis.

Ventīdius Bassus, P., a celebrated Roman general, was a native of Picenum, and was taken prisoner by Pompeius Strabo in the Social war (B. C. 89), and carried to Rome. When he grew up to man's estate, he got a poor living by undertaking to furnish mules and vehicles for those magistrates who went from Rome to administer a province. In this humble employment he became known to C. Julius Caesar, whom he accompanied into Gaul. In the Civil war he executed Caesar's orders with ability, and became a favourite of his great commander. He obtained the rank of tribune of the plebs, and was made a praetor for B. C. 43. After Caesar's death Ventidius sided with M. Antony in the war of Mutina (43), and in the same year was made consul suffectus. In 39 Antony sent Ventidius into Asia, to oppose Labienus and the Parthians. He conducted this war with distinguished ability and success. In the 1st campaign (39) he defeated the Parthians and Labienus. the latter of whom was slain in his flight after the battle ; and in the 2nd campaign (38) Ventidius gained a still more brilliant victory over the Parthians, who had again invaded Syria. Pacorus, the king's son, fell in this battle. Antony, however, far from being pleased with the success of Ventidius, showed great jealousy of him, and dismissed him from his employment. Yet his services were too great to be overlooked ; and he had a triumph in November, 38. Nothing more is known of him. Ventidius was often cited as an instance of a man who rose from the lowest condition to the highest honours ; a captive became a Roman consul and enjoyed a triumph ; but this was in a period of revolution.

Venus, the goddess of love among the Romans. Before she was identified with the Greek Aphrodite, she was one of the least important divinities in the religion of the Romans ; but still her worship seems to have been established at Rome at an early time. There was a stone chapel with an image of Venus *Murtea* or *Murcia* in the Circus near the spot where the altar of Consus was concealed. This surname was said to be the same as Myrtea (from *myrtus*, a myrtle), and to indicate the fondness of the goddess for the myrtle-tree. In ancient times there is said to have been a myrtle-grove in front of her sanctuary below the Aventine. Another ancient surname of Venus was *Cloacina*, which is said to have been derived from her image having been found in the great sewer (*cloaca*) ; but this tale is nothing but an etymological inference from the name. It is supposed by modern writers that this surname signifies the "Purifier" from *cloare* or *cluere* "to wash" or "purify." The statue of Venus under this surname was set up by T. Tatius in a temple near the forum. A 3rd ancient surname of Venus is Calva, under which she had 2 temples in the neighbourhood of the Capitol. Some believed that one of them had been built by Ancus Marcius, because his wife was in danger of losing her hair ; others thought that it was a monument of a patriotic act of the Roman women, who during the siege of the Gauls cut off their hair and gave it to the men to make strings for their bows ; and others again supposed it to refer to the fancies and caprices of lovers, *calvere* signifying "to tease.'

But it probably refers to the fact that on her wedding day the bride, either actually or symbolically, cut off a lock of hair to sacrifice it to Venus. In these, the most ancient surnames of Venus, we must recognise her primitive character and attributes. — In later times her worship became much more extended, and her identification with the Greek Aphrodite introduced various new attributes. At the beginning of the second Punic war, the worship of Venus Erycina was introduced from Sicily, and a temple was dedicated to her on the Capitol, to which subsequently another was added outside the Colline gate. In the year B.C. 114, a Vestal virgin was killed by lightning ; and as the general moral corruption, especially among the Vestals, was believed to be the cause of this disaster, the Sibylline books, upon being consulted, commanded that a temple should be built to Venus Verticordia (the goddess who turns the hearts of men) on the via Salaria. After the close of the Samnite war, Fabius Gurges founded the worship of Venus Obsequens and Postvorta ; Scipio Africanus the younger, that of Venus Genitrix, in which he was afterwards followed by Caesar, who added that of Venus Victrix. The worship of Venus was promoted by Caesar, who traced his descent from Aeneas, who was supposed to be the son of Mars and Venus. The month of April, as the beginning of spring, was thought to be peculiarly sacred to the goddess of love. Respecting the Greek goddess see APHRODITE.

Vĕnūsĭa (Venusinus : *Venosa*), an ancient town of Apulia, S. of the river Aufidus, and near Mt. Vultur, situated in a romantic country, and memorable as the birthplace of the poet Horace. It was originally a town of the Hirpini in Samnium ; and after its original Sabellian inhabitants had been driven out by the Romans, it was colonised by the latter, B.C. 291, and formed an important military station. Here the remnants of the Roman army took refuge after the fatal battle of Cannae, 216.

Verăgri or Varăgri, a people in Gallia Belgica, on the Pennine Alps, near the confluence of the Dranse and the Rhone.

Verbānus Lacus (*Lago Maggiore*), a lake in Gallia Cisalpina, and the largest lake in all Italy, being about 40 miles in length from N. to S.: its greatest breadth is 8 miles. It is formed by the river Ticinus and other streams descending from the Alps ; and the river Ticinus issues from its southern extremity.

Vercellae (Vercellensis : *Vercelli*), the chief town of the Libici in Gallia Cisalpina, and subsequently a Roman municipium, and a place of considerable importance.

Vercingetŏrix, the celebrated chieftain of the Arverni, who carried on war with great ability against Caesar in B.C. 52. The history of this war occupies the 7th book of Caesar's Commentaries on the Gallic war. Vercingetorix fell into Caesar's hands on the capture of Alesia, was subsequently taken to Rome, where he adorned the triumph of his conqueror in 45, and was afterwards put to death.

Verĕtum (Veretinus : *Alessano*), more anciently called Baris, a town in Calabria, on the road from Leuca to Tarentum, and 600 stadia S. E. of the latter city.

Vergae, a town in the interior of Bruttium, of uncertain site.

Vergellus, a rivulet in Apulia crossing the plain of Cannae, which is said to have been choked by the dead bodies of the Romans slain in the memorable battle against Hannibal.

Vergilĭus. [VIRGILIUS.]

Verginĭus. [VIRGINIUS.]

Verolamĭum or Verulamĭum (*Old Verulam*, near St. Albans), the chief town of the Catuellani in Britain, probably the residence of the king Cassivellannus, which was conquered by Caesar. It was subsequently made a Roman municipium. It was destroyed by the Britons under Boadicea, in their insurrection against the Romans, but was rebuilt and continued to be an important place.

Veromandui, a people in Gallia Belgica, between the Nervii and Suessiones, in the modern *Vermandois*. Their chief town was Augusta Veromanduorum (*St. Quentin*).

Vĕrōna (Veronensis : *Verona*), an important town in Gallia Cisalpina, on the river Athesis, was originally the capital of the Euganei, but subsequently belonged to the Cenomani. At a still later time it was made a Roman colony, with the surname Augusta ; and under the empire it was one of the largest and most flourishing towns in the N. of Italy. It was the birthplace of Catullus ; and, according to some accounts, of the elder Pliny, though others make him a native of Comum. It is celebrated on account of the battle fought in its neighbourhood in the Campi Raudii, by Marius against the Cimbri, and also by the victory of Theodoric the Great over Odoacer. Theodoric took up his residence in this town, whence it is called by the German writers of the middle ages Dietrichs Bern, to distinguish it from Bern in Switzerland. There are still many Roman remains at Verona, and among others an amphitheatre in a good state of preservation.

Verres, C., was quaestor B. c. 82, to Cn. Papirius Carbo, and therefore at that period belonged to the Marian party. He, however, deserted Carbo and went over to Sulla, who sent him to Beneventum, where he was allowed a share of the confiscated estates. Verres next appears as the legate of Cn. Cornelius Dolabella, praetor of Cilicia in 80 —79, and one of the most rapacious of the provincial governors. On the death of the regular quaestor C. Malleolus, Verres became the pro-quaestor of Dolabella. In Verres Dolabella found an active and unscrupulous agent, and, in return, connived at his excesses. But the pro-quaestor proved as faithless to Dolabella as he had been to Carbo, and turned evidence against him on his prosecution by M. Scaurus in 78. Verres was praetor urbanus in 74, and afterwards propraetor in Sicily, where he remained nearly 3 years (73—71). The extortions and exactions of Verres in the island have become notorious through the celebrated orations of Cicero. No class of the inhabitants of Sicily was exempted from his avarice, his cruelty, or his insults. The wealthy had money or works of art to yield up ; the middle classes might be made to pay heavier imposts ; and the exports of the vineyards, the arable land, and the loom, he saddled with heavier burdens. By capricious changes or violent abrogation of their compacts, Verres reduced to beggary both the producers and the farmers of the revenue. His three years' rule desolated the island more effectually than the two recent Servile wars, and than the old struggle between Carthage and Rome for the possession of the island. So diligently did he employ his opportunities, that he boasted of having amassed enough for a life of opulence, even if he were compelled to disgorge two-thirds of his plunder, in stifling inquiry or purchasing an acquittal. As soon as he left Sicily, the inhabitants resolved to bring him to trial. They committed the prosecution to Cicero, who had been Lilybaean quaestor in Sicily in 75, and had promised his good offices to the Sicilians whenever they might demand them. Cicero heartily entered into the cause of the Sicilians, and spared no pains to secure a conviction of the great criminal. Verres was defended by Hortensius, and was supported by the whole power of the aristocracy. At first his partisans attempted to stop the prosecution by bribes, flatteries, and menaces ; but finding this to be impossible, they endeavoured to substitute a sham prosecutor in the place of Cicero. Hortensius therefore offered as prosecutor Q. Caecilius Niger, who had been quaestor to the defendant, had quarrelled with him, and had consequently, it was alleged, the means of exposing officially his abuse of the public money. But the Sicilians rejected Caecilius altogether, not merely as no match for Hortensius, but as foisted into the cause by the defendant or his advocate. By a technical process of the Roman law, called *Divinatio*, the judices, without hearing evidence, determined from the arguments of counsel alone, who should be appointed prosecutor. They decided in Cicero's favour. The oration which Cicero delivered on this occasion, was the *Divinatio in Q. Caecilium*. The pretensions of Caecilius were thus set aside. Yet hope did not yet forsake Verres and his friends. Evidence for the prosecution was to be collected in Sicily itself. Cicero was allowed 110 days for the purpose. Verres once again attempted to set up a sham prosecutor, who undertook to impeach him for his former extortions in Achaia, and to gather the evidence in 108 days. But the new prosecutor never went even so far as Brundisium in quest of evidence, and the design was abandoned. Instead of the 110 days allowed, Cicero, assisted by his cousin Lucius, completed his researches in 50, and returned with a mass of evidence and a crowd of witnesses gathered from all parts of the island. Hortensius now grasped at his last chance of an acquittal, and it was not an unlikely one. Could the impeachment be put off to the next year, Verres was safe. Hortensius himself would then be consul, with Q. Metellus for his colleague, and M. Metellus would be praetor urbanus. For every firm and honest judex whom the upright M. Acilius Glabrio, then praetor urbanus, had named, a partial or venal substitute would be found. Glabrio himself would give place as quaesitor or president of the court to M. Metellus, a partisan, if not a kinsman, of the defendant. It was already the month of July. The games to be exhibited by Cn. Pompey were fixed for the middle of August, and would occupy a fortnight ; the Roman games would immediately succeed them, and thus 40 days intervene between Cicero's charge and the reply of Hortensius, who again, by dexterous adjournments, would delay the proceedings until the games of Victory, and the commencement of the new year. Cicero therefore abandoned all thought of eloquence or display, and merely introducing his case in the first of the Verrine orations, rested all his hopes of success on the weight of testimony alone. Hortensius was quite unprepared with counter-evidence, and after

the first day he abandoned the cause of Verres. Before the nine days occupied in hearing evidence were over, Verres quitted the city in despair, and was condemned in his absence. He retired to Marseilles, retaining so many of his treasures of art as to cause eventually his proscription by M. Antony in 43. Of the 7 Verrine orations of Cicero, 2 only, the *Divinatio* and the *Actio Prima*, were spoken, while the remaining 5 were compiled from the depositions after the verdict. Cicero's own division of the impeachment is the following :

1. Preliminary {
1. In Q. Caecilium or Divinatio.
2. Proemium — Actio Prima — Statement of the Case.
}

These alone were spoken.

2. Orations founded on the Depositions. {
3. Verres's official life to B. C. 73.
4. Jurisdictio Siciliensis.
5. Oratio Frumentaria.
6. —— De Signis.
7. —— De Suppliciis.
}

These were circulated as documents or manifestoes of the cause after the flight of Verres.

Verrūgo, a town of the Volsci in Latium, of uncertain site.

Vertīcordïa. [VENUS.]

Vertumnus or **Vortumnus**, is said to have been an Etruscan divinity whose worship was introduced at Rome by an ancient Vulsinian colony occupying at first the Caelian hill, and afterwards the vicus Tuscus. The name is evidently connected with *verto*, and formed on the analogy of *alumnus* from *alo*, whence it must signify "the god who changes or metamorphoses himself." For this reason the Romans connected Vertumnus with all occurrences to which the verb *verto* applies, such as the change of seasons, purchase and sale, the return of rivers to their proper beds, &c. But in reality the god was connected only with the transformation of plants and their progress from blossom to fruit. Hence the story, that when Vertumnus was in love with Pomona, he assumed all possible forms, until at last he gained his end by metamorphosing himself into a blooming youth. Gardeners accordingly offered to him the first produce of their gardens and garlands of budding flowers. The whole people celebrated a festival to Vertumnus on the 23rd of August, under the name of the *Vortumnalia*, denoting the transition from the beautiful season of autumn to the less agreeable one. He had a temple in the vicus Tuscus, and a statue of him stood in the vicus Jugarius near the altar of Ops. The story of the Etruscan origin seems to be sufficiently refuted by his genuine Roman name, and it is much more probable that the worship of Vertumnus was of Sabine origin. The importance of the worship of Vertumnus at Rome is evident from the fact, that it was attended to by a special flamen (*flamen Vortumnalis*).

Verulae (Verulanus : *Veroli*), a town of the Hernici in Latium, S. E. of Aletrium, and N. of Frusino, subsequently a Roman colony.

Verulamium. [VEROLAMIUM.]

Vērus, L. Aurēlius, the colleague of M. Aurelius in the empire, A. D. 161—169. He was born in 130, and his original name was L. Ceionius Commodus. His father L. Ceionius Commodus was adopted by Hadrian in 136; and on the death of his father in 138, he was, in pursuance of the command of Hadrian, adopted, along with M. Aurelius, by M. Antoninus. On the death of

Antoninus in 161, he succeeded to the empire along with M. Aurelius. The history of his reign is given under AURELIUS. Verus died suddenly at Altinum in the country of Veneti, towards the close of 169. He had been married to Lucilla, the daughter of his colleague.

Vescinus Ager. [SUESSA AURUNCA.]

Vĕsĕvus. [VESUVIUS.]

Vesontĭo (*Besançon*), the chief town of the Sequani in Gallia Belgica, situated on the river Dubis (*Doubs*), which flowed around the town, with the exception of a space of 600 feet, on which stood a mountain, forming the citadel of the town, and connected with the latter by means of walls. Vesontio was an important place under the Romans, and still contains ruins of an aqueduct, a triumphal arch, and other Roman remains.

Vespāsĭānus, T. Flāvĭus Sabīnus, Roman emperor, A. D. 70—79, was born in the Sabine country on the 17th of November, A. D. 9. His father was a man of mean condition, of Reate, in the country of the Sabini. His mother, Vespasia Polla, was the daughter of a praefectus castrorum, and the sister of a Roman senator. She was left a widow with 2 sons, Flavius Sabinus and Vespasian. Vespasian served as tribunus militum in Thrace, and was quaestor in Crete and Cyrene. He was afterwards aedile and praetor. About this time he took to wife Flavia Domitilla, the daughter of a Roman eques, by whom he had 2 sons, both of whom succeeded him. In the reign of Claudius he was sent into Germany as legatus legionis; and in 43 he held the same command in Britain, and reduced the Isle of Wight. He was consul in 51, and proconsul of Africa under Nero. He was at this time very poor, and was accused of getting money by dishonourable means. But he had a great military reputation, and he was liked by the soldiers. Nero afterwards sent him to the East (66), to conduct the war against the Jews. His conduct of the Jewish war had raised his reputation, when the war broke out between Otho and Vitellius after the death of Galba. He was proclaimed emperor at Alexandria on the 1st of July 69, and soon after all through the East. Vespasian came to Rome in the following year (70), leaving his son Titus to continue the war against the Jews. Titus took Jerusalem after a siege of 5 months; and a formidable insurrection of the Batavi, headed by Civilis, was put down about the same period. Vespasian, on his arrival at Rome, worked with great industry to restore order in the city and in the empire. He disbanded some of the mutinous soldiers of Vitellius, and maintained discipline among his own. He co-operated in a friendly manner with the senate in the public administration. The simplicity and frugality of his mode of life formed a striking contrast with the profusion and luxury of some of his predecessors, and his example is said to have done more to reform the morals of Rome than all the laws which had ever been enacted. He lived more like a private person than a man who possessed supreme power; he was affable and easy of access to all persons. The personal anecdotes of such a man are some of the most instructive records of his reign. He was never ashamed of the meanness of his origin, and ridiculed all attempts to make out for him a distinguished genealogy. When Vologeses, the Parthian king, addressed to him a letter commencing in these terms, "Arsaces, king

of kings, to Flavius Vespasianus," the answer began, "Flavius Vespasianus to Arsaces, king of kings." If it be true, as it is recorded, that he was not annoyed at satire or ridicule, he exhibited an elevation of character almost unparalleled in one who filled so exalted a station. He knew the bad character of his son Domitian, and as long as he lived he kept him under proper restraint. The stories that are told of his avarice and of his modes of raising money, if true, detract from the dignity of his character; and it seems that he had a taste for little savings, and for coarse humour. Yet it is admitted that he was liberal in all his expenditure for purposes of public utility. In 71 Titus returned to Rome, and both father and son triumphed together on account of the conquest of the Jews. The reign of Vespasian was marked by few striking events. The most important was the conquest of North Wales and the island of Anglesey by Agricola, who was sent into Britain in 78. In the summer of 79 Vespasian, whose health was failing, went to spend some time at his paternal house in the mountains of the Sabini. By drinking to excess of cold water he damaged his stomach, which was already disordered. But he still attended to business, just as if he had been in perfect health; and on feeling the approach of death, he said that an emperor should die standing; and in fact he did die standing in this attitude, on the 24th of June 79, being 69 years of age.

Vesta, one of the great Roman divinities, identical with the Greek **Hestia,** both in name and import. She was the goddess of the hearth, and therefore inseparably connected with the Penates; for Aeneas was believed to have brought the eternal fire of Vesta from Troy, along with the images of the Penates; and the praetors, consuls, and dictators, before entering upon their official functions, sacrificed, not only to the Penates, but also to Vesta at Lavinium. In the ancient Roman house, the hearth was the central part, and around it all the inmates daily assembled for their common meal (*coena*); every meal thus taken was a fresh bond of union and affection among the members of a family, and at the same time an act of worship of Vesta, combined with a sacrifice to her and the Penates. Every dwelling-house therefore was, in some sense, a temple of Vesta; but a public sanctuary united all the citizens of the state into one large family. This sanctuary stood in the Forum, between the Capitoline and Palatine hills, and not far from the temple of the Penates. The temple was round with a vaulted roof, like the impluvium of private houses, so that there is no reason to regard that form as an imitation of the vault of heaven. The goddess was not represented in her temple by a statue, but the eternal fire burning on her hearth or altar was her living symbol, and was kept up and attended to by the Vestals, her virgin priestesses. As each house, and the city itself, so also the country had its own Vesta, and the latter was worshipped at Lavinium, the metropolis of the Latins, where she was worshipped and received the regular sacrifices at the hands of the highest magistrates. The goddess herself was regarded as chaste and pure like her symbol, the fire; and the Vestals who kept up the sacred fire were likewise pure maidens. Respecting their duties and obligations, see *Dict. of Antiq.* art. *Vestales.* On the 1st of March in every year her sacred fire, and the laurel tree which shaded her hearth, were renewed, and on the 15th of June her temple was cleaned and purified. The dirt was carried into an angiportus behind the temple, which was locked by a gate that no one might enter it. The day on which this took place was a *dies nefastus*, the first half of which was thought to be so inauspicious, that the priestess of Juno was not allowed to comb her hair or to cut her nails, while the second half was very favourable to contracting a marriage or entering upon other important undertakings. A few days before that solemnity, on the 9th of June, the Vestalia was celebrated in honour of the goddess, on which occasion none but women walked to the temple, and that with bare feet. On one of these occasions an altar had been dedicated to Jupiter Pistor. Respecting the Greek goddess see HESTIA.

Vestini, a Sabellian people in central Italy, lying between the Apennines and the Adriatic sea, and separated from Picenum by the river Matrinus, and from the Marrucini by the river Aternus. They are mentioned in connexion with the Marsi, Marrucini, and Peligni; but they subsequently separated from these peoples, and joined the Samnites in their war against Rome. They were conquered by the Romans, B. C. 328, and from this time appear as the allies of Rome. They joined the other allies in the Marsic war, and were conquered by Pompeius Strabo in 89. They made a particular kind of cheese, which was a great favourite with the Romans.

Vestilus. [ALPES.]

Vesuvius, also called **Vesevus, Vesbius,** or **Vesvius**, the celebrated volcanic mountain in Campania, rising out of the plain S. E. of Neapolis. There are no records of any eruption of Vesuvius before the Christian era, but the ancient writers were aware of its volcanic nature from the igneous appearance of its rocks. The slopes of the mountain were extremely fertile, but the top was a rough and sterile plain, on which Spartacus and his gladiators were besieged by a Roman army. In A. D. 63 the volcano gave the first symptoms of agitation in an earthquake, which occasioned considerable damage to several towns in its vicinity; and on the 24th of August A. D. 79, occurred the first great eruption of Vesuvius, which overwhelmed the cities of Stabiae, Herculaneum, and Pompeii. It was in this eruption that the elder Pliny lost his life. [PLINIUS.] There have been numerous eruptions since that time, which have greatly altered the shape of the mountain. Its present height is 3200 feet.

Vetera or **Castra Vetera.** [CASTRA, No. 5.]

Vetranio, commanded the legions in Illyria and Pannonia, at the period (A. D. 350) when Constans was treacherously destroyed, and his throne seized by Magnentius. Vetranio was proclaimed emperor by his troops; but at the end of 10 months he resigned his pretensions in favour of Constantius, by whom he was treated with great kindness, and permitted to retire to Prusa, in Bithynia, where he passed the remaining 6 years of his life.

Vettius, L., a Roman eques, in the pay of Cicero in B. C. 63, to whom he gave some valuable information respecting the Catilinarian conspiracy. He again appears in 59, as an informer. In that year he accused Curio, Cicero, L. Lucullus, and many other distinguished men, of having formed a conspiracy to assassinate Pompey. This conspiracy was a sheer invention for the purpose of injuring Cicero, Curio, and others; but there is difficulty

in determining who were the inventors of it. Cicero regarded it as the work of Caesar, who used the tribune Vatinius as his instrument. At a later period, when Cicero had returned from exile, and feared to provoke the triumvir, he threw the whole blame upon Vatinius. Vettius gave evidence first before the senate and on the next day before the assembly of the people; but his statements were regarded with great suspicion, and on the following morning he was found strangled in prison, to which the senate had sent him. It was given out that he had committed suicide; but the marks of violence were visible on his body, and Cicero at a later time charged Vatinius with the murder.

Vettius Scato. [SCATO.]

Vettones or **Vectones**, a people in the interior of Lusitania, E. of the Lusitani and W. of the Carpetani, extending from the Durius to the Tagus.

Vetulonia, Vetulonium, or **Vetulonii**, an ancient city of Etruria, and one of the 12 cities of the Etruscan confederation. From this city the Romans are said to have borrowed the insignia of their magistrates — the fasces, sella curulis, and toga praetexta — as well as the use of the brazen trumpet in war. After the time of the Roman kings we find no further mention of Vetulonia, except in the catalogues of Pliny and Ptolemy, both of whom place it among the inland colonies of Etruria. Pliny also states that there were hot springs in its neighbourhood not far from the sea, in which fish were found, notwithstanding the warmth of the water. The very site of the ancient city was supposed to have been entirely lost; but it has been discovered within the last few years near a small village called *Magliano*, between the river Osa and the Albegna, and about 8 miles inland. It appears to have had a circuit of at least 4½ miles.

Veturia Gens, anciently called **Vetusia**, patrician and plebeian. The Veturii rarely occur in the later times of the republic, and after B. C. 206, when L. Veturius Philo was consul, their name disappears from the Fasti. The most distinguished families in the gens bore the names CALVINUS, CICURINUS, and PHILO.

Veturius Mamurius is said to have been the armourer who made the 11 ancilia exactly like the one that was sent from heaven in the reign of Numa. His praises formed one of the chief subjects of the songs of the Salii. Even the ancients themselves doubted in the reality of his existence: Varro interpreted his name as equivalent to *vetus memoria*. Some modern writers regard Mamurius Veturius as an Etruscan artist, because he is said to have made a brazen image of the god Vertumnus.

Vetus, Antistius. 1. Proprietor in Further Spain about B. C. 68, under whom Caesar served as quaestor. — 2. C., son of the preceding, quaestor in 61, and tribune of the plebs in 57, when he supported Cicero in opposition to Clodius. In the Civil war he espoused Caesar's party, and we find him in Syria in 45, fighting against Q. Caecilius Bassus. In 34 Vetus carried on war against the Salassi, and in 30 was consul suffectus. He accompanied Augustus to Spain in 25, and on the illness of the emperor continued the war against the Cantabri and Astures, whom he reduced to submission. — 3. C., son of No. 2, consul B. C. 6; and as he lived to see both his sons consuls, he must have been alive at least as late as A. D. 28.

He was a friend of Velleius Paterculus. — 4. L. grandson of No. 3, and consul with the emperor Nero, A. D. 55. In 58 he commanded a Roman army in Germany, and formed the project of connecting the Mosella (*Moselle*) and the Arar (*Saone*) by a canal, and thus forming a communication between the Mediterranean and the Northern Ocean, as troops could be conveyed down the Rhone and the Saone into the Moselle through the canal, and down the Moselle into the Rhine, and so into the Ocean. Vetus put an end to his life in 65, in order to anticipate his sentence of death, which Nero had resolved upon. Vetus was the father-in-law of Rubellius Plautus.

Viădus (*Oder*), a river of Germany, falling into the Baltic.

Vibius Pansa. [PANSA.]

Vibius Sequester. [SEQUESTER.]

Vibo (Vibonensis: *Bivona*), the Roman form of the Greek town **Hippōnium** ('Ιππώνιον: 'Ιππωνιάτης), situated on the S. W. coast of Bruttium, and on a gulf called after it **Sinus Vibonensis** or **Hipponiates.** It is said to have been founded by the Locri Epizephyrii; but it was destroyed by the elder Dionysius, who transplanted its inhabitants to Syracuse. It was afterwards restored; and at a later time it fell into the hands of the Bruttii, together with the other Greek cities on this coast. It was taken from the Bruttii by the Romans, who colonised it B. C. 194, and called it **Vibo Valentia.** Cicero speaks of it as a municipium; and in the time of Augustus it was one of the most flourishing cities in the S. of Italy.

Vibulānus, the name of the most ancient family of the **Fabia Gens.** It was so powerful in the early times of the republic, that 3 brothers of the family held the consulship for 7 years in succession, B. C. 485—479. The last person of the gens who bore this surname was Q. Fabius Vibulanus, consul 412. This Vibulanus assumed the agnomen of Ambustus; and his descendants dropt the name of Vibulanus and took that of Ambustus in its place. In the same way Ambustus was after a time supplanted by that of Maximus. — 1. **Q. Fabius Vibulanus,** consul 485, when he carried on war with success against the Volsci and Aequi, and consul a 2nd time in 482. In 480 he fought under his brother Marcus [No. 31] against the Etruscans, and was killed in battle. — 2. **K.,** brother of the preceding, was quaestor parricidii in 485, and along with his colleague L. Valerius accused Sp. Cassius Viscellinus, who was in consequence condemned by the votes of the populus. He was consul in 484, when he took an active part in opposing the agrarian law, which the tribunes of the people attempted to bring forward. In 481 he was consul a 2nd time, and in 479 a 3rd time, when he espoused the cause of the plebeians, to whom he had become reconciled. As his propositions were rejected with scorn by the patricians, he and his house resolved to quit Rome altogether, where they were regarded as apostates by their own order. They determined to found a settlement on the banks of the Cremera, a small stream that falls into the Tiber a few miles above Rome. According to the legend, the consul Kaeso went before the senate and said, that the Fabii were willing to carry on the war against the Veientes, alone and at their own cost. Their offer was joyfully accepted, for the patricians were glad to see them expose themselves voluntarily to such dangers. On

the day after Kaeso had made the proposal to the senate, 306 Fabii, all patricians of one gens, assembled on the Quirinal at the house of Kaeso, and from thence marched with the consul at their head through the Carmental gate. They proceeded straight to the banks of the Cremera, where they erected a fortress. Here they took up their abode along with their families and clients, and for 2 years continued to devastate the territory of Veii. They were at length destroyed by the Veientes in 477. Ovid says that the Fabii perished on the Ides of February; but all other authorities state that they were destroyed on the day on which the Romans were subsequently conquered by the Gauls at the Allia, that is, on the 15th before the Kalends of Sextilis, June the 18th. The whole Fabia gens perished at the Cremera with the exception of one individual, the son of Marcus, from whom all the later Fabii were descended. — 3. **M.,** brother of the 2 preceding, was consul 483, and a 2nd time 480. In the latter year he gained a great victory over the Etruscans, in which however his colleague the consul Cincinnatus and his brother Q. Fabius were killed. — 4. **Q.,** son of No. 3, is said to have been the only one of the Fabii who survived the destruction of his gens at the Cremera, but he could not have been left behind at Rome on account of his youth, as the legend relates, since he was consul 10 years afterwards. He was consul 467, a 2nd time in 465, and a 3rd time in 459. Fabius was a member of the 2nd decemvirate (450), and went into exile on the deposition of the decemvirs.

Vibullius Rufus, L., a senator and a friend of Pompey, who made him praefectus fabrûm in the Civil war. He was taken prisoner by Caesar at Corfinium (49), and a 2nd time in Spain later in the year. When Caesar landed in Greece in 48, he despatched Vibullius to Pompey with offers of peace. Vibullius made the greatest haste to reach Pompey, in order to give him the earliest intelligence of the arrival of his enemy in Greece.

Vicentia or **Vicetia,** less correctly **Vincentia** (Vicentinus: *Vicenza*), a town in Venetia in the N. of Italy, and a Roman municipium on the river Togisonus.

Victor, Sex. Aurēlius, a Latin writer, flourished in the middle of the 4th century under the emperor Constantius and his successors. He was born of humble parents, but rose to distinction by his zeal in the cultivation of literature. Having attracted the attention of Julian when at Sirmium, he was appointed by that prince governor of one division of Pannonia. At a subsequent period, he was elevated by Theodosius to the high office of city praefect, and he is perhaps the same as the Sex. Aurelius Victor, who was consul along with Valentinian in A. D. 373. The following works, which present in a very compressed form a continuous record of Roman affairs, from the fabulous ages down to the death of the emperor Theodosius, have all been ascribed to this writer; but the evidence upon which the determination of authorship depends, is very slender, and in all probability the 3rd alone belongs to the Sex. Aurelius Victor whom we have noticed above: — 1. *Origo Gentis Romanae,* in 23 chapters, containing the annals of the Roman race, from Janus and Saturnus down to the era of Romulus. It is probably a production of some of the later grammarians who were desirous of prefixing a suitable introduction to the series.

2. *De Viris illustribus Urbis Romae*, in 86 chapters, commencing with the birth of Romulus and Remus, and concluding with the death of Cleopatra. **3.** *De Caesaribus*, in 42 chapters, exhibiting short biographies of the emperors, from Augustus to Constantius. **4** *Epitome de Caesaribus*, in 48 chapters, commencing with Augustus and concluding with Theodosius. These lives agree for the most part almost word for word with the preceding, but variations may here and there be detected. Moreover, the first series terminates with Constantius, but the second comes down as low as Arcadius and Honorius. The best edition of these 4 pieces is by Arntzenius, Amst. et Traj. Bat. 1733, 4to.

Victor, Publius, the name prefixed to an enumeration of the principal buildings and monuments of ancient Rome, distributed according to the regions of Augustus, which has generally been respected as a work of great authority by Italian antiquaries. The best modern scholars, however, are agreed that this work, and a similar production ascribed to SEXTUS RUFUS, cannot be received in their present state as ancient at all, but must be regarded as mere pieces of patchwork, fabricated not earlier than the 15th century.

Victoria, the personification of victory among the Romans. It is said that Evander by the command of Minerva dedicated on mount Palatine a temple of Victoria, the daughter of Pallas. On the site of this ancient temple a new one was built by L. Postumius, during the war with the Samnites; and M. Porcius Cato added to it a chapel of Victoria Virgo. In later times there existed 3 or 4 sanctuaries of Victory at Rome. Respecting the Greek goddess of Victory see NICE.

Victoria or **Victorina**, the mother of Victorinus, after whose death she was hailed as the mother of camps (*Mater Castrorum*); and coins were struck, bearing her effigy. Feeling herself unequal to the weight of empire, she transferred her power first to Marius, and then to Tetricus, by whom some say that she was slain, while others affirm that she died a natural death.

Victorinus. 1. One of the Thirty Tyrants, was the 3rd of the usurpers who in succession ruled Gaul during the reign of Gallienus. He was assassinated at Agrippina by one of his own officers in A. D. 268, after reigning somewhat more than a year. — **2.** Bishop of Pettaw on the Drave in Styria, hence distinguished by the epithet *Petavionensis*, or *Pictaviensis*, flourished A. D. 270—290, and suffered martyrdom during the persecution of Diocletian, probably in 303. He wrote commentaries on the Scriptures, but all his works are lost. — **3.** C. **Marius Victorinus**, surnamed *Afer* from the country of his birth, taught rhetoric at Rome in the middle of the 4th century, with so much reputation that his statue was erected in the forum of Trajan. In his old age he embraced Christianity; and when the edict of Julian, prohibiting Christians from giving instruction in polite literature, was promulgated, Victorinus chose to shut up his school rather than deny his religion. Besides his commentaries on the Scriptures, and other theological works, many of which are extant, Victorinus wrote : — *Commentarius s. Expositio in Ciceronis libros de Inventione*, the best edition of which is in the 5th volume of Orelli's edition of Cicero. 2. *Ars Grammatica de Orthographia et*

Ratione Metrorum, a complete and voluminous treatise upon metres, in 4 books, printed in the *Grammaticae Latinae Auctores Antiqui* of Putschius, Hannov. 1605. The fame enjoyed by Victorinus as a public instructor does not gain any accession from his works. The exposition of the *De Inventione* is more difficult to comprehend than the text which it professes to explain. — **4. Maximus Victorinus.** We possess three short tracts — 1. *De Re Grammatica*; 2. *De Carmine Heroico*; 3. *De Ratione Metrorum*; all apparently the work of the same author, and usually ascribed in MSS. to a Maximus Victorinus; but whether we ought to consider him the same with the rhetorician who flourished under Constantius, or as an independent personage, it is impossible to decide. They were printed in the collection of Putschius, Hannov. 1605, and in that of Lindemann, Lips. 1831.

Victrix. [VENUS.]

Viducasses, a tribe of the Armorici in Gallia Lugdunensis, S. of the modern *Caen*.

Vienna (Viennensis : *Vienne*), the chief town of the Allobroges in Gallia Lugdunensis, situated on the Rhone, S. of Lugdunum. It was subsequently a Roman colony, and a wealthy and flourishing town. Under the later emperors it was the capital of the province called after it Gallia Viennensis. The modern town contains several Roman remains, of which the most important is a temple, supposed to have been dedicated to Augustus, and now converted into a museum.

Villius Annalis. [ANNALIS.]

Viminalis. [ROMA.]

Vincentius, surnamed **Lirinensis**, from the monastery in the island of Lerina, where he officiated as a presbyter. He was by birth a native of Gaul, and died in the reign of Theodosius and Valentinian, about A. D. 450. His fame rests upon a treatise against heretics, composed in 434. It commonly bears the title *Commonitorium pro Catholicae fidei antiquitate et universitate adversus profanas omnium Haereticorum novitates*. The standard edition is that of Baluzius, 8vo. Paris, 1663, 1669, 1684.

Vindalum, a town of the Cavares in Gallia Narbonensis, situated at the confluence of the Sulgas and the Rhone.

Vindelicia, a Roman province S. of the Danube, bounded on the N. by the Danube, which separated it from Germany, on the W. by the territory of the Helvetii in Gaul, on the S. by Rhaetia, and on the E. by the river Oenus (*Inn*), which separated it from Noricum, thus corresponding to the N.E. part of Switzerland, the S.E. of Baden, the S. of Würtemberg and Bavaria, and the N. part of the Tyrol. It was originally part of the province of Rhaetia, and was conquered by Tiberius in the reign of Augustus. At a later time Rhaetia was divided into two provinces, *Rhaetia Prima* and *Rhaetia Secunda*, the latter of which names was gradually supplanted by that of Vindelicia. It was drained by the tributaries of the Danube, of which the most important were the Licias, or Licus (*Lech*), with its tributary the Vindo, Vinda, or Virdo (*Werlach*), the Isarus (*Isar*), and Oenus (*Inn*). The E. part of the Lacus Brigantinus (*Lake of Constance*) also belonged to Vindelicia. The greater part of Vindelicia was a plain, but the S. portion was occupied by the N. slopes of the Alpes Rhaeticae. It derived its name from its chief inhabitants, the **Vindělici,** a warlike people dwelling in the S. of the country. Their name is said to have been formed from the 2 rivers, Vinda and Licus ; but it is more likely connected with the Celtic word *Vind,* which is found in the names *Vindobona, Vindomagus, Vindonissa,* &c. The Vindelici were a Celtic people, and were closely connected with the Rhaeti, with whom they are frequently spoken of by the ancient writers, and along with whom they were subdued by Tiberius, as is mentioned above. The other tribes in Vindelicia were the Brigantii on the Lake of Constance, the Licatii or Licates on the Lech, and the Breuni in the N. of Tyrol on the Brenner. The chief town in the province was Augusta Vindelicorum (*Augsburg*), at the confluence of Vindo and the Licus, which was made a Roman colony, A. D. 14, and was the residence of the governor of the province. This town, together with the other towns of Vindelicia, fell into the hands of the Alemanni in the 4th century, and from this time the population of the country appears to have been entirely Germanized.

Vindex, C. Jŭlĭus, propraetor of Gallia Celtica in the reign of Nero, was the first of the Roman governors who disowned the authority of Nero (A. D. 68). He did not, however, aspire to the empire himself, but offered it to Galba. Virginius Rufus, the governor of Upper Germany, marched with his army against Vindex. The two generals had a conference before Vesontio (*Besançon*), in which they appear to have come to some agreement ; but as Vindex was going to enter the town, he was attacked by the soldiers of Virginius, and put an end to his own life.

Vindicĭus, a slave, who is said to have given information to the consuls of the conspiracy, which was formed for the restoration of the Tarquins, and who was rewarded in consequence with liberty and the Roman franchise. He is said to have been the first slave manumitted by the *Vindicta,* the name of which was derived by some persons from that of the slave ; but it is unnecessary to point out the absurdity of this etymology.

Vindili. [VANDILI.]

Vindilis (*Belle Isle*), one of the islands of the Veneti off the N. W. coast of Gaul.

Vindĭus or **Vinnĭus,** a mountain in the N. W. of Hispania Tarraconensis, forming the boundary between the Cantabri and Astures.

Vindobona (*Vienna,* Engl. ; *Wien,* Germ.), a town in Pannonia, on the Danube, was originally a Celtic place, and subsequently a Roman municipium. Under the Romans it became a town of importance ; it was the chief station of the Roman fleet on the Danube, and the head quarters of a Roman legion. It was taken and plundered by Attila, but continued to be a flourishing town under the Lombards. It was here that the emperor M. Aurelius died, A. D. 180.

Vindonissa (*Windisch*), a town in Gallia Belgica, on the triangular tongue of land between the Aar and Reuss, was an important Roman fortress in the country of the Helvetii. Several Roman remains have been discovered on the site of the ancient town ; and the foundations of walls, the traces of an amphitheatre, and a subterranean aqueduct, are still to be seen.

Vinĭus, T., consul in A. D. 69 with the emperor Galba, and one of the chief advisers of the latter during his brief reign. He recommended Galba

to choose Otho as his successor, but he was notwithstanding killed by Otho's soldiers, after the death of Galba.

Vipsānĭa Agrippīna. 1. Daughter of M. Vipsanius Agrippa by his first wife Pomponia, the daughter of T. Pomponius Atticus, the friend of Cicero. Augustus gave her in marriage to his step-son Tiberius, by whom she was much beloved ; but after she had borne him a son, Drusus, Tiberius was compelled to divorce her by the command of the emperor, in order to marry Julia, the daughter of the latter. Vipsania afterwards married Asinius Gallus. She died in A. D. 20. — 2. Daughter of M. Vipsanius Agrippa by his second wife Julia, better known by the name of Agrippina. [AGRIPPINA.]

Vipsānĭus Agrippa, M. [AGRIPPA.]

Virbĭus, a Latin divinity worshipped along with Diana in the grove at Aricia, at the foot of the Alban Mt. He is said to have been the same as Hippolytus, who was restored to life by Aesculapius at the request of Diana. He was placed by this goddess under the care of the nymph Aricia, and received the name of Virbius. By this nymph he became the father of a son, who was also called Virbius, and whom his mother sent to the assistance of Turnus against Aeneas.

Virdo. [VINDELICIA.]

Virgīlĭus or **Vergīlĭus Maro, P.,** the Roman poet, was born on the 15th of October, B. C. 70, at Andes (*Pietola*), a small village near Mantua in Cisalpine Gaul. Virgil's father probably had a small estate which he cultivated : his mother's name was Maia. He was educated at Cremona and Mediolanum (*Milan*), and he took the toga virilis at Cremona on the day on which he commenced his 16th year in 55. It is said that he subsequently studied at Neapolis (*Naples*) under Parthenius, a native of Bithynia, from whom he learned Greek. He was also instructed by Syron an Epicurean, and probably at Rome. Virgil's writings prove that he received a learned education, and traces of Epicurean opinions are apparent in them. The health of Virgilius was always feeble, and there is no evidence of his attempting to rise by those means by which a Roman gained distinction, oratory and the practice of arms. After completing his education, Virgil appears to have retired to his paternal farm, and here he may have written some of the small pieces, which are attributed to him, the *Culex, Ciris, Moretum,* and others. After the battle of Philippi (42) Octavian assigned to his soldiers lands in various parts of Italy ; and the neighbourhood of Cremona and Mantua was one of the districts in which the soldiers were planted, and from which the former possessors were dislodged. Virgil was thus deprived of his property. It is said that it was seized by a veteran named Claudius or Clodius, and that Asinius Pollio, who was then governor of Gallia Transpadana, advised Virgil to apply to Octavian at Rome for the restitution of his land, and that Octavian granted his request. It is supposed that Virgilius wrote the Eclogue which stands first in our editions, to commemorate his gratitude to Octavian. Virgil became acquainted with Maecenas before Horace was, and Horace (*Sat.* i. 5, and 6. 55, &c.) was introduced to Maecenas by Virgil. Whether this introduction was in 41, or a little later, is uncertain ; but we may perhaps conclude from the name of Maecenas not

Head of Olympian Zeus (Jupiter).
(Visconti, Mus. Pio. Clem., vol. 6, tav. 1.) Page 830.

Zeus (Jupiter). (A Medal of M. Aurelius in
British Museum.) Page 830.

Zeus (Jupiter) and the Giants. (Neapolitan Gem.) Page 830.

Cronus (Saturnus).
(From a Painting at Pompeii.) Page 197.

Zeus (Jupiter) holding a thunderbolt in his right
hand, and with the aegis wrapt round the left
arm. (From an ancient Cameo.) Page 830.

[To face p. 816.

Valentinian I., Roman Emperor, A.D. 364—375. Page 802.

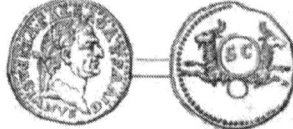

Vespasian, Roman Emperor, A.D. 70—79. Page 812.

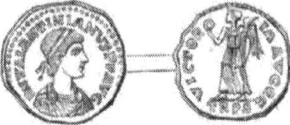

Valentinian II., Roman Emperor, A.D. 375—392. Page 803.

Vetranio, Roman Emperor, A.D. 350. Page 813.

Valentinian III., Roman Emperor, A.D. 425—455.

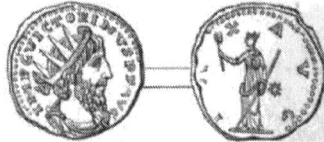

,Victorinus, one of the Thirty Tyrants, A.D. 265. Page 815.

Galeria Valeria, daughter of Diocletian, ob. A.D. 315.
Page 803.

Vitellius, Roman Emperor, A.D. 69. Page 819.

Valerian, Roman Emperor, A.D. 253—260. Page 803.

Volusianus, Roman Emperor, A.D. 251—254. Page 821.

L. Aurelius Verus, Roman Emperor, A.D. 161—169. Page 811.
To face p. 817.}

Zenobia, Queen of Palmyra. Page 829.

being mentioned in the Eclogues of Virgil, that he himself was not on those intimate terms with Maecenas which ripened into friendship, until after they were written. Horace, in one of his Satires (*Sat.* i. 5), in which he describes the journey from Rome to Brundusium, mentions Virgil as one of the party, and in language which shows that they were then in the closest intimacy. The most finished work of Virgil, his *Georgica*, an agricultural poem, was undertaken at the suggestion of Maecenas (*Georg.* iii. 41). The concluding lines of the Georgica were written at Naples (*Georg.* iv. 559), and the poem was completed after the battle of Actium B. C. 31, while Octavian was in the East. (Comp. *Georg.* iv. 560, and ii. 171.) His Eclogues had all been completed, and probably before the Georgica were begun (*Georg.* iv. 565). The epic poem of Virgil, the *Aeneid*, was probably long contemplated by the poet. While Augustus was in Spain (27), he wrote to Virgil to express his wish to have some monument of his poetical talent. Virgil appears to have commenced the Aeneid about this time. In 23 died Marcellus, the son of Octavia, Caesar's sister, by her first husband; and as Virgil lost no opportunity of gratifying his patron, he introduced into his 6th book of the Aeneid (883) the well-known allusion to the virtues of this youth, who was cut off by a premature death. Octavia is said to have been present when the poet was reciting this allusion to her son and to have fainted from her emotions. She rewarded the poet munificently for his excusable flattery. As Marcellus did not die till 23, these lines were of course written after his death, but that does not prove that the whole of the 6th book was written so late. A passage in the 7th book (606) appears to allude to Augustus receiving back the Parthian standards, which event belongs to 20. When Augustus was returning from Samos, where he had spent the winter of 20, he met Virgil at Athens. The poet, it is said, had intended to make a tour of Greece, but he accompanied the emperor to Megara and thence to Italy. His health, which had been long declining, was now completely broken, and he died soon after his arrival at Brundusium on the 22d of September, 19, not having quite completed his 51st year. His remains were transferred to Naples, which had been his favourite residence, and placed on the road from Naples to Puteoli (*Pozzuoli*), where a monument is still shown, supposed to be the tomb of the poet. The inscription said to have been placed on the tomb.

" Mantua me genuit, Calabri rapuere, tenet nunc
     Parthenope. Cecini pascua, rura, duces,"

we cannot suppose to have been written by the poet. Virgil named, as heredes in his testament, his half-brother Valerius Proculus, to whom he left one-half of his property, and also Augustus, Maecenas, L. Varius and Plotius Tucca. It is said that in his last illness he wished to burn the Aeneid, to which he had not given the finishing touches, but his friends would not allow him. Whatever he may have wished to be done with the Aeneid, it was preserved and published by his friends Varius and Tucca. The poet had been enriched by the liberality of his patrons, and he left behind him a considerable property and a house on the Esquiline Hill near the gardens of

Maecenas. He used his wealth liberally, and his library, which was doubtless a good one, was easy of access. He used to send his parents money every year. His father, who became blind, did not die before his son had attained a mature age. Two brothers of Virgil also died before him. In his fortunes and his friends Virgil was a happy man. Munificent patronage gave him ample means of enjoyment and of leisure, and he had the friendship of all the most accomplished men of the day, among whom Horace entertained a strong affection for him. He was an amiable good-tempered man, free from the mean passions of envy and jealousy; and in all but health he was prosperous. His fame, which was established in his lifetime, was cherished after his death, as an inheritance in which every Roman had a share; and his works became school-books even before the death of Augustus, and continued such for centuries after. The learned poems of Virgil soon gave employment to commentators and critics. Aulus Gellius has numerous remarks on Virgil, and Macrobius, in his Saturnalia, has filled four books (iii—vi.) with his critical remarks on Virgil's poems. One of the most valuable commentaries of Virgil, in which a great amount of curious and instructive matter has been preserved, is that of Servius [SERVIUS]. Virgil is one of the most difficult of the Latin authors, not so much for the form of the expression, though that is sometimes ambiguous enough, but from the great variety of knowledge that is required to attain his meaning in all its fulness. Virgil was the great poet of the middle ages too. To him Dante paid the homage of his superior genius, and owned him for his master and his model. Among the vulgar he had the reputation of a conjurer, a necromancer, a worker of miracles: it is the fate of a great name to be embalmed in fable. — The 10 short poems called *Bucolica* were the earliest works of Virgil, and probably all written between 41 and 37. These Bucolica are not Bucolica in the same sense as the poems of Theocritus, which have the same title. They have all a Bucolic form and colouring, but some of them have nothing more. They are also called Eclogae or Selections, but this name may not have originated with the poet. Their merit consists in their versification, which was smoother and more polished than the hexameters which the Romans had yet seen, and in many natural and simple touches. But as an attempt to transfer the Syracusan muse into Italy, they are certainly a failure, and we read the pastorals of Theocritus and of Virgil with a very different degree of pleasure. The 4th Eclogue, entitled Pollio, which may have been written in 40, after the peace of Brundusium, has nothing of the pastoral character about it. It is allegorical, mystical, half historical and prophetical, aenigmatical, anything in fact but Bucolic. The 1st Eclogue is Bucolic in form and in treatment, with an historical basis. The 2nd Eclogue, the Alexis, is an amatory poem, with a Bucolic colouring, which indeed is the characteristic of all Virgil's Eclogues, whatever they may be in substance. The 3rd, the 5th, the 7th, and the 9th are more clearly modelled on the form of the poems of his Sicilian prototype; and the 8th, the Pharmaceutria, is a direct imitation of the original Greek. The 10th, entitled Gallus, perhaps written the last of all, is a love poem, which, if written in elegiac verse, would be more appropriately called an elegy than a Bucolic.—The *Georgica* or "Agricultural Poem" in 4 books is a didactic poem, which Virgil dedicated to his patron Maecenas. He treats of the cultivation of the soil in the first book, of fruit trees in the second, of horses and other cattle in the third, and of bees in the fourth. In this poem Virgil shows a great improvement both in his taste and in his versification. Neither in the Georgics nor elsewhere has Virgil the merit of striking originality; his chief merit consists in the skilful handling of borrowed materials. His subject, which was by no means promising, he treated in a manner both instructive and pleasing; for he has given many useful remarks on agriculture and diversified the dryness of didactic poetry by numerous allusions and apt embellishments, and some occasional digressions without wandering too far from his main matter. In the first book he enumerates the subjects of his poem, among which is the treatment of bees; yet the management of bees seems but meagre material for one fourth of the whole poem, and the author accordingly had to complete the fourth book with matter somewhat extraneous—the long story of Aristaeus. The Georgica is the most finished specimen of the Latin hexameter which we have; and the rude vigour of Lucretius and the antiquated rudeness of Ennius are here replaced by a versification, which in its kind cannot be surpassed. The Georgica are also the most original poem of Virgil, for he found little in the *Works and Days* of Hesiod that could furnish him with hints for the treatment of his subject, and we are not aware that there was any work which he could exactly follow as a whole. For numerous single lines he was indebted to his extensive reading of the Greek poets.—The *Aeneid*, or adventures of Aeneas after the fall of Troy, is an epic poem on the model of the Homeric poems. It was founded upon an old Roman tradition that Aeneas and his Trojans settled in Italy, and were the founders of the Roman name. In the 1st book we have the story of Aeneas being driven by a storm on the coast of Africa, and being hospitably received by Dido queen of Carthage, to whom he relates in the episode of the 2nd and 3rd books the fall of Troy and his wanderings. In the 4th book the poet has elaborated the story of the attachment of Dido and Aeneas, the departure of Aeneas in obedience to the will of the gods, and the suicide of the Carthaginian queen. The 5th book contains the visit to Sicily, and the 6th the landing of Aeneas at Cumae in Italy, and his descent to the infernal regions, where he sees his father Anchises, and has a prophetic vision of the glorious destinies of his race and of the future heroes of Rome. In the first 6 books the adventures of Ulysses in the Odyssey are the model, and these books contain more variety of incident and situation than those which follow. The critics have discovered an anachronism in the visit of Aeneas to Carthage, which is supposed not to have been founded until two centuries after the fall of Troy, but this is a matter which we may leave without discussion, or admit without allowing it to be a poetical defect. The last 6 books, the history of the struggles of Aeneas in Italy, are founded on the model of the battles of the Iliad. Latinus, the king of the Latini, offers the Trojan hero his daughter Lavinia in marriage, who had been be-

trothed to Turnus, the warlike king of the Rutuli. The contest is ended by the death of Turnus, who falls by the hand of Aeneas. The fortunes of Aeneas and his final settlement in Italy are the subject of the Aeneid, but the glories of Rome and of the Julian house, to which Augustus belonged, are indirectly the poet's theme. In the first book the foundation of Alba Longa is promised by Jupiter to Venus (*Aeneid*, i. 254), and the transfer of empire from Alba to Rome; from the line of Aeneas will descend the "Trojan Caesar," whose empire will only be limited by the ocean, and whose glory by the heavens. The future rivalry between Rome and Carthage, and the ultimate triumphs of Rome are predicted. The poems abound in allusions to the history of Rome; and the aim of the poet to confirm and embellish the popular tradition of the Trojan origin of the Roman state, and the descent of the Julii from Venus, is apparent all through the poem. It is objected to the Aeneid that it has not the unity of construction either of the Iliad or of the Odyssey, and that it is deficient in that antique simplicity which characterises these two poems. Aeneas, the hero, is an insipid kind of personage, and a much superior interest is excited by the savage Mezentius, and also by Turnus, the unfortunate rival of Aeneas. Virgil imitated other poets besides Homer, and he has occasionally borrowed from them, especially from Apollonius of Rhodes. If Virgil's subject was difficult to invest with interest, that is his apology; but it cannot be denied that many parts of his poem are successfully elaborated, and that particular scenes and incidents are treated with true poetic spirit. The historical colouring which pervades it, and the great amount of antiquarian learning which he has scattered through it, make the Aeneid a study for the historian of Rome. Virgil's good sense and taste are always conspicuous, and make up for the defect of originality. As a whole, the Aeneid leaves no strong impression, which arises from the fact that it is not really a national poem, like the Iliad or the Odyssey, the monument of an age of which we have no other literary monument; it is a learned poem, the production of an age in which it does not appear as an embodiment of the national feeling, but as a monument of the talent and industry of an individual. Virgil has the merit of being the best of the Roman epic poets, superior both to Ennius who preceded him, and on whom he levied contributions, and to Lucan, Silius Italicus, and Valerius Flaccus, who belong to a later age. The passion for rhetorical display, which characterises all the literature of Rome, is much less offensive in Virgil than in those who followed him in the line of epic poetry.—The larger editions of Virgil contain some short poems, which are attributed to him, and may have been among his earlier works. The *Culex* or Gnat is a kind of Bucolic poem in 413 hexameters, often very obscure; the *Ciris*, or the mythus of Scylla the daughter of Nisus, king of Megara, in 541 hexameters, has been attributed to Cornelius Gallus and others; the *Moretum*, in 123 verses, the name of a compound mess, is a poem in hexameters, on the daily labour of a cultivator, but it contains only the description of the labours of the first part of the day, which consist in preparing the Moretum; the *Copa*, in elegiac verse, is an invitation by a female tavern keeper or servant attached to a Caupona, to passengers to come in and enjoy themselves. There are also 14 short pieces in various metres, classed under the general name of *Catalecta*. That addressed " Ad Venerem " shows that the writer, whoever he was, had a talent for elegiac poetry. Of the numerous editions of Virgil the best are by Burmann, Amsterdam, 1746, 4 vols. 4to.; by Heyne, 1767—1775, Lips. 4 vols. 8vo., of which the 4th edition contains important improvements, by Wagner, Lips. 1830, 4 vols. 8vo.; and by Forbiger, Lips. 1845—1846, 3 vols. 8vo.

Virginia, daughter of L. Virginius, a brave centurion, was a beautiful and innocent girl, betrothed to L. Icilius. Her beauty excited the lust of the decemvir Appius Claudius, who got one of his clients to seize the damsel and claim her as his slave. The case was brought before the decemvir for decision; her friends begged him to postpone his judgment till her father could be fetched from the camp, and offered to give security for the appearance of the maiden. Appius, fearing a riot, agreed to let the cause stand over till the next day; but on the following morning he pronounced sentence, assigning Virginia to his freedman. Her father, who had come from the camp, seeing that all hope was gone, prayed the decemvir to be allowed to speak one word to the nurse in his daughter's hearing, in order to ascertain whether she was really his daughter. The request was granted; Virginius drew them both aside, and snatching up a butcher's knife from one of the stalls, plunged it in his daughter's breast, exclaiming, " There is no way but this to keep thee free." In vain did Appius call out to stop him. The crowd made way for him; and holding his bloody knife on high, he rushed to the gate of the city, and hastened to the Roman camp. The result is known. Both camp and city rose against the decemvirs, who were deprived of their power, and the old form of government was restored. L. Virginius was the first who was elected tribune, and he hastened to take revenge upon his cruel enemy. By his orders Appius was dragged to prison to await his trial, and he there put an end to his own life in order to avoid a more ignominious death.

Virginia or **Verginia Gens**, patrician and plebeian. The patrician Virginii frequently filled the highest honours of the state during the early years of the republic. They all bore the cognomen of *Tricostus*, but none of them are of sufficient importance to require a separate notice.

Virginius, L., father of Virginia, whose tragic fate occasioned the downfall of the decemvirs, B. C. 149. [VIRGINIA.]

Virginius Rufus, consul A. D. 63, and governor of Upper Germany at the time of the revolt of Julius Vindex in Gaul (68). The soldiers of Virginius wished to raise him to the empire; but he refused the honour, and marched against Vindex, who perished before Vesontio. [VINDEX.] After the death of Nero, Virginius supported the claims of Galba, and accompanied him to Rome. After Otho's death, the soldiers again attempted to proclaim Virginius emperor, and in consequence of his refusal of the honour, he narrowly escaped with his life. Virginius died in the reign of Nerva, in his 3rd consulship, A. D. 97, at 83 years of age. He was honoured with a public funeral, and his panegyric was pronounced by the historian Tacitus, who was then consul. The younger

Pliny, of whom Virginius had been the tutor or guardian, also mentions him with praise.

Viriáthus, a celebrated Lusitanian, is described by the Romans as originally a shepherd or huntsman, and afterwards a robber, or, as he would be called in Spain in the present day, a guerilla chief. His character is drawn very favourably by many of the ancient writers, who celebrate his justice and equity, which was particularly shown in the fair division of the spoils he obtained from the enemy. Viriathus was one of the Lusitanians who escaped the treacherous and savage massacre of the people by the proconsul Galba in B. C. 150. [GALBA, No. 2.] He was destined to be the avenger of his country's wrongs. He collected a formidable force, and for several successive years he defeated one Roman army after another. At length, in 140, the proconsul Fabius Servilianus concluded a peace with Viriathus, in order to save his army, which had been enclosed by the Lusitanians in a mountain pass, much in the same way as their ancestors had been by the Samnites at the Caudine Forks. The treaty was ratified by the senate; but Servilius Caepio, who had succeeded to the command of Further Spain in 140, renewed the war, and shortly afterwards procured the assassination of Viriathus by bribing 3 of his friends.

Viridomarus. 1. Or **Britomartus**, the leader of the Gauls, slain by Marcellus. [MARCELLUS, No. 1.] — 2. Or **Virdumarus**, a chieftain of the Aedui, whom Caesar had raised from a low rank to the highest honour, but who afterwards joined the Gauls in their great revolt in B. C. 52.

Virtus, the Roman personification of manly valour. She was represented with a short tunic, her right breast uncovered, a helmet on her head, a spear in her left hand, a sword in the right, and standing with her right foot on a helmet. A temple of Virtus was built by Marcellus close to one of Honor. [HONOR.]

Viscellinus, Sp. Cassius. [CASSIUS, No. 1.]

Vistula (*Vistula*, Engl.; *Weichsel*, Germ.), an important river of Germany, forming the boundary between Germany and Sarmatia, rising in the Hercynia Silva and falling into the Mare Suevicum or the Baltic.

Visurgis (*Weser*), an important river of Germany, falling into the German Ocean. Ptolemy makes it rise in M. Meliboeus, because the Romans were not acquainted with the southern course of the Weser below Minden.

Vitellius. 1. L., father of the emperor, was a consummate flatterer, and by his arts he gained promotion. After being consul in A. D. 34, he had been appointed governor of Syria, and had made favourable terms of peace with Artabanus. But all this only excited Caligula's jealousy, and he sent for Vitellius to put him to death. The governor saved himself by his abject humiliation and the gross flattery which pleased and softened the savage tyrant. He paid the like attention to Claudius and Messalina, and was rewarded by being twice consul with Claudius, and censor. — 2. L., son of the preceding, and brother of the emperor, was consul in 48. He was put to death by the party of Vespasian on his brother's fall. — 3. A., Roman emperor, from January 2nd to December 22nd, A. D. 69, was the son of No. 1. He was consul during the first 6 months of 48, and his brother Lucius during the 6 following months. He had some knowledge of letters and some eloquence. His vices made him a favourite of Tiberius, Caius Caligula, Claudius, and Nero, who loaded him with favours. People were much surprised when Galba chose such a man to command the legions in Lower Germany, for he had no military talent. His great talent was eating and drinking. The soldiers of Vitellius proclaimed him emperor at Colonia Agrippinensis (*Cologne*) on the 2nd of January, 69. His generals Fabius Valens and Caecina marched into Italy, defeated Otho's troops at the decisive battle of Bedriacum, and thus secured for Vitellius the undisputed command of Italy. The soldiers of Otho, after the death of the latter, took the oath of fidelity to Vitellius. Vitellius reached Rome in July. He did not disturb any person in the enjoyment of what had been given by Nero, Galba, and Otho; nor did he confiscate any person's property. Though some of Otho's adherents were put to death, he let the next of kin take their property. But though he showed moderation in this part of his conduct, he showed none in his expenses. He was a glutton and an epicure, and his chief amusement was the table, on which he spent enormous sums of money. Meantime Vespasian, who had at first taken the oath of allegiance to Vitellius, was proclaimed emperor at Alexandria on the 1st of July. Vespasian was speedily recognised by all the East; and the legions of Illyricum under Antonius Primus entered the N. of Italy and declared for Vespasian. Vitellius despatched Caecina with a powerful force to oppose Primus; but Caecina was not faithful to the emperor. Primus defeated the Vitellians in two battles, and afterwards took and pillaged the city of Cremona. Primus then marched upon Rome, and forced his way into the city, after much fighting. Vitellius was seized in the palace, led through the streets with every circumstance of ignominy, and dragged to the Gemoniae Scalae, where he was killed with repeated blows. His head was carried about Rome, and his body was dragged into the Tiber; but it was afterwards interred by his wife Galeria Fundana. A few days before the death of Vitellius, the Capitol had been burnt in the assault made by his soldiers upon this building, where Flavius Sabinus, the brother of the emperor Vespasian, had taken refuge.

Vitruvius Pollio, M., the author of the celebrated treatise on Architecture, of whom we know nothing except a few facts contained in scattered passages of his own work. He appears to have served as a military engineer under Julius Caesar, in the African war, B. C. 46, and he was broken down with age when he composed his work, which is dedicated to the emperor Augustus. (The name of the emperor is not mentioned in the dedication, but there can be no doubt that it was Augustus.) The object of his work appears to have had reference to himself, as well as to his subject. He professes his intention to furnish the emperor with a standard by which to judge of the buildings he had already erected, as well as of those which he might afterwards erect; which can have no meaning, unless he wished to protest against the style of architecture which prevailed in the buildings already erected. That this was really his intention appears from several other arguments, and especially from his frequent references to the unworthy means by which architects obtained wealth and favour, with which he contrasts his own moderation and contentment in his more obscure position. In a word, comparatively unsuccessful as an architect, for we have no building of his mentioned except the basilica at Fanum, he attempted to establish his reputation as a writer upon the theory of his art; and in this he has been tolerably successful. His work is a valuable compendium of those written by numerous Greek architects, whom he mentions chiefly in the preface to his 7th book, and by some Roman writers on architecture. Its chief defects are its brevity, of which Vitruvius himself boasts, and which he often carries so far as to be unintelligible, and the obscurity of the style, arising in part from the natural difficulty of technical language, but in part also from the author's want of skill in writing, and sometimes from his imperfect comprehension of his Greek authorities. His work is entitled *De Architectura Libri X*. In the *First Book*, after the dedication to the emperor, and a general description of the science of architecture, and an account of the proper education of an architect, he treats of the choice of a proper site for a city, the disposition of its plan, its fortifications, and the several buildings within it. The *Second Book* is on the materials used in building. The *Third* and *Fourth Books* are devoted to temples and the four orders of architecture employed in them, namely, the Ionic, Corinthian, Doric, and Tuscan. The *Fifth Book* relates to public buildings, the *Sixth* to private houses, and the *Seventh* to interior decorations. The *Eighth* is on the subject of water; the mode of finding it; its different kinds; and the various modes of conveying it for the supply of cities. The *Ninth Book* treats of various kinds of sun-dials and other instruments for measuring time; and the *Tenth* of the machines used in building, and of military engines. Each book has a preface, upon some matter more or less connected with the subject; and these prefaces are the source of most of our information about the author. The best editions of Vitruvius are those of Schneider, 3 vols. Lips. 1807, 1808, 8vo.; of Stratico, 4 vols., Udine, 1825–30, with plates and a *Lexicon Vitruvianum*; and of Marini, 4 vols., Rom. 1836, fol.

Vocātes, a people in Gallia Aquitanica, dwelling in the neighbourhood of the Tarusates, Sossiates, and Elusates, probably in the modern *Tursan* or *Teursan*.

Vocetīus (*Bözberg*), a mountain in Gallia Belgica, an eastern branch of the Jura.

Voconīus Saxa. [SAXA.]

Vocontii, a powerful and important people in Gallia Narbonensis, inhabiting the S. E. part of Dauphiné, and a part of Provence between the Drac and the Durance, bounded on the N. by the Allobroges, and on the S. by the Salyes and Albioeci. Their country contained large and beautiful valleys between the mountains, in which good wine was grown. They were allowed by the Romans to live under their own laws, and, though in a Roman province, they were the allies and not the subjects of Rome.

Vŏgĕsus or **Vosgĕsus** (*Vosges*), a range of mountains in Gaul in the territory of the Lingones, running parallel to the Rhine, and separating its basin from that of the Mosella. The rivers Sequana (*Seine*), Arar (*Saône*), and the Mosella (*Moselle*), rise in these mountains.

Volandum, a strong fortress in Armenia Major,

some days' journey W. of Artaxata, mentioned by Tacitus (*Ann.* xiii. 39).

Vŏlǎterrae (Volaterranus: *Volaterra*), called by the Etruscans Velathri, one of the 12 cities of the Etruscan Confederation, was built on a lofty hill, about 1800 English feet above the level of the sea, rising from a deep valley, and precipitous on every side. The city was about 4 or 5 miles in circuit. It was the most N.-ly city of the Confederation, and possessed an extensive territory. Its dominions extended E.-ward as far as the territory of Arretium, which was 50 miles distant ; W.-ward as far as the Mediterranean, which was more than 20 miles off ; and S.-ward at least as far as Populonia, which was either a colony or an acquisition of Volaterrae. In consequence of possessing the 2 great ports of Luna and Populonia, Volaterrae, though so far inland, was reckoned as one of the powerful maritime cities of Etruria. Volaterrae is mentioned as one of the 5 cities which, acting independently of the rest of Etruria, determined to aid the Latins against Tarquinius Priscus ; but its name is rarely mentioned in connection with the Romans, and we have no record of its conquest by the latter. Volaterrae, like most of the Etruscan cities, espoused the Marian party against Sulla ; and such was the strength of its fortifications, that it was not till after a siege of two years that the city fell into Sulla's hands. Cicero speaks of Volaterrae as a municipium, and a military colony was founded in it under the triumvirate. It continued to be a place of importance even after the fall of the Western Empire ; and it was for a time the residence of the Lombard kings, who fixed their court here on account of the natural strength of the site. The modern town covers but a small portion of the area occupied by the ancient city. It contains, however, several interesting Etruscan remains. Of these the most important, in addition to the ancient walls, are the family tomb of the Caecinae, and a double gateway, nearly 30 feet deep, united by parallel walls of very massive character.

Volaterrāna Vada. [VADA, No. 3.]

Volcae, a powerful Celtic people in Gallia Narbonensis, divided into the 2 tribes of the Volcae Tectosages and Volcae Arecomici, extending from the Pyrenees and the frontiers of Aquitania along the coast as far as the Rhone. They lived under their own laws, without being subject to the Roman governor of the province, and they also possessed the Jus Latii. The Tectosages inhabited the western part of the country from the Pyrenees as far as Narbo, and the Arecomici the E. part from Narbo to the Rhone. The chief town of the Tectosages was TOLOSA. A portion of the Tectosages left their native country under Brennus, and were one of the 3 great tribes into which the Galatians in Asia Minor were divided. [GALATIA.]

Volcatĭus Sedigĭtus. [SEDIGITUS.]

Volci or Vulci. 1. (Volcientes, pl. : *Vulci*), an inland city of Etruria, about 18 miles N. W. of Tarquinii, was about 2 miles in circuit, and was situated upon a hill of no great elevation. Of the history of this city we know nothing. It is only mentioned in the catalogues of the geographers, and in the Fasti Capitolini, from which we learn that its citizens, in conjunction with the Volsinienses, were defeated by the consul Tib. Coruncanius, B. C. 280. But its extensive sepulchres, and the vast treasures of ancient art which they contain, prove that Vulci must at one time have been a powerful

and flourishing city. These tombs were only discovered in 1828, and have yielded a greater number of works of art than have been discovered in any other parts of Etruria. — 2. (Volcentes, Volcentani, pl. ; *Vallo*), a town in Lucania, 36 miles S. E. of Paestum, on the road to Buxentum.

Volero Publĭlĭus. [PUBLILIUS.]

Vologeses, the name of 5 kings of Parthia. [ARSACES XXIII., XXVII., XXVIII., XXIX., XXX.]

Volsci, an ancient people in Latium, but originally distinct from the Latins, dwelt on both sides of the river Liris, and extended down to the Tyrrhene sea. Their language was nearly allied to the Umbrian. They were from an early period engaged in almost unceasing hostilities with the Romans, and were not completely subdued by the latter till B. C. 338, from which time they disappear from history.

Volsĭnĭi or Vulsĭnĭi (Volsiniensis : *Bolsena*), called Velsna or Velsuna by the Etruscans, one of the most ancient and most powerful of the 12 cities of the Etruscan Confederation, was situated on a lofty hill on the N. E. extremity of the lake called after it, Lacus Volsiniensis and Vulsiniensis (*Lago di Bolsena*). Volsinii is first mentioned in B. C. 392, when its inhabitants invaded the Roman territory, but were easily defeated by the Romans, and were glad to purchase a 20 years' truce on humiliating terms. The Volsinienses also carried on war with the Romans in 311, 294, and 280, but were on each occasion defeated, and in the last of these years appear to have been finally subdued. On their final subjugation their city was rased to the ground by the Romans, and its inhabitants were compelled to settle on a less defensible site in the plain. The new city, on which stands the modern *Bolsena*, also became a place of importance. It was the birth-place of Sejanus, the favourite of Tiberius. Of the ancient city there are scarcely any remains. It occupied the summit of the highest hill, N. E. of Bolsena, above the remains of a Roman amphitheatre. From the Lacus Volsiniensis the river Marta issues ; and the lake contains 2 beautiful islands.

Volturcĭus, or Vulturcĭus, T., of Crotona, one of Catiline's conspirators, was sent by Lentulus to accompany the ambassadors of the Allobroges to Catiline. Arrested along with the ambassadors on the Mulvian bridge, and brought before the senate by Cicero, Volturcius turned informer upon obtaining the promise of pardon.

Volumnĭa, wife of Coriolanus. [CORIOLANUS.]

Volupĭa, or Voluptas, the personification of sensual pleasure among the Romans, who was honoured with a temple near the porta Romanula.

Volusiānus, son of the emperor Trebonianus Gallus, upon whom his father conferred the title of Caesar in A. D. 251, and of Augustus in 252. He was slain along with his father in 254. [GALLUS.]

L. Vŏlūsĭus Maecĭānus, a jurist, was in the consilium of Antoninus Pius, and was one of the teachers of M. Aurelius. Maecianus wrote several works ; and there are 44 excerpts from his writings in the Digest. A treatise, *De Asse et Ponderibus*, is attributed to him, but there is some doubt about the authorship. It is edited by Böcking, Bonn, 1831.

Vŏlūsus or Vŏlĕsus, the reputed ancestor of the Valeria gens, who is said to have settled at Rome with Titus Tatius. [VALERIA GENS.]

Vomānus (*Vomano*), a small river in Picenum.

3 G 3

Vŏnŏnĕs, the name of two kings of Parthia. [ARSACES XVIII., XXII.]

Vŏpiscus, a Roman praenomen, signified a twin-child, who was born safe, while the other twin died before birth. Like many other ancient Roman praenomens, it was afterwards used as a cognomen.

Vŏpiscus, Flăvĭus, a native of Syracuse, and one of the 6 *Scriptores Historiae Augustae*, flourished about A. D. 300. His name is prefixed to the biographies of — 1. Aurelianus; 2. Tacitus; 3. Florianus; 4. Probus; 5. The four tyrants, Firmus, Saturninus, Proculus, and Bonosus; 6. Carus; 7. Numerianus; 8. Carinus; at this point he stops, declaring that Diocletian, and those who follow, demand a more elevated style of composition. For editions, see CAPITOLINUS.

Vosgĕsus. [VOGESUS.]

Votiĕnus Montănus. [MONTANUS.]

Vulcānĭae Insŭlae. [AEOLIAE INSULAE.]

Vulcānus, the Roman god of fire, whose name seems to be connected with *fulgere*, *fulgur*, and *fulmen*. His worship was of considerable political importance at Rome, for a temple is said to have been erected to him close by the comitium as early as the time of Romulus and Tatius, in which the 2 kings used to meet and settle the affairs of the state, and near which the popular assembly was held. Tatius is reported to have established the worship of Vulcan along with that of Vesta, and Romulus to have dedicated to him a quadriga after his victory over the Fidenatans, and to have set up a statue of himself near the temple. According to others the temple was built by Romulus himself, who also planted near it the sacred lotus-tree which still existed in the days of Pliny. These circumstances, and what is related of the lotus-tree, show that the temple of Vulcan, like that of Vesta, was regarded as a central point of the whole state, and hence it was perhaps not without a meaning that the temple of Concord was subsequently built within the same district. The most ancient festival in honour of Vulcan seems to have been the Fornacalia or Furnalia, Vulcan being the god of furnaces; but his great festival was called Vulcanalia, and was celebrated on the 23d of August. The Roman poets transfer all the stories which are related of the Greek Hephaestus to their own Vulcan, the two divinities having in the course of time been completely identified. Respecting the Greek divinity, see HEPHAESTUS.

Vulci. [VOLCI.]

Vulgientes, an Alpine people in Gallia Narbonensis, whose chief town was Apta Julia (*Apt*).

Vulsinii. [VOLSINII.]

Vulso, Manlĭus. 1. L., consul B. C. 256 with M. Atilius Regulus. He invaded Africa along with his colleague. [For details see REGULUS, No. 3.] Vulso returned to Italy at the fall of the year with half of the army, and obtained the honour of a triumph. In 250 Vulso was consul a second time with T. Atilius Regulus Serranus, and with his colleague commenced the siege of Lilybaeum. — 2. Cn., curule aedile 197, praetor with Sicily as his province 195, and consul 189. He was sent into Asia in order to conclude the peace which Scipio Asiaticus had made with Antiochus, and to arrange the affairs of Asia. He attacked and conquered the Gallograeci or Galatians in Asia Minor without waiting for any formal instructions from the senate. He set out on his return to Italy

in 188, but in his march through Thrace he suffered much from the attacks of the Thracians, and lost a considerable part of the booty he had obtained in Asia. He reached Rome in 187. His triumph was a brilliant one, but his campaign in Asia had a pernicious influence upon the morals of his countrymen. He had allowed his army every kind of licence, and his soldiers introduced into the city the luxuries of the East.

Vultur, a mountain dividing Apulia and Lucania near Venusia, is a branch of the Apennines. It is celebrated by Horace as one of the haunts of his youth. From it the S. E. wind was called Vulturnus by the Romans.

Vulturnum (*Castel di Volturno*), a town in Campania, at the mouth of the river Vulturnus, was originally a fortress erected by the Romans in the 2nd Punic war. At a later time it was made a colony.

Vulturnus (*Volturno*), the chief river in Campania, rising in the Apennines in Samnium, and falling into the Tyrrhene sea. Its principal affluents are the Calor (*Calore*), Tamarus (*Tamaro*), and Sabatus (*Sabato*).

X.

Xanthippĕ (Ξανθίππη), wife of Socrates, said to be a woman of a peevish and quarrelsome disposition.

Xanthippus (Ξάνθιππος). 1. Son of Ariphron and father of Pericles. In B. C. 490, he impeached Miltiades on his return from his unsuccessful expedition against the island of Paros. He succeeded Themistocles as commander of the Athenian fleet in 479, and commanded the Athenians at the decisive battle of Mycale. — 2. The elder of the 2 legitimate sons of Pericles, Paralus being the younger. For details, see PARALUS. — 3. The Lacedaemonian, who commanded the Carthaginians against Regulus. For details, see REGULUS, No. 3. Xanthippus appears to have left Carthage a short time after his victory over Regulus.

Xanthus (Ξάνθος). 1. A lyric poet, older than Stesichorus, who mentioned him in one at least of his poems, and who borrowed from him in some of them. Xanthus may be placed about B. C. 650. No fragments of his poetry survive. — 2. A celebrated Lydian historian, older than Herodotus, who flourished about B. C. 480. The genuineness of the *Four Books of Lydian History* which the ancients possessed under the name of Xanthus, and of which some considerable fragments have come down to us, was questioned by some of the ancient grammarians themselves. There has been considerable controversy respecting the genuineness of this work among modern scholars. It is certain that much of the matter in the extant fragments is spurious; and the probability appears to be that the work from which they are taken is the production of an Alexandrian grammarian, founded upon the genuine work of Xanthus.

Xanthus (Ξάνθος), rivers. 1. [SCAMANDER.] — 2. (*Eschen Chai*), the chief river of Lycia, rises in M. Taurus, on the borders of Pisidia and Lycia, and flows S. through Lycia, between M. Cragus and M. Massicytus, in a large plain called the Plain of Xanthus (τὸ Ξάνθιον πεδίον), falling at last into the Mediterranean Sea, a little W. of Patara. Though not a large river, it is navigable for a considerable part of its course.

Xanthus (Ξάνθος: Ξάνθιος, Xanthius: *Gunik*, Ru.), the most famous city of Lycia, stood on the W. bank of the river of the same name, 60 stadia from its mouth. Twice in the course of its history it sustained sieges, which terminated in the self-destruction of the inhabitants with their property, first against the Persians under Harpagus, and long afterwards against the Romans under Brutus. The city was never restored after its destruction on the latter occasion. Xanthus was rich in temples and tombs, and other monuments of a most interesting character of art. Among its temples the most celebrated were those of Sarpedon and of the Lycian Apollo; besides which there was a renowned sanctuary of Latona (τὸ Λητῷον), near the river Xanthus, 10 stadia from its mouth, and 60 stadia from the city. The splendid ruins of Xanthus have recently been thoroughly explored by Sir C. Fellowes and his coadjutors, and several important remains of its works of art are now exhibited in the British Museum under the name of the Xanthian Marbles.

Xenarchus (Ξέναρχος). 1. Son of Sophron, and, like his father, a celebrated writer of mimes. He flourished during the Rhegian War (B. C. 399—389), at the court of Dionysius. — 2. An Athenian comic poet of the Middle Comedy, who lived as late as the time of Alexander the Great.— 3. Of Seleucia in Cilicia, a Peripatetic philosopher and grammarian, in the time of Strabo, who heard him. He taught first at Alexandria, afterwards at Athens, and last at Rome, where he enjoyed the friendship of Augustus.

Xeniades (Ξενιάδης), a Corinthian, who became the purchaser of Diogenes the Cynic, when he was taken by pirates and sold as a slave.

Xenippa (prob. *Uratippa*), a city of Sogdiana, mentioned by Curtius.

Xenocles (Ξενοκλῆς). 1. An Athenian tragic poet, son of Carcinus, who was also a tragic poet, and a contemporary of Aristophanes, who attacks him on several occasions. His poetry seems to have been indifferent, and to have resembled the worse parts of Euripides; but he obtained a victory over Euripides, B. C. 415. There was another tragic poet of the name of Xenocles, a grandson of the preceding, of whom no particulars are recorded. — 2. An Athenian architect, of the demos of Cholargos, was one of the architects who superintended the erection of the temple of Demeter, at Eleusis, in the time of Pericles.

Xenocrates (Ξενοκράτης). 1. The philosopher, was a native of Chalcedon. He was born B. C. 396, and died 314 at the age of 82. He attached himself first to Aeschines the Socratic, and afterwards, while still a youth, to Plato, whom he accompanied to Syracuse. After the death of Plato he betook himself, with Aristotle, to Hermias, tyrant of Atarneus; and, after his return to Athens, he was repeatedly sent on embassies to Philip of Macedonia, and at a later time to Antipater during the Lamian war. He is said to have wanted quick apprehension and natural grace; but these defects were more than compensated by persevering industry, pure benevolence, freedom from all selfishness, and a moral earnestness which obtained for him the esteem and confidence of the Athenians of his own age. Yet he is said to have experienced the fickleness of popular favour, and being too poor to pay the protection-money (μετοίκιον), to have been saved only by

the courage of the orator Lycurgus. He became president of the Academy even before the death of Speusippus, who was bowed down by sickness, and he occupied that post for 25 years. — The importance of Xenocrates is shown by the fact that Aristotle and Theophrastus wrote upon his doctrines, and that Panaetius and Cicero entertained a high regard for him. Of his numerous works only the titles have come down to us. — 2. A physician of Aphrodisias in Cilicia, lived about the middle of the 1st century after Christ. Besides some short fragments of his writings there is extant a little essay by him, entitled Περὶ τῆς ἀπὸ τῶν Ἐνύδρων Τροφῆς, " De Alimento ex Aquatilibus," which is an interesting record of the state of Natural History at the time in which he lived. Edited by Franz, 1774, Lips., and by Coray, 1794, Neap., and 1814, Paris. — 3. A statuary of the school of Lysippus, was the pupil either of Tisicrates or of Euthycrates. He also wrote works upon the art. He flourished about B. C. 260.

Xenocritus (Ξενόκριτος), of Locri Epizephyrii, in Lower Italy, a musician and lyric poet, was one of the leaders of the second school of Dorian music, which was founded by Thaletas, and was a composer of Paeans.

Xenophanes (Ξενοφάνης), a celebrated philosopher, was a native of Colophon, and flourished between B. C. 540 and 500. He was a poet as well as a philosopher, and considerable fragments have come down to us of his elegies, and of a didactic poem " On Nature." According to the fragments of one of his elegies, he had left his native land at the age of 25, and had already lived 67 years in Hellas, when, at the age of 92, he composed that elegy. He quitted Colophon as a fugitive or exile, and must have lived some time at Elea (Velia) in Italy, as he is mentioned as the founder of the Eleatic school of philosophy. He sung in one of his poems of the foundation of Velia. Xenophanes was usually regarded in antiquity as the originator of the Eleatic doctrine of the oneness of the universe. The Deity was in his view the animating power of the universe, which is expressed by Aristotle in the words, that, directing his glance on the whole universe, Xenophanes said, " God is the One."

Xenophon (Ξενοφῶν). 1. The Athenian, was the son of Gryllus, and a native of the demus Erchia. The time of his birth is not known, but it is approximated to by the fact that Xenophon fell from his horse in the flight after the battle of Delium, and was taken up by Socrates, the philosopher, on his shoulders and carried a distance of several stadia. The battle of Delium was fought B. C. 424 between the Athenians and Boeotians, and Xenophon therefore could not well have been born after 444. The time of his death also is not mentioned by any ancient writer. Lucian says that he attained to above the age of 90, and Xenophon himself mentions the assassination of Alexander of Pherae, which happened in 357. Between 424 and 357, there is a period of 67 years, and thus we have evidence of Xenophon being alive nearly 70 years after Socrates saved his life at Delium. Xenophon is said to have been a pupil of Socrates at an early age, which is consistent with the intimacy which might have arisen from Socrates saving his life. The most memorable event in Xenophon's life is his connection with the Greek army, which marched under Cyrus against Artaxerxes in 401. Xenophon himself mentions (*Anab.* iii. 1) the circumstances under which he joined this army. Proxenus, a friend of Xenophon, was already with Cyrus, and he invited Xenophon to come to Sardis, and promised to introduce him to the Persian prince. Xenophon consulted his master Socrates, who advised him to consult the oracle of Delphi, for it was rather a hazardous matter for him to enter the service of Cyrus, who was considered to be the friend of the Lacedaemonians and the enemy of Athens. Xenophon went to Delphi, but he did not ask the god whether he should go or not: he probably had made up his mind. He merely asked to what gods he should sacrifice in order that he might be successful in his intended enterprise. Socrates was not satisfied with his pupil's mode of consulting the oracle, but as he had got an answer, he told him to go; and Xenophon went to Sardis, which Cyrus was just about to leave. He accompanied Cyrus into Upper Asia. In the battle of Cunaxa, Cyrus lost his life, his barbarian troops were dispersed, and the Greeks were left alone on the wide plains between the Tigris and the Euphrates. It was after the treacherous massacre of Clearchus and other of the Greek commanders by the Persian satrap Tissaphernes, that Xenophon came forward. He had held no command in the army of Cyrus, nor had he in fact served as a soldier. He was now elected one of the generals, and took the principal part in conducting the Greeks in their memorable retreat along the Tigris over the high table lands of Armenia to Trapezus (Trebizond), on the Black Sea. From Trapezus the troops were conducted to Chrysopolis, which is opposite to Byzantium. The Greeks were in great distress, and some of them under Xenophon entered the service of Seuthes, king of Thrace. As the Lacedaemonians under Thimbron were now at war with Tissaphernes and Pharnabazus, Xenophon and his troops were invited to join the army of Thimbron, and Xenophon led them back out of Asia to join Thimbron 399. Xenophon, who was very poor, made an expedition into the plain of the Caicus with his troops before they joined Thimbron, to plunder the house and property of a Persian named Asidates. The Persian, with his women, children, and all his moveables was seized; and Xenophon, by this robbery, replenished his empty pockets (*Anab.* vii. 8. 23). He tells the story himself as if he were not ashamed of it. Socrates was put to death in 399, and it seems probable that Xenophon was banished either shortly before or shortly after that event. Xenophon was not banished at the time when he was leading the troops back to Thimbron (*Anab.* vii. 7. 57), but his expression rather seems to imply that his banishment must have followed soon after. It is not certain what he was doing after the troops joined Thimbron. As we know nothing of his movements, the conclusion ought to be that he stayed in Asia, and probably with Thimbron and his successor Dercyllidas. Agesilaus, the Spartan king, was commanding the Lacedaemonian forces in Asia against the Persians in 396, and Xenophon was with him at least during part of the campaign. When Agesilaus was recalled (394), Xenophon accompanied him; and he was on the side of the Lacedaemonians in the battle which they fought at Coronea (394) against the Athenians. It seems that he went to Sparta with

Agesilaus after the battle of Coronea, and soon after he settled at Scillus in Elis not far from Olympia, a spot of which he has given a description in the *Anabasis* (v. 3. 7, &c.). Here he was joined by his wife Philesia and his children. His children were educated in Sparta. Xenophon was now an exile, and a Lacedaemonian so far as he could become one. His time during his long residence at Scillus was employed in hunting, writing, and entertaining his friends; and perhaps the *Anabasis* and part of the *Hellenica*, were composed here. The treatise on hunting and that on the horse were probably also written during this time, when amusement and exercise of that kind formed part of his occupation. Xenophon was at last expelled from his quiet retreat at Scillus by the Eleans after remaining there about 20 years. The sentence of banishment from Athens was repealed on the motion of Eubulus, but it is uncertain in what year. In the battle of Mantinea, which was fought 362, the Spartans and the Athenians were opposed to the Thebans, and Xenophon's 2 sons, Gryllus and Diodorus, fought on the side of the allies. Gryllus fell in the same battle in which Epaminondas lost his life. There is no evidence that Xenophon ever returned to Athens. He is said to have retired to Corinth after his expulsion from Scillus, and as we know nothing more, we assume that he died there. The *Hipparchicus* was written after the repeal of the decree of banishment, and the treatise on the revenues of Athens. The events alluded to in the Epilogus to the *Cyropaedia* (viii. 8. 4) show that the Epilogus at least was written after 362. The time of his death may have been a few years later. The following is a list of Xenophon's works. 1. The *Anabasis* ('Aνάβασις) or the History of the Expedition of the Younger Cyrus, and of the retreat of the Greeks, who formed part of his army. It is divided into 7 books. This work has immortalised Xenophon's name. It is a clear and pleasing narrative, written in a simple style, free from affectation; and it gives a great deal of curious information on the country which was traversed by the retreating Greeks, and on the manners of the people. It was the first work which made the Greeks acquainted with some portions of the Persian empire, and it showed the weakness of that extensive monarchy. The skirmishes of the retreating Greeks with their enemies and the battles with some of the barbarian tribes are not such events as elevate the work to the character of a military history, nor can it as such be compared with Caesar's Commentaries. 2. The *Hellenica* ('Ελληνικά) of Xenophon are divided into 7 books, and comprehend the space of 48 years, from the time when the history of Thucydides ends [THUCYDIDES] to the battle of Mantinea, 362. The *Hellenica* is generally a dry narrative of events, and there is nothing in the treatment of them which gives a special interest to the work. Some events of importance are briefly treated, but a few striking incidents are presented with some particularity. 3. The *Cyropaedia* (Κυροπαιδεία) in 8 books, is a kind of political romance, the basis of which is the history of Cyrus, the founder of the Persian monarchy. It shows how citizens are to be made virtuous and brave; and Cyrus is the model of a wise and good ruler. As a history it has no authority at all. Xenophon adopted the current stories as to Cyrus and the chief events of his reign, without any intention of subjecting them to a critical examination ; nor have we any reason to suppose that his picture of Persian morals and Persian discipline is any thing more than a fiction. Xenophon's object was to represent what a state might be, and he placed the scene of his fiction far enough off to give it the colour of possibility. His own philosophical notions and the usages of Sparta were the real materials out of which he constructed his political system. The *Cyropaedia* is evidence enough that Xenophon did not like the political constitution of his own country, and that a well-ordered monarchy or kingdom appeared to him preferable to a democracy like Athens. 4. The *Agesilaus* ('Αγησίλαος) is a panegyric on Agesilaus II., king of Sparta, the friend of Xenophon. 5. The *Hipparchicus* ('Ιππαρχικός) is a treatise on the duties of a commander of cavalry, and it contains many military precepts. 6. The *De Re Equestri*, a treatise on the Horse ('Ιππική), was written after the *Hipparchicus*, to which treatise he refers at the end of the treatise on the Horse. The treatise is not limited to horsemanship, as regards the rider: it shows how a man is to avoid being cheated in buying a horse, how a horse is to be trained, and the like. 7. The *Cynegeticus* (Κυνηγετικός) is a treatise on hunting ; and on the dog, and the breeding and training of dogs ; on the various kinds of game, and the mode of taking them. It is a treatise written by a genuine sportsman, who loved the exercise and the excitement of the chase ; and it may be read with delight by any sportsman who deserves the name. 8, 9. The *Respublica Lacedaemoniorum* and *Respublica Atheniensium*, the 2 treatises on the Spartan and Athenian states (Λακεδαιμονίων Πολιτεία, and 'Αθηναίων Πολιτεία), were not always recognised as genuine works of Xenophon, even by the ancients. They pass, however, under his name, and there is nothing in the internal evidence that appears to throw any doubt on the authorship. The writer clearly prefers Spartan to Athenian institutions. 10. The *De Vectigalibus*, a treatise on the Revenues of Athens (Πόροι ἤ περὶ Προσόδων) is designed to show how the public revenue of Athens may be improved. 11. The *Memorabilia* of Socrates, in 4 books ('Απομνημονεύματα Σωκράτους), was written by Xenophon to defend the memory of his master against the charge of irreligion and of corrupting the Athenian youth. Socrates is represented as holding a series of conversations, in which he developes and inculcates moral doctrines in his peculiar fashion. It is entirely a practical work, such as we might expect from the practical nature of Xenophon's mind, and it professes to exhibit Socrates as he taught. It is true that it may exhibit only one side of the Socratic argumentation, and that it does not deal in those subtleties and verbal disputes which occupy so large a space in some of Plato's dialogues. Xenophon was a hearer of Socrates, an admirer of his master, and anxious to defend his memory. The charges against Socrates for which he suffered were, that "Socrates was guilty of not believing in the gods which the state believed in, and in introducing other new daemons (δαιμόνια) : he was also guilty of corrupting the youth." Xenophon replies to these two charges specifically ; and he then goes on to show what Socrates' mode of life was. The whole treatise is intended to be an answer to the charge for which Socrates was executed, and it is,

therefore, in its nature, not intended to be a complete exhibition of Socrates. That it is a genuine picture of the man, is indisputable, and it is the most valuable memorial that we have of the practical philosophy of Socrates. 12. The *Apology of Socrates* ('Απολογία Σωκράτους πρὸς τοὺς δικαστάς) is a short speech, containing the reasons which induced Socrates to prefer death to life. It is not a first-rate performance ; and is considered by some critics not to have been written by Xenophon. 13. The *Symposium* (Συμπόσιον), or Banquet of Philosophers, in which Xenophon delineates the character of Socrates. The speakers are supposed to meet at the house of Callias, a rich Athenian, at the celebration of the great Panathenaea. Socrates and others are the speakers. The piece is interesting as a picture of an Athenian drinking party, and of the amusement and conversation with which it was diversified. The nature of love and friendship is discussed. 14. The *Hiero* ('Ιέρων ἤ Τυραννικός) is a dialogue between king Hiero and Simonides, in which the king speaks of the dangers and difficulties incident to an exalted station, and the superior happiness of a private man. The poet, on the other hand, enumerates the advantages which the possession of power gives, and the means which it offers of obliging and doing services. 15. The *Oeconomicus* (Οἰκονομικός) is a dialogue between Socrates and Critobulus, in which Socrates gives instruction in the art called Oeconomic, which relates to the administration of a household and of a man's property. This is one of the best treatises of Xenophon. — All antiquity and all modern writers agree in allowing Xenophon great merit as a writer of a plain, simple, perspicuous, and unaffected style. His mind was not adapted for pure philosophical speculation : he looked to the practical in all things ; and the basis of his philosophy was a strong belief in a divine mediation in the government of the world. The best edition of Xenophon's complete works is by Schneider, Lips. 1815, 6 vols. 8vo. — 2. The Ephesian, the author of a romance, still extant, entitled *Ephesiaca*, or the Loves of Anthia and Abrocomas ('Εφεσιακά, τὰ κατὰ 'Ανθίαν καὶ 'Αβροκόμην). The style of the work is simple, and the story is conducted without confusion, notwithstanding the number of personages introduced. The adventures are of a very improbable kind. The age when Xenophon lived is uncertain. He is probably the oldest of the Greek romance writers. The best editions of his work are by Peerlkamp, Harlem, 1818, and by Passow, Lips. 1833.

Xerxes (Ξέρξης). I. King of Persia B. C. 485—465. The name is said by Herodotus (vi. 98) to signify the warrior, but it is probably the same word as the Zend *ksathra* and the Sanscrit *kshatra*, "a king." Xerxes was the son of Darius and Atossa. Darius was married twice. By his first wife, the daughter of Gobryas, he had 3 children before he was raised to the throne ; and by his second wife, Atossa, the daughter of Cyrus, he had 4 children after he had become king. Artabazanes, the eldest son of the former marriage, and Xerxes, the eldest son of the latter, each laid claim to the succession ; but Darius decided in favour of Xerxes, no doubt through the influence of his mother Atossa, who completely ruled Darius. Xerxes succeeded his father at the beginning of 485. Darius had died in the midst of his preparations against Greece, which had been interrupted by the revolt of the Egyptians. The first care of Xerxes was to reduce the latter people to subjection. He accordingly invaded Egypt at the beginning of the 2d year of his reign (B. C. 484), compelled the people again to submit to the Persian yoke, and then returned to Persia, leaving his brother Achaemenes governor of Egypt. The next 4 years were devoted to preparations for the invasion of Greece. In the spring of 480 he set out from Sardis on his memorable expedition against Greece. He crossed the Hellespont by a bridge of boats, and continued his march through the Thracian Chersonese till he reached the plain of Doriscus, which is traversed by the river Hebrus. Here he resolved to number both his land and naval forces. Herodotus has left us a most minute and interesting catalogue of the nations comprising this mighty army with their various military equipments and different modes of fighting. The land forces contained 46 nations. (Herod. vii. 61, foll.) In his march through Thrace and Macedonia, Xerxes received a still further accession of strength; and when he reached Thermopylae the land and sea forces amounted to 2,641,610 fighting men. This does not include the attendants, the slaves, the crews of the provision ships, &c., which according to the supposition of Herodotus were more in number than the fighting men; but supposing them to have been equal, the total number of male persons who accompanied Xerxes to Thermopylae reach the astounding figure of 5,283,220 ! Such a vast number must be dismissed as incredible; but, considering that this army was the result of a maximum of effort throughout the empire, and that provisions had been collected for 3 years before along the line of march, we may well believe that the numbers of Xerxes were greater than were ever assembled in ancient times, or perhaps at any known epoch of history. After the review of Doriscus Xerxes continued his march through Thrace. On reaching Acanthus, near the isthmus of Athos, Xerxes left his fleet, which received orders to sail through the canal that had been previously dug across the isthmus—and of which the remains are still visible [ATHOS]—and await his arrival at Therme, afterwards called Thessalonica. After joining his fleet at Therme, Xerxes marched through Macedonia and Thessaly without meeting with any opposition till he reached Thermopylae. Here the Greeks resolved to make a stand. Leonidas, king of Sparta, conducted a land force to Thermopylae; and his colleague Eurybiades sailed with the Greek fleet to the N. of Euboea, and took up his position on the N. coast, which faced Magnesia, and was called Artemisium from the temple of Artemis belonging to the town of Hestiaea. Xerxes arrived in safety with his land forces before Thermopylae, but his fleet was overtaken by a violent storm and hurricane off the coast of Sepias in Magnesia, by which at least 400 ships of war were destroyed, as well as an immense number of transports. Xerxes attempted to force his way through the pass of Thermopylae, but his troops were repulsed again and again by Leonidas; till a Malian, of the name of Ephialtes, showed the Persians a pass over the mountains of Oeta, and thus enabled them to fall on the rear of the Greeks. Leonidas and his Spartans disdained to fly, and were all slain. [LEONIDAS.] On the same day on which Leonidas was fighting with the land forces of

Xerxes, the Greek ships at Artemisium attacked the Persian fleet. In the first battle, the Greeks had the advantage, and in the following night the Persian ships suffered still more from a violent storm. Two days afterwards the contest was renewed; and both sides fought with the greatest courage. Although the Greeks at the close still maintained their position, and had destroyed a great number of the enemy's ships, yet their own loss was considerable, and half the Athenian ships were disabled. Under these circumstances the Greek commanders abandoned Artemisium and retired to Salamis, opposite the S. W. coast of Attica. It was now too late to send an army into Boeotia, and Attica thus lay exposed to the full vengeance of the invader. The Athenians removed their women, children, and infirm persons to Salamis, Aegina, and Troezen. Meantime Xerxes marched through Phocis and Boeotia, and at length reached Athens. About the same time as Xerxes entered Athens, his fleet arrived in the bay of Phalerum. He now resolved upon an engagement with the Greek fleet. The history of this memorable battle, of the previous dissensions among the Greek commanders, and of the glorious victory of the Greeks at the last, is related elsewhere. [THEMISTOCLES.] Xerxes witnessed the battle from a lofty seat, which was erected for him on the shore of the mainland on one of the declivities of Mount Aegaleos, and thus beheld with his own eyes the defeat and dispersion of his mighty armament. Xerxes now became alarmed for his own safety, and resolved to leave Greece immediately. He was confirmed in his resolution by Mardonius, who undertook to complete the conquest with 300,000 of his troops. Xerxes left Mardonius the number of troops which he requested, and with the remainder set out on his march homewards. He reached the Hellespont in 45 days from the time of his departure from Attica. On arriving at the Hellespont, he found the bridge of boats destroyed by a storm, and he crossed over to Asia by ship. He entered Sardis towards the end of the year 480. In the following year, 479, the war was continued in Greece; but Mardonius was defeated at Plataea by the combined forces of the Greeks, and on the same day another victory was gained over the Persians at Mycale in Ionia. Next year, 478, the Persians lost their last possession in Europe by the capture of Sestos on the Hellespont. Thus the struggle was virtually brought to an end, though the war still continued for several years longer. We know little more of the personal history of Xerxes. He was murdered in 465, after a reign of 20 years, by Artabanus, who aspired to become king of Persia. Xerxes was succeeded by his son ARTAXERXES I. — II. The only legitimate son of Artaxerxes I., succeeded his father as king of Persia in 425, but was murdered after a short reign of only 2 months by his half-brother Sogdianus, who thus became king.

Xiphilīnus (Ξιφιλῖνος), of Trapezus, was a monk at Constantinople, and made an abridgement of Dion Cassius from the 36th to the 80th book at the command of the emperor Michael VII. Ducas, who reigned from A. D. 1071 to 1078. The work is executed with carelessness, and is only of value as preserving the main facts of the original, the greater part of which is lost. It is printed along with Dion Cassius.

Xiphōnia (Ξιφωνία: *Capo di S. Croce*), a promontory on the E. coast of Sicily, above Syracuse, with a harbour (Ξιφώνειος λιμήν).

Xŏïs or Chŏïs (Ξόϊς, Ξόης, Χόϊς), an ancient city of Lower Egypt, N. of Leontopolis, on an island of the Nile, in the Nomos Sebennyticus, the seat, at one time, of a dynasty of Egyptian kings. It appears to have entirely perished under the Roman empire, and its site is very doubtful. Some identify it with the Papremis of Herodotus.

Xūthus (Ξοῦθος), son of Hellen by the nymph Orseïs, and a brother of Dorus and Aeolus. He was king of Peloponnesus, and the husband of Creusa, the daughter of Erechtheus, by whom he became the father of Achaeus and Ion. Others state that after the death of his father Hellen, Xuthus was expelled from Thessaly by his brothers, and went to Athens, where he married the daughter of Erechtheus. After the death of Erechtheus, Xuthus being chosen arbitrator, adjudged the kingdom to his eldest brother-in-law, Cecrops, in consequence of which he was expelled by the other sons of Erechtheus, and settled in Aegialus in Peloponnesus.

Xylinē, a town of Pisidia, between Corbasa and Termessus, mentioned by Livy (xxxviii. 15).

Xynia or Xyniae (Ξυνία: Ξυνιεύς: Taukli), a town of Thessaly in the district Phthiotis, E. of the lake of the same name (ἡ Ξυνίας λίμνη: Nizero or Dereli).

Xypětē (Ξυπέτη: Ξυπεταιών, Ξυπετέων, Ξυπεταιωνεύς, Ξυπετεύς, Ξυπέτιος), said to have been anciently called Troja, a demus of Attica belonging to the tribe Cecropis, near Piraeus.

Z.

Zabătus (Ζάβατος). [LYCUS, No. 5.]

Zabē (Ζάβη), a name applied, under the later emperors, to the S. part of Numidia, as far as the border of the Great Desert.

Zăcynthus (Ζάκυνθος: Ζακύνθιος, Zacynthius: Zante), an island in the Ionian sea off the coast of Elis, about 40 miles in circumference. It contained a large and flourishing town of the same name upon the E. coast, the citadel of which was called Psophis. There are 2 considerable chains of mountains in the island. The ancient writers mention M. Elatus, which is probably the same as the modern Scopo in the S. E. of the island, and which rises to the height of 1509 feet. Zacynthus was celebrated in antiquity for its pitch wells, which were visited by Herodotus, and which still supply a large quantity of bitumen. About 100 tons of bitumen are at the present day annually extracted from these wells. — Zacynthus was inhabited by a Greek population at an early period. It is said to have derived its names from Zacynthus, a son of Dardanus, who colonised the island from Psophis in Arcadia; and according to an ancient tradition, the Zacynthians founded the town of Saguntum in Spain. [SAGUNTUM.] The island is frequently mentioned by Homer, who speaks of it as the "woody Zacynthus." It was afterwards colonised by Achaeans from Peloponnesus. It formed part of the maritime empire of Athens, and continued faithful to the Athenians during the Peloponnesian war. At a later time it was subject to the Macedonian monarchs, and on the conquest of Macedonia by the Romans passed into the hands of the latter. It is now one of the Ionian islands under the protection of Great Britain.

Zadracarta (Ζαδράκαρτα), one of the capital cities and royal residences in Hyrcania, lay at the N. foot of the chief pass through M. Coronus. (Comp. TAPAE.)

Zagreus (Ζαγρεύς), a surname of the mystic Dionysus (Διόνυσος χθόνιος), whom Zeus, in the form of a dragon, is said to have begotten by Persephone (Proserpina), before she was carried off by Pluto. He was torn to pieces by the Titans; and Athena carried his heart to Zeus.

Zagros or -us (ὁ Ζάγρος and τὸ Ζάγριον ὄρος, Mts. of Kurdistan and Louristan), the general name for the range of mountains forming the S. E. continuation of the Taurus, and the E. margin of the Tigris and Euphrates valley, from the S. W. side of the Lake Arsissa (Van) in Armenia, to the N. E. side of the head of the Persian Gulf, and dividing Media from Assyria and Susiana. More specifically, the name Zagros was applied to the central part of the chain, the N. part being called the mountains of the Cordueni or Gordyaei, and the S. part Parachoathras.

Zaitha or Zautha (Ζανθά), a town of Mesopotamia, on the E. bank of the Euphrates, 20 Roman miles S. of Circesium, remarkable as the place at which a monument was erected to the murdered emperor Gordian by his soldiers.

Zăleucus (Ζάλευκος), the celebrated lawgiver of the Epizephyrian Locrians, is said by some to have been originally a slave, but is described by others as a man of good family. He could not however have been a disciple of Pythagoras, as some writers state, since he lived upwards of 100 years before Pythagoras. The date of the legislation of Zaleucus is assigned to B. C. 660. His code is stated to have been the first collection of written laws that the Greeks possessed. The general character of his laws was severe; but they were observed for a long period by the Locrians, who obtained, in consequence, a high reputation for legal order. Among other enactments we are told that the penalty of adultery was the loss of the eyes. There is a celebrated story of the son of Zaleucus having become liable to this penalty, and the father himself suffering the loss of one eye that his son might not be utterly blinded. It is further related that among his laws was one forbidding any citizen under penalty of death, to enter the senate house in arms. On one occasion, however, on a sudden emergency in time of war, Zaleucus transgressed his own law, which was remarked to him by one present; whereupon he fell upon his own sword, declaring that he would himself vindicate the law. Other authors tell the same story of Charondas, or of Diocles.

Zalmoxis or Zamolxis (Ζάλμοξις, Ζάμολξις), said to have been so called from the bear's skin (Ζάλμος) in which he was clothed as soon as he was born. He was, according to the story current among the Greeks on the Hellespont, a Getan, who had been a slave to Pythagoras in Samos, but was manumitted, and acquired not only great wealth, but large stores of knowledge from Pythagoras, and from the Egyptians, whom he visited in the course of his travels. He returned among the Getae, introducing the civilisation and the religious ideas which he had gained, especially regarding the immortality of the soul. He was said to have lived in a subterraneous cave for 3 years, and after that to have again made his appearance among the Getae. Herodotus inclines to place the age of Zalmoxis a long time before Pythagoras, and expresses a doubt not only about the story itself, but as to whether Zalmoxis were a man, or an indigenous Getan deity. The latter appears to have been the real state of the case. The Getae believed that the departed went to him.

Zāma Regīa (Zάμα : Zamensis : Zowareen, S. E. of *Kaff*), a strongly fortified city in the interior of Numidia, on the borders of the Carthaginian territory. It was the ordinary residence of King Juba, who had here his treasury and his harem. It was the scene of one of the most important battles in the history of the world, that in which Hannibal was defeated by Scipio, and the 2nd Punic War was ended, B. C. 202. Strabo tells us that it was destroyed by the Romans; but if so, it must have been restored, for we find it mentioned under the empire as a colony and a bishop's see. Pliny and Vitruvius speak of a fountain in its neighbourhood. — There were unimportant places of the same name in Cappadocia and Mesopotamia.

Zanclē. [MESSANA.]

Zapaortēne, a city in the S. E. of Parthia, in the mountains of the Zapaorteni.

Zaradrus (*Sutlej*), a river of N. India, now the S. boundary of the *Punjab*. It rises from 2 principal sources beyond the *Himalaya*, and falls into the Hyphasis (*Gharra*).

Zarangae or **-i**, or **Sarangae** (Ζαράγγοι, Σαράγγαι), a people in the N. of Drangiana, on the confines of Aria. The close resemblance of their name to the generic name of all the people of Drangiana, that is, Drangae, suggests a doubt whether they ought to be specifically distinguished from them.

Zarax or **Zarex** (Ζάραξ, Ζάρηξ). 1. The central part of the chain of mountains, extending along the E. coast of Laconica from Mt. Parnon, on the frontiers of Argolis, down to the promontory Malea. — 2. (*Jeraka*), a town on the E. coast of Laconica, at the foot of the mountain of the same name.

Zariaspe. [BACTRA.]

Zariaspis, an earlier, probably the native name for the river on which Bactra stood, and which is usually called Bactrus. [BAC.RA.] The people on its banks were called Zariaspae.

Zēla or **Ziela** (τὰ Ζῆλα : *Zilleh*), a city in the S. of Pontus, not far S. of Amasia, and 4 days' journey E. of Tavium. It stood on an artificial hill, and was strongly fortified. Near it was an ancient and famous temple of Anaïtis and other Persian deities, in which great religious festivals were held. The surrounding district was called Zelētis or Zelītis. At Zela the Roman general Valerius Triarius was defeated by Mithridates; but the city is more celebrated for another great battle, that in which Julius Caesar defeated Pharnaces, and of which he wrote this despatch to Rome: — VENI: VIDI: VICI.

Zelasīum, a Thessalian town in the district Phthiotis of uncertain site.

Zelīa (Ζέλεια), an ancient city of Mysia, at the foot of M. Ida, and on the river Aesepus, 80 stadia from its mouth, belonging to the territory of Cyzicus. At the time of Alexander's invasion the head-quarters of the Persian army were fixed here.

Zēlus (Ζῆλος), the personification of zeal or strife, is described as a son of Pallas and Styx, and a brother of Nice.

Zēno, Zēnon (Ζήνων). 1. The founder of the Stoic philosophy, was a native of Citium in Cyprus, and the son of Mnaseas. He began at an early age to study philosophy through the writings of the Socratic philosophers, which his father was accustomed to bring back from Athens when he went thither on trading voyages. At the age of 22, or, according to others, of 30 years, Zeno was shipwrecked in the neighbourhood of Piraeus; whereupon he was led to settle in Athens, and to devote himself entirely to the study of philosophy. According to some writers he lost all his property in the shipwreck; according to others, he still retained a large fortune; but whichever of these accounts is correct, his moderation and contentment became proverbial, and a recognition of his virtues shines through even the ridicule of the comic poets. The weakness of his health is said to have first determined him to live rigorously and simply; but his desire to make himself independent of all external circumstances seems to have been an additional motive, and to have led him to attach himself to the cynic Crates. In opposition to the advice of Crates, he studied under Stilpo of the Megaric school; and he subsequently received instruction from the 2 other contemporary Megarics, Diodorus Cronus and Philo, and from the Academics, Xenocrates and Polemo. The period which Zeno thus devoted to study is said to have extended to 20 years. At its close, and after he had developed his peculiar philosophical system, he opened his school in the porch adorned with the paintings of Polygnotus (*Stoa Poecile*), which, at an earlier time, had been a place in which poets met. From this place his disciples were called *Stoics*. Among the warm admirers of Zeno was Antigonus Gonatas, king of Macedonia. The Athenians likewise placed the greatest confidence in him, and displayed the greatest esteem for him; for although the well-known story that they deposited the keys of the fortress with him, as the most trustworthy man, may be a later invention, there seems no reason for doubting the authenticity of the decree of the people by which a golden crown and a public burial in the Ceramicus were awarded to him. The Athenian citizenship, however, he is said to have declined, that he might not become unfaithful to his native land, where in return he was highly esteemed. We do not know the year either of Zeno's birth or death. He is said to have presided over his school for 58 years, and to have died at the age of 98. He is said to have been still alive in the 130th Olympiad (B. C. 260). Zeno wrote numerous works; but the writings of Chrysippus and the later Stoics seem to have obscured those of Zeno, and even the warm adherents of the school seem seldom to have gone back to the books of its founder. Hence it is difficult to ascertain how much of the later Stoic philosophy really belongs to Zeno. — 2. The Eleatic philosopher, was a native of Elea (Velia) in Italy, son of Teleutagoras, and the favourite disciple of Parmenides. He was born about B. C. 488, and at the age of 40 accompanied Parmenides to Athens. [PARMENIDES.] He appears to have resided some time at Athens, and is said to have unfolded his doctrines to men like Pericles and Callias for the price of 100 minae. Zeno is said to have taken part in the legislation of Parmenides, to the maintenance of which the citizens of Elea had pledged themselves every year by an oath. His love of freedom is shown by the courage with which he exposed his life in order to deliver his native country from a tyrant. Whether he perished in the attempt, or survived the fall of the tyrant, is a point on which the authorities vary. They also state the name of the tyrant differently. Zeno devoted all his energies to explain and develop the philosophical system of Parmenides. [PARMENIDES.] — 3. An Epicurean philosopher, a native of Sidon, was a contemporary of Cicero, who heard him when at Athens. He was sometimes termed *Coryphaeus Epicureorum.* He seems to have been noted for the disrespectful terms in which he spoke of other philosophers. For instance, he called Socrates the Attic buffoon. He was a disciple of Apollodorus, and is described as a clear-headed thinker and perspicuous expounder of his views.

Zěnōbǐa, queen of Palmyra. After the death of her husband, Odenathus, whom, according to some accounts, she assassinated (A. D. 266), she assumed the imperial diadem, as regent for her sons, and discharged all the active duties of a sovereign. But not content with enjoying the independence conceded by Gallienus and tolerated by Claudius, she sought to include all Syria, Asia, and Egypt within the limits of her sway, and to make good the title which she claimed of Queen of the East. By this rash ambition she lost both her kingdom and her liberty. She was defeated by Aurelian, taken prisoner on the capture of Palmyra (273), and carried to Rome, where she adorned the triumph of her conqueror (274). Her life was spared by Aurelian, and she passed the remainder of her years with her sons in the vicinity of Tibur (*Tivoli*). Longinus lived at her court, and was put to death on the capture of Palmyra. [LONGINUS.]

Zěnōbǐa (Ζηνοβία: *Chelebi* or *Zelebi*), a city of Chalybonitis, in Syria, on the W. bank of the Euphrates, 3 days' journey both from Sura and from Circesium. It was founded by Zenobia.

Zěnōbǐus (Ζηνόβιος), lived at Rome in the time of Hadrian, and was the author of a collection of proverbs in Greek, which have come down to us. In this collection the proverbs are arranged alphabetically, and divided into hundreds. The last division is incomplete, the total number collected being 552. It is printed in the collection of Schottus (Παροιμίαι Ἑλληνικαί, Antwerp, 1612).

Zěnōdōrus, a Greek artist, who made for Nero the colossal statue of that emperor, which he set up in front of the golden house, and which was afterwards dedicated afresh by Vespasian as a statue of the Sun. It was 110 feet in height.

Zěnōdŏtǐum or **-ǐa** (Ζηνοδότιον, Ζηνοδοτία), a fortress in the N. of Mesopotamia, on the small tributary of the Euphrates called Bilecha, a little above Nicephorium, and below Ichnae. It was a Macedonian settlement, and the only one of the Greek cities of Mesopotamia which did not revolt from the Parthians at the approach of Crassus.

Zěnōdōtus (Ζηνόδοτος). 1. Of Ephesus, a celebrated grammarian, was the first superintendent of the great library at Alexandria, and flourished under Ptolemy Philadelphus about B. C. 208. Zenodotus was employed by Philadelphus together with his 2 great contemporaries, Alexander the Aetolian and Lycophron the Chalcidian, to collect and revise all the Greek poets. Alexander, we are told, undertook the task of collecting the tragedies, Lycophron the comedies, and Zenodotus the poems of Homer, and of the other illustrious poets. Zenodotus, however, devoted his chief attention to the Iliad and Odyssey. Hence he is called the first *Reviser* (Διορθητής) of Homer, and his recension (Διόρθωσις) of the Iliad and Odyssey obtained the greatest celebrity. The corrections which Zenodotus applied to the text of Homer were of three kinds. 1. He expunged verses. 2. He marked them as spurious, but left them in his copy. 3. He introduced new readings or transposed or altered verses. The great attention which Zenodotus paid to the language of Homer caused a new epoch in the grammatical study of the Greek language. The results of his investigations respecting the meaning and the use of words were contained in two works which he published under the title of a Glossary (Γλῶσσαι), and a Dictionary of barbarous or foreign phrases. — 2. Of Alexandria, a grammarian, lived after Aristarchus, whose recension of the Homeric poems he attacked.

Zephyra. [HALICARNASSUS.]

Zephyrium (Ζεφύριον, sc. ἀκρωτήριον, i. e. *the W. promontory*), the name of several promontories of the ancient world, not all of which, however, faced the W. The chief of them were the following: — I. In Europe. 1. (*C. di Brussano*), a promontory in Bruttium, forming the S. E. extremity of the country, from which the Locri, who settled in the neighbourhood, are said to have obtained the name of *Epizephyrii.* [See p. 387, b.] — 2. A promontory on the W. coast of Cyprus. II. In Asia. 1. In Pontus (*C. Zefreh*), a headland W. of TRIPOLIS, with a fort and harbour of the same name. — 2. [CARIA.] — 3. In Cilicia (prob. *C. Cavaliere*), a far-projecting promontory, W. of Prom. Sarpedon. Some make it the headland E. of Prom. Sarpedon, and just S. of the mouth of the Calycadnus, which Polybius, Appian, and Livy call by the same name as the river, Calycadnus. — III. In Africa (*Kasser Maarah*), a headland on the N. E. coast of Cyrenaïca, W. of Darnis.

Zephyrus (Ζέφυρος), the personification of the W. wind, is described by Hesiod as a son of Astraeus and Eos. Zephyrus and Boreas are frequently mentioned together by Homer, and both dwelt together in a palace in Thrace. By the Harpy Podarge, Zephyrus became the father of the horses Xanthus and Balius, which belonged to Achilles; but he was married to Chloris, whom he had carried off by force, and by whom he had a son Carpus.

Zerynthus (Ζήρυνθος, Ζηρύνθιος), a town of Thrace in the territory of Aenos, with a temple of Apollo and a cave of Hecate, who are hence called *Zerynthius* and *Zerynthia* respectively. Some writers, however, place the Zerynthian cave of Hecate in Samothrace.

Zětēs (Ζήτης) and **Călăis** (Κάλαϊς), sons of Boreas and Orithyia, frequently called the **Borĕădae,** are mentioned among the Argonauts, and are described as winged beings. Their sister Cleopatra, who was married to Phineus, king of Salmydessus, had been thrown with her sons into prison by Phineus at the instigation of his second wife. Here she was found by Zetes and Calais, when they arrived at Salmydessus in the Argonautic expedition. They liberated their sister and his children, gave the kingdom to the latter, and sent the second wife of Phineus to her own country, Scythia. Others relate that the Boreadae delivered Phineus from the Harpies; for it had been foretold that the Harpies might be killed by the sons of Boreas, but that the sons of Boreas must die, if they should not be able to overtake the Harpies. Others again state that the Boreadae perished in their pursuit of the Harpies, or that Hercules killed them with his arrows near the island of Tenos. Different stories were related to account for the anger of Hercules against the Boreadae. Their tombs were said to be in Tenos, adorned with sepulchral stelae, one of which moved whenever the wind blew from the north. .Calais is also mentioned as the founder of the Campanian town of Cales.

Zethus (Ζῆθος), son of Zeus and Antiope, and brother of Amphion. For details see Amphion.

Zeugis, Zeugitana Regio (ἡ Ζευγιτανή: N. part of *Tunis*), the N. district of Africa Propria. [Africa.]

Zeugma (Ζεῦγμα, i. e. *Junction*: prob. *Rumkaleh*), a city of Syria, on the borders of Commagene and Cyrrhestice, built by Seleucus Nicator, on the W. bank of the Euphrates, at a point where the river was crossed by a bridge of boats, which had been constructed by Alexander the Great: hence the name. Afterwards, when the ford of Thapsacus became impassable for travellers, on account of the hordes of Arabs who infested the banks of the Lower Euphrates, the bridge at Zeugma gave the only passage over the river.

Zeus (Ζεύς), called **Jupiter** by the Romans, the greatest of the Olympian gods, was a son of Cronos and Rhea, a brother of Poseidon, Hades (Pluto), Hestia, Demeter, Hera, and was also married to his sister Hera. When Zeus and his brothers distributed among themselves the government of the world by lot, Poseidon obtained the sea, Hades the lower world, and Zeus the heavens and the upper regions, but the earth became common to all. According to the Homeric account Zeus dwelt on Mt. Olympus in Thessaly, which was believed to penetrate with its lofty summit into heaven itself. He is called the father of gods and men, the most high and powerful among the immortals, whom all others obey. He is the supreme ruler, who with his counsel manages everything; the founder of kingly power, and of law and of order, whence Dice, Themis, and Nemesis are his assistants. For the same reason he protects the assembly of the people (ἀγοραῖος), the meetings of the council (βουλαῖος), and as he presides over the whole state, so also over every house and family (ἑρκεῖος). He also watched over the sanctity of the oath (ὅρκιος) and the laws of hospitality (ξένιος), and protected suppliants (ἱκέσιος). He avenged those who were wronged, and punished those who had committed a crime, for he watched the doings and sufferings of all men (ἐπόψιος). He was further the original source of all prophetic power, from whom all prophetic signs and sounds proceeded (πανομφαῖος). Every thing good as well as bad comes from Zeus; according to his own choice he assigns good or evil to mortals; and fate itself was subordinate to him. He is armed with thunder and lightning, and the shaking of his aegis produces storm and tempest: a number of epithets of Zeus in the Homeric poems describe him as the thunderer, the gatherer of clouds, and the like. He was married to Hera, by whom he had two sons, Ares and Hephaestus, and one daughter, Hebe. Hera sometimes acts as an independent divinity; she is ambitious and rebels

against her lord, but she is nevertheless inferior to him, and is punished for her opposition; his amours with other goddesses or mortal women are not concealed from her, though they generally rouse her jealousy and revenge. During the Trojan war, Zeus, at the request of Thetis, favoured the Trojans, until Agamemnon repaired the wrong he had done to Achilles. Zeus, no doubt, was originally a god of a portion of nature. Hence the oak with its eatable fruit and the fertile doves were sacred to him at Dodona and in Arcadia. Hence also rain, storms, and the seasons were regarded as his work; and hence, likewise, the Cretan stories of milk, honey, and cornucopia. In the Homeric poems, however, this primitive character of a personification of certain powers of nature is already effaced to some extent, and the god appears as a political and national divinity, as the king and father of men, as the founder and protector of all institutions hallowed by law, custom, or religion. Hesiod also calls Zeus the son of Cronos and Rhea, and the brother of Hestia, Demeter, Hera, Hades, and Poseidon. Cronos swallowed his children immediately after their birth, but when Rhea was pregnant with Zeus, she applied to Uranus and Ge to save the life of the child. Uranus and Ge therefore sent Rhea to Lyctos in Crete, requesting her to bring up her child there. Rhea accordingly concealed Zeus in a cave of Mount Aegaeon, and gave to Cronos a stone wrapped up in cloth, which he swallowed in the belief that it was his son. Other traditions state that Zeus was born and brought up on Mount Dicte or Ida (also the Trojan Ida), Ithome in Messenia, Thebes in Boeotia, Aegion in Achaia, or Olenos in Aetolia. According to the common account, however, Zeus grew up in Crete. In the meantime Cronos by a cunning device of Ge or Metis was made to bring up the children he had swallowed, and first of all the stone, which was afterwards set up by Zeus at Delphi. The young god now delivered the Cyclopes from the bonds with which they had been fettered by Cronos, and they in their gratitude provided him with thunder and lightning. On the advice of Ge, Zeus also liberated the hundred-armed Gigantes, Briareos, Cottus, and Gyes, that they might assist him in his fight against the Titans. The Titans were conquered and shut up in Tartarus, where they were henceforth guarded by the Hecatoncheires. Thereupon Tartarus and Ge begot Typhoeus, who began a fearful struggle with Zeus, but was conquered. Zeus now obtained the dominion of the world, and chose Metis for his wife. When she was pregnant with Athena, he took the child out of her body and concealed it in his head, on the advice of Uranus and Ge, who told him that thereby he would retain the supremacy of the world. For if Metis had given birth to a son, this son (so fate had ordained it) would have acquired the sovereignty. After this Zeus became the father of the Horae and Moerae, by his second wife Themis; of the Charites by Eurynome; of Persephone by Demeter; of the Muses by Mnemosyne; of Apollo and Artemis by Leto; and of Hebe, Ares, and Ilithyia by Hera. Athena was born out of the head of Zeus; while Hera, on the other hand, gave birth to Hephaestus without the co-operation of Zeus. The family of the Cronidae accordingly embraces the 12 great gods of Olympus, Zeus (the head of them all), Poseidon, Apollo, Ares, Hermes, Hephaestus, Hestia, Demeter, Hera, Athena, Aphrodite, and Artemis. These 12 Olympian gods, who in some places were worshipped as a body, were recognised not only by the Greeks, but were adopted also by the Romans, who, in particular, identified their Jupiter with the Greek Zeus. In surveying the different local traditions about Zeus, it would seem that originally there were several, or at least 3, divinities which in their respective countries were supreme, but which in the course of time became united in the minds of the people into one great national divinity. We may accordingly speak of an Arcadian, Dodonaean, Cretan, and a national Hellenic Zeus. 1. The *Arcadian Zeus* (Ζεὺς Λυκαῖος) was born, according to the legends of the country, in Arcadia, either on Mt. Parrhasium, or on Mt. Lycaeus. He was brought up there by the nymphs Thisoa, Neda, and Hagno. Lycaon, a son of Pelasgus, erected a temple to Zeus Lycaeus on Mt. Lycaeus, and instituted the festival of the Lycea in honour of him [LYCAEUS; LYCAON]. No one was allowed to enter this sanctuary of Zeus Lycaeus on Mt. Lycaeus. 2. The *Dodonaean Zeus* (Ζεὺς Δωδωναῖος or Πελασγικός) possessed the most ancient oracle in Greece, at Dodona in Epirus, from which he derived his name. At Dodona Zeus was mainly a prophetic god, and the oak tree was sacred to him ; but there too he was said to have been reared by the Dodonaean nymphs (Hyades). Respecting the Dodonaean oracle of Zeus, see *Dict. of Antiq.* art. *Oraculum.* 3. The *Cretan Zeus* (Ζεὺς Δικταῖος or Κρηταγενής). We have already given Hesiod's account of this god. He was brought up in a cave of mount Dicte, by the Curetes and the nymphs Adrastia and Ida, the daughters of Melisseus. They fed him with the milk of the goat Amalthea, and the bees of the mountain provided him with honey. Crete is called the island or nurse of the great Zeus, and his worship there appears to have been very ancient. 4. The *national Hellenic Zeus*, near whose temple at Olympia in Elis, the great national panegyris was celebrated once in 4 years. There too Zeus was regarded as the father and king of gods and men, and as the supreme god of the Hellenic nation. His statue there was executed by Phidias, a few years before the outbreak of the Peloponnesian war, the majestic and sublime idea of this statue having been suggested to the artist by the words of Homer (*Il.* i. 527). [PHIDIAS.]—The Greek and Latin poets give to Zeus or Jupiter an immense number of epithets and surnames, which are derived partly from the places where he was worshipped, and partly from his powers and functions. The eagle, the oak, and the summits of mountains were sacred to him, and his sacrifices generally consisted of goats, bulls, and cows. His usual attributes are, the sceptre, eagle, thunderbolt, and a figure of Victory in his hand, and sometimes also a cornucopia. The Olympian Zeus sometimes wears a wreath of olive, and the Dodonaean Zeus a wreath of oak leaves. In works of art Zeus is generally represented as the omnipotent father and king of gods and men, according to the idea which had been embodied in the statue of the Olympian Zeus by Phidias. Respecting the Roman god see JUPITER.

Zeuxidamus (Ζευξίδαμος). 1. King of Sparta, and 10th of the Eurypontidae. He was grandson of Theopompus, and father of Anaxidamus, who succeeded him. — 2 Son of Leotychides, king of Sparta. He was also named Cyniscus. He died before his father, leaving a son, Archidamus II.

Zeuxis (Ζεῦξις), the celebrated Greek painter, who excelled all his contemporaries except Parrhasius, was a native of Heraclea (probably of the city of this name on the Euxine), and flourished B. C. 424 — 400. He came to Athens soon after the beginning of the Peloponnesian War, when he had already achieved a great reputation, although a young man. He passed some time in Macedonia, at the court of Archelaüs, for whom he decorated the royal palace at Pella with paintings, probably soon after 413. He must have spent some time in Magna Graecia, as we learn from the story respecting the picture of Helen, which he painted for the city of Croton ; and it is also probable that he visited Sicily, as we are told that he gave away one of his pictures to the Agrigentines. His travels through Greece itself were no doubt extensive. We find him at Olympia, where he made an ostentatious display, before the eyes of all Greece, of the wealth which his art had brought him, by appearing in a robe embroidered with his own name in letters of gold. After acquiring a great fortune by the exercise of his art, he adopted the custom of giving away his pictures, because no adequate price could be set upon them. The time of his death is unknown. The masterpiece of Zeuxis was his picture of Helen, in painting which he had as his models the 5 most beautiful virgins of Croton, whom he was allowed to select for this purpose from among all the virgins of the city. It was painted for the temple of Juno at Croton. This picture and its history were celebrated by many poets, who preserved the names of the 5 virgins upon whom the choice of Zeuxis fell. The accurate imitation of inanimate objects was a department of the art which Zeuxis and his younger rival Parrhasius appear to have carried almost to perfection. The well-known story of the trial of skill in that species of painting between these two artists, if not literally true, indicates the opinion which was held in ancient times of their powers of imitation. In this contest the picture of Zeuxis represented a bunch of grapes, so naturally painted that the birds flew at the picture to eat the fruit ; upon which the artist, confident in this proof of his success, called upon his rival no longer to delay to draw aside the curtain and show his picture : but the picture of Parrhasius was the curtain itself, which Zeuxis had mistaken for real drapery. On discovering his error, Zeuxis honourably yielded the palm to Parrhasius, saying that he himself had deceived birds, but Parrhasius an artist. Besides this accuracy of imitation, many of the works of Zeuxis displayed great dramatic power. This appears to have been especially the case with his *Infant Hercules strangling the Serpent*, where the chief force of the composition consisted in the terror of Alcmena and Amphitryon, as they witnessed the struggle. Another picture, in which he showed the same dramatic power, applied to a very different subject, was his *Female Hippocentaur*, and which was lost in a shipwreck off Cape Malea, on its way to Rome, whither it had been sent by Sulla.

Ziklag (Σίκελλα, Σίκελα), a town in the S.W. of Palestine, belonging to the Philistines of Gath, whose king Achish gave it to David for a residence during his exile from the court of Saul. On David's accession to the kingdom, it was united to Judah.

Zioberis (*Jinjeran*), a river of Parthia.

Zion. [JERUSALEM.]

Zoar or **Tsoar, Zoăra** or **Zoăras** (Ζόαρ, Ζόαρα ; LXX. Σηγώρ and Ζόγορα: prob. Rn. in *Ghor el Mezraa* on the *Wady el Deraah*), originally called **Bĕla**, a city on the S. E. of the Dead Sea, belonging first to the Moabites, and afterwards to the Arabs. In the time of Abraham it was the smallest of the "cities of the plain," and was saved, at the intercession of Lot, from the destruction which fell upon Sodom and Gomorrha.

Zoetĭum or **Zoetĕum** (Ζοίτιον, Ζοίτειον ; Ζοιτειεύς), a town of Arcadia in the district Eutresia, N. of Megalopolis.

Zŏĭlus (Ζωΐλος), a grammarian, was a native of Amphipolis, and flourished in the time of Philip of Macedon. He was celebrated for the asperity with which he assailed Homer. He found fault with him principally for introducing fabulous and incredible stories in his poems. From the list that we have of his writings, it also appears that he attacked Plato and Isocrates. His name became proverbial for a captious and malignant critic.

Zŏnăras, Joannes ('Ιωάννης ὁ Ζωναρᾶς), a celebrated Byzantine historian and theologian, lived in the 12th century under the emperors Alexus I. Comnenus and Calo-Joannes. Besides his theological works there are still extant : 1. *Annales* (χρονικόν), in 18 books, from the creation of the world to the death of Alexis in 1118. It is compiled from various Greek authors, whose very words Zonaras frequently retains. The earlier part is chiefly taken from Josephus ; and in the portion which relates to Roman history he has for the most part followed Dion Cassius. In consequence of the latter circumstance the Annals of Zonaras are of great importance in studying the early history of Rome. Of the first 20 books of Dion Cassius we have nothing but the abstract of Zonaras ; and even of the later books, of which Xiphilinus has made a more full epitome, Zonaras has preserved many statements of Dion which are entirely omitted by Xiphilinus. The best editions are by Du Fresne Du Cange, Paris, 1686, fol. ; and by Pinder, Bonn, 1841, 8vo. 2. A *Lexicon*, edited by Tittmann, Lips. 1808, 4to.

Zŏnē (Ζώνη : Ζωναῖος), a town of Thrace on a promontory of the same name in the Aegaean, where Orpheus is said to have sung.

Zŏpўrus (Ζώπυρος). 1. A distinguished Persian, son of Megabyzus. After Darius Hystaspis had besieged Babylon for 20 months in vain, Zopyrus resolved to gain the place for his master by the most extraordinary self-sacrifice. Accordingly, one day he appeared before Darius, with his body mutilated in the most horrible manner ; both his ears and nose were cut off, and his person otherwise disfigured. After explaining to Darius his intentions, he fled to Babylon as a victim of the cruelty of the Persian king. The Babylonians gave him their confidence, and placed him at the head of their troops. He soon found means to betray the city to Darius, who severely punished the inhabitants for their revolt. Darius appointed Zopyrus satrap of Babylon for life, with the enjoyment of its entire revenues. — 2. The Physiognomist, attributed many vices to Socrates in an assembly of his disciples, who laughed at him and at his art in consequence ; but Socrates admitted

that such were his natural propensities, but said that they had been overcome by philosophy. — 3. A surgeon at Alexandria, the tutor of Apollonius Citiensis and Posidonius, about the beginning o the 1st century B.C. He invented an antidote, used by Mithridates, king of Pontus.

Zŏrŏaster or **Zoroastres** (Ζωροάστρης), the Zarathustra of the Zendavesta, and the Zerdusht of the Persians, was the founder of the Magian religion. The most opposite opinions have been held both by ancient and modern writers respecting the time in which he lived ; but *it* is quite impossible to come to any conclusion on the subject. As the founder of the Magian religion he must be placed in remote antiquity, and it may even be questioned whether such a person ever existed. This religion was probably of Bactrian origin, and from thence spread E.-ward ; and the tradition which represents Zoroaster a Mede sprang up at a later time, when the chief seat of his religion was in Media, and no longer in the further East. There were extant in the later Greek literature several works bearing the name of Zoroaster ; but these writings were forgeries of a later age, and belong to the same class of writings as the works of Hermes Trismegistus, Orpheus, &c. There is still extant a collection of oracles ascribed to Zoroaster, which are of course spurious. They have been published by Morell, Paris, 1595 ; by Obsopaeus, Paris, 1507, and by others.

Zŏsĭmus (Ζώσιμος), a Greek historian, who lived in the time of the younger Theodosius. He wrote a history of the Roman empire in 6 books, which is still extant. This work must have been written after A. D. 425, as an event is mentioned in it which took place in that year. The 1st book comprises a sketch of the history of the early emperors, down to the end of the reign of Diocletian (305). The 2d, 3d, and 4th books are devoted to the history of the 4th century, which is treated much less concisely. The 5th and 6th books embrace the period from 395 to 410, when Attalus was deposed. The work of Zosimus is mainly (though not altogether) an abridgment or compilation of the works of previous historians. His style is concise, clear, pure, and not unpleasing. His chief fault as an historical writer is his neglect of chronology. Zosimus was a pagan, and comments severely upon the faults and crimes of the Christian emperors. Hence his credibility has been assailed by several Christian writers. There are no doubt numerous errors of judgment to be found in the work, and sometimes (especially in the case of Constantine) an intemperate expression of opinion, which somewhat exaggerates, if it does not distort the truth. But he does not seem fairly chargeable with deliberate invention or wilful misrepresentation. The best edition is by Reitemeier, Lips. 1784.

Zostēr (*C. of Vari*), a promontory on the W. of Attica, between Phalerum and Sunium. It was a sacred spot, and contained altars of Leto, Artemis, and Apollo.

Zygantes or **Gygantes** (Ζύγαντες, Γύγαντες), a people of Libya, whom Herodotus places on the W. side of the lake Triton. Others mention a city Zygantis and a people Zyges on the coast of Marmarica.

Spottiswoode & Co., Printers, New-street Square and 30 Parliament Street.

Lightning Source UK Ltd.
Milton Keynes UK
UKHW022225160820
368356UK00002B/11